W9-CNI-688

STRAND PRICE
$ 5.00

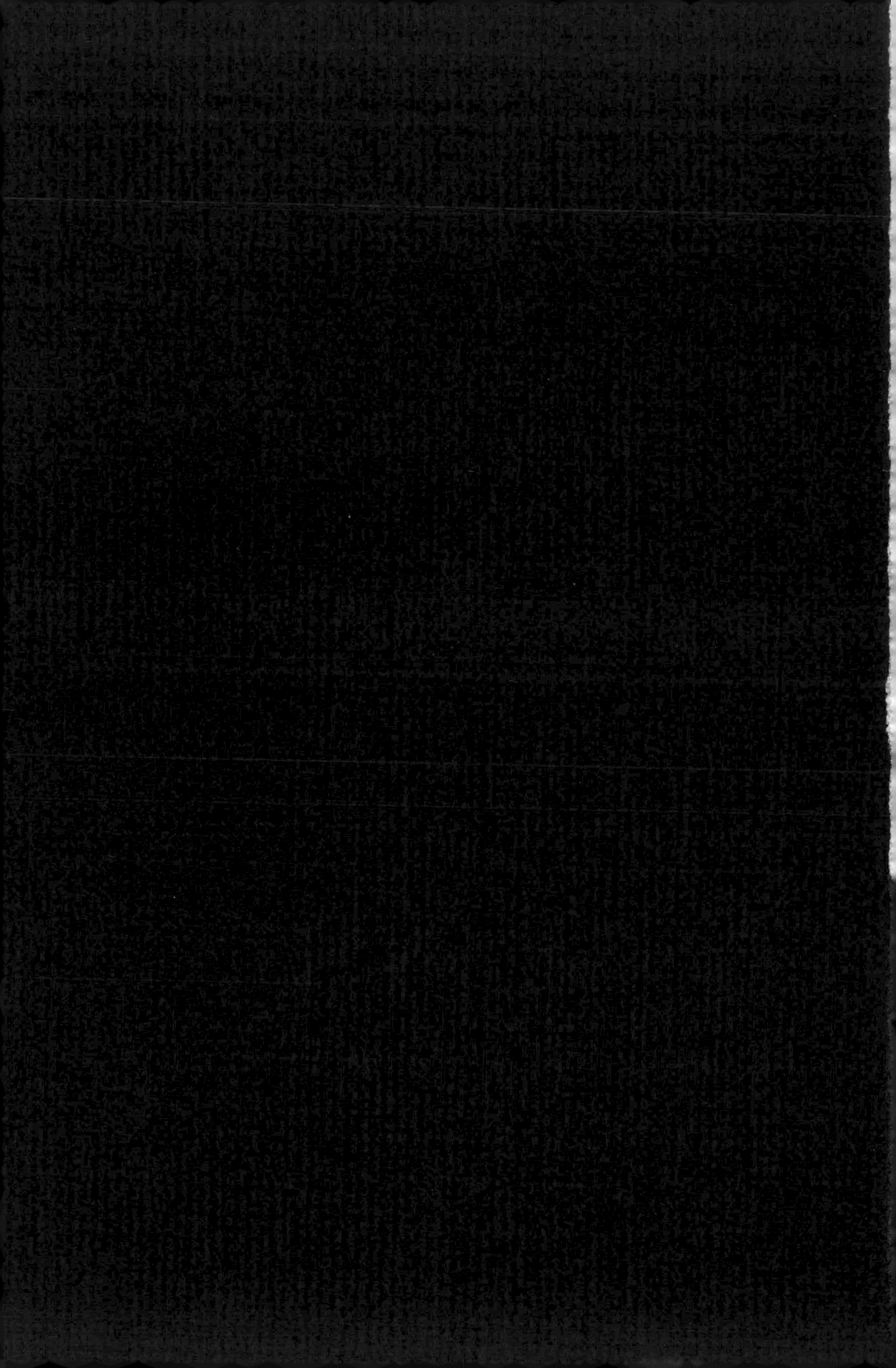

THE RANDOM HOUSE CROSS-WORD PUZZLE DICTIONARY

Random House New York

All inquiries should be addressed to Reference Department, Random House, Inc., 201 East 50th Street, New York, N.Y. 10022. Published in the United States by Random House, Inc., New York, and simultaneously in Canada by Random House of Canada Limited, Toronto.

Prepared for Random House, Inc., by Sachem Publishing Associates, Inc., Stephen P. Elliott, President; Elizabeth J. Jewell, Managing Editor.

Library of Congress Cataloging-in-Publication Data

The Random House crossword puzzle dictionary.

1. Crossword puzzles—Glossaries, vocabularies, etc.
GV1507.C7R28 1989 793.73'2'0321 88-32554
ISBN 0-394-53513-8

Book design: Charlotte Staub
Manufactured in the United States of America
a.o/se

PREFACE

Although various word games and puzzles have existed almost since the beginnings of language, the modern crossword puzzle is a 20th-century innovation. The first newspaper crossword appeared on December 21, 1913, in the New York *World,* and this new type of word puzzle quickly captured the public's fancy. Within a decade, crossword puzzles were featured in most American newspapers, and they soon became the rage in England as well. Since the 1920s, crossword puzzles have been a standard feature of daily newspapers and have proved enormously popular when collected in book form.

Now found in almost every language and in variations ranging from theme puzzles to diagramless puzzles, crosswords are available for almost any age and vocabulary level. Those who solve crossword puzzles invariably relish the challenge of completing a puzzle, of "getting it right." When faced with a clue they cannot answer, they resist "cheating"—looking at the puzzle's solution. One way out of this difficulty is to consult a reference work, yet neither a dictionary nor an encyclopedia nor an almanac contains the necessary information in a useful, quick-reference format. A standard dictionary might give a few synonyms for a word, an encyclopedia would give information about countries or historical figures, and an almanac usually has information about sports figures or the Academy awards, but only a crossword puzzle dictionary combines in one handy volume the information that might be found in all three. Equally important, it does so without extraneous information and with the convenience of an arrangement by the number of letters in each word.

The Random House Crossword Puzzle Dictionary, drawing on the resources of the Random House dictionaries and thesauruses, with research into a host of other topics, answers the need of crossword puzzlers for one single-purpose reference work. In addition to general vocabulary and synonyms, there are entries covering history; the natural and physical sciences; literature; music, painting, and other arts; religion; mythology; sports; popular culture; and current affairs, among others. Highlighted boxed items provide easy-to-find detailed information on the continents and countries of the world, states of the United States, U.S. presidents, the months of the year, and other facts of special interest.

While *The Random House Crossword Puzzle Dictionary*'s primary purpose is to meet the needs of the growing numbers of people who find crosswords both relaxing and challenging, even a cursory glance will demonstrate the book's usefulness as a reference for trivia buffs. From who won the Academy Award for best actress in 1970 (Glenda Jackson) to the name of a coffee grown in Jamaica (Blue Mountain), it's all here.

A volume of this scope is necessarily the work of many researchers, editors, and proofreaders. We would like to acknowledge the invaluable contributions made by Julianna Arbo, Suzanne Stone Burke, Francine Esposito, Gretchen Ferrante, Jan Jamilkowski, Rebecca Lyon, Julie E. Marsh, Blaine Merritt, Laurie Romanik, Christine Lindberg Stevens, and Diane Bell Surprenant; and by Patricia W. Ehresmann, Typographic Director and Production Manager, Random House, Inc., and Rita Rubin, Administrative Assistant.

HOW TO USE THIS BOOK

The main entries in *The Random House Crossword Puzzle Dictionary* are words or phrases likely to appear as crossword puzzle clues. Each entry consists of a clue word or phrase and a list of answer words, arranged first by the number of letters in each word and then alphabetically. For example, if the main entry—**banal**—is the clue for a five-letter answer, the answer—"trite"—will be found alphabetically listed under the five-letter answer words. For phrases, such as **contracted form,** the answer could be "digest," "summary," or "synopsis." Entries may also contain indented subheads and secondary subheads. If, for instance, the clue is a phrase, like **cotton fabric,** the word **cotton** will be found as a main entry in the dictionary, and **fabric** will be found as a subhead under it, with such possible answer words as "terry," "poplin," and "gingham." In some cases, the answer can be found in more than one place. For example, if the clue is **Mexican coin,** the answer could be found by looking under the main entry **Mexico** and the subhead **monetary unit,** or by looking under the main entry **coin/currency** and the subhead **of Mexico.**

Longer entries are set off in highlighted boxes so they can be found more quickly. All continents and countries of the world, states of the United States, presidents of the United States, and months of the year appear as boxed items, as do many other major entries.

There are also cross references for alternate spellings (**Epicaste** *see* **7** Jocasta) and very closely related items (**Epeans** *see* **5** Epeus—a look at **Epeus** reveals that **Epeans** are descendants of this king of the Peloponnesus).

The main entries, subheads, secondary subheads, and numbers all appear in boldface type; the answer words are in regular roman type. Most punctuation and accent marks have been omitted, since they are not used in puzzle answers; occasionally, apostrophes and other marks have been included in answers to make them more readable.

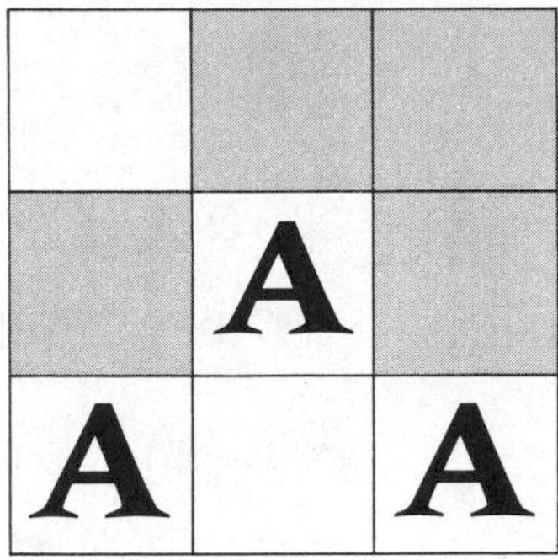

aardvark
also: 7 ant bear **8** anteater
family: 15 Orycteropodidae
species: 15 Orycteropus afer
order: 13 Tubulidentata
native to: 6 Africa
food: 4 ants **8** termites
name comes from:
9 Africaans
meaning: **8** earth hog, earth pig

Aaron
brother: 5 Moses
father: 5 Amram
mother: 8 Jochebed
sister: 6 Miriam
son: 5 Abihu, Nadab **7** Eleazar, Ithamar
wife: 8 Elisheba
successor: 7 Eleazar
deathplace: 3 Hor **8** Mount Hor
priestly descendant of:
8 Aaronite
set up: 10 golden calf

Aaron, Henry (Hank)
sport: 8 baseball
position: 10 outfielder
record: 8 homeruns
team: 13 Atlanta Braves
15 Milwaukee Braves
16 Milwaukee Brewers

Aaron's Rod 21 miraculously blossomed
yielded: 7 almonds
herb: 21 Thermopsis caroliniana

Aatam *see* **4** Pima

Ab 16 fifth Hebrew month

Abaddon 4 hell **8** Appolyon

abaft 6 behind **11** to the rear of **12** to the stern of

Abagtha 6 eunuch
served: 9 Ahasuerus

abandon 4 dash, drop, elan, jilt, junk, quit, stop **5** ardor, cease, forgo, gusto, leave, let go, scrap, verve, waive **6** desert, give up, spirit **7** discard, forfeit, forsake, freedom **8** abdicate, evacuate, forswear, get rid of, renounce, run out on **9** animation, cast aside, repudiate, surrender **10** depart from, enthusiasm, exuberance, relinquish, wantonness **11** discontinue, impetuosity, leave behind, spontaneity, unrestraint **12** immoderation, intemperance, recklessness, withdraw from
13 impulsiveness

abandoned 4 lewd, wild
5 loose **6** impure, jilted, sinful, vacant, wanton, wicked **7** debased, immoral **8** cast away, degraded, deserted, desolate, forsaken, marooned, rejected, unchaste **9** cast aside, debauched, discarded, dissolute, neglected, reprobate, shameless **10** dissipated, left behind, licentious, profligate, unoccupied **11** unrepentant **12** disreputable, incorrigible, irreformable, relinquished, unprincipled **13** irreclaimable

abandon oneself to 7 yield to **8** give in to, give up to
9 indulge in

Abantes
tribe: 7 Euboean

Abaris
origin: 5 Greek
form: 4 sage

Abas
mentioned in: 5 Iliad
king of: 7 Argolis
father: 6 Celeus **7** Lynceus
9 Eurydamas
mother: 8 Metanira
12 Hypermnestra
wife: 6 Aglaia
son: 7 Proetus **8** Acrisius
daughter: 7 Idomene
changed into: 4 bird **6** lizard
mocked: 7 Demeter
protected by: 11 magic shield
companion: 8 Diomedes
killed by: 8 Diomedes

a bas 8 down with **11** to the bottom

abase 4 mock **5** shame **6** debase, defame, demean, humble, malign, vilify **7** cheapen, degrade, mortify, put down, vitiate **8** badmouth, belittle, besmirch, bring low, cast down, disgrace, dishonor
9 denigrate, devaluate, discredit, downgrade, humiliate
13 bring down a peg, cut down to size

abash 4 dash **5** daunt **6** deject, dismay **7** depress **8** dispirit
9 discomfit, embarrass **10** discompose, disconcert, discourage, dishearten

abashed 3 shy **5** cowed, fazed
7 ashamed, bashful, crushed, daunted, humbled, subdued
8 confused, dismayed, overawed **9** chagrined, mortified
10 bewildered, confounded, humiliated, nonplussed, taken aback **11** dumbfounded, embarrassed, intimidated **12** disconcerted, disheartened
13 self-conscious

abashment 3 awe **6** wonder
9 confusion **12** discomfiture, discomposure **13** embarrassment **14** disconcertment

abate 3 ebb **4** cool, dull, ease, fade, slow, wane **5** allay, blunt, lower, quell, quiet, slack **6** dampen, go down, lessen, pacify, recede, reduce, soften, soothe, temper, weaken **7** assuage, curtail, decline, dwindle, fall off, lighten, mollify, relieve, slacken, subside
8 decrease, diminish, fade away, fall away, mitigate, moderate, palliate, restrain, restrict, slack off, slow down, taper off **9** alleviate

abatement 3 cut, ebb **5** break

6 ebbing, waning **8** decrease, discount, soothing **9** lessening, reduction, weakening **10** concession, mitigation, moderation, slackening, subsidence **11** assuagement, curtailment **13** mollification

Abba
means: **6** father

Abbe Faria
character in: **21** The Count of Monte Cristo
author: **5** Dumas (pere)

abbey **6** cenoby, chapel, church, friary, priory **7** convent, nunnery **8** cloister, seminary **9** cathedral, hermitage, monastery

Abbey, Edwin Austin
born: **14** Philadelphia PA
artwork: **21** Quest of the Golden Grail **23** The Quest for the Holy Grail **37** Richard Duke of Gloucester and the Lady Anne

Abbott, Bud
real name: **14** William A Abbott
partner: **11** Lou Costello
born: **12** Asbury Park NJ
roles: **11** Who's on First **12** Buck Privates **13** Hold that Ghost **33** Abbott and Costello Meet Frankenstein

abbreviate **3** cut **4** clip, trim **6** reduce **7** abridge, curtail, cut down, shorten **8** boil down, compress, condense, contract, cut short, diminish, truncate **9** summarize, synopsize

abbreviated **5** brief, short **7** limited, summary **8** abridged **9** condensed, curtailed, shortened **10** compressed, summarized

abbreviation **5** brief **6** digest **7** cutting, pruning, summary **8** abstract, clipping, synopsis, trimming **9** lessening, reduction, short form **10** abridgment, diminution, shortening **11** abstraction, compression, contraction, curtailment, cut-down form, reduced form **12** condensation **13** condensed form, shortened form **14** compressed form, contracted form

Abderus
father: **6** Hermes
killed by: **5** mares **13** Diomedes mares

abdicate **4** cede, quit **5** forgo, waive, yield **6** abjure, give up, resign **7** abandon **8** abnegate, renounce **9** surrender **10** relinquish **15** vacate the throne

abdomen **3** gut, pot **5** belly, tummy **6** paunch, venter **7** stomach **8** pot belly **9** bay window **11** breadbasket, epigastrium **14** visceral cavity

Abdon **11** Hebrew judge
father: **5** Micah **6** Achbor, Jehiel **7** Shashak
city of: **5** Asher

abduct **5** seize, steal **6** kidnap **7** bear off **8** carry off, take away **10** run off with **11** make off with

Abduction from the Harem, The
also: **25** Die Entfuhrung aus dem Serail
opera by: **6** Mozart
character: **5** Osmin **6** Blonde **8** Belmonte, Pedrillo **9** Constanze **10** Pasha Selim

Abdul-Jabbar, Kareem
formerly: **11** Lew Alcindor **22** Lewis Ferdinand Alcindor
sport: **10** basketball
position: **6** center
team: **8** LA Lakers **10** UCLA Bruins **14** Milwaukee Bucks **16** Los Angeles Lakers
shot: **7** sky hook

Abednego
companion: **6** Daniel
friend: **8** Meschach, Shadrach
former name: **7** Azariah

Abel
father: **4** Adam
mother: **3** Eve
brother: **4** Cain, Seth
killer: **4** Cain

Abel, Niels Henrik
field: **11** mathematics
nationality: **9** Norwegian
theorem: **8** binomial
theory of: **19** elliptical functions

Abe Lincoln in Illinois
author: **14** Robert Sherwood
director: **12** John Cromwell
cast: **10** Alan Baxter, Mary Howard, Ruth Gordon (Mary Todd Lincoln) **11** Dorothy Tree, Minor Watson **12** Gene Lockhart **13** Howard da Silva, Raymond Massey (Abraham Lincoln)

Abelmeholah
home of: **6** Elisha

aberrance **6** oddity **7** anomaly **8** rambling, straying **9** wandering **10** aberration **11** abnormality, peculiarity **12** eccentricity, irregularity **13** nonconformity

aberrant **3** odd **7** unusual **8** abnormal, atypical, peculiar, uncommon **9** anomalous, eccentric, irregular

aberration **5** lapse, quirk **6** lunacy, oddity **7** anomaly, madness **8** delusion, illusion, insanity, mutation, rambling, straying **9** aberrance, aberrancy, curiosity, departure, deviation, exception, wandering **10** digression, distortion, divergence **11** abnormality, derangement, incongruity, mental lapse, peculiarity, singularity, strangeness **12** eccentricity, idiosyncrasy, irregularity, unconformity **13** hallucination, nonconformity, self-deception

abet **3** aid **4** back, goad, help, spur, urge **5** egg on **6** assist, incite, lead on, second, uphold, urge on **7** advance, endorse, promote, support, sustain **8** advocate, join with, sanction **9** encourage, instigate

abettor **4** ally **6** cohort **7** partner **9** accessory, associate, colleague **10** accomplice **11** confederate **12** collaborator

ab extra **11** from outside, from without

abeyance **5** delay, on ice, pause **6** hiatus, recess **7** latency **8** deferral, dormancy, inaction **9** cessation, remission **10** quiescence, suspension **11** adjournment **12** intermission, postponement **13** in cold storage, on a back burner, waiting period **14** discontinuance

abhor **4** hate, shun **5** scorn **6** detest, eschew, loathe **7** despise, disdain, dislike **8** execrate, recoil at **9** abominate, can't stand, shudder at **10** shrink from **11** can't stomach **12** be revolted by **13** be nauseated by, find repulsive

abhorred **5** hated **8** despised, detested, disliked **10** abominated

abhorrence **4** hate **5** odium, scorn **6** hatred **7** disdain, disgust, dislike **8** aversion, contempt, distaste, loathing **9** antipathy, revulsion **10** repugnance **11** abomination

abhorrent **4** foul, vile **6** odious **7** hateful **8** accursed **9** execrable, loathsome, repellent, repugnant, repulsive, revolting **10** abominable, despicable, disgusting, nauseating

Abiathar
companion: **5** David
father: **9** Ahimelech
banished to: **7** Anatoth
conspired to overthrow: **5** David

abide **3** sit **4** bear, last, live, stay, stop **5** brook, dwell, stand, tarry, visit **6** accept, endure, linger, remain, reside, suffer **7** sojourn, stomach **8** stand for, submit to, tolerate

abide by **4** obey **6** follow **8** accede to, adhere to, submit to **9** conform to **10** comply with **11** go along with

abiding **4** fast, firm **6** steady **7** durable, eternal, lasting **8** constant, enduring, unending **9** immutable, permanent, steadfast **10** changeless, continuing, unchanging, unshakable **11** everlasting **12** indissoluble, wholehearted **13** unquestioning

Abidjan
capital of: **10** Ivory Coast

Abigail
husband: **5** David, Nabal
brother: **5** David

Abihu
father: **5** Aaron
mother: **8** Elisheba
brother: **5** Nadab **7** Eleazar, Ithamar
killed with: **5** Nadab
accompanied to Mt Sinai: **5** Moses

Abijah
father: **8** Rehoboam
grandfather: **7** Solomon
grandmother: **6** Naamah

ability **4** bent, gift **5** flair, knack, power, skill **6** acumen, genius, talent **7** faculty, know-how, mind for **8** aptitude, capacity, facility **9** adeptness, expertise, potential **10** adroitness, capability, competence **11** proficiency **12** potentiality **13** qualification

Abimelech
king of: **5** Gerar
means: **15** the father is king
father: **6** Gideon **8** Abiathar
brother: **6** Jotham
army commander: **7** Phichol

ab initio **16** from the beginning

Abinoam
father: **4** Saul
son: **5** Barak

ab intra **10** from inside, from within

Abishag
comforted: **5** David

abject **3** low **4** base, mean, vile **6** sordid **7** ignoble **8** complete, cringing, hopeless, horrible, terrible, thorough, wretched **9** groveling, miserable **10** deplorable, despicable, spiritless **11** inescapable **12** contemptible

abjuration **7** refusal **8** eschewal **9** rejection **10** abnegation, disclaimer, retraction **11** repudiation **12** renunciation

abjure **6** desert, give up, recant, reject **7** abandon, disavow **8** disallow, disclaim, forswear, renounce **9** repudiate **10** relinquish

ablaze **5** afire, eager, fiery **6** aflame, alight, ardent, fervid, on fire, red-hot **7** blazing, burning, excited, fervent, flaming, flushed, glowing, ignited, zealous **8** feverish, hopped-up, in flames, turned-on **10** passionate, switched-on **11** conflagrant, impassioned, intoxicated

able **3** apt, fit **4** good **5** adept **6** adroit, expert, fitted **7** capable, equal to, learned **8** adequate, skillful, talented **9** competent, effective, efficient, masterful, practiced, qualified **10** proficient **11** experienced **12** accomplished

able-bodied **5** beefy, hardy, husky, lusty, thewy **6** brawny, hearty, robust, rugged, strong, sturdy **8** athletic, muscular, powerful, stalwart, vigorous **9** herculean, strapping, well-built **15** broad-shouldered

ablution **4** bath, wash **7** bathing, washing **8** cleaning, lavation **9** cleansing **12** purification **13** ritual washing **17** ceremonial washing

Abnaki (Wabanaki)
language family: **9** Algonkian **10** Algonquian
tribe: **6** Micmac **8** Malecite **9** Penobscot **13** Norridgewock, Passamaquoddy
location: **5** Maine **6** Canada, Quebec **7** Old Town **9** Norumbega **10** New England **12** New Brunswick

abnegate **5** forgo, waive **6** abjure, eschew, give up, refuse **7** abstain, forbear **8** renounce **9** repudiate **10** relinquish **11** deny oneself

abnegation **7** refusal **8** eschewal, giving up **9** rejection, sacrifice, surrender **10** abstinence, continence, forbearing, self-denial, temperance **11** forbearance, resignation **12** renunciation **14** relinquishment

Abner
commanded: **9** Saul's army
father: **3** Ner
cousin: **4** Saul

abnormal **3** odd **4** rare **5** queer, weird **7** bizarre, curious, deviant, strange, unusual **8** aberrant, atypical, deformed, freakish, peculiar, uncommon **9** anomalous, eccentric, grotesque, irregular, monstrous, unheard of, unnatural **10** inordinate, outlandish, unexpected **11** exceptional **12** unaccustomed **13** extraordinary **14** unconventional

abnormality **6** oddity **7** anomaly **9** aberrance, curiosity, deformity, deviation **10** aberration, perversion **11** peculiarity **12** eccentricity, idiosyncrasy, irregularity, malformation, unconformity

abode **3** pad **4** home, nest **5** house **7** address, habitat, lodging **8** domicile, dwelling **9** residence **10** habitation **13** dwelling place **14** living quarters

abolish **3** end **5** annul, erase, quash **6** cancel, repeal, revoke **7** blot out, nullify, rescind, squelch, vitiate, wipe out **8** abrogate, set aside, stamp out **9** eliminate, eradicate, extirpate, repudiate, terminate **10** annihilate, do away with, extinguish, invalidate, obliterate, put an end to **11** exterminate **18** declare null and void

abolishment **7** voiding **8** recision **9** abolition, annulment **10** extinction, rescinding, revocation **11** destruction, eradication **12** cancellation **13** doing away with, nullification

abolition **6** ending, repeal **9** annulment, vitiation **10** abrogation, extinction, rescinding, retraction, revocation **11** abolishment, dissolution, elimination, eradication, recantation, repudiation, termination **12** cancellation, invalidation **13** nullification

abominable **4** base, evil, foul, vile **5** awful, lousy **6** cursed, horrid, odious **7** hateful, heinous, hellish **8** accursed, damnable, horrible, infamous, terrible, wretched **9** abhorrent, atrocious, execrable, loathsome, miserable, repellent, repugnant, repulsive, revolting **10** deplorable, despicable, detestable, disgusting, unsuitable, villainous **11** ignominious **12** contemptible, disagreeable **13** reprehensible

abominate **4** hate **5** abhor, scorn **6** detest, loathe **7** despise **8** execrate **9** can't stand **10** recoil from, shrink from **11** can't stomach **12** be revolted by **13** find repugnant, find repulsive

abomination **4** evil, hate **6** hatred, horror, plague **7** bugbear, disgust, torment

8 anathema, aversion, disgrace, loathing 9 annoyance, antipathy, bete noire, obscenity, revulsion 10 abhorrence, affliction, defilement, repugnance 11 detestation

aboriginal 5 first, prime 6 native 7 ancient, endemic, primary 8 earliest, original, primeval 9 primitive 10 indigenous, primordial 13 autochthonous

aborigine 6 native 16 indigenous person 18 original inhabitant 19 primitive inhabitant

abort 3 end 4 fail, halt, stop 7 call off 8 miscarry 9 terminate

abortion 6 ending, fiasco 7 failure, halting 8 disaster 10 calling off 11 miscarriage, termination 16 fruitless attempt 19 unsuccessful attempt

abortive 4 vain 6 futile 7 sterile, useless 8 bootless 9 fruitless, nonviable, worthless 10 profitless, unavailing, unfruitful 11 ineffective, ineffectual, unrewarding 12 unproductive, unprofitable, unsuccessful 13 inefficacious

abound 4 gush, teem 5 swarm 6 thrive 7 run wild 8 be filled, be rich in, flourish, overflow 9 be flooded, luxuriate, spill over 10 be numerous 11 be plentiful, superabound, proliferate

abounding 4 rich, rife 5 ample 6 lavish, plenty 7 profuse, replete, teeming 8 abundant, brimming, swarming 9 bounteous, bountiful 11 overflowing, running over 14 more than enough

about 2 in, of, on 4 near 5 astir, circa 6 abroad, almost, around, circum, nearby, nearly 7 close to 9 proximate, regarding 10 concerning, in regard to 13 approximately, connected with 14 associated with

about-face 5 shift 6 switch 7 reverse 8 reversal 9 disavowal, turnabout, volte-face 10 retraction, rightabout, turnaround 11 recantation 13 change of heart 14 tergiversation

above 4 atop, over 5 aloft, north, supra 6 before, beyond, dorsal, excess, heaven, higher 7 earlier 8 in heaven, overhead, superior, upstairs 9 exceeding 10 surpassing

above all 4 most 9 most of all 10 especially 12 particularly

aboveboard 4 just, open 5 blunt, frank, moral, plain 6 candid, direct, honest, public, square 7 artless, ethical, sincere, upright 8 revealed, straight, truthful, virtuous 9 disclosed, guileless, ingenuous, righteous 10 forthright, foursquare 11 unconcealed 12 on the up and up, plain-dealing, out in the open 13 square-dealing, undissembling 15 straightforward 16 straight-shooting

ab ovo 10 from the egg 16 from the beginning

abracadabra 5 charm, magic, spell 6 voodoo 7 sorcery 8 exorcism 10 hocus-pocus, invocation, magic spell, mumbo-jumbo, open sesame, witchcraft 11 incantation

abrade 3 rub 4 file, fray, fret, rasp 5 chafe, erode, grate, grind 6 scrape 8 irritate, wear down

Abraham
former name: 5 Abram
founded: 12 Hebrew nation
father: 5 Terah
wife: 5 Sarah, Sarai 7 Keturah
brother: 5 Haran, Nahor
son: 5 Isaac 6 Midian 7 Ishmael
nephew: 3 Lot
birthplace: 15 Ur of the Chaldees
received: 17 law of circumcision
sacrificed Isaac at: 6 Moriah
burial place: 6 Hebron
tomb buried in: 9 Machpelah

Abraham Lincoln
author: 12 Carl Sandburg

Abraham's bosom 6 heaven

Abram *see* 7 Abraham

Abramovitz, Max
architect of: 13 ALCOA Building (Pittsburgh PA, with Wallace Harrison) 15 Avery Fisher Hall (Lincoln Center NYC)

Abrams, Creighton
served in: 4 WWII 10 Vietnam War
rank: 16 army chief of staff

abrasion 6 lesion, scrape 7 chafing, erosion, grating, rubbing, scratch 8 friction, scouring, scraping 11 excoriation, scraped spot

abrasive 5 harsh, nasty, rough, sharp 6 biting, coarse 7 caustic, chafing, cutting, galling, grating, hurtful, rasping 8 annoying 10 irritating 11 excoriating 16 grinding material, scouring material, scraping material

abreast 6 in rank 7 aligned 10 side by side 11 in alignment

abridge 3 cut 4 trim 5 limit 6 digest, lessen, reduce 7 curtail, cut down, shorten 8 compress, condense, decrease, diminish, pare down, restrict, take away, truncate 9 scale down, telescope 10 abbreviate

abridgment 6 digest 8 decrease 9 lessening, reduction, restraint 10 diminution, limitation, truncation 11 curtailment, diminishing, restriction 12 abbreviation, condensation 13 condensed form, shortened form

abroad 3 out 4 rife 5 astir, forth 7 at large, outside 8 overseas 9 all around 10 out of doors 13 in circulation, out of the house, round and about 15 making the rounds, out in the open air, out of the country

abrogate 3 end 4 junk, undo, void 5 annul, quash 6 abjure, cancel, negate, recall, repeal, revoke 7 abolish, nullify, rescind, retract, reverse, vitiate 8 dissolve, override, renounce, set aside, throw out, withdraw 9 repudiate, terminate 10 do away with, invalidate, put an end to 11 countermand

abrogation 6 repeal 7 junking 8 recision, reneging, reversal 9 abolition, annulment 10 rescinding, retraction, revocation 11 abolishment, going back on, repudiation 12 cancellation 13 nullification

abrupt 4 curt, rude 5 blunt, brisk, crisp, gruff, hasty, quick, rapid, rough, sharp, sheer, short, steep, swift 6 sudden 7 brusque, uncivil 8 impolite 9 impulsive 10 unexpected, unforeseen, ungracious 11 precipitate, precipitous, unannounced, unlooked for 12 discourteous 13 instantaneous, unanticipated, unceremonious

Absalom
father: 5 David
mother: 6 Maacah
sister: 5 Tamar
brother: 7 Solomon 8 Adonijah
half-brother: 5 Amnon

defeated at: **6** Gilead
killed by: **4** Joab

Absalom, Absalom!
author: **15** William Faulkner
character: **5** Henry **6** Judith **10** Charles Bon **13** Rosa Coldfield **14** Quentin Compson, Shreve McCannon **16** Goodhue Coldfield **19** Colonel Thomas Sutpen **20** Ellen Coldfield Sutpen

Absalom and Achitophel
author: **10** John Dryden

abscond **3** fly **4** flee, skip **5** split **6** escape, run off, vanish **7** make off, run away, take off **8** steal off **9** disappear, steal away **10** take flight

absence **3** cut **4** lack, want **6** dearth **7** truancy **8** scarcity **10** deficiency, scantiness **11** absenteeism, nonpresence **12** nonexistence **13** insufficiency, nonappearance, nonattendance **14** unavailability

Absence of Malice
director: **13** Sydney Pollack
based on story by: **11** Kurt Luedtke
cast: **10** Bob Balaban, Paul Newman, Sally Field **13** Melinda Dillon
setting: **5** Miami

absent **3** cut, out **4** away, gone **5** blank, empty, vague **6** dreamy, musing, truant, vacant **7** faraway, missing, out of it, removed, unaware **8** heedless, keep away, stay away, tuned out **9** not appear, not show up, oblivious **10** distracted, nonpresent, not present, out to lunch, play truant, unthinking **11** inattentive, preoccupied, unconscious **12** nonattendant

absentee **6** no show, truant **10** nonpresent **11** nonattendee, nonpresence **12** nonattendant **13** nonattendance

absenteeism **5** hooky **7** truancy **11** nonpresence **13** nonappearance **19** absence without cause

absent-minded **5** blank, vague **6** dreamy **9** oblivious **10** abstracted, distracted **11** preoccupied **14** out in left field **17** out of it

Absent Without Leave
author: **12** Heinrich Boll

absinthe
ingredient: **8** licorice, wormwood **9** aromatics, star anise
color: **11** yellow green
substitute: **4** Ouzo **6** Pastis, Pernod **8** Anisette

absolute **4** full, pure, real, sure **5** sheer, total, utter **7** certain, genuine, perfect, supreme **8** complete, decisive, definite, outright, positive, reliable, thorough **9** confirmed, out-and-out, unbounded, unlimited **10** conclusive, consummate, infallible, undeniable **11** unequivocal, unmitigated, unqualified **12** unrestrained, unrestricted **13** unadulterated, unconditional **14** unquestionable **17** through and through

Absolute, Sir Anthony
character in: **9** The Rivals
author: **8** Sheridan

absolutely **5** truly **6** indeed, really, wholly **7** utterly **8** entirely **9** certainly, decidedly **10** completely, definitely, positively, thoroughly **11** indubitably, undoubtedly **13** unequivocally **14** unquestionably **15** unconditionally **17** without limitation

absolution **5** mercy **6** pardon **7** amnesty, release **9** acquittal, clearance, quittance, remission **10** indulgence, liberation **11** deliverance, exculpation, exoneration, forgiveness, vindication **12** dispensation

absolve **4** free **5** clear, loose **6** acquit, exempt, pardon, shrive **7** deliver, forgive, release, set free **9** discharge, exculpate, exonerate, vindicate **10** excuse from **13** find not guilty, judge innocent

absolved **5** freed **6** exempt, spared **7** cleared, excused **8** forgiven, pardoned, released, relieved **9** acquitted **10** discharged, exonerated, vindicated **13** found innocent

absorb **3** fix **5** rivet **6** arrest, digest, engage, enwrap, ingest, occupy, soak up, suck up, take up **7** consume, drink in, engross, immerse **8** sponge up **9** fascinate, preoccupy, swallow up **10** assimilate **11** incorporate

absorbed **4** deep **8** immersed, involved, soaked up, sucked up **9** blotted up, engrossed

absorbent **6** porous, spongy **7** osmotic, thirsty **8** bibulous, pervious **9** permeable **10** absorptive, penetrable **12** assimilative

absorbing **8** engaging, exciting **9** thrilling **10** engrossing, intriguing **11** captivating, fascinating, interesting

abstain **5** avoid, forgo **6** desist, eschew, refuse, resist **7** decline, forbear, refrain

abstainer **3** dry **7** ascetic **10** nondrinker, self-denier, teetotaler

abstemious **3** dry **5** sober **7** ascetic, austere, sparing, spartan **8** teetotal **9** abstinent, continent, temperate **10** forbearing **11** abstentious, self-denying, straitlaced, teetotaling **12** nonindulgent **15** self-disciplined

abstention **7** refusal **8** eschewal **9** avoidance, desisting, eschewing **10** abstaining, refraining, resistance **11** forbearance, holding back **13** nonindulgence **14** denying oneself **16** nonparticipation

abstinence **8** chastity, sobriety **10** abstention, continence, discipline, self-denial, temperance **11** forbearance, self-control **13** nonindulgence, self-restraint

abstinent **3** dry **5** sober **6** chaste **8** celibate, virginal **9** continent **10** abstemious, forbearing

abstract **4** take **5** brief **6** arcane, digest, precis, remote, remove, resume, subtle **7** abridge, extract, general, isolate, obscure, outline, summary, take out **8** abstruse, compress, condense, esoteric, profound, separate, synopsis, withdraw **9** imaginary, recondite, summarize, synopsize, theoretic, unapplied, visionary **10** abridgment, conceptual, dissociate, indefinite, intangible **11** generalized, impractical, nonspecific, theoretical **12** condensation, hypothetical, intellectual **14** recapitulation

abstruse **4** deep **6** arcane, remote, subtle **7** complex, obscure **8** abstract, esoteric, profound, puzzling **9** enigmatic, recondite **10** perplexing **11** complicated **12** unfathomable **16** incomprehensible

absurd **4** wild **5** crazy, funny, inane, kooky, silly **6** screwy, stupid **7** asinine, comical, foolish, idiotic **8** farcical **9** illogical, laughable, ludicrous, senseless **10** irrational, ridiculous **11** nonsensical **12** preposterous, unreasonable

absurdity **6** drivel, idiocy **7** fallacy, inanity **8** delusion, nonsense **9** asininity, falsehood, silliness **10** buffoonery **11** comicalness, foolishness

13 irrationality 14 ridiculousness 15 unbelievability 16 unreasonableness

Absyrtus *see* 8 Apsyrtus

Abu Dhabi
capital of: 18 United Arab Emirates

Abuja
capital of: 7 Nigeria

abundance 4 glut, heap 5 flood 6 bounty, excess, plenty, wealth 7 surfeit, surplus 8 plethora, richness 9 plenitude, profusion, repletion 10 cornucopia 11 copiousness, full measure, sufficiency

abundant 4 rich, rife 5 ample 6 enough, galore, lavish, plenty 7 copious, profuse, replete, teeming 8 brimming, prolific 9 abounding, bounteous, bountiful, luxuriant 10 sufficient

ab urbe condita 24 from the founding of the city

abuse 4 harm, hurt, slur 5 curse, scold 6 berate, carp at, defame, deride, ill-use, injure, injury, insult, malign, misuse, rail at, revile, tirade, vilify 7 assault, bawl out, beating, carping, censure, cruelty, cursing, exploit, harming, insults, railing, slander, torment, upbraid 8 badmouth, belittle, berating, denounce, derision, diatribe, ill-treat, maltreat, mistreat, reproach, ridicule, scolding, sneering, torments 9 castigate, criticism, criticize, denigrate, disparage, excoriate, invective 10 belittling, defamation, impose upon, imposition, oppression, speak ill of, upbraiding 11 castigation 12 exploitation, maltreatment, mistreatment, vilification 13 disparagement, misemployment, tongue-lashing 14 inveigh against, misapplication 15 take advantage of

abusive 4 rude, vile 5 cruel, gross, harsh 7 harmful, hurtful, obscene 8 critical, improper, reviling, scornful 9 injurious, insulting, maligning, offensive, vilifying 10 censorious, defamatory, derogatory, scurrilous, slanderous 11 acrimonious, castigating, deprecatory, disparaging, foulmouthed 12 vituperative

abusive word 5 curse 6 insult 7 epithet 9 blasphemy, expletive, invective, obscenity

abut 4 join, meet 5 touch 6 adjoin, border

abutment 4 prop, stay 5 brace, union 7 contact, meeting, support 8 buttress, junction, shoulder, touching 9 adjacency

abutting 6 next to 7 joining, meeting 8 adjacent, touching 9 bordering 10 contiguous, juxtaposed 12 conterminous

abysmal 4 deep, vast 7 endless, extreme, immense 8 complete, enormous, profound, thorough, unending 9 boundless 10 bottomless, incredible, stupendous 12 unfathomable, unbelievable, unimaginable

abyss 4 gulf, void 5 depth, gorge, gully, nadir 7 fissure 8 crevasse 9 vast chasm 13 bottomless pit

Abyssinia *see* 8 Ethiopia

Acacallis
father: 5 Minos
mother: 8 Pasiphae
son: 11 Amphithemis

acacia
family: 6 legume 11 leguminosae
also called: 5 thorn 6 mimosa, wattle

academic 4 moot 6 remote, school 7 bookish, erudite, general, learned 8 abstract, educated, pedantic, studious 9 scholarly 10 collegiate, scholastic, university 11 conjectural, educational, liberal-arts, presumptive, speculative, theoretical 12 hypothetical, ivory-towered, nontechnical, not practical 13 nonvocational, suppositional 14 nonspecialized 18 college-preparatory

Academus
origin: 8 Arcadian
owned: 6 estate
located in: 6 Athens
served as meeting place for: 12 philosophers

Academy Award ***see box***

Acanthopholis
type: 8 dinosaur 10 ornithopod

Acastus
member of: 9 Argonauts
father: 6 Pelias
mother: 10 Phylomache
sister: 8 Alcestis
wife: 8 Cretheis
daughter: 7 Sterope 8 Laodemia, Sthenele

Acawai, Akawai
language family: 7 Cariban
location: 7 Guianas 12 South America

Accad
kingdom of: 6 Nimrod
location: 13 Plain of Shinar
captured by: 6 Sargon (I)

Acca Larentia
form: 7 goddess
corresponds to: 6 Dea Dia

accede 5 admit, grant 6 accept, permit 7 abide by, agree to, approve, concede, defer to, endorse, inherit, yield to 8 assent to, submit to 9 acquiesce, conform to, consent to, succeed to 10 comply with, concur with 11 acknowledge, subscribe to, surrender to

accede to the throne 4 keep 5 claim, usurp 6 ascend 7 possess, succeed 8 take over 9 be crowned 15 ascend the throne

accelerando
music: 15 becoming quicker

accelerate 4 rush, spur 5 hurry, impel 6 hasten, step up 7 advance, augment, further, promote, quicken, speed up 8 expedite 9 intensify 10 facilitate, to go faster 11 pick up speed, precipitate

accelerator 3 gas 4 goad, prod, spur 8 gas pedal 13 encouragement

accent 4 hint, tone 5 drawl, touch, twang 6 detail, stress 7 feature 8 emphasis, ornament, tonality, trimming 9 adornment, emphasize, highlight, punctuate, spotlight, underline 10 accentuate, inflection, intonation, modulation, underscore 11 enunciation 12 articulation 13 embellishment, primary stress, pronunciation

accentuate 6 accent, stress 7 feature, point up 9 emphasize, punctuate, underline 10 underscore

accentuation 6 accent, stress 8 emphasis

accept 3 buy 4 avow, bear 5 admit 6 assume 7 agree to, fall for, swallow 8 accede to, assent to 9 consent to, undertake 11 acknowledge, go along with

acceptable 4 fair, good, so-so 6 proper, worthy 8 adequate, passable, suitable 9 agreeable, allowable, tolerable 10 admissible 12 satisfactory

acceptable person
Latin: 12 persona grata

acceptance 6 belief, taking 7 consent, receipt 8 approval, sanction 9 accepting, agreement, receiving, reception 10 concession, permission

Academy Award
also called: 5 Oscar
1927-28:
actor: **12** Emil Jannings
actress: **11** Janet Gaynor
director: **12** Frank Borzage **14** Lewis Milestone
picture: **5** Wings
1928-29:
actor: **12** Warner Baxter
actress: **12** Mary Pickford
director: **10** Frank Lloyd
picture: **14** Broadway Melody
1929-30:
actor: **12** George Arliss
actress: **12** Norma Shearer
director: **14** Lewis Milestone
picture: **25** All Quiet on the Western Front
1930-31:
actor: **15** Lionel Barrymore
actress: **13** Marie Dressler
director: **12** Norman Taurog
picture: **8** Cimarron
1931-32:
actor: **12** Fredric March
actress: **10** Helen Hayes
director: **12** Frank Borzage
picture: **10** Grand Hotel
1932-33:
actor: **15** Charles Laughton
actress: **16** Katharine Hepburn
director: **10** Frank Lloyd
picture: **9** Cavalcade
1934:
actor: **10** Clark Gable
actress: **16** Claudette Colbert
director: **10** Frank Capra
picture: **18** It Happened One Night
1935:
actor: **14** Victor McLaglen
actress: **10** Bette Davis
director: **8** John Ford
picture: **17** Mutiny on the Bounty
1936:
actor: **8** Paul Muni
actress: **11** Luise Rainer
director: **10** Frank Capra
picture: **16** The Great Ziegfeld
1937:
actor: **12** Spencer Tracy
actress: **11** Luise Rainer
director: **10** Leo McCarey
picture: **15** Life of Emile Zola
1938:
actor: **12** Spencer Tracy
actress: **10** Bette Davis
director: **10** Frank Capra
picture: **20** You Can't Take It with You
1939:
actor: **11** Robert Donat
actress: **11** Vivien Leigh
director: **13** Victor Fleming
picture: **15** Gone with the Wind
1940:
actor: **12** James Stewart
actress: **12** Ginger Rogers
director: **8** John Ford
picture: **7** Rebecca
1941:
actor: **10** Gary Cooper
actress: **12** Joan Fontaine
director: **8** John Ford
picture: **19** How Green Was My Valley
1942:
actor: **11** James Cagney
actress: **11** Greer Garson
director: **12** William Wyler
picture: **10** Mrs Miniver
1943:
actor: **9** Paul Lukas
actress: **13** Jennifer Jones
director: **13** Michael Curtiz
picture: **10** Casablanca
1944:
actor: **10** Bing Crosby
actress: **13** Ingrid Bergman
director: **10** Leo McCarey
picture: **10** Going My Way
1945:
actor: **10** Ray Milland
actress: **12** Joan Crawford
director: **11** Billy Wilder
picture: **14** The Lost Weekend
1946:
actor: **12** Fredric March
actress: **17** Olivia de Haviland
director: **12** William Wyler
picture: **22** The Best Years of Our Lives
1947:
actor: **12** Ronald Colman
actress: **12** Loretta Young
director: **9** Elia Kazan
picture: **19** Gentleman's Agreement
1948:
actor: **15** Laurence Olivier
actress: **9** Jane Wyman
director: **10** John Huston
picture: **6** Hamlet
1949:
actor: **17** Broderick Crawford
actress: **17** Olivia de Haviland
director: **17** Joseph L Mankiewicz
picture: **14** All the King's Men
1950:
actor: **10** Jose Ferrer
actress: **12** Judy Holliday
director: **17** Joseph L Mankiewicz
picture: **11** All About Eve
1951:
actor: **14** Humphrey Bogart
actress: **11** Vivien Leigh
director: **13** George Stevens
picture: **17** An American in Paris
1952:
actor: **10** Gary Cooper
actress: **12** Shirley Booth
director: **8** John Ford
picture: **19** Greatest Show on Earth
1953:
actor: **13** William Holden
actress: **13** Audrey Hepburn
director: **13** Fred Zinnemann
picture: **18** From Here to Eternity
1954:
actor: **12** Marlon Brando
actress: **10** Grace Kelly
director: **9** Elia Kazan
picture: **15** On the Waterfront
1955:
actor: **14** Ernest Borgnine
actress: **11** Anna Magnani
director: **11** Delbert Mann
picture: **5** Marty
1956:
actor: **10** Yul Brynner
actress: **13** Ingrid Bergman
director: **13** George Stevens
picture: **26** Around the World in Eighty Days
1957:
actor: **12** Alec Guinness
actress: **14** Joanne Woodward
director: **9** David Lean
picture: **23** The Bridge on the River Kwai
1958:
actor: **10** David Niven
actress: **12** Susan Hayward
director: **16** Vincente Minnelli
picture: **4** Gigi
1959:
actor: **14** Charlton Heston
actress: **14** Simone Signoret
director: **12** William Wyler
picture: **6** Ben-Hur
1960:
actor: **13** Burt Lancaster
actress: **15** Elizabeth Taylor
director: **11** Billy Wilder
picture: **12** The Apartment
1961:
actor: **16** Maximilian Schell
actress: **11** Sophia Loren
director: **10** Robert Wise **13** Jerome Robbins
picture: **13** West Side Story

(*continued*)

Academy Award (*continued*)
1962:
actor: **11** Gregory Peck
actress: **12** Anne Bancroft
director: **9** David Lean
picture: **16** Lawrence of Arabia
1963:
actor: **13** Sidney Poitier
actress: **12** Patricia Neal
director: **14** Tony Richardson
picture: **8** Tom Jones
1964:
actor: **11** Rex Harrison
actress: **12** Julie Andrews
director: **11** George Cukor
picture: **10** My Fair Lady
1965:
actor: **9** Lee Marvin
actress: **13** Julie Christie
director: **10** Robert Wise
picture: **15** The Sound of Music
1966:
actor: **12** Paul Scofield
actress: **15** Elizabeth Taylor
director: **13** Fred Zinnemann
picture: **17** A Man for All Seasons
1967:
actor: **10** Rod Steiger
actress: **16** Katharine Hepburn
director: **11** Mike Nichols
picture: **19** In the Heat of the Night
1968:
actor: **14** Cliff Robertson
actress: **15** Barbra Streisand and **16** Katharine Hepburn
director: **12** Sir Carol Reed
picture: **6** Oliver!
1969:
actor: **9** John Wayne
actress: **11** Maggie Smith
director: **15** John Schlesinger
picture: **14** Midnight Cowboy
1970:
actor: **12** George C Scott
actress: **13** Glenda Jackson
director: **17** Franklin Schaffner
picture: **6** Patton
1971:
actor: **11** Gene Hackman
actress: **9** Jane Fonda
director: **15** William Friedkin
picture: **19** The French Connection
1972:
actor: **12** Marlon Brando
actress: **11** Liza Minnelli
director: **8** Bob Fosse
picture: **12** The Godfather
1973:
actor: **10** Jack Lemmon
actress: **13** Glenda Jackson
director: **13** George Roy Hill
picture: **8** The Sting
1974:
actor: **9** Art Carney
actress: **12** Ellen Burstyn
director: **18** Francis Ford Coppola
picture: **12** The Godfather (Part II)
1975:
actor: **13** Jack Nicholson
actress: **14** Louise Fletcher
director: **11** Milos Forman
picture: **25** One Flew Over the Cuckoo's Nest
1976:
actor: **10** Peter Finch
actress: **11** Faye Dunaway
director: **13** John G Avildsen
picture: **5** Rocky
1977:
actor: **15** Richard Dreyfuss
actress: **11** Diane Keaton
director: **10** Woody Allen
picture: **9** Annie Hall
1978:
actor: **9** Jon Voight
actress: **9** Jane Fonda
director: **13** Michael Cimino
picture: **13** The Deer Hunter
1979:
actor: **13** Dustin Hoffman
actress: **10** Sally Field
director: **12** Robert Benton
picture: **14** Kramer vs Kramer
1980:
actor: **12** Robert De Niro
actress: **11** Sissy Spacek
director: **13** Robert Redford
picture: **14** Ordinary People
1981:
actor: **10** Henry Fonda
actress: **16** Katharine Hepburn
director: **12** Warren Beatty
picture: **14** Chariots of Fire
1982:
actor: **11** Ben Kingsley
actress: **11** Meryl Streep
director: **19** Richard Attenborough
picture: **6** Gandhi
1983:
actor: **12** Robert Duvall
actress: **15** Shirley MacLaine
director: **12** James L Brooks
picture: **17** Terms of Endearment
1984:
actor: **14** F Murray Abraham
actress: **10** Sally Field
director: **11** Milos Forman
picture: **7** Amadeus
1985:
actor: **11** William Hurt
actress: **13** Geraldine Page
director: **13** Sydney Pollack
picture: **11** Out of Africa
1986:
actor: **10** Paul Newman
actress: **12** Marlee Matlin
director: **11** Oliver Stone
picture: **7** Platoon
1987:
actor: **14** Michael Douglas
actress: **4** Cher
director: **18** Bernardo Bertolucci
picture: **14** The Last Emperor

11 affirmation, approbation, endorsement, recognition **12** acquiescence, confirmation **14** acknowledgment **15** stamp of approval

accepted **5** usual **6** common, normal **7** regular **8** approved, standard **9** confirmed, customary, universal **10** acceptable, agreed upon **11** established, time-honored **12** acknowledged, conventional

access **3** way **4** path, road **5** entry **6** avenue, course, entree **7** gateway, passage **8** entrance **10** admittance, an approach, passageway

accessible **5** handy, ready **6** at hand, nearby, on hand **8** possible **9** available, reachable **10** attainable, obtainable **11** within reach **12** approachable

accession **7** seizure **9** induction **10** arrogation, assumption, investment, taking over, usurpation **11** inheritance **12** inauguration, installation

accessory **4** plus **6** accent, cohort, detail **7** adjunct, partner **8** addition **9** adornment, assistant, associate, auxiliary, colleague, component, extension **10** accomplice, attachment, complement, decoration, supplement **11** confederate, contributor **13** accompaniment

accident **4** fate, luck **5** crash, fluke, wreck **6** chance, mishap **7** smashup **8** fortuity **9** collision, mischance **10** misfortune **11** good fortune, serendipity **12** happenstance, misadventure

accidental **6** chance, random **9** haphazard, unplanned, unwitting **10** fortuitous, incidental, unexpected, unforeseen **11** inadvertent **12** uncalculated **13** serendipitous, unanticipated, unintentional **14** unpremeditated

acclaim **4** hail, laud **5** cheer, exalt, extol, honor, kudos **6** bravos, praise, salute **7** applaud, commend, ovation **8** applause, cheering, eulogize, plaudits **9** celebrate, rejoicing **10** compliment, enthusiasm **11** acclamation, endorsement

acclamation **6** cheers, homage **7** acclaim, hurrahs, ovation, tribute **8** cheering, hosannas, plaudits **9** adulation **10** salutation **11** approbation

acclimate **5** adapt, inure **6** adjust **8** accustom **9** get used to, habituate, reconcile **11** accommodate **16** become seasoned to

acclimation **9** seasoning **10** adaptation, adjustment **11** habituation

acclimatize **5** adapt **6** attune **8** accustom **9** acclimate, get used to

acclivity **4** hill, rise **6** ascent **9** elevation **11** upward slope

accolade **5** award, honor, prize **6** praise, trophy **7** acclaim, tribute **8** citation **10** admiration, compliment, decoration **11** recognition, testimonial **12** commendation

accommodate **3** aid, fit **4** help, hold **5** adapt, board, house, lodge, put up **6** adjust, assist, billet, modify, oblige, supply **7** bed down, conform, contain, furnish, provide, quarter, shelter **8** accustom **9** acclimate, entertain, get used to, harmonize, lend a hand, reconcile

accommodating **4** kind **6** polite **7** helpful **8** gracious, obliging, yielding **9** courteous **10** hospitable, neighborly **11** considerate **12** conciliatory

accommodation **5** rooms **7** concord, housing **8** lodgings, quarters **9** agreement **10** adjustment, compromise, settlement **12** arrangements **14** reconciliation

accommodative **8** friendly **9** appeasing, pacifying, placatory **10** mollifying **11** peacemaking, reconciling **12** conciliatory

accompaniment **6** escort **7** support **8** ornament **9** accessory, adornment **10** incidental

accompany **5** guard, usher **6** attend, back up, convoy, escort, follow **7** conduct, support **8** chaperon

accomplice **4** aide, ally **5** crony **6** cohort, helper, stooge **7** abettor, comrade, partner **8** henchman, sidekick **9** accessory, assistant, associate, colleague, supporter **11** confederate, participant, subordinate **12** collaborator **13** co-conspirator **14** partner-in-crime

accomplish **2** do **6** attain, finish **7** achieve, execute, fulfill, get done, perform, produce, realize **8** carry out, complete, expedite, knock off **9** succeed at **10** bring about

accomplished **3** apt **4** able, deft, fine **6** adroit, expert, gifted, proved, proven **7** capable, eminent, skilled **8** accepted, effected, existing, finished, masterly, polished, realized, seasoned, skillful, talented **9** brilliant, completed, concluded, practiced, qualified **10** cultivated, proficient **11** consummated, established, experienced, well-trained

accomplished fact
French: **12** fait accompli

accomplishment **3** act **4** deed, feat, gift **5** skill **6** talent **7** exploit, success, triumph, victory **9** execution **10** attainment, capability **11** achievement, carrying out, culmination, fulfillment, proficiency, realization, tour de force **12** consummation

accomplishments
Latin: **9** res gestae

accord **4** cede, give, jibe **5** agree, allow, award, grant, match, tally **6** bestow, concur, render, square, tender, unison **7** concede, concert, conform, harmony, present, rapport **8** be in tune, bequeath, sympathy **9** agreement, harmonize, unanimity, vouchsafe **10** accordance, be in unison, comply with, conformity, consonance, correspond, uniformity **11** concurrence, go along with **19** mutual understanding

accordant **4** like **7** similar **8** parallel **10** consistent **11** homogeneous

accordingly **2** so **4** ergo, then, thus **5** hence **6** thence, whence **8** suitably **9** as a result, therefore, wherefore, whereupon **11** conformably, in due course, in which case **12** consequently **15** correspondingly

according to
Latin: **8** secundum

according to fact
Latin: **7** ex facto

according to form
Latin: **8** pro forma

according to law
Latin: **6** de jure

accost **3** nab **4** hail, halt, stop **5** greet **6** call to, salute, waylay **7** address, solicit **8** approach, confront **10** buttonhole **11** proposition

accouchement **10** childbirth **11** confinement

accoucheur **12** obstetrician **25** assistant during childbirth

accoucheuse **7** midwife **25** assistant during childbirth

account **3** use **4** deem, hold, note, rank, rate, sake, tale **5** basis, books, cause, count, gauge, honor, judge, merit, score, story, think, value, weigh, worth **6** esteem, import, reason, reckon, record, regard, report, repute, view as **7** believe, clarify, dignity, explain, grounds, history, justify, recital, version **8** appraise, consider, estimate, megillah, standing **9** calculate, chronicle, narration, narrative, statement **10** accounting, commentary, illuminate, importance **11** bookkeeping, consequence, description, distinction, enumeration, explanation **12** significance **13** consideration **15** financial record **18** financial statement
French: **11** compte rendu

accountable **6** guilty, liable **7** at fault, to blame **8** beholden, culpable **9** obligated **10** answerable, chargeable **11** blameworthy, responsible

accountant **3** CPA **7** actuary, auditor **10** bookkeeper **25** certified public accountant

account for **6** excuse **7** explain, justify **9** answer for

accounting **5** cause **6** answer, motive, reason **7** warrant **10** motivation **11** explanation

account rendered
French: 11 compte rendu

accoutrements 4 gear 7 apparel 8 supplies 9 equipment, trappings 11 accessories, furnishings 13 paraphernalia

Accra, Akkra
capital of: 5 Ghana

accredit 6 assign, credit 7 ascribe, certify, empower, endorse, license 8 sanction 9 attribute, authorize, guarantee 10 commission 19 officially recognize 22 furnish with credentials

accredited 8 ascribed, assigned, endorsed, licensed 9 authentic, certified, empowered 10 attributed, authorized, recognized, sanctioned 12 commissioned 20 officially recognized

accretion 4 rise 6 growth 7 accrual 8 addition, increase 9 expansion, extension, increment 10 supplement 11 enlargement 12 accumulation, augmentation 13 amplification

accrue 4 grow 5 add up, amass 6 pile up 7 build up, collect 8 increase 10 accumulate

accumulate 4 grow 5 amass, hoard 6 accrue, garner, gather, heap up, pile up, save up 7 collect, store up 8 assemble, cumulate 9 aggregate 10 congregate 14 gather together

accumulation 4 heap, mass, pile 5 hoard, stack, stock, store 6 pile-up, supply 7 accrual 8 amassing, hoarding 9 acquiring, gathering, stockpile 10 assemblage, collecting, collection 11 aggregation 13 agglomerating 14 conglomeration

accuracy 5 truth 6 verity 8 fidelity 9 exactness, precision 10 exactitude 11 correctness 12 accurateness, faithfulness

accurate 4 true 5 exact, right 7 careful, correct, perfect, precise 8 faithful, truthful, unerring 9 authentic, faultless 10 meticulous, scrupulous 11 punctilious 12 without error

accursed 4 base, foul, vile 6 cussed, horrid, odious 7 hellish 8 damnable, horrible, infamous 9 abhorrent, atrocious, execrable, loathsome, revolting 10 abominable, despicable, detestable, disgusting 12 contemptible

accusation 6 charge 8 citation 9 complaint 10 allegation, imputation, indictment 11 insinuation 13 incrimination

accuse 4 cite 5 blame 6 charge, indict 7 arraign, upbraid 8 reproach 10 take to task 13 call to account 22 lodge a complaint against

accuser 8 attacker 11 complainant 13 finger pointer

accustomed 3 set 5 fixed, prone, trite, usual 6 cliche, common, inured, normal, used to, wonted 7 general, given to, regular, routine 8 everyday, expected, familiar, habitual, hardened, ordinary, seasoned 9 customary, hackneyed, ingrained, prevalent, well-known 10 acclimated, habituated, prevailing 11 commonplace, established 12 conventional, familiarized

ace 2 A-1 3 top 4 star 5 crack, super 6 expert, master, tip-top, victor, winner 8 champion, medalist, terrific, top-rated 9 excellent, first-rate, headliner 10 first-class 11 crackerjack, outstanding 12 front-ranking

Aceldama
means: 12 field of blood
purchased by: 5 Judas

Acerbas *see* 8 Sychaeus

acerbity 7 acidity, sarcasm 8 acridity, acrimony, pungency, sourness, tartness 9 nastiness, sharpness 10 bitterness 11 astringency, brusqueness 12 irascibility

aces 2 A-1 4 fine, tops 5 great, prime, super 6 grade-A, superb, tip-top 8 peerless, superior, terrific, top-notch 9 excellent, first-rate, marvelous, matchless, superfine, wonderful 10 first-class, tremendous 11 outstanding, superlative 13 extraordinary

Acesius
epithet of: 6 Apollo
means: 6 healer

Acessamenus
origin: 8 Thracian
mentioned in: 5 Iliad
form: 4 king

Acetes
origin: 6 Lydian
duty: 8 helmsman
protected: 8 Dionysus

Achaeus
founder of: 6 Achaea
father: 6 Xuthus
mother: 6 Creusa
brother: 3 Ion

Achan
punishment: 13 stoned to death

Acharnians
author: 12 Aristophanes
character: 7 Demigod 8 Lamachus 11 Dikaiopolis

Achates
mentioned in: 6 Aeneid
companion of: 6 Aeneas
position: 11 armorbearer

ache 4 hurt, need, pain, pang, want 5 covet, crave, mourn, smart, throb, yearn 6 be sore, desire, grieve, hanker, hunger, lament, sorrow, suffer, twinge 7 agonize, long for 8 soreness 10 discomfort

Achech
origin: 8 Egyptian
form: 8 creature
body of: 4 lion
wings of: 4 bird

Achelous
form: 3 god
habitat: 5 river
father: 7 Oceanus
mother: 6 Tethys
daughter: 6 Sirens 8 Castalia 10 Callirrhoe
defeated by: 8 Hercules
struggled over: 8 Deianira

Acheron
river in: 5 Hades
ferryman: 6 Charon
carries: 4 dead

Acheson, Dean
author of: 20 Present at the Creation

a cheval 7 by horse 11 on horseback

achieve 2 do 3 get, win 4 earn, gain 5 reach 6 attain, effect, finish, obtain 7 acquire, fulfill, procure, realize 8 arrive at, carry out, complete, dispatch 9 succeed in 10 accomplish, bring about, effectuate 11 bring to pass

achievement 3 act 4 coup, deed, fear 5 skill 6 effort 7 command, exploit, mastery 9 expertise 10 attainment 11 acquirement, fulfillment, realization, tour de force 14 accomplishment

achieve recognition 6 arrive, make it 7 succeed 8 make good 10 be somebody 11 reach the top

Achilles
mentioned in: 5 Iliad
father: 6 Peleus
mother: 6 Thetis
foster father: 7 Phoenix
grandfather: 6 Aeacus
teacher: 6 Chiron

charioteer: **9** Automedon
friend: **9** Patroclus
warrior in: **9** Trojan War
vulnerability: **4** heel
killed: **6** Hector
killed by: **5** Paris

Achish
king of: **4** Gath
gave refuge to: **5** David

Achomawi
language family: **5** Hokan
location: **8** Pit River **10** California **12** Shasta County
related to: **8** Atsugewi

Achsah
father: **5** Caleb
grandfather: **9** Jephunneh
husband: **7** Othniel

acid **4** sour, tart **5** acrid, harsh, nasty, sharp **6** biting, bitter, ironic **7** acerbic, caustic, crabbed, cutting, pungent **8** scalding, scathing, stinging, vinegary **9** acidulous, irascible, sarcastic, satirical, vitriolic **10** astringent, vinegarish **11** acrimonious

acidity **8** acerbity, pungency, sourness, tartness **9** sharpness **10** bitterness **11** astringency **13** nonalkalinity

Acis
lover: **7** Galatea
killed by: **10** Polyphemus

Acis and Galatea
opera by: **6** Handel

Acis et Galatee
opera by: **5** Lully

acknowledge **3** own **5** admit, allow, grant, yield **6** accede, accept, answer, assent, concur **7** concede, confess, own up to, reply to **8** call upon, thank for **9** recognize, respond to

acknowledged **7** acceded **8** accepted, admitted, answered, called on, conceded **9** replied to **10** agreed upon, called upon, recognized, thanked for **11** established, responded to

acknowledgment **5** reply **6** answer, credit, thanks **8** response **9** admission, gratitude **10** concession, confession **11** affirmation, recognition **12** appreciation, recognizance

acme **4** apex, peak **5** crest, crown **6** apogee, climax, height, heyday, summit, zenith **8** pinnacle **9** flowering, high point **11** culmination **12** highest point
Latin: **11** ne plus ultra

Acmon
companion: **8** Diomedes
changed into: **4** bird
defied: **9** Aphrodite

acolyte **3** fan **6** helper, novice **7** admirer, devotee, groupie **8** adherent, altar boy, follower **9** assistant, attendant

Acoma
language family: **6** Pueblo
location: **3** Ako **4** Acus **8** Valencia **9** New Mexico
noted for: **7** pottery

acorn
from: **3** oak
shape: **8** balanoid

a couvert **9** sheltered **10** under cover

acquaint **4** meet, tell **6** advise, inform, notify, reveal **7** apprise **8** disclose **9** divulge to, enlighten, introduce, make aware **11** familiarize

acquaintance **8** dealings **9** awareness, knowledge **10** cognizance, friendship **11** association, conversance, familiarity **12** relationship

acquiesce **5** admit, agree, allow, bow to, grant, yield **6** accede, assent, comply, concur, give in, submit **7** concede, conform, consent **10** capitulate, fall in with **13** resign oneself **16** reconcile oneself

acquiescence **5** leave **7** consent **8** approval, giving in, sanction **10** permission, submission **11** concurrence

acquiescent **7** willing **8** amenable, yielding **9** agreeable **10** submissive

acquire **3** get, win **4** earn, gain **6** attain, obtain, pick up, secure **7** achieve, capture, procure, realize **9** cultivate

acquirement **4** gain **5** prize **7** earning **10** attainment, obtainment, possession **11** achievement, acquisition, procurement

acquisition **4** gain **5** prize **8** property, purchase **10** attainment, obtainment, possession **11** achievement, acquirement, procurement

acquisitive **6** greedy **7** selfish **8** covetous, grasping **10** avaricious, possessive **13** materialistic

acquit **3** act **5** clear **6** behave, excuse, exempt, let off, pardon **7** absolve, comport, conduct, deliver, release, relieve, set free **8** liberate, reprieve **9** discharge, exculpate, exonerate, vindicate

Acraea
epithet of: **9** Aphrodite
means: **6** height

acre
one-fourth: **4** rood
one-half: **3** erf **5** erven
two-thirds: **5** cover
ten: **6** decare **7** furlong
one hundred: **7** hectare
one hundred twenty: **4** hide

Acres, Bob
character in: **9** The Rivals
author: **8** Sheridan

acrid **4** acid **5** harsh, nasty, sharp **6** biting, bitter, ironic, smelly **7** burning, caustic, pungent **8** stinging **9** sarcastic, satirical, vitriolic **10** irritating, malodorous **11** acrimonious **12** foul-smelling

acrimonious **4** sour **5** nasty, testy **6** bitchy, biting, bitter **7** caustic, cutting, peevish **8** venomous, spiteful **9** corrosive, irascible, rancorous, sarcastic, splenetic, vitriolic **10** ill-natured

acrimony **5** anger, scorn, spite **6** animus, rancor, spleen **7** ill will **8** asperity, derision **9** animosity, hostility, malignity **10** antagonism, bitterness, malignancy **12** hard feelings, spitefulness

Acrisius
king of: **5** Argos
father: **4** Abas
mother: **6** Aglaia
twin brother: **7** Proetus
daughter: **5** Danae
grandson: **7** Perseus
killed by: **7** Perseus

acrophobia
fear of: **7** heights

acrostic **6** cipher, puzzle **7** acronym

act **2** do **3** bit, gig, law **4** bill, deed, do it, fake, feat, move, play, pose, show, skit, step, work **5** edict, enact, feign, front, order, put-on **6** action, affect, behave, decree, stance **7** execute, exploit, go about, mandate, measure, operate, perform, portray, posture, press on, routine, statute **8** carry out, function, pretense, put forth, simulate **9** enactment, ordinance, represent **10** pretension, resolution **11** achievement, affectation, counterfeit, impersonate, legislation, performance, pretend to be **14** accomplishment

Actaeon
form: 6 hunter
father: 9 Aristaeus
mother: 7 Autonoe
changed into: 4 stag
transformed by: 5 Diana
killed by: 6 hounds
killed at: 9 Gargaphia

acting 5 drama 6 deputy, ersatz, pro tem 7 interim, theater 8 the stage 9 dramatics, simulated, surrogate, temporary 10 dramaturgy, stagecraft, substitute, the theater 11 dramatic art, officiating, provisional, thespianism 12 stage playing

actinium
chemical symbol: 2 Ac

action 3 act 4 deed, feat, move, step, suit, work 5 force, power 6 battle, combat, effect, effort, motion 7 exploit, process, warfare 8 activity, conflict, endeavor, exertion, fighting, movement, progress 9 adventure, execution, influence, operation 10 enterprise, excitement, performing, production 11 achievement, functioning, performance, prosecution 14 accomplishment

Actis
father: 6 Helius
mother: 5 Rhoda
crime: 10 fratricide
taught: 9 astrology
fled to: 5 Egypt
memorial: 16 Colossus of Rhodes

activate 4 stir 5 drive, impel, start 6 prompt, propel, turn on 7 actuate 8 energize, mobilize, motivate, vitalize 9 stimulate

activated 5 drive 7 started 8 impelled, in action, in effect, turned on 9 effective, energized, mobilized, operative, vitalized 10 stimulated 11 in operation

active 4 busy, spry 5 agile, alert, alive, peppy, quick 6 acting, at work, frisky, lively, nimble 7 engaged, in force, on the go, working, zealous 8 animated, diligent, forceful, occupied, spirited, vigorous 9 ambitious, assertive, effectual, energetic, go-getting, operative, sprightly, strenuous 10 aggressive, productive 11 functioning, imaginative, industrious 12 enterprising 13 indefatigable

active person 4 doer 6 dynamo 7 hustler 8 activist, go-getter

activist 4 doer 6 zealot 7 apostle 8 advocate, exponent 9 proponent, supporter

activity 4 fuss, stir 6 action, bustle, flurry, hustle, tumult 7 project, pursuit, venture 8 endeavor, exercise, exertion, function, goings on, movement, vivacity 9 agitation, animation, avocation, commotion 10 assignment, enterprise, hurly-burly, liveliness, occupation 11 undertaking 13 sprightliness

act of the faith
Spanish: 8 auto da fe, auto de fe

act of war 4 raid 6 attack, strike 7 assault, offense 8 invasion 10 aggression, hostile act

actor 3 ham 4 doer, star 6 player, walk on 7 starlet, trouper 8 thespian 9 bit player, performer 11 functionary, participant, perpetrator 14 dramatic artist 15 supporting actor
type: 4 hero 7 feature, leading 9 character 10 supporting

Actor
king of: 6 Phthia
father: 8 Myrmidon
mother: 8 Pasidice
brother: 6 Augeas
son: 7 Cteatus, Eurytus

actual 4 real, sure, true 7 certain, current, factual, genuine, present 8 bona fide, concrete, existent, existing, physical, tangible 9 authentic, confirmed, corporeal 10 legitimate, prevailing, true-to-life, verifiable

actuality 4 fact, life 5 being, truth 6 effect, living, verity 7 reality 8 existing 9 existence, plain fact, substance 10 brutal fact 11 point of fact

actually 5 truly 6 indeed, in fact, really, verily 9 genuinely, literally
Latin: 7 ex facto

actually existing
Latin: 6 in esse 7 de facto

actuary 5 clerk 9 tabulator 12 statistician

actuate 4 move, stir 5 cause, drive, impel, rouse 6 arouse, excite, incite, induce, prompt 7 animate, inspire, trigger 8 activate, motivate 9 influence, instigate, stimulate 10 bring about

acumen 6 wisdom 7 insight 8 keenness, sagacity 9 acuteness, ingenuity, smartness 10 astuteness, cleverness, perception, shrewdness 11 discernment 12 intelligence, perspicacity 13 sound judgment 15 clearheadedness

acute 4 keen 5 sharp 6 clever, fierce, peaked, severe 7 intense, very bad 8 critical, piercing, powerful 9 agonizing, ingenious, intuitive, sensitive, very great 10 discerning, perceptive 11 distressing, penetrating 12 excruciating, needle-shaped 14 discriminating

acuteness 6 acumen 8 keenness 9 sharpness, smartness 10 astuteness, cleverness, shrewdness

acute suffering 5 agony 7 anguish, torment, torture 8 distress

adage 3 saw 4 quip, wise 5 axiom, maxim, motto 6 cliche, dictum, old saw, saying, truism 7 epigram, precept, proverb 8 aphorism 9 platitude 11 observation

adagio
music: 4 slow

Adah
also: 9 Bashemath
husband: 4 Esau 6 Lamech
son: 5 Jabal, Jubal 7 Eliphaz

Adam
wife: 3 Eve
son: 4 Abel, Cain, Seth
home: 4 Eden
grandson: 4 Enas 5 Enoch

adamant 3 set 4 firm 5 fixed, rigid, tough 7 uptight 8 obdurate, resolute, stubborn 9 immovable, insistent, unbending 10 determined, hard as rock, inexorable, inflexible, unyielding 12 intransigent 14 uncompromising

Adamas
ally of: 7 Trojans
plotted against: 10 Antilochus
thwarted by: 8 Poseidon

Adamawa-Eastern
language family: 16 Niger-Kordofanian
group: 10 Niger-Congo
includes: 5 Sango, Zande

Adam Bede
author: 11 George Eliot
character: 8 Seth Bede 11 Dinah Morris, Hetty Sorrel 12 Martin Poyser 17 Arthur Donnithorne

Adams, Henry
author of: 6 Esther 9 Democracy 14 Chapters of Erie 24 History of the United States (Under the Jefferson and Adams Administration), The Education of Henry Ad-

ams **26** Mont-Saint Michel and Chartres **34** The Degradation of the Democratic Dogma

Adams, John ***see box***

Adams, John Quincy ***see box, p. 14***

Adams, Parson
character in: 13 Joseph Andrews
author: 8 Fielding

Adams, Richard
author of: 4 Maia **7** Shardik **12** Girl in a Swing **13** The Plague Dogs, Watership Down

Adam's Rib
director: 11 George Cukor
script by: 10 Ruth Gordon **11** Garson Kanin
cast: 8 Tom Ewell **9** Jean Hagen **10** David Wayne **12** Judy Holliday, Spencer Tracy **16** Katharine Hepburn

Adapa
origin: 8 Akkadian
form: 4 sage
forfeits: 4 food **5** water **11** immortality
offered by: 3 Anu
patron: 2 Ea

adapt 3 fit **4** suit **5** alter, frame, shape **6** adjust, change, modify, rework **7** conform, convert, fashion, make fit, remodel, reshape **8** attune to **9** acclimate, harmonize, recompose, reconcile, transform **10** assimilate, coordinate **11** accommodate, acculturate **12** make suitable

adaptable 6 pliant, usable **7** unrigid **8** amenable, flexible, obliging **9** alterable, compliant, easygoing, malleable, tractable **10** adjustable, applicable, changeable, open-minded **11** conformable, serviceable **13** accommodating, accommodative

adaptation 5 shift **6** change **8** revision **9** refitting, reshaping, reworking **10** adjustment, alteration, conversion, remodeling **12** modification **13** metamorphosis

Adar 18 twelfth Hebrew month

add 4 join **5** affix, sum up, total **6** append, attach, join on, reckon, tack on **7** combine, compute, count up, enlarge, include **8** figure up, increase **9** calculate, enlarge by **10** increase by, supplement

Addams, Frankie
character in: 19 A Member of the Wedding
author: 15 Carson McCullers

Addams Family, The
character: 5 Gomez, Lurch **7** Pugsley **8** Morticia **9** Grandmama, Wednesday **11** Uncle Fester
cast: 9 John Astin **10** Lisa Loring, Ted Cassidy **11** Blossom Rock **12** Carolyn Jones, Jackie Coogan **13** Ken Weatherwax

add details 6 expand **7** clarify **9** elaborate, embellish **13** particularize

added 5 extra **6** joined **7** totaled **8** appended, attached, computed, included, joined on, reckoned, summed up, tacked on **9** counted up **10** additional, enlarged by, enumerated **11** increased by **13** supplementary

addendum 7 codicil **8** addition **9** appendage **10** attachment, postscript, supplement **12** afterthought

addict 3 fan, nut **4** buff, head, hook, user **5** freak, hound **6** junkie, submit, turn on, votary **7** acolyte, devotee, druggie, habitue **8** adherent **9** dope fiend, indulge in, surrender

addiction 5 craze, mania, quirk **6** fetish, hangup **8** fixation **9** cocainism, obsession **10** alcoholism, compulsion, dipsomania, morphinism **11** barbiturism, enslavement **12** addictedness, enthrallment **13** preoccupation

adding machine
invented by: 6 Pascal **9** Burroughs

Addis Ababa
capital of: 8 Ethiopia

Addison, Joseph
author of: 4 Cato **9** The Tatler **12** The Spectator **13** The Freeholder
co-author: 13 Richard Steele

addition 4 wing **5** annex, extra **6** adding **7** adjunct, joining **8** addendum, additive, annexing, increase, totaling **9** adjoining, appendage, appending, attaching, embracing, expansion, extending, extension, including, increment, reckoning, summation, summing up **10** counting up, increasing **11** enlargement, enumeration **12** appurtenance, augmentation, encompassing

additional 5 added, extra, spare **7** added on **8** appended

---

Adams, John
nickname: 19 Atlas of Independence
presidential rank: 6 second
party: 10 Federalist
state represented: 2 MA
defeated: 9 Jefferson
vice president: 9 Jefferson
cabinet:
***state:* 8** (John) Marshall **9** (Timothy) Pickering
***treasury:* 6** (Samuel) Dexter **7** (Oliver) Wolcott
***war:* 6** (Samuel) Dexter **7** (James) McHenry
***attorney general:* 3** (Charles) Lee
***navy:* 8** (Benjamin) Stoddert
born: 2 MA **9** Braintree
***town now called:* 6** Quincy
died/buried: 6 Quincy
education: 7 Harvard
religion: 9 Unitarian
author: 18 Discourses on Davila **20** Thoughts on Government
political career: 13 vice president **24** First Continental Congress **25** Second Continental Congress
***minister:* 11** Netherlands **12** Great Britain
civilian career: 6 lawyer
notable events of lifetime/term: 9 XYZ Affair
***act:* 9** Judiciary **16** Alien and Sedition
father: 4 John
mother: 7 Susanna (Boylston)
siblings: 5 Elihu **13** Peter Boylston
wife: 7 Abigail (Smith)
children: 7 Charles, Susanna **10** John Quincy (6th president) **13** Abigail Amelia **14** Thomas Boylston

Adams, John Quincy
nickname: **14** Old Man Eloquent
presidential rank: **5** sixth
party: **4** Whig **10** Federalist **20** Democratic-Republican
state represented: **2** MA
defeated: **4** (Henry) Clay **7** (Andrew) Jackson **8** (William H) Crawford
vice president: **7** (John C) Calhoun
cabinet:
state: **4** (Henry) Clay
treasury: **4** (Richard) Rush
war: **6** (Peter Buell) Porter **7** (James) Barbour
attorney general: **4** (William) Wirt
navy: **8** (Samuel Lewis) Southard
born: **2** MA **9** Braintree
town now called: **6** Quincy
died: **2** DC **10** Washington
buried: **2** MA **6** Quincy
education:
studied in: **5** Paris **9** Amsterdam **11** Latin School
University of: **6** Leyden
College: **7** Harvard
religion: **9** Unitarian
author: **7** Memoirs **14** Eulogy to Monroe, The Adams Papers **17** Eulogy to Lafayette **18** Letters from Silesia
political career: **8** US Senate **19** Massachusetts Senate **24** US House of Representatives
secretary of: **5** state
minister: **6** Russia **7** Prussia **8** Portugal **11** Netherlands **12** Great Britain
civilian career: **6** lawyer
notable events of lifetime/term: **19** Pan-American Congress **20** Tariff of Abominations
father: **4** John
mother: **7** Abigail (Smith)
siblings: **7** Abigail, Charles, Susanna **14** Thomas Boylston
wife: **6** Louisa (Catherine Johnson)
children: **4** John **14** Charles Francis **15** Louisa Catherine **16** George Washington

12 over-and-above **13** supplementary

additional feature **5** extra **7** adjunct **10** attachment, complement, supplement **12** appurtenance **13** accompaniment

additive **5** extra **8** addition **10** adulterant, supplement **12** augmentation, preservative

addle **5** mix up **6** muddle **7** confuse, nonplus, stupefy **8** befuddle

addled **5** silly **7** foolish, mixed-up, muddled **8** confused **9** befuddled, nonplused **10** nonplussed

add on **5** affix **6** append, attach, tack on **7** include **10** increase by

address **4** talk **5** greet, orate **6** salute, speech, talk to **7** lecture, oration, speak to, write to **8** dwelling, locality, location **9** discourse, statement

Address to the Deil
author: **11** Robert Burns

add to **6** expand, extend, pad out **7** amplify, augment, bolster, enlarge **8** compound, increase, lengthen **10** strengthen, stretch out, supplement

Ade, George
author of: **13** Fables in Slang **15** The College Widow **17** The County Chairman

Aden
capital of: **10** South Yemen

adept **3** apt **4** able, good **6** adroit, expert, gifted, master **7** skilled **8** skillful **9** dexterous, ingenious, masterful, practiced **10** proficient **12** accomplished

adequacy **7** fitness **11** sufficiency **16** satisfactoriness

adequate **3** fit **4** so-so **5** ample **6** enough **7** fitting **8** passable, suitable **9** tolerable **10** sufficient **12** satisfactory

a deux **6** for two **10** two at a time

ad extremum **6** at last **7** finally **12** to the extreme

ad fin **8** at the end **12** toward the end

adhere **3** fix **4** glue, hold, keep **5** cling, paste, stick **6** be true, cement, cleave, fasten, glue on, keep to **7** abide by, be loyal, stand by **8** maintain **9** stick fast **10** be constant, be faithful

adherence **6** fealty **7** loyalty **8** adhesion, devotion, fidelity **9** constancy, keeping to, obedience **10** allegiance, attachment, observance, stickiness **12** adhesiveness, faithfulness

adherent **3** fan **4** ally **5** gummy, pupil **6** sticky, viscid **7** acolyte, devotee, viscous **8** adhering, adhesive, advocate, champion, clinging, disciple, follower, partisan, sticking, upholder **9** supporter

adhesion **9** adherence **10** attachment, sticking to

adhesive **4** glue **5** epoxy, gummy, paste **6** cement, gummed, mortar, solder, sticky **7** stickum **8** adherent, adhering, clinging, sticking **12** mucilaginous, rubber cement

ad hoc **17** with respect to this **18** for this purpose only

ad hominem **8** to the man **17** against an opponent **20** appealing to prejudice

adieu **4** by-by, ciao, ta-ta **5** adios, aloha **6** bye-bye, goodby, so long **7** a demain, cheerio, goodbye, good day **8** a bientot, au revoir, farewell, godspeed, toodle-oo **10** take it easy **11** leavetaking, see you later, valediction **14** Auf Wiedersehen

ad infinitum **9** endlessly **10** infinitely, to infinity, unendingly **11** boundlessly, ceaselessly, limitlessly, unceasingly **12** continuously, interminably, without limit

ad initium **14** at the beginning

ad interim **13** in the meantime

adios **4** by-by, ciao, ta-ta **5** adieu, aloha **6** bye-bye, goodby, so long **7** a demain, cheerio, goodbye, good day **8** a bientot, au revoir, farewell, godspeed, toodle-oo **10** take it easy **11** leavetaking, see you later, valediction **14** Auf Wiedersehen

adjacency **5** union **7** contact, meeting **8** abutment, junction, touching **11** proximation **13** juxtaposition

adjacent **6** beside, next to **8** abutting, touching **9** bordering, proximate **10** contiguous, juxtaposed, next door to, tangential **12** conterminous

adjoining **6** joined **7** joining **8** next-door, touching **9** connected **10** contiguous **14** interconnected

adjourn **3** end **4** move **5** close **6** put off, recess, remove, repair **7** dismiss, suspend **8** break off, dissolve, postpone, withdraw **9** depart for, interrupt **11** discontinue

adjournment **6** recess **7** removal **8** abeyance **9** dismissal **10** suspension **12** postponement

adjudge **4** rule **5** judge **6** decide, decree, ordain, rule on, settle, umpire **7** referee **8** consider **9** arbitrate, determine, pronounce **10** adjudicate

adjudicate **4** rule **5** judge **6** settle **7** adjudge **9** arbitrate

adjunct **9** accessory, auxiliary, secondary **10** complement, incidental, subsidiary, supplement **12** appurtenance

adjuration **4** oath, plea, suit **6** appeal **8** advising, entreaty **12** supplication

adjure **3** beg **5** plead **6** charge, enjoin, exhort **7** beseech, command, entreat, implore, solicit **8** appeal to, petition **9** importune **10** supplicate

adjust **3** fix, set **4** move **5** adapt, alter, order **6** attune, change, modify **7** conform **8** accustom, regulate **9** acclimate, reconcile **11** accommodate

adjustable **7** movable **9** adaptable, alterable **11** rectifiable, regulatable **12** controllable

adjusting **8** adapting, altering **9** modifying **10** regulating **11** acclimating, controlling

adjusting device **5** lever, tuner, valve **6** handle **7** adapter **8** governor **9** modulator, regulator **11** control knob

adjustment **6** fixing **7** control, setting **8** adapting, focusing **9** adjusting, alignment, regulator **10** alteration, regulating, regulation, settlement, settling in **11** acclimation, orientation **12** modification **13** justification, rectification, straightening **14** reconciliation

adjutant **4** aide **9** assistant, right hand **10** aide-de-camp **12** right-hand man

ad-lib **6** make up **9** improvise **11** extemporize **13** improvisation **14** speak impromptu **15** speak off the cuff **21** speak extemporaneously **23** extemporaneous wisecrack

ad loc, ad locum **10** at the place, to the place

Admah
destroyed with: **5** Sodom **6** Zeboim **8** Gomorrah

ad majorem Dei gloriam **23** for the greater glory of God

Admete
father: **10** Eurystheus
received: **12** golden girdle
belonged to: **4** Ares
received from: **8** Hercules
stolen from: **9** Hippolyte

Admeto, Re di Tessaglia
also: **21** Admetus King of Thessaly
opera by: **6** Handel

Admetus
king of: **8** Thessaly
member of: **9** Argonauts
father: **6** Pheres
wife: **8** Alcestis

administer **3** run **4** boss, give **5** apply **6** direct, govern, manage, tender **7** oversee **8** dispense **9** supervise **11** preside over, superintend **12** administrate

administering **7** bossing, running, tending **8** managing **9** directing, executing **10** dispensing, governance, overseeing **11** carrying out, supervising, supervision **14** administration, superintending

administrate **3** run **6** direct, govern, manage **9** supervise **10** administer **11** superintend

administration **5** brass **8** officers **9** execution, governing, tendering **10** executives, government, leadership, management, overseeing **11** application **12** dispensation, distribution **13** administering, governing body **15** superintendence

administrative **9** executive **10** management, managerial **11** supervisory **14** organizational

administrative head **7** manager **8** chairman, director **9** executive, president **10** supervisor **13** administrator **14** superintendent

admirable **6** worthy **8** laudable **9** estimable, venerable **11** commendable **12** praiseworthy

Admirable Crichton, The
author: **12** James M Barrie

admiration **5** honor **6** esteem, praise **7** respect **8** approval **10** high regard, veneration **11** high opinion **12** commendation

admire **5** prize, value **6** esteem, praise **7** respect

admirer **3** fan **5** swain **6** suitor, votary **7** acolyte, devotee **8** adherent, advocate, champion, disciple, follower, partisan **9** attendant **10** aficionado

admissible **7** allowed **8** passable **9** allowable, permitted, tolerable, tolerated **10** acceptable, admittable, legitimate **11** permissible

admission **3** fee **5** entry **6** access, assent, charge, entree, tariff, ticket **8** entrance **10** admittance, concession, confession, profession **11** affirmation, declaration, entrance fee **14** acknowledgment

admit **3** let **5** allow, grant, let in, own up **6** induct, invest, permit **7** appoint, concede, confess, declare, profess, receive, welcome **8** let enter **11** acknowledge

admittable **7** allowed **9** allowable, permitted, tolerable, tolerated **10** acceptable, admissible **11** permissible

admittance **5** entry **6** access, entree **7** ingress **8** entrance **9** admission

admixture **4** mess **5** blend **6** jumble, medley **7** amalgam, melange, mixture **8** compound, mishmash **9** composite, confusion, potpourri **10** commixture, hodgepodge, salmagundi **11** combination, commingling, gallimaufry **12** amalgamation, intermixture **13** intermingling **14** conglomeration

admonish **4** warn **5** chide, scold **6** advise, enjoin, rebuke, tip off **7** caution, censure, chasten, counsel, reprove, upbraid **8** reproach **9** criticize, reprimand **10** put on guard, take to task **11** remonstrate **13** call to account **16** rap on the knuckles

admonition 6 advice, rebuke **7** chiding, warning **8** reproach, scolding **9** reprimand **11** mild reproof **12** remonstrance **16** rap on the knuckles

admonitor 7 advisor **9** counselor **10** admonisher

Adnah
deserted from: 4 Saul
deserted to: 5 David
fought against: 10 Amalekites
commander for: 10 Jehosaphat

ado 4 fuss, stir, to-do **5** furor **6** bother, bustle, flurry, fracas, furore, hubbub, pother, racket, tumult, uproar **7** flutter, trouble, turmoil **9** agitation, commotion, confusion **10** hurlyburly

adobe 3 mud **4** clay, silt, tile **5** brick, marly **6** earthy **7** clayish **13** sun-dried brick

adolescence 5 teens, youth **7** puberty **10** pubescence

adolescent 3 lad **4** lass, teen **5** minor, youth **6** boyish, callow, lassie **7** babyish, girlish, puerile **8** childish, immature, juvenile, teenager, young man, youthful **9** fledgling, pubescent, schoolboy, stripling, young teen **10** schoolgirl, sophomoric, young woman **11** undeveloped

Adolf Hitler 9 der Fuhrer **10** der Fuehrer

Adonai 3 God **6** my Lord

Adonia
event: 8 festival
honors: 6 Adonis

Adonijah
father: 5 David
mother: 7 Haggith
brother: 5 Amnon **7** Absalom, Chileab
executed by: 7 Solomon
conspired to overthrow: 5 David

Adonis
represents: 15 vegetation cycle
father: 7 Cinyras
mother: 6 Myrrha, Smyrna
favorite of: 9 Aphrodite
killed by: 4 boar
festival in honor of: 6 Adonia

adopt 3 use **4** take **6** accept, affect, assume, choose, employ, follow, take up **7** approve, embrace, espouse, utilize **9** conform to **11** acknowledge, appropriate

adorable 6 divine **7** darling, likable, lovable, winsome **8** charming, engaging, fetching, pleasing, precious **9** appealing **10** delightful **11** captivating **12** irresistible

adoration 5 honor **7** worship **8** devotion **9** adulation, reverence **10** exaltation, veneration, worshiping **11** idolization **13** glorification, magnification

adore 4 like, love **5** exalt, fancy, prize **6** admire, dote on, revere **7** cherish, glorify, idolize, worship **8** hold dear, venerate

adorer 3 fan **5** lover **7** admirer **8** follower **9** worshiper

adorn 5 array **6** bedeck **7** bejewel, deck out, furbish **8** beautify, decorate, ornament **9** embellish

adornment 6 attire, finery **7** jewelry **8** ornament **10** decoration **13** embellishment, ornamentation

ad patres 4 dead

Adrammelech 13 Sepharvite god
father: 11 Sennacherib
killed: 11 Sennacherib

Adrastea
also: 7 Nemesis
origin: 5 Greek
goddess of: 17 divine retribution
father: 9 Melisseus
reared: 4 Zeus
entrusted by: 4 Rhea

Adrastos *see* **8** Adrastus

Adrastus
also: 8 Adrastos
king of: 5 Argos
son: 8 Aegialus
leader of: 18 Seven against Thebes
companions: 6 Tydeus **8** Capaneus **9** Polynices **10** Amphiaraus, Hippomedon **13** Parthenopaeus
horse: 5 Arion

ad rem 9 pertinent **15** straightforward **17** without digression

Adrian, Edgar Douglas
field: 8 medicine **10** physiology
nationality: 7 British
discovered function of: 10 nerve cells
awarded: 10 Nobel Prize

Adriana
character in: 17 The Comedy of Errors
author: 11 Shakespeare

adrift 4 lost **5** at sea **6** afloat, aweigh **8** confused, drifting, unmoored, unstable **9** perplexed, uncertain, unsettled **10** bewildered, irresolute, unanchored

adroit 3 apt **4** deft **5** slick **6** artful, clever, expert, facile, nimble **7** cunning, skilled **8** skillful **9** dexterous, masterful **10** proficient

adroitness 7 aptness **8** deftness, facility **9** dexterity, handiness **10** cleverness **11** proficiency **12** skillfulness
French: 11 savoir-faire

adulation 7 fawning **8** flattery **9** adoration **11** fulsomeness **13** fulsome praise

adulatory 7 fulsome **8** admiring **10** flattering **13** complimentary

adult 3 big, man **5** elder, of age, woman **6** father, granny, mature, mother, parent, senior **7** grandma, grandpa, grownup, oldster **8** seasoned **9** developed, full-grown **11** experienced, grandfather, grandmother **13** senior citizen

adulterate 3 cut **4** thin **5** water **9** water down **10** depreciate **11** contaminate

adulterated 3 cut **6** impure, watery **7** debased, diluted, thinned, watered **8** doctored, weakened **11** watered down

adultery 9 carnality, cuckoldry **10** unchastity **11** fornication, promiscuity **14** unfaithfulness **17** marital infidelity **18** illicit intercourse **21** extramarital relations

adulthood 8 maturity, ripeness **10** full growth **11** age of reason

adumbrate 3 dim **6** darken, sketch **7** obscure, outline **8** intimate **9** prefigure **10** foreshadow, overshadow

adumbrated 3 dim **5** murky **7** shadowy **8** darkened **9** intimated **10** indistinct, prefigured **12** foreshadowed, overshadowed

advance 3 pre **4** gain, pass, step **5** add to, offer, prior **6** assign, binder, growth, move up, pay now, propel, send up **7** bring up, forward, further, improve, in front, lay down, press on, proffer, promote, upgrade, up front **8** foremost, increase, multiply, overture, previous, progress **9** go forward, promotion **10** furthering, move onward, prepayment, put up front

11 advancement, down payment, improvement, preliminary, proposition 12 breakthrough, bring forward, pay on account

advanced 7 extreme, far gone, radical 10 avant-guard 12 farther along, further along 14 industrialized

advanced in years 3 old 4 aged 5 hoary, older 7 ancient, antique, elderly 8 outmoded 9 senescent, venerable 10 antiquated, gray-haired

advancement 4 rise 5 boost 9 bettering, elevation, promotion 10 betterment, forwarding 11 improvement, progression

Advancement of Learning
author: 12 Francis Bacon

advance slowly 4 inch 5 crawl, creep

advantage 3 aid 4 boon, edge, help 5 asset, clout 6 profit 7 benefit, comfort, service, success, support 8 blessing 9 dominance, upper hand 10 precedence 11 convenience, superiority

advantageous 6 useful 7 helpful 8 enviable, superior, valuable 9 favorable, fortunate 10 auspicious, beneficial, dominating, profitable

advent 5 onset, start 6 coming 7 arrival 9 appearing, beginning, emergence, opening up 10 appearance, occurrence 12 commencement

adventitious 5 alien 6 exotic 7 foreign, strange 9 adventive, extrinsic 10 accidental

adventure 5 quest 7 emprise, venture 8 escapade 10 enterprise 11 undertaking

adventurer 4 hero 7 heroine 8 romantic, vagabond 9 buccaneer, daredevil 11 giant-killer 12 dragonslayer, swashbuckler 16 soldier of fortune

Adventures of Robin Hood, The
director: 13 Michael Curtiz 15 William Keighley
cast: 8 Alan Hale (Little John) 10 Errol Flynn (Robin Hood) 11 Claude Rains (Prince John) 13 Basil Rathbone 17 Olivia de Havilland (Lady Marion)
Oscar for: 5 score (Erich Wolfgang Korngold)

Adventures of Sherlock Holmes
author: 16 (Sir) Arthur Conan Doyle
character: 9 Mrs Hudson 10 Irene Adler 12 Dr John Watson 13 Mycroft Holmes 14 Sherlock Holmes 17 Inspector Lestrade, Professor Moriarty 21 Baker Street Irregulars

adventuresome 4 bold 6 daring 9 audacious, daredevil 11 adventurous

adventurous 4 bold 5 brave, risky 6 daring 7 valiant 8 intrepid, perilous 9 audacious, dangerous, hazardous 10 courageous 11 challenging, venturesome

adventurousness 6 daring 8 audacity, boldness 11 intrepidity

ad verbum 8 verbatim 9 to the word

adversary 3 foe 5 enemy, rival 8 opponent 10 antagonist, competitor

adverse 7 harmful, hostile 8 contrary, inimical, negative, opposing 9 difficult, injurious 10 pernicious, unfriendly 11 detrimental, unfavorable 12 antagonistic, unpropitious

adversity 3 woe 5 trial 6 mishap 7 bad luck, trouble 8 calamity, disaster, distress, hardship 9 suffering 10 affliction, ill-fortune, misfortune 11 catastrophe, tribulation

advertise 4 show, tout 5 vaunt 6 reveal 7 display 8 proclaim 9 broadcast, publicize 11 noise abroad

advertisement 5 blurb, flier, pitch, promo 6 notice, poster, want ad 7 leaflet, placard, trailer 8 circular, handbill 9 billboard, broadside, throwaway 10 commercial 12 announcement, classified ad, public notice

advice 4 news, view, word 6 report 7 account, counsel, message, opinion, tidings 8 guidance 10 advisement, suggestion 11 information 12 intelligence, notification 13 communication 14 recommendation

advisable 3 fit 4 best, wise 5 smart, sound 6 proper, seemly 7 fitting, prudent 8 a good bet, suitable 9 expedient, judicious 13 recommendable

advise 4 tell, urge, warn 6 enjoin, exhort, inform, notify, report 7 apprise, caution, commend, counsel, suggest 8 admonish 9 encourage, make known, recommend, suggest to 10 give notice 11 communicate

advise against 8 dissuade 10 discourage, disincline

advisement 5 study 7 thought 12 deliberation 13 consideration

adviser, advisor 4 aide 5 coach, guide, tutor 6 mentor 7 monitor, teacher 8 director 9 admonitor, assistant, counselor, preceptor, surrogate 10 consultant, idea person, instructor

advisory 7 guiding, warning 10 admonitory, cautionary, counseling 11 informative, instructive 12 consultative, consultatory 13 informational

advisory board 7 cabinet, council 8 ministry

advocaat
type: 7 liqueur
origin: 7 Holland

advocacy 5 aegis 7 backing, defense, support 8 auspices, espousal 9 patronage, promotion 10 furthering, supporting 11 advancement, endorsement, pressing for, propagation, sponsorship 12 championship 14 campaigning for, recommendation

advocate 4 back, urge 5 favor 6 advise, backer, lawyer, patron 7 advance, apostle, counsel, endorse, espouse, further, pleader, promote, propose, push for, support 8 argue for, attorney, believer, champion, defender, press for, promoter, upholder 9 apologist, barrister, counselor, encourage, prescribe, propagate, proponent, recommend, solicitor, spokesman, supporter 10 mouthpiece, stand up for 11 campaign for, speak out for 12 legal adviser, propagandist, spokesperson 13 attorney-at-law

advocatus diaboli 14 devil's advocate

adz 2 ax 3 axe 5 addis 7 hatchet

Aeacides
descendants of: 6 Aeacus

Aeacus
form: 5 judge
habitat: 5 Hades
father: 4 Zeus
mother: 6 Aegina
brother: 12 Rhadamanthys
wife: 6 Endeis
son: 6 Peleus, Phocus 7 Telamon
grandson: 8 Achilles

Aechmagoras
father: 8 Hercules
mother: 6 Phialo

Aedon
father: 9 Pandareus
sister: 8 Chelidon
husband: 11 Polytechnus
transformed into: 11 nightingale
transformed by: 4 Zeus

Aeetes
king of: 7 Colchis
custodian of: 12 Golden Fleece
father: 6 Helios
mother: 5 Perse
sister: 5 Circe 8 Pasiphae
wife: 5 Idyia 9 Asterodea
son: 8 Absyrtus, Apsyrtus
daughter: 5 Medea 9 Chalciope

Aegaeon *see* 8 Briareus

Aegean Sea
branch of: 13 Mediterranean
islands: 5 Chios, Crete, Samos 6 Euboea, Lesbos, Rhodes 8 Cyclades 10 Dodecanese 16 Northern Sporades
rivers into: 6 Struma, Vardar 7 Maritsa 8 Menderes
surrounding countries: 6 Greece, Turkey

Aegeon
character in: 17 The Comedy of Errors
author: 11 Shakespeare

Aegeria *see* 6 Egeria

Aegesta *see* 6 Egesta

Aegeus
king of: 6 Athens
son: 6 Medeus 7 Theseus

Aegialeus
father: 8 Adrastus
killed by: 8 Laodamas

Aegicores
father: 3 Ion

Aegimius
king of: 5 Doris 7 Dorians
father: 5 Dorus
son: 5 Dymas 9 Pamphylus

Aegina
father: 6 Asopus
mother: 6 Metope
son: 6 Aeacus
abducted by: 4 Zeus

Aeginaea
epithet of: 7 Artemis
means: 11 goat goddess

Aegiochus
epithet of: 4 Zeus
means: 11 aegis bearer

Aegipan
form: 3 god 4 goat
related to: 3 Pan

Aegir
origin: 6 Nordic
form: 5 giant
god of: 3 sea
wife: 3 Ran

aegis 4 wing 5 favor, guard 6 surety 7 backing, shelter, support 8 advocacy, auspices, guaranty 9 patronage 10 protection 11 sponsorship 12 championship, guardianship

Aegis
form: 6 shield
shield of: 4 Zeus 6 Athena

Aegisthus
father: 8 Thyestes
mother: 7 Pelopia
cousin: 9 Agamemnon
daughter: 7 Erigone
seduced: 12 Clytemnestra
killed by: 7 Orestes

Aegle
member of: 8 Heliades 10 Hesperides
mother of: 6 Graces

Aegyptus
king of: 5 Egypt
father: 5 Belus
twin brother: 6 Danaus
number of sons: 5 fifty

Aella
form: 6 Amazon
gift: 9 swiftness
killed by: 8 Hercules

Aello
member of: 7 Harpies

aelurophobia
fear of: 4 cats

Aemilia
character in: 17 The Comedy of Errors
author: 11 Shakespeare

Aeneas
hero of: 4 Troy
father: 8 Anchises
mother: 5 Venus
grandfather: 5 Capys
son: 5 Iulus 7 Silvius 8 Ascanius
ancestor of: 6 Romans

Aeneas Silvius
king of: 9 Alba Longa

Aeneid
author: 6 Virgil
character: 4 Gyas 5 Amata, Dares, Nisus 6 Arruns, Iarbas, Lausus, Pallas, Salius, Turnus 7 Acestes, Allecto, Camilla, Celaeno, Drances, Evander, Harpies, Helenus, Juturna, Latinus, Lavinia, Tarchon, Trojans, Venulus, Virbius 8 Ascanius, Entellus, Euryalus, Messapus 9 Cloanthus, Mezentius, Mnestheus, Palinurus, Sergestus 10 Andromache 12 Cumaean Sibyl
gods: 4 Juno 5 Diana, Venus 6 Vulcan 7 Jupiter, Neptune
Queen of Carthage: 4 Dido
Aeneas' father: 8 Anchises
Aeneas' mother: 9 Aphrodite
Aeneas' wife: 6 Creusa
Aeneas' son: 5 Iulus
Aeneas meets in underworld: 6 Charon 8 Cerberus 9 Palinurus
parts of the underworld: 7 Elysium 8 Tartarus 9 Ivory Gate
river: 4 Styx 5 Lethe
Aeneas plucks: 11 Golden Bough
Aeneas visits: 5 Crete, Delos 6 Latium, Sicily, Thrace 8 Carthage

Aenius
ally of: 4 Troy
killed by: 8 Achilles

Aeolides
descendants of: 6 Aeolus

Aeolus
ruler of: 5 winds
founder of: 8 Aeolians
father: 6 Hellen
mother: 6 Orseis
brother: 5 Dorus 6 Xuthus
wife: 7 Enarete
son: 5 Deion 6 Magnes 7 Athamas, Misenus 8 Cretheus, Macareus, Perieres, Sisyphus 9 Salmoneus
daughter: 6 Calyce, Canace 7 Alcyone 8 Cleobule, Perimede, Pisidice

aerate 3 air 9 ventilate 10 mix with air 11 expose to air

aerial 3 air 4 airy 5 by air, lofty 6 dreamy, flying, unreal 7 antenna, elusive, soaring, tenuous 8 airborne, ethereal, fanciful, in the air 9 ephemeral, imaginary, visionary 10 by aircraft, from the air, of aircraft 11 atmospheric, impractical, wind-created 13 unsubstantial 15 capable of flight

aerobatic group 10 Blue Angels

aeronautics 6 flight, flying 8 aviation

Aerope
father: 7 Catreus, Cerheus
husband: 6 Atreus 10 Plisthenes
sister: 9 Clymene
son: 8 Menelaus 9 Agamemnon

aerophobia
fear of: 6 flying

aeroplane **5** plane **8** aircraft, airplane

Aesacus
father: **5** Priam
lover: **8** Hesperia

Aeschylus
author of: **8** Oresteia **9** Agamemnon, Choephori (The Libation-bearers), Eumenides **11** The Persians **13** The Suppliants **15** Prometheus Bound **16** The House of Atreus **18** Seven Against Thebes

Aesculapius
origin: **5** Roman
god of: **7** healing **8** medicine
corresponds to: **9** Asclepius

Aesepus
mother: **9** Abarbarea
twin brother: **7** Pedasus
fought in: **9** Trojan War
killed by: **8** Euryalus

Aesir
also: **4** Asar
origin: **12** Scandinavian
leader: **4** Odin **5** Othin
home: **6** Asgard
conflicting with: **5** Vanir

aesthetic *see* **8** Esthetic

Aesyetes
son: **7** Antenor

Aethalides
member of: **9** Argonauts
father: **6** Hermes
trait: **6** memory

Aether
origin: **5** Greek
personifies: **3** air, sky

Aetheria
member of: **8** Heliades
father: **6** Helius
mother: **7** Clymene

Aethra
father: **8** Pittheus
son: **7** Theseus

Aethylla
brother: **5** Priam

Aetolus
founder of: **7** Aetolia
father: **8** Endymion
brother: **5** Epeus, Paeon
wife: **6** Pronoe
son: **7** Calydon, Pleuron
killed: **8** Laodocus

Afars and the Issas *see* **8** Djibouti

affability **9** geniality **10** amiability, cordiality **11** sociability **12** friendliness, pleasantness **13** compatibility

affable **4** open, warm **5** civil **6** genial **7** amiable, cordial **8** friendly, gracious, mannerly, pleasant, sociable **9** agreeable, congenial, courteous, easygoing **10** compatible **11** good-humored, good-natured

affair **5** amour, event, party **6** effort, matter **7** concern, episode, liaison, pursuit, romance, shindig **8** activity, business, function, incident, interest, intrigue, occasion **9** adventure, festivity, happening, operation **10** love affair, occurrence, proceeding **11** celebration, transaction, undertaking **12** circumstance, relationship **14** social function **15** social gathering

affaire d'honneur **4** duel **13** affair of honor

affect **4** fake, move, stir **5** act on, adopt, alter, fancy, feign, put on, touch **6** assume, change, modify, regard **7** embrace, concern, imitate, impress **8** interest, relate to, simulate **9** impinge on, influence, pertain to, pretend to **10** tend toward **11** counterfeit

affectation **4** airs, sham **5** put-on **6** facade **8** false air, pretense **10** pretension **11** insincerity **13** artificiality, false mannerism

affected **4** vain **5** moved, phony, sorry, upset **6** harmed, unreal **7** assumed, changed, grieved, injured, pompous, stirred, studied, touched **8** impaired, mannered, troubled **9** acted upon, afflicted, concerned, conceited, contrived, impressed, pertinent, sorrowful, unnatural **10** artificial, distressed, influenced, interested, not genuine **11** pretentious **12** vainglorious

affectedness **4** airs **7** hauteur, tension **9** formality **10** constraint **11** haughtiness, pretensions **12** affectations **15** pretentiousness

affection **4** love **6** liking, malady, warmth **7** ailment, disease, illness **8** disorder, fondness, sickness **10** proclivity, tenderness

affectionate **4** fond, warm **6** ardent, caring, doting, loving, tender **11** warmhearted **13** demonstrative, tenderhearted

affectionate term **7** pet name **8** nickname **9** sobriquet **10** endearment

Affery
character in: **12** Little Dorrit
author: **7** Dickens

affettuoso
music: **8** tenderly

affiance **6** engage, pledge **7** betroth **13** engage to marry **15** solemnly promise

affiancing **5** troth **8** pledging **9** betrothal **10** engagement

affiche **6** poster **12** public notice

affidavit **4** oath **8** document **11** affirmation **14** sworn statement

affiliate **3** arm **4** ally, join, part **5** merge, unite **6** branch **7** chapter, connect, consort **8** division **9** associate, colleague **10** amalgamate, fraternize **11** incorporate, subdivision **12** band together

affiliated **6** allied, joined, united **9** connected **10** associated **12** incorporated

affiliation **5** union **8** alliance **10** connection **11** association **12** relationship

affinity **4** bent **5** fancy **6** liking **7** leaning, rapport **8** fondness, homology, likeness, penchant, relation, sympathy, tendency **10** connection, partiality, proclivity, propensity, similarity **11** inclination, parallelism **13** compatibility

affirm **4** aver, avow, hold **5** claim **6** allege, assert, ratify, uphold **7** approve, confirm, contend, declare, endorse, profess, support, sustain, warrant **8** maintain, proclaim, validate

affirmation **6** avowal **7** consent **8** approval **11** declaration, endorsement **12** confirmation, ratification **13** certification

affirmative **3** yes **8** emphatic, positive **9** affirming, approving, assenting, ratifying **10** conclusive, concurring, confirming **11** affirmatory, categorical **12** confirmatory **13** corroborative

affix **3** fix, tag **4** glue, seal **5** add on, paste, put on, set to, stick **6** attach, fasten, tack on

afflict **5** beset **6** plague **7** oppress, torment **8** distress

afflicted **6** cursed **7** plagued **8** affected, troubled **9** tormented **10** distressed

affliction **4** pain **5** curse, trial **6** misery, ordeal **7** anguish, torment, trouble **8** calamity, distress, hardship **9** adversity **10** misfortune, oppression **11** tribulation **12** wretchedness

affluence **5** money **6** plenty, riches, wealth **7** success **10** prosperity **14** prosperousness, successfulness

affluent **4** rich **6** loaded **7** moneyed, wealthy, well-off **8** well-to-do **9** well-fixed **10** prosperous, well-heeled

afford **4** bear, give, lend, risk **5** grant, offer, yield **6** chance, impart, manage, supply **7** command, furnish, provide, support, sustain

affray **4** fray **5** brawl, melee **6** fracas **7** contest, scuffle **8** conflict **9** encounter **11** altercation

affright **4** fear **5** alarm, dread, panic, scare **6** dismay, fright, horror, terror **8** frighten

affront **4** slur **5** abuse, wrong **6** injury, insult, offend, slight **7** offense, outrage, provoke, put-down **8** disgrace, dishonor, ignominy, rudeness **9** indignity, insolence **11** discourtesy, humiliation **12** ill-treatment, impertinence **13** mortification **16** contemptuousness

afghan **5** shawl, throw **7** blanket **8** covering, coverlet

Afghanistan ***see box***

aficionado **3** fan, nut **5** freak, pupil **7** devotee, pursuer, student **8** disciple

afield **5** amiss **6** abroad, astray **10** off the mark **11** out of the way **16** off the right track

afire **5** fiery **6** ablaze, aflame, alight, ardent, fervid, fuming, on fire **7** blazing, burning, fervent, flaming, flaring, glowing, ignited, smoking, zealous **8** aflicker, in flames, inspired **10** flickering, smoldering

afloat **5** at sea **6** adrift, wafted **7** sailing, wafting **8** drifting, floating

afoot **5** astir **8** underway **10** in the works

a fortiori **10** all the more

afraid **5** sorry **6** scared **7** alarmed, anxious, chicken, fearful, panicky, unhappy **8** cowardly, timorous **9** regretful, terrified **10** apologetic, frightened **11** lily-livered **12** apprehensive, disappointed, fainthearted **13** anxiety-ridden, panic-stricken **14** chicken-hearted, chicken-livered, terror-stricken

Afreet
also: **5** Afrit
origin: **7** Arabian
form: **5** demon

afresh **4** anew **5** again **11** from scratch **16** from the beginning
Latin: **6** de novo

Africa ***see box***

Africaine, L'
also: **14** The African Girl
opera by: **9** Meyerbeer

African Queen, The
director: **10** John Huston
cast: **12** Robert Morley **14** Humphrey Bogart **16** Katharine Hepburn
setting: **5** Congo
Oscar for: **5** actor (Bogart)

Afrit *see* **6** Afreet

Afghanistan
other name: **6** Ariana, Aryana
capital/largest city: **5** Kabul
others: **3** Rui **4** Jurm, Nani, Wama **5** Asmar, Balkh, Doshi, Farah, Herat, Kunar, Makur, Maruf, Matun, Pahra, Tagab, Tulak, Urgan **6** Chaman, Gardez, Ghazni, Haibak, Kunduz, Nauzad, Panjao, Rustak, Sangan, Sarobi, Tukzar, Washir **7** Andkhui, Baghlan, Bamiyan, Dilaram, Ghurian, Girishk **8** Charikar, Faizabad, Kandahar **9** Jalalabad **10** Daulatabad, Pul-i-Khumri, Shibarghan **12** Mazar-i-Sharif
government:
parliament: **10** Loya-Jirgah
leader: **4** amir, emir **5** ameer, emeer **6** sharif, sherif
measure: **3** paw, sir **5** jerib, karoh **6** khurds **7** kharwar
monetary unit: **3** pul **5** abaze, riyal, rupee **6** abbasi, amania **7** afghani
weight: **3** pau, paw, ser, sir
lake: **13** Hamud-i-Helmand
mountain: **3** Koh **5** Safeo **6** Chagai, Pamirs **7** Nowshak **8** Koh-i-Baba, Safed Koh, Sulaiman **9** Himalayas, Hindu Kush **11** Khwaja Amran, Paropamisus
highest point: **9** Istoro Nal
river: **4** Lora, Oxus **5** Cabul, Indus, Kabul, Kunar **6** Kokcha, Kunduz **7** Hari Rud, Helmand, Helmund, Murghab, Taleqan **8** Amu Darya, Farah Rud, Harut Rud, Khash Rud **9** Arghandab
sea: **5** Darya
physical feature:
desert: **8** Registan
panhandle: **6** Wakhan
pass: **6** Khyber
wind: **9** Afghanets
people: **5** Aimak, Aymak, Kafir, Nuris **6** Baloch, Baluch, Chahar, Durani, Hasara, Hazara, Kaffir, Kirgiz, Pathan, Tajiks, Uzbeks **7** Beluchi, Belucki, Ghilzai, Pakhton, Pakhtun, Pashtun, Pukhtun, Pushtun, Sistani, Taimani, Taimuri **8** Jamshidi, Siah Push **9** Firuzkuhi, Safed Push, Safid Push
dynasty: **8** Barakzai
leader: **7** Mohmand **12** Babrak Karmal **14** Hafizullah Amin **17** Mohammad Zahir Shah, Mohammed Daoud Khan **18** Noor Mohammed Taraki
language: **4** Dari **5** Farsi **6** Afghan, Pashto, Pushtu **7** Balochi, Baluchi, Persian
religion: **5** Islam
place:
dam: **6** Boghra **7** Kajakai **9** Arghandab
feature:
clothing: **7** chaderi
coat: **6** chapan
dance: **5** attan
game: **8** buz-kashi
guest room: **5** hujra
hat: **7** karakul
head-cloth: **7** chawdar
house with tower: **4** qala
medicinal plant: **9** asafetida
wrestling: **6** ghosai
food:
potluck meal: **6** sohbat

Africa
country: **4** Chad, Mali, Togo **5** Benin, Congo, Egypt, Gabon, Ghana, Kenya, Libya, Niger, Sudan, Zaire **6** Angola, Guinea, Malawi, Rwanda, Uganda, Zambia **7** Algeria, Burkina, Burundi, Comoros, Lesotho, Liberia, Morocco, Namibia, Nigeria, Reunion, Senegal, Somalia, Tunisia **8** Botswana, Cameroon, Djibouti, Ethiopia, Tanzania, Zimbabwe **9** Cape Verde, The Gambia, Mauritius, Swaziland **10** Ivory Coast, Madagascar, Mauritania, Mozambique, Seychelles **11** Sierra Leone, South Africa **12** Guinea-Bissau **13** Canary Islands, Western Sahara **15** South-West Africa **16** Equatorial Guinea **18** Sao Tome and Principe **22** Central African Republic
people: **2** Ga **3** Ibo, Kru, Luo, San, Tiv, Yao **4** Arab, Beja, Bobo, Boer, Fang, Hutu, Kota, Kuba, Luba, Nuba, Nuer, Nupe, Teda, Tibu, Zulu **5** Bemba, Dinka, Galla, Hausa, Kamba, Makua, Masai, Mende, Mongo, Negro, Pygmy, Rundi, Serer, Shona, Sotho, Swazi, Temne, Tigre, Tutsi, Wolof, Xhosa **6** Bateke, Berber, Fulani, Herero, Ibibjo, Kikuyu, Mau Mau, Nubian, Ovambo, Rwanda, Senufo, Sidamo, Somali, Tswana, Tuareg, Yoruba, Watusi **7** Ashanti, Baganda, Bambara, Bushmen, Chaamba, Makonde, Mashoma, Ndebele, Nilotic, Oshogbo, Songhai, Turkana **8** Khoikhoi, Mangbetu, Matabele **9** Africaner, Hottentot
desert: **5** Namib **6** Sahara **8** Kalahari
island: **5** Bioko, Pemba **6** Canary **7** Comoros, Madeira, Mayotte, Reunion **8** St Helena, Zanzibar **9** Ascension, Cape Verde, Mauritius **10** Madagascar, Seychelles
ancient people/empire: **3** Oyo **4** Kush, Mali, Toro **5** Aksum, Benin, Ghana, Kongo, Mossi, Nubia, Wadai **6** Ankole, Tekrur **7** Ashanti, Buganda, Bunyoro, Dahomey, Songhai **8** Baguirmi, Carthage **10** Kanem-Bornu, Monomotapa **11** Ife and Benin
ancient city: **5** Kilwa, Meroe **8** Timbuktu
language: **4** Afar, Peul, Teda **5** Bantu, Bemba, Click, Hausa, Masai, Wolof **6** Arabic, Berber, French, Kanuri, Tsonga **7** Amharic, Khoisan, Lingala, Nilotic, Songhai, Swahili, Turkana **8** Cushitic, Mandingo **9** Afrikaans
river: **4** Juba, Nile, Sudd **5** Congo, Kasai, Niger **6** Kwango, Orange, Ubangi **7** Senegal, Zambezi **8** Blue Nile **9** White Nile
lake: **4** Chad, Kivu, Tana **5** Assal, Nyasa **6** Albert, Edward, Kariba, Malawi, Nassar, Red Sea, Rudolf **8** Victoria **10** Tanganyika **12** Chott Melrhir
falls: **8** Victoria
mountain/mountain range: **3** Air **4** Bihu, Meru **5** Atlas, Elgon, Kenya **6** Hoggar **7** Ahaggar, Crystal, Tibesti, Toubkal **8** Cameroon **9** Emi Koussi, Munchinga, Ruwenzori **10** Futa Jallon **11** Drakensberg, Kilimanjaro **13** Tibesti Massif
lowest point: **17** Qattari Depression
mineral/natural resource: **3** oil, tin **4** gold **5** ivory **6** cloves, copper, rubber **7** diamond, palm oil, uranium
disease: **4** AIDS **7** malaria **9** bilharzia **11** yellow fever **16** sleeping sickness
homeland: **5** Venda **6** Ciskei **8** Transkei **14** Bophuthatswana
game reserve: **5** Tsavo **6** Kruger **8** Amboseli **9** Serengeti
tree: **4** cork, teak **5** cedar, ebony, olive **6** acacia, baobab, okoume, rubber **7** juniper, oil palm **8** date palm, mahogany, tamarisk **10** silk-cotton
animal: **4** lion **5** bongo, hippo, hyena, zebra **6** jackal, monkey **7** buffalo, cheetah, giraffe, gorilla, leopard, wild pig **8** aardvark, antelope, elephant **9** crocodile **10** chimpanzee, rhinoceros **11** wildebeeste **12** hippopotamus
bird: **5** heron, stork **6** falcon **7** bustard, ostrich, pelican **8** flamingo, hornbill **10** kingfisher
fly: **6** tsetse
snake: **5** cobra, mamba **6** python

after **4** next, post **5** later **6** behind **9** afterward, following **10** conclusion, subsequent, succeeding

aftereffect **6** result **11** consequence

After Hours
director: **14** Martin Scorsese
cast: **12** Griffin Dunne **15** Rosanna Arquette

Afterlife
god of: **4** Gwyn

aftermath **6** payoff, result, sequel, upshot **7** outcome **8** follow-up, offshoot **9** byproduct **11** consequence

afterpart **4** back, tail **6** far end **7** back end, rear end, tail end **8** backside, hind part **9** posterior

after the fact **4** late **5** tardy **7** belated, delayed, too late **10** behindhand, behind time

After the Fall
author: **12** Arthur Miller

after this, therefore because of it
Latin: **21** post hoc ergo propter hoc
describes: **14** logical fallacy

afterword **4** coda **8** addendum, epilogue **10** conclusion

Agacles
king of: **9** Myrmidons

Agag
king of: **10** Amalekites
captured by: **4** Saul
killed by: **6** Samuel

again **4** also, anew, more **7** besides **8** moreover, once more **10** in addition, repetition **11** another time, duplication, furthermore **12** additionally
Latin: **6** de novo

against **7** adverse, opposed **8** conflict, contrary, opposite **10** opposition **11** unfavorable

against an opponent
Latin: **9** ad hominem

Against Our Will
author: **16** Susan Brownmiller

against the property
Latin: **5** in rem
describes: **15** legal proceeding

against the thing
Latin: **5** in rem

Agamede
father: **6** Augeas
husband: **6** Mulius
gift: **7** healing
healed with: **5** herbs

Agamemnon
author: **9** Aeschylus
mentioned in: **5** Iliad
king of: **7** Mycenae
leader of: **6** Greeks
fought in: **9** Trojan War
father: **6** Atreus
brother: **8** Menelaus
sister: **8** Anaxibia
wife: **12** Clytemnestra
daughter: **7** Electra **9** Iphigenia **12** Chrysothemis
son: **7** Orestes
cousin: **9** Aegisthus
captive: **9** Cassandra
Clytemnestra's lover: **9** Aegisthus
killed by: **12** Clytemnestra

Aganippe **8** fountain
location: **6** Greece **7** Helicon
sacred to: **5** Muses

Aganus
father: **5** Paris
mother: **5** Helen

agape **4** agog **6** amazed, gaping **8** wide open **9** awestruck, stupefied **10** astonished, dumbstruck, spellbound **11** dumbfounded **12** wonderstruck **13** flabbergasted

Agassiz, Jean Louis Rodolphe
field: **7** zoology
worked on: **7** fossils **8** glaciers **14** classification

Agastrophus
father: **5** Paeon
killed by: **8** Diomedes

agate
species: **6** quartz
variety of: **10** chalcedony
type: **3** eye **4** moss, onyx, ring **9** landscape **13** fortification
source: **4** Ider **6** Brazil **7** Uruguay **9** Oberstein **14** Rio Grande de Sul

Agathon
father: **5** Priam

Agathyrsus
father: **8** Hercules

Agave
father: **6** Cadmus
mother: **8** Harmonia
sister: **3** Ino **6** Semele **7** Autonoe
husband: **6** Echion
son: **8** Pentheus

age **3** eon, era **4** date **5** epoch, phase, ripen **6** mature, mellow, period, season **7** develop, forever, make old **8** life span, lifetime **9** adulthood, a long time, grow older, seniority **10** generation, millennium **11** stage of life, stage of time
French: **6** siecle

aged **3** old **4** ripe **6** mature, mellow **7** ancient, as old as, elderly, ripened **8** enduring, grown old **9** developed, full-grown, long-lived

Agee, James
author of: **10** Agee on Film **17** A Death in the Family **23** Let Us Now Praise Famous Men
screenwriter for: **15** The African Queen **19** The Night of the Hunter

Agelaus
mentioned in: **5** Iliad **7** Odyssey
occupation: **8** herdsman
father: **8** Hercules, Phradmon
mother: **7** Omphale
courted: **8** Penelope
raised: **5** Paris
employer: **5** Priam

ageless **7** classic, eternal **8** enduring, timeless

agency **5** force, means, power **6** action, bureau, charge **8** activity **9** influence, mediation, operation **10** department, instrument **12** intervention **15** instrumentality

agenda **6** docket **7** program **8** schedule **9** timetable

Agenor
mentioned in: **5** Iliad
king of: **9** Phoenicia
father: **7** Antenor **8** Poseidon
mother: **5** Libya **6** Theano
twin brother: **5** Belus
wife: **10** Telephassa
son: **5** Cilix **6** Cadmus **7** Phoenix
daughter: **6** Europa
gift: **7** bravery

agent **4** doer **5** cause, envoy, force, means, mover, power **6** agency, author, deputy, worker **7** vehicle **8** advocate, emissary, executor, operator **9** go-between, performer **10** instrument, negotiator **11** perpetrator **12** intermediary, practitioner **14** representative

Age of Innocence, The
author: **12** Edith Wharton
character: **10** May Welland **12** Ellen Olenska **13** Newland Archer

age-old **4** aged **7** ancient, antique, very old **9** venerable

agglomerate **4** clot, mass **5** amass, bunch, clump, rally **6** gather, heap up, muster, pile up **7** cluster, collect **8** assemble, condense, mobilize **10** accumulate, collection **12** accumulation, conglomerate, heap together, lump together **14** conglomeration **15** gather into a mass

agglomeration **4** heap, mass, pile **5** bunch, clump **7** cluster **10** collection **12** accumulation **14** conglomeration

aggrandize **5** bloat, exalt, widen **6** beef up, blow up, dilate, expand, extend, puff up, step up **7** amplify, broaden, build up, distend, enhance, enlarge, inflate, magnify, stretch **8** escalate, increase **9** intensify **10** strengthen

aggrandizement **8** increase, widening **9** expansion, extension **10** broadening, escalation, exaltation, stepping up **11** enhancement, enlargement **13** amplification, magnification **15** intensification

aggravate **3** vex **4** rile **5** anger, annoy **6** nettle, worsen **7** affront, inflame **8** heighten, increase, irritate **9** intensify, make worse **10** exacerbate, exasperate

aggravating **7** irksome **9** inflaming, vexatious, worsening **10** irritating **11** heightening **12** exacerbating, exasperating, intensifying

aggregate **3** mix **4** mass **5** blend, union **7** mixture **8** amassing, compound **9** composite, gathering, summation **10** collection **11** combination **12** accumulation, conglomerate **14** conglomeration

aggregation **3** mob **4** army, band, bevy, crew, gang, host, mass, pack **5** crowd, horde, swarm **6** throng **7** cluster **9** multitude **10** collection

aggression **4** raid **7** assault, offense **8** act of war, invasion **9** hostility, pugnacity **11** viciousness **12** belligerence **13** combativeness

aggressive **4** bold **5** harsh, pushy **7** dynamic, hostile, intense, vicious, warlike, warring, zealous **8** forceful, militant **9** ambitious, assailant, assertive, attacking, combative, energetic **10** pugnacious

11 belligerent, competitive, contentious, quarrelsome **12** antagonistic, enterprising **13** self-assertive **15** tending to attack

aggressiveness **9** hostility, pugnacity **10** antagonism **12** belligerence **13** combativeness

aggressor **7** invader **8** attacker **9** assailant **11** belligerent **12** antagonistic

aggrieved **3** sad **4** hurt **5** stung **6** abused, pained **7** injured, put upon, tearful, wounded, wronged **8** grieving, mournful, offended, saddened, troubled **9** affronted, disturbed, sorrowful **10** distressed, ill-treated, maltreated, persecuted **11** imposed upon **13** grief-stricken

aghast **6** amazed **7** shocked, stunned **8** appalled **9** astounded, horrified, terrified **10** astonished, fear-struck, frightened **12** horror-struck **13** thunderstruck

agile **4** keen, spry **5** alert, fleet, lithe, quick, swift **6** active, clever, limber, nimble, supple **8** athletic, graceful **9** dexterous

agility **8** alacrity, spryness **9** dexterity, quickness, swiftness **10** limberness, nimbleness **12** gracefulness

agitate **3** jar, mix **4** beat, goad, rock, stir **5** alarm, churn, shake, upset **6** excite, foment, stir up, work up **7** disturb, provoke, shake up, trouble **8** disquiet

agitated **6** uneasy **7** anxious, frantic, nervous **8** confused, seething **9** disturbed, perturbed, unsettled **10** disquieted, distracted, distraught **11** discomfited, discomposed **12** disconcerted

agitation **7** anxiety **9** confusion **10** discomfort, uneasiness **11** disquietude, distraction, nervousness **12** discomfiture, discomposure, perturbation

agitato
music: **8** agitated

agitator **7** inciter **8** fomentor, inflamer, provoker **9** firebrand **10** incendiary, instigator **11** provocateur **12** rabble-rouser, troublemaker **13** mischief-maker, revolutionary **16** agent provocateur

Aglaia
member of: **6** Graces
father: **7** Jupiter
mother: **8** Eurynome
sister: **6** Thalia **10** Euphrosyne
husband: **4** Abas
son: **7** Proteus **8** Acrisius
daughter: **7** Idomene

Aglauros *see* **8** Agraulos

Aglaus
father: **8** Thyestes
mother: **5** naiad
killed by: **6** Atreus

aglow **4** warm **5** fiery **6** ablaze, red-hot **7** blazing, glowing, radiant, shining

Agnes Grey
author: **10** Anne Bronte
character: **8** Mr Weston **13** Rosalie Murray

agnostic **5** pagan **7** atheist, doubter, heathen, heretic, infidel, skeptic **10** empiricist, free spirit, secularist, unbeliever **11** disbeliever, freethinker, nonbeliever **14** doubting Thomas

ago **4** gone, over, past **5** since **6** gone by **7** earlier **8** backward **15** retrospectively

agog **5** astir **7** excited **8** thrilled, worked up **9** awestruck **10** enthralled **11** openmouthed

Agon
ballet by: **10** Stravinsky

agonize **5** labor, sweat, worry **6** strain, suffer **7** anguish, wrestle **8** struggle

agonizing **6** severe **7** painful, racking **8** grievous, worrying **9** suffering, torturous **10** tormenting, unbearable **11** distressing, intolerable, unendurable **12** excruciating, insufferable

agony **3** woe **4** pain **5** trial **6** effort, misery, sorrow, strain, throes **7** anguish, anxiety, torment, torture **8** distress, striving, struggle **9** suffering **10** affliction **11** tribulation

Agony and the Ecstasy, The
author: **11** Irving Stone

Agoraea
epithet of: **6** Athena
means: **16** of the marketplace

Agoraeus
epithet of: **4** Zeus **6** Hermes
means: **16** of the marketplace

agoraphobia
fear of: **10** open spaces

Agraeus
epithet of: **6** Apollo
means: **6** hunter

agrarian **5** rural **7** farming **8** pastoral **11** agronomical, crop-raising **12** agricultural

Agraulos
also: **8** Aglauros
father: **7** Actaeus
husband: **7** Cecropa
daughter: **9** Pandrosos

agree **4** jibe **5** admit, allow, chime, grant, match, tally **6** accede, accept, accord, assent, concur, settle, square **7** concede, conform, consent, support **8** coincide, side with **9** harmonize, subscribe **10** correspond, think alike

agreeable **7** fitting **8** amenable, in accord, pleasant, pleasing, suitable **9** approving, complying, congenial **10** acceptable, concurring, consenting, gratifying **11** appropriate
German: **9** gemutlich

agreeableness **7** amenity **9** geniality **10** amiability **11** sociability **12** pleasantness

agreed
French: **7** d'accord

agreed upon **6** common, normal **8** accepted, approved **9** confirmed, customary **10** acceptable **11** established **12** acknowledged

agreement **4** deal, pact **6** accord **7** analogy, bargain, compact, concert, concord, harmony, promise **8** affinity, alliance, contract, covenant **10** accordance, compliance, conformity, settlement, similarity **11** arrangement, concordance, conformance **13** compatibility **14** correspondence

agricultural **4** farm **5** rural **7** farming **8** agrarian **9** gardening **11** agronomical, crop-raising **13** nonindustrial

agriculture **7** farming, tillage **8** agronomy **9** geoponics, husbandry **10** agronomics **11** crop-raising, cultivation **15** market gardening

Agriculture
god of: **4** Dago **5** Dagan, Dagon, Picus **6** Saturn **12** Bonus Eventus
goddess of: **5** Ceres **6** Brigit, Dea Dia, Vacuna

Agriope *see* **8** Eurydice

Agrius
member of: **8** Gigantes
form: **7** centaur
mother: **5** Circe
father: **8** Odysseus
son: **9** Thersites
attacked: **8** Hercules

agronomics **7** farming, tillage **8** agronomy **9** geoponics **11** agriculture, crop-raising

agronomy **7** farming **9** gardening, husbandry **11** agriculture, cultivation

Agrotera
epithet of: **7** Artemis
means: **8** huntress

aground **5** stuck **6** ashore **7** beached **8** grounded, stranded **9** foundered

ague **5** chill, fever **7** malaria, shivers **12** sweating fits

Aguecheek, Sir Andrew
character in: **12** Twelfth Night
author: **11** Shakespeare

Agyius
epithet of: **6** Apollo
means: **15** god of the streets

Ah, But Your Land Is Beautiful
author: **9** Alan Paton

Ah! Wilderness
author: **12** Eugene O'Neill

Ahab
character in: **8** Moby Dick
author: **8** Melville

Ahab
father: **4** Omri
wife: **7** Jezebel
son: **7** Ahaziah
daughter: **8** Athaliah
opposed: **6** Elijah
killed by: **4** Aram

Ahasuerus
known as: **6** Xerxes **8** Cyaxares
wife: **6** Esther
divorced: **6** Vashti
son: **6** Darius
eunuchs: **6** Biztha, Carcas, Zethar **7** Abagtha, Harbona, Mehuman
servant: **7** Abagtha
conqueror of: **7** Nineveh

Ahaz
father: **6** Jotham

Ahaziah
father: **4** Ahab **7** Jehoram
mother: **7** Jezebel **8** Athaliah
uncle: **7** Jehoram
defeated by: **6** Hazael
killed by: **4** Jehu
died at: **7** Megiddo

ahead of time **5** early **6** before, in time, sooner **7** betimes, earlier **9** before now, in advance **10** beforehand, in good time **13** before the fact

Ahib **16** first Hebrew month

Ahiezer
father: **11** Ammishaddai

Ahimelech
father: **6** Ahitub
son: **8** Abiathar
killed by: **4** Saul
friend: **8** Ahuzzath

Ahithophel
counseled: **5** David
rebelled with: **7** Absalom
granddaughter: **9** Bathsheba

Ahuzzath
friend: **9** Abimelech
visited: **5** Isaac

Aias *see* **4** Ajax

aid **4** abet, alms, dole, help **5** serve **6** assist, foster, relief **7** advance, charity, further, promote, subsidy, support, sustain **8** donation, minister **9** allowance **10** assistance, contribute, facilitate **11** accommodate, helping hand **12** contribution

Aida
opera by: **5** Verdi
character: **4** Aida **6** Ramfis **7** Amneris, Radames **8** Amonasro, Rhadames

aide **5** gofer **6** deputy, helper **7** abettor, acolyte **8** adherent, adjutant, follower, retainer, sidekick **9** assistant, associate, auxiliary, man Friday **10** aide-de-camp, apprentice, girl Friday, lieutenant **11** helping hand, subordinate **12** right-hand man

aide-de-camp **4** aide **6** helper **8** adjutant **9** assistant, man Friday, right hand **12** right-hand man

aide memoire **4** memo, note **10** memorandum

aider **4** aide **6** helper **7** abettor **9** assistant **11** helping hand

Aidos
origin: **5** Greek
personifies: **10** conscience

Aiken, Conrad Potter
author of: **6** Ushant **10** Blue Voyage **12** Reviewer's ABC **14** The Charnel Rose **15** Earth Triumphant

Aiken, Howard H
field: **11** mathematics
designed: **15** digital computer

ail **4** pain **5** annoy, be ill, upset, worry **6** be sick, bother, sicken **7** afflict, make ill, trouble **8** be infirm, be unwell, distress **12** be indisposed, fail in health

ailing **3** ill **4** sick **6** infirm, sickly, unwell **8** delicate

ailment **6** malady **7** disease, illness **8** disorder, sickness, weakness **9** complaint, infection, infirmity **10** affliction, disability, discomfort **13** indisposition

ailurophobia
fear of: **4** cats

aim **3** try **4** beam, goal, mean, plan, seek, want, wish **5** essay, focus, level, point, sight, slant **6** aiming, design, desire, direct, intend, intent, object, scheme, strive, target **7** attempt, be after, purpose, take aim, train on **8** ambition, aspire to, endeavor **9** intention **10** aspiration, have in mind, have in view, work toward **11** have an eye to, line of sight **12** marksmanship

aim at **4** seek **6** pursue, target **8** aspire to, shoot for

aimless **6** chance, random **7** erratic, wayward **8** unguided **9** frivolous, haphazard, hit-or-miss, pointless, unfocus(s)ed **10** accidental, rudderless, undirected **11** purposeless, unorganized **12** inconsistent, unsystematic **13** directionless, unpredictable **14** indiscriminate

aine **5** elder **6** eldest

Ainsworth, William Harrison
author of: **8** Boscobel, Crichton, Rookwood **9** Guy Fawkes **10** Old St Paul's **12** Jack Sheppard **13** Windsor Castle **16** The Flitch of Bacon, The Tower of London **17** The Miser's Daughter, The South Sea Bubble **20** The Lancashire Witches

Ainu
language spoken in: **8** Hokkaido, Sakhalin

air, airs **3** lay, sky **4** aura, look, mood, puff, song, tell, tone, tune, vent, waft, wind **5** blast, carol, ditty, draft, ozone, style, swank, utter, voice, whiff **6** aerate, ballad, breath, breeze, expose, manner, melody, reveal, spirit, strain, zephyr **7** declare, display, divulge, exhibit, express, feeling, hauteur, quality **8** ambience, disclose, pretense, proclaim **9** arrogance, publicize, ventilate **10** appearance, atmosphere, make public **11** haughtiness, pretensions **12** affectations, affectedness, stratosphere **16** superciliousness
god of: **5** Enlil
goddess of: **6** Ninlil

airborne **5** aloft **6** aerial **8** in flight **12** off the ground

aircraft **3** jet, SST **4** bird **5** blimp, crate, plane **6** copter, glider **7** balloon, chopper, prop-jet, zepplin **8** airplane, jumbo jet **10** helicopter, whirlybird

air current **4** puff, wind

5 blast, draft, whiff **6** breeze, zephyr **11** breath of air

airdrome, aerodrome 7 air-base, airport, jet base **8** air-field **11** flying field **12** landing field

airfield 7 air base, airport, jet base **8** airstrip **11** flying field **12** landing field, landing strip

airfoil
insect: 4 wing

airless 8 stifling **10** overheated, sweltering **16** poorly ventilated

airplane ***see box***

airport 5 field **7** air base, jet base **8** airdrome, airfield, air-strip **9** aerodrome **11** flying field **12** landing field, landing strip

airship 5 blimp **7** balloon **9** dirigible **19** lighter-than-air craft

airship, rigid dirigible
invented by: 8 Zeppelin

airstrip 6 runway **12** landing field, landing strip

air weapon
German: 9 Luftwaffe

airy 5 light, merry, sunny, windy **6** breezy, cheery, drafty, dreamy, jaunty, lively **8** cheerful, ethereal, fanciful, gossamer, illusory, spacious **9** idealized, imaginary, sprightly **10** frolicsome, immaterial **11** unrealistic **12** light-hearted, light-of-heart **13** unsubstantial **14** well-ventilated

aisle 3 way **4** lane, path, walk **5** alley **6** avenue **7** passage, walkway **8** cloister, corridor **10** ambulatory, passageway

Aius Locutius
form: 5 voice
warned: 6 Romans
warned of: 14 Gallic invasion

ajar 4 open **5** agape **6** gaping **8** unclosed **10** partly open

Ajax
also: 4 Aias
called: 9 Great Ajax **10** Oilean Ajax **11** Locrian Ajax **13** Ajax the Lesser **14** Telamonian Ajax
king of: 7 Locrius
father: 6 Oileus **7** Telamon
mother: 8 Periboea
brother: 6 Teucer
author: 9 Sophocles
character: 8 Achilles, Odysseus **9** Agamemnon
***son:* 9** Eurysaces
***slave:* 8** Tecmessa
***seer:* 7** Calchas
rescued body of: 8 Achilles
violated shrine of: 6 Athena
killed in: 9 shipwreck

Akawai *see* **6** Acawai

Akela
character in: 14 The Jungle Books
author: 7 Kipling

Akeldama *see* **8** Aceldama

airplane 3 jet **4** bird **5** crate, plane **7** airship, prop-jet **8** air-craft **9** aeroplane **11** flying jenny **19** heavier-than-air craft **20** propeller-driven plane
invented by:
***automatic pilot:* 6** Sperry
***jet engine:* 5** Ohain
***with motor:* 12** Wilbur Wright **13** Orville Wright **14** Wright Brothers
***hydro:* 7** Curtiss
first: 5 Flyer
part: 3 fin **4** flap, nose, tail, wing **5** cabin, cargo, pylon **6** rudder **7** aileron, cockpit, turbine **8** elevator, fuel tank, fuselage, throttle, turbofan, turbojet **9** empennage, propeller, turboprop **10** flight deck, power plant, stabilizer **11** landing gear **13** undercarriage
kind: 3 MIG **4** Zero **5** Eagle, Gotha, Piper, Sabre **6** Boeing, Cessna, Fokker, Mirage **7** Concorde, Piper Cub **10** Beechcraft, Dornier Do-X **11** Piper Navajo **12** Lockheed Vega, Sopwith Camel **13** Boeing Clipper, Messerschmitt, Piper Cherokee, Super Fortress **14** Cessna Citation, Flying Fortress, Grumman Hellcat, Stratofortress **15** Hawker Hurrican **16** De Havilland Comet
variation: 3 SST **4** STOL, VTOL **5** blimp, drone, VSTOL **6** bomber, glider **7** airship, fighter **8** zeppelin **10** hang glider, helicopter, supersonic
battle: 8 dog fight

Akh
origin: 8 Egyptian
transfiguration of: 4 dead

akin 3 kin **4** like **5** alike **6** allied **7** kindred, related, similar, uniform **8** agreeing, parallel **9** analogous, congenial, connected, identical **10** affiliated, comparable, resembling **11** correlative **13** corresponding **14** consanguineous

Akkad *see* **5** Accad

Akkadian Mythology *see* **19** Babylonian Mythology

Akutagawa, Ryunosuke
author of: 5 Kappa **8** Rashomon **13** The Hell Screen

a la 9 in honor of **13** in the manner of

Alabama ***see box, p. 26***

Alabama, Alibamu
language family: 9 Muskogean
location: 5 Texas **9** Louisiana **10** Polk County **12** Alabama River
related to: 7 Koasati

Alacaluf
location: 5 Chile **12** South America

alacrity 4 zeal **6** fervor **7** agility, avidity **8** dispatch **9** alertness, briskness, eagerness, readiness **10** enthusiasm, liveliness, nimbleness, promptness **11** willingness **13** sprightliness

Aladdin
character in: 27 Arabian Nights' Entertainments

Al Aiun, El Aaiun
capital of: 13 Western Sahara

Alalcomenean Athena *see* **6** Athena
reared by: 12 Alalcomeneus

Alalcomeneus
first: 3 man

a la mode 12 in the fashion, in the style of **13** in the manner of

Alarcon, Pedro Antonio de
author: 10 The Scandal **12** Captain Venom **14** El Nino de la Bola **19** The Three-Cornered Hat

alarm 4 fear **5** alert, panic, scare **6** appall, dismay, fright, terror, war cry **7** agitate, disturb, terrify, trouble, unnerve, warning **8** affright, distress, frighten **9** agitation, hue and cry, misgiving **11** trepidation **12** apprehension, perturbation **13** consternation

alarmed 6 afraid, scared

Alabama
abbreviation: **2** AL **3** Ala
nickname: **6** Cotton **12** Heart of Dixie, Yellowhammer
capital: **10** Montgomery
largest city: **10** Birmingham
others: **5** Selma **6** Athens, Dothan, Marion, Mobile **7** Decatur, Gadsden **8** Anniston **10** Huntsville, Tuscaloosa
colleges: **5** Miles **6** Auburn **7** Alabama **8** Tuskegee **9** Talladega **10** Huntingdon
explorer: **12** Hernan DeSoto
feature:
festival: **11** Azalea Trail
statue: **6** Vulcan
tribe: **5** Creek **6** Tohome **7** Alabamu, Alibamu, Koasati **8** Tuskegee
people: **8** Joe Louis **9** Hank Aaron, Hugo Black **10** Willie Mays **11** Helen Keller, Nat King Cole **13** George Wallace, William C Handy, William Gorgas
lake: **12** Guntersville
land rank: **11** twenty-ninth
physical feature:
gulf: **6** Mexico
highest point: **6** Cheaha
highlands: **11** Appalachian
river: **3** Pea **5** Coosa **6** Mobile **7** Alabama **9** Tombigbee, Tennessee **10** Tallapoosa **13** Chattahoochee
state admission: **12** twenty-second
state bird: **7** flicker **12** yellowhammer
state fish: **6** tarpon
state flower: **8** camellia **9** goldenrod
state motto: **21** We Dare Defend Our Rights
state song: **7** Alabama
state tree: **20** southern longleaf pine

7 anxious, fearful, panicky, worried **8** dismayed **9** concerned, terrified **10** frightened **12** apprehensive **13** panic-stricken **14** terror-stricken

alarming **5** awful, dread **7** fearful **8** dreadful **10** horrifying, terrifying **11** frightening, hair-raising

alas
expresses: **4** pity **5** grief **6** sorrow **7** concern **9** weariness **11** unhappiness **12** wretchedness

Alaska ***see box***

Alaskan Adventures
author: **8** Rex Beach

Alastor
epithet of: **4** Zeus **5** demon **11** avenging god
means: **7** avenger
father: **13** Neleus of Pylos
brother: **6** Nestor
wife: **9** Harpalyce
killed by: **8** Hercules

Albach-Retty, Rosemarie
real name of: **13** Romy Schneider

Albania ***see box, p. 28***

Albanian
language family: **12** Indo-European
spoken in: **7** Balkans

Albee, Edward
author of: **3** Box **7** All Over **8** Seascape, Zoo Story **9** Tiny Alice **10** The Sandbox **16** A Delicate Balance, The American Dream **18** The Lady from Dubuque **21** The Ballad of the Sad Cafe, The Death of Bessie Smith **25** Who's Afraid of Virginia Woolf?
identified with: **18** theater of the absurd

Albeniz, Isaac
born: **5** Spain **9** Camprodon
composer of: **6** Iberia **12** The Magic Opal **13** Henry Clifford

Alberich
origin: **8** Teutonic
king of: **6** dwarfs
possessed treasure of: **8** Niblungs **9** Nibelungs
also possessed: **9** Tarnkappe

Albert, Eddie
real name: **21** Eddie Albert Heimberger
wife: **5** Margo
born: **12** Rock Island IL
roles: **8** Oklahoma **10** Brother Rat, Green Acres **11** Room Service **12** Roman Holiday **13** The Longest Day **16** The Heartbreak Kid **19** The Boys from Syracuse

Alberta
abbreviation: **4** Alta
capital/largest city: **8** Edmonton
others: **7** Calgary, Reddeer **10** Lethbridge **11** Medicine Hat
lakes: **5** Banff, Claire **6** Jasper **8** Waterton **9** Athabasca **11** Lesser Slave
rivers: **3** Bow **4** Milk **6** Oldman, Wapiti **9** Athabasca **12** Saskatchewan
religion: **13** Roman Catholic **20** United Church of Canada **22** Anglican Church of Canada
people: **5** Dutch **6** French, German **7** British, English **9** Ukrainian **12** Scandinavian

Albert Herring
opera by: **7** Britten

Alberti, Leon Battista
architect of: **15** Palazzo Rucellai **18** Church of Sant' Andrea, Temple Malatestiano **20** Church of San Sebastian **25** Church of Santa Maria Novello

Albertosaurus
type: **8** dinosaur, theropod
period: **10** Cretaceous

Albertson, Jack
born: **8** Malden MA
roles: **14** Chico and the Man **15** The Sunshine Boys **18** Days of Wine and Roses, The Subject Was Roses

Albion *see* **7** England

album **2** LP **4** book **6** record **8** register **9** portfolio, scrapbook

Albunea
origin: **5** Roman
form: **5** nymph
habitat: **8** fountain

Alcaeus
father: **9** Androgeus
mother: **9** Andromeda
grandfather: **5** Minos
brother: **9** Sthenelus

Alcaids
descendants of: **7** Alcaeus

Alcandre
husband: **7** Polybus
received: **5** Helen **8** Menelaus

Alceste
opera by: **5** Gluck

Alaska
abbreviation: **2** AK **4** Alas
nickname: **9** Great Land, Sourdough **12** Last Frontier **20** Land of the Midnight Sun
capital: **6** Juneau
largest city: **9** Anchorage
others: **4** Nome **5** Sitka **6** Barrow, Kodiak **7** Cordova, Douglas, Skagway **9** Fairbanks, Ketchikan
feature: **5** Alcan **13** Alaska Highway
national park: **13** Mount McKinley
tribe: **3** Han **5** Aleut, Haida **6** Ahtena, Akkhas, Eskimo, Karluk, Tetlin **7** Amerind, Ingalik, Kayukon, Khotana, Kutchin, Tanaina, Tlingit, Tlinkit, Venetie **9** Tsimshian, Unakalett
island: **4** Adak, Atka **5** Aleut **6** Kodiak, Unimak **7** Diomede, Nunivak **8** Aleutian, Pribilof **9** Alexander
lake: **6** Naknek **7** Iliamna **8** Becharof **9** Teshekpuk
land rank: **5** first
mountain: **3** Ada **4** Muir **5** Coast **6** Alaska, Brooks **7** Foraker, St Elias **8** Aleutian, Wrangell **9** Blackburn
highest point: **8** McKinley
physical feature:
bay: **7** Glacier, Prudhoe
channel: **9** Gastineau
glacier: **9** Malaspina
pass: **8** Chilkoot
peninsula: **5** Kenai **6** Alaska, Seward
rapids: **10** Whitehorse
sea: **6** Arctic **8** Beaufort
strait: **6** Bering
river: **5** Kobuk, Yukon **6** Copper, Noatak, Tanana **7** Koyukuk, Susitna **8** Colville **9** Kuskokwim, Matanuska, Porcupine
state admission: **10** forty-ninth
state bird: **15** willow ptarmigan
state fish: **10** king salmon
state flower: **11** forget-me-not
state motto: **16** North to the Future
state song: **11** Alaska's Flag
state symbol: **9** bald eagle
state tree: **11** sitka spruce

Alcestis
author: **9** Euripides
character: **6** Apollo **7** Admetus **8** Heracles, Thanatos

Alcestis
father: **6** Pelias
mother: **8** Anaxibia **10** Phylomache
husband: **7** Admetus
son: **7** Eumelus **8** Hippasus
returned from: **5** Hades
returned by: **8** Hercules

Alchemist, The
author: **9** Ben Jonson
character: **4** Face **5** Surly **6** Dapper, Subtle **7** Ananias, Drugger, Kastril, Love-wit **9** Dol Common **10** Dame Pliant **16** Sir Epicure Mammon **20** Tribulation Wholesome

alchemy **5** magic **7** sorcery **8** wizardry **10** conversion, witchcraft **11** magic appeal **13** transmutation **17** medieval chemistry
god of: **6** Hermes

Alcides *see* **8** Hercules

Alcidice
husband: **10** Salmoneaus
daughter: **4** Tyro

Alcimede
father: **8** Phylacus
mother: **7** Clymene
husband: **5** Aeson
son: **5** Jason

Alcimedon
origin: **8** Arkadian
mentioned in: **5** Iliad
father: **7** Laerces
daughter: **6** Philao
captain of: **9** Myrmidons

Alcina
opera by: **6** Handel
character: **6** Alcina **8** Ruggiero

Alcindor, Lew
former name of: **17** Kareem Abdul-Jabbar

Alcinous
origin: **5** Greek
mentioned in: **7** Odyssey
king of: **10** Phaeacians
father: **10** Nausithous
mother: **8** Periboea
brother: **8** Rhexenor
wife: **5** Arete
son: **8** Laodamas
daughter: **8** Nausicaa
niece: **5** Arete

Alcis
father: **10** Antipoenus
sister: **9** Androclea

Alcithoe
father: **6** Minyas
mocked: **8** Dionysus

Alcmaeon
father: **10** Amphiaraus
mother: **8** Eriphyle
brother: **11** Amphilochus
wife: **10** Callirrhoe
son: **7** Acarnan **10** Amphoterus
daughter: **9** Tisiphone
commanded: **7** Thebans

Alcmaon
father: **7** Thestor
wounded by: **7** Glaucus
killed by: **8** Sarpedon

Alcmene
father: **9** Electryon
mother: **5** Anaxo
husband: **10** Amphitryon **12** Rhadamanthys
twin sons: **8** Hercules, Iphicles

alcohol **3** ale **4** beer, wine **5** drink **6** liquor **7** whiskey **9** the bottle
Latin: **9** aqua vitae

alcoholic **3** sot **4** hard, lush, soak **5** drunk, rummy, souse, toper **6** barfly, boozer, strong **7** guzzler, imbiber, tippler **8** drunkard **9** distilled, fermented, inebriate **10** spirituous **11** dipsomaniac, hard drinker, inebriating, inebriative, whiskey head **12** intoxicating

alcoholism **3** DT's **9** oenomania **10** dipsomania **12** intemperance **15** delirium tremens

Alcon
form: **6** archer, Trojan **7** warrior
aided: **8** Hercules
wounded: **8** Odysseus
abducted: **13** Geryons cattle
killed by: **8** Odysseus

Alcott, Louisa May
author of: **7** Jo's Boys **9** Lit-

Albania
other name: **8** Shqiperi **9** Shqiprija, Shqyptare
capital/largest city: **6** Tirana, Tirane
others: **3** Opp **4** Fier, Klos, Puka, Puke **5** Berat, Dukat, Korce, Kruje, Pecin, Peqin, Qukes, Rubic, Spash, Vlore **6** Avlona, Bitsan, Dardhe, Durrcs, Karaje, Preshe, Valona **7** Chimara, Coritza, Durazzo, Elbasan, Koritsa, Preyesa, Scutari, Shkoder **8** Tepeleni **11** Gjirokaster
monetary unit: **3** lek **5** franc **6** qintar **7** quintar
island: **6** Saseno
lake: **4** Ulze **5** Matia, Ohrid **6** Prespa **7** Ochrida, Scutari, Shkoder **8** Ohridsko
mountain: **5** Shala **6** Pindus **8** Koritnjk **12** Albanian Alps
highest point: **10** Mount Korab
river: **3** Mat **4** Arta, Drin **5** Byene, Erzen, Seman **6** Bojana, Bojane, Vijosa, Vijosa, Vijose **7** Drin-i-ci, Shkumbi
sea: **6** Ionian **8** Adriatic
physical feature:
bay: **5** Vlore
cape: **6** Glossa
gulf: **4** Drin
lagoon: **10** Kara Vastas
peninsula: **6** Balkan
promontory: **13** acroceraunium
strait: **7** Otranto
wind: **4** bora
people: **3** Geg **4** Cham, Gheg, Gueg, Tosk **6** Arnaut, Arnout **8** Illyrian, Skipetar
king: **3** Zog **9** Ahmet Zogu
leader: **5** Hoxha **10** Scanderbeg, Skenderbeg **13** Bishop Fan Noli
language: **3** Geg **4** Cham, Gheg, Hish, Tosk **5** Greek **8** Albanian
religion: **5** Islam **7** Bektash **13** Roman Catholic **15** Eastern Orthodox
place:
square: **10** Skenderbeg
feature:
lute: **6** luhata
soldier: **7** palikar
stone house: **4** kula
food:
cheese: **8** kackaval

tle Men **11** Little Women **12** Eight Cousins, Flower Fables **15** Aunt Jo's Scrap-Bag **18** An Old-Fashioned Girl

alcove **3** bay **4** nook **5** niche **6** corner, recess **7** cubicle, opening **11** compartment

Alcyone
also: **7** Halcyon
father: **6** Aeolus
husband: **4** Ceyx
son: **6** Anthas
transformed into: **10** kingfisher

Alcyoneus
form: **5** giant
hurled: **5** stone
victim: **8** Hercules
killed by: **8** Hercules

Alda, Alan
born: **9** New York NY
father: **10** Robert Alda
real name: **15** Alfonso D'Abruzzo
roles: **4** MASH **9** Paper Lion **13** Hawkeye Pierce **14** The Four Seasons **16** Same Time Next Year, The Mephisto Waltz

Alden, Roberta
character in: **17** An American Tragedy
author: **7** Dreiser

al dente **10** to the tooth **24** neither too soft nor too firm

alder **5** Alnus
varieties: **3** Red **5** Black, Hazel, White, Witch **6** Oregon, Smooth, Yellow **7** Italian, Seaside **8** Japanese, Mountain, Speckled **9** Caucasian **10** Manchurian **13** American green, European green

Aldiss, Brian W
author of: **7** Non-Stop **9** Greybeard **13** The Saliva Tree **19** Frankenstein Unbound, The Billion Year Spree, The Eighty Minute Hour

ale **4** beer, brew **5** stout **12** malt beverage **15** English festival

Alea
epithet of: **6** Athena
means: **9** sanctuary

Alebion
father: **8** Poseidon
brother: **8** Dercynus
killed by: **8** Hercules

Alecto
member of: **6** Furies

alehouse **3** pub **6** saloon, tavern **7** taproom **11** public house

Aleichem, Sholom
author of: **12** The Great Fair **14** Tevye's Daughter

Alembert, Jean le Rond d'
field: **11** mathematics
nationality: **6** French
studied: **13** fluid dynamics **18** celestial mechanics **28** partial differential equations

Aleph and Other Stories
author: **15** Jorge Luis Borges

alert **4** warn, wary **5** alarm, aware, quick, siren **6** active, inform, lively, nimble, notify, signal **7** careful, heedful, on guard, warning **8** diligent, forewarn, keen-eyed, vigilant, watchful **9** attentive, observant, sprightly, wideawake **10** perceptive **11** intelligent

alertness **8** alacrity, dispatch **9** awareness, readiness, vigilance **10** liveliness **12** watchfulness

Alethia
origin: **5** Greek
personifies: **5** truth

Aleus
king of: **5** Tegea
father: **7** Aphidas
brother: **6** Pereus
cousin: **6** Neaera
wife: **6** Neaera
son: **7** Cepheus **8** Lycurgus **10** Amphidamas
daughter: **4** Auge

Aleut
language family: **6** Eskimo
tribe: **4** Atka **8** Unalaska
location: **6** Alaska **15** Shumagin Islands **17** Aleutian Peninsula
noted for: **7** hunting

Aleutians
islands: **3** Fox, Rat **4** Near

9 Andreanof 25 Islands of the Four Mountains
state: 6 Alaska
people: 6 Aleuts
language: 5 Atkan 9 Unalaskan

Alexander, Jane
real name: 11 Jane Quigley
born: 8 Boston MA
roles: 9 Testament 17 The Great White Hope 18 Eleanor and Franklin 19 All the President's Men

Alexander's Feast
author: 10 John Dryden

Alexander the Great
battle: 5 Issus 9 Gaugamela
birthplace: 5 Pella
conquered: 6 Darius, Persia
father: 8 Philip II
founded: 10 Alexandria
friend: 11 Hephaestion
general: 7 Cleitus 8 Philotas 9 Parmenion
horse: 10 Bucephalus
mother: 8 Olympias
nationality: 10 Macedonian
tutor: 9 Aristotle
wife: 6 Roxana

Alexandra *see* 9 Cassandra

Alexandrinus 16 Greek unical codex

alexandrite
species: 11 chrysoberyl
source: 8 Sri Lanka
color: 3 red 5 green

Alexiares
father: 8 Hercules
mother: 4 Hebe

Alexicacus
epithet of: 6 Apollo
means: 13 averter of evil

Alfader *see* 7 Alfadir

Alfadir
also: 7 Alfader
origin: 12 Scandinavian
epithet of: 4 Odin 5 Othin

Alfheim
origin: 12 Scandinavian
dwelling place of: 5 elves
location: 11 above ground

Alfie
director: 12 Lewis Gilbert
based on play by: 12 Bill Naughton
cast: 12 Michael Caine 14 Shelley Winters

alga, algae 6 fungus 8 pond scum
contains: 4 agar 5 algin 11 carrageenan, chlorophyll
type: 3 red 5 brown, green 9 blue-green, euglenids 11 golden-brown, yellow-green 15 dinoflagellates
forms: 4 kelp 5 dulse 7 diatoms, seaweed 8 plankton, rockweed 9 Irish moss, stonewort

Alger, Horatio
author of: 10 Ragged Dick 11 Tattered Tom 12 Luck and Pluck

Algeria ***see box***

Algiers
Arabic: 8 al-Jazair
building: 11 Great Mosque
capital of: 7 Algeria
center of city: 6 Casbah

Algeria
other name: 7 Algerie, Numidia, Pomaria 9 al-Djazair
capital/largest city: 7 Algiers
others: 4 Bona, Bone, Oran 5 Aflou, Arzew, Batna, Blida, Medea, Saida, Setif, Tenes 6 Abadla, Annaba, Aumale, Barika, Bechar, Bejaia, Benoud, Biskra, Bougie, Dellys, Djanet, Djelfa, Dzioua, Eloued, Frenda, Guelma, Skikda 7 Boghari, Mascara, Miliana, Negrine, Nemours, Ouargla, Tebessa, Tlemcen 8 Ghardaia, Laghouat 9 Touggourt 11 Constantine 12 Sidi-bel-abbes
division: 4 Oran 6 Annaba 7 Algiers 11 Constantine
leader: 3 bey, dey 6 disawa 9 beylerbey
measure: 3 pik 5 rebis, tarri 6 termin
monetary unit: 5 dinar 7 centime
weight: 4 rotl
lake: 5 Hodna 6 Sabkha 7 Cherqui, Fedjadj, Meirhir 10 Azzel Matti, Mekerrhane
mountain: 5 Aissa, Atlas, Aures, Dahra 6 Chelia 7 Ahaggar, Kabylia, Mouydir 8 Djurjura 9 Djurdjura, Tell Atlas 12 Saharan Atlas
highest point: 5 Tahat
river: 6 Shelif 7 Cheliff 8 Medjerda 15 Cheliffmedjerda
sea: 13 Mediterranean
physical feature: 14 Tropic of Cancer
desert: 6 Sahara
giant sand dune: 3 erg
grass: 4 diss 7 esparto
hill: 4 tell
oasis: 4 Mzab
oil field: 7 Edjeleh, El Gassi 10 Zarzaitine 13 Hassi Messaoud (happy spring), Tiguentourine
plain: 7 Cheliff, Mitidja
rocky plateau: 7 hammada
salt basin: 5 chott, shatt
wind: 7 sirocco
people: 4 Arab 6 Berber, Kabyle, Shawia, Tuareg 7 Haratin
author: 3 Dib 5 Camus, Fanon 6 Yacine
leader: 9 Bendjedid 10 Abd al-Qadir, Abd-al-Kadir, Abd-el-Kader 11 Boumedienne 13 Ahmed Ben Bella
ruler: 8 Jugurtha 9 Masinissa
language: 6 Arabic, Berber, French, Zenata 7 Senhaja
religion: 5 Islam
place:
monastery: 5 Ribat
ruins: 7 Djemila
feature:
camel: 6 mehari
cavalry man: 5 spahi 6 spahee
commune: 5 setif
dwelling: 6 gourbi
French settler/landowner: 5 colon 8 piednoir
holy man: 8 marabout
kingdom: 7 Numidia
native quarter: 6 casbah, kasbah
pirate: 7 corsair
ship: 5 xebec, zebec
slum: 10 bidonville
food:
dish: 8 couscous
fruit drink: 5 syrop
seasoning: 4 mint 5 anise, cumin 6 cloves, fennel, ginger, pepper 7 parsley, pimento 8 cinnamon 9 coriander

French: 5 Alger
hills: 5 Sahel
Roman: 7 Icosium
ruled by: 5 Turks 6 French 7 Berbers 10 Free French 14 Barbary Pirates
sea: 13 Mediterranean

Algonkian-Mosan
language branches: 5 Mosan 7 Kutenai 15 Algonkian-Ritwan

Algonkian-Ritwan
language family: 14 Algonkian-Mosan
subgroup: 3 Fox 4 Cree, Sauk 5 Wiyot, Yurok 6 Ojibwa 7 Abenaki, Arapaho, Mohican 8 Cheyenne, Delaware, Menomini 9 Blackfoot

Algonkin, Algonquin
language family: 9 Algonkian 10 Algonquian
tribe: 7 Abitibi 8 Algonkin 9 Nipissing 11 Temiscaming
location: 6 Canada 11 Ottawa River
spirit of nature: 7 Manitou

Algonquian, Algonkian
tribe: 3 Fox, Sac 4 Cree, Innu, Sauk 5 Miami 6 Abnaki, Atsina, Micmac, Ojibwa, Ottawa, Pequot 7 Arapaho, Mahican, Mohegan, Mohican, Ojibway, Shawnee 8 Algonkin, Cheyenne, Chippawa, Delaware, Haaninin, Iliniwek, Illinois, Kickapoo, Menomini, Merrimac, Powhatan, Puyallop 9 Algonquin, Blackfeet, Blackfoot, Massasoit, Menominee, Menomonie, Mesquakie, Pennacook, Penobscot, Pokanoket, Twightwee, Wampanoag 10 Leni-Lenape, Potawatomi 11 Gros Ventres 12 Narragansett 17 Montagnais-Naskapi

algophobia
fear of: 4 pain

Algum 13 red sandalwood

Ali, Muhammad
formerly: 11 Cassius Clay
sport: 6 boxing
class: 11 heavyweight
won: 8 Olympics 16 heavyweight title

alias 9 pseudonym 11 assumed name, nom de guerre

Ali Baba
character in: 27 Arabian Nights' Entertainments

Alibamu *see* 7 Alabama

alibi 3 out 6 excuse 7 pretext 11 explanation 13 justification

Alice Adams
author: 15 Booth Tarkington
character: 6 Mr Lamb 11 Virgil Adams, Walter Adams 13 Arthur Russell, Mildred Palmer

Alice's Adventures in Wonderland
author: 12 Lewis Carroll
character: 5 Alice 7 Duchess 9 Mad Hatter, March Hare 10 Mock Turtle 11 Cheshire Cat, White Rabbit 12 King of Hearts 13 Queen of Hearts

Alice Sit-by-the-Fire
author: 12 James M Barrie

alien 6 exotic, remote, unlike 7 distant, foreign, opposed, strange 8 contrary, newcomer, outsider, stranger 9 different, estranged, foreigner, immigrant, not native, outlander, separated, unrelated 10 dissimilar, outlandish 11 conflicting, incongruous, unconnected 12 incompatible, inconsistent 13 contradictory
German: 9 Auslander

alienate 7 divorce 8 estrange, separate, turn away

alienation 5 exile 7 divorce 9 isolation 10 separation, withdrawal 13 repulsiveness

alight 4 land 6 get off 7 deplane, descend, detrain, get down 8 come down, dismount 9 climb down, disembark, thump down, touch down

align 4 ally, even, join, side 6 even up, line up 9 affiliate, associate 10 straighten

alignment 7 allying, evening 9 evening up 13 straightening

alike 4 akin, even, same 5 equal 6 evenly 7 equally, kindred, uniform 8 of a piece, parallel 9 analogous, identical, similarly, uniformly 10 equivalent, synonymous 11 homogeneous, identically 13 corresponding

Alisande (Sandy)
character in: 36 A Connecticut Yankee in King Arthur's Court
author: 5 Twain

alive 4 spry 5 alert, aware, eager, quick, vital 6 active, extant, lively, living, viable 7 animate, in force, not dead 8 animated, possible, spirited, vigorous 9 breathing, energetic, operative, vivacious 10 subsisting, unquenched 11 above ground, in existence, in operation 14 unextinguished

alive to 5 alert, awake, aware 7 heedful, mindful 8 watchful 9 attentive, conscious, wide-awake

alkaline 5 salty 7 antacid 9 nonacidic

alkaloid 7 alkaline, codeine, guinine 8 morphine, nicotine 16 colorless complex

all 4 each, full, very 5 any of, every, fully, total, utter, whole 6 each of, entire, to a man, utmost, wholly 7 highest, perfect, totally, utterly 8 any one of, complete, entirely, everyone, greatest, the sum of, the total, the whole 9 every item 10 altogether, completely, every one of, everything, the total of, the whole of 11 every member, every part of, exceedingly, the entirety

All About Eve
director: 17 Joseph L Mankiewicz
cast: 10 Anne Baxter, Bette Davis 11 Celeste Holm, Gary Merrill 12 Thelma Ritter 13 George Sanders, Marilyn Monroe
Oscar for: 7 picture 8 director 10 screenplay 15 supporting actor (George Sanders)

Allan-a-Dale, Alan-a-Dale
character in: 9 Robin Hood

allargando
music: 13 getting slower

all around 6 abroad 7 all over 10 everywhere, far and wide 15 making the rounds

all-around 5 broad 6 adroit, gifted 8 flexible 9 adaptable, many-sided, versatile 11 well-rounded 12 ambidextrous, multifaceted 13 comprehensive

allay 4 calm, dull, ease, hush 5 blunt, check, quell, quiet, slake 6 lessen, pacify, quench, reduce, smooth, soften, soothe, subdue 7 appease, assuage, lighten, mollify, relieve, slacken 8 diminish, mitigate, moderate 9 alleviate, put to rest 14 cause to subside

all but 6 almost, nearly 7 close to 8 not quite 10 not far from, very nearly 14 except everyone, within an inch of 16 everything except

all by oneself 5 alone 7 unaided **9** on one's own **10** unassisted **13** unaccompanied

all-consuming **3** hot **5** fiery **6** ardent, fervid, raging, red-hot **7** burning, fanatic, fervent, frantic, glowing, intense, zealous **8** frenzied **10** passionate **11** impassioned

allegation **5** claim **6** avowal, charge **9** assertion, statement **10** accusation, contention, indictment, profession **11** declaration

allege **3** say **4** aver, avow **5** claim, state **6** accuse, affirm, assert, charge, impugn, impute **7** contend, declare, profess **8** maintain

allegiance **6** fealty, homage **7** loyalty **8** devotion, fidelity **9** adherence, constancy, deference, obedience **12** faithfulness

allegory **5** fable **7** parable

allegro
music: **4** fast

all-embracing **5** broad **6** all-out **7** general, overall **8** complete, sweeping, thorough **9** expansive, extensive, universal, unlimited **10** exhaustive, widespread **11** far-reaching, wide-ranging **12** all-inclusive, encyclopedic **13** comprehensive

Allen, Arabella
character in: **14** Pickwick Papers
author: **7** Dickens

Allen, Ethan
served in: **16** Revolutionary War
commander of: **17** Green Mountain Boys
captured: **15** Fort Ticonderoga

Allen, Fred
real name: **20** John Florence Sullivan
born: **11** Cambridge MA
roles: **11** What's My Line **16** The Fred Allen Show

Allen, Steve
real name: **12** Stephen Allen
wife: **12** Jayne Meadows
nickname: **10** Mr Midnight
born: **9** New York NY
roles: **13** I've Got a Secret **14** The Tonight Show

Allen, William Hervey
author of: **7** Israfel **14** Anthony Adverse

Allen, Woody
author of: **11** Getting Even, Side Effects **15** Without Feathers
real name: **22** Allen Stewart Konigsberg
wife: **12** Louise Lasser
born: **10** Brooklyn NY
roles: **5** Zelig **7** Bananas, Sleeper **9** Annie Hall, Manhattan **16** Stardust Memories **19** Hannah and Her Sisters
director of: **5** Zelig **7** Bananas, Sleeper **9** Annie Hall (Oscar), Interiors, Manhattan **16** Stardust Memories **19** Hannah and Her Sisters **20** The Purple Rose of Cairo

alleviate **4** dull, ease, quit **5** abate, allay, blunt, check, slake **6** lessen, quench, reduce, soften, subdue, temper **7** assuage, lighten, mollify, relieve, slacken **8** diminish, mitigate, moderate

alleviation **6** easing, relief **9** lessening **10** palliation

alley **4** lane **5** byway **7** passage, pathway **10** passageway **16** narrow back street

Alley Oop
creator: **14** Vincent T Hamlin
character:
girlfriend: **4** Oola
dinosaur: **5** Dinny
king: **6** Guzzle
scientist: **8** Dr Wonmug
place:
kingdom of: **3** Moo

All for Love
author: **10** John Dryden
character: **6** Antony, Caesar **7** Octavia **9** Cleopatra, Dolabella, Ventidius

All God's Chillun Got Wings
author: **12** Eugene O'Neill
character: **6** Mickey **9** Jim Harris **10** Ella Downey

alliance **4** pact **5** union **6** league, treaty **7** compact, company **9** agreement, coalition, concordat **10** federation **11** affiliation, association, confederacy, partnership **13** confederation **15** entente cordiale

allied **4** akin, like **5** alike, joint **6** united **7** cognate, kindred, related, similar **8** combined **9** corporate, federated **10** affiliated, associated, resembling **11** amalgamated **12** incorporated

all in **4** beat **5** spent, tired, weary **6** bushed, done in, pooped **7** drained, wearied, worn out **8** dog tired, fatigued, tired out **9** bone weary, dead tired, exhausted, played out

all in all **5** in sum **10** on the whole **20** when all is said and done

all-inclusive **5** broad **6** all-out, entire **7** general, overall **8** absolute, complete, sweeping, thorough **9** expansive, extensive, universal, unlimited **10** altogether, exhaustive, widespread **11** far-reaching, wide-ranging **12** all-embracing **13** comprehensive

All in the Family
character: **10** Joey Stivic, Mike Stivic (Meathead) **11** Edith Bunker (Dingbat) **12** Archie Bunker **18** Gloria Bunker Stivic
cast: **9** Rob Reiner **13** Jean Stapleton **14** Carroll O'Connor, Sally Struthers
spinoffs: **5** Maude **12** Archie's Place **13** The Jeffersons

allocate **5** allot, allow **6** assign, budget **7** earmark **8** set aside **9** apportion, designate **11** appropriate

allocation **5** quota, share **7** measure, portion **8** division **9** allotment, meting out **10** dealing out **11** consignment, designation **12** apportioning, dispensation, distribution **13** apportionment

Allosaurus *see* **10** Antrodemus

allot **5** allow, grant **6** assign **7** appoint, consign, dole out, earmark, give out, mete out, provide **8** allocate, dispense, divide up **9** apportion, parcel out **10** distribute, portion out

allotment **5** grant, quota, share **6** ration **7** measure, portion **9** allowance **10** allocation **11** consignment **12** dispensation **13** apportionment, appropriation

all-out **5** broad, total **7** full-out, maximum **8** complete, sweeping, thorough **9** extensive, full-scale **11** unqualified, unremitting **12** all-embracing, all-inclusive **13** comprehensive, thoroughgoing

all over **5** ended, kaput **8** finished **9** concluded **10** everywhere **11** universally

All Over
author: **11** Edward Albee

allow **3** let **4** give **5** allot, grant **6** assign, permit **7** agree to, approve, concede, provide **8** allocate, sanction **9** authorize

allowable **7** allowed **8** accepted **9** permitted, tolerable, tolerated **10** acceptable, admissible, admittable, authorized, sanctioned **11** permissible

allowance **5** grant **6** bounty, income, ration **7** annuity, payment, pension, stipend, subsidy **8** discount **9** allotment, deduction, reduction **10** concession **11** subtraction

allow to go **4** free **5** let go **6** excuse **7** dismiss, release, set free **8** liberate **9** discharge

allow to pass
French: **13** laissez passer

alloy **3** mix **5** admix, blend **6** commix, dilute, fusion, impair **7** amalgam, combine, mixture **8** compound, intermix **9** admixture, composite, synthesis **10** adulterate, commixture, interblend **12** conglomerate

alloyed **5** mixed **6** impure **7** debased

All Quiet on the Western Front
author: **18** Erich Maria Remarque
character: **6** Muller, Tjaden **10** Paul Baumer **11** Albert Kropp, Haie Westhus **20** Stanislaus Katczinsky (Kat)
director: **14** Lewis Milestone
cast: **8** Lew Ayres **12** Louis Wolheim **14** Russell Gleason
setting: **3** WWI
Oscar for: **7** picture

all right **2** OK **3** yes **4** fair, hale, safe, well **6** hearty **7** healthy **8** properly, unharmed **9** certainly, correctly, uninjured **10** absolutely, acceptably, unimpaired **14** satisfactorily
Spanish: **5** bueno

All Said and Done
author: **16** Simone de Beauvoir

allspice
botanical name: **7** pimenta, p dioica **12** p officinalis
also called: **7** pimento
origin: **7** Jamaica **16** Caribbean Islands
flavor: **5** clove **6** nutmeg **8** cinnamon
use: **6** baking

Allston, Washington
born: **10** Waccamaw SC
artwork: **9** The Deluge **13** Uriel in the Sun **16** Belshazzar's Feast, Moonlit Landscape **20** Spanish Girl in Reverie

All's Well That Ends Well
author: **18** William Shakespeare
character: **5** Diana **6** Helena **7** Bertram **8** Parolles **12** King of France **14** Duke of Florence **19** Countess of Rousillon

All That Jazz
director: **8** Bob Fosse
cast: **9** Ben Vereen **11** Ann Reinking, Cliff Gorman, Roy Scheider **12** Jessica Lange, Leland Palmer

All the King's Men
author: **16** Robert Penn Warren
character: **10** Jack Burden, Judge Irwin, Sadie Burke **11** Adam Stanton, Willie Stark **12** Annie Stanton
director: **12** Robert Rossen
cast: **9** Joanne Dru, John Derek **11** John Ireland **17** Broderick Crawford **19** Mercedes McCambridge
Oscar for: **5** actor (Crawford) **7** picture **17** supporting actress (McCambridge)

all the more
Latin: **9** a fortiori

All the President's Men
author: **11** Bob Woodward **13** Carl Bernstein
subject: **16** Watergate scandal
newspaper: **14** Washington Post
director: **11** Alan J Pakula
cast: **10** Jack Warden **11** Hal Holbrook **12** Jason Robards, Martin Balsam **13** Dustin Hoffman (Carl Bernstein), Jane Alexander, Robert Redford (Bob Woodward)
Oscar for: **12** screenwriter **15** supporting actor (Robards)

all the same **5** alike **7** however, uniform **8** unvaried **9** identical **11** homogeneous

all together **7** en masse, in a body **8** as a group, in a group, in unison
French: **12** tout ensemble

all told **5** in sum, total **6** in toto **7** totally **8** as a whole **10** altogether

allude **4** hint **5** refer **7** mention, speak of, suggest **8** intimate **9** touch upon

allure **4** bait, lure **5** charm, tempt **6** entice, lead on, seduce **7** attract, beguile, enchant, glamour **8** intrigue **9** captivate, fascinate **10** attraction, enticement, temptation **11** enchantment, fascination

allurement **4** draw, lure **5** charm **9** magnetism **10** attraction **11** fascination

alluring **4** sexy **8** charming, enticing, magnetic **10** attractive **11** fascinating

allusion **4** hint **7** mention **9** reference **10** suggestion

Allworthy, Squire
character in: **8** Tom Jones
author: **8** Fielding

ally **5** unite **6** league **7** combine, partner **8** confrere **9** accessory, affiliate, associate, colleague **10** accomplice, join forces **11** confederate **12** band together, bind together, collaborator, join together

Allyson, June
real name: **11** Ella Geisman
husband: **10** Dick Powell
born: **9** New York NY
roles: **8** Good News **9** Interlude, The Shrike **11** Little Women **12** My Man Godfrey **16** The Stratton Story **18** The Glen Miller Story

Almagest
author: **7** Ptolemy
title means: **11** the greatest
subject: **9** astronomy

Al Maghrib *see* **7** Morocco

almandite
species: **6** garnet
color: **3** red

Almaviva, Count and Countess
author: **12** Beaumarchais
characters in: **18** The Barber of Seville **19** The Marriage of Figaro

Almayer's Folly
author: **12** Joseph Conrad

almighty **7** supreme **8** absolute, infinite **9** sovereign, unlimited **10** invincible, omnipotent **11** all-powerful **12** transcendent

Almira
opera by: **6** Handel

almond **12** Prunus dulcis
varieties: **4** Wild **5** Earth, Green, Sweet **6** Bitter, Desert, Indian **8** Tropical **9** Flowering **12** Dwarf Russian
candy: **8** marzipan
liqueur: **6** orgeat **7** ratafia

almost **5** about **6** all but, nearly **7** close to **8** not quite, well-nigh **9** just about **10** not far from, very nearly **11** practically, on the verge of **13** approximately **14** within an inch of

almost alike **5** close **7** similar **10** resembling **11** approaching, much the same **15** nearly identical

alms **3** aid **4** dole, gift **5** mercy **6** relief **7** charity, handout, largess, present, subsidy, tribute **8** donation, gratuity, offering, pittance **9** baksheesh **10** assistance

11 benefaction, beneficence **12** contribution

almshouse 6 asylum **9** poorhouse, workhouse

almsman 5 tramp **6** beggar **9** mendicant **10** panhandler

Almug 13 red sandalwood

aloft 2 up **5** above, way up **6** high up, on high **7** skyward **8** in the air, in the sky, overhead **10** heavenward

Aloha state
nickname of: 6 Hawaii

Aloidae
name: 4 Otus **9** Ephialtes
form: 5 giant
father: 8 Poseidon
mother: 9 Iphimedia
raised by: 6 Aloeus

alone 4 only, sole **6** lonely, single, singly, solely, unique **7** forlorn, unaided **8** deserted, desolate, forsaken, isolated, lonesome, peerless, singular, solitary, uniquely **9** abandoned, matchless, nonpareil, separated, unmatched, unrivaled **10** friendless, separately, singularly, solitarily, unassisted, unattended, unequalled, unescorted **11** unsurpassed, without help **12** incomparable, unchaperoned, unparalleled, without peers **13** unaccompanied, without others **14** single-handedly
Latin: 4 sola **5** solus
French: 4 seul

along 2 on **4** over **6** beside, during, onward **7** abreast, forward, through

alongside 2 at, by **6** beside, next to **7** abreast, close by **9** at the side **10** parallel to **12** collaterally, parallelwise **13** equidistantly

aloof 4 cold, cool **5** above, apart **6** chilly, formal, remote **7** distant, haughty, high-hat **8** detached, reserved **10** unsociable **11** at a distance, indifferent, standoffish, unconcerned **12** uninterested, unresponsive **13** unsympathetic **14** unapproachable

aloofness 7 reserve **8** coldness, coolness **9** formality **10** detachment, remoteness **11** haughtiness **12** indifference **13** unsociability **15** standoffishness

Alope
father: 7 Cercyon
son: 10 Hippothous
attacked by: 8 Poseidon

Alopecus
origin: 7 Spartan
form: 6 prince

aloud 7 audibly

alphabet 4 ABCs **6** schema **7** grammar, letters **8** elements **9** rudiments, tablature **10** characters, principles **13** writing system

Alphesiboea
also: 7 Arsinoe
form: 5 nymph
father: 4 Bias **7** Phegeus **9** Leucippus
mother: 9 Philodice
husband: 8 Alcmaeon
son: 6 Adonis
rejected: 8 Dionysus
nurse for: 7 Orestes

Alpheus
father: 7 Oceanus
mother: 6 Tethys
loved: 8 Arethusa
changed into: 5 river

Alphonse and Gaston
creator: 14 Frederick Opper
saying: 22 After you my dear Alphonse, No after you my dear Gaston

alpine 5 alpen, lofty **6** aerial **8** elevated, snow-clad, towering **9** subalpine **10** alpestrine, sky-kissing, snow-capped **11** cloud-capped, mountainous **13** cloud-piercing, cloud-touching **14** heaven-touching

Alps, Alpine
country: 5 Italy **6** France **7** Austria, Germany **10** Yugoslavia **11** Switzerland **13** Liechtenstein
range: 6 Carnic, Graian, Julian, Otztal **7** Bernese, Cottian, Pennine **8** Bavarian, Ligurian, Maritime, Rhaetian **9** Dolomites, Lepontine **10** Hohe Tauern
peak: 4 Rosa **5** Eiger, Monch **8** Jungfrau **10** Karawanken, Matterhorn, Piz Bernina **13** Grossglockner
highest point: 5 Blanc
pass: 7 Brenner, Simplon, Splugen, Stelvio **9** Semmering **10** St Gotthard **14** Great St Bernard
lake: 4 Como **6** Alpine, Geneva **7** Lucerne **8** Maggiore **9** Constance
resort: 7 Zermatt **8** Chamonix, Salzburg, St Moritz **9** Innsbruck **13** Berchtesgaden
wind: 6 foehns

already 5 early, so far **6** before **8** formerly, hitherto, until now **10** heretofore, previously

already seen
French: 6 deja vu

also 3 and, too **4** more, plus **5** extra **6** as well **7** besides **8** moreover **9** including **10** in addition **12** additionally

Altaic
language branches: 6 Turkic **8** Tungusic **9** Mongolian

altar 5 bomos **6** hestia, scribis **7** eschara **8** credence **9** holy table, prothesis **10** Lord's table

Altar
constellation of: 3 Ara

Altdorfer, Albrecht
born: 7 Germany **10** Regensburg
artwork: 16 Susanna at the Bath **20** St George and the Dragon, Susannah and the Elders **24** Landscape with a Footbridge **39** The Battle of Alexander and Darius on the Issus

alter 4 vary **5** amend **6** change, modify, recast, revise **7** convert, remodel **9** transform **13** make different

alterable 7 unfixed **8** variable **9** adaptable **10** adjustable, changeable, modifiable **11** convertible

alteration 6 change **10** adjustment, conversion, remodeling **12** modification **13** transmutation **14** transformation

altercation 3 row **4** spat **5** brawl, broil, fight, melee, scene **6** affray, fracas, rumpus, scrape **7** discord, dispute, quarrel, scuffle **8** argument **9** bickering, wrangling **10** falling-out **11** controversy **12** disagreement

alter ego 4 twin **5** match **6** double **9** duplicate, other self, semblable **10** complement, other image, second self, simulacrum **11** counterpart **12** Doppelganger

alternate 3 sub **4** vary **5** alter, proxy **6** backup, change, deputy, rotate, second **7** another, standby, stand-in **9** surrogate, take turns **10** every other, reciprocal, substitute, successive, understudy **11** alternating, consecutive, every second, interchange, intersperse, pinch hitter

alternative 6 choice, option, way out **8** recourse **9** selection **10** substitute **11** other choice

Altes
origin: 5 Greek
mentioned in: 5 Iliad
king of: 7 Leleges
daughter: 7 Laothoe

Althaea
father: **8** Thestius
brother: **9** Plexippus
husband: **6** Oeneus
son: **6** Toxeus, Tydeus **8** Meleager
daughter: **5** Gorge **8** Deianira

Althaemenes
father: **7** Catreus
sister: **9** Apemosyne
killed: **7** Catreus **9** Apemosyne

although **3** but, yet **4** even **5** still **7** however **11** nonetheless **12** nevertheless **15** notwithstanding

altitude **4** apex **6** height, vertex, zenith **8** eminence, tallness **9** elevation, loftiness, sublimity **10** prominence

Altman, Robert
director of: **4** MASH **9** Nashville

altogether **5** fully, in all, in sum, quite **6** in toto, wholly **7** all told, totally, utterly **8** all in all, as a whole, entirely **9** in general, out and out, perfectly **10** absolutely, completely, in sum total, on the whole, thoroughly **12** all inclusive, collectively

altruism **7** charity **10** generosity **11** benevolence **12** philanthropy, public spirit **13** unselfishness **14** bigheartedness, charitableness **15** humanitarianism

altruistic **8** generous **9** unselfish **10** benevolent, charitable **12** humanitarian, largehearted **13** philanthropic **14** public-spirited

aluminum
chemical symbol: **2** Al

alumnus **8** graduate **12** male graduate **13** former student

Alverio, Rosita Dolores
real name of: **10** Rita Moreno

always **7** forever **8** evermore **9** eternally, every time, regularly **10** for all time, invariably **11** continually, incessantly, perpetually, unceasingly **12** consistently **13** everlastingly, unremittingly **14** forever and ever

Amadan
origin: **5** Irish
form: **5** fairy

Amadeus
director: **11** Milos Forman
cast: **8** Tom Hulce (Wolfgang Amadeus Mozart) **14** F Murray Abraham (Antonio Salieri)
choreography: **10** Twyla Tharp
Oscar for: **5** actor (Abraham) **7** picture **8** director

Amadis of Gaul
author: **16** Garcia de Montalvo
character: **6** Oriana, Perion **7** Elisena **8** Garinter, Lisuarte

Amado, Jorge
author of: **14** Tent of Miracles **15** Home Is the Sailor **19** Shepherds of the Night **24** Gabriela Clove and Cinnamon **25** Dona Flor and Her Two Husbands **30** The Two Deaths of Quincas Wateryell

Amahl and the Night Visitors
opera by: **7** Menotti

Amalek
father: **7** Eliphaz
mother: **6** Timnah
grandfather: **4** Esau
descendant of: **9** Amalekite

amalgam **5** alloy, blend, combo, union **6** fusion, league, merger **7** joining, mixture **8** alliance, compound, mishmash **9** admixture, composite **10** assemblage, commixture **11** combination **12** amalgamation, intermixture

amalgamate **3** mix **4** fuse **5** blend, merge, unify, unite **7** combine **8** coalesce, federate **9** commingle, integrate **10** synthesize **11** consolidate, incorporate **12** join together

Amalthaea
form: **4** goat **5** nymph
raised: **4** Zeus

Amarcord
director: **15** Federico Fellini
cast: **10** Bruno Zanin, Magali Noel **13** Pupella Maggio

amaretto
type: **7** liqueur
origin: **5** Italy
flavor: **6** almond
with vodka: **9** Godmother

Amaryllis
character in: **9** Ecologues
author: **6** Virgil
represented: **11** shepherdess

Amarynceus
origin: **5** Greek
mentioned in: **5** Iliad
king of: **7** Messene
ruled: **4** Elis
ruled with: **6** Augeas
killed by: **6** Nestor

Amasa
father: **6** Jether
mother: **7** Abigail
uncle: **5** David
commander for: **5** David **7** Absalom
killed by: **4** Joab

amass **6** gather, heap up, pile up **7** acquire, collect, compile, round up **8** assemble **10** accumulate

amassing **7** heaping, piling **8** piling up **9** aggregate, compiling, gathering **10** assemblage, assembling, collecting **11** compilation **12** accumulating

Amata
husband: **7** Latinus
daughter: **7** Lavinia

amateur **4** tyro **6** novice **7** dabbler **8** beginner, hobbyist, inexpert, neophyte **9** greenhorn, unskilled **10** dilettante, unpolished **13** inexperienced **14** unprofessional **15** nonprofessional

amateurish **5** inept **6** clumsy **7** awkward **8** inexpert, mediocre **9** unskilled, untrained **10** unskillful **11** incompetent, ineffective, unpracticed **13** inexperienced **14** unaccomplished, unprofessional

amatory **3** hot **4** fond, sexy **6** ardent, doting, erotic, loving, sexual, steamy, tender **7** adoring, amorous, devoted, fervent, sensual, sexed-up **8** lovesick, romantic, yearning **9** libidinal, loverlike, rapturous **10** infatuated, lascivious, passionate **11** impassioned, languishing

amaxophobia
fear of: **7** driving **8** vehicles

amaze **3** awe **4** daze, stun **5** shock **7** astound, stagger, stupefy **8** astonish, surprise **9** dumbfound **11** flabbergast

amazement **3** awe **5** shock **6** wonder **8** surprise **9** disbelief **11** incredulity **12** astonishment, bewilderment, stupefaction

Amaziah
father: **5** Joash
opposed: **7** Jehoash
captured at: **11** Bethshemesh
killed at: **7** Lachish

Amazon
occupation: **7** warrior
sex: **6** female
queen: **9** Hippolyta

amazonite
species: **8** feldspar

Amazonomachia
battle between: **6** Greeks **7** Amazons

ambassador **5** agent, envoy **6** consul, deputy, legate, nuncio **7** attache, courier **8** diplomat, emissary, minister **9** go-between **11** diplomatist **12** intermediary **13** consul general **14** representative

Ambassadors, The
author: **10** Henry James
character: **8** Strether, Waymarsh **10** Mrs Newsome **11** Mamie Pocock, Sarah Pocock **12** Maria Gostrey **15** Chadwick Newsome **17** Comtesse de Vionnet

amber
formed from: **5** resin
color: **6** yellow
Greek: **8** elektron

ambiance **3** air **4** aura, mood, tone **5** tenor **6** spirit, flavor, milieu, temper **7** climate, setting **9** character **10** atmosphere **11** environment **12** surroundings

ambiguity **9** vagueness **11** uncertainty **12** abstruseness, doubtfulness, equivocation **14** indefiniteness
French: **13** double entente

ambiguous **5** vague **7** cryptic, unclear **8** doubtful, puzzling **9** enigmatic, equivocal, uncertain **10** indefinite, misleading

ambition **3** aim **4** goal, hope, plan, push, zeal **5** dream, drive **6** design, desire, intent **7** longing, purpose **8** striving, yearning **9** objective **10** aspiration

ambitious **4** avid **5** eager **6** ardent, intent **7** arduous, zealous **8** aspiring, desirous **9** difficult, energetic, grandiose, strenuous **10** determined **11** industrious **12** enterprising

ambivalent **5** mixed **7** warring **8** clashing, confused, opposing, wavering **9** equivocal, undecided, unfocused **10** wishy-washy **11** conflicting, fluctuating, vacillating **13** contradictory

amble **6** ramble, stroll **7** meander, saunter **15** wander aimlessly

Ambler, Eric
author of: **11** The Levanter **12** A Kind of Auger **13** The Care of Time **14** The Night-Comers, Uncommon Danger **15** Journey Into Fear, The Dark Frontier **16** The Light of the Day **19** A Coffin for Dimitrios **22** The Siege of the Villa Lipp

Ambling Alp, The
nickname of: **12** Primo Carnera

ambrosial **5** balmy **8** fragrant, luscious, perfumed **9** delicious **13** sweet-smelling

ambrosia of the gods
4 food **5** drink **6** nectar **7** perfume

ambulance chaser **4** beak **6** lawyer **8** attorney **9** counselor **10** mouthpiece **12** legal advisor

ambulatory **6** mobile, moving **7** walking **10** up and about **11** peripatetic

ambush **4** trap **5** blind, cover **6** attack, entrap, hiding, lay for, waylay **7** assault **8** hideaway, surprise **9** ambuscade **11** concealment, hiding place **13** stalking-horse

Ameche, Don
real name: **17** Dominic Felix Amici
born: **9** Kenosha WI
roles: **6** Cocoon (Oscar) **13** Heaven Can Wait, Moon Over Miami, Silk Stockings **14** That Night in Rio **16** Down Argentine Way **18** The Three Musketeers **29** The Story of Alexander Graham Bell

Amelia
author: **13** Henry Fielding
character: **10** Dr Harrison **11** Mrs Atkinson **12** Miss Matthews **19** Captain William Booth

ameliorate **4** heal, help, mend **5** amend, fix up **6** better, perk up, pick up, reform, remedy, revise **7** advance, correct, improve, patch up, promote, rectify **8** palliate, progress **9** come along, get better **10** grow better **11** improve upon

ameliorative **8** remedial **9** improving **10** corrective, palliative **11** therapeutic **12** compensatory

amen **5** truly **6** it is so, so be it, verily **8** hear hear **9** let it be so, yes indeed **11** so shall it be **17** would that it were so

Amen
also: **4** Amon **5** Ammon
origin: **8** Egyptian
king of: **4** gods
worshiped at: **6** Thebes
personifies: **3** air **6** breath
represented by: **3** ram **5** goose
patron of: **6** Thebes
corresponds to: **4** Jove, Zeus **6** Amen Ra, Amon Ra **7** Jupiter

amenable **4** open **7** cordial, willing **8** obliging, yielding **9** agreeable, tractable **10** open-minded, responsive, submissive **11** acquiescent, complaisant, cooperative, persuadable, sympathetic **17** favorably disposed

amend **3** fix **4** mend **5** alter, emend **6** better, change, modify, polish, reform, remedy, revise **7** correct, develop, enhance, improve, perfect, rectify

amendment **6** change, reform **7** adjunct **8** addition, revision **10** alteration, correction, emendation **11** improvement **12** modification **13** rectification

amends **7** apology, defense, payment, redress **8** requital **9** atonement, expiation **10** recompense, reparation **11** explanation, restitution, restoration, retribution, vindication **12** compensation, satisfaction **13** justification, peace offering **14** acknowledgment **15** indemnification

amenity, amenities **8** civility, mildness, niceties **9** geniality, gentility **10** affability, amiability, courtesies, gentleness, politeness, refinement **11** gallantries, good manners **12** friendliness, graciousness, pleasantness **13** agreeableness

Amen Ra
also: **6** Amon Ra
origin: **8** Egyptian
god of: **8** universe
corresponds to: **4** Amen, Amon, Jove, Zeus **5** Ammon **7** Jupiter

America
author: **19** Stephen Vincent Benet

America, North ***see box, p. 36***

America, South ***see box, p. 37***

American, The
author: **10** Henry James
character: **8** Mrs Bread **10** Mr Tristram **11** Mrs Tristram **12** Noemie Nioche **13** Count Valentin **14** Claire de Cintre **17** Christopher Newman **25** Marquis Urbain de Bellegarde
setting: **5** Paris

American Caesar
author: **17** William Manchester

American Claimant, The
author: **9** Mark Twain

American Dreams
author: **11** Studs Terkel

American Graffiti
director: **11** George Lucas
cast: **9** Paul Le Mat, Ron

America, North
country: **4** Cuba **5** Haiti **6** Belize, Canada, Mexico, Panama **8** Honduras **9** Costa Rica, Guatemala, Nicaragua **10** El Salvador **12** United States **17** Dominican Republic
island: **5** Banks **6** Baffin, Kodiak **7** Bahamas, Bermuda **8** Victoria **9** Alexander, Anticosti, Ellesmere, Greenland, Vancouver **10** Aleutians, Cape Breton, Long Island, West Indies **11** Southampton **12** Newfoundland, Prince Edward **13** Prince of Wales **14** Queen Charlotte
mountain: **5** Coast, Rocky **6** Brooks **7** Cascade **9** Mackenzie **10** Bitterroot **11** Appalachian **12** Sierra Nevada
highest point: **8** McKinley
lowest point: **11** Death Valley
river: **3** Red **4** Ohio **5** Yukon **6** Copper, Fraser, Hudson, Nelson **8** Arkansas, Colorado, Columbia, Delaware, Missouri **9** Mackenzie **10** Coppermine, Sacramento, San Joaquin, St Lawrence **11** Connecticut, Mississippi
lake: **4** Erie **5** Huron **6** Carson, Walker **7** Nipigon, Ontario **8** Manitoba, Michigan, Reindeer, Superior, Winnipeg **9** Athabasca, Champlain, Great Bear, Great Salt **10** Great Slave **11** Yellowstone
animal: **3** bat, rat **4** bear, lynx, puma, wolf **5** bison, moose, skunk **6** beaver, musk ox **7** bighorn, caribou **8** sewellel **9** pronghorn, white goat
bird: **4** hawk **5** eagle, snipe **8** bobwhite, woodcock, wood ibis **9** blue heron, ptarmigan
sea: **6** Bering **7** Chukchi, Lincoln **8** Beaufort **9** Caribbean
religion: **7** Judaism **10** Protestant **13** Roman Catholic **27** Eastern Orthodox Christianity
people: **6** Eskimo **8** European **12** African Negro **14** American Indian
language: **6** French **7** English, Spanish

Howard **10** Candy Clark **11** Wolfman Jack **12** Harrison Ford **13** Cindy Williams **15** Richard Dreyfuss **17** MacKenzie Phillips

American in Paris, An
director: **16** Vincente Minnelli
cast: **8** Nina Foch **9** Gene Kelly **11** Leslie Caron, Oscar Levant **14** Georges Guetary
score: **14** George Gershwin
Oscar for: **7** picture

Americanization of Emily
director: **12** Arthur Hiller
script by: **14** Paddy Chayefsky
cast: **11** James Coburn, James Garner **12** Julie Andrews **13** Melvyn Douglas

American Tragedy, An
author: **15** Theodore Dreiser
character: **12** Roberta Alden **14** Clyde Griffiths, Sondra Finchley **15** Samuel Griffiths

America's Sweetheart
nickname of: **12** Mary Pickford

amethyst
species: **6** quartz
color: **6** purple
month: **8** February

Amfortas
leader of: **7** knights
in search of: **9** holy grail

ami, amie **6** friend

amiability **10** good nature, kindliness **12** agreeability, friendliness, pleasantness

amiable **6** genial, kindly, polite **7** affable, cordial, winning **8** amicable, charming, engaging, friendly, gracious, obliging, pleasant, pleasing, sociable **9** agreeable, congenial **10** attractive **11** good-natured

amicability **5** amity **7** concord **8** good will **9** affection **10** cordiality, friendship **12** friendliness **14** neighborliness

amicable **4** kind **5** civil **6** kindly, polite **7** amiable, cordial **8** amenable, friendly, sociable **9** agreeable, courteous, peaceable **10** benevolent, harmonious, neighborly **11** kindhearted

Amici, Dominic Felix
real name of: **9** Don Ameche

amicus curiae **17** a friend of the court

amigo, amiga **6** friend

Amis, Kingsley
author of: **8** Ending Up, Lucky Jim **10** Colonel Sun, Jake's Thing **11** I Like It Here, The Green Man **16** One Fat Englishman, Take A Girl Like You **18** Russian Hide-and-Seek, The Anti-Death League **20** That Uncertain Feeling

amiss **4** awry **5** askew, false, wrong **6** astray, faulty **7** falsely, mixed-up, off base, wrongly **8** faultily, improper, mistaken, untoward **9** erroneous, incorrect, out of line **10** fallacious, improperly, mistakenly, out of order, unsuitable, unsuitably, untowardly **11** erroneously, incorrectly **12** inaccurately **13** inappropriate **15** inappropriately

Amittai
son: **5** Jonah

amity **6** accord **7** concord, harmony **8** good will, sympathy **9** agreement **10** cordiality, fellowship, fraternity, friendship **11** brotherhood, cooperation **13** understanding

Ammishaddai
son: **7** Ahiezer

Ammon
father: **3** Lot
descendants: **9** Ammonites

Ammon *see* **4** Amen

Ammonite god **6** Molech, Moloch

ammunition **4** ammo, arms **5** shell **6** bullet, rocket **7** missile, torpedo **9** artillery, cartridge, small arms **11** iron rations **13** powder and shot

ammunition dump **7** arsenal **8** magazine **18** military storehouse, munitions warehouse

amnesia **4** daze **5** fugue **6** stupor **7** agnosia **8** blackout **9** memory gap **11** anterograde, trance state

amnesty **6** pardon **8** immunity, reprieve **10** absolution **11** forgiveness **14** reconciliation

amoeba, ameba **4** dyad, germ, mold **5** spore, virus **6** fungus **7** ciliate, microbe **8** bacteria, reovirus **9** bacterium, echovirus **13** microorganism
part: **7** nucleus **8** membrane **9** pseudopod **10** protoplasm **11** food vacuole **18** contractile vacuole
reproduction by: **7** fission

amok *see* **5** amuck

Amon *see* **4** Amen

America, South
country: **4** Peru **5** Chile **6** Brazil, Guyana **7** Bolivia, Ecuador, Uruguay **8** Colombia, Paraguay, Suriname **9** Argentina, Venezuela
city: **4** Lima **5** Quito **6** Bogota, Recife **7** Caracas **8** Salvador, Santiago, Sao Paulo **10** Montevideo **11** Buenos Aires, Porto Alegre **12** Rio de Janeiro **13** Belo Horizonte
island: **6** Chiloe, Chonos, Marajo **9** Galapagos **10** Wellington **11** Madre de Dios **13** Juan Fernandez, Reina Adelaida **14** Tierra del Fuego
sea: **9** Caribbean
lake: **5** Patos, Poopo, Mirim **6** Viedma **8** Titicaca **9** Maracaibo, San Martin **10** Concepcion
mountain: **6** Andes **9** Pakaraima **12** Monte Fitz Roy **14** Cerro Aconcagua, Monte Sarmiento **15** Serra dos Parecis **16** Monte San Valentin, Serra do Espinhaco
highest point: **9** Aconcagua
lowest point: **15** Peninsula Valdes
river: **3** Ica **4** Beni, Iaco, Jari, Meta, Napo **5** Abuna, Cauca, Chico, Iriri, Ituxi, Jurua, Jutai, Negro, Palma, Pardo, Purus, Tiete, Tigre, Xingu **6** Amazon, Arauca, Branco, Chubut, Cumina, Curaco, Cuyuni, Grande, Gurupi, Iguacu, Japura, Javari, Mamore, Maroni, Mortes, Parana, Salado, Vaupes **7** Bermejo, Caqueta, Deseado, Guapore, Jamunda, Juruena, Madeira, Mapuera, Maranon, Orinoco, Oyapock, Ucayali, Vichada **8** Amazonas, Araguaia, Colorado, Guaviare, Jamachim, Paraguay, Parnaiba, Putumayo, Tapajoz, Urubamba, Uruguay **9** Essequibo, Jaguaribe, Paranaiba, Saladillo, Sao Manuel, Tocantins **10** Courantyne **12** Sao Francisco
animal: **3** bat **4** bear, deer **5** llama, sloth, tapir **6** alpaca, monkey, ocelot, weasel **7** opossum, peccary, raccoon **8** capybara, javelina **9** armadillo
bird: **3** owl **4** hawk, rhea **5** eagle **6** condor, falcon, jabiru **7** hoatzin **8** flamingo **11** hummingbird
people: **6** Indian **7** African, Chibcha, Mestizo, Mulatto, Spanish **10** Araucanian, Portuguese
religion: **7** Judaism **10** Protestant **13** Roman Catholic
language: **5** Dutch **7** English, Spanish **10** Portuguese

among **2** at **3** mid **4** amid, with **6** amidst **7** amongst, between, betwixt **12** in the midst of

among other persons
Latin: **10** inter alios

among others **8** attended, escorted, in a crowd, in a group, together **11** accompanied

among other things
Latin: **9** inter alia

among themselves
Latin: **7** inter se

Amon Ra *see* **6** Amen Ra

Amopaon
mentioned in: **5** Iliad
form: **7** warrior
army: **6** Trojan
killed by: **6** Teucer

Amor *see* **5** Cupid

Amore dei Tre Re, L'
opera by: **10** Montemezzi

Amoretti
author: **13** Edmund Spenser

amorous **4** fond **6** ardent, doting, loving, tender **8** enamored, lovesick **10** passionate **11** impassioned **12** affectionate

amorousness **4** love **5** ardor **6** warmth **7** passion

amor patriae **10** patriotism **13** love of country

amorphous **5** vague **8** formless, unshapen **9** anomalous, shapeless, undefined **11** nondescript **12** undelineated **13** characterless, indeterminate

Amos
father: **4** Naum

Amos 'n' Andy
character: **8** Lightnin' **9** Amos Jones, Andy Brown **13** George (the King Fish) Stevens **15** Sapphire Stevens
cast: **8** Tim Moore **13** Ernestine Wade, Horace Stewart **14** Alvin Childress **15** Spencer Williams

amount **3** sum **4** bulk, mass **5** total **6** extent, volume **7** measure **8** quantity, sum total **9** aggregate, magnitude

amour **6** affair **7** liaison, romance **8** intrigue **10** love affair

amour propre **8** self-love **10** self-esteem **11** self-respect

Ampelos
form: **5** satyr

Ampere, Andre-Marie
field: **7** physics **11** mathematics
nationality: **6** French
founded: **15** electrodynamics **16** electromagnetism

Amphiaraus
father: **6** Oicles
mother: **12** Hypermnestra
wife: **8** Eriphyle
son: **8** Alcmaeon **11** Amphilochus
daughter: **9** Demonassa
member: **18** Seven against Thebes
charioteer: **5** Baton

amphibian **8** seaplane **10** hydroplane, vertebrate **14** aerohydroplane
kind: **4** frog, newt, toad **9** caecilian **10** salamander
young: **6** larvae **7** tadpole **8** polliwog

Amphidamas
king of: **7** Cythera
father: **5** Aleus
brother: **7** Cepheus
member of: **9** Argonauts

Amphilochus
form: **4** seer
father: **10** Amphiaraus
mother: **8** Eriphyle
brother: **8** Alcmaeon

Amphimachus
origin: **5** Greek
mentioned in: **5** Iliad
chief of: **6** Epeans
father: **13** Cteatus of Elis
killed by: **6** Hector

Amphimarus
father: **8** Poseidon
son: **5** Linus
vocation: **8** musician

Amphinome
form: **6** maiden
father: **6** Pelias
sister: **6** Evadne
deceived by: **5** Medea
killed: **6** Pelias

Amphinomus
suitor of: **8** Penelope

Amphion
father: **4** Zeus

mother: 7 Antiope
twin brother: 6 Zethus
wife: 5 Niobe
daughter: 7 Chloris
built: 11 Theban walls

Amphisbaena
form: 7 serpent
number of heads: 3 two

amphitheater 4 bowl 5 arena 7 gallery, stadium 8 coliseum 10 auditorium
Roman: 9 Colosseum

Amphithemis
also: 7 Garamas
father: 6 Apollo
mother: 9 Acacaelis
son: 8 Nausamon 9 Caphaurus

Amphitrite
origin: 5 Greek
goddess of: 3 sea
father: 6 Nereus
mother: 5 Doris
husband: 8 Poseidon

Amphitruo (Amphitryon)
author: 7 Plautus
character: 4 Zeus 7 Alcmena, Jupiter, Mercury 10 Amphitryon

Amphitryon
father: 7 Alcaeus
grandfather: 7 Perseus
uncle: 9 Electryon, Sthenelus
wife: 7 Alcmene
son: 8 Iphicles
daughter: 8 Perimede

Amphitryon 38
author: 13 Jean Giraudoux

Amphius
ally of: 7 Trojans

amphora 3 jar, jug, urn 4 vase

Amphoterus
father: 8 Alcmaeon
mother: 10 Callirrhoe
brother: 7 Acarnan

ample 3 big 4 huge, vast, wide 5 broad, large, roomy 6 enough, plenty 7 copious, immense, liberal, profuse 8 abundant, adequate, extended, generous, spacious 9 bountiful, capacious, expansive, extensive, outspread, plentiful 10 commodious, sufficient, voluminous 11 substantial 12 satisfactory 14 more than enough

amplification 7 raising 8 increase, widening 9 expansion, extension 10 developing, filling out, increasing 11 added detail, development, elaboration, enlargement, expatiation, fleshing out, heightening, lengthening, rounding out 12 augmentation 13 magnification 14 aggrandizement 15 supplementation

amplify 5 add to, raise, widen 6 deepen, expand, extend 7 augment, broaden, develop, enlarge, fill out 8 complete, heighten, increase, lengthen 9 elaborate (on), expatiate, intensify 10 illustrate, strengthen, supplement

amplitude 4 bulk, mass, size 5 range, reach, scope, sweep, width 6 extent, volume 7 bigness, breadth, compass, expanse 8 fullness, plethora, richness, vastness 9 abundance, dimension, largeness, magnitude, plenitude, profusion 11 copiousness 12 completeness, spaciousness 13 capaciousness

amply 5 fully 6 richly 8 lavishly 9 copiously, liberally, profusely 10 abundantly, adequately, completely, generously, thoroughly 11 bountifully, plentifully 12 sufficiently, unstintingly 14 satisfactorily

amputate 5 sever 6 cut off, excise, lop off, remove 9 dismember

Ampycides
epithet of: 6 Mopsus
means: 12 son of Ampycus

Amram
father: 4 Bani 6 Dishon
son: 5 Aaron, Moses
daughter: 6 Miriam

Amsterdam
airport: 8 Schiphol
canal: 11 Herengracht 13 Keizersgracht, Prinsengracht
capital of: 7 Holland 11 Netherlands
landmark: 8 Oude Kerk 10 Nieuwe Kerk
museum: 7 Van Gogh 9 Stedelijk 11 Rijksmuseum
nickname: 16 Venice of the North
waters: 6 Amstel 7 Ij River 9 Zuiderzee 10 Ijsselmeer 13 North Sea

amuck 4 amok, nuts 6 wildly 7 berserk, bonkers 8 crackers, insanely 9 in a frenzy 10 frenziedly, maniacally 11 ferociously, murderously 14 uncontrollably

amulet 5 charm 6 fetish 8 talisman 10 lucky piece

Amulius
father: 5 Proca
brother: 7 Numitor

amuse 5 cheer 6 absorb, divert, occupy, please 7 beguile, engross, enliven, gladden 8 interest 9 entertain

amusement 3 fun 4 game, play 5 hobby, revel 7 delight, pastime 8 pleasure 9 avocation, diversion, enjoyment, merriment 10 recreation 11 distraction 13 entertainment

amusing 5 droll, funny, witty 7 comical, waggish 8 cheering, farcical, humorous, pleasant, pleasing 9 absorbing, beguiling, diverting 10 delightful, engrossing 11 interesting, pleasurable 12 entertaining

Amy, Gilbert
composer of: 9 Alpha-Beth 10 Epigrammes, Mouvements 11 Antiphonies 12 Trajectories

Amyclas
father: 7 Amphion 10 Lacedaemon
mother: 5 Niobe 6 Sparta

Amymone
father: 6 Danaus
son: 8 Nauplius
lover: 8 Poseidon

Amyntor
king of: 8 Ormenium
father: 7 Ormenus
wife: 8 Cleobule
son: 7 Phoenix
daughter: 9 Astydamia
concubine: 6 Phthia
killed by: 8 Hercules

Amythaon
father: 4 Tyro
mother: 8 Cretheus
wife: 7 Idomene
son: 4 Bias 8 Melampus

An
origin: 8 Sumerian
god of: 6 heaven
corresponds to: 3 Anu

Anadyomene *see* 9 Aphrodite

anagram 4 code 6 cipher

Anakim 11 giant people

analects 8 extracts 9 gleanings 10 miscellany, selections 11 collectanea, miscellanea

Analects of Confucius, The
author: 9 Confucius

analeptic 9 stimulant 11 restorative

analgesic 4 drug 6 opiate 7 anodyne 8 narcotic 10 anesthetic, painkiller

analogous 4 akin, like 7 similar 8 parallel 10 comparable, equivalent 11 correlative 13 corresponding

analogy 6 simile 8 likeness, metaphor 10 comparison, similarity, similitude 11 correlation, equivalence, parallelism, resemblance **14** correspondence

analysis **4** test **5** assay, brief, study **6** digest, precis, review, search **7** breakup, inquiry, outline, summary, therapy **8** abstract, judgment, synopsis, thinking **9** appraisal, breakdown, diagnosis, partition, reasoning, reduction **10** dissection, estimation, evaluation, resolution, separation **11** examination, observation, speculation **12** dissociation **13** investigation, psychotherapy **14** interpretation, psychoanalysis

analyst **5** judge **6** shrink, tester **8** examiner, observer **9** appraiser, estimator, evaluator **12** headshrinker, investigator **13** psychoanalyst

analytic, analytical **7** logical, testing **8** rational, studious **9** inquiring, organized, searching **10** diagnostic, systematic **14** problem-solving

analyze **5** assay, judge, study **6** search **7** examine **8** appraise, consider, diagnose, evaluate, question **9** reason out **11** investigate **12** think through

Anammelech **13** Sepharvite god

Ananais
father: **8** Nebedeus
wife: **8** Sapphira
sent to: **4** Paul, Saul
lied to: **5** Peter

anarchist **5** rebel **8** mutineer, nihilist **9** insurgent, terrorist **11** syndicalist **13** revolutionary

anarchy **5** chaos **6** utopia **8** disorder **11** lawlessness **13** the millennium **19** absence of government

Anastasia
director: **13** Anatole Litvak
cast: **10** Helen Hayes, Yul Brynner **12** Akim Tamiroff **13** Ingrid Bergman
Oscar for: **7** actress (Bergman)

anathema **3** ban **5** curse, taboo **7** censure **11** abomination, malediction **12** condemnation, denunciation, proscription **13** unmentionable **15** excommunication

Anathema
author: **14** Leonid Andreyev

anathematize **4** damn **7** accurse, condemn **8** execrate, maledict **9** abominate **13** excommunicate **17** hold in abomination

Anatolia *see* **7** Armenia

Anatolian
language family: **12** Indo-European
spoken in: **9** Asia Minor
spoken by: **8** Hittites

anatomist **12** morphologist
American: **5** Allen, Evans **7** Herrick **8** Stockard
Arabian: **8** Avicenna
British: **4** Owen **5** Hooke **6** Harvey
Dutch: **10** Swammerdam
French: **6** Buffon, Cuvier
German: **5** Wolff **7** Schwann
Greek: **5** Galen **9** Aristotle **10** Herophilus **12** Erasistratus
Italian: **8** Malpighi
Scottish: **5** Brown

anatomize **7** analyze, dissect **18** separate into pieces

anatomy **4** body **8** analysis **9** structure **10** dissection **11** examination

Anatomy Lesson, The
author: **10** Philip Roth

Anatomy of a Murder
director: **13** Otto Preminger
cast: **8** Eve Arden **9** Lee Remick **10** Ben Gazzara **12** George C Scott, James Stewart, Kathryn Grant **14** Arthur O'Connell
score: **13** Duke Ellington

Anatomy of Melancholy, The
author: **12** Robert Burton

Anatosaurus
type: **8** dinosaur **10** ornithopod
period: **10** Cretaceous
characteristic: **10** duck-billed
location: **12** North America

Anax
member of: **8** Gigantes
son: **8** Asterius

Anaxarete
form: **8** princess

Anaxibia
father: **6** Atreus
mother: **6** Aerope
brother: **8** Menelaus **9** Agamemnon
husband: **6** Nestor **9** Strophius
son: **7** Pylades

Anaximander
field: **11** mathematics
nationality: **5** Greek
doctrine: **11** single-world
first: **22** geometric universe model

Ancaeus
father: **8** Poseidon
member: **9** Argonauts
ship: **4** Argo
vocation: **8** helmsman
gift: **8** strength

ancestor **8** begetter, forebear **9** precursor, prototype **10** antecedent, forefather, forerunner, procreator, progenitor **11** predecessor

ancestry **4** line, race **5** house, stock **6** family, origin **7** descent, lineage **8** heredity, pedigree **9** ancestors, blood line, genealogy, parentage **10** derivation, extraction, family tree **11** progenitors

Anchesmius *see* **4** Zeus

Anchiale
form: **5** nymph

Anchinoe
father: **5** Nilus
husband: **5** Belus
son: **6** Danaus **8** Aegyptus

Anchisaurus
type: **8** dinosaur
location: **17** Connecticut Valley

Anchises
prince of: **4** Troy
father: **5** Capys
mother: **8** Themiste
grandfather: **9** Assaracus
uncle: **8** Laomedon
brother: **7** Laocoon
son: **5** Lyrus **6** Aeneas

anchor **3** fix **4** hook, moor **5** affix, basis **6** fasten, secure **7** bulwark, defense, mooring, support **8** mainstay, security **9** safeguard **10** foundation **12** ground tackle

anchorage **3** key **4** bund, dock, pier, port, quay, slip **5** berth, haven, jetty, wharf **6** harbor, marina **7** dockage, mooring, seaport **9** harborage, roadstead

ancient **3** old **4** aged **5** early, hoary, Greek, olden, passe, Roman **6** age-old, bygone, old hat, remote **7** antique, archaic, very old **8** long past, obsolete, outmoded, primeval, timeworn **9** classical, out-of-date, primitive **10** antiquated, fossilized, Greco-Roman **11** obsolescent, prehistoric **12** old-fashioned, out-of-fashion

ancientness **8** great age **9** antiquity **11** advanced age

ancient times **9** antiquity **10** days of yore **12** the Golden Age

Ancile
origin: **5** Roman
form: **6** shield
given to: **13** Numa Pompilius
given by: **4** Mars
purpose: **10** protection
copied by: **8** Mamurius

ancillary **5** minor **7** adjunct

8 inferior **9** accessory, auxiliary, dependent, secondary **10** additional, subsidiary **11** subordinate, subservient **12** contributory **13** supplementary

Ancius
form: **7** centaur

Ancus Marcius
king of: **4** Rome

and **3** too **4** also, more, plus **10** in addition

andante
music: **4** even **14** moderately slow

Andean
language family: **16** Andean-Equatorial
group: **3** Ona **6** Aymara, Yahgan, Zaparo **7** Quechua **10** Araucanian

Andean-Equatorial
language branch: **6** Andean **10** Equatorial

Andersen, Hans Christian
author of: **10** Thumbelina **11** The Red Shoes **12** The Snow Queen, The Swineherd, The Tinder Box **14** The Nightingale **15** The Ugly Duckling **16** The Little Mermaid **18** The Little Match Girl **20** The Princess and the Pea **21** The Emperor's New Clothes **22** The Steadfast Tin Soldier **25** The Shepherdess and the Sweep

Anderson, Frances Margaret
real name of: **14** Judith Anderson

Anderson, Judith
real name: **23** Frances Margaret Anderson
born: **8** Adelaide **9** Australia
roles: **5** Medea **6** Hamlet, Salome **7** Macbeth, Rebecca **8** Kings Row **16** Cat on a Hot Tin Roof

Anderson, Maxwell
author of: **7** High Tor **8** Key Largo **9** Winterset **11** Valley Forge **14** Both Your Houses, Lost in the Stars, Mary of Scotland, What Price Glory? **17** Elizabeth the Queen **20** Knickerbocker Holiday

Anderson, Sherwood
author of: **9** Poor White **12** Beyond Desire, Dark Laughter, Horses and Men **13** Many Marriages, Winesburg Ohio **15** Death in the Woods **18** The Triumph of the Egg

Anderson, Sparky (George Lee)
sport: **8** baseball
position: **7** manager
team: **9** Minnesota **14** Cincinnati Reds

Andersonville
author: **15** MacKinlay Kantor

Andersson, Bibi
born: **6** Sweden **9** Stockholm
roles: **14** The Seventh Seal **16** Wild Strawberries **19** Scenes from a Marriage **20** Smiles of a Summer Night

Andes
Spanish: **20** Cordillera de los Andes
peak: **6** Pissis, Sajama, Sorata **7** Illampu **8** Cotopaxi, Illimani **9** Huascaran **10** Chimborazo **14** Cristobal Colon
highest point: **9** Aconcagua
volcano: **6** Sangay, Tolima **8** Cotopaxi **10** Tungurahua
country: **4** Peru **5** Chile **6** Panama **7** Bolivia, Ecuador **8** Colombia **9** Argentina, Venezuela
river: **5** Cauca **6** Amazon, Parana **7** Orinoco, Ucayali **9** Magdalena
lake: **5** Poopo **8** Titicaca
animal: **5** llama **6** alpaca, condor, huemul **10** chinchilla

And I Worked at the Writer's Trade
author: **13** Malcolm Cowley

Andorra ***see box***

Andorra-la-Vella
capital of: **7** Andorra

and others **3** etc **4** et al **6** et alii **7** and so on **8** et cetera **10** and so forth, and the rest

And Quiet Flows the Don
author: **15** Mikhail Sholokov
character: **6** Piotra **7** Bunchuk, Natalia **14** Gregor Melekhov **16** Aksinia Astakhova

Andrea del Sarto
real name: **32** Andrea Domenico d'Agnolo di Francesco
born: **5** Italy **8** Florence
artwork: **7** Caritas **9** A Young Man **16** Birth of the Virgin, Journey of the Magi **19** Madonna of the Harpies, Portrait of a Sculptor

Andrea del Sarto
author: **14** Robert Browning

Andress, Ursula
husband: **9** John Derek
born: **5** Bern **11** Switzerland
roles: **3** She **4** Dr No **12** Casino Royale, Four for Texas

Andorra
other name: **13** Valls d'Andorra **16** Valleys of Andorra
capital/largest city: **14** Andorra-la-Vella
others: **3** Pal **5** Ramio **6** Ordino, Soldeu **7** Canillo, Certers **9** La Massana **11** Les Escaldes **16** San Julian de Loria
division: **6** Encamp, Ordino **7** Andorra, Camillo **9** La Massana, Sant Julia
heads of state: **13** Bishop of Urgel (Spain) **17** President of France
head of government: **11** First Syndic
monetary unit: **5** franc **6** peseta
lake: **11** Engolasters
mountain: **6** d'Etats **8** l'Estanyo, Pyrenees **10** Cataperdis
highest point: **11** Como Pedrosa
river: **6** Ariege, Valira
people: **7** Catalan **8** Andosian
language: **6** French **7** Catalan, Spanish
religion: **13** Roman Catholic
place: **12** Casa de la Vall
Moorish ruin: **4** Ceca, Meka
feature:
co-princes' representative: **7** vigueer, viguier
fiesta: **13** Bal de Morratxa
food payment to bishop: **9** la quistia

Andrew **7** apostle
brother: **5** Peter, Simon

Andrews, Dana
real name: **17** Carver Dana Andrews
brother: **12** Steve Forrest
born: **9** Collins MS
roles: **5** Laura **9** State Fair **12** Elephant Walk **13** A Walk in the Sun, Ox-Bow Incident **15** Two for the Seesaw **22** The Best Years of Our Lives

Andrews, Julie
real name: **19** Julia Elizabeth Wells
husband: **12** Blake Edwards
born: **7** England **14** Walton-on-Thames

roles: **10** My Fair Lady **11** Mary Poppins (Oscar) **14** Victor Victoria **15** The Sound of Music

Andreyev, Leonid Nikolaevich
author of: **3** S O S **5** Savva **7** Lazarus, Silence **8** Anathema **10** To the Stars **11** The Red Laugh **12** The Life of Man **16** He Who Gets Slapped **18** Love of One's Neighbor **19** Seven That Were Hanged

Andria
author: **7** Terence

Androclea
father: **18** Antipoenus of Thebes

Androcles
origin: **5** Roman
position: **5** slave

Androcles and the Lion
author: **17** George Bernard Shaw

Androgeus
father: **5** Minos
mother: **8** Pasiphae
son: **7** Alcaeus **9** Sthenelus
battled: **6** Athens

androgenous
14 hermaphroditic

Andromache
father: **6** Eetion
husband: **6** Hector
son: **6** Pielus **8** Astyanax, Molossus, Pergamus **9** Cestrinus
author: **9** Euripides
character: **6** Peleus, Thetis **7** Orestes **8** Menelaus
mistress of: **11** Neoptolemus
rival: **8** Hermione
son: **8** Molossus
setting: **8** Thessaly

Andromaque
author: **18** Jean Baptiste Racine
character:
son: **8** Astyanax
king: **7** Pyrrhus
setting: **6** Epirus

Andromeda
father: **7** Cepheus
mother: **10** Cassiopeia
husband: **7** Perseus
son: **6** Mestor, Perses **7** Alcaeus, Heleius **9** Electryon, Sthenelus
daughter: **10** Gorgophone
rescued from: **10** sea monster
rescued by: **7** Perseus

Andromeda Strain, The
author: **15** Michael Crichton

androphobia
fear of: **3** men

Androsphinx
form: **6** sphinx
head of: **3** man

and so forth **3** etc **7** and so on **8** et cetera **9** and others **10** and the rest

and so on **3** etc **8** et cetera **9** and others **10** and so forth, and the rest

And Then There Were None
director: **9** Rene Clair
based on novel by: **14** Agatha Christie
cast: **11** Roland Young **12** Louis Hayward, Walter Huston **15** Barry Fitzgerald
remade as: **16** Ten Little Indians

and thou, Brutus
Latin: **9** et tu Brute
spoken by: **12** Julius Caesar

Andvari
origin: **6** Nordic
form: **5** dwarf

Andy Capp
creator: **14** Reginald Smythe
character: **5** Vicar
wife: **3** Flo
plays: **7** snooker

Andy Griffith Show, The
character: **10** Andy Taylor, Barney Fife, Goober Pyle, Helen Crump, Opie Taylor **11** Floyd Lawson **12** Otis Campbell **13** Aunt Bee Taylor, Howard Sprague
cast: **8** Hal Smith **9** Don Knotts, Ron (Ronny) Howard **10** Jack Dodson **12** Andy Griffith, Anita Corsaut, Howard McNear **13** Frances Bavier, George Lindsey
setting: **8** Mayberry
Andy's job: **7** sheriff

anecdote **4** tale, yarn **5** story **6** sketch **12** brief account, reminiscence

anemic, anaemic **3** wan **4** dull, pale, weak **5** quiet **6** feeble, pallid **7** subdued **9** colorless **11** thin-blooded **13** characterless

anemone **4** lily **5** plant **6** flower

Anemotis
epithet of: **6** Athena
means: **5** winds

Anesidora
epithet of: **7** Demeter
means: **15** sender up of gifts

anesthesia, anaesthesia, anesthesis **6** stupor **8** numbness **11** insentience **13** loss of feeling **15** unconsciousness

anesthetic, anaesthetic **4** drug **5** ether, local **6** caudal, opiate, spinal **7** general **8** narcotic, procaine **9** analgesic, enflurane, halothane, lidocaine, peridural **10** chloroform, isoflurane, painkiller, tetracaine, thiopental **11** acupuncture, laughing gas **12** nitrous oxide **15** sodium pentothal

anesthetize **4** dope, drug, numb **6** deaden, sedate

anew **5** again, newly **6** afresh **8** once more **9** over again **11** from scratch
Latin: **6** de novo

a new order of the ages is born
Latin: **17** novus ordo seclorum
author: **6** Virgil
work: **8** Eclogues
motto of: **11** US great seal

angel **3** gem **4** doll **5** jewel, power, saint **6** cherub, patron, seraph, throne, virtue **7** sponsor **8** cherabim, seraphim, treasure **9** archangel **10** benefactor, domination **11** underwriter **12** principality **14** celestial being, heavenly spirit, messenger of God **15** financial backer

Angel, fallen **5** Satan **6** Azazel **7** Lucifer

angelic **4** good, pure **5** ideal **6** divine, lovely **7** saintly **8** adorable, beatific, cherubic, ethereal, heavenly, innocent, seraphic **9** angel-like, beautiful, celestial, rapturous, spiritual **10** entrancing **11** enrapturing

Angelic Doctor
nickname of: **15** St Thomas Aquinas

Angelico, Fra
real name: **13** Guido di Pietro
born: **7** Vicchio **14** Castell Vecchio
artwork: **12** Annunciation **15** Madonna Annalena **19** Descent from the Cross **21** Coronation of the Virgin **29** Madonna of the Linen Drapers' Guild

Angelo
character in: **17** Measure for Measure
author: **11** Shakespeare

Angel of Fire, The
also: **13** The Fiery Angel
opera by: **9** Prokofiev

anger **3** ire, vex **4** bile, fury, gall, rage, rile **5** annoy, chafe, pique, wrath **6** choler, dander, enmity, enrage, hatred, madden, nettle, rankle, ruffle, spleen, temper **7** incense, inflame, outrage, provoke, umbrage **8** acrimony, embitter, irritate, vexation **9** animosity, annoyance, displease, hostility, hot temper, ill temper, infuriate, petulance **10** antagonism, antagonize, exacerbate, exasperate, irritation, resentment **11** displeasure, indignation **12** exasperation, make bad blood **14** disapprobation **15** get one's dander up **16** cause ill feelings **18** ruffle one's feathers

Anger
author: **9** May Sarton

Angerboda
also: **9** Angrbodha, Angurboda
origin: **12** Scandinavian
form: **8** giantess
children: **3** Hel **6** Fenrir, Fenris **11** Iormungandr, Jormungandr **14** Midgard Serpent

Angerona
origin: **5** Roman
goddess of: **7** anguish

angle **4** bend, cusp, edge, side, turn **5** focus, slant **6** aspect, corner **7** outlook **8** position **9** viewpoint **10** divergence, standpoint **11** perspective, point of view
kind: **5** acute, right **6** obtuse **8** straight
point: **6** vertex
measure: **7** degrees

angled **4** bent **6** fished **7** crooked, slanted **8** diverged

Anglo-Frisian
language family: **12** Indo-European
branch: **8** Germanic
group: **15** Western Germanic
language: **7** English, Frisian

Angola ***see box***

Angrbodha *see* **9** Angerboda

angry **3** mad **5** huffy, irate, riled, vexed **6** fuming, galled, piqued, raging **7** annoyed, boiling, burnt up, enraged, furious, hateful, hostile, nettled **8** incensed, inflamed, offended, outraged, petulant, provoked **9** affronted, indignant, irascible, irritated, resentful, splenetic, turbulent **10** displeased, embittered, infuriated **11** acrimonious, exasperated, ill-tempered **12** antagonistic

angst **5** dread **6** unease **7** anxiety **10** foreboding, uneasiness **12** apprehension

angstrom
abbreviation: **1** A

Angstrom, Anders Jon
field: **7** physics **9** astronomy
founded: **12** spectroscopy
mapped: **11** solar system
angstrom unit: **17** wavelength of light

anguish **3** woe **4** pain **5** agony, grief **6** misery, sorrow **7** anxiety, despair, remorse, torment **8** distress **9** heartache, suffering

Anguish
goddess of: **8** Angerona

anguished **6** pained **7** anxious, fearful **9** tormented **10** distressed **11** heartbroken

angular **4** bent, bony, lank, lean **5** gaunt, lanky, spare **6** jagged **7** crooked, scrawny **8** rawboned **13** sharp-cornered

Angurboda *see* **9** Angerboda

Angus Og
origin: **5** Irish
god of: **4** love **5** youth **6** beauty

Anicetus
father: **8** Hercules
mother: **4** Hebe

animadversion **4** flak **7** nagging, quibble **9** aspersion, criticism, pestering **12** faultfinding **14** censoriousness

animal **3** pet **5** beast, brute **6** mammal **8** creature, nonhuman, organism **9** quadruped
group: **4** bird, fish, worm **6** insect, mammal, sponge **7** primate, reptile, rotifer **8** ruminant **9** amphibian **10** vertebrate **12** invertebrate

Animal Crackers
director: **13** Victor Heerman
cast: **5** Chico, Harpo, Zeppo **7** Groucho **11** Lillian Roth **12** Marx Brothers **14** Margaret Dumont
song: **25** Hooray for Captain Spaulding

Animal Farm
author: **12** George Orwell
character: **5** Boxer **7** Mr Jones **8** Napoleon, Snowball

Animals in that Country, The
author: **14** Margaret Atwood

Angola
other name: **7** Bakongo **20** Portuguese West Africa
capital/largest city: **6** Luanda
others: **5** Dundo **6** Ambriz, Huambo, Lobito **7** Cabinda, Kampala, Malange, Malanje, Salazar **8** Benguela, Cassinga, Vila Luso **9** Ambrizete, Mocamedes **10** Mossamedes, Nova Lisboa, Silva Porto
division: **3** Bie **4** Uige **5** Huila, Lunda, Zaire **6** Cunene, Huambo, Luanda, Moxico **7** Cabinda, Malanje **8** Benguela **9** Cuanza Sul, Mocamedes **11** Cuanza Norte **13** Cuando Cubango
monetary unit: **6** escudo, macuta, macute **7** angolar, centavo
mountain: **5** Chela **6** Loviti **16** Humpata Highlands
highest point: **4** Moco
river: **4** Cuvo **5** Congo, Cuito, Longa **6** Cassai, Coanza, Cuando, Cuanza, Cunene, Kunene, Kwango, Kwanza, Luando **7** Chiumbe, Cubango, Zambezi **11** Lungue-Bungo
sea: **6** Indian **8** Atlantic
physical feature:
basin: **8** Okavango
desert: **9** Mocamedes
falls: **15** Catarata Ruacana, Duque de Braganca
plain: **8** Planalto
plateau: **4** Rand **5** Huila **11** Benguela Bie, Lunda Divide
people: **5** Bantu, Kongo, Lundu **6** Chokwe, Herero, Mbundu, Ovambo **7** Bakongo, Kangela, Kikongo **8** Kimbundu, Kwangare **9** Ovinbundu **12** Nyaneka-Humbi
leader: **13** Agostinho Neto
language: **5** Bantu **8** Kimbundu, Oumbundu **9** Ovimbundu **10** Portuguese
religion: **7** animism **10** Protestant **13** Roman Catholic
place:
fortress: **9** Sao Miguel
feature:
mahogany: **5** khaya
weed: **6** archil

animate **4** fire, goad, move, stir, urge, warm **5** alive, impel, set on **6** arouse, excite, fire up, incite, moving, prompt, spur on, vivify, work up **7** actuate, enliven, inspire, provoke, quicken **8** activate, energize, vitalize **9** instigate, make alive, stimulate **10** invigorate, make lively **11** add spirit to **12** give energy to

animated **3** gay, hot **4** airy **5** brisk, quick, vivid **6** active, ardent, blithe, breezy, bright, elated, lively **7** buoyant, dynamic, fervent, glowing, vibrant, zealous, zestful **8** exciting, spirited, sportive, vigorous **9** ebullient, energetic, sprightly, vivacious **10** passionate **12** invigorating

animation **3** vim **4** fire, glow, life, zest **5** ardor, verve, vigor **6** action, gaiety, spirit **7** elation **8** activity, alacrity, buoyancy, vibrancy, vitality, vivacity **9** alertness, briskness, eagerness, good cheer **10** brightness, ebullience, enthusiasm, excitement, liveliness **12** exhilaration, sportiveness **13** sprightliness

animosity **4** hate **5** anger **6** enmity, hatred, malice, rancor, strife **7** dislike, ill will **8** acrimony **9** antipathy, hostility, malignity **10** antagonism, bitterness, resentment **11** malevolence **14** unfriendliness

animus **5** anger, spite, venom **6** enmity, hatred, malice, rancor **7** disdain, dislike, ill will **8** acrimony, bad blood **9** animosity, antipathy, hostility **10** antagonism, bitterness, ill feeling, resentment **12** hard feelings

anise
botanical name: **16** Pimpinella Anisum
origin: **5** Egypt, India **13** Mediterranean
flavor: **8** licorice
use: **5** cakes, fruit, rolls **7** cookies
plant with similar flavor: **9** star anise
legend:
safeguards against: **7** evil eye **10** nightmares **11** indigestion
antidote to: **12** scorpion bite

anisette
type: **7** liqueur
origin: **6** France
flavor: **5** anise
drink: **17** Suissesse cocktail
with gin: **8** Snowball **11** Bachio Punch
substitute for: **8** Absinthe

Ankylosaurus
type: **8** dinosaur **10** ornithopod
location: **12** North America
period: **10** Cretaceous
characteristic: **7** armored

Anna
husband: **5** Tobit
daughter: **4** Mary
sister: **4** Dido
corresponds to: **11** Anna Perenna
died by: **8** drowning

Annabel Lee
author: **13** Edgar Allan Poe

Anna Christie
author: **12** Eugene O'Neill
character: **6** Marthy **8** Mat Burke **19** Chris Christopherson
ship: **14** Simeon Winthrop

Anna Karenina
author: **10** Leo Tolstoy
character: **12** Count Vronsky **13** Alexei Karenin **15** Konstantin Levin **19** Kitty Shcherbatskaya **20** Prince Stepan Oblonsky
setting: **6** Moscow, Russia **12** St Petersburg
director: **13** Clarence Brown
cast: **9** May Robson **10** Greta Garbo (Anna Karenina) **13** Basil Rathbone (Karenin), Frederic March (Vronsky) **16** Maureen O'Sullivan **18** Freddie Bartholomew
earlier film version: **4** Love

annals **7** history, minutes, records **8** archives **9** registers **10** chronicles, chronology **13** yearly records **15** historical rolls **20** chronological records

Annam *see* **7** Vietnam

Anna Marie
character in: **16** Giants of the Earth
author: **7** Rolvaag

Anna of the Five Towns
author: **13** Arnold Bennett

Anna Perenna
origin: **5** Roman
goddess of: **9** longevity

anneal **6** harden, temper **7** toughen

Anne of Geierstein (or, The Maiden of the Mist)
author: **14** Sir Walter Scott

annex **3** add **4** grab, join **5** affix, merge, seize **6** adjoin, append, attach, tack on **7** acquire, connect, subjoin **8** addition **9** appendage **10** attachment **11** appropriate, expropriate, incorporate

Annfwn
also: **5** Annwn
origin: **5** Welsh
means: **8** paradise

Annie Hall
director: **10** Woody Allen
cast: **9** Carol Kane, Paul Simon **10** Woody Allen **11** Diane Keaton, Tony Roberts **13** Shelley Duvall **15** Colleen Dewhurst
Oscar for: **7** actress (Keaton), picture **8** director (Allen) **10** screenplay

annihilate **3** end **5** erase, waste **7** abolish, destroy, wipe out **8** decimate, demolish, lay waste **9** eradicate, extirpate, liquidate **10** extinguish, obliterate **11** exterminate

annihilation **9** abolition, wiping out **11** destruction, extirpation, laying waste, liquidation **12** obliteration **13** extermination

anniversary **4** fete **7** holiday, name day **8** birthday, feast day **9** centenary **10** centennial **11** bicentenary, celebration **12** bicentennial **13** commemoration, golden jubilee **16** sesquicentennial

Ann-Margret
real name: **16** Ann-Margret Olsson
husband: **10** Roger Smith
born: **6** Sweden **9** Valsjobyn
roles: **5** Tommy **12** Bye-Bye Birdie **15** Carnal Knowledge

anno mundi **19** in the year of the world

anno regni **19** in the year of the reign

annotate **5** gloss **6** remark **7** comment, explain, expound **8** construe, footnote **9** elucidate, explicate, interpret **10** commentate

annotation **4** note **5** gloss **6** remark **7** comment **8** exegesis, footnote **10** commentary, marginalia **11** elucidation, explication, observation

announce **5** augur **6** herald, reveal, signal **7** betoken, declare, divulge, give out, portend, presage, publish, signify, trumpet **8** disclose, foretell, proclaim **9** advertise, broadcast, harbinger **10** promulgate **11** disseminate

announcement **9** broadcast, statement **11** declaration **12** proclamation

annoy **3** irk, nag, tax, vex **4** gall, rile **5** harry, tease, worry **6** badger, bother, harass, heckle, hector, nettle, pester, plague, ruffle **7** disturb, provoke, torment, trouble **8** distract, irritate **10** exasperate **13** inconvenience

annoyance **6** bother **8** irritant, nuisance, vexation **10** irritation **11** distraction, disturbance

annoyed **5** irked, upset, vexed **9** disturbed, irritated, perturbed **11** discomposed **12** disconcerted

Ann Sothern Show, The
character: **6** Johnny **10** Olive Smith **11** James Devery, Katy O'Connor **13** Jason Macauley
cast: **9** Don Porter **10** Ann Sothern, Ann Tyrrell **11** Ernest Truex **12** Jack Mullaney

annual **4** weed **5** plant **6** flower, serial **7** gazette, journal, reports **8** bulletin, magazine, notebook, periodic **9** vegetable **10** periodical, record book

annuity **6** income **7** pension, stipend **9** allowance

annul **4** undo, void **6** cancel, negate, recall, repeal, revoke **7** abolish, nullify, rescind, retract, reverse **8** abrogate, dissolve **10** invalidate

annulment **6** recall, repeal **7** undoing, voiding **8** reversal **9** abolition **10** abrogation, retraction, revocation **11** dissolution, repudiation **12** cancellation, invalidation **13** nullification

annus mirabilis **13** year of wonders

Annwn *see* **6** Annfwn

anodyne **4** balm **6** solace **7** comfort **9** comforter **10** palliative

anoint **3** oil **5** crown **6** ordain **8** put oil on **9** pour oil on

Anointed One **5** Jesus **7** Messiah

anomalous **3** odd **7** bizarre, strange **8** abnormal, atypical, peculiar **9** irregular, monstrous **11** incongruous **12** out of keeping

anomaly **6** oddity, rarity **9** deviation **10** aberration **11** abnormality, incongruity, peculiarity **12** eccentricity, irregularity **18** exception to the rule

anon **4** soon, then **5** again, later **7** by and by, shortly **8** tomorrow **9** afterward, presently **10** before long **11** immediately, in the future

anonymous **7** unnamed **8** nameless, unsigned **12** unidentified **13** bearing no name **14** unacknowledged **19** of unknown authorship

anoplura
class: **8** hexopoda
phylum: **10** arthropoda
group: **11** sucking lice

another **4** else, more **5** extra, other **7** further, renewed **9** accessory, otherwise **10** additional **12** supplemental **13** something else, supplementary **14** different thing

Anouilh, Jean
author of: **6** Becket **8** Antigone, Eurydice, Leocadia, L'hermine **11** Dear Antoine **14** Time Remembered **15** Le Bal des Voleurs, Thieves' Carnival **16** Point of Departure, Ring Round the Moon **19** Waltz of the Toreadors **20** L'Invitation au Chateau **23** Traveller Without Luggage

answer **3** say **4** fill, meet, suit **5** reply, serve, solve, write **6** be like, rejoin, retort **7** conform, fulfill, react to, resolve, respond **8** be enough, response, solution **9** be similar, rejoinder **10** be adequate, correspond, pass muster, resolution **11** acknowledge, explanation **12** be correlated, be equivalent, be sufficient, do well enough **14** acknowledgment, be satisfactory

answerable **6** liable **8** beholden **10** chargeable **11** accountable, responsible

Answer as a Man
author: **14** Taylor Caldwell

ant
caste: **4** male **5** queen **6** worker **7** soldier
kind: **3** red **4** army, fire **5** dairy, thief **6** beggar, farmer, velvet, weaver **7** formica, janitor, pharaoh **8** honeypot, mushroom **9** Argentine, carpenter, cornfield, harvester, legionary **10** leaf cutter **11** little black **12** fungus grower, odorous house, southern fire **13** mound building **14** Texas harvester
group of: **6** colony

Antaea
epithet of: **4** Rhea **6** Cybele **7** Demeter
means: **6** prayer

Antaeus
form: **5** giant
father: **8** Poseidon
mother: **2** Ge
gift: **13** invincibility
power derived from: **5** Earth
crushed by: **8** Hercules
crushed in: **3** air
home: **6** Africa

antagonism **5** spite **6** animus, enmity, hatred, rancor, strife **7** discord, dislike, rivalry **8** aversion, clashing, conflict, friction **9** animosity, antipathy, hostility **10** bitterness, dissension, opposition, resentment **11** detestation

antagonist **3** foe **5** enemy, rival **7** opposer **8** attacker, opponent **9** adversary, assailant, disputant **10** competitor, contestant

antagonistic **7** hostile **8** contrary, inimical **9** rancorous **10** antisocial, unfriendly **11** belligerent **12** antipathetic, disputatious

antagonize **5** repel **6** offend **8** alienate, estrange

Antagoras
occupation: **8** shepherd
home: **3** Cos
challenged: **8** Hercules

Antananarivo, Tananarive
capital of: **10** Madagascar

Antarctica ***see box***

ante **3** bet, pot **5** stake, wager **12** beginning bet

anteater **5** sloth **7** echidna **8** aardvark **9** armadillo

antecede **7** precede, predate **8** go before, preexist **10** anticipate

ante Christum **12** before Christ
abbreviation: **2** AC

antedate **7** precede, predate **8** antecede, go before **9** come first **10** anticipate **12** happen before

Antediluvian **14** before the flood

antediluvian **7** antique, archaic **8** obsolete **10** antiquated

antelope **8** ruminant
family: **7** Bovidae
kind: **3** doe, gnu **4** buck, deer, fawn, kudu, oryx, roan **5** bongo, eland, moose, sable **6** dik-dik, duiker, impala, lechwe, nilgai **7** gazelle, gemsbok, gerenuk **8** bluebuck, bontebok, steinbok **9** blackbuck, sitatunga, springbok, waterbuck **10** four-horned **12** Klipspringer
habitat: **4** Asia **6** Africa

Antelope State
nickname of: **8** Nebraska

Antarctica
division: **10** Wilkes Land **13** Marie Byrd Land, Queen Maud Land **14** Edith Ronne Land **17** Ellsworth Highland
island: **4** Ross **5** Peter, Scott **6** Biscoe, Hearst **7** Ballery, Charcot **8** Adelaide, Elephant **9** Alexander, Joinville, Roosevelt **10** Coronation, King George **11** South Orkney **13** South Shetland
mountain: **8** Sentinel **9** Pensacola **14** Transantarctic **23** Executive Committee Range
valley: **6** Wright
river: **4** Onyx
natural resource/mineral: **4** coal
plant life: **4** moss **5** algae, fungi **6** lichen, pollen **8** bacteria
animal: **4** lice, mite, tick **5** whale **7** fur seal **8** ross seal **9** crabeater **11** weddell seal, wingless fly
bird: **4** skua **6** fulmar, petrel **7** penguin **10** cape pigeon
sea: **4** Ross **5** Davis **6** Scotia **7** Weddell **8** Amundsen **14** Bellingshausen

antenna **6** aerial, feeler

anterior **5** front, prior **7** forward, in front **8** previous **9** precedent **10** antecedent **12** placed before

Anteros
brother: **4** Eros
avenger of: **14** unrequited love

Antevorta
also: **6** Prorsa **7** Porrima
form: **5** nymph
member of: **7** Camenae
gift: **8** prophecy

Anthas
father: **8** Poseidon
mother: **7** Alcyone

Anthea
epithet of: **4** Hera
means: **7** flowery

Antheil, George
born: **9** Trenton NJ
autobiography: **13** Bad Boy of Music
composer of: **7** Volpone **12** Helen Retires, Jazz Symphony **13** Sonata Sauvage, Transatlantic **14** Airplane Sonata **15** Ballet Mecanique

anthem **4** hymn, song **5** carol, ditty, music, paean, psalm **6** ballad, sacred **7** cantata **8** doxology **11** church music

Anthesteria
origin: **5** Greek
festival of: **4** wine **6** spring **7** flowers

Antheus
father: **7** Antenor
killed by: **5** Paris

anthology **6** choice, digest **7** garland **8** analects, chapbook, extracts, treasury **9** gleanings, scrapbook **10** collection, compendium, miscellany, selections **11** collectanea, compilation, florilegium, miscellanea **15** commonplace book

Anthony Adverse
author: **18** William Hervey Allen

anthophobia
fear of: **7** flowers

anthropologist
American: **4** Boas, Mead **5** Lowie, Sapir **6** Geertz, Linton, Morgan **7** Kroeber **8** Benedict
British: **5** Leach, Tylor **6** Fortes, Leakey, Rivers **14** Evans-Pritchard, Radcliffe-Brown
French: **5** Mauss **8** Durkheim **11** Levi-Strauss
Polish: **10** Malinowski

anthropology
term: **4** myth **6** custom, ritual **7** culture, kinship **8** artifact **9** ethnology, evolution, field work **11** ethnography **16** natural selection
type/related study: **5** legal, urban **6** social **7** applied, medical **8** cultural, economic, physical **9** political **11** linguistics **12** human ecology **13** psychological **19** structural-symbolist
famous study: **3** San **4** Kung **7** Eskimos, Samoans, Tasaday **10** Aborigines **16** Pacific Islanders

anthropophobia
fear of: **6** people

Antia
husband: **7** Proetus
daughter: **7** Lysippe
slandered: **11** Bellerophon

antibiotic **4** drug **5** venom **6** poison **8** curative **9** antidotal, antitoxic, pesticide **10** wonder drug **11** insecticide, miracle drug
kind: **8** neomycin, subtilin **9** mycomycin **10** ampicillin, penicillin **12** erythromycin

antic, antics **5** larks, sport **6** pranks, tricks **9** escapades **10** buffoonery, skylarking, tomfoolery **11** shenanigans **12** clownishness, monkeyshines **14** practical jokes

anticipate **5** await **6** expect **7** count on, foresee, long for, look for, predict **8** envision, forecast, foretell **9** pin hope on **10** look toward **13** look forward to

anticipation **4** hope **10** expectancy **11** expectation, preparation

anticlimax **7** letdown **8** comedown **14** disappointment

antidote **4** cure **6** remedy **9** antitoxin **10** antipoison, corrective **12** counteragent, countervenom **13** counterpoison **14** countermeasure

Antigone
author: **9** Sophocles **11** Jean Anouilh
character: **6** Ismene **8** Tiresias
father: **7** Oedipus
mother: **7** Jocasta
brother: **8** Eteocles **9** Polynices
sister: **6** Ismene
uncle: **5** Creon
cousin/lover: **6** Haemon
defied: **5** Creon

Antigua and Barbuda ***see box, p. 46***

anti-intellectual **5** yahoo **7** lowbrow **9** ignoramus, vulgarian **10** illiterate, philistine

Antilochus
father: **6** Nestor
brother: **11** Thrasymedes
friend: **8** Achilles

Antimachus
origin: **5** Greek
mentioned in: **5** Iliad
chieftain of: **7** Trojans

antimony
chemical symbol: **2** Sb

Antinous
suitor of: **8** Penelope
killed by: **8** Odysseus

Antiochus
father: **8** Hercules
mother: **4** Meda

Antiope
form: **6** Amazon
father: **7** Nycteus
sister: **9** Hippolyte
son: **6** Zethus **7** Amphion **10** Hippolytus
mistress of: **7** Theseus

Antigua and Barbuda
capital/largest city: **7** St John's
government:
member of: **26** West Indies Associated States
head of state: **14** British monarch **15** governor-general
island: **4** Long **5** Guana **7** Antigua, Barbuda, Redonda
highest point: **9** Boggy Peak
sea: **9** Caribbean
physical feature:
cove: **5** Royal
harbor/harbour: **7** English
people: **7** African, British **8** Lebanese **10** Portuguese
language: **7** English
religion: **8** Anglican, Moravian **13** Roman Catholic
feature: **15** Nelson's Dockyard

antipathetic **6** averse **7** hostile **8** inimical **9** rancorous **11** ill-disposed

antipathy **6** enmity, rancor **7** disgust, dislike, ill will **8** aversion, distaste, loathing **9** animosity, hostility, repulsion **10** abhorrence, antagonism, repugnance **14** unfriendliness

Antiphas
father: **7** Laocoon

Antiphates
origin: **5** Greek
mentioned in: **5** Iliad **7** Odyssey
father: **8** Melampus
chief of: **10** Laestrygon
occupation: **7** warrior **9** chieftain
killed by: **8** Leonteus

Antipholus
character in: **17** The Comedy of Errors
author: **11** Shakespeare

antiphony **6** chorus **7** refrain **8** response

Antiphus
origin: **5** Greek
mentioned in: **5** Iliad **7** Odyssey
form: **5** nymph
father: **5** Priam **10** Talaemenes
half-brother: **4** Isus
ally of: **4** Troy
devoured by: **10** Polyphemus

antipode **8** contrary, opposite **10** antithesis

Antipoenus
daughter: **5** Alcis **9** Androclea
home: **6** Thebes
descendant of: **6** Sparti

Antiquary, The
author: **14** Sir Walter Scott

antiquated **5** dated, passe **7** antique, archaic **8** obsolete, outdated, outmoded **9** out-of-date **11** obsolescent **12** old-fashioned

antique **3** old **5** curio, relic **6** rarity **7** bibelot, trinket **9** objet d'art **10** antiquated, memorabile **11** memorabilia

antiquities **6** relics **8** artifact **9** monuments

antiquity **7** oldness **8** great age **11** ancientness **12** ancient times

antiseptic **7** aseptic, sterile **8** germ-free **9** germicide **10** germ killer **11** bactericide **12** disinfectant, prophylactic

antisocial **7** asocial, hostile **8** menacing, retiring, unsocial **9** alienated **10** disruptive, rebellious, unfriendly, unsociable **11** belligerent, sociopathic **12** antagonistic, misanthropic

antithesis **7** inverse, reverse **8** antipode, contrary, contrast, converse, opposite

antithetical **8** contrary, opposing, opposite **10** discrepant, refutatory **11** conflicting, disagreeing **13** contradictory **14** countervailing, irreconcilable

antitoxin **5** serum **8** antidote **9** antivenom **12** counteragent **13** counterpoison

antler **4** horn, knob, rack **5** spike **6** shovel **8** deerhorn, troching
part: **3** bay **4** brow **5** crown, royal

ant lion
also: **8** lacewing **9** doodlebug
kind: **6** owlfly **9** dusty wing, mantidfly **12** spongillafly **13** brown lacewing, giant lacewing, green lacewing **14** beaded lacewing **15** ithonid lacewing **16** pleasing lacewing

Antonello da Messina
born: **5** Italy **7** Messina
artwork: **8** Ecce Homo **11** Three Angels **13** Il Condottiere (Portrait of a Man), Salvador Mundi **21** Saint Jerome in his Study

Antonio
character in: **12** Twelfth Night **19** The Merchant of Venice
author: **11** Shakespeare

Antonioni, Michelangelo
director of: **6** Blowup **8** The Night **10** The Eclipse **12** The Adventure, The Passenger **14** Zabriskie Point

Antony, Mark
also: **14** Marcus Antonius
member of: **11** triumvirate
other triumvirs: **7** Lepidus **8** Octavian (Caesar Augustus)
lover: **9** Cleopatra
cousin: **12** Julius Caesar
wife: **7** Octavia
battle: **6** Actium **8** Philippi **9** Pharsalus
invaded: **7** Parthia
died by: **7** suicide

Antony and Cleopatra
author: **18** William Shakespeare
character: **7** Octavia **9** Cleopatra **10** Mark Antony **14** Octavius Caesar
setting: **5** Egypt
Cleopatra bitten by: **3** asp

antonym **8** opposite **10** antithesis
abbreviation: **3** ant

Antrodemus
type: **8** dinosaur, therapod
also called: **10** Allosaurus
period: **8** Jurassic **10** Cretaceous

Anu
origin: **8** Akkadian
god of: **6** heaven
corresponds to: **2** An

Anubis
origin: **8** Egyptian
god of: **5** tombs **9** embalming
weigher of: **15** hearts of the dead
represented by head of: **6** jackal

Anunnaki
origin: **8** Sumerian
member of: **14** divine assembly
assembly headed by: **2** An **5** Enlil

anvil **5** block, incus **9** converter **11** transformer

anxiety **4** fear **5** alarm, angst, dread, worry **6** unease **7** anguish, concern, tension **8** disquiet, distress, suspense **9** misgiving **10** foreboding, solicitude, uneasiness **11** disquietude, fretfulness **12** apprehension

anxiety-ridden **7** anxious, fearful, nervous **10** distraught

11 worried sick
12 apprehensive

anxious **4** avid, keen **5** eager, tense **6** ardent, intent, uneasy **7** alarmed, earnest, fearful, fervent, fretful, itching, uptight, wanting, worried, zealous **8** desirous, troubled, yearning **9** anguished, concerned, disturbed, expectant, impatient **10** disquieted, distressed **11** overwrought **12** apprehensive

any **3** all, one **4** each, lone, sole, some **5** every **6** single, unique **8** anything, singular, solitary **9** something **10** individual, quantifier

anybody **3** any **6** anyone **8** anything

anyhow *see* **6** anyway

anything **3** any **4** some **5** aught **6** anyone **7** anybody

anyway **6** anyhow **8** sloppily **9** at any rate, in any case **10** carelessly, in any event, regardless **11** haphazardly, just the same, nonetheless **12** nevertheless **13** indifferently **14** without concern

anywhere **8** anyplace, wherever **11** wheresoever

Aoede
muse of: **4** song

Ao-men *see* **5** Macao

A-1 **3** ace **4** aces, fine, tops **5** great, prime, super **6** choice, grade-A, superb, tip-top **7** capital **8** sterling, superior, topnotch **9** excellent, first-rate, superfine **10** first-class, tremendous **11** crackerjack, outstanding, superlative

Aornis
tributary of: **4** Styx

Aornum
entrance to: **5** Hades
used by: **7** Orpheus

Aotearoa *see* **10** New Zealand

apace **4** fast **7** flat-out, hastily, quickly, rapidly, swiftly **8** speedily **9** posthaste **10** at top speed **11** double-quick, on the double **12** lickety-split **13** expeditiously, precipitately **18** hell bent for leather

Apache
language family: **10** Athabascan, Athapaskan
band: **9** Jacarilla, Mescalero, San Carlos **13** White Mountain
location: **7** Arizona **8** Oklahoma **9** New Mexico
leader: **7** Cochise **8** Geronimo
noted for: **8** basketry

apart **4** afar **5** alone, aloof, aside **6** cut off **7** asunder, distant **8** by itself, divorced, isolated, separate **9** by oneself, into parts, to one side **10** into pieces, separately

apartment **3** pad **4** flat **5** rooms, suite

Apartment, The
director: **11** Billy Wilder
cast: **10** Jack Lemmon, Ray Walston **13** Fred MacMurray **15** Shirley MacLaine
Oscar for: **7** picture

apathetic **4** cold **7** unmoved **9** impassive, unfeeling **10** disengaged, impossible, phlegmatic, spiritless **11** emotionless, indifferent, passionless, uncommitted, unconcerned, unemotional **12** uninterested, unresponsive

apathy **8** coolness, lethargy, numbness **9** lassitude, unconcern **11** impassivity, inattention, passiveness **12** indifference **13** impassibility, lack of feeling **14** lack of interest **15** emotionlessness **16** unresponsiveness

apatite
source: **5** Burma, Mogok

Apatosaurus *see* **12** Brontosaurus

ape **4** copy, echo, mock **5** mimic **6** follow, mirror, monkey, parody, parrot **7** emulate, imitate, primate **8** travesty **9** burlesque **10** caricature
family: **8** Pongidae
combining form: **8** pithecus
study of: **11** pithecology
kind: **6** gibbon **7** gorilla, siamang **9** orangutan **10** chimpanzee
famous: **8** Godzilla, King Kong

Apemius
epithet of: **4** Zeus
means: **13** averter of ills

Apemosyne
father: **7** Catreus
brother: **11** Althaemenes
ravished by: **6** Hermes
killed by: **11** Althaemenes

Apepi *see* **7** Apophis

apercu **6** glance **7** glimpse, insight, outline, summary

aperture **3** gap **4** hole, rent, rift, slit, slot **5** chink, cleft, space **6** breach **7** fissure, opening, orifice **10** interstice

apex **3** cap, tip **4** acme, peak **5** crest, crown **6** apogee, climax, height, summit, vertex, zenith **8** pinnacle **11** culmination **12** consummation, highest point **13** crowning point

Aphareus
king of: **8** Messenia
father: **8** Perieres
mother: **10** Gorgophone
grandfather: **7** Perseus
brother: **9** Leucippus
wife: **5** Arene
son: **4** Ides **7** Lynceus

aphasic **4** dumb, mute **12** inarticulate **17** incapable of speech

Aphesius
epithet of: **4** Zeus
means: **8** releaser

aphid
variety: **3** pea **4** pine, rose **5** apple, grape, peach, tulip **6** cereal, cotton, potato, spruce **7** adelgid, cabbage **8** pear root **9** elm woolly, plant lice, water lily **10** gall-making, phylloxera

Aphidas
father: **5** Arcas
son: **5** Aleus

aphorism **5** adage, axiom, maxim **6** dictum, old saw, saying, slogan, truism **7** epigram, proverb **8** apothegm

aphrodisiac **4** sexy **6** carnal, erotic **7** fleshly, philter, raunchy **8** prurient **9** cantharis **10** love potion **11** cantharides, magic potion, stimulating

Aphrodite
also: **6** Urania **7** Cyprian, Paphian **8** Cytherea **10** Anadyomene
origin: **5** Greek
goddess of: **4** love **6** beauty
husband: **10** Hephaestus
lover: **4** Ares
son: **5** Lyrus **6** Deimos, Phobus, Rhodus **7** Priapus
daughter: **8** Harmonia
corresponds to: **5** Venus
epithet: **6** Acraea, Scotia **7** Doritis, Erycina, Limenia **8** Melaenis, Nymphaea, Pandemos **9** Migonitis **11** Aphrogeneia, Apostrophia

Aphrogeneia
epithet of: **9** Aphrodite
means: **8** foam born

Apia
capital of: **12** Western Samoa

apiary **4** hive **7** beehive

apiece **4** each **9** severally **12** individually, respectively

a pied **6** on foot **7** walking

Apis
origin: **8** Egyptian
also: **3** Hap **4** Hapi
form: **4** bull
from: **7** Memphis

father: **6** Apollo **9** Phoroneus
mother: **8** Teledice
sister: **5** Niobe
nephew: **5** Argus
rid Argos of: **8** serpents
killed by: **7** Aetolus
worshipped at: **7** Memphis

aplomb **5** poise **7** balance **8** calmness, coolness **9** composure, sang-froid, stability **10** confidence, equanimity **11** intrepidity, savoir faire **13** self-assurance, self-composure **14** self-confidence, self-possession **15** level-headedness **16** imperturbability

Apocalypse Now
director: **18** Francis Ford Coppola
based on: **15** Heart of Darkness
novel by: **12** Joseph Conrad
cast: **11** Martin Sheen **12** Marlon Brando, Robert Duvall **16** Frederick Forrest
setting: **7** Vietnam

apocalyptic **4** dire **7** ominous **8** oracular **9** far-seeing, ill-boding, ill-omened, prescient, prophetic, revealing **10** disclosing, eye-opening, foreboding, portentous, predictive, revelatory **11** prophetical **12** inauspicious, revelational **15** prognosticative

apocryphal **7** dubious **8** disputed, doubtful, mythical, spurious **10** fabricated, fictitious, unofficial, unverified **11** unauthentic, uncanonical **12** questionable, unauthorized **14** probably untrue **15** unauthenticated, unsubstantiated

apogee **3** top **4** acme, apex, peak **5** crest, crown **6** climax, summit, vertex, zenith **8** meridian, pinnacle **9** high point **11** culmination **12** highest point

Apollo
also: **7** Phoebus, Pythius **9** Musagetes
origin: **5** Greek, Roman
god of: **5** light, music **6** beauty, poetry **7** healing **8** prophecy
father: **4** Zeus
mother: **4** Leto
twin sister: **7** Artemis
sons: **5** Iamus **8** Laodocus **9** Aristaeus, Asclepius, Philammon **10** Polypoetes
corresponds to: **5** Paeon **8** Hyperion
epithet: **6** Loxias **7** Acesius, Agraeus, Agyieus, Carneus, Phyteus, Spodius **8** Grynaeus **9** Parnopius, Smintheus **10** Alexicacus, Archegetes, Boedromius, Delphinius **11** Argyrotoxus, Epibaterius **12** Platanistius

Apollyon **4** hell **7** Abaddon

apologetic **5** sorry **8** contrite, penitent **9** defensive, regretful **10** excusatory, mitigatory, remorseful **11** exonerative, extenuatory, vindicatory **12** apologetical **13** justificatory, making excuses **15** self-reproachful

Apologia pro Vita Sua
author: **15** John Henry Newman (Cardinal)

Apologie for Poetrie (Defense for Poetry)
author: **15** Sir Philip Sidney

apologist **7** pleader **8** advocate, defender **9** supporter

apologize **9** beg pardon **11** make apology **13** express regret

apology **6** excuse **7** defense **11** explanation, vindication **13** begging pardon, justification

Apomyius
epithet of: **4** Zeus
means: **14** averter of flies

Apophis
also: **5** Apepi
form: **7** serpent
habitat: **8** darkness
destroyed daily by: **4** Dawn

Apophthegms New and Old
author: **12** Francis Bacon

apostasy **7** atheism, perfidy **8** unbelief **9** defection, disbelief, recreancy **10** disloyalty, infidelity, irreligion **11** godlessness **13** double-dealing

apostate **6** bolter **7** heretic, seceder, traitor **8** defector, deserter, recanter, recusant, renegade, turncoat **9** dissenter, dissident, turnabout **10** backslider **13** nonconformist, tergiversator

apostle **5** envoy **6** zealot **7** pioneer, witness **8** activist, advocate, disciple, emissary, exponent, preacher **9** messenger, proponent, supporter **10** evangelist, missionary, propagator **12** propagandist, proselytizer, spokesperson

Apostle, The
author: **10** Sholem Asch

Apostles **4** John, Jude, Levi, Paul **5** Jacob, James, Peter, Simon **6** Andrew, Philip, Thomas **7** Matthew **8** Barnabas, Matthais **9** Nathanael, Thaddaeus **11** Bartholomew **12** James the Less **13** Judas Iscariot

apostle to the Gentiles: **4** Paul
apostle to the English: **9** Augustine
apostle to the Irish: **7** Patrick
apostle to the Goths: **7** Ulfilas
apostle to the Germans: **8** Boniface
apostle to the French: **5** Denis
apostle to the American Indians: **9** John Eliot

Apostrophia
epithet of: **9** Aphrodite
means: **24** rejecter of sinful passions

apothegm **5** adage, axiom, maxim, motto **6** dictum **7** epigram, proverb **8** aphorism **9** catchword

apotheosis **7** epitome, essence **9** elevation **10** embodiment, exaltation **11** deification **12** canonization, consecration, enshrinement, idealization, quintessence **13** dignification, glorification, magnification **15** immortalization

Appalachian Spring
ballet by: **7** Copland

appall **4** stun **5** abash, alarm, repel, shock **6** dismay, offend, revolt, sicken **7** disgust, horrify, outrage, terrify, unnerve **8** frighten, nauseate **10** dishearten

appalled **6** aghast **7** alarmed, shocked **8** dismayed, outraged, repelled, revolted **9** disgusted, horrified, nauseated

appalling **4** dire, grim **5** awful **6** horrid **7** fearful, ghastly **8** alarming, dreadful, horrible, horrific, shocking, terrible **9** dismaying, frightful, repellent, repulsive, revolting, sickening **10** abominable, disgusting, horrifying, nauseating, outrageous, terrifying **11** frightening, intolerable **12** insufferable **13** disheartening

apparatus **4** gear **5** gismo, setup, tools **6** device, gadget, outfit, system, tackle **7** machine **8** material, utensils **9** appliance, equipment, machinery, materials, mechanism **10** implements **11** contraption, contrivance, instruments **12** organization **13** paraphernalia

apparatus criticus **8** exegesis **10** annotation **11** elucidation, explication **14** interpretation

apparel **4** duds, garb, gear, togs **5** array, dress, habit, robes **6** attire **7** clothes, costume, raiment, threads, vesture **8** clothing, garments **9** equipment, trappings, vestments **13** accouterments

appareled **4** clad **5** robed **6** garbed, suited **7** attired, clothed, covered, dressed

apparent **4** open **5** clear, overt, plain **6** likely, marked, patent **7** blatant, evident, obvious, seeming, visible **8** clear-cut, distinct, manifest, probable **10** clear as day, ostensible, presumable **11** conspicuous, discernible, perceivable, perceptible, self-evident, unequivocal **12** unmistakable **14** understandable

apparently
Latin: **7** ex facie

apparition **5** ghost, shade, spook **6** spirit, wraith **7** phantom, specter **8** phantasm, presence, revenant **10** phenomenon **13** manifestation **15** materialization

appeal **3** beg, SOS **4** plea, pull, suit **5** apply, charm, plead, sue to, tempt **6** adjure, allure, engage, entice, excite, invite, invoke **7** attract, beseech, entreat, implore, request, solicit **8** call upon, charisma, entreaty, interest, petition **9** fascinate **10** adjuration, attraction, supplicate **11** fascination **12** solicitation, supplication

appealing **7** likable, lovable **8** adjuring, charming, engaging, enticing, fetching, inviting, pleading, pleasing, tempting **10** attractive, entreating, requesting, soliciting **11** charismatic, petitioning **12** irresistable, supplicating

appear **4** look, seem, show **5** arise **6** crop up, emerge, loom up, show up, turn up **7** be clear, be plain, come out, perform, surface **8** be patent **9** be evident, be obvious **10** be apparent, be manifest **11** be published, come to light, materialize

appearance **4** look **5** guise, image **6** advent, aspect, coming **7** arrival, pretext **8** pretense **9** appearing, emergence, showing up, turning up **10** impression **11** outward show **13** manifestation **15** materialization

appear at **6** attend, show up **8** peform at

appease **4** calm, dull, ease, lull **5** abate, allay, blunt, quell, quiet, slake, still **6** pacify, quench, solace, soothe, temper **7** assuage, compose, mollify, placate, relieve, satisfy **8** mitigate **9** alleviate **10** conciliate, propitiate **11** accommodate

appeasement **6** easing **7** abating, dulling **8** allaying, blunting, giving in **9** abatement, assuasion, quenching **10** mitigation, submission **11** alleviation, assuagement **12** conciliation, pacification, propitiation, satisfaction **13** accommodation, gratification, mollification

appellation **3** tag **4** name **5** title **6** handle **7** epithet, moniker **8** cognomen **9** sobriquet **11** designation, nom de guerre

append **3** add **4** join **5** affix **6** attach, hang on, tack on **7** subjoin, suspend **10** supplement

appendage **3** arm, leg **4** limb, tail **6** branch, feeler, member **7** adjunct **8** addition, offshoot, tentacle **9** accessory, auxiliary, extension, extremity **10** attachment, supplement

appendix **7** codicil **8** addendum, addition **10** back matter, postscript, supplement

appertain **7** apply to, concern, refer to **8** bear upon, be part of, belong to, inhere in, relate to **9** touch upon

appetite **4** zest **5** gusto **6** desire, hunger, liking, relish, thirst **7** craving, passion, stomach **8** fondness, penchant, yearning **10** proclivity **11** inclination

appetizer **6** canape, dainty, savory, tidbit **8** aperitif, cocktail, delicacy **9** antipasto **11** bonne bouche, hors d'oeuvre

appetizing **6** savory **8** alluring, enticing, inviting, tempting **9** appealing, palatable, succulent **10** attractive **11** tantalizing **13** mouth-watering

applaud **4** clap, hail, laud **5** extol **6** praise **7** acclaim, commend **8** eulogize **10** compliment **12** congratulate

applaudable **8** laudable **9** admirable, desirable, excellent **11** commendable, meritorious, outstanding **12** praiseworthy

applause **5** kudos **6** praise **7** acclaim, ovation **8** approval, clapping, plaudits **9** accolades **11** compliments

apple **5** Malus **15** Malus Sylvestris
varieties/fruit: **4** Crab, Lodi **6** Pippin **7** Baldwin, Stayman, Winesap **8** Ben Davis, Cortland, Jonathan, McIntosh **9** Delicious **10** Rome Beauty **11** Granny Smith, Gravenstein, Northern Spy, Summer Rambo **12** Grimes Golden, York Imperial **13** Yellow Newtown **14** Stayman Winesap **15** Yellow Delicious **17** Esopus Spitzenberg, Yellow Transparent **19** Rhode Island Greening
varieties/tree: **2** Wi **3** Kai, Kau, Sea, Wax **4** Cane, Java, Jew's, Pond, Rose, Star **5** Adam's, Baked, Belle, Blade, Chess, Conch, Malay, Melon, Thorn **6** Balsam, Indian, Mammee, Possum **7** Chinese, Custard, Dead Sea, Mexican **8** Elephant, Kangaroo, Otaheite, Paradise, Peruvian **11** Soulard crab, Toringo crab **12** Siberian crab
beverage: **5** cider **8** Calvados **9** Applejack

apple brandy
drink: **8** Jack Rose **12** Jack-in-the-Box
with rum: **6** Bolero **8** Apple Pie

applejack
type: **6** brandy
origin: **6** Canada **10** New England
flavor: **10** apple cider
drink: **11** Frozen Apple **13** Harvard Cooler

Apple of discord
color: **6** golden
thrown by: **4** Eris
awarded to: **9** Aphrodite
awarded by: **5** Paris
inscription: **13** for the fairest

apple of one's eye **11** pride and joy **15** light of one's life

applesauce **3** rot **4** bull, bunk **5** hokum, hooey **6** bunkum **7** baloney, hogwash, spinach **8** tommyrot **9** poppycock **12** fiddlesticks **13** horsefeathers **16** stuff and nonsense

Apples of the Hesperides
color: **6** golden
given to: **4** Hera
kept by: **5** Ladon **10** Hesperides

appliance **4** gear **6** device **7** fixture, machine **9** apparatus, equipment, implement, mechanism **11** contraption, contrivance

applicable **3** apt, fit **6** useful **7** apropos, fitting, germane **8** relevant, suitable **9** adaptable, befitting, pertinent

applicant **7** hopeful **8** aspirant, claimant **9** candidate, job seeker, suppliant **10** petitioner

application **4** balm, form, suit, wash **5** claim, salve **6** appeal, lotion **7** request, unguent **8** dressing, entreaty, industry, ointment, petition, poultice, solution **9** assiduity, attention, diligence, emollient, putting on, relevance **10** commitment, dedication, pertinence **11** germaneness, persistence, requisition, suitability **12** appositeness, perseverance, solicitation **13** attentiveness

Appling, Luke (Lucius Benjamin)
nickname: **16** Old Aches and Pains
sport: **8** baseball
position: **9** shortstop
team: **15** Chicago White Sox

apply **3** fit, use **4** suit **5** adapt, lay on, put on, refer **6** devote, direct, employ, relate **7** address, pertain, request, utilize **8** dedicate, exercise, petition, practice, spread on **9** implement

apply oneself **6** attend **10** buckle down **13** give oneself to **15** give it all one has **16** put one's heart into

appoint **3** fix, set **4** name **5** equip **6** assign, choose, engage, fit out, select, settle, supply **7** arrange, furnish, provide **8** decide on, delegate, deputize, nominate **9** designate, determine, establish, prescribe **10** commission

appointment **3** job **4** date, post, spot **5** berth, place **6** naming, office **7** meeting, station **8** choosing, position **9** placement, selection, situation **10** assignment, engagement, nomination, rendezvous **11** designation, meeting time **13** commissioning

Appointment in Samarra
author: **9** John O'Hara
character: **8** Al Grecco, Caroline **11** Harry Reilly **13** Julian English

appointments **4** gear **6** outfit **8** equipage **9** equipment, furniture **11** furnishings **13** accouterments

apportion **5** allot, share **6** divide, ration **7** consign, deal out, dole out, mete out, prorate **8** allocate, disperse **9** parcel out, partition **10** measure out

apportioning **8** alloting, dividing **9** doling out, meting out **10** allocating, consigning, dealing out, dispensing **12** distributing

apportionment **5** quota **6** ration **7** measure, portion **8** division **9** allotment **10** allocation **11** consignment **12** distribution, pro rata share

apposite **3** apt **7** apropos, fitting, germane **8** material, relevant, suitable **9** pertinent **10** applicable **11** appropriate

appositeness **9** relevance **10** pertinence **11** germaneness **15** appropriateness

appraisal **8** estimate, judgment **9** valuation **10** assessment, evaluation **14** estimated value

appraise **5** assay, judge, value **6** assess, review, size up **7** examine, inspect **8** evaluate

appreciable **7** evident, obvious **8** clear-cut, definite **10** detectable, noticeable, pronounced **11** discernible, perceivable, perceptible, significant, substantial **12** recognizable **13** ascertainable

appreciate **4** like **5** prize, savor, value **6** admire, esteem, relish **7** cherish, enhance, improve, inflate, realize, respect **8** perceive, treasure **9** recognize **10** comprehend, sympathize, understand **11** acknowledge

appreciation **4** rise **6** growth, liking, regard, relish, thanks **7** advance **8** sympathy **9** awareness, elevation, gratitude **10** admiration, cognizance **12** gratefulness, thankfulness **13** comprehension, understanding

apprehend **3** bag, nab, see **4** know **5** catch, grasp, seize, sense **6** arrest, collar **7** capture, discern, realize **8** perceive **9** recognize **10** comprehend, understand **12** take prisoner **15** take into custody

apprehension **5** alarm, dread, worry **6** arrest, dismay **7** anxiety, capture, concern, seizure **8** disquiet, distress, mistrust **9** misgiving, suspicion **10** foreboding, perception, uneasiness **11** premonition **12** presentiment **13** comprehension, understanding **16** apprehensiveness

apprehensive **6** afraid, scared, uneasy **7** alarmed, anxious, fearful, jittery, nervous, worried **9** concerned, misgiving **10** disquieted, distressed, suspicious **11** distrustful

apprehensiveness **5** dread, worry **6** dismay **7** anxiety **9** misgiving **10** foreboding, uneasiness **12** apprehension

apprentice **4** tyro **5** pupil **6** novice **7** learner, student **8** beginner, neophyte **19** indentured assistant

apprise **4** tell **6** advise, inform, notify **8** disclose **9** enlighten, make aware

approach **3** way **4** come, near, road **5** begin, equal, match **6** access, avenue, be like, method, system **7** advance, compare, passage, solicit **8** attitude, come near, draw near, embark on, gain upon, initiate, resemble, set about, sound out **9** come close, enter upon, procedure, technique, undertake **10** move toward, passageway **11** approximate

approachable **9** available, reachable **10** accessible

approbation **6** praise **7** acclaim, support **8** applause, approval, sanction **9** laudation **10** acceptance, compliment **11** endorsement **12** commendation, ratification **14** congratulation

appropriate **3** apt **4** take **5** allot **6** assign, proper, seemly **7** apropos, correct, earmark, fitting, germane **8** allocate, relevant, set apart, suitable **9** apportion, befitting, belonging, congruous, opportune, pertinent **10** confiscate, to the point, well-chosen, well-suited **11** expropriate **12** to the purpose **14** characteristic

appropriateness **7** aptness, fitness **9** congruity, propriety, relevance **10** pertinence **11** correctness, suitability

appropriation **6** taking **9** allotment **10** allocation, arrogation, usurpation **12** confiscation **13** expropriation, money set aside **16** misappropriation

approval **5** favor, leave **6** esteem, liking, regard **7** acclaim, consent, license, mandate, respect **8** sanction **9** agreement **10** acceptance, admiration, compliance, permission **11** approbation, concurrence, countenance, endorsement, good opinion **12** acquiescence, appreciation, confirmation **13** authorization **14** acknowledgment

approve **4** like, pass **5** allow **6** accept, affirm, defend, esteem, permit, praise, ratify, second, uphold **7** condone, confirm, endorse, respect, sustain **8** accede to, advocate, assent to, concur in, sanction **9** authorize, consent to **10** appreciate **11** countenance, go along with, rubber-stamp, subscribe to

approved 8 official **9** canonical **10** authorized, sanctioned

approving 9 endorsing, favorable **10** concurring **11** affirmative, sanctioning **12** appreciative

approximate 5 guess, rough **6** reckon **7** inexact, verge on **8** approach, border on, estimate, look like, relative, very near **9** estimated

approximately 5 circa **6** almost, around **7** close to **9** generally, just about **10** more or less, not far from, very nearly

appurtenance 4 wing **5** annex, extra **7** adjunct **8** addendum, addition **9** accessory, appendage, extension **10** attachment

Apres-midi d'un Faune, L' (The Afternoon of a Faun)
author: 16 Stephane Mallarme

April ***see box***

April Fool's Day
French: 9 April Fish

April
event: 11 Black Monday (13)
flower: 5 daisy **8** sweet pea
French: 5 Avril
gem: 7 diamond
German: 5 April
holiday: 6 Easter **11** All Fool's Day (1) **13** April Fool's Day (1)
Italian: 6 Aprile
Latin: 7 Aprilis
number of days: 6 thirty
origin of name: 4 aper (wild boar) **6** aparas (following) **7** aperire (to open) **9** Aphrodite
place in year:
***Gregorian:* 6** fourth
***Roman:* 6** second
saying: 24 April is the cruellest month **27** April showers bring May flowers
Spanish: 5 Abril
zodiac signs: 5 Aries **6** Taurus

a priori 6 theory **7** opinion **11** of reasoning

apron 3 bib **5** smock **8** covering **10** stagefront

apropos 3 apt **6** seemly **7** correct, fitting, germane, related **8** relevant, suitable **9** befitting, congruous, opportune, pertinent **10** applicable, to the point, well-suited **11** appropriate **12** just the thing

apry
type: 7 liqueur
origin: 6 France
flavor: 7 apricot

Apsyrtus
also: 8 Absyrtus
father: 6 Aeetes
sister: 5 Medea
killed by: 5 Medea

apt 5 prone **6** bright, clever, gifted, liable, likely, proper, seemly **7** apropos, fitting, germane, given to **8** inclined, relevant, suitable **9** befitting, congruous, opportune, pertinent **10** disposed to, well-suited **11** appropriate, intelligent, predisposed

aptitude 4 bent, gift, turn **5** flair, knack, skill **6** genius, talent **7** ability, faculty, leaning **8** capacity, facility, penchant, tendency **9** endowment, proneness, quickness **10** capability, cleverness, proclivity, propensity **11** inclination, proficiency **12** predilection **14** predisposition

aptness 4 bent, gift **5** flair, knack **6** talent **7** ability, faculty **8** aptitude, facility **11** suitability **15** appropriateness

Apuleius
author of: 12 The Golden Ass **13** Metamorphoses

aqua 4 blue **5** water **6** bluish **9** turquoise **10** aquamarine **12** greenish-blue

aquamarine 4 aqua, blue **5** beryl **9** turquoise **12** greenish-blue
color: 9 blue-green

aquaphobia
fear of: 5 water

aquarelle 10 watercolor

Aquarius
symbol: 11 water bearer **12** water-carrier
planet: 6 Saturn, Uranus
rules: 5 hopes **7** friends
born: 7 January **8** February

aquatic 6 marine **7** abyssal, fluvial, neritic, oceanic, pelagic **8** littoral **9** thalassic **10** fluviatile, lacustrine

aquavit
type: 6 spirit
origin: 11 Scandinavia
flavor: 4 dill **7** caraway **9** coriander
drink: 5 Glogg

aqua vitae 7 alcohol **11** water of life

aqueduct 4 duct, race **7** channel, conduit **11** watercourse **18** artificial waterway

aqueous 4 damp **5** moist **6** liquid, serous, watery **7** hydrous **8** waterish **9** lymphatic

Aqueus
epithet of: 4 Zeus
means: 6 watery

Aquilo *see* **6** Boreas

Aquinas, St Thomas
nickname: 13 Angelic Doctor
followers: 8 Thomists
author of: 15 Summa Theologica **21** Summa Totius Theologiae **34** Summa Catholicae Fidei contra Gentiles

Arab
clothing: 3 fez **4** veil
country: 4 Iraq, Oman **5** Egypt, Libya, Qatar, Sudan, Syria, Yemen **6** Jordan, Kuwait **7** Algeria, Bahrain, Lebanon, Morocco, Tunisia **11** Saudi Arabia **18** United Arab Emirates
habitat: 6 desert
Holy City: 5 Mecca **6** Medina
language: 6 Arabic
people: 7 Semitic
religion: 6 Muslim **7** Islamic
tribe: 4 Kurd **6** Berber, Nubian, Tuareg

Arabella
opera by: 7 (Richard) Strauss

Arabia
ancient name: 14 Jazirat al-Arab
ancient people: 6 Sabean **8** Egyptian **10** Babylonian
bounded by: 5 Syria **6** Jordan, Red Sea **10** Gulf of Aden, Gulf of Oman **11** Indian Ocean, Persian Gulf
country: 4 Oman **5** Qatar, Yemen **6** Kuwait **11** Saudi Arabia **18** United Arab Emirates
highest peak: 11 Jabal Shayib
holy book: 5 Koran
Holy City: 5 Mecca **6** Medina
island: 7 Bahrain, Socotra **9** Laccadive
language: 6 Arabic
mineral/natural resource: 3 oil **4** goat **5** sheep, wheat **6** barley, millet **7** iron ore, granite **8** porphyry **9** manganese, petroleum

nomadic tribe: 5 Maaza 6 Ababda
prophet: 8 Muhammad
religion: 6 Muslim 7 Islamic
river: 4 Nile, Oxus 5 Indus 6 Tigris 9 Euphrates
sea: 3 Red 7 Arabian 11 Persian Gulf 13 Mediterranean

Arabian Nights
director: 17 Pier Paolo Pasolini
based on: 20 Thousand and One Nights
cast: 11 Franco Citti 13 Ninetto Davoli 14 Ines Pellegrina

Arabian Nights' Entertainments, The (The Thousand and One Nights)
author: 7 unknown
storyteller: 12 Scheherazade

Arabic
national language in: 4 Iraq 5 Syria 6 Jordan 7 Lebanon 11 North Africa 16 Arabian Peninsula
also spoken in: 6 Israel 12 North America, South America 17 Soviet Central Asia, Sub-Saharan Africa
language of: 5 Koran

arable 6 fecund 7 fertile 8 farmable, fruitful, plowable, tillable 10 cultivable, productive

Arachne
origin: 6 Lydian
challenged: 6 Athena
contest: 7 weaving
changed into: 6 spider

arachnid
class: 4 mite, tick 6 spider 8 scorpion 13 daddy-long-legs
phylum: 9 Arthropod
pairs of legs: 4 four
respiratory organ: 12 pulmonary sac, tracheal tube
dwelling: 4 land 5 water
body part: 15 anterior prosoma 20 posterior opisthosoma
way of feeding: 8 parasite, predator 9 scavenger

arachnophobia
fear of: 7 spiders

Aram *see* 5 Syria

Aramis
character in: 18 The Three Musketeers
author: 5 Dumas (pere)

Arapaho
language family: 9 Algonkian 10 Algonquian
tribe: 6 Atsine 11 Gros Ventres 15 Northern Arapaho, Southern Arapaho
location: 6 Plains 8 Colorado, Red River
related to: 8 Cheyenne
ceremony: 8 sun dance

Aras
first king of: 8 Phliasia

Arawak
language family: 8 Arawakan
tribe: 5 Taino 6 Igneri, Lucayo
location: 4 Cuba 5 Haiti 6 Guyana 8 Antilles, Colombia 9 Venezuela 12 South America

Arawakan
tribe: 6 Arawak 8 Boriquen 9 Borinquen

Arawn
lord of: 6 Annfwn

arbiter 5 judge 6 pundit, umpire 7 referee 9 authority 10 arbitrator 11 connoisseur

arbitrary 6 chance, random 7 summary, willful 8 absolute, despotic, fanciful, personal 9 frivolous, imperious, unlimited, whimsical 10 autocratic, capricious, peremptory, subjective 12 inconsistent, uncontrolled, unrestrained

arbitrate 5 judge 6 decide, settle, umpire 7 adjudge, mediate, referee 9 reconcile 10 adjudicate 12 bring to terms 13 sit in judgment

Arbitration, The
author: 8 Menander

arbitrator 5 judge 6 umpire 7 arbiter, referee 8 mediator 9 go-between, moderator 10 negotiator 11 adjudicator 12 intermediary

arbor 5 bower, folly, kiosk 6 gazebo, grotto 7 pergola 8 pavilion 9 belvedere 10 shaded walk 11 summerhouse

arc 3 bow 4 arch 5 curve 8 crescent, half-moon 10 semicircle

arcade 6 loggia, piazza 7 archway, areaway, gallery, skywalk 8 cloister, overpass 9 breezeway, colonnade, peristyle, underpass

Arcadia, The
author: 15 Sir Philip Sidney
character: 5 Mopsa 6 Pamela 7 Dametas, Gynecia, Zelmane 8 Basilius, Cecropia, Pyrocles 9 Amphialus, Musidorus, Philoclea, Plexistus

Arcadian stag *see* 8 Cerynean

Arcanan
father: 8 Alcmaeon
mother: 10 Callirrhoe
brother: 10 Amphoterus

arcane 6 mystic, occult 7 obscure 8 abstruse, esoteric, hermetic, mystical 9 enigmatic, recondite 10 mysterious

Arcas
father: 4 Zeus
mother: 8 Callisto
wife: 5 Erato
son: 6 Elatus
ancestor of: 9 Arcadians
set among: 5 stars
placed by: 4 Zeus

Arce
father: 7 Thaumas
sister: 4 Iris 7 Harpies
Zeus took: 5 wings
aided: 6 Titans

Arcesius
father: 4 Zeus
mother: 8 Euryodia
son: 7 Laertes
grandson: 8 Odysseus

arch 3 arc, bow, sly 4 bend, dome, main, span, wily 5 chief, curve, major, saucy, vault 7 cunning, primary, roguish 8 bow shape 9 curvature, designing, principal 10 curved span 11 mischievous

archaeologist
American: 7 Bingham 8 Douglass, Stephens
British: 5 Evans 6 Carter, Childe, Layard, Leakey, Petrie, Wooley 7 Lubbock, Ventris, Wheeler 9 Rawlinson 10 Pitt-Rivers 13 Caton-Thompson
Danish: 7 Thomsen, Worsaae
French: 5 Botta 8 Cousteau 11 Champollion
German: 5 Conze 7 Curtius 8 Dorpfeld, Koldewey 9 Grotefend 10 Schliemann 11 Winckelmann
Italian: 8 Fiorelli
Swedish: 4 Geer 9 Montelius

archaic 5 passe 6 bygone 7 ancient, antique 8 obsolete 9 out-of-date 10 antiquated 11 obsolescent 12 old-fashioned

archangel 5 Satan, Uriel 7 Gabriel, Michael, Raphael

arched 4 bent 5 bowed 6 curved

Archegetes
epithet of: 6 Apollo
means: 7 founder

Archelaus
father: 7 Temenus
descendant of: 8 Hercules

Archelochus
mentioned in: 5 Iliad
father: 7 Antenor
mother: 6 Theano
killed by: 14 Telamonian Ajax

Archemorus *see* 8 Opheltes

archenemy **3** foe **7** archfoe, bugbear, nemesis, scourge **8** opponent **9** adversary, assailant, bete noire, combatant, disputant **10** antagonist

archeology
term: **3** dig **6** midden **9** earthwork **11** burial mound **17** aerial photography
type: **7** salvage **8** American, medieval **9** classical, text-aided **10** Egyptology, industrial, underwater **11** Assyriology, prehistoric **12** Mesopotamian
ages: **4** Iron **6** Bronze
Old Stone Age: **11** Paleolithic
Middle Stone Age: **10** Mesolithic
New Stone Age: **9** Neolithic
dating method: **5** cross **8** absolute, carbon-14 **13** geochronology **16** dendrochronology **18** thermoluminescence **28** potassium-argon varved deposits
site/artifact: **2** Ur **4** Giza, Troy **5** Copan, Crete, Delos, Minos **6** Amarna, Carnac, Nimrud, Nippur, Tiryns **7** Alalakh, Babylon, Ephesus, Knossos, Mycenae, Nineveh, Olympia, Pompeii, Rio Azul **8** Behistun, Kuyunjik, Pergamum, pyramids **9** Arikamedu, Hissarlik, Khorsabad, New Grange, Tarquinia, Woodhenge **10** Carchemish, Persepolis, Samothrace, Stonehenge **11** Herculaneum, Machu Picchu, Mohenjodaro **12** Easter Island, Hadrian's Wall, Olduvai Gorge, Rosetta Stone **13** Avebury Circle, Zimbabwe Ruins **14** Dead Sea Scrolls, Laocoon statues **15** temple of Artemis **16** Valley of the Kings **18** Ostrava-Petrokovice, Royal Palace of Minos
tomb: **11** Tutankhamen **15** Ch'in Shih Huang Ti

Archeptolemus
mentioned in: **5** Iliad
father: **7** Iphitus
charioteer of: **6** Hector

archer **6** bowman **8** spearman
famous: **5** Cupid **9** Robin Hood **11** William Tell

Archer
constellation of: **11** Sagittarius

Archer, Isabel
character in: **18** The Portrait of a Lady
author: **5** James

Archer, Miles
character in: **16** The Maltese Falcon
author: **7** Hammett

Archer, Newland
character in: **17** The Age of Innocence
author: **7** Wharton

Archer in Jeopardy
author: **13** Ross MacDonald

archery
athlete: **10** Linda Myers, Luanne Ryon **11** Darrell Pace

archetypal **5** model **7** classic **8** original **9** classical, exemplary **10** definitive, prototypal, protypical

archetype **5** model **7** classic **8** exemplar, original **9** prototype **12** prime example

Archias
founder of: **8** Syracuse
location: **6** Sicily
descendant of: **8** Hercules

Archie
creator: **10** Bob Montana **13** John Goldwater
character: **5** Betty, Moose **6** Reggie **7** Sabrina **8** Big Ethel, Veronica **11** Mr Weatherby **12** Jughead Jones
place: **9** Riverdale

Archimago
character in: **15** The Faerie Queene
author: **7** Spenser

Archipenko, Alexsandr
born: **4** Kiev **6** Russia
artwork: **8** Medranos **9** Gondolier, Medrano II, Pregnancy, The Bather **11** Boxing Match **12** Archipentura, Walking Woman **15** Geometric Statue **18** Wilhelm Furtwangler **19** Woman Combing Her Hair

architect **6** author, shaper **7** creator, deviser, founder, planner **8** designer, engineer **9** artificer, contriver, draftsman, innovator **10** instigator, originator, prime mover **13** master builder **16** building designer
name **3** Pei **4** Hunt, Mead, Pope, Root, Wren **5** Hoban, Jones, Le Vau, McKim, Mills, Roche, Stone, Tange, White, Wyatt **6** Breuer, Fuller, Owings, Smirke, Wright **7** Bernini, Burnham, Gilbert, Gropius, Johnson, Latrobe, Mansart, Merrill, Renwick **8** Bramante, Harrison, Palladio, Saarinen, Skidmore, Sullivan, Yamasaki **9** Jefferson **10** Richardson **11** Le Corbusier **12** Brunelleschi, Michelangelo **14** Mies van der Rohe **15** Hardouin-Mansart
legendary first: **8** Daedalus
designed: **18** Minotaur's Labyrinth
Roman: **9** Vitruvius

architecture **5** style **6** design **11** structuring **12** construction **14** architectonics **16** structural design

archives **6** annals, museum, papers **7** library, records **9** documents **10** chronicles, depository **11** memorabilia

arctic **3** icy **5** gelid, polar **6** bitter, frigid, frozen **7** glacial, ice-cold **8** freezing, icebound **9** North Pole **10** frostbound **11** far-northern, hyperborean **13** septentrional

Arden, Eve
real name: **13** Eunice Quedens
born: **12** Mill Valley CA
roles: **13** Mildred Pierce, Our Miss Brooks

ardent **4** keen **5** eager, fiery, lusty **6** fierce **7** earnest, fervent, intense, zealous **8** feverish, spirited, vehement **10** passionate **11** impassioned, tempestuous **12** enthusiastic

ardor **4** love, zeal **5** gusto, verve, vigor **6** fervor, spirit **7** feeling, passion, rapture **8** devotion **9** eagerness, intensity, vehemence **10** enthusiasm, excitement, fierceness **11** amorousness **12** feverishness

Ardrey, Robert
author of: **17** The Social Contract

arduous **4** hard **5** heavy, tough **6** severe, tiring, trying **7** onerous **8** toilsome, vigorous **9** difficult, energetic, fatiguing, Herculean, laborious, strenuous, wearisome **10** burdensome, exhausting, formidable **11** troublesome

arduousness **5** trial **8** tough job **10** difficulty, rough going, uphill work **12** hard sledding, toilsomeness **13** laboriousness, wearisomeness

area **4** turf, zone **5** arena, field, range, realm, scope, space, tract **6** domain, extent, region, sphere **7** expanse, portion, section, stretch, terrain **8** district, locality, precinct, province **9** territory

Areithous
origin: **5** Greek
mentioned in: **5** Iliad
king of: **7** Arcadia

son: **10** Menesthius
nickname: **7** maceman
weapon: **8** iron mace
killed by: **8** Lycurgus

Areius *see* **5** Areus

arena **4** area, bowl, ring **5** field, lists, realm, scene, stage **6** circus, domain, sector, sphere **7** stadium, theater **8** coliseum, platform, province **9** gymnasium, territory **10** hippodrome **11** battlefield, marketplace **12** amphitheater, battleground, playing field

Arendt, Hannah
author of: **10** On Violence **12** On Revolution **13** Life of the Mind **17** The Human Condition **19** Crises of the Republic, Eichmann in Jerusalem **27** The Origins of Totalitarianism

Arene
son: **4** Idas **7** Lynceus

Arensky, Anton Stepanovich (Antony)
born: **6** Russia **8** Novgorod
composer of: **7** Tempest **13** Egyptian Night **18** Variations on Legend

Areopagitica
author: **10** John Milton

Ares
also: **8** Theritas
origin: **5** Greek
god of: **3** war
father: **4** Zeus
mother: **4** Hera
sister: **4** Hebe
son: **5** Molus **6** Cycnus, Deimos, Phobos, Tereus **8** Diomedes, Eurytion, Meleager, Oenomaus, Phlegyas, Thestius **10** Ascalaphus
daughter: **7** Alcippe **8** Harmonia **9** Melanippe **11** Penthesilea
nurse: **5** Thero
corresponds to: **4** Mars
epithet: **8** Enyalius **14** Gynaecothoenas

Arete
father: **8** Rhexenor
husband: **8** Alcinous
daughter: **8** Nausicaa
personifies: **7** courage

Arethusa
form: **5** nymph
changed into: **6** spring
saved from: **7** Alpheus

Aretus
father: **5** Priam
killed by: **9** Automedon

Areus
also: **6** Areius
father: **4** Bias
mother: **4** Pero
brother: **6** Talaus **8** Leodocus
member of: **9** Argonauts
epithet of: **4** Zeus
means: **7** warlike

Are You There, God? It's Me, Margaret
author: **9** Judy Blume

Argades
father: **3** Ion

Argeiphontes
also: **11** Argiphontes
epithet of: **6** Hermes
means: **13** slayer of Argus

argent **5** white **6** silver **7** shining, silvery

Argentina ***see box***

Arges
member of: **8** Cyclopes

Argia
also: **5** Aegia
father: **7** Oceanus
mother: **6** Tethys
husband: **7** Polybus
son: **5** Argus

Argiope
form: **5** nymph
father: **8** Teuthras
husband: **6** Agenor **8** Telephus
son: **6** Cadmus
daughter: **6** Europa

Argiphontes *see* **12** Argeiphontes

Argive
pertaining to: **5** Argos

Argo
ship of: **4** Argo

argon
chemical symbol: **2** Ar

Argonauts
searchers for: **12** Golden Fleece
leader: **5** Jason
ship: **4** Argo
sailed to: **7** Colchis

argot **4** cant **5** idiom, lingo, slang **6** jargon, patois **10** vernacular

arguable **7** at issue **9** debatable **10** disputable **12** questionable **13** controversial, problematical

argue **4** hold, show **5** claim, imply, plead **6** assert, bicker, debate, denote, evince, reason **7** contend, display, dispute, exhibit, express, point to, quarrel, quibble, wrangle **8** indicate, maintain, manifest **11** demonstrate, expostulate, remonstrate

argument **3** row **4** case, gist, plot, spat, tiff **5** clash, fight, story **6** debate, reason **7** dispute, outline, quarrel, summary **8** abstract, contents, squabble, synopsis **9** bickering, imbroglio **10** war of words **11** altercation, central idea, controversy, embroilment **12** disagreement

argumentation **6** debate **7** dispute **8** argument **10** discussion

argumentative **5** testy **7** peevish, scrappy **8** contrary, petulant, snappish **9** combative, fractious, litigious, querulous **11** belligerent, contentious, quarrelsome **12** cantankerous, disputatious

Argus
form: **5** giant
father: **7** Phrixus
mother: **9** Chalciope
builder of: **4** Argo
number of eyes: **10** one hundred
epithet: **8** Panoptes

Argyra
form: **5** nymph
habitat: **6** spring
loved: **8** Selemnus

Argyrotoxus
epithet of: **6** Apollo
means: **18** lord of the silver bow

aria **3** air **4** solo, song, tune **6** melody, number **7** arietta, excerpt, section **9** selection **10** canzonetta **13** aria cantabile

Aria
form: **5** nymph
son: **7** Miletus
fathered by: **6** Apollo

Ariadna *see* **7** Ariadne

Ariadne
also: **7** Ariadna
father: **5** Minos
mother: **8** Pasiphae
husband: **8** Dionysus
son: **8** Oenopion
gave thread to: **7** Theseus
deserted by: **7** Theseus

Ariadne auf Naxos
also: **14** Ariadne on Naxos
opera by: **7** (Richard) Strauss
character: **7** Bacchus, Theseus **8** Composer **10** Zerbinetta

Ariana *see* **11** Afghanistan

Ariane et Barbe-Bleu
also: **19** Ariadne and Bluebeard
opera by: **5** Dukas
character: **7** Ariadne **9** Bluebeard

Arianrhod
origin: **5** Welsh
form: **7** goddess
brother: **7** Gwydion

Argentina
name means: **6** silver
capital/largest city: **11** Buenos Aires
others: **4** Acha, Azul, Goya, Oran, Puan, Rosa **5** Jujuy, Junin, Lanus, Lujan, Metan, Monte, Salta, Tigre **6** Parana, Rufino, Zarate **7** Bolivar, Caseros, Cordoba, Dolores, Formosa, LaBanda, LaPlata, LaRioja, Mendoza, Neuquen, Posadas, Quilmes, Rafaela, Rosario, San Juan, Santa Fe, Tucuman **9** Catamarca, Rio Cuerto **10** Avellaneda, Corrientes **11** Bahai Blanca, Mar del Plata, Resistencia **17** Santiago del Estero **20** San Carlos de Bariloche
division: **5** Andes, Chaco, Pampa **9** Patagonia **11** Mesopotamia **14** Tierra del Fuego
measure: **4** sino **5** legua **6** cuadra, lastre **7** manzana
monetary unit: **4** peso **7** centavo **9** argentino
weight: **4** last **5** libra **7** quintal **8** tonelada
island: **14** Tierra del Fuego
lake: **6** Viedma **7** Cardiel, Fagnano, Musters **11** Buenos Aires, Mar Chiquita, Nahuel Huapi
mountain: **4** Toro **5** Andes, Chato, Laudo, Potro **6** Bonete, Conico, Pissis, Rincon **8** Famatina, Murallon, Olivares, Tronador, Zapaleri **9** Aconcagua, Tupungato **10** Cordillera **13** Ojos del Salado **15** Cerro Mercedario, Sierra de Cordoba
highest point: **9** Aconcagua
river: **4** Sali **5** Atuel, Chico, Coyle, Dulce, Limay, Negro, Plata, Teuco **6** Blanco, Chubut, Cuarto, Flores, Grande, Iguazu, Parana, Quinto, Salado **7** Bermejo, Deseado, Iguassu, Mendoza, Tercero, Tunuyan, Uruguay **8** Colorado, Paraguay, Picomayo, Senguerr **9** Pilcomayo
sea: **8** Atlantic
physical feature:
falls: **6** Grande, Iguazu **7** Iguassu
lowland: **5** chaco
plains: **6** pampas
plateau: **4** Puna **6** Parana
salt flat: **14** Salinas Grandes
volcano: **5** Lanin, Maipo **6** Domuyo **7** Peteroa
wind: **5** Zonda **7** Pampero
people: **3** Api **4** Lule **5** Vejoz **6** Abipon, Vilela **7** Guarani, Puelche, Ranquel, Taluhet **8** Querandi, Querendy
artist: **6** Borges
author: **4** Wast **6** Banchs, Borges **7** Lugones **9** Guiraldes, Hernandez **10** Echeverria
leader: **4** Roca **5** Illia, Mitre, Peron, Rosas **6** Videla **7** Urquiza **8** Aramburu, Belgrano, Eva Peron, Frondici, Galtieri **9** San Martin, Sarmiento **11** Isabel Peron
language: **7** Spanish
religion: **13** Roman Catholic
place:
opera house: **11** Teatro Colon
world's southernmost town: **7** Ushuaia
feature:
bird: **6** chunga
cowboy: **6** gaucho **7** vaquero
dance: **5** samba, tango, zamba **6** cuando, gaucho **7** milonga **9** chacarera
farm: **6** quinta
knife: **5** facon
metal straw: **8** bombilla
ranch: **8** estancia
school smock: **9** delantale
shawl: **6** poncho
trousers: **9** bombachas
weapon: **4** bola
food:
cocktail: **7** clarito
dish: **4** luna **7** criollo, puchero **8** chivitos, empanada **10** parrillada

mistress of: **7** Gwydion
son: **14** Llew Llew Gyffes
cursed: **14** Llew Llew Gyffes

arid **3** dry **4** dull **5** vapid **6** barren, dreary, jejune **7** dried-up, parched, tedious **8** lifeless, pedantic **9** colorless, dry as dust, waterless **10** desertlike, uninspired **13** unimaginative, uninteresting **15** drought-scourged

aridity **6** dearth **7** drought, dryness **8** aridness, dullness **10** barrenness **12** lifelessness, rainlessness **17** unimaginativeness

aridness **6** dearth **7** aridity, drought, dryness **8** dullness **10** barrenness **12** lifelessness, rainlessness **17** unimaginativeness

arid region **6** desert **9** wasteland **16** barren wilderness

Ariel
author: **11** Shakespeare, Sylvia Plath
character in: **10** The Tempest

Aries
symbol: **3** ram
planet: **4** Mars
rules: **11** personality
born: **5** April, March

Arimaspians
member of: **9** Scythians
number of eyes: **3** one

Arion
form: **11** winged horse
father: **8** Poseidon
mother: **7** Demeter

Ariosto, Ludovico
author of: **14** Orlando Furioso

Arisbe
father: **6** Teucer
husband: **5** Priam **8** Dardanus, Hyrtacus

arise **4** dawn, go up, rise, wake **5** awake, begin, climb, ensue, get up, mount, occur, set in, start **6** appear, ascend, crop up, emerge, result, wake up **7** emanate, stand up **8** commence, spring up, stem from **9** originate **11** come to light

Aristaeus
origin: **5** Greek
god of: **9** husbandry **10** beekeeping, winemaking
father: **6** Apollo
mother: **6** Cyrene
wife: **7** Autonoe
son: **7** Actaeon
caused death of: **8** Eurydice

aristocracy **5** elite **6** gentry **7** peerage, society **8** nobility **9** beau monde **10** patricians, upper class, upper crust **11** high society

aristocrat **4** duke, earl, lady, lord, peer **5** noble **7** Brahmin, duchess, grandee, marquis **8** countess, marquess, nobleman **9** blue blood, gentleman, patrician **10** noblewoman **11** gentlewoman **12** silk stocking

aristocratic **5** noble, regal, royal **6** lordly, titled **7** courtly, genteel, refined **8** highborn, highbred, wellborn **9** dignified, patrician **10** of high rank, upper-class **11** blue-blooded, gentlemanly **12** silk-stocking **13** of gentle blood

Aristodemus
member of: **10** Heraclidae
father: **12** Aristomachus
son: **7** Procles **11** Eurysthenes
killed by: **9** lightning

Aristomachus
member of: **10** Heraclidae
son: **7** Temenus **11** Aristodemus, Cresphontes
granddaughter: **8** Hyrnetho
invaded: **12** Peloponnesus

Aristophanes
author of: **6** Plutus **8** The Birds, The Frogs, The Peace, The Wasps **9** The Clouds **10** Lysistrata, The Knights **13** Ecclesiazusae, The Acharnians

Aristotle
author of: **7** Physics, Poetics **8** On Plants, Politics, Rhetoric, Sophisms **9** On the Soul **10** Generation **11** Metaphysics **12** On the Heavens **14** Parts of Animals, Prior Analytics **17** Nicomachean Ethics **18** Posterior Analytics **23** On Beginning and Perishing

Arizona ***see box***

ark **3** box **4** ship **5** barge, chest **8** flatboat **9** houseboat **10** Noah's boat

Arkansas ***see box***

Arkin, Alan
born: **9** New York NY
roles: **7** Catch-22 **13** Wait Until Dark **21** Last of the Red-Hot Lovers **23** The Heart Is a Lonely Hunter **40** The Russians Are Coming The Russians Are Coming

Ark of the Covenant
gold covering: **9** mercy seat **12** propitiatory

arm, arms **4** guns **5** brace, crest, equip, prime **6** branch, outfit, sector **7** forearm, fortify, prepare, protect, section, weapons **8** armament, blazonry, division, firearms, insignia, materiel, offshoot, ordnance, weaponry **9** appendage, make ready, upper limb **10** coat of arms, department, detachment, obtain arms, projection, strengthen, take up arms **12** anterior limb **13** prepare for war **14** heraldic emblem **18** furnish with weapons

armada **4** navy **5** fleet **8** flotilla, squadron **10** escadrille

armadillo
family: **11** Dasypodidae
order: **8** Edentata
body: **5** armor **6** plates
habitat: **12** South America, United States **14** Central America
habit: **9** nocturnal

Armageddon **8** doomsday **11** final battle **13** great conflict
author: **8** Leon Uris

armagnac
type: **6** brandy **7** liqueur
origin: **6** France

Arizona
abbreviation: **2** AZ **4** Ariz
nickname: **11** Grand Canyon
capital/largest city: **7** Phoenix
others: **3** Ajo **4** Eloy, Mesa, Naco, Yuma **5** Globe, Leupp, Tempe **6** Bisbee, McNary, Salome, Toltec, Tucson **7** Cortaro **8** Chandler, Glendale, Prescott **9** Flagstaff **10** Scottsdale
college: **11** Grand Canyon **12** Southwestern
explorer: **8** Coronado **12** Marcos de Niza
feature:
dam: **6** Hoover **8** Coolidge **9** Roosevelt
national park: **11** Grand Canyon **15** Petrified Forest
tribe: **4** Hano, Hopi, Pima **6** Apache, Navaho, Navajo, Papago
people: **7** Cochise **8** Geronimo **14** Barry Goldwater
lake: **4** Mead **6** Havasu, Mohave, Mormon, Powell **9** Roosevelt
land rank: **5** sixth
mountain: **5** White **6** Lemmon **7** Hualpai **8** Mazatzal **9** Baldy Peak **13** Santa Catalina
highest point: **13** Humphreys Peak
physical feature:
canyon: **5** Grand
desert: **6** Sonora **7** Painted
forest: **9** Petrified
river: **4** Gila, Salt, Zuni **5** Verde **6** Puerco **8** Colorado **12** Bill Williams **14** Little Colorado
state admission: **11** forty-eighth
state bird: **10** cactus wren
state flower: **13** saguaro cactus
state motto: **11** God Enriches
state song: **7** Arizona
state tree: **9** palo verde

armament **4** arms, guns **7** weapons **8** ordnance, weaponry **9** equipment, munitions **10** outfitting **13** military might **16** war-making machine

Armenia ***see box***

Armenian
- **language family:** **12** Indo-European
- **spoken in:** **4** USSR **6** Russia **7** Armenia

Armida
- **opera by:** **5** Gluck, Haydn, Lully **6** Dvorak **7** Rossini **10** Eszterhazy

Armies **7** Sabaoth

Armies of the Night
- **author:** **12** Norman Mailer

armistice **5** peace, truce **9** cease-fire **23** suspension of hostilities

armlet **6** bangle **8** bracelet, ornament

arm of the sea **5** bight, firth, fjord (fiord), inlet **6** strait **7** channel, estuary, narrows

armoire **8** cupboard, wardrobe **12** clothespress

armor **4** mail **5** chain **6** shield **7** bulwark **10** coat of mail, protection **11** suit of armor **18** protective covering

armorial bearings **4** arms **5** crest **10** coat of arms, escutcheon

armory **7** arsenal **9** arms depot **13** ordnance depot

Arms and the Man
- **author:** **17** George Bernard Shaw

arms depot **6** armory **7** arsenal **13** ordnance depot **18** military storehouse

Armstrong, Henry
- **sport:** **6** boxing
- **class:** **11** lightweight **12** welterweight

army **3** mob **4** band, bevy, crew, gang, host, mass, pack **5** crowd, force, horde, swarm **6** legion, throng, troops **7** legions, militia **8** military, soldiers, soldiery **9** land force, multitude **10** land forces **11** aggregation, fighting men **12** congregation **13** military force **15** military machine

Arnaeus
- **also:** **4** Irus
- **origin:** **5** Greek
- **mentioned in:** **7** Odyssey
- **form:** **6** beggar **9** errandboy
- **errandboy for:** **16** Penelopes suitors

Arkansas
- **abbreviation:** **2** AR **3** Ark
- **nickname:** **4** Bear **9** Bowie Land **17** Land of Opportunity
- **capital/largest city:** **10** Little Rock
- **others:** **3** Coy, Cuy, Keo, Ola, Roe, Ulm **4** Alma, Bono, Casa, Dell, Diaz, Moro **5** Enola, Perla, Rondo **6** Alicia, Camden **8** El Dorado **9** Fort Smith, Jonesboro, Pine Bluff, Texarkana **10** Hot Springs **11** Blytheville **12** Fayetteville
- **feature:**
  - ***national park:*** **10** Hot Springs
- **tribe:** **5** Caddo, Osage **6** Quapaw **7** Choctaw, Wichita **8** Cherokee
- **people:** **8** Alan Ladd **10** Dick Powell **16** Douglas MacArthur
- **lake:** **6** Beaver, Chicot, Conway, Nimrod **7** Greeson, Norfork **8** Maumelle, Ouachita **10** Bull Shoals **11** Greers Ferry **12** Blue Mountain
- **land rank:** **13** twenty-seventh
- **mountain:** **4** Blue **5** Ozark **6** Boston, Gaylor **7** Fourche **8** Magazine, Ouachita
  - ***highest point:*** **8** Magazine
- **river:** **3** Red **5** Black, White **6** Saline **7** Buffalo, Current **8** Arkansas, Cossatot, Ouachita **9** St Francis **11** Mississippi
- **state admission:** **11** twenty-fifth
- **state bird:** **11** mockingbird
- **state flower:** **12** apple blossom
- **state motto:** **13** (Let) The People Rule
- **state song:** **8** Arkansas
- **state tree:** **13** shortleaf pine

Armenia
- **other name:** **5** Minni **6** Urartu **8** Anatolia **31** Armenian Soviet Socialist Republic
- **capital/largest city:** **6** Erivan **7** Yerevan
- **ancient capital:** **3** Ani **8** Artashat, Artaxata
- **others:** **3** Van **5** Sivas **7** Trabzon **9** Kirovakan, Leninakan, Trabizond **13** Bitlisarzurum
- **head of state:** **41** President of the Presidium of the Supreme Soviet
- **head of government:** **31** Chairman of the Council of Ministers
- **monetary unit:** **5** ruble
- **lake:** **3** Van **5** Sevan, Urmia **8** Urumiyah
- **mountain:** **6** Ararat, Taurus **7** Aladagh **8** Karabakh
- **highest peak:** **12** Mount Aragats
- **river:** **3** Ara **4** Aras, Kura **5** Araks, Cyrus, Halys, Zanga **6** Araxes, Razdan, Tigris **9** Euphrates **10** Kizil-Irmak
- **physical feature:**
  - ***volcano:*** **7** Aragats
- **people:** **5** Armen, Ermyn, Gomer, Hadji
  - ***apostle:*** **7** Gregory
  - ***gypsy:*** **5** bosha
  - ***hero:*** **4** haik **6** vartan
  - ***me:*** **3** ara
  - ***saint:*** **5** Sahak **6** Mesrop
- **language:** **7** Russian **8** Armenian
- **religion:** **16** Armenian Orthodox
- **feature:**
  - ***cap:*** **6** calpac
  - ***fortress:*** **7** erebuni
  - ***game:*** **7** barbout
  - ***kingdom:*** **6** Urartu, Vannic **7** Cilicia, Sophene **8** Ardsruni
- **food:**
  - ***bread:*** **4** peda
  - ***cucumber:*** **4** guta
  - ***dish:*** **7** lahvosh **9** paraghatz, sou-beoreg

Arne
author: **20** Bjornstjerne Bjornson

Arne
son: **6** Aeolus **7** Boeotus
foster father: **9** Desmontes

Arne, Thomas Augustine
born: **6** London **7** England
composer of: **6** Alfred, Judith **8** Rosamond, Tom Thumb **10** Artaxerxes **14** Love in a Village, Thomas and Sally

Arness, James
real name: **12** James Aurness
brother: **11** Peter Graves
born: **13** Minneapolis MN
roles: **8** Gunsmoke **10** Matt Dillon

Arnljot Gelline
author: **20** Bjornstjerne Bjornson

Arnold, Matthew
author of: **7** Thyrsis **10** Dover Beach **15** Sohrab and Rustum, The Scholar-Gypsy **16** Empedocles on Etna **17** Culture and Anarchy, Essays in Criticism **18** On Translating Homer

aroma **4** odor **5** savor, scent, smell **7** bouquet **9** fragrance, redolence

aromatic **5** spicy **7** odorous, piquant, pungent, scented **8** fragrant, perfumed, redolent **11** odoriferous

Aron Kodesh **7** Holy Ark

Aronnax, Professor Pierre
character in: **32** Twenty Thousand Leagues Under the Sea
author: **10** Jules Verne

around **4** near **5** about, circa **10** encircling, on all sides, roundabout **11** surrounding

Around the World in Eighty Days
author: **10** Jules Verne
director: **15** Michael Anderson
character: **11** Phileas Fogg **12** Passepartout
cast: **10** Cantinflas, David Niven **12** Robert Newton **15** Marlene Dietrich, Shirley MacLaine
score: **11** Victor Young
Oscar for: **5** score **7** picture

arouse **3** fan **4** goad, move, spur, warm, whet **5** pique, rouse, waken **6** awaken, bestir, excite, foment, foster, heat up, incite, kindle, stir up, wake up **7** provoke, quicken, sharpen **8** summon up **9** stimulate

Arowhena
character in: **7** Erewhon
author: **6** Butler

arpeggio **5** chord, scale **8** flourish **13** musical device

arraign **6** accuse, charge, impute, indict **7** censure **8** denounce **9** criticize

arrange **4** file, plan, plot, pose, rank, sort **5** adapt, array, fix up, group, order, range, score **6** assort, design, devise, lay out, line up, map out, set out, settle **7** agree to, marshal, prepare, provide **8** classify, contrive, organize, schedule **9** methodize **11** orchestrate, systematize

arrangement **5** order **8** arraying, disposal, grouping, ordering **10** assortment **12** distribution, organization **13** methodization **14** categorization, classification **15** systematization
German: **9** Ausgleich

arrangements **5** plans, score, terms **7** compact **8** measures **9** agreement **10** adaptation, provisions, settlement **12** preparations **13** orchestration

arrant **4** rank **5** utter **7** extreme **8** flagrant, outright, thorough **9** confirmed, downright, egregious, notorious, out-and-out **11** undisguised, unmitigated **13** thoroughgoing

array **4** deck, garb, pose, rank, robe, show, wrap **5** adorn, align, dress, group, order, place, range **6** attire, bedeck, clothe, deploy, finery, fit out, outfit, parade, set out, supply **7** apparel, arrange, display, marshal, raiment **8** clothing, garments, organize **9** pageantry **10** assortment, collection, exhibition, marshaling **11** arrangement, disposition

arrears **5** debit **9** liability **10** balance due, obligation, unpaid debt **11** overdue debt **12** indebtedness **15** outstanding debt

arrest **3** end, fix, nab **4** bust, halt, hold, slow, stay, stop **5** block, catch, check, delay, pinch, rivet, roust, seize, stall **6** absorb, collar, detain, engage, hinder, occupy, retard, secure **7** attract, capture, engross, inhibit, seizure, slowing, staying **8** blocking, checking, hold back, restrain, stoppage, stopping, suppress **9** apprehend, interrupt, retention **10** inhibiting **11** holding back **12** apprehension, take prisoner

Arrhenius, Svante August
field: **7** physics **9** chemistry
nationality: **7** Swedish
theory of: **24** electrolytic dissociation

arriere pensee **12** hidden motive **17** mental reservation

arrival **5** comer **6** advent, coming **7** entrant, visitor **8** approach, arriving, entrance, newcomer, visitant **10** appearance

arrive **4** come, near **5** get to, occur, reach **6** appear, befall, happen, show up, turn up **7** succeed **8** approach, make good

arrivederci, a rivederci
7 goodbye **8** farewell **16** until we meet again

arrogance **5** scorn **6** egoism, vanity **7** bluster, conceit, disdain, swagger **8** contempt **9** assurance, insolence, loftiness, vainglory **10** lordliness, pretension **11** braggadocio, haughtiness, presumption **13** imperiousness **14** self-importance

arrogant **4** vain **6** lordly **7** haughty, pompous **8** insolent, scornful **9** conceited, imperious **10** disdainful, egoistical, swaggering **11** egotistical, overbearing, overweening, pretentious **12** contemptuous, presumptuous, self-assuming, supercilious, vainglorious **13** high-and-mighty, self-important

arrogate **5** adopt, claim, seize, usurp **6** assume **7** preempt **8** take over **10** commandeer **11** appropriate

arrogation **6** taking **7** seizure **10** assumption, usurpation **12** confiscation **13** appropriation, expropriation

arrow **3** bow **4** bolt, dart **5** shaft **7** pointer **9** direction **12** pointed shaft

Arrow
constellation of: **7** Sagitta

Arrowsmith
author: **13** Sinclair Lewis
character: **10** Leora Tozer **11** Max Gottlieb **12** Terry Wickett **14** Capitola McGurk **15** Gustaf Sondelius **16** Martin Arrowsmith **18** Dr Almus Pickerbaugh

arroyo **4** wadi **5** gorge, gully **6** ravine, trench

arsenal **6** armory **7** weapons **8** magazine **9** arms depot **11** arms factory **13** ordnance depot **14** ammunition dump

arsenic
chemical symbol: 2 As

Arsenic and Old Lace
director: 10 Frank Capra
cast: 9 Cary Grant **10** Jack Carson, Peter Lorre **13** Josephine Hull, Priscilla Lane, Raymond Massey

Arsinoe *see* **11** Alphesiboea

Arsinous
son: 8 Aecamede

Arsippe
father: 6 Minyas
mocked: 8 Dionysus

ars longa, vita brevis 20 art is long life is short

Ars Poetica
author: 5 Homer

art, arts 5 craft, knack, skill **6** genius **7** finesse, mastery, methods **8** artistry, facility, strategy **9** dexterity, expertise, technique **10** fine points, humanities, principles, subtleties, virtuosity
goddess of: 6 Athena, Athene, Pallas, Saitis **7** Minerva **11** Tritogeneia **12** Pallas Athena **18** Alalcomenean Athena

Artacia
origin: 5 Greek
mentioned in: 7 Odyssey
means: 6 spring
in the land of: 10 Laestrygon

Artegall
character in: 15 The Faerie Queene
author: 7 Spenser

Artemis
also: 7 Cynthia **9** Astrateia
origin: 5 Greek
form: 6 virgin **7** goddess **8** huntress
habitat: 4 moon
mother: 4 Leto
twin brother: 6 Apollo
companion: 4 Opis **5** Oread
corresponds to: 5 Diana **6** Phoebe, Selene **11** Britomartis
epithet: 6 Orthia **7** Euripa, Laphria, Limnaea, Pyronia **8** Aeginaea, Agrotera, Calliste, Caryatis, Daphnaea **9** Hemerasia, Lygodesma **10** Polymastus **11** Leucophryne

Artemision
shrine of: 7 Artemis

artery 3 way **4** path, road, vein **5** aorta **6** street **7** channel, highway **11** blood vessel

artful 3 apt, sly **4** able, deft, foxy, wily **5** adept, quick, sharp, smart **6** adroit, astute, clever, crafty, gifted, shifty, shrewd, subtle, tricky **7** cunning, knowing, politic **8** masterly, scheming, skillful, talented **9** deceitful, deceptive, designing, dexterous, ingenious, inventive, strategic, underhand **10** contriving, diplomatic, proficient **11** imaginative, machinating, maneuvering, resourceful **12** disingenuous

artfulness 5 guile **6** deceit **7** cunning, slyness **8** artifice, foxiness, scheming, subtlety, trickery, wiliness **10** craftiness **11** machination

Arthur
director: 11 Steve Gordon
cast: 11 Dudley Moore, John Gielgud **12** Liza Minnelli **19** Geraldine Fitzgerald
Oscar for: 15 supporting actor (Gielgud)

Arthur
began: 10 Round Table
father: 14 Uther Pendragon
half-sister: 11 Morgan le Fay
home: 7 Camelot
island: 6 Avalon
knights: 3 Kay **6** Gareth, Gawain **7** Geraint **8** Bedivere, Lancelot, Percival, Tristram **9** Launcelot
knights sought: 9 Holy Grail
mother: 7 Igraine, Ygaerne
nephew: 6 Modred
sword: 9 Excalibur
given by: **13** Lady of the Lake
wife: 9 Guinevere
wizard: 6 Merlin

Arthur, Chester Alan ***see box, p. 60***

artichoke 14 Cynara Scolymus
varieties: 5 Globe **7** Chinese **8** Japanese **9** Jerusalem **14** White Jerusalem

article 4 item, part, term **5** count, essay, paper, piece, point, story, theme, thing **6** clause, detail, matter, object, review, sketch **7** portion, product, proviso, write-up **8** division **9** commodity, condition, paragraph, provision, substance **10** commentary, particular **11** proposition, stipulation

articulate 4 join **5** hinge, state, utter, voice **6** convey, facile, fluent, hook up **7** connect, enounce, express **8** eloquent, organize **9** enunciate, formulate, pronounce **10** enunciated, expressive, meaningful, speechlike **12** intelligible

articulation 5 hinge, joint **7** diction **8** juncture **9** elocution, utterance **10** connection **11** enunciation **13** pronunciation

artifact 4 tool **7** manmade **9** arrowhead

artifice 4 hoax, ruse, trap, wile **5** blind, dodge, feint, guile, trick **6** deceit, device, tactic **7** cunning, slyness **8** foxiness, intrigue, maneuver, scheming, trickery, wiliness **9** deception, duplicity, falsehood, imposture, ingenuity, invention, stratagem **10** artfulness, cleverness, craftiness, subterfuge **11** contrivance, machination **13** inventiveness

artificer 7 artisan, deviser **9** contriver, craftsman

artificial 4 fake, mock, sham **5** false, phony, stagy **6** ersatz, forced **7** feigned, labored, manmade, stilted **8** affected, mannered, specious, spurious **9** imitation, insincere, pretended, simulated, synthetic, unnatural **10** factitious, nonnatural, theatrical **11** counterfeit **12** manufactured

artillery 6 cannon **7** big guns **8** ordnance **11** mounted guns

artisan 6 master **9** craftsman **10** technician **14** handicraftsman

art is long life is short
Latin: 18 ars longa vita brevis

artist 6 expert, master **8** virtuoso

artistic 7 elegant, stylish **8** graceful, handsome, tasteful **9** aesthetic, cxquisite **10** attractive

artistic ability 6 talent **7** mastery **8** artistry **10** virtuosity

artistry 5 taste, touch **6** talent **7** mastery **10** virtuosity **11** proficiency, sensibility **14** accomplishment

artless 4 open, pure, true **5** crude, frank, naive, plain **6** candid, honest, humble, simple **7** natural, sincere **8** innocent, trusting **9** guileless, ingenuous, primitive, unadorned **10** inartistic, lacking art, unaffected, untalented **11** open-hearted, undesigning **13** unpretentious **15** straightforward, unselfconscious, unsophisticated

artlessness 6 candor **7** honesty, naivete **8** openness **9** frankness, sincerity **10** simplicity **11** naturalness **13** guilelessness, ingenuousness **14** unaffectedness

art object
French: 9 objet d'art

Arthur, Chester Alan
nickname: 4 Chet **16** The Gentleman Boss
presidential rank: 11 twenty-first
party: 10 Republican
state represented: 2 NY
defeated: 5 no-one
succeeded upon death of: **8** Garfield
vice president: 4 none
cabinet:
state: **6** (James Gillespie) Blaine **13** (Frederick Theodore) Frelinghuysen
treasury: **6** (Charles James) Folger, (William) Windom **7** (Walter Quintin) Gresham **9** (Hugh) McCulloch
war: **7** (Robert Todd) Lincoln
attorney general: **8** (Benjamin Harris) Brewster, (Isaac Wayne) MacVeagh
navy: **4** (William Henry) Hunt **8** (William Eaton) Chandler
postmaster general: **4** (Timothy Otis) Howe **5** (Thomas Lemuel) James **6** (Frank) Hatton **7** (Walter Quinton) Gresham
interior: **6** (Henry Moore) Teller **8** (Samuel Jordan) Kirkwood
born: 2 VT (or Canada) **9** Fairfield
died: 2 NY **11** New York City
buried: 2 NY **6** Albany
education:
college: **5** Union
studied: **3** law
religion: 12 Episcopalian
interests: 8 good food (an epicure) **13** salmon fishing
political career: 13 vice president **26** customs collector for New York
civilian career: 6 lawyer **7** teacher
military service: 8 Civil War
quartermaster general of: **12** state militia (New York)
notable events of lifetime/term: 5 Panic (of 1883)
Act: **9** Pendleton **16** Chinese Exclusion **19** Edmunds Anti-Polygamy
father: 7 William
mother: 7 Malvina (Stone)
siblings: 4 Jane, Mary **6** Almeda, George, Regina **7** Malvina, William **8** Ann Eliza
wife: 5 Ellen (Lewis Herndon)
nickname: **4** Nell
children: 11 Chester Alan **12** Ellen Herndon **19** William Lewis Herndon

Art of Living, The
author: 11 John Gardner

Art of Love, The (Ars Amatoria)
author: 4 Ovid

arty 6 dainty **7** foppish **8** affected, highbrow, overnice, precious **9** dandified, overblown **10** effeminate **11** overrefined, pretentious **12** artsy-craftsy, bluestocking, high-sounding

Aruns
killer of: 7 Camilla

Arval
also: 13 Arval Brothers **14** Fratres Arvales
priests of: 6 Dea Dia
number of priests: 6 twelve

Arval Brothers *see* **5** Arval

Aryan
modern name: 13 Indo-European
origin: 10 North India **11** Central Asia
family of languages: 5 Hindi **7** Bengali, Panjabi **9** Sinhalese
religion: 8 Hinduism
originated: 11 caste system

Aryana *see* **11** Afghanistan

as 4 that, when **5** while **7** because, equally

Asa
father: 6 Abijah
grandfather: 8 Rehoboam
grandmother: 6 Maacah
deposed: 6 Maacah
defeated: 6 Baasha

as above
Latin: 7 ut supra

as a group 7 en masse, in a body **8** as a whole, together **11** all together

as a matter of form
Latin: 8 pro forma

Asar *see* **5** Aesir

as a result 2 so **5** due to **7** because **9** therefore, wherefore, whereupon **11** accordingly **12** consequently **13** in consequence

as a whole 8 all in all **10** altogether **19** all things considered
French: 6 en bloc

as below
Latin: 7 ut infra

Ascalabus
form: 5 youth
mocked: 7 Demeter
changed into: 6 lizard

Ascalaphus
occupation: 6 sentry **8** gardener
location: 10 underworld
father: 4 Ares
brother: 8 Ialmenus
member of: 9 Argonauts
killed by: 9 Deiphobus
changed into: 3 owl
changed by: 7 Demeter

Ascanius
also: 5 Iulus
father: 6 Aeneas
mother: 6 Creusa
founder of: 9 Alba Longa

ascend 4 rise **5** climb, mount, scale **7** inherit **9** succeed to

ascendancy, ascendance **4** edge, rule, sway **5** power, reign **7** command, control, mastery **8** whip hand **9** advantage, authority, dominance, influence, supremacy, upper hand **10** domination, leadership **11** preeminence, sovereignty, superiority **12** predominance

ascension 6 ascent, rising **7** scaling **8** climbing, mounting **10** ascendancy

ascent 4 rise **5** climb, grade, slope **6** rising **7** advance, incline, scaling, upgrade **8** climbing, gradient, mounting, progress **9** ascension **11** advancement, progression

ascertain 5 learn **6** detect, verify **7** certify, find out, unearth **8** discover **9** determine, establish, ferret out

ascertainable 10 detectable

11 discernible, perceivable, perceptible

ascetic **3** nun **4** monk, yogi **5** fakir, stern **6** hermit, strict **7** austere, dervish, eremite, recluse, Spartan **8** celibate, cenobite, rigorous, solitary **9** abstainer, anchorite, religious **10** abstemious, flagellant, self-denier **11** self-denying **13** self-mortifier **14** self-mortifying

Asch, Sholem
author of: **4** Mary **5** Moses **8** A Village **10** The Apostle, The Prophet **11** The Nazarene, Three Cities **15** Song of the Valley **17** The God of Vengeance

Asclepiade
descendants of: **9** Asclepius

Asclepius
origin: **5** Greek
god of: **7** healing **8** medicine
father: **6** Apollo
mother: **7** Coronis
wife: **6** Epione
son: **7** Machaon **10** Podalirius
daughter: **4** Iaso **6** Hygeia
nurse: **6** Trygon
corresponds to: **11** Aesculapius
epithet: **8** Cotyleus

ascribe **6** assign, credit, impute, relate **7** trace to **8** accredit, charge to **9** attribute

Ascus
form: **5** giant
helped: **8** Lycurgus
chained: **8** Dionysus

asea **4** lost **6** addled, adrift **7** puzzled **8** confused **10** bewildered

Asenath
father: **10** Potipherah
husband: **6** Joseph
son: **7** Ephraim **8** Manasseh

Asgard
home of: **4** Asar **5** Aesir
origin: **12** Scandinavian
connected to earth by: **7** bifrost **13** rainbow bridge
location of: **8** Valhalla

ash **4** dust **6** cinder **7** residue **12** powdered lava
family: **5** olive
genus: **8** Fraxinus
climatic zone: **17** northern temperate
varieties: **3** Pop, Red, Sea **4** Blue **5** Black, Green, Manna, Texas, Wafer, Water, White **6** Alpine, Ground, Shamel, Syrian, Velvet **7** Arizona, Modesto, Prickly **8** Carolina, Stinking **9** Evergreen, Flowering **10** Manchurian, Montebello **18** Yellow-topped mallee
use: **4** fuel **6** timber **7** barrels **8** landscape **9** furniture **10** motor parts, sport goods
most common species: **8** white ash

ashamed **3** shy **7** abashed, bashful, prudish **9** chagrined, mortified, squeamish **10** chapfallen, distressed, humiliated, shamefaced **11** crestfallen, discomfited, embarrassed **12** disconcerted **13** guilt-stricken **18** conscience-stricken

Ashby, Hal
director of: **10** Being There, Coming Home

ashen **3** wan **4** gray, pale **5** livid, pasty **6** anemic, leaden, pallid **8** blanched

Asher
father: **5** Jacob
mother: **6** Zilpah
brother: **3** Dan, Gad **4** Levi **5** Judah **6** Joseph, Reuben, Simeon **7** Zebulun **8** Benjamin, Issachar, Nephtali
sister: **5** Dinah
city in: **8** Manasseh
descendant of: **8** Asherite

Ashkenaz
father: **6** Japhet
mother: **5** Gomer

Ashley, Lady Brett
character in: **15** The Sun Also Rises
author: **9** Hemingway

ashore **6** on land **7** aground **9** on dry land

Ashton-Warner, Sylvia
author of: **5** Three **6** Myself **7** Teacher **8** Spinster **10** Greenstone

Ashtoreth
origin: **7** Semitic
corresponds to: **6** Inanna, Ishtar **7** Astarte, Mylitta

Ash-Wednesday
author: **7** T S Eliot

ashy **3** wan **4** pale **5** ashen, pasty, white **6** pallid, sallow **7** ghastly, ghostly **8** blanched **9** colorless

Asia *see box, p. 62*

aside **4** away **5** apart **6** aslant, beside **7** whisper

As I Lay Dying
author: **15** William Faulkner
character:
Bundren family: **4** Anse, Cash, Darl **5** Addie, Jewel **9** Dewey Dell

Asimov, Isaac
author of: **6** I Robot **10** Foundation (trilogy) **12** Caves of Steel, Robots of Dawn **17** The Gods Themselves
character: **12** Elijah Bailey **13** R Daneel Olivaw

asinine **5** silly **6** absurd, insane, stupid **7** foolish, idiotic, moronic, witless **9** brainless, imbecilic, senseless **10** halfwitted, irrational, muddlehead, ridiculous **11** lamebrained, thickheaded, thick-witted **12** dunderheaded, feebleminded, simpleminded, thickskulled

asininity **5** folly **8** dumbness **9** silliness, stupidity **10** imbecility **11** doltishness, foolishness **16** simplemindedness

as it should be
French: **11** comme il faut

Asius
origin: **5** Greek
mentioned in: **5** Iliad
king of: **7** Percote
father: **8** Hyrtacus
killed by: **9** Idomeneus

ask **3** beg, bid, sue **4** call, pump, quiz, seek, urge **5** apply, claim, grill, plead, press, query **6** appeal, charge, demand, desire, expect, invite, summon **7** beseech, entreat, implore, inquire, request, solicit **8** petition, question, sound out **10** supplicate **11** interrogate

Ask
origin: **6** Nordic
first: **3** man
made from: **7** ash tree
made by: **4** gods

askance **11** skeptically **12** disdainfully, suspiciously **13** distrustfully, mistrustfully **14** disapprovingly

askew **4** awry **6** aslant **7** crooked **8** cockeyed, lopsided, sleeping **9** crookedly

Askkimey *see* **6** Eskimo

aslant **4** awry **5** askew **7** crooked **8** cockeyed, lopsided **9** crookedly, obliquely, slantwise

asleep **6** dozing **7** napping **10** slumbering **13** taking a siesta **14** dead to the world

as much as this
Latin: **8** quoad hoc

Asner, Ed
born: **12** Kansas City KS
roles: **5** Roots **8** Lou Grant **14** Rich Man Poor Man **18** Mary Tyler Moore Show

asocial **8** unsocial **9** nonsocial, reclusive **10** antisocial **12** misanthropic

Asia
country: **4** Iran, Iraq, Laos, Oman **5** Burma, China, India, Japan, Macao, Nepal, Qatar, Syria, Tibet, Yemen **6** Bhutan, Brunei, Cyprus, Israel, Jordan, Sikkim, Taiwan, Turkey **7** Bahrain, Kashmir, Lebanon, Siberia, Vietnam **8** Hong Kong, Malaysia, Maldives, Mongolia, Pakistan, Sri Lanka, Thailand, Uzbek SSR **9** Indonesia, Kampuchea, Kazakh SSR, Singapore **10** Bangladesh, Kirghiz SSR, North Korea, Seychelles, South Korea, Tadzhik SSR, Turkmen SSR **11** Afghanistan, Armenia SSR, Georgian SSR, Saudi Arabia **13** Azerbaijan SSR, Inner Mongolia **14** Papua New Guinea **15** Sinkiang-Uighur **18** United Arab Emirates
desert: **4** Gobi, Thar **6** Syrian **7** Arabian, Karakum **8** Kyzylkum **10** Takla Makan
island: **5** Kuril, Japan **6** Taiwan **7** Hai-nan **8** Sri Lanka **9** Indonesia: **3** Aru **4** Java, Sulu **5** Ceram, Sumba, Timor **6** Borreo, Flores **7** Celebes, Sumatra **8** Moluccas, Tanimbar **9** Halmaherd, New Guinea **11** Philippines
ancient people/empire: **4** Elam, Thai **5** Akkad, Aryan, Indus, Khmer, Media, Shang **6** Mongol, Ohoman, Semite **7** Amorite, Assyria, Hwang Ho, Parthia, Persian **8** Sumerian **9** Babylonia, Dravidian, Sassanian **11** Hephthalite, Mesopotamia
ancient city: **2** Ur **5** Pagan, Sumer **6** Anyang **7** Ayuthia, Harappa **8** Mandalay **12** Mohenjo-daro
ancient leader: **5** Asoka, Kassi **6** Darius **9** Anawratha, Zoroaster **13** Cyrus the Great **17** Alexander the Great
religion: **5** Islam **6** Muslim, Shinto, Taoism **7** Jainism, Judaism **8** Buddhism, Hinduism **12** Christianity, Confucianism **13** Protestantism **16** Roman Catholicism
language: **5** Hindi **6** Arabic, French **7** Chinese, English, Russian, Spanish
Chinese dialects: **2** Wu **3** Min **5** Hakka **8** Mandarin **9** Cantonese
river: **2** Ob **3** Amu, Hsi, Syr **4** Amur, Lena **5** Indus **6** Ganges, Mekong, Tigris **7** Hwang Ho, Salween, Yangtze, Yenisei **9** Euphrates, Irrawaddy **11** Brahmaputra **16** Tigris-Euphrates
lake: **6** Baikal **7** Aral Sea **8** Balkhash **10** Caspian Sea
mountain/mountain range: **5** Altai, Urals **6** Kunlon, Pamirs, Taurus, Zagros **8** Caucasus, Sulaiman, Tien Shan **9** Himalayas, Hindu Kush, Karakoram **10** Arakan Yoma
highest point: **12** Mount Everest
lowest point: **7** Dead Sea
mineral/natural resources: **3** oil, tin **4** coal, mica, talc, zinc **7** bauxite, iron ore, mercury **8** chromium, graphite, selenium, tungsten **9** manganese **10** natural gas
largest city: **8** Shanghai
vegetation: **3** fir, sal **4** moss, pine, teak **5** larch **6** bamboo, lichen, spruce **8** ironwood
animal: **3** elk, yak **4** bear, wolf **5** camel, panda, sable, takin, tiger **6** ermine, kuland **7** markhor **8** antelope, elephant, reindeer **9** arctic fox, polar bear
people: **4** Huis, Kurd, Thai, Turk **5** Aryan, Khmer, Malay, Tungu **6** Buryat, Chuang, Kalmyk, Mongol, Semite, Vighor **7** Baluchi, Burmese, Chinese, Chukchi, Persian, Russian, Tadzhik, Tibetan **8** Armenian, Filipino, Japanese **9** Dravidian **10** Han Chinese, Indonesian, Vietnamese **15** European Russian

Asopus
form: **3** god
habitat: **5** river
father: **7** Oceanus
mother: **6** Tethys
wife: **6** Metope
son: **7** Ismenus, Pelagon
number of daughters: **6** twenty

asparagus
varieties: **4** Cape **6** Common, Garden, Smilax **7** Cossack **8** Prussian, Sprenger

aspect **3** air **4** look, side **5** angle, facet, point **7** feature **10** appearance **13** consideration

aspen **7** Populus
varieties: **7** Chinese, Quaking **8** European, Japanese **9** Trembling **12** Large-toothed

asperity **5** rigor **6** rancor **8** acrimony, hardship, severity **9** harshness, hostility, roughness **10** difficulty

Aspern Papers, The
author: **10** Henry James

aspersion **4** slur **5** abuse, smear **7** calumny, censure, obloquy, railing, slander **8** reproach, reviling **10** defamation, detraction **11** deprecation **12** vilification **13** disparagement

Asphalius *see* **8** Poseidon

Asphodel Fields
meadow of: **10** dead heroes

asphyxiate **5** choke **6** stifle **7** smother **9** suffocate **11** strangulate

aspirant **7** hopeful, nominee **9** applicant, candidate **10** competitor, contestant

aspiration **3** end **4** hope, mark, wish **6** design, desire, intent, object **7** craving, longing, purpose **8** ambition, daydream, endeavor, yearning **9** hankering, intention, objective

aspire **4** seek **5** aim at, covet, crave **6** desire, pursue **7** hope for, long for, pine for, wish for **8** yearn for **9** pant after **10** hunger over **11** hanker after, thirst after

ass **4** dolt, fool, jerk **5** booby, burro, dunce, idiot, moron, ninny **6** donkey, dum-dum, nitwit **7** half-wit, jackass **8** bonehead, imbecile, lunkhead, numskull **9** blockhead, lamebrain **10** dunderhead, nincompoop **11** male jackass

assail **5** fly at **6** attack **7** assault, lunge at, set upon **9** pitch into **11** descend upon

assailant **6** mugger **8** assailer, attacker, molester **9** aggressor, assaulter

assailer **8** attacker **9** aggressor, assailant, assaulter

Assamese
language family: **12** Indo-European
branch: **11** Indo-Iranian
group: **5** Indic
spoken in: **5** (northern) India

Assaracus
origin: **5** Greek
mentioned in: **5** Iliad
father: **4** Tros
son: **5** Capys
founder of: **10** royal house

assassin **6** hit man, killer, slayer **8** murderer **11** executioner

assassinate **4** kill, slay **6** murder, rub out **7** bump off **9** do to death, liquidate **10** put to death **11** exterminate

assault **4** push, raid **5** drive, fly at, foray, lunge, sally, siege, storm **6** assail, attack, charge, invade, strike, thrust **7** besiege, bombard, lunge at, offense, set upon **8** fall upon, invasion, storming, strike at, thrust at **9** assailing, lash out at, onslaught **10** aggression **11** bombardment

assaulter **6** mugger **8** assailer, attacker **9** aggressor, assailant

assay **3** try **4** rate, test **5** essay, prove **6** assess **7** analyze, attempt **8** appraise, endeavor, estimate, evaluate **9** undertake

assemblage **4** body, heap, herd, mass, pack, pile **5** batch, bunch, clump, flock, group, stock, store **6** throng **7** cluster, company **8** assembly, conclave **9** aggregate, amassment, gathering **10** collection **11** aggregation **12** accumulation, congregation

assemble **4** join, meet **5** amass, flock, rally **6** gather, heap up, muster, pile up, summon **7** collect, compile, connect, convene, convoke, marshal, round up **9** construct, fabricate **10** accumulate, congregate **11** fit together, put together **12** call together, come together **13** bring together, group together

assembly **4** body, herd, mass, pack **5** crowd, flock, group, troop **6** throng **7** cluster, company, council **8** conclave, congress **9** aggregate, gathering **10** assemblage, collection **11** aggregation, convocation, legislature **12** congregation

assembly hall **8** auditory **10** auditorium **11** concert hall, lecture hall, meeting hall

assent **5** agree, allow, grant, yield **6** accept, accord, comply, concur, permit **7** approve, concede, consent, defer to **8** approval, sanction **9** acquiesce, admission, agreement **10** acceptance, compliance, concession, fall in with **11** affirmation, approbation, concurrence, endorsement, recognition, subscribe to **12** acquiescence, confirmation, ratification, verification **13** corroboration **14** acknowledgment

assent to **4** okay **5** allow **6** accept, permit **7** approve **8** sanction, say yes to **9** agree with, authorize **11** acquiesce to, go along with

assert **4** aver, avow **5** argue, claim, state, swear **6** accent, affirm, avouch, insist, stress, uphold **7** advance, contend, declare, profess **8** advocate, maintain, propound, set forth **9** emphasize **10** put forward

assertion **5** claim **6** avowal, dictum **8** argument, averment **9** statement, upholding **10** allegation, contention **11** declaration, maintaining **12** protestation

assertion without proof
Latin: **9** ipse dixit

assertive **5** pushy **8** cocksure, decisive, emphatic, forceful, positive **9** confident, insistent, outspoken **10** aggressive **11** domineering, self-assured **12** strong-willed

assertiveness **10** insistence **11** forwardness **12** cocksureness, forcefulness, positiveness **13** agressiveness, outspokenness **14** self-confidence

assess **3** tax **4** levy **5** judge, value **6** charge **8** appraise, consider, estimate, evaluate, look over

assessment **3** fee, tax **4** dues, fine, rate, toll **6** charge, impost, tariff **8** judgment **9** appraisal **10** estimation, evaluation

asset **3** aid **4** boon, help, plus **7** benefit, service **9** advantage

assets **4** cash **5** goods, means, money **6** wealth **7** capital, effects **8** property, reserves **9** resources **10** belongings **11** possessions

asseverate **4** aver, avow **5** state, swear **6** affirm, assert, attest, avouch, insist **7** certify, contend, declare, protect **8** maintain, proclaim **9** emphasize, pronounce

as shown below
Latin: **7** ut infra

assiduity **8** industry, tenacity **9** diligence **10** dedication, doggedness **11** application, persistence **13** determination

assiduous **6** dogged **7** earnest **8** constant, diligent, sedulous, tireless, untiring **9** laborious, steadfast, tenacious **10** determined, persistent, unflagging **11** hardworking, industrious, persevering, unremitting **13** indefatigable

assign **3** fix, set **4** give, name **5** allot, grant **6** charge, choose, invest **7** appoint, consign, entrust, mete out, specify **8** allocate, delegate, dispense, set apart **9** apportion, designate, determine, prescribe, stipulate **10** commission, distribute

assignation **4** date **5** tryst **7** meeting **10** rendezvous **11** appointment

assignment **3** job **4** duty, post, task **5** chore **6** lesson **8** exercise, homework **9** allotment **10** allocation, commission **11** appointment, designation **12** distribution **13** apportionment

assimilate **6** absorb, digest, imbibe, ingest, take in **9** integrate **10** metabolize **11** incorporate

Assiniboine, Assiniboin
language family: **6** Siouan
location: **9** Minnesota **12** Lake Winnipeg, Saskatchewan
related to: **7** Dakotas

assist **3** aid **4** abet, hand, help **5** boost, serve **6** back up, uphold, wait on **7** benefit, support, sustain **9** cooperate, lend a hand, reinforce **11** accommodate, collaborate, helping hand

assistance **3** aid **4** alms, help **6** relief **7** charity, service, stipend, subsidy, support **10** sustenance **11** cooperation, helping hand **12** contribution **13** collaboration, reinforcement **16** financial support

assistant **3** aid **4** aide, ally **5** aider **6** helper **7** partner **8** adjutant, co-worker, sidekick **9** accessory, associate, auxiliary, colleague, subaltern, supporter **10** accomplice, apprentice, cooperator, lieutenant **11** confederate, helping hand, subordinate **12** collaborator **15** second-in-command

associate **3** mix, pal, tie **4** ally, bind, chum, club, join, link, mate, pair, peer, yoke **5** buddy, crony, merge, unite **6** allied, couple, fellow, friend, hobnob, league, mingle, relate **7** combine, comrade, connect, consort, hang out, partner, related **8** confrere, coworker, identify, intimate, sidekick **9** affiliate, colleague, companion, confidant, correlate, pal around, rub elbows, run around **10** accomplice, affiliated, fraternize **11** confederate, subordinate **12** collaborator

associated 6 allied, joined, united **9** connected **10** affiliated **11** amalgamated

association 3 tie **4** body, bond, club, meld **5** blend, group, union **6** clique, league **7** combine, company, linkage, mixture, society **8** alliance, intimacy, mingling, relation **9** coalition, community, relations, syndicate **10** assemblage, connection, federation, fellowship, fraternity, friendship, membership **11** affiliation, camaraderie, combination, confederacy, corporation, correlation, familiarity, partnership **12** acquaintance, friendliness, organization, relationship **13** collaboration, companionship, confederation, participation **14** fraternization, identification

assorted 5 mixed **6** motley, sundry, varied **7** diverse, various **9** different **11** diversified **13** heterogeneous, miscellaneous

assortment 5 array, stock, store **6** medley, motley **7** melange, mixture, sorting, variety **8** grouping, quantity **9** arranging, assorting, diversity, potpourri, selection **10** collection, hodgepodge, miscellany **11** arrangement, classifying, disposition **14** classification, conglomeration

as stated below
Latin: 7 ut infra

assuage 4 calm, ease **5** allay, quiet, still **6** lessen, pacify, soften, soothe, temper **7** appease, lighten, mollify, relieve **8** mitigate, tone down **9** alleviate **14** take the edge off

assuagement 6 easing, relief, solace **7** comfort **8** blunting, easement **9** abatement, lessening, tempering **10** mitigation **11** appeasement **13** mollification

assume 4 take **5** fancy, guess, infer, judge, seize, think, usurp **6** accept, deduce, gather, take on, take up **7** believe, imagine, presume, suppose, surmise, suspect **8** arrogate, shoulder, take over, theorize **9** postulate, speculate, undertake **10** commandeer, conjecture, understand **11** appropriate, expropriate, hypothesize **14** take for granted

assumed 4 fake **5** bogus, false, phony **6** made-up **8** presumed, supposed **9** falsified **10** fictitious **11** make-believe, presupposed, pseudonymic **12** pseudonymous

assumed name 5 alias **7** pen name **9** pseudonym **13** false identity
French: 10 nom de plume **11** nom de guerre

assuming 4 bold **5** nervy, pushy **6** brazen, cheeky **7** forward, haughty **8** arrogant, insolent **9** audacious, presuming **11** overbearing **12** presumptuous **13** self-assertive

assumption 6 belief, taking, theory **7** premise, seizure **8** assuming, taking on, taking up **9** accepting, postulate **10** acceptance, arrogation, hypothesis, usurpation **11** postulation, presumption, shouldering, supposition, undertaking **13** appropriating **14** presupposition

assurance 3 vow **4** oath **5** poise **6** binder, pledge **7** promise **8** averment, boldness, coolness, sureness, warranty **9** certainty, certitude, guarantee **10** confidence, profession **11** affirmation, assuredness, word of honor **12** self-reliance **14** aggressiveness, self-confidence, self-possession

assure 5 vow to **6** clinch, ensure, secure **7** confirm, promise **8** pledge to **9** guarantee **11** make certain **14** give one's word to

assured 4 sure **5** fixed **6** poised, secure **7** certain, settled **8** positive **9** confident, undoubted **10** dependable, guaranteed **11** indubitable, irrefutable **12** indisputable **13** self-confident, self-possessed **14** unquestionable

Astaire, Fred
real name: 19 Frederick Austerlitz
partner: 12 Ginger Rogers
born: 7 Omaha NE
roles: 6 Top Hat **9** Funny Face, Let's Dance, Swing Time **10** Holiday Inn **12** Easter Parade, Royal Wedding, Shall We Dance **14** The Gay Divorcee

Astarte
origin: 7 Semitic
goddess of: 9 fertility **12** reproduction
habitat: 4 moon
corresponds to: 6 Inanna, Ishtar **7** Mylitta **9** Ashtoreth

aster 12 Callistephus
varieties: 4 Tree **5** Black, China, Heath **6** Annual, Golden, Mojave, Stoke's **7** Italian **8** Blue-wood **9** Tartarian, White wood **10** New England **11** White upland

Asteria
form: 8 Titaness
father: 5 Coeus
mother: 6 Phoebe
sister: 4 Leto
husband: 6 Perses
son: 8 Paropeus
daughter: 6 Hecate
changed into: 5 Delos **6** island

Asterion
also: 8 Asterius
father: 7 Cometes
member of: 9 Argonauts

Asterius
also: 8 Asterion
form: 5 giant **8** minotaur
king of: 5 Crete
father: 4 Anax **8** Tectamus **10** Cretan Bull, Hyperasius
mother: 8 Pasiphae
wife: 6 Europa
adopted sons: 5 Minos **8** Sarpedon **12** Rhadamanthys
daughter: 5 Crete
member of: 9 Argonauts

astern 3 aft **5** abaft **6** behind **9** to the rear

Asterodia
form: 5 nymph
type of nymph: 9 Caucasian

asteroid 6 debris **9** meteorite, planetoid

Asteropaeus
origin: 5 Greek
mentioned in: 5 Iliad
father: 7 Pelegon
ally of: 4 Troy
killed by: 8 Achilles

Asterope *see* **7** Sterope

astir 2 up **5** afoot, awake **6** active, roused **8** in motion, out of bed **10** up and about

astonish 4 daze, stun **5** amaze, shock **6** dazzle **7** astound, confuse, perplex, stagger, startle, stupefy **8** bewilder, confound, dumfound, surprise **9** electrify, overwhelm, take aback **10** strike dumb **11** flabbergast **15** make one's eyes pop **18** take one's breath away

astonishing 7 amazing **8** dazzling, shocking, striking **9** confusing, startling **10** astounding, impressive, perplexing, staggering, stupefying, surprising **11** bewildering, confounding **12** breathtaking, electrifying, overpowering, overwhelming

astonishment **3** awe **5** shock **6** wonder **8** surprise **9** amazement, confusion **10** perplexity, wonderment **12** bewilderment, stupefaction

Astor, Mary
real name: **28** Lucille Vasconcellos Langhanke
born: **8** Quincy IL
roles: **6** Marmee **11** Little Women, The Great Lie **15** Meet Me in St Louis **16** The Maltese Falcon **17** The Palm Beach Story **18** The Prisoner of Zenda

astound **4** daze, stun **5** amaze, shock **6** dazzle **7** stagger, startle, stupefy **8** astonish, dumfound, surprise, take back **9** electrify, overwhelm **10** strike dumb **11** flabbergast **15** make one's eyes pop **18** take one's breath away

Astrabacus
origin: **5** Greek **7** Spartan
form: **6** prince
found: **11** wooden image
hidden by: **7** Orestes
co-finder: **8** Alopecus

Astraea
also: **6** Astrea
goddess of: **7** justice
father: **4** Zeus
mother: **6** Themis

Astraeus
form: **5** Titan
consort of: **3** Eos
father of: **4** wind **5** stars

astral **6** starry **9** celestial **12** astronomical

astraphobia
fear of: **9** lightning

Astrateia *see* **7** Artemis

astray **3** off **5** amiss **6** afield **10** off the mark **12** off the course **16** off the right track

Astrea *see* **7** Astraea

astringent **4** acid, keen, sour, tart **5** brisk, sharp, stern, tonic **6** biting, severe **7** acerbic, austere, bracing, puckery, styptic **8** curative, incisive, piercing, salutary, stabbing, vinegary **10** antiseptic, salubrious **11** contracting, penetrating, restorative **12** invigorating

astrology **6** Zodiac **9** horoscopy, starcraft **10** astromancy, astrometry, stargazing **11** genethliacs **13** mathematicals **14** astrodiagnosis
belief in: **8** siderism
term: **4** sign **5** house, trine **6** alnath, apheta, aspect **7** almuten, anareta, mansion, mundane, sextile **8** alkahest, nativity, quartile, synastry **9** planetary **10** opposition **11** conjunction

astronomer **4** Bode, Gold **5** Adams, Baade, Bayer, Bethe, Gould, Hoyle, Royer **6** Bessel, Halley, Hubble, Jansky, Kepler, Newton, Piazzi **7** Bradley, Celcius, Galileo, Huggins, Huygens, Kapteyn, Laplace, Ptolemy, Russell, Shapley, Slipher **8** Angstrom, Einstein, Herschel, Hevelius, Lacaille, Lemaitre, Mercator **9** Eddington, Leverrier **10** Copernicus, Hipparchus, Tycho Brahe **11** Aristarchus, Hertzsprung **13** Petrus Apianus

astronomy
term: **5** comet, orbit **6** apogee, meteor, nebula, parsec, quasar **7** azimuth, eclipse, equinox, perigee, transit **8** aphelion, asteroid, ecliptic, meridian, solstice **9** meteorite, satellite **10** perihelion, precession **11** declination, occultation **12** perturbation, spectroscopy **16** celestial equator
type/related study: **9** cosmogony, cosmology **10** astrometry, photometry **12** astrophysics **18** celestial mechanics
see also: **4** star

Astrophel and Stella
author: **15** Sir Philip Sidney

astute **3** sly **4** able, foxy, keen, wily **5** acute, sharp, smart **6** adroit, artful, bright, clever, crafty, shrewd, subtle **7** cunning, knowing, politic **9** designing, sagacious **10** discerning, keen-minded, perceptive **11** calculating, intelligent, penetrating **13** Machiavellian, perspicacious

astuteness **6** acumen **8** keenness **9** acuteness, smartness **10** cleverness, shrewdness **12** perspicacity

Astyanax
also: **11** Scamandrius
father: **6** Hector **9** Strophius
mother: **10** Andromache
thrown from: **11** Trojan walls
thrown by: **6** Greeks
slain by: **8** Menelaus

Astydamia
father: **7** Amyntor
husband: **7** Acastus
daughter: **8** Laodamia
abducted by: **8** Hercules

Asuncion
capital of: **8** Paraguay

asunder **4** rent **5** apart **8** in pieces, to shreds **9** torn apart **11** broken apart

asylum **4** home **5** haven **6** harbor, refuge **7** retreat, shelter **8** madhouse, preserve **9** almshouse, orphanage, poorhouse, sanctuary **10** sanatorium, sanitarium **11** institution **13** children's home, state hospital **14** mental hospital **15** place of immunity **17** mental institution **23** eleemosynary institution

Asynjur
origin: **12** Scandinavian
goddesses of: **4** Asar **5** Aesir
leader: **3** Fri **5** Frigg, Frija **6** Frigga

As You Like It
author: **18** William Shakespeare
character: **5** Celia (Aliena) **6** Audrey, Jaques, Oliver **7** Orlando **8** Rosalind (Ganymede) **9** Frederick **10** Touchstone

Atabyrian *see* **4** Zeus

at a distance **4** afar, away **5** above, aloof, apart **6** far off **9** separated

Atala
author: **21** Francois Chateaubriand

Atalanta
also: **8** Atalante
form: **6** virgin **8** huntress
father: **5** Iasus
mother: **7** Clymene
son: **13** Parthenopaeus
wounded: **14** Calydonian boar
lost race to: **10** Hippomenes

Atalanta in Calydon
author: **24** Algernon Charles Swinburne

Atalante *see* **8** Atalanta

at any rate **6** anyhow, anyway **9** in any case **10** in any event

at cross purposes **7** counter, opposed **8** contrary, converse, inimical, opposite **9** disparate **10** at variance, discordant **11** conflicting **12** antithetical, incompatible **13** contradictory

Ate
origin: **5** Greek
form: **7** goddess
personifies: **12** recklessness **16** divine punishment

at ease **4** calm, cool **6** at rest,

serene **7** content, relaxed, unmoved **8** composed **9** at leisure, confident, unruffled **10** complacent, nonchalant, unbothered, untroubled **11** comfortable, unconcerned

a tergo 9 at the back **10** from behind

at fault 6 guilty **8** culpable **10** implicated **11** blameworthy, responsible

at full length
Latin: 9 in extenso

Athabascan, Athapascan (Slave Indians)
language family: 10 Athabascan, Athapaskan
location: 6 Canada **14** Great Slave Lake
dominated by: 4 Cree
related to: 9 Chipewyan
tribe: 4 Dine **5** Slave **6** Apache, Navaho, Navajo **9** Mescalero **10** Athabascan

Athaliah
father: 4 Ahab
mother: 7 Jezebel
husband: 7 Jehoram
son: 7 Ahaziah

Athalie
author: 18 Jean Baptiste Racine

Athamas
king of: 6 Thebes
father: 6 Aeolus
wife: 3 Ino **7** Nephele
son: 5 Ptous **6** Leucon **7** Phrixus **8** Learchus **10** Melicertes
daughter: 5 Helle

at hand 4 near, nigh **5** close, handy, on tap, ready **6** nearby **7** close by **8** imminent **9** available, impending **10** accessible, convenient **11** at one's elbow, forthcoming **14** at one's disposal **15** within arm's reach

atheism 8 apostasy, unbelief **9** disbelief **10** irreligion **11** godlessness

atheist 7 infidel **10** unbeliever **11** disbeliever, nonbeliever **13** godless person

Athena
also: 6 Athene, Pallas, Saitis **11** Tritogeneia **12** Pallas Athena **18** Alalcomenean Athena
origin: 5 Greek
goddess of: 4 arts **6** wisdom **7** warfare **9** fertility
father: 4 Zeus **6** Triton
mother: 5 Metis
sprang from head of: 4 Zeus
raised by: 12 Alalcomeneus
symbol: 3 owl
corresponds to: 7 Minerva
epithet: 4 Alea **5** Meter, Xenia **6** Ergane, Itonia, Polias **7** Agoraea, Cissaea, Paeonia, Pronaus, Pronoea **8** Anemotis, Poliates, Zosteria **9** Oxyderces, Parthenia, Poliuchus, Promachus **10** Axiopoenus, Chalinitis, Cyparissia **11** Promachorma

Athens
capital of: 6 Greece
Greek: 7 Athinai
hills: 9 Acropolis **14** Hagios Georgios
landmark: 4 Stoa **9** Areopagus, Parthenon **10** Erechtheum, Propylaeum **17** Theater of Dionysus
marketplace: 5 Agora
mountain: 6 Parnes **8** Aigaleos, Hymettus **10** Pentelikon
named for: 6 Athena
port: 7 Piraeus
river: 7 Ilissus
sea: 6 Aegean **11** Saronic Gulf
square: 8 Syntagma (Constitution)

Athens Graces 4 Auxe **8** Hegemone

athirst 4 avid, keen **5** eager **6** raring **7** longing, panting **8** yearning

athlete 4 jock **8** champion **9** contender, sportsman **10** contestant, game player

athletic 5 burly, hardy, husky, manly **6** brawny, robust, strong, sturdy, virile **8** muscular, powerful, stalwart, vigorous **9** masculine, strapping **10** able-bodied

athletics 5 games **6** sports **8** exercise **9** exercises **10** gymnastics

at home 6 at ease, inside, shut in **7** indoors **8** confined **10** in the house **11** comfortable
French: 4 chez

Athos
character in: 18 The Three Musketeers
author: 5 Dumas (pere)

athwart 6 across **7** astride **8** sideways, sidewise **9** crossways, crosswise **12** transversely

Atlanta
baseball team: 6 Braves
basketball team: 5 Hawks
football team: 7 Falcons

Atlantean
pertaining to: 5 Atlas

Atlantic
pertaining to: 10 Titan Atlas

Atlantic City
director: 10 Louis Malle
cast: 8 Kate Reid **13** Burt Lancaster, Michel Piccoli, Susan Sarandon

at large 5 astir, loose **6** abroad **8** as a whole, at length **9** at liberty, in general **10** on the loose, unconfined **11** out and about **13** in circulation **14** around and about **15** making the rounds

Atlas
form: 5 Titan
father: 7 Iapetus
mother: 7 Clymene
brother: 9 Menoetius **10** Epimetheus, Prometheus
wife: 7 Pleione
daughters: 6 Hyades **7** Calypso **8** Pleiades **10** Hesperides
supported: 3 sky
identified with: 14 Atlas Mountains

Atlas Shrugged
author: 7 Ayn Rand
character: 8 John Galt **11** Hank Reardon **12** Dagny Taggart, James Taggart

at last
Latin: 10 ad extremum

at leisure 4 idle **7** off duty **8** inactive **9** at liberty **10** unemployed, unoccupied

Atli
origin: 12 Scandinavian
sister: 8 Brynhild
wife: 6 Gudrun, Kudrun **7** Guthrun
killed by: 6 Gudrun, Kudrun **7** Guthrun
represents: 6 Atilla

atmosphere 3 air **4** aura, feel, mood, tone **5** color **6** spirit **7** feeling, quality **8** ambience **11** environment **12** surroundings

atmospheric 3 air **4** airy **8** ethereal

at odds 6 unlike **8** contrary **9** different **10** at variance, discordant, discrepant, dissimilar **11** contrasting

at odds with 9 counter to **10** contrary to **14** at variance with

atom 3 bit, dot, jot **4** iota, mite, mote, whit **5** crumb, grain, scrap, shred, speck, trace **6** morsel, tittle **7** smidgen **8** fragment, particle **9** scintilla **10** smithereen

atomic 6 cobalt **7** fission, neutron, nuclear, uranium **8** hydrogen **9** molecular, plutonium, subatomic, unseeable **10** impalpable **11** fissionable, microcosmic, microscopic, superatomic **13** imperceptible, indiscernible, infinitesimal, thermonuclear

atom part **6** proton **7** neutron **8** electron

at once
French: **11** tout de suite

atone **6** pay for, redeem, repent, shrive **7** expiate **9** make up for **10** compensate, recompense, remunerate **12** do penance for **13** make amends for **17** make reparation for

atonement **6** amends, shrift **7** penance, redress **9** expiation **10** recompense, redemption, reparation, repentance **12** compensation, satisfaction **14** penitential act

at one's disposal **5** handy **6** at hand, on hand **9** available **10** accessible, convenient **11** at one's elbow, ready for use **13** at one's service

at one's elbow **5** handy **6** at hand, nearby **9** available **10** accessible, convenient

Atrax
father: **6** Peneus

at rest **5** quiet, still **6** asleep, at ease, serene **7** at peace, content **8** in repose **9** quiescent **10** motionless

Atreus
father: **6** Pelops
mother: **10** Hippodamia
sister: **7** Nicippe
wife: **6** Aerope
son: **8** Menelaus **9** Agamemnon **10** Plisthenes
daughter: **8** Anaxibia
killed: **6** Aglaus

Atridae
descendants of: **6** Atreus
family name of: **8** Anaxibia, Menelaus **9** Agamemnon **10** Plisthenes

atrium **4** hall **6** cavity **7** auricle **8** entrance **13** Roman entrance

atrocious **3** bad, low **4** dark, evil, rude, vile **5** black, cruel **6** brutal, savage, tawdry, vulgar **7** heinous, hellish, inhuman, uncouth, vicious **8** dreadful, enormous, fiendish, flagrant, grievous, horrible, infamous, infernal, pitiless, ruthless, terrible **9** barbarous, execrable, merciless, monstrous, nefarious, tasteless **10** diabolical, outrageous, villainous

atrociousness **6** infamy **7** cruelty **8** enormity, vileness **9** barbarity, brutality, depravity **11** heinousness, viciousness **13** monstrousness, offensiveness **14** outrageousness

atrocity **6** horror **7** outrage **8** enormity, savagery, villainy **9** barbarism, barbarity, brutality **10** inhumanity **11** heinousness

atrophy **7** decline **8** decaying, drying up **9** lack of use, withering **10** emaciation, shriveling **11** wasting away **12** degeneration **13** deterioration

Atropos
member of: **5** Fates
cuts thread of: **4** life

Atsina (Gros Ventres, Haaninin)
language family: **9** Algonkian **10** Algonquian
location: **6** Canada **7** Montana **9** Milk River **12** Saskatchewan **13** Missouri River
related to: **7** Arapaho

attach **3** fix **4** join **5** affix, allot, annex **6** append, assign, couple, detail, secure **7** connect, destine, earmark **8** allocate, be fond of, fasten to, make fast **9** affiliate, associate, designate

attache **4** aide **5** envoy **6** consul **8** adjutant, diplomat, emissary, minister **9** assistant **10** ambassador, vice consul **11** diplomatist, subordinate **12** ambassadress **13** consul general

attachment **4** bond, love **6** fixing, liking, regard **7** adjunct, fixture, respect **8** addendum, addition, affinity, affixing, appendix, coupling, devotion, fondness, securing **9** accessory, affection, appendage, attaching, fastening **10** connection, friendship, supplement, tenderness **12** predilection

attack **3** fit **4** damn, go at **5** abuse, blame, fault, fly at, onset, spasm, spell **6** assail, charge, impugn, strike, stroke, tackle **7** assault, censure, lunge at, offense, seizure **8** denounce, fall upon, invasion, paroxysm **9** criticism, criticize, denigrate, disparage, incursion, offensive, onslaught, pitch into, undertake **10** aggression, impugnment **11** denigration **13** disparagement

attacker **6** mugger **7** accuser **8** assailer, opponent **9** adversary, aggressor, assailant **10** antagonist **11** belligerent

attain **3** win **4** earn, gain, reap **5** reach **6** effect, obtain, secure **7** achieve, acquire, procure, realize **10** accomplish

attainable **6** at hand **9** available, reachable **10** accessible, achievable, realizable **11** within reach

attainment **5** skill **6** talent **7** earning, gaining, getting, mastery, success, winning **8** securing **9** acquiring, attaining, obtaining, procuring **10** competence **11** achievement, acquirement, acquisition, fulfillment, procurement, proficiency, realization **14** accomplishment

attempt **3** aim, try **4** seek **5** essay **6** attack, effort, hazard, strive, tackle, work at **7** assault, venture **8** endeavor **9** have a go at, onslaught, undertake **11** undertaking **12** make an effort, take a crack at, take a whack at

Attenborough, Richard
director of: **6** Gandhi (Oscar) **12** Young Winston **13** A Bridge Too Far

attend **4** go to, heed, mark, mind, note **5** serve, usher, visit **6** convoy, escort, follow, show up, squire, tend to **7** care for, conduct, observe, oversee, service **8** appear at, consider, frequent, harken to, listen to, wait upon **9** accompany **11** superintend
French: **4** oyez
cry used by: **10** court crier
preceded: **12** proclamation

attendance **4** gate **5** crowd, house **8** audience, presence **10** appearance, assemblage, being there

attendant **3** aid **6** escort, flunky, helper, lackey, menial **7** related, servant **8** adherent, chaperon, follower **9** accessory, assistant, companion, underling **10** associated, consequent **12** accompanying

attention **4** care, heed, mind, note, suit **5** court **6** homage, notice, regard, wooing **7** concern, respect, service, thought **8** civility, courtesy, devotion, wariness **9** alertness, deference, diligence, vigilance **10** observance, politeness **11** assiduities, compliments, gallantries **12** deliberation **13** concentration, consideration, contemplation **14** thoughtfulness

attentive **5** alert, awake **6** intent, polite **7** devoted, heedful, mindful, zealous **8** diligent, obliging **9** courteous, dedicated, listening, observant, wide awake **10** respectful, thoughtful **11** considerate, deferential, painstaking **13** accommodating

attentiveness **7** concern **8** devotion, industry **9** alertness, attention, diligence **10** commitment, dedication **11** application, devotedness, heedfulness, mindfulness **14** thoughtfulness

attenuate **6** dilute, impair, lessen, reduce, weaken **7** draw out, spin out **8** decrease, diminish, enervate, enfeeble **9** water down **10** adulterate

attest **4** show **5** prove **6** affirm, assert, assure, evince, verify **7** bear out, certify, confirm, declare, display, exhibit, support, swear to, testify, warrant **8** vouch for **11** bear witness, corroborate, demonstrate **12** substantiate

attestation **9** testimony **10** deposition **11** declaration

at the back
Latin: **6** a tergo

at the beginning
Latin: **9** ad initium

at the bottom
French: **6** au fond

At the Edge of the Body
author: **9** Erica Jong

at the end
Latin: **5** ad fin

at the place
Latin: **5** ad loc **7** ad locum

At the Sign of the Reine Pedauque
author: **13** Anatole France

attic **4** loft **6** garret **7** mansard **8** cockloft **10** clerestory
French: **7** grenier
German: **9** Dachboden
Spanish: **9** guardilla

attire **3** don **4** duds, garb, gown, robe, togs **5** array, dress **6** bedeck, clothe, finery, fit out, invest, outfit, rig out **7** apparel, clothes, costume, deck out, raiment, turn out **8** clothing, garments, glad rags, wardrobe **9** vestments **11** habiliments

Attis
also: **4** Atys
form: **5** youth
home: **7** Phrygia
loved: **6** Cybele
driven mad by: **6** Cybele

attitude **3** air **4** pose **6** manner, stance **7** outlook, posture **8** demeanor, position **11** disposition, frame of mind, perspective, point of view

attorney **4** beak **6** lawyer **7** counsel **8** advocate **9** barrister, counselor, solicitor **10** mouthpiece **12** legal adviser **14** member of the bar **15** ambulance chaser

attract **4** draw, lure, pull **5** cause, charm, evoke **6** allure, beckon, entice, induce, invite **7** bewitch, enchant, provoke **8** appeal to, interest **9** captivate, fascinate **11** precipitate

attraction **4** lure, pull **5** charm **6** allure, appeal **7** glamour **8** affinity, charisma, tendency **9** magnetism **10** enticement, inducement, temptation **11** captivation, enchantment, fascination **12** drawing power

attractive **4** chic, fair **6** lovely, pretty **7** elegant, likable, sightly, winning **8** alluring, becoming, charming, engaging, enticing, fetching, handsome, inviting, pleasant, pleasing, tasteful, tempting **9** agreeable, appealing, beautiful, seductive **10** bewitching, delightful, enchanting **11** captivating, charismatic, fascinating

attractiveness **5** charm **6** beauty **9** good looks **11** pulchritude **12** handsomeness

attribute **4** gift **5** facet, grace, lay to, trait **6** aspect, assign, credit, impute, talent, virtue **7** ability, ascribe, blame on, cause by, faculty, feature, quality, trace to **8** charge to, property **9** character, endowment, set down to **10** account for, attainment, derive from, saddle with **11** acquirement, bring home to, distinction **14** accomplishment, characteristic

attrition **4** loss **7** erosion **8** abrasion, decrease, friction, grinding, scraping **9** reduction **10** decimation **11** wearing away, wearing down **14** disintegration

attune **5** adapt **6** adjust, tailor **8** accustom **9** acclimate **11** acclimatize

attune to **3** fit **5** adapt **6** adjust **7** conform **9** harmonize **11** accommodate

at variance **7** counter, opposed **8** contrary, converse, inimical, opposite **9** disparate **10** discordant **11** conflicting **12** antithetical, incompatible **13** contradictory **15** at cross purposes

Atwood, Margaret
author of: **8** Survival **9** Surfacing **10** Bodily Harm, Lady Oracle **11** Second Words **13** Life Before Man, Power Politics, The Circle Game **23** The Animals in That Country

at work **4** busy **5** in use **6** active **7** engaged, working **8** occupied

Atymnius
mentioned in: **5** Iliad
companion of: **8** Sarpedon
killed by: **10** Antilochus

atypical **7** unusual **8** abnormal, contrary, uncommon **9** anomalous, irregular, unnatural, untypical **10** nontypical **11** uncustomary, unlooked for **12** out of keeping **16** unrepresentative

Atys *see* **5** Attis

Auber, Daniel Francois Esprit
born: **4** Caen **6** France
composer of: **6** Haydee **7** La Macon **10** Fra Diavolo **12** Le Domino Noir **14** The Bronze Horse **16** Le Cheval de Bronze, The Crown Diamonds **17** La Muette de Portici **19** La Bergere Chatelaine **20** The Dumb Girl of Portici **22** Le Premier Jour de Bonheur **23** Les Diamants de la Couronne

auberge **3** inn **6** tavern

auburn **5** henna, tawny **6** russet **8** cinnamon, nutbrown **11** golden-brown, rust-colored **12** reddish-brown **13** copper-colored **15** chestnut-colored

Aucassin and Nicolette
author: **7** unknown

Auchincloss, Louis
author of: **10** Watchfires **11** The Dark Lady, The Partners **12** Second Chance, The Embezzler **14** A World of Profit **16** Powers of Attorney, Tales of Manhattan, The Country Cousin **17** The Rector of Justin **19** The Winthrop Covenant **20** Portrait in Brownstone

au contraire **13** on the contrary

au courant **8** up-to-date

auction **3** sale **7** bidding **8** offering

Auction Block, The
author: **8** Rex Beach

audacious **4** bold, pert, rash, rude, wild **5** bossy, brave, fresh, gutsy, risky, saucy **6** brazen, cheeky, daring, plucky **7** defiant, forward, valiant **8** assuming, fearless, heedless, impudent, insolent, intrepid, reckless, stalwart, unafraid, valorous **9** breakneck, daredevil, dauntless, desperate, foolhardy, hotheaded, imprudent, shameless, unabashed **10** courageous, outrageous, self-willed **11** adventurous, impertinent, injudicious, lionhearted, venturesome **12** death-defying, devil-may-care, discourteous, enterprising, presumptuous, stouthearted **13** disrespectful

audaciousness **6** daring **8** audacity, boldness **11** forwardness **13** assertiveness **14** aggressiveness **15** adventurousness

audacity **4** gall, grit, guts **5** brass, cheek, nerve, pluck, spunk, valor **6** daring, mettle **7** bravery, courage **8** backbone, boldness, chutzpah, rashness, temerity **9** brashness, derring-do, impudence, insolence **10** brazenness, effrontery **11** forwardness, presumption **12** fearlessness, impertinence, recklessness **13** bumptiousness, foolhardiness, shamelessness **15** venturesomeness

Auden, W H
author of: **11** Another Time, Thank You Fog **12** Homage to Clio, The Dyer's Hand **13** About the House, Journey to a War **15** For the Time Being, The Age of Anxiety **16** City Without Walls, Epistle to a Godson **17** In Memory of W B Yeats, Musee des Beaux Arts **20** The Dog Beneath the Skin **22** Forewords and Afterwords

Audhumbla
also: **8** Audhumla
origin: **12** Scandinavian
form: **3** cow
owner: **4** Ymir
birth from: **3** ice
uncovered: **4** Buri

Audhumla *see* **9** Audhumbla

audible **5** clear, heard **8** distinct **11** discernible, perceptible

audience **4** talk **5** house **6** market, parley, public **7** hearing, meeting **8** assembly, audition **9** following, interview, listeners, onlookers, reception **10** conference, discussion, readership, spectators **12** congregation, constituency, consultation

audit **5** check **6** go over, review, verify **7** balance, examine, inspect **10** inspection, scrutinize **11** examination, investigate, take stock of **12** scrutinizing, verification **13** investigation

audition **6** tryout **7** hearing **15** test performance

auditor **8** listener **10** accountant, bookkeeper **11** comptroller **17** financial examiner

auditorium **4** hall **5** arena **7** theater **8** auditory, coliseum **11** concert hall, lecture hall, meeting hall **12** assembly hall

Audrey
character in: **11** As You Like It
author: **11** Shakespeare

Audubon
author: **16** Robert Penn Warren

Audubon, John James
born: **8** Les Cayes **12** Santo Domingo
artwork: **14** Birds of America **34** Viviparous Quadrupeds of North America

Auel, Jean M
author of: **17** The Mammoth Hunters, The Valley of Horses **20** The Clan of the Cave Bear

Auerbach, Arnold (Red)
sport: **10** basketball
position: **5** coach
team: **13** Boston Celtics

au fait **6** expert, versed **11** experienced **13** knowledgeable

Aufklarung **13** enlightenment **16** the Enlightenment

au fond **9** basically, in reality **11** at the bottom

auf Wiedersehen **7** goodbye **8** farewell **16** until we meet again

Auge
priestess of: **6** Athena
father: **9** King Aleus
mother: **6** Neaera
son: **8** Telephus
assaulted by: **8** Hercules

Augean stables
owned by: **10** King Augeas
number of oxen: **13** three thousand
cleaned by: **8** Hercules
river running through: **7** Alpheus

Augeas
king of: **6** Epeans
realm: **4** Elis
member of: **9** Argonauts
brother: **5** Actor
son: **7** Eurytus, Phyleus **10** Agasthenes
daughter: **7** Agamede
grandson: **9** Polyxenus

auger **4** bore **5** drill **6** pierce **10** boring tool

aught **3** all, zip **4** love, nada, null, zero **6** naught **7** a cipher, nothing **8** goose egg **11** horse collar

augment **5** add to, boost, raise, swell, widen **6** deepen, expand, extend **7** amplify, build up, enlarge, inflate, magnify **8** flesh out, heighten, increase, lengthen **9** intensify

augmentation **5** boost, extra, raise **8** addition, increase, swelling, widening **9** deepening, expansion, extension, inflation **10** supplement **11** elaboration, enlargement, heightening, lengthening **13** amplification, magnification **15** intensification

augur **4** bode, seer **6** herald, oracle **7** diviner, portend, predict, presage, promise, prophet, signify **8** forecast, foretell, forewarn, intimate, prophesy **9** be a sign of **10** be an omen of, foreshadow, soothsayer **13** prognosticate **14** prognosticator

augury **4** omen, sign **5** token **6** herald **7** auspice, portent, promise, warning **8** prophecy **9** harbinger, precursor, sortilege **10** divination, forerunner, indication **11** forewarning, soothsaying **14** fortunetelling **15** prognostication

august **5** grand, lofty, noble, regal **6** solemn, superb **7** eminent, exalted, stately, sublime, supreme **8** glorious, imposing, majestic **9** dignified, estimable, grandiose, venerable **10** impressive, monumental **11** high-ranking, illustrious, magnificent **12** awe-inspiring **13** distinguished

August *see box, p. 70*

Augustine, St (of Hippo)
author of: **10** Civitas Dei **11** Confessions, Enchiridion **12** The City of God

augustness **7** dignity, majesty **8** eminence, nobility **9** loftiness **11** distinction **13** monumentality **15** illustriousness

August 1914
author: **23** Aleksandr Solzhenitsyn Jr

au naturel **4** nude **8** uncooked **15** in a natural state

Auntie Mame
author: **13** Patrick Dennis

Aunt Jo's Scrap-Bag
author: **15** Louisa May Alcott

August
Anglo-Saxon: 10 Weod-Monath
characteristic: 7 dog days
flower: 5 poppy
French: 4 Aout
gem: 7 peridot **8** sardonyx **9** carnelian
German: 6 August
holiday:
England/Scotland: **11** Harvest Home (I)
Italian: 6 Agosto
number of days: **9** thirty-one
original name: 8 Sextilis **12** Metageitnion
origin of name: 6 Augere (Latin to open) **8** Augustus (Roman emperor)
place in year:
Roman: **5** sixth
Gregorian: **6** eighth
Spanish: 6 Agosto
zodiac sign: 3 Leo **5** Virgo

Aunt Julia and the Scriptwriter
author: 16 Mario Vargas Llosa

au pair 4 maid **5** nanny **9** governess **13** mother's helper

aura 3 air **4** feel, mood **5** aroma **7** essence, feeling, quality **8** ambience **9** character, emanation **10** atmosphere, suggestion

Aura
companion of: 7 Artemis
bore: 5 twins
fathered by: **9** Dionysius
changed into: 6 spring
changed by: **4** Zeus

au revoir 7 goodbye **8** farewell **16** until we meet again

Aurness, James
real name of: 11 James Arness

Aurora
origin: 5 Roman
goddess of: 4 dawn
corresponds to: 3 Eos

Aurora Leigh
author: 24 Elizabeth Barrett Browning

Ausgleich 10 compromise **11** arrangement **12** equalization

Auslander 5 alien **9** foreigner, outlander

auspice 4 omen, sign **6** augury **7** portent, warning **10** indication **15** prognostication

auspices 4 care **5** aegis **6** charge **7** control, support **8** advocacy, guidance **9** authority, influence, patronage **10** protection **11** countenance, sponsorship **12** championship

auspicious 4 good **5** happy, lucky **6** benign, timely **7** hopeful **9** favorable, fortunate, opportune, promising, red-letter **10** felicitous, heartening, propitious, reassuring, successful **11** encouraging

Austen, Jane
author of: 4 Emma **10** Persuasion **13** Mansfield Park **15** Northanger Abbey **17** Pride and Prejudice **19** Sense and Sensibility

austere 5 rigid, spare, stark, stern **6** chaste, severe, simple, strict **7** ascetic, Spartan **8** rigorous **10** abstemious, forbidding **11** self-denying, strait-laced

Austerlitz, Frederick
real name of: 11 Fred Astaire

Australia *see box*

Austria *see box, p. 72*

Austroasiatic
language subfamily: 5 Khasi, Munda **8** Annamite, Mon-Khmer **9** Palaung-Wa **10** Nicobarese **11** Semang-Sakai **13** Annamite-Muong
spoken in: 5 Burma, India **7** Nicobar, Vietnam **8** Cambodia, Malaysia **9** Kampuchea

authentic 4 pure, real, true **5** valid **6** actual **7** factual, genuine **8** accurate, attested, bona fide, faithful, original, reliable, verified **9** veritable **10** accredited, dependable, legitimate **11** trustworthy **12** unquestioned **13** authoritative, unadulterated

authenticate 6 attest, avouch, verify **7** certify, confirm, endorse, warrant **8** document, validate, vouch for **9** guarantee **11** corroborate **12** substantiate

authenticated 7 genuine **8** attested, verified **9** validated **10** accredited, vouched for **13** substantiated

authentication 7 voucher **10** validation **11** certificate **12** verification **13** authorization, certification

author 4 poet **5** maker **6** father, framer, writer **7** creator, founder, planner **8** essayist, inventor, novelist, producer **9** initiator, innovator, organizer **10** originator, playwright, prime mover **16** short-story writer
see author under each country

authoritarian 5 harsh **6** severe, strict, tyrant **7** austere, fascist **8** autocrat, dogmatic, martinet **9** by the book, by the rule **10** inflexible, tyrannical, unyielding **11** dictatorial, doctrinaire **12** disciplinary, rule follower **14** disciplinarian, little dictator, uncompromising

authoritative 5 sound, valid **6** lordly, ruling **7** factual, learned **8** arrogant, decisive, dogmatic, imposing, official, reliable **9** authentic, masterful, scholarly, sovereign **10** autocratic, commanding, definitive, dependable, imperative, impressive, peremptory, sanctioned, tyrannical **11** dictatorial, trustworthy **14** administrative

authoritativeness 6 belief **9** authority **10** conviction **11** credibility **14** conclusiveness

authorities 6 expert, police, pundit **7** scholar **10** mastermind, specialist **11** connoisseur, officialdom **12** powers that be

authority 4 rule, sway **5** clout, force, might, power **6** esteem, weight **7** command, control, respect **8** dominion, prestige, strength **9** influence, supremacy **10** domination, importance **12** jurisdiction **14** administration

authorization 7 license **8** approval, sanction **10** commission, imprimatur, permission **11** entitlement **12** confirmation, legalization **13** accreditation, certification

authorize 5 allow **6** enable, invest, permit **7** approve, certify, charter, confirm, empower, entitle, license, warrant **8** accredit, sanction, vouch for **9** give leave **10** commission

authorized 8 approved, official **9** canonical **10** sanctioned

Autobiography of Alice B Toklas
author: 13 Gertrude Stein

Autobiography of Miss Jane Pittman, The
author: 13 Ernest J Gaines

Australia
other name: **9** Down Under
name means: **19** unknown southern land
capital: **8** Canberra
largest city: **6** Sydney
others: **3** Ayr **4** Yass **5** Dubbo, Perth **6** Albury, Cairns, Casino, Coburg, Darwin, Hobart **7** Bendigo, Geelong, Kogarah, Mildura, Mitcham, Whyalla **8** Adelaide, Ballarat, Bathurst, Brighton, Brisbane, Essendon, Randwick, Ringwood **9** Melbourne, Newcastle, Port Pirie, Toowoomba **10** Broken Hill, Kalgoorlie, Waggawagga, Wollongong **11** Collingwood, Rockhampton **12** Alice Springs
division: **8** Tasmania, Victoria **10** Queensland **13** New South Wales **14** South Australia **16** Western Australia **17** Northern Territory **26** Australian Capital Territory
head of state: **14** British monarch **15** governor general
measure: **4** arna, naut, saum
monetary unit: **4** dump, tray, zack **5** pound **6** dollar **8** shilling
island: **4** Cato, King **5** Cocos, Green, Timor **6** Barrow, Koolan **7** Coringa, Keeling, Neptune, Norfolk **8** Flinders, Kangaroo, Lacepede, Melville, Rottnest, Tasmania, Thursday **9** Admiralty
lake: **4** Eyre **5** Carey, Cowan, Frome, Moore, Wells **6** Austin, Barlee, Bulloo, Dundas, Harris, Mackay **7** Amadeus, Blanche, Everard, Torrens **8** Carnegie, Gairdner **9** MacDonald **10** Yammayamma **14** Disappointment
mountain: **3** Ise **4** Blue, Olga, Ossa, Zeil **5** Bruce, Snowy **6** Cradle, Doreen, Garnet, Gawler, Magnet, Morgan **7** Bongong, Gregory, Herbert **8** Augustus, Brockman, Cuthbert, Jusgrave, Mulligan, Surprise **9** Murchison, Woodroffe **14** Australian Alps **15** New England Range **18** Great Dividing Range
highest point: **9** Kosciusko
river: **3** Hay **4** Avon, Daly, Swan, Yule **5** Bullo, Comet, Drava, Naomi, Paroo, Roper, Yarra **6** Barcoo, Barwon, Bulloo, Culgoa, Degrey, Hunter, Isaacs, Murray, Norman **7** Darling, Derwent, Fitzroy, Georges, Gilbert, Lachlan, Staaten, Warrego **8** Belyando, Brisbane, Burdekin, Clarence, Drysdale, Flinders, Gascoyne, Georgina, Mitchell, Thompson, Victoria, Weeribee, Wooramel **9** Ashburton, Fortescue, Hawksbury, MacKenzie, Macquarie, Murchison, Saltwater **10** Diamantina, Shoalhaven **12** Murrambidgee
sea: **5** Coral, Timor **6** Indian, Tasman **7** Arafura, Pacific
physical feature:
bay: **5** Bight, Shark **6** Botany **7** Moreton **11** Port Phillip
cape: **4** Howe, York **5** Byron **9** Southeast
channel: **5** Cowal **9** Anabranch, Billabong
desert: **6** Arunta, Gibson, Stuart, Tanami **7** Simpson **10** Great Sandy **13** Great Victoria
gulf: **8** Spencers **9** Van Dieman **11** Carpentaria **15** Joseph Bonaparte **20** Great Australian Bight
peninsula: **4** Eyre
reef: **12** Great Barrier
strait: **4** Bass
people: **3** Abo **4** Koko, Mara, Wong **5** Anzac, Binge, Dieri, Maori, Myall **6** Aranda, Arunta, Aussie, Binghi, Digger, Kipper, Papuan **7** Arawong, Ilpirra **8** Antipode, Barkinji, Billijim, Euahlayi, Warragal, Warrigal **9** Aborigine **10** Australoid, Melanesian, Sandgroper **12** Jindyworobak
actor: **9** Judy Davis, Mel Gibson, Paul Hogan **10** Bryan Brown
author: **4** West **5** White **7** Russell **10** Richardson
explorer: **4** Bass, Cook **6** Mawson, Tasman **7** Wilkins
nurse: **11** Sister Kenny
language: **7** English
religion: **7** Judaism **8** Anglican **10** Protestant **13** Roman Catholic
place: **7** outback **9** billabong **11** back country
aborigine area: **9** Arhemland
beach: **5** Manly
dam: **4** Hume
possession: **12** Cocos Islands **13** Norfolk Island **16** Christmas Islands
feature:
animal: **5** dingo **6** kelpie **7** wallaby **8** anteater, kangaroo **9** koala bear **18** duckbilled platypus
bird: **3** emu **10** kookaburra
cowboy: **6** waddie **8** jackaroo
dance: **6** dreher
flower: **7** boronia, fuchsia, waratah **9** coachwood **12** kangaroo paws
game: **3** sye **10** tambaroora
tree: **3** gum **10** eucalyptus
weapon: **5** kiley, kyley **7** wommera **9** boomerang
food: **3** kai **6** tucker
cake: **6** damper **7** brownie
dish: **8** coolamon
drink: **9** arkaloola
fruit: **5** nonda **7** kumquat **11** desert-lemon

Austria

other name: **10** Osterreich

name means: **12** eastern state

capital/largest city: **6** Vienna

others: **4** Enns, Graz, Lech, Linz, Ried, Wels **5** Krems, Steyr, Traun **6** Leoben **7** Bregenz, Modling, Spittal, Villach **8** Bad Ischl, Dornbirn, Salzburg **9** Innsbruck, Semmering **10** Kapfenberg, Klagenfurt **11** Sankt Polten **14** Wiener Neustadt

division: **5** Tirol, Tyrol **6** Istria, Styria, Triest **7** Bohemia, Galicia, Moravia, Silesia **8** Bukowina, Dalmatia, Earniola, Gradisca **9** Earinthia **10** Burgenland, Vorarlberg **12** Lower Austria, Upper Austria

Roman province: **6** Raetia **7** Noricum **8** Pannonia

government:

legislature: **9** Bundesrat, Reichsrat **10** Herrenhaus, Reichsrath

head of government: **10** Chancellor

other leader: **7** emperor **12** burgomeister

measure: **4** fass, fuss, joch, mass, muth, yoke **5** halbe, linie, meile, metze, pfiff, punkt **6** achtel, becher, leipoa, seidel **7** dlafter, viertel **8** dreiling **12** futtermassel

monetary unit: **4** lira **5** crown, ducat, krone **6** florin, gulden, heller, zehner **8** albertin, groschen, kreutzer **9** schilling

weight: **4** marc, unze **5** denat, karch, stein **7** centner, pfennig **8** vierling **9** quantchen

lake: **6** Almsee **7** Fertoto, Mondsee **8** Bodensee, Traunsee **9** Constance **10** Neusiedler

mountain: **4** Alps **6** Stubai, Tirols, Tyrols **8** Eisenerz, Rhatikon **9** Dolomites, Kitzbuhel **10** Hohe Tauern **14** Silvretta Group

highest point: **13** Grossglockner

river: **3** Inn, Mur **4** Drau, Elbe, Enns, Iser, Kamp, Lech, Murz, Raab **5** Donau, Drava, Drave, March, Salza, Thaya, Traun **6** Danube, Moldau

physical feature:

basin: **7** Styrian
canal: **6** Danube
mountain pass: **7** Brenner
wind: **6** Foehen
woods: **6** Vienna

people: **5** Poles **6** Croats, Czechs **7** Germans, Gypsies **8** Slovenes **10** Hungarians

botanist: **6** Mendel
composer: **5** Haydn **6** Czerny, Mahler, Mozart, Webern **7** Amadeus, Strauss **8** Bruckner, Schubert **9** Beethoven **10** Schoenberg
emperor: **7** Charles, Francis **9** Ferdinand, Habsburgs, Hapsburgs **10** Franz Josef
philosopher: **12** Wittgenstein
psychiatrist: **5** Adler, Freud, Reich
statesman: **10** Metternich **12** Kurt Waldheim

language: **5** Czech **6** German, Magyar **8** Croatian **9** Slovenian

religion: **7** Judaism **10** Protestant **13** Roman Catholic

place:

boulevard: **3** Kai **11** Ringstrasse
cathedral: **9** St Stephen
city hall: **7** Rathaus
fortress: **13** Hochosterwitz, Hohensalzburg
imperial palace: **7** Hofburg
monastery: **4** Melk **8** Gottweig **14** Klosterneuburg
museum: **6** Mozart **9** Johanneum
people's garden: **11** Volksgarten
resort: **5** Baden **7** Bregenz **8** Bad Ischl **9** Innsbruck, Semmering

feature: **8** yodelers **11** ice grottoes

clothing: **5** loden **10** lederhosen
dance: **5** waltz **6** dreher **7** landler **13** schuhplattler **14** grand polonaise
festival: **8** Salzburg
horse: **10** Lippizaner
pastry shop: **12** konditoreien

food:

breaded veal cutlet: **15** Wiener schnitzel
cake: **11** linzer torte, sacher torte
cookie: **7** kipferl
roll: **10** golatschen

autochthonous **5** first **6** native, primal **7** ancient **8** earliest, original, primeval **10** aboriginal, indigenous, primordial

autocracy **7** czarism, tyranny **8** autarchy, monarchy **9** Caesarism, despotism, Hitlerism, kaiserism, monocracy, Stalinism **10** absolutism **11** Bonapartism **12** dictatorship **14** tyrannical rule **15** totalitarianism **16** absolute monarchy

autocrat **5** ruler **6** despot, tyrant **7** monarch **8** dictator, overlord **13** absolute ruler

autocratic **8** despotic **9** czaristic, imperious, tyrannous **10** iron-handed, oppressive, repressive, tyrannical **11** dictatorial, monarchical **13** authoritarian

auto da fe, auto de fe
13 act of the faith **17** burning of heretics
from: **18** Spanish Inquisition

autograph **4** mark, sign **5** x-mark **9** John Henry, signature **11** endorsement, handwriting, inscription, John Hancock **16** countersignature

Autolycus
character in: **14** The Winter's Tale
author: **11** Shakespeare

Autolycus
form: **5** thief
father: **6** Hermes
mother: **6** Chione
half-brother: **9** Philammon
wife: **9** Amphithea
daughter: **8** Anticlea
grandson: **8** Odysseus
gift: **12** invisibility **13** shape changing

automated **9** automatic **10** mechanical, mechanized **15** machine-operated

automatic **6** reflex **7** natural, routine **8** electric, habitual, inherent, unwilled **9** automated **10** mechanical, push-button, self-acting, self-moving **11** instinctive, involuntary, spontaneous, unconscious **12** uncontrolled **13** nonvolitional, self-operating **14** self-propelling

automaton **4** pawn, tool **5** patsy, robot **6** puppet, stooge **7** android, cat's-paw, fall guy, machine **10** fantoccino, marionette

Automedon
charioteer of: **8** Achilles

automobile
invented by:
differential gear: **4** Benz
electric: **8** Morrison
gasoline: **6** Duryea **7** Daimler
muffler: **5** Maxim
self-starter: **9** Kettering
see also: car

Automobile state
nickname of: **8** Michigan

Autonoe
father: **6** Cadmus
mother: **8** Harmonia
sister: **3** Ino **5** Agave **6** Semele
husband: **9** Aristaeus
son: **7** Actaeon
daughter: **6** Macris

autonomous **4** free **9** sovereign **11** independent, self-reliant **13** self-governing **14** self-determined, self-sufficient

autonomy **7** freedom **8** home rule, self-rule **10** liberation **11** sovereignty **12** independence **14** self-government **17** self-determination

auto racing
driver: **6** A J Foyt **7** Al Unser **8** Tom Sneva **9** Niki Lauda **10** Bobby Unser, Juan Fangio **11** Jack Brabham **12** Bobby Allison, Janet Guthrie, Richard Petty **13** Jackie Stewart, Mario Andretti **14** Barney Oldfield, Cale Yarborough, Craig Breedlove **16** Johnny Rutherford

Autry, Gene
horse: **8** Champion
born: **7** Tioga TX
roles: **11** Melody Ranch **16** The Singing Cowboy **19** Tumbling Tumbleweeds **22** Springtime in the Rockies

autumn **4** fall **11** harvest time **12** Indian summer **15** autumnal equinox

auxiliary **6** backup, helper **7** partner, reserve **9** accessory, ancillary, assistant, associate, companion, emergency, secondary **10** accomplice, subsidiary, supplement **11** subordinate **13** supplementary

avail **3** aid, use **4** help **5** serve **6** assist, profit **7** benefit, purpose, service, success, utilize **9** advantage **10** usefulness

available **4** free, open **5** handy, on tap **6** at hand, on hand **9** in reserve **10** accessible, convenient, obtainable

avalanche **4** heap, mass, pile **5** flood **6** deluge **7** barrage, cascade, torrent **8** blizzard **9** cataclysm, rockslide, snowslide **10** earthslide, inundation **11** bombardment

Avalon
island of: **8** Paradise
burial place for: **6** heroes **10** King Arthur

avant-garde **7** leaders **8** pioneers, vanguard **10** innovators **11** forerunners, originators, tastemakers **12** advance guard, trailblazers, trendsetters

avarice **5** greed **6** penury **8** rapacity, venality **9** parsimony **10** greediness, stinginess **11** miserliness **12** covetousness, graspingness **13** money-grubbing, niggardliness, penny-pinching **15** close-fistedness

Ave Maria **8** Hail Mary

avenge **5** repay **6** injure, punish **7** revenge **9** retaliate

Avengers, The
character: **8** Emma Peel, Tara King **9** John (Jonathan) Steed
cast: **9** Diana Rigg **12** Linda Thorson **13** Patrick Macnee

avenue **3** way **4** gate, path, road **5** means, route **6** access, chance, course, outlet **7** gateway, parkway, passage, pathway **8** approach **9** boulevard, concourse, direction, esplanade **10** passageway **11** opportunity **12** thoroughfare

aver **4** avow **5** state, swear **6** affirm, assert, avouch, insist, verify **7** certify, contend, declare, profess, protest **8** maintain, proclaim **9** emphasize, guarantee, pronounce, represent **10** asseverate

average **3** par **4** fair, mean, norm, so-so **5** ratio, usual **6** common, medial, median, medium, normal, not bad **7** the rule, typical **8** mediocre, midpoint, moderate, ordinary, passable, standard, standing, the usual **9** tolerable **10** mean amount **11** indifferent, rank and file **12** run-of-the-mill

averment **5** claim **6** avowal **8** argument **9** assertion, assurance **10** allegation, contention, profession **11** affirmation

averse **5** loath **7** opposed **8** inimical **9** reluctant, unwilling **10** indisposed, unamenable **11** disinclined, ill-disposed, unfavorable **12** antipathetic, recalcitrant

aversion **6** hatred, horror **7** disgust, dislike **8** distaste, loathing **9** animosity, antipathy, hostility, prejudice, repulsion, revulsion **10** abhorrence, opposition, reluctance, repugnance **11** detestation **13** unwillingness **14** disinclination

avert 4 turn **5** avoid, deter, shift **7** beat off, deflect, fend off, keep off, prevent, ward off **8** preclude, stave off, turn away **9** forestall, frustrate, keep at bay, sidetrack **11** nip in the bud

aviary 4 cage **9** birdhouse, enclosure

aviation 6 flight, flying **11** aeronautics **12** aerodynamics

aviator, aviatrix 4 bird **5** flyer, pilot **6** airman, flyboy **7** birdman

avid 4 keen **5** eager, rabid **6** ardent, greedy, hungry **7** anxious, devoted, fanatic, intense, zealous **8** covetous, desirous, grasping **9** rapacious, voracious **10** avaricious, insatiable **11** acquisitive **12** enthusiastic

avidity 4 zeal **5** greed **6** fervor, hunger **8** rapacity, voracity **9** eagerness **10** enthusiasm, fanaticism, greediness **12** covetousness **15** acquisitiveness

Avignon Papacy 15 Babylonian Exile **19** Babylonian Captivity

avocado 9 dark green **13** alligator pear, tropical fruit
origin: 6 Mexico **12** South America **14** Central America
family: 9 Lauraceae
used to make: 9 guacamole

avocation 5 hobby **7** pastime **8** sideline **9** diversion **10** recreation **11** distraction **13** entertainment

Avogadro, Amedeo
field: 7 physics **9** chemistry
nationality: 7 Italian
formulated: 19 molecular hypothesis

avoid 4 shun **5** avert, dodge, elude, evade, skirt **6** escape, eschew **7** boycott, forbear, forsake **8** sidestep **10** fight shy of **11** refrain from **12** steer clear of

avoidance 7 eluding, evasion **8** shirking, shunning, skirting

avoid the issue 4 duck **5** dodge, evade, hedge, stall **10** equivocate **17** beat around the bush

a votre sante 12 to your health

avouch 5 argue, swear **6** affirm **7** declare **8** advocate, maintain

avow 3 own **4** aver **5** admit, state, swear **6** affirm, assert, reveal **7** confess, declare, profess **8** announce, disclose, proclaim **11** acknowledge

avowal 4 word **8** averment **9** admission, assertion, assurance, statement **10** confession, profession **11** affirmation, declaration **12** proclamation, protestation **14** acknowledgment

avowed 5 sworn **8** admitted, declared **9** confessed, professed **12** acknowledged, self-declared **14** self-proclaimed

await 6 attend, expect **7** look for **10** anticipate

awake 5 alert, aware, spark **6** arouse, awaken, bestir, excite, incite **7** alive to, heedful, inspire, mindful, provoke **8** open-eyed, vigilant, watchful **9** attentive, conscious, stimulate

Awake and Sing!
author: 13 Clifford Odets

awaken 3 fan **4** fire **6** arouse, excite, kindle, revive, stir up **9** stimulate

awakening 7 arising, arousal **8** sparking, stirring **11** stimulation

award 4 give **5** allot, allow, grant, honor, medal, prize **6** accord, assign, bestow, decree, trophy **7** appoint, concede, laurels, tribute **8** citation, confer on **10** decoration

aware 6 with it **7** alert to, alive to, awake to, mindful **8** apprised, informed, sensible, sentient **9** cognizant, conscious, tuned in to **10** conversant **11** enlightened **12** familiar with **13** knowledgeable

awareness 9 acuteness, alertness, appraisal, knowledge **10** cognizance, perception **11** familiarity, information, mindfulness, realization, recognition, sensibility **12** acquaintance **13** consciousness, understanding

away 3 far **4** gone **6** absent, at once, way off **8** distance **9** elsewhere

awe 3 cow **4** fear **5** abash, alarm, amaze, dread, panic, shock **6** dismay, fright, horror, terror, wonder **7** perturb, quaking, respect, terrify **8** astonish, disquiet, frighten **9** abashment, adoration, amazement, quivering, reverence, solemnity, trembling **10** exaltation, intimidate, veneration **11** disquietude, trepidation **12** apprehension, astonishment, perturbation **13** consternation

awe-inspiring 5 giant, grand, great, noble **6** august, mighty **7** eminent, exalted, mammoth, sublime, supreme, titanic **8** colossal, enormous, gigantic, glorious, imposing, majestic, wondrous **9** excessive **10** impressive, incredible, monumental, prodigious, stupendous, tremendous **11** astonishing, extravagant, illustrious, magnificent, spectacular **12** breathtaking, over-whelming

awesome 6 solemn **7** amazing, fearful **8** alarming, dreadful, fearsome, majestic, wondrous **9** inspiring **10** formidable, perturbing, stupefying, terrifying **11** astonishing, disquieting, frightening, magnificent **12** breathtaking, intimidating, overwhelming

awestruck 6 humble **8** overcome **11** reverential

awful 3 bad, low **4** base, dire, mean, ugly **5** lousy **6** solemn **7** amazing, awesome, fearful, ghastly, heinous, hideous **8** alarming, dreadful, fearsome, gruesome, horrible, majestic, shocking, terrible, wondrous **9** appalling, frightful, monstrous, revolting **10** deplorable, despicable, formidable, horrendous, horrifying, stupefying, terrifying, unpleasant **11** displeasing, disquieting, distressing, redoubtable **12** awe-inspiring, contemptible, disagreeable **13** reprehensible

awfully 4 very **5** quite **8** horribly, terribly **9** extremely, immensely **10** dreadfully **11** excessively **13** exceptionally

awkward 5 inept **6** clumsy, touchy, trying **7** unhandy **8** bungling, delicate, inexpert, ticklish, ungainly, unwieldy **9** difficult, graceless, maladroit **10** blundering, cumbersome, unpleasant, unskillful **11** troublesome **12** embarrassing, inconvenient, unmanageable **13** disconcerting, uncomfortable, uncoordinated
French: 6 gauche

Awkward Age, The
author: 10 Henry James

awkwardness 9 gaucherie **10** clumsiness, difficulty, ineptitude **12** ungainliness, unwieldiness **13** embarrassment, inconvenience

awl **4** nail **6** gimlet **11** leather tool, sharp device

awning **4** hood **6** canopy **7** marquee **8** covering, sunshade

awry **5** amiss, askew, wrong **6** astray, uneven **7** crooked, twisted **8** unevenly **9** crookedly, obliquely **11** out of kilter

axe, ax **3** can **4** chop, fire, oust, sack **5** let go, split **6** bounce, cut out, delete, remove **7** cut down, dismiss **8** get rid of, tomahawk **9** discharge, terminate **11** send packing
type: **4** pick **6** poleax **7** hatchet **8** tomahawk

Axe, The
author: **12** Sigrid Undset

Axelrod, Julius
field: **9** chemistry
studied: **24** nerve-impulse transmission
awarded: **10** Nobel Prize

axiom **3** law **5** basic **7** precept **9** postulate, principle **10** assumption **14** fundamental law

axiomatic **5** banal, given **6** cliche **7** assumed **8** accepted, manifest **9** apodictic **10** aphoristic **11** self-evident **12** demonstrable, epigrammatic, indisputable, unquestioned **13** incontestable, platitudinous

Axiopoenus
epithet of: **6** Athena
means: **12** just requital

axis **4** stem **5** pivot, shaft **7** compact, entente, spindle **8** alliance **9** alignment, coalition **10** center line **11** affiliation **12** pivotal point **13** confederation **14** line of rotation, line of symmetry

axle **3** bar, pin **5** shaft, wheel **7** spindle **8** crossbar **10** turning bar

ayah **4** maid **5** nurse

aye **3** yea, yes **11** affirmative

Aykroyd, Dan
born: **6** Canada, Ottawa **7** Ontario
roles: **12** Ghostbusters **13** Doctor Detroit, Trading Places **16** The Blues Brothers, The Great Outdoors **17** Saturday Night Live

Aymara
location: **4** Peru **7** Bolivia **12** South America

Ayres, Lew
wife: **8** Lola Lane **12** Ginger Rogers
born: **13** Minneapolis MN
roles: **7** Holiday, The Kiss **9** Dr Kildare **25** All Quiet on the Western Front

azalea **12** Rhododendron
varieties: **4** Cork, Mock, Snow **5** Coast, Dwarf, Early, Flame, Hiryu, Hoary, Luchu, Royal, Sims's, Swamp, Sweet, Torch **6** Alpine, Balsam, Clammy, Indian, Korean, Kurume, Kyushu, Oconee, Pontic, Smooth, Spider, Summer, Yellow **7** Alabama, Chinese, Maries's, Mt Amagi, Oldham's, Western **8** Five-leaf, Japanese, Piedmont, Rusticum, Yodogawa **9** Kirishima, Mayflower, Pink-shell, Rose-shell, Wild-thyme **10** Cumberland, Macranthum, Plum-leaved, White swamp **11** Gable hybrid, Ghent hybrid, Molle hybrid **12** Arnold hybrid, Florida flame, Sander hybrid **13** Indicum hybrid **15** Glenn Dale hybrid, Kaempferi hybrid, Knapp Hill hybrid **16** Rutherford hybrid **24** Rusticum Flore Pleno hybrid

Azan
father: **5** Arcas
mother: **5** Erato

Azariah
also: **6** Uzziah
father: **4** Jehu **5** Ethan **6** Nathan **7** Hilkiah, Jehoram, Johanan **11** Jehoshaphat
son: **4** Joel
known as: **8** Abednego
companion: **6** Daniel
friend: **7** Meshach **8** Shadrach
succeeded: **5** Zadok

Azazel **9** scapegoat **11** fallen angel

Aziz, Dr
character in: **15** A Passage to India
author: **7** Forster

Aztec (Nahua, Mexica)
language family: **7** Nahuatl **10** Uto-Aztecan
location: **6** Mexico, Puebla **8** Guerrero, Veracruz **9** Guatemala, Michoacan **11** Lake Texcoco **14** Central America
leader: **9** Montezuma
worshipped: **12** Quetzalcoatl
capital: **12** Tenochtitlan

Azuela, Mariano
author of: **8** The Flies **9** The Bosses **12** The Underdogs **26** Trials of a Respectable Family

azure **5** lapis **6** cobalt **7** sky blue **8** cerulean **9** clear blue, cloudless **11** lapis lazuli

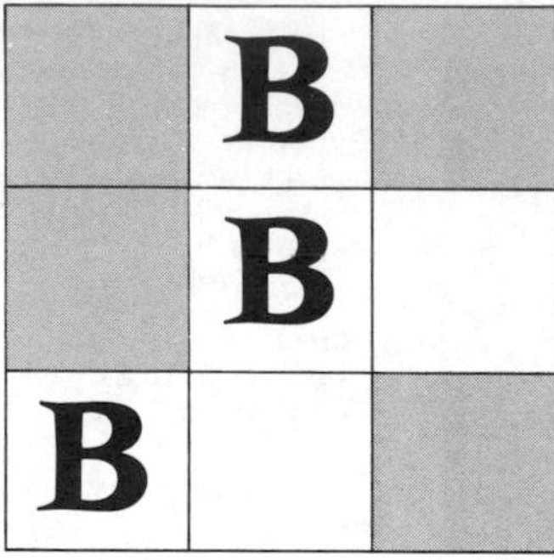

Baade, Walter
field: **9** astronomy
discovered: **15** Hidalgo asteroid

Baal **3** god **5** deity

Baal Merodach *see* **6** Marduk

Babbage, Charles
field: **11** mathematics
nationality: **7** British, English
first: **15** actuarial tables
inventor of: **13** adding machine **18** calculating machine
invented forerunner of: **15** digital computer
planned: **10** calculator

Babbitt **9** bourgeois **10** conformist, middlebrow, philistine

Babbitt
author: **13** Sinclair Lewis
character: **11** Myra Babbitt, Seneca Deane **12** Paul Riesling **15** Mrs Tanis Judique **22** George Folansbee Babbitt

babble **3** coo, din, gab, hum **4** blab, talk **5** prate **6** burble, clamor, drivel, gabble, gibber, gurgle, hubbub, jabber, murmur **7** blabber, blather, chatter, prattle, twaddle **8** chitchat, rattle on **9** jabbering, murmuring **14** chitter-chatter

babbling **6** drivel, hubbub **7** blabber, twaddle **8** burbling, gabbling, gurgling, nonsense **9** clamoring, gibberish, jabbering, murmuring

babe **3** tot **4** baby **5** child **6** infant

babe in arms **4** baby **6** infant **7** neonate, newborn

babe in the woods **8** innocent **9** fledgling, greenhorn **10** tenderfoot

babel, Babel **3** din **6** bedlam, clamor, hubbub, tumult, uproar **7** turmoil **9** confusion **10** hullabaloo **11** pandemonium

Babel, Isaac
author of: **9** Benia Krik **11** Odessa Tales **13** The Red Cavalry

Babe Ruth
nickname of: **16** George Herman Ruth

Babe the Blue Ox
character in: **10** Paul Bunyan

baboon **6** monkey
breeding: **9** year round
characteristic: **4** mane, pads **6** muzzle
diet: **6** plants **8** scorpion **12** small animals
dwelling: **5** Egypt, Sudan **6** Africa, Arabia **7** Somalia **8** Ethiopia
family: **15** cercopithecidae
habitat: **5** hills **6** plains
largest genus: **6** Chacma
most sacred: **6** Anobis
smallest genus: **7** Western

babushka **4** baba, veil **5** scarf, stole **8** kerchief

baby **3** wee **4** babe, tiny **5** dwarf, humor, pygmy, small, spoil, young **6** bantam, coddle, coward, infant, little, midget, minute, pamper, petite **7** crybaby, indulge, neonate **8** dwarfish, sniveler **9** miniature, youngster **10** babe in arms, diminutive **11** mollycoddle, overindulge, pocket-sized

Baby
nickname of: **12** Lauren Bacall

baby carriage **4** cart, pram **6** cradle **12** perambulator

babyish **7** puerile **8** childish, immature, juvenile **9** infantile

babylike **3** wee **4** tiny **5** small **9** infantile **10** diminutive

Babylonian Captivity **13** Avignon Papacy **15** Babylonian Exile

Babylonian god **3** Bel **6** Marduk

Babylonian Mythology *see box*

Baby Roo
character in: **13** Winnie-the-Pooh
author: **5** Milne

Baby Snookums
character in: **12** The Newlyweds

Bacall, Lauren
real name: **15** Betty Joan Perske

Babylonian Mythology
chief of gods: **6** Marduk **8** Merodach **12** Baal Merodach
demon: **6** Namtar
goddess of air: **6** Ninlil
goddess of death: **10** Ereshkigal
goddess of love/war/fertility: **6** Ananna, Inanna, Ishtar **7** Astarte, Mylitta **9** Ashtoreth
god of air: **5** Enlil
god of dead: **6** Nergal
god of fire: **5** Ishum
god of heaven: **2** An **3** Anu
god of moon: **3** Sin
god of pastures/vegetation: **6** Dumuzi
god of pestilence: **4** Irra
god of shepherds: **6** Tammuz
god of sun: **3** Utu **7** Shamash
god of wisdom: **4** Enki
hero: **5** Ninib **7** Ninurta
king: **9** Gilgamesh
king of gods: **5** Enlil
mother of gods: **5** Nammu
queen of heaven: **6** Ishtar
world of dead: **3** Kur

husband: **12** Jason Robards **14** Humphrey Bogart
nickname: **4** Baby
born: **9** New York NY
roles: **8** Applause, Key Largo **11** Dark Passage, The Big Sleep **12** Cactus Flower **16** To Have and Have Not **22** How to Marry a Millionaire

Bacchae
form: **11** priestesses
attendants of: **7** Bacchus
participants in: **11** Bacchanalia

Bacchae, The
author: **9** Euripides
character: **4** Zeus **5** Agave **6** Cadmus, Semele **8** Dionysus, Pentheus, Tiresias

bacchanal **4** orgy **5** feast, revel, spree **6** frolic **7** carouse, debauch, revelry, wassail **8** carnival, carousal, festival **10** debauchery, Saturnalia **11** merrymaking

Bacchanalia
festival honoring: **7** Bacchus

Bacchant
priest who worships: **7** Bacchus

Bacchante
also: **6** Thyiad
priestess who worships: **7** Bacchus

Bacchus
also: **5** Evius **8** Dionysus
god of: **4** wine **5** drama **9** fertility
father: **4** Zeus
mother: **6** Semele
son: **6** Phlias **7** Narcaus, Priapus **8** Oenopion
epithet: **6** Lyaeus **7** Bromius, Cresius **8** Thyoneus, Triambus **9** Pyrigenes **11** Dithyrambus, Mitrephorus

Bach, Carl (Karl) Philipp Emanuel
born: **6** Weimar **7** Germany
father: **19** Johann Sebastian Bach
composer of: **14** Prussian Sonata **19** Wurtembergian Sonata

Bach, Johann Sebastian
born: **7** Germany **8** Eisenach
composer of: **8** Chaconne **10** Giant Fugue, Inventions, Magnificat, Wedge Fugue **11** Dorian Fugue, Fiddle Fugue, Little Fugue **12** Corelli Fugue, French Suites, Fuga alla Giga, German Suites, St Anne's Fugue **13** Coffee Cantata, English Suites, St John Passion **14** Alla Breve Fugue, Easter Oratorio, Peasant Cantata, Wedding Cantata **15** Jesu Meine Freude, Musical Offering **16** St Matthew Passion, The Art of the Fugue **17** Christmas Oratorio **18** Goldberg Variations **20** Brandenburg Concertos **22** The Well-Tempered Clavier **24** The Wise and Foolish Virgins **30** The Dispute Between Phoebus and Pan

Bach, Richard
author of: **25** Jonathan Livingston Seagull

bachelor **6** single **9** single man, unmarried **12** unmarried man

Bachelor Father
character: **9** Peter Tong **10** Kelly Gregg **12** Bentley Gregg **13** Ginger Farrell
cast: **10** Sammee Tong **12** John Forsythe **14** Noreen Corcoran **17** Bernadette Withers

bachelorhood **8** celibacy **13** baccalaureate **14** unmarried state

bacillus **3** bug **4** germ **7** microbe **8** pathogen **9** bacterium **13** microorganism

Bacis
origin: **8** Boeotian
form: **7** prophet

back ***see box***

back away from **7** back off **11** retreat from **12** draw back from, withdraw from

backbiter **5** scold **6** carper, critic **7** reviler **8** vilifier **9** slanderer

backbiting **5** abuse, catty **6** gossip, malice **7** abusive, calumny, gossipy, hurtful, obloquy, slander **8** libeling, reviling **9** aspersion, cattiness, censuring, contumely, injurious, invective, malicious, maligning, vilifying **10** belittling, bitchiness, calumnious, defamation, defamatory, derogating, detracting, detraction, scandalous, scurrility, slanderous, traduction **11** badmouthing, denigrating, deprecating, disparaging, traducement **12** backstabbing, calumniation, vilification, vituperation **13** disparagement, maliciousness **16** scandal-mongering

backbone **4** grit, guts, sand **5** basis, chine, nerve, pluck, spine, spunk **6** dorsum, mettle, spirit **7** bravery, courage, resolve **8** firmness, mainstay, strength, tenacity **9** character, fortitude, manliness, vertebrae **10** foundation, resolution **11** intrepidity **12** resoluteness, spinal column **13** dauntlessness, steadfastness **15** vertebral column **19** strength of character

> **back** **3** aid, ebb **4** abet, gone, help, hind, late, past, rear, tail **5** after, guard, minor, rural, spine, tardy **6** affirm, assist, attest, behind, bygone, caudal, dorsal, dorsum, far end, former, hinder, hold up, praise, recede, recoil, remote, retire, return, revert, second, succor, tergal, uphold, verify **7** belated, bolster, certify, confirm, delayed, distant, earlier, elapsed, endorse, expired, far side, finance, not paid, overdue, promote, protect, rear end, rebound, retract, retreat, reverse, sponsor, support, sustain, tail end, warrant **8** advocate, backbone, hind part, hindmost, maintain, move away, obsolete, previous, sanction, secluded, turn tail, validate, vouch for, withdraw **9** afterpart, encourage, in arrears, out-of-date, patronize, posterior, reinforce, subsidize **10** retrogress, testify for, underwrite, untraveled **11** bear witness, corroborate, countenance, countrified, countryside, farthermost, furthermost, reverse side, undeveloped, unimportant, unpopulated **12** beat a retreat, hindquarters, spinal column, substantiate **13** take sides with

back-country **4** farm **5** rural **6** rustic **7** farming **10** provincial

back down **7** back off **8** draw back, move away **9** withdrawn

backdrop **4** flat **7** curtain, scenery **10** background

backer **4** ally **5** angel **6** patron **7** sponsor **8** adherent, advocate, champion, follower, investor, promoter **9** financier, guarantor, supporter **10** well-wisher **11** underwriter

backfire **4** flop, miss **5** crash **6** fizzle, go awry **8** backlash, lay an egg, miscarry, ricochet **9** boomerang **10** bounce back, disappoint **11** come to grief, fall through **12** come to naught **13** come to nothing

background **3** set **4** past, rear **5** flats **6** milieu **7** context, history, rearing, setting **8** backdrop, breeding, distance, heritage, training **9** education, grounding, landscape, life story **10** experience, upbringing **11** antecedents, credentials, environment, mise-en-scene, preparation **13** circumstances

backhanded **7** awkward **8** reversed **9** insincere

backing **3** aid **4** core, help **5** aegis **6** succor **7** support **8** advocacy, interior, sanction **9** patronage, prompting **10** assistance, inner layer, sustenance **11** championing, cooperation, endorsement, helping hand, sponsorship **13** encouragement

backlash **4** flop, snag **5** crash, ravel **6** fizzle, go away, recoil **7** rebound **8** backfire, kick back, miscarry, ricochet, snap back **9** animosity, boomerang, hostility, reversion **10** antagonism, bounce back, opposition, resistance **11** come to grief, fall through **12** come to naught **13** come to nothing, counteraction, recalcitrance

backlog **5** hoard, stock, store **6** assets, excess, supply **7** nest egg, reserve, savings **9** abundance, amassment, inventory, reservoir, stockpile **12** accumulation **13** reserve supply **14** superabundance

back matter **5** index **8** addendum, appendix **10** supplement **12** bibliography

back off **7** retreat **8** back down, pull back, withdraw

backpack **4** hike, load **5** pouch **6** bundle **8** knapsack

backside **3** can **4** buns, butt, duff, prat, rear, rump, seat, tail **5** fanny **6** behind, bottom, settee, setter, sitter **7** keister, rear end **8** buttocks, derriere **9** fundament, posterior

backslide **5** lapse **6** revert **7** relapse **10** recurrence, regression **11** deteriorate **14** slip from virtue

back street **5** alley, byway **8** alleyway **13** secondary road

Back Street
director:
1941 version: **15** Robert Stevenson
1961 version: **11** David Miller
based on story by: **11** Fannie Hurst
cast:
1932 version: **9** John Boles **10** Irene Dunne
1941 version: **12** Charles Boyer **16** Margaret Sullavan
1961 version: **9** John Gavin, Vera Miles **12** Susan Hayward

back talk **3** jaw, lip **4** gall, guff, rude, sass **5** cheek **8** pertness, rudeness **9** impudence, insolence, sassiness, sauciness **12** impertinence

Back to the Future
director: **14** Robert Zemeckis
cast: **11** Lea Thompson, Michael J Fox **16** Christopher Lloyd

backup **6** second **7** reserve, standby, stand-in **9** alternate, auxiliary, emergency, secondary **10** substitute, understudy **11** pinch-hitter **13** supplementary

back up **4** abet **6** assist, uphold **9** reinforce **11** corroborate

backward, backwards **3** shy **4** dull, slow **5** dense, tardy, timid, wrong **6** behind, ebbing, remiss, toward **7** bashful, impeded, laggard, messily, reverse, the rear **8** inverted, rearward, receding, reserved, retarded, reticent, reversed, sluggish **9** in retreat, in reverse, inside out, returning, slow-paced, to the past, to the rear, withdrawn **10** disorderly, improperly, regressive, retreating, retrograde, slow-witted, topsy-turvy, upside down **11** chaotically, undeveloped, withdrawing **12** wrong side out **13** retrogressive **15** uncommunicative
French: **9** en arriere

backwash **4** burg, wake **6** result, sticks, upshot **7** boonies, outcome **8** frontier, tank town **9** aftermath, backwater, boondocks, provinces, upcountry **10** hinterland **11** aftereffect, backcountry, consequence

backwater **3** ebb **5** slack **7** retreat, reverse **8** holdback, stagnant, withdraw

backwoods **5** rural, wilds **6** rustic, simple, sticks **7** boonies, country **8** woodland **9** boondocks, rural area **10** hinterland, provincial **11** back-country, countryside, hinterlands **15** unsophisticated

bacon **3** pig **4** pork **6** gammon **8** porkslab **10** smoked pork **11** porkbellies
measure: **6** rasher

Bacon, Francis
author of: **6** Essays **11** New Atlantis **12** Novum Organum **14** Maxims of the Law **16** Instauratio Magna **17** History of Henry VII **18** De Sapientia Veterum **20** Apophthegms New and Old **21** Advancement of Learning **25** Reading on the Statute of Uses

Bacon, Francis
born: **6** Dublin **7** Ireland
artwork: **15** Henrietta Moraes **35** Three Studies at the Base of a Crucifixion **44** Studies After Velazquez' Portrait of Pope Innocent X

Bacon, Henry
architect of: **15** Lincoln Memorial

bacteria **3** bug **4** germ **5** virus **7** microbe **8** bacillus, pathogen **13** microorganism

bactericide **9** germicide **10** antiseptic, germ killer **12** disinfectant

bacteriologist
American: **4** Reed
British: **7** Fleming
German: **4** Koch **7** Behring, Ehrlich **10** Wassermann
Japanese: **7** Noguchi **8** Kitasato

bad ***see box***

bad faith **7** perfidy, treason **8** betrayal **9** falseness, treachery, two timing **10** disloyalty **11** double-cross **13** breach of faith, double-dealing **14** unfaithfulness

badge **4** mark, seal, sign **5** brand, stamp, token **6** device, emblem, ensign, shield, symbol **7** earmark **8** hallmark, insignia **9** medallion

badger **3** nag, vex **4** bait, goad **5** annoy, beset, bully, chafe, harry, hound, tease **6** coerce, harass, hector, nettle, pester, plague **7** provoke, torment, trouble **8** irritate **9** persecute
group of: **4** cete

Badger State
nickname of: **9** Wisconsin

badinage **5** chaff **6** banter, joking **7** jesting, joshing, kidding, ragging, ribbing, waggery **8** chaffing, raillery, repartee, word play

bad judgment **5** folly **10** imprudence **11** foolishness **12** carelessness **13** senselessness **15** thoughtlessness **16** shortsightedness, unperceptiveness

bad **3** ill, sad, sin **4** base, dire, evil, foul, glum, grim, mean, poor, rank, sick, sour, vile **5** acrid, acute, angry, awful, cross, false, fetid, grave, harsh, lousy, moldy, nasty, risky, sorry, unfit, wrong **6** ailing, bitter, crimes, faulty, gloomy, guilty, infirm, odious, putrid, rancid, rotten, severe, sickly, sinful, touchy, tragic, turned, unwell, wicked, wrongs **7** baneful, beastly, corrupt, decayed, harmful, hurtful, immoral, joyless, lacking, naughty, not good, noxious, painful, searing, serious, spoiled, tainted, unsound, useless **8** below par, contrite, criminal, dreadful, grievous, inferior, menacing, mildewed, offenses, polluted, terrible, troubled, villainy, wretched **9** agonizing, dangerous, defective, deficient, erroneous, frightful, hazardous, imperfect, incorrect, injurious, irascible, irritable, loathsome, miserable, nefarious, obnoxious, offensive, regretful, repugnant, repulsive, revolting, sad events, sickening, troubling, unethical, unhealthy, unnerving, unwelcome, valueless **10** calamitous, decomposed, deplorable, detestable, disastrous, disgusting, distressed, disturbing, fallacious, immorality, inadequate, indisposed, melancholy, misfortune, nauseating, not correct, perfidious, putrescent, remorseful, second-rate, unpleasant, villainous, wickedness **11** detrimental, discouraged, distasteful, distractive, distressing, ineffective, inefficient, opprobrious, regrettable, substandard, troublesome, unpalatable **12** contaminated, disagreeable, discouraging, disreputable, excruciating, questionable, unprincipled, unproductive **13** below standard, disappointing, disheartening, harmful things, nonproductive, reprehensible, short-tempered **14** disappointment **15** disadvantageous, under the weather **18** conscience-stricken

bad luck **6** mishap **7** ill wind **8** bad break **9** adversity, mischance **10** ill fortune, misfortune

badly **5** wrong **6** basely, poorly, sorely, vilely **7** acutely, greatly, ineptly, not well, wrongly **8** faultily, horribly, severely, shoddily, sinfully, sloppily, terribly, very much, wickedly **9** corruptly, extremely, immorally, intensely, unsoundly **10** carelessly, criminally, dreadfully, improperly, wretchedly **11** defectively, deficiently, desperately, erroneously, exceedingly, frightfully, imperfectly, incorrectly, nefariously, offensively, unethically **12** disreputably, inadequately, villainously **13** incompetently, in the worst way **16** unsatisfactorily

bad manners **8** rudeness **9** surliness **10** incivility **11** boorishness, discourtesy **12** impoliteness

bad mark **4** blot **7** demerit **9** poor grade

badminton
racket: **10** battledore
racket used to hit: **4** bird **7** shuttle **11** shuttlecock
Indian version: **5** poona
stroke: **4** drop **5** clear, smash **7** service **13** backhand drive, forehand drive

badmouthing **5** barbs **7** insults, slander **9** criticism, insulting **10** slandering **11** criticizing

bad taste **9** crudeness, vulgarity **10** coarseness, garishness, tawdryness

bad tasting **4** sour **5** nasty **6** bitter **7** spoiled **9** medicinal, revolting **10** disgusting **11** unpalatable

bad-tempered **5** cross, testy **6** grumpy **7** grouchy **8** choleric, churlish **9** difficult, irascible, irritable **10** ill-natured **11** acrimonious **12** disagreeable

bad times **4** bust **5** slump **9** hard times, recession **10** depression

bad turn **4** harm, hurt **5** wrong **6** injury **7** ill turn **8** disfavor **9** injustice **10** disservice **11** discourtesy

Baekleland, Leo Hendrik
field: **9** chemistry
invented: **8** Bakelite **32** artificial light photographic paper

Baer, Max (Maximillian Adalbert)
nickname: **17** Livermore Larruper
sport: **6** boxing
class: **11** heavyweight

Baeyer, Johann Friedrich Wilhelm Adolph von
field: **9** chemistry
nationality: **6** German
synthesized: **6** indigo
discovered: **13** phthalein dyes
awarded: **10** Nobel Prize

baffle **3** bar **4** daze, dull, foil, stop **5** amaze, check, stump **6** deaden, muddle, puzzle, reduce, thwart **7** astound, confuse, inhibit, mystify, nonplus, perplex **8** astonish, befuddle, bewilder, confound, dumfound, minimize, restrain, surprise **10** disconcert

baffling **7** elusive **8** puzzling **9** confusing, enigmatic **10** mysterious, mystifying, perplexing **11** confounding **16** incomprehensible

bag **3** get, sag **4** hunt, kill, sack, take, trap **5** bulge, catch, droop, pouch, purse, shoot, snare **6** bundle, entrap, obtain, packet **7** acquire, capture, collect, ensnare **8** paper bag, protrude, suitcase **10** receptacle

bagatelle **6** trifle **7** nothing, trinket **10** knickknack, light music **11** unimportant

baggage **4** bags, gear **5** grips **6** trunks **7** bundles, effects, luggage, valises **8** movables, packages **9** apparatus, equipment, suitcases, trappings **10** belongings **11** impedimenta **13** accouterments, paraphernalia

baggy **4** limp **5** loose, slack **6** droopy, flabby, puffed **7** bloated, bulbous, flaccid, paunchy, sagging, swollen **9** unpressed, unshapely **12** loose-fitting

Baghdad
capital of: **4** Iraq
founder: **8** (Caliph) al-Mansur
landmark:
minaret: **10** Suq al-Ghazi
mosque: **8** Madrasah **14** al-Mustansiriya
means: **8** God-given
river: **6** Tigris

Bagheera
character in: **14** The Jungle Books
author: **7** Kipling

bagnio **4** bath, stew **5** house **6** bordel, prison **7** brothel **8** bordello, cathouse **10** bawdy house, fancy house, whorehouse **13** sporting house **14** house of ill fame **16** house of ill repute **19** house of prostitution

Bagnold, Enid
author of: **14** National Vel-

vet, The Chalk Garden **23** The Chinese Prime Minister

Bagstock, Joe
character in: 12 Dombey and Son
author: 7 Dickens

Bahamas
capital/largest city: 6 Nassau
others: 8 Freeport **9** Rock Sound **10** George Town **11** Mastic Point **12** Spanish Wells
head of state: 14 British monarch **15** governor general
island: 3 Cat **4** Long **5** Berry, Exuma **6** Andros, Bimini, Caicos, Rum Cay **7** Crooked, Harbour, Watling **9** Eleuthera, Mayaguana **10** Great Abaco **11** Grand Bahama, Great Inagua, Great Ragged, San Salvador **13** New Providence
sea: 8 Atlantic **9** Caribbean
physical feature:
***strait:* 7** Florida
***swamp:* 8** mangrove
people: 5 black **7** Haitian
language: 6 Creole **7** English
religion: 12 Christianity
place:
***harbor:* 9** Governors
***naval base:* 9** Mayaguana
feature:
***key:* 3** cay
***native:* 5** conch

Bahrain ***see box***

bail 3 dip **4** bond, lade **5** ladle, scoop, spoon **6** surety **9** guarantee **11** post bond for

bailiff 6 deputy **8** marshall, overseer **9** assistant, constable **12** court officer

bailiwick 4 area, beat, turf **5** arena, orbit, place, realm **6** domain, sphere **7** compass **8** dominion, province **9** territory **10** department **12** neighborhood

Baird, Spencer Fullerton
field: 7 zoology
authority on: 5 birds **7** mammals
established: 30 US Commission of Fish and Fisheries

Bahrain
capital/largest city: 6 Manama
others: 5 Rifaa **7** Jidhafs **8** Muharraq
head of state/government: 4 emir
monetary unit: 4 fils **5** dinar
island: 5 Hawar, Jidda **6** Sitrah **7** Bahrain **9** Umm Nassan **10** al-Muharraq **11** An Nabi Salih
physical feature:
***gulf:* 7** Bahrain, Persian
people: 4 Arab **6** Indian **7** Persian **8** American, European **9** Pakistani
***ruling family:* 9** al-Khalifa
language: 4 Urdu **5** Farsi **6** Arabic **7** English, Persian
religion: 5 Islam

laboratory at: 11 Woods Hole MA

bait 3 vex **4** lure, ride, worm **5** annoy, bribe, harry, hound, tease, worry **6** allure, badger, come-on, harass, heckle, hector, magnet, needle **7** provoke, torment **9** put bait on, tantalize **10** allurement, antagonize, attraction, enticement, inducement, temptation

bake 3 fry **4** boil, burn, cook, sear, stew **5** grill, roast, saute, toast **6** braise, pan-fry, scorch, simmer **7** parboil, swelter

Baked Bean State
nickname of: 13 Massachusetts

Baker, Norma Jean Mortenson
real name of: 13 Marilyn Monroe

Baking
goddess of: 6 Fornax

Balaam
father: 4 Beor
brother: 4 Bela
lived at: 4 Aram **6** Pethor
commanded by: 5 Balak
killed by: 6 Israel

Balak
father: 6 Zippor
commanded: 6 Balaam

Balakiref, Mily
born: 6 Russia **13** Nijni-Novgorod
member of: 7 Kutchka, The Five
composer of: 6 Russia, Tamara, Thamar **7** Islamey **8** King Lear (overture)

balance, balances 3 pay **4** cool, mean, rest **5** poise, ratio, scale, sum up, tally, total, tot up, weigh **6** aplomb, equate, offset, parity, ponder, reckon, scales, set off, square, steady, weight **7** compare, compute, harmony, opinion, reflect, remnant, residue **8** cogitate, consider, contrast, coolness, equality, estimate, evaluate, judgment, leftover, level off, parallel, presence, symmetry **9** appraisal, calculate, composure, equipoise, juxtapose, make level, remainder, stability, stabilize **10** amount owed, comparison, counteract, deliberate, equanimity, evaluation, keep steady, neutralize, proportion, steadiness **11** equilibrium **12** counterpoise, equalization, middle ground **13** compensate for, consideration, judiciousness **14** amount credited, self-possession, unflappability **15** level-headedness **16** imperturbability
constellation of: 5 Libra

balanced 4 fair, just **9** equitable, impartial **12** unprejudiced **13** disinterested

balance out 6 cancel, offset **9** make up for **10** neutralize **13** compensate for **14** counterbalance

Balanchine, George
choreographer of: 4 Agon **6** Jewels **8** Episodes, Ivesiana, Serenade **15** Concerto Barocco **16** Allegro Brillante

balcony 4 deck **5** boxes, foyer, loges **6** loggia **7** portico, terrace, veranda **9** mezzanine

bald 4 bare, flat, open **5** blunt, naked, plain, stark, utter **6** barren, simple, smooth **7** denuded, obvious **8** flagrant, glabrous, hairless, outright, treeless **9** depilated, out-and-out, unadorned **11** categorical, undisguised, unqualified, unvarnished **12** without cover **13** unembellished, unequivocable **15** straightforward

Balder
also: 5 Baldr **6** Baldur
origin: 6 Nordic
god of: 6 beauty **8** radiance
father: 4 Odin **5** Othin
mother: 3 Fri **5** Frigg, Frija **6** Frigga
twin brother: 5 Hoder, Hodur
killed by: 5 Hoder, Hodur

balderdash 3 rot **4** bosh, bull,

bunk **5** crock, trash **6** bunkum, drivel, hot air **7** twaddle **8** buncombe, claptrap, flummery, nonsense, tommyrot **9** gibberish, poppycock **10** double-talk, tomfoolery **11** obfuscation **16** stuff and nonsense

baldheaded **8** hairless **9** baldpated, depilated **10** skinheaded **11** chrome-domed

Baldr
see: **6** Balder

Baldung Grien, Hans
born: **6** Alsace **10** Weyersheim
artwork: **9** Todentanz **17** Death and the Maiden **19** Death Kissing a Maiden **21** The Bewitched Stable Boy **24** Rest on the Flight into Egypt

Baldur
see: **6** Balder

Baldwin, James
author of: **13** Giovanni's Room, The Amen Corner **14** Another Country **15** Just Above My Head, The Fire Next Time **17** Going to Meet the Man, Nobody Knows My Name, No Name in the Street **21** Blues for Mister Charlie, Go Tell It on the Mountain

bale **4** case, load, pack **6** bundle, packet, parcel **7** package **11** bound bundle

balefire **6** beacon **9** watchfire **10** signal fire

baleful **3** icy **4** cold, dire, evil **6** deadly, malign **7** baneful, furious, harmful, hurtful, ominous **8** sinister, spiteful, venomous **9** malicious, malignant **10** malevolent **11** coldhearted, threatening

Balfe, Michael William
born: **6** Dublin **7** Ireland
composer of: **15** The Bohemian Girl, The Maid of Artois **17** I rivali di se stessi **18** The Siege of Rochelle

Balfour, David
character in: **9** Kidnapped
author: **9** Stevenson

Bali
province of: **9** Indonesia
capital: **8** Denpasar
city: **10** Singaraja
island: **11** Lesser Sunda
highest peak: **6** Agoeng
climate: **3** dry **7** monsoon
tree: **8** waringin
animal: **4** deer **5** tiger
people: **7** Malayan
religion: **8** Hinduism
agriculture: **3** pig **4** corn, rice **6** cattle, coffee **7** tobacco

Balius
horse of: **8** Achilles
gift: **11** immortality

balk **3** bar **4** foil, shun **5** block, check, demur, evade, shirk, spike, stall **6** baffle, defeat, derail, eschew, hinder, impede, recoil, refuse, resist, stymie, thwart **7** inhibit, prevent **8** draw back, hang back, hesitate, obstruct **9** forestall, frustrate **10** shrink from

Balkan **16** Forested mountain
agriculture: **5** grain **6** cotton, grapes, olives **7** tobacco
ancient people: **4** Slav **5** Greek, Roman **8** Illyrian, Thracian
language: **9** Slovenian **10** Macedonian **14** Serbo-Croatian
mountain: **6** Balkan, Massif **7** Rhodope **10** Carpathian **11** Dinaric Alps **13** Transylvanian
religion: **5** Islam **8** Orthodox **13** Roman Catholic
river: **6** Danube, Morava, Vardar
sea boundary: **5** Black **6** Aegean, Ionian **8** Adriatic **13** Mediterranean
state: **6** Greece, Turkey **7** Albania, Romania **8** Bulgaria **10** Yugoslavia

balky **6** mulish, ornery, unruly **7** restive, wayward, willful **8** contrary, perverse, stubborn **9** fractious, obstinate, pigheaded **10** rebellious, refractory **11** disobedient, intractable **12** recalcitrant, unmanageable

ball **3** hop, orb **4** prom, shot **5** dance, globe **6** pellet, soiree, sphere **7** bullets, globule **8** spheroid **9** cotillion, promenade **11** projectiles

Ball, Lucille
husband: **9** Desi Arnaz
children: **4** Desi **5** Lucie
born: **11** Jamestown NY
roles: **9** Here's Lucy, I Love Lucy **11** The Lucy Show

Balla, Giacomo
born: **5** Italy, Turin
artwork: **8** The Sewer **11** The Mad Woman **18** Speeding Automobile **20** Rhythm of the Violinist **22** Dynamism of a Dog on a Leash **26** The Street Light—Study of Light **29** Mercury Passing in Front of the Sun **40** Swifts Paths of Movement and Dynamic Sequences

ballad **3** lay **4** song **5** carol, ditty **6** chanty **8** folk song **12** rhyming story **13** narrative poem **14** narrative verse

Ballad of Reading Gaol, The
author: **10** Oscar Wilde

Ballads and Poems
author: **19** Stephen Vincent Benet

ballast **6** weight **7** balance, control **9** equipoise **10** ballasting, dead weight, makeweight, stabilizer **12** counterpoise **13** counterweight **14** counterbalance **19** stabilizing material

Ballesteros, Severiano
nickname: **4** Seve
sport: **4** golf
nationality: **7** Spanish

ballet *see box, p. 82*

Ball of Fat
author: **15** Guy de Maupassant

balloon **4** grow **5** belly, bloat **6** billow, blow up, dilate, expand **7** distend, enlarge, fill out, inflate, puff out **8** increase, swell out

ballot **4** poll, vote **5** slate **6** ticket, voting **7** polling **13** round of voting **16** list of candidates

ballyhoo **4** hype, puff, push, tout **6** herald, hoopla **7** buildup, promote, puffery, trumpet **8** proclaim **9** advertise, promotion, publicity, publicize **10** hullabaloo, propaganda **11** advertising **15** public relations

balm **5** cream, salve **6** balsam, lotion, solace **7** anodyne, comfort, unguent **8** curative, narcotic, ointment, sedative **9** comforter, emollient **10** palliative **11** restorative **12** tranquilizer

balmy **3** odd **4** calm, fair, mild, soft, warm **5** bland, kooky, weird **6** easing, gentle **7** calming, clement, summery **8** aromatic, fragrant, perfumed, pleasant, redolent, soothing **9** agreeable, ambrosial, eccentric, temperate **10** refreshing, salubrious

Balnibari
fictional land in: **16** Gulliver's Travels
author: **5** Swift

baloney **3** rot **4** bull, bunk **5** hokum, hooey, stuff **6** bunkum, hot air, humbug **7** hogwash, sausage, spinach **8** claptrap, nonsense, tommyrot **9** poppycock **10** applesauce **11** foolishness

ballet **4** Agon **5** Manon, Rodeo **6** Apollo, Parade **7** Giselle, Orpheus **8** Coppelia, Episodes, Ivesiana, Les Noces, Serenade, Swan Lake, The Doves **9** Anastasia, Fancy Free, Interplay, Petrushka, The Jewels **10** La Sylphide, Petrouchka **11** Billy the Kid, Lilac Garden, Soccer Dance, Symphony in C, The Firebird **12** Pillar of Fire, Sailor's Dance, Spring Waters, The Partisans **13** The Nutcracker **14** Romeo and Juliet **15** Concerto Barocco, Fall River Legend, The Rite of Spring **16** Allegro Brillante, La Fille Mal Gardee, Specter of the Rose **17** The Sleeping Beauty **18** Raymonda Variations **19** The Afternoon of a Faun, The Four Temperaments **24** Stravinsky Violin Concerto
- **ballet company:** **5** Kirov, Royal **7** Bolshoi, Joffrey **9** Marinsky, Maryinsky **11** New York City **13** Ballets Russes **20** Dance Theater of Harlem **21** American Ballet Theater **22** National Ballet of Canada
- **choreographer:** **9** Hanya Holm, Lev Ivanov **10** John Weaver **11** Jules Perrot **12** Agnes de Mille, Igor Moiseyev, Marius Petipa, Michel Fokine **13** Jean Dauberval, Jerome Robbins, Leonid Massine **15** Arthur Saint-Leon **16** George Balanchine, Kenneth MacMillan **18** August Bournonville, Bronislava Nijinska, Jean Georges Noverre, Sir Frederick Ashton
- **chorus:** **8** ensemble **13** corps de ballet
- **dancer:** **9** Karen Kain **10** Anton Dolin, Marie Lieta, Serge Lifar **11** Allegra Kent, Anna Pavlova, Anthony Blum, Lucile Grahn, Lynn Seymour, Nadia Nerina **12** Fanny Cerrito, Marie Camargo, Peter Martins **13** Alicia Markova, Andre Eglevsky, Anthony Dowell, Carlotta Grisi, Frank Augustyn, Galina Ulanova, Margot Fonteyn, Marie Taglioni, Melissa Hayden, Patricia Neary, Rudolf Nureyev **14** Arthur Mitchell, Cynthia Gregory, Edward Villella, Gelsey Kirkland, Leonide Massine, Maria Tallchief, Suzanne Farrell, Vaslav Nijinsky **15** Jacques D'Amboise, Martine Van Hamel, Maya Plisetskaya, Natalia Makarova, Patricia McBride, Tamara Karsavina **16** Antoinette Sibley, Olga Spessivtseva **17** Alexandra Danilova, Marina Kondratieva **18** Mikhail Baryshnikov
- **fast movement:** **7** allegro
- **first ballet:** **22** Ballet Comique de la Reine
- **impresario:** **12** Marie Rambert **15** Ninette de Valois, Sergei Diaghilev
- **kick:** **9** battement
- **modern dancer/choreographer:** **8** Ted Shawn **9** Eliot Feld **10** Mary Wigman, Paul Draper, Twyla Tharp **11** Anna Sokolow, Antony Tudor, Eric Hawkins, Ruth St Denis **12** Martha Graham **13** Alwin Nikolais, Doris Humphrey, Isadora Duncan **14** Charles Weidman **15** Merce Cunningham
- **position/step:** **4** jete, plie, tour **5** saute **6** releve **7** en avant, fouette, on point, pas seul, turnout **8** batterie, cabriole, en dedans, en dehors, glissade **9** arabesque, developpe, en arriere, entrechat, pas de chat, pas-de-deux, pirouette **10** demi-pointe, port de bras, tour en l'air **11** rond de jambe, terre-a-terre **12** pas de bourree, saut de basque **17** changement de pieds
- **principal female dancer:** **9** ballerina **14** prima ballerina
- **principal male dancer:** **12** danseur noble
- **skirt:** **4** tutu
- **slow movement:** **6** adagio
- **term:** **4** coda **5** barre **6** ballon **14** divertissement

Baloo
- **character in:** **14** The Jungle Books
- **author:** **7** Kipling

balsam **3** fir **4** balm **5** cream, salve **7** unguent **8** ointment **9** Impatiens
- **varieties:** **2** He **3** Fir, She **4** Rose, Wild **6** Garden **8** Zanzibar

Balsam, Martin
- **born:** **9** New York NY
- **roles:** **6** Psycho **7** Catch-22 **15** A Thousand Clowns, On the Waterfront

Baltic
- **language family:** **12** Indo-European
- **group:** **11** Balto-Slavic
- **subgroup:** **7** Latvian **10** Lithuanian

Baltimore
- **baseball team:** **7** Orioles
- **football team:** **5** Stars

Baltimore, David
- **field:** **12** microbiology
- **studied:** **11** animal cells **13** viral genetics
- **awarded:** **10** Nobel Prize

Balto-Slavic
- **language family:** **12** Indo-European
- **branch:** **6** Baltic, Slavic

baluster **4** post, rail **6** column, pillar **7** support, upright **8** pilaster

balustrade **7** railing **8** baluster, banister, handrail

Balzac, Honore de
- **author of:** **7** Gobseck **10** La Vendetta **11** Cousin(e) Bette **12** Father Goriot, Le Cousin Pons, Le Pere Goriot **13** Lost Illusions **14** Eugenie Grandet, The Human Comedy **15** The Wild Ass's Skin **16** La Comedie Humaine **23** The Physiology of Marriage

Bamako
- **capital of:** **4** Mali

Bambi
- **author:** **11** Felix Salten
- **character:** **6** Faline, Flower **7** Thumper

bamboo **4** Sasa **7** Bambusa **9** Shibataea **10** Pseudosasa **11** Arundinaria **13** Phyllostachys **14** Chimonobambusa **15** Semiarundinaria
- **varieties:** **4** Moso **5** Arrow, Black, Dwarf, Giant, Hardy, Hedge, Henon, Meyer, Pygmy, Simon, Stake **6** Buddha, Common, Forage, Oldham, Sacred, Sickle, Square, Tonkin **7** Allgold, Beechey, Mexican **8** Calcutta, Feathery, Heavenly, Narihira **9** Canebrake, Castillon **10** Red-berried, Square-stem **11** Punting-pole **12** Alphonse Karr, Yellow-groove **13** Dwarf fern-leaf, Fern-leaf hedge, Oriental hedge **14** Chinese-goddess **16** Dwarf white-stripe **17** Silver-stripe hedge **18** Stripe-stem fern-leaf

bamboozle **3** con, gyp **4** coax, dupe, fool, gull, hoax, lure, rook, take **5** cheat, cozen, trick **6** delude **7** beguile, deceive, defraud, mislead, swindle **8** hoodwink **9** victimize

ban 3 bar **5** debar, taboo **6** banish, enjoin, forbid **7** barring, embargo, exclude **8** disallow, prohibit, stoppage, suppress **9** exclusion, interdict, proscribe, restraint **10** banishment, censorship **11** forbiddance, prohibition, restriction **12** interdiction, proscription

banal 4 dull **5** corny, stale, stock, tired, trite, vapid **6** jejune **7** humdrum, insipid, prosaic **8** bromidic, everyday, ordinary, shopworn **9** hackneyed **10** pedestrian, threadbare, unexciting, unoriginal **11** commonplace, stereotyped **12** cliche-ridden, conventional **13** platitudinous, unimaginative, uninteresting

banality 6 cliche **7** bromide **9** platitude, staleness, triteness **10** insipidity

banana 4 Musa
varieties: 3 Fe'i **4** Fehi, Koae **5** Dwarf **6** Edible **7** Chinese **9** Flowering **10** Abyssinian, Ladyfinger **12** Canary Island, Chinese dwarf
similar to: 8 plantain

Bananas
director: 10 Woody Allen
cast: 10 Woody Allen **12** Howard Cosell, Louise Lasser **15** Carlos Montalban

Bancroft, Anne
real name: 23 Anna Maria Louise Italiano
husband: 9 Mel Brooks
born: 7 Bronx NY
roles: 11 Mrs Robinson, The Graduate **15** The Pumpkin Eater, The Turning Point, Two for the Seesaw **16** The Miracle Worker (Oscar)

band 3 set **4** belt, body, club, crew, gang, hoop, join, pack, ring, sash **5** bunch, crowd, group, junta, party, strap, strip, swath, thong, troop, unite **6** caucus, circle, clique, collar, fillet, gather, girdle, league, ribbon, streak, stripe, throng **7** bandeau, binding, circlet, company, society **8** assembly, cincture, ensemble **9** multitude, orchestra, surcingle **10** fellowship, sisterhood **11** association, brotherhood, confederacy, consolidate **13** confederation

bandage 4 bind **5** dress **7** binding, plaster **8** compress, dressing

bandanna, bandana 5 scarf **8** kerchief **10** silk square **11** neckerchief **12** handkerchief

Bandar Seri Begawan
capital of: 6 Brunei

bandeau 3 bra **4** band **6** fillet **7** binding, circlet **9** brassiere

bandit 4 thug **5** crook, thief **6** badman, outlaw, robber **7** brigand, burglar, footpad, ladrone **8** blackleg **9** desperado, road agent **10** highwayman

bandleader 6 master **7** maestro **8** director **9** conductor
famous: 11 Glenn Miller, Tommy Dorsey **12** Lawrence Welk

Band of Merry Men
followers of: 9 Robin Hood

band together 5 unify, unite **6** league **7** combine **10** join forces **11** consolidate

bandy 4 swap **5** trade **6** barter **7** shuffle **8** exchange **9** toss about **11** interchange **16** toss back and forth

bandying 4 swap **5** trade **8** exchange **9** tit for tat **10** quid pro quo **11** give and take

bane 3 woe **4** ruin **5** curse, toxin, venom **6** blight, burden, canker, plague, poison **7** scourge, torment, tragedy **8** calamity, disaster, downfall, nuisance **9** destroyer, detriment, ruination **10** affliction **13** pain in the neck **14** thorn in the side **16** fly in the ointment

baneful 4 evil **6** deadly, malign, woeful **7** harmful, noxious **8** venomous **9** injurious, malignant, poisonous **10** malevolent **11** destructive

bang 3 box, hit, pop, rap, tap **4** beat, blow, boom, clap, cuff, kick, lick, slam, slap, sock **5** burst, clout, crash, knock, smack, thump, whack **6** buffet, charge, report, thrill, thwack, wallop **7** delight **8** good time, headlong, pleasure, suddenly **9** enjoyment, explosion **10** crashingly, excitement

Bangkok, Bankok
also: 9 Krung Thep
capital of: 8 Thailand
landmark: 5 Wat Po **11** Grand Palace **16** Wat Emerald Buddha
means: 12 City of Angels
nickname: 15 Venice of the East
port: 8 Klongtoi
river: 10 Chao Phraya

Bangladesh
other name: 10 East Bengal **12** East Pakistan
capital/largest city: 5 Dacca
others: 6 Khulna, Sylhet **7** Comilla, Jessore, Rangpur, Saidpur **8** Jamalpur, Rajshahi **9** Madaripur **10** Chittagong **11** Narayanganj **12** Brahmanbaria
monetary unit: 4 taka **5** paisa
island: 10 Sundarbans
mountain: 15 Chittagong Hills
highest point: 10 Keokradong
river: 5 Padna **6** Ganges, Meghna **10** Burhi Ganga, Karnaphuli **11** Brahmaputra
physical feature:
***bay:* 6** Bengal
people: 7 Bengali
***guerrillas:* 11** muktibahini
***leader:* 6** Ershad **11** Ziaur Rahman **19** Sheikh Mujibur Rahman
language: 6 Bihari **7** Bengali, English
religion: 5 Hindu, Islam
feature:
***clothing:* 4** sari **5** lungi

bangle 3 fob **5** chain, charm **6** armlet, bauble, gewgaw, tinsel **7** bibelot, fribble, trinket **8** bracelet, gimcrack, ornament, wristlet **10** knickknack **11** junk jewelry **14** costume jewelry

Bangui
capital of: 22 Central African Republic

banish 3 ban, bar **4** drop, oust **5** eject, erase, evict, exile, expel **6** deport, dispel, outlaw, reject, remove **7** cast out, discard, dismiss, exclude, put away, shut out, turn out **8** cast away, dislodge, drive out, get rid of, send away, shake off **9** discharge, eliminate, eradicate, extradite **13** excommunicate **14** send to Coventry

banished person 5 exile **6** emigre, pariah **7** outcast **8** deportee, expellee **10** expatriate **14** deported person **15** displaced person

banishment 3 ban **5** exile **6** ouster **7** removal **8** eviction

9 dismissal, exclusion, expulsion **11** deportation **12** expatriation **14** transportation **15** excommunication

Banjo Eyes
nickname of: **11** Eddie Cantor

Banjul, Bathurst
capital of: **9** The Gambia

bank **3** bar, row, tip **4** dike, dune, edge, file, flat, fund, heap, hill, keep, line, mass, pile, rank, reef, rise, save, side, tier, tilt **5** amass, array, brink, chain, knoll, mound, ridge, shelf, shoal, shore, slant, slope, stack, store, train **6** barrow, line up, margin, pile up, series, strand, string, supply **7** deposit, parapet, reserve, savings, shallow, terrace **8** keyboard, sandbank **9** exchequer, reservoir, stockpile **10** depository, embankment, repository, storehouse, succession **12** accumulation, trust company **14** savings and loan

Bank Dick, The
director: **10** Eddie Cline
cast: **8** W C Fields **9** Una Merkel **15** Cora Witherspoon

Bankhead, Tallulah
father: **16** William B Bankhead
born: **12** Huntsville AL
roles: **8** Lifeboat **14** The Little Foxes **17** The Skin of Our Teeth

banknote **4** bill **9** greenback **11** certificate, legal tender **12** currency note, treasury note **17** silver certificate

bank of pity
French: **11** mont-de-piete
literal name for: **10** pawnbroker

bankrupt **5** broke **6** busted, failed, ruined **8** depleted, indigent, in the red, wiped out **9** destitute, exhausted, insolvent, penniless **12** impoverished, without funds

Bankruptcy, A
author: **20** Bjornstjerne Bjornson

Banks, Ernie
nickname: **5** Mr Cub
sport: **8** baseball
noted for: **7** hitting
team: **11** Chicago Cubs

banner **4** flag **6** burgee, colors, ensign, record **7** leading, notable, pendant, pennant, winning **8** standard, streamer **9** red-letter **10** profitable **11** outstanding **14** most successful

Bannock
language family: **10** Shoshonean
location: **5** Idaho

banquet **4** dine **5** feast, revel **6** dinner, repast **9** symposium

Banquo
character in: **7** Macbeth
author: **11** Shakespeare

bantam **3** hen, wee **4** cock, fowl, tiny **5** dwarf, pygmy, runt, small, teeny, weeny **6** little, midget, minute, petite **7** chicken, dwarfed, rooster, stunted **9** miniature **10** diminutive, pocket-size, teeny-weeny **11** Lilliputian, pocket-sized

banter **3** kid, rib **4** dish, josh, mock, ride, twit **5** chaff, jolly, taunt, tease **6** joking, needle **7** jesting, joshing, kidding, ragging, ribbing, teasing, waggery **8** badinage, chaffing, raillery, repartee, word play

Banting, Frederick Grant
field: **8** medicine
nationality: **8** Canadian
extracted: **7** insulin
awarded: **10** Nobel Prize

Bantu
means: **9** the people
dwelling: **6** Africa
tribe: **5** Xosas, Zulus **6** Swazis **7** Basutos, Kalanga

baptism **9** beginning, immersion, sacrament **10** initiation, sprinkling **11** christening **12** introduction, purification **13** rite of passage **16** spiritual rebirth

baptize **3** dub **4** name **8** christen

bar **3** ban, pub, rib, rod **4** band, bank, beam, belt, bolt, cake, curb, flat, line, lock, oust, pale, pole, rail, reef, snag, spar, spit, stay, stop **5** block, catch, check, court, debar, eject, evict, exile, expel, forum, ingot, jimmy, lever, limit, shelf, shoal, slice, sprit, stake, stick, strip, taboo **6** banish, enjoin, fasten, forbid, impede, lounge, paling, ribbon, saloon, secure, streak, stripe, stroke, tavern **7** barrier, block up, canteen, cast out, close up, crowbar, exclude, grating, lock out, measure, prevent, sandbar, shallow, shut out, taproom **8** alehouse, crossbar, disallow, judgment, obstacle, obstruct, preclude, prohibit, restrain, restrict, tribunal **9** barricade, blackball, blacklist, hindrance, long table, lunchroom, restraint, speakeasy **10** constraint, crosspiece, impediment, injunction, limitation **11** obstruction, public house, restriction **14** cocktail lounge, serving counter, stumbling block **15** legal profession

Bara, Theda
real name: **16** Theodosia Goodman
nickname: **7** The Vamp
born: **12** Cincinnati OH
roles: **6** Carmen, Salome **7** Camille **8** The Vixen **9** Cleopatra **13** A Fool There Was, Madame Du Barry

Barabbas **6** robber **8** murderer

Barak
father: **7** Abinoam
summoned by: **7** Deborah
defeated: **6** Sisera

barb **3** cut, dig, nib **4** cusp, jibe, snag, spur, tine **5** point, prong, spike **6** insult **7** affront, barbule, bristle, prickle, putdown, sarcasm, spicule **9** complaint, criticism **11** badmouthing

Barbados ***see box***

barbarian **4** boor, hood, lout, punk **5** alien, bully, crude, rowdy, tough, yahoo **6** savage, vandal **7** boorish, hoodlum, lowbrow, peasant, ruffian, uncouth **8** hooligan **9** ignoramus, outlander, roughneck, vulgarian **10** delinquent, illiterate, philistine, provincial, troglodyte, uncultured **11** know-nothing **12** uncultivated **15** unsophisticated **16** anti-intellectual

barbaric **4** rude, wild **5** crude **6** coarse, savage, vulgar **7** boorish, uncouth, untamed **9** barbarian, barbarous **10** unpolished **11** ill-mannered, uncivilized

barbarism **7** cruelty **8** savagery **9** brutality **10** inhumanity **11** viciousness

barbarity **7** cruelty **9** brutality **10** savageness **12** ruthlessness

barbarous **4** mean **5** crass, crude, cruel, harsh, rough **6** brutal, coarse, vulgar **7** inhuman, vicious **8** barbaric, impolite **10** outrageous

barber **3** cut **4** trim **5** dress, shave, style **7** arrange, stylist, tonsure **10** haircutter **11** hairdresser

Barber, Samuel
born: **13** West Chester PA
composer of: **7** Vanessa **10** Dover Beach **16** Adagio for Strings **17** Capricorn

Barbados
capital/largest city: **10** Bridgetown
others: **7** Oistins **8** Boscabel, Crab Hill, Hastings, Holetown, Portland, Worthing **9** Bathsheba **10** Martin's Bay **11** Belleplaine **12** Speightstown
school: **10** Codrington
head of state: **14** British monarch **15** governor general
mountain: **6** Chalky
highest point: **7** Hillaby
river: **12** Constitution
sea: **8** Atlantic **9** Caribbean
physical feature:
bay: **4** Foul, Long **8** Carlisle
beach: **5** Crane
gully: **12** Welchman Hall
hill: **10** Cherry Tree
point: **5** North, South **6** Ragged **8** Harrison, Kitridge
people: **5** Bajan **9** Barbadian
leader: **5** Adams
language: **7** English
religion: **8** Anglican
place:
airport: **7** Seawell
castle: **8** Sam Lords
church: **7** St Johns
feature:
sea crab: **7** shagger

Concerto **19** Anthony and Cleopatra, The School for Scandal

Barber of Seville, The
author: **12** Beaumarchais
opera by: **7** Rossini
character: **6** Bazile, Figaro, Rosine, Rosina **8** Almaviva, Bartholo **9** Dr Bartolo **13** Count Almaviva

barbette **5** mound **7** bastion, rampart **8** platform **9** earthwork **10** breastwork

barbiturate **8** euphoria, hypnotic, sedative **10** depressive **13** anesthesiatic **14** barbituric acid
kind: **7** seconal **10** thiopental **11** amobarbital **12** secobarbital **13** phenobarbital

barbule **4** barb **11** feather part

Barchester Towers
author: **15** Anthony Trollope
sequel to: **9** The Warden
character: **7** Mr Slope, Mrs Bold **8** Mr Arabin **9** Dr Proudie, Mr Harding **10** Mrs Proudie **11** Mr Quiverful **13** Canon Stanhope **17** Archdeacon Grantly **18** Signora Vesey-Neroni

bard **4** poet **6** rhymer, writer **8** epic poet, minstrel, poetizer **9** poetaster, rhymester, troubador, versifier **10** poet-singer **13** narrative poet

Bardell, Mrs
character in: **14** Pickwick Papers
author: **7** Dickens

Bardot, Brigitte
husband: **10** Roger Vadim
born: **5** Paris **6** France
roles: **18** And God Created Woman

bare **4** bald, mere, nude, open, show, thin, void, worn **5** basic, blank, empty, naked, offer, plain, scant, stark, strip **6** denude, divest, expose, meager, peeled, reveal, simple, unclad, unmask, unveil, vacant **7** austere, exposed, hapless, uncover, undrape, undress, unrobed **8** disrobed, in the raw, marginal, stripped **9** endurable, essential, unadorned, unclothed, uncolored, uncovered, undressed, unsheathe **10** elementary, just enough, threadbare **11** fundamental, supportable, undecorated, undisguised, unvarnished **12** unelaborated, unornamented **13** unembellished **15** straightforward

barefaced **4** bald, bold, flip **5** brash, fresh, sassy **6** brazen, cheeky, snotty **7** forward **8** flippant, impudent, insolent, palpable **9** shameless, unabashed **11** transparent

barefoot **6** unshod **8** shoeless **9** discalced **10** unsandaled **11** discalceate

Barefoot Boy
author: **21** John Greenleaf Whittier

Barefoot in the Park
director: **8** Gene Saks
based on play by: **9** Neil Simon
cast: **9** Jane Fonda **12** Charles Boyer **13** Robert Redford

barely **4** just **6** almost, hardly **7** faintly, scantly **8** meagerly, only just, scarcely, slightly **9** almost not, just about, sparingly **10** no more than **20** by the skin of one's teeth

bareness **6** nudity **9** bleakness, emptiness, nakedness **10** barrenness

Baresark
origin: **12** Scandinavian
form: **7** warrior
trait: **7** courage

Baretta
character: **7** Rooster **11** Billy Truman, (Det) Tony Baretta, (Lt) Hal Brubaker
cast: **8** Tom Ewell **11** Robert Blake **12** Edward Grover **15** Michael D Roberts
Tony's pet: **8** cockatoo
named: **4** Fred

barfly **3** sot **4** lush, soak **5** drunk, rummy, souse, toper **7** tippler **8** drunkard **9** alcoholic **11** dipsomaniac

bargain **4** deal, pact **5** steal **6** accord, barter, dicker, haggle, higgle, pledge, treaty **7** compact, entente, good buy, promise **8** contract, covenant, good deal **9** agreement, negotiate **10** settlement **11** arrangement, transaction **13** understanding
French: **9** bon marche

bargain for **6** expect **7** foresee **8** envision, reckon on **11** contemplate

barge **4** bust, scow, ship **6** launch, vessel **7** freight, intrude

barium
chemical symbol: **2** Ba

bark **3** bay, cry, rub, yap, yip **4** flay, hide, howl, hull, husk, peel, rind, roar, skin, woof, yell, yelp **5** crust, scale, shout, strip **6** abrade, arf-arf, bellow, bow-wow, casing, cry out, holler, scrape **7** howling **8** covering, periderm **9** sheathing

Barker, Lex
real name: **25** Alexander Crichlow Barker Jr
wife: **10** Arlene Dahl, Lana Turner
born: **5** Rye NY
roles: **6** Tarzan **11** La Dolce Vita

Barkis
character in: **16** David Copperfield
author: **7** Dickens

Barkley, Catherine
character in: **15** A Farewell to Arms
author: **9** Hemingway

Barlach, Ernst
born: **5** Wedel **7** Germany **8** Holstein
artwork: **9** Expellees **10** Seated Girl, Singing Man **11** Man in a Stock **13** Mater Dolorosa **14** Crippled Beggar, The Hovering

One **16** Man Drawing a Sword **25** The Community of the Holy Ones

barn 4 mews **6** corral, stable

Barnabas
companion: 4 Paul

Barnaby Jones
character: 7 J R (Jedediah Romano) Jones **8** Lt Biddle **10** Betty Jones
cast: 9 Mark Shera **10** Buddy Ebsen, John Carter **13** Lee Meriwether

Barnaby Rudge
author: 14 Charles Dickens
character: 8 Mrs Rudge **9** Miss Miggs **10** John Willet **11** Dolly Varden **12** Emma Haredale **13** Edward Chester, Gabriel Varden **14** Reuben Haredale, Simon Tappertit, Sir John Chester **16** Dennis the Hangman, Geoffrey Haredale
subject: 11 Gordon riots

Barnard, Christiaan
field: 7 surgery **8** medicine
nationality: 12 South African
performed first: 15 heart transplant

Barnard, Edward Emerson
field: 9 astronomy
named for him: 12 red dwarf star

Barnes, Jake
character in: 15 The Sun Also Rises
author: 9 Hemingway

Barney Google
creator: 11 Billy DeBeck
character: 11 Snuffy Smith
***baby:* 5** Bunky
***horse:* 9** Spark Plug

Barney Miller
character: 8 (Det) Phil Fish **9** (Det) Ron Harris **10** (Det Wojo) Wojohowicz, (Det) Nick Yamana, (Officer) Carl Levitt **14** Inspector Luger, (Det) Arthur Dietrich
cast: 7 Jack Soo **8** Ron Carey, Ron Glass **9** Abe Vigoda, Hal Linden **11** Maxwell Gail **12** James Gregory **15** Steve Landesberg

Barnstock *see* **9** Branstock

Baroja y Nessi, Pio
author of: 15 Caesar or Nothing **23** The Struggle for Existence **26** Memorias de un Hombre de Accion

barometer
invented by: 10 Torricelli

baroque 6 florid, ornate **10** flamboyant **11** extravagant

Barrack-Room Ballads
author: 14 Rudyard Kipling

barracks 3 BOQ **4** base, camp **7** lodging **8** garrison

barrage 5 blast, burst, salvo, spray **6** ack-ack, deluge, shower, stream, volley **7** battery, torrent **8** shelling **9** cannonade, fusillade **10** outpouring **11** bombardment

barrel 3 keg, tub, tun, vat **4** butt, cask, drum, tube **8** hogshead
abbreviation: 3 bar, bbl

barren 3 dry **4** arid, dull **5** stale, waste **6** farrow, futile **7** austere, prosaic, sterile, useless **8** depleted, desolate, infecund **9** fruitless, infertile **10** lackluster, unfruitful **11** ineffectual, uninspiring, unrewarding **12** unproductive **13** uninformative, uninstructive, uninteresting

barrenness 8 bareness **9** bleakness, emptiness **10** desolation

barren wilderness 6 desert **9** wasteland

barricade 5 block, fence **7** barrier, bulwark, rampart **8** blockade, obstacle, obstruct **10** impediment **11** obstruction

Barrie, Sir James M
author of: 7 The Will **8** Mary Rose, Peter Pan **10** Dear Brutus **13** Quality Street **15** Margaret Ogilvie, The Wedding Guest **17** Alice Sit-By-the-Fire, The Little Minister **18** A Kiss for Cinderella, The Twelve-Pound Look **19** What Every Woman Knows **20** Shall We Join the Ladies?, The Admirable Crichton
character: 8 Peter Pan **10** Tinkerbell **11** Captain Hook
***Darling children:* 4** John **5** Wendy **7** Michael
***nurse/Newfoundland dog:* 4** Nana
***setting:* 14** Never-Never Land

barrier 3 bar **4** moat, wall **5** ditch, fence, hedge **6** hurdle, trench **7** rampart **8** blockade, handicap, obstacle **9** barricade, hindrance **10** difficulty, impediment, limitation **11** obstruction, restriction **13** fortification **14** stumbling block

Barrier, The
author: 8 Rex Beach

barring 3 but **4** save **6** except, saving **7** besides **9** excepting, excluding, other than **11** exclusive of

barrister 6 lawyer **7** counsel **8** advocate, attorney **9** counselor **10** mouthpiece **13** attorney-at-law

barroom 3 bar, pub, **6** bistro, lounge, saloon, tavern **7** taproom

barrow 4 heap, pile **5** mound **7** tumulus **8** handcart, pushcart **11** wheelbarrow

Barrow, Joe Louis
real name of: 8 Joe Louis

Barry, Gene
real name: 11 Eugene Klass
born: 9 New York NY
roles: 9 Burke's Law **11** Thunder Road **12** Bat Masterson **16** The Name of the Game **17** The War of the Worlds

Barry, John
served in: 16 Revolutionary War
commander of ship: 7 Raleigh **8** Alliance **9** Effingham, Lexington
ship captured: 6 Edward

Barry, Redmond
character in: 11 Barry Lyndon
author: 9 Thackeray

Barry, Sir Charles
architect of: 8 Cliveden **14** City Art Gallery (Manchester) **18** Houses of Parliament (London)

Barry Lyndon
author: 25 William Makepeace Thackeray
character: 12 Redmond Barry **14** Lord Bullingdon **17** Lady Honoria Lyndon (Countess of Lyndon) **19** Chevalier de Balibari
director: 14 Stanley Kubrick
cast: 9 Ryan O'Neal **11** Hardy Kruger **12** Patrick Magee **14** Marisa Berenson

Barrymore, Ethel
real name: 14 Ethel Mae Blythe
brother: 4 John **6** Lionel
born: 14 Philadelphia PA
roles: 11 A Doll's House **14** The Corn Is Green **16** Portrait of Jennie **19** Trelawney of the Wells **21** None But the Lonely Heart, Rasputin and the Empress

Barrymore, John
real name: 10 John Blythe
brother: 6 Lionel
sister: 5 Ethel
son: 17 John Drew Barrymore
daughter: 14 Diana Barrymore
nickname: 12 Great Profile

born: **14** Philadelphia PA
roles: **6** Hamlet **7** Don Juan **8** Moby Dick, Svengali **9** Richard IV **10** Grand Hotel **11** Beau Brummel **13** Dinner at Eight **17** Dr Jekyll and Mr Hyde **21** Rasputin and the Empress

Barrymore, Lionel
real name: **12** Lionel Blythe
brother: **4** John
sister: **5** Ethel
born: **14** Philadelphia PA
roles: **7** The Jest **9** A Free Soul (Oscar), Dr Kildare **11** Dr Gillespie **13** Peter Ibbitson, The Copperhead **21** Rasputin and the Empress

Barsabbas *see* **6** Joseph

Barstad, John
character in: **16** A Tale of Two Cities
author: **7** Dickens

Bart, Lily
character in: **15** The House of Mirth
author: **7** Wharton

barter **4** swap **5** trade **8** exchange **11** interchange

Bartered Bride, The
opera by: **7** Smetana
character: **5** Jenik, Kecal, Micha, Vasek **7** Marenka

Barth, John
author of: **7** Chimera **12** Giles Goat-Boy **15** The End of the Road **16** The Floating Opera, The Sot-Weed Factor **17** Lost in the Funhouse

Barthelme, Donald
author of: **7** Sadness **8** City Life **9** Great Days, Snow White **12** Sixty Stories **13** The Dead Father **15** Guilty Pleasures **18** Come Back Dr Caligari **33** Unspeakable Practices Unnatural Acts

Bartholdi, Frederic-Auguste
born: **6** Alsace, Colmar
artwork: **13** Lion of Belfort **26** Liberty Enlightening the World (Statue of Liberty)

Bartholo, Dr
character in: **18** The Barber of Seville **19** The Marriage of Figaro
author: **12** Beaumarchais

Bartholomew **7** apostle
also called: **9** Nathanael

Bartholomew Fair
author: **9** Ben Jonson

Bartok, Bela
born: **7** Hungary **15** Nagyszentmiklos
composer of: **9** Wrestling **11** Mikrokosmos **12** Divertimento **14** Cantata Profana **15** The Wooden Prince **20** Duke Bluebeard's Castle **21** The Miraculous Mandarin

Bartolommeo, Fra
born: **5** Italy **8** Florence
real name: **31** Bartolommeo di Pagolo del Fattorino
artwork: **5** Jonah **6** Isaiah **13** Salvator Mundi **15** The Last Judgment **17** Vision of St Bernard **24** Madonna della Misericordia **30** The Mystic Marriage of St Catherine

Barton, Benjamin Smith
field: **6** botany
noted for first American: **14** botany textbook

Bartram, John
field: **6** botany
noted for first American: **12** hybrid plants

Baruch
father: **5** Judah **6** Neriah
friend and scribe of: **8** Jeremiah

basal **3** key **4** easy **5** basic, vital **6** simple **7** initial, minimal, primary **8** cardinal **9** beginning, essential, intrinsic, necessary **10** elementary, lower-level, simplified **11** fundamental, rudimentary **12** prerequisite **13** indispensable

bas bleu **12** bluestocking

base **3** bad, bed, key, low **4** camp, core, foul, mean, post, root, vile **5** basis, dirty, gross, heart, petty, place, stand **6** abject, billet, bottom, craven, ground, impure, locate, scurvy, sinful, sneaky, sordid, source, vulgar, wicked **7** alloyed, corrupt, debased, essence, found on, ignoble, immoral, install, model on, scrubby, situate, station, support **8** backbone, cowardly, degraded, depraved, garrison, infamous, inferior, pedestal, rudiment, shameful, spurious, unworthy **9** dastardly, dissolute, establish, faithless, insidious, nefarious, principle **10** degenerate, derive from, despicable, detestable, evil-minded, foundation, groundwork, iniquitious, villainous **11** adulterated, disgraceful, ignominious, poor quality, scoundrelly **12** black-hearted, contemptible, dishonorable, disreputable, installation, substructure, underpinning, unprincipled **13** discreditable, reprehensible

baseball
athlete/coach: **6** Mel Ott, Ty Cobb **7** Al Lopez, Cy Young, Jim Rice **8** Al Kaline, Babe Ruth, Lou Brock, Pete Rose, Rod Carew, Vida Blue **9** Alvin Dark, Bob Feller, Bob Gibson, Bowie Kuhn, Dizzy Dean, Ford Frick, Gil Hodges, Hank Aaron, Hank Bauer, Jim Palmer, Jimmy Foxx, Joe Morgan, Lou Gehrig, Luis Tiant, Nellie Fox, Nolan Ryan, Ralph Houk, Ron Guidry, Ted Turner, Tom Seaver, Tommy John, Yogi Berra **10** Boog Powell, Connie Mack, Duke Snider, Earl Weaver, Ernie Banks, John McGraw, Lefty Grove, Maury Wills, Ralph Kiner, Roger Maris, Sparky Lyle, Stan Musial, Whitey Ford, Willie Mays **11** Billy Martin, Carl Hubbell, Dave Kingman, Don Drysdale, George Brett, George Weiss, Honus Wagner, Joe DiMaggio, Joe McCarthy, Johnny Bench, Leo Durocher, Luke Appling, Mark Fidrych, Mike Schmidt, Pee Wee Reese, Phil Rizzuto, Rich Gossage, Sandy Koufax, Ted Williams, Tris Speaker, Warren Spahn **12** Branch Rickey, Casey Stengel, Craig Nettles, Dave Winfield, Dennis McLain, Dick Williams, Eddie Mathews, Elston Howard, Gaylord Perry, George Sisler, Mickey Mantle, Satchel Paige, Steve Carlton, Tommy Lasorda **13** Catfish (Jim) Hunter, Frank Robinson, Reggie Jackson, Rocky Colavito, Rogers Hornsby, Roy Campanella, Thurman Munson, Walter Johnson, Walter O'Malley, Willie McCovey **14** Al Schoendienst, Brooks Robinson, Jackie Robinson, Keith Hernandez, Peter Ueberroth, Sparky Anderson, Willie Stargell **15** Carl Yastrzemski, Charly Gehringer, Harmon Killebrew, Rickey Henderson, Roberto Clemente **16** Christy Mathewson, Darryl Strawberry **18** Fernando Valenzuela, George Steinbrenner **21** Kenesaw Mountain Landis **24** Grover Cleveland Alexander

baseball leagues
National: **11** Chicago Cubs, New York Mets **13** Atlanta Braves, Houston Astros, Montreal Expos **14** Cincinnati Reds, San Diego Padres **16** St Louis Cardi-

nals **17** Los Angeles Dodgers, Pittsburgh Pirates **18** San Francisco Giants **20** Philadelphia Phillies
American: **9** Oakland A's **12** Boston Red Sox, Texas Rangers **13** Detroit Tigers **14** Minnesota Twins, New York Yankees **15** Chicago White Sox, Seattle Mariners, Toronto Blue Jays **16** Baltimore Orioles, California Angels, Cleveland Indians, Kansas City Royals, Milwaukee Brewers

baseball team ***see box***

baseless **7** unsound **9** unfactual, unfounded **10** groundless, ungrounded **11** unjustified, unsupported **12** without basis **13** unjustifiable **14** uncorroborated **15** unsubstantiated

basement **5** below **6** bottom, cellar **15** underground room

baseness **7** lowness **8** meanness, vileness **9** depravity **11** ignobleness **14** iniquitousness **16** contemptibleness

base of operations
Greek: **6** pou sto

bash **4** blow **5** blast, clout, crack, knock, party, whack **7** clopper **8** wingding **9** bacchanal

Bashemath *see* **4** Adah

bashful **3** shy **5** timid **6** demure, modest **8** blushing, reserved, reticent, retiring, sheepish, skittish, timorous **9** diffident, shrinking, uncertain **10** shamefaced **11** constrained, unconfident

bashfulness **7** shyness **10** diffidence **12** sheepishness **14** self-effacement **15** unassertiveness

basic **3** key **4** base, core **5** prime, vital **7** bedrock, primary **8** rudiment **9** essential, intrinsic **10** elementary, foundation **11** fundamental, rudimentary **12** foundational, prerequisite, underpinning

basically
French: **6** au fond

basic ideas **6** basics **7** essence, factors, origins **8** elements, features **9** rudiments **10** principles **11** foundations

basic need **9** essential, necessity, requisite, vital part **10** key element, sine qua non

basic part **4** unit **7** element **9** component **10** ingredient **11** constituent **13** building block

baseball team
Atlanta: **6** Braves
stadium: **7** Atlanta
Baltimore: **7** Orioles
stadium: **8** Memorial
Boston: **6** Red Sox
stadium: **10** Fenway Park
California: **6** Angels
stadium: **7** Anaheim
Chicago: **4** Cubs
stadium: **12** Wrigley Field
Chicago: **8** White Sox
stadium: **12** Comiskey Park
Cleveland: **7** Indians
stadium: **9** Municipal
Cincinnati: **4** Reds
stadium: **10** Riverfront
Detroit: **6** Tigers
stadium: **5** Tiger
Houston: **6** Astros
stadium: **9** Astrodome
Kansas City: **6** Royals
stadium: **6** Royals
Los Angeles: **7** Dodgers
stadium: **6** Dodger **18** Los Angeles Coliseum
Milwaukee: **7** Brewers
stadium: **6** County
Minnesota: **5** Twins
stadium: **12** Metropolitan **24** Hubert H Humphrey Metrodome
Montreal: **5** Expos
stadium: **7** Olympic
New York: **4** Mets
stadium: **4** Shea
New York: **7** Yankees
stadium: **6** Yankee
Oakland: **2** A's
stadium: **7** Oakland
Philadelphia: **8** Phillies
stadium: **8** Veterans
Pittsburgh: **7** Pirates
stadium: **11** Three Rivers
St Louis: **9** Cardinals
stadium: **13** Busch Memorial
San Diego: **6** Padres
stadium: **10** Jack Murphy
San Francisco: **6** Giants
stadium: **15** Candlestick Park
Seattle: **8** Mariners
stadium: **8** Kingdome
Texas: **7** Rangers
stadium: **9** Arlington
Toronto: **8** Blue Jays
stadium: **10** Exhibition

basic quality **6** nature **7** essence **9** principle, substance **12** quintessence

basics **8** elements **9** rudiments **10** principles **11** nitty-gritty **12** fundamentals

basil
also called: **6** tulasi
botanical name: **6** Ocimum **8** O minimum **10** O basilicum
means: **5** royal **6** kingly, lizard (basilisk)
nickname: **14** kiss-me-Nicholas
origin: **5** India
sacred to: **6** Vishnu **7** Krishna, Lakshmi
symbol of: **4** hate, love
use: **10** vegetables

basilica **6** church **10** house of God **14** house of worship

Basiliensis **16** Greek unical codex

Basilisk
form: **6** dragon

basin **3** pan, tub, vat **4** bowl, dale, dell, font, glen, sink **5** gulch, gully, stoup **6** crater, hollow, lavabo, ravine, tureen, valley **7** dishpan, washtub **8** lavatory, sinkhole, washbowl **9** porringer, washbasin, washstand **10** depression, finger bowl

Basin, footed **5** laver

basis, bases **4** base, root **6** ground **7** bedrock **9** essential, principle **10** foundation, touchstone **11** cornerstone, fundamental **12** underpinning **13** starting point

bask **5** revel, savor **6** relish, wallow **7** delight **8** sunbathe **9** luxuriate **11** warm oneself **12** soak up warmth, toast oneself

basket **5** crate **6** barrel, hamper **7** carrier, pannier **8** bassinet, canister

basketball
athlete/coach: **7** A C Green, K C Jones **8** Bob Cousy, Hal Greer, Joe Fulks, Sam Jones **9** Bob Davies, Bob McAdoo, Bob Pettit, Jerry West, Jo Jo White, Larry Bird, Rick Barry, Ted Turner, Wes Unseld **10** Bill Walton, Bryon Scott, Danny Ainge, Dave Cowens, Earl Monroe, Elvin Hayes, John Wooden, Kurt Rambis, Paul Arizin, Red Holzman, Willis Reed **11** Alex English, Bernard King, Bill Bradley, Bill Lambeer, Bill Russell, Bill Sharman, Dick Barnett, El-

gin Baylor, George Mikan, James Worthy, Kevin McHale, Lew Alcindor, Moses Malone, Red Auerbach, Scott Wedman, Walt Frazier **12** Calvin Murphy, Dolph Schayes, Gail Goodrich, George Gervin, Isaiah Thomas, Jamaal Wilkes, John Havlicek, Julius (Dr J) Erving, Larry Spriggs, Lenny Wilkens, Patrick Ewing, Richie Guerin, Robert Parish, Slater Martin **13** Akeem Olajuwon, Cedric Maxwell, Connie Hawkins, Dennis Johnson, Earvin (Magic) Johnson, Emmette Bryant, George Yardley, Maurice Cheeks, Michael Jordan, Nate Archibald, Terry Cummings **14** Oscar Robertson, Sidney Moncrief **15** Billy Cunningham, Dave DeBusschere, Wilt Chamberlain **17** Kareem Abdul-Jabbar **20** Nat Sweetwater Clifton

basketball team
league: 3 NBA **29** National Basketball Association
Atlanta: 5 Hawks
Boston: 7 Celtics
Chicago: 5 Bulls
Cleveland: 9 Cavaliers
Dallas: 9 Mavericks
Denver: 7 Nuggets
Detroit: 7 Pistons
Golden State: 8 Warriors
Houston: 7 Rockets
Indiana: 6 Pacers
Kansas City: 5 Kings
Los Angeles: 6 Lakers **8** Clippers
Milwaukee: 5 Bucks
New Jersey: 4 Nets
New York: 14 Knickerbockers
Philadelphia: 5 76ers **13** Seventy-sixers
Phoenix: 4 Suns
Portland: 12 Trail Blazers
San Antonio: 5 Spurs
Seattle: 11 Supersonics
Utah: 4 Jazz
Washington: 7 Bullets

Basque
language spoken in: 5 Italy, Spain **6** France

bas-relief
Italian: 12 basso-rilievo

bass 3 low **4** alto **5** basso **7** harmony **8** baritone, bass clef

bass
types: 3 sea **4** rock **5** black **6** calico **7** striped, sunfish
characteristic: 10 forked-tail **12** spiny-finned

Bassanio
character in: 19 The Merchant of Venice
author: 11 Shakespeare

basso-rilievo 9 bas-relief

Bast, Jacky and Leonard
characters in: 10 Howard's End
author: 9 E M Forster

bastard 6 impure **8** inferior, spurious **9** imperfect, irregular, love child **12** natural child **17** illegitimate child

bastardize 6 debase, weaken **7** degrade **9** downgrade

baste 3 sew **4** drip **5** roast **6** cudgel, flavor, stitch, thrash **15** temporary stitch

bastinado 4 beat, blow, cane, drub **5** whale **7** beating **8** drubbing

bastion 4 fort **5** tower **6** pillar **7** bulwark, citadel, rampart **8** barbette, fortress **10** breastwork, stronghold

bat 3 hit, rod **4** cane, clip, club, cuff, mace, slug, sock **5** baton, billy, knock, smack, staff, stick, whack **6** buffet, cudgel, mallet, strike, thwack, wallop **7** clobber **8** bludgeon **9** blackjack, truncheon **10** shillelagh

batch 3 lot **5** bunch, crowd, group, stock **6** amount, number **8** quantity **9** aggregate **10** collection

Bates, Alan
born: 7 England **9** Allestree **10** Derbyshire
roles: 8 The Fixer **10** Georgy Girl **12** King of Hearts **13** Zorba the Greek **16** An Unmarried Woman **22** Far From the Madding Crowd

Bates, Miss
character in: 4 Emma
author: 6 Austen

Bateson, William
field: 7 biology
nationality: 7 British
founded: 8 genetics

bath 3 dip, tub **4** wash **5** sauna **6** douche, shower **7** washing **8** ablution, lavement **9** cleansing, immersion, steam bath **10** irrigation
type: 2 hip **4** sitz **5** steam **6** shower, sponge **7** Turkish bath

bathe 3 dip, tub, wet **4** lave, soak, wash **5** douse **6** douche, shower, sponge **7** cleanse **8** irrigate

bathing 3 dip, tub **6** laving, plunge **7** washing **8** swimming **9** ablutions, immersion

bathos 4 corn, mush **5** slush **8** schmaltz **9** mushiness, soppiness **10** maudlinism, slushiness **11** false pathos, mawkishness **14** sentimentalism, sentimentality

bathroom 2 W C **3** can, loo **4** head, john **5** biffy **6** toilet **7** commode, latrine **8** facility, lavatory, men's room, restroom, washroom **10** ladies' room, powder room **11** water closet **14** little boys' room **15** little girls' room

Bathsheba
also: 8 Bathshua
father: 5 Eliam
husband: 5 David, Uriah
son: 7 Solomon
grandfather: 10 Ahithophel

Bathshua *see* **9** Bathsheba

Bathurst
see: Banjul

Batia
form: 5 nymph
father: 6 Teucer
husband: 8 Dardanus
son: 12 Erichthonius

Batman
character: 6 Alfred **7** Egghead, King Tut **8** Catwoman, The Joker **10** Bruce Wayne (Batman), Chief O'Hara, The Penguin, The Riddler **11** Dick Grayson (Robin) **13** Barbara Gordon (Batgirl) **17** Aunt Harriet Cooper **24** Police Commissioner Gordon
cast: 8 Adam West, Burt Ward **9** John Astin **10** Alan Napier, Eartha Kitt, Madge Blake **11** Cesar Romero, Julie Newmar, Victor Buono, Yvonne Craig **12** Frank Gorshin, Neil Hamilton, Stafford Repp, Vincent Price **13** Lee Meriwether **15** Burgess Meredith
city: 10 Gotham City
nickname: 9 Boy Wonder **10** Dynamic Duo **13** Caped Crusader
gimmick: 6 Batlab **8** Batphone **9** Batmobile, Batsignal

Bat Masterson
cast: 9 Gene Barry

baton 3 bat, rod **4** club, mace, wand **5** billy, crook, staff, stick **6** cudgel, fasces **7** crosier, scepter, war club **8** bludgeon, caduceus **9** billy club, truncheon **10** nightstick, shillelagh

Baton
charioteer of: 10 Amphiaraus

batter 4 beat, lash, maul **5** break, crush, pound, smash, smite **6** beat up, buffet, mangle, pummel **7** clobber, shatter

battercake 6 waffle **7** biscuit, pancake

battered 4 shot **6** beat-up, ruined, shabby **8** decrepit **11** dilapidated **12** disreputable

battery 3 set **4** army, band, pack, team **5** block, cadre, force, group, suite, troop **6** caning, cannon, convoy, legion, lineup, outfit, series **7** beating, brigade, company, hitting, hurting, maiming, phalanx, section **8** armament, cannonry, clubbing, division, drubbing, flogging, ordnance, squadron, whipping, wounding **9** cudgeling, spearhead, strapping, thrashing

battle 3 war **4** bout, duel, feud, fray, meet **5** argue, brawl, clash, fight, siege **6** action, affray, combat, debate, engage, tussle **7** contend, contest, crusade, dispute, quarrel, warfare **8** campaign, conflict, skirmish, struggle **9** agitation, encounter, firefight **10** engagement **11** altercation, controversy **13** confrontation

Battle, final
place: 10 Armageddon

battle cry 6 war cry **8** Geronimo, war whoop **9** Rebel yell

Battle Cry
author: 8 Leon Uris

battlefield 5 arena, lists **8** the front, war arena **9** front line **10** battle line, no man's land **11** battlefront **12** battleground

battleground 5 arena, lists **11** battlefield, battlefront

Battle of the Books
author: 13 Jonathan Swift

battle-ready 5 armed **7** arrayed **8** prepared **9** fortified

battleship 4 Iowa **5** Maine **6** Oregon **7** carrier, warship **8** Missouri **9** Ironsides, New Jersey, Wisconsin **10** bluish-gray **11** Dreadnought **12** Constitution
first: 7 Gloire
largest: 6 Yamato

Battus
ruler of: 5 Libya
form: 7 peasant
witness to: 11 cattle theft
thief: 6 Hermes
turned to: 5 stone
cured of: 16 speech impediment

batty 4 nuts **5** crazy, loony, queer, wacko, wacky **6** cuckoo, crazed **7** bat-like, cracked

bauble 3 toy **4** bead **6** geegaw, trifle **7** trinket **8** gimcrack, ornament

Baucis
form: 7 peasant
home: 7 Phrygia
husband: 8 Philemon
offered hospitality to: 4 Zeus **6** Hermes

Baudelaire, Charles
author of: 13 Flowers of Evil **14** Les Fleurs du Mal

Baugh, Sammy
nickname: 13 Slinging Sammy
sport: 8 football
position: 11 quarterback
team: 18 Washington Redskins

Bauhin, Gaspard
field: 6 botany
nationality: 5 Swiss
devised: 14 binomial system
described: 14 ileocecal valve

Baum, Lyman Frank
author of: 13 The (Wonderful) Wizard of Oz **18** Father Goose His Book, Mother Goose in Prose

Baum, Vicki
author of: 8 Shanghai **10** Grand Hotel, Grand Opera **12** Men Never Know **13** A Tale from Bali, And Life Goes On

Baumer, Paul
character in: 25 All Quiet on the Western Front
author: 8 Remarque

Baumgarner, James
real name of: 11 James Garner

Bauto
nurse of: 6 Celeus

bawdy 4 blue, lewd, sexy **5** dirty, gross, lusty **6** coarse, earthy, ribald, risque, sexual, vulgar **7** raunchy **8** immodest, improper, indecent, off-color **10** indecorous, indelicate, licentious, suggestive

bawdy house 7 brothel **8** bordello, cathouse **10** fancy house, whorehouse **13** sporting house **14** house of ill fame **16** house of ill repute **19** house of prostitution

bawl 3 cry **4** call, howl, roar, wail, weep, yell, yowl **5** shout **6** bellow, clamor, cry out, squall **7** blubber, call out

bawling out 6 rebuke **7** censure, chiding, reproof **8** reproach, scolding **9** reprimand **10** chewing out, upbraiding **11** castigation, reprobation **12** dressing-down, remonstrance **13** tongue-lashing

bawl out 5 scold **6** berate, rail at, rebuke, yell at **7** censure, chew out, reprove, upbraid **8** admonish, reproach **9** castigate, dress down, reprimand **10** take to task, tongue-lash **14** read the riot act

Bax, Arnold Edward Trevor
born: 6 London **7** England
composer of: 8 Tintagel **13** November Woods **14** Mater Ora Filium **15** The Garden of Fand **27** Overture to a Picaresque Comedy

Baxter, Anne
grandfather: 16 Frank Lloyd Wright
born: 14 Michigan City IN
roles: 8 Applause **11** All About Eve **13** The Razor's Edge

Baxter, Jody
character in: 11 The Yearling
author: 8 Rawlings

Baxter, William Sylvanus
character in: 9 Seventeen
author: 10 Tarkington

bay 3 cry, yap **4** bank, bark, cove, gulf, howl, nook, road, yelp **5** basin, bayou, bight, fiord, firth, inlet, niche, sound **6** alcove, bellow, clamor, lagoon, recess, strait **7** barking, estuary, howling, narrows, yapping, yelling, yelping **9** bellowing **11** compartment **13** natural harbor

bay (at bay) 7 trapped **8** cornered

bay leaf
botanical name: 12 Pimenta acris
expression: 16 to win one's laurels
from tree: 9 bay laurel
***transformation of:* 6** Daphne
***tree sacred to:* 6** Apollo
***laurel berries called:* 10** bacca lauri
***source of:* 13** baccalaureate
gives gift of: 8 prophecy
helps girls win back: 12 errant lovers
origin: 5 Italy
protects against: 5 death **6** poison **7** sorcery **11** evil spirits
symbol of: 7 victory (laurel wreath)
use: 4 fish, fowl, meat, soup, stew

bayou **4** slew **5** creek, inlet, marsh, river, swamp **6** outlet, slough, stream **9** backwater **13** stagnant marsh

Bayou State
nickname of: **9** Louisiana **11** Mississippi

Bay Psalm Book
author: **9** John Eliot

Bay State
nickname of: **13** Massachusetts

bazaar, bazar **4** fair, mart **6** market **8** carnival, exchange **11** charity fair, charity sale, marketplace

Bazile
character in: **18** The Barber of Seville
author: **12** Beaumarchais

Bazzard, Deputy
character in: **22** The Mystery of Edwin Drood
author: **7** Dickens

B C
creator: **10** Johnny Hart
character: **3** Tor **4** Grog **5** Peter **8** anteater **10** Clumsy Carp **11** the Fat Broad
poet: **5** Wiley
era: **11** Neanderthal, prehistoric

be **4** last, live, stay **5** exist, occur **6** befall, endure, happen, remain **7** persist, subsist **8** continue **9** be present, take place **10** come to pass

be absent **4** miss **12** fail to attend

beach **5** coast, shore **6** strand **8** littoral, seashore **10** water's edge

Beach, Rex
author of: **6** The Net **7** Oh Shoot **8** Pardners **9** Going Some **10** Jungle Gold, The Barrier **11** Don Careless, The Spoilers **12** Son of the Gods **13** The Goose Woman, The Ne'er-do-well **15** The Auction Block **17** Alaskan Adventures

beached **7** aground **8** grounded, stranded **11** shipwrecked **12** washed ashore

beacon **4** beam **5** light **6** pharos, signal **7** seamark **8** bale-fire, landmark **9** watch fire **10** lighthouse, watchtower **11** lighted buoy

bead **3** dot **4** blob, drop, pill **5** speck **6** bubble, pellet **7** droplet, globule **8** particle, spherule

be adequate **2** do **6** answer **8** be enough **10** pass muster **12** be sufficient, do well enough **14** be satisfactory

be afraid of **4** fear **5** dread **7** cower at **8** cringe at **10** shrink from

beak **3** neb, tip **4** bill, nose, pike, prow **5** lorum, snout, spout **7** process, rostrum, snozzle **8** hooknose **9** headmaster, proboscis **10** magistrate

beaker **3** cup **5** glass **6** vessel **9** container

beam **3** ray **4** emit, glow, prop, spar, stud **5** brace, glare, gleam, glint, joist, shine, width **6** girder, rafter, streak, stream, timber **7** breadth, expanse, glimmer, glitter, radiate, trestle **8** transmit **9** broadcast, radiation

bean **9** Phaseolus
varieties: **3** Goa, Pea, Soy, Wax, Yam **4** Jack, Lima, Moth, Mung, Rice, Seim, Snap, Soja, Soya, Tick, Wild **5** Azuki, Black, Broad, Civet, Coral, Field, Green, Horse, Lubia, Pinto, Salad, Screw, Sewee, Sieva, Snail, Sword, Tonka **6** Butter, Castor, Common, French, Indian, Kaffir, Kidney, Lablab, Locust, Manila, Mescal, Nicker, Potato, Romano, Runner, Sacred, String, Tepary, Velvet, Winged, Wonder **7** Cluster, English, Sarawak, Windsor **8** Bovanist, Bush lima, Carolina, Cherokee, European, Egyptian, Hyacinth, Yard-long **9** Algarroba, Asparagus, Bonavista, Dwarf lima, Java glory **10** Dwarf sieva, Giant stock, Hottentot's **12** Italian queen, Scarlet flame **13** African locust, Florida velvet, Scarlet runner **14** Dutch case-knife **16** White Dutch runner

be a party to **3** aid **4** abet **7** support **9** connive in **11** cooperate in **13** be accessory to, participate in

be apparent **6** appear **7** be clear, be plain **8** be patent **9** be evident, be obvious **10** be manifest

bear **4** bend, drop, give, haul, have, lead, push, show, take, tend, tote, turn, wear **5** abide, admit, allow, apply, brace, brave, bring, brook, carry, curve, drive, force, hatch, press, refer, spawn, stand, whelp, yield **6** affect, aim for, convey, convoy, create, endure, escort, go with, harbor, invite, permit, relate, render, suffer, take on, uphold **7** bolster, cherish, concern, conduct, contain, deliver, develop, deviate, display, diverge, exhibit, pertain, possess, produce, stomach, support, sustain, undergo, warrant **8** bear down, engender, generate, maintain, manifest, shoulder, submit to, tolerate, transfer, underpin **9** accompany, appertain, encourage, germinate, hold close, propagate, put up with, reproduce, touch upon, transport **10** bring forth, keep in mind **11** give birth to, hold up under

bear
combining form: **4** arct, ursi **5** arcto
constellation: **4** ursa **9** ursa major, ursa minor
family: **7** Ursidae
group of: **6** sleuth
kind: **3** sun **5** black, brown, koala, malay, panda, polar, sloth **6** kodiak, wombat **7** grizzly **9** roachback, silvertip **10** spectacled, thalarctos
male: **4** boar
mythological: **8** Callisto
order: **9** carnivora
young: **3** cub

beard **4** dare, defy, face, trap **5** brave **6** corner **7** stubble **8** bristles, confront, whiskers **10** bring to bay **16** five-o'clock shadow

bearded **5** bushy, hairy **6** shaggy **7** bristly, hirsute **8** unshaven **9** whiskered **11** bewhiskered

bear down **4** push **5** press **13** apply pressure

bear down upon **6** assail, attack, come at **7** assault **11** descend upon

Beardsley, Aubrey Vincent
born: **7** England **8** Brighton
artwork: **6** Salome **10** Lysistrata **12** Morte d'Arthur

Beard's Roman Women
author: **14** Anthony Burgess

bearer **5** Atlas **6** holder, porter **7** carrier **8** conveyer, producer **9** messenger **13** beast of burden **16** one holding a check
Spanish: **8** escudero, portador

bear fruit **4** bear **6** mature **7** develop, prosper **8** fructify

bearing **3** air **4** mien, port **5** sense **6** import, manner **7** concern, meaning **8** attitude, behavior, breeding, carriage, demeanor, presence, relation **9** producing, reference, relevance **10** conception, connection, deportment, importance, pertinence **11** application, association, comportment, germination, giving birth, procreation, propagation, reproducing **12** relationship, reproduction, significance **13** applicability

bearing no name 7 unnamed **8** unsigned **9** anonymous

bearings 3 way **6** course **8** position **9** direction **11** orientation **16** sense of direction

bearish 5 cross, gruff, surly, testy **6** crusty, sullen **7** brusque, crabbed, grouchy **8** churlish **9** crotchety, irascible **10** ill-humored, out of sorts **11** ill-tempered, pessimistic **12** cantankerous

bear off 5 seize, steal **6** abduct, convey, kidnap

bear out 5 prove **6** verify **7** confirm **11** corroborate **12** substantiate

Bear State
nickname of: 8 Arkansas

bear up under 4 bear, take **5** abide, brave, brook, stand **6** endure, suffer **7** stomach, undergo, weather **9** go through, withstand

bear witness 4 back **6** attest **7** confirm, testify **11** corroborate, demonstrate **12** give evidence, substantiate

beast 3 cad, cur, pig, rat **4** ogre **5** brute, swine **6** animal, mammal, savage **8** creature **9** barbarian, quadruped

beastly 3 bad **4** vile **5** awful, cruel, gross, lousy, nasty **6** brutal, coarse, savage **7** bestial, brutish, inhuman, swinish **8** degraded, dreadful, terrible **9** barbarous, loathsome, monstrous **10** abominable, deplorable, disgusting, unpleasant **12** contemptible, disagreeable

beat 3 bat, hit, mix, rap, tap, way **4** area, bang, best, blow, cane, club, drub, flap, flog, flop, lick, maul, path, rout, slap, time, whip, zone **5** clout, count, crush, flail, knock, meter, outdo, pound, pulse, punch, quake, quell, realm, repel, route, shake, smack, smite, strap, throb, whack **6** accent, batter, course, defeat, domain, hammer, master, pummel, quiver, rhythm, rounds, stress, strike, stroke, subdue, switch, thrash, thwack, twitch, wallop **7** cadence, circuit, clobber, conquer, destroy, eclipse, flutter, pulsate, put down, repulse, scourge, shellac, surpass, trounce, vibrate, win over **8** overcome, vanquish **9** excel over, fluctuate, go pit-a-pat, overpower, palpitate, pulsation, territory **10** win out over **11** predominate, prevail over, triumph over **14** stir vigorously

beat a retreat 6 beat it **7** back off **8** turn tail, withdraw **10** high tail it

beat around the bush
5 dodge, evade, hedge, stall **10** equivocate, mince words

beatific 4 rapt **6** divine, serene **7** angelic, exalted, saintly, sublime **8** blissful, ecstatic, glorious, heavenly **9** rapturous **10** enraptured **14** transcendental

beat it 2 go **3** out **4** away, scat, shoo **5** be off, leave, scram **6** begone, cut out, depart, get out, go away **7** get lost, vamoose **10** hit the road, make tracks

beatitude 5 bliss **7** ecstasy, rapture **8** euphoria, felicity **10** exaltation **11** blessedness, exaltedness, saintliness **13** transcendence **15** transfiguration

be at loggerheads 5 clash **7** quarrel **8** disagree

be at odds 6 differ **7** dispute, diverge **8** conflict, disagree

beat rhythmically 3 rap, tap **4** drum **6** tattoo **7** pulsate

Beatrice
character in: 12 Divine Comedy
author: 5 Dante

Beatrice
character in: 19 Much Ado About Nothing
author: 11 Shakespeare

Beatrice et Benedict
opera by: 7 Berlioz

Beat the Clock
host: 10 Bud Collyer

Beattie, Ann
author of: 11 Distortions **14** Falling in Place **15** The Burning House **19** Secrets and Surprises **20** Chilly Scenes of Winter

Beatty, Warren
real name: 11 Warren Beaty
sister: 15 Shirley MacLaine
born: 10 Richmond VA
roles: 4 Reds **11** All Fall Down **13** Heaven Can Wait **14** Bonnie and Clyde **18** Splendor in the Grass **24** The Roman Spring of Mrs Stone
director of: 4 Reds (Oscar)

beat up 3 mug **4** lick, maul, whip **6** batter, pummel **7** assault, clobber

beat-up 4 shot **6** shabby **7** worn-out **8** battered **10** broken-down **11** dilapidated

Beaty, Shirley MacLean
real name of: 15 Shirley MacLaine

Beaty, Warren
real name of: 12 Warren Beatty

beau, beaux 3 fop, guy, nob **4** buck, dude, love, stud, toff **5** blade, dandy, flame, lover, Romeo, spark, swain, swell, wooer **6** adorer, escort, fellow, fiance, garcon, squire, steady, suitor **7** admirer, beloved, courter, coxcomb, cupidon, Don Juan, gallant, playboy **8** cavalier, courtier, gay blade, Lothario, paramour, popinjay, true love, young man **9** betrothed, boyfriend, courtesan, gentleman, inamorta, ladies' man **10** sweetheart, young blood **15** gentleman caller, gentleman friend
nickname of: 14 George Brummell

Beauchamp's Career
author: 14 George Meredith

Beau Geste
author: 6 P C Wren **15** Christopher Wren
director: 14 William Wellman
cast: 10 Gary Cooper, Ray Milland **12** Brian Donlevy, Susan Hayward **13** Robert Preston
silent version starred: **12** Ronald Colman
setting: 19 French Foreign Legion

Beaumarchais, Pierre Augustin Caron de
author of: 18 The Barber of Seville **19** The Marriage of Figaro

beau monde 5 elite **6** gentry **7** society **10** upper class, upper crust **11** aristocracy, high society **15** beautiful people

Beaumont, Ned
character in: 11 The Glass Key
author: 7 Hammett

Beauregard, P G T (Pierre Gustave Toutant)
served in: 8 Civil War
side: 11 Confederate
rank: 7 general

ordered firing on: 8 Ft Sumter
battle: 7 Bull Run

beaut 4 lulu 5 daisy, dandy 6 beauty 7 stunner 8 knockout 10 good-looker

beautification 9 adornment 10 decoration 13 embellishment, ornamentation

beautiful 4 fair, fine 5 bonny, great 6 comely, lovely, pretty, seemly, superb, worthy 7 radiant 8 alluring, gorgeous, handsome, pleasing, splendid, very good 9 admirable, beauteous, enjoyable, estimable, excellent, exquisite, first-rate, ravishing, wonderful 10 attractive, stupendous 11 captivating, commendable, fine-looking, good-looking, resplendent 15 pulchritudinous

beautify 4 do up 5 adorn, grace 7 dress up, enhance, gussy up, improve 8 ornament 9 embellish, glamorize

beauty 4 boon, doll 5 asset, beaut, belle, grace, Venus 6 eyeful, looker 7 benefit, feature, goddess, stunner 8 knockout, radiance, splendor 9 advantage, good looks, good thing 10 attraction, excellence, good-looker, loveliness 11 pulchritude 12 handsomeness, magnificence, resplendence 14 attractiveness
goddess of: 6 Graces 7 Gratiae 9 Aphrodite, Charities
god of: 5 Baldr 6 Apollo, Balder, Baldur 7 Angus Og, Phoebus, Pythias 9 Musagetes

Beauvoir, Simone de
author of: 12 The Mandarins, The Second Sex 14 A Very Easy Death, All Said and Done, The Coming of Age, The Prime of Life 17 Ethics of Ambiguity 22 The Force of Circumstance 25 Memoirs of a Dutiful Daughter 34 Brigitte Bardot and the Lolita Syndrome

beaver
young: 3 kit

Beaver State
nickname of: 6 Oregon

be blessed with 3 own 4 have 5 enjoy 7 possess 16 have the benefit of

because 2 so 3 for 4 that, then, thus 5 cause, hence, since 6 whence 7 whereas 8 inasmuch 9 therefore 10 seeing that 11 considering

Bechuanaland
now called: 8 Botswana

beck 3 bid 4 call 7 bidding, summons 9 summoning

Becket
author: 11 Jean Anouilh 18 Alfred Lord Tennyson
director: 14 Peter Glenville
cast: 11 John Gielgud, Peter O'Toole (King Henry II) 13 Richard Burton (Becket)

Beckett, Samuel
author of: 4 Not I, Play, Watt 6 Embers, Molloy 7 Endgame 8 That Time 9 Footfalls, Happy Days 10 Malone Dies 11 All that Fall, The Lost Ones 13 The Unnameable 15 Waiting for Godot 16 Mercier and Camier 20 Murphy Krapp's Last Tape 25 Stories and Texts for Nothing

Beckmann, Max
born: 7 Germany, Leipzig
artwork: 6 Kasbek 7 Perseus 8 Acrobats, The Night 9 The Actors 11 View of Genoa 12 Charnel House, The Argonauts, The Departure 13 Blindman's Buff, Family Picture 14 Double Portrait 17 David and Bathsheba 18 Odysseus and Calypso 19 Sinking of the Titanic 20 Destruction of Messina 22 The Descent from the Cross

beckon 4 call, coax, draw, lure, pull 6 allure, entice, invite, motion, signal, summon, wave at, wave on 7 attract, gesture 11 gesticulate 14 crook a finger at

be clear 6 appear 7 be plain 8 be patent 9 be evident, be obvious 10 be apparent, be manifest

becloud 3 fog 4 blur, hide, veil 5 befog, cloud 6 muddle, screen, shroud 7 confuse, cover up, eclipse, obscure 8 confound, make hazy, overcast 9 obfuscate 10 camouflage, overshadow 14 make indistinct

become 3 get 4 grow, suit, turn 6 go with 7 enhance, flatter, get to be 8 come to be 9 agree with, begin to be 10 complement 11 be reduced to, turn out to be

become apparent 4 dawn, loom 5 arise 6 appear, crop up, emerge, turn up 7 develop, surface

become bigger 4 grow 5 swell 6 expand 7 develop, enlarge, inflate 8 increase

become irrational 5 break, crack 7 crack up 9 break down, fall apart, go berserk 10 go to pieces 11 lose control 12 lose one's mind

become one 3 wed 4 fuse 5 blend, marry, merge, unite 7 combine 8 coalesce 10 amalgamate 11 consolidate

become seasoned to 5 adapt, inure 6 adjust 8 accustom 9 acclimate, get used to, habituate 15 learn to live with

become smaller 6 lessen, shrink 7 decline, dwindle, shrivel 8 decrease, diminish

become visible 4 loom, show 6 appear, crop up, emerge, show up, turn up 7 surface 11 come to light 12 come into view

becoming 3 apt, fit 4 meet 6 pretty, proper, seemly, worthy 7 fitting 8 suitable 9 befitting, congenial, congruous, enhancing, in keeping 10 attractive, compatible, consistent, flattering, harmonious 11 appropriate, good-looking

Becquerel, Antoine Henri
field: 7 physics
nationality: 6 French
discovered: 13 radioactivity
awarded: 10 Nobel Prize

bed 3 cot, hay 4 band, bank, base, belt, bunk, crib, lode, plot, sack, seam, zone 5 berth, floor, layer, patch 6 bottom, cradle, pallet 7 deposit, stratum 8 bedstead 10 foundation

bedazzle 4 daze 6 dazzle 7 astound, confuse, enchant, fluster, nonplus, stagger, stupefy 8 befuddle, bewilder, confound, dumfound 9 captivate, overpower, overwhelm 10 disconcert 11 flabbergast 19 sweep one off one's feet

bed chamber 7 bedroom, boudoir

bed down 5 sleep 7 lie down, sack out 8 doss down 10 hit the hay, settle down 11 accommodate, hit the sack

bedeck 4 deck, trim 5 adorn, array 7 garnish 8 decorate, ornament 9 embellish

be deficient in 4 fail, lack, want 7 be scant 9 be short of 10 have too few

be deprived of 4 lack, lose, want

be deserving of 4 earn, rate

5 merit 7 deserve 10 be worthy of 12 be entitled to

bedevil 3 dog 5 annoy, hound, worry 6 badger, harass, pester, plague 9 beleaguer

be devoted to 4 love 5 adore 6 dote on 7 cherish 8 be fond of

bedim 4 blur 6 darken 7 obscure

Bedivere
character in: 16 Arthurian romance

bedizen 5 adorn, array 6 bedeck, rig out 7 bejewel, costume

bedlam 5 chaos 6 tumult, uproar 7 turmoil 8 madhouse 11 pandemonium

bed of justice
French: 12 lit de justice

Bedouin, Beduin
also: 4 Absi, Arab 5 nomad 7 bedawee
Arabic: 6 badawi
means: 13 desert dweller
found in: 5 Egypt, Syria 6 Arabia 11 North Africa
religion: 5 Islam

bedraggled 4 limp 5 dirty, dowdy, messy, seedy, soggy, tacky, tatty 6 blowsy, frowsy, frumpy, matted, ragtag, sloppy, soiled, untidy 7 unkempt 8 frumpish, sluttish, tattered 10 disarrayed, disordered, disheveled, slatternly, threadbare 11 disarranged 13 draggletailed 14 down-at-the-heels, out-at-the-elbows

bedridden 7 invalid 8 disabled, immobile 13 incapacitated

bedroom 7 boudoir, chamber 10 bedchamber

bedspread 5 quilt 8 bedcover, coverlet 9 comforter

bedstead 3 bed 8 bed frame 10 four poster

bee
caste: 5 drone, queen 6 worker
classification: 6 social 8 solitary
communication: 13 dance language
family: 6 Apidae 7 Apoidea 8 Bombidae 10 Andrenidae, Halictidae 11 Meliponidae, Xylocopidae 12 Megachilidae
group of: 5 grist, swarm
order: 11 Hymenoptera
scent: 10 pheromones
variety: 5 mason, miner 6 alkali, cuckoo 8 burrower, honeybee 9 bumblebee, carpenter, plasterer 10 leafcutter 11 yellow-faced

beech 5 Fagus
varieties: 4 Blue 5 Water 6 Copper, Purple 7 Cut-leaf, Weeping 8 American, European, Fern-leaf, Japanese

Beedle, William Franklin, Jr.
real name of: 13 William Holden

beef 4 heft, kick, meat 5 brawn, gripe, steer 6 cattle, grouch, grouse 7 grumble 8 complain 9 bellyache, complaint, criticize, find fault

Beef State
nickname of: 8 Nebraska

beefy 5 bulky, burly, hefty 6 brawny, robust 8 thickset 9 strapping

beehive 4 hive 6 apiary 9 busy place 10 powerhouse

Beehive State
nickname of: 4 Utah

Beekeeping
god of: 9 Aristaeus

Beelzebub
character in: 12 Paradise Lost
author: 6 Milton

be enough 2 do 6 answer 7 suffice

be entitled to 4 rate 5 merit 7 deserve 10 be worthy of 13 be deserving of

beer-bust 4 toot 5 binge, drunk, spree 6 bender 8 carousal 9 bacchanal

Beery, Noah
brother: 7 Wallace
son: 6 Noah Jr
born: 12 Kansas City MO
roles: 7 Lord Jim, The Dove 9 Beau Geste 10 The Sea Wolf 14 The Mark of Zorro

Beery, Wallace
brother: 4 Noah
nephew: 6 Noah Jr
wife: 13 Gloria Swanson
born: 12 Kansas City MO
roles: 8 The Champ (Oscar) 9 The Bowery, Viva Villa 10 Grand Hotel 11 The Big House 13 Dinner at Eight 14 Treasure Island 15 The Mighty Barnum 16 A Message to Garcia

beet 12 Beta vulgaris
varieties: 3 Red, Sea 4 Leaf, Wild 5 Sugar 6 Garden, Yellow 7 Spinach

Beethoven, Ludwig van
born: 4 Bonn 7 Germany
composer of: 5 Laube (sonata) 6 Egmont, Eroica (symphony no 3), Spring (sonata) 7 Fidelio, Leonore 8 Coriolan, Dramatic (sonata), Kreutzer (sonata), Pastoral (symphony no 6), The Storm 9 Moonlight (sonata), Pastorale (sonata), Waldstein (sonata) 10 Bagatellen, Great Fugue (no 133), Pathetique

beer 3 ale, keg, mum 4 bier, bock, brew, dark, faro, flip, gail, grog, gyle, hops, kvas, malt, mild, quas, scud, suds 5 chang, chica, draft, grout, kvass, lager, light, quass, scuds, stout, weiss 6 bitter, chicha, double, gatter, porter, spruce, stingo, swanky, swipes, wallop, zythum 7 bottled, cerveza, pangasi, pharaoh, Pilsner, tankard, taplash, tapwort 8 bock beer, cervisia, near beer, pilsener 10 malt liquor
add to beer: 7 krausen
bad/inferior beer: 4 tack 5 belch 6 swanky 7 taplash
brand: 5 Beck's, Coors, Pabst, Piels 6 Miller, Molson, Stroh's 7 Schlitz 8 Bud Light, Michelob 9 Budweiser, Lowenbrau 10 Miller Lite, Molson Gold 13 Guinness Stout 15 Pabst Blue Ribbon
cask: 4 butt
cup: 3 mug 4 toby 5 glass, stein 6 flagon, seidel 7 tankard 8 schooner 9 blackjack
hot beer and gin: 4 purl
ingredient: 4 hops, malt 5 yeast 6 barley
maker: 6 brewer 8 brewster, maltster
mythological inventor: 9 Gambrinus
quantity of: 3 keg 4 case 7 six-pack
small beer: 4 tiff 5 grout
sour beer: 4 kuas, kvas 5 quash, quass 8 beeregar
thin beer: 6 pritch, swipes
Tibetan beer: 5 chang
warm beer and oatmeal: 6 storry
with whiskey: 11 Boilermaker

(sonata), Spirit Trio **11** Grosse Fugue (no 133), Harp Quartet (no 74), Namensfeier **12** Appassionata (sonata), Archduke Trio, Konig Stephan **13** Hammerklavier (sonata), Missa Solemnis **15** Emperor Concerto (No 5) **16** Christus am Olberg, The Mount of Olives, The Ruins of Athens **17** Die Ruinen von Athen, Die Weihe des Hauses **18** An die ferne Geliebte, Rage over a Lost Penny **20** Rasoumoffsky Quartets (no 59) **24** The Creatures of Prometheus **25** Die Geschopfe des Prometheus

beetle
variety: 3 bog, may, sap **4** bark, bean, flea, leaf, mold, moss, pill, rove, sand, stag **5** cedar, click, flour, grain, marsh, penny, tiger, water **6** beaver, diving, flower, fungus, ground, hister, lizard, spider, weevil **7** bessbug, blister, burying, carrion, firefly, goldbug, goliath, ladybug, soldier **8** elephant, glowworm, hercules, Japanese, ladybird, tortoise **9** ant loving, bombadier, burrowing, checkered, fruitworm, goldsmith, grassroot, scavenger, tumblebug, whirligig **10** deathwatch, false clown, longhorned, mammal nest, shiptimber **11** reticulated, trout stream **12** antlike stone, lightning bug **13** feather winged, horseshoe crab

Beetle Bailey
creator/artist: 9 Dik Browne **10** Mort Walker **12** Bob Gustafson
character: 5 Cosmo, Plato **6** Killer, Lt Flap, Lt Fuzz **10** Miss Buxley **12** Gen Halftrack **17** Sgt Orville Snorkel
***chef:* 6** Cookie
place: 10 Camp Swampy

be evident 6 appear **7** be clear, be plain **8** be patent **9** be obvious **10** be apparent, be manifest

befall 5 ensue, occur **6** betide, chance, follow, happen **10** come to pass **11** materialize

befitting 3 apt, fit **5** right **6** decent, proper, seemly **8** becoming, relevant, suitable **11** appropriate

be fond of 6 dote on **11** be devoted to **12** be in love with

before 3 ere, yet **5** afore, ahead, prior **6** rather, sooner **7** already, earlier, vis-a-vis **8** erewhile, until now **9** in advance, in front of, in sight of **10** face-to-face, previously

before Christ
abbreviation: 2 BC
Latin: 2 AC **12** ante Christum

beforehand 6 in time, sooner **7** earlier **9** in advance **11** ahead of time

before now 6 in time, sooner **7** earlier **9** in advance

before the fact 6 in time **9** in advance **10** beforehand **11** ahead of time

before the public
Latin: 11 coram populo

befoul 4 soil **5** dirty, smear, stain, sully, taint **6** defile, poison **7** blacken, corrupt, pollute, tarnish **8** besmirch **9** desecrate **11** contaminate

befriend 4 help **6** assist, defend, succor, uphold **7** comfort, embrace, help out, protect, stand by, stick by, support, sustain, welcome **8** side with **9** give aid to, look after **10** minister to **11** consort with **13** associate with **14** fraternize with, sympathize with **17** take under one's wing

be friends 7 consort **9** associate, pal around **10** fraternize

befringe 3 hem **4** bind, edge, trim **6** border **7** festoon **8** decorate

befuddle 4 daze **5** addle, mix up **6** baffle, muddle, puzzle, rattle **7** confuse, fluster, perplex, stupefy **8** bewilder, confound, unsettle **9** disorient, inebriate, make drunk, make tipsy **10** intoxicate, make groggy **11** disorganize

beg 3 bum, sue **4** pray, shun **5** avert, avoid, cadge, dodge, evade, mooch, parry, plead, shirk **6** escape, eschew, hustle, sponge **7** beseech, entreat, fend off, implore, solicit **8** appeal to, petition, sidestep **9** importune, panhandle **10** supplicate

beg, bey 4 lord **6** prince **8** governor

beget 3 get **4** sire **5** breed, cause, spawn **6** effect, father, lead to **7** produce **8** engender, generate, occasion, result in **9** call forth, procreate, propagate **10** bring about, give rise to

begetter 4 sire **6** father **7** creator **9** generator **10** progenitor

beggar 3 bum, guy **4** chap **5** devil, tramp **6** baffle, fellow **7** almsman, moocher, sponger, surpass **8** be beyond **9** challenge, mendicant **10** panhandler

Beggar 7 Lazarus

Beggar's Opera, The
author: 7 John Gay
form: 11 ballad opera
character: 6 Lockit **10** Lucy Lockit **12** Polly Peachum **15** Captain Macheath

begin 5 arise, found, start **6** be born, crop up, emerge, launch, set out **8** break out, commence, embark on, initiate **9** establish, institute, introduce, originate, undertake **10** burst forth, inaugurate **11** set in motion **16** take the first step

beginner 4 babe, tyro **6** author, father, novice, rookie **7** creator, founder, learner, starter, student **8** freshman, neophyte **9** fledgling, greenhorn, initiator, organizer **10** apprentice, originator, prime mover, tenderfoot **11** inaugurator **14** babe in the woods

beginning 3 new **4** germ, seed **5** birth, onset, start **6** embryo, novice, origin, outset, source, spring **7** kickoff, student, untried **8** neophyte, zero hour **9** embryonic, inception, incipient, launching **10** foundation, wellspring **11** preliminary, springboard **12** commencement, fountainhead, inauguration, introduction **13** inexperienced, starting point
Latin: 12 terminus a quo

Beginning of Wisdom, The
author: 19 Stephen Vincent Benet

Beginnings
god of: 5 Janus

begone 3 out **4** away, scat, shoo **5** be off, leave, scram **6** beat it, depart, get out, go away **7** get lost, vamoose

begonia
varieties: 3 Rex, Wax **4** Fern, King, Star, Wild **5** Hardy, Trout **6** Bamboo, Kidney, Shrimp, Winter, Zigzag **7** Bedding, Dewdrop, Elmleaf, Eyelash, Fuchsia, Leopard, Lily-pad, Swedish **8** Climbing, Fern-leaf, Fireking, Lorraine, Palm-leaf, Pond-lily, Star-leaf, Trailing **9** Alder-leaf, Angel-wing, Beefsteak, Calla-lily, Christmas, Crazy-leaf, Grape-leaf,

Grapevine, Hollyhock, Holly-leaf, Honey-bear, Iron-cross, Maple-leaf, Miniature, Pennywort, Trout-leaf, Whirlpool **10** Bronze-leaf, Castor-bean, Finger-leaf, Guinea-wing, Seersucker, Strawberry **11** Fairy-carpet, Lettuce-leaf, Painted-leaf **12** Blooming-fool, Elephant's Ear, Metallic-leaf **13** Peanut-brittle **14** Hybrid tuberous, Nasturtium-leaf, Youth-and-old-age **15** Winter-flowering **16** Manda's woolly-bear, Philodendron-leaf **17** Miniature pond-lily **18** Trailing watermelon

beg pardon **6** excuse **9** apologize **13** express regret, say one is sorry

be grateful **9** be obliged **10** appreciate, be beholden, be thankful **11** be obligated

begrime **4** soil **5** dirty, muddy, smear, stain, sully **6** smudge, soot up **7** besmear, tarnish

begrimed **5** dirty, grimy, muddy **6** filthy, grubby, soiled **7** unclean **8** unwashed **9** tarnished

begrudge **4** envy **5** covet **6** grudge, resent **11** be jealous of, hold against

beguile **4** dupe, hoax, lull, lure **5** amuse, charm, cheat, cheer, trick **6** delude, divert, occupy, please **7** bewitch, deceive, enchant, ensnare **8** distract, hoodwink **9** bamboozle, captivate, entertain **10** lead astray

beguiling **7** winning, winsome **8** charming, magnetic **9** appealing, disarming **10** bewitching, entrancing **11** captivating **12** ingratiating, irresistible

behalf **3** aid, for **4** part, side **5** favor **7** benefit, by proxy, defense, in aid of, support **8** interest

Behan, Brendan
author of: **10** Borstal Boy, The Hostage **12** The Scarperer **14** The Quare Fellow **25** Confessions of an Irish Rebel

be handed down **4** pass **7** descend **11** be inherited

behave **3** act **13** acquit oneself, deport oneself **14** comport oneself, conduct oneself, control oneself

behavior **4** acts **5** deeds **6** action, habits, manner **7** actions, bearing, conduct, control **8** activity, attitude, demeanor, practice, reaction, response **9** operation **10** deportment **11** comportment, functioning, performance, self-control

behead **9** decollate **10** decapitate, guillotine **15** bring to the block

behest **4** fiat **5** edict, order, say-so **6** charge, decree, ruling **7** bidding, command, dictate, mandate **9** direction, ultimatum **10** injunction **11** instruction

behind **4** rump, seat, slow **5** abaft, after, fanny **8** backward, buttocks, in back of **9** fundament, in arrears **11** to the rear of **12** hindquarters

behind closed doors **7** sub rosa **8** in secret, secretly **9** in private, privately

behindhand **4** late, slow **5** tardy **7** belated **8** backward **10** unpunctual

behind the times **5** passe **7** archaic **9** out-of-date **10** antiquated **12** old-fashioned

behind time **4** late, slow **5** tardy **7** belated, delayed **12** after the fact

behold **3** see **4** heed, look, mark, note, scan, view **5** watch **6** attend, gaze at, look at, notice, regard, survey **7** discern, examine, inspect, observe, stare at, witness **8** look upon **10** scrutinize **11** contemplate **12** pay attention

beholden **5** bound **6** liable **7** obliged **8** indebted **9** obligated **10** answerable, in one's debt **11** accountable, responsible **15** under obligation

behold the man
Latin: **8** ecce homo
said by: **13** Pontius Pilate
spoken of: **6** Christ

behoove **4** suit **5** be apt, befit **6** become, be wise **7** benefit **8** be proper **9** be fitting **11** be advisable, be necessary **13** be appropriate **14** be advantageous

Behring, Emil Adolph von
field: **12** bacteriology
nationality: **6** German
developed: **19** diphtheria antitoxin
awarded: **10** Nobel Prize

beige **3** tan **4** ecru, fawn **6** greige **8** brownish

be ill **3** ail **6** be sick **8** be unwell **12** be indisposed **13** be in ill health

be in a class with **5** equal, match **6** be up to **7** compare **8** approach **10** be as good as **11** compete with **12** be comparable, be on a par with **13** hold a candle to **14** bear comparison

being **4** core, life, soul **5** human **6** living, mortal, nature, person, psyche, spirit **7** essence, persona, reality **8** creature, existing **9** actuality, existence **10** individual, occurrence **11** subsistence

Being There
author: **13** Jerzy Kosinski
director: **8** Hal Ashby
cast: **10** Jack Warden **12** Peter Sellers **13** Melvyn Douglas **15** Shirley MacLaine
Oscar for: **15** supporting actor (Douglas)

be inherited **4** pass **7** descend **12** be handed down

be in short supply **4** lack, want **8** be scanty, be scarce **9** fall short

be intemperate **7** carouse, debauch **9** dissipate **11** overindulge

be in tune **4** jibe **5** agree, match, tally **6** accord, square **7** conform **9** harmonize **10** be in unison

Beirut, Beyrouth
capital of: **7** Lebanon
Phoenician name: **7** Berytus
sea: **13** Mediterranean
settled by: **11** Phoenicians
square: **15** Place des Martyrs

be jealous of **4** envy **6** resent **8** begrudge

Bekesy, Georg von
field: **7** physics
researched: **3** ear **7** cochlea, hearing
awarded: **10** Nobel Prize

Bel **3** god **5** deity

Bela
father: **4** Beor
brother: **6** Balaam

belabor **6** rehash, repeat **7** dwell on **9** reiterate **11** pound away at **12** hammer away at, recapitulate **14** beat a dead horse, go on and on about

Bel-Ami
author: **15** Guy de Maupassant

Belasco, David
author of: **7** DuBarry **15** Madame Butterfly **21** The Return of Peter Grimm **22** The Girl of the Golden West

belated **4** late, slow **5** tardy **6** behind **7** delayed, overdue, past due **8** deferred **10** behindhand, behind time, unpunctual **12** after the fact

belch **4** burp, emit, gush, spew, vent **5** eject, eruct, erupt, expel, issue, spout, spurt, vomit **7** cough up, issuing **8** disgorge, ejection, emission, eruption **9** discharge, roar forth, send forth **10** eructation

Belch, Sir Toby
character in: **12** Twelfth Night
author: **11** Shakespeare

beleaguer **3** vex **5** annoy **6** assail, badger, bother, harass, hector, pester, plague **7** besiege, bombard **8** blockade, surround

bel-esprit **3** wit **12** intellectual

belfry **4** dome **5** spire **7** steeple **9** bell tower, campanile

Belgian Congo *see* **5** Zaire

Belgium
other name: **13** Gallia Belgica **15** Cockpit of Europe **16** Koninkrijk Belgie **17** Royaume de Belgique
capital/largest city: **8** Brussels **9** Bruxelles
others: **2** As **3** Aat, Ans, Ath, Hal, Huy, Mol, Spa **4** Aath, Amay, Asse, Boom, Bree, Doel, Gaud, Geel, Genk, Gent, Hoei, Lier, Looz, Mons, Vise, Waha, Zele **5** Aalst, Alost, Arlon, Ciney, Ecklo, Essen, Eupen, Evere, Genck, Ghent, Heist, Ieper, Jette, Jumet, Liege, Namur, Ronse, Tielt, Uccle, Vorst, Wezet, Ynoir, Ypres **6** Aarlen, Anvers, Bergen, Bilzen, Bruges, Deurne, Izegem, Leuven, Lierre, Merxem, Opwijk, Ostend **7** Antwerp, Ardooie, Berchem, Brabant, Hainaut, Herstal, Hoboken, Ixelles, Leliven, Limburg, Louvain, Malmedy, Mechlin, Roulers, Seraing, Tournai **8** Bastogne, Courtrai, Doorwick, Flanders, Kortrijk, Mouscron, Turnhout, Verviers, Waterloo **9** Antwerpen, Charleroi **10** Anderlecht, Borgerhout, Luxembourg, Quatrebras, Schaerbeek
school: **7** Louvain
division: **5** Liege, Namur **7** Antwerp, Brabant, Hainaut, Limburg **8** Flanders, Wallonia
head of state: **4** king
measure: **3** vat **4** aune, pied **5** carat **6** perche **8** boisseau
monetary unit: **5** belga, franc **7** brabant, centime, crocard
weight: **4** last **5** carat, livre **6** charge **7** chariot **8** esterlin
mountain: **8** Ardennes
highest point: **16** Signal de Botrange
river: **3** Lys **4** Dyle, Leie, Maas, Mark, Yser **5** Boucq, Demer, Lesse, Meuse, Nethe, Rupel, Senne **6** Dender, Escaut, Manjel, Ourthe, Sambre, Semois, Vesdre, Warche **7** Ambleve, Schelde, Scheldt
sea: **5** North
physical feature:
canal: **4** Yser **5** Union **6** Albert **7** Campine
cave: **7** Furfooz **8** Grenelle
forest: **8** Ardennes
plateau: **8** Hohevenn
people: **4** Remi **6** Nervii **7** Belgian, Fleming, Flemish **8** Walloons **9** Bellovaci
artist: **5** Ensor **6** Rubens **7** Delvaux, Vandyke, Van Eyck **8** Brueghal, Magritte
author: **6** Coster **7** Simenon **9** Verhaeren **10** Conscience, Ghelderode **11** Maeterlinck
composer: **6** Franck
king: **7** Leopold **8** Baudouin
leader: **5** Spaak **9** Tindemans
language: **5** Dutch **6** French, German **7** Flemish
religion: **13** Roman Catholic
place:
battleground: **5** Bulge **8** Waterloo
breadhouse: **9** Broodhuis
castle: **5** Steen
cathedral: **5** Ghent **13** Saint Rombauts
city hall: **12** Hotel de Ville
home for elderly women: **9** Beguinage
museum: **9** Beaux Arts
palace: **10** Gruuthuuse
features:
horse: **9** Brabancon
lace: **5** fichu **6** Bruges **7** Malines, Mechlin **8** Brussels
lawn bowling: **6** boules
linen: **7** brabant
musical instrument: **8** carillon
religious procession: **9** Holy Blood
tapestry: **9** oudenarde
food:
cheese: **9** Limburger
gingerbread: **12** pain d'espices
raisin bread: **8** cramique
soup: **9** Waterzooi

Belgrade, Beograd
capital of: **10** Yugoslavia
landmark:
fortress: **10** Kalemegdan
parliament house: **9** Skupstina
name means: **11** white forest
river: **4** Sava **6** Danube
Roman fort: **10** Singidinum
Serbian: **7** Beograd

Belial
character in: **12** Paradise Lost
author: **6** Milton

belie **4** defy, deny, mask **5** cloak **6** betray, negate, refute **7** conceal, falsify, gainsay **8** disguise, disprove **9** repudiate **10** camouflage, contradict, controvert, invalidate **12** misrepresent

belief **4** view **5** faith, guess, trust **6** theory **7** feeling, opinion **8** judgment, reliance **9** assurance, certitude, deduction, inference **10** assumption, conclusion, confidence, conviction, firm notion, hypothesis, impression, persuasion **11** expectation, presumption, supposition

beliefs **5** canon, creed, dogma, faith, tenet **6** ethics, gospel, morals **8** doctrine, morality **9** principle, teachings **10** conviction, persuasion

believable **8** credible, knowable, possible **9** plausible, thinkable **10** acceptable, convincing, imaginable, supposable **11** conceivable, perceivable

believe **4** hold **5** guess, infer, judge, think, trust **6** assume, credit, deduce, rely on **7** count on, fall for, imagine, presume, suppose, surmise, suspect, swallow, swear by **8** be sure of, consider, depend on, maintain, theorize **9** speculate **10** conjecture, presuppose, put faith in **11** hypothesize

believe in **5** trust **6** accept, esteem **7** approve, go in for, respect **11** have faith in **16** have confidence in

Believe It or Not
author: **13** Robert L Ripley

believer **7** admirer **8** advocate, disciple, partisan **9** supporter **16** faithful adherent

be like **5** equal, match **8** approach, resemble

Bel-Imperia
character in: **17** The Spanish Tragedy
author: **3** Kyd

Belinda
character in: **16** The Rape of the Lock
author: **4** Pope

belittle **5** knock, scorn **6** deride, malign **7** disdain, put down, run down, sneer at **8** minimize, mitigate, play down, pooh-pooh **9** deprecate, disparage, underrate **10** depreciate, undervalue **11** make light of **13** underestimate **16** cast aspersions on

belittling **5** snide **10** derogatory **11** deprecating, disparaging, unfavorable **12** depreciating **15** uncomplimentary

Belize
other name: **15** British Honduras
capital: **8** Belmopan
largest city/former capital: **10** Belize City
head of state: **13** prime minister **14** British monarch **15** governor-general
monetary unit: **6** dollar
island: **8** Turneffe
mountain range: **4** Maya
highest point: **12** Victoria Peak
river: **3** New **4** Moho **6** Belize, Monkey
sea: **9** Caribbean
physical feature:
gulf: **8** Honduras
peninsula: **7** Yucatan
swamp: **8** mangrove
people: **5** Mayan **6** Indian, Syrian **7** African, Chinese **15** Spanish-American
language: **7** English

bell **4** gong, peal **5** chime **6** tocsin **7** ringing **8** carillon **16** tintinnabulation

Bell, Alexander Graham
born: **8** Scotland
inventor of: **9** telephone **14** record cylinder
saying: **24** Mr Watson come here I want you

Bellamann, Henry
author of: **8** King's Row

Bellamy, Edward
author of: **8** Equality **15** Looking Backward

Bellamy, Ralph
born: **9** Chicago IL
roles: **11** Ellery Queen, Mike Barnett **13** The Awful Truth **14** Detective Story **15** Man Against Crime, State of the Union **19** Sunrise at Campobello

Bellarius
character in: **9** Cymbeline
author: **11** Shakespeare

Bellaston, Lady
character in: **8** Tom Jones
author: **8** Fielding

bell buoy **5** float **6** signal **13** channel marker

belle **4** star **5** queen **6** beauty **7** charmer **12** heart-stopper

Belle Dame Sans Merci, La
author: **9** John Keats

Bellefleur
author: **15** Joyce Carol Oates

Belle Helene, La
also: **14** Beautiful Helen
operetta by: **9** Offenbach

Bellerophon
form: **4** hero
brother: **8** Deliades
son: **11** Hippolochus
home: **7** Corinth
rode: **7** Pegasus
killed: **7** Chimera

Bell for Adano, A
author: **10** John Hersey
director: **9** Henry King
cast: **10** John Hodiak **11** Gene Tierney **13** William Bendix

bellicose *see* **11** belligerent

belligerence, belligerency **9** animosity, hostility, pugnacity **10** aggression, antagonism **11** bellicosity **12** warmongering **13** combativeness **14** aggressiveness, unfriendliness

belligerent **7** fighter, hostile, martial, warlike, warring **8** attacker, inimical **9** adversary, aggressor, bellicose, combatant, combative, irascible, irritable, truculent **10** aggressive, antagonist, pugnacious, unfriendly **11** bad-tempered, contentious, quarrelsome **12** antagonistic, cantankerous

belligerent state **3** foe **5** enemy **9** aggressor **13** hostile nation

Bellini, Gentile
born: **5** Italy **6** Venice
father: **6** Jacopo
brother: **8** Giovanni
artwork: **24** The Miracle of the True Cross **26** A Procession in St Mark's Square, The Miracle at Ponte di Lorenzo **27** St Mark Preaching in Alexandria **38** A Procession of Relics in the Piazza San Marco

Bellini, Giovanni (Giambellino)
born: **5** Italy **6** Venice
father: **6** Jacopo
brother: **7** Gentile
artwork: **8** St Jerome **16** Venus with a Mirror **18** St Francis in Ecstasy, The Madonna and Child **19** Allegory of Purgatory, The Agony in the Garden, The Barberini Madonna

Bellini, Jacopo
born: **5** Italy **6** Venice
son: **7** Gentile **8** Giovanni
artwork: **11** Crucifixion **16** Christ on the Cross **35** The Madonna and Child with Lionello d'Este

Bellini, Vincenzo
born: **5** Italy **7** Catania
composer of: **5** Norma, Zaira **8** Il Pirata **9** I Puritani **11** La Straniera **12** La Sonnambula **15** Bianca e Fernando

Bell Jar, The
author: **11** Sylvia Plath

Bellona
origin: **5** Roman
goddess of: **3** war
husband: **4** Mars
brother: **4** Mars
corresponds to: **4** Enyo

bellow **4** bawl, roar, yell **5** shout, whoop **6** holler, scream, shriek

Bellow, Saul
author of: **6** Herzog **13** Dean's December, Humboldt's Gift, Mosby's Memoirs **15** The Last Analysis **16** Mr Sammler's Planet **18** To Jerusalem and Back **25** The Adventures of Augie March

Bellows, George Wesley
born: **10** Columbus OH
artwork: **8** Lady Jean **11** Billy Sunday, Edith Cavell, Floating Ice, Up the Hudson **12** Forty-Two Kids **13** Men of the Docks **14** Rain on the River, Stag at Sharkey's **16** The Cliff Dwellers **18** Emma and her Children **21** Both Members of This Club

Bells Are Ringing
director: **16** Vincente Minnelli
cast: **9** Fred Clark **10** Dean Martin **12** Judy Holliday
song: **10** Just in Time **13** The Party's Over

Bells in Winter
author: **13** Czeslaw Milosz

Bells of St Mary's, The
director: **10** Leo McCarey
cast: **10** Bing Crosby (Father O'Malley) **12** Henry Travers **13** Ingrid Bergman
sequel to: **10** Going My Way
song: **20** Aren't You Glad You're You

bell tower **5** spire **6** belfry **7** steeple **9** campanile

Belluschi, Pietro
architect of: **21** Bank of America Building (San Francisco) **22** Juilliard School of Music (NYC) **31** Pan American World Airways Building (NYC, with Gropius)

bellwether **4** lead **5** doyen, guide, pilot **6** leader **8** director, shepherd **9** conductor, guidepost, precursor **10** forerunner, pacesetter **14** standard-bearer

belly **3** gut, yen **4** guts **5** taste, tummy **6** bowels, depths, desire, hunger, liking, paunch, vitals **7** abdomen, insides, midriff, stomach **8** appetite, interior, recesses **11** breadbasket

bellyache **4** beef, kick **5** gripe **6** grouch, grouse, squawk **7** grumble **8** complain **9** tummy ache **11** stomach ache **12** upset stomach

belong **6** go with **7** concern **8** attach to, be held by, be part of **9** be owned by, pertain to **10** be allied to **11** be a member of **12** be included in **15** be connected with, be the property of

belongings **4** gear, junk **5** goods, stuff **6** things **7** effects **8** movables **11** possessions **13** accouterments, paraphernalia **16** personal property

beloved **4** beau, dear, love, wife **5** loved, lover **6** adored, fiance, spouse, steady **7** admired, darling, dearest, fiancee, husband, revered **8** endeared, esteemed, loved one, precious **9** betrothed, boyfriend, cherished, respected, treasured **10** girlfriend, sweetheart

below **4** less **5** lower, under **6** in hell **7** beneath, on earth, short of **8** inferior, unworthy **9** at a low ebb, downwards **10** downstairs, downstream, second-rate, underneath **11** at a discount, at the foot of, indifferent, subordinate, underground

below par **3** bad **4** poor **8** inferior **9** imperfect **10** second-rate **12** below average, not up to snuff

below standard **3** bad **4** poor **5** lousy **6** faulty, shoddy **8** below par, inferior, slipshod, terrible **9** imperfect **10** second-rate **12** not up to snuff

Belshazzar
father: **9** Nabonidus **14** Nebuchadnezzar

belt **4** area, band, land, sash, zone **5** cinch, layer, strip **6** circle, girdle, region, stripe **7** country **8** district, encircle **9** waistband **10** cummerbund

Belteshazzar
Babylonian name of: **6** Daniel
friend: **7** Meshach **8** Abednego, Shadrach

Belus
king of: **7** Chemmis
father: **8** Poseidon
mother: **5** Libya
twin brother: **6** Agenor
wife: **8** Anchinoe
son: **6** Danaus **8** Aegyptus
daughter: **4** Dido

Belushi, John
born: **9** Chicago IL
roles: **9** Neighbors **11** Animal House **16** The Blues Brothers **17** Saturday Night Live

be manifest **6** appear **7** be clear, be plain **8** be patent **9** be evident, be obvious **10** be apparent

bemoan **3** rue **5** mourn **6** bewail, lament, regret **7** cry over **8** weep over **9** whine over **10** grieve over

bemused **5** dazed, fuzzy **7** muddled, stunned **8** confused **9** engrossed, stupefied **10** bewildered, dull-witted, thoughtful **11** preoccupied **12** absent-minded

be nauseated by **4** hate **5** abhor **6** detest, loathe **7** despise **8** execrate **9** abominate **11** can't stomach **13** be disgusted by, find repulsive, find revolting, find sickening

Benbow, Horace
character in: **9** Sanctuary
author: **8** Faulkner

Ben Casey
character: **12** Dr David Zorba, Dr Ted Hoffman **13** Nick Kanavaras **14** Dr Maggie Graham
cast: **8** Sam Jaffe **10** Nick Dennis **12** Harry Landers, Vince Edwards **14** Bettye Ackerman

bench **3** pew **4** seat **5** board, court, stool, table **6** settee **7** counter, take out, trestle **8** sideline, tribunal **9** judiciary, workbench, worktable **10** second team **11** judge's chair, substitutes **12** second string

Benchley, Peter
author of: 4 Jaws **7** The Deep

Benchley, Robert
author of: 14 From Bed to Worse **21** Benchley Beside Himself, My Ten Years in a Quandary

benchmark 4 norm **5** gauge, guide, model **7** example, measure **8** exemplar, paradigm, standard **9** criterion, principle, prototype, reference, yardstick **10** touchstone

bend 3 arc, bow **4** flex, hook, lean, loop, mold, sway, turn, warp, wind **5** crook, curve, defer, force, shape, stoop, twist, yield **6** accede, attend, buckle, coerce, compel, crouch, give in, relent, submit **7** bow down, contort, control, succumb **9** genuflect, influence, surrender **10** buckle down, capitulate **11** make crooked

Bend in the River, The
author: 9 V S Naipaul

Bendix, William
born: 9 New York NY
roles: 8 Hostages, Lifeboat **11** The Hairy Ape **13** A Bell for Adano **14** The Life of Riley **16** Guadalcanal Diary, The Babe Ruth Story

bend to one's own will
4 tame **5** break, train **6** master, subdue **8** overcome **10** discipline **12** show who's boss **18** have under one's thumb

beneath 5 below, lower, under **9** covered by **10** inferior to, underneath, unworthy of **11** subordinate, underground **16** below one's dignity

Benedick
character in: 19 Much Ado About Nothing
author: 11 Shakespeare

benedictine
type: 6 brandy, cognac **7** liqueur
flavor: 4 herb
with brandy: 5 B and B
with bourbon: 9 Twin Hills **13** Brighton Punch
with whiskey: 10 Frisco Sour

benediction 6 prayer **7** benison **8** blessing **10** invocation **12** consecration **13** closing prayer

benefaction 4 alms, gift **5** grant **7** charity **8** bestowal, donation, offering **9** endowment **10** almsgiving **12** contribution, dispensation, philanthropy

benefactor 5 angel, donor **6** backer, friend, helper, patron **7** sponsor **8** upholder **9** supporter **11** contributor **14** fairy godmother

beneficent 6 benign, kindly **7** liberal **8** generous, salutary **10** beneficial, benevolent, charitable **11** magnanimous **13** philanthropic

beneficial 6 useful **7** good for, healing, helpful **8** valuable **9** favorable, healthful **10** productive, profitable, propitious **12** advantageous, contributive

beneficiary 4 heir **7** grantee, heiress, legatee **8** receiver **9** inheritor, recipient

benefit 3 aid, use **4** gain, good, help **5** asset, avail, serve, value, worth **6** assist, behalf, better, profit **7** advance, be aided, service **8** be helped, be served, blessing, interest **9** advantage, do good for **10** be useful to, betterment, profit from **13** charity affair **18** charity performance

Benet, Stephen Vincent
author of: 7 America **8** Tiger Joy **11** Western Star **14** John Brown's Body, Thirteen O'Clock, Young Adventure **16** Five Men and Pompey **19** Tales Before Midnight, The Headless Horseman **20** The Beginning of Wisdom **24** The Devil and Daniel Webster

benevolence 7 charity **8** good will, kindness **9** benignity **10** compassion, generosity, kindliness, liberality **13** bountifulness **14** charitableness **15** humanitarianism, kindheartedness

benevolent 3 kin **6** benign, humane, tender **7** liberal **8** generous **9** benignant, bounteous, bountiful, unselfish **10** bighearted, charitable **11** considerate, kindhearted, warmhearted **12** humanitarian **13** compassionate, philanthropic

Bengali
language family: 12 Indo-European
branch: 11 Indo-Iranian
group: 5 Indic
spoken in: 5 (northern) India

Ben-Hur
author: 10 Lew Wallace
character: 4 Iras, Isas **5** Jesus **6** Esther **7** Messala **9** Balthasar, Simonides **11** Judah Ben-Hur
director: 12 William Wyler
cast: 11 Jack Hawkins, Stephen Boyd **12** Hugh Griffith **14** Charlton Heston (Judah Ben-Hur)
setting: 9 Palestine
Oscar for: 5 actor (Heston) **7** picture **8** director **14** cinematography **15** supporting actor (Griffith)

benighted 4 dumb **5** crude, unhip **8** backward, ignorant, untaught **9** primitive, untutored **10** illiterate, uncultured, uneducated, uninformed, unlettered, unschooled **11** empty-headed, know-nothing, uncivilized **12** uncultivated **13** unenlightened

benign 4 good, kind, mild, nice, soft **5** balmy, lucky **6** genial, gentle, humane, kindly, tender **7** affable **8** gracious, harmless, pleasant, salutary **9** favorable, healthful, innocuous, temperate **10** auspicious, benevolent, propitious **11** encouraging, kindhearted, softhearted **13** tender-hearted

benignant 4 kind **6** benign, humane, kindly, tender **9** forgiving **10** benevolent **11** kindhearted **13** compassionate, tenderhearted

benignity 8 good will, kindness **10** compassion, kindliness **11** benevolence **15** kindheartedness

Benin ***see box***

Benito Cereno
author: 14 Herman Melville

Benjamin
father: 5 Jacob
mother: 6 Rachel
also known as: 6 Benoni
brother: 3 Dan, Gad **4** Levi **5** Asher, Judah **6** Joseph, Reuben, Simeon **7** Zebulun **8** Issachar, Naphtali
sister: 5 Dinah
descendant of: 11 Benjaminite

Bennet family
characters in: 17 Pride and Prejudice
members: 4 Jane, Mary **5** Kitty, Lydia **9** Elizabeth
author: 6 Austen

Bennett, Arnold
author of: 8 Accident **10** Clayhanger, Lord Raingo, Milestones, These Twain **11** Buried Alive **13** Hilda Lessways, Riceyman Steps **15** The Old Wives' Tale **18** Anna of the Five Towns

Benny, Jack
real name: 16 Benjamin Kubelsky
born: 10 Waukegan IL
roles: 12 Charley's Aunt

Benin
other name: **17** Republic of Dahomey
capital: **9** Porto-Novo
largest city: **7** Cotonou
others: **4** Pobe **5** Kandi, Kerou, Ketou, Porga **6** Abomey, Ouidah **7** Parakou, Savalou **8** Aplahoue
government: **30** Military Council of the Revolution
monetary unit: **5** franc **7** centime
lake: **5** Aheme **6** Nokoue
mountain: **7** Atakora
river: **4** Mono **5** Niger, Oueme **6** Couffo
sea: **8** Atlantic
physical feature:
gulf: **6** Guinea
plains: **6** Borgou
people: **3** Fon, Pla **4** Adja, Aizo, Mina, Peul **5** Pedah, Peuhl, Somba **6** Bariba, Fulani, Yoruba **8** Pilapila **9** Dahomeyan
language: **3** Fon **5** Dendi **6** Bariba, French, Fulani, Yoruba
religion: **5** Islam **6** tribal **7** animism **13** Roman Catholic
food:
tapioca: **4** gari

13 Jack Benny Show, To Be or Not To Be **16** Artists and Models

Benoni *see* **8** Benjamin

Benson
character: **5** Kraus **12** (Lt Gov) Benson DuBois **13** (Gov) Eugene Gatling
cast: **10** James Noble **11** Inga Swenson **15** Robert Guillaume

bent **4** bias, gift, mind **5** bowed, flair, knack **6** angled, arched, curved, genius, liking, talent **7** ability, aptness, crooked, faculty, hunched, leaning, stooped, twisted **8** aptitude, capacity, facility, fondness, penchant, tendency **9** contorted, endowment **10** attraction, partiality, proclivity, propensity **11** disposition, inclination **12** predilection **14** predisposition

bent into folds **6** fluted, ridged **7** creased, grooved, pleated **8** crinkled, furrowed, puckered, wrinkled **10** corrugated

Benton, Robert
director of: **14** Kramer vs Kramer (Oscar) **16** Places in the Heart

Benton, Thomas Hart
born: **8** Neosho MO
artwork: **7** Bubbles **8** Boomtown **9** Homestead **12** American Life **13** Arts of the West, Cotton Pickers **14** Threshing Wheat **19** Louisiana Rice Fields, The Lord Is My Shepherd

Benue-Congo
language family: **16** Niger-Kordofanian
group: **10** Niger-Congo
includes: **3** Tiv **4** Zulu **5** Bantu, Jukun **6** Chwana, Nyanja **7** Kikongo, Luganda, Swahili

benumb **4** daze, dull **5** blunt **6** deaden **7** stupefy **15** make insensitive

Benvolio
character in: **14** Romeo and Juliet
author: **11** Shakespeare

Benz, Karl
nationality: **6** German
inventor of: **22** electric ignition engine **26** differential gear automobile
built first practical: **10** automobile

be obvious **6** appear **7** be clear, be plain **8** be patent **9** be evident **10** be apparent, be manifest

be off **2** go **5** leave, scram **6** beat it, begone, cut out, depart, go away, set out **8** set forth, withdraw **10** make tracks

be of one mind **5** agree **6** accord, concur **10** think alike **11** see eye to eye

be of use **3** aid **4** help **5** serve **6** assist **7** benefit

be on a par with **5** equal **6** be up to **7** compare **10** be as good as **12** be comparable **14** be in a class with

be on the sick list **3** ail **5** be ill **6** be sick **8** be unwell **12** be indisposed **13** be in ill health **17** be under the weather

Beor
son: **4** Bela **6** Balaam

Beothuk (Red Indians)
location: **6** Canada **12** Newfoundland
intermixed with: **7** Naskapi

Beowulf
author: **7** unknown
character: **4** Finn **5** Breca, Hnaef, Oslaf, Scyld **6** Wiglaf **7** Guthlaf, Hengest, Higelac, Hrethel, Unferth **8** Aeschere, Heardred, Hondscio, Hrothgar **9** Hildeburh
great hall: **6** Heorot
monster: **7** Grendel **14** Grendel's mother
tribe: **5** Danes, Geats **8** Frisians
Beowulf tears from Grendel: **3** arm

bequeath **4** will **5** endow, leave **6** impart **7** consign **8** hand down

bequest **6** legacy **8** bestowal **9** endowment **10** settlement **11** inheritance

be part of **4** form **6** make up **8** belong to **9** appertain, pertain to **10** constitute

be patent **6** appear **7** be clear, be plain **9** be evident, be obvious **10** be apparent, be manifest

be pertinent to **4** bear **5** apply, refer **6** affect, relate **7** concern, pertain **9** appertain, touch upon

be plain **6** appear **7** be clear **8** be patent **9** be evident, be obvious **10** be apparent, be manifest

be pleased with **4** like **5** favor **7** approve

berate **5** scold **6** rail at, rebuke **7** bawl out, chew out, reprove, upbraid **8** reproach **9** castigate, criticize, reprimand **10** take to task, tongue-lash

Berber
language family: **11** Afro-asiatic **13** Hamito-Semitic
spoken in: **6** Sahara **11** North Africa

Berchta *see* **7** Perchta

bereave **3** rob **5** strip **6** divest **7** deprive **10** dispossess

Berecyntia *see* **6** Cybele

Berenice's Hair
constellation of: **13** Coma Berenices

be resigned to **6** accept **8** tolerate

Beret
character in: **16** Giants of the Earth
author: **7** Rolvaag

be revolted by **4** hate **5** abhor **6** detest, loathe **7** despise **8** execrate **9** abominate **10** recoil from, shrink from **11** can't stomach **13** find repulsive

berg **4** floe **7** glacier, iceberg, icefloe
South African: **8** mountain
French: **4** neve **5** serac

Berg, Alban
born: **6** Vienna **7** Austria
composer of: **4** Lulu **7** Wozzeck

Bergen, Candace
father: **11** Edgar Bergen
born: **14** Beverly Hills CA
roles: **8** The Group **15** Carnal Knowledge

Berger, Thomas
author of: **7** The Feud **9** Neighbors **10** Vital Parts **11** Killing Time **12** Little Big Man, Sneaky People **15** Regiment of Women

Bergman, Ingmar
director of: **14** The Seventh Seal **16** Cries and Whispers, Wild Strawberries **17** Fanny and Alexander **19** Scenes from a Marriage **20** Smiles of a Summer Night

Bergman, Ingrid
born: **6** Sweden **9** Stockholm
roles: **8** Gaslight (Oscar) **9** Anastasia (Oscar), Joan of Arc, Notorious **10** Casablanca, Intermezzo, Spellbound **17** A Woman Called Golda, The Bells of St Mary's **19** For Whom the Bell Tolls **24** Murder on the Orient Express **25** The Inn of the Sixth Happiness

Berith, Berit, Brith, Brit
8 covenant **12** circumcision

Berle, Milton
real name: **15** Milton Berlinger
nickname: **11** Uncle Miltie **12** Mr Television
born: **9** New York NY
roles: **17** The Texaco Star Hour **18** Who's Minding the Mint **23** Always Leave Them Laughing

Berlin (East, West)
landmark: **14** Humboldt Castle **15** Gruenwald Castle **16** Berlin Opera House, Markisches Museum **21** Scharlottenburg Castle **29** Kaiser-Wilhelm-Gedachtniskirche
river: **5** Spree
square: **14** Alexander-Platz

Berlin, Elaine
real name of: **9** Elaine May

Berlinger, Milton
real name of: **11** Milton Berle

Berlioz, (Louis) Hector
born: **6** France **13** La Cote St Andre
composer of: **6** Rob Roy, Te Deum **7** Requiem, **8** Herminie, King Lear, Waverley **9** Cleopatra, Nuits d'Ete **10** Le Corsaire, Les Troyens, The Trojans **11** Sardanapale **13** Harold in Italy **14** Les Francs Juges, Romeo and Juliet **16** Benvenuto Cellini, Damnation of Faust, Le Carnaval Romain, L'Enfance du Christ **18** Beatrice et Benedict **20** Symphonie Fantastique **28** Symphonie Funebre et Triomphale

Bermuda
other name: **13** Somers Islands
capital/largest city: **8** Hamilton
others: **8** St George
head of state: **14** British monarch **15** governor general
island: **4** Boaz **5** Coney **7** Bermuda, Ireland, Watford **8** Somerset, St Davids **9** St Georges
highest point: **8** Town Hill
sea: **8** Atlantic
physical feature:
harbor: **6** Castle
hill: **5** Gibbs
people:
discoverer: **14** Juan de Bermudez
language: **7** English
religion: **8** Anglican **10** Protestant **15** Church of England
feature:
dancers: **6** Gombey

Bern
capital of: **11** Switzerland
landmark: **10** Clock Tower **12** Nydegg Church
river: **4** Aare

Bernard, Henriette-Rosine
real name of: **14** Sarah Bernhardt

Bernhardt, Sarah
real name: **22** Henriette-Rosine Bernard
nickname: **11** Divine Sarah
born: **5** Paris **6** France
roles: **6** Phedre **7** Hernani, Ruy Blas **8** King Lear **14** Queen Elizabeth **17** La Dame aux Camelias

Bernini, Gianlorenzo (Giovanni Lorenzo)
born: **5** Italy **6** Naples
father: **6** Pietro
artwork: **7** Montoya **8** Louis XIV, Vigevano **10** Bellarmine, St Longinus **13** Cathedra Petri, Francis I d'Este, The Assumption **15** Apollo and Daphne **18** Costanza Buonarelli **19** The Rape of Proserpina **21** Saints Andrew and Thomas, The Ecstasy of St Theresa **24** Blessed Lodovica Albertoni **25** Aeneas Anchises and Ascanius
architect of: **12** Santa Bibiana **16** Piazza of St Peter's (Rome) **19** Palazzo Montecitorio **21** Sant' Andrea al Quirinale **22** Palazzo Chigi-Odescalchi **23** Fountain of the Four Rivers **24** Santa Maria dell' Assunzione

Bernoulli, Daniel
field: **11** mathematics
nationality: **5** Swiss
theory of: **5** gases **6** fluids **18** Bernoulli's Equation

Bernstein, Carl
author of: **12** The Final Days (with Bob Woodward) **19** All the President's Men (with Bob Woodward)
newspaper reporter for: **14** Washington Post

Bernstein, Leonard
born: **10** Lawrence MA
composer of: **4** Mass **7** Candide, Kaddish **8** Jeremiah **9** Facsimile, Fancy Free, On the Town **13** West Side Story, Wonderful Town **15** The Age of Anxiety, Trouble in Tahiti **16** Chichester Psalms

Beroe
father: **6** Adonis
mother: **9** Aphrodite
nurse of: **6** Semele

Berowne
character in: **16** Love's Labour's Lost
author: **11** Shakespeare

Berra, Yogi (Lawrence Peter Berra)
sport: **8** baseball
position: **5** coach **7** catcher
team: **14** New York Yankees

berry **3** egg **4** seed **5** fruit, grain, grape **6** dollar, kernel, tomato, banana **7** currant **8** allspice, bayberry, mulberry **9** blueberry, cranberry, raspberry **10** blackberry, gooseberry, peppercorn, strawberry **11** boysenberry, huckleberry, pomegranate **12** checkerberry
poisonous: **9** baneberry

Berryman, John
author of: **8** Recovery **9** Delusions **11** Love and Fame **12** 77 Dream Songs **13** The Dream Songs **16** Berryman's Sonnets **19** The Freedom of

the Poet **21** His Toy His Dream His Rest **26** Homage to Mistress Bradstreet

berserk **4** amok, wild **5** crazy **6** insane **7** frantic, violent **8** demented, deranged, frenzied, maniacal, wild-eyed **9** desperate **10** distracted, distraught **12** out of control

Berserker
origin: **6** Nordic
form: **7** warrior

berth **3** bed, job **4** bunk, dock, pier, post, quay, slip, spot **5** haven, niche, place, wharf **6** billet, employ, office **8** position **9** anchorage, situation **11** appointment **12** resting place **13** sleeping place

Berthollet, Claude Louis
field: **9** chemistry
nationality: **6** French
researched: **7** ammonia **8** chlorine

Bertram
character in: **20** All's Well That Ends Well
author: **11** Shakespeare

Bertram family
characters in: **13** Mansfield Park
members: **3** Tom **5** Julia, Maria **6** Edmund **9** Sir Thomas
author: **6** Austen

beryl
color: **5** green **6** yellow

Berzelius, Jons Jakob
field: **9** chemistry
nationality: **7** Swedish
developed: **15** chemical symbols
discovered: **6** cerium **7** silicon, thorium **8** selenium, titanium **9** zirconium
founded: **15** modern chemistry

be satisfactory **2** do **6** answer **7** suffice **8** be enough **10** be adequate, pass muster **12** be sufficient, do well enough

be scant **4** lack, want **8** be skimpy **9** fall short **14** be insufficient **15** be in short supply

beseech **3** beg **4** pray **6** adjure **7** entreat, implore **9** plead with **10** supplicate

beset **3** dog, set **4** bead, deck, stud **5** annoy, array, hem in, hound, worry **6** assail, badger, harass, pester, plague **7** bedevil, besiege, set upon **8** surround **9** beleaguer, embellish

be sick **3** ail **5** be ill **8** be unwell **12** be indisposed **13** be in ill health

beside **2** by **4** near **5** saved **6** except, nearby, unless **7** abreast, barring, without **8** let alone **9** adjoining, alongside, aside from, other than **10** on a par with, side by side **12** compared with, in addition to

beside oneself **4** wild **6** elated, joyful, joyous, raging **7** berserk, exalted, frantic, furious, ranting **8** agitated, blissful, distrait, ecstatic, frenetic, frenzied **9** delirious, in a frenzy, overjoyed, rapturous **10** distracted, distraught, distressed, enraptured **11** carried away, overwrought, transported **13** out of one's wits

besides **3** but **4** also, save **6** as well, except, saving **7** barring **8** moreover **9** excepting, excluding, other than **11** exclusive of, furthermore

besiege **3** dog **5** annoy, beset, hound **6** assail, badger, harass, pester, plague **7** assault, bedevil **9** beleaguer **10** lay siege to

besmear **4** soil **5** dirty, muddy, smear, stain, sully **6** mess up, slop up, smudge **7** begrime, tarnish **8** besmirch

besmeared **5** dirty, grimy, messy **6** grubby, smudgy **7** muddied, sullied **8** begrimed **10** besmirched

besmirch **4** soil **5** smear, stain, sully, taint **6** defame, defile **7** blacken, corrupt, debauch, degrade, slander, tarnish **8** discolor, disgrace, dishonor **9** discredit

besotted **5** drunk **6** sodden, soused, wasted, zapped, zonked **7** smashed **9** plastered **10** inebriated, infatuated **11** intoxicated **17** under the influence **20** three sheets to the wind

bespangle **3** dot **4** gild, star, stud **5** adorn, jewel **6** bedeck **7** dress up, festoon, garnish **8** decorate, ornament **9** embellish **10** illuminate

bespatter **4** blot, soil, spot **5** decry, dirty, libel, smear, stain, sully, taint **6** debase, defame, defile, smudge, splash **7** condemn, slander, smotter, tarnish **8** denounce, reproach **9** deprecate, fling dirt **10** calumniate, disapprove

Bessemer, Sir Henry
nationality: **7** English
inventor of manufacturing process for: **5** steel

best **3** top **4** most, pick **5** cream, elite **6** choice, finest, nicest, utmost **7** hardest, largest **8** foremost, greatest, superior, topnotch **9** greetings, loveliest, most fully, most of all, unequaled, unrivaled **10** unexcelled **11** compliments, unsurpassed **13** most competent, most desirable, most excellent **14** highest quality, kindest regards

Best, Charles Herbert
field: **10** physiology
nationality: **8** Canadian
discovered: **7** insulin

best group **3** top **5** cream, elite **6** choice **9** chosen few **10** select body **14** cream of the crop, creme de la creme

bestial **5** cruel **6** brutal, savage **7** beastly **8** barbaric, depraved, inhumane, ruthless **9** barbarous, merciless

bestir **4** goad, spur, stir, urge **5** rouse, speed **6** arouse, excite, hasten **7** quicken **8** activate **9** get moving

bestir oneself **5** rouse **8** be active **9** make haste **10** get up early, lose no time **11** keep moving **15** make short work of **19** seize the opportunity

bestow **3** use **4** give, mete **5** apply, award, grant, lay on, spend **6** accord, confer, devote, donate, employ, expend, impart, occupy, render **7** consign, consume, deal out, deliver, hand out, present, utilize **8** dispense, give away **9** apportion **10** settle upon, turn over to

bestowal **4** alms, gift **5** bonus, favor, grant **6** reward **7** charity, present, tribute **8** donation, gratuity, offering **9** endowment **10** conferment, recompense **11** benefaction **12** contribution, dispensation

best society
French: **10** grand monde

Best Years of Our Lives, The
director: **12** William Wyler
based on story by: **15** MacKinlay Kantor
script: **14** Robert Sherwood
cast: **8** Myrna Loy **11** Dana Andrews **12** Teresa Wright, Virginia Mayo **13** Frederic March, Harold Russell **15** Hoagy Carmichael
Oscar for: **5** actor (March) **7** picture **8** director

be sufficient **6** answer **7** suffice **8** be enough **10** be adequate, pass muster **12** do well enough **14** be satisfactory

bet **4** ante, risk **5** stake, wager **6** chance, gamble, hazard, plunge **7** venture **8** make a bet **9** speculate **11** speculation

bete noir **5** bogey **6** plague **7** bugaboo, bugbear **8** anathema, bogeyman **9** annoyance **10** black beast

be thankful **8** thank God **10** appreciate **11** thank heaven **19** thank one's lucky stars

Bethe, Hans Albrecht
field: **7** physics
developed: **8** atom bomb
awarded: **10** Nobel Prize

be the same **5** agree, equal, match **6** equate **7** balance **11** be identical

Bethuel
son: **5** Laban

betide **4** fall **5** occur **6** befall, chance, happen **10** come to pass

betimes **5** early **10** in good time

betoken **4** show **5** augur **6** attest, denote **7** portend, presage, signify **8** foretell

betray **4** dupe, fink, jilt, show, tell **5** rat on, trick **6** expose, reveal, squeal, tell on, unmask **7** abandon, deceive, divulge, lay bare, let down, let slip, sell out, two-time, uncover, violate **8** blurt out, disclose, give away **9** play Judas **10** be disloyal **11** double-cross **12** be unfaithful **13** inform against, play false with **14** break faith with

betrayal **7** perfidy, telling, treason **8** bad faith, sedition, trickery **9** chicanery, deception, duplicity, falseness, treachery, two-timing, violation **10** disclosure, disloyalty, divulgence, revelation **11** double-cross **13** breach of faith, double-dealing **14** unfaithfulness

betrayal of trust **7** falsity, perfidy **8** apostasy, cheating **9** falseness, recreancy **10** disloyalty, infidelity **11** inconstancy **13** deceitfulness, double-dealing, faithlessness **14** unfaithfulness

Betrayer **13** Judas Iscariot

betroth **6** commit, engage, pledge **7** espouse, promise **8** affiance, contract

betrothal **5** troth **8** espousal **10** affiancing, betrothing, engagement

betrothed **6** fiance **7** engaged, fiancee **8** promised **9** affianced

Bettelheim, Bruno
author of: **15** Love Is Not Enough **16** The Informed Heart **20** The Uses of Enchantment

better **3** top **4** more **5** finer, outdo, raise **6** bigger, enrich, exceed, fitter, larger, longer, refine, uplift **7** advance, elevate, enhance, farther, forward, further, greater, improve, mending, promote, surpass, upgrade **8** heighten, improved, increase, outstrip, stronger, superior **9** cultivate, healthier, improving **10** preferable, recovering, strengthen **11** more healthy, progressing

bettering **9** elevation **10** betterment **11** advancement, improvement

betterment **4** good **6** reform **7** benefit **8** revision **9** advantage, amendment, promotion **10** correction, enrichment **11** advancement, improvement **12** amelioration, regeneration **13** rectification **14** reconstruction

better than average **2** A-1 **3** A-OK **4** aces, fine, good, tops **5** great, prime, super **6** choice, grade-A, superb **7** capital, special **8** peerless, sterling, superior, terrific, topnotch **9** excellent, first-rate, marvelous, matchless, wonderful **10** first-class, inimitable, preeminent, remarkable, tremendous **11** exceptional, outstanding, superlative **12** incomparable **13** extraordinary

between **4** amid **5** among, entre **6** amidst, atwixt, shared **7** betwixt, joining **9** in the midst **10** connecting

between ourselves
French: **9** entre nous
Latin: **8** inter nos

Between the Battles
author: **20** Bjornstjerne Bjornson

between themselves
Latin: **7** inter se

between us **9** entre nous, privately **14** confidentially **15** between you and me **16** between me and thee, between ourselves

betwixt and between **4** so-so **7** average **8** confused **9** in between, undecided **14** halfway between **21** neither one nor the other

Beulah, Land of
place in: **16** Pilgrim's Progress
author: **6** Bunyan

be unlike **4** vary **6** differ **7** deviate, diverge **8** conflict, disagree **12** be at variance, be discordant, be dissimilar

be unwell **3** ail **5** be ill **6** be sick **12** be indisposed **13** be in ill health

be unwilling to pursue
Latin: **13** nolle prosequi

bevel **4** blow, cant, ream, tool **5** angle, bezel, miter, mitre, slant, slope, snape, splay **6** aslant **7** incline, oblique **8** slanting

beverage **3** ade, ale, cup, nog, pop, tea **4** beer, brew, dram, grog, milk, soda, soup, wine **5** broth, cider, cocoa, draft, drink, juice, julep, lager, leban, punch, toddy, water **6** bishop, coffee, cordial, eggnog, liquid, liquor, potion **7** limeade, seltzer, spirits, wassail **8** aperitif, cocktail, highball, lemonade, libation, potation **9** champagne, chocolate, orangeade

Beverley, Constance de
character in: **7** Marmion
author: **5** Scott

Beverly Hillbillies, The
character: **11** Jed Clampett **12** Jane Hathaway, Jethro Bodine **14** Granny Clampett, Milton Drysdale **16** Ellie May Clampett
cast: **9** Irene Ryan, Max Baer Jr, Nancy Kulp **10** Buddy Ebsen **12** Donna Douglas **13** Raymond Bailey

Beverly Hills Cop
director: **11** Martin Brest
cast: **11** Eddie Murphy **13** Judge Reinhold, Lisa Eilbacher

bevy **4** band, body, herd, host, pack **5** brood, covey, crowd, drove, flock, group, horde, party, shoal, swarm **6** clutch, flight, gaggle, school, throng **7** company, coterie **9** gathering, multitude **10** assemblage, collection

bewail **3** rue **5** mourn **6** bemoan, lament, regret **7** cry over, deplore **8** moan over, weep over **10** grieve over

beware **4** mind **6** be wary **7** look out **8** take care, take heed **9** be careful **11** take warning, watch out for **12** be on the alert, guard against **15** take precautions

beware of the dog
Latin: **9** cave canem

bewhiskered **5** bushy, hairy **6** shaggy **7** bearded, bristly, hirsute **8** unshaven **11** mustachioed

bewilder **5** addle, mix up **6** baffle, bemuse, muddle, puzzle **7** confuse, fluster, mystify, nonplus, perplex, stupefy **8** befuddle **10** disconcert

bewildered **7** at a loss, up a tree **8** all at sea, confused **9** perplexed **10** confounded, nonplussed **12** disconcerted

bewilderment **9** confusion **10** perplexity, puzzlement **11** frustration **13** mystification

bewitch **4** jinx **5** charm, spook **6** turn on **7** bedevil, beguile, delight, enchant **8** entrance **9** captivate, enrapture, fascinate **12** cast a spell on **14** put under a spell

bewitched **7** charmed, seduced **8** beguiled **9** bedeviled, enchanted, entranced **10** captivated, enraptured, fascinated, spellbound **11** under a spell

Bewitched
character: **6** Endora, Serena **7** Maurice **9** Aunt Clara, Esmerelda, Larry Tate **11** Uncle Arthur **12** Abner Kravitz **13** Gladys Kravitz **14** Darrin Stephens **15** Tabitha Stephens **16** Samantha Stephens
cast: **8** Dick York **9** Paul Lynde **10** David White **11** Dick Sargent, Marion Lorne, Sandra Gould **12** George Tobias, Maurice Evans **13** Alice Ghostley **14** Agnes Moorehead **19** Elizabeth Montgomery

bewitching **8** alluring, charming, enticing, fetching, tempting **9** appealing, beguiling, disarming, seductive **10** enchanting, entrancing **11** captivating, fascinating **12** irresistible

be worthy of **4** earn, rate **5** merit **7** deserve

bey, beg **4** lord **6** prince **8** governor

beyond **2** by **4** over, past **5** above, later, ultra **6** abroad, except, yonder **7** beneath, besides, farther, further, outside, passing **8** superior **9** exceeding, hereafter **10** out of range, out of reach **11** at a distance, in addition to

Beyond Desire
author: **15** Maxwell Anderson

beyond hope **8** hopeless **9** desperate **10** despairing

Beyond Human Power
author: **20** Bjornstjerne Bjornson

beyond one's means **10** immoderate **11** extravagant **15** too high on the hog

beyond question **4** sure **6** surely **7** certain, decided, settled **9** certainly, decidedly **10** absolutely, positively **12** without doubt

Bharat (Varsha) *see* **5** India

Bhot *see* **5** Tibet

Bhutan ***see box***

Bia
origin: **5** Greek
personifies: **5** force
father: **11** Titan Pallas
mother: **4** Styx
brother: **5** Zelos **6** Cratus
sister: **4** Nike

Biadice
husband: **8** Cretheus

Bianca
character in: **19** The Taming of the Shrew
author: **11** Shakespeare

Bianchi, Mose
born: **5** Italy, Milan
artwork: **11** Snow in Milan **21** Return from the Festival

bias **4** bent, sway **5** angle, slant **7** bigotry, feeling, leaning **8** tendency **9** fixed idea, prejudice, proneness **10** narrow view, partiality, predispose, proclivity, propensity, unfairness **11** inclination, intolerance **12** diagonal line, one-sidedness, predilection **13** preconception **16** narrow-mindedness, preconceived idea

Bias
father: **8** Amythaon
mother: **7** Idomene
brother: **8** Melampus
wife: **4** Pero **10** Iphianassa
son: **6** Talaus
daughter: **8** Anaxibia
secured: **6** cattle
cattle owned by: **8** Phylacus

biased **6** unfair, unjust **7** bigoted, slanted **8** inclined **9** arbitrary **10** intolerant, prejudiced **11** close-minded, opinionated **12** narrow-minded

bibelot **5** curio **7** trinket **8** ornament **9** objet d'art

bible **5** guide **6** manual **8** handbook **9** authority, guidebook **13** reference book

Bible **6** Gospel **7** the Book **8** good book, Holy Writ **10** Scriptures **11** bibliotheca, the Good Book **13** holy scripture **14** Holy Scriptures, sacred writings

Bible, books of
Old Testament: **3** Job **4** Amos, Ezra, Joel, Osee, Ruth **5** Hosea, Jonah, Jonas, Josue, Kings, Micah, Nahum, Tobit **6** Abdias, Aggeus, Baruch, Daniel, Esdras, Esther, Exodus, Haggai, Isaiah, Isaias, Joshua, Judges, Judith, Psalms, Samuel, Sir-

---

Bhutan
other name: **7** Druk-Yul **15** Kingdom of Bhutan, Land of the Dragon
capital/largest city: **6** Thimbu **7** Thimphu
others: **4** Paro **12** Phuntsholing **14** Wangdu Phedrang
government:
assembly: **7** Tsongdu
head of state/government:
hereditary king: **10** dragon king, druk gyalpo
other leader:
spiritual leader: **10** dharma raja
temporal ruler: **7** deb raja
monetary unit: **5** paisa, rupee **8** chetrums, ngultrum
mountain: **5** Black **9** Himalayas **10** Chomo Lhari
highest point: **10** Kula Kangri
river: **4** Kuru, Paro **5** Machu, Manas, Pachu, Torsa **6** Amochu, Raidak, Tongsa **7** Sankosh, Thinchu
physical feature:
plain: **5** Duars
people: **5** Monpa **6** Bhutia **7** Tibetan **8** Assamese, Nepalese
dragon people: **7** Drukpas
language: **5** Hindi, Lhoke **7** Tibetan **8** Dzongkha, Nepalese
religion: **15** Tibetan Buddhism
place:
fortress (dzong): **4** Paro **6** Bya Kar, Tongsa **8** Tashi Cho
feature:
pony: **6** Tangun

ach, Tobias, Wisdom **7** Ezekiel, Genesis, Habacuc, Malachi, Micheas, Numbers, Obadiah **8** Ezechiel, Habakkuk, Jeremiah, Jeremias, Nehemiah, Proverbs **9** Leviticus, Maccabees, Machabees, Malachias, Sophonias, Zacharias, Zechariah, Zephaniah **10** Chronicles **11** Deuteronomy, Song of Songs **12** Ecclesiastes, Lamentations **13** Paralipomenon, Song of Solomon **14** Ecclesiasticus **19** Canticle of Canticles
New Testament: **4** Acts, John, Jude, Luke, Mark **5** James, Peter **6** Romans **7** Hebrews, Matthew, Timothy **9** Ephesians, Galatians **10** Colossians, Revelation **11** Corinthians, Philippians **13** Thessalonians, Titus Philemon
first five books called: **3** Law **5** Torah **10** Pentateuch
first seven books called: **10** Heptateuch

Bible scholar **7** biblist **9** biblicist

Bible version **6** The Way **7** Vulgate **8** Peshitta **9** Gutenberg, Jerusalem, King James **10** New English **11** New American, Rheims-Douay **14** The Living Bible **15** American revised, revised standard

Biblical animal **7** unicorn

Biblical gemstone **6** ligure **7** sardius **8** sardonyx

Biblical instrument **7** sackbut

Biblical length
reed: **9** six cubits

Biblical measure **3** cab, cor **4** epah, omet, reed, seah **5** cubit, epheh, homer **6** shekel **9** half homer

Biblical personage **9** patriarch

Biblical plant **6** hyssop **12** Rose of Sharon

Biblical precept
Hebrew: **7** mitsvah, mitzvah

Biblical tree **5** algum, almug **6** storax **7** juniper **8** sycamire **10** gopherwood **11** shittim wood **12** opobalsammum **13** red sandalwood

Biblical weed **4** tare **6** darnel

Biblical weight **6** talent

Biblicist **12** Bible scholar

Bibliotheca **5** Bible **14** sacred writings

Biblist **12** Bible scholar

Bickel, Ernest Frederick McIntyre
real name of: **13** Frederic March

bicker **4** spar, spat **5** argue, fight **6** haggle **7** dispute, quarrel, wrangle **8** disagree, squabble

bickering **4** spat **5** fight **7** arguing, dispute, quarrel **8** argument, fighting **9** wrangling **10** quarreling, squabbling **12** disagreement

Bickford, Charles
born: **11** Cambridge MA
roles: **12** Anna Christie **13** Johnny Belinda **16** Song of Bernadette **18** The Farmer's Daughter

bicycle **4** bike, ride **5** cycle, moped **10** two-wheeler
invented by: **7** Starley

Bicycle Thief, The
director: **14** Vittorio De Sica
cast: **14** Lianella Carell **18** Lamberto Maggiorani

bid **3** ask, say, try **4** call, tell, wish **5** greet, offer, order **6** beckon, charge, demand, direct, effort, enjoin, insist, invite, ordain, summon, tender **7** attempt, command, proffer, propose, request, require **8** call upon, endeavor, instruct, offering, proposal **10** invitation

bidding **4** beck, call **5** offer, order **6** behest, charge, demand, offers **7** command, dictate, mandate, request, summons **8** offering, proposal **9** direction, summoning, tendering **10** injunction, invitation, proffering **11** instruction

bide **4** stay, wait **5** abide, dwell, stand, tarry **6** endure, linger, remain, suffer **8** tolerate **9** put up with

Bierce, Ambrose
author of: **15** Can Such Things Be? **16** In the Midst of Life **19** The Devil's Dictionary

Bierstadt, Albert
born: **7** Germany **8** Solingen
artwork: **11** Laramie Park **13** Mount Corcoran **17** The Rocky Mountains **20** Discovery of the Hudson, Storm on the Matterhorn **21** Sunrise Yosemite Valley **22** Settlement of California **31** Thunderstorm in the Rocky Mountains

bifocal lenses
invented by: **8** Franklin

Bifrost
origin: **12** Scandinavian
form: **6** bridge
bridge of: **4** gods
made of: **7** rainbow
from: **6** Asgard
to: **5** earth

bifurcate **4** fork **5** split **6** branch, divide **7** diverge **8** separate

big **3** top **4** head, high, huge, just, kind, main, vast **5** adult, ample, bulky, chief, great, grown, heavy, husky, large, major, noble, prime, vital **6** heroic, humane, mature **7** eminent, grown-up, haughty, hulking, immense, leading, liberal, mammoth, massive, notable, pompous, sizable, weighty **8** abundant, arrogant, boastful, bragging, colossal, enormous, generous, gigantic, gracious, princely **9** conceited, grandiose, honorable, important, momentous, prominent, strapping **10** benevolent, chivalrous, high-minded, monumental, prodigious **11** magnanimous, pretentious, significant, substantial **12** considerable **13** consequential

Big Apple
nickname of: **11** New York City

Big Bend State
nickname of: **9** Tennessee

Big Chill, The
director: **14** Laurence Kasdan
cast: **10** Kevin Kline **11** William Hurt

Big Daddy
character in: **16** Cat on a Hot Tin Roof
author: **8** Williams

Big E
nickname of: **10** Elvin Hayes

Bigfoot **4** Yeti **9** Sasquatch **17** Abominable Snowman

big guns **4** VIPs **5** brass **6** cannon **7** bigwigs, top dogs **8** big shots, ordnance **9** artillery **14** heavy artillery, high mucky-mucks **15** important people

bighearted **6** lavish **7** liberal **8** generous, handsome, princely, prodigal **9** bounteous, bountiful, unselfish **10** beneficent, benevolent, charitable, free-handed, open-handed, unstinting **11** magnanimous, open-hearted **12** humanitarian

bight **3** bay **4** bend, cave, road

Biglow Papers
author: **18** James Russell Lowell

Big Money, The
author: **13** John Dos Passos

bigness **4** bulk **8** enormity, hugeness **9** amplitude, great size, greatness, largeness, magnitude **11** massiveness

Big O, The
nickname of: **14** Oscar Robertson

bigoted **6** biased **10** intolerant, prejudiced **12** closed-minded, narrow-minded

bigotry **4** bias **6** racism **9** prejudice **10** unfairness **11** intolerance **14** discrimination **16** closed-mindedness, narrow-mindedness

Big Parade, The
director: **9** King Vidor
cast: **11** John Gilbert, Renee Adoree **14** Hobart Bosworth

big shot **3** VIP **4** name **5** mogul, nabob, wheel **6** big gun, bigwig, fat cat, tycoon **7** big deal, magnate, notable **8** somebody **9** big cheese, dignitary, personage **13** high-muck-a-muck, wheeler-dealer

Big Six
nickname of: **16** Christy Mathewson

Big Sky, The
author: **11** A B Guthrie Jr

Big Sky State
nickname of: **7** Montana

Big Sleep, The
author: **15** Raymond Chandler
director: **11** Howard Hawks
cast: **12** Elisha Cook Jr, Lauren Bacall **13** Dorothy Malone, Martha Vickers **14** Humphrey Bogart (Philip Marlowe)
setting: **10** Los Angeles

Big Train
nickname of: **13** Walter Johnson

Big Valley, The
character: **11** Nick Barkley **12** Audra Barkley, Heath Barkley **13** Jarrod Barkley **15** Victoria Barkley
cast: **9** Lee Majors **10** Linda Evans, Peter Breck **11** Richard Long **15** Barbara Stanwyck

bigwig **3** vip **7** big shot, notable **9** dignitary, personage

bikini **8** two-piece **11** bathing suit
topless: **8** monokini
type: **6** string

Bikini **5** atoll **9** Namu islet **10** West Pacific **15** Marshall Islands

Bilah, Bilhah
concubine of: **5** Jacob
son: **3** Dan **8** Maphtali, Naphtali
served: **6** Rachel

Bildad
friend: **3** Job **5** Elihu **6** Zophar **7** Eliphaz

bile **4** gall, rage **5** anger, venom, wrath **6** choler, spleen

bilge **3** rot **4** bosh, bull, bunk, tosh **5** hooey, tripe **6** drivel, humbug, jabber, piffle **7** baloney, hogwash, rubbish, twaddle **8** malarkey, nonsense **9** gibberish **10** balderdash **11** foolishness, jabberwocky **13** horsefeathers **16** stuff and nonsense

bilious **4** sick **5** angry, cross, huffy, nasty, testy **6** crabby, cranky, grumpy, queasy, sickly, touchy **7** grouchy, peevish **8** bilelike, greenish, nauseous, petulant, snappish **9** irritable, sickening **10** ill-humored, out of sorts **11** ill-tempered **12** cantankerous **13** short-tempered **15** green at the gills

bilk **3** gyp **4** dupe, gull, rook, take **5** cheat, cozen, trick **6** fleece, rip off **7** deceive, defraud, swindle **8** hoodwink **9** bamboozle, victimize

bill **3** act, fee, law **4** card, chit, list **5** tally **6** agenda, charge, decree, docket, poster, roster, ticket **7** account, catalog, charges, invoice, leaflet, measure, placard, program, statute **8** banknote, brochure, bulletin, calendar, circular, handbill, proposal, register, schedule **9** greenback, inventory, ordinance, reckoning, statement **10** regulation **12** treasury note **13** advertisement **17** silver certificate

billet **3** job **4** base, bunk, camp, digs, note, post **5** berth, house, lodge, place, put up **6** letter, office **7** bed down, lodging, quarter, shelter **8** domicile, dwelling, lodgment, position, quarters **9** residence, situation **11** accommodate, appointment **13** accommodation

billfold *see* **6** wallet

billiards
player: **11** Willie Hoppe **13** Minnesota Fats, Willie Mosconi

Bill of Divorcement, A
director: **11** George Cukor
cast: **11** Billie Burke **13** John Barrymore **16** Katharine Hepburn

billow **4** roll, wave **5** belly, cloud, crest, surge, swell **6** puff up **7** balloon, breaker

Billy Budd
author: **14** Herman Melville
character: **8** Claggart **11** Captain Vere

billyclub **3** bat **5** billy, stick **8** bludgeon **9** truncheon

bin **3** box **4** cart, crib, silo **5** crate, frame, hatch **6** barrel, basket, bunker, hamper, holder, trough, vessel **9** container, inclosure **10** receptacle

binate **4** dual **6** double **7** coupled, two fold **14** growing in pairs

bind **3** rim, tie **4** edge, gird, glue, join, lash, rope, trim, wrap **5** affix, chafe, cover, cramp, force, frame, hitch, paste, stick, strap, tie up, truss **6** attach, border, coerce, compel, encase, fasten, fringe, oblige, secure, swathe **7** bandage, confine, require **8** encumber, obligate **9** prescribe **11** necessitate

binder **4** glue, roux **5** paste **6** cement **8** notebook **9** assurance, guarantee **11** down payment **12** earnest money **17** looseleaf notebook

binding **4** band, face, tape **5** valid **6** edging, ribbon **7** styptic **8** fastener, ligative **9** stringent **10** compulsory, obligatory, peremptory **12** constricting

binge **3** jag **4** bust, orgy, tear, toot **5** blast, drunk, fling, revel, spree **6** bender **7** carouse **8** beer bust, carousal **11** bacchanalia **12** drunken spree

Bingham, George Caleb
born: **15** Augusta County VA
artwork: **13** Stump Speaking **17** The Trapper's Return **18** Verdict of the People **19** The Jolly Flatboatman **20** Raftsmen Playing Cards **31** Fur Traders Descending the Missouri

Bingley, Mr
character in: **17** Pride and Prejudice
author: **6** Austen

biochemist **17** biological chemist
American: **4** Cori **5** Bloch, Moore, Ochoa **7** Axelrod, Lipmann **8** Kornberg
English: **5** Krebs **6** Porter, Sanger **8** Mitchell
French: **5** Monod **7** Duclaux
German: **5** Lynen

biogenesis
discoverer: **12** Louis Pasteur

biography **3** bio **4** life, vita **6** memoir **7** account, history **9** life story

biologist
American: **6** Carson, Yerkes **7** Burbank **8** Delbruck
British: **6** Darwin, Huxley **7** Bateson, Medawar
French: **5** Jacob, Monod **7** Lamarck
German: **7** Schwann
Swiss: **6** Haller

biology
branch: **6** botany **7** zoology
classification: **15** Carolus Linnaeus

birch **6** Betula
varieties: **3** Low, Red **4** Fire, Gray **5** Black, Canoe, Dwarf, Paper, River, Swamp, Sweet, Water, White **6** Cherry, Yellow **7** Monarch **8** Mahogany, Old-field **10** West Indian **13** European white, Japanese white, Young's weeping **14** Japanese cherry

Birches
author: **11** Robert Frost

bird ***see box***

Bird, Larry
sport: **10** basketball
position: **7** forward
team: **13** Boston Celtics

bird
anatomy: **3** bec, neb, nib **4** beak, bill, cere, crop, lora, lore, mala, nape, rump, tail, tuft, wing **5** alula, crest, crown, flank, larum, lorum, pilea, rosta **6** breast, gullet, pecten, pileum, pinion, syrinx, tarsus **7** ambiens, crissum, gizzard, rostrum **8** gigerium, pectines, scapular **9** auchenium, gastraeum **10** cordylanus
aquatic/water: **3** auk, cob, ern, mew **4** cobb, coot, duck, erne, gony, gull, ibis, loon, rail, shag, skua, sora, swan, teal, tern **5** booby, cahow, crane, diver, goose, grebe, heron, murre, ousel, rotch, snipe, solan, stilt, stork **6** avocet, curlew, cygnet, dipper, fulmar, gannet, godwit, hagdon, jabiru, jacana, osprey, petrel, plover, puffin, rotche, scoter, wigeon **7** anhinga, bidcock, bittern, bustard, dovekey, dovekie, finfoot, mallard, moorhen, pelican, penguin, seriema, skimmer, widgeon **8** alcatras, baldpate, dabchick, flamingo, murrelet, umbrette **9** albatross, baptornis, cormorant, gallinule, guillemot, kittiwake, phalarope, snakebird, spoonbill **10** gaviformes, kingfisher, shearwater, sheathbill, yellowlegs **13** whooping crane
bird cage/home: **4** cote, mews, nest **5** roost **6** aviary, volary, volery **7** rookery
bird of freedom: **9** bald eagle
bird of ill-omen: **5** raven
bird of Jove: **5** eagle
bird of June: **7** peacock
bird of Minerva: **3** owl
bird of peace: **4** dove
bird of prey: **3** owl **4** gled, hawk, kite **5** buteo, eagle, glead, glede, harpy, saker **6** condor, elanet, elenet, falcon, musket, osprey, raptor **7** buzzard, goshawk, harrier, kestrel, stooper, vulture **8** caracara **9** accipiter, gyrfalcon, peregrine **11** accipitrine, lammergeier
bird of wonder/rebirth: **7** phoenix
carrion-eater: **4** aura **5** urubu **6** condor **7** buzzard, vulture
class: **4** Aves
combining form: **3** avi **4** orni **5** ornis **6** ornith **7** ornitho **8** ornithes
crow family: **3** daw, jay, kae **4** crow, rook **5** crake, raven **6** chough, corbie, magpie **7** corvine, jackdaw
duck family: **4** clee, coot, lory, smew, teal, wood **5** eider, goose **6** scoter **7** gadwall, mallard, Muscovy, pintail, pochard **8** baldpate, redshank, shoveler **9** merganser **10** bufflehead, canvasback
extinct: **3** auk, jib, moa **4** dodo, jibi, mamo **5** didus **8** Diatryma **9** aepyornis, apatornis, gastornis, hespornis, solitaire **11** archaeornis
flightless: **3** emu, ihi, moa **4** dodo, gorb, kagu, kiwi, rhea, weka **5** nandu **6** callow, kakapo, moorup, ratite, takahe **7** apteryx, horling, ostrich, peacock, penguin, roatelo **8** notornis **9** cassowary
game: **4** duck, guan, rail, sora, teal **5** brant, goose, quail, snipe **6** chukar, colima, grouse, pigeon, plover, turkey **7** bustard, chicken, flapper, gadwall, mallard, pintail, prairie, widgeon **8** baldpate, bobwhite, moorfowl, pheasant, shoveler, tragopan, wildfowl, woodcock **9** merganser, partridge, ptarmigan **10** canvasback
group of birds: **3** nye **4** bank, bevy, cast, nide, sord **5** aerie, brood, covey, drove, flock, plump **6** covert, flight, gaggle, litter, spring
largest: **7** ostrich **11** lammergeier
legendary: **3** roc **6** simurg **7** phoenix, simurgh **9** feng-huang, feng-hwang
loss of feathers: **7** molting
smallest: **11** hummingbird
nocturnal: **3** owl **5** cahow, owlet, potoo **7** bullbat, dorhawk **8** guacharo, nightjar **9** nighthawk, thickknee **10** goatsucker **11** nightingale
pet: **4** myna **5** mynah **6** canary, parrot, pigeon **8** cockatoo, lovebird, parakeet
plumage: **8** ptilosis
poultry: **3** hen **4** duck **5** goose **6** pigeon, turkey **7** chicken, rooster **8** pheasant **14** Cornish game hen
talking: **4** myna **5** mynah **6** parrot

Birdman of Alcatraz
director: **17** John Frankenheimer
cast: **10** Karl Malden **12** Edmond O'Brien, Neville Brand, Thelma Ritter **13** Burt Lancaster (Robert Stroud)

Bird of Paradise
constellation of: **4** Apus

Birds, The
author: **12** Aristophanes
character: **4** Iris **5** Meton **8** Basileia, Cinesias **9** Euelpides **10** King Tereus, Prometheus **12** Peithetairos

Birds, The
director: **15** Alfred Hitchcock
based on story by: **15** Daphne du Maurier
cast: **9** Rod Taylor **11** Tippi Hedren **12** Jessica Tandy **16** Suzanne Pleshette
setting: **10** California

Birds Fall Down, The
author: **15** Dame Rebecca West

Birkin, Rupert
character in: **11** Women in Love
author: **8** Lawrence

Birmingham
football team: **9** Stallions

Birmingham, Stephen
author of: **8** Our Crowd

wingless: **4** kiwi, weka **7** apteryx
young: **4** eyas, gull **5** chick, piper, poult, squab **6** gorlin, pullus **7** flapper, nestler **8** birdikin, nestling **9** fledgling
of Africa: **4** coly, fink, taha, tock **5** crane, paauw **6** barbet, bulbul, cuckoo, jabiru, quelea, whidah **7** courser, finfoot, marabou, ostrich, touraco **8** hornbill, oxpecker, parakeet, umbrette **9** beefeater, broadbill, francolin, napecrest, trochilus **10** hammerhead, weaverbird
of Antarctic/Arctic: **3** auk **4** gull, knot, skua, xema **5** brant, murre, rotch **6** dunlin, falcon, fulmar, jaeger, rotche **7** dovekey, dovekie, penguin **8** grayling **9** guillemot, gyrfalcon, ptarmigan **10** sheathbill
of Asia: **4** kora, myna, ruff, smew **5** mynah, pewit, pitta **6** bulbul, chukar, drongo, dunlin, hoopoe, linnet **7** boobook, courser, hill tit, lapwing, peacock, sirgang **8** accentor, dotterel, hornbill, leaf bird, parakeet, tragopan, wheatear **9** brambling, francolin, muted swan
of Australia: **3** emu **4** kahu, kiwi, koel, koil, lory **5** arara, galah, lowan, pitta **6** drongo, leipoa **7** boobook, bustard, figbird, grinder, waybung **8** bellbird, bushlark, cockatoo, ganggang, lorikeet, lyrebird, megapode, manucode, morepork, parakeet, platypus **9** bowerbird, cassowary, coachwhip, cockatiel, frogmouth, pardalote, thornbird **10** kookaburra
of Central America: **4** guan, ibis **5** booby, macaw **6** barbet, jabiru, quezal, toucan **7** bittern, cotinga, jacamar, quetzal, tinamou **8** curassow, puffbird, troupial
of Cuba: **6** trogon **8** tocororo **14** bee hummingbird
of England: **4** kite, rook **9** cormorant **11** carrion crow
of Europe: **3** dar, mag, mew, nun **4** clee, gled, mall, merl, pope, rook, ruff, shag, smew, wren **5** amsel, crake, egret, finch, glede, merle, ousel, ouzel, pewit, pipit, stilt, stork, swift, tarin, terek, whaup **6** cuckoo, dunlin, godwit, grouse, hoopoe, linnet, martin, merlin, missel, redleg, roller, siskin, thrush **7** bittern, bustard, jackdaw, kestrel, lapwing, martlet, ortolan, redwing, ruddock, skylark, sparrow, starnel, wagtail, wryneck **8** bee eater, blackcap, brantail, daychick, dotterel, garganey, nightjar, nuthatch, peesweep, redstart, reedling, starling, throstle, wheatear, whimbrel, whinchat, whinshat, woodcock **9** brambling, chaffinch, crossbill, field fare, gallinule, sheldrake, stonechat **10** chiffchaff, goatsucker, kingfisher, lammergeir, turtledove **11** lammergeier, nightingale, wallcreeper **12** capercaillie
of Hawaii: **2** io **3** ava, ioa, iwa, poe **4** nene, iiwi, koae, mamo, moho, omao **6** parson **7** frigate
of India: **4** baya, kala, koel, koil **5** sarus, shama **6** argala, bulbul, homrai, luggar **7** peacock **8** adjutant, amadavat, pheasant, tragopan **11** red hornbill
of Jamaica: **7** vervain
of Java: **7** sparrow **8** rice bird **9** fruit dove
of Madagascar: **6** drongo **7** anhinga, kirombo, roatelo
of Mexico: **6** jacana
of New Guinea: **9** cassowary **14** bird of paradise
of New Zealand: **3** ihi, kea, moa, poe, tui **4** huia, kaka, kaki, kiwi, koko, kuku, ruru, titi, weka **6** kakapo **7** apteryx **8** morepork, notornis
of North America: **3** ani, auk, tit **4** coot, crow, dove, ibis, lark, loon, pape, rook, sora, stib, swan, tern, wamp, wren **5** booby, brant, colin, crane, egret, finch, grebe, junco, murre, quail, robin, snipe, swift, veery, vireo **6** chebec, cuckoo, curlew, darter, dunlin, fulmar, grouse, hagdon, magpie, martin, oriole, phoebe, plover, shrike, thrush, towhee, turkey, verdin, willet **7** anhinga, bittern, blue jay, catbird, flicker, goshawk, grackle, lapwing, pelican, sparrow, swallow, tanager, warbler **8** bluebird, bobolink, bobwhite, cardinal, grosbeak, killdeer, nuthatch, poorwill, starling, thrasher, titmouse, wheatear **9** blackbird, chickadee, crossbill, goldfinch, gyrfalcon, nighthawk, partridge, sandpiper, snakebird **10** bufflehead, kingfisher, meadowlark, woodpecker **11** hummingbird, mockingbird **12** whippoorwill
of South America: **3** ara, hia **4** anna, guan, jacu, loro, mitu, rhea, soco, toco, yeni **5** egret, macaw, potoo, sylph **6** barbet, chatja, chunga, cracid, jabiru, motmot, sappho, toucan **7** cariama, cotinga, hoatzin, jacamar, limpkin, manakin, seriema, tinamou, warrior **8** boatbill, caracara, curassow, guacharo, hoactzin, screamer, tapacolo, tapaculo, terutero, troupial **9** campanero, trumpeter **11** scarlet ibis
of West India: **3** ani **4** tody

11 The Grandees **14** The Right People **15** Life at the Dakota

Birnbaum, Nathan
real name of: 11 George Burns

birth 5 blood, start, stock **6** family, origin, source, strain **7** bearing, descent, genesis, lineage **8** ancestry, breeding, delivery **9** beginning, being born, emergence, genealogy, inception, parentage **10** background, beginnings, childbirth, derivation, extraction **11** confinement, parturition **12** commencement

Birth of a Nation, The
director: 10 D W Griffith
cast: 8 Mae Marsh **11** Lillian Gish **14** Henry B Walthall

Birth of Tragedy, The
author: 18 Friedrich Nietzsche

birthstones
January: 6 garnet
February: 8 amethyst
March: 6 jasper **10** aquamarine, bloodstone
April: 7 diamond **8** sapphire
May: 5 agate **7** emerald
June: 5 pearl **7** emerald **9** moonstone **11** alexandrite
July: 4 onyx, ruby **8** star ruby
August: 7 peridot **8** sardonyx **9** carnelian
September: 8 sapphire **10** chrysolite **12** star sapphire
October: 4 opal **5** beryl **10** aquamarine, tourmaline
November: 5 topaz
December: 4 ruby **6** zircon **9** turquoise

biscuit 3 bun **4** cake, roll **5** cooky, scone, wafer **6** bisque, cookie, muffin, parking, simnel **7** cracker, dogbone **8** hardtack, zwieback **9** pale-brown **10** crisp bread, quick bread **15** unglazed pottery

bisect 5 cross, split **8** cut in two **9** cut in half, intersect

bishop 4 abba, pope **5** punch **6** cleric, despot, priest **7** pontiff, prelate, primate **8** overseer **9** clergyman, patriarch **10** chesspiece, high priest
of Rome: 4 pope
Greek: 9 episkopos
***means:* 8** overseer
district: 7 diocese
headdress: 5 miter, mitre

Bismarck, Otto von
nickname: 14 Iron Chancellor
unified: 7 Germany
chancellor / minister for: 15 Emperor William I
policy: 12 "iron and blood"

bison 4 urus **6** wild ox, wisent **7** aurochs, buffalo
native to: 6 Europe **12** North America

Bissau
capital of: 12 Guinea-Bissau

Bisset, Jacqueline
real name: 22 Jacqueline Fraser Bisset
born: 7 England **9** Weybridge
roles: 5 Class **7** Airport, The Deep **11** Day for Night **12** Anna Karenina **16** The Mephisto Waltz **24** Murder on the Orient Express

bistro 3 bar **4** cafe **6** tavern **7** cabaret **9** nightclub **10** supper club
French: 9 estaminet

bit 3 dab **4** chip, drop, iota, mite, snip, whit **5** crumb, grain, pinch, scrap, shred, speck, spell, trace **6** dollop, moment, morsel, paring, trifle **7** droplet, granule, shaving, smidgen **8** fragment, particle **9** short time **10** short while, small piece, smithereen, sprinkling
type: 5 auger, drill **6** gimlet, wimble **7** bradawl **11** brace and bit

bitch 3 nag **5** botch, brood, cheat, fault, shrew, spoil, witch, whine **6** kvetch, virago **7** blunder, bungle, grouse **8** complain, harridan **9** complaint, female dog, termagant

bitchy 4 mean **5** catty, cruel, nasty **6** wicked **7** hateful, vicious **8** spiteful **9** heartless, malicious **10** backbiting, malevolent, vindictive

bite 3 bit, dab, dig, nip **4** gnaw, grip, snip **5** champ, crumb, gnash, prick, scrap, shred, smart, speck, sting, taste **6** morsel, nibble, pierce **7** eat into **8** mouthful, stinging, take hold **10** small piece, tooth wound **12** small portion

biting 5 harsh, sharp **6** bitter **7** caustic, cutting, mordant, nipping **8** piercing, scathing, smarting, stinging **9** sarcastic, trenchant, withering **12** sharp-tongued

Biton
father: 7 Cydippe

bit player 5 extra **6** walk on **14** minor character

bitte 6 please **12** you're welcome **14** I beg your pardon

bitter 4 acid, mean, sour, tart **5** acrid, angry, cruel, harsh, sharp **6** biting, morose, severe, sullen **7** acerbic, caustic, crabbed, painful **8** grievous, piercing, scornful, smarting, spiteful, stinging, wretched **9** rancorous, resentful **10** astringent **11** distressing

bitterness 5 anger, scorn, spite **6** animus, rancor, spleen **7** ill will **8** acerbity, acrimony, sourness **9** animosity, harshness, hostility, malignity, sharpness **10** antagonism, malignancy **11** astringency **12** hard feelings, spitefulness **14** unpleasantness

bitters
type: 6 spirit
flavor: 6 orange **7** gentian
brand: 9 Angostura

bivalve 4 clam **5** pinna **6** cockle, mussel, mollusk, scallop **8** mollusca **9** pelecypod **13** lamellibranch

bivouac 4 camp **5** tents **10** campground, encampment

bizarre 3 odd **5** kinky, kooky, queer, weird **7** strange, unusual **8** freakish **9** fantastic, grotesque **10** outlandish

Bizet, Georges
real name: 26 Alexandre Cesar Leopold Bizet
born: 5 Paris **6** France
composer of: 4 Roma (suite) **6** Carmen, Patrie **8** Djamileh **11** Don Procopio, L'Arlesienne **12** Jeux d'enfants, Pearl Fishers **14** Children's Games **15** Ivan the Terrible **16** Le Docteur Miracle **18** The Fair Maid of Perth

Biztha 6 eunuch

Bjornson, Bjornstjerne
author of: 4 Arne **7** The King **8** Magnhild **9** A Happy Boy, In God's Way, Lame Hulda, The Editor **10** King Sverre **11** A Bankruptcy, The Bankrupt **12** Sigurd Slembe **14** Arnljot Gelline, Beyond Our Power **15** The Fisher Maiden, The Newly Married **16** Beyond Human Might, Sigurd the Bastard **17** Between the Battles **20** Mary Stuart in Scotland **24** Paul Lange and Tora Parsberg **27** Flags Are Flying in Town and Port

blab 3 rat **6** babble, tattle **7** blabber, prattle **9** tell tales **13** spill the beans **20** let the cat out of the bag

blabber 3 gab, gas, yak **4** blab, bull **5** prate **6** babble, drivel, gabble, gibber, gossip, jabber **7** blather, chatter, palaver, prattle, twaddle **8** blah-blah, chitchat, idle talk **9** jabbering **10** mumbo-jumbo **12** gobbledegook **14** chitter-chatter

blabbermouth **6** gabber, gossip, prater **7** blabber **8** bigmouth, busybody, gossiper, informer, jabberer, liverlip, prattler, quidnunc **9** chatterer **10** chatterbox, talebearer, tattletale **11** rumormonger **12** gossipmonger **13** scandalmonger

black, Black **3** bad, dim, jet **4** dark, evil, grim, inky **5** angry, ebony, murky, Negro, raven, sable **6** dismal, gloomy, somber, sullen, wicked **7** colored, furious, hostile, stygian, sunless, swarthy **8** moonless **9** coal-black, lightless, nefarious, unlighted **10** calamitous **11** dark-skinned, threatening **12** Afro-American **13** unilluminated

Black Arrow, The
author: **20** Robert Louis Stevenson

blackball **3** ban, bar, cut **4** snub **5** debar **6** banish, outlaw, reject **7** boycott, exclude, keep out, shut out **8** pass over, turndown **9** blacklist, ostracize, proscribe **11** vote against **12** cold-shoulder **14** send to Coventry

black beast
French: **9** bete noire

blackberry **5** Rubus
variety: **4** Sand **5** Swamp **7** Cut-leaf, Pacific, Running, Sow-teat **9** Evergreen **13** Parsley-leaved **18** Evergreen thornless

Blackberry Winter
author: **12** Margaret Mead

blackbird **4** crow **5** raven, slave **6** thrush **7** cowbird, grackle, redwing **8** song bird **9** slave ship **11** slave trader **17** kidnapped islander, plantation laborer
kind: **9** red-winged **12** yellow-headed
family: **8** Turdidae **9** Icteridae

Blackboard Jungle, The
director: **13** Richard Brooks
based on novel by: **10** Evan Hunter
cast: **9** Glenn Ford, Vic Morrow **11** Anne Francis **12** Louis Calhern, Paul Mazursky, Richard Kiley **13** Sidney Poitier **14** Warner Anderson

Black Boy
author: **13** Richard Wright

blacken **5** libel, smear, stain, sully **6** befoul, darken, defame, defile, revile, vilify **7** slander, tarnish **8** besmirch, disgrace, dishonor **9** denigrate, discredit **10** stigmatize

Blackfoot, Blackfeet
language family: **9** Algonkian **10** Algonquian
tribe: **6** Bloods, Kainah, Piegan, Pikuni **7** Siksika
location: **6** Canada **7** Alberta, Montana **12** Saskatchewan

blackguard **3** cad, rat, SOB **5** knave, louse, rogue, scamp **6** rascal **7** bastard, villain **9** miscreant, scoundrel

blackhearted **4** base, vile **6** sinful, wicked **7** ignoble **10** despicable, evil-minded, villainous **11** scoundrelly **12** unprincipled **13** reprehensible

blackjack
also known as: **9** twenty-one
French: **9** vingt-et-un
play against: **6** dealer
additional card: **3** hit

Black Lamb and Grey Falcon
author: **15** Dame Rebecca West

Black Land, The *see* **5** Egypt

blackleg **7** cheater **8** swindler **9** trickster

blacklist **3** ban, bar **4** shun **5** debar **6** reject **7** exclude, lock out, shut out **8** preclude **9** blackball, ostracize

blacklisting **7** boycott **8** spurning **9** exclusion, ostracism, rejection **12** blackballing

black magic **7** sorcery **10** witchcraft

blackmail **5** force **6** coerce, extort, payoff **7** squeeze, tribute **8** threaten **9** extortion, hush money, shakedown

black mark **4** blot **5** stain **6** bruise **7** blemish, demerit **9** contusion

Blackmore, Richard Doddridge
author of: **10** Lorna Doone **11** Springhaven **13** The Maid of Sker

black mountain *see* **10** Montenegro

Black Narcissus
author: **11** Rumer Godden
director: **13** Michael Powell **17** Emeric Pressburger
cast: **4** Sabu **11** David Farrar, Deborah Kerr, Jean Simmons
setting: **9** Himalayas

blackness **4** dark **5** gloom, shade **7** dimness **8** darkness

Blackpool, Stephen
character in: **9** Hard Times
author: **7** Dickens

Black Prince, The
author: **11** Iris Murdoch

Blackstone, Sir William
author of: **12** Commentaries (on the Laws of England)

Black Uhlan
nickname of: **12** Max Schmeling

Blackwater State
nickname of: **8** Nebraska

Blackwell, Elizabeth
first American: **11** woman doctor

bladder **3** bag, sac **4** cyst **5** pouch **7** blister, pustule, saccule, utricle **10** receptacle

blade **4** leaf **5** frond, knife, razor, sword **6** cutter, needle, switch **7** scalpel **10** sled runner **11** cutting edge, skate runner

blah **4** bosh, dull, flat, guff, so-so **5** bland, ho-hum, hooey, vapid **6** boring, bunkum, dreary, hot air, humbug **7** blather, eyewash, humdrum, nothing, tedious, twaddle **8** claptrap, lifeless, listless, nonsense **9** gibberish **10** balderdash, monotonous, pedestrian **11** uninspiring **13** characterless, unimaginative, uninteresting, unstimulating

Blaik, Earl H
sport: **8** football
position: **5** coach
team: **4** Army **9** Dartmouth
military rank: **7** colonel

Blair, Eric Arthur
real name of: **12** George Orwell

Blake, Robert
real name: **28** Michael James Vijencio Gubitosi
born: **8** Nutley NJ
roles: **7** Baretta, Our Gang **8** Red Ryder **11** In Cold Blood **12** Little Beaver **23** Tell Them Willie Boy Is Here **24** The Treasure of Sierra Madre

Blake, William
born: **6** London **7** England
author of: **6** Milton, Tiriel **9** Jerusalem **13** The Book of Thel **14** Prophetic Books **15** The Book of Urigen **16** Songs of Innocence **17** Songs of Experience **21** Little Lamb Who Made Thee **23** Marriage of Heaven and Hell, Tiger Tiger Burning Bright
artwork: **6** Milton **9** Book of

Job, Jerusalem **11** The Four Zoas **12** Book of Urizen, Divine Comedy **16** Songs of Innocence **17** Songs of Experience **23** Marriage of Heaven and Hell

blamable 10 censurable, deplorable, punishable, reprovable **11** blameworthy **12** reproachable **13** reprehensible

Blamauer, Karoline
real name of: 10 Lotte Lenya

blame 4 onus **5** fault, guilt **6** accuse, burden, charge, rebuke **7** censure, condemn, reproof, reprove **8** reproach **9** castigate, criticism, criticize, liability **10** accusation, disapprove **11** castigation, culpability **12** condemnation, denunciation, remonstrance **13** find fault with, recrimination **14** accountability, responsibility **15** hold responsible

blameless 5 clear **8** innocent, spotless **9** guiltless, not guilty, unspotted, unstained, unsullied, untainted **10** inculpable, not at fault, unblamable **11** unblemished, uncorrupted **13** unimpeachable **14** irreproachable, not responsible

blameless in life
Latin: 12 integer vitae

blame on 7 trace to **8** charge to **9** set down to **11** attribute to **14** lay at the door of

blameworthy 8 blamable **10** censurable, deplorable, punishable, reprovable **12** reproachable **13** reprehensible

blanch 4 fade **6** bleach, whiten **7** lighten **8** turn pale

blanched 3 wan **4** pale **5** ashen, faded **6** chalky, pallid **8** bleached **9** bloodless

bland 4 blah, calm, dull, even, flat, mild **5** balmy, quiet, vapid **6** benign, smooth **7** calming, humdrum, nothing, prosaic, tedious **8** moderate, peaceful, soothing, tiresome, tranquil **9** peaceable, temperate, unruffled **10** monotonous, unexciting, untroubled **11** uninspiring **13** nonirritating, uninteresting, unstimulating

blandish 4 coax, lure, urge **5** charm, tempt **6** cajole, entice, prompt **7** blarney, flatter, wheedle **8** inveigle, persuade

blandishment, blandishments 7 blarney, coaxing **8** cajolery, flattery **9** sweet talk, wheedling **12** ingratiation, inveiglement

Blandois, Monsieur
character in: 12 Little Dorrit
author: 7 Dickens

blank 3 gap **4** dull, idle, void **5** clean, clear, empty, inane, plain, space **6** futile, hollow, unused, vacant, vacuum, wasted **7** useless, vacancy, vacuous **8** unmarked **9** emptiness, fruitless, valueless, worthless **10** empty space, hollowness, profitless **11** meaningless, thoughtless, unrewarding **12** inexpressive **14** expressionless

blanket 4 coat, film **5** cloak, cover, quilt, throw **6** afghan, carpet, mantle, veneer **7** coating, overlay **8** covering, coverlet **9** comforter

blare 4 honk, peal, roar **5** blast **6** bellow, scream **7** resound, trumpet

blarney 4 fibs, line **5** pitch, spiel **6** hot air **7** coaxing, fawning, snow job, stories **8** cajolery, flattery **9** hyperbole, wheedling **10** inveigling, overpraise, sweet words **12** exaggeration, honeyed words **13** blandishments, overstatement

blase 4 full **5** bored, jaded **6** gorged **7** glutted **9** apathetic, satisfied, saturated, surfeited, unexcited, unmovable **10** insouciant, nonchalant, spiritless, world-weary **11** indifferent, unconcerned **12** uninterested **14** unenthusiastic

Blasko, Bela
real name of: 10 Bela Lugosi

blaspheme 5 curse, swear **6** revile **7** profane **10** take in vain

blasphemous 7 godless, impious, profane, ungodly **10** irreverent **11** irreligious **12** sacrilegious

blasphemy 7 cursing, impiety **8** swearing **9** profanity, sacrilege **11** impiousness, irreverence, profanation

blast 4 bomb, boom, bore, gale, gust, honk, peal, roar, rush, toot **5** blare, bleat, burst, level, shell, surge **6** bellow, blow up, report, scream, shriek **7** explode, resound, torpedo **8** dynamite, eruption **9** discharge, explosion, loud noise **10** detonation **11** sound loudly

blasting material 3 TNT **8** dynamite **9** explosive

blatant 4 loud **5** cheap, clear, crass, crude, gross, harsh, noisy, overt **6** brazen, coarse, tawdry, vulgar **7** blaring, glaring, obvious, uncouth **8** flagrant, piercing, unsubtle **9** clamorous, deafening, obtrusive, offensive, prominent, tasteless, ungenteel, unrefined **10** indelicate, unpolished **11** conspicuous, ill-mannered, undignified **12** ear-splitting, unmistakable

blather 4 stir **7** chatter, prattle **8** nonsense **9** commotion

Blatty, William P
author of: 11 The Exorcist

Blaue Reiter 10 Blue Riders
group of: 13 German artists

blaze 3 ray **4** beam, burn, fire, glow, rush **5** blast, burst, flame, flare, flash, glare, gleam, shine **6** flames **7** glisten, glitter, shimmer, torrent **8** eruption, outbreak, outburst, radiance **9** explosion **10** brightness, brilliance, effulgence **12** resplendence **13** conflagration

blazer 4 coat **6** jacket **12** sports jacket

blazing 3 hot **5** fiery, afire **6** firing, on fire **7** burning, flaming, flaring, glaring, glowing, intense, shining **8** bursting, bleaming, shooting, shouting **9** brilliant

Blazing Saddles
director: 9 Mel Brooks
cast: 9 Mel Brooks **10** Alex Karras, Dom DeLuise, Gene Wilder **11** Slim Pickens **12** Harvey Korman, Madeline Kahn **13** Cleavon Little, John Hillerman **15** David Huddleston

blazon 5 blare, boast **7** trumpet **8** proclaim **10** coat of arms, make public **16** armorial bearings

blazonry 4 arms **5** crest **6** blazon **8** insignia **10** coat of arms **14** heraldic emblem **16** heraldic bearings

bleach 4 fade **6** blanch, whiten **7** lighten, wash out **8** make pale

bleak 3 icy, raw **4** bare, cold, grim **5** chill **6** barren, biting, bitter, dismal, dreary, frosty, gloomy, somber, wintry **7** nipping **8** desolate, piercing **9** cheerless, windswept **10** depressing, forbidding **11** distressing, unpromising **13** weather-beaten

Bleak House
author: 14 Charles Dickens
character: 2 Jo (the crossing

sweeper) **4** Nemo **5** Guppy, Krook **6** Bucket, Guster **7** Snagsby **8** Ada Clare, Chadband **9** Miss Flite **10** Mrs Jellyby, Turveydrop **11** Dr Woodcourt, Lady Dedlock, Tulkinghorn **12** John Jarndyce **13** Captain Rawdon **14** Harold Skimpole **15** Esther Summerson, Richard Carstone **19** Sir Leicester Dedlock
satire of: **3** law **6** courts **8** chancery
case: **19** Jarndyce and Jarndyce

bleakness **8** bareness, grimness **10** barrenness, desolation, dreariness, gloominess **13** cheerlessness

bleat **3** baa, cry, maa **5** whine **7** whimper

bleb **6** bubble **7** blister

bleed **3** run, tap **4** leak, soak **5** drain, valve **6** fleece, suffer **7** diffuse, extract, **8** let blood **9** draw blood, sacrifice **10** hemorrhage, overcharge **12** phlebotomize

Blefuscu
fictional land in: **16** Gulliver's Travels
author: **5** Swift

blemish **3** mar, zit **4** blot, blur, flaw, mark, spot **5** spoil, stain, sully, taint **6** blotch, defect, smirch, smudge **7** tarnish **9** disfigure **12** imperfection **13** disfigurement

blend **3** mix **4** fuse **5** merge, unite **6** fusion, go well, merger, mingle **7** amalgam, combine, mixture **8** coalesce, compound, mergence, mingling **9** harmonize **10** amalgamate, complement, concoction **11** combination, incorporate, intermingle

bless **4** give **5** endow, favor, grace, guard, honor **6** anoint, bestow, hallow, oblige, ordain **7** baptize, benefit, protect, support **8** dedicate, sanctify **9** watch over **10** consecrate

blessed **4** holy **5** happy, lucky **6** adored, graced, joyful, joyous, sacred **7** endowed, favored, revered **8** blissful, hallowed **9** fortunate, venerated, wonderful **10** felicitous, sanctified **11** consecrated

Blessed Damozel, The
author: **20** Dante Gabriel Rossetti

blessedness **5** bliss **8** felicity **9** beatitude **11** saintliness

blessing **4** gain, gift, good **5** favor, grace, leave **6** bounty, profit, regard **7** backing, benefit, consent, support **8** approval, sanction **9** advantage, hallowing **10** dedication, good wishes, invocation, permission **11** benediction, concurrence, good fortune **12** consecration, thanksgiving **14** sanctification

blessings **4** joys **5** gifts **6** favors **7** success **8** benefits, delights **10** advantages **11** good fortune

Blifil, Master
character in: **8** Tom Jones
author: **8** Fielding

Bligh, Captain William
character in: **17** Mutiny on the Bounty
authors: **4** Hall **8** Nordhoff

blight **3** pox, rot **4** harm, kill, ruin, rust **5** blast, crush, curse, decay, smash, spoil, wreck **6** cancer, canker, dry rot, fungus, injure, mildew, plague, thwart, wither **7** cripple, destroy, scourge, shrivel **8** demolish **9** frustrate **10** affliction, corruption, pestilence **12** plant disease **13** contamination

Blimber, Dr
character in: **12** Dombey and Son
author: **7** Dickens

blind **4** dull, ruse **5** cover, dodge, front, shade **6** hidden, insane, obtuse, screen **7** obscure, pretext, unaware **8** disguise, heedless, ignorant, mindless, unseeing **9** concealed, deception, senseless, sightless, sun shield, unfeeling, unknowing, unmindful, unnoticed **10** camouflage, insouciant, irrational, masquerade, neglectful, subterfuge, unthinking **11** inattentive, incognizant, indifferent, insensitive, smoke screen, unconcerned, unconscious, unobservant, unobserving **12** imperceptive, uncontrolled, undiscerning, uninterested, unnoticeable, unperceptive, unreasonable **13** unenlightened **14** uncontrollable **15** uncomprehending

blind alley **7** closure, dead-end, impasse **8** blockade, cul-de-sac, dead lock, no escape **9** hindrance, stone wall **10** impassable, standstill **11** obstruction

blinder **4** hood **5** blind, shade **6** screen **7** blinker **9** blindfold

blindfold **6** darken **7** bandage, blinder, obscure **8** covering heedless, reckless **11** strike blind

blind seer **8** Tiresias

blink **4** wink **5** flash, shine, waver **6** falter, flinch, squint **7** flicker, glimmer, shimmer, sparkle, twinkle **9** nictitate, vacillate

blinker(s) **3** eye **6** peeper **7** blinder, flasher, goggles **8** black eye **13** warning signal

blintz, blintze **4** blin **5** crepe **6** blints **7** pancake

blip **3** dot, tap **4** spot **5** bleep, image **6** censor **7** replace

bliss **3** joy **4** glee **6** heaven, luxury **7** delight, ecstasy, rapture **8** gladness, paradise **9** happiness **10** exaltation, jubilation **12** exhilaration

blissful **5** happy **6** divine, joyful, joyous **7** blessed, sublime **8** beatific, ecstatic, glorious, heavenly **9** rapturous

blithe **3** gay **4** airy, glad **5** blind, happy, jolly, merry, sunny **6** casual, cheery, jaunty, jovial, joyous, lively **7** gleeful, radiant **8** carefree, careless, cheerful, debonair, exaltant, heedless, mirthful, uncaring **9** ebullient, sprightly, unfeeling, unmindful **10** blithesome, frolicking **11** indifferent, insensitive, thoughtless, unconcerned, unconscious **12** lighthearted **13** inconsiderate

Blithedale Romance, The
author: **18** Nathaniel Hawthorne

blithesome **3** gay **5** light, merry, sunny **6** breezy, jaunty, lively **7** buoyant **8** animated, carefree, cheerful **11** free and easy

Blixen-Finecke, Karen
real name of: **11** Isak Dinesen

blizzard **4** blow, gale **5** blast **6** flurry, squall **7** tempest **8** snowfall **9** snowstorm **11** winter storm

Blizzard State
nickname of: **11** South Dakota

bloat **5** swell **6** blow up, dilate, expand, puff up **7** balloon, distend, enlarge, inflate

blob **4** daub, drop, mass **7** globule, splotch

bloc **4** body, ring, wing **5** cabal, group, union **6** clique **7** combine, faction **8** alliance **9** coalition **11** combination

Bloch, Ernest
born: **6** Geneva **11** Switzerland

composer of: **7** Macbeth, Solomon **8** Baal Shem, Schelomo **13** Sacred Service **14** Avodath Hakdesh, Israel Symphony **16** American Symphony **19** Concerto Symphonique **20** Voice in the Wilderness

block **3** bar, jam **4** cube, form, halt, mold **5** brick, check, choke, shape **6** hinder, impede, re-form, square, stop up, thwart **7** barrier, prevent, reshape **8** blockade, blockage, obstacle, obstruct **9** hindrance **10** impediment **11** obstruction **12** interference

blockade **3** bar, dam **4** dike **5** block, check, levee **6** hurdle **7** barrier, parapet, rampart **8** blockage, obstacle, obstruct, stockade, stoppage **9** barricade, hindrance, roadblock **10** checkpoint, earthworks, impediment **11** obstruction, restriction **13** fortification

blockage **3** jam **8** obstacle **9** hindrance **10** impediment **11** obstruction

blockhead **3** ass **4** clod, dolt, fool, yutz **5** booby, dummy, dunce, idiot, klutz, moron, ninny **6** dum-dum, nitwit **7** fathead, half-wit, jackass **8** bonehead, dumb-dumb, dumm kopf, imbecile, lunkhead, mushhead, numskull **9** harebrain, lamebrain, simpleton **10** chowerhead, dunderhead, nincompoop, noodlehead **12** featherbrain

block out **3** hew **5** carve **6** chisel, devise, map out, sculpt, sketch **7** outline **8** indicate **9** formulate

block up **3** bar **4** clog **6** stop up **7** brick up **9** barricade

blond, blonde **4** fair, gold, pale **5** light **6** flaxen, golden, yellow **8** light tan **9** yellowish **10** fair-haired **11** fair-skinned **12** light-colored

Blonde Bombshell
nickname of: **10** Jean Harlow

Blondell, Joan
husband: **8** Mike Todd **10** Dick Powell
born: **9** New York NY
roles: **8** The Champ **11** Blonde Crazy, Gold Diggers, The Blue Veil **14** Blondie Johnson, The Public Enemy **20** A Tree Grows in Brooklyn

Blondie
creator: **9** Chic Young
character:
husband: **15** Dagwood Bumstead
children: **6** Cookie **9** Alexander **12** Baby Dumpling
boss: **6** Julius **9** Mr Dithers
boss's wife: **4** Cora
neighbor: **11** Herb Woodley **14** Tootsie Woodley
dog: **5** Daisy

blood **4** gore **5** birth, stock **6** family, source, spirit, temper **7** descent, lineage, passion **8** ancestry, heritage, vitality **9** lifeblood **10** extraction, family line, vital fluid, vital force **11** temperament **13** consanguinity **14** vital principle

Blood, field of **8** Aceldama

Blood, Sweat and Tears
author: **17** Winston S Churchill

bloodless **4** pale **5** ashen **6** anemic, pallid **7** insipid **8** blanched, lifeless, peaceful **9** colorless, deathlike, washed out

bloodline **6** family **8** ancestry, pedigree **9** genealogy **10** family tree

Bloodline
author: **13** Sidney Sheldon

bloodshed **4** gore **6** murder, pogrom **7** carnage, killing, slaying **8** butchery, massacre **9** blood bath, blood feud, slaughter **10** mass murder **12** bloodletting, manslaughter **15** spilling of blood

Bloodsmoor Romance, A
author: **15** Joyce Carol Oates

bloodstone
month: **5** March

blood system
part: **5** blood, liver **6** spleen **9** lymph node **10** bone marrow

bloodthirsty **5** cruel **6** bloody, brutal, fierce, savage **7** bestial, demonic, inhuman, vicious **8** barbaric, demoniac, fiendish, pitiless, ruthless **9** atrocious, barbarous, cutthroat, heartless, homicidal, merciless, murdering, murderous **10** demoniacal, sanguinary **11** sanguineous

blood vessel **4** vein **5** aorta **6** artery **7** carotid **9** capillary
prefix: **5** angio

Blood Wedding
author: **19** Federico Garcia Lorca

bloody **3** red **4** gory, rude, vevy **5** cruel, lurid **6** cursed, damned **7** crimson, scarlet **8** bleeding **9** merciless, murderous **10** sanguinary

Bloody Shame *see* **10** Virgin Mary (drink)

bloom **3** bud **4** glow, grow, zest **5** flare, flush, prime, shine, vigor **6** beauty, flower, heyday, luster, sprout, thrive **7** blossom, burgeon, develop, prosper, succeed **8** fare well, flourish, fructify, radiance, rosiness, strength **9** bear fruit, flowerage, flowering, germinate **10** blossoming **11** florescence, flourishing

Bloom, Claire
real name: **11** Claire Blume
husband: **10** Rod Steiger
born: **6** London **7** England
roles: **6** Charly **9** Limelight **10** Richard III **15** Look Back in Anger **26** The Spy Who Came in from the Cold

Bloom, Leopold and Molly
characters in: **7** Ulysses
author: **5** Joyce

bloomers **8** knickers, trousers **9** plus fours, underwear **10** underpants **15** knickerbockers

blooming **3** fit **4** pert, rosy **5** utter **6** abloom, robust, strong **7** healthy **8** vigorous **9** healthful **10** blossoming **11** flourishing **12** efflorescent, fit as a fiddle **15** picture of health

blooper **4** goof, slip **5** boner, botch, error, fluff, gaffe, lapse **6** bobble, booboo, slip-up **7** blunder, mistake, screwup

blossom **4** grow **5** bloom **6** flower, thrive **7** burgeon, develop **8** flourish, progress

Blossomed miraculously
9 Aaron's rod

blossoming **5** bloom **8** blooming, thriving **9** flowering **10** burgeoning, developing **11** florescence, flourishing

blot **3** dry **4** flaw, mark, spot **5** smear, stain, taint **6** absorb, blotch, remove, smirch, smudge, soak up, stigma, take up **7** bad mark, blemish, splotch **8** besmirch **13** discoloration

blotch **4** blot, mark, spot **7** splotch

Blot on the 'Scutcheon, The
author: **14** Robert Browning

blot out **5** erase **6** remove, rub out **7** abolish, eclipse, expunge **9** eliminate, eradicate **10** obliterate

blotting out **7** eclipse, erasing **9** expunging, wiping out **11** eradicating, eradication **12** annihilation, obliterating, obliteration **13** overshadowing

blouse **4** coat **5** drape, tunic, shirt, smock **6** camise, billow **7** blouson **8** casaquin

blow **3** box, hit, jab, pop **4** bang, bash, belt, cuff, gale, gust, honk, jolt, play, puff, sock, toot, wind **5** blast, burst, clout, crack, knock, punch, shock, smack, sound, storm, thump, upset, whack **6** exhale, rebuff, squall, wallop **7** breathe, explode, tempest, tragedy, whistle **8** calamity, disaster, expel air, reversal **9** detriment, windstorm **10** affliction, misfortune **11** catastrophe **14** disappointment

blow from the hand
French: **10** coup de main

blowhard **6** gascon **7** boaster, bragger, egotist **8** braggart **9** big talker **11** braggadocio

blow of mercy
French: **11** coup de grace

blow out **5** burst **7** rupture **10** extinguish

blowsy, blowzy **5** messy **6** frowzy, mussed, sloppy, untidy **7** unkempt **10** disarrayed, disheveled, disordered, disorderly, in disorder **11** disarranged

blow up **5** bloat, burst **6** billow, dilate, expand **7** balloon, distend, enlarge, explode, inflate, puff out **8** dynamite, swell out **12** lose one's cool **14** lose one's temper

Blowup
director: **21** Michelangelo Antonioni
cast: **8** Verushka **10** Sarah Miles **13** David Hemmings **15** Vanessa Redgrave

blowy **5** gusty, windy **6** breezy **7** squally **8** blustery

blubber **3** cry, fat, sob **4** bawl, flab, wail, weep **6** boohoo

Blubber
author: **9** Judy Blume

bludgeon **3** bat, hit **4** club **5** billy, clout, stick **6** cudgel **7** clobber **9** billyclub, truncheon

blue **3** low, sad **4** aqua, down, navy **5** azure **6** bluish, cobalt, gloomy, indigo, morose **7** doleful **8** cerulean, dejected, downcast, sapphire **9** depressed, turquoise **10** aquamarine, despondent, melancholy **11** downhearted, lapis lazuli, ultra-marine **12** disconsolate **14** down in the dumps, down in the mouth

Blue Angel, The
director: **17** Josef von Sternberg
based on novel by: **12** Heinrich Mann
cast: **10** Kurt Gerron **12** Emil Jannings **15** Marlene Dietrich (Lola-Lola)
song: **18** Falling in Love Again

Bluebeard
characteristic: **9** many wives

bluebell **9** Mertensia **18** Mertensia Virginica **21** Campanula rotundifolia
variety: **7** English, Spanish **8** Virginia **10** Australian, California **11** Clanwilliam

blueberry **9** Vaccinium
variety: **3** Low **4** Male **5** Swamp **7** Lowbush, Sourtop, Western **8** Creeping, Elliott's, Highbush, Low sweet **9** Late sweet, Rabbiteye **10** Velvet-leaf **13** Black highbush

blueblood **4** peer **5** noble **8** nobleman **9** patrician, socialite **10** aristocrat, noblewoman **14** peer of the realm

blue-blooded **5** noble, regal, royal **6** titled **7** courtly **8** highbred, wellborn **9** patrician **10** upper-class **12** aristocratic, of royal blood

blue bloods **5** elite **8** nobility **9** haut monde **10** patricians **11** aristocracy, high society **14** creme de la creme

bluegrass **3** Poa
varieties: **3** Big **4** Wood **5** Rough, Texas **6** Annual, Canada **7** Bulbous, English **8** Kentucky, Sandberg **10** Rough-stalk

Bluegrass State
nickname of: **8** Kentucky

Blue Hen State
nickname of: **8** Delaware

Blue Knight, The
author: **14** Joseph Wambaugh

Blue Law State
nickname of: **11** Connecticut

blue-pencil **3** cut **4** edit, trim **6** censor, cut out, delete, digest, reduce **7** abridge, shorten **8** boil down, condense, pare down **9** expurgate **10** abbreviate

blueprint **4** plan **5** chart **6** design, scheme **7** diagram **9** schematic

Blue Riders
German: **11** Blaue Reiter
group of: **7** artists

blues **5** dumps **8** doldrums **10** depression, low spirits, melancholy **11** despondency

bluestocking
French: **7** bas bleu

bluff **3** lie **4** bank, bold, crag, curt, dupe, fake, fool, hoax, liar, open, peak, sham **5** blunt, boast, cliff, faker, frank, fraud, ridge, rough **6** abrupt, candid, crusty, delude, direct, humbug **7** bluffer, boaster, brusque, deceive, fake out, mislead, pretend **8** bragging, headland, headlong, palisade, pretense **9** bamboozle, deception, idle boast, outspoken, precipice, pretender **10** escarpment, forthright, promontory, subterfuge **11** braggadocio, counterfeit, plainspoken **13** unceremonious, straightforward

bluffer **5** bluff, faker, fraud, phony **6** humbug **9** pretender

bluish **7** off-blue **12** somewhat blue

Blume, Claire
real name of: **11** Claire Bloom

Blume, Judy
author of: **5** Wifey **6** Deenie **7** Blubber, Forever **19** Then Again Maybe I Won't **22** It's Not the End of the World **26** Tales of a Fourth Grade Nothing **27** Are You There God? It's Me Margaret

Blumenbach, Johann Friedrich
field: **7** anatomy **10** physiology
nationality: **6** German
father of: **20** physical anthropology

blunder **4** goof, slip **5** boner, error, gaffe **6** booboo, bumble, bungle, slip up **7** faux pas, mistake, stagger, stumble **8** flounder **9** gaucherie **11** impropriety, make a booboo **12** indiscretion

blunt **4** curt, dull, numb, open **5** frank, rough, thick **6** abrupt, benumb, candid, deaden, dulled, soften, weaken **7** brusque, lighten, stupefy **8** edgeless, explicit, mitigate, moderate, tactless **9** outspoken, unpointed **10** to the point

11 insensitive, unsharpened **15** straightforward

bluntness **6** candor **10** directness **14** forthrightness **15** plainspokenness

blur **3** dim, fog, run **4** blot, haze, veil **5** bedim, befog, cloud, smear **6** blotch, darken, smudge, spread **7** becloud, obscure, splotch **9** confusion, obscurity

blurb **2** ad **4** rave, spot **5** brief **10** commercial **13** advertisement

blurred **3** dim **5** vague **6** blurry **7** smeared **10** ill-defined, indefinite, indistinct

blurt out **4** blab, sing **7** confess, divulge, let slip **8** give away **9** come clean

blush **5** color, flush **6** redden **7** grow red, turn red **8** rosy tint **9** reddening

blushing **3** coy, red **4** rosy **5** fresh, timid **6** demure, modest **7** colored, bashful, flushed, glowing **8** blooming, sheepish **9** rosaceous **10** embarrassed **11** flourishing

bluster **4** brag, crow, rant **5** bluff, boast, bully, gloat, noise, storm **7** bombast, bravado, crowing, protest, ranting, swagger **8** boasting, gloating, threaten **9** noisy talk **10** swaggering **14** boisterousness

blustery **5** blowy, gusty, windy **6** breezy **7** squally

Blythe, Ethel Mae
real name of: **14** Ethel Barrymore

Blythe, John
real name of: **13** John Barrymore

Blythe, Lionel
real name of: **15** Lionel Barrymore

Boadicea
Latin name: **8** Boudicca
queen of: **5** Iceni
husband: **10** Prasutagus
ruled: **7** Norfolk (England)
fought: **6** Romans
died: **7** suicide

Boanerges
means: **13** sons of thunder
name given to: **4** John **5** James

boar
group of: **7** sounder

board **3** bed **4** deal, feed, food, slat **5** enter, get on, house, lodge, meals, panel, plank, put up **6** batten, billet, embark, go onto **7** council, quarter **8** tribunal **9** clapboard, directors **10** daily meals

board game **4** Clue, Life, ludo **5** chess **7** Othello **8** checkers, cribbage, dominoes, draughts, fanorona, Monopoly, Scrabble **9** Alquerque **10** backgammon **14** Trivial Pursuit **15** Chinese checkers
Egyptian: **5** Senat
Korean: **5** Nyout, Pa-tok
Indian: **7** pachisi **8** parchesi, shatranj **9** ashtapada **10** shaturanga
Japanese: **2** Go **3** I-go **5** Shogi
Chinese: **6** Ma-jong, wei-ch'i **7** Ma-jongg
Swedish: **6** tablut

boast **4** brag, crow, have **5** vaunt **6** flaunt **7** contain, exhibit, possess, show off, talk big **15** blow one's own horn

boaster **6** gascon **7** bragger, egotist **8** blowhard, braggart **9** big talker **11** braggadocio

boastful **5** cocky **7** crowing, pompous, swollen **8** bragging, cocksure, inflated, puffed up, vaunting **9** conceited **11** braggadocio, exaggerated, pretentious **12** vainglorious

boastfulness **7** conceit, egotism **8** bragging **9** cockiness, immodesty, pomposity, vainglory **10** self-praise **11** braggadocio **12** cocksureness

boastful soldier
Latin: **14** miles gloriosus

boat **4** ship **5** craft **6** vessel

Boaz
father: **5** Salma **6** Salmon
wife: **4** Ruth
son: **4** Obed
kinsman of: **5** Naomi **9** Elimelech

bob **3** cut, hop, nod **4** clip, crop, dock, duck, leap, trim **5** dance, shear **6** bounce **7** shorten

Bobadill
character in: **19** Every Man in His Humour
author: **6** Jonson

bobbin **3** pin **4** coil, cord, reel **5** quill, spool **6** piping **7** ratchet, spindle, torchon **8** cylinder

bobcat **3** cat **4** lynx **7** wildcat

Bob Cummings Show, The
later name: **11** Love That Bob
character: **10** Bob Collins **14** Chuck MacDonald **15** Charmaine (Shultzy) Shultz **17** Margaret MacDonald
cast: **9** Ann B Davis **11** Bob Cummings **13** Dwayne Hickman **14** Rosemary DeCamp

Bob Newhart Show, The
character: **12** Elliot Carlin, Emily Hartley, Howard Borden **13** Jerry Robinson, Robert (Bob) Hartley **20** Carol Kester Bondurant
cast: **9** Bill Daily, Jack Riley **11** Peter Bonerz **13** Marcia Wallace **16** Suzanne Pleshette

Boccaccio, Giovanni
author of: **10** Filostrato, Il Filocopo **11** Life of Dante **12** The Decameron

Boccherini, Luigi
born: **5** Italy, Lucca
composer of: **8** La Divina **9** The Aviary **10** Clementina **11** L'Uccelliera

Boccioni, Umberto
born: **5** Italy **12** Reggio Emilia **16** Reggio di Calabria
artwork: **10** Elasticity **12** The City Rises **15** Charge of Lancers **18** Dynamism of a Cyclist, The Forces of a Street **21** Fusion of Head and Window **30** Unique Forms of Continuity in Space

Bock, Hier
field: **6** botany
nationality: **6** German
founded: **12** modern botany
classified: **6** plants
author of: **15** Neu Kreutterbuch

Bocklin, Arnold
born: **5** Basel **7** Germany
artwork: **13** Pan in the Reeds **16** The Isle of the Dead

Bod *see* **5** Tibet

bode **4** omen **5** augur **6** herald **7** betoken, ominate, point to, portend, predict, presage, signify **8** forecast, foretell, precurse **9** foreshadow, prefigure

bodega **9** warehouse **12** grocery store

bodice **3** top **5** stays, waist **6** bolero, corset, girdle **7** corsage **8** camisole, corselet **9** stomacher **10** underwaist

bodily **8** corporal, physical

Bodily Harm
author: **14** Margaret Atwood

bodkin **3** awl **4** pick, tool **5** auger, borer, drill, point, probe **6** dagger, lancet, needle, reamer **7** hair pin, piercer **8** puncheon, stiletto

body **3** mob **4** bloc, bulk, form, mass **5** being, build, force, frame, group, shape, stiff, thing, torso, trunk **6** corpse, figure, league, person, throng **7** cadaver, carcass, combine, council, faction, remains, society **8** assembly, cohesion, congress, deceased, main part, majority, physique, quantity **9** coalition, multitude, stiffness, thickness **10** federation **11** brotherhood, consistency **13** confederation

Body and Soul
director: **12** Robert Rossen
cast: **10** Anne Revere **11** Hazel Brooks, Lilli Palmer **12** John Garfield **13** William Conrad

bodybuilder **12** Charles Atlas **20** Arnold Schwarzenegger

Boedromius
epithet of: **6** Apollo
means: **7** rescuer

Boeotus
father: **8** Poseidon
mother: **4** Arne

Boer, Boor **6** farmer **9** Afrikaner
language: **9** Afrikaans
ancestry: **5** Dutch
inhabitants of: **9** Transvaal **11** South Africa **15** Orange Free State

Boethius, Anicius Manlius Severinus
also called: **5** Boece
author of: **23** Consolation of Philosophy

Boffin
character in: **15** Our Mutual Friend
author: **7** Dickens

bog **3** fen **4** mire, sink **5** marsh, swamp **6** morass **7** be stuck **8** quagmire, wetlands **9** marshland, swampland

Bogaerde, Derek Van den
real name of: **11** Dirk Bogarde

Bogarde, Dirk
real name: **19** Derek Van den Bogaerde
born: **6** London **7** England **9** Hempstead
roles: **6** Victim **7** Darling **10** The Servant **13** Death in Venice **14** Song Without End, The Night Porter **16** A Tale of Two Cities

Bogart, Humphrey
nickname: **5** Bogie
wife: **12** Lauren Bacall
born: **9** New York NY
roles: **8** Key Largo **10** Casablanca, High Sierra **11** The Big Sleep **14** The Caine Mutiny **15** The African Queen (Oscar) **16** The Maltese Falcon, To Have and Have Not **18** The Petrified Forest **27** The Treasure of the Sierra Madre

Bogdanovich, Peter
director of: **4** Mask **9** Paper Moon **18** The Last Picture Show

boggle **3** shy **4** balk, muff **5** botch, demure, hover, waver **6** bungle, shrink, wobble **7** blunder, stumble **8** flounder, frighten, hesitate, hold back **9** overwhelm **11** make a mess of

boggy **3** wet **4** soft **5** foggy, mossy, soggy **6** marshy, spongy, swampy **7** squashy

Bogie
nickname of: **14** Humphrey Bogart

Bogota
capital of: **8** Colombia

bogus **4** fake, sham **5** dummy, false, phony **6** ersatz, forged, pseudo **7** feigned, pretend **8** spurious **9** imitation, simulated, synthetic **10** artificial, fraudulent **11** counterfeit, make-believe

Boheme, La
also: **12** Bohemian Life
opera by: **7** Puccini
character: **4** Mimi **7** Colline, Musetta, Rodolfo **8** Marcello **9** Schaunard

bohemian, Bohemian **6** hippie **7** beatnik **10** unorthodox **13** nonconformist **14** unconventional

Bohr, Niels
field: **7** physics
nationality: **6** Danish
developed: **8** atom bomb **13** quantum theory, uranium theory

Boiardo, Matteo Maria
author of: **17** Orlando Innamorato

boil **4** brew, burn, foam, fume, rage, rant, rave, sore, stew, toss **5** chafe, churn, froth, storm **6** bubble, fester, quiver, seethe, simmer, sizzle, well up **7** abscess, bristle, parboil, pustule, smolder **8** furuncle **9** carbuncle, fulminate

boil down **3** cut **6** reduce **7** abridge, cut down, shorten **8** condense, contract **10** abbreviate

boiler **6** copper, geyser, heater, kettle **7** alembic, caldron, furnace

Boilermaker, the
nickname of: **20** James Jackson Jeffries

boisterous **4** loud, wild **5** noisy, rowdy **6** unruly **9** clamorous, out-of-hand **10** disorderly, uproarious **12** obstreperous, uncontrolled, unrestrained

boite, boite de nuit **7** cabaret **9** nightclub

Bojer, Johan
author of: **12** Folk by the Sea, The Emigrants **14** The Great Hunger, The Power of a Lie **16** Last of the Vikings

bold **3** hot **4** loud, rude **5** brash, brave, fiery, fresh, saucy, vivid **6** brazen, cheeky, daring, flashy, heroic **7** defiant, forward, valiant **8** colorful, creative, fearless, impudent, insolent, intrepid, spirited, stalwart, striking, unafraid, valorous **9** audacious, daredevil, dauntless **10** courageous **11** eye-catching, imaginative, impertinent, indomitable, lionhearted, unshrinking **12** stouthearted **13** adventuresome

boldfaced **5** brash, saucy **6** brassy, brazen **7** forward **8** immodest, impudent, insolent **9** audacious, barefaced, shameless, unabashed

boldness **4** grit **5** nerve, pluck, spunk **6** daring, mettle **7** bravery, courage **8** audacity **9** brashness, hardihood **10** brazenness **13** audaciousness, determination, self-assurance **14** courageousness **15** adventurousness

Bolger, Ray
born: **12** Dorchester MA
roles: **9** Scarecrow **10** On Your Toes **13** The Wizard of Oz, Where's Charley

Bolivia ***see box, p. 118.***

Bolkonsky, Andrei
character in: **11** War and Peace
author: **7** Tolstoy

Boll, Heinrich
author of: **8** The Clown **12** The Safety Net **18** Absent Without Leave **21** Group Portrait With Lady **27** The Lost Honor of Katharina Blum **28** Missing Persons and Other Essays

bolster **3** aid **4** help **5** add to, brace **6** assist, cradle, hold up, pillow, prop up, uphold **7** cushion, shore up, support, sustain **8** buttress, maintain,

Bolivia

named for: 12 Simon Bolivar

capital:
***administrative:* 5** La Paz
***legal:* 5** Sucre

largest city: 5 La Paz

others: 3 Ivo **4** Icla, Itau, Mojo, Saya, Yaco, Yato, Yura **5** Cliza, Llica, Oruro, Quime, Uyuni, Zongo **6** Guaqui, Potosi, Tiraja, Tupiza **8** Pulacayo **9** Santa Cruz **10** Chuquisaca, Cochabamba **11** Vallegrande, Villa Montes

school: 6 Xavier **8** St Andrew **12** San Francisco

division: 6 Valles **7** Oriente, Valleys **8** Montanas **9** Altiplano

measure: 6 league **7** celemin

monetary unit: 7 centavo **13** peso boliviano

weight: 5 libra, marco

lake: 5 Poopo **7** Allagas, Coipasa, Rogagua **8** Titicaca **10** Desaguader

mountain: 4 Jara **5** Andes, Cusco, Cuzco **6** Pupuya, Sajama, Sorata, Sunsas **7** Illampu **8** Illimani, Mururata, Sansimon, Santiago, Zapaleri **12** Eastern Range, Western Range **18** Cordillera Oriental **20** Cordillera Occidental

highest point: 8 Ancohuma

river: 4 Beni, Yata **5** Abuna, Lauca, Orton **6** Blanco, Ichilo, Itenez, Madidi, Mamore, Mizque, Yacuma **7** Guapore, Machupo **8** Inambari, Itonamas **9** Pilcomayo, Rio Grande, San Miguel **11** Desaguadero, Madre de Dios

physical features:
***lowlands:* 6** Llanos
***plateau:* 9** Altiplano
***swamp:* 6** Izozog
***valley:* 5** Yunga
***volcano:* 7** Ollague

people: 6 Aymara **7** mestizo, Quechua
***author:* 7** Mendoza **8** Arguedas **11** Costa du Rels
***leader:* 5** Busch, Sucre **6** Candia, Ortuno **7** Bolivar **9** Melgarejo, Santa Cruz **10** Barrientos, Estenssoro

language: 6 Aymara **7** Quechua, Spanish

religion: 13 Roman Catholic

place:
***church:* 9** St Francis, St Michael **10** San Lorenzo
***monument:* 11** La Coronilla
***ruins:* 10** Tiahuanaco
***tower:* 6** Chulpa

feature:
***animal:* 5** llama **6** alpaca, vicuna
***bar/club:* 7** boliche
***boat:* 5** balsa
***dance/song:* 5** cueca **7** huainos, pasillo **8** morenada **9** taquirari **10** palla-palla **11** cacharpayas, waka-tokonis
***devil dance:* 8** Diablado
***guitar:* 8** charango
***skirt:* 7** pollera
***wind instrument:* 4** kena, sicu **5** erque, quena, tarka **6** pututu **9** pinquillo

food:
***chicken dish:* 14** picante de pollo
***corn:* 4** mote
***corn drink:* 3** api **14** chicha taratena
***dish:* 11** plato paceno **14** sajta de gallina
***dried meat:* 7** charque
***pancakes:* 7** bunulos
***potato:* 5** chuno

shoulder **9** reinforce **10** strengthen

bolster one's spirits 5 cheer **7** cheer up, comfort, hearten **8** inspirit **9** buoy one up, encourage

bolt 3 bar, fly, peg, pin, rod, run **4** dart, dash, flee, gulp, jump, leap, lock, roll, rush, tear, wolf **5** bound, brand, catch, dowel, flash, hurry, latch, rivet, scoot, shaft, speed **6** fasten, gobble, hasten, hurtle, length, secure, spring, sprint, stroke **8** fastener **12** swallow whole

bolt down 4 wolf **5** scarf **6** devour, gobble **8** gulp down

bomb 3 dud, egg **4** bust, fail, flop, mine **5** lemon **6** fiasco, fizzle **7** bombard, grenade, failure, washout

bombard 5 beset, hound, shell, worry **6** assail, attack, batter, harass, pepper, pester, strafe **7** assault, barrage, besiege **8** fire upon **9** cannonade

bombardment 5 blitz, siege **7** air raid, assault, barrage, bombing **10** blitzkrieg

bombast 3 pad **4** puff, rant **6** cotton **7** bluster, fustian, palaver **8** boasting, flummery, rhapsody, tall talk, verbiage **9** bavardage **10** balderdash **12** braggadocio, exaggeration **13** magniloquence, overstatement **14** grandiloquence **17** sesquipedalianism

bombastic 5 tumid, windy, wordy **6** padded, turgid **7** pompous, verbose **8** inflated **12** magniloquent **13** grandiloquent

Bombay
area: 7 Trombay **8** Salsette **12** Bombay Island
called: 14 Gateway to India
creek: 7 Bassein
landmark: 9 High Court **13** Taj Mahal Hotel **14** Gateway of India **16** Victoria Terminus **17** Rajabai Clock Tower
rock formation: 10 Deccan Trap
sea: 7 Arabian

Bona Dea
also: 5 Fauna
origin: 5 Roman
goddess of: 8 chastity **9** fertility
worshipped by: 5 women
father: 6 Faunus
brother: 6 Faunus
husband: 6 Faunus

bona fide 4 real, true **5** legal **6** actual, honest, lawful **7** genuine, sincere **9** authentic, honorable **10** legitimate **11** in good faith

bon ami **5** lover **10** good friend

bonanza **8** gold mine, windfall

Bonanza
character: **3** Ben **4** Adam, Hoss **5** Candy **7** Hop Sing **9** Little Joe
family: **10** Cartwright
cast: **10** Dan Blocker **11** David Canary, Lorne Greene **13** Michael Landon, Victor Sen Yung **14** Pernell Roberts
ranch: **9** Ponderosa

Bonanza State
nickname of: **7** Montana

bon appetit **14** hearty appetite

Bonario
character in: **7** Volpone
author: **6** Jonson

bonbon **5** candy, sweet **7** fondant **9** sweetmeat **10** confection, sugar candy **13** confectionery **14** chocolate cream

bond, bonds **3** tie **4** cord, knot, link, rope **5** irons, scrip, union **6** chains, pledge **7** compact, fetters, promise **8** affinity, bindings, manacles, security, shackles **9** agreement, guarantee, handcuffs **10** allegiance, attachment, connection, fastenings, obligation **11** certificate, stipulation

Bond, James
actor: **10** Roger Moore **11** Sean Connery **12** Peter Sellers **13** George Lazenby, Timothy Dalton
appears in: **4** Dr No **9** Moonraker, Octopussy **10** Goldfinger **11** Thunderball **12** A View To A Kill **13** Live and Let Die **15** For Your Eyes Only **16** The Spy Who Loved Me, You Only Live Twice **18** Diamonds Are Forever, From Russia with Love, Never Say Never Again, The Living Daylights **22** The Man with the Golden Gun **26** On Her Majesty's Secret Service
author: **10** Ian Fleming
drink: **12** vodka martini **16** shaken not stirred
employer: **3** MI-6 **20** British Secret Service
foe: **7** Blofeld, SPECTRE
office staff: **1** M, Q **14** Miss Moneypenny
university: **6** Oxford
wife: **5** Tracy

bondage **4** yoke **6** chains **7** fetters, serfdom, slavery **8** shackles **9** captivity, servitude, vassalage **11** enslavement

bone
comprise: **8** skeleton
contain: **6** marrow **9** cartilage **11** blood vessel
fitted together by: **5** joint
held by: **8** ligament
pulled by: **6** muscle
specific: **3** rib **4** ulna **5** femur, skull, tibia **6** carpal, fibula, pelvis, radius, sacrum, tarsal **7** humerus, patella, scapula, sternum **8** clavicle, vertebra **9** vertebrae

bone chilling **3** icy **4** cold **5** harsh, sharp **6** arctic, biting, bitter, frigid **7** cutting, glacial **8** piercing, stinging **11** penetrating **15** teeth-chattering

bonehead **3** ass **4** clod, dolt, fool **5** booby, dunce, idiot, moron, ninny **6** dimwit, nitwit **7** fathead, half-wit **8** dumb-dumb, imbecile, lunkhead **9** blockhead, lamebrain, numbskull **10** dunderhead, nincompoop **11** chowderhead

boner **4** goof, slip **5** error **6** boo-boo, slip-up **7** blooper, blunder, mistake

boneyard **4** dump **7** ossuary **8** Boot Hill, cemetery, junkyard **9** graveyard **10** churchyard **12** burial ground **13** burying ground

Bonheur, Rosa
real name: **19** Marie Rosalie Bonheur
born: **6** France **8** Bordeaux
artwork: **12** The Horse Fair **23** Ploughing in the Nivernais

bonjour **5** hello **7** good day

Bonjour Tristesse
author: **14** Francoise Sagan

bon marche **7** bargain

bon mot **4** quip **7** epigram **9** witticism

Bonn
capital of: **11** West Germany
landmark: **10** Bundeshaus **11** Munsterkerk
museum: **18** Ludwig van Beethoven
river: **5** Rhine
Roman fort: **15** Castra Bonnensia

Bonnard, Pierre
born: **6** France **16** Fontenay-aux-Roses
artwork: **8** Intimist, Luncheon **9** The Review **13** Nude in the Bath, The Open Window, Women with a Dog **14** After the Shower, Farm at Le Cannet **16** The Breakfast Room **17** The Terrasse Family **22** Figure Before a Fireplace

bonne amie **5** lover **6** friend **10** good friend

bonne nuit **9** good night

bonnet **3** cap, hat **4** cowl, hood, sail **5** cover, toque **7** chapeau, commode **8** headgear **9** headdress

Bonnie and Clyde
director: **10** Arthur Penn
cast: **11** Faye Dunaway (Bonnie Parker), Gene Hackman **12** Warren Beatty (Clyde Barrow) **15** Michael J Pollard

bonny **4** fair **6** comely, lovely, pretty, seemly **7** winning, winsome **8** engaging, fetching, handsome, pleasing **9** beautiful, exquisite, ravishing **10** attractive

bon soir **9** good night **11** good evening

bonus **4** gift **5** prize **6** bounty, reward **7** benefit, premium **8** dividend, gratuity **10** honorarium

Bonus Eventus
also: **7** Eventus
origin: **5** Roman
god of: **4** luck **10** prosperity **11** agriculture

bon vivant **7** epicure, gourmet **8** gourmand, sybarite **10** gastronome

bony **4** lean **5** gaunt, lanky, spare **6** skinny **7** angular, scrawny **11** full of bones **12** skin-and-bones

boo **3** pan **4** hiss **5** taunt **6** deride, heckle, revile **7** catcall **8** ridicule **9** criticize, shout down **11** give the bird **16** give the raspberry

boo-boo **4** goof, slip **5** boner, error **6** slip-up **7** blunder, mistake

boobtube **2** TV **3** box **8** idiot box **13** television set

booby **4** bird, dope, fool **5** dummy, dunce, idiot, moron, ninny **6** dimwit, gannet, nitwit **7** fathead, halfwit **8** bonehead, dumb-dumb, imbecile, lunkhead, numskull **9** blockhead, lamebrain, simpleton **10** nincompoop **11** chowderhead

Booby, Lady
character in: **13** Joseph Andrews
author: **8** Fielding

boodle **4** loot, swag **5** booty, bribe, crowd, graft, group

7 plunder 10 collection 11 stolen goods

Boog
nickname of: 10 John Powell

boohoo 3 cry, sob 4 bawl, weep 7 blubber 9 shed tears

book 4 bill, file, list, note, opus, post, tome 5 album, enter, index, slate 6 accuse, charge, engage, enroll, indict, insert, line up, record, tablet, volume 7 catalog, procure, program, put down, reserve 8 mark down, notebook, register, schedule, treatise 9 bound work, write down 10 arrange for 11 publication, written work 16 make reservations

bookish 7 erudite, learned, stilted 8 academic, educated, informed, literary, pedantic, studious, well-read 9 scholarly 11 pedagogical, impractical 12 intellectual

bookkeeper 5 clerk 7 auditor 10 accountant 11 comptroller

booklet 5 folio 7 leaflet, program 8 brochure, circular, pamphlet

Book of Common Prayer
author: 10 Joan Didion

Book of Lights, The
author: 10 Chaim Potok

Book of Manuel
author: 13 Julio Cortazar

Book of Odes
author: 9 Confucius

Book of psalms 12 psalter

Book of Sand, The
author: 15 Jorge Luis Borges

Book of the Duchess, The
author: 15 Geoffrey Chaucer

boom 3 bar 4 bang, beam, gain, grow, push, roar, spar 5 blast, boost, shaft, spurt 6 growth, rumble, thrive, thrust, upturn 7 advance, develop, prosper, thunder, upsurge 8 flourish, increase 9 expansion, good times

Boom Boom
nickname of: 15 Bernie Geoffrion

boomerang 5 kalie, kiley, kylie, wango 6 atlatl, recoil 7 rebound, womerah, woomera 8 backfire, ricochet, trombush 9 bound back, solitaire 10 projectile

Boomer State
nickname of: 8 Oklahoma

boon 3 fun, gay 4 gift 5 favor, jolly, merry 6 kindly 7 benefit, bequest 8 blessing, donation, offering, pleasant 9 advantage, congenial, convivial, endowment 11 full of cheer, good-natured

boon companion 3 pal 4 chum 5 buddy, crony 6 friend 7 comrade 8 confrere, intimate 9 confidant 10 bosom buddy

boondocks 4 bush, veld 6 Podunk, sticks 7 boonies, country, outback 8 frontier 9 backwater, backwoods, provinces 10 hinterland 11 backcountry, countryside 12 squaresville 13 nowheresville 14 wide open spaces

Boone, Richard
born: 12 Los Angeles CA
roles: 5 Medic 6 Hombre 7 Paladin 8 The Alamo 11 The Shootist 12 Ten Wanted Men, The Desert Fox 17 Have Gun Will Travel

boonies 6 sticks 7 country 9 backwoods, boondocks, provinces 10 hinterland 11 countryside

boor 3 oaf 4 hick, lout, rube 5 brute, churl, yokel 6 rustic 7 bumpkin, hayseed, peasant 9 vulgarian 10 clodhopper, philistine 11 guttersnipe

boorish 4 rude 5 crude 6 coarse, gauche, oafish, rustic, vulgar 7 loutish, uncouth 9 unrefined 10 unpolished 11 peasantlike

boorishness 8 rudeness 9 surliness, vulgarity 10 bad manners, coarseness, incivility, oafishness 12 churlishness, impoliteness

boost 4 hike, laud, lift, plug, push, rise 5 add to, extol, heave, hoist, pitch, raise, shove 6 expand, foster, free ad, growth, pickup, praise, upturn, urge on 7 acclaim, advance, develop, elevate, enlarge, forward, further, improve, nurture, promote, root for, support, sustain, upsurge, upswing 8 addition, applause, good word, increase, propound 9 expansion, increment, promotion 10 compliment, give a leg up, stick up for 11 development, enlargement, improvement, speak well of

boot
French: 9 chaussure

booth 3 pen 4 coop, nook, tent 5 hutch, stall, stand, table 7 counter 9 cubbyhole, enclosure 11 compartment

Booth, Shirley
real name: 15 Thelma Booth Ford
born: 9 New York NY
roles: 5 Hazel 13 The Matchmaker 19 Come Back Little Sheba (Oscar)

bootleg 5 hooch 7 illegal, illicit 8 unlawful 9 moonshine 12 football play

bootless 6 futile 7 useless 11 ineffective, ineffectual 12 unproductive, unprofitable

bootlick 4 fawn 5 toady 6 cringe, grovel 7 flatter, truckle

bootmaker 7 cobbler 9 shoemaker

booty 4 gain, loot 5 prize 6 boodle, spoils 7 pillage, plunder, takings 8 pickings, winnings

booze 4 bout, soak 5 drink, hooch, spree 6 guzzle, liquor, tipple 7 alcohol, spirits, swizzle 8 cocktail 10 intoxicant 14 drink like a fish
type: 3 gin, rum, rye 4 beer, wine 5 vodka 6 scotch 7 bourbon, whiskey

boozer 3 sot 4 lush 5 drunk, souse, toper 7 tippler 8 drunkard 9 alcoholic, inebriate 11 hard drinker

bordello, bordel 4 stew 5 house 6 bagnio 7 brothel 8 cathouse 10 bawdy house, fancy house, whorehouse 13 sporting house 14 house of ill fame 16 house of ill repute 19 house of prostitution

border 3 hem, rim 4 abut, bind, brim, curb, edge, join, line, pale, trim 5 brink, flank, frame, limit, skirt, touch, verge 6 adjoin, fringe, margin 8 befringe, be next to, boundary, frontier, outskirt 9 extremity, perimeter, periphery 13 circumference

borderline 4 open 5 vague 7 halfway, inexact, obscure, unclear 8 marginal 9 ambiguous, equivocal, uncertain, undecided, unsettled 10 ambivalent, indefinite 11 indefinable, problematic 13 indeterminate

bore 4 drag, drip, sink, tire 5 drill, drive, weary 6 burrow, pierce, tunnel 7 caliber, exhaust, fatigue, wear out 8 gouge out 9 hollow out 10 wet blanket 14 inside diameter

Boreadae
decendants of: 6 Boreas

Boreal
pertaining to: **6** Boreas

Boreas
origin: **5** Greek
personifies: **9** north wind
father: **8** Astraeus
mother: **3** Eos
twin sons: **5** Zetes **6** Calais
daughter: **6** Chione **9** Cleopatra

bored **5** jaded **7** wearied **12** discontented, uninterested

boredom **6** tedium **8** doldrums, dullness, monotony **9** weariness **11** tediousness
French: **5** ennui

Borges, Jorge Luis
author of: **8** The Aleph **10** Labyrinths **11** Dreamtigers **13** The Book of Sand **18** A Personal Anthology, In Praise of Darkness **19** Doctor Brodie's Report, Fervor of Buenos Aires **25** A Universal History of Infamy

Borghild
origin: **12** Scandinavian
mentioned in: **8** Volsunga
husband: **7** Sigmund

Borgia, Alfonso de **16** Pope Callistus III

Borgia, Rodrigo de **15** Pope Alexander VI

Borglum, (John) Gutzon
born: **10** Bear Lake ID
artwork: **7** Lincoln **18** Mt Rushmore Memorial, The Mares of Diomedes

Borgnine, Ernest
real name: **18** Ermes Effron Borgnine
wife: **11** Ethel Merman
born: **8** Hamden CT
roles: **5** Marty (Oscar) **8** Barabbas **11** McHale's Navy **12** The Wild Bunch **13** The Dirty Dozen **17** Bad Day at Black Rock **18** From Here to Eternity **20** The Poseidon Adventure

boring **4** dull, flat **5** stale **6** tiring **7** humdrum, insipid, tedious **8** tiresome **9** wearisome **10** monotonous, unexciting **11** repetitious **13** uninteresting

boring tool **3** bit **5** auger, drill **11** brace and bit

Borinquen *see* **10** Puerto Rico

Boriquen, Borinquen
language family: **8** Arawakan
location: **10** Puerto Rico
related to: **5** Taino

Boris Godunov
author: **16** Alexander Pushkin
opera by: **10** Mussorgsky **12** Shostakovich **14** Rimsky-Korsakov
character: **6** Dmitri, Feodor, Maryna **7** Gregory, Grigory **8** Basmanov, Otrepyev

born **6** innate **7** natural **9** delivered, intuitive **12** brought forth

Born, Max
field: **7** physics
nationality: **7** British
worked on: **13** quantum theory
awarded: **10** Nobel Prize

borne **6** afloat, braved **7** carried, endured **9** put up with, tolerated **11** gone through, went through **12** given birth to

Borneo ***see box***

Born Yesterday
director: **11** George Cukor
cast: **12** Judy Holliday **13** William Holden **17** Broderick Crawford
Oscar for: **7** actress (Holliday)

Borodin, Alexander
born: **6** Russia **12** St Petersburg
member of: **7** The Five
composer of: **8** Bogatyri **10** Prince Igor **25** In the Steppes of Central Asia

boron
chemical symbol: **1** B

borough **4** burg, town **5** borgo, shire **6** county, parish **7** village **8** district, precinct, province, township **12** municipality
of New York City: **5** Bronx **6** Queens **8** Brooklyn **9** Manhattan **12** Staten Island

Borromini, Francesco
architect of: **10** San Carlino **17** Palazzo Falconieri **20** Sant' Ivo della Sapienza **23** Oratory of San Filippo Neri **24** Collegio di Propaganda Fide **26** San Carlo alle Quattro Fontane (Rome)

borrow **3** get, use **4** copy, take **5** filch, steal, usurp **6** obtain, pilfer, pirate **7** acquire **10** commandeer, plagiarize, take on loan **11** appropriate

Borrow, George Henry
author of: **8** Lavengro **9** Romany Rye, Wild Wales **10** The Zincali **15** The Bible in Spain

Bors
character in: **16** Arthurian romance

Bosch, Hieronymus
real name: **13** Jerome van

Borneo
other name: **10** Kalimantan
largest city: **12** Bandjermasin
others: **5** Kumai **6** Sambas, Sampit **7** Malinau, Pagatan, Sanggau, Sintang, Tarakan **8** Ketapang **9** Pontianak **10** Balikpapan
division of island:
independent: **6** Brunei
Malaysian state: **5** Sabah **7** Sarawak
part of Indonesia: **10** Kalimantan
measure: **7** gantang
weight: **4** para **6** chapah
mountain: **4** Iran, Raja **5** Saran **6** Kapuas, Muller, Nijaan, Tebang **8** Kinibalu, Schwaner
highest point: **8** Kinabalu
river: **4** Arut, Iwan **5** Bahau, Berau, Kajan, Padas, Pawan **6** Barito, Kapuas, Rajang, Sebuku **7** Kahajan, Mahakam, Mendawi **8** Pembuang
sea: **4** Java, Sulu **7** Celebes **10** South China
physical feature:
bay: **5** Adang, Kumai **6** Sampit
cape: **3** Aru **4** Datu **5** Lojar **6** Puting, Sambar **7** Selatan
port: **4** Miri **5** Balik, Papan **6** Brunei **9** Pontianak **12** Bandjermasin
strait: **8** Macassar
people: **4** Iban **5** Bukat, Dajak, Dayak, Dusan, Malay, Punan **6** Illano **7** Bakatan, Chinese, Illanum
language: **5** Malay **6** tribal **7** Chinese, English
religion: **5** Islam **7** animism **12** Christianity
feature:
tree: **5** kapor, kapur **7** billian

Aken **14** Jerome van Aeken **17** Jeroen Anthoiszoon **artwork: 7** Hay-Wain **11** Ship of Fools **14** The Crucifixion **19** Adoration of the Kings **21** The Crowning with Thorns **26** The Garden of Earthly Delights

Boscobel
author: 16 William Ainsworth

bosh 3 rot **4** bunk **6** bunkum, drivel **7** twaddle **8** claptrap, nonsense, tommyrot **10** balderdash, tomfoolery **11** foolishness **16** stuff and nonsense

Bosinney, Philip
character in: 14 The Forsyte Saga
author: 10 Galsworthy

bosky 5 bushy, drunk, shaded, tipsy, treed **6** wooded

bosom 4 bust, core, dear, soul **5** chest, close, heart, midst **6** breast, center, spirit **7** beloved, nucleus **8** intimate **9** cherished **11** inner circle

bosom buddy 4 chum **5** crony **6** cohort **7** best pal, comrade **8** alter ego, intimate, sidekick **9** companion, confidant **10** best friend

bosomy 5 busty, buxom **6** zaftig **11** full-figured **13** large-breasted

boss 4 head, push **5** chief, order **6** leader, master **7** command, foreman, kingpin, manager **8** employer **9** big cheese, executive **10** supervisor **13** administrator **14** superintendent

bossy 3 cow **9** imperious **10** commanding, tyrannical **11** dictatorial, domineering

Boston
airport: 5 Logan
area: 7 Back Bay **10** Bunker Hill, Fenway Park **11** Faneuil Hall **14** Kennedy Library, Old North Church
baseball team: 6 Red Sox
basketball team: 7 Celtics
dish: 10 baked beans
hockey team: 6 Bruins
landmark: 10 Beacon Hill
leader: 7 Brahmin
nickname: 8 Bean town
river: 7 Charles

Bostonians, The
author: 10 Henry James

Boston Strong Boy
nickname of: 13 John L Sullivan

Boswell, James
author of: 22 The Life of Samuel Johnson

botanist
American: 6 Barton, Torrey **7** Bartram
Austrian: 6 Mendel
Dutch: 7 DeVries
German: 4 Bock, Cohn
Scottish: 5 Brown
Swedish: 8 Linnaeus
Swiss: 6 Bauhin

botch 3 err, mar **4** blow, fail, flop, flub, goof, hash, mess, muff, ruin **5** spoil **6** bungle, foul up, fumble **7** blunder, butcher, failure, louse up **8** butchery **9** mismanage **11** make a mess of

bother 3 ado, irk, nag, tax, try, vex **4** care, drag, fret, fuss, load, onus, stir **5** annoy, harry, trial, upset, worry **6** dismay, flurry, harass, pester, racket, rumpus, strain, stress, tumult **7** attempt, disturb, problem, trouble **8** disquiet, distress, hardship, headache, irritate, nuisance, vexation **9** aggravate, commotion, hindrance **10** affliction, difficulty, impediment, irritation **11** aggravation, disturbance, encumbrance **12** make an effort **13** inconvenience, pain in the neck **14** responsibility

bothersome 6 taxing, vexing **8** annoying **9** worrisome **10** disturbing **11** aggravating, disquieting, distressing, troublesome **12** inconvenient

Both Your Houses
author: 15 Maxwell Anderson

Botswana ***see box***

Botticelli, Sandro
real name: 30 Alessandro di Mariano dei Filipepi
born: 5 Italy **8** Florence
artwork: 12 Birth of Venus **14** Mystic Nativity **16** Calumny of Apelles **18** Adoration of the Magi **22** Pallas Subduing a Centaur **25** The Madonna of the Magnificat

bottle 3 jar **4** vial **5** flask, phial **6** carafe, flagon, vessel **7** canteen

bottleneck 3 bar, jam **4** clog, stop **5** block **6** detour **7** barrier, embolus **8** blockage, embolism, gridlock, obstacle, stoppage, thrombus **10** congestion, impediment, infarction **11** costiveness, obstruction

bottom 3 can **4** base, core, foot, gist, root, rump, seat, sole **5** basis, belly, cause, fanny, heart, lower **6** center, deeper, depths, ground, lowest, origin, source, spring **7** deepest, essence **8** backside, buttocks, pedestal, riverbed **9** beginning, fundament, principle, rudiments, substance, underpart, underside **10** foundation, mainspring, wellspring **12** quintessence

Bottom
character in: 21 A Midsummer Night's Dream
author: 11 Shakespeare

bottomless 4 deep **7** abysmal **8** profound **11** measureless **12** immeasurable, unfathomable

Bouchardon, Edme
born: 6 France **8** Chaumont
artwork: 14 Philippe Stosch **31** Cupid Making a Bow from Hercules' Club

Boucher, Francois
born: 5 Paris **6** France
artwork: 9 The Rising

Botswana
other name:
12 Bechuanaland
capital/largest city:
8 Gaborone
9 Gaberones
others: 5 Kanye, Orapa, Tsane **6** Serowe **7** Lobatse, Lobotsi, Mochudi, Palapye, Thamaga **10** Molepolole **11** Francistown, Selebi-Pikwe
monetary unit: 4 pula, rand
lake: 3 Dow, Xau **5** Ngami
highest point: 11 Tsodilo Hill
river: 4 Nata, Okwa **5** Chobe, Nosob **6** Cuando, Molopo, Shashi **7** Cubango, Limpopo **8** Botletle, Okovango **9** Okovanggo
physical feature:
***desert:* 8** Kalahari
salt pans: **10** Makarikari
***swamp:* 8** Okavango
people: 5 Bantu **6** Tswana **7** Bakatla, Bakwena, Bushman **8** Bamalete, Baralong, Batawana, Batlokwa, Botswana **10** Bamangwato **11** Bangwaketse
language: 5 Bantu, Click **6** Tswana **7** English, Khoisan **8** Setswana
religion: 7 animism **10** Protestant **12** Christianity

13 Madame Boucher, Reclining Girl 16 Evening Landscape, Rinaldo and Armida, The Toilet of Venus 17 Chinese Tapestries, The Triumph of Venus 18 The Setting of the Sun

boudoir 7 bedroom 10 bedchamber 12 dressing room

bough 4 limb 6 branch

bougie 3 dip, wax 5 light, taper 6 candle, cierge, tallow

boulder, bowlder 3 nob 4 crag, knob, rock 5 block, stone 6 gibber 7 dornick 8 megalith

boulevard 6 avenue 7 parkway 9 concourse

bouleversement 7 turmoil 9 confusion, upsetting 11 overturning

bounce 3 bob, hop, pep 4 bump, life 5 bound, thump, verve, vigor 6 energy, jounce, recoil, spirit 7 rebound 8 dynamism, ricochet, vitality, vivacity 9 animation 10 liveliness

bouncing 3 big 4 full 5 jolly, large, lusty, plump 6 chubby, lively, robust, strong 7 healthy 8 animated, vigorous 12 in good health

bound 3 bob, orb, rim 4 area, edge, jump, leap, line, mark, pale, romp, sure, tied 5 dance, fated, hedge, limit, orbit, range, realm, vault 6 border, bounce, define, domain, doomed, forced, fringe, gambol, liable, prance, region, spring, tied up 7 certain, compass, confine, covered, encased, enclosed, flounce, going to, in bonds, limited, obliged, rebound, secured, trussed, wrapped 8 beholden, boundary, confined, destined, district, encircle, fastened, province, required, resolute, resolved, surround, tethered 9 bailiwick, committed, demarcate, extremity, periphery, territory 10 determined, restrained 11 demarcation 12 circumscribe

Boundaries
god of: 8 Terminus

boundary 3 rim 4 edge, line, pale 6 border, margin 7 barrier 8 frontier, landmark 9 extremity, periphery 11 demarcation 12 dividing line

boundary line 4 edge 5 bound 6 border 8 sideline

bounder 3 cad, rat 4 heel 5 knave, louse, rogue 6 rascal, rotter 7 caitiff, dastard, villain 9 scoundrel 10 blackguard

Bounderby, Mr
character in: 9 Hard Times
author: 7 Dickens

boundless 4 vast 7 endless, immense 8 infinite, unending 9 limitless, perpetual, unbounded, unlimited 10 without end 11 everlasting, measureless 12 immeasurable, incalculable, unrestricted 13 inexhaustible

bounteous, bountiful 4 free, full, rich 5 ample, large 6 lavish 7 copious, liberal, profuse, teeming 8 abundant, generous, prolific 9 abounding, plenteous, plentiful, unsparing 10 beneficent, benevolent, charitable, munificent, unstinting 11 magnanimous, overflowing

Bountiful, Lady
character in: 17 The Beaux Stratagem
author: 8 Farquhar

bountifulness 10 liberality, generosity 11 benevolence, magnanimity, munificence 14 charitableness 15 humanitarianism

bounty 3 aid 4 gift, help 5 bonus, favor, grant 6 giving, reward 7 charity, present, tribute 8 bestowal, donation, gratuity 9 endowment 10 almsgiving, assistance, generosity, liberality, recompense 11 benefaction, benevolence, munificence 12 contribution, philanthropy 14 charitableness, openhandedness

bouquet 4 odor 5 aroma, scent, spray 7 essence, garland, nosegay, perfume 9 fragrance 11 boutonniere

bouquet garni
ingredient: 5 basil, thyme 6 celery, savory 7 bay leaf, chervil, parsley 8 rosemary, tarragon

bourbon
variety of: 7 whiskey
origin: 7 America
ingredient: 4 corn
type: 7 blended 8 straight
drink: 9 Mint Julep 10 Boston Sour 11 John Collins 12 Old Fashioned
with Benedictine: 9 Twin Hills
with brandy and Benedictine: 13 Brighton Punch
with Cointreau: 10 Temptation
with rum: 14 Artillery Punch
with sloe gin: 9 Black Hawk
with Southern Comfort: 14 Blended Comfort
with triple sec: 10 Chapel Hill
with vermouth: 9 Allegheny

bourgeois 6 square 7 Babbitt, burgher 8 commoner, ordinary 11 middle-class 12 conventional 13 unimaginative

Bourgeois Gentleman, The
author: 7 Moliere
character: 6 Lucile, Nicole 7 Cleonte, Dorante 8 Covielle, Dorimene 14 Madame Jourdain 16 Monsieur Jourdain

Bourget, Charles Joseph Paul
author of: 11 The Disciple 12 A Cruel Enigma 14 The Night Cometh

Bourgh, Lady Catherine de
character in: 17 Pride and Prejudice
author: 6 Austen

Bourjaily, Vance
author of: 11 The Violated 14 The End of My Life 18 Brill Among the Ruins 22 Now Playing at Canterbury

Bourne Identity, The
author: 12 Robert Ludlum

bout 4 fray, term, tilt, turn 5 brush, clash, cycle, fight, match, set-to, siege, spell, spree 6 affair, battle, course, period, series 7 contest, go-round, scuffle, session, tourney 8 conflict, interval, skirmish, struggle 9 encounter 10 contention, engagement 11 boxing match, embrollment

boutonniere 4 posy 7 nosegay 16 buttonhole flower

bow 3 arc 4 bend, knot, prow, stem 5 agree, curve, defer, front, stoop, yield 6 archer, comply, curtsy, give in, kowtow, relent, salaam, submit, weapon 7 concede, succumb, crescent 9 acquiesce, genuflect, surrender 10 capitulate, forward end 12 genuflection, knuckle under

Bow, Clara
nickname: 6 It Girl
born: 10 Brooklyn NY
roles: 2 It 7 Mantrap 12 The Wild Party

bowdlerize 6 censor 9 expurgate 10 blue-pencil

bow down 5 yield 6 give in, submit 9 surrender 10 capitulate 12 knuckle under

bowed 4 bent 6 arched,

curved, nodded **7** hunched, stooped

bowels **3** gut, pit **4** core, guts, womb **5** abyss, belly, bosom, heart, midst **6** depths, hollow, vitals **7** innards, insides, stomach, viscera **8** entrails, interior, recesses **10** intestines **11** vital organs **13** innermost part

Bowen, Elizabeth
author of: **8** Eva Trout, The Hotel **10** To the North **11** Bowen's Court, Little Girls, The Cat Jumps **12** A World of Love **15** The Heat of the Day, The House in Paris **18** The Death of the Heart

Bowen's Court
author: **14** Elizabeth Bowen

bower **4** jack, joker, nook **5** arbor **6** alcove, anchor, pandal **7** bedroom, chamber, cottage, enclose, retreat, sanctum, shelter **8** dwelling, snuggery

Bowie, David
real name: **16** David Robert Jones
born: **6** London **7** England
roles: **9** Cat People, The Hunger **20** The Man Who Fell to Earth **24** Merry Christmas Mr Lawrence

Bowie Land, Bowie State
nickname of: **8** Arkansas

bowl **4** boat **5** arena, basin **6** cavity, hollow, tureen, valley, vessel **7** dishful, helping, portion, stadium **8** coliseum, deep dish **9** container, porringer **10** depression, receptacle **12** amphitheater

bowler **11** Earl Anthony

bowling
variation: **7** tenpins **8** duckpins, fivepins **10** candlepins
term: **4** miss **5** frame, spare, split **6** strike **10** gutterball
perfect score: **12** three hundred

bow-shape **3** arc **4** arch, bend **5** curve **9** curvature

bow to **5** yield **6** give in, give up, submit **9** acquiesce

box **3** bat, hit, rap **4** belt, cuff, slap, spar **5** booth, caddy, chest, crate, fight, punch, stall, whack **6** buffet, carton, coffer, strike, thwack **8** thumping **9** container **10** receptacle **11** compartment **13** exchange blows

boxer **7** Max Baer **8** Joe Louis **10** Barney Ross, Gene Tunney, Joe Frazier, Joe Walcott, Leon Spinks **11** Archie Moore, Jack Dempsey, Jack Johnson, Jake LaMotta, Larry Holmes, Muhammad Ali, Sonny Liston **12** Benny Leonard, James Corbett, John Sullivan, Johnny Dundee, Max Schmeling, Mickey Walker, Primo Carnera, Roberto Duran, Thomas Hearns **13** Carmen Basilio, Ezzard Charles, George Foreman, James Jeffries, Rocky Graziano, Rocky Marciano **14** Bob Fitzsimmons, Floyd Patterson, Henry Armstrong **15** Maxie Rosenbloom, Sugar Ray Leonard **16** Sugar Ray Robinson

boy **3** lad **5** youth **8** man child **9** male child, stripling, youngster
French: **6** garcon

Boy
character in: **6** Tarzan
author: **9** Burroughs

boycott **5** spurn **6** reject **7** exclude **8** spurning **9** blackball, blacklist, exclusion, ostracism, ostracize, rejection **12** blackballing, blacklisting

Boyd, James
author of: **5** Drums **8** Long Hunt **9** Roll River **10** Marching On

Boyd, William
born: **13** Hendrysburg OH
roles: **15** Hopalong Cassidy

Boyer, Charles
born: **6** Figeac, France
roles: **7** Algiers **8** Conquest, Gaslight **10** Back Street **11** Lost Horizon **16** The Garden of Allah **19** All This and Heaven Too

boyfriend **3** man **4** beau, date **5** flame, lover, swain, wooer **6** escort, fellow, old man, squire, steady, suitor **7** admirer, beloved, Don Juan **8** cavalier, Lothario, paramour, truelove, young man **9** companion, inamorato **10** sweetheart **15** gentleman caller

boyish **5** boyey, fresh **6** callow, tender **7** boylike, puerile **8** childish, immature, innocent, juvenile, youthful **9** childlike **10** sophomoric

Boylan, Blazes
character in: **7** Ulysses
author: **5** Joyce

Boyle, Robert
field: **9** chemistry
nationality: **7** British
father of: **9** chemistry
advocated: **20** experimental approach
established: **9** Boyle's Law

boylike **5** fresh, young **6** boyish, callow **7** puerile **8** childish, immature, innocent, juvenile, youthful **9** childlike

Boys Town
director: **12** Norman Taurog
cast: **9** Henry Hull **12** Mickey Rooney, Spencer Tracy (Father Flanagan)
Oscar for: **5** actor (Tracy)
sequel: **13** Men of Boys Town

Boy Wonder
nickname of: **5** Robin **6** Mel Ott

brace **3** duo **4** pair, prop, stay **5** shore, strut, truss **6** bracer, couple, hold up, prop up, steady **7** bolster, bracket, fortify, prepare, shore up, support, sustain, twosome **8** buttress **9** reinforce, stanchion **10** strengthen **13** reinforcement

bracelet **6** armlet, bangle

bracer **10** stiff drink, stimulator, wristguard **11** invigorator **12** strengthener, strong drink

Brachiosaurus
type: **8** dinosaur, sauropod
location: **10** East Africa **12** United States
period: **8** Jurassic

bracing **8** arousing, reviving **10** energizing, fortifying, refreshing **11** restorative, stimulating **12** exhilarating, invigorating **13** strengthening

Brack, Judge
character in: **11** Hedda Gabler
author: **5** Ibsen

bracken **4** fern **5** brake, brush, ferns **10** underbrush **11** undergrowth

bracket **4** prop, rank, stay **5** brace, class, group, range, shore, strut, truss **6** prop up, status **7** shore up, support **8** category, classify, division, grouping **9** designate, stanchion **10** categorize **11** designation **14** classification

brackish **4** salt **5** briny, salty **6** saline

Bracknell, Lady Augusta
character in: **27** The Importance of Being Earnest
author: **5** Wilde

bract **4** leaf

Bradbury, Ray
author of: **13** Dandelion Wine, Fahrenheit 451 **17** The Illustrated Man **20** The Martian Chronicles **27** Something Wicked This Way Comes

Bradford, Barbara Taylor
author of: **17** A Woman of Substance

Bradford, Richard
author of: **15** Red Sky at Morning

Bradley, Bill (William Warren)
nickname: **10** Dollar Bill
sport: **10** basketball
team: **13** New York Knicks
elected: **7** Senator
from: **9** New Jersey

Bradstreet, Anne
author of: **35** The Tenth Muse Lately Sprung Up in America

Brady Bunch, The
character: **3** Jan **4** Greg **5** Alice, Bobby, Cindy, Peter **6** Marcia **9** Mike Brady **10** Carol Brady
cast: **8** Eve Plumb **9** Ann B Davis **10** Robert Reed, Susan Olsen **13** Barry Williams **14** Mike Lookinland **16** Maureen McCormick **17** Christopher Knight, Florence Henderson

brag **4** crow **5** boast, vaunt **7** big talk, crowing, talk big **8** boasting, bragging **10** exaggerate, self-praise **12** boastfulness, exaggeration **15** blow one's own horn **19** pat oneself on the back

Brage *see* **5** Bragi

Bragg, William Henry and William Lawrence
field: **7** physics
nationality: **7** British
determined: **16** crystal structure
by: **15** X-ray diffraction
established: **9** Bragg's Law
awarded: **10** Nobel Prize

braggadocio **5** pride **6** egoism, vanity **7** bluster, conceit, swagger **9** cockiness, vainglory **10** pretension **14** self-importance

braggart **7** boaster, bragger **8** blowhard **9** big talker

Bragi
also: **5** Brage
origin: **6** Nordic
god of: **5** music **6** poetry
father: **4** Odin **5** Othin
wife: **4** Idun **5** Iduna, Ithun **6** Ithunn
mother: **3** Fri **5** Frigg, Frija **6** Frigga

Brahe, Tycho
field: **9** astronomy
nationality: **6** Danish
built: **11** observatory

Brahman
country: **5** India
religion: **8** Hinduism
system: **5** caste
rank: **7** highest
function: **6** leader, priest **7** teacher

Brahms, Johannes
born: **7** Germany, Hamburg
composer of: **7** Rinaldo **10** Rain Sonata **11** Triumphlied, Volkslieder **12** Thuner-Sonate **13** German Requiem, Song of Destiny, Song of Triumph **14** Schicksalslied, Song of the Fates, Tragic Overture **15** Gesang der Parzen, Hungarian Dances **19** Liebeslieder Waltzes, Meistersinger Sonata **24** Academic Festival Overture **31** Variations on the St Anthony Chorale

braid **4** knit, lace **5** plait, ravel, twine, twist, weave **7** entwine, wreathe **9** interlace **10** intertwine

brain
part: **7** medulla **8** cerebrum **9** pituitary **10** cerebellum

brainchild **8** creation **9** invention **12** original work **15** imaginative work

braininess **6** genius **9** smartness **10** brightness, brilliance, cleverness **12** intelligence

brainless **4** dumb **6** stupid **7** asinine, foolish, idiotic, moronic, witless **8** mindless **9** imbecilic **10** half-witted **11** lamebrained **12** feeble-minded, simple-minded

brain power **4** mind **9** intellect **12** intelligence **14** mental capacity

Brainworm
character in: **19** Every Man in His Humour
author: **6** Jonson

brainy **5** smart **6** bright, clever **9** brilliant **11** intelligent

brake **4** curb, drag, halt, rein, slow, stay, stop **5** check **6** arrest **7** control **9** restraint **10** constraint **11** reduce speed

Bramante, Donato
architect of: **9** Tempietto **14** Belvedere Court (the Vatican), Palazzo Caprini **19** Santa Maria della Pace **21** Santa Maria della Grazie

bramble **4** bush, vine **5** rough, shrub **7** thicket **8** prickers **13** raspberry bush **14** blackberry bush

Bramble, Matthew
character in: **14** Humphry Clinker
author: **8** Smollett

Bran
origin: **5** Welsh
king of: **7** Britain
habitat: **3** sea
saint in: **12** Christianity
brother: **9** Evnissyen **10** Manawyddan
sister: **7** Branwen
head buried in: **6** London

branch **3** arm, leg **4** fork, limb, part, wing **5** bough, prong, spray **6** agency, bureau, divide, feeder, member, office, ramify **7** channel, chapter, diverge, radiate, section, segment **8** division, offshoot, separate, shoot off **9** bifurcate, component, extension, tributary **10** department **11** subdivision **12** ramification

branched **6** forked, parted **7** divided **8** extended **9** spread out

Branchus
father: **6** Apollo
power of: **6** augury
power given by: **6** Apollo

Brancusi, Constantin
born: **7** Romania **13** Pestisani Gorj
artwork: **4** Fish **7** Chimera, The Kiss, The Seal **9** Sorceress **10** Adam and Eve, Prometheus **11** Bird in Space, Prodigal Son **12** Flying Turtle, Sleeping Muse **13** Endless Column **20** Sculpture for the Blind

brand **4** blot, kind, make, mark, sear, sign, slur, sort, spot, type **5** class, grade, label, smear, stain, stamp, taint **6** burn in, emblem, smirch, stigma **7** blemish, quality, variety **8** besmirch, disgrace **9** discredit, trademark **10** imputation, stigmatize **11** manufacture

brandish **4** wave **5** shake, swing, wield **6** flaunt, waggle **7** display, exhibit, show off **8** flourish

brand new **5** fresh, young **6** unused

Brando, Marlon
born: **7** Omaha NE
roles: **8** Sayonara **10** The Wild One, Viva Zapata **12** Julius Caesar, The Godfather (Oscar refused) **13** Apocalypse Now **15** On the Waterfront (Oscar) **16** Last Tango in Paris **17** Mutiny on the Bounty **21** A Streetcar Named Desire

brandy **6** cognac, grappa, kahlua, kirsch, metaxa **8** Calvados, Tia Maria **9** applejack, Slivovitz **12** Grand Marnier, Peter

Heering **14** forbidden fruit
French: 8 eau de vie

Brangwen, Ursula and Gudrun
characters in: 11 Women in Love
author: 8 Lawrence

Branstock
also: 9 Barnstock
origin: 12 Scandinavian
mentioned in: 8 Volsunga
form: 3 oak **4** tree
location: 7 Volsung
house of: 7 Volsung
Odin (Othin) thrusts: 4 Gram **5** sword

Brant, Captain Adam
character in: 22 Mourning Becomes Electra
author: 6 O'Neill

Branwen
origin: 5 Welsh
brother: 4 Bran
husband: 10 Matholwych
son killed by: 9 Evnissyen

Braque, Georges
born: 6 France **18** Argenteuil sur Seine
artwork: 7 Atelier, Grand Nu (Great Nude), The Echo **8** The Table **13** The Portuguese **14** Man with a Guitar **16** Violin and Palette, Violin and Pitcher **18** Woman with a Mandolin

brash 4 bold, rash, rude **5** fresh, hasty, sassy **6** brazen, cheeky, madcap **7** forward **8** careless, heedless, impudent, reckless **9** foolhardy, impetuous, imprudent, know-it-all **10** incautious **11** impertinent, precipitous, smart-alecky **12** unconsidered **13** overconfident

brashness 4 gall **5** brass, cheek, nerve **8** audacity, boldness, chutzpah, temerity **10** brazenness, effrontery **11** forwardness, presumption

Brasilia
capital of: 6 Brazil

brass 4 gall, sand, VIPs **5** cheek, nerve **8** audacity, boldness, chutzpah, officers, temerity **9** impudence **10** brazenness, effrontery **11** forwardness, presumption

Brass, Sampson
character in: 19 The Old Curiosity Shop
author: 7 Dickens

brass instrument 4 tuba **5** bugle **6** cornet **7** trumpet **8** trombone **9** euphonium **10** French horn, sousaphone
ancient: 3 lur **7** Alphorn, buisine, serpent **10** ophicleide

brass tacks 4 crux, meat **7** details **9** realities, substance **10** essentials **11** nitty-gritty **15** sum and substance

brassy 4 bold **5** brash, cocky, sassy, saucy **6** brazen **7** forward **8** arrogant, impudent, insolent, overbold **9** barefaced, outspoken, shameless, unabashed **10** unblushing **11** impertinent

brat 3 imp **4** chit **5** whelp **6** hoyden, rascal **9** rude child **12** spoiled child

Brauhaus 6 tavern **7** brewery

Brautigan, Richard
author of: 15 Sombrero Fallout **18** The Hawkline Monster **21** Trout Fishing in America **38** The Pill Versus the Springhill Mine Disaster

bravado 7 big talk, blowing, bluster, bombast, bravura, crowing, puffery, swagger **8** boasting, bragging **9** cockiness **10** swaggering **11** braggadocio **12** boastfulness **13** show of courage

brave 4 bear, dare, defy, face, game, take **5** abide, brook, gutsy, stand **6** breast, endure, gritty, heroic, plucky, spunky, suffer **7** doughty, stomach, sustain, undergo, valiant, weather **8** confront, fearless, intrepid, stalwart, tolerate, unafraid, valorous **9** challenge, dauntless, outbrazen, put up with, stand up to, undaunted, withstand **10** courageous **11** lionhearted, unflinching, unshrinking **12** stouthearted

brave deed 4 feat **7** exploit **9** heroic act **11** achievement

Brave New World
author: 12 Aldous Huxley
character: 4 John **11** Bernard Marx **12** Lenina Crowne, Mustapha Mond

bravery 4 grit **5** pluck, spunk, valor **6** daring, mettle, spirit **7** courage, heroism **8** audacity, boldness **11** intrepidity **12** fearlessness **13** dauntlessness

Bravo, The
author: 19 James Fenimore Cooper

brawl 3 row **4** fray, tiff **5** broil, clash, fight, melee, scrap, set-to **6** battle, fracas, ruckus, rumpus, uproar **7** dispute, quarrel, scuffle, wrangle **8** squabble **9** imbroglio **11** altercation, embroilment

brawn 5 might, power **7** muscles, stamina **8** strength **9** beefiness, huskiness **10** robustness, ruggedness, sturdiness **19** muscular development

brawny 5 burly, husky **6** mighty, robust, rugged, strong, sturdy **8** muscular, powerful **9** strapping

Bray, Madeline
character in: 16 Nicholas Nickleby
author: 7 Dickens

brazen 4 bold, open **5** brash, saucy **6** brassy, cheeky **7** forward **8** arrogant, immodest, impudent, insolent **9** audacious, barefaced, boldfaced, shameless, unabashed

brazenness 4 gall **5** brass, cheek, nerve **8** audacity, boldness, chutzpah **9** impudence **10** effrontery, fowardness **11** presumption

Brazil *see box*

Brazil
director: 12 Terry Gilliam
cast: 8 Ida Lowry **9** Kim Greist **12** Robert De Niro **13** Jonathan Pryce

Brazilian Bombshell
nickname of: 13 Carmen Miranda

Brazzaville
capital of: 5 Congo

breach 3 gap **4** gash, hole, rent, rift, slit **5** break, chink, cleft, crack, split **7** crevice, failure, fissure, neglect, opening, rupture **8** defiance, trespass **9** disregard, violation **10** infraction **11** dereliction **12** disobedience, infringement **13** noncompliance, nonobservance, transgression

breach of faith 7 perfidy **8** bad faith, betrayal **9** falseness, treachery, two-timing **10** disloyalty **11** double-cross **13** double-dealing

breach of order 4 riot **6** fracas, mutiny, ruckus, uproar **7** turmoil **8** uprising **9** commotion, rebellion **10** dissension **11** disturbance, pandemonium **18** disturbance of peace

breach of trust 7 falsity, perfidy **9** falseness, treachery **10** disloyalty, infidelity **13** deceitfulness, double-dealing

bread 3 rye **4** food, pita **5** bucks, dough, money, wheat **6** staple **9** sourdough **10** livelihood, sustenance **11** staff of life **12** pumpernickel

bread and butter 3 job **6** ca-

Brazil

capital: **8** Brasilia

former capital: **12** Rio de Janeiro

largest city: **8** Sao Paulo

others: **5** Bahia, Belem **6** Recife, Sabara, Santos **7** Vitoria **8** Salvador **9** Ouro Preto, Paranagua **10** Diamantina **11** Porto Alegre **13** Belo Horizonte, Cruzeiro do Sul

school:
junior high: **7** ginasio
senior high: **7** colegio

measure: **2** pe **4** moio, sack, vara **5** braca, legoa, milha, tonel **6** canada, cuarto, quarto, tarefa **7** garrafa **8** alqueire

monetary unit: **3** joe **4** reis **5** dobra **7** centara, halfjoe, milreis **8** cruzeiro

weight: **3** bag **4** onca **5** libra **6** arroba, oitava **7** quilate, quintal **8** tonelada

island: **6** Maraca, Marajo **7** Bananal, Cardoso, Caviana, Mexiana **8** Comprida

lake: **4** Aima, Feia **5** Mirim **13** Logo dos Platos

mountain: **3** Mar **5** Geral, Organ, Piaui **6** Acarai, Gurupi, Parima, Urucum **7** Amambai, Carajas, Gradaus, Oragaos, Roraima **8** Bandeira, Itatiaja, Roncador, Tombador **9** Pacaraima, Sugar Loaf **10** Tumuc-Humac

highest point: **7** Neblina

river: **3** Apa, Ica **4** Doce, Geio, Ivai, Jari, Para, Paru, Sono, Tefe **5** Abuna, Anaua, Apore, Capim, Claro, Corua, Icana, Iriri, Itapi, Jurua, Jutai, Manso, Negro, Pardo, Piaui, Preto, Tiete, Turvo, Urubu, Verde, Xingu **6** Ajuana, Amazon, Arinos, Balsas, Branco, Canuma, Contas, Cuiaba, Demini, Grajau, Grande, Gurupi, Ibicui, Iguacu, Japura, Javari, Mearim, Mortes, Mucuri, Parana, Purpus, Ronuro, Sangue, Tacutu, Tibagi, Uatuma, Uaupes **7** Corumba, Iguassu, Madeira, Madiera, Orinoco, Paraiba, Sucuriu, Tapajos, Taquari, Teodoro, Uruguai, Uruguay, Velhass **8** Araguaia, Padauiri, Paracatu, Paraguay, Parnaiba, Solimoes, Tarauaca **9** Tocantins **12** Sao Francisco

sea: **8** Atlantic

physical feature:
bay: **9** All Saints
cape: **4** Frio **6** Blanco, Buzios, Gurupy, Orange **7** Saotome **8** Saoroque
dam: **6** Furnas **7** Peixoto
estuary: **4** Para
rain forest: **5** selva
waterfall: **6** Guaira, Iguacu **7** Iguassu **11** Paulo Afonso

people: **2** Ge **4** Anta **5** Acroa, Arara, Araua, Bravo, Carib, Guana, Negro **6** Arawak, Caraja **7** Carayan, Javahai, Tariana **8** Botocudo, Chambioa **9** Caucasian, mamelucos, mulattoes **10** Portuguese **11** Tupi-Guarani
architect: **8** Niemeyer
artist: **6** Segall **9** Portinari **10** Cavalcenti
author: **5** Amado, Bilac, Ramos **6** Freyre
composer: **10** Villalobos
discoverer: **6** Cabral
leader: **6** Aranha, Branco, Geisel, Medici, Vargas **7** Goulart
sculptor: **11** Aleijadinho

language: **10** Portuguese

religion: **10** Protestant **13** Roman Catholic

place:
beach: **7** Ipanema **9** Boa Viagem **10** Copacabana

feature:
bird: **4** mitu **5** mitua
dance: **5** frevo, samba **6** maxixe **9** bossa nova
fish: **7** piranha
gourd: **4** cuia
plantation: **7** fazenda
slums: **7** favelas
tree: **5** icica **6** ucuuba **7** arariba

food:
dish: **6** vatapa **8** feijoada
dried salted beef: **7** charque
drink: **4** acai **9** cafezinho
tea: **4** mate
turtle soup: **16** cas quinho de mucua

reer, living **7** calling **8** business, vocation **9** life's work **10** livelihood **14** means of support

Bread and Wine
author: **13** Ignazio Silone

breadbasket **3** gut **5** belly, tummy **6** paunch **7** abdomen, labonza, midriff, Midwest, stomach **11** solar plexus

breadth **4** area, size, span **5** range, reach, scope, width **6** extent, spread **7** compass, expanse, measure, stretch **8** latitude, wideness **9** broadness **10** dimensions **13** extensiveness

break ***see box***

breakable **5** frail, shaky **6** flimsy **7** brittle, crumbly, fragile **8** delicate

break apart **7** crumble, shatter **8** collapse **9** fall apart **12** disintegrate, fall to pieces

breakdown **6** mishap **7** crackup, decline, failure **8** analysis, collapse, disorder, division **12** detailed list **13** deterioration **14** categorization

break down **6** divide **7** dissect **8** collapse, separate **9** decompose **11** deteriorate

breaker **4** cask, wave **6** comber **7** crusher **8** boat cask **9** destroyer

break faith with **6** betray **7** do wrong **9** play false **11** double-cross **12** be unfaithful **13** be treacherous **16** sell down the river

Breakfast at Tiffany's
author: **12** Truman Capote
director: **12** Blake Edwards
cast: **10** Buddy Ebsen **12** Mickey Rooney, Patricia Neal **13** Audrey Hepburn (Holly Golightly), George Peppard
score: **12** Henry Mancini
song: **9** Moon River

Breakfast Club, The
director: **10** John Hughes
cast: **10** Ally Sheedy **13** Emilio Estevez, Molly Ringwald **18** Anthony Michael Hall

Breakfast of Champions
author: **12** Kurt Vonnegut

break free **4** bolt, flee, skip **6** escape **7** get away, make off, run away **9** cut and run **10** fly the coop **12** make a getaway

breakfront **5** hutch **7** cabinet **8** bookcase, cupboard **12** china cabinet

break in **5** train **7** intrude **8** accustom, initiate **9** acclimate, interrupt **10** burglarize **12** indoctrinate

break-in **5** theft **7** robbery **8** burglary, stealing **12** burglarizing **13** housebreaking **19** breaking and entering

Breaking Away
director: **10** Peter Yates
screenplay: **11** Steve Tesich
cast: **10** Paul Dooley **11** Daniel Stern, Dennis Quaid **13** Barbara Barrie **16** Jackie Earle Haley **17** Dennis Christopher

setting: **7** Indiana **11** Bloomington

break loose **4** bolt, flee, skip **6** escape **7** get away, make off **9** cut and run **10** fly the coop **12** make a getaway

breakneck **4** rash **5** risky **8** reckless, very fast **9** dangerous, daredevil **12** death-defying

break of day **4** dawn **5** sunup **7** dawning, sunrise **8** daybreak **11** crack of dawn

break off **3** end **4** halt **5** cease **6** recess **7** adjourn, snap off, suspend **8** conclude, shut down **11** discontinue

breakout **6** escape, flight **7** getaway **10** decampment

break out **4** bolt, skip **5** begin, erupt **6** escape **7** bust out, get away **10** burst forth, fly the coop **12** make a getaway

Break the Bank
host: **9** Bert Parks **10** Bud Collyer

break the habit **4** kick, quit, stop **6** eschew, give up **8** renounce, withdraw **14** quit cold turkey

breakthrough **7** advance **11** advancement, improvement, penetration, step forward

breakup **5** split **7** crackup **9** dispersal, splitting **10** separation **14** disintegration

break with **5** leave **8** be untrue, part from **10** be disloyal **11** divorce from **12** fall away from, separate from

breast **4** bust, core **5** bosom, chest, heart **10** very marrow
Italian: **5** petto

breastwork **7** bastion, rampart **8** barbette **9** earthwork **13** fortification

breath **4** wind **6** spirit **9** animation, breathing, lifeblood, life force **10** exhalation, inhalation, vital spark **11** divine spark, respiration, vital spirit **12** vitalization

breathe **4** gasp, huff, pant, puff **5** utter **6** impart, murmur **7** respire, whisper **9** draw in air **10** draw breath **15** inhale and exhale

breathe in **6** inhale **7** inspire, respire

breathe out **4** huff, pant, puff **6** exhale, expire **7** respire

breathing **4** live **5** alive **6** living **7** animate **11** respiratory **13** drawing breath

---

break **3** cap, end, fly, gap, off, run, top **4** beat, bust, chip, dash, defy, flee, gash, halt, hole, rend, rent, rest, rift, rive, ruin, snap, stop, tame, tear, tell **5** burst, cease, cleft, crack, crush, erupt, excel, lapse, occur, outdo, pause, sever, shirk, smash, split, train **6** appear, better, breach, chance, cleave, detach, divide, escape, exceed, happen, hiatus, ignore, inform, lessen, master, powder, recess, reveal, soften, subdue, sunder, weaken **7** control, cushion, destroy, disobey, divulge, eclipse, fissure, fortune, give out, lighten, neglect, opening, pull off, respite, run away, rupture, shatter, surpass, suspend, tear off, violate, wipe out **8** announce, bankrupt, burst out, cracking, demolish, diminish, disclose, disjoint, division, fracture, fragment, go beyond, interval, outstrip, overcome, proclaim, renege on, separate, shut down, slip away, splinter **9** dismember, disregard, granulate, interlude, interrupt, make a dash, pulverize, splitting, transcend **10** discipline, disconnect, fall back on, fly the coop, fracturing, impoverish, infringe on, make public, overshadow, separation, shattering, take flight, wrench away **11** discontinue, get away from, opportunity, pay no heed to **12** be derelict in, disintegrate, intermission, interruption, make a getaway, stroke of luck **13** strap for funds **14** bend to one's will, take the force of **15** take to one's heels

Breathless
director: **14** Jean-Luc Goddard
written by: **16** Francois Truffaut
cast: **10** Jean Seberg **16** Jean-Paul Belmondo
setting: **5** Paris

breathtaking **7** amazing, awesome **8** exciting **9** startling **10** surprising **11** astonishing

Brecht, Bertolt
author of: **13** Mother Courage **15** Drums in the Night **18** The Threepenny Opera **21** St Joan of the Stockyards **23** The Caucasian Chalk Circle **27** The Resistable Rise of Arturo Ui **29** The Private Life of the Master Race

Breck, Alan
character in: **9** Kidnapped
author: **9** Stevenson

breech **4** rump, seat **6** behind **8** buttocks, haunches, hind part **9** fundament, posterior **12** hindquarters

breeches **5** pants **8** trousers

breed **4** bear, grow, kind, race, sire, sort, type **5** beget, cause, order, raise, spawn, stock **6** family, father, foster, lead to, mother, strain **7** develop, nurture, produce, promote, species, variety **8** generate, multiply, occasion **9** cultivate, give forth, procreate, propagate, reproduce **10** bring forth, give rise to **11** proliferate **16** produce offspring

breeding **4** line **5** grace **6** mating, polish **7** bearing, descent, growing, lineage, manners, raising, rearing **8** ancestry, courtesy, hatching, heredity, pedigree, spawning, training **9** begetting, bloodline, genealogy, gentility, parentage, producing **10** background, extraction, family tree, generation, politeness, production, refinement, upbringing **11** cultivation, germination, multiplying, procreation, propagation **12** reproduction

breeze **4** flit, pass, sail, waft **5** coast, float, glide, sweep **6** zephyr **9** light gust, light wind **10** gentle wind, puff of wind

breezy **3** gay **4** airy, pert, spry **5** blowy, brisk, fresh, gusty, light, merry, peppy, sunny, windy **6** bouncy, casual, frisky, jaunty, lively **7** buoyant, squally **8** animated, blustery, carefree, cheerful, debonair, spirited **9** energetic, resilient, sprightly, vivacious, windswept **10** blithesome **11** free and easy

Brennan, Walter
born: **12** Swampscott MA
roles: **8** Kentucky **12** Come and Get It, The Westerner **13** The Real McCoys **16** To Have and Have Not

Brent, George
real name: **18** George Brendan Nolan
wife: **11** Ann Sheridan **14** Ruth Chatterton
born: **7** Ireland **14** Shannonsbridge
roles: **7** Jezebel **11** Dark Victory, The Great Lie **17** Forty-Second Street

Bres
origin: **5** Irish
king of: **7** Ireland

Breton, Andre
author of: **5** Nadja **21** Manifesto of Surrealism

Breuer, Marcel
architect of: **17** IBM Research Center (La Gaude France) **18** UNESCO headquarters (Paris) **25** St John's Abbey and University (Collegeville MN) **26** Whitney Museum of American Art (NYC)

brevity **9** briefness, pithiness, quickness, shortness, terseness **10** transience **11** conciseness **12** ephemerality, impermanence, succinctness

brew **3** ale **4** beer, boil, cook, form, make, plan, plot, soak **5** begin, drink, hatch, ripen, start, steep, stout **6** cook up, devise, foment, gather, porter, scheme, seethe **7** arrange, concoct, ferment, mixture, prepare, produce, think up **8** beverage, contrive, initiate **9** formulate, germinate, originate **10** concoction, malt liquor

brewery
German: **8** Brauhaus

Brian de Bois, Sir
character in: **7** Ivanhoe
author: **5** Scott

Briareus
also: **7** Aegaeon
member of: **13** Hecatonchires

bribe **5** graft **6** buy off, grease, pay off, payola, suborn **9** hush money **10** inducement **11** illegal gift **15** grease the hand of, grease the palm of
French: **7** douceur

bric-a-brac **7** baubles, gewgaws **8** bibelots, trinkets **9** gimcracks, kickshaws, ornaments **11** knickknacks

Brick
character in: **16** Cat on a Hot Tin Roof
author: **8** Williams

Bricks
god of: **5** Kulla

bridal **7** nuptial, wedding **8** marriage **11** matrimonial

Bridehead, Sue
character in: **14** Jude the Obscure
author: **5** Hardy

Bride of Lammermoor, The
author: **14** Sir Walter Scott
character: **10** Lady Ashton, Lucy Ashton, Ravenswood **14** Laird of Bucklaw **16** Sir William Ashton

Brideshead Revisited
author: **11** Evelyn Waugh
character: **5** Celia, Julia **8** Cordelia **9** Sebastian **10** Brideshead (Bridey), Rex Mottram **12** Boy Mulcaster, Charles Ryder **13** Lady Marchmain, Lord Marchmain **14** Anthony Blanche

bridge **3** tie **4** band, bind, bond, link, span **5** cross, unify, union **6** go over **7** catwalk, connect, liaison, viaduct **8** alliance, overpass, traverse **9** cross over **10** connection, passageway **11** association, reach across **12** extend across

bridge
derived from: **5** whist
variation: **14** contract bridge
partnership: **9** East/West **11** North/South
cards/hand: **8** thirteen
no cards of a suit: **4** void
one card of a suit: **9** singleton
two cards of a suit: **9** doubleton
rule book by: **5** Goren

Bridge of San Luis Rey, The
author: **14** Thornton Wilder
character: **5** Clara, Jaime **6** Manuel, Pepita **7** Esteban, Viceroy **8** Uncle Pio **11** La Perichole **14** Brother Juniper **20** Marquesa de Montemayor

Bridge on the River Kwai, The
director: **9** David Lean
based on story by: **12** Pierre Boulle
cast: **11** Jack Hawkins **12** Alec Guinness **13** Wil-

liam Holden **14** Sessue Hayakawa
Oscar for: 5 actor (Guinness) **7** picture

Bridges, Beau
real name: 21 Lloyd Vernet Bridges III
father: 5 Lloyd
brother: 4 Jeff
born: 12 Los Angeles CA
roles: 5 Space **8** Norma Rae **11** The Landlord **25** The Other Side of the Mountain

Bridges, Jeff
father: 5 Lloyd
brother: 4 Beau
born: 12 Los Angeles CA
roles: 4 Tron **7** Starman **8** King Kong **10** Jagged Edge **13** Kiss Me Goodbye **14** Against All Odds **18** The Last Picture Show

Bridges, Lloyd
son: 4 Beau, Jeff
born: 12 San Leandro CA
roles: 7 Sea Hunt **8** Airplane, High Noon

Bridges at Toko-ri, The
author: 13 James Michener

Bridget
character in: 19 Every Man in His Humour
author: 6 Jonson

Bridge Too Far, A
author: 13 Cornelius Ryan

Bridgetown
capital of: 8 Barbados

bridle 3 gag **4** curb, rule **5** check **6** arrest, direct, draw up, flinch, hinder, manage, master, muzzle, rear up, recoil **7** control, harness, inhibit, repress **8** draw back, restrain, restrict, suppress **9** constrain, restraint **11** bit and brace, head harness

brief 4 case **5** hasty, pithy, quick, short, swift, terse **6** advise, inform, precis, resume **7** capsule, compact, concise, defense, limited, prepare, summary **8** abridged, abstract, argument, fill in on, fleeting, instruct, succinct **9** condensed, curtailed, momentary, shortened, temporary, thumbnail, transient **10** abridgment, compressed, contention, describe to, short-lived, summarized, transitory **11** abbreviated **12** legal summary

brief account 6 precis, sketch **7** outline, summary **8** anecdote

brier, briar 4 Rosa **5** Rubus, thorn **6** Smilax **7** bramble
varieties: 3 Cat, Dog, Hag, Saw **4** Bull **5** Green, Horse, Sweet **7** Jackson **8** Austrian **9** Sensitive **14** Austrian copper

brigade 4 crew, team, unit **5** corps, force, group, squad **6** legion, outfit **7** company **9** regiments, squadrons **10** army groups, battalions, contingent, detachment

Brigadoon
director: 16 Vincente Minnelli
based on Broadway hit by: 14 Lerner and Loewe
cast: 9 Gene Kelly **10** Van Johnson **11** Cyd Charisse

brigand 5 thief **6** bandit, gunman, looter, outlaw, pirate, robber, vandal **7** corsair, hoodlum, ruffian, rustler, spoiler **8** marauder, pilferer, pillager **9** buccaneer, cutthroat, desperado, despoiler, plunderer, privateer **10** highwayman

bright 3 gay **4** glad, good, keen, rosy, sage, warm, wise **5** acute, alert, aware, grand, great, happy, jolly, merry, quick, sharp, smart, sunny, vivid **6** astute, blithe, brainy, clever, gifted, joyful, joyous, lively, shrewd **7** beaming, blazing, capable, glowing, healthy, hopeful, intense, lambent, radiant, shining **8** cheerful, dazzling, exciting, gleaming, luminous, lustrous, profound, splendid, talented **9** brilliant, competent, effulgent, excellent, favorable, ingenious, inventive, masterful, promising, sagacious, sparkling, wide-awake **10** auspicious, discerning, glittering, optimistic, perceptive, proficient, propitious, prosperous, remarkable, shimmering, successful **11** clearheaded, illuminated, illustrious, intelligent, light-filled, magnificent, outstanding, quick-witted, resourceful, resplendent **12** exhilarating

brighten 4 lift **5** boost, cheer, light **6** buoy up, lift up, perk up **7** animate, enliven, gladden, lighten **9** make happy, stimulate **10** illuminate

bright-eyed 5 alert, awake **9** wide-awake **12** on the qui vive

Bright Flows the River
author: 14 Taylor Caldwell

brightness 4 glow **5** glare, gleam, shine **6** dazzle, luster **7** glitter, sparkle **8** radiance **9** lightness **10** brilliance, luminosity **12** intelligence

bright spot 3 joy **6** solace **7** comfort **8** pleasure **13** consolidation

Brigit
origin: 5 Welsh
goddess of: 4 fire **6** wisdom **9** fertility, household **11** agriculture

Brigitte Bardot & the Lolita Syndrome
author: 16 Simone de Beauvoir

Brill Among the Ruins
author: 14 Vance Bourjaily

brilliance, brilliancy 4 gift, glow **5** blaze, gleam, sheen, shine **6** acuity, dazzle, genius, luster, talent, wisdom **7** glitter, shimmer, sparkle **8** grandeur, keenness, radiance, sagacity, splendor **9** alertness, awareness, greatness, ingenuity, intensity, quickness, sharpness, smartness, vividness **10** braininess, brightness, capability, cleverness, competence, effulgence, excellence, luminosity, perception, profundity, shrewdness **11** discernment, distinction, proficiency **12** intelligence, magnificence, resplendence **13** inventiveness, masterfulness **15** clearheadedness, illustriousness, resourcefulness

brilliant *see* **6** bright

brim 3 fill, lip, rim **5** brink, flood, ledge, verge **6** border, fill up, margin, well up **8** overflow

brimless hat 3 cap **5** beret **6** beanie **11** stocking cap, tam o'shanter

brimming 4 full **7** flooded, teeming **8** overfull, swarming **11** overflowing

Brimo
origin: 5 Greek
form: 7 goddess
corresponds to: 6 Hecate **7** Demeter **10** Persephone

brine 6 the sea **8** sea water **9** salt water **12** salt solution **14** saline solution **16** pickling solution

bring 4 bear, make, take, tote **5** begin, carry, cause, fetch, force, start **6** compel, convey, create, effect, induce **7** deliver, produce, sell for, usher in

8 convince, engender, generate, initiate, persuade, result in **9** accompany, institute, originate, transport **10** bring about

bring about **2** do **4** form, open **5** begin, cause, found, set up, start **6** attain, create, effect, lead to **7** achieve, execute, produce **8** carry out, generate, initiate, organize **9** establish, institute, succeed at **10** accomplish, effectuate, inaugurate **11** bring to pass, precipitate **18** bring into existence

bring back **6** return **7** restore **8** recreate **9** surrender **10** return with

bring down a peg **5** abase **6** humble **7** mortify **9** humiliate **13** cut down to size

bring down to earth **10** disenchant **11** disenthrall, disillusion, open the eyes **13** break the spell **14** burst the bubble **20** shatter one's illusions

bring forth **4** bear **5** breed, elicit, evoke, hatch, spawn, whelp **7** deliver, produce **9** reproduce **10** make appear **11** give birth to

bring home to **7** blame on, clarify **11** attribute to **15** place emphasis on

bringing together **7** joining, wedding **8** amassing **9** combining, gathering, including **10** assembling, collecting **12** accumulating **13** incorporating

Bringing Up Baby
director: **11** Howard Hawks
cast: **9** Cary Grant **14** Charlie Ruggles **16** Katharine Hepburn

Bringing Up Father
creator: **13** George McManus
character: **5** Jiggs **6** Maggie
daughter: **5** Rosie
brother-in-law: **5** Bimmy
place: **11** Dinty Moore's
favorite dish: **20** corned beef and cabbage

bring into being **4** bear, form, make **5** erect, hatch, spawn, whelp **6** create, design, devise, invent, render **7** concoct, deliver, develop, fashion, produce **8** contrive, generate **9** construct, fabricate, formulate, originate **10** bring forth **11** give birth to

bring into existence **4** form **5** begin, set up, start **6** create **8** organize **9** establish, institute **10** bring about, inaugurate

bring into line **5** adapt **6** adjust **7** conform, shape up **9** harmonize, reconcile **10** discipline **11** accommodate **13** whip into shape

bring into question **11** cast doubt on **18** throw suspicion upon

bring into relief **6** accent, stress **7** dwell on, feature, point up **9** emphasize, press home, underline **10** accentuate, underscore

bring low **5** abase, shame **6** humble **8** cast down **9** denigrate, humiliate

bring off **4** gain **6** attain, effect, secure **7** achieve **10** accomplish

bring to an end **5** cease **6** finish **8** break off, conclude **9** call a halt, terminate **11** discontinue

bring to a standstill **3** end **4** halt, stay, stop **5** block, check **6** arrest **12** bring to a halt

bring to bay **4** trap, tree **6** corner **8** confront, hunt down

bring to bear **5** apply **6** employ **7** utilize **9** implement

bring together **5** amass **6** gather, muster **7** collect, marshal, round up **8** assemble **10** accumulate

bring to light **6** expose, reveal, unveil **7** clarify, divulge, explain, uncover **8** disclose **9** explicate, make known, make plain **10** illuminate, make public

bring to one's senses **3** jar **5** alarm, alert, shock **9** make aware

bring to pass **5** cause **6** create, effect **8** carry out **10** bring about, effectuate

bring to terms **6** settle **7** mediate **9** arbitrate, reconcile

bring to view **5** dig up **6** reveal **7** exhibit, uncover, unearth **8** disclose, retrieve **10** come up with

bring word **4** tell **6** advise, convey, inform, notify, relate, reveal **7** divulge, publish **8** announce, disclose, proclaim **9** apprise of, broadcast, make known, publicize **11** communicate

brink **3** rim **4** bank, brim, edge **5** point, shore, skirt, verge **6** border, margin **9** threshold

briny **4** salt **5** salty **6** saline

brio, con
music: **9** with vigor **10** with spirit

Briseis
origin: **5** Greek
mentioned in: **5** Iliad
father: **18** Briseus of Lyrnessus
husband: **5** Mynes
captured by: **8** Achilles
caused: **7** quarrel
between: **8** Achilles **9** Agamemnon

Briseus
origin: **5** Greek
mentioned in: **5** Iliad
daughter: **7** Briseis
death by: **7** suicide

Brisingamen **8** necklace
origin: **12** Scandinavian
trait: **5** magic
owned by: **5** Freia, Freya

brisk **4** busy, spry **5** alert, fresh, peppy, quick, swift **6** active, breezy, lively, snappy **7** bracing, chipper, dynamic, rousing **8** animated, bustling, spirited, stirring, vigorous **9** energetic, sprightly, vivacious, vivifying **10** refreshing **11** stimulating **12** exhilarating, invigorating

briskness **3** pep **5** vigor **6** energy **8** alacrity, spryness **9** quickness, swiftness **13** sprightliness

bristle **4** hair **5** quill **7** stiffen, whisker

bristles **5** barbs **6** quills **7** stubble **8** prickles, whiskers

bristletail
variety: **7** jumping **8** firebrat **9** primitive **10** nicoletiid, silverfish

bristly **5** rough **6** barbed, coarse **7** prickly, stubbly **8** unshaven **9** whiskered **11** bewhiskered

Britannia *see* **7** England

British **6** Breton, Briton **7** English **8** Brittany

British Columbia
bordered by: **5** Idaho, Yukon **6** Alaska **7** Montana **10** Washington **12** Pacific Ocean, United States **20** Northwest Territories
country: **6** Canada
Indian: **5** Haida **6** Nootka, Salish **8** Kwakiutl **9** Tsimshian **10** Bella Coola
island: **9** Vancouver **14** Queen Charlotte
mountain: **5** Coast, Rocky **7** Cascade **8** Columbia

11 Cordilleran **14** Cassiar Omineca
nickname: **2** BC
park: **7** Glacier
rank in size: **5** sixth
river: **6** Fraser
section: **8** province

British Guiana *see* **6** Guyana

British Honduras *see* **6** Belize

British Mythology
god of rebirth/afterlife: **4** Gwyn
chief of gods: **5** Woden
island of paradise: **6** Avalon

Britomart
character in: **15** The Faerie Queene
author: **7** Spenser

Britomartis
origin: **6** Cretan
goddess of: **7** hunters, sailors **9** fishermen
father: **4** Zeus
mother: **5** Carme
corresponds to: **7** Artemis **8** Dictynna

Briton **4** Celt **6** Celtic **7** British

Brittany
coast: **5** Armor
country: **6** France
inhabitant: **5** Celts **6** French, Romans
interior: **6** Argoat
land form: **9** peninsula
language: **6** Breton
other name: **5** Breiz **6** Breton **8** Bretagne

Britten, (Edward) Benjamin
born: **7** England **9** Lowestoft
composer of: **8** Gloriana **9** Billy Budd **10** Paul Bunyan, War Requiem **11** Curlew River, Peter Grimes, Winter Words **12** Owen Wingrave, The Poet's Echo **13** Albert Herring, Death in Venice **14** The Prodigal Son, Turn of the Screw **15** Phantasy Quartet **17** A Ceremony of Carols, A Charm of Lullabies, Sinfonia da Requiem, The Rape of Lucretia **18** Holderlin Fragments **20** Cantata Misericordium **21** A Midsummer Night's Dream, Sonnets of Michelangelo **22** The Burning Fiery Furnace

brittle **7** crumbly, fragile, friable **9** breakable, frangible

Brize
form: **6** gadfly
sent by: **4** Hera
sent to annoy: **2** Io

Brizo
origin: **5** Greek
goddess of: **7** sailors
prophesied through: **6** dreams

broach **4** pose **6** launch, open up, submit **7** advance, bring up, mention, propose, suggest, touch on **9** institute, introduce

broad **4** full, open, wide **5** ample, clear, large, plain, rangy, roomy, thick **7** general, immense, obvious, sizable **8** extended, spacious, sweeping **9** capacious, expansive, extensive, inclusive, outspread, universal, unlimited **10** undetailed **11** far-reaching, nonspecific, wide-ranging **12** all-embracing, encyclopedic **13** comprehensive

broadcast **4** beam, show, talk **5** cable, radio, relay **7** program, send out **8** televise, transmit **9** statement **10** distribute **11** disseminate, put on the air **12** announcement

broaden **5** boost, raise, swell, widen **6** dilate, expand, extend **7** advance, amplify, augment, build up, develop, distend, enlarge, improve, stretch **8** increase **9** intensify, reinforce, spread out **10** strengthen, supplement

broadened **7** dilated, swelled, swollen, widened **8** enlarged, expanded, extended **9** distended, spread out

broad-minded **7** liberal **8** amenable, catholic, flexible, tolerant, unbiased **9** receptive, unbigoted **10** charitable, open-minded, undogmatic **11** magnanimous **12** unprejudiced, unprovincial

Broadway Joe
nickname of: **9** Joe Namath

Brobdingnag
fictional land in: **16** Gulliver's Travels
author: **5** Swift

Brobdingnagian **4** huge **5** giant **7** immense, mammoth **8** colossal, enormous, gigantic **10** gargantuan, tremendous **11** elephantine

broccoli **9** vegetable **12** Brassica rapa **16** Brassica oleracea (Botyris Group) **17** Brassica septiceps
variety: **6** Turnip **7** Italian **9** Asparagus, Sprouting

brochure **5** flier **6** folder **7** booklet, leaflet **8** circular, handbill, pamphlet **9** throwaway

Brockton Blockbuster
nickname of: **13** Rocky Marciano

Broglie, Louis Victor de
field: **7** physics
nationality: **6** French
developed: **13** wave mechanics
awarded: **10** Nobel Prize

broil **3** fry **4** bake, burn, cook, sear **5** parch, roast, toast **6** scorch **7** blister

broiler **3** hot, pan **4** rack **5** grill **6** cooker **8** scorcher **12** young chicken

broke **8** bankrupt, strapped, wiped out **9** insolvent, penniless **10** down and out **12** impoverished, on one's uppers, without funds **16** strapped for funds

broken **4** torn **5** rough, split, tamed **6** ruined, uneven **7** crushed, damaged **8** bankrupt, in pieces, ruptured **9** fractured, separated, shattered **10** incomplete **11** fragmentary, interrupted

Broken Commandment, The
author: **14** Toson Shimazaki

broken-down **6** beat-up, ruined **7** rickety, worn-out **8** battered, decrepit **10** ramshackle **11** dilapidated **12** deteriorated

broken-hearted **3** sad **6** gloomy, woeful **7** crushed, doleful, forlorn, unhappy **8** dejected, desolate, downcast, mournful, wretched **9** depressed, long-faced, miserable, sorrowful, woebegone **10** despairing, despondent, melancholy **11** heartbroken **12** disconsolate, inconsolable

Brom Bones
also: **12** Brom Van Brunt
character in: **23** The Legend of Sleepy Hollow
author: **6** Irving

Brome
form: **5** nymph
cared for: **8** Dionysus

Bromfield, Louis
author of: **11** Early Autumn, Malabar Farm **12** The Rains Came **13** Mrs Parkington, Night in Bombay **14** Wild Is the River **15** The Green Bay Tree **31** The Strange Case of Miss Annie Spragg

bromide **6** cliche **8** banality **9** platitude **10** stereotype **11** trite phrase **19** hackneyed expression

bromidic **4** dull **5** banal, corny, stale, tired, trite, vapid **6** jejune **7** humdrum, insipid **8** ordinary **9** hackneyed **10** pedestrian, unexciting, unoriginal **13** platitudinous, unimaginative

bromine
chemical symbol: 2 Br

Bromius
epithet of: 8 Dionysus
means: 7 thunder

Bronson, Charles
real name: 16 Charles Buchinsky
wife: 11 Jill Ireland
born: 11 Ehrenfeld PA
roles: 9 Death Wish **13** The Dirty Dozen **14** The Great Escape **16** Battle of the Bulge, The Valachi Papers **19** The Magnificent Seven

Bronte, Anne
author of: 9 Agnes Grey **23** The Tenant of Wildfell Hall

Bronte, Charlotte
author of: 7 Shirley **8** Jane Eyre, Villette **12** The Professor

Bronte, Emily
author of: 16 Wuthering Heights

Brontes
member of: 8 Cyclopes

brontophobia
fear of: 7 thunder

Brontosaurus
also: 11 Apatosaurus
type: 8 dinosaur, sauropod
period: 8 Jurassic

Bronx Bull
nickname of: 11 Jake La Motta

bronze 3 tan **5** metal **8** brownish, chestnut **10** reddish-tan **12** reddish-brown **13** copper-colored

brooch 3 pin **5** clasp

brood 4 chew, fret, mope, mull, sulk **5** cover, dwell, hatch, spawn, worry, young **6** chicks, family, litter **7** agonize, sit upon **8** children, incubate **9** offspring **10** hatchlings

brook 3 run **4** bear, rill, take **5** abide, allow, creek, stand **6** accept, endure, stream, suffer **7** rivulet, stomach **8** tolerate **9** put up with, streamlet

Brooks, Gwendolyn
author of: 4 Riot **10** Annie Allen **14** Family Pictures

Brooks, James L
director of: 17 Terms of Endearment (Oscar)

Brooks, Mel
real name: 14 Melvin Kaminsky
wife: 12 Anne Bancroft
born: 10 Brooklyn NY
director of/roles: 11 High Anxiety, Silent Movie **12** The Producers **14** Blazing Saddles **17** Young Frankenstein **20** The History of the World

Brooks, Richard
director of: 11 Elmer Gantry, In Cold Blood **16** Cat on a Hot Tin Roof, Sweet Bird of Youth **19** The Blackboard Jungle

broom 4 bush **5** besom, brush, whisk **7** sweeper

Broteas
father: 8 Tantalus
devotee of: 6 Cybele
denied divinity of: 7 Artemis

broth 5 stock **8** bouillon, consomme **9** clear soup

brothel 4 stew **5** house **6** bagnio, bordel **8** bordello, cathouse **10** bawdy house, fancy house, whorehouse **11** maison close **13** maison de passe, sporting house **14** house of ill fame **16** house of ill repute **19** house of prostitution

brother 3 pal **4** chum, monk, peer **5** buddy, friar **6** cleric **7** comrade, kinsman, partner, sibling **8** confrere, landsman, monastic, relative, relation **9** associate, colleague, companion, fellowman **10** countryman **11** male sibling **12** fellow member **13** fellow citizen
French: 5 frere

brotherhood 4 club **5** amity, lodge **10** fellowship, fraternity, friendship **11** association

Brother Juniper
character in: 21 The Bridge of San Luis Rey
author: 6 Wilder

Brothers Karamazov, The
author: 10 Dostoevsky **17** Fyodor Dostoyevsky
character: 4 Ivan **6** Dmitri **7** Alyosha (Alexey), Zossima **8** Katerina **9** Grushenka **10** Smerdyakov **15** Fyodor Karamazov

brougham 3 car **8** carriage **10** automobile

brought 6 caused **7** carried, fetched, sold for **8** conveyed **9** conducted, convinced, persuaded

brow 3 rim **4** brim, edge, side **5** brink, verge **6** border, margin **8** boundary, forehead **9** periphery

browbeat 3 cow **5** abash, bully, cower **6** badger, harass, hector **7** henpeck **8** bulldoze, domineer, frighten, threaten **9** terrorize, tyrannize **10** intimidate

browbeater 5 bully **6** despot **7** coercer **9** oppressor, tormenter, tormentor **11** intimidator, petty tyrant

browbeating 8 bullying **11** threatening, tyrannizing **12** intimidation

brown 3 bay, dun, fry, tan **4** buff, cook, drab, fawn, puce, roan, rust **5** beige, camel, cocoa, hazel, khaki, saute, tawny, toast, umber **6** auburn, bronze, brunet, coffee, copper, ginger, russet, sorrel, walnut **8** brunette, chestnut, cinnamon, mahogany **9** chocolate, olive drab **10** terra-cotta **11** dirt-colored, sand-colored **12** liver-colored

Brown, Angeline
real name of: 14 Angie Dickinson

Brown, Berenice Sadie
character in: 19 A Member of the Wedding
author: 9 McCullers

Brown, Charles Brockden
author of: 6 Ormond **7** Wieland **11** Edgar Huntly **12** Arthur Mervyn

Brown, Claude
author of: 16 The Children of Ham **25** Manchild in the Promised Land

Brown, Dee
author of: 15 Creek Mary's Blood **24** Bury My Heart at Wounded Knee

Brown, Helen Gurley
author of: 19 Sex and the Single Girl
editor of: 12 Cosmopolitan

Brown, Helen Hayes
real name of: 10 Helen Hayes

Brown, Jim (Jimmy)
sport: 8 football
position: 8 fullback
team: 15 Cleveland Browns
actor in: 10 Dirty Dozen

Brown, Robert
field: 6 botany
nationality: 8 Scottish
established: 16 Brownian movement

Brown Bomber
nickname of: 8 Joe Louis

Browne, Dik
creator/artist of: 9 Hi and Lois **12** Beetle Bailey **16** Hagar the Horrible

Browne, Sir Thomas
author of: **9** Urn Burial **12** Hydriotaphia **13** Religio Medici **16** The Garden of Cyrus

brownie **3** elf **4** cake, puck **5** fairy, pixie **6** sprite **10** leprechaun

Browning, Elizabeth Barrett
author of: **11** Aurora Leigh **14** How Do I Love Thee **16** Casa Guidi Windows **24** Sonnets from the Portuguese

Browning, Robert
author of: **8** Sordello **10** Paracelsus **11** Pippa Passes **13** Fra Lippo Lippi, My Last Duchess **14** Andrea del Sarto **17** The Ring and the Book **20** The Pied Piper of Hamlin **29** Soliloquy of the Spanish Cloister **30** Childe Roland to the Dark Tower Came

brownish **3** tan **5** taupe **6** bronze **8** chestnut **13** copper-colored

Brownlow, Mr
character in: **11** Oliver Twist
author: **7** Dickens

Brownmiller, Susan
author of: **14** Against Our Will

Brown's Descent
author: **11** Robert Frost

browse **3** eat **4** feed, scan, skim **5** graze **6** nibble, peruse, survey **7** dip into, pasture **8** look over **9** check over **11** look through **13** glance through

Bruckner, Anton
born: **7** Austria **9** Ansfelden
composer of: **6** Te Deum **7** Psalm CL **11** Grosse Messe **16** Romantic Symphony **26** Intermezzo for String Quartet

Brueghel, Pieter (the Elder)
born: **5** Breda **8** Flanders
nickname: **14** Peasant Bruegel
son: **11** Jan Brueghel
artwork: **9** Blue Cloak, The Months **10** Dulle Griet (Mad Meg) **12** Fall of Icarus, Peasant Dance, Tower of Babel **14** Children's Games, The Misanthrope **15** Return of the Herd **16** Hunters in the Snow **17** The Triumph of Death **19** Peasant Wedding Dance **21** Peasant Wedding Banquet, The Magpie on the Gallows **22** Massacre of the Innocents **23** The Blind Leading the Blind, The Fall of the Rebel Angels

Brueghel, Jan
born: **8** Brussels, Flanders
nickname: **6** Velvet
father: **13** Pieter Bruegel
artwork: **12** Four Elements **13** Village Street **15** The Garden of Eden (with Rubens) **17** The Battle of Arbela

Brueghel, Pieter (the Younger)
born: **8** Brussels, Flanders
nickname: **12** Hell Brueghel **19** The Infernal Brueghel
father: **13** Pieter Bruegel (the Elder)
artwork: **11** Village Fair **14** The Crucifixion **16** The Burning of Troy

Brugh, Spangler Arlington
real name of: **12** Robert Taylor

bruise **3** mar **4** hurt, mark **5** abuse, wound **6** damage, injure, injury, offend **7** blacken, blemish **8** discolor **9** black mark, contusion **13** discoloration

bruit **3** din **5** noise, rumor **6** clamor, hubbub, racket, report, uproar **7** clangor **10** clattering, noise about **11** voice abroad

Brunei
capital/largest city: **17** Bandar Seri Begawan
others: **4** Labi **5** Badas, Danau, Muara, Seria **6** Bangar, Tutong **7** Kampong **10** Kuala Abang, Kuala Balai **11** Kuala Belait
head of state/government: **6** sultan
island: **6** Borneo **8** Sipitang
mountain: **6** Teraja **9** Ulu Tutong
highest point: **10** Pagon Priok
river: **6** Belait, Brunei, Tutong **9** Temburong
sea: **10** South China
physical feature:
bay: **6** Brunei
people: **4** Iban **5** Dayak, Malay **7** Chinese, Kadazan
language: **4** Iban **5** Malay **7** Chinese, English
religion: **5** Islam **6** Taoism **7** animism **8** Buddhism **12** Christianity
feature: **3** oil

Brunelleschi, Filippo
architect of: **10** San Lorenzo **11** Pazzi Chapel (Santa Croce), Pitti Palace **12** Santo Spirito **14** Badia Fiesolana **15** Duomo of Florence **16** Palazzo Quaratesi **21** Santa Maria degli Angeli **22** Ospedale degli Innocenti **23** Dome of Florence Cathedral

brunet, brunette **4** dark **5** black **9** brown-eyed, dark brown **10** dark-haired **11** brown-haired, dark-skinned **12** olive-skinned **16** dark-complexioned

Brunhild
origin: **8** Germanic
Scandinavian: **8** Brynhild
character in: **14** Nibelungenlied
queen of: **8** Isenland
husband: **7** Gunther
won by: **9** Siegfried

brunt **5** force **6** impact, stress, thrust **8** violence **9** full force, main shock

brush **4** bush, dust, fern, wash **5** clean, copse, flick, graze, groom, paint, run-in, scrub, sedge, set-to, shine, sweep, touch, whisk **6** battle, bushes, caress, duster, forest, fracas, polish, shrubs, stroke **7** bracken, cleanse, dusting, grazing, meeting, scuffle, thicket, varnish **8** skirmish, woodland **9** encounter, shrubbery, woodlands **10** engagement, underbrush, whiskbroom **11** bush country, undergrowth **12** bristled tool **13** confrontation
type: **4** hair, nail, shoe, wash **5** paint, scrub, tooth **7** clothes

brush aside **6** slight **7** neglect **8** pass over **9** disregard

brush-off **3** cut **4** snub **5** brush **6** rebuff, slight **7** put-down, squelch **9** disregard, rejection **11** repudiation **12** cold shoulder

brusque **4** curt, rude, tart **5** bluff, blunt, gruff, harsh, rough, short **6** abrupt, crusty **7** bearish **8** impolite, ungentle **10** ungracious **12** discourteous **13** unceremonious

Brussels
canal: **9** Charleroi **10** Willebroek
capital of: **7** Belgium
cathedral: **26** Saint Michel and Sainte Gudule
early name: **10** Bruoc-sella
means: **16** marshy settlement
Flemish: **7** Brussel

French: **9** Bruxelles
headquarters of: **3** EEC **4** NATO **12** Common Market **25** European Economic Community
landmark: **11** Royal Palace **15** Palace of Justice **17** Palace of the Nation
province: **7** Brabant
river: **5** Senne, Zenne
square: **11** Grande Place

brutal **5** crude, cruel, harsh **6** bloody, coarse, fierce, savage **7** brutish, hellish, inhuman, vicious **8** barbaric, pitiless, ruthless **9** atrocious, barbarous, heartless, merciless, unfeeling **10** demoniacal **11** hardhearted, remorseless **12** bloodthirsty

brutality **7** cruelty **8** ferocity, savagery **9** barbarity, harshness **10** inhumanity, savageness **11** brutishness, viciousness **12** ruthlessness

brute **5** beast, demon, devil, fiend, swine **6** animal, savage **7** monster **9** barbarian **10** wild animal **11** cruel person **12** dumb creature

brutish **5** cruel, feral **6** bloody, brutal, fierce, savage **7** inhuman **8** barbaric **9** barbarous, ferocious, unfeeling **11** remorseless

brutishness **8** ferocity, savagery **9** barbarity, brutality **10** bestiality, coarseness, inhumanity, savageness **11** viciousness **15** remorselessness

Brutus
also: **12** Marcus Brutus
character in: **12** Julius Caesar
author: **11** Shakespeare

Bruxelles *see* **8** Brussels

Bryan, C D B
author of: **12** Friendly Fire **24** Ugly Scenes Beautiful Women

Bryant, Bear (Paul)
sport: **8** football
position: **5** coach
team: **7** Alabama **11** Crimson Tide

Brynhild
origin: **12** Scandinavian
Germanic: **8** Brunhild
husband: **6** Gunnar
won by: **6** Sigurd
position: **8** Valkyrie

Brynhildr Sigrdrifa *see* **9** Sigrdrifa

Brynner, Yul
real name: **10** Taidje Khan
born: **14** Sakhalin Island
roles: **9** Anastasia, West World **11** The King and I (Oscar) **18** The Ten Commandments **19** The Magnificent Seven **20** The Brothers Karamazov **23** Invitation to a Gunfighter

Brythonic
language family: **12** Indo-European
group: **5** Welsh **6** Breton **7** Cornish, Pictish

Bschliessmayer, Oskar Josef
real name of: **11** Oskar Werner

Bubba Smith
nickname of: **17** Charles Aaron Smith

bubble, bubbles **4** bleb, boil, fizz, foam **5** froth **6** burble, fizzle, gurgle, seethe **7** air ball, blister, droplet, globule, sparkle **9** percolate **10** effervesce **13** effervescence

bubbliness **9** fizziness, foaminess **10** ebullience, enthusiasm, frothiness, liveliness **11** high spirits **13** effervescence

bubbling **5** fizzy, foamy **6** frothy **7** fizzing, foaming **9** sparkling **12** effervescent

bubbly **5** fizzy, foamy **6** frothy, lively **7** fizzing, foaming **9** champagne, sparkling **12** effervescent, high-spirited

Bubona
origin: **5** Roman
protectress of: **4** cows, oxen

buccaneer **6** pirate **7** corsair **9** privateer **10** freebooter

Buchan, John (Baron Tweedsmuir)
author of: **10** John Macnab **11** Greenmantle, Pilgrim's Way **17** John Burnet of Barns **18** The Thirty-Nine Steps

Buchanan, Daisy
character in: **14** The Great Gatsby
author: **10** Fitzgerald

Buchanan, Edgar
born: **13** Humansville MO
roles: **5** Shane, Texas **7** Arizona **8** Cimarron **9** McLintock **13** Penny Serenade **17** Petticoat Junction **18** Ride the High Country

Buchanan, James *see box, p. 136*

Bucharest
capital of: **7** Romania, Rumania
founder: **5** Bucur
landmark: **8** Scinteia **13** Village Museum
river: **9** Dimbovita
Rumanian: **9** Bucuresti

Buchinsky, Charles
real name of: **14** Charles Bronson

buck **3** man **4** beau, deer, dude, kick, male **5** dandy **6** dollar, oppose **7** coxcomb **8** cavalier, gay blade **9** go against **10** young blood

Buck
character in: **16** The Call of the Wild
author: **6** London

Buck, Pearl S
author of: **8** The Exile **9** Other Gods **10** Dragon Seed **12** The Good Earth **13** A House Divided

bucket **3** can, hod, tub **4** cask, pail **5** scoop **6** vessel **7** pailful, pitcher, scuttle **9** container **10** receptacle

Buckeye State
nickname of: **4** Ohio

buckle **3** sag **4** bend, clip, curl, hasp, hook, warp **5** bulge, catch, clasp **6** cave in, couple, fasten, secure **7** contort, crinkle, crumple, distort, wrinkle **8** belly out, collapse, fastener

buckle down **6** attend **12** apply oneself

Buckley, William F Jr
author of: **11** Who's on First? **15** God and Man at Yale, God Save the Queen

Buck Rogers
creator: **14** Richard Calkins
character: **5** Alura, Buddy, Dercu, Kayla, Wilma **6** Ardala **10** Killer Kane

bucolic **4** idyl, poem **5** idyll, rural **6** poetic, rustic **7** eclogue, idyllic, peasant **8** pastoral, shepherd

Bucolion
father: **8** Laomedon
son: **7** Aesepus
wife: **9** Abarbarea

bud **4** open **5** shoot **6** flower, sprout **7** blossom, burgeon, develop

Bud, Rosa
character in: **22** The Mystery of Edwin Drood
author: **7** Dickens

Budapest
area: **4** Buda, Pest **5** Obuda
capital of: **7** Hungary
cathedral: **13** Saint Matthias
hill: **10** Castle Hill
island: **6** Csepel
river: **6** Danube
Roman town: **8** Aquincum

Buddenbrooks
author: **10** Thomas Mann

Buchanan, James
nickname: 7 Old Buck
presidential rank: 9 fifteenth
party: 8 Democrat
state represented: 2 PA
defeated: 7 (John Charles) Fremont 8 (Millard) Fillmore
vice president: 12 (John Cabell) Breckinridge
cabinet:
state: 4 (Lewis) Cass 5 (Jeremiah Sullivan) Black
treasury: 3 (John Adams) Dix 4 (Howell) Cobb 6 (Philip Francis) Thomas
war: 4 (Joseph) Holt 5 (John Buchanan) Floyd
attorney general: 5 (Jeremiah Sullivan) Black 7 (Edwin McMasters) Stanton
navy: 6 (Isaac) Toucey
postmaster general: 4 (Horatio) King, (Joseph) Holt 5 (Aaron Venable) Brown
interior: 8 (Jacob) Thompson
born: 11 Cove Gap PA (near Mercersburg)
died/buried: 11 Lancaster PA
education:
Academy: 8 Old Stone
College: 9 Dickinson
studied: 3 law
religion: 12 Presbyterian
political career: 13 state assembly 24 US House of Representatives
secretary of: 5 State
minister: 6 Russia 12 Great Britain
civilian career: 6 lawyer
notable events of lifetime/term: 5 Panic (of 1857) 11 English Bill, Pony Express
raid by: 9 John Brown
raid on: 12 Harper's Ferry
Supreme Court case: 9 Dred Scott
father: 5 James
mother: 9 Elizabeth (Speer)
siblings: 4 Jane, John, Mary 5 Maria, Sarah 7 Harriet 9 Elizabeth 11 Edward Young 12 William Speer 16 George Washington
wife: 4 none
children: 4 none

Buddha
also called: 5 Butsu
born: 11 Kapilavastu
father: 11 Suddhodhana
founded: 8 Buddhism
means: 15 enlightened one
message: 6 dharma
name for: 17 Siddhartha Gautama
son: 6 Rahula
tree: 2 bo 5 bodhi
wife: 9 Yasodhara

Buddhism
action: 5 karma
branch: 8 Mahayana 9 Theravada 12 Great Vehicle 14 way of the elders
doctrine: 6 duhkha 7 nirvana 9 suffering 13 eightfold path 15 four noble truths 17 pratityasamutpada
founded by: 6 Buddha 17 Siddhartha Gautama
monk: 7 bhikshu
nun: 9 bhikshuni
rebirth: 7 samsara
religious community: 6 sangha

buddy 3 pal 4 chum, mate 5 amigo, crony 6 cohort, fellow, friend 7 brother, comrade, partner 8 confrere, intimate, playmate, sidekick 9 associate, colleague, companion, confidant 10 playfellow 11 confederate

buddy-buddy 5 close, palsy 6 chummy 8 friendly, intimate 10 palsy-walsy

budge 4 move, push, roll, stir, sway 5 shift, slide 6 change 8 convince, dislodge, persuade 9 dislocate, influence

budget 4 cost, plan 5 funds, means 6 moneys, ration 7 arrange 8 allocate, schedule 9 allotment, allowance, apportion, resources 10 allocation, portion out 12 spending plan 13 financial plan

budgetary 6 fiscal 8 economic, monetary 9 financial, pecuniary

buenas noches 9 good night

bueno 4 good

Buenos Aires
capital of: 9 Argentina
landmark: 11 Teatro Colon 16 Saavedra Monument, San Martin Theater 17 Wildestein Gallery, Witcomb Art Gallery 18 Church of El Salvador 27 Christopher Columbus Monument
park: 7 Palermo
people: 8 portenos
means: 15 people of the port
river: 12 Rio de la Plata

buff 3 bug, fan, nut, rub, tan 4 swab 5 freak, hound, mavin, sandy, straw, tawny 6 addict, dauber, polish, smooth, the raw 7 admirer, burnish, devotee, leather 8 bare skin, follower, polisher 9 nakedness, yellowish 10 aficionado, enthusiast 11 buffalo hide, connoisseur 14 yellowish-brown

buffalo 5 bison 6 puzzle 7 mystify 10 intimidate
kind: 7 African 10 Asian water
African: 14 syncerus caffer
Asian water: 14 bubalus bubalis

Buffalo
football team: 5 Bills
hockey team: 6 Sabres

buffer 6 bumper, fender, shield 7 cushion 9 protector

buffet 3 box, hit, jab, rap 4 bang, beat, bump, cuff, meal, push, slap 5 baste, knock, pound, shove, thump 6 pummel, strike, supper, thrash, thwack, wallop 7 cabinet, counter 8 credenza 9 cafeteria, sideboard 11 smorgasbord

Buffone, Carlo
character in: 22 Every Man out of His Humour
author: 6 Jonson

buffoon 3 wag 4 fool, zany 5 clown, comic, joker, mimic, Punch 6 jester, madcap 7 Pierrot 8 comedian, funnyman 9 harlequin, pantaloon, prankster, trickster 10 Scaramouch, silly-billy 11 merry-andrew, punchinello, Scaramouche

buffoonery 6 antics, comedy 7 foolery, inanity 8 zaniness 9 asininity, horseplay, silliness, slapstick 10 tomfoolery 11 foolishness, loutishness

12 clownishness, monkeyshines, prankishness
14 clowning around, playing the fool

bug **3** nag **4** flaw, germ **5** annoy, fault, virus **6** badger, bother, defect, insect, pester **7** wiretap **8** drawback, listen in, weakness **9** eavesdrop, Hemiptera **11** Heteroptera
variety: **3** bat, bed, red **4** gnat, lace, leaf, seed, toad **5** negro, plant, shore, stilt, stink, water **6** ambush, damsel, fungus, pirate, ripple **7** boatman, stainer **8** assassin, burrower, creeping **9** royal palm **10** leaf footed **11** ashgray leaf, backswimmer, broadheaded, jumping tree, velvet water **12** velvety shore, water strider, water treader **13** jumping ground, water measurer, water scorpion **14** scentless plant **17** terrestrial turtle

bugaboo **5** scare **6** fright **7** anxiety

bugbear **4** ogre **5** bogey **6** goblin **7** bugaboo **8** bogeyman **9** bete noire

buggy **4** cart **5** wagon **7** vehicle **8** carriage **10** conveyance

bugle **4** horn **10** instrument

Bugs Bunny
creator: **15** Leon Schlesinger
character: **9** Elmer Fudd
voice of: **8** Mel Blanc
saying: **10** what's up doc

build **4** body, form, make, mold, open **5** begin, brace, erect, forge, found, put up, raise, renew, set up, shape, start, steel **6** create, extend, figure, harden, launch **7** amplify, augment, develop, enhance, enlarge, fashion, greaten, improve, produce **8** embark on, increase, initiate, multiply, physique **9** construct, establish, fabricate, institute, intensify, originate, reinforce, structure, undertake **10** inaugurate, strengthen, supplement **11** manufacture, put together **12** construction

building **7** edifice **9** structure **12** construction

building front **6** facade **8** frontage

build up **5** amass **7** develop, promote **8** increase **10** accumulate

Bujold, Genevieve
born: **6** Canada **8** Montreal
roles: **4** Coma **9** Monsignor, Obsession **12** King of Hearts **21** Anne of the Thousand Days

Bujumbura
capital of: **7** Burundi

Bul **17** eighth Hebrew month

bulb **3** bud **4** corm, seed **5** plant, tuber **8** swelling

Bulfinch, Charles
architect of: **7** Capitol (Washington DC) **16** Hartford City Hall (CT) **23** Massachusetts State House (Boston)
style: **7** Federal

Bulgakov, Mikhail
author of: **9** Black Snow **13** The White Guard **14** The Heart of a Dog **19** The Days of the Turbins **21** The Master and Margarita

Bulgaria ***see box***

bulge **3** bag, sag **4** bump, lump **5** curve, swell **6** excess **7** distend, project, puff out, sagging **8** protrude, stand out, stick out, swelling, swell out **9** bagginess **10** projection, prominence, protrusion **12** protuberance

bulk **4** body, mass, most, size **6** extent, volume, weight **7** bigness, measure **8** enormity, hugeness, main part, majority, quantity **9** amplitude, greatness, largeness, magnitude, major part, plurality, substance **10** better part, dimensions, lion's share **11** greater part, massiveness, proportions **13** preponderance

bulky **3** big **4** huge **5** large **6** clumsy **7** awkward, hulking, immense, lumpish, massive, sizable, unhandy **8** enormous, ungainly, unwieldy **9** capacious, extensive **10** cumber-

Bulgaria
capital/largest city: **5** Sofia
others: **3** Lom **4** Rila, Ruse **5** Aytos, Butan, Byclu, Elena, Iskra, Stara, Varna **6** Bleven, Burgas, Devnia, Dulovo, Levsky, Pernik, Pleuna, Pleven, Plevna, Shumen, Shumla, Sliven, Slivno, Widden, Yambol, Zagora **7** Gabrovo, Karlovo, Plovdiv, Sistova, Tirnova **8** Khaskovo, Rustchuk, Svishtov **9** Ruse Vidin, Silistria **11** Kolorovgrad **12** Dimitrovgrad
school: **5** Sofia **7** Plovdiv **13** Veliko Turnovo
measure: **3** oka, oke **5** krine, lekhe, likhe
monetary unit: **3** lev **8** stotinki
weight: **3** oka, oke **5** tovar
mountain: **3** Kom **5** Botev, Pirin, Sapka **6** Balkan, Sredna **7** Vikhren **11** Rila-Rhodope
highest point: **6** Musala **8** Musallah
river: **3** Lom, Vit **4** Arda, Osma **5** Isker, Iskur, Mesta **6** Danube, Marica, Ogosta, Struma, Yantra **7** Maritsa, Stryama, Tundzha
sea: **5** Black
physical feature:
cape: **5** Emine, Sabla **7** Kuratan
gulf: **5** Burga
plateau: **6** Danube
resort: **9** Pyassatzi **13** Slunchev Bryay
valley: **7** Maritsa
people: **4** Slav, Turk **5** Gypsy, Pomak, Tatar **6** Bulgar, Slavic **7** Chuvash **9** Cheremiss **10** Macedonian
language: **9** Bulgarian
religion: **5** Islam **24** Bulgarian Eastern Orthodox
place:
church: **9** St Nedelja
monastery: **4** Rila **6** Rilski
monument: **7** Red Army
mosque: **10** Banya Bashi
museum: **21** Revolutionary Movement
square: **5** Lenin
valley of roses: **8** Kazanluk
feature:
dance: **4** horo
holiday: **12** St Georges Day
newspaper: **17** Rabot Nichesko Delo
food:
stew: **8** giuvetch

some, voluminous 12 unmanageable

bull 2 ox **4** male
male of the: 3 elk **4** seal **5** moose, whale **6** bovine **8** elephant
constellation of: 6 Taurus
Spanish: 4 toro

bulldoze 3 cow **4** bump, fell, push, rage, raze **5** abash, bully, drive, force, level, press, shove **6** coerce, hector, jostle, propel, subdue, thrust **7** buffalo, dragoon, flatten **8** bludgeon, browbeat, domineer, shoulder **9** push about, tyrannize **10** intimidate

Bullen, Frank T
author of: 19 Told in the Dry Watches **22** The Cruise of the Cachalot

bullet 4 ball, lead, shot, slug **7** missile **8** buckshot

bulletin 4 note **6** report **7** account, message, release **8** dispatch **9** statement **10** communique, news report **12** notification **13** communication

Bullet Park
author: 11 John Cheever

bull fighter 6 torero **7** matador, picador **8** toreador **10** El Cordobes **15** Miguel Dominguin

Bullion State
nickname of: 8 Missouri

Bullitt
director: 10 Peter Yates
cast: 9 Don Gordon **12** Robert Duvall, Robert Vaughn, Steve McQueen **16** Jacqueline Bisset
setting: 12 San Francisco

bullock 2 ox **4** beef, bull **5** steer

bullocks 4 kine, oxen **5** beefs, bulls **6** beeves, cattle, steers

bull session 3 rap **4** talk **7** gabfest, palaver **8** dialogue **9** discourse **10** discussion **12** conversation **13** confabulation

bull's-eye 5 black **6** center **7** exactly **8** on target **9** dead center, precisely

bully 3 cow **4** good **5** annoy, swell, tough **6** cheers, coerce, despot, harass, hurrah, hurray **7** coercer, right on, ruffian, tread on **8** browbeat, bulldoze, domineer, frighten, ride over, well done **9** oppressor, terrorize, tormentor, tyrannize **10** browbeater, intimidate **11** intimidator

bullying 7 torment **8** coercion **9** despotism **10** harassment, tormenting **11** browbeating, domineering, tyrannizing **12** intimidation

bulrush 5 plant, sedge **7** cattail, papyrus

bulwark 5 guard **7** barrier, parapet, rampart, support, defense **8** mainstay **9** earthwork **10** embankment

Bulwer-Lytton, Edward
author of: 6 Harold, Pelham, Rienzi **9** Richelieu **13** The Coming Race **16** Kenelm Chillingly **18** The Last of the Barons **20** The Last Days of Pompeii

bum 3 beg **4** grub, hobo **5** cadge, idler, mooch, tramp **6** borrow, loafer, sponge **7** drifter, vagrant **8** derelict, vagabond

bumble 6 bungle **7** blunder, stagger, stumble **8** flounder

Bumble
character in: 11 Oliver Twist
author: 7 Dickens

bumcombe, bunkum 3 rot **4** bosh, bunk **6** drivel **7** twaddle **8** nonsense, tommyrot **10** balderdash **16** stuff-and-nonsense

bump 3 hit, jar, rap **4** bang, blow, butt, hump, jolt, knob, knot, lump, node, poke, slam, slap, sock **5** bulge, clash, crack, crash, gnarl, knock, punch, shake, smack, smash, thump, whack **6** bounce, buffet, impact, jostle, jounce, nodule, rattle, strike, wallop **7** collide, run into **8** swelling **9** collision, crash into, smash into **11** excrescence **12** protuberance

bump into 4 meet **7** collide, run into **9** encounter

bumpkin 3 oaf **4** boor, lout **5** churl, yokel **8** ship beam **10** clodhopper

bump off 4 do in, kill, slay **6** murder, rub out **7** execute, gun down **8** dispatch **11** assassinate **12** take for a ride

bumptious 4 bold **5** cocky, pushy **6** brazen **7** forward, haughty **8** arrogant, boastful, cocksure, impudent, insolent **9** bodacious, conceited, obtrusive **10** aggressive, swaggering **11** impertinent, overbearing **12** presumptuous **13** overconfident, self-assertive

bumptiousness 4 gall **5** cheek **8** audacity, boldness **9** impudence **11** forwardness, presumption **12** impertinence **13** obtrusiveness **17** self-assertiveness

bumpy 5 lumpy, rocky, rough **6** uneven **10** undulating

bun 4 coil, knot, roll **8** soft roll **9** sweet roll

Bunaea
epithet of: 4 Hera
refers to: 6 temple

bunch 3 lot, mob **4** band, bevy, gang, heap, herd, host, knot, mass, pack, pile, team **5** array, batch, clump, crowd, flock, group, shock, stack, tribe, troop **6** amount, bundle, gather, huddle, number, string **7** cluster, collect, company **8** assemble, assembly, quantity **9** gathering, multitude **10** assortment, collection, congregate **12** accumulation

bundle 3 lot **4** bale, bind, heap, mass, pack, pile, wrap **5** array, batch, bunch, group, sheaf, stack, truss **6** amount, packet, parcel **7** package **8** quantity **9** multitude **10** assortment, collection **11** tie together **12** accumulation

Bundren family
characters in: 11 As I Lay Dying
member: 4 Anse, Cash, Darl **5** Addie, Jewel **9** Dewey Dell
author: 8 Faulkner

bungalow 5 cabin, house, lodge **7** cottage

bungle 3 mar **4** flub, goof, miff, ruin **5** botch, spoil **6** foul up, mess up, muddle **7** blunder, butcher, do badly, louse up, screw up **8** misjudge **9** mismanage, misreckon **10** miscompute **11** make a mess of, misestimate **12** miscalculate

Bunin, Ivan Alekseyevich
author of: 10 The Village **15** The Elagin Affair **17** The Life of Arseniev **28** The Gentleman from San Francisco

bunk 3 bed, cot, rot **4** bull **5** berth, hokum, hooey, stuff **6** bunkum, hot air, humbug, pallet **7** baloney, blather, bombast, hogwash, inanity, malarky, spinach **8** claptrap, nonsense, tommyrot **9** poppycock **10** applesauce, balderdash **11** foolishness **16** stuff and nonsense

Bunsen, Robert Wilhelm
nationality: 6 German
inventor of: 9 gas burner

10 photo meter **12** Bunsen burner, spectroscope **24** electromechanical battery

Bunshaft, Gordon
architect of: **10** Lever House (NY) **23** Beinecke Rare Book Library (Yale) **33** Hirshhorn Museum and Sculpture Garden (Washington DC) **34** Lyndon Baines Johnson Memorial Library (Austin TX)

Bunus
father: **6** Hermes
mother: **9** Aleidamea
raised temple honoring: **4** Hera
location of temple: **7** Corinth

Bunyan, John
author of: **10** The Holy War **16** Pilgrim's Progress **25** The Life and Death of Mr Badman **33** Grace Abounding to the Chief of Sinners

buona notte **9** good night

buona sera **11** good evening

buon giorno **7** good day **11** good morning

Buono, Victor
born: **10** San Diego CA
roles: **11** The Stranger **12** Four for Texas **22** Hush Hush Sweet Charlotte **26** Whatever Happened to Baby Jane

buoy **4** bell, lift **5** boost, cheer, float, raise **6** beacon, uplift **7** cheer up, elevate, gladden, lighten **8** brighten **10** keep afloat **14** floating marker

buoyancy, buoyance **4** glee **6** gaicty **7** jollity **8** gladness, vivacity **9** animation, good humor, joviality, lightness, sunniness **10** brightness, cheeriness, enthusiasm, floatiness, joyousness **11** good spirits **12** cheerfulness, exhilaration, floatability **14** weightlessness **16** lightheartedness

buoyant **3** gay **4** glad **5** happy, jolly, light, merry, peppy, sunny **6** afloat, breezy, bright, elated, joyful, joyous, lively **7** hopeful **8** animated, carefree, cheerful, floating, sportive **9** energetic, floatable, sprightly, vivacious **10** blithesome, optimistic, weightless **11** exhilarated, free and easy **12** enthusiastic, lighthearted

buoyed **6** elated **7** exalted, pleased **8** elevated **9** confident, heartened, reassured **10** inspirited

buoy up **4** warm **6** assure, uplift **7** comfort, hearten, inspire **8** inspirit, reassure **9** encourage

Buphagus
father: **7** Iapetus
slain by: **7** Artemis
epithet of: **8** Hercules
means: **7** ox-eater

Burbank, Luther
field: **7** biology
developed: **13** plant breeding

burble **6** babble, bubble, gurgle, murmur **8** babbling

Burce, Suzanne
real name of: **10** Jane Powell

Burchill, Mr
character in: **19** The Vicar of Wakefield
author: **9** Goldsmith

burden **3** tax, try, vex **4** care, load, onus, pack **5** cargo **6** hamper, hinder, strain, stress, weight **7** afflict, anxiety, freight, oppress, trouble **8** encumber, handicap, hardship, load with, obligate, overload **9** press down, weigh down **10** saddle with **11** encumbrance **14** responsibility

Burden, Jack
character in: **14** All the King's Men
author: **6** Warren

burden of proof
Latin: **12** onus probandi

burdensome **4** hard **5** heavy **6** tiring **7** arduous, onerous **8** wearying **9** Herculean, laborious **10** exhausting

bureau **6** agency, branch, office **7** cabinet, commode, dresser, service, station **8** division **10** chiffonier, department **14** administration, chest of drawers

bureaucrat **8** mandarin, official, politico **9** penpusher **10** politician **11** apparatchik, functionary, rubber stamp **12** civil servant, officeholder **13** public servant

burgee **4** flag **6** banner, colors, ensign **7** pennant

burgeon **3** wax **4** blow, grow, open **5** bloom **6** expand, flower, spread, thrive **7** augment, blossom, develop, enlarge, prosper, shoot up, succeed **8** escalate, flourish, fructify, increase, mushroom, spring up **9** bear fruit **10** effloresce **11** proliferate

Burgess, Anthony
author of: **2** MF **13** Man of Nazareth, Time for a Tiger **14** Enderby Outside, The Wanting Seed **16** A Clockwork Orange, Beard's Roman Women **17** Nothing Like the Sun **20** The End of the World News

burgher **7** citizen **9** bourgeois **11** townsperson

burglar **3** cat **4** yegg **5** thief **6** robber **7** prowler **8** pilferer **9** cracksman, purloiner **12** housebreaker **14** second-story man

burglary **5** theft **6** felony **7** break-in, larceny, robbery **8** filching, stealing **9** pilfering **10** purloining **13** housebreaking **19** breaking and entering

burgundy **3** red **4** wine **5** color **13** reddish-purple

Burgundy
ancient city: **5** Autun
city: **5** Dijon
district: **5** Youne **6** Nievre **7** Cote d' Or **12** Saone-et-Loire
French: **9** Bourgogne
location: **6** France
river: **5** Rhone, Saone
tribe: **9** Burgundii

Buri
origin: **12** Scandinavian
first: **3** god
revealed by: **8** Audhumla **9** Audhumbla

burial **5** rites **7** funeral **9** interment, obsequies **10** entombment, inhumation

burial ground **7** ossuary **8** boneyard, Boot Hill, catacomb, cemetery **9** graveyard **10** churchyard, necropolis **12** potter's field

buried **4** laid, sunk **6** hidden **7** covered, inhumed, immured **9** concealed, deep sixed **10** laid to rest **11** underground

Buried Alive
author: **13** Arnold Bennett

Burke, Francis
character in: **21** The Master of Ballantrae
author: **9** Stevenson

burlap **3** bag **4** hemp, jute **5** cloth **6** fabric **8** material

burlesque **5** farce, spoof **6** comedy, parody, satire **7** mockery, takeoff **8** ridicule, travesty **10** buffoonery, caricature **15** slapstick comedy

burly **3** big **5** beefy, bulky, hefty, large **6** brawny, stocky, strong, sturdy **7** hulking, sizable **8** thickset **9** ponderous, strapping

Burma
other name: **16** Land of the Pagodas
capital: **7** Rangoon
ancient capital: **3** Ava **4** Pegu **8** Mandalay
largest city: **7** Rangoon
others: **2** Ye **3** Ava **4** Pegu **5** Akyab, Bhamo, Katha, Minbu, Namtu, Papun, Prome, Tavoy **6** Hsenwi, Hsipaw, Lashio, Maymyo, Monywa, Shwebo **7** Bassein, Henzada, Pakokku, Toungoo **8** Moulmein, Myingyan
measure: **2** ly **3** dha, gon, mau, sao, tao, tat **4** byee, phan, seit, taun, that **5** shita, thuoc **6** lamany, palgat **7** chaivai **8** okthabah
monetary unit: **3** pya **4** kyat
weight: **2** ta **3** can, pai, vis **4** binh, kyat, ruay, viss **5** behar, candy, ticul **6** abucco **7** peiktha
lake: **4** Inle
mountain: **4** Chin, Naga, Pegu, Popa **5** Davna **6** Arakan, Kachin, Lushai, Patkai **7** Karenni **8** Nattaung, Peguyoma, Saramati, Victoria **10** Tenasserim **11** Manipur Hill **12** Tanen Taunggi
highest point: **11** Hkakabo Razi
river: **3** Hka **6** Salwin, Sutang **7** Irawadi, Kaladan, Myitnge, Salween, Schweli, Sittang **8** Chindwin, Indawgyi **9** Irrawaddy
sea: **7** Andaman
physical feature:
bay: **4** Siam **6** Bengal, Hunter **7** Heanzay **8** Thailand
gulf: **8** Martaban
plateau: **4** Shan
port: **5** Akyab **7** Bassein, Henzada **8** Moulmein
people: **2** Ao, Vu, Wa **3** Kaw, Lai, Lao, Mon, Pyu, Tai, Was **4** Akha, Chin, Juki, Kadu, Laos, Lolo, Miao, Naga, Sema, Shan, Thai, Tsin **5** Karen, Lhota **6** Birman, Burman, Kachin, Peguan, Rengma **7** Akhlame, Burmese, Kakhyen, Palauna, Palaung, Siamese **8** Mon-Khmer **9** Arakanese **12** Tibeto-Berman
language: **3** Lai **4** Chin, Kuki, Pegu, Shan **5** Karen **6** Kachin **7** Burmese, English
religion: **5** Hindu, Islam **8** Buddhism **12** Christianity
place:
mines: **6** Mawchi **7** Bawdwin
pagoda: **9** Shwe Dagon
road: **4** Ledo **5** Burma **9** Stillwell
feature:
ball game: **7** chin-lon
festival: **5** Water **6** Lights **10** Thadin-gyut
silk head band: **10** gaungbaung
skirt: **6** longyi
traveling theatrical group: **4** Pwes

burn **3** nip, tan **4** bite, char, fire, glow, hurt, pain, sear, skin **5** be hot, blaze, brown, chafe, flame, flare, flash, parch, prick, scald, singe, smart, smoke, sting **6** abrade, bronze, flames, ignite, kindle, nettle, scorch, scrape, suntan, tingle, wither **7** blister, consume, cremate, flicker, oxidize, prickle, shrivel, smolder, sunburn, swelter **8** abrasion, be ablaze, be on fire, charring, irritate, kindling **9** be flushed, reddening, set fire to, set on fire, use as fuel **10** be feverish, be in flames, blistering, incandesce, incinerate, irritation, smoldering **12** incineration **13** reduce to ashes

burnable **9** flammable, ignitable **10** combustive **11** combustible, inflammable **13** conflagrative

Burne-Jones, Sir Edward Coley
born: **7** England **10** Birmingham
artwork: **11** Laus Veneris **15** The Golden Stairs **16** The Mirror of Venus **18** The Star of Bethlehem **28** King Cophetua and the Beggar Maid

burner, gas
invented by: **6** Bunsen

Burnett, Carol
born: **12** San Antonio TX
roles: **14** The Four Seasons **19** The Carol Burnett Show

Burnett, Frances H
author of: **20** Little Lord Fauntleroy

Burney, Fanny
author of: **7** Camilla, Diaries, Evelina

Burnham, Daniel Hudson
partner: **16** John Wellborn Root
architect of: **7** Rookery **12** Union Station (Washington DC) **15** Calumet Building **16** Flatiron Building (NYC), Reliance Building **17** Monadnock Building **25** World's Columbian Exposition

burning **3** hot **5** acrid, afire, aglow, eager, fiery, sharp **6** aflame, ardent, biting, fervid, heated, raging, red-hot **7** blazing, boiling, caustic, earnest, fanatic, fervent, flaming, flaring, frantic, glowing, ignited, intense, kindled, painful, pungent, sincere, smoking, zealous **8** flashing, frenzied, piercing, resolute, sizzling, smarting, stinging, tingling **9** corroding, prickling **10** astringent, compelling, flickering, irritating, passionate, smoldering **11** impassioned **12** all-consuming

burnish **3** wax **4** buff **5** rub up, shine **6** polish, smooth

burnished **5** shiny **6** bright, buffed, shined **8** lustrous, polished, smoothed

burnoose **4** cape, robe **5** cloak **6** mantle **7** pelisse

burn out **3** pop **4** blow **7** exhaust **10** exhaustion, extinguish

Burns, George
real name: **14** Nathan Birnbaum
wife: **11** Gracie Allen
born: **9** New York NY
roles: **5** Oh God **12** Going in Style **15** The Sunshine Boys **17** Burns and Allen Show

Burns, Robert
author of: **8** To a Louse, To a Mouse **11** A Red Red Rose, Tam O'Shanter **12** Auld Lang Syne **16** Address to the Deil, Coming Thro the Rye **17** Holy Willie's Prayer **20** Flow Gently Sweet Afton **22** My Heart's in the Highlands **23** The Cotter's Saturday Night **32** Poems Chiefly in the Scottish Dialect

Burnt Norton
author: **7** T S Eliot

burp **5** belch, eruct **10** eructation

burr **4** buhr, rock **5** notch, stone **9** whetstone **13** pronunciation

Burr
author: **9** Gore Vidal

Burr, Raymond
born: **6** Canada **14** New Westminster **15** British Columbia
roles: **8** Ironside **10** Perry Mason, Rear Window

burro **3** ass **4** mule **6** donkey, onager **7** jackass

Burroughs, Edgar Rice
author of: **15** Tarzan of the Apes

Burroughs, William S
author of: **6** Junkie **13** The Naked Lunch

Burroughs, William Seward
nationality: **8** American
inventor of: **13** adding machine
grandson: **17** William S Burroughs (author)

burrow **3** den, dig **4** cave, hole, lair **6** covert, dugout, furrow, tunnel **8** excavate, scoop out **9** hollow out

Burrows, Abe
author of: **41** How to Succeed in Business without Really Trying

bursa **3** bag, sac **5** pouch, purse **6** cavity

bursar **6** purser **7** cashier **9** paymaster, treasurer **10** cashkeeper

burst **3** fly, pop, run **4** bang, bust, rend, rush **5** barge, blast, break, crack, erupt, split, spout **6** blow up, detach, divide, sunder **7** disjoin, explode, rupture, shatter, torrent **8** breaking, break out, cracking, crashing, detonate, eruption, fly apart, fracture, fragment, outbreak, separate, splinter **9** break open, discharge, explosion, gush forth, pull apart, splitting, tear apart **10** detonation, disconnect, outpouring, shattering **11** spring forth **12** disintegrate

burst forth **5** arise, begin, erupt, start **6** arrive, emerge **8** break out, commence

Burstyn, Ellen
real name: **14** Edna Rae Gillooly
born: **9** Detroit MI
roles: **11** The Exorcist **16** Same Time Next Year **18** The Last Picture Show **26** Alice Doesn't Live Here Anymore (Oscar)

Burton, Richard
real name: **22** Richard Walter Jenkins Jr
wife: **15** Elizabeth Taylor
born: **5** Wales **11** Pontrhydfen Wales
roles: **6** Becket, Hamlet **7** Camelot, The Robe **9** Cleopatra **14** My Cousin Rachel **19** The Night of the Iguana, The Taming of the Shrew **21** Anne of the Thousand Days **25** Who's Afraid of Virginia Woolf **26** The Spy Who Came in from the Cold

Burton, Robert
author of: **22** The Anatomy of Melancholy

Burundi
capital/largest city: **9** Bujumbura
others: **5** Ngozi **6** Bururi, Gitega, Kitega, Rutana, Ruyigi **7** Kibumbu, Muyinga
monetary unit: **5** franc **7** centime
lake: **7** Rugwero **8** Tshohoha **10** Tanganyika
mountain: **9** Nyamisana
highest point: **8** Nyarwana
river: **6** Akanya, Ruvuvu, Ruzizi **8** Rukagera **10** Malagarasi
people: **3** Twa **4** Hutu **5** Bantu, Batwa, Pygmy, Tutsi **6** Bahutu, Watusi **7** Barundi
language: **6** French **7** Kirundi, Swahili
religion: **5** Islam **7** animism **10** Protestant **13** Roman Catholic
feature:
king: **4** mwam
food:
coffee: **7** Arabica

Burushaski
language spoken in: **7** Kashmir

bury **4** hide **5** cache, cover, inter **6** encase, engulf, entomb, inhume **7** conceal, cover up, enclose, immerse, secrete **8** submerge, submerse **13** lay in the grave **17** consign to the grave

Bury My Heart at Wounded Knee
author: **8** Dee Brown

bush **4** veld **5** brush, hedge, plant, shrub, woods **6** forest, jungle **7** barrens **9** shrubbery, woodlands

Bush, George Herbert Walker
presidential rank: **10** forty-first
party: **10** Republican
state represented: **2** TX **5** Texas
defeated: **7** (Michael) Dukakis
vice president: **6** (Daniel) Quayle
born: **8** Milton MA
education: **4** Yale **7** Andover
religion: **12** Episcopalian
vacation spot: **5** Maine **13** Kennebunkport
political career: **13** vice president **14** representative **21** Ways and Means Committee
ambassador to: **2** UN **13** United Nations
chairman of: **27** Republican National Committee
head of: **3** CIA
liaison with: **5** China
civilian career: **3** oil **14** Zapata Offshore
military career: **5** pilot **6** US Navy
vice president under: **12** Ronald Reagan
father: **15** Prescott Sheldon
mother: **13** Dorothy Walker
wife: **13** Barbara Pierce
children: **4** John, Neil **5** Robin (died 1953) **6** George, Marvin **7** Dorothy

bush country **5** scrub, wilds **7** outback **10** wilderness

bushed **4** beat **5** all in, spent, tired, weary **6** done it, pooped **7** drained, wearied, worn out **8** dog tired, fatigued, tired out **9** dead tired, exhausted, played out

bushel
abbreviation: **2** bu **4** bush

bushes **5** brush **6** shrubs **9** brushwood, shrubbery **10** underbrush **11** undergrowth

bushy **5** hairy **6** fluffy, shaggy **7** hirsute **9** overgrown

business **3** job **4** case, duty,

firm, line, shop, task, work **5** chore, field, place, point, store, topic, trade **6** affair, career, living, matter, office, racket **7** affairs, calling, company, concern, dealing, factory, mission, problem, pursuit, subject, venture **8** activity, commerce, function, industry, position, province, question, vocation **9** procedure, situation, specialty **10** assignment, bargaining, employment, enterprise, livelihood, occupation, profession, walk of life **11** corporation, negotiation, partnership, transaction, undertaking **13** establishment, manufacturing, merchandising **14** bread and butter, responsibility

businesslike **7** careful, correct, orderly, regular, serious **8** diligent, sedulous, thorough **9** assiduous, efficient, organized, practical **10** methodical, systematic **11** industrious, painstaking **12** professional

Busiris
king of: **5** Egypt
father: **8** Poseidon
mother: **10** Lysianassa

Busoni, Ferruccio
born: **5** Italy **6** Empoli
composer of: **8** Turandot **10** Arlecchino **11** Doctor Faust, Doktor Faust **12** Die Brautwahl **14** Comedy Overture **25** Fantasia Contrappuntistica

bus station **5** depot **8** terminal, terminus

Bus Stop
director: **11** Joshua Logan
cast: **9** Don Murray **10** Betty Field **13** Eileen Heckart, Marilyn Monroe **14** Arthur O'Connell

bust **3** nab **4** head, raid **5** bosom, chest, seize **6** arrest, breast, collar **7** capture **9** apprehend, sculpture **12** take prisoner **15** take into custody

Buster Brown
creator: **10** RF Outcault
bulldog: **4** Tige
trademark: **9** sailor hat **10** wide collar

bustle **3** ado, fly **4** dash, flit, fuss, rush, stir, tear, to-do **5** hurry **6** bestir, flurry, hustle, pother, scurry, tumult **7** be quick, fluster, flutter, press on, scamper, scuttle **8** activity, be active, scramble **9** agitation, commotion, make haste **10** excitement, hurly-burly

busy **4** full **6** active, employ, engage, intent, occupy, on duty, work at **7** engaged, labor at, slaving, toiling, working **8** absorbed, bustling, employed, laboring, occupied **9** engrossed, in harness, strenuous **10** hard at work **11** industrious **12** be absorbed in, keep occupied **13** be engrossed in

busybody **3** pry **5** snoop **6** gossip **7** blabber, meddler, Paul Pry **8** telltale **10** chatterbox, newsmonger, talebearer, tattletale **12** blabbermouth **13** scandalmonger

busy place **4** hive **6** warren **7** anthill, beehive

but **3** yet **4** save, than that **5** if not, still **6** except, saving, unless **7** however, outside, that not **9** excepting, other than, otherwise **10** except that **14** on the other hand

Butch Cassidy and the Sundance Kid
director: **13** George Roy Hill
cast: **10** Paul Newman (Butch) **13** Katharine Ross (Etta Place), Robert Redford (The Kid)
score: **13** Burt Bacharach
Oscar for: **5** score
song: **27** Raindrops Keep Fallin' on My Head

butcher **4** goof, kill, muff, ruin, slay **5** botch, purge, spoil **6** boggle, bungle, fumble, hack up, hit man, killer, mess up, murder **7** louse up, screw up **8** assassin, decimate, homicide, massacre, murderer **9** liquidate, manhandle, mishandle, slaughter **10** annihilate, hatchet man, liquidator **11** assassinate, exterminate, make a mess of, slaughterer **12** exterminator, mass-murderer **15** homicidal maniac

butchery **4** flop, mess **5** botch **8** massacre **9** slaughter

Butes
father: **6** Boreas **7** Pandion
mother: **8** Zeuxippe
brother: **8** Lycurgus **10** Erechtheus
sister: **6** Procne **9** Philomela
son: **4** Eryx
priest of: **6** Athena **8** Poseidon
member of: **9** Argonauts
stricken with: **8** insanity
enticed by: **6** Sirens
leaped into: **3** sea
rescued by: **9** Aphrodite

Butkus, Dick (Richard Marvin)
sport: **8** football
position: **10** linebacker
team: **12** Chicago Bears

Butler, Rhett
character in: **15** Gone With the Wind
author: **8** Mitchell

Butler, Samuel
author of: **7** Erewhon **8** Hudibras **16** The Way of All Flesh **20** The Elephant in the Moon

butt **3** end, hit, jab, ram, rap **4** buck, bump, bunt, dupe, goat, mark, push, slap, stub **5** knock, shank, shove, smack, stump, thump **6** bottom, buffet, jostle, object, strike, target, thrust, thwack, victim **8** blunt end **13** laughingstock

buttercup **10** Ranunculus
variety: **4** Tall **5** Early **6** Common **7** Bermuda, Bulbous, Persian **8** Colombia, Creeping **11** Yellow water

butterfingered **5** inept **6** clumsy **7** awkward **8** bungling **9** maladroit **10** ungraceful

butterfly
pupa: **9** chrysalis **10** chrysalids **11** chrysalides
variety: **4** blue **5** giant, nymph, satyr, snout, tiger, zebra **6** alpine, apollo, arctic, kalima **7** alfalfa, budwing, dogface, monarch, peacock, viceroy **9** Baltimore, bathwhite, brimstone, christmas, metalmark, orange tip, wood nymph **10** Parnassian **11** painted lady, spring azure **12** blue mountain, cabbage white, clouded white, silver stripe, white admiral **13** chalkhill blue, mourning cloak, pearl crescent **14** American copper, gulf fritillary, tailed birdwing **15** longtail skipper, regal fritillary **16** black swallowtail, black veined white, camberwell beauty, green veined white, Leonardus skipper, red-spotted purple **18** orchard swallowtail **19** European swallowtail **20** spicebush swallowtail, variegated fritillary **21** great purple hairstreak, questionmark anglewing, white admiral wood nymph

butter up **4** coax **6** cajole **7** flatter, wheedle **8** soft-soap

buttocks **4** buns, butt, rear, rump, seat **5** fanny, nates **6** behind, bottom **7** keister, rear end **8** backside, derriere, haunches **9** fundament, posterior **12** hindquarters

buttonhole **4** halt, slit, stop **6** accost, waylay **7** solicit **8** approach, confront

button one's lip **7** keep mum **10** keep silent **16** keep one's trap shut **18** keep one's lips sealed

Buttons, Red
real name: **11** Aaron Chwatt
born: **9** New York NY
roles: **8** Sayonara **13** The Longest Day **20** The Poseidon Adventure **23** They Shoot Horses Don't They

buttress **4** arch, prop, stay **5** boost, brace, shore, steel **6** prop up **7** bolster, shore up, support **8** abutment, shoulder **9** reinforce, stanchion **10** strengthen

buxom **5** plump **6** bosomy, chesty, robust, zaftig **9** strapping **10** voluptuous **13** large-breasted, well-developed

buy **3** get **4** deal, gain **5** bribe **6** buy off, obtain, pay for, suborn **7** acquire, bargain, corrupt, procure **8** invest in, purchase **9** influence

buy and sell **4** deal **5** trade **6** market

buy off **5** bribe **6** pay off **13** grease the palm

Buzi
son: **7** Ezekiel

Buz Sawyer
creator: **8** Roy Crane
sidekick: **7** Sweeney

Buzuhov, Pierre
character in: **11** War and Peace
author: **7** Tolstoy

buzz **3** hum **4** whir **5** drone **6** murmur **7** whisper

by **4** near, over, past **5** along **6** beside, beyond, during, toward **7** through **9** alongside **10** concerning, on or before **11** according to, no later than

by air
French: **8** par avion

Byam, Roger
character in: **17** Mutiny on the Bounty
authors: **4** Hall **8** Nordhoff

Byblis
father: **7** Miletus
mother: **6** Cyanea
twin brother: **6** Caunus
loved: **6** Caunus
changed into: **8** fountain

by few words
Latin: **12** paucis verbis

bygone **4** past **5** olden **6** former, gone by, of yore **7** ancient, earlier **8** departed, obsolete, previous **10** antiquated

by horse
French: **7** a cheval

Byington, Spring
born: **17** Colorado Springs CO
roles: **7** Jezebel **11** Little Women **13** December Bride, Heaven Can Wait **17** Mutiny on the Bounty **20** The Devil and Miss Jones, You Can't Take It with You **26** The Charge of the Light Brigade

by itself **4** solo **5** alone, aloof, apart **8** isolated **13** unaccompanied

Byng, Admiral
character in: **7** Candide
author: **8** Voltaire

by oneself **4** solo **5** alone, aloof **8** isolated **10** solitarily **13** unaccompanied
Latin: **4** sola **5** solus

by operation of law
Latin: **8** ipso jure

bypass **4** go by **5** avert, avoid, dodge **8** go around **10** circumvent **12** detour around

bypath **3** way **4** lane **5** alley, byway, track, trail **6** bypass **7** footway, pathway, towpath, walkway **8** back road, dirt road, footpath, shortcut, side road **10** beaten path, bridle path, garden path

by-product **8** offshoot **9** aftermath **16** incidental result

by right
Latin: **6** de jure

Byron, Lord (George Gordon)
author of: **7** Don Juan, Manfred **10** The Corsair **19** The Vision of Judgment **20** The Prisoner of Chillon **23** Childe Harold's Pilgrimage

byrrh
type: **8** aperitif
origin: **6** France
flavor: **6** orange **7** quinine

bystander **6** viewer **7** watcher, witness **8** attender, beholder, looker-on, observer, onlooker, passerby **9** spectator

by the book **9** by the rule **13** authoritarian **16** according to Hoyle

by the fact itself
Latin: **9** ipso facto

by the grace of God
Latin: **9** Dei gratia

by the law itself
Latin: **8** ipso jure

by the month
Latin: **9** per mensem

by the rule **9** by the book **11** as specified **13** authoritarian

by the skin of one's teeth **6** barely, hardly **8** only just, scarcely **11** by an eyelash

by the very nature of the deed
Latin: **9** ipso facto

by the way
French: **9** en passant

by virtue and arms
Latin: **13** virtute et armis
motto of: **11** Mississippi

byway **4** lane **5** alley **6** detour, street **8** shunpike

by what right?
Latin: **7** quo jure

byword **3** law, saw **4** rule **5** adage, axiom, maxim, motto, truth **6** dictum, saying, slogan **7** precept, proverb **8** aphorism, apothegm **9** catchword, pet phrase, principle, watchword **10** shibboleth

Byzantine **6** complex **8** scheming **9** expedient, intricate **13** Machiavellian

Byzas
founder of: **9** Byzantium
father: **8** Poseidon

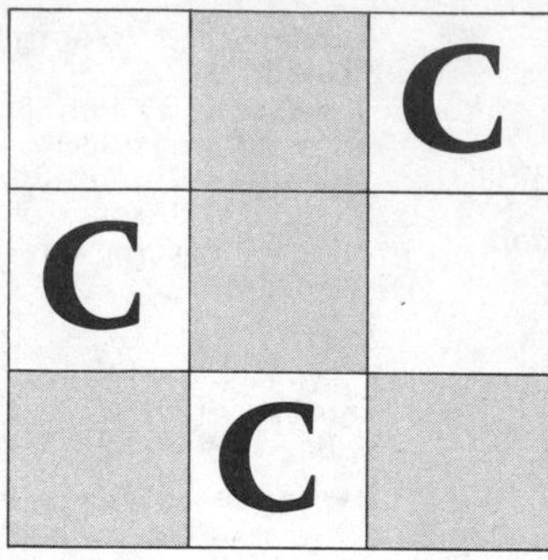

Caan, James
born: **9** New York NY
roles: **9** Funny Lady **10** Brian's Song, Rollerball **12** Brian Piccolo, The Godfather **13** Sonny Corleone **17** Cinderella Liberty

Caanthus
father: **7** Oceanus
sister: **5** Melia
killed by: **6** Apollo

cab **4** hack, taxi **7** taxi cab

Cab **15** Biblical measure

cabal **4** band, plan, plot, ring **5** junta **6** design, league, scheme **7** faction **8** intrigue **10** connivance, conspiracy **11** combination, machination

cabalistic **6** arcane, mystic, occult, secret **7** cryptic, obscure, strange **8** abstruse, esoteric, mystical **10** mysterious, unknowable **11** inscrutable **12** impenetrable, supernatural, unfathomable **16** incomprehensible

cabaret **4** cafe, club **6** bistro **9** nightclub **10** supper club
French: **5** boite **11** boite de nuit

Cabaret
director: **8** Bob Fosse
based on stories by: **20** Christopher Isherwood
cast: **8** Joel Grey **11** Fritz Wepper, Helmut Griem, Michael York **12** Liza Minnelli (Sally Bowles) **14** Marisa Berenson
Oscar for: **7** actress (Minnelli) **8** director **15** supporting actor (Grey)
song: **12** The Money Song

cabbage **16** Brassica oleracea (Capitata Group)
varieties: **3** Cow **4** Deer, Head, Wild **5** John's, Savoy, Skunk **6** Celery **7** Chinese **9** Flowering, Tronchuda **10** Portuguese **11** Yellow skunk **12** Western skunk

Cabecar
language family: **10** Talamancan
location: **9** Costa Rica **12** Sixaola River **14** Central America, Talamanca Plain
intermixed with: **6** Bribri

Cabell, James Branch
author of: **6** Jurgen **12** The High Place **14** Figures of Earth **17** The Cream of the Jest

cabin **3** hut **4** room **5** hutch, lodge, shack **6** shanty **7** cottage **8** bungalow, log cabin, quarters **9** stateroom **11** compartment

cabinet **3** box **4** case, file **5** chest **6** bureau **7** council **8** advisors, cupboard, ministry **10** breakfront, counselors, receptacle **11** china closet **13** advisory board **14** chest of drawers

cable **4** cord, line, rope, wire **5** chain, wires **6** hawser **7** mooring **8** wire line, wire rope **12** electric wire **16** overseas telegram

Cable, George W
author of: **8** Dr Sevier **13** Old Creole Days **15** The Grandissimes

cablegram **4** wire **5** cable **7** message **8** wireless **16** overseas telegram

Cabot, Ephraim
character in: **18** Desire Under the Elms
author: **6** O'Neill

Caca
origin: **5** Roman
goddess of: **6** hearth
corresponds to: **5** Vesta

Cacambo
character in: **7** Candide
author: **8** Voltaire

cache **4** heap **5** hoard, stock, store **8** hideaway **9** stockpile **11** hiding place, secret place

cachet **4** mark, seal **5** stamp, wafer **6** design, slogan **7** capsule

cackle **7** chatter **10** harsh laugh **11** shrill laugh
sound made by: **3** hen **4** chicken

cacophonous **5** harsh **6** off-key **7** grating, jarring, raucous **8** off-pitch, screechy, strident **9** dissonant, out of tune, unmusical **10** discordant **11** unmelodious **12** inharmonious, nonmelodious **13** disharmonious

cacophony **7** discord **9** harshness **10** disharmony, dissonance

cactus ***see box***

Cacus
form: **5** giant
father: **6** Vulcan
eats: **3** men
killed by: **8** Hercules

cad **3** cur, rat **4** heel, lout **5** churl, knave, louse, rogue **6** rascal, rotter **7** bounder, caitiff, dastard, villain **9** scoundrel

cadaver **4** body **5** stiff **6** corpse **7** remains **8** dead body, deceased

cadaverous **4** pale **5** ashen, gaunt **6** chalky, pallid **7** deathly, ghastly **8** blanched **9** bloodless, deathlike **10** corpselike

caddisfly
variety: **5** micro **8** northern **9** fingernet, primitive, snailcase **10** longhorned, trumpetnet, tubemaking **11** netspinning

Caddoan
tribe: **6** Pawnee **14** Chahiksichhiks

cactus
varieties: **3** Cob, Sun **4** Ball, Cane, Chin, Claw, Club, Comb, Crab, Hook, Lace, Leaf, Moon, Rose, Star, Toad, Vine, Yoke **5** Agave, Apple, Brain, Chain, Coral, Crown, Devil, False, Giant, Leafy, Melon, Paper, Plain, Prism, Snake, Spice, Torch **6** Barrel, Button, Cholla, Dagger, Dollar, Easter, Hatpin, Hot-dog, Myrtle, Nipple, Old-man, Orchid, Peanut, Pencil, Ribbon, Spider **7** Cushion, Eve's pin, Feather, Hatchet, Hat-rack, Jumping, Old-lady, Popcorn, Rainbow, Rattail, Redbird, Serpent, Thimble, Whisker **8** Cinnamon, Dumpling, Fishbone, Fishhook, Flapjack, Gold lace, Golf-ball, Hedgehog, Old-woman, Polka-dot, Pond-lily, Snowball, Snowdrop, Starfish, Tortoise, Turk's-cap **9** Bird's nest, Chain-link, Christmas, Cow-tongue, Electrode, Fire-crown, Hairbrush, Lamb's-tail, Mistletoe, New old-man, Organ-pipe, Porcupine, Red orchid, Sea-urchin, Spineless, Teddy-bear, Toothpick, Totem-pole, Turk's-head, White chin **10** Bluebarrel, Candelabra, Cotton-pole, Easter-lily, Golden ball, Golden-star, Living-rock, Powder-puff, Silver ball, Strawberry, Unguentine, White torch, Wickerware **11** Frilled lace, Grizzly-bear, Joseph's coat, Large barrel, Scarlet ball, Woolly torch **12** Dancing-bones, Golden barrel, Mule-crippler, Scarlet crown, Thanksgiving **13** Colombian ball, Creeping-devil, Dutchman's pipe, Peruvian apple, Peruvian torch, Silver cluster **15** Golden bird's nest **16** Mexican dwarf tree **17** Burbank's spineless **18** Fishhook pincushion

caddy **3** box, can, tin **5** chest **6** coffer

cadence **4** beat, lilt **5** meter, pulse, swing, tempo, throb **6** accent, rhythm **7** measure

Caderousse
character in: **21** The Count of Monte Cristo
author: **5** Dumas (pere)

cadet **5** plebe **7** recruit, student **11** youngest son **14** military student

cadge **3** beg, bum **5** mooch **6** hustle, peddle, sponge **7** solicit, scrounge **9** panhandle

cadmium
chemical symbol: **2** Cd

Cadmus
form: **6** prince
realm: **9** Phoenicia
father: **6** Agenor
mother: **10** Telephassa
brother: **5** Cilix **7** Phoenix
sister: **6** Europa
wife: **8** Harmonia
son: **8** Illyrius **9** Polydorus
daughter: **3** Ino **5** Agave **6** Semele **7** Autonoe
introduced to the Greeks: **7** writing
founded: **6** Thebes
planted: **12** dragons teeth

Caduceus
staff of: **7** Mercury

Caeneus
also: **6** Caenis
member of: **9** Argonauts
gift: **15** invulnerability
former identity: **6** Caenis

Caenis
also: **7** Caeneus
father: **6** Elatus
violated by: **8** Poseidon
changed into: **3** man
subsequent identity: **7** Caeneus

caesar, Caesar **5** ruler **6** despot, tyrant **7** emperor **8** autocrat, dictator

Caesar, Julius *see box*

Caesar, Sid
partner: **11** Imogene Coca
born: **9** Yonkers NY
roles: **15** Your Show of Shows

Caesar and Cleopatra
author: **17** George Bernard Shaw

Caesar or Nothing
author: **9** Pio Baroja

caesura **5** break, pause **6** hiatus **12** interruption

cafe **3** bar, inn **5** diner **6** bistro, eatery, nitery, tavern **7** automat, beanery, cabaret **9** cafeteria, chophouse, hash house, lunchroom, nightclub **10** restaurant, supper club **11** bar and grill, coffeehouse, discotheque **12** luncheonette
French: **9** estaminet

cafe au lait **10** light brown **14** coffee with milk

cafe noir **11** black coffee

cage **3** pen **4** coop **5** pen in **6** coop up, encage, lock up, shut in **7** confine, impound **8** imprison, restrain, restrict **9** enclosure

cagey **3** sly **4** foxy, keen, wary, wily **5** alert, chary, leery, sharp **6** artful, crafty, shifty, shrewd **7** careful, cunning, heedful, prudent **8** cautious, discreet, watchful

Cagliari
capital of: **8** Sardinia

Cagney, James
nickname: **5** Jimmy
born: **9** New York NY
roles: **7** Ragtime **14** The Public Enemy **17** Yankee Doodle Dandy (Oscar) **19** Man of a Thousand Faces

Cagney and Lacey
cast: **8** Tyne Daly **11** Sharon Gless

Cahita
tribe: **5** Yaqui

Cain
father: **4** Adam
mother: **3** Eve
brother: **4** Abel, Seth
home: **4** Eden
son: **5** Enoch
killed: **4** Abel
traveled to: **3** Nod

Caesar, Julius
adopted son: **8** Octavian **14** Caesar Augustus
author of: **13** On the Civil War **14** On the Gallic War
battle: **4** Zela **5** Munda **7** Durazzo, Thapsus **8** Mytilene **9** Pharsalus **11** Dyrrhachium
conquered: **4** Gaul
crossed: **7** Rubicon (river)
defeated: **6** Pompey
lover: **9** Cleopatra
member of: **16** First Triumvirate
murdered by: **5** Casca **6** Brutus **7** Cassius
murdered on: **11** Ides of March
other triumvirs: **6** Pompey **7** Crassus
saying: **9** Et tu Brute? (Even you Brutus?) **12** Veni vidi vici (I came I saw I conquered)
wife: **7** Pompeia **8** Cornelia **9** Calpurnia

Caine, Michael
real name: **24** Maurice Joseph Micklewhite
born: **6** London **7** England
roles: **4** Zulu **5** Alfie **6** Sleuth **9** Deathtrap **13** Educating Rita **14** The Ipcress File

Caine Mutiny, The
author: **10** Herman Wouk
director: **13** Edward Dmytryk
cast: **7** May Wynn **9** Lee Marvin **10** E G Marshall, Jose Ferrer, Van Johnson **13** Fred MacMurray, Robert Francis **14** Humphrey Bogart (Captain Queeg)

Caingua *see* **7** Guarani

Cairo
Arab camp: **8** al-Fustat
Arabic: **9** al-Qahirah
capital of: **5** Egypt
island: **5** Rodah **7** Zamalik
landmark:
mosque: **7** al-Azhar **11** Muhammed Ali
statue: **8** Ramses II
museum: **8** Egyptian
river: **4** Nile
Roman fortress: **7** Babylon
rulers: **5** Turks **7** British, Saladin **8** Fatimids **9** Mamelukes **11** Ismail Pasha, Muhammed Ali **12** Ottoman Turks
university: **7** Al-Azhar **8** Ain Shams, American

Cairo, Joel
character in: **16** The Maltese Falcon
author: **7** Hammett

caitiff **3** cad, cur, rat **4** heel **5** churl, knave, louse, rogue **6** rascal, rotter **7** bounder, dastard, villain **9** scoundrel **10** blackguard

cajole **4** coax **7** beguile, deceive, flatter, wheedle **8** blandish, inveigle, persuade

cajolery **7** blarney, coaxing, fawning **8** flattery, promises, soft soap **9** adulation, sweet talk, wheedling **10** enticement, inveigling, persuasion **11** beguilement **12** blandishment

cake **3** bar, bun, dry **4** lump, mass **5** block, crust, tort **6** cookie, eclair, gateau, harden, pastry, **7** congeal, cupcake, thicken **8** compress, solidify **9** coagulate, sweet roll **11** consolidate

Cakes and Ale
author: **16** W Somerset Maugham

cakewalk **5** cinch, dance **9** promenade **12** dance contest

calaboose **3** pen **4** jail, stir **6** prison **7** slammer **8** hoosegow

Calah
founder: **6** Nimrod

Calais
origin: **5** Greek
member of: **9** Argonauts
father: **6** Boreas
mother: **8** Orithyia
twin brother: **5** Zetes

calamitous **5** fatal **6** tragic, woeful **7** adverse, baleful, harmful, ruinous, unlucky **8** dreadful **9** blighting **10** disastrous, pernicious **11** cataclysmic, deleterious, destructive, detrimental, distressful, unfortunate **12** catastrophic

calamity **3** ill, woe **4** blow, ruin **5** trial **6** misery, mishap **7** bad luck, failure, ill wind, reverse, scourge, tragedy, trouble, undoing **8** disaster, distress, downfall, hardship **9** adversity, cataclysm, mischance **10** affliction, ill fortune, misfortune **11** catastrophe, tribulation **13** sea of troubles **15** stroke of ill luck

calando
music: **22** getting weaker and slower

Calchas
vocation: **10** soothsayer
father: **7** Thestor
burial place: **6** Notium

calcium
chemical symbol: **2** Ca

calculate **4** mean, plan **5** add up, aim at, count, judge, sum up **6** design, devise, figure, intend, reckon **7** compute, measure, predict, project, surmise, work out **8** estimate **9** ascertain, determine **10** conjecture

calculated **7** planned **10** deliberate, purposeful, thought out **11** intentional, prearranged **12** premeditated

calculating **3** sly **4** foxy, wily **6** artful, crafty, shrewd, tricky **7** cunning, devious **8** plotting, scheming **9** designing **10** contriving, intriguing **12** manipulative **13** Machiavellian

calculating machine
invented by: **7** Babbage

calculation **6** answer, result **8** figuring, judgment **9** reckoning **10** estimation **11** computation

calculator **6** abacus **7** counter, thinker **8** computer, reckoner

Calcutta
captured by: **5** Clive
founded by: **23** British East India Company
landmark: **10** Jain Temple **12** Howrah Bridge, Indian Museum **16** Botanical Gardens, Victoria Memorial **17** Zoological Gardens **18** Dakshineswar Temple
opposite city: **6** Howrah
river: **7** Hooghly
state: **10** West Bengal

Calder, Alexander
born: **14** Philadelphia PA
sculptures also called: **7** mobiles
artwork: **3** Man **5** Whale **6** Spiral **10** Teodelapio **12** Ticket Window **13** La Grande Voile **14** The Brass Family **23** Lobster Traps and Fish Tail

Calderon de la Barca, Pedro
author of: **12** Life Is a Dream

caldron, cauldron **3** pot **6** boiler, kettle

Caldwell, Erskine
author of: **10** Georgia Boy **11** Tobacco Road **14** God's Little Acre

Caldwell, Taylor
author of: **12** Answer as a Man **13** A Pillar of Iron **14** Great Lion of God **17** Testimony of Two Men, The Devil's Advocate **19** Bright Flows the River **20** Glory and the Lightning **22** The Captains and the Kings **24** Dear and Glorious Physician

Caleb
father: **8** Jepunneh
brother: **5** Kenaz
daughter: **6** Achash
nephew: **7** Othniel
descendant: **8** Calebite

Caleb Williams
author: **13** William Godwin

Caledonia *see* **8** Scotland

calendar **4** list **5** chart, diary, table **6** agenda, docket **7** day book, program **8** register, schedule

Caletor
origin: **5** Greek
mentioned in: **5** Iliad
cousin: **6** Hector
killed by: **14** Telamonian Ajax

calf **4** veal **5** dogie **6** weaner **7** leg part
young of: **3** cow **4** bull, seal **5** whale **8** elephant

Calgary
hockey team: **6** Flames

Calhern, Louis
real name: **13** Carl Henry Vogt
born: **10** Brooklyn NY
roles: **8** King Lear **12** Julius Caesar **15** Annie Get Your Gun **16** The Asphalt Jungle **20** The Magnificent Yankee

Calhoun, Rory
real name: **20** Francis Timothy Durgin
born: **12** Los Angeles CA
roles: **8** The Texan **21** Treasure of Pancho Villa **22** How to Marry a Millionaire, Requiem for a Heavyweight

Caliban
character in: **10** The Tempest
author: **11** Shakespeare

caliber **4** bore, rank **5** gifts, merit, place, power, scope, skill, worth **6** repute, talent **7** ability, quality, stature **8** capacity, diameter, eminence, position, prestige **10** capability, competence, estimation, excellence, importance, prominence, reputation **11** achievement, distinction

California ***see box***

Calinieff, Martin
real name of: **13** Michael Callan

Calinky State
nickname of: **13** South Carolina

calisay
type: **7** liqueur
origin: **5** Spain **9** Catalonia
flavor: **5** herbs **7** quinine

Calkins, Richard
creator/artist of: **10** Buck Rogers

call **3** ask, bid, cry, dub, tag **4** bawl, buzz, hail, name, need, plea, ring, roar, stop, term, yell **5** cause, claim, label, order, phone, rally, right, shout, style, title, visit **6** appeal, ask for, bellow, charge, clamor, cry out, decree, demand, direct, drop in, excuse, gather, halloo, holler, invite, invoke, know as, muster, notice, outcry, pray to, reason, scream, stop by, summon **7** collect, command, contact, convene, convoke, declare, entitle, entreat, grounds, refer to, request, require, specify, stop off, summons, warrant

California
abbreviation: **2** CA **3** Cal **5** Calif
nickname: **6** Golden **8** Eldorado **12** Promised Land
capital: **10** Sacramento
largest city: **10** Los Angeles
others: **4** Lodi **5** Azusa, Chico, Chino, Indio **6** Blythe, Carmel, Covina, Eureka, Fresno, Lompoc, Merced, Oxnard, Pomona, Sonoma, Tulare **7** Alameda, Anaheim, Burbank, Gardena, Needles, Oakland, Salinas, Vallejo, Visalia **8** Altadena, Berkeley, Palo Alto, Pasadena, Redlands, San Diego, Stockton **9** Cucamonga, Long Beach **11** Palm Springs, Santa Monica **12** Beverly Hills, San Francisco, Santa Barbara
college: **3** USC **4** UCLA **5** Mills **6** Pitzer, Pomona **7** Caltech, Chapman, Scripps **8** Stanford, Whittier **10** Occidental, Pepperdine
explorer: **6** Cortez
feature:
amusement park: **10** Disneyland **15** Knotts Berry Farm
area: **9** Hollywood **15** Fishermans Wharf
dam: **6** Hoover, Shasta **7** Boulder
island prison: **8** Alcatraz
mill: **7** Sutters
national park: **7** Redwood, Sequoia **8** Yosemite **11** Kings Canyon **14** Channel Islands, Lassen Volcanic
parade: **4** Rose
prison: **6** Folsom **10** San Quentin
tribe: **4** Hupa, Pomo, Yana, Yuki **5** Karok, Maidu, Miwok, Wappo, Wiyot, Yurok **6** Patwin, Shasta, Tolowa, Yokuts **7** Chumash, Luiseno, Salinan, Serrano **8** Diegueno
people: **6** Sutter **10** Earl Warren **11** Robert Frost **13** George S Patton, John Steinbeck **14** William Saroyan
island: **4** Goat, Mare **7** Anacapo, Channel **8** Alcatraz, Catalina, Coronado **9** Farallone
lake: **4** Mono, Soda **5** Clear, Eagle, Owens, Tahoe **6** Salton, Tulare **7** Almanor **8** Elsinore **9** Berryessa
land rank: **5** third
mountain: **4** Muir **5** Coast **6** Lassen, Shasta, Wilson **7** Cascade, Klamath, Palomar, Whitney **10** Peninsular, Transverse **12** Sierra Nevada
highest point: **7** Whitney
physical feature:
bay: **8** Monterey, San Diego **12** San Francisco
cape: **9** Mendocino
desert: **6** Mohave, Mojave **8** Colorado
fault: **10** San Andreas
glacier: **8** Palisade
sea: **6** Cortez **7** Pacific
tree: **7** redwood
valley: **5** Death
volcano: **6** Lassen
wind: **7** Collada **8** Santa Ana
president: **13** Richard M Nixon, Ronald W Reagan
river: **3** Eel, Mad, Pit **4** Kern **5** Kings, Owens, Putah, Smith, Stony **6** Little, Merced, Salmon **7** Feather, Klamath, Rubicon, Russian, Salinas, Trinity, Truckee **10** Sacramento, San Jacinto, San Joaquin, Stanislaus
state admission: **11** thirty-first
state bird: **21** California Valley quail
state fish: **21** California golden trout
state flower: **11** golden poppy
state motto: **6** Eureka (I have found it)
state song: **18** I Love You California
state symbol: **11** grizzly bear
state tree: **17** California redwood
baseball team: **6** Angels, Padres **7** Dodgers
basketball team: **6** Lakers **8** Clippers **19** Golden State Warriors
football team: **4** Rams **7** Raiders **8** Chargers **11** Forty-Niners

8 announce, appeal to, assemble, christen, entreaty, identify, instruct, look in on, occasion, petition, proclaim **9** crying out, designate, direction, pay a visit, telephone **10** describe as, invitation, supplicate **11** declaration, instruction **12** announcement, call together, characterize, proclamation, supplication **13** justification

Callan, Michael
real name: 15 Martin Calinieff
born: 14 Philadelphia PA
roles: 9 Cat Ballou **10** The Interns **18** Gidget Goes Hawaiian, The Flying Fontaines **23** The Magnificent Seven Ride

call for 4 need **6** demand, pick up **7** request, require

call forth 4 spur **5** evoke, raise **6** arouse, awaken, excite, incite, invoke, kindle, stir up **7** command, conjure, provoke **8** summon up **9** make aware, stimulate **10** make appear

Callidice
form: 5 queen
realm: 10 Thesprotia
husband: 8 Odysseus
son: 10 Polypoetes

calling 3 job **4** line, work **5** craft, field, forte, trade **6** career, crying, living, metier, outcry **7** hailing, mission, passion, yelling **8** activity, business, devotion, function, province, shouting, vocation **9** bellowing, crying out, first love, hallooing, life's work, screaming, specialty **10** assignment, attachment, dedication, employment, enthusiasm, livelihood, occupation, profession, walk of life **14** bread and butter, means of support, specialization

calling off 6 ending **7** halting **8** giving up **11** termination **12** backing out of, cancellation

calling oneself thus
French: 9 soi-disant

Calliope
member of: 5 Muses
presided over: 10 epic poetry
father: 4 Zeus
mother: 9 Mnemosyne
son: 7 Orpheus

Callipolis
father: 9 Alcathous

Callirrhoe, Callirhoe
father: 6 Oeneus **8** Achelous
husband: 4 Tros **8** Alcmaeon
son: 4 Ilus **8** Ganymede **10** Amphoterus

ended plague in: 7 Calydon
death by: 9 sacrifice

Calliste
epithet of: 7 Artemis
means: 7 fairest

Callisto
form: 5 nymph
attended: 7 Artemis
loved: 4 Zeus
changed into: 4 bear
killed by: 7 Artemis

call off 3 end **4** halt **5** abort **6** cancel, give up **8** postpone **9** back out of, terminate **10** summon away **12** dispense with

Call of the Wild, The
author: 10 Jack London
dog: 4 Buck
master: 12 John Thornton

callous 4 cold, hard **5** cruel, horny, tough **6** inured **8** hardened, uncaring **9** apathetic, heartless, unfeeling **11** hardhearted, indifferent, insensitive **12** thick-skinned, unresponsive **13** dispassionate, unsympathetic **14** pachydermatous

call out 3 cry **4** bawl, hail, yell **5** shout **6** bellow, cry out, holler, summon **9** challenge

callow 3 raw **5** crude, green, naive **7** artless, awkward, puerile, shallow, untried **8** childish, ignorant, immature, juvenile **9** infantile **10** sophomoric, uninformed, unschooled, unseasoned **11** uninitiated **13** inexperienced **15** unsophisticated

call to 4 hail **5** greet **6** accost, salute **7** address, shout at

call to account 5 chide, scold **6** accuse, charge, rebuke **7** arraign, bawl out, censure, chasten, reprove, upbraid **8** admonish, denounce, reproach **9** criticize, dress down, reprimand **10** take to task **11** remonstrate

call to arms 6 war cry **9** battle cry **11** rallying cry

call to order 4 open **6** muster **7** convene, convoke

call upon 3 ask, bid **4** urge **5** visit **6** charge, enjoin, exhort, invite, invoke **7** beseech, entreat, request, require **8** appeal to, petition, summon up **9** encourage **11** acknowledge

callused 4 hard **5** horny, tough **8** hardened **12** thick-skinned **14** pachydermatous

calm 4 cool, ease, mild **5** allay, balmy, bland, quell, quiet, still **6** becalm, gentle, lessen, pacify, placid, reduce, repose, sedate, serene, smooth, soothe, subdue **7** assuage, collect, compose, cool off, halcyon, mollify, pacific, placate, relaxed, relieve **8** composed, coolness, diminish, mitigate, moderate, peaceful, serenity, tranquil, unshaken **9** alleviate, collected, composure, impassive, placidity, quietness, stillness, unexcited, unruffled **10** cool-headed, motionless, simmer down, smoothness, unagitated, untroubled **11** impassivity, passionless, restfulness, self-control, tranquility, tranquilize, undisturbed, unflappable, unperturbed **12** peacefulness, tranquillity, windlessness **13** imperturbable, self-possessed, stormlessness **14** self-possession **16** imperturbability

calmness 5 poise **6** aplomb **8** coolness, serenity **9** composure, placidity, sangfroid, stillness **10** equanimity, steadiness **11** self-control, tranquility **12** peacefulness, tranquillity **14** presence of mind, self-possession **16** imperturbability

Calpurnia
character in: 12 Julius Caesar
author: 11 Shakespeare

calumnious 8 libelous **9** maligning, vilifying **10** defamatory, derogatory, slanderous **11** disparaging

calumny 4 barb, slur **5** libel, smear **6** malice **7** slander **8** innuendo **9** aspersion **10** backbiting, defamation, derogation, revilement **11** denigration, deprecation, insinuation **12** backstabbing, calumniation, depreciation, vilification **13** animadversion, disparagement, malicious lies

calvados
type: 6 brandy
origin: 6 France **8** Normandy
flavor: 5 apple
aged in: 3 oak

Calvary 8 Golgotha
means: 10 skull place

Calyce
father: 6 Aeolus
mother: 7 Enarete
son: 8 Endymion

Calydonian boar
sent by: 5 Diana
killed by: 8 Meleager

Calydonian hunt
pursuit of: 4 boar

Calypso
form: 5 nymph

home: **6** Ogygia
father: **10** Titan Atlas
detained: **8** Odysseus
for: **10** seven years

calyx **4** husk **5** sepal

cam **3** cog **4** disk **8** cylinder **10** projection
located on: **5** shaft, wheel
motion: **7** rocking **8** circular **12** back and forth

Cambodia
other name: **7** Camboja **8** Cambodge **9** Kampuchea
capital/largest city: **8** Pnom-Penh
others: **3** Som **4** Ream **5** Takeo **6** Kampot, Kratie, Pursat **7** Kohnieh, Kompong, Kracheh, Rovieng, Samrong **8** Siem Reap, Sisophon **10** Battambang, Stung Treng **11** Kompong Cham **12** Krungkoh Kong **13** Sihanoukville
head of state: **8** Chairman
monetary unit: **3** sen **4** quan, riel **6** puttan **7** piaster
weight: **4** mace, tael
island: **4** Kong, Rong
lake: **8** Tonle Sap
mountain: **3** Pan **7** Dangrek, Dong Rek **8** Cardamom, Elephant
highest point: **10** Phnom Aoral, Phnom Aural
river: **3** San, Sen **5** Sreng **6** Bassac, Chinit, Mekong, Porong, Pursat, Srepok **7** Kamlong, Sekhong **8** Tonle Sap
physical feature:
bay: **10** Kompongsom
cape: **5** Samit
gulf: **4** Siam **8** Thailand
people: **4** Cham, Thai **5** Khmer **7** Chinese **10** Vietnamese
leader: **6** Pol Pot **12** Khieu Samphan
language: **5** Khmer **6** French **9** Cambodian **10** Vietnamese
religion: **7** animism **8** Buddhism **12** Christianity
places:
ruins/temple: **6** Angkor **9** Angkor Wat
feature:
Communist group: **10** Khmer Rouge

camaraderie **7** jollity **8** bonhomie, good will **10** affability, clubbiness, fellowship, friendship **11** brotherhood, comradeship, sociability **12** congeniality, conviviality, friendliness **13** companionship, esprit de corps **14** good-fellowship

Camarasaurus
type: **8** dinosaur, sauropod
location: **12** United States
period: **8** Jurassic

Cambodia ***see box***

Cambria *see* **5** Wales

cambric **5** cloth, linen **6** cotton, fabric **8** material

camel
called: **13** beast of burden **15** ship of the desert
chews: **3** cud
group: **4** herd
habitat: **4** Asia **6** Africa, desert
kind: **7** Arabian **8** Bactrian **9** dromedary
number of humps: **3** one, two
species: **6** mammal
type of: **8** ruminant
young: **4** calf

camellia
varieties: **5** Silky **6** Common **8** Mountain, Sasanqua

Camenae
means: **11** foretellers
form: **6** nymphs **7** deities
gift: **8** prophecy
names: **6** Egeria **8** Carmenta **9** Antevorta, Postvorta
habitat: **8** fountain
correspond to: **5** Muses

camera
invented by:
Kodak: **6** Walker **7** Eastman
Polaroid: **4** Land
photography: **6** Niepce, Talbot **8** Daguerre
film, celluloid: **6** Edison **11** Reichenbach
film, transparent: **7** Eastman, Goodwin
color photo: **4** Ives

Cameroon ***see box***

Camilla
form: **5** woman
occupation: **7** warrior
father: **7** Metabus
mother: **7** Casmila
fought with: **6** Turnus
fought against: **6** Aeneas

Camille
also: **17** La Dame aux camelias
author: **14** Alexander Dumas (fils)
character: **6** Nanine **11** Armand Duval **17** Marguerite Gautier (Camille)
director: **11** George Cukor
cast: **10** Greta Garbo (Camille) **12** Henry Daniell, Robert Taylor (Armand) **14** Elizabeth Allan, Laura Hope Crews **15** Lionel Barrymore

Cameroon
capital: **7** Yaounde
largest city: **6** Douala
others: **3** Wum **4** Bali, Buea, Edea, Tiko **5** Kumba, Lomie, Mamfe **6** Garona, Maroua **7** Batouri, Dschang, Ebolowa, Foumban **8** Victoria **10** N'Gaoundere, N'Kongsamba
monetary unit: **5** franc **7** centime
island: **5** Nanny **8** Fernando
lake: **4** Chad
mountain: **5** Mbabo **7** Bambuto, Kapsiki, Mandara **8** Batandji **9** Atlantika
highest point: **8** Cameroon
river: **3** Dja, Lom **4** Faro, Mbam, Vina **5** Benue, Campo, Cross, Kadei, Mbere, Nyong, N'Goko, Sanga, Shari **6** Djerem, Ivindo, Logone, Sanaga
sea: **8** Atlantic
physical feature:
cape: **10** Debundscha
gulf: **6** Guinea
plateau: **7** Adamawa **8** Mambilla
people: **3** Abo, Edo, Ibo **4** Beti, Bulu, Ekoi, Ijaw, Sara **5** Bantu, Bassa, Kirdi, Pygmy, Tikar **6** Bamoun, Donala, Ewondo, Fulani, Ibibio **7** Bakweri **8** Bamileke
Fulani chief: **7** Lamidos
language: **4** Bulu **5** Bantu, Bassa, Hausa **6** Douala, Ewondo, French, Fulani **7** English **8** Bamileke, Fulfulde
religion: **5** Islam **7** animism **12** Christianity
places:
home of prime minister: **7** Schloss

Camillo
character in: **14** The Winter's Tale
author: **11** Shakespeare

Camirus
origin: **5** Greek
grandfather: **6** Helios, Helius

camisole **3** top **4** slip **6** jacket **10** underwaist

camouflage **4** hide, mask, veil **5** blind, cloak, cover, front **6** screen, shroud **7** conceal, cover up **8** disguise **10** masquerade, subterfuge **11** concealment

camouflaged **6** hidden, masked **7** cloaked **8** shrouded **9** concealed, disguised

camp **4** tent **5** tents **7** bivouac, lodging, rough it **8** army base, barracks, quarters **10** pitch a tent

campaign **3** run **4** push **5** drive, stump **6** action, effort **7** crusade **8** endeavor, move-

Canada
capital: **6** Ottawa
largest city: **8** Montreal
others: **4** Hull **5** Banff, Laval **6** Dawson, Guelph, London, Oshawa, Quebec, Regina, Sarnia, Val d'or **7** Calgary, Halifax, Moncton, Nanaimo, Sudbury, Toronto, Welland, Windsor **8** Edmonton, Hamilton, Kingston, Moose Jaw, Victoria, Winnipeg **9** Saskatoon, Vancouver **10** Port Arthur, Sherbrooke **11** Fredericton **12** Niagara Falls, Peterborough, Prince Albert, Prince George **13** Charlottetown **21** St Catherines Stratford
school: **3** UBC **5** Laval, Simon **6** Fraser, McGill, Queens **7** Toronto **8** McMaster, Montreal **9** Concordia, Dalhousie
division: **5** Yukon **6** Quebec **7** Alberta, Ontario **8** Manitoba **10** Nova Scotia **12** Newfoundland, New Brunswick, Saskatchewan **15** British Columbia **18** Northwest Territory, Prince Edward Island
head of state: **14** British monarch **15** governor general
measure: **3** ton **5** minot, perch, point **6** arpent **7** chainon
island: **4** Read **5** Banks, Bylot, Coats, Devon, Grand, Manan, Parry, Sable **6** Baffin, Breton, Mansel, Middle **7** Belcher **8** Bathurst, Magdalen, Victoria **9** Anticosti, Ellesmere, Vancouver **10** Campobello, Manitoulin **11** Southampton **14** Queen Charlotte
lake: **4** Cree, Erie, Gras, Seul **5** Garry, Huron, Rainy **6** Louise, St John **7** Abitibi, Dubawnt, Nipigon, Ontario, Testlin **8** Kootenay, Manitoba, Okanagan, Reindeer, Superior, Winnipeg **9** Athabaska, Great Bear, Nipissing **10** Great Slave, Mistassini **13** Winnepeogosis
mountain: **5** Coast, Royal **6** Robson, Skeena **7** Cariboo, Cascade, Purcell, Rockies, Selkirk, St Elias **8** Columbia, Hazelton, Monashee **9** Mackenzie, Notre Dame, Tremblant **10** Laurentian, Richardson, Shickshock **14** Jacques Cartier
highest point: **5** Logan
river: **3** Hay, Red **4** Peel **5** Liard, Peace, Slave, Yukon **6** Albany, Fraser, Nelson, Nicola, Ottawa, Skeena, St John, Thames, Thelon **7** St Marys **8** Columbia, Gatineau, Kootenay, Petawawa, Saguenay **9** Athabasca, Athapaska, Churchill, Mackenzie, Richelieu **10** Coppermine, St Lawrence **11** Assiniboine, **12** Saskatchewan
sea: **6** Arctic **7** Pacific **8** Atlantic, Labrador
physical features:
bay: **5** Basin, Fundy, Hecla, James, Minas **6** Baffin, Griper, Hudson, Ungava **8** Georgian
canal: **3** Soo **7** Welland **10** Wellington
cape: **5** Canso
falls: **7** Niagara **9** Horseshoe
gulf: **10** St Lawrence
pass: **8** Chilkoot
peninsula: **5** Gaspe **7** Botthia **8** Labrador, Melville
plain: **11** Barren lands
port: **6** Quebec **7** St Johns **8** Hamilton, Victoria **9** Churchill
strait: **5** Cabot, Davis, Dease **6** Hecate, Hudson **7** Georgia **9** Belle Isle **10** Juan de Fuca
people: **6** Canuck, Eskimo, French, Innuit **7** English
explorer: **5** Cabot **6** Fraser, Joliet **7** Cartier, LaSalle, Selkirk **8** Thompson **9** Champlain, MacKenzie, Marquette
leader: **4** King, Riel **5** Clark **6** Borden **7** Laurier, Trudeau **9** Macdonald, St Laurent **11** Diefenbaker
language: **6** Eskimo, French **7** English
religion: **8** Anglican **13** Roman Catholic **20** United Church of Canada
places:
battlefield: **15** Plains of Abraham
national park: **4** Yoho **5** Banff, Lakes **6** Acadia, Jasper **7** Glacier **8** Kootenay, Waterton **9** Elk Island **10** Laurentian, Revelstoke **11** Wood Buffalo **12** Prince Albert
resort: **5** Banff **10** Lake Louise
feature:
airport: **6** Gander
emblem: **9** maple leaf
fish: **5** charr, trout
flower: **10** Juneflower
police: **8** Mounties **12** Royal Mounted
food:
soup: **7** rubaboo

ment **9** offensive, operation **11** electioneer, whistle-stop **12** battle series, beat the drums, solicit votes

campanile **6** belfry **9** bell tower

campari
type: **7** bitters **8** aperitif
origin: **5** Italy

Campe
form: **8** old woman
occupation: **6** jailer
place: **8** Tartarus

campground **7** bivouac **8** tent city **16** temporary shelter

Campin, Robert
born: **8** Flanders
also known as/identified with: **14** Master of Merode **16** Master of Flemalle
artwork: **10** St Veronica, The Trinity **13** The Entombment **16** Merode Altarpiece (Merode Triptych) **17** The Virgin and Child **18** The Thief on the Cross

Camptosaurus
type: **8** dinosaur **10** ornithopod
location: **12** North America
period: **8** Jurassic
characteristic: **10** duck-billed

Camus, Albert
author of: **4** L'ete **6** Summer **7** The Fall **8** Caligula, The Rebel **9** The Plague **11** A Happy Death, The Stranger **12** Cross Purpose **17** The Myth of Sisyphus

can **3** tin **4** buns, fire, rump, seat **5** fanny, put up **6** bottom **8** backside, buttocks, preserve **9** container, fundament, give the ax

Canaan
father: **3** Ham
brother: **4** Cush
grandfather: **4** Noah
known as: **12** promised land
see also **6** Israel

Canace
father: **6** Aeolus
brother: **8** Macareus
death by: **7** suicide

Canada ***see box***

canaille **6** proles, rabble **8** riffraff **9** commoners, hoi polloi **11** proletariat **13** great unwashed

canal **4** duct, tube **7** channel, conduit, passage **8** aqueduct

Canaletto
real name: **20** Giovanni Antonio Canal
born: **5** Italy **6** Venice
artwork: **18** The Stonemason's Yard

canard **4** hoax **5** rumor **7** slander **9** falsehood **12** exaggeration

Canary Islands
other name: **14** Fortunate Isles **15** Isles of the Blest
named for: **3** dog **5** canis **6** canine
capital: **9** Las Palmas **19** Santa Cruz de Tenerife
largest city: **9** Las Palmas
others: **4** Icod **6** Laguna **7** Orotava **8** Arrecife, Valverde **12** San Sebastian
government: **16** overseas province
of: **5** Spain
measure: **8** fanegada
monetary unit: **6** peseta
island: **4** Roca **5** Clara, Ferro, Lobos, Rocca **6** Gomera, Hierro **7** Inferno, La Palma **8** Graciosa, Tenerife **9** Lanzarote **10** Lanzarotte **11** Gran Canaria **13** Fuerteventura
mountain: **6** La Cruz **8** El Cumbre, Tenerife
highest point: **5** Teide, Teyde
sea: **8** Atlantic
people: **7** Spanish
language: **7** Spanish
religion: **13** Roman Catholic

canasta
number of players: **4** four
cards/hand: **6** eleven
meld: **12** three of a kind
wild card: **5** deuce, joker

Canberra
capital of: **9** Australia
territory: **13** New South Wales **26** Australian Capital Territory
lake: **13** Burley Griffin

cancel **4** void **5** annul, erase, quash **6** delete, offset, recall, recant, repeal, revoke **7** abolish, call off, nullify, rescind, retract, vitiate **8** abrogate, call back, set aside **9** repudiate **10** balance out, blue-pencil, do away with, invalidate, neutralize **11** countermand **12** dispense with **13** compensate for **14** counterbalance **18** declare null and void

cancellation **6** repeal **9** abolition **10** abrogation, effacement, rescinding, revocation **11** abolishment, eradication, repudiation, termination

cancer **3** rot **6** plague **7** sarcoma, scourge **8** neoplasm, sickness **9** carcinoma **10** malignancy **14** malignant tumor **15** malignant growth

Cancer
symbol: **4** crab
planet: **4** Moon
rules: **4** home **6** family
born: **4** July, June

Cancer Ward, The
author: **21** Aleksandr Solzhenitsyn

candelabrum **7** menorah **8** dikerion **9** girandole, trikerion **11** candlestick **12** candleholder

Candia *see* **5** Crete

candid **4** fair, free, just, open **5** blunt, frank, plain **6** direct, honest **7** genuine, natural, relaxed, sincere, unposed **8** informal, outright, truthful **9** downright, impromptu, outspoken **10** forthright **11** plain spoken, spontaneous, unvarnished **14** extemporaneous **15** straightforward

Candida
author: **17** George Bernard Shaw

candidate **7** hopeful, nominee **8** aspirant, eligible **9** applicant, contender, job seeker **10** competitor, contestant **11** possibility **12** office seeker

Candid Camera
host: **9** Allen Funt
co-host: **11** Bess Myerson **12** Durward Kirby **13** Arthur Godfrey

Candide
author: **8** Voltaire
character: **6** Martin **7** Cacambo **8** Pangloss **9** Cunegonde **11** Admiral Byng **17** Thunder-ten-Tronckh

candidness **6** candor **7** honesty, openess **9** frankness, sincerity **10** directness **12** truthfulness **13** guilelessness

candle **3** dip, wax **5** light, taper **6** bougie, cierge, tallow **9** rush light

candleholder, candlestick **6** sconce **7** menorah **8** dikerion **9** girandole, trikerion **10** chandelier **11** candelabrum

candor **7** honesty **8** fairness, justness, openness **9** bluntness, frankness, sincerity **10** directness **11** artlessness **12** impartiality, truthfulness **14** forthrightness **15** plainspokenness **19** straightforwardness

candy **3** bar **4** kiss **5** cream, fudge, jelly, sweet, taffy **6** bonbon, comfit, dainty, nougat, sweets, toffee **7** brittle, caramel, fondant, gumdrop, praline **8** lollipop **9** chocolate, jellybean, sweetmeat **10** confection **12** all-day sucker **13** confectionery, peanut brittle

cane **3** hit, rap, rod, tan **4** beat, drub, flog, lash, whip **5** baste, flail, smite, staff, stick, whack **6** strike, switch, thrash, wallop **7** trounce **12** walking stick

cane **11** Arundinaria
varieties: **4** Dumb, Wild **5** Arrow, Sugar **6** Rattan, Switch, Tobago, Tonkin **7** Tsingli **8** Southern **11** Spotted dumb **12** Chinese sweet **14** Yellow-leaf dumb

Canea
capital of: **5** Crete

Canens
father: **5** Janus
mother: **7** Venilia
betrothed to: **5** Picus
cried over: **5** Picus
death by: **6** crying

Canephora
form: **7** maidens
carried: **7** baskets

Canetti, Elias
author of: **8** Auto da Fe **12** Tower of Babel **14** Crowds and Power **15** The Torch in My Ear **16** Kafka's Other Trial, The Tongue Set Free

Caniff, Milton
creator/artist of: **10** Dickie Dare **11** Steve Canyon **14** The Gay Thirties **18** Terry and the Pirates

canine **3** cur, dog, fox, pup **4** mutt, wolf **5** hound, hyena, puppy **6** coyote, cuspid, jackal **7** mongrel **8** eyetooth

canker **4** sore **5** ulcer **6** blight, cancer, lesion **9** mouth sore **12** inflammation

Cannibal Galaxy, The
author: **12** Cynthia Ozick

cannon **3** bit, gun **4** bone **5** carom **6** mortar **7** battery **8** field gun, howitzer, ordnance **9** artillery **10** field piece, mounted gun, pickpocket

Cannon
character: **11** Frank Cannon
cast: **13** William Conrad

Cannon, Dyan
real name: **19** Samille Diane Friesen
husband: **9** Cary Grant
born: **8** Tacoma WA
roles: **6** Shamus **9** Deathtrap **13** Heaven Can Wait **15** Such Good Friends **19** Bob & Carol & Ted & Alice **23** Revenge of the Pink Panther

cannonade **5** burst, salvo **6** volley **7** barrage, battery **8** shelling **9** fusillade **11** bombardment

canny **4** foxy, wary, wily, wise **5** cagey, sharp **6** artful, astute, clever, crafty, shrewd, subtle **7** careful, cunning, knowing **8** skillful **9** judicious, sagacious **10** convincing **11** circumspect, intelligent **13** perspicacious

Cano, Alonso
born: **5** Spain **7** Granada
artwork: **16** Granada Cathedral (facade) **18** Madonna of the Rosary **20** Immaculate Conception **23** The Seven Joys of the Virgin

canoe **4** boat **5** bungo, kayak **6** dugout **7** pirogue

canoeing
athlete: **11** Marcia Smoke

canon **3** law **4** code, rule **5** dogma, edict, model, order **6** decree **7** pattern, precept, statute **8** doctrine, standard **9** bench mark, criterion, ordinance, principle, yardstick **10** regulation, touchstone

canonical **6** proper **8** accepted, approved, official orthodox **9** authentic, customary **10** authorized, legitimate, recognized, sanctioned **12** conventional **13** authoritative

Canonization, The
author: **9** John Donne

canopy **4** hood **5** cover **6** awning, tester **8** covering

Canova, Antonio
born: **5** Italy **8** Possagno
artwork: **7** Perseus **12** Venus Victrix (Pauline Bonaparte Borghese) **14** Cupid and Psyche **16** Letizia Bonaparte **17** Daedalus and Icarus

Cansino, Margarita Carmen
real name of: **12** Rita Hayworth

cant **4** sham, talk **5** argot, lingo, slang **6** humbug, jargon **8** parlance, pretense **9** hypocrisy **10** lip service, vernacular **11** insincerity **15** pretentiousness **17** sanctimoniousness

cantabile
music: **7** flowing, singing **8** songlike

cantaloupe **5** fruit, melon **9** muskmelon

cantankerous **4** mean **5** cross, huffy, short, sulky, surly, testy **6** cranky, crusty, grumpy, morose, sullen, touchy **7** bearish, crabbed, fretful, grouchy, peevish, waspish **8** choleric, churlish, contrary, snappish **9** irascible, irritable, splenetic **10** ill-humored, ill-natured **11** contentious, ill-tempered, quarrelsome **12** disagreeable **13** argumentative

cantatrice **6** singer **9** chanteuse **10** songstress **18** professional singer

canteen **2** PX **4** club **5** flask **6** bottle **10** commissary **11** pocket flask **12** post exchange

canter **4** gait, lope, trot **6** gallop, singer, whiner

Canterbury Tales, The
author: **15** Geoffrey Chaucer
starting point: **9** Southwark, Tabard Inn
goal:
tomb of: **6** Becket
character/tale: **3** Nun **4** Cook, Dyer, Monk **5** Canon, Friar, Reeve, Webbe **6** Knight, Miller, Parson, Squire, Yeoman **7** Shipman, Tapicer **8** Franklin, Manciple, Merchant, Pardoner, Prioress, Summoner **9** Carpenter, Ploughman **10** Wife of Bath **11** Haberdasher **13** Clerk of Oxford, Sergeant of Law **14** Doctor of Physic

Canthus
member of: **9** Argonauts

Cantor, Eddie
real name: **21** B Edward Israel Iskowitz
nickname: **9** Banjo Eyes
wife: **9** Ida Tobias
born: **9** New York NY
roles: **7** Whoopee **8** Kid Boots **9** Banjo Eyes

cantor of a synagogue
Hebrew: **5** hazan

Cantos
author: **9** Ezra Pound

can't stand **4** hate **5** abhor **6** detest, eschew, loathe **7** despise **8** execrate **9** abominate, can't abide **11** can't stomach **14** hate the sight of

can't stomach **4** hate **5** abhor **6** detest, loathe **7** despise **8** execrate **9** abominate, can't abide, can't stand

10 shrink from 13 find repulsive

canvas 4 duck 7 painting 8 painting 9 sailcloth, tarpaulin, tent cloth

canvass 4 poll, scan, sift 5 study, tally 6 survey 7 analyze, discuss, examine, explore, inquiry, inquire, inspect, solicit 8 analysis, campaign, scrutiny 10 evaluation, scrutinize 11 enumeration, exploration, inquire into, investigate, take stock of 13 give thought to, investigation

canyon 3 col, cut, gap 4 draw, pass, wadi, wash 5 break, chasm, cleft, crack, gorge, gulch, gully, notch 6 arroyo, coulee, defile, divide, ravine, valley 7 fissure, opening 8 corridor, crevasse, water gap

cap 3 lid, top 4 seal 5 cover, outdo 6 better, exceed, top off 7 surpass 8 headgear, outstrip 9 headdress 10 visored hat

capability 3 art 4 gift 5 flair, knack, power, skill 6 talent 7 ability, faculty, know-how 8 capacity, efficacy, facility 9 potential 10 attainment, competence, competency 11 proficiency 12 potentiality 13 qualification

capable 3 apt 4 able, deft 5 adept 6 adroit, artful, clever, expert, gifted 7 skilled 8 masterly, skillful, talented 9 competent, effective, ingenious 10 proficient 11 efficacious, intelligent 12 accomplished

capable of assuming legal responsibility
Latin: 8 sui juris

Capable of Honor
author: 10 Allan Drury

capable of managing one's own affairs
Latin: 8 sui juris

capacious 3 big 4 huge, vast, wide 5 ample, broad, large, roomy 7 mammoth, massive 8 gigantic, spacious 9 expansive, extensive 10 commodious, expandable, tremendous, voluminous 13 amplitudinous

capaciousness 9 amplitude, roominess 12 spaciousness 14 commodiousness

capacitate 5 allow 6 enable, permit 7 empower, qualify 8 make able

capacity 4 mind, role, room, size 5 gifts, limit, might, power, range, scope, space 6 extent, talent, volume 7 ability, faculty 8 aptitude, facility, function, judgment, position, sagacity, strength 9 amplitude, endowment, intellect, potential 10 brain power, capability 11 discernment 12 intelligence, perspicacity 15 maximum contents

Capaneus
member of: 18 Seven against Thebes
father: 9 Hipponous
mother: 8 Astynome
wife: 6 Evadne
son: 9 Sthenelus
crime: 9 blasphemy
destroyed by: 4 Zeus

caparison 5 adorn, equip 6 bedeck 9 equipment, trappings

cape 4 spit 5 cloak, manta, point, shawl 6 mantle, poncho, serape, tabard, tongue 7 pelisse 8 headland 9 peninsula 10 promontory

Capek, Karel
author of: 3 R U R 8 Hordubal, Krakatit 9 The Mother 13 Power and Glory 18 The War with the Newts

caper 3 hop 4 jape, jump, lark, leap, romp, skip 5 antic, bound, fling, frisk, prank, spree, stunt, trick 6 bounce, cavort, frolic, gambol, prance 7 caprice 8 escapade 9 adventure, high jinks 10 carrying on 11 shenanigans 14 monkey business

Cape Verde *see box*

capital 4 cash, fine 5 great, money, super 6 center, riches, superb, wealth 7 supreme 9 excellent, financing, first-rate, majuscule, matchless, principal, resources 10 cash on hand, first-class 11 large letter, wherewithal 12 headquarters 13 working assets 14 available means 15 investment funds, upper-case letter

capital city (of countries) *see box, p. 154*

capital city (of states) *see* 13 state capitals

capitalism 14 free enterprise

capitalist 5 mogul 6 tycoon 8 investor 9 financier, plutocrat 14 businessperson

capitalize 4 back, fund 5 stake 7 exploit, finance, support, trade on, utilize 8 bankroll, cash in on, profit by 9 subsidize 11 foot the bill 13 make the most of 17 turn an honest penny 23 strike while the iron is hot 24 make hay while the sun shines

Cape Verde
capital: 5 Praia
largest city: 7 Mindelo
others: 6 Sal Rei 7 Espargo 8 Assomada, Palmeira, Tarrafal 9 Pedra Lume, Sao Filipe 10 Nova Sintra, Santa Maria 11 Porto Ingles 13 Ribeira Grande 16 Vila de Nova Sintra 18 Vila de Ribeira Brave
division: 9 Solavento 10 Barlavento 14 Leeward Islands 15 Windward Islands
monetary unit: 6 escudo 7 centavo
island: 3 Sal 4 Fogo, Maio, Razo 5 Brava, Secos 6 Branco 8 Boa Vista, Sao Tiago 10 Santa Luzia, Santo Antao, Sao Nicolau, Sao Vicente
mountain: 4 Fogo
highest point: 4 Cano 10 Pico de Cano
sea: 8 Atlantic
physical feature:
volcano: 4 Cano
people: 6 Creole 7 mulatto 8 Africans 9 Europeans 10 Portuguese
language: 7 Crioulo 10 Portuguese 13 Verdean Creole
religion: 13 Roman Catholic

capitalize on 7 exploit, utilize 8 profit by 13 turn to account 14 use to advantage

capitol 10 statehouse 11 legislature 15 government house

capitulate 5 yield 6 accede, give in, give up, relent, submit 7 succumb 8 cry quits 9 acquiesce, surrender 11 come to terms, sue for peace 15 lay down one's arms 17 acknowledge defeat, hoist the white flag

capitulation 8 giving in, giving up, quitting, yielding 9 surrender 10 submission

Capote, Truman
author of: 11 In Cold Blood 12 A Tree of Night 19 Breakfast at Tiffany's
character: 14 Holly Golightly

Capp, Al
real name: 18 Alfred George Caplin
creator/artist of: 8 Li'l Abner

Cappotas
epithet of: 4 Zeus
means: 8 reliever

Capra, Frank
director of: 11 Lady for a Day, Lost Horizon **15** State of the Union **17** Arsenic and Old Lace, It's a Wonderful Life, Mr Deeds Goes to Town (Oscar) **18** It Happened One Night (Oscar) **20** You Can't Take It with You (Oscar) **23** Mr Smith Goes to Washington

caprice 3 fad **4** lark, whim **5** antic, caper, craze, fancy, fling, prank, quirk, spree, stunt **6** notion, oddity, vagary **7** impulse **8** crotchet, escapade **10** erraticism **11** peculiarity **12** eccentricity, idiosyncrasy

capricious 6 fickle, fitful, quirky, uneven **7** erratic, faddish, flighty **8** fanciful, skittish, unstable, unsteady, variable, wavering **9** eccentric, impulsive, mercurial, uncertain, undecided **10** changeable, indecisive, irresolute **11** vacillating **12** inconsistent **13** irresponsible **15** shilly-shallying

capriciousness 7 caprice **10** fickleness **11** instability **12** irresolution **13** impulsiveness, inconsistency **15** shilly-shallying

Capricorn
symbol: 4 goat
planet: 6 Saturn
rules: 6 career
born: 7 January **8** December

capsicum peppers
origin: 15 tropical America
color: 3 red **5** green, white **6** violet, yellow
variety: 7 cayenne, paprika **9** red pepper **11** chili pepper, chili powder, curry powder, sweet pepper
flavor: 3 hot
use: 5 chili, curry, pizza **8** barbecue **9** paprikash

capsize 5 upset **6** invert **7** tip over **8** flip over, keel over, overturn, turn over **10** turn turtle

capsule 4 case, pill **6** ampule **7** cockpit **8** covering **9** spore case **12** condensation

captain 4 boss, head **5** chief, pilot **6** leader, master, old man **7** headman, skipper **9** chieftain, commander **10** commandant **12** chief officer **16** company commander **17** commanding officer

Captain Blood
director: 13 Michael Curtiz

capital city (of countries)
of Afghanistan: 5 Kabul
of Albania: 6 Tirana, Tirane
of Algeria: 7 Algiers
of Andorra: 14 Andorra-la-Vella
of Angola: 6 Luanda
of Antigua and Barbuda: 7 St John's
of Argentina: 11 Buenos Aires
of Armenia: 6 Erivan **7** Yerevan
of Australia: 8 Canberra
of Austria: 6 Vienna
of the Bahamas: 6 Nassau
of Bahrain: 6 Manama
of Bangladesh: 5 Dacca
of Barbados: 10 Bridgetown
of Belgium: 8 Brussels **9** Bruxelles
of Belize: 8 Belmopan
of Benin: 9 Porto-Novo
of Bermuda: 8 Hamilton
of Bhutan: 6 Thimbu **7** Thimphu
of Bolivia: 5 Sucre
of Botswana: 8 Gaborone **9** Gaberones
of Brazil: 8 Brasilia **12** Rio de Janeiro
of Brunei: 17 Bandar Seri Begawan
of Bulgaria: 5 Sofia
of Burma: 7 Rangoon
of Burundi: 9 Bujumbura
of Cambodia: 8 Pnom-Penh
of Cameroon: 7 Yaounde
of Canada: 6 Ottawa
of the Canary Islands: 9 Las Palmas **19** Santa Cruz de Tenerife
of Cape Verde: 5 Praia
of the Central African Republic: 6 Bangui
of Chad: 8 Fort-Lamy, N'Djamena
of Chile: 8 Santiago
of China: 6 Peking
of Colombia: 6 Bogota
of Comoros: 6 Moroni
of the Congo: 11 Brazzaville
of Costa Rica: 7 San Jose
of Crete: 5 Canea **8** Iraklion
of Cuba: 6 Havana **8** Le Habana
of Cyprus: 7 Nicosia
of Czechoslovakia: 6 Prague
of Denmark: 10 Copenhagen
of Djibouti: 8 Djibouti
of the Dominican Republic: 12 Santo Domingo **14** Ciudad Trujillo
of Ecuador: 5 Quito
of Egypt: 5 Cairo
of El Salvador: 11 San Salvador
of England: 6 London
of Equatorial Guinea: 6 Malabo
of Estonia: 7 Tallinn
of Ethiopia: 10 Addis Ababa
of Fiji: 4 Suva
of Finland: 8 Helsinki **11** Helsingfors
of France: 5 Paris
of the Gabon Republic: 10 Libreville
of The Gambia: 6 Banjul **8** Bathurst
of Germany (East): 10 East Berlin
of Germany (West): 4 Bonn
of Ghana: 5 Accra, Akkra
of Greece: 6 Athens
of Greenland: 3 Nuk **8** Godthaab, The Point
of Grenada: 9 St Georges
of Guatemala: 13 Guatemala City
of Guinea: 7 Conakry
of Guinea-Bissau: 6 Bissau
of Guyana: 10 Georgetown
of Haiti: 12 Port-au-Prince
of Honduras: 11 Tegucigalpa
of Hong Kong: 8 Victoria
of Hungary: 8 Budapest
of Iceland: 9 Reykjavik
of India: 8 New Delhi
of Indonesia: 7 Jakarta **8** Djakarta
of Iran: 6 Tehran **7** Teheran
of Iraq: 7 Baghdad
of Ireland: 6 Dublin
of Israel: 9 Jerusalem
of Italy: 4 Roma, Rome
of the Ivory Coast: 7 Abidjan
of Jamaica: 8 Kingston
of Japan: 3 Edo **5** Tokyo
of Java: 7 Jakarta **8** Djakarta
of Jordan: 5 Amman
of Kenya: 7 Nairobi
of Kiribati: 6 Tarawa
of Korea (North): 9 Pyongyang
of Korea (South): 5 Seoul
of Kuwait: 10 Kuwait City
of Laos: 9 Viengchan, Vientiane
of Latvia: 4 Riga
of Lebanon: 6 Beirut **8** Beyrouth
of Lesotho: 6 Maseru
of Liberia: 8 Monrovia
of Libya: 7 Tripoli

of Liechtenstein: 5 Vaduz
of Lithuania: 5 Vilna 6 Kausas 7 Vilnius
of Luxembourg: 10 Luxembourg
of Madagascar: 10 Tananarive 12 Antananarivo
of Malawi: 8 Lilongwe
of Malaysia: 11 Kuala Lumpur
of Maldives: 4 Male
of Mali: 6 Bamako
of Malta: 8 Valletta
of Mauritania: 10 Nouakchott
of Mauritius: 9 Port Louis
of Mexico: 10 Mexico City
of Monaco: 11 Monaco-Ville
of Mongolia: 9 Ulan Bator
of Montenegro: 7 Cetinje 8 Titograd 9 Podgorica
of Morocco: 5 Rabat 6 Rabbat
of Mozambique: 6 Maputo 15 Lourenco Marques
of Namibia: 8 Windhoek
of Nauru: 13 Yaren District
of Nepal: 8 Katmandu 9 Kathmandu
of Netherlands: 8 The Hague 9 Amsterdam
of New Guinea: 11 Port Moresby
of New Zealand: 10 Wellington
of Nicaragua: 7 Managua
of Niger: 6 Niamey
of Nigeria: 5 Abuja, Lagos
of Norway: 4 Oslo 11 Christiania
of Oman: 6 Masqat, Muscat
of Pakistan: 9 Islamabad
of Panama: 10 Panama City
of Paraguay: 8 Asuncion
of Peru: 4 Lima
of the Philippines: 6 Manila
of Poland: 6 Warsaw
of Portugal: 6 Lisbon
of Puerto Rico: 7 San Juan
of Qatar: 4 Doha 7 al-Dawha
of Rumania: 9 Bucharest
of Russia: 6 Moscow
of Rwanda: 6 Kigali
of Samoa (American): 8 Pago Pago
of Samoa (Western): 4 Apia
of San Marino: 9 San Marino
of Sao Tome and Principe: 7 Sao Tome
of Sardinia: 8 Cagliari
of Saudi Arabia: 6 Riyadh
of Scotland: 9 Edinburgh
of Senegal: 5 Dakar
of Seychelles: 8 Victoria
of Sicily: 7 Palermo
of Sierra Leone: 8 Freetown
of Sikkim: 7 Gangtok
of Singapore: 9 Singapore
of the Solomon Islands: 7 Honiara
of Somalia: 9 Mogadishu 10 Mogadiscio
of South Africa: 8 Cape Town, Pretoria 12 Bloemfontein
of Spain: 6 Madrid
of Sri Lanka: 7 Colombo
of the Sudan: 8 Khartoum
of Suriname: 10 Paramaribo
of Swaziland: 7 Mbabane
of Sweden: 9 Stockholm
of Switzerland: 4 Bern
of Syria: 8 Damascus
of Taiwan: 6 Taipei
of Tanzania: 11 Dar es Salaam
of Thailand: 6 Bankok 7 Bangkok 8 Thonburi 9 Ayutthaya
of Tibet: 5 Lassa, Lhasa
of Togo: 4 Lome
of Tongo: 9 Nukualofa
of Trinidad and Tobago: 11 Port of Spain
of Tunisia: 5 Tunis
of Turkey: 6 Ankara
of Tuvalu: 8 Funafuti
of Uganda: 7 Kampala
of United Arab Emirates: 8 Abu Dhabi
of United States: 12 Washington DC
of Upper Volta: 11 Ouagadougou
of Uruguay: 10 Montevideo
of Vanuatu: 4 Vila
of Venezuela: 7 Caracas
of Vietnam: 5 Hanoi 6 Saigon
of Wales: 7 Cardiff
of Western Sahara: 6 Al Aiun 7 El Aaiun
of Western Samoa: 4 Apia
of Yemen (North): 4 Sana 5 Sanaa
of Yemen (South): 4 Aden 14 Madinat al-Shaab
of Yugoslavia: 7 Beograd 8 Belgrade
of Zaire: 8 Kinshasa
of Zambia: 6 Lusaka
of Zimbabwe: 6 Harare 9 Salisbury

cast: 10 Errol Flynn 12 Lionel Atwill 13 Basil Rathbone 17 Olivia de Havilland

Captain Carpenter
author: 15 John Crowe Ransom

Captain Craig
author: 22 Edwin Arlington Robinson

Captain Hook
character in: 8 Peter Pan
author: 6 Barrie

Captain Horatio Hornblower
author: 10 C S Forester

Captains Courageous
author: 14 Rudyard Kipling
director: 13 Victor Fleming
cast: 12 Mickey Rooney, Spencer Tracy 13 John Carradine, Melvyn Douglas 15 Lionel Barrymore 18 Freddie Bartholomew
Oscar for: 5 actor (Tracy)

Captain's Daughter, The
author: 16 Alexander Pushkin

Captain Video and His Video Rangers
character: 7 Dr Pauli 9 The Ranger 12 Captain Video
cast: 7 Al Hodge 10 Hal Conklin 11 Don Hastings 13 Richard Coogan
slogan: 29 Guardian of the Safety of the World
villain: 4 Atar 7 Nargola 8 Dahoumie, Kul of Eos 9 Dr Clysmok 12 Heng Foo Seeng 14 Mook the Moon Man
gimmick: 5 Tobor 9 Discatron 11 Atomic Rifle 16 Barrier of Silence, Radio Scillograph 17 Cosmic Ray Vibrator 18 Opticon Scillometer 19 Cloak of Invisibility, Trisonic Compensator
spaceship: 6 Galaxy

caption 5 title 6 legend 7 heading, subhead 8 headline, subtitle 11 explanation

captious 4 mean 5 picky, testy 6 ornery 7 carping, cutting, peevish 8 caviling, contrary, niggling, perverse, petulant, picayune, snappish 9 fractious, querulous 10 belittling, censorious, nitpicking 11 deprecating 12 cantankerous, faultfinding 13 hypercritical

captivate 4 lure 5 charm 6 dazzle, enamor, seduce 7 attract, bewitch, delight, enchant, win over 8 enthrall 9 carry away, enrapture, fascinate, hypnotize, infatuate, mesmerize, transport 13 turn the head of 14 take the fancy of

captivated **7** charmed, pleased **9** delighted, enchanted **10** enraptured, enthralled, spellbound

captivating **7** winning, winsome **8** adorable, charming, dazzling, engaging, fetching, magnetic **9** appealing, beguiling, disarming **10** attractive, bewitching, delightful, enchanting, entrancing **11** enthralling, fascinating, mesmerizing **12** ingratiating, irresistible

captive **5** caged **6** penned **7** hostage **8** confined, enslaved, interned, locked up, prisoner **9** oppressed **10** imprisoned, subjugated **12** incarcerated

captivity **7** bondage, holding, slavery **9** servitude **10** detainment **12** imprisonment

capture **3** bag, nab **4** bust, grab, snag, take, trap **5** catch, grasp, pinch, seize, snare **6** arrest, collar, taking **7** bagging, ensnare, procure, seizure, snaring **8** catching, trapping **9** apprehend, collaring, ensnaring, lay hold of **12** apprehension, laying hold of, take prisoner **14** taking prisoner **15** take into custody

Capulet family
characters in: **14** Romeo and Juliet
author: **11** Shakespeare

Capys
father: **9** Assaracus
son: **7** Laocoon **8** Anchises
grandson: **6** Aeneas
founded: **5** Capua
warned against: **11** Trojan horse

car **4** auto, heap **5** buggy, coach, diner, motor **6** boxcar, hot rod, jalopy, wheels **7** flivver, machine, sleeper, vehicle **8** carriage **9** tin lizzie **10** automobile **12** motor vehicle
kind: **4** coal **5** cable, horse, motor **6** cattle, dining, parlor, street **7** baggage, freight, Pullman, railway **8** sleeping

Car
father: **9** Phoroneus
mother: **5** Cerdo
founder of: **6** Megara

carabiniere **9** policeman

Caracas
birthplace of: **12** Simon Bolivar
capital of: **9** Venezuela
founder: **13** Diego de Losada
museum: **7** Bolivar **8** Criolan **11** Colonial Art, Raul Santana
river: **6** Guaire

carafe **5** flask **6** bottle, vessel **9** container

carapace **4** case **5** shell **6** lorica, shield **7** carapax **8** calipash, covering **11** turtle shell

Caravaggio, Michelangelo Merisi da
born: **5** Italy **10** Caravaggio
artwork: **12** Young Bacchus **14** Burial of St Lucy **16** Raising of Lazarus **17** The Supper at Emmaus **18** Calling of St Matthew, The Life of St Matthew **20** St Matthew and the Angel **21** The Conversion of St Paul **23** The Crucifixion of St Peter **30** The Beheading of St John the Baptist

caravan **4** band, file, line **5** queue, train, troop **6** coffle, column, convoy, parade, string **7** company, cortege, retinue **9** cavalcade, chain gang, entourage, motorcade **10** procession, wagon train

caravansary **3** inn **5** hotel **8** hostelry

caraway
botanical name: **10** Carum carvi
origin: **6** Europe **9** Asia Minor **14** the Netherlands
liqueur: **6** Kummel
candy-covered caraway seeds: **6** comfit **12** whiskykiller
use: **4** pork, soup, stew **8** rye bread

carbohydrate
consists of: **5** water **6** carbon, oxygen **8** hydrogen **13** carbon dioxide
kinds: **5** sugar **6** simple, starch, xylose **7** complex, glucose, lactose, maltose, sucrose **8** dextrose, fructose **9** cellulose

carbon **4** coal, coke, copy **8** charcoal **9** lampblack
chemical symbol: **1** C

carbon copy **5** clone **7** replica **9** duplicate, facsimile **12** reproduction

carbonize **4** burn, char, sear **5** singe **6** scorch **10** incinerate

carbuncle **4** boil, sore **11** excrescence **12** inflammation

carcass **4** body, bouk, husk, wall **5** shell, stiff, trunk **6** corpse **7** cadaver, carrion, remains **8** dead body, fireball, skeleton **9** framework

carcinoma **5** tumor **6** cancer **8** neoplasm **10** malignancy **15** malignant growth

card **4** bill **6** ticket **7** program **8** postcard
kind: **7** calling, get-well, playing **8** birthday, business, greeting **9** Christmas, Valentine

cardamon
botanical name: **19** Elettaria cardamomum
origin: **4** Asia **5** India **13** southeast Asia
related to: **6** ginger
color: **5** black
use: **5** curry **7** dessert **12** Danish pastry

Cardea
origin: **5** Roman
goddess of: **6** family **10** door hinges

Cardew, Cecily
character in: **27** The Importance of Being Earnest
author: **5** Wilde

card game ***see box***

Cardiff
capital of: **5** Wales

cardigan **5** corgi **6** jacket, wampus **7** sweater **10** Welsh corgi

cardinal **3** key, top **4** head, main **5** basic, chief, first, prime, vital **6** cherry, claret **7** carmine, central, deep-red, highest, leading, primary, scarlet **8** blood-red, dominant, foremost, greatest **9** essential, intrinsic, necessary, paramount, principal, uppermost **10** elementary, preeminent, underlying **11** fundamental, outstanding, predominant, wine-colored **13** indispensable, most important

care **4** heed, load, mind, want, wish **5** grief, pains, worry **6** bother, charge, desire, effort, misery, regard, sorrow, strain, stress **7** anguish, anxiety, caution, concern, control, custody, keeping, sadness, thought, trouble **8** distress, hardship, nuisance, pressure, vexation **9** annoyance, attention, be worried, diligence, exactness, heartache, vigilance **10** affliction, management, precaution, protection, solicitude **11** application, be concerned, bother about, carefulness, supervision, tribulation, unhappiness **12** ministration, trouble about, watchfulness **13** attentiveness, consideration **14** be interested in, circumspection, discrimination, fastidiousness, meticulousness, responsibility, scrupulousness **17** conscientiousness

card game **3** loo, war **4** brag, fish, skat, vint **5** ombre, poker, rummy, whist **6** boston, bridge, casino, chemmy, ecarte, euchre, go fish, hearts, memory, piquet, pocher **7** bezique, canasta, cooncan, Old Maid, plafond, primero **8** baccarat, conquian, cribbage, gin rummy, napoleon, patience, pinochle, slapjack **9** blackjack, pelmanism, solitaire, spoil five, twenty-one **11** chemin de fer, crazy eights **13** concentration **14** contract bridge **16** beggar-my-neighbor, trente et quarante
card names: **3** ace **4** fool, jack, king, trey **5** joker, queen
combination of cards: **4** meld
one hand or round: **5** trick
rulebook by: **5** Hoyle
suits: **4** club **5** heart, spade **7** diamond
French: **5** coeur, pique **6** trefle **7** carreau
German: **4** grun, herz, piks **5** karos, treff **6** eichel **7** schelle
Italian: **5** coppa, cuori, fiori, spada **6** denaro, picchi, quadri **7** bastone
Spanish: **3** oro **4** copa **5** basto **6** espada

Careas **6** eunuch

careen **3** tip, yaw **4** lean, list, sway, tilt, veer **5** heave, slant, slope **7** capsize **8** lean over, overturn

career **3** job **4** line, work **7** calling, pursuit **8** activity, business, lifework, vocation **10** employment, livelihood, occupation, profession, walk of life

care for **4** like, mind, tend **5** fancy **7** oversee **8** attend to, wait upon **9** look after, watch over **10** minister to, provide for

carefree **3** gay **4** glad **5** happy, jolly, sunny **6** breezy, elated, jaunty, joyous **7** buoyant, gleeful, radiant, relaxed, smiling **8** careless, cheerful, jubilant, laughing **9** easygoing **10** full of life, optimistic, untroubled **11** free-and-easy **12** happy-go-lucky, light-hearted, without worry **13** in high spirits **23** without a worry in the world
French: **9** sans souci

careful **4** fine, nice, wary **5** alert, chary, exact, fussy **7** correct, guarded, heedful, mindful, on guard, precise, prudent, tactful **8** accurate, cautious, diligent, discreet, vigilant, watchful **9** attentive, concerned, judicious, observant, regardful **10** fastidious, meticulous, particular, scrupulous, solicitous, thoughtful **11** circumspect, painstaking, punctilious **13** conscientious

carefulness **7** caution **10** steadiness **12** deliberation **14** circumspection

careless **3** lax **4** rash **5** messy, slack **6** casual, sloppy, untidy **7** inexact, offhand **8** heedless, mindless, slapdash, slipshod, slovenly **9** forgetful, imprecise, incorrect, negligent, unmindful **10** disorderly, inaccurate, neglectful, nonchalant, unthinking, untroubled **11** indifferent, thoughtless, unconcerned **12** absent-minded, devil-may-care **13** inconsiderate, lackadaisical

carelessness **6** laxity **7** neglect **9** messiness, slackness **10** inaccuracy, negligence, sloppiness, untidiness **11** imprecision, inexactness **12** heedlessness, indiscretion, slovenliness **13** unmindfulness **14** disorderliness **15** thoughtlessness **16** absentmindedness, irresponsibility

Care of Time, The
author: **10** Eric Ambler

caress **3** hug, pat, pet **5** clasp, touch **6** cuddle, fondle, stroke **7** embrace, petting, toy with **8** fondling, stroking **11** gentle touch

caretaker **6** keeper, porter, warden **7** curator, janitor, steward **8** overseer, watchman **9** concierge, custodian **10** gatekeeper **14** superintendent

careworn **7** haggard, worried **8** fatigued, troubled **11** pessimistic

cargo **4** load **5** goods **6** burden, lading **7** freight **8** shipment **11** consignment, merchandise

Carib
language family: **7** Cariban
location: **7** Guianas **9** Caribbean, Venezuela **12** South America
custom: **11** cannibalism

Cariban
tribe: **5** Carib **6** Acawai, Akawai

Caribbean **3** sea
channel: **7** Yucatan
city: **6** Havana **7** San Juan **8** Santiago **10** Guantanamo **12** Port au Prince **13** Santo Domingo **15** Charlotte Amalie
Indian: **5** Carib **6** Arawak
island: **4** Cuba **5** Aruba, Haiti, Nevis **6** Cayman, Nassau, Tobago, Virgin **7** Antigua, Bahamas, Barbuda, Curacao, Grenada, Jamaica, Leeward **8** Anguilla, Dominica, Trinidad, Windward **9** Saint John **10** Guadeloupe, Hispaniola, Martinique, Montserrat, Puerto Rico, Saint Kitts, Saint Lucia **11** Saint Thomas **12** Saint Vincent **14** Lesser Antilles **15** Greater Antiiles **19** Dominican Republic, Netherlands Antilles
language: **6** gullah **10** papiamento
product: **3** rum **5** fruit, spice, sugar **6** coffee

caricature **4** mock **6** parody, satire **7** lampoon, mockery, takeoff **8** satirize, travesty **9** absurdity, burlesque **10** distortion **12** exaggeration

Carker
character in: **12** Dombey and Son
author: **7** Dickens

Carlisle, Kitty
real name: **13** Katherine Conn
husband: **8** Moss Hart
born: **12** New Orleans LA
roles: **13** She Loves Me Not **14** To Tell the Truth **16** A Night at the Opera **19** Murder at the Vanities

Carlton, Steve (Steven Norman)
nickname: **5** Lefty
sport: **8** baseball
position: **7** pitcher
team: **20** Philadelphia Phillies

Carlyle, Thomas
author of: **8** Cromwell **14** Sartor Resartus **17** Frederick the Great **19** The French Revolution **20** Heroes and Hero-Worship

Carmanor
king of: **5** Crete
purified: **6** Apollo **7** Artemis

Carme
daughter: **11** Britomartis

Carmen
author: **14** Prosper Merimee
opera by: **5** Bizet
setting: **7** Seville

character: **7** Don Jose **9** Escamillo, Frasquita

Carmen Jones
director: **13** Otto Preminger
based on opera by: **5** Bizet (Carmen)
adaptation by: **18** Oscar Hammerstein II
cast: **11** Pearl Bailey **14** Harry Belafonte **16** Dorothy Dandridge

Carmenta
origin: **5** Roman
member of: **7** Camanae
protectress of: **10** childbirth
husband: **7** Evander
son: **7** Evander

carmine **3** red **6** cherry **7** crimson, deep red, scarlet **8** blood red **9** bright red

carnage **8** butchery, massacre **9** blood bath, slaughter

carnal **4** lewd **6** erotic, impure, sexual, sinful, wanton **7** fleshly, immoral, lustful, sensual **8** prurient, sensuous, unchaste, venereal **9** lecherous, salacious **10** lascivious, libidinous, voluptuous

Carnegie, Dale
author of: **33** How To Win Friends and Influence People

carnelian
species: **6** quartz

Carnera, Primo
nickname: **13** the Ambling Alp
sport: **6** boxing
class: **11** heavyweight

Carneus
epithet of: **6** Apollo
alludes to: **11** cornel trees

Carney, Art
real name: **26** Arthur William Matthew Carney
partner: **13** Jackie Gleason
born: **13** Mount Vernon NY
roles: **8** Ed Norton **13** Harry and Tonto (Oscar) **15** The Honeymooners

carnival **4** fair, fete, gala **6** circus **7** holiday, jubilee **8** festival, jamboree, sideshow **9** Mardi Gras **11** celebration

carnivore **3** cat, dog, fox **4** bear, lion, lynx, mink, puma, wolf **5** civet, dingo, fossa, hyena, otter, panda, skunk, tayra, tiger **6** badger, bobcat, coyote, ferret, grison, hyaena, jackal, jaguar, marten, olingo, weasel **7** polecat, raccoon, suricat **8** aardwolf, kinkajou, mongoose **9** meat eater, wolverine **10** cacomistle, coatimundi, flesh eater

carnivorous **9** predatory **10** meat-eating, predaceous **11** flesh-eating

Carnus
occupation: **4** seer
seer of: **6** Apollo
killed by: **10** Heraclidae

carol **4** hymn, noel, sing **5** paean **6** warble **8** canticle **9** song of joy **12** song of praise

Caroline Islands
district: **3** Yap **4** Truk **5** Palau **6** Ponape
inhabitant: **10** Polynesian **11** Micronesian
island: **3** Yap **6** Ponape, Ulithi **8** Nukuroro **10** Babelthuap **14** Kapinamarangi
language: **7** English **10** Polynesian **11** Micronesian
ocean: **7** Pacific

carom **6** bounce, strike **7** collide, rebound, **8** billiard, ricochet **9** bounce off

Caron, Leslie
born: **6** France **19** Boulogne-Billancourt
roles: **4** Gaby, Gigi, Lili **5** Fanny **11** Father Goose **13** Daddy Longlegs **14** The L-Shaped Room **17** An American in Paris

Carothers, Wallace Hume
field: **9** chemistry
discovered: **5** nylon

carousal **4** orgy **5** binge, drunk, spree **7** debauch **9** bacchanal **10** debauchery, saturnalia

carouse **5** drink, party, quaff, revel **6** guzzle, imbibe, tipple **7** roister, wassail **8** live it up **9** make merry **10** go on a binge **11** make whoopee

Carousel
director: **9** Henry King
based on: **6** Liliom
adaptation by: **21** Rodgers and Hammerstein
cast: **12** Gordon MacRae (Billy Bigelow), Shirley Jones **15** Cameron Mitchell
song: **9** Soliloquy **11** If I Loved You **19** You'll Never Walk Alone

carp **3** nag **5** cavil, chide, decry, knock **6** deride, impugn, jibe at, pick on **7** censure, condemn **8** belittle, complain, reproach **9** criticize, deprecate, disparage, fault-find, find fault **10** disapprove

Carpaccio, Vittore
born: **5** Italy **6** Venice
artwork: **13** Two Courtesans **18** The Dream of St Ursula **19** The Legend of St Ursula **21** St Augustine in his Study **24** St George Killing the Dragon **28** St Augustine's Vision of St Jerome **29** The Arrival of St Ursula at Cologne

carpal
bone of: **5** wrist

carpe diem **11** seize the day **15** enjoy the present

carpenter **6** fitter, joiner **7** builder **8** repairer **10** woodworker **12** cabinetmaker
ant: **10** camponotus
bee: **8** xylocopa
bird: **10** woodpecker
fish: **10** hammerhead
moth: **10** prinoxysus

Carpenter, Harlean
real name of: **10** Jean Harlow

carper **6** critic **7** caviler **9** nitpicker **11** fault-finder

carpet **3** mat, rug **5** cover, layer, sheet **7** blanket, matting **8** covering

Carpetbaggers, The
author: **13** Harold Robbins

Carpo
origin: **5** Greek
member of: **5** Horae
goddess of: **11** summer fruit

Carpophorus
epithet of: **7** Demeter **10** Persephone
means: **11** fruit bearer

Carr, Emily
born: **6** Canada **8** Victoria **15** British Columbia
artwork: **3** Sky **8** Big Raven **14** Blunden Harbour, Kispiax Village **15** Woods and Blue Sky **17** Forest Landscape II **36** Cape Mudge An Indian Family with Totem Pole

Carra, Carlo
born: **5** Italy **9** Quargneto
artwork: **13** Lot's Daughters **16** Metaphysical Muse **20** Patriotic Celebration **29** The Funeral of the Anarchist Galli

Carradine, David
father: **4** John
half-brothers: **5** Keith **6** Robert
born: **11** Hollywood CA
roles: **6** Kung Fu **13** Bound for Glory **14** The Serpent's Egg

Carradine, John
real name: **21** Richmond Reed Carradine
son: **5** David, Keith **6** Robert

born: 18 Greenwich Village NY
roles: 9 Cleopatra, Kidnapped 10 Stagecoach 12 Count Dracula 15 The Invisible Man 18 Captains Courageous, The Three Musketeers

Carradine, Keith
father: 4 John
brother: 6 Robert
half-brother: 5 David
born: 10 San Mateo CA
roles: 9 Nashville 10 Pretty Baby

Carraway, Nick
character in: 14 The Great Gatsby
author: 10 Fitzgerald

Carrere, John Merven
partner: 14 Thomas Hastings
architect of: 19 House Office Building (Washington DC) 20 New York Public Library, Senate Office Building (Washington DC) 21 Henry Clay Frick mansion (now Frick Collection NYC)
style: 18 French neo-classical, Spanish Renaissance

carriage 3 air, rig 4 mien 5 buggy, coach, poise, wagon 6 aspect, manner 7 bearing, posture, vehicle 8 attitude, behavior, demeanor, presence 10 appearance, conveyance, deportment 11 comportment

Carrie
author: 11 Stephen King

carried away 7 excited, frantic, seduced 8 ecstatic, frenzied, overcome 9 delirious 10 fascinated, infatuated 11 transported

carrier 3 bus, car 4 rack, wave 5 agent, barge, plane, coach, drain, ferry, train, truck, wagon 6 bearer, boxcar, pigeon, porter 7 airline, channel, mailman, postman, trucker, vehicle 8 airplane, aircraft, carriage, catalyst, railroad 9 messenger 11 transmitter, wheelbarrow

carrion 5 bones, offal, waste 6 corpse, refuse 7 cadaver, carcass, garbage, remains, wastage 8 crowbait, dead body, leavings

Carroll, Leo G
born: 6 Weedon 7 England
roles: 6 Topper 7 Rebecca 9 Suspicion 10 Spellbound 11 Cosmo Topper 15 A Christmas Carol, The Man from UNCLE, The Paradine Case 16 Father of the Bride, North by Northwest

Carroll, Lewis
real name: 22 Charles Lutwidge Dodgson
author of: 11 Jabberwocky 22 Through the Looking Glass 28 Alice's Adventures in Wonderland

carrousel 4 ride, tray 8 conveyor 9 quadrille, whirligig 10 tournament 12 merry-go-round

carry 3 lug, run 4 bear, cart, haul, lift, move, prop, ship, take, tote 5 brace, bring, fetch, offer, print, shift, stock 6 convey, hold up, supply, uphold 7 conduct, deliver, display, publish, release, support, sustain 8 displace, maintain, shoulder, transfer, transmit 9 broadcast, transport 10 keep on hand 11 communicate, disseminate

carry away 4 lure 6 abduct, kidnap, seduce 7 attract 9 captivate, fascinate, infatuate, transport

carry off 5 seize, steal 6 abduct, kidnap 7 bear off 9 succeed at 11 get away with

carry out 2 do 6 effect, wind up 7 achieve, execute, fulfill, perform, realize 8 complete, conclude, dispatch 9 discharge, dispose of, succeed at 10 accomplish, bring about 11 bring to pass

carry through 6 effect, finish 7 achieve, develop, execute, fulfill, perform, realize 8 complete, conclude 9 discharge 10 accomplish, consummate, effectuate, perpetuate 13 put into effect

Carson, Rachel Louise
field: 7 biology
studied: 9 pollution
author of: 12 Silent Spring 14 The Sea Around Us 15 The Edge of the Sea

Carstone, Richard
character in: 10 Bleak House
author: 7 Dickens

cart 3 gig, lug 4 bear, dray, haul, move, take, tote, trap 5 bring, carry, fetch, truck, wagon 6 barrow, convey 7 schlepp, tumbrel 8 curricle, transfer, transmit 9 transport 10 handbarrow, transplant, two-wheeler 11 wheelbarrow
kind: 2 go 3 dog, tip 4 dump, hand, push

carte blanche 7 license 9 a free hand, free reign 10 blank check 12 open sanction 13 full authority 18 unconditional power

cartel 4 pool 5 chain, trust 7 combine 8 monopoly 9 syndicate 10 consortium, federation 11 corporation

Carter, Charles
real name of: 14 Charlton Heston

Carter, James Earl, Jr *see box, p. 160*

Carthage *see* 7 Tunisia

carton 3 box 4 case 5 crate 9 container 11 packing case 12 cardboard box, packing crate 18 cardboard container

Carton, Sydney
character in: 16 A Tale of Two Cities
author: 7 Dickens

cartoon 5 comic 6 design, satire, sketch 7 drawing, funnies, picture 8 animated 10 caricature, comicstrip

cartoonist 6 artist, drawer 7 gagster 12 caricaturist
famous: 6 Al Capp, C C Beck, Ted Key 8 Herblock (Herbert L. Block), Jim Davis, Roy Crane 9 Bud Fisher, Chic Young, Dik Browne, Frank King, Hal Foster, Ham Fisher, Walt Kelly 10 Bob Montana, Harold Gray, Johnny Hart, Mort Walker, Paul Conrad, Thomas Nast, Walt Disney 11 Alex Raymond, Bill Mauldin, Dale Messick, David Levine, Ding Darling, Elzie C. Segar, Hank Ketcham, Max Beerbohm, Rollin Kirby 12 Brad Anderson, Chester Gould, Garry Trudeau, James Thurber, Jeff MacNelly, Jules Feiffer, Milton Caniff, Rube Goldberg, Rudolph Dirks, Virgil Partch 13 Charles Addams, Charles Schulz, George McManus, Honore Daumier, Joseph Keppler, Saul Steinberg 14 Homer Davenport, William Hogarth 15 Ernie Bushmiller, Patrick Oliphant, Richard Outcault 16 Benjamin Franklin, George Cruikshank

cartridge 3 dud 4 case, tape 5 blank, shell 6 holder 7 capsule, package 8 cassette, cylinder 9 container

Cartwright, Edmund
nationality: 7 English
inventor of: 9 power loom 18 wool-combing machine

carve 3 hew, saw 4 etch, form, hack, mold, rend, turn, work 5 allot, cleve, cut up, model, shape, slash, slice, split 6 chisel, divide, incise, sculpt

Carter, James Earl, Jr
nickname: **3** Hot **5** Jimmy **7** Hotshot
presidential rank: **11** thirty-ninth
party: **10** Democratic
state represented: **2** GA **7** Georgia
defeated: **4** (Gerald R) Ford **8** (Eugene) McCarthy
vice president: **7** (Walter Frederick "Fritz") Mondale
cabinet:
state: **5** (Cyrus R) Vance **6** (Edmund S) Muskie
treasury: **6** (G William) Miller **10** (W Michael) Blumenthal
defense: **5** (Harold) Brown
attorney general: **4** (Griffin B) Bell **9** (Benjamin R) Civiletti
interior: **6** (Cecil D) Andrus
agriculture: **8** (Robert S) Bergland
commerce: **5** (Juanita Morris) Kreps **9** (Philip M) Klutznick
labor: **8** (F Ray) Marshall
HEW: **6** (Patricia Roberts) Harris **8** (Joseph A) Califano (Jr)
HUD: **6** (Patricia Roberts) Harris **8** (Moon) Landrieu
transportation: **5** (Brockman) Adams **11** (Neil E) Goldschmidt
education: **10** (Shirley) Hufstedler
born: **2** GA **6** Plains
education: **14** US Naval Academy **26** Georgia Southwestern College **28** Georgia Institute of Technology
religion: **15** Southern Baptist
interests: **5** track **6** tennis **7** fishing, hunting **8** football, softball **10** basketball **12** cross country **13** square dancing **17** collecting bottles
music: **8** folk rock **9** classical
author: **13** Why Not the Best?
political career: **12** state senator
governor of: **7** Georgia
civilian career: **12** peanut farmer
military service: **6** US Navy
notable events of lifetime/term: **6** SALT II **9** Love Canal, recession
deaths at: **9** Jonestown
eruption of: **13** Mount St Helens
first baby from: **8** test tube
hostages taken in: **4** Iran
nuclear accident: **15** Three Mile Island
pipeline: **5** Alcan
scandal/investigation: **6** Abscam **9** Bert Lance, Koreagate **11** Billy Carter
Supreme Court case: **5** Bakke
treaty: **11** Panama Canal **16** Camp David Accords
father: **11** James Earl Sr
mother: **7** Lillian (Gordy)
nickname: **11** Miss Lillian
siblings: **6** Gloria **17** William "Billy" Alton **19** Ruth Carter Stapleton
wife: **8** Rosalynn (Smith)
children: **7** Amy Lynn **11** John William (Jack) **12** James Earl III (Chip) **13** Donnel Jeffrey (Jeff)
first lady: **36** Presidential Commission on Mental Health
author: **19** First Lady from Plains

7 engrave, fashion, pattern, quarter **8** block out, dissever **9** apportion, sculpture

Carver, George Washington
field: **9** chemistry
worked in: **11** agriculture
studied: **6** peanut **7** soybean **11** sweet potato

carving **5** cameo **8** intaglio, triptych **9** sculpture

Carya
origin: **8** Laconian
form: **6** maiden
home: **7** Laconia
changed into: **10** walnut tree
changed by: **8** Dionysus

Caryatis
epithet of: **7** Artemis
means: **15** of the walnut tree

Casablanca
director: **13** Michael Curtiz
cast: **10** Peter Lorre **11** Claude Rains (Louis), Conrad Veidt, Paul Henreid (Victor Laslo) **12** Dooley Wilson (Sam), **13** Ingrid Bergman (Ilsa Lund) **14** Humphrey Bogart (Rick) **17** Sydney Greenstreet
Oscar for: **7** picture
song: **12** As Time Goes By

Casanova **3** cad, rip **4** beau, lech, roue, wolf **5** lover, Romeo, swain, wooer **6** chaser, lecher, suitor **7** admirer, bounder, Don Juan, gallant, rounder **8** cavalier, Lothario, lover boy, paramour **9** ladies' man, libertine, womanizer **10** lady-killer, profligate **11** philanderer

Casby
character in: **12** Little Dorrit
author: **7** Dickens

cascade **4** fall, gush, pour, rush **5** chute, falls, surge **6** plunge, rapids, tumble **7** Niagara **8** cataract **9** waterfall

case **3** bin, box **4** plea, suit, tray **5** cause, chest, cover, crate, event **6** action, affair, appeal, carton, debate, injury, jacket, matter, sheath, victim **7** cabinet, concern, disease, dispute, episode, example, hearing, housing, inquiry, invalid, lawsuit, overlay, patient, wrapper **8** argument, business, covering, envelope, incident, instance, sufferer **9** condition, container, happening, incidence, sheathing, situation **10** litigation, occurrence, proceeding, protection, receptacle, sick person **11** controversy **12** circumstance, illustration

case in point **7** example **8** instance **12** illustration

Case of Sergeant Grischa, The
author: **11** Arnold Zweig

Casey
nickname of: **20** Charles Dillon Stengel

cash **5** bills, bread, coins, dough, money **6** change, redeem **8** currency, exchange **9** bank notes **10** paper money **11** legal tender **13** turn into money **14** coin of the realm

cashier **6** banker, bursar, purser, teller **9** treasurer **10** bank teller

cash register
invented by: **5** Ritty

casing **4** skin **5** frame **9** sheathing

Casino Royale
author: **10** Ian Fleming

cask **3** keg, tub, tun, vat **4** butt, pipe **6** barrel **8** hogshead

casket **4** case, pall **5** chest **6** coffer, coffin **8** jewel box **11** sarcophagus

Cask of Amontillado, The
author: **13** Edgar Allan Poe
character: **9** Fortunato, Montresor

Cassandra
also: **9** Alexandra
father: **5** Priam
mother: **6** Hecuba
brother: **5** Paris
concubine of: **9** Agamemnon
son: **6** Pelops **9** Teledamus
cursed by: **6** Apollo
violated by: **4** Ajax
killed by: **12** Clytemnestra

Cassatt, Mary
born: **15** Allegheny City PA
artwork: **6** La Loge **7** The Bath **11** The Cup of Tea **12** After the Bath, Woman Bathing **14** Gathering Fruit **15** Reading Le Figaro **20** Girl Arranging Her Hair, Woman and Child Drawing

Cassavetes, John
wife: **12** Gena Rowlands
born: **9** New York NY
roles/films: **8** Husbands **10** The Tempest **13** Rosemary's Baby, The Dirty Dozen **23** A Woman Under the Influence

casserole **4** dish, food, mold **6** tureen, vessel **8** saucepan

Cassio
character in: **7** Othello
author: **11** Shakespeare

Cassiopeia
husband: **7** Cepheus
daughter: **9** Andromeda
offended: **7** Nereids

Cassius
also: **12** Caius Cassius
character in: **12** Julius Caesar
author: **11** Shakespeare

Cass Timberlane
author: **13** Sinclair Lewis
character: **11** Bradd Criley **24** Jinny Marshland Timberlane

cast **3** set, sow **4** fire, form, hurl, look, mien, mint, mold, pick, shed, toss **5** fling, heave, model, pitch, shape, shoot, sling, stamp, throw **6** actors, assign, casing, choose, direct, launch, let fly, propel, sculpt, spread, troupe **7** appoint, company, deposit, diffuse, pattern, players, project, scatter **8** catapult, disperse **9** broadcast, circulate, discharge, launching, semblance **10** appearance, distribute, impression, performers, propulsion **11** disseminate, give parts to **16** dramatis personae

Castalia
origin: **5** Greek
sacred: **6** spring
location: **14** Mount Parnassus
sacred to: **5** Muses **6** Apollo
source of: **11** inspiration

Castalides *see* **5** Muses

cast aside **4** junk, shed **6** desert, reject **7** abandon, discard, forsake, neglect **8** get rid of, renounce, throw out **9** repudiate, throw away **11** discontinue

cast a spell on **5** charm **7** bewitch, conjure, enchant **8** entrance **11** work magic on

cast aspersions on **5** knock, scorn **6** deride, malign **7** disdain, put down, run down, sneer at **8** belittle, pooh-pooh **9** criticize, disparage **13** find fault with

castaway **3** bum **4** hobo, waif **5** exile, leper, nomad, rover, stray **6** outlaw, pariah **7** Ishmael, outcast, vagrant **8** deportee, derelict, renegade, unperson, vagabond, wanderer **9** foundling, nonperson **10** expatriate **11** beachcomber, offscouring, untouchable **12** down-and-outer **15** knight-of-the-road

cast away **4** junk **6** launch, propel, reject **7** abandon, discard, toss out **8** get rid of, pitch out, throw out **9** throw away

cast down **5** abase, droop, lower **6** abased, deject, droopy, humble, sadden **7** depress, humbled, lowered **8** bring low, dejected, disgrace, saddened **9** depressed, disgraced, humiliate **10** brought low, dishearten, humiliated **11** crestfallen **12** disheartened

caste **4** rank **6** status **7** lineage, station **8** position **9** condition
Hindu: **5** sudra, varna **6** vaisya **7** brahman **9** kshatriya

castigate **5** chide, scold **6** berate, punish, rebuke **7** bawl out, censure, chasten, chew out, correct, reprove, upbraid **8** admonish, chastise, penalize, reproach **9** criticize, dress down, reprimand **10** discipline, take to task **15** call on the carpet **16** haul over the coals

castigation **9** reprimand **10** chastening, correction, discipline, penalizing, punishment **12** chastisement

Castiglione, Baldassare
author of: **20** The Book of the Courtier

castle **4** hall, keep **5** manor, tower, villa **6** palace **7** chateau, citadel, mansion **8** fortress **10** stronghold

Castle, The
author: **10** Franz Kafka
character: **1** K

Castle of Otranto, The
author: **13** Horace Walpole
character: **6** Conrad **7** Alfonso, Manfred, Matilda **8** Isabella, Theodore **12** Father Jerome

Castle Rackrent
author: **14** Maria Edgeworth

cast off **4** shed **6** reject **7** discard, set sail, toss out **8** throw off, throw out **9** repudiate, throw away **11** weigh anchor

Castor and Pollux
also: **8** Dioscuri **10** Polydeuces, Tyndaridae
form: **8** twin sons
mother: **4** Leda
father: **4** Zeus
sister: **5** Helen **12** Clytemnestra
members of: **9** Argonauts
protectors of: **6** seamen

cast out **4** oust **5** eject, evict, exile, expel **6** banish, reject **7** discard, dismiss, turn out **8** drive out, send away, throw out

cast up **4** spew **5** eject, expel, vomit **6** spew up **7** cough up, throw up **8** disgorge

casual **4** cool, so-so **5** blase, vague **6** chance, random, sporty **7** offhand, passing, relaxed **8** informal **9** easygoing, haphazard, non-dressy, unplanned **10** accidental, fortuitous, incidental, nonchalant, unarranged, undesigned, undirected, unexpected, unforeseen **11** half-hearted, indifferent, unlooked for **13** lackadaisical, serendipitous, unintentional **14** indiscriminate, unpremeditated

Casuals of the Sea
author: **12** William McFee

casualty **6** injury, victim **7** injured **8** fatality

casuistry **5** guile **6** deceit **7** fallacy, sophism **8** subtlety **9** Jesuitism, quibbling, sophistry **10** nitpicking **12** equivocation, pettifoggery, speciousness **13** deceptiveness, hair-splitting **14** sophistication

casus belli **10** cause of war

Casy, Jim
character in: **16** The Grapes of Wrath
author: **9** Steinbeck

cat ***see box***

cat **3** pet **4** puss, whip **5** kitty, pussy, tabby **6** feline, kitten, mouser, tomcat
anatomy: **3** paw **4** loin, nape, rump, tail **5** break, flank, shank **6** feeler **7** dewclaw, leather, whisker **8** vibrissa **10** metatarsus
breed/kind: **3** tom **4** coon, Eyra, lion, lynx, Manx, puma **5** alley, civet, hyena, kitty, Korat, tabby, tiger **6** Angola, angora, bobcat, cougar, jaguar, ocelot, serval **7** Burmese, caracal, cheetah, leopard, linsang, Maltese, panther, Persian, polecat, Siamese, Turkish, wildcat **8** Balinese, Cheshire, Egyptian, ringtail **9** Himalayan, shorthair **10** Abyssinian, chinchilla **11** Russian blue **13** tortoise-shell
combining form: **5** aelur, ailur, felin **6** aeluro, ailuro, felino
Egyptian goddess of: **4** Bast
extinct: **10** saber-tooth
family: **7** Felidae
famous: **6** Morris **8** Cheshire, Garfield, Kilkenny **9** Mehitabel **10** Heathcliff
fastest: **7** cheetah
fear of: **12** aelurophobia, ailurophobia
female: **5** queen **7** lioness, tigress **8** wheencat **9** grimalkin
genus: **5** Felis
grinning: **8** Cheshire
group: **7** clowder, clutter
group of kittens: **6** kendle, kindle
lover: **11** aelurophile, ailurophile
male: **3** gib, tom **6** tomcat
ring-tailed: **6** serval **10** cacomistle
tailless: **4** Manx
young: **6** kitten

cataclysm **4** blow **7** debacle **8** calamity, disaster, upheaval **11** catastrophe, devastation

cataclysmic **4** dire **6** tragic **7** ruinous **10** calamitous, disastrous **12** catastrophic, earth-shaking

catacomb **4** tomb **7** ossuary **8** cemetery **10** passageway **12** burial ground

Cataebates
epithet of: **4** Zeus
means: **9** descender

catafalque **3** box **4** pall **6** casket, coffin

catalog, catalogue **4** file, list, post, roll **5** index **6** record, roster **7** listing **8** classify, register, syllabus, tabulate **9** directory, enumerate, inventory

Catamitus *see* **8** Ganymede

Cat and Mouse
author: **11** Gunter Grass

catapult **4** cast, hurl, toss **5** fling, heave, pitch, shoot, sling, throw **6** hurtle, propel **9** slingshot **13** hurling engine

cataract **5** falls, flood **6** deluge, rapids **7** cascade, torrent **8** downpour **9** waterfall **10** inundation

catastrophe **4** blow **5** havoc **6** mishap, ravage **7** debacle, scourge, tragedy **8** calamity, disaster **9** cataclysm **10** affliction, misfortune **11** devastation

catastrophic **6** tragic **7** ruinous **10** calamitous, disastrous **11** cataclysmic

catcall **3** boo **4** gibe, hiss, hoot, jeer **7** whistle **8** heckling **9** raspberry **10** Bronx cheer

catch **3** bag, bat, get, hit, nab **4** bait, bang, belt, bump, bust, dupe, feel, find, fool, grab, hasp, haul, hoax, hook, lock, lure, make, snag, snap, spot, take, trap **5** booty, break, charm, clasp, crack, get to, grasp, hitch, latch, prize, reach, seize, sense, smack, smite, snare, trick, whack, yield **6** allure, arrest, betray, buffet, collar, corner, corral, dazzle, deceit, delude, descry, detect, expose, fasten, fathom, kicker, snatch, strike, take in, turn on, unmask **7** attract, bewitch, capture, closure, deceive, delight, discern, enchant, ensnare, find out, gimmick, mislead, rasping, seizure **8** catching, come upon, contract, coupling, discover, drawback, enthrall, hoodwink, overtake, perceive, pickings, surprise **9** apprehend, bamboozle, captivate, carry away, enrapture, fastening, intercept, lay hold of, play false, recognize, transport **10** comprehend, understand **11** take captive **12** break out with, come down with, disadvantage, seize and hold, take off guard **14** stumbling block **15** take into custody **18** become infected with

catch-as-catch-can **7** cursory **9** haphazard, hit-or-miss, unplanned **10** disorderly, incomplete **11** superficial, unorganized **12** disorganized, unsystematic

Catcher in the Rye, The
author: **10** J D Salinger
character: **15** Holden Caulfield

catching **10** contagious, infectious **12** communicable **13** transmittable

catch on to **3** get **5** grasp, savvy **6** absorb, digest, fathom, pick up **10** assimilate, comprehend, get the idea, understand

catch sight of **3** see **4** espy **6** behold, descry, detect, notice **7** discern, make out, observe, pick out **8** perceive

Catch-22
author: **12** Joseph Heller
character: **9** Yossarian

catchword **5** motto **6** byword, cliche, slogan, war cry **8** password **9** battle cry, guide word, pet phrase, watchword **10** shibboleth

categorical **4** flat, sure **7** certain, express **8** absolute, definite, emphatic, explicit **10** pronounced, unreserved **11** unequivocal, unqualified **12** unmistakable **13** unconditional

categorically **10** absolutely, definitely, positively **12** conclusively

categorization **5** order **11** arrangement **14** classification

category **5** class, group **8** division, grouping **14** classification

cater **5** humor **6** pamper, pander, please **7** gratify, indulge, satisfy

caterpillar **4** moth, worm **5** larva **7** cutworm, tractor, webworm **8** hangworm, silkworm, wortworm **9** butterfly, woolybear **10** astragalus

caterwaul 3 cry **4** bawl, howl, wail, yelp **5** whine **6** clamor, scream, shriek, squawk, squeal **7** screech **10** rend the air

catfish 4 barb **5** banjo **6** dorado, madtom, mudcat, sucker **7** ariidae, bluecat **8** bagridae, bullhead, claridae, electric, flathead **9** siluridae **10** channel cat, cuttlefish, mochocidae, plotosidae, spotted cat **11** ictaluridae, pimelodidae, schilbeidae **12** aspredinidae, ostariophysi **14** malapteruridae **16** trichomycteridae

Catfish
nickname of: 9 Jim Hunter

catharsis 7 purging, release, venting **9** cleansing **12** purification

Catharsius
epithet of: 4 Zeus
means: 8 purifier

cathartic 5 purge **6** physic **8** aperient, evacuant, laxative **9** castor oil, purgative, purifying

cathedral 3 see **6** church, temple **7** lateran **8** basilica, official **9** authority **10** pontifical
Italian: 5 duomo

Cather, Willa
author of: 9 A Lost Lady, My Antonia, One of Ours, O Pioneers! **13** My Mortal Enemy **16** Shadows on the Rock, The Song of the Lark **18** The Professor's House **23** Sapphira and the Slave Girl **26** Death Comes for the Archbishop

cathode ray tube
abbreviation: 3 CRT
invented by: 7 Crookes

catholic, Catholic 5 broad **7** liberal **9** universal, worldwide **12** all-embracing, all-inclusive **13** comprehensive

cathouse 4 stew **5** house **6** bagnio, bordel **7** brothel **8** bordello **10** bawdy house, fancy house, whorehouse **13** sporting house **14** house of ill fame **16** house of ill repute **19** house of prostitution

Cat Jumps, The
author: 14 Elizabeth Bowen

catlike 5 catty, lithe **7** sinuous **8** stealthy **14** light on the feet

Catlin, George
born: 13 Wilkes-Barre PA
artwork: 16 Gallery of Indians

catnap 3 nap **4** doze **6** siesta, snooze **10** forty winks, light sleep

Cato
author: 13 Joseph Addison

Cat on a Hot Tin Roof
author: 17 Tennessee Williams
director: 13 Richard Brooks
cast: 8 Burl Ives (Big Daddy) **10** Jack Carson, Paul Newman (Brick) **14** Judith Anderson **15** Elizabeth Taylor (Maggie)

Catreus
king of: 5 Crete
father: 5 Minos
mother: 8 Pasiphae
son: 11 Althaemenes
daughter: 6 Aerope **7** Clymene **9** Apemosyne
grandson: 8 Menelaus

cats-eye
species: 11 chrysoberyl
source: 8 Sri Lanka

cat's paw 4 dupe, pawn, tool **5** patsy **7** fall guy

cattle 4 cows, kine, oxen **5** beefs, bulls, stock **6** beeves, calves, dogies, steers **8** bullocks, milk cows **9** livestock
family: 7 Bovidae
group of: 5 drove
kind: 2 ox **3** yak **4** Zebu **5** Angus **6** Ankole, Jersey **7** Brahman **8** Ayrshire, Guernsey, Hereford, Highland, Holstein **9** Charolais **12** water buffalo **13** Texas Longhorn **16** English Shorthorn, Holstein-Friesian
young: 4 calf **6** heifer **8** yearling

Catton, Bruce
author of: 22 A Stillness at Appomattox

catty 4 mean **7** catlike **8** spiteful **9** malicious, malignant **10** malevolent

catwalk 6 bridge **7** walkway **10** passageway

Caucasian
language branch: 5 Ubykh **9** Daghestan **10** Circassian **11** Khartvelian

Caucon
brought mysteries to: 8 Messenia

caucus 6 parley, powwow **7** council, meeting, session **8** assembly, conclave **10** conference

caudal 4 back, tail **7** tail-end

cauldron *see* **7** caldron

Caulfield, Holden
character in: 18 The Catcher in the Rye
author: 8 Salinger

Caulfield, Joan
real name: 21 Beatrice Joan Caulfield
born: 8 Orange NJ
roles: 8 Dear Ruth **17** My Favorite Husband

Caunus
brother: 6 Byblis

causation 4 root **5** cause **6** author, origin, reason, source **7** creator, genesis **8** etiology, inventor, stimulus **9** generator, invention **10** antecedent, conception, mainspring, originator **11** determinant, inspiration, origination

cause 4 goal, make, root, side **5** ideal, impel, tenet **6** belief, create, effect, incite, lead to, motive, object, origin, reason, source, spring, stir up **7** genesis, grounds, incline, inspire, produce, provoke, purpose **8** etiology, generate, motivate, occasion, stimulus **9** incentive, principle, stimulate **10** aspiration, bring about, conviction, foundation, give rise to, inducement, initiation, mainspring, motivation, persuasion, prime mover **11** bring to pass, inspiration, instigation, precipitate, provocation

cause of war
Latin: 10 casus belli

cause to appear 6 expose, reveal **7** uncover **8** disclose **12** bring to light **13** bring into view

caustic 4 tart **5** acrid, harsh, sharp **6** biting, bitter **7** burning, cutting, erosive, gnawing **8** scathing, stinging **9** corroding, corrosive, sarcastic **10** astringent **11** acrimonious

caution 4 care, heed, warn **5** alarm, alert **6** advise, caveat, exhort, notify, regard, tip-off **7** concern, thought, warning **8** admonish, forewarn, prudence, wariness **9** alertness, restraint, vigilance **10** admonition, discretion, precaution **11** carefulness, forewarning, guardedness, heedfulness, mindfulness **12** deliberation, watchfulness **14** circumspection, put on one's guard

cautionary 7 warning **8** advisory **10** admonitory **11** admonishing

cautious 4 wary **5** alert, cagey **7** careful, guarded, prudent **8** discreet, vigilant, watchful

9 attentive, judicious **11** circumspect

cavalcade **5** troop **6** column, parade **7** caravan, retinue **10** procession

Cavalcade
director: **10** Frank Lloyd
based on play by: **10** Noel Coward
cast: **10** Clive Brook **11** Ursula Jeans **12** Diana Wynyard **13** Herbert Mundin **15** Margaret Lindsay
Oscar for: **7** picture

cavalier **3** fop **4** beau **5** blade, cocky, dandy, swell **6** hussar, lancer **7** cursory, dragoon, gallant, haughty, offhand, playboy **8** arrogant, courtier, gay blade, horseman, uncaring **9** easygoing **10** cavalryman, disdainful, nonchalant **11** indifferent, thoughtless

cavalry **7** hussars, lancers **8** dragoons **10** mounted men **11** horse troops **13** horse soldiers, mounted troops

cavalryman **6** hussar, lancer **7** dragoon **8** cavalier, horseman **12** horse soldier, horse trooper **14** mounted soldier

cave **3** den **4** lair, sink **6** burrow, cavern, cavity, dugout, grotto, hollow
growth: **10** stalactite, stalagmite
explorer: **9** spelunker

caveat **5** alarm, alert, aviso **6** tip-off **7** caution, red flag, warning **8** high sign, red light **10** admonition, danger sign, yellow jack **11** forewarning **12** admonishment, flea in the ear **13** word to the wise **20** handwriting on the wall

caveat emptor **17** let the buyer beware

cave canem **14** beware of the dog

cave in **6** buckle, fall in, give up, submit **7** crumple, give way, implode **8** collapse **10** capitulate **12** fall to pieces

Cavendish, Henry
field: **7** physics **9** chemistry
nationality: **7** British
discovered: **8** hydrogen
determined composition of: **3** air **5** water **10** nitric acid
method: **19** Cavendish experiment

cavernous **4** huge, vast **5** roomy **6** gaping **7** chasmal, immense, yawning **8** cavelike, enormous, spacious **10** tremendous

cavil **6** deride **7** nitpick, quibble **8** belittle, complain **9** criticize, deprecate, discredit, disparage, faultfind, find fault **12** pick to pieces

cavity **3** dip, pit **4** bore, dent, hole, sink **5** basin, niche **6** burrow, crater, hollow, pocket, tunnel **7** opening, orifice, vacuity **8** aperture **9** concavity **10** depression, excavation

cavort **4** play, romp **5** bound, caper, frisk **6** frolic, gambol, prance

Cawdor
author: **15** Robinson Jeffers

Caxtons, The
author: **12** Bulwer Lytton

Cayster
river in: **5** Lydia

Cayuga
language family: **9** Iroquoian
location: **4** Ohio **6** Canada **7** New York **8** Oklahoma **9** Wisconsin
branch of: **10** Six Nations **19** Iroquois Confederacy, League of the Iroquois

cease **3** end **4** halt, pass, quit, stop **5** abate, pause **6** desist, finish **7** adjourn, die away, forbear, suspend **8** break off, conclude, leave off **9** terminate **11** abstain from, discontinue, refrain from **12** bring to an end

cease-fire **5** truce **9** armistice

ceaseless **7** endless, eternal **8** constant, enduring, unending **9** continual, incessant, permanent, perpetual, unceasing **10** continuous, protracted **11** everlasting, never-ending, unremitting **12** interminable **13** uninterrupted

cease to be **3** die, end **6** die out, expire, vanish **9** disappear, evaporate **13** become extinct

Cebriones
father: **5** Priam
brother: **6** Hector
charioteer for: **6** Hector

Cecilia (Memoirs of an Heiress)
author: **11** Fanny Burney

Cecrops
also: **8** Cecropia
form: **3** man **6** dragon
founder of: **6** Attica
king of: **6** Attica
father: **14** King Erechtheus
brother: **6** Metion, Orneus
wife: **8** Aglaurus
son: **11** Erysichthon
daughter: **5** Herse **8** Aglaurus **9** Pandrasos
renamed Attica: **8** Cecropia

Cedalion
occupation: **5** smith
forge owner: **10** Hephaestus
served as guide for: **5** Orion

cedar **6** Cedrus
varieties: **3** red **4** pink, salt **5** Atlas, giant, white **6** Alaska, Cyprus, ground, Mlanje **7** Bermuda, incense, Russian, Spanish **8** Barbados, cigar-box, creeping, Japanese, stinking **10** Ozark white, Port Orford, swamp white, western red, West Indian, Willowmore **11** Clanwilliam, Colorado red, southern red **13** Atlantic white, southern white **14** Chilean incense, Formosa incense **17** California incense

cede **4** give **5** grant, leave, yield **6** tender **7** abandon, deliver, release **8** hand over, transfer **9** deliver up, surrender **10** relinquish

cedez
music: **8** slow down

Cedreatis
epithet of: **7** Artemis
means: **14** of the cedar tree

Cedric the Saxon
character in: **7** Ivanhoe
author: **5** Scott

ceiling **3** top **4** roof **5** cover, limit **6** canopy, cupola, lining **7** maximum **8** altitude **10** upperlimit

Celaeno
member of: **7** Harpies **8** Pleiades

Celebes
also: **8** Sulawesi
bordered by: **6** Borneo **8** Moluccas **10** Celebes Sea, Kalimantan **12** Flores Strait **14** Makassar Strait
city: **4** Poso **6** Manado **7** Kendari, Madjene **8** Bonthain, Donggala, Makassar **9** Gorontalo
location: **9** Indonesia
people: **4** Bugi, Laki, Mori, Muna, Napu, Palu, Peso, Seko, Wana **5** Besoa, Buton, Toala **6** Bungku, Butung, Parigi, Sadang, Sangir, Toland **7** Banggai, Bolaang, Kabaena, Loinang, Toradja **8** Balantak, Buginese, Mongondu, Rongkong, Sanghike **9** Gorontalo **11** Makassarese
province: **13** North Sulawesi, South Sulawesi **15** Central Sulawesi **17** Southeast Sulawesi

celebrate **4** laud **5** bless, cheer, exalt, extol, honor **6** hallow, praise, revere **7** acclaim, applaud, commend, glorify, observe **8** proclaim, sanctify, venerate **9** broadcast, ritualize, solemnize **10** consecrate **11** commemorate **13** ceremonialize

celebrated **5** famed, noted **6** famous, prized **7** eminent, honored, notable, revered **8** lionized, renowned **9** acclaimed, important, prominent, respected, treasured, venerable, well-known **11** illustrious, outstanding **13** distinguished

Celebrated Jumping Frog of Calaveras County, The
author: **9** Mark Twain

celebration **4** fete, gala **5** feast, party **6** ritual **7** jubilee, revelry **8** carnival, ceremony, festival **9** festivity, hallowing **10** ceremonial, observance **13** commemoration, solemnization **14** sanctification **15** memorialization

celebrity **3** VIP **4** fame, name, note, star **5** glory, wheel **6** bigwig, renown **7** big shot, notable, stardom **8** eminence, luminary **9** dignitary, notoriety, personage **10** notability, popularity, prominence **11** distinction, personality **12** famous person, person of note

celerity **5** haste, hurry, speed **6** hustle **8** alacrity, dispatch, fast clip, fastness, legerity, rapidity **9** briskness, quickness, swiftness **10** expedition, snappiness, speediness **12** precipitance **14** lightning speed **15** expeditiousness

celery seed
also called: **8** smallage
origin: **13** Mediterranean
use: **4** soup **5** salad, sauce **6** pickle **10** vegetables

celestial **3** sky **5** solar **6** astral, divine **7** angelic, elysian, stellar, sublime **8** beatific, blissful, empyrean, ethereal, hallowed, heavenly, seraphic **9** planetary, unearthly **12** astronomical, otherworldly, paradisiacal

celestial being **3** god **5** angel, deity **7** goddess **8** divinity **11** divine being

Celestial City
place in: **16** Pilgrim's Progress
author: **6** Bunyan

Celia (Aliena)
character in: **11** As You Like It
author: **11** Shakespeare

celibacy **8** chastity **9** virginity **10** abstinence, continence **12** bachelorhood, spinsterhood

celibate **4** pure **5** unwed **6** chaste, single **8** bachelor, spinster, virginal **9** abstinent, continent, unmarried

Celine, Louis-Ferdinand
author of: **12** Guignol's Band **25** Death on the Installment Plan, Journey to the End of the Night

cell
part: **7** nucleus **8** membrane **9** cytoplasm
made of: **3** fat **4** salt **5** water **7** protein **9** compounds **12** carbohydrate
theory of: **7** (Rudolf) Virchow, (Theodor) Schwann

cellar **3** den **4** cave **6** dugout **8** basement **10** downstairs

Cellini, Benvenuto
born: **5** Italy **8** Florence
artwork: **7** Cosimo I, Perseus **13** Bindo Altoviti **18** The Crucified Christ **20** Nymph of Fontainebleau
autobiography: **22** Life of Benvenuto Cellini

Celsius
abbreviation of: **1** C

Celt **4** Gaul, Kelt, Manx, Scot **5** Irish, Welsh **6** Breton, Briton, chisel **8** Scottish **10** Highlander

Celtic
language group: **6** Gaelic **9** Brythonic
family: **12** Indo-European
language of: **5** Gauls

cement **3** fix, set **4** bind, fuse, glue, join, seal, weld **5** paste, stick, unite **6** mortar, secure **8** concrete

cemetery **7** ossuary **8** boneyard, Boot Hill, catacomb **9** graveyard **10** churchyard, necropolis **12** burial ground, memorial park, potter's field **13** burying ground

Cenaean *see* **4** Zeus

Cenchrias
father: **8** Poseidon
mother: **6** Pirene
killed by: **7** Artemis

Cenci, The
author: **18** Percy Bysshe Shelley

cenobite **4** monk **7** ascetic **8** celibate **9** religious

censor **4** blip, edit **5** amend, judge, purge **6** critic, delete, excise **7** amender, clean up **8** black out, examiner, reviewer, suppress **9** expurgate, inspector **10** blue-pencil, bowdlerize, expurgator, suppressor **11** bowdlerizer, faultfinder, scrutinizer **12** investigator **17** custodian of morals **25** guardian of the public morals

censorious **5** picky **7** abusive, carping **8** critical **10** defamatory **12** faultfinding

censurable **8** blamable **10** deplorable, punishable, reprovable **11** blameworthy **12** reproachable **13** reprehensible

censure **3** pan, rap **5** chide, scold **6** berate, rebuke **7** bawl out, chew out, chiding, condemn, reproof, reprove, upbraid **8** admonish, denounce, reproach, scolding **9** castigate, complaint, criticism, criticize, reprehend, reprimand **10** admonition, bawling-out, chewing-out, disapprove, upbraiding **11** castigation, disapproval, reprobation **12** condemnation, dressing-down, remonstrance **13** tongue-lashing **14** disapprobation **16** rap on the knuckles, take over the coals
god of: **5** Momos, Momus

census **3** tax **4** data, list, poll **5** count **6** amount, number **11** enumeration **12** registration

Centaur
form: **3** man **5** horse **7** monster **16** half-man half-horse
constellation of: **9** Centaurus
famous: **6** Chiron
represents: **11** Sagittarius

Centaurus
father: **5** Ixion
mother: **7** Nephele
father of: **8** Centaurs

Centennial
author: **13** James Michener

Centennial State
nickname of: **8** Colorado

center, centre **3** fix, hub, mid **4** axis, core, crux **5** focus, heart, pivot, point **6** direct, gather, middle **7** address, essence, nucleus **8** converge, interior **9** middle **10** focal point **11** concentrate

centered **4** even, true **5** right **7** focused **8** straight **10** pinpointed **12** concentrated

centigrade **5** scale **6** degree **7** celcius **11** thermometer

centigram
abbreviation of: **2** cg

centiliter
abbreviation of: **2** cl

Centimani *see* **13** Hecatonchires

centimeter
abbreviation of: **2** cm

centipede **4** boat **5** shrub **6** earwig, insect **8** chilopod, multiped **9** arthropod **13** muehlenbeckia

central **3** key **4** main **5** basic, chief, focal, inner, major, prime **6** inmost, middle **7** leading, midmost, pivotal, primary **8** dominant, foremost, interior **9** essential, paramount, principal **10** middlemost **11** fundamental, predominant **13** most important

Central African Republic
other name: **11** Ubangi-Chari **20** Central African Empire
capital/largest city: **6** Bangui
others: **3** Obo **4** Bria, Ippy **5** Birao, Bouar, Kembe, Ndele, Ngoto, Paoua, Rafai, Zemio **6** Baboua, Bakala, Bozoum, Mbaiki **7** Bambari, Grimari, Zemongo **9** Bangassou, Berberati, Bossangoa, Fort-Sibut
monetary unit: **5** franc **7** centime
lake: **4** Chad
mountain: **5** Karre, Tinga **6** Mongos **9** Dar Challa
highest point: **11** Kayagangiri
river: **4** Bomu, Nana **5** Chari, Kotto, Mbari, Mpoko, Ouaka **6** Chinko, Lobaye, Mbomou, Ubangi **11** Upper Sangha
people: **4** Baya, Sara **5** Banda, Bwaka, Sango **6** Azande, Yakoma **7** Banziri, Mandjia, Nzakara
language: **5** Sango, Zande **6** French
religion: **5** Islam **7** animism **12** Christianity **13** Roman Catholic
place:
plaza: **13** Edouard Renard
food:
tapioca: **6** manioc **7** cassava

Central America *see box*

Central Amerind
language branch: **9** Oto-Mangue **10** Uto-Aztecan **11** Kiowa-Tanoan

Central America
land form: **7** isthmus
countries: **6** Belize, Panama **8** Honduras **9** Costa Rica, Guatemala, Nicaragua **10** El Salvador
bordered by: **6** Mexico, **8** Colombia **12** Caribbean Sea, North America, Pacific Ocean, South America
capital city: **7** Managua, San Jose **8** Belmopan **10** Panama City **11** San Salvador, Tegucigalpa **13** Guatemala City
river: **3** New **4** Axul, Coco, Sico, Tuma, Ulua, Wawa **5** Aguan, Chepo, Hondo, Lempa, Wauks **6** Chixoy, Grande, Pasion, Patuca, Sulaco, Waspuk **7** Motagua, Paulaya, San Juan, Sarstun, Segovia **8** Kukalaya **9** Choluteca, Escondido **10** Chucunague **11** Prinzapolca
lake: **5** Gatun, Guija, Yojoa **7** Atitlan, Managua **9** Nicaragua, Peten Itza
mountain: **4** Maya, Pija **5** Colon, Huapi, Minas, Pando **6** Blanco **7** Dipilto, Gongora, San Blas **8** Brewster, Dariense, Isabelia, San Pablo, Santa Ana **9** Esperanza **14** Chirripo Grande
people: **3** Mam **5** Zambo **6** Indian, Ladino, Quiche **7** mestizo **8** Miskitas **10** Black Carib, Cakchiquel
animal: **5** tapir **6** agouti **7** opossum, peccary **8** anteater, kinkajou, marmoset **9** armadillo, porcupine, tree sloth **12** howler monkey, spider monkey **14** capuchin monkey

central city **8** core city, downtown **9** inner city, urban area **10** metropolis **16** business district, metropolitan area

central idea **3** nut **4** core, crux, gist, meat **5** heart, theme **6** kernel **7** essence **9** main point

centralization **5** focus **11** convergence **13** concentration, consolidation

centralize **5** focus, unify **6** center, gather **7** collect, compact **8** center on, coalesce, converge, pinpoint **9** integrate **10** congregate **11** concentrate, consolidate

central part **4** core, crux, gist, pith **5** heart **6** center, kernel **7** nucleus

century
abbreviation of: **4** cent
French: **6** siecle

cephalopod **5** squid **7** mollusk, octopus **8** nautilus **10** cuttlefish

Cephalus
father: **6** Hermes
mother: **5** Herse
brother: **5** Ceryx
wife: **7** Clymene, Procris

Cephas *see* **5** Peter

Cepheus
king of: **8** Ethiopia
wife: **10** Cassiopeia
daughter: **9** Andromeda

Cerambus
form: **6** beetle

ceramic ware **5** china, glass **7** pottery **8** crockery **9** chinaware, glassware, porcelain, stoneware **10** enamelware **11** earthenware

ceratopsid
type of: **8** dinosaur
member: **10** Torosaurus **11** Monoclonius, Triceratops **13** Protoceratops, Styracosaurus **14** Psittacosaurus

Ceratosaurus
type: **8** dinosaur
period: **8** Jurassic

Cerberus
form: **3** dog
father: **6** Typhon
mother: **7** Echidna
sibling: **5** Hydra **7** Orthrus **8** Chimaera **10** Nemean lion **12** Theban Sphinx
number of heads: **5** three
guarded: **10** Underworld

Cercopes
race of: **6** Gnomes

Cercyon
king of: **7** Arcadia
daughter: **5** Alope

cereal **4** corn, oats, rice, seed **5** grain, grass, gruel, plant, wheat **6** barley, pablum **7** oatmeal, pabulum **8** porridge

cerebellum
part of: **5** brain
controls: **7** balance **8** movement

cerebrum
part of: **5** brain
controls: **6** seeing **7** hearing, tasting **8** deciding, feelings, learning, smelling, thinking, touching **9** awareness **11** remembering

ceremonial **4** rite **6** formal, ritual **7** liturgy, service **8** ceremony **9** formality, sacrament **10** liturgical, observance **11** celebration, ritualistic

ceremonialize **7** observe **9** celebrate, ritualize **11** commemorate

ceremonious **5** exact, fussy, rigid, stiff **6** formal, proper, solemn **7** careful, correct, pompous, precise **8** starched **9** dignified **10** methodical, meticulous **11** punctilious

ceremony **4** rite **6** custom, nicety, ritual **7** amenity, decorum, pageant, service **8** function, protocol **9** etiquette, formality, propriety **10** observance, politeness **11** celebration, formalities **13** commemoration

Cerenkov, Pavel Alekseevich
field: **7** physics
nationality: **7** Russian
discovered: **12** cause of light **14** Cerenkov effect

Ceres
origin: **5** Roman
goddess of: **11** agriculture
corresponds to: **7** Demeter

certain **4** sure **5** valid **6** secure **7** assured, express, settled, special **8** absolute, cocksure, definite, positive, reliable, specific **9** confident, convinced, satisfied **10** conclusive, individual, inevitable, particular, undeniable, undisputed, undoubtful, undoubting, unshakable **11** indubitable, inescapable, irrefutable, unalterable, unequivocal, unqualified **12** indisputable, unchangeable, unmistakable, well-grounded **13** bound to happen, incontestable **14** unquestionable **16** incontrovertible

certainly **5** truly **6** indeed, surely **7** for sure **8** of course **9** decidedly **10** absolutely, definitely, positively **11** indubitably, undoubtedly **13** unequivocally, without a doubt **14** unquestionably **21** beyond a shadow of a doubt

Certain Smile, A
author: **14** Francoise Sagan

certainty **4** fact **5** faith, trust **6** belief, surety **7** reality, sure bet **8** sureness **9** actuality, assurance, certitude, sure thing **10** confidence, conviction **11** presumption **12** positiveness **13** inevitability **14** conclusiveness, inescapability **17** authoritativeness

certificate **4** deed **6** permit **7** diploma, license, voucher **8** document, warranty **9** affidavit **10** credential **11** testimonial **13** authorization **14** authentication

certification **7** voucher **8** approval **10** validation **11** endorsement **12** confirmation, ratification, verification **13** authorization, corroboration **14** authentication, substantiation

certify **4** aver **5** swear, vouch **6** assure, attest, ratify, second, verify **7** confirm, declare, endorse, support, warrant, witness **8** notarize, sanction, validate **9** authorize, guarantee, testify to **10** underwrite **11** corroborate **12** authenticate, give one's word, substantiate

certitude **5** faith, trust **6** belief, surety **8** reliance, sureness **9** assurance, certainty **10** confidence **12** positiveness **14** conclusiveness

cerulean **4** blue **5** azure **6** cobalt **7** sky blue **9** clear blue

Cervantes Saavedra, Miguel de
author of: **20** Don Quixote de la Mancha

Cerynean stag
also: **12** Arcadian stag
home: **7** Arcadia
captured by: **8** Hercules

Ceryx
herald of: **4** gods
father: **6** Hermes
mother: **5** Herse
brother: **8** Cephalus

Cesar Birotteau
author: **14** Honore de Balzac

cessation **3** end **4** halt, stay, stop **5** pause **6** ending, recess **7** ceasing, halting, respite **8** quitting, stopping, surcease **9** desisting **10** concluding, leaving off, suspension **11** adjournment, breaking off, termination **12** interruption **13** coming to a halt, discontinuing **14** discontinuance

c'est la vie **9** that's life **10** such is life

Cestrinus
father: **7** Helenus
mother: **10** Andromache

Cestus
girdle of: **5** Venus

cetacean **4** apod **5** whale **6** beluga, mammal **7** cetacea, dolphin, dowfish, grampus, narwhal **8** porpoise, sturgeon **9** blue whale **11** baleen whale, killer whale

Cetinje
capital of: **10** Montenegro

Ceto
father: **6** Pontus
mother: **4** Gaea
brother: **7** Phorcys
husband: **7** Phorcys
mother of: **6** Graeae **7** Gorgons
children called: **8** Phorcids

Ceylon *see* **8** Sri Lanka

Ceyx
father: **9** Eosphorus
wife: **7** Alcyone

Cezanne, Paul
born: **6** France **13** Aix-en-Provence
artwork: **7** Bathers **11** Card Players **13** The Black Clock, The Railway Out **14** Uncle Dominique **15** La Maison du Pendu **16** The Suicide's House **17** Grandes Baigneuses **19** Woman with a Coffee Pot **36** Mont-Sainte-Victoire with Large Pine Trees

Chabrier, (Alexis) Emmanuel
born: **6** Ambert, France
composer of: **6** Espana **7** L'Etoile **10** Gwendoline **13** Marche Joyeuse **14** Le Roi Malgre Lui **18** King Despite Himself **19** Une Education Manquee

Chad
other name: **5** Tchad
capital/largest city: **8** Fort-Lamy, N'Djamena
others: **3** Ati, Bol, Lai, Mao **4** Fada, Faya, Sarh **5** Mongo **6** Abeche, Bongor **7** Largeau, Moundou **8** Moussoro
monetary unit: **5** franc **7** centime
lake: **4** Chad
mountain: **7** Tibesti, Touside
highest point: **9** Emi Koussi
river: **5** Chari **6** Logone **8** Bahraouk
physical feature:
plateau: **6** Ennedi
people: **4** Arab, Daza, Maba, Sara, Teda, Tubu **5** Barma, Hakka, Kreda, Massa **6** Fulani, Kotoko, Toubou, Wadaii **7** Kamadja, Kanembu, Moundan
language: **4** Sara **5** Turku **6** Arabic, French
religion: **5** Islam **7** animism **12** Christianity

Chadband
character in: **10** Bleak House
author: **7** Dickens

Chadic
language family: **11** Afroasiatic **13** Hamito-Semitic
includes: **5** Hausa
spoken in: **6** Africa **8** Lake Chad

Chadwick, James
field: **7** physics
nationality: **7** British
discovered: **7** neutron
awarded: **10** Nobel Prize

chafe **3** rub **4** boil, burn, foam, fume, rage, rasp **6** abrade, rankle, scrape, seethe **7** scratch **9** be annoyed **11** be irritated

chaff **3** bug, kid, rag, rib **4** josh, junk, pods, razz, ride, slag, twit **5** dross, hulls, husks, jolly, trash, waste **6** banter, debris, litter, refuse, rubble, shells, shoddy, shucks **7** kidding, ragging, remnant, residue, ribbing, rubbish, waggery **8** badinage, chaffing, leavings, raillery, ridicule **9** sweepings **9** give and take

chaffing **6** banter **7** jesting, joshing, kidding, ragging, ribbing, waggery **8** badinage, raillery

chafing **5** harsh **6** fuming **7** rasping, rubbing **8** abrading, abrasive **10** irritating

Chagall, Marc
born: **6** Liosno, Liozno, Russia
artwork: **8** Birthday, Cockcrow **9** The Circus, The Red Sun **10** The Juggler **11** Over Vitebsk **12** The Violinist **14** Double Portrait, I and the Village **16** The Jewish Wedding **17** Lovers with Rooster **20** Paris Through My Window

chagrin **5** shame **6** dismay **8** distress **11** humiliation **13** embarrassment, mortification

chagrined **7** abashed, ashamed **9** mortified **10** humiliated **11** embarrassed

Chahiksichhiks *see* **6** Pawnee

chain **3** fob **5** cable, links **7** shackle **8** necklace **10** metal links **11** linked cable
abbreviation: **2** ch

Chain, Ernst Boris
field: **12** biochemistry
nationality: **7** British
discovered: **10** penicillin
worked with: **6** Florey **7** Fleming
awarded: **10** Nobel Prize

Chained Lady
constellation of: **9** Andromeda

chains **3** tie **4** bind, lash, moor **5** bonds, irons, tie up, train **6** fasten, fetter, secure, series, string, tether **7** bondage, fetters, manacle, serfdom, shackle, slavery **8** leg irons, manacles, sequence, shackles **9** handcuffs, servitude, thralldom **10** put in irons, succession **11** enslavement, subjugation

chair **4** seat **5** bench, couch, sedan stool **6** chaise, lounge, rocker, settee, throne **7** conduct, ottoman **11** preside over **16** presiding officer

chairman **4** head **5** chair, emcee **6** leader **7** manager, speaker **8** director **9** chairlady, executive, moderator **10** chairwoman, supervisor **11** chairperson, toastmaster **13** administrator **16** presiding officer **18** master of ceremonies

Chair of Forgetfulness
form: **4** seat
made of: **5** stone
location: **10** Underworld

chaise **3** gig **4** shay **5** chair **6** daybed, lounge **7** calesin **8** carriage, duchesse

chalcedony **3** gem **4** onyx, opal, sard **5** agate, prase **6** jasper, plasma, quartz, silica **7** catseye, mineral, opaline, sardius **8** hematite, sardonyx **9** carnelian **10** bloodstone, heliotrope **11** chrysoprase **12** semiprecious **14** silicon dioxide

Chalcis
father: **6** Asopus
mother: **6** Metope

Chaldean **4** seer **5** magic **6** Syriac **7** Aramaic, semitic **8** magician **9** astrology, enchanter, Nabonidus **10** astrologer, Babylonian, soothsayer **12** Nabopolassar **14** Nebuchadnezzar

chalice **3** cup **5** grail **6** goblet, vessel

Chalinitis
epithet of: **6** Athena
means: **7** bridler

chalk **4** draw **6** crayon, pastel, sketch **9** limestone

chalk up **4** earn **5** score **6** attain, charge, credit **7** achieve, ascribe

chalky **3** wan **4** pale **5** ashen, white **6** pallid **7** powdery **8** blanched **9** bloodless

challenge **3** bid, tax, try **4** dare, defy, gage, test **5** doubt, trial **6** demand, impute, summon **7** defiant, dispute, summons **8** question **15** take exception to **20** fling down the gauntlet

chamber **4** diet, hall, room **5** board, court, house, salon **6** office, parlor **7** bedroom, boudoir, council **8** assembly, congress **9** apartment

Chamberlain, Owen
field: **7** physics
developed: **8** atom bomb
awarded: **10** Nobel Prize

Chamberlain, Richard
real name: **24** George Richard Chamberlain
born: **12** Los Angeles CA
roles: **6** Shogun **9** Dr Kildare **10** Wallenberg **13** The Thorn Birds **17** The Bourne Identity **21** The Count of Monte Cristo

Chamberlain, Wilt (Wilton Norman)
nickname: **6** Dipper **12** Wilt the Stilt
sport: **10** basketball
position: **5** coach **6** center
team: **16** Los Angeles Lakers **17** Philadelphia 76ers **20** Philadelphia Warriors, San Francisco Warriors **21** San Diego Conquistadors

chambermaid
French: **14** femme de chambre

chambord
type: **7** liqueur
origin: **6** France
flavor: **9** raspberry

chameleon **4** newt **6** lizard **8** renegade, turncoat **10** fickleness **14** changeableness

champ **4** bite, chew, gnaw **5** chomp, crush, grind, munch **6** crunch **8** champion

champagne
type: **4** wine
drink: **7** the Pope
with white wine: **8** Cold Duck
with orange juice: **6** Mimosa
measure: **6** magnum **8** jeroboam, rehoboam **9** balthazar **10** methuselah, salmanazar **14** Nebuchadnezzar

Champaigne, Philippe de
born: **7** Belgium **8** Brussels
artwork: **6** Ex Voto **17** Cardinal Richelieu **26** The Adoration of the Shepherds

champion **3** aid **4** abet, back **6** backer, defend, master, uphold, victor, winner **7** espouse, paragon, promote, support **8** advocate, defender, fight for, laureate, promoter, speak for, upholder **9** battle for, conqueror, protector, supporter **10** stand up for, vanquisher **11** protagonist, title holder

Champion
constellation of: 7 Perseus

championship 3 cup **5** crown, title **7** backing, defense, support, winning **8** advocacy, espousal

Chamyne
epithet of: 7 Demeter

chance 3 try **4** fall, fate, luck, risk **5** lucky, occur **6** befall, danger, gamble, happen, hazard, random **7** attempt, destiny, fortune, turn out, venture **8** accident, jeopardy, occasion **9** come about, fortunate, unplanned **10** accidental, fortuitous, likelihood, likeliness, providence, undesigned, unexpected, unforeseen **11** opportunity, possibility, probability, speculation, unlooked for **12** happenstance **13** unintentional **14** unpremeditated

chance upon 4 find, meet **7** learn of, run into **8** come upon, discover **9** encounter, light upon **10** happen upon **11** stumble upon

chancy 4 iffy **5** dicey, risky **6** touchy, tricky **7** dubious, erratic, unsound **8** doubtful **9** hazardous, uncertain, whimsical **10** capricious, precarious **11** speculative, venturesome **13** problematical, unpredictable

chandelier 11 hanging lamp **12** candleholder **15** lighting fixture

Chandler, Jeff
real name: 10 Ira Grossel
born: 10 Brooklyn NY
roles: 7 Cochise **11** Broken Arrow **17** Merrill's Marauders

Chandler, Raymond
author of: 11 The Big Sleep **14** The Long Goodbye **16** Farewell My Lovely
character: 13 Philip Marlowe
screenplay: 13 The Blue Dahlia **15** Double Indemnity **17** Strangers on a Train

Chaney, Lon
real name: 12 Alonso Chaney
son: 9 Creighton (Lon Chaney Jr)
nickname: 19 Man of a Thousand Faces
born: 17 Colorado Springs CO
roles: 14 The Unholy Three **18** Tell It to the Marines **20** Hunchback of Notre Dame, The Phantom of the Opera

Chaney, Lon Jr
real name: 9 Creighton
father: 3 Lon
born: 14 Oklahoma City OK
roles: 6 Lennie **8** The Mummy **10** The Wolf Man **12** Of Mice and Men, Son of Dracula **20** Frankenstein's Monster

change 4 swap, turn, vary **5** alter, coins, shift, trade **6** modify, mutate, recast, reform, silver, switch **7** convert, novelty, remodel, replace, restyle, shuffle, variety, veering **8** pin money, swapping, transfer **9** deviation, diversion, exception, restyling, transform, transmute, turn about, variation **10** alteration, conversion, difference, remodeling, reorganize, revolution, small coins, substitute **11** fluctuation, pocket money, reformation **12** metamorphose, modification, substitution **13** make different, metamorphosis, revolutionize, transmutation, transposition **14** reorganization, transformation **15** transfiguration

changeable 6 fickle, fitful **7** erratic, flighty, mutable, varying **8** unstable, unsteady, variable, volatile **9** deviating, irregular, mercurial, uncertain **10** capricious, inconstant, modifiable, reversible **11** alternating, convertible, fluctuating, vacillating **13** transformable

change in plan
French: 8 demarche

changeless 4 fast **5** fixed **6** stable **7** abiding, certain, durable, eternal, lasting **8** constant, enduring **9** immutable, steadfast, unvarying **10** unshakable **11** everlasting, unalterable **12** indissoluble

changelessness 9 certainty, constancy, stability **10** durability, permanence **12** immutability **13** steadfastness

change of heart 10 conversion **16** change of attitude

changeover 10 conversion

channel 3 cut **4** gash, lead, send **5** guide, route, steer **6** convey, course, direct, furrow, groove, gutter, strait, trough **7** narrows, passage **11** watercourse **21** avenue of communication

Channing, Carol
born: 9 Seattle WA
roles: 10 Hello Dolly **22** Gentlemen Prefer Blondes, Thoroughly Modern Millie

chanson 4 song

Chanson de Roland
also: 12 Song of Roland
author: 7 unknown
character: 4 Aude **6** Turpin **7** Ganelon, Marsile, Olivier **11** Charlemagne, Twelve Peers
foe: 8 Saracens

chant 3 ode **4** hymn, lied, sing, song **5** carol, croon, dirge, elegy, psalm, theme, trill, troll **6** chorus, intone, melody, monody, strain **7** chanson, chorale, descant **8** canticle, doxology, threnody, vocalize **9** homophony, monophony, offertory, plainsong **11** Gloria Patri **14** Gregorian chant

chanteuse 6 singer (female)

Chants de Maldoror, Les
author: 18 Comte de Lautreamont

Chaon
father: 5 Priam
mother: 6 Hecuba
brother: 5 Paris **6** Hector **7** Helenus
sister: 8 Polyxena **9** Cassandra

chaos 4 mess **5** furor **6** bedlam, jumble, muddle, tumult, uproar **7** turmoil **8** disarray, disorder, upheaval **9** agitation, commotion, confusion **10** turbulence **11** pandemonium **12** discomposure **14** disarrangement **15** disorganization

Chaos
origin: 5 Greek
personifies: 9 confusion

chaotic 7 jumbled, mixed-up, muddled, tangled **8** confused **9** confusing, illogical, turbulent **10** disjointed, incoherent, in disarray **11** unorganized **12** disorganized **13** disharmonious

chap 3 boy, dry, guy, jaw, lad, man, rap **4** chop, gent **5** bloke, buyer, crack, knock, split **6** fellow, redden, split, stroke **7** fissure, roughen **8** customer **9** purchaser

chapbook 7 garland **8** treasury **9** anthology **10** collection **11** florilegium

chapeau 3 hat

chapel 6 church, shrine **7** oratory **9** sanctuary **10** house of God, tabernacle **14** place of worship

chaperon, chaperone
5 guard, watch **6** duenna, es-

cort **7** oversee **8** guardian, shepherd **9** accompany, attendant, custodian, protector, safeguard **11** keep an eye on

chaperoned **7** oversaw **8** attended, escorted **10** supervised **11** accompanied

chapfallen **6** droopy **8** cast down, dejected **9** depressed

chaplain **4** abbe **5** padre, rabbi, vicar **6** cleric, curate, father, parson, pastor, priest, rector **7** Holy Joe **8** minister, preacher, reverend, sky pilot **9** churchman, clergyman **12** ecclesiastic

chaplet **4** band **6** fillet, wreath **7** circlet, coronet

Chaplin, Charlie
real name: **24** Sir Charles Spencer Chaplin
nickname: **14** the Little Tramp
wife: **10** Oona O'Neill **15** Paulette Goddard
daughter: **9** Geraldine
born: **6** London **7** England
director of/roles: **6** The Kid **8** The Tramp **9** Limelight **10** City Lights **11** Modern Times, The Gold Rush **15** Monsieur Verdoux **16** The Great Dictator

Chaplin, Geraldine
father: **14** Charlie Chaplin
mother: **17** Oona O'Neill Chaplin
born: **13** Santa Monica CA
roles: **12** The Hawaiians **13** Doctor Zhivago

chapter **3** era **4** body, part, span, unit **5** group, phase **6** branch, clause, period **7** episode, portion, section **8** division **9** affiliate **11** subdivision

Chapters of Erie
author: **10** Henry Adams

char **4** burn, sear **5** singe **6** scorch **9** carbonize **10** incinerate

character **4** part, role, self **5** being, honor **6** makeup, nature, person, traits, weirdo **7** honesty, oddball, persona **8** goodness, morality, original, specimen **9** eccentric, integrity, odd person, qualities, rectitude **10** attributes, individual, one-of-a-kind **11** personality, uprightness **13** individuality, moral strength **15** distinctiveness **16** dramatis personae

characteristic **4** mark **5** trait **6** aspect **7** earmark, feature, quality, typical **8** property, symbolic **9** attribute, mannerism, specialty, trademark **10** emblematic, indicative **11** distinctive, peculiarity **14** distinguishing, representative

characterization **8** portrait **9** depiction, picturing, portrayal **11** delineation, description **12** representing **14** representation

characterize **4** mark **5** class **6** define, depict, typify **7** earmark, portray **8** classify, describe, indicate **9** designate, represent **11** distinguish

characterless **4** weak **5** vague **6** anemic **11** nondescript **13** indeterminate **14** expressionless

Characters of Shakespeare's Plays, The
author: **14** William Hazlitt

Charcot, Jean Martin
nationality: **6** French
father of: **9** neurology

Chardin, Jean Baptiste Simeon
born: **5** Paris **6** France
artwork: **7** The Kiss **8** The Grace **14** Young Governess **16** The Copper Cistern **17** Attributes of Music **19** Attributes of the Arts **28** Rayfish Cat and Kitchen Utensils

charge **3** ask, bid, fee **4** care, cost, duty, fill, heap, lade, levy, load, pack, pile, rate, rush, toll **5** beset, blame, debit, exact, onset, order, price, stack, storm, stuff **6** accuse, advice, amount, assail, assess, assign, attack, come at, demand, direct, enjoin, impute, indict, sortie, summon **7** ascribe, assault, bidding, command, control, custody, dictate, expense, keeping, payment, require **8** call upon, instruct, storming **9** attribute, complaint, direction, enjoining, onslaught **10** accusation, allegation, assessment, indictment, injunction, management, protection **11** arraignment, incriminate, instruction, safekeeping, supervision **12** delay payment, guardianship, jurisdiction **14** administration, lay the blame for, request payment **15** superintendence **16** put on one's account

chargeable **6** liable **10** answerable **11** responsible

charged **5** taxed, tense **6** blamed, filled, levied, loaded, priced **7** accused, ordered, uptight **8** assessed, attacked, exhorted, mandated, prepared **9** commanded, entrusted **10** accusation, allegation, indictment

Charge of the Light Brigade, The
author: **18** Alfred Lord Tennyson
director: **13** Michael Curtiz
cast: **10** David Niven, Errol Flynn, Nigel Bruce **11** Donald Crisp **13** Patric Knowles **15** Henry Stephenson **17** Olivia de Havilland
setting: **6** Russia

charger **5** horse, mount, steed **6** vessel **7** accuser, platter **8** warhorse

charge with **5** trust **6** assign, commit **7** consign, entrust **8** delegate, hand over, turn over **9** authorize

Chariclo
husband: **6** Chiron
son: **8** Tiresias
companion of: **6** Athena

chariot **3** car **5** buggy **7** phaeton, vehicle **8** carriage

Charioteer
constellation of: **6** Auriga

Chariots of Fire
director: **10** Hugh Hudson
cast: **7** Ian Holm **8** Ben Cross (Harold Abrahams) **11** John Gielgud, Nigel Havers **12** Ian Charleson (Eric Liddell)
Oscar for: **5** score (Vangelis) **6** script **7** picture

Charis
member of: **6** Graces
husband: **10** Hephaestus

charisma **5** charm **6** allure, appeal **7** glamour **8** presence, witchery **9** magnetism, sex appeal **10** bewitchery **11** enchantment, fascination **14** attractiveness

charitable **4** kind **6** giving, kindly **7** lenient, liberal **8** generous, gracious, tolerant **9** bounteous, bountiful, forgiving, indulgent **10** almsgiving, benevolent, munificent, openhanded **11** considerate, kindhearted, magnanimous, sympathetic, warmhearted **12** eleemosynary, sympathizing **13** philanthropic, understanding

charitableness **10** liberality **11** benevolence, generousity **12** philanthropy **13** bountifulness **14** openhandedness **15** humanitarianism

Charites *see* **6** Graces

charity **3** aid **4** alms, fund, gift, help, love **6** bounty, giving **7** handout **8** altruism, donating, good will, goodness, humanity, kindness, offering, sympathy **9** benignity, donations, endowment, tolerance **10** alms-giving, assistance, compassion, generosity **11** benefaction, benevolence, fundraising, munificence **12** graciousness, philanthropy **13** contributions, financial help, love of mankind **14** open-handedness

charlatan **4** fake **5** cheat, fraud, quack **7** cozener **8** deceiver, imposter, impostor, swindler **9** trickster **10** mountebank **16** confidence artist

Charles, Nick and Nora
characters in: **10** The Thin Man
author: **7** Hammett

Charles O'Malley
author: **12** Charles Lever

Charleston **5** dance **13** ballroom dance
capital of: **9** W Virginia

Charlie's Angels
character: **10** Jill Monroe, John Bosley, Kris Munroe **12** Kelly Garrett **13** Sabrina Duncan **15** Charlie Townsend
cast: **10** Cheryl Ladd, David Doyle **11** Jaclyn Smith, Kate Jackson **18** Farah Fawcett-Majors
voice of Charlie: **12** John Forsythe

Charlotte's Web
author: **7** E B White

Charly
director: **11** Ralph Nelson
based on story by: **11** Daniel Keyes (Flowers for Algernon)
cast: **10** Leon Janney, Lilia Skala **11** Claire Bloom **13** Dick van Patten **14** Cliff Robertson
Oscar for: **5** actor (Robertson)

charm **4** draw, grip, lure, take **5** magic, spell **6** allure, amulet, bauble, cajole, engage, please, seduce, turn on **7** attract, beguile, bewitch, conjure, delight, enchant, gratify, sorcery, trinket, win over **8** charisma, enthrall, entrance, ornament, talisman **9** captivate, enrapture, fascinate, magnetism **10** allurement, attraction, cast a spell, lucky piece **11** conjuration, enchantment, fascination, incantation, work magic on

charmer **4** vamp **5** belle, siren **9** enchanter, temptress **11** enchantress, femme fatale, spellbinder

charming **6** lovely **7** likable, winning, winsome **8** alluring, engaging, enticing, fetching, graceful, magnetic, pleasing **9** agreeable **10** attractive, bewitching, delightful, enchanting, entrancing **11** captivating, charismatic, enthralling, fascinating **12** irresistible

charmless **4** dull **5** blunt **6** dreary **9** repulsive, unlikable, unlovable **10** unpleasant **12** disagreeable, unattractive

Charon
father: **6** Erebus
mother: **3** Nyx
occupation: **8** ferryman
river: **4** Styx

Charops
epithet of: **8** Hercules
means: **14** with bright eyes

Charpentier, Gustave
born: **6** Dieuze, France
composer of: **6** Julien, Louise **18** Impressions of Italy

chart **3** map **4** plan, plot **5** draft, graph, table **6** design, draw up, lay out, map out, scheme, sketch **7** diagram, outline **8** tabulate **9** blueprint, delineate **10** tabulation

charter **3** let **4** deed, hire, rent **5** grant, lease **6** employ, engage, permit **7** compact, license **8** contract, covenant, sanction **9** agreement, authority, authorize, franchise **10** commission, concession

Charterhouse of Parma, The
author: **23** Marie Henri Beyle Stendhal
character: **8** Marietta **10** Count Mosca **11** Clelia Conti **14** Gina Pietranera **16** Fabrizio del Dongo

chartreuse
type: **7** liqueur
origin: **6** France **15** Carthusian monks
flavor: **4** herb
color: **5** green **6** yellow
with apricot brandy: **13** Golden Slipper
with gin: **5** Bijou **9** Green Lady

chary **3** shy **4** wary **5** alert, cagey, leery **7** careful, guarded, heedful, prudent, sparing **8** cautious, hesitant, vigilant, watchful **10** economical, suspicious **11** circumspect, distrustful

Charybdis
form: **7** monster
father: **8** Poseidon
mother: **4** Gaea
identified with: **9** whirlpool

chase **3** dog **4** hunt, oust, rout, shoo, tail **5** drive, evict, hound, quest, stalk, track, trail **6** dispel, follow, pursue, shadow **7** cast out, go after, hunting, pursuit, repulse, scatter **8** pursuing, run after, send away, stalking, tracking **9** drive away, following **11** put to flight, send packing

Chase, Chevy
real name: **19** Cornelius Crane Chase
born: **9** New York NY
roles: **8** Foul Play, Vacation **10** Caddyshack **17** Saturday Night Live

chasm **3** gap, pit **4** gulf, hold, rift **5** abyss, break, cleft, crack, gorge, gulch, split **6** breach, cavity, crater, divide, ravine **7** fissure **8** crevasse

chasseur **6** hunter

chaste **4** pure **5** clean **6** decent, modest, severe, strict **7** austere, classic, precise, sinless **8** virginal, virtuous **9** continent, righteous, unadorned, unsullied, untainted, wholesome **10** immaculate, restrained **11** clean-living, uncorrupted **12** unornamented **13** unembellished

chasten **5** chide, scold **6** berate, punish, rebuke **7** censure, reprove, upbraid **8** admonish, chastise, reproach **9** reprimand **10** discipline, take to task

chastened **7** humbled **8** contrite, penitent **9** repentant **10** remorseful **18** conscience-stricken

chastise **4** beat, flog, whip **5** chide, roast, scold, spank, strap **6** berate, punish, rebuke, thrash **7** censure, chasten, correct, reprove, scourge, upbraid **8** admonish, call down, penalize, reproach **9** castigate, criticize, reprimand **10** discipline, take to task, tongue-lash **15** call on the carpet **16** fulminate against, haul over the coals

chastisement **10** correction, discipline, punishment **11** castigation **12** reprimanding

chastity **6** purity **8** celibacy **9** innocence, virginity **10** abstinence, continence, singleness **12** bachelorhood, spinsterhood **14** abstemiousness
goddess of: **5** Diana, Fauna **7** Artemis, Bona Dea

chasuble **6** casual **7** garment **8** vestment

Chasuble, Reverend Canon
character in: **27** The Importance of Being Earnest
author: **5** Wilde

chat **3** gab, rap **4** talk **5** prate **7** chatter, palaver, prattle **8** chitchat, converse **10** chew the fat, chew the rag, rap session **11** talk session **12** conversation **13** confabulation **16** heart-to-heart talk

chateau **4** wine **6** castle, estate **7** mansion **8** chatelet **12** country house

Chateaubriand, Francois Rene
author of: **4** Rene **5** Atala **10** Los Natchez, The Martyrs **19** Memoires d'Outre-tombe **24** Memoirs from Beyond the Tomb

Chateau d'If
prison in: **21** The Count of Monte Cristo
author: **5** Dumas (pere)

Chateaupers, Phoebus de
character in: **23** The Hunchback of Notre Dame
author: **4** Hugo

chattel **4** gear **6** things **7** effects **8** movables **9** trappings **10** belongings **13** accouterments, paraphernalia **15** personal effects **19** personal possessions

chatter **3** gas **4** blab, talk **5** clank, click, prate **6** babble, gabble, gibber, gossip, jabber, patter **7** blabber, blather, clatter, palaver, prattle, talking, twaddle **8** blabbing, chitchat, idle talk, talk idly **11** confabulate **14** chitterchatter

chatterbox **6** gabber, gasbag, gossip, talker **7** babbler, tattler, windbag **8** jabberer, prattler, tell tale **9** chatterer **10** talebearer, tattle tale **12** blabbermouth, blatherskite, hot-air artist **13** chatterbasket

chatty **5** gabby, gassy, gushy, talky, windy **7** gossipy, gushing, prating, verbose, voluble **8** babbling, chatting, effusive **9** garrulous, jabbering, talkative **10** blabbering, long-winded, loquacious **11** loose-lipped **12** loose-tongued **13** tongue-wagging

Chaucer, Geoffrey
author of: **18** The Canterbury Tales, Troilus and Criseyde **19** The Book of the Duchess **20** The Legend of Good Women, The Parlement of Fowles

Chauchoin, Claudette Lily
real name of: **16** Claudette Colbert

chauffeur **6** driver

chaussure **4** boot, shoe **8** footwear

chauvinism **8** jingoism **10** flag-waving, militarism, patriotism **11** nationalism **15** ethnocentricity, superpatriotism

cheap **4** base, easy, mean, poor **5** close, gaudy, petty, tacky, tight **6** common, flashy, meager, paltry, shabby, shoddy, sordid, stingy, tawdry, trashy, two-bit, vulgar **7** ignoble, immoral, miserly **8** costless, gimcrack, indecent, inferior, wretched **9** inelegant, low-priced, penurious, worthless **10** despicable, economical, effortless, in bad taste, reasonable, second-rate **11** inexpensive, tightfisted **12** contemptible

Cheaper by the Dozen
author: **14** Frank B Gilbreth (with Ernestine Gilbreth Carey)

cheat **3** con, gyp **4** bilk, dupe, fake, foil, fool, gull, hoax, rook, take **5** cozen, crook, fraud, quack, shark, trick **6** baffle, betray, defeat, delude, dodger, escape, fleece, humbug, outwit, thwart **7** deceive, defraud, mislead, swindle **8** chiseler, deceiver, hoodwink, imposter, impostor, swindler **9** bamboozle, charlatan, con artist, frustrate, trickster, victimize **10** circumvent, mountebank **11** short-change **13** break the rules, double-crosser

check **3** bar, end, fit, gag **4** curb, halt, hold, jibe, mesh, rein, slow, stay, stop, test **5** agree, block, brake, chime, choke, limit, probe, stall, study, tally **6** arrest, bridle, impede, look at, muzzle, peruse, rein in, retard, review, search, survey, thwart **7** barrier, conform, control, examine, explore, harness, inhibit, inspect, perusal, prevent, smother **8** hold back, look into, look over, obstacle, obstruct, restrain, scrutiny, stoppage, suppress **9** cessation, constrain, frustrate, harmonize, hindrance, restraint **10** circumvent, constraint, correspond, impediment, inspection, limitation, prevention, repression, scrutinize **11** examination, exploration, investigate, obstruction, prohibition, restriction, take stock of **13** investigation **18** bring to a standstill

checkered **4** pied **6** fitful, motley, seesaw, uneven, varied **7** checked, dappled, mottled, piebald **9** irregular, up-and-down **10** inconstant, variegated **11** fluctuating, vacillating **12** parti-colored

checkmate **4** rout, stop **6** corner, defeat, outwit, stymie, thwart **8** deadlock **9** frustrate, overthrow **11** countermove

cheder, heder **12** Jewish school

cheek **4** jowl **5** brass, nerve **8** audacity, boldness, temerity **9** arrogance, brashness, impudence, insolence **10** brazenness, effrontery **11** forwardness **12** impertinence

cheep **4** peep **5** chirp, tweet **7** chirrup, chitter, twitter

cheer **3** cry, fun, joy **4** glee, hail, hope, root, warm, yell **5** bravo, shout **6** assure, buoy up, gaiety, hooray, hurrah, huzzah, shriek, uplift **7** acclaim, animate, comfort, delight, enliven, fortify, gladden, hearten, inspire, revelry **8** brighten, buoyance, buoyancy, gladness, optimism, pleasure, reassure, vivacity **9** animation, assurance, encourage, festivity, geniality, joviality, merriment, rejoicing **10** joyfulness, jubilation, liveliness **11** acclamation, high spirits, hopefulness, merrymaking, reassurance **13** encouragement

cheerful **3** gay **4** airy, glad **5** happy, jolly, merry, sunny **6** blithe, breezy, bright, cheery, elated, jaunty, jovial, joyful, joyous, lively **7** buoyant, gleeful **8** gladsome, pleasant **9** agreeable, sparkling, sprightly **10** optimistic **11** in high humor **12** high-spirited, lighthearted

cheerfulness **5** gaity **7** jollity **8** buoyancy, optimism **9** joviality, merriment **10** brightness, cheeriness **11** high spirits **16** lightheartedness

cheerless **3** sad **4** dull, glum, gray, grim **5** bleak **6** dismal, dreary, gloomy, morose, rueful, solemn, somber, sullen, woeful **7** austere, doleful, forlorn, joyless, sunless, unhappy **8** dejected, desolate, dolorous, downcast, funereal, mournful **9** miserable, saturnine, woebegone **10** depressing, despondent, dispirited, lugubrious, melancholy, spiritless, uninviting **11** comfortless, downhearted **12** disconsolate, heavy-hearted

Cheers
location: **3** bar **6** Boston
character: **4** Norm **5** Cliff, Coach, Woody **5** Lilith **7** Rebecca **9** Sam Malone **13** Carla Tortelli, Diane Chambers
cast: **9** Ted Danson **11** George Wendt, Rhea Perlman, Shelley Long **12** Kirstie Alley **13** Kelsey Grammer **14** Woody Harrelson **16** John Ratzenberger

cheer up **5** pep up **6** buoy up **7** comfort, enliven, hearten **8** brighten, inspirit **9** bolster up, encourage **18** bolster one's spirits

cheery **3** gay **5** happy, jolly, merry, sunny **6** bright, joyful **9** sprightly **12** lighthearted

Cheeryble Brothers
nephew: **5** Frank
characters in: **16** Nicholas Nickleby
author: **7** Dickens

cheese
French: **7** fromage
kind: **4** bleu, blue, brie, edam, feta, jack **5** brick, colby, cream, gouda, Swiss **6** romano, samsoe **7** cheddar, cottage, fontina, gjetost, gruyere, limburg, munster, ricotta, sapsago, stilton **8** American, bel paese, cheshire, emmental, muenster, parmesan, port wine, raclette **9** camembert, jarlsberg, limburger, port salut, provolone, roquefort **10** caerphilly, Danish blue, Gloucester, gorgonzola, mozzarella, neufchatel **11** emmenthaler, liederkranz, petit suisse, port du salut, wensleydale **12** monterey jack

Cheever, John
author of: **8** Falconer **10** Bullet Park **16** The Enormous Radio, The World of Apples **17** The Wapshot Scandal **19** The Wapshot Chronicle **20** The Way Some People Live **22** Oh What a Paradise It Seems

Chekhov, Anton
author of: **6** Ivanov **10** The Sea Gull, Uncle Vanya **15** The Three Sisters **16** The Cherry Orchard

Chelciope
father: **6** Aeetes
mother: **5** Idyia
sister: **5** Medea
husband: **7** Phrixus
son: **5** Argus, Melas **8** Phrontis **9** Thessalus **10** Cytissorus

Chelidon
sister: **5** Aedon
brother-in-law: **11** Polytechnus
changed into: **7** swallow
changed by: **7** Artemis

chemical symbols
actinium: **2** Ac
aluminum: **2** Al
antimony: **2** Sb
argon: **2** Ar
arsenic: **2** As
barium: **2** Ba
boron: **1** B
bromine: **2** Br
cadmium: **2** Cd
calcium: **2** Ca
carbon: **1** C
chlorine: **2** Cl
chromium: **2** Cr
cobalt: **2** Co
columbium: **2** Cb
copper: **2** Cu
fluorine: **1** F
gold: **2** Au
hafnium: **2** Hf
helium: **2** He
hydrogen: **1** H
iodine: **1** I
iron: **2** Fe
krypton: **2** Kr
lead: **2** Pb
lithium: **2** Li
magnesium: **2** Mg
manganese: **2** Mn
mercury: **2** Hg
molybdenum: **2** Mo
neon: **2** Ne
nickel: **2** Ni
nitrogen: **1** N
oxygen: **1** O
phosphorus: **1** P
platinum: **2** Pt
plutonium: **2** Pu
potassium: **1** K
radium: **2** Ra
radon: **2** Rn
rhodium: **2** Rh
rubidium: **2** Rb
silicon: **2** Si
silver: **2** Ag
sodium: **2** Na
sulfur: **1** S
thorium: **2** Th
tin: **2** Sn
titanium: **2** Ti
tungsten: **1** W
uranium: **1** U
xenon: **2** Xe
zinc: **2** Zn
zirconium: **2** Zr

chemise **4** slip **5** dress, shift, shirt, smock **6** blouse **7** garment **8** camisole, lingerie, unbelted **12** undergarment

chemist
American: **4** Urey **5** Tatum **6** Carver **7** Axelrod, Lipmann, Pauling **8** Kornberg, Langmuir, McMillan **9** Carothers **10** Baekleland
British: **4** Davy **5** Boyle, Chain, Soddy **6** Dalton, Ramsay **7** Faraday **8** Smithson **9** Cavendish, Priestley, Wollaston
Dutch: **4** Hoff
French: **5** Curie, Le Bel **6** Cuvier, Dulong **7** Pasteur **9** Gay-Lussac, Lavoisier **10** Berthollet **11** Joliot-Curie
German: **4** Hahn **5** Krebs **6** Baeyer, Wohler **7** Glauber, Ostwald
Italian: **8** Avogadro
Russian: **9** Mendeleev **10** Mendeleyev
Scottish: **5** Dewar
Swedish: **7** Scheele **9** Arrhenius, Berzelius
Swiss: **6** Muller

Chemosh **10** Moabite god

Chennault, Claire L
served in: **4** WWII **15** Sino-Japanese War
commander of: **12** Flying Tigers
general in: **12** Army Air Force
air advisor to: **13** Chiang Kai-shek

cherchez la femme **15** look for the woman

cherie **4** dear **10** sweetheart

cherish **4** love **5** honor, nurse, prize, value **6** dote on, esteem, revere, succor **7** care for, idolize, nourish, nurture, shelter, sustain **8** hold dear, treasure, venerate **10** appreciate, take care of

cherished **4** dear **5** loved **7** beloved, darling, dearest **8** favorite, held dear, precious **9** treasured

Cherokee
language family: **9** Iroquoian
location: **7** Alabama, Georgia **8** Oklahoma, Virginia **9** Tennessee **13** North Carolina, South Carolina
associated with: **12** Trail of Tears
scholar: **7** Sequoya

cherry
varieties: **3** pie, pin, rum **4** bing, bird, duke, fire, sand, sour, wild **5** black, brush, choke, dwarf, Higan, Naden, sweet **6** bitter, Brazil, ground, Indian, Madden, Oregon, Taiwan, winter **7** bastard, Cayenne, Morello, Nanking, Potomac, prairie, rosebud, sargent, Spanish, St

Lucie, wild red, Windsor, Yoshino **8** Barbados, Catalina, oriental, perfumed, Suriname **9** christmas, cornelian, evergreen, Jerusalem, wild black **10** west indian **11** downy ground, Hansen's bush, holly-leaved, western sand **12** clammy ground, European bird, Japanese bush, purple ground **13** European dwarf **14** European ground, false Jerusalem, purple-leaf sand **15** Australian brush **17** Japanese cornelian, Japanese flowering, north Japanese hill
drink: **6** kirsch

cherry brandy **6** kirsch **12** Peter Heering

Cherry Orchard, The
author: **12** Anton Chekhov
character: **4** Anya, Gaev **5** Fiers, Varya, Yasha **7** Pischin **8** Dunyasha, Lopakhin, Trofimov **9** Charlotta **16** Madame Ranevskaya

cherub **4** amor **5** angel, child, cupid, youth **6** moppet **8** cherubim **13** heavenly being

cherubic **7** angelic **8** innocent **9** spiritual

Cherubin
character in: **19** The Marriage of Figaro
author: **12** Beaumarchais

chervil
botanical name: **20** Anthriscus cerefolium
origin: **6** Europe, Russia
use: **4** soup **5** salad **11** fines herbes, potato salad

Chesapeake
author: **13** James Michener

Cheshire Cat
character in: **28** Alice's Adventures in Wonderland
author: **7** Carroll

chess *see box*

chest
Italian: **5** petto

Chester, Edward
character in: **12** Barnaby Rudge
author: **7** Dickens

chesterfield **4** coat, sofa **5** couch **8** overcoat **9** davenport

Chesterton, G K (Gilbert Keith)
author of: **20** The Man Who Was Thursday **24** The Napoleon of Notting Hill **25** The Innocence of Father Brown

chess
also called: **9** Royal Game
chess champion: **4** Euwe, Fine, Tahl **6** Karpov, Lasker **7** Fischer, Kashdan, Smyslov, Spassky **8** Alekhine, Kasparov, Philador, Steinitz **9** Anderssen, Botvinnik, Petrosian, Reshevsky **10** Capablanca
French: **6** echecs
German: **11** schachspiel
horizontal rows: **4** rank
international chess federation: **4** FIDE
patron goddess / muse: **6** Caissa
piece: **4** king, pawn, rook **5** queen **6** bishop, castle, knight **8** chessman, material
Russian: **8** shakhmat
Spanish: **7** Ajedrez
term: **3** pin **4** fork, hole **5** check, tempo **6** center **7** isolani, outpost **8** castling, majority, open file, queening, zugzwang **9** checkmate, en passant, promotion **10** fianchetto **11** zwischenzug
tied game: **4** draw **9** stalemate
vertical rows: **4** file

chestnut **8** Castanea
varieties: **4** Cape, Wild **5** Horse, Water **6** Guiana, Marron **7** Chinese, Spanish **8** American, Eurasian, European, Japanese, Red horse **10** Dwarf horse, Moreton Bay **11** Common horse **12** Chinese water **13** European horse, Japanese horse **15** California horse

chestnut-colored **6** auburn, russet, sienna **8** cinnamon, nut-brown **11** golden-brown, rust-colored **12** reddish-brown

chest of drawers **5** chest **6** bureau, lowboy **7** cabinet, commode, dresser, highboy, tallboy **10** chiffonier

cheval **5** horse

chevalier **4** lord **5** cadet, noble **6** knight **7** gallant **8** cavalier

Chevalier, Maurice
born: **5** Paris **6** France
roles: **4** Gigi **5** Fanny **6** Can-Can **13** The Love Parade, The Merry Widow **18** Love in the Afternoon

chew **4** gnaw **5** champ, crush, grind, munch **6** crunch, nibble **8** ruminate **9** masticate

Chew
character in: **21** The Master of Ballantrae
author: **9** Stevenson

chewing-out **6** rebuke **7** censure, chiding, reproof **8** reproach, scolding **9** reprimand **10** bawling-out, upbraiding **11** castigation, reprobation **12** dressing-down, remonstrance **13** tongue-lashing

chew noisily **4** gnaw **5** chomp, gnash, grind, munch **6** crunch

chew out **5** scold **6** berate, rail at, rebuke **7** bawl out, reprove, upbraid **8** reproach **9** castigate, reprimand **10** take to task, tongue-lash **14** read the riot act

chew the fat **3** gab, gas **4** blab, chat, talk **5** prate **6** gossip, patter **7** blather, chatter, palaver, prattle, twaddle **8** chitchat, converse, talk idly **10** chew the rag **11** confabulate **14** chitterchatter

chew the rag **3** gab, gas, jaw, rap **4** chat, chin, talk **5** prate **7** chatter, palaver, prattle **8** chitchat, converse **10** chew the fat **11** confabulate

Cheyenne
language family: **9** Algonkian **10** Algonquian
location: **6** Platte **7** Montana, Wyoming **8** Oklahoma, Red River **9** Minnesota **11** South Dakota
allied with: **7** Arapaho

Cheyenne
character: **6** Smitty **13** Cheyenne Bodie
cast: **7** L Q Jones **11** Clint Walker

chez **4** with **6** at home

Chiang Kai-shek
leader of: **5** China **6** Taiwan
ally: **9** Sun Yat-sen
party: **10** Kuomintang **11** Nationalist
defeated by: **10** Communists
wife: **12** Soong Mei-ling

Chibcha (Muisca)
location: **6** Bogota, Panama **8** Colombia **12** South America
associated with: **8** El Dorado

Chibchan
language family: **13** Macro-Chibchan
group: **4** Cuna, Paya, Rama **5** Lenca, Xinca **7** Chibcha

chic **5** natty, ritzy, smart, swank **6** classy, modish, snazzy, swanky **7** elegant, stylish, voguish **11** fashionable

Chicago
author: **12** Carl Sandburg

Chicago ***see box***

Chicago
airport: **5** O'Hare **6** Midway
baseball team: **4** Cubs **8** White Sox
basketball team: **5** Bulls
downtown area: **4** Loop
football team: **5** Bears
fort: **8** Dearborn
hockey team: **10** Black Hawks
lake: **4** Wolf **7** Calumet **8** Michigan
landmark: **10** Meigs Field, Sears Tower **12** Board of Trade, Comiskey Park, Humboldt Park, Soldier Field, Wrigley Field **13** Shedd Aquarium **15** Lincoln Monument, Merchandise Mart, Newberry Library, Wrigley Building **16** Adler Planetarium **17** Holy Name Cathedral, John Hancock Center **18** Mercantile Exchange, Prudential Building **20** Midwest Stock Exchange **21** Art Institute of Chicago **23** Museum of Contemporary Art **26** Museum of Science and Industry **27** Field Museum of Natural History
mayor: **5** Byrne, Daley **10** Washington
nickname: **9** Windy City
river: **7** Chicago **10** Des Plaines
street: **11** Wacker Drive **13** Chicago Skyway **14** Lake Shore Drive
university: **6** DePaul, Loyola **9** Roosevelt **12** Northwestern **29** Illinois Institute of Technology

chicanery **4** ruse, wile **5** craft, fraud, guile **6** deceit, duping **7** cunning, gulling, knavery, roguery **8** artifice, cozenage, trickery, villainy **9** deception, duplicity, rascality, sophistry **10** craftiness, hocus-pocus, humbuggery, subterfuge **11** hoodwinking **12** pettifoggery **13** double-dealing

chichi **4** arty **5** fussy, showy **6** flashy, frilly, garish, prissy, vulgar **7** finical, pompous, splashy **8** affected, gimcrack, overnice, precious, sissyish **9** arty-tarty, grandiose, nasty-nice **10** flamboyant **11** overrefined, pretentious **12** artsy-craftsy, ostentatious

chick
group of: **5** brood **6** clutch

Chickasaw
language family: **10** Muskhogean
location: **8** Oklahoma **9** Tennessee **11** Mississippi
related to: **7** Choctaw
member of: **19** Five Civilized Tribes

chicken, chickenhearted **3** hen **4** cock, fowl **5** layer, timid **6** afraid, coward, craven, pullet, scared, yellow **7** caitiff, dastard, fearful, gutless, rooster **8** cowardly, poltroon, timorous **9** flinching, fraidy-cat, shrinking **11** lily-livered, yellow-belly **12** fainthearted **13** pusillanimous, yellow-bellied **22** showing the white feather

chickenheartedness **8** timidity **9** cowardice **10** yellowness **11** fearfulness, poltroonery **12** timorousness **13** pusillanimity **16** faintheartedness

chide **5** scold **6** berate, rebuke **7** censure, chasten, reprove, upbraid **8** admonish, denounce, reproach **9** criticize, find fault, reprimand **10** take to task

chief **3** key **4** boss, head, lord, main **5** first, major, prime, ruler **6** leader, master, ruling **7** captain, highest, leading, monarch, primary, supreme **8** cardinal, chairman, crowning, director, dominant, foremost, greatest, overlord, overseer **9** chieftain, commander, governing, number-one, paramount, potentate, principal, sovereign, uppermost **10** prevailing, ringleader, supervisor **11** outstanding, predominant **12** preponderant **13** administrator

chief good
Latin: **11** summum bonum

chiefly **5** first **6** mainly, mostly **8** above all **9** expressly, in the main, most of all, primarily **10** especially **11** principally **12** particularly **13** predominantly

chieftan **4** boss, head **6** leader **7** captain, head man

chiffonier **6** bureau **7** dresser **8** cupboard **14** chest of drawers

chignon **3** bun **4** knot, roll **6** hairdo **9** hairpiece, hairstyle

child **3** boy, kid, lad, son, tad, tot **4** baby, girl, lass, tyke **5** youth **6** infant, moppet **7** toddler **8** daughter, juvenile **9** little one, offspring, youngster

childbearing **5** birth **11** parturition

childbirth **8** delivery **11** confinement, parturition
French: **12** accouchement
goddess of: **4** Upis **5** Parca **6** Lucina, Matuta **7** Artemis **8** Ilithyia **10** Eileithyia

Childe Harold's Pilgrimage
author: **21** George Gordon Lord Byron

Childe Roland to the Dark Tower Came
author: **14** Robert Browning

childhood **5** youth **7** boyhood **8** girlhood **10** school days **11** adolescence, nursery days

childish **5** naive, silly **6** callow, simple **7** asinine, babyish, foolish, puerile **8** immature, juvenile **9** infantile **10** adolescent

childlike **8** childish, immature, innocent **9** ingenuous

child prodigy
German: **10** Wunderkind

children **4** boys, kids, sons, tads, tots **5** girls, issue, young **6** babies, result, youth **7** infants, product, progeny **9** daughters, juveniles **11** descendants

Children of God
author: **12** Vardis Fisher

Children of Paradise
director: **11** Marcel Carne
cast: **7** Arletty **11** Albert Remay **14** Pierre Brasseur **17** Jean-Louis Barrault

Child's Garden of Verses, A
author: **20** Robert Louis Stevenson

Chile ***see box, p. 176***

chill, chilly **3** icy, nip, raw **4** bite, cold, cool, keen **5** aloof, brisk, crisp, fever, harsh, nippy, sharp, stiff, stony **6** arctic, biting, bitter, frigid, frosty, frozen, wintry

Chile

other name: **6** Tchile

name means: **21** deepest part of the Earth

capital/largest city: **8** Santiago

others: **4** Boco, Cuya, Lebu, Lota, Ocoa, Tome **5** Angol, Arica, Cobya, Talca **6** Arauco, Calama, Curico, Gatico, Osorno, Ovalle, Serena, Temuco, Vicuna, Yumbel, Yungay **7** Caldera, Chillan, Copiapo, Iquique, Valdiva **8** Coquimbo, Rancagua, Santiago, Vallenar **9** Cauquenes **10** Concepcion, Coquembana, Valparaiso, Vina del Mar **11** Antofagasta, Puerto Montt, Punta Arenas, San Bernardo

measure: **4** vara **5** legua, linea **6** cuadra, fanega

monetary unit: **4** peso **5** libra **6** condor, escudo

weight: **5** grano, libra **7** quintal

island: **3** Luz **4** Prat **5** Byron, Guafo, Hoste, Mocha, Nueva, Nunez, Vidal **6** Chiloe, Chonos, Dawson, Easter, Lennox, Piazzi, Picton, Quilan, Riesco, Stosch, Talcan **7** Angamos, Campana, Hanover, Hermite, Pajaros, Refugio, Tranqui **8** Chauques, Clarence, Huamblin, Nalcayec, Navarino, Traiguen **13** Juan Fernandez **14** Tierra del Fuego

lake: **5** Ranco **6** Yelcho **7** Puyehue, Rupanco **8** Cochrane **10** General Paz, Llanquihue **11** Buenos Aires

mountain: **4** Maca, Toro **5** Chato, Maipo, Maipu, Paine, Potro, Pular, Torre, Yogan **6** Apiwan, Burney, Conico, Jervis, Poquis, Rincon **7** Chaltel, Copiapo, Fitzroy, Palpana, Velluda **8** Cochrane, Tronador, Yanteles **9** Tupungato

highest point: **13** Ojos del Salado

river: **3** Loa **4** Laja, Yali **5** Alhue, Azapa, Bravo, Bueno, Elqui, Lauca, Lluta, Maipo, Maule, Puelo, Rahue, Rapel, Stata, Vitor **6** Biobio, Camina, Choapa, Choros, Cisnes, Colina, Huasco, Limari, Morado, Palena, Poscua, Tolten **7** Copiapo **8** Valdivia

sea: **7** Pacific

physical features:
- ***bay:*** **4** Cook, Eyre, Nena, Tarn **5** Lomas, Otway, Sarco **6** Darwin, Inutil, Moreno, Stokes, Tongoy **7** Dyneley, Inglesa, Skyring **8** Desolate
- ***cape:*** **4** Dyer, Horn **6** Choros, Falsos, Hornos, Quilan, Tablas **7** Deseado **10** Tres Montes
- ***channel:*** **5** Ancho, Cheap **6** Beagle **8** Cockburn, Moraleda
- ***desert:*** **7** Atacama
- ***gulf:*** **5** Ancud, Guafo, Penas **6** Arauco
- ***isthmus:*** **5** Ofqui
- ***peninsula:*** **5** Hardy, Lacuy **6** Taitao, Tumbes
- ***point:*** **4** Toro **5** Gallo, Liles, Lobos, Loros, Morro, Talca, Tetas, Vieja **6** Cachos, Galera, Molles **7** Angamos, Lavapie
- ***strait:*** **6** Nelson **8** Magellan
- ***volcano:*** **5** Lanin, Maipo **6** Antuco, Llaima, Oyahue, Tacora **7** Peteroa, Socomap

people: **3** Ona **4** Auca, Inca, Onan **6** Arauca, Chango, Yahgan **7** Mapuche, mestizo, Moluche, Pampean, Patagon, Puegian, Ranquel **8** Alikuluf, Picunche, Tsonecan
- ***author:*** **5** Bello **6** Donoso, Neruda **7** Mistral
- ***conqueror:*** **7** Valdiva
- ***explorer:*** **8** Magellan
- ***leader:*** **7** Allende **8** O'Higgins, Pinochet **9** San Martin **10** Alessandri

language: **7** Spanish

religion: **13** Roman Catholic

places:
- ***copper mine:*** **12** Chuquicamata
- ***resort:*** **8** Portillo **10** Vina del Mar

possession: **12** Easter Island **20** Juan Fernandez Islands

feature:
- ***cowboy:*** **5** huaso
- ***dance:*** **5** cueca **6** pequen **9** resbalosa
- ***shrub:*** **5** litre
- ***slum:*** **9** callempas
- ***tree:*** **5** rauli
- ***wind instrument:*** **4** sicu

food:
- ***drink:*** **5** pisco **6** chicha
- ***hot red pepper:*** **3** aji
- ***meat pie:*** **8** empanada
- ***soup:*** **7** cazuela **8** caldillo

7 callous, coolish, cutting, glacial, hostile, iciness, rawness, shivery 8 coolness, uncaring 9 crispness, frigidity, sharpness, unfeeling 10 forbidding, frostiness, unfriendly 11 indifferent, passionless, penetrating 12 unresponsive

chilled 4 cold, iced 6 cooled, frozen 7 frosted 8 hardened 10 dispirited 11 discouraged 12 refrigerated

chilling 3 icy, raw 5 nippy, on ice 6 frigid 7 bracing, cooling 10 unfriendly

Chillingworth, Roger
character in: 16 The Scarlet Letter
author: 9 Hawthorne

chime 4 gong, peal, ring, toll 5 knell, sound 6 jingle, tinkle 7 pealing, ringing 8 carillon, ding-dong, tinkling, tollings 10 set of bells 14 tintinnabulate 16 tintinnabulation

Chimene
character in: 6 The Cid
author: 9 Corneille

chimera 5 dream, fancy 6 bubble, mirage 7 fantasy, monster, phantom 8 daydream, delusion, idle whim, illusion 9 pipe dream 10 self-deceit, she-monster 12 will-o'-the-wisp 13 castle in Spain, fool's paradise, hallucination, self-deception 14 castle in the air 24 figment of one's imagination

Chimera
form: 7 monster
father: 6 Typhon
mother: 7 Echidna
breathes: 4 fire

Chimera
author: 9 John Barth

chimerical 6 absurd, unreal 7 utopian 8 delusive, ethereal, fabulous, fanciful, illusory, mythical quixotic 9 fantastic, imaginary, visionary 10 impossible, phantasmal, 11 nonexistent

chimney 4 flue, tube, vent 5 cleft, gully, spout, stack 6 funnel, hearth 7 opening 9 stovepipe 10 smokestack

chimpanzee 3 ape 6 animal, baboon, monkey

chin 3 gab, jaw, rap 4 chat, talk 7 chatter, palaver 8 chitchat, converse 10 chew the fat, chew the rag 11 confabulate

china 6 dishes, plates 7 pottery 8 crockery 9 chinaware, porcelain, stoneware, tableware 11 ceramic ware, earthenware 14 cups and saucers

China *see box, p. 178*

China Syndrome, The
director: 12 James Bridges
cast: 9 Jane Fonda 10 Jack Lemmon, Scott Brady 14 Michael Douglas
setting: 17 nuclear power plant

Chinatown
director: 13 Roman Polanski
cast: 10 John Huston 11 Faye Dunaway 13 Jack Nicholson
Oscar for: 5 story 10 screenplay

chinaware 6 dishes, plates 7 pottery 8 crockery 9 porcelain, stoneware, tableware 11 ceramic ware, earthenware 14 cups and saucers

chine 5 spine 6 dorsum 8 backbone

Chinese book of divination 6 I Ching

Chingachgook
character in: 13 The Pathfinder 20 The Last of the Mohicans
author: 6 Cooper

chink 3 cut, gap 4 gash, hole, rent, rift, ring, slit 5 break, clank, cleft, clink, crack, fault, split 6 breach, jangle, jingle, rattle, tinkle 7 crevice, fissure, opening 8 aperture

Chinook (Flathead)
language family: 9 Chinookan
location: 7 Pacific 10 Washington
ritual: 15 head deformation

Chinookan
tribe: 7 Chinook 8 Flathead

chintzy 5 cheap, close, dowdy, tacky, tatty, tight 6 frowzy, frumpy, shabby, sleazy, stingy 7 miserly 8 grudging, schlocky, stinting 9 niggardly, penurious 11 closefisted 12 parsimonious 13 penny-pinching

Chione
father: 6 Boreas 9 Daedalion
mother: 8 Orithyia
son: 9 Autolycus, Philammon

chip 3 bit, cut, hew 4 chop, gash, hack, nick 5 chunk, crumb, flake, scrap, shred, slice, split, wafer 6 chisel, morsel, paring, sliver 7 cutting, shaving, whittle 8 fragment, splinter

chipmunk 6 chippy, gopher, rodent 8 chipmuck, squirrel 14 ground squirrel 16 chipping squirrel

chipper 3 gay 4 pert, spry 5 alive, brisk, peppy 6 frisky, jaunty, lively 8 animated, carefree, cheerful, spirited 9 easygoing, energetic, sprightly, vivacious 12 high-spirited, light-hearted

Chippewa (Ojibwa, Ojibway)
language family: 9 Algonkian 10 Algonquian
tribe: 4 Cree 6 Ottawa 8 Chippewa 10 Missisauga
location: 6 Canada 9 Lake Huron 11 North Dakota 12 Lake Superior, Niagara Falls
leader: 7 Pontiac

CHiPS
character: 8 (Officer) Jon Baker 10 (Sgt) Joe Getraer 16 (Officer) Frank (Ponch) Poncherello
cast: 10 Robert Pine 11 Erik Estrada, Larry Wilcox

Chirico, Giorgio de
born: 5 Volos 6 Greece
artwork: 15 Enigma of the Hour 19 Enigma of an Afternoon 21 Enigma of an Autumn Night 22 Nostalgia of the Infinite 32 The Melancholy and Mystery of a Street

Chiron
also: 7 Cheiron
form: 7 centaur
father: 6 Cronos, Cronus, Kronos
mother: 7 Philyra
wife: 8 Chariclo
daughter: 6 Endeis
grandson: 6 Peleus
occupation: 7 teacher

chirp 4 peep, sing 5 cheep, chirr, tweet 7 chirrup, chitter, peeping, twitter 8 cheeping

chirrup 4 peep 5 cheep, chirp, tweet 7 chitter, twitter

chisel 3 cut, gyp 4 gull, hoax, rook, tool 5 blade, cheat, slice 6 incise
type: 4 cape, cold, wood 7 v-shaped

Chisel
constellation of: 6 Caelum

chiseler 4 fake 5 cheat, fraud, quack 7 cheater 8 swindler

Chislev 16 ninth Hebrew month

chit 3 IOU, tab 4 note 5 check 7 voucher

chitchat 3 gab 4 chat 5 prate 6 drivel, gossip 7 chatter, palaver, prattle 8 converse 9 small talk 10 chew the fat, chew the rag 11 confabulate 13 confabulation

China

other name: **3** PRC **13** Middle Kingdom **14** Flowery Kingdom **22** People's Republic of China

capital: **6** Peking **7** Beijing

largest city: **8** Shanghai

others: **3** Bai, Noh **4** Ahpa, Amoy, Fuyu, Guma, Hami, Huma, Ipin, Kian, Kisi, Lini, Loho, Luta, Moho, Moyu, Niya, Noho, Omin, Rima, Saka, Sian, Taku, Tali, Tayu, Wuhu, Yaan **5** Chiai, Fusin, Kirin, Koklu, Linyu, Macao, Penki, Shasi, Soche, Taian, Talai, Tihwa, Tuyun, Wuhan, Wusih, Yenan, Yenki, Yulin, Yumen **6** Anshan, Antung, Canton, Dairen, Fuchau, Fuchow, Fushun, Hankow, Harbin, Ilhasa, Kalgan, Loyang, Lushun, Mukden, Nanhai, Ningpo, Singan, Sining, Taipei, Tsinan, Yangku, Yunnan **7** Fuskhih, Hanyang, Kunming, Lanchow, Lioyang, Mengtze, Nanking, Nanning, Paoshan, Peiping, Soochow, Taiyuan, Tat-shan, Urumchi, Urumsti, Waichow, Wuchang, Yenping **8** Chinchow, Fengkiek, Fengtien, Hangchow, Kingchow, Nanchang, Shanghai, Shenyang, Siangtan, Tientsin, Tungchow, Wan-chuan, Wanhsien **9** Chungking, Kiangling, Tsingyuan **10** Chiangling, Port Arthur

school: **5** Futan **6** Peking **7** Nanking **8** Hangchow **9** Sun Yat-sen **16** Cheng-tu Technical

division:

province: **5** Honan, Hunan, Hupei, Kansu **6** Anhwei, Fukien, Shansi, Shensi, Yunnan **7** Kiangsi, Kiangsu **8** Chekiang, Kweichow, Shantung, Szechwan, Tientsin, Tsinghai **9** Kwangtung, Manchuria

measure: **3** cho, fan, fen, pau, tou, tun, yan, yin **4** chek, chih, fang, kish, papa, quei, shih, teke, tsan, tsun **5** catty, chang, ching, sheng, shing **6** chupak, gungli, kungho, kungmu, tching **7** kungfen, kungyin **8** kungchih, kungshih, **9** kungching

monetary unit: **4** cash, cent, fyng, mace, tael, tiao, yuan **5** sycee **12** jen nin piao pu

weight: **3** fan, fen, hao, kin, ssu, tan, yin **4** chee, chin, dong, shih, tael, tsin **5** catty, chien, picul, tchin, tsien **6** kungli **7** haikwan, kungfen, kungssu, kungtun **8** kungchin **9** candareen **10** kupingtael

island: **4** Amoy **5** Macao, Matsu, Namki, Taipa **6** Chusan, Hainan, Pratas, Quemoy, Taiwan, Tinian, Yuhwan **7** Coloane, Formosa, Hungtow, Tungsha **8** Ching Hai, Chouchan, Kulangsu, Staunton

lake: **3** Tai **4** Chao, Na-mu **5** Kaoyu, Oling, Telli **6** Bamtso, Bornor, Ebinor, Erhhai, Khanka, Lopnor, Namtso, Poyang **7** Chaling, Hungtse, Karanor, Kokonor **8** Hulunnor, Montcalm, Tar-oktso, Tellinor, Tienchih, Tsinghai, Tungting

sea: **6** Yellow **9** East China **10** South China

physical features:

bay: **7** Laichow **8** Hangchow
cape: **7** Olwanpi
channel: **5** Bashi
desert: **4** Gobi **5** Ordos, Shamo **7** Alashan **10** Takla Makan
dry lake: **6** Lopnor
gulf: **5** Pohai **6** Chihli, Tonkin **7** Pechili **8** Liaotung
peninsula: **6** Leichu **7** Luichow **8** Liaotung
plateau: **5** Loess **7** Tibetan
port: **4** Amoy, Wuhu **5** Aigun, Shasi **6** Antung, Canton, Chefoo, Dairen, Ichang, Ningpo, Pakhoi, Swatow, Wuchow **7** Foochow, Hunchun, Luichow, Nanking, Samshui, Santuao, Soochow, Wenchow, Yinkkow, Yungkia **8** Changsha, Hangchow, Kiukiang, Kongmoon, Shanghai, Tengyueh, Tientsin, Tsingtao, Wanhsien **9** Kwangchow, Weihaiwei **10** Tsingkiang
rains: **4** plum **5** Mai-yu
reservoir: **7** Sungari
strait: **6** Hainan, Taiwan **7** Formosa

people: **3** Han, Yis **4** Huis, Lolo, Miao, Pu-is **5** Hakka, Hoklo, Seres, Sinic **6** Cataia, Chuang, Johnny, Korean, Manchu, Mongol, Serian, Uighun **7** Sinaean, Tibetan
leader: **9** Sun Yat-sen **10** Kublai Khan, Mao Tse-tung **11** Genghis Khan **13** Chiang Kai-shek
philosopher: **6** Lao-tzu **9** Confucius

language: **7** Chinese **8** Mandarin, Shanghai **9** Cantonese

religion: **5** Islam **6** Taoism **8** Buddhism **12** Christianity, Confucianism

place:

palace: **6** Summer **8** Imperial **13** Forbidden City
ruins: **9** Ming Tombs
wonder: **9** Great Wall

feature:

boat: **4** junk
dynasty: **3** Han, Sui **4** Chou, Ch'in, Ming, Sung, T'ang **5** Ch'ing, Shang **6** Manchu
military academy: **7** whompoa
watercolor: **8** shan shiu

Chitimacha
language family: **6** Tunica
location: **9** Louisiana
noted for: **8** basketry

chitter **4** peep **5** cheep, chirp, tweet **7** chatter, chirrup, twitter

chitter-chatter **3** gab **4** blab **6** babble, drivel, gabble, jabber **7** blabber, prattle, twaddle **8** chitchat **9** jabbering **16** idle conversation

chivalrous **6** polite **7** courtly, gallant **8** mannerly

chivalry **8** courtesy **9** gallantry **10** knighthood, politeness **11** courtliness

Chivery, Young John
character in: **12** Little Dorrit
author: **7** Dickens

chivy **3** nag **4** hunt, race **5** annoy, chase, chevy, hound, trail, worry **6** badger, bother, harass, pursue **7** scamper, torment

Chlidanope
form: **5** Naiad

Chloe
epithet of: **7** Demeter
means: **5** green

chloride **7** muriate **8** chemical, compound

chlorine
chemical symbol: **2** Cl

Chloris
father: **7** Amphion
mother: **5** Niobe
daughter: **4** Pero

chocolate **5** brown, candy, cacao, cocoa, drink **6** bon bon **10** confection

Choctaw
language family: **10** Muskhogean
location: **7** Alabama **11** Mississippi
related to: **9** Chickasaw

Choephoroe
author: **9** Aeschylus
character: **6** Furies **7** Electra, Orestes, Pylades **9** Aegisthus **12** Clytemnestra

choice **3** say **4** A-one, best, fine, pick, vote **5** array, elite, prime, prize, stock, store, voice **6** better, opting, option, select, supply, tip-top **7** display, special, variety **8** choosing, deciding, decision, superior **9** excellent, exclusive, first-rate, preferred, selection, top drawer **10** assemblage, assortment, collection, consummate, discretion, first-class, preferable, preference, well-chosen **11** alternative, appointment, exceptional, superlative **13** determination, extraordinary

choice food **5** treat **8** delicacy

choicest part
French: **14** creme de la creme

choir **4** band **5** quire **6** angels, chorus **7** chorale, singers **10** choristers

Choirboys, The
author: **14** Joseph Wambaugh

choke **3** dam, gag **4** clog, plug **5** block, check, dam up, stuff **6** arrest, bridle, hamper, hinder, impede, plug up, retard, stifle, stop up **7** congest, garrote, inhibit, repress, smother **8** blockade, hold back, obstruct, restrain, strangle, suppress, throttle **9** constrain, constrict, suffocate **10** asphyxiate

choler **3** ire **4** fury, rage **5** anger, wrath **6** spleen, temper

choleric **3** mad **5** angry, irate, testy, vexed **6** cranky, grumpy, shirty, touchy **7** enraged, furious, grouchy, peevish, waspish **8** snappish, wrathful **9** dyspeptic, indignant, irritable, irascible, splenetic **10** infuriated, short-fused **11** contentious, hot-tempered, ill-tempered, thin-skinned **12** cantankerous, sour-tempered **13** quick-tempered, short-tempered

choose **3** opt **4** like, pick, take, wish **5** adopt, elect **6** decide, desire, intend, opt for, prefer, see fit, select **7** call out, embrace, espouse, extract, fix upon, pick out, resolve **8** decide on, settle on **9** determine, single out **10** be inclined **13** commit oneself **14** make up one's mind

choosy **5** fussy, picky **7** finicky **9** selective **10** fastidious, particular **14** discriminating

chop **3** cut, hew, hit, lop **4** blow, chip, crop, cube, dice, fell, gash, hack **5** cut up, mince, slash, slice, split, swipe, whack **6** cleave, cutlet, stroke, sunder **8** fragment, rib slice **9** cotelette, pulverize

Chopin, Frederic Francois
born: **6** Poland **12** Zelazowawola
companion: **10** George Sand
composer of: **5** Etude **7** Ballade **8** Berceuse, Cat Valse, Dog Valse, Fantasie **9** Ecossaise **10** Barcarolle **11** Minute Valse **15** Andante Spianato, Heroic Polonaise (No 6), Raindrop Prelude, Winter Wind Etude **16** Shepherd Boy Etude **17** Impromptu Fantasie, Rondo a la Krakowiak **18** Revolutionary Etude **20** Butterfly's Wings Etude

choral ode
Greek: **7** parodos **8** stasimon

chord **4** cord, line, note, tone **5** music, triad **6** accord, string, tendon **7** cadence, emotion, feeling, harmony **9** harmonize

chore **3** job **4** duty, task, work **5** stint **6** burden, errand, strain **8** farm task, small job **10** assignment **13** household task **14** responsibility

choreography **5** dance **12** stage dancing **16** dance composition

chorister **6** singer **7** changer **8** choirboy

chortle **5** laugh **7** chuckle

chorus **5** choir, unity **6** accord, unison **7** concert, concord, refrain **8** glee club, one voice, response **9** antiphony, consensus, unanimity **11** concordance **12** singing group

chosen **5** elite **6** picked, sorted **7** elected **8** selected **9** picked out

Chosen, The
author: **10** Chaim Potok

Choson *see* **5** Korea

Chouans, The
author: **14** Honore de Balzac

chough
group of: **10** chattering

Chowbok
character in: **7** Erewhon
author: **6** Butler

Christ, the *see* **5** Jesus

christen **3** dip, dub **4** name **6** launch **7** baptize, immerse **8** dedicate, sprinkle **9** designate

Christian
character in: **16** Pilgrim's Progress
author: **6** Bunyan

Christian, Fletcher
character in: **17** Mutiny on the Bounty
authors: **4** Hall **8** Nordhoff

Christian, Linda
real name: **16** Blanca Rosa Welter
husband: **11** Tyrone Power **12** Edmund Purdom
born: **6** Mexico **7** Tampico
roles: **6** Athena **15** Slaves of Babylon **18** Green Dolphin Street

Christiania
capital of: **6** Norway

Christie, (Dame) Agatha
author of: **7** Curtain **12** The Mousetrap **14** Death on the Nile **15** The Mirror Crack'd **16** Ten Little Indians **19** Murder at the Vicarage **20** And Then There Were None **22** What Mrs McGillicuddy Saw! **23** The Murder of Roger Ackroyd **24** Murder on the Orient Express, Witness for the Prosecution **27** The Mysterious Affair at Styles
character: **10** Jane Marple **13** Hercule Poirot

Christie, Julie
born: **5** Assam, India **6** Chukua
roles: **7** Darling (Oscar), Shampoo **9** Billy Liar **11** Heat and Dust **13** Doctor Zhivago, Fahrenheit 451, Heaven Can Wait **18** McCabe and Mrs Miller **22** Far From the Madding Crowd

Christine
author: **11** Stephen King

Christmas
also: **4** Noel, Yule **8** Yuletide
feature/symbol: **4** bell, star, tree **5** angel, gifts, holly **6** candle, carols, creche, manger, sleigh, wreath **7** Yule log **8** presents **9** evergreen, mistletoe, snowflake, stockings **10** Santa Claus

Christmas, Joe
character in: **13** Light in August
author: **8** Faulkner

Christmas Carol, A
author: **14** Charles Dickens
character: **7** Tiny Tim **8** Fezziwig **11** Bob Cratchit **12** Marley's Ghost **15** Ebenezer Scrooge
ghosts of: **13** Christmas Past **15** Christmas Future **16** Christmas Present
director: **17** Brian Desmond Hurst
cast: **10** Jack Warner **11** Alistair Sim (Ebenezer Scrooge), Mervyn Johns **14** Michael Hordern **16** Kathleen Harrison

Chrome Yellow
author: **12** Aldous Huxley

chromium
chemical symbol: **2** Cr

chronic **7** abiding, lasting **8** constant, enduring, habitual, periodic **9** confirmed, continual, ingrained, perennial, recurrent, recurring **10** continuous, deep-rooted, deep-seated, inveterate, persistent, persisting **12** intermittent, longstanding

chronicle **3** log **4** epic, list, note, post, saga **5** diary, enter, story **6** annals, docket, record, relate, report **7** account, history, journal, narrate, recount, set down **8** archives **9** narrative **10** chronology

Chronicles of England, Scotland, and Ireland
author: **17** Raphael Hollinshed

chronological **5** dated **6** serial **7** ordered, sequent **10** sequential, succeeding, successive **11** consecutive, progressive, time-ordered **12** chronometric, chronoscopic **13** chronographic

chronology **6** annals, record **7** history **9** chronicle **13** order of events

chronometer **5** clock **8** horologe **9** timepiece

chrysanthemum
varieties: **3** Max **4** Corn **5** Daisy, Tansy **6** Nippon **7** Garland **8** Florist's, Tricolor **10** Portuguese

Chrysaor
father: **8** Poseidon
mother: **6** Medusa
brother: **7** Pegasus

Chryseis
father: **7** Chryses
concubine of: **9** Agamemnon

Chryses
priest of: **6** Apollo
daughter: **8** Chryseis

Chrysippus
father: **6** Pelops
abducted by: **5** Laius
half-brother: **6** Atreus **8** Thyestes

chrysoberyl
variety: **7** cat's-eye **11** alexandrite

chrysolite **4** iron, lava **5** beryl, green, stone **6** yellow **7** mineral, olivine, peridot **8** silicate **9** magnesium **10** aquamarine

chrysoprase
species: **6** quartz
color: **5** green

Chrysothemis
father: **9** Agamemnon
mother: **12** Clytemnestra
brother: **7** Orestes
sister: **7** Electra **9** Iphigenia
daughter: **5** Rhoeo

Chthonian
form: **5** deity **6** spirit
habitat: **10** underworld

Chthonius
member of: **6** Sparti
epithet of: **4** Zeus
means: **15** of the underworld

Chuang-tzu, Chwang-tse
author: **9** Chuang-tzu

chubby **3** fat **5** buxom, plump, podgy, pudgy, stout, tubby **6** chunky, flabby, fleshy, portly, rotund, stocky, zaftig **7** paunchy **8** heavyset, roly-poly, thickset **9** corpulent **10** overweight **15** pleasingly plump

chuck **3** pat, pet, tap **4** cast, toss **5** fling, heave, pitch, sling, throw **6** tickle

chuckle **3** big **5** cluck, laugh **6** clumsy **7** blokish, cackle, chortle, snicker

chum **3** pal **5** buddy, crony **6** cohort, friend **7** comrade **8** intimate, playmate, sidekick **9** companion, confidant **10** bosom buddy, playfellow **11** close friend

chummy **5** close, palsy **7** devoted **8** familiar, friendly, intimate **9** congenial **10** buddy-buddy, palsy-walsy **12** affectionate

chump **4** dolt, dupe, fool, goof, goon, head **5** champ, munch **6** sucker **9** blockhead

chunk **3** gob, wad **4** clod, hunk, lump, mass **5** batch, block, piece **6** nugget, square

chunky **5** beefy, dumpy, lumpy, pudgy, squat, stout, thick **6** chubby, portly, stocky, stodgy, stubby **7** squabby **8** heavyset, thickset **11** thick-bodied

church **4** cult, sect **5** faith **6** belief, chapel, mosque, temple **7** service **8** basilica, religion **9** cathedral, devotions, synagogue **10** house of God, Lord's house, persuasion, tabernacle **11** affiliation **12** denomination **13** divine worship **14** house of worship

Church, Frederick Edwin
born: **10** Hartford CT
artwork: **14** Andes of Ecuador, Falls of Niagara (Niagara Falls) **18** The Heart of the Andes **19** Morning in the Tropics

Churchill, Frank
character in: **4** Emma
author: **6** Austen

Churchill, Sarah
father: **19** Sir Winston Churchill
born: **6** London **7** England
roles: **12** Royal Wedding

Churchill, Winston Spencer
born: 7 England 14 Blenheim Palace
father: 8 Randolph
mother: 12 Jennie Jerome
wife: 16 Clementine Hosier
daughter: 5 Sarah
school: 6 Harrow 9 Sandhurst
captured by: 5 Boers
position: 13 prime minister
author of: 11 Marlborough, My Early Life 14 The World Crisis 17 The Second World War 35 A History of the English-Speaking Peoples

churchly 8 clerical, pastoral, priestly 9 parochial 11 ministerial 14 ecclesiastical

churchman 5 vicar 6 bishop, cleric, curate, deacon, parson, pastor, priest, rector 7 prelate 8 chaplain, minister, preacher 9 clergyman 12 ecclesiastic

church official 5 elder 6 beadle, deacon 9 presbyter

churchyard 8 cemetery 9 graveyard 12 burial ground 13 burying ground

churl 3 cad, oaf 4 boor, lout 7 bounder

churlish 4 rude, sour, tart 5 crude, surly, testy 6 crusty, sullen 7 bearish, bilious, boorish, brusque, crabbed, grouchy, ill-bred, uncivil, uncouth, waspish 8 arrogant, captious, choleric, impolite, impudent, insolent, petulant 9 dastardly, insulting, irascible, irritable, obnoxious, rancorous, splenetic 10 unmannerly 11 ill-mannered, ill-tempered, quarrelsome 12 contemptible, discourteous

churn 4 beat, foam, rage, roil, roll, toss, whip 5 heave, shake, swirl, whisk 6 stir up 7 agitate, disturb, pulsate, shake up, vibrate 8 convulse 9 palpitate

chute 5 rapid, slide, slope 7 incline, passage 9 parachute

chutzpa, chutzpah 4 gall 5 brass, cheek, nerve 8 audacity, boldness, temerity 9 brashness, impudence 10 brazenness, effrontery 11 forwardness, presumption

Chwatt, Aaron
real name of: 10 Red Buttons

ciao 2 hi 5 hello 6 so long 7 goodbye 11 see you later

Cicero, Marcus Tullius
lived in: 11 ancient Rome
noted as: 6 author, lawyer, orator 9 statesman 11 philosopher 12 letter writer
position: 6 aedile, consul 7 praetor
author of: 9 De finibus, De oratore 10 De amicitia, De officiis 11 De re publica, De senectute, In Catilinam 14 De natura deorum, Pro lege Manilia 23 Tusculanae Disputationes

cicerone 5 guide, pilot 8 conductor 9 explainer

cicisbeo 5 lover

Cid, The
also: 11 Poema del Cid
author: 7 unknown 15 Pierre Corneille
character: 7 Chimene 8 Rodrigue
Cid also called: 14 el Cid Campeador 18 Rodrigo Diaz de Bivar
horse: 7 Babieca

ci-devant 6 former 7 retired 10 heretofore

cierge 3 dip, wax 5 light, taper 6 bougie, candle, tallow

cigar 4 toby 5 claro 6 corona, havana, maduro, stogie 7 cheroot 8 panatela, panetela, perfecto 9 cigarillo, panatella
ingredient: 11 tobacco leaf
part: 6 binder, filler 7 wrapper
made in: 4 Cuba 6 Havana
kept in: 7 humidor

cigarette, cigaret 3 cig, fag 4 biri 5 smoke 6 gasper, reefer 10 coffin nail
ingredient: 3 tar 7 menthol, tobacco 8 nicotine

Cilissa
nurse of: 7 Orestes

Cilix
father: 6 Agenor
sister: 6 Europa
searched for: 6 Europa

Cilla
brother: 5 Priam
killed by: 5 Priam

Cillus
charioteer of: 6 Pelops

Cimabue
real name: 11 Cenni di Pepi
born: 5 Italy 8 Florence
artwork attributed: 18 The S Trinita Madonna 29 Madonna Enthroned with St Francis 45 Madonna and Child Enthroned with Angels and Prophets

Cimarron
author: 10 Edna Ferber
director: 13 Wesley Ruggles
cast: 10 Irene Dunne, Richard Dix 13 Estelle Taylor
Oscar for: 7 picture 10 screenplay

Cimarron Strip
character: 8 (US Marshal) Jim Crown 9 Mac Gregor 12 Francis Wilde 17 Dulcey Coopersmith
cast: 10 Randy Boone 12 Jill Townsend, Percy Herbert 13 Stuart Whitman

Cimino, Michael
director of: 11 Heaven's Gate 13 The Deer Hunter (Oscar)

Cimmerian
mentioned by: 5 Homer
form: 10 Westerners
live in: 8 darkness

cinch 4 band, snap 5 girth 6 clinch, ensure, girdle, shoo-in 8 lead-pipe 9 pull tight, sure thing 11 piece of cake

Cincinnati
baseball team: 4 Reds
football team: 7 Bengals

cincture 4 band, belt, cord, sash 6 girdle

cinder 3 ash 4 slag 5 ashes, dross, ember 6 embers, scoria 8 clinkers, iron slag 10 burned coal, burned wood

Cinderella
author: 7 unknown
source: 8 Perrault
character: 14 Fairy Godmother, Handsome Prince 15 Ugly Stepsisters 16 Wicked Stepmother
coach: 7 pumpkin
horses: 9 white mice
footman: 4 frog
loses: 12 glass slipper

cinema 5 films 6 flicks, movies 7 theater 14 motion pictures, moving pictures

cinnamon 5 spice
botanical name: 20 Cinnamomum zeylanicum
variety: 6 cassia, Ceylon 10 zeylanicum
color: 4 buff 5 tawny 6 auburn 8 nut-brown 11 golden-brown, yellow-brown 12 reddish-brown 13 chestnut-brown 14 yellowish-brown
origin: 5 China 7 Vietnam 9 Indonesia 10 East Indies

Cinyras
king of: 6 Cyprus
son: 5 Melus
daughter: 6 Myrrha
introduced worship of: 9 Aphrodite
crime: 6 incest
death by: 7 suicide

cipher 3 nil, zip 4 code, zero 5 aught 6 naught, nobody 7 anagram, nothing, nullity 8 acrostic, goose egg 9 nonentity, obscurity **10** cryptogram **11** cryptograph

Cipus
origin: **5** Roman
occupation: **7** praetor

Circe
form: **11** enchantress
father: **6** Helios
mother: **5** Perse
brother: **6** Aeetes
son: **6** Agrius **7** Latinus **9** Telegonus
home: **5** Aeaea
turned men into: **4** pigs **5** swine

circle **3** orb, set **4** belt, curl, gird, girt, halo, hoop, knot, loop, reel, ring, turn **5** arena, bound, cabal, crowd, curve, cycle, field, girth, group, hem in, orbit, pivot, range, reach, realm, round, sweep, swing **6** border, bounds, clique, cordon, corona, course, domain, girdle, region, sphere **7** circlet, circuit, company, compass, coterie, enclose, envelop, hedge in, revolve, ringlet, society, theater **8** dominion, encircle, province, sequence, surround **9** bailiwick, encompass, territory, wind about **10** move around, revolution, ring around **11** curve around, progression **12** circumrotate, circumscribe **13** revolve around **14** circumnavigate

Circle **6** gilgal

circlet **4** band, halo, ring **5** tiara **6** diadem, fillet, wreath **7** chaplet, coronet, ringlet

circuit **3** lap, run **4** area, beat, edge, tour, trek, walk **5** jaunt, limit, round, route **6** border, bounds, course, margin, sphere **7** compass, confine, journey **8** circling, frontier, orbiting, pivoting **9** excursion, extremity, perimeter, revolving, territory **10** revolution **13** circumference **14** distance around

circuitous **7** devious, turning, winding **8** circular, indirect, rambling, tortuous, twisting **10** meandering, roundabout, serpentine **12** labyrinthine **14** circumlocutory

circular **4** bill **5** flier, round **6** curved, notice, rotary **7** coiling, curling, leaflet, rocking, rolling, rounded, turning, winding **8** bulletin, gyrating, handbill, pivoting, spinning, twirling **9** revolving, spiraling, swiveling, throwaway **10** circuitous, ring-shaped **12** announcement **13** advertisement

circulate **4** flow **5** issue, strew **6** circle, course, spread, travel **7** give out, go forth, journey, publish, radiate, scatter **8** announce, disperse, go around, put about **9** broadcast, get abroad, make known, move about, publicize **10** distribute, make public, move around, pass around, put forward **11** disseminate, pass through, visit around **13** make the rounds

circulation **4** flow **6** motion **7** flowing **8** circling, rotation **9** diffusion, radiation **10** dispersion **11** propagation **12** distribution, promulgation, transmission **13** dissemination

circulatory system
part: **4** vein **5** heart **6** artery **9** capillary **15** lymphatic vessel
carries: **6** plasma **9** platelets **13** red blood cells **15** white blood cells

circumcision
Hebrew: **4** Brit **5** Berit, Brith **6** Berith

circumference **3** rim **4** edge **5** girth **6** border, bounds, fringe, girdle, limits, margin **7** circuit, compass, outline **8** boundary **9** extremity, perimeter, periphery **14** distance around

circumlocution **8** rambling, verbiage **9** garrulity, verbosity, wordiness **10** digression, meandering **14** discursiveness, long-windedness, roundaboutness

circumlocutory **5** wordy **7** diffuse, verbose **8** rambling **9** wandering **10** digressive, discursive, maundering, roundabout

circumnavigate **5** skirt **6** bypass, circle **8** encircle, go around **10** circumvent

circumnavigation **8** circling, skirting **9** bypassing **11** going around **12** encirclement **13** circumvention

circumscribe **3** fix **4** curb **5** check, hem in, limit **6** bridle, circle, corset, define, impede **7** confine, enclose, outline **8** encircle, restrain, restrict, surround **9** constrain, delineate, encompass, proscribe

circumscribed **6** narrow **7** limited **10** restricted

circumscription **5** limit **7** outline **9** hemming in, restraint **10** constraint **11** confinement **12** encirclement **14** restrictedness

circumspect **4** sage, wary **5** alert **7** careful, guarded, prudent **8** cautious, discreet, vigilant, watchful **9** judicious, sagacious, wide-awake **10** deliberate, discerning, particular, thoughtful **13** contemplative, perspicacious **14** discriminating

circumspection **4** care, heed **7** caution **8** prudence **10** discretion, precaution, steadiness **11** carefulness, heedfulness, mindfulness **12** deliberation

circumstance **4** fact, item **5** event, point, thing **6** detail, factor, matter, ritual **7** element **8** ceremony, incident, splendor **9** condition, formality, happening, pageantry **10** brilliance, occurrence, particular, phenomenon **11** vicissitude **12** happenstance, magnificence, resplendence **14** state of affairs

circumstances **5** state **9** situation **11** environment **16** living conditions

circumstantial **4** full **6** minute **7** deduced, hearsay, implied, precise **8** accurate, complete, detailed, explicit, inferred, presumed, thorough **9** secondary **10** blow-by-blow, evidential, exhaustive, extraneous, incidental, particular, unabridged **11** conjectural, inferential, provisional **12** nonessential

circumvent **4** miss, shun **5** avoid, dodge, elude, evade, skirt **6** bypass, circle, escape, outwit, thwart **8** go around **9** frustrate **12** keep away from **14** circumnavigate

circumvention **7** dodging, ducking, eluding, evasion **9** avoidance, bypassing **11** frustration **12** sidestepping

circus **4** ring **5** arena **6** big top, circle, uproar **8** carnival, coliseum **9** spectacle **10** exhibition, hippodrome **11** ampitheater **12** intersection
act: **5** clown, flyer **7** acrobat, juggler, trapeze **8** side show **9** lion tamer, menagerie **10** equestrian **13** flying trapeze
famous: **6** Astley **12** Cirque d'Hiver **15** Barnum and Bailey **16** Ringling Brothers

Cissaea
epithet of: **6** Athena
means: **10** ivy goddess

Cist
form: **9** sacred box
used for: **8** utensils

cistern **3** box, tub, vat **4** tank,

well **6** cavity, vessel **8** aqueduct **9** reservoir

citadel 4 fort **7** bastion, rampart **8** fortress **10** stronghold **13** fortification

citation 4 cite **5** award, honor, kudos, medal, quote **7** example, excerpt, extract, passage **8** instance **9** quotation **12** commendation, illustration **14** official praise

cite 4 name, note **5** honor, quote **6** praise **7** advance, commend, mention, present, refer to, specify **8** allude to, document, indicate **9** enumerate, exemplify **12** bring forward **13** give as example

Cithaeron
brother: 7 Helicon
crime: 6 murder
changed into: 8 mountain

Cithaeronian *see* **4** Zeus

citified 5 urban **6** urbane **12** cosmopolitan **13** sophisticated

citizen 6 native **7** denizen, subject **8** national, resident **10** inhabitant
French: 7 citoyen

Citizen Kane
director: 11 Orson Welles
script: 11 Orson Welles **17** Herman J Mankiewicz
cast: 11 Orson Welles **12** Joseph Cotten **13** Everett Sloane **14** Agnes Moorehead
score: 15 Bernard Herrmann
sled: 7 Rosebud

citizenry 4 folk **6** people, public **7** society **8** populace **9** community **10** population

citoyen 7 citizen

citrine
species: 6 quartz
color: 6 yellow

citron 3 rue **4** lime, rind **5** lemon **6** cedrat, orange, yellow **8** Rutaceae **9** tangerine **10** watermelon **12** citrus medica
Jewish: 6 ethrog

city 4 burg, town **7** big town **8** denizens, township **9** residents **10** metropolis **11** inhabitants, megalopolis, townspeople **12** municipality **16** incorporated town, metropolitan area

city hall
French: 12 hotel de ville

City Life
author: 15 Donald Barthelme

City Lights
director: 14 Charles Chaplin
cast: 8 Hank Mann **10** Harry Myers **14** Charlie Chaplin **16** Virginia Cherrill

City of God, The (De Civitate Dei)
author: 11 St Augustine

City of the Lion *see* **9** Singapore

city slicker 4 dude **8** urbanite **11** cosmopolite **12** sophisticate

City Without Walls and Other Poems
author: 7 W H Auden

Ciudad Trujillo
capital of: 17 Dominican Republic

Civ 17 second Hebrew month

civic 5 local **6** public **8** citizen's, communal **9** community

civil 3 lay **4** city **5** civic, state **6** genial, polite, public **7** affable, amiable, citizen, cordial, secular **8** citizen's, communal, decorous, gracious, mannerly, obliging **9** civilized, community, courteous, municipal **10** individual, neighborly, respectful **11** gentlemanly, nonmilitary **12** conciliatory, well-mannered

Civil Disobedience
author: 17 Henry David Thoreau

civilian 9 lay person **14** private citizen **17** nonmilitary person **18** nonuniformed person

civility 4 tact **7** manners, respect **8** courtesy **10** affability, amiability, cordiality, good temper, politeness **11** good manners **12** graciousness, pleasantness **13** agreeableness, courteousness **14** respectfulness

civilization 7 culture, society **10** refinement **11** cultivation, worldliness **13** enlightenment **14** sophistication

civilize 5 edify, teach, train **6** inform, polish, refine **7** culture, develop, educate, elevate **8** humanize, instruct **9** cultivate, enlighten **11** acculturate **12** sophisticate

civil law
Latin: 9 jus civile

clad 6 garbed **7** arrayed, attired, clothed, dressed **9** outfitted

Claggart
character in: 9 Billy Budd
author: 8 Melville

claim 3 ask **4** avow, call, plea, take **5** exact, right, title **6** access, affirm, allege, assert, avowal, charge, demand, pick up **7** call for, collect, command, declare, profess, request **8** exaction, insist on, maintain, proclaim **9** assertion, ownership, seek as due, statement **10** allegation, lay claim to, pretension, profession **11** affirmation, declaration, postulation, requirement **12** proclamation, protestation

claimant 6 suitor **9** applicant, pretender **10** petitioner

clairvoyant 7 psychic **8** divining, oracular **9** prescient, prophetic **10** telepathic **11** foreknowing, telekinetic **12** extrasensory, precognitive, psychometric **13** psychokinetic, second-sighted

clam 4 vise **5** clamp, clasp **6** dollar, marine **7** bivalve, mollusk
kind: 5 pismo, razor **6** butter, quahog **7** geoduck, steamer **10** little neck **11** cherrystone
part: 4 foot, palp **5** gills, shell, valve **6** mantle, siphon **7** sinuses **8** ligament
habitat: 3 mud **4** sand
relative: 6 mussel, oyster

clamber up 5 climb, mount, scale **10** scramble up, struggle up

clamminess 4 damp **7** wetness **8** dampness, dankness **10** stickiness, sweatiness

clammy 3 wet **4** damp **5** pasty, slimy **6** sticky, sweaty **10** perspiring **11** cold and damp

clamor 3 cry, din **4** call, howl, yell **5** blast, chaos, noise, shout, storm **6** bedlam, bellow, cry out, hubbub, jangle, outcry, racket, rumpus, tumult, uproar **7** bluster, call out, clangor, thunder **8** brouhaha, shouting **9** commotion, hue and cry **10** hullabaloo, vociferate, wild chorus

clamorous 4 loud **5** noisy **10** boisterous, uproarious

clamp 4 clip, grip, vise **5** brace, clasp **6** clench, clinch, fasten, secure **7** bracket **8** fastener

clan 4 gang, knot, line, ring **5** breed, cabal, crowd, group, guild, house, party, stock **6** circle, league, strain **7** company, dynasty, lineage, society **8** alliance, pedigree **10** fraternity **11** affiliation, association, brotherhood, family group, lineal group **12** tribal family

clandestine 6 covert, hidden, masked, secret, veiled **7** cloaked, furtive, private **8** secluded, sneaking, stealthy **9** concealed, secretive, underhand **10** undercover, unrevealed **11** underground, underhanded, undisclosed **12** confidential **13** surreptitious

clang **3** din **4** bong, gong, peal, toll **5** chime, clank, clash, knell **6** jangle **7** clangor, resound, ringing, tolling **8** clashing **10** resounding, ring loudly

clangor **3** din **5** noise **6** clamor, hubbub, jangle, racket, uproar

clank **5** chink, clang, clash, clink **6** jangle, rattle **7** clangor, clatter **8** clashing

clannish **4** cold **5** aloof **6** narrow **7** distant, insular **8** cliquish, snobbish **9** exclusive, parochial, sectarian **10** provincial, restricted, unfriendly **11** unreceptive

Clan of the Cave Bear, The
author: **9** Jean M Auel

clap **3** bat, hit, rap, tap **4** bang, bump, cast, cuff, dash, hurl, peal, push, roar, rush, slam, slap, swat, toss **5** burst, clack, crack, drive, fling, force, pitch, shove, smack, smite, thump, whack **6** buffet, plunge, propel, strike, thrust, thwack, wallop **7** applaud, clatter **9** explosion **11** set suddenly

claptrap **3** rot **4** bosh, bull, bunk, sham, **5** bilge, hokum, hooey, stuff, trash, tripe **6** bunkum, drivel, hot air, humbug, tinsel **7** baloney, blarney, fustian, hogwash, spinach, twaddle **8** buncombe, nonsense, quackery, tommyrot **9** gaudiness, poppycock, staginess **10** applesauce, flapdoodle, tawdriness, tomfoolery **12** foolishiness **15** pretentiousness **16** stuff and nonsense

claque **10** sycophants **15** cheering section

Clare, Ada
character in: **10** Bleak House
author: **7** Dickens

claret **3** red **7** carmine, deep red, red wine **8** blood-red, Bordeaux, cardinal **11** purplish red, wine-colored

clarification **10** commentary **11** elucidation, explanation, explication **14** further comment
French: **15** eclaircissement

clarify **5** clear, purge, solve **6** purify, refine **7** clear up, explain, lay open, resolve **9** elucidate, explicate, make clear, make plain **10** illuminate **11** disentangle, shed light on **12** bring to light **18** make understandable

clarinet **4** wind **8** woodwind **11** transposing
mouthpiece: **4** reed
ancestor: **9** chalumeau
musician: **12** Benny Goodman

clarion **5** acute, clear, sharp **6** shrill **7** blaring, ringing **8** distinct, piercing, resonant, sonorous, stirring **10** commanding, compelling, imperative **11** high-pitched

Clarissa Harlowe
author: **16** Samuel Richardson
character: **8** Miss Howe **11** John Belford **14** Robert Lovelace **20** Colonel William Morden

clarity **6** purity **8** lucidity, radiance **9** clearness, exactness, plainness, precision **10** brightness, brilliance, directness, effulgence, glassiness, luminosity, simplicity **12** explicitness, translucence, transparency **15** intelligibility **17** comprehensibility

Clark, Mark W
served in: **3** WWI **4** WWII **9** Korean War
rank: **22** allied commander in Italy **24** commander of forces in Korea **30** chief of staff of army ground forces **42** commander of Allied occupation forces in Austria
president of: **7** Citadel

Clark, Walter Van Tilburg
author of: **16** The Ox-Bow Incident

Clarke, Arthur C
author of: **10** (2010) Odyssey Two **13** (2001) A Space Odyssey, Childhood's End

clash **4** bang, boil, feud, fray, tiff **5** argue, clang, clank, crash, fight, set-to **6** battle, combat, fracas, jangle, rattle, tussle **7** clangor, clatter, contend, contest, discord, dispute, grapple, jarring, quarrel, wrangle **8** conflict, crashing, friction, skirmish, squabble, struggle **9** altercate, encounter, lock horns **10** antagonism, difference, disharmony, dissidence, opposition **11** cross swords **12** disagreement **13** exchange blows

clash of arms **5** fight **6** battle, combat **8** conflict, skirmish, struggle **9** encounter **10** engagement

clash with **9** fight with **12** do battle with **14** contend against **15** cross swords with

clasp **3** hug **4** bolt, clip, grip, hasp, hold, hook, link, lock, snap **5** catch, clamp, grasp, latch, press **6** buckle, clinch, clutch, couple, fasten, secure **7** coupler, embrace, grapple, squeeze **8** fastener **9** fastening

clasp in the arms **3** hug **4** hold **6** enfold **7** embrace

class **3** set **4** form, kind, rank, rate, size, sort, type **5** brand, breed, caste, genre, genus, grade, group, index, label, order, state **6** circle, clique, codify, course, lesson, number, sphere, status **7** arrange, catalog, section, session, species, station, variety **8** category, classify, division, pedigree, position **9** condition, designate **10** categorize, pigeonhole, social rank **11** set of pupils **13** social stratum **14** classification **15** departmentalize, graduating group

classic, classical **4** epic **5** model **6** heroic **7** ageless, paragon **8** absolute, accepted, enduring, masterly **9** archetype, excellent, exemplary, first-rate, prototype **10** archetypal, consummate, definitive, first-class, Greco-Roman, prototypal **11** masterpiece, outstanding, traditional **12** ancient Greek, ancient Roman, standard work **13** authoritative, distinguished **14** distinguishing **17** first-class example

classification **4** kind, rank, sort, type **5** class, genus, group, order **6** family, series **7** section, species **8** category, classing, division, grouping, labeling, ordering, taxonomy **9** arranging, gradation **10** assortment, organizing **11** arrangement, designation, disposition **12** categorizing, codification, organization **14** categorization **15** systematization

classified **5** secret **6** sorted **7** classed **8** assorted **10** restricted **11** categorized **12** confidential

classify **3** tag **4** list, rank, rate, size, type **5** brand, class, grade, group, index, label, order, range **6** assort, codify, number, ticket **7** arrange, catalog **8** organize **9** segregate **10** categorize, pigeonhole **11** distinguish

classy **4** chic, posh, tony **5** nifty, nobby, ritzy, smart, swank, swell **6** dressy, modish, spiffy, swanky **7** elegant, genteel, opulent, refined, stylish **8** cultured, polished, tasteful

9 high-class **10** ultrasmart **11** fashionable, in good taste **12** aristocratic, well-mannered

clatter **4** bang **5** clack, clang, clank, clash, clink, clump, crash **6** clamor, jangle, racket, rattle **7** chatter **8** crashing, rattling

clattering **3** din **6** clamor, hubbub, racket, uproar **7** clangor

Claude
real name: **12** Claude Gellee
also called: **14** Claude Lorraine
born: **6** France **8** Chamagne
artwork: **7** The Mill **16** Hagar and the Angel **18** Ascanius and the Stag, The Enchanted Castle **27** The Rest on the Flight into Egypt **31** The Embarkation of the Queen of Sheba

Claudel, Paul
author of: **6** L'Otage **10** The Hostage **13** Partage de Midi **15** The Satin Slipper **20** Tidings Brought to Mary

Claudia Quinta
freed: **12** grounded ship
feat proved: **8** chastity

Claudio
character in: **17** Measure for Measure **19** Much Ado About Nothing
author: **11** Shakespeare

Claudius
character in: **6** Hamlet
author: **11** Shakespeare

Claudius the God
author: **12** Robert Graves

clause **4** term **7** article, proviso **8** covenant **9** condition, provision **11** proposition, stipulation **13** specification **14** simple sentence

claustrophobia
fear of: **12** closed spaces **14** confined spaces

Clavell, James
author of: **6** Shogun, Tai-Pan **7** King Rat **9** Whirlwind **10** Noble House

clavicle
bone of: **10** collarbone

claw **3** paw **4** foot, grip, maul, tear **5** seize, slash, talon **6** clutch, pincer, scrape **7** scratch **8** lacerate **10** animal nail

Clay, Cassius
former name of: **11** Muhammad Ali

Clayburgh, Jill
born: **9** New York NY
roles: **9** Semi-Tough **12** Starting Over **16** An Unmarried Woman, North Dallas Forty **21** I'm Dancing as Fast as I Can

Clayhanger Trilogy, The
author: **13** Arnold Bennett

clean **3** mop **4** dust, fine, neat, pure, tidy, trim, wash **5** bathe, clear, fresh, moral, order, scour, scrub, sweep **6** bathed, chaste, decent, neaten, tidy up, vacuum, washed **7** cleaned, cleanse, healthy, launder, orderly, perfect, scoured, shampoo, upright **8** cleansed, decorous, flawless, innocent, sanitary, scrubbed, spotless, unsoiled, virtuous, well-made **9** exemplary, faultless, honorable, laundered, stainless, undefiled, unspotted, unstained, unsullied, untainted, wholesome **10** immaculate, uninfected, unpolluted **11** unblemished **13** unadulterated **14** uncontaminated

cleaner, cleanser **4** soap **5** borax **6** washer **7** ammonia, janitor **8** purifier, scrubber **9** detergent **14** scouring powder

cleaning **7** bathing, washing **8** scouring **9** cleansing, going-over, scrubbing, tidying up **10** laundering

cleanse **3** rid **4** free, wash **5** bathe, clean, clear, erase, flush, scour, scrub **7** absolve, deliver, expunge, launder, release, shampoo **8** sweep out, unburden **9** expurgate

clean-shaven **6** smooth **9** unbearded **11** unwhiskered **12** smooth-shaven

cleansing **7** bathing, healing, purging, washing **8** flushing, scouring **9** expunging, purifying, scrubbing **10** absolution

cleanup **4** gain **6** profit **8** windfall
baseball: **12** fourth batter

clear *see box*

clearance **4** room, sale **6** margin, permit **7** removal **8** clearing **10** offsetting **11** elimination **13** authorization, certification

clear as day **5** plain **7** obvious **8** apparent, clear-cut, manifest **11** self-evident

clear-cut **4** open **5** exact, lucid, plain **6** patent **7** evident, express, obvious, precise **8** definite, detailed, distinct, explicit, manifest **10** clear as day, unconfused, undeniable **11** appreciable, conspicuous, self-evident, substantial, unambiguous, undisguised, unequivocal, well-defined **12** crystal-clear, unmistakable **14** comprehensible, understandable **15** straightforward

clear **3** rid **4** fair, free, keen, make, open **5** alert, clean, empty, gauzy, lucid, plain, sharp, sunny **6** acquit, bright, patent, remove, serene, unstop, wholly **7** absolve, audible, audibly, certain, clearly, evident, express, fly over, glowing, halcyon, hop over, lighten, obvious, plainly, radiant, unblock **8** apparent, brighten, clear-cut, dazzling, definite, distinct, entirely, explicit, gleaming, leap over, luminous, manifest, pass over, pellucid, positive, skip over, unhidden **9** all the way, bound over, brilliant, cloudless, exculpate, exonerate, sparkling, unblocked, unclouded, unimpeded, unmuddled, vindicate, wide-awake **10** articulate, become fair, completely, diaphanous, discerning, distinctly, glistening, pronounced, unconfused, undeniable, unobscured **11** crystalline, inescapable, self-evident, translucent, transparent, unambiguous, unconcealed, undisguised, unequivocal, unqualified **12** articulately, intelligible, recognizable, unencumbered, unmistakable, unobstructed **14** comprehensible **15** distinguishable, straightforward

clearheaded **5** acute, alert, awake, aware, sharp **6** astute **8** rational, sensible **9** on the ball, practical, realistic, wide-awake **10** discerning, insightful, on one's toes, on the stick, perceptive **13** perspicacious

clearheadedness **7** insight **8** sagacity **9** alertness, sharpness **10** perception **11** discernment **12** perspicacity

clearing **5** glade

clearly **6** surely **7** plainly **8** markedly, palpably, patently **9** assuredly, certainly, decidedly, evidently, obviously **10** distinctly, manifestly, noticeably, observably, undeniably **11** beyond doubt, indubitably, perceptibly, undoubtedly **12** recognizably, unmistakably **13** unequivocally **14** beyond question, unquestionably

clearly expressed 8 coherent **10** articulate **11** unambiguous **12** intelligible

clearness 7 clarity **10** brightness, brilliance **12** explicitness **15** unmistakability

clear-sighted 4 sage, wise **5** acute, sharp **6** astute, shrewd **8** piercing **9** judicious, sagacious, sensitive **10** discerning, perceptive **11** intelligent, keen-sighted, penetrating **12** sharp-sighted **13** perspicacious

clear up 6 settle **7** clarify, unsnarl **8** untangle **11** disentangle **12** uncomplicate **13** straighten out

Cleary, Beverly
author of: 6 Ramona **7** Fifteen **12** Henry Huggins **13** Jean and Johnny **15** Beezus and Ramona **16** Sister of the Bride

cleat 5 block, chock, spike, wedge **6** batten **7** bollard

cleavage 3 gap **4** rent, rift, slit **5** cleft, crack, notch, split **6** furrow, trench, trough **7** crevice, fissure, opening **8** crevasse

cleave 3 cut, hew **4** chop, fuse, hack, hold, open, part, plow, rend, rive, slit, tear **5** cling, crack, halve, sever, slash, slice, split, stick, unite **6** adhere, be true, bisect, cut off, detach, divide, furrow, sunder, uphold **7** abide by, chop off, disjoin, lay open, stand by **8** be joined, break off, hold fast, separate **9** disengage, dismember

cleaver 3 axe **4** tool **5** knife ridge

cleft 3 gap **4** rent, rift, slit **5** break, crack, notch, split **6** breach, cloven, cranny, divide, forked, furrow, trench, trough **7** crevice, divided, fissure, notched, opening, slotted **8** aperture, bisected, branched, cleavage, crevasse, division **10** separation **11** indentation

clemency 5 mercy **7** charity **8** humanity, kindness, leniency, mildness, softness, sympathy **9** tolerance **10** compassion, indulgence, moderation, temperance **11** benevolence, forbearance, magnanimity **12** mercifulness, pleasantness **13** forgivingness

clement 4 kind, mild, warm **5** balmy **6** benign, gentle, humane **7** lenient **8** merciful, tolerant **9** not severe, not strict **10** benevolent **13** compassionate

clench 3 set **4** grip **5** clasp, tense **6** clinch, clutch **7** stiffen, tighten **8** fasten on, hold fast **11** grasp firmly, strain tight **12** close tightly

Clennam, Arthur
character in: 12 Little Dorrit
author: 7 Dickens

Cleobis
mother: 7 Cydippe
brother: 5 Biton

Cleodaeus
father: 6 Hyllus
mother: 4 Iole
grandfather: 8 Hercules

Cleone
father: 6 Asopus

Cleopas *see* **4** Mary

Cleopatra
queen of: 5 Egypt
father: 7 Ptolemy
brother/husband: 7 Ptolemy
lover: 10 Mark Antony **12** Julius Caesar
son: 9 Caesarion **15** Alexander Helios **19** Ptolemy Philadelphos
daughter: 15 Cleopatra Selene
death by: 3 asp **7** suicide

Cleopatra
director:
***1934 version:* 13** Cecil B DeMille
***1963 version:* 17** Joseph L Mankiewicz
cast:
***1934 version:* 13** Henry Wilcoxon, Warren William **16** Claudette Colbert
***1963 version:* 11** Rex Harrison **13** Richard Burton, Roddy McDowall **15** Elizabeth Taylor

Cleothera
father: 9 Pandareus

clergy 6 rabbis **7** clerics, pastors, priests **8** ministry, prelates, the cloth **9** churchmen, clergymen, clericals, ministers, pastorate, preachers, rabbinate, the church, the pulpit **10** priesthood **14** the first estate

clergyman 5 padre, rabbi **6** cleric, father, parson, pastor, priest **7** prelate **8** chaplain, minister, preacher, reverend, sky pilot **9** churchman **13** man of the cloth

cleric 6 parson, pastor **8** chaplain, preacher **9** churchman, clergyman **13** man of the cloth

clerical 6 cleric, filing, office, typing **7** clerkly **8** churchly, of clerks, pastoral, priestly **10** accounting, rabbinical **11** bookkeeping, ministerial **13** recordkeeping **14** ecclesiastical

clerical worker 5 clerk **6** typist **9** file clerk **10** bookkeeper, keypuncher **12** office worker **13** data processor

clerk 6 typist **8** salesman **9** file clerk **10** bookkeeper, salesclerk, saleswoman **11** salesperson **12** office worker

Cleta
member of: 6 Graces
worshipped at: 6 Sparta

Cleveland
baseball team: 7 Indians
basketball team: 9 Cavaliers
football team: 6 Browns

Cleveland, Grover ***see box***

clever 4 able, cute, deft, keen **5** acute, quick, sharp, smart, witty **6** adroit, artful, astute, bright, crafty, expert, shrewd **8** creative, humorous, original **9** ingenious, inventive **11** imaginative, intelligent, quick-witted, resourceful

cleverly 6 deftly **7** sharply, smartly, wittily **8** adroitly, artfully, craftily, expertly **10** creatively, humorously **11** ingeniously, inventively **13** imaginatively, intelligently

cleverness 3 wit **6** acumen **8** ableness, deftness, keenness **9** expertise, ingenuity, quickness, sharpness, smartness **10** adroitness, artfulness, astuteness, brightness, craftiness **12** intelligence, skillfulness **13** inventiveness **15** imaginativeness, quick-wittedness

clew *see* **4** clue

Clew
thread in: 9 Labyrinth
showed way to: 7 Theseus
given by: 7 Ariadne

cliche 3 saw **6** old saw **7** bromide **8** banality, old story **9** platitude **10** stereotype **11** trite phrase

cliche-ridden 5 corny, stale, tired, trite, vapid **6** jejune **8** bromidic **9** hackneyed **10** unoriginal **13** platitudinous, unimaginative

click 3 tap **4** clap, snap **5** clack, clink, crack **6** rattle **7** crackle

Clide
form: 5 nymph
habitat: 5 Naxos

Cleveland, Grover
name at birth: **22** Stephen Grover Cleveland
nickname: **5** Grove
presidential rank: **12** twenty-fourth, twenty-second
party: **8** Democrat
state represented: **2** NY
defeated: **4** (Simon) Wing **6** (Benjamin Franklin) Butler, (James Baird) Weaver, (James Gillespie) Blaine, (John Pierce) St John **7** (John) Bidwell **8** (Belva Ann Bennett) Lockwood, (Benjamin) Harrison
vice president: **9** (Adlai Ewing) Stevenson, (Thomas Andrews) Hendricks
cabinet:
state: **5** (Richard) Olney **6** (Thomas Francis) Bayard **7** (Walter Quinton) Gresham
treasury: **7** (Daniel) Manning **8** (John Griffin) Carlisle **9** (Charles Stebbins) Fairchild
war: **6** (David Scott) Lamont **8** (William Crowninshield) Endicott
attorney general: **5** (Richard) Olney **6** (Judson) Harmon **7** (Augustus Hill) Garland
navy: **7** (Hilary Abner) Herbert, (William Collins) Whitney
postmaster general: **5** (William Freeman) Vilas **6** (William Lyne) Wilson **7** (Wilson Shannon) Bissell **9** (Donald McDonald) Dickinson
interior: **5** (Hoke) Smith, (Lucius Quintus Cincinnatus) Lamar, (William Freeman) Vilas **7** (David Rowland) Francis
agriculture: **6** (Julius Sterling) Morton, (Norman Jay) Colman
born: **2** NJ **8** Caldwell
died/buried: **2** NJ **9** Princeton
education:
high school: **16** Liberal Institute
religion: **12** Presbyterian
interests: **7** fishing **8** shooting **13** gun collecting
author: **15** Good Citizenship **20** Presidential Problems **26** Fishing and Shooting Sketches
political career:
mayor of: **7** Buffalo
governor of: **7** New York
civilian career: **6** lawyer
president of University Board of Trustees: **9** Princeton
notable events of lifetime/term: **5** Panic (of 1893) **10** gold crisis (of 1895)
Act: **6** Tariff **14** Dawes Severalty **18** Interstate Commerce
strike: **7** Pullman
father: **13** Richard Falley
mother: **4** Anne (Neal)
siblings: **7** Ann Neal **9** Mary Allen **11** Susan Sophia, William Neal **12** Richard Cecil **13** Rose Elizabeth **14** Lewis Frederick **20** Margaret Louise Falley
wife: **7** Frances (Folsom)
children: **4** Ruth **6** Esther, Marion **13** Francis Grover, Richard Folsom

client **5** buyer **6** patron **7** advisee, shopper **8** customer **9** purchaser **17** person represented

cliff **3** tor **4** crag **5** bluff, ledge **8** palisade **9** precipice **10** promontory

Cliff Dwellers *see* **6** Pueblo

Clift, Montgomery
real name: **21** Edward Montgomery Clift
nickname: **5** Monty
born: **7** Omaha NE
roles: **9** The Search **10** The Heiress, The Misfits **14** A Place in the Sun **18** From Here to Eternity, Suddenly Last Summer

Clifton, Nathaniel
nickname: **10** Sweetwater
sport: **10** basketball
team: **13** New York Knicks **14** Detroit Pistons **19** Harlem Globetrotters

climactic **7** crucial **8** critical, dramatic **11** sensational, suspenseful

climate **3** air **4** mood, tone **5** pulse **6** spirit, temper **7** quality, weather **8** ambience, attitude **9** character, condition **10** atmosphere **11** disposition, frame of mind, weather zone **12** usual weather **13** weather region **14** general feeling, weather pattern

climax **4** acme, apex, peak **5** crown **6** crisis, height, summit **8** best part, pinnacle **9** high point **10** denouement **11** culmination **12** highest point, turning point **13** critical point, crowning point, decisive point, supreme moment **18** moment of revelation

climb **4** go up, rise **5** mount, scale **6** ascend, ascent, come up **8** climbing **9** clamber up **10** scramble up

climb down **6** go down **7** descend **8** back down, come down

clinch **3** cap, fix, win **4** bind, bolt, grip, nail **5** cinch, clamp, clasp, close, crown, grasp, screw **6** assure, clutch, couple, decide, fasten, obtain, secure, settle, verify, wind up **7** confirm, grapple **8** complete, conclude, make fast, make sure **9** culminate, establish, finish off **10** grab hold of, hold firmly **12** seize and hold **13** ensure victory

cling **3** hug **4** fuse, grip, hold **5** clasp, grasp, stick **6** adhere, be true, cleave, clutch **7** stand by **8** hang on to, hold fast, hold on to, maintain **9** stay close **10** be constant, be faithful, grab hold of

clinging **6** sticky **7** holding **8** adherent, adhering, adhesive, clasping, cleaving, grasping, gripping, sticking **9** hanging on, holding on **11** holding fast **12** grabbing hold

clinic **9** infirmary **10** polyclinic **13** medical center **15** outpatients' ward

Clinis
form: **3** man
home: **11** Mesopotamia
loved by: **6** Apollo **7** Artemis

clink **4** ting **5** clack, clank, click **6** jangle, jingle, rattle, tinkle **11** ring sharply

clinkers **4** duds, slag **5** dross, flops **6** cinder, scoria **8** failures

Clio
muse of: **7** history

clip **3** bob, cut, fix **4** crop, grip, hook, snip, trim **5** clamp, clasp, shear **6** attach, buckle, clinch, couple, cut off, cut out, fasten, paring, secure, staple **7** cutting, shorten **8** clipping, cropping, cut short, fastener, shearing, snipping

clipper **4** boat, ship **6** cutter, shears **8** aircraft, airplane, sailboat, scissors **9** racehorse

clipping **7** cutting, pruning, snippet **8** trimming

clique **3** set **4** clan, gang **5** crowd, group **6** circle **7** coterie, faction

cliquish **4** cold **5** aloof **7** distant **8** clannish, snobbish **9** exclusive **10** unfriendly **11** unreceptive

Clite
father: **6** Merops
husband: **7** Cyzicus
killed by: **7** hanging, suicide

Clitus
father: **7** Mantius
loved by: **3** Eos
abducted by: **3** Eos

cloak **4** cape, hide, mask, robe, veil, wrap **5** cover, tunic **6** mantle, screen, shield, shroud **7** conceal, curtain, pelisse, secrete **8** burnoose, disguise **10** camouflage **11** concealment

cloaked **7** covered, muffled, wrapped **9** disguised

cloaking **7** masking, veiling **8** covering **9** obscuring **10** disguising

cloakroom **8** anteroom, coatroom

Cloanthus
origin: **5** Roman
companion of: **6** Aeneas

clobber **3** hit **4** beat, belt, drub, lick, maul, rout, slug, sock, trim, whip **5** clout, pound, punch, smash, smear, whack **6** batter, beat up, strike, subdue, thrash, wallop **7** conquer, shellac, trounce **8** beat up on, lambaste

clock **5** watch **8** horologe **9** timepiece **11** chronometer

Clock
constellation of: **10** Horologium

clock, pendulum
invented by: **7** Huygens

Clockwork Orange, A
author: **14** Anthony Burgess
director: **14** Stanley Kubrick
cast: **12** Patrick Magee **13** Adrienne Corri **15** Malcolm McDowell

clod **3** oaf, wad **4** boor, dolt, dope, glob, hunk, lout, lump, rube **5** chunk, clown, clump, dummy, dunce, moron, yokel **7** bumpkin, fathead **8** imbecile, numskull **9** blockhead, ignoramus, simpleton

clodhopper **3** oaf **4** boot, clod, hick, lout, rube, slob **5** booby, clown, yokel **6** galoot, lubber, lummox, rustic **7** bumpkin, hayseed, peasant, plowboy, redneck **8** clodpole, lunkhead **9** heavy shoe, hillbilly **10** provincial

Cloelia
origin: **5** Roman
form: **6** maiden
escaped from: **11** Lars Porsena **12** Etruscan king
escaped by: **13** swimming Tiber

clog **4** stop **5** block, check, choke, close, dam up **6** stop up **7** barrier, congest **8** blockage, obstacle, obstruct, stoppage **9** restraint **10** impediment **11** obstruction

clogged **6** choked, halted, jammed **7** clotted, impeded **8** choked up, filled up, hampered, hindered, restrained **10** encumbered, obstructed, overloaded

cloister **4** stoa, walk **5** abbey, aisle **6** arcade, closet, coop up, friary, hole up, immure, shut up, wall up **7** conceal, confine, convent, embower, gallery, nunnery, passage, portico, seclude, walkway **8** shut away **9** colonnade, courtyard, monastery, promenade, sequester **10** ambulatory, passageway

Cloister and the Hearth, The
author: **12** Charles Reade

cloistered **5** alone, aloof, apart **6** hidden **7** immured, recluse **8** closeted, confined, detached, isolated, secluded, secreted, separate, solitary **9** concealed, insulated, sheltered, withdrawn **11** dissociated, sequestered

clone **4** copy **5** robot **6** double **7** android, replica **9** automaton, duplicate, replicate **10** carbon copy **12** doppelganger **13** identical copy

close *see box*

closed **6** secret **7** private **9** exclusive

closed-minded **5** rigid **7** adamant, uptight **8** obdurate, stubborn **9** hidebound, obstinate, pig-headed, unbending **10** inflexible, unyielding **12** intransigent **14** uncompromising

Close Encounters of the Third Kind
director: **15** Steven Spielberg
cast: **8** Teri Garr **13** Melinda Dillon **15** Richard Dreyfuss **16** Francois Truffaut
score: **12** John Williams

closefisted **4** mean **5** cheap, close, mingy, tight **6** stingy **7** miserly **8** grudging **9** niggardly, penurious **10** economical, ungenerous **11** close-handed, tightfisted

close **3** end, hot, pen **4** akin, clog, fast, fill, firm, fuse, halt, join, keen, link, near, neat, nigh, plug, shut, stop, trim, warm **5** alert, block, cease, dense, fixed, humid, muggy, pen in, sharp, short, solid, stuff, tight, unite **6** allied, at hand, clog up, coop up, couple, ending, fill in, fill up, finale, finish, hard by, intent, jammed, loving, narrow, nearby, next to, plug up, recess, secure, shut in, shut up, smooth, stingy, stop up, stuffy, windup **7** adjourn, careful, close up, closing, compact, confine, connect, cramped, crowded, devoted, dismiss, enclose, intense, miserly, pinched, seal off, shut off, similar, stuffed, suspend, teeming **8** attached, blockade, break off, conclude, confined, familiar, friendly, grudging, imminent, intimate, leave off, obstruct, populous, shut down, squeezed, stagnant, stifling, stinting, swarming, thorough, vigilant, watchful **9** attentive, congested, impending, niggardly, penurious, scrimping, terminate **10** almost like, completion, compressed, conclusion, nearly even, nip-and-tuck, resembling, restricted, sweltering, ungenerous **11** almost alike, approaching, approximate, close-fisted, discontinue, forthcoming, impermeable, in proximity, inseparable, nearly equal, neighboring, suffocating, termination, tight-fisted, well-matched **12** bring to an end, impenetrable, parsimonious, unventilated **13** bring together, near to the skin, penny-pinching, uncomfortable **14** thick as thieves

12 parsimonious 13 penny-pinching

close-fitting 4 snug 5 tight 9 skintight 11 constricted, form-fitting 12 constricting, tight-fitting 15 like a second skin

close friend 3 pal 4 chum, mate 5 buddy, crony 6 cohort 7 best pal 8 alter ego, intimate 9 companion, confidant 10 bosom buddy 17 intimate confidant

close loudly 4 bang, clap, slam

closely 6 keenly 7 alertly, sharply 8 intently 9 carefully, heedfully, intensely 10 diligently, vigilantly, vigorously, watchfully 11 attentively

close-mouthed 3 shy 4 cool 5 terse 7 bashful, distant 8 reserved, reticent, retiring, taciturn 9 diffident, secretive, withdrawn 11 tight-lipped 15 uncommunicative

closeness 8 meanness, nearness 10 stinginess 11 familiarity, miserliness 15 tightfistedness

close of day 3 eve 4 dusk, even 6 sunset 7 evening, sundown 8 eventide, gloaming, twilight 9 nightfall

closet 2 WC 4 eury, safe 5 ambry, cuddy 6 covert, hidden, locker pantry, secret, toilet 7 cabinet, private 8 coatroom, cupboard, imprison, secluded 9 cloakroom, storeroom, visionary 11 speculative, theoretical, unpractical, water closet

close tightly 3 set 4 seal, slam 5 latch 6 clench, secure 13 press together

close to 4 near 6 almost, around 9 just about 12 on the point of 13 approximately

closure 3 lid, tap 4 bung, cork, plug, stop 5 cover 6 ending, faucet, finish, spigot 7 barring, bolting, closing, cloture, locking, sealing, stopper 8 securing, shutting, stoppage 9 cessation 10 conclusion, stoppering 11 termination 14 discontinuance 15 discontinuation

clot 3 gob 4 lump, mass 7 congeal, thicken 8 embolism, solidify, thrombus 9 coagulate, occlusion 11 coagulation

Cloten
character in: 9 Cymbeline
author: 11 Shakespeare

cloth 5 goods 6 fabric 7 textile 8 dry goods, material 9 yard goods 10 piece goods

clothe 3 don 4 case, coat, deck, garb, robe, veil, wrap 5 array, cloak, cloud, cover, drape, dress 6 attire, bedeck, encase, enwrap, outfit, rig out, screen, shroud 7 bedizen, costume, deck out, envelop, sheathe, swaddle 8 accouter

clothed 4 clad 5 robed 6 draped 7 cloaked, couched, covered, dressed, mantled, wearing 8 equipped, provided 9 expressed, furnished

clothes 4 duds, garb, rags, togs, wear 5 dress 6 attire, finery 7 apparel, costume, raiment, regalia 8 clothing, ensemble, garments, wardrobe 11 habiliments

clotheshorse 3 fop 5 dandy, model 12 Beau Brummell, fashion plate, man of fashion, sharp dresser 14 woman of fashion

clothing *see* 7 clothes

Clotho
member of: 5 Fates
spinner of: 12 thread of life

cloud 3 dim, mar 4 blur, hide, veil 5 blind, cloak, cover, muddy, shade, sully, upset 6 darken, impair, muddle, screen, shadow, shroud 7 conceal, confuse, curtain, distort, disturb, eclipse, obscure, tarnish 8 overcast 9 discredit, make vague 10 overshadow 11 cast doubt on 14 call to question 19 place under suspicion

cloudburst 6 deluge 8 downpour, rainfall 9 rainstorm

clouded 3 dim 5 dusky, murky 7 blurred, obscure, sullied, tainted, unclear 8 confused, darkened, obscured 10 ill-defined, indistinct

cloudless 4 fair 5 clear, sunny 6 bright 7 halcyon 8 sunshiny 9 unclouded 10 unobscured

Clouds
goddess of: 3 Fri 5 Frigg, Frija 6 Frigga

Clouds, The (Nephelai)
author: 12 Aristophanes
character: 8 Just Plea, Socrates 10 Unjust Plea 11 Strepsiades 12 Pheidippides

cloudy 4 dark, gray, hazy 5 murky, vague 6 dreary, gloomy, leaden, veiled 7 clouded, obscure, sunless, unclear 8 confused, nebulous, overcast 9 confusing, undefined 10 indefinite, mysterious 11 overclouded

Clouet, Jean
born: 8 Flanders
artwork attributed: 13 Guillaume Bude 16 Madame de Canaples, Man with Gold Coins 17 The Count of Brissac, The Dauphin Francis 22 Man with a Book by Petrarch

clout 3 box, hit, jab 4 bash, belt, blow, pull, sock 5 crack, knock, punch, smack, thump, whack 6 wallop 9 influence 10 importance

clove
botanical name: 16 Eugenia aromatica 18 Syzygium aromaticum
origin: 5 Pemba 7 Far East 8 Moluccas, Zanzibar 9 Mauritius 10 Madagascar
use: 3 ham 8 pickling, pomander 16 yellow vegetables

cloven 5 cleft, split 7 divided, notched, slotted 8 bisected

clover 9 Trifolium
varieties: 3 bur, elk, hop, low, pin, red 4 bush, holy, Kura, musk, owl's, tick 5 Alyce, Hubam, lucky, sweet, water, white 6 Alsike, cow hop, indoor, Korean, Ladino, yellow 7 Bukhara, crimson, Italian, mammoth, Mexican, Persian, prairie 8 Japanese, large hop, reversed, small hop, stinking 9 Hungarian 10 strawberry, toothed bur, white Dutch, white sweet 11 yellow sweet 12 silky prairie, subterranean, white prairie 13 European water 16 strawberry-headed

clown 3 wag, wit 4 card, fool, jest, joke, mime, zany 5 comic, cut up, joker 6 jester, madcap 7 buffoon 8 comedian, humorist 9 harlequin, kid around 10 comedienne, fool around 11 funny person, merry-andrew

Clown, The
author: 12 Heinrich Boll

clownishness 6 antics 10 buffoonery, tomfoolery 12 monkeyshines 14 playing the fool

Clowns of God, The
author: 11 Morris L West

cloy 3 gag 4 bore, glut, pall, sate, tire 5 choke, weary 6 benumb, overdo 7 exhaust, satiate, surfeit 8 nauseate, saturate

cloying 5 sweet 6 sugary 9 excessive, satiating 10 saccharine

club **3** bat, hit **4** bash, beat, flog, slug **5** billy, flail, group, guild, lay on, lodge, stick, union **6** batter, buffet, cudgel, league, pommel, pummel, strike **7** society **8** alliance, bludgeon, sorority **9** billyclub, clubhouse, truncheon **10** fraternity, shillelagh, sisterhood **11** affiliation, association, brotherhood, country club

clubhouse **4** club, hall **5** lodge **11** locker rooms **12** meeting house

clue **3** cue, key **4** clew, hint, mark, sign **5** guide, scent, trace **7** glimmer, inkling, pointer **8** evidence **9** indicator, inference **10** indication, intimation, suggestion **11** insinuation

clump **4** bulb, bump, knob, knot, lump, mass, plod, thud **5** batch, bunch, clomp, clunk, copse, group, grove, plunk, shock, stamp, stomp, thump, tramp **6** lumber **7** cluster, thicket **9** aggregate **10** assemblage, collection

clumsiness **9** gawkiness **10** ineptitude **11** awkwardness **12** carelessness, ungainliness **13** gracelessness, maladroitness

clumsy **5** bulky, crude, gawky, inept, rough **6** klutzy **7** awkward, unhandy **8** bungling, careless, ungainly, unwieldy **9** graceless, makeshift, maladroit, unskilled **10** blundering, cumbersome, ungraceful **11** heavy-handed **12** ill-contrived, unmanageable **14** butterfingered **21** like a bull in a china shop

cluster **4** band, bevy, heap, herd, knot, mass, pack, pile **5** amass, batch, block, bunch, clump, crowd, flock, group, sheaf, shock, swarm **6** gather, muster, throng **7** collect, company **8** assemble, converge **9** aggregate **10** accumulate, assemblage, collection, congregate **12** accumulation, congregation **13** agglomeration **14** conglomeration

cluster around **6** gather **7** collect **10** congregate **12** herd together **13** flock together

clutch **3** hug **4** grip, hold **5** clasp, grasp **6** clench **7** cling to, embrace, squeeze **8** hang on to

clutter **4** fill, heap, mess, pile **5** chaos, strew **6** jumble, litter, tangle **7** scatter **8** disarray, disorder **9** confusion **10** hodgepodge

cluttered **5** messy **7** chaotic, crowded, jumbled, muddled **8** confused, littered **9** scattered **10** disordered, disorderly

Clymene
origin: **5** Greek
mentioned in: **5** Iliad
form: **5** nymph
habitat: **5** ocean
father: **6** Mimyas, Minyas **7** Catreus, Oceanus
mother: **6** Tethys
husband: **7** Iapetus **8** Cephalus, Phaethon, Phylacus
son: **4** Oeax **5** Atlas **8** Iphiclus, Phaethon **9** Palamedes **10** Epimetheus, Nausimedon, Prometheus
daughter: **8** Alcimede
attended: **11** Helen of Troy
sold to: **8** Nauplius
beloved of: **3** Sun

Clymenus
king of: **10** Orchomenus
grandfather: **7** Phrixus
son: **7** Erginus
daughter: **9** Harpalyce
violated: **9** Harpalyce
home: **7** Arcadia

Clytemnestra
father: **9** Tyndareus
mother: **4** Leda
brother: **6** Castor, Pollux
sister: **5** Helen **8** Timandra
cousin: **8** Perilaus
husband: **9** Agamemnon
son: **7** Orestes
daughter: **7** Electra, Erigone **9** Iphigenia **12** Chrysothemis
lover: **9** Aegisthus
killed: **9** Agamemnon
killed by: **7** Orestes

Clytie
form: **5** nymph
habitat: **5** water
loved: **6** Apollo
changed into: **10** heliotrope

Clytius
member of: **8** Gigantes
father: **8** Laomedon
brother: **5** Priam
companion of: **5** Jason
killed by: **8** Hercules

coach **3** bus **5** drill, guide, sedan, stage, teach, train, tutor **6** advise, direct, mentor **7** omnibus, trainer **8** carriage, instruct **9** limousine, preceptor **10** automobile, four-in-hand, motor coach, stagecoach **11** four-wheeler, second class **12** economy class **14** private teacher **16** athletic director

coachman **3** fly **4** jehu, whip **5** pilot **6** driver **10** charioteer

Coactrice **14** poisonous snake

coagulate **3** gel, set **4** clot, jell **6** curdle, harden **7** congeal, jellify, thicken **8** solidify

coagulation **3** gob **4** clot, mass **8** clotting, curdling, thrombus **10** thickening

coal **4** ash, bass, char, coke, coom, culm, dust, fuel, slag, smut, swad **5** ember **6** cannel, cinder **7** lignite, clinker **8** charcoal **10** fossil fuel **11** charred wood
box: **3** hod **7** scuttle
made from: **6** carbon
type: **4** hard, soft **7** lignite **10** anthracite, bituminous
mining method: **4** deep **8** opencast **10** strip auger **11** underground
mine: **5** drift, shaft, slope, strip
size: **3** egg, nut, pea **5** stove

coal-black **3** jet **4** dark, inky **5** black, ebony, raven, sable **9** pitch-dark

coalesce **3** mix **4** ally, form, fuse, join, meld **5** blend, merge, unify, unite **6** cohere **7** combine **9** become one, integrate **10** amalgamate, join forces **11** agglutinate, consolidate **12** band together, come together **14** form an alliance

coalition **5** union **6** fusion, league **7** society **8** alliance **9** syndicate **10** federation **11** affiliation, association, combination, confederacy, partnership **12** amalgamation **13** agglomeration, consolidation **14** conglomeration

Coal Miner's Daughter
director: **12** Michael Apted
cast: **9** Levon Helm **11** Sissy Spacek (Loretta Lynn) **13** Tommy Lee Jones **14** Beverly D'Angelo
Oscar for: **7** actress (Spacek)
screenplay: **10** Tom Rickman

Coaluitecan
tribe: **6** Payaya

coarse **4** lewd, rude, vile **5** crass, crude, dirty, gross, harsh, rough **6** common, nubbly, odious, ribald, shaggy, sordid, vulgar **7** boorish, bristly, brutish, ill-bred, loutish, obscene, prickly, uncouth **8** impolite, improper, indecent, scratchy **9** bristling, inelegant, offensive, repulsive, revolting, sandpaper, unrefined **10** disgusting, indecorous, indelicate, lascivious, licentious, scurrilous, unladylike, unpolished **11** foul-mouthed, ill-mannered **12** lacking taste **13** rough-textured, ungentlemanly

coarse-grained **5** crude, harsh,

nubby, rough **6** coarse, grainy, shaggy **7** bristly **8** scratchy **9** unrefined **13** rough-textured

coarseness **9** crudeness, grossness, roughness, vulgarity **10** indelicacy, inelegance **11** boorishness **16** lack of refinement

coast **4** skim, slip, waft **5** drift, float, glide, shore, slide, sweep **6** strand **7** seaside **8** glissade, littoral, seaboard, seacoast, seashore **9** shoreline

coaster **3** mat **4** ship, sled, tray **5** wagon **6** cradle, glider, slider **8** toboggan **9** tray stand **13** decanter stand, roller coaster

coat **3** fur **4** hair, hide, pelt, wrap **5** cover, glaze, layer, paint, smear **6** blazer, enamel, encase, jacket, spread **7** coating, encrust, envelop, lacquer, overlay, plaster, slicker, topcoat **8** covering, laminate, mackinaw, overcoat, raincoat **9** whitewash **10** mackintosh, sports coat

coating **4** coat, film, skin **5** layer, sheet **6** veneer **7** overlay **8** covering, envelope

coat of arms **4** arms **5** crest **6** creast **8** insignia **9** blaconwry **10** escutcheon **14** heraldic emblem **16** armorial bearings

coat of mail **4** mail **5** armor **9** chain mail **11** suit of armor

Coat of Varnish, A
author: **6** C P Snow

coax **6** cajole **7** wheedle **8** butter up, inveigle, soft-soap, talk into **9** sweet-talk

cobalt **4** blue **5** azure **7** element, sky blue **10** bright blue **12** greenish blue
chemical symbol: **2** Co

Cobb, Lee J
born: **9** New York NY
roles: **10** Willy Loman **12** The Virginian **14** Twelve Angry Men **15** On the Waterfront **16** Death of a Salesman

Cobb, Ty (Tyrus Raymond)
nickname: **12** Georgia Peach
sport: **8** baseball
position: **8** outfield
team: **13** Detroit Tigers

cobbler **3** pie **9** bootmaker, shoemaker **12** shoe repairer **16** deepdish fruit pie

cobra
also: **3** asp **5** mamba **11** hooded snake
native to: **4** Asia **6** Africa
kind: **4** king **6** hooded, Indian **8** Egyptian
enemy: **8** mongoose

Coburn, Charles
born: **10** Savannah GA
roles: **9** Boss Tweed **17** The More the Merrier

Coburn, James
born: **8** Laurel NE
roles: **11** In Like Flint, Our Man Flint **14** The Great Escape **19** The Magnificent Seven

Coca, Imogene
partner: **9** Sid Caesar
born: **14** Philadelphia PA
roles: **15** Your Show of Shows

Cocalus
king of: **6** Sicily

Coccygius
epithet of: **4** Zeus
means: **6** cuckoo

cock **3** tip **4** knob **5** raise, valve **6** faucet, handle, perk up **7** rooster, stand up **8** cockerel, male bird, set erect **9** bristle up **11** chanticleer **13** turn to one side **16** raise the hammer of **17** draw back the hammer

cockade **4** knot **5** badge **6** ribbon **7** rosette **8** ornament **10** party badge

Cockade State
nickname of: **8** Maryland

cock-and-bull story **3** fib, lie **4** myth, yarn **5** fable **7** fiction, untruth, whopper **9** fairy tale, falsehood, fish story, invention, tall story **11** fabrication **13** prevarication

Cockcroft, John Douglas
field: **7** physics
nationality: **7** British
developed: **24** Cockcroft-Walton generator
worked with: **6** Walton
awarded: **10** Nobel Prize

cockeyed **3** mad **4** awry, wild **5** askew, crazy, goofy, inane, nutty, weird **6** absurd, aslant, insane, tilted **7** crooked, foolish, twisted **8** lopsided, sideways **9** irregular, off-center, senseless **10** cockamamie, out of whack, ridiculous, unbalanced **11** nonsensical **12** asymmetrical, preposterous

Cockpit of Europe *see* **7** Belgium

cockscomb **4** comb **5** crest **7** celosia, coxcomb **8** amaranth, caruncle

cocksure **4** pert, smug, vain **5** brash, cocky, pushy **6** cheeky, snooty **8** arrogant, positive **9** assertive, audacious, bumptious, conceited **10** aggressive, swaggering **11** overbearing, self-assured, swellheaded **13** overconfident, self-confident

cocktail **5** drink, fruit, horse **6** shrimp **10** docked tail, semiformal
type: **4** grog **6** brandy, gibson, gimlet, mai tai, rob roy, zombie **7** gin fizz, martini, sidecar, stinger **8** daiquiri, highball, hot toddy, pink lady **9** cuba libre, hurricane, gin rickey, manhattan, margarita, mint julep, rusty nail **10** bloody mary, tom collins **11** boilermaker, gin and tonic, grasshopper, screwdriver, sloe gin fizz **12** black russian, old-fashioned, tom and jerry, whiskey sour **13** planter's punch **15** brandy alexander
mixer: **4** soda **5** tonic, water **7** bitters, seltzer **9** ginger ale
garnish: **4** lime **5** lemon, olive, orange, twist **16** maraschino cherry

cocktail lounge **3** bar **6** saloon, tavern **7** gin mill, taproom

cocky **5** brash, saucy **6** jaunty **8** arrogant, cocksure, impudent **9** conceited, egotistic **10** swaggering

Cocles *see* **8** Horatius

Coco, James
born: **9** New York NY
roles: **11** Sancho Panza **13** Man of La Mancha **21** Last of the Red Hot Lovers

cocoa **5** brown, cacao **9** chocolate **12** hot chocolate

cocoon
covering for: **5** larva
stage: **5** pupal
made of: **4** silk

Cocteau, Jean
author of: **7** Orpheus **8** Antigone **12** Blood of a Poet **18** The Infernal Machine **19** Les Enfants Terribles, Les Parents Terribles **20** The Beauty and the Beast

Cocytus
river in: **5** Hades

coddle **3** pat, pet **4** baby **5** humor, spoil **6** caress, cuddle, dote on, fondle, pamper **7** indulge **11** mollycoddle

code **4** laws **5** rules **6** cipher **7** statute **8** precepts **9** ordinance, standards **10** cryptogram, guidelines, principles **11** cryptograph, proprieties, regulations **13** secret writing **14** secret language

codger **5** crank, miser **6** oddity, old man **9** eccentric, odd person

codicil **5** rider **8** addendum, addition, appendix **9** extension, subscript **10** postscript, supplement **11** added clause

codify **4** rank, rate **5** grade, group, index, order **7** arrange, catalog **8** classify, organize, tabulate **9** methodize **10** categorize, coordinate, regularize **11** systematize

coelenterate **5** coral, hydra, polyp **6** Medusa **7** acaleph, radiate **8** acalephe **9** jellyfish **10** sea anemone
habitat: **5** ocean **9** salt water

Coelophysis
type: **8** dinosaur, therapod
location: **7** Arizona
period: **8** Triassic

coequal **5** equal **10** coordinate **16** equally important

coequality **6** parity **8** equality, evenness, sameness **10** uniformity **11** equivalency **14** correspondence

coerce **3** cow **4** make **5** bully, drive, force **6** compel, oblige **7** dragoon **8** browbeat, bulldoze, pressure, threaten **9** constrain, strong-arm **10** intimidate

coercer **5** bully **9** oppressor, tormenter, tormentor **10** browbeater **11** intimidator, petty tyrant

coercion **5** force **6** duress **7** threats **8** bullying, pressure **10** compulsion, constraint **11** browbeating **12** intimidation

coercive **8** enforced, forcible **10** compulsory, obligatory **11** threatening

Coeus
form: **5** Titan
father: **6** Uranus
mother: **4** Gaea
daughter: **4** Leto **7** Asteria

coexist with **12** go hand in hand, go side by side, live together **13** go hand in glove

coffee **6** Coffea **13** Coffea arabica
varieties: **4** Java, Kona, Wild **5** Irish, Mocha **6** Almond, Common **7** Arabian, Arabica, Robusta, Vanilla **8** Liberian, Liberica, Zanzibar **9** Colombian **11** French Roast, Wild robusta **13** Decaffeinated **20** Jamaican Blue Mountain
beverage: **6** kahlua **8** espresso **10** cafe au lait, cappuccino
small cup: **9** demitasse

coffee (black)
French: **8** cafe noir **10** cafe nature

coffee brandy **6** Kahlua **8** Tia Maria

coffee with milk
French: **10** cafe au lait

coffer **3** box **4** case **5** chest **9** strongbox **10** depository, repository **13** treasure chest

coffers **5** safes **6** vaults **8** treasury **9** cash boxes **11** money supply

coffin **3** box **4** pall **6** casket **10** catafalque **11** sarcophagus

cog **3** cam, lie **4** gear **5** cheat, cozen, tenon, tooth, wedge, wheel **8** small boat **10** projection

cogent **5** sound, valid **6** potent **7** weighty **8** forceful, powerful **9** effective, trenchant **10** compelling, convincing, persuasive, undeniable **11** meritorious, well-founded **12** well-grounded **16** incontrovertible

cogitate **5** study, think, weigh **6** ponder **7** reflect **8** meditate, mull over, ruminate **9** think over **10** deliberate, think about **11** contemplate, reflect upon **18** consider thoroughly

cogito ergo sum **18** I think therefore I am
said by: **9** Descartes

cognac
type: **6** brandy **7** liqueur
origin: **6** France
brand: **7** Bisquit, Martell **8** Hennessy **10** Remy Martin **11** Courvoisier
label: **2** VO (very old), VS (very special), XO (extra old) **3** XXO (extra extra old) **4** VSOP (very superior old pale) **8** Napoleon (5 year premium)
drink: **9** Andalusia
with Cointreau: **10** Rolls Royce
with Triple Sec: **7** Chicago **10** Rolls Royce
with vodka: **7** Cossack

cognate **4** akin, like **5** alike, close **7** kindred, related, similar **8** familial, parallel, relative **9** affiliate **10** derivative **11** consanguine

cognition **7** knowing **9** awareness, knowledge **11** familiarity **13** comprehension, understanding

cognizance **4** heed, note **5** grasp **6** notice, regard **8** scrutiny **9** attention, awareness, cognition, knowledge **10** perception **11** familiarity, observation, recognition, sensibility **12** apprehension **13** comprehension, consciousness, understanding

cognizant **5** aware **6** posted **7** knowing, mindful **8** familiar, informed, versed in **9** conscious **10** acquainted, conversant, instructed **11** enlightened **13** knowledgeable, understanding

cognomen **4** name **6** handle **7** epithet, moniker, surname **11** appellation, designation

cognoscenti **6** judges **7** experts **8** insiders **11** authorities **12** connoisseurs **14** those in the know

cohere **3** fit, set **4** bind, fuse, glue, hold, jibe, join **5** agree, cling, match, stick, tally, unite **6** cement, concur, square **7** combine, conform, congeal **8** coalesce, coincide, dovetail, solidify **9** coagulate, harmonize **10** correspond **11** consolidate, synchronize **12** hold together **13** stick together

coherence **5** logic, unity **7** clarity, concord, harmony **8** cohesion **9** congruity **10** accordance, conformity, consonance **11** consistency, rationality **12** organization

coherent **5** clear, lucid **7** logical, orderly **8** cohesive, rational **9** congruous, connected, in keeping, organized **10** articulate, consistent, harmonious, meaningful, systematic **11** in agreement **12** intelligible **13** corresponding **14** comprehensible, understandable

cohesion **4** bond **5** union, unity **7** bonding **8** adhesion **10** attraction, solidarity

cohesive **3** set **5** solid **6** sticky **7** viscous **8** cemented, coherent, cohering, sticking **9** connected **11** indivisible, inseparable **12** consolidated **13** agglutinative

Cohn, Ferdinand Julius
field: **6** botany
nationality: **6** German
founded: **12** bacteriology

Cohn, Robert
character in: **15** The Sun Also Rises
author: **9** Hemingway

cohort **3** pal **4** chum **5** buddy, crony **6** fellow, friend **7** comrade **8** follower, myrmidon **9** associate, companion **10** accomplice

coif **3** cap **4** hood, veil **6** beggin, burlet, hairdo **8** biggonet, coiffure, skull cap **9** head-dress

coiffed **6** capped, styled **7** dressed **8** arranged

coiffeur **7** stylist **11** hairdresser **15** male hairdresser

coiffure **2** DA, GI **3** bob, bun **4** Afro, coif, perm, shag, trim, wave **6** hairdo **7** beehive, blowcut, comb-out, flattop, haircut, pageboy, upsweep **8** cold wave, cornrows, ducktail **9** hairstyle, permanent, pompadour

coil **4** curl, loop, ring, roll, wind **5** braid, twine, twist **6** circle, spiral, writhe **7** entwine **8** encircle

coin **4** mint **5** hatch, money, piece **6** change, create, devise, invent, make up, silver, strike **7** concoct, dream up, think up **8** conceive **9** fabricate, originate

coin/currency ***see box***

coincide **3** fit **4** jibe, meet **5** agree, cross, match, tally **6** accord, concur, square **7** conform **8** converge, dovetail **9** harmonize **10** correspond **11** synchronize **12** be concurrent, come together **19** occur simultaneously

coincidence **4** fate, luck **6** chance **8** accident **11** concurrence, synchronism **12** happenstance **22** simultaneous occurrence

coincident **10** coexistent, concurrent **12** contemporary, simultaneous **15** contemporaneous

---

coin/currency
- **of Afghanistan:** **3** pul **5** abaze, riyal, rupee **6** abbasi, amania **7** afghani
- **of Albania:** **3** lek **5** franc **6** qintar **7** quintar
- **of Algeria:** **5** dinar **7** centime
- **of Andorra:** **5** franc **6** peseta
- **of Angola:** **6** escudo, kwanza, macuta, macute **7** angolar, centavo
- **of Argentina:** **4** peso **7** centavo **9** argentino
- **of Armenia:** **5** ruble
- **of Australia:** **4** dump, tray, zack **5** pound **6** dollar **8** shilling
- **of Austria:** **4** lira **5** crown, ducat, krone **6** florin, gulden, heller, zehner **8** albertin, groschen, kreutzer **9** schilling
- **of Bahrain:** **5** dinar
- **of Bangladesh:** **4** taka **5** paisa
- **of Belgium:** **5** belga, franc **7** brabant, centime, crocard
- **of Benin:** **5** franc **7** centime
- **of Bhutan:** **5** paisa, rupee **7** chetrum **8** ngultrum
- **of Bolivia:** **4** peso **7** centavo **13** peso boliviano
- **of Botswana:** **4** pula, rand
- **of Brazil:** **3** joe **4** reis **5** dobra **7** centara, halfjoe, milreis **8** cruzeiro
- **of Bulgaria:** **3** lev **8** stotinki
- **of Burma:** **3** pya **4** kyat
- **of Burundi:** **5** franc **7** centime
- **of Cambodia:** **3** sen **4** quan, riel **6** puttan **7** piaster
- **of Cameroon:** **5** franc **7** centime
- **of Canary Islands:** **6** peseta
- **of Cape Verde:** **6** escudo **7** centavo
- **of Central African Republic:** **5** franc **7** centime
- **of Chad:** **5** franc **7** centime
- **of Chile:** **4** peso **5** libra **6** condor, escudo
- **of China:** **4** cash, cent, fyng, mace, tael, tiao, yuan **5** sycee **12** jen nin piao pu
- **of Colombia:** **4** peso, real **6** condor, peseta **7** centavo
- **of Comoros:** **5** franc **7** centime
- **of Congo:** **5** franc **7** centime
- **of Costa Rica:** **5** colon **6** colone **7** centimo
- **of Crete:** **7** drachma
- **of Cuba:** **4** peso **7** centavo **8** cuarenta
- **of Cyprus** **4** para **5** pound
- **of Czechoslovakia:** **5** crown, ducat **6** heller, koruna
- **of Denmark:** **3** one, ora, ore **4** fyrk **5** krone **8** frederik, skilling **9** rigsdaler
- **of Djibouti:** **5** franc **7** centime
- **of Dominican Republic:** **3** oro **4** peso **6** franco
- **of Ecuador:** **5** sucre **7** centavo
- **of Egypt:** **4** fils, kees, para **5** asper, dinar, fodda, gersh, girsh, medin, pound, riyal **6** ahmadi, dirham, foddah, guinea, junayh, maidin, medine, medino **7** piaster, piastre, tallard **8** bedidlik, millieme
- **of El Salvador:** **4** peso **5** colon **7** centavo
- **of England:** **3** ora **4** rial **5** achey, crown, groat, noble, pence, penny, pound **6** bawbee, florin, guinea **7** angelet, hapenny **8** farthing, shilling, sixpence, tuppence, tuppenny **13** pound sterling
- **of Equatorial Guinea:** **6** ekuele, peseta **7** centimo
- **of Estonia:** **3** lat **4** sent **5** kroon **7** estmark
- **of Ethiopia:** **4** besa, birr, harf **5** amole, girsh **6** dollar, kharaf, levant, pataca, talari **7** ashrafi, menelik, piaster, tallero **12** maria theresa
- **of Fiji:** **6** dollar
- **of Finland:** **4** mark **5** penni **6** markka **7** markkaa
- **of France:** **5** franc **7** centime **8** napoleon
- **of Gabon Republic:** **5** franc **7** centime
- **of the Gambia:** **5** pound **6** butbut, dalasi
- **of Germany:** **4** mark **7** Ostmark, pfennig **12** Deutsche mark
- **of Ghana:** **4** cedi, cidi **5** ackey
- **of Greece:** **5** lepta **7** drachma
- **of Greenland:** **3** ore **5** krone
- **of Guatemala:** **4** peso **7** centavo, quetzal

(*continued*)

coin / currency (*continued*)
of Guinea: 4 iliy, syli **5** franc **6** cauris
of Guinea-Bissau: 4 peso **6** escudo **7** centavo
of Haiti: 6 gourde **7** centime
of Honduras: 4 peso **7** centavo, lempira
of Hungary: 4 gara **5** balas, krone, pengo **6** filler, forint, gulden, korona, ongara, ungara
of Iceland: 5 aurar, eyrir, krona **6** kronur
of India: 3 lac, pie **4** anna, fels, lakh, pice, tara **5** abidi, crore, paisa, rupee
of Indonesia: 3 sen **6** rupiah
of Iran: 3 pul **4** asar, gran, lari, rial **5** bisti, daric, dinar, larin, shahi, toman **6** stater **7** ashrafi, kasbeke, pahlavi
of Iraq: 4 fils **5** dinar
of Ireland: 3 rap **4** real **5** pence, pound **6** turney **8** shilling
of Israel: 3 mil **5** agora, agura, pound, pruta **6** agorot, shekel
of Italy: 4 lira, lire, tara **5** grano, paoli, paolo, scudo, soldo **6** danaro, denaro, ducato, sequin **7** testone **8** zecchino **9** centesini
of Ivory Coast: 5 franc **7** centime
of Jamaica: 7 quattie
of Japan: 2 bu **3** mon, rin, rio, sen, shu, yen **4** cash, mibu, oban **5** koban, obang, tempo **6** cobang, ichebu, ichibu, itzebu, kogang **7** itzeboo, itziboo
of Jordan: 4 fils **5** dinar
of Kenya: 4 cent **5** pound **8** shilling
of Kiribati: 4 cent **6** dollar
of Korea: 3 woh, won **4** chun, hwan, kwan
of Kuwait: 4 fils **5** dinar
of Laos: 2 at **3** att, kip
of Latvia: 3 lat **4** latu **6** rublis, santim **7** kapeika, santima
of Lebanon: 5 livre, pound **7** piastre
of Lesotho: 4 cent, rand **6** maloti
of Liberia: 4 cent **6** dollar
of Libya: 5 dinar
of Liechtenstein: 5 franc **6** rappen **7** franken
of Lithuania: 3 lit **5** litas, marka **6** centas, fennig **7** ostmark, skatiku **8** auksinas, skatikas
of Luxembourg: 5 franc **7** centime
of Macao: 3 avo **6** pataca, pataco
of Madagascar: 5 franc **7** centime
of Malawi: 6 kwacha **7** tambala
of Malaysia: 3 sen, tra **4** taro, trah **7** ringgit, tampang
of Maldives: 5 laree, rupee **7** rufiyaa
of Mali: 5 franc **7** centime
of Malta: 4 cent **5** grain, grano, pound
of Mauritania: 5 khoum **7** ouguiya
of Mauritius: 4 cent **5** rupee
of Mexico: 4 onza, peso **5** adobe, claco, tlaco **6** azteca, cuarto, dinero **7** centavo, piaster
of Monaco: 5 franc **7** centime
of Mongolia: 5 mongo, mungo **6** tugrik **7** tughrik
of Montenegro: 4 para **6** florin **7** perpera
of Morocco: 4 flue, okia, rial **5** floos, franc, okieh, ounce **6** dirham, miskal **8** mouzouna
of Mozambique: 6 escudo **7** centavo, metical
of Namibia: 4 cent, rand
of Nauru: 4 cent **6** dollar
of Nepal: 4 anna, pice **5** mohar, rupee
of the Netherlands: 4 doit, oord, raps **5** crown, daler, rider, ryder **6** florin, gulden, stiver, suskin **7** daalder, ducaton, escalan, escalin, guilder, stooter, stuiver **8** albertin, ducatoon **9** dubbeltje **12** rijksdaalder **13** albertustaler
of New Guinea: 4 kina, toea
of New Zealand: 4 cent **6** dollar
of Nicaragua: 4 peso **7** centavo, cordoba
of Niger: 5 franc **7** centime
of Nigeria: 4 kobo **5** naira
of Norway: 3 ore **5** krone **6** kroner
of Oman: 3 gaj, gaz **4** rial **5** baiza, ghazi **7** mahmudi
of Pakistan: 4 anna, pice **5** paisa, rupee
of Panama: 4 cent **6** balboa **9** centesimo
of Paraguay: 4 peso **7** centimo, guarani
of Peru: 3 sol **5** libra **6** dinero, reseta **7** centavo
of the Philippines: 4 peso **6** conant, peseta **7** centavo
of Poland: 4 abia **5** dalar, ducat, grosz, marka, zloty **6** fening, groszy, gulden, halerz, korona **8** groschen
of Portugal: 3 avo, joe **4** peca, real **5** conto, crown, dobra, indio, justo, rupia **6** escudo, macuta, octave, pataca, testad, tostao, vintem **7** angalar, centavo, crusado, miereis, moidore, testone **8** equipaga, johannes
of Qatar: 5 riyal **6** dirham
of Rumania: 3 ban, lei, leu, lev, ley **4** bani **5** uncia **6** triens
of Russia: 5 altin, bisti, copec, genga, grosh, kopek, ruble, shaur **6** abassi, copeck, grivna, kopeck, piatak, rouble **7** poltina, valiuta **8** auksinas, deneshka, imperial, polushka **9** poltinnik **10** altininik, chervonets
of Rwanda: 5 franc **7** centime
of San Marino: 4 lira, lire **9** centesimi
of Samoa: 4 tala
of Sao Tome and Principe: 5 dobra **6** escudo **7** centavo
of Sardinia: 7 carline
of Saudi Arabia: 5 girsh, gursh, pound, riyal
of Scotland: 3 ecu **4** demy, doit, lion, mark, rial, ryal **5** bodle, broad, groat, plack, rider, turne **6** bawbee, folles **7** unicorn **8** atchison, hardhead **9** halfpenny **11** bonnetpiece
of Senegal: 5 franc **7** centime
of Sicily: 5 litra, oncia, uncia **6** carlin **7** carline, oncetta

of Sierra Leone: 4 cent 5 leone
of Singapore: 4 cent 6 dollar
of Solomon Islands: 4 cent 6 dollar
of Somalia: 4 besa 6 somalo 8 shilling 9 centesimi
of South Africa: 4 cent, pond, rand 5 pound 6 florin 7 daalder 9 krugerand
of Spain: 3 cob 4 duro, peso, real 5 dobla 6 cuarto, dinero, doblon, escudo, peseta 7 alfonso, centimo, pistole, realdor 8 doubloon
of Sri Lanka: 4 cent 5 rupee
of Sudan: 5 pound 7 piastre
of Suriname: 4 cent 7 guilder
of Swaziland: 4 rand 9 lilangeni
of Sweden: 3 ore 5 krona, krone 7 carolin 8 skilling 9 rigsdaler
of Switzerland: 5 franc, rappe 6 hallar, rappen 7 angster, centime, duplone 8 baetzner, blaffert
of Syria: 4 lira 5 pound 6 talent 7 piaster
of Taiwan: 4 yuan 6 dollar
of Tanzania: 4 cent 8 shilling
of Thailand: 2 at 3 att 4 baht 5 cutty, fuang, tical 6 pynung, salung, satang 11 bullet money
of Tibet: 5 tanga
of Togo: 5 franc 7 centime
of Tongo: 6 paanga, seniti
of Trinidad and Tobago: 4 cent 6 dollar
of Tunisia: 5 dinar 6 dollar 7 millime
of Turkey: 4 lira, para 5 akcha, asper, attun, kurus, pound, rebia 6 akcheh, sequin, zequin 7 aetilik, beshlik, pataque, piaster 8 medjidie, zecchino
of Tuvalu: 4 cent 6 dollar
of Uganda: 4 cent 8 shilling
of United Arab Emirates: 3 fil 6 dirham
of Upper Volta: 5 franc 7 centime
of Uruguay: 4 peso 9 centesimo, centisimo
of Vanuatu: 5 franc 6 dollar
of Venezuela: 4 peso, real 5 medio 6 fuerte 7 bolivar, centimo 8 morocota 10 venezolano
of Vietnam: 2 xu 4 dong 7 piaster
of Western Samoa: 4 sene, tala
of Yemen: 4 fils, rial 5 dinar, riyal
of Yugoslavia: 4 para 5 dinar
of Zaire: 5 zaire 6 makuta
of Zambia: 5 ngwee 6 kwacha
of Zimbabwe: 4 cent 6 dollar

coincidental 6 chance 9 unplanned 10 accidental, contiguous, synchronal 11 concomitant, synchronous 12 happenstance, simultaneous

cointreau
type: 7 liqueur
variety: 7 curacao 9 triple sec
origin: 6 France
flavor: 6 orange
drink: 8 Applecar
with bourbon: 10 Temptation
with brandy: 7 Sidecar
with cognac: 10 Rolls Royce
with gin: 7 Florida 9 White Lady 13 Sweet Patootie 14 Flying Dutchman
with rum: 8 Acapulco 10 Casa Blanca 11 Beachcomber 12 Blue Hawaiian
with rye: 10 Temptation
with tequila: 9 Margarita
with whiskey: 16 Canadian Cocktail

Colavito, Rocky (Rocco Domenico)
sport: 8 baseball
team: 16 Cleveland Indians

Colbert, Claudette
real name: 22 Claudette Lily Chauchoin
born: 5 Paris 6 France
roles: 8 Tovarich 9 Cleopatra 14 Palm Beach Story 18 It Happened One Night (Oscar)

cold *see box*

cold-blooded 4 evil, hard 5 cruel, harsh, stiff, stony 6 brutal, flinty, formal, frigid, inured, savage, steely 7 callous, demonic, inhuman, passive, satanic, unmoved 8 detached, fiendish, hardened, inhumane, pitiless, reserved, ruthless, uncaring 9 barbarous, heartless, impassive, merciless, unfeeling, unpitying, unstirred 10 deliberate, diabolical, disdainful, impervious, implacable, unfriendly, unmerciful, villainous 11 calculating, hard-hearted, indifferent, insensitive, passionless, unconcerned, unemotional, unexcitable 12 bloodthirsty, contemptuous, uninterested, unresponsive 13 disinterested, unimpassioned, unimpressible, unsympathetic 16 unimpressionable

cold-hearted 5 cruel 9 heartless, unfeeling 11 hardhearted 13 unsympathetic

cold 3 icy, old 4 cool, dead, flat, hard 5 aloof, brisk, chill, crisp, cruel, faded, faint, gelid, harsh, nippy, polar, sharp, stale, stiff, stony 6 arctic, biting, bitter, chilly, cooled, frigid, frosty, frozen, inured, numbed, remote, severe, snappy, steely, wintry 7 callous, chilled, cutting, distant, frosted, glacial, haughty, nipping, passive, unmoved 8 chilling, coolness, detached, freezing, hardened, piercing, reserved, reticent, stinging, uncaring, unheated, unloving, unwarmed 9 apathetic, heartless, impassive, insensate, unfeeling, unstirred 10 disdainful, forbidding, impervious, insensible, phlegmatic, unfriendly 11 frozen stiff, indifferent, passionless, penetrating, unconcerned, unconscious, unemotional, unexcitable 12 antipathetic, bone-chilling, inaccessible, supercilious, uninterested, unresponsive 13 uninteresting, unsympathetic 14 marrow-chilling, unapproachable 15 teeth-chattering, uncommunicative, undemonstrative 16 chilled to the bone, unimpressionable 18 chilled to the marrow

coldness **5** chill **7** iciness **9** aloofness **10** chilliness, frostiness **12** indifference **13** unfeelingness **14** unfriendliness **15** hardheartedness

Cole, Janet
real name of: **9** Kim Hunter

Cole, Thomas
born: **7** England **13** Bolton-le-Moors
artwork: **8** The Ox-Bow **15** The Voyage of Life **17** The Course of Empire

coleoptera
class: **8** hexopoda
phylum: **10** arthropoda
group: **6** beetle, weevil

Coleridge, Samuel
author of: **9** Kubla Khan **10** Christabel **14** Dejection An Ode, Lyrical Ballads (with Wordsworth) **19** Biographia Literaria **26** The Rime of the Ancient Mariner

Colette (Sidonie)
author of: **4** Gigi, Sido **5** Cheri **8** Claudine **11** La Vagabonde **14** The Evening Star

coliseum **4** bowl **5** arena **6** circus **7** stadium, theater **10** hippodrome **12** amphitheater **14** exhibition hall

collaborate **4** join **5** unite **6** assist, team up **7** collude **9** cooperate **10** join forces **12** work together **14** work side by side

collaborationist **6** puppet **7** traitor **8** quisling

collaborator **4** ally **6** puppet **7** traitor **8** co-worker, quisling, teammate **9** associate, colleague, co-partner **11** confederate

collapse **4** coma, fail, fall, flop, fold **5** faint, swoon **6** attack, buckle, cave-in, fizzle **7** break up, crack-up, crumple, failure, give way, seizure **8** be in vain, buckling, downfall, flounder, keel over, take sick **9** become ill, break down **10** be stricken, break apart, run aground **11** fall through **12** disintegrate, falling apart, fall helpless, fall to pieces **13** come to nothing, sudden illness **14** disintegration **17** become unconscious

collapsed **4** limp **7** caved in, compact **8** deflated, fallen in, folded up **13** disintegrated

Collapse of the Third Republic, The
author: **14** William L Shirer

collapsible **7** folding **8** foldable **10** deflatable

collar **3** nab **4** eton, grab **5** catch, fichu, pinch, seize **6** arrest, bertha **7** capture **9** apprehend, neckpiece **12** take prisoner **15** take into custody

collate **5** order **6** bestow, verify **7** compare **8** assemble, organize **9** integrate **11** put together

collateral **4** bond **5** extra **6** pledge, surety **7** warrant **8** parallel, security, warranty **9** accessory, ancillary, auxiliary, guarantee, insurance, secondary **10** additional, incidental, supporting, supportive **11** endorsement, subordinate **12** contributory **13** supplementary

collation **3** tea **4** meal **5** lunch **6** brunch, repast, sermon **7** address, reading **8** hotchpot, luncheon, treatise **10** comparison **11** description

colleague **4** mate **6** fellow **7** partner **8** confrere, co-worker, teammate **9** associate, co-partner **11** confederate **12** collaborator, fellow worker

collect **3** get **4** calm, meet **5** amass, raise, rally **6** gather, heap up, muster, obtain, pick up, pile up, summon **7** call for, compile, compose, control, convene, marshal, prepare, receive, solicit **8** assemble, gather up, scrape up **9** aggregate, get hold of **10** accumulate, congregate **11** concentrate, get together

collectanea **8** analects, treasury **9** anthology, gleanings **10** collection, miscellany, selections **11** miscellanea

collected **4** calm, cool **5** quiet **6** placid, poised, serene, steady **8** composed, peaceful, tranquil **9** confident, unruffled **10** cool-headed, restrained **11** level-headed, self-assured, undisturbed, unemotional, unflappable, unperturbed **12** even-tempered **13** self-possessed **14** self-controlled

collection **3** mob **4** bevy, body, gift, heap, mass, pack, pile **5** array, bunch, clump, crowd, drove, flock, group, hoard, store, swarm **6** corpus, jumble, muster, throng **7** cluster, clutter, variety **8** amassing, assembly, oblation, treasury **9** anthology, gathering, offertory, receiving **10** assemblage, assortment, hodgepodge, miscellany, soliciting **11** aggregation, compilation **12** accumulating, accumulation

Collection of Ten Thousand Leaves (Manyoshu)
author: **7** unknown

collective **5** joint **6** common, mutual, united **7** unified **8** combined, gathered **9** aggregate, composite **10** cumulative, integrated **11** accumulated, cooperative

collector **6** grouper **7** dustman **8** antiquer, compiler, composer, gatherer, zamindar **9** assembler **10** garbageman **11** anthologist

Collector, The
author: **10** John Fowles

college **7** academy **8** seminary **9** institute **10** university **11** institution

college-preparatory **4** prep **8** academic **11** liberal-arts **12** nontechnical **13** nonvocational

collegiate **8** academic **10** scholastic, university **11** educational

collembola
class: **8** hexopoda
phylum: **10** arthropoda
group: **10** springtail

collide **3** hit **4** meet **5** clash, crash, smash **7** crack up, diverge, run into **8** bump into, conflict, disagree **9** knock into **10** meet head on **11** beat against **13** hurtle against, strike against

Collier, Lucille Ann
real name of: **9** Ann Miller

Collins, Mary Catherine
real name of: **7** Bo Derek

Collins, Mr
character in: **17** Pride and Prejudice
author: **6** Austen

Collins, Wilkie
author of: **6** No Name **12** The Moonstone **15** The Woman in White

collision **4** bump **5** clash, crash, fight, smash **6** battle, combat, impact **7** smash-up **8** accident, conflict, skirmish, struggle **9** encounter **10** engagement **11** clash of arms

colloquial **5** homey, plain **6** casual, chatty, common, folksy **8** everyday, familiar, homespun, informal, ordinary, workaday **9** idiomatic **10** vernacular **14** conversational **15** unsophisticated

colloquy **4** chat, talk **6** caucus, parley **7** council, palaver, seminar **8** commerce, congress, converse, dialogue **9** communion, discourse **10** conference, discussion, rap session **11** interchange, intercourse **12** conversation **13** confabulation

collude **4** plot **7** connive **8** conspire, intrigue **9** cooperate **11** collaborate

collusion **5** fraud **7** treason **8** intrigue **10** complicity, connivance, conspiracy **13** collaboration **15** secret agreement **17** guilty association

Colman, Ronald
born: **7** England **8** Richmond
roles: **9** Beau Geste **10** Arrowsmith **11** A Double Life (Oscar), Lost Horizon **16** A Tale of Two Cities

cologne **5** scent **7** essence, perfume **9** fragrance **11** toilet water

Colomba
author: **14** Prosper Merimee

Colombia ***see box***

Colombo
capital of: **8** Sri Lanka

colon **4** coin **6** farmer, vitals **7** pioneer, planter, settler, viscera **9** hemistich, intestine **15** plantation owner, punctuation mark

colonize **5** found, plant **6** gather, settle **7** migrate **8** establish **10** infiltrate

colonnade **3** row **4** stoa **5** porch **6** arcade, piazza **7** portico, terrace **8** cloister **9** peristyle

colony **3** set **4** band, body **5** flock, group, swarm **7** mandate **8** dominion, province **9** community, territory **10** dependency, possession, settlement **12** protectorate **14** satellite state

colophon **6** design, device, emblem **7** insigne **8** insignia **11** inscription

color **3** dye, hue **4** bias, burn, cast, glow, mood, tint, tone, warp, wash **5** bloom, blush, chalk, drift, flame, flush, force, paint, sense, shade, slant, stain, taint, tinge, twist **6** affect, aspect, crayon, effect, import, intent, redden, spirit, stress **7** distort, feeling, meaning, pervert, pigment, redness, skin hue **8** dyestuff, rosiness **9** go crimson, influence, intention, prejudice **10** intimation **11** connotation, implication, insinuation **12** become florid, pigmentation, significance **17** natural complexion

Colorado ***see box, p. 198***

Colombia
other name: **6** Darien **10** New Granada
capital/largest city: **6** Bogota
others: **3** Ten **4** Amza, Buga, Cali, Mitu, Muzo, Paez, Sipi, Tado, Tolu, Yari **5** Bello, Chinu, Guapi, Neiva, Pasto, Tulua, Tunja **6** Cucuta, Ibaque, Lorica, Quibdo, Sangil, Tumaco **7** Cartago, Ipiates, Leticia, Palmira, Pereira, Popayan **8** Girardot, Maganque, Medellin, Monteria **9** Cartagena, Manizales **10** Santa Marta **11** Bucaramanga **12** Barranquilla, Buenaventura
school: **5** Andes, Valle **20** Instituto Caro y Cuervo **21** Industrial de Santander
measure: **4** vara **7** azumbre, celemin
monetary unit: **4** peso, real **6** condor, peseta **7** centavo
weight: **3** bag **4** saco **5** libra **7** quintal
island: **4** Baru **5** Naipo **6** Fuerte **7** Gorgona, Malpelo **8** Cusachon **9** San Andres **11** Providencia
lake: **4** Tota
mountain: **5** Abibe, Andes, Baudo, Chita, Cocuy, Huila, Pasto **6** Ayapel, Perija, Purace, Tolima, Tunahi **7** Chamusa, del Ruiz **8** Oriengal **10** Santa Marta **17** Central Cordillera, Eastern Cordillera, Western Cordillera
highest point: **14** Cristobal Colon
river: **3** Uva **4** Bita, Meta, Muco, Sinu, Tomo, Yari **5** Cauca, Cesar, Isana, Mesai, Nechi, Pauto, Sucio **6** Amazon, Arauca, Ariari, Atrato, Atroto, Caguan, Pattia, Yapura **7** Apapois, Caqueta, Guainia, Inirida, Truando, Vichada **8** Casanare, Guaviara, Putumayo **9** Magdalena
sea: **7** Pacific **9** Caribbean
physical feature:
cape: **4** Vela **5** Aguja, Marzo, Punta **7** Augusta **8** Gallinas
falls: **10** Tequendama
gulf: **5** Uraba **6** Cupica, Darien, Tibuga **8** Tortugas
inlet: **6** Tumaco
plains: **6** Ilanos
point: **6** Cruces, Lacruz, Solano **8** Caribana, Gallinas
people: **4** Boro, Cuna, Duit, Hoka, Macu, Muso, Muzo, Paez, Tama, Tapa **5** Carib, Catio, Choco, Cofan, Cogui, Cubeo, Guane, Haida, Mocoa, Paeze, Pijao, Seona, Yagua **6** Arawak, Betoya, Calima, Colima, Ingano, Mirana, Saliva, Tahami, Ticunu, Tucano, Tunebo, Witoto, Yahuna **7** Achagua, Andaqui, Chibcha, Chimila, Churoya, Guahibo, Guajiro, Panches, Puinave, Puitoto, Quechua, Shuswap, Tairona, Telembi **8** Coconuco, Guarauno, mestizos, Motilone, Puinavis, Quimbaya, Sinsigas **9** Cocanucos, Coconucan, mulattoes, Panaquita **10** Bellacoola
leader: **7** Bolivar
language: **7** Spanish
religion: **13** Roman Catholic
place:
museum: **4** Gold **8** Colonial
palace: **11** Inquisition
feature:
dance: **7** bambuco **8** merengue
game: **4** tejo
guitar: **5** tiple
poncho: **5** ruana
shoes: **10** alpargatas
shoulder bag: **7** carriel
tree: **8** arboloco
woven hat: **5** jipas

colored **4** dyed, hued **5** dusky **6** biased, shaded, tinged, tinted **7** blushed, excused, flushed, glossed, labeled, painted, stained **8** affected, labelled, reddened **9** chromatic, distorted, pigmented **10** influenced, prejudiced **12** complexioned **13** characterized **14** misrepresented

colorful **3** gay **4** loud **5** showy, vivid **6** bright, florid, unique **7** dynamic, graphic, unusual, vibrant, zestful **8** animated, forceful, spirited, vigorous

Colorado
abbreviation: **2** CO **4** Colo
nickname: **10** Centennial
capital/largest city: **6** Denver
others: **4** Vail **5** Aspen, Delta, Lamar, Ouray **6** Arvada, Aurora, Denver, Golden, Pueblo, Salida **7** Alamosa, Boulder, Durango, Greeley, Manassa, Manitou **8** Gunnison, Loveland, Trinidad **9** Purgatory, Silverton, Telluride **11** Central City **12** Cripple Creek **13** Grand Junction **15** Colorado Springs
college: **5** Regis **6** Denver **7** Boulder **17** US Air Force Academy
feature: **11** Four Corners **15** Garden of the Gods **17** Continental Divide
national monument: **8** Dinosaur **14** Great Sand Dunes
national park: **5** Estes **9** Mesa Verde **13** Rocky Mountain
tribe: **3** Ute **7** Arapaho **8** Cheyenne
people: **11** Jack Dempsey **12** Ralph Edwards **14** Scott Carpenter **18** Douglas Fairbanks Sr
lake: **6** Frozen
land rank: **6** eighth
mountains: **5** Longs, Rocky **7** San Juan **9** Pikes Peak **14** Sangre de Cristo
highest point: **6** Elbert
physical feature:
canyon: **5** Black
gorge: **5** Royal
plains: **5** Great
wind: **7** Chinook
river: **4** Gila **5** Yampa **6** Platte **7** Dolores **8** Apishapa, Arikaree, Arkansas, Gunnison **9** Rio Grande **10** Purgatoire
state admission: **12** thirty-eighth
state bird: **11** lark bunting
state flower: **22** Rocky Mountain columbine
state motto: **24** Nothing Without Providence
state song: **22** Where the Columbines Grow
state tree: **18** Colorado blue spruce

9 brilliant, full-toned, vivacious **10** compelling, variegated **11** distinctive, interesting, many-colored, picturesque **12** multicolored, particolored

coloring **3** dye **4** tint **5** color, shade, stain **10** coloration, complexion

colorless **3** wan **4** ashy, drab, dull, flat, pale **5** ashen, dingy, faded, pasty, vapid, white **6** anemic, boring, dreary, grayed, pallid, sallow, sickly, undyed **7** ghastly, ghostly, insipid, natural, neutral, prosaic **8** blanched, bleached, lifeless, ordinary, whitened **9** bloodless, washed out **10** cadaverous, lackluster, monotonous, spiritless, unanimated, unexciting, uninspired **11** commonplace **13** uninteresting

Color Purple, The
author: **11** Alice Walker
director: **15** Steven Spielberg
cast: **11** Danny Glover **12** Adolph Caesar, Oprah Winfrey **13** Margaret Avery **14** Whoopi Goldberg

colors **4** flag, jack **6** banner, ensign, pennon **7** pennant **8** standard

colossal **4** huge, vast **5** giant, grand, great **6** mighty **7** extreme, immense, mammoth, massive, titanic **8** enormous, gigantic, imposing **9** exceeding, excessive **10** incredible, inordinate, monumental, prodigious, tremendous **11** extravagant, spectacular **12** awe-inspiring, overwhelming

Colossus of Rhodes
statue of: **6** Apollo

colt **4** foal **5** horse **6** novice **8** equuleus, yearling **9** fledgling, youngster
constellation of: **8** Equuleus

columbium
chemical symbol: **2** Cb

Columbo
character: **9** Lt Columbo
cast: **9** Peter Falk

column **3** row **4** file, line, post **5** pylon, queue, shaft, train **6** parade, pillar, string **7** caravan, phalanx, support, upright **8** pilaster **9** cavalcade, formation **10** procession **11** vertical row **12** vertical list

columnist **6** writer **7** analyst
famous: **7** Heloise **8** Dear Abby, Herb Caen **9** HL Mencken, Jack Smith **10** Ann Landers **11** Miss Manners **15** Abigail van Buren

coma **6** stupor, torpor **8** collapse **15** unconsciousness

Comaetho
form: **9** priestess
father: **9** Pterelaus
loved: **10** Amphitryon
lover: **10** Melanippus
killed by: **10** Amphitryon

Comanche
language family: **10** Shoshonean
location: **5** Texas **6** Kansas, Mexico **8** Oklahoma
noted as: **8** horsemen

comatose **3** lax **4** dull, idle, lazy **5** inert **6** leaden, torpid **7** drugged, languid, passive **8** inactive, indolent, lifeless, listless, slothful, sluggish **9** apathetic, catatonic, lethargic, stuporous **10** cataleptic, insensible, narcotized, phlegmatic, spiritless **11** indifferent, unconcerned, unconscious **12** unresponsive

comb **4** card, tuft **5** curry, dress, groom, plume, scour, style **6** search **7** arrange, explore, panache, ransack, topknot **8** head tuft, hunt over, untangle **9** cast about, cockscomb, currycomb **11** look through **14** rummage through

combat **5** clash, fight **6** action, attack, battle, oppose, resist **7** contest, go to war, wage war **8** conflict, fighting, skirmish, struggle **9** encounter **10** contention, engagement, war against **11** come to blows, grapple with, make warfare, work against **12** do battle with, march against **13** confrontation **14** military action

Combat
character: **4** Caje (Caddy Cadron) **5** Kirby **8** (Pvt) Braddock **9** Doc Walton, (Lt) Gil Hanley **12** (Sgt) Chip Saunders
cast: **9** Jack Hogan, Rick Jason, Vic Morrow **12** Shecky Greene, Steven Rogers **13** Pierre Jalbert

combatant **7** fighter, soldier, warrior **9** man-at-arms **10** serviceman **11** fighting man

combating **8** battling, clashing, fighting, opposing **9** waging war **10** contention, contesting, opposition, struggling **11** doing battle **13** grappling with **17** coming to blows with

combative **6** bantam **8** militant **9** agonistic, bellicose **10** aggressive, pugnacious **11** belligerent, contentious **12** antagonistic

combativeness **9** hostility, pugnacity **10** antagonism **12** belligerence **14** aggressiveness **15** contentiousness

combination **3** mix **5** alloy, blend, union **6** fusion, league, medley, merger, mixing **7** amalgam, joining, mixture, pooling, variety **8** alliance, blending, compound **9** coalition, composite, synthesis **10** assortment, coalescing, federation **11** association, composition, confederacy **12** amalgamation **13** confederation

combine **3** mix **4** fuse, join, pool **5** blend, merge, unify, unite **6** couple, league, mingle **8** compound **9** commingle **10** amalgamate, synthesize **11** consolidate, incorporate

combo **4** band **5** group **11** aggregation, combination

comb out **4** curl **5** dress **7** arrange, unsnarl **8** untangle

combustible **8** burnable **9** flammable, ignitable **10** combustive, incendiary **11** inflammable **13** conflagrative

combustion **6** firing **7** burning, flaming **8** ignition, kindling **12** incineration **13** conflagration

combustive **8** burnable **9** flammable, ignitable **11** combustible, inflammable **13** conflagrative

come **2** be, go **3** bud **4** fall, loom, rise **5** arise, issue, occur, range, reach **6** appear, arrive, be made, drop in, emerge, extend, follow, happen, impend, show up, spread, spring, turn up **7** advance, descend, emanate, stretch **8** approach, draw near, go toward, grow to be **9** be a native, germinate, take place **10** be imminent, move toward **11** be a resident, be in the wind, materialize, originate in, spring forth

come about **5** occur **6** chance, happen **7** turn out **10** come to pass

come afterward **5** ensue **6** derive, follow, result **7** succeed

come apart **6** detach **7** disjoin, unstick **8** separate

come back **5** rally **6** answer, retort, return **7** rebound **8** recovery

Come Back Little Sheba
director: **10** Daniel Mann
based on play by: **11** William Inge
cast: **10** Terry Moore **12** Shirley Booth **13** Burt Lancaster
Oscar for: **7** actress (Booth)

come clean **4** sing **5** own up **7** confess **14** unbosom oneself **18** make a clean breast of

come close to **7** verge on **8** approach, border on **11** approximate, nearly equal

comedian **3** wag **4** fool, zany **5** clown, comic, cutup, joker **6** jester, madcap **7** buffoon **8** humorist, jokester **9** prankster **10** comedienne, comic actor **14** practical joker

comedown **4** drop **8** lowering **10** anticlimax

come down **4** dive, drop, fall, sink **6** plunge, tumble **7** descend, plummet **8** decrease

come down a peg **5** deign, stoop **6** unbend **7** descend **10** condescend **12** lower oneself **13** humble oneself

comedy **3** fun, wit **5** farce, humor **6** banter, joking, pranks, satire **7** foolery, jesting **8** drollery, raillery, travesty **9** burlesque, cutting up, horseplay, silliness **10** buffoonery, pleasantry, tomfoolery **13** fooling around

Comedy of Errors, The
author: **18** William Shakespeare
character: **6** Aegeon, Dromio **7** Adriana, Aemilia, Luciana, Solinus **10** Antipholus

come face to face with **4** meet **8** confront **9** encounter

come first **7** precede, predate **8** antecede, antedate, go before **10** anticipate

come into being **4** dawn, show **5** arise, begin, occur, set in, start **6** appear, be born, crop up, emerge, sprout **8** commence, spring up **9** germinate, originate **11** come to light

come into port **4** dock **5** berth

come into view **4** show **6** appear, come up, emerge, show up **7** surface **11** come to light **13** become visible

come loose **5** let go **6** detach, loosen **7** slip off **8** break off, separate, unfasten **9** break away **10** come undone, come untied, disconnect **11** come unglued, come unstuck

comely **4** fair, nice **5** bonny **6** pretty, proper, seemly, simple **7** correct, fitting, natural, sightly, winning, winsome **8** becoming, blooming, charming, decorous, engaging, fetching, pleasant, pleasing, suitable, tasteful **9** agreeable, appealing, wholesome **10** attractive, unaffected **11** well-favored

come near **4** loom, near **6** appear **8** approach **9** draw close **10** move toward

come-on **4** bait, hook, lure, trap **5** decoy, snare **6** magnet **9** seduction **10** allurement, attraction, bewitchery, enticement, inducement, seducement, temptation **12** inveiglement

comestibles **5** foods **7** edibles **8** victuals **10** foodstuffs, provisions

Cometes
lover of: **8** Aegialia

come to a decision **6** decide, settle **7** resolve **8** conclude **9** determine

come to an understanding **5** agree **6** settle **11** come to terms **12** agree to marry **16** reach an agreement

come to a standstill **4** halt, quit, stop **5** abate, cease **7** die away **8** quit cold

come to blows **5** fight **7** contest **8** do battle **9** square off **12** start to fight

come together **4** meet **5** flock, group, rally **6** gather **7** collect, convene **8** assemble **10** congregate **11** get together

come to light **4** dawn **5** arise **6** appear, crop up, emerge, evolve, show up, turn up, unfold **7** develop, surface, turn out

come to nothing **4** fail, flop, fold **6** fizzle **8** be in vain, collapse **9** break down **11** fall through **12** come to naught **17** fail to materialize

come to pass **5** ensue, occur **6** arrive, befall, follow, happen **9** take place

come to terms **5** agree, yield **6** give up, settle **7** succumb **8** contract, cry quits **9** make a deal, negotiate, surrender **10** capitulate, compromise **11** come to grips, meet halfway, sue for peace **13** resign oneself **14** strike a bargain **15** lay down one's arms **16** reach an agreement **17** acknowledge defeat, hoist the white flag **18** split the difference

come unglued 6 detach, loosen **8** separate **9** fall apart **11** come unstuck

come unstuck 4 lift **6** detach, loosen **8** break off, unfasten **9** break away, come apart, come loose, fall apart **11** come unglued

come up 4 rise **5** arise **7** quicken, sharpen **8** heighten, increase **9** intensify **10** accelerate, strengthen **12** be referred to

come upon 4 find, meet **7** learn of, run into **8** discover **9** encounter

comfit 5 candy, sweet **9** sweetmeat **10** confection, sugar candy **13** confectionery

comfort 4 calm, ease, help **5** cheer, peace, quiet **6** luxury, relief, solace, soothe, succor, warmth **7** cheer up, compose, console, hearten **8** coziness, opulence, pleasure, reassure, serenity, snugness **9** bolster up, comforter, composure, encourage, well-being **10** cheering up, relaxation **11** consolation, contentment, reassurance **12** satisfaction **13** encouragement, gratification **14** quiet one's fears **16** source of serenity **17** lighten one's burden **18** bolster one's spirits

Comfort, Alex
author of: 11 The Joy of Sex **12** More Joy of Sex

comfortable 4 cozy, easy **6** at ease, at home, serene **7** relaxed **8** adequate, pleasant, suitable **9** agreeable, congenial, contented **10** giving ease, gratifying, untroubled **11** pleasurable, undisturbed **12** satisfactory **16** free from distress

comforter 4 balm, puff **5** quilt, scarf **6** afghan, solace **7** anodyne, blanket, comfort, soother **8** coverlet **10** palliative

comic, comical 4 rich **5** droll, funny, merry, silly, witty **6** absurd, jocose, jovial **7** amusing, jocular, risible **8** farcical, humorous, mirthful **9** facetious, laughable, ludicrous, whimsical **10** ridiculous **11** nonsensical **12** nimble-witted

coming 4 next **6** advent, future, in view, to come **7** arrival, nearing **8** approach, arriving, imminent, on the way **9** advancing, emergence, imminence, impending, in the wind, proximity **10** appearance, occurrence, subsequent **11** approaching, forthcoming, prospective **12** on the horizon **13** materializing

Coming Home
director: 8 Hal Ashby
cast: 9 Bruce Dern, Jane Fonda, Jon Voight **15** Robert Carradine
Oscar for: 5 actor (Voight) **7** actress (Fonda) **10** screenplay

Coming into the Country
author: 10 John McPhee

Coming of Age, The
author: 16 Simone de Beauvoir

Coming of Age in Samoa
author: 12 Margaret Mead

Coming Race, The
author: 18 Edward Bulwer-Lytton

command 3 bid, get **4** boss, call, draw, fiat, grip, head, hold, lead, rule **5** edict, evoke, grasp, guide, order, power **6** adjure, behest, charge, compel, decree, demand, direct, elicit, enjoin, govern, incite, induce, kindle, manage, ordain, prompt, summon **7** call for, conduct, control, deserve, extract, inspire, mastery, provoke, receive, require, summons **8** call upon, instruct, motivate **9** authority, call forth, direction, directive, governing, knowledge, ordinance, supervise, ultimatum **10** administer, be master of, domination, injunction, leadership, management **11** familiarity, instruction, superintend, supervision **12** have charge of **13** comprehension, understanding **14** administration **17** have authority over

commandant 7 captain **9** commander **12** chief officer

commandeer 4 take **5** seize, usurp **8** shanghai **11** appropriate, expropriate

commander 4 boss, head **5** chief, ruler **6** leader **7** manager **8** director **9** conductor

commanding 4 head **5** chief, grand, lofty **6** ruling, senior, strong **7** dynamic, leading, ranking, stately **8** forceful, gripping, imposing, powerful, striking, towering **9** arresting, directing, governing, important, prominent **10** compelling, dominating, impressive **11** controlling, significant **13** authoritative, distinguished, overshadowing

commandment
Hebrew: 7 mitsvah, mitzvah

comme il faut 6 proper **7** fitting **12** as it should be

commemorate 4 hail, mark **5** extol, honor **6** hallow, revere, salute **7** acclaim, glorify, observe **8** venerate **9** celebrate, solemnize **11** acknowledge, memorialize, pay homage to **12** pay tribute to

commence 5 begin, start **8** get going, initiate **10** get started, inaugurate, originated

commencement 4 dawn **5** birth, onset, start **6** outset **7** genesis, morning **9** beginning, first step, inception **10** graduation, initiation **11** origination **12** inauguration **13** graduation day **20** graduation ceremonies

commend 2 OK **4** back, give, laud **5** extol **6** commit, confer, convey, praise **7** acclaim, approve, consign, endorse, entrust, stand by, support **8** delegate, give over, hand over, pass over, relegate, transfer **13** speak highly of

commendable 6 worthy **7** notable **8** laudable **9** admirable, deserving, estimable, exemplary, honorable **10** creditable **11** meritorious **12** praiseworthy

commendation 5 honor **6** praise **7** support **8** approval **10** acceptance **11** acclamation, approbation

commendatory 8 admiring, praising **9** laudatory, praiseful **10** plauditory **13** complimentary **14** congratulatory

commensurate, commensurable 4 even, meet **5** equal **6** square **7** fitting **8** balanced, in accord, parallel, relative, suitable **10** comparable, compatible, consistent, equivalent **11** appropriate, in agreement **13** corresponding, proportionate **14** on a proper scale

comment 4 note, word **6** remark **7** clarify, discuss, explain, expound **8** expand on **9** assertion, criticism, elucidate, shed light, statement, talk about, touch upon, utterance

10 annotation, expression, reflection 11 elucidation, explanation, explication, observation 13 clarification 15 exemplification

commentary 6 review 8 critique, scholium, treatise 9 criticism 10 exposition 11 explanation, explication 12 dissertation 14 interpretation 16 explanatory essay

commentator 6 critic, writer 7 speaker 8 panelist, reporter, reviewer 9 columnist, explainer 10 newscaster 11 interpreter, news analyst

comment upon 7 clarify, clear up, explain 8 spell out 9 delineate, elucidate, explicate, interpret, make plain 10 illuminate, illustrate 14 throw light upon

commerce 5 trade 6 barter 7 trading, traffic 8 business, exchange, industry 12 mercantilism 16 buying and selling
god of: 6 Hermes 7 Mercury

commercial 2 ad 5 sales, trade 8 business 10 mercantile, sales pitch 12 profit-making 13 advertisement 16 buying-and-selling

commingle 3 mix 4 fuse 5 blend, merge, unify 7 combine 10 amalgamate

commiserate 7 feel for 8 show pity 10 grieve with, lament with 13 express sorrow 14 sympathize with 15 share one's sorrow 17 have compassion for

commiseration 4 pity 8 sympathy 10 compassion, tenderness 13 fellow feeling

commission *see box*

commissioner 5 envoy, trier 7 officer, pristaw 8 delegate, official 9 authority, commissar

commissioning 10 assignment, delegation 11 appointment, designation, entrustment 13 authorization

commit 2 do 3 act, put 4 bind, pull 5 enact, place 6 assign, decide, effect, engage, intern, pursue 7 confine, consign, deliver, deposit, entrust, execute, perform, pull off, resolve 8 carry out, give over, obligate, practice, transact, transfer 9 determine 10 make liable, perpetrate 13 participate in 16 institutionalize

commitment 3 vow 4 bond, word 5 stand 6 pledge 7 promise 8 decision, delivery, transfer, warranty 9 assurance, detention, guarantee, liability, restraint 10 assignment, giving over, internment, obligation, resolution 11 confinement, consignment, dispatching 12 imprisonment 13 determination, incarceration 14 responsibility 18 institutionalizing

commit oneself 3 act 7 resolve 8 dedicate, obligate 9 determine

commission 3 act, bid, cut, fee 4 duty, hire, name, rank, role, task 5 board, doing, order, piece, power, proxy, trust 6 agency, assign, charge, direct, employ, engage, office 7 appoint, certify, charter, conduct, council, empower, license, mandate, mission, portion, rake-off, stipend, warrant 8 capacity, contract, delegate, dividend, document, exercise, function, position 9 acting out, allotment, allowance, authority, authorize, committal, committee 10 assignment, commitment, committing, delegation, deputation, entrusting, percentage, performing 11 appointment, carrying out, certificate, performance, transacting 12 officer's rank, perpetration 13 authorization, written orders 14 give the go-ahead 15 representatives 16 piece of the action 17 appointment papers, grant officer's rank

committed 6 active, liable 8 confined, detained, interned 9 concerned, delivered, entrusted, obligated 10 interested, responsive 11 responsible 17 institutionalized

committee 4 body, jury 5 bench, board, group, junta, table 6 bureau, soviet 7 cabinet, council 9 gathering, syndicate 10 assemblage 12 organization

commode 6 bureau 7 cabinet, dresser 9 washstand 14 chest of drawers

commodious 5 ample, large, roomy 8 spacious 9 capacious, uncramped 11 unconfining

commodity 4 ware 5 asset, goods, stock 6 staple 7 chattel, holding, product 8 property 9 advantage, belonging 10 possession 11 convenience, merchandise 14 article of trade 17 article of commerce

common *see box*

commoners 5 plebs 6 masses 8 plebians

common law
Latin: 13 lex non scripta

commonly 5 often 6 widely 7 as a rule, usually 8 normally, of course 9 generally, in general, most often, popularly, regularly, routinely 10 by and large, familiarly, frequently, habitually, informally, ordinarily, repeatedly 11 customarily 13 traditionally 14 by force of habit, conventionally, for the most part 15 in most instances 17 generally speaking

common people 5 demos, plebs 6 masses 8 populace

common 3 bad, low 4 base, lewd, mean, rude, vile 5 brash, cheap, crass, crude, gross, joint, lowly, minor, plain, stock 6 brazen, brutal, coarse, lesser, normal, old-hat, public, ribald, shared, simple, smutty, tawdry, vulgar 7 average, boorish, callous, general, ignoble, ill-bred, loutish, low-bred, obscene, obscure, popular, prosaic, regular, routine, settled, uncouth, unknown, worn-out 8 communal, everyday, familiar, frequent, homespun, impolite, informal, mediocre, middling, nameless, ordinary, plebeian, shameful, standard, workaday, worn thin 9 bourgeois, customary, deficient, household, low-minded, moth-eaten, obnoxious, offensive, pervasive, shameless, tasteless, unexalted, universal, unnoticed, unrefined, well-known 10 collective, colloquial, despicable, dime-a-dozen, inglorious, threadbare, unblushing, uncultured, unpolished, widespread 11 disgraceful, established, ill-mannered, insensitive, middle-class, oft-repeated, subordinate, traditional, unimportant, widely known, without rank 12 contemptible, conventional, disagreeable 13 garden-variety, insignificant 15 undistinguished

9 hoi polloi, plebeians 11 bourgeoisie

commonplace 3 old 4 dull 5 adage, banal, stale, trite, usual 6 cliche, old-hat, truism 7 bromide, general, humdrum, regular, routine, worn out 8 banality, everyday, familiar, ordinary, standard, worn thin 9 customary, hackneyed, moth-eaten, platitude 10 pedestrian, threadbare, unoriginal, widespread 11 oft-repeated, stereotyped, traditional 12 received idea, run-of-the-mill 13 unimaginative, uninteresting

commonplace book 9 anthology, gleanings, scrapbook

Common Sense
author: 11 Thomas Paine

common-sense 5 sound 8 everyday, sensible 9 mother wit, practical, pragmatic, realistic 10 no-nonsense 11 down-to-earth, levelheaded, serviceable, utilitarian 12 matter-of-fact

commonwealth 5 state 6 nation 8 republic
Latin: 10 res publica

commotion 3 ado 4 fuss, stir, to-do 5 furor 6 bustle, racket, ruckus, tumult, uproar 7 clatter, turmoil 9 agitation 10 excitement, hullabaloo 11 disturbance 12 perturbation

communal 5 joint 6 common, mutual, public, shared 9 community 10 collective

commune 3 gab, rap, yak 4 chat, chin, talk 5 visit 6 babble, confer, gossip, parley, powwow 7 chatter, palaver, prattle 8 converse, schmooze 9 discourse 10 chew the fat, chew the rag 11 communicate, confabulate 14 shoot the breeze

communicable 8 catching 10 contagious, infectious 12 transferable 13 transmissible, transmittable

communicate 3 say 4 give, show, talk, tell 5 state, write 6 advise, convey, impart, notify, pass on, relate, reveal 7 declare, divulge, exhibit, mention, publish, signify 8 announce, converse, disclose, inform of, proclaim, transmit 9 apprise of, bring word, broadcast, make known, publicize 10 correspond

communication 4 news, note, wire 5 cable 6 letter, missal, report 7 liaison, message, missive, notices, rapport, writing 8 bulletin, dispatch, document, speaking, telegram 9 broadcast, cablegram, directive, statement 10 communique 11 declaration, information 12 conversation, intelligence, proclamation, radio message 13 telephone call 14 correspondence

communicative 4 open 5 frank 6 candid, chatty 7 voluble 8 friendly, outgoing, sociable 9 revealing, talkative 10 expressive, forthright, free-spoken, loquacious, revelatory, unreserved 11 informative

communion, Communion 6 accord 7 concord, harmony, rapport, sharing 8 affinity, sympathy 9 agreement 12 the Eucharist 13 communication, contemplation

communique 4 note, wire 5 aviso, cable, flash 6 report, letter, notice 7 epistle, message, missive, release, telegram 8 bulletin, dispatch 9 directive, statement 10 memorandum 12 announcement, intelligence, notification 13 communication

Communist 3 red 6 soviet 7 comrade, marxist 8 Leninist 9 bolshevik, socialist 10 bolshevist 12 totalitarian

Communist Manifesto
author: 8 Karl Marx 15 Friedrich Engels

community 4 area, folk, town 5 arena, field, group, range, realm, scope 6 locale, people, public, sphere, suburb 7 quarter, society 8 affinity, district, environs, likeness, populace, province, sameness, vicinity 9 agreement, citizenry 10 population, similarity 11 environment, social group 12 commonwealth, neighborhood, surroundings

commute 4 ride, trip 5 alter 6 adjust, change, redeem, soften, switch, travel 7 convert, journey, replace, reverse 8 diminish, exchange, mitigate 9 alleviate, supersede, transform, transmute, transpose 10 substitute 11 transfigure 12 metamorphose, transmogrify

comodo
music: 9 leisurely

Comoros *see box*

Comoros
other name: 26 lost pearls of the Indian Ocean
capital/largest city: 6 Moroni
others: 6 Bambao 7 Fomboni 8 Dzaoudzi 9 Mutsamudu 11 Mitsamiouli
monetary unit: 5 franc 7 centime
island: 6 Moheli 7 Anjouan, Mayotte 12 Grande Comoro
highest point: 7 Kartala 8 Karthala
sea: 6 Indian
physical feature:
channel: 10 Mozambique
people: 4 Arab 5 Bantu, Malay 7 African 8 Malagasy
language: 6 Arabic, French 7 Swahili 8 Malagasy
religion: 5 Islam 13 Roman Catholic

compact 4 bond, cram, deal, pack, pact, snug, tidy 5 close, dense, press, small, stuff 6 little, treaty 7 bargain, crammed, pressed, squeeze, stuffed 8 alliance, compress, contract, covenant 9 agreement, clustered, concordat 10 compressed 11 arrangement, pack closely 12 concentrated 13 tightly packed, understanding

compactness 7 density 8 snugness 9 smallness 10 littleness 11 compression 13 concentration

companion 3 pal 4 chum, mate 5 buddy, crony 6 escort, friend, helper 7 comrade 9 assistant, associate, attendant

companionable 6 social 7 amiable, cordial 8 friendly, sociable 9 agreeable, congenial, convivial

companionate 4 warm 6 genial 7 cordial 8 amicable, friendly, platonic, suitable 9 accordant, agreeable, consonant, easygoing, nonsexual, spiritual, unfleshly 10 compatible, concordant, harmonious 11 nonphysical, passionless, warm-hearted 12 affectionate 13 companionable

companionship 4 pals 5 chums 7 buddies, company, friends 8 comrades 10 associates, companions, fellowship, friendship 11 camaraderie, comradeship, familiarity, sociability 17 close acquaintance, friendly relations

company 3 mob 4 band, firm,

gang **5** bunch, group, guest, party **6** guests, outfit, people, throng **7** callers, concern, friends, society, visitor **8** assembly, comrades, presence, visitors **9** gathering, multitude, syndicate **10** assemblage, companions, fellowship, friendship **11** camaraderie, comradeship, corporation, sociability **12** conglomerate, congregation **13** companionship, establishment **15** business concern

comparable **4** like, up to **5** close, equal **6** akin to **7** similar **8** as good as, parallel **9** a match for, analogous **10** equivalent, on a par with, tantamount **11** approaching, approximate **12** commensurate, in a class with **13** commensurable

comparative **4** near **8** relative **11** approximate

compare **5** equal, liken, match **6** be up to, equate, relate **7** vie with **8** approach, contrast **9** correlate **11** compete with **12** be on a par with **13** hold a candle to **14** be in a class with **20** draw a parallel between

compare notes **6** confer **7** consult **8** talk over **13** exchange views

comparison **7** analogy, kinship **8** contrast, equality, likeness, parallel, relation **10** connection, similarity **11** correlation, resemblance **13** comparability

compartment **3** box, pew **4** brig, cell, crib, hold, hole, nook, room **5** berth, booth, cabin, crypt, niche, stall, vault **6** alcove, bunker, closet **7** chamber, cubicle, section **8** anteroom, roomette **9** cubbyhole **10** pigeonhole **11** antechamber

compass **5** bound, range, reach, scope, sweep **6** domain, extent **8** boundary, province **13** circumference

Compass, Mariner's Compass
constellation of: **5** Pyxis

Compasses, Pair
constellation of: **8** Circinus

compassion **4** pity **5** heart **7** empathy, feeling **8** humanity, sympathy **10** tenderness **13** commiseration, fellow feeling **17** tender-heartedness
Latin: **12** misericordia

compassionate **4** kind **6** humane **7** pitying **8** merciful **10** benevolent, charitable **11** kindhearted, sympathetic **13** tender-hearted

compatibility **6** accord **7** concord, harmony, rapport **8** affinity **9** agreement, unanimity **12** congeniality **14** like-mindedness

compatible **3** apt, fit **6** seemly **7** fitting **8** in accord, suitable **9** congenial, in harmony, in keeping **10** like-minded **11** appropriate

compel **4** make **5** drive, force **6** oblige **7** require **11** necessitate

compelled **4** must **5** bound, urged **6** driven, forced **7** coerced, obliged, pressed **8** commanded, dragooned, enforced, impelled, obsessed, pressured, required **11** constrained, overpowered

compelling **7** driving, dynamic **8** forceful **10** commanding **12** overwhelming

compel obedience to **5** force **6** coerce **7** enforce **8** carry out, insist on **10** administer

compendium **4** list **5** brief **6** apercu, digest, precis, survey **7** abstract, capsule, catalog, epitome, summary **8** syllabus, synopsis **9** catalogue **11** abridgement, compilation **12** condensation

compensate **3** pay **5** cover, repay **6** make up, offset, redeem, square **7** balance, pay back, redress **9** indemnify, reimburse **10** make amends, recompense, remunerate **14** counterbalance **15** make restitution

compensation **3** fee, pay **4** gain **5** wages **6** income, profit, return, reward, salary **7** payment, redress **8** benefits, earnings, gratuity **9** indemnity, repayment **10** recompense, settlement **11** restitution **12** remuneration, satisfaction **13** consideration, reimbursement

compete **3** vie **5** fight **6** battle, combat, oppose **7** contend, contest **8** be rivals **9** lock horns, match wits

competence **5** skill **7** ability, know-how, mastery **8** ableness **9** expertise **10** capability, competency, expertness **11** proficiency

competent **3** fit **6** expert, versed **7** skilled, trained **8** skillful **9** efficient, practiced, qualified **10** dependable, proficient **11** experienced, responsible, trustworthy

competition **4** game **5** event, match, rival **7** contest, rivalry, tourney **8** conflict, opponent, struggle **9** contender **10** contention, opposition, tournament

competitive **8** fighting, opposing, striving **9** combative **10** aggressive, contending

competitor **5** rival **7** fighter **8** opponent **9** adversary, contender **10** contestant, opposition

compilation **4** body **5** group **9** collating, garnering, gathering, mustering **10** assemblage, assembling, assortment, collecting, collection, compendium, marshaling **11** aggregating, aggregation, marshalling **12** accumulating, accumulation

compile **5** amass **6** garner, gather, heap up, muster **7** collate, collect, marshal **8** assemble **10** accumulate

complacent **4** smug **6** at ease **7** content **9** contented **10** self-secure, unbothered, untroubled **13** self-satisfied

complain **3** nag **4** beef, carp, kick, moan, pick **5** cavil, gripe, whine **6** grouch, grouse, squawk **7** grumble **9** bellyache, criticize, find fault **15** state a grievance

complaint **4** beef, kick **5** gripe **6** malady, squawk, tirade **7** ailment, illness, protest **8** debility, disorder, sickness **9** criticism, grievance, infirmity, objection **10** impairment **12** faultfinding **15** dissatisfaction

complaisance **7** pliancy **8** docility **10** affability, amiability, compliance **12** acquiescence

complaisant **4** warm **7** affable, amiable, cordial **8** friendly, gracious, obliging, pleasant, pleasing **9** agreeable, compliant, congenial, easygoing **10** solicitous **11** good-humored, good-natured

Compleat Angler, The
author: **11** Izaak Walton

complement **3** cap **5** crown, match, total, whole **7** balance, perfect **8** ensemble, entirety, parallel, round out **9** aggregate, companion **10** completion, consummate, full amount, full number, supplement **11** counterpart, rounding-out **12** consummation **14** required number

complementary **7** matched **8** integral, opposite **9** companion **10** additional, compatible, completing **11** correlative **12** interrelated, supplemental **13** correspondent, corresponding

complete **3** cap, end **4** full **5** crown, total, utter, whole **6** entire, finish, intact, settle, wrap up **7** achieve, execute, fulfill, perfect, perform, plenary, settled **8** absolute, achieved, carry out, conclude, executed, round out, thorough, unbroken **9** discharge, make whole, performed, polish off, terminate, undivided **10** accomplish, carried out, complement, conclusive, consummate, unabridged **11** consummated **12** accomplished

completed **4** done **5** ended, whole **6** closed, entire, filled **7** matured, through **8** achieved, finished, realized **9** concluded, executed, fulfilled, perfected **10** terminated, wrapped up **11** consummated **12** accomplished

completeness **8** fullness, richness **9** wholeness **10** perfection **12** thoroughness

completion **3** end **5** close **6** ending, finish, windup **7** closing **9** finishing **10** concluding, conclusion, expiration **11** fulfillment, terminating, termination **12** consummation

complex **4** maze **5** mixed **6** knotty, system **7** network, tangled **8** compound, involved, manifold, multiple, puzzling **9** aggregate, composite, difficult, enigmatic, fixed idea, intricate, obsession **10** perplexing, variegated **11** bewildering, complicated **12** conglomerate, labyrinthian, labyrinthine, multifarious **13** preoccupation

complexion **3** hue **4** look, tone **5** color, guise, image, slant **6** aspect **7** outlook **8** coloring **9** character **10** appearance, coloration, impression **11** countenance, skin texture **12** pigmentation, skin coloring

complexity **6** puzzle **9** intricacy, obscurity **10** bafflement, involution, perplexity **11** crabbedness, elaboration, involvement **12** complication, entanglement **15** inextricability **17** unintelligibility **19** incomprehensibility

compliance **6** assent **7** pliancy **8** docility, giving in, meekness, yielding **9** deference, obedience, passivity **10** conforming, conformity, submission **12** acquiescence, complaisance **13** nonresistance

compliant **8** flexible, yielding **9** agreeable **10** submissive

complicate **4** knot **5** ravel, snarl **6** muddle, tangle **7** confuse, involve **8** confound, entangle **11** make complex **13** make difficult, make intricate

complicated **7** complex **8** involved **9** elaborate, intricate

complication **4** snag **5** hitch **7** dilemma, problem **8** drawback, handicap, obstacle, quandary **9** hindrance **10** difficulty, impediment, perplexity **11** aggravation, obstruction, predicament **12** disadvantage **14** stumbling block

complicity **8** abetment, intrigue, plotting, schemery, scheming **9** collusion, finagling **10** connivance, conspiracy **11** confederacy, contrivance, implication, involvement **12** entanglement

compliment **5** honor, kudos **6** homage, praise **7** tribute **8** flattery **9** adulation, laudation **11** acclamation **12** commendation **14** congratulation

complimentary **4** free **6** gratis **8** admiring, praising **9** adulatory, extolling, laudatory, panegyric, praiseful **10** flattering, gratuitous, plauditory **12** appreciative, commendatory **13** without charge **14** congratulatory

compliments **4** best, laud **5** exalt, extol, toast **6** homage, praise, salute **7** applaud, commend, regards **8** respects **9** greetings **10** best wishes, good wishes **11** salutations **13** felicitations **15** congratulations

comply **3** bow **4** bend, meet, mind, obey **5** defer, yield **6** accede, adhere, follow, give in, submit **7** abide by, conform, consent, fulfill, observe, satisfy **9** acquiesce, surrender

component **4** item, part **5** piece **6** detail, member, module **7** element, modular, segment **8** material **9** composing, elemental, essential, intrinsic **10** elementary, ingredient, particular **11** constituent, fundamental **13** component part

component part **4** item, part **5** piece **6** detail, member **7** element **10** ingredient, particular **11** constituent, fundamental

comport **3** act **4** bear **5** carry **6** acquit, behave, deport **7** conduct

comportment **7** bearing, conduct **8** attitude, behavior, carriage, demeanor, presence **9** acquittal **10** appearance, deportment

comport oneself **3** act **6** behave **13** acquit oneself **14** conduct oneself

compose **4** calm, form, lull, make **5** frame, quell, quiet, relax, shape, write **6** create, devise, make up, pacify, settle, soothe **7** collect, fashion, placate **8** be part of, belong to, comprise, conceive, modulate **9** formulate **10** constitute

composed **4** calm, cool **5** quiet **6** at ease, placid, poised, sedate, serene, steady **8** peaceful, tranquil **9** collected, quiescent, unexcited, unruffled **10** controlled, coolheaded, restrained, unagitated, untroubled **11** level-headed, undisturbed, unemotional, unflappable, unperturbed **12** even-tempered **13** dispassionate, imperturbable **15** undemonstrative

composer **4** bard, poet **6** author, writer **7** creator **8** musician, producer **10** compositor, typesetter

composite **6** mosaic **7** blended **8** combined, compound **10** compounded

composition **4** form, opus, work **5** essay, etude, piece **6** design, layout, make-up, making **7** forming, framing, product, shaping **8** creating, creation, devising, exercise **9** framework, structure **10** concoction, fashioning, organizing, production **11** arrangement, combination, compilation, formulation, preparation **12** constitution, organization **13** configuration

compos mentis **4** sane **13** mentally sound

composure **4** calm, cool, ease **5** poise **6** aplomb **7** control, dignity **8** calmness, coolness, patience, serenity **9** sangfroid **10** equanimity **11** self-control **13** self-assurance, self-restraint **14** cool-headedness, self-possession, unexcitability, unflappability **15** levelheadedness **16** even-temperedness, imperturbability

compound **3** mix **4** fuse, make **5** add to, alloy, blend, boost, mixed, union, unite **6** devise, fusion, mingle **7** amalgam, amplify, augment, blended, combine, complex, concoct, enlarge, magnify, mixture, prepare **8** combined, heighten, increase **9** composite, fabricate, formulate, reinforce **10** synthesize **11** combination, complicated, composition, incorporate, put together **12** conglomerate **14** conglomeration

comprehend **3** dig, get **5** catch, grasp, savvy **6** absorb, digest, fathom **7** make out **8** conceive, perceive **9** penetrate **10** appreciate, assimilate, understand

comprehensible **5** clear, plain **7** evident **8** apparent **11** unambiguous **12** intelligible

comprehension **5** grasp **7** insight **9** awareness **10** conception, perception **11** realization **12** acquaintance, appreciation, apprehension **13** consciousness, understanding

comprehensive **4** full **5** broad **7** copious, general, overall **8** complete, sweeping, thorough **9** expansive, extensive, universal **10** exhaustive, widespread **11** compendious **12** all-embracing, all-inclusive

compress **4** cram, pack **5** press **6** reduce, shrink **7** abridge, bandage, compact, curtail, plaster, shorten, squeeze **8** condense, dressing **10** abbreviate

compressed **5** dense **6** jammed, packed **7** crowded **8** squashed, squeezed **9** compacted **12** concentrated

compressed form **6** digest **7** summary **8** cake form, synopsis **10** shortening **11** abridgement, contraction, curtailment **12** abbreviation, condensation

compression **9** narrowing, squeezing, stricture, tightness **10** compaction, constraint **12** constriction

compressor **4** pump **7** presser, reducer **8** squeezer **9** compactor, condenser

comprise **4** form **6** make up **7** compose, contain, include **8** be made of **9** consist of **10** constitute **12** be composed of

compromise **4** risk **5** agree, truce **6** settle **7** balance, compact, imperil **8** endanger, undercut **9** agreement, discredit, embarrass, implicate, make a deal, prejudice **10** adjustment, jeopardize, settlement **11** arrangement, come to terms, happy medium, make suspect, meet halfway **12** conciliation **13** accommodation, rapprochement **14** make vulnerable, strike a bargain **16** mutual concession **18** split the difference **21** come to an understanding
German: **9** Ausgleich

compromising **7** risking **8** settling **9** adjusting **10** bargaining **11** give and take, making a deal **12** embarrassing, jeopardizing **13** accommodating, coming to terms **14** meeting halfway

Compsognathus
type: **8** dinosaur, theropod
characteristic: **8** smallest
location: **6** Europe **7** Bavaria
period: **8** Jurassic

Compson, Quentin
character in: **14** Absalom Absalom **18** The Sound and the Fury
author: **8** Faulkner

Compson family
characters in: **18** The Sound and the Fury
member: **5** Benjy, Caddy, Jason **7** Candace, Quentin **8** Benjamin
author: **8** Faulkner

compte rendu **6** record, report, review **7** account **15** account rendered

comptroller **7** auditor **9** treasurer **10** accountant, bookkeeper, controller

compulsion **5** force **6** demand, duress, urging **8** coercion, pressure **9** necessity **10** obligation **11** domineering, requirement

compulsive **6** driven, hooked **7** driving, fanatic **8** addicted, habitual **9** compelled, obsessive **10** compelling **14** unable to resist, uncontrollable

compulsory **7** binding **8** coercive, demanded, enforced, forcible, required **9** mandatory, requisite **10** compulsive, imperative, obligatory **11** unavoidable **12** prescriptive

compunction **5** demur, qualm, shame **6** regret, unease **7** anxiety, concern, remorse, scruple **9** misgiving **10** contrition **16** pang of conscience

computation **5** tally, total **8** figuring **9** numbering, reckoning **10** numeration **11** calculation, enumeration

compute **3** add **5** add up, sum up, tally, total **6** figure, reckon **7** count up, work out **9** ascertain, calculate, figure out

computer **5** adder **9** processor **10** calculator
language: **3** ADA **4** LOGO **5** ALGOL, BASIC, COBOL **6** PASCAL **7** FORTRAN
term: **2** PC **3** bit, CAD, CAM, CPU, RAM, ROM **4** boot, byte, chip, hack **5** drive, input, modem, pixel, queue **6** analog, glitch, hacker, memory, online, output **7** digital, network, offline, program **8** database, hardware, lightpen, printout, software, terminal **9** interface, mainframe **10** binary code, floppy disk **12** minicomputer **13** microcomputer, word processor **14** microprocessor

comrade **3** pal **4** ally, chum **5** buddy, crony **6** friend **7** partner **8** confrere, coworker, helpmate, intimate **9** associate, colleague, companion, confidant **10** bosom buddy **11** confederate **12** collaborator **13** boon companion
Russian: **8** tovarich

comradeship **8** alliance **10** fellowship, friendship **11** association, camaraderie **13** companionship

comte **5** count

Comte Ory, Le
also: **8** Count Ory
opera by: **7** Rossini
character: **13** Countess Adele

Comus
author: **10** John Milton

Comus
origin: **5** Roman
god of: **7** revelry **8** drinking

con **3** gyp **4** anti, bilk, coax, fool, gull, hoax, lure, rook **5** cheat, cozen, felon, trick **6** delude **7** against, beguile, convict, defraud, mislead, swindle **8** hoodwink, jailbird, prisoner, yardbird **9** bamboozle

Conakry
capital of: **6** Guinea

concatenation **4** link **5** union **6** hookup **7** joining, linking, reunion **8** coupling, junction **10** bracketing, confluence, connection **11** conjunction **12** interlinking **15** interconnection **16** interassociation **18** intercommunication

concave **6** hollow, sunken **8** indented **9** depressed **13** curving inward

conceal **4** hide, mask **5** cloak, cover **6** screen, shield **7** cover up, obscure, secrete **8** disguise **10** camouflage, keep secret

concealed **5** blind, doggo **6** covert, hidden, latent, masked, perdue, secret, veiled **7** cloaked, covered, obscure, unknown, wrapped **8** abstruse, shrouded, ulterior **9** disguised, incognito **11** clandestine

concealment **5** cover **6** hiding **7** hideout, masking **8** covering, hideaway **9** screening, secreting, secretion **10** covering up, under cover

concede **3** own **4** cede **5** admit, agree, allow, grant, yield **6** accept, give up, resign, tender **7** abandon, confess, deliver **8** hand over **9** acquiesce, recognize, surrender, vouchsafe **10** relinquish **11** acknowledge, be persuaded

conceit **5** pride **6** vanity **7** ego trip, egotism **8** bragging, self-love **9** vainglory **10** self-esteem **12** boastfulness **14** self-importance

conceited **4** smug, vain **7** stuck-up **8** arrogant, boasting, bragging, puffed up **9** bombastic, overproud, strutting **11** egotistical, swell-headed **12** vainglorious **13** self-important

conceivable **8** credible, knowable, possible **9** thinkable **10** believable, imaginable, supposable **11** perceivable

conceive **4** form **5** frame, hatch, start **6** create, invent **7** concoct, dream up, imagine, produce, think of, think up **8** consider, contrive, envisage, envision, initiate **9** originate **10** comprehend, understand

concentrate **4** mass **5** amass, bunch, focus, hem in **6** center, gather, heap up, reduce **7** close in, cluster, pay heed, thicken **8** assemble, attend to, condense, converge, fasten on **10** accumulate, congregate **11** bring to bear **12** direct toward

concentrated **5** dense **7** crowded, focused, thought **8** centered **10** compressed

concentration **4** mass **5** focus **7** cluster **9** diligence, gathering, reduction **10** absorption, assemblage, collection, intentness, thickening **11** aggregation, boiling down, convergence, deep thought, engrossment **12** accumulation **13** concentrating, consolidation **14** centralization

concept **4** idea, view **5** image **6** belief, notion, theory **7** opinion, surmise, thought **9** postulate **10** conviction, hypothesis, impression **11** supposition

conception **4** idea **5** birth, image, start **6** notion **7** forming, genesis, inkling, picture **8** creating, devising, hatching **9** beginning, formation, imagining, inception, invention, launching **10** conceiving, concocting, initiation, perception **11** envisioning, formulation, originating **12** apprehension **13** fertilization, understanding **16** becoming pregnant

conceptual **8** abstract **9** visionary **11** conjectural, ideological, speculative, theoretical **12** experimental, hypothetical **15** impressionistic

concern **3** job **4** care, duty, firm, heed **5** chore, house, store, touch, worry **6** affair, affect, charge, matter, occupy, regard **7** anxiety, apply to, company, disturb, involve, mission, trouble **8** bear upon, business, distress, interest, relate to **9** attention, pertain to **10** disconcert, enterprise, solicitude **11** appertain to, corporation, disturbance, involvement, undertaking **12** apprehension **13** consideration, establishment **14** thoughtfulness

concerned **5** upset **6** active, caring, uneasy **7** alarmed, anxious, engaged, fearful, worried **8** involved, troubled **9** attentive, committed, disturbed **10** disquieted, distressed, interested, solicitous **12** apprehensive **13** participating

concerning **2** of, on, re **3** for **4** as to, over, upon **5** about, anent **7** apropos **8** engaging, touching, worrying **9** affecting, involving, mattering, regarding **10** relating to, respecting

concert **5** union, unity **6** accord, settle **7** concord, harmony **8** teamwork **9** agreement, congruity, unanimity **10** accordance, complicity **11** association, cooperation **13** collaboration **14** correspondence **18** musical performance

concerted **5** joint **6** united **7** planned **8** by assent **10** agreed upon **11** cooperative, prearranged **12** premeditated **13** predetermined

concert hall **9** music hall **10** auditorium **12** symphony hall

concession **5** lease **6** assent **8** giving in, yielding **9** admission, franchise, privilege **10** adjustment, compromise, indulgence **12** acquiescence, modification **14** acknowledgment

Conch
form: **7** trumpet
made of: **5** shell
owned by: **7** Tritons

Conchobar
origin: **5** Irish
king of: **6** Ulster
nephew: **10** Cuchulainn

concierge **7** janitor **9** custodian **10** doorkeeper

conciliate **6** pacify **7** appease, placate **9** make peace, reconcile **11** accommodate

conciliation **11** appeasement, peacemaking **12** propitiation **13** accommodation **14** reconciliation

conciliatory **8** friendly **9** appeasing, pacifying, placatory **10** mollifying, reassuring **11** peacemaking, reconciling **13** accommodative

concise **5** brief, pithy, short, terse **7** compact **8** succinct **9** condensed **10** to the point **11** abbreviated

conciseness **7** brevity **9** terseness **11** compactness **12** condensation, succinctness

conclave **6** parley, powwow **7** council, meeting, session **8** assembly **10** conference, convention **11** convocation **13** secret council

conclude **3** end **4** halt, stop **5** close, infer, judge **6** decide, deduce, effect, finish, gather, reason, settle **7** arrange, resolve, surmise **8** break off, carry out, complete **9** determine, terminate **10** accomplish **11** bring to pass, discontinue **12** draw to a close

concluded **5** bound, ended, guess **6** closed, judged **7** decided, deduced, expired, settled, wound up **9** completed **10** culminated, determined, restrained, terminated

conclusion **3** end **5** close **6** finale, finish, result, upshot, windup **7** finding, outcome **8** decision, judgment **9** agreement, deduction, final part, inference, summation

10 completion, denouement, resolution, settlement, working out **11** arrangement, presumption, termination **13** determination

conclusive **5** clear **6** patent **7** certain, obvious **8** absolute, decisive, definite, manifest, palpable **9** clinching **10** compelling, convincing, undeniable **11** categorical, determining, inescapable, irrefutable **12** demonstrable, unanswerable **13** incontestable, unimpeachable **14** unquestionable **16** incontrovertible

concoct **3** mix **4** brew **5** frame, hatch **6** cook up, create, devise, invent, make up **7** think up **8** compound, contrive **9** fabricate, formulate

concoction **4** brew **5** blend **6** jumble, medley **7** mixture **8** compound, creation **9** invention, potpourri **11** contrivance, fabrication **14** conglomeration

concomitant **7** related **9** accessory, attendant, connected, corollary, secondary **10** additional **12** accompanying, contributing, supplemental **13** complementary

concord **5** amity, peace **6** accord **7** harmony **8** goodwill **9** agreement **10** friendship **11** amicability, cooperation **16** cordial relations **19** mutual understanding

concordance **5** index **6** accord **7** concord **9** agreement, consensus, unanimity **17** meeting of the minds

concordant **6** unison **7** calming **8** agreeing, unifying **9** assenting, consonant **10** concurrent, harmonious

concordat **4** pact **8** covenant **9** agreement

Concordia
origin: **5** Roman
goddess of: **5** peace **7** harmony

concourse **7** conflux, joining, linkage, meeting **8** junction **9** amassment **10** assembling, concursion, confluence **11** aggregation, association, convergence **12** congregation, focalization **13** concentration **14** conglomeration **15** flowing together **16** flocking together

concrete **4** real **5** solid **6** cement **7** express, factual, precise **8** definite, distinct, explicit, material, specific, tangible **10** particular **11** fused stones, substantial **12** alloyed rocks

concupiscence **4** itch, lust **6** desire **7** craving, lechery, longing, passion **8** appetite, hot pants, lewdness, satyrism **9** horniness, lubricity, prurience, randiness **10** wantonness **11** goatishness, libertinism, lustfulness **12** sexual desire **13** lecherousness **14** lasciviousness, libidinousness

concur **5** agree, match, tally **6** square **7** conform **8** coincide, hold with **9** be uniform **10** be in accord, correspond **11** go along with **12** go hand in hand

concur in **7** approve **9** agree with **11** go along with

concurrence, concurrency **6** accord **7** concord, consent, harmony **8** approval **9** agreement, consensus, unanimity **10** acceptance, conformity **11** affirmation, coexistence, coincidence, conjuncture, cooperation, synchronism **12** acquiescence **13** collaboration, mutual consent **14** correspondence **15** working together **17** meeting of the minds **22** simultaneous occurrence

concurrent **5** at one **6** allied **7** aligned **8** agreeing, matching **9** congenial, congruous, consonant **10** coexisting, coincident, coinciding, compatible, harmonious **11** in agreement, sympathetic, synchronous **12** commensurate, contemporary, in accordance, simultaneous **13** correspondent, of the same mind **15** contemporaneous

concurring **8** agreeing **10** consenting **11** affirmative, in agreement, synchronous **12** coincidental, simultaneous **13** corresponding

concussion **3** jar **4** blow, bump **5** clash, shock **6** buffet, impact **7** shaking **8** pounding **9** agitation, collision **11** brain injury

condemn **4** damn, doom **5** decry **6** rebuke **7** censure **8** denounce, sentence **9** criticize, proscribe, reprehend **10** disapprove

condemnation **6** rebuke **7** censure, reproof **8** judgment, reproach, sentence **9** criticism **10** conviction, punishment **11** disapproval **12** denunciation, reprehension **14** disapprobation **20** pronouncement of guilt

condensation **6** digest **9** reduction **10** abridgment **13** shortened form **16** condensed version

condense **3** cut **4** trim **6** digest, reduce **7** abridge, compact, liquefy, shorten, thicken **8** boil down, compress, contract, pare down **10** abbreviate, blue-pencil **11** concentrate, consolidate, precipitate

condensed form **6** digest **7** summary **8** synopsis **10** shortening **11** abridgement, compression, contraction, curtailment **12** abbreviation

condescend **5** deign, stoop **6** submit, unbend **7** descend, disdain **9** patronize **10** look down on, talk down to **12** come down a peg, lower oneself **13** humble oneself

condescending **7** high-hat **8** superior **10** disdainful **11** overbearing, patronizing

condescension **4** airs **7** disdain, hauteur, modesty **8** humility **9** deference, loftiness **10** humbleness **11** haughtiness **12** graciousness **13** self-abasement **14** self-effacement **19** patronizing attitude **20** assumption of equality **21** high-and-mighty attitude

condign **3** due **4** fair, just, meet **5** right **6** earned, proper, worthy **7** fitting, merited **8** deserved, suitable **9** warranted **11** appropriate

condiment **4** herb **5** sauce, spice **8** dressing, flavorer, seasoner **9** seasoning
kind: **3** bay **4** dill, mace, mint, sage, salt **5** caper, clove, curry, onion, thyme **6** catsup, garlic, ginger, nutmeg, pepper, pickle, relish **7** caraway, chutney, ketchup, mustard, parsley, oregano, paprika, pimento, tabasco, vinegar **8** cardamon, marjoram, turmeric **9** pimpernel **10** bell pepper, mayonnaise

condition **3** fit **4** term **5** adapt, equip, ready, shape, state, train **6** demand, fettle, malady, status, tone up **7** ailment, prepare, problem, proviso **8** accustom, position, standing **9** agreement, complaint, provision, requisite, situation **10** limitation, make used to, put in shape **11** arrangement, contingency, malfunction, reservation, restriction, stipulation **12** prerequisite **13** circumstances, qualification, state of health **14** state of affairs **15** physical fitness

conditional **7** limited **9** dependent, qualified, tentative **10** contingent, restricted **11** provisional, stipulative **16** with reservations

condolence **4** pity **6** solace **7** comfort **8** sympathy **10** compassion **11** consolation **13** commiseration

Condon, Richard
author of: **11** Winter Kills **18** Death of a Politician **22** The Manchurian Candidate

condonation **11** forgiveness, overlooking **12** disregarding **13** putting up with

condone **6** excuse, forget, ignore, pardon, wink at **7** absolve, forgive, justify, let pass **8** overlook **9** disregard, put up with

conduce **3** aid **4** help, lead, tend **5** bring, favor, guide **6** effect **7** advance, forward, further, promote **10** contribute

conducive **7** helpful **8** salutary **9** favorable, promotive **10** beneficial **11** expeditious **12** contributive, contributory, instrumental **19** calculated to produce **22** helpful in bringing about

conduct **3** act **4** bear, lead, rule, ways **5** carry, chair, deeds, enact, guide, pilot, steer, usher **6** action, attend, behave, convey, convoy, direct, escort, govern, manage, manner **7** carry on, comport, control, execute, marshal, operate, perform **8** behavior, carry out, dispatch, guidance, regulate, transact **9** accompany, direction, discharge, look after, supervise **10** administer, deportment, government, leadership, management **11** comportment, generalship, preside over, superintend, supervision **14** administration

conduct oneself **3** act **6** behave **13** acquit oneself **14** comport oneself

conductor **3** cad **5** guide **6** carman, escort, leader **7** cathode, channel, maestro, manager **8** aqueduct, batonist, cicerone, conveyor, director, operator, stickman, trainman **9** collector, drum major **10** impresario, supervisor **11** choirmaster, transmitter **13** concert master

conduit **4** duct, main, pipe, tube **5** canal, drain, flume, sewer **6** gutter, trough **7** channel, passage **8** aqueduct **11** watercourse

cone **5** bevel, shape, spire **6** bobbin, conoid, funnel **7** pyramid, volcano **8** pyramid
kind: **3** fir **4** pine **5** larch **7** conifer, retinal **8** ice cream

confabulate **4** chat, talk **6** confer, patter **7** chatter, discuss **8** chitchat, converse, talk idly

confabulation **4** chat, talk **8** chitchat **10** conference, discussion **12** conversation

confection **3** jam **5** candy **6** pastry **7** dessert **8** conserve, delicacy **9** preserves, sweetmeat **10** sugar candy

confectionery **5** candy **6** sweets **7** goodies, pasties **10** sugar candy, sweetmeats

confederacy, Confederacy **3** CSA **4** band, bloc **5** guild, union **6** fusion, league **7** combine, society **8** alliance, the South **9** coalition, syndicate **10** federation **11** association **13** confederation **14** Southern states **18** secessionist states **26** Confederate States of America

confederate **4** ally **5** merge, unite **6** cohort, helper **7** abettor, comrade, partner **8** coalesce, coworker **9** accessory, affiliate, associate, colleague, companion **10** accomplice, cooperator, join forces **11** consolidate, helping hand **12** band together, collaborator, right hand man **17** fellow conspirator

Confederates
author: **14** Thomas Keneally

confederation **4** band **5** guild, union **6** fusion, league **7** combine, society **8** alliance **9** coalition, syndicate **10** federation **11** association, confederacy

confer **4** give **5** award **6** accord, parley **7** consult, discuss, palaver **8** converse **9** present to **10** bestow upon **12** compare notes, talk together **15** hold a conference **18** deliberate together

conference **4** talk **6** parley **7** council, meeting, seminar **8** conclave **9** symposium **10** convention, discussion **12** consultation, deliberation

conferment **4** gift **5** award **8** bestowal **12** presentation

confess **4** avow, sing **5** admit, own up **6** expose, reveal **7** declare, divulge, lay bare **8** blurt out, disclose **9** come clean, make known **11** acknowledge **12** bring to light **14** unbosom oneself **18** make a clean breast of

confessed **6** avowed **8** admitted **9** professed **12** self-declared **14** self-proclaimed

confession **6** avowal, shrift **9** admission **10** disclosure, divulgence, revelation **11** declaration **12** confessional **14** acknowledgment

Confessions of an English Opium Eater
author: **15** Thomas DeQuincey

Confessions of Nat Turner, The
author: **13** William Styron

confidant, confidante **5** crony **6** friend **8** intimate **10** bosom buddy **15** trusty companion

confide **6** impart, reveal **7** confess, divulge, lay bare, let in on, let know **8** disclose **9** make known **12** tell secretly **13** tell privately **14** unbosom oneself

confidence **4** grit, guts **5** faith, nerve, pluck, spunk, trust **6** belief, daring, mettle, secret, spirit **7** courage **8** audacity, boldness, credence, intimacy, reliance **9** certainty, certitude **10** conviction **11** intrepidity **12** self-reliance **13** private matter, self-assurance **14** faith in oneself **17** inside information

confidence man **5** cheat **6** con man **8** swindler **9** charlatan, trickster **10** mountebank

confident **4** bold, sure **5** cocky **6** daring, secure **7** assured, certain **8** cocksure, intrepid, positive **9** convinced, dauntless, expectant **10** optimistic **11** self-assured, self-reliant **13** sure of oneself

confidential **5** privy **6** secret **7** private **8** hush-hush **9** top-secret **10** classified **11** undisclosed **12** off-the-record **16** not to be disclosed

confidentially **7** sub rosa **8** in secret, secretly **9** privately **16** between ourselves **17** behind closed doors
French: **9** entre nous

confiding **6** trusty **7** reliant **8** trustful, trusting **9** confident **11** trustworthy

configuration **4** form **6** design, makeup **11** arrangement, composition

confine **3** pen, tie **4** bind, cage, hold, jail, keep **5** limit **6** coop up, govern, keep in, lock up, shut in, shut up **7** fence in, impound **8** imprison, regulate, restrain, restrict **9** sequester **11** incarcerate **13** hold in custody

confined **5** close, tight **6** jailed, narrow **7** cramped **8** locked up **10** imprisoned, restricted

confinement **7** custody, lying in **9** cooping up, detention, restraint **10** childbirth, constraint, limitation, shutting in **11** parturition, restriction **12** accouchement, imprisonment **13** incarceration **15** circumscription

confines **4** edge **6** border, bounds, limits **7** margins **8** precinct **10** boundaries **13** circumference

confirm **5** prove **6** accept, clinch, ratify, uphold, verify **7** agree to, approve, bear out, certify, sustain **8** make firm, validate **9** authorize, establish **11** acknowledge, corroborate, make binding, make certain **12** authenticate, substantiate

confirmation **5** proof **6** assent **8** approval, sanction **9** agreement **10** acceptance, validation **11** affirmation, endorsement **12** ratification, verification **13** corroboration **14** authentication, substantiation

confirmed **3** set **5** fixed **7** chronic **8** hardened, verified **9** ingrained, validated **10** deep-rooted, deep-seated, inveterate, proven true **11** established **12** corroborated **13** authenticated, dyed-in-the-wool, substantiated

confiscate **4** take **5** seize **7** impound, possess, preempt **8** take over **9** sequester **10** commandeer **11** appropriate, expropriate

confiscation **7** seizure **10** impounding, preemption **13** appropriation, commandeering, expropriation

conflagration **4** fire **5** blaze **7** bonfire, inferno **8** conflict, fighting, wildfire **9** brush fire, firestorm, holocaust **10** forest fire, raging fire, wall of fire **11** sea of flames **12** sheet of flame

conflagrative **8** burnable **9** flammable, ignitable **10** combustive, incendiary **11** combustible, inflammable

conflict **4** fray **5** clash, fight, melee, set-to **6** action, battle, combat, fracas, oppose, strife, tussle **7** collide, discord, dissent, scuffle, warfare **8** disagree, division, friction, skirmish, struggle, variance **9** encounter, hostility **10** antagonism, be contrary, difference, dissension, engagement **12** disagreement **13** confrontation **14** be inharmonious **15** be contradictory
Spanish: **9** mano a mano

conflicting **7** warring **8** clashing, opposing **10** ambivalent **13** contradictory

confluence **5** union **7** conflux, joining, linkage, meeting **8** junction, juncture **9** concourse, gathering **10** assembling, concursion **11** association, convergence **13** concentration **14** coming together **15** flowing together

conform **3** fit **4** obey **5** adapt **6** adjust, follow **8** adhere to, jibe with, submit to **9** agree with, reconcile, tally with **10** be guided by, comply with, fall in with, square with **11** acquiesce in **12** correspond to

conformable **8** amenable **9** agreeable, malleable **10** submissive **12** in compliance

conformance **7** harmony **9** agreement **10** accordance, compliance, conformity **13** compatibility

conformation **4** form **5** build, shape **6** figure **7** anatomy **9** formation, framework, structure **11** arrangement **13** configuration

conformist **12** well-adjusted **13** unadventurous

conformity **6** accord, assent **7** harmony **8** likeness **9** agreement, obedience **10** compliance, observance, similarity, submission, uniformity **11** resemblance **12** acquiescence **14** correspondence **15** conventionality

confound **5** amaze, mix up **6** baffle, puzzle, rattle **7** astound, confuse, fluster, mystify, nonplus, perplex, startle **8** astonish, bewilder, dumfound, surprise, unsettle **10** disconcert **11** flabbergast **16** strike with wonder, throw off the scent

confounded **8** confused **10** bewildered, nonplussed **11** dumbfounded **12** disconcerted

confraternity **4** body **5** guild, union **7** society **8** sodality **9** confrairy **11** association, brotherhood

confrere **3** pal **4** ally, chum **5** buddy **6** friend **7** brother, comrade, partner **9** associate, colleague

confront **4** dare, defy, face, meet **5** brave **8** cope with, face up to **9** challenge, encounter, withstand

confrontation **5** clash, run-in, set-to **6** battle, combat, debate **7** contest, dispute, face-off **8** conflict, showdown, skirmish **9** encounter **10** engagement, opposition **11** controversy **17** face-to-face meeting
Spanish: **9** mano a mano

Confucius
author of: **10** Book of Odes **11** The Analects

confuse **5** addle, befog, mix up, stump **6** baffle, muddle, puzzle, rattle **7** fluster, mistake, mystify, nonplus, perplex **8** befuddle, bewilder, confound, unsettle **10** discompose, disconcert **11** make unclear **12** make baffling **14** make perplexing **17** throw into disorder

confused **5** fazed **6** addled **7** abashed, baffled, chaotic, jumbled, mixed-up, muddled, tangled **8** rambling **9** befuddled, illogical, perplexed, unsettled **10** bewildered, disjointed, distracted, incoherent, nonplussed **11** dumbfounded **12** disconcerted, disorganized **13** disharmonious, heterogeneous

confusing **7** addling **8** baffling, blinding, blurring, dizzying, jumbling, mixing up, muddling **9** deranging, mistaking **10** befuddling, disorderly, flustering, mystifying, perplexing, stupefying **11** bewildering, confounding **13** disconcerting, unintelligible

confusion **4** mess, riot **5** chaos, snarl **6** bedlam, hubbub, jumble, muddle, tangle, tumult, uproar **7** clutter, ferment, turmoil **8** disarray, disorder, madhouse, shambles, upheaval **9** abashment, commotion **10** bafflement, hodgepodge, hullabaloo, perplexity, puzzlement, untidiness **11** disturbance, pandemonium **12** bewilderment, discomposure, stupefaction **13** mystification **14** disarrangement, disconcertment **15** disorganization
French: **14** bouleversement

confutation **6** denial **7** counter **8** negation, rebuttal **10** refutation **13** contradiction

confute **4** deny **5** rebut **6** impugn, oppose, refute **7** counter, gainsay **10** contradict, controvert **12** be contrary to

congeal **3** set **4** clot, jell **6** curdle, freeze, harden **7** stiffen, thicken **8** solidify **9** coagulate **10** gelatinize

congenial **4** like **6** genial, social **7** affable, cordial, kindred, related, similar **8** agreeing, amenable, gracious, pleasant, pleasing, sociable **9** agreeable, convivial **10** compatible, consistent, harmonious, well-suited **11** sympathetic **13** companionable, corresponding
French: **9** en rapport
German: **9** gemutlich

congeniality **7** harmony, rapport **8** affinity **11** sociability **12** conviviality, friendliness, pleasantness **13** compatibility **14** like-mindedness

congenital **6** inborn, inbred, innate, native **7** natural **8** inherent **9** ingrained, inherited, intrinsic **10** hereditary

congested **6** filled, gorged, jammed, packed **7** crowded **9** saturated **11** overcrowded

congestion **3** jam, mob **4** mass **5** snarl **6** pile-up **8** crowding **10** bottleneck **11** obstruction **12** overcrowding

conglomerate **4** heap, mass, pile **5** amass, blend, stack **7** mixture **8** assemble **9** aggregate **10** accumulate, assemblage **12** accumulation **16** large corporation

conglomeration **6** jumble, medley **7** mixture **8** mishmash **9** aggregate, potpourri **10** assortment, collection, hodgepodge **11** aggregation, combination **13** agglomeration

Congo ***see box***

congratulate **4** hail **6** salute **10** compliment, felicitate, wish one joy **11** rejoice with **18** give one's best wishes **28** wish many happy returns of the day

congratulations **6** salute **9** blessings, greetings **10** best wishes, good wishes **11** well-wishing **13** felicitations **24** many happy returns of the day

congregate **4** mass **5** amass, flock, swarm **6** gather, throng **7** cluster, collect **8** assemble **12** come together **13** crowd together

congregation **5** crowd, flock, group, horde, laity **6** parish, throng **8** assembly, audience, brethren **9** gathering, multitude **12** parishioners **16** church membership **17** religious assembly

congress, Congress **4** diet **6** caucus **7** council **8** assembly **9** delegates, gathering **10** conference, convention, parliament **11** legislature **14** federal council **15** discussion group, legislative body, national council, representatives **17** chamber of deputies

Congreve, William
author of: **11** Love for Love **15** The Double-Dealer **16** The Mourning Bride, The Way of the World

congruity **7** harmony **9** agreement, coherence **10** consonance **11** consistency **12** congeniality **13** compatibility **14** correspondence **15** appropriateness

congruous **4** meet **6** seemly **7** apropos **8** becoming, relevant, suitable **9** congenial, consonant, in keeping **10** harmonious **11** appropriate, in agreement **13** corresponding

conifer
means: **11** cone bearing
order: **11** coniferales
class: **10** gymnosperm
kind: **3** fir, yew **4** pine **5** cedar, larch, pinal **6** ginkgo, pinale, spruce, torrey **7** cypress, hemlock, juniper, redwood, sequoia **8** softwood **9** evergreen

Coningsby
author: **16** Benjamin Disraeli

conjectural **7** reputed **8** abstract, academic, doubtful, putative, supposed, surmised **11** inferential, speculative, theoretical **12** hypothetical **13** suppositional **14** supposititious

conjecture **4** idea, view

Congo
other name: **10** Moyen Congo **11** Middle Congo
capital/largest city: **11** Brazzaville
others: **3** Ewo **4** Boko **5** Epena, Kayes, Kelle, Okoyo, Sembe **6** Dongou, Komono, Makoua, Matadi, M'Binda, M'Vouti, Ouesso, Sibiti, Zanaga **7** Cabinda, Dolisie, Etoumbi, Gamboma, Kinkala, Loubomo, Loudima, Madingo, Mossaka, Souanke **8** Djambala, Impfondo, Kibangou, Madingou, Mindouli **9** Mossendjo **11** Fort-Rousset, Pointe-Noire **17** Mayombe Escarpment
school: **13** Marien Ngoubai
monetary unit: **5** franc **7** centime
lake: **5** Mweru, Tumba **6** Albert, Nyanza, Upemba **7** Leopold **11** Stanley Pool
highest point: **6** Leketi
river: **3** Dja **4** Uele **5** Alima, Congo, Kasal, Kwilu, Lulua, Ngoko, Niari, Sanga, Swilu, Wamba, Zahir, Zaire **6** Kwango, Kwenge, Loange, Lobaye, Lomami, Ogooue, Ubangi **7** Aruwima, Kouilou, Lualaba, Luapula, N'Gounie **8** Itimbiri, Likouala, Lubilash
sea: **8** Atlantic
physical feature:
plateau: **6** Bateke
people: **3** Rua **4** Akka, Susa, Teke, Vili **5** Amadi, Bantu, Figot, Kongo, Mantu, Pygmy, Sanga, Warua, Zambi **6** Ababua, Bafyot, Bateke, Mbochi, Nzambi, Wabuma **7** Bacongo, Bakongo, Bangala, Batetla, Manyema **10** Binga Pygmy
discoverer: **3** Cam
language: **4** Susu **5** Bantu, Fiote **6** French, Kituba **7** Bangala, Lingala
religion: **5** Islam **7** animism **10** Protestant **13** Roman Catholic
place:
church: **9** Saint Anne
stadium: **5** Eboue
feature:
tree: **5** limba

5 fancy, guess, infer, judge, think **6** augury, notion, reckon, theory **7** imagine, opinion, presume, suppose, surmise **8** estimate, forecast, judgment, theorize **9** calculate, deduction, guesswork, inference, speculate, suspicion **10** assumption, guestimate, hypothesis, presuppose **11** guess-timate, hypothesize, speculation, supposition **13** shot in the dark

conjoin **4** join, knit, link **5** touch, unite **7** combine, connect, overlap **8** together **9** associate

conjoined **6** joined, linked, united **7** knitted, meeting **8** combined, touching **9** connected **10** associated **11** overlapping **14** joined together

conjugal **6** wedded **7** marital, married, nuptial, spousal **9** connubial **11** matrimonial

conjugate **4** join, pair, yoke **5** mated, unite, yoked **6** couple, joined, paired, united **7** connect, coupled, related **9** connected **10** paronymous

conjunction **5** union **7** joining, meeting **11** association, coincidence, combination, concurrence

conjuration **5** charm, spell, trick **11** incantation

conjure **5** allay, charm, raise **6** invoke, summon **7** bewitch, command, enchant **8** call away, call upon **9** call forth **10** cast a spell, make appear **13** make disappear **15** practice sorcery

conjurer **6** wizard **8** magician

conk **3** die, hit **4** bean, blow, fail, head **5** decay, faint, sleep, stall **6** fungus, strike **7** bracket **8** knock out **9** break down **10** straighten

Conn, Katherine
real name of: **13** Kitty Carlisle

connect **3** tie **4** join **5** hinge, merge, unite **6** attach, couple, relate **7** combine, compare **9** associate, correlate **14** fasten together

connected **4** tied **6** joined, merged, united **7** coupled **8** abutting, adjacent, attached, combined, touching **9** bordering, proximate **10** connecting, contiguous, juxtaposed **12** conterminous **16** fastened together

connected group **5** cycle **6** series **8** sequence **11** progression

Connecticut
abbreviation: **2** CT **4** Conn
nickname: **6** Nutmeg **7** Blue Law **9** Freestone **12** Constitution **18** Land of Steady Habits
capital/largest city: **8** Hartford
others: **4** Avon **6** Bethel, Canaan, Cos Cob, Darien, Hamden, Mystic, Sharon, Storrs **7** Ansonia, Bristol, Danbury, Enfield, Madison, Meriden, Milford, Niantic, Norwalk, Norwich, Shelton, Tolland, Windsor **8** Guilford, New Haven, Simsbury, Stamford, Westport **9** Greenwich, Naugatuck, New London, Stratford, Waterbury **10** Bridgeport, Manchester, New Britain, Torrington **11** Wallingford
college: **4** Yale **7** Trinity **8** Hartford, St Joseph, Wesleyan **9** Fairfield **10** Bridgeport, Quinnipiac **11** Sacred Heart **12** U S Coast Guard
feature: **10** Charter Oak
museum: **8** PT Barnum
seaport: **6** Mystic
theater: **27** American Shakespeare Festival
tribe: **6** Pequot **7** Mohegan, Niantic **10** Quinnipiac
people: **8** PT Barnum **9** John Brown **10** Nathan Hale **11** Noah Webster **12** Thomas Hooker **19** Harriet Beecher Stowe
lake: **10** Candlewood
land rank: **11** forty-eighth
mountain: **4** Bear **7** Taconic
hills: **10** Berkshires
highest point: **8** Frissell
physical feature: **15** Long Island Sound
river: **6** Thames **9** Naugatuck **10** Housatonic **11** Connecticut
state admission: **5** fifth
state bird: **5** robin
state flower: **14** mountain laurel
state motto: **30** He Who Transplanted Still Sustains
state song: **12** Yankee Doodle
state tree: **8** white oak

Connecticut Yankee in King Arthur's Court, A
author: **9** Mark Twain
character: **5** Sandy **6** Merlin **8** Alisande, Clarence **11** Morgan le Fay **12** Hello-Central **18** Sir Kay the Seneschal

connection **3** kin, tie **4** bond, link **5** nexus **6** family, friend **7** contact, coupler, kinfolk, kinsman, linkage **8** affinity, alliance, coupling, junction, kinsfolk, relation, relative **9** associate, connector, fastening **10** attachment, kith and kin **11** association, correlation **12** acquaintance, relationship **13** flesh and blood, interrelation

Connelly, Marc
author of: **16** The Green Pastures
with Frank Elser: **19** The Farmer Takes a Wife
with George S Kaufman: **5** Dulcy **11** To the Ladies **17** Beggar on Horseback, Merton of the Movies

Connery, Sean
real name: **13** Thomas Connery
born: **8** Scotland **9** Edinburgh
roles: **6** Marnie **14** Robin and Marian **15** The Untouchables **16** The Molly Maguires **20** The Man Who Would Be King **28** Darby O'Gill and the Little People
James Bond: **4** Dr No **10** Goldfinger **11** Thunderball **16** You Only Live Twice **18** Diamonds Are Forever, From Russia with Love, Never Say Never Again

connivance **4** plot **5** cabal **6** design, scheme **8** intrigue **9** collusion **10** complicity, conspiracy **11** machination

connive **3** aid **4** abet, plan, plot **5** allow **6** wink at **7** collude **8** conspire **10** be a party to **13** be accessory to, lend oneself to **14** shut one's eyes to **17** be in collusion with, cooperate secretly

conniving **4** wily **6** artful,

crafty **7** cunning **8** plotting, scheming **9** designing **10** intriguing **11** calculating

connoisseur **5** judge, maven, mavin **6** expert **7** epicure, gourmet **9** authority **11** cognoscente **17** person of good taste

Connolly, Maureen
nickname: **8** Little Mo
sport: **6** tennis

Connor, Dale
creator/artist of: **9** Mary Worth

connotation **5** drift **6** import, spirit **8** coloring **9** evocation, undertone **10** intimation, suggestion **11** implication, insinuation **12** significance

connote **5** imply **6** hint at **7** suggest **8** intimate **9** insinuate **11** bring to mind

connubial **6** wedded **7** marital, married, nuptial **8** conjugal **11** matrimonial

conquer **4** beat, best, drub, lick, rout, rule, trim, whip **5** floor, quell **6** defeat, humble, master, occupy, subdue, thrash **7** possess, win over **8** overcome, surmount, vanquish **9** overpower, rise above, subjugate **11** prevail over, triumph over **14** get the better of

conqueror **6** victor, winner **7** subduer **8** champion **10** subjugator, vanquisher **12** conquistador

conquest **3** fan **4** sway **5** lover **6** adorer, defeat **7** captive, mastery, triumph, victory, winning **8** adherent, follower, whip hand **9** upper hand **10** ascendancy, conquering, domination, overcoming **11** acquisition, subjugation **12** vanquishment **17** captured territory

Conrad, Joseph
real name: **29** Josef Teodor Konrad Korzeniowski
author of: **6** Chance **7** Lord Jim, Typhoon, Victory **8** Nostromo **13** Almayer's Folly **14** The Secret Agent **15** Heart of Darkness **16** Under Western Eyes **21** An Outcast of the Islands **23** The Nigger of the Narcissus

consanguine **4** akin **7** cognate, kindred, related **8** relative

consanguineous **3** kin **4** akin **7** kindred, related **9** connected **21** having a common ancestor

conscience **8** scruples **10** moral sense, principles **15** ethical feelings **20** sense of right and wrong

conscience-stricken **6** guilty **7** ashamed **8** contrite, penitent **9** chastened, regretful, repentant **10** remorseful **13** guilt-stricken

conscientious **5** exact **6** honest **7** careful, dutiful, ethical, upright **10** fastidious, meticulous, particular, scrupulous **11** painstaking, responsible, trustworthy **12** conscionable **14** high-principled

conscious **5** aware **7** alert to, alive to, awake to, studied **8** noticing, sensible, sentient **9** cognizant, in the know, observing **10** calculated, deliberate, discerning, perceiving **12** apperceptive, premeditated **13** knowledgeable

consciousness **4** mind **6** senses **8** feelings, thoughts **9** awareness **10** cognizance, perception **11** discernment, sensibility

conscript **3** PFC **4** boot, hire, levy **5** draft **6** call up, employ, engage, enlist, enroll, induct, muster, rookie, seaman, select, take on **7** draftee, impress, private, recruit **8** enlistee, inductee, mobilize, register, selectee, shanghai **9** conscribe **11** buck private

consecrate **5** bless **6** hallow **7** glorify **8** sanctify **10** make sacred **11** immortalize **13** declare sacred

consecrated **4** holy **7** blessed **8** hallowed **10** sanctified

consecutive **6** in turn, serial **8** unbroken **10** continuous, sequential, successive **11** progressive **13** uninterrupted **19** following one another

consensus **6** accord **7** concord **9** unanimity **11** concurrence **13** common consent **14** general opinion **15** majority opinion **16** general agreement

consent **5** agree, allow, yield **6** accede, accept, accord, assent, concur, permit, ratify, submit **7** approve, concede, concord, confirm, endorse **8** approval, sanction **9** acquiesce, agreement **10** acceptance, fall in with, permission **11** concurrence, endorsement, willingness **12** acquiescence, confirmation, ratification

Consenting Adults
author: **12** Peter DeVries

consent to **2** OK **4** okay **6** permit **7** approve **8** accede to **10** concur with **11** acquiesce to, go along with **14** give the go-ahead

consequence **3** end **4** note **5** avail, fruit, issue, value, worth **6** import, moment, result, sequel, upshot **7** account, gravity, outcome **9** aftermath, influence, magnitude, outgrowth **10** importance, notability, prominence, usefulness **11** development, distinction, seriousness **12** significance

consequent **7** ensuing **8** eventual **9** following, resulting

consequential **7** crucial, epochal **8** historic **9** important, momentous **10** meaningful **11** significant

consequently **2** so **4** ergo, then **5** and so, hence, later **9** as a result, therefore **11** accordingly **12** subsequently

conservation **4** care **6** upkeep **9** husbandry **10** careful use, protection **11** maintenance, safekeeping **12** preservation

conservative **5** quiet **6** square **7** old-line **8** cautious, moderate, undaring **9** right-wing **10** nonliberal, unchanging **11** reactionary, right-winger, traditional **13** unprogressive **15** middle-of-the-road **16** opponent of change **17** middle-of-the-roader **22** champion of the status quo

conservatoire **11** music school **12** conservatory, music academy

conservatory **7** nursery **8** hothouse **9** arboretum **10** glasshouse, greenhouse **11** music school **12** music academy **13** conservatoire

conserve **4** save **5** guard **7** care for, cut back, husband, use less **8** maintain, not waste, preserve **9** safeguard **12** use sparingly

consider **4** deem, hold, note **5** gauge, honor, judge, opine, study, think, weigh **6** ponder, regard, review **7** believe, examine, pay heed, respect **8** appraise, envision, hold to be, mull over **9** be aware of, reflect on **10** bear in mind, cogitate on, think about **11** contemplate **12** deliberate on **17** make allowances for **18** turn over in one's mind

considerable **4** tidy **5** ample, great, large **6** goodly **7** notable, sizable **8** not small **9** estimable, important **10** impressive, noteworthy, noticeable, of some size, remarkable **11** a good deal of, significant, substantial

considerably **5** amply **7** greatly, largely, notably, sizably **9** estimably **10** abundantly, noticeably, remarkably **13** significantly, substantially

considerate **4** kind **6** kindly **7** mindful **8** obliging **9** attentive, concerned **10** solicitous, thoughtful

consideration **4** heed, tact **5** cause, honor, point, study **6** factor, ground, motive, notice, reason, regard, review **7** concern, respect, thought **8** interest, judgment **9** attention **10** advisement, cogitation, inducement, kindliness, meditation, reflection, solicitude **11** examination **12** deliberation **13** contemplation **14** thoughtfulness **15** considerateness

consider closely **7** pay heed **11** concentrate **12** pay attention **13** put one's mind to **21** give one's full attention

considered **5** mused **6** deemed, heeded, judged, mulled **7** advised, express, honored, noticed, studied, thought, weighed, willful **8** believed, esteemed, looked on, pondered, regarded, supposed **9** reflected, respected, ruminated **10** considered, deliberate, looked upon, thought out **11** deliberated, entertained, intentional **12** contemplated, premeditated, thought about

consign **5** remit **6** assign, commit, convey, remand **7** deliver, entrust **8** delegate, hand over, relegate, transfer **9** commend to **11** deposit with

consignment **8** delivery, shipment, transfer **10** assignment, committing, consigning, delegation, depositing, entrusting, relegation **11** handing over **12** goods for sale, goods shipped **19** goods sent on approval

consist **3** lie **6** reside **7** contain, include **10** be made up of **11** to be found in **13** be comprised of **14** to be composed of

consistency, consistence **4** body **5** unity **6** makeup **7** density, harmony, texture **8** firmness **9** agreement, coherence, congruity, stiffness, structure, thickness, viscosity **10** accordance, conformity, connection, uniformity **11** compactness, composition, persistence **12** construction, faithfulness, steady effort **13** compatibility, steadfastness **14** correspondence **16** uniform standards **19** constant performance, undeviating behavior

consistent **4** meet **6** steady **7** regular, unified **8** agreeing, constant, of a piece, suitable **9** congenial, congruous, consonant **10** compatible, harmonious, persistent, unchanging **11** in agreement, undeviating **13** correspondent **16** conforming to type

consolation **4** help **5** cheer **6** relief, solace, succor **7** comfort, support **8** easement, soothing, sympathy **10** condolence **11** alleviation, assuagement **13** encouragement

Consolation of Philosophy (De Consolatione Philosophiae)
author: **31** Anicius Manlius Severinus Boethius

console **4** calm, ease **5** cheer **6** soothe, succor **7** comfort, support, sustain **10** lament with, sympathize **11** condole with **13** express sorrow **15** commiserate with **18** express sympathy for

consolidate **4** fuse, join **5** merge, unify, unite **6** league **7** combine, fortify **8** coalesce, compress, condense, federate, make firm, make sure, solidify **9** integrate, make solid **10** amalgamate, centralize, strengthen **11** concentrate, incorporate **12** band together **13** bring together

consolidation **5** union **6** fusion, merger **8** alliance **9** coalition **11** unification **12** amalgamation **13** agglomeration **14** conglomeration

consomme **4** soup **5** broth **9** madrilene

consonance **5** amity, unity **6** accord, unison **7** concord, harmony, oneness **9** agreement, coherence, congruity, unanimity **10** accordance, conformity, congruence, consonancy **11** concordance, consistency, homogeneity **13** compatibility **14** correspondence, like-mindedness

consonant **8** in accord **9** agreeable, congruous, in harmony **10** concordant, consistent **11** in agreement

consort **3** mix **4** club, mate, wife **6** mingle, spouse **7** hang out, husband, pair off, partner **8** go around, sidekick **9** accompany, associate, companion, other half, pal around, rub elbows **10** fraternize **11** keep company

conspicuous **5** clear, great, plain **6** famous, patent **7** eminent, evident, glaring, notable, obvious **8** distinct, flagrant, glorious, manifest, renowned, splendid, striking **9** arresting, brilliant, memorable, notorious, prominent, well-known **10** celebrated, easily seen, remarkable **11** illustrious, outstanding, standing out **13** distinguished, easily noticed, highly visible

conspicuousness **9** celebrity, flagrance, notoriety **10** prominence, visibility **11** obviousness **13** noticeability

conspiracy **4** plot **7** treason **8** intrigue, sedition **9** collusion, treachery **10** connivance, secret plan **11** machination **12** criminal plan **14** treasonous plan

conspirator **7** plotter, schemer, traitor **8** conniver **9** intriguer **10** subversive

conspire **5** unite **6** concur, scheme **7** collude, combine, connive **8** intrigue **9** cooperate, machinate **11** plot treason **12** work together

Constable, John
born: **7** England **12** East Bergholt
artwork: **10** The Haywain **12** Cloud Studies **14** Hadleigh Castle **39** Salisbury Cathedral from the Bishop's Grounds

constancy **6** fealty **7** loyalty **8** devotion **9** fixedness, stability **10** allegiance, permanence **12** faithfulness, immutability **13** dependability, invariability, steadfastness **15** trustworthiness **16** unchangeableness

constant **4** even, true **5** fixed, loyal **6** stable, steady, trusty **7** abiding, devoted, endless, eternal, regular, staunch, uniform **8** diligent, enduring, faithful, resolute, stalwart, unbroken, unvaried **9** ceaseless, continual, immutable, incessant, permanent, perpetual, steadfast, sustained, unceasing, unfailing **10** dependable, invariable, persistent, unchanging, unflagging, unswerving, unwavering **11** everlasting, never-ending, trustworthy, unalterable, undeviating, unrelenting **12** interminable, tried-and-true **13** uninterrupted

Constant Nymph, The
director: **14** Edmund Goulding
cast: **11** Alexis Smith **12** Charles Boyer, Joan Fontaine **14** Brenda Marshall

constellation ***see box***

consternation **5** alarm, panic, shock **6** dismay, fright, horror, terror **11** trepidation **12** apprehension

constituent **4** atom, part **5** piece, voter **6** factor, member **7** elective, element, essence **8** electing, integral, making up **9** component, formative, principal, supporter **10** appointing, ingredient

constitute **4** form, make, name **5** found, set up **6** create, invest, make up **7** appoint, compose, empower, produce **8** compound, delegate **9** authorize, establish, institute **10** commission

constitution **6** figure, health, make-up, mettle **7** charter, stamina, texture **8** physique, strength, vitality **9** basic laws, formation, structure **10** figuration **11** composition **12** construction **13** configuration **16** governing charter **17** physical condition **21** fundamental principles

constitutional **4** turn, walk **5** basic **6** inborn, ramble, stroll, vested **7** natural, organic **8** inherent, internal, physical **9** chartered, intrinsic **10** congenital **11** fundamental

Constitution State
nickname of: **11** Connecticut

constrain **4** curb, urge **5** check, crush, drive, force, quash **6** coerce, compel, oblige, subdue **7** confine, enforce, put down, repress, squelch **8** hold back, pressure, restrain, restrict, suppress **9** fight down, necessity, strong-arm **14** put the screws on

constrained **3** shy **5** timid **6** forced **7** bashful **8** reserved, reticent **9** compelled, diffident **10** restricted **11** embarrassed

constraint **5** force **6** duress **7** reserve **8** coercion, pressure **9** restraint **10** compulsion, diffidence, inhibition, obligation **11** enforcement **13** necessitation

constrict **4** bind **5** choke, cramp, pinch **6** shrink **7** squeeze **8** compress, contract, strangle **11** strangulate

constriction **7** binding, choking **8** cramping, pinching **9** narrowing, shrinking, squeezing, stricture, tightness **10** constraint, strangling **11** compression, contraction

construct **4** form, make **5** build, erect, frame, set up, shape **6** create, design, devise **7** arrange, fashion **8** organize **9** fabricate, formulate

construction **4** form, make **5** build, style **6** format **7** edifice, raising, reading, rearing, version **8** building, creation, erecting **9** rendition, structure **10** fashioning, production **11** composition, elucidation, explanation, explication, fabrication, manufacture **12** conformation, constructing **13** configuration **14** interpretation **15** putting together

constructive **5** handy **6** useful **7** helpful **8** valuable **9** practical **10** beneficial, productive **12** advantageous

construe **4** read, take **7** explain, make out **8** decipher **9** elucidate, figure out, interpret, translate **10** comprehend, understand

Consuelo
author: **10** George Sand

consul **5** envoy **8** emissary, minister **14** foreign officer, representative **15** diplomatic agent

Consul, The
opera by: **7** Menotti
character: **10** Magda Sorel

consult **6** confer, parley, regard **7** refer to **8** consider, talk over **9** inquire of **11** ask advice of, have an eye to **12** compare notes **13** exchange views **15** discuss together, seek counsel from, take into account **16** seek the opinion of **18** deliberate together

consultant **6** expert **7** adviser, advisor, counsel **9** discusser

consultation **7** council, hearing, meeting, palaver **9** interview **10** conference, discussion **12** deliberation

consumable **6** edible **7** eatable **10** comestible

consume **3** eat **4** gulp **5** drain, eat up, spend, use up, waste **6** absorb, devour, expend, guzzle, ravage **7** deplete, destroy, drink up, engross, exhaust **8** demolish, lay waste, squander **9** devastate, dissipate, swallow up **10** annihilate

consumed **4** used **5** burnt, drank, drunk, eaten, spent **6** used up, wasted **7** drained, outworn **8** absorbed, burned up, expended, perished **9** destroyed, engrossed, exhausted, swallowed **10** squandered **11** annihilated

consume greedily **6** devour **7** stuff in **8** bolt down, gobble up, gulp down, wolf down **12** swallow whole **13** eat ravenously **14** eat voraciously

consumer **4** user **5** buyer, drain **6** client, patron, waster **7** spender **8** customer **9** purchaser **10** dissipater, squanderer

consummate **2** do **5** sheer, total, utter **6** effect, finish **7** achieve, execute, fulfill, perfect, perform, realize, supreme **8** absolute, carry out, complete, finished, thorough **9** faultless **10** accomplish,

---

constellation **4** host **5** group, rally **6** circle, galaxy, nebula, spiral, throng **7** cluster, company, pattern **9** gathering **10** assemblage, collection **12** spiral nebula **13** configuration **14** island universe
name: **3** Ara, Leo **4** Apus, Crux, Grus, Lynx, Lyra, Pavo, Vela **5** Aries, Cetus, Draco, Hydra, Indus, Lepus, Libra, Lupus, Mensa, Musca, Norma, Orion, Pyxis, Virgo **6** Antlia, Aquila, Auriga, Bootes, Caelum, Cancer, Carina, Corvus, Crater, Cygnus, Dorado, Fornax, Gemini, Hydrus, Octans, Pictor, Pisces, Puppis, Scutum, Taurus, Tucana, Volans **7** Cepheus, Columba, Lacerta, Pegasus, Perseus, Phoenix, Sagitta, Serpens, Sextans **8** Aquarius, Circinus, Equuleus, Eridanus, Hercules, Leo Minor, Scorpius, Sculptor **9** Andromeda, Centaurus, Delphinus, Monoceros, Ophiuchus, Reticulum, Ursa Major, Ursa Minor, Vulpecula **10** Canis Major, Canis Minor, Cassiopeia, Chamaeleon, Horologium, Triangulum **11** Capricornus, Sagittarius, Telescopium **12** Microscopium **13** Canes Venatici, Coma Berenices **14** Camelopardalis, Corona Borealis **15** Corona Australis, Piscis Austrinus **18** Triangulum Australe

bring about, undisputed **11** unmitigated **12** accomplished, unquestioned **13** unconditional **17** through-and-through

consummation 3 end **5** close **6** finish **9** execution **10** attainment, completion, conclusion **11** achievement, culmination, fulfillment, realization **14** accomplishment

consumption 2 TB **3** use **7** using up **9** consuming, depletion **10** exhaustion **11** expenditure, utilization **12** exploitation, tuberculosis

Consus
origin: 5 Roman
god of: 11 good counsel, horse racing
protector of: 5 grain
corresponds to: 3 Ops

contact 4 join, meet **5** reach, touch, union **7** connect, meeting **8** abutment, junction, touching **9** adjacency, get hold of **10** connection **11** association **13** communication **14** get in touch with **15** communicate with

contagion 7 disease **8** epidemic, outbreak **9** infection, spreading **13** contamination

contagious 8 catching **9** spreading **10** infectious, spreadable **12** communicable **13** transmittable

contain 4 curb, hold **5** check **6** embody, hold in **7** control, embrace, enclose, include, inhibit, involve, repress **8** hold back, keep back, restrain, suppress **11** accommodate, incorporate **12** keep the lid on **16** keep within bounds

container 3 bag, box, can, jar, vat **4** pail **6** barrel, bottle, bucket, carton, holder, vessel **10** receptacle

containment 7 control **9** restraint, retention

contaminate 4 foul, soil **5** dirty, spoil, taint **6** befoul, blight, debase, defile, infect, poison **7** corrupt, pollute **8** besmirch **10** adulterate, make impure

contamination 5 filth **7** fouling, soiling **8** dirtying, foulness, impurity, spoiling **9** dirtiness, poisoning, polluting, pollution, putridity **10** defilement **11** uncleanness **12** adulteration

Conte, Richard
real name: 18 Nicholas Peter Conte
born: 12 Jersey City NJ
roles: 8 Barabbas **13** A Bell for Adano **24** The Greatest Story Ever Told

contemplate 4 note, plan, scan **5** weigh **6** expect, gaze at, intend, ponder, regard, survey **7** examine, imagine, inspect, observe, project, stare at, think of **8** aspire to, envision, mull over, ruminate **9** muse about **10** anticipate, cogitate on, have in view, meditate on, think about **11** reflect upon **12** deliberate on **13** consider fully, look at fixedly, look forward to **14** speculate about **15** view attentively

contemplation 5 study **6** gazing, musing, seeing, survey **7** looking, reverie, thought, viewing **8** scanning, thinking **9** pondering **10** cogitation, inspection, meditation, reflection, rumination **11** examination, observation **12** deliberation **13** consideration

contemplative 6 musing **7** pensive **8** studious **9** engrossed **10** cogitative, meditative, reflective, ruminating, thoughtful **11** speculative **13** introspective, lost in thought

contemporaneous 6 coeval **10** coexistent, coincident, concurrent **11** synchronous **12** contemporary, simultaneous

contemporary 3 new **4** late **6** modern, recent, with-it **7** current **8** advanced, brand-new, up-to-date **10** coexistent, coincident, concurrent, newfangled, present day **11** ultra modern **12** simultaneous **13** of the same time, up-to-the-minute **15** contemporaneous

contempt 4 hate **5** scorn, shame **6** hatred **7** disdain, disgust **8** aversion, derision, disfavor, disgrace, dishonor, distaste, ignominy, loathing, ridicule **9** antipathy, disregard, disrepute, revulsion **10** abhorrence, repugnance **11** detestation, humiliation

contemptible 3 low **4** base, mean, vile **5** cheap **6** abject, paltry, shabby **8** shameful, unworthy, wretched **9** miserable, repugnant, revolting **10** despicable, detestable, disgusting **11** ignominious

contemptuous 6 lordly **7** haughty, pompous **8** arrogant, derisive, insolent, scornful, snobbish **10** disdainful **12** supercilious **13** condescending, disrespectful

contemptuousness 5 scorn **7** disdain **8** contempt, rudeness **9** arrogance, insolence

contend 3 vie, war **4** aver, avow, hold, spar **5** argue, claim, clash, fight **6** allege, assert, battle, combat, debate, insist, jostle, strive, tussle **7** compete, contest, declare, dispute, grapple, quarrel, wrestle **8** be a rival, maintain, propound, skirmish, struggle **10** put forward

content 4 area, core, gist, load, size, text **5** cheer, happy, heart, ideas, peace **6** at ease, at rest, matter, please, serene, thesis, volume **7** appease, comfort, essence, gratify, insides, meaning, pleased, satisfy, suffice, unmoved **8** capacity, make easy, pleasure, serenity, thoughts **9** contented, gratified, happiness, satisfied, set at ease, substance **10** complacent, untroubled **11** comfortable, contentment, peace of mind, unconcerned **12** satisfaction **13** gratification

contented 5 happy **6** at ease, serene **7** at peace, content, pleased **9** gratified, satisfied **11** comfortable

contentedness 4 ease **5** peace **7** comfort, content **8** pleasure, serenity **9** happiness **11** contentment **12** satisfaction **13** gratification

contention 5 clash, fight **6** battle, combat, strife **7** contest, discord, dispute, rivalry **8** argument, conflict, disunity, fighting, friction, skirmish, struggle, variance **9** assertion, encounter, wrangling **10** dissension, quarreling **11** competition, discordance **12** disagreement **13** confrontation

contentious 5 angry, cross **7** bateful, scrappy **8** captious **9** bellicose **10** pugnacious **11** belligerent, competitive, quarrelsome **12** cantankerous, disputatious **13** argumentative, controversial

contentment 4 ease **5** peace **7** comfort, content **8** pleasure, serenity **9** happiness **12** satisfaction **13** contentedness, gratification

conterminous 8 abutting, adjacent, touching **9** bordering **11** right beside **14** contiguous with

contest 3 war **4** bout, game **5** fight, match **6** battle, combat, debate, oppose, vie for **7** dispute, rivalry, tourney

8 conflict, fight for, object to, struggle **9** battle for, challenge, combat for, encounter **10** compete for, contend for, controvert, engagement, tournament **11** competition, struggle for **12** argue against **14** call in question

contestant 5 rival **6** player **7** entrant, fighter **8** competer, prospect **9** combatant, contender **10** challenger, competitor

context 6 milieu **7** climate, meaning, setting **8** ambience **9** framework, precincts, situation **10** atmosphere, background, conditions, connection **11** environment **12** relationship, surroundings **13** circumstances **16** frame of reference

contiguous 5 close, handy **6** nearby **7** close-by, tangent **8** abutting, adjacent, next-door, touching **9** adjoining, bordering, in contact **10** juxtaposed **11** neighboring **12** conterminous

continence 6 purity **8** chastity, sobriety **10** abstinence, moderation, temperance **11** forbearance **13** self-restraint

continent 4 Asia, pure **6** Africa, chaste, Europe **8** celibate, land mass, mainland, virginal **9** abstinent, Australia, temperate **10** abstemious, Antarctica **12** North America, South America

contingency 7 urgency **8** accident **9** emergency, extremity **10** likelihood **11** possibility, predicament **15** unforeseen event

contingent 9 dependent, subject to **11** conditioned **12** controlled by

continual 7 endless, eternal **8** constant, frequent, habitual, unbroken, unending **9** ceaseless, incessant, perennial, perpetual, recurring, unceasing **10** continuous, persistent **11** everlasting, never-ending, oft-repeated, unremitting **12** interminable **13** uninterrupted

continually 3 aye **4** ever **6** always, steady **7** endless, eternal, forever, on and on **8** steadily **9** recurring **10** constantly, frequently, repeatedly

continuance 4 stay, term **6** extent, period **7** lasting **8** duration **9** extension **10** continuing, permanence **11** adjournment, persistence, protraction **12** continuation, perseverance, prolongation

continuation 6 sequel **8** addition, sequence **9** extension **10** continuing, supplement **11** continuance, protraction **12** prolongation

continue 4 go on, last, stay **5** abide **6** drag on, endure, extend, keep on, keep up, remain, resume, stay on **7** carry on, persist, proceed **9** persevere

continued 6 kept on, kept up, lasted, went on **7** endured **8** extended **9** carried on, persisted, proceeded, prolonged **10** persevered, protracted

continuing 6 steady **7** abiding, eternal, ongoing **8** constant, enduring, extended, unbroken, unending **9** ceaseless, incessant, perpetual, prolonged **10** dragged out, persistent, protracted **11** persevering, unremitting **12** interminable **13** uninterrupted

continuity 4 flow **5** chain **9** continuum **10** succession **11** continuance, progression **12** continuation

continuous 6 linked, steady **7** endless, eternal, lasting **8** constant, enduring, unbroken **9** ceaseless, connected, continual, extensive, incessant, perpetual, prolonged, unceasing **10** continuing, persistent, protracted, successive **11** consecutive, everlasting, persevering, progressive, unremitting **12** interminable **13** uninterrupted

continuum 4 flow **5** chain **8** sequence **10** continuity, succession **11** continuance, progression **12** continuation

contort 4 bend, warp **5** twist **6** deform **7** distort **11** be misshapen

contorted 4 bent **7** crooked, twisted **8** deformed **9** distorted

contortion 7 bending **8** twisting **10** distortion **11** crookedness

contour 4 form **5** lines, shape **6** figure **7** outline, profile **10** silhouette **11** physiognomy

contraband 11 bootlegging **13** smuggled goods **14** illegal exports, illegal imports **15** unlicensed goods **17** black-marketeering **18** prohibited articles **19** unlawful trafficking

contract 3 get **4** pact, take **5** agree, incur **6** absorb, assume, narrow, pledge, reduce, shrink, treaty **7** acquire, compact, develop, dwindle, promise, shorten, tighten **8** compress, condense, covenant, engender **9** constrict, enter into, negotiate, undertake **11** arrangement, come to terms **12** draw together, make a bargain **13** become smaller, legal document **15** sign an agreement **16** written agreement

contracted form 6 digest **7** summary **8** synopsis **9** short form **11** abridgement, compression **12** abbreviation, condensation

contraction 8 decrease **9** drawing in, lessening, narrowing, reduction, shrinkage **10** shortening, shriveling, tightening **11** compression **12** abbreviation, condensation, constriction

contradict 4 deny **5** belie, rebut **6** impugn, oppose, refute **7** confute, counter, dispute, gainsay **8** disprove **10** controvert **12** be contrary to, disagree with

contradiction 6 denial **7** counter **8** negation, rebuttal **10** refutation **11** confutation **12** disagreement

contradictory 8 contrary, opposing **10** discrepant, dissenting, refutatory **11** conflicting, disagreeing **12** antithetical, inconsistent **14** countervailing, irreconcilable

contradistinction 8 contrast **10** difference **13** dissimilarity

contraption 6 device, gadget **9** apparatus, invention **11** contrivance

contrariety 9 deviation **10** difference, divergence **13** contradiction

contrary 5 balky **7** adverse, counter, froward, hostile, opposed, wayward, willful **8** converse, inimical, opposite, stubborn, untoward **9** disparate, obstinate, unfitting **10** at variance, discordant, headstrong, refractory, unsuitable **11** conflicting, disagreeing, intractable, unfavorable **12** antagonistic, antithetical, disagreeable, inauspicious, incompatible, recalcitrant, unpropitious **13** contradictory **15** at cross purposes, unaccommodating

contrast 6 depart, differ **7** deviate, diverge **8** variance **9** disparity **10** comparison, difference, divergence, unlikeness **11** distinction **12** disagree with **13** differentiate, dissimilarity **15** differentiation, set in opposition

contrasting **8** clashing, dividing, opposing **9** comparing, differing **10** discordant, juxtaposed **14** distinguishing **15** differentiating

contravene **4** deny **5** annul, fight, spurn **6** abjure, breach, combat, disown, negate, offend, oppose, reject, resist **7** disobey, exclude, gainsay, infract, nullify, violate **8** abrogate, disclaim, overstep **9** overreach, repudiate **10** act against, contradict, infringe on, transgress **12** encroach upon **15** trespass against

contretemps **4** spat **5** clash, set-to **7** dispute, quarrel **8** argument, squabble **10** difference, falling out **12** disagreement **18** embarrassing mishap

contribute **4** give **5** endow, grant **6** bestow, confer, donate, lead to **7** advance, forward, hand out, present **9** bear a part, influence **11** have a hand in **13** be conducive to **14** help bring about

contribution **4** alms, gift **5** grant **7** charity, subsidy **8** bestowal, donation, offering **9** endowment **11** benefaction **12** dispensation

contributive **8** valuable **9** favorable **10** beneficial

contributory **9** accessory, ancillary, auxiliary **13** supplementary

contrite **6** rueful **7** humbled **8** penitent **9** chastened, regretful, repentant, sorrowful **10** apologetic, remorseful **18** conscience-stricken

contrition **6** regret **7** penance, remorse **9** atonement, penitence **10** repentance **11** compunction **12** self-reproach **18** qualms of conscience

contrivance **4** plan, plot, tool **5** gizmo, trick **6** design, device, doodad, gadget **7** machine, measure **8** artifice, intrigue **9** apparatus, implement, invention, mechanism, stratagem **10** instrument **11** contraption, machination, thingamajig

contrive **4** plan, plot **6** create, design, devise, invent, manage, scheme **7** concoct **8** maneuver **9** improvise **11** devise a plan **17** effect by stratagem

contrived **7** labored, studied **8** mannered **9** unnatural **10** artificial

contriver **7** creator, deviser **8** designer, inventor **9** architect

control **4** curb, rule, sway **5** brake, steer **6** bridle, charge, govern, manage, master, subdue **7** command, contain, mastery, repress **8** dominate, dominion, regulate, restrain, restrict **9** authority, direction, reign over, restraint, supervise **10** domination, management, manipulate, regulation **11** superintend, supervision, suppressant **12** have charge of, jurisdiction

controlled **5** ruled **6** curbed, steady, swayed **7** checked, managed, powered, servile, subdued **8** directed, governed, held back, kept down, reserved, verified **9** commanded, contained, dominated, moderated, regulated, repressed **10** authorized, regimented, restrained, supervised **11** manipulated

controlling **6** ruling **8** dominant **9** governing **10** commanding **11** influencing, predominant **13** predominating

controversial **7** at issue **8** arguable **9** debatable, polemical **10** disputable **12** questionable **13** causing debate **15** widely discussed **16** open to discussion

controversy **6** debate **7** dispute, quarrel, wrangle **8** argument, squabble **10** contention, discussion, dissension **11** altercation **12** disagreement

controvert **4** deny **5** belie, rebut **6** negate, oppose, refute **7** confute, dispute, gainsay, protest **8** confound, disprove, question **9** challenge, disaffirm **10** contradict, contravene, invalidate **12** give the lie to

contumacious **6** unruly **7** froward **8** contrary, factious, insolent, mutinous, perverse **9** fractious, seditious **10** headstrong, rebellious, refractory **11** disobedient, intractable **12** ungovernable, unmanageable **13** disrespectful, insubordinate

contumely **5** abuse, insult, scorn **7** disdain, obloquy **8** contempt, diatribe, reproach, rudeness **9** arrogance, insolence, invective, pomposity **10** opprobrium, scurrility **11** brusqueness, haughtiness **12** billingsgate, vituperation **15** overbearingness

contusion **4** hurt, mark, sore **5** mouse **6** bruise, injury, shiner **7** blemish **8** abrasion, black eye **9** black mark **13** discoloration **16** black-and-blue mark

conundrum **5** poser, rebus **6** enigma, puzzle, riddle **7** arcanum, mystery, paradox, problem, puzzler, stopper, stumper **11** brain-teaser **13** Chinese puzzle

convalesce **4** mend **5** rally **6** revive **7** improve, recover, restore **8** progress **9** get better **10** recuperate

convalescence **7** recruit **8** recovery **11** restoration **12** recuperation **14** return to health

convene **6** gather, muster, summon **7** collect, convoke, round up **8** assemble **12** call together, come together, hold a session **13** bring together

convenience **3** use **4** ease **6** chance **7** benefit, comfort, service, utility **8** facility, pleasure **9** appliance, enjoyment, handiness, work saver **10** usefulness **11** opportunity **12** availability, satisfaction, suitable time **13** accessibility, accommodation

convenient **5** handy **6** at hand, nearby, suited, useful **7** adapted, helpful **8** suitable **9** easy to use **10** beneficial **11** serviceable **12** advantageous **16** easily accessible

convent **7** nunnery **8** cloister **13** society of nuns

convention **4** code **6** caucus, custom **7** meeting, precept **8** assembly, conclave, congress, practice, propriety, protocol, standard **9** formality, gathering **10** conference, social rule **11** convocation

conventional **5** usual **6** common, normal, proper **7** regular, routine **8** accepted, orthodox, standard **9** customary **11** traditional

converge **4** meet **5** focus **8** approach **11** concentrate **12** come together **13** bring together

convergence **6** accord **8** junction **9** congruity **10** confluence **12** meeting place **14** correspondence

conversant **4** up on **5** aware **6** au fait **7** erudite, privy to, skilled, tutored **8** familiar, informed, sensible, sentient **9** au courant, cognizant, practiced **10** acquainted, proficient **12** well-informed **13** knowledgeable

conversation **3** rap **4** chat,

talk **7** gabfest, palaver **8** chitchat, dialogue **9** discourse, tete-a-tete **11** bull session **13** confabulation
Italian: 13 conversazione

Conversation, The
director: 18 Francis Ford Coppola
cast: 10 John Cazale **11** Gene Hackman **13** Allen Garfield

conversational 6 casual, chatty **8** everyday, informal **9** idiomatic **10** colloquial, vernacular

conversazione 12 conversation

converse 3 gab, jaw, rap **4** chat, chin, talk **7** palaver, reverse **8** chitchat, contrary, opposite **10** antithesis, chew the fat, chew the rag **11** confabulate **13** speak together **14** shoot the breeze

conversely 12 contrariwise **14** antithetically, on the other hand

conversion 6 change **10** changeover **12** modification **13** change of heart, metamorphosis, transmutation **14** transformation **15** change in beliefs, transfiguration **16** change of religion

convert 4 turn **6** change, modify, novice **8** neophyte **9** proselyte, transform **11** proselytize

convex 7 bulging, rounded **11** protuberant **13** curved outward

convey 4 bear, cede, deed, give, move, tell, will **5** bring, carry, grant, leave **6** impart, relate, reveal **7** conduct, consign, deliver, divulge **8** bequeath, disclose, dispatch, transfer, transmit **9** confide to, make known, transport **11** communicate

conveyance 3 bus, car, rig, van **4** cart **5** buggy, truck, wagon **7** vehicle **8** carriage, carrying, movement, transfer **9** conveying, transport **12** transmission **14** transportation

convict 3 con **4** doom **5** felon **7** condemn **8** jailbird, prisoner, yardbird **10** find guilty **11** prove guilty **13** declare guilty

conviction 4 view, zeal **5** ardor, creed, dogma, faith, fever, tenet **6** belief, fervor **7** opinion **8** doctrine, judgment, position **9** assurance, certainty, certitude, intensity, principle, viewpoint **10** persuasion **11** earnestness **13** steadfastness

convince 4 sway **6** assure **7** satisfy, win over **8** persuade **9** influence **11** bring around, prevail upon

convincing 5 sound, valid **6** cogent, potent **7** evident **8** assuring, forceful, powerful **9** plausible **10** persuading, persuasive, satisfying

convivial 5 merry **6** genial, jovial **7** affable, festive **8** friendly, sociable **9** agreeable, fun-loving **10** gregarious **13** companionable

convocation 6 caucus, muster, roster **7** council, meeting, roundup **8** assembly, conclave, congress **9** gathering **10** conference, convention **11** ingathering

convoke 4 meet, open **6** gather, muster **8** assemble, converse **11** call to order **12** call together

convolute 4 coil, wave, wavy, wind **5** twirl, twist **6** coiled, rolled, spiral, tangle **7** contort, sinuous, twisted **8** involved, spiraled **9** intricate **11** complicated **12** turn and twist

convolution 4 coil, maze **5** twist **7** coiling, winding **8** twisting **9** labyrinth, sinuosity **10** contortion, undulation **11** sinuousness **12** tortuousness

convoy 5 fleet, usher **6** column, escort **7** conduct **9** accompany, formation, safeguard **10** armed guard, protection

convulse 4 rock, stir **5** laugh, shake, spasm, wring **6** excite **7** agitate, disturb, perturb, trouble **8** double up

convulsion 3 fit **5** spasm **6** tumult **7** seizure **8** outburst, paroxysm **9** agitation, commotion **10** contortion **11** disturbance

convulsive 6 fitful **7** hurtful, rending, shaking **8** exciting, stirring **9** agitating, epileptic, spasmodic, troubling **10** disturbing

Conway, Tim
real name: 18 Thomas Daniel Conway
born: 12 Willoughby OH
roles: 11 McHale's Navy **16** Carol Burnett Show **17** The Steve Allen Show

coo 6 babble, gurgle, murmur **20** whisper sweet nothings

Coogan, Jackie
real name: 16 Jack Leslie Coogan
wife: 11 Betty Grable
born: 12 Los Angeles CA
roles: 6 The Kid **9** Tom Sawyer **11** Oliver Twist, Peck's Bad Boy **15** Huckleberry Finn

cook 3 fix **4** chef, fire, heat, make **5** occur **6** cookie, doctor, happen, seethe **7** concoct, falsify, prepare, process **8** work well **9** improvise
method: 3 fry **4** bake, boil, brew, sear, stew **5** baste, broil, grill, poach, roast, saute, scald, shirr, steam **6** braise, coddle, simmer **7** parboil **8** barbecue **9** fricassee

Cooke, Alistair
author of: 14 One Man's America **18** A Generation on Trial **26** Around the World in Fifty Years
TV host of: 18 Masterpiece Theatre

cooked sufficiently 4 done **5** ready **7** al dente **11** done to a turn

cookie 3 bar, gal, gul **4** cake, cook **5** wafer **6** person **7** biscuit, brownie **10** shortbread
type: 4 oreo **5** sugar **7** oatmeal **8** macaroon, molasses **9** girl scout, tollhouse **10** gingersnap, lorna doone **12** peanut butter **13** chocolate chip

cooking, fine/gourmet
French: 12 haute cuisine

cooking term 3 a la, cut, dot, fry **4** bake, beat, boil, chop, coat, cube, dice, dust, flan, fold, lard, roux, sear, snip, stew, toss, whip **5** aspic, au jus, baste, blend, bread, broil, brush, candy, cream, crepe, devil, dough, flake, glace, glaze, grate, grill, knead, plank, puree, roast, saute, scald, score, shirr, steep, stock, torte **6** au lait, blanch, braise, coddle, devein, dredge, fillet, flambe, fondue, render, simmer, skewer, sliver **7** a la mode, compote, crouton, garnish, goulash, liquefy, parboil, precook, preheat, rissole, scallop, stir-fry **8** aperitif, au gratin, barbecue, conserve, consomme, julienne, marinate, pot roast **9** brochette, demitasse, drippings, forcemeat, fricassee, lyonnaise, macedoine **10** caramelize, cracklings
boneless strips of meat/fish: 6 fillet
clear soup: 8 bouillon, consomme

cubed toasted bread: 7 crouton
food cooked and served in foil or paper: 11 en papillote
fruit preserve with nuts/raisins: 8 conserve
fruits in syrup: 7 compote
in the fashion: 7 a la mode
remove veins: 6 devein
skewered meat: 5 kebab 9 brochette
small cup of black coffee: 9 demitasse
thin strips: 6 sliver 8 julienne
with cheese: 8 au gratin
with ice cream: 7 a la mode
with juice/with its own juices: 5 au jus
with milk: 6 au lait

cook up 3 mix 4 brew 5 hatch 6 create, devise, invent, make up 7 concoct, think up 8 compound, contrive 9 fabricate, formulate

cool 3 icy 4 calm, cold 5 aloof, chill 6 chilly, frosty, offish, serene 7 distant, not warm 8 composed, lose heat, make cool, reserved 9 collected, impassive, uncordial, unexcited 10 become cool, cool-headed, deliberate, nonchalant, unfriendly, unsociable, untroubled 11 indifferent, standoffish, undisturbed, unemotional, unflappable 12 slightly cold, somewhat cold, unresponsive 13 dispassionate, imperturbable, self-possessed

cooler 3 ade, can, fan, jug 4 coop, icer, jail 5 drink, icier 6 calmer, icebox, lockup, prison 11 refrigerant 12 refrigerator 14 air conditioner

Cool Hand Luke
director: 15 Stuart Rosenberg
cast: 8 J D Cannon 10 Jo Van Fleet, Lou Antonio, Paul Newman 12 Anthony Zerbe, Dennis Hopper 13 George Kennedy 14 Strother Martin
Oscar for: 15 supporting actor (Kennedy)

Coolidge, Calvin ***see box***

coolness 5 chill 7 dislike 8 distance 9 aloofness, composure, sangfroid 10 chilliness, detachment, frostiness 11 impassivity 12 indifference 13 lack of emotion, lack of feeling 14 unfriendliness 15 emotionlessness, standoffishness 16 imperturbability, unresponsiveness

coop 3 car, mew, pen, sty 4 auto, cage, cote 5 cramp, hutch 6 encase, prison 7 confine 8 imprison 9 enclosure 11 cooperation, cooperative

Cooper, Gary
real name: 16 Frank James Cooper
born: 8 Helena MT
roles: 8 High Noon (Oscar) 9 Beau Geste 12 Sergeant York (Oscar), The Virginian 15 A Farewell to Arms 17 Mr Deeds Goes to Town 19 For Whom the Bell Tolls, The Cowboy and the

Coolidge, Calvin
name at birth: 18 John Calvin Coolidge
nickname: 9 Silent Cal
presidential rank: 9 thirtieth
party: 10 Republican
state represented: 2 MA
succeeded: 7 Harding
defeated: 5 (Frank Thomas) Johns, (Herman P) Faris, (John William) Davis 6 (William Zebulon) Foster 7 (Gilbert O) Nations, (William James) Wallace 10 (Robert Marion) La Follette
vice president: 4 none (first term) 5 (Charles Gates) Dawes
cabinet:
state: 6 (Charles Evans) Hughes 7 (Frank Billings) Kellogg
treasury: 6 (Andrew William) Mellon
war: 5 (Dwight Filley) Davis, (John Wingate) Weeks
attorney general: 5 (Harlan Fiske) Stone 6 (Charles B) Warren 7 (John Garibaldi) Sargent 9 (Harry Micajah) Daugherty
navy: 5 (Edwin) Denby 6 (Curtis Dwight) Wilbur
postmaster general: 3 (Harry Stewart) New
interior: 4 (Hubert) Work, (Roy Owen) West
agriculture: 4 (Howard Mason) Gore 7 (Henry Cantwell) Wallace, (William Marion) Jardine
commerce: 6 (Herbert Clark) Hoover 7 (William Fairfield) Whiting
labor: 5 (James John) Davis
born: 2 VT 13 Plymouth Notch
died: 2 MA 11 Northampton
buried: 2 VT 8 Plymouth
education:
College: 7 Amherst
later studied: 3 law
religion: 17 Congregationalist
vacation spot: 10 Black Hills
author: 32 The Autobiography of Calvin Coolidge
political career: 13 vice president
state senator/lieutenant governor/governor of: 2 Ma 13 Massachusetts
civilian career: 6 lawyer 17 bank vice president 18 newspaper columnist
notable events of lifetime/term: 22 Pennsylvania coal strike
Act: 8 Volstead 10 Boulder Dam 11 Immigration 17 Japanese Exclusion
bribery case: 8 Elks Hill
conference: 11 Geneva Naval
flight by: 16 Charles Lindbergh
Lindbergh's plane: 15 Spirit of St Louis
Pact: 13 Kellogg-Briand
trial: 6 Scopes 12 Scopes monkey
quote: 35 (After all) the chief business of America is business 43 Spend less than you make and make more than you spend
father: 10 John Calvin
mother: 8 Victoria (Josephine Moor)
stepmother: 8 Caroline (Brown)
sibling: 13 Abigail Gratia
wife: 5 Grace (Anna Goodhue)
children: 4 John 6 Calvin

Lady **20** The Pride of the Yankees **22** North West Mounted Police

Cooper, James Fenimore
author of: 6 The Spy **8** The Bravo, The Pilot **9** Wyandotte **10** The Prairie **11** The Pioneers, The Red Rover **13** The Deerslayer, The Pathfinder, The Water-Witch **20** Leatherstocking Tales, The Last of the Mohicans
character: 4 Cora **5** Alice, Magua, Uncas **7** Hawkeye **11** Natty Bumppo **12** Chingachgook

cooperate 4 join **5** unite **7** go along, pitch in, share in **8** take part **9** join hands **10** act jointly, bear part in, join forces **11** collaborate, participate **12** pull together, work together **14** work side by side

cooperation 7 concert, detente **8** teamwork **9** agreement **10** accordance **11** concurrence, cooperating, give and take, joint action **13** collaboration, participation **15** pulling together, working together

coop up 3 pen **4** cage **5** pen in **6** closet, encage, shut in **7** confine, impound **8** restrain, restrict

coordinate 4 mesh **5** equal, match, order **6** relate **7** arrange, coequal **8** organize, parallel **9** correlate, harmonize **11** correlative, systematize **16** equally important

coordination 4 bond **5** skill **6** accord **7** harmony, liaison **10** adaptation, adjustment **12** equalization, organization **15** synchronization

cop 3 bag, nab, rob, win **4** bull, grab, take **5** bobby, catch, filch, pinch, snare, steal, swipe **6** peeler, pilfer, snatch **7** capture **8** gendarme, purchase **9** policeman **11** acquisition, policewoman **13** police officer

cope 4 face, spar **6** hurdle, manage, strive, tussle **7** contend, wrestle **8** struggle **11** hold one's own

copious 4 full **5** ample **6** lavish **7** liberal, profuse **8** abundant, generous **9** bountiful, extensive, plenteous, plentiful

copiousness 6 bounty, plenty, wealth **7** surfeit **8** fullness, plethora **9** abundance, ampleness, plenitude, profusion **10** lavishness, oversupply

Copland, Aaron
born: 10 Brooklyn NY
composer of: 5 Rodeo **9** Quiet City **10** Statements **11** Billy the Kid **12** Connotations **13** Dance Symphony, El Salon Mexico, The Tender Land **15** Outdoor Overture **17** Appalachian Spring **18** Music for a Great City, Music for the Theater

Copley, John Singleton
born: 8 Boston MA
artwork: 11 Samuel Adams **19** The Siege of Gibraltar **21** The Boy with the Squirrel **22** Brook Watson and the Shark, The Death of Major Pierson **26** The Death of the Earl of Chatham

copper
chemical symbol: 2 Cu

copper-colored 5 henna **6** auburn, russet **11** golden-brown, rust-colored **12** reddish-brown

coppice 4 bosk, wood **5** bluff, copse, firth, grove **6** forest, growth **7** boscage, thicket

Coppola, Francis Ford
director of: 12 The Godfather (Part I) (Part II, Oscar) **13** Apocalypse Now, The Cotton Club **15** The Conversation

Copreus
father: 6 Pelops
son: 10 Periphetes
herald of: 14 King Eurystheus

copse 5 brush, clump, grove **6** forest **7** coppice, thicket **8** woodland

copy 3 ape **4** fake, sham, text **5** clone, mimic, story, Xerox **6** follow, mirror, parody, repeat **7** emulate, forgery, imitate, replica **8** likeness **9** duplicate, facsimile, imitation, photostat, reportage, reproduce **10** carbon copy, manuscript **11** counterfeit, make a copy of **12** reproduction **14** representation **15** written material

coquette 4 vamp **5** flirt, tease **12** heart-breaker

coquettish 3 coy **9** kittenish **11** flirtatious

Cor 15 Biblical measure

Cora *see* **10** Persephone

coral 3 red **4** fire, pink, rose **5** horny, polyp, snake **6** orange, sea fan **8** acropora, hydrozoa, staghorn **9** gorgonian **10** sea feather **12** coelenterata

coram populo 8 publicly **15** before the public

corban 8 offering

Corbett, James (John)
nickname: 12 Gentleman Jim
sport: 6 boxing
class: 11 heavyweight

cord 5 braid, twine **8** thin rope **11** heavy string
abbreviation: 2 cd

Cordelia
character in: 8 King Lear
author: 11 Shakespeare

cordial 4 warm **6** genial, hearty **7** affable, amiable, sincere **8** friendly, gracious **9** heartfelt **11** good-natured **12** affectionate, wholehearted

cordiality 6 warmth **8** goodwill **9** affection, geniality, sincerity **10** affability, amiability, heartiness **11** amicability, earnestness **12** friendliness, graciousness, pleasantness **13** agreeableness

cordial relations 5 amity **6** accord **7** concord, harmony **8** goodwill **9** agreement **10** friendship **11** amicability **15** entente cordiale

cordon 4 cord, ring, rope **6** circle **8** encircle

cordon bleu 4 bird **5** finch **7** waxbill **10** red cheeked **11** estrildidae
school for: 5 chefs **7** cooking
***where:* 5** Paris **6** France
***founded by:* 13** Marthe Distell
***means:* 10** blue ribbon

core 3 nub **4** crux, gist, guts, meat, pith **5** heart **6** center, kernel **7** essence, nucleus **9** substance **10** brass tacks **11** central part, nitty-gritty **13** essential part, innermost part **15** sum and substance

Corelli, Arcangelo
born: 5 Imola, Italy
composer of: 7 La Folia (sonata No 12) **14** Concerti Grossi

Coresus
form: 6 priest
father: 6 Asopus
loved: 10 Callirrhoe
rejected by: 10 Callirrhoe

coriander
botanical name: 17 Coriandrum sativum
origin: 13 Mediterranean
color: 5 brown, white **6** yellow
flavor: 4 sage **5** cumin **7** caraway **9** lemon peel
candy: 6 comfit

Corinth, Lovis
born: 6 Tapiau **7** Prussia
artwork: 6 Salome **8** Ecce

Homo **10** Apocalypse **29** The Walchensee with a Yellow Field

Corinthus
founder of: 7 Corinth
possible father: 4 Zeus **8** Marathon

Coriolanus
author: 18 William Shakespeare
character: 8 Cominius, Virgilia, Volumnia **12** Junius Brutus, Titus Lartius **14** Tullus Aufidius **15** Menenius Agrippa, Sicinius Velutus **22** Caius Marcius Coriolanus

cork 3 bob, oak **4** bark, bung, plug, seal, stop **5** check, close, float **7** confine, filling stopper, stopple **8** restrain, suppress **10** insulation

corker 3 ace **4** whiz **7** stopper **8** clencher, striking, top notch **9** excellent, humdinger **10** remarkable **11** astonishing

corkscrew 4 coil, curl **5** twist **6** spiral **7** winding **10** serpentine **12** bottle opener

Corleone family
characters in: 12 The Godfather
author: 4 Puzo
member: 5 Sonny **7** Don Vito, Freddie, Michael

corn 4 cure **5** grain **6** callus **7** Zea Mays **8** preserve, schmaltz **9** vegetable
varieties: 3 Pod **4** Crow, Dent, Rice, Sand **5** Broom, Flint, Kafir, maize, Sugar, Sweet **6** Indian, Turkey **8** Egyptian, Squirrel
bread/cake: 4 pone **7** hoecake **8** tortilla **9** hushpuppy **10** johnnycake
beverage: 7 bourbon, whiskey

Corncracker State
nickname of: 8 Kentucky

Corneille, Pierre
author of: 5 Cinna, Le Cid, Medea, Medee **6** Horace, The Cid **8** Nicomede **9** Polyeucte

Cornelius, Peter von (van)
born: 7 Germany **10** Dusseldorf
artwork: 12 Last Judgment **24** The Wise and Foolish Virgins **30** The Four Horsemen of the Apocalypse

Cornell, Katharine
nickname: 21 first lady of the theater
born: 6 Berlin **7** Germany
roles: 8 Dear Liar **9** Saint Joan **18** Antony and Cleopatra **26** The Barretts of Wimpole Street

corner 3 fix, jam, nab **4** bend, grab, hole, nail, nook, spot, trap **5** angle, seize **6** collar, pickle, plight, scrape **7** dead end, dilemma, impasse **10** blind alley, pigeonhole **11** predicament

cornerstone 4 base **5** basis **9** principle **10** foundation **11** fundamental

cornet 4 cone, horn **7** trumpet **9** cornopean

Cornhuskers, The
author: 12 Carl Sandburg

Cornhusker State
nickname of: 8 Nebraska

cornice 4 drip **5** ancon, crown **7** molding, valance **8** astragal

Cornopian *see* **8** Hercules

Cornwallis, Charles
also: 10 second Earl **13** first Marquess
nationality: 7 British
served in: 5 India **7** Ireland **18** American Revolution
battle: 8 Yorktown **10** Brandywine
captured: 10 Charleston **12** Philadelphia
surrendered at: 8 Yorktown

Cornwell, David
real name of: 11 John Le Carre

corny 5 banal, hokey, inane, stale, tired, trite, vapid **6** jejune, square **7** fatuous, insipid **8** bromidic, ordinary, shopworn **9** hackneyed **10** threadbare, unoriginal **11** commonplace, stereotyped **12** cliche-ridden, old-fashioned **13** platitudinous, unimaginative **15** unsophisticated

Coroebus
form: 4 hero
home: 5 Argos
father: 6 Mygdon
built: 6 temple
temple honored: **6** Apollo
killed: 5 Poena
killed by: 8 Diomedes

corona 4 halo, ring **5** cigar **6** circle, nimbus

coronet 5 tiara **6** diadem **7** chaplet, circlet **10** small crown

Coronis
form: 5 nymph **8** princess
father: 9 Phylegyas
husband: 6 Ischys
son: 9 Asclepius
cared for: 8 Dionysus
killed by: 6 Apollo

Coronus
king of: 7 Lapiths
father: 7 Caeneus
son: 8 Leonteus
daughter: 10 Anaxirrhoe
companion: 5 Jason

Corot, Jean-Baptiste-Camille
born: 5 Paris **6** France
artwork: 9 Pastorale **11** Ville d'Avray, Woman in Blue **15** Woman with a Pearl **16** The Farnese Garden, Woman in the Studio **21** Memory of Mortefontaine **23** Souvenir de Mortefontaine

corporal 6 bodily **8** physical **9** corporeal

corporation 7 combine, company **9** syndicate **11** association **14** conglomeration

corporeal 6 bodily, mortal **7** worldly **8** material, physical **11** perceptible **12** nonspiritual

corps 4 band, crew, team **5** force, party, squad, troop **6** outfit

corpse 4 body **5** stiff **7** cadaver, remains **8** dead body

corpselike 4 pale **5** ashen **6** pallid **9** bloodless, deathlike **10** cadaverous

corpulent 3 fat **5** dumpy, hefty, obese, plump, pudgy, stout **6** chubby, chunky, fleshy, portly, rotund **7** lumpish, well-fed **8** roly-poly **10** overweight, well-padded

corral 4 herd **5** pen in **6** shut in **7** enclose, fence in, round up

correct 3 fit, fix **4** true **5** alter, amend, chide, exact, right, scold **6** adjust, berate, change, modify, proper, punish, rebuke, remedy, repair, revamp, revise, rework, seemly **7** censure, chasten, factual, fitting, improve, lecture, perfect, precise, rectify, reprove **8** accurate, admonish, becoming, chastise, flawless, regulate, suitable, unerring **9** castigate, dress down, faultless, make right, reprimand **10** acceptable, discipline, take to task **11** appropriate **12** conventional **16** haul over the coals, read the riot act to

correction 6 change **8** revision **10** adjustment, alteration, discipline, emendation, punishment **11** castigation, improvement, reformation **12** chastisement, modification **13** rectification

corrective 7 counter **8** remedial **9** improving **10** palliative, rectifying **11** reformatory, restorative, therapeutic **12** ameliorative, compensatory **13** counteractive **16** counterbalancing

correctness **8** accuracy **9** exactness, precision, propriety, rightness **10** exactitude, seemliness **11** suitability **12** becomingness, flawlessness **13** acceptability

Correggio
real name: **14** Antonio Allegri
born: **5** Italy **6** Emilia **9** Correggio
artwork: **5** Danae **12** Jupiter and Io **14** Leda and the Swan **17** The Rape of Ganymede **21** The Madonna of St Francis **23** Adoration of the Shepherds **28** Mystic Marriages of St Catherine

correlate **7** compare, connect **8** parallel **10** correspond

correlation **8** parallel **10** comparison, connection **14** correspondence

correlative **4** akin **7** related **8** agreeing, parallel **9** analogous **10** comparable, connecting, equivalent **13** corresponding

correspond **3** fit **4** jibe, suit **5** agree, match, tally **6** accord, be like, concur, equate, square **7** conform **8** coincide, dovetail, parallel **9** harmonize **11** communicate, drop a line to, keep in touch

correspondence **4** mail **7** analogy, letters **8** epistles, missives, relation **9** bulletins **10** dispatches, similarity **11** association, communiques, resemblance

corresponding **4** akin **5** alike, equal **7** similar **8** agreeing, matching, tallying **9** according **10** equivalent **11** correlative **12** proportional

corridor **3** way **4** hall, road **5** aisle **6** artery **7** hallway, passage **8** approach **10** passageway

Corridors of Power
author: **6** C P Snow

corroborate **4** back **5** prove **6** affirm, back up, uphold, verify **7** bear out, certify, confirm, endorse, support, sustain **8** validate **9** vindicate **12** authenticate, substantiate

corroborated **6** backed, proved, proven, upheld **7** factual **8** affirmed, backed up, borne out, verified **9** certified, confirmed, supported, sustained, validated **10** vindicated **11** well-founded **12** well-grounded **13** authenticated, substantiated

corroboration **5** proof **7** support **8** evidence **10** validation **11** affirmation, endorsement, vindication **12** confirmation, verification **13** certification, documentation **14** authentication, substantiation

corroborative **7** proving **9** affirming, backing up, upholding, verifying **10** bearing out, concurring, confirming, supporting, validating **11** affirmative **12** confirmative **14** substantiating

corrode **4** rust **7** oxidize **12** disintegrate

corrosive **4** acid **7** burning, caustic, erosive, mordant **8** abrasive **9** corroding **11** destructive

corrugated **6** fluted, ridged **7** creased, grooved, pleated **8** crinkled, furrowed, puckered, wrinkled **10** crenulated

corrupt **3** low **4** base, evil, mean **5** shady **6** debase, poison, seduce, sinful, wicked **7** crooked, debased, debauch, deprave, immoral, pervert, subvert **8** depraved **9** dishonest, unethical **10** fraudulent, iniquitous **11** contaminate **12** dishonorable, unprincipled, unscrupulous

corruption **4** vice **5** fraud, graft **7** bribery **8** iniquity **9** decadence, depravity, looseness, turpitude **10** debauchery, degeneracy, dishonesty, immorality, perversion, sinfulness, wickedness, wrongdoing **11** malfeasance

corsair **6** pirate, sea dog, Viking **7** brigand, sea wolf **8** marauder, picaroon, sea rover **9** buccaneer, plunderer, privateer, sea looter, sea robber **10** Blackbeard, freebooter **11** Captain Kidd **14** Long John Silver

corset **5** laces **6** girdle **8** corselet **17** foundation garment

Corsica **6** island
located in: **16** Mediterranean Sea
capital: **7** Ajaccio
colony of: **4** Rome
purchased by: **6** France
birthplace of: **8** Napoleon
industry: **7** tourism **10** wine making **12** sheep raising, cheese making

Corsican Brothers, The
author: **14** Alexandre Dumas (pere)

Cortazar, Julio
author of: **7** Rayuela **9** A Model Kit, Bestiario, Hopscotch **10** The Winners **12** Book of Manuel, End of the Game **15** All Fires the Fire **18** We Love Glenda So Much

cortege **4** line **5** court, staff, suite, train **6** column, escort, parade, string **7** caravan, company, retinue **9** cavalcade, entourage, following, motorcade **10** attendants, procession **17** funeral procession

corundum
variety: **4** ruby **8** sapphire, star ruby **12** star sapphire

coruscate **4** beam **5** flash, gleam **7** glimmer, glitter, shimmer, sparkle

Corybant
attendant of: **6** Cybele

Corycia
form: **5** nymph
bore son to: **6** Apollo

Corynetes
also: **8** Pelasgus
epithet of: **10** Periphetes
means: **12** cudgel bearer

Coryphaeus
epithet of: **4** Zeus
means: **7** highest

Corythosaurus
type: **8** dinosaur **10** ornithopod
period: **10** Cretaceous
characteristic: **10** duck-billed

Corythus
father: **5** Priam
mother: **6** Oenone
adopted son: **8** Telephus
loved: **5** Helen
killed by: **5** Priam
birthplace of: **8** Dardanus

Cosby, Bill
born: **14** Philadelphia PA
roles: **4** I Spy **12** The Cosby Show **19** Mother Juggs and Speed, Uptown Saturday Night

Cosby Show, The
character: **4** Rudy, Theo **6** Denise, Sondra **7** Vanessa **13** Clair Huxtable, (Dr) Cliff (Heathcliff) Huxtable
cast: **9** Bill Cosby, Lisa Bonet **14** Sabrina LeBeauf **15** Tempestt Bledsoe **18** Malcolm Jamal-Warner **19** Keshia Knight Pulliam, Phylicia Ayers-Rashad

Cosi fan tutte
also: **11** So Do They All **16** Women Are Like That
opera by: **6** Mozart
character: **7** Despina **8** Ferrando **9** Dorabella, Guglielmo **10** Don Alfonso, Fiordiligi

Cosmetas
epithet of: **4** Zeus
means: **7** orderer

cosmetic **5** paint, rouge **6** powder **7** mascara, surface **8** artifice, eyeliner, lipstick **9** cold cream, eye shadow **10** foundation, nail polish **11** beautifying **13** eyebrow pencil

cosmic **4** vast **7** immense **8** colossal, enormous, infinite **9** grandiose, universal **10** stupendous, widespread **12** interstellar **14** interplanetary **16** extraterrestrial

cosmopolitan **6** urbane **7** worldly **8** traveler **11** broadminded, worldly-wise **12** globe trotter, sophisticate **13** international, sophisticated

cosmos **5** stars **8** universe **9** macrocosm **10** starry host **13** vault of heaven

Cosmos
author: **9** Carl Sagan

Cossack **7** czarist, Russian, trooper **8** horseman **10** cavalry man

Cossacks, The
author: **10** Leo Tolstoy

cosset **3** pet **6** caress, coddle, fondle, pamper

cost **3** fee, run, tab **4** bill, harm, hurt, loss, pain, take, toll **5** fetch, go for, price, value, worth **6** amount, burden, charge, come to, damage, injure, injury, outlay **7** bring in, expense, penalty, sell for, set back **8** amount to, distress **9** face value, sacrifice, suffering, valuation, weigh down **11** expenditure, market price

Costa-Gavras, Constantine
director of: **7** Missing

Costard
character in: **16** Love's Labour's Lost
author: **11** Shakespeare

Costa Rica ***see box***

Costello, Lou
real name: **21** Louis Francis Cristillo
partner: **9** Bud Abbott
born: **10** Paterson NJ
roles: **11** Who's on First

Costa Rica
name means: **9** rich coast
other name: **19** Land of Eternal Spring
capital/largest city: **7** San Jose
others: **5** Canas, Limon, Vesta **6** Boruca, Nicoya **7** Cartago, Golfito, Heredia, Liberia, Negrita **8** Alajuela, Colorado, Guapiles **9** Turrialba **10** Puntarenas
measure: **4** vara **5** cafiz, cahiz **6** fanega, tercia **7** cajuela, cantaro, manzana **10** caballeria
monetary unit: **5** colon **7** centimo
weight: **3** bag **4** caja **5** libra
island: **4** Cano, Coco
lake: **6** Arenal
mountain: **4** Poas **5** Barba, Irazu **6** Blanco **7** Central, Gongora **9** Talamanca, Turrialba **10** Guanacaste
highest point: **14** Chirripo Grande
river: **4** Poas **5** Irazu **6** Matina **7** San Juan, Sixaola, Tenoria **8** Tarcoles
sea: **7** Pacific **9** Caribbean
physical feature:
bay: **7** Salinas **8** Coronada
cape: **5** Velas **6** Blanco **8** Matapalo **10** Santa Elena
crater: **4** Poas
gulf: **5** Dulce **6** Nicoya **8** Papagayo
hot springs spa: **12** Agua Caliente
peninsula: **3** Osa **6** Nicoya
point: **5** Judas **6** Blanca, Burica, Quepos **7** Cahuito, Galonos, Guionos, Llerena
valley: **8** Tarcoles **10** Reventazon
people: **4** Voto **6** Boruca, Bribri, Guaymi **7** Guatuso, mestizo, Spanish
explorer: **8** Columbus, Coronado
language: **7** Spanish
religion: **13** Roman Catholic
place:
shrine: **18** Our Lady of the Angels
theater: **14** Teatro Nacional
feature:
barbecue: **5** asado
dance: **6** torito **9** botijuela, zapateado **11** baile suelto **17** punto guanacasteco
drum: **8** quijonga
gourd: **4** caro
outdoor concerts: **7** retreta
plantation: **5** finca
wind instrument: **8** chirimia
food:
hearts of palm salad: **7** palmito
pudding: **10** tamal asado

costly **4** dear **5** steep, stiff **7** harmful **8** damaging, precious **9** expensive **10** disastrous, exorbitant, high-priced **11** deleterious, extravagant **12** catastrophic

costume **4** garb **5** dress **6** attire, livery, outfit **7** apparel, clothes, raiment, uniform **8** clothing, garments

costuming **8** disguise **10** masquerade

cot **3** bed, hut, pen **4** coop, crib **5** cover, stall **7** cottage

cotelette **3** cut **4** chop **5** slice **6** cutlet

coterie **3** set **4** band, camp, clan, club, crew, gang **5** crowd, group **6** circle, clique **7** faction

cottage **3** cot, hut **5** lodge, shack **6** chalet **8** bungalow

Cotten, Joseph
born: **12** Petersburg VA
roles: **8** Gaslight **11** Citizen Kane, The Third Man **12** Duel in the Sun **14** Shadow of a Doubt **15** Journey into Fear **16** Portrait of Jennie **23** The Magnificent Ambersons

Cotter's Saturday Night, The
author: **11** Robert Burns

cotton **9** Gossypium
varieties: **3** bog **4** tree, wild **6** kidney, levant, upland **8** lavender **9** sea island **11** Arizona wild
fabric: **4** duck, jean, lawn, pima **5** baize, chino, denim, drill, khaki, lisle, pique, scrim, terry, twill **6** burlap, calico, canvas, chintz, dimity, madras, muslin, nankin, oxford, poplin, sateen **7** batiste, buckram, cambric, flannel, fustian, gingham, holland, jaconet, oilskin, organdy, percale, ticking **8** chambray, cretonne, sheeting **9** crinoline, sailcloth **10** broadcloth, hopsacking, printcloth, seersucker, terrycloth **11** cheesecloth, dotted Swiss

Cotton Club, The
director: **18** Francis Ford Coppola
cast: **9** Diane Lane **11** Richard Gere **12** Gregory Hines

cotton gin
invented by: **7** Whitney

Cotton State
nickname of: **7** Alabama

cottonwood **7** Populus **16** Populus deltoides
varieties: **5** black, Jack's, swamp **7** Fremont **9** Rio Grande **10** Wislizenus **11** Great Plains

Cottus
member of: **13** Hecatonchires

Cotyleus
epithet of: **9** Asclepius
means: **13** of the hip joint

Cotys, Cotytto
origin: **8** Thracian
form: **7** goddess
corresponds to: **6** Cybele **11** Great Mother

couch **3** put **4** sofa, word **5** divan, draft, frame, state, utter, voice **6** daybed, draw up, lounge, phrase, settee **7** express **8** love seat, set forth **9** davenport **12** chesterfield

cougar **3** cat **4** lion, puma **7** panther **9** catamount **12** mountain lion

cough **4** hack **6** tussis **9** pertussis

cough up **3** pay **5** eject, expel **7** deliver **8** disgorge, hand over **9** surrender **11** regurgitate

Coulomb, Charles Augustin de
field: **7** physics
nationality: **6** French
invented: **14** torsion balance
discovered: **16** inverse square law

council **5** board, panel, synod **7** cabinet, chamber **8** assembly, colloquy, conclave, congress, ministry **9** committee, gathering, sanhedrin **10** conference, convention **11** convocation **12** congregation **15** representatives

counsel **4** urge, warn **6** advice, advise, charge, lawyer, prompt **7** call for, caution, opinion, suggest **8** admonish, advocate, attorney, guidance, instruct **9** barrister, counselor, recommend, solicitor **10** advisement, suggestion **12** consultation **14** recommendation

counsel house
German: **7** Rathaus

Counsellor-at-Law
director: **12** William Wyler
based on play by: **9** Elmer Rice
cast: **11** Bebe Daniels, Doris Kenyon **12** Isabel Jewell **13** John Barrymore, Melvyn Douglas, Onslow Stevens

counselor, counsellor **5** tutor **6** lawyer, mentor **7** adviser **8** advocate, attorney, minister **9** barrister, solicitor **10** instructor

counselor-at-law **6** lawyer **8** advocate, attorney **9** barrister, solicitor **10** mouthpiece

count **4** deem, hold, lord, rate, tell **5** add up, judge, noble, tally, total **6** impute, look on, matter, number, reckon, regard **7** ascribe, include, tick off **8** consider, estimate, look upon, numerate **9** attribute, enumerate, numbering, reckoning **10** numeration **11** calculation, computation, enumeration
German: **4** Graf
French: **5** comte
Italian: **5** conte

countenance **3** aid, air **4** back, face, help, look, mien **5** build, favor **6** aspect, permit, traits, uphold, visage **7** advance, approve, condone, endorse, forward, further, profile, promote, support, work for **8** advocacy, advocate, approval, auspices, champion, contours, features, presence, sanction **9** promotion **10** appearance, assistance, expression, silhouette **11** approbation, physiognomy **12** championship, moral support **13** encouragement

counter **3** bar, man **4** defy, disk **5** piece, stand, table **6** buffet, contra, offset, oppose, resist **7** against, get even, hit back, opposed, pay back, reverse **8** contrary, fountain, opposite **9** fight back, retaliate **11** conflicting **13** contradictory

counteract **4** curb, undo **5** check, fight **6** defeat, hinder, negate, offset, oppose, resist, thwart **7** assuage, nullify, repress **8** overcome, restrain **9** alleviate, frustrate, overpower **10** annihilate, contravene, neutralize

counteraction **8** negation **10** offsetting, opposition **13** contravention, nullification **14** neutralization

counteractive **7** adverse **8** inimical **10** corrective **11** unfavorable **12** antagonistic, neutralizing

counteractor **7** negator **9** nullifier, offsetter **11** neutralizer

counteragent **8** antidote **9** antitoxin **10** antipoison **11** double agent

counterbalance **5** amend, check **6** cancel, offset, redeem, set off **7** correct, rectify **8** atone for, equalize, make good, outweigh **9** make up for **10** balance out, neutralize, outbalance, recompense **12** compensation

counterfeit **4** copy, fake, sham **5** bogus, fraud, phony **6** ersatz, forged **7** feigned, forgery **8** spurious **9** facsimile, imitation, simulated **10** artificial, fraudulent, substitute **11** make-believe

Counterfeiters, The
author: **9** Andre Gide

countermand **4** void **5** annul, quash **6** cancel, recall, repeal, revoke **7** abolish, nullify, rescind, retract, reverse **8** abrogate, call back, disenact, override, overrule, set aside, withdraw, write off **12** disestablish

counterpart **4** copy, mate, twin **5** equal, match **6** double, fellow **8** parallel **9** duplicate **11** correlative **12** doppelganger **13** correspondent, spitting image

counterpoise **7** balance **9** stability **11** equilibrium

countersign **4** sign **7** certify, confirm, endorse **8** validate **9** authorize **11** corroborate **12** authenticate

countess
French: **8** comtesse
Italian: **8** contessa

countless **6** myriad, untold **7** endless **8** infinite **9** limitless, unlimited **10** numberless, unnumbered **11** innumerable, measureless **12** immeasurable, incalculable **13** multitudinous

Count of Monte Cristo, The
author: **14** Alexandre Dumas (pere)
character: **6** Albert, Haydee, Morrel **7** Fernand (Comte de Morcerf) **8** Danglars, Mercedes **9** Abbe Faria, Valentine, Villefort **10** Caderousse, Maximilian **12** Edmond Dantes
prison: **10** Chateau d'If

count on **6** expect **7** hope for **10** anticipate

countrified **5** rural **6** rustic **9** backwoods **15** unsophisticated

country **4** area, farm, land **5** realm, rural, state **6** nation, people, public, region, rustic, simple, sticks **7** boonies, farming, kingdom, natives, scenery, terrain **8** citizens, district, homeland, populace **9** backwoods, boondocks, community, landscape, territory **10** fatherland, native land, native soil, population, provincial, rural areas **11** farming area, hinterlands, inhabitants, nationality **12** commonwealth **15** unsophisticated

Country Cousin
author: **16** Louis Auchincloss

Country Girl, The
director: **12** George Seaton
based on play by: **13** Clifford Odets
cast: **10** Bing Crosby, Grace Kelly **11** Anthony Ross **13** William Holden
Oscar for: **7** actress (Kelly)

countryman **4** hick, rube **5** yokel **6** farmer, rustic **7** bumpkin, hayseed, peasant **8** landsman **10** clodhopper, compatriot, provincial

Country of the Pointed Firs, The
author: **15** Sarah Orne Jewett

country place **4** farm **5** manor **6** estate

countryside **6** sticks **7** boonies **9** backwater, backwoods, boondocks, rural area **10** hinterland

count up **3** add **5** tally, total **6** reckon **7** compute **9** calculate

count upon **6** expect **7** foresee **10** anticipate

coup **3** act **4** blow, deed, feat **6** stroke **12** master stroke

coup de grace **9** deathblow **11** mercy stroke **12** decisive blow **15** finishing stroke
literally: **11** blow of mercy

coup de main **14** surprise attack **17** sudden development
literally: **15** blow from the hand

coup d'etat **6** mutiny **8** uprising **9** overthrow, rebellion **10** revolution, subversion

coup de theatre **15** theatrical trick

coup d'oeil **11** quick glance
literally: **14** stroke of the eye

Couperin, Francois (Le Grand)
born: **5** Paris **6** France
composer of: **9** La Sultane, Les Fastes (de la grande et ancienne) **13** Concert Royaux **16** Apotheose de Lulli, Pieces de Clavecin **17** Lecons des Tenebres **20** Les Follies Francoises **31** Le Parnasse on l'Apotheose de Corelli

couple **3** duo, tie **4** bind, join, link, pair, yoke **5** hitch **6** fasten **7** connect, doublet, twosome **10** man and wife **11** man and woman **14** husband and wife

coupler **4** link, lock **5** clasp, hitch **6** buckle **8** fastener **9** fastening

Couples
author: **10** John Updike

coupling **5** clasp, hatch **6** hookup, yoking **7** joining, pairing **8** hitching **9** attaching, fastening **10** attachment, connecting, connection

courage **4** grit, guts, sand **5** nerve, pluck, spunk, valor **6** daring, mettle **7** bravery **8** boldness **9** derring-do, fortitude **11** intrepidity **12** fearlessness **13** dauntlessness **16** stoutheartedness

courageous **4** bold **5** brave, manly **6** dogged, heroic **7** dashing, doughty, gallant, valiant **8** fearless, intrepid, resolute, stalwart, unafraid, valorous **9** dauntless **10** chivalrous **11** indomitable **12** bold-spirited **13** stronghearted

Courbet, Jean Desire Gustave
born: **6** France, Ornans
artwork: **16** The Artist's Studio, The Stonebreakers **17** The Burial at Ornans **19** The Peasants of Flagey **25** Self-Portrait with a Black Dog

courier **4** mule **5** envoy **6** herald, legate, runner **7** Gabriel, mailman, Mercury, postman **8** emissary **9** go-between, harbinger, messenger, postrider **11** herald angel, internuncio

course **3** run, way **4** flow, gush, mode, path, pour, race, road **5** march, orbit, round, route, surge, track **6** action, circle, method, policy, stream **7** channel, circuit, classes, conduct, lessons, passage, subject **8** behavior, lectures, sequence **9** direction, procedure, unfolding **10** curriculum, racecourse, trajectory **11** development, progression

court **3** bar, woo **4** hall, quad, seek, suit, yard **5** bench, manor, plaza, staff, train **6** atrium, castle, homage, induce, invite, palace, pursue, wooing **7** address, attract, chateau, cortege, council, flatter, hearing, meeting, provoke, retinue, session **8** advisers, assembly, audience, blandish, fawn upon, pander to, respects, run after **9** entourage, following **10** attendants, quadrangle **13** solicitations

Courtenay, Tom
born: **4** Hull **7** England
roles: **9** Billy Liar **10** The Dresser **36** The Loneliness of the Long Distance Runner

courteous **4** kind, mild **5** civil **6** polite **7** refined, tactful **8** gracious, mannerly, well-bred **10** diplomatic, respectful, soft-spoken **11** considerate, well-behaved **12** well-mannered

courtesy **5** favor **7** manners, regards, respect **8** civility, kindness, respects **9** deference, gallantry, gentility **10** indulgence, politeness, refinement **11** cultivation **12** graciousness **13** consideration

courtier **4** beau **7** gallant **8** cavalier **9** attendant **18** gentleman-in-waiting

Courtier, The
author: **21** Baldassare Castiglione

Court Jester
director: **11** Melvin Frank **12** Norman Panama

cast: **9** Danny Kaye **11** Glynis Johns **13** Basil Rathbone **14** Angela Lansbury

courtly **5** suave **6** polite **7** elegant, gallant, genteel, refined, stately **8** debonair, decorous, highbred, ladylike, mannerly, polished **9** civilized, courteous, dignified **10** chivalrous **11** blue-blooded, gentlemanly **12** aristocratic **14** silk-stockinged

courtship **4** suit **6** wooing **14** keeping company

Courtship of Eddie's Father, The
character: **4** Tina **10** Tom Corbett **12** Eddie Corbett, Norman Tinker **13** Mrs Livingston
cast: **9** Bill Bixby **11** Brandon Cruz, James Komack **12** Miyoshi Umeki **15** Kristina Holland

Courtship of Miles Standish, The
author: **24** Henry Wadsworth Longfellow
character: **9** John Alden, Priscilla

courtyard **4** area, quad **9** curtilage, enclosure **10** quadrangle

cousin **7** kinsman **8** relation, relative **9** kinswoman

Cousin Bette
author: **14** Honore de Balzac
character: **6** Crevel **7** Adeline **10** Baron Hulot **11** Mme Marneffe **13** Hortense Hulot, Marechal Hulot **14** Lisbeth Fischer **23** Count Wenceslas Steinbock

Cousin Pons
author: **14** Honore de Balzac

Cousy, Bob
nickname: **12** Mr Basketball
sport: **10** basketball
position: **5** guard
team: **13** Boston Celtics

couturier, couturiere **8** designer **9** midinette **10** dressmaker, seamstress

cove **3** bay **5** inlet **6** lagoon **7** estuary

covenant **3** vow **4** bond, oath, pact **6** pledge, treaty **7** bargain, promise **8** contract **9** agreement **15** solemn agreement
Hebrew: **4** Brit **5** Berit, Brith **6** Berith

Covenant, The
author: **13** James Michener

cover ***see box***

cover **3** cap, lid, top **4** case, hide, hood, mask, veil, wrap **5** cloak, cross, guard, lay on, put on, quilt **6** asylum, clothe, defend, embody, enwrap, jacket, refuge, report, screen, sheath, shield, shroud, take in, tell of **7** binding, blanket, conceal, contain, defense, embrace, envelop, include, involve, obscure, overlay, protect, put over, secrete, sheathe, shelter, wrapper, write up **8** comprise, deal with, describe, disguise, envelope, pass over, traverse **9** chronicle, comforter, eiderdown, encompass, sanctuary **10** camouflage, comprehend, encasement, protection **11** concealment, hiding place

coverage **7** payment **8** analysis **9** indemnity, reporting **10** protection, publishing **11** description **12** broadcasting **13** reimbursement

covered **4** clad **6** hidden **7** aimed at, cloaked, guarded, insured **8** included, overlaid, screened **9** blanketed, concealed, protected, sheltered, traversed **10** overspread

covering **6** casing, sheath **7** wrapper **8** envelope, wrapping **11** descriptive, explanatory **12** introductory

coverlet **5** quilt, throw **6** afghan, spread **7** blanket **9** bedspread, comforter

Coverly, Sir Roger de
character in: **12** The Spectator
authors: **6** Steele **7** Addison

covert **6** hidden, secret, veiled **7** sub rosa, unknown **9** concealed, disguised **11** clandestine **13** surreptitious

cover up **4** hide, mask, veil **6** hush up **7** conceal **8** disguise, keep back, suppress, withhold **9** gloss over, whitewash

cover-up **4** mask **5** blind **6** screen **8** disguise **9** whitewash **11** concealment

covet **4** want **5** crave, fancy **6** desire **7** long for

covetous **6** greedy **7** craving, envious, jealous, lustful, selfish **8** desirous, grasping, yearning **9** mercenary, rapacious **10** avaricious

covetousness **4** envy **5** greed **7** avarice **8** jealousy, rapacity **10** greediness **12** graspingness **13** mercenariness

covey **4** bevy **5** flock, group **6** family

cow **4** beef **5** abash, bossy, bully, deter, scare **6** bovine, cattle, dismay **7** terrify **8** browbeat, bulldoze, frighten, threaten **9** terrorize **10** discourage, dishearten, intimidate, make cringe
young: **4** calf **6** heifer

coward **3** cad **5** sissy **6** craven **7** caitiff, chicken, dastard, milksop **8** poltroon **11** Milquetoast, mollycoddle, yellowbelly

Coward, Sir Noel
author of: **8** Hay Fever **9** Cavalcade **10** Sigh No More **12** Blithe Spirit, Private Lives **14** In Which We Serve, Nude with Violin **15** Design for Living

cowardliness **8** timidity **10** yellowness **12** irresolution **13** pusillanimity, spinelessness **18** chicken-heartedness

cowardly **5** shaky, timid **6** afraid, craven, yellow **7** anxious, fearful, gutless, nervous **8** timorous **9** dastardly, tremulous **10** frightened **11** lily-livered **12** apprehensive, fainthearted, uncourageous **13** pusillanimous, yellow-bellied **14** chicken-hearted

Cowardly Lion
character in: **13** The Wizard of Oz
author: **4** Baum

cowboy **6** drover, gaucho **7** vaquero **8** buckaroo **10** roughrider **12** broncobuster, cattle-herder

cowed **5** fazed **7** abashed, crushed, subdued **8** dismayed **11** intimidated **12** disconcerted **14** under one's thumb

cower **5** crawl, quail, toady **6** cringe, flinch, grovel, recoil, shrink **7** tremble, truckle **8** bootlick, draw back

cowl **4** cope, hood **5** cloak

Cowley, Malcolm
author of: **12** Exile's Return **16** A Second Flowering **27** And I Worked at the Writer's Trade **28** The Dream of the Golden Mountains

coworker **7** partner **8** teammate **9** associate, colleague **10** accomplice **11** confederate **12** collaborator

Cowper, William
author of: **7** The Task **11** The Cast-Away

Cowperwood, Frank
character in: **8** The Titan **12** The Financier
author: **7** Dreiser

coxcomb **3** fop **4** beau **5** dandy **8** popinjay

coy **3** shy **5** timid **6** demure, modest **7** bashful, prudish **8** blushing, sheepish, skittish, timorous **9** diffident, kittenish, shrinking **10** coquettish, overmodest

Coyote State
nickname of: **11** South Dakota

cozen **3** con, gyp **4** bilk, coax, dupe, gull, rook **5** cheat, trick **6** fleece **7** deceive, defraud, swindle, wheedle **9** bamboozle, victimize

cozener **4** fake **5** cheat, fraud, quack **6** con man **8** deceiver, swindler **9** charlatan, trickster **10** mountebank **13** confidence man

coziness **6** warmth **7** comfort **8** intimacy, snugness **11** contentment

cozy **4** easy, snug **5** comfy, homey **7** restful **8** homelike, relaxing **9** gemutlich, simpatico **11** comfortable **16** snug as a bug in a rug
French: **6** intime

Cozzens, James Gould
author of: **12** Guard of Honor **15** By Love Possessed

CPA **7** auditor **10** accountant, bookkeeper **25** certified public accountant

crab **4** carp **5** crank, gripe, grump **6** grouch, grouse **8** complain, sourball **9** shellfish **10** crustacean, curmudgeon
constellation of: **6** Cancer

Crabbe, Buster
real name: **20** Clarence Linden Crabbe
nickname: **16** King of the Serials
born: **9** Oakland CA
roles: **6** Tarzan **10** Buck Rogers **11** Flash Gordon **15** King of the Jungle

crabbed **4** mean, sour **6** cranky, morose **7** grouchy, peevish, pinched **8** churlish, spiteful **9** irascible, irritable, rancorous

crabby **5** cross, testy **6** cranky, touchy **7** grouchy, peevish **8** petulant, snappish **9** irritable **10** ill-humored, out of sorts **11** ill-tempered **12** cantankerous

crack **3** gag, jab, pop **4** chip, clap, gash, gibe, jest, joke, quip, rent, rift, slit, snap **5** break, burst, cleft, split, taunt **6** cleave, insult, report **7** crackle, crevice, fissure, give way, rupture, thunder **8** fracture, splinter **9** break down, wisecrack, witticism **10** go to pieces

cracked **3** mad **4** daft, nuts **5** crazy, nutty **6** crazed, insane **8** demented, deranged, unhinged **10** unbalanced **12** mad as a hatter **13** off one's rocker, out of one's head **14** off one's trolley **15** mad as a March hare

cracker **5** snack, wafer **7** biscuit, redneck **10** party favor **11** backsettler **12** backwoodsman

crackerjack **2** A-1 **3** ace **4** a-one, fine **5** super **6** superb, tip-top **8** splendid, terrific **9** excellent, fantastic, first-rate, wonderful **10** first-class

Cracker State
nickname of: **7** Georgia

crackle **4** snap **5** craze, crink **9** crepitate

crackpot **3** nut, odd **4** fool, kook **5** balmy, crank, flake, freak, kinky, kooky, loony, nutty, wacko **6** freaky, insane, looney, madman, maniac, weirdo **7** dingbat, foolish, lunatic, oddball **9** character, eccentric, screwball **11** impractical

cracksman **4** yegg **7** burglar **10** cat burglar **14** second-story man

crackup **5** crash, smash, split, wreck **6** mishap, pileup **7** breakup, debacle, smashup **8** accident, calamity, collapse, disaster **9** breakdown, collision, splitting **10** exhaustion, shellshock **11** catastrophe, prostration **14** disintegration

cradle **3** hug **4** crib, font, rock **6** cuddle, enfold, origin, source, spring **7** nursery, snuggle **8** bassinet, fountain **10** birthplace, wellspring **12** fountainhead

craft **3** art **4** boat, ruse, ship, wile **5** guile, knack, plane, skill, trade **6** deceit, vessel **7** ability, calling, cunning, know-how, mastery, perfidy, pursuit **8** airplane, artifice, business, commerce, deftness, fineness, industry, intrigue, trickery, vocation **9** adeptness, chicanery, deception, duplicity, expertise, technique **10** adroitness, artfulness, competency, craftiness, employment, expertness, handicraft, occupation **11** proficiency

craftiness **4** ruse, wile **5** guile **7** cunning, slyness **8** artifice, foxiness, scheming, trickery, wiliness **9** chicanery **10** artfulness **11** machination

craftsman **4** hand **5** smith **6** worker, wright **7** artisan **8** mechanic

crafty **3** sly **4** foxy, wily **5** canny, sharp **6** artful, astute, shifty, shrewd, tricky **7** cunning, devious **8** guileful, plotting, scheming **9** deceitful, deceptive, designing, dishonest, underhand, unethical **10** intriguing, perfidious, suspicious **11** calculating

crag **3** tor **4** rock **5** bluff, cliff **9** precipice

craggy **5** rocky, rough, sheer, steep, stony **6** abrupt, jagged, ragged, rugged, snaggy **7** scraggy **8** bouldery **9** rockbound **10** rock-ribbed **11** precipitous

Crain, Jeanne
born: **9** Barstow CA
roles: **5** Pinky **6** Margie **9** State Fair **17** Cheaper by the Dozen **19** A Letter to Three Wives

cram **3** jam **4** fill, pack **5** crowd, force, grind, press, stuff **7** congest, squeeze **8** compress **9** overcrowd, study hard

Cram, Ralph
architect of: **17** US Military Academy (West Point) **29** Cathedral of Saint John the Divine (NYC)
style: **13** Gothic Revival

crammed **4** full **6** filled, packed **7** studied, stuffed **9** jam-packed **11** overflowing, well-stocked

cramp **4** pang **5** block, check, crick, limit, spasm **6** hamper, hinder, stitch, stymie, thwart **7** prevent, seizure **8** handicap, obstruct, restrain, restrict **9** frustrate **12** charley horse

cramped **5** close, tight **6** narrow **7** compact, pinched **8** confined **10** compressed, restrained, restricted

Cranach, Lucas (Lukas) (the Elder)
born: **7** Kronach, Germany
artwork: **6** Luther **10** Adam and Eve **11** Crucifixion **14** Apollo and Diana

15 Rest on the Flight
18 The Judgment of Paris
22 Duke and Duchess of Saxony

Cranaus
king of: 6 Athens, Attica
wife: 6 Pedias
daughter: 6 Atthis, Cranae
renamed Athens: 6 Attica

cranberry 9 Vaccinium
19 Vaccinium vitis-idaea
20 Vaccinium macrocarpon
varieties: 3 bog **4** rock, tree **5** large, small **8** American, European, highbush, mountain **10** Australian

crane 4 bird, boom **5** davit, heron **7** derrick **10** wading bird
group of: 5 sedge, siege
constellation of: 4 Grus

Crane, Bob
born: 11 Waterbury CT
roles: 12 Colonel Hogan, Hogan's Heroes

Crane, Hart
author of: 9 The Bridge
14 White Buildings

Crane, Ichabod
character in: 23 The Legend of Sleepy Hollow
author: 6 Irving

Crane, Roy
creator/artist of: 9 Buz Sawyer, Wash Tubbs **11** Captain Easy

Crane, Stephen
author of: 11 The Open Boat **20** The Red Badge of Courage **23** Maggie: A Girl of the Streets **24** The Bride Comes to Yellow Sky

Cranford
author: 10 Mrs Gaskell

cranium 4 head **5** skull **6** noggin **8** brain box, brainpan **9** brain case

crank 4 turn, whim **5** brace, winch **6** grouch, handle **7** fanatic **8** crotchet **9** eccentric

cranky 5 cross, testy **6** crabby, touchy **7** bearish, grouchy, peevish, waspish **8** captious, petulant **9** crotchety, irascible, splenetic **10** ill-humored, out of sorts **11** ill-tempered **12** cantankerous

cranny 3 gap **4** nook, slit **5** break, chink, cleft, crack, notch, split **7** crevice, fissure **8** cleavage

crash 3 din **4** bang, boom, bump, dash, ruin **5** crack, slump, smash, wreck **6** hurtle, invade, pileup, plunge, racket, slip in, topple, tumble **7** bumping, clangor, clatter, collide, crackup, decline, failure, hitting, intrude, setback, shatter, smashup, sneak in **8** accident, smashing, toppling, tumbling **9** collision, recession **10** bankruptcy, depression, shattering

crass 5 crude, cruel, gross **6** coarse, oafish, vulgar **7** boorish **8** uncaring **9** inelegant, unfeeling, unrefined **10** unpolished **11** hardhearted, insensitive **13** unsympathetic

crassness 9 crudeness, grossness, vulgarity **10** coarseness, inelegance, oafishness **11** boorishness **13** insensitivity

Crataeis
daughter: 6 Scylia

Cratchit, Bob
character in: 15 A Christmas Carol
author: 7 Dickens

crate 3 box, car **4** auto, case, pack **5** plane **6** jalopy, pallet **8** airplane **9** container

crater 3 pit **4** hole **6** cavity **10** depression

Cratus
origin: 5 Greek
personifies: 8 strength

cravat 3 tie **5** ascot, scarf, stock **7** necktie **11** neckerchief

crave 4 need, want **5** covet **6** desire **7** hope for, long for, pine for, require, sigh for, wish for **8** yearn for **9** hunger for, lust after, thirst for **11** hanker after, have a yen for **13** have a fancy for

craven 3 low **4** base **5** timid **6** scared, yellow **7** fearful, lowdown **8** cowardly, timorous **9** dastardly **10** frightened **11** lily-livered **12** mean-spirited **13** pusillanimous **14** chicken-hearted

craving 3 yen **4** need **6** desire, hunger, thirst **7** longing **9** hankering

Crawford, Broderick
real name: 24 William Broderick Crawford
wife: 11 Jan Sterling
born: 14 Philadelphia PA
roles: 6 The Mob **10** The Interns **12** Of Mice and Men **13** Born Yesterday, Highway Patrol **14** All the King's Men (Oscar)

Crawford, Henry
character in: 13 Mansfield Park
author: 6 Austen

Crawford, Joan
real name: 17 Lucille Fay Le Sueur
husband: 12 Franchot Tone **18** Douglas Fairbanks Jr
daughter: 6 Cheryl **9** Christina
born: 12 San Antonio TX
biography: 13 Mommie Dearest
roles: 8 The Women **10** Grand Hotel **13** Mildred Pierce (Oscar) **26** What Ever Happened to Baby Jane

crawl 4 drag, inch, poke, worm **5** creep, mosey **6** squirm, wiggle, writhe **7** slither, wriggle

Crawley, Rawdon
character in: 10 Vanity Fair
author: 9 Thackeray

crayon 5 chalk, draft **6** pastel, pencil, sketch **7** drawing **8** charcoal

craze 3 fad **4** rage **5** furor, mania **6** dement **7** derange, passion, unhinge **11** infatuation

crazed 3 mad **6** insane **7** cracked, lunatic **8** demented, deranged

crazy 3 mad, odd **4** avid, daft, gaga, keen, nuts, wild **5** nutty, rabid, silly, weird **6** absurd, far-out, insane, stupid, unwise **7** berserk, bizarre, cracked, excited, foolish, frantic, idiotic, strange, touched, unusual, zealous **8** demented, deranged, maniacal, peculiar, uncommon, unhinged **9** fanatical, foolhardy, imprudent, laughable, senseless **10** hysterical, infatuated, outrageous, passionate, ridiculous, unbalanced **11** smitten with **12** enthusiastic, mad as a hatter **13** out of one's head **15** mad as a March hare

creak 4 rasp **5** grate, grind **6** scrape, screak, squeak **7** screech

Creakle
character in: 16 David Copperfield
author: 7 Dickens

cream 3 top **4** beat, best, drub **5** elite **6** choice, flower **7** the pick, trounce **8** greatest, off-white **14** creme de la creme

Cream, Arnold Raymond
real name of: 10 Joe Walcott

cream of the cream
French: 14 creme de la creme

Cream of the Jest, The
author: 17 James Branch Cabell

creamy 5 thick, foamy **6** smooth, yellow **8** emulsive

crease **4** fold **5** crimp, pleat, ridge **6** furrow, pucker, ruffle, rumple **7** crimple, crinkle, wrinkle **9** corrugate **11** corrugation

create **4** form, make, mold **5** cause, erect, found, set up **6** design, devise, invent **7** appoint, concoct, develop, fashion **8** conceive, contrive, organize **9** construct, establish, fabricate, formulate, institute, originate

creation **5** world **6** making, nature **8** building, devising, erection, founding **9** all things, formation, handiwork, invention **10** brainchild, conception, concoction, fashioning, production **11** development, fabrication, institution, origination **12** construction **13** establishment

Creation
author: **9** Gore Vidal

creative **8** fanciful, original **9** ingenious, inventive **11** imaginative, resourceful

creator **5** maker **6** author, father, framer **7** founder **8** begetter, designer, inventor, producer **9** architect, generator, initiator **10** originator

creature **3** man **4** bird, fish **5** beast, human **6** animal, insect, mammal, mortal, person **7** critter, reptile **9** earthling, quadruped **10** individual, vertebrate **12** invertebrate

credence **5** faith, trust **6** belief, credit **8** reliance **9** certainty, certitude **10** confidence **11** reliability **13** believability **14** acceptableness, dependableness **15** trustworthiness

credentials **6** permit **7** diploma, license, voucher **9** reference **11** certificate, testimonial **13** authorization

credenza **5** shelf, table **6** buffet **8** bookcase **9** sideboard

credible **6** likely **7** tenable **8** possible, probable, reliable **9** plausible, thinkable **10** believable, dependable, imaginable, reasonable **11** conceivable, trustworthy

credit **3** buy **4** time **5** glory, honor, trust **6** accept, assign, esteem, rely on **7** acclaim, ascribe, believe, fall for, swallow **9** allowance, attribute, recognize **10** prepayment **11** acknowledge, recognition **12** commendation **14** acknowledgment

creditable **6** worthy **8** laudable **9** admirable, estimable, reputable **11** commendable, meritorious, respectable **12** praiseworthy

credo **4** code, rule **5** maxim, motto, tenet **8** doctrine **10** philosophy

credulous **5** naive **8** gullible, trusting **9** believing **12** overtrustful, unsuspecting, unsuspicious **13** unquestioning **15** unsophisticated

Cree
language family: **9** Algonkian **10** Algonquian
tribe: **10** Plains Cree **13** Woodlands Cree
location: **6** Canada **8** Manitoba
related to: **8** Chippewa

creed **5** dogma **6** belief, canons, gospel **8** doctrine

creek **3** run **4** rill **5** brook **6** branch, spring, stream **7** freshet, rivulet **10** millstream, small river

Creek
language family: **10** Muskhogean
location: **7** Alabama, Florida, Georgia **11** Mississippi
leader: **8** Red Eagle **15** William McIntosh **20** Alexander McGillivray

Creek Mary's Blood
author: **8** Dee Brown

creep **4** inch, worm **5** crawl, sneak, steal **6** dawdle, squirm, writhe **7** slither, wriggle

creeper **3** ivy **4** bird, iron, vine, worm **5** snake **7** climber, crawler, grapnel, trailer

creepy **4** eery **5** eerie, scary **6** crawly, spooky, uneasy **12** apprehensive

cremate **4** burn, char, fire, sear **5** roast **6** ignite, kindle, scorch **8** enkindle **10** incinerate **11** conflagrate **17** consume with flames

creme de banane
type: **7** liqueur
flavor: **6** banana
color: **6** yellow

creme de cacao
type: **6** brandy **7** liqueur
origin: **6** France
flavor: **9** chocolate
color: **5** brown, white
drink: **11** Fifth Avenue
with rum: **6** Panama
with tequila: **8** Toreador
with vodka: **9** Ninotchka **11** Russian Bear **12** Velvet Hammer, White Russian

creme de cassis
type: **7** liqueur
origin: **6** France **8** Burgundy
flavor: **12** black currant
with gin: **8** Parisian

creme de fraise
type: **7** liqueur
flavor: **10** strawberry

creme de framboise
type: **7** liqueur
flavor: **9** raspberry

creme de la creme **3** top **4** best **5** cream, elite **6** choice, flower **8** choicest, very best **12** choicest part **15** cream of the cream

creme de menthe
type: **7** liqueur
flavor: **4** mint
color: **5** green, white
with brandy: **7** Stinger
with cream: **11** Grasshopper
with gin: **6** Caruso, Virgin

creme de noyau
type: **7** liqueur
flavor: **6** almond

creme de violette
type: **7** liqueur
flavor: **7** violets
color: **8** lavender

creme Yvette
type: **7** liqueur
origin: **12** United States
flavor: **7** violets
with gin: **9** Union Jack

Crenna, Richard
born: **12** Los Angeles CA
roles: **9** Death Ship **13** Our Miss Brooks, The Real McCoys

Creole **6** patois **7** criollo, dialect, Haitian **10** West Indian

Creole State
nickname of: **9** Louisiana

Creon
king of: **6** Thebes **7** Corinth
father: **9** Lycaethus, Menoeceus
sister: **7** Jocasta
daughter: **6** Creusa, Glauce
nephew: **7** Oedipus **8** Eteocles **9** Polynices
niece: **6** Ismene **8** Antigone
defeated: **18** Seven against Thebes

crescendo
music: **22** gradually getting louder
abbreviation: **5** cresc

crescent **3** arc, bow **4** arch **5** curve **8** half-moon

crescit eundo **15** it grows as it goes
motto of: **9** New Mexico

Cresius
epithet of: **8** Dionysus
means: **6** Cretan

Cresphontes
member of: **8** Heraclid

father: **12** Aristomachus
brother: **7** Temenus **11** Polyphontes
wife: **6** Merope
father-in-law: **8** Cypselus
son: **7** Aepytus
controlled: **8** Messenia
invaded: **12** Peloponnesus

Cressida
also: **8** Criseyde **9** Crisseyde
based on characters of: **7** Bryseis **8** Chryseis
setting: **9** Trojan War
loved: **7** Troilus
deserted Troilus for: **8** Diomedes

crest **3** tip, top **4** apex, arms, comb, peak, tuft **5** crown, plume **6** emblem, height, summit **7** topknot **8** pinnacle **10** coat of arms, escutcheon

crestfallen **8** dejected, downcast **9** depressed, woebegone **10** despondent, dispirited **11** discouraged, downhearted, low-spirited **12** disappointed, disheartened

Creta
daughter: **8** Pasiphae

Cretaceous period
dinosaur from: **9** Euhelopus, Iguanodon **10** Allosaurus, Antrodemus **11** Anatosaurus, Ankylsaurus, Deinonychus, Gorgosaurus, Triceratops **12** Lambeosaurus, Ornithomimus **13** Albertosaurus, Corythosaurus, Hypselosaurus, Hypsilophodon, Palaeoscincus, Protoceratops, Struthiomimus, Styracosaurus, Tyrannosaurus **14** Psittacosaurus, Thescelosaurus **15** Parasaurolophus, Procheneosaurus

Cretan bull
also: **15** Marathonian bull
form: **4** bull
son: **8** Minotaur
captured on: **5** Crete
captured by: **8** Hercules
roamed: **8** Marathon
recaptured by: **7** Theseus

Cretan Mythology
goddess of fishermen/hunters/sailors: **11** Britomartis
corresponds to Greek: **7** Artemis
goddess of the sea: **8** Dictynna
maze: **9** labyrinth
monster: **8** Minotaur

Crete *see box*

Cretheis
husband: **7** Acastus
killed by: **6** Peleus

Cretheus
founder of: **6** Iolcus
father: **6** Aeolus
mother: **7** Enarete
brother: **9** Salmoneus
wife: **4** Tyro
son: **5** Aeson **6** Pheres **8** Amythaon
companion: **6** Aeneas

Creusa
also: **6** Glauce
father: **5** Creon, Priam **8** Cychreus **10** Erechtheus
mother: **6** Hecuba
husband: **6** Aeneas **7** Telamon
son: **3** Ion **8** Ascanius
bride of: **5** Jason
killed by: **5** magic, Medea

crevasse **3** gap **4** rift **5** abyss, break, chasm, cleft, gorge, gulch, gully, split **6** breach, divide **7** fissure

crevice **4** rent, rift, slit **5** chasm, cleft, crack, split **6** breach **7** fissure **8** crevasse, fracture

crew **3** mob **4** band, body, herd, mass, pack, team **5** corps, force, group, hands, horde, party, squad, troop **6** seamen, throng **7** company, sailors **8** mariners **9** multitude, seafarers **10** assemblage, complement

crib **3** bed, bin, cot, hut, key **4** pony **5** cheat, shack, stall, steal **6** creche, manger **7** purloin **8** bassinet **10** plagiarize, plagiarism

cribbage
score kept on: **5** board
points/game: **8** sixty-one
third hand (of discards) called: **4** crib

Crich, Gerald
character in: **11** Women in Love
author: **8** Lawrence

Crichton, Michael
author of: **5** Congo **14** The Terminal Man **18** The Andromeda Strain **20** The Great Train Robbery

cricket *see box*

cricket
variety: **4** bush, cave, sand, tree **5** camel, field, house **6** ground **9** Jerusalem, pygmy mole

Cries and Whispers
director: **12** Ingmar Bergman
cast: **10** Liv Ullmann **12** Ingrid Thulin **16** Harriet Andersson

crime **3** sin **4** tort **5** wrong **6** felony **7** misdeed, offense, outrage **8** foul play, iniquity, villainy **10** misconduct, wrongdoing **11** abomination, lawbreaking, malfeasance, misdemeanor **13** transgression

Crime and Punishment
author: **16** Fyodor Dostoevsky
character: **5** Sonya **6** Dounia **7** Porfiry **9** Razumihin **11** Raskolnikov

Crete
other name: **5** Kriti **6** Candia
capital/largest city: **5** Canea **8** Iraklion
others: **3** Hag **4** Lato **5** Khora, Sitia, Zakro **6** Anoyia, Candia, Khania, Lisamo, Mallia, Meleme, Retimo **7** Malerni **8** Kastelli, Nikolaos, Sphakion **9** Heraclion, Heraklion, Rethymnon, Tympakion **11** Palaiophora
government: **15** belongs to Greece
monetary unit: **7** drachma
mountain: **3** Ida **5** Dikte, Phino **6** Juktas **7** Lasithi, Madaras **8** Leuka Ori, Theodore, Thriphte **9** Psiloriti
highest point: **3** Ida
sea: **5** Crete **6** Aegean **13** Mediterranean
physical feature:
bay: **4** Suda **5** Kanca **6** Kisamo, Mesara
cape: **4** Buza **5** Liano **6** Salome, Sidero, Spatha **7** Stavros **8** Lithinon, Sidheros
gulf: **6** Khania **9** Merabello
people: **7** Candiot, Cretans, Minoans **9** Caphtorim, Sphakiots **11** Philistines
artist: **7** El Greco
author: **11** Kazantzakis
conqueror: **8** Metellus
king: **5** Minos
language: **5** Greek **6** Minoan **7** Linear A, Linear B
religion: **14** Greek Orthodoxy
place:
ruins: **15** Palace at Knossos

cricket
players/team: **6** eleven
equipment: **3** bat **4** bail, ball **5** stump **6** wicket
position: **5** gully, mid on, slops **6** bowler, long on, mid off **7** batsman, fine leg, long off **8** third man **9** mid wicket, square leg **10** cover point, extra cover, silly mid on **11** silly mid off **12** wicket keeper **13** deep mid wicket **16** backward short leg
lines: **7** creases
period of play: **4** over **7** innings
championship game: **9** test match
England/Australia match: **8** the Ashes

criminal **4** hood **5** crook, felon, wrong **6** guilty, outlaw **7** crooked, culprit, illegal, illicit, lawless **8** culpable, offender, unlawful, wasteful **9** felonious, senseless, wrongdoer **10** abominable, delinquent, indictable, lawbreaker, malefactor, outrageous, villainous **11** blameworthy, disgraceful, lawbreaking **12** transgressor

crimp **4** curl, fold, kink, wave **5** clamp, flute, frill, frizz **7** crinkle, frizzle, wrinkle **8** obstacle

crimple **4** curl **6** pucker **7** crinkle, crumple, wrinkle **9** corrugate

crimson **3** red **5** blush, flush **6** redden **7** carmine, scarlet

cringe **4** duck **5** cower, dodge, quail, toady **6** blench, flinch, grovel, recoil, shrink **7** truckle

cringing **6** abject **7** fawning, ignoble, servile, wincing **8** cowering, toadying **9** flinching, groveling, shrinking, sniveling

crinkle **5** crush **6** rumple, rustle **7** crumple, wrinkle

crinkly **4** wavy **5** curly, kinky **6** crimpy, frizzy **7** cockled, crimped, crimply, puckery, ruffled, rumpled, twisted, wrinkly **8** crimpled, frizzled, puckered, wrinkled **9** shriveled

crinoline **4** hoop **5** skirt **9** hoopskirt, petticoat **10** underskirt

Criophorus
epithet of: **6** Hermes
means: **9** ram bearer

cripple **4** gimp, halt, harm, maim, stop **6** damage, impair **7** disable **8** make lame, paralyze **9** hamstring **10** debilitate, inactivate **12** incapacitate

Crises of the Republic
author: **12** Hannah Arendt

crisis **6** climax **9** emergency

Crisis, The
author: **23** Winston Spencer Churchill

crisp **5** brisk, fresh, nippy, sharp, terse, witty **6** candid, chilly, crispy, lively, snappy **7** bracing, brittle, crunchy, pointed **8** incisive **9** energetic, sparkling, vivacious **10** refreshing **12** invigorating

Crisparkle, Mr
character in: **22** The Mystery of Edwin Drood
author: **7** Dickens

crisscross **4** awry **5** cross **8** confused, traverse

Crisseyde *see* **8** Cressida

Cristillo, Louis Francis
real name of: **11** Lou Costello

criterion **3** law **4** norm, rule **5** gauge, model **7** example, measure **8** standard **9** guidepost, precedent, principle, yardstick **10** touchstone

critic **5** judge, mavin, scold **6** carper, censor, expert, rapper **7** analyst, arbiter, knocker, reviler **8** attacker, vilifier, virtuoso **9** authority, backbiter, detractor, evaluator **10** antagonist, criticizer **11** cognoscente, commentator, connoisseur, faultfinder

Critic, The
author: **23** Richard Brinsley Sheridan

critical **5** fussy, grave, hairy, picky, risky, vital **6** urgent **7** carping, crucial, finicky, judging, nagging, serious **8** caviling, decisive, perilous, pressing **9** dangerous, harrowing, hazardous, judicious, momentous, sensitive **10** analytical, censorious, derogatory, diagnostic, nitpicking, precarious **11** disparaging **12** disapproving, faultfinding **13** hairsplitting, perspicacious **14** discriminating

critical situation **3** jam **4** mess **6** crisis, pickle **7** straits, trouble **8** hot water **9** deep water **10** difficulty **11** predicament

critical stage **6** climax, crisis **9** emergency

critical success
French: **13** succes d'estime

criticism **4** fire, flak, slam **5** blame, knock **6** review **7** censure, comment **8** analysis, critique, judgment **9** aspersion, stricture **10** commentary, evaluation **12** faultfinding

criticize **4** carp, fuss, pick **5** cavil, nag at **7** censure, nitpick, reprove **8** denounce, reproach **9** disparage

critique **6** review **8** analysis

Critique of Pure Reason
author: **12** Immanuel Kant

Crna Gora *see* **10** Montenegro

croak **3** caw, die **4** kill, moan, roup **7** grumble, kick off **8** complain, harsh cry **13** kick the bucket

Crocetti, Dino Paul
real name of: **10** Dean Martin

crocodile **4** croc **6** cayman, gavial, lizard **7** reptile, asurian

crock **3** jar, pot **9** container

crockery **5** china **6** dishes, plates **7** pottery **8** clayware **9** chinaware, tableware **11** ceramic ware, earthenware **14** cups and saucers

Crock of Gold
author: **13** James Stephens

crocus
varieties: **4** fall, wild **5** dutch **6** autumn, scotch **7** Chilean, saffron **8** tropical **9** celandine **12** iris-flowered

Crocus
form: **5** youth
changed into: **12** saffron plant

Crome Yellow
author: **12** Aldous Huxley

Crommyonian sow
also: **5** Phaea
killed by: **7** Theseus

Cromwell, Oliver
also: **13** Lord Protector
served in: **15** English Civil War
fought against: **8** Charles I **9** Cavaliers
fought for: **10** Parliament, Roundheads
regiment: **9** Ironsides
battle: **6** Naseby, Oxford **7** Preston **11** Marston Moor

crone **3** hag **5** witch **6** beldam **7** beldame, old wife

Cronia
festival in: **6** Athens

Cronus
also: **6** Cronos, Kronos
form: **5** Titan
father: **6** Uranus
mother: **4** Gaea
sister: **4** Rhea
wife: **4** Rhea
son: **4** Zeus **5** Hades **8** Poseidon
daughter: **4** Hera **6** Hestia **7** Demeter
corresponds to: **6** Saturn

crony **3** pal **4** ally, chum, mate **5** buddy **6** bunkie, cohort, friend **7** comrade **8** bunkmate, intimate, shipmate, sidekick **9** accessory, associate, companion, old friend **10** accomplice, bosom buddy **11** confederate **12** acquaintance, collaborator **13** coconspirator

Cronyn, Hume
wife: **12** Jessica Tandy
born: **6** London **7** Canada, Ontario
roles: **13** The Fourposter **17** Phantom of the Opera **19** Sunrise at Campobello

crook **3** arc, bow **4** bend, hook, thug, turn **5** angle, cheat, curve, knave, thief, twist **6** bandit, outlaw, robber **7** burglar **8** criminal, swindler **9** curvature, embezzler

crooked **4** awry, bent, wily **5** askew, bowed, shady **6** crafty, curved, hooked, shifty, sneaky, spiral, warped, zigzag **7** corrupt, sinuous, twisted, winding **8** criminal, deformed, tortuous, twisting, unlawful **9** deceitful, deceptive, dishonest, distorted, nefarious, unethical **10** fraudulent, meandering, perfidious, serpentine **11** underhanded **12** dishonorable, unscrupulous

crookedness **10** dishonesty **11** deviousness **13** deceitfulness, double-dealing

Crookes, William
nationality: **7** British
invented: **8** thallium **10** radiometer **11** Crookes tube

croon **3** hum **4** sing **6** murmur, warble

crop **3** bob, cut, lop **4** clip, snip, trim **5** prune, shear, yield **6** growth **7** harvest, reaping **8** cut short, gleaning **9** gathering **10** production

crop-raising **7** farming, tillage **11** agriculture **12** agribusiness, truck farming **15** market gardening

crop up **5** arise, ensue, occur **6** appear **7** develop, surface **11** come to light

croquet
equipment: **4** hoop **6** mallet, wicket
variation: **5** roque
term: **5** rover

Crosby, Bing
real name: **17** Harry Lillis Crosby
partner: **7** Bob Hope **10** Hedy Lamarr **13** Dorothy Lamour
nickname: **8** Der Bingle
wife: **8** Dixie Lee **12** Kathryn Grant
born: **8** Tacoma WA
roles: **10** Going My Way (Oscar), Holiday Inn **11** High Society **14** The Country Girl, White Christmas **17** The Bells of St Mary's **22** Christmas in Connecticut
Road to: **3** Rio **4** Bali **7** Morocco **8** Hong Kong, Zanzibar **9** Singapore

cross **3** mad, mix **4** crux, ford, meet, rood **5** angry, blend, erase, gruff, surly, testy, trial **6** burden, cancel, cranky, delete, go over, hybrid, ordeal, shirty, touchy **7** amalgam, annoyed, athwart, grouchy, oblique, peevish, trouble, waspish **8** captious, choleric, churlish, contrary, crucifix, distress, intermix, pass over, petulant, snappish, traverse **9** adversity, crotchety, half-breed, hybridize, intersect, irascible, irritable, querulous, splenetic, strike out, suffering **10** affliction, difficulty, ill-humored, interbreed, misfortune, obliterate, out of sorts, transverse **11** combination, ill-tempered, intractable, tribulation **12** cantankerous, disagreeable, intersecting

crossbar **3** bar **4** spar **5** sprit **6** stripe

crossbreed **3** mix **8** intermix **9** hybridize **10** interbreed

cross-fertilize **9** hybridize

crossing **4** pass **7** mixture, passage **8** blocking, opposing, traverse **9** thwarting **10** traversing **11** hybridizing, intersection **13** hybridization

cross over **4** span **5** cross **6** bridge **8** traverse

crosspiece **3** bar **4** spar **5** sprit

cross-pollinate **9** hybridize

crossroad **12** intersection, turning point

cross swords **5** clash, fight **6** battle, combat, tussle **7** contend, contest **8** skirmish

crossways **7** athwart **12** transversely

crosswise **6** across **7** athwart **8** sideways, traverse **10** transverse

crotchet **4** bent, whim **5** habit, quirk, trait **6** foible, hang-up, oddity, vagary, whimsy **7** caprice **8** quiddity **9** mannerism **10** erraticism **11** peculiarity **12** eccentricity, idiosyncrasy, irregularity **14** characteristic

crotchety **3** odd **5** fussy **6** cranky **7** erratic, grouchy **8** contrary, peculiar **9** eccentric

Crotopus
king of: **5** Argos
daughter: **8** Psamathe
killed: **8** Psamathe

Crotus
father: **3** Pan
skilled in: **7** archery
companion of: **5** Muses

crouch **4** bend, duck **5** cower, squat, stoop **6** cringe, recoil, shrink **9** hunch over **10** hunker down **11** scrooch down, scrunch down

crow **3** daw, jay, kae **4** blow, brag, rook **5** boast, crake, exult, gloat, raven, strut, vaunt **6** cackle, chough, corbie, magpie **7** corvine, jackdaw, rejoice, swagger, triumph, trumpet **8** jubilate **14** cock-a-doodle-doo
group of: **6** murder

Crow
constellation of: **6** Corvus

Crow
language family: **6** Siouan
tribe: **9** River Crow **12** Mountain Crow
location: **7** Montana, Wyoming
related to: **7** Hidatsa

crowbar **3** bar, pry **5** jimmy, lever

crowd **3** jam, mob, set **4** cram, gang, herd, host, mass, push **5** crush, flock, group, horde, press, shove, surge, swarm **6** circle, claque, clique, gather, huddle, legion, throng **7** cluster, coterie, elbow in, squeeze **8** assemble **9** gathering, multitude **10** assemblage, congregate **11** concentrate **12** congregation

Crowd, The
director: **9** King Vidor
cast: **9** Bert Roach **11** James

Murray **15** Eleanor Boardman

crowded **4** full **6** filled, jammed, mobbed, packed **7** crammed, teeming **8** swarming, thronged **9** congested, jampacked **11** overflowing

Crowders
character in: 8 Hudibras
author: 6 Butler

crowd out **8** displace **9** overwhelm

crown **3** cap, top **4** acme, apex, head, pate, peak **5** crest, tiara **6** climax, diadem, noggin, noodle, summit, top off, wreath, zenith **7** chaplet, circlet, coronet, fulfill, garland, perfect, royalty **8** complete, monarchy, pinnacle, round out **11** sovereignty

Crowne, Lenina
character in: 13 Brave New World
author: 6 Huxley

crowning point **3** cap, tip **4** apex, peak **6** summit, vertex, zenith **8** pinnacle

crown of thorns **4** bane **5** cross **6** burden, ordeal **7** torment **8** vexation **10** affliction **11** tribulation

crow over **5** gloat **9** brag about **10** boast about

crucial **5** grave **6** knotty, urgent **7** serious, weighty **8** critical, decisive, pressing **9** essential, important, momentous **11** determining, significant

Crucible, The
author: 12 Arthur Miller

crude **3** raw **5** crass, gross, rough **6** coarse, vulgar **7** obscene, sketchy, uncouth **9** imperfect, tasteless, unrefined **10** incomplete, unfinished, unpolished, unprepared **11** uncompleted, undeveloped, unprocessed

crudeness **7** rawness **8** bad taste **9** crassness, grossness, obscenity, vulgarity **10** coarseness, indelicacy **13** tastelessness

cruel **6** brutal, savage **7** inhuman, vicious **8** inhumane, pitiless, ruthless, sadistic **9** heartless, merciless, unfeeling **10** unmerciful **11** cold-blooded, hardhearted, remorseless **15** uncompassionate

cruelty **6** sadism **8** ferocity, savagery **9** barbarity, brutality **10** bestiality, inhumanity **11** viciousness **12** ruthlessness **13** heartlessness

cruet **3** jar, jug **6** bottle **7** urceole **9** dispenser

cruise **4** sail, scud, skim **5** coast, drift, float, glide, sweep **6** stream, voyage **7** seafare **8** navigate

Cruise of the Cachalot, The
author: 12 Frank T Bullen

crumb **3** bit **5** grain, scrap, shred, speck **6** morsel, sliver **8** fragment, particle

crumble **5** crush, decay, grate, grind **6** powder **8** fragment, splinter **9** decompose, pulverize **12** disintegrate

crumbly **7** brittle, friable **9** breakable

Crummles, Vincent
character in: 16 Nicholas Nickleby
author: 7 Dickens

crummy **5** awful, lousy **6** rotten **8** terrible

crumple **4** fall **5** crush **6** cave in, crease, pucker, rumple **7** crimple, crinkle, wrinkle **8** collapse **9** corrugate

crunch **4** chew, gnaw **5** chomp, gnash, grind, munch **9** masticate

Cruncher, Jerry
character in: 16 A Tale of Two Cities
author: 7 Dickens

crunchy **3** dry **5** crisp **6** crispy **7** crackly

crusade, Crusade **5** drive, rally **8** movement

crusader, Crusader **6** knight, zealot **7** pilgrim, Templar **8** champion **11** Hospitaller

crush **4** mash **5** break, press, quash, quell, smash **6** enfold, quench, squash, subdue **7** crumble, crumple, embrace, put down, shatter, squeeze, squelch **8** compress, overcome, suppress **9** granulate, overpower, overwhelm, pulverize **10** extinguish

crushed **3** sad **5** cowed **6** broken, mashed, woeful **7** abashed, doleful, forlorn, pressed, put down, quashed, quelled, smashed, subdued **8** crumbled, crumpled, dejected, desolate, overcame, overcome, quenched, squashed, squeezed, wretched **9** flattened, miserable, squelched, woebegone **10** compressed, despondent, pulverized, suppressed **11** overpowered, overwhelmed **12** disconsolate, extinguished, inconsolable **13** broken-hearted

crushing **7** mashing **8** decisive, quelling, smashing **10** shattering **11** humiliating, putting down, stamping out, suppression **12** obliterating, overwhelming **13** pulverization

crust **4** coat, gall, hull, rind, scab **5** brass, nerve, shell **6** harden **7** coating **8** chutzpah, covering, pie shell **9** impudence **11** pastry shell

crustacean **4** crab, flea **5** louse, prawn **6** isopod, shrimp **7** lobster **8** barnacle, crawfish, crayfish **9** shellfish, water flea

crusty **4** curt **5** blunt, gruff, rough, short, stern, surly, testy **6** abrupt, crabby, cranky, shirty, snippy, sullen **7** brusque, peevish, waspish **8** choleric, snappish, snippety **9** irascible, splenetic **10** ill-natured **11** ill-tempered **13** short-tempered

crux **3** nub **4** core, gist **5** basis, heart **7** essence **9** essential **10** brass tacks **11** nitty-gritty

Cruyff, Johan
nickname: 14 Flying Dutchman
sport: 6 soccer
position: 7 forward **10** midfielder
nationality: 5 Dutch

cry **3** beg, sob, sue **4** bawl, call, hawk, howl, keen, moan, plea, roar, wail, weep, yell, yelp **5** blare, cheer, groan, mourn, plead, shout, utter, whoop **6** appeal, bellow, blazon, boohoo, clamor, hurrah, huzzah, lament, outcry, prayer, scream, shriek, snivel **7** blubber, call out, exclaim, implore, request, screech, trumpet, whimper **8** entreaty, petition, proclaim **9** advertise, importune **10** adjuration, promulgate **11** exclamation **12** solicitation, supplication

Cry, the Beloved Country
author: 9 Alan Paton
locale: 11 South Africa

cry out **4** bark, bawl, call, howl, roar, yell **5** shout **6** bellow, clamor, holler **7** exclaim **8** proclaim **9** ejaculate **10** vociferate

cry over **5** mourn **6** bemoan, bewail, lament

crypt **4** tomb **5** vault **8** catacomb **9** mausoleum, sepulcher

cryptic **4** dark **5** vague **6** arcane, hidden, occult, secret **7** obscure, strange **8** esoteric, mystical, puzzling **9** ambiguous **10** cabalistic, mysterious, perplexing **11** enigmatical

cryptogram **4** code **6** cipher

cryptograph **4** code **6** cipher, encode

crystal **3** ice **5** clear, flake, glass, lucid **6** quartz **7** diamond **8** stemware **9** glassware, snowflake, watch part **10** rhinestone **11** transparent

crystallize **3** fix, gel **4** firm, jell **5** candy **6** harden **8** solidify **9** granulate

Csonka, Larry (Lawrence Richard)
nickname: **9** Lawnmower
sport: **8** football
position: **8** fullback
team: **13** Miami Dolphins, New York Giants

Cteatus
origin: **5** Greek
mentioned in: **5** Iliad
father: **5** Actor
mother: **7** Molione

Ctesippus
father: **8** Hercules
suitor of: **8** Penelope

Ctesius
epithet of: **4** Zeus
means: **9** god of gain

cub **3** boy, pup **4** bear, lion **5** scout, whelp **6** novice **8** reporter **9** youngling, youngster **10** apprentice

Cuba ***see box***

cubbyhole **4** nook **5** niche **6** cranny **10** pigeonhole **11** compartment

cube of deep-fried pork
American Spanish: **10** cuchifrito

cubic centimeter
abbreviation: **4** cu cm

cubic dekameter
abbreviation: **5** cu dkm

cubic foot
abbreviation: **4** cu ft

Cuba
other name: **18** pearl of the Antilles
capital/largest city: **6** Havana **8** Le Habana
others: **5** Bauta, Colon, Duabi, Guane, Manes **6** Baines, Bayamo, Gibara, Guines, Mayari **7** Antilla, Baracoa, Fomento, Holguin, Holquin, Jiguani, Niquero, Palmira, Sanhuis **8** Artemisa, Camaguey, Cardenas, Guaimaro, Guayabal, Marianao, Matanzas, Nuevitas, Varadero, Yaguajay **9** Cabaiguan, Camajuani, Cienfuego **10** Cienfuegos, Guanabacoa, Guantanamo, Manzanillo, Santa Clara **11** Campechuela, Pinar del Rio, Puerto Padre **12** Ciego de Avila **13** Sagua de Tanamo **14** Sancti Spiritus, Santiago de Cuba **17** Aguada de Pasajeros, Consolacion del Sur
measure: **4** vara **5** bocoy, cocoy, tarea **6** cordel, fanega **10** caballeria
monetary unit: **4** peso **7** centavo **8** cuarenta
weight: **5** libra **6** tercio
island: **5** Pines, Pinos **6** Sabana **8** Camaguey, Juventud **9** Canarreos **17** Jardines de la Reina
cay: **4** Coco **5** Largo **6** Romano **7** Guajaba, Rosareo, Sabinal **8** Cantiles **9** San Felipe **10** Santa Maria
mountain: **6** Copper **7** Cristal, Maestra, Organos **8** Camaguey, Trinidad **9** Las Villas **11** Pinar del rio **12** Guaniguanico **14** Sancti-Spiritus
highest point: **8** Turquino
river: **4** Zaza **5** Cauto **8** San Pedro
sea: **8** Atlantic **9** Caribbean
physical feature:
bay: **4** Nipe, Pigs **6** Jiguey **8** Cochinos **10** Buena Vista, Guantznamo
cape: **4** Cruz **5** Maisi **8** Lucrecia **10** Corrientes, San Antonio
channel: **8** Nicholas **9** Old Bahama
falls: **3** Toa **7** Agabama, Caburni
gulf: **6** Mexico **7** Cazones **8** Anamaria, Batabano **12** Guancanayabo
inlet: **4** Broa **10** Corrientes
peninsula: **6** Zapata
point: **7** Guarico
swamp: **6** Zapata
people: **5** Carib, Negro, Taino, white **6** Arawak **7** Ciboney, mestizo **8** Ciboneye
conqueror: **9** Velazquez
explorer: **8** Columbus
leader: **6** Castro **7** Batista **10** Che Guevara
language: **7** Spanish
religion: **13** Roman Catholic
cult: **6** Chango, Yemaya
places:
castle: **5** Morro
cathedral: **8** Santiago
feature:
dance: **5** conga, rumba **6** danzon, rhumba **8** guaracha, pachanga
harvest: **5** zafra
peasant: **7** guajiro
tree: **5** jique, jiqui
witch doctor: **7** nanigos
food:
dish: **6** paella
drink: **4** pina

cubic inch
abbreviation: **4** cu in

cubicle **3** bay **4** cell, nook **5** booth, niche **6** alcove, recess

cubic meter
abbreviation: **3** cu m

cubic millimeter
abbreviation: **4** cu mm

cubic yard
abbreviation: **4** cu yd

cubit **15** Biblical measure

cuchifrito **19** cube of deep-fried pork

Cuchulainn
origin: **5** Irish
hero of: **6** Ulster
uncle: **9** Conchobar
guarded house of: **10** Smith Culan
killed by: **6** Lugaid

cuckoo **3** ani **4** bats, bird, fool, gaga, nuts **5** balmy, batty, crazy, daffy, dotty, goofy, loony, nutty, silly, wacky **6** screwy **7** idiotic **9** screwball **12** crackbrained **13** off one's rocker **14** off one's trolley

cucumber **14** Cucumis sativus
varieties: **3** bur **4** mock, star, wild **6** bitter **7** prickly, serpent **9** squirting **13** African horned

cuddle **3** pet **5** clasp **6** caress, curl up, fondle, huddle, nestle, nuzzle **7** cling to, embrace, lie snug, snuggle

Cuddly Dudley
nickname of: **11** Dudley Moore

cudgel **4** club **5** baton, staff, stick **8** bludgeon **9** billy club, blackjack, truncheon **10** shillelagh **12** quarterstaff

cue **3** key, tip **4** clue, hint, sign **6** signal **7** inkling **10** intimation, suggestion **11** insinuation

cuff **3** box, hit, rap **4** blow **5** clout, smack, thump, whack **6** thwack, wallop

cui bono **10** for what use, of what good **15** for whose benefit

cuisine **4** fare, food, menu **5** table **6** viands **7** cookery, cooking, edibles **8** victuals, vittles **11** comestibles

Cukor, George
director of: **7** Camille **8** Adam's Rib, Gaslight, The Women **10** My Fair Lady (Oscar) **11** A Double Life, A Star Is Born, Little Women **13** Born Yesterday, Dinner at Eight **14** Romeo and Juliet **16** David Copperfield **18** A Bill of Divorcement **20** The Philadelphia Story

cul-de-sac **6** pocket **7** dead-end, impasse **10** blind alley

cull **4** junk, pick, sift, take **5** dross, glean, scrap, trash, waste **6** choose, divide, garner, gather, jetsam, reject, second, select, winnow **7** castoff, collect, discard, excerpt, extract, leaving **8** abstract, scouring, separate **9** segregate

culminate **3** cap, end, top **5** crown, end up **6** climax, finish, result, top off, wind up **8** complete, conclude **9** terminate **10** consummate

culmination **4** acme, apex, peak **6** apogee, climax, height, zenith **7** epitome **8** pinnacle **10** conclusion **11** fulfillment, realization **12** consummation

Culp, Robert
born: **10** Berkeley CA
roles: **4** I Spy **20** Greatest American Hero

culpability **4** onus **5** blame, fault, guilt **9** liability **14** accountability, responsibility

culpable **6** guilty, liable **7** at fault, to blame **8** blamable **10** censurable **11** blameworthy

culprit **5** felon **6** sinner **8** criminal, evildoer, offender **9** miscreant, wrongdoer **10** lawbreaker, malefactor **12** transgressor

cult **4** sect **7** faction, zealots **8** admirers, devotees, devotion **9** disciples, followers **10** admiration

cultivable **6** arable **7** fertile, friable **8** farmable, plowable, tillable

cultivate **3** dig, hoe, sow **4** farm, grow, plow, seek, till, weed **5** court, plant, spade **6** enrich, garden **7** acquire, advance, develop, elevate, enhance, improve

cultivated **3** dug **4** fine, grew, hoed **6** farmed, forked, sought, spaded, tilled, weeded **7** courted, planted **8** advanced, cultured, elevated, enhanced, enriched, finished, improved, polished **9** developed

cultivation **5** grace **6** polish, sowing **7** farming, manners, tilling **8** agronomy, planting **9** elevation, gardening, gentility, good taste, husbandry **10** refinement **11** agriculture

culture **3** art **5** music **7** the arts **8** learning **9** erudition, knowledge **10** enrichment, literature, refinement **12** civilization **13** enlightenment **15** accomplishments

Culture and Anarchy
author: **13** Matthew Arnold

cultured **7** elegant, erudite, genteel, learned, refined **8** polished, well-bred, well-read **11** enlightened **12** accomplished, well-educated **13** sophisticated

culvert **5** ditch, drain, sewer **6** trench **7** channel, conduit, fox-hole

Cumaean sibyl
prophetess of: **5** Cumae
guided: **6** Aeneas

cumbersome **5** bulky, hefty **6** clumsy **7** awkward **8** cumbrous, ungainly, unwieldy **9** ponderous **12** unmanageable

cum grano salis **15** not too seriously **16** with a grain of salt

cumin
botanical name: **14** Cuminum cyminum
other name: **6** comino, jiraka, kummel
origin: **5** Egypt
family: **7** parsley
symbol of: **5** greed
guards against straying: **7** pigeons **8** chickens, husbands
use: **4** fish, meat, rice, soup, stew **5** bread, curry **6** cheese **7** pickles, sausage **8** potatoes **11** chili powder

cum laude **10** with praise

cummings, e e (Edward Estlin)
author of: **12** in just spring **15** The Enormous Room **17** Tulips and Chimneys **18** Chansons Innocentes

Cummings, Robert
real name: **29** Clarence Robert Orville Cummings
born: **8** Joplin MO
roles: **8** King's Row **14** Dial M for Murder **18** The Bob Cummings Show

cumulate **5** amass **6** gather, heap up, pile up **10** accumulate

cumulative **7** amassed, piled up **8** additive, heaped up **9** aggregate **10** collective **12** accumulative, conglomerate

Cunegonde
character in: **7** Candide
author: **8** Voltaire

Cunina
origin: **5** Roman
goddess of: **15** sleeping infants

cunning 3 art, sly **4** foxy, wily **5** canny, craft, guile, knack, skill **6** artful, crafty, deceit, genius, shifty, shrewd, talent, tricky **7** ability, devious, finesse, slyness **8** aptitude, artifice, deftness, foxiness, guileful, subtlety, trickery, wiliness **9** chicanery, deceitful, deception, deceptive, dexterity, duplicity, ingenious, underhand **10** adroitness, artfulness, cleverness, craftiness, expertness, shrewdness **11** deviousness **13** Machiavellian
god of: 6 Hermes

Cunning Little Vixen, The
opera by: 7 Janacek

cup 3 cup **5** glass, grail, stein **6** beaker, goblet, vessel **7** chalice, tankard **8** schooner
abbreviation: 1 c

Cup
constellation of: 6 Crater

Cupava
companion of: 6 Aeneas

cupbearer of gods
8 Ganymede

cupboard 6 buffet, bureau, closet **7** armoire, cabinet **9** sideboard, storeroom **10** chiffonier **11** china closet **12** clothespress

Cupid
also: 4 Amor
origin: 5 Roman
god of: 4 love
mother: 5 Venus
corresponds to: 4 Eros

cupidity 5 greed **7** avarice, avidity **8** rapacity **10** greediness **11** selfishness **12** covetousness, graspingness **13** concupiscence, insatiability, rapaciousness **14** avariciousness **15** acquisitiveness

cupola 4 dome, roof **5** tower, vault **6** belfry, turret **7** ceiling

cur 3 cad **4** mutt **5** rogue **6** rascal, varlet, wretch **7** mongrel, varmint, villain **9** scoundrel **10** blackguard

curacao
type: 7 liqueur
origin: 19 Netherlands Antilles
flavor: 6 orange
with gin: 8 Blue Moon, Napoleon **9** Blue Devil **14** Flying Dutchman
with rum: 6 Mai-Tai **8** Blue Lady **12** Blue Hawaiian
with vodka: 8 Aqueduct

curate 5 vicar **6** cleric, deacon, parson, pastor, priest, rector **8** minister, preacher **9** churchman, clergyman **12** ecclesiastic

curative 4 balm **7** healing **11** restorative

curator 5 doyen **6** keeper **8** director, overseer **9** caretaker, custodian

curb 3 rim **4** edge, rein **5** brink, check, ledge, limit **6** border, bridle, halter, retard, slow up **7** control, harness, inhibit, repress, slacken **8** hold back, moderate, restrain, restrict, slow down, suppress **9** curbstone, hindrance, restraint **10** decelerate, limitation **11** restriction, retardation

curdle 3 rot **4** clot, curd, sour, turn **5** decay, go bad, go off, spoil **7** clabber, congeal, ferment, putrefy, thicken **8** putresce, solidify **9** coagulate **11** deteriorate

cure 3 dry **4** heal, salt **5** smoke **6** remedy **8** antidote, make well, preserve **10** corrective

cure-all 4 balm **6** elixir, remedy **7** panacea **10** catholicon

cured 5 dried **6** healed, mended, smoked **8** made well, remedied **9** preserved, recovered

Curetes
form: 8 demigods
attendants of: 4 Zeus

Curiatii *see* **7** Horatii

Curie, Marie Sklodowska and Pierre
field: 7 physics **9** chemistry
discovered: 6 radium **8** polonium **13** radioactivity
awarded: 10 Nobel Prize

curio 7 bibelot, trinket **9** bric-a-brac, objet d'art

curiosity 5 freak, sight **6** marvel, oddity, prying, rarity, wonder **7** novelty **8** interest, nosiness **10** phenomenon, rare object **11** questioning **15** inquisitiveness

curious 3 odd **4** nosy, rare **5** funny, novel, queer, weird **6** prying, quaint, unique **7** bizarre, strange, unusual **8** peculiar, singular, snooping, uncommon **9** inquiring, searching **11** inquisitive, questioning

Curitis
epithet of: 4 Juno
means: 10 of the spear

curl 4 coil, lock, wave, wind **5** crimp, frizz, swirl, twirl, twist **6** spiral **7** frizzle, ringlet, scallop **8** curlicue **9** corkscrew

curled 3 set **5** kinky, waved, wound **6** coiled, frizzy spiral **7** crimped, frizzed, twisted **8** crinkled, scrolled **9** curlicued

curlicue 4 coil **5** twist **6** spiral **8** flourish

curly 4 wavy **5** kinky **6** frizzy **7** rippled **8** crinkled **9** ringleted

curmudgeon 4 crab **5** crank, grump **6** grouch **8** grumbler, sourball

currant 5 Ribes
varieties: 3 red **5** black, fetid, skunk, squaw, stink **6** alpine, cherry, common, garden, Indian, Sierra **7** Buffalo **8** Missouri, mountain, swamp red **9** chaparral, wild black **11** northern red **12** bristly black **13** American black, European black, northern black, white-flowered **15** California black

currency 4 cash, coin **5** bills, money, vogue **7** coinage **9** bank notes **10** acceptance, popularity, prevalence **12** predominance, universality

current 3 now **4** flow, flux, mood, tide **5** draft, drift, trend **6** modern, spirit, stream, with-it **7** feeling, in style, in vogue, popular, present **8** existing, tendency, up-to-date **9** prevalent, zeitgeist **10** atmosphere, present-day, prevailing **11** inclination **12** contemporary, undercurrent

current of air 4 wind **5** draft **6** breeze, zephyr

curricle 3 gig **4** cart, trap **6** chaise **8** carriage

curry powder
origin: 5 India
ingredient: 5 cumin **6** cloves **8** capsicum, turmeric **9** coriander, fenugreek, red pepper **13** cayenne pepper
use: 5 kebab, kebob, kofta, malai **6** kormas **7** curries, pea soup **8** meat loaf, vindaloo, zucchini **11** potato salad

curse 3 vex **4** bane, cuss, damn, oath **5** blast, cross, swear, trial **6** burden, ordeal, plague, whammy **7** afflict, condemn, evil eye, scourge, swear at, torment, trouble **8** anathema, denounce, execrate, swearing, vexation **9** annoyance, blasphemy, damnation, evil spell, expletive, obscenity, profanity **10** affliction, execration, misfortune **11** imprecation, malediction, tribulation **12** anathematize, denunciation

cursory 5 brief, hasty, quick, swift **6** casual, random **7** hurried, offhand, passing **8** careless **9** desultory, haphazard

11 inattentive, perfunctory, superficial

curt 4 rude **5** bluff, blunt, gruff, short, terse **6** abrupt, crusty, snappy **7** brusque, summary **8** petulant **10** peremptory

curtail 3 cut **4** clip, trim **6** reduce **7** abridge, shorten **8** condense, contract, cut short, decrease, diminish, pare down **10** abbreviate

curtailed 3 cut **7** checked, concise, cut back, reduced, slashed **8** abridged, cut short **9** shortened **10** retrenched

curtailment 7 cutback, cutting, halting, pruning **8** clipping, decrease, trimming **9** lessening, reduction, restraint **10** limitation, shortening **11** abridgement, contraction **12** abbreviation, condensation

curtain 3 end **4** mask, veil **5** blind, cover, drape, shade, sheet **6** screen, shroud **7** conceal, drapery, hanging **8** portiere

Curtis, Tony
real name: 15 Bernard Schwartz
wife: 10 Janet Leigh
daughter: 8 Jamie Lee
born: 9 New York NY
roles: 7 Houdini, Trapeze **12** The Great Race **13** Some Like It Hot **14** The Defiant Ones **16** The Great Imposter **18** The Boston Strangler **22** The Sweet Smell of Success

Curtius
also: 6 Marcus
volunteered as: 17 sacrificial victim

Curtiz, Michael
director of: 10 Casablanca (Oscar), The Sea Hawk **12** Captain Blood **13** Mildred Pierce **14** Life with Father **17** Yankee Doodle Dandy **24** The Adventures of Robin Hood (with William Keighley) **26** The Charge of the Light Brigade **34** The Private Lives of Elizabeth and Essex

curtsy, curtsey 3 bob, bow, dip **5** honor **6** homage **9** obeisance, reverence **11** bend the knee

curvature 3 arc **4** arch, bend **5** crook **6** bowing

curve 3 arc, bow **4** arch, bend, coil, hook, loop, turn, wind **5** crook, twist **6** spiral, swerve

curved 4 bent **5** bowed **6** arched, looped, turned

curved span 3 bow **4** arch, dome **5** vault **6** bridge

Curve of Binding Energy, The
author: 10 John McPhee

curving 4 bent **5** bowed **6** arched **7** bending, looping, turning, winding **8** twisting

curving inward 6 hollow, sunken **7** concave **8** hollowed **9** depressed

curving outward 5 bowed **6** convex **7** bulging, rounded **8** bellying **11** protuberant

Cuscatlan *see* **10** El Salvador

Cush
father: 3 Ham
grandfather: 4 Noah
brother: 6 Canaan
son: 6 Nimrod
Hebrew for: 8 Ethiopia

cushion 3 mat, pad **4** damp **5** quiet **6** dampen, deaden, muffle, pillow, soften, stifle **7** bolster **8** suppress

Cushitic
language family: 11 AfroAsiatic **13** Hamito-Semitic
branch: 6 Somali **8** Gallinya
spoken in: 7 Somalia **8** Ethiopia, Tanzania

cusp 4 apex, barb, horn, peak **5** angle, point, tooth **6** corner

custard 4 flan, fool **5** creme **6** junket **7** dessert, pudding **8** flummery **10** blanc-mange, zabaglione

Custer, George A
served in: 8 Civil War **10** Indian Wars
side: 5 Union
battle: 13 Little Big Horn
defeated: 11 Black Kettle
defeated by: 10 Crazy Horse

custodian 6 duenna, keeper, warden **7** janitor **8** chaperon, guardian, watchman **9** attendant, caretaker, chaperone, concierge **14** superintendent

custody 4 care **5** watch **6** charge **9** detention **10** possession, protection **11** confinement, safekeeping, trusteeship **12** conservation, guardianship, preservation

custom 4 form, mode **5** habit, usage **7** fashion **10** convention

customarily 7 as a rule, usually **8** commonly, normally **9** generally, regularly **10** frequently, habitually, ordinarily **13** traditionally

customary 5 usual **6** common, normal, wonted **7** general, regular, routine, typical **8** everyday, habitual, ordinary **10** accustomed **11** traditional **12** conventional

customer 5 buyer **6** client, patron **7** habitue, shopper **9** purchaser

customs 4 duty, levy, toll **6** excise, tariff **9** import tax **10** assessment

cut 3 mow, saw **4** chop, clip, crop, cube, dice, fall, gash, hack, move, nick, pare, part, rent, rive, slit, snip, snub, trim **5** carve, cross, lance, mince, piece, prune, sever, share, shave, shear, slash, slice, split, wound **6** bisect, course, delete, divide, furrow, hollow, ignore, incise, pierce, reduce, sunder, trench **7** abridge, channel, curtail, decline, dissect, opening, passage, portion, section, segment **8** condense, contract, decrease, diminish, incision, lacerate **9** abatement, intersect, lessening, reduction, shrinkage **10** abbreviate, diminution, excavation, shortening **11** contraction, curtailment, indentation

cut and run 4 bolt, flee, skip **6** escape **7** abscond, get away, make off, run away **8** slip away **9** break free **10** break loose, fly the coop **12** make a getaway

cut apart 7 dissect **9** anatomize

cutback 8 decrease, trimming **9** reduction **11** abridgement, curtailment

cut back 4 trim **5** prune **6** reduce **7** abridge, curtail **8** decrease

cut costs 4 save **5** skimp, stint **6** scrimp **7** husband **8** conserve **9** economize **15** tighten one's belt

cut down 4 kill, trim **5** limit **6** lessen, reduce **7** abridge, curtail, destroy, disable, remodel, shorten **8** condense, decrease, diminish, restrict **10** abbreviate

cut-down form 6 digest, precis **7** summary **8** synopsis, trimming **10** shortening **11** abridgement, contraction, curtailment **12** abbreviation, condensation

cut down to size **5** abase **6** humble **7** mortify **8** belittle, bring low, disgrace **9** humiliate **13** bring down a peg

cute **5** sweet **6** dainty, pretty **7** darling, lovable **8** adorable, handsome, precious **9** beautiful **10** attractive

cut expenses **4** save **5** skimp, stint **6** scrimp **8** conserve **9** economize **12** pinch pennies **15** tighten one's belt

cut in half **5** halve **6** bisect

cut in two **5** halve, sever **6** bisect

cutlet **3** cut **4** chop **5** slice **9** cotelette, croquette

cut off **4** dock, trim **5** apart, sever **6** detach, remove **7** chop off, divorce, isolate **8** amputate, divorced, isolated, separate **10** disconnect

cut out **2** go **4** blow, exit **5** be off, erase, leave, scram, split **6** beat it, delete, depart, escape, excise, go away, remove, set out **7** abolish **8** designed, get rid of, set forth **9** eliminate **10** do away with, hit the road, make tracks **11** exterminate, take a powder

cut short **4** clip, crop, dock, trim **7** abridge, shorten **8** truncate **10** abbreviate

cutter **4** boat **5** blade, hewer, knife **6** sledge, sleigh, tailor **11** cutting edge

cutthroat **5** cruel **6** outlaw **7** brigand, hoodlum, ruffian **8** ruthless **9** merciless

cutting **3** raw **4** acid, cold **5** harsh, nasty, sharp **6** biting, bitter **7** acerbic, caustic, nipping, pruning, searing **8** clipping, derisive, piercing, scathing, smarting, snubbing, stinging, trimming **9** reduction, sarcastic, stringent **11** abridgement, acrimonious, compression, contraction, curtailment, disparaging, penetrating **12** abbreviation, condensation

cutting edge **5** blade **8** vanguard **9** forefront

cutting off **8** severing **9** severance **10** detachment, separation **13** disconnection, disengagement

cutting remark **3** dig **4** gibe, jeer **5** taunt

Cuttle
character in: **12** Dombey and Son
author: **7** Dickens

cut up **4** chop, hack, maim, rend **5** caper, carve, halve, mince, slash, slice, split **6** cleave, deface, deform, divide **7** portion, quarter **8** dissever, mutilate **9** apportion, kid around **10** fool around **11** clown around, play the fool

Cuvier, Georges
field: **7** geology, zoology
nationality: **6** French
founded: **12** paleontology **18** comparative anatomy

Cyane
form: **5** nymph **8** princess
violated by: **6** father
unsuccessful rescuer of: **10** Persephone

Cyaxares *see* **9** Ahasuerus

Cybele
also: **9** Dindymene **10** Berecyntia, Magna Mater **11** Great Mother **12** Mater Turrita **17** Great Idaean Mother
origin: **8** Phrygian **9** Asia Minor
goddess of: **6** nature
priest: **5** Galli **10** Corybantes
corresponds to: **3** Ops **4** Rhea
epithet: **6** Antaea

Cychreus
king of: **7** Salamis
father: **8** Poseidon
mother: **7** Salamis
daughter: **6** Glauce

Cyclades **3** Dos, Zea **4** Keos, Nios, Sira, Syra **5** Delos, Melos, Naxos, Paros, Siros, Syros, Tenos, Tinos **6** Andros **7** Amorgos, islands, Kythnos **13** Aegean islands

cycle **3** run **6** series **8** sequence **10** succession **11** progression **14** connected group

cyclone **4** gale, gust, wind **5** storm **7** tornado, twister, typhoon **9** whirlwind, windstorm
Australian: **10** willy-nilly

Cyclone (Cy)
nickname of: **15** Denton True Young

Cyclops, Cyclopes
form: **5** giant
number of eyes: **3** one
father: **6** Uranus
mother: **2** Ge
blinded by: **8** Odysseus

Cycnus
father: **4** Ares
killed in: **4** duel
killed by: **8** Hercules
changed into: **4** swan

Cydippe
priestess of: **4** Hera
location: **5** Argos
father: **7** Ochimus
son: **5** Biton **7** Cleobis

cylinder **3** can, tin **4** drum, pipe, roll, tube **5** spool **6** barrel, column, pillar, piston, platen, roller **13** piston chamber

cylindrical **5** round **6** tarete **7** tubular **8** columnar

Cyllene
form: **5** nymph
nursed: **6** Hermes

Cyllenian
pertains to: **6** Hermes **12** Mount Cellene

Cymbeline
author: **18** William Shakespeare
character: **6** Cloten, Imogen **7** Iachimo, Pisanio **9** Bellarius **17** Leonatus Posthumus

Cymodoce
mentioned in: **6** Aeneid
form: **4** ship
fleet of: **6** Aeneas
changed by: **6** Cybele
changed into: **8** sea nymph

Cymru *see* **5** Wales

cynic **7** scoffer, skeptic **9** pessimist **10** misogynist **11** faultfinder, misanthrope

cynical **8** derisive, sardonic, scoffing, scornful, sneering **9** misogynic, sarcastic, skeptical **12** misanthropic

Cynortes
father: **7** Amyclas
mother: **7** Diomede

Cynosura
nurse of: **4** Zeus

Cynthia *see* **7** Artemis

Cynurus
father: **7** Perseus

Cyparissia
epithet of: **6** Athena
means: **14** cypress goddess

Cyparissus
killed: **4** stag
changed into: **11** cypress tree

cypress **8** Taxodium **9** Cupressus
varieties: **3** toy **4** bald, berg, pond **5** false, Gowen, Modoc, Piute **6** Bhutan, Hinoki, Lawson, MacNab, Nootka, Sawara, summer, Tecate **7** African, Arizona, Italian, Mexican, Sargent **8** Cuyamaca, golf-ball, Monterey, mourning, Siskiyou, standing **9** Guadalupe, Mendocino, Montezuma, red summer, Santa Cruz **10** Portuguese, tennis-ball **12** Chinese swamp **18** rough-barked Arizona **19** smooth-barked Arizona

Cyprian *see* **9** Aphrodite

Cyprus
biblical name: **6** Kittim
capital/largest city: **7** Nicosia
city: **6** Paphos **7** Kyrenia, Larnaca **8** Limassol **9** Famagusta
monetary unit: **4** para **5** pound
mountain: **7** Kyrenia, Troodos
highest point: **7** Olympus
river: **6** Pedias
sea: **13** Mediterranean
physical feature:
bay: **8** Episkopi
cape: **4** Gata **5** Greco **7** Andreas, Arnauti **9** Kormakiti
peninsula: **6** Karpas
plain: **8** Mesaoria **9** Messaoria
people: **5** Greek, Turks **9** Cypriotes
ruler: **5** Turks **6** Greeks, Romans **7** British **9** Egyptians, Lusignans, Venetians **10** Byzantines **11** Phoenicians
language: **5** Greek **7** Turkish
religion: **5** Islam **6** Muslim **13** Greek Orthodoxy **16** Eastern Orthodoxy

Cypselus
king of: **7** Arcadia
father: **7** Aepytus
daughter: **6** Merope
son-in-law: **11** Cresphontes
grandson: **7** Aepytus

Cyrano de Bergerac
director: **13** Michael Gordon
author: **13** Edmond Rostand
cast: **10** Jose Ferrer (Cyrano), Mala Powers **13** William Powers
character: **6** Roxane **22** Christian de Neuvillette
setting: **5** Paris
Oscar for: **9** best actor (Ferrer)

Cyrano de Bergerac, Savinien
author of: **25** Voyages to the Moon and the Sun
play based on his life by: **13** Edmond Rostand

Cyrene
father: **7** Hypseus
mother: **6** Creusa
lover: **6** Apollo
son: **5** Idmon **9** Aristaeus

Cytherea *see* **9** Aphrodite

Cytissorus
father: **7** Phrixus
mother: **9** Chalciope
brother: **5** Argus, Melas **8** Phrontis

cytology
study of: **5** cells

czar, tsar **4** king **5** ruler **6** caesar, despot, tyrant **7** emperor, monarch **8** dictator, overlord **9** potentate, sovereign

czarina **7** empress

czaristic **10** autocratic **11** all-powerful, dictatorial, monarchical

Czechoslovakia ***see box***

Czechoslovakia
capital/largest city: **5** Praha **6** Prague
others: **2** As **4** Asch, Brno, Cheb, Eger, Most **5** Brunn, Nitra, Opava, Plzeu, Tabor, Tuzla **6** Aussig, Bilina, Kladus, Kosice, Pilsen, Presov, Sadowa, Trnava, Vsetin **7** Budwies, Jihlava, Liberee, Ostrava, Teplitz **8** Carlsbad, Jachymov, Karlsbad, Olomoric **9** Pressburg **10** Austerlitz, Bratislava, Koniggratz **11** Reichenberg
university: **7** Charles
division: **7** Bohemia, Moravia, Silesia **8** Ruthenia, Slovakia
measure: **3** Lan **4** Mira **5** Korec, Liket, Stopa **6** Merice, Strych
monetary unit: **5** crown, ducat **6** heller, Koruna
mountain: **3** Erz, Ore **5** Giant, Tatra **6** Sumava **7** Sudeten, Sudetes **8** Krkonose **10** Carpathian
highest point: **7** Gerlach **11** Gerlachovka
river: **2** Uh, **3** Mze, Vag, Bah **4** Dyje, Eger, Elbe, Gran, Hron, Ipel, Isar, Iser, Labe, Nisa, Oder, Odra, Ohre, Olse, Waag **5** Becva, Dunaj, March, Nitra, Slana, Tisza **6** Danube, Moldau, Morava, Ondava, Sazava, Torysa, Vltava **7** Laborec, Luznice **8** Berounka
physical feature:
plateau: **8** Bohemian **11** Sudetenland
people: **4** Slav **5** Czech **6** Slovak **8** Bohemian, Moravian
author: **5** Capek, Hasek, Havel **7** Kundera, Seifert
composer: **6** Dvorak **7** Janacek, Martinu, Smetana
director: **11** Milos Forman
philosopher/reformer: **8** Comenius, John Huss
language: **5** Czech **6** German, Magyar, Slovak **7** Russian **9** Hungarian
religion: **6** Uniate **8** Lutheran **9** Orthodoxy **13** Roman Catholic
place:
castle: **8** Hradcany
cathedral: **7** St Vitus **10** St Nicholas
resort/spa: **8** Carlsbad, Piestany **9** Marienbad **10** Luhacovice **11** Karlovy Vary **14** Marianske Lazne
square: **9** Wenceslas
feature:
dance: **5** polka **6** redowa, talian **7** furiant
gymnastics festival: **11** spartakiada
song: **7** Ma Vlast
food:
beer: **6** pilsen
sausage: **5** parky **6** vursty

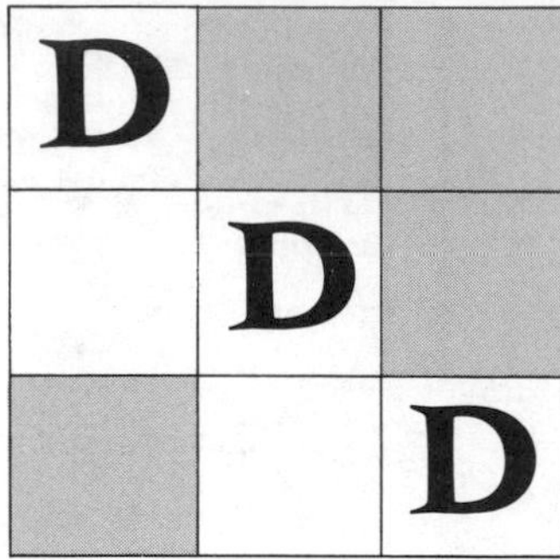

dab **3** bit, pat, tap **6** stroke **7** smidgen, soupcon

dabble **5** slosh **6** fiddle, putter, splash **7** spatter, toy with **8** sprinkle

dabbler **7** amateur, trifler **10** dilettante **12** experimenter **15** nonprofessional

da capo
music: **22** repeat from the beginning
abbreviation: **2** D C

Dacca
capital of: **10** Bangladesh

d'accord **2** OK **6** agreed **7** granted

Dactyls
also: **7** Daktyls
dwellers of: **8** Mount Ida

dad **2** da, pa **3** pop **4** papa, pops, sire **5** daddy, pappy, pater **6** father, parent **11** the old man

Daedala
festival in: **7** Boeotia

Daedalion
father: **9** Eosphorus
mother: **10** Phosphorus
daughter: **6** Chione
leaped off: **9** Parnassus
changed into: **4** hawk

Daedalus
occupation: **9** architect
father: **6** Metion
son: **5** Iapyx **6** Icarus
nephew: **5** Talos **6** Perdix
killed: **5** Talos
built: **9** labyrinth
for: **5** Minos
made: **5** wings

daffodil **9** Narcissus **24** Narcissus pseudonarcissus
varieties: **3** sea **6** winter **8** Peruvian **9** petticoat **13** hoop-petticoat

daft **3** mad **4** loco **5** balmy, batty, crazy, daffy, dizzy, goofy, loony, nutty, silly, wacky **6** cuckoo, insane, screwy **7** foolish, lunatic, witless

Dagan
origin: **12** Mesopotamian
god of: **5** earth **11** agriculture
corresponds to: **5** Dagon

dagger **4** dirk, snee **5** blade, knife **6** weapon **7** poniard **8** stiletto

Dagon
origin: **10** Philistine, Phoenician
god of: **5** earth **11** agriculture
corresponds to: **5** Dagan

Daguerre, Louis J M
nationality: **6** French
inventor of: **11** photography **13** daguerreotype

dahlia
varieties: **3** sea **4** tree **6** common, garden **7** bedding **8** bell tree **10** candelabra

Dahomey, Republic of *see* **5** Benin

daily **7** diurnal, per diem **9** circadian, quotidian

Daimler, Gottlieb
nationality: **6** German
inventor of: **10** carburetor, motorcycle **14** gasoline engine **18** gasoline automobile **25** compression ignition engine

daimyo **4** lord **10** feudal lord

dainty **4** fine **5** fussy, tasty **6** choice, choosy, lovely, pretty, savory **7** choosey, elegant, refined **8** delicate, pleasing **9** beautiful, delicious, exquisite **10** attractive, fastidious, particular

Daira
father: **7** Oceanus

dais **5** stage **6** podium **7** rostrum **8** platform

daisy **6** Bellis **23** Chrysanthemum frutescens **25** Chrysanthemum leucanthemum
varieties: **4** blue, cape, high, lazy **5** crown, giant, globe, oxeye, Paris, veldt, white **6** butter, Easter, Nippon, shasta, sleepy, Tahoka **7** African, English, painted, seaside, turfing **8** Dahlberg, mountain, panamint **9** Barberton, Englemann, Swan River, Transvaal **10** Kingfisher, Michaelmas, Portuguese **11** Clanwilliam, Livingstone, Namaqualand **12** Boston yellow, double orange **15** blue-eyed African

Daisy Miller
author: **10** Henry James
character: **10** Giovanelli **12** Winterbourne

Dakar
capital of: **7** Senegal

Dakota (Sioux)
language family: **6** Siouan
tribe: **5** Teton **6** Lakota, Nakota, Santee **7** Yankton **8** Sisseton, Wahpeton, Wiciyela **9** Wahpekute, Yanktonai **11** Mdewakanton
location: **7** Montana **9** Minnesota **11** North Dakota, South Dakota
leader: **4** Gall **10** Crazy Horse **11** Sitting Bull **13** Jashunca-Uiteo
noted for: **15** military prowess
deity: **10** Wakan Tanka

Daktyls *see* **7** Dactyls

dale **4** dell, dene, glen, vale **6** dingle, hollow, valley

D'Alembert
author of: **12** Encyclopedia

Dali, Salvador
born: **5** Spain **7** Figuras
artwork: **10** Last Supper **17** Atomic Leda and Swan **19** Persistence of Memory **22** Accommodations of De-

sire **24** Christ of St John of the Cross

Dalibor
opera by: 7 Smetana
character: 6 Milada

Dallas
airport: 23 Dallas-Fort Worth Regional
basketball team: 4 Mavs **9** Mavericks
football team: 7 Cowboys
landmark: 15 Turtle Creek Park **16** Museum of Fine Arts **19** Dallas Theater Center **25** Margo Jones Memorial Theater
river: 7 Trinity
stadium: 10 Cotton Bowl
university: 3 SMU **13** Bishop College **17** Southern Methodist

Dallas
character: 7 JR Ewing **9** Jack Ewing, Jenna Wade, Jock Ewing, Miss Ellie, Ray Krebbs **10** Bobby Ewing **11** Christopher, Cliff Barnes, Mandy Winger, Mark Graison **12** Digger Barnes **13** Clayton Farlow, John Ross Ewing, Sue Ellen Ewing **16** Donna Culver Krebs **17** Pamela Barnes Ewing **22** Eleanor Southworth Ewing
cast: 8 John Beck **9** Dack Rambo, Linda Gray **10** Howard Keel **11** Larry Hagman, Steve Kanaly, Susan Howard **12** Ken Kercheval, Patrick Duffy **16** Barbara Bel Geddes, Priscilla Presley **17** Victoria Principal
ranch: 9 Southfork
business: 3 oil **8** Ewing Oil

dalliance 6 affair, toying **7** romance **8** fiddling, trifling **10** flirtation, lovemaking

dally 3 toy **4** play **5** flirt **6** dawdle, loiter, trifle

Dalmatia *see* **10** Yugoslavia

Dalton, John
field: 7 physics **9** chemistry
nationality: 7 British
formulated: 12 atomic theory
first: 18 atomic weights table
described: 14 color blindness

dam 3 bar, cow **4** clog, mare, plug, stop, wall **5** bitch, block, check **6** bridle, hinder, hold in, impede, plug up, stanch, stop up **7** barrier, block up, confine, congest, inhibit, repress, stopper, stuff up **8** blockade, hold back, obstruct, restrain **9** barricade, hindrance **11** obstruction

damage, damages 3 mar **4** cost, harm, hurt, loss **6** impair, injure, injury, ravage **10** impairment, reparation, settlement **11** destruction **12** compensation, despoliation

damaging 7 harmful, hurtful, ruinous **9** injurious **11** destructive, detrimental

Damascus
ancient kingdom: 8 Aramaean
Arabic: 7 Dimashq
capital of: 5 Syria
monastery: 22 Suleiman the Magnificent
mosque: 5 Great **7** Umayyad
mount: 6 Qasyun
museum: 8 National **9** Qasr al-Azm
river: 4 Awaj **6** Barada
rulers: 5 Arabs, Timur **6** Romans **7** Mongols, Saladin **8** Assyrian **9** Caliphate, Seleucids **12** Ottoman Turks **15** Byzantine Empire **17** Alexander the Great
tomb: 7 Saladin

Damastes *see* **10** Procrustes

Dame Pliant
character in: 12 The Alchemist
author: 6 Jonson

Damia
spirit of: 9 fertility

damn 4 doom **5** blast **6** rail at **7** censure, condemn **8** denounce **9** criticize, disparage

damned 4 lost **6** cursed, darned, doomed, fallen **7** doggone, dratted, godless **8** accursed, doggoned **9** condemned, execrated, reprobate **12** unregenerate

Damocles
offended: 9 Dionysius
seated under: 14 suspended sword

Damon
friend: 7 Pythias

damp 3 wet **4** curb, dank, dash, dewy, dull, mist **5** check, foggy, humid, misty, moist, muggy, rainy, soggy, spoil **6** clammy, deaden, hamper, hinder, reduce, soaked, sodden **7** depress, drizzly, inhibit, sopping, wettish **8** dankness, diminish, dripping, humidity, moisture, restrain **9** mugginess, restraint **10** clamminess, discourage **14** discouragement

dampen 3 wet **7** moisten, wet down

dampen one's spirits 5 daunt, unman **6** deject **7** depress **10** discourage, dishearten

damper 4 curb **8** obstacle **9** hindrance, restraint **10** constraint, impediment, wet blanket **14** discouragement

damsel 4 girl, lass **6** maiden **9** young lady

damselfly
varieties: 8 forktail **10** civil-bluet **11** black-winged, broad-winged **12** narrow-winged, spread-winged, violet dancer

dam up 4 clog, plug **5** block, choke **6** plug up, stop up **7** congest **8** obstruct

Damysus
member of: 8 Gigantes

Dan
means: 5 judge
father: 5 Jacob
mother: 6 Bilhah
brother: 3 Gad **4** Levi **5** Asher, Judah **6** Joseph, Reuben, Simeon **7** Zebulun **8** Benjamin, Issachar, Naphtali
sister: 5 Dinah
descendant of: 6 Danite

Dana *see* **4** Danu

Dana, Richard Henry
author of: 21 Two Years Before the Mast

Danae
form: 6 maiden
father: 8 Acrisius
mother: 8 Eurydice
imprisoned by: 8 Acrisius
lover: 4 Zeus
son: 7 Perseus

Danai
members of: 6 Greeks **7** Argives

Danaides
daughters of: 6 Danaus
number of daughters: 5 fifty

Dan August
character: 9 (Sgt) Joe Rivera **14** (Sgt) Charles Wilentz **16** (Chief) George Untermeyer
cast: 9 Ned Romero **10** Nor-

man Fell **12** Burt Reynolds **15** Richard Anderson

Danaus
ruler of: 5 Argos
father: 5 Belus
twin brother: 8 Aegyptus
daughters called: 8 Danaides
number of daughters: 5 fifty

dance ***see box***

dance of death
French: 12 danse macabre

Dandelion Wine
author: 11 Ray Bradbury

dander 5 anger, Irish **6** temper

Dandie Dinmont terrier 24 soft-coated wheaten terrier, Staffordshire bull terrier, West Highland white terrier

dandy 3 fop **4** beau, dude, fine **5** beaut, great, super, swell **6** beauty, superb **7** coxcomb, peacock **8** terrific **9** excellent **12** clotheshorse

danger 4 risk **5** peril **6** hazard, menace, threat **8** jeopardy **12** endangerment

dangerous 5 hairy, risky **6** chancy, unsafe **8** menacing, perilous **9** hazardous **10** precarious **11** threatening, treacherous

danger signal 5 alarm, alert **7** red flag, warning

dangle 3 sag **4** drag, hang, sway **5** droop, swing, trail **6** depend **7** draggle, hang out, suspend **8** hang down, hang over **9** oscillate

Daniel
Babylonian name: 12 Belteshazzar
companion: 7 Meshach **8** Abednego, Shadrach

Daniel Boone
character: 5 Mingo **6** Yadkin **11** Cincinnatus, Israel Boone, Jemima Boone **12** Rebecca Boone
cast: 6 Ed Ames **10** Fess Parker **11** Albert Salmi, Dal McKennon, Darby Hinton **13** Patricia Blair **18** Veronica Cartwright

Danielovitch, Issur
real name of: 11 Kirk Douglas

dank 3 wet **4** cold, damp **5** humid, moist, muggy, soggy **6** chilly, clammy, sodden, sticky

danke 8 thank you

danke schon 16 thank you very much

dankness 4 damp **7** wetness **8** dampness, humidity **9** humidness, moistness, mugginess **10** clamminess

Danner, Blythe
born: 14 Philadelphia PA
roles: 8 Betrayal **15** The Great Santini **16** Man Woman and Child

Danny Deever
story in: 18 Barrack-Room Ballads
author: 14 Rudyard Kipling

Danny Thomas Show, The
character: 6 Clancy **12** Uncle Tonoose **13** Danny Williams, Linda Williams, Rusty Williams, Terry Williams **16** Mrs Kathy Williams **18** Uncle Charley Halper
cast: 9 Sid Melton **10** Rusty Hamer **11** Hans Conried **12** Marjorie Lord, Penney Parker **13** Sherry Jackson **16** Angela Cartwright

danse macabre 12 dance of death

Dante (Alighieri)
author of: 9 Vita Nuova **15** The Divine Comedy
Divine Comedy Part I: **10** The Inferno

---

dance 3 hop **4** ball, jump, leap, prom, reel, skip **5** lindy, party, polka, twist **6** bounce, cavort, frolic, gambol, prance, square **7** fox-trot, perform **8** cakewalk **9** jitterbug **10** Charleston **11** Boston waltz **12** choreography, Virginia reel **15** hesitation waltz
Renaissance/17th century: 3 jig **5** galop, gigue **6** branle, pavane, redowa **7** bourree, gavotte, lancers, lavolta, mazurka **8** canaries, chaconne, courante, galliard, rigadoon, rigaudon, tourdion **9** allemande, passepied, polonaise, sarabande **10** danse basse, danse haute
18th century: 6 minuet **9** cotillion **11** contre danse **12** country dance
19th century: 5 waltz **9** quadrille
early 1900's: 7 foxtrot, one-step, two-step **8** bunny hug **10** turkey trot **11** grizzly bear
1920's: 5 tango **6** shimmy, toddle **10** Charleston **11** black bottom
1930's: 4 shag **5** conga, rumba, samba, Suzy-Q **7** pecking **8** big apple, lindy hop, trucking **9** jitterbug
1940's: 5 mambo **6** cha-cha
1950's and 1960's: 4 frug, go-go **5** twist **6** monkey **9** rock-'n'-roll
1970's: 5 disco
Argentine: 5 tango
Austrian: 13 schuhplattler
Balinese: 6 legong
Brazilian: 5 samba **6** maxixe
Cuban: 5 conga, rumba **6** cha-cha
Czech: 5 polka
Dominican: 8 marengue, merengue
folk: 6 Morris **7** maypole
French: 6 can-can **8** galliard **9** ecossaise
German: 11 schottische
Indian: 6 kathak **8** manipuri **9** kathakali **13** bharata nat yam
Japanese: 6 bugaku **7** dengaku **8** sarugaku
dance/theater: **2** no **3** noh **6** kabuki
Mexican: 3 hat
Polish: 7 mazurka **9** krakoviak, polonaise **11** varsovienne
Scottish: 5 sword
Siamese: 10 wayang wong
Spanish: 4 jota **6** bolero **8** flamenco **9** sevillana **10** seguidilla
modern dancer/choreographer: 4 Juba **8** Ted Shawn **9** Eliot Feld, Gene Kelly, Ray Bolger **10** Mary Wigman, Paul Draper, Twyla Tharp **11** Anna Sokolow, Antony Tudor, Eric Hawkins, Fred Astaire, Irene Castle, Ruth St Denis **12** Bill Robinson, Ginger Rogers, Martha Graham, Vernon Castle **13** Alwin Nikolais, Doris Humphrey, Isadora Duncan **14** Charles Weidman **15** Merce Cunningham
see also: **6** ballet

Divine Comedy Part II: 9 Purgatory
Divine Comedy Part III: 8 Paradise
heroine: 8 Beatrice

Dantes, Edmond
character in: 21 The Count of Monte Cristo
author: 5 Dumas (pere)

Danton, Ray
born: 9 New York NY
roles: 14 I'll Cry Tomorrow 18 The George Raft Story 27 The Rise and Fall of Legs Diamond

Danu
also: 4 Dana
origin: 5 Irish
mother of: 14 Tuatha De Danann

Danvers, Mrs
character in: 7 Rebecca
author: 9 Du Maurier

Daphnaea
epithet of: 7 Artemis
means: 11 of the laurel

Daphne
form: 5 nymph
father: 5 Ladon 6 Peneus
pursued by: 6 Apollo 9 Leucippus
changed into: 7 bay tree

Daphnephoria
festival of: 6 Apollo

Daphnis
occupation: 7 cowherd 8 shepherd
father: 6 Hermes
originated: 14 pastoral poetry
blinded by: 5 Nomia

Daphnis and Chloe
characters in: 12 Greek romance
author: 6 Longus

Daphnis et Chloe
ballet by: 5 Ravel
choreographer: 12 Michel Fokine

dapper 4 neat, trim 5 natty, smart 6 jaunty, modish, spiffy, sporty, spruce 7 stylish

dapple 3 dab, dot 4 spot 6 mottle

dappled 7 flecked, mottled, spotted 10 variegated

Darcy, Fitzwilliam
character in: 17 Pride and Prejudice
author: 6 Austen

Dardanus
father: 4 Zeus
mother: 7 Electra
twin brother: 6 Iasion
wife: 6 Myrina
son: 12 Erechthonius
ancestor of: 7 Trojans

dare 3 bet 4 defy 5 taunt 7 venture 9 challenge 11 provocation

daredevil 4 bold, rash 5 risky 8 heedless, reckless 9 audacious, breakneck, risk-taker 11 adventurous 12 death-defying, devil-may-care 13 adventuresome

daredevilry 6 daring 8 rashness 9 derring-do 10 imprudence 12 carelessness, heedlessness, recklessness 13 foolhardiness

Dares
companion of: 6 Aeneas
noted for: 6 boxing

Dares Phrygius
priest of: 10 Hephaestus

Dar es Salaam
former capital of: 8 Tanzania

Darien *see* 8 Colombia

daring 4 bold, game 5 brave 6 plucky 7 bravery, courage, gallant, valiant 8 audacity, boldness, intrepid 9 audacious, dauntless, undaunted 10 courageous 11 adventurous, venturesome 13 audaciousness 15 adventurousness

daring deed 4 feat 7 exploit 11 achievement

dark 3 dim 4 deep, evil, inky 5 angry, black, bleak, dingy, dusky, murky, night, shady 6 dismal, dreary, gloomy, hidden, opaque, secret, somber, sullen, wicked 7 evening, joyless, obscure, ominous, shadowy, sunless 8 eventide, frowning, hopeless, overcast, sinister, twilight 9 concealed, nightfall, nighttime, sorrowful 10 forbidding 11 threatening 12 discouraging 13 disheartening

darken 3 dim, dye 4 tint 5 cloud, color 6 sadden 7 blacken, obscure 8 dispirit

darkened 3 dim 5 dusky, unlit 6 cloudy, gloomy 7 clouded 9 blackened, tenebrous, unlighted 10 blacked out 13 unilluminated

darkening 7 eclipse, shading 8 clouding, lowering 9 obscuring, shadowing 10 blackening 12 clouding over

Dark Frontier, The
author: 10 Eric Ambler

dark-hued 5 black, dusky, ebony, raven 6 somber 7 swarthy

Dark Is Light Enough, The
author: 14 Christopher Fry

Dark Lady, The
author: 16 Louis Auchincloss

Dark Laughter
author: 16 Sherwood Anderson

darkness 4 dusk 5 night, shade 7 dimness, evening 8 eventide, twilight 9 blackness, nightfall, nighttime

Darkness at Noon
author: 14 Arthur Koestler

Darkness Visible
author: 14 William Golding

Dark Victory
director: 14 Edmund Goulding
cast: 10 Bette Davis 11 George Brent 12 Ronald Reagan 14 Humphrey Bogart 19 Geraldine Fitzgerald
remade as: 11 Stolen Hours

darling 4 cute, dear, love 5 loved, sweet 6 adored, lovely 7 beloved, dearest, lovable 8 adorable, charming, precious 9 cherished 10 attractive, enchanting, sweetheart 11 captivating

Darling
director: 15 John Schlesinger
cast: 11 Dirk Bogarde 13 Julie Christie 14 Laurence Harvey
Oscar for: 6 script 7 actress (Christie)

Darling, Wendy
character in: 8 Peter Pan
author: 6 Barrie

darn 4 damn, dang, dash, drat, mend 5 blast, patch, sew up 6 hang it, stitch 7 consarn, doggone, goldang 8 confound 10 confound it

Darnay, Charles
character in: 16 A Tale of Two Cities
author: 7 Dickens

darnel 12 Biblical weed

Darnell, Linda
real name: 20 Monetta Eloyse Darnell
born: 8 Dallas TX
roles: 12 Blood and Sand, Forever Amber 14 The Mark of Zorro 17 Unfaithfully Yours

Darren, James
real name: 13 James Ercolani
born: 14 Philadelphia PA
roles: 6 Gidget 13 The Time Tunnel

dart 3 run 4 bolt, dash, flit, jump, leap, race, rush, tear 5 bound, fling, hurry, spear, spurt 6 hasten, spring, sprint 7 javelin, missile 10 projectile

D'Artagnan
character in: **18** The Three Musketeers
author: **5** Dumas (pere)

Dartle, Rosa
character in: **16** David Copperfield
author: **7** Dickens

Darwin, Charles
author of: **15** The Descent of Man **18** The Origin of Species **20** The Voyage of the Beagle
studied: **16** Galapagos Islands
field: **6** nature **7** biology
nationality: **7** British
theory of: **9** evolution **16** natural selection
ship: **6** Beagle

Dascylus
member of: **9** Argonauts
father: **5** Lycus

dash **3** bit, run, zip **4** bolt, dart, drop, elan, foil, hurl, race, ruin, rush, slam, tear, zeal **5** bound, crash, flair, fling, hurry, oomph, pinch, smash, speed, spoil, throw, touch, verve, vigor **6** dampen, energy, hasten, pizazz, spirit, splash, sprint, thrust, thwart **7** a little, panache, shatter, soupcon, spatter **8** splatter, splinter, vivacity **9** animation, frustrate **10** disappoint, discourage

dashing **4** bold **5** brave **6** daring, plucky **7** gallant **8** fearless, spirited, unafraid **9** audacious, impetuous **10** courageous **13** swashbuckling

dash one's hopes **5** daunt, unman **6** deject **7** depress **8** dispirit **10** discourage, dishearten

Dashwood, Elinor and Marianne
characters in: **19** Sense and Sensibility
author: **6** Austen

DaSilva, Howard
real name: **17** Harold Silverblatt
born: **11** Cleveland OH
roles: **8** Oklahoma **12** Sergeant York **14** The Great Gatsby **20** Abe Lincoln in Illinois

Dass, Secundra
character in: **21** The Master of Ballantrae
author: **9** Stevenson

dastard **3** cad **6** coward, craven **7** bounder, caitiff, chicken **8** poltroon **11** yellow-belly

dastardly **3** low **4** base, mean, vile **6** sneaky **8** cowardly, shameful **9** atrocious **10** despicable

data **4** dope, info **5** facts **7** dossier, figures **8** evidence **9** documents **11** information

Datchery, Mr
character in: **22** The Mystery of Edwin Drood
author: **7** Dickens

date **3** age, era **5** court, epoch, stage **6** escort, period **7** partner, take out **9** companion, originate **10** engagement, rendezvous **11** appointment

date **18** Phoenix dactylifera
varieties: **5** cliff **6** Ceylon **7** Chinese **9** Jerusalem **12** Canary Island

dated **5** passe **6** old hat **8** obsolete, outmoded **9** out-of-date **10** antiquated **12** old-fashioned **13** unfashionable

daub **4** blot, coat, soil, spot **5** cover, dirty, paint, smear, stain **6** blotch, smirch, smudge **7** splotch

Daudet, Alphonse
author of: **6** Sappho **15** The Woman of Arles **17** Letters from My Mill **18** Tartarin of Tarascon

Daughter of the Regiment, The
opera by: **9** Donizetti

Daumier, Honore
born: **6** France **10** Marseilles
artwork: **7** Bathers **9** Gargantua **12** Men of Justice **13** Bluestockings **14** The Washerwoman **16** The Good Bourgeois **18** The Legislative Body **19** Professors and Pupils **20** Stories from Antiquity **21** The Third-Class Carriage

daunt **3** cow **4** dash, faze **5** abash, alarm, scare **6** deject, dismay, menace, subdue **7** depress, unnerve **8** affright, browbeat, frighten, threaten **10** discourage, dishearten, intimidate

dauntless **4** bold **5** brave, gutsy **6** daring, heroic **7** gallant, valiant **8** fearless, resolute, unafraid, valorous **10** courageous **12** stouthearted

dauntlessness **4** grit, guts, sand **5** nerve, pluck, spunk, valor **6** daring, mettle **7** bravery, courage, resolve **8** boldness **9** fortitude **10** resolution **12** fearlessness, resoluteness **16** stout-heartedness

Davers, Lady
character in: **6** Pamela
author: **10** Richardson

David
king of: **6** Israel
father: **5** Jesse
wife: **6** Maacah, Michal **7** Abigail, Ahinoam, Haggith **9** Bathsheba
son: **5** Amnon **7** Absalom, Chileab, Solomon **8** Adonijah
daughter: **5** Tamar
brother: **5** Eliab **7** Shammah **8** Abinadab
sister: **7** Abigail
friend: **5** Abner **8** Jonathan
nephew: **5** Amasa
city of: **9** Bethlehem, Jerusalem
anointed by: **6** Samuel
killed: **7** Goliath
wrote: **6** Psalms
comforter: **7** Abishag
conspirators against: **4** Joab **8** Abiathar, Adonijah
pertaining to: **7** Davidic

David, Jacques-Louis
born: **5** Paris **6** France
artwork: **13** Mme de Verninac **15** The Death of Marat **19** The Oath of the Horatii **23** The Coronation of Napoleon **26** View of the Luxembourg Gardens **31** The Intervention of the Sabine Women

David Copperfield
author: **14** Charles Dickens
character: **3** Ham **6** Barkis, Mr Dick **7** Creakle **8** Traddles **9** Mr Spenlow, Uriah Heep **10** Aunt Betsey, Little Em'ly, Mr Micawber, Rosa Dartle, Steerforth **11** Dora Spenlow, Little Emily, Mr Murdstone, Mr Wickfield, Mrs Gummidge **13** Clara Peggotty **14** Agnes Wickfield, Betsey Trotwood
director: **11** George Cukor
cast: **8** W C Fields **10** Madge Evans **11** Frank Lawton, Roland Young **13** Basil Rathbone, Edna May Oliver **15** Lionel Barrymore **16** Maureen O'Sullivan **18** Freddie Bartholomew

David Harum
author: **19** Edward Noyes Westcott

Davies, Arthur Bowen
born: **7** Utica NY

artwork: **5** Dream **8** Unicorns **9** Crescendo **13** Every Saturday **15** Dancing Children, Sacramental Tree **17** Along the Erie Canal **18** Leda and the Dioscuri

Davies, Marion
real name: **19** Marion Cecilia Douras
lover: **21** William Randolph Hearst
born: **10** Brooklyn NY
roles: **12** Cain and Mable **13** Runaway Romany **15** Tillie the Toiler

Davis, Bette
real name: **18** Ruth Elizabeth Davis
husband: **11** Gary Merrill
born: **8** Lowell MA
roles: **7** Jezebel (Oscar) **9** Dangerous (Oscar), The Letter **10** Now Voyager, The Old Maid **11** All About Eve, Dark Victory **14** Of Human Bondage, The Little Foxes **18** The Petrified Forest **22** Hush Hush Sweet Charlotte **26** What Ever Happened to Baby Jane?

Davis, H L
author of: **14** Honey in the Horn

Davis, Ossie
wife: **7** Ruby Dee
born: **9** Cogdell GA
author: **16** Purlie Victorious
roles/films: **7** Jamaica **15** A Raisin in the Sun **18** No Time for Sergeants **19** Cotton Comes to Harlem

Davis, Sammy Jr
wife: **8** May Britt
group: **14** Will Master Trio
born: **9** New York NY
autobiography: **7** Yes I Can
roles: **11** Mr Wonderful **12** Porgy and Bess **20** The Benny Goodman Story

Davis, Stuart
born: **14** Philadelphia PA
artwork: **4** Visa **9** Eggbeater **11** Lucky Strike, Ready to Wear **11** Owh! In Sao Pao **12** The Mellow Pad **14** Colonial Cubism **15** Cigarette Papers

Davy, Humphrey
field: **9** chemistry
nationality: **7** British
isolated: **5** boron **6** barium, sodium **7** calcium **8** chlorine **9** magnesium, potassium, strontium
invented: **8** Davy lamp **10** miner's lamp

dawdle **4** idle, loaf **5** dally, delay **6** loiter **10** dillydally **12** putter around **13** procrastinate

dawdler
French: **7** flaneur

dawdling
French: **8** flanerie

dawn **4** rise **5** begin, birth, occur, start, sunup **6** advent, appear, Aurora, emerge, origin, strike, unfold **7** develop, sunrise **8** commence, daybreak, daylight **9** beginning, emergence, inception, unfolding **12** commencement
god of: **8** Heimdall
goddess of: **3** Eos **6** Aurore, Matuta

dawning **5** sunup **7** morning, sunrise **8** daybreak, daylight

Dawn Patrol, The
director: **14** Edmund Goulding
cast: **10** David Niven, Errol Flynn **11** Donald Crisp **13** Basil Rathbone **14** Melville Cooper **15** Barry Fitzgerald

day **3** age **4** date, time **5** epoch **6** period

Day, Clarence (Jr)
author of: **14** God and My Father, Life with Father, Life with Mother

Day, Doris
real name: **18** Doris von Kappelhoff
born: **12** Cincinnati OH
autobiography: **19** Doris Day Her Own Story
roles: **10** Pillow Talk **12** Calamity Jane **13** The Pajama Game **15** Move Over Darling, The Doris Day Show **23** Please Don't Eat the Daisies

daybed **5** couch **6** lounge **12** chaise longue

day book **5** diary **6** agenda **7** journal **8** calendar, schedule

daybreak **4** dawn **5** sunup **7** sunrise

daydream **4** muse **5** fancy **7** fantasy, imagine, reverie **9** fantasize **10** wool-gather **14** castle in the air

Day for Night
director: **16** Francois Truffaut
cast: **15** Jean-Pierre Leaud **16** Francois Truffaut, Jacqueline Bisset, Jean-Pierre Aumont
Oscar for: **11** foreign film

daylight **4** dawn **5** sunup **7** morning, sunrise **8** full view, openness, sunlight, sunshine

Days and Nights
author: **17** Konstantin Simonov

day's end **3** eve **4** dusk, even **6** sunset **7** evening, sundown **8** gleaming, twilight **9** nightfall

Days of Heaven
director: **14** Terrence Malick
cast: **9** Linda Manz **10** Sam Shepard **11** Brooke Adams, Richard Gere
Oscar for: **14** cinematography

Days of Wine and Roses
director: **12** Blake Edwards
cast: **9** Lee Remick **10** Jack Lemmon **11** Jack Klugman **15** Charles Bickford
score: **12** Henry Mancini

daze **4** numb, stun **5** amaze, shock **6** benumb, dazzle, excite, muddle, stupor **7** astound, confuse, stagger, startle, stupefy **8** astonish, bewilder, surprise **9** disorient, electrify **11** flabbergast **12** astonishment, bewilderment, blow one's mind **14** discombobulate

dazed **5** woozy **6** groggy **7** confused, dazzled, stunned **9** befuddled, stupefied **10** bewildered, punch-drunk

dazzle **3** awe **4** blur, daze **5** blind **6** excite **7** confuse, overawe **9** electrify, overpower, overwhelm

dazzling **7** radiant **8** blinding **9** sparkling **10** impressive, staggering **11** coruscating **12** breathtaking, electrifying, overwhelming **14** flabbergasting

deacon **6** cleric **9** churchman, clergyman **12** ecclesiastic

deactivate **6** defuse **9** switch off **10** neutralize

dead, the dead **4** beat, cold, dull, flat **5** depth, exact, midst, quiet, spent, tired, total, utter, vapid **6** entire, middle, unused **7** defunct, expired, extinct, insipid, precise, useless, utterly, worn-out **8** abruptly, absolute, complete, deceased, entirely, inactive, lifeless, obsolete, perished, stagnant, suddenly, thorough, unerring **9** exhausted, inanimate, inorganic **10** absolutely, completely, lackluster, unemployed, unexciting **11** ineffectual, inoperative **12** unproductive, unprofitable
Latin: **8** ad patres
god of: **6** Osiris **7** Veiovis

dead body **5** stiff **6** corpse **7** cadaver, remains

deaden **4** dope, drug, dull, mute, numb **5** abate, blunt **6** lessen, muffle, soothe, subdue, weaken **7** assuage, smother **8** diminish, mitigate, moderate **9** alleviate **11** anesthetize

deadened 5 muted **6** dulled, numbed **7** muffled, subdued

Dead Father, The
author: 15 Donald Barthelme

Dea Dia
origin: 5 Roman
goddess of: 11 agriculture
corresponds to: 13 Acca Laurentia

deadlock 7 impasse **8** standoff **9** stalemate **10** standstill

deadly 3 wan **4** dull **5** ashen, awful, fatal, fully, undue **6** boring, lethal, mortal, pallid **7** awfully, baneful, destroy, extreme, ghostly, tedious, totally **8** dreadful, entirely, horribly, terrible, terribly, tiresome **9** excessive, malignant, wearisome **10** cadaverous, completely, implacable, inordinate, relentless, thoroughly **11** destructive, unrelenting

deadpan 5 sober **8** detached **9** impassive **11** unemotional **13** straight-faced

dead ringer 4 copy, mate, twin **6** double **9** duplicate **11** counterpart **13** spitting image

Dead Souls
author: 12 Nikolai Gogol

dead to the world 6 asleep **7** out cold **9** konked out **10** fast asleep, slumbering **11** sound asleep

dead weight 7 ballast **9** inert mass

Dead Zone, The
author: 11 Stephen King

deal 3 act **4** give, hand **5** round, see to, trade, treat **6** behave, handle, market **7** bargain, concern, deliver, dole out, give out, mete out, oversee **8** consider, dispense **9** agreement, apportion **10** administer, distribute, **11** arrangement **12** distribution **13** apportionment

dealer 5 agent **6** monger, trader, vendor **8** merchant **10** trafficker **11** distributor

dealing, dealings 5 trade **7** traffic **8** business, practice **9** relations, treatment **12** transactions

dealing out 8 dividing **9** allotting, bestowing **10** conferring, consigning, dispensing **12** apportioning, distributing

Dea Marica *see* **6** Marica

Dean, Dizzy (Jay Hanna)
sport: 8 baseball
position: 7 pitcher
team: 16 St Louis Cardinals
part of: 12 Gashouse Gang
brother: 4 Paul

Dean, James (Jimmy)
real name: 14 James Byron Dean
born: 8 Marion IN
roles: 5 Giant **10** East of Eden **18** Rebel Without a Cause

Deane, Seneca
character in: 7 Babbitt
author: 5 Lewis

Dean's December
author: 10 Saul Bellow

dear 4 love **5** angel, loved **6** costly **7** beloved, darling **8** esteemed, favorite, precious **9** cherished, expensive, respected **10** sweetheart
French: 5 cheri **6** cherie

Dear Antoine
author: 11 Jean Anouilh

Dear Brutus
author: 12 James M Barrie

dearest 7 beloved, darling

dearth 4 lack **7** paucity **8** scarcity, shortage **10** deficiency

death, Death 5 dying **6** demise **7** decease, passing **9** departure **10** expiration, grim reaper
goddess of: 3 Hel **7** Berchta, Perchta **10** Ereshkigal

Death Be Not Proud
author: 9 John Donne

death blow
French: 11 coup de grace

Death Comes for the Archbishop
author: 11 Willa Cather
character: 7 Jacinto **9** Kit Carson **16** Bishop Jean Latour **20** Father Joseph Vaillant

death-dealing 5 fatal **6** lethal, mortal **7** killing **11** destructive

death-defying 4 bold, rash **5** risky **6** daring **8** reckless **9** audacious, breakneck, daredevil

Death in the Family, A
author: 9 James Agee

Death in Venice
director: 15 Luchino Visconti
author: 10 Thomas Mann
cast: 9 Mark Burns **11** Dirk Bogarde **14** Marisa Berenson

deathless 7 eternal **8** immortal **9** perpetual **11** everlasting

deathlike 3 wan **4** pale **5** ashen **6** pallid **7** ghastly **9** bloodless **10** cadaverous, corpselike

deathly 4 very **7** extreme, intense **8** terrible **9** extremely **12** overwhelming **15** resembling death

Death of a Salesman
director: 12 Laslo Benedek
author: 12 Arthur Miller
character: 4 Biff **5** Happy, Linda **7** Bernard, Charley **8** Uncle Ben **10** Willy Loman
cast: 13 Frederic March, Kevin McCarthy **14** Mildred Dunnock **15** Cameron Mitchell

Death of Ivan Ilyich, The
author: 10 Leo Tolstoy

Death of the Gods, The
author: 17 Dmitri Merejkowski

Death of the Heart
author: 14 Elizabeth Bowen

Death on the Nile
author: 14 Agatha Christie

Death Takes a Holiday
director: 14 Mitchell Leisen
cast: 11 Guy Standing **13** Evelyn Venable, Frederic March (Death)

Death Valley Days
host: 12 Robert Taylor, Ronald Reagan **13** Dale Robertson **14** Stanley Andrews

debacle 4 rout, ruin **5** havoc, wreck **8** collapse, disaster, downfall **9** breakdown, cataclysm, overthrow, ruination **10** bankruptcy **11** catastrophe, devastation, dissolution **12** vanquishment **14** disintegration

debar 3 ban **6** reject **7** exclude, keep out **8** preclude, prohibit **9** blackball, blacklist

debark 4 land

debarment 7 removal **8** omission **9** exception, exclusion, exemption, rejection **11** elimination, prohibition **12** nonadmission

debase 5 lower **6** befoul, defile **7** corrupt, degrade **8** disgrace, dishonor **9** desecrate **10** adulterate **11** deteriorate **16** impair the worth of **18** reduce the quality of

debased 4 vile **6** impure **7** corrupt, defiled, lowered **8** degraded, depraved **9** debauched, disgraced, dissolute, perverted **10** degenerate, dissipated **11** adulterated

debasement 9 decadence, depravity **10** corruption, debauchery, degeneracy, immorality, perversion **13** dissoluteness

debatable 4 iffy **6** unsure **7** dubious **8** arguable, doubtful **9** uncertain, undecided **10** disputable **12** questionable **13** problematical

debate 5 argue **6** ponder **7** discuss, dispute, reflect **8** argument, cogitate, consider, hash over **10** cogitation, deliberate, discussion, meditation, reflection, think about **12** deliberation, meditate upon **13** consideration

debauch 4 orgy **5** revel, spree **6** debase **7** carouse, corrupt, deprave, revelry, subvert **8** carousal **9** bacchanal **10** lead astray, saturnalia

debauched 4 lewd **6** wanton **7** corrupt, debased, immoral **8** degraded, depraved, perverse, vitiated **9** abandoned, corrupted, dissolute, lecherous, led astray, perverted, reprobate, shameless **10** degenerate, dissipated, lascivious, libidinous, licentious, profligate **12** disreputable

debauchery 6 excess **11** dissipation **12** immoderation, intemperance **14** self-indulgence

DeBeck, Billy
creator/artist of: 12 Barney Google **20** Parlor Bedroom and Sink

debilitate 6 weaken **7** wear out **8** enervate **10** devitalize, make feeble **17** deprive of strength

debilitated 5 frail **6** feeble, infirm **7** worn out **8** delicate, weakened **9** enervated **11** devitalized

debilitation 8 handicap, weakness **9** infirmity **10** affliction, disability, impairment, inadequacy **11** disablement

debility 7 fatigue, frailty **8** asthenia, handicap, senility, weakness **9** infirmity, lassitude, weakening **10** affliction, enervation, exhaustion, feebleness, impairment, invalidism, sickliness **11** decrepitude, prostration

Debir
conqueror: 7 Othniel

debit 4 debt **6** red ink **7** account, payable **9** liability **10** balance due, obligation **11** ledger entry, shortcoming

debonair 5 suave **6** dapper, jaunty, urbane **7** buoyant, elegant, genteel, refined **8** carefree, charming, gracious, wellbred **9** sprightly **11** free and easy **12** lighthearted **13** sophisticated

Deborah 11 Hebrew judge
companion: 7 Rebekah
summoned: 5 Barak

debouch 5 drain **6** emerge, let out **7** flow out **9** discharge

debris 4 crap, junk **5** dreck, dregs, dross, ruins, scrap, trash, waste **6** litter, rubble, shards **7** clutter, garbage, rubbish **8** detritus, wreckage **9** fragments

debt 4 bill **5** debit **7** arrears **9** liability **10** obligation **15** deferred payment, that which is owed

debunk 4 bare **5** strip **6** expose, send up, show up, unmask **7** deflate, lampoon, take off, uncloak, uncover **8** ridicule, satirize **9** burlesque, demystify, disparage **13** demythologize

Debussy, Claude Achille
born: 6 France **15** St Germain-en-Laye
composer of: 5 La Mer **6** Gigues, Iberia, Images **8** Estampes **9** Nocturnes, Printemps **11** Clair de Lune **13** En Blanc et Noir **15** Children's Corner, L'Enfant prodigue **16** La Demoiselle Elue, Suite Bergamasque **17** Rondes de Printemps, The Blessed Damozel **18** Pelleas et Melisande **24** The Girl with the Flaxen Hair **26** Prelude a l'apres-midi d'un faune **28** Prelude to the Afternoon of a Faun

debut 9 coming out **12** presentation

decadence 5 decay **7** decline **10** corruption, debasement, degeneracy, immorality **12** degeneration **13** deterioration

decadent 7 corrupt, debased, immoral **8** decaying, depraved, perverse **9** debauched, dissolute, perverted **10** degenerate
French: 11 fin de siecle

Decalogue 15 Ten Commandments

Decameron, The
author: 17 Giovanni Boccaccio

decamp 7 move off, run away, take off **8** march off, sneak off

decampment 6 escape, flight **7** getaway

decant 4 pour **7** draw off, pour out

decanter 6 bottle, carafe, vessel

decathlon winner 11 Bruce Jenner

Decatur, Stephen
served in: 11 Algerine War, Barbary Wars **13** Tripolitan War **19** War of Eighteen Twelve
commander of ship: 12 United States
defeated ship: 10 Macedonian (British)
saying: 22 "Our country right or wrong"

decay 3 rot **5** spoil **7** corrode, putrefy, rotting **8** spoiling **9** decompose **12** disintegrate, putrefaction **13** decomposition
goddess of: 4 Hour **5** Horae

decayed 3 bad **6** putrid, rotted, rotten, ruined **7** corrupt, gone bad, spoiled **10** decomposed **12** deteriorated **13** disintegrated

deceased *see* **4** dead

deceit 5 fraud **8** cheating, trickery **9** duplicity **10** dishonesty, trickiness **11** fraudulence **13** double-dealing **15** underhandedness **17** misrepresentation

deceitful 5 false **6** crafty, sneaky, tricky **7** cunning **9** dishonest, insincere **11** duplicitous, treacherous, underhanded **12** hypocritical **13** double-dealing, untrustworthy

deceitfulness 5 fraud **7** cunning, slyness **9** falseness, hypocrisy, treachery **10** craftiness, dishonesty, sneakiness, trickiness **11** insincerity **15** underhandedness **17** untrustworthiness

deceive 3 con **4** fool **5** cheat, put on, trick **6** delude **7** defraud, mislead, swindle

deceiver 4 fake **5** cheat, fraud, quack **6** con man **7** cozener **8** impostor, swindler **9** charlatan, trickster **10** mountebank **13** confidence man

decelerate 5 brake **8** slow down

deceleration 7 braking, slowing

December *see box, p. 248*

decency 7 decorum, modesty **9** propriety **14** respectability **15** appropriateness

decent 4 fair, nice **5** ample **6** proper, seemly **7** correct, fitting **8** adequate, gracious, obliging, passable, suitable

December
event: **11** Pearl Harbor (7), Winter solstice (21, 22)
flower: **5** holly **9** narcissus
French: **8** Decembre
gem: **4** ruby **6** zircon **9** turquoise
German: **8** Dezember
holiday: **8** Hanukkah **9** Boxing Day (26), Christmas (25) **16** Saint Nicholas Day (6)
Italian: **8** Dicembre
number of days: **9** thirty-one
origin of name: **5** decem (Latin meaning ten)
place in year:
Gregorian: **7** twelfth
Roman: **5** tenth
Julian: **7** twelfth
Spanish: **9** Diciembre
Zodiac sign: **9** Capricorn **11** Sagittarius

9 courteous **10** acceptable, sufficient **11** appropriate **12** satisfactory **13** accommodating

deception **5** fraud, trick **7** cunning **8** artifice, illusion, trickery **9** duplicity, treachery **10** trickiness **11** fraudulence, insincerity **13** double-dealing

deceptive **5** phony **9** dishonest **10** fraudulent, misleading

deceptiveness **5** fraud **11** fraudulence

decibel
abbreviation: **2** dB

decide **4** rule **5** elect, judge **6** choose, decree, select, settle **7** resolve **9** determine

decided **4** firm **7** certain **8** clear-cut, definite, emphatic, resolute **9** assertive **10** deliberate, determined, unwavering **12** indisputable, strong-willed, unhesitating, unmistakable **14** unquestionable

decidedly **9** certainly **10** absolutely **11** indubitably, undoubtedly **12** indisputably, unmistakably **13** unequivocally **14** unquestionably

decidedness **7** purpose, resolve **10** resolution **12** resoluteness **13** determination **14** purposefulness

decide on **5** adopt, elect **6** choose, opt for, select, settle **7** appoint, arrange, embrace, espouse, pick out **8** settle on **9** determine, establish, single out

decigram
abbreviation: **2** dg

deciliter
abbreviation: **2** dL

decimate **6** reduce **7** destroy **8** massacre **9** slaughter **13** greatly reduce

decimeter
abbreviation: **2** dm

decipher **5** solve **6** decode, deduce, render **7** decrypt, dope out, explain, make out, unravel **8** construe, untangle **9** interpret, translate **12** cryptanalyze

decision **6** decree, ruling **7** finding, outcome, purpose, resolve, verdict **8** judgment **10** conclusion, resolution **12** resoluteness **13** determination **14** purposefulness

decisive **4** firm **5** final **8** absolute, definite, positive, resolute **10** conclusive, convincing, definitive, determined, undeniable **12** indisputable

decisive blow **9** deathblow **11** coup de grace

decisiveness **7** purpose, resolve **10** resolution **12** resoluteness **14** purposefulness

decisive point **3** nut **4** core, crux, gist **5** basis, heart **6** kernel **7** essence **9** essential

deck **4** garb, trim **5** adorn, array, dress, prank **6** clothe, doll up, enrich, outfit, tog out **7** apparel, bedizen, festoon, furbish, garnish, gussy up **8** accouter, beautify, ornament, spruce up **9** embellish

Decker, Mary
sport: **7** running
married name: **6** Slaney

deck out **5** adorn, array, dress **6** attire, clothe, fit out, outfit, rig out **7** costume

declaim **4** rail **5** orate **6** recite **7** inveigh **9** sermonize **11** pontificate

declaration **6** avowal, notice **8** document **9** assertion, statement, testimony **10** deposition **11** affirmation, attestation, publication **12** announcement, notification, proclamation **14** acknowledgment

declare **4** show **6** affirm, reveal **7** express **8** announce, proclaim **9** pronounce

declare null and void **6** cancel, repeal, revoke **7** abolish, rescind, retract **8** abrogate, set aside **9** repudiate **10** invalidate **11** countermand

declare untrue **4** deny **9** repudiate **10** contradict

decline **3** ebb **4** drop, fail, flag, sink, wane **5** decay, slump, spurn **6** balk at, eschew, lessen, refuse, reject, weaken, worsen **7** dwindle **8** decrease, diminish, downfall **9** downgrade, downswing **11** deteriorate **13** deterioration

Decline and Fall
author: **11** Evelyn Waugh

Decline and Fall of the Roman Empire, The
author: **12** Edward Gibbon

declivity **4** drop **5** slant, slope **6** plunge **7** descent

decompose **3** rot **5** decay, spoil **7** putrefy **8** separate **10** go to pieces **12** disintegrate

decomposed **6** putrid, rotted, rotten **7** decayed, spoiled **9** putrefied **13** disintegrated

decontaminate **6** purify **9** disinfect, sterilize

decor **13** ornamentation

decorate **4** trim **5** adorn, array, honor **7** festoon, garnish **8** beautify, ornament **9** embellish

decorated **5** fancy **6** decked, ornate **7** adorned, trimmed **8** bedecked **9** bemedaled, bedizened, garnished **10** ornamented **11** embellished

decoration **4** trim **5** award, badge, medal **6** emblem, ribbon **7** garnish **8** ornament, trimming **9** adornment **13** embellishment, ornamentation **14** beautification

decorous **3** fit **6** decent, polite, proper, seemly **7** correct **8** becoming, mannerly, suitable **9** dignified **10** respectful **11** appropriate

decorum **4** tact **5** taste **7** dignity **8** good form **9** gentility, propriety **10** politeness **14** respectability

decoy **4** bait, lure **5** plant, snare **6** allure, come-on, entice **10** enticement, inducement **11** smoke screen

decrease **4** drop, ease, loss **5** abate, taper **6** lessen, reduce **7** cutback, decline, dwindle, fall-off, slacken, subside **8** diminish **9** abatement, dwindling, lessening, reduction **10** de-escalate, diminution **12** de-escalation

decree **3** law **5** edict, order

6 dictum, ruling 7 command, mandate, statute 8 proclaim 9 authorize 12 proclamation

decrepit 7 rickety 8 battered 10 broken-down 11 dilapidated

decrescendo
music: 22 gradually getting softer
abbreviation: 4 decr

decry 7 censure, condemn 8 denounce 9 criticize, deprecate, disparage

Dedalus, Stephen
character in: 7 Ulysses 30 Portrait of the Artist as a Young Man
author: 5 Joyce

dedicate 6 commit, devote, launch, pledge 7 address, present 8 inscribe

dedication 8 devotion 10 commitment 11 devotedness 16 prefatory address 20 prefatory inscription

Dedlock, Sir Leicester and Lady
characters in: 10 Bleak House
author: 7 Dickens

deduce 5 infer 6 gather, reason 8 conclude 10 comprehend, understand

deduct 4 take 6 remove 8 subtract, take from, withdraw 10 decrease by

deduction 5 guess 6 belief, credit, rebate 7 removal 8 analysis, decrease, discount, judgment, markdown, rollback 9 abatement, allowance, exemption, gathering, inference, lessening, reasoning, reduction 10 assumption, concession, conclusion, diminuition, hypothesis, reflection, taking away, withdrawal 11 calculation, presumption, speculation, subtraction, supposition 13 comprehension, consideration, understanding 14 interpretation

Dee, Ruby
real name: 14 Ruby Ann Wallace
husband: 10 Ossie Davis
born: 11 Cleveland OH
roles: 15 A Raisin in the Sun 16 Purlie Victorious

Dee, Sandra
real name: 13 Alexandra Zuck
husband: 10 Bobby Darin
born: 9 Bayonne NJ
roles: 6 Gidget 12 A Summer Place 15 Tammy Tell Me True

deed 3 act 4 feat 5 title 6 action, effort 11 achievement 14 accomplishment

deeds are manly, words are womanish
Italian: 24 fatti maschii parole femine
motto of: 8 Maryland

deem 4 hold, view 5 judge, think 6 regard 7 believe 8 consider

de-emphasize 8 play down 9 underplay

deep 3 far, sea 4 dark, late, lost, rich, wise 5 far in, midst, ocean, vivid 6 astute, strong 7 extreme, intense, learned 8 absorbed, immersed, involved, profound, resonant, sonorous 9 engrossed, sagacious 10 discerning 11 intelligent 13 philosophical

Deep, The
author: 13 Peter Benchley

deeply 6 richly 7 acutely, gravely, greatly, vividly 8 entirely 9 intensely, seriously 10 completely, profoundly, resonantly, sonorously, thoroughly 12 passionately

deeply felt 6 ardent, fervid 7 earnest, fervent, intense, sincere, zealous 9 heartfelt 10 passionate 11 impassioned 12 wholehearted

deepness 10 profundity

deep-rooted 7 abiding, lasting 8 enduring 9 confirmed, ingrained

deep-seated 7 abiding, lasting 8 enduring 9 confirmed, ingrained

deep thought 10 absorption, brown study, intentness 11 engrossment 13 concentration

deep water 3 jam 4 mess 5 ocean 6 pickle 7 trouble 8 distress 10 difficulty 11 dire straits, predicament 12 over one's head

deer
young: 4 fawn
female: 3 doe

Deer Hunter, The
director: 13 Michael Cimino
cast: 10 John Cazale, John Savage 11 Meryl Streep 12 Robert De Niro 17 Christopher Walken
Oscar for: 7 picture 8 director 15 supporting actor (Walken)

Deerslayer, The
author: 19 James Fenimore Cooper
first of: 20 Leatherstocking Tales
character: 4 Hist 5 Hetty 6 Judith 10 Hurry Harry 11 Natty Bumppo (Deerslayer) 12 Chingachgook, Thomas Hutter

de-escalate 5 limit 6 lessen, narrow 8 contract, minimize

deface 3 mar 4 mark, scar 5 spoil 6 bruise, damage, impair, injure 9 disfigure

de facto 4 real 6 actual, really 8 actually

defalcate 8 embezzle 14 misappropriate

defamation 5 libel 7 calumny, slander 12 vilification 13 disparagement

defamatory 8 libelous 9 vilifying 10 calumnious, derogatory, slanderous 11 disparaging

defame 5 libel 6 malign, vilify 7 degrade, slander 8 derogate 9 denigrate, discredit, disparage 10 calumniate

Defarge, Madame
character in: 16 A Tale of Two Cities
author: 7 Dickens

default 10 nonpayment

defeat 4 foil, loss, rout 5 cream, crush, elude, quell 6 baffle, thwart 7 conquer, setback, shellac, trounce 8 confound, overcome, vanquish 9 frustrate, overpower, overthrow, overwhelm, thwarting 11 frustration 14 disappointment

defeated 4 beat 5 upset 6 beaten, bested, licked, routed 7 outdone, whipped, worsted 8 overcame 9 conquered, overthrew, put to rout 10 frustrated, overthrown 11 overpowered, overwhelmed 12 hors de combat

defect 4 flaw, scar, spot 5 break, crack, fault, stain 6 blotch, foible 7 blemish, default, failing, frailty 8 omission, weakness 10 deficiency 11 shortcoming 12 imperfection 14 incompleteness

defective 6 broken, faulty, flawed 7 lacking, wanting 8 abnormal, impaired 9 deficient, imperfect, subnormal 10 inadequate, out of order 11 inoperative 12 insufficient

Defence of Poetry
author: 18 Percy Bysshe Shelley

defend 5 guard 6 secure, shield, uphold 7 endorse, protect, shelter, stand by, support, sustain **8** advocate, champion, maintain, preserve **9** safeguard

defender **8** advocate, champion, guardian, upholder **9** protector, supporter

Defender of the Faith
Latin: **13** Fidei Defensor
title of: **17** English sovereigns

Defenders, The
character: **10** Joan Miller **14** Helen Donaldson, Kenneth Preston **15** Lawrence Preston
cast: **10** E G Marshall, Robert Reed **11** Joan Hackett, Polly Rowles

defense **4** care **5** guard **7** custody, support **8** advocacy, security **9** barricade, safeguard, upholding **10** protection, stronghold **11** maintenance, safekeeping **12** preservation **13** fortification, justification

defenseless **7** unarmed **8** helpless **10** on one's back, vulnerable, weaponless **11** unprotected, unresisting

defensible **3** fit **5** valid **6** proper **7** tenable **8** sensible, suitable **9** allowable, excusable **10** admissible, condonable, forgivable, pardonable, vindicable **11** justifiable, permissible, supportable, warrantable

defer **4** obey **5** delay, table, yield **6** accede, give in, put off, shelve, submit **7** respect, suspend **8** postpone **10** capitulate

deference **5** honor **6** esteem, regard **7** respect **9** obedience, reverence **12** capitulation **13** consideration

deferential **5** civil **6** polite **7** dutiful **8** obedient, reverent **9** courteous, regardful **10** respectful, submissive **11** acquiescent, considerate, reverential

deferment **4** stay **5** delay **9** extension **12** postponement

deferral **5** pause **6** hiatus, recess **8** abeyance **10** suspension **12** postponement **14** discontinuance

defiance **9** hostility, obstinacy, rebellion **12** disobedience **14** rebelliousness

defiant **4** bold **9** truculent **10** aggressive, rebellious **11** disobedient, provocative

Defiant Ones, The
director: **13** Stanley Kramer
cast: **10** Tony Curtis **11** Lon Chaney Jr **12** Cara Williams **13** Charles McGraw, Sidney Poitier, Theodore Bikel
Oscar for: **10** screenplay

deficiency **4** flaw **6** defect **7** failing, frailty **8** shortage, weakness **10** inadequacy **11** shortcoming **12** imperfection **13** insufficiency

deficient **4** weak **6** flawed **7** lacking, short on **8** inferior **9** defective **10** inadequate **11** substandard **12** insufficient **14** unsatisfactory

deficit **8** shortage **9** shortfall **10** deficiency

de fide **10** of the faith

defile **4** soil **5** dirty, smear, spoil, stain, taint **6** befoul, debase **7** degrade, profane, tarnish **8** besmirch, disgrace, dishonor **9** desecrate

defiled **5** dirty **6** fouled, impure, soiled **7** debased, dirtied, stained, sullied, tainted, unclean **8** befouled, polluted, ravished, smirched, violated **9** blackened, corrupted, tarnished **10** besmirched **12** contaminated

define **5** state **7** clarify, explain, specify **8** describe, spell out **9** delineate, designate

definite **3** set **4** sure **5** exact, fixed **7** certain, precise **8** clear-cut, positive

definitely **5** truly **6** indeed, surely **7** for sure, no doubt **9** assuredly, certainly, decidedly, doubtless, expressly **10** absolutely, decisively, explicitly, positively, undeniably **11** indubitably, inescapably, unavoidably, undoubtedly **12** unmistakably **13** categorically, unequivocally **14** unequivocally, unquestionably **16** incontrovertibly

definiteness **8** sureness **9** certainty, precision **10** exactitude **11** unambiguity

definition **6** limits **7** clarity, purpose **11** description **15** distinctiveness

definitive **5** exact **7** decided, perfect **8** complete, decisive, reliable **10** conclusive, consummate

deflate **6** reduce **7** flatten **8** contract **9** devaluate

deflect **6** divert, swerve

Defoe, Daniel
author of: **6** Roxana **11** Colonel Jack **12** Moll Flanders **14** Robinson Crusoe **23** A Journal of the Plague Year

DeForest, Lee
invented/worked on: **10** audion tube, television **13** sound pictures

deform **3** mar **4** maim **5** twist **6** mangle **7** contort, distort **9** disfigure

deformation **9** deformity **10** distortion **12** malformation **13** disfigurement

deformed **6** marred, warped **7** defaced, mangled, spoiled, twisted **8** crippled **9** misshapen, monstrous **10** disfigured

deformity **12** malformation

defraud **3** con **4** bilk, rook **5** cheat **6** fleece, rip off **7** swindle

defray **3** pay **5** cover **11** foot the bill

deft **3** apt **4** able, sure **5** quick **6** adroit, expert **8** skillful **9** dexterous

deftness **5** knack, skill **7** ability **8** facility **9** adeptness, dexterity, handiness **10** adroitness, competency **11** proficiency **12** skillfulness

defunct **4** dead **7** extinct

defy **5** spurn **6** oppose, resist **7** disdain **8** confront **9** challenge, disregard, withstand

degage **4** easy **8** detached **10** disengaged **13** unconstrained

Degas, (Hilaire Germain) Edgar
born: **5** Paris **6** France
artwork: **14** The Ballet Class, The Morning Bath **15** Ballet Rehearsal **16** The Millinery Shop **17** The Glass of Absinth **23** Woman with Chrysanthemums **30** The Little Fourteen-Year-Old Dancer

degeneracy **9** decadence, depravity **10** debasement, debauchery, immorality, perversion **11** dissolution

degenerate **3** rot **4** base, sink, vile **5** decay **6** revert, wanton, wicked, worsen **7** corrupt, debased, decline, go to pot, immoral, pervert, vicious **8** decadent, degraded, depraved **9** abandoned, backslide, debauched, dissolute, perverted **10** dissipated, go downhill, profligate, retrograde, retrogress **11** deteriorate, hit the skids **12** disintegrate

degeneration **7** decline **9** depravity **10** corruption, debasement, immorality, perversion **11** degradation, dissolution, viciousness **13** deterioration

degradation **8** disgrace **11** humiliation

Degradation of the Democratic Dogma, The
author: **10** Henry Adams

degrade **5** lower, shame **6** debase, demote **7** corrupt **8** disgrace, dishonor

degraded **4** vile **6** wicked **7** corrupt, debased, lowered **8** depraved, shameful, unworthy **9** debauched, perverted, reprobate **10** degenerate **11** undignified **12** unregenerate

degrading **3** low **6** menial **8** shameful **11** humiliating

degree **4** mark, step, unit **5** grade, level, order, phase, point, stage **8** division, interval
abbreviation: **3** deg

De Guiche, Lillian
real name of: **11** Lillian Gish

de gustibus non est disputandum **29** there is no disputing about tastes

De Havilland, Joan de Beauvoir
real name of: **12** Joan Fontaine

De Havilland, Olivia
sister: **12** Joan Fontaine
born: **5** Japan, Tokyo
roles: **7** Melanie **10** The Heiress (Oscar) **11** The Snake Pit **12** Captain Blood, To Each His Own (Oscar) **14** Anthony Adverse, My Cousin Rachel **15** Gone With the Wind, Hold Back the Dawn **16** Light in the Piazza **22** Hush Hush Sweet Charlotte **24** The Adventures of Robin Hood

dehydrate **3** dry **5** parch **6** dry out

dehydrated **3** dry **7** parched, thirsty **8** dried-out **9** shriveled **10** desiccated

Deianira
father: **6** Oeneus
mother: **7** Althaea
brother: **8** Meleager
husband: **8** Heracles
killed: **8** Heracles

Deicoon
father: **8** Hercules
mother: **6** Megara
killed by: **8** Hercules

Deidamia
father: **9** Lycomedes
lover: **8** Achilles
son: **11** Neoptolemus

deification **7** worship **8** idolatry **10** exaltation **13** glorification

deify **5** exalt **7** glorify, idolize, worship

Deighton, Len
author of: **4** SS-GB **14** The Ipcress File **15** Funeral in Berlin **16** Catch a Falling Spy

deign **4** deem **5** stoop **6** see fit **7** consent **8** think fit **10** condescend

Dei gratia **15** by the grace of God

Deimos
origin: **5** Greek
father: **4** Ares
mother: **9** Aphrodite
brother: **6** Phobus
personifies: **4** fear

Deino
member of: **6** Graeae, Graiae

Deinonychus
type: **8** dinosaur
period: **10** Cretaceous

Deiope
father: **11** Triptolemus

Deiphobe
form: **5** sibyl
father: **7** Glaucus

Deiphobus
father: **5** Priam
mother: **6** Hecuba
brother: **6** Hector
wife: **5** Helen
killed by: **8** Menelaus

Deipyle
father: **8** Adrastus
husband: **6** Tydeus
son: **8** Diomedes

Deipylus
grandfather: **5** Priam

Deirdre
origin: **5** Irish
husband: **6** Naoise
father-in-law: **6** Usnach
uncle: **9** Conchobar

Deirdre of the Sorrows
author: **19** John Millington Synge

deity, the Deity **3** god **4** idol **7** goddess, godhead, Jehovah **8** Almighty, divinity, immortal, Olympian

deja vu **11** already seen

dejected **3** low, sad **4** blue, down **7** doleful, unhappy **8** desolate **9** depressed, sorrowful **10** despondent, dispirited, spiritless **11** discouraged, downhearted, low-spirited **12** disconsolate, disheartened

dejection **5** gloom **7** sadness **10** depression, low spirits, melancholy **11** despondency **15** dispiritedness, downheartedness

dejeuner **5** lunch

de jure **7** by right **14** according to law

dekagram
abbreviation: **3** dkg

dekaliter
abbreviation: **3** dkL

dekameter, decameter
abbreviation: **3** dkm

Dekker, Thomas
author of: **11** Westward Ho! (with John Webster) **20** The Shoemaker's Holiday

de Kooning, Willem
born: **9** Rotterdam **14** The Netherlands
artwork: **5** Woman **8** Painting **15** Woman and Bicycle

Delacroix, Eugene
born: **6** France **18** Charenton-St Maurice
artwork: **8** Paganini **14** Women of Algiers **15** Massacre at Chios **16** The Barque of Dante **19** Chopin and George Sand **20** Dante and Virgil in Hell **22** Liberty at the Barricades, The Death of Sardanapalus

Delaroche, Paul
born: **5** Paris **6** France
artwork: **24** The Death of Queen Elizabeth, The Death of the Duke of Guise, **26** The Execution of Lady Jane Grey **36** Children of Edward Imprisoned in the Tower

Delaunay, Robert
born: **5** Paris **6** France
artwork: **5** Disks **6** Cities, Rhythm **7** Runners, Windows **10** Cathedrals **11** City of Paris, Eiffel Tower **14** The Cardiff Team **19** Cosmic Circular Forms **28** Simultaneous Prismatic Windows

Delaware ***see box, p. 252***

Delaware (Lenni-Lenape)
language family: **9** Algonkian **10** Algonquian
tribe: **5** Munsi, Unami **6** Munsee **11** Unalachtigo
location: **7** New York **8** Delaware **9** Manhattan, New Jersey **10** Long Island **12** Pennsylvania, Staten Island
leader: **7** Tamanen, Tammany
deity: **11** Kitanitowet

delay **4** slow, stay **5** check, table, tarry **6** dawdle, detain, hamper, hinder, hold up, impede, linger, put off, retard, shelve **7** inhibit, slowing, sus-

Delaware
abbreviation: 2 DE **3** Del
nickname: 5 First **7** Blue Hen, Diamond
capital: 5 Dover
largest city: 10 Wilmington
others: 5 Acoma, Lewes **6** Easton, Newark, Smyrna **7** Bris-ton, Elsmere, Milford **8** Claymont **9** New Castle **10** Georgetown
college: 6 Wesley **10** Brandywine, Wilmington **12** Goldey Beacom
feature: 10 Winterthur **15** Old Swedes Church **17** E I du Pont de Nemours
tribe: 4 Leni **5** Lenni **6** Lenape, Munsee
people: 10 Howard Pyle
island: 7 Fenwick
land rank: 10 forty-ninth
physical feature:
bay: **8** Delaware, Rehoboth
sea: **8** Atlantic
river: 8 Delaware **9** Christina, Nanticoke **10** Brandywine
state admission: 5 first
state bird: 14 blue hen chicken
state flower: 12 peach blossom
state motto: 22 Liberty and Independence
state song: 11 Our Delaware
state tree: 13 American holly

pend **8** dawdling, obstruct, postpone, reprieve, stoppage, tarrying **9** deferment, lingering, loitering **10** suspension **12** postponement, prolongation **13** procrastinate

delayed 4 late **6** put off, slowed **7** held up, stalled, tarried **8** arrested, deferred, detained, retarded **9** postponed, slackened **12** dillydallied **14** procrastinated **15** dragged one's feet

Delbruck, Max
field: 7 biology **17** molecular genetics
researched: 20 genetic recombination
awarded: 10 Nobel Prize

delectable 8 pleasant **9** agreeable, delicious, enjoyable **10** delightful, gratifying **11** pleasurable

delegate 4 give, name **5** agent, envoy, proxy **6** assign, charge, deputy **7** entrust **8** give over, transfer **9** authorize, designate **10** commission **14** representative

delegation 11 designation, entrustment **13** authorization, commissioning

delete 3 cut **4** omit **5** erase **6** cancel, remove

deleterious 7 harmful, hurtful, ruinous **9** dangerous, injurious **11** destructive, detrimental

Delia
festival of: 6 Apollo

deliberate 4 easy, slow, wary **5** weigh **6** confer, debate **7** careful, discuss, examine, express, planned, prudent, willful **8** cautious, cogitate, consider, measured, meditate, mull over **9** leisurely, unhurried **10** calculated, considered, purposeful, thoughtful **11** circumspect, contemplate, intentional, prearranged **12** premeditated

deliberate together 6 confer **7** consult, discuss

deliberation 4 care **6** debate **10** conference, discussion, steadiness **11** calculation, carefulness, forethought **13** premeditation **14** circumspection

Delibes, C P (Clement Philibert) Leo
born: 6 France **14** St Germain-du-Val
composer of: 5 Lakme **6** Sylvia **8** Coppelia **10** Le Roi l'a dit

delicacy 4 tact **5** taste **7** frailty **8** accuracy, elegance, fineness, softness, weakness **9** fragility, frailness, lightness, precision **10** perfection, smoothness **11** savoir-faire, sensibility, sensitivity, unsoundness **13** consideration, exquisiteness, sensitiveness **14** discrimination

delicate 4 fine, soft **5** frail, muted **6** ailing, dainty, feeble, flimsy, infirm, minute, savory, sickly, touchy, unwell **7** careful, elegant, fragile, refined, subdued, tactful **8** detailed, luscious, tasteful, ticklish, weakened **9** breakable, delicious, difficult, exquisite, palatable, sensitive, toothsome **10** appetizing, diplomatic, fastidious, perishable, precarious, scrupulous **11** debilitated

Delicate Balance, A
author: 11 Edward Albee

delicious 5 tasty **6** joyful, savory **8** charming, luscious, pleasant **9** palatable **10** appetizing, delectable, delightful **11** pleasurable **13** mouth-watering

delight 3 joy **5** amuse, charm, cheer, revel **6** please **7** enchant, gratify, rapture **8** pleasure **9** enjoyment, fascinate, happiness **13** gratification

delighted 6 elated **7** pleased **8** ecstatic **9** enchanted **10** captivated, enraptured, enthralled

delightful 6 peachy **7** amiable, amusing **8** charming, engaging, pleasing **9** agreeable, congenial, enjoyable **10** enchanting **11** pleasurable **12** entertaining

delight in 4 love **5** adore, eat up, enjoy, fancy, savor **6** dote on, relish **7** cherish **8** treasure **10** appreciate

Delilah
lover: 6 Samson
betrayed: 6 Samson

delineate 4 draw **5** draft **6** define, depict, design, lay out, sketch **7** outline, portray **8** describe **9** represent **12** characterize

delineation 9 depiction, portrayal **11** description **12** illustration **14** representation **16** characterization

delineavit 6 he drew (this) **7** she drew (this)

delinquency 7 misdeed **10** misconduct, negligence **11** dereliction, misbehavior **19** neglect of obligation

delinquent 3 due **4** late **6** remiss **7** hoodlum, misdoer, overdue **8** derelict **9** in arrears, miscreant, negligent, wrongdoer **10** neglectful

delirious 6 raving **7** excited, frantic **8** ecstatic, frenzied **10** incoherent **11** carried away **13** hallucinating

delirium 5 fever **6** frenzy, raving **7** madness, ranting **8** insanity **10** brain fever

Deliro
character in: **22** Every Man Out of His Humour
author: **6** Jonson

Delisle, Guillaume
field: **9** geography
nationality: **6** French
founder of: **15** modern geography

Delius, Frederick
born: **7** England **8** Bradford
composer of: **5** Paris **6** Koanga **7** Eventyr, Irmelin **8** Sea-Drift **9** Brigg Fair **10** Appalachia **11** A Mass of Life, Sur les Cimes **17** Fennimore and Gerda **20** North Country Sketches **22** A Village Romeo and Juliet, Over the Hills and Far Away

deliver **3** aim, say **4** bear, deal, free, give, save **5** bring, carry, throw, utter **6** convey, direct, launch, rescue, strike **7** release, set free **8** give over, hand over, liberate, proclaim, turn over **9** surrender **10** emancipate

deliverance **6** rescue **7** release **9** salvation **10** liberation **12** emancipation

Deliverance
director: **11** John Boorman
author: **11** James Dickey
cast: **8** Ronny Cox **9** Jon Voight, Ned Beatty **12** Burt Reynolds
song: **13** Dueling Banjos

deliver up **4** cede, give **5** grant, yield **8** fork over, hand over, transfer **9** surrender **10** relinquish

delivery **8** transfer **11** transferral, transmittal **12** transmission

dell **4** dale, dene, glen, vale **5** glade **6** dingle, hollow, valley

Della Robbia, Luca
born: **5** Italy **8** Florence
artwork: **8** Cantoria (Singing Gallery) **12** The Ascension **13** Altman Madonna **15** Madonna and Child, The Resurrection

Dello Joio, Norman
born: **9** New York NY
composer of: **7** The Ruby **12** Psalm of David **15** New York Profiles, The Trial at Rouen, Triumph of St Joan **20** Proud Music of the Storm, The Lamentation of Saul

Delon, Alain
born: **6** France, Sceaux
roles: **10** Purple Noon, The Leopard **13** The Black Tulip **14** Is Paris Burning? **19** Rocco and His Brothers

Delphic
pertains to: **6** Apollo, Delphi

Delphic oracle
oracle of: **6** Apollo
located at: **6** Delphi
priestess: **6** Pythia

Delphinia
festival of: **6** Apollo

Delphinius
epithet of: **6** Apollo
means: **7** dolphin

Delphinus
function: **12** intermediary
persuaded Amphitrite to marry: **8** Poseidon

Delphus
father: **8** Poseidon
mother: **8** Melantho

Delphyne
also: **6** Python
form: **7** monster
guarded: **4** Zeus **5** chasm
location: **6** Delphi
killed by: **6** Apollo

Del Rio, Dolores
real name: **21** Lolita Dolores Negrette
born: **6** Mexico **7** Durango
roles: **11** The Fugitive **13** Madame duBarry **15** Flying Down to Rio, Journey into Fear, Maria Candelaria

Delta Wedding
author: **11** Eudora Welty

delude **3** con **4** dupe, fool **5** put on, trick **7** deceive, mislead

deluge **4** bury, glut **5** drown, flood, spate, swamp **6** engulf **7** barrage, torrent **8** inundate, overflow, submerge **10** inundation

DeLuise, Dom
born: **10** Brooklyn NY
roles: **5** Fatso **6** The End **11** Silent Movie **14** Blazing Saddles

delusion **8** illusion **9** misbelief **10** aberration **11** derangement **13** hallucination, irrationality, misconception, self-deception

Delusions, Etc. of John Berryman
author: **12** John Berryman

deluxe **4** fine, posh **5** grand **6** choice, classy **7** elegant **8** splendid **9** luxurious

delve **5** probe **6** search **7** examine, explore **8** look into

demagogue **6** ranter **7** hothead, spouter **8** agitator, fomenter, inflamer **9** firebrand, haranguer **10** incendiary, malcontent, tub-thumper **12** rabble-rouser, troublemaker

demand **4** call, need, want **5** exact, order **7** command, require **11** requirement

demanding **4** hard **5** harsh, rigid **6** strict **8** exacting **9** difficult

demantoid
species: **6** garnet

demarche **4** gait, plan

demean **5** lower, shame **6** debase, humble **7** degrade **8** disgrace **9** humiliate

demeanor **6** manner **7** bearing, conduct **8** behavior, presence **10** appearance, deportment **11** comportment

demented **3** mad **4** nuts **5** crazy **6** crazed, cuckoo, insane **7** lunatic **8** deranged

dementia praecox **13** schizophrenia

dementophobia
fear of: **8** insanity

demesne **4** land **5** realm **6** domain, estate **8** property

Demeter
origin: **5** Greek
goddess of: **5** earth **9** fertility
protectress of: **8** marriage **11** social order
father: **6** Cronus
mother: **4** Rhea
daughter: **10** Persephone
corresponds to: **5** Brimo, Ceres **8** Despoena
epithet: **5** Chloe, Lusia, Mysia **6** Antaea, Erinys, Stiria **7** Chamyne, Thesmia **8** Stiritis **9** Anesidora, Thermasia **11** Carpophorus **13** Thesimophorus

Demetrius
character in: **21** A Midsummer Night's Dream
author: **11** Shakespeare

DeMille, Cecil B
director of: **9** Cleopatra **18** The Ten Commandments **22** The Greatest Show on Earth

Demiphon
form: **4** king
sacrificed: **7** maidens
to prevent: **6** plague

demise **3** end **4** fall, ruin **5** death **7** decease, passing **8** collapse **10** expiration

demobilization **7** release **9** discharge **10** disbanding

demobilize **7** disband, release **9** discharge

Democoon
father: **5** Priam
birth: **12** illegitimate
killed by: **8** Odysseus

democracy **8** equality, fairness

Democracy
author: **10** Henry Adams

Democracy in America
author: **19** Alexis de Tocqueville

Democratic Party
symbol: **6** donkey
president belonging to: **4** Polk **6** Carter, Pierce, Truman, Wilson **7** (Lyndon Baines) Johnson, Jackson, Kennedy **8** Buchanan, Van Buren **9** Cleveland, (Franklin D) Roosevelt

Democratic Republican Party
president belonging to: **5** (John Quincy) Adams **6** Monroe **7** Madison **9** Jefferson

demode **8** outmoded **13** unfashionable

Demodocus
minstrel of: **8** Alcinous

Demogorgon
object of: **3** awe **4** fear

demoiselle **4** girl

demolish **4** raze, ruin **5** level, total, wreck **7** destroy **9** devastate

demolition **6** razing **8** leveling, wrecking **11** destruction

demon **5** devil, fiend **7** monster **8** go-getter

Demonassa
father: **10** Amphiaraus
mother: **8** Eriphyle
husband: **10** Thersander
son: **9** Tisamenus

demonic, demoniacal **6** hectic **7** frantic, hellish **8** devilish, fiendish, frenzied

demonstrable **7** evident **8** apparent, manifest, palpable **11** supportable

demonstrate **4** show **5** march, prove, teach **6** parade, picket, reveal **7** display, exhibit, explain **8** describe, manifest **9** establish **10** illustrate

demonstration **5** march, rally **6** parade **7** display **9** picketing **10** exhibition, exposition, expression **12** illustration, presentation **13** manifestation

demonstrative **7** gushing **8** effusive **12** affectionate

demonstrativeness **9** gushiness **12** effusiveness, emotionalism

Demophon
father: **7** Theseus
mother: **7** Phaedra
brother: **6** Acamas
wife: **7** Phyllis

Demophoon
father: **6** Celeus
mother: **8** Metanira
nursed by: **7** Demeter

demoralize **8** dispirit **9** undermine **10** disconcert, discourage, dishearten **11** disorganize

de mortuis nil nisi bonum **26** of the dead say nothing but good

demos **5** plebs **6** masses **7** commons **8** populace **9** commoners

demote **4** bust **7** degrade

Dempsey, Jack (William Harrison)
nickname: **13** Manassa Mauler
sport: **6** boxing
class: **11** heavyweight

demur **5** qualm **6** object **7** protest, scruple **8** disagree **9** misgiving, objection **10** hesitation **11** compunction

demure **3** shy **4** prim **6** modest **7** bashful **8** reserved

demurrer **5** doubt, qualm **7** dissent, protest, scruple **8** objector, question, rebuttal **9** challenge, exception, misgiving, objection, protester, protestor, stricture **11** compunction **12** remonstrance

den **4** lair **5** haunt, study **6** hotbed **7** hangout, library, retreat, shelter **9** sanctuary

denial **7** refusal **9** disavowal, disowning, rejection **10** disclaimer

denigrate **4** soil **5** abuse, smear, sully **6** defame, dump on, malign, revile, vilify **7** asperse, blacken, degrade, run down, slander, traduce **8** backbite, badmouth, belittle, besmirch, tear down **9** call names, discredit, disparage, downgrade **10** calumniate, stigmatize

De Niro, Robert
born: **9** New York NY
roles: **10** Raging Bull (Oscar), Taxi Driver **11** Mean Streets **13** The Deer Hunter **14** New York New York, The Godfather II **15** The King of Comedy, True Confessions **17** Bang the Drum Slowly

denizen **7** dweller **8** resident **10** inhabitant

Denmark ***see box***

Dennis, Patrick
author of: **10** Auntie Mame

Dennis, Sandy
real name: **16** Sandra Dale Dennis
born: **10** Hastings NE
roles: **12** Any Wednesday **15** A Thousand Clowns **18** Up the Down Staircase **25** Who's Afraid of Virginia Woolf?

Dennis the Hangman
character in: **12** Barnaby Rudge
author: **7** Dickens

Dennis the Menace
creator: **11** Hank Ketcham
character: **9** Mrs Elkins **10** John Wilson **12** Eloise Wilson, George Wilson, Joey McDonald, Martha Wilson **13** Alice Mitchell, Henry Mitchell, Tommy Anderson **14** Dennis Mitchell
dog: **4** Ruff
cast: **8** Gil Smith, Jay North **10** Billy Booth, Gale Gordon, Sara Seeger **11** Gloria Henry, Irene Tedrow, Sylvia Field **12** Joseph Kearns **15** Herbert Anderson

denomination **4** name, sect, size **5** class, value **8** category, grouping **10** persuasion **11** designation

denotation **4** mark, name, sign **6** symbol **7** meaning **10** indication

denote **4** mark, mean, name **6** signal **7** signify **8** indicate

denouement **3** end **6** finale, upshot **7** outcome **8** solution **10** conclusion **11** termination

denounce **6** accuse, vilify **7** censure, condemn **9** criticize

denouncement **7** censure **12** condemnation, denunciation

de novo **4** anew **5** again **6** afresh **16** from the beginning

dense **4** dull, dumb, slow **5** close, heavy, thick **6** stupid **7** compact, crowded, intense **8** ignorant **9** dimwitted **10** compressed **11** thickheaded **12** concentrated, impenetrable

Densher, Merton
character in: **17** The Wings of the Dove
author: **5** James

density **4** mass **6** weight

Denmark

other name: 17 Kongeriget Danmark

capital/largest city: 9 Kobenhavn **10** Copenhagen

others: 3 Hov **4** Hals, Koge, Nibe, Ribe, Soro **5** Arhus, Kosor, Vejle **6** Aarhus, Abenra, Alborg, Dorsor, Dragor, Nyberg, Odense, Skagen, Struer, Viborg **7** Aalborg, Esbjerg, Horsens, Kolding, Morsens, Randers **8** Ballerup, Elsinore, Gentofte, Glostrup, Hillerod, Naestred, Roskilde, Slagelse **9** Haderslev, Helsingor, Svendborg **10** Fredericia **13** Frederikshavn

school:

university institute of: **18** Theoretical Physics
folk high school: **14** folkehojskoler
continuation school: **11** efterskoler

division: 3 Fyn **7** Jutland, Lolland **9** Schleswig, Sjaelland

measure: 3 ell, fod, mil, pot **4** alen, favn, last, rode **5** album, anker, kande, linje, paegl, tomme **6** achtel, paegel, skeppe **7** landmil, oltonde, ortonde, skieppe, viertel **8** fjerding **9** ottingkar **10** korntonmde

monetary unit: 3 one, ora, ore **4** fyrk **5** krone **8** frederik, skilling **9** rigsdaler

weight: 2 es **3** lod, ort, vog **4** last, mark, pund, unze **5** carat, kvint, pound, quint, tonde **6** toende **7** centner, lispund, quintin **8** lispound, skippund **9** skibslast, skippound **10** bismerpund

island: 2 Oe **3** Als, Fyn, Mon, Rum, Thy **4** Aaro, Aero, Fano, Fohr, Moen, Mors, Romo **5** Baago, Faero, Faroe, Funen, Laeso, Samso, Sando **6** Amager, Sandoy, Sejero, Sudero **7** Faeroes, Falster, Hesselo, Laaland, Lolland, Seeland, Zealand **8** Bornholm, Eysturoy, Sudhuroy **9** Greenland, Langeland, Sjaelland **10** Vendsyssel

lake: 6 Arreso

hill: 12 Ejer Bavnehoj **14** Himmelbjaerget

highest point: 12 Yding Skovhoj

river: 3 Asa **4** Holm, Omme, Stor **5** Skive, Susaa, Varde **6** Gelsaa, Gudena, Vorgod **7** Gudenaa, Lilleaa, Lonborg

sea: 5 North **6** Baltic **7** Oresund **8** Atlantic, Kattegat **9** Skagerrak

physical feature:

fjord: **3** Ise **4** Isse **5** Lamme
inlet: **3** Ise **5** Fjord, Vejle **6** Nissum, Odense **7** Horsens, Logstor **8** Limfjord, Mariager
peninsula: **7** Jutland
strait: **7** Otesund **8** Kattegat **9** Skagerrak

people: 4 Dane, Jute **5** Angle **6** Cimbri, Eskimo, German, Ostmen, Teuton, Viking **12** Scandinavian

astronomer: **10** Tycho Brahe
author: **11** Isak Dinesen **21** Hans Christian Andersen
founder: **4** Axel **7** Absalon
king: **4** Hans, Knud **6** Canute **8** Frederik **9** Christian **10** Gorm the Old **15** Harold Bluetooth
philosopher: **11** Kierkegaard
physicist: **9** Niels Bohr
queen: **9** Margrethe **12** Thyra Danebod
sculptor: **11** Thorvaldsen
teacher: **4** Kold

language: 4 Odan **6** Danish, German **8** Faeroese **11** Greenlander

religion: 19 Evangelical Lutheran

place:

airport: **7** Kastrup
castle: **7** Egeskov **8** Kronborg **13** Frederiksborg
museum: **6** Rebild **9** Glyptotek **11** Thorvaldsen **15** Rosenborg Castle
park: **10** Langelinie **13** Tivoli Gardens
royal palace: **11** Amalienborg
statue: **13** Little Mermaid
stock exchange: **5** Borse **6** Borsen

feature:

dance: **6** sextur
drink: **5** glogg **7** aquavit

food:

beer: **6** Tuborg **9** Carlsberg
cheese: **3** Ost **4** Blue, Tybo **5** Esrom, Samso **6** Samsoe **7** Havarti, Mycella
meat patty: **11** frikadeller
pudding: **15** rodgrod med flode

7 opacity 8 dullness, solidity 9 stupidity, thickness 10 obtuseness, opaqueness 11 compactness

dent 3 pit 4 nick 6 hollow 10 depression 11 indentation

denude 4 bare 5 strip 6 divest 7 lay bare 8 unclothe

denuded 4 bare 5 naked 6 barren 8 stripped 9 unclothed, uncovered

denunciation 7 censure 12 condemnation, denouncement 13 attack against

Denver
basketball team: 7 Nuggets
football team: 4 Gold 7 Broncos

deny 6 refuse, refute 7 disavow 8 disallow, disclaim 9 disaffirm 10 contradict

deny oneself 5 avoid, forgo 6 eschew, give up, refuse 7 abstain, forbear 8 renounce 9 sacrifice

deny responsibility 7 disavow

Deo gratias 13 thanks be to God

Deo volente 10 God willing

DePalma, Brian
director of: 6 Carrie 13 Dressed to Kill

depart 2 go 4 exit 5 leave 7 deviate, digress

departed 4 dead, gone, late, left, past, went 6 at rest, bygone 7 gone off 8 gone away 10 passed away 11 gone to glory 12 late-lamented 20 gone the way of all flesh

depart for 8 leave for 9 adjourn to, set off for, set out for 10 head toward, move toward

depart hastily 3 fly 4 flee 6 decamp, escape 7 abscond 9 skedaddle

department 4 unit 6 branch, bureau, sector 7 section 8 district, division, province

departure 4 exit 5 going 6 exodus 7 leaving 9 deviation 10 digression, divergence

depend 4 rely, rest 5 count, hinge 6 hang on

dependable 4 sure, true 5 loyal 6 steady, trusty 7 trusted 8 faithful, reliable 9 steadfast, unfailing 11 trustworthy

dependence 5 trust 8 reliance 10 confidence, dependency

dependency 10 dependence

dependent 7 reliant

depict 4 draw, limn 5 carve, chart, draft, paint 6 define, detail, map out, recite, record, relate, sculpt, sketch 7 diagram, narrate, picture, portray, recount 8 describe 9 chronicle, delineate, dramatize, represent, verbalize 10 illustrate 12 characterize

depiction 6 sketch 7 drawing, picture 8 portrait 9 picturing, portrayal 11 delineation 12 illustration 14 representation 16 characterization

deplete 5 drain, use up 6 lessen, reduce 7 consume, exhaust 8 decrease 10 impoverish

depleted 5 empty, spent, waste 6 barren, used up 7 drained, emptied, reduced, worn out 8 bankrupt, consumed, expended, lessened 9 exhausted, infertile 10 unfruitful

depletion 5 drain 7 using up 8 decrease 9 lessening, reduction 10 exhaustion 11 consumption

deplorable 5 awful 8 wretched 9 miserable 11 blameworthy 13 reprehensible 17 deserving reproach

deplore 5 mourn 6 bemoan, bewail, lament 7 censure, condemn 9 grieve for 12 disapprove of

deport 3 act 4 oust 5 carry, exile, expel 6 banish, behave 7 cast out 10 expatriate 14 conduct oneself

deported person 2 DP 5 exile 8 deportee 10 expatriate 14 banished person

deportment 7 conduct 8 behavior, demeanor 11 comportment

depose 4 oust 6 unseat 8 dethrone 16 remove from office

deposit 3 put 4 pile 5 place 7 put down, set down 8 sediment 10 accumulate 11 down payment, give in trust, installment 12 accumulation 14 partial payment

deposition 7 deposit 9 statement, testimony 11 declaration 12 accumulation

depository 4 bank, safe 5 vault 6 museum 7 library 8 archives 10 storehouse

depot 4 dump 8 terminal, terminus 10 bus station 15 railroad station 20 military storage place

depraved 4 vile 6 wicked 7 corrupt, debased 8 degraded 9 debauched, perverted 10 degenerate

depravity 8 vileness 9 decadence 10 corruption, debasement, debauchery, degeneracy, immorality, perversion, wickedness 11 degradation, dissolution

deprecate 7 condemn, protest 8 belittle, object to, play down 10 depreciate 15 take exception to

deprecated 7 defamed, put down 8 despised 9 belittled, derogated, disdained

deprecation 4 slur 5 abuse 7 protest, put-down 9 aspersion 10 aspersions, belittling, defamation, derogation 11 disapproval 12 condemnation 13 disparagement

deprecatory 8 critical 9 maligning, vilifying 10 belittling, defamatory, derogatory, slanderous 11 disparaging 12 disapproving

depreciate 5 scorn 7 run down 8 belittle, diminish 9 denigrate, disparage, downgrade, lose value 13 reduce in value, lower the value

depreciation 5 scorn 7 disdain 8 contempt 9 criticism, deflation 10 belittling, disrespect 11 devaluation 13 disparagement

depredation 4 sack 6 rapine, ravage 7 looting, pillage, plunder, robbery, sacking 8 spoiling 9 marauding 10 brigandage, ravishment, spoliation 11 desecration, devastation, freebooting, laying waste

depress 5 lower 6 deject, lessen, reduce, sadden, weaken 7 cut back 8 diminish, dispirit 9 press down 10 dishearten 14 lower in spirits

depressed 3 sad 4 blue 7 unhappy 8 dejected, downcast 10 despondent, dispirited, melancholy 11 low-spirited 12 disconsolate, inconsolable

depressing 3 sad 6 gloomy 8 lowering 9 dejecting, saddening 10 oppressing 11 casting down, dispiriting, melancholic, pushing down 12 discouraging, pressing down, weighing down 14 causing sadness

depression 5 gloom 6 dimple, hollow 7 sadness 9 dejection, recession 10 desolation, melancholy 11 despondency, indentation, melancholia

14 discouragement 15 downheartedness, economic decline

deprive 5 strip 6 divest 8 take from 10 confiscate, dispossess

deprived 8 divested, stripped 11 handicapped 12 dispossessed, impoverished 13 disadvantaged 15 underprivileged

deprive of honor 5 abase, shame, sully 6 defame 7 blacken, tarnish 8 disgrace, dishonor 9 discredit 10 stigmatize

deprive of strength 6 hinder, weaken 7 disable, wear out 8 enervate, enfeeble, handicap 10 debilitate, devitalize

de profundis 13 from the depths

depth 6 timbre 8 deepness 10 profundity 19 downward measurement 24 perpendicular measurement

depths 4 deep 6 bowels 8 interior, recesses

deputation 9 committee 10 commission, delegation 15 representatives

deputize 6 assign 7 appoint 8 delegate 10 commission

deputy 4 aide 5 agent, envoy, proxy 6 second 8 delegate, emissary, minister 9 alternate, assistant, go-between, messenger, middleman, surrogate 10 ambassador, substitute 11 pinch hitter 12 spokesperson 14 representative 15 second-in-command

DeQuincey, Thomas
author of: 19 The English Mail-Coach 31 On the Knocking at the Gate in Macbeth 32 Confessions of an English Opium-Eater

derail 3 bar 4 balk, foil 5 block, check, spike 6 hinder, impede, thwart 7 inhibit, prevent 8 obstruct 14 throw off course

deranged 5 crazy 6 insane 8 demented 10 irrational, unbalanced

derangement 6 lunacy 7 madness 8 insanity 9 craziness 11 peculiarity 13 irrationality, mental illness 14 mental disorder

Der Bingle
nickname of: 10 Bing Crosby

Derek, Bo
husband: 4 John
roles: 3 Ten (10) 6 Bolero, Tarzan

derelict 3 bum 4 hobo 5 tramp 6 remiss 7 outcast, vagrant 8 careless, deserted 9 abandoned, negligent 10 delinquent, neglectful

dereliction 7 failure, neglect 9 disregard 10 negligence 11 delinquency 13 noncompliance, nonobservance

De rerum natura
author: 9 Lucretius

deride 4 mock 5 scoff, scorn 7 sneer at 8 ridicule

de rigueur 11 fashionable 16 strictly required

derision 5 scorn 7 disdain, mockery 8 ridicule, sneering

derivation 5 stock 6 origin, source 7 descent, getting, lineage 8 ancestry, deriving, heritage 9 acquiring, etymology, parentage 10 background, beginnings, extraction 21 historical development

derive 4 gain 5 arise, enjoy, glean 6 obtain 7 descend 8 stem from 9 originate

dermaptera
class: 8 hexapoda
phylum: 10 arthropoda
group: 6 earwig

dermatitis 4 rash 6 eczema 9 psoriasis 12 inflammation

Dern, Bruce
born: 9 Chicago IL
roles: 6 Marnie, Tattoo 10 Coming Home, Family Plot 11 Black Sunday 13 The Wild Angels 14 The Great Gatsby 22 The King of Marvin Gardens

dernier 4 last 5 final 8 ultimate

dernier cri 9 latest cry 10 latest word 13 latest fashion

derogate 4 blot 5 taint 6 smirch 8 disgrace 9 disparage

derogation 4 blot 5 odium, stain 7 blemish 8 contempt, disfavor, disgrace, ignominy 9 disesteem, disrepute 10 disrespect 11 humiliation 13 disparagement

derogatory 9 injurious 10 belittling 11 disparaging, unfavorable 12 unflattering 15 uncomplimentary

derrick 3 rig 5 crane, hoist, tower 9 framework
kind: 3 oil 6 sheers 7 gin-pole
part: 3 gin, leg 4 boom, mast 6 pulley 7 guy line

derring-do 6 daring 8 audacity, boldness 11 daredevilry 12 daredeviltry, recklessness 15 venturesomeness

dervish 5 fakir 6 Muslim 7 ascetic

De Sapientia Veterum
author: 12 Francis Bacon

Descartes, Rene
author of: 17 Discourse on Method
field: 11 mathemathics
nationality: 6 French
developed: 18 analytical geometry
quote: 13 Cogito ergo sum 18 I think therefore I am

descend 3 dip 4 drop, pass 5 slant, slope, swoop 6 go down, invade 7 incline 8 come down, inherited 11 come in force 12 be handed down, move downward

descendant 5 issue 7 progeny 9 offspring

descend upon 6 assail, attack, charge 7 assault, set upon 12 bear down upon

descent 4 drop, fall, raid 5 slant, slope 6 origin 7 assault, decline, lineage 8 ancestry 9 declivity, incursion 10 coming down 11 sneak attack, sudden visit

describe 4 draw 5 trace 6 depict, detail, recite, relate 7 explain, mark out, narrate, outline, portray, recount, speak of 9 delineate 10 illustrate 12 characterize

description 3 ilk 4 kind, sort, type 5 brand, class, genus 6 manner, nature 7 account, species, variety 9 depiction, narration, portrayal 12 illustration 16 characterization

descry 3 see 4 spot 6 behold, notice 7 discern, observe, pick out 8 discover 12 catch sight of

Desdemona
character in: 7 Othello
author: 11 Shakespeare

desecrate 6 defile 7 profane, violate 8 dishonor

desecration 8 dishonor 9 violation 10 defilement 11 profanation

desert 3 dry 4 arid, wild 5 leave, waste 6 barren 7 abandon, forsake 8 desolate, untilled 9 infertile, wasteland 10 arid region 11 run away from, uninhabited 12 uncultivated 16 barren wilderness

deserted 4 AWOL, left 5 empty 6 lonely, vacant 7 cast off, forlorn, reneged 8 defected, desolate, forsaken, marooned 9 abandoned, absconded **12** quit one's post **14** left in the lurch

desertedness **9** emptiness **10** desolation **13** uncrowdedness

Deserted Village, The
author: **15** Oliver Goldsmith

desertion **8** quitting **9** forsaking **11** abandonment **14** relinquishment

desertlike **3** dry **4** arid **5** sandy **6** barren **7** dried up, parched **9** waterless

deserts **3** due **5** worth **6** reward **7** payment

deserve **4** rate **5** merit **7** warrant **9** earn as due **10** be worthy of, qualify for **12** be entitled to **13** be deserving of

deserving **6** worthy **9** qualified

deserving reproach **8** blamable **10** deplorable, punishable, reprovable **11** blameworthy **12** reproachable **13** reprehensible

De Sica, Vittorio
director of: **15** The Bicycle Thief **27** The Garden of the Finzi-Continis

desiccate **5** dry up, parch **6** wither **7** shrivel **9** dehydrate

design **3** aim, end **4** draw, form, goal, plan, plot **5** draft, motif, set up **6** devise, intend, scheme, sketch, target **7** destine, diagram, drawing, fashion, outline, pattern, project, purpose **8** conceive, intrigue **9** blueprint, intention, objective **11** arrangement **14** draw up plans for

designate **4** call, name, term **5** elect, label **6** assign, choose, select **7** appoint, signify, specify **8** identify, indicate, nominate, pinpoint

designation **5** label **6** naming **10** delegation **11** appointment **13** specification **14** identification

designer **7** creator, deviser, planner **9** contriver **10** originator

designing **4** wily **6** artful, crafty **7** cunning **8** plotting, scheming **9** conniving

desirable **4** fine **8** in demand, pleasing **9** advisable **10** beneficial **11** worth having **12** advantageous

desire **4** need, urge, want, wish **5** crave **6** ask for, hunger, thirst **7** craving, longing, long for, request **8** yearning, yearn for **9** hunger for, thirst for

Desire Under the Elms
author: **12** Eugene O'Neill
character: **4** Eben **5** Peter **6** Simeon **11** Abbie Putnam **12** Ephraim Cabot

desirous **4** avid, keen **5** eager **7** hopeful, longing, wishful **8** yearning

desist **4** stop **5** cease **6** lay off **7** suspend **8** leave off **11** discontinue, refrain from

Desk Set
director: **10** Walter Lang
cast: **8** Gig Young **11** Dina Merrill **12** Joan Blondell, Spencer Tracy **16** Katharine Hepburn

Desmontes
foster son: **4** Arne

desolate **3** sad **4** bare, ruin **5** bleak, empty **6** barren, grieve, ravage, sadden **7** depress, destroy, forlorn **8** dejected, demolish, deserted, distress, downcast, forsaken, lay waste, wretched **9** abandoned, depressed, devastate, miserable, sorrowful **10** despondent, discourage, dishearten, melancholy **11** downhearted, uninhabited

desolating **6** tragic **7** ruinous **8** dreadful, grievous, terrible **10** calamitous, horrendous **11** devastating **12** catastrophic

desolation **4** ruin **6** misery, sorrow **7** sadness **8** bareness, distress, solitude **9** bleakness, dejection, emptiness, seclusion **10** barrenness, depression, dreariness, loneliness, melancholy, wilderness **11** destruction, devastation, unhappiness **12** solitariness

despair **5** gloom, trial **6** burden, ordeal **9** lose heart **10** depression, have no hope **11** despondency, lose faith in **12** hopelessness **14** discouragement

despair of **5** doubt **8** give up on **10** have no hope

desperado **4** thug **5** rowdy **6** bandit, gunman, outlaw **7** brigand, convict, hoodlum, ruffian **8** criminal, fugitive, hooligan **9** terrorist **10** lawbreaker

desperate **4** dire, rash, wild **5** grave, great **6** daring, urgent **7** extreme, frantic, serious **8** critical, hopeless, reckless, wretched **9** dangerous, incurable **10** beyond hope, despairing, despondent

Desperate Hours, The
director: **12** William Wyler
cast: **8** Gig Young **11** Dewey Martin, Martha Scott **13** Arthur Kennedy, Frederic March **14** Humphrey Bogart

Desperately Seeking Susan
director: **14** Susan Seidelman
cast: **7** Madonna **15** Rosanna Arquette

desperation **7** despair **12** hopelessness, recklessness

despicable **4** base, mean, vile **10** detestable, outrageous **11** disgraceful **12** contemptible **13** reprehensible

despise **5** abhor, scorn **6** detest, loathe **7** contemn, disdain, dislike **10** look down on

Despoena
origin: **5** Greek
father: **8** Poseidon
mother: **7** Demeter
corresponds to: **10** Persephone

despoil **3** rob **4** loot **6** ravage **7** pillage, plunder

despoiler **6** looter, robber, vandal **7** brigand **8** pillager **9** plunderer

despondency **5** gloom **6** dismay **7** despair, sadness **9** dejection, pessimism **10** depression, desolation, low spirits, melancholy **11** melancholia **12** hopelessness **14** discouragement **15** downheartedness

despondent **3** low **4** blue, down **8** dejected, downcast, hopeless **9** depressed **11** discouraged, downhearted **12** disconsolate, disheartened

despot **6** tyrant **8** autocrat, dictator **9** oppressor

despotic **9** imperious **10** autocratic, tyrannical **11** dictatorial **13** authoritarian

despotism **7** tyranny **9** autocracy **10** absolutism

dessert **3** pie **4** cake, nuts, tart **5** fruit, sweet **8** ice cream **11** final course

destination **3** aim, end **4** goal, plan **6** object, target **7** purpose **8** ambition **9** objective **11** journey's end

destiny **3** lot **4** fate **5** karma, moira **6** future, kismet **7** fortune **9** necessity
goddess of: **5** Fates, Morae, Parca **6** Moerae, Moirai, Parcae

destitute **4** poor **5** broke, needy **6** busted **8** indigent **9** penniless **15** poverty-stricken

destitution **4** lack, want **6** penury **7** beggary, poverty **9** indigence, privation **11** extreme want **13** pennilessness **14** impoverishment

destroy **4** ruin **5** waste, wreck **6** ravage **8** demolish **9** devastate

destroy completely **3** end **7** abolish, wipe out **8** lay waste **9** eradicate, extirpate, liquidate **10** annihilate, obliterate **11** exterminate

destroyer **4** bane **6** blight, killer **7** gunboat, warship **10** affliction **11** annihilator

destruct **3** gut **4** raze, ruin **5** wreck **7** despoil, destroy, wipe out **8** decimate, demolish, desolate, pull down, tear down **9** devastate **10** lay in ruins

destruction **4** ruin **5** havoc **8** wreckage, wrecking **10** demolition **11** devastation

destructive **7** harmful, hurtful, ruinous **8** damaging **9** injurious **11** detrimental, devastating **15** not constructive

Destry Rides Again
director: **14** George Marshall
based on a story by: **8** Max Brand
cast: **12** Brian Donlevy, James Stewart **15** Marlene Dietrich **16** Charles Winninger
song: **35** See What the Boys in the Back Room Will Have

desultory **6** casual, chance, fitful, random **7** aimless, cursory **9** haphazard **10** without aim **11** unconnected

detach **5** sever **6** loosen **7** unhitch **8** separate, unfasten **9** disengage **10** disconnect **11** disentangle

detached **4** fair **5** aloof **7** distant, neutral, severed **8** reserved, unbiased **9** impartial, objective, separated, uncoupled, unhitched **10** disengaged, fair-minded, unfastened **11** indifferent, unconnected **12** disconnected, unprejudiced **13** disinterested, dispassionate
French: **6** degage

detachment **4** unit **5** force **8** coolness, fairness, severing **9** aloofness, isolation, severance **10** cutting off, neutrality, separation **11** objectivity **12** impartiality, indifference **13** disconnection, disengagement, preoccupation **16** special task force

detail **4** fact, iota, item **6** aspect, relate **7** appoint, feature, itemize, recount, respect, specify **9** component, delineate, designate, enumerate **10** detachment, particular **11** special duty **13** assign to a task, particularize **14** special service **20** particular assignment

detailed **6** minute **8** itemized, thorough **10** item by item **12** point by point

detailed list **9** breakdown **11** itemization **14** categorization

detain **4** hold, slow, stop **5** delay **6** arrest, hinder, retard, slow up **7** confine **8** slow down **13** keep in custody

detainment **7** custody, holding **9** detention **11** confinement **12** imprisonment **13** incarceration

detect **3** see **4** espy, note, spot **5** catch **6** notice **7** observe, uncover **8** discover, perceive

detectable **10** noticeable **11** appreciable, discernible, perceivable, perceptible **13** ascertainable

detective **2** PI **6** shamus, sleuth **7** gumshoe **10** private eye **12** investigator **19** special investigator

detention **7** custody, holding **9** keeping in **10** detainment **11** confinement, holding back **12** imprisonment **13** incarceration

deter **4** stop **5** daunt **6** divert, hinder, impede **7** prevent **8** dissuade **10** discourage

deteriorate **3** ebb **4** fade, wane **5** decay, lapse **6** worsen **7** crumble, decline, fall off **10** degenerate **12** disintegrate

deteriorated **6** shabby **7** rickety **8** decaying, worsened **9** crumbling **10** broken-down, tumble-down **11** dilapidated, in disrepair **13** disintegrated

deterioration **5** decay, lapse **6** fading, waning **7** decline **9** crumbling, decadence, worsening **12** degeneration, dilapidation **14** disintegration

determination **4** grit **5** pluck, power, spunk **6** fixing **7** finding, resolve, verdict **8** boldness, decision, judgment, settling, solution, tenacity **9** reasoning, resolving **10** conclusion, resolution **11** determining, persistence **12** perseverance, resoluteness **13** act of deciding, steadfastness **16** stick-to-it-iveness

determine **5** learn **6** affect, decide, detect, settle **7** control, find out, resolve **8** conclude, discover, regulate **9** ascertain, establish, figure out, influence **15** come to a decision, give direction to

determined **7** dead set, decided, settled **8** found out, obdurate, resolute, stubborn **9** obstinate, tenacious **10** figured out **11** ascertained, established **15** come to a decision

deterrent **4** curb **5** check **9** hindrance, restraint **14** discouragement

detest **4** hate **5** abhor **6** loathe **7** despise **10** recoil from **16** dislike intensely

detestable **4** vile **6** odious **7** hateful **9** abhorrent, loathsome, obnoxious, offensive, repulsive, revolting **10** disgusting, unpleasant **12** disagreeable

detestation **4** hate **6** hatred **7** disgust, dislike **8** aversion, distaste, loathing **9** antipathy, repulsion, revulsion **10** abhorrence, repugnance

dethrone **4** oust **6** depose, unseat

detonate **4** fire **5** blast, burst, erupt, go off, shoot **6** blow up, ignite, report, set off **7** explode **8** touch off **9** discharge, fulminate

detonation **5** blast, burst **6** report **9** discharge, explosion

detour **5** skirt **6** bypass, byroad, divert **7** digress **9** deviation, diversion **10** digression

detract **5** lower **6** lessen, reduce **8** diminish **12** subtract from, take away from

detraction **4** flaw **11** shortcoming **12** disadvantage

detractor **5** enemy **6** critic **8** opponent **9** adversary, belittler, slanderer **10** antagonist, bad mouther, disparager

detriment **4** harm, loss **6** damage, injury **10** impairment **12** disadvantage

detrimental **7** adverse, harmful **8** damaging **9** injurious **10** pernicious **11** deleterious, destructive, unfavorable **15** disadvantageous

Detroit
baseball team: **6** Tigers
basketball team: **7** Pistons
football team: **5** Lions
hockey team: **8** Redwings

de trop **7** too many, too

much **8** in the way **9** not wanted

Deucalion
father: 10 Prometheus
mother: 7 Pronoia
wife: 6 Pyrrha
son: 6 Hellen
founded: 9 human race
after: 6 deluge

deus ex machina 15 god from a machine **18** improbable solution

Deus vobiscum 12 God be with you

Deus vult 8 God wills (it)
cry of: 9 Crusaders

devaluate 6 lessen, reduce **7** deflate, degrade **10** depreciate

devaluation 4 drop **7** decline **12** depreciation

devalue 5 lower, taint **6** debase, defile, infect **7** cheapen, corrupt, degrade, pervert, pollute, revalue **8** mark down **9** devaluate, underrate, write down **10** adulterate, degenerate, demonetize, depreciate, remonetize **11** contaminate

devastate 4 ruin **5** level, spoil, waste, wreck **6** ravage **7** despoil, destroy **8** demolish, desolate, lay waste

devastating 7 ruinous **8** damaging **9** injurious **10** calamitous, disastrous **11** cataclysmic, destructive, detrimental **12** catastrophic

devastation 4 ruin **9** ruination **10** demolition **11** destruction

develop 4 grow **5** print, ripen **6** evolve, expand, finish, flower, mature, pick up, unfold **7** acquire, advance, amplify, augment, broaden, build up, convert, enlarge, improve, process, turn out **8** contract, energize **9** cultivate **10** come to have **11** come to light, elaborate on

development 5 event **6** growth, result **7** advance, history **8** progress **9** evolution

deviant 4 warp **5** shift **7** deviate, pervert **8** aberrant, abnormal **9** deflected, divergent

deviate 4 part, vary, veer **5** stray **6** depart, swerve, wander **8** go astray **9** sidetrack, turn aside

deviation 6 change **7** veering **8** rambling, straying **9** wandering **10** aberration, digression, divergence **11** abnormality, fluctuation

device 4 plan, plot, ploy, ruse, wile **5** angle, trick **6** design, gadget, scheme **7** gimmick **8** artifice, strategy **9** apparatus, invention, mechanism, stratagem **11** contraption, contrivance

devil, the Devil 3 guy **5** rogue, Satan, thing **6** Azazel, fellow, wretch **7** hellion, Lucifer, ruffian, serpent, villain **8** creature **9** Archfiend, Beelzebub, scoundrel **11** unfortunate **12** spirit of evil **13** mischief-maker **16** prince of darkness

Devil and Daniel Webster, The
author: 19 Stephen Vincent Benet
director: 15 William Dieterle
character: 5 Devil **7** Webster **9** Mr Scratch
cast: 10 James Craig **11** Anne Shirley **12** Edward Arnold, Walter Huston
score: 15 Bernard Herrmann
Oscar for: 5 score
also titled: 18 All That Money Can Buy

devilish 4 evil **6** wicked **7** demonic, heinous, impious, satanic, vicious **8** demoniac, fiendish **9** nefarious **10** demoniacal, diabolical, villainous

devil-may-care 4 bold, rash, wild **5** risky **6** daring, rakish **8** heedless, reckless **9** audacious, daredevil

devil's advocate
Latin: 16 advocatus diaboli

Devil's Advocate
author: 14 Taylor Caldwell

Devil's Disciple, The
author: 17 George Bernard Shaw

Devine, Andy
real name: 16 Jeremiah Schwartz
born: 11 Flagstaff AZ
roles: 7 Jingles **9** Andy's Gang **14** Wild Bill Hickok

devious 3 sly **4** wily **6** sneaky, tricky **7** crooked **9** deceitful, dishonest **11** treacherous **12** dishonorable **13** double-dealing

devise 4 plot **5** forge, frame **6** design, invent, map out **7** concoct, prepare, think up **8** block out, conceive, contrive **9** construct, formulate

deviser 6 author, framer **7** creator, planner **8** inventor **9** architect, contriver **10** originator

devitalize 4 kill **6** deaden, weaken **8** enervate **10** debilitate

devoid 5 empty **6** barren **7** lacking, wanting, without **8** bereft of **9** destitute **11** unblest with

devote 5 apply **6** direct **7** address, utilize **8** dedicate **10** consecrate, give over to **11** concentrate **15** give oneself up to **22** center one's attentions on

devoted 4 fond, true **5** loyal **6** ardent, loving **7** earnest, staunch, zealous **8** adhering, faithful **9** dedicated, steadfast **10** passionate, unwavering **17** strongly committed

devotedness 8 devotion **10** commitment, dedication **13** attentiveness **17** earnest attachment

devoted to luxury 9 sybaritic **10** hedonistic, voluptuous

devotee 3 fan **6** rooter **7** booster **8** adherent, advocate, champion, disciple, follower **10** aficionado, enthusiast **11** afficionado

devotion, devotions 4 love, zeal **5** ardor, piety **6** fealty, regard **7** loyalty **8** fondness, holiness **9** adherence, godliness, reverence **10** allegiance, commitment, concern for, dedication, devoutness, meditation **11** religiosity **12** faithfulness, spirituality **13** attentiveness, prayer service **15** religious fervor **17** earnest attachment **19** religious observance

De Voto, Bernard A
author of: 21 Across the Wide Missouri

devour 7 stuff in **8** bolt down, gobble up, gulp down, knock off, wolf down **9** go through **10** read widely **14** eat voraciously **15** absorb oneself in, consume greedily **16** read compulsively, take in ravenously **17** become engrossed in

devout 5 pious **6** ardent **7** earnest, fervent, intense, serious, zealous **8** orthodox, reverent **9** religious **10** passionate, worshipful

devoutness 5 piety **8** devotion, holiness **9** godliness, reverence **12** spirituality **15** religious fervor

DeVries, Hugo
field: 6 botany
nationality: 5 Dutch
researched: 8 heredity, mutation

DeVries, Peter
author of: 16 Consenting Adults **24** Slouching Toward Kalamazoo

dew **8** moisture **12** condensation **18** droplets of moisture

Dewar, James
field: **7** physics **9** chemistry
nationality: **8** Scottish
liquified: **8** hydrogen
solidified: **8** hydrogen
developed: **7** cordite **10** Dewar flask **12** liquid oxygen

Dewey, George
served in: **18** Spanish-American War
battle: **9** Manila Bay
destroyed: **12** Spanish fleet

Dewhurst, Colleen
husband: **12** George C Scott
born: **6** Canada **8** Montreal
roles: **12** The Nun's Story **18** Desire Under the Elms **22** A Moon for the Misbegotten

De Wilde, Brandon
born: **10** Brooklyn NY
roles: **3** Hud **5** Shane **11** All Fall Down

dewy **4** damp **5** moist **7** bedewed

Dexamenus
form: **7** centaur
king of: **6** Olenus

dexterity **8** deftness, facility **9** handiness **10** adroitness, nimbleness **11** manual skill, proficiency

dexterous **4** able, deft **5** agile, quick **6** active, adroit, gifted, nimble **8** skillful **9** efficient, ingenious **11** resourceful

Dhegiha
tribe: **5** Omaha

Dia
father: **7** Eioneus
husband: **5** Ixion
son: **9** Pirithous

diabolic, diabolical **4** evil, foul **6** wicked **7** baleful, demonic, heinous, impious, satanic, vicious **8** devilish, fiendish **9** monstrous, nefarious **10** malevolent, villainous

diadem **4** halo **5** crown **7** circlet, coronet **8** headband

diagnosis **5** study **8** analysis, scrutiny **11** examination **13** investigation, medical report **16** scientific report **22** conclusion from symptoms, specification of illness

diagonal line **4** bias **5** angle, slant

diagram **3** map **4** plan **5** chart **6** sketch **7** drawing, outline **9** breakdown **11** line drawing **12** illustration **14** representation **15** rough projection

dialect **5** argot, idiom, lingo **6** jargon, patois **8** localism **10** vernacular **11** regionalism **13** colloquialism, provincialism **15** language variety

Dial M for Murder
director: **15** Alfred Hitchcock
based on play by: **14** Frederick Knott
cast: **10** Grace Kelly, Ray Milland **14** Robert Cummings

dialogue, dialog **4** talk **5** lines **6** parley, speech **8** conclave **10** conference **12** conversation **14** verbal exchange **15** personal meeting **16** formal discussion

diamond
characteristic: **7** hardest
color: **4** blue, pink **9** blue-white **12** canary yellow
element: **6** carbon
famous: **4** Hope **6** Jonker **8** Cullinan, Idol's Eye, Koh-i-Noor **9** Excelsior **12** Star of Africa **13** Star of the East **17** Star of Sierra Leone
quality: **3** cut **4** fire **5** color **7** clarity **10** brilliance
source: **5** Congo, India **6** Africa, Borneo, Brazil, Guyana **8** Tanzania **9** Australia, Venezuela **11** South Africa, Soviet Union **12** South America **15** South West Africa
weight: **5** carat, point

Diamond State
nickname of: **8** Delaware

Diana
origin: **5** Roman
goddess of: **4** moon **6** slaves **7** hunting
protectress of: **5** women
corresponds to: **6** Phoebe **7** Artemis
epithet: **10** Nemorensis
means: **10** of the grove

Diana of the Crossways
author: **14** George Meredith
character: **9** Mr Warwick **11** Diana Merion, Percy Dacier **12** Lady Dunstane **14** Thomas Redworth **15** Lord Dannisburgh

diaphanous **5** filmy, gauzy, lucid, sheer **6** flimsy, limpid **8** gossamer, pellucid **11** translucent, transparent

diary **3** log **7** daybook, journal **9** chronicle **12** daily journal **14** day-to-day record

Diary of Anne Frank, The
author: **9** Anne Frank
director: **13** George Stevens
cast: **6** Ed Wynn **9** Lou Jacobi **10** Diane Baker **13** Millie Perkins, Richard Beymer **14** Shelley Winters (Mrs Van Daan) **17** Joseph Schildkraut (Father Frank)
Oscar for: **17** supporting actress (Winters)

Diasia
festival of: **4** Zeus

diatribe **6** tirade **9** contumely, invective **11** castigation **12** vituperation **13** stream of abuse **14** bitter harangue **18** accusatory language **19** violent denunciation

dice **4** chop, cube **5** bones, cubes, cut up, mince
singular: **3** die

Dice
also: **4** Dike
origin: **5** Greek
member of: **5** Horae
goddess of: **7** justice
father: **4** Zeus
mother: **6** Themis

Dick, Mr
character in: **16** David Copperfield
author: **7** Dickens

Dickens, Charles
author of: **9** Hard Times **10** Bleak House **11** Oliver Twist **12** Barnaby Rudge, Dombey and Son, Little Dorrit **14** Pickwick Papers **15** A Christmas Carol, Our Mutual Friend **16** A Tale of Two Cities, David Copperfield, Martin Chuzzlewit, Nicholas Nickleby **17** Great Expectations **19** The Old Curiosity Shop **22** The Mystery of Edwin Drood

dicker **4** deal **6** haggle, higgle, outbid **7** bargain, chaffer, quibble, wrangle **8** beat down, talk down, underbid **9** negotiate **17** drive a hard bargain

Dickey, James
author of: **9** The Zodiac **11** Deliverance **16** Strength of Fields **17** Buckdancer's Choice

Dickinson, Angie
real name: **13** Angeline Brown
husband: **13** Burt Bacharach
born: **6** Kulm ND
roles: **8** Rio Bravo **11** Police Woman **13** Dressed to Kill **19** The Sins of Rachel Cade

Dick Tracy
creator: **12** Chester Gould
character: **8** BO Plenty, Moonmaid **12** Gravel Gertie **13** Sparkle Plenty **16** Jeremiah Truehart
wife: **12** Tess Truehart
daughter: **11** Bonny Braids
assistant: **9** Pat Patton

protege: **6** Junior
villain: **5** Itchy **6** B-B Eyes **7** Flattop, Flyface, Measles, Mumbles, The Brow, The Mole **8** The Blank **9** Pruneface, The Midget, The Rodent
equipment: 16 two-way wristradio

Dick Van Dyke Show, The
character: 9 Alan Brady, Rob Petrie **11** Jerry Helper, Laura Petrie, Sally Rogers **12** Buddy Sorrell, Melvin Cooley, Millie Helper **13** Ritchie Petrie
cast: 9 Rose Marie **10** Carl Reiner, Jerry Paris **13** Larry Matthews, Richard Deacon **14** Mary Tyler Moore, Morey Amsterdam **17** Ann Morgan Guilbert

dictate 4 rule **5** edict, order **6** decree, dictum, direct, enjoin, impose, ordain, ruling, urging **7** bidding, counsel, lay down, mandate **8** set forth **9** determine, ordinance, prescribe, prompting, pronounce, stricture **11** exhortation, inclination, requirement

dictator 4 czar, duce **6** caesar, despot, fuhrer, kaiser, tyrant **7** emperor **8** autocrat **13** absolute ruler
Argentinian: 5 Peron
German: 6 Hitler
Italian: 9 Mussolini
Russian: 5 Lenin **6** Stalin
Spanish: 6 Franco

dictatorial 6 lordly **7** haughty, willful **8** absolute, arrogant, despotic **9** arbitrary, imperious, unlimited **10** autocratic, peremptory, tyrannical **11** categorical, domineering, magisterial, overbearing **12** supercilious, unrestricted **13** authoritative **17** inclined to command

diction 7 wording **8** delivery, rhetoric, verbiage **9** elocution **10** intonation, use of idiom, vocabulary **11** enunciation, phraseology, verbal style **12** articulation **13** choice of words, pronunciation **16** turn of expression **17** command of language **18** manner of expression

dictum 3 saw **4** fiat **5** adage, axiom, edict, maxim, order **6** decree, saying, truism **7** dictate, precept, proverb **11** commandment **13** pronouncement **15** dogmatic bidding **22** authoritative statement

Dictynna
origin: 6 Cretan
goddess of: 3 sea
corresponds to: 11 Britomartis

Dictys
occupation: 9 fisherman
found: 5 chest
containing: **5** Danae **7** Perseus

didactic 7 donnish, preachy **8** academic, edifying, pedantic, tutorial **9** doctrinal, homiletic, pedagogic **10** expository, moralizing **11** educational, instructive, lecturelike, overbearing **12** prescriptive **17** inclined to lecture

didactics 8 teaching **9** education, teachings **10** pedagogics **11** instruction

Diderot, Denis
author of: 12 Encyclopedia **13** Rameau's Nephew

Didion, Joan
author of: 8 Salvador **10** White Album **14** Play It as It Lays **19** A Book of Common Prayer **24** Slouching Toward Bethlehem

Dido
queen of: 8 Carthage
father: 5 Mutto
brother: 9 Pygmalion
sister: 4 Anna
husband: 8 Sychaeus
lover: 6 Aeneas
corresponds to: 6 Elissa

Dido and Aeneas
opera by: 7 Purcell
character: 4 Dido (Queen of Carthage) **6** Aeneas

Didymaea
festival of: 4 Zeus **6** Apollo

Didymus *see* **6** Thomas

die 3 ebb, rot **4** ache, fade, fail, long, pass, stop, wane **5** croak, yearn **6** depart, expire, go flat, pass on, perish, recede, run out, wither **7** be eager, decline, die away, go stale, run down, subside **8** fade away, melt away, pass away, pass over, wear away **9** be anxious, break down, lose force, lose power, meet death **10** degenerate, want keenly **11** come to an end, suffer death **12** wish ardently **13** come to one's end, desire greatly, go to one's glory, kick the bucket **14** leave this world, pine with desire, become inactive **15** slowly disappear **17** become inoperative
plural: 4 dice

die away 4 fade **5** abate, cease **8** diminish

die down 5 abate **7** subside **8** diminish, slack off

die out 6 vanish **9** cease to be, disappear **13** become extinct

Diesel, Rudolf
field: 11 engineering
invented: 12 Diesel engine

diet 5 board, synod **7** edibles, nurture **8** congress, victuals **9** nutriment, nutrition **10** assemblage, convention, parliament, provisions, sustenance **11** comestibles, convocation, legislature, nourishment, subsistence **12** eating habits, eat sparingly **13** eating regimen, lawmaking body **14** eat judiciously **15** eat abstemiously, eat restrictedly, general assembly **16** limitation of fare, regulate one's food **17** bicameral assembly **18** nutritional regimen, representative body, restrict one's intake

Dietrich, Marlene
real name: 22 Maria Magdalene Dietrich
born: 7 Germany
roles: 8 Lola Lola **11** Blonde Venus **12** The Blue Angel **15** Rancho Notorious **16** Destry Rides Again, The Garden of Allah **17** The Scarlet Empress **24** Witness for the Prosecution

Dietrich von Bern
origin: 8 Germanic
king of: 10 Ostrogoths
Latin name: 9 Theodoric

Diety 3 Bel, God **4** Baal **6** Marduk, Molech, Moloch, Yahweh **7** Chemosh, Jehovah **10** Anammelech **11** Adrammelech

Dieu et mon droit 13 God and my right
motto of: 18 royal arms of England

differ 5 demur **7** dispute, dissent **8** be unlike, contrast, disagree **9** take issue **10** be distinct, depart from, stand apart **11** be disparate, deviate from, diverge from **12** be at variance, be dissimilar, stand opposed

difference 4 spat **5** clash, set-to **7** dispute, quarrel **8** argument, contrast, squabble **9** deviation, disparity, variation **10** divergence, falling out, unlikeness **11** contrariety, contretemps, discrepancy, distinction **12** disagreement **13** contradiction, dissimilarity, dissimilitude **17** contradistinction, lack of resemblance

different 4 rare **6** divers, sundry, unique, unlike **7** bizarre, diverse, foreign, several, strange, unusual, various

8 aberrant, atypical, distinct, manifold, not alike, peculiar, separate, singular, uncommon 9 anomalous, disparate, divergent, other than, unrelated 10 dissimilar, individual, variegated 11 contrasting, distinctive, diversified, not ordinary 12 not identical 13 miscellaneous 14 unconventional

differential 8 contrast 11 distinction

differentiate 6 set off 8 contrast, separate, set apart 11 distinguish, draw the line 12 discriminate 13 make different

differentiation 8 contrast 10 comparison, separation 11 discernment, distinction

differing 6 unlike 7 variant 8 distinct, opposing 9 deviating, disparate, dissident, divergent 10 dissenting, dissimilar 11 contrasting, disagreeing

difficult 4 grim, hard 5 hairy, rough, tough 6 knotty, thorny, trying, unruly, uphill 7 arduous, complex, forward, not easy, onerous, tedious, willful 8 critical, exacting, perverse, stubborn, ticklish, toilsome 9 demanding, enigmatic, fractious, Herculean, intricate, laborious, obstinate, Sisyphean, strenuous, wearisome 10 burdensome, exhausting, fastidious, formidable, inflexible, perplexing, unyielding 11 bewildering, complicated, hard to solve, intractable, troublesome 12 hard to manage, hard to please, obstreperous, rambunctious, recalcitrant, unmanageable 13 hard to satisfy, problematical, unpredictable 14 hard to deal with 15 unaccommodating

difficulty 3 jam 4 mess, snag 5 trial 6 crisis, muddle, pickle, puzzle 7 barrier, dilemma, problem, straits, trouble 8 hot water, obstacle, quandary, tough job 9 deep water, hindrance, intricacy 10 impediment, perplexity, rough going, uphill work 11 arduousness, obstruction, predicament 12 hard sledding 13 laboriousness 14 stumbling block 15 troublesomeness 17 critical situation

diffidence 7 reserve, shyness 8 meekness, timidity 9 hesitancy, timidness 10 constraint, humbleness, insecurity, reluctance 11 bashfulness 12 introversion, sheepishness, timorousness 14 extreme modesty 15 unassertiveness 19 lack of self-assurance, retiring disposition

diffident 3 shy 6 modest 7 anxious, bashful 8 doubtful, hesitant, reserved, reticent, retiring 11 distrustful, unassertive 12 apprehensive

diffuse 5 wordy 7 verbose 8 rambling 9 desultory, dispersed, scattered, spread out, wandering 10 digressive, discursive, disjointed, long-winded, maundering, meandering, roundabout 14 circumlocutory, extended widely, unconcentrated, vaguely defined 15 not concentrated 18 lacking conciseness

diffuseness 8 rambling 9 prolixity, verbosity, wandering, wordiness 10 dispersion 11 indirection 14 circumlocution, long-windedness

diffusion 6 spread 8 rambling, verbiage 9 dispersal, prolixity, verbosity, wordiness 10 maundering, scattering 11 indirection, profuseness 14 circumlocution, discursiveness, disjointedness, roundaboutness

dig 3 jab 4 gibe, jeer, poke, prod, slur 5 aside, drive, gouge, punch, taunt 6 exhume, thrust 7 put-down, salvage, unearth 8 disinter, excavate, pinpoint, retrieve, scoop out 9 extricate, find among, hollow out 10 come up with, excavation, wry comment 11 bring to view 12 verbal thrust 13 cutting remark, search and find

digest 3 dig 5 grasp 6 absorb, fathom, precis, resume 7 realize, summary 8 abstract, dissolve, synopsis 10 abridgment, appreciate, assimilate, comprehend, understand 12 condensation, take in wholly 14 take in mentally

digestive system
component: 5 liver, mouth, teeth 6 tongue 7 stomach 8 appendix, pancreas 9 esophagus, intestine 11 gall bladder 13 salivary gland

dig in 4 root 5 embed, imbed, plant 6 anchor 7 pitch in 8 entrench, go to work 10 begin to eat 12 apply oneself

digit 3 one, six, two, toe 4 five, four, nine, unit, zero 5 light, seven, three 6 cipher, figure, finger, number 7 integer, numeral

dignified 5 proud 6 august, proper 7 upright 8 decorous, reserved 9 honorable 10 upstanding 11 circumspect 13 distinguished 14 self-respecting

dignify 5 raise 6 uplift 7 elevate, inflate, promote

dignitary 3 VIP 7 notable 8 luminary 9 personage 12 person of note

dignity 5 honor 7 decorum, majesty, station 9 loftiness, solemnity 10 augustness, importance 11 comportment, stateliness 12 high position, lofty bearing 13 proud demeanor 14 self-possession

digress 5 stray 6 back up, wander 7 deviate 8 divagate 9 turn aside 15 go off on a tangent 17 depart from subject

digression 6 detour 8 straying 9 departure, deviation, diversion, wandering 10 divagation, divergence, side remark 12 obiter dictum

digressive 7 diffuse 9 wandering 10 disjointed, maundering, roundabout 11 off the point 14 circumlocutory

dig up 6 locate 7 find out, root out, uncover, unearth 8 discover 9 ferret out 12 bring to light

dike 4 bank 5 levee, ridge 10 embankment

Dike *see* 4 Dice

dikerion 11 candelabrum, candlestick 12 candleholder

dilapidated 4 shot 6 beat-up, ruined, shabby 7 rickety, rundown, worn-out 8 battered, decaying, decrepit 10 broken-down, ramshackle, tumble-down 11 in disrepair 12 deteriorated, falling apart 15 falling to pieces

dilate 5 swell, widen 6 expand, extend 7 broaden, distend, enlarge, inflate, puff out 9 make wider

dilation 8 swelling, widening 9 expansion 10 broadening, distension, distention

dilatory 4 lazy, slow 5 tardy 6 remiss 8 dawdling, indolent, slothful, sluggish 9 negligent, reluctant 10 phlegmatic 13 lackadaisical 15 inclined to delay, procrastinating

dilemma 4 bind 6 crunch, plight 7 impasse, problem 8 deadlock, quandary 9 stalemate 11 predicament 13 Hobson's choice 15 difficult choice

dilettante **7** amateur, dabbler, trifler **12** experimenter **16** cultured hobbyist

diligence **4** zeal **8** industry **10** commitment, dedication **11** persistence **12** perseverance

diligent **6** active **7** careful, earnest, patient, zealous **8** plodding, sedulous, studious, thorough, untiring **9** assiduous, concerted **10** persistent **11** hardworking, industrious, painstaking, persevering **12** pertinacious **15** well-intentioned

dill
botanical name: **17** Anethum graveolens
origin: **9** Asia Minor **13** Mediterranean
family: **7** parsley
guards against: **7** Evil Eye **10** witchcraft
use: **6** sauces **7** pickles **10** vegetables

Dillon, Matt
roles: **3** Tex **10** Rumblefish **12** The Outsiders

dillydally **3** lag **4** idle, loaf **5** dally, delay **6** dawdle, loiter **8** kill time **9** waste time **10** fool around **13** procrastinate

Dilsey
character in: **18** The Sound and the Fury
author: **8** Faulkner

dilute **4** thin, weak **6** reduce, temper, watery, weaken **7** diffuse, diluted, thin out **8** decrease, diminish, make weak, mitigate, weakened **9** attenuate, liquidify, water down **10** add water to, adulterate, thinned out **11** adulterated, make thinner, watered down

diluted **4** weak **6** dilute, watery **8** weakened **10** thinned out **11** adulterated, watered down

dilution **8** thinning **9** weakening **12** watering down

dim **3** low **4** hazy, soft, weak **5** dusky, faint, foggy, murky, muted, vague **6** blurry, feeble, gloomy, remote **7** blurred, clouded, muffled, shadowy **8** darkened, nebulous, obscured **9** not bright, tenebrous **10** adumbrated, ill-defined, indefinite, indistinct, intangible **13** unilluminated

DiMaggio, Joe
nickname: **9** Joltin Joe
sport: **8** baseball
position: **8** outfield
team: **14** New York Yankees
wife: **13** Marilyn Monroe

dime-a-dozen **6** common **7** humdrum **8** ordinary, workaday **9** plentiful **10** ubiquitous **11** commonplace **12** easy to come by **13** garden-variety **15** undistinguished

dimension, dimensions **4** bulk, mass, size **5** range, scope, width **6** extent, height, length, volume, weight **7** measure **9** amplitude, greatness, magnitude, thickness **10** importance, proportion **11** massiveness **12** measurements **14** physical extent

diminish **3** ebb **4** wane **5** abate, lower **6** lessen, narrow, reduce, shrink **7** decline, dwindle, fall off, shorten, shrivel, subside **8** decrease, peter out **9** be reduced **11** make smaller **13** become smaller

diminuendo
music: **22** gradually getting softer
abbreviation: **3** dim

diminution **6** ebbing, waning **7** decline **8** decrease, lowering **9** dwindling, lessening, reduction, shrinkage **10** falling off, shortening, shriveling, subsidence **11** petering out, slacking off

diminutive **3** wee **4** tiny **5** elfin, short, small, teeny **6** little, minute, petite, slight **7** pet name, stunted **8** dwarfish, half-pint, nickname **9** miniature, short form **10** pocket-size, undersized, vest-pocket **11** lilliputian, small-scale, unimportant **13** insignificant **14** inconsiderable

Dimmesdale, Arthur
character in: **16** The Scarlet Letter
author: **9** Hawthorne

dimness **4** dusk **5** gloom, shade **8** darkness **14** indistinctness

dimwit **4** fool **5** dummy, dunce, idiot, moron **6** cretin, nitwit **7** dingbat, dullard, dumbell, pinhead **8** dumbbell, dummkopf, imbecile, meathead, numskull **9** birdbrain, blockhead, ding-a-ling, lamebrain, numbskull, simpleton **11** chowderhead, knucklehead

dim-witted **4** dull, dumb **5** dense **6** stupid **7** foolish, idiotic, moronic, witless **8** retarded **9** cretinous, imbecilic

din **4** stir, to-do **5** bruit **6** babble, clamor, hubbub, racket, ruckus, tumult, uproar **7** clangor **9** commotion **10** clattering, hullabaloo

Dinah
father: **5** Jacob
mother: **4** Leah
brother: **3** Dan, Gad **4** Levi **5** Asher, Judah **6** Joseph, Reuben, Simeon **7** Zebulun **8** Benjamin, Issachar, Naphtali
violated by: **7** Shechem

Dindymene *see* **6** Cybele

dine **3** eat, sup **4** feed **5** feast, lunch **6** fall to, supper **7** banquet, partake **9** breakfast, eat dinner **10** break bread, gluttonize, have dinner **11** gourmandize **14** take sustenance

Dine *see* **6** Navajo

Dinesen, Isak
real name: **18** Karen Blixen-Finecke
author of: **9** Last Tales **11** Out of Africa **12** Winter's Tales **16** Seven Gothic Tales

dinghy **5** skiff **7** rowboat **8** sailboat **9** small boat

dingy **4** dull **5** dusty, grimy, murky, tacky **6** dismal, dreary, gloomy, shabby **12** dirty and drab

dining room
French: **12** salle a manger

dinner **4** food, meal **5** beano, feast **6** repast, supper **7** banquet
French: **8** dejeuner **10** table d'hote

Dinner at Eight
director: **11** George Cukor
author: **10** Edna Ferber **14** George S Kaufman
cast: **8** Lee Tracy **10** Jean Harlow **11** Billie Burke **12** Wallace Beery **13** John Barrymore, Marie Dressler **15** Lionel Barrymore

dinosaur ***see box***

dint **4** push, will **5** drive, force, labor, might, power **6** charge, effort, energy, strain, stress **8** endeavor, exertion, strength, struggle **10** insistence **12** forcefulness **13** determination **14** relentlessness

diocese **3** see **7** eparchy **9** bishopric **14** church district
jurisdiction of: **6** bishop

Diomedes
king of: **6** Thrace
father: **4** Ares **6** Tydeus
mother: **6** Cyrene **7** Deipyle
member of: **7** Epigoni
kept: **9** wild mares
fed mares on: **10** human flesh
death planned by: **8** Hercules

dinosaur
means: **14** fearfully great, terrible lizard
subclass: **11** Archosauria
characteristic: **7** diapsid **14** teeth in sockets, two-arched skull **18** three-element pelvis
group: **11** Saurischian **13** Ornithischian
flesh-eating biped: **8** therapod
plant-eating quadruped: **8** sauropod
plant-eating biped: **10** ornithopod
armored: **10** ceratopsid
of Africa: **9** Iguanodon **13** Brachiosaurus **17** Heterodontosaurus
of Asia: **13** Hypselosaurus, Protoceratops
of Europe: **9** Iguanodon **12** Plateosaurus **13** Compsognathus, Hypselosaurus, Hypsilophodon
of North America: **10** Diplodocus, Edmontonia, Nodosaurus **11** Anatosaurus, Anchisaurus, Gorgosaurus, Monoclonius, Saurolophus, Scolosaurus, Stegosaurus, Triceratops **12** Ankylosaurus, Camarasaurus, Camptosaurus, Coelophysics, Lambeosaurus, Paleoscincus **13** Brachiosaurus, Styracosaurus, Tyrannosaurus **14** Thescelosaurus **15** Parasaurolophus, Procheneosaurus
of South America: **12** Pisanosaurus

Dione
consort of: **4** Zeus

Dionysia
festival of: **8** Dionysus

Dionysus *see* **7** Bacchus

Diores
father: **10** Amarynceus
fought against: **7** Trojans

Dioscuri *see* **15** Castor and Pollux

dip **4** bail, dish, dunk, sink, skim, soak **5** droop, ladle, scoop, slope, spoon **6** dabble, dish up, peruse, shovel **7** decline, descend, dish out, run over **8** drop down, glance at, submerge, turn down **13** study slightly **14** immerse briefly, lift by scooping, try tentatively **15** incline downward

dip into **4** scan, skim **5** ladle **6** browse, peruse **7** deplete **8** look over **13** glance through, make inroads in

Diplodocus
type: **8** dinosaur, sauropod
period: **8** Jurassic
location: **12** North America

diplomacy **4** tact **5** craft, skill **7** finesse **8** delicacy, prudence, subtlety **10** artfulness, discretion **11** maneuvering, savoir-faire **13** statesmanship **14** foreign affairs **16** artful management **18** foreign negotiation **21** international politics

diplomat **5** envoy **6** consul **7** attache **8** emissary, minister **9** statesman **10** ambassador, negotiator **12** interlocutor **13** tactful person
acceptable: **12** persona grata
unacceptable: **15** persona non grata

diplomatic **5** adept, suave **6** artful, urbane **7** attuned, politic, prudent, tactful **8** discreet **9** sensitive, strategic **13** ambassadorial **14** foreign-service **15** state-department

Dipolia
festival of: **4** Zeus
location: **6** Athens
slaughter of: **2** ox

Dipper
nickname of: **15** Wilt Chamberlain

Dipsas
form: **7** serpent

dipsomaniac **3** sot **4** lush, soak, wino **5** drunk, rummy, souse, toper **6** barfly, boozer **7** tippler **8** drunkard **9** alcoholic, inebriate

diptera
class: **8** hexapoda
phylum: **10** arthropoda
group: **7** true fly

Dirae *see* **6** Furies

dire **4** grim **5** awful, grave **6** dismal, urgent, woeful **7** crucial, extreme, fearful, ominous, ruinous **8** critical, dreadful, horrible, terrible **9** appalling, desperate, harrowing, ill-boding, ill-omened **10** calamitous, disastrous, portentous **11** apocalyptic, cataclysmic **12** catastrophic, inauspicious

direct **3** aim **4** head, lead, urge **5** blunt, clear, focus, frank, guide, order, pilot, usher **6** advise, candid, charge, enjoin, handle, head-on, honest, manage **7** address, command, conduct, control, earmark, forward, level at, oversee, pointed, sincere, train at **8** explicit, indicate, instruct, navigate, personal **9** conduct to, designate, firsthand, intend for, supervise **10** administer, face-to-face, forthright, point-blank, show the way, unmediated **11** plain-spoken, point the way, point toward, preside over, superintend **15** straightforward

direction **3** aim, way **4** bent, care, path **5** drift, order, route, track, trend **6** charge, course, recipe **7** bearing, command, control, current **8** guidance, headship, tendency **9** alignment **10** guidelines, leadership, management, regulation **11** inclination, instruction, line of march, supervision **12** line of action, prescription, surveillance **13** line of thought **14** administration, point of compass **15** superintendence

directive **5** ukase **8** bulletin **9** statement **10** communique **11** declaration **12** instructions, proclamation **13** communication

directly **4** soon **6** at once, openly **7** exactly, frankly **8** candidly, honestly, in person, promptly, straight **9** forthwith, precisely, presently, right away **10** face-to-face, in a beeline, personally **11** immediately, momentarily **12** in plain terms, not obliquely, unswervingly **13** unambiguously, unequivocally **14** as the crow flies **15** in a straight line **16** as soon as possible **17** on a straight course, straightforwardly

directness **6** candor **9** bluntness, frankness **10** candidness **14** forthrightness **19** straightforwardness

direct opposite **7** reverse **8** converse **10** antithesis

director **4** boss, head **5** chief **6** leader, master **7** curator, foreman, manager **8** chairman, governor, overseer **9** commander, conductor, organizer **10** controller, supervisor **13** administrator **14** superintendent

dirge **6** lament **7** requiem **8** threnody **9** death song **10** burial hymn, death march **11** funeral song **13** mournful sound **19** mournful composition

dirigo **7** I direct
motto of: **5** Maine

dirk **3** sny **4** snee, stab **5** knife, skean **6** dagger, skiver **7** poniard
origin: **8** Scotland

Dirks, Rudolph
creator/artist of: **12** Hans and Fritz **17** Captain and the Kids **19** The Katzenjammer Kids

dirt **3** mud **4** dust, loam, mire, muck, scum, slop, smut, soil, soot **5** dross, earth, filth, grime, humus, offal, rumor, slime, trash **6** gossip, ground, refuse, sludge, smudge **7** garbage, rubbish, scandal, slander **8** impurity, leavings, vileness **9** excrement, indecency, obscenity, profanity, sweepings **10** foul matter, moral filth, scurrility **11** pornography, scuttlebutt, squalidness **12** scabrousness **13** salaciousness **14** defamatory talk **15** filthy substance, unclean language **17** sensational expose

dirt-cheap **6** a steal **7** bargain **11** inexpensive **14** very reasonable **15** bargain-basement

dirty **4** base, foul, hard, lewd, mean, soil, spot, vile **5** grimy, messy, muddy, nasty, smear, stain, sully **6** coarse, filthy, grubby, mess up, muck up, risque, rotten, shabby, slop up, smudge, smudgy, smutty, soiled, sordid, untidy, vulgar **7** begrime, besmear, blacken, corrupt, crooked, devious, illegal, illicit, immoral, low-down, muddied, obscene, pollute, squalid, sullied, tarnish, unclean **8** befouled, begrimed, indecent, off-color, polluted, prurient, scabrous, unwashed **9** besmeared, deceitful, difficult, dishonest, tarnished, unsterile **10** despicable, fraudulent, licentious, perfidious, unpleasant, villainous **11** distasteful, treacherous **12** contemptible, disagreeable, dishonorable, pornographic, unscrupulous **14** morally unclean

Dirty Dozen, The
director: **13** Robert Aldrich
cast: **8** Jim Brown **9** Lee Marvin **10** Robert Ryan, Trini Lopez **11** Clint Walker **13** George Kennedy **14** Charles Bronson, Ernest Borgnine, John Cassavetes, Richard Jaeckel **16** Donald Sutherland

Dis
also: **8** Dis Pater
means: **5** Hades
god of: **10** underworld
corresponds to: **5** Orcus, Pluto

disability **5** minus **6** defect **8** handicap, weakness **9** infirmity, unfitness **10** affliction, impairment, impediment, inadequacy **11** shortcoming **12** debilitation, disadvantage **16** disqualification

disable **6** damage, hinder, impair, weaken **7** cripple **8** handicap **12** incapacitate

disabled
French: **12** hors de combat

disabuse **8** set right **9** relieve of **10** disenchant **11** disillusion, set straight

disaccord **7** discord **10** disharmony **12** disagreement **15** incompatibility

disacknowledge **4** deny **6** disown **7** disavow **8** disallow, disclaim **9** repudiate

disadvantage **4** flaw **6** burden **7** trouble **8** drawback, handicap, hardship, nuisance, weakness **9** detriment, hindrance, in arrears, weak point **10** impediment **12** weak position **13** inconvenience **16** fly in the ointment

disadvantaged **8** deprived, emergent, emerging, troubled **10** struggling **11** handicapped **12** impoverished **14** underdeveloped **15** underprivileged

disadvantageous **7** harmful **9** injurious **11** detrimental, inadvisable, inexpedient, undesirable, unfavorable, unfortunate

disaffect **4** wean **8** alienate, estrange **10** drive apart

disaffected **5** upset **7** hostile **8** agitated, inimical **9** alienated, disturbed, estranged, withdrawn **10** unfriendly **11** belligerent, discomposed, disgruntled, quarrelsome **12** antipathetic, discontented, dissatisfied **14** irreconcilable

disaffection **7** dislike **8** aversion, distaste **9** antipathy **10** alienation, discontent, disloyalty **12** estrangement

disaffirm **4** deny **5** annul **6** disown **7** decline, disavow **8** abnegate, disclaim, forswear, renounce **9** repudiate **15** wash one's hands of

disaffirmation **6** denial **9** annulment, disavowal **10** abnegation, disclaimer **11** repudiation **12** renunciation **13** contradiction

disagree **4** vary **5** clash, upset **6** depart, differ **7** deviate, diverge, make ill **8** be unlike, conflict, distress **9** discomfit **10** disconcert, stand apart **11** be injurious, fail to agree, not coincide **12** be at variance, be discordant, be dissimilar **13** cause problems **14** be unreconciled **15** be at loggerheads, differ in opinion **16** oppose one another, think differently

disagreeable **5** cross, harsh, nasty, surly, testy **7** grating, grouchy, peevish **8** churlish, petulant **9** difficult, irascible, irritable, obnoxious, offensive, repellent, repugnant, repulsive, unamiable, unwelcome **10** disgusting, ill-natured, uninviting, unpleasant **11** acrimonious, bad-tempered, displeasing, distasteful, ill-tempered, uncongenial, unpalatable **13** uncomfortable

disagreeing **6** at odds **7** deviant, varying **8** clashing **9** deviating, differing, disputing **10** quarreling **11** conflicting **13** at loggerheads

disagreement **5** clash, fight **7** discord, dispute, quarrel **8** argument, squabble, variance **9** deviation, disaccord, disparity, diversity **10** difference, divergence, falling-out, unlikeness **11** discrepancy, incongruity **13** dissimilarity, dissimilitude, lack of harmony **15** incompatibility **16** misunderstanding

disallow **4** deny, veto **6** abjure, forbid, refuse, reject **8** prohibit **9** repudiate

disallowance **4** veto **6** denial **7** refusal **9** rejection **11** prohibition, repudiation

disallowed **6** vetoed **7** abjured, refused **8** rejected **9** forbidden **10** repudiated **12** inadmissible, unacceptable

disappear **2** go **3** end **4** exit, fade, flee **5** leave **6** be gone, depart, die out, retire, vanish **8** be no more, fade away, melt away, withdraw **9** evaporate **12** be lost to view, cease to exist, leave no trace **13** cease to appear, cease to be seen **14** become obscured, cease to be known, pass out of sight **15** vanish from sight

disappearance **9** vanishing **11** evanescence **16** passing from sight

disappoint **4** foil **6** hinder, sadden, thwart **7** chagrin, let down, mislead **9** frustrate **10** dishearten **11** disillusion

disappointing 11 frustrating **12** unfulfilling **13** dissatisfying **14** unsatisfactory

disappointment 3 dud **4** bomb, loss **6** defeat, fiasco, fizzle **7** failure, letdown, setback, washout **8** disaster **9** the knocks **11** frustration **13** unfulfillment, unrealization **15** disillusionment, dissatisfaction

disapprobation 7 censure **8** disfavor **9** criticism, disesteem, objection **11** disapproval, displeasure **12** condemnation **15** dissatisfaction

disapprove 4 veto **5** decry **6** refuse, reject **7** censure, condemn, deplore, dislike **8** denounce, disallow, object to, turn down **9** criticize, deprecate, disparage, frown upon **10** think ill of **13** look askance at, regard as wrong **14** discountenance, refuse assent to **15** take exception to **16** find unacceptable, view with disfavor

disapprove of 7 censure, condemn, deplore **8** object to

disarm 4 move, sway **5** charm **6** entice **7** attract, bewitch, enchant, win over **8** convince, persuade **9** captivate, fascinate, influence, prevail on

disarming 7 melting, winning, winsome **8** charming, magnetic **9** appealing, beguiling, ingenuous, seductive **10** bewitching, entrancing **11** captivating **12** ingratiating, irresistible

disarrange 5 mix up, upset **6** jumble, mess up, muddle, ruffle, rumple **7** confuse, scatter **8** disarray, dishevel, disorder, displace, put askew, scramble **11** disorganize **13** put out of order **14** turn topsy-turvy

disarranged 5 messy **6** mussed, sloppy, untidy **7** jumbled, ruffled, rumpled, tousled, unkempt **8** uncombed **9** cluttered **10** disarrayed, disheveled, disordered, disorderly, in disorder **11** in a shambles

disarrangement 4 mess **5** chaos, mix-up, upset **6** jumble, mixing, muddle **7** clutter **8** disarray, disorder, scramble, shambles **9** confusion, messiness, messing up **10** disharmony, disruption, sloppiness, untidiness **12** dishevelment **14** disorderliness **15** disorganization, heaping together

disarray 5 chaos, mix-up, upset **6** jumble **7** clutter **8** disorder, scramble, shambles **9** confusion, messiness **10** disharmony, sloppiness, untidiness **12** dishevelment **14** disarrangement **15** disorganization

disarrayed 5 messy **6** mussed, sloppy, untidy **7** chaotic, jumbled, mixed up **10** disheveled, disordered, disorderly, in disorder **11** disarranged

disarticulate 6 detach **7** unhinge **8** disjoint, disunite, separate **9** disengage, dislocate **10** disconnect **13** put out of joint

disarticulated 5 apart **7** divided **8** unhinged **9** disunited, separated **10** disengaged, disjointed, dislocated, unattached **11** unconnected **12** disconnected **13** helter-skelter

disassemble 7 disband, scatter **8** disperse **9** knock down, take apart

disassociate 7 divorce **8** separate **10** disconnect **12** disaffiliate

disassociation 5 break, split **6** schism **7** divorce **8** division **10** separation

disaster 4 harm **5** wreck **6** blight, fiasco **7** scourge, tragedy, trouble **8** accident, calamity **9** adversity, cataclysm, ruination **10** misfortune **11** catastrophe, great mishap **12** misadventure

disastrous 4 dire **5** fatal **6** tragic **7** adverse, hapless, harmful, ruinous **8** dreadful, grievous, ill-fated, terrible **9** harrowing **10** calamitous, desolating, horrendous, ill-starred **11** destructive, devastating, unfortunate **12** catastrophic, inauspicious

disavow 4 deny **6** abjure, disown, recant, reject **7** gainsay, retract **8** denounce **9** repudiate **10** contradict

disavowal 6 denial **8** demurrer **9** rejection **10** abjuration, disclaimer, refutation **11** repudiation **13** contradiction

disband 7 adjourn, dismiss, scatter **8** disperse, dissolve **11** disassemble

disbelief 5 doubt **7** dubiety **8** distrust, mistrust, unbelief **10** skepticism **11** incredulity **12** doubtfulness **14** lack of credence

disbelieve 5 doubt **6** refuse, reject **7** suspect **8** discount, distrust **9** discredit, unbelieve **10** misbelieve

disbeliever 7 atheist, skeptic **8** apostate

disbursable 7 payable **9** available, spendable **10** expendable

disburse 6 lay out, pay out **7** fork out **8** allocate, shell out **10** distribute

disbursement 6 outlay **7** payment **8** spending **9** paying out **10** dispensing **11** expenditure **12** dispensation, distribution

discard 4 drop, dump, junk, shed **5** scrap **6** remove, shelve **7** abandon, weed out **8** get rid of, jettison, throw out **9** cast aside, dispose of, eliminate, throw away **10** relinquish **11** thrust aside **12** dispense with, have done with **14** throw overboard

discarded 6 dumped, junked **7** cast off, dropped **8** deserted, forsaken, rejected, scrapped **9** abandoned, cast aside, tossed out **10** jettisoned, left behind, thrown away

discern 3 see **4** espy **6** behold, descry, detect, notice **7** make out, observe, pick out **8** perceive **9** ascertain **12** catch sight of

discernible 7 visible **8** apparent **10** detectable, noticeable **11** perceivable, perceptible

discerning 4 sage, wise **5** acute, sharp **6** astute, shrewd **8** piercing **9** judicious, sagacious, sensitive **10** perceptive **11** intelligent, keen-sighted, penetrating **12** clear-sighted, sharp-sighted **13** perspicacious **14** discriminating

discernment 6 acumen, senses **7** insight **8** feelings, sagacity, thoughts **10** cognizance, discretion, perception **11** distinction **13** consciousness, judiciousness **14** discrimination **15** differentiation

discharge 3 axe, can **4** emit, fire, flow, free, gush, ooze, oust, sack, shot **5** blast, burst, eject, expel, exude, issue, let go, shoot **6** bounce, firing, launch, lay off, let fly, propel, report, set off **7** cashier, dismiss, explode, fire off, project, release, seepage, set free, trigger **8** activate, detonate, drainage, emission, get rid of, liberate, throw off, touch off **9** allow to go, exploding, explosion, firing off, fusillade, give forth, pour forth, secretion, send forth, terminate **10** activating, detonating, detonation, triggering **11** send packing, suppuration **13** give the gate to, walking papers **14** demobilization **15** release document **16** remove from office

disciple **3** nut **5** freak, pupil **7** admirer, convert, devotee, pursuer, student **8** adherent, believer, follower, neophyte, partisan **9** proselyte, supporter **10** aficionado **11** afficionado

Disciple, The
author: **11** Paul Bourget

disciplinarian **8** martinet **13** authoritarian **16** stickler for rules, strict taskmaster

disciplinary **8** punitive **9** punishing **10** corrective **13** authoritarian

discipline **5** drill, prime, rigor, train **6** method, punish **7** break in, chasten, regimen **8** chastise, drilling, instruct, practice, training **9** schooling **11** preparation **14** indoctrination **15** prescribed habit, teach by exercise **16** course of exercise

disclaim **4** deny **6** disown **7** decline, disavow **8** abnegate, forswear, renounce **9** disaffirm, repudiate

disclaimer **6** denial **8** demurrer **9** disavowal **10** abnegation **11** repudiation **12** renunciation

disclose **4** bare, leak, show, tell **6** expose, impart, reveal, unveil **7** divulge, lay bare, publish, uncover **9** broadcast, make known **10** make public **11** communicate **12** bring to light **13** allow to be seen, bring into view, cause to appear

discolor **4** spot **5** stain, tinge **6** bleach, streak **7** tarnish

discoloration **4** blot, mark, spot **5** smear, stain **6** blotch, bruise, smudge **7** blemish **9** contusion

discolored **4** doty **5** dingy, dirty, faded, livid **6** soiled, tinged **7** bruised, stained **9** tarnished

discomfit **5** upset **6** thwart **7** chagrin **8** confound, distress **9** embarrass, frustrate **10** disconcert

discomfited **5** upset **6** uneasy **7** ashamed **8** thwarted **9** chagrined, ill at ease **10** distressed **11** embarrassed **12** disconcerted

discomfiture **7** anxiety **9** agitation, confusion **10** uneasiness **11** disquietude, distraction, nervousness **12** discomposure, perturbation **13** embarrassment

discomfort **3** try **4** ache, hurt, pain **5** trial **6** misery **7** malaise, trouble **8** disquiet, distress, hardship, nuisance, soreness, vexation **9** annoyance, discomfit, embarrass **10** affliction, discompose, irritation, make uneasy **11** disquietude

discompose **5** abash, upset **6** rattle **7** agitate, confuse, disturb, fluster, nonplus, perturb, trouble, unnerve **8** disquiet, distract, distress, unsettle **9** discomfit, embarrass **10** disconcert

discomposed **5** upset **6** jolted, rocked, shaken, uneasy **7** anxious, nervous, worried **8** agitated, confused, troubled **9** disturbed, flustered, perturbed **10** disquieted, distracted **11** discomfited, uncollected

discomposure **6** flurry **7** anxiety **8** disquiet **9** agitation, confusion **10** discomfort, uneasiness **11** awkwardness, disquietude, distraction, nervousness **12** discomfiture, perturbation **13** embarrassment **17** self-consciousness

disconcert **5** abash, annoy, upset **6** rattle, ruffle **7** agitate, confuse, disturb, nonplus, perturb, trouble **8** unsettle **10** discompose

disconcerted **5** fazed, upset **7** annoyed, rattled, ruffled **8** agitated, confused, troubled **9** disturbed, perturbed, thrown off, unsettled **10** distracted, nonplussed

disconcertment **8** rattling **9** abashment, agitation, confusion **11** disturbance **12** discomposure

disconnect **6** detach **8** separate, uncouple **9** disengage

disconnected **5** split **6** cut off **7** jumbled, mixed-up, severed **8** confused, detached, rambling **9** illogical, separated, uncoupled **10** disengaged, disjointed, incoherent, irrational, unattached, unfastened **12** disorganized

disconnection **8** severing **9** severance **10** cutting off, detachment, separation **13** disengagement

disconsolate **3** sad **4** blue, down **6** woeful **7** crushed, doleful, forlorn, unhappy **8** dejected, desolate, downcast, wretched **9** depressed, miserable, sorrowful, woebegone **10** despondent, dispirited, melancholy **11** discouraged, low-spirited, pessimistic **12** heavy-hearted, inconsolable **13** brokenhearted **14** down in the dumps, down in the mouth

discontent **9** displease **10** discomfort, disgruntle **11** displeasure, unhappiness **15** dissatisfaction

discontented **5** bored **7** fretful, unhappy **9** miserable, regretful **10** displeased, malcontent **11** disgruntled **12** dissatisfied

discontinuance **3** end **4** halt, stop **6** ending, recess **7** ceasing, halting **8** abeyance, giving up, quitting, stoppage, stopping, surcease **9** cessation, desisting **10** concluding, leaving off, suspension **11** abandonment, breaking off, termination

discontinue **3** end **4** drop, quit, stop **5** cease **6** desist, give up **7** abandon, abstain, suspend **8** break off, leave off **9** interrupt, terminate **10** put an end to

discontinuous **8** discrete, episodic, sporadic **9** segmented, spasmodic **10** occasional **11** interrupted **12** disconnected, intermittent

discord **6** strife **7** dispute **8** clashing, conflict, disunity, division, friction **9** cacophony, harshness, wrangling **10** contention, disharmony, dissension, dissonance, quarreling **11** being at odds, differences, discordance **12** disagreement, grating noise **13** lack of concord **15** incompatibility **16** unpleasant sounds
goddess of: **4** Eris **9** Discordia

discordance **6** strife **7** discord, dispute **8** clashing, conflict, disunity, division, friction **9** wrangling **10** contention, disharmony, dissension, quarreling **12** disagreement **15** incompatibility

discordant **6** at odds **9** disparate, dissonant **10** at variance, discrepant **11** conflicting, disagreeing **12** unharmonious

Discordia
origin: **5** Roman

goddess of: 7 discord
corresponds to: 4 Eris

discount 3 cut 5 break 6 rebate 7 cut rate 9 abatement, allowance, deduction, exemption, reduction 10 concession 11 subtraction

discountenance 7 condemn, despise, disdain, dislike 8 object to 9 frown upon 10 disapprove, think ill of 12 look down upon 13 look askance at, regard as wrong 14 hold in contempt 15 take exception to

discourage 4 do in 5 daunt, deter, unman 6 deject, dismay 7 depress, unnerve 8 decimate, dispirit, dissuade, keep back, restrain 9 disparage, prostrate 10 dishearten, disincline, divert from 13 advise against, dash one's hopes 17 dampen one's spirits

discouraged 3 low 7 daunted 8 dejected, downcast, hopeless 9 depressed 10 despondent, dispirited 11 downhearted, pessimistic 12 disconsolate, disheartened

discouragement 4 curb 5 gloom, worry 6 damper, dismay 7 despair 8 obstacle 9 dejection, hindrance, pessimism, restraint 10 constraint, depression, impediment, low spirits, melancholy, moroseness 11 despondency 12 hopelessness, lack of spirit 13 consternation 15 downheartedness

discourse 3 gab 4 chat, talk 5 essay 6 confer, sermon, speech 7 address, discuss, lecture, oration 8 colloquy, converse, dialogue, diatribe, harangue, treatise 10 discussion 11 intercourse 12 conversation, dissertation, talk together 16 formal discussion

Discourse on Method
author: 13 Rene Descartes

discourteous 4 rude 5 fresh, surly 6 cheeky 7 boorish, ill-bred, uncivil, uncouth 8 impolite, impudent, insolent 9 uncourtly, ungallant 10 ill-behaved, ungracious, unladylike, unmannerly 11 ill-mannered, impertinent 13 disrespectful, ungentlemanly

discourtesy 8 rudeness 9 impudence, insolence 10 incivility 11 boorishness 12 impoliteness

discover 3 see 4 find, spot 5 dig up 6 detect, locate, notice 7 discern, find out, learn of, realize, root out, uncover, unearth 8 come upon, perceive 9 ascertain, determine, ferret out, light upon, recognize 10 chance upon 11 gain sight of, stumble upon 12 bring to light

discredit 4 deny, slur 5 abuse, smear, sully, taint 6 debase, defame, demean, reject, smirch, vilify 7 degrade, dispute, tarnish, vitiate 8 disallow, disgrace, dishonor, disprove, question 9 challenge, disparage, undermine 10 prove false, stigmatize 16 shake one's faith in 17 drag through the mud

discreditable 8 shameful, shocking 9 appalling 10 outrageous, scandalous 11 disgraceful, ignominious 12 dishonorable, disreputable

discreet 6 polite 7 careful, politic, prudent, tactful 8 cautious 9 judicious, sensitive 10 diplomatic, thoughtful 11 circumspect

Discreet Charm of the Bourgeoisie, The
director: 10 Luis Bunuel
cast: 11 Fernando Rey 14 Delphine Seyrig, Stephane Audran
Oscar for: 11 foreign film

discrepancy 3 gap 8 variance 9 disparity 10 difference, divergence 11 discordance, incongruity 12 disagreement 13 dissimilarity, inconsistency

discrepant 6 at odds 8 contrary, opposing 9 disparate 10 at variance, discordant, dissimilar, refutatory 11 conflicting, contrasting, disagreeing 12 antithetical, inconsistent 13 contradictory 14 countervailing, irreconcilable

discrete 7 several, various 8 detached, distinct, separate 9 different 10 unattached 11 disjunctive, independent 12 disconnected, unassociated 13 discontinuous

discretion 4 tact 6 acumen, option 8 judgment, prudence, sagacity, volition 9 good sense 10 preference 11 discernment, inclination 12 good judgment, predilection 13 judiciousness, sound judgment 14 discrimination 15 power of choosing 16 individual choice

discretionary 8 optional 9 voluntary 10 nonbinding 11 nonrequired, unnecessary 12 nonrequisite, unimperative 13 nonobligatory

discriminate 7 disdain 8 separate 11 distinguish 12 disfranchise 13 differentiate

discriminating 5 acute 6 astute, biased, shrewd 7 bigoted, refined 9 judicious, sensitive 10 cultivated, discerning, fastidious 11 intelligent, prejudicial 13 perspicacious 15 differentiating

discrimination 4 bias 5 taste 6 acumen 7 bigotry 8 inequity, judgment, keenness, sagacity 9 prejudice 10 astuteness, discretion, favoritism, refinement, shrewdness 11 discernment, distinction 12 perspicacity 21 differential treatment

discursive 7 diffuse 8 rambling 9 wandering 10 circuitous, digressive, long-winded, meandering, roundabout

discursiveness 8 rambling 10 digression, meandering 14 circumlocution

discuss 6 debate, parley, review 7 dissect, examine, speak of 8 consider, talk over 9 talk about 13 converse about, exchange views 14 discourse about

discussion 3 rap 4 talk 6 debate, parley, powwow, review 7 inquiry 8 analysis, argument, colloquy, dialogue, scrutiny 9 discourse 10 hashing-out 11 disputation 12 deliberation 13 consideration, investigation

disdain 4 snub 5 abhor, scorn, spurn 6 deride, detest, loathe 7 despise, dislike 8 contempt, distaste 9 frown upon 10 abhorrence, brush aside, disrespect 11 intolerance 12 icy aloofness, look down upon 14 deem unbecoming, discountenance

disdained 7 derided, scorned, spurned 8 abhorred, despised 10 deprecated, disparaged 14 held in contempt

disdainful 4 cold 5 aloof 7 haughty, high-hat 8 derisive, scornful, superior 11 overbearing, patronizing 12 contemptuous, supercilious 13 condescending

disease 6 malady 7 ailment, illness 8 sickness 9 ill health, infirmity 10 affliction 15 morbid condition 16 physical disorder

disembark 4 land 7 deplane, detrain, pile out 10 leave a ship 11 get off a ship

disenchant 6 put off 7 turn off 8 alienate, disabuse, turn away 9 undeceive 11 disenthrall, disillusion 12 open one's eyes 13 break the spell

15 burst one's bubble 16 bring down to earth

disencumber 8 unburden 9 disburden, extricate 11 disentangle

disengage 5 sever 6 detach 7 disjoin 8 separate 9 extricate 10 disconnect

disengaged 7 unmoved 8 detached 9 apathetic, disjoined, separated 11 indifferent, uncommitted, unconcerned 12 disconnected, unresponsive French: 6 degage

disengagement 6 apathy 8 severing 9 severance, unconcern 10 detachment, separation 12 indifference 13 disconnection 16 unresponsiveness

disentangle 4 free 6 detach, loosen, remove 7 unravel 9 extricate

disenthrall 9 undeceive 10 disenchant 11 disillusion 12 open one's eyes 13 break the spell 15 burst one's bubble 16 bring down to earth

disesteem 7 dislike 8 disfavor 9 disrepute 11 disapproval, displeasure 14 disapprobation

disfavor 5 odium 7 dislike, ill turn 8 disgrace, ignominy 9 disesteem, disregard 10 disrespect, disservice, harmful act 11 disapproval, discourtesy, displeasure 14 disapprobation 15 dissatisfaction 16 unacceptableness

disfigure 3 mar 4 maim, scar 5 cut up 6 damage, deface, deform, impair 7 blemish, scarify 8 make ugly, mutilate

disfigurement 4 blot, flaw, mark, scar, spot 6 blotch, defect 7 blemish 12 imperfection

disfranchise, disenfranchise 15 deprive of a right 19 discriminate against

disgorge 4 spew 5 eject, expel, spout, vomit 6 cast up, spew up 7 cough up, throw up 8 dislodge 9 discharge 10 vomit forth 11 regurgitate

disgrace 4 blot 5 abase, shame, stain, taint 6 debase, smirch 7 blemish, degrade, eyesore, scandal, tarnish 8 contempt, derogate, disfavor, dishonor, ill favor, reproach 9 discredit, disparage, disrepute, embarrass, humiliate 13 embarrassment, in the doghouse 14 bring shame upon

disgraceful 3 low 4 base, mean, vile 6 odious 8 infamous, shameful, shocking, unseemly, unworthy 9 appalling, degrading, obnoxious 10 despicable, detestable, inglorious, outrageous, scandalous, unbecoming 11 ignominious, opprobrious 12 dishonorable, disreputable 13 discreditable, reprehensible

disgruntled 5 sulky, testy, vexed 6 grumpy, shirty, sullen 7 grouchy, peevish 8 petulant 9 irritated 10 displeased, malcontent 12 discontented, dissatisfied

disguise 4 garb, hide, mask, pose, sham, veil 5 blind, cloak, cover, feign, getup, guise 6 facade, muffle, screen, shroud, veneer 7 conceal, cover-up, dress up, falsify 8 pretense, simulate 9 costuming, dissemble, gloss over 10 camouflage, false front, masquerade 11 concealment, counterfeit 12 misrepresent 13 false identity 15 false appearance

disguised 6 masked, veiled 7 cloaked 9 dressed up, incognito 10 undercover 11 camouflaged 14 unrecognizable

disgust 5 repel 6 appall, hatred, offend, put off, revolt, sicken 7 dislike 8 aversion, contempt, distaste, loathing, nauseate 9 antipathy, disrelish, repulsion, revulsion 10 abhorrence, repugnance 11 detestation, displeasure 12 disaffection 13 be repulsive to, cause aversion 15 turn one's stomach

disgusting 4 vile 5 hasty 6 horrid, odious 7 hateful 9 abhorrent, appalling, loathsome, offensive, repellent, repugnant, repulsive, revolting, sickening 10 abominable, despicable, nauseating 13 reprehensible

dish 4 dole, fare, food 5 ladle, place, plate, scoop, serve, spoon 6 recipe, saucer, vessel 7 bowlful, dishful, edibles, helping, platter, portion, serving 8 dispense, plateful, transfer, victuals 10 comestible 11 shallow bowl

dishabille 7 undress 8 bathrobe, disarray, disorder, informal, negligee 9 housecoat

disharmonious 7 chaotic 8 clashing, confused 9 dissonant, illogical 10 discordant, incoherent 11 conflicting, contentious 12 incompatible 13 heterogeneous

disharmony 5 chaos 6 strife 7 discord 8 clashing, conflict, disarray, disunity, division, friction 9 cacophony, confusion, disaccord, harshness 10 contention, dissension, dissonance 11 discordance 12 disagreement, grating noise 15 disorganization, incompatibility

dishearten 4 dash, faze 5 abash, crush, daunt 6 deject, dismay, sadden 7 depress 8 dispirit 10 discourage

disheartened 3 low 6 dismal 8 dejected, desolate, downcast 9 depressed 10 despondent, dispirited 11 discouraged 12 disconsolate

disheartening 4 dark 7 adverse 8 hopeless 11 dispiriting 12 discouraging, inauspicious

disheveled 5 messy 6 blowsy, frowzy, mussed, sloppy, untidy 7 ruffled, rumpled, tousled, unkempt 8 uncombed 10 bedraggled, disarrayed, disorderly, in disorder 11 disarranged

dishevelment 5 chaos, mix-up, upset 6 jumble 7 clutter 8 disarray, disorder, scramble, shambles 9 messiness 10 sloppiness, untidiness 14 disarrangement 15 disorganization

dishonest 5 false 7 corrupt, crooked 8 cheating, specious, spurious, two-faced 9 deceitful, deceptive, faithless, insincere, not honest 10 fraudulent, mendacious, misleading, perfidious, untruthful 11 underhanded 12 disingenuous, false-hearted, unprincipled, unscrupulous 13 untrustworthy

dishonesty 8 cheating 9 duplicity, falseness, mendacity 10 corruption 11 crookedness 12 speciousness 14 untruthfulness

dishonor 4 blot 5 abase, odium, shame, stain, sully 6 debase, defame, infamy, insult, slight, stigma 7 affront, blacken, blemish, degrade, offense, scandal, tarnish 8 disfavor, disgrace, ignominy 9 discredit, disparage, disrepute, humiliate, ill repute 10 derogation, stigmatize 11 discourtesy, humiliation 12 bring shame on 14 public disgrace

dishonorable 4 base 7 debased, ignoble 8 shameful 10 despicable 12 contemptible, disreputable 13 reprehensible

dishonorableness 4 blot 5 odium, shame, stain 6 stigma 7 blemish 8 disfavor, disgrace, ignominy 9 discredit, disrepute, ill repute **10** derogation **11** humiliation

dishonoring **8** disgrace **10** debasement **11** degradation, humiliation

dish up **3** dip **5** ladle, serve, spoon **7** dish out, serve up

disillusion **6** clue in **8** disabuse **9** undeceive **10** disenchant **11** disenthrall **13** break the spell, open the eyes of **14** burst the bubble **16** bring down to earth

disinclination **8** aversion **9** hesitancy **10** reluctance **13** indisposition, unwillingness

disincline **5** deter **8** dissuade, keep back, restrain **10** discourage, divert from **13** advise against **16** attempt to prevent

disinclined **5** loath **6** averse **8** hesitant **9** reluctant, unwilling **10** indisposed

disinfect **6** purify **7** cleanse **8** sanitize **9** kill germs, sterilize **13** decontaminate **15** destroy bacteria

disinfectant **9** germicide **10** antiseptic, germ killer **11** bactericide

disinherit **6** cut off, disown **15** deprive of rights

disintegrate **7** break up, crumble, shatter **8** splinter **9** fall apart **10** break apart, go to pieces

disintegration **4** ruin **5** decay **7** breakup, erosion **8** biolysis **9** crumbling **10** dispersion, dissolving, separation **11** decomposing **12** falling apart **13** decomposition, deterioration, pulverization

disinter **5** dig up **6** exhume **7** unearth

disinterest **6** apathy **9** disregard, unconcern **12** indifference

disinterested **7** neutral, outside **8** unbiased **9** impartial **10** impersonal, uninvolved **12** free from bias, unprejudiced **13** dispassionate

disinterment **9** digging up **10** exhumation, unearthing

disjecta membra **15** disjointed parts **16** scattered members

disjoin **4** part, undo **5** break, sever **6** detach, divide **8** disunite, separate **9** disengage

disjoint **6** detach **7** unhinge **8** disunite, separate **9** dislocate **10** disconnect **13** disarticulate

disjointed **5** apart, split **7** chaotic, divided, jumbled, mixed-up, tangled **8** confused, detached, rambling **9** illogical, spasmodic **10** incoherent, irrational, unattached **11** unconnected **12** disconnected, disorganized **13** discontinuous, disharmonious, helter-skelter, heterogeneous **14** disarticulated

disjointedness **8** rambling **11** indirection **14** discursiveness **16** disconnectedness

disjointed parts
Latin: **14** disjecta membra

disk, disc **3** cam **4** aten, coin, dial, face, plow, puck **5** plate, wafer, wheel **6** harrow, record, sequin **7** discuss **8** diskette **9** cultivate, videodisc **11** discotheque
type: **4** hard **5** fixed **6** floppy **8** magnetic **10** Winchester

dislike **4** hate **5** abhor, scorn **6** animus, detest, enmity, hatred, loathe, malice, rancor **7** despise, disdain, disgust, not like **8** aversion, distaste, loathing, object to **9** abominate, animosity, antipathy, hostility, repulsion, revulsion **10** abhorrence, antagonism, repugnance **11** abomination, detestation **12** disaffection

disliked **5** hated **7** loathed, unloved **8** abhorred, despised, detested **10** abominated

dislike intensely **4** hate **5** abhor **6** detest, loathe **7** despise **9** abominate **10** recoil from

dislocate **6** uproot **7** unhinge **8** disjoint, disunite, separate **9** disengage **10** disconnect **13** disarticulate, put out of joint

dislodge **4** oust **5** eject, expel **6** dig out, dispel, remove, uproot **7** disturb **8** displace, force out **9** extricate **11** disentangle

disloyal **6** untrue **8** recreant **9** faithless, seditious, undutiful **10** inconstant, perfidious, subversive, traitorous, unfaithful **11** treacherous, treasonable **12** dishonorable

disloyalty **7** falsity, perfidy, treason **8** apostasy, betrayal, sedition **9** falseness, rebellion, recreancy, treachery **10** infidelity, subversion **11** inconstancy **12** insurrection **13** breach of trust, deceitfulness, double-dealing, faithlessness **14** lack of fidelity, perfidiousness, unfaithfulness **15** betrayal of trust, breaking of faith **18** subversive activity

dismal **3** sad **4** drab, grim, poor **5** awful, bleak **6** dreary, gloomy, morbid, rueful, somber, woeful **7** abysmal, doleful, forlorn, joyless, unhappy, very bad, visaged **8** dejected, desolate, dolorous, downcast, dreadful, hopeless, horrible, mournful, terrible **9** cheerless, depressed, long-faced, sorrowful, woebegone **10** abominable, despondent, in the dumps, lugubrious, melancholy **11** pessimistic **12** disconsolate, disheartened, heavy-hearted **13** unmentionable **14** down-in-the-mouth

dismantle **5** strip **6** denude, divest **9** take apart

dismay **3** cow **5** abash, alarm, daunt, dread, panic, scare **6** appall, fright, horror, put off, terror **7** anxiety, concern, horrify, unnerve **8** affright, distress, frighten **10** disappoint, discourage, dishearten, intimidate **11** disillusion, trepidation **12** apprehension, exasperation, intimidation, perturbation **13** consternation **14** disappointment, discouragement **15** disillusionment

dismayed **7** abashed, daunted **8** appalled **10** confounded, nonplussed **12** disconcerted

dismember **4** limb **6** hack up **8** disjoint **16** tear limb from limb

dismiss **3** can **4** fire, free, oust, sack **5** let go **6** bounce, excuse, reject **7** adjourn, cashier, disband, discard, release **8** disclaim, disperse, dissolve, lay aside, liberate, pink-slip, set aside **9** disregard, eliminate, repudiate, send forth, terminate **10** permit to go **11** send packing **12** allow to leave, put out of a job, put out of mind **14** give the heave-ho **17** remove from service, give walking papers **19** discharge from office

dismissal **6** firing **7** release **9** discharge, dispersal, disregard **10** disclaimer **11** adjournment, repudiation

Disney, Walt
creator/artist of: **10** Donald Duck **11** Mickey Mouse

disobedience **8** defiance **9** rebellion **10** resistance **13** noncompliance, nonconformity **14** rebelliousness

disobedient **6** unruly **7** defiant, froward, haughty, wayward **8** contrary, mutinous, perverse, stubborn **9** fractious, insurgent, obstinate, seditious, undutiful

10 disorderly, rebellious, refractory, unyielding 11 intractable 12 noncompliant, recalcitrant, ungovernable, unmanageable, unsubmissive 13 insubordinate

disobey 4 defy 5 break 6 ignore, resist 7 violate 8 overstep 9 disregard 10 infringe on, transgress 11 go counter to 12 rebel against

disoblige 5 annoy 6 bother 7 trouble 13 inconvenience

disobliging 4 rude 8 churlish 9 unhelpful 13 inconsiderate

disorder 4 mess, riot 5 chaos 6 fracas, jumble, malady, muddle, ruckus, uproar 7 ailment, clutter, disease, illness, turmoil 8 disarray, sickness 9 commotion, complaint, confusion 10 affliction, disruption, dissension 11 disturbance 13 indisposition, minor uprising 14 disarrangement 15 disorganization

disordered 7 jumbled 8 confused, messed up 9 haphazard 11 disarranged 12 disorganized

disorderliness 4 mess 5 chaos 6 muddle 8 disarray 9 confusion 10 disruption 14 disarrangement 15 disorganization

disorderly 3 bad 4 wild 5 messy, noisy, rowdy 6 sloppy, unruly, untidy 7 chaotic, jumbled, lawless, riotous, unkempt, wayward 8 careless, confused, improper, pell-mell, rowdyish, slipshod, slovenly, unlawful, unsorted 10 boisterous, disheveled, disordered, disruptive, rebellious, straggling, topsy-turvy 11 disarranged 12 disorganized, disreputable, obstreperous, unrestrained, unsystematic 13 helter-skelter, undisciplined 14 rough-and-tumble, unsystematized

disorganization 4 mess 5 chaos, upset 6 jumble, muddle 7 clutter 8 disarray, disorder, shambles 9 confusion, messiness 10 disharmony, disruption, sloppiness, untidiness 12 dishevelment 14 disarrangement, disorderliness

disorganize 5 mix up, upset 6 jumble, mess up, muddle 7 confuse, scatter 8 disarray, disorder, put askew, scramble 10 disarrange 13 put out of order 14 turn topsy-turvy

disorganized 5 messy, upset 7 chaotic, jumbled, mixed-up, muddled 8 confused, rambling 9 haphazard, illogical 10 disordered, disorderly, incoherent, in disarray, irrational 12 unsystematic 16 at sixes and sevens

disoriented 7 mixed-up 8 confused, unstable 10 distracted, out of joint, out of touch 11 not adjusted

disown 6 reject 7 cast off, disavow, forsake 8 denounce, disclaim, renounce 9 repudiate 10 disinherit 17 refuse to recognize 19 refuse to acknowledge

disparage 4 mock 6 demean, slight 7 put down, run down 8 belittle, derogate, ridicule 9 denigrate, discredit, underrate 10 depreciate, undervalue 11 detract from

disparaged 7 ran down 9 belittled, ridiculed 10 denigrated, deprecated 11 depreciated

disparagement 5 abuse, libel 7 slander 8 ridicule 9 criticism 10 belittling, defamation, derogation, detraction 11 denigration, putting down 12 vilification 17 defamatory remarks

disparaging 5 snide 10 belittling, derogatory 11 unfavorable 15 uncomplimentary

disparate 6 at odds, unlike 9 different 10 at variance, discordant, discrepant, dissimilar 11 contrasting

disparity 3 gap 8 contrast, imparity, variance 10 difference, divergence, inequality, unlikeness 11 discrepancy, incongruity 12 disagreement, dissemblance 13 contradiction, disproportion, dissimilarity, dissimilitude, inconsistency

dispassion 6 apathy 8 coolness 10 detachment 12 indifference

dispassionate 4 calm, cool, fair 6 serene 7 neutral, unmoved 8 composed, detached, unbiased 9 collected, impartial, unexcited, unruffled 10 impersonal, uninvolved 11 levelheaded, undisturbed, unemotional 12 unprejudiced 13 disinterested, imperturbable

dispatch 4 item, kill, post, slay 5 flash, haste, piece, speed, story 6 finish, letter, murder, report, settle, wind up 7 bump off, execute, forward, message, missive, send off 8 alacrity, bulletin, carry out, celerity, complete, conclude, expedite, massacre, rapidity 9 finish off, quickness, slaughter, swiftness 10 communique, expedition, promptness, put an end to, put to death 11 assassinate, news account 12 send on the way 14 execute quickly, summarily shoot, swift execution 15 make short work of, transmit rapidly 16 carry out speedily, dispose of rapidly 18 telegraphic message 21 official communication

Dis Pater *see* 3 Dis

dispel 4 rout 5 allay, expel, repel 6 banish, remove 7 diffuse, dismiss, resolve, scatter 8 drive off 9 dissipate, drive away, eliminate 10 put an end to 11 disseminate 13 make disappear

dispensable 8 nonvital 9 accessory, extrinsic, secondary 10 disposable, expendable, extraneous 11 superfluous, unessential, unimportant, unnecessary 12 nonessential

dispensation 6 decree 8 approval, bestowal, division 9 allotment, diffusion, exemption, meting out 10 allocation, conferment, credential, dealing out, dispensing, permission, reparation 11 consignment, designation 12 apportioning, distribution, remuneration 13 authorization, dissemination

dispense 6 confer 7 dole out, mete out 8 allocate 9 apportion 10 administer, distribute

dispense with 4 drop, dump, junk, shed 5 scrap 6 shelve 7 abandon, discard 9 dispose of

dispensing 9 bestowing, doling out, meting out 10 allocating, conferring 12 distributing

dispersal 7 breakup, parting 9 dismissal 10 breaking up, scattering 12 distributing, distribution

disperse 4 rout 6 dispel 7 diffuse, disband, scatter, send off 8 drive off 9 dissipate 10 distribute 11 disseminate 13 send scurrying 16 spread throughout

dispersed 7 diffuse 9 scattered, spread out 10 dissipated 11 distributed 14 extended widely, unconcentrated

dispersion 9 dispersal 10 disbanding, scattering 11 dissipation 12 distribution

dispirit 5 cloud 6 darken, deject, sadden 7 depress 10 demoralize, dishearten

dispirited 3 sad 4 blue, down, glum 5 moody 6 morose

7 forlorn, unhappy 8 dejected, downcast, listless 9 cheerless, depressed 10 melancholy 11 crestfallen, demoralized, discouraged, downhearted, pessimistic 12 disconsolate, disheartened 14 down in the dumps, down in the mouth, unenthusiastic

dispiriting 4 cold, dark 6 chilly, dismal, gloomy 9 dampening 10 depressing 12 discouraging 13 disheartening

displace 4 bump, move, oust 5 shift 6 unseat 7 replace 8 crowd out, dislodge, force out, supplant 9 dislocate, supersede

displaced person 2 DP 5 exile 6 emigre 7 refugee 8 expellee 10 expatriate

display 4 show 6 reveal 7 exhibit 8 manifest 10 exhibition 11 demonstrate, make visible 12 presentation 13 bring into view, demonstration, manifestation 15 put in plain sight

display case 7 cabinet, vitrine 8 showcase

displease 3 irk 5 annoy, pique 6 offend 7 disturb, incense, provoke 8 irritate

displeasing 8 annoying 9 loathsome, offensive, repellent, repugnant 10 irritating 11 distasteful, distressing 12 disagreeable

displeasure 5 wrath 7 dislike 8 vexation 9 annoyance 10 irritation 11 disapproval, indignation 15 dissatisfaction

disport 3 act 4 play, romp 5 amuse, caper, sport 6 divert, frolic, gambol 7 display, pastime 9 amusement, entertain 10 recreation 13 entertainment

disposal 5 array, order, power 7 command, control, dumping, junking, pattern, ridding 8 grouping, riddance 9 authority, clearance, direction, placement 10 discarding, government, management, regulation, settlement 11 arrangement, destruction, disposition, supervision 12 distribution, organization, throwing away 13 authorization, configuration, juxtaposition 14 administration

dispose 4 rank 5 array, order, place 7 arrange, deal out, incline 8 classify, get rid of, motivate, organize 9 be willing 10 distribute

dispose of 4 dump 5 scrap 6 unload 7 discard 8 get rid of, throw out 9 cast aside, throw away

disposition 6 nature, spirit 7 control 8 bestowal, grouping, tendency 9 placement 11 arrangement, inclination, temperament 12 distribution, organization 14 predisposition 15 final settlement

dispossess 4 oust 5 evict, expel 8 take away, take back 9 deprive of

disproportionate 7 unequal 9 disparate 10 dissimilar, unbalanced

disprove 6 refute 9 discredit 10 controvert

disputable 7 dubious 8 doubtful 9 debatable, uncertain 12 questionable 14 controvertible

disputant 5 rival 7 opposer 8 opponent 9 adversary 10 antagonist, competitor, contestant

disputation 6 debate, review 8 argument, dialogue 10 discussion

dispute 4 feud 5 argue, clash, doubt 6 debate, impugn 7 quarrel, wrangle 8 argument, question, squabble 9 bickering, challenge 10 contradict 11 altercation, controversy 12 disagreement

disputed 6 argued 8 wrangled 9 debatable, in dispute, quarreled 10 in question, unverified 12 questionable 13 controversial 15 unsubstantiated

disqualification 5 minus 8 handicap 10 disability 11 shortcoming 13 ineligibility

disqualify 7 disable 9 make unfit 17 declare ineligible, deny participation

disquiet, disquietude 3 awe 6 unease 7 anxiety 8 distress 9 agitation 10 uneasiness 11 fretfulness, trepidation 12 apprehension, discomposure, perturbation 13 consternation

disquieted 6 uneasy 7 anxious, worried 9 concerned 10 distressed 12 apprehensive

disquieting 6 vexing 8 annoying 9 troubling, upsetting 10 bothersome, disturbing, irritating, perturbing, unsettling 11 distressing 13 disconcerting

disquisition 8 tractate, treatise 9 discourse, monograph 12 dissertation

disregard 6 ignore 8 overlook 11 pay no heed to 13 lack of respect 14 take no notice of 15 lack of attention 16 willful oversight

disregardful 8 careless, heedless 9 unmindful 11 insensitive, thoughtless 13 inconsiderate

disreputable 5 shady 8 infamous, shameful, shocking 9 notorious 10 scandalous 11 disgraceful 12 dishonorable, unprincipled 14 not respectable, of bad character

disrespect 8 contempt, dishonor, rudeness 9 disregard 11 discourtesy, irreverence 12 impoliteness

disrespectful 4 rude 8 impolite 11 impertinent 12 contemptuous, discourteous

disrobe 5 strip 7 undress 16 divest of clothing

disrupt 5 upset 9 interrupt 13 interfere with 17 throw into disorder

disruption 5 upset 8 disorder 9 confusion 11 disturbance 12 interference, interruption 14 disarrangement 15 disorganization

dissatisfaction 4 veto 7 protest 9 rejection 10 discontent 11 disapproval, displeasure, unhappiness

dissatisfied 7 unhappy 10 displeased 12 discontented

dissect 5 study 7 analyze, lay open 8 cut apart, separate 9 anatomize, break down

dissemble 4 hide, mask 5 feign 7 conceal 8 disguise 10 camouflage 11 dissimulate

disseminate 6 spread 7 diffuse, scatter 8 disperse 9 broadcast, circulate

dissemination 9 diffusion, dispersal, spreading 10 scattering 12 broadcasting, distribution

dissension 7 discord, dispute 8 conflict, disunity, division 9 rebellion 10 contention, disharmony, quarreling 11 discordance 12 disagreement 14 rebelliousness

dissent 6 object, oppose 7 discord, protest 8 disagree 10 difference, dissension, opposition 12 disagreement 14 withhold assent 16 withhold approval

dissenter 5 rebel 9 dissident, protester 13 nonconformist

dissenting 9 differing, dissident **11** disagreeing

dissertation 6 memoir, thesis **8** tractate, treatise **9** discourse, monograph **12** disquisition

disservice 4 harm, hurt **5** wrong **6** injury **7** bad turn **9** injustice

dissever 3 saw **4** hack, rend **5** carve, sever, slash, slice, split **6** cleave, divide **8** disunite, separate

dissident 5 rebel **8** agitator, opposing **9** differing, dissenter **10** dissenting **11** disagreeing

dissimilar 6 unlike **8** distinct **9** different, disparate

dissimilarity 8 contrast, variance **9** disparity **10** difference, dissonance, divergence, inequality, unlikeness **11** discrepancy **12** disagreement **13** inconsistency **17** lack of resemblance

dissimilitude 8 variance **9** disparity **10** difference, unlikeness **11** incongruity **12** disagreement **17** lack of resemblance

dissimulate 4 hide, mask **7** conceal **8** disguise **9** dissemble **10** camouflage

dissipate 5 waste **6** dispel **7** carouse, deplete, scatter **8** disperse, misspend, squander **11** fritter away, overindulge **13** be intemperate **14** spend foolishly

dissipated 6 wasted **8** misspent **9** abandoned, debauched, dispelled, dispersed, dissolute, scattered **10** squandered **11** intemperate **12** disreputable **13** frittered away

dissipater 5 waste **7** wastrel **8** prodigal **10** profligate, squanderer **11** spendthrift

dissipation 6 excess **7** wasting **9** dispersal **10** debauchery, dispelling, scattering **11** dissolution, loose living **12** immoderation, intemperance **14** disintegration, frittering away, self-indulgence

dissociate 8 separate **10** disconnect **12** break off with

dissociation 7 breakup **10** separation

dissolute 5 loose **7** corrupt, immoral **9** abandoned, debauched **10** dissipated **12** unrestrained

dissolution 9 annulment **10** separation **11** termination **14** disintegration

dissolve 3 end, run **4** fade, melt, thaw, void **5** annul, sever **6** finish, render, soften, vanish **7** break up, disband, liquefy, thaw out **8** abrogate, conclude, evanesce **9** disappear, dissipate, terminate **10** deliquesce **12** disintegrate **13** dematerialize

dissonance 5 clash **7** discord **9** cacophony, harshness **10** difference, disharmony **11** discordance **12** disagreement **13** dissimilarity

dissonant 5 harsh **7** grating, hostile, jarring, raucous, warring **8** clashing, jangling **10** discordant, discrepant **11** cacophonous, disagreeing, incongruent, incongruous, unmelodious **12** incompatible, inconsistent, inharmonious **13** contradictory **14** irreconcilable

dissuade 9 urge not to **10** discourage **13** advise against, persuade not to

distance 3 gap **4** span **7** reserve, stretch **8** coldness, coolness, interval **9** aloofness, formality, restraint, stiffness **11** reservation **16** intervening space

distant 3 far **4** cold, cool **5** aloof **6** far-off, remote **7** faraway **8** detached, reserved **10** far-removed, restrained, unfriendly **11** standoffish **17** not closely related

Distant Mirror, A
author: 15 Barbara W Tuchman

distaste 7 disgust, dislike **8** aversion **9** antipathy **10** repugnance **11** displeasure

distasteful 9 loathsome, repugnant **10** disgusting, unpleasant **11** displeasing **12** disagreeable

distastefulness 13 offensiveness **14** unpleasantness **16** disagreeableness

distasteful work 8 drudgery **11** menial labor

distend 5 bloat, bulge, swell **6** billow, expand **7** inflate, puff out **8** swell out

distended 4 full, taut **5** puffy, tumid **7** blown up, bloated, dilated, swelled, swollen **8** enlarged, expanded, extended, inflated, patulant **9** edematous, stretched

distill 7 draw out, extract **8** condense, vaporize **9** draw forth, evaporate

distillate 7 essence, extract **11** concentrate **13** concentration

distilled 9 condensed, extracted, vaporized **10** evaporated

distinct 5 clear, lucid, plain **7** diverse, supreme **8** clear-cut, definite, explicit, separate **9** different **10** dissimilar, individual **11** unmitigated, well-defined **12** not identical, unmistakable **13** extraordinary **14** unquestionable

distinction 6 renown **8** contrast, eminence **9** greatness **10** difference, excellence, importance, notability, prominence, separation **11** discernment, preeminence, superiority **12** differential **14** discrimination **15** differentiation

distinctive 6 unique **7** special **8** atypical, original, singular, uncommon **9** different **10** individual **13** extraordinary **14** characteristic

distinctiveness 7 clarity **9** character **10** definition, uniqueness **11** personality **13** individuality

distingue 13 distinguished

distinguish 6 decide, define **7** discern **8** set apart **9** single out **10** make famous **12** characterize, discriminate **13** differentiate, make prominent, make well known **14** make celebrated **15** make distinctive, note differences

distinguished 5 grand, great **6** famous, superb **7** elegant, eminent, notable, refined **8** renowned, splendid **9** acclaimed, dignified, distingue, prominent **10** celebrated **11** illustrious, magnificent
French: 9 distingue

distort 6 deform **7** contort **8** misshape **9** disfigure **11** misconstrue **12** misrepresent **15** twist out of shape, twist the meaning

distorted 4 awry **5** askew **6** belied, loaded, warped **7** altered, colored, crooked, twisted **8** cockeyed, deformed, wrenched **9** contorted, falsified, grotesque, irregular, misshapen, misstated, perverted **13** unsymmetrical **14** misrepresented **15** misproportioned

distortion 7 skewing **8** twisting **10** aberration, caricature **11** crookedness, deformation **12** malformation **17** misrepresentation

distract 5 amuse, craze,

worry **6** divert, madden **7** agitate, confuse, disturb, perplex, torment, trouble **8** bewilder, disorder **9** entertain

distracted 3 mad **4** wild **6** amused, crazed, insane, raving **7** frantic, pleased, puzzled **8** agitated, confused, deranged, diverted, frenzied, harassed, heedless, occupied **9** disturbed, stirred up **10** bewildered, distraught, irrational **11** entertained, turned aside

distraction 5 fazed, upset **6** frenzy **7** frantic, madness, pastime, rattled, ruffled **8** agitated, confused **9** amusement, diversion, unsettled **10** distraught, distressed, nonplussed, recreation **11** desperation **12** disconcerted **13** entertainment **14** mental distress

distractive 9 confusing **10** disturbing, unsettling **11** distressing, troublesome

distraught 3 mad **7** anxious, frantic **8** agitated, frenzied, seething **10** distracted, distressed **13** beside oneself

distress 4 need, pain, want **5** agony, upset **6** danger, grieve **7** anguish, disturb, torment, torture, trouble **14** acute suffering

distressed 5 upset **7** anxious, fearful, frantic, grieved, unhappy, worried **8** agitated, troubled **9** anguished, concerned, disturbed, tormented **10** distracted, distraught

distressing 5 acute **7** nagging, painful **8** grevious **9** agonizing, upsetting **10** disturbing, tormenting, unpleasant **11** displeasing, troublesome, unfortunate **13** uncomfortable

distribute 5 allot, class **6** divide, parcel **7** arrange, catalog, deliver, dole out, give out, scatter **8** classify, dispense, disperse, separate, tabulate **9** apportion, circulate, methodize, spread out **11** disseminate, systematize

distribution 7 sorting **8** division, grouping **9** allotment, spreading **10** allocation, dispersion, scattering **11** arrangement, circulation, disposition **12** organization **13** apportionment, dissemination

distribution center
French: 8 entrepot

district 4 area, ward **6** parish, region **8** precinct **12** neighborhood

distrust 5 doubt **7** suspect **8** question **9** misgiving, suspicion **11** lack of faith

distrustful 3 shy **4** wary **5** leery **7** dubious, jealous **8** cautious, doubtful, doubting **9** diffident **10** suspicious, untrusting **11** incredulous, mistrustful **12** disbelieving

disturb 5 annoy, upset, worry **6** bother **7** disrupt, perturb, trouble **8** distress, unsettle **9** dislocate, interrupt, intrude on **10** disarrange **11** disorganize

disturbance 5 upset, worry **6** bother, hubbub, ruckus, tumult, uproar **7** rioting, turmoil **8** disorder, distress, outbreak **9** annoyance **11** distraction **12** interruption, perturbation

disturbance of peace 4 riot **6** fracas, ruckus, uproar **7** turmoil **8** disorder **9** commotion **13** breach of order

disturbed 5 upset **6** uneasy **7** annoyed, anxious, nervous, rattled **8** agitated, confused, troubled **9** perturbed **10** disquieted **11** discomfited **12** disconcerted

disunion 7 divorce **8** division **9** secession **10** separation **14** disintegration

disunite 4 part **6** divide **7** divorce **8** separate **9** disengage **10** disconnect **12** disintegrate **13** disarticulate

disunited 6 parted **8** diverged, divorced, unallied **9** came apart, dispersed, separated **10** uncombined **13** disassociated

disunity 6 strife **7** discord **8** clashing, conflict, division, friction **9** wrangling **10** contention, dissension, separation **11** being at odds, discordance **12** disagreement **15** incompatibility

ditat Deus 11 God enriches
motto of: 7 Arizona

ditch 3 pit **4** junk **5** scrap **6** hollow, trench **7** abandon, discard **8** get rid of **10** excavation

dither 4 flap, fuss **5** tizzy, waver, whirl **6** bother, flurry, lather, quiver, shiver, thrill **7** fluster, tremble, twitter **8** hesitate **9** agitation, commotion, confusion, vacillate, vibration **10** excitement

Dithyrambus
epithet of: 8 Dionysus
means: 20 child of the double door

ditty 3 lay **4** song, tune **6** ballad **7** refrain

Dius Fidius
origin: 5 Roman
god of: 5 oaths **11** hospitality **20** international affairs
corresponds to: 6 Sancus **10** Semo Sancus

divagation 8 straying **9** wandering **10** digression, divergence

divan 4 book, hall, poem, room, salon, seat, sofa **5** couch, court **6** canape, daybed, leewan, lounge, settee **7** chamber, council, ottoman, davenport

dive 4 dash, fall, jump, leap **5** lunge **6** plunge **7** gin mill **9** honky-tonk, shabby bar **15** sleazy nightclub

Diver, Dick and Nicole
characters in: 16 Tender Is the Night
author: 10 Fitzgerald

diverge 6 differ, swerve **7** deflect, deviate **8** be at odds, conflict, disagree, separate, split off

divergence 7 parting **8** conflict, rambling, straying, variance **9** deviation, disparity, wandering **10** difference, separation **11** discrepancy, incongruity **13** dissimilarity, inconsistency

divergent 8 separate **9** different **11** conflicting, disagreeing **12** drawing apart, splitting off

diverse 6 sundry, varied **8** eclectic, far-flung, opposite **9** different, differing, disparate **10** dissimilar **11** conflicting, of many kinds **13** contradictory

diversified 6 divers **7** various **8** manifold **9** different, unrelated **13** miscellaneous

diversify 4 vary **7** diffuse **8** divide up **9** spread out, variegate

diversion 5 hobby **7** pastime **9** amusement, avocation **10** deflection **11** distraction, drawing away **12** turning aside
French: 14 divertissement

diversity 7 variety **8** variance **10** assortment, difference **13** heterogeneity

divert 5 amuse **7** deflect **8** distract **9** entertain, sidetrack, turn aside

diverting 7 amusing **10** deflecting **11** distracting **12** entertaining, sidetracking

divertissement 9 diversion **13** entertainment

divest **3** rid **4** free **5** strip **7** deprive, disrobe, peel off, take off **8** get out of **10** dispossess **14** remove clothing

divest oneself of **6** give up **7** take off **8** get rid of, give over, hand over, put aside, strip off **9** surrender **10** relinquish

divide **4** part, sort **5** share, split **7** arrange, deal out, divvy up **8** allocate, classify, disunite, separate **9** apportion, partition **10** distribute, put in order

divide and rule
Latin: **14** divide et impera
maxim of: **11** Machiavelli

divided **5** apart, split **6** parted **8** meted out **9** disunited, separated **10** unattached **11** apportioned **12** disconnected, portioned out

divide et impera **13** divide and rule
maxim of: **11** Machiavelli

divide in two **5** halve, split **6** bisect **8** cut in two, separate **9** cut in half **10** break in two **11** split in half **18** split down the middle

dividing line **4** edge **5** brink, verge **6** border, margin **8** boundary **9** threshold

divination **5** guess **6** augury **8** prophecy **10** conjecture, foreboding, prediction, prescience **11** premonition, soothsaying **15** prognostication

divine **4** holy **5** guess **6** fathom, sacred **7** predict, surmise, suspect **8** forecast, foretell, heavenly, prophesy **9** admirable, celestial, excellent, marvelous, wonderful

divine being **3** god **5** deity **7** goddess **8** divinity **14** celestial being

Divine Comedy
author: **14** Dante Alighieri
part: **7** Inferno **8** Paradiso **10** Purgatorio
guide: **6** Virgil **8** Beatrice

diviner **4** seer **5** augur **10** soothsayer **14** prognosticator

Divine retribution
goddess of: **7** Nemesis **8** Adrastea

Divine Sarah
nickname of: **14** Sarah Bernhardt

divinity **3** god **5** deity **7** goddess **8** holiness, religion, theology **9** theosophy **12** science of God **14** celestial being

division **4** part, unit, wing **5** split **6** branch **7** discord, divider, section **8** disunion, variance **9** partition **10** department, difference, divergence, separation **11** splitting up **12** disagreement

divorce **4** rift **5** split **6** breach, divide **7** rupture **8** disunite, separate **9** segregate **10** dissociate, separation

divulge **4** tell **6** impart, relate, reveal **8** disclose **9** make known **11** communicate

divulgence **7** telling **8** exposure **9** imparting **10** disclosure, giving away, laying open, revelation **13** communication **15** bringing to light **17** bring out in the open

divulge to **4** tell **6** advise, inform, notify, reveal **7** apprise **8** acquaint, disclose **9** enlighten, make aware **11** familiarize **13** spill the beans **20** let the cat out of the bag

Dix, Otto
born: **7** Germany **11** Unterhausen
artwork: **6** The War **7** The City **12** The Procuress **15** Sylvia von Harden **18** Parents of the Artist **39** Prague Street—Dedicated to My Contemporaries

Dixie Dugan
creator: **8** J P McEvoy **13** John H Striebel

dizzy **5** fleet, giddy, quick, rapid, shaky, swift **6** whirly **7** confuse, reeling **8** bewilder, unsteady **9** make giddy **11** lightheaded, vertiginous **12** make unsteady

Djawa *see* **4** Java

Djebel al-Tarik *see* **9** Gibraltar

Djibouti ***see box***

do **3** act **4** fare **5** clean, cover, get on, serve, visit **6** behave, finish, look at, stop in **7** achieve, arrange, carry on, conduct, execute, fulfill, make out, perform, prepare, proceed, suffice **8** be enough, carry out, complete, conclude, organize **10** accomplish, administer, bring about, put in order **13** travel through **14** be satisfactory, comport oneself, conduct oneself

do a favor **4** help **6** assist, oblige **7** help out **11** accommodate, do a kindness

do away with **3** end **4** junk, kill, void **5** erase, quash **6** banish, cancel, cut out, give up, remove, repeal, revoke, rub out **7** abolish, blot out, nullify, rescind, weed out, wipe out **8** abrogate, stamp out, throw out **9** eliminate, eradicate, terminate **10** annihilate, put an end to **11** exterminate

Djibouti
other name: **16** French Somaliland **39** The French Territory of the Afars and the Issas
capital/largest city: **8** Djibouti
others: **5** Obock **6** Dikhil **8** Tadjoura **9** Ali-Sabieh
monetary unit: **5** franc **7** centime
lake: **4** Abbe **5** Assal
mountain: **5** Gouda
highest point: **9** Moussa Ali
sea: **3** Red
physical feature:
gulf: **4** Aden **8** Tadjoura
strait: **11** Bab el-Mandeb
people: **4** Afar, Arab **5** Issas **6** French **8** European
language: **4** Afar **6** Arabic, French, Somali
religion: **5** Islam

Dobbin, Captain William
character in: **10** Vanity Fair
author: **9** Thackeray

Dobie Gillis, The Many Loves of
character: **11** Zelda Gilroy **13** Maynard G Krebs **14** Herbert T Gillis, Milton Armitage, Winifred (Winnie) Gillis **15** Thalia Menninger **19** Chatsworth Osborne Jr
cast: **9** Bob Denver **11** Frank Faylen, Sheila James, Tuesday Weld **12** Warren Beatty **13** Dwayne Hickman **14** Florida Friebus, Stephen Franken
Dobie imitated pose of: **7** Thinker

do business **4** deal **5** trade **10** buy and sell

docile **4** tame **7** willing **8** obedient, obliging **9** agreeable, compliant, tractable **10** manageable **11** complaisant

docility **7** pliancy **8** meekness **9** passivity **10** placidness **12** acquiescence, complaisance **13** nonresistance

dock **4** crop, join, pier, quay **5** berth, wharf **6** couple, cut off, deduct, hook up, link up **7** landing **8** cut short **10** waterfront **12** come into port **13** subject to loss **14** fasten together

dock **5** Rumux
varieties: **3** Bur **4** Sour **5** Green **6** Golden **7** Prairie, Spinach, Tanner's, Western **8** Patience **9** Purple-wen **10** Giant water

docket **4** bill, card, list **5** slate **6** agenda, lineup, roster **7** program **8** calendar, schedule **9** timetable **14** things to be done **15** order of business

doctor **2** GP, MD **3** PhD **5** alter, treat **6** change **7** dentist, falsify, surgeon **9** internist, osteopath, physician **10** podiatrist, tamper with **11** pathologist **12** gynecologist, obstetrician, pediatrician, psychiatrist, veterinarian **15** ophthalmologist **17** apply medication to **19** general practitioner, medical practitioner

Doctor Brodie's Report
author: **15** Jorge Luis Borges

Doctor Faustus
author: **10** Thomas Mann **18** Christopher Marlowe

Doctor Grimshaw's Secret
author: **18** Nathaniel Hawthorne

Doctor J
nickname of: **12** Julius Erving

Doctorow, E L
author of: **7** Ragtime **15** The Book of Daniel

Doctor's Dilemma, The
author: **17** George Bernard Shaw

Doctor Zhivago
director: **9** David Lean
author: **14** Boris Pasternak
cast: **10** Omar Sharif (Zhivago), Rod Steiger **12** Alec Guinness, Tom Courtenay **13** Julie Christie (Lara) **14** Rita Tushingham **15** Ralph Richardson **16** Geraldine Chaplin

doctrinaire **5** rigid **6** mulish **8** absolute, dogmatic, stubborn **9** arbitrary, imperious, pigheaded **10** bullheaded, inflexible, pontifical **11** dictatorial, opinionated, overbearing, stiff-necked **12** narrow-minded **13** authoritarian **14** disciplinarian

doctrinal **8** didactic, dogmatic, edifying, tutorial **11** educational, instructive **12** prescriptive

doctrine **5** dogma, tenet **6** belief, gospel **7** precept **8** teaching **9** principle **10** conviction, philosophy

document **6** back up, record, verify **7** certify, support **9** legal form **10** instrument **12** give weight to, substantiate **13** official paper

documentation **5** proof **7** support **8** evidence **12** verification **13** corroboration **14** substantiation

doddering **4** weak **6** feeble, senile **7** shaking **8** decrepit **9** tottering, trembling

dodge **4** duck, wile **5** avoid, elude, evade, hedge, trick **6** device, swerve **7** fend off **8** sidestep **9** jump aside, stratagem, turn aside **10** equivocate **11** machination

dodging **7** ducking, eluding, evading **8** shunning **12** sidestepping **13** circumventing

Dodgson, Charles Lutwidge
real name of: **12** Lewis Carroll

Dodoma
capital of: **8** Tanzania

Dodonian
epithet of: **4** Zeus

Dodsworth
director: **12** William Wyler
author: **13** Sinclair Lewis
character: **4** Fran **12** Arnold Israel **14** Edith Cortright, Renee de Penable **15** Samuel Dodsworth **16** Kurt von Obersdorf **17** Major Clyde Lockert
cast: **9** Mary Astor, Paul Lukas **10** David Niven **12** Walter Huston **14** Ruth Chatterton

doer **6** dynamo **7** hustler **8** activist, go-getter **12** active person

doff **4** bare, drop, junk, shed **5** scrap, strip **6** put off, remove **7** abandon, cast off, discard, disrobe, take off, toss off, undress **8** throw off, throw out **9** eliminate, step out of **10** do away with

dog ***see box, p. 278***

Dogberry
character in: **19** Much Ado About Nothing
author: **11** Shakespeare

Dog Day Afternoon
director: **11** Sidney Lumet
cast: **8** Al Pacino **10** John Cazale **14** Charles Durning

dogged **8** stubborn **9** tenacious **10** determined, persistent **11** unremitting

dogie **4** calf **14** motherless calf

dogies **6** calves, cattle **16** motherless calves

dogma **5** credo, tenet **7** beliefs **8** doctrine **9** teachings **10** philosophy, principles **11** convictions

dogmatic **6** biased **8** stubborn **9** arbitrary, doctrinal, imperious, obstinate **10** prejudiced **11** dictatorial, domineering, opinionated

Dog Star
constellation of:
Hunting Dogs: **13** Canes Venatici
Larger Dog: **10** Canis Major
Smaller Dog: **10** Canis Minor

dogwood **6** Cornus
varieties: **5** Brown, Creek, False, Giant, Silky, Stiff **6** Pagoda, Poison **7** Chinese **8** American, Jamaican, Mountain, Panicled, Red-osier, Siberian, Tatarian **9** Blood-twig, Flowering, Tartarian **10** Golden-twig, West Indian **11** Round-leaved **13** White Mountain

Doha, al-Dawha
capital of: **5** Qatar

do in **4** kill **6** murder **7** destroy, exhaust, tire out

Doktor Faust
opera by: **6** Busoni
character: **5** Faust **14** Duchess of Parma **14** Mephistopheles

dolce
music: **7** sweetly

dolce far niente **18** pleasing inactivity **20** it is sweet to do nothing

dolce vita **9** sweet life

Dol Common
character in: **12** The Alchemist
author: **6** Jonson

doldrums **5** blues, dumps, gloom **10** depression, melancholy

dole **4** deal, give **5** share **6** parcel **7** charity, handout, welfare **9** allotment **10** allocation **13** apportionment

doleful **3** sad **6** dismal, dreary, gloomy, woeful **7** joyless, unhappy **9** sorrowful

dolente
music: **9** sorrowful

dog **3** cur, pup **4** heel, mutt **5** beast, puppy **6** canine **7** mongrel, villain **9** scoundrel **10** blackguard

Alaskan: **5** husky **8** malamute, malemute

anatomy: **3** hip, lip, pad, paw, toe **4** arch, back, hock, loin, rump, stop **5** cheek, crest, croup, flews, skull **6** carpus, dewlap, muzzle, stifle, tarsus **7** brisket, cushion, knuckle, occiput, pastern, withers **8** heelknob, shoulder **10** metacarpus, metatarsus

Australian: **5** dingo **8** warragal

barkless: **7** basenji

breed:

herding group: **5** pulik **6** briard, collie **13** bearded collie **14** German Shepherd **15** Belgian malinois, Belgian sheepdog, Belgian tervuren **16** Shetland sheepdog **18** Cardigan Welsh corgi, Old English sheepdog, Pembroke Welsh corgi **19** Australian cattle dog, Bouviers des Flandres

hound group: **6** beagle, borzoi, saluki **7** basenji, harrier, whippet **9** dachshund, greyhound **10** bloodhound, otter hound **11** Afghan hound, basset hound, Ibizan hound **12** pharaoh hound **14** Irish wolfhound **15** English foxhound **16** American foxhound **17** Norwegian elkhound, Scottish deerhound **18** Rhodesian ridgeback **20** black and tan coonhound

nonsporting group: **6** poodle **7** bulldog **8** chow chow, keeshond **9** dalmatian, lhasa apso **10** keeshonden, schipperke **11** Bichon frise **13** Boston terrier, French bulldog **14** Tibetan spaniel, Tibetan terrier

sporting group: **6** vizsla **7** pointer **8** Brittany **10** weimaraner **11** Irish setter **12** field spaniel, Gordon setter **13** cocker spaniel, English setter, Sussex spaniel **14** Clumber spaniel **15** golden retriever **17** Irish water spaniel, Labrador retriever **19** flat-coated retriever **20** American water spaniel, curly-coated retriever, English cocker spaniel, Welsh springer spaniel **22** Chesapeake Bay retriever, English springer spaniel **23** German wirehaired pointer **24** German shorthaired pointer **25** wirehaired pointing griffon

terrier group: **10** fox terrier **11** bull terrier, Skye terrier **12** Cairn terrier, Irish terrier, Welsh terrier **13** border terrier **14** Norfolk terrier, Norwich terrier, wire fox terrier **15** Airedale terrier, Lakeland terrier, Scottish terrier, Sealyham terrier **16** Kerry blue terrier, smooth fox terrier **17** Australian terrier, Bedlington terrier, Manchester terrier **18** miniature schnauzer **20** Dandie Dinmont terrier **24** soft-coated wheaten terrier, Staffordshire bull terrier, West Highland white terrier **28** American Staffordshire terrier

toy group: **3** pug **7** Maltese, shih tzu **8** papillon **9** chihuahua, pekingese, toy poodle **10** pomeranian **12** Japanese chin, silky terrier **13** affenpinscher **15** Brussels griffon **16** Italian greyhound, Yorkshire terrier **17** English toy spaniel, Manchester terrier, miniature pinscher

working group: **5** akita, boxer **7** mastiff, samoyed **8** kuvaszok **9** great Dane, St Bernard **10** komondorok, rottweiler **11** bullmastiff **12** Newfoundland **13** great Pyrenees, Siberian husky **14** giant schnauzer **15** Alaskan malamute **16** doberman pinscher **17** standard schnauzer **18** Bernese mountain dog, Portuguese water dog

Buster Brown's: **4** Tige

Chinese: **7** shih tzu

coach: **9** dalmatian

combining form: **3** cyn **4** cani, cyno

constellation: **12** Canis Majoris

Dorothy's: **4** Toto

family: **7** Canidae

FDR's: **4** Fala **5** Falla

female: **3** dam, gip, gyp **4** slut **5** bitch, brach **7** brachet

genus: **5** Canis

group: **4** pack **5** leash **6** kennel

"His Master's Voice": **6** Nipper

Hungarian: **4** puli **6** kuvasz, vizsla

Indian: **5** dhole

Japanese: **5** akita

Little Orphan Annie's: **5** Sandy

male: **3** dog

movie/TV: **4** Asta, Lady **5** Benji, Tramp **6** Lassie **9** Old Yeller, Rin Tin Tin

mythical: **8** Cerberus

Nixon's: **8** Checkers

Punch and Judy's: **4** Toby

Russian: **6** borzoi **7** samoyed

star: **6** Sirius **8** Canicula

Welsh: **5** corgi

wild: **5** adjag, dhole, dingo, guara, rabid **6** jackal **7** agouara **8** cimarron

young: **3** pup **5** puppy, whelp

dole out **4** give, mete **5** allot **6** parcel **7** portion **8** allocate, dispense **9** apportion **10** distribute

doling out **7** dealing **9** allotment, parceling **10** allocation, assignment **12** distribution **13** apportionment

Dolius
epithet of: **6** Hermes
means: **6** crafty
form: **5** slave
given to: **8** Penelope

doll **5** dolly, dummy, honey **6** beauty, puppet **7** darling, rag doll **8** baby doll, figurine, golliwog **9** teddy bear **10** marionette, sweetheart **11** pretty child

dollar **3** one **4** bean, bill, buck, coin, note, skin, yuan **5** money, tater, token **6** single **7** ironman, smacker **8** cartwheel, simolean

Dollar A Second
host: **9** Jan Murray

Dollar Bill
nickname of: **11** Bill Bradley

dollop **3** dab **4** blob, dash, lump **11** small amount

Doll's House, A
author: **11** Henrik Ibsen
character: **8** Krogstad **10** Nora Helmer **13** Torvald Helmer

dolly **3** toy **4** cart, doll **9** plaything **15** wheeled platform

Dolon
mentioned in: **5** Iliad
father: **7** Eumedes
killed by: **8** Diomedes, Odysseus

dolor **5** grief **6** sorrow **7** anguish, sadness

dolorous **3** sad **6** rueful, woeful **7** doleful, tearful, unhappy **8** dejected, downcast, grievous, mournful, pathetic, pitiable, wretched **9** anguished, cheerless, harrowing, miserable, sorrowful, woebegone **10** calamitous, despondent, lamentable, melancholy **11** distressing **12** disconsolate, heavy-hearted **13** grief-stricken

Dolphin
constellation of: **9** Delphinus

Dolphin, The
author: **12** Robert Lowell

dolt **4** clod, fool, jerk **5** idiot, moron **6** nitwit **7** half-wit, jackass **8** bonehead, imbecile, numskull **9** blockhead

doltish **4** dumb, slow **5** thick **6** simple, stupid **7** asinine, foolish, idiotic, moronic, witless **8** ignorant, retarded **9** brainless, imbecilic **10** half-witted, slow-witted **12** dunderheaded, muddleheaded, simpleminded **13** rattlebrained **14** featherbrained

domain **4** area, fief, land **5** field **6** empire, estate, region, sphere **7** kingdom **8** dominion, property, province **9** bailiwick, territory

Dombey and Son
author: **14** Charles Dickens
character: **4** Paul **5** Toots **6** Carker, Cuttle **8** Florence, Mr Dombey **9** Dr Blimber, Walter Gay **11** Joe Bagstock, Susan Nipper **12** Cousin Feenix, Edith Granger, Solomon Gills

dome
Italian: **5** duomo

Domenichino
real name: **16** Domenico Zampieri
born: **5** Italy **7** Bologna
artwork: **11** Hunt of Diana **16** Monsignor Agucchi **18** The Four Evangelists, The Life of St Cecilia **23** Last Communion of St Jerome **30** Landscape with Tobias and the Angel

domestic **4** cook, maid, tame **6** butler, native **7** endemic, servant **8** homemade, houseboy **9** attendant, home-grown **10** indigenous, not foreign **11** housebroken, native-grown, not imported **12** domesticated, hearth-loving **13** household help

domesticated **4** tame **11** housebroken

domicile **4** home **5** house **8** dwelling **9** residence **14** legal residence

dominance **4** edge **8** hegemony **9** advantage, authority, upper hand **10** precedence **11** preeminence, superiority

dominant **5** chief, major **6** ruling **8** superior **9** principal **10** commanding **11** controlling, outstanding **13** authoritative, most important, most prominent

dominate **4** rule **5** dwarf **6** direct, govern **7** command, control **8** domineer **9** tower over **11** preside over

dominating **6** lordly, ruling **7** topmost **8** dominant **9** directing, governing, principal, prominent **10** commanding **11** controlling, domineering, outstanding **12** advantageous **13** authoritative, most important **15** most outstanding

domination **4** rule **5** power **7** command, control, mastery **9** authority **11** superiority

domineer **7** control **8** dominate, lord over **9** dictate to, tyrannize

domineering **8** arrogant, despotic, dogmatic **9** imperious **10** commanding, oppressive, tyrannical **11** dictatorial, overbearing **13** authoritative

Dominican Republic *see box, p. 280*

dominion **4** land, rule **5** realm **6** domain, empire, region **7** command, mastery **9** authority, supremacy, territory **11** sovereignty **12** jurisdiction
Hindu: **3** raj

Dominus **3** God **4** Lord

Dominus vobiscum **16** the Lord be with you

don **4** wear **5** put on **6** pull on **7** dress in, get into

Don
origin: **5** Welsh
form: **7** goddess
son: **7** Gwydion
daughter: **8** Arianrod

dona **4** lady **5** madam

Dona Flor and Her Two Husbands
author: **10** Jorge Amado

Donalbain
father: **6** Duncan
brother: **7** Malcom

Donald Duck
creator: **10** Walt Disney
character:
girlfriend: **5** Daisy
nephew: **4** Huey **5** Dewey, Louie
uncle: **7** Scrooge

Donar
origin: **8** Germanic
god of: **7** thunder

donate **4** give **6** bestow **7** present **8** bequeath **10** contribute **11** make a gift of

Donatello
real name: **15** Donato di Niccolo
born: **5** Italy **9** Florence
artwork: **5** David **6** St Mark **7** Zuccone **8** Jeremiah, St George **11** Gattamelata **12** Mary Magdalen **19** Judith and Holofernes, St John the Evangelist **22** Cavalcanti Annunciation

donation **4** gift **7** present **12** contribution

Dominican Republic
capital/largest city: **12** Santo Domingo **14** Ciudad Trujillo
others: **4** Azua, Bani, Moca, Pena, Polo **5** Bonao, Cotui, Nagua, Neiba, Nizao, Sosua **6** Higuey, La Vega, Oviedo **7** Sanchez **8** Barahona, Santiago **11** Puerto Plata **17** San Pedro de Macoris **21** San Francisco de Macoris
measure: **3** ona **5** tarea **6** fanega
monetary unit: **3** oro **4** peso **6** franco
island: **5** Beata, Saona **8** Altovelo, Catalina **10** Hispaniola
lake: **10** Enriquillo
mountain: **4** Tina **5** Gallo, Neiba **7** Baoruco, Central **8** Bahoruco, Oriental **13** Sententrional
highest point: **6** Duarte
river: **4** Yuna **5** Ozama **11** Yaque del Sur **13** Yaque del Norte
sea: **8** Atlantic **9** Caribbean
physical feature:
bay: **4** Ocoa, Yuma **5** Neiba **6** Rincon, Samana **7** Isabela **8** Calderas, Escocesa
cape: **5** Beata, Falso **6** Cabron, Engano **7** Caucedo, Isabela, Macoris
valley: **4** Real **5** Neyba
people: **5** Negro, Taino **6** Indian **7** mulatto, Spanish **9** Caucasian
discoverer: **8** Columbus
language: **6** French **7** English, Spanish
religion: **13** Roman Catholic
feature:
dance: **8** merengue
religious pilgrimage: **8** romerias
food:
dessert: **8** pinonate
fish/meat pastry: **10** pastelitos
stew: **8** sancocho

Don Careless
author: **8** Rex Beach

Don Carlos
author: **14** Johann Schiller
opera by: **5** Verdi
character: **7** Rodrigo **8** Philip II **9** Don Carlos **13** Princess Eboli **15** Grand Inquisitor **17** Elizabeth de Valois

Dondi
creator: **8** Gus Edson **10** Irwin Hasen
dog: **7** Queenie

done **5** ready **8** finished, prepared **9** completed **12** cooked enough **18** cooked sufficiently

done for **4** dead, gone, over, sunk **5** all up, ended, kaput, spent **6** beaten, doomed, ruined **7** all over, damaged, through **8** finished **9** exhausted

done in **4** beat **5** all in, slain, spent, tired, weary **6** bushed, killed, pooped **7** drained, wearied, worn out **8** dog tired, fatigued, murdered, tired out **9** bone weary, dead tired, played out **10** knocked off

Don Giovanni
also: **7** Don Juan **15** The Rake Punished
opera by: **6** Mozart
setting: **7** Seville
character: **7** Masetto, Zerlina **9** Donna Anna, Leporello **10** Don Ottavio **11** Donna Elvira **15** The Commendatore

Donizetti, Gaetano
born: **5** Italy **7** Bergamo
composer of: **10** Anna Bolena, La Favorita **11** Don Pasquale **12** Elixir of Love, Maria Stuarda **13** L'elisir d'amore, Marino Faliero, Torquato Tasso **14** Lucrezia Borgia **15** Roberto Devereux **16** Linda di Chamounix **17** Lucia di Lammermoor **21** Daughter of the Regiment

Don Juan **3** man **4** beau, wolf **5** Romeo, swain, wooer **6** fellow, squire, steady, suitor **7** admirer, courter, gallant, pursuer **8** Casanova, lothario, lover boy, paramour, young man **9** boyfriend, Lochinvar **10** lady-killer **15** gentleman caller

Don Juan
author: **21** George Gordon Lord Byron
character: **6** Haidee **9** Donna Inez **10** Donna Julia

donkey **3** ass **4** fool, mule **5** burro, idiot **7** jackass

Donlevy, Brian
wife: **12** Marjorie Lane
born: **7** Ireland **9** Portadown
roles: **9** Beau Geste **15** The Great McGinty **21** Two Years Before the Mast

Donn, Arabella
character in: **14** Jude the Obscure
author: **5** Hardy

donna **4** lady **5** madam

Donna Reed Show, The
character: **9** Jeff Stone, Mary Stone **10** Donna Stone **11** Dr Alex Stone, Midge Kelsey, Trisha Stone **12** Dr Dave Kelsey
cast: **8** Bob Crane, Carl Betz **9** Ann McCrea, Donna Reed **12** Paul Peterson **13** Patty Peterson **14** Shelley Fabares

Donne, John
author of: **7** Sermons **10** The Ecstasy, The Extasie **11** Holy Sonnets **15** Death Be Not Proud, Songs and Sonnets, The Canonization **20** Paradoxes and Problems **30** A Valediction Forbidding Mourning

donnish **7** preachy **8** academic, didactic, pedantic **9** pedagogic

Donnithorne, Arthur
character in: **8** Adam Bede
author: **5** Eliot

donnybrook **3** row **4** fray **5** brawl, fight, melee, set-to **6** affray, dustup, fracas, ruckus, rumpus **7** ruction, scuffle **8** skirmish **10** free-for-all **19** knock-down-and-drag-out

donor **5** giver **10** benefactor **11** contributor **12** humanitarian **14** philanthropist

do-nothing **5** idler **6** loafer **14** good-for-nothing

do not prosecute
Latin: **13** nolle prosequi

do not repeat
Latin: **12** non repetatur

Don Pasquale
opera by: **9** Donizetti
character: **6** Norina **7** Ernesto **11** Dr Malatesta

Don Quixote de la Mancha
also: **38** El ingenioso hidalgo Don Quijote de la Mancha
author: **17** Miguel de Cervantes (Saavedra)
character: **10** Pedro Perez

11 Sancho Panza **17** Dulcinea del Toboso
horse: **9** Rosinante
musical: **13** Man of La Mancha

doodad **5** gizmo **6** device, gadget **8** ornament **9** doohickey **10** decoration **11** contraption, contrivance, thingamabob, thingamajig **15** whatchamacallit

doohickey **5** gizmo, thing **6** device, dingus, gadget, object, widget **7** dojiggy, whatsis **8** dojigger **9** thingummy **11** thingamabob, thingamajig **14** thingamadoodle **15** whatchamacallit

Dooley, Thomas Anthony
founded: **6** MEDICO **31** Medical International Corporation
worked in: **13** Southeast Asia

Doolittle, Eliza
character in: **9** Pygmalion **10** My Fair Lady
author: **4** Shaw

doom **3** end, lot **4** fate, ruin **5** death, judge **7** condemn, convict, destiny, portion, verdict **8** judgment **10** Armageddon **11** destruction, Judgment Day **13** consign to ruin, end of the world, pronouncement **15** resurrection day, the Last Judgment **17** mark for demolition

doomed **5** fated **6** damned, ruined **8** ill-fated **9** condemned

doomsday **11** Judgment Day **13** Day of Judgment, end of the world **15** the Last Judgment

do one's best **3** try **6** strive **7** attempt **8** endeavor, go all out **9** take pains **12** make an effort **13** give all one has **15** knock oneself out

Doonesbury
creator: **12** Garry Trudeau
character: **2** B D **5** Honey, Rufus **6** Calvin **7** Boopsie **9** Uncle Duke **12** Joanie Caucus **14** Mark Slackmeyer **18** Michael J Doonesbury

door **4** exit **5** entry **6** egress, portal **7** hallway, ingress **8** entrance **11** entranceway

Door hinges
goddess of: **6** Cardea

doorway **5** entry **7** ingress, opening **8** entrance

Doorways
god of: **5** Janus

dope **3** tip **4** drip, drug, fool, jerk, nerd, news **5** creep, drugs, dummy, klutz, scoop **6** sedate, uppers **7** downers, opiates **8** additive **9** narcotics, narcotize, substance **10** antiseptic, astringent, medication **11** anesthetize, preparation **12** disinfectant **17** inside information

dope fiend **4** head, user **5** doper, freak **6** addict, junkie **7** hophead **8** cokehead **10** dope addict, drug abuser, drug addict

do penance **5** atone **7** expiate **10** make amends

dopey **4** dumb **6** leaden, stupid, torpid **7** asinine, idiotic, witless **8** comatose, mindless, sluggish **9** brainless, lethargic **10** dull-witted, slow-witted, slumberous **11** block-headed, thickheaded **12** simple-minded

Doppelganger **6** double **13** ghostly double
literally: **12** double-walker

Doppler, Christian Johann
field: **7** physics
nationality: **8** Austrian
discovered: **13** Doppler Effect

Dorcas
also called: **7** Tabitha
revived by: **5** Peter
hometown: **5** Joppa

Doris
father: **7** Oceanus
mother: **6** Tethys
husband: **6** Nereus
mother of: **7** Nereids

Doritis
epithet of: **9** Aphrodite
means: **9** bountiful

dormancy **7** latency **8** inaction **10** inactivity, quiescence, somnolence **11** hibernation

dormant **4** idle **8** inactive, sleeping **9** quiescent, somnolent **11** hibernating

Dorothy
character in: **13** The Wizard of Oz
author: **4** Baum

Dorset, Bertha and George
characters in: **15** The House of Mirth
author: **7** Wharton

dorsum **5** chine, spine **8** backbone

Dorus
father: **6** Apollo, Hellen
mother: **6** Orseis, Phthia
killed by: **7** Aetolus

dose **2** OD **3** cut, nip **4** dram, pill, shot, slug **5** quota, share, slice **6** amount, needle, ration, tablet **7** capsule, measure, portion, section, segment **8** division, overdose, quantity **9** allotment, allowance, daily dose, injection **10** percentage

Dos Passos, John
author of: **3** U S A **11** The Big Money **13** Three Soldiers **16** Nineteen Nineteen **17** Manhattan Transfer **22** The Forty-Second Parallel

dossier **4** file **5** brief **6** record **9** portfolio **14** detailed report

Dostoevsky, Fyodor Mikhailovich
author of: **8** The Idiot **9** The Double **10** The Gambler **12** The Possessed **18** Crime and Punishment **20** The Brothers Karamazov **23** Notes from the Underground

dot **3** dab **4** mark, spot **5** fleck, point, speck **6** dapple, period **9** small spot

dotage **8** senility **15** second childhood **16** feeblemindedness

dote **8** be senile, fuss over

dote on **5** adore, prize, spoil, value **6** pamper **7** cherish, indulge **8** fuss over, treasure **15** lavish affection

doting **4** fond **6** loving **9** indulgent, pampering **12** affectionate

double **4** dual, twin **5** clone **6** paired **7** replica, two-part **8** two-sided **9** ambiguous, duplicate **10** dead ringer **11** again as much, counterpart, meant for two, twice as much **12** twice as great **13** multiply by two, spitting image **15** increase twofold
German: **12** Doppelganger

Double, The
author: **16** Fyodor Dostoevsky

double-cross **5** rat on **6** betray, do dirt, tell on, turn in **7** abandon, deceive, let down, sell out, two-time **8** denounce, inform on, run out on, snitch on **9** play Judas **10** be disloyal **13** be treacherous, inform against, play false with **14** break faith with **16** blow the whistle on, sell down the river

double-crosser **5** cheat **7** traitor **8** betrayer, deceiver, informer

Double-Dealer, The
author: **15** William Congreve

double-dealing **5** false **6** deceit, sneaky, tricky **7** crooked, devious, perfidy **8** bad faith, betrayal, disloyal **9** deceitful, duplicity, falseness, treachery, two-timing **10** disloyalty, perfidious, sneakiness **11** crookedness, double-cross, duplicitous, treacherous **12** dishonorable **13** breach of faith, faithlessness

double entendre **12** off-color joke, risque remark **18** ambiguous statement

double entente **9** ambiguity

Double Indemnity
director: **11** Billy Wilder
cast: **13** Fred MacMurray **15** Barbara Stanwyck, Edward G Robinson
script: **9** James Cain **15** Raymond Chandler

Double Life, A
director: **11** George Cukor
cast: **10** Signe Hasso **12** Edmond O'Brien, Ronald Colman **14** Shelley Winters
Oscar for: **5** actor (Colman)
script: **10** Ruth Gordon **11** Garson Kanin

double meaning **9** ambiguity
French: **13** double entente **14** double entendre

doublet **4** pair **5** tunic **6** couple, jacket **10** two of a kind

double-talk **4** bunk, jazz **5** hokum **6** bunkum, drivel, gabble, jabber **7** baloney, blather, palaver, prattle, twaddle **8** flimflam, flummery, nonsense **9** gibberish **10** balderdash, hocus-pocus, mumbo jumbo **11** obfuscation **12** gobbledygook

double-walker
German: **12** Doppelganger

Double X
nickname of: **9** Jimmy Foxx

doubt **5** qualm **6** wonder **7** suspect **8** distrust, mistrust, question **9** misgiving, skeptical, suspicion **10** be doubtful, indecision **11** uncertainty **12** apprehension **13** feel uncertain **14** waver in opinion **15** have doubts about **16** lack confidence in, lack of conviction

Doubter *see* **6** Thomas

doubtful **5** vague **7** dubious, obscure, suspect, unclear **9** tentative, uncertain, undecided, unsettled **10** hesitating, irresolute, suspicious **11** unconvinced **12** inconclusive, questionable

doubtfulness **5** doubt **7** dubiety **8** distrust, mistrust, unbelief **9** disbelief, suspicion **10** skepticism **11** incredulity **14** lack of credence

Doubting *see* **6** Thomas

doucement
music: **6** gently

douceur **3** tip **5** bribe **8** gratuity **9** sweetness

dough **4** cash, duff, spud **5** bread, crust, money, paster **6** batter, change, leaven, noodle **8** doughboy **11** infantryman

doughnut **4** cake, tire **5** bagel, torus **6** cymbal, dunker, sinker **7** beignet, cruller, twister

doughty **4** bold **5** brave **6** strong **8** fearless, intrepid, unafraid **9** confident, dauntless **10** courageous, determined **12** stout-hearted

Douglas, Archibald
character in: **7** Marmion
author: **5** Scott

Douglas, Kirk
real name: **17** Issur Danielovitch
son: **7** Michael
born: **11** Amsterdam NY
roles: **8** Champion **9** Spartacus **10** The Vikings **11** Lust for Life **14** Detective Story, Seven Days in May **17** The Glass Menagerie, Young Man with a Horn **18** Letter to Three Wives **22** Mourning Becomes Electra

Douglas, Lloyd C
author of: **7** The Robe **23** The Magnificent Obsession

Douglas, Melvyn
real name: **23** Melvyn Edouard Hesselberg
wife: **12** Helen Gahagan
born: **7** Macon GA
roles: **3** Hud **9** Ninotchka **10** Being There

Douglas, Michael
father: **4** Kirk
roles: **4** Coma **10** Wall Street **11** Star Chamber **14** Jewel of the Nile **15** Fatal Attraction (Oscar) **16** The China Syndrome **17** Romancing the Stone

dour **4** sour **6** gloomy, morose, solemn, sullen **9** cheerless **10** forbidding, unfriendly

Douras, Marion Cecilia
real name of: **12** Marion Davies

douse **4** soak **5** souse **6** drench **7** immerse **8** saturate, submerge **15** plunge into water

Dove, Noah's
constellation of: **7** Columba

Dover Beach
author: **13** Matthew Arnold

dovetail **4** jibe, join **5** match, tally, unite **8** coincide **9** harmonize **11** fit together **12** interlocking

dowager **5** widow **6** relict **7** elderly

dowdy **4** drab **5** tacky **6** frumpy, shabby, sloppy **8** slovenly **12** unattractive

dowel **3** peg, pin, rod **4** pole **5** stick **7** spindle

down **3** ill **4** blue, deck, drop, fell, gulp, sick **5** drink, floor **6** ailing **7** put away, swallow **8** dejected, downcast, feathers **9** depressed **10** dispirited **12** disheartened

down-and-out **4** sick **5** broke **9** penniless **12** impoverished, on one's uppers **13** incapacitated **15** under the weather

downcast **3** low, sad **4** blue **7** unhappy **8** dejected **9** cheerless, depressed **11** discouraged **12** disconsolate, disheartened

downfall **4** fall, ruin **6** shower **8** collapse, downpour **9** rainstorm, ruination **10** rain shower **11** destruction

downgrade **4** drop **5** lower **6** debase **7** decline, descent, way down **8** belittle, minimize **9** declivity, denigrate, devaluate **10** depreciate

downhearted **3** sad **7** unhappy **8** dejected, downcast **9** depressed, sorrowful **10** dispirited **11** discouraged **12** disheartened

downheartedness **5** gloom **6** dismay **7** despair, sadness **9** dejection, pessimism **10** depression, low spirits, melancholy **11** despondency **12** hopelessness **14** discouragement

down in the dumps **4** blue, glum **6** gloomy **7** in a funk **9** depressed **10** despondent **13** in the doldrums

down in the mouth **3** sad **6** dismal, woeful **7** joyless, unhappy **8** dejected, downcast **9** depressed, sorrowful, woebegone **10** lugubrious **12** disconsolate

downpayment **6** binder **7** advance, deposit **9** money down

downpour **6** shower **9** rainstorm **10** cloudburst, rain shower

downright **4** open **5** blunt, frank, total, utter **6** candid, direct, honest, really **7** in truth, plainly, sincere, utterly **8** absolute, actually, complete

9 out-and-out **10** aboveboard, completely, thoroughly **12** unmistakably **13** thoroughgoing, unequivocally **15** straightforward

Downright
character in: **19** Every Man in His Humour
author: **6** Jonson

downstairs **5** below **6** cellar **8** basement **10** first floor **11** ground floor

down the drain **4** gone, lost **9** up in smoke **12** out the window

down-to-earth **5** crass, plain, sober, solid **6** casual, coarse, earthy, simple **7** relaxed **8** informal, sensible **9** practical, pragmatic, realistic **10** hardheaded, hard-boiled, nononsense **11** plain-spoken, substantial **12** matter-of-fact, unidealistic **13** unsentimental

downtown **9** inner city, urban area **10** center city, metropolis **16** business district, metropolitan area

downtrodden **9** exploited, oppressed **10** tyrannized **11** subservient **12** harshly ruled

downturn **3** dip, sag **4** drop, fall, skid, slip **5** slide, slump **6** plunge, waning **7** decline, reverse, setback **8** decrease **9** downslide, downswing, downtrend, dwindling, recession **10** depression, diminution **12** degeneration **13** deterioration

Down Under *see* **9** Australia

down with
French: **4** a bas

downy **4** soft **5** fuzzy, nappy, plumy, quiet **6** fleecy, fluffy **7** cunning, knowing **8** feathery **9** featherbed

do wrong **3** err, sin **8** go astray **9** misbehave **10** transgress

Doyle, Sir Arthur Conan
author of: **13** The Sign of Four **15** A Study in Scarlet, The White Company **25** The Hound of the Baskervilles **26** Adventures of Sherlock Holmes
character: **12** Dr John Watson **13** Mycroft Holmes **14** Sherlock Holmes **17** Inspector Lestrade, Professor Moriarty

doze **3** nap **6** catnap, siesta, snooze **10** forty winks, light sleep **12** sleep lightly

dozy **4** lazy **6** drowsy, sleepy **7** languid **9** lethargic, somnolent

D P **5** exile **6** emigre **7** outcast, refugee **8** deportee **10** expatriate **14** banished person, deported person **15** displaced person **16** political refugee

drab **4** dull, gray **5** dingy **6** dismal, dreary, gloomy, somber **9** cheerless, dull brown **10** lackluster

drabness **8** dullness **9** dinginess **10** dreariness, gloominess **13** colorlessness

Dracula
author: **10** Bram Stoker
character: **8** Dr Seward **10** Mina Murray **12** Count Dracula, Dr Van Hesling, Lucy Westenra **14** Arthur Holmwood, Jonathan Harker

draft **4** drag, gulp, haul, pull, wind **5** drink **6** breeze, induct, sketch **7** diagram, outline, swallow **9** conscript, induction **10** money order **11** postal order, rough sketch **12** conscription, current of air **15** military service **16** drawing from a cask **18** preliminary version **22** call for military service

drafty **6** breezy, chilly

drag **3** lug **4** bore, haul, pull **5** bring, crawl, trail **6** dredge **7** be drawn **9** inch along **10** creep along, move slowly, spoilsport, wet blanket **11** party-pooper

Dragnet
character: **8** (Sgt) Ed Jacobs **9** (Sgt) Ben Romero, (Sgt) Joe Friday **10** (Officer) Bill Gannon, (Officer) Frank Smith
cast: **8** Jack Webb **9** Herb Ellis **11** Harry Morgan **12** Ben Alexander **14** Barney Phillips **16** Barton Yarborough
setting: **10** Los Angeles

Dragon **14** Leviathan
constellation of: **5** Draco

drag on **4** last **6** endure, keep on, keep up **7** persist **8** continue **9** persevere

drag one's feet **5** crawl, creep **6** dawdle **9** waste time **10** move slowly **13** procrastinate

dragonfly
varieties: **5** biddy **6** darner **7** skimmer **8** clubtail, grayback **9** amberwing **12** elisa skimmer

Dragon Seed
author: **10** Pearl S Buck

Dragon's teeth
sown by: **6** Cadmus
location: **6** Thebes
grew into: **8** warriors

dragoon **5** bully, force **6** coerce, compel **7** trooper **8** browbeat, bulldoze, cavalier, horseman, pressure **9** strongarm **10** cavalryman **12** horse soldier, horse trooper **14** mounted soldier

drag through the mud **5** smear, sully, taint **6** debase, defame, smirch, vilify **7** degrade, tarnish, vitiate **8** disgrace, dishonor **9** discredit, disparage **10** stigmatize

drain **3** sap **4** drag, pipe, tube **5** empty, sewer, use up **6** outlet, strain **7** channel, conduit, debouch, deplete, flow out, pump off **8** empty out **9** depletion, discharge, dissipate **10** impoverish

drainage **4** flow **9** discharge

drained **4** beat **5** all in, empty, spent, tired, weary **6** bushed, done in, pooped, used up **7** emptied, wearied, worn out **8** consumed, depleted, dog tired, expended, fatigued, finished, tired out **9** dead tired, enervated, exhausted, played out

Drake, Stan
creator/artist of: **21** The Heart of Juliet Jones

Drake, Temple
character in: **9** Sanctuary
author: **8** Faulkner

dram
abbreviation: **2** dr

drama **4** play **6** acting **8** the stage **9** direction, vividness **10** excitement, the theater **11** mise-en-scene **15** dramatic quality, intense interest, theatrical piece
god of: **7** Bacchus

dramatic **8** striking **9** climactic, emotional **10** theatrical **11** sensational, suspenseful **12** melodramatic **13** for the theater

dramatics **6** acting **7** emoting **9** theatrics **10** dramaturgy, stagecraft **11** hamming it up, histrionics, thespianism

dramatis personae **4** cast **6** actors **7** players **10** performers **16** cast of characters, list of performers

dramaturgy **5** drama **7** theater **10** stagecraft **11** dramatic art

Drambuie
type: **7** liqueur

origin: **8** Scotland
flavor: **5** herbs, honey
with scotch: **9** Rusty Nail

Drances
enemy of: **6** Turnus

drape **4** deck, garb, veil, wrap **5** adorn, array, cloak, cover, dress **6** attire, bedeck, enrobe, enwrap, shroud, swathe, wrap up **7** apparel, bedight, envelop, festoon, sheathe, swaddle **8** enshroud, enswathe

drastic **4** dire, rash **7** bizarre, extreme, radical **8** dreadful **9** dangerous **10** outlandish **11** deleterious

Dravidian
language group: **3** Kui **5** Ghond, Tamil **6** Teluga **8** Kanarese **9** Malayalam
spoken in: **5** India **6** Ceylon **8** Sri Lanka

draw **3** get, tie, tow **4** drag, etch, haul, limn, lure, pick, pull, take **5** charm, draft, drain, evoke, infer, write **6** allure, come-on, deduce, elicit, entice, extend, make up, siphon, sketch **7** attract, distort, draw out, extract, make out, pick out, pull out, pump out, stretch, suck dry, take out, wrinkle **8** contract, deadlock, elongate, protract **9** attenuate, pull along, stalemate **10** attraction, bring forth, enticement, inducement, make appear **14** make a picture of

draw away **2** go **5** leave **6** go back, shrink **7** retreat **8** withdraw

drawback **8** handicap, obstacle **9** detriment, hindrance **10** impediment **12** disadvantage **14** stumbling block

draw back **6** flinch, recoil **7** back off, retreat **8** move away, withdraw

draw close **3** hug **4** come, near **6** arrive, enfold **7** embrace **8** approach, come nigh, gain upon **10** move toward

drawers **5** pants **6** shorts **7** panties **8** bloomers, calzoons, trousers **9** pantalets, underwear **10** underpants

draw forth **5** evoke **6** elicit **7** distill, extract

drawing **5** study **6** sketch **7** lottery, picture **9** depiction, selection **11** delineation **12** illustration

drawing apart **8** dividing **9** diverging **10** separating **12** splitting off

drawing out **9** expansion, extension **10** elongation, stretching **11** attenuation, lengthening, protraction **12** prolongation

drawing power **4** pull **6** allure, appeal **9** magnetism **10** attraction, enticement **11** fascination

drawing room **5** salon **6** parlor **10** living room **11** sitting room **13** reception room

drawn out **4** long **7** lengthy **8** extended **9** elongated, prolonged **10** lengthened, protracted

draw out **5** educe, evoke **6** elicit, expand, extend, extort **7** distill, enlarge, extract, prolong, spin out, stretch **8** elongate, lengthen, protract **9** attenuate, call forth **10** stretch out

draw the line **5** limit **8** contrast, separate **12** fix a boundary **13** differentiate

draw to a close **3** end **6** finish **8** conclude **11** come to an end

draw together **4** herd, mass, pack **5** bunch, crowd, flock, group **6** gather, huddle **7** cluster, collect, tighten **8** assemble, compress, contract **9** constrict **10** congregate

draw up **3** map **5** draft **6** make up, map out **7** charter, diagram, outline **9** blueprint

draw up plans **5** draft **6** design, sketch **7** outline

dray **4** cart **5** wagon **7** tipcart, tumbrel **8** dumpcart

dread **4** fear **5** awful **6** fright, terror **7** anguish, anxiety, cower at, fearful **8** alarming, cringe at **10** be afraid of, horrifying, shrink from, terrifying **11** fearfulness, frightening, trepidation **12** apprehension **20** anticipate with horror

dreaded object
French: **9** bete noire

dreadful **5** awful **6** tragic **7** fearful **8** alarming, horrible, shocking, terrible **9** frightful **11** distressing

dream **3** joy **4** goal, hope, muse, wish **5** think **6** desire, vision **7** delight, fantasy, hope for, incubus, reverie, think up **8** consider, pleasure, prospect **9** nightmare **11** expectation, have as a goal **13** look forward to, lost in thought

Dream Merchants, The
author: **13** Harold Robbins

Dream of the Golden Mountains, The
author: **13** Malcolm Cowley

Dreams
god of: **6** Icelus, Oniros **7** Oneiros **8** Morpheus **9** Phantasus

Dream Songs, The
author: **12** John Berryman

dream up **5** frame, hatch **6** create, invent **7** concoct **8** conceive, contrive

dreamy **4** airy **5** blank, empty, vague **6** absent, musing, unreal **8** ethereal, fanciful, illusory, soothing **9** fantastic, wonderful **10** delightful **11** preoccupied, unrealistic **13** unsubstantial **14** out of this world

dreariness **9** bleakness **10** desolation, dismalness, gloominess, melancholy **13** cheerlessness

dreary **3** sad **4** drab **5** bleak **6** dismal, gloomy **7** forlorn **8** mournful **9** cheerless **10** depressing, melancholy

dregs **6** rabble **7** deposit, grounds, residue **8** canaille, riffraff, sediment **9** settlings, worst part **11** lower depths

Dreiser, Theodore
author of: **8** The Titan **12** Sister Carrie, The Financier **17** An American Tragedy

drench **3** wet **4** soak **5** douse **8** saturate

dress **4** curl, deck, do up, garb, gown, robe, trim **5** adorn, frock, groom, treat **6** attire **7** apparel, arrange, bandage, cleanse, clothes, comb out, costume, garnish **8** clothing, decorate, ornament **9** disinfect, embellish **12** put on clothes **13** clothe oneself

Dressed to Kill
director: **12** Brian De Palma
cast: **10** Nancy Allen **11** Keith Gordon **12** Michael Caine **14** Angie Dickinson

dressed up **7** adorned, duded up **8** costumed, dolled up, tarted up **9** decorated, disguised, in costume **10** ornamented **11** embellished

dresser **6** bureau **7** cabinet, commode **8** cupboard **10** chiffonier **14** chest of drawers

dressing-down **6** rebuke **7** censure, chiding, reproof **8** reproach, scolding **9** reprimand **10** bawling-out, chewing-out, upbraiding **11** castigation, reprobation **12** remonstrance **13** tongue-lashing

dressing-gown
French: **13** robe-de-chambre

dressmaker **9** couturier, midinette **10** couturiere, seamstress

dress up **5** adorn **6** doll up **7** enhance, improve **8** beautify, ornament, spruce up **9** embellish, embroider, smarten up **10** exaggerate

Dreyfuss, Richard
born: **10** Brooklyn NY
roles: **4** Jaws **6** Tin Men **8** Stakeout **14** The Goodbye Girl (Oscar) **15** Moon Over Parador **16** American Graffiti **24** Down and Out in Beverly Hills **29** Close Encounters of the Third Kind **31** The Apprenticeship of Duddy Kravitz

dribble **4** drip, kick **6** bounce **7** drizzle, trickle **11** fall in drops, run bit by bit

driblet **4** drip, drop, tear **7** droplet, globule

dried up **4** arid **7** drained, parched **9** prunelike, shriveled **10** dehydrated, desiccated

drift **3** aim **4** flow, gist, heap, mass, pile **5** amass, amble, sense **6** course, gather, object, pile up, ramble, stream, wander **7** current, meander, meaning, purpose, scatter **8** movement **9** direction, intention, objective **10** accumulate **11** implication, peregrinate **12** accumulation, be borne along

drifter **3** bum **4** hobo **5** idler, tramp **6** loafer **8** derelict, vagabond **16** ne'er-do-well

drill **4** bore **5** punch, train **6** pierce **8** exercise, practice, puncture, training, work with **10** boring tool, repetition **11** instruction **17** repeated exercises
type: **4** hand **5** twist **8** electric

drilling **4** rote **6** boring **8** practice, training **9** schooling **10** discipline **11** preparation

drink **3** sip **4** gulp, swig **5** booze, taste, toast **6** absorb, imbibe, ingest, salute, take in **7** alcohol, swallow **8** beverage, libation **9** partake of, the bottle **10** alcoholism **11** drunkenness **15** alcoholic liquor **17** liquid refreshment
type of: **3** cup, fix **4** fizz, flip, mull, puff, sour **5** daisy, julep, punch, shrub, sling, smash **6** cooler, frappe, rickey **7** cobbler, stinger **8** highball

drinker **3** sot **4** lush, wino **5** dipso, drunk, rummy, souse **6** bibber, boozer, sponge **7** guzzler, imbiber, tippler, waterer **8** drunkard **9** alcoholic, inebriate

drink in **6** absorb, digest, soak up, take in **10** assimilate **14** immerse oneself

Drinking
god of: **5** Comus

drinking spree **4** orgy, toot **5** binge, drunk **6** bender **8** beer-bust, carousal **9** bacchanal

drink up **4** gulp **5** quaff **6** absorb, guzzle, soak up **7** consume, swallow

drip **3** ass **4** bore, jerk, nerd **5** creep, dummy, klutz **6** splash **7** dribble, drizzle, trickle **8** sprinkle

dripping **3** wet **4** damp **5** soggy **6** soaked, sodden **10** soaking wet

drive **4** goad, lead, mean, move, prod, push, ride, rush, spur, urge **5** force, guide, impel, motor, press, steer, surge **6** coerce, compel, incite, intend, outing **7** advance, conduct, go by car, impulse, operate, suggest **8** ambition, campaign, motivate **9** excursion, insinuate, trip by car, urge along **10** motivation

drive apart **8** alienate, estrange **9** disaffect

drive away **4** rout, shoo **5** chase, deter, repel **6** rebuff **7** repulse **8** alienate **11** put to flight, send packing

drive home **7** impress **8** hammer at

drivel **5** drool **6** babble, ramble, slaver **7** dribble, slobber **8** babbling, nonsense, rambling **9** gibberish **12** talk nonsense **13** senseless talk, talk foolishly

drive out **4** fire **5** chase, depel, eject, evict, exile, expel, force, roust **6** compel, remove **7** dismiss, repulse **8** discharge, exorcise

driver **6** cowboy, drover **8** herdsman **9** chauffeur

drizzle **3** fog **4** mist, rain **7** dribble **8** sprinkle

drizzly **3** wet **4** damp **5** foggy, misty, rainy

Dr Jekyll and Mr Hyde
author: **20** Robert Louis Stevenson
character: **5** Poole **10** Mr Utterson **13** Dr Henry Jekyll **14** Dr Hastie Lanyon

Dr Kildare
character: **14** Dr James Kildare **18** Dr Leonard Gillespie
cast: **13** Raymond Massey **18** Richard Chamberlain
hospital: **12** Blair General

Dr No
author: **10** Ian Fleming

Dr Strangelove or How I Learned to Stop Worrying and Love the Bomb
director: **14** Stanley Kubrick
cast: **9** Peter Bull **10** Keenan Wynn **11** Slim Pickens **12** George C Scott, Peter Sellers **14** James Earl Jones, Sterling Hayden

Dr Zhivago
author: **14** Boris Pasternak
character: **4** Lara
setting: **17** Russian Revolution

droll **5** funny **7** offbeat, strange **8** humorous **9** eccentric, laughable, whimsical **12** oddly amusing

drollery **3** wit **5** humor **6** banter, comedy, whimsy **7** jesting

Dromio
character in: **17** The Comedy of Errors
author: **11** Shakespeare

drone **3** hum **4** buzz, whir **5** idler **6** loafer **7** vibrate **8** parasite **9** murmuring, vibration **10** lazy person

drool **6** drivel, slaver **7** dribble, slobber **8** salivate **15** water at the mouth

droop **3** dim, sag **4** flag, sink **5** lower **6** weaken, wither **8** diminish, hang down **9** lose vigor **14** hang listlessly **15** incline downward

droopy **4** bent, blue, down, limp **5** baggy, bowed, slack **6** dashed, pining **7** doleful, sagging, subdued **8** cast down, dangling, dejected, downcast **9** depressed **10** despairing, despondent, dispirited, spiritless, world-weary **11** downhearted, hanging down, languishing **14** down in the mouth

drop **3** can, dab **4** bead, dash, deck, dive, drip, fall, fell, fire, omit, sack, sink, tear **5** abyss, floor, leave, lower, pinch, slide, slope, smack, trace **6** give up, lessen, plunge **7** abandon, decline, descend, descent, dismiss, dribble, driblet, dwindle, forsake, globule, plummet, slacken, smidgen, soupcon, trickle **8** decrease, diminish, leave out, lowering **9** declivity, discharge, knock down, precipice, terminate **10** sprinkling **12** bring to an end **13** fail to include **15** cease to consider, fail to pronounce

drop anchor 4 dock, moor **5** tie up

drop in 4 call, come **5** visit **6** appear, come by, look in, show up, stop by, turn up **7** stop off **9** pay a visit

droplet 4 bead, drip, tear **7** driblet, globule **8** spherule

droplets of moisture 3 dew, fog **4** mist **5** sweat **12** condensation

drop out 4 quit **5** leave **6** resign, retire

dross 4 scum, slag **5** waste **6** cinder, scoria **8** clinkers, impurity

drought, drouth 4 lack, need, want **6** dearth **7** aridity, paucity **8** scarcity, shortage **10** deficiency, dry weather, lack of rain **13** insufficiency

drover 6 cowboy, driver **7** cowpoke **8** herdsman, shepherd **10** cowpuncher

drown 4 soak **5** flood **6** deluge, drench, engulf **7** immerse **8** inundate, overcome, submerge **9** overpower, overwhelm, suffocate, swallow up **10** asphyxiate

drowse 3 nap, nod **4** doze, laze **5** dover, drone, sleep **6** snooze **7** slumber **8** languish **10** sleepiness

drowsy 4 dozy, lazy, slow **5** tired **6** sleepy **7** languid **8** hypnotic, listless, sluggish, soothing **9** lethargic, somnolent, soporific

drub 3 hit **4** beat, cane, flog, whip **5** whale **6** thrash **9** bastinado

drubbing 6 caning **7** beating, licking, tanning **9** trouncing **11** shellacking

drudge 4 grub, hack, plod, toil **5** labor, slave **6** lackey, menial, toiler **7** grubber **8** inferior, struggle **9** underling **11** subordinate

drudgery 4 toil **5** grind **7** travail **8** hack work **11** menial labor **15** distasteful work

Druk-Yul *see* **6** Bhutan

drum 3 din, keg, rap, tap, tub **4** beat, cask, roar, roll **5** expel, force **6** barrel, harp on, rumble, tattoo **7** dismiss, pulsate **8** drive out, hammer at **9** discharge, drive home, reiterate **11** beat a tattoo, din in the ear, reverberate

Drums
author: 9 James Boyd

Drums Along the Mohawk
author: 14 Walter D Edmonds
character: 4 Lana **9** Blue Black, John Wolff **11** Joseph Brant, Mark Demooth **12** Mrs McKlennan **13** Gilbert Martin **20** Magdelena Borst Martin

drunk 3 sot **4** bust, lush, soak **5** binge, rummy, souse, tipsy, toper **6** barfly, bender, looped, sodden, soused, stewed, zapped, zonked **7** smashed **8** beer-bust, besotted, carousal **9** alcoholic, plastered **10** inebriated **11** dipsomaniac, intoxicated **13** drinking spree, under the influence

drunkard 3 sot **4** lush, soak, wino **5** rummy, souse, toper **6** barfly **9** alcoholic **11** dipsomaniac

drunkenness 10 alcoholism **11** inebriation **12** intoxication

Drury, Allen
author of: 14 Capable of Honor, Return to Thebes **15** The Promise of Joy **16** Advise and Consent **19** Come Nineveh Come Tyre

dry 4 arid, blot, dull, wipe **5** droll **6** boring, low-key **7** deadpan, parched, tedious, thirsty **8** rainless **9** dehydrate, desiccate, shrivel up, wearisome **10** dehydrated, monotonous **13** uninteresting

Dryad
form: 5 deity, nymph
location: 5 woods

Dryas
father: 8 Lycurgus
killed by: 8 Lycurgus

dry as dust 4 arid, dull, sere **7** parched **8** pedantic, withered **9** shriveled **13** unimaginative

Dryden, John
author of: 10 All for Love **11** Mac Flecknoe **14** Annus Mirabilis **15** Alexander's Feast, Marriage-a-la-Mode **20** Absalom and Achitophel, Essay on Dramatic Poesy, The Hind and the Panther **22** Fables Ancient and Modern

dry goods 5 cloth, goods **6** fabric **8** material **9** yard goods **10** piece goods

dryness 7 aridity, drought **8** aridness **11** dehydration

Dryope
form: 5 nymph
changed into: 6 poplar

Dry Salvages
author: 7 T S Eliot

dry up 6 wither **7** shrivel **9** dehydrate, desiccate, evaporate

dual 6 double **7** twofold, two-part

dub 4 call, name **5** label **6** knight **7** baptize **8** christen, nickname **9** designate

dubiety 5 doubt **8** unbelief **9** disbelief **10** skepticism **11** incredulity **12** doubtfulness **14** lack of credence

Dubin's Lives
author: 14 Bernard Malamud

dubious 5 shady **6** unsure **7** suspect **8** doubtful **9** skeptical, uncertain **10** suspicious, unreliable **11** unconvinced **12** questionable, undependable **13** untrustworthy

Dublin
brewery: 8 Guinness
capital of: 7 Ireland
Irish: 8 Dubh Linn (black pool) **15** Baile Atha Cliath (town of the Hurdle Ford)
landmark: 10 Four Courts **11** Custom House **12** Abbey Theater, Christ Church, Dublin Castle **13** Leinster House **18** Kilmainham **19** St Patrick's Cathedral
mountain: 7 Wicklow
museum: 8 National **10** James Joyce
park: 7 Phoenix
river: 6 Liffey
rulers: 7 English, Vikings
scene of: 12 Easter Rising (1916)
university: 14 Trinity College

Dubliners
author: 10 James Joyce

DuBois, Blanche
character in: 21 A Streetcar Named Desire
author: 8 Williams

Du Bois, W E B
founded: 5 NAACP
author of: 19 The Souls of Black Folk

Dubonnet
type: 8 aperitif
origin: 6 France

ingredient: **7** quinine, red wine
with gin: **3** BVD **8** Napoleon
with rum: **10** Bushranger

duc **4** duke

Duccio di Buoninsegna
born: **5** Italy **6** Sienna
artwork: **6** Maesta **18** The Rucellai Madonna (attributed)

duce, il duce **6** despot, tyrant **8** dictator **9** Mussolini

Duchamp, Marcel
born: **6** France **8** Normandy **10** Blainville
artwork: **5** LHOOQ **9** Given That **11** Etant Donnes **12** Bicycle Wheel **13** The Large Glass (The Bride Stripped Bare by Her Bachelors Even) **24** Nude Descending a Staircase **37** The King and Queen Surrounded by Swift Nudes

Duchess of Malfi, The
author: **11** John Webster
character: **6** Bosola **7** Antonio **8** Giovanna **9** Ferdinand **11** The Cardinal

duck **4** clee, coot, lory, smew, teal, veer **5** avoid, dodge, drake, eider, elude, evade, goose, ruddy, shirk, stoop **6** canard, canvas, crouch, gannet, Peking, scoter, swerve **7** gadwall, mallard, Muscovy, pintail, pochard **8** baldpate, freckled, redshank, shelduck, shoveler, sidestep, submerge **9** merganser, whistling **10** bufflehead, canvasback **11** wood steamer **13** give the slip to
male: **5** drake
group of: **5** brace

Duck Soup
director: **10** Leo McCarey
cast: **5** Chico, Harpo, Zeppo **7** Groucho (Rufus T Firefly) **12** Louis Calhern, Raquel Torres **14** Margaret Dumont
setting: **9** Freedonia

duct **4** pipe, tube **6** vessel **7** channel, conduit

ductile **6** docile, pliant, supple **7** elastic, plastic, pliable, tensile **8** amenable, bendable, flexible, formable, moldable, shapable, swayable **9** adaptable, compliant, malleable, tractable **10** extensible, manageable, submissive **11** complaisant, manipulable, stretchable, susceptible

dud **3** dog **4** bomb, bust, flop, hash **5** botch, lemon, loser **6** bummer, fiasco, fizzle **7** clinker, debacle, failure, washout **11** lead balloon, miscarriage **14** disappointment

dude **3** fop **4** beau **5** dandy **7** peacock **11** city dweller, city slicker **12** Beau Brummell

Dudevant, Aurore
real name of: **10** George Sand

duds **4** togs **5** flops **6** attire **7** apparel, clothes, fizzles, threads **8** clothing, failures, garments

due **4** owed **5** ample, owing **6** enough, proper, unpaid **7** fitting, merited **8** adequate, becoming, deserved, expected, plenty of, rightful, suitable **9** in arrears, scheduled **10** sufficient **11** appropriate, outstanding

duel
French: **15** affaire d'honneur

Duel, The
author: **15** Alexander Kuprin

duenna **8** guardian **9** attendant, chaperone, custodian, protector

dues **4** fees **7** charges **10** assessment

Duessa
character in: **15** The Faerie Queene
author: **7** Spenser

duet **3** duo, two **4** pair **6** couple **7** twosome

Dufy, Raoul
born: **6** France **7** Le Havre
artwork: **7** The Palm **15** Riders in the Wood **16** Chateau and Horses **18** Deauville Racetrack, Posters at Trouville

dugout **3** den **4** cave **5** canoe **6** cavity, hollow **7** shelter

Duino Elegies
author: **16** Rainer Maria Rilke

Dukas, Paul
born: **5** Paris **6** France
composer of: **6** La Peri **18** Ariane et Barbe-Bleue **19** Ariadne and Bluebeard **22** The Sorcerer's Apprentice

duke
French: **3** duc

Duke
nickname of: **9** John Wayne

Duke, Patty (Patty Duke Astin)
real name: **13** Anna Marie Duke
husband: **9** John Astin
born: **10** Elmhurst NY
roles: **11** Helen Keller **16** The Miracle Worker, The Patty Duke Show, Valley of the Dolls

Dukenfield, William Claude
real name of: **8** W C Fields

Duke Snider
nickname of: **11** Edwin Snider

dulcet **7** lyrical, musical, tuneful **8** pleasing, sonorous **9** melodious **11** mellifluous

Dulcinea del Toboso
character in: **10** Don Quixote
author: **9** Cervantes

dull **4** slow **5** blunt, dense, muted, quiet, thick, trite, vapid **6** boring, obtuse, stupid **7** muffled, not keen, prosaic, subdued, vacuous **8** deadened, inactive, not brisk, not sharp **9** dimwitted **10** indistinct, lackluster, uneventful **13** unimaginative, uninteresting

Dull
character in: **16** Love's Labour's Lost
author: **11** Shakespeare

dullard **4** dolt **5** dummy, dunce **6** nitwit **7** halfwit **8** dumbbell, imbecile

Dullea, Keir
born: **11** Cleveland OH
roles: **12** David and Lisa **18** Butterflies Are Free **27** Two Thousand One: A Space Odyssey

dullness **6** idiocy, tedium **8** dumbness, lethargy, monotony, slowness **9** bluntness, ignorance, stupidity, vapidness **10** boringness, imbecility, obtuseness **11** tediousness **13** dim wittedness **15** thickheadedness

dull-witted **5** dazed, fuzzy **7** bemused, muddled, stunned **8** confused **9** stupefied

Dulong, Pierre-Louis
field: **7** physics **9** chemistry
nationality: **6** French
discovered: **19** nitrogen trichloride
studied: **4** heat **13** atomic weights

duly **6** on time **8** properly, suitably **9** correctly **10** deservedly, punctually, rightfully **13** appropriately **15** at the proper time

Dumaine
character in: **16** Love's Labour's Lost
author: **11** Shakespeare

Dumas, Alexandre (fils)
author of: **7** Camille **11** Le Demi-Monde **17** La Dame

aux Camelias **21** The Lady of the Camellias
Camille inspired: 10 La Traviata
opera by: **5** Verdi

Dumas, Alexandre (pere)
author of: 17 The Queen's Necklace **18** The Three Musketeers **19** The Man in the Iron Mask **21** The Count of Monte Cristo **22** The Vicomte de Bragelonne

Du Maurier, Daphne
author of: 7 Rebecca **10** Jamaica Inn **11** Don't Look Now **14** My Cousin Rachel **15** Frenchman's Creek **19** The House on the Strand

Du Maurier, George
author of: 6 Trilby **10** The Martian **13** Peter Ibbetson

dumb 3 mum **4** dull, mute **5** dense, dopey **6** silent, stupid **7** foolish, aphasic **8** aphasiac **9** dim-witted **13** unintelligent **17** incapable of speech

dumbbell 3 oaf **4** clod, dolt, dope, fool **5** booby, clown, dummy, dunce, idiot, moron **6** dimwit, nitwit **7** dullard, halfwit **8** dumb-dumb, dummkopf, imbecile, lunkhead, meathead, numskull **9** birdbrain, blockhead, ignoramus, lamebrain, numbskull, simpleton **10** noodlehead

dumb-dumb 3 ass **4** dope, fool **5** booby, dunce, idiot, moron, ninny **6** dimwit, nitwit **7** halfwit **8** bonehead, imbecile, lunkhead, numskull **9** blockhead, lamebrain, numbskull **10** nincompoop

dumbfound, dumfound 4 stun **5** amaze **7** startle **8** astonish **11** flabbergast

dumbfounded 5 agape **6** amazed **7** stunned **9** astounded, stupefied **10** astonished, speechless **11** openmouthed **13** flabbergasted

dumbness 6 idiocy **8** dullness **9** asininity, stupidity, thickness **10** imbecility **11** witlessness **12** wordlessness **14** speechlessness **15** thickheadedness

dumbstruck 5 agape **6** amazed, gaping **7** riveted **9** awestruck, stupefied **10** speechless **11** electrified, open-mouthed **13** flabbergasted

dummy 3 oaf **4** dolt, form **5** clown, idiot, klutz, model **6** figure **9** blockhead, mannequin, simpleton **10** dunderhead **11** chowderhead, knucklehead

dump 3 hut **4** hole, toss **5** empty, hovel, shack **6** shanty, unload **8** get rid of, junkyard **9** dispose of **10** refuse pile **11** rubbish heap

dumpy 5 squat **7** lumpish **13** short and stout

Dumuzi
origin: 8 Sumerian
god of: 8 pastures **10** vegetation
consort of: 6 Inanna

Dunaway, Faye
real name: 18 Dorothy Faye Dunaway
born: 8 Bascom FL
roles: 6 Barfly, Milady **7** Network (Oscar) **8** The Champ **9** Chinatown **13** Mommie Dearest **14** Bonnie and Clyde **15** Towering Inferno **17** The Four Musketeers **18** The Three Musketeers

Duncan
character in: 7 Macbeth
author: 11 Shakespeare

Duncan, Sandy
born: 11 Henderson TX
roles: 8 Peter Pan **9** Funny Face **12** The Boyfriend

dunce 4 fool **5** dummy, idiot, moron **6** dimwit, nitwit **8** imbecile, numskull **9** blockhead, numbskull, simpleton

Dunciad, The
author: 13 Alexander Pope

dunderhead 3 ass **4** dolt, fool **5** booby, dunce, idiot, moron, ninny **6** dimwit, nitwit **7** dullard, fathead, halfwit **8** bonehead, dumb-dumb, imbecile, lunkhead, numskull **9** blockhead, dumb bunny, lamebrain, numbskull **10** nincompoop **11** chowderhead

dune 4 bank **5** mound **8** sandbank, sandpile

dunk 3 dip, sop **4** duck, soak **5** bathe, douse, drown, slosh, souse, steep **6** deluge, drench, engulf, plunge **7** baptize, immerse **8** inundate, saturate, submerge

Dunne, John Gregory
author of: 11 Dutch Shea Jr **18** Quintana and Friends

Dunnock, Mildred
born: 11 Baltimore MD
roles: 8 Baby Doll **12** The Nun's Story **14** The Corn Is Green **16** Butterfield Eight, Cat on a Hot Tin Roof, Death of a Salesman

duo 4 pair **5** combo **6** couple **7** twosome **11** combination

duomo 4 dome **9** cathedral

dupe 4 fool, pawn **5** patsy, trick **6** humbug, sucker **7** cat's paw, deceive, fall guy, mislead **8** hoodwink **9** bamboozle

duplicate 4 copy **5** clone, match **6** repeat **7** replica **8** parallel **9** facsimile, imitation, make again, photocopy, photostat **10** carbon copy **12** reproduction

duplicity 5 fraud, guile **6** deceit **7** cunning **9** deception, falseness **10** dishonesty **13** deceitfulness

Du Pont Labs
founder: 17 E I du Pont de Nemours
inventor of: 5 nylon

Duquesnoy, Francois
born: 8 Brussels, Flanders
nickname: 11 Il Fiammingo
artwork: 8 St Andrew **9** St Susanna

dur
musical term: 5 major **8** major key

durability 7 stamina **8** strength **9** endurance, toughness **10** sturdiness

durable 5 sound, tough **6** strong, sturdy **7** lasting **8** enduring **11** long-wearing, substantial

Durand, Asher Brown
born: 18 Jefferson Village NJ
artwork: 14 Kindred Spirits

Durant, Will and Ariel
authors of: 20 The Story of Philosophy **21** Rousseau and Revolution **22** The Story of Civilization

Durante, Jimmy
real name: 19 James Francis Durante
nickname: 10 Schnozzola **15** Inka Dinka Doo Man
born: 9 New York NY
roles: 5 Jumbo **21** It's a Mad Mad Mad Mad World

duration 4 term **6** extent, period **11** continuance **12** continuation

Durdles
character in: 22 The Mystery of Edwin Drood
author: 7 Dickens

Durer, Albrecht
born: 7 Germany **9** Nuremberg
artwork: 10 Adam and Eve, Apocalypse, The Triumph **11** Wehlsch Pirg **12** Four Apostles, Large Passion, Melancholia I **13** Castle of Trent **15** Life of the Virgin **18** St Jerome in his Study **19** Virgin with the Siskin

21 Christ Among the Doctors 22 Knight Death and the Devil 24 Crowned Death on a Thin Horse 25 The Feast of the Rose Garlands 28 The Festival of the Rose Garlands

duress 5 force 6 threat 8 coercion, pressure 10 compulsion, constraint

Durgin, Francis Timothy
real name of: 11 Rory Calhoun

during litigation
Latin: 12 pendente lite

Durocher, Leo
nickname: 9 Leo the Lip
sport: 8 baseball
position: 7 manager
team: 11 Chicago Cubs 13 New York Giants 15 Brooklyn Dodgers
saying: 18 Nice guys finish last

Durrenmatt, Friedrich
author of: 5 Traps 8 The Visit 9 The Pledge, The Quarry 13 The Physicists 21 The Judge and His Hangman 27 The Marriage of the Mississippi

Durrie, James and Henry
character in: 21 The Master of Ballantrae
author: 9 Stevenson

dusk 6 sunset 7 sundown 8 twilight 9 nightfall

dusky 3 dim 4 dark 5 murky 6 cloudy, gloomy, veiled 7 swarthy 8 dark-hued

dust 4 dirt, lint 5 brush, motes 8 sprinkle

duster 3 rag 4 coat, robe 5 brush, cloth, whisk 9 housecoat 10 whisk broom

Dutch Guiana *see* 8 Suriname

Dutch Shea, Jr
author: 16 John Gregory Dunne

dutiful 5 loyal 8 diligent, faithful, obedient 9 compliant 13 conscientious

duty 3 tax 4 levy, onus, task 6 charge, excise, tariff 7 customs 8 business, function, province 10 assignment, obligation 14 responsibility

Duval, Armand
character in: 7 Camille
author: 5 Dumas (fils)

Duvall, Robert
born: 10 San Diego CA
roles: 4 MASH 11 Godfather II 12 The Godfather 13 Apocalypse Now, Tender Mercies (Oscar) 15 The Great Santini, True Confessions 18 To Kill a Mockingbird

Duvall, Shelley
born: 9 Houston TX
roles: 6 Popeye 9 Nashville 10 The Shining, Three Women 15 Brewster McCloud

Dvorak, Antonin
born: 11 Nelahozeves 14 Czechoslovakia
composer of: 5 Dumky 6 Hymnus, Te Deum 8 Carnival (overture) 10 St Ludmilla 11 Stabat Mater 15 American Quartet, From the New World (Symphony in E Minor) 16 The Specter's Bride 17 The Bells of Zlonice

dwarf 3 dim, elf, imp 4 baby, tiny 5 fairy, gnome, pixie, pygmy, small, troll 6 bantam, goblin, petite, sprite 8 diminish 9 miniature 10 diminutive, leprechaun, overshadow

dwarfish 3 wee 4 tiny 5 pygmy, short, small 6 bantam, little, midget 7 compact, squatty 10 diminutive, undersized 13 foreshortened

dwell 4 live 5 abide 6 harp on, reside 7 inhabit 10 linger over

dwelling 4 home 5 abode, house 8 domicile 9 residence 10 habitation

dwelling place 4 home 5 abode, house 7 habitat, lodging 8 domicile 9 residence 10 habitation 14 living quarters

dwell on 6 accent, stress 7 feature, iterate 9 emphasize, press home

dwindle 4 fade, wane 6 lessen, shrink 7 decline 8 decrease, diminish 13 become smaller

dye 4 tint 5 color, shade, stain 8 coloring 10 coloration

dyed-in-the-wool 9 confirmed, ingrained 10 deep-rooted, inveterate 11 established

dyestuff 14 coloring matter

Dymas
home: 4 Troy
fought with: 6 Aeneas
fought against: 6 Greeks

dynamic 5 vital 6 active 7 driving 8 forceful, powerful, vigorous 9 energetic

dynamism 3 pep 4 life 5 verve, vigor 6 energy, spirit 8 vitality, vivacity 9 animation 10 liveliness

dynamite 4 raze, ruin 5 blast, trash, wreck 6 blow up, charge 7 destroy, shatter, wipe out 8 decimate, demolish 9 devastate, dismantle, eradicate, explosive 10 annihilate, extinguish, obliterate 11 exterminate

dynamo 4 doer 7 hustler 8 activist, go-getter 9 generator 12 active person 14 bundle of energy, mover and shaker

Dynasts, The
author: 11 Thomas Hardy
subject: 17 Napoleon Bonaparte

dynasty 4 line 5 crown, reign 6 regime 7 lineage, regency 8 dominion, hegemony, kingship, monarchy, regnancy 9 authority 10 government, suzerainty 11 ruling house 12 jurisdiction 14 administration

Dynasty
character: 9 Dex Dexter, Jeff Colby 12 Alexis (Morel Carrington Colby) Dexter 14 Adam Carrington 15 Blake Carrington 16 Amanda Carrington, Steven Carrington 17 Krystle Carrington 18 Dominique Devereaux, Krystina Carrington 21 Fallon Carrington Colby
cast: 9 John James 10 Linda Evans 11 Joan Collins 12 John Forsythe
setting: 6 Denver 8 Colorado
hotel: 8 La Mirage

dyspeptic 4 mean 6 crabby, grumpy, ornery, shirty, touchy 7 grouchy, waspish 8 choleric 9 crotchety, fractious, irascible, irritable 10 ill-humored, ill-natured 11 bad-tempered, contentious, hot-tempered 12 cantankerous, sour-tempered 13 short-tempered

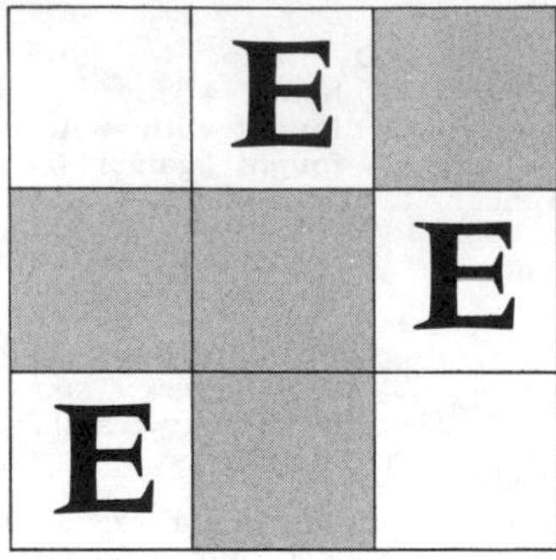

Ea
origin: 8 Akkadian
god of: 6 wisdom
father: 4 Apsu
son: 6 Marduk **8** Merodach **12** Baal Merodach
corresponds to: 4 Enki

each 5 every **6** apiece **7** that one, this one **8** everyone, separate **12** respectively

Eagels, Jeanne
born: 12 Kansas City MO
roles: 4 Rain **8** Jealousy **9** The Letter **13** Sadie Thompson **14** Man Woman and Sin

eager 4 agog, avid, keen **6** ardent, fervid, intent, raring **7** athirst, earnest, excited, fervent, intense, longing, zealous **8** desirous, diligent, resolute, spirited, yearning **9** ambitious, hungering, impatient, thirsting **10** aggressive, passionate **11** hardworking, impassioned, industrious, persevering **12** enterprising, enthusiastic

eagerly 6 avidly, keenly **8** ardently, desiring, fervidly, intently **9** anxiously, earnestly, fervently, zealously **16** enthusiastically

eagerness 4 zeal, zest **5** ardor **6** fervor **7** avidity **9** readincss **10** enthusiasm **11** willingness

eagle
young: 6 eaglet

Eagle
constellation of: 6 Aquila

Eakins, Thomas
born: 14 Philadelphia PA
artwork: 11 Agnew Clinic **13** Mrs Edith Mahon **14** The Gross Clinic **24** Max Schmitt in a Single Scull

ear
section: 5 inner, outer **6** middle
part: 4 drum **5** anvil, canal **6** hammer **7** cochlea, stirrup **8** hair cell **14** eustachian tube

earl 4 lord, peer **5** noble **8** nobleman
wife: 8 countess

earlier 6 before, in time, sooner **9** before now, in advance **10** beforehand **11** ahead of time **13** before the fact

earliest 5 first **6** oldest, primal **7** ancient, initial, primary, soonest **8** original, primeval **9** beginning, primitive **10** aboriginal, indigenous **11** fundamental

Earl of Baltimore
nickname of: 10 Earl Weaver

Earl the Pearl
nickname of: 10 Earl Monroe

early 5 first **6** primal **7** ancient, archaic, betimes, initial, too soon, very old **8** primeval **9** in advance, premature, primitive **10** beforehand, in good time, primordial **11** ahead of time, prehistoric, prematurely

Early Autumn
author: 14 Louis Bromfield

early man 6 Peking **9** Cro-Magnon, Steinheim **11** Neanderthal **18** Trobriand Islanders **24** Australopithecus robustus **25** Australopithecus africanus

earmark 3 tag **4** band, hold, sign **5** allot, label, stamp, token, trait **6** aspect, assign **7** feature, put away, quality, reserve **8** allocate, property, set aside **9** attribute, designate **11** peculiarity, singularity **14** characteristic

earn 3 get, net **4** draw, gain, make, rate, reap **5** clear, merit **6** attain, pick up, secure **7** achieve, collect, deserve, realize, receive, warrant **9** bring home **12** be entitled to

earn as due 4 rate **5** merit **7** deserve **10** be worthy of **12** be entitled to **13** be deserving of

earnest 4 firm **5** eager, fixed, grave, sober, staid **6** ardent, fervid, honest, intent, sedate, solemn, stable, steady, urgent **7** devoted, fervent, intense, serious, sincere, zealous **8** constant, diligent, resolute, spirited, vehement **9** ambitious, assiduous, heartfelt, insistent **10** deeply felt, determined, passionate, purposeful, thoughtful **11** hardworking, impassioned, industrious, persevering **12** enthusiastic, wholehearted

earnest attachment 4 love **6** regard **7** concern **8** devotion, fondness **9** reverence **10** commitment, dedication **11** devotedness **13** attentiveness

earnest request 4 plea **6** appeal **8** entreaty, petition **11** importunity **12** supplication

earnings 3 pay **5** wages **6** income, salary **7** payment, profits **8** proceeds, receipts **12** compensation

Earnshaw, Catherine
character in: 16 Wuthering Heights
author: 6 Bronte

ear-splitting 7 blaring **8** piercing **9** clamorous, deafening **10** thunderous

earth 3 sod **4** clay, dirt, dust, land, loam, soil, turf **6** ground **7** topsoil
god of: 3 Geb, Keb **5** Dagan, Dagon **10** Trophonius
goddess of: 2 Ge **4** Gaea, Gaia **6** Hecate, Hekate, Tellus

earthen pot
Spanish: **4** olla

earthenware **5** china **7** pottery **8** clayware, crockery **11** ceramic ware

earthly **6** bodily **7** mundane, secular, ungodly, worldly **8** feasible, material, physical, possible, temporal **9** corporeal, practical **10** imaginable **11** conceivable, terrestrial **12** nonspiritual **13** materialistic

earthquake **5** quake, seism, shock **6** tremor **8** tremblor, upheaval **11** earth tremor

earth tremor **5** quake, seism, shock **6** tremor **8** tremblor, upheaval **10** earthquake

earthy **5** bawdy, crude, dirty, funky, gross, lusty, rough **6** coarse, filthy, ribald, robust, smutty, vulgar **7** obscene, peasant, raunchy **8** indecent **9** primitive, unrefined **10** unblushing, uncultured **12** uncultivated

Earwicker family
characters in: **13** Finnegans Wake
author: **5** Joyce

earwig
variety: **5** black **6** little **10** long horned

ease **4** calm, rest, slip **5** abate, allay, poise, quiet, slide, still **6** aplomb, lessen, luxury, pacify, plenty, relief, repose, solace, soothe **7** assuage, comfort, console, leisure, lighten, mollify, relieve **8** diminish, easement, easiness, facility, maneuver, mitigate, palliate, security, serenity **9** abundance, affluence, alleviate, composure, disburden, readiness **10** confidence, prosperity, relaxation **11** assuagement, naturalness, peace of mind, restfulness **12** tranquillity, unconstraint **13** luxuriousness, move carefully, relaxed manner **14** effortlessness, handle with care, unaffectedness

easement **4** ease **6** relief, solace, succor **7** comfort **8** soothing **10** right of way **11** assuagement

easily **5** by far **6** freely, surely **7** clearly, handily, lightly, plainly, readily **8** facilely, smoothly, with ease **9** certainly **10** far and away, undeniably **11** beyond doubt, undoubtedly **12** effortlessly, with facility **13** without a hitch **14** beyond question, without trouble **17** without difficulty **23** beyond the shadow of a doubt

easily embarrassed **3** shy **5** timid **7** bashful **8** blushing, skittish, timorous **9** diffident, shrinking **11** constrained, unconfident

easily noticed **5** clear, plain **6** patent **7** evident, glaring, obvious, visible **8** flagrant, striking **9** arresting, prominent **10** noticeable **11** conspicuous, outstanding

easily ruffled **9** emotional, excitable **11** hot-tempered **13** quick-tempered

easiness **4** ease **10** equanimity, simplicity **11** naturalness **12** indifference **13** impassiveness

East, the **4** Asia **9** the Orient **10** the Far East **11** the Near East **17** Eastern Hemisphere

East Bengal *see* **10** Bangladesh

East Berlin
capital of: **11** East Germany

East Coker
author: **7** T S Eliot

Eastern Slavic
language family: **12** Indo-European
group: **11** Balto-Slavic
branch: **6** Slavic
language: **7** Russian **9** Ukrainian **12** White Russian

Easter Parade
director: **14** Charles Walters
based on musical by: **12** Irving Berlin
cast: **9** Ann Miller **11** Fred Astaire, Judy Garland **12** Peter Lawford

East Germany *see* Germany, East

Eastman, George
nationality: **8** American
founder of: **14** Eastman Kodak Co
inventor of: **9** Kodak film **11** Kodak camera **20** transparent photo film

East of Eden
author: **13** John Steinbeck
director: **9** Elia Kazan
cast: **8** Burl Ives **9** James Dean **10** Jo Van Fleet **11** Julie Harris **13** Raymond Massey
Oscar for: **17** supporting actress (Van Fleet)

East Pakistan *see* **10** Bangladesh

East wind
associated with: **5** Eurus **9** Volturnus

Eastwood, Clint
born: **14** San Francisco CA
roles: **7** Firefox, Rawhide **10** Dirty Harry, Hang Em High **11** Magnum Force, The Dead Pool **12** Coogan's Bluff, Kelly's Heroes, Sudden Impact **14** Play Misty for Me **15** Where Eagles Dare **17** A Fistful of Dollars, Any Which Way You Can, High Plains Drifter **18** Escape from Alcatraz, For a Few Dollars More **21** Two Mules for Sister Sara **23** The Good the Bad and the Ugly
mayor of: **6** Carmel

easy **4** calm, mild, open, soft **5** cushy, frank, light, naive **6** benign, calmly, candid, docile, easily, gentle, secure, serene, simple **7** lenient, natural, not hard, relaxed, restful, wealthy **8** affluent, carefree, composed, friendly, gracious, gullible, informal, outgoing, painless, peaceful, pleasant, scarcely, serenely, tranquil, unforced, well-to-do, yielding **9** compliant, indulgent, leisurely, luxurious, tractable, unworried **10** effortless, peacefully, permissive, unaffected, untroubled **11** comfortable, comfortably **12** not difficult, unsuspicious **13** accommodating, unconstrained

easygoing **4** calm **6** casual **7** offhand, patient, relaxed **8** carefree **9** unruffled, unworried **10** insouciant, nonchalant **11** unconcerned, unexcitable **12** even-tempered, happy-go-lucky, mild-tempered

Easy Rider
director: **12** Dennis Hopper
cast: **10** Karen Black, Peter Fonda **11** Luana Anders **12** Dennis Hopper, Robert Walker **13** Jack Nicholson

easy to use **7** adapted, helpful **9** adaptable **10** convenient **11** serviceable **12** advantageous

eat **3** sup **4** bolt, dine, feed, gulp, rust, take **5** feast, lunch **6** devour, gobble, ingest, nibble **7** consume, corrode **8** dispatch, dissolve, wear away, wolf down **9** breakfast, take a meal, waste away **10** break bread, gormandize **14** take sustenance **15** take nourishment

eatable **4** food **6** edible **8** fit to eat **10** comestible, consumable

eat away **4** rust **5** erode **7** corrode, oxidize

eating habits **4** diet **13** eating regimen

eating regimen **4** diet **12** eating habits

eat into **4** bite **5** erode **6** nibble **7** consume, corrode **8** wear away **9** swallow up

eat one's fill **5** feast, gorge **6** pig out **7** banquet **12** stuff oneself

eat rapidly **4** bolt, gulp, wolf **5** scarf **6** gobble **12** swallow whole

eat up **5** enjoy, savor **6** devour, relish **7** consume, swallow **9** delight in, rejoice in **13** be pleased with, get a kick out of **14** take pleasure in

eat voraciously **6** cram in, devour, gobble **7** stuff in **8** bolt down, gulp down, wolf down **10** gormandize **12** swallow whole

eau, eaux **5** water

eau de vie **6** brandy **11** water of life

eavesdrop **3** bug, pry, spy, tap **5** snoop **6** attend, harken **7** monitor, wiretap **8** listen in, overhear **9** bend an ear **11** cock one's ear **14** strain one's ears **15** prick up one's ears

ebb **5** abate, go out **6** go down, lessen, recede, shrink, weaken **7** decline, dwindle, retreat, slacken, subside **8** decrease, diminish, fade away, fall away, flow away, flow back, move back, withdraw **9** waste away **10** degenerate **11** deteriorate

ebony **3** jet **4** dark, inky **5** black, raven, sable **8** hardwood **9** coal-black **15** Diospyros Ebenum
 varieties: **5** Green, Texas **8** Macassar, Mountain **10** East Indian, Queensland

Ebsen, Buddy
 real name: **23** Christian Rudolph Ebsen Jr
 born: **12** Belleville IL
 roles: **12** Barnaby Jones, Davy Crockett **21** The Beverly Hillbillies

ebullience **3** zip **7** elation **8** buoyancy **9** animation **10** enthusiasm, exuberance, joyousness, liveliness **11** high spirits **12** exhilaration **13** effervescence

ebullient **6** elated, joyful, joyous **9** exuberant **11** exhilarated **12** effervescent, enthusiastic, high-spirited

ecce homo **12** behold the man
 said by: **13** Pontius Pilate
 spoken of: **6** Christ

eccentric **3** nut, odd **4** kook, rash, sick **5** curio, flake, funny, kooky, nutty, queer, weird **6** freaky, insane, quaint, unique, weirdo **7** bizarre, curious, erratic, oddball, offbeat, strange, unusual, weirdie **8** aberrant, abnormal, crackpot, freakish, peculiar, quixotic, singular, uncommon **9** character, irregular, odd person, off center, parabolic, psychotic, screwball, unnatural, whimsical **10** capricious, elliptical, outlandish, unorthodox **13** extraordinary **14** unconventional

eccentricity **6** oddity, whimsy **7** caprice **9** deviation, queerness **10** aberration **11** abnormality, peculiarity, strangeness **12** idiosyncrasy, irregularity

ecclesiastic, ecclesiastical **5** rabbi, vicar **6** cleric, curate, deacon, parson, pastor, priest, rector **7** prelate **8** chaplain, churchly, clerical, minister, pastoral, preacher **9** churchman, clergyman, episcopal, parochial, religious

Echecles
 father: **5** Actor
 wife: **8** Polymela
 raised child of Polymela and: **6** Hermes

echelon **4** file, line, rank, rung, tier **5** grade, level **6** office **8** position **9** authority, hierarchy

Echemus
 king of: **7** Arcadia
 father: **7** Cepheus
 wife: **8** Timandra
 son: **8** Laodocus
 delayed: **18** Heraclidan invasion
 killed: **6** Hyllus

Echetus
 king of: **6** Epirus
 daughter: **8** Amphissa
 blinded: **8** Amphissa

Echidna
 form: **7** monster
 mother of: **5** Hydra **6** Sphinx **7** Chimera **8** Cerberus
 slain by: **5** Argus

echinoderm **9** sea animal
 characteristic: **10** spiny shell
 form: **6** radial
 kind: **6** cystid **7** crinoid **8** starfish **9** sea urchin **10** basket star **11** sea cucumber

Echion
 member: **6** Sparti
 wife: **5** Agave
 son: **8** Pentheus

echo **3** ape **4** copy, ring **5** match **6** follow, mirror, parrot, repeat **7** imitate, reflect, resound **8** parallel, simulate **9** duplicate, reproduce, take after **11** reverberate **13** reverberation

Echo
 form: **5** nymph
 location: **8** mountain
 loved: **9** Narcissus
 loved by: **3** Pan
 changed into: **4** echo

eclair **6** pastry **7** dessert **9** creampuff

eclaircissement **11** explanation **13** clarification, (the) Enlightenment

eclipse **3** dim **4** hide, loss, mask **5** cloak, cover, excel, outdo **6** darken, exceed **7** blot out, conceal, erasing, masking, obscure, surpass, veiling, wipe out **8** cloaking, clouding, covering, outrival, outshine **9** darkening, shadowing, transcend **10** obliterate, overshadow, tower above **11** blotting out, diminishing, eradicating, obscuration **12** annihilation, obliteration **13** overshadowing

eclogue **4** idyl, poem **5** idyll **7** bucolic **8** dialogue, pastoral

Eclogues
 author: **6** Vergil, Virgil

ecole **6** school

economic **6** fiscal **8** material, monetary **9** budgetary, financial, pecuniary **10** productive **12** distributive

economical **5** chary, cheap **6** frugal, modest, saving **7** careful, prudent, sparing, spartan, thrifty **8** economic **9** low-priced, niggardly, penurious, scrimping **10** reasonable **11** closefisted, tightfisted **12** parsimonious

economic decline **8** downturn **9** recession **10** depression

economics
 term: **3** GNP **5** labor **7** capital, Marxism, surplus **8** property **9** commodity, Communism, inflation, Keynesian, recession **10** capitalism, monetarist, supply-side **11** bourgeoisie, central bank, competition, consumption, marketplace, proletariat, stagflation **12** distribution, econometrics, fiscal policy, interest rate, laissez-faire, mercantilism **14** federal deficit, macroeconomics, microeconomics, monetary policy **17** trickle-down the-

ory **20** gross national product

economist
American: **6** George, Hansen, Sumner, Veblen **7** Commons **8** Friedman, Laughlin **10** Schumpeter
British: **4** Mill **5** Smith **6** Keynes **7** Malthus, Ricardo **8** Marshall
French: **3** Say **7** Quesnay
German: **4** Marx **7** Schacht
Italian: **6** Pareto
Scottish: **5** Smith

economize **4** save **5** pinch, skimp, stint **6** scrimp **7** husband **8** be frugal, conserve, cut costs **9** be prudent **10** avoid waste **11** cut expenses **12** be economical, use sparingly **14** be parsimonious **15** practice economy, tighten one's belt

economizing **10** conserving **11** cutting down **13** penny-pinching **14** belt-tightening **15** pinching pennies **18** tightening one's belt

economy **6** thrift **8** prudence **9** frugality **10** providence **11** thriftiness **15** financial status, productive power

ecstasy **3** joy **5** bliss **6** frenzy, thrill, trance **7** delight, emotion, madness, rapture **8** delirium, gladness, pleasure **9** happiness, transport **10** enthusiasm, exultation

ecstatic **4** glad, rapt **5** happy **6** elated, joyful, joyous **7** exalted, excited **8** blissful **9** delighted, delirious, ebullient, entranced, overjoyed, rapturous **10** enraptured **11** transported **12** enthusiastic **13** beside oneself

Ecuador ***see box***

ecumenical **6** global **7** general **8** catholic **9** communist, planetary, universal, worldwide **10** heavenwide **11** communalist **12** all-embracing, all-including, all-inclusive, all-pervading, collectivist, cosmopolitan **13** communitarian, comprehensive, international

eczema **4** rash **8** eruption **10** dermatitis **12** inflammation

eddy **6** vortex **9** maelstrom, whirlpool **14** countercurrent

Eddy, Nelson
partner: **17** Jeanette MacDonald
born: **12** Providence RI
roles: **9** Rose Marie **15** Naughty Marietta **16** Northwest Outpost

Ecuador
name means: **7** equator
other name: **5** Quito
capital: **5** Quito
largest city: **9** Guayaquil
others: **4** Jama, Loja, Napo, Puyo, Tena **5** Guano, Manta, Pajan, Pinas, Piura, Pojan, Yaupi **6** Ambato, Cuenca, Ibarra, Tulcan, Zaruma **7** Azogues, Cayambe, Guamote, Guapulo, Machala, Pelileo, Pillaro, Salinas **8** Riobamba **10** Esmeraldas, Portoviejo
division: **5** Costa **6** Sierra **7** Oriente
measure: **5** libra **6** cuadra, fanega
monetary unit: **5** sucre **7** centavo
weight: **5** libra
island: **4** Puna, Wolf **5** Colon, Mocha, Pinta **6** Baltra, Chaves, Darwin, Pinzon, Rabida, Wenman **7** Isabela, La Plata, Sante Fe, Tortuga **8** Espanola, Floreana, Genovesa, Marchena, Santiago **9** Culpepper, Galapagos, Santa Cruz **10** Fernandina, Santa Maria **11** San Salvador **12** San Cristobal
mountain: **5** Andes **6** Condor, Sangay **7** Cayambe **8** Antisana, Cotopaxi **9** Cotacachi, Pichincha
highest point: **10** Chimborazo
river: **4** Coca, Mira, Napo **5** Cocoa, Daule, Paute, Pindo, Tigre **6** Blanco, Guayas, Tumbes, Zamora **7** Conambo, Curaray, Jubones, Pastaza, Puyango **8** Aguarico, Bobonaza, Cononaco, Naranjal, Putumayo **9** San Miguel **10** Esmeraldas, Nangaritza **12** Guaillabamba
sea: **7** Pacific
physical feature:
bay: **5** Manta **7** Isabela **9** Elizabeth **11** Santa Elenas **15** Ancon de Sardinas
cape: **4** Rosa **6** Pasado **8** Marshall, Puntilla **10** San Lorenzo
channel: **7** Jambeli
gulf: **9** Guayaquil, Pichincha
peninsula: **10** Santa Elena
point: **4** Jama **5** Essex **6** Galera **9** Albemarle **10** Christobal
people: **4** Cara, Cixo, Inca **5** Ardan, Aucas, Macoa, Maina, Palta, Quitu, Yumbo **6** Canelo, Jibaro, Jivaro, Puruha **7** Cayapas, Jivaros, mestizo, mulatto **8** Barbacoa, Colorado, Montuvio, Serranos **9** Montubios
artist: **4** Egas **8** Santiago **9** Caspicara **10** Guayasamin
author: **6** Espejo **14** Carrera Andrade
conqueror: **7** Pizarro **10** Benalcazar **11** Huayna-Capac
god: **5** umina
leader: **6** Alfaro, Flores **10** Plaza Lasso, Rocafuerte **12** Garcia Moreno **13** Velasco Ibarra
language: **6** Jibaro **7** Quechua, Spanish
religion: **13** Roman Catholic
feature:
animal: **6** vicuna
dictator: **8** caudillo
estate: **8** hacienda
festival: **5** Yamor
hat: **6** Panama **8** jipijapa, toquilla
tree: **5** balsa
food:
baked guinea pig: **3** cuy
corn tamale: **6** humita
drink: **6** chicha
marinated raw shrimp/fish: **7** ceviche, seviche
potato/cheese patty: **11** llapingacho
potato soup: **5** locro

Eden **8** Paradise
see also: **4** Adam

edentate **5** manis, sloth **7** antbear **8** aardvark, anteater **9** armadillo, toothless

Edgar Huntly
author: **20** Charles Brockden Brown

edge **3** hem, rim **4** bind, inch, line, side, trim **5** bound, brink, creep, limit, sidle, slink, sneak, steal, verge **6** border, fringe, margin **7** contour, outline **9** extremity, periphery, threshold **12** boundary line, dividing line, move sideways

Edgeworth, Maria
author of: **7** Belinda **11** The Absentee **14** Castle Rackrent

edging **3** hem **4** trim **5** limit **6** border, fringe, margin, ruffle **7** binding, curbing, salvage **8** boundary, fringing, trimming

edgy **5** sharp, testy **7** anxious, nervous **8** snappish **9** excitable, impatient, irascible, irritable **10** highstrung

edible **7** eatable **10** comestible, consumable, digestible **12** fit to be eaten, nonpoisonous **13** safe for eating

edict **3** law **4** bull, fiat **5** order, ukase **6** decree, dictum, ruling **7** command, dictate, mandate, statute **9** enactment, manifesto, ordinance, prescript **10** injunction, regulation **12** proclamation, public notice **13** pronouncement **14** pronunciamento

edification **8** guidance, teaching **9** direction, education, elevation, uplifting **11** advancement, information, instruction **13** enlightenment **14** indoctrination

edifice **8** building **9** structure **12** construction

edify **5** teach **6** inform **7** educate, improve **8** instruct **9** enlighten

edifying **8** didactic, tutorial **11** educational, instructive **12** enlightening

Edinburgh
bay: **12** Firth of Forth
capital of: **8** Scotland
Celtic: **11** Dune-eideann (Eidin's Fort)
church: **7** St Giles
landmark: **14** Holyrood Palace **15** Edinburgh Castle
port: **5** Leith
rocks: **10** Castle Rock **11** Arthur's Seat

Edison, Thomas Alva
nickname: **17** Wizard of Menlo Park
inventor of: **6** (wax cylinder) record **9** light bulb, (quadruplex) telegraph **10** phonograph **11** kinetoscope, stock ticker **14** movie projector **16** incandescent lamp **18** automatic telegraph (transmitter and receiver) **21** flexible celluloid film **22** alkaline storage battery

edit **5** adapt, emend **6** censor, polish, redact, revise **7** abridge, clean up, correct, expunge, rewrite, touch up **8** annotate, condense, copy-edit, rephrase **9** expurgate **10** blue-pencil, bowdlerize

edition **4** book, copy, kind **5** issue **6** number **7** imprint, version **8** printing **9** redaction

editor **2** ed **6** writer **7** newsman, reviser **8** compiler, redactor **10** journalist

Edmonds, Walter D
author of: **8** Rome Haul **19** Drums Along the Mohawk

Edmonton
hockey team: **6** Oilers

Edmontonia
type: **8** dinosaur **10** ornithopod
location: **12** North America

Edmund Campion
author: **11** Evelyn Waugh

Edom
name given: **4** Esau
descendants: **8** Edomites

Edson, Gus
creator/artist of: **5** Dondi **8** The Gumps

Ed Sullivan Show, The
regular cast: **17** June Taylor Dancers **23** Ray Bloch and His Orchestra
noted appearances: **7** Beatles, Bob Hope **10** Walt Disney **12** Elvis Presley **14** Martin and Lewis

educate **5** coach, edify, teach, train, tutor **6** inform, school **7** develop **8** civilize, instruct **9** enlighten

education **5** study **7** culture **8** learning, pedagogy, teaching, training, tutelage **9** didactics, erudition, knowledge, schooling **10** pedagogics **11** cultivation, edification, information, instruction, scholarship **13** enlightenment

Education of Henry Adams, The
author: **10** Henry Adams

educe **5** evoke **6** elicit, extort **7** draw out, extract **8** bring out **9** draw forth **12** bring to light

Edward II
author: **18** Christopher Marlowe

Edwards, Blake
director of: **3** SOB, Ten **14** The Pink Panther, Victor Victoria **18** Days of Wine and Roses **19** Breakfast at Tiffany's

Edwards, Vince
real name: **18** Vincent Edward Zoimo
roles: **8** Ben Casey **13** Devil's Brigade **14** The Desperadoes **15** Three Faces of Eve

Edwin Drood, The Mystery of
author: **14** Charles Dickens
character: **7** Durdles, Mr Tatar, Rosa Bud **8** Mr Sapsea **10** John Jasper, Mr Datchery **11** Mr Grewgious **12** Mr Crisparkle **13** Deputy Bazzard **14** Helena Landless, Miss Twinkleton, Mr Honeythunder **15** Neville Landless

eel
young: **5** elver

eerie **3** odd **5** queer, weird **6** creepy, spooky, uneasy **7** bizarre, fearful, ghostly, ominous, strange, uncanny **10** mysterious, portentous **11** frightening **12** apprehensive

Eetion
king of: **6** Thebes **7** Cilicia
daughter: **10** Andromache

Eeyore
character in: **13** Winnie-the-Pooh
author: **5** Milne

efface **4** raze **5** erase **6** cancel, delete, excise, rub out **7** blot out, destroy, expunge, wipe out **9** eradicate, extirpate **10** annihilate, obliterate

effect, effects **4** fact, gist, make **5** cause, drift, force, goods, power, tenor, truth **6** action, assets, attain, create, impact, import, intent, result, sequel, things, upshot, weight **7** achieve, essence, execute, meaning, outcome, perform, produce, purport, reality, realize **8** carry out, chattels, efficacy, function, holdings, movables, validity **9** actuality, aftermath, execution, furniture, influence, intention, operation, outgrowth, trappings **10** accomplish, bring about, impression **11** commodities, consequence, development, enforcement, general idea, implication, possessions **12** significance **14** accomplishment

effective **4** real **6** active, actual, cogent, moving, potent, strong, useful **7** capable, current, dynamic, telling **8** a reality, eloquent, forceful, forcible, incisive, powerful, striking **9** activated, competent, effectual, efficient, operative **10** compelling, convincing, impressive, persuasive, productive, successful **11** efficacious, influential, in operation, serviceable

effectiveness **5** power **6** effect, impact **7** potency **8** efficacy, strength **9** influence **10** efficiency, usefulness **14** serviceability

effectual **6** acting, active, useful **7** working **8** adequate **9** effective, efficient, operative **11** efficacious, functioning

effectuate **6** effect **7** achieve, execute, realize **8** carry out, complete **9** discharge **10** accomplish, consummate, perpetrate **12** carry through **13** put into effect

effeminate **7** unmanly **8** sissyish, womanish **9** sissified

effervesce **4** fizz, foam **5** froth **6** bubble, fizzle **7** sparkle

effervescence **3** zip **4** dash, fizz, life **5** froth, vigor **6** fizzle, gaiety, spirit **7** foaming **8** bubbling, buoyancy, vitality, vivacity **9** animation, fizziness **10** bubbliness, bubbling up, ebullience, enthusiasm, liveliness

effervescent **3** gay **5** fizzy, merry **6** bubbly, lively **7** fizzing, foaming **8** animated, bubbling **9** ebullient, exuberant, sparkling, vivacious **13** irrepressible

effete **5** spent **6** barren, wasted **7** sterile, worn-out **8** decadent, depraved **9** enervated, exhausted **10** degenerate, unprolific **12** unproductive

efficacious **9** effective, effectual, efficient

efficacy **6** impact **10** efficiency **13** effectiveness

efficiency **5** skill **6** energy **8** efficacy, facility **9** apartment **10** competence **11** proficiency **13** effectiveness

efficient **3** apt **7** capable **8** skillful **9** competent, effective, effectual **10** productive, proficient, timesaving, unwasteful, work-saving **11** crackerjack, efficacious, workmanlike **12** businesslike

effigy **4** doll **5** dummy, image **6** puppet, statue **8** likeness, straw man **9** mannequin, scarecrow **10** marionette **14** representation

effluence **6** efflux **7** outflow, outpour **8** effluent **9** discharge

effluent **5** waste **6** efflux, sewage **7** outflow **9** effluence

effluvium **4** aura, odor, ooze, reek **5** vapor **6** efflux, flatus **8** outgoing

efflux **7** outflow **8** effluent, emission **9** discharge, effluence

effort **3** try **4** toil, work **5** force, labor, pains, power **6** energy, strain, stress **7** attempt, travail, trouble **8** endeavor, exertion, industry, struggle **11** elbow grease

effortless **4** easy **6** facile, simple, smooth **8** graceful, painless **12** not difficult **13** uncomplicated

effortlessness **4** ease **8** easiness, facility **9** readiness **12** painlessness

effrontery **4** gall **5** brass, cheek, nerve **8** audacity, temerity **9** arrogance, brashness, impudence, insolence **10** brazenness **11** presumption **12** impertinence **13** shamelessness
Yiddish: **7** chutzpa **8** chutzpah

effulgence **6** dazzle **8** radiance, splendor **10** brilliance **12** resplendence

effulgent **6** bright **7** radiant **8** dazzling, splendid **9** brilliant **11** resplendent

effusive **5** gushy **6** lavish **7** copious, gushing, profuse **9** ebullient, expansive, exuberant **10** unreserved **11** extravagant, free-flowing, overflowing **12** unrestrained

eft **4** newt **5** again **6** lizard **9** afterward

egalitarian **10** democratic **11** equal-rights **14** constitutional

egalite **8** equality

Egeria
also: **7** Aegeria
member of: **7** Camenae
husband: **13** Numa Pompilius
instructed: **13** Numa Pompilius

Egesta
also: **7** Aegesta
home: **4** Troy
position: **5** slave
sold by: **8** Laomedon
rescued by: **9** Aphrodite

egg **3** ova, roe **4** bomb, goad, mine, oval, ovum, seed, spur **6** embryo, fellow, incite, person **7** albumen **9** instigate, stimulate

Eggar, Samantha
born: **6** London **7** England
roles: **12** The Collector, Walking Stick **15** Doctor Doolittle, The Lady in the Car **16** The Molly Maguires

egghead **8** highbrow **13** intellectual

Eggleston, Edward
author of: **15** The Circuit Rider **19** The Hoosier Schoolboy **22** The Hoosier Schoolmaster

egg on **4** abet, back, goad, spur **6** exhort, incite **8** talk into **9** encourage

egg-shaped **4** oval **5** ovoid **7** oviform **10** elliptical

Egmont
author: **12** Johann Goethe

egocentric **8** egoistic **11** egomaniacal, egotistical, on an ego trip, self-seeking, self-serving **12** narcissistic, self-absorbed, self-centered, self-involved, self-obsessed **13** self-concerned **14** megalomaniacal, stuck on oneself **18** wrapped up in oneself

egoism **6** vanity **8** self-love **10** narcissism **14** self-absorption, self-importance **16** overweening pride, self-centeredness

egoist **10** narcissist, selfish one **13** selfish person **18** self-centered person

Egoist, The
author: **14** George Meredith

egoistic **7** selfish **12** narcissistic, self-centered

egotism **6** vanity **7** conceit **8** bragging, smugness **9** arrogance, immodesty, vainglory **10** self-praise **11** braggadocio **12** boastfulness

egotist **6** gascon **7** boaster, peacock **8** blowhard, braggart **9** swaggerer **11** braggadocio

egotistic **4** vain **10** egocentric **12** self-centered **13** self-important

egregious **5** gross **7** extreme, glaring, heinous **8** flagrant, grievous, shocking **9** monstrous, notorious **10** outrageous **11** intolerable **12** insufferable

Egypt

other name: **3** UAR **5** Kemet **6** To-meri **11** The Two Lands **12** The Black Land

capital/largest city: **5** Cairo

others: **3** Tor **4** Edfu, Gaza, Giza, Idfu, Said, Suez **5** Altur, Aswan, Tanta **6** Boolak, Dumyat, Faiyum, Quseir, Safaga, Sallum **7** Alemein, Memphis, Raschid, Rosetta, Zagazig **8** Damietta, Hurghada, Ismailia, Mansurah **10** Alexandria

school: **5** Cairo **7** Al-Azhar **8** American

division: **5** Lower, Nubia, Upper

measure: **3** apt, dra, hen, rob **4** arab, dira, draa, khet, nief, ocha, roub, theb, wudu **5** abdat, ardab, cubit, farde, fedan, keleh, kerat, kilah, sahme **6** artaba, aurure, baladi, kantar, keddah, robhah, schene **7** choryos, daribah, malouah, roubouh, toumnah **8** kassabah, kharouba **10** diramimari, diribaladi

monetary unit: **4** fils, kees, para **5** asper, dinar, fodda, gersh, girsh, medin, pound, riyal **6** ahmadi, dirham, foddah, guinea, junayh, maidin, medine, medino **7** piaster, piastre, tallard **8** bedidlik, millieme

weight: **3** kat, ket, oka, oke **4** dera, heml, khar, okia, rotl **5** artal, artel, deben, kerat, minae, minas, okieh, pound, ratel, uckia **6** hamlah, kantar **7** drachma, quintal

island: **4** Roda **6** Philae **7** Shadwan **11** Elephantine

lake: **4** Edku, Idku **5** Qarun **6** Maryut, Moeris, Nasser **7** Manzala **8** Burullus, Mareotis

mountain: **5** Sinai, Uekia **6** Gharib **13** Shayib al-Banat

highest point: **8** Katerina **9** Katherina

river: **4** Bahr, Nile
Nile branch: **7** Rosetta **8** Damietta

sea: **3** Red **13** Mediterranean

physical feature:
cape: **4** Sudr **5** Banas **8** Rasbanas
desert: **3** Tih **5** Dakla, Scete, Sinai, Skete **6** Libyan, Nubian, Sahara **7** Arabian
gulf: **4** Suez **5** Aqaba
isthmus: **4** Suez
oasis: **4** Siwa **6** Dakhel, Dakhla, Kharga **7** Farafra, Khargeh **8** Bahariya **9** Bahariyeh **12** Wahel-Khargeh
peninsula: **5** Sinai **6** Pharos
plain: **7** Asaseff
plateau: **3** Tih

people: **3** Kem **4** Arab, Copt, Misr, Wafd **5** Gippy, Gyppy, Gypsy, Nilot **6** Ababda, Berber, Hyksos, Nubian, Tasian **7** Mizraim, Pharian **8** Badarian, Bisharin, Memphian
leader: **5** Jawar, Sadat **6** Nasser **7** Saladin **10** King Farouk **11** Ismail Pasha, Mohammed Ali, Tawfiq Pasha
pharaoh: **5** Khufu, Menes, Zoser **6** Khafre, Ptulol, Ramses **8** Horemheb, Menkaure **9** Akhenaten, Amenemhet, Amenhotep **10** Mentuhotep **11** Tutankhamen
queen: **9** Cleopatra, Nefertari, Nefertiti **10** Hatshepsut, Hetepheres

language: **6** Arabic, French **7** English
for liturgy: **6** Coptic

religion: **5** Islam **18** Coptic Christianity
ancient god: **2** Ra **3** Geb, Nut, Shu **4** Aton, Atum, Isis, Ptah, Seth **5** Horus, Thoth **6** Anubis, Hathor, Osiris, Tefnut **8** Nephthys

place:
dam: **4** Sadd, Sudd **5** Aswan **6** Assuan
mosque: **5** Rifai **9** Alabaster **11** Sultan Hasan
palace: **6** Kubbeh
pyramids: **4** Giza **5** Khufu **6** Cheops **7** Saqqara
ruins: **5** Miroe **6** Abydos, Sphinx, Thebes **7** Memphis **8** Berenice **9** Abu Simbel **13** Valley of Kings, Valley of Tombs
temple: **4** Idfu **5** Edoon, Luxor, Thoth **6** Abydos, Karnak, Osiris **7** Dendera

feature:
dynasty: **5** Saite **7** Ayyubid, Fatimid **8** Mameluke **9** Ptolemaic
long robe: **10** gallabiyea
peasant: **6** fellah **8** fellahin **9** fellaheen
sacred bird: **4** benu, ibis **5** bennu
sailboat: **7** felucca
statue: **6** Sphinx **15** Colossi of Memnon

food:
bean: **5** lotus
beer: **6** zythum
bread: **6** herisa
dish: **3** ful
drink: **4** bosa, boza **5** bozah

egress **4** exit, vent **5** issue **6** escape, outlet, way out **7** leakage, outflow, seepage **8** aperture **9** departure, discharge **10** passage out, withdrawal

Egypt ***see box***

Egyptian
language family: **11** Afro-Asiatic **13** Hamito-Semitic
later form: **6** Coptic

Egyptian cross **4** ankh

Egyptian Mythology ***see box***

Ehrlich, Paul
field: **12** bacteriology
nationality: **6** German
studied: **6** toxins **8** immunity **10** antitoxins
discovered: **9** salvarsan
coined term: **12** chemotherapy
awarded: **10** Nobel Prize

Ehud **11** Hebrew judge

Eichenor
mentioned in: **5** Iliad
father: **8** Polyidus
fought with: **6** Greeks
slain by: **5** Paris

Eichmann in Jerusalem
author: **12** Hannah Arendt

eiderdown **4** puff **5** cover, quilt **8** coverlet **9** comforter **10** featherbed

Eight and a half, 8 1/2
director: **15** Federico Fellini
cast: **10** Anouk Aimee **16** Claudia Cardinale **19** Marcello Mastroianni

Eighteen Seventy-Six, 1876
author: **9** Gore Vidal

Eijkman, Christiaan
nationality: **5** Dutch
discovered: **19** antineuritic vitamin
researched: **8** beriberi
awarded: **10** Nobel Prize

Eileithyia
also: **8** Ilithyia
origin: **5** Greek
goddess of: **10** childbirth
father: **4** Zeus
mother: **4** Hera
corresponds to: **6** Lucina

Einstein, Albert
field: **7** physics
theory of: **10** relativity **14** uranium fission
awarded: **10** Nobel Prize

Eioneus
son: **6** Rhesus
daughter: **3** Dia

Eire *see* **7** Ireland

Eisenhower, Dwight David ***see box, p. 298***

ejaculate **4** howl, yell, yelp **5** shout **6** bellow, cry out **7** exclaim **10** vociferate

ejaculation **3** cry **4** howl, yell, yelp **5** shout **6** bellow, outcry, shriek, squeal **7** screech **11** exclamation **12** vociferation

eject **4** emit, oust, spew **5** evict, exile, expel, exude, spout **6** banish, bounce, deport, remove **7** cast out, kick out, spit out, turn out **8** disgorge, drive out, force out, throw out **9** discharge **10** dispossess

ejection **4** gush **5** spurt **6** ouster **7** issuing, removal **8** emission, eruption, eviction **9** dismissal, expelling, expulsion **10** banishment **11** throwing out

Ekdal, Hjalmar
character in: **11** The Wild Duck
author: **5** Ibsen

eke **3** add **4** also **7** augment, enlarge, stretch **8** increase, lengthen, likewise, moreover **10** in addition, supplement

elaborate **5** fancy, gaudy, showy **6** expand, flashy, garish, ornate **7** clarify, complex, elegant, labored, specify **8** involved, overdone **9** embellish, intricate **10** add details **11** complicated, painstaking **12** ostentatious **13** particularize

elaborate on **6** expand **7** amplify, develop **9** embellish **10** supplement **11** expatiate on

elaboration **11** added detail, rounding out **12** augmentation **13** amplification, embellishment

Elaine
character in: **16** Arthurian romance

Elais
father: **5** Anius
mother: **7** Dorippe
changed things into: **3** oil

elan **4** dash, zeal **5** flair, verve, vigor **6** energy, spirit **8** vivacity **9** animation **10** enthusiasm

eland **3** elk **8** antelope **11** taurotragus

elapse **4** go by, pass **5** lapse **6** pass by, roll by, slip by **7** glide by, slide by **8** slip away **9** intervene

Elara
mother of: **6** Tityus

elastic **6** pliant, supple **7** pliable, rubbery, springy **8** flexible, tolerant, yielding **9** adaptable, recoiling, resil-

Egyptian Mythology
deities: **6** Ennead
eight gods: **3** Heh **6** Ogdoad
goddess of evil: **7** Sekhmet
goddess of fertility: **2** Io **4** Isis
goddess of law/righteousness: **4** Maat
goddess of love/joy/music/dance: **6** Hathor
goddess of sky: **3** Nut
goddess personifying sky: **6** Hathor
god of bricks: **5** Kulla
god of creation: **4** Ptah
god of dead/Nile: **6** Osiris
god of earth: **3** Geb, Keb
god of ocean: **3** Nun **4** Nunu
god of sun: **2** Ra, Re **5** Horus
corresponds to Greek: **10** Harcorates
god of tombs/embalming: **6** Anubis
god of wisdom/magic/learning: **5** Thoth
corresponds to Greek: **6** Hermes
immortal spirit: **2** Ka
judge of dead: **6** Osiris
king of dead: **6** Osiris
king of gods: **4** Amen, Amon **5** Ammon **6** Amen Ra, Amon Ra
corresponds to Greek: **4** Zeus
corresponds to Roman: **4** Jove **7** Jupiter
personification of femininity: **5** Neith
corresponds to Greek: **6** Athena
ram god: **5** Khnum
vulture: **7** Nekhbet

Eisenhower, Dwight David
nickname: **3** Ike
changed name from: **21** David Dwight Eisenhower
presidential rank: **12** thirty-fourth
party: **10** Republican
state represented: **2** NY
defeated: **4** (Eric) Hass, (Harry Flood) Byrd **5** (Farrell) Dobbs **6** (Darlington) Hoopes, (William Ezra) Jenner **7** (Stuart) Hamblen, (Thomas Coleman) Andrews **8** (Enoch Arden) Holtwick, (Vincent William) Hallinan **9** (Adlai Ewing) Stevenson
vice president: **5** (Richard Milhous) Nixon
cabinet:
state: **6** (Christian Archibald) Herter, (John Foster) Dulles
treasury: **8** (George Magoffin) Humphrey, (Robert Bernard) Anderson
defense: **5** (Thomas Sovereign) Gates (Jr) **6** (Charles Erwin) Wilson **7** (Neil Hesler) McElroy
attorney general: **6** (William Pierce) Rogers **8** (Herbert) Brownell (Jr)
postmaster general: **11** (Arthur Ellsworth) Summerfield
interior: **5** (Douglas) McKay **6** (Frederick Andrew) Seaton
agriculture: **6** (Ezra Taft) Benson
commerce: **5** (Sinclair) Weeks **7** (Frederick Henry) Mueller, (Lewis Lichtenstein) Strauss
labor: **6** (Martin Patrick) Durkin **8** (James Paul) Mitchell
HEW: **5** (Oveta Culp) Hobby **6** (Marion Bayard) Folsom **8** (Arthur Sherwood) Flemming
born: **9** Denison TX
died: **12** Washington DC
buried: **9** Abilene KS
education: **9** West Point **17** US Military Academy
religion: **12** Presbyterian
interest: **4** golf **6** flying **7** fishing, hunting **8** football, painting
vacation spot: **2** CA **11** Palm Springs
author: **11** Waging Peace **15** Crusade in Europe **16** Mandate for Change **27** At Ease: Stories I Tell to Friends
political career: **4** none (prior to presidency)
civilian career:
president of: **18** Columbia University
military service: **7** general **9** World War I **10** World War II **16** Army Chief of Staff
supreme commander of: **6** Allies **15** European Defense (NATO) **18** US occupation forces (Europe)
head of: **18** Joint Chiefs of Staff
notable events of lifetime/term: **4** D-Day, NATO
Acts: **11** Civil Rights
battle of the: **5** Bulge
conference: **7** Big Four **10** NATO Summit **11** Paris Summit
Cuba taken over by: **11** Fidel Castro
invasion: **8** Normandy
trial/execution of: **14** Ethel Rosenberg **15** Julius Rosenberg
USSR shot down: **9** U-Two plane
father: **10** David Jacob
mother: **3** Ida (Elizabeth Stover)
siblings: **3** Roy **4** Earl, Paul **5** Edgar **6** Arthur, Milton
wife: **5** Marie (Geneva Doud)
nickname: **5** Mamie
children: **10** Doud Dwight **15** John Sheldon Doud

ient **10** rebounding, responsive **11** complaisant, stretchable **12** recuperative **13** accommodating

elate **5** cheer, exalt **6** excite, lift up, please **7** animate, delight, elevate, enliven, gladden, gratify, inspire **10** exhilarate

elated **4** glad **5** happy, proud **6** joyful, joyous **7** exalted, excited, gleeful, pleased **8** animated, blissful, ecstatic, jubilant **9** overjoyed, rejoicing **10** delightful **11** exhilarated **13** in high spirits **18** flushed with success

elation **3** joy **4** glee **5** pride **7** triumph **8** gladness **9** happiness **10** excitement, exultation, jubilation **12** cheerfulness

Elatus
father: **5** Arcas
son: **6** Pereus **10** Polyphemus

elbow grease **4** work **5** force, labor **6** effort, energy, muscle **8** exertion, hard work **11** application

elbow in **4** push **5** force, press, shove **6** horn in **7** crowd in

El Cordobes (Manuel Benitez Perez)
sport: **12** bullfighting

elder **4** head **5** older **6** senior **8** old-timer **9** firstborn, patriarch, presbyter **14** church official **15** church dignitary
French: **4** aine

elder, elderberry **8** Sambucus
varieties: **3** Box **4** Blue **5** Dwarf, Sweet **6** Ground, Poison, Yellow **8** American, European, Stinking **10** Redberried **11** American red, European red **15** Pacific Coast red

elderly **3** old **4** aged **9** venerable **11** over the hill **13** past one's prime

Eldorado
nickname of: **10** California

Eleanor and Franklin
author: **11** Joseph P Lash

Eleazar
father: **4** Dodo **5** Aaron, Elind, Mahli **6** Parosh **7** Phineas **8** Abinadab
mother: **8** Elisheba
brother: **5** Abihu, Nadab **7** Ithamar
succeeded: **5** Aaron

elect **4** pick **5** adopt **6** choose, opt for, select, take up **7** embrace, espouse, fix upon, pick out **8** decide on, settle on **9** single out

election **4** poll, vote **6** choice, option, voting **7** resolve **8** decision **9** balloting, selection **10** resolution **11** alternative **13** determination

electioneer **3** run **5** stump **8** campaign **11** whistle-stop **12** beat the drums, solicit votes

elective **8** optional **9** selective, voluntary **11** not required **12** open to choice, passed by vote **13** discretionary, not obligatory

Electra
author: **9** Euripides, Sophocles
character: **7** Orestes, Pylades **8** Dioscuri **9** Aegisthus **12** Clytemnestra
father: **9** Agamemnon
mother: **12** Clytemnestra
brother: **7** Orestes
sister: **9** Iphigenia **12** Chrysothemis
husband: **7** Pylades
son: **5** Medon **9** Strophius

electric **7** dynamic, rousing **8** exalting, exciting, spirited, stirring **9** inspiring, thrilling **10** full of fire **11** galvanizing, power-driven, stimulating **12** electrifying, soul-stirring

electric battery
invented by: **5** Volta

electricity measure **3** ohm **4** volt, watt **5** joule **6** ampere **10** horsepower

Electric Kool-Aid Acid Test, The
author: **8** Tom Wolfe

Electrides
form: **7** islands
color: **5** amber

electrify **4** daze, stir, stun **5** amaze, rouse **6** dazzle, excite, fire up, thrill **7** animate, astound, quicken, startle **8** astonish, surprise **9** fascinate, galvanize, stimulate **18** take one's breath away

electrifying **8** dazzling, shocking, stunning **10** astounding, stupefying **11** astonishing

electromagnet
invented by: **8** Sturgeon

Electryon
king of: **7** Mycenae
father: **7** Perseus
mother: **9** Andromeda
brother: **6** Mestor **9** Sthenelus
wife: **5** Anaxo
son: **9** Licymnius
daughter: **7** Alcmene
grandson: **8** Hercules

eleemosynary **10** altruistic, beneficent, benevolent, charitable **13** philanthropic **15** nonprofitmaking

elegance **5** class, grace, taste **6** purity **7** balance **8** delicacy, grandeur, richness, symmetry **10** refinement **12** gracefulness **13** exquisiteness, luxuriousness, sumptuousness

elegant **4** fine, rich **5** grand **6** classy, dapper, lovely, ornate, polite, urbane **7** classic, courtly, genteel, refined, stylish **8** artistic, charming, debonair, delicate, graceful, gracious, handsome, polished, tasteful, well-bred **9** beautiful, dignified, exquisite, luxurious, sumptuous **10** attractive, cultivated **11** fashionable, symmetrical **16** well-proportioned

elegiac **3** sad **8** funereal, mournful **10** melancholy

elegy **7** requiem, sad poem **11** funeral song **14** melancholy poem **16** lament for the dead **17** poem of lamentation, song of lamentation **22** melancholy piece of music

Elegy Written in a Country Churchyard
author: **10** Thomas Gray

Elektra *see* **7** Electra

element, elements **3** air **4** fire **5** earth, water **6** basics, member, milieu **7** essence, factors, origins **8** original **9** basic part, basic unit, component, rudiments **10** basic ideas, ingredient, principles, simple body **11** constituent, environment, foundations, native state, subdivision **13** building block, component part, natural medium **14** natural habitat

elemental **5** basal, basic **10** elementary **11** fundamental, rudimentary

elementary **4** easy **5** basal, basic, crude, first, plain **6** simple **7** primary **8** original **9** elemental, primitive **11** fundamental, rudimentary, undeveloped **13** uncomplicated

elephant
group of: **4** herd

elephantine **4** huge **7** immense, mammoth, titanic **8** colossal, enormous, gigantic **9** ponderous **10** gargantuan, tremendous **14** Brobdingnagian

Elephant Man, The
director: **10** David Lynch
cast: **8** John Hurt **11** John Gielgud, Wendy Hiller **12** Anne Bancroft **14** Anthony Hopkins

Eleusinia
origin: **5** Greek
form: **8** festival

Eleusinian mysteries
in memory of: **10** Persephone
in honor of: **7** Bacchus, Demeter
celebrated at: **6** Athens **7** Eleusis
founded by: **8** Eumolpus
god of: **7** Bacchus

Eleutherius
epithet of: **4** Zeus
means: **12** god of freedom

elevate **4** lift **5** boost, cheer, elate, heave, hoist, raise **6** better, excite, lift up, move up, perk up, refine, uplift **7** advance, animate, dignify, enhance, ennoble, improve, inspire, promote, upraise **8** heighten **9** place high **10** exhilarate, raise aloft

elevated **4** high **5** lofty **6** raised **7** exalted **8** improved, uplifted **9** prominent **10** heightened

elevation **4** hill, lift, rise **5** boost **6** ascent, height **8** altitude, mountain **9** acclivity, bettering, high place, promotion **10** prominence, refinement **11** advancement, cultivation, improvement

elevator **4** cage, lift, silo, wing **5** hoist **7** granary **10** dumbwaiter

elevator brake
invented by: **4** Otis

elf **4** puck **5** fairy, gnome, pixie, troll **6** goblin, sprite **7** brownie, gremlin **9** hobgoblin **10** leprechaun

elfin **3** wee **4** tiny **7** pixyish **9** fairylike **10** diminutive

Elgar, Sir Edward William
born: **7** England **10** Broadheath
composer of: **8** Falstaff **9** Cockaigne, Froissart **10** Caractacus, The Kingdom **11** The Apostles **14** The Black Knight, The Light of Life **16** Enigma Variations **19** Pomp and Circumstance, The Banner of St George, The Dream of Gerontius **30** Scenes from the Bavarian Highlands

Eli
son: **6** Hophni **7** Phineas
home: **6** Shiloh

Eli, Eli, Lama sabachthani
means: **31** My God My God why hast thou forsaken me?

elicit **5** cause, educe, evoke, exact, fetch, wrest **6** derive, extort **7** draw out, extract **9** call forth, draw forth **10** bring forth **12** bring to light

Elicius
origin: **5** Roman
epithet of: **7** Jupiter

elide **4** omit, slur **5** annul **6** delete **7** neglect **8** slur over, suppress **9** eliminate, strike-out **10** abbreviate

Eliezar
father: **5** Moses
mother: **8** Zipporah
brother: **7** Gershom

eligible **6** proper **7** fitting **8** suitable **9** desirable, qualified **10** acceptable, applicable, authorized, worthwhile **11** appropriate

Elihu
brother: **5** David
friend: **3** Job **6** Bildad, Zophar **7** Eliphaz

Elijah
opposed: **4** Ahab, Baal **7** Jezebel
successor: **6** Elisha

Elimelech
wife: **5** Naomi

eliminate **4** drop, omit, oust **5** eject, erase, exile, expel **6** banish, cut out, delete, except, reject, remove, rub out **7** abolish, cast out, dismiss, exclude, weed out **8** get rid of, leave out, stamp out, throw out **9** eradicate **10** annihilate, do away with **11** exterminate

Eliot, George
real name: **13** Mary Anne Evans
author of: **6** Romola **8** Adam Bede **11** Middlemarch, Silas Marner **17** The Mill on the Floss

Eliot, John
author of: **12** Bay Psalm Book

Eliot, T S
author of: **9** East Coker, Gerontion, Hollow Men **11** Burnt Norton, Dry Salvages **12** Ash Wednesday, Four Quartets, The Waste Land **13** Little Gidding, The Sacred Wood **16** The Family Reunion **20** Murder in the Cathedral **27** Sweeney Among the Nightingales **28** The Love Song of J Alfred Prufrock

Eliphaz
father: **4** Adah, Esau
friend: **3** Job **5** Elihu **6** Bildad, Zophar

Elisabeth *see* **9** Elizabeth

Elisha
home: **11** Abelmeholah
succeeded: **6** Elijah

Elissa
origin: **10** Phoenician
corresponds to: **4** Dido

elite **3** top **4** best **5** cream **6** choice, flower **7** bigwigs, society, the pick, wealthy **8** big shots, notables **9** haut monde **10** blue bloods, personages, select body, upper class **11** aristocracy, celebrities, high society **14** creme-de-la-creme

elixir **7** essence, extract, spirits **8** tincture **11** concentrate **17** alcoholic solution

Eliza
character in: **14** Uncle Tom's Cabin
author: **5** Stowe

Elizabeth
husband: **9** Zacharias, Zechariah
son: **14** John the Baptist

Elizabeth I
queen of: **7** England
father: **10** Henry Tudor **14** Henry the Eighth
mother: **10** Anne Boleyn
sister: **4** Mary **10** Bloody Mary
brother: **14** Edward the Sixth
advisor: **5** Cecil **8** Burghley **10** Walsingham
suitor: **5** Essex **6** Dudley **9** Leicester
victory over: **13** Spanish Armada

Elizabeth II
father: **14** George the Sixth
mother: **9** Elizabeth
husband: **17** Philip Mountbatten
son: **6** Andrew, Edward **7** Charles
daughter: **4** Anne

Elizabeth the Queen
author: **15** Maxwell Anderson

elk
group of: **4** gang

Ellas *see* **6** Greece

Elli
origin: **12** Scandinavian
personifies: **5** aging
defeated: **4** Thor
sport: **9** wrestling

Ellice Islands *see* **6** Tuvalu

Ellington, Duke
real name: **22** Edward Kennedy Ellington
born: **12** Washington DC
composer of: **10** Mood Indigo **14** Creole Love Call, Creole Rhapsody, Hot and Bothered **17** Concerto for Cootie **18** Black and Tan Fantasy

Elliot family
characters in: **10** Persuasion
member: **4** Anne **7** William **9** Elizabeth, Sir Walter
author: **6** Austen

Ellison, Harlan
author of: **7** Paingod **10** Spider Kiss **13** A Boy and His Dog **16** Deathbird Stories **19** Approaching Oblivion **20** Alone Against Tomorrow

Ellison, Ralph
author of: **15** The Invisible Man

elm **5** Ulmus
varieties: **3** red **4** bush, cork, rock, vase, wych **5** cedar, Dutch, dwarf, globe, wahoo, water, white **6** Exeter, horned, Jersey, moline, Scotch, willow, winged **7** Belgian, Chinese, Cornish, English, Holland **8** American, fern-leaf, Guernsey, Japanese, Siberian, slippery, tabletop, wheatley **9** September **10** camperdown, Chichester, Huntingdon, smooth-leaf **11** small-leaved **13** European white

Elmer Gantry
author: **13** Sinclair Lewis
director: **13** Richard Brooks
cast: **10** Dean Jagger **11** Jean Simmons **12** Shirley Jones **13** Arthur Kennedy, Burt Lancaster
Oscar for: **5** actor (Lancaster) **17** supporting actress (Jones)

elocution **6** speech **7** diction, oratory **10** intonation **11** enunciation **12** articulation **13** pronunciation **14** public speaking

Elohim **3** God

Eloisa to Abelard
author: **13** Alexander Pope

Elon **11** Hebrew judge

elongate **6** extend **7** draw out, prolong **8** lengthen, protract **10** stretch out

elongated **4** long **8** drawn out, extended **9** prolonged **10** attenuated, lengthened, protracted **12** stretched out

eloquence **5** force, grace **7** fluency, oratory **8** rhetoric **9** elocution, speakwell, vividness **10** expression **12** silver tongue
god of: **4** Ogma **6** Ogmios **7** Mercury

eloquent **5** vivid **6** moving, poetic **8** emphatic, forceful, spirited, stirring, striking **10** articulate, passionate, persuasive **11** impassioned

Elpenor
companion of: 7 Ulysses **8** Odysseus

El Salvador *see box*

Elscheimer, Adam
born: 7 Germany **15** Frankfurt am Main
artwork: 17 Tobias and the Angel **21** The Stoning of St Stephen **24** Rest on the Flight into Egypt

else 3 and, too **4** also, more **5** if not, other **7** besides, instead **9** different, otherwise **10** additional, contrarily, in addition

elsewhere 4 away **6** except **7** absence, not here

Elsinore
castle in: 6 Hamlet
author: 11 Shakespeare

Elton, Mr
character in: 4 Emma
author: 6 Austen

elucidate 6 detail **7** clarify, clear up, explain, expound **8** describe, spell out **9** delineate, explicate, interpret, make plain **10** illuminate, illustrate **11** comment upon **14** throw light upon

elucidation 7 account **10** commentary **11** description, explanation, explication **13** clarification **14** interpretation **15** exemplification

elude 4 shun **5** avoid, dodge, evade **6** escape, slip by **10** circumvent, fight shy of **11** get away from, keep clear of

eluding 7 dodging, ducking, evading, evasion **8** avoiding **9** avoidance **12** escaping from, sidestepping **13** circumventing **15** getting away from

Elul 16 sixth Hebrew month

elusive 4 foxy, wily **6** crafty, shifty, tricky **7** evasive **8** baffling, puzzling, slippery **11** hard to catch, hard to grasp

elusory 4 wily **6** shifty **7** devious, dodging, elusive, evasive, hedging **8** slippery **9** ambiguous, deceitful, deceptive, equivocal **10** misleading **12** equivocating

Elvsted, Thea
character in: 11 Hedda Gabler
author: 5 Ibsen

elysian 7 sublime **8** blissful, empyreal, empyrean, ethereal, heavenly **9** celestial, unearthly **12** otherworldly, paradisiacal

Elysium
also: 17 islands of the blest
afterworld of the: 7 blessed

Elytis, Odysseus
real name: 19 Odysseus Alepoudelis
author of: 10 Seemly It Is **20** Heroic and Elegiac Song

emaciated 4 lank, lean, thin **5** gaunt **6** sickly, skinny, wasted **7** haggard, scrawny, wizened **8** skeletal, starving, underfed **10** cadaverous **14** undernourished

emanate 4 flow, rise, stem, well **5** exude, issue **6** spring **7** give off, proceed **8** come from **9** come forth, originate, send forth

emanation 6 coming **7** arising, flowing, issuing **8** effusion **9** effluence, radiation, springing **10** exhalation **11** coming forth

emancipate 4 free **7** manumit, release, set free, unchain **8** liberate, unfetter **9** unshackle **12** set at liberty

emancipation 7 freedom, liberty **10** liberation **11** manumission **12** independence

emasculate 4 geld **5** alter **6** soften, weaken **8** castrate **9** undermine **10** devitalize

Emathion
father: 8 Tithonus
mother: 3 Eos
brother: 6 Memnon

El Salvador
other name: 9 Cuscatlan
capital/largest city: 11 San Salvador
others: 6 Cutuco, Izalco **7** Corinto, Metapan **8** Acajutla, Libertad, Santa Ana, Usulutan **9** San Miguel, Sonsonate **10** San Vicente, Santa Tecla **11** Union-Cutuco **12** Chalatenango
school: 15 Jose Simeon Canas **16** Alberto Masferrer
measure: 4 vara **5** cafiz, cahiz **6** fanega **7** batella, botella, cantara, manzana
monetary unit: 4 peso **5** colon **7** centavo
weight: 3 bag **4** caja **5** libra
lake: 5 Guiha, Guija **8** Ilopango **10** Coatepeque
mountain: 6 Izalco
highest point: 8 Santa Ana
river: 5 Jiboa, Lempa, Lopaz **6** Torola **7** de la Paz **9** Goascoaran **17** Grande de San Miguel
sea: 7 Pacific
physical feature:
***bay:* 10** Jiquilisco
***coast:* 6** Balsam
***gulf:* 7** Fonseca
***point:* 7** Amapala **8** Remedios
***valley:* 7** Hamacas
people: 5 Lenca, Pipil **6** Indian, Mangue **7** mestizo, Spanish **9** Matagalpa
***artist:* 8** Salarrue **10** Mejia Vides
***author:* 8** Salarrue **14** Antonio Gavidia
***conqueror:* 8** Alvarado
***leader:* 6** Osorio **8** Jose Arce **13** Matias Delgado **15** Manuel Rodriguez **17** Hernandez Martinez
***philosopher/journalist:* 9** Masferrer
language: 7 Spanish
religion: 13 Roman Catholic
place:
***ruins:* 7** Tazumal
feature:
***blouse:* 9** volcanena
***dance:* 7** pasillo **15** los historiantes
***drum:* 8** huehuetl
***estate:* 5** finca
***musical instrument:* 7** caramba
food:
***bread:* 10** quesadilla
***cheese pancake:* 6** pupusa

Emaux et Camees
author: **16** Theophile Gautier

Embalming
god of: **6** Anubis

embankment **4** bank, dike, wall **5** levee

embargo **3** ban **8** shutdown, stoppage **10** impediment, inhibition, injunction, quarantine, standstill **11** prohibition, restriction **12** interdiction, proscription **16** restraint of trade

embark **5** begin, board, start **6** launch, set out **7** enplane, entrain **8** commence, go aboard **9** board ship, enter upon

embark on **5** begin, start **8** approach, commence, initiate, set about **9** enter upon, undertake

embarras de richesses **13** overabundance **21** embarrassment of riches

embarrass **4** faze **5** abash, shame, upset **6** rattle **7** agitate, chagrin, confuse, fluster, mortify, nonplus **8** distress **9** discomfit **10** discompose, disconcert **13** make ill at ease **14** discountenance **17** make self-conscious

embarrassed **7** abashed **8** red-faced **9** chagrined, mortified **10** nonplussed **11** discomfited **13** self-conscious

embarrassing **7** awkward **8** confused, crushing **9** bothering **10** disturbing, mortifying, unpleasant **12** demoralizing, discomfiting **13** discomforting, disconcerting, uncomfortable

embarrassment **4** blot **5** stain **6** smirch **7** blemish, scandal, tarnish **8** disgrace **9** discredit **19** financial difficulty

embarrassment of riches
French: **19** embarras de richesses

embattled **8** fighting **9** embroiled, fortified **11** battle-ready, hard-pressed

embed **3** fix, set **4** bond **5** plant **6** fasten **8** ensconce **9** establish

embedded **3** set **5** fixed **6** bonded **7** engaged, planted **8** immersed, inserted **9** ensconced **11** established

embellish **4** gild **5** adorn, color **6** set off **7** dress up, enhance, fancy up, garnish, gussy up **8** beautify, decorate, ornament **9** elaborate, embroider **10** exaggerate

embellished **6** ornate **7** adorned, flowery **8** brocaded **9** decorated **10** beautified, elaborated, ornamented, rhetorical **11** embroidered

embellishment **5** frill **6** accent **7** garnish **8** furbelow, ornament, trimming **9** adornment **10** decoration, embroidery **11** elaboration **14** beautification **15** fuss and feathers

ember **3** ash **4** slag **6** cinder **7** clinker **8** live coal

embezzle **4** bilk, rook **5** cheat, filch **6** fleece **7** defraud, swindle **9** defalcate **14** misappropriate

embezzler **5** cheat, crook, thief **8** swindler

Embezzler, The
author: **16** Louis Auchincloss

embitter **4** sour **6** rankle **7** envenom **10** make bitter **11** make cynical **13** make rancorous, make resentful **15** make pessimistic

embittered **6** soured **7** cynical **9** rancorous, resentful **11** acrimonious

Embla
origin: **12** Scandinavian
first: **5** woman
made by: **4** gods
made from: **4** tree

emblem **4** sign **5** badge **6** design, device, symbol **7** insigna **8** colophon, hallmark

emblematic **7** typical **8** symbolic **10** indicative **11** distinctive **14** characteristic, representative

embodiment **7** epitome, essence **14** representation **15** exemplification, personification

embody **4** fuse **5** blend, merge **6** typify **7** collect, contain, embrace, express, include, realize **8** manifest, organize **9** exemplify, personify, represent, symbolize **10** assimilate **11** consolidate, incorporate **12** substantiate

embolden **7** fortify, hearten, inspire **8** inspirit **9** encourage

emboldened **6** poised **7** assured, unfazed **9** confident, heartened, unabashed **10** courageous, encouraged, inspirited

embonpoint **9** plumpness, stoutness **15** in good condition

emboss **4** knob, knot, stud **5** adorn, chase **6** indent **7** engrave, exhaust **8** decorate

embossed **4** bold **6** raised **7** adorned, antique, knotted **8** engraved, indented **9** decorated, exhausted

embrace **3** hug **5** adopt, clasp, cover, grasp **6** accept, embody **7** contain, espouse, include, involve **8** comprise **9** encompass **10** comprehend **11** consolidate, incorporate

embroider **5** color **7** dress up **9** elaborate, embellish, fabricate **10** exaggerate **11** romanticize

embroidery **8** tapestry **9** adornment, gros point **10** crewelwork, decoration, needlework, petit point **11** imagination **12** exaggeration **13** ornamentation

embroil **4** trap **6** enmesh **7** ensnare, involve **8** entangle **10** complicate

embroiled **8** enmeshed **9** embattled, entangled **11** hard-pressed

embroilment **3** row **4** fray, tilt **5** brawl, brush, clash, melee **6** fracas, ruckus, rumpus, uproar **7** scuffle **8** conflict, disorder, struggle **9** confusion, imbroglio **10** contention **11** altercation **12** entanglement

embryo **3** bud, egg **4** germ **5** fetus, larva, ovule **6** budding, source **8** immature, rudiment **9** beginning **11** rudimentary, undeveloped

embryonic **5** rough **6** unborn **7** nascent **8** immature, inchoate **9** beginning, imperfect, incipient **10** incomplete, unfinished **11** rudimentary, undeveloped

emend **6** change, revise **7** correct, improve, rectify

emendation **8** revision **10** alteration, correction **11** improvement

emerald
species: **5** beryl
source: **4** Muzo **5** Egypt, India **6** Chivor **8** Colombia, Rhodesia, Zimbabwe **11** South Africa, Soviet Union **13** Ural Mountains
color: **5** green

Emerald City
setting in: **13** The Wizard of Oz
author: **4** Baum

Emerald Isle *see* **7** Ireland

emerge **3** run **4** dawn, emit, flow, gush, loom, pour, rise **5** arise, issue **6** appear, come up, crop up, escape, stream, turn up **7** develop, surface **9** come forth, discharge

11 come to light **12** come into view **13** become visible **14** become apparent, become manifest

emergence **4** dawn **7** dawning **10** appearance **11** development **13** coming to light, manifestation **15** materialization

emergency **5** pinch **6** crisis **7** urgency **8** exigency **11** contingency, predicament **16** unforeseen danger

Emergency
character: **8** (Dr) Joe Early, (Paramedic) John Gage **9** (Paramedic) Roy DeSoto **11** (Nurse) Dixie McCall **13** (Dr) Kelly Brackett
cast: **10** Bobby Troup, Kevin Tighe **11** Julie London **12** Robert Fuller **16** Randolph Mantooth

Emerson, Ralph Waldo
nickname: **13** Sage of Concord
author of: **4** Fate **6** Brahma, Nature **10** Friendship, The Rhodora **12** Compensation, Self-Reliance **14** The Concord Hymn **18** The American Scholar
philosophy: **17** Transcendentalism

emeute **4** riot

emigrant **6** emigre **8** wanderer, wayfarer **10** expatriate

Emigrants, The
author: **10** Johan Bojer

emigrate **4** move, quit **5** leave **6** depart, remove **7** migrate

emigration **5** exile **6** exodus **12** expatriation

emigre **2** DP **5** alien, exile **7** evacuee, refugee **8** defector, emigrant, expellee, fugitive **9** immigrant **10** expatriate **15** displaced person **16** political refugee

Emile
author: **19** Jean Jacques Rousseau
treatise on: **9** education

Emilia
character in: **7** Othello
author: **11** Shakespeare

eminence **4** fame, hill, note, peak, rise **5** bluff, cliff, glory, knoll, ridge **6** height, repute, summit, upland **7** hillock, hummock **8** mountain, standing **9** celebrity, elevation, greatness, high place, high point **10** excellence, importance, notability, prominence, promontory, reputation **11** distinction, preeminence **12** elevated rank, high position, public esteem **15** conspicuousness

eminence grise **15** unofficial power
literally: **12** gray eminence

eminent **3** top **5** grand, great, noted **6** famous, signal, utmost **7** exalted, notable, unusual **8** elevated, esteemed, glorious, imposing, laureate, renowned **9** important, memorable, paramount, prominent, well-known **10** celebrated, noteworthy, preeminent, remarkable **11** high-ranking, illustrious, outstanding **13** distinguished, extraordinary

emir **4** amir, Arab, Turk **5** chief, emeer, ruler **6** leader, prince **9** chieftain, commander, dignitary

emissary **5** agent, envoy **6** deputy, herald, legate **7** courier **8** delegate **9** go-between, messenger **10** ambassador **14** representative

emission **5** fumes, smoke, waste **8** ejection, emitting, impurity, issuance, voidance **9** discharge, emanation, excretion, expulsion, extrusion, pollutant **10** sending out **11** throwing out **12** transmission

emit **4** beam, give, shed, vent **5** expel, issue **7** cast out, excrete, secrete, send out **8** dispatch, throw out, transmit **9** discharge, give forth, pour forth

Emma
author: **10** Jane Austen
character: **7** Mr Elton **9** Miss Bates, Mrs Weston **11** Jane Fairfax **12** Harriet Smith, Robert Martin **13** Emma Woodhouse **14** Frank Churchill **15** George Knightley

Emmanuel **7** Messiah **11** Jesus Christ
means: **9** God with us

emollient **3** oil **4** balm **5** balmy, cream, salve **6** lotion **7** calming, easeful, healing, unguent **8** allaying, lenitive, ointment, relaxing, soothing **9** assuasive, lubricant, relieving **10** palliative **11** alleviative, restorative

emolument **3** fee, pay **4** gain, wage **6** income, profit, salary **7** benefit, stipend **9** advantage **10** honorarium **12** compensation, remuneration

emotion **4** fear, hate, heat, love, zeal **5** anger, ardor, pride **6** fervor, sorrow, warmth **7** concern, despair, passion, sadness **8** jealousy **9** agitation, happiness, sentiment, vehemence **10** excitement **12** satisfaction

emotional **4** warm **5** fiery **6** ardent, moving **7** fervent, zealous **8** stirring, touching **9** excitable, impetuous, thrilling, wrought-up **10** high-strung, hysterical, passionate, responsive, vulnerable **11** impassioned, sentimental, tear-jerking **12** enthusiastic, heart-warming, heart-rending, soul-stirring **13** demonstrative, temperamental **14** hypersensitive

emotionalism **8** hysteria **9** gushiness, hysterics, melodrama, theatrics **11** mawkishness **13** melodramatics, show of emotion **14** sentimentality **17** demonstrativeness

emotionless **6** stolid **7** unmoved **9** apathetic, impassive, unfeeling **11** passionless, unemotional

emperor, empress **4** czar, king, shah **5** queen, ruler **6** caesar, kaiser, mikado, sultan **7** czarina, monarch, sultana **9** sovereign **14** dowager empress

Emperor Jones, The
author: **12** Eugene O'Neill
character: **4** Jeff **8** Smithers **11** Brutus Jones

Emperor's New Clothes, The
author: **21** Hans Christian Andersen

emphasis **6** accent, stress, weight **7** feature **10** focal point **12** accentuation, underscoring

emphasize **6** accent, stress **7** dwell on, feature, iterate, point up **9** press home, punctuate, underline **10** accentuate, underscore

emphatic **4** flat **6** marked, strong **7** certain, decided, express, telling **8** absolute, decisive, definite, distinct, forceful, striking, vigorous **9** assertive, insistent, momentous **10** pronounced, undeniable, unwavering, unyielding **11** categorical, conspicuous, significant, unequivocal, unqualified **12** unmistakable

empire **4** rule **5** realm **6** domain **8** dominion, imperium **11** sovereignty **12** commonwealth

Empire State
nickname of: 7 New York

Empire State of the South
nickname of: 7 Georgia

Empire Strikes Back, The
director: 13 Irvin Kershner
cast: 10 Kenny Baker, Mark Hamill (Luke Skywalker) 11 David Prowse, Peter Mayhew 12 Alec Guinness, Carrie Fisher (Princess Leia), Harrison Ford (Han Solo) 14 Anthony Daniels (C3P0) 16 Billy Dee Williams (Lando Calrissian)
sequel to: 8 Star Wars
sequel: 15 Return of the Jedi

empirical 9 firsthand, practical, pragmatic 12 experiential, experimental

employ 3 use 4 hire 5 apply 6 devote, engage, occupy, retain, take on 7 service, utilize 8 exercise, keep busy, put to use 9 make use of 10 commission, employment 12 retainership

employee 6 member, worker 8 hireling 9 job holder, underling 10 wage earner

employer 4 boss, firm 6 outfit 7 company 8 business 10 proprietor 12 organization 13 establishment

employment 3 job, use 4 line, task, work 5 chore, field, trade, using 6 employ 7 calling, pursuit, service 8 business, exercise, exertion, vocation 9 employing 10 engagement, occupation, profession 11 application, utilization 13 preoccupation

emporium 5 store 6 bazaar, market 9 warehouse 10 large store 12 general store 15 department store

empower 4 vest 5 allow, endow 6 enable, invest, permit 7 license 8 delegate, sanction 9 authorize 10 commission

empress 5 queen, ruler 7 czarina, monarch, sultana 9 sovereign

emprise 7 venture 9 adventure 10 enterprise 11 undertaking

emptied 6 used up 7 drained, vacated 8 consumed, depleted, finished 9 evacuated, exhausted

emptiness 4 void 6 vacuum 7 vacancy 8 bareness 10 barrenness, desolation, hollowness

empty 4 bare, dump, flow, idle, void 5 banal, drain, inane 6 futile, hollow, vacant 7 aimless, debouch, insipid, pour out, shallow, trivial, vacuous 8 evacuate 9 discharge, frivolous, worthless 10 unoccupied 11 meaningless, purposeless, unfulfilled, uninhabited 13 insignificant

empty space 3 gap 4 void 5 blank 6 cavity, lacuna, vacuum 7 vacancy

Empusae
form: 7 monster
eats: 3 man

empyrean 7 elysian, sublime 8 blissful, heavenly 9 celestial 12 paradisiacal

emu
also: 4 emeu
form: 4 bird
characteristic: 9 nonflying, three toed

emulate 3 ape 4 copy 5 mimic, rival 6 follow 7 imitate

emulative 5 model 9 exemplary

enable 3 aid 5 allow 6 assist, permit 7 benefit, empower, qualify, support 8 make able 10 capacitate, facilitate 15 make possible for

enact 4 pass 6 decree, ratify 7 approve 8 proclaim, sanction 9 authorize, institute, legislate 11 pass into law 12 vote to accept

enactment 3 law 4 bill 5 canon, edict, ukase 6 decree 7 statute 9 ordinance, prescript 11 legislation 12 proclamation, ratification

Enalus
loved: 7 Phineis
saved by: 7 dolphin

enamel 4 coat 5 paint 7 coating 12 glossy finish, tooth coating

enamor 5 charm 6 allure, attach, draw to, excite 7 bewitch, enchant 8 enthrall, entrance 9 captivate, enrapture, fascinate, infatuate 12 take a fancy to

enamored 6 in love 7 amorous 8 lovesick 10 infatuated

en arriere 8 backward

en avant 6 onward 7 forward

en bloc 8 as a whole

encage 3 pen 4 cage 5 pen in 6 coop up, lock up, shut in 7 confine 8 restrain 11 incarcerate

encamp 4 camp 7 bivouac 9 set up camp 10 pitch a tent

encampment 4 camp 5 tents 7 bivouac 8 tent city

encase 4 wrap 5 cover 6 enfold, enwrap 7 enclose, envelop, sheathe

enceinte 8 pregnant

Enceladus
form: 5 giant
hit by: 5 stone
stone flung by: 6 Athena
location: 6 Sicily
buried under: 9 Mount Etna

enchain 7 enslave, shackle 8 enthrall 11 put in chains 13 hold in bondage

enchant 5 charm 7 bewitch, delight 8 enthrall, entrance 9 captivate, enrapture, fascinate, hypnotize, mesmerize, transport 14 cast a spell over 16 place under a spell

enchanted 7 charmed, pleased 9 bewitched, delighted, entranced 10 captivated, enraptured, enthralled, spellbound 11 under a spell

enchanting 8 charming, pleasant 9 agreeable, wonderful 10 bewitching, delightful, entrancing 11 captivating, enthralling, fascinating, hypnotizing 12 spellbinding 15 casting a spell on 17 casting a spell over

enchantment 5 spell 6 allure, appeal 9 magnetism 10 attraction 11 captivation, fascination

enchantress 4 vamp 5 siren, witch 7 charmer, vampire 9 sorceress, temptress 10 seductress 11 femme fatale

Enchiridion
author: 11 St Augustine

encircle 4 gird, ring, wall 5 fence, hem in 6 circle, girdle 7 enclose, wreathe 8 surround 9 encompass 12 circumscribe

enclose, inclose 4 ring 6 circle, girdle, insert, wall in 7 close in, fence in, include 8 encircle, surround 9 encompass, send along 12 circumscribe

enclosed area 4 quad 5 court, patio 6 atrium 9 courtyard 10 quadrangle

enclosure 3 sty 4 cage, coop, jail, wall 5 fence, hedge, stall 6 corral, kennel, pigsty 7 paddock, wrapper 8 envelope, stockade 9 cartridge, inclosure 10 receptacle

encomium 5 paean 6 eulogy 7 plaudit, tribute 8 citation

9 laudation, panegyric **11** acclamation

encompass 4 hold, ring **5** cover, hem in **6** circle, embody, girdle, take in, wall in **7** contain, embrace, enclose, fence in, include, involve, touch on **8** comprise, encircle, surround **11** incorporate **12** circumscribe

encounter 4 bout, face, meet **5** brush, clash, fight **6** affray, battle, combat, endure, fracas, suffer **7** run into, sustain, undergo **8** come upon, confront, meet with, skirmish **9** clash with **10** chance upon, engagement, experience **11** grapple with **12** do battle with, meet and fight, skirmish with **13** confrontation **14** contend against, engage in combat, hostile meeting **18** come face to face with

Encounters with the Archdruid
author: 10 John McPhee

encourage 3 aid **4** help, spur, sway **5** boost, cheer, egg on, favor, impel, rally **6** assist, exhort, foster, induce, prompt **7** advance, forward, further, hearten, inspire, promote **8** embolden, inspirit, reassure **10** give hope to

encouragement 4 lift **5** boost **6** praise **7** backing, support **11** approbation, encouraging, reassurance **12** shot in the arm **13** reinforcement

encroach 6 invade **7** impinge, intrude, overrun, violate **8** infringe, overstep, trespass **9** break into, interfere **10** transgress **11** make inroads

encumber 3 tax **4** lade, load **6** burden, hinder, impede, saddle **8** handicap, load down, obstruct, slow down **9** weigh down **13** inconvenience

encumbrance 4 load, onus **6** burden **9** hindrance **10** impediment **11** obstruction **13** inconvenience

Encyclopedia
author: 9 D'Alembert **12** Denis Diderot

encyclopedic 5 broad **7** erudite **9** scholarly, universal **10** exhaustive **11** wide-ranging **13** comprehensive **15** all-encompassing

end 3 aim **4** edge, goal, halt, kill, ruin, stop **5** cease, close, death, issue, limit, scrap **6** border, demise, design, effect, ending, finale, finish, object, result, run out, upshot, windup **7** destroy, outcome, purpose, remnant **8** boundary, conclude, fragment, leave off, leftover, terminus **9** cessation, eradicate, extremity, finish off, intention, objective, terminate **10** annihilate, completion, conclusion, denouement, expiration, extinction, extinguish, put an end to, settlement **11** consequence, culmination, destruction, exterminate, fulfillment, termination **12** annihilation, consummation, draw to a close **13** extermination **19** bring down the curtain

endanger 4 risk **6** expose, hazard **7** imperil **8** threaten **10** compromise, jeopardize **11** put in danger

endear 8 make dear **10** ingratiate **11** make beloved

endearment 7 pet name **9** sweet talk **10** loving word **12** sweet nothing **13** fond utterance

endeavor 3 aim, job, try **4** seek, work **5** essay, labor **6** aspire, career, effort, strive, work at **7** attempt **8** exertion, interest, striving, struggle, vocation **9** take pains, undertake **10** do one's best, enterprise, occupation **11** undertaking **12** make an effort **13** preoccupation

ended 4 done, over **6** ceased, closed, halted, runout **7** expired, stopped, wound up **8** finished, over with, resulted **9** completed, concluded, destroyed **10** terminated **11** annihilated **12** discontinued, exterminated

Endeis
father: 6 Sciron
husband: 6 Aeacus
son: 6 Peleus **7** Telamon
stepson: 6 Phocus

Enderby
author: 14 Anthony Burgess

end from which
Latin: 12 terminus a quo

ending 3 end **5** close **6** finale, finish, windup **9** cessation **10** completion, conclusion, expiration **11** culmination, termination **12** consummation

ending point
Latin: 14 terminus ad quem

Ending Up
author: 12 Kingsley Amis

endless 7 eternal **8** constant, infinite, unbroken, unending **9** boundless, continual, perpetual, unlimited **10** continuous, persistent, without end **11** everlasting, measureless, never-ending **12** interminable **13** uninterrupted

endlessly 7 forever **10** constantly **11** ceaselessly, continually, perpetually **12** continuously
Latin: 11 ad infinitum

endocrine system
component: 5 ovary **6** testes, thymus **7** adrenal, thyroid **9** pituitary **11** parathyroid

endocuticle
consists of: 6 chitin

end of the century
French: 11 fin de siecle

End of the Road, The
author: 9 John Barth

end of the world 8 doomsday **10** Armageddon **11** Judgment Day **13** Day of Judgment **15** the Last Judgment

End of the World News, The
author: 14 Anthony Burgess

endorse, indorse 2 OK **4** back, sign **6** affirm, ratify, second **7** approve, certify, support **8** advocate, champion, sanction, validate, vouch for **9** authorize, recommend **11** countersign, stand behind, subscribe to **14** lend one's name to

endorsement 2 OK **7** support **8** approval **9** signature **10** acceptance **12** commendation, ratification **14** seal of approval **16** official sanction

endow 4 will **5** award, bless, equip, favor, grace, grant, leave **6** accord, bestow, confer, invest, supply **7** furnish, provide **8** bequeath, settle on

endowed 6 graced **7** blessed, favored **8** bestowed, enriched, provided **10** bequeathed

endowment 4 gift **5** award, flair, grant **6** legacy, talent **7** ability, bequest, faculty **8** aptitude, donation **9** attribute **10** capability **11** benefaction, natural gift

end to which
Latin: 14 terminus ad quem

endue 5 dress, endow, equip, indue, put on **6** bestow, clothe, outfit, supply **7** furnish

endurable 8 bearable **9** tolerable **11** sustainable

endurance 7 stamina **8** strength, tenacity **9** fortitude, hardihood, stability **10** durability, permanence, resolution **11** durableness, persistence **12** immutability, perseverance, staying power **13** tenaciousness **14** changelessness **16** stick-to-itiveness

endure **4** bear, last, live **5** brave, brook, stand **6** live on, remain, suffer **7** persist, prevail, sustain, undergo, weather **8** continue, cope with, tolerate **9** go through, withstand **10** experience **11** bear up under, countenance

enduring **7** abiding, durable, eternal, lasting **8** constant, unending **9** immutable, permanent, steadfast **10** changeless, continuing, unchanging **11** everlasting, long-lasting **12** indissoluble

Endymion
author: **9** John Keats
form: **5** youth
father: **8** Aethlios
mother: **6** Calyce
loved by: **4** Moon **6** Selene
son: **5** Epeus, Paeon **7** Aetolus
number of daughters: **5** fifty
granddaughter: **7** Hyrmina

enemy **3** foe **5** rival **7** nemesis **8** armed foe, attacker, opponent **9** adversary, assailant, detractor **10** antagonist, competitor

Enemy of the People, An
author: **11** Henrik Ibsen

energetic **5** alert, brisk, peppy, zippy **6** active, lively, robust **7** dynamic **8** animated, forceful, restless, spirited, vigorous **9** go-getting **11** hard-working, high-powered, industrious, quick-witted **12** enthusiastic

energize **7** animate, enliven, quicken **8** vitalize **9** galvanize, stimulate **10** invigorate, strengthen

energy **2** go **3** pep, vim, zip **4** elan, zeal, zest **5** drive, force, power, verve, vigor **6** hustle **8** dynamism, vitality, vivacity **9** animation **10** enterprise, liveliness

enervate **3** fag **4** bush, tire **5** weary **6** tucker, weaken **7** deplete, disable, exhaust, fatigue, wash out **8** enfeeble **9** prostrate **10** debilitate, devitalize **13** sap one's energy

enervated **5** spent **6** effete, wasted **7** languid, worn-out **8** fatigued, listless, sluggish, unmanned, unnerved, weakened **9** enfeebled, exhausted, lethargic, washed out **11** debilitated, devitalized, emasculated

enervation **7** fatigue **9** tiredness, weariness **10** exhaustion

en famille **11** in the family

Enfants Terribles, Les
author: **11** Jean Cocteau

enfant terrible **16** indiscreet person **17** incorrigible child **19** irresponsible person

enfeeble **3** sap **6** impair, weaken **8** enervate **10** debilitate

enfin **7** finally **8** in the end **12** in conclusion

enfold **4** veil, wrap **5** cloak, cover **6** encase, enwrap, shroud **7** blanket, contain, embrace, enclose, envelop, sheathe **8** surround

enforce **5** apply, exact **6** defend, impose **7** execute, support **8** carry out, insist on **9** implement **10** administer

enforcement **5** force **6** duress **7** defense, support **8** coercion, pressure **9** execution **10** compulsion, constraint, imposition, obligation **11** carrying out **13** necessitation, strengthening **14** implementation

engage **4** hire **6** absorb, combat, employ, occupy, pledge, retain, secure, take on **7** betroth, engross, involve, partake, promise, war with **8** affiance, embark on, set about, takepart **9** enter into, fight with, undertake **10** commission **11** busy oneself, participate **12** give battle to **15** take into service

engaged **5** hired, in use **6** active, took on **7** partook, pledged, secured **8** absorbed, employed, involved, occupied, promised, retained, took part **9** affianced, betrothed, engrossed, undertook **10** embarked on **11** entered into, particpated **15** took into service

engagement **3** gig, job **4** bout, date, duty, fray, post **5** banns, berth, brush, fight, troth **6** action, battle, billet, combat **7** contest, meeting, scuffle **8** conflict, position, skirmish **9** betrothal, encounter, situation **10** affiancing, commitment, employment, obligation **11** appointment, arrangement

engage pleasantly **5** amuse, charm **6** divert, please **7** beguile, delight **8** enthrall, interest **9** entertain

engaging **7** likable, lovable, winning, winsome **8** charming, fetching, pleasing **9** agreeable, appealing, disarming **10** attractive, enchanting **11** captivating **12** ingratiating

Engels, Friedrich
author of: **18** Communist Manifesto (with Karl Marx)

engender **5** beget, breed, cause **7** produce **8** generate, occasion **10** bring about, give rise to **11** precipitate

engine
inventor:
of compression ignition: **7** Daimler
of electric ignition: **4** Benz
of gas (compound): **10** Eickemeyer
of gasoline: **7** Brayton, Daimler
of piston steam: **4** Watt **8** Newcomen

engineer **5** pilot **6** driver, hogger **7** builder, hoghead, planner **8** maneuver, motorman, operator **10** accomplish

England ***see box***

Engles, Friedrich
author of: **18** Communist Manifesto (with Karl Marx)

English, Julian
character in: **20** Appointment in Samarra
author: **5** O'Hara

English Mail-Coach, The
author: **15** Thomas DeQuincey

engrave **3** cut **4** etch **5** carve, stamp **6** chisel **7** decorate, stipple

engraving **3** cut, die **5** print, stamp **7** etching, gravure **9** woodblock **11** copperplate, lithography **12** photogravure

engross **4** hold **6** absorb, arrest, engage, occupy, take up **7** immerse, involve **9** preoccupy

engrossed **4** busy, deep **6** intent **7** engaged **8** absorbed, immersed, involved, occupied **11** preoccupied

engrossing **8** engaging, exciting **9** absorbing, arresting, thrilling **10** intriguing **11** captivating, fascinating, interesting

engrossment **9** immersion **10** absorption, intentness **11** involvement **13** concentration, preoccupation

engulf **4** bury **5** swamp **6** deluge **7** envelop, immerse, overrun **8** inundate, submerge **9** swallow up

enhance **4** lift **5** add to, boost, raise **7** augment, elevate, magnify **8** heighten, redouble **9** embellish, intensify **10** complement

England

other name: 6 Albion **7** Britain **9** Britannia **12** Great Britain

capital/largest city: 6 London

others: 3 Ely **4** Bath, Deal, Hull, Ryde, Ware, York **5** Blyth, Brent, Derby, Dover, Erith, Flint, Leeds, Ripon, Truro, Wigan **6** Barnet, Bolton, Bootle, Camden, Durham, Ealing, Exeter, Henley, Jarrow, Leyton, Oldham, Oxford, Yeovil **7** Bristol, Bromley, Burnley, Chelsea, Croydon, Enfield, Grimsby, Halifax, Hornsey, Ipswich, Lambeth, Newport, Norwich, Preston, Salford, Seaford, Westham **8** Bradford, Brighton, Cornwall, Coventry, Dewsbury, Hastings, Plymouth **9** Greenwich, Liverpool, Newcastle, Sheffield **10** Birmingham, Manchester **15** Stratford-on-Avon

school: 4 Eton **5** Leeds, Rugby **6** Harrow, London, Oxford **9** Cambridge, Sandhurst **23** London School of Economics

division: 4 Avon, Kent **5** Devon, Essex, Salop **6** Dorset, Durham, Surrey, Sussex **7** Cambria, Norfolk, Suffolk **8** Cheshire, Cornwall, Hereford, Somerset **9** Hampshire, Wiltshire, Worcester, Yorkshire **10** Derbyshire, Humberside, Lancashire **11** Oxfordshire, Tyne and Wear **12** Bedfordshire, Lincolnshire, Warwickshire, West Midlands **13** Hertfordshire, Staffordshire **14** Cambridgeshire, Leicestershire, Northumberland **15** Buckinghamshire, Gloucestershire, Nottinghamshire **16** Northamptonshire

head of state: 4 king **5** queen **7** monarch

measure: 3 cut, lea, pin, rod, ton, tun, vat **4** acre, bind, butt, comb, coom, foot, gill, goad, hand, hank, heer, hide, inch, last, line, mile, nail, pace, palm, peck, pint, pipe, pole, pool, rood, rope, sack, seam, span, trug, typp, wist, yard, yoke **5** bodge, chain, coomb, cubit, digit, float, floor, fluid, hutch, jugum, minim, ounce, perch, point, prime, quart, skein, stack, truss **6** barrel, bovate, bushel, cranne, fathom, firkin, gallon, hobbet, hobbit, league, manent, oxgang, pottle, runlet, square, strike, sulung, thread, tierce **7** auchlet, furlong, kenning, quarter, rundlet, seamile, spindle, tertian, virgate **8** carucate, chaldron, hogshead, landyard, puncheon, quadrant, standard

monetary unit: 3 ora **4** rial **5** ackey, crown, groat, noble, pence, penny, pound, sprat, unite **6** bawbee, florin, guinea, seskin **7** angelet, hapenny **8** farthing, shilling, sixpence, tuppence

weight: 3 bag, kip, tod, ton **4** keel, last, mast, maun **5** barge, fagot, grain, pound, score, stone, truss **6** bushel, cental, fangot, fother, fotmal, pocket **7** quarter, sarpler

island: 3 Man **4** Holy **5** Farne, Lundy, Wight **6** Coquet, Mersea, Scilly, Thanet, Tresco, Walney **7** Bardsey, Channel, Hayling, Ireland, Sheppey **8** Anglesea, Anglesey, Foulness, Holyhead

lake: 8 Grasmere **9** Ennerdale, Ullswater, Wastwater **10** Buttermere, Windermere **12** Derwentwater **13** Coniston Water

mountain: 5 Black **7** Pennine, Snowdon **8** Cambrian, Cumbrian

***hill:* 6** Formby, Lizard, Mendip **7** Brendon, Cemmaes, Trevose

highest point: 11 Scafell Pike

river: 3 Cam, Dee, Don, Esk, Exe, Lea, Nen, Ure, Wye **4** Aire, Avon, Eden, Lune, Nene, Nidd, Ouse, Penk, Tame, Tees, Till, Tyne, Wear, Yare **5** Anker, Colne, Deben, Stour, Swale, Tamar, Tawar, Trent, Tweed **6** Humber, Kennet, Mersey, Rother, Severn, Thames, Wharfe, Witham **7** Derwent, Parrett, Waveney, Welland **8** Torridge **9** Yorkshire **12** Wensum Ribble

sea: 5 Irish, North **6** Celtic **8** Atlantic

physical feature:

***bay:* 3** Tor **4** Lyme, Wash **5** Start **6** Mounts **7** Bigbury **8** Bideford, Cardigan, Falmouth, Tremadoc, Weymouth

***chalk cliffs:* 5** Dover

***channel:* 6** Solent **7** Bristol, English **8** Spithead

***firth:* 6** Solway

***forest:* 5** Arden **6** Exmoor **8** Dartmoor, Sherwood

***peninsula:* 8** Portland

***point:* 4** Naze **5** Lynas, Morte, Sales **6** Dodman, Lizard, Prawle **8** Hartland, Landsend

***region:* 5** Weald **8** Midlands **10** West Riding **11** North Riding **12** Lake District

***valley:* 4** Coom, Eden, Tees, Tyne **5** Combe, Coomb **6** Coquet

people: 4 Celt, Pict **5** Jutes, Norse, Saxon **6** Angles, Briton, Norman, Viking

***artist:* 6** Romney, Turner **7** Hogarth **8** Reynolds, Rossetti **9** Constable **12** Gainsborough

***author:* 3** Kyd **4** Bede, Hume, Pope, Shaw **5** Auden, Bacon, Blake, Burke, Byron, Defoe, Donne, Eliot, Hardy, Joyce, Keats, Scott, Swift, Waugh, Wilde, Woolf **6** Austen, Bronte, Bunyan, Conrad, Dryden, Gibbon, Jonson, Milton, Newton, Ruskin, Sterne, Thomas **7** Boswell, Chaucer, Dickens, Kipling, Marlowe, Shelley, Spenser, Walpole **8** Browning, Fielding, Lawrence, Sheridan, Smollett, Tennyson, Trollope **9** Churchill, Coleridge, Stevenson, Thackeray **10** Galsworthy, Richardson, Thomas More, Wordsworth **11** Shakespeare

***king:* 3** Hal **4** Cnut, John, Lear **5** Henry, James **6** Alfred, Arthur, Canute, Edmund, Edward, Egbert, George, Harold **7** Charles, Richard, Stephen, William **9** Cymbeline **18** Richard Coeur de Lion **19** Richard the Lionheart

***leader:* 4** Eden, Grey, Lamb, Peel, Pitt **5** Heath **6** Attlee, Wilson **7** Baldwin, Balfour, Canning, Fitzroy, Spencer, Stanley, Walpole **8** Disraeli, Stanhope, Thatcher **9** Cavendish, Churchill, Gladstone, Grenville, MacDonald, Macmillan **10** Palmerston, Wellington **11** Chamberlain, Douglas-Home, Lloyd George

***queen:* 3** Mab **4** Anne, Bess, Jane, Mary **7** Eleanor **8** Boadicea, Victoria **9** Catherine, Charlotte, Elizabeth, Guinivere **10** Bloody Mary **11** Jane Seymour

(*continued*)

England *(continued)*
language: **7** English
religion: **6** Jewish **8** Anglican **9** Methodist, Unitarian **13** Roman Catholic **15** Church of England
place:
bridge: **5** Tower **6** London **11** Westminster
cathedral: **4** York **6** Exeter **7** St Pauls **8** St Albans **9** Salisbury **10** Canterbury, Winchester **16** Westminster Abbey
clock: **6** Big Ben
fortification: **12** Hadrian's Wall
museum: **4** Tate **7** British **9** Ashmolean **17** Madame Tussauds Wax
palace: **7** St James, Windsor **10** Buckingham **12** Hampton Court
racetrack: **5** Ascot
ruins: **10** Stonehenge
street: **5** Fleet **12** Threadneedle **16** Piccadilly Circus
tower: **6** London
feature:
dance: **6** morris
food:
bacon: **6** gammon, rasher **7** streaky
beer: **5** grout, stout
cookie: **7** biscuit
dessert: **6** trifle **11** plum pudding
dish: **12** fish and chips **14** Cornish pasties **15** bubble and squeak **16** Yorkshire pudding
drink: **3** ale, tea **6** squash

enhancement **11** heightening, improvement **15** intensification

Enid
character in: **12** The Mabinogion **15** Idylls of the King **16** Arthurian romance
author: **8** Tennyson

enigma **6** puzzle, riddle, secret **7** mystery **8** question **9** conundrum **10** perplexity

enigmatic, enigmatical **7** cryptic, elusive **8** baffling, puzzling **9** ambiguous, equivocal, secretive **10** mysterious, perplexing **11** inscrutable, paradoxical **12** unfathomable **14** indecipherable

Eniopeus
mentioned in: **5** Iliad
charioteer of: **6** Hector
slain by: **8** Diomedes

enjoin **3** ask, ban, bar, beg, bid **4** urge, warn **6** advise, charge, direct, forbid **7** command, counsel, entreat **8** admonish, call upon, instruct, prohibit, restrain, restrict **9** interdict, proscribe

enjoy **3** own **4** have, like **5** eat up, fancy, savor **6** admire, relish **7** possess **9** delight in, rejoice in **10** appreciate **11** think well of **13** be blessed with, be pleased with, get a kick out of **14** take pleasure in **16** have the benefit of

enjoyable **8** pleasant, pleasing **9** agreeable, fun-filled, rewarding **10** delightful, gratifying, satisfying **11** pleasurable

enjoyment **3** fun, joy **4** zest **5** gusto, right **6** relish **7** benefit, delight **8** blessing, exercise, good time, pleasure **9** advantage, amusement, diversion, happiness, privilege **10** possession, recreation **11** prerogative **12** satisfaction **13** entertainment, gratification

Enki
origin: **8** Sumerian
god of: **6** wisdom
habitat: **5** water
corresponds to: **2** Ea

Enkidu
origin: **8** Sumerian
servant of: **9** Gilgamesh
friend of: **9** Gilgamesh

enlarge **4** grow **5** add to, swell, widen **6** expand, extend **7** amplify, augment, broaden, develop, expound, inflate, magnify **8** elongate, increase, lengthen, multiply **9** discourse, elaborate, expatiate

enlarged **7** swollen, widened **8** expanded, extended, inflated **9** amplified, broadened, distended, elongated, magnified

enlargement **6** growth **8** addition, increase, swelling, widening **9** expansion, extension, inflation **10** broadening, elongation **11** development, elaboration, expatiation, lengthening **12** augmentation **13** amplification, magnification **14** multiplication

enlighten **5** edify **6** advise, inform, wise up **7** apprise, clarify, educate **8** civilize, instruct **9** make aware **10** illuminate **12** sophisticate

enlightenment **8** learning **9** erudition, knowledge **11** edification, instruction
French: **15** Eclaircissement
German: **10** Aufklarung

Enlil
origin: **8** Sumerian
king of: **4** gods
god of: **3** air
son: **5** Ninib **7** Ninurta

enlist **4** join **6** engage, enroll, join up, obtain, secure, sign up **7** procure, recruit **8** register **9** volunteer **19** gain the assistance of

enlistment **9** signing up **10** admittance, enrollment, recruiting

enliven **4** fire **5** pep up, renew **6** excite, vivify, wake up **7** animate, cheer up, quicken **8** brighten, vitalize **10** make lively, rejuvenate

enlivened **7** revived **8** animated, vivified **9** refreshed **11** invigorated

en masse **7** in a body **8** as a group, as a whole, in a group, together **11** all together

enmesh **4** trap **5** catch, snare, snarl **6** tangle **7** embroil, ensnare, entwine, involve **8** entangle

enmity **6** animus, hatred, malice, rancor, strife **7** ill will

8 acrimony, bad blood **9** animosity, antipathy, hostility **10** bitterness

Ennead **7** dieties
origin: **8** Egyptian
number: **4** nine

ennoble **5** raise **6** refine **7** dignify, elevate

Ennomus
vocation: **6** angler
joined: **7** Trojans

Ennosigaeus
epithet of: **8** Poseidon
means: **11** earth shaker

ennui **6** apathy, tedium **7** boredom, languor **9** lassitude, weariness **12** indifference, listlessness
Latin: **12** taedium vitae

Enoch
father: **4** Cain **5** Jared
son: **10** Methuselah
grandfather: **4** Adam

Enoch Arden
author: **18** Alfred Lord Tennyson
character: **8** Annie Lee **9** Philip Ray **10** Miriam Lane

enormity **8** baseness, evilness, hugeness, vastness, vileness, villainy **9** depravity, immensity, largeness, malignity **10** wickedness **11** heinousness, viciousness **12** enormousness **13** atrociousness, monstrousness, offensiveness **14** outrageousness

enormous **4** huge, vast **7** immense, mammoth, massive, titanic **8** colossal, gigantic **10** gargantuan, prodigious, tremendous **11** elephantine **14** Brobdingnagian

enormousness **8** enormity, hugeness, vastness **9** amplitude, immensity, largeness **11** massiveness

Enormous Room, The
author: **10** e e cummings

Enos
father: **4** Seth
grandfather: **4** Adam

enough **5** ample, amply **6** plenty **7** copious **8** abundant, adequate, passably **9** tolerably **10** abundantly, adequately, competence, plentitude, reasonably, sufficient **11** ample supply, full measure, sufficiency **12** sufficiently **14** satisfactorily

enounce **8** set forth **9** enunciate **10** articulate

en passant **8** by the way **9** in passing

enrage **5** anger **6** madden **7** incense, inflame **9** aggravate, infuriate **11** make furious **13** make one see red **14** throw into a rage **17** make one's blood boil

enraged **3** mad **5** angry, irate **7** angered, furious, violent **8** incensed, inflamed, maddened, provoked **9** irritated **10** aggravated, infuriated **11** exasperated

en rapport **8** in accord **9** congenial **10** in sympathy **11** in agreement

enrapture **5** charm **6** thrill **7** beguile, bewitch, delight, enchant **8** enthrall, entrance, hold rapt **9** captivate, transport

enraptured **4** rapt **8** beatific, blissful, ecstatic **9** delighted, enchanted **10** enthralled **11** transported

enravel **5** snare, snarl, twist **6** enmesh, tangle **7** ensnare, ensnarl, entwine **8** entangle **10** intertwine

enrich **5** adorn, endow **6** refine **7** elevate, enhance, fortify, improve, upgrade **8** make rich **9** embellish **10** ameliorate **11** make wealthy **15** feather one's nest

enroll **4** join **5** admit, enter **6** accept, engage, enlist, join up, sign up, take on **7** recruit **8** register

enrollment **6** roster **9** enrolling, signing up **10** admittance, enlistment, recruiting **12** registration **13** matriculation

en route **8** on the way **9** in transit, on the road

ensconce **4** bury, hide, seat **5** lodge **6** settle **7** conceal, secrete, shelter **9** establish

ensemble **5** getup **6** attire, outfit, troupe **7** company, costume **8** assembly, entirety, grouping, totality **9** aggregate

ensign **4** flag, jack, mark, sign **5** badge **6** banner, colors, emblem, pennon, symbol **7** pennant **8** insignia, standard

enslave **6** addict, subdue **7** capture, control, enchain, shackle **8** dominate, enthrall **9** indenture, subjugate **13** hold in bondage, put in shackles

enslavement **4** yoke **6** chains, thrall **7** bondage, serfdom, slavery **9** captivity, servitude, thralldom, vassalage **11** subjugation

ensnare **4** trap **5** catch **6** enmesh, entrap, tangle **7** enravel **8** entangle

Ensor, James
born: **6** Ostend **7** Belgium
artwork: **8** Intrigue **19** Bourgeois Living Room **25** Entry of Christ into Brussels **26** The Tribulations of St Anthony **29** Self-Portrait Surrounded by Masks

enstatite
source: **5** Burma, Mogok

ensue **6** derive, follow, result **7** succeed **10** come to pass **13** come afterward

ensuing **8** eventual **9** following, resulting **10** consequent, succeeding

en suite **6** in a set **9** in a series **12** in succession

ensure, insure **5** guard **6** assure, clinch, secure **7** protect, warrant **8** be sure of, make safe, make sure **9** guarantee, safeguard **13** make certain of

entail **6** demand **7** call for, include, involve, require **8** occasion **11** incorporate, necessitate

entangle **4** trap **5** catch, mix up, snare, snarl **6** enmesh, foul up, muddle, tangle **7** confuse, embroil, enravel, ensnare, involve **8** encumber **9** embarrass, implicate **10** complicate, compromise, intertwine

entanglement **5** mixup, snarl **6** foul-up, muddle **7** problem **9** confusion, imbroglio **10** difficulty, entrapment **11** embroilment **12** complication

Entellus
vocation: **5** boxer
home: **6** Sicily
defeated: **5** Dares

entente **4** pact **6** accord, treaty **7** compact **8** alliance, covenant **9** agreement, consensus, unanimity **10** consortium **12** conciliation **13** rapprochement, understanding **14** likemindedness

entente cordiale **21** friendly understanding

enter **4** go in, join, list, post **6** arrive, come in, record **8** enlist in, enroll in, inscribe, pass into, set out on, trespass **9** penetrate, sign up for **10** embark upon, take part in

enterprise **4** push, task, zeal **5** drive, vigor **6** daring, effort, energy, spirit **7** attempt, program, project, venture **8** ambition, boldness, campaign, endeavor, industry **9** alertness, eagerness, ingenuity, operation **10** enthusiasm, initiative **11** undertaking, willingness **14** aggressiveness **15** adventurousness

enterprising **4** bold, keen **5** alert, eager **6** active **7** earnest, zealous **8** intrepid **9** ambitious, energetic, inventive, wide-awake **10** aggressive **11** hardworking, industrious, self-reliant, up-and-coming, venturesome **12** enthusiastic

entertain **4** heed **5** admit, amuse, charm **6** absorb, divert, foster, harbor, please, ponder, regale **7** beguile, delight, dwell on, engross, imagine, nurture, support **8** consider, enthrall, interest, muse over, play host **10** cogitate on, give a party, have guests, keep in mind, think about **11** contemplate **13** keep open house

entertainer **4** host **5** actor **6** amuser, artist, dancer, singer **7** hostess **8** magician, musician **9** performer

entertaining **3** fun **7** amusing, hosting **8** charming, pleasing **9** beguiling, diverting, enjoyable **10** delightful, hostessing **11** playing host **12** having guests **14** having people in

entertainment **3** fun **4** play **7** novelty, pastime **8** good time, pleasure **9** amusement, diversion, enjoyment **10** recreation **11** distraction **12** satisfaction
French: **14** divertissement

enter upon **5** begin **6** assume **9** undertake

enthrall, enthral **5** charm, rivet **6** seduce, thrill **7** beguile, bewitch, enchant, enslave **8** entrance, intrigue, transfix **9** captivate, enrapture, fascinate, hypnotize, overpower, spellbind, subjugate, transport **13** keep in bondage **14** put into slavery

enthralled **4** rapt **8** beguiled, enslaved **9** bewitched, enchanted, entranced, in bondage, intrigued **10** captivated, enraptured, fascinated, hypnotized, spellbound, subjugated

enthusiasm **4** love, rage, zeal, zest **5** ardor, craze, hobby, mania **6** fervor, relish **7** elation, passion **8** devotion, interest, keenness **9** diversion, eagerness **10** excitement, exuberance, hobbyhorse **11** distraction, pet activity **12** anticipation

enthusiast **3** bug, fan, nut **4** buff **5** freak **6** addict **7** devotee, fanatic **10** aficionado

enthusiastic **5** eager **6** ardent, fervid **7** fervent, zealous **8** spirited **9** exuberant **10** passionate, unstinting **11** unqualified **12** wholehearted

entice **4** coax, lure **5** tempt **6** allure, incite, induce, seduce **7** attract, beguile, wheedle **8** inveigle, persuade

enticement **4** bait, draw, lure **6** allure **9** seduction, siren song **10** attraction, temptation

entire **4** full **5** gross, total, whole **6** in toto, intact **8** absolute, complete, thorough, unbroken **9** undamaged **10** unimpaired **12** all-inclusive

entirely **5** fully **6** wholly **7** totally, utterly **10** absolutely, altogether, completely, thoroughly **12** unreservedly **13** unqualifiedly
French: **9** tout a fait

entitle **3** dub, tag **4** call, name **5** allow, label, style, title **6** enable, permit **7** qualify **9** authorize, designate **12** make eligible

entity **4** body **5** being, thing **6** matter, object **7** article **8** creature, presence, quantity **9** real thing, structure, substance **10** individual

entomb **4** bury **5** inter **7** confine

entombment **6** burial **9** interment **10** inhumation

Entommeures, Frere Jean des
character in: **22** Gargantua and Pantagruel
author: **8** Rabelais

entourage **5** court, staff, suite, train **6** convoy, escort **7** cortege, retinue **9** followers, following **10** associates, attendants, companions

entrails **4** guts **5** offal **6** bowels **7** innards, insides, viscera **10** intestines

entrance **4** door, gate **5** charm, entry, way in **6** access, entree, portal **7** beguile, bewitch, delight, doorway, gateway, gladden, ingress, opening **8** approach, coming in, enthrall **9** captivate, enrapture, fascinate, hypnotize, mesmerize, spellbind, transport **10** admittance, appearance, passageway **12** introduction

entranced **4** rapt **7** charmed **8** beguiled **9** entralled, rapturous **10** enraptured, fascinated, spellbound **11** carried away, transported

entranceway **5** entry, foyer, way in **7** doorway, ingress **8** entryway **9** front hall, vestibule

entrancing **6** lovely **8** adorable, charming **9** appealing, beautiful, beguiling, disarming **10** bewitching, delightful **11** captivating, fascinating **12** irresistible

entrap **3** bag, nab **4** hook, land, nail **5** catch, snare, tempt **6** allure, collar, drag in, draw in, entice, rope in, seduce, suck in **7** beguile, capture, ensnare **8** inveigle

entreat **3** beg **6** adjure, enjoin, exhort **7** beseech, implore, request **8** appeal to, petition **9** importune, plead with **10** supplicate

entreaty **4** plea **6** appeal, prayer **8** petition **11** importunity **12** supplication

entree **4** pull **5** entry **6** access **7** ingress **8** entrance, main dish **9** admission **10** acceptance, admittance, main course

entremets **8** side dish

entrench, intrench **3** fix, set **4** root **5** dig in, embed, plant **6** anchor **7** implant, ingrain, install, solidly **8** ensconce **12** establish

entrenched leaders **11** ruling class **12** powers that be **13** Establishment **14** power structure

entre nous **9** between us, privately **14** confidentially **15** between you and me **16** between me and thee, between ourselves **18** in strict confidence

entrepot **5** depot **9** warehouse **18** distribution center

entrepreneur **7** manager **8** director **9** organizer **10** impresario **11** coordinator

entrust, intrust **5** trust **6** assign, commit **7** consign **8** delegate, hand over, turn over **9** authorize **10** charge with

entrustment **10** delegation **13** authorization, commissioning

entry **3** way **4** door, gate, item, memo, note **5** foyer, way in **6** access, entree, minute, portal, record **7** account, doorway, gateway, ingress, jotting **8** approach, entrance **9** admission, vestibule **10** admittance, appearance, competitor, contestant, memorandum, passageway **11** entranceway **12** entrance hall, introduction, registration

entwine, intwine 4 fold, lace, wind **5** braid, plait, twine, twist, weave **9** interlace **10** interweave

enumerable 6 finite **7** limited **11** denumerable

enumerate 3 add **4** cite, list **5** add up, count, sum up, tally, total **6** detail, number, relate **7** count up, recount, specify, tick off **8** numerate, spell out, tabulate

enumeration 4 list **5** tally **7** account, listing **8** adding up, addition, citation, tallying, totaling **9** checklist, detailing, numbering, reckoning, summing up **10** counting up, recounting, tabulation, ticking off **11** spelling out

enunciate 5 sound, speak, voice **8** vocalize **10** articulate **15** utter distinctly **16** pronounce clearly

enunciation 6 accent, speech **7** diction **9** utterance **12** articulation **13** pronunciation

envelop 4 hide, veil, wrap **5** cloak, cover **6** encase, enfold, engulf, enwrap, shroud, swathe **7** blanket, conceal, contain, enclose, obscure, sheathe, swaddle **8** encircle, surround **9** encompass

envelope 5 cover **6** jacket **8** covering, wrapping

envenom 4 sour **6** rankle **8** embitter **13** make poisonous

enviable 5 lucky **8** salutary **9** agreeable, covetable, desirable, excellent, fortunate **10** beneficial **12** advantageous

envious 5 green **7** jealous **8** covetous, grudging, spiteful **9** jaundiced, resentful

enviousness 4 envy **8** jealousy **10** resentment **12** covetousness **13** resentfulness **19** the green-eyed monster

environment 5 scene **6** locale, medium, milieu **7** climate, element, habitat, setting **8** ambience **9** situation **10** atmosphere, background **12** surroundings **13** circumstances
French: 11 mise en scene

environs 6 exurbs **7** suburbs **8** vicinity **9** outskirts, precincts **11** outer limits **12** outlying area **15** surrounding area

envisage 5 fancy **7** dream of, dream up, imagine, picture **8** conceive, envision **9** conjure up, visualize **11** contemplate **13** conceptualize **14** have a picture of **16** picture to oneself

envoy 5 agent **6** deputy, legate **7** attache, courier **8** delegate, emissary, minister **9** messenger, middleman **10** ambassador **12** intermediary **14** representative

envy 5 greed, spite **6** resent **8** begrudge, grudging, jealousy **10** resentment **11** be jealous of, enviousness, malevolence **12** covetousness **13** resentfulness **16** be spiteful toward **19** the green-eyed monster

enwrap 6 absorb, engage, enrobe **7** engross, envelop **9** preoccupy

Enyalius
epithet of: 4 Ares
means: 14 slayer of heroes

Enyeus
king of: 6 Scyrus

Enyo
origin: 5 Greek
goddess of: 3 war
companion of: 4 Ares
member of: 6 Graeae, Graiae
corresponds to: 7 Bellona

enzyme 7 protein **8** molecule **13** macromolecule
function: 8 catalyst
acts on: 9 substrate
kind: 5 amino, malic **6** lactic, lipase, pepsin, rennin, urease **7** amylase, glucose, trypsin **8** aldehyde, glutamic, glycolic, lipozyme, thrombin, xanthine **9** cellulase **12** ribonuclease

eon 3 age, era **8** eternity, long time **9** many years **15** one billion years

Eos
origin: 5 Greek
goddess of: 4 dawn
father: 8 Hyperion
mother: 5 Theia
brother: 6 Helios
sister: 6 Selene
husband: 8 Astraeus, Tithonus **10** Eosophorus
son: 6 Memnon **8** Phaethon, Zephyrus **10** Eosophorus
horse: 6 Lampos **8** Phaethon
mother of: 5 stars, winds
corresponds to: 6 Aurore **7** Hermera

Epaphus
king of: 5 Egypt
father: 4 Zeus
mother: 2 Io
wife: 7 Memphis
daughter: 5 Lybia **10** Lysianassa

Epeans *see* **5** Epeus

Epeus
king of: 12 Peloponnesus
father: 8 Endymion, Panopeus
brother: 5 Paeon **7** Aetolus
wife: 10 Anaxirrhoe
noted for: 9 cowardice
built: 11 Trojan horse
helped by: 6 Athena
descendants: 6 Epeans

Epheh 15 Biblical measure

ephemeral 5 brief **7** passing **8** fleeting, flitting, fugitive, temporal **9** fugacious, momentary, temporary, transient **10** evanescent, fly-by-night, inconstant, nondurable, short-lived, transitory, unenduring **11** impermanent **21** here today gone tomorrow

ephemeroptera
class: 8 hexapoda
phylum: 10 arthropoda
group: 6 mayfly

Ephialtes
form: 5 giant
member of: 7 Aloidae
father: 8 Poseidon
mother: 9 Iphimedia
brother: 5 Oteus

Ephraim
father: 6 Joseph
mother: 7 Asenath
brother: 8 Manasseh
blessed by: 5 Jacob
descendant of: 10 Ephraimite

Ephraimi 16 Greek unical codex

Epibaterius
epithet of: 6 Apollo
means: 9 seafaring

epic 4 saga **5** drama, great, noble **6** fabled, heroic **7** exalted, storied **8** fabulous, imposing, majestic **9** legendary **10** heroic poem, superhuman

Epicaste *see* **7** Jocasta

epicure 7 glutton, gourmet **8** gourmand, hedonist, sybarite **9** bon vivant **10** gastronome

epicurean 4 rich **6** lavish **7** gourmet, sensual **8** hedonist, Lucullan, sybarite **9** libertine, luxurious, sybaritic **10** hedonistic, sensualist, voluptuary, voluptuous **11** intemperate **13** self-indulgent

epidemic 4 rife **6** plague **7** rampant, scourge **8** catching, outbreak, pandemic **9** contagion, infection, pervasive, prevalent **10** infectious, pestilence, prevailing, widespread **11** far-reaching

Epigoni
sons of: 18 Seven against Thebes

epigram 4 quip **5** adage, maxim **6** bon mot **8** aphorism, apothegm **9** witticism

epilogue 4 coda **5** rider **7** codicil **8** addendum **9** afterword **10** supplement **12** final section

Epimetheus
father: 7 Iapetus
brother: 5 Atals **9** Menoetius **10** Prometheus
wife: 7 Pandora
daughter: 6 Pyrrha

Epione
husband: 9 Asclepius

episcopal 8 churchly, diocesan, pastoral **12** ecclesiastic(al)

episode 4 part **5** event, scene **6** affair, period **7** chapter, passage, section **8** incident **9** adventure, happening, milestone **10** experience, occurrence **11** installment

Episode of Sparrows, An
author: 11 Rumer Godden

episodic 7 halting **8** rambling **9** segmented, wandering **10** digressive, discursive, meandering **13** discontinuous

epistle 6 letter **7** message, missive **10** encyclical

Epistle to a Godson and Other Poems
author: 7 W H Auden

Epistle to Dr Arbuthnot
author: 13 Alexander Pope

Epithalamion
author: 13 Edmund Spenser

epithet 5 curse **6** insult **8** nickname **9** blasphemy, expletive, obscenity, sobriquet **10** ascription **11** appellation, designation

Epithet ***see box***

epitome 4 peak **5** ideal, model **6** height **7** essence, summary **9** summation **10** embodiment **12** typification **14** representation **15** exemplification, sum and substance

e pluribus unum 12 out of many one
motto of: 12 United States

epoch 3 age, era **4** time **6** period **8** interval

epochal 7 weighty **8** historic **9** important, momentous **11** significant **13** consequential

Eppie
character in: 11 Silas Marner
author: 5 Eliot

Epstein, Sir Jacob
born: 9 New York NY
artwork: 4 Adam **7** Genesis **8** Ecce Homo, Einstein **9** Rock Drill **10** Visitation **11** Night and Day, Paul Robeson **12** Behold the Man, Joseph Conrad **13** Haile Selaisse **14** Consummatum Est **19** Social Consciousness **20** Monument to Oscar Wilde, St Michael and his (the) Devil

equable 4 calm, even **5** sunny **6** placid, serene, stable, steady **7** regular, uniform **8** constant, pleasant, tranquil, unvaried **9** agreeable, easygoing, unruffled **10** consistent, dependable, unchanging **11** good-natured, predictable, unexcitable, unflappable **12** even-tempered **13** imperturbable

equably
Latin: 9 pari passu

equal 4 even, like, peer **5** match **7** matched, the same, uniform **8** balanced, be even to, equalize, jibe with, of a piece, parallel **9** agree with, identical, tally with **10** accord with, comparable, equate with, equivalent, square with, tantamount **11** balance with, be

Epithet
of Aphrodite: 6 Acraea, Scotia **7** Doritis, Erycina, Limenia **8** Melaenis, Nymphaea, Pandemos **9** Migonitis **11** Aphrogeneia, Apostrophia
of Apollo: 6 Loxias **7** Acesius, Agraeus, Agyieus, Carneus, Phyteus, Spodius **8** Grynaeus **9** Parnopius, Smintheus **10** Alexicacus, Archegetes, Boedromius, Delphinius **11** Argyrotoxus, Epibaterius **12** Platanistius
of Ares: 8 Enyalius **14** Gynaecothoenas
of Argus: 8 Panoptes
of Artemis: 6 Orthia **7** Eurippa, Laphria, Limnaea, Pyronia **8** Aeginaea, Agrotera, Calliste, Caryatis, Daphnaea **9** Hemerasia, Lygodesma **10** Polymastus **11** Leucophryne
of Asclepius: 8 Cotyleus
of Athena: 4 Alea **5** Meter, Xenia **6** Ergane, Itonia, Polias **7** Agoraea, Cissaea, Paeonia, Pronaus, Pronoea **8** Anemotis, Poliates, Zosteria **9** Oxyderces, Parthenia, Poliuchus, Promachus **10** Axiopoenus, Chalinitis, Cyparissia **11** Promachorma
of Cybele: 6 Antaea
of Demeter: 5 Chloe, Lusia, Mysia **6** Antaea, Erinys, Stiria **7** Chamyne, Thesmia **8** Stiritis **9** Anesidora, Thermasia **11** Carpophorus **12** Thesmophorus
of Dionysus: 6 Lyaeus **7** Bromius, Cresius **8** Thyoneus, Triambus **9** Pyrigenes **11** Dithyrambus, Mitrephorus
of Hera: 6 Anthea, Bunaea **8** Henioche **9** Prodromia
of Hercules: 7 Charops **8** Buphagus **9** Ipoctonus
of Hermes: 6 Dolius **8** Agoraeus **9** Spelaites **10** Criophorus **11** Argiphontes **12** Argeiphontes, Psychopompus
of Icelus: 8 Phobetor
of Juno: 6 Moneta **7** Curitis, Pronuba, Sospita
of Jupiter: 5 Ultor **7** Elicius, Pluvius
of Mopsus: 9 Ampycides
of Nestor: 7 Nelides
of Odin: 7 Alfader, Alfadir
of Odysseus: 10 Laertiades
of Persephone: 11 Carpophorus
of Pheriphetes: 9 Corynetes
of Poseidon: 11 Ennosigaeus, Hippocurius **12** Prosclystius
of Rhea: 6 Antaea
of Sinis: 12 Pityocamptes
of Vulcan: 8 Mulciber
of Zeus: 5 Areus, Soter **6** Aqueus, Areius, Nemean, Philus **7** Alastor, Apemius, Ctesius, Lycaeus, Polieus, Stenius **8** Agoraeus, Aphesius, Apomyius, Cappotas, Cosmetas, Dodonian, Herceius, Leucaeus, Tropaean **9** Aegiochus, Chthonius, Coccygius, Hecaleius, Lecheates, Mechaneus **10** Cataebates, Catharsius, Coryphaeus, Homagyrius, Laphystius, Meilichius **11** Eleutherius **12** Panhellenius

the same as, correlative, counterpart, symmetrical **12** commensurate, correspond to, proportional **13** be identical to, corresponding, evenly matched, one and the same

equality 6 parity **7** balance, justice **8** evenness, fair play, fairness, sameness **10** similarity, uniformity **11** equivalency **12** impartiality **13** fair treatment **14** correspondence
French: 7 egalite

Equality
author: 13 Edward Bellamy

Equality State
nickname of: 7 Wyoming

equalization 7 balance **9** stability **11** equilibrium **14** counterbalance
German: 9 Ausgleich

equalize 7 balance **9** make equal **11** make uniform **13** compensate for

equal to 3 fit **4** able, up to **5** adept **7** capable **8** adequate, master of **9** competent, qualified

equanimity 4 cool **5** poise **6** aplomb **8** calmness, coolness **9** composure, sangfroid **10** steadiness **11** self-control, tranquility **12** tranquillity **14** presence of mind, self-possession **16** imperturbability

equate 5 liken, match **7** average, balance, compare, even out **8** equalize, equal out **9** think of as **10** consider as **14** be commensurate, be equivalent to **17** be proportionate to

Equatorial
language family: 16 Andean-Equatorial
group: 8 Arawakan **11** Tupi-Guarani

Equatorial Guinea ***see box***

equilibrium 7 balance **8** symmetry **9** equipoise, stability **14** sense of balance

equip 3 rig **5** stock **6** fit out, outfit, supply **7** appoint, furnish, prepare, provide **8** accoutre **9** caparison, provision

equipage 4 gear **6** outfit **8** carriage **9** equipment **13** accoutrements

equipment 4 gear **5** stuff **6** tackle **8** equipage, material, materiel, supplies **9** apparatus **11** furnishings, outfittings **13** accoutrements, paraphernalia

equipoise 7 balance **9** stability **11** equilibrium

equitable 3 due **4** fair, just **6** proper **8** unbiased **9** impartial **10** evenhanded, reasonable **12** unprejudiced

equity 4 cash **5** value **6** assets, profit **7** justice **8** fairness, justness **9** cash value **10** investment **12** fair dealings, impartiality **14** evenhandedness, fairmindedness, reasonableness

equivalency 6 parity **7** balance **8** equality **10** coequality, uniformity **14** correspondence

equivalent 4 even, peer **5** equal, match **8** of a piece, parallel **9** the same as **10** comparable, tantamount **11** correlative, counterpart, equal amount

equivocal 4 hazy **5** vague **7** dubious **8** doubtful **9** ambiguous, enigmatic, imprecise, qualified, uncertain, undecided **10** ambivalent, indefinite, suspicious **11** nonspecific **12** undetermined **13** indeterminate

equivocate 5 dodge, evade, fudge, hedge, stall **9** pussyfoot **10** mince words **11** be ambiguous, prevaricate **13** avoid the issue **16** straddle

Equatorial Guinea
other name: 13 Spanish Guinea
capital/largest city: 6 Malabo
others: 4 Bata **9** Rio Benito
division: 5 Bioko **7** Rio Muni
monetary unit: 6 ekuele, peseta **7** centimo
island: 5 Bioko **6** Pagalu **7** Corisco **11** Chico Elobey **12** Grande Elobey
mountain: 5 Mitra
highest point: 11 Santa Isabel
river: 5 Mbini
physical feature:
gulf: **6** Guinea
people: 4 Bubi, Fang **5** Benge, Combe **6** Bujeba **10** Fernandino
explorer: **2** Po
leader: **12** Nguema Biyogo
language: 4 Bubi, Fang **7** Spanish **13** pidgin English
religion: 7 animism **10** Protestant **13** Roman Catholic

the fence **17** beat around the bush

equivocating 6 shifty **7** devious, dodging, elusive, elusory, evasive, hedging **8** stalling **9** ambiguous, deceptive, equivocal **10** misleading **11** dissembling

era 3 age **4** time **5** epoch **6** period **8** interval

eradicate 5 erase **6** remove **7** abolish, blot out, destroy, expunge, wipe out **8** get rid of **9** eliminate, extirpate, liquidate **10** annihilate, do away with, extinguish, obliterate **11** exterminate

eradication 7 erasure, removal **9** abolition **11** blotting out, destruction, elimination **12** obliteration

erase 6 delete, remove, rub out **7** expunge, scratch **8** wipe away **9** eliminate, eradicate, strike out

Erasistratus
field: 10 physiology
nationality: 5 Greek
described: 5 brain, heart

Erasmus, Desiderius
author of: 14 Encomium Moriae **16** The Praise of Folly

Erato
muse of: 10 love poetry

Ercolani, James
real name of: 11 James Darren

Erebus
location: 10 underworld
means: 8 darkness

Erechtheus
king of: 6 Athens
father: 7 Pandion
wife: 9 Praxithea
son: 6 Metion, Orneus, Sicyon **7** Cecrops **8** Pandorus, Thespius **9** Eupalamus
daughter: 6 Creusa **7** Otionia, Procris **8** Chthonia, Orithyir **10** Protogonia

erect 5 build, put up, raise, rigid, stiff **6** unbent **7** stand up, upright **8** straight, vertical **9** construct, unstooped **12** place upright

erection 7 raising **8** building **9** putting up **11** fabrication **12** construction

eremite 4 monk **6** hermit **7** ascetic, recluse **9** anchorite, religious

Ereshkigal
origin: 8 Akkadian, Sumerian
goddess of: 5 death
consort of: 6 Nergal

Ereuthalion
mentioned in: **5** Iliad
vocation: **7** warrior
home: **7** Arcadia
dueled with: **6** Nestor

Erewhon
author: **12** Samuel Butler
title anagram of: **7** nowhere
character: **5** Higgs **6** Strong **7** Chowbok **8** Arowhena

Ergane
epithet of: **6** Athena
means: **6** worker

ergo **4** work **6** hence **7** because **9** therefore **11** accordingly

Eriboea
husband: **6** Aloeus

Erigone
father: **7** Icarius **9** Aegisthus
mother: **12** Clytemnestra
brother: **6** Aletes
death by: **7** suicide

Eriking
origin: **8** Germanic **12** Scandinavian
form: **6** spirit
personifies: **6** nature
works: **8** mischief

Erin *see* **7** Ireland

Erin go bragh **14** Ireland forever

Erinys
also: **6** Furies
epithet of: **7** Demeter
means: **4** fury

Eris
origin: **5** Greek
goddess of: **7** discord
brother: **4** Ares
threw: **14** apple of discord
corresponds to: **9** Discordia

ermine **3** fur **4** duty, rank **6** weasel **7** ermalin **8** position **14** muste la erminea

Ernani
opera by: **5** Verdi
setting: **6** Aragon
character: **6** Ernani **11** Donna Elvira

Ernst, Max
born: **5** Bruhl **7** Germany
co-founder of: **7** Dadaism **10** Surrealism
artwork: **7** Moon Man **8** Lady Bird **11** A Little Calm, Femme Oiseau **12** The Whole City **13** The Table Is Set, Totem and Taboo **14** Lunar Asparagus **15** La Femme 100 Tetes, Mundus est Fabula **16** A Chinaman Fargone, The Parisian Woman **18** Europe after the Rain, Fiat Modes Pereat Ars, The Elephant (of the) Celebes **22** Men Will Make Nothing of It, The Spirit of the Bastille **24** The Temptation of St Anthony **26** The King Playing With the Queen

erode **5** spoil, waste **6** ravage **7** corrode, despoil, eat away **8** wear away **12** disintegrate

Eros
origin: **5** Greek
god of: **4** love
mother: **9** Aphrodite
corresponds to: **4** Amor **5** Cupid

erosion **8** abrasion, ravaging **9** corrosion **10** eating away **11** wearing away, wearing down

erosive **7** burning, caustic **9** corrosive

erotic **3** hot **4** lewd, sexy **5** bawdy, lusty **6** ardent, carnal, impure, ribald, risque, sexual, wanton **7** amatory, amorous, obscene, raunchy **8** immodest, indecent, unchaste **9** salacious **10** lascivious, passionate, suggestive

err **3** sin **6** mess up, slip up **7** blunder, do wrong **8** go astray **9** be in error, misbehave **10** transgress **12** make a mistake, miscalculate **13** slip from grace

errand **4** duty, task **6** office **7** mission **10** assignment **11** undertaking

errant **5** wrong **6** arrant, astray, erring, roving **7** erratic, wayward **8** mistaken, straying **9** incorrect, wandering, wayfaring **11** adventurous

errare humanum est **12** to err is human

erratic **3** odd **5** queer **6** fitful **7** strange, unusual, wayward **8** aberrant, abnormal, peculiar, shifting, unstable, variable **9** eccentric, unnatural **10** capricious, changeable **11** vacillating **12** inconsistent **13** unpredictable

erroneous **5** false, wrong **6** all wet, faulty, untrue **7** off base, unsound **8** mistaken, spurious **9** incorrect, unfounded **10** fallacious, inaccurate **12** full of hot air **13** unsupportable

error **4** flaw **5** boner, botch, fault **6** boo-boo, bungle, howler **7** blooper, fallacy, mistake **9** oversight **10** inaccuracy **13** misconception **14** miscalculation **15** misapprehension **16** misunderstanding **17** misinterpretation

ersatz **4** fake, sham **5** bogus, phony **9** imitation, pretended, synthetic **10** artificial, not genuine **11** counterfeit

Erse **4** Celt, Gael, Scot **5** Irish **6** Celtic, Gaelic **7** Ireland **8** Scottish **10** Highlander

erstwhile **2** ex **4** past **6** bygone, former **8** previous

eruct **4** burp **5** belch

eructation **4** burp **5** belch

erudite **4** wise **7** learned, sapient **8** cultured, literate, well-read **9** scholarly **10** cultivated, thoughtful, well-versed **11** intelligent **12** well-educated, well-informed, well-reasoned

erudition **5** skill **7** culture **8** learning, literacy **9** education, expertise, knowledge, schooling **10** refinement **11** cultivation, learnedness, scholarship **12** book learning **13** enlightenment

Erulus
king of: **5** Italy
mother: **7** Feronia
gift: **10** three lives

erupt **4** emit, gush, vent **5** eruct **6** blow up **7** explode **8** break out, throw off **9** be ejected, discharge, flow forth, pour forth **10** belch forth, burst forth

eruption **4** rash **6** eczema **7** flare-up, gushing, venting **8** ejection, emission, outbreak, outburst **9** blowing up, discharge, explosion, festering **10** dermatitis, outpouring **11** breaking out **12** flowing forth, inflammation, pouring forth **13** belching forth, bursting forth

Erving, Julius
nickname: **7** Doctor J
sport: **10** basketball
position: **7** forward
team: **11** New York Nets **15** Virginia Squires **25** Philadelphia Seventy Sixers

Erycina
epithet of: **9** Aphrodite

Erymanthian boar
form: **4** boar
plagued: **7** Arcadia
captured by: **8** Hercules

Erysichthon
cut sacred tree of: **7** Demeter

Erytheis
member: **10** Hesperides
changed into: **3** elm

erythrophobia
fear of: **8** blushing

Eryx
vocation: **5** boxer

challenged: **8** Hercules
killed by: **8** Hercules

Esau
also called: **4** Edom
father: **5** Isaac
mother: **7** Rebekah
twin brother: **5** Jacob
wife: **6** Judith **8** Makalath
son: **7** Eliphaz
birthright sold to: **5** Jacob

escadrille **6** armada **8** flotilla, squadron

escalate **4** rise **5** boost, mount, swell **6** ascend, expand, extend, step up **7** advance, amplify, broaden, elevate, enlarge, magnify **8** increase **9** intensify **10** accelerate, aggrandize

Escalus
character in: **17** Measure for Measure
author: **11** Shakespeare

escapade **4** lark **5** antic, caper, fling, prank, revel, spree, trick **7** caprice **8** mischief **9** adventure **11** high old time

escape **4** bolt, exit, flee, flow, gush, leak, seep, shun, skip **5** avert, avoid, dodge, elude, issue, skirt **6** efflux, egress, emerge, eschew, exodus, flight, stream **7** abscond, emanate, getaway, leakage, make off, outflow, outpour, run away, seepage **8** breakout, emission, outburst, slip away, steal off **9** be emitted, break free, cut and run, discharge, diversion, effluence, pour forth **10** break loose, decampment, fly the coop **11** avoid danger, deliverance, distraction, extrication, safe getaway **12** make a getaway

escargot **5** snail

escarpment **4** bank, crag **5** bluff, cliff, ridge, slope **8** headland, palisade **9** precipice **10** promontory

eschew **4** shun **5** avoid, forgo **6** give up **7** forbear **9** keep shy of **11** abstain from **12** steer clear of

eschewal **7** refusal **8** forgoing, shunning **9** avoidance **10** abnegation, abstention, self-denial **11** forbearance **13** nonindulgence **16** nonparticipation

escort **4** date, take **5** guard, guide, train, usher **6** squire **7** company, conduct, cortege, retinue **8** chaperon **9** companion, conductor, entourage **10** attendants, lead the way

escritoire **4** desk **5** table **9** secretary **10** secretaire **11** writing desk

escutcheon **4** arms **5** crest **6** shield **10** coat of arms **16** armorial bearings

Eskimo (Eskimantsic, Askkimey, Inuit, Yuit)
tribe: **5** Aleut
location: **6** Alaska, Arctic, Canada **9** Greenland
noted for: **7** fishing **9** mechanics

Eskimo-Aleut
language branch: **5** Aleut, Yupik
spoken in: **6** Alaska **7** Siberia **15** Aleutian Islands

Esmeralda
character in: **23** The Hunchback of Notre Dame
author: **4** Hugo

esoteric **6** arcane, covert, hidden, occult, secret, veiled **7** cloaked, cryptic, obscure, private **8** abstruse, mystical **9** concealed, enigmatic, recondite **10** inviolable, mysterious **11** inscrutable, undisclosed **12** confidential **16** incomprehensible

espanol **7** Spanish **13** Spanish person **15** Spanish language

especial *see* **7** special

especially **6** really **7** notably **9** expressly, intensely, primarily, unusually **10** singularly, uncommonly **11** exclusively, principally **12** particularly, specifically **13** exceptionally, outstandingly **15** extraordinarily

espiegle **7** playful, roguish

espieglerie **12** playful trick

esplanade **4** mall, path, walk **5** drive **9** boardwalk **10** quadrangle

espousal **7** backing, support, wedding **8** adoption, advocacy, marriage, taking up **9** betrothal, promotion **10** supporting **12** championship

espouse **3** wed **4** back, tout **5** adopt, boost, marry **6** take up **7** embrace, further, promote, support **8** advocate, champion, side with **10** stand up for

espressivo
music: **12** expressively
abbreviation: **4** espr

esprit de corps **10** fellowship, group pride, group unity, high morale, solidarity, team spirit **11** camaraderie

espy **3** see, spy **4** spot, view **6** behold, descry, detect, locate, notice **7** discern

essay **3** try **5** paper, theme, tract **6** effort, take on **7** article, attempt, venture **8** critique, endeavor, treatise **9** editorial, undertake **10** commentary, experiment **11** make a stab at, undertaking **12** dissertation, take a crack at, take a fling at **14** make an effort at **16** short composition

Essay on Criticism, An
author: **13** Alexander Pope

Essay on Man, An
author: **13** Alexander Pope

Essays
author: **12** Francis Bacon

Essays in Criticism
author: **13** Matthew Arnold

esse **5** being **9** existence

essence **4** core, germ, gist, pith, soul **5** heart, point, scent **6** elixir, nature, spirit **7** cologne, extract, meaning, perfume, spirits **8** tincture **9** fragrance, lifeblood, principle, substance **11** concentrate, toilet water **12** basic quality, quintessence, significance **15** sum and substance

essential, essentials **3** key **4** main **5** basic, vital **6** basics, needed **7** crucial, leading **8** cardinal, inherent **9** basic need, important, ingrained, intrinsic, necessary, necessity, principal, requisite, rudiments, vital part **10** key element, principles **11** fundamental, nitty-gritty **12** fundamentals **13** indispensable

essential ingredient **9** necessity **10** sine qua non **22** indispensable component

establish **3** fix **4** form, open, show **5** begin, found, prove, set up, start **6** create, settle, uphold, verify **7** confirm, implant, install, justify, situate, sustain, warrant **8** initiate, organize, validate **9** institute **10** bring about, inaugurate, make secure **11** corroborate, demonstrate **12** authenticate **16** win acceptance for **18** bring into existence

established **6** common **7** regular **8** accepted, familiar **9** customary **10** recognized

establishment, Establishment **4** firm **5** plant **6** office, outfit, system **7** company, concern, factory **8** building, business, creation, founding **9** formation, setting up **10** foundation **11** corporation, development, instituting, institution, ruling class **12** organization, powers that be **13** bringing about

estaminet **4** cafe **6** bistro

estate **4** rank, will **5** class, grade, manor, money, order, state **6** assets, legacy, status, wealth **7** bequest, fortune, station **8** compound, holdings, property **9** condition, situation **10** belongings, plantation **11** inheritance **12** country place

esteem **4** deem, hold **5** honor, judge, prize, think, value **6** admire, reckon, regard, revere **7** believe, cherish, respect **8** approval, consider, estimate, look up to, treasure, venerate **9** calculate, reverence **10** admiration, set store by, veneration **12** appreciation **13** think highly of **16** favorable opinion, hold in high regard **18** attach importance to

esteemed **5** great, noted **6** prized, valued, worthy **7** admired, eminent, honored, notable, revered **9** admirable, important, respected **10** looked up to, preeminent **11** illustrious **13** distinguished, well thought of **14** highly regarded

Estella
character in: **17** Great Expectations
author: **7** Dickens

Estevez, Ramon
real name of: **11** Martin Sheen

Esther
author: **10** Henry Adams

Esther
Persian name of: **8** Hadassah
father: **7** Abihail
grandfather: **6** Shimei
cousin: **8** Mordecai
husband: **9** Ahasuerus
displaced: **6** Vashti
enemy: **5** Haman

Esther Waters
author: **11** George Moore

esthetic **7** refined **8** artistic **9** sensitive **10** cultivated, fastidious **12** aesthetic **14** discriminating

estimable **4** good **6** prized **7** admired, revered **8** laudable **9** admirable, honorable, important, reputable, respected, treasured **10** worthwhile **11** commendable **12** praiseworthy **14** highly regarded

estimate **4** view **5** assay, guess, judge, opine, think, value **6** assess, belief, figure, reckon **7** believe, opinion, surmise **8** appraise, conclude, consider, evaluate, judgment, thinking **9** appraisal, calculate, reckoning **10** assessment, conjecture, evaluation **11** calculation

estimation **4** view **6** belief, esteem, regard **7** opinion, respect **8** approval, judgment **9** appraisal, reckoning **10** admiration, evaluation **13** consideration

estimator **7** analyst **8** assessor **9** appraiser, evaluator **10** calculator

Estonia ***see box***

estop **3** bar **4** fill, plug, stop **7** prevent **8** obstruct

esto perpetua **17** may she live forever
motto of: **5** Idaho

Estragon
character in: **15** Waiting for Godot
author: **7** Beckett

estrange **4** part **8** alienate **9** disaffect **10** antagonize, dissociate, drive apart

estranged **5** aloof **6** cut off **7** distant **8** detached, divorced **9** alienated, separated **10** unfriendly

Estonia
capital/largest city: **7** Tallinn
others: **5** Narva, Paide, Parnu, Tartu, Valga **6** Dorpat **7** Petseri **8** Paldiski **11** Kohtla-Jarve
government: **24** Republic of the Soviet Union
measure: **3** tun **4** elle, liin, sund, toll, toop **5** verst **6** sagene, versta **7** kulimet **8** tonnland
monetary unit: **3** lat **4** sent **5** kroon **7** estmark
weight: **4** lood, nael, puud
island: **4** Dago, Muhu **5** Kihnu, Oesel, Saare **6** Sarema, Vormsi **7** Hiiumaa **8** Saaremaa
lake: **5** Pskov **6** Peipus **9** Vortsjarv
highest point: **8** Munamagi
river: **3** Ema **5** Narva, Parnu
sea: **6** Baltic
physical feature:
gulf: **4** Riga **5** Parnu **7** Finland
strait: **4** Irbe
people: **4** Esth, Finn **5** Aesti **6** Jewish **8** Estonian **9** Ukrainian **11** Belorussian
language: **5** Tartu **10** Finno-Ugric
religion: **8** Lutheran

estrangement **8** coolness **10** alienation **12** disaffection

estuary **5** firth, inlet **10** river mouth, tidal basin

etagere **7** whatnot **11** open shelves

etc (&c) **4** et al **7** and so on, whatnot **8** et cetera, whatever **9** and others **10** and so forth, and the rest

etch **3** cut, fix **5** carve, stamp **7** corrode, engrave, impress, scratch

Eteocles
father: **7** Oedipus
mother: **7** Jocasta **10** Euryganeia
uncle: **5** Creon
brother: **9** Polynices
sister: **6** Ismene **8** Antigone
son: **8** Laodamas
slain by: **9** Polynices

eternal **7** abiding, endless **8** constant, immortal, infinite, timeless, unending **9** ceaseless, continual, perpetual **10** persistent, relentless, without end **11** everlasting, never-ending **12** interminable **13** uninterrupted

eternity **4** Zion **6** Heaven **7** forever, nirvana **8** infinity, paradise **11** ages and ages, endlessness, eons and eons, immortality **12** New Jerusalem, the hereafter, the next world **13** the afterworld **14** the world to come, time without end **15** everlasting life

Ethan Frome
author: **12** Edith Wharton
character: **5** Zeena **7** Zenobia **12** Mattie Silver

Ethanim **18** seventh Hebrew month

ether **5** ester, ethyl, ozone, vapor **7** diethyl, solvent **10** anesthetic **11** refrigerant

ethereal **4** airy, rare **6** aerial **7** elusive, refined, sublime **8** delicate, rarefied **9** celestial, exquisite, unearthly, unworldly

ethical **4** fair, just **5** moral, right **6** decent, kosher, proper **7** correct, fitting, upright **8** virtuous **9** honorable **10** aboveboard, scrupulous **15** straightforward **17** open and aboveboard

ethical feelings **9** integrity **10** conscience, moral sense **16** incorruptibility

ethics, ethic **8** morality **9** integrity, moral code **10** conscience, principles **11** moral values, sense of duty **14** moral standards, rules of conduct

Ethics of Ambiguity
author: **16** Simone de Beauvoir

Ethiopia ***see box***

ethnic **6** native, racial, unique **8** cultural, national, original **10** indigenous

ethnic group ***see box, p. 318***

etiquette **5** usage **7** decorum, manners **8** behavior, courtesy, good form, protocol **9** amenities, gentility, good taste **10** civilities, politeness **11** conventions, proprieties **15** rules of behavior

etoile **4** star

Ettarre
character in: **16** Arthurian romance

ET The Extra-Terrestrial
director: **15** Steven Spielberg
cast: **10** Dee Wallace **11** Henry Thomas, Peter Coyote **13** Drew Barrymore **17** Robert MacNaughton

et tu, Brute **13** and thou Brutus
spoken by: **12** Julius Caesar

etymology **7** history **10** derivation

Etzel
origin: **8** Germanic
mentioned in: **14** Nibelungenlied
represents: **6** Attila
wife: **9** Kriemhild

Euaechme
parent: **8** Megareus
husband: **9** Alcathous

Euboean *see* **7** Abantes

Eubuleus
father: **9** Trochilus
helped: **7** Demeter

Eucharist **8** viaticum **9** Communion, sacrament **13** Holy Communion

euchre
number of players: **3** two **4** four **5** three
derived from: **8** triomphe
five tricks won: **5** march
jack of trump: **10** right bower
second highest trump: **9** left bower

Euclid
field: **11** mathematics
nationality: **5** Greek
founder of: **8** geometry
author of: **8** Elements

Eugene Onegin
author: **16** Alexander Pushkin

Ethiopia
Biblical name: **4** Cush
other name: **9** Abyssinia
capital/largest city: **10** Addis Ababa
others: **3** Edd **4** Axum, Bako, Dori, Goba, Gore, Thio **5** Adola, Adowa, Aduwa, Aksum, Assab, Awash, Dimtu, Elfud, Harar, Jidda, Jimma, Kecha, Meroe, Mojjo **6** Antalo, Asmara, Dessye, Dunkur, Gondar, Harrar, Makale, Napata **7** Ankober, Gambela, Gardula, Magdala, Massawa, Nakamti **8** Dire Dawa, Lalibala, Mustahil
school: **13** Haile Selassie
division: **6** Amhara, Ogaden **7** Eritrea
measure: **3** tat **4** cubi, kuba **5** derah, messe **6** cabaho, sinjer, sinzer, tanica **7** entelam, farsakh, farsang, ghebeta
monetary unit: **4** besa, birr, harf **5** amole, girsh **6** dollar, kharaf, levant, pataca, talari **7** ashrafi, menelik, plaster, tallero **12** maria theresa
weight: **3** pek **4** kasm, natr, oket, rotl **5** alada, artal, mocha, neter, ratel, wakea **6** wogiet **8** farasula **9** mutagalla
island: **6** Dahlak
lake: **3** Abe **4** Tana **5** Abaya, Shola, Tanna, Tsana, Tzana, Zeway **6** Dambea, Dembea **7** Rudolph **8** Stefanie **11** The Blue Nile
mountain: **4** Amba, Batu, Guge, Guna, Talo **5** Ahmar, Choke **9** Rasdashan
highest point: **9** Ras Deshen
river: **3** Omo **4** Baro, Dawa, Gibe, Gila, Juba **5** Abbai, Akoho, Albai, Awash, Fafan, Mareb, Mofer, Rahad, Webbe **6** Tekeze **7** Tacazze, Takkaze **8** Gashgash, Shebante **11** The Blue Nile
sea: **3** Red
physical feature:
desert: **17** Danakil Depression
falls: **7** Tisisat **8** Blue Nile
valley: **4** Rift
people: **4** Afar, Agau, Beja, Doko, Kafa, Kala, Saho, Shoa **5** Afara, Agows, Galas, Galla, Negro, Tigre **6** Abigar, Amhara, Annuak, Gondar, Hamite, Harari, Sidama, Sidamo, Somali, Tigrai, Wolamo **7** Cushite, Danakil, Donakus, Falasha, Somalis **8** Assamite, Blemmyes **10** Abyssinian, Troglodyte
language: **3** Giz **4** Afar, Agow, Geez, Saho **5** Geeze, Ghese, Smali, Tigre **6** Arabic, Harari **7** Amharic, English, Italian, Russian **8** Gallinya, Irob-Saho, Tigrinya
religion: **5** Islam **7** Falasha, Judaism **18** Ethiopian Orthodoxy
place:
cathedral: **8** St George
hall: **6** Africa
palace: **7** Jubilee **9** Menelik II
park: **4** Lion
feature:
flower: **7** brayera
game: **5** dulla **8** shum-shir
garment: **4** toga **5** kamis **6** barnos, chamma, netela, shamma
tree: **4** koho, koso **5** cusso
food:
banana: **4** musa **6** ensete
beer: **5** talla
bread dish: **6** injera
cereal: **4** teff
honey liquor: **3** tej
spicy sauce: **3** wat

ethnic group

of Afghanistan: 5 Aimak, Aymak, Kafir, Nuris **6** Baloch, Baluch, Chahar, Durani, Hasara, Hazara, Kaffir, Kirgiz, Pathan, Tajiks, Uzbeks **7** Beluchi, Belucki, Ghilzai, Pakhton, Pakhtun, Pashtun, Pukhtun, Pushtun, Sistani, Taimani, Taimuri **8** Jamshidi, Siah Push **9** Firuzkuhi, Safed Push, Safid Push

of Albania: 3 Geg **4** Cham, Gheg, Gueg, Tost **6** Arnaut, Arnout **8** Illyrian, Skipetar

of Algeria: 4 Arab **6** Berber, Kabyle, Shawai, Tuareg **7** Haratin

of Andorra: 7 Catalan

of Angola: 5 Bantu, Kongo, Lundu **6** Chokwe, Herero, Mbundi, Ovambo **7** Bakongo, Kangela, Kikongo **8** Kimbundu, Kwangare **9** Ovinbundu **12** Nyaneka-Humbi

of Antigua and Barbuda: 7 African, British **8** Lebanese **10** Portuguese

of Argentina: 3 Api **4** Lule **5** Vejoz **6** Abipon, Vilela **7** Guarani, Puelche, Ranquel, Taluhet **8** Querandi, Querendy

of Armenia: 5 Armen, Ermyn, Gomer, Hadji

of Australia: 3 Abo **4** Koko, Mara, Wong **5** Anzac, Bieri, Binge, Maori, Myall **6** Aranda, Arunta, Aussie, Binghi, Digger, Kipper, Papuan **7** Arawong, Billjim, Ilpirra **8** Antipode, Barkinji, Euahlayi, Warragal, Warrigal **9** Aborigine **10** Austroloid, Melanesian, Sandgroper **12** Jindyworobak

of Austria: 4 Pole **5** Croat, Czech, Gypsy **6** German **7** Slovene **9** Hungarian

of the Bahamas: 5 black **7** Haitian

of Bahrain: 4 Arab **6** Indian **7** Persian **8** European **9** Pakistani

of Bangladesh: 7 Bengali

of Barbados: 5 Bajan **9** Barbadian

of Belgium: 4 Remi **6** Nervii **7** Belgian, Fleming, Flemish, Walloon **9** Bellovaci

of Benin: 3 Fon, Pla **4** Adja, Aizo, Mina, Peul **5** Pedah, Peuhl, Somba **6** Bariba, Fulani, Yoruba **8** Pilapila **9** Dahomeyan

of Bhutan: 5 Monpa **6** Bhutia **7** Tibetan **8** Assamese, Nepalese

of Bolivia: 6 Aymara **7** mestizo, Quechua

of Borneo: 4 Iban **5** Bukat, Dajak, Dayak, Dusan, Malay, Punan **6** Illano **7** Bakatan, Chinese, Illanum

of Botswana: 5 Bantu **6** Tswana **7** Bakatla, Bakwena, Bushman **8** Bamalete, Baralong, Batawana, Batlokwa, Botswana **10** Bamangwato **11** Bangwaketse

of Brazil: 2 Ge **4** Anta **5** Acroa, Arara, Araua, Bravo, Carib, Guana, Negro **6** Arawak, Caraja **7** Carayan, Javahai, mulatto, Tariana **8** Botocudo, Chambioa, mameluco **9** Caucasian **10** Portuguese **11** Tupi-Guarani

of Brunei: 4 Iban **5** Dayak, Malay **7** Chinese, Kadazan

of Bulgaria: 4 Slav, Turk **5** Gypsy, Pomak, Tatar **6** Bulgar, Slavic **7** Chuvash **9** Cheremiss **10** Macedonian

of Burundi: 3 Twa **4** Hutu **5** Bantu, Batwa, Pygmy, Tutsi **6** Bahutu, Watusi **7** Barundi

of Cambodia: 4 Cham, Thai **5** Khmer **7** Chinese **10** Vietnamese

of Cameroon: 3 Abo, Edo, Ibo **4** Beti, Bulu, Ekoi, Ijaw, Sara **5** Bantu, Bassa, Kirdi, Pygmy, Tikar **6** Bamoun, Donala, Ewondo, Fulani, Ibibio **7** Bakweri **8** Bamileke

of Canada: 6 Canuck, Eskimo, French, Innuit **7** English

of the Canary Islands: 7 Spanish

of Cape Verde: 6 Creole **7** African, mulatto **8** European **10** Portuguese

of Central African Republic: 4 Baya, Sara **5** Banda, Bwaki, Sango **6** Azande, Yakoma **7** Banziri, Mandjia, Nzakara

of Chad: 4 Arab, Daza, Maba, Sara, Teda, Tubu **5** Barma, Hakka, Kroda, Massa **6** Fulani, Kotoko, Toubou, Wadaii **7** Kamadja, Kanembu **8** Moundang

of Chile: 3 Ona **4** Auca, Inca, Onan **6** Arauca, Chango, Yahgan **7** Mapuche, mestizo, Moluche, Pampean, Patagon, Puegian, Ranquel **8** Alikuluf, Picunche, Tsonecan

of China: 3 Han, Yis **4** Huis, Lolo, Miao, Pu-is **5** Hakka, Hoklo, Seres, Sinic **6** Cataia, Chuang, Johnny, Korean, Manchu, Mongol, Serian, Uighun **7** Sinaean, Tibetan

of Colombia: 4 Boro, Cuna, Duit, Hoka, Macu, Muso, Muzo, Paez, Tama, Tapa **5** Carib, Catio, Choco, Cofan, Cogui, Cubeo, Guane, Haida, Mocoa, Paeze, Pijao, Seona, Yagua **6** Arawak, Betoya, Calima, Colima, Ingano, Mirana, Saliva, Tahami, Ticunu, Tucano, Tunebo, Witoto, Yahuna **7** Achagua, Andaqui, Chibcha, Chimila, Churoya, Guahibo, Guajiro, mestizo, mulatto, Panches, Puinave, Puitoto, Quechua, Shuswap, Tairona, Telembi **8** Coconuco, Guarauno, Motilone, Puinavis, Quimbaya, Sinsigas **9** Cocanucos, Coconucan, Panaquita **10** Bellacoola

of Comoros: 4 Arab **5** Bantu, Malay **7** African **8** Malagasy

of the Congo: 3 Rua **4** Akka, Susa, Teke, Vili **5** Amadi, Bantu, Figot, Kongo, Mantu, Pygmy, Sanga, Warua, Zambi **6** Ababua, Bafyot, Bateke, Mbochi, Nzambi, Wabuma **7** Bacongo, Bakongo, Bangala, Batetla, Manyema **10** Binga Pygmy

of Costa Rica: 4 Voto **6** Boruca, Bribri, Guaymi **7** Guatuso, mestizo, Spanish

of Crete: 6 Cretan, Minoan **7** Candiot **8** Sphakiot **9** Caphtorim **10** Philistine

of Cuba: 5 Carib, Negro, Taino **6** Arawak **7** Ciboney, mestizo **8** Ciboneye **9** Caucasian

of Czechoslovakia: 4 Slav **5** Czech **6** Slovak **8** Bohemian, Moravian

of Denmark: 4 Dane, Jute **5** Angle **6** Cimbri, Eskimo, German, Ostmen, Teuton, Viking **12** Scandinavian

of Djibouti: 4 Afar, Arab **5** Issas **6** French **8** European

of Dominican Republic: 5 Negro, Taino **6** Indian **7** mulatto, Spanish **9** Caucasian

of Ecuador: 4 Cara, Cixo, Inca **5** Ardan, Aucas, Macoa, Maina, Palta, Quitu, Yumbo **6** Canelo,

Jibaro, Jivaro, Puruha **7** Cayapas, Jivaros, mestizo, mulatto **8** Barbacoa, Colorado, Montuvio, Serranos **10** Montubious

of Egypt: **3** Kem **4** Arab, Copt, Misr, Wafd **5** Gippy, Gyppy, Gypsy, Nilot **6** Ababda, Berber, Hyksos, Nubian, Tasian **7** Mizraim, Pharian **8** Badarian, Bisharin, Memphian

of El Salvador: **5** Lenca, Pipil **6** Indian, Mangue **7** mestizo, Spanish **9** Matagalpa

of England: **4** Celt, Jute, Pict **5** Norse, Saxon **6** Angles, Briton, Norman, Viking

of Equatorial Guinea: **4** Bubi, Fang **5** Benge, Combe **6** Bujeba **10** Fernandino

of Estonia: **4** Esth, Finn **5** Aesti **6** Jewish **8** Estonian **9** Ukrainian **11** Belorussian

of Ethiopia: **4** Afar, Agau, Beja, Doko, Kafa, Kala, Saho, Shoa **5** Afara, Agows, Galas, Galla, Negro, Tigre **6** Abigar, Amhara, Annuak, Gondar, Hamite, Harari, Sidama, Sidamo, Somali, Tigrai, Wolamo **7** Cushite, Danakil, Donakus, Falasha **8** Assamite, Blemmyes **10** Abyssinian, Troglodyte

of Fiji: **6** Fijian, Indian **7** Chinese **10** Melanesian, Polynesian **11** Micronesian

of Finland: **3** Jew, Vod, Vot, Yak **4** Avar, Finn, Hame, Lapp, Turk, Veps **5** Fioun, Gypsy, Ijore, Inger, Suomi, Vepse, Zyrin **6** Magyar, Ostiak, Ostyak, Tarast, Tavast, Ugrian **7** Lappish, Mordvin, Permiak, Samoyed, Uralian **8** Cheremis, Estonian, Karelian, Livonian, Swekoman **9** Tavastian **11** Karjalaiset, Suomalaiset

of France: **5** Frank

of the Gabon Republic: **4** Fang **6** Adouma, Bakota, Bateke, Echira, Okande, Omyene **7** Eshiras **8** Bandjabi, Bapounou

of the Gambia: **4** Fula, Jola **5** Foula, Wolof **6** Fulani **8** Mandingo, Serahuli **9** Seranuleh

of Germany: **3** Hun **4** Slav, Sorb, Wend **5** Saxon

of Ghana: **2** Ga **3** Ewe **4** Akan, Akim, Akra, Aksa **5** Ahafo, Brong, Inkra **7** Akwapim, Ashanti, Dagomba, Maprusi **11** Mole-Dagbani

of Gibraltar: **6** Jewish **7** British, Italian, Maltese, Spanish **10** Portuguese

of Greece: **5** Greek **6** Achean, Dorian, Ionian **7** Aeolian, Hellene

of Greenland: **3** Ita **6** Eskimo **8** European

of Grenada: **5** Negro **6** Indian

of Guatemala: **3** Mam **4** Chol, Itza, Ixil, Maya **5** Xinca **6** Caribe, Quiche **7** ladinos, mestizo, Pocomam **13** Guatemaltecos

of Guinea: **4** Koma, Loma, Nalu, Susu, Toma **5** Kissi, Manon **6** Fulani, Guerzi **7** Landoma, Malinke **8** Kouranke, Landuman **11** Kissi-Sherbo **12** Guerze-Kpelle

of Guinea-Bissau: **6** Fulani **7** Balanta, Balante, mulatto **8** Mandingo, Mandyako

of Guyana: **6** Akawai, Arawak, Creole, Taruma **7** African, Chinese, mulatto **10** Portuguese

of Haiti: **5** Taino **7** African, mulatto

of Honduras: **4** Maya, Paya, Sumo, Ulva **5** Carib, Lenoa, Pipil **6** Tauira **7** Jicaque, mestizo, Miskito **8** Mosquito

of Hong Kong: **5** Hakka, Haklo, Punti, Tanka **7** British, Chinese **8** American, Japanese **9** Cantonese **10** Portuguese

of Hungary: **3** Hun **4** Serb **5** Croat, Gypsy **6** Cigany, Magyar, Slovak, Ugrian

of Iceland: **6** Celtic, Viking **8** Norseman **9** Norwegian

of India: **2** Ao **3** Gor **4** Bhil **5** Aryan **6** Badaga, Pathan **7** Sherani **9** Dravidian **10** Andamanese

of Indonesia: **4** Dyak **5** Batak, Dayak, Malay **6** Battak, Papuan, Toraja **7** Chinese, Igorots **8** Acehnese, Achinese, Balinese, Javanese, Madurese, Sudanese **11** Minang Kabau

of Iran: **3** Lur, Tat **4** Arab, Kurd, Turk **5** Medes **6** Galcha, Gilani, Jewish, Shugni **7** Baluchi, Persian **8** Armenian, Bactrian, Bartangi, Parthian, Scythian **9** Bakhtiari **11** Azerbaijani, Mazandarani

of Iraq: **4** Arab, Kurd **7** Bedouin

of Ireland: **4** Celt, Erse, Gael **5** Irish **6** Celtic **9** Hibernian

of Israel: **3** Jew **4** Arab **5** Druze **10** Circassian

of Italy: **5** Latin **6** Sabine **7** Italian, Lombard **8** Etruscan

of Ivory Coast: **3** Abe, Dan, Kru, Kwa **4** Akan, Bete, Dida, Guro, Koua, Lobi, Wobe **5** Abron, Abure, Attie, Baule, Guere, Mande, Mossi **6** Baoule, Lagoon, Senufo, Senufu **7** Kroumen, Malinke, Voltaic **8** Dan-Gouro **10** Anyi-Baoule **11** Lobi-Kulango **12** Agnis-Ashanti

of Jamaica: **7** African, Chinese **10** East Indian

of Japan: **3** Eta **6** Korean **8** Japanese, Okinawan **10** Buramkumin

of Java: **5** Krama, Kromo **6** Kalang **8** Javanese, Madurese, Sudanese

of Jordan: **4** Arab, Kurd **7** Bedouin, Checher **8** Armenian, Assyrian **10** Circassian **11** Palestinian

of Kenya: **3** Luo **4** Arab, Meru **5** Bantu, Elgey, Galla, Kamba, Kisii, Luhya, Masai, Nandi, Tugen **6** Kikuyu, Ogaden, Somali **7** Baluyha, Hamitic, Hilotic, Kipsigi, Swahili, Turkana **8** Kalenjin, Marakwet

of Kiribati: **8** Banabans **10** Polynesian **11** Micronesian

of Korea: **6** Korean

of Kuwait: **4** Arab **5** Iraqi, Saudi **6** Indian **7** Bedouin **8** Egyptian **9** Pakistani **11** Palestinian

of Laos: **2** Lu **3** Kha, Lao, Man, Meo, Tai, Yao, Yun **4** Miao, Thai **5** Hmong **8** Lao Teung **10** Phoutheung

of Latvia: **3** Kur, Liv **4** Balt, Cour, Lett **7** Latgale, Latvian, Russian, Zemgale

of Lebanon: **4** Arab **9** Canaanite **10** Phoenician **11** Palestinian

of Lesotho: **4** Zulu **5** Bantu, Tembu **6** Basuto **7** Basotho

(*continued*)

ethnic group (*continued*)

of Liberia: 2 Gi **3** Gio, Kra, Kru, Kwa, Vai, Vei **4** Gola, Kroo, Krou, Loma, Mano, Toma **5** Bassa, Gibbi, Gissi, Grebo **6** Gbande, Kpelle, Kpuesi, Krooby, Kruman **7** Krooboy, Krooman **8** Mandingo **15** Americo-Liberian

of Libya: 4 Arab, Tebu **6** Berber, Tuareg **7** Gaetuli **8** Getulans, Harratin

of Liechtenstein: 8 Alamanni, Alemanni

of Lithuania: 4 Balt, Lett, Pole **5** Zhmud **6** Jewish, Litvak **7** Aistian, Russian, Yatvyag **10** Lithuanian, Samogitian **11** Belorussian

of Luxembourg: 6 French, German **12** Luxembourger

of Macao: 6 Macaon **7** Chinese **10** Portuguese

of Madagascar: 4 Arab, Bara, Hova **5** Malay **6** Merina, Tanala **7** African **8** Betsileo, Mahafaly, Malagasy, Sakalava **9** Antaimoro, Antaisaka, Antandroy, Tsimihety **10** Indonesian, Polynesian **13** Betsimisaraka

of Malawi: 3 Yao **4** Sena **5** Bantu, Lomwe, Ngoni **6** Cheiva, Maravi, Ngonde, Nyanja **7** Tumbuka

of Malaysia: 4 Iban **5** Dayak, Malay **6** Indian **7** Chinese, Kadazan **9** Pakistani, Sri Lankan **10** Bangladesh, Indonesian

of Maldives: 4 Arab **6** Indian **9** Sinhalese **10** Singhalese

of Mali: 3 Bwa **4** Fula, Kyan, Moor, Peul **5** Dogon, Dyula, Fulbe, Marka **6** Berber, Dognon, Fulani, Senufo, Tuareg **7** Bembara, Fellata, Malinke, Miniaka, Songhai, Soninke **8** Khasonke, Mandingo, Senoulfo

of Malta: 7 Maltese

of Mauritania: 4 Arab, Fula, Moor **5** Black, Fulbe, Wolof **6** Bafour, Berber, Fulani **7** African, Soninke, Tukulor **8** Sarakole **9** Sarakolle **10** Toucouleur **12** Halphoolaren

of Mauritius: 6 Creole, French, Indian **7** African, Chinese **8** European **13** Indo-Mauritian

of Mexico: 3 Ixe, Mam, Mie, Ser **4** Chol, Cora, Jova, Meco, Mixe, Pame, Pima, Roto, Seri, Teca, Teco, Texo, Xova **5** Aztec, Chizo, Chora, Mayan, Nahua, Opata, Otomi, Zoque **6** Eudeve, Indian, Mixtec, Pueblo, Toltec, Zotzil **7** Chincha, mestizo, Nahuatl, Nayarit, Spanish, Tehueco, Tepanec, Totonac, Zacatec, Zapotec **8** Lagunero, Mazateca, Tezcucan, Totonaco, Tzapotec, Yucateco, Zacateco, Zapoteca **9** Tlascalan **10** Coahuiltec, Cuitlateco, Tarahumara

of Monaco: 6 French **7** Italian **10** Monagasque

of Mongolia: 5 Oirat, Tungu **6** Buryat, Darbet, Khoton, Mongol **7** Kazakhs, Khalkha **8** Tuvinian **9** Dariganga

of Montenegro: 4 Serb, Slav **11** Montenegrin

of Morocco: 4 Arab, Moor **6** Berber, French **7** Spanish

of Mozambique: 3 Yao **5** Bantu, Chopi, Lomue, Lomwe, Macua, Makua, Ngoni, Nguni, Shona **6** Maravi, Thouga **7** Maconde, Makonde **10** Portuguese

of Namibia: 4 Nama **5** Bantu **6** Damara, Herero, Ovambo, Tswara **7** Bushman, Colored **8** Okavango **9** Hottentot

of Nauru: 7 Chinese **10** Melanesian, Polynesian **11** Micronesian

of Nepal: 3 Rai **4** Aoul **5** Limbu, Magar, Murmi, Newar, Tharu **6** Gurkha, Gurung, Nepali, Sherpa, Tamang **7** Bhutias, Kiranti **8** Gorkhali, Nepalese

of the Netherlands: 5 Dutch **7** Frisian **9** Hollander **10** Surinamese **12** Netherlander **13** South Moluccan

of New Guinea: 5 Pygmy **6** Papuan **7** Negrito **10** Melanesian

of New Zealand: 3 Ati **5** Arawa, Dutch, Maori **7** British, Ringatu **10** Polynesian

of Nicaragua: 4 Mico, Mixe, Rama, Smoo, Ulva **5** Cukra, Diria, Lenca, Sambo, Toaca **6** Mangue **7** mestizo, Miskito **8** Mosquito **9** Matagalpa

of Niger: 4 Daza, Idjo, Idyo, Idzo, Peul, Teda **5** Hausa, Warri **6** Djerma, Fulani, Kanuri, Songha, Toubou, Tuareg **13** Djerma-Songhai

of Nigeria: 3 Abo, Aro, Djo, Ebo, Edo, Ibo, Ijo, Tiv, Vai **4** Beni, Bini, Eboe, Efik, Egba, Ejam, Ekoi, Idyo, Igbo, Ijaw, Nupe **5** Angas, Benin, Gwari, Hausa **6** Chamba, Fulani, Ibibio, Kanuri, Yoruba **11** Hausa-Fulani

of Norway: 4 Lapp **5** Samme **6** Nordic, Viking

of Oman: 4 Arab

of Pakistan: 5 Sindi, Wazir **6** Afridi, Bengal, Mahsud, Pathan, Puktun, Sindhi **7** Baluchi, Brahuis, Punjabi, Pushtun, Sherani **8** Khattack, Shinwari, Yusefazi **11** Mohammedzai

of Panama: 4 Cuna **5** Choco **6** Guaymi **7** mestizo

of Qatar: 4 Arab **6** Pushtu, Yemeni **7** Baluchi, Iranian **9** Pakistani

of Rumania: 6 Dacian **8** Romanian, Rumanian

of Russia: 4 Slav **5** Ersar, Kulak, Tatak, Uzbec **6** Jewish, Kazakh, Soviet, Velika **7** Chukchi, Cossack, Kirghiz, Latvian, Russian, Tadzhik, Turkmen **8** Armenian, Estonian, Georgian, Siberian, Ukranian **9** Moldavian **10** Lithuanian **11** Azerbaijani, Belorussian

of Rwanda: 3 Twa **4** Hutu **5** Batwa, Pygmy, Tutsi **6** Bahutu, Watusi **7** Batutsi

of Samoa: 6 Samoan **10** Polynesian

of San Marino: 7 Italian **11** San Marinese

of Sao Tome and Principe: 7 African **10** Portuguese **11** Cape Verdean

of Saudi Arabia: 4 Arab **7** Bedouin

of Scotland: 4 Gael, Pict, Scot **5** Norse

of Senegal: 4 Lebu, Peul, Soce **5** Diola, Dyola, Foula, Laobe, Peulh, Serer, Wolof **6** Fulani, Serere **7** Bambara, Malinke, Tukuler, Tukulor **8** Mandingo

of Seychelles: 5 Asian **6** Creole, French, Indian **7** African, Chinese

of Sicily: 5 Elymi, Sican, Sicel **6** Sicani, Siculi

of Sierra Leone: **3** Vai **4** Kono, Loko, Susu **5** Bulom, Kissi, Limba, Mande, Mendi, Temne **6** Creole, Fulani, Syrian **7** Gallina, Koranko, Kuranko, Sherbro, Yalunka **8** Lebanese, Mandingo
of Sikkim: **4** Rong **5** Bhote **6** Bhotia, Bhutia, Indian, Lepcha **7** Tibetan **8** Nepalese **9** Mongoloid
of Singapore: **5** Malay **6** Indian **7** Chinese **9** Malaysian, Pakistani, Sri Lankan
of the Solomon Islands: **7** Chinese **8** European **10** Melanesian, Polynesian
of Somalia: **3** Sab **4** Asha **5** Galla **6** Hawiya, Isbaak, Somali **7** Danakil, Hamitic, Marehan, Samaale, Shuhali **8** Rahanwin
of South Africa: **4** Boer, Yosa, Zulu **5** Asian, Bantu, Namas, Nguni, Pondo, Sotho, Swazi, Tembu, Venda **6** Damara, Kaffir **7** African, British, Bushmen, English, Swahili **8** Bechuana, Coloured, Khoikhoi, San Xhosa **9** Afrikaner, Hottentot
of Spain: **4** Pict **5** Diego, Gente, Latin **6** Basque, Espana **7** Catalan, Espanol, Iberian **8** Galician, Gallegos, Maragato
of Sri Lanka: **5** Malay, Tamil, Vedda **6** Veddah, Weddah **7** Burgher, Mahinda, Malabar **8** Eurasian **9** Cingalese, Dravidian, Sinhalese **10** Ginghalese **12** Bandaranaike
of the Sudan: **3** Bor, Dor, Fur **4** Arab, Bari, Beri, Bobo, Daza, Egba, Fula, Golo, Nuba, Nuer, Poul, Sere **5** Anuak, Bongo, Dinka, Fulah, Hausa, Joluo, Junje, Mosgu, Mossi, Negro, Tibbu, Volta **6** Acholi, Azande, Gurusi, Hamite, Lotuho, Makari, Nilote, Nubian, Senufo, Surhai, Taureg **7** Balante, Baqqara, Gubayna, Jaaliin, Nilotes, Shilluk, Songhai, Songhay, Songhoi, Sourhai **8** Kababish, Mandingo, Menkiera **9** Sarakille **10** Gurmantshi, Shaiquiyya
of Suriname: **4** Boni, Bush, Trio **5** Djuka, Dutch **6** Creole, Wayana **7** African, Chinese **10** Amerindian, Boschneger, West Indian **11** Asian Indian
of Swaziland: **5** Asian, Bantu, Swazi **10** Eurafrican
of Sweden: **4** Lapp **5** Norse, Swede **6** Viking
of Switzerland: **5** Swiss, **6** Franks **8** Alamanni, Alemanni, Italians **12** Rhaeto-Romans
of Syria: **4** Arab, Kurd, Turk **5** Alawi, Aptal, Druse, Druze **6** Afshar, Aissor, Aushar, Avshar, Awshar **7** Amorite, Ansarie, Bedouin, Nosaris, Saracen, Shemite **8** Ansarieh, Armenian **9** Ansariyah **10** Circassian **12** Khachaturian
of Taiwan: **4** Yami **5** Hakka, Hoklo **7** Chinese, Malayan **9** Fukienese, Taiwanese **10** Indonesian, Polynesian **12** Kwangtungese
of Tanzania: **2** Ha **4** Arab, Gogo, Goma, Haya, Hehe **5** Asian, Bantu, Masai **6** Arusha, Chagga, Sukuma, Wagogo, Wagoma **7** African, Makonde, Sambara, Sandawe, Shirazi, Swahili, Wabunga, Zongora **8** Nyakyusa, Nyamwezi
of Thailand: **3** Lao, Mon **4** Lawa, Shan, Thai **5** Malay **6** Indian, Khymer **7** Chinese, Siamese **9** Cambodian **10** Vietnamese
of Tibet: **5** Asian, Balti, Bodpa, Drupa **6** Bhotia, Champa, Drokpa, Khamba, Khambu, Mongol, Panaka, Sherpa, Tangut **7** Bhotiya, Bhutani, Gyarung, Taghlik, Tibetan
of Togo: **3** Ana, Ewe, Twi **4** Mina **5** Hausa **6** Akposa, Kabrai **7** Bassari, Cabrais, Kabrais, Ouatchi **8** Konkomba, Kotokoli, Lotokoli
of Tongo: **10** Polynesian
of Trinidad and Tobago: **5** Irish **6** French, Syrian **7** African, Chinese, English, Spanish **8** European, Lebanese **10** East Indian, Portuguese, Venezuelan **11** Asian Indian **13** Latin American
of Tunisia: **4** Arab **6** Berber, Jewish
of Turkey: **4** Arab, Kurd, Turk **6** Seljuk
of Tuvalu: **6** Samoan **10** Polynesian
of Uganda: **4** Alur, Gisu, Soga, Teso **5** Ateso, Bantu, Chiga, Ganda, Langi, Lango, Nkole, Pygmy **6** Acholi, Ankole, Bagisu, Bakega, Basoga, Batoro **7** Baganda, Banyoro, Bunyoro, Hamitic, Lugbara, Nilotic, Sudanic **9** Nyoro-Toro **10** Banyankole, Karamojong
of United Arab Emirates: **4** Arab **6** Indian **7** African, Iranian **9** Pakistani **10** South Asian
of Upper Volta: **4** Bobo, Lobi, Samo **5** Bella, Bissa, Dyula, Fulbe, Hausa, Mande, Marka, Mossi, Puehl **6** Fulani, Senufo, Tuareg **7** Grunshi, Voltaic, Yatenga **8** Mandingo **9** Gourounsi **15** Bunsansi Gambaga
of Uruguay: **4** Yaro **5** Swiss **6** Indian **7** Italian, mestizo, Russian, Spanish **8** Charruas
of Vanuatu: **8** European **10** Melanesian, Polynesian **11** Micronesian
of Venezuela: **4** Bare, Pume **5** Bello, Carib, pardo, zambo **6** Arawak, Creole, Timote **7** Charoya, Guahibo, Kaliana, mestizo, mulatto, Otomaca, Timotex **8** Caquetio, Guarauno, Matilone **11** Maquiritare
of Vietnam: **3** Hoa, Man, Meo, Tai, Tay **4** Cham, Kinh, Nung, Thai **5** Khmer, Malay, Muong **7** Chinese **8** Annamese, Annamite **9** Cambodian **10** montagnard, Vietnamese
of Wales: **4** Celt, Kelt **5** Cymry, Kymry, Welsh **7** Brython, Silures, Taffies **8** Awabokal, Cambrian **9** Siluridan
of Western Sahara: **4** Arab **6** Berber
of Western Samoa: **6** Samoan **10** Melanesian, Polynesian
of Yemen: **4** Arab **5** Zaidi **6** Shafai, Yemeni **8** Yemenite
of Yugoslavia: **4** Serb, Slav **5** Croat **7** Bosnian, Slovene **8** Albanian, Croatian **9** Hungarian **10** Macedonian **11** Montenegrin **13** Herzegovinian
of Zaire: **4** Kuba, Luba, Yaka **5** Bantu, Bashi, Bemba, Kongo, Lulue, Lunda, Mongo, Pygmy **6** Azande, Baluba, Watusi **7** Bakongo, Nilotes, Tshokwe **8** European, Mangbetu, Sudanese
of Zambia: **4** Lozi **5** Bantu, Bemba, Ngoni, Tonga
of Zimbabwe: **3** Ila **4** Sena **5** Asian, Bantu, Bemba, Sotho, Tongo, white **6** Indian **7** Barotse, Chinese, English, Mashoma, Mashona, Ndebele **8** Coloured, Japanese, Matabele **9** Afrikaner **10** Balakwakwa

opera by: 11 Tchaikovsky
character: 4 Olga 6 Lensky, Onegin 7 Tatyana 12 Prince Gremin, Tatyana Larin 14 Vladimir Lensky

Eugenie Grandet
author: 14 Honore de Balzac
character: 5 Nanon 7 Charles, Eugenie 11 Mme d'Aubrion

Euhelopus
type: 8 dinosaur, sauropod
period: 10 Cretaceous

Euhemerism
theory of: 9 Euhemerus
reduced deification of: 4 gods

Euippe
origin: 5 Roman
form: 6 maiden
parent: 6 Daunus
husband: 8 Diomedes
changed into: 5 horse

Euler, Leonhard
field: 7 physics 11 mathematics
nationality: 5 Swiss
first: 12 calculus book

eulogize 4 hail, laud, tout 5 boost, exalt, extol 7 acclaim, commend, glorify, magnify 9 celebrate 10 compliment, panegyrize 12 pay tribute to, praise highly

eulogy 5 paean 6 homage 7 hosanna, plaudit, tribute 8 citation, encomium 9 laudation, panegyric 10 high praise 11 acclamation

Eumedes
father: 5 Dolon
companion of: 6 Aeneas
vocation: 6 herald

Eumelus
member of: 7 Trojans
commander of: 13 Thessalonians
lost race to: 8 Diomedes
wife: 8 Iphthime
companion: 6 Aeneas

Eumenides
author: 9 Aeschylus
character: 6 Apollo, Athene, Furies 7 Orestes *see* 6 Furies

Eumolpus
king of: 6 Thrace
father: 8 Poseidon
mother: 6 Chione
son: 7 Ismarus
founded: 19 Eleusinian mysteries
supported accusations of: 9 Phylonome

Euneus
father: 5 Jason
mother: 9 Hypsipyle

Eunice
son: 7 Timothy

Eunomia
member of: 5 Horae
personifies: 5 order

Eunomus
father: 10 Architeles
cup bearer of: 6 Oeneus
slain by: 8 Hercules

Eunuch 6 Biztha, Careas, Zethar 7 Abagtha, Harbona, Mehuman

Eunuch, The
author: 7 Terence

euphemism 11 prudishness, refined term 12 delicate term, overdelicacy 13 prudish phrase 14 mild expression, overrefinement

Euphemus
father: 8 Poseidon
mother: 6 Europa
aided: 9 Argonauts

Euphorbus
father: 8 Panthous
brother: 9 Hyperenor, Polydemas
fought with: 7 Trojans

euphoria 7 ecstasy, elation, rapture 9 well-being

Euphorion
father: 8 Achilles
mother: 5 Helen

Euphrosyne
member of: 6 Graces

Euphues
character in: 20 Euphues and His England 22 Euphues The Anatomy of Wit
author: 4 Lyly

Euripides
author of: 3 Ion 5 Medea 6 Hecuba 7 Electra, Orestes 8 Alcestis, Heracles 10 Andromache, Heraclidae, Hippolytus, Phoenissae, The Bacchae 13 The Suppliants 14 The Trojan Women 16 Iphigenia in Aulis 17 Iphigenia in Tauris 21 The Children of Heracles

Eurippa
epithet of: 7 Artemis
means: 18 delighting in horses

Europa
also: 6 Europe
father: 6 Agenor
mother: 10 Telephassa
brother: 5 Cilix 6 Cadmus 7 Phoenix
son: 5 Minos 8 Sarpedon 12 Rhadamanthus
daughter: 5 Crete
abducted by: 4 Zeus

Europe *see* 6 Europa

Europe *see box*

Eurotes
father: 5 Myles

Eurus
origin: 5 Greek
personifies: 8 east wind 13 southeast wind

Euryale
member of: 7 Gorgons

Euryanthe
opera by: 5 Weber
character: 6 Adolar 7 Lysiart 9 Eglantine

Eurybates
companion of: 8 Odysseus

Eurybia
father: 6 Pontus
mother: 4 Gaea
mated with: 5 Crius

Euryclea
nurse of: 10 Telemachus

Eurydamas
member of: 9 Argonauts

Eurydice
also: 7 Agriope
form: 5 dryad
husband: 7 Orpheus
daughter: 8 Themiste
pursued by: 9 Aristaeus

Euryganeia
son: 8 Eteocles 9 Polynices

Eurylochus
companion of: 8 Odysseus

Eurynome
father: 7 Oceanus
mother: 6 Tethys
sister: 6 Thetis
daughters: 6 Graces

Eurypylus
origin: 5 Greek
occupation: 7 warrior
father: 8 Poseidon, Telephus
mother: 8 Astyoche
uncle: 5 Priam
killed by: 8 Hercules 11 Neoptolemus

Eurysaces
father: 14 Telamonian Ajax
mother: 8 Tecmessa
inherited: 6 shield

Eurysthenes
origin: 7 Spartan
father: 11 Aristodemus
twin brother: 7 Procles
shared: 6 throne
shared throne with: 7 Procles

Eurystheus
king of: 6 Tiryns 7 Mycenae
father: 9 Sthenelus
mother: 7 Nicippe
cousin: 8 Hercules
son: 9 Perimedes
imposed: 6 labors
number of labors: 6 twelve
imposed on: 8 Hercules

Europe
country: **4** USSR **5** Italy, Malta, Spain, Wales **6** France, Greece, Monaco, Norway, Poland, Russia, Sweden **7** Albania, Andorra, Austria, Belgium, Denmark, England, Hungary, Iceland, Ireland, Rumania **8** Bulgaria, Portugal, Scotland **9** San Marino **10** Luxembourg, Yugoslavia **11** East Germany, Netherlands, Soviet Union, Switzerland, Vatican City, West Germany **13** Liechtenstein **14** Czechoslovakia
city: **4** Bern, Bonn, Oslo, Rome **5** Paris, Sofia, Vaduz **6** Athens, Dublin, Lisbon, London, Madrid, Moscow, Prague, Tirana, Vienna, Warsaw **7** Cardiff **8** Belgrade, Brussels, Budapest, Helsinki, Valletta **9** Amsterdam, Bucharest, Edinburgh, Reykjavik, San Marino, Stockholm **10** Copenhagen, East Berlin, Luxembourg **11** Monaco-ville **14** Andorra la Vella
river: **3** Don **4** Ebro, Elbe, Oder **5** Loire, Neman, Rhine, Rhone, Seine, Tagus, Volga **6** Danube, Thames **7** Dnieper, Pechora, Vistula **8** Dniester
island: **3** Man **4** Skye **5** Crete, Malta **6** Faeroe, Sicily **7** Corsica, Iceland, Ireland **8** Balearic, Sardinia **12** British Isles
mountain/mountain range: **4** Alps **7** Balkans **8** Caucasus, Pyrenees **9** Apennines **11** Carpathians **12** Sierra Nevada
highest point: **11** Mount Elbrus
lowest point: **10** Caspian Sea
sea: **4** Aral, Azov, Kara **5** Black, North, White **6** Aegean, Baltic **7** Caspian, Marmara **8** Adriatic **13** Mediterranean
people: **3** Hun **4** Gael, Pict, Serb **5** Celts, Croat, Danes, Dutch, Jutes, Kymry, Marur, Poles, Scots, Slavs, Tatar, Welsh **6** Czechs, Franks **7** Basques, Britons, Gypsies, Iberian, Magyars, Slovaks, Slovene **8** Alamanni, Cossacks, Tyrolean, Walloons
language: **5** Czech **6** Danish, German, French, Polish **7** English, Italian, Romance, Russian, Spanish, Swedish **8** Germanic **9** Bulgarian, Portugese **11** Balto-slavic
religion: **5** Islam **6** Jewish, Muslim **8** Anglican, Lutheran **9** Methodist **10** Protestant **12** Presbyterian **13** Dutch Reformed, Greek Orthodox, Roman Catholic **15** Church of England, Eastern Orthodox
holiday: **11** Bastille Day, National Day **12** Guy Fawkes Day **13** Liberation Day, St Patricks Day **14** Queens Birthday **15** Independence Day **19** Heroes of the Republic

Eurytion
form: **7** centaur
father: **4** Ares **5** Actor
companion of: **6** Aeneus
guarded cattle of: **6** Geryon
killed by: **6** Peleus **8** Hercules

Eurytus
form: **5** giant
father: **5** Actor **7** Auglaus **8** Melaneus
twin brother: **7** Cteatus
noted for: **7** archery
slain by: **8** Hercules

Euterpe
member of: **5** Muses
muse of: **5** music **11** lyric poetry

evacuate **4** quit **5** leave **6** desert, remove, vacate **7** abandon, forsake, move out, take out **8** order out **12** withdraw from

evade **4** duck, shun **5** avoid, dodge, elude, hedge, parry **6** escape, eschew **7** fend off **8** sidestep **10** circumvent, equivocate **12** steer clear of

Evadne
father: **6** Pelias **8** Poseidon
mother: **6** Pitana
sister: **9** Amphinome
husband: **8** Capaneus

evaluate **4** rate **5** assay, gauge, judge, value, weigh **6** assess, size up **8** appraise, estimate

evaluation **4** test **8** analysis, judgment **9** appraisal **10** assessment, estimation

evaluator **5** judge **6** critic, tester **7** analyst, arbiter **8** assessor, reviewer **9** appraiser, estimator

Evander
father: **6** Hermes **9** Carmentis
mother: **6** Themis
daughter: **4** Roma
allied with: **6** Aeneas

evanesce **6** vanish **8** fade away, pass away **9** disappear, dissipate, evaporate

evanescence **9** vanishing **10** fading away **12** ephemerality **13** disappearance **14** transitoriness

evanescent **8** fleeting **9** ephemeral, transient **10** short-lived, transitory

Evangeline
author: **24** Henry Wadsworth Longfellow
character: **17** Gabriel Lajeunesse **23** Evangeline Bellefontaine

evangelist **4** John, Luke, Mark **7** apostle, Matthew **8** disciple, minister, preacher, reformer **9** apostolic, missioner, soul-saver **10** missionary, revivalist **12** Bible Thumper, propagandist, proselytizer **17** religious crusader

Evan Harrington
author: **14** George Meredith
character: **6** Louisa **10** Jack Raikes **11** Rose Jocelyn **12** Tom Cogglesby **13** Count de Saldar, Juliana Bonner **14** Caroline Strike **15** Andrew Cogglesby, Ferdinand Laxley, Melville Jocelyn **16** Countess de Saldar, Harriet Cogglesby **21** Melchisedek Harrington

Evans, Dame Edith
born: **6** London **7** England
roles: **8** Tom Jones **11** A Doll's House **13** The Whisperers **14** The Chalk Garden **27** The Importance of Being Earnest

Evans, Mary Anne
real name of: **11** George Eliot

Evans, Maurice
born: **6** Dorset **7** England **10** Dorchester
roles: **9** Saint Joan **13** Rosemary's Baby **14** Man and Superman, Romeo and Juliet **15** Heartbreak House, Planet of the Apes **17** The Devil's Disciple **18** Gilbert and Sullivan **19** Androcles and the Lion

evaporate **5** dry up **6** dispel, vanish **7** scatter **8** dissolve, evanesce, fade away, melt away, vaporize **9** dehydrate, desiccate, disappear, dissipate

evasion **7** dodging, ducking, eluding **8** shunning **9** avoidance **12** sidestepping **13** circumventing, shrinking from **15** attempt to escape

evasive **6** shifty **7** devious, dodging, elusive, elusory, hedging **9** ambiguous, deceitful, deceptive, equivocal **10** misleading **11** dissembling **12** equivocating

Eva Trout
author: **14** Elizabeth Bowen

eve **4** dusk **6** female, sunset **7** evening, sunset **8** eventide **9** day before

Eve
husband: **4** Adam
son: **4** Abel, Cain, Seth
home: **4** Eden

Evelina
author: **11** Fanny Burney

even **4** calm, fair, flat, just, true **5** equal, flush, level, plane, plumb **6** placid, smooth, square, steady **7** balance, equable, flatten, regular, the same, uniform **8** balanced, constant, equalize, matching, parallel, straight, unbiased **9** equitable, identical, impartial, make flush, unruffled, unvarying **10** straighten, unwavering **11** make uniform, unexcitable **12** even-tempered, make parallel **13** dispassionate

evening **3** eve **4** dusk, even **6** sunset **7** day's end, sundown **8** eventide, gloaming, twilight **9** nightfall **10** close of day

evenly matched **5** equal **8** of a piece **9** identical **10** well suited **13** one and the same

evenness **7** balance **8** calmness, equality, fairness, flatness, sameness **9** placidity **10** regularity, smoothness, steadiness, uniformity **11** equivalency

event **4** bout, game **7** contest, episode **8** incident, occasion **9** happening, milestone **10** experience, occurrence, tournament **11** competition

even-tempered **4** calm **6** serene **7** equable, patient **11** good-natured, unflappable **12** mild-tempered, well-adjusted

eventful **7** crucial, epochal, fateful, notable, weighty **8** critical, exciting, historic **9** important, memorable, momentous, thrilling **10** noteworthy **11** significant **13** consequential, unforgettable

eventide **4** dusk **6** sunset **7** evening, sundown **8** gloaming, twilight **9** nightfall

eventual **5** final, later **6** coming, future **7** ensuing **8** imminent, ultimate, upcoming **9** following, impending, resulting **10** consequent, subsequent **11** prospective

eventually **6** one day **7** finally **8** in the end, sometime **10** ultimately **12** in the long run **13** sooner or later **17** in the course of time **20** when all is said and done

Eventus *see* **12** Bonus Eventus

even up **3** tie **5** align **8** make even **10** straighten

Evenus
father: **4** Ares
mother: **8** Demonice
daughter: **8** Marpessa

Eve of St Agnes, The
author: **9** John Keats

ever **5** at all **6** always **7** forever **9** at any time, eternally, in any case **10** at all times, constantly **11** incessantly, perpetually **12** continuously

Everdene, Bathsheba
character in: **22** Far From the Madding Crowd
author: **5** Hardy

Everes
son: **8** Tiresias

Everglade State
nickname of: **7** Florida

evergreen **3** fir, yew **4** pine **5** heath, holly **6** jujube, laurel, myrtle, needle, privet **7** arbutus, casiope, conifer, jasmine, juniper **8** camellia, hawthorn, oleander, rosemary **9** mistletoe, sugarbush **11** conebearing **12** rhododendrum

Evergreen State
nickname of: **10** Washington

everlasting **7** durable, endless, eternal, lasting, tedious, undying **8** constant, immortal, infinite, timeless, tiresome **9** ceaseless, continual, incessant, perpetual, unceasing, wearisome **10** continuous, ever-living **11** long-lasting, never-ending **12** imperishable, interminable **14** indestructible

evermore **6** always **7** forever **9** eternally **10** for all time **13** everlastingly

ever upward
Latin: **9** excelsior
motto of: **7** New York (state)

everybody
French: **11** tout le monde

everyday **4** dull **5** daily, stock, trite, usual **6** common, square **7** mundane, regular, routine **8** familiar, ordinary, workaday **9** customary, hackneyed, quotidian **11** commonplace, day after day, established, stereotyped **12** conventional, run-of-the-mill **13** unimaginative

Everyman
author: **7** unknown
character: **3** God **5** Death, Goods **6** Beauty **7** Kindred **8** Strength **9** Good Deeds, Knowledge, Messenger **10** Fellowship

every man for himself
French: **12** sauve qui peut

Every Man in His Humour
author: **9** Ben Jonson
character: **6** Kitely **7** Bridget **8** Bobadill, Wellbred **9** Brainworm, Downright **13** Edward Knowell **14** Justice Clement

Every Man out of His Humour
author: **9** Ben Jonson
character: **6** Deliro **7** Fungoso, Sordido **9** Macilente, Sogliardo **10** Puntarvolo **12** Carlo Buffone **15** Fastidious Brisk

everyone
French: **11** tout le monde

everywhere **7** all over **10** every place, far and near, far and wide, throughout **11** extensively, in all places, universally **12** the world over, ubiquitously **14** to the four winds

evict **4** oust **5** eject, expel **6** remove **7** kick out, turn out **8** dislodge, get rid of, throw out **10** dispossess

evidence **4** fact, sign **5** proof, token **7** exhibit, grounds **9** testimony **10** indication **11** affirmation **12** confirmation, illustration **13** corroboration, documentation, material proof **14** authentication, substantiation **15** exemplification

evident **5** clear, plain **6** patent **7** certain, obvious, visible **8** apparent, manifest, tangible **10** noticeable, undeniable **11** conspicuous, perceptible **12** demonstrable, unmistakable **14** unquestionable **24** plain as the nose on your face

evidently **7** clearly, plainly **9** assumedly, certainly, doubtless, obviously **10** apparently, undeniably **11** doubtlessly **12** unmistakably **14** unquestionably **16** to all appearances

evil **3** bad, sin **4** base, vice, vile **5** venal **6** sinful, wicked **7** heinous, immoral, vicious **8** baseness, iniquity, sinister **9** depravity, malicious, malignant, nefarious, turpitude **10** corruption, immorality, iniquitous, malevolent, pernicious, villainous, wickedness, wrongdoing **12** black-hearted, unprincipled, unscrupulous
goddess of: **7** Sekhmet

evildoer **6** sinner **7** culprit, villain **9** miscreant, wrongdoer **10** malefactor **12** transgressor

evil-minded **4** base **5** nasty **6** wicked **7** ignoble, immoral **8** depraved **10** despicable, iniquitous, villainous **12** dishonorable, unprincipled

evilness **6** malice **7** cruelty **8** villainy **9** barbarity, malignity **10** sinfulness, wickedness

evince **4** show **6** convey, reveal **7** display, exhibit, express **11** communicate, demonstrate **12** give evidence

Evius *see* **7** Bacchus

Evnissyen
origin: **5** Welsh
brother: **4** Bran **10** Manawyddan
sister: **7** Branwen
caused: **3** war
between: **5** Irish **7** British
killed: **6** nephew

evoke **4** stir **5** rouse, waken **6** arouse, awaken, call up, elicit, excite, induce, invite, invoke, summon **7** produce, provoke, suggest **9** call forth, conjure up, stimulate **10** bring forth

evolution **4** rise **6** change, growth **8** fruition, increase **9** expansion, unfolding **10** maturation **11** development, enlargement, progression **13** metamorphosis
founder of theory: **13** Charles Darwin
forerunner of theory: **12** Charles Lyell **18** Chevalier de Lamarck

evolve **4** grow **5** ripen **6** expand, mature, unfold, unroll **7** develop, enlarge **8** increase

Ewell, Tom
real name: **14** Yewell Tompkins
born: **11** Owensboro KY
roles: **8** Adam's Rib **9** State Fair **14** The Great Gatsby **16** Tender Is the Night, The Seven Year Itch

ewer **3** jug, urn **5** basin **6** vessel **7** pitcher

Ewing, Patrick
sport: **10** basketball
team: **13** New York Knicks **15** Georgetown Hoyas

exacerbate **3** irk **5** anger **6** deepen, worsen **7** inflame, magnify, provoke, sharpen **8** heighten, increase, irritate **9** aggravate, intensify **10** exaggerate **12** fan the flames **16** pour oil on the fire **17** add insult to injury **18** add fuel to the flames **19** rub salt into the wound

exact **4** take, true **5** claim, force, mulct, right, wrest **6** compel, demand, extort, strict **7** careful, correct, extract, literal, precise, require, squeeze **8** accurate, clear-cut, exacting, explicit, specific **9** on the head, on the nose **10** methodical, meticulous, scrupulous, systematic **11** painstaking, punctilious, to the letter, unequivocal

exacting **4** hard **5** harsh, rigid, stern, tough **6** severe, strict, trying **7** arduous **8** critical **9** demanding, difficult, hard-nosed, strenuous, unbending, unsparing **10** hard-headed, meticulous, no-nonsense

exactly **4** just **5** fully, quite, truly **6** indeed, just so, wholly **7** quite so **8** entirely, of course, strictly **9** assuredly, certainly, correctly, literally, precisely **10** absolutely, accurately, definitely, explicitly, that's right **12** specifically

exactness **8** accuracy **9** precision **10** exactitude **12** accurateness

exact satisfaction **6** avenge, punish **7** get back, get even, revenge **9** retaliate **14** get one's own back

exaggerate **5** boast **6** overdo **7** amplify, lay it on, magnify, stretch **9** embellish, embroider, enlarge on, overstate **11** hyperbolize

exaggerated **7** extreme, intense **10** inordinate, overstated **14** overemphasized

exalt **4** laud **5** cheer, elate, extol, honor **6** praise, uplift **7** acclaim, applaud, commend, elevate, ennoble, glorify, inspire, magnify, worship **8** venerate **9** celebrate, stimulate **10** exhilarate, make much of **12** pay tribute to

exaltation **4** high **5** bliss, glory, honor **6** praise **7** dignity, ecstasy, elation, rapture, tribute, worship **8** grandeur, nobility, praising **9** happiness, panegyric, transport **10** eulogizing, exultation, veneration **11** celebration, deification **12** exhilaration

exalted **2** up **5** grand, happy, lofty, noble **6** august, elated, lordly **7** excited, notable **8** blissful, ecstatic, elevated, glorious, inspired, uplifted **9** dignified, honorable, rapturous, venerable **10** heightened **11** high-ranking, illustrious, magnificent

exaltedness **5** bliss **6** height **7** ecstasy, elation, heights, rapture **8** highness, nobility **9** elevation, loftiness, transport

examination **4** exam, quiz, test **5** assay, audit, final, orals, probe, study **6** review, survey **7** midterm, perusal **8** analysis, scrutiny **10** inspection **11** looking over **13** investigation **15** physical checkup

examine **4** pump, quiz, scan, test, view **5** audit, grill, probe, query, study **6** peruse, ponder, review, survey **7** explore, inspect, observe **8** consider, look into, look over, question **10** scrutinize **11** inquire into, interrogate, investigate, take stock of

examiner **6** tester **8** inquirer, reviewer, surveyor **12** interrogator, investigator

example **5** ideal, model **6** sample **7** paragon, pattern **8** exemplar, specimen, standard **9** archetype, prototype **11** case in point **12** illustration **14** representation **15** exemplification

exasperate **3** bug, irk, vex **4** rile **5** anger, annoy, chafe, pique **6** bother, enrage, harass, madden, offend, rankle, ruffle **7** incense, provoke, turn off **8** irritate **9** aggravate, infuriate **15** try one's patience

exasperating **7** irksome **8** annoying **9** vexatious **10** irritating **11** infuriating

ex cathedra **12** from the chair **13** with authority **22** from the seat of authority

excavate **3** dig **4** mine **5** dig up, gouge **6** burrow, cut out, dig out, furrow, groove, quarry, tunnel **7** uncover, unearth **8** scoop out **9** hollow out **11** make a hole in

excavation **3** dig, pit **4** hole, mine, sump **5** ditch, grave, shaft, space **6** cavity, dugout, trench, trough **7** digging, opening

exceed **4** pass **5** excel **6** go over, outrun, overdo **7** outpace, outrank, surpass **8** go beyond, outreach, outrival, outstrip, surmount **9** come first, overshoot, transcend **10** be superior **11** predominate

exceedingly **4** very **6** vastly **7** greatly, notably **9** amazingly, eminently, extremely, supremely, unusually **10** enormously, especially, unwontedly, very highly **11** excessively **12** immeasurably, impressively, inordinately, preeminently, surpassingly **13** astonishingly, outstandingly, superlatively **15** extraordinarily

excel **5** outdo **6** exceed **7** prevail, surpass **8** outrival, outstrip **9** rank first **10** tower above **11** predominate, take the cake **20** walk off with the honors

excellence **5** merit **7** quality **8** eminence **9** greatness **10** perfection **11** distinction, high quality, preeminence, superiority **13** transcendence

excellent **4** aces, A-one, fine, tops **5** great, nifty, prime, super, swell **6** bang-up, choice, grade A, superb **7** capital, classic, notable **8** peerless, sterling, superior, terrific, top-notch **9** admirable, exemplary, first-rate, matchless, superfine, wonderful **10** first-class, preeminent, tremendous **11** exceptional, outstanding, superlative

excelsior **10** ever upward
motto of: **7** New York (state)

Excelsior State
nickname of: **7** New York

except **3** ban, bar, but **4** omit, save **6** enjoin, excuse, exempt, reject, remove, saving **7** barring, besides, exclude, shut out **8** count out, disallow, pass over **9** eliminate, excepting, excluding, other than **11** exclusive of

excepted **6** exempt **7** excused **8** excluded **11** not included

exception **6** oddity, rarity **7** anomaly, removal **8** omission **9** debarment, deviation, exclusion, exemption, isolation, rejection, seclusion **10** difference, leaving out, separation **11** elimination, peculiarity, repudiation, segregation, shutting out, special case **12** disallowment, irregularity, renunciation **13** inconsistency

exceptional **3** odd **4** rare **5** great, queer **6** unique **7** special, strange, unusual **8** aberrant, abnormal, atypical, freakish, peculiar, singular, superior, terrific, uncommon, unwonted **9** anomalous, excellent, irregular, marvelous, unheard of, unnatural, wonderful **10** first-class, inimitable, noteworthy, out-of-sight, phenomenal, remarkable **11** outstanding **12** incomparable **13** extraordinary, unprecedented **17** better than average

exception to the rule
7 anomaly **11** abnormality **12** irregularity

excerpt **4** part **5** piece **7** extract, portion, section **8** abstract, fragment **9** quotation, selection **13** quoted passage

excess **4** glut **5** extra, flood, spare **7** residue, surfeit, surplus, too much **8** fullness, overflow, plethora **9** avalanche, excessive, profusion, remainder, repletion **10** inundation, lavishness, oversupply **11** undue amount **13** overabundance **14** superabundance

excessive **5** undue **6** excess **7** extreme, profuse, too much **8** needless **9** senseless **10** immoderate, inordinate **11** exaggerated, extravagant, superfluous, unnecessary **12** overabundant, unreasonable **16** disproportionate

excessively **5** enorm **7** greatly **9** extremely, intensely **11** exceedingly, fanatically **12** boisterously, exorbitantly, inordinately **14** overabundantly

exchange **4** swap **5** trade **6** barter, switch **8** bandying, trade off **9** tit for tat **10** quid pro quo **11** convert into, give-and-take, interchange, reciprocate, reciprocity

exchange blows **3** box **5** clash, fight **6** battle, combat, tussle **7** contend, contest, grapple **8** skirmish **11** cross swords

exchange of viewpoints
6 debate, parley **8** dialogue **10** conference, discussion

exchange views **6** confer, debate **7** consult, discuss **8** consider, talk over **12** compare notes

excise **3** tax **4** duty **6** cut off, cut out, impost, remove **7** extract **8** pluck out **9** eradicate, surcharge

excitable **4** edgy **5** jumpy **7** jittery, nervous **8** feverish, frenzied, skittish **9** flappable, hotheaded **10** highstrung, passionate **11** combustible, inflammable

excite **4** fire, move, whet **5** evoke, pique, rouse, waken **6** arouse, awaken, elicit, foment, incite, kindle, spur on, stir up, thrill **7** agitate, animate, inflame, provoke **8** energize **9** electrify, galvanize, instigate, stimulate, titillate **13** get a kick out of

excited **4** daft **5** afire, astir **6** ablaze **7** aroused **8** agitated, ecstatic, frenzied, inflamed, turned on **9** disturbed, stirred up **10** magnetized **11** electrified

excitement **3** ado **4** flap, stir, to-do **5** furor, kicks **6** action, flurry, frenzy, hoopla, thrill, tumult **7** elation, ferment, flutter, turmoil **8** activity, brouhaha, interest **9** adventure, agitation, animation, commotion, fireworks **10** enthusiasm **11** stimulation

exciting **5** spicy **6** moving, risque **7** rousing, zestful **8** dazzling, stirring **9** affecting, impelling, inspiring, thrilling **11** hair-raising, provocative, sensational, stimulating, titillating **12** breathtaking, electrifying **13** spine-tingling

exclaim **4** howl, yell **5** shout **6** bellow, cry out **7** call out **8** proclaim **9** ejaculate **10** vociferate

exclamation **3** cry **4** howl, yell, yelp **5** shout **6** bellow, outcry, shriek, squeal **7** screech **9** expletive **11** ejaculation **12** interjection, vociferation

exclude **3** ban, bar **4** omit, oust **5** eject, evict, expel **6** banish, except, forbid, refuse, reject, remove **7** boycott, keep out, rule out, shut out **8** disallow, leave out, prohibit, set aside, throw out **9** blackball, repudiate **13** shut the door on

excluding **3** but **4** save **6** except, saving **7** banning, barring, besides **9** excepting, other than **10** keeping out

exclusion **6** ouster **7** barring, refusal, removal **8** ejection, eviction **9** debarment, dismissal, expelling, expulsion, rejection, restraint **10** banishment, keeping out, preclusion, prevention **11** prohibition, throwing out **12** nonadmission

exclusive **4** full, posh, sole **5** aloof, total **6** closed, entire, single **7** private **8** absolute, clannish, cliquish, complete, snobbish, unshared **9** undivided, selective **10** restricted **11** restrictive

exclusive of **3** but **4** save **6** except, saving **7** barring, besides **9** excepting, excluding, other than

excommunicate **3** ban **4** oust **5** eject, expel **6** banish, remove **8** unchurch **12** anathematize

excommunication **3** ban **6** ouster **8** anathema **10** banishment **12** proscription

excoriate **4** flay **5** curse **6** berate, revile **7** censure **8** denounce, execrate **9** skin alive

excrescence **4** bump, hump, knob, knot, lump **5** bulge, gnarl **6** nodule **8** swelling **10** protrusion **12** protuberance

excrete **4** void **5** expel **8** evacuate **9** discharge, eliminate

excruciating **5** acute **6** fierce, severe **7** cutting, extreme, intense, racking, violent **9** agonizing, exquisite, torturous **10** lacerating, tormenting, unbearable **11** unendurable **12** insufferable

exculpate **5** clear **6** acquit, excuse, pardon **7** absolve **9** exonerate, let one off, vindicate

excursion **4** hike, ride, tour, trek, trip, walk **5** drive, jaunt, sally, tramp **6** cruise, flight, junket, outing, ramble, sortie, stroll, voyage **10** expedition **12** pleasure trip

excusatory **9** defensive **10** apologetic **11** extenuatory, vindicatory **13** justificatory

excuse **4** free **5** alibi, clear, spare **6** acquit, defend, exempt, let off, pardon, reason **7** absolve, condone, defense, explain, forgive, indulge, justify, release **8** argument, bear with, mitigate, overlook, palliate, pass over **9** disregard, exculpate, exemption, exonerate, extenuate, gloss over, let one off, relieve of, vindicate, whitewash **10** absolution **11** exoneration, vindication **12** apologize for **13** justification **16** make allowance for **17** accept one's apology

execrable **4** vile **5** awful **8** dreadful, terrible **9** atrocious, revolting **10** abominable

execrate **4** hate **5** abhor **6** detest, loathe **7** despise **9** abominate, can't stand, excoriate **10** shrink from **11** can't stomach **12** be revolted by **13** be nauseated by, find repulsive **15** be disgusted with **20** regard with repugnance

execration **4** hate **6** hating **7** disgust **8** loathing **9** despising, repulsion, revulsion **10** repugnance **11** abomination, detestation

execute **2** do **3** act **4** kill, play, slay **5** enact **6** effect, murder, render **7** achieve, enforce, fulfill, perform, realize, sustain **8** carry out, complete, massacre **9** discharge **10** accomplish, administer, consummate, effectuate, perpetrate, put to death **11** assassinate **12** carry through **13** put into effect

execution **5** doing **7** killing, slaying **9** discharge, effecting, rendition **10** completion **11** achievement, carrying out, fulfillment, performance, realization, transaction **14** accomplishment, administration, implementation, interpretation, putting to death

executioner **6** hit man, killer, slayer **7** butcher, hangman **8** assassin, murderer

Executioner's Song, The
author: **12** Norman Mailer

executive **7** manager **8** chairman, director, overseer **9** president **10** leadership, managerial, supervisor **11** directorial, supervisory **13** administrator **14** administrative, superintendent

executives **7** leaders **8** managers, officers **9** directors **13** governing body **14** administration

executor **4** doer **5** agent **9** performer **13** administrator

exegesis **10** exposition **11** explanation **14** interpretation **18** explication de texte

exemplar **5** ideal, model **7** example, pattern **8** original, standard **9** archetype, prototype

exemplary **5** ideal, model **6** sample **7** typical **8** laudable, sterling **9** admirable, emulative, estimable, nonpareil **10** noteworthy **11** commendable, meritorious **12** illustrative, praiseworthy **14** characteristic, representative

exemplification **7** epitome, essence, example **8** citation, evidence **10** embodiment **11** case in point **12** illustration **13** documentation **14** representation **15** personification

exemplify **6** depict, embody, typify **8** instance **9** epitomize, personify, represent **10** illustrate **11** demonstrate **12** characterize

exempli gratia **6** such as **10** for example **19** for the sake of example
abbreviation: **2** eg

exempt **4** free **5** clear, freed, spare **6** except, excuse, immune, pardon, spared **7** absolve, cleared, excused, release, relieve **8** absolved, excepted, relieved **9** not liable, privilege **10** privileged

exemption **6** excuse **7** expense, freedom, release **8** immunity **9** allowance, deduction, exception **10** absolution **12** dispensation

exercise **3** use **4** show **5** apply, drill, exert, teach, train, tutor, wield **6** employ, school, warmup **7** break in, develop, display, execute, exhibit, perform, prepare, program, utilize, workout **8** accustom, aerobics, carry out, ceremony, movement, practice, training **9** discharge, inculcate, schooling **10** daily dozen, discipline, employment, gymnastics, isometrics **11** application, demonstrate, give lessons, performance, utilization **12** calisthenics **14** do calisthenics

exert **3** use **5** apply, wield **6** employ, expend **7** utilize **8** exercise, put forth, resort to **9** discharge, make use of **11** put in action, set in motion

exertion **4** toil, work **5** labor, pains **6** effort, energy **7** travail, trouble **8** activity, endeavor, industry, strength, struggle **11** application, elbow grease

ex facie **9** on the face **10** apparently **11** from the face

ex facto **8** actually **15** according to fact

exhalation **4** puff **6** breath, wheeze, whoosh **10** expiration **12** breathing out

exhale **4** huff, pant, puff **6** expire **7** breathe, respire **10** breathe out

exhaust **3** fag, tax **4** bush, poop, tire **5** drain, empty, spend, use up **6** expend, finish, strain, weaken **7** consume, deplete, disable, draw off, draw out, fatigue, wear out **8** enervate, overtire **9** dissipate **10** debilitate, devitalize, run through **13** sap one's energy

exhausted 4 beat, gone **5** all in, spent **6** bushed, done in, pooped, used up **7** drained, emptied, wearied, worn out **8** bankrupt, consumed, depleted, expended, fatigued, finished, tired out **9** dead tired, enervated, played out **11** devitalized **12** impoverished

exhausting 5 tough **6** tiring, uphill **7** arduous **8** toilsome **9** difficult, fatiguing, Herculean, laborious, Sisyphean, wearisome **10** burdensome

exhaustion 7 fatigue, using up **8** draining, spending **9** depletion, tiredness, weariness **10** enervation **11** consumption

exhaustive 6 all-out **7** in-depth **8** complete, profound, sweeping, thorough **9** intensive **12** all-embracing, all-inclusive **13** comprehensive

exhibit 3 air **4** show **6** flaunt, parade, reveal, unveil **7** display **8** brandish **9** put on view **10** exhibition, exposition, make public **11** demonstrate **12** bring to light **13** public showing

exhibition 4 show **5** array **7** display, exhibit, showing **9** unveiling **10** exposition **13** demonstration, public showing

exhibitionist 7 flasher, show-off **15** attention-seeker

exhilarate 4 lift **5** cheer, elate **6** excite, perk up **7** animate, delight, enliven, gladden, hearten, quicken **9** stimulate **10** invigorate

exhilaration 6 gaiety **7** delight, elation **8** gladness, vivacity **9** animation **10** exaltation, excitement, joyousness, liveliness **11** high spirits **16** lightheartedness

exhort 3 bid **4** goad, prod, spur, urge **5** egg on, press **6** advise, enjoin **7** beseech, implore **8** admonish, advocate, appeal to, persuade **9** encourage, plead with, recommend **14** give a pep talk to

exhortation 6 sermon, urging **7** bidding, lecture, pep talk **8** dictates, harangue, prodding **9** prompting

exhumation 9 digging up **12** disinterment **13** disentombment

exhume 5 dig up **8** disinter

exigency 3 fix, jam **5** needs, pinch **6** crisis, pickle, plight, scrape, strait **7** demands **8** hardship, quandary **9** emergency, extremity, urgencies **10** difficulty **11** constraints, contingency, necessities, predicament **12** circumstance, requirements

exigent 5 vital **6** urgent **8** critical, exacting, pressing **9** demanding, difficult, necessary

exile 2 DP **4** oust **5** eject, expel **6** banish, deport, emigre, pariah **7** outcast, refugee **8** drive out, expellee **9** expulsion **10** banishment, expatriate

Exile, The
author: 9 Pearl Buck

exiled person 5 exile **6** emigre **7** outcast **8** expellee **10** expatriate

Exile's Return
author: 13 Malcolm Cowley

exist 4 last, live, stay **5** abide, ensue, occur **6** endure, happen, obtain, remain **7** breathe, prevail, survive

existence 4 life **5** being **7** reality **8** presence, survival **9** actuality, animation, endurance **11** continuance, materiality, subsistence, tangibility

existent 4 real **5** alive **6** actual, extant, living **7** present **8** existing, tangible **9** surviving, to be found **11** in existence

existing 4 real **5** being **6** actual, extant, living **7** ongoing, present **9** existence, surviving, to be found **10** continuing, prevailing **11** established, in existence **12** accomplished

exit 4 blow **5** go out, leave, split **6** cut out, depart, egress, escape, exodus, way out **7** retreat **8** withdraw **9** departure **10** withdrawal **11** take a powder

ex libris 15 out of the books of **16** from the library of

ex nihilo nihil fit 25 out of nothing nothing is made **27** nothing is created from nothing

exocuticle
consists of: 9 sclerotin

exodus 4 exit **5** exile **6** flight, hegira **9** departure, migration **10** emigration, going forth

Exodus
author: 8 Leon Uris
story of founding of: 6 Israel

exonerate 4 free **5** clear **6** acquit **7** absolve, forgive **9** exculpate, vindicate **12** find innocent

exoneration 8 clearing **10** absolution **11** exculpation, vindication

exorbitant 4 dear **5** undue **6** costly **7** extreme **8** enormous **9** egregious, excessive, expensive, out-of-line **10** high-priced, inordinate, oppressive, outrageous, overpriced **11** extravagant **12** extortionate, preposterous, unreasonable

exorcise 5 expel **7** cast out **8** get rid of

Exorcist, The
author: 18 William Peter Blatty
director: 15 William Friedkin
cast: 8 Lee J Cobb **10** Linda Blair **11** Jason Miller, Max von Sydow **12** Ellen Burstyn
Oscar for: 10 screenplay

exoskeleton
of insect: 5 shell **8** body wall
part: 10 epicuticle, exocuticle **11** endocuticle

exoteric 4 open **6** public, simple **7** popular **8** exterior, external, outsider

exotic 5 alien **6** quaint, unique **7** foreign, strange, unusual **8** colorful, peculiar, striking **9** different, not native **10** from abroad, intriguing, outlandish, unfamiliar **11** exceptional **13** not indigenous

expand 4 grow, open **5** swell, widen **6** dilate, evolve, extend, fatten, spread, unfold, unfurl, unroll **7** amplify, augment, develop, distend, enlarge, inflate, magnify, stretch, unravel **8** heighten, increase, multiply **9** outspread, spread out **10** aggrandize

expanded 4 grew **5** grown **7** dilated, swelled, swollen, widened **8** enlarged, extended, unfolded, unfurled, unrolled **9** augmented, broadened, increased, outspread, spread out, stretched **10** heightened **11** aggrandized

expanse 4 area **5** field, range, reach, space, sweep **6** extent **7** breadth, compass, stretch **9** magnitude

expansion 6 growth **8** dilation, increase, swelling, widening **9** enlarging, extension, spreading **10** amplifying, distention, magnifying, stretching **11** development, enlargement, lengthening, multiplying

12 augmentation 13 amplification

expansive 4 free, open, vast, wide 5 broad 6 genial 7 affable, amiable, general, liberal 8 effusive, generous, outgoing 9 bounteous, bountiful, capacious, extensive, exuberant 10 voluminous 11 extroverted, far-reaching, uninhibited, unrepressed, wide-ranging 12 unrestrained 13 comprehensive

expatiate 6 expand 7 amplify, enlarge, expound 9 discourse, elaborate

expatriate 2 DP 5 exile 6 emigre, pariah 7 outcast, refugee 15 displaced person

expatriation 5 exile 9 expulsion 10 banishment

expect 5 guess, trust 6 assume, demand, plan on, reckon 7 believe, count on, foresee, hope for, imagine, look for, presume, require, suppose, surmise 8 envision, reckon on, rely upon 9 calculate 10 anticipate, bargain for, conjecture, reckon upon 11 contemplate 13 look forward to

expectancy 11 expectation 12 anticipation

expectant 4 agog 5 eager, ready 7 anxious, hopeful, waiting 9 expecting 10 looking for, optimistic 12 anticipating, apprehensive

expectation 4 hope 5 trust 6 belief, chance 8 prospect, reliance 9 assurance 10 confidence, expectancy, likelihood 11 presumption 12 anticipation 13 contemplation

expedient 4 help, wise 5 means 6 resort, tactic, useful 7 benefit, helpful, measure, politic, selfish, stopgap 9 advantage, advisable, conniving, desirable, effective, judicious, makeshift, opportune, practical, strategem 10 beneficial, instrument, profitable, worthwhile 11 calculating, self-seeking, self-serving 12 advantageous 14 self-interested

expedite 4 rush 5 hurry 6 hasten 7 advance, forward, further, promote, quicken, speed up 8 dispatch 10 accelerate, facilitate 11 precipitate, push through

expedition 4 trek 6 voyage 7 journey, mission 8 campaign, voyagers 9 explorers, travelers, wayfarers 10 enterprise 11 adventurers, exploration

expeditious 4 fast 5 alert, awake, hasty, quick, rapid, ready, swift 6 prompt, snappy, speedy 7 instant 8 punctual 9 effective, immediate 10 bright-eyed 11 efficacious

expel 4 fire, oust, sack, spew, void 5 eject, evict, exile 6 banish, bounce, remove 7 cashier, cast out, dismiss, drum out, excrete 8 dislodge, drive out, evacuate, force out, throw out 9 discharge, eliminate

expellee 2 DP 5 exile 14 banished person 15 displaced person

expend 3 pay 4 give 5 drain, empty, spend, use up 6 donate, lay out, pay out 7 consume, exhaust, fork out, wear out 8 disburse, dispense, shell out, squander 9 dissipate, go through 10 contribute

expendable 7 payable 9 available, forgoable, spendable 10 consumable, extraneous 11 disbursable, dispensable, replaceable, superfluous 12 nonessential 14 relinquishable

expended 5 spent 6 used up 7 drained, emptied, paid out 8 consumed 9 disbursed, exhausted 10 dissipated

expenditure 3 use 4 cost 5 price 6 charge, outlay, output 7 payment 8 exertion, expenses, spending 9 expending, paying out 10 employment, money spent 11 application, consumption 12 disbursement

expense 4 cost, rate 5 drain, price 6 amount, charge, figure, outlay 8 depletion, quotation

expensive 4 dear 6 costly 9 excessive 10 exorbitant, high-priced, immoderate, overpriced 11 extravagant 12 uneconomical, unreasonable 15 beyond one's means

experience 3 see 4 bear, feel, know, meet, view 5 doing, event, sense 6 affair, behold, endure, suffer 7 episode, observe, sustain, undergo 8 exposure, incident, perceive, practice, training 9 adventure, encounter, go through, happening, seasoning, withstand 10 occurrence 11 familiarity, live through, observation 17 personal knowledge 18 firsthand knowledge

experienced 4 able, wise 6 expert, master 7 capable, knowing, skilled, trained, veteran 8 seasoned 9 competent, efficient, practical, qualified 10 well-versed 11 worldly-wise 12 accomplished 13 sophisticated

experiential 9 empirical, first-hand, practical

experiment 4 test 5 assay, flier, trial 6 feeler, try out 7 analyze, examine, explore, venture 8 analysis, research 11 examination, investigate 12 seek proof for, verification 13 investigation 14 mess around with

experimental 3 new 4 test 5 fresh, rough, trial 7 radical 9 tentative 10 conceptual, first-draft 11 conjectural, speculative 13 developmental, trial-and-error

experimentation 7 testing 8 analysis, research 10 experiment 11 examination, exploration 13 investigation, trial and error

experimenter 6 tester 10 researcher 15 experimentalist

expert 3 ace, apt, pro, wiz 4 able, deft, whiz 5 adept, crack, doyen, maven, mavin, shark 6 adroit, artist, facile, master, wizard 7 artiste, capable, perfect, skilled, trained, veteran 8 masterly, skillful, virtuoso 9 authority, competent, masterful, practiced, qualified 10 first-class, past-master, proficient, specialist 11 connoisseur, crackerjack, experienced 12 accomplished, professional 13 knowledgeable **French:** 6 au fait

expertise 5 savvy, skill 7 know-how 10 expertness 12 special skill 14 specialization 15 professionalism

expertness 5 savvy, skill 7 ability, know how 8 training 9 expertise 10 capability, competence, experience 11 proficiency 12 special skill 13 qualification 14 accomplishment, specialization 15 professionalism

expiate 7 appease 8 atone for 13 make amends for 16 pay the penalty for

expiation 6 amends, shrift 7 penance 9 atonement 11 appeasement 16 paying the penalty

expiration 3 end 5 death, dying 6 demise, ending, finish 7 passing, closing 8 decrease, exhaling 10 conclusion 11 termination 12 breathing out

expire 3 die, end 5 cease, lapse 6 finish, perish, run out 7 decease, kick off, succumb

8 conclude, pass away 9 terminate 11 come to an end, discontinue 13 kick the bucket 14 give up the ghost

expired 4 dead, died 6 lapsed, ran out, run out 7 defunct, laspsed 8 deceased, lifeless, perished 10 passed away 11 came to an end, come to an end 14 gave up the ghost

explain 6 fathom 7 clarify, clear up, justify, resolve 8 describe, spell out 9 elucidate, explicate, interpret, make clear, make plain 10 account for, illuminate, illustrate 11 demonstrate, rationalize 14 give a reason for 20 give an explanation for

explainer 6 critic 7 analyst 8 reviewer 10 translator 11 commentator, interpreter

explanation
French: 15 eclaircissement

explicate 7 analyze, clarify, develop, explain 8 annotate 9 elucidate, interpret 10 elucidated, illuminate, illustrate

explication 8 analysis 10 commentary 11 elucidation, explanation 12 illumination 13 clarification 14 interpretation

explication de texte 8 exegesis 11 explanation 14 interpretation 17 literary criticism

explicit 5 blunt, clear, exact, frank, plain 6 candid, direct 7 certain, express, pointed, precise 8 absolute, definite, distinct, specific 9 outspoken 10 unreserved 11 categorical, unequivocal, unqualified 15 straightforward 16 clearly expressed

explicitness 7 clarity 9 clearness, precision 11 unambiguity

explode 5 belie, blast, burst, erupt, go off 6 blow up, expose, refute, set off 7 destroy 8 detonate, disprove 9 discredit, repudiate 10 invalidate, prove false, prove wrong 11 burst loudly 12 utter noisily 14 burst violently, express noisily 18 discharge violently 19 burst out emotionally

exploit 4 feat 5 abuse 6 misuse 7 utilize 8 profit by, put to use 9 adventure, brave deed, heroic act, make use of 10 daring deed 11 achievement 12 capitalize on 14 accomplishment, use to advantage 15 take advantage of 16 make selfish use of 21 take unfair advantage of 22 turn to practical account

exploited 6 abused 7 ill used, misused 11 downtrodden 15 took advantage of 16 taken advantage of

exploration 5 probe 7 inquiry 8 scrutiny 9 discovery 10 expedition, experiment 11 examination 12 scouting trip 13 investigation

explore 3 try 5 plumb, probe, scout 6 survey, try out 7 analyze, examine, feel out, pry into 8 look into, research, traverse 9 delve into, penetrate, range over 10 scrutinize, search into, travel over 11 inquire into, investigate, reconnoiter 14 experiment with

explorer *see box*

explosion 3 fit 4 clap 5 blast, burst, crack 6 report 7 tantrum 8 eruption, outbreak, outburst, paroxysm 9 blowing up, discharge 10 detonation 11 fulmination

explosive 5 shaky, tense 6 touchy 7 keyed up 8 critical, perilous, strained, ticklish, unstable, volatile 9 dangerous, emotional 10 ammunition, precarious 12 pyrotechnics

exponent 6 backer 8 advocate, champion, defender, promoter 9 expounder, proponent, spokesman, supporter 12 propagandist

export 7 send out 8 dispatch 10 sell abroad 11 foreign sale 12 ship overseas

expose 4 bare, risk, show 5 brand, offer, strip 6 betray, denude, divest, hazard, let out, reveal, submit 7 display, divulge, exhibit, imperil, let slip, subject, uncover, unearth 8 denounce, disclose, endanger 10 jeopardize, reveal to be 12 acquaint with, bring to light 16 leave unprotected

expose 6 baring 8 exposure 10 divulgence, revelation

exposed 4 open 5 bared 8 divulged, laid open, revealed, unmasked 9 denounced, disclosed, displayed, uncovered, unearthed 11 unprotected, unsheltered

exposition 4 expo, fair, mart, show 6 bazaar, market 7 account, display, exhibit, picture 8 exegesis 9 trade fair, trade show 10 commentary, exhibition, world's fair 11 description, elucidation, explanation, explication 12 illustration, presentation 13 clarification, demonstration 14 interpretation

expostulate 5 argue 6 enjoin, exhort, object, reason 7 caution, counsel, protest 8 forewarn 9 plead with 11 remonstrate 13 cry out against, reason against 14 inveigh against

exposure 4 view 5 vista 6 expose 7 outlook 8 frontage, prospect 9 divulging, unmasking 10 disclosure, divulgence, laying bare, laying open, reve-

explorer
American: 4 Byrd, Pike 5 Boone, Clark, Lewis, Peary, Perry
Australian: 4 Hume 5 Sturt 6 Stuart 8 Mitchell
British: 4 Bell, Cook, Park 5 Baker, Bligh, Bruce, Cabot, Davis, Drake, Grant, Puget, Scott, Smith, Speke 6 Baffin, Burton, Hudson, Lander 7 Raleigh, Stanley 8 Franklin 9 Frobisher, MacKenzie, Vancouver 11 Livingstone
Danish: 6 Bering 7 Niebuhr
Dutch: 6 Tasman 7 Barents, Le Maire 8 Schouten 10 Linschoten
French: 6 Joliet 7 Cartier, Jolliet, La Salle 9 Champlain, Marquette 12 Bougainville
Italian: 8 Columbus 9 Marco Polo, Verrazano 15 Amerigo Vespucci
Moslem: 10 Ibn Battuta
Norwegian: 8 Amundsen
Portuguese: 3 Cam, Cao 4 Dias, Diaz 6 Cabral, Da Gama 7 Almeida 8 Covilhao, Magellan 11 Albuquerque 23 Prince Henry the Navigator
Russian: 10 Middendorf 11 Przhevalsky
Spanish: 6 Balboa, Cortes, De Soto 7 Pizarro 8 Coronado, Orellana, Valdivia 11 Ponce de Leon
Swedish: 12 Nordenskjold
Viking: 10 Eric the Red 11 Leif Ericson

lation, subjection, submission, uncovering **11** perspective **12** public notice **15** bringing to light

expound **6** defend, uphold **7** explain **8** describe **9** elucidate, explicate, hold forth, make clear

express **3** say **4** fast, show, word **5** clear, couch, exact, lucid, plain, quick, rapid, speak, state, swift, utter, vivid, voice **6** convey, direct, evince, phrase, relate, reveal **7** certain, declare, divulge, exhibit, nonstop, precise **8** definite, describe, disclose, evidence, explicit, forceful, specific, vocalize **9** high-speed, make known, verbalize **10** articulate, particular **11** categorical, communicate, unequivocal **12** put into words

expression **4** look, mien, term, tone, word **5** idiom, style **6** airing, aspect, phrase, saying **7** emotion, meaning, stating, telling, venting, voicing, wording **8** language, locution, phrasing, relating, speaking, uttering **9** assertion, eloquence **10** appearance, modulation **11** countenance, declaration, enunciation, phraseology **12** articulation, setting forth, turn of phrase **13** communication

expressionless **5** blank, empty **6** vacant **7** deadpan **12** inexpressive

expressive **5** vivid **6** moving **7** telling **8** eloquent, forceful, poignant, powerful, striking **9** effective **10** compelling, indicative, meaningful, thought ful **11** significant **14** characteristic

expressly **7** clearly, plainly **9** decidedly, pointedly, precisely, specially **10** definitely, distinctly, explicitly **12** particularly, specifically **13** categorically, unequivocally **18** in no uncertain terms

express sorrow **3** cry **4** weep **6** grieve, lament **7** condole, console **10** sympathize **11** commiserate

expropriate **4** take **5** seize **8** take over **10** commandeer, confiscate **11** appropriate

expropriation **7** seizure **10** arrogation, taking over **12** confiscation **13** commandeering

expulsion **5** exile **6** ouster **7** ousting, removal **8** ejection, eviction **9** debarment, discharge, dismissal, exclusion, expelling **10** banishment **11** elimination, prohibition, throwing out **12** proscription

expunge **5** erase **6** delete, efface, rub out **7** blot out, destroy, wipe out **9** eradicate, strike out **10** obliterate

expurgate **3** cut **4** blip, edit **5** purge **6** censor, cut out, delete, excise, remove **8** bleep out **10** blue-pencil, bowdlerize

exquisite **4** fine **5** dainty **6** choice, lovely, superb **7** elegant, perfect **8** delicate, flawless, peerless, precious, splendid **9** admirable, excellent, faultless, matchless **10** consummate, fastidious, impeccable, meticulous **11** superlative **12** incomparable **14** discriminating

exquisiteness **6** beauty **8** delicacy, elegance, fineness **10** loveliness, perfection **12** flawlessness

extant **6** living **7** present **8** existent, existing **9** surviving, to be found **11** in existence

Extasie, The
author: **9** John Donne

extemporaneous **5** ad-lib **7** offhand **9** extempore, impromptu **10** improvised, off the cuff, unprepared **11** extemporary, spontaneous, unrehearsed **12** without notes **13** without notice **14** unpremeditated **15** spur-of-the-moment **19** off the top of one's head

extemporary **5** ad-lib **9** extempore, impromptu **10** improvised, off the cuff, unprepared **14** extemporaneous **19** off the top of one's head

extempore **5** ad-lib **7** offhand **9** impromptu **10** improvised, off the cuff, unprepared **11** extemporary, unrehearsed **12** without notes **14** extemporaneous, unpremeditated **15** spur-of-the-moment **19** off the top of one's head

extemporize **5** ad-lib **6** make up **9** improvise **14** speak impromptu **15** speak off the cuff

extend **4** give **5** grant, offer, widen **6** bestow, expand, impart, put out, spread, submit **7** advance, amplify, augment, broaden, draw out, enlarge, hold out, proffer, prolong, stretch **8** continue, elongate, increase, lengthen, protract, reach out **10** make longer, stretch out **12** stretch forth

extended **4** long **7** widened **8** drawn out, enlarged, expanded, thorough, unfolded, unfurled **9** broadened, continued, extensive, prolonged, spread out **10** lengthened, protracted, widespread **12** stretched out **13** comprehensive

extending **8** full form **9** expansion **10** drawing out, elongation, proffering, stretching **11** enlargement, lengthening **12** putting forth

extension **3** arm **4** wing **5** annex, delay **6** branch, length, outlay **7** adjunct **8** addition, appendix, increase **9** appendage, expansion, outgrowth **10** drawing out, proffering **11** enlargement, lengthening **12** continuation, postponement, prolongation

extensive **4** huge, long, vast, wide **5** broad, great, large **7** lengthy **8** enormous, extended, far-flung, thorough **9** capacious, universal **10** protracted, voluminous **12** all-inclusive, considerable **13** comprehensive

extensiveness **4** span **5** range, reach, scope **6** extent, spread **7** breadth, compass, expanse, stretch

extent **4** area, size, time **5** range, reach, scope, sweep **6** amount, degree, length **7** breadth, compass, expanse, stretch **8** duration **9** amplitude, magnitude **10** dimensions

extenuate **6** excuse, temper **7** explain, justify, qualify **8** mitigate, moderate

extenuating **9** lessening, tempering **10** mitigating, moderating, qualifying **11** attenuating, diminishing, explanatory, justifiable

exterior **4** face, skin **5** alien, outer, shell **6** exotic, facade, finish, manner **7** bearing, coating, foreign, outside, outward, surface **8** covering, demeanor, external **9** extrinsic, outer side, outermost **10** extraneous **11** superficial

exterminate **3** zap **4** kill **5** erase, waste **7** abolish, destroy, expunge, root out, wipe out **8** demolish, massacre **9** eliminate, eradicate, slaughter **10** annihilate, extinguish

external **5** alien, outer **7** foreign, outside, outward, surface **8** exterior **9** extrinsic, outermost **10** extraneous **11** superficial

extinct **4** dead, gone, lost **6** put out **7** defunct, died out, gone out **8** quenched, vanished **12** extinguished

extinction **5** death **7** eclipse **9** wiping out **11** destruction, eradication **13** disappearance

extinguish **3** end, zap **4** dash, do in, kill **5** crush, douse, quash **6** cancel, dispel, put out, quench, stifle **7** abolish, blow out, destroy, smother, wipe out **8** demolish, snuff out **9** eliminate, eradicate, suffocate

extinguished **6** put out **7** gone out **8** quenched **15** no longer burning

extirpate **5** erase **7** abolish, destroy, extract, pull out, root out, wipe out **8** demolish **9** eradicate **10** annihilate, extinguish, obliterate **11** exterminate

extol **4** laud **6** praise **7** acclaim, applaud, commend, glorify **8** eulogize **9** celebrate **10** compliment **16** sing the praises of

extort **5** educe, exact **6** coerce, elicit **7** extract **9** shake down

extortion **5** force, graft **6** payola, ransom **7** threats, tribute **8** coercion **9** blackmail, hush money, shakedown **14** forced payments

extortionate **5** undue **7** extreme **9** excessive, out-of-line **10** exorbitant, inordinate **12** unreasonable

extra **4** more **5** spare **7** adjunct, further, surplus **9** accessory, auxiliary, redundant, unusually **10** additional, attachment, complement, especially, remarkably, uncommonly **11** superfluous, unnecessary **12** additionally, appurtenance, particularly, supplemental **13** exceptionally **15** extraordinarily

extract **3** get **4** cite, cull **5** educe, evoke, exact, gleen, juice, quote, wrest **6** choose, deduce, derive, elicit, obtain, pry out, remove, select **7** copy out, distill, draw out, essence, excerpt, passage, pull out, root out, take out **8** abstract, bring out, citation, pluck out, press out, separate **9** extirpate, extricate, quotation, selection **10** distillate, squeeze out **11** concentrate

extraction **5** stock **7** descent, removal **8** ancestry **10** derivation, drawing out, pulling out

extraneous **5** alien **6** exotic **7** foreign, strange **9** extrinsic, unrelated **10** immaterial, incidental, irrelevant, not germane **11** superfluous **12** adventitious, inadmissible, nonessential, not pertinent **13** inappropriate

extraordinary **3** odd **4** rare **5** queer **6** unique **7** amazing, notable, strange, unusual **8** uncommon **9** fantastic, monstrous, unheard of **10** incredible, phenomenal, remarkable **11** exceptional **12** unbelievable **13** inconceivable

extraterrestrial **6** cosmic **10** outer-space **12** interstellar, otherworldly **14** interplanetary

extravagance **5** folly, waste **6** excess **7** caprice **9** absurdity **10** profligacy **11** prodigality, squandering, unrestraint **12** immoderation, improvidence, overspending, recklessness, wastefulness **13** excessiveness **14** capriciousness **16** inordinate outlay, unreasonableness

extravagant **4** wild **6** absurd, costly, unreal **7** foolish **8** fabulous, lavishly, prodigal, spending, wasteful **9** excessive, expensive, fantastic, high-flown, imprudent **10** exorbitant, high-priced, immoderate, inordinate, openhanded, outlandish, outrageous, overpriced, profligate **11** improvident, spendthrift, squandering **12** overspending, preposterous, unreasonable, unrestrained

extravaganza **4** fair **5** opera **6** ballet **7** pageant **8** carnival, operetta **9** spectacle, stage show **10** exposition, vaudeville **11** opera bouffe, spectacular **12** Broadway show, opera comique, son et lumiere, wild west show **14** phantasmagoria **17** sound and light show

extreme **3** end **5** depth **6** excess, height, severe **7** intense, radical, unusual **8** advanced, boundary, farthest, uncommon **9** excessive, extremity, nth degree, outermost, very great **10** avant-garde, immoderate, inordinate, outrageous **11** exaggerated, extravagant, most distant **13** extraordinary

extremely **4** very **5** quite **7** awfully **8** terribly **9** curiously, intensely, unusually **10** abnormally, especially, freakishly, peculiarly, remarkably, singularly, uncommonly **11** exceedingly, excessively, unnaturally **12** immoderately, surprisingly **13** exceptionally **15** extraordinarily

extremely painful **7** racking **9** agonizing, torturous **10** tormenting, unbearable **11** intolerable, unendurable **12** excruciating, insufferable

extremity **3** arm, end, leg, tip, toe **4** edge, foot, hand, limb **5** bound, brink, limit, reach **6** border, finger, margin **7** confine, extreme **8** boundary, terminus **9** outer edge, periphery

extricate **4** free **5** loose **6** get out, rescue **7** deliver, release **8** liberate, untangle **9** disengage **11** disencumber, disentangle **12** wriggle out of

extrication **6** escape **7** loosing, release **10** liberation **11** deliverance **13** disengagement **15** disentanglement

extrinsic **5** alien **7** foreign **9** accessory **10** accidental, extraneous, incidental **11** dispensable **12** nonessential

extrovert **7** show-off **13** exhibitionist **14** life of the party **17** hail-fellow-well-met

extroverted **8** outgoing, sociable **9** expansive **10** gregarious **12** unrestrained

extrude **4** spew **5** eject, expel **7** project, push out **8** force out, protrude, stickout **9** thrust out

exuberance **3** zip **4** elan, life, zeal **5** vigor **6** energy, spirit **8** buoyancy, vitality, vivacity **9** animation, eagerness **10** enthusiasm, excitement, liveliness **13** effervescence, sprightliness

exuberant **4** lush, rich **5** eager **6** lavish, lively **7** copious, excited, profuse, zealous **8** abundant, animated, spirited, vigorous **9** bounteous, energetic, luxuriant, plenteous, plentiful, sprightly **12** enthusiastic **13** superabundant

exudation **3** sap, tar **4** ooze **5** pitch, sweat **7** leakage, seepage **8** bleeding, drainage **9** discharge, excretion

exude **4** drip, emit, ooze **5** sweat **7** secrete **9** discharge

exult **4** crow **5** gloat, glory **7** rejoice **8** be elated **10** be jubilant, jump for joy **11** be delighted **13** be exhilarated **15** be in high spirits

exultant **5** happy **6** elated, joyful **7** crowing **8** boasting, ecstatic, euphoric, gloating, jubilant **9** rapturous, rejoicing **10** triumphant

exultation **3** joy **7** elation, ovation, rapture, triumph **9** rejoicing **10** jubilation

Eyck, Jan van
born: **8** Flanders, Maaseyck **10** Maastricht
artwork: **9** Timotheos **15** Ghent Altarpiece **18** Adoration of the Lamb, The Man in a Red Turban, The Virgin in a Church **20** The Arnolfini Marriage **24** Arnolfini Wedding Portrait **29** The Madonna with Chancellor Rolin **30** The Madonna with Canon van der Paele

eye **3** orb **4** scan, view **5** sight, study, taste, watch **6** behold, gaze at, look at, peeper, regard, survey, take in, vision **7** inspect, observe, stare at **8** eyesight, glance at **10** perception, scrutinize **14** discrimination
part: **4** iris, lens, rods **5** cones, nerve, pupil **6** cornea, muscle, retina **11** blood vessel

eyeful **4** doll **5** beaut, peach, Venus **6** beauty **7** stunner **8** knockout **10** good-looker **13** beautiful girl **14** beautiful woman

eyeglass, eyeglasses **4** lens **5** specs **6** eyecup, lenses **7** goggles, monocle **8** cheaters, contacts, pincenez **9** lorgnette **10** spectacles

Eye of the Needle
author: **10** Ken Follett

eyesight **4** eyes **5** sight **6** vision

eyewitness **5** gaper, gazer **6** gawker, viewer **7** witness **8** attester, attestor, beholder, informer, looker-on, observer, onlooker, passerby **9** bystander, spectator, testifier **10** rubberneck

Ezekiel
father: **4** Buzi

Ezra
father: **7** Seraiah

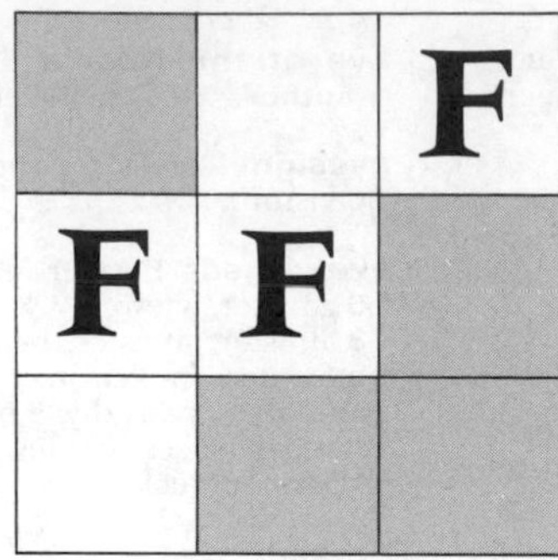

Fabares, Ruby Bernadette Nanette
real name of: **13** Nanette Fabray

fable **3** fib, lie **4** hoax, myth, tale, yarn **6** legend **7** fiction, leg-pull, parable, romance, untruth, whopper **8** allegory **9** fairy tale, falsehood, invention, tall story **11** fabrication

fabled **6** unreal **7** storied **8** fabulous, fanciful, mythical **9** imaginary, legendary **10** fictitious **12** mythological

Fables
author: **16** Jean de La Fontaine

Fabray, Nanette
real name: **28** Ruby Bernadette Nanette Fabares
partner: **9** Sid Caesar
born: **10** San Diego CA
roles: **7** Baby Nan **12** The Band Wagon **13** Sid Caesar Hour **15** High Button Shoes, Our Gang comedies

fabric ***see box***

fabricate **4** fake, form **5** build, erect, feign, forge, frame, hatch, shape **6** design, devise, invent, make up **7** compose, concoct, falsify, fashion, produce, trump up **8** assemble, contrive, simulate **9** construct, embroider, formulate **11** counterfeit, manufacture

fabrication **3** fib, lie **4** myth, yarn **5** fable **6** makeup **7** fiction, forgery, untruth **8** building, creation, erection **9** fairy tale, falsehood, invention **10** assemblage, concoction, fashioning, production **11** composition, manufacture **12** constructing, construction **13** prevarication **16** cock-and-bull story

Fabritius, Carel
real name: **13** Carel Pietersz
born: **14** Midden-Beemster, The Netherlands
artwork: **11** View of Delft **12** The Goldfinch **19** The Raising of Lazarus

fabulous **5** great **6** fabled, superb **7** amazing, storied **8** fanciful, invented, mythical, smashing **9** fantastic, imaginary, legendary, marvelous, wonderful **10** apocryphal, astounding, fictitious, incredible, stupendous **11** astonishing, spectacular **12** mythological, unbelievable **13** extraordinary

facade **4** face, mask **6** veneer **8** frontage, pretense **9** front view **10** false front **13** building front

face **3** air, mug, pan **4** coat, gall, grit, look, pout, puss, sand **5** brass, cheek, cover, front, image, nerve, pluck, spunk **6** aspect, daring, facade, kisser, mettle, repute, visage **7** bravado, dignity, front on, grimace, obverse, overlay, surface **8** boldness, confront, features, forepart, frontage, good name, overlook, prestige **9** encounter, hardihood, impudence, semblance **10** appearance, confidence, effrontery, expression, give toward, look toward, reputation,

---

fabric **5** cloth, frame, stuff **6** makeup **7** textile, texture **8** dry goods, material **9** framework, structure, substance, yard goods **10** foundation **12** organization, substructure **14** infrastructure, superstructure
cotton: **4** duck **5** denim, drill, scrim, terry **6** burlap, calico, canvas, chintz, dimity, madras, muslin, oxford, poplin **7** batiste, buckram, flannel, gingham, organdy, percale, ticking **8** chambray **9** crinoline, sailcloth **10** broadcloth, printcloth, seersucker **11** cheesecloth, dotted Swiss
linen: **6** canvas, damask **7** butcher, cambric **8** birds-eye **9** huckaback
natural: **4** jute, silk, wool **5** linen **6** cotton **8** asbestos
silk: **3** raw **4** tram **7** organza **8** organzie **9** organzine
synthetic: **5** nylon, orlon, rayon **6** olefin **7** acetate, acrylic **9** polyester
type: **4** felt, lace, lame **5** crepe, gauze, moire, serge, voile **6** damask, faille, jersey, melton, velour, velvet **7** brocade, chiffon, flannel, foulard, gingham, taffeta **8** chenille, corduroy, tapestry **9** gabardine, velveteen
wool: **4** felt **5** crepe, serge, tweed, twill **6** boucle, covert, faille, melton, woolen **7** challis, doeskin, Donegal, worsted **8** homespun, Shetland **9** Astrakhan, gabardine, sharkskin **10** hopsacking **11** Harris tweed, herringbone
from goats: **8** cashmere
sheep: **5** Iraqi **6** Hirrik, merino, Romney, Somali **7** Lincoln **8** Cotswold, Tatarian **9** Hampshire, Southdown **10** Corriedale, Dorset Down, Dorset Horn, Shropshire, Sikkim Bera **13** Hampshire Down
other wool-bearing animals: **5** camel, llama **6** alpaca, vicuna

turn toward **11** countenance, physiognomy, self-respect

Face
character in: 12 The Alchemist
author: 6 Jonson

facet 3 cut **4** part, side **5** angle, phase, plane **6** aspect **7** surface

facetious 5 comic, droll, funny, witty **6** clever, jocose, joking, jovial **7** amusing, comical, jesting, jocular, playful **8** humorous **12** wisecracking

face-to-face 6 direct **8** personal **9** firsthand

facile 3 apt **4** glib **5** adept, handy, quick, slick **6** adroit, artful, casual, clever, fluent, smooth **7** cursory, shallow **8** careless, skillful **10** effortless, proficient **11** superficial

facilitate 3 aid **4** ease **6** foster, help in, smooth **7** advance, forward, further, lighten, promote, speed up **8** expedite, simplify **10** accelerate, make easier

facility 3 aid **4** bent, ease **5** knack, means, skill **7** aptness, fluency **8** deftness, easiness, resource **9** advantage, appliance, dexterity, readiness **10** adroitness, capability, competence, efficiency, expertness, smoothness **11** convenience, proficiency **14** effortlessness, practicability

facsimile 4 copy **5** clone **7** replica, reprint **8** likeness **9** duplicate, imitation, photostat **10** transcript **12** reproduction

fact 3 act **4** deed **5** event, truth **6** verity **7** reality **8** incident, specific **9** actuality, certainty, happening, thing done **10** occurrence, particular **12** circumstance

faction 3 set **4** bloc, gang, ring, sect, side, unit **5** cabal, clash, group, split **6** breach, circle, clique, schism, strife **7** combine, coterie, discord, rupture, section **8** conflict, division, minority, sedition **9** rebellion **10** contention, disruption, dissension, dissidence, insurgency, quarreling **11** subdivision **12** disagreement **13** splinter group **15** incompatibility

factious 7 warring **8** divisive, fighting, mutinous **9** alienated, bickering, combative, estranged **10** contending, rebellious **11** belligerent, contentious, disaffected, disagreeing, dissentious, quarrelsome **12** disputatious **13** at loggerheads, insubordinate **15** insurrectionary **16** at sixes and sevens

factitious 4 sham **5** phony **9** pretended, synthetic, unnatural **10** artificial **12** manufactured

factor 4 part **5** cause **6** reason **7** element **9** component, influence **11** constituent **12** circumstance **13** consideration

factory 4 mill, shop **5** plant, works **8** workshop **11** manufactory

factotum 8 handyman **9** gal Friday, guy Friday, man Friday **10** girl Friday **12** right-hand man **15** jack-of-all-trades

factual 4 real, true **5** exact, plain **6** actual **7** certain, correct, genuine, literal **8** accurate, concrete, definite, faithful **9** authentic, unadorned **10** scrupulous, verifiable

faculty, faculties 4 bent, gift, wits **5** flair, knack, power, skill **6** genius, reason, talent **7** quality **8** aptitude, capacity, function, penchant, teachers **9** adeptness, endowment **10** capability, professors **12** mental powers, skillfulness **13** teaching staff

fad 4 mode, rage, whim **5** craze, fancy, mania, vogue **6** whimsy **7** fashion **10** dernier cri, latest word **11** latest thing

faddish 2 in **6** trendy **10** innovative **11** fashionable

fade 3 die, dim, ebb **4** blur, dull, fail, flag, pale, wane **5** droop, taper **6** bleach, lessen, recede, whiten, wither **7** crumble, decline, dwindle, fall off, grow dim, shrivel **8** diminish, dissolve, evanesce, languish, make pale, melt away, pass away **9** disappear dissipate, evaporate, lose color

fade away 3 die, ebb **6** recede **7** subside **8** diminish

faded 4 drab, dull, pale **5** dingy **6** grayed **7** died out **8** bleached, dwindled, whitened, withered **9** colorless, shriveled, washed out

Faerie Queene, The
author: 13 Edmund Spenser
character: 3 Una **5** Guyon **6** Duessa **8** Artegall, Gloriana (the Faerie Queen) **9** Archimago, Britomart **12** Prince Arthur **14** Red Cross Knight

Fafnir
origin: 12 Scandinavian
form: 6 dragon
father: 8 Hreidmar
brother: 5 Otter, Regin
killed: 8 Hreidmar
killed by: 6 Sigurd

fag 4 bush, butt, poop, tire, weed **5** weary **6** tucker **7** exhaust **9** cigarette

Fagin
character in: 11 Oliver Twist
author: 7 Dickens

Fahrenheit
abbreviation: 1 F

Fahrenheit 451
author: 11 Ray Bradbury

Fahrenheit, Gabriel Daniel
field: 7 physics
nationality: 6 German
invented: 16 thermometer scale **18** alcohol thermometer, mercury thermometer

fail 3 die, ebb **4** bomb, flag, flop, fold, wane **5** abort, crash, droop, flunk **6** desert, slip up **7** decline, dwindle, forsake, founder, give out, go under, let down, misfire **8** be in vain, collapse, fade away, languish, lay an egg, miscarry **9** disappear, fall short, fizzle out **10** end in smoke, go bankrupt, not succeed, run aground **11** be stillborn, come to grief, deteriorate, fall through, go up in smoke, miss the mark **12** come to naught, turn out badly **13** come to nothing **15** go out of business **16** meet one's Waterloo, meet with disaster

fail at 11 fall short of **12** be defeated in, not succeed at **16** be unsuccessful at

failed
French: 6 manque

failing 4 weak **5** shaky **6** defect, ebbing, waning **7** folding, frailty **8** drooping, flagging, giving up, slipping, weakness **9** deficient, dwindling, giving out, weakening, weak point **10** deficiency, going under **11** shortcoming **12** unsuccessful **13** insufficiency

fail to include 4 drop, omit **8** leave out

failure 3 dud **4** bomb, flop, mess, ruin **5** botch, crash, loser **6** fizzle, mishap, muddle **7** decline, default, failing, folding, misfire, washout **8** collapse, downfall **9** breakdown, ruination **10** bankruptcy, ne'er-do-well

Fainall, Mrs
character in: 16 The Way of the World
author: 8 Congreve

faint **3** dim, low **4** pale, soft, thin, weak **5** dizzy, faded, frail, giddy, muted, small, swoon, timid **6** dulcet, feeble, little, meager, remote, slight, subtle, torpid **7** fearful, fragile, languid, muffled, obscure, pass out, worn out **8** black out, collapse, cowardly, delicate, drooping, fatigued, timorous **9** exhausted, inaudible, lethargic, whispered **10** indistinct **11** lightheaded, lily-livered, vertiginous **13** inconspicuous **17** lose consciousness

fainthearted **4** weak **5** timid **6** feeble **8** cowardly **10** irresolute **11** halfhearted, indifferent, lily-livered

faintheartedness **9** cowardice **12** cowardliness, yellow streak **13** pusillanimity, yellow feather **17** pusillanimousness **18** chickenheartedness

fair **4** fine, just, pale, so-so **5** blond, bonny, sunny **6** bright, comely, creamy, decent, honest, justly, kosher, lovely, medium, pretty, proper, square **7** average, legally, not dark, upright **8** adequate, candidly, carnival, honestly, mediocre, middling, moderate, ordinary, passable, pleasant, rainless, squarely, sunshiny, unbiased **9** beautiful, cloudless, equitable, ethically, honorable, honorably, impartial, justified, objective, tolerable, unclouded **10** aboveboard, attractive, evenhanded, exhibition, legitimate, pretty good, reasonable, truthfully **11** indifferent, respectable **12** forthrightly, light-colored, light-skinned, on the up-and-up, run-of-the-mill, satisfactory, unprejudiced **13** disinterested, dispassionate **19** according to the rules

Fair, A A
pseudonym of: **18** Erle Stanley Gardner

Fairbanks, Douglas
real name: **17** Douglas Elton Ulman
wife: **12** Mary Pickford
son: **18** Douglas Fairbanks Jr
born: **8** Denver CO
roles: **9** Robin Hood **11** The Iron Mask **14** The Black Pirate, The Mark of Zorro **16** The Thief of Bagdad **18** The Three Musketeers **23** The Private Life of Don Juan

Fairbanks, Douglas Jr
father: **16** Douglas Fairbanks
wife: **12** Joan Crawford
born: **9** New York NY
roles: **8** Gunga Din **12** Little Caesar **15** Sinbad the Sailor **16** That Lady in Ermine **17** Catherine the Great **18** The Prisoner of Zenda **19** The Corsican Brothers

fair dealing **7** honesty **8** fairness **15** trustworthiness

Fairfax, Gwendolen
character in: **27** The Importance of Being Earnest
author: **5** Wilde

Fairfax, Jane
character in: **4** Emma
author: **6** Austen

Fairfax, Mrs
character in: **8** Jane Eyre
author: **6** Bronte

Fair Land, Fair Land
author: **11** A B Guthrie Jr

fairly **5** fully **6** justly, rather, really **7** rightly **8** actually, honestly, passably, properly, somewhat, squarely **9** equitably, honorably, so to speak, tolerably **10** absolutely, completely, moderately, positively, reasonably **11** impartially, objectively **12** evenhandedly, legitimately **15** dispassionately **19** in a manner of speaking
Latin: **9** pari passu

fairness **7** balance, honesty, justice **8** equality, fair play **11** objectivity **12** impartiality **14** even-handedness **16** equal opportunity

fair play **7** justice **8** equality, fairness **12** impartiality **16** equal opportunity

fair-skinned **4** pale **5** blond, light **6** blonde **17** light-complexioned

fairy **3** elf **5** pixie **6** sprite **10** leprechaun

fairy tale **3** fib **4** myth **5** fable **6** legend **7** fantasy, fiction **8** tall tale **9** invention **11** fabrication **16** cock-and-bull story
German: **7** Marchen

fait accompli **16** accomplished fact, thing already done

faith **4** sect **5** creed, trust **6** belief, church, fealty **7** loyalty, promise **8** credence, fidelity, reliance, religion, security **9** assurance, certainty, certitude, constancy **10** confidence, conviction, obligation, persuasion

faithful **4** true **5** close, exact, loyal, tried **6** honest, strict, trusty **7** devoted, factual, precise, similar, staunch, upright **8** accurate, constant, lifelike, reliable, resolute, truthful **9** steadfast **10** dependable, scrupulous, true-to-life, unswerving, unwavering, verifiable **11** trustworthy **13** conscientious, incorruptible

faithfulness **6** fealty **7** loyalty **8** devotion, fidelity **9** constancy **10** allegiance **11** reliability **13** steadfastness

faithless **5** false **6** fickle **8** disloyal **10** inconstant, perfidious, unreliable **11** treacherous **13** untrustworthy

faithlessness **5** doubt **7** perfidy **9** disbelief, falseness, treachery **10** disloyalty, fickleness, infidelity, skepticism **11** inconstancy **13** unreliability **14** perfidiousness, unfaithfulness

fake **4** hoax, ruse, sham **5** bogus, dodge, dummy, faker, false, feign, forge, fraud, phony, put-on, quack, trick **6** deceit, forged, humbug, poseur, pseudo **7** falsify, forgery, not real, pretend, trump up **8** artifice, contrive, deceiver, delusion, imposter, invented, simulate, specious, spurious **9** charlatan, concocted, contrived, deception, dissemble, fabricate, imitation, imposture, pretender, simulated **10** artificial, fabricated, fictitious **11** contrivance, counterfeit, dissimulate, fabrication, make-believe

faker **5** fraud, phony **6** humbug **8** imposter **9** charlatan, pretender

fakir **5** Hindu **6** Muslim **7** ascetic, dervish

falcon **5** hobby, saker **6** desert, lanner, merlin **7** goshawk, kestrel, prairie, shaheen, tiercel **8** caracara, falconet **9** gyrfalcon, peregrine

Falcon and the Snowman, The
author: **13** Robert Lindsey
director: **15** John Schlesinger
cast: **8** Sean Penn (Andrew Daulton Lee, the Snowman) **13** Timothy Hutton (Christopher John Boyce, the Falcon)

Falconer
author: **11** John Cheever

Falconet, Etienne-Maurice
born: **5** Paris **6** France
artwork: **9** The Bather **12** Bathing Nymph **13** Milo of Crotona, Peter the Great **19** Pygmalion and Galatea

falconry **7** hawking
equipment: **4** lure **5** cadge **6** jesses **7** creance

Falk, Lee
creator/artist of: 10 The Phantom **19** Mandrake the Magician

Falk, Peter
born: 9 New York NY
roles: 7 Columbo **9** Murder Inc **12** The Great Race **13** Murder by Death **17** The Cheap Detective **19** Pocketful of Miracles **21** It's a Mad Mad Mad Mad World, Robin and the Seven Hoods

fall, falls 3 die, ebb, err, sin **4** drop, plop, ruin, slip, wane **5** droop, lapse, occur, slope, slump, spill **6** autumn, crop up, defeat, happen, perish, plunge, topple, tumble **7** be slain, be taken, capture, cascade, cheapen, come off, crumple, decline, descend, descent, falling, plummet, sinking, succumb **8** cataract, collapse, come down, decrease, diminish, disgrace, downfall, drop down, dropping, go astray, hang down, lowering **9** crash down, overthrow, reduction, surrender, take place, waterfall **10** capitulate, come to pass, corruption, debasement, depreciate, diminution, subsidence, subversion, transgress **11** be destroyed, harvest time **12** capitulation, depreciation, Indian summer **15** loss of innocence

Fall, The
author: 11 Albert Camus

Falla, Manuel de
born: 5 Cadiz, Spain
composer of: 11 El Amor Brujo, La Atlantida, La Vida Breve, Life Is Short **14** Fantasia Betica **15** Love the Magician **19** The Three-Cornered Hat **21** El sombrero de tres picos **25** Nights in the Gardens of Spain

fallacious 5 false, wrong **6** faulty, flawed, untrue **8** delusive, mistaken **9** deceptive, erroneous, illogical, incorrect **10** inaccurate, misleading, untruthful

fallacy 4 flaw **5** catch, error, fault **7** mistake, pitfall **8** delusion, illusion **9** misbelief **10** faultiness **11** false belief, false notion **13** inconsistency, misconception **15** misapprehension

fall apart 5 decay **7** break up, crumble, shatter **8** fragment, splinter **10** go to pieces **11** fragmentize **12** disintegrate

fall away 4 fade, wane **5** abate **7** drop off, slacken, subside **8** mitigate, taper off

fall back 6 recede **7** back off, retreat

fallen 4 dead **5** loose, slain **6** ousted, ruined, sinful **7** debased, deposed, dropped, immoral, spilled, toppled, tumbled **8** sprawled **9** butchered, disgraced, massacred, turned out **10** discharged, overthrown **11** slaughtered

fallen short
French: 6 manque

fall for 7 believe, swallow

fall guy 4 dupe, pawn, tool **5** patsy **7** cat's-paw

fallible 5 frail, human **6** faulty, mortal, unsure **9** imperfect **10** unreliable

fall in drops 4 drip, rain **7** dribble, drizzle **8** sprinkle

falling apart 6 ruined, shabby **7** rickety, run-down **8** decaying, decrepit **9** crumbling **10** broken-down, collapsing, ramshackle, tumbledown **11** dilapidated **13** deteriorating

Falling in Place
author: 10 Ann Beattie

falling into decay 6 ruined, shabby **7** rotting, run-down **8** decrepit **9** crumbling, moldering **10** broken-down, tumbledown **11** dilapidated, in disrepair **13** deteriorating

falling off 3 ebb **4** fall, wane **7** decline **8** decrease **9** dwindling, lessening, reduction **10** diminution **13** deterioration

falling out 4 spat **7** dispute, quarrel **8** argument, squabble **10** difference **12** disagreement

fall in with 6 concur **7** conform **8** accede to **9** acquiesce **11** go along with

fall off 4 drop, wane **6** lessen, plunge, reduce, topple **7** decline, drop off, plummet, slacken, subside **8** decrease, diminish, moderate, peter out

Fall of the House of Usher, The
author: 13 Edgar Allan Poe
character: 8 Narrator **13** Madeline Usher, Roderick Usher

fallow 4 arid, idle **5** inert **6** barren, unused **7** dormant, unsowed, worn out **8** depleted, inactive, untilled **9** exhausted, unplanted **10** unfruitful **12** uncultivated, unproductive

fall short 6 be less, fail at, give up **9** be lacking, lag behind **10** have too few **11** fail to reach, miss the mark **12** be inadequate **14** be insufficient

fall to one's lot 4 fall **5** occur **6** befall, chance, happen **7** turn out **9** come about **10** come to pass

fall upon 5 fly at **6** assail, attack, dive at **7** embrace, lunge at, set upon **8** thrust at, tuck into

false 4 fake, sham **5** bogus, phony, wrong **6** ersatz, faulty, forged, pseudo, tricky, unreal, untrue **7** devious, feigned, inexact, invalid, unsound **8** delusive, disloyal, mistaken, spurious, two-faced **9** deceitful, deceiving, deceptive, dishonest, erroneous, faithless, imitation, incorrect, unfounded **10** apocryphal, artificial, factitious, fallacious, inaccurate, inconstant, misleading, not correct, perfidious, traitorous, unfaithful, untruthful **11** counterfeit, make-believe, treacherous **12** hypocritical **13** double-dealing

false front 4 mask, sham, show **6** facade, screen, veneer **8** pretense

false-hearted 8 two-faced **9** deceitful, deceiving, faithless **10** perfidious **13** double-dealing, untrustworthy

falsehood 3 fib, lie **5** lying, story **6** canard, deceit **7** fiction, figment, perfidy, perjury, untruth, whopper **8** bad faith, white lie **9** deception, duplicity, hypocrisy, invention, mendacity **10** dishonesty, distortion, inaccuracy **11** dissembling, fabrication, insincerity **12** misstatement, two-facedness **13** deceptiveness, dissimulation, double-dealing, falsification **17** misrepresentation

falseness 5 fraud **6** deceit **7** perfidy **9** duplicity, treachery **10** dishonesty **12** spuriousness **13** deceitfulness, double-dealing, faithlessness **14** untruthfulness

falsified 5 false, phony **6** forged, made-up **7** assumed **10** fictitious

falsify 4 fake **5** belie, rebut **6** doctor, misuse, refute **7** confute, distort, pervert **8** disprove **10** tamper with **12** misrepresent

Falstaff
opera by: 5 Verdi
character: 4 Anne **6** Fenton, Pistol **7** Dr Caius **8** Bardolph **11** Dame Quickly **12** Mistress Ford, Mistress Page **15** Mistress Quickly, Sir John Falstaff

Falstaff, Sir John
character in: **22** The Merry Wives of Windsor
author: **11** Shakespeare

falter **3** lag **4** halt, reel **5** demur, waver **6** dodder, mumble, shrink, teeter, totter **7** shamble, shuffle, stagger, stammer, stumble, stutter **8** hesitate **9** fluctuate, vacillate **10** dilly-dally **11** be undecided **12** be irresolute, show weakness **14** blow hot and cold

fame **4** note **5** glory **6** renown, repute **7** laurels **8** eminence, prestige **9** celebrity, notoriety **10** notability, popularity, prominence, reputation **11** distinction, preeminence **15** illustriousness

famed **5** noted **6** famous **7** notable **8** renowned **9** prominent, well-known **10** celebrated

familiar **3** pal **4** bold, chum, cozy, free, snug **5** buddy, close, crony, known, stock, usual **6** chummy, common, friend **7** forward, general **8** accepted, amicable, at home in, everyday, frequent, friendly, habitual, informal, intimate, ordinary, seasoned, versed in **9** abreast of, brotherly, confidant, customary, fraternal, gemutlich, intrusive, simpatico, skilled in, well-known **10** accessible, accustomed, acquainted, apprised of, conversant, proverbial, unreserved **11** cognizant of, commonplace, impertinent, traditional **12** confidential, conventional, hand and glove, no stranger to, proficient at **13** boon companion, companionable, disrespectful **15** taking liberties

familiarity **4** ease **5** amity, skill **7** know-how, mastery **8** coziness, intimacy **9** closeness, impudence, indecorum, knowledge, unreserve **10** casualness, chumminess, cognizance, disrespect, experience, fellowship, fraternity, friendship **11** association, brotherhood, conversance, forwardness, impropriety, informality, naturalness, presumption, proficiency **12** acquaintance, impertinence, unconstraint, undue liberty, unseemliness **13** brotherliness, comprehension, intrusiveness, understanding, undue intimacy **16** acquaintanceship

familiarize **5** edify, teach, tutor **6** inform, school, season **7** educate **8** accustom, acquaint, instruct **9** enlighten, habituate, inculcate **11** acclimatize

family **3** kin, set **4** clan, kind, line, race **5** blood, breed, brood, class, group, house, issue, order, stock, tribe **7** dynasty, kinfolk, kinsmen, lineage, progeny **8** ancestry, category, division, kinsfolk **9** forebears, genealogy, offspring, parentage, relations, relatives **10** extraction, kith and kin **11** forefathers **14** classification
goddess of: **6** Cardea

Family Affair
character: **4** Jody **5** Buffy, Cissy **8** Mr (Giles) French **9** Bill Davis
cast: **10** Brian Keith **11** Anissa Jones, Kathy Garver **14** Sebastian Cabot **15** Johnnie Whitaker

family line **7** lineage **8** ancestry **9** blood line, genealogy, parentage

Family Moskat, The
author: **19** Isaac Bashevis Singer

Family Reunion, The
author: **7** T S Eliot

Family Ties
character: **4** Nick **5** Ellen **6** Skippy **10** Alex Keaton **11** Elyse Keaton **12** Andrew Keaton, Steven Keaton **13** Mallory Keaton **14** Jennifer Keaton
cast: **9** Marc Price **11** Michael J Fox, Tina Yothers **12** Michael Gross **14** Justine Bateman **20** Meredith Baxter-Birney

family tree **7** lineage **8** ancestry, pedigree **9** blood line, genealogy

famine **4** lack, want **6** dearth **7** paucity, poverty **8** scarcity **9** depletion **10** deficiency, exhaustion, famishment, meagerness, scantiness, starvation **11** destitution, half rations, short supply **13** acute shortage, extreme hunger, insufficiency

famish **6** hunger, starve

famous **5** noted **7** eminent, notable **8** far-famed, renowned, well-known **9** notorious, prominent **10** celebrated **11** conspicuous, illustrious **13** distinguished

famous person **4** name, star **7** notable **8** luminary, somebody **9** celebrity, personage, superstar **11** personality

fan **3** bug, nut **4** buff **5** fiend, freak **6** addict, rooter, zealot **7** booster, fanatic **8** follower, partisan

fanatic **5** crazy **6** maniac, zealot **7** hothead, radical **8** activist, militant **9** extremist **10** enthusiast **24** member of the lunatic fringe

fanaticism **6** fervor **8** activism, zealotry **9** dogmatism, extremism, monomania, obsession **10** enthusiasm, radicalism **11** extreme zeal, militantism **12** intemperance **13** ruling passion **15** opinionatedness

fancied **5** liked **6** dreamt, took to, unreal **7** assumed, desired, dreamed, thought **8** imagined, supposed **9** conceived, imaginary, preferred

fanciful **3** odd **6** unreal **7** bizarre, curious, flighty, unusual **8** fabulous, humorous, illusory, mythical, quixotic, romantic **9** eccentric, fantastic, imaginary, invective, legendary, visionary, whimsical **10** apocryphal, capricious, chimerical, fictitious **11** imaginative

fanciful talk **7** blarney **9** hyperbole, tall tales **11** fish stories **12** exaggeration

fancy **3** yen **4** fine, idea, like, want **5** crave, dream, enjoy, favor, opine, showy, taste, think **6** assume, custom, deluxe, desire, florid, liking, notion, ornate, relish, rococo, take it, take to, vagary, vision, whimsy **7** baroque, caprice, conceit, dream of, elegant, fantasy, figment, gourmet, imagine, leaning, longing, long for, picture, presume, reverie, special, suppose, surmise, suspect, unusual **8** be fond of, crotchet, daydream, fondness, illusion, not plain, penchant, superior, weakness, yearn for **9** elaborate, epicurean, expensive, hankering, superfine **10** be bent upon, conceive of, conjecture, decorative, high-priced, ornamental, partiality **11** distinctive, exceptional, extravagant, gingerbread, hanker after, have a mind to, imagination, inclination **12** have an eye for, predilection **13** be pleased with, take a liking to

fancy house **4** stew **5** house **6** bagnio **7** brothel **8** bordello, cathouse **10** bawdy house, whorehouse **13** sporting house **14** house of ill fame **16** house of ill repute **19** house of prostitution

fang **4** claw, nail, root, take, tang, tusk **5** prong, seize, tooth **6** obtain **7** capture, procure **8** eyetooth **9** chelicera

fanny **4** buns, rump, seat **6** behind, bottom **8** backside, buttocks **9** fundament

Fanny
author: **9** Erica Jong

Fanny
character in: **13** Joseph Andrews
author: **8** Fielding

fan out **7** scatter **8** disperse **9** spread out

fantasize **5** dream, fancy **7** imagine **8** daydream

fantastic **3** mad, odd **4** huge, wild **5** antic, crazy, great, queer, weird **6** absurd, superb **7** amazing, bizarre, extreme, strange **8** enormous, fabulous, fanciful, freakish, illusory, quixotic, romantic, terrific **9** grotesque, imaginary, marvelous, visionary, wonderful **10** chimerical, far-fetched, incredible, irrational, outlandish, ridiculous, tremendous **11** extravagant, implausible, sensational **12** preposterous, unbelievable

fantasy **4** mind **5** dream, fancy **6** mirage, notion, vision, whimsy **7** caprice, chimera, fiction, figment, phantom, reverie **8** daydream, illusion, phantasm **9** imagining, invention, nightmare, unreality **10** apparition **11** fabrication, imagination, make-believe, supposition **13** hallucination, realm of dreams, visionary idea

Fantasy Island
character: **6** Tattoo **8** Mr Roarke
cast: **16** Herve Villechaize, Ricardo Montalban

far **4** afar, much **6** deeply, remote, way-off, yonder **7** distant, greatly **11** beyond range, out-of-the-way **12** considerably, immeasurably, incomparably

Faraday, Michael
field: **7** physics **9** chemistry
worked in: **11** electricity
developed: **9** generator **12** electrolysis
liquified: **8** chlorine
discovered: **6** carbon **7** benzene **24** electromagnetic induction
named for him: **5** farad

far and near **10** every place, everywhere, far and wide **11** in all places

far and wide **10** every place, everywhere, far and near **11** in all places

Far Away and Long Ago
author: **8** W H Hudson

farce **4** sham **6** parody **7** mockery **8** drollery, nonsense, pretense, travesty **9** absurdity, burlesque, horseplay, low comedy **10** buffoonery, tomfoolery **11** broad comedy, make-believe **12** harlequinade **14** ridiculousness

farceur **3** wag **5** joker

farcical **5** droll, funny, silly **6** absurd, stupid **7** asinine, comical, foolish **8** humorous **9** laughable, ludicrous, senseless **10** irrational, ridiculous

fare **2** do **3** fee **4** diet, food, menu **5** board, get on, rider, table **6** charge, client, manage **7** make out, perform, regimen, turn out **8** customer, get along, victuals **10** provisions **11** comestibles, ticket price **12** food and drink, passage money **15** paying passenger **20** cost of transportation

farewell **6** so long **7** good-bye, parting **8** Godspeed **9** departing, departure **11** leave-taking, parting wish, valediction **17** parting compliment
French: **5** adieu **8** au revoir
German: **14** auf Wiedersehen
Hawaiian: **5** aloha
Italian: **4** ciao **5** addio **11** arrivederci
Japanese: **8** sayonara
Latin: **4** vale
Spanish: **5** adios

Farewell to Arms, A
author: **15** Ernest Hemingway
character: **13** Frederic Henry **16** Catherine Barkley

far-fetched **7** dubious **8** doubtful, strained, unlikely **10** cockamamie, improbable **11** implausible **12** preposterous, unconvincing

Far From the Madding Crowd
author: **11** Thomas Hardy
character: **10** Fanny Robin, Gabriel Oak **12** Sergeant Troy **14** Farmer Boldwood **17** Bathsheba Everdene
setting: **6** Wessex

farina **4** meal, mush **5** flour **6** cereal, pollen, starch **8** semolina

farm **3** sow **4** plow, reap **5** plant, ranch, tract **6** grange, spread **7** harvest **9** cultivate **10** plantation **11** till the soil **12** country place

farmable **6** arable **7** friable **8** plowable, tillable **10** cultivable

farm animal **2** ox **3** cow, ewe, hen, hog, pig, ram, sow **4** bull, goat **5** beast, brute, horse, sheep **7** chicken, rooster

farm boundaries
god of: **8** Silvanus, Sylvanus

farmer **6** grower, raiser, reaper **7** granger, planter, rancher **8** agrarian **9** harvester **10** agronomist, husbandman **12** sharecropper **13** agriculturist, truck gardener **15** tiller of the soil

farming
god of: **4** Thor

far-off **6** remote **7** distant, faraway **11** unreachable **12** inaccessible **13** unforeseeable

farouche **3** shy **6** fierce, sullen **10** unsociable

far-out **3** mad **4** wild **5** crazy, weird **7** bizarre, strange **10** outlandish **14** fantastic

Far Pavilions, The
author: **6** M M Kaye

Farragut, David
served in: **8** Civil War **10** Mexican War **19** War of Eighteen Twelve
captured: **9** Mobile Bay **10** New Orleans
saying: **30** Damn the torpedoes full speed ahead

far-reaching **4** wide **5** broad **8** sweeping **9** expansive, extensive, universal, unlimited **11** wide-ranging

Farrell, James T
author of: **11** Judgment Day **12** Studs Lonigan, Young Lonigan **29** The Young Manhood of Studs Lonigan

far-removed **6** far-off, remote **7** distant, faraway

farrow **6** barren **7** piglets, sterile **9** infertile **10** unpregnant

Farrow, Mia
real name: **27** Maria de Lourdes Villier Farrow
father: **10** John Farrow
mother: **16** Maureen O'Sullivan
husband: **11** Andre Previn **12** Frank Sinatra
born: **12** Los Angeles CA
roles: **5** Zelig **11** John and Mary, Peyton Place **12** The Hurricane **13** Rosemary's Baby **14** The Great Gatsby **16** Allison MacKenzie **19** Hannah and Her Sisters **20** The Purple Rose of Cairo

far side **4** back **7** reverse **8** back side

Far Side, The
creator/artist: **10** Gary Larson

farsighted **4** wise **5** acute **6** shrewd **7** prudent **9** farseeing, hyperopic, judicious, prescient, provident **10** forehanded, foreseeing **11** clairvoyant, levelheaded

farther **6** beyond, deeper, longer **7** further, remoter **9** lengthier **10** more remote **11** more distant, more removed

farthermost **7** extreme **8** farthest, furthest **11** furthermost, most distant

farthest **3** end **4** most **7** extreme, longest **8** furthest, remotest, ultimate **9** uttermost **11** farthermost, furthermost

fascia **4** band, sash **5** board, strip **6** fillet, girdle, ribbon, tissue **7** bandage **8** membrane **9** dashboard

fascinate **5** charm, rivet **6** absorb, allure **7** beguile, bewitch, delight, enchant, engross **8** enravish, enthrall, entrance, transfix **9** captivate, enrapture, overpower, spellbind **14** hold spellbound

fascinating **8** alluring, charming, gripping, riveting **9** absorbing, beguiling **10** bewitching, delightful, enchanting, engrossing, entrancing **11** captivating, enthralling, interesting **12** overpowering, spellbinding

fascination **4** draw, lure **5** charm **6** allure **9** magnetism **10** attraction **11** captivation

fascism **6** Nazism **9** autocracy, oligarchy **10** plutocracy **11** corporatism, police state **13** corporativism **14** corporate state **15** totalitarianism **17** national socialism **21** right-wing dictatorship

fascist **9** right-wing **10** repressive, tyrannical **11** dictatorial, doctrinaire

fashion **3** air, fad, hew, way **4** form, make, mode, mold, rage **5** carve, craze, forge, frame, habit, shape, style, tenor, trend, usage, vogue **6** create, custom, design, devise, manner **7** compose, pattern, produce **8** attitude, behavior, contrive, demeanor **9** construct, fabricate **10** convention **11** manufacture

fashionable **2** in **3** hip **4** chic **5** smart **6** modish, with-it **7** current, in style, in vogue, popular, stylish, voguish **9** in fashion **10** all the rage, prevailing
French: **9** de rigueur

fashionable world
French: **10** grand monde

fashion designer **4** (Christian) Dior **5** Kenzo, (Jean) Patou **6** Adolfo, Lanvin, Poiret, (Coco) Chanel **7** Galanos, Halston, Missoni, (Pierre) Balmain **8** Givenchy **9** Courreges, Mary Quant, Valentino **10** Balenciaga, Mainbocher, Perry Ellis **11** Calvin Klein, Emilio Pucci, Ralph Lauren **12** Liz Claiborne, Lucien Lelong, Norman Norell, Pierre Cardin, Schiaparelli **13** Karl Lagerfeld, Rudi Gernreich **14** Pauline Trigere **15** Claire McCardell **16** Gloria Vanderbilt, Yves Saint-Laurent
Empress Eugenie's: **5** (Charles Frederick) Worth
Marie Antoinette's: **10** Rose Bertin
Empress Josephine's: **19** Louis Hippolyte Leroy

fashioned **4** made **5** built **6** formed, framed, molded, shaped, styled **7** adapted, crafted, created, devised, managed, modeled **9** contrived, patterned **11** constructed **12** accommodated

fashion plate **4** dude **5** dandy **12** Beau Brummell, clotheshorse, man of fashion, sharp dresser **14** woman of fashion

fast **4** firm, taut, true, wild **5** ahead, brisk, fleet, fully, hasty, loose, loyal, quick, rapid, rigid, swift, tight **6** famish, firmly, flying, rakish, secure, speedy, stable, starve, steady, wanton, winged **7** abiding, devoted, durable, fasting, fast day, fixedly, hastily, hurried, immoral, lasting, lustful, quickly, rapidly, solidly, soundly, staunch, swiftly, tightly **8** constant, enduring, faithful, fastened, go hungry, immodest, reckless, resolute, securely, speedily, unfading **9** debauched, dissolute, hurriedly, immovable, immovably, in advance, permanent, resistant, steadfast **10** completely, dissipated, firmly tied, lascivious, licentious, profligate, starvation, stationary, unswerving, unwavering **11** accelerated, expeditious, extravagant, intemperate, pleasure-mad, tenaciously **12** hunger strike, ineradicable, lickety-split

Fast, Howard
author of: **9** Spartacus **11** Freedom Road **13** The Immigrants **15** Citizen Tom Paine

fasten **3** bar, fix, pin, tie, wed **4** bind, bolt, clip, fuse, hold, hook, join, lash, link, lock, moor, snap, weld, yoke **5** affix, clamp, clasp, dowel, focus, hitch, close, latch, rivet, screw, stick, truss, unite **6** adhere, anchor, attach, button, cement, couple, direct, pinion, secure, solder, tether **7** connect **8** dovetail **11** put together

fastener **3** peg, pin, tie **4** clip, glue, grip, hook, line, nail, snap, tack **5** catch, clamp, clasp, cleat, latch, screw, strap, truss **6** buckle, button, cement, staple, thread, zipper **7** bracket **8** barrette **9** fastening, safety pin, thumbtack **10** clothespin, connection, hook and eye

fastening **4** snap **5** clasp **8** coupling **9** attaching **10** attachment, connection

fasten together **3** tie **4** dock, join **6** couple, hook up, link up

fastidious **5** fussy, picky **6** choosy, dainty, proper, queasy **7** finicky **8** exacting, precious **9** difficult, squeamish **10** meticulous, particular **11** overprecise, overrefined, persnickety **12** hard to please, overdelicate **13** hypercritical

Fastidious Brisk
character in: **22** Every Man out of His Humour
author: **6** Jonson

fastidious connoisseur **7** epicure, gourmet **9** bon vivant **10** gastronome

fastidiousness **4** care **12** exactingness **14** discrimination **15** persnicketiness

fat **4** full, oily **5** beefy, fatty, flush, heavy, obese, palmy, plump, pudgy, stout, suety **6** chubby, fleshy, grease, greasy, portly, rotund **7** copious, fertile, lumpish, paunchy, replete, stuffed **8** abundant, blubbery, chockful, fruitful, thickset, unctuous **9** animal fat, corpulent, fortunate, lucrative, plenteous, plentiful, rewarding **10** overweight, potbellied, productive **11** well-stocked **12** remunerative

fatal **6** deadly, lethal, mortal **7** ruinous **8** terminal, virulent **10** calamitous, disastrous **11** destructive **12** catastrophic, causing death

fatalism **8** stoicism **11** resignation **12** acquiescence, helplessness **13** powerlessness **14** predestination

fatality **5** death **8** casualty **9** lethality, mortality **10** deadliness, malignancy **11** banefulness

fatal woman
French: **11** femme fatale

fate **3** lot **4** doom **5** karma, moira **6** effect, future, kismet, upshot **7** chances, destiny, fortune, outcome, portion **8** prospect **10** providence **11** consequence **12** will of heaven **14** predestination

fated **4** sure **5** bound, meant **6** doomed **7** certain **8** destined

fateful **5** fatal **7** crucial, ominous **8** critical, decisive **9** momentous **10** disastrous, portentous **11** significant

Fates
also: **5** Morae **6** Moerae, Moirai, Parcae
named: **6** Clotho **7** Atropos **8** Lachesis
goddesses of: **7** destiny
number of goddesses: **5** three
called: **12** weird sisters
parents: **4** Zeus **5** Night **6** Themis

father **3** dad, pop **4** abbe, cure, papa, sire **5** beget, begin, daddy, found, hatch, maker, padre, pater **6** author, create, design, old man, parson, pastor, priest **7** creator, founder **8** ancestor, begetter, designer, engender, forebear, inventor, preacher **9** architect, confessor, originate, procreate **10** forefather, male parent, originator, progenitor
French: **4** pere

Father **4** Abba

Father, The
author: **16** August Strindberg

Father Knows Best
character: **11** Jim Anderson **13** Betty Anderson (Princess), Kathy Anderson (Kitten) **15** James Anderson Jr (Bud) **16** Margaret Anderson
cast: **9** Billy Gray, Jane Wyatt **11** Robert Young **12** Lauren Chapin **13** Elinor Donahue

fatherland **6** Heimat, patria, patrie **8** homeland **10** birthplace, motherland, native land, native soil **13** mother country, native country

fatherly **6** benign, kindly, tender **8** parental, paternal **9** indulgent **10** beneficent, benevolent

father of his country
Latin: **12** Pater Patriae

father of stars/wind
8 Astraeus

Father of the Bride
director: **16** Vincente Minnelli
cast: **11** Billie Burke, Joan Bennett, Leo G Carroll **12** Spencer Tracy **15** Elizabeth Taylor
sequel: **21** Father's Little Dividend

father of the family
Latin: **13** paterfamilias

Father of the Rivers *see* **4** Nile

Fathers and Sons
author: **12** Ivan Turgenev
character: **5** Katya, Pavel **6** Arkady, Vasily **8** Bazaroff, Fenichka **9** Kirsanoff **15** Madame Odintzoff

fathom **5** probe **6** divine, follow **7** hunt out, root out, uncover, unravel **8** discover **9** ferret out, figure out, penetrate **10** comprehend, understand **16** get to the bottom of

fathom
abbreviation: **4** fath

fatigue **3** fag **4** bush, tire **5** drain, weary **6** tedium, tucker, weaken **7** exhaust, languor, wear out **8** enervate, overtire **9** heaviness, lassitude, tiredness, weariness **10** debilitate, drowsiness, enervation, exhaustion **12** debilitation, listlessness **13** overtiredness

fatigued **4** beat **5** all in, jaded, spent, tired, weary **6** bushed, done in, fagged, pooped **7** worn out **8** dog-tired, weakened **9** dead tired, enervated, exhausted, overtaxed **10** overworked **11** debilitated, tuckered out

fatiguing **6** tiring **7** arduous, tedious **8** tiresome **9** wearisome **10** exhausting

Fatima
character in: **9** Bluebeard

fatti maschii, parole femine **29** deeds are manly words are womanish
motto of: **8** Maryland

fatty **4** oily **5** lardy, suety **6** greasy **7** buttery **8** blubbery **9** shortened

fatuous **5** inane, silly, vapid **6** obtuse, simple, stupid **7** asinine, foolish, idiotic, moronic, puerile, vacuous, witless **8** besotted, imbecile **9** brainless, senseless **10** ridiculous

faucet **3** tap **4** cock **5** spout, valve **6** nozzle, outlet, spigot **7** bibcock

Faulkland
character in: **9** The Rivals
author: **8** Sheridan

Faulkner, William
author of: **7** The Bear **8** Sartoris **9** Sanctuary, The Hamlet **10** The Reivers **11** As I Lay Dying **13** Light in August **15** Absalom Absalom! **17** Intruder in the Dust **18** The Sound and the Fury
fictional county: **13** Yoknapatawpha

fault **3** bug, sin **4** flaw, slip, snag **5** blame, crime, error, guilt, stain, taint, wrong **6** defect, foible, glitch, impugn **7** blemish, blunder, censure, failing, frailty, misdeed, mistake, offense, reprove **8** drawback, weakness **9** criticize, infirmity, oversight, weak point **10** deficiency, impediment, negligence, peccadillo, wrongdoing **11** culpability, dereliction, misdemeanor, shortcoming **12** imperfection, indiscretion **13** answerability, transgression **14** accountability, responsibility

faultfind **3** nag **4** beef, carp, kick **5** cavil, gripe, knock **6** deride, squawk **7** nitpick **8** complain **9** criticize

faultfinder **3** nag **4** bear, crab **5** crank **6** carper, censor, critic, grouch **7** caviler, grouser **8** quibbler, sorehead **9** derogator, detractor, Mrs Grundy, nitpicker **10** bellyacher, complainer, curmudgeon, fuddy-duddy, fussbudget

faultfinding **4** beef, kick **5** gripe **6** squawk **7** beefing, carping, griping, kicking, nagging **9** complaint, criticism, squawking **10** nitpicking **11** complaining, criticizing

faultless **5** ideal **7** correct, perfect **8** accurate, flawless **9** exemplary **10** immaculate, impeccable **11** unblemished **13** unimpeachable **14** irreproachable, without blemish

faulty **3** bad **4** awry **5** amiss, false, wrong **7** injured, unsound **8** impaired, inferior, mistaken **9** defective, deficient, erroneous, imperfect, incorrect **10** inadequate, out of order, unreliable **14** unsatisfactory

faun
form: **5** deity
location: **5** rural

Fauna *see* **7** Bona Dea

Faunus
origin: **5** Roman
form: **5** deity

location: 5 woods
also called: 5 Inuus 6 Fatuus
king of: 6 Latium
father: 5 Picus
son: 7 Latinus
corresponds to: 3 Pan

Faure, Gabriel Urbain
born: 6 France 7 Pamiers
composer of: 5 Dolly 6 Pavane 7 Ballade, Mirages, Requiem, Shylock 8 Penelope 9 Fantaisie, Promethee 12 Le Jardin Clos 13 La Chanson d'Eve 14 La Bonne Chanson 18 L'Horizon Chimerique, Pelleas et Melisande 21 Masques et Bergamasques

Faust
author: 12 Johann Goethe
character: 6 Wagner 8 Gretchen 10 Homunculus 11 Helen of Troy 14 Mephistopheles

Faust
opera by: 6 Gounod
character: 9 Valentine 10 Marguerite 14 Mephistopheles

Faustulus
vocation: 8 herdsman, shepherd
raised: 5 Remus 7 Romulus

faute de mieux 24 for lack of something better

faux pas 4 goof 5 boner, error, gaffe, lapse 6 boo-boo, howler, slip-up 7 blooper, blunder, mistake 9 false step 11 impropriety 12 indiscretion

favela 4 slum 10 shanty town

Favell, Jack
character in: 7 Rebecca
author: 9 Du Maurier

Favonius
origin: 5 Roman
personifies: 8 west wind

favor 3 aid 4 abet, back, gift, help, like 5 be for, fancy, humor 6 assist, esteem, foster, oblige, pamper, prefer, succor, uphold 7 approve, commend, endorse, go in for, indulge, kind act, memento, present, service, support 8 advocacy, approval, courtesy, espousal, good deed, good turn, goodwill, largesse, look like, resemble, sanction, side with, souvenir 9 encourage, patronage, patronize, smile upon, take after, use gently 10 act of grace, use lightly 11 accommodate, approbation, be partial to, benefaction, countenance, good opinion 12 be the image of, championship, commendation, dispensation, kindly regard 13 accommodation, goodwill token

favorable 4 fair, good, kind 6 benign, timely 7 helpful, hopeful 8 amicable, friendly, salutary 9 approving, conducive, opportune, promising 10 auspicious, beneficial, convenient, propitious 11 predisposed, serviceable, sympathetic 12 advantageous, commendatory, well-disposed

favorable opinion 6 esteem, regard 7 respect 8 approval 10 admiration 12 appreciation

favorably disposed 7 willing 8 amenable, inclined, obliging 9 agreeable 11 sympathetic

favorite 3 pet 5 fancy, jewel 6 choice 7 darling, special 9 best-liked, preferred 11 frontrunner, most popular 13 fairhaired one 14 apple of one's eye

favoritism 4 bias 10 partiality 12 one-sidedness, partisanship

Fawley, Jude and Drusilla
characters in: 14 Jude the Obscure
author: 5 Hardy

fawn 5 toady 6 pander 7 flatter, truckle 8 pay court 9 be servile, seek favor 12 be obsequious, bow and scrape

fawning 7 servile 8 flattery, toadying 9 adulating, adulation, truckling 10 flattering, obsequious 11 sycophantic 12 ingratiating 14 obsequiousness

faze 4 fret 5 abash, daunt, upset, worry 6 bother, flurry, rattle 7 disturb, fluster, perturb 8 confound 9 discomfit, embarrass 10 discompose, disconcert

fazed 5 upset 7 abashed, ruffled 8 agitated, bothered, confused 9 chagrined, unsettled 10 confounded, distracted, nonplussed 11 embarrassed 12 disconcerted

FBI, The
character: 10 Arthur Ward 21 Inspector Lewis Erskine
cast: 12 Philip Abbott 16 Efrem Zimbalist Jr

fealty 7 loyalty 8 devotion, fidelity 9 adherence, constancy 10 allegiance, attachment 12 faithfulness

fear 3 awe 4 care 5 alarm, bogey, dread, panic, qualm, worry 6 dismay, esteem, fright, horror, phobia, revere, terror, threat, wonder 7 anxiety, bugaboo, bugbear, concern, quaking, specter 8 affright, venerate 9 cowardice, nightmare, reverence, shudder at, tremble at 10 be afraid of, be scared of, feel awe for, foreboding, take fright, veneration 11 trepidation 12 apprehension, perturbation 13 consternation 14 be frightened of

fearful 4 dire 5 awful, dread, eerie, lurid, timid 6 afraid, aghast, horrid, scared, uneasy 7 alarmed, anxious, ghastly, macabre, nervous, ominous, panicky, worried 8 alarming, dreadful, horrible, shocking, sinister, skittish, terrible, timorous 9 appalling, concerned, diffident, frightful, tremulous 10 formidable, frightened, portentous, terrifying 11 distressing, frightening, intimidated 12 apprehensive, fainthearted 13 panic-stricken 14 chickenhearted

fearfulness fear 5 alarm, dread, panic 6 fright, terror 7 anguish, anxiety 8 timidity 11 trepidation 12 apprehension

fearless 4 bold 5 brave 6 daring, gritty, heroic, plucky 7 doughty, gallant, valiant 8 intrepid, unafraid, valorous 9 audacious, confident, dauntless, unabashed, undaunted 10 courageous, undismayed 11 adventurous, indomitable, lionhearted, unflinching, unshrinking, venturesome, without fear 12 stout-hearted

fearlessness 4 grit 5 pluck, valor 7 bravery, courage 8 boldness 10 confidence 13 dauntlessness

Fear of Flying
author: 9 Erica Jong

feasible 6 viable 7 fitting, politic 8 possible, suitable, workable 9 advisable, desirable 10 achievable, attainable, reasonable 11 appropriate, conceivable, practicable

feast 4 dine, fete 5 festa, gorge 6 bounty 7 banquet, holiday, jubilee, surplus 8 feast day, festival 9 bacchanal, saint's day 10 gluttonize, gormandize, have a feast, rich supply 11 celebration, eat one's fill, elegant meal, wine and dine

feat 3 act 4 deed, task 6 action, stroke 7 exploit, triumph 8 maneuver 9 adventure 10 attainment, enterprise 11 achievement, performance, tour de force 14 accomplishment

feather **4** down, kind, sort **5** adorn, eider, plume, quill **7** bristle, plumage, variety **9** character, turn an oar

featherbrained **4** dumb **5** silly **6** simple, stupid **7** foolish, witless **9** brainless **12** muddleheaded, simple-minded **13** rattle-brained **14** scatterbrained

feather in one's cap **5** honor **6** credit **11** distinction

feather one's nest **6** enrich **15** fill one's pockets

feature, features **3** see **4** mark, star **5** fancy, trait **6** aspect, play up, visage **7** display, earmark, imagine, picture, present, quality **8** envision, hallmark, headline, main item, property **9** attribute, character, highlight, specialty, spotlight **10** conceive of, lineaments **14** characteristic

February ***see box***

Fechner, Gustav Theodore
nationality: **6** German
founder of: **22** experimental psychology

fecit **6** he made (it) **7** she made (it)

feckless **3** lax **5** slack **6** remiss **8** careless, heedless **9** negligent, worthless **10** neglectful **11** thoughtless **13** irresponsible

Fecundity
goddess of: **5** Freia, Freya

Federalist Party
president belonging to: **5** Adams **10** Washington

federate **5** unite **7** combine **12** join together

federation **5** union **6** league **7** combine **8** alliance **9** coalition, syndicate **10** sisterhood **11** association, brotherhood, confederacy **12** amalgamation **13** confederation

fee **4** fare, hire, toll, wage **5** price **6** charge, salary, tariff **7** payment, stipend **9** emolument **10** commission, honorarium **12** compensation, remuneration **13** consideration

feeble **4** flat, lame, poor, puny, tame, thin, weak **5** faint, frail, vapid **6** ailing, flabby, flimsy, infirm, meager, paltry, senile, sickly, slight **7** fragile, insipid **8** decrepit, delicate, disabled, impotent, weakened **9** colorless, declining, doddering, enervated, enfeebled, forceless, not strong, powerless **10** inadequate, spiritless, wishy-washy **11** debilitated, ineffective, ineffectual

feeble-minded **4** dull **6** senile, stupid **7** moronic **8** backward, childish, retarded **9** imbecilic, senseless, subnormal **10** half-witted, weak-minded **12** mentally slow

feeble-mindedness **6** dotage, idiocy **8** dullness, senility, slowness **9** denseness, stupidity **11** retardation

feed **3** eat **4** fare, fuel, mash **5** cater, feast, graze **6** devour, fodder, forage, foster, viands **7** augment, bolster, consume, gratify, nourish, nurture, pasture, satisfy, support, sustain **8** maintain, take food, victuals **9** encourage, foodstuff, provender **10** minister to, provisions, strengthen **11** comestibles, nourishment, wine and dine

feeder **6** branch **7** channel **9** tributary

feel **3** paw, see **4** know **5** grope, press, probe, reach, sense, think, touch **6** finger, fumble, handle, makeup, notice **7** believe, discern, feeling, observe, palpate, texture **8** perceive **9** be aware of, be moved by, character, sensation **10** comprehend, experience, manipulate, suffer from, understand **11** be convinced, be stirred by, be touched by, composition

feel aversion toward **4** hate **5** abhor **6** detest **7** despise **9** abominate, can't abide, can't stand **11** can't stomach **12** be revolted by **13** find repugnant, find repulsive **14** view with horror

feeler **7** antenna **8** proposal, tentacle **10** experiment **12** trial balloon

feel indebted **10** appreciate, be beholden, be grateful **13** feel obligated

feeling **4** aura, pity, view, zeal **5** ardor, gusto, sense, verve **6** fervor, spirit, thrill, warmth **7** concern, emotion, opinion, passion **8** attitude, instinct, reaction, response, sympathy **9** affection, awareness, intuition, sensation, sentiment, vehemence **10** atmosphere, compassion, enthusiasm, impression **11** earnestness, inclination, point of view, sensibility, sensitivity

feeling life is wearisome
Latin: **12** taedium vitae

feelings **3** ego **5** pride **8** emotions, passions **10** self-esteem **13** sensibilities, sensitivities **16** susceptibilities

feel pain **4** ache, hurt **5** smart **6** suffer **7** agonize **9** be in agony **11** be tormented **12** be in distress

Feenix, Cousin
character in: **12** Dombey and Son
author: **7** Dickens

feet **4** dogs, pads, paws **5** hoofs **6** hooves **8** gunboats, tootsies

feign **4** fake, sham **5** forge, put on **6** affect, assume, cook up, invent, make up **7** concoct, pretend **8** simulate **9** fabricate **11** counterfeit, make a show of, make believe

feigned **4** fake, sham **5** bogus, phony **6** ersatz **8** spurious **9** imitation, insincere, pretended, simulated **10** artificial **11** counterfeit, make-believe

feint **4** hoax, mask, move, pass, ploy, ruse, wile **5** blind, bluff, dodge, trick **6** gambit **7** pretext **8** artifice, maneuver, pretense **9** stratagem **10** subterfuge **13** feigned attack

---

February
event: **4** Lent **5** Purim **8** Leap year **9** Mardi Gras **12** Ash Wednesday, Groundhog Day (2)
flower: **6** violet **8** primrose
French: **7** Fevrier
gem: **8** amethyst
German: **7** Februar
holiday: **9** Candlemas (2) **13** Valentine's Day (14) **14** Chinese New Year **16** Lincoln's Birthday (12) **19** Washington's Birthday (22)
Italian: **8** Febbraio
Latin: **6** Februa
number of days: **10** twenty-nine (every 4 years) **11** twenty-eight
origin of name: **7** Februus
Roman god of: **12** purification
place in year:
Gregorian: **6** second
Roman: **7** twelfth
Spanish: **7** Febrero
Zodiac signs: **6** Pisces **8** Aquarius

Feldman, Marty
born: **6** London **7** England
roles: **11** Silent Movie **17** Young Frankenstein **24** The Last Remake of Beau Geste

feldspar
varieties: **8** sunstone **9** amazonite, moonstone

felicitate **4** hail **6** salute **10** wish one joy **11** rejoice with **12** congratulate **18** give one's best wishes **28** wish many happy returns of the day

felicitations **3** joy **6** cheers **9** blessings, greetings **10** best wishes, good wishes **11** compliments, salutations **12** pat on the back **15** congratulations **24** many happy returns of the day

felicitous **3** apt **5** happy **6** joyful, joyous **7** fitting, germane, well-put **8** inspired, pleasing, relevant, suitable, well-said **9** effective, fortunate, pertinent **10** propitious, well-chosen **11** appropriate

felicity **5** bliss, charm, grace, knack, skill **6** heaven, nicety **7** aptness, delight, ecstasy, fitness **8** paradise **9** beatitude, happiness **12** blissfulness **13** effectiveness **15** appropriateness

Felix the Cat
creator: **11** Pat Sullivan

fell **4** raze **5** level **7** cut down, destroy, hew down **8** demolish **9** knock down, prostrate

Feller, Bob (Robert)
nickname: **11** Rapid Robert
sport: **8** baseball
position: **7** pitcher
team: **16** Cleveland Indians

Fellini, Federico
director of: **8** Amarcord, Casanova, La Strada **11** La Dolce Vita **15** Nights of Cabiria **18** Juliet of the Spirits

fellow **3** boy, guy, man, pal **4** chap, chum, dude, mate, peer **5** equal **6** friend **7** comrade, consort **8** coworker **9** associate, colleague, companion **10** compatriot

fellow-conspirator **4** ally **6** cohort **7** abettor **8** henchman **9** accessory **11** confederate **12** collaborator

fellow creature **6** mortal, person **10** individual

fellow feeling **6** regard **7** kinship **8** affinity, fondness **10** attraction, partiality

fellowship **5** amity **7** society **8** intimacy **10** affability, cordiality, fraternity, friendship **11** amicability, association, brotherhood, comradeship, familiarity, sociability **12** friendliness **13** companionship

felon **5** crook, cruel, thief **6** fierce, outlaw, wicked **7** convict, illegal, villain, whitlow **8** criminal, gangster, jailbird, murderer **10** lawbreaker, malefactor **11** public enemy **12** inflammation

felony **5** arson, crime **6** murder **7** assault, misdeed, offense, robbery **8** burglary **9** blackmail **10** kidnapping, wrongdoing **12** capital offense

female **3** cow, dam, hen, sow **4** girl, mare **5** bitch, tabby, woman **6** heifer **7** distaff, womanly **8** feminine, ladylike **9** womanlike

feminine **4** soft **5** woman **6** dainty, female, gentle **7** distaff, girlish, womanly **8** delicate, ladylike **10** femalelike, like a woman **14** of the female sex

femininity **8** softness **10** femaleness, gentleness **11** girlishness, womanliness **12** feminineness **13** female quality

femme **4** wife **5** woman

femme de chambre **9** lady's maid **11** chambermaid

femme fatale **4** vamp **5** siren **7** charmer **10** fatal woman, seductress **11** enchantress

femur
bone of: **5** thigh **8** upper leg

fen **3** bog **4** moor, sump **5** marsh, swale, swamp **6** bottom, morass, slough **7** lowland, wetland **8** quagmire

fence **3** pen **4** coop, duel, gird, rail **5** hedge, hem in **6** corral, secure, wall in **7** barrier, confine, palings **8** encircle, palisade, stockade, surround **9** barricade, encompass **11** cross swords

fencing
equipment: **4** epee, foil, mask **5** saber, sword **8** plastron
part of weapon: **5** blade, forte, guard **6** foible, handle, medium, pommel
term: **3** hit **5** prime, sixte, touch **6** octave, quarte, quinte, tierce **7** on guard, seconde, septime
deceptive move: **5** feint
movement: **4** beat **5** lunge, parry **6** double, fleche, thrust **7** advance, cutover, recover, retreat, riposte **9** disengage **11** froissement

fend **2** do **5** avert, avoid, parry, repel, shift **6** manage **7** keep off, make out, provide, repulse, support, survive, ward off **8** push away

fender **3** pad **4** curb **5** guard **6** buffer, bumper, shield, sluice **7** cushion, railing **9** fireguard, protector **10** cowcatcher, fire screen, protection, wheel guard

fend off **5** avert, dodge, evade, parry, repel **6** escape **7** ward off **8** sidestep, stave off

fennel
botanical name: **17** Foeniculum vulgare
family: **7** parsley
varieties: **3** dog **4** wild **5** giant **8** Florence **9** common dog **11** common giant
mythical aid to: **9** fortifier **11** aphrodisiac, slenderizer **12** rejuvenation, stops hiccups **16** restores eyesight
use: **4** duck, fish **5** bread, rolls **7** chicken **8** apple pie **16** seafood casserole

Fenrir
also: **6** Fenris
origin: **12** Scandinavian
form: **4** wolf **7** monster
father: **4** Loki
mother: **9** Angerboda, Angrbodha, Angurboda
sister: **3** Hel
brother: **11** Iormungandr, Jormungandr **14** Midgard Serpent
ate: **4** Odin **5** Othin
killed by: **5** Vidar

Fenris *see* **6** Fenrir

Fenton
character in: **22** The Merry Wives of Windsor
author: **11** Shakespeare

feral **4** wild **6** brutal, deadly, ferine, fierce, savage **7** bestial, untamed, vicious **9** ferocious **12** uncultivated **14** undomesticated

Ferber, Edna
author of: **5** Giant, So Big **8** Cimarron, Show Boat **9** Ice Palace, Stage Door (with George S Kaufman) **13** Dinner at Eight (with George S Kaufman), Saratoga Trunk **14** The Royal Family (with George S Kaufman)

Ferdinand
character in: **10** The Tempest
author: **11** Shakespeare

Ferdinand
character in: **16** Love's Labour's Lost
author: **11** Shakespeare

Ferd'nand
creator: **3** Mik **13** Dahl Mikkelsen

Feria
origin: **5** Roman
form: **7** holiday

Fermat, Pierre de
field: **11** mathematics
nationality: **6** French
discovered: **16** analytic geometry

ferment **4** foam, mold, sour, turn **5** froth, yeast **6** enzyme, fester, leaven, seethe, tumult, unrest, uproar **7** agitate, inflame, smolder, turmoil **8** bubble up, disquiet **9** agitation, commotion, leavening **10** disruption, effervesce, turbulence **11** be turbulent, fomentation

fermented **6** soured, worked **7** seethed **8** agitated

Fermi, Enrico
field: **7** physics
nationality: **7** Italian
developed: **10** atomic bomb **20** uranium fission theory
awarded: **10** Nobel Prize

fern ***see box***

fernet-branca
type: **8** aperitif
origin: **5** Italy
flavor: **4** herb

Fern Hill
author: **11** Dylan Thomas

ferocious **6** brutal, deadly, fierce, savage **7** bestial, brutish, enraged, violent **8** fiendish, maddened, ravening, ruthless **9** atrocious, barbarous, merciless, murderous, predatory, rapacious **10** relentless **11** cold-blooded **12** bloodthirsty

ferocity **7** cruelty **8** savagery **9** barbarity, brutality, harshness **10** fierceness, inhumanity, savageness **11** brutishness, viciousness **12** ruthlessness

Ferrer, Jose
real name: **33** Jose Vincente Ferrer de Otero y Cintron
wife: **8** Uta Hagen **15** Rosemary Clooney
born: **8** Santurce **10** Puerto Rico
roles: **7** I Accuse **9** Joan of Arc **11** Moulin Rouge, Ship of Fools **14** The Caine Mutiny **16** Cyrano de Bergerac (Oscar), Lawrence of Arabia **24** The Greatest Story Ever Told

fern
varieties: **3** air, cup, lip, man, oak, saw **4** ball, blue, claw, deer, dish, felt, fire, gold, hand, iron, king, lace, lady, male, moss, nest, pine, sago, tara, tree, wall, wart, wood **5** beard, beech, chain, cloak, fancy, glade, glory, grape, grass, hedge, holly, marsh, plume, royal, strap, swamp, sweet, sword, table, water, whisk **6** adder's, bamboo, basket, Boston, button, carrot, coffee, cotton, cuplet, dagger, ladder, meadow, mother, ribbon, shield, silver, tongue, turnip, winter **7** bladder, boulder, brittle, bulblet, crested, emerald, feather, Fee's lip, fragile, Goldie's, hacksaw, Halberd, hammock, leather, New York, ostrich, parsley, peacock, rainbow, walking **8** bear-foot, bear's-paw, cinnamon, climbing, elk's-horn, fishtail, floating, florist's, fragrant, hairy lip, Hartford, licorice, mosquito, Nebraska, Savannah, snuffbox, soft tree, staghorn **9** asparagus, bird's-nest, black tree, blond tree, Christmas, common cup, deer's-foot, downy wood, flowering, glossy cup, hare's foot, long beech, sensitive, vegetable, Venus hair, viscid lip, wavy cloak, woolly lip **10** Alabama lip, Boott's wood, broad beech, deer-tongue, Duff's sword, erect sword, five-finger, hay-scented, lady ground, maidenhair, scented oak, shoestring, silver tree, silver-back, silver-lace, silver-leaf, slender lip, strawberry, upside-down, woolly tree **11** Braun's holly, coastal wood, Coville's lip, crested felt, crested wood, dwarf Boston, elephant-ear, Fendler's lip, hart's-tongue, interrupted, Jamaica gold, leatherleaf, leatherwood, narrow beech, netted chain, Northern oak, Parry's cloak, Pursh's holly, rabbit's-foot, rattlesnake, Sierra water, walking leaf **12** Adder's-tongue, American wall, berry bladder, Clinton's wood, Dudley's holly, Eaton's shield, English hedge, Hawaiian tree, Java staghorn, limestone oak, mountain wood, Northern lady, resurrection, Southern lady, squirrel-foot, toothed sword, Western holly, Western sword **13** California lip, Cleveland's lip, Dudley's shield, European chain, fan maidenhair, Fendler's cloak, Florida ribbon, leathery grape, Malay climbing, mountain holly, Northern holly, prickly shield, Prince-of-Wales, spinulose wood, Tasmanian tree, triangle water, Virginia chain, wild bird's nest **14** Anderson's holly, Australian tree, bulblet bladder, California gold, common staghorn, dissected grape, dwarf asparagus, hen-and-chickens, imbricate sword, silver-king tree, West Indian tree **15** American parsley, California cloak, California holly, Delta maidenhair, East Indian holly, European parsley, mountain bladder, mountain parsley **16** black-stemmed tree, daisy-leaved grape, Farley maidenhair, Tassel maidenhair, Tracy's maidenhair **17** Bermuda maidenhair, brittle maidenhair, climbing bird's nest, walking maidenhair **18** Aleutian maidenhair, American maidenhair, Barbados maidenhair, Northern maidenhair, Trailing maidenhair, Triangular staghorn **20** Australian maidenhair, California maidenhair

ferret out **5** dig up **6** detect **7** find out, root out, uncover, unearth **8** discover **9** ascertain

fertile **4** rich **5** loamy **6** fecund **8** creative, fruitful, original, prolific **9** fructuous, ingenious, inventive, luxuriant, plenteous **10** fecundated, fertilized, fructified, generative, productive, vegetative **11** imaginative, resourceful **12** reproductive

Fertility
god of: **7** Bacchus, Mutinus **8** Lupercus, Picumnus
goddess of: **4** Isis **5** Fauna **6** Athena, Athene, Brigit, Libera, Pallas, Saitis, Tellus **7** Astarte, Berchta, Bona Dea, Demeter, Perchta **11** Tritogeneia **12** Pallas Athena **16** Alalcomean Athena

fertilize **6** enrich, manure **8** fructify **9** fecundate, pollinate **10** impregnate, inseminate

fertilizer **4** dung, muck **5** guano **6** manure, potash **7** compost **8** bonemeal, dressing **10** enrichener **14** superphosphate

fervent **4** keen **5** eager, fiery **6** ardent, devout, fervid, fierce, hearty, heated **7** burning, earnest, intense, zealous **8** spirited, vehement **9** heartfelt **10** passionate **11** impassioned, warmhearted **12** enthusiastic, wholehearted

fervid **5** eager **6** ardent, raging **7** burning, earnest, fanatic, fervent, intense, zealous **8** spirited **10** passionate **11** impassioned **12** all-consuming

fervor **4** fire, zeal, zest **5** ardor, gusto, piety, verve **6** warmth **7** passion **9** animation, eagerness, intensity, vehemence **10** devoutness, enthusiasm, heartiness **11** earnestness, seriousness **14** purposefulness

Feste
character in: **12** Twelfth Night
author: **11** Shakespeare

fester **3** rot, vex **4** fret, gall, grow, rile **5** chafe, pique **6** nettle, plague, rankle **7** blister, form pus, inflame, putrefy, smolder, torment **8** irritate, ulcerate **9** intensify, suppurate

festering **6** putrid **7** rotting **8** infected, inflamed, rankling **10** putrefying **11** suppurating

festina lente **15** make haste slowly

festival **4** fete, gala **5** feast **6** fiesta **7** gala day, holiday, jubilee **8** carnival, jamboree **11** celebration, festivities

festival of ***see box***

festive **3** gay **4** gala **5** jolly, merry **6** festal, joyous **7** larkish, playful **8** sportive **9** convivial **10** frolicsome **11** celebratory **12** lighthearted

festivity **3** joy **4** fete, gala **5** feast, mirth **6** fiesta, gaiety, levity **7** fanfare, jollity, jubilee, revelry **8** festival, jamboree **9** merriment, rejoicing **11** celebration, merrymaking

festoon **3** lei **4** swag **5** chain, curve **6** wreath **7** garland, hanging **8** decorate

fetch **3** get **4** cost **5** bring, go for, yield **6** afford, obtain **7** procure, realize, sell for **8** amount to, retrieve

fetching **6** divine, lovely **8** adorable, becoming, charming, engaging, pleasing **9** appealing **10** attractive, delightful **11** captivating

fete **4** gala **5** feast, party, treat **6** regale **7** banquet, holiday **8** carnival, festival **9** bal masque **11** celebration, garden party, wine and dine **13** fete champetre

fete champetre **11** garden party **15** outdoor festival

fetid **4** foul, gamy, rank **5** fusty, moldy, musty, nasty **6** putrid, rancid, rotten **7** noisome, stenchy, tainted **8** mephitic, stifling, stinking **9** stenchful **10** malodorous **11** ill-smelling, suffocating

fetish **4** idol, joss **5** charm, craze, image, mania, totem **6** amulet, scarab **7** passion **8** idee fixe, talisman **9** obsession **10** golden calf, phylactery **11** magic object **12** superstition **13** preoccupation

fetter **4** bind, bond, cage, curb, yoke **5** chain, tie up **6** duress, hamper, hinder, hobble, impede, shut in, tether **7** confine, durance, manacle, pin down, shackle, tie down, trammel, truss up, bracelet, encumber, handcuff, hold back, restrain **9** hindrance, restraint **13** put into bilbos **15** bind hand and foot

Festival of
Adonis: **6** Adonia
Apollo: **5** Delia **8** Didymaea **9** Delphinia **12** Daphnephoria
Athena: **6** Lenaea **8** Diipolia **9** Pyanepsia **11** Oschophoria
Attica: **13** Rural Dionysia **14** Lesser Dionysia
Bacchus: **11** Bacchanalia
Boeotians: **7** Daedala **13** Little Doedala
Demeter: **5** Haloa
Dionysus: **5** Haloa **8** Dionysia
flowers: **11** Anthesteria
Greeks: **6** Heraea **9** Pyanepsia **11** Scirophoria, Skirophoria **13** Thesmorphoria
Persephone: **5** Haloa
Roman: **8** Floralia, Matralia **9** Lemuralia, Liberalia **10** Larentalia, Lupercalia, Matronalia, Parentalia, Saturnalia
spring: **11** Anthesteria
wine: **11** Anthesteria
Zeus: **6** Diasia **8** Didymaea

feud **3** row **4** fuss, spat, tiff **5** argue, brawl, clash, set-to **6** affray, bicker, breach, enmity, fracas, schism, strife **7** discord, dispute, faction, ill will, quarrel, rupture, wrangle **8** argument, bad blood, be at odds, clashing, conflict, disagree, squabble, vendetta **9** animosity, bickering, hostility **10** falling out **11** altercation, controversy **12** disagreement, hard feelings

Feud, The
author: **12** Thomas Berger

feudal lord
Japanese: **6** daimyo

Feuerbach, Anselm
born: **6** Speyer **7** Germany
artwork: **9** Iphigenia **15** Judgment of Paris, Plato's Symposium **18** The Fall of the Titans

fever **4** fire, heat **5** ardor, craze, flush, furor **6** desire, frenzy, warmth **7** ferment, illness, pyrexia **8** delirium, sickness **9** agitation **10** enthusiasm, excitement **11** temperature **12** restlessness

feverish **3** hot **5** fiery **6** ardent, red-hot **7** burning, excited, fanatic, febrile, fervent, fevered, flushed, parched, pyretic, zealous **8** frenzied, inflamed, restless **9** impatient, overeager, wrought-up **10** high-strung, passionate **11** impassioned

few **4** rare, some, thin **5** scant **6** meager, paltry, scanty, scarce, skimpy, sparse, unique **7** handful, limited, not many, several, unusual **8** exiguous, piddling, sporadic, uncommon **9** hardly any **10** infrequent, occasional **11** scarcely any, small number **13** infinitesimal, insignificant **14** inconsiderable

Fezziwig
character in: **15** A Christmas Carol
author: **7** Dickens

fiance, fiancee **6** future **7** engaged, pledge **8** intended, promised **9** affianced, betrothed, bride-to-be, groom-to-be **10** bride-elect, groom-elect

fiasco **4** bomb, flop **5** botch **6** fizzle **7** debacle, washout **8** disaster **10** nonsuccess

fiat **3** act, law **4** rule **5** edict, order, ukase **6** decree, dictum, ruling **7** command, mandate **11** commandment

fiat lux **15** let there be light

fib **3** lie **5** hedge **7** fiction, untruth **8** white lie **9** half-truth, invention **10** equivocate **11** fabrication, harmless lie, prevaricate **13** falsification, prevarication, tell a white lie **15** stretch the truth **17** misrepresentation

fiber **4** hemp, jute, silk **5** fibre, linen, nylon, rayon, shred, sinew, sisal **6** cotton, dacron, manila, nature, strand, thread **7** quality, texture **8** filament **9** character, polyester, structure

fibrolite
source: **5** Burma, Mogok

fibula
bone of: **8** lower leg

fickle **5** giddy **6** fitful **7** erratic, flighty **8** shifting, unstable, unsteady, variable, volatile, wavering **9** frivolous, mercurial, spasmodic, whimsical **10** capricious, changeable, inconstant, irresolute, unreliable **11** fluctuating, light-headed, vacillating **12** inconsistent **13** feather-headed, unpredictable, untrustworthy **14** feather-brained

fiction **3** fib, lie **4** play, tale, yarn **5** fable, novel **7** fantasy, forgery, novella, romance, whopper **8** tall tale **9** falsehood, invention, narrative **10** concoction, short novel, short story **11** fabrication, imagination, made-up story **12** storytelling **13** prevarication **16** cock-and-bull story

fictional **6** made-up **8** invented, literary, mythical **9** storybook **10** fictitious **11** theoretical **12** hypothetical

fictitious **4** fake, sham **5** bogus, false, phony **6** forged, made-up, unreal, untrue **7** assumed, feigned **8** fanciful, invented, mythical, spurious **9** imaginary, legendary, simulated, trumped-up, unfounded **10** apocryphal, artificial, fabricated, fraudulent, not genuine **11** counterfeit **14** supposititious

fiddle **3** bow, saw, toy **4** fool **5** cheat, dally, fraud **6** dawdle, monkey, potter, putter, tamper, trifle, violin **7** falsify, finagle, fritter, swindle **9** deception **10** fool around, mess around **12** monkey around

Fidei Defensor **18** Defender of the Faith
title of: **17** English sovereigns

Fidelio
opera by: **9** Beethoven
character: **5** Rocco **7** Leonora (Fidelio), Pizarro **8** Fernando **9** Florestan

fidelity **5** honor **6** fealty **7** honesty, loyalty, probity **8** accuracy, devotion **9** adherence, closeness, constancy, exactness, good faith, integrity, precision, sincerity **10** allegiance, exactitude **11** earnestness, reliability, staunchness **12** faithfulness, truthfulness **14** correspondency **15** trueheartedness, trustworthiness

Fides
origin: **5** Roman
personifies: **9** good faith

fidget **4** fret, fuss, jerk, stew, toss **5** chafe, worry **6** jiggle, squirm, twitch, wiggle, writhe **7** twiddle, wriggle

fidgety **5** antsy, fussy, jerky, jumpy **6** uneasy **7** jittery, nervous, restive, squirmy, twitchy, unquiet **8** restless **9** impatient, irritable, tremulous **12** apprehensive

fief **4** land **6** domain, estate **9** territory

field **3** lea **4** area, grab, lawn, line, mead, turf, yard **5** arena, catch, court, front, glove, green, heath, lists, orbit, range, reach, realm, scope, sward, sweep **6** circle, common, course, domain, extent, meadow, pick up, region, sphere **7** acreage, calling, diamond, expanse, pasture, run down, stretch **8** clearing, province, retrieve, spectrum **9** bailiwick, grassland, territory **10** department, occupation, profession **12** battleground

Field, Sally
born: **10** Pasadena CA
roles: **5** Sybil **6** Gidget **8** Norma Rae (Oscar) **9** Punchline, Surrender **12** The Flying Nun **14** Murphy's Romance **15** Absence of Malice **16** Places in the Heart (Oscar) **18** Smokey and the Bandit

Fielding, Cecil
character in: **15** A Passage to India
author: **7** Forster

Fielding, Henry
author of: **6** Amelia **7** Shamela **8** Tom Jones, Tom Thumb **12** Jonathan Wild **13** Joseph Andrews

Field of Blood **8** Aceldama

Fields, W C
real name: **23** William Claude Dukenfield
born: **14** Philadelphia PA
roles: **5** Poppy **8** Micawber **11** The Bank Dick **16** David Copperfield **17** My Little Chickadee **27** Never Give a Sucker an Even Break

Fields of Mourning
location: **10** underworld
inhabited by: **14** shades of lovers
lovers who died by: **7** suicide

Fields of Visions, The
author: **12** Wright Morris

fiend **5** beast, brute, demon, devil, Satan **6** dybbuk **7** incubus, monster, villain **8** succubus **9** barbarian, hellhound, scoundrel **10** evil spirit **12** wicked person **14** devil incarnate **16** prince of darkness

fiendish **4** evil, foul **5** cruel **6** wicked **7** demonic, heinous, impious, satanic, vicious **8** barbaric, demoniac, devilish **9** monstrous, nefarious **10** demoniacal, diabolical, villainous

fierce **4** fell, wild **5** cruel, feral, fiery **6** brutal, fervid, raging, savage, strong **7** enraged, extreme, fearful, fervent, furious, intense, leonine, untamed, violent **8** horrible, menacing, powerful, ravening, ravenous, terrible, tigerish, uncurbed, vehement **9** barbarous, bellicose, ferocious, impetuous, merciless, truculent, unbridled, voracious **10** immoderate, inordinate, passionate **11** threatening **12** bloodthirsty, overpowering, overwhelming, unrestrained
French: **8** farouche

fierceness **4** zeal **7** passion **8** ferocity, wildness **9** pugnacity, vehemence **10** savageness

fiery **5** afire, angry, irate **6** ablaze, alight, ardent, fervid, fierce, red-hot, torrid **7** blazing, burning, febrile, fervent, fevered, flaming, glaring, glowing, peppery, pyretic, violent, zealous **8** choleric, feverish, flashing, headlong, inflamed, spirited, vehement, wrathful **9** excitable, hotheaded, impetuous, impulsive, irascible, irritable **10** full of fire, high-strung, mettlesome, passionate, sweltering **11** hot-tempered, impassioned, precipitate **12** enthusiastic

fiesta **4** fete, gala **5** feast, party **6** picnic **7** funfair **8** carnival, feast day, festival, jamboree **9** saint's day **10** block party, observance, street fair **11** celebration **13** commemoration **15** festive occasion

fig 5 Ficus
varieties: 3 keg, sea **4** bush, cape, Java, Zulu **5** cedar, clown, Congo, rusty **6** common, Devil's, exotic, golden, Indian, Kaffir, Mysore, sacred **7** Barbary, cluster, oakleaf, spotted, weeping **8** climbing, creeping, Dracaena, mulberry, sycamore **9** Hottentot, mistletoe, strangler **10** East Indian, fiddleleaf, glossy-leaf, little-leaf, Moreton Bay, Philippine **11** Port Jackson **16** West Indian laurel

Figaro
character in: 18 The Barber of Seville **19** The Marriage of Figaro
author: 12 Beaumarchais

fight 3 box, row, war **4** bout, duel, feud, fray, grit, spar, spat, tiff, tilt, wage **5** argue, brawl, brush, clash, event, joust, match, melee, pluck, round, scrap, set-to **6** battle, bicker, combat, engage, fracas, mettle, oppose, resist, spirit, strife, tussle **7** carry on, conduct, contend, contest, discord, dispute, go to war, quarrel, repulse, scuffle, tourney, wage war, wrangle **8** confront, dogfight, gameness, skirmish, squabble, struggle **9** bickering, encounter, pugnacity, scrimmage, toughness, wrangling **10** contention, difference, dissension, prizefight, strive with, tournament **11** altercation, armed action, battle royal, bellicosity, clash of arms, controversy **12** belligerency, do battle with, rise up in arms, struggle with **13** armed conflict, combativeness, confrontation, exchange blows, pitched battle

fight back 7 counter, get even, hit back, pay back **9** retaliate **10** strike back **13** counterattack

fighter 5 boxer **7** soldier, sparrer, warrior **8** pugilist, scrapper **9** combatant **10** militarist **11** belligerent

fighting 3 war **4** fray **5** brawl, melee **6** action, battle, bicker, combat, rumpus, tumult, tussle **7** contest, dispute, quarrel, warfare **8** battling, brawling, conflict, skirmish, squabble **9** bickering, disputing **10** engagement, quarreling, squabbling **11** clash of arms, controversy, hostilities

Fighting Marine
nickname of: 10 Gene Tunney

fighting men 4 army **6** legion, troops **7** legions, militia **8** military, soldiers, soldiery **13** military force **15** military machine

fighting spirit 9 animosity, hostility, pugnacity **10** antagonism **11** bellicosity **12** belligerence **14** aggressiveness

fight shy of 5 avoid, dodge, elude, evade, skirt **6** escape **8** sidestep

figment 5 fable, fancy, story **6** canard **7** fantasy, fiction, product **8** creation **9** falsehood, invention **10** concoction **11** fabrication

figuration 4 form **7** outline **9** formation, structure **12** constitution

figurative 6 florid, ironic, ornate **7** flowery **8** humorous, symbolic **9** satirical **10** not literal **11** allegorical **12** hyperbolical, metaphorical

figure, figures 3 cut, man, sum **4** body, cast, cost, foot, form, mark, plan, rate, sign, sums **5** add up, adorn, build, count, digit, force, frame, guess, judge, motif, price, shape, think, total, tot up, value, woman **6** amount, appear, assess, cipher, design, device, emblem, factor, leader, number, person, reckon, schema, symbol **7** anatomy, believe, compute, contour, count up, diagram, drawing, imagine, notable, numeral, outline, pattern, presume, suppose **8** appraise, be placed, eminence, estimate, ornament, physique, presence **9** calculate, character, diversify, embellish, have a part, personage, play a part, quotation, variegate **10** arithmetic, conjecture, shine forth, silhouette **11** be mentioned, be prominent **12** calculations, computations, illustration

figurehead 4 tool **5** dummy, front, token **6** cipher, puppet **8** ornament **9** nonentity

figure out 6 reckon **7** compute, find out, work out **8** discover **9** ascertain, calculate, determine

figure roughly 5 guess **6** reckon **8** estimate **11** approximate, make a stab at

figure up 3 add **5** add up, total, tot up **6** reckon **7** compute, count up **9** calculate

> **Fiji**
> **capital/largest city: 4** Suva
> **others: 3** Mba **4** Mbua **5** Navua **6** Labasa **7** Lautoka, Nausori, Vaileka, Vunisea **8** Korolevu, Savusavu **9** Singatoka
> **school: 12** South Pacific
> **head of state: 14** British monarch **15** governor general
> **monetary unit: 6** dollar
> **island: 4** Ngau **6** Ovalau, Rotuma, Yasawa **7** Kandavu, Taveuni **8** Viti Levu **9** Vanua Levu
> **highest point: 8** Victoria **9** Tomaniivi
> **river: 4** Rewa **8** Ndreketi
> **sea: 4** Koro **7** Pacific
> **people: 6** Fijian, Indian **7** Chinese **10** Melanesian, Polynesian **11** Micronesian
> **language: 5** Hindi **6** Fijian **7** English
> **religion: 5** Hindu, Islam **9** Methodist **13** Roman Catholic
> **feature:**
> ***cluster houses:***
> **5** mbure

figurine 7 bibelot **8** ornament **9** statuette

Fiji ***see box***

filament 4 hair, line, wire **5** fiber, fibre **6** cilium, ribbon, strand, string, thread

filbert 7 Corylus
varieties: 3 red **4** cork, Momi, plum **5** azure, China, giant, Greek, joint, Nikko, noble, white **6** alpine, balsam, Fraser, Korean, needle, Scotch, silver, summer **7** cascade, Douglas, lowland, Spanish **8** Algerian, Japanese, Sakhalin, Southern **9** Himalayan, Shasta Red **10** dwarf Nikko, Santa Lucia **11** bristle-cone **13** Pacific silver **14** Southern balsam

filch 3 cop, rob **4** copy, crib, hook, lift **5** boost, heist, steal, swipe **6** pilfer, pirate **7** purloin **8** arrogate **10** plagiarize **11** appropriate, expropriate

file 3 row **4** data, line, list, rank, tier **5** apply, chain, index, put in, queue, store

6 drawer, folder, record, stacks, string **7** catalog, dossier, put away, records, request **8** archives, classify, petition **9** catalogue, chronicle
type: 4 mill, nail, rasp, wood **5** round **9** half-round **13** three-cornered

filial 7 dutiful, sonlike **10** daughterly, respectful

fill 3 act **4** cram, glut, lade, load, meet, pack, puff, sate **5** crowd, gorge, lay by, lay in, serve, stock, store **6** answer, assign, blow up, charge, dilate, do duty, expand, infuse, make up, occupy, outfit, supply, take up **7** distend, execute, furnish, inflate, pervade, preside, provide, satiate, satisfy, suffuse, surfeit **8** carry out, function, permeate, saturate **9** discharge, provision, replenish **10** full amount, impregnate, overspread

filled in 7 stood in **9** completed, **11** substituted

filled out 6 marked **7** matured **9** completed

fillet 4 band **5** slice, strip **6** ribbon **7** bandeau, circlet

fillip 3 tap **4** flip, snap, toss **5** flick, tonic **6** buffet **8** stimulus

Fillmore, Millard ***see box***

fill with air 5 bloat **6** billow, blow up, expand **7** balloon, distend, inflate, puff out **8** swell out

fill with dread 5 alarm, panic **6** dismay **7** perturb, terrify, unnerve **8** disquiet, frighten

fill with gloom 6 darken, sadden **8** dispirit

fill with wonder 3 awe **5** amaze **7** astound **8** astonish **9** fascinate

film, films 4 coat, haze, mist, skin, veil **5** cloud, flick, movie, sheet, shoot **6** cinema, flicks, movies, screen **7** coating **8** membrane

filmy 3 dim **4** fine, hazy, thin **5** gauzy, misty, sheer, wispy **8** cobwebby, finespun, gossamer **10** diaphanous

fils 3 son

filter 4 leak, ooze, seep **5** drain, exude, sieve **6** effuse, purify, refine, screen, strain **7** clarify, cleanse, dribble, trickle, well out **8** filtrate, strainer

filth 3 mud **4** dirt, dung, mire, muck, slop, smut **5** feces, offal, slime, slush, trash **6** manure, ordure, refuse, sewage, sludge **7** carrion, excreta, garbage, squalor **8** impurity, lewdness, ribaldry, vileness **9** excrement, grossness, indecency, nastiness, obscenity, pollution **10** corruption, defilement, immorality, indelicacy, putridness **11** pornography, squalidness **13** contamination **14** suggestiveness

filthy 4 foul, vile **5** black, dirty, grimy, gross, messy, nasty **6** grubby, impure, odious, soiled **7** defiled, dirtied, obscene, smirchy, squalid, unclean **8** befouled, slovenly, unwashed **9** repulsive **10** besmirched, disgusting **12** contaminated

finagle 3 con, gyp **4** plot, rook **5** cheat, mulct, trick **6** chisel, fleece, scheme, wangle **7** defraud, swindle **8** engineer, intrigue, maneuver

final 4 last, rear **6** ending, latest **7** closing, extreme **8** complete, decisive, finished, hindmost, rearmost, terminal, thorough, ultimate **10** concluding, conclusive, definitive, exhaustive, hindermost **11** irrevocable, terminating **12** unappealable, unchangeable **13** determinative
French: 7 dernier

finale 3 end **5** close, finis **6** finish, windup **7** curtain **8** epilogue, last part, swan song **10** conclusion **11** culmination, termination

final limit
Latin: 14 terminus ad quem

finally 6 lastly **10** eventually, inexorably, ultimately **11** inescapably **12** conclusively, definitively, in conclusion **16** incontrovertibly
French: 5 enfin
Latin: 10 ad extremum

Fillmore, Millard
presidential rank: 10 thirteenth
party: 4 Whig
state represented: 2 NY
defeated: 5 no one
succeeded upon death of: **6** Taylor
vice president: 4 none
cabinet:
State: **7** (Daniel) Webster, (Edward) Everett
Treasury: **6** (Thomas) Corwin
War: **6** (Charles Magill) Conrad
Attorney General: **10** (John Jordan) Crittenden
Navy: **6** (William Alexander) Graham **7** (John Pendleton) Kennedy
Postmaster General: **4** (Nathan Kelsey) Hall **7** (Samuel Dickinson) Hubbard
Interior: **6** (Alexander Hugh Holmes) Stuart
born: 7 Locke NY
died/buried: 9 Buffalo NY
education:
college: **4** none
studied: **3** law
religion: 9 Unitarian
interests: 5 civic
first chancellor of University of: **7** Buffalo
founder: **22** Buffalo General Hospital **24** Buffalo Historical Society
author: 21 Millard Fillmore Papers
political career: 13 state assembly, Vice President **24** US House of Representatives
civilian career: 6 lawyer (New York Supreme Court) **7** teacher **10** wool carder **12** cloth dresser
notable events of lifetime/term: 25 Compromise of Eighteen-Fifty
act: **13** Fugitive Slave
father: 9 Nathaniel
mother: 6 Phoebe (Millard)
siblings: 5 Cyrus, Julia **11** Phoebe Maria **12** Almon Hopkins, Calvin Turner **13** Charles DeWitt **14** Darius Ingraham, Olive Armstrong
wife: 7 Abigail (Powers) **8** Caroline (Carmichael McIntosh)
children: 11 Mary Abigail **13** Millard Powers

final section **4** coda **5** rider **6** ending **7** last act **8** addendum, epilogue **9** afterword **10** conclusion

final settlement **8** solution **11** disposition

finance **6** pay for **7** banking **8** accounts **9** economics **10** underwrite

financial backer **5** angel **6** patron **7** sponsor **9** supporter **10** benefactor

financial support **7** backing, subsidy **10** assistance **12** contribution

financier **5** angel **6** backer, banker, broker **7** rich man **10** capitalist **11** millionaire, underwriter

Financier, The
author: **15** Theodore Dreiser
character: **12** Aileen Butler, Edward Butler **15** Henry Cowperwood **16** Frank A Cowperwood **23** Lillian Semple Cowperwood

Finch, Peter
real name: **15** Peter Ingle-Finch
born: **6** London **7** England
roles: **7** Network (Oscar) **11** Lost Horizon **12** The Nun's Story **15** The Pumpkin Eater **18** Sunday Bloody Sunday

Finchley, Sondra
character in: **17** An American Tragedy
author: **7** Dreiser

find **3** get, see, win **4** earn, espy, gain, meet, rule, spot **5** award, catch, dig up, judge, learn **6** attain, come by, decide, decree, detect, expose, locate, regain **7** achieve, acquire, adjudge, bargain, bonanza, discern, get back, godsend, good buy, hit upon, procure, recover, uncover, unearth **8** bump into, come upon, discover, disinter, lucky hit, meet with, retrieve, windfall **9** ascertain, determine, discovery, encounter, pronounce, repossess **10** adjudicate **11** acquisition

fin de siecle **8** decadent **15** end of the century

find fault **3** nag **4** beef, carp **5** blame, cavil, gribe **6** grouse, squawk **7** nitpick **8** complain **9** bellyache, criticize, disparage **10** disapprove

find guilty **5** blame **6** indict **7** condemn, convict **8** sentence **9** implicate

finding **6** decree, ruling **7** verdict **8** decision

find innocent **5** clear **6** acquit **9** exonerate

find out **5** learn **6** detect, locate **7** uncover, unearth **8** discover **9** ascertain, determine, establish

find repulsive **4** hate **5** abhor **6** detest, loathe **7** despise **8** execrate, recoil at **9** abominate

fine **4** airy, chic, fair, keen, neat, nice, rare, thin **5** bonny, clear, dandy, gauzy, mulct, nifty, sharp, sheer, silky, small, smart, sunny, swell **6** assess, bonnie, bright, charge, choice, comely, dainty, flimsy, ground, lovely, minute, modish, pretty, silken, slight, spiffy, subtle, superb **7** damages, elegant, forfeit, fragile, penalty, perfect, powdery, precise, refined, slender, stylish, tenuous **8** cobwebby, delicate, ethereal, flawless, gossamer, handsome, penalize, pleasant, polished, powdered, rainless, skillful, splendid, superior, tasteful **9** admirable, beautiful, brilliant, cloudless, excellent, exquisite **10** assessment, attractive, consummate, diaphanous, fastidious, pulverized, swimmingly **11** excellently, exceptional, lightweight, magnificent, transparent, well-favored **12** accomplished **13** hairsplitting, unsubstantial
music: **3** end

fine clothes **8** glad rags **10** Sunday best **16** best bib and tucker

fine-looking **4** fair **5** bonny **6** bonnie, comely, lovely, pretty, seemly **8** gorgeous, handsome **9** beauteous, beautiful, exquisite, ravishing **10** attractive **11** resplendent **15** pulchritudinous

fineness **6** beauty **8** delicacy, elegance, thinness **10** perfection, smoothness **12** flawlessness **13** exquisiteness

fine points **3** art **7** finesse, nuances **8** niceties **10** subtleties **11** refinements **12** distinctions

finer **6** better **8** superior

finery **6** frills, tinsel **7** baubles, gaudery, gewgaws **8** frippery, spangles, trinkets **9** trappings, trimmings **13** paraphernalia

finesse **4** ruse, tact, wile **5** craft, dodge, guile, savvy **7** cunning **8** artifice, delicacy, intrigue, trickery **9** deception, stratagem **10** artfulness, discretion, subterfuge
French: **11** savoir-faire

fine workmanship **8** delicacy **9** precision **13** craftsmanship

finger **3** paw **4** feel, poke **5** digit, punch, thumb, touch **6** caress, feeler, handle **7** pointer, squeeze, toy with, twiddle **8** play with **10** manipulate

finicky **5** fussy, picky **6** choosy **8** niggling **10** fastidious, meticulous, nitpicking, overprecise, particular, pernickety **11** persnickety **14** discriminating, overparticular

finish **3** end **4** coat, face, gild, goal, kill, last, seal, stop **5** cease, close, glaze, use up **6** clinch, defeat, devour, ending, finale, settle, veneer, wind up **7** achieve, coating, consume, curtain, destroy, fulfill, get done, lacquer, realize, surface, varnish **8** carry out, complete, conclude, dispatch, epilogue, exterior, get rid of, knock off, make good **9** discharge, eradicate, objective, polishing, terminate **10** accomplish, completion, conclusion, consummate, denouement **11** discontinue, exterminate, termination

finished **4** full **5** ended, final, ideal, whole **6** entire, urbane **7** classic, elegant, perfect, refined, shapely, skilled, trained, well-set **8** complete, flawless, polished, well-bred **9** beautiful, completed, concluded, exquisite, faultless **10** consummate, cultivated, impeccable **11** consummated **12** accomplished

finishing stroke **9** death blow
French: **11** coup de grace

finish off **4** kill, slay **7** destroy, execute, wipe out **8** complete, dispatch **9** eradicate, polish off **10** annihilate **11** exterminate

finite **7** bounded, limited **8** confined, temporal **9** countable **10** measurable, restricted, short-lived, terminable **13** circumscribed

Finland ***see box***

Finn
also: **5** Fionn **13** Fionn MacCumal
origin: **5** Irish
king of: **4** gods **14** Tuatha De Danann
son: **6** Ossian
father: **5** Cumal **6** Comhal

Finnegan's Wake
author: **10** James Joyce
family: **9** Earwicker

Finney, Albert
wife: **10** Anouk Aimee
born: **7** England, Salford
roles: **5** Annie **7** Scrooge **8** Tom Jones **10** The Dresser **12** Shoot the Moon **13** Two for the Road **17** Under the Volcano **29** Saturday Night and Sunday Morning

Finnish Mythology *see* **21** Scandinavian Mythology

Finland
other name: **5** Suomi **15** Suomen Tasavalta
capital/largest city: **8** Helsinki **11** Helsingfors
others: **3** Aba, Abo, Kem **4** Kemi, Ouli, Oulu, Ouou, Pori, Vasa **5** Enare, Espoo, Kotka, Lahti, Rauma, Turku, Vaasa **6** Imatra, Kuopio **7** Joensuu, Kajaani, Kokkola, Mikkeli, Tampere, Tapiola **9** Jyvaskyla, Mariehamn, Rovaniemi **12** Lappeenranta
measure: **5** kannu, verst **6** fathom, kannor **8** otlinger, skalpund, tunnland
monetary unit: **4** mark **5** penni **6** markka
island: **5** Aland, Karlo **6** Aaland **7** Hailuto **9** Vallgrund **10** Ahvenanmaa
lake: **3** Juo, Muo **4** Kemi, Kiui, Nasi, Oulu, Puru, Pyha, Simo **5** Enara, Enare, Hauki, Inari, Kalla, Lappa, Lesti, Puula, Saima **6** Ladoya, Lentua, Saimaa, Sounne, Syvari **7** Koitere, Nilakka, Pielien **9** Kallavesi, Pielavesi
mountain: **7** Laltiva **10** Saari Selka
highest point: **6** Haltia **11** Haldetsokka
river: **4** Kala, Kemi, Kymi, Oulu, Pats, Simo, Teno **5** Ivalo, Lotta, Ounas, Siika, Torne **6** Iijoki, Lapuan, Muonio, Pasvik, Tornoi, Vuoski **7** Kitinen **8** Kokemaki
sea: **6** Baltic **8** Atlantic
physical feature:
gulf: **7** Bothnia, Finland
isthmus: **7** Karelia
peninsula: **13** Fennoscandian
people: **3** Jew, Vod, Vot, Yak **4** Avar, Finn, Hame, Lapp, Turk, Veps **5** Fioun, Gypsy, Ijore, Inger, Suomi, Vepse **6** Magyar, Ostiak, Ostyak, Tarast, Tavast, Ugrian, Zyrian **7** Lappish, Mordvin, Permiak, Samoyed, Uralian **8** Cheremis, Estonian, Karelian, Livonian, Swekoman **9** Tavastian **11** Karjalaiset, Suomalaiset
athlete: **10** Paavo Nurmi
composer: **8** Sibelius
designer: **9** Marimekko
language: **4** Avar, Lapp **5** Karel, Ugric, Vogul **6** Magyar, Ostyak, Tarast **7** Finnish, Olonets, Samoyed, Swedish **8** Estonian **10** Olonetsian
religion: **19** Evangelical Lutheran
place:
canal: **6** Saimaa
castle: **10** Saint Olaf's **11** Olavinlinna
fortress: **8** Sveaborg **11** Suomenlinna
memorial: **8** Sibelius
pine ridge: **10** Punkaharju
feature:
game: **9** pesapallo
food:
dish: **11** Karelian pie
fruit: **16** yellow cloudberry
liqueur: **9** Mesimarja

Finno-Ugric
language family: **6** Uralic
Finnic group: **4** Lapp **6** Votyak, Zyryan **7** Finnish, Mordvin, Permian **8** Estonian **9** Cheremiss
Ugric group: **5** Vogul **6** Ostyak **7** Ob-Ugric **9** Hungarian

Fionn, Fionn MacCumal *see* **4** Finn

fiord, fjord **5** firth, inlet **7** estuary

fir **4** pine **5** cedar, larch **6** alpine, balsam, linden, spruce **7** conifer, cypress, douglas **9** evergreen

Firbolg
origin: **5** Greek, Irish
defeated by: **9** Fomorians
ousted by: **4** gods **14** Tuatha De Danann

fire ***see box***

Fire and Ice
author: **11** Robert Frost

firearm **3** gun, rod **5** piece, rifle **6** pistol **7** shotgun **8** revolver **10** machine gun **12** shooting iron **13** submachine gun **20** Saturday-night special

fire **3** can, vim **4** bake, boot, burn, cook, dash, dump, elan, hurl, oust, sack, stir **5** ardor, blaze, eject, flame, flare, flash, force, gusto, let go, light, power, punch, rouse, salvo, shell, shoot, spark, verve, vigor **6** arouse, bounce, depose, excite, fervor, foment, genius, ignite, incite, kindle, luster, spirit, stir up, vivify, volley **7** animate, bombard, bonfire, cashier, dismiss, inferno, inflame, inspire, project, quicken, sniping, trigger **8** enfilade, fervency, inspirit, radiance, splendor, vivacity **9** broadside, cannonade, discharge, eagerness, fusillade, galvanize, holocaust, instigate, intensity, stimulate, vehemence **10** brilliance, effulgence, enthusiasm **11** bombardment, earnestness, inspiration **13** conflagration, sharpshooting **15** imaginativeness
god of: **4** Loki **5** Ishum **6** Vulcan **10** Hephaestus, Hephaistos
goddess of: **6** Brigit

firefight **5** clash **6** battle, combat **8** skirmish

firefly **8** glowworm, lampyrid **9** candlefly **12** lightning bug

Fire Next Time, The
author: **12** James Baldwin

fire off **5** eject, shoot **6** launch **8** detonate **9** discharge

Fireside Theatre
host: **9** Jane Wyman **11** Frank Wisbar, Gene Raymond

Firestarter
author: **11** Stephen King

fire up **4** fuel, rile **5** anger, light, rouse **6** arouse, excite, ignite, incite, kindle **7** animate, enthuse, inspire **8** activate, energize, irritate, vitalize **9** galvanize, stimulate

firm **4** bent, fast, grim, hard, taut **5** close, dense, fixed, house, rigid, rocky, solid, stiff, stony, tight, tough **6** dogged, flinty, intent, moored, rooted, secure, stable, steady, steely **7** compact, company, dead set, decided, earnest, serious, settled, staunch **8** anchored, business, constant, definite, fearless, obdurate, resolute, resolved, unshaken **9** confirmed, hardnosed, immovable, obstinate, steadfast, tenacious, unbending **10** adamantine, compressed, determined, inexorable, inflexible, invincible, persistent, unwavering, unyielding **11** corporation, established, partnership, unalterable, unfaltering, unflinching **12** conglomerate, indissoluble, organization **13** establishment

firmament **3** air, sky **5** ether, space, vault **6** canopy, welkin **7** heavens, the blue, the void **10** outer space

firmness **8** tenacity **9** obstinacy **10** resolution **11** persistence, staunchness **12** resoluteness **13** determination, inflexibility, steadfastness

first **4** head, main **5** basic, prime, start, vital **6** before, eldest, maiden, outset, primal, rather, sooner **7** highest, leading, premier, primary, ranking, supreme **8** earliest, foremost, original, primeval, superior **9** beginning, essential, inception, initially, paramount, primitive, principal **10** aboriginal, elementary, preeminent, preferably, primordial **11** fundamental, rudimentary **12** commencement, introduction, introductory

first among equals
Latin: **16** primus inter pares

first appearance **4** dawn **5** debut **9** beginning **12** introduction

firstborn **5** elder, older **6** eldest, oldest

Firstborn, The
author: **14** Christopher Fry

First Circle
author: **23** Aleksandr Solzhenitsyn Jr

first god *see* **8** god, first

firsthand **6** direct **8** personal **9** empirical **10** unmediated **12** experimental

First Lady of the Theater
nickname of: **10** Helen Hayes **16** Katherine Cornell

first-line **4** main **5** chief **7** primary **8** foremost

first man *see* **8** man, first

first moving thing
Latin: **12** primum mobile

first-rate **3** ace **4** A-one, best, fine, tops **5** crack, elite, great, prime **6** choice, finest, select **7** top-hole **8** splendid, superior, top-notch, very good **9** admirable, estimable, excellent, exclusive, nonpareil, top drawer, topflight, wonderful **10** noteworthy, stupendous **11** commendable, outstanding **12** above-average, incomparable **13** distinguished

First State
nickname of: **8** Delaware

first step **5** start **9** beginning **12** commencement

first woman *see* **10** woman, first

firth **5** fjord, inlet **7** estuary

fiscal **8** economic, monetary **9** budgetary, financial, pecuniary

fish **3** net **4** cast, hook, hunt **5** angle, grope, seine, trawl, troll **6** ferret, search **7** rummage

fish ***see box***

Fisher, Bud
creator/artist of: **11** Mutt and Jeff

Fisher, Carrie
father: **11** Eddie Fisher
mother: **13** Debbie Reynolds
roles: **7** Shampoo **8** Star Wars **12** Princess Leia **18** The Return of the Jedi **19** The Empire Stikes Back

Fisher, Ham
creator/artist of: **10** Joe Palooka

fish
class: **7** Agnatha **12** Osteichthyes **14** Chondrichthyes
fin: **4** anal, tail **6** caudal, dorsal, median, paired, pelvic **7** adipose, ventral **8** pectoral
kind: **3** cod, eel, gar, ray **4** bass, carp, hake, opah, pike, tuna **5** brill, perch, shark, skate, sword, trout **6** bichir, blenny, marlin, minnow, mullet, salmon, tarpon **7** anchovy, catfish, dogfish, dolphin, hagfish, herring, lamprey, piranha, sunfish **8** bluefish, cavefish, crayfish, flounder, goldfish, lungfish, mackerel, menhaden, moray eel, pilchard, sea horse, squirrel, sturgeon **9** killifish, pygmy goby, swordfish **10** coelacanth, flying fish, paddlefish, rabbit fish, rocksucker, whale shark **11** anemonefish, electric eel, electric ray, lanternfish, long-nose gar **13** butterflyfish **14** largemouth bass
part: **3** fin **4** gill **5** scale **6** cirrhi **10** gas bladder **11** swim bladder **12** rete mirabile
shellfish:
crustacean: **4** crab **6** shrimp **7** lobster **8** blue crab, king crab, snow crab **9** langouste **11** langoustine **13** Dungeness crab, horseshoe crab
mollusk: **4** clam **6** mussel, oyster, quahog **8** surf clam **9** horse clam, razor clam **11** geoduck clam
young: **3** fry **10** fingerling

Fisher, Vardis
author of: 10 The Mothers **13** Children of God **17** The Testament of Man

fisherman 5 eeler **6** angler, caster, jacker, netter, seiner **7** trawler, troller **8** piscator **9** flycaster, Waltonian **17** the compleat angler

Fishermen
goddess of: 11 Britomartis

Fishes
constellation of: 6 Pisces

fish story 3 fib, lie **7** fiction, whopper **9** falsehood, tall story **16** cock-and-bull story

fishy 3 odd **4** dull **5** blank, queer, shady, weird **6** vacant **7** dubious, strange, suspect **8** doubtful, peculiar, slippery **9** dishonest **10** farfetched, glassy-eyed, improbable, suspicious, unreliable **11** exaggerated, extravagant **12** questionable, unscrupulous **14** expressionless

fission 7 atomize **8** breaking, cleavage, scission **9** severance, splitting **10** breaking up, sunderance **12** disseverance, reproduction

fissure 3 gap **4** rift, slit **5** chink, cleft, crack, gully, split **6** breach, cranny, groove, hiatus **8** aperture, cleavage

fit ***see box***

fitful 4 weak **6** broken, random, uneven **7** erratic **8** listless, off-and-on, periodic, sporadic, unsteady, variable **9** irregular, spasmodic **10** capricious, changeable, convulsive **11** fluctuating **12** disconnected, intermittent

fitness
Hebrew: 7 kashrut **8** kashruth

fit out 4 robe **5** array, dress, equip **6** attire, clothe, supply **7** appoint, prepare

fitting 3 apt **4** meet **6** proper, seemly **8** decorous, suitable **9** congruous **11** appropriate
French: 11 comme il faut

fit to be eaten 6 edible **9** palatable **10** comestible, consumable, digestible

fit together 4 join **5** hinge, unite **6** hook up **7** connect **8** dovetail **9** interlock **10** articulate

Fitzgerald, Barry
real name: 20 William Joseph Shields
born: 6 Dublin **7** Ireland
roles: 10 Going My Way **11** The Quiet Man **19** How Green Was My Valley

FitzGerald, Edward
author of: 24 The Rubaiyat of Omar Khayyam (translation)

Fitzgerald, F Scott
wife: 10 Zelda Sayre
author of: 10 The Crack-Up **13** The Last Tycoon **14** The Great Gatsby **16** Tender Is the Night **18** This Side of Paradise **24** The Beautiful and the Damned

Fitzgerald, George Francis
field: 7 physics
nationality: 5 Irish
theory of: 24 electromagnetic radiation

Fitzgerald, Geraldine
born: 6 Dublin **7** Ireland
roles: 11 Dark Victory **12** Ah Wilderness, Rachel Rachel **15** Watch on the Rhine **16** Wuthering Heights **24** Long Day's Journey into Night

Fitzsimmons, Bob (Robert Prometheus)
sport: 6 boxing

FitzSimons, Maureen
real name of: 12 Maureen O'Hara

fit 4 able, good, hale, meet, ripe, suit, well, whim **5** adapt, agree, alter, burst, equal, equip, hardy, match, ready, right, shape, sound, spasm, spell, train **6** access, accord, adjust, become, concur, enable, in trim, mature, primed, proper, robust, seemly, strong, timely, worthy **7** adapted, apropos, capable, caprice, conform, correct, empower, fashion, healthy, prepare, qualify, rectify, seizure, toned up, trained **8** apposite, becoming, coincide, crotchet, decorous, eligible, graduate, grand mal, outbreak, outburst, paroxysm, petit mal, prepared, relevant, suitable **9** calibrate, competent, consonant, deserving, efficient, explosion, harmonize, initiated, opportune, pertinent, qualified **10** acceptable, applicable, capacitate, convenient, convulsion, correspond, seasonable **11** appropriate, capacitated

Five, The
group of: 16 Russian composers
member: 3 Cui **7** Borodin **9** Balakirev **10** Mussorgsky **14** Rimsky-Korsakov

Five Easy Pieces
director: 11 Bob Rafelson
cast: 10 Karen Black **11** Fannie Flagg **12** Susan Anspach **13** Jack Nicholson **14** Billy Breen Bush, Sally Struthers

Five Men and Pompey
author: 19 Stephen Vincent Benet

five-o'clock shadow 5 beard **7** stubble **8** bristles, whiskers

fix 3 jam, put, set **4** bind, make, mend, mess, moor, spot **5** place, rivet **6** adjust, anchor, attach, decide, fasten, harden, impose, muddle, pickle, plight, repair, scrape, secure, settle **7** congeal, connect, correct, dilemma, impasse, implant, patch up, prepare, rebuild **8** assemble, hot water, make fast, make firm, quandary, regulate, renovate, set right, solidify **9** establish, prescribe, retaliate, stabilize **10** difficulty **11** consolidate, involvement, predicament **12** entanglement

fixation 5 quirk **6** fetish **7** complex **8** crotchet, delusion **9** monomania, obsession **13** preoccupation

fixed 3 set **4** fast, firm **5** rigid, still **6** intent, rooted, stable, steady **8** constant, fastened, resolute, unpliant **9** immovable, unbending **10** determined, inflexible, motionless, persistent, stationary, unwavering

fixed idea 4 bias **5** slant **9** obsession **13** preconception
French: 8 idee fixe

fixedness 8 firmness **9** constancy, stability **10** immobility **12** immutability **16** unchangeableness

fixed regard 7 staring **9** diligence **10** absorption, intentness **11** engrossment **13** concentration

Fixer, The
author: 14 Bernard Malamud

fixing 6 repair **7** mending, mooring, placing, putting, setting **8** deciding, imposing, righting, riveting, settling, trimming **9** adjusting, anchoring, attaching, fastening, hardening, preparing, repairing **10** adjustment, assembling, congealing, connecting, correcting, implanting, rectifying, regulating, regulation **11** determining, prescribing, solidifying, stabilizing **12** establishing **13** consolidating

fixture 6 addict **7** devotee, habitue, regular **8** equipage **9** apparatus, appendage, appliance, equipment **10** attachment **11** appointment **12** appurtenance **13** paraphernalia

fix up 4 plan **6** design, devise **7** arrange, prepare **8** renovate, schedule

fix upon 4 pick **6** choose, opt for, select **7** call out, extract, pick out

fizz 4 foam **5** froth **7** bubbles **11** carbonation **13** effervescence

fizziness 9 foaminess **10** bubbliness, frothiness **13** effervescence

fizzing 6 bubbly **7** foaming **8** bubbling **9** sparkling **12** effervescent, effervescing

fizzle 3 dog, dud **4** bomb, fail, flop, hiss, mess **5** abort, botch **6** bubble, fiasco, gurgle, muddle, turkey **7** failure, founder, misfire, sputter, washout **8** collapse, disaster, miscarry

fizzy 6 bubbly **8** bubbling **9** sparkling **12** effervescent

flabbergast 4 stun **5** amaze, shock **6** puzzle **7** astound, stagger, stupefy **8** astonish, bewilder, bowl over, confound, overcome **9** dumbfound

flabbergasted 5 agape **6** amazed, gaping **9** awestruck, stupefied **10** astonished, dumbstruck, spellbound **11** dumbfounded **12** hornswoggled **13** thunderstruck

flabby 4 lame, limp, soft, weak **5** baggy, slack **6** doughy, effete, feeble, flimsy, floppy, spongy **7** flaccid **8** impotent, listless, yielding **9** enervated, inelastic **10** spiritless **11** adulterated, emasculated

flag 3 ebb, sag **4** fade, fail, pall, sink, tire, wane, warn, wave, wilt **5** abate, faint, slump **6** banner, colors, dodder, emblem, ensign, signal, totter **7** decline, give way, pennant, subside, succumb **8** grow weak, languish, Old Glory, standard, streamer **9** grow weary, Union Jack **12** Stars and Bars **15** Stars and Stripes

flagellant 7 ascetic **8** penitent **13** self-mortifier

flagon 3 gun, jug, mug **4** ewer **5** flask, stein **6** bottle, carafe, vessel **7** canteen **8** schooner

flagrant 5 gross, sheer **6** arrant, brazen, crying **7** blatant, glaring, heinous, obvious **8** immodest **9** audacious, barefaced, flaunting, monstrous, notorious, shameless **10** outrageous, scandalous **11** conspicuous

Flaherty, Margaret (Pegeen)
character in: 24 Playboy of the Western World
author: 5 Synge

flail 4 beat, lash, whip **5** swing **6** thresh **7** scourge

flair 4 bent, dash, feel, gift **5** knack, style, taste, touch, verve **6** genius, talent **7** faculty, feeling, panache **8** aptitude, capacity **9** ingenuity **11** discernment

flake 3 bit **4** chip, peel **5** fleck, layer, patch, scale, sheet, strip **7** chip off, crumble, peel off, shaving **8** scale off

flaky 4 bats, gaga, nuts **5** balmy, batty, crisp, daffy, dotty, goofy, loony, nutty, scaly, short, wacky **6** scabby, screwy, scurfy **8** scabious, squamous **9** eccentric **10** flocculent

flamboyant 4 wild **5** gaudy, jazzy, showy **6** flashy, florid, garish, ornate, rococo **7** baroque, dashing **8** colorful, exciting **10** theatrical **11** sensational **12** ostentatious

flame 4 beau, fire, glow **5** ardor, blaze, blush, flare, flash, flush, glare, gleam, light, lover, spark, swain **6** fervor, ignite, kindle, redden, warmth **7** passion **8** fervency **9** affection, boyfriend, intensity **10** enthusiasm, excitement, girlfriend, sweetheart **13** conflagration

flaming 5 afire, fiery **6** ablaze, alight, ardent, bright, fervid, stormy **7** blazing, burning, fervent, glaring, glowing, igneous, intense, shining, violent **8** flagrant, vehement **9** brilliant, egregious **10** passionate, smoldering **11** conspicuous, inflammable

flammable 7 igneous **10** combustive, incendiary **11** combustible, inflammable

flan 3 pie **4** gust, puff, tart **6** expand, pastry **7** custard, dessert **12** creme caramel

flanerie 8 dawdling, idleness

flaneur 5 idler **6** loafer **7** dawdler

flank 3 hip **4** edge, line, loin, side, wing **5** cover, skirt **6** border, fringe, haunch, screen, shield

Flannagan, John Bernard
born: 7 Fargo ND
artwork: 6 New One, Not Yet **9** Beginning **11** Dragon Motif **15** Triumph of the Egg **16** Jonah and the Whale

flap 3 bat, fly, tab **4** bang, beat, flop **5** apron, shake, skirt **6** lappet **7** agitate, banging, flutter, vibrate **9** oscillate

flare 4 burn, glow **5** blaze, erupt, flame, flash, glare, gleam, taper, torch, widen **6** blow up, dilate, expand, ignite, signal, spread **7** bell out, broaden, distend, explode, stretch **8** boil over, break out **9** coruscate **10** incandesce

flash 4 glow, wink **5** blaze, blink, burst, flame, flare, glare, gleam, jiffy, shake, shine, spark, touch, trice **6** minute, moment, second, streak **7** flicker, glimmer, glisten, glitter, instant, sparkle **8** instance, outburst, radiance **9** coruscate **10** occurrence **11** coruscation, fulmination, scintillate **13** incandescence

Flash Gordon
creator: 8 Dan Berry **11** Alex Raymond **12** Austin Briggs
character:
***companion:* 4** Dale

flashy 4 loud **5** gaudy, jazzy, showy, smart **6** garish, sporty, tawdry, tinsel, vulgar **7** raffish **8** dazzling **9** bedizened **10** flamboyant, tricked out **11** pretentious **12** ostentatious

flask 6 bottle **7** canteen **9** container

flat, flats 3 low **4** dead, dull **5** clear, equal, flush, level, marsh, plain, plane, prone, shoal, shoes, stale, total, vapid **6** direct, planar, smooth, supine **7** blowout, exactly, insipid, laid low, leveled, levelly, loafers, prairie, regular, shallow **8** absolute, complete, definite, lowlands, positive, puncture, thorough, unbroken **9** apartment, downright, precisely, prostrate, reclining, recumbent, tasteless **10** flavorless, horizontal, peremptory

11 unequivocal, unpalatable, unqualified **12** deflated tire, horizontally, unmistakable

flatfish 3 ray **4** sole **5** brill, fluke **6** turbot **7** halibut, sand dab, sunfish, teleost **8** flounder

Flathead *see* **5** Salis **7** Chinook

flatness 8 dullness **9** levelness, staleness **10** insipidity **13** tastelessness **14** flavorlessness

flatten 4 deck, even, fell **5** crush, floor, level, plane **6** defeat, ground, smooth **7** deflate **8** compress, overcome **9** overwhelm, prostrate

flatter 4 fool, laud **5** court, extol, honor, toady **6** become, cajole, delude **7** adulate, beguile, deceive, mislead, wheedle **8** blandish, bootlick, butter up, eulogize, soft-soap **9** brown-nose, sweet-talk, truckle to **10** compliment, overpraise, panegyrize

flatterer 5 toady **6** fawner, yes man **8** eulogist, truckler, wheedler **9** sycophant **10** bootlicker **11** lickspittle **13** apple-polisher

flattering 7 lauding **8** praising **9** extolling, favorable, laudatory **10** gratifying **13** complimentary

flattering attention 5 court **7** fawning

flattery 6 eulogy **7** blarney, fawning, snow job **8** cajolery, encomium, jollying, soft soap, toadying, toadyism **9** adulation, panegyric, servility, truckling, wheedling **10** sycophancy **12** blandishment **14** obsequiousness

Flaubert, Gustave
author of: 8 Salammbo **12** Madame Bovary **21** A Sentimental Education **24** The Temptation of St Anthony

flaunt 3 air **4** brag, wave **5** boast, sport, strut, vaunt **6** blazon, dangle, parade **7** exhibit, show off **8** brandish, flourish **9** advertise, broadcast

flavor 4 aura, lace, soul, tang, tone **5** gusto, imbue, savor, spice, style, tenor **6** aspect, infuse, lacing, relish, season, spirit **7** essence, instill **8** ambience, piquancy **9** attribute, seasoning

flavorful 4 rich **5** nutty, sapid, spicy, tangy, tasty, zesty **6** savory **7** peppery, piquant **8** aromatic **9** palatable, toothsome **10** appetizing

flavoring 4 herb, salt **5** spice **6** pepper **7** essence, extract, vanilla **8** additive, seasoner **9** chocolate, condiment, seasoning

flavorless 4 dull, flat, thin, weak **5** bland, stale, vapid **6** watery **7** insipid **9** tasteless

flaw 3 mar **4** blot, harm, spot, vice **5** error, fault, speck, stain **6** blotch, deface, defect, foible, impair, injure, injury, smudge, weaken **7** blemish, failing, fallacy, frailty, mistake **8** weak spot, weakness **9** deformity, disfigure **10** compromise, defacement **11** shortcoming **12** imperfection **13** disfigurement

flawed 6 faulty **8** impaired **9** defective, imperfect

flawless 5 sound **7** perfect **9** errorless, faultless **10** immaculate, impeccable

flawlessness 8 accuracy **10** perfection **11** correctness **14** immaculateness

flay 4 bark, pare, peel, skin **5** scalp, scold, strip **6** assail, fleece, punish, rebuke **7** plunder, upbraid **9** castigate, excoriate **11** decorticate

flea
varieties: 3 bat, dog, rat **5** mouse **6** rodent **9** carnivore **10** sticktight

fleck 3 dot, jot **4** drop, mark, mole, spot **5** flake, speck **6** bespot, dapple, mottle, streak, tittle **7** blemish, freckle, spatter, speckle, stipple **8** particle, small bit **9** bespeckle **10** besprinkle

Fledermaus, Die
also: 6 The Bat
operetta by: 7 (Johann) Strauss
character: 5 Adele, Falke, Frank **6** Alfred **9** Rosalinda **14** Prince Orlofsky **18** Baron von Eisenstein

fledgling 4 tyro **6** novice **8** beginner, freshman **9** greenhorn **10** apprentice, tenderfoot

flee 4 shun, skip **5** avoid, dodge, elude, evade, split **6** decamp, desert, vanish **7** abscond, fly away, make off **8** speed off **9** cut and run, disappear **10** fly the coop

fleece 3 gyp **4** bilk, dupe, gull, rook, wool **5** cheat, cozen, trick **7** deceive, defraud, swindle **9** bamboozle, victimize

fleet 3 run **4** band, fade, fast, flow, navy, skim, spry, swim, unit **5** agile, array, brief, creek, drift, float, hasty, inlet, light, quick, rapid, shift, ships, short, swift **6** abound, active, armada, nimble, number, speedy, sudden, vanish **7** caravan, cursory, hurried **8** flotilla, squadron **9** disappear, momentary, transient **10** evanescent, transitory **11** expeditious **13** instantaneous

fleeting 5 brief, quick **7** passing **8** flitting, fugitive, temporal **9** ephemeral, fugacious, momentary, temporary, transient **10** evanescent, perishable, transitory **11** impermanent, precarious, unenduring

Fleming, Alexander
field: 12 bacteriology
nationality: 7 British
discovered: 10 penicillin
awarded: 10 Nobel Prize

Fleming, Henry
character in: 20 The Red Badge of Courage
author: 5 Crane

Fleming, Ian
author of: 4 Dr No **9** Moonraker **10** Goldfinger **11** Thunderball **12** Casino Royale **13** Live and Let Die **15** For Your Eyes Only **16** The Spy Who Loved Me, You Only Live Twice **18** From Russia with Love
character: 1 M, Q **6** Oddjob **7** SPECTRE (organization) **9** James Bond **14** Miss Moneypenny **15** Auric Goldfinger

Fleming, Victor
director of: 13 The Wizard of Oz **14** Treasure Island **15** Gone With the Wind (Oscar) **18** Captains Courageous

flesh 3 fat, man **4** body, meat, pulp **5** brawn, power, vigor **6** embody, fatten, people **7** fatness, fill out, mankind, realize **8** humanity, physique, strength **9** carnality, substance **10** sensuality **11** materiality **13** individualize, particularize

flesh and blood 3 kin **4** real **5** a body, child **6** family **7** kindred **8** children **9** corporeal, offspring, relations, relatives **10** kith and kin **11** substantial

flesh-eating 9 predatory **10** predaceous **11** carnivorous

fleshy 3 fat **5** beefy, obese,

plump, stout, tubby **6** chubby, portly, rotund, stocky **7** paunchy **8** roly-poly, thickset **9** corpulent, succulent **10** overweight, potbellied

Fletcher, Louise
born: 12 Birmingham AL
roles: 17 The Cheap Detective **25** One Flew Over the Cuckoo's Nest (Oscar)

Fletcher, Susannah Yolande
real name of: 12 Susannah York

flex 4 bend **5** curve

flexible 4 mild, soft **5** lithe **6** docile, genial, gentle, limber, pliant, supple **7** amiable, ductile, elastic, plastic, pliable, springy **8** bendable, yielding **9** adaptable, compliant, malleable, resilient, tractable **10** changeable, extensible, manageable, responsive, submissive **11** complaisant

Flibbertigibbet
character in: 10 Kenilworth
author: 5 Scott

flick 4 film **5** brush, graze, movie, sweep, whisk

flicker 4 flit, glow, sway **5** blaze, flame, flare, flash, gleam, glint, shake, spark, throb, trace, waver **6** quaver, quiver, waggle **7** flutter, glimmer, glisten, glitter, modicum, pulsate, shimmer, sparkle, tremble, vestige, vibrate, wriggle **8** undulate **9** coruscate, fluctuate, oscillate, scintilla, vacillate

Flickertail State
nickname of: 11 North Dakota

flicks 5 films **6** cinema, grazes, movies, sweeps, whisks **7** brushes

flier 4 bill **5** pilot **6** notice **7** aviator, leaflet, venture **8** brochure, bulletin, circular, handbill **10** experiment **12** announcement **13** advertisement

flight 4 rout, rush, wing **5** flock **6** escape, exodus, flying, hegira **7** fleeing, retreat, soaring, winging **8** squadron **10** withdrawal **11** aeronautics

flighty 5 dizzy, giddy **6** fickle **8** quixotic, reckless, unstable, volatile **9** frivolous, mercurial, whimsical **10** capricious, changeable, inconstant, indecisive, irresolute **11** harebrained, impractical, light-headed, thoughtless **13** irresponsible **14** scatterbrained

flimsy 4 poor, thin, weak **5** cheap, filmy, frail, gauzy, petty, sheer **6** feeble, shabby, shoddy, sleazy, slight, trashy **7** foolish, fragile, ill-made, shallow, trivial **8** cobwebby, delicate, gossamer, trifling **9** frivolous, worthless **10** diaphanous, inadequate, jerry-built, ramshackle **11** dilapidated, superficial **13** unsubstantial

flinch 3 fly, shy **4** jerk **5** cower, quail, quake, start, wince **6** blench, cringe, falter, quaver, quiver, recoil, shiver, shrink **7** contort, grimace, retreat, shudder

fling 2 go **3** try **4** ball, bash, cast, dash, emit, hurl, lark, toss **5** eject, expel, heave, pitch, sling, spree, trial **6** let fly, propel **7** attempt **8** bit of fun **11** precipitate

Flintstones, The
character: 7 Pebbles **8** Bamm Bamm **11** Betty Rubble **12** Barney Rubble **14** Fred Flintstone **15** Dino the Dinosaur, Wilma Flintstone
voice: 8 Alan Reed, Mel Blanc **10** Don Messick **12** Bea Benaderet, Gerry Johnson **13** Jean Vander Pyl
city: 7 Bedrock
creator: 12 Hanna-Barbera

Flintwinch
character in: 12 Little Dorrit
author: 7 Dickens

flinty 4 cold, hard **5** cruel, harsh, stern, stony **6** inured, steely **7** callous **8** hardened **10** unyielding **11** hardhearted, insensitive

flip 3 tap **4** bold, pert, spin, toss, turn **5** brash, flick, fresh, throw, thumb **6** cheeky, fillip **8** impudent, insolent, turn over **9** unabashed

flippant 4 glib, pert, rude **5** brash, lippy, saucy **6** cheeky, nimble **7** voluble **8** impudent, insolent, trifling **9** bumptious, frivolous, talkative **11** impertinent **12** presumptuous **13** disrespectful

Flipper
character: 8 Bud Ricks **10** Sandy Ricks **11** Porter Ricks
cast: 10 Brian Kelly, Luke Halpin **11** Tommy Norden
Flipper played by: 4 Suzy

flirt 3 toy **4** play, vamp **5** dally, tease **6** trifle **8** coquette **12** heartbreaker

flit 4 dart, scud, skim, wing **5** speed **6** hasten, scurry **7** flicker, flutter

Flitch of Bacon, The
author: 16 William Ainsworth

Flite, Miss
character in: 10 Bleak House
author: 7 Dickens

flivver 3 car **4** auto, heap **5** motor **6** jalopy, wheels **7** machine, vehicle **8** motorcar **9** tin lizzie **10** automobile

float 3 bob **4** waft **5** drift, hover, slide **6** bear up, buoy up, hold up, launch **8** levitate

floating 4 free **5** awash, loose **6** adrift, afloat, errant **7** buoyant, wafting **8** drifting **9** fluctuant, wandering **10** unattached

flock 2 go **3** mob, run **4** band, bevy, gang, herd, mass, pack, rush **5** bunch, crowd, crush, drove, group, surge, troop **6** clique, gather, huddle, muster, stream, throng **7** cluster, company, coterie **8** converge **9** gathering, multitude **10** assemblage, collection, congregate **11** aggregation **12** congregation
of fish: 6 school
of game birds: 5 covey
of geese: 6 gaggle
of insects: 5 swarm
of lions: 5 pride
of seals or whales: 3 pod
of young birds: 5 brood

flocks
god of: 3 Pan

flock together 6 gather, mingle **7** convene **8** assemble **9** associate **10** congregate

flog 4 beat, cane, club, cuff, drub, hide, lash, maul, whip **5** birch, flail, smite, strap **6** cudgel, paddle, strike, switch, thrash **7** scourge **8** lambaste **9** horsewhip **10** flagellate

flood 4 flow, glut, gush, tide **6** deluge, drench, shower, stream **7** cascade, current, torrent **8** downpour, flow over, inundate, overflow, saturate, submerge, wash over **9** overwhelm **10** cloudburst, inundation, outpouring, oversupply
period before: 12 antediluvian

Flood
author: 16 Robert Penn Warren

flooded 6 flowed, surged **7** deluged, glutted, overran, swamped **8** drenched, engulfed **9** inundated, outpoured, washed out **10** downpoured, overflowed

floor 4 base, deck, fell, tier **5** level, stage, story **6** bottom, ground **7** minimum, parquet **8** base rate, flooring, pavement **9** prostrate

flop 4 bomb, bust, drop, fail, fold, plop **5** close **6** fiasco, fizzle, topple, tumble, turkey **7** failure, go under, shutter, washout **8** disaster, lay an egg **14** disappointment

Flora
origin: 5 Roman
goddess of: 7 flowers

floral 6 bloomy **7** verdant **8** blossomy **9** botanical **10** herbaceous

Floralia
origin: 5 Roman
form: 8 festival

Florence ***see box***

florescence 5 bloom **9** flowerage **10** blossoming

Florence
artist: 6 Giotto **7** Cimabue **8** Ghiberti **9** Donatello **10** Michelozzi **11** della Robbia **12** Brunelleschi, Michelangelo
capital of: 7 Tuscany **15** Firenze province
cathedral/church: 10 San Lorenzo, San Miniato, Santa Croce **18** Santa Maria del Fiore
Italian: 7 Firenze
landmark: 5 Pieta **6** Uffizi **8** Bargello **11** Pitti Palace **12** Ponte Vecchio **13** Boboli Gardens **14** Loggia dei Lanzi, Palazzo Vecchio **19** Piazza della Signoria **22** Baptistry of San Giovanni, Ospedale degli Innocenti
mountain: 9 Apennines
religious reformer: 10 Savonarola
river: 4 Arno
ruler: 5 Goths **6** Medici, Romans **8** Lombards **9** Etruscans **15** Byzantine Empire
tomb of: 7 Galileo, Rossini **11** Machiavelli **12** Michelangelo **15** Lorenzo de Medici

florid 4 rosy **5** gaudy, ruddy, showy **6** blowsy, hectic, ornate, rococo **7** baroque, flowery, flushed, reddish **8** inflamed, red-faced, rubicund, sanguine **9** elaborate **10** flamboyant, ornamented **12** ostentatious **13** grandiloquent

Florida ***see box***

florilegium 7 garland **8** chapbook, treasury **9** anthology

Florizel
character in: 14 The Winter's Tale
author: 11 Shakespeare

floruit 12 he flourished **13** she flourished

flotilla 5 fleet **6** armada

Flotow, Friedrich von
born: 7 Germany **11** Mecklenburg
composer of: 6 Martha **11** Die Matrosen **19** Alessandro Stradella

flotsam 4 junk **6** debris, refuse **7** garbage **8** castoffs

flounce 3 hem **4** edge, leap, skip, trim, trip **5** bound, caper, frill, stamp, stomp, storm, strut **6** bounce, edging, fringe, gambol, prance, ruffle, sashay, spring **7** valance **8** furbelow, ornament, skirting, trimming

flounder 4 fish, flop, halt, limp **5** lurch, waver **6** falter, hobble, muddle, totter, tumble, wallow, welter **7** blunder,

Florida
abbreviation: 2 FL **3** Fla
nickname: 6 Flower **8** Sunshine **10** Peninsular
capital: 11 Tallahassee
largest city: 12 Jacksonville
others: 4 Tice **5** Cocoa, Miami, Ocala, Tampa **7** Hialeah, Orlando, Palatka, Sebring **8** Sarasota **9** Bradenton, Palm Beach, Pensacola **10** Clearwater **11** Brooksville, Coral Gables, Gainesville, St Augustine **12** Daytona Beach, Ft Lauderdale, St Petersburg
college: 4 Nova **5** Barry, Miami, Tampa **6** Eckerd **7** Rollins, Stetson
explorer: 11 Ponce de Leon
feature:
amusement park: **5** Epcot **10** Marineland **11** Disney World
canal: **5** Miami **7** Tamiami
museum: **8** Ringling
national park: **10** Everglades
tribe: 3 Ais **5** Ocale, Utina **6** Calusa, Chatot, Potano **7** Timucua **8** Seminole
people: 5 conch **7** cracker, Osceola
island: 7 Bahamas, Sanibel **8** Biscayne
key: **4** Long, Vaca, West **5** Largo **7** Big Pine **8** Biscayne **9** Sugarloaf
lake: 4 Dora **6** Apopka, Harney, Jessup, Newnan **7** Ledwith **8** Arbuckle **9** Kissimmee **10** Okeechobee
land rank: 12 twenty-second
physical feature:
bay: **8** Biscayne **9** Apalachee **10** Waccasassa
cape: **5** Sable **7** Kennedy **9** Canaveral
gulf: **6** Mexico
sea: **8** Atlantic
springs: **6** Silver **7** Rainbow
swamp: **10** Everglades, Okefenokee
river: 6 Banana, Indian **7** Aucilla, Manatee, Scambia, St Johns, Suwanee **9** Ochlawaha **12** Apalachicola
state admission: 13 twenty-seventh
state bird: 11 mockingbird
state fish: 16 Atlantic sailfish
state mammal: 7 dolphin
state flower: 13 orange blossom
state motto: 12 In God We Trust
state song: 11 Swanee River **14** Old Folks at Home
state tree: 13 sabal palmetto **15** cabbage palmetto

shamble, stagger, stumble **8** flatfish, hesitate, struggle

Flounder, The
author: 11 Gunter Grass

flourish 4 curl, dash, grow, pomp, rant, show, turn **5** bloom, bluff, get on, shake, strut, sweep, swing, swish, twirl, twist, wield **6** flaunt, flower, hot air, parade, splash, thrive, waving **7** blossom, bravado, burgeon, cadenza, fanfare, fustian, glitter, prosper, shaking, succeed, swagger **8** boasting, brandish, curlicue, fare well, get ahead, swinging, vaunting, wielding **9** agitation, grace note, thrashing **10** decoration **11** braggadocio, brandishing, fanfaronade, ostentation **12** appoggiatura **13** embellishment, magniloquence, swashbuckling **14** grandiloquence

flourishing 8 swinging, swishing, thriving, wielding **9** flaunting **10** prospering, successful **11** brandishing

flout 3 rag **4** defy, mock, twit **5** chaff, scorn, spurn, taunt **6** gibe at, insult

flow 3 jet, run **4** flux, gush, pass, pour, rush, seep, tide **5** drain, drift, float, flood, glide, issue, spout, spurt, surge, sweep, swirl, train **6** abound, course, deluge, efflux, effuse, filter, plenty, rapids, stream **7** cascade, current, debouch, torrent, well out **8** effusion, millrace, plethora, sequence **9** abundance, discharge, effluence, emanation **10** outpouring, succession **11** debouchment, progression

flower 3 bud **4** best, blow, open, pick, posy **5** bloom, cream, elite, ripen **6** mature **7** blossom, bouquet, burgeon, develop, nosegay, prosper **8** flourish **11** aristocracy

flower arranging, art of
Japanese: 7 ikebana

Flower Fables
author: 15 Louisa May Alcott

flowering 4 peak **5** bloom **6** height, heyday **8** blooming, maturing **10** blossoming, developing, prospering **11** flourishing

Flowering Judas
author: 19 Katherine Anne Porter

flowers
goddess of: 5 Flora

Flowers of Evil
author: 17 Charles Baudelaire

Flower State
nickname of: 7 Florida

flowery 5 fancy **6** floral, florid, ornate **8** blooming **10** blossoming, burgeoning, euphuistic, figurative, florescent, ornamental, rhetorical **11** embellished **12** efflorescent, magniloquent **13** grandiloquent

Flowery Kingdom *see* **5** China

flowing 4 flux **5** fluid **6** ebbing, fluent, smooth **7** current, copious, gliding, running **8** abundant **9** liquefied, plentiful **10** continuity, pouring out, proceeding

fluctuate 4 sway, vary, veer **5** shift, swing, waver **6** dawdle, falter, wobble **8** hesitate, undulate **9** alternate, oscillate, vacillate **10** dillydally

fluctuation 5 shift **6** change **7** veering **8** shifting, swinging **9** deviation, variation **11** alternation, oscillation, vacillation

flue 3 net **4** barb, down, pipe, tube, vent **5** fluff, fluke, shaft **6** funnel **7** channel, chimney, passage **9** smokejack

fluent 4 glib **5** vocal **6** facile **7** voluble **8** effusive, eloquent **9** garrulous, talkative **10** articulate, effortless

fluff 3 err, nap **4** down, flub, fuzz, lint, miss, puff, slip, soft **5** botch, floss, froth, primp **6** forget **7** blunder **8** feathers

fluffy 5 downy, fuzzy, nappy, wooly **6** fleecy, woolly **8** feathery

fluid 6 liquid, watery **7** unfixed **8** flexible, floating, shifting, solution, unstable **9** adaptable, liquefied, unsettled **10** adjustable, changeable, indefinite

fluid ounce
abbreviation: 4 fl oz

fluke 3 hap **5** freak **6** chance **7** miracle **8** accident, windfall **9** mischance **11** vicissitude **12** stroke of luck

flummery 7 dessert, pudding **9** gibberish **10** doubletalk, mumbo jumbo **11** obfuscation

flunky 6 lackey, menial, minion **7** servant **9** attendant, underling

fluorine
chemical symbol: 1 F

flurry 3 ado **4** fuss, gust, heat, puff, stir **5** alarm, fever, flush, haste, panic **6** breeze, bustle, pother, rattle, shower, squall, tumult **7** agitate, confuse, disturb, fidgets, fluster, flutter, perturb **8** confound, disquiet **9** agitation, commotion, confusion **10** discompose, disconcert, turbulence **11** disturbance, hurry-scurry, trepidation **12** discomposure, perturbation, restlessness

flush 4 even, glow, swab, tint, wash **5** bloom, blush, color, elate, flood, level, rinse, scour, scrub, shock, spray **6** access, dampen, deluge, douche, drench, excite, puff up, quiver, redden, sponge, thrill, tremor **7** animate, flutter, glowing, impulse, moisten, redness, wash out **8** rosiness, rosy glow, squarely, strength **9** freshness, make proud, ruddiness **10** exultation, jubilation

flushed 3 hot, red **4** rosy, ruby **5** aglow, **6** florid, torrid **7** crimson, excited, scarlet **8** blushing, feverish **10** prosperous

flushed with success
5 proud **6** elated

fluster 4 daze **5** shake, upset **6** dither, flurry, hubbub, muddle, ruffle **7** agitate, confuse, disturb, flutter, perplex, perturb, startle, turmoil **8** befuddle, bewilder **9** agitation, commotion, confusion, discomfit **10** discompose, disconcert **12** bewilderment, discomfiture, discomposure **14** discombobulate

flute 4 fife, fold, pipe, roll, tube, wind **5** crimp **6** furrow, groove **7** piccolo, whistle **8** recorder **9** wine glass **14** champagne glass

flutter 3 bob **4** flap, flit, soar, stir, wave, wing **5** hurry, shake, throb **6** flurry, quiver, ripple, thrill, tremor, wobble **7** beating, flitter, fluster, pulsate, tremble, twitter **8** flapping, tingling **9** agitation, commotion, confusion, palpitate, sensation, vibration **12** perturbation

fluvial 7 aquatic

fluviatile 7 aquatic

flux 4 flow, tide **5** flood **6** course, motion, stream, unrest **7** current **8** mutation, shifting **10** alteration, transition **11** fluctuation **12** modification **14** transformation

fly 4 flap, flee, sail, skip, soar, wave, wing **5** coast, float, glide, hover, hurry, split, swoop **6** hasten, hustle **7** flutter, run away, take off, vibrate **8** take wing, undulate

fly
varieties: **3** bat, bot **4** blow, deer, dung, gnat, horn, moth, rust, sand **5** beach, black, crane, dance, drone, flesh, fruit, horse, house, march, marsh, midge, mydas, punky **6** bee fly, cactus, maggot, pomace, robber, stable, tsetse, warble, window **7** chalcid, seaweed, skipper, soldier, tachima **8** lousefly, mosquito, stiletto **9** leaf miner **10** flat-footed, fungus gnat, hump-backed **11** thickheaded **14** black scavenger

fly apart **5** burst **6** blow up **7** explode, shatter **8** detonate, fragment

fly at **6** assail, attack

fly-by-night **5** shady **6** shifty **7** crooked **8** unstable, untrusty **9** dishonest **10** unreliable **12** disreputable, undependable **13** irresponsible, untrustworthy

Flying Dutchman, The
opera by: **6** Wagner
character: **4** Erik **5** Senta **6** Daland **11** The Dutchman

Flying Fish
constellation of: **6** Volans

Flying Nun, The
character: **9** Sister Ana **11** Sister Sixto **13** Carlos Ramirez **14** Mother Superior **15** Sister Bertrille **16** Sister Jacqueline
cast: **10** Sally Field **12** Alejandro Rey, Linda Dangcil, Marge Redmond **14** Shelly Morrison **17** Madeleine Sherwood

fly in the ointment **5** hitch **7** problem, trouble **8** drawback, nuisance **9** hindrance **10** impediment **12** disadvantage

Flynn, Errol
real name: **17** Leslie Thomas Flynn
born: **6** Hobart **8** Tasmania
roles: **10** The Sea Hawk **12** Captain Blood **14** Too Much Too Soon **15** The Sun Also Rises **24** The Adventures of Robin Hood **26** The Charge of the Light Brigade

fly off the handle **6** see red

fly the coop **4** bolt, flee **6** escape, run off **7** abscond, get away, make off, run away, skip out, take off

foal **4** cade, colt **5** filly, young **9** fledgling

foam **4** fizz, head, scum, suds **5** froth, spume **6** lather **7** sparkle **8** bubbling **13** effervescence

foaming **5** sudsy **6** bubbly, frothy **7** lathery **8** bubbling, frothing

foamy **5** fizzy **6** frothy **7** lathery **8** bubbling **9** sparkling **12** effervescent

fob **5** chain, medal, strap **6** ribbon **8** ornament **9** medallion

focal **3** key **4** main **5** chief **7** central, pivotal **8** foremost **9** principal

Foch, Ferdinand
served in: **3** WWI
nationality: **6** French
rank: **7** marshal **16** commander-in-chief
battle: **5** Marne, Somme

Foch, Nina
real name: **20** Nina Consuelo Maud Fock
born: **6** Leyden **11** Netherlands
roles: **9** Spartacus **14** Executive Suite, Song to Remember **17** An American in Paris, My Name Is Julia Ross **18** The Ten Commandments

Fock, Nina Consuelo Maud
real name of: **8** Nina Foch

focus **3** aim, fix, hub **4** core **5** haunt, heart **6** adjust, center, direct, middle, resort **7** nucleus, retreat **8** converge **9** limelight, spotlight **10** rendezvous **11** concentrate **12** headquarters

focusing **6** aiming **9** adjusting, centering, directing **10** adjustment, converging **11** pinpointing **13** concentrating

fodder **4** feed, food **6** forage, silage **7** rations **9** provender

foe **5** enemy, rival **8** attacker, opponent **9** adversary, assailant, combatant, contender, disputant **10** antagonist, competitor

fog **3** dim **4** daze, haze, smog, soup **5** brume, cloud **6** darken, muddle, stupor, trance **7** confuse, obscure, pea soup, perplex **8** bewilder **9** murkiness **10** cloudiness **12** bewilderment

Fogg, Phileas
character in: **26** Around the World in Eighty Days
author: **10** Jules Verne

foggy **3** dim **4** dark, hazy **5** dusky, filmy, fuzzy, misty, murky, musty, soupy, vague **6** cloudy, smoggy, spacey **7** brumous, clouded, obscure, shadowy, unclear **8** confused, nebulous, overcast, vaporous **9** beclouded **10** indistinct

foible **4** kink **5** quirk **6** defect, whimsy **7** failing, frailty **8** crotchet, weak side, weakness **9** infirmity **10** deficiency **11** shortcoming **12** imperfection

Foible
character in: **16** The Way of the World
author: **8** Congreve

foil **3** nip **4** balk, film, leaf **5** check, flake, match, sheet, wafer **6** hinder, lamina, set off, thwart **7** enhance, prevent **8** backdrop, contrast **9** frustrate **10** antithesis, complement, supplement **11** correlative, counterpart

foist **6** impose, unload **7** palm off, pass off

fold **3** hug, lap, pen, sty **4** bend, curl, sect, tuck, wrap, yard **5** clasp, close, crimp, flock, group, layer, pleat **6** corral, crease, dog-ear, double, encase, enfold, furrow, gather, parish, pucker, ruffle, rumple, wrap up **7** crinkle, crumple, embosom, embrace, entwine, envelop, flounce, overlap, wrinkle **8** barnyard, compound, doubling, stockade **9** community, corrugate, enclosure **12** congregation

folder **7** booklet, leaflet **8** brochure, circular, pamphlet **9** portfolio

foliage **6** leaves **7** leafage, verdure

folklore **5** myths **6** fables **7** legends **10** traditions

folks **3** kin **6** family, people **7** kinsmen, parents **8** everyone **9** relatives **10** kith and kin

folksy **6** casual, chatty **8** familiar, friendly, homespun, informal, sociable **10** neighborly **14** conversational **15** unsophisticated

folk tale
German: **7** Marchen

Follett, Ken
author of: **14** Eye of the Needle **15** On Wings of Eagles, The Key to Rebecca **22** The Man from St Petersburg

follow **3** dog **4** copy, heed, hunt, mind, note, obey, tail **5** aim at, chase, grasp, hound, stalk, trace, track, trail, watch **6** attend, notice, pursue, regard, shadow, take up **7** cherish, emulate, imitate, observe, replace, succeed **8** practice, supplant **9** accompany, cultivate, prosecute **10** comprehend, understand

follower **3** fan **4** tail **5** pupil, toady **6** chaser, hunter, shadow, stooge **7** admirer, apostle, convert, devotee, protege, pursuer, servant, stalker **8** adherent, advocate, disciple, hanger-on, henchman, parasite, partisan, retainer, servitor **9** accessory, attendant, dependent, proselyte, satellite, supporter, sycophant

following **4** next **5** below, suite, train **6** public **7** ensuing, retinue **8** audience **9** adherents, clientele, entourage, partisans, patronage **10** attendance, consequent, sequential, subsequent, succeeding, successive **11** consecutive

Follow the Fleet
director: **12** Mark Sandrich
cast: **11** Fred Astaire **12** Ginger Rogers **13** Randolph Scott **21** Harriet Hilliard Nelson
song: **11** We Saw the Sea **13** Let Yourself Go **24** Let's Face the Music and Dance

follow-up **7** ensuing **8** sequence **9** aftermath **10** subsequent

folly **6** idiocy, levity **7** inanity, mistake **8** nonsense, trifling **9** absurdity, asininity, frivolity, giddiness, silliness **10** imbecility, imprudence, tomfoolery **11** doltishness, fatuousness, foolishness **12** indiscretion **13** brainlessness, irrationality, senselessness

foment **4** goad, spur, urge **5** rouse **6** arouse, excite, foster, incite, kindle, stir up **7** agitate, inflame, promote, provoke, quicken **8** irritate **9** aggravate, galvanize, instigate, stimulate **10** exacerbate

Fomorian
origin: **5** Irish
form: **5** demon **6** pirate
habitat: **3** sea
raided: **7** Ireland
personifies: **13** hostile nature

fond **5** naive **6** ardent, doting, loving, tender **7** amorous, devoted **8** desirous, enamored, harbored, held dear **9** cherished, indulgent, preserved, sustained **10** infatuated, passionate **11** impassioned, sentimental **12** affectionate **16** overaffectionate

Fonda, Henry
wife: **16** Margaret Sullavan
son: **5** Peter
daughter: **4** Jane
born: **13** Grand Island NE
roles: **7** Jezebel, Warlock **8** Fail Safe **10** Fort Apache, In Harm's Way, The Best Man, The Lady Eve **12** On Golden Pond (Oscar) **13** Mister Roberts, Ox-Bow Incident, The Longest Day **14** Twelve Angry Men, Young Mr Lincoln **16** Advise and Consent, Battle of the Bulge, How the West Was Won, The Grapes of Wrath **18** The Boston Strangler **19** My Darling Clementine, The Immortal Sergeant **21** Sometimes a Great Notion

Fonda, Jane
father: **5** Henry
brother: **5** Peter
husband: **9** Tom Hayden **10** Roger Vadim
born: **9** New York NY
roles: **5** Julia, Klute (Oscar) **10** Barbarella, Coming Home (Oscar) **11** A Doll's House **12** Any Wednesday, On Golden Pond **13** China Syndrome **17** Barefoot in the Park **23** They Shoot Horses Don't They?

Fonda, Peter
father: **5** Henry
sister: **4** Jane
born: **9** New York NY
roles: **7** The Trip **9** Easy Rider **13** The Wild Angels

fondle **3** hug, pet **5** spoon **6** caress, cuddle, nestle, nuzzle, smooch, stroke **7** embrace, make out **10** bill and coo

fondness **4** bent, care, love **5** ardor, fancy **6** desire, liking **7** passion **8** devotion, penchant, weakness **9** affection **10** attachment, partiality, preference, propensity, tenderness **11** amorousness, inclination **12** predilection **14** susceptibility

fond utterance **9** sweet talk **10** endearment **12** sweet nothing

Fons
origin: **5** Roman
god of: **7** springs

fons et origo **15** source and origin

Fontaine, Joan
real name: **25** Joan de Beauvoir de Havilland
sister: **17** Olivia de Havilland
husband: **11** Brian Aherne
born: **5** Japan, Tokyo
roles: **3** Ivy **7** Ivanhoe, Rebecca **8** Casanova, Gunga Din, Jane Eyre, The Women **9** Suspicion (Oscar) **12** The Devil's Own **15** Frenchman's Creek, September Affair **16** Tender Is the Night, The Constant Nymph

Fontanne, Lynn
husband: **10** Alfred Lunt
born: **6** London **7** England
roles: **8** The Visit **9** Quadrille, The Pirate **10** The Sea Gull **13** O Mistress Mine **15** Design for Living **18** The Great Sebastians **19** The Taming of the Shrew

food **4** chow, feed, grub **5** board **6** fodder, forage, silage, viands **7** edibles, nurture, pasture, rations **8** eatables, victuals **9** nutrition, pasturage, provender **10** provisions, sustenance **11** comestibles, nourishment, subsistence

food, miraculous **5** manna

fool **3** ass, con, oaf **4** bilk, clod, dolt, dupe, gull, hoax, jest, joke **5** cheat, chump, clown, cozen, cut up, dummy, dunce, feign, goose, idiot, klutz, moron, ninny, tease, trick **6** diddle, fleece, frolic, humbug, jester, nitwit, rip off, stooge **7** beguile, buffoon, deceive, defraud, half-wit, Pierrot, pretend **8** bonehead, dummkopf, flimflam, hoodwink, imbecile, lunkhead, meathead, numskull **9** bamboozle, blockhead, harlequin, ignoramus, numbskull, simpleton **10** dunderhead, nincompoop, scaramouch **11** Punchinello

fool around **3** toy **4** idle **5** clown, dally **6** dawdle, loiter, trifle

foolhardy **4** rash **5** brash, hasty **6** madcap **8** careless, heedless, reckless **9** daredevil, hotheaded, impetuous, imprudent, impulsive **10** headstrong, incautious **11** harebrained, thoughtless

foolish **5** inane, silly **6** absurd, stupid, unwise **7** asinine, fatuous, idiotic, moronic, witless **9** brainless, imbecilic, imprudent, ludicrous, senseless **10** boneheaded, incautious, indiscreet, ridiculous **12** preposterous **13** irresponsible, unintelligent

foolishness **5** folly **6** idiocy, lunacy **8** unwisdom **9** absurdity, asininity, puerility, silliness, stupidity **10** imbecility, imprudence **11** fatuousness, witlessness **12** childishness, extravagance, indiscretion

13 brainlessness, senselessness **14** ridiculousness **15** injudiciousness **16** irresponsibility, preposterousness

Fool of Quality, The
author: **11** Henry Brooke

foot **3** dog, pad, paw **4** base, hoof **6** bottom, tootsy **7** trotter **8** infantry **10** foundation
abbreviation: **2** ft

football
athlete/coach: **8** Don Shula, Jim Brown, Kyle Rote, Lou Groza, Y A Tittle **9** Amos Stagg, Bart Starr, Bob Griese, Chuck Noll, Dan Marino, Don Hutson, Earl Blaik, Joe Greene, Joe Namath, Len Dawson, Lou Little, O J Simpson, Red Grange, Tom Landry **10** Bear Bryant, Bubba Smith, Dick Butkus, Joe Montana, Joe Paterno, Ken Stabler, Larry Brown, Otto Graham, Sammy Baugh, Walter Camp, Weeb Ewbank **11** Ahmad Rashad, Craig Morton, Deacon Jones, Earl Morrall, Ernie Nevers, Floyd Little, Gayle Sayers, George Halas, Jan Stenerud, Jim Plunkett, John Riggins, Knute Rockne, Larry Csonka, Merlin Olsen, Paul Hornung, Pete Rozelle, Richard Todd, Tony Dorsett **12** Bud Wilkinson, Earl Campbell, Franco Harris, Frank Gifford, George Blanda, Joe Thiesmann, Johnny Unitas, Lance Alworth, Ozzie Newsome, Raymond Berry, Roman Gabriel, Walter Payton, William Perry **13** Ara Parseghian, Eric Dickerson, Fran Tarkenton, Roger Staubach, Terry Bradshaw, Vince Lombardi **14** Bronco Nagurski, Lydell Mitchell, Sonny Jurgensen **15** Norm Van Brocklin

football bowl games **3** Sun (El Paso) **4** Rose (Pasadena) **5** Aloha (Honolulu), Gator (Jacksonville), Peach (Atlanta), Sugar (New Orleans), Super **6** Cotton (Dallas), Fiesta (Tempe), Orange (Miami) **7** Holiday (San Diego), Liberty (Memphis) **10** Bluebonnet (Houston), California (Fresno) **12** Independence (Shreveport) **13** Florida Citrus (Orlando)

football leagues
National Football League (NFL): **11** New York Jets **12** Buffalo Bills, Chicago Bears, Detroit Lions **13** Dallas Cowboys, Denver Broncos, Houston Oilers, Miami Dolphins, New York Giants **14** Atlanta Falcons, Los Angeles Rams **15** Cleveland Browns, Green Bay Packers, Seattle Seahawks **16** Kansas City Chiefs, Minnesota Vikings, New Orleans Saints, Phoenix Cardinals (formerly St Louis), San Diego Chargers **17** Cincinnati Bengals, Indianapolis Colts (formerly Baltimore), Los Angeles Raiders (formerly Oakland) **18** New England Patriots, Philadelphia Eagles, Pittsburgh Steelers, Tampa Bay Buccaneers, Washington Redskins
United States Football League (USFL): **10** Denver Gold **12** Chicago Blitz **14** Baltimore Stars, Boston Breakers **15** Houston Gamblers, Oakland Invaders, Oklahoma Outlaws, Tampa Bay Bandits **16** Arizona Wranglers, Memphis Showboats, Michigan Panthers, Orlando Renegades, Portland Breakers **17** Jacksonville Bulls, Los Angeles Express, New Jersey Generals, Philadelphia Stars **18** Washington Federals **19** Birmingham Stallions **21** San Antonio Gunslingers **23** San Francisco Forty-niners

football team ***see box***

footfall **3** pad **4** pace, step **5** tread **8** footstep

foothold **4** grip, hold **7** support **8** purchase

footloose **4** free **8** carefree **9** fancy-free **10** unattached **11** uncommitted **12** unencumbered

footnote **5** gloss **9** reference **10** annotation **11** explanation **12** afterthought

footpad **5** thief **6** bandit, mugger, outlaw, robber **10** highwayman

football team
Buffalo: **5** Bills
stadium: **4** Rich
Cincinnati: **7** Bengals
stadium: **10** Riverfront
Cleveland: **6** Browns
stadium: **9** Cleveland
Dallas: **7** Cowboys
stadium: **5** Texas
Denver: **7** Broncos
stadium: **8** Mile High
Houston: **6** Oilers
stadium: **9** Astrodome
Indianapolis: **5** Colts
stadium: **11** Hoosier Dome
formerly in: **9** Baltimore
Kansas City: **6** Chiefs
stadium: **9** Arrowhead
Los Angeles: **7** Raiders
stadium: **16** Memorial Coliseum
formerly in: **7** Oakland
Miami: **8** Dolphins
stadium: **10** Orange Bowl
New England: **8** Patriots
stadium: **8** Schaefer
New York: **4** Jets
stadium: **4** Shea
6 Giants
Pittsburgh: **8** Steelers
stadium: **11** Three Rivers
San Diego: **8** Chargers
stadium: **8** San Diego
Seattle: **8** Seahawks
stadium: **8** Kingdome
Atlanta: **7** Falcons
stadium: **13** Atlanta-Fulton
Chicago: **5** Bears
stadium: **12** Soldier Field
Detroit: **5** Lions
stadium: **12** Lambeau Field **17** Pontiac Silverdome
Green Bay: **7** Packers
stadium: **9** Milwaukee
Los Angeles: **4** Rams
stadium: **7** Anaheim
Minnesota: **7** Vikings
stadium: **12** Metropolitan
New Orleans: **6** Saints
stadium: **18** Louisiana Superdome
New York: **6** Giants
stadium: **6** Giants
Philadelphia: **6** Eagles
stadium: **8** Veterans
Phoenix: **9** Cardinals
stadium: **8** Sun Devil
formerly in: **7** St Louis
San Francisco: **11** Forty-Niners
stadium: **15** Candlestick Park
Tampa Bay: **10** Buccaneers
stadium: **5** Tampa
Washington: **8** Redskins
stadium: **14** Robert F Kennedy

footpath **4** lane, ramp **5** jetty, trail **8** sidewalk

foot soldiers **8** infantry **10** fusilliers, musketeers

footstool **6** buffet **7** hassock, ottoman **8** footrest

footwear
French: **9** chaussure

fop **4** beau, dude **5** dandy, swell **7** coxcomb **8** popinjay **9** prettyboy **11** Beau Brummel

foppish **4** vain **5** gaudy, showy **6** ornate **7** finical **8** affected, dandyish **9** dandified **12** ostentatious **13** overelaborate

forage **4** feed, food, hunt, raid, seek **6** fodder, ravage, search, silage **7** despoil, explore, pasture, plunder, rummage **8** scavenge, scrounge **9** pasturage, provender **10** provisions

foray **4** raid **5** sally **6** attack, inroad, invade, ravage, thrust **7** pillage, plunder, venture **8** invasion **9** incursion **10** expedition **11** depredation

forbear **4** quit, stop **5** cease, forgo **6** desist, endure, eschew, forego, give up, suffer **7** abstain, refrain **8** abnegate, renounce, tolerate

forbearance **4** pity **5** mercy **6** pardon **8** clemency, eschewal, leniency, meekness, mildness, patience **9** endurance, tolerance **10** abstention, abstinence, continence, indulgence, moderation, submission, temperance **11** longanimity, resignation **12** mercifulness

forbearing **6** denial **7** lenient, refusal **8** eschewal, tolerant **9** indulgent **10** abnegation, abstention, abstinence, permissive, refraining **13** nonindulgence **16** nonparticipation

forbid **3** ban, bar **4** veto **5** taboo **6** enjoin, hinder, impede, oppose, refuse, reject **7** exclude, gainsay, inhibit, obviate, prevent **8** disallow, obstruct, preclude, prohibit, restrain **9** interdict, proscribe

forbiddance **3** ban **5** taboo **7** barring, embargo **9** exclusion, interdict **11** prohibition **12** interdiction, proscription

forbidden **5** taboo **6** banned **8** debarred **10** prohibited, proscribed
German: **8** verboten

forbidden fruit
type: **6** brandy **7** liqueur
origin: **7** America
flavor: **5** honey **6** orange **10** grapefruit

forbidden marriage
goddess of: **4** Lofn

forbidding **4** dour, grim, ugly **6** odious **7** hideous, ominous **8** horrible, sinister **9** abhorrent, offensive, repellent, repulsive **10** unfriendly, unpleasant **11** prohibitive, prohibitory, threatening **12** disagreeable, inhospitable **14** unapproachable

force **3** pry, vim **4** army, body, coax, crew, drag, gang, make, pull, push, team, unit, urge **5** break, clout, corps, drive, group, impel, might, power, press, squad, value, vigor, wrest **6** coerce, compel, duress, effect, elicit, energy, enjoin, extort, impact, import, impose, induce, oblige, propel, stress, thrust, weight, wrench **7** cogency, intrude, meaning, obtrude, potency, require, squeeze, stamina **8** charisma, coercion, division, efficacy, emphasis, momentum, persuade, pressure, squadron, strength, validity, violence, vitality **9** animation, battalion, constrain, magnetism, overpower, puissance **10** attraction, compulsion, constraint, detachment **11** necessitate, weightiness **12** significance **13** effectiveness
Latin: **3** vis

forced **5** slave **7** binding, coerced, labored, obliged **8** affected, enslaved, grudging, mannered, required, strained **9** compelled, impressed, insincere, mandatory, unwilling **10** artificial, compulsory, obligatory **11** constrained, involuntary

forceful **5** pithy, valid, vivid **6** cogent, potent, robust, strong, virile **7** dynamic, intense **8** emphatic, powerful, puissant, vigorous **9** effective, energetic **10** impressive

forceless **4** weak **8** impotent

force measurement **4** dyne **6** newton **7** poundal

Force of Circumstance
author: **16** Simone de Beauvoir

Force of Destiny, The
also: **17** La Forza del Destino
opera by: **5** Verdi
character: **7** Leonora **8** Don Carlo **9** Don Alvaro

forcible **8** coercive **10** compulsory

ford **3** car **4** span, wade **5** cross, edsel, shoal **6** bridge, model T, stream **7** passage **8** crossing, tin lizzy

Ford, Gerald Rudolph ***see box***

Ford, Glenn
real name: **11** Gwyllyn Ford
wife: **13** Eleanor Powell
born: **6** Canada, Quebec
roles: **4** Rage **5** Gilda, Jubal **6** Santee **8** Cimarron **11** The Rounders **14** Is Paris Burning? **17** Interrupted Melody **18** Don't Go Near the Water **19** The Blackboard Jungle **23** Teahouse of the August Moon

Ford, Harrison
born: **9** Chicago IL
roles: **7** Frantic, Witness **8** Star Wars **11** Blade Runner **15** Return of the Jedi **16** American Graffiti **19** Raiders of the Lost Ark **20** The Empire Strikes Back **30** Indiana Jones and the Temple of Doom

Ford, John
author of: **13** Perkin Warbeck **17** 'Tis Pity She's a Whore **19** The Lover's Melancholy

Ford, John
director of: **10** Stagecoach **11** The Informer (Oscar), The Quiet Man (Oscar) **12** The Hurricane, The Searchers **13** Grapes of Wrath (Oscar), Mister Roberts (with Mervyn LeRoy), The Lost Patrol **17** The Long Voyage Home **19** How Green Was My Valley (Oscar), My Darling Clementine **27** The Man Who Shot Liberty Valence

Ford, Thelma Booth
real name of: **12** Shirley Booth

Ford and Mistress Ford
characters in: **22** The Merry Wives of Windsor
author: **11** Shakespeare

fore **5** front **7** frontal **8** anterior, headmost

forearm **4** ulna **5** prime, ready **7** prepare

forebear **8** ancestor, begetter **10** antecedent, procreator, progenitor

foreboding **4** omen **5** dread **6** augury, boding **7** portent **9** intuition, misgiving **10** prescience, prognostic **11** premonition **12** apprehension, presentiment

Ford, Gerald Rudolph
born: **17** Leslie Lynch King Jr
adopted by/named after: **10** stepfather
nickname: **5** Jerry **7** Mr Clean
presidential rank: **12** thirty-eighth
party: **10** Republican
state represented: **2** MI
defeated: **5** no one
elected to neither: **10** presidency **14** vice presidency
vice president: **11** (Nelson A) Rockefeller
cabinet:
state: **9** (Henry A) Kissinger
treasury: **5** (William E) Simon
defense: **8** (Donald H) Rumsfeld **11** (James) Schlesinger
attorney general: **4** (Edward H) Levi **5** (William B) Saxbe
interior: **6** (Rogers Clark Ballard) Morton, (Thomas S) Kleppe **8** (Stanley K) Hathaway
agriculture: **4** (Earl Lauer) Butz **6** (John A) Knebel
commerce: **4** (Frederick B) Dent **6** (Rogers Clark Ballard) Morton **10** (Elliot L) Richardson
labor: **5** (W J) Usery (Jr) **6** (John T) Dunlop **7** (Peter J) Brennan
HEW: **7** (F David) Mathews **10** (Caspar W) Weinberger
HUD: **4** (James T) Lynn **5** (Carla Anderson) Hills
transportation: **7** (William T) Coleman (Jr) **8** (Claude S) Brinegar
born: **7** Omaha NE
education:
University: **8** Michigan
Law School: **4** Yale
religion: **12** Episcopalian
interests: **4** golf **6** boxing, skiing **8** football, swimming
vacation spot: **2** CO **4** Vail
author: **21** Portrait of the Assassin (with John R Stiles) **27** A Time To Heal: An Autobiography
political career: **13** vice president **19** House minority leader **24** US House of Representatives
civilian career: **6** lawyer
assistant football coach at: **4** Yale
military service: **6** US Navy **10** lieutenant, World War II
notable events of lifetime/term: **9** recession **12** Bicentennial
assassination attempts on: **4** Ford
clemency for: **12** draft dodgers, draft evaders
kidnapping/trial/conviction of: **11** Patty Hearst
scandal: **8** Lockheed **10** Hays Affair
talks: **4** SALT
quotes: **19** I am a Ford not a Lincoln **41** Indebted to no man—the president of all the people **50** Our long national nightmare is over Our constitution works
father:
natural: **15** Leslie Lynch King
adoptive: **17** Gerald Rudolph Ford
mother: **7** Dorothy (Gardner King Ford)
siblings:
half-brothers: **12** James Francis **13** Thomas Gardner **14** Richard Addison
wife: **9** Elizabeth (Bloomer Warren)
nickname: **5** Betty
children: **4** John **5** Susan **6** Steven **7** Michael

forecast **5** augur **6** augury, divine, expect **7** outlook, portend, predict, presage, project **8** envisage, envision, prophesy **9** calculate, prevision, prognosis **10** anticipate, conjecture, prediction, prescience, projection **11** extrapolate **12** anticipation, precognition, presentiment **13** prognosticate **15** prognostication

forefather **6** author **8** ancestor, begetter **9** patriarch, precursor **10** antecedent, originator, procreator, progenitor **12** primogenitor

forefront **4** fame, head, lead **8** vanguard **9** celebrity

foreign **5** alien **6** exotic, remote **7** distant, strange, unknown, unusual **8** imported **9** barbarous, extrinsic, irregular, unrelated **10** extraneous, heathenish, introduced, irrelevant, outlandish, unfamiliar **11** incongruous, inconsonant, unconnected **12** antipathetic, inadmissible, inapplicable, incompatible, inconsistent **13** inappropriate **16** uncharacteristic

Foreign Correspondent
director: **15** Alfred Hitchcock
cast: **10** Joel McCrea, Laraine Day **13** George Sanders **14** Robert Benchley **15** Albert Basserman, Herbert Marshall

foreigner **5** alien, pagan **6** emigre **8** newcomer, outsider, stranger **9** barbarian, immigrant, nonnative, outlander
German: **9** Auslander

foreign officer **6** consul **8** diplomat, minister **10** ambassador **14** representative **15** charge d'affaires

foreknowledge **9** intuition, prevision **10** prescience **11** premonition **12** anticipation, apprehension, clairvoyance, precognition, presentiment

foreman **4** boss **7** manager **8** chairman, overseer **9** president, spokesman **10** supervisor **11** coordinator **14** superintendent

foremost **4** head, main **5** chief, vital **7** capital, leading, supreme **8** cardinal **9** essential, paramount, principal **10** preeminent

forerunner **4** omen, sign **5** token **6** augury, herald **7** portent, presage **8** ancestor **9** harbinger, precursor, prototype **10** progenitor, prognostic **11** predecessor, premonition

foresee **5** augur **6** divine, expect **7** predict, presage **8** envision, prophesy **10** anticipate **13** prognosticate

foreshadow **5** augur **7** presage, promise **9** prefigure

foresight **6** wisdom **8** planning, prudence, sagacity **9** prevision **10** discretion, precaution, prescience, providence, shrewdness **12** anticipation, clairvoyance, perspicacity, precognition, preparedness **13** premeditation **14** farsightedness

forest **4** bush, wood **5** copse, grove, stand, woods **6** jungle **7** thicket **8** wildwood, woodland **10** timberland, wilderness

forestall **5** avert, avoid, block, deter **6** thwart **7** head off, obviate, prevent, ward off **8** preclude **10** anticipate, circumvent, counteract

Forester, C S (Cecil Scott)
author of: **6** The Gun **14** A Ship of the Line **15** Payment Deferred, The African Queen **24** Captain Horatio Hornblower

forests
god of: **3** Pan **7** Silenus, Virbius

foretell **5** augur **6** divine **7** portend, predict, presage **8** prophesy, soothsay **9** apprehend **13** prognosticate

forethought **4** heed **7** caution **8** prudence, sagacity, wariness **10** discretion, precaution, providence, shrewdness **11** carefulness **12** anticipation, deliberation **13** consideration, premeditation **14** circumspection, farsightedness

forever **6** always **9** eternally, undyingly **10** constantly **11** ceaselessly, continually, incessantly, perpetually, unceasingly **12** interminably **13** everlastingly, unremittingly
Latin: **11** in perpetuum

forewarn **4** bode **5** alert **6** advise, notify, signal, tip off **7** caution, portend, presage, prewarn **8** cry havoc

foreword **7** preface, prelude **8** preamble, prologue **12** introduction

Forewords and Afterwords
author: **7** W H Auden

for example
Latin: **2** eg **13** exempli gratia

forfeit **4** fine, miss **5** waive, waste, yield **6** waiver **7** damages, default, let slip, penalty **8** squander **9** surrender **10** assessment

Forfeit
author: **11** Dick Francis

forge **4** copy, form, make **5** clone, shape **6** devise, hearth, smithy **7** falsify, fashion, furnace, imitate, produce, turn out **8** contrive, simulate **9** fabricate, ironworks **11** counterfeit, manufacture

forgery **4** copy, fake, hoax, sham **5** clone, fraud **7** cloning **9** deception, imitation **11** counterfeit, fraudulence **13** falsification **14** counterfeiting **17** misrepresentation

forget **6** slight **7** neglect **8** overlook, pass over **9** disregard

forgetful **6** remiss **7** out of it **8** amnesiac, careless, heedless, mindless **9** negligent, oblivious, unmindful **10** neglectful **11** inattentive

forget-me-not **8** Myosotis
varieties: **5** white **6** alpine, garden **7** Chinese **8** creeping

forgive **5** clear **6** acquit, excuse, pardon **7** absolve, condone, release, set free **8** overlook, reprieve **9** discharge, exculpate, exonerate

forgiveness **6** pardon **7** amnesty **9** remission **10** absolution

forgiving **6** benign, kindly **8** excusing **9** benignant, pardoning **11** kindhearted

forgo, forego **4** skip **5** waive, yield **6** eschew, give up **8** abnegate, renounce **9** sacrifice, surrender **10** relinquish

fork **4** bend, stab **5** angle, elbow, split **6** branch, crotch, divide, impale, pierce, ramify, skewer **7** diverge, trident **8** division **9** bifurcate, pitchfork **10** divergence, separation **11** bifurcation **12** intersection

forked **5** cleft **6** horned, zigzag **7** angular, divided, pronged **8** branched **9** ambiguous, deceitful, equivocal **10** bifurcated

For Kicks
author: **11** Dick Francis

fork out **5** spend **6** expend **8** disburse, dispense

for lack of something better
French: **12** faute de mieux

forlorn **4** lone **6** abject, bereft, dismal, dreary, lonely **7** unhappy **8** bereaved, dejected, deserted, desolate, forsaken, helpless, hopeless, lonesome, pathetic, pitiable, solitary, wretched **9** abandoned, depressed, desperate, destitute, forgotten, miserable, woebegone **10** despairing, despondent, dispirited, friendless **11** comfortless **12** disconsolate, inconsolable **13** brokenhearted

form ***see box***

formal **4** cool, prim **5** aloof, fancy, fixed, grand, legal, rigid, smart, stiff **6** dressy, lawful, proper, solemn, strict **7** distant, outward, pompous, prudish, regular, settled, stilted, stylish **8** decorous, definite, explicit, external, official, positive, reserved, starched **9** customary **10** ceremonial, inflexible, prescribed **11** ceremonious, highfalutin, perfunctory, punctilious, ritualistic, standoffish, straitlaced **12** conventional **13** authoritative **14** uncompromising

formal discussion **6** debate, parley **8** dialogue **10** conference

formality **4** rite **6** custom, motion, ritual **7** decorum, reserve **8** ceremony, coolness **9** etiquette, propriety, punctilio **10** ceremonial, convention **15** conventionality

Forman, Milos
director of: **7** Amadeus (Oscar), Ragtime **25** One Flew

form **3** cut, hew, way **4** body, cast, kind, make, mode, mold, plan, rite, rule, sort, trim, type **5** being, brand, build, carve, class, forge, found, frame, genre, genus, guise, habit, image, model, order, phase, set up, shape, stamp, style, usage **6** aspect, chisel, create, custom, design, devise, fettle, figure, manner, matrix, person, ritual, sculpt, system **7** acquire, anatomy, compose, conduct, contour, decorum, develop, fashion, fitness, harmony, liturgy, manners, outline, pattern, produce, species, variety **8** ceremony, comprise, contract, likeness, physique, practice, presence, roughhew, symmetry **9** character, construct, establish, etiquette, fabricate, framework, propriety, sculpture, semblance, structure **10** appearance, constitute, deportment, figuration, proceeding, proportion, regularity **11** arrangement, description, incarnation, manufacture, orderliness, shapeliness **12** denomination **13** configuration, manifestation **15** conventionality

Over the Cuckoo's Nest (Oscar)

formation **3** set **6** makeup **7** genesis **8** building, creation **9** structure **10** generation, production **11** arrangement, composition, development, fabrication, manufacture **12** organization **13** configuration, constellation, establishment

formative **7** plastic, shaping **9** sensitive **10** accessible **11** susceptible **13** determinative **14** impressionable

former **2** ex **4** gone, past **5** olden, prior **6** bygone, gone by, lapsed, of yore, whilom **7** ancient, earlier, elapsed, old-time, quondam **8** anterior, previous **9** aforesaid, erstwhile, preceding **10** antecedent, first-named **14** aforementioned
French: **8** ci-devant

formerly **4** once **5** of old **6** ere now, lately, of yore, whilom **7** long ago **8** hitherto **9** anciently **10** originally, previously

former student **6** alumna **7** alumnus, dropout **8** graduate

formidable **6** taxing **7** awesome, fearful, mammoth, onerous **8** alarming, dreadful, imposing, menacing, terrific **9** dangerous, demanding, difficult **10** forbidding, impressive, portentous, terrifying **11** threatening **12** overpowering, overwhelming

formless **5** vague **9** amorphous, shapeless

Formosa *see* **6** Taiwan

formula **4** cant, plan, rule **5** chant **6** cliche, recipe, saying, slogan **7** precept **9** blueprint, guideline, platitude, principle, rigmarole **10** pleasantry **11** incantation **12** prescription

formulate **5** draft, frame, state **6** define, devise, invent **7** compose, itemize, specify **11** systematize **13** particularize

Fornax
origin: **5** Roman
goddess of: **6** baking

fornication **8** adultery

for one's country
Latin: **9** pro patria

Forrest, Nathan Bedford
served in: **8** Civil War
side: **11** Confederate
known for: **12** cavalry raids

forsake **4** deny, drop, flee, quit **5** leave, spurn, waive, yield **6** abjure, depart, desert, give up, reject, resign, vacate **7** abandon, cast off, disavow, discard, lay down **8** abdicate, disclaim, go back on, jettison, part with, renounce **9** repudiate, surrender **10** relinquish

forsaken **4** bare **5** empty **8** deserted, desolate, rejected **9** abandoned, discarded, neglected **11** uninhabited

Forsete *see* **7** Forseti

Forseti
also: **7** Forsete
origin: **12** Scandinavian
god of: **7** justice
father: **5** Baldr **6** Balder, Baldur
mother: **5** Nanna
dwelling place: **7** Glitnir

Forster, E M (Edward Morgan)
author of: **7** Maurice **10** Howard's End **14** A Room with a View **15** A Passage to India **17** The Longest Journey **22** Where Angels Fear to Tread
member of: **15** Bloomsbury Group

forswear, foreswear **4** deny **5** spurn **6** abjure, disown, eschew, give up, recant, reject, revoke **7** disavow, gainsay, retract **8** abdicate, disclaim, renounce, take back **9** disaffirm, repudiate **10** contravene

Forsyte Saga, The
author: **14** John Galsworthy
trilogy including: **5** To Let **10** In Chancery **16** The Man of Property
character: **3** Jon **4** June **5** Fleur **6** Dartie **7** Annette **8** Winifred **9** Old Jolyon **11** Young Jolyon **12** Irene Forsyte **13** Soames Forsyte **14** Philip Bosinney

Forsythe, John
real name: **17** John Lincoln Freund
born: **12** Penn's Grove NJ
roles: **5** Topaz **7** Dynasty, Madame X **11** In Cold Blood **14** Bachelor Father, Charlie's Angels **15** Blake Carrington **16** And Justice for All **19** The Trouble with Harry **23** Teahouse of the August Moon

fort **4** base, camp **6** castle **7** bastion, bulwark, citadel, station **8** fastness, garrison **10** stronghold

forte **4** bent **5** knack, skill **8** strength **9** specialty **11** proficiency
music: **4** loud
abbreviation: **1** f

forth **5** ahead **6** onward **7** outward

forthcoming **5** handy, on tap **6** at hand **7** helpful **8** imminent **9** available, impending **10** accessible, obtainable, openhanded **11** approaching, cooperative, prospective

for the greater glory of God
Latin: **19** ad majorem Dei gloriam

for the public good
Latin: **14** pro bono publico

for the time being
Latin: **10** pro tempore

For the Time Being
author: **7** W H Auden

for this purpose only
Latin: **5** ad hoc

forthright **4** open **5** blunt, frank **6** candid, direct, openly **7** bluntly, frankly, up-front **8** candidly, directly, straight **9** outspoken **10** truthfully **11** outspokenly, plain-spoken **15** straightforward **17** straightforwardly

forthrightness **6** candor **7** honesty **8** openness **9** frankness, sincerity **19** straightforwardness

forthwith **6** at once, pronto **7** quickly **8** directly, in a jiffy, promptly, right off **9** instantly **11** immediately **12** straightaway

fortification **5** tower **7** bastion, bulwark, citadel, rampart **8** fortress, garrison **9** earthwork **10** breastwork, stronghold

fortify **4** lace **5** boost, brace, cheer **6** buoy up, enrich, harden, secure, shield, urge on **7** build up, bulwark, hearten, protect, shore up, stiffen, support, sustain **8** buttress, embolden, garrison, reassure **9** encourage, reinforce, stimulate **10** invigorate, strengthen

fortissimo
music: **8** very loud
abbreviation: **2** ff

fortitude **4** dash, grit, guts, sand **5** nerve, pluck, spunk, valor **6** daring, mettle, spirit **7** bravery, courage, heroism, prowess **8** backbone, boldness, firmness, tenacity **9** endurance, hardihood **10** resolution **11** intrepidity **12** fearlessness, resoluteness **13** dauntlessness, determination

Fortitude
author: **11** Hugh Walpole

Fort-Lamy
capital of: **4** Chad

fortress **7** bastion, bulwark, citadel, rampart **8** buttress **9** acropolis **10** stronghold

Fortress, The
author: **11** Hugh Walpole

fortuitous **5** happy, lucky, stray **6** casual, chance, random **9** haphazard, hit-or-miss **10** accidental, incidental, undesigned, unexpected, unintended, unpurposed **11** inadvertent **12** adventitious **13** serendipitous, unintentional **14** unpremeditated

fortuity **6** chance **8** accident **12** happenstance

Fortuna
origin: **5** Roman
goddess of: **7** fortune
corresponds to: **5** Tyche

fortunate **4** fair, rich, rosy **5** happy, lucky, palmy **6** benign, bright, timely **7** blessed, booming, favored, halcyon, well-off **8** well-to-do **9** favorable, opportune, promising **10** auspicious, convenient, felicitous, profitable, propitious, prosperous, successful **11** encouraging, flourishing **12** advantageous, providential

Fortunate Isles *see* **13** Canary Islands

Fortunato
character in: **20** The Cask of Amontillado
author: **3** Poe

fortune, fortunes **3** lot **4** doom, fate, luck, mint, pile, star **5** means **6** chance, estate, income, kismet, riches, wealth **7** bonanza, capital, destiny, godsend, portion, revenue **8** accident, fatality, gold mine, good luck, lady luck, opulence, property, treasure, windfall **9** affluence, haphazard, substance **10** prosperity, providence **12** circumstance **13** circumstances
goddess of: **5** Tyche **7** Fortuna

Fortunes of Nigel, The
author: **14** Sir Walter Scott

fortuneteller **4** seer **5** augur, Gypsy, sibyl **6** medium, oracle **7** palmist, prophet **8** magician **10** soothsayer **11** chiromancer, clairvoyant **12** crystal gazer

for two
French: **5** a deux

Forty Days of Musa Dagh, The
author: **11** Franz Werfel

42nd Parallel, The
author: **13** John Dos Passos

Forty-Second Street
director: **10** Lloyd Bacon
cast: **9** Guy Kibbee, Una Merkel **10** Dick Powell, Ruby Keeler **11** Bebe Daniels, George Brent **12** Ginger Rogers, Warner Baxter
choreographer: **13** Busby Berkeley
song: **15** Young and Healthy **17** Forty-second Street **19** Shuffle Off to Buffalo **28** You're Getting to Be a Habit with Me

Forty Thieves, The
author: **7** unknown
character: **7** Ali Baba
code word: **10** Open Sesame

forty winks **3** nap **4** doze **6** catnap, snooze

forum **6** medium, outlet **7** rostrum, seminar **8** platform **9** symposium **10** colloquium

forward, forwards **3** out **4** back, bold **5** ahead, brash, fresh, relay, sassy **6** assist, brazen, cheeky, hasten, onward, pass on, send on, spread **7** advance, frontal, further, go-ahead, promote, quicken, reroute **8** anterior, champion, immodest, impudent, insolent, up-to-date **9** advancing, barefaced, intrusive, offensive, presuming, readdress, shameless **10** accelerate, unmannerly **11** impertinent, progressive **12** enterprising, presumptuous **13** overconfident
French: **7** en avant

forwardness **4** gall **5** brass, cheek **8** audacity, boldness **10** brazenness, effrontery **11** presumption **13** bumptiousness, obtrusiveness

for what use
Latin: **7** cui bono

For Whom the Bell Tolls
author: **15** Ernest Hemingway
director: **7** Sam Wood
character: **5** Maria, Pablo, Pilar **6** Andres, Rafael **7** Anselmo, El Sordo **8** Augustin, Fernando **12** Robert Jordan
cast: **10** Gary Cooper **12** Akim Tamiroff **13** Ingrid Bergman, Joseph Calleia, Katina Paxinou **15** Arturo de Cordova
score: **11** Victor Young
Oscar for: **17** supporting actress (Paxinou)

for whose benefit
Latin: **7** cui bono

For Your Eyes Only
author: **10** Ian Fleming

Fosse, Bob
director of: **5** Lenny **7** Cabaret (Oscar) **11** All That Jazz

fossil **4** fogy, rock **5** fogey, oldie, relic, stone **7** imprint, antique **9** remainder **13** petrification

foster **3** aid **4** back, feed, rear, tend **5** favor, nurse, raise **6** foment, harbor, mother, rear up, take in **7** advance, bring up, care for, cherish, forward, further, nourish, nurture, promote, protect, support, sustain **8** advocate, befriend, hold dear, sanction, side with, treasure **9** encourage, patronize, stimulate **11** accommodate, countenance

Foster, Alicia Christian
real name of: **11** Jodie Foster

Foster, Harold
creator/artist of: **6** Tarzan **13** Prince Valiant

Foster, Jodie
real name: **21** Alicia Christian Foster
born: **7** Bronx NY
roles: **9** Tom Sawyer **10** Taxi Driver **11** Bugsy Malone

Foster, Stephen Collins
born: **15** Lawrenceville PA
composer of: **11** Swanee River **13** Camptown Races **16** Beautiful Dreamer **17** My Old Kentucky Home, The Old Folks at Home **27** Jeanie with the Light Brown Hair

Foucault, Jean Bernard Leon
field: **7** physics
nationality: **6** French
proved: **19** Earth spins on its axis
measured: **15** velocity of light
named for him: **16** Foucault currents

foul ***see box***

foul-mouthed **4** lewd, rude, vile **5** dirty, gross **6** coarse, filthy, vulgar **7** abusive, obscene, profane **9** offensive **10** indelicate

foul play **5** crime **6** murder **8** violence **9** treachery

foul-smelling **4** rank **5** acrid, fetid, musty **6** putrid, smelly **7** noisome, reeking **8** stinking **10** malodorous

foul up **3** mar **4** goof, muff, ruin **5** botch, mix up, spoil **6** bungle, mess up, muddle **7** blunder, butcher, confuse, louse up, screw up **9** mismanage

foul **3** wet **4** base, clog, evil, lewd, soil, vile **5** dirty, foggy, grimy, gross, gusty, misty, muddy, murky, nasty, rainy, sully, taint **6** choked, cloudy, coarse, defile, filthy, grubby, odious, putrid, risque, scurvy, smelly, smutty, soiled, sordid, stormy, tangle, turbid, vulgar, wicked **7** abusive, begrime, drizzly, ensnare, hateful, heinous, impeded, obscene, pollute, profane, smeared, squalid, squally, stained, sullied, tangled, unclean **8** begrimed, besmirch, blustery, ensnared, entangle, immodest, indecent, infamous, stinking, unseemly **9** atrocious, besmeared, entangled, insulting, loathsome, monstrous, nefarious, notorious, obnoxious, repulsive, revolting **10** abominable, bedraggled, detestable, disgusting, encumbered, flagitious, indelicate, malodorous, putrescent, scurrilous, villainous **11** blasphemous, disgraceful **12** contemptible

found **4** base, rear, rest **5** build, erect, raise, set up, start **6** create, ground, locate, settle **7** develop, sustain **8** colonize, organize **9** construct, establish, institute, originate

foundation **3** bed **4** base, foot, fund, rock, root **5** basis, cause **6** bottom, cellar, ground, motive, origin, reason, source **7** charity, premise, purpose, support **8** basement, creation, pedestal **9** endowment, rationale **10** assumption, groundwork, settlement **11** benefaction, institution **12** commencement, installation, philanthropy, substructure, underpinning **13** establishment, justification **14** infrastructure, understructure

foundational **3** key **4** base, core **5** basic, prime **7** primary **9** essential **10** elementary

foundation garment **6** corset, girdle **8** corselet

founder **4** fall, limp, reel, sink, trip **5** abort, drown, lurch, swamp **6** author, father, go down, go lame, hobble, perish, plunge, sprawl, topple, tumble **7** break up, builder, capsize, creator, go under, planner, stagger, stumble, succumb **8** collapse, miscarry **9** architect, organizer, shipwreck **10** originator, strategist **12** disintegrate

foundered **4** sank **6** failed **7** beached, swamped **8** capsized, went down **9** collapsed

founding **5** birth **8** creation, settling **9** beginning **11** institution, origination **12** introduction, organization **13** establishment

found on **6** base on **7** model on **8** stem from **10** derive from **11** establish on

fountain **3** jet **4** flow, gush, well **5** birth, cause, spout **6** cradle, feeder, origin, reason, source, spring **7** genesis **8** purveyor, supplier **9** beginning, reservoir, upswelling **10** derivation, wellspring

fountainhead **4** font **6** origin, source, spring **9** beginning **10** wellspring

Fountainhead, The
author: **7** Ayn Rand

fourgon **3** van **7** tumbril

Four Horsemen of the Apocalypse, The
author: **19** Vicente Blasco Ibanez
based on: **10** Revelation

400 Blows, The
director: **16** Francois Truffaut
cast: **10** Albert Remy **13** Claire Maurier **14** Patrick Auffray **15** Jean-Pierre Leaud

Four Quartets
author: **7** T S Eliot

Four-Season Recreation State
nickname of: **7** Vermont

fowl **3** hen **4** cock, duck, game **5** banty, capon, chick, goose, quail **6** bantam, grouse, pigeon, turkey **7** chicken, cornish, leghorn, poultry **8** duckling

Fowles, John
author of: **8** Mantissa, The Magus **10** The Aristos **12** Daniel Martin, The Collector **13** The Ebony Tower **25** The French Lieutenant's Woman

fox **9** scavenger
young: **3** kit, pup
group of: **5** leash, skulk

Fox (Mesquakie, Red Earth People)
language family: **9** Algonkian **10** Algonquian
location: **4** Iowa **9** Wisconsin
allied with: **4** Sauk **8** Kickapoo

Fox, Fontaine
creator/artist of: **16** Toonerville Folks **18** Toonerville Trolley

foxglove **9** digitalis
varieties: **5** false, rusty **6** common, yellow **7** Grecian, Mexican **10** downy false **12** willow-leaved

foxiness **5** guile **7** cunning, slyness **8** artifice, trickery, wiliness **10** craftiness, shrewdness

fox-trot **5** dance **13** ballroom dance

Foxx, Jimmy (James Emory)
nickname: **7** Double X
sport: **8** baseball
team: **12** Boston Red Sox **21** Philadelphia Athletics

Foxx, Redd
real name: **16** John Elroy Sanford
born: **9** St Louis MO
roles: **13** Sanford and Son **19** Cotton Comes to Harlem

foxy **3** sly **4** wily **5** canny, sharp, slick **6** artful, astute, clever, crafty, shifty, shrewd, sneaky, tricky **7** cunning, devious, oblique **8** guileful, scheming, stealthy **9** conniving, deceitful, deceptive, designing, insidious, underhand **10** intriguing

foyer **4** hall **5** lobby **6** loggia **8** anteroom **9** vestibule **11** antechamber

fracas **3** row **4** fray, to-do **5** brawl, broil, clash, fight, melee, scrap **6** battle, ruckus, rumpus, strife, uproar **7** scuffle **9** imbroglio **10** donnybrook, free-for-all **11** altercation, embroilment

fraction **3** bit, few **4** chip **5** crumb, piece, ratio, scrap **6** morsel, trifle **7** cutting, portion, section, segment, shaving **8** fragment, particle, quotient **10** proportion **11** subdivision

fractious **5** cross, huffy **6** shirty, touchy, unruly **7** fretful, grouchy, peevish, pettish, waspish, wayward, willful **8** contrary, perverse, petulant, shrewish, snappish **9** irascible, irritable, querulous **10** rebellious, refractory

11 quarrelsome **12** disputatious, recalcitrant, unmanageable

fracture **4** rend, rift **5** break, crack, fault, sever, split **6** breach, cleave **7** disrupt, rupture, shatter **8** cleavage, division **9** severance **10** separation

Fra Diavolo, ou L'Hotellerie de Terracine
also: **31** Brother Devil or The Inn at Terracina
comic opera by: **5** Auber
character: **7** Lorenzo, Zerlina **11** Lady Allcash, Lord Allcash **17** Marquis di San Marco

fragile **4** soft, weak **5** crisp, frail **6** dainty, feeble, flimsy, infirm, sleazy, slight, tender **7** brittle, crumbly, friable, rickety, shivery **8** decrepit, delicate **9** breakable, ephemeral, frangible, splintery **10** evanescent, tumbledown **11** dilapidated **13** unsubstantial

fragility **7** frailty **8** delicacy, weakness **9** frailness **10** feebleness **11** brittleness **12** frangibility

fragment **3** bit **4** chip, snip **5** crumb, cut up, piece, scrap, shard, shred, trace **6** chop up, divide, morsel **7** break up, crumble, portion, remnant, section, segment, shatter, vestige **8** disunite, fraction, separate, splinter, survival **12** disintegrate

fragmentary **6** broken, choppy **7** scrappy **8** detached **9** piecemeal, scattered, segmented **10** disjointed, fractional, incomplete, unfinished **12** disconnected

Fragonard, Jean-Honore
born: **6** France, Grasse
artwork: **8** The Swing **10** Stolen Kiss, The Bathers, The Warrior **12** Le Billet Doux **14** Progress of Love **16** La Chemise Enlevee **18** Storming the Citadel **40** Coresus Sacrificing Himself to Save Callirhoe

fragrance **4** aura, balm **5** aroma, scent **7** bouquet, incense, perfume **9** redolence, sweetness

fragrant **5** balmy, spicy **7** odorous **8** aromatic, perfumed, redolent **11** odoriferous

France
other name: **4** Gaul
anthem: **14** La Marseillaise
capital/largest city: **5** Paris
others: **4** Nice **5** Brest, Lille, Lyons, Rouen, Vichy **6** Amiens, Calais, Cannes, Carnac, Cognac, Dieppe, Grasse, Nantes, Prades, Rheims **7** Antibes, Avignon, Bayonne, Dunkirk, Le Havre, Les Baux **8** Bordeaux, Boulogne, Chartres, Grenoble, Poitiers, Toulouse **9** Cherbourg, Roquefort **10** La Rochelle, Marseilles, Saint-Denis, Strasbourg **12** Saint-Nazaire **13** Aix-en-Provence, Fontainebleau
school: **8** Grenoble, Saint Cyr, Sorbonne **10** Montpelier
division: **5** Anjou, Bearn, Berry, Maine, Savoy **6** Alsace, Artois, Marche, Poitou **7** Gascony, Guienne, Picardy **8** Auvergne, Bordeaux, Brittany, Burgundy, Dauphine, Flanders, Lorraine, Lyonnais, Normandy, Provence, Touraine **9** Aquitaine, Champagne, Languedoc **11** Ile de France **12** Bourbonnaise, Franche-Comte
measure: **3** pot, sac **4** aune, mine, muid, pied, velt **5** arpen, carat, ligne, minot, pinte, point, pouce, velte **6** arpent, hemine, league, quarte, setier
monetary unit: **5** franc **7** centime
weight: **3** sol **4** gros, kilo, once **5** carat, livre, pound, tonne **6** gramme **7** tonneau **8** esterlin **9** esterling
island: **2** Re **3** Yeu **4** Cite **5** Groix, Hyere **6** Comoro, Oleron, Tahiti, Ushant **7** Corsica, Leeward, Reunion **8** Windward **10** Guadeloupe, Martinique **12** New Caledonia
lake: **6** Annecy, Cazaux, Geneva
mountain: **4** Jura **5** Pelat **6** Vosges **8** Ardennes, Pyrenees **10** French Alps **11** Pic Montcalm
highest point: **5** Blanc **9** Mont Blanc
river: **3** Lys **4** Yser **5** Aisne, Eiser, Isere, Loire, Meuse, Rhine, Rhone, Saone, Seine **7** Garonne, Gironde
sea: **5** North **8** Atlantic **13** Mediterranean
physical feature:
bay: **6** Biscay **7** Arachon
beach: **5** Omaha
cape: **5** Hague, Talma
channel: **7** English **8** La Manche
gulf: **4** Lion
people: **6** Franks
artist: **5** Corot, David, Degas, Manet, Monet **6** Braque, Ingres, Millet, Renoir, Seurat **7** Cezanne, Daumier, Gauguin, Matisse, Utrillo **8** Pissarro **9** Delacroix, Fragonard, Gericault
author: **4** Gide, Hugo, Zola **5** Camus, Dumas **6** France, Proust, Racine, Sartre, Villon **7** Moliere **8** Rabelais, Rousseau, Voltaire **9** Corneille, Descartes, Giraudoux, Montaigne **10** Baudelaire
composer: **5** Bizet, Ravel, Satie **6** Franck, Gounod **7** Berlioz, Debussy, Poulenc
king: **5** Henri, Louis **6** Clovis, Philip **7** Charles **9** Hugh Capet **11** Charlemagne **13** Louis Philippe **14** Henry of Navarre
leader: **6** Danton, Petain **7** Colbert, Mazarin **8** de Gaulle, D'Estaing, Pompidou **9** Joan of Arc, Richelieu **10** Mitterrand **11** Robespierre **17** Napoleon Bonaparte

Fragrant Harbor *see* **8** Hong Kong

frail 4 puny, weak **6** feeble, flimsy, infirm, sleazy, slight, weakly **7** brittle, crumbly, fragile, rickety, shivery **8** decrepit, delicate, fallible **9** breakable, frangible, splintery **10** perishable, vulnerable **11** dilapidated **13** unsubstantial

frailness 8 delicacy, weakness **9** fragility **11** unsoundness

frailty 3 sin **4** flaw, vice **5** fault **6** defect, foible **7** blemish, failing **11** fallibility **12** imperfection **14** susceptibility

Fra Lippo Lippi
author: 14 Robert Browning

frame 3 rim, set **4** body, case, cast, form, make, mold, mood, plan **5** build, draft, hatch, humor, set up, shape, state **6** border, casing, design, devise, edging, figure, indite, invent, map out, nature, scheme, sketch, system, temper **7** anatomy, backing, chassis, concoct, contour, housing, outline, setting **8** attitude, conceive, contrive, mounting, organize, physique, skeleton **9** formulate, structure **11** disposition, scaffolding, systematize, temperament **12** constitution, construction

frame of mind 4 mood **7** climate **8** attitude **10** atmosphere **11** disposition

framer 6 author, shaper **7** creator, planner **10** formulator

framework 5 shell, truss **7** carcass **8** skeleton, template **9** structure **10** foundation **11** scaffolding **14** infrastructure

Framley Parsonage
author: 15 Anthony Trollope

France ***see box***

France, Anatole
real name: 30 Jacques Anatole Francois Thibault
author of: 5 Thais **12** Golden Verses **13** My Friend's Book, Penguin Island **17** The Gods Are Athirst **20** The Revolt of the Angels **25** Le Crime de Sylvestre Bonnard **27** At the Sign of the Reine Pedauque

franchise 5 grant, right **6** ballot **7** charter, freedom, license

---

***queen:* 7** Eugenie **9** Josephine **13** Marie de Medici **15** Marie Antoinette
language: 6 French
religion: 5 Islam **7** Judaism **8** Huguenot **10** Protestant **13** Roman Catholic
place:
***cathedral:* 6** Rheims **8** Chartres **9** Madeleine, Notre Dame **10** Sacre-Coeur **14** Sainte-Chapelle **15** Mont-Saint-Michel
***chapel:* 8** Ronchamp
***gardens:* 9** Tuileries
***hall of mirrors:* 16** Galerie des Glaces
***museum:* 6** Louvre
***palace:* 6** Elysee **10** Luxembourg, Versailles **12** Grand Trianon, Petit Trianon, **13** Fontainebleau
***prison:* 8** Bastille
***racetrack:* 6** Le Mans **7** Auteuil **10** Longchamps
***resort:* 3** Pau **5** Vichy **6** Cannes, Menton **7** Antibes, Mentone, Riviera **8** Biarritz, Chamonix, Grenoble **9** Cote d'Azur **11** Aix-les-Bains
***section of Paris:* 8** Left Bank **9** Right Bank **10** Montmartre, Rive Droite, Rive Gauche **12** Latin Quarter
***street:* 13** Champs-Elysees **17** Place de la Concorde
***woods:* 14** Bois de Boulogne **15** Bois de Vincennes
possession: 12 French Guiana
***island:* 6** Futuna, Hoorne, Wallis **7** Reunion **8** Miquelon **10** Guadeloupe, Martinique **11** Saint Pierre **12** New Caledonia **15** French Polynesia
feature:
***airport:* 4** Orly **9** Le Bourget **15** Charles de Gaulle
***bicycle race:* 12** Tour de France
***dance:* 5** gavot **6** branle, canary, cancan **7** boutade, gavotte
***fortification:* 11** Maginot Line
***holiday:* 11** Bastille Day
***monument:* 13** Arc de Triomphe **14** Tomb of Napoleon
***national theater:* 16** Comedie Francaise
***sightseeing boat:* 12** bateau mouche
***tower:* 6** Eiffel
food:
***cheese:* 4** bleu, Brie **6** bonbel **7** boursin **8** Muenster **9** camembert, marcillat, port-salut, Roquefort **11** coulommiers
***dessert:* 6** mousse
***dish:* 4** pate **5** crepe **6** canape, quiche **7** souffle **8** escargot, piperade, pot au feu **9** cassoulet, tournedos **14** pate de foie gras
***drink:* 6** cognac **8** bordeaux, burgundy **9** champagne
***french fries:* 12** pommes frites
***pastry:* 7** brioche **8** napoleon **9** croissant
***soup:* 8** a l'oignon **13** bouillabaisse
***steak:* 7** bifteck

8 immunity, suffrage **9** privilege **10** permission **11** prerogative **13** authorization

Franciosa, Anthony
real name: 14 Anthony Papales
born: 9 New York NY
wife: 14 Shelley Winters
roles: 12 The Naked Maja **13** A Hatful of Rain, Long Hot Summer, Name of the Game, Wild Is the Wind **15** Assault on a Queen

Francis, Dick
author of: 4 Bolt, Risk **5** Nerve, Proof **6** Banker, Reflex **7** Break In, Enquiry, Forfeit, Rat Race **8** Dead Cert, For Kicks, Slayride, Trial Run, Twice Shy, Whip Hand **9** Bonecrack, The Danger, Knockdown **10** Blood Sport, High Stakes, In the Frame **11** Smokescreen **12** Flying Finish

Franck, Cesar
born: 5 Liege **7** Belgium
composer of: 4 Ruth **5** Hulda **6** Psyche **7** Rebecca **8** Ghiselle **9** Les Djinns **10** Les Eolides, Redemption **13** La Tour de Babel, Les Beatitudes, The Beatitudes **16** Le Chasseur Maudit **17** The Accursed Hunter

Franglais 13 French-English **14** French-American

frank 4 bold, free, open **5** clear, plain, round **6** candid, direct, honest, patent **7** artless, evident, genuine, natural, sincere, up-front **8** apparent, distinct, explicit, manifest **9** downright, ingenuous, outspoken **10** aboveboard, forthright, unreserved **11** plainspoken, transparent, unambiguous, undisguised, unequivocal **12** unmistakable **15** straightforward

Frank, Anne
author of: 19 The Diary of Anne Frank

Frankenstein
author: 17 Mary Godwin Shelley
character: 7 Clerval, Justine, William **9** Elizabeth **10** The Monster **12** Robert Walton **18** Victor Frankenstein

Franklin, Benjamin
author of: 20 Poor Richard's Almanack
inventor of: 12 lightning rod **13** bifocal lenses, Franklin stove

frankness 6 candor **7** honesty **8** openness **9** bluntness, sincerity **10** directness **11** artlessness **13** guilelessness **14** forthrightness **19** straightforwardness

frantic 3 mad **4** wild **5** crazy, rabid **6** hectic, insane, raging, raving **7** berserk, excited, furious, nervous, violent **8** agitated, deranged, frenetic, frenzied **9** delirious **10** distracted, distraught, infuriated **11** impassioned, overwrought **12** ungovernable

fraternal 6 hearty, loving, social **7** devoted, kindred, related **8** amicable, friendly **9** brotherly **11** warmhearted **12** affectionate **14** consanguineous

fraternity 4 clan, club **5** union **6** circle, clique, league **7** company, coterie, kinship, society **8** alliance **9** coalition **10** federation **11** association, brotherhood, confederacy, propinquity **13** brotherliness, consanguinity, interrelation

Fraternity
author: 14 John Galsworthy

fraternize 3 mix **5** unite **6** concur, hobnob, mingle **7** combine, consort **8** coalesce **9** associate, cooperate, harmonize, pal around, socialize **10** sympathize **11** confederate

Fratres Arvales *see* **5** Arval

frau 4 lady, wife **12** married woman

fraud 4 fake, hoax, hype, ruse, sham **5** cheat, craft, guile, knave, quack, rogue, trick **6** deceit, humbug, rascal **7** swindle **8** artifice, cheating, cozenage, impostor, swindler, trickery **9** charlatan, chicanery, con artist, deception, duplicity, imposture, pretender, stratagem, swindling, treachery **10** dishonesty, mountebank, subterfuge **11** counterfeit, four-flusher, machination **13** dissimulation

fraudulence 6 deceit **8** trickery **9** deception **13** deceitfulness, deceptiveness **17** misrepresentation

fraudulent 4 sham, wily **5** bogus, false **6** crafty, tricky **7** crooked, cunning, knavish **8** cheating, guileful, spurious **9** deceitful, deceptive, dishonest **11** counterfeit, treacherous, underhanded **12** dishonorable, unprincipled

fraught 4 full **5** heavy, laden **6** filled, loaded **7** charged, replete, teeming **8** attended, pregnant **9** abounding **11** accompanied

fraulein 9 young lady **14** unmarried woman

Fraunhofer, Joseph von
field: 7 physics
nationality: 6 German
established: 12 spectroscopy

fray 3 rub **4** fret, fuss, riot, spat, tiff **5** brawl, chafe, fight, melee, ravel, set-to **6** battle, combat, fracas, rumble, rumpus, strain, tatter, tumult, tussle **7** contest, dispute, frazzle, quarrel, scuffle, warfare, wear out, wrangle **8** conflict, skirmish, squabble **9** bickering, commotion **10** contention, dissension, engagement **11** altercation, controversy **12** disagreement

Frazer, Sir James G
author of: 14 The Golden Bough

freak 3 fad, odd **4** kink, turn, whim **5** craze, fancy, humor, queer, quirk, sport, twist **6** marvel, oddity, vagary, whimsy, wonder **7** anomaly, bizarre, caprice, erratic, monster, strange, unusual **8** crotchet, mutation, peculiar **9** curiosity, deviation **10** aberration **11** abnormality, monstrosity **12** irregularity

freakish 3 odd **5** queer, weird **7** bizarre, strange, unusual **8** peculiar, singular, uncommon **9** eccentric, fantastic **10** outlandish **13** extraordinary

Frederick
character in: 11 As You Like It
author: 11 Shakespeare

Frederick I
nickname: 10 Barbarossa
position: 16 Holy Roman Emperor
dynasty: 12 Hohenstaufen
wife: 7 Beatrix
battle: 7 Legnano

Frederick II
position: 12 king of Sicily **13** king of Germany **16** Holy Roman Emperor
battle: 8 Bouvines

Frederick the Great
nickname: 8 Old Fritz
position: 13 King of Prussia
invaded: 7 Silesia
war: 13 Seven Years' War **18** Austrian Succession

free ***see box***

free-and-easy 6 breezy, casual, jaunty **7** buoyant, relaxed **8** debonair, informal

free 3 big, lax **4** able, bold, easy, idle, idly, open, save **5** clear, extra, let go, loose, rid of, spare **6** daring, devoid, exempt, giving, gratis, lavish, parole, ransom, redeem, unbond, uncage, wanton **7** allowed, assured, forward, liberal, loosely, manumit, release, unchain, unleash **8** at no cost, careless, costless, devoid of, familiar, fearless, generous, handsome, immune to, informal, let loose, liberate, prodigal, released, unfasten **9** abandoned, audacious, available, boundless, bounteous, bountiful, confident, delivered, discharge, disengage, dissolute, expansive, extricate, footloose, lacking in, leisurely, liberated, permitted, unblocked, unbridled, unchained, unclogged, unimpeded, unmuzzled, unshackle **10** autonomous, bighearted, carelessly, chargeless, emancipate, gratuitous, licentious, manumitted, munificent, openhanded, unattached, unconfined, unfettered, unhampered, unoccupied, unreserved, unshackled **11** emancipated, enfranchise, independent, uncluttered, uncommitted, uninhibited, unrepressed **12** enfranchised, overfamiliar, uncontrolled, unencumbered, unobstructed, unrestrained **13** complimentary, unceremonious, unconstrained

12 lighthearted, presumptuous, unrestrained **13** unconstrained

freed 6 exempt, loosed, spared **7** cleared, excused **8** absolved, let loose, released, relieved **11** emancipated

freedom 4 play **5** range, scope, sweep, swing **6** candor, margin **7** abandon, license, release **8** autonomy, boldness, latitude, openness, rudeness **9** bluntness, frankness, impudence, indecorum **10** directness, disrespect, liberation **11** abandonment, forwardness, impropriety, informality, manumission, naturalness, sovereignty, unrestraint **12** emancipation, impertinence, unconstraint **13** downrightness **14** unreservedness **15** enfranchisement

Freedom of the Poet, The
author: 12 John Berryman

free-flowing 7 copious, gushing, profuse **8** effusive

free-for-all 3 row **4** fray **5** brawl, fight, melee, scrap **6** affray, fracas, ruckus, tussle **7** rhubarb, ruction, wrangle **9** brannigan **10** donnybrook

free from bias 7 neutral **9** impartial, unbigoted **12** unprejudiced **13** disinterested

free from moisture 3 dry **4** arid, sere **5** parch **6** dry out **7** parched **8** dried out, rainless **9** dehydrate **10** dehydrated, desertlike, desiccated

free hand 12 carte blanche, open sanction **13** full authority

free rein 12 carte blanche, open sanction **13** full authority

free-spoken 6 chatty **7** voluble **9** talkative **10** loquacious, unreserved **13** communicative

Free State
nickname of: 8 Maryland

Freestone State
nickname of: 11 Connecticut

Free to Choose
author: 14 Milton Friedman (with Rose Friedman)

Freetown
capital of: 11 Sierra Leone

freeze 3 nip **4** bite, cool, halt, stop **5** chill, frost, sting **6** arrest, benumb, harden, pierce **7** ceiling, congeal, terrify **8** glaciate, solidify **11** anesthetize, refrigerate, restriction

freezing 3 icy **6** arctic, frigid **7** glacial

Frege, Gottlieb
field: 11 mathematics
nationality: 6 German
founded: 13 symbolic logic

Freia *see* **5** Freya

freight 4 haul, lade, load, ship **5** cargo, carry, goods **6** burden, charge, convey, lading **7** baggage, cartage, luggage, portage **8** transmit, truckage **9** transport **10** conveyance **13** transshipment

Freischutz, Der
also: 11 The Marksman
opera by: 5 Weber
character: 3 Max **6** Agathe, Caspar, Samiel

Freki
origin: 12 Scandinavian
form: 4 wolf
owner: 4 Odin **5** Othin
received: 4 food
exception: 4 meat
fellow wolf: 4 Geri

French, Daniel Chester
born: 8 Exeter NH
artwork: 7 (seated) Lincoln (at Lincoln Memorial) **21** The Minute Man of Concord

French-American
French: 9 Franglais

French civil code 12 Code Napoleon

French Connection, The
director: 15 William Friedkin
cast: 11 Fernando Rey, Gene Hackman (Popeye Doyle), Roy Scheider
Oscar for: 5 actor (Hackman) **7** editing, picture **8** director **10** screenplay
sequel: 21 The French Connection II

French-English
French: 9 Franglais

French Guinea *see* **6** Guinea

French Indonesia *see* **7** Vietnam

French is spoken here
French: 18 ici on parle francais

French Lieutenant's Woman, The
director: 10 Karel Reisz
author: 10 John Fowles
cast: 9 Leo McKern **11** Hilton McRae, Jeremy Irons, Meryl Streep
script: 12 Harold Pinter

French national anthem 12 Marseillaise

French national theater 16 Comedie Francaise

French parliament
formal sessions: 12 lit de justice

French Somaliland *see* **8** Djibouti

French Sudan, Soudan *see* **4** Mali

French Togoland *see* **4** Togo

frenzied 3 mad **4** wild **7** excited, frantic, furious **8** agitated, ecstatic **9** delirious

frenzy 3 fit **4** fury **5** craze, furor, mania, state **6** access **7** mad rush, madness, seizure, turmoil **8** delirium, hysteria, outburst **9** obsession, transport **11** distraction

Frenzy
director: **15** Alfred Hitchcock
cast: **8** Jon Finch **10** Anna Massey **11** Barry Foster **16** Barbara Leigh-Hunt

frequency **9** iteration **10** recurrence, regularity, repetition **11** persistence, reiteration

frequent **5** daily, haunt, usual **6** common, wonted **7** regular **8** constant, everyday, familiar, habitual, numerous, ordinary, resort to **9** continual, customary, incessant, perpetual, recurrent **10** accustomed **11** reiterative

frequently **5** often **7** usually **8** ofttimes **9** generally **10** constantly, habitually, ordinarily, repeatedly **11** continually, customarily, incessantly, perpetually, recurrently

frere **4** monk **5** friar **7** brother

Frescobaldi, Girolamo
born: **5** Italy **7** Ferrara
composer of: **13** Fiori Musicali **14** Musical Flowers

fresh ***see box***

freshen **4** wash **5** brace, calve, clean, groom, renew **6** air out, breeze, desalt, revive **7** cool off, sweeten **8** renovate, spruce up **9** deodorize

fresh **3** fit, hot, new **4** bold, cool, fair, keen, late, pert, pure, rare, rosy, rude **5** alert, brisk, chill, clear, green, nervy, novel, ready, ruddy, sassy, saucy, stiff, sweet **6** active, biting, brassy, brazen, bright, cheeky, lively, modern, recent, rested, snotty, unique, unused, unworn **7** bracing, cutting, forward, glowing, just out, nipping, strange, uncured, undried, unfaded, untried, unusual **8** assuming, blooming, brand-new, creative, flippant, gleaming, impudent, insolent, original, stinging, unabated, undimmed, unsalted, unsmoked, unwilted, up-to-date **9** energetic, inventive, obtrusive, refreshed, sparkling, undecayed, unpickled, unspoiled, unwearied, wholesome **10** meddlesome, newfangled, refreshing, unfamiliar, unimpaired, unwithered **11** flourishing, invigorated, modernistic, smart-alecky, untarnished **12** presumptuous, unaccustomed

freshet **5** crest, flood **11** overflowing

Freshman, The
director: **9** Sam Taylor **12** Fred Newmeyer
cast: **11** Harold Lloyd **13** Jobyna Ralston **14** Brooks Benedict

Fresnel, Augustin Jean
field: **7** physics
nationality: **6** French
worked in: **6** optics

fret **3** eat, rub, vex **4** fray, fume, gall, gnaw, mope, pine, pout, stew, sulk **5** brood, chafe, erode, sulks, worry **6** abrade, lament, ruffle, tatter **7** agonize, corrode, fidgets **8** disquiet, distress, irritate, vexation, wear away **9** annoyance, excoriate **10** irritation **11** displeasure, peevishness **12** discomposure

fretful **5** cross, huffy, sulky, tense **6** cranky, shirty, touchy **7** grouchy, nervous, peevish, pettish, waspish **8** contrary, petulant, snappish **9** crotchety, irritable, querulous **11** complaining **12** cantankerous

fretfulness **5** worry **6** unease **7** anxiety **10** crankiness **11** peevishness **12** irritability

Freud, Sigmund
lived in: **6** Vienna
collaborator: **6** Breuer
disciple: **4** Jung **5** Adler
daughter: **4** Anna
method: **15** free association **19** dream interpretation
coined: **2** id **8** superego **14** psychoanalysis
author of: **13** Totem and Taboo **22** Interpretation of Dreams **37** Group Psychology and the Analysis of the Ego, Jokes and Their Relation to the Unconscious

Freund, John Lincoln
real name of: **12** John Forsythe

Frey
also: **5** Freyr
origin: **12** Scandinavian
god of: **5** peace **8** marriage **10** prosperity
race: **5** Vanir
father: **5** Niord, Njord
home: **7** Alfheim

Freya
also: **5** Freia
origin: **8** Teutonic
goddess of: **4** love **6** beauty **9** fecundity
race: **5** Vanir
leader of: **9** Valkyries
father: **5** Niord, Njord

Fri *see* **5** Frigg

friable **7** crumbly **9** breakable, frangible

friar
French: **5** frere

Friar Lawrence
character in: **14** Romeo and Juliet
author: **11** Shakespeare

Friar Tuck
character in: **9** Robin Hood

friary **5** abbey **6** priory **8** cloister **9** hermitage, monastery

friction **6** strife **7** chafing, discord, grating, quarrel, rubbing **8** abrasion, bad blood, conflict, fretting **9** animosity, attrition, hostility **10** antagonism, contention, dissension, dissidence, opposition, resentment, resistance **12** disagreement **13** counteraction

Friday
character in: **14** Robinson Crusoe
author: **5** Defoe

Friday
from: **5** Freya, Frigg
heavenly body: **5** Venus
French: **8** vendredi
Italian: **7** venerdi
Spanish: **7** viernes
German: **7** freitag

Friedan, Betty
author of: **19** The Feminine Mystique
co-founder of: **3** NOW **28** National Organization for Women

Friedkin, William
director of: **11** The Exorcist **19** The French Connection (Oscar)

Friedman, Milton
author of: **12** Free to Choose (with Rose Friedman) **20** Capitalism and Freedom

Friedrich, Caspar David
born: **7** Germany **10** Greifswald
artwork: **22** The Cross on the Mountains **26** Man and Woman Gazing at the Moon, The Ruined Monastery of Eldena, Two Men Contemplating the Moon

friend ***see box***

friendliness **5** amity **8** bonhomie, good will **9** geniality **10** affability, amiability, cordiality, fraternity **11** amicability, camaraderie, sociability **14** neighborliness **16** companionability

friend **3** pal **4** ally, beau, chum, date, mate **5** amigo, buddy, crony, lover **6** backer, cohort, escort, fellow, intime, minion, patron **7** brother, comrade, consort, partner **8** adherent, advocate, confrere, coworker, defender, favorite, follower, henchman, intimate, mistress, myrmidon, paramour, partisan, playmate, retainer, sidekick, soul mate **9** associate, bedfellow, colleague, companion, confidant, copartner, supporter **10** benefactor, encourager, playfellow, well-wisher **12** acquaintance
French: **3** ami **4** amie **9** bonne amie
Spanish: **5** amiga, amigo

friendly **4** kind **6** allied, ardent, benign, chummy, clubby, genial, kindly, loving, social **7** affable, amiable, cordial, devoted, helpful **8** amicable, familiar, generous, gracious, intimate, salutary **9** brotherly, convivial, favorable, fortunate, fraternal, opportune **10** accessible, auspicious, beneficial, hospitable, neighborly, not hostile, propitious **11** kindhearted, sympathetic, warmhearted **12** advantageous, affectionate **13** companionable

Friendly Fire
author: **8** C D B Bryan

Friendly Islands *see* **5** Tongo

Friendly Persuasion
director: **12** William Wyler
author: **12** Jessamyn West
cast: **10** Gary Cooper **11** Richard Eyer **12** Marjorie Main **14** Anthony Perkins, Dorothy McGuire
score: **14** Dimitri Tiomkin

friendly understanding
French: **15** entente cordiale

friend of the court
Latin: **12** amicus curiae

friendship **5** amity **6** accord, comity **7** concord, harmony **8** close tie, goodwill, intimacy, sympathy **10** consonance, cordiality, fellowship, fraternity **11** brotherhood, comradeship, familiarity **12** amicableness **13** companionship, understanding **14** neighborliness **16** acquaintanceship

Friesen, Samille Diane
real name of: **10** Dyan Cannon

Frigg
also: **3** Fri **5** Frija **6** Frigga
origin: **8** Teutonic
goddess of: **3** sky **6** clouds **8** marriage
husband: **4** Odin **5** Othin
race: **4** Asar **5** Aesir

Frigga *see* **5** Frigg

fright **4** fear, funk **5** alarm, dread, panic, scare **6** dismay, horror, terror, tremor **7** anxiety, concern, flutter, quaking **8** cold feet **9** misgiving, quivering, the creeps **10** the jitters, the willies **11** disquietude, palpitation, trepidation **12** apprehension, intimidation, perturbation **13** consternation

frighten **5** alarm, daunt, scare, shock **6** affray, excite **7** agitate, horrify, petrify, startle, terrify **8** disquiet **9** terrorize **10** intimidate

frightened **6** afraid, scared **7** alarmed, panicky **9** horrified, petrified, terrified **10** terrorized

frightening **5** awful, dread **7** fearful **8** alarming, dreadful **10** horrifying, terrifying **11** hair-raising

frightful **5** awful, lurid, nasty **6** grisly, horrid **7** baleful, extreme, fearful, ghastly, hideous, macabre, ogreish **8** alarming, dreadful, fearsome, freakish, gruesome, horrible, horrific, shocking, sinister, terrible, terrific **9** appalling, loathsome, monstrous, offensive, repellent, repulsive, revolting **10** abominable, detestable, disgusting, horrendous **12** insufferable

frigid **3** icy, raw **4** cold, cool, prim **5** aloof, bleak, gelid, stiff **6** biting, bitter, chilly, formal, frosty **7** austere, cutting, distant, glacial, nipping **8** freezing, piercing **10** forbidding **11** straitlaced **12** unresponsive

frigidity **7** iciness **8** coldness **9** aloofness **10** frostiness **16** unresponsiveness

Frija *see* **5** Frigg

frill **3** air **6** edging, fringe, ruffle **7** flounce **8** falderal, frippery, furbelow, ornament **9** gathering, mannerism **10** decoration **11** affectation, superfluity **13** embellishment

fringe **3** hem, rim **4** edge, mane **5** limit, skirt **6** border, edging, margin, tassel **7** enclose, outline, selvage **8** decorate, frontier, skirting, surround, trimming **9** embellish, periphery

frisk **3** hop **4** jump, lark, leap, romp, skip, trip **5** bound, caper, cut up, dance, sport **6** bounce, cavort, frolic, gambol, prance, search, spring **7** disport, examine, inspect, ransack **8** look over

frisky **4** spry **5** agile, peppy **6** active, lively, nimble **7** jocular, playful, waggish **8** animated, mirthful, prankish, spirited, sportive **9** vivacious **10** frolicsome, rollicking

fritter **4** blow **5** use up, waste **7** deplete **8** fool away, idle away, squander **9** dissipate

fritter away **4** blow **5** waste **6** misuse **8** misspend, squander **9** dissipate

fritter away time **4** idle **6** dawdle **10** dillydally

Fritzi Ritz
also named: **5** Nancy
creator: **15** Ernie Bushmiller **16** Larry Whittington
character: **4** Phil **5** Nancy **6** Sluggo

frivolity **3** fun **4** jest, play **5** folly, sport **6** levity, whimsy **7** abandon **8** airiness, dallying, frippery **9** emptiness, flippancy, giddiness, lightness **10** fickleness, triviality, wantonness **11** flightiness **15** thoughtlessness

frivolous **4** airy, vain **5** barmy, dizzy, empty, inane, light, minor, petty, silly **6** flimsy, frothy, paltry, slight, stupid **7** fatuous, flighty, foolish, trivial, witless **8** careless, flippant, heedless, niggling, piddling, trifling **9** brainless, imprudent, pointless, senseless, unserious, worthless **10** insouciant **11** extravagant, harebrained, impractical, improvident, nonsensical, superficial, unimportant **13** insignificant, rattlebrained **14** shallowbrained

frizzle **4** curl **5** crimp

frock **4** coat, gown, robe, suit **5** cloak, dress, smock **6** blouse **7** cassock, soutane **8** chasuble, surplice, vestment **9** clericals **10** canonicals

frog **3** pad, pod **4** knot, wood **5** frosh, hitch, track **6** holder, peeper, toggle **7** crawler, croaker, cushion, leopard, tadpole **8** bullfrog, fastener, pickerel, pollywog **9** amphibian, plow frame **12** flower holder

Frogs, The
author: **12** Aristophanes

character: **5** Pluto **6** Charon **7** Bacchus **8** Dionysus, Hercules, Xanthias **9** Aeschylus, Euripides

Froissart, Jean
author of: **8** Meliador **10** Chronicles

frolic **3** fun **4** lark, play, romp, skip **5** act up, antic, caper, frisk, mirth, prank, sport, spree **6** cavort, gaiety, gambol **7** disport, jollity, make hay **8** escapade **9** amusement, festivity, joviality, merriment **10** buffoonery, pleasantry, recreation, skylarking, tomfoolery **11** merrymaking **13** entertainment

frolicsome **5** antic, jolly, merry **6** cheery, jaunty, lively **7** playful **8** cheerful, mirthful, prankish **9** sprightly **12** lighthearted

Frollo, Claude
character in: **23** The Hunchback of Notre Dame
author: **4** Hugo

from **2** de, ex, of **3** for, fro **5** off of, out of **7** against **8** starting **9** beginning

from abroad **5** alien **6** exotic **7** foreign **8** imported

fromage **6** cheese

from behind
Latin: **6** a tergo

From Here to Eternity
director: **13** Fred Zinnemann
author: **10** James Jones
cast: **9** Donna Reed **11** Deborah Kerr **12** Frank Sinatra, George Reeves **13** Burt Lancaster **14** Ernest Borgnine **15** Montgomery Clift
setting: **11** Pearl Harbor
Oscar for: **7** picture **8** director **12** screenwriter **15** supporting actor (Sinatra) **17** supporting actress (Reed)

from inside
Latin: **7** ab intra

from outside
Latin: **7** ab extra

From Russia With Love
author: **10** Ian Fleming

from scratch **4** anew **14** from ground zero **16** from the beginning **20** from fresh ingredients

from side to side **4** over, sway **5** cross **7** athwart, swaying, zigzag **12** back and forth

from the beginning
Latin: **5** ab ovo **6** de novo **8** ab initio

from the chair
Latin: **10** ex cathedra

from the depths
Latin: **11** de profundis

from the face
Latin: **7** ex facie

from the fact
Latin: **7** de facto

from the founding of the city
Latin: **13** ab urbe condita

from the library of
Latin: **8** ex libris

from the seat of authority
Latin: **10** ex cathedra

front **3** air, top **4** face, fore, head, lead, mask, mien **5** first **6** facade, give on, regard **7** bearing, initial, look out **8** anterior, carriage, demeanor, presence, pretense, trenches, vanguard **9** beginning, semblance

Front, The
director: **10** Martin Ritt
cast: **10** Lloyd Gough, Woody Allen, Zero Mostel **13** Joshua Shelley, Michael Murphy **16** Herschel Bernardi

frontage **7** outlook **8** exposure, prospect

frontier **4** edge **5** march, verge **6** border, limits **7** extreme, marches **8** boundary, confines, outposts **9** backlands, backwoods, outskirts, perimeter **10** hinterland **11** territories

front matter **8** foreword **9** title page **12** introduction **15** table of contents **20** introductory material

Front Page, The
author: **8** Ben Hecht **16** Charles MacArthur
director: **11** Billy Wilder **14** Lewis Milestone
actor: **9** Mae Clarke, Mary Brian, Pat O'Brien **10** Jack Lemmon, David Wayne **12** George E Stone, Carol Burnett **13** Adolphe Menjou, Allen Garfield, Susan Sarandon, Walter Catlett, Walter Matthau **14** Charles Durning **15** Andrew Pendleton, Vincent Gardenia **19** Edward Everett Horton
character: **4** Earl **5** Burns, Grant, Hildy, Peggy **6** Walter **7** Hartman, Johnson **8** Williams

frost **4** rime **5** chill **7** iciness **8** coolness, distance **9** aloofness, cold spell, frigidity **10** chilliness, glaciality **13** inhospitality **14** unfriendliness

Frost, Robert
author of: **7** Birches **10** Fire and Ice, Home Burial **11** Mending Wall **13** Brown's Descent **15** The Road Not Taken **17** After Apple-Picking **21** The Death of the Hired Man **30** Stopping by Woods on a Snowy Evening

frostiness **3** nip **4** bite **5** chill **7** iciness **8** coldness, coolness **9** crispness, frigidity, hoariness, sharpness **10** chilliness, wintriness

frosting **3** mat **4** trim **5** glass, icing **7** cooling, topping **8** chilling, divinity, freezing, trimming **13** embellishment, ornamentation

frosty **3** icy **4** cold, cool **5** bleak, chill, hoary **6** frigid, wintry **8** freezing

froth **4** bosh, fizz, foam, fume, head, scum, suds, surf **5** spume, trash, yeast **6** lather, trivia **7** bubbles, rubbish **8** flummery, frippery, nonsense, trumpery, whitecap **9** frivolity **10** balderdash, triviality **12** fiddle-faddle

frothy **5** fizzy, foamy, light **6** bubbly **7** trivial **9** frivolous **15** inconsequential

froward **5** balky **6** unruly **7** wayward, willful **8** contrary, perverse, stubborn **9** difficult, fractious, obstinate **10** headstrong, refractory **11** disagreeing, intractable **12** recalcitrant **13** contradictory **15** unaccommodating

frown **4** fret, mope, muse, pout, sulk **5** glare, scowl **6** glower, ponder **14** discountenance

frowning **4** dark **5** angry **6** gloomy, somber, sullen **8** scowling **9** glowering

frown upon **7** condemn, dislike **8** object to **14** discountenance

frowsy, frowzy **5** fusty, musty, stale **6** sloppy, untidy **7** tousled, unkempt **8** slovenly

frozen **3** icy **4** cold, iced, numb **5** chill, gelid, polar **6** arctic, chilly, cooled, wintry **7** chilled, clogged, glacial, stymied **8** benumbed, hibernal, icebound **10** obstructed, stalemated **11** frostbitten, immobilized **12** refrigerated

fructify **5** bloom **6** sprout, thrive **7** blossom, prosper, succeed **8** flourish

frugal **4** slim **5** scant, tight **6** skimpy, stingy **7** ascetic, sparing, thrifty **9** niggardly, penny-wise **10** abstemious, economical, unwasteful **12** parsimonious

frugality **6** thrift **7** economy **8** prudence, stinting **9** parsimony **10** scantiness, stinginess **11** thriftiness **12** cheeseparing **13** niggardliness, penny-pinching **16** parsimoniousness

fruit **4** crop **5** award, issue, yield, young **6** effect, profit, result, return, reward, upshot **7** benefit, harvest, outcome, produce, product, progeny, revenue **8** earnings **9** advantage, emolument, offspring, outgrowth **10** production **11** consequence **12** remuneration

fruitful **6** fecund **7** fertile **8** blooming, prolific, yielding **9** effective **10** productive, profitable, successful **11** efficacious **12** advantageous, fructiferous

fruition **8** maturity, ripeness **10** attainment **11** achievement, fulfillment, realization **12** consummation, satisfaction **13** actualization, gratification **15** materialization

fruitless **4** arid, vain **5** empty, inept **6** barren, futile, hollow **7** sterile, useless **8** abortive, bootless, nugatory **9** infertile, pointless, worthless **10** profitless, unavailing, unprolific **11** incompetent, ineffective, ineffectual, inoperative, purposeless, unrewarding **12** unproductive, unprofitable, unsuccessful **13** inefficacious

fruit trees
goddess of: **6** Pomona

frumpy **4** drab **5** dowdy **8** slovenly **10** slatternly **12** unattractive

frustrate **3** bar **4** balk, foil **5** block, check, upset **6** baffle, cancel, defeat, hinder, impede, thwart **7** counter, cripple, fluster, inhibit, nullify, prevent **8** dispirit, obstruct, prohibit, suppress **9** forestall, hamstring, undermine **10** circumvent, disappoint, disconcert, discourage, dishearten

frustration **6** defeat **7** balking, chagrin, failure, foiling, letdown **8** futility **9** hindrance, thwarting **10** bafflement, inhibition, nonsuccess **11** obstruction **12** discomfiture, interference **13** contravention, counteraction **14** disappointment, nonfulfillment **15** dissatisfaction

fry **4** cook **5** brown, grill, saute **7** frizzle **9** fricassee

Fry, Christopher
author of: **9** Yard of Sun **12** The Firstborn **13** Venus Observed **20** The Dark Is Light Enough **21** The Lady's Not for Burning

frying pan **3** wok **6** frypan **7** browner, griddle, skillet

fuchsia
varieties: **4** cape, tree **5** hardy **10** California **11** honeysuckle

fuddled **5** bosky, dopey, drunk, tipsy **6** boozed, groggy **7** maudlin, muddled, sozzled, tippled **8** confused **9** stupefied **10** inebriated **11** intoxicated

fudge **3** lie **4** bosh, fake **5** candy, cheat, evade, hedge, hunch, patch, welch **7** falsify, penuche **8** divinity

fuel **3** fan, gas, oil **4** coal, feed, fire, wood **5** light, means, stoke **6** charge, fill up, fodder, ignite, incite, kindle **7** impetus, inflame, sustain **8** activate, energize, gasoline, material, recharge, stimulus **9** petroleum, stimulate **10** ammunition, motivation, sustenance **11** inspiration, wherewithal

fugitive **4** hobo **5** brief, exile, hasty, nomad, rover, short, tramp **6** errant, fading, flying, loafer, outlaw **7** cursory, elusive, erratic, escaped, escapee, fleeing, hurried, passing, refugee, runaway, summary, vagrant **8** apostate, deserter, escaping, fleeting, flitting, renegade, shifting, unstable, vagabond, volatile, wanderer **9** ephemeral, fugacious, itinerant, momentary, straggler, temporary, transient, uncertain **10** evanescent, expatriate, short-lived, transitory **11** impermanent

Fugitive, The
character: **9** Donna Taft **11** Fred Johnson (one-armed man) **12** (Lt) Philip Gerard **13** (Dr) Richard Kimble
cast: **10** Barry Morse, Bill Raisch **12** David Janssen **15** Jacqueline Scott

fuhrer, Fuhrer, der fuhrer **4** Nazi **6** Hitler, leader, tyrant **8** dictator **11** Adolf Hitler

fulfill **2** do **4** heed, keep, meet, obey, suit **6** answer, effect, follow, redeem **7** achieve, execute, observe, perfect, perform, realize, satisfy **9** discharge, establish, implement **10** accomplish, consummate, effectuate

fulfillment, fulfilment **7** delight **8** crowning, pinnacle, pleasure **9** execution, happiness **10** attainment, completion **11** achievement, contentment, culmination, realization **12** effectuation, satisfaction **13** contentedness, establishment, gratification **14** accomplishment, implementation

Fulks, Sarah Jane
real name of: **9** Jane Wyman

full **3** big **4** rich, very, wide **5** ample, broad, flush, laden, large, plump, quite, round, sated, total, whole **6** entire, gorged, intact, loaded, mature, packed, rotund **7** brimful, crammed, exactly, fraught, glutted, heaping, maximum, perfect, plenary, replete, shapely, stuffed, teeming **8** brimming, bursting, complete, resonant, swarming, thorough **9** abounding, capacious, perfectly, precisely, saturated, surfeited **10** unabridged, voluminous

full amount **3** all, sum **5** total, whole **8** entirety, totality **9** aggregate **10** complement

full-bodied **3** fat **4** rich **5** ample, lofty **6** hearty, mature, robust **9** flavorful **10** meaningful

Fuller, R Buckminster
architect of: **10** US Pavilion (Expo '67 Montreal) **13** Dymaxion House
form: **12** geodesic dome

full-fledged **5** adept **6** expert, mature **7** skilled, trained **8** complete, masterly, schooled **9** qualified, topflight **10** proficient **11** experienced **13** authoritative

full form **9** extension **10** elongation **11** enlargement **12** augmentation **13** amplification

full-grown **4** ripe **5** adult, manly, of age, matured, womanly **9** developed

full measure **6** enough, plenty **9** abundance, plenitude **10** competence **11** sufficiency

Full Moon
author: **11** P G Wodehouse

fullness **7** satiety **8** richness **9** amplitude, roundness, satiation **12** completeness **14** voluminousness

full of fire **7** rousing **8** electric, exciting, spirited **9** thrilling **11** galvanizing, stimulating **12** electrifying, soul-stirring

full of life **5** vital **8** animated, spirited, vigorous **9** ebullient, energetic, exuberant, vivacious

full of pep **5** vital **6** lively **8** animated

full of vim and vigor **5** peppy **6** lively **11** invigorated

full view **7** the open **8** daylight, openness

fully **5** amply, quite **6** richly, wholly **7** totally, utterly **8** entirely **9** copiously, perfectly **10** abundantly, altogether, completely, positively, throughout **11** plentifully **12** sufficiently **13** substantially

fully realized **7** perfect **8** achieved, complete, executed, finished **9** completed, perfected, performed **11** consummated **12** accomplished

fulminate **4** boil, rage, rant **7** explode **8** denounce

fulminate against **5** roast **6** berate **7** scourge **8** call down, chastise **9** castigate

fulmination **7** violent **8** bursting, eruption **9** discharge, explosion

fulsome **3** fat **4** foul **5** suave **6** lavish, odious **7** cloying, lustful, noisome, obscene **8** overdone, unctuous **9** excessive, obnoxious, offensive, repulsive, tasteless **10** disgusting, obsequious

Fulton, Robert
nationality: **8** American
inventor of: **9** steamboat (Clermont), submarine **13** marine torpedo

fumble **3** err, mar **4** blow, muff **5** grope, spoil **6** bobble, boggle, bollix, bungle, goof up, mess up, muddle **7** butcher, louse up, screw up **9** mishandle

fume **3** gas **4** boil, burn, emit, foam, haze, puff, rage, rant, rave, reek, waft **5** exude, scent, smell, smoke, stink, vapor **6** billow, exhale, miasma, seethe, stench **7** carry on, explode, flame up, flare up, smolder **10** exhalation

fun **3** gas **4** ball, game, jest, lark, play, romp, trip **5** antic, blast, cheer, mirth, prank, sport, spree **6** frolic, gaiety, joking **7** jollity, revelry, whoopee **8** escapade, good time, pleasure **9** amusement, diversion, enjoyment, horseplay, joviality, merriment **10** buffoonery, recreation, relaxation, skylarking, tomfoolery **11** distraction, playfulness, waggishness **13** entertainment

Funafuti
capital of: **6** Tuvalu

function **3** act, job **4** duty, fete, gala, help, role, task, work **5** feast, field, niche, party, place, power, range, scope, serve **6** affair, behave, do duty, office, soiree, sphere **7** banquet, benefit, concern, faculty, operate, perform, purpose **8** activity, business, capacity, ceremony, occasion, province **9** festivity, objective, operation, reception **13** entertainment

functional **6** useful **7** working **8** operable **9** operative, practical **11** serviceable, utilitarian

functionary **8** employee, official **10** bureaucrat **13** administrator

functioning **5** in use **6** active, at work, usable **7** working **9** effectual, operating, operative

fund **3** pot **4** bank, foot, lode, mine, pool, vein, well **5** endow, float, fount, hoard, kitty, stock, store **6** pay for, spring, supply **7** finance, nest egg, reserve, savings, support **8** treasure **9** endowment, patronize, reservoir **10** foundation, investment, repository, storehouse, underwrite **12** accumulation

fundament **3** can **4** buns, rump, seat **5** fanny **6** behind, bottom **8** backside, buttocks, haunches **9** posterior **12** hindquarters

fundamental **3** key **4** ABC's, base, main **5** axiom, basic, basis, chief, first, major, vital **7** central, crucial, element, primary **8** cardinal, integral **9** component, essential, necessary, principal, principle, requisite **10** elementary, foundation, groundwork, underlying **11** cornerstone **13** indispensable

funds **4** cash, jack, pelf **5** bread, dough, lucre, means, money, moola **6** assets, income, wampum, wealth **7** capital, scratch **8** finances, property **9** resources **11** wherewithal

funeral **4** wake **5** rites **6** burial **7** requiem **9** cremation, interment, obsequies **10** entombment, inhumation

funeral song **5** dirge, elegy **6** lament **7** requiem **8** threnody **11** lamentation

funereal **3** sad **4** grim **5** weepy **6** dismal, dreary, gloomy, solemn, somber, woeful **7** doleful **8** desolate, dirgeful, grieving, mournful **9** cheerless, woebegone **10** depressing, lachrymose, lugubrious **13** brokenhearted

fun-filled **5** happy **6** joyful, joyous **8** pleasant, pleasing **9** enjoyable **10** delightful **11** pleasurable

Fungoso
character in: **22** Every Man Out of His Humour
author: **6** Jonson

fungus, fungi **4** mold, myco, rust, smut **5** ergot, yeast **6** mildew **7** truffle **8** mushroom **9** toadstool **11** thallophyte

fun-loving **5** jolly, merry **6** genial, jovial **7** affable **8** sociable **9** convivial **10** gregarious

funnel **4** cone, duct, flue, pipe, pour **5** focus, shaft **6** direct, filter, siphon **7** channel, chimney, conduit **9** stovepipe **10** smokestack, ventilator **11** concentrate

funny **3** odd **5** antic, comic, droll, merry, queer, weird, witty **6** absurd, jocose **7** amusing, bizarre, comical, curious, jesting, jocular, offbeat, strange, unusual, waggish **8** farcical, humorous, mirthful, peculiar, sporting, uncommon **9** diverting, facetious, hilarious, laughable, ludicrous **10** outlandish, ridiculous

Funny Girl
director: **12** William Wyler
cast: **8** Lee Allen **10** Kay Medford, Omar Sharif **11** Anne Francis **13** Walter Pidgeon **15** Barbra Streisand (Fanny Brice)
score: **9** Jule Styne **10** Bob Merrill
sequel: **9** Funny Lady
song: **6** People **18** Don't Rain on My Parade

funnyman **3** wag, wit **4** card, fool, mime, zany **5** clown, comic, joker **6** jester, madcap **7** buffoon **8** comedian, humorist, jokester **9** harlequin

fuoco, con
music: **8** with fire

fur **3** fox **4** down, hair, lamb, mink, pelt, seal **5** coney, lapin, otter, sable **6** beaver, fleece, jaguar, kit fox, nutria, rabbit, red fox **7** blue fox, cheetah, leopard, muskrat, opossum, raccoon **8** black fox, cross fox, squirrel, white fox **9** silver fox **10** animal skin, chinchilla **11** karakul lamb, Persian lamb **13** broadtail lamb **14** mouton-dyed lamb

furbelow 5 frill **6** fringe **7** falbala, flounce **8** trimming

furbish 4 buff **5** renew, shine **6** polish **7** burnish **8** renovate

Furiae *see* **6** Furies

Furies
also: 5 Dirae **6** Erinys, Furiae, Semnai **7** Allecto, Erinyes, Megaera **9** Eumenides, Tisiphone
corresponds to: 3 Ker

furious 3 mad **4** wild **5** angry, fiery, irate, rabid **6** enrage, fierce, fuming, raging, savage, stormy **7** intense, rampant, violent **8** frenetic, frenzied, heedless, maddened, provoked, reckless, up in arms, vehement, wrathful **9** fanatical, irascible, turbulent **10** infuriated, passionate, tumultuous, unbalanced **11** tempestuous **12** ungovernable, unrestrained

furl 4 coil, curl, fold, roll, wrap **5** truss **6** curl up, fold up, furdle, roll up, spiral

furlong
abbreviation: 3 fur

furnace 4 kiln, oven **5** forge, stove **6** boiler, heater **11** incinerator

Furnace
constellation of: 6 Fornax

furnish 3 arm, rig **4** gird, give, vest **5** array, dress, endow, equip, favor, fit up, grant, stock **6** fit out, outfit, purvey, render, supply **7** appoint, indulge, prepare, provide **8** accoutre, bestow on **9** provision **11** accommodate

furnishings 9 equipment **11** accessories **12** haberdashery

furnish room for 5 lodge, put up **6** billet **7** shelter **11** accommodate

furniture 7 effects **8** chattels, movables, property **11** possessions **12** appointments

furor 3 fad **4** flap, rage, to-do, word **5** craze, mania, noise, thing, vogue **6** fervor, frenzy, hoopla, lunacy, raving, uproar **7** fashion, madness, passion **8** brouhaha, insanity, reaction **9** agitation, commotion, obsession, transport **10** dernier cri, enthusiasm, excitement, fanaticism

furrow 3 cut, dig, rut **4** knit, line, plow, rift, seam **5** cleft, crack, ditch, ridge, track **6** crease, groove, pucker, trench, trough **7** channel, crevice, fissure, wrinkle **10** depression **11** corrugation

furry 4 soft **5** downy, hairy, scary **6** cuddly, fleecy, pelted, shaggy **8** fearsome, horrible **11** hair-raising

further 3 aid, new, too, yet **4** also, back, help, more **5** again, extra, favor, fresh, other, spare, speed **6** abroad, assist, back up, beyond, foster, hasten, oblige, to boot, yonder **7** advance, afar off, besides, farther, forward, promote, quicken, stand by, work for **8** champion, expedite, likewise, moreover **9** accessory, ancillary, auxiliary, encourage, propagate **10** accelerate, additional, strengthen **11** accommodate **12** additionally, contributory, supplemental **13** supplementary

furtherance 3 aid **4** help, lift **5** favor **6** succor **7** advance, defense, support **8** advocacy, interest **9** patronage, promotion **10** assistance **11** advancement, cooperation, countenance **12** championship

furthering 3 aid **6** aiding, growth **8** abetting, advocacy, espousal **9** assisting, fostering, promoting, promotion **10** assistance, supporting **11** advancement, encouraging, propagating, propagation **12** accelerating, acceleration, encouragement **13** strengthening

furthermore 3 too **4** also **6** as well, to boot **7** besides **8** likewise, moreover **10** in addition **12** additionally

furthermost 7 extreme **8** farthest **11** farthermost

furtive 3 sly **4** wily **5** shady **6** covert, crafty, hidden, masked, secret, shifty, sneaky, unseen, veiled **7** cloaked, elusive, evasive, private **8** secluded, shrouded, skulking, sneaking, stealthy **9** collusive, secretive, underhand **10** mysterious, undercover, unrevealed **11** clandestine **12** confidential **13** surreptitious **14** conspiratorial

fury 3 fit, hag, ire, pet **4** gall, huff, rage, snit **5** force, might, shrew, vixen, wrath **6** attack, choler, frenzy, spleen, virago **7** assault, bluster, dudgeon, hellcat, tantrum **8** acerbity, acrimony, ferocity, outburst, severity, she-devil, spitfire, violence **9** intensity, termagant, vehemence, virulence **10** excitement, fierceness, turbulence **11** impetuosity

Fury
form: 8 divinity
sex: 6 female
mother: 4 Gaea
father: 6 Uranus
born of the blood of: 6 Uranus
Greek name: 6 Erinys **7** Erinyes **9** Eumenides
Roman name: 5 Dirae **6** Furiae

fuse 4 join, link, meld, melt, weld, wick **5** blend, merge, smelt, torch **6** league, mingle, solder **7** combine **8** coalesce, federate, ignition, solidify **9** associate, detonator **10** amalgamate, assimilate **11** confederate, consolidate, incorporate, intermingler

fusillade 4 hail, rain **5** salvo, spray **6** volley **7** barrage, battery **8** drumfire, enfilade **9** broadside, cannonade **11** bombardment

fusion 5 blend, union **6** league **7** combine, melding, melting, merging **8** alliance, blending, compound, smelting **9** coalition, synthesis **10** commixture, dissolving, federation **11** association, coalescence, combination, commingling, confederacy, unification **12** amalgamation, intermixture, liquefaction **13** agglomeration, confederation

fuss 3 ado, nag **4** carp, fool, fret, fume, pomp, spat, stew, stir, tiff, to-do **5** annoy, cavil, labor, set-to, worry **6** bother, bustle, excite, fidget, flurry, hubbub, hustle, niggle, pester, pother, potter, putter, rattle, scurry, tinker **7** agitate, confuse, dispute, fluster, flutter, nitpick, quarrel, quibble, perturb, trouble, turmoil **8** ceremony **9** agitation, commotion, confusion **10** disconcert, hurly-burly, turbulence **11** disturbance, superfluity **12** perturbation **15** ceremoniousness
Yiddish: 7 tzimmes

fuss over **6** dote on

fussy **4** busy **6** ornate **7** finical, finicky, nervous **8** bustling, critical, exacting **9** assiduous, cluttered, crotchety, demanding, squeamish **10** compulsive, fastidious, meticulous, nitpicking, old-maidish, particular, scrupulous **11** painstaking, persnickety

fusty **5** moldy, musty, stale **6** foisty, rancid, stuffy **8** obsolete **9** out of date **10** malodorous **12** old fashioned

Futabatei, Shimei
author of: **16** The Drifting (Floating) Cloud

futile **4** idle, vain **5** empty, petty **7** trivial, useless **8** abortive, bootless, nugatory, trifling **9** frivolous, fruitless, valueless, worthless **10** profitless, unavailing **11** ineffective, ineffectual, unimportant **12** unprofitable, unsuccessful **13** insignificant

future **4** hope **5** after, later **6** coming, latter, morrow, offing, to come **7** by-and-by, ensuing, outlook **8** eventual, prospect, tomorrow, ultimate **9** following, hereafter, impending, projected **10** in prospect, subsequent, succeeding **11** anticipated, expectation, opportunity, prospective **12** anticipation
Spanish: **6** manana

Future Shock
author: **12** Alvin Toffler

fuzz **4** down, lint **5** fluff

fuzzy **3** dim **4** hazy **5** downy, foggy, linty, misty, murky, vague, wooly **6** fluffy, frizzy, woolly **7** blurred, obscure, shadowy, unclear **8** confused **9** pubescent **10** indefinite, indistinct

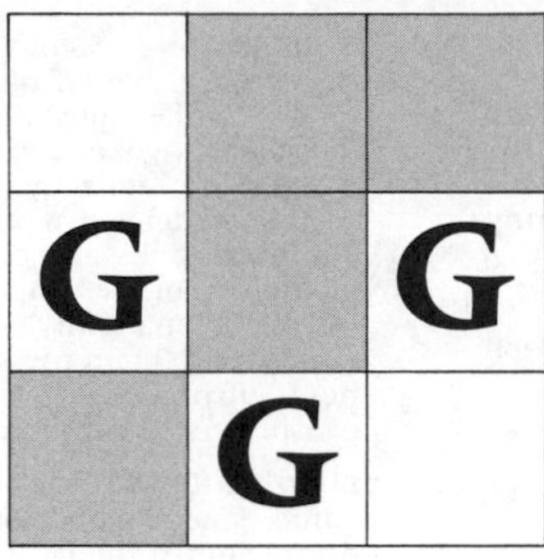

gab **3** jaw, rap **4** blab, chat **5** prate **6** babble, gibber, gossip, jabber, patter **7** baloney, blarney, blather, chatter, prattle **8** chitchat, idle talk, talk idly **10** balderdash **12** conversation

gabble **3** rap **4** blab **5** prate **6** babble, drivel, gossip, jabber **7** blather, chatter, prattle, twaddle **8** babbling, chitchat, idle talk **9** gibbering, jabbering **10** blathering, chattering **14** chitterchatter

gabfest **3** rap **4** chat, talk **7** palaver **8** chitchat **10** discussion **12** conversation **13** confabulation

gable **4** edge, peak, roof, wall **6** detail, dormer, pinion **7** aileron **8** pediment, triangle

Gable, Clark
- **real name:** **17** William Clark Gable
- **wife:** **13** Carole Lombard
- **nickname:** **7** The King
- **born:** **7** Cadiz OH
- **roles:** **7** Red Dust **8** Saratoga **10** The Misfits **11** Rhett Butler **15** Gone With the Wind **18** It Happened One Night (Oscar)

Gabo, Naum
- **real name:** **17** Naum Neemia Pevsner
- **born:** **6** Russia **7** Brainsk
- **founder:** **14** Constructivism
- **artwork:** **6** Column **11** Spiral Theme **16** Sculptural Models **19** Kinetic Construction **24** Variations of Spheric Theme

Gabon Republic *see box*

Gabor, Eva
- **mother:** **5** Jolie
- **sister:** **5** Magda **6** Zsa Zsa
- **born:** **7** Hungary **8** Budapest
- **roles:** **4** Gigi **10** Green Acres **12** My Man Godfrey **13** A Royal Scandal, Forced Landing **15** Youngblood Hawke **18** The Truth About Women **20** The Last Time I Saw Paris

Gabor, Sari
- **real name of:** **11** Zsa Zsa Gabor

Gabor, Zsa Zsa
- **real name:** **9** Sari Gabor
- **mother:** **5** Jolie
- **sister:** **3** Eva **5** Magda
- **husband:** **10** Nick Hilton **13** George Sanders
- **born:** **7** Hungary **8** Budapest
- **roles:** **4** Lili **11** Moulin Rouge **14** Lovely To Look At **20** The Story of Three Loves

Gaboriau, Emile
- **author of:** **9** File No 113

Gaborone, Gaberones
- **capital of:** **8** Botswana

Gabriel **9** archangel
- **means:** **8** man of God **11** God is strong
- **spoke to:** **4** Mary **9** Zacharias, Zechariah

Gad
- **father:** **5** Jacob
- **mother:** **6** Zilpah
- **brother:** **3** Dan **4** Levi **5** Asher, Judah **6** Joseph, Reuben, Simeon **7** Zebulun **8** Benjamin, Issachar, Naphtali
- **sister:** **5** Dinah
- **descendant of:** **6** Gadite

gadget **4** tool **6** device, doodad, jigger **7** gimmick, novelty **9** accessory, doohickey **10** attachment **11** contraption, contrivance, thingamabob, thingamajig

Gaea
- **also:** **2** Ge **4** Gaia
- **origin:** **5** Greek
- **goddess of:** **5** earth
- **husband:** **6** Uranus
- **children:** **6** Pontus, Titans, Uranus **7** Cyclops, Erinyes **9** mountains **13** Hecatonchires
- **son:** **6** Nereus **7** Iapetus, Oceanus
- **daughter:** **4** Rhea **5** Theia **6** Phoebe, Tethys, Themis **9** Mnemosyne
- **corresponds to:** **6** Tellus

Gabon Republic
- **capital/largest city:** **10** Libreville
- **others:** **4** Oyem **5** Bongo, Kango **6** Mitzic, Moanda, Mouila, Omvane **7** Makokou, Mounana **9** Lambarene **10** Port-Gentil **11** Franceville
- **monetary unit:** **5** franc **7** centime
- **lake:** **7** Anengue, Azinguo
- **mountain:** **5** Mpele **7** Chaillu, Cristal, Mikongo **8** Balaquri, Birougou
- **highest point:** **8** Iboundji
- **river:** **4** Como **6** Abanga, Ivindo, Ogooue **7** Ngounie
- **sea:** **8** Atlantic
- **physical feature:**
  - ***cape:*** **5** Lopez
- **people:** **4** Fang **6** Adouma, Bakota, Bateke, Echira, Okande, Omyene **7** Eshiras **8** Bandjabi, Bapounou
  - ***leader:*** **3** Mba **5** Bongo
  - ***philanthropist:*** **16** Albert Schweitzer
- **language:** **6** French
- **religion:** **5** Islam **7** animism **10** Protestant **13** Roman Catholic
- **feature:**
  - ***tree:*** **6** okoume
- **food:** **6** manioc **9** Dika bread

Gaelic
language family: **12** Indo-European
branch: **6** Celtic
subgroup: **4** Manx **5** Irish **8** Scottish

gaffe **4** goof **5** boner **6** boo-boo **7** blunder **11** impropriety **12** indiscretion
French: **7** faux pas **9** gaucherie

gag **4** hoax, hush, jest, joke, stop **5** block, choke, heave, retch **6** muffle, muzzle, stifle **7** cloture, foolery, silence, smother **8** stoppage, suppress **9** horseplay, restraint **13** facetiousness

Gaia *see* **4** Gaea

gaiety, gayety **3** fun **4** show **5** mirth **6** frolic, tinsel **7** elation, glitter, jollity, spirits **8** airiness, frippery, trumpery, vivacity **9** amusement, animation, brummagem, gaudiness, merriment, showiness **10** brightness, brilliance, garishness, jauntiness, joyousness, liveliness **11** celebration, merrymaking **12** cheerfulness, colorfulness, exhilaration, sportiveness **13** effervescence, sprightliness

gain, gains **3** add, bag, get, hit, net, win **4** jump, leap, plus, reap **5** bloom, bonus, fetch, glean, put on, reach, wages, yield **6** attain, come to, gather, income, obtain, pick up, profit, return, salary, secure, thrive **7** achieve, acquire, blossom, capture, collect, improve, procure, produce, prosper, recover, revenue **8** addition, arrive at, black ink, dividend, earnings, flourish, increase, overtake, proceeds, winnings **9** accretion, advantage, increment **10** attainment **11** improvement **12** accumulation, compensation, remuneration

Gaines, Ernest J
author of: **33** The Autobiography of Miss Jane Pittman

gainful **4** rich **6** paying **9** lucrative **10** productive, profitable **12** remunerative

gainfully **8** usefully **10** profitably **11** lucratively **12** productively **14** remuneratively

gain recognition **9** establish

gainsay **4** deny **6** abjure, oppose, refute **7** disavow, dispute **9** repudiate **10** contradict, controvert

Gainsborough, Thomas
born: **7** England, Sudbury
artwork: **10** The Blue Boy **14** The Morning Walk **15** Mr and Mrs Andrews, The Hon Mrs Graham **16** Viscount Ligonier **26** Peasant Girl Gathering Sticks

gait **4** pace, step, walk **5** tread **6** stride **7** bearing **8** carriage **10** deportment
French: **8** demarche

gaiter **4** boot, shoe, spat, vamp **5** chaps, strad **6** gaskin, hugger, puttee **7** legging **8** cuttikin, overshoe

gala **3** gay **5** grand, party **7** benefit, festive, opulent **8** festival, majestic, splendid **9** festivity, glamorous, sumptuous **10** ceremonial, fancy-dress, glittering **11** celebration, celebratory, magnificent, spectacular, star-studded
French: **4** fete

Galahad
character in: **16** Arthurian romance

Galatea
form: **6** maiden, statue **8** sea nymph
father: **6** Nereus
mother: **5** Doris
courted by: **10** Polyphemus
lover: **4** Acis
killed: **4** Acis
statue carved by: **9** Pygmalion
brought to life by: **9** Aphrodite
son: **6** Paphos

gale **3** fit **4** blow, gust, stir **6** flurry, squall, tumult, uproar **7** cyclone, tempest **8** eruption, outbreak, outburst **9** agitation, commotion, windstorm

Galeus
form: **6** lizard
father: **6** Apollo

Galileo Galilei
nationality: **7** Italian
inventor of: **6** sector **11** thermometer
studied: **6** motion **8** pendulum
discovered: **18** Jupiter's satellites
constructed: **9** telescope
formulated: **18** law of falling bodies
author of: **8** Dialogue **10** Discourses **18** The Starry Messenger

Galinthias
handmaiden of: **7** Alcmene

gall **3** bug, irk, vex **4** bile, flay, fret, miff, rile **5** anger, annoy, brass, chafe, cheek, gripe, nerve, score, sting, venom **6** abrade, bruise, enrage, harass, injure, nettle, offend, rancor, ruffle, spleen **7** affront, incense, provoke, rub sore **8** acrimony, audacity, boldness, irritate, rudeness, temerity **9** animosity, assurance, displease, excoriate, impudence, insolence, malignity, sauciness, virulence **10** bitterness, brazenness, effrontery, exacerbate, exasperate **11** presumption

gallant **3** fop **4** bold, dude, game, stud **5** blood, brave, dandy, gutsy, noble, suave, swell **6** daring, heroic, kindly, plucky, polite, urbane **7** courtly, dashing, valiant **8** cavalier, fearless, gay blade, intrepid, mannerly, obliging, resolute, stalwart, valorous, well-bred **9** attentive, courteous, dauntless **10** chivalrous, courageous, thoughtful **11** considerate, gentlemanly, lionhearted **12** stouthearted

gallantries **10** attentions **11** compliments **12** pleasantries

gallantry **4** grit, sand **5** nerve, pluck, valor **6** daring, mettle, spirit **7** bravery, courage, dashing, heroism, prowess, suavity **8** chivalry, courtesy, urbanity **9** derring-do, fortitude, gentility **10** politeness **11** courtliness, intrepidity **12** fearlessness, resoluteness **13** attentiveness, dauntlessness, determination **14** courageousness

gallery **4** stoa **5** salon **6** arcade, loggia, piazza **7** balcony, passage, portico **8** cloister, corridor **9** bleachers, colonnade, mezzanine, triforium **10** ambulatory, grandstand, passageway

Gallia Belgica *see* **7** Belgium

galliano
type: **7** liqueur
origin: **5** Italy
flavor: **5** herbs, spice
color: **6** yellow
with creme de cacao: **14** Golden Cadillac
with rum: **9** Bossa Nova
with vodka: **16** Harvey Wallbanger

gallinule **3** hen **4** coot, fowl, rail, sora **7** moorhen **8** dabchick, hyacinth, rallidae, ricebird, swamphen

Gallipoli
director: **9** Peter Weir
cast: **7** Mark Lee **8** Bill Kerr **9** Mel Gibson **11** Robert Grubb

gallivant, galavant **3** gad **4** kite, roam, rove **5** jaunt, range, stray **6** ramble, travel, wander **7** gallant, meander, traipse, **8** gad about **9** philander

gallon
abbreviation: 3 gal

gallop 3 fly, hie, jog, run **4** bolt, dart, dash, flit, race, rush, scud, skim, trot, whiz **5** bound, hurry, scoot, shoot, speed, whisk **6** hasten, scurry, spring, sprint **7** mad dash, scamper, scuttle, tear off **8** fast clip, fast gait **9** skedaddle

Galloping Ghost
nickname of: 9 Red Grange

gallows 4 rope **5** noose **6** gibbet, halter **8** scaffold

galore 7 aplenty, to spare

galosh, galoche 4 boot, clog, shoe **6** arctic, patten, rubber **8** overshoe

Galsworthy, John
author of: 5 To Let **6** Strife **7** Justice **9** Loyalties **10** In Chancery **11** The Skin Game **13** A Modern Comedy **14** The Forsyte Saga **15** End of the Chapter **16** The Man of Property **22** Indian Summer of a Forsyte

Galt, John
character in: 13 Atlas Shrugged
author: 4 Rand

galvanize 4 fire, move, stir, wake **5** rally, rouse, treat **6** arouse, awaken, charge, excite, foment, spur on, thrill **7** inspire, provoke, quicken **8** activate, energize, vitalize **9** electrify, stimulate

galvanizing 7 rousing **8** electric, exciting, spirited **9** inspiring, thrilling **11** stimulating **12** electrifying, soul-stirring

Galveston Giant
nickname of: 11 Jack Johnson

Gamaliel
father: 6 Simeon **8** Pedahzur
grandfather: 6 Hillel
taught: 4 Paul

Gambia, The ***see box***

gambit 4 ploy, ruse **5** feint, trick **6** scheme **8** artifice, maneuver **9** stratagem

gamble 3 bet **4** back, risk **5** flyer, wager **6** chance, hazard, toss-up **7** trust in, venture **9** speculate **11** speculation, uncertainty

gambler 5 dicer, shark, sharp, sport **6** banker, bettor, bookie, dealer, player **7** hustler **8** gamester, hazarder **10** speculator

Gambler, The
author: 16 Fyodor Dostoevsky
character: 6 Astley, Polina **10** The General **11** Mlle Blanche **15** Marquis de Grieux **16** Alexey Ivanovitch **22** Antonida Tarasyevitchev

gambol 3 hop **4** leap **5** bound, caper, frisk, sport, vault **6** bounce, cavort, frolic, prance, spring **7** disport, rollick

game ***see box, p. 382***

gamete 3 egg **4** ovum **5** sperm **6** oocyte, zygote **8** germ cell, oosphere **12** spermatozoan, spermatozoon

Gamow, George
field: 7 physics **9** cosmology
proponent of: 13 big bang theory
deciphered: 11 genetic code
proposed: 13 quantum theory
established: 17 Gamow-Teller theory

Gamp, Sarah
character in: 16 Martin Chuzzlewit
author: 7 Dickens

gamut 3 ken **5** reach, scope, sweep **6** extent **7** compass, purview

Gandhi
director: 19 Richard Attenborough
cast: 11 Ben Kingsley **13** Candice Bergen
Oscar for: 5 actor (Kingsley) **7** picture

gang 3 mob **4** band, body, crew, pack, pals, ring, team **5** chums, crowd, flock, group, party, relay, shift, squad, troop **6** clique, outfit **7** buddies, company, coterie, cronies, friends, phalanx **8** comrades **9** coworkers, neighbors **10** associates, classmates, companions, contingent, detachment **11** schoolmates

gangster 4 goon, hood, thug **5** crook, felon, tough **6** bandit, gunman **7** hoodlum, mafioso, mobster, ruffian **8** criminal, hooligan **9** racketeer

Gant, Eugene
character in: 17 Look Homeward Angel, Of Time and the River
author: 5 Wolfe

Ganymede
also: 9 Catamitus
cupbearer of: 4 gods

gap 3 cut **4** gash, hole, rent, rift, slit, slot, void **5** abyss, break, chasm, chink, cleft, crack, gulch, gully, notch, pause **6** breach, canyon, cavity, divide, hiatus, lacuna, ravine, recess, vacuum, valley **7** crevice, fissure, interim, opening **8** aperture, crevasse, fracture, interval, puncture **9** disparity, interlude **10** difference, divergence **12** intermission, interruption

gape 4 gasp, gawk, gaze, ogle, part, peer, yawn **5** split, stare **6** cleave, expand **7** fly open **8** wide open, separate **10** rubberneck

gaping 6 astare **7** gawking, staring, yawning **13** rubbernecking

Garamas *see* **11** Amphithemis

garb 3 rig **4** gear, gown, robe, suit, togs **5** dress, getup, habit **6** attire, finery, livery, outfit **7** apparel, clothes, costume, raiment, uniform, vesture **8** clothing, garments, vestment, wardrobe **9** trappings **11** habiliments

garbage 4 dirt, junk **5** offal, swill, trash, waste **6** debris, litter, refuse **7** carrion, rubbish **9** sweepings

garble 5 mix up **6** jumble **7** confuse, distort **8** fragment

Garbo, Greta
real name: 21 Greta Louisa Gustaffson

Gambia, The
capital/largest city: 6 Banjul **8** Bathurst
others: 5 Bakau, Basse, Mansa **7** Bintang, Brikama, Kuntaur **10** Georgetown
monetary unit: 5 butut, pound **6** dalasi
island: 7 Ft James, St Mary's **8** Elephant
river: 3 Bao **6** Gambia **7** Bintang, Nianija **9** Sandougou
sea: 8 Atlantic
people: 4 Fula, Jola **5** Foula, Wolof **6** Fulani **8** Mandingo, Serahuli **9** Seranuleh
language: 4 Fula **5** Wolof **6** Fulani **7** English, Malinke **8** Mandingo
religion: 5 Islam **10** Protestant **13** Roman Catholic

game **3** bad, fun **4** golf, halt, lame, lark, play, polo, pool, prey, romp **5** antic, brave, cocky, darts, gimpy, jacks, match, rugby, sport, spree **6** boccie, boxing, daring, frolic, gaiety, gambol, heroic, plucky, quarry, soccer, spunky, squash, tennis **7** archery, bowling, contest, crooked, croquet, curling, fencing, frisbee, gallant, hawking, hunting, hurling, jai alai, limping, pastime, tourney, valiant, willing **8** baseball, crippled, deformed, disabled, fearless, football, handball, hobbling, intrepid, lacrosse, ping pong, resolute, skittles, spirited, valorous, wild fowl **9** amusement, badminton, billiards, dauntless, diversion, festivity, merriment, wrestling **10** basketball, courageous, determined, horseshoes, ice-skating, lawn tennis, recreation, tournament, volleyball **11** competition, distraction, merrymaking, racquetball, table tennis, unflinching **12** shuffleboard **13** entertainment, incapacitated, roller-skating
board game: **4** Clue, Life, ludo **5** chess **7** Othello **8** checkers, cribbage, dominoes, draughts, fanorona, Monopoly, Scrabble **10** backgammon **14** Trivial Pursuit
Chinese: **6** Ma-jong, wei-ch'i **7** mahjong **8** Mah-jongg
Egyptian: **5** Senat
Indian: **7** pachisi **8** parchesi, shatranj **9** ashtapada, parcheesi **10** shaturanga
Japanese: **2** Go **3** I-go **5** Sho-gi
Korean: **5** Nyout, Pa-tok
Swedish: **6** tablut
card game: **3** loo, war **4** brag, fish, skat, vint **5** ombre, poker, rummy, tarot, whist **6** boston, bridge, casino, chemmy, ecarte, euchre, go fish, hearts, memory, piquet, pocher **7** bezique, canasta, cooncan, old maid, plafond, primero **8** baccarat, conquian, cribbage, gin rummy, napoleon, patience, pinochle, slapjack **9** blackjack, pelmanism, solitaire, spoil five, twenty-one **11** chemin de fer, crazy eights **13** concentration **14** contract bridge **16** beggar-my-neighbor, trente et quarante

born: **6** Sweden **9** Stockholm
roles: **4** Love **7** Camille **8** Conquest, Mata Hari **9** Ninotchka **10** Grand Hotel **12** Anna Christie, Anna Karenina **13** Queen Cristina, Two-Faced Woman **14** The Painted Veil **16** Flesh and the Devil

Garcia Lorca, Federico
author of: **5** Yerma **12** Blood Wedding, Gypsy Ballads **19** House of Bernarda Alba

Garcia Marquez, Gabriel
author of: **9** Leaf Storm **23** The Autumn of the Patriarch **25** One Hundred Years of Solitude

garcon **3** boy **6** waiter **7** servant

garden **4** Eden, lawn, plot, yard **7** Arcadia **8** paradise **10** Gethsemane
type: **4** herb, rock, rose **5** truck **6** flower, formal **7** kitchen **9** botanical, vegetable

gardenia
varieties: **5** crape **9** butterfly

Garden of Cypress, The
author: **15** Sir Thomas Browne

Garden of the Finzi-Continis, The
director: **14** Vittorio De Sica
author: **11** Rumer Godden
cast: **10** Fabio Testi **11** Romolo Valli **12** Helmut Berger **14** Dominique Sanda **15** Lino Capolicchio
Oscar: **11** foreign film

Garden of the West
nickname of: **6** Kansas

garden party
French: **13** fete champetre

gardens
god of: **9** Vertumnus
goddess of: **5** Venus

Garden State
nickname of: **9** New Jersey

garden variety **5** plain **6** common, simple **7** regular **8** everyday, familiar, ordinary **11** commonplace

Gardner, Ava
husband: **9** Artie Shaw **12** Frank Sinatra, Mickey Rooney
born: **12** Smithfield NC
roles: **7** Mogambo **8** Show Boat **9** Mayerling, Naked Maja **10** On the Beach **15** The Sun Also Rises **18** Snows of Kilimanjaro **19** The Barefoot Contessa, The Night of the Iguana

Gardner, Erle Stanley
character: **9** Paul Drake **10** Perry Mason **11** Della Street **14** Hamilton Burger
also wrote as: **6** A A Fair

Gardner, John
author of: **7** Grendel **12** October Light **14** Nickel Mountain, The Art of Living, The King's Indian **17** Michelsson's Ghosts **20** The Sunlight Dialogues, The Wreckage of Agathon

Gareth
character in: **16** Arthurian romance

Garfield, James Abram *see box*

Garfield, John
real name: **15** Julius Garfinkle
born: **9** New York NY
roles: **6** Juarez **10** Humoresque **11** Body and Soul **26** The Postman Always Rings Twice

Garfinkle, Julius
real name of: **12** John Garfield

Gargamelle
character in: **22** Gargantua and Pantagruel
author: **8** Rabelais

Gargantua and Pantagruel
author: **16** Francois Rabelais
character: **7** Panurge **10** Gargamelle, Grangosier, Picrochole **23** Frere Jean des Entommeures

gargantuan **4** huge, vast **5** great **7** hulking, immense, mammoth, massive, titanic **8** colossal, enormous, gigantic, lubberly, towering **9** herculean, monstrous, overgrown **10** prodigious, stupendous, tremendous **11** elephantine **13** amplitudinous

Gargaphia
death place of: **7** Actaeon

Gargery, Joe
character in: **17** Great Expectations
author: **7** Dickens

garish **4** loud **5** cheap, gaudy, showy **6** brassy, bright, flashy, tawdry, tinsel, vulgar **7** blatant, glaring **9** flaunting, obtrusive **11** pretentious **12** ostentatious **13** overelaborate

Garfield, James Abram
presidential rank: **9** twentieth
party: **10** Republican
state represented: **2** OH
defeated: **3** (Neal) Dow **6** (James Baird) Weaver, (John Wolcott) Phelps **7** (Winfield Scott) Hancock
vice president: **6** (Chester Alan) Arthur
cabinet:
state: **6** (James Gillespie) Blaine
treasury: **6** (William) Windom
war: **7** (Robert Todd) Lincoln
attorney general: **8** (Isaac Wayne) MacVeagh
navy: **4** (William Henry) Hunt
postmaster general: **5** (Thomas Lemuel) James
interior: **8** (Samuel Jordan) Kirkwood
born: **2** OH **6** Orange **8** log cabin
died: **9** Elberon NJ
died by: **13** assassination
buried: **11** Cleveland OH
education:
seminary: **6** Geauga
college: **5** Hiram (Eclectic Institute) **8** Williams
studied: **3** law
religion: **17** Disciples of Christ
political career: **8** US Senate (declined seat) **11** state Senate **24** US House of Representatives
civilian career: **6** lawyer **7** teacher **11** lay preacher
military service: **6** US Army **8** Civil War **12** major general
notable events of lifetime/term:
exposure of: **15** Star Route frauds
father: **7** Abraham
mother: **5** Eliza (Ballou)
siblings: **4** Mary **5** James **6** Thomas **9** Mehitabel
wife: **8** Lucretia (Rudolph)
nickname: **5** Crete
children: **4** Mary **5** Abram, Eliza **6** Edward **12** James Rudolph **13** Harry Augustus, Irvin McDowell

garland **3** bay, lei **4** halo **5** crown **6** corona, diadem, fillet, laurel, wreath **7** chaplet, circlet, coronet, festoon **8** chapbook, headband, treasury **9** anthology **10** collection **11** florilegium

Garland, Hamlin
author of: **18** Main-Travelled Roads **20** Rose of Dutcher's Coolly

Garland, Judy
real name: **11** Frances Gumm
husband: **7** Sid Luft **16** Vincente Minnelli
daughter: **9** Lorna Luft **12** Liza Minnelli
costar: **12** Mickey Rooney
born: **13** Grand Rapids MN
roles: **7** Dorothy **11** A Star Is Born, Babes in Arms **12** Easter Parade **13** The Wizard of Oz **14** The Harvey Girls **15** A Child Is Waiting, Meet Me in St Louis

garlic
botanical name: **13** Allium sativum
origin: **4** Asia **13** Mediterranean
charm against: **7** poverty, witches **13** whooping cough
use: **4** fish, fowl, meat **5** salad **10** vegetables **13** Italian dishes, salad dressing
varieties: **4** crow, hog's, wild **5** bear's, false, field, giant, grace, mouse, stag's, sweet **6** levant **7** serpent, society, Spanish, striped **8** daffodil, oriental **11** great-headed, round-headed **16** fragrant-flowered

Garm
origin: **12** Scandinavian
form: **8** watchdog
watches over: **3** Hel
location: **8** Niflheim

garment, garments **4** garb, gear, togs **5** dress, habit **6** attire, outfit **7** apparel, clothes, costume, raiment **8** clothing, vestment **10** habiliment

garner **4** reap **5** amass, hoard **6** gather, heap up **7** acquire, collect **8** assemble **10** accumulate

Garner, James
real name: **15** James Baumgarner
born: **8** Norman OK
roles: **8** Maverick, Sayonara **11** Jim Rockford **12** Bret Maverick, Hour of the Gun **13** Darby's Rangers, Rockford Files **14** Murphy's Romance, Victor Victoria **23** Support Your Local Sheriff **25** The Americanization of Emily

garnet
varieties: **6** syrope **9** almandite, demantoid, hessonite, rhodolite **12** grossularite
month: **7** January

Garnett, David
author of: **11** Lady into Fox

garnish **4** deck, gild, trim **5** adorn, array **6** bedeck, doll up, set off **7** festoon, furbish, smarten **8** beautify, decorate, emblazon, ornament, spruce up, trimming **9** adornment, embellish, embroider **10** decoration **13** embellishment

garret **4** loft **5** attic

garrison **4** fort **5** guard **6** patrol, secure **7** battery, bivouac, brigade, platoon, station **8** division, regiment, squadron **10** detachment, escadrille **13** fortification

garrulity **8** verbiage **9** loquacity, prosiness, verbosity, wordiness **13** talkativeness

garrulous **5** gabby, windy, wordy **6** chatty **7** gossipy, prating, verbose, voluble **8** babbling, chattery, effusive **9** prattling, talkative **10** loquacious

Garry Moore Show, The
cast: **9** Allen Funt, Denise Lor, John Byner, Ken Carson **11** Chuck McCann, Marion Lorne **12** Carol Burnett, Durward Kirby, Jackie Vernon, Pete Barbutti **13** Dorothy Loudon

Garson, Greer
born: **7** Ireland **10** County Down
roles: **10** Mrs Miniver (Oscar) **11** Madame Curie **12** Her Twelve Men **13** Mrs Parkington, Random Harvest **14** Goodbye Mr Chips **16** That Forsyte Woman **17** Pride and Prejudice **19** Sunrise at Campobello

gas **4** fuel, fume **5** vapor **6** petrol **7** essence

gascon **7** boaster, bragger, egotist **8** blowhard, braggart **9** swaggerer **11** braggadocio

gasconade 4 brag, crow **5** boast **7** bravado **8** boasting **11** braggadocio

gash 4 hack, rend, rent, slit, tear **5** carve, cleft, crack, lance, slash, slice, split, wound **6** cleave, incise, pierce **7** dissect, fissure, quarter **8** incision, lacerate

Gaskell, Elizabeth
author of: 4 Ruth **8** Cranford **10** Mary Barton **13** North and South **24** The Life of Charlotte Bronte

Gaslight
director: 11 George Cukor
cast: 10 Terry Moore **12** Charles Boyer **13** Dame May Whitty, Ingrid Bergman **14** Angela Lansbury **15** Halliwell Hobbes

Gasoline Alley
creator: 9 Bill Perry, Frank King **10** Dick Moores
character: 3 Eve **4** Adam, Hope **6** Clovia, Gideon, Nubbin **7** Chipper, Gabriel **10** Walt Wallet
***wife:* 14** Phyllis Blossom
***children:* 4** Judy **5** Corky **7** Skeezix
***daughter-in-law:* 9** Nina Clock
***dog:* 5** Punky

gasp 4 gulp, pant, puff **5** blurt **6** suck in, wheeze **10** vociferate

Gasterocheires
companions of: 7 Proteus

gastronome 7 epicure, gourmet **9** bon vivant

gastronomy 9 epicurism

gastropod, gasteropod
4 slug **5** cowry, snail, whelk **6** cowrie, limpet, nerite **7** abalone, mollusk **8** univalve

gate 3 tap **5** crowd, house, valve **6** portal, sluice, spigot **7** doorway **8** audience, hatchway **9** turnstile **10** attendance

gateau 4 cake **7** dessert

gatekeeper 5 guard **6** porter **8** watchman

Gates, Horatio
served in: 16 Revolutionary War **18** French and Indian War
battle: 6 Camden **8** Saratoga
defeated: 8 Burgoyne
defeated by: 10 Cornwallis

gateway 4 adit **5** entry **6** access, portal **7** doorway, opening **8** entrance, entryway **10** passageway

Gath 14 Philistine city

gather 4 fold, mass **5** amass, group, infer, learn, pleat, shirr, stack **6** assume, deduce, heap up, muster, pile up, pucker, ruffle **7** cluster, collect, convene, marshal, observe **8** assemble, conclude **9** stockpile **10** accumulate, congregate, understand **11** concentrate

gathering 3 mob **4** gang, pack **5** bunch, crowd, crush, drove, flock, horde, party, press **6** throng **7** company, meeting, roundup, turnout **8** assembly, conclave **9** concourse, multitude **10** assemblage, collection, conference, convention **11** aggregation, convergence, convocation **12** accumulation, congregation **13** concentration

gather together 4 herd **5** amass, hoard, rally **6** muster **7** collate, collect, compile, marshal, round up, sweep up **8** assemble, shepherd **9** aggregate, stockpile **10** accumulate, congregate

Gatling, Richard Jordan
nationality: 8 American
inventor of: 10 machine gun **16** steam-powered plow

gatophobia
fear of: 4 cats

gauche 5 inept **6** clumsy, oafish **7** awkward, boorish, ill-bred, uncouth **8** bungling, plebeian, tactless **9** inelegant, maladroit, tasteless, unrefined **10** blundering, uncultured, ungraceful, unmannerly, unpolished **11** proletarian **13** ungentlemanly

gaucherie 5 gaffe **7** blunder, faux pas **11** impropriety **12** indiscretion

Gaudeamus igitur 22 Let us therefore be joyful

gaudy 4 loud, sham **5** cheap, showy, vivid **6** flashy, flimsy, garish, tawdry, tinsel, vulgar **7** glaring, intense **8** colorful, dazzling, lustrous, striking **9** brilliant, sparkling, tasteless, worthless **10** bespangled, glittering **11** pretentious **12** ostentatious

gauge, gage 4 rate, size **5** guess, judge, meter **6** assess **7** adjudge, measure **8** appraise, estimate, evaluate, standard **9** ascertain, calculate, criterion, yardstick **11** measurement
type: 4 ring **5** bevel

Gauguin, Paul Eugene Henri
born: 5 Paris **6** France
artwork: 9 Nevermore **12** The Tahitians **13** The White Horse **15** The Yellow Christ **18** Horsemen on the Beach **23** The Vision after the Sermon (Jacob Wrestling with the Angel) **25** Be in Love and You Will Be Happy **26** The Spirit of the Dead Watching **36** Where Do We Come From? Who Are We? Where Do We Go?
book: 6 Noa Noa

Gaul *see* **6** France

gaunt 4 bony, grim, lank, lean, slim, thin **5** bleak, lanky, spare **6** barren, meager, skinny, wasted **7** haggard, pinched, scraggy, scrawny, slender, spindly, starved **8** deserted, desolate, forsaken, rawboned, skeletal, withered **9** emaciated, shriveled **10** cadaverous, forbidding **14** spindle-shanked

Gauss, Carl Friedrich
field: 7 physics **9** astronomy **11** mathematics
nationality: 6 German
worked in: 9 magnetism **11** electricity **12** number theory
named for him: 9 Gauss's Law

Gautier, Marguerite
character in: 7 Camille
author: 5 Dumas (fils)

Gautier, Theophile
author of: 6 La Peri **7** Giselle **8** Albertus **11** Young France **13** Emaux et Camees **16** Enamels and Cameos **20** Mademoiselle de Maupin, The Romance of the Mummy
doctrine: 14 Art for art's sake

gauzy 5 filmy, sheer **6** flimsy, sleazy **10** diaphanous **11** translucent, transparent

gave up 4 quit **5** ceded **7** dropped, forsook, yielded **8** forswore, resigned **9** abandoned, abdicated, forfeited, renounced **11** surrendered **12** discontinued, relinquished

Gawain
character in: 16 Arthurian romance

gawk 4 gape, gaze, peer **10** rubberneck

gawky 6 clumsy, klutzy **7** awkward, lumpish **8** bungling, fumbling, lubberly, ungainly, unwieldy **9** all thumbs, graceless, ham-fisted, ham-handed, maladroit **10** blundering, ungraceful

gay 3 fun **4** airy, glad **5** happy, jolly, merry, showy, sunny, vivid **6** blithe, bright, cheery, elated, frisky, genial, jaunty, jocose, jovial, joyful, joyous, lively, social **7** buoyant, chipper, coltish, dashing, festive, gleeful, glowing, intense, jocular, playful, smiling, waggish **8** animated, cheerful, colorful, exultant, gladsome, humorous, jubilant, lustrous, skittish, spirited, splendid, sportive, volatile **9** brilliant, convivial, frivolous, hilarious, rejoicing, sparkling, sprightly, sumptuous, vivacious **10** flamboyant, frolicsome, glittering, insouciant, theatrical, variegated **12** effervescent, lighthearted, multicolored

Gay, John
author of dialogue/lyrics for: 15 The Beggar's Opera

Gay, Walter
character in: 12 Dombey and Son
author: 7 Dickens

gay blade 3 fop **4** beau **5** blade, dandy **7** playboy **8** cavalier **9** ladies' man **12** boulevardier, man-about-town

Gay Divorcee, The
director: 12 Mark Sandrich
cast: 10 Alice Brady, Erik Rhodes **11** Betty Grable, Fred Astaire **12** Ginger Rogers **19** Edward Everett Horton
song: 11 Continental, Night and Day

Gay-Lussac, Joseph
field: 7 physics **9** chemistry
nationality: 6 French
discovered: 24 law of combining gas volumes
invented: 10 hydrometer

Gaynor, Mitzi
real name: 20 Franceska Mitzi Gerber
husband: 8 Jack Bean
born: 9 Chicago IL
roles: 8 Les Girls **10** Golden Girl **12** Anything Goes, South Pacific **14** The Joker Is Wild **32** There's No Business Like Show Business

gaze 3 eye **4** gape, ogle, peek, peer, scan **5** glare, lower, stare, study, watch **6** behold, glance, glower, peruse, regard, survey **7** examine, inspect, observe, witness **8** look long, pore over, scrutiny **10** rubberneck, scrutinize **11** contemplate

gaze at 4 view **5** watch **6** behold, look at **7** stare at **8** look upon **11** contemplate

Gazza Ladra, La
also: 17 The Thieving Magpie
opera by: 7 Rossini

Ge *see* **4** Gaea

gear 3 cam, rig **4** duds, garb, togs **5** dress, tools **6** attire, outfit, tackle, things **7** apparel, clothes, rigging **8** clothing, cogwheel, flywheel, garments, material, property **9** apparatus, equipment, trappings **10** belongings, implements **11** accessories, instruments **12** contrivances **13** accoutrements, paraphernalia

Geb
also: 3 Keb
origin: 8 Egyptian
god of: 5 earth
daughter: 4 Isis
son: 6 Osiris
sister: 3 Nut

Gedaliah
means: 14 Jehovah is great
father: 6 Ahikam, Pashur **8** Jeduthun
descendant: 9 Zephaniah

Geer, Will
born: 11 Frankfort IN
roles: 7 Grandpa **10** The Waltons **11** In Cold Blood

Gehenna 4 hell

Gehrig, Lou (Henry Louis)
nickname: 9 Iron Horse
sport: 8 baseball
position: 9 first base
team: 14 New York Yankees

Geisman, Ella
real name of: 11 June Allyson

Geist 4 mind **6** spirit

gelatin 4 agar, glue **5** aspic, gelee, jelly **6** glutin, pectin **7** protein, sericin

gelatinize 3 set **4** jell **7** congeal, stiffen, thicken **9** coagulate

gelatinous 7 colloid, viscous **8** muculent **9** jelly-like

geld 5 alter **8** castrate **10** emasculate

gelid 3 icy **6** frigid, frozen **8** freezing

Gelonus
father: 8 Hercules

gem ***see box***

Gemini
symbol: 5 twins
planet: 7 Mercury
rules: 14 communications
born: 3 May **4** June

Gemini Contenders, The
author: 12 Robert Ludlum

Gem State
nickname of: 5 Idaho

gemutlich 4 easy **9** agreeable, congenial, simpatico **11** comfortable

gendarme 9 policeman

gender 3 sex **4** kind, male, sort, type **5** class **6** female, neuter **8** feminine **9** masculine

Gendre, Louis
real name of: 12 Louis Jourdan

genealogy 4 line **5** birth, house, stock **7** lineage **8** ancestry, pedigree **9** parentage **10** derivation, extraction

Gene Autry Show, The
cast: 10 Pat Buttram
horse: 8 Champion
theme song: 20 Back in the Saddle Again

general 5 basic, broad, usual, vague **6** common, normal,

gem 4 dear, doll, rock **5** beaut, bijou, jewel, peach, prize **6** marvel, wonder **8** treasure
type: 4 jade, opal, ruby, sard **5** agate, amber, beryl, coral, pearl, topaz **6** garnet, pyrope, quartz, spinel, zircon **7** apatite, cat's-eye, citrine, diamond, emerald, jadeite, kunzite, olivine, peridot **8** amethyst, corundum, feldspar, hematite, lazurite, nephrite, sapphire, steatite, sunstone **9** almandite, amazonite, carnelian, demantoid, enstatite, fibrolite, malachite, moonstone, morganite, rhodolite, scapolite, spodumene, tiger's-eye, turquoise **10** aquamarine, bloodstone, chalcedony, hessionite, rose quartz, tourmaline **11** alexandrite, chrysoberyl, chrysocolla, chrysoprase, lapis lazuli, rock crystal, topaz quartz **12** grossularite

public, wonted **7** blanket, current, generic, inexact, natural, overall, popular, regular, typical **8** everyday, frequent, habitual, ordinary, pandemic, sweeping **9** customary, extensive, imprecise, panoramic, prevalent, universal, worldwide **10** accustomed, collective, ecumenical, prevailing, widespread **11** unspecified **12** conventional, nonexclusive, nontechnical **13** comprehensive, miscellaneous

General Electric Theater
host: **12** Ronald Reagan

general idea **4** gist **5** drift, tenor **6** effect, import **7** purport **10** impression **11** implication

generality **6** cliche, truism **9** platitude **12** universality **14** collectiveness **17** miscellaneousness **18** indiscriminateness

generalization **3** law **5** axion **7** bromide **9** inference, statement

generalize **5** infer, judge **8** conclude

generally **5** often **6** always, mainly, mostly **7** as a rule, chiefly, largely, usually **9** currently, typically **10** frequently, habitually, ordinarily, repeatedly **11** extensively, principally, universally

general/military leader *see box*

generate **4** bear, coin, form, make, sire **5** beget, breed, cause, frame, spawn, yield **6** create, evolve, father, induce, invent **7** develop, fashion, produce **8** contrive, engender, fructify, occasion **9** construct, fabricate, fecundate, fertilize, institute, originate, procreate, propagate, reproduce **10** effectuate, impregnate **11** proliferate

generation **3** kin **4** clan, line, race **5** breed, house, issue, stock, tribe **6** family, growth, strain **7** genesis, lineage, progeny **8** breeding, creation **9** begetting, causation, evolution, formation, offspring **10** production **11** development, engendering, origination, procreation, propagation **12** impregnation, reproduction **13** fertilization, proliferation

generic **6** common **7** general **8** sweeping **9** universal **10** collective **11** generalized, unspecified **12** nonexclusive **13** comprehensive **14** nonrestrictive

generosity **6** bounty **7** charity **8** altruism, courtesy, kindness, largesse **9** abundance, nobleness **10** liberality **11** benevolence, hospitality, magnanimity

generous **5** ample, large, lofty, noble **6** humane, lavish **7** copious, liberal **8** abundant, effusive, obliging, princely, prodigal **9** bounteous, bountiful, honorable, plenteous, plentiful, plethoric, unselfish, unstinted **10** altruistic, beneficent, benevolent, bighearted, charitable, freehanded, freegiving, high-minded, hospitable, munificent, openhanded, ungrudging, unstinting **11** considerate, extravagant, magnanimous, overflowing **12** humanitarian, largehearted, unrestricted **13** accommodating, philanthropic

genesis **4** rise, root **5** birth **6** origin **8** creation **9** begetting, beginning, inception **10** generation **11** engendering **12** commencement

geneticist
American: **5** Temin **6** Morgan, Muller

genetics
science of: **8** heredity
researcher: **6** Mendel

Genetyllis
origin: **5** Greek
protectress of: **6** births

Genghis Khan
also: **11** Jenghiz Khan
name means: **14** universal ruler
position: **13** Mongol emperor

general/military leader
American:
Revolutionary War: **3** (Light Horse Harry) Lee **5** Allen, Barry, Gates, Jones, Wayne **6** Arnold, Greene, Marion, Morgan **10** Washington
War of 1812: **4** Hull **5** Perry, Scott **7** Decatur
Mexican War: **5** Scott **6** Kearny
Civil War: **3** Lee **5** Early, Grant, Meade **6** Thomas, (JEB) Stuart **7** Forrest, Pickett, Sherman, (Stonewall) Jackson **8** Farragut, Sheridan **9** McClellan **10** Beauregard, Longstreet
Indian Wars: **6** Custer **7** Houston **10** Crazy Horse
WWI: **4** Sims **8** Mitchell, Pershing
WWII: **4** King **5** Clark **6** Arnold, Halsey, Nimitz, Patton **7** Bradley, Merrill **8** Marshall, Stilwell **9** Chennault, Doolittle, MacArthur **10** Eisenhower, Wainwright
Korean War: **5** Clark **9** MacArthur
Vietnam War: **6** Abrams **12** Westmoreland
British: **4** Byng, Haig, Howe, Slim **5** Wolfe **6** French, Gordon, Harris, Nelson, Wavell **7** Allenby, Clinton, Dowding, Wingate **8** Braddock, Burgoyne, Cromwell, Jellicoe, Lawrence **9** Alexander, Kitchener **10** Cornwallis, Montgomery, Wellington **11** Marlborough, Mountbatten
Carthagenian: **8** Hannibal **13** Hamilcar Barca
French: **3** Ney **4** Foch **5** Murat **6** Giraud, Joffre, Petain, Roland **7** Nivelle **8** De Gaulle, Montcalm, Napoleon **9** Lafayette **10** Bernadotte
German: **5** Kluck **6** Moltke, Paulus, Rommel, Scheer **7** Blucher, Goering, Tirpitz **8** Bismarck, Goebbels, Guderian **9** Rundstedt **10** Falkenhayn, Hindenburg, Kesselring, Ludendorff, Schlieffen **17** Frederick the Great
Israeli: **5** Dayan
Japanese: **10** Tojo Hideki **15** Yamamoto Isoroku
Macedonian: **7** Ptolemy **8** Philip II **9** Alexander (the Great)
Norman: **7** William (the Conqueror)
Roman: **5** Sulla **6** Brutus, Pompey, Seneca, Trajan **7** Crassus, Hadrian, Lepidus **8** Gracchus, Octavian (Caesar Augustus), Tiberius **9** Vespasian **10** Flamininus, Mark Antony **11** Gaius Marius **12** Julius Caesar **15** Cassius Longinus, Scipio Africanus **18** Tarquinius Superbus
Russian: **6** Zhukov **7** Kutuzov, Voronov **8** Brusilov, Kerensky, Kornilov, Samsonov **9** Bagration **10** Timoshenko, Vasilevsky

defeated: **6** Russia **10** Chin empire
occupied: **6** Peking

genial **3** gay **4** glad, kind, warm **5** civil, happy, jolly, merry, sunny **6** bright, cheery, hearty, jaunty, jocund, jovial, joyful, joyous, kindly, lively, social **7** affable, amiable, chipper, cordial, festive **8** cheerful, friendly, gracious, mirthful, pleasant, sociable **9** agreeable, congenial, convivial, courteous, expansive, sparkling, vivacious **10** neighborly **12** lighthearted **13** companionable

geniality **10** affability, cordiality **11** sociability **12** conviviality, friendliness **13** expansiveness

genius **3** ace, wit **4** bent, gift, mind, whiz **5** brain, flair, knack **6** expert, master, wisdom **7** faculty, insight, prodigy **8** aptitude, judgment, penchant, sagacity, wizardry **9** ingenuity, intuition, invention **10** mastermind, perception, proclivity, propensity **11** imagination, percipience **12** intelligence, predilection **13** understanding

Genius, The
author: **15** Theodore Dreiser

genius loci **16** guardian of a place

Genoveva
opera by: **8** Schumann
character: **4** Golo **15** Prince Siegfried

genre **4** kind, sort, type **5** breed, class, genus, group, order, style **6** school **7** fashion, species, variety **8** category, division **11** description **14** classification

genteel **4** tony **5** civil, elite, ritzy, swank, swell **6** modish, poised, polite, urbane **7** courtly, elegant, high-hat, refined, stylish **8** cultured, decorous, ladylike, mannerly, polished, well-bred **9** courteous, high-class, high-toned, patrician **10** cultivated, well-spoken **11** fashionable, gentlemanly, highfalutin, overrefined, pretentious **12** aristocratic, silk-stocking, thoroughbred

gentian **8** Gentiana
varieties: **5** blind, green, horse **6** alpine, bottle, closed, Sierra, yellow **7** crested, fringed, prairie, spurred **8** Catesby's, soapwort, stemless **9** Mendocino **10** pine barren

gentil **4** kind **5** noble **6** gentle

gentile
Yiddish: **3** goy
man: **7** shegetz
woman: **6** shiksa

gentility **6** polish **7** decorum, suavity **8** breeding, chivalry, civility, courtesy, urbanity **9** gallantry, propriety, punctilio **10** refinement **11** cultivation, savoir-faire **12** mannerliness

gentle **3** low **4** calm, easy, kind, meek, mild, soft, tame **5** balmy, bland, light, quiet **6** benign, broken, docile, kindly, placid, serene, slight, smooth, tender **7** lenient, pacific, subdued **8** harmless, merciful, moderate, peaceful, tolerant, tranquil **9** indulgent, temperate, tractable **10** manageable, thoughtful, untroubled **11** considerate, sympathetic **12** domesticated **13** compassionate, tenderhearted
French: **6** gentil

gentleman **3** don, guy, man, one **4** chap, gent **5** swell **6** fellow, person, squire **7** esquire, hidalgo **8** cavalier **9** caballero, chevalier, patrician **10** aristocrat, individual

Gentleman Jim
nickname of: **12** James Corbett

gentlemanly **6** polite **7** courtly, gallant, refined **8** cultured, decorous, mannerly, polished, well-bred **9** courteous, dignified **10** cultivated

Gentleman's Agreement
director: **9** Elia Kazan
based on novel by: **12** Laura Z Hobson
cast: **10** Anne Revere **11** Celeste Holm, Gregory Peck **12** John Garfield **14** Dorothy McGuire
Oscar for: **7** picture **17** supporting actress (Holm)

Gentlemen Prefer Blondes
author: **9** Anita Loos

gentleness **8** calmness, docility, mildness, serenity, tameness **10** compassion, tenderness **12** mercifulness, peacefulness, tractability

gentle wind **4** waft **6** breath, breeze, zephyr

gently **6** easily, kindly, meekly, mildly, softly, tamely **7** amiably, lightly **8** benignly, placidly, smoothly, tenderly **9** gradually **10** delicately, moderately, pleasantly, soothingly **15** compassionately, sympathetically

gentry **5** elite **7** society **8** nobility **10** blue bloods, gentlefolk **11** aristocracy, aristocrats

genuflect **4** bend **6** kowtow

genuine **4** open, pure, real, true **5** frank, naive, plain, solid **6** actual, candid, honest, proven, simple **7** artless, earnest, natural, sincere **8** bona fide, sterling, true-blue **9** authentic, guileless, heartfelt, ingenuous, simon-pure, unalloyed, veritable **10** legitimate, unaffected **13** unadulterated **15** straightforward, unsophisticated

genuineness **7** honesty **9** frankness, sincerity **10** candidness, simplicity **11** artlessness **13** guilelessness **14** unaffectedness **19** straightforwardness

genus **4** kind, sort, type **5** class, group **7** variety **8** category, division **14** classification

Geoffrion, Bernie (Bernard)
nickname: **8** Boom Boom
sport: **9** ice hockey
team: **14** New York Rangers **17** Montreal Canadiens

geographer
French: **7** Delisle

geologist
British: **4** Hall
German: **6** Werner
Scottish: **6** Hutton

geoponics **7** tillage **8** agronomy **9** husbandry **10** agronomics **11** agriculture, cultivation

George Burns and Gracie Allen Show, The
character: **9** Mr Beasley (Mailman) **11** Harry Morton **13** Blanche Morton
cast: **8** Hal March **9** Fred Clark, John Brown **11** Bill Goodwin, Ralph Seadan, Ronnie Burns **12** Bea Benaderet, Harry Von Zell, Larry Keating
theme song: **8** Love Nest

Georgetown
capital of: **6** Guyana

Georgia ***see box, p. 388***

Georgia Peach
nickname of: **6** Ty Cobb

Georgics, The
author: **6** Vergil, Virgil
called: **17** agricultural poems

Georgia
abbreviation: 2 GA
nickname: 5 Peach 7 Cracker 21 Empire State of the South
capital/largest city: 7 Atlanta
others: 4 Rome 5 Jesup, Macon 6 Albany, Athens, Dalton, Plains, Sparta 7 Augusta, Conyers, Cordele, Decatur, Griffen, Vidalia 8 Columbus, LaGrange, Marietta, Moultrie, Savannah, Valdosta, Waycross 9 Brunswick 11 College Park, Gainesville, Thomasville 13 Andersonville
college: 4 Tift 5 Clark, Emory, Paine 6 Mercer 7 Atlanta, Spelman 8 Wesleyan 9 Morehouse 10 Agnes Scott 11 Georgia Tech
explorer: 15 James Oglethorpe
feature: 16 Little White House
amusement park: 19 Six Flags Over Georgia
national cemetery: 13 Andersonville
national monument: 8 Ocmulgee 11 Fort Pulaski 13 Fort Frederica
tribe: 5 Creek, Guale, Yuchi 6 Chiaha, Oconee, Uchean 7 Yamasee 8 Hitchiti
people: 6 Ty Cobb 7 cracker 10 Bobby Jones 11 Juliette Low 15 Erskine Caldwell 16 Margaret Mitchell 18 Joel Chandler Harris
island: 3 Sea 6 Jekyll, Sapelo 7 Ossabaw 10 Cumberland
lake: 6 Lanier, Martin 7 Harding, Nottely 8 Bankhead, Hartwell, Sinclair
land rank: 11 twenty-first
mountain: 5 Stone 7 Lookout 8 Kennesaw 9 Blue Ridge 11 Alleghenies 13 High Point Peak
highest point: 17 Brasstown Bald Peak
physical feature:
sea: 8 Atlantic
springs: 4 Warm
swamp: 10 Okefenokee
president: 11 Jimmy Carter
river: 3 Pea 5 Flint 6 Etowah, Oconee, Pigeon 7 Conecuh, Satilla, St Mary's, Tugaloo 8 Altamaha, Ocmulgee, Ogeechee, Savannah, Suwannee 9 Chattooga 13 Chattahoochie
state admission: 6 fourth
state bird: 13 brown thrasher
state fish: 14 largemouth bass
state flower: 12 Cherokee rose
state motto: 6 Wisdom 20 Justice and Moderation
state song: 7 Georgia
state tree: 7 live oak

Ge-Pano-Carib
language branch: 7 Macro-Ge 10 Macro-Carib 11 Macro-Panoan

gephyrophobia
fear of: 7 bridges

Geraint
character in: 16 Arthurian romance

geranium 11 Pelargonium
varieties: 3 ivy 4 fish, lime, mint, pine, rock, rose, show, wild 5 apple, fancy, house, lemon, regal, zonal 6 almond, alpine, cactus, jungle, nutmeg, orange 7 apricot, bedding, coconut, feather, hanging, knotted, polecat 8 crowfoot, fern-leaf, horsehoe 9 beefsteak, oak-leaved 10 California, gooseberry, peppermint, strawberry, sweetheart, village-oak 11 grape-leaved, herb-scented, maple-leaved, rose-scented 12 silver-leaved, southernwood, sweet-scented 13 black-flowered, pansy-flowered, pheasant's-foot 14 Lady Washington, little-leaf rose 15 mint-scented rose 16 Martha Washington 17 English finger-bowl

Gerber, Franceska Mitzi
real name of: 11 Mitzi Gaynor

Gerd, Gerda
origin: 12 Scandinavian
husband: 4 Frey 5 Freyr

Gere, Richard
roles: 5 Yanks 10 Breathless, Cotton Club 12 Days of Heaven 14 American Gigolo 19 Looking for Mr Goodbar 22 An Officer and a Gentleman

Geri
origin: 12 Scandinavian
form: 4 wolf
owner: 4 Odin 5 Othin
received: 4 food
exception: 4 meat
fellow wolf: 5 Freki

germ 3 bud, bug, egg 4 ovum, root, seed 5 ovule, spark, spore, virus 6 embryo, origin, source, sprout 7 microbe, nucleus, seed bud 8 bacillus, offshoot, rudiment 9 bacterium, beginning 12 fountainhead 13 microorganism

German 3 Hun 4 balt, Goth 5 boche, heine, jerry, kraut, Saxon 6 Teuton 7 tedesco 8 Prussian, Teutonic 9 deutscher
article: 3 das, dem, den, der, des, die, ein 4 eine
empire: 5 reich
man: 4 herr
storm and stress: 13 sturm und drang
thank you: 5 danke 10 danke schon
toast: 6 prosit
woman: 4 frau 8 fraulein

German-Dutch
language family: 12 Indo-European
branch: 8 Germanic
group: 15 Western Germanic
language: 9 Low German 10 High German

germane 3 apt, fit 6 native, proper 7 apropos, fitting, related 8 material, relative, relevant, suitable 9 connected, intrinsic, pertinent 10 applicable 11 appropriate 12 appertaining

germaneness 9 relevance 10 pertinence 13 applicability 15 appropriateness

Germanic
language family: 12 Indo-European
group: 6 Gothic 15 Western Germanic

Germanic Mythology *see box*

German is spoken here
German: 25 hier wird Deutsch gesprochen

German literary movement (18th cent) 13 sturm und drang

Germanic Mythology
chief of gods: **5** Wotan
corresponds to Scandinavian: **4** Odin
dwarf: **15** Rumpelstiltskin
dwarves: **8** Niblungs **9** Nibelungs
emperor: **15** Dietrich von Bern
epic: **14** Nibelungenlied
goddess of clouds/sky/marriage: **3** Fri **5** Frigg, Frija **6** Frigga
goddess of death/fertility: **7** Berchta, Perchta
goddess of love/beauty/fecundity: **5** Freya
goddess of moon/witch: **5** Holle
god of thunder: **5** Donar
god of winter sports: **4** Ullr **5** Uller
hero: **6** Sigurd **9** Siegfried
heroine: **6** Gudrun, Kudrun **7** Guthrun **8** Brunhild **9** Kriemhild
king: **7** Siggeir
king of dwarves: **8** Alberich
knight of the holy grail: **9** Lohengrin
magic cloak: **9** Tarnkappe
maidens: **9** Valkyries
nature spirit: **7** Eriking
nymph: **7** Lorelei, Lurelei
water spirit: **3** Nix

Germany *see box*

Germany, East *see box*

Germany, West *see box, p. 390*

germicide **11** bactericide **12** disinfectant

Germinal
author: **9** Emile Zola

germinate **3** bud **4** blow, open **5** bloom, shoot **6** flower, push up, sprout **7** blossom, burgeon, develop **8** generate, spring up, vegetate

germination **9** sprouting **11** propagation

Gershom
means: **13** stranger there
father: **5** Moses
mother: **8** Zipporah
brother: **12** Eliezar

Gershwin, George
born: **10** Brooklyn NY

Germany
people: **3** Hun **4** Slav, Sorb, Wend **5** Saxon
artist: **4** Marc **5** Durer **7** Barlach, Cranach, Gropius, Holbein **9** Grunewald **14** Mies van der Rohe
author: **4** Mann, Marx **5** Grass **6** Brecht, Elsner, Goethe **7** Johnson, Lessing **8** Hochhuth
composer: **4** Bach **5** Weill **6** Brahms, Handel, Wagner **7** Strauss **8** Schumann **9** Beethoven, Hindemith **11** Mendelssohn
conductor: **5** Henze **6** Walter **9** Klemperer **11** Furtwangler, Stockhausen
leader: **6** Hitler, Kaiser **8** Bismarck **10** Barbarossa
Prussian noble: **6** Junker
religious leader: **6** Luther
language: **6** German **10** High German **11** Hochdeutsch
religion: **8** Lutheran **10** Protestant **13** Roman Catholic **17** Evangelical Church
food:
bread: **12** pumpernickel
dish: **9** lebkuchen **15** wiener schnitzel
dumpling: **6** knodel
frankfurter: **15** wiener wurstchen
fruit bread: **7** stollen
ham: **11** Westphalian
potato salad: **14** kartoffelsalat
pot roast: **11** sauerbraten
sausage: **5** wurst **9** blutwurst, bratwurst **10** brockwurst, knackwurst, leberwurst
sole: **8** seezunge

Germany, East
capital/largest city: **10** East Berlin
others: **4** Jena **5** Halle, Waren **6** Erfurt, Weimar **7** Cottbus, Dresden, Leipzig, Meissen, Potsdam, Rostock, Schwedt, Wannsee, Zwickau **9** Frankfurt, Magdeburg **10** Angermunde, Warnemunde, Wittenberg **11** Neustrelitz **13** Karl-Marx-Stadt (Chemnitz)
school: **8** Humboldt
division: **6** Saxony **9** Thuringia **11** Brandenburg, Mecklenburg **12** Saxony-Anhalt
government: **11** Volkskammer (Peoples' Chamber)
monetary unit: **4** mark **7** Ostmark, pfennig
lake: **6** Muritz
mountain: **3** Ore **4** Harz **10** Erzgebirge
highest point: **11** Fichtelberg
river: **4** Elbe, Oder **5** Havel, Saale, Spree **6** Neisse, Warnow
sea: **6** Baltic
physical feature:
forest: **10** Thuringian
place: **10** Berlin Wall **17** Checkpoint Charlie
castle: **9** Sans Souci
church: **8** St Thomas **12** Thomaskirche
city center: **13** Karl Marx Platz **14** Alexanderplatz, Neubrandenberg
comic opera: **12** Komische Oper
gate: **11** Brandenburg
museum: **7** Zwinger **8** Pergamon **10** Goethe Haus
opera house: **18** Deutsche Staatsoper
feature:
china: **7** Dresden
fair: **7** Leipzig
theater company: **16** Berliner Ensemble

Germany, West

capital: **4** Bonn

largest city: **10** West Berlin

others: **4** Kiel **5** Essen, Mainz, Trier **6** Aachen, Bochum, Bremen, Kassel, Lubeck, Minden, Munden, Munich **7** Cologne, Hamburg, Hanover, Krefeld, Munster **8** Augsburg, Biberach, Dortmund, Duisberg, Duisburg, Freiburg, Mannheim, Solingen **9** Darmstadt, Karlsruhe, Nuremberg, Oldenburg, Stuttgart, Wiesbaden, Wuppertal **10** Dusseldorf, Heidelberg, Steingaden **11** Saarbrucken **12** Oberammergau **13** Gelsenkirchen **15** Frankfurt am Main **16** Mulheim an der Ruhr

school: **4** Bonn **7** Hamburg **10** Heidelberg **16** Ludwig-Maximilian

division: **4** Saar **5** Baden, Hesse **6** Bremen **7** Bavaria **9** Rhineland **10** Palatinate, Westphalia **11** Lower Saxony, Wurttemberg **17** Schleswig-Holstein

head of government: **10** chancellor

monetary unit: **4** mark **7** pfennig **12** Deutsche mark

island: **11** East Frisian **12** North Frisian

lake: **9** Constance **11** Inner Alster, Outer Alster

mountain: **4** Harz **8** Feldberg **11** Black Forest **12** Bavarian Alps

highest point: **9** Zugspitze

river: **3** Ems **4** Elbe, Main, Nahe, Ruhr, Saar, Wese **5** Rhine, Weser **6** Danube, Neckar **7** Moselle, Pegnitz

sea: **5** North **6** Baltic

physical feature:
canal: **4** Kiel **10** Mittelland
forest: **5** Black **7** Bohemia **9** Teu Toburg

place: **17** Checkpoint Charlie
botanical garden: **18** Pflantzen und Blumen
boulevard: **14** Kurfurstendamm
church: **12** Frauenkirche (Cathedral of Our Lady) **13** Kaiser Wilhelm **16** Gadachtniskirche
city center: **11** Marienplatz
fortress: **9** Marksburg
fountain: **14** Schoner Brunnen
garden: **10** Englischer
hall: **9** Beethoven
museum: **8** Residenz **9** Durer Haus **12** Schatzkammer **14** Alte Pinakothek
opera house: **18** Deutsches Opern Haus
park/zoo: **18** Hagenbecks Tierpark
residential district: **11** Hansa Vierte **12** Hanse Viertel
resort (on Baltic): **10** Travemunde
theater: **9** Cuvillies

feature:
beer cellar: **11** bierkellern
beer garden: **10** biergarten
beer hall: **10** bierhallen
beer room: **10** bierstuben
cars: **3** BMW **7** Porsche **10** Volkswagen **12** Mercedes-Benz
children: **6** kinder
city hall: **5** Romer **7** Rathaus
festival: **11** Oktoberfest
folk songs: **11** volkslieder
kitchen: **5** kuche
old city: **8** Altstadt
pre-Lent carnival: **8** Fasching
secondary school: **9** gymnasium
states: **6** lander
wine street: **11** Weinstrasse

partner/lyricist: **11** Ira Gershwin
composer of: **9** Funny Face **11** Of Thee I Sing **12** Porgy and Bess **13** Cuban Overture **14** Rhapsody in Blue **15** Strike Up the Band **17** An American in Paris

Gertrude
character in: **6** Hamlet
author: **11** Shakespeare

Gervin, George
nickname: **6** Iceman
sport: **10** basketball
team: **15** San Antonio Spurs

Geryon
form: **7** monster
father: **8** Chrysaor
mother: **10** Callirrhoe
home: **7** Erythea
possessed: **6** cattle
color of cattle: **3** red
herdsman: **8** Eurytion
dog: **7** Orthrus
killed by: **8** Heracles
cattle stolen by: **8** Heracles

Gesta Romanorum
author: **7** unknown

gestation **9** evolution, pregnancy **10** epigenesis, generation, incubation, maturation **11** development, propagation

gesticulate **3** nod **4** wink **5** nudge, shrug **6** beckon, motion, signal **8** indicate **9** pantomime

gesture **3** nod **4** sign, wave, wink **5** nudge, shrug, touch **6** beckon, motion, signal **8** courtesy, dumb show, flourish, high sign **9** formality, pantomime **13** demonstration

get **3** bag, fix, net, wax, win **4** beat, coax, earn, gain, grab, grip, grow, have, hear, move, reap, sway, take, turn **5** annoy, catch, fetch, glean, grasp, learn, reach, seize, sense, upset **6** arrive, attain, baffle, become, collar, come by, come to, enlist, entrap, fathom, follow, induce, obtain, pick up, pocket, prompt, puzzle, secure, snatch, suborn, take in, turn to **7** achieve, acquire, capture, confuse, contact, dispose, ensnare, go after, incline, inherit, mystify, perplex, prepare, procure, realize, receive, wheedle, win over **8** bewilder, confound, contract, irritate, perceive, persuade **9** influence, transport **10** comprehend, disconcert, predispose, understand

get a kick out of **4** like **5** eat

up, enjoy, fancy, savor **6** relish **10** appreciate

getaway **6** escape, exodus, flight **10** decampment

get done **2** do **6** finish **8** complete **10** accomplish

get even **6** avenge **7** counter, hit back, pay back, revenge **9** retaliate

Gethsemane **6** garden

get into **3** don **5** enter, put on

get in touch with **5** reach **7** contact

get lost **4** scat, shoo **5** be off, leave, scram **6** beat it, begone, depart, go away **7** vamoose

get one's dander up **4** gall, rile **5** anger **6** enrage, madden, nettle, ruffle **7** incense, inflame, outrage **9** infuriate

get out of bed **4** rise **5** arise **12** rise and shine

get rid of **4** drop, dump, junk, shed **5** ditch, scrap **6** banish, cut out, delete, remove, unload **7** abolish, discard, weed out **8** jettison, stamp out, throw out **9** eliminate, eradicate **10** annihilate **11** exterminate

Get Smart
character: **5** Hymie (CONTROL robot) **7** Agent 99, Carlson, Starker **8** Larrabee, The Chief (Thaddeus) **12** Maxwell Smart (Agent 86) **15** Conrad Siegfried
cast: **8** Don Adams **9** King Moody **10** Stacy Keach **11** Dave Ketchum, Dick Gautier, Edward Platt **12** Bernie Kopell **13** Barbara Feldon **14** Robert Karvelas
Max worked for: **7** CONTROL
foe: **4** KAOS

get the better of **4** foil, rout **5** crush, quell **6** baffle, defeat, thwart **7** conquer **8** confound, overcome **9** frustrate, overthrow

get the upper hand of **5** quell **6** master **7** conquer **8** dominate, overcome, surmount

get the worst of **4** fail, fall, lose

Getting Even
author: **10** Woody Allen

get to **5** reach **8** approach

get-together **2** do **3** bee **4** meet **5** agree, party, visit **6** affair, gather, hobnob **7** meeting **8** assemble, assembly **9** gathering

getup **3** rig **6** attire, outfit **7** costume **8** disguise, ensemble

get up **4** find, rise **5** arise, rouse, stand **8** assemble

get used to **5** adapt, inure **6** adjust **8** accustom **9** acclimate, habituate

gewgaws **7** baubles, doodads, trifles **8** trinkets **9** bric-a-brac, gimcracks, kickshaws, ornaments **11** knickknacks

Ghana ***see box***

ghastly **3** wan **4** grim, ugly **5** ashen, pasty, weird **6** dismal, glassy, grisly, horrid, odious, pallid **7** fearful, ghostly, haggard, hideous, uncanny **8** blanched, dreadful, gruesome, horrible, shocking, spectral, terrible **9** appalling, colorless, deathlike, frightful, ghostlike, loathsome, repellent, repulsive, revolting **10** cadaverous, corpselike, forbidding, horrendous, lackluster, terrifying

Ghiberti, Lorenzo
born: **5** Italy **8** Florence
artwork: **9** St Matthew, St Stephen **15** Gates of Paradise (baptistry doors) **16** St John the Baptist **19** The Sacrifice of Isaac

ghost **4** hint **5** demon, shade, spook, trace **6** goblin, shadow, sprite, wraith **7** banshee, chimera, phantom, specter **8** phantasm **9** hobgoblin, phantasma, semblance **10** apparition, suggestion **12** Doppelganger **13** manifestation **15** materialization

Ghost and Mrs Muir, The
character: **11** Candice Muir, Martha Grant **12** Jonathan Muir **13** Claymore Gregg **14** Mrs Carolyn Muir **18** Captain Daniel Gregg
TV cast: **8** Reta Shaw **9** Hope Lange **13** Edward Mulhare **14** Harlen Carraher, Kellie Flanagan **19** Charles Nelson Reilly
setting: **11** Gull Cottage
director: **17** Joseph L Mankiewicz
movie cast: **8** Edna Best **11** Gene Tierney, Rex Harrison **13** George Sanders

Ghostbusters
director: **11** Ivan Reitman
screenplay: **10** Dan Ackroyd **11** Harold Ramis
cast: **10** Bill Murray, Dan Ackroyd **11** Harold Ramis **15** Sigourney Weaver

ghostly **4** pale **5** eerie, weird **6** spooky, unreal **7** ghastly, phantom, shadowy, uncanny **8** illusive, spectral **9** unearthly **10** phantasmal, wraithlike

Ghana
other name: **9** Gold Coast
capital/largest city: **5** Accra, Akkra
others: **3** Oda **4** Axim, Fian, Keta, Tala, Tema **5** Bawku, Enchi, Lawra, Legon, Sampa, Yapei **6** Dunkwa, Karaga, Kpandu, Kumasi, Nsawam, Obuasi, Swedru, Tamale, Tarkwa, Wasipe **7** Antubia, Damongo, Mampong, Prestea, Sekondi, Sunyani, Winneba **8** Akosombo, Kintampo, Takoradi **9** Cape Coast **15** Sekondi-Takoradi
school: **6** Kumasi **9** Cape Coast
monetary unit: **4** cedi **5** ackey
lake: **5** Volta **8** Bosumtwi
mountain: **12** Akwapim Hills
highest point: **8** Afadjato
river: **3** Oti, Pra **4** Daka, Tano **5** Afram, Volta **7** Ankobra, Kulpawn **10** Black Volta, White Volta
sea: **8** Atlantic
physical feature:
gulf: **6** Guinea
people: **2** Ga **3** Ewe **4** Akan, Akim, Akra, Aksa **5** Ahafo, Brong, Inkra **7** Akwapim, Ashanti, Dagomba **8** Mamprusi **11** Mole-Dagbani
language: **2** Ga **3** Ewe, Gur, Kwa, Twi **5** Fanti, Hausa **7** Dagomba, English
religion: **5** Islam **7** animism **13** Roman Catholic
feature:
castle: **14** Christiansborg
dam: **8** Akosombo
national dress: **5** kente

11 phantomlike 12 supernatural

ghostly double
German: 12 Doppelganger

Ghosts
author: 11 Henrik Ibsen
character: 7 Manders 12 Oswald Alving 14 Jacob Engstrand, Mrs Helen Alving 15 Regina Engstrand

ghoulish 5 eerie, scary, weird 7 demonic, hellish, macabre, ogreish, satanic 8 diabolic, fiendish, gruesome, infernal, sinister 9 monstrous 10 horrifying, zombielike 11 hair-raising, necrophilic

Giacometti, Alberto
born: 11 Switzerland 12 Stampa-Tessin
artwork: 3 Dog 7 The Cage 8 Caroline 10 City Square 11 Head of Diego, Man Pointing 14 Reclining Woman 17 The Palace at Four Am 19 Hands Holding the Void

Gianni Schicchi
opera by: 7 Puccini
character: 11 Buoso Donati

giant 3 big 4 huge 5 titan 7 Goliath, spanker, thumper, whopper 8 behemoth, colossus, strapper 9 Gargantua 14 Brobdingnagian

Giant
director: 13 George Stevens
author: 10 Edna Ferber
cast: 9 James Dean 10 Chill Wills, Rock Hudson 11 Jane Withers 12 Carroll Baker 15 Elizabeth Taylor
setting: 5 Texas
Oscar for: 8 director

Giant *see* 8 Gigantes

giant people 6 Anakim

Giants in the Earth
author: 9 O E Rolvaag
character: 3 Ole 5 Beret 8 Per Hanea 9 Anna Marie 12 Hans Kristian 15 Peder Victorious

gibber 3 gab 4 blab 5 prate 6 babble, gabble, jabber 7 blabber, blather, chatter, prattle 8 chitchat

gibberish 4 blab, bosh 6 babble, drivel, gabble 7 blather, twaddle 8 nonsense 10 balderdash, double-talk, flapdoodle, hocus-pocus, mumbo-jumbo 12 gobbledegook

Gibbon, Edward
author of: 33 The (History of the) Decline and Fall of the Roman Empire

gibbous 6 convex, curved, humped 7 bulging, rounded, swollen 8 swelling 10 humpbacked, protuberant

Gibbs family
characters in: 7 Our Town
member: 6 George 7 Rebecca
author: 6 Wilder

gibe, jibe 3 rag 4 jeer, mock, quip, razz, twit 5 chaff, flout, knock, toast, scoff, sneer, taunt 6 deride, needle, rail at 7 mockery, poke fun, sarcasm 8 brickbat, derision, ridicule, taunting 9 criticism, wisecrack

Gibraltar
other name: 11 rock of Tarik 13 Djebel al-Tarik 15 rock of Gibraltar
largest city: 9 Gibraltar
government: 18 British crown colony
head of government: 15 governor general
mountain: 6 Misery
sea: 13 Mediterranean
physical feature:
bay: 5 Ceuta, Rosia, Sandy 6 Catlan 9 Algeciras
cliffs: 17 Pillars of Hercules
people: 6 Jewish 7 British, Maltese, Spanish 8 Italians 10 Portuguese
language: 7 English, Spanish
feature: 12 King's Bastion
gardens: 7 Alameda

Gibson, Mel
roles: 6 Mad Max 9 Gallipoli, The Bounty 12 Lethal Weapon 14 The Road Warrior 26 The Year of Living Dangerously

Giddens, Regina
character in: 14 The Little Foxes
author: 7 Hellman

giddy 5 dizzy, faint, silly 6 fickle, fitful 7 awesome, erratic, flighty, muddled, reeling 8 careless, dizzying, fainting, fanciful, reckless, swimming, unsteady, volatile, whirling 9 befuddled, frivolous, impulsive, mercurial, whimsical 10 capricious, changeable, inconstant 11 hare-brained, harum-scarum, lightheaded, thoughtless, vacillating, vertiginous 12 inconsistent, overpowering 13 irresponsible, rattlebrained

Gide, Andre
author of: 13 The Immoralist 15 Strait Is the Gate 17 The Counterfeiters 18 Lafcadio's Adventure (The Vatican Swindle) 19 The Pastoral Symphony

Gideon 11 Hebrew judge
father: 5 Joash, Ophra
son: 9 Abimelech
also called: 9 Jerubbaal

Gidget
character: 5 Larue 10 Anne Cooper, John Cooper 16 Francine (Gidget) Lawrence 21 Professor Russ Lawrence
cast: 9 Don Porter 10 Peter Deuel, Sally Field 11 Betty Conner 13 Lynette Winter

Gielgud, Sir John
born: 6 London 7 England
roles: 6 Arthur, Becket, Hamlet 7 Macbeth 9 Saint Joan 26 The Barretts of Wimpole Street 27 The Importance of Being Earnest

gift 3 aid, dot, fee, sop, tip 4 alms, bent, boon, dole, help, turn 5 award, bonus, bribe, craft, dower, dowry, favor, flair, forte, graft, grant, knack, power, prize, skill 6 genius, legacy, talent, virtue 7 aptness, bequest, faculty, handout, largess, premium, present, quality, tribute 8 aptitude, capacity, donation, facility, gratuity, offering, property 9 attribute, endowment, expertise, ingenuity 10 adroitness, capability, competency 11 benefaction, proficiency 12 contribution 13 consideration, qualification

gifted 4 able, deft 5 adept, crack, handy, quick, slick 6 adroit, bright, clever, expert, facile, master, wizard 7 capable, skilled 8 finished, masterly, polished, superior, talented 9 brilliant, ingenious, inventive, practiced, qualified 10 proficient 11 crackerjack, experienced, resourceful 12 accomplished

Gift From the Sea, The
author: 19 Anne Morrow Lindbergh

gig 3 job 4 trap 5 stint 6 chaise 7 dogcart 8 carriage, curricle 10 engagement

Gigantes
single member: 5 giant
father: 6 Uranus
mother: 4 Gaea

heads of: 3 men
bodies of: 8 serpents
attacked: 4 gods

gigantic 4 huge, vast 5 bulky, jumbo 6 mighty 7 hulking, immense, lumpish, mammoth, massive, titanic 8 colossal, enormous, lubberly, towering, unwieldy 9 herculean, monstrous, ponderous, strapping 10 gargantuan, prodigious, stupendous, tremendous, voluminous 11 elephantine

Gigantomachia
war of: 6 giants

giggle 6 cackle, hee-hee, simper, tee-hee, titter 7 chuckle, snicker, snigger, twitter

Gigi
director: 16 Vincente Minnelli
based on story by: 7 Colette
cast: 8 Eva Gabor 11 Leslie Caron 12 Louis Jourdan 15 Hermione Gingold, Jacques Bergerac 16 Maurice Chevalier
score: 14 Lerner and Loewe
Oscar for: 7 picture 8 director
song: 4 Gigi 15 I Remember It Well 25 Thank Heaven for Little Girls 29 The Night They Invented Champagne

Gilbert, Cass
architect of: 14 US Customs House (NYC) 17 Woolworth Building (NYC) 20 Supreme Court Building (Washington DC) 21 Minnesota State Capitol (St Paul) 22 George Washington Bridge

Gilbert, John
real name: 11 John Pringle
wife: 9 Ina Claire 11 Leatrice Joy 13 Virginia Bruce
born: 7 Logan UT
roles: 4 Love 12 The Big Parade 13 The Merry Widow 15 A Woman of Affairs 16 Flesh and the Devil

Gilbert, William
field: 7 physics
nationality: 7 British
father of: 11 electricity
named for him: 27 CGS unit of magnetomotive force

Gilbert, W S, and Sullivan, Arthur Seymour
composers of: 7 Ivanhoe 8 Iolanthe, Patience 9 Ruddigore, The Mikado 11 H M S Pinafore, Princess Ida, The Sorcerer, Trial by Jury 12 The Grand Duke 13 The Gondoliers, Utopia Limited 19 The Yeoman of the Guard 20 The Pirates of Penzance 24 Thespis or The Gods Grown Old

Gilbert Islands *see* 8 Kiribati

Gil Blas (of Santillane)
author: 11 Alain LeSage
character: 6 Scipio 11 Don Alphonso

Gilbreth, Frank B, Jr
author of: 17 Cheaper by the Dozen (with Ernestine Gilbreth Carey)

gild 4 bend 5 slant, twist 7 cover up, stretch, touch up 10 exaggerate

Gilded Age, The
authors: 9 Mark Twain 19 Charles Dudley Warner

gilded youth
French: 13 jeunesse doree

Gileadite password
10 Shibboleth

Giles Goat-Boy
author: 9 John Barth

Gilgal 5 wheel 6 circle

Gilgamesh
origin: 8 Sumerian
king of: 4 Uruk 5 Erech
servant: 6 Enkidu

gill
abbreviation: 2 gi

Gilligan's Island
character: 7 Skipper (Jonas Grumby) 8 Gilligan 9 Mrs Howell (Lovey), Professor (Roy Hinkley) 11 Ginger Grant 14 Mary Ann Summers 17 Thurston Howell III
cast: 9 Bob Denver, Dawn Wells, Jim Backus 10 Alan Hale Jr, Tina Louise 14 Natalie Schafer, Russell Johnson
ship: 6 Minnow

Gillooly, Edna Rae
real name of: 12 Ellen Burstyn

Gills, Solomon
character in: 12 Dombey and Son
author: 7 Dickens

Gilyak
language spoken in: 4 Amur 8 Sakhalin

gimcrack 5 bijou, curio 6 bauble, gewgaw, trifle 7 trinket, whatnot 8 kickshaw, ornament 9 bagatelle, plaything 10 knickknack 11 contrivance, thingamabob, thingamajig

gimmick 4 plan, ploy, ruse, wile 5 angle, dodge, stunt 6 design, device, gadget, scheme 7 wrinkle 9 stratagem 10 subterfuge 11 contrivance

gin ***see box, p. 394***

ginger 3 pep, tan 5 brown, spice 6 energy
varieties: 3 red 4 wild 5 crape, crepe, shell, torch, white 6 canton, common, Kahili, orchid, spiral, yellow 9 butterfly 10 small shell, variegated
botanical name: 8 Zingiber 12 Z officinales
Sanskrit: 9 singabera
origin: 4 Asia 5 China, India 7 Jamaica
use: 6 tongue 7 vinegar 9 beef stock 11 baked dishes, gingerbread 12 chicken stock

gingerly 6 warily 7 charily, timidly 8 daintily 9 carefully, finically, guardedly, heedfully, mincingly, prudently 10 cautiously, delicately, discreetly, hesitantly, vigilantly, watchfully 11 squeamishly 12 fastidiously, suspiciously 13 circumspectly

gingham 5 cloth 6 cotton, fabric, striped 8 chambray 9 checkered

gin mill 4 dive 9 honky-tonk, roadhouse

Ginnungagap
origin: 12 Scandinavian
void filled with: 4 mist
between: 9 Nifelheim 10 Muspelheim

Ginsberg, Allen
author of: 4 Howl 7 Kaddish 10 Planet News 11 Mind Breaths 16 The Fall of America 20 Reality and Sandwiches

Giono, Jean
author of: 6 Regain 7 Colline, Harvest 13 Hill of Destiny 18 The Hussar on the Roof

Giordano, Umberto
born: 5 Italy 6 Foggia
composer of: 6 Fedora 8 Mala Vita 13 Andrea Chenier 14 Madame Sans-Gene

Giorgione da Castelfranco
born: 5 Italy 12 Castelfranco
artwork: 10 The Tempest 13 Ordeal of Moses, Sleeping Venus 17 Judgment of Solomon 19 The Concert Champetre (disputed) 20 The Three Philosophers 23 Adoration of the Shepherds

Giotto di Bondone
born: 5 Italy 8 (near) Florence
artwork attributed: 17 Ognissanti Madonna 31 Presentation of Christ in the Temple 32 St Francis Surrounded by his Brothers

gin
origin: **11** Netherlands
ingredient: **6** grains **12** juniper berry
type: **6** Geneva **8** Plymouth **9** London dry
drink: **5** Allen **6** Gibson, gimlet **7** Belmont, Bennett, gin Fizz, swizzle **8** Pink Lady **9** Gin Rickey **10** Tom Collins **11** Alabama Fizz, gin and tonic **12** Grand Passion **14** Casino Cocktail
with anisette: **8** Snowball **11** Bachio Punch
with apricot brandy: **14** Boston Cocktail
with brandy: **15** Bermuda Highball
with Chartreuse: **5** Bijou **9** Green Lady
with cherry brandy: **14** Singapore Sling
with Cointreau: **7** Florida **9** White Lady **13** Sweet Patootie **14** Flying Dutchman
with creme de cacao: **9** Alexander
with creme de cassis: **8** Parisian
with creme de menthe: **6** Caruso, Virgin
with creme Yvette: **9** Union Jack
with Curacao: **8** Blue Moon, Napoleon **9** Blue Devil **14** Flying Dutchman
with Dubonnet: **3** BVD **8** Napoleon
with Grand Marnier: **7** Red Lion
with grapefruit juice: **8** Salty Dog
with kirsch, kirschwasser: **7** Florida **10** Lady Finger
with onions: **6** Gibson
with orange juice: **5** Abbey **13** Orange Blossom
with Pernod: **7** Dubarry
with rum: **3** BVD
with scotch: **12** Barbary Coast
with sherry: **11** Renaissance
with strawberries: **10** Bloodhound
with Swedish Punch: **5** Biffy
with vermouth: **5** Bijou, Bronx, Tango **6** Caruso **7** Bermuda, Cabaret, Martini **10** Bloodhound
with vodka: **15** Russian Cocktail

Giovanelli
character in: **11** Daisy Miller
author: **5** James

Giovanni's Room
author: **12** James Baldwin

Giraffe
constellation of: **14** Camelopardalis

girandole **11** candelabrum, candlestick **12** candleholder

Girardon, Francois
born: **6** France, Troyes
artwork: **13** Bathing Nymphs **14** Galley of Apollo, Virgin of Troyes **16** Rape of Persephone **17** (tomb for) Cardinal Richelieu **23** Apollo Tended by the Nymphs

Giraudoux, Jean
author of: **5** Bella **6** Judith, Ondine, Racine **7** Electra **12** Amphitryon 38 **15** Tiger at the Gates **18** Madwoman of Chaillot **20** My Friend from Limousin

gird **3** pen, tie **4** belt, girt, loop, ring **5** brace, hem in, hitch, steel, strap, truss **6** circle, fasten, girdle, harden, secure, wall in **7** besiege, confine, enclose, fortify, hedge in, prepare, stiffen, sustain, tighten **8** blockade, buttress, encircle, lay siege, surround **9** encompass **10** strengthen **12** circumscribe

girder **4** beam **5** brace, truss **6** binder, rafter **7** support, tiebeam

girdle **3** hem **4** band, belt, ring, sash **5** girth, hedge, stays **6** bodice, circle, corset **7** baldric, circlet, contour **8** boundary, cincture, corselet **9** surcingle, waistband **10** cummerbund **12** waist cincher **17** foundation garment

girl **4** bird, cook, help, lass, maid, minx, miss **5** angel, chick, nymph, wench **6** damsel, kitten, lassie, maiden, pigeon, virgin **7** baggage, colleen, darling, fiancee, ingenue, nymphet **8** daughter, domestic, handmaid, lady love, mistress, scullion **9** affianced, betrothed, inamorata, lady's maid, soubrette **10** sweetheart **11** maidservant
French: **10** demoiselle, jeune fille

girl Friday **4** aide **6** helper **9** assistant, secretary **10** amanuensis **12** office worker **23** administrative assistant

girlfriend **6** steady **7** beloved, sweetie **8** best girl **10** one and only, sweetheart

Girl in a Swing
author: **12** Richard Adams

girlish **8** girl-like, maidenly, youthful **10** maidenlike

Girl of the Golden West, The
opera by: **7** Puccini
setting: **8** Gold Rush **10** California
character: **6** Minnie **7** Johnson, Sheriff

girt **4** belt, bind, gird, ring **5** bound, girth **6** belted, circle, girdle, ringed **7** circled, girdled **9** encircled

girth **5** cinch **9** perimeter **10** saddle band **13** circumference

Giselle
ballet by: **4** (Adolphe Charles) Adam

Gish, Lillian
real name: **12** Lillian Gishi **15** Lillian de Guiche
born: **13** Springfield OH
roles: **8** La Boheme **10** Enoch Arden **11** Annie Laurie, Intolerance, Way Down East **12** Duel in the Sun **13** Scarlet Letter **14** Broken Blossoms **16** Portrait of Jennie **17** Orphans of the Storm, The Birth of a Nation

Gissing, George
author of: **5** Demos **13** New Grub Street **14** The Nether World

gist **4** core, crux, meat, pith **5** drift, force, heart, sense, tenor, theme **6** burden, center, effect, import, kernel, marrow, spirit **7** essence, purport **8** main idea **9** main point, substance **11** implication **12** significance

Giuki
also: **5** Gjuki
origin: **12** Scandinavian
mentioned in: **8** Volsunga
form: **4** king
wife: **8** Grimhild
daughter: **6** Gudrun, Kudrun **7** Guthrun
son: **6** Gunnar

Giukung
also: **7** Gjukung

origin: **12** Scandinavian
family member of: **5** Giuki, Gjuki

Giulio Romano
architect of: **12** Palazzo del Te
style: **9** Mannerist

give ***see box***

give aid to **4** help **6** assist, succor **7** help out **8** befriend **9** look after **10** minister to

give a leg up **3** aid **4** help, lift **5** boost, hoist, raise **6** assist **7** elevate

give and take **8** exchange **10** compromise **11** interchange, reciprocity

give a pep talk to **4** goad, prod, spur **5** press **6** exhort **9** encourage

give a reason for **7** clarify, clear up, explain, justify **9** elucidate **10** account for

give as security **4** pawn **6** pledge **7** deposit, pay down, put down

give away **6** bestow, betray, donate, reveal **7** hand out

give birth **4** bear **5** hatch **6** create, invent **7** deliver, develop **9** originate **10** bring forth

give confidence to **7** inspire **8** embolden, inspirit **9** encourage

give courage **5** brace **6** buck up **7** hearten **8** inspirit, motivate

give energy to **7** animate, enliven **8** activate, energize, vitalize **9** stimulate **10** invigorate

give enjoyment **5** amuse, charm **6** divert, please **7** beguile, delight **8** enthrall **9** entertain

give forth **4** emit, gush **5** exude, issue **7** send out **8** throw off, transmit **9** discharge

give full attention **7** pay heed **8** fasten on **11** concentrate

give in **5** defer, yield **6** accede, cave in, submit **7** succumb **9** surrender **10** capitulate **12** knuckle under

give in to **7** yield to **9** indulge in, partake of **16** abandon oneself to

give leave **3** let **5** allow **6** permit **8** sanction **9** authorize **14** give permission

give moral support to **3** aid **4** abet, back, help **6** assist, uphold **7** support, sustain **8** sanction **9** encourage

given **3** apt **4** wont **5** prone **6** likely, wonted **7** awarded, donated, granted, offered **8** accorded, bestowed **9** committed, conferred, entrusted, presented **10** accustomed, handed over, in the habit **11** contributed **13** furnished with, made a donation, presented with **17** made a contribution

give new life to **3** fan **4** fire **6** awaken, revive **8** revivify **10** rejuvenate **11** reincarnate

give oneself to **8** dedicate **10** buckle down, consecrate

give one's word **3** vow **5** swear **6** assure, pledge **7** certify, promise, warrant **9** guarantee

give one walking papers **3** axe, can **4** fire, oust, sack **5** let go **6** bounce, lay off **7** cashier, dismiss, release **8** get rid of **9** discharge, terminate **11** give the gate, send packing

give out **4** quit, tell, tire **6** assign, inform, reveal, run out **7** divulge, dole out, mete out **8** allocate, announce, disclose, dispense, proclaim **9** apportion, broadcast, parcel out **10** distribute, make public, portion out **11** disseminate

give over **4** cede **5** yield **9** surrender **10** relinquish

give permission **3** let **5** allow **6** accede, permit **7** approve **8** sanction **9** acquiesce, authorize, give leave

give rise to **4** sire **5** breed, cause **6** lead to **7** produce **8** engender, generate, occasion **9** call forth **10** bring about

give support to **3** aid **4** abet **5** serve **6** defend, prop up, second **7** bolster, comfort, sustain **8** buttress, champion **10** contribute, minister to, provide for, stick up for

give the go-ahead **4** okay **5** order **6** direct **7** appoint, charter, empower **8** contract **9** authorize **10** commission

give the lie to **5** belie **8** disprove **9** repudiate **10** contradict, controvert

give the raspberry **3** boo, pan **4** razz **6** deride, hoot at **8** ridicule **11** give the bird **17** give the Bronx cheer

give the right to **5** allow **6** permit **7** entitle, qualify **9** authorize

give the slip **4** duck **5** avoid, dodge, elude, evade

give up **4** cede, drop, lose, quit, skip **5** forgo, let go, waive, yield **6** eschew, resign **7** abandon, forfeit, forsake **8** abdicate, forswear, renounce **9** sacrifice, surrender **10** relinquish **11** discontinue

give up the ghost **3** die **6** expire, pass on, perish **7** decease **8** pass away **15** breathe one's last

give vent **4** free **5** let go **7** release **8** let loose, liberate **12** give free rein

give way **4** fall **6** buckle, cave in **7** crumple **8** collapse **10** break apart

giving birth **7** bearing **8** creating, creation, delivery, hatching **9** inventing, invention **10** childbirth, delivering

---

give **3** buy, pay, tip **4** bend, ease, emit, hire, lend, show, sink **5** admit, allot, allow, apply, award, bribe, deign, endow, grant, issue, leave, offer, relax, utter, voice, yield **6** accord, addict, afford, assign, attach, bestow, bounce, commit, confer, convey, devote, donate, enable, enrich, hand to, impart, loosen, notify, open on, permit, recede, relent, render, shrink, supply, tender, unbend, vest in **7** concede, consign, deliver, entrust, fork out, furnish, hand out, let know, present, proffer, provide, requite, retreat, slacken **8** announce, bequeath, collapse, dispense, exchange, fork over, hand over, lead on to, make over, move back, put forth, shell out **9** apportion, break down, dispose of, equip with, favor with, look out on, present to, pronounce, subscribe, surrender, vouchsafe **10** articulate, become soft, compensate, contribute, deliquesce, distribute, recompense, remunerate, resilience, supply with **11** communicate, flexibility, provide with, springiness

---

11 originating, origination, parturition

giving up 7 refusal **8** dropping, quitting, yielding **9** resigning **10** abandoning, abdicating, abdication, abstinence, continence, forbearing, forfeiting, forfeiture, self-denial **11** abandonment, forswearing, resignation **12** renunciation, surrendering **14** relinquishment

gizmo 4 tool **6** device, doodad, gadget **9** apparatus, implement, invention, mechanism **10** instrument **11** contraption, contrivance, thingamabob, thingamajig

Gjuki *see* **5** Giuki

Gjukung *see* **7** Giukung

glacial 3 icy, raw **4** cold **5** chill, gelid, polar **6** arctic, biting, bitter, frigid, frosty, frozen, wintry **7** hostile **8** freezing, inimical, piercing **9** congealed **10** disdainful, unfriendly **12** antagonistic, bone-chilling, contemptuous

Glackens, William James
born: 14 Philadelphia PA
artwork: 9 Promenade **11** Chez Mouquin **15** Nude with an Apple **16** Washington Square (A Holiday in the Park) **17** Luxembourg Gardens

glad 5 happy **6** elated, joyful, joyous **7** elating, gleeful, pleased, tickled **8** blissful, cheerful, cheering, pleasing, rejoiced **9** contented, delighted, joy-giving **10** delightful, entrancing, gratifying **11** exhilarated, tickled pink **12** exhilarating

gladden 5 cheer, elate **6** please **7** animate, cheer up, delight, enliven, gratify, hearten, rejoice **8** inspirit, pleasure **9** make happy **10** exhilarate

gladdened 5 happy **6** joyful, joyous **8** cheerful

glade 4 dell, glen, lawn, vale, wood **5** grove, marsh, vista **6** canada, hollow, valley **7** opening **8** clearing

gladness 3 joy **4** glee **5** bliss, cheer, mirth **7** delight, gaiety, jollity **8** pleasure **9** happiness **10** joyfulness **11** contentment **12** cheerfulness

glad rags 5 array **6** attire, finery **10** Sunday best

Gladsheim
origin: 12 Scandinavian
palace of: 4 Odin **5** Othin
location: 8 Valhalla

gladsome 3 gay **5** happy, merry **6** cheery, joyful, joyous **8** cheerful **12** lighthearted

glamor, glamour 5 charm, magic **6** allure **7** glitter, romance **8** illusion **9** adventure, challenge, magnetism **10** excitement **11** enchantment, fascination **14** attractiveness

glamorous, glamourous 8 alluring, charming, dazzling, exciting, magnetic **10** attractive, bewitching, enchanting **11** captivating, charismatic, fascinating

glance 4 kiss, peek, peep, scan, skim, slip **5** brush, graze, shave, touch **6** bounce, careen, squint **7** glimpse, rebound **8** ricochet **9** brief look, quick look, quick view
French: 6 apercu

glance through 4 scan, skim **6** browse, peruse **7** dip into **8** look over **9** check over

gland
part of: 15 endocrine system
type: 4 duct **8** ductless
kind: 3 oil **5** sweat **7** adrenal, thyroid **8** pancreas **9** pituitary **11** parathyroid
ductless gland secretes: 8 hormones

glare 4 glow **5** blaze, flame, flare, flash, gleam, glint, gloss, lower, scowl, sheen **6** dazzle, glower **7** flicker, glimmer, glisten, glitter, radiate, shimmer, sparkle, twinkle **8** radiance **9** angry look, black look, dirty look **10** brightness, harsh light, luminosity **12** resplendence

glaring 4 rank **5** gross, harsh, vivid **6** arrant, bright, strong **7** blatant, flaring, intense, obvious **8** blinding, dazzling, flagrant, piercing **9** audacious, brilliant, egregious **10** glittering, outrageous, shimmering **11** conspicuous, penetrating, resplendent, unconcealed, undisguised **12** unmistakable

Glasgow, Ellen
author of: 10 Vein of Iron **12** Barren Ground **13** In this Our Life, Sheltered Life **18** They Stooped to Folly **20** The Romantic Comedians

glass 6 beaker, goblet **7** chalice, tumbler **10** tumblerful
type of: 4 fizz, sour **5** flute, tulip **6** jigger, sherry **7** balloon, collins, cordial, red wine, snifter **8** cocktail, highball **9** champagne, white wine **10** hollow-stem, pousse cafe **12** old-fashioned

glasshouse 7 nursery **8** hothouse **10** greenhouse **12** conservatory

glassiness 7 clarity **8** dullness, flatness **9** shininess **10** brilliance, luminosity **12** lifelessness, transparency

Glass Key, The
author: 15 Dashiell Hammett
character: 9 Shad O'Rory **10** Janet Henry, Opal Madvig, Paul Madvig **11** Ned Beaumont **12** Senator Henry **13** Bernie Despain

Glass Menagerie, The
director: 12 Irving Rapper
author: 17 Tennessee Williams
character: 5 Laura **6** Amanda **12** Tom Wingfield
cast: 9 Jane Wyman **11** Kirk Douglas **13** Arthur Kennedy **16** Gertrude Lawrence

glassware 5 agata **6** aurene **7** crystal, favrile, steuben, vitrics **8** amerina, stemware
worker: 7 glazier

glassy 4 dull **5** clear, shiny **6** glazed, smooth **8** lifeless **10** glittering **11** transparent

Glauber, Johann Rudolf
field: 9 chemistry
nationality: 6 German
prepared: 12 tartar emetic **13** sodium sulfate (Glauber's salt) **16** hydrochloric acid

Glauce *see* **6** Creusa

Glaucus
god of: 3 sea
father: 5 Minos
ally of: 7 Trojans
loved by: 5 Circe **6** Scylla **10** Amphitrite

glaze 4 blur **5** gloss **6** enamel, finish **7** grow dim, varnish **8** film over **9** glass over

glazed 4 iced **5** filmy **6** coated, glassy, shined, smooth **7** glossed, sugared **8** enameled, lustrous, polished **9** burnished, varnished

Glazunoff, Alex K (Glazunov, Alexander Konstantinovich)
born: 6 Russia **12** St Petersburg
composer of: 10 Chopiniana, The Seasons **11** Stenka Razin **13** Hymn to Pushkin **15** Memorial Cantata

gleam 3 bit, jot, ray **4** beam, drop, glow, hint, iota **5** blink, flare, flash, glare, glint, gloss, grain, sheen, shine, spark, speck, trace **6** luster, streak

7 flicker, glimmer, glimpse, glisten, glitter, inkling, shimmer, sparkle, tiny bit, twinkle 8 least bit, radiance 9 coruscate 10 brightness, brilliance, effulgence 11 coruscation, scintillate

gleaming 5 clear, shiny 6 bright, flashy, glossy 7 shining, radiant 8 dazzling, glinting, luminous, lustrous, polished, splendid 9 brilliant, burnished, sparkling 10 glistening

glean 4 cull 5 amass 6 gather, pick up 7 harvest 10 accumulate 13 piece together 14 scrape together

gleanings 8 analects, extracts 10 miscellany, selections 11 collectanea, miscellanea 15 commonplace book

Gleason, Jackie
real name: 18 Herbert John Gleason
nickname: 15 Mr Saturday Night
born: 10 Brooklyn NY
roles: 5 Gigot 6 The Toy 10 The Hustler 11 Life of Riley, The Poor Soul 12 Ralph Kramden 15 Joe the Bartender, The Honeymooners 17 Don't Drink the Water, Jackie Gleason Show, The Time of Your Life 22 Requiem for a Heavyweight 24 Reggie Van Gleason the Third

glebe 3 sod 4 clod, land, plot, soil 5 earth, field 6 termon 8 kirktown 10 church land

glee 3 joy 5 mirth, verve 6 gaiety 7 delight, ecstasy, jollity, rapture 8 gladness, hilarity, laughter 9 joviality, merriment 10 exultation, jocularity, joyfulness, joyousness, liveliness 11 playfulness 12 cheerfulness, exhilaration, sportiveness 13 jollification, sprightliness

glee club 6 chorus 12 singing group 13 choral society

gleeful 3 gay 4 glad 5 happy, jolly, merry 6 elated, jocund, jovial, joyful, joyous, lively 7 festive 8 blissful, cheerful, exultant, mirthful 9 delighted 11 exhilarated 12 lighthearted

Gleipnir
origin: 12 Scandinavian
chain that bound: 6 Fenrir, Fenris

glen 4 dale, dell, vale 6 bottom, hollow

Glencaire Cycle
author: 12 Eugene O'Neill

glib 4 oily 5 gabby, quick, ready, suave 6 facile, fluent, smooth 7 devious, voluble 8 flippant, slippery, unctuous 9 insincere, talkative

glide 3 run 4 flow, roll, sail, skim, slip, soar 5 coast, drift, float, issue, skate, slide, steal 6 elapse, stream 7 proceed 8 glissade

glider 5 swing 7 aviator 9 sailplane 10 hydroplane

glimmer 3 bit, ray 4 beam, drop, glow, hint 5 blink, flare, flash, glare, gleam, grain, shine, speck, trace 7 flicker, glimpse, glisten, glitter, shimmer, sparkle, twinkle 9 coruscate, scintilla 10 flickering, intimation 11 scintillate

glimpse 3 see, spy 4 espy, peek, peep, spot 6 glance, peek at, peep at, squint 9 brief look, quick look, quick view 12 catch sight of, fleeting look
French: 6 apercu

Glinka, Mikhail Ivanovich
born: 6 Russia 8 Smolensk
composer of: 12 Ivan Sussanin, Karaminskaya 13 Jota Aragonesa 18 Russlan and Ludmilla

glint 4 gaze, look, peep 5 flash, gleam, sheen, shine, stare 6 glance 7 appear, glimmer, glimpse, glisten, glitter, shimmer, sparkle, twinkle 9 coruscate 11 scintillate

glissade 5 coast, glide, slide

glissando
music: 7 sliding

glisten 4 glow 5 flash, gleam, glint, shine 7 flicker, glimmer, glister, glitter, radiate, shimmer, sparkle, twinkle 9 coruscate 11 scintillate

glitter 4 fire, glow, pomp, show 5 flare, flash, gleam, glint, sheen, shine 6 luster, thrill, tinsel 7 beaming, display, glamour, glimmer, glisten, radiate, sparkle, twinkle 8 grandeur, radiance, splendor 9 pageantry, showiness 10 brilliance, excitement, refulgence 11 electricity

glittering 6 bright 7 radiant, shining 8 luminous, lustrous 9 brilliant, sparkling 11 coruscating

gloaming 4 dusk 7 evening 8 twilight

gloat 4 bask, brag 5 exult, strut, vaunt 7 revel in, swagger, triumph 8 crow over 9 glory over

global 5 world 6 all-out 7 general 9 planetary, unbounded, universal, unlimited, worldwide 10 widespread 13 comprehensive, international 16 intercontinental

globe 3 orb 4 ball 5 Earth, world 6 planet, sphere 7 globule 8 spheroid, spherule 9 biosphere

globule 4 ball, bead, bleb, blob, drop 5 globe 6 bubble, pellet, sphere 7 blister, droplet 8 particle, spheroid

glogg
type: 5 punch
origin: 6 Sweden

gloom 3 woe 4 dark, dusk, murk 5 blues, dolor, grief, shade 6 misery, sorrow 7 despair, dimness, sadness, shadows 8 darkness, distress, doldrums 9 blackness, dejection, dinginess, duskiness, murkiness, obscurity 10 cloudiness, depression, gloominess, low spirits, melancholy, mopishness, moroseness, oppression 11 despondency, forlornness, unhappiness 12 hopelessness 13 cheerlessness 16 disconsolateness, heavy-heartedness

gloomy 3 dim, sad 4 dark, dour, down, dull, glum, grim, mopy, sour 5 dusky, moody, mopey, murky, shady 6 cloudy, dismal, dreary, morbid, morose, shaded, somber 7 doleful, forlorn, shadowy, sunless, unhappy 8 dejected, desolate, downcast, frowning, funereal, overcast 9 cheerless, depressed, heartsick, miserable, sorrowful, woebegone 10 chapfallen, despondent, dispirited, ill-humored, melancholy 11 comfortless, crestfallen, discouraged, downhearted, low-spirited, pessimistic 12 disconsolate, disheartened, heavy-hearted 13 in the doldrums 14 down in the dumps, down in the mouth

Gloria in Excelsis Deo
22 Glory in the highest to God

Gloriana
character in: 15 The Faerie Queene
author: 7 Spenser

Gloriana
opera by: 7 Britten
character: 10 Elizabeth I 11 Earl of Essex

glorification 7 worship 8 devotion 9 adoration, adulation

10 exaltation, veneration **13** magnification

glorify 4 laud **5** adore, deify, exalt, extol, honor **6** praise, revere **7** beatify, dignify, elevate, ennoble, idolize, worship **8** canonize, enshrine, sanctify, venerate **9** celebrate, glamorize **10** consecrate **11** apotheosize, immortalize, romanticize

glorious 4 fine **5** grand, great, noble, noted **6** august, divine, famous, superb **7** eminent, glowing, honored, notable, radiant, shining, stately, sublime, supreme **8** dazzling, gorgeous, imposing, lustrous, majestic, renowned, splendid **9** beautiful, brilliant, dignified, excellent, marvelous, sparkling, wonderful **10** celebrated, delightful, impressive, preeminent **11** illustrious, magnificent, resplendent **12** praiseworthy **13** distinguished

glory 4 fame, mark, name **5** boast, honor, revel, vaunt **6** esteem, homage, praise, renown, repute **7** dignity, majesty, worship **8** blessing, eminence, grandeur, nobility, prestige, splendor **9** adoration, celebrity, gratitude, solemnity, sublimity **10** admiration, excellence, notability, veneration **11** benediction, distinction, preeminence, stateliness **12** magnificence, resplendence, thanksgiving **14** impressiveness **15** illustriousness

Glory in the highest to God
Latin: 19 Gloria in Excelsis Deo

gloss 4 glow, mask, veil **5** cloak, color, glaze, gleam, japan, sheen, shine **6** enamel, excuse, luster, polish, veneer **7** cover up, lacquer, shimmer, varnish **8** annotate, disguise, mitigate, radiance **9** whitewash **10** annotation, brightness, brilliance, commentary, smooth over **11** explain away, explanation, rationalize **12** luminousness, treat lightly **14** interpretation

gloss over 4 hide, mask, veil **7** conceal, cover up **9** dissemble, whitewash **12** misrepresent

glossy 5 photo, shiny, showy, silky, sleek, slick **6** bright, satiny, smooth **7** picture, shining **8** gleaming, lustrous, magazine, polished **9** burnished

glove 3 kid **4** cuff, mitt **5** catch, thumb **6** gusset, mitten, muffle **7** chevron **8** gauntlet

glow 4 fill, heat **5** ardor, bloom, blush, color, flush, gleam, gusto, shine **6** fervor, thrill, tingle, warmth **7** flicker, glimmer, glisten, glitter, radiate, shimmer, smolder, twinkle **8** radiance **9** eagerness, intensity, radiation, reddening, vividness **10** brightness, enthusiasm **11** earnestness

glower 4 pout, sulk **5** frown, glare, lower, scowl, stare

glowing 3 hot, red **4** rave **5** ruddy, vivid **6** ardent, bright, florid, raving **7** fervent, flaming, flushed **8** ecstatic, exciting **9** rhapsodic, thrilling **10** passionate **11** luminescent, sensational, stimulating **12** enthusiastic

Glubbdubdrib
fictional land in: 16 Gulliver's Travels
author: 5 Swift

Gluck, Christoph Willibald (von)
born: 7 Bavaria **8** Neumarkt
composer of: 5 Orfeo **6** Armide **7** Alceste **13** Paride ed Elena **14** Echo et Narcisse **17** Iphigenie en Aulide **18** Iphigenie en Tauride

glue 3 fix, gum **5** affix, epoxy, paste, putty, stick **6** adhere, cement, fasten, mortar **7** plaster, stickum **8** adherent, adhesive, concrete, fixative, mucilage **11** agglutinate

gluey 5 gooey, gummy, mucid, ropey, slimy, tacky, thick, **6** sticky, viscid **7** stringy, viscous **8** adhesive **12** mucilaginous

glum 6 gloomy, morose **8** dejected **9** cheerless **10** melancholy **14** down in the mouth

glut 4 bolt, clog, cram, drug, fill, gulp, jade, load, sate **5** choke, flood, gorge, stuff **6** burden, deluge, devour, excess, gobble **7** congest, overeat, satiate, surfeit, surplus **8** gobble up, obstruct, overdose, overfeed, overload, plethora, saturate **10** gormandize, oversupply, saturation **11** obstruction, superfluity **13** overabundance, supersaturate **14** superabundance

glutinous 5 gluey, bummy, mucid, ropey, slimy, tacky, thick **6** sticky, viscid **7** viscous **8** adhesive **10** gelatinous **12** musilaginous

glutton 3 hog, pig **6** gorger **7** stuffer **8** gourmand **9** chowhound, overeater **10** bellyslave **11** gormandizer, trencherman

gluttonous 6 greedy **7** hoggish, piggish, swinish **8** edacious, grasping, ravening, ravenous **9** excessive, voracious **10** insatiable, omnivorous **11** intemperate

gluttony 8 rapacity, voracity **10** overeating **11** gormandism, hoggishness, piggishness **12** gormandizing, intemperance, ravenousness **13** voraciousness

gnarled 6 knotty, rugged, snaggy **7** crooked, knotted, nodular, twisted **8** leathery, wrinkled **9** contorted, distorted **11** full of knots **13** weather-beaten

gnash 4 gnaw **5** chomp

gnat 7 no-see-um
group of: 5 cloud, horde

gnaw 4 bite, chew, fret, gall **5** chafe, chomp, eat at, grate, graze, munch, worry **6** browse, crunch, harrow, nibble, rankle **7** torment, trouble **8** distress, nibble at, ruminate **9** eat away at, masticate

gnome 3 elf **4** pixy **5** dwarf, troll **6** goblin, sprite **10** leprechaun

gnostic 4 sage, wise **6** clever, shrewd **7** knowing **8** mandaean, simonian **10** insightful

gnothi seauton 11 know thyself

gnu 7 brindle **8** antelope **10** wildebeest
type: 5 C gnou **9** C taurinus **12** Connochaetes

go ***see box***

goad 4 move, prod, push, spur, urge, whet **5** drive, egg on, impel, press, prick, set on **6** arouse, exhort, fillip, incite, motive, propel, stir up **8** pressure, stimulus **9** constrain, incentive, stimulant, stimulate **10** cattle prod, inducement, motivation **11** instigation

goal 3 aim, end **4** home, mark, wire **5** point, score, tally **6** design, intent, object, target **7** end line, purpose **8** ambition, goal line, terminus **9** intention, objective **10** finish line

go along with 5 usher **6** assent, convoy, escort **8** accede to, shepherd **9** accompany, agree with, chaperone, consent to **10** comply with

go 3 act, end, fit, fly, pep, run, try, vim **4** blow, dash, elan, fare, flee, flow, jibe, lead, life, pass, quit, stir, turn, wend, work **5** agree, begin, be off, blend, drive, force, get on, lapse, leave, reach, scram, slide, split, steam, tally, trial, verve, vigor, whirl **6** accord, beat it, be used, belong, chance, decamp, depart, effort, elapse, energy, expire, extend, mettle, pass by, repair, result, retire, spirit **7** advance, attempt, be given, be known, comport, fall out, glide by, move out, operate, perform, proceed, slip off, take off, turn out, vamoose, work out **8** ambition, endeavor, function, move away, progress, slip away, sneak off, spread to, start for, steal off, vitality, vivacity, withdraw **9** animation, harmonize, terminate, transpire **10** enterprise, experiment, initiative

go ashore 4 land **6** debark **9** disembark

go astray 3 err, sin **6** wander **7** deviate, do wrong **9** misbehave **10** transgress **13** fall from grace

goat ***see box***

Goat, Horned Goat
constellation of: **11** Capricornus

goat god 3 Pan **5** satyr

go away 3 ebb **4** fade, scat, wane **5** abate, leave, scram **6** depart, lessen, retire **8** withdraw **9** disappear

gob 3 dab, tar **4** clot, glob, lump, mass **6** sailor **7** Jack Tar

go back 6 return **7** retreat

gobble 3 caw **4** bolt, gulp, wolf **5** raven, stuff **6** cackle, devour, gabble, gaggle **8** bolt down, cram down, gulp down

gobbledygook 4 bosh, bunk, cant, tosh **6** jargon **7** rubbish, twaddle **8** buncombe, nonsense, tommyrot **9** gibberish, moonshine **10** balderdash, double-talk, hocus-pocus, mumbo jumbo **11** foolishness **12** fiddle-faddle

gobble up 6 devour **8** bolt down, gulp down, wolf down

go before 7 precede, predate **8** antecede, antedate **9** come first, go ahead of **10** anticipate

go-between 5 agent, envoy, fixer, proxy **6** deputy, second **7** arbiter **8** delegate, emissary, mediator **9** messenger, middleman, moderator **10** arbitrator, interceder, negotiator **12** intermediary **13** intermediator **14** representative

goblet 3 cup **5** glass **6** vessel **7** chalice

goblin 4 ogre **5** bogey, demon, troll **7** gremlin **8** bogeyman

Gobseck
author: **14** Honore de Balzac

go by 4 pass **6** elapse, pass by, roll by, rush by, slip by **7** glide by, slide by **8** slip away

go by car 4 ride **5** drive, motor

go-cart 4 cart **5** buggy **6** barrow **8** carriage, handcart, pushcart, stroller **11** wheelbarrow

go crimson 4 burn, glow **5** blush, color, flame, flush **6** redden

goat 3 kid **4** buck, butt **5** billy, nanny **6** victim **7** fall guy **9** scapegoat **11** whipping boy **13** laughingstock
breed: **6** Angora, Chamal, Nubian, Saanen **7** Granada **8** La Mancha **10** Toggenburg **11** Anglo-Nubian **12** French Alpine **13** British Alpine
combining form: **4** aego **5** capri
family: **7** Bovidae
female: **3** doe **5** capra, nanny **7** doeling
genus: **5** Capra
goat-boy: **5** Giles
goat-milk cheese: **7** chevret
goat-man: **5** satyr
god: **3** Pan **5** satyr **7** Aegipan
group of: **4** herd **5** tribe
hair: **5** kasha, tibet
hair of Angora goat: **6** mohair
male: **4** buck **5** billy
meat: **7** cabrito
star: **7** capella
young: **3** kid

God, god 4 Lord **5** Allah, deity, Jeveh **6** Elohim, Yahweh **7** Holy One, Jehovah, Skaddai **8** divinity, the Deity **9** Our Father **10** the Creator, the Godhead **11** divine being, God Almighty, the Almighty **13** the Omnipotent, the Omniscient **14** the All-Merciful, the Man Upstairs **15** the Supreme Being
Hebrew: **6** Adonai
Latin: **7** Dominus

god, first
origin: **12** Scandinavian
known as: **7** Forsete, Forseti

God and Man at Yale
author: **17** William F Buckley Jr

God and my right
French: **14** Dieu et mon droit
motto of: **18** royal arms of England

God be with us
German: **10** Gott mit uns

God be with you
Latin: **12** Deus vobiscum

Godbole, Professor
character in: **15** A Passage to India
author: **7** Forster

Goddard, Jean-Luc
director of: **10** Breathless

Goddard, Paulette
real name: **10** Marion Levy
husband: **14** Charlie Chaplin **15** Burgess Meredith **18** Erich Maria Remarque
born: **11** Great Neck NY
roles: **11** Modern Times, Unconquered **15** So Proudly We Hail **16** Standing Room Only, The Great Dictator **19** Diary of a Chambermaid

Goddard, Robert Hutchings
nationality: **8** American
inventor of: **12** rocket engine **22** liquid propellant rocket

Godden, Rumer
author of: **8** The River **14** Black Narcissus, Kitchen Madonna **16** The Peacock Spring **18** In This House of Brede, The Greengage Summer **19** An Episode of Sparrows **23** The Battle of Villa Fiorita

God enriches
Latin: **9** ditat Deus
motto of: **7** Arizona

Godfather, The
author: **9** Mario Puzo
family: **8** Corleone
director: **18** Francis Ford Coppola
cast: **8** Al Pacino (Michael) **9** James Caan (Sonny)

10 John Marley **11** Diane Keaton **12** Marlon Brando (Don Vito Corleone), Richard Conte, Robert Duvall **14** Sterling Hayden **17** Richard Castellano
Oscar for: 5 actor (Brando) **7** picture **10** screenplay
sequel: 18 The Godfather Part II

Godfather, The, Part II
director: 18 Francis Ford Coppola
cast: 8 Al Pacino **10** John Cazale, Talia Shire **11** Diane Keaton **12** Lee Strasberg, Robert DeNiro, Robert Duvall
Oscar for: 7 picture **10** screenplay **15** supporting actor (DeNiro)
sequel to: 12 The Godfather

godforsaken 5 bleak **6** lonely, remote **8** deserted, desolate, wretched **9** abandoned, neglected

god from a machine
Latin: 13 deux ex machina

God is with us
German: 10 Gott mit uns

godless 4 evil **6** wicked **7** heathen, impious, profane, ungodly **8** agnostic, depraved **9** atheistic **10** unhallowed **11** blasphemous, irreligious, unrepentant, unrighteous **12** sacrilegious, unsanctified

godlessness 7 atheism **8** apostasy, unbelief **9** disbelief **10** irreligion

godlike 4 holy **5** godly, pious **6** deific, divine, sacred **8** immortal, olympian

godliness 5 piety **8** devotion, holiness **9** reverence **10** devoutness **12** spirituality

godly 4 good, holy **5** moral, pious **6** devout, divine, sacred **7** devoted, saintly **8** faithful, hallowed, reverent **9** believing, God-loving, pietistic, religious, righteous, spiritual **10** God-fearing, sanctified **11** consecrated, pure in heart, reverential

God of Vengeance, The
author: 10 Sholem Asch

go down 3 ebb **4** drop, fade, wane **5** abate, lower, slide **6** lessen, plunge, reduce, weaken **7** descend, plummet, slacken, subside **8** decrease, diminish, moderate

God Save the Queen
author: 17 William F Buckley Jr

God's Grace
author: 14 Bernard Malamud

God's Little Acre
author: 15 Erskine Caldwell

Godthaab
capital of: 9 Greenland

God willing
Latin: 10 Deo volente

God wills it
Latin: 8 Deus vult
cry of: 9 Crusaders

Godwin, William
author of: 13 Caleb Williams **35** An Enquiry Concerning Political Justice

Goes, Hugo van der
born: 5 Ghent **8** Flanders
artwork: 7 The Fall **14** The Lamentation **19** The Death of the Virgin **21** The Adoration of the Magi **22** The Adoration of the Child **26** The Adoration of the Shepherds

Goethe, Johann
author of: 5 Faust **6** Egmont **24** The Sorrows of Young Werther **29** Wilhelm Meister's Apprenticeship

go-getter 4 doer **7** hustler **8** achiever, live wire

go-getting 7 driving, dynamic **8** forceful, hustling **9** ambitious, assertive, energetic **10** aggressive **11** hard-driving, hard-working, industrious

Gogol, Nikolai
author of: 7 The Nose **9** Dead Souls **10** Taras Bulba **11** The Overcoat **19** The Inspector-General

go hand in hand 5 match, tally **6** concur, square **7** coexist **9** accompany

go hungry 4 fast **6** famish, starve **7** abstain

Going My Way
director: 10 Leo McCarey
cast: 10 Bing Crosby (Father O'Malley) **12** Gene Lockhart **15** Barry Fitzgerald
Oscar for: 4 song **5** actor (Crosby) **7** picture **8** director **15** supporting actor (Fitzgerald)
song: 15 Swinging on a Star

gold 3 bar **4** gilt **5** aurum, ingot **6** beauty, nugget, purity, yellow **7** bullion **8** goodness, goodwill, humanity, kindness **11** beneficence
chemical symbol: 2 Au

gold and silver
Spanish: 9 oro y plata
motto of: 7 Montana

Gold Bug, The
author: 13 Edgar Allan Poe

Gold Coast *see* **5** Ghana **11** Sierra Leone

golden 4 best, gilt, rosy **5** blest, blond, great, happy, palmy **6** bright, gilded, joyous, timely **7** aureate, halcyon, richest, shining **8** beatific, glorious, happiest, splendid **9** favorable, opportune, priceless, promising **10** auspicious, delightful, propitious, seasonable **11** exceptional, flourishing, resplendent **12** advantageous, bright-yellow **13** extraordinary

Golden Age
first age of: 3 man
world ruled by: 6 Cronus, Saturn

Golden Ass, The
author: 14 Lucius Apuleius
character: 4 Milo **5** Fotis **6** Lucius **8** Charites, Pamphile **9** Lepolemus **10** Thrasillus

Goldenberg, Emmanuel
real name of: 15 Edward G Robinson

Golden Bough, The
branch of: 9 mistletoe
sacred to: 10 Proserpina
used by: 6 Aeneas
at shrine of: 5 Diana **7** Virbius
author: 15 Sir James G Frazer

Golden Bowl, The
author: 10 Henry James
character: 8 Mr Verver **12** Maggie Verver, Mrs Assingham **13** Prince Amerigo **14** Charlotte Stant

Golden Boy
nickname of: 11 Paul Hornung

golden brown 3 tan **5** tawny, toast **6** sienna **7** tobacco **8** chestnut

Golden Cockerel, The
also: 8 Le Coq d'Or **15** Zolotoy Petushok
opera by: 14 Rimsky-Korsakov
character: 9 King Dodon **14** Queen of Shemaka

golden egg-layer
form: 5 goose
made of: 4 gold

Golden Fleece
made of: 4 gold
kept at: 7 Colchis
kept by: 10 King Aeetes
stolen by: 5 Jason **9** Argonauts
accomplice: 5 Medea

Golden Legend
author: **13** William Caxton

goldenrod **8** Solidago
varieties: **5** sweet, white **6** Wreath **7** seaside **8** bluestem, European **10** California

Golden State
nickname of: **10** California

golden youth
French: **13** jeunesse doree

goldfinch
group of: **5** charm

Goldfinger
director: **11** Guy Hamilton
author: **10** Ian Fleming
cast: **9** Gert Frobe (Auric Goldfinger) **10** Bernard Lee (M) **11** Lois Maxwell (Miss Moneypenny) **12** Harold Sakata (Oddjob), Shirley Eaton **13** Honor Blackman (Pussy Galore), Sean Connery (James Bond, 007)

Golding, William
author of: **8** Free Fall **13** A Moving Target **14** Lord of the Flies, Rites of Passage **15** Darkness Visible

gold mine **7** bonanza **10** mother lode

Gold Rush, The
director: **14** Charlie Chaplin
cast: **9** Mack Swain, Tom Murray **11** Georgia Hale **14** Charlie Chaplin (Little Tramp)
setting: **5** Yukon

Goldsmith, Oliver
author of: **18** She Stoops to Conquer, The Deserted Village **19** The Vicar of Wakefield

Goldstein, Elliott
real name of: **12** Elliott Gould

goldwasser
form: **7** liquor
origin: **6** France **7** Germany
flavor: **4** herb **5** spice **7** caraway
flecked with: **8** gold leaf

golf ***see box***

golfer **8** Ben Hogan, Lee Elder, Sam Snead **9** Carol Mann, Hale Irwin, Patty Berg, Tom Watson **10** Betsy Rawls, Bobby Jones, Deane Beman, Gary Player, Hubie Green, Jim Demaret, Judy Rankin, Lee Trevino, Nancy Lopez **11** Ben Crenshaw, Billy Casper, Byron Nelson, Calvin Peete, Donna Caponi, Gene Sarazen, Julius Boros, Tom Weiskopf, Walter Hagen **12** Arnold Palmer, Jack Nicklaus, Joanne Carner, Johnny Miller, Mickey Wright, Sandra Haynie **14** Cary Middlecoff, Kathy Whitworth **16** Roberto De-Vicenzo **19** Susie Maxwell Berning **20** Severiano Ballesteros **21** Babe Didrikson Zaharias

Golgotha **7** Calvary
means: **10** skull place

Goliath
killed by: **5** David

golliwogg **3** toy **4** doll **9** plaything

Gomer
father: **7** Diblaim
husband: **5** Hosea

Gomer Pyle USMC
character: **5** Bunny **7** Frankie **9** Corp Boyle **11** Duke Slayter, (Sgt) Vince Carter
cast: **9** Jim Nabors, Roy Stuart **10** Ted Bessell **11** Frank Sutton **12** Ronnie Schell **13** Barbara Stuart

Gomorrah
destroyed with: **5** Sodom **6** Zeboim **10** Admah

Gondoliers, The
operetta by: **18** Gilbert and Sullivan
character: **4** Luiz **5** Tessa **7** Casilda **8** Gianetta **13** Marco Palmieri **15** Duke of Plaza-Toro **16** Giuseppe Palmieri

gone **3** ago, out **4** away, dead, left, lost, past **6** absent, ruined, used up **7** defunct, died out, extinct, missing **8** departed, finished, hopeless, vanished **11** disappeared

Goneril
character in: **8** King Lear
author: **11** Shakespeare

Gone With the Wind
author: **16** Margaret Mitchell
character: **5** Mammy **6** Big Sam, Prissy **7** Dr Meade **10** Ellen (Robillard) O'Hara **11** Gerald O'Hara, Honey Wilkes, India Wilkes **12** Ashley Wilkes, Aunt Pittypat, Belle Watling **13** Scarlett O'Hara, Tarleton twins **15** Mrs Merriweather **21** Melanie Hamilton Wilkes
Scarlett's husband: **11** Rhett Butler **12** Frank Kennedy **15** Charles Hamilton
Scarlett's children: **4** Emma, Wade **6** Bonnie
Scarlett's sister: **7** Carreen, Suellen
director: **13** Victor Fleming
cast: **9** Ona Munson **10** Clark Gable (Rhett Butler) **11** Evelyn Keyes, Vivien Leigh (Scarlett O'Hara) **12** Leslie Howard (Ashley Wilkes) **13** Ann Rutherford **14** Hattie McDaniel (Mammy), Thomas Mitchell (Gerald O'Hara) **16** Butterfly McQueen (Prissy) **17** Olivia de Havilland (Melanie Hamilton Wilkes)
score: **10** Max Steiner
Oscar for: **7** actress (Leigh), picture **8** director **12** screenwriter **17** supporting actress (McDaniel)
producer: **14** David O Selznick

golf
average number strokes to reach a hole: **3** par
ball in another's path: **6** stymie
championship: **6** US Open **9** Grand Slam **11** British Open **17** Masters' Tournament
club: **4** iron, wood **6** driver, putter **7** brassie **8** long iron **9** sand wedge, short iron **10** middle iron **13** pitching wedge
club carrier: **6** caddie
course also called: **5** links
golf ball formerly called: **6** guttie **8** feathery
hole scored in one stroke: **3** ace **9** hole-in-one
one stroke less than par: **6** birdie
one stroke more than par: **5** bogey
part of the course: **3** cup, tee **4** hole **5** apron, green, rough **6** bunker, hazard **7** fairway **8** sand trap
position: **3** lie
stance: **4** open **6** closed, square **7** address
two strokes less than par: **5** eagle
type of competition: **5** match **6** stroke
uprooted turf: **5** divot
warning cry: **4** fore

good **3** ace, fit, new **4** best, boon, fine, full, gain, kind, pure, real **5** ample, crack, favor, great, large, merit, moral, pious, prize, right, solid, sound, sunny, valid, value, worth **6** adroit, choice, devout, entire, genial, honest, humane, kindly, lively, newest, profit, proper, seemly, select, tiptop, useful, virtue, wealth, worthy **7** adapted, benefit, capable, capital, dutiful, fitting, genuine, godsend, healthy, orderly, service, sizable, skilled, success, upright, welfare **8** adequate, becoming, blessing, bonafide, cheerful, complete, decorous, gracious, innocent, interest, kindness, obedient, obliging, pleasant, precious, reliable, salutary, skillful, smartest, sociable, splendid, suitable, thorough, topnotch, valuable, virtuous, windfall **9** admirable, advantage, agreeable, authentic, convivial, deserving, efficient, enjoyable, enjoyment, excellent, exemplary, expensive, favorable, first-rate, happiness, healthful, honorable, priceless, qualified, religious, righteous, unsullied, untainted, wholesome, wonderful **10** altruistic, beneficent, beneficial, benevolent, excellence, first-class, legitimate, proficient, prosperity, sufficient, worthwhile **11** appropriate, commendable, considerate, improvement, kindhearted, substantial, sympathetic, well-behaved **12** advantageous, considerable, praiseworthy, satisfactory **13** companionable, conscientious, righteousness
French: **3** bon **4** bien
Spanish: **5** bueno
German: **3** gut

Good as Gold
author: **12** Joseph Heller

Good Book **5** Bible

good breeding **5** grace **6** polish **7** manners **9** gentility **10** refinement **11** cultivation

good buy **4** deal **5** steal **7** bargain

good-by, good-bye **3** bye **6** bye-bye, bye now, so long **7** parting, send-off **8** farewell, Godspeed **9** departure **10** separation **11** be seeing you, leave-taking, see you later **12** God be with you **15** till we meet again
French: **5** adieu **8** au revoir
German: **14** auf Wiedersehen
Hawaiian: **5** aloha
Italian: **4** ciao **5** addio **11** arrivederci
Japanese: **8** sayonara
Latin: **4** vale
Spanish: **5** adios **12** hasta la vista

Goodbye, Darkness
author: **17** William Manchester

Goodbye, Mr Chips
director: **7** Sam Wood
author: **11** James Hilton
cast: **11** Greer Garson, Paul Henreid (von Henreid), Robert Donat
Oscar for: **5** actor (Donat)
character: **7** Mr Chips **10** Mrs Wickett **12** Kathy Bridges
school: **10** Brookfield

Goodbye Girl, The
director: **11** Herbert Ross
based on play by: **9** Neil Simon
cast: **11** Marsha Mason **13** Quinn Cummings **15** Richard Dreyfuss
Oscar for: **5** actor (Dreyfuss)

Good Companions, The
author: **11** J B Priestley

good counsel
god of: **6** Consus

good day
French: **7** bonjour
German: **8** guten tag
Spanish: **10** buenos dias
Italian: **10** buon giorno

good deal **3** buy **5** steal **7** bargain

good deed **8** kindness **11** benefaction **12** philanthropy
Hebrew: **7** mitsvah, mitzvah

Good Earth, The
author: **10** Pearl S Buck
character: **4** O-Lan **6** Nung En **7** Nung Wen, The Fool **8** Wang Lung **11** Pear Blossom **12** Lotus Blossom
director: **14** Sidney Franklin
cast: **8** Keye Luke, Paul Muni **10** Tilly Losch **11** Jessie Ralph, Luise Rainer **14** Walter Connolly **15** Charley Grapewin
Oscar for: **7** actress (Rainer)

good feelings **8** good will **11** benevolence **12** friendliness

good form **9** etiquette, good taste **10** politeness **11** good manners

good-for-nothing **5** idler **6** loafer **7** useless **9** no-account, shiftless, worthless

good fortune **4** luck **7** bonanza **8** fortuity, lady luck, windfall **9** blessings **10** lucky break

good friend
French: **6** bon ami **9** bonne amie

good health **5** vigor **7** fitness **8** vitality **10** robustness

Goodhue, Bertram Grosvenor
architect of: **13** St Bartholomew (NYC) **14** St Thomas Church (NYC) **25** Chapel at US Military Academy (West Point), National Academy of Sciences (Washington DC) **28** Nebraska State Capitol Building (Lincoln)
style: **13** Gothic Revival **15** Spanish Colonial

good humor **10** affability, amiability, cheeriness, kindliness, mellowness **12** cheerfulness, complaisance, pleasantness **15** kindheartedness

good-humored **4** mild, warm **6** cheery, genial, gentle, kindly, mellow **7** affable, amiable **8** cheerful, pleasant **9** congenial, easygoing **11** complaisant

good-looker **3** fox **4** doll, hunk **5** beaut, Venus **6** Adonis, beauty, eyeful **7** stunner **8** knockout **11** handsome Dan

good-looking **4** fair, foxy, sexy **5** bonny **6** comely, lovely, pretty **8** alluring, clean-cut, gorgeous, handsome, stunning **9** beauteous, beautiful, exquisite, ravishing **10** attractive, bewitching, enchanting **11** captivating, eye-catching, well-favored **15** pulchritudinous

good looks **6** beauty **10** comeliness, loveliness **11** pulchritude **12** handsomeness **14** attractiveness

good luck
Yiddish: **8** mazel tov

goodly **4** tidy **5** ample, large **7** sizable **11** substantial **12** considerable

Goodman, Theodosia
real name of: **9** Theda Bara

good manners **8** courtesy **9** amenities, etiquette, gentility **10** politeness, refinement

good name **4** face **5** image **10** reputation **11** self-respect

good nature **6** warmth **9** geniality, good humor **10** affability, amiability, cordiality, likability **12** complaisance, pleasantness **13** agreeableness

good-natured **4** warm **5** sunny **6** genial, kindly **7** affable, amiable **8** cheerful, friendly, obliging, pleasant **9** agreeable, congenial, easygoing **11** complaisant, good-humored, warm-hearted **13** accommodating

goodness **3** boy, gee, hey, say, wow **5** favor, honor, mercy, merit, piety, value, worth, wowee **6** profit, purity, virtue **7** benefit, decorum, gee whiz, heavens, honesty, probity, service **8** boy-oh-boy, devotion, gracious, kindness, morality **9** advantage, innocence, integrity, land alive, landsakes, nutrition, propriety, rectitude **10** generosity, kindliness, sakes alive, usefulness **11** benevolence, nourishment **12** virtuousness **13** righteousness, wholesomeness **14** heavens to Betsy

good night
French: **7** bon soir **9** bonne nuit
German: **9** gute nacht
Spanish: **12** buenas noches
Italian: **10** buona notte

Good Old Boy
author: **12** Willie Morris

good opinion **6** esteem, regard **7** respect **8** approval **10** admiration

good person **4** dear, love **5** angel **7** darling **10** sweetheart

goods **4** gear **5** cloth, stock, wares **6** fabric, things **7** effects, fabrics **8** chattels, material, movables, property, textiles **9** inventory, trappings **11** commodities, furnishings, merchandise, possessions **13** appurtenances, paraphernalia

good sense **6** brains, wisdom **8** judgment **12** intelligence

good taste **10** refinement **11** cultivation, discernment **14** discrimination

good-tempered **5** sunny **7** amiable, smiling **8** cheerful **12** sweet-natured

good time **3** fun **9** amusement, diversion, enjoyment **13** entertainment

good times **4** boom **8** fat years

good turn **5** favor **7** service **8** good deed

goodwill **5** amity **8** kindness **9** benignity **10** cordiality, kindliness **11** amicability, benevolence **12** friendliness **15** kindheartedness

Goodwin, Lee
character in: **9** Sanctuary
author: **8** Faulkner

good wishes **4** best **5** favor **6** regard **7** consent, regards **8** approval, blessing, respects, sanction **11** compliments **15** congratulations

Goodwood, Caspar
character in: **18** The Portrait of a Lady
author: **5** James

good word **6** praise **10** compliment **11** approbation **12** commendation **14** congratulation

Goodyear, Charles
nationality: **8** American
developed: **16** vulcanized rubber

goof **3** err **4** boob, flub, fool, mess **5** botch, error, gum up **6** bollix, boo-boo, bungle, fumble, slip up **7** blunder, mistake **9** oversight

Goolagong Cawley, Evonne
sport: **6** tennis
heritage: **19** Australian Aborigine

go on all fours **5** crawl, creep

goose
young: **7** gosling
group of: **5** flock, skein **6** gaggle

goose egg **3** nil, zip **4** zero **5** aught **6** cipher, naught **7** nothing **11** horse collar

go over **5** audit, check **6** review **7** examine, inspect **10** scrutinize **11** investigate

Gopher State
nickname of: **9** Minnesota

Gorbachev, Mikhail Sergeyevich
party: **9** Communist
country: **4** USSR **6** Russia **31** Union of Soviet Socialist Republics
born: **9** Stavropol **10** Privolnoye **16** Krasnogvardeisky
education: **21** Moscow State University
political career: **9** Politburo **16** General Secretary **20** Agriculture Secretary **23** Stavropol Communist Party **35** Deputy Supreme Soviet Central Committee
policy: **8** glasnost **11** perestroika
distinguishing characteristic: **19** strawberry birthmark (head)
wife: **15** Raisa Maksimovna
occupation: **7** teacher
daughter: **5** Irisa
occupation: **6** doctor **9** physician
grandchild: **6** Oksana

Gorboduc
author: **12** Thomas Norton **15** Thomas Sackville

Gorcey, Leo
born: **9** New York NY
roles: **4** Spit **10** Bowery Boys **11** Dead End Kids

Gordimer, Nadine
author of: **11** July's People **12** The Lying Days **13** A Guest of Honor **15** Burger's Daughter **16** A Soldier's Embrace **21** The Late Bourgeois World

Gordon, Caroline
author of: **18** The Strange Children **19** Aleck Maury Sportsman

Gordon, Ruth
real name: **15** Ruth Gordon Jones
husband: **11** Garson Kanin
born: **11** Wollaston MA
roles: **11** Where's Poppa? **13** Rosemary's Baby **14** Harold and Maude **17** Inside Daisy Clover **20** Abe Lincoln in Illinois

gore **5** blood **7** carnage **8** butchery **9** bloodshed, slaughter

Gorgas, William Crawford
field: **8** medicine
position: **18** army surgeon general
conquered: **7** malaria **11** yellow fever
location: **11** Panama Canal

gorge **3** gap, ire **4** bolt, cram, craw, dale, dell, fill, glen, glut, gulp, pass, sate, vale **5** abyss, anger, blood, chasm, cleft, gulch, gully, mouth, stuff, wrath **6** canyon, defile, devour, gobble, gullet, hatred, hollow, muzzle, nausea, ravine, throat **7** disgust, indulge, overeat, satiate **8** crevasse **9** animosity, esophagus, repulsion, revulsion **10** gluttonize, gormandize, repugnance **11** overindulge

gorgeous **4** fine, rich **5** grand **6** bright, costly, lovely **7** elegant, opulent, shining **8** dazzling, glorious, imposing, splendid, stunning **9** beautiful, brilliant, exquisite, luxurious, ravishing, sumptuous **10** attractive, glittering, impressive **11** good-looking, magnificent, resplendent, splendorous **13** splendiferous

Gorgons
form: **7** maidens **8** monsters
names: **6** Medusa, Stheno **7** Euryale, Sthenno
father: **7** Phorcys
mother: **4** Ceto
protectress: **6** Graeae, Graiae
hair of: **6** snakes
hands of: **5** brass
turned viewers to: **5** stone

Gorgophone
father: **7** Perseus
mother: **9** Andromeda
husband: **7** Oebalus **8** Perieres
son: **9** Leucippus

Gorgosaurus
type: **8** dinosaur, theropod
location: **7** Alberta **12** North America
period: **10** Cretaceous

Gorgythion
mentioned in: **5** Iliad
father: **5** Priam
killed by: **6** Teucer

gorilla
group of: **4** band

Gorky, Arshile
real name: **21** Vosdanig Manoog Adokian
born: **7** Armenia **11** Khorkomvari
artwork: **5** Agony **15** Diary of a Seducer **17** Making the Calendar **21** The Artist and his Mother, Water of the Flowery Hill **22** The Liver is the Cock's Comb

Gorky, Maxim (Maksim)
real name: **25** Alekseimaksimovich Peshkov
author of: **7** V I Lenin **11** My Childhood **14** The Lower Depths **18** The Small Town Okurov **20** City of the Yellow Devil, Twenty-six Men and a Girl **27** The Life of Matthew Kozhemyakin

gormandize **5** feast, raven **6** devour

Gortys
father: **10** Stymphalus **12** Rhadamanthys

gory **5** scary **6** bloody, creepy **9** murderous **10** horrifying, sanguinary, terrifying **11** bloodsoaked, ensanguined, frightening **12** bloodstained, bloodthirsty **13** bloodcurdling

gospel, Gospel **5** credo, creed **8** doctrine **11** the good news, the last word **12** the final word **13** the whole truth, ultimate truth
the first four books of the New Testament: **4** Luke, John, Mark **7** Matthew

Gospel writers **4** John, Luke, Mark **7** Matthew **9** synoptist

gospodin **2** Mr **6** Mister

gossamer **5** filmy, gauzy, sheer **8** cobwebby **10** diaphanous **13** insubstantial

gossip **4** news **6** babble, report, tattle **7** comment, hearsay, prattle, scandal, twaddle **8** idle talk **10** backbiting **12** tittle-tattle **13** newsmongering

gossiper **3** pry **4** blab **5** prate, snoop, yenta **6** gabble, magpie, meddle, tattle **7** babbler, meddler, prattle, snooper, tattler **8** busybody **9** chatterer **10** chatterbox, newsmonger, talebearer, tattletale **11** rumormonger **12** blabbermouth, gossipmonger **13** scandalmonger

go stale **3** die

Go Tell It on the Mountain
author: **12** James Baldwin

Gothic
language family: **12** Indo-European

go through **4** bear **6** endure, suffer **7** sustain, undergo **9** encounter, withstand **10** experience

go to **3** see **5** visit **6** attend **8** appear at, frequent

go to bed **6** retire, turn in **7** lie down, sack out **8** flake out **9** hit the hay **10** call it a day, hit the sack **11** catch some z's

go to pieces **5** break, crack **7** break up, crack up, crumble, give way, shatter **8** splinter **9** break down, fall apart **11** lose control **12** disintegrate

go to work on **6** attack, tackle **8** set about **9** undertake

go to wrack and ruin **5** decay **7** crumble **9** fall apart **12** disintegrate

Gotterdammerung **17** Twilight of the Gods
see: **8** Ragnarok

Gott mit uns **11** God be with us, God is with us

gouge **5** carve, drill, scoop **6** chisel, extort **10** overcharge

gouge out **5** drill **6** hollow **8** carve out, scoop out **9** chisel out, hollow out **10** whittle out

Gould, Chester
creator/artist of: **9** Dick Tracy

Gould, Elliott
real name: **16** Elliott Goldstein
wife: **15** Barbra Streisand
born: **10** Brooklyn NY
roles: **4** MASH **13** Little Murders **14** The Long Goodbye **15** California Split, Getting Straight **19** Bob & Carol & Ted & Alice

Goulding, Edmund
director of: **10** Grand Hotel **11** Dark Victory **13** The Dawn Patrol

go under **4** fail, fall, sink **9** go belly up **10** go bankrupt

Gounod, Charles Francois
born: **5** Paris **6** France
composer of: **5** Faust **6** Gallia, Sappho, Te Deum **8** Cinq-Mars, Mireille **9** La Colombe, Polyeucte **10** Mors et Vita **11** Marie Stuart, Stabat Mater **13** La Reine de Saba **14** Romeo and Juliet **16** La Nonne Sanglante, Philemon et Baucis **17** La Tribute de Zamora **18** Le Medecin Malgre Lui

gourd **9** Cucurbita **13** Cucurbita pepo
varieties: **3** ash, ivy, rag, wax **4** club **5** snake, white **6** bitter, bottle, dipper, sponge, teasel, viper's **7** figleaf, Malabar, serpent, trumpet **8** calabash, hedgehog, Missouri **9** dishcloth **10** goareberry, gooseberry, knob-kerrie, silver-seed **11** sugar-trough **12** Hercules'-club **14** scarlet-fruited

gourmand **7** glutton **8** big eater **9** bon vivant, chowhound **11** gormandizer, trencherman

gourmet **7** epicure **9** bon vivant **10** gastronome **11** connoisseur, gastronomer **12** gastronomist

gourmet cooking
French: **12** haute cuisine

Gourmont, Remy de
author of: **18** A Night in Luxembourg

gout **5** style, taste **10** preference

govern **3** run **4** boss, curb, form, head, lead, rule, sway, tame **5** check, guide, pilot, steer **6** bridle, direct, manage **7** command, control, incline, inhibit, oversee **8** dominate, restrain **9** influence, supervise **10** administer, discipline, hold in hand **11** hold in check, superintend **13** be at the helm of **14** pull the strings **16** keep under control **17** exercise authority **18** be in the driver's seat

governed **3** led **5** ruled **6** guided **7** steered, subject **8** directed **9** dependent **10** controlled, supervised **12** administered **13** superintended

governing **6** ruling **7** curbing, guiding, heading, leading, swaying **8** bridling, checking, managing, piloting, reigning, steering **9** directing, inclining **10** inhibiting, management, overseeing **11** controlling, influencing, restraining, supervision **13** administering **14** administrating, administration, superintending

governing body **10** government, management, parliament **12** powers that be **14** administration **16** board of directors, board of governors **18** executive committee

government **3** law **4** rule **5** state **6** regime **7** command, control **8** dominion, guidance **9** authority, direction **10** domination, management, regulation **11** supervision **13** governing body, statesmanship **14** administration

governor
Turkish: **3** beg, bey

Gowan
character in: **12** Little Dorrit
author: **7** Dickens

go with **6** convey, convoy, escort **7** conduct **9** accompany

gown **4** robe **5** dress, frock **10** nightdress

goy **6** non-Jew **7** Gentile

Goya (y Lucientes, Francisco Jose de)
born: **5** Spain **13** Fuente de todos
artwork: **8** Proverbs **10** Disparates **11** Tauromaquia **12** Los Caprichos, The Naked Maja **15** Majas on a Balcony **17** The Disasters of War **21** Charles IV and his Family

grab **3** bag, nab **4** grip, hold, pass **5** catch, clasp, grasp, lunge, pluck, seize **6** clutch, collar, snatch **7** capture

grace **4** deck, love, tact, trim **5** adorn, charm, endow, exalt, favor, honor, mercy, merit, piety, skill, taste **6** beauty, bedeck, enrich, pardon, polish, set off, virtue **7** charity, culture, decorum, dignify, dress up, elevate, enhance, garnish, glorify, manners, smarten, suavity **8** beautify, clemency, decorate, elegance, felicity, fluidity, God's love, holiness, lenience, ornament, reprieve, sanctity, spruce up, urbanity **9** embellish, endowment, etiquette, exemption, extra time, God's favor, good looks, propriety **10** aggrandize, comeliness, devoutness, excellence, indulgence, refinement **11** cultivation, forgiveness, lissomeness, pulchritude, saintliness, willowiness **12** dispensation, gracefulness, mannerliness, mercifulness **14** accomplishment, divine goodness
French: **11** savoir faire

graceful **5** lithe **6** comely, limber, lovely **7** elegant, lissome, shapely, sinuous, willowy **8** delicate **9** beautiful, lithesome, sylphlike **10** attractive **11** light-footed

gracefulness **8** delicacy, fluidity **10** suppleness **11** lissomeness

graceless **5** gawky, inept **6** clumsy **7** awkward **10** ungraceful **11** heavy-handed

Graces
also: **7** Gratiae **9** Charities
goddesses of: **6** beauty
father: **4** Zeus
mother: **8** Eurynome
names: **4** Auxo **5** Cleta **6** Aglaia, Thalia **7** Phaenna **8** Hegemone **10** Euphrosyne

gracious **2** my **3** boy, gee, wow **4** kind **5** civil, mercy, oh boy **6** benign, humane, kindly, polite, tender, ye gods **7** affable, amiable, clement, cordial, courtly, gee whiz, lenient, my stars **8** friendly, goodness, merciful, obliging, pleasant **9** benignant, courteous, landsakes **10** benevolent, charitable, chivalrous, hospitable **11** good heavens, good natured, kindhearted **13** compassionate **14** heavens to Betsy

gradation **4** step **5** stage **6** degree **7** shading **8** grouping, ordering **9** arranging **11** arrangement **12** organization **14** classification

grade **4** bank, even, hill, mark, ramp, rank, rate, sort, step **5** brand, caste, class, level, order, pitch, place, slope, stage, value **6** degree, estate, rating, smooth, sphere, status **7** flatten, incline, quality, station **8** classify, gradient, position, standing **9** acclivity, condition, declivity, intensity

grade-A **2** A-1 **4** aces, a-one, fine, tops **5** grade, great, prime, super **6** choice, superb, tip-top **7** capital **8** peerless, sterling, superior, top-notch **9** excellent, first-rate, matchless, superfine **10** first-class, preeminent, tremendous **11** outstanding, superlative

Gradgrind, Thomas and Louisa
characters in: **9** Hard Times
author: **7** Dickens

gradient **4** ramp, tilt **5** pitch, slant, slope **6** ascent **7** incline, leaning **9** steepness **11** inclination

gradual **4** slow **6** gentle, steady **7** regular **8** measured **9** graduated, piecemeal **10** continuous, deliberate, drop-by-drop, inch-by-inch, step-by-step, successive **11** incremental, progressive **13** imperceptible, slow-but-steady **14** little-by-little

graduate **5** grade **6** alumna **7** alumnus, mark off **9** calibrate **10** measure out **14** grant a degree to, receive a degree

Graduate, The
director: **11** Mike Nichols
cast: **12** Anne Bancroft (Mrs Robinson) **13** Dustin Hoffman, Katharine Ross **14** Murray Hamilton, William Daniels
score: **17** Simon and Garfunkel
Oscar for: **8** director

Graeae
also: **6** Graiae
goddesses of: **3** sea
number: **5** three
names: **4** Enyo **5** Deino **9** Pemphredo
father: **7** Phorcys
mother: **4** Ceto
sisters: **7** Gorgons
protectresses of: **7** Gorgons
personified: **6** old age
three shared: **6** one eye **8** one tooth
eye stolen by: **7** Perseus
corresponds to: **4** Enyo

Graeme, Alison
character in: **21** The Master of Ballantrae
author: **9** Stevenson

Graf 5 count

graft 3 bud 4 join, last, slip, swag 5 booty, infix, inset, plant, scion 6 bribes, payola, splice, spoils, sprout 7 bribery, implant, ingraft, payoffs, plunder, rake-off 8 kickback 9 hush money 10 corruption, transplant 12 implantation 13 inserted shoot

Graham, Bruce
architect of: 17 John Hancock Center (Chicago)

Grahame, Kenneth
author of: 19 The Wind in the Willows

Graiae *see* 6 Graeae

grain 3 bit, dot, jot, rye 4 atom, corn, dash, iota, mite, oats, seed, whit 5 crumb, grist, maize, ovule, pinch, spark, speck, touch, trace, wheat 6 barley, cereal, kernel, millet, morsel, pellet, tittle, trifle 7 granule, modicum 8 fragment, molecule, particle 9 scintilla
abbreviation: 2 gr
god of: 7 Robigus
goddess of: 6 Ribigo

Grain Coast *see* 11 Sierra Leone

Grainger, Percy Aldridge
born: 9 Australia, Melbourne
composer of: 14 Country Gardens 17 Handel in the Strand 19 Rosenkavalier Ramble

gram
abbreviation of: 1 g

Gram
origin: 12 Scandinavian
mentioned in: 8 Volsunga
form: 5 sword
owned by: 7 Sigmund
used by: 6 Sigurd
killed: 6 Fafnir

grand 2 A-1 3 big 4 fine, full, good, head, huge, keen, main 5 chief, fancy, great, large, lofty, noble, regal, royal, showy, super, swell 6 august, choice, groovy, kingly, lordly, superb 7 dashing, elegant, exalted, haughty, mammoth, opulent, pompous, queenly, stately, sublime, supreme 8 arrogant, complete, elevated, fabulous, glorious, imperial, imposing, majestic, palatial, princely, real cool, real gone, smashing, splendid, striking, terrific 9 admirable, dignified, excellent, first-rate, grandiose, luxurious, marvelous, principal, sumptuous, wonderful 10 impressive, monumental, out-of-sight 11 highfalutin, magnificent, pretentious, sensational 12 ostentatious 13 comprehensive, distinguished

Grand Canyon State
nickname of: 7 Arizona

grande dame 9 great lady

grandee 5 noble 8 nobleman 9 blue blood 10 aristocrat

Grandees
author: 17 Stephen Birmingham

grandeur 4 fame, pomp 5 glory, state 6 luster 7 dignity, majesty 8 eminence, nobility, splendor 9 celebrity, loftiness, solemnity, sublimity 10 augustness, excellence, importance 11 distinction, stateliness 12 magnificence, resplendence 14 impressiveness

Grand Hotel
author: 9 Vicki Baum
character: 9 Miss Flamm 12 Baron Gaigern 14 Dr Otternschlag, Otto Kringelein 27 Herr Generaldirektor Preysing 32 Elisaveta Alexandrovna Grusinskaya
director: 14 Edmund Goulding
cast: 10 Greta Garbo 12 Joan Crawford, Wallace Beery 13 John Barrymore 15 Lionel Barrymore
setting: 6 Berlin

Grand Illusion
director: 10 Jean Renoir
cast: 5 Dalio 7 Carette 9 Dita Parlo, Jean Gabin 13 Pierre Fresnay 16 Erich von Stroheim

grandiloquent 5 lofty 6 florid, turgid 7 flowery, pompous, stilted, swollen 8 inflated 9 bombastic, grandiose, high-flown 10 rhetorical 11 highfalutin, pretentious 12 high-sounding, magniloquent

grandiose 5 grand 7 pompous, splashy 8 affected 9 high-flown 10 flamboyant, theatrical 11 extravagant, highfalutin, pretentious

Grand Marnier
type: 6 brandy, cognac 7 liqueur
origin: 6 France
flavor: 6 orange
with gin: 7 Red Lion

grand monde 10 great world 11 best society 16 fashionable world

grand prix 10 grand prize

grand prize
French: 9 grand prix

Grange, Red (Harold)
nickname: 14 Galloping Ghost
sport: 8 football
team: 11 U of Illinois 12 Chicago Bears

Granger, Edith
character in: 12 Dombey and Son
author: 7 Dickens

Grangosier
character in: 22 Gargantua and Pantagruel
author: 8 Rabelais

Granite State
nickname of: 12 New Hampshire

grant 4 boon, cede, gift, give 5 admit, allot, allow, award, endow, favor, yield 6 accord, assign, bestow, confer, donate, permit 7 agree to, bequest, concede, consent, deal out, largess, present, subsidy, tribute 8 accede to, allocate, bestowal, dispense, donation, gratuity, offering 9 allotment, allowance, apportion, consent to, endowment, vouchsafe 10 assignment, concession, indulgence 11 benefaction 12 contribution, presentation 13 appropriation

Grant, Cary
real name: 23 Archibald Alexander Leach
wife: 10 Dyan Cannon 13 Barbara Hutton
born: 7 England 8 Bristol
roles: 6 Topper 9 Dream Wife, Houseboat 10 Indiscreet 11 Blonde Venus, Father Goose 13 To Catch a Thief 14 Bringing Up Baby, Monkey Business, The Bishop's Wife 15 She Done Him Wrong 16 North by Northwest 17 Arsenic and Old Lace, I Was a Male War Bride 18 Operation Petticoat 20 The Philadelphia Story 21 None But the Lonely Heart

Grant, Lee
real name: 21 Lyova Haskell Rosenthal
born: 9 New York NY
roles: 7 Shampoo 10 Plaza Suite 11 Peyton Place, The Landlord 14 Detective Story 19 In the Heat of the Night 20 Divorce American Style

Grant, Ulysses Simpson ***see box***

granted
French: 7 d'accord

grantee 8 receiver 9 recipient 11 beneficiary

Grant, Ulysses Simpson
real name: 17 Hiram Ulysses Grant
nickname: 3 Sam **4** Lyss **27** Unconditional Surrender Grant
presidential rank: 10 eighteenth
party: 10 Republican
state represented: 2 IL
defeated: 5 (David) Davis, (James) Black **6** (Charles) O'Conor **7** (Horace) Greeley, (Horatio) Seymour **9** (William Slocomb) Groesbeck
vice president: 5 (Thomas W) Ferry (acting) **6** (Henry) Wilson (died in office 1875), (Schuyler) Colfax
cabinet:
state: **4** (Hamilton) Fish **9** (Elihu Benjamin) Washburne
treasury: **7** (Alexander Turney) Stewart, (Benjamin Helm) Bristow, (Lot Myrick) Morrill **8** (George Sewall) Boutwell **10** (William Adams) Richardson
war: **4** (Alphonso) Taft **7** (James Donald) Cameron, (John Aaron) Rawlins, (William Worth) Belknap
attorney general: **4** (Alphonso) Taft, (Ebenezer Rockwood) Hoar **7** (Amos Tappan) Akerman **8** (George Henry) Williams **10** (Edwards) Pierrepont
navy: **5** (Adolph Edward) Borie **7** (George Maxwell) Robeson
postmaster general: **5** (James Noble) Tyner **6** (Marshall) Jewell **8** (James William) Marshall, (John Angel James) Creswell
interior: **3** (Jacob Dolson) Cox **6** (Columbus) Delano **8** (Zachariah) Chandler
born: 15 Point Pleasant OH
died: 15 Mount McGregor NY
buried: 9 New York NY
education: 9 West Point **17** US Military Academy
religion: 9 Methodist
author: 24 Personal Memoirs of US Grant **30** Around the World with General Grant
political career:
secretary of: **3** War (interim appointment)
civilian career: 6 farmer
military service: 6 US Army **8** Civil War **10** Mexican War **18** Illinois Volunteers **20** Commander of Union Army
notable events of lifetime/career: 5 Panic (of 1873) **11** Black Friday (gold panic) **16** Custer's Last Stand
Act: **10** Salary Grab
conspiracy: **11** Whiskey Ring
scandal: **14** Credit Mobilier
quote: 60 "No terms except unconditional and immediate surrender can be accepted"
father: 9 Jesse Root
mother: 6 Hannah (Simpson)
siblings: 5 Clare **10** Orvil Lynch **11** Mary Frances **13** Samuel Simpson, Virginia Paine
wife: 5 Julia (Boggs Dent)
children: 5 Ellen **9** Jesse Root **13** Frederick Dent **14** Ulysses Simpson

grant immunity to 4 free **5** clear, spare **6** except, excuse, exempt **7** absolve, release, relieve **9** privilege

grantor 5 giver **8** bestower **10** benefactor

granulate 5 crush **6** powder **9** pulverize **11** crystallize

granulated 6 ground **7** crushed **8** powdered **10** pulverized **12** crystallized

granule 5 grain **7** crystal **8** particle

grape ***see box***

Grapes of Wrath, The
author: 13 John Steinbeck
character: 4 Noah **6** Connie, Ma Joad, Pa Joad **7** Jim Casy, Tom Joad **12** Rose of Sharon
director: 8 John Ford
cast: 10 Henry Fonda **11** Jane Darwell **12** Dorris Bowden **13** John Carradine **15** Charley Grapewin
Oscar for: 17 supporting actress (Darwell)

graphic 4 seen **5** clear, drawn, lucid, vivid **6** visual **7** painted, printed, visible, written **8** distinct, explicit, forcible, lifelike, pictured, striking **9** pictorial, realistic, trenchant **10** expressive **11** descriptive, picturesque **12** illustrative

grappa
type: 6 brandy **7** liqueur
origin: 5 Italy
made from: 9 grape pulp

grapple 4 face, grip, hold, meet **5** catch, clasp, fight, grasp, seize **6** breast, clutch, combat, engage, fasten, tackle, take on **7** contend, grapnel, wrestle **8** confront, deal with, do battle, make fast, struggle **9** encounter, large hook, lay hold of **11** hold tightly

grape 5 Vitis **13** Vitis vinifera
varieties: 3 cat, red, sea **4** amur, blue, bush, cape, rock, sand, tail **5** bear's, bunch, frost, Javan, sugar, veldt **6** canyon, Damson, Miller, Oregon, pigeon, possum, summer, winter **7** African, Bullace, catbird, chicken, Concord, Spanish **8** European, mountain **9** evergreen, panhandle, river-bank **10** silverleaf **11** southern fox **13** sweet mountain
wine: 5 Gamay **6** Cayuga, Duriff, Merlot, Muscat, Shiraz **7** Barbera, Catawba **8** Baco Noir, Dolcetto, Labrusca, Nebbiolo, Verduzzo **9** Aglianico, Fume Blanc, Huxelrebe, Pinot Noir, Primitivo, Trebbiano, Zinfandel **10** Chardonnay, Sangiovese **11** Chenin Blanc, Petite Sirah, Pinot Bianco, Seyval Blanc **13** Cabernet Franc, Montepulciano **14** Sauvignon Blanc **15** Gewurztraminer **17** Cabernet Sauvignon **20** Johannisberg Riesling

grasp **3** get, ken **4** grab, grip, hold, sway, take **5** catch, clasp, infer, power, range, reach, savvy, scope, seize, sense, skill, sweep **6** clinch, clutch, deduce, fathom, follow, master, snatch, take in, talent **7** catch at, compass, control, embrace, grapple, mastery, seizing, seizure **8** clutches, gripping, perceive **9** handclasp, knowledge, seize upon **10** comprehend, perception, understand **13** comprehension, understanding

grasping **5** venal **6** greedy **7** hoggish, miserly, selfish, wolfish **8** covetous **9** mercenary, predatory, rapacious **10** avaricious **11** acquisitive

graspingness **5** greed **7** avarice **8** rapacity, venality **10** greediness **12** covetousness

grass *see box*

Grass, Gunter
author of: **6** Floods **8** Dog Years **10** The Tin Drum **11** Cat and Mouse, The Flounder **16** Local Anaesthetic **18** The Meeting at Telgte **20** From the Diary of a Snail **33** Headbirths or The Germans Are Dying Out

grasshopper
variety: **5** pygmy **6** meadow, monkey **7** katydid **10** band winged, cone headed, longhorned, slant-faced **11** bush katydid, leaf-rolling, shorthorned **12** shield-backed, spur-throated

grassland **3** lea **4** farm, vale, veld **5** field, pampa, plain, range, veldt **6** meadow **7** pasture, prairie, savanna **8** farmland, flatland, savannah **10** plantation

grate **3** irk, jar, rub, vex **4** bars, burr, buzz, gall, rasp **5** annoy, chafe, clack, grill, grind, mince, shred **6** abrade, gnaw at, hearth, jangle, rankle, scrape, scream, screen **7** firebed, firebox, grating, lattice, scratch, screech **8** irritate **9** fireplace, pulverize **10** exasperate, firebasket **11** latticework

grateful **7** obliged **8** beholden, indebted, thankful **9** gratified, obligated **12** appreciative

gratefulness **6** thanks **9** gratitude **12** appreciation, thankfulness

Gratiae *see* **6** Graces

Gratiano
character in: **19** The Merchant of Venice
author: **11** Shakespeare

gratification **3** joy **4** glee, kick **5** bliss **6** relish, solace, thrill **7** comfort, delight, ecstasy, elation, rapture **8** gladness, humoring, pleasing, pleasure, soothing **9** enjoyment, happiness, transport **10** indulgence, jubilation, satisfying **11** contentment, enchantment **12** exhilaration, satisfaction

gratified **5** happy **7** content, pleased **9** satisfied **11** comfortable

gratify **4** suit **5** amuse, favor, humor **6** coddle, divert, pamper, please, regale, soothe, thrill, tickle **7** appease, delight, enchant, flatter, gladden, indulge, refresh, satisfy **8** enthrall, entrance, interest, recreate **9** enrapture, entertain, transport **10** compliment, exhilarate

gratifying **8** humoring, pleasant, pleasing, soothing **9** agreeable, enjoyable, indulging, pampering, rewarding **10** delightful, satisfying **11** pleasurable

grating **4** bars, fret, grid **5** grate, harsh, raspy **6** creaky, grille, shrill **7** jarring, lattice, rasping, raucous, squeaky, tracery, trellis **8** abrasive, annoying, filigree, fretwork, gridiron, jangling, piercing,

grass
varieties: **3** cup, cut, dog, eel, elk, mat, nut, oat, oil, pin, rib, rye, Uva **4** barn, bear, bent, blue, chee, cord, crab, deer, fish, hair, lace, love, Lyme, moor, Nard, palm, Para, rice, rush, silk, star, tape, worm, yard **5** arrow, Bahia, beach, beard, Brome, Carib, China, cloud, curly, Ditch, fever, goose, lemon, Means, Melic, Mondo, natal, quack, sedge, shave, shore, Smilo, spike, squaw, Sudan, sword, Vasey, wheat, white, witch, zebra **6** Aleppo, alkali, basket, Bengal, Buffel, Canary, carpet, Dallis, Dudder, finger, gallow, Guinea, Indian, Korean, Manila, Napier, orange, orchid, Pampas, Rescue, Rhodes, ribbon, ripple, scurvy, signal, starry, switch, Tobosa, velvet, vernal, viper's, Zoysia **7** Bermuda, Brahman, Bristle, Buffalo, Esparto, Harding, Johnson, Kleberg, Pangola, poverty, pudding, quaking, Ravenna, sea lyme, serpent, tall oat, Wallaby, Widgeon **8** Angleton, blue-eyed, blue love, Boer love, elephant, fountain, hairy cup, lazy-man's, molasses, Ree wheat, sand love, scorpion, tuber oat **9** blue conch, centipede, common rye, hairy crab, hare's-tail, Hungarian, Malojilla, Mascarene, Oregon rye, rancheria, tall wheat, water star, yellow nut **10** Amur silver, beavertail, big quaking, blue finger, citronella, English rye, false wheat, golden-eyed, Indian rice, Italian rye, Korean lawn, Kuma bamboo, purple-eyed, rabbit-foot, rabbit-tail, reed canary, tufted hair, Washington, western rye, yellow-eyed **11** annual beard, branched cup, desert wheat, domestic rye, dwarf meadow, feather love, giant finger, green needle, Lehmann love, Nepal silver, Pentz finger, prairie cord, ringed beard, St Augustine, sweet vernal, Texas needle, Texas winter, weeping love **12** Common carpet, crested wheat, crinkled hair, European dune, Indian basket, Japanese lawn, Japanese love, Korean velvet, perennial rye, slender wheat, squirreltail, western wheat **13** American beach, Australian rye, billion-dollar, European beach, Himalaya fairy, Japanese sedge, little quaking, Paraguay Bahia, plains bristle, Siberian wheat **14** African Bermuda, bluebunch wheat, Japanese carpet, Pensacola Bahia, perennial veldt, pubescent wheat, Saint Augustine, stiff-hair wheat **15** European feather, Wilmington Bahia **16** creeping windmill, Pacey's English rye **17** Australian feather, intermediate wheat, Mediterranean salt, Transvaal dog-tooth **18** Australian windmill, California blue-eyed, Mexican everlasting **19** Fairway crested wheat **20** standard crested wheat

scraping, strident **9** offensive, vexatious **10** discordant, gate of bard, irritating, unpleasant **11** cacophonous, displeasing, high-pitched **12** disagreeable, exacerbating, exasperating

grating noise **7** discord, rasping **8** grinding **9** cacophony, harshness **10** disharmony, dissonance

gratis **4** free **10** gratuitous, on the house **13** complimentary, without charge

gratitude **6** thanks **10** obligation **11** recognition **12** appreciation, beholdenness, gratefulness, thankfulness, thanksgiving **14** acknowledgment

gratuitous **4** free **6** gratis, wanton **7** donated, willing **8** baseless, unproven **9** unfounded, voluntary **10** free of cost, groundless, irrelevant, unasked for, unprovoked **11** conjectural, impertinent, presumptive, spontaneous, uncalled for, unjustified, unwarranted **13** complimentary, unrecompensed

gratuity **3** tip **4** gift **8** donation
French: **7** douceur **9** pourboire

Graustark
author: **20** George Barr McCutcheon

grave **4** dour, sage, tomb **5** acute, crypt, mound, quiet, sober, staid, vault, vital **6** gloomy, sedate, solemn, somber, urgent **7** crucial, earnest, ossuary, serious, subdued, weighty **8** catacomb, cenotaph, critical, frowning, pressing **9** dignified, important, long-faced, mausoleum, momentous, sepulcher **10** thoughtful **11** burial ground, grim visaged, significant **13** consequential, philosophical **16** last resting place, place of interment
music: **6** solemn **7** serious

Graves, Robert
author of: **9** I Claudius, King Jesus **14** Claudius the God **15** The White Goddess **16** Goodbye to All That

graveyard **7** charnel, ossuary **8** boneyard, boot hill, cemetery **10** churchyard, necropolis **12** memorial park, potter's field **13** burying ground

gravitate **4** fall, head, move, sink, tend **6** settle **7** be drawn, descend, incline **8** converge, zero in on **9** be prone to **10** lean toward

gravity **4** pull **6** danger, import, moment **7** concern, dignity, urgency **8** calmness, enormity, grimness, serenity, sobriety **9** emergency, magnitude, solemnity, staidness **10** attraction, gloominess, importance, sedateness, solemnness, somberness **11** consequence, earnestness, gravitation, seriousness **12** significance, tranquillity **13** consideration, crucial nature **14** critical nature, pull of the earth, thoughtfulness **16** mutual attraction

gray, grey **3** dun **4** ashy, dark, drab, pale **5** ashen, foggy, hoary, misty, murky, slate **6** cloudy, dismal, gloomy, silver, somber **7** clouded, grayish, grizzly, neutral, silvery, sunless **8** overcast **9** cheerless, pearl-gray **10** depressing, gray-haired, gray-headed **11** dove-colored, hoary-headed **12** mouse-colored, silver-haired **13** salt and pepper

Gray, Harold
creator/artist of: **17** Little Orphan Annie

Gray, Thomas
author of: **32** Elegy Written in a Country Churchyard

grayness **4** murk **6** pallor **8** drabness **9** bleakness **10** somberness

Grayson, Kathryn
real name: **19** Zelma Kathryn Hedrick
born: **14** Winston-Salem NC
roles: **8** Show Boat **10** Kiss Me Kate **13** Anchors Aweigh, The Desert Song **15** The Vagabond King

graze **3** rub **4** crop, rasp, skim, skin **5** brush, grind, swipe **6** abrade, browse, bruise, glance, scrape **7** pasture, scratch **8** abrasion, eat grass **16** turn out to pasture

grease **3** fat, oil **4** balm, lard **5** salve **6** anoint, tallow **7** unguent **8** ointment **9** drippings, lubricant, lubricate

grease the palm **3** tip **5** bribe **6** buy off, pay off

greasy **3** fat **4** oily, waxy **5** fatty, lardy, slick **7** buttery **8** slippery, slithery **10** lardaceous, oleaginous

great ***see box***

Great Ajax
origin: **5** Greek
hero of: **9** Trojan War

greater **4** more **5** finer **6** better, bigger, larger **8** superior

Great Escape, The
director: **11** John Sturges
cast: **11** James Coburn, James Garner **12** Steve McQueen **13** David McCallum **14** Charles Bronson **15** Donald Pleasance **19** Richard Attenborough
setting: **7** Germany, POW camp

greatest **4** best, most **5** ultra **6** picked, select, utmost **7** extreme, highest, maximal, maximum, noblest, supreme **8** champion **9** first-rate **11** superlative, unsurpassed

Greatest Show on Earth, The
director: **13** Cecil B DeMille
cast: **11** Betty Hutton, Cornel Wilde **12** James Stewart

great **3** apt, big **4** able, a-one, fine, good, high, huge, kind, many, vast, well **5** chief, crack, grand, grave, gross, heavy, large, noble, noted, super, swell **6** adroit, choice, expert, famous, groovy, humane, loving, strong, superb **7** crucial, decided, eminent, extreme, grandly, immense, leading, mammoth, notable, serious, titanic, weighty **8** abundant, colossal, critical, enormous, esteemed, fabulous, generous, gigantic, glorious, gracious, manifold, renowned, skillful, smashing, splendid, superbly, superior, terrific, very well **9** boundless, countless, cyclopean, excellent, fantastic, first-rate, important, marvelous, momentous, monstrous, prominent, unlimited, wonderful **10** altruistic, celebrated, gargantuan, high-minded, inordinate, out-of-sight, prodigious, proficient, pronounced, remarkable, splendidly, stupendous, tremendous, voluminous **11** crackerjack, excellently, extravagant, illustrious, magnanimous, magnificent, outstanding, sensational, significant, superlative, wonderfully **12** considerable **13** consequential, distinguished, inexhaustible, magnificently, multitudinous **14** out of this world

Greece

other name: **5** Ellas **16** Hellenic Republic

capital/largest city: **6** Athens

others: **4** Enor **5** Canea, Corfu, Pylos, Volos **6** Delphi, Patras, Sparta **7** Chalcis, Corinth, Olympia, Piraeus **8** Salonika, Thessaly **9** Epidaurus, Gallipoli **10** Herakleion **11** Hermoupolis

school: **5** Crete **6** Athens, Patras, Thrace **8** Ioannina, Salonika

division: **6** Attica, Epirus, Thrace **7** Boeotia **8** Thessaly **9** Macedonia

measure: **3** pik **4** bema, piki, pous **5** baril, chous, cubit, diote, doron, maris, pekhe, podos, pygon, xylon **6** acaena, bacile, barile, cotula, dichas, gramme, hemina, koilon, lichas, milion, orgyia, palame, pechys, schene, xestes **7** amphora, bacvhel, chenica, choenix, cyathos, diaulos, metreta, stadium, stremma **8** condylos, daktylos, dekapode, dolichos, medimnos, medimnus, metretes, palaiste, plethron, plethrum, stathmos **9** hemiekton, oxybaphon

monetary unit: **5** lepta **7** drachma

weight: **3** mna, oke **4** mina, obol **5** livre, pound **6** diobol, kantar, obolos, obolus, talent **7** chalcon, drachma **8** diobolon

island: **3** Ios **5** Chios, Corfu, Crete, Delos, Melos, Naxos, Paros, Samos, Syros, Tenos, Thera, Zante **6** Andros, Euboea, Ionian, Ithaca, Lemnos, Lesbos, Patmos, Rhodes, Skyros, Thasos **7** Mykonos **8** Cyclades, Mytilene, Skiathos, Skopelos **9** Alonnisos **10** Cephalonia, Dodecanese, Samothrace **16** Northern Sporades

lake: **5** Karla, Volve **6** Copais, Kopais, Prespa, Voweis **8** Ioannina, Koroneia, Vistonis **9** Trichonis, Vegoritis

mountain: **3** Ida **4** Idhi, Oeta, Oite, Ossa **5** Athos **6** Ithome, Peleon, Pelion, Pindus **7** Grammos, Helicon, Rhodope **8** Hymettos, Smolikas, Taygetos, Taygetus **9** Parnassus **10** Hagion Oros, Lycabettus, Pentelicus

highest point: **7** Olympus

river: **4** Arta **6** Peneus, Struma, Vardar **7** Hellada, Maritsa **8** Achelous, Aliakmon

sea: **5** Crete **6** Aegean, Ionian **7** Mirtoon **13** Mediterranean

physical feature:

gulf: **7** Corinth, Saronic

peninsula: **6** Balkan **10** Chalcidice **12** Peloponnesus

plain: **7** Boeotia **8** Thessaly

plateau: **7** Arcadia

valley: **5** Nemea

people: **5** Greek **6** Achean, Dorian, Ionian **7** Aeolian, Hellene

artist: **7** El Greco

author: **5** Homer **6** Hesiod, Pindar **8** Menander **9** Aeschylus, Euripides, Sophocles **11** Kazantzakis **12** Aristophanes

god: **4** Ares, Hera, Leto, Zeus **5** Cupid **6** Apollo, Cronus, Hermes, Hestia **7** Artemis, Demeter **8** Dionysus, Poseidon **9** Aphrodite **10** Hephaestus, Persephone **12** Pallas Athena **13** Phoebus Apollo

historian: **9** Herodotus **10** Thucydides

king: **11** Constantine

lawmaker: **5** Draco, Solon **8** Lycurgus, Pericles

leader: **10** Papandreou

mathematician: **6** Euclid **10** Archimedes, Pythagoras

mythological: **5** Atlas, Helen, Jason, Medea, Paris **6** Hector, Medusa **7** Ariadne, Chimera, Pandora, Pegasus, Perseus, Theseus **8** Achilles, Heracles, Minotaur, Odysseus **9** Agamemnon, Andromeda, Iphigenia, King Minos **10** Prometheus **11** Bellerophon

orator: **11** Demosthenes

philosopher: **5** Plato **8** Socrates **9** Aristotle

physician: **11** Hippocrates

sculptor: **5** Myron **7** Phidias **10** Praxiteles

tycoon: **7** Onassis

language: **5** Greek

religion: **14** Greek Orthodoxy

place:

ruins: **5** Delos, Pella, Pylos, Samos **6** Delphi, Sparta, Thebes, Tiryns **7** Corinth, Eleusis, Elevsis, Knossos, Mycenae, Olympia **9** Acropolis, Epidaurus, Parthenon **13** Palace of Minos

feature:

coffeeshop: **7** kaphene

marketplace: **5** agora

port **7** Piraeus

presidential guard: **7** Evzones

village square: **7** plateia

food:

dish: **7** mousaka **8** moussaka, souvlaka, dolmades, souvlakia **10** shish kabob

liquor: **4** ouzo

wine: **7** retsina

13 Dorothy Lamour, Gloria Grahame **14** Charlton Heston
Oscar for: 7 picture

Great Expectations
author: 14 Charles Dickens
character: 3 Pip **7** Estella **9** Compeyson, Mr Jaggers **10** Joe Gargery **12** Abel Magwitch, Miss Havisham **13** Herbert Pocket
director: 9 David Lean
cast: 9 John Mills **11** Martita Hunt **12** Alec Guinness, Bernard Mills **13** Valerie Hobson **16** Francis L Sullivan

Great Gatsby, The
author: 16 F Scott Fitzgerald
character: 9 Jay Gatsby **11** Tom Buchanan **12** Myrtle Wilson, Nick Carraway **13** Daisy Buchanan

Great God Brown, The
author: 12 Eugene O'Neill

Great Idean Mother *see* **6** Cybele

great lady
French: 10 grande dame

Great Lake 4 Erie **5** Huron **7** Ontario **8** Michigan, Superior

Great Land
nickname of: 6 Alaska

greatly 6 vastly **7** largely, notably **8** markedly, mightily, very much **9** immensely **10** abundantly, enormously, infinitely, powerfully, remarkably **12** considerably, immeasurably, tremendously

great mishap 5 wreck **6** blight, fiasco **7** tragedy **8** calamity, disaster **9** cataclysm, ruination **11** catastrophe

greatness 8 eminence, nobility **9** loftiness **10** excellence, importance, notability, prominence **11** preeminence, superiority **12** magnificence **15** illustriousness

Great Profile
nickname of: 13 John Barrymore

Great Railway Bazaar, The
author: 11 Paul Theroux

great world
French: 10 grand monde

Great Ziegfeld, The
director: 14 Robert Z Leonard
cast: 8 Myrna Loy **10** Fanny Brice **11** Frank Morgan, Luise Rainer (Anna Held) **13** Virginia Bruce, William Powell
Oscar for: 7 actress (Rainer), picture

grebe 4 bird, fowl, loon **5** diver **6** dipper **7** henbill **8** dabchick **9** hell-diver **10** water witch

Grecco, Al
character in: 20 Appointment in Samarra
author: 5 O'Hara

Greco, El Greco
real name: 23 Domenikos Theotokopoulos
born: 5 Crete **6** Candia
artwork: 7 Espolio (Disrobing of Christ), Laocoon **12** View of Toledo **19** Cleaning of the Temple **20** Healing of the Blind Man **21** Burial of the Count Orgaz **27** Christ Stripped of his Garments **28** San Ildefonso at his Writing Desk **29** Cardinal Fernando Nino de Guevara **42** Christ Driving the Money-Changers from the Temple

Greece ***see box***

greed 7 avarice, avidity, craving **8** cupidity, rapacity **11** itching palm, money-hunger, piggishness, selfishness **12** covetousness **13** rapaciousness **14** avariciousness

greediness 7 avarice **8** gluttony, rapacity, voracity **12** covetousness, graspingness **15** acquisitiveness

greedy 4 avid **5** eager **6** ardent, hungry **7** anxious, burning, craving, fervent, hoggish, piggish, selfish, swinish, wolfish **8** covetous, famished, grasping, ravenous **9** devouring, impatient, mercenary, predatory, rapacious, thirsting, voracious **10** avaricious, gluttonous, insatiable **11** acquisitive, money-hungry **12** gormandizing

Greek
language family: 12 Indo-European
ancient branch: 5 Doric, Ionic **6** Aeolic

Greek alphabet ***see box***

Greek Anthology, The
author: 8 Cephalas, Meleager

Greek measure 4 mina **5** cubit **6** obolos, talent **7** drachma, stadion

Greek Mythology ***see box, p. 412***

Greek uncial codex 4 Syri **6** Regius **8** Ephraemi **9** Laudianus, Vaticanus **10** Sinaiticus **11** Basiliensis **12** Alexandrinus, Sangallensis **13** Koridethianus

green 3 raw **4** jade, lawn, lime, turf **5** crude, heath, olive, rough, sward, young **6** callow, campus, common, tender, unripe **7** awkward, emerald, verdant, verdure **8** greenish, gullible, ignorant, immature, inexpert, not cured, not dried, pea-green, sea-green, unsmoked, untanned, unversed **9** blue-green, credulous, grassplot, lime-green, unfledged, unskilled, untrained **10** aquamarine, chartreuse, golf course, grass-green, greensward, kelly-green, olive green, uninformed, unmellowed, unpolished, unseasoned **11** cobalt green, forest green, undeveloped, yellow-green **12** easily fooled, green-colored, not fully aged, putting green, village green **13** inexperienced, undisciplined **14** underdeveloped **15** unsophisticated

Green Acres
character: 7 Mr Haney **8** Eb Dawson **10** Fred Ziffel, Sam Drucker **11** Doris Ziffel, Hank Kimball, Lisa Douglas **20** Oliver Wendell Douglas
cast: 8 Eva Gabor, Fran Ryan **9** Alvy Moore, Frank Cady, Tom Lester **10** Pat Buttram **11** Eddie Albert **13** Barbara Pepper, Hank Patterson
pig: 6 Arnold
town: 11 Hooterville

green at the gills 6 queasy, sickly **7** bilious **8** nauseous **9** nauseated, sickening

greenback 4 bill **8** banknote **12** treasury note **15** legal-

Greek alphabet
a: 5 alpha
b: 4 beta
ch/kh: 3 chi
d: 5 delta
e: 3 eta **7** epsilon
g: 5 gamma
i: 4 iota
k: 5 kappa
l: 6 lambda
m: 2 mu
n: 2 nu
o: 5 omega **7** omicron
p: 2 pi
ph: 3 phi
ps: 3 psi
r: 3 rho
s: 5 sigma
t: 3 tau
th: 5 theta
x: 2 xi
y: 7 upsilon
z: 4 zeta

tender note **17** silver certificate

Green Bay
football team: **7** Packers

Green Bay Tree, The
author: **14** Louis Bromfield

Greene, Graham
author of: **11** The Third Man **12** Brighton Rock, Ways of Escape **14** The Human Factor **16** Monsignor Quixote, **17** The End of the Affair, The Ministry of Fear, Travels with My Aunt **19** The Heart of the Matter, The Power and the Glory

Greene, Joe
nickname: **7** Mean Joe
sport: **8** football
position: **7** lineman
team: **18** Pittsburgh Steelers

Greene, Lorne
born: **6** Canada, Ottawa **7** Ontario
roles: **5** Adama **7** Bonanza **11** Peyton Place **12** Autumn Leaves, The Buccaneer **13** Ben Cartwright **16** The Silver Chalice **19** Battlestar Galactica

Greene, Nathanael
served in: **16** Revolutionary War
rank: **16** brigadier general **20** quartermaster general
battle: **7** Cowpens, Trenton **12** Eutaw Springs, Hobkirk's Hill **18** Guilford Court House

green-eyed monster **4** envy **8** jealousy **12** covetousness

Green for Danger
director: **13** Sidney Gilliat
cast: **7** Leo Genn **9** Sally Gray **11** Alastair Sim **12** Rosamund John, Trevor Howard

greenhorn **4** rube, tyro **6** novice, rookie **7** learner **8** beginner, neophyte, newcomer **9** fledgling **10** apprentice, tenderfoot **14** babe in the woods

Green Hornet, The
character: **4** Kato **9** Britt Reid (The Green Hornet)
cast: **8** Bruce Lee **11** Van Williams
car: **11** Black Beauty
creator: **11** Bert Whitman
sidekick: **4** Kato

Green House, The
author: **16** Mario Vargas Llosa

Greening of America, The
author: **12** Charles Reich

greenish **6** sickly **7** bilious

Greek Mythology
afterworld of the blessed: **7** Elysium
amber islands: **10** Electrides
architect of labyrinth: **8** Daedalus
blood-sucking monster: **5** Lamia
cupbearer to the gods: **8** Ganymede **9** Catamitus
dragon: **8** basilisk
drink of the gods: **6** nectar
eagle/lion monster: **7** griffin, griffon, gryphon
enchantress: **5** Circe
female warrior: **6** Amazon
fire-breathing monster: **7** Chimera
first man: **12** Alalcomeneus
food/drink/perfume of the gods: **8** ambrosia
the Furies: **5** Dirae **6** Erinys, Furiae, Semnai **7** Erinyes **9** Eumenides
names: **7** Allecto, Megaera **9** Tisiphone
goat god: **7** Aegipan
goddess of beauty: **6** Graces **7** Gratiae **9** Charities
names: **4** Auxo **5** Cleta **6** Aglaia, Thalia **7** Phaenna **8** Hegemone **10** Euphrosyne
goddess of childbirth: **8** Ilithyia **10** Eileithyia
corresponds to Roman: **6** Lucina
goddess of the dawn: **3** Eos
corresponds to Roman: **6** Aurora
goddesses of destiny: **5** Fates, Morae **6** Moerae, Moirai
names: **5** Moira **6** Clotho **8** Lachesis
corresponds to Roman: **6** Parcae
goddess of discord: **4** Eris
corresponds to Roman: **9** Discordia
goddess of divine punishment/recklessness: **3** Ate
goddess of divine retribution: **8** Adrastea
goddess of the earth: **2** Ge **4** Gaea, Gaia
corresponds to Roman: **6** Tellus
goddess of earth/fertility: **7** Demeter
corresponds to Roman: **5** Ceres
goddess of earth/Hades: **5** Brimo **6** Hecate, Hekate
goddess of fortune: **5** Tyche
corresponds to Roman: **7** Fortuna
goddess of healing: **4** Iaso
goddess of health: **6** Hygeia
corresponds to Roman: **5** Salus
goddess of the hearth: **6** Hestia
corresponds to Roman: **5** Vesta
goddess of justice: **4** Dice, Dike **6** Astrea **7** Astraea
goddesses of literature/the arts: **5** Muses **7** the Nine **8** Pierides **10** Castalides
names: **4** Clio **5** Aoede, Erato, Mneme **6** Melete, Thalia, Urania **7** Euterpe **8** Calliope **9** Melpomene **10** Polyhymnia **11** Terpsichore
corresponds to Roman: **7** Camenae
muse of astronomy: **6** Urania
muse of dancing/choral song: **11** Terpsichore
muse of history: **4** Clio
muse of idyllic poetry/comedy: **6** Thalia
muse of love poetry: **5** Erato
muse of meditation: **6** Melete
muse of memory: **5** Mneme
muse of music/lyric poetry: **7** Euterpe
muse of poetry/epic: **8** Calliope
muse of sacred music/dance: **10** Polyhymnia
muse of song: **5** Aoede
muse of tragedy: **9** Melpomene
goddess of love/beauty: **6** Urania **7** Cyprian, Paphian **8** Cytherea **9** Aphrodite **10** Anadyomene
corresponds to Roman: **5** Venus
goddess of memory: **9** Mnemosyne
goddess of the night: **3** Nox, Nyx
goddess of peace: **5** Irene
corresponds to Roman: **3** Pax
goddess of the rainbow: **4** Iris

goddess of sailors: 5 Brizo
goddess of the sea: 10 Amphitrite
goddesses of the sea: 6 Graeae, Graiae
names: **4** Enyo **5** Deino **9** Pemphredo
goddesses of seasons/growth/decay/social order: **4** Hour **5** Horae
names: **4** Dice, Dike **5** Carpo, Irene **6** Thallo **7** Eunomia
goddess of spring flowers: 6 Thallo
goddess of summer fruit: 5 Carpo
goddess of victory: 4 Nike
corresponds to Roman: **6** Athena **8** Victoria
goddess of war: 4 Enyo
corresponds to Roman: **7** Bellona
goddess of wisdom/fertility/arts/warfare: 6 Athena, Athene, Pallas, Saitis **11** Tritogeneia **12** Pallas Athena **18** Alalcomenean Athena
corresponds to Roman: **7** Minerva
goddess of youth/spring: 4 Hebe
god of beekeeping/winemaking/husbandry: 9 Aristaeus
god of censure/ridicule: 5 Momos, Momus
god of dreams: 6 Icelus, Oniros **7** Oneiros **8** Morpheus
god of earth: 10 Trophonius
god of Eleusinian mysteries: 7 Bacchus
god of erotic desire: 7 Himeros
god of fire/metalworking/handicrafts: 10 Hephaestus, Hephaistos
corresponds to Roman: **6** Vulcan
god of the heavens: 4 Zeus
corresponds to Roman: **4** Jove **7** Jupiter
corresponds to Egyptian: **4** Amen, Amon **5** Ammon **6** Amen Ra, Amon Ra
god of light/healing/music/poetry/prophecy/beauty: **6** Apollo
god of love: 4 Eros
corresponds to Roman: **4** Amor **5** Cupid
god of male power/procreation: 7 Priapus
corresponds to Roman: **7** Mutinus
god of marriage: 5 Hymen **9** Hymenaeus
corresponds to Roman: **8** Talassio
god of medicine/healing: 9 Asclepius
corresponds to Roman: **11** Aesculapius
god of oaths: 6 Horcus
god of recovery from illness: 11 Telesphorus
god of sea/caused earthquakes: 8 Poseidon
corresponds to Roman: **7** Neptune
god of shepherds/flocks/pastures/forests: 3 Pan **7** Sinoeis
god of sleep: 6 Hypnos, Hypnus
corresponds to Roman: **6** Somnus
god of the sun: 6 Helios **8** Hyperion
corresponds to Roman: **3** Sol
god of the underworld: 6 Infiri
god of war: 4 Ares **8** Theritas
corresponds to Roman: **4** Mars
god of wine/fertility/drama: 5 Evius **7** Bacchus **8** Dionysus
Gorgon monster: 6 Medusa
hundred-headed monster: 5 Ladon **8** Typhoeus
islands of the blessed: 10 Hesperides
man/horse monster: 7 centaur
messenger of gods/god of roads/commerce/invention/cunning/thieves: 6 Hermes
corresponds to Roman: **7** Mercury
monster that asked riddles: 6 Sphinx
monsters that turn people to stone: 7 Gorgons
moon goddess/huntress/virgin: 6 Phoebe, Selene **7** Artemis
corresponds to Roman: **5** Diana
corresponds to Cretan: **11** Britomartis
nine-headed water serpent: 5 Hydra
nymph: 7 Calypso

(*continued*)

Greenland ***see box, p. 415***

Green Mansions
author: 8 W H Hudson
character: 4 Rima **5** Nuflo **6** Mr Abel

Greenmantle
author: 10 John Buchan

Green Mountain State
nickname of: 7 Vermont

Greenough, Horatio
born: 8 Boston MA
artwork: 16 George Washington **18** The Chanting Cherubs

Green Pastures, The
author: 12 Marc Connelly

Greenstreet, Sydney
born: 7 England **8** Sandwich
roles: 9 The Fat Man **10** Casablanca **16** The Maltese Falcon **19** Passage to Marseilles

green with envy 7 envious, jealous **8** covetous

greet 4 hail, meet **5** admit **6** accept, accost, salute **7** receive, speak to, welcome **9** , smile upon, recognize **10** bid welcome

greeting 6 salute **7** welcome **8** saluting **9** reception, welcoming **10** salutation **12** introduction, presentation

greetings 4 best **5** hello **7** regards **8** respects **10** best wishes, good wishes, salutation **11** compliments, remembrance, well-wishing **13** felicitations
Latin: 5 salve

gregarious 6 genial, lively, social **7** affable **8** friendly, outgoing, sociable **9** convivial, talkative, vivacious **11** extroverted **13** companionable

gremlin 3 imp **5** demon, gnome **6** goblin

Grenada ***see box, p. 415***

grenade 7 missile **9** pineapple

Grendel
character in: 7 Beowulf
author: 7 unknown

Grewgious, Mr
character in: 22 The Mystery of Edwin Drood
author: 7 Dickens

Grey, Joel
real name: 8 Joel Katz
born: 13 Cleveland Ohio
roles: 7 Cabaret, George M **13** Come September **23** The Seven Percent Solution

Greek Mythology *(continued)*
one-eyed giant: 7 Cyclops
oracle of Apollo: 13 Delphic oracle
personification of death: 4 Mors **8** Thanatos
personification of punishment/revenge: 5 Poena, Poine
personification of soul: 6 Psyche
physician to gods of Olympia: 5 Paeon
prophetess: 9 Alexandra, Cassandra
queen of heaven: 4 Hera, Here
***corresponds to Roman:* 4** Juno
race of gods: 6 Titans
***names:* 4** Rhea, Thia **5** Coeus, Crius **6** Cronus, Phoebe, Tethys, Themis **7** Iapetus, Oceanus **8** Hyperion **9** Mnemosyne
river god: 6 Asopus, Peneus, Simois **7** Inachus, Pelegon **8** Achelous
river in Hades: 4 Styx **5** Lethe **7** Acheron, Cocytus
***ferryman:* 6** Charon
***river of forgetfulness:* 5** Lethe
ruler of the winds: 6 Aeolus
satyr/god of the forest: 7 Silenus
sea god: 6 Nereus, Triton **7** Glaucus, Phorcys, Proteus
sea monster: 6 Scylla
seer: 6 Mopsus **8** Tiresias
serpent: 6 dipsas
serpent of darkness: 5 Apepi **7** Apophis
seven against Thebes: 6 Tydeus **8** Adrastus, Capaneus **9** Polynices **10** Amphiaraus, Hippomedon **13** Parthenopaeus
seven sisters: 8 Pleiades
***names:* 4** Maia **6** Merope **7** Alcyone, Celaeno, Electra, Sterope, Taygete
sorceress: 5 Medea
spirits of disease/evil/old age/death: 5 Keres
three-headed dog that guards underworld: 8 Cerberus
twins: 8 Dioscuri **15** Castor and Pollux
two-headed serpent: 11 Amphisbaena
underworld: 5 Hades, Pluto
***corresponds to Roman:* 3** Dis **5** Orcus **8** Dis Pater
underworld darkness: 6 Erebus
underworld spirit: 9 Chthonian
virgin huntress: 8 Atalanta, Atalante
whirlpool: 9 Charybdis
winged horse: 5 Arion **7** Pegasus
woman/beast monster: 6 Python **8** Delphyne
woman/bird monster: 5 Harpy
woman/serpent monster: 7 Echidna
wood nymph: 5 dryad

Grey, Zane
author of: 18 Valley of Wild Horses **20** The Spirit of the Border **21** Riders of the Purple Sage, The Last of the Plainsmen

greyhound
group of: 5 leash

Greystoke, Lord
real identity of: 6 Tarzan

griddle cake 6 blintz, waffle **7** crumpet, hot cake, pancake **8** corncake, flapcake, flapjack **10** battercake **11** flannel cake **13** buckwheat cake
French: 5 crepe **12** crepe suzette
German: 11 pfannkuchen
Hungarian: 10 palacsinta
Indian: 8 chapatty

Gride, Arthur
character in: 16 Nicholas Nickleby
author: 7 Dickens

grief 3 woe **4** care **5** agony, worry **6** burden, misery, ordeal, sorrow **7** anguish, anxiety, concern, despair, remorse, sadness, trouble **8** distress, grieving, hardship, nuisance, vexation **9** grievance, heartache, suffering **10** affliction, desolation, discomfort, heartbreak **11** despondency, tribulation **12** wretchedness **13** inconvenience

griefstricken 7 joyless, unhappy **8** saddened, wretched **9** sorrowful **13** brokenhearted

Grieg, Edvard Hagerup
born: 6 Bergen, Norway
composer of: 5 I Host **8** Bergljot, In Autumn, Peer Gynt **11** Lyric Pieces **12** Landjaenning **14** Fra Holbergs Tid, Lyriske Stykker **15** Sigurd Jorsalfar **16** From Holberg's Time **17** Recognition of Land **18** Foran Sydens Kloster **22** At a Southern Convent Gate

grievance 4 beef, hurt **5** wrong **6** injury **7** outrage **8** hardship, iniquity **9** complaint, injustice **10** affliction, bone to pick, disservice

grieve 3 cry, rue, sob **4** moan, pain, wail, weep **5** be sad, mourn **6** bemoan, deject, harass, lament, sadden, sorrow **7** afflict, agonize, depress, oppress, torture **8** disquiet, distress **10** discomfort **11** be anguished

grieve over 5 mourn **6** bemoan, bewail, lament **7** cry over **8** moan over, weep over

grievous 3 sad **5** acute, grave, harsh, heavy **6** severe, tragic, woeful **7** crucial, glaring, harmful, heinous, painful, serious, very bad **8** critical, shameful, shocking **9** agonizing, appalling, atrocious, monstrous, nefarious, sorrowful **10** burdensome, calamitous, deplorable, iniquitous, lamentable, outrageous, unbearable **11** destructive, distressing, intolerable, significant **12** insufferable **13** heartbreaking

griffin
also: 7 griffon, gryphon
form: 7 monster
head of: 5 eagle
wings of: 5 eagle
body of: 4 lion
guards of: 4 gold
location: 7 Scythia

Griffith, Andy
real name: 20 Andrew Samuel Griffith
born: 8 Mt Airy NC
roles: 7 Matlock **13** Will Stockdale **15** A Face in the Crowd, Angel in My Pocket **18** No Time for Sergeants **19** The Andy Griffith Show

Griffith, D W
director of: 11 Intolerance

Greenland
capital/largest city: **3** Nuk **8** Godthaab, The Point
others: **4** Etah, Nord **5** Thule **6** Umanak **7** Godhavn, Ivigtut **10** Nanortalik **11** Julianehaab **12** Angmagssalik, Sukkertoppen **14** Christianshaab
government: **20** home rule under Denmark
monetary unit: **3** ore **5** krone
island: **5** Disko
mountain: **5** Forel, Payer **7** Khardyu **8** Peterman **15** Petermannsbjerg
highest point: **9** Gunnbjorn **16** Gunnbjornsfjaeld
sea: **6** Arctic **9** Greenland
physical feature: **9** Inland Ice
bay: **5** Disko **6** Baffin **8** Melville
cape: **4** Jaal **6** Grivel, Walker **8** Bismarck, Brewster, Farewell, Lowenorn **11** Morris Jesup
glacier: **10** Jacobshavn
strait: **5** Davis **7** Denmark
people: **3** Ita **6** Eskimo **8** European
explorer: **10** Eric the Red
language: **6** Danish, Eskimo **11** Greenlandic
religion: **19** Evangelical Lutheran
feature:
airbase: **4** Etah **5** Thule
animal: **7** caribou

14 Broken Blossoms **17** Orphans of the Storm, The Birth of a Nation

Griffith, Hugh
born: **5** Wales **8** Anglesey **10** Marian Glas
roles: **6** Ben-Hur **8** Lucky Jim, Tom Jones

Griffiths, Clyde
character in: **17** An American Tragedy
author: **7** Dreiser

griffon *see* **7** griffin

grill **3** fry **4** cook, grid, pump, quiz, sear **5** broil, query **7** broiler, grating, griddle **8** gridiron, question **9** crossbars **11** interrogate **12** cross-examine **18** give the third degree

grim **4** foul, hard, ugly **5** cruel, harsh, lurid, stern, sulky **6** brutal, fierce, gloomy, grisly, grumpy, horrid, morose, odious, severe, somber, sullen **7** austere, ghastly, hideous, inhuman, macabre, squalid, vicious **8** dreadful, fiendish, gruesome, horrible, resolute, scowling, shocking, sinister **9** appalling, ferocious, frightful, heartless, loathsome, merciless, obstinate, repellent, repugnant, repulsive, revolting **10** determined, forbidding, implacable, inexorable, relentless, unyielding **11** unrelenting **12** cantankerous

grimace **4** face **5** scowl, smirk, sneer **6** glower **7** wry face
French: **4** moue

grime **4** dirt, dust, smut, soil, soot **5** filth **6** smudge

Grimhild
origin: **12** Scandinavian
mentioned in: **8** Volsunga
form: **9** sorceress
husband: **5** Giuki, Gjuki
daughter: **6** Gudrun, Kudrun **7** Guthrun
son: **6** Gunnar
tricked Sigurd to marry: **6** Gudrun, Kudrun **7** Guthrun

Grimm Brothers (Jakob and Wilhelm)
editors of: **15** Hansel and Gretel **16** Grimm's Fairy Tales

grim reaper **5** death **12** angel of death

grim-visaged **8** frowning, scowling **9** long-faced **10** stern-faced

grin **4** beam **5** smile, smirk **6** rictus, simper **11** crack a smile

grind **4** file, grit, mill, rasp, whet **5** chore, crush, gnash, grate **6** abrade, drudge, polish, powder, scrape **7** crammer, hard job, plodder, sharpen, slavery **8** bookworm, drudgery **9** granulate, pulverize, triturate

Gringoire
character in: **23** The Hunchback of Notre Dame
author: **4** Hugo

grip **3** bag **4** grab, hilt, hold **5** clasp, grasp, rivet, seize **6** clench, clutch, handle, retain, snatch, valise **7** attract, control, impress, mastery, satchel **8** clutches, hold fast, suitcase **9** gladstone, handclasp, handshake, retention, spellbind **10** domination, perception **12** traveling bag **13** comprehension, understanding

gripe, gripes **4** beef, carp, fret, kick, pain, pang, rail **5** cavil, colic, spasm, whine **6** cramps, grouch, grouse, kvetch, mutter, squawk, twinge, twitch **7** grumble, protest, whining **8** complain, distress, grousing, bellyache, complaint, find fault, grievance, grumbling **10** affliction **11** stomachache **12** faultfinding

grisly **4** foul, gory, grim **5** lurid **6** horrid, odious **7** ghastly, hideous, macabre **8** dreadful, gruesome, horrible, shocking, sinister **9** abhorrent, appalling, frightful, loathsome, repellent, repugnant, repulsive, revolting **10** abominable, forbidding, horrendous

Grenada
other name: **11** Isle of Spice
capital/largest city: **9** St Georges
others: **8** Sauteurs
head of state: **14** British monarch **15** governor general
island: **8** Windward **9** Carriacon **10** Grenadines
lake: **10** Grand Etang
highest point: **11** St Catherine
sea: **9** Caribbean
physical feature:
bay: **9** St Georges'
people: **5** Black, Negro **6** Indian
discoverer: **8** Columbus
language: **7** English
religion: **8** Anglican **10** Protestant **13** Roman Catholic
food:
spice: **4** mace **6** nutmeg

grit **3** rub **4** dirt, dust, guts, muck, rasp, sand, soot **5** filth, gnash, grate, nerve, pluck, spunk **6** crunch, mettle, scrape **7** courage, stamina **8** backbone, tenacity **9** fortitude **10** doggedness, resolution **12** perseverance **13** determination, grind together

Grizzly Bear State
10 California

groan **4** howl, moan, roar, wail **5** bleat, crack, creak, whine **6** bellow, bemoan, lament, murmur, squeak **7** grumble, screech, whimper **8** complain

grocery store
Spanish: **6** bodega

groggy **5** dazed, dizzy, dopey, shaky, woozy **6** addled, punchy **7** muddled, reeling, stunned **8** confused, sluggish, unsteady **9** befuddled, lethargic, perplexed, stupefied **10** bewildered, punch-drunk, staggering

groom **4** comb, wash **5** boots, brush, curry, dress, drill, preen, prime, primp, train, valet **6** flunky, lackey, spouse **7** clean up, consort, develop, educate, footman, freshen, hostler, husband, prepare, refresh, rub down, servant **8** exercise, initiate, make neat, make tidy, practice, spruce up **9** currycomb, make ready, stableboy **10** bridegroom, manservant **12** indoctrinate **13** livery servant

groove **3** cut, rut, use **4** rule **5** flute, habit, score, usage **6** custom, furrow, gutter, hollow, trench **7** channel, cutting, scoring **8** practice **9** procedure **10** beaten path, convention **11** corrugation **12** fixed routine, second nature

grope **3** paw **5** probe **6** finger, fumble **7** fish for, venture **9** feel about **11** feel one's way, move blindly, try one's luck **13** search blindly

Gropius, Walter
architect of: **5** Fagus (factory) **7** Bauhaus (Dessau) **13** Pan Am Building (NYC) **31** Harvard University Graduate Center

gross **3** bag, big, fat **4** bulk, earn, huge, lewd, mass, rank, reap, vast **5** bulky, crude, great, heavy, large, obese, plain, sheer, total, utter, whole **6** carnal, coarse, earthy, entire, pick up, ribald, smutty, sordid, take in, vulgar **7** glaring, heinous, immense, lump sum, massive, obscene, obvious, titanic, uncouth **8** colossal, complete, enormous, flagrant, gigantic, improper, indecent, manifest, unseemly, unwieldy **9** aggregate, downright, egregious, lecherous, monstrous, offensive, unrefined **10** gargantuan, indelicate, lascivious, licentious, outrageous, overweight, prodigious, stupendous **11** unequivocal, unmitigated, unqualified

Grossel, Ira
real name of: **12** Jeff Chandler

grossness **7** obesity **8** hugeness, lewdness, ribaldry **9** crudeness, heaviness, indecency, obscenity, roughness, vulgarity **10** coarseness, indelicacy, inelegance **14** lasciviousness

grossularite
species: **6** garnet

Gros Ventre *see* **7** Hidatsa

grotesque **3** odd **4** wild **5** antic, weird **6** absurd, exotic, far-out, rococo, way-out **7** baroque, bizarre, strange **8** deformed, fanciful, peculiar **9** contorted, distorted, eccentric, fantastic, misshapen, odd-shaped, unnatural **10** outlandish **11** extravagant, incongruous **12** preposterous

grotto **4** cave **6** burrow, cavern, hollow, recess, tunnel **8** catacomb

grouch **3** cry **4** beef, carp, crab, fret, kick, mope, pout, rail, sulk **5** cavil, crank, gripe, growl, moper, whine **6** grouse, mutter, pouter **7** grumble, killjoy, protest **8** complain, grumbler **9** bellyache, find fault **10** complainer, curmudgeon, spoilsport, wet blanket

grouchy **5** cross, testy **6** crabby, cranky, grumpy, touchy **8** snappish **10** ill-humored, out of sorts **11** ill-tempered **12** cantankerous **13** short-tempered

ground, grounds **3** set, sod **4** area, base, call, dirt, farm, land, loam, soil, turf, yard **5** acres, basis, beach, cause, dregs, drill, earth, field, found, lawns, realm, teach, train **6** campus, domain, estate, excuse, inform, motive, object, reason, region, secure, settle, sphere, strand **7** account, confirm, deposit, dry land, educate, founder, gardens, habitat, prepare, purpose, support, terrain **8** district, exercise, firm land, initiate, instruct, occasion, organize, practice, premises, property, province, sediment, the earth **9** arguments, bailiwick, establish, fix firmly, institute, principle, rationale, settlings, territory **10** discipline, inducement, real estate, terra firma **11** pros and cons **12** indoctrinate **14** considerations

grounded **5** based **6** kept in, taught **7** aground, beached, bounded, drilled, founded, secured, trained **8** informed, prepared, stranded **9** foundered, initiated **10** kept at home, instructed, restricted **11** disciplined, established **12** washed ashore **13** indoctrinated

grounding **8** training **9** education **10** background, experience **11** preparation **14** indoctrination **15** familiarization

groundless **4** idle **5** empty, false **6** faulty, flimsy, unreal, untrue **8** baseless, needless, unproved **9** erroneous, illogical, imaginary, unfounded **10** chimerical, fallacious, gratuitous **11** uncalled for, unjustified, unsupported, unwarranted **13** unjustifiable, without reason

groundwork **4** base, root **5** basis **6** cradle, ground, origin, source, spring **7** bedrock, footing, grounds, taproot **8** keystone, learning, planning, practice, training **9** spadework **10** foundation **11** cornerstone, fundamental, preparation **12** fundamentals, underpinning **14** apprenticeship, indoctrination

group **3** set **4** band, clan, file, gang, herd, pack, sift, size, sort **5** align, bunch, class, crowd, flock, grade, hoard, index, party, place, range, swarm, tribe, troop **6** assign, branch, circle, clique, family, hobnob, league, line up, mingle, throng **7** arrange, catalog, cluster, combine, company, consort, coterie, faction, marshal, section, species, variety **8** classify, division, graduate, organize, register **9** associate, gathering **10** assemblage, collection, coordinate, detachment, fraternity, fraternize **11** aggregation, alphabetize, association, brotherhood, subdivision **12** congregation **14** classification, representation

Group, The
author: **12** Mary McCarthy

grouping **7** sorting **8** arraying, ordering **10** assemblage, assortment **11** arrangement, disposition **12** distribution, organization

group of performers **6** troupe **7** company **8** ensemble

Group Portrait of a Lady
author: **12** Heinrich Boll

grouse **4** beef, crab, fret, fume, fuss, kick **5** gripe **6** grouch, mutter, squawk, take on **7** carry on, grumble **8** complain, gamebird **9** bellyache

grove **4** bosk **5** brake, copse **6** forest, pinery, timber **7** coppice, orchard, thicket, wood lot **8** wildwood, woodland **9** shrubbery **10** plantation

grovel **4** fawn **5** cower, crawl, stoop, toady **6** cringe, kowtow, snivel **7** flatter, truckle **12** bow and scrape **13** demean oneself, humble oneself **14** lick the boots of

groveling **6** abject **7** fawning, servile **8** cowering, crawling, cringing, toadying **9** kowtowing, truckling **11** bootlicking **17** bowing and scraping

grow **3** bud, sow, wax **4** boom, farm, rise, till **5** bloom, breed, plant, raise, ripen, surge, swell, widen **6** become, expand, extend, flower, garden, mature, spread, sprout, thrive **7** advance, amplify, blossom, develop, enlarge, fill out, get to be, improve, magnify, produce, prosper, shoot up, stretch, succeed **8** come to be, flourish, fructify, increase, mushroom, progress, spring up, vegetate **9** cultivate, germinate, propagate, skyrocket **10** aggrandize

Growing Up in New Guinea
author: **12** Margaret Mead

growl **4** fret, snap **5** croak, grind, gripe, groan, grunt, snarl, whine **6** grouse, murmur, mutter, rumble **7** grumble **8** complain, talk back

grown-up **3** big, man **4** lady, ripe **5** adult, of age, woman **6** mature, senior **7** worldly **9** full-blown, full-grown, gentleman **11** full-fledged **13** sophisticated

growth **4** crop, hump, lump, rise **5** gnarl, prime, surge, swell, tumor **6** sowing, spread **7** advance, harvest, produce, success **8** increase, maturity, planting, progress **9** expansion, extension, flowering, increment **10** burgeoning, matureness, production, prospering **11** advancement, cultivation, development, enlargement, excrescence, flourishing; improvement, propagation **12** augmentation, mass of tissue **13** amplification
goddess of: **4** Hour **5** Horae

Groza, Lou
nickname: **6** The Toe
sport: **8** football
team: **15** Cleveland Browns

grub **3** bum, dig **4** food, toil, worm **5** cadge, dig up, larva, mooch, slave **6** drudge, sponge **7** rummage

grubber **5** slave **6** drudge, toiler **7** laborer

grubby **4** foul **5** dirty, grimy, messy, muddy, nasty, seedy, tacky **6** beat-up, filthy, frowzy, frumpy, shabby, shoddy, sloppy, smudgy, soiled, sordid **7** squalid, unclean, unkempt **8** begrimed, slovenly, unwashed **9** besmeared **10** bedraggled

grudge **4** envy **5** pique, spite **6** animus, hatred, malice, rancor, resent **7** dislike, ill will **8** aversion, begrudge **9** animosity **10** resentment **11** malevolence **12** hard-feelings

grudging **7** envious **8** hesitant, spiteful **9** reluctant, resentful, unwilling **10** ungenerous **13** penny-pinching

grueling **4** hard **6** brutal, tiring **7** racking **9** fatiguing, punishing, torturous **10** exhausting

gruesome **4** gory, grim **5** awful **6** grisly, horrid **7** fearful, ghastly, hideous, macabre **8** horrible, shocking, terrible **9** frightful, loathsome, repellent, repulsive, revolting **10** forbidding, horrendous, horrifying **13** bloodcurdling, spine-chilling

gruff **4** curt, rude, sour, tart **5** bluff, blunt, harsh, husky, raspy, rough, sharp, short, stern, sulky, surly **6** abrupt, croaky, crusty, grumpy, hoarse, ragged, sullen **7** bearish, brusque, caustic, crabbed, cracked, grouchy, peevish, throaty, uncivil, waspish **8** churlish, guttural, impolite, snarling, strident **9** bristling, insulting **10** ill-humored, ill-natured, ungracious **11** ill-tempered **12** discourteous

grumble **4** fret **5** chafe, gripe, growl **6** grouch, grouse, mutter **8** complain **9** find-fault

grump **4** crab **5** crank **6** grouch **8** grumbler, sourball **10** curmudgeon

grumpy **4** sour **5** moody, sulky, surly, testy **6** crabby, cranky, crusty, sullen **7** grouchy, peevish, pettish **8** churlish **9** irritable, splenetic **10** ill-humored, out of humor, out of sorts **11** disgruntled, ill-disposed, ill-tempered **12** cantankerous

grunt **3** cry **4** bark, call, gasp, howl **5** burro, croak, groan, snort, utter **6** bellow, grouch, mumble, murmur, mutter, shriek **7** howling, whisper **8** complain **9** ululation **11** foot soldier, infantryman

Grunwald, Matthais (Grunewald, Mathis)
real name: **23** Mathis Gothardt Neithardt
born: **7** Germany **8** Wurzburg
artwork: **14** The Crucifixion **15** The Resurrection **20** Altarpiece at Isenheim

Grushenka
character in: **20** The Brothers Karamazov
author: **11** Dostoyevsky

Gryce, Percy
character in: **15** The House of Mirth
author: **7** Wharton

Grynaeus
epithet of: **6** Apollo

gryphon *see* **7** griffin

Guam ***see box, p. 418***

Guarani (Caingua)
language family: **7** Guarani
location: **6** Brazil **8** Paraguay **9** Argentina **12** South America
allied to: **4** Tupi

guarantee, guaranty **4** avow, bail, bond, pawn, word **5** swear **6** affirm, allege, assure, attest, avowal, insure, pledge, surety **7** deposit, endorse, promise, sponsor, testify, voucher, warrant **8** contract, covenant, security, vouch for, warranty **9** agreement, answer for, assurance, insurance, testimony **10** collateral, underwrite **11** affirmation, endorsement, word of honor **12** give one's word

guard **4** mind, save, tend **5** watch **6** attend, convoy, defend, escort, patrol, picket, screen, secure, sentry, shield, warder **7** conduct, defense, protect, shelter **8** defender, garrison, guardian, keep safe, preserve, security, sentinel, watchdog, watchman **9** bodyguard, concierge, custodian, guardsman, protector, safe-

Guam
capital: **5** Agana
largest city: **8** Tamuning
others: **4** Agat, Apra, Toto, Yigo **5** Magua **6** Dededo, Merizo **8** Inarajan, Mangilao, Mongmong, Sinajana, Talofofo, Tamuning **9** Barrigada, Finegayan, Santa Rita
member of: **7** Mariana (islands)
mountain: **5** Tenjo
highest point: **6** Lamlam
sea: **7** Pacific **10** Philippine
people: **7** Spanish **8** American, Chamorro, Filipino **11** Micronesian
explorer: **8** Magellan
ruler: **5** Japan, Spain **12** United States
language: **7** English **8** Chamorro
religion: **16** Roman Catholicism
feature: **7** typhoon **9** coral reef
Air Force base: **8** Andersen
product: **5** copra **6** banana, papaya

guard, watch over **10** doorkeeper, gatekeeper, protection **12** preservation **13** keep watch over

guard against **6** beware **10** look out for **11** take warning, watch out for

guarded **4** wary **5** cagey, chary, leery **7** careful, heedful, mindful, prudent **8** cautious, discreet, hesitant **9** in custody, protected, tentative **10** restrained, suspicious, under guard **11** circumspect, on one's guard

guardian **5** guard **6** convoy, escort, keeper, patrol, patron, picket, sentry, warden, warder **7** curator, trustee **8** advocate, champion, defender, sentinel, shepherd, wardsman, watchdog **9** attendant, bodyguard, caretaker, conductor, custodian, preserver, protector, safeguard, vigilante **10** benefactor **11** conservator **13** friend at court, guardian angel **14** legal custodian

guardian of a place
Latin: **10** genius loci

guardianship **4** care **6** charge **7** custody, keeping **10** protection **11** safekeeping, supervision, trusteeship

Guatemala ***see box***

guava **7** Psidium **16** Psidium guineense
varieties: **5** apple **6** common, purple, yellow **7** Cattley, Chilean **9** pineapple **10** Costa Rican, strawberry **13** yellow cattley **16** purple strawberry, yellow strawberry

Gubitosi, Michael James Vijencio
real name of: **11** Robert Blake

Gudrun
also: **6** Kudrun **7** Guthrun
origin: **12** Scandinavian
mentioned in: **8** Volsunga
father: **5** Giuki, Gjuki **6** Hertel
mother: **8** Grimhild
brother: **6** Gunnar
husband: **4** Atli **6** Herwig, Sigurd
killed: **4** Atli
corresponds to: **9** Kriemhild

Guerrillas
author: **9** V S Naipaul

guess **4** deem, view **5** fancy, judge, opine, think **6** assume, belief, deduce, divine, gather, reckon, regard, theory **7** believe, daresay, feeling, imagine, opinion, predict, suppose, surmise, suspect, venture **8** conclude, estimate, theorize **9** postulate, speculate, suspicion **10** assumption, conjecture, divination, hypothesis, prediction **11** hypothesize, make a stab at, postulation, presumption, speculation, supposition

guesswork **7** surmise **10** con-

Guatemala
capital/largest city: **13** Guatemala City
others: **4** Ocos **5** Coban, Vieja **6** Chahal, Chisec, Cuilco, Flores, Iztapa, Jalapa, Salama, Solola, Tacana, Tecpan, Yaloch, Zacapa **7** Antigua, Cuilapa, Jutiapa, San Jose **8** Progreso **9** Escuintla, Tiquisate **10** Livingston **11** Totonicapan **13** Puerto Barrios, Quezaltenango **14** San Pedro Carcha **16** Chichicastenango
school: **9** San Carlos
measure: **4** vara **6** cuarta, tercia **7** cajuela, manzana **10** caballeria
monetary unit: **4** peso **7** centavo, quetzal
weight: **4** caja **5** libra
lake: **5** Dulce, Guija, Peten **6** Izabal **7** Atitlan **9** Amatitlan, Peten Itza
mountain: **4** Agua, Mico **5** Fuego, Madre **6** Pacaya, Tacana **7** Atitlan, Toliman **8** La Candon, Las Minas **10** Acatenango, Santa Maria **12** Cuchumatanes
highest point: **8** Tajumuko **9** Tajamulco
river: **4** Azul **5** Bravo, Dulce, Lapaz **6** Belize, Chixoy, Negino, Pasion, Samala **7** Chiapas, Motagua, Sarstun, Sastoon **8** Polochic, Rio Dulce, Sarstoon **10** Usumacinta
sea: **7** Pacific **8** Atlantic **9** Caribbean
physical feature:
bay: **8** Amatique
gulf: **8** Honduras
people: **3** Mam **4** Chol, Itza, Ixil, Maya **5** Xinca **6** Caribe, Quiche **7** ladinos, mestizo, Pocomam **13** Guatemaltecos
language: **6** Quiche **7** Spanish
religion: **13** Roman Catholic
place:
church: **10** Santo Tomas
ruins: **5** Mayan, Tikal **8** Uaxactun
feature:
bird: **7** quetzal
clarinet: **8** chirimta
dance: **5** elson **8** guarimba
flute: **3** xul
military dictator: **8** Caudillo
food:
dish: **6** pepian **10** enchiladas **13** gallo en chicha
fruit: **4** anay

jecture, hypothesis **11** supposition **13** shot in the dark

guest **5** diner **6** caller, client, friend, inmate, lodger, patron, roomer **7** boarder, company, habitue, invitee, patient, visitor **8** customer **9** sojourner **10** frequenter **14** paying customer

Guest, Edgar A
author of: **12** A Heap of Livin'

Guest, Judith
author of: **14** Ordinary People

guffaw **4** howl **6** scream **10** belly laugh, horse laugh

Guglielmi, Rodolfo
real name of: **16** Rudolph Valentino

Guicciardini, Francesco
author of: **13** Storia d'Italia

guidance **3** tip **4** clue, help, hint, lead **6** advice, escort **7** conduct, counsel, pointer **8** auspices **9** direction **10** leadership, management, protection, suggestion **11** information, instruction, supervision **12** intelligence **13** enlightenment

guide **4** lead, rule **5** model, pilot, steer, usher **6** beacon, convoy, direct, escort, govern, handle, leader, manage, marker, master, mentor **7** adviser, command, conduct, control, example, marshal, monitor, oversee, pattern, steerer, teacher **8** chaperon, cicerone, director, engineer, helmsman, landmark, lodestar, maneuver, polestar, regulate, shepherd, signpost **9** accompany, attendant, conductor, counselor **10** manipulate

guidebook **5** bible **6** manual **8** Baedeker, handbook **13** reference book

Guidry, Ron (Ronald Ames)
nickname: **18** Louisiana Lightning
sport: **8** baseball
position: **7** pitcher
team: **14** New York Yankees

guild **5** order, union **6** league **7** company, society **8** alliance **9** coalition **10** craft union, federation, fraternity, labor union, sisterhood, trade union **11** association, brotherhood, confederacy, corporation

Guildenstern
character in: **6** Hamlet
author: **11** Shakespeare

guile **5** craft, fraud **6** deceit, tricks **7** cunning, slyness **8** artifice, strategy, trickery, wiliness **9** chicanery, deception, duplicity, treachery **10** artfulness, craftiness, dishonesty, hanky-panky, stratagems, trickiness **11** fraudulence **13** sharp practice

guileless **4** open **5** frank, naive **6** candid, honest, simple **7** artless, natural, sincere **8** harmless, innocent, truthful **9** ingenuous, innocuous **10** aboveboard, unaffected **11** undesigning, unoffending **15** straightforward, unselfconscious, unsophisticated

guilelessness **6** candor **9** innocence, sincerity **10** candidness, directness **11** artlessness **13** ingenuousness

guilt **3** sin **4** blot, vice **5** shame, wrong **6** infamy, stigma **7** misdeed **8** disgrace, dishonor, misdoing, trespass **9** black mark, turpitude **10** guiltiness, misconduct, sinfulness, wrongdoing **11** criminality, culpability, degradation, delinquency, dereliction, humiliation, misbehavior, self-disgust **13** transgression

guiltless **4** good, pure **5** clean **6** chaste **7** angelic, sinless **8** innocent, unfallen, virtuous **9** blameless, childlike, faultless **10** immaculate, inculpable, unblamable **11** uncorrupted
French: **12** sans reproche

guilt-stricken **7** ashamed

guilty **5** sorry, wrong **6** erring, sinful **7** ashamed, corrupt, hangdog, immoral **8** blamable, contrite, criminal, culpable, penitent, sheepish **9** offensive, regretful, repentant **11** blameworthy **18** conscience-stricken

Guilty Pleasures
author: **15** Donald Barthelme

Guinea ***see box***

Guinea-Bissau ***see box, p. 420***

Guinevere
character in: **16** Arthurian romance
husband: **6** Arthur
lover: **8** Lancelot

Guinness, Sir Alec
born: **6** London **7** England
roles: **8** Star Wars **11** Oliver Twist **13** Doctor Zhivago **14** Our Man in Havana, The Ladykillers **15** A Passage to India, Ben Obi Wan Kenobi, Lavender Hill Mob **16** Lawrence of Arabia **17** Great Expectations **21** Kind Hearts and Coronets **22** Tinker Tailor Soldier Spy **23** The

Guinea
other name: **12** French Guinea **13** Rivieres du Sud
capital/largest city: **7** Conakry
others: **4** Boke, Fria, Labe **5** Beyla **6** Dabola, Kankan, Kin dia **7** Dubreka, Siguiri **8** Kerouane **9** Kouroussa, Nzerekore
measure: **7** jacktan
monetary unit: **4** iliy, syli **5** franc **6** cauris
weight: **4** akey, piso, uzan **5** benda, seron **6** quinto **8** aguirage
island: **3** Los **5** Tombo **7** Tristao
mountain: **4** Loma **6** Tamgue **11** Fouta Djalon
highest point: **5** Nimba
river: **4** Milo **5** Kogon, Niger **6** Bafing, Faleme, Gambia **7** Kolente, Senegal **8** Konkoure, Tinkisso **13** Great Scarcies
sea: **8** Atlantic
physical feature:
cape: **5** Verga
people: **4** Koma, Loma, Nalu, Susu, Toma **5** Kissi, Manon **6** Fulani, Guerzi **7** Landoma, Malinke **8** Kouranke, Landuman **11** Kissi-Sherbo **12** Guerze-Kpelle
language: **5** Fulbe, Mande **6** Arabic, French, Fulani **7** English
religion: **5** Islam **7** animism
feature:
plant: **11** globeflower
tree: **4** akee **5** dalli

Guinea-Bissau
other name: **16** Portuguese Guinea
capital/largest city: **6** Bissau
others: **4** Buba **5** Catio, Farim **6** Bafata, Bolama, Cacheu, Cacine, Dandum, Mansoa **7** Bissora, Bubaque, San Joav **9** Fulacunda **10** Nova Lamego **11** Madina do Boe, Madine do Boe, Sao Domingos
monetary unit: **4** peso **6** escudo **8** centavos
island: **4** Roxa **6** Orango **7** Bijagos, Formosa
river: **4** Geba **6** Cacheu, Mansoa **7** Corubal
sea: **8** Atlantic
people: **6** Fulani **7** Balanta, Balante, mulatto **8** Mandingo, Mandyako
language: **5** Fulah **7** Balante, Crioulo **8** Mandingo **10** Portuguese **21** Cape Verde-Guinea Creole
religion: **5** Islam **7** animism **12** Christianity

Bridge on the River Kwai (Oscar)

guise **4** garb, mode **5** dress, habit **6** attire **7** apparel, clothes, costume, fashion **8** clothing, disguise, pretense **10** masquerade

Gujarati
language family: **12** Indo-European
branch: **11** Indo-Iranian
group: **5** Indic
spoken in: **5** (northern) India

Gulag Archipelago, The
author: **23** Aleksandr Solzhenitsyn Jr

gulch **3** gap **4** rift **5** abyss, chasm, cleft, crack, gorge, gully, split **6** arroyo, breach, divide, ravine **8** crevasse

gulf **4** cove, rent, rift **5** abyss, chasm, cleft, firth, fjord, gully, inlet, split **6** canyon, lagoon **7** estuary, opening **8** crevasse **10** separation

gull **3** gyp **4** dupe, rook **5** cozen, trick **7** deceive, defraud, sea gull, sea bird, swindle **9** bamboozle, victimize

gullet **3** maw **4** craw, crop **5** belly, gorge, tummy **6** dewlap, throat **7** abdomen, channel, stomach, weasand **9** beer belly, esophagus

gullible **5** green, naive **6** simple **8** innocent, trustful, trusting **9** credulous **11** easily duped **12** easily fooled, overtrusting, unsuspicious **13** easily cheated, inexperienced **14** easily deceived **15** unsophisticated

Gulliver's Travels
author: **13** Jonathan Swift
character: **14** Lemuel Gulliver
visited: **6** Laputa, Yahoos **8** Blefuscu, Lilliput, Luggnagg **9** Balnibari **10** Houyhnhnms **11** Brobdingnag **12** Glubbdubdrib

gully **3** gap **5** ditch, gorge, gulch **6** defile, furrow, gutter, ravine, trench **7** channel **11** small canyon, small valley, watercourse **13** drainage ditch

gulp **4** bolt, swig, wolf **5** quaff, swill **6** devour, guzzle **7** swallow, toss off **8** mouthful

gulp down **4** bolt **6** devour, gobble **7** swallow **8** gobble up, wolf down

gum **3** wax **5** latex, resin **6** chicle **8** mucilage **10** Eucalyptus
varieties: **3** cup, red **4** blue, cape, gray, rose, snow, sour **5** apple, black, cider, coral, giant, gully, Karri, Manna, sugar, swamp, sweet **6** cotton, Deane's, desert, gimlet, salmon, snappy, Tupelo **7** Barbary, cabbage, Fuchsia, maiden's, Morocco, scarlet, spotted **8** Formosan, Lehmann's, mountain, scribbly, spinning **9** forest red, Murray red, steedman's **10** Australian, candle-bark, red-spotted, Sydney blue, Timor white, tumble-down, urn-fruited **11** Blakely's red, blue weeping, salmon white, small-leaved, strickland's **12** lemon-scented, red-flowering, silver-dollar **13** American sweet, Oriental sweet, Tasmanian blue, Tasmanian snow **14** yellow-flowered **15** Omeo round-leaved, round-leaved snow **16** rough-barked manna, scarlet-flowering **17** heart-leaved silver **20** silver-leaved mountain

Gumm, Frances
real name of: **11** Judy Garland

gummed **5** glued, gummy, stuck **6** sticky **8** adhering, adhesive

Gummidge, Mrs
character in: **16** David Copperfield
author: **7** Dickens

gummy **5** gluey, gooey, gunky **6** gloppy, sticky, viscid **7** rubbery, viscous **8** adhesive **10** gelatinous **12** mucilaginous

gumption **3** zip **4** dash, push **5** drive, spunk, verve **6** energy, hustle, pizazz, spirit **7** courage **10** enterprise, get-up-and-go, initiative **12** forcefulness **14** aggressiveness **15** resourcefulness

gumshoe **4** dick **6** shamus **9** detective **10** private eye **12** investigator

gun **3** aim, gat, rod, try **4** Colt, hunt, iron **5** piece, rifle, shoot **6** cannon, Magnum, mortar, musket, pistol **7** attempt, carbine, firearm, Gatling, go after, Long Tom, shotgun **8** howitzer, ordnance, revolver **9** automatic, Big Bertha, derringer, equalizer, flintlock, forty-five, twenty-two, Remington **10** fieldpiece, machine gun, six-shooter, three-fifty, Walther PPK, Winchester **11** blunderbuss, thirty-eight, trusty-rusty **12** fowling piece, muzzle loader, shooting iron **13** Kentucky rifle **14** artillery piece, Smith and Wesson
invented by:
breechloader: **8** Thornton
magazine: **9** Hotchkiss
silencer: **5** Maxim

Gunga Din
story in: **18** Barrack-Room Ballads
author: **14** Rudyard Kipling
director: **13** George Stevens
cast: **8** Sam Jaffe **9** Cary Grant **12** Joan Fontaine **14** Victor McLaglen **18** Douglas Fairbanks Jr
setting: **5** India
remade as: **13** Soldiers Three **14** Sergeants Three

gunman **6** bandit, outlaw, robber, sniper **7** hoodlum **9** assailant, desperado, holdup man

Gunn, Ben
character in: **14** Treasure Island
author: **9** Stevenson

Gunnar
origin: **12** Scandinavian
father: **5** Giuki, Gjuki
mother: **8** Grimhild
sister: **6** Gudrun, Kudrun **7** Guthrun
wife: **8** Brynhild
Brynhild won by: **6** Sigurd

Gunsmoke
character: **3** Sam (the bartender) **8** Doc (Dr Galen) Adams **10** Quint Asper **11** Newly O'Brien **12** Chester Goode, Festus Haggen, Kitty Russell (Miss Kitty) **18** Marshall Matt Dillon **24** Clayton Thaddeus (Thad) Greenwood
cast: **9** Ken Curtis **10** Buck Taylor, Roger Ewing **11** Amanda Blake, James Arness **12** Burt Reynolds, Dennis Weaver, Glenn Strange, Milburn Stone
setting: **9** Dodge City
saloon: **10** Longbranch

Guns of August, The
author: **15** Barbara W Tuchman

Guns of Navarone, The
director: **12** J Lee Thompson
based on novel by: **15** Alistair MacLean
cast: **10** David Niven **11** Gregory Peck, James Darren **12** Anthony Quinn, Stanley Baker **13** Anthony Quayle

Gunther
origin: **8** Germanic
mentioned in: **14** Nibelungenlied
king of: **8** Burgundy
wife: **8** Brunhild
sister: **9** Kriemhild
killed by: **9** Kriemhild

Guppy
character in: **10** Bleak House
author: **7** Dickens

Gurdin, Natasha
real name of: **11** Natalie Wood

gurgle **5** plash **6** babble, bubble, burble, murmur, ripple **7** sputter **8** bubbling, gurgling

guru **5** guide **6** leader, master **7** teacher **9** preceptor **10** instructor

gush **3** gab, gas, jet, run **4** blab, bull, rush, well **5** issue, prate, spout, spurt **6** babble, burble, drivel, hot air, splash, squirt, stream **7** baloney, blabber, blather, chatter, pour out, prattle, rubbish, torrent, twaddle **8** nonsense, outburst, rattle on **10** outpouring **11** mawkishness **12** emotionalism **14** sentimentalism, talk effusively **16** run off at the mouth

gushiness **12** effusiveness, emotionalism **17** demonstrativeness

gushing **6** lavish **7** pouring, profuse **8** effusive, spurting **10** flattering **11** free-flowing **12** demonstrative, unrestrained **16** overenthusiastic

gushy **8** effusive **12** unrestrained **13** demonstrative **16** overenthusiastic

gussy up **5** adorn **7** dress up, enhance **8** beautify, decorate, ornament **9** embellish

gust **3** fit **4** blow, puff, wind **5** blast, burst, draft **6** breeze, flurry, squall, zephyr **8** outbreak, outburst, paroxysm **9** explosion

Gustaffson, Greta Louisa
real name of: **10** Greta Garbo

Guster
character in: **10** Bleak House
author: **7** Dickens

gusto **3** joy **4** zeal, zest **5** savor **6** fervor, relish **7** delight **8** appetite, pleasure **10** enthusiasm **12** appreciation, exhilaration, satisfaction

gusto, con
music: **9** with style, with taste

gusty **5** blowy, windy **6** breezy **7** squally **8** blustery

gut **4** raze **5** belly, clean, level, tummy **6** bowels, paunch, ravage **7** abdomen, consume, midriff, stomach, viscera **8** entrails, lay waste **9** bay window, beer belly, spare tire **10** disembowel, eviscerate, intestines, midsection **11** breadbasket

guten abend **11** good evening

Gutenberg
nationality: **6** German
inventor of: **11** movable type
printer of: **14** Gutenberg Bible

guten morgen **11** good morning

guten tag **7** good day

Guthrie, A B Jr
author of: **6** Arfive **9** The Big Sky **10** The Way West **13** The Last Valley **16** Fair Land Fair Land, The Blue Hen's Chick, The Thousand Hills

Guthrun *see* **6** Gudrun

Gutman, Casper
character in: **16** The Maltese Falcon
author: **7** Hammett

guts **4** dash, grit **5** nerve, pluck, spunk **6** bowels, daring, mettle, spirit, vitals **7** bravado, bravery, courage, gizzard, innards, insides, viscera **8** audacity, backbone, boldness **9** fortitude **10** intestines **11** intrepidity

gutsy **4** game **5** brave **6** heroic, plucky **7** doughty, valiant **8** fearless, intrepid, stalwart, unafraid, valorous **9** dauntless, undaunted **10** courageous **11** lionhearted, unflinching **12** stouthearted

guttural **3** low **4** deep **5** gruff, harsh, husky, raspy, thick **6** hoarse **7** throaty **8** croaking **12** inarticulate

guy **3** boy, joe, kid, man **4** body, chap, dude, gent, rope **5** bloke, human, joker **6** fellow, hombre, person **8** blighter, upholder **9** supporter **10** individual

Guyana
name means: **12** land of waters
other name: **13** British Guiana
capital/largest city: **10** Georgetown
others: **7** Charity **8** Hyde Park, Rosignol **9** Mackenzie **12** New Amsterdam, Spring Garden
island: **6** Leguan **8** Wakenaam
mountain: **5** Amuku, Ariwa, Kamoa **6** Akarai, Kanuku **7** Caburai **9** Pacaraima
highest point: **7** Roraima
river: **5** Waini **6** Barama **7** Amakura, Baruima, Berbice **8** Demerara, Mazaruni, Rupununi **9** Essequibo **10** Burro-Burro
sea: **8** Atlantic
physical feature:
falls: **5** Great, Tiger **7** Kamaria **8** Kaieteur **9** Serikoeng **10** Surwakwima **15** Fredrik Willem IV
people: **6** Akawai, Arawak, Creole, Taruma **7** African, Chinese, mulatto **10** Portuguese
language: **5** Hindi **7** English
religion: **5** Hindu, Islam **8** Anglican **13** Roman Catholic

Guy Fawkes
author: 16 William Ainsworth

Guy Mannering
author: 14 Sir Walter Scott

Guyon
character in: 15 The Faerie Queene
author: 7 Spenser

Guys and Dolls
director: 17 Joseph L Mankiewicz
based on story by: 11 Damon Runyon
cast: 10 Stubby Kaye **11** Jean Simmons **12** Frank Sinatra, Marlon Brando, Vivian Blaine
setting: 11 New York City
score: 12 Frank Loesser
song: 11 Luck Be a Lady **12** Guys and Dolls **26** Sit Down You're Rocking the Boat

guzzle 4 bolt, swig **5** quaff, swill **6** devour, imbibe, tipple **7** toss off **8** gulp down

guzzler 5 drunk **6** boozer **7** imbiber, tippler **8** devourer, drunkard **9** alcoholic

Gwawl
origin: 5 Welsh
mentioned in: 10 Mabinogion
rival of: 5 Pwyll
sought hand of: 8 Rhiannon

Gwydion
origin: 5 Welsh
son: 14 Llew Llaw Gyffes
sister: 9 Arianhrod
lover: 9 Arianhrod

Gwyn
origin: 7 British
god of: 7 rebirth **9** afterlife

Gyas
companion of: 6 Aeneas

Gyes *see* **5** Gyges

Gygaea, Gyge
form: 5 nymph
location: 4 lake

Gyges
also: 4 Gyes
member of: 13 Hecatonchires

gymnasium 5 arena **6** circus **7** stadium **10** hippodrome

gymnast 10 Olga Korbut **13** Mary Lou Retton, Nadia Comaneci

gymnastics 9 exercises **10** acrobatics **11** contortions **16** physical training

Gynaecothoenas
epithet of: 4 Ares
means: 17 feasted by the women

gynophobia
fear of: 5 women

gyp 3 con **4** bilk, burn, fake, hoax, rook, scam, soak **5** cheat, cozen, fraud, phony, trick **6** diddle, fleece, humbug, ripoff **7** con game, defraud, swindle **8** flimflam, hoodwink **9** bamboozle, deception

gypsy
Italian: 7 zingara, zingaro

gyrate 5 swirl, twirl, wheel, whirl **6** circle, rotate, spiral **7** revolve **9** pirouette **10** spin around

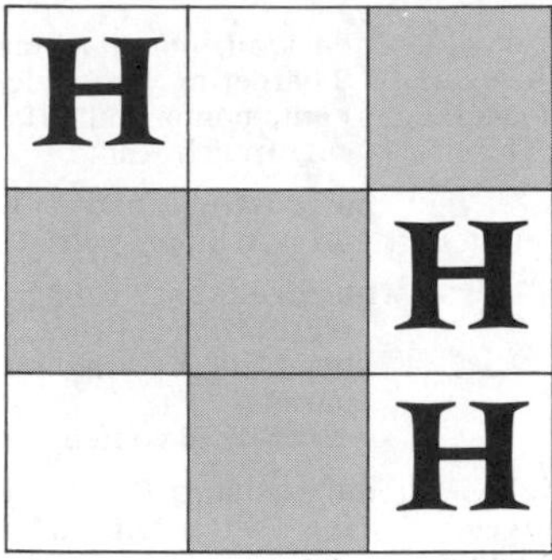

habeas corpus **11** have the body **23** produce the person in court
legal writ guards against: **19** illegal imprisonment

habiliments **4** garb, wear **5** dress **6** attire, outfit **7** clothes, costume, raiment, regalia **8** clothing, wardrobe **9** vestments

habit **3** rut, way **4** garb, gear, robe, rule, wont **5** dress, trait **6** attire, custom, groove, livery, manner, outfit **7** apparel, clothes, costume, garment, leaning, raiment, routine, uniform, vesture **8** clothing, fondness, habitude, practice **9** mannerism, trappings **10** beaten path, convention, observance, partiality, proclivity, propensity **11** habiliments, inclination, peculiarity **12** predilection, second nature **13** accoutrements, fixed practice **14** matter of course, predisposition **15** behavior pattern

habitat **3** pad **4** digs, home, spot, zone **5** abode, haunt, place, range, realm, roost **6** domain, locale, milieu, region **7** housing, lodging, setting, terrain **8** domicile, dwelling, home base, lodgment, precinct, quarters **9** territory **10** habitation **11** environment, natural home **12** place of abode **13** dwelling place **14** stamping ground **15** natural locality **17** native environment

habitation **3** pad **4** digs, home **5** abode, haunt, house, roost **6** colony **7** habitat, housing, lodging, shelter, tenancy **8** domicile, dwelling, lodgment, quarters **9** community, occupancy, residence **10** occupation, settlement **12** place of abode **13** dwelling place, temporary stay **16** place of residence

Habit of Being, The
author: **15** Flannery O'Connor

habitual **5** fixed, usual **6** common, normal, wonted **7** chronic, natural, regular, routine, typical **8** addicted, constant, expected, familiar, frequent, periodic, repeated **9** confirmed, continual, customary, incessant, ingrained, perpetual, recurrent **10** accustomed, deep-rooted, deep-seated, inveterate, methodical, systematic **11** established, traditional **12** conventional, second nature **14** by force of habit

habitual practice **4** wont **5** habit **6** custom

habituate **5** adapt, drill, imbue, inure, train **6** harden, school, season **7** break in, instill **8** accustom, initiate **9** inculcate **10** discipline, make used to **12** indoctrinate

habitue **7** regular **10** frequenter **13** regular patron **15** frequent visitor **16** constant customer

hack **3** cab, cut, hew, nag **4** bark, chip, chop, gash, plug, rasp, slit, taxi **5** coach, cut up, notch, slash, slice, whack **6** cleave, mangle **7** hackney, taxicab **8** lacerate, mutilate **9** cart horse, dray horse, scribbler, workhorse **10** cough drily, cut roughly, draft horse, hired horse, shaft horse **11** common horse, penny-a-liner **12** hackney coach, worn-out horse **13** carriage horse **16** grubstreet writer **18** horse-drawn carriage

hackle **3** peg **4** card, comb, hack, hook, ruff **5** curry, plume, quill **6** heckle, mangle **7** bristle, feather, plumage

Hackman, Gene
born: **15** San Bernardino CA
roles: **8** Superman **11** Popeye Doyle **14** Bonnie and Clyde **15** The Conversation **19** The French Connection (Oscar) **20** The Poseidon Adventure

hackneyed **4** dull, worn **5** banal, inane, stale, stock, trite, vapid **6** common, jejune **7** cliched, humdrum, insipid, routine, worn-out **8** bromidic, ordinary, shopworn, well-worn **9** moth-eaten **10** pedestrian, threadbare, uninspired **11** commonplace, stereotyped **12** conventional **13** platitudinous, unimaginative

Hadassah **6** Esther

Hades **4** hell
also: **5** Pluto **10** lower world, Underworld
corresponds to: **5** Orcus
god of: **5** Orcus, Pluto
goddess of: **6** Hecate, Hekate

Haemon
father: **5** Creon
loved: **8** Antigone
died at tomb of: **8** Antigone
death by: **7** suicide

Haenigsen, Harry
creator/artist of: **5** Penny **7** Our Bill

hafnium
chemical symbol: **2** Hf

hag **3** bat, nag **4** drab, fury **5** biddy, crone, frump, harpy, shrew, vixen, witch **6** beldam, gorgon, ogress, virago **7** hellcat **8** battle-ax, harridan **9** termagant

Hagar
servant of: **5** Sarah
husband: **7** Abraham
son: **7** Ishmael

Hagar the Horrible
creator: **9** Dik Browne

Hagen
origin: **8** Germanic

mentioned in: 14 Nibelungenlied
killed by: 9 Kriemhild
killed: 9 Siegfried

haggard 4 beat, wild, worn 5 gaunt, spent, tired, upset, weary 6 bushed, fagged, pooped, raging, wasted 7 ranting 8 careworn, drooping, fatigued, flagging, frenzied, harassed, harrowed, overcome, toilworn, wild-eyed 9 exhausted, woebegone 10 hollow-eyed 11 debilitated, overwearied, overwrought, tuckered out, wild-looking 12 tired-looking

Haggard, H Rider
author of: 3 She 17 King Solomon's Mines

haggle 6 barter, bicker, dicker, higgle 7 bargain, dispute, quarrel, quibble, wrangle 8 beat down, squabble

Hagiographa
Hebrew: 7 Ketubim

hagiographer 19 writer of saints' lives

Hagman, Larry
mother: 10 Mary Martin
born: 13 Weatherford TX
roles: 6 Dallas 7 J R Ewing 15 I Dream of Jeannie

Hagno
origin: 8 Arcadian
form: 5 nymph
location: 6 spring

Hahn, Otto
field: 9 chemistry
nationality: 6 German
discovered: 13 protoactinium 14 nuclear isomers
awarded: 10 Nobel Prize

Haida
language family: 6 Masset, Na-Dene 10 Skidegatta
tribe: 7 Kaigani
location: 6 Alaska 15 British Columbia 21 Queen Charlotte Islands
related to: 7 Tlingit 9 Tsimshian
associated with: 9 totem pole 13 wood sculpture

hail 4 call 5 cheer, exalt, extol, greet, hello, honor, shout 6 accost, call to, esteem, salute 7 acclaim, address, applaud, commend, glorify, receive, shout at, usher in, welcome 8 cry out to, eulogize, greeting 9 accosting 10 calling out, compliment, panegyrize, salutation 11 make welcome
German: 4 heil
Latin: 5 salve

Hailey, Arthur
author of: 5 Hotel 6 Wheels 7 Airport 12 In High Places 14 Final Diagnosis 16 The Moneychangers

hail-fellow-well-met 8 familiar, friendly, intimate, outgoing, sociable 9 extrovert 10 gregarious

Hail Mary
Latin: 8 Ave Maria

Hail the Conquering Hero
director: 14 Preston Sturges
cast: 10 Ella Raines 12 Eddie Bracken 14 Raymond Walburn 15 William Demarest 16 Franklin Pangborn

hail to victory
German: 8 Sieg Heil

hair 3 fur, mop 4 coat, down, iota, mane, pelt, wool 5 bangs, curls, locks 6 fleece 7 tresses 8 ringlets 12 narrow margin

haircut, hairdo 3 bob, bun, cut 4 Afro, clip, crop, perm, shag, trim 5 bangs, braid, butch, swirl 6 boogie, mohawk 7 beehive, chignon, cornrow, crewcut, flattop, fuzz cut, natural, pachuco, page boy, pigtail, shingle, tonsure 8 bouffant, brushcut, coiffure, ducktail, ponytail, razorcut 9 barbering, hairstyle, permanent, pompadour 10 feathercut, french knot

haircutter 6 barber 11 hairdresser, hair stylist

hairdresser 8 coiffeur 9 coiffeuse 10 beautician, haircutter 11 beauty salon 12 beauty parlor
French: 8 coiffeur

hair-raising 8 exciting 9 thrilling 10 terrifying 11 astonishing 12 breathtaking, electrifying

hairsplitting 4 fine 6 minute, subtle 7 carping 8 caviling, delicate, hairline, niggling 9 minuscule, quibbling 10 nitpicking, unapparent 12 faultfinding, overcritical 13 imperceptible, inappreciable, infinitesimal 15 inconsequential

hairy 5 bushy, furry, wooly 6 fleecy, pilose, shaggy, woolly 7 hirsute

Hairy Ape, The
author: 12 Eugene O'Neill

Haiti *see box*

Hakenkreuz 11 hooked cross 12 Nazi swastika

Haiti
name means: 15 mountainous land
other name: 12 Santo Domingo
capital/largest city: 12 Port-au-Prince
others: 5 Aquin, Furcy, Limbe 6 Hinche, Jacmel, St Marc 7 Jeremie, Leogane, Saltrou 8 Gonaives, Kenscoff, Les Cayes 10 Cap-Haitien
monetary unit: 6 gourde 8 centimes
island: 5 Vache 6 Gonave, Tortue 7 Navassa, Tortuga 8 Caymites 10 Hispaniola 14 Grande Cayemite 15 Greater Antilles
lake: 8 Saumatre
mountain: 4 Nord 5 Cahos 6 Macaya, Noires 7 Lahotte 8 Troudeau
highest point: 7 La Selle, Laselle
river: 9 Guayamoul 10 Artibonite
sea: 8 Atlantic 9 Caribbean
physical feature:
gulf: 6 Gonave
passage: 8 Windward
people: 5 Taino 7 African, mulatto
discoverer: 8 Columbus
liberator: 19 Toussaint Louverture
ruler: 8 Duvalier
language: 6 Creole, French, patois
religion: 6 voodoo 13 Roman Catholic
feature:
dance: 5 mambo
festival: 9 Mardi Gras
fortress: 10 La Ferriere 24 Citadelle du Roi Christophe
security force: 8 bogeymen 15 Tontons Macoutes
food:
sweet potato: 6 batata

Hakluyt, Richard
author of: 7 Voyages **15** Hakluyt's Voyages

HAL
character in: 14 Two Thousand One (2001)
author: 6 Clarke

Halas, George
nickname: 8 Papa Bear
sport: 8 football
position: 5 coach
team: 12 Chicago Bears

halcyon 4 calm, fair **5** happy, quiet, sunny **6** blithe, golden, hushed, joyous, placid, serene **7** pacific **8** carefree, cheerful, peaceful, tranquil **9** cloudless, contented, reposeful, unclouded, unruffled **10** unagitated, untroubled

Halcyon *see* **7** Alcyone

hale 3 fit **4** well **5** hardy, sound **6** hearty, robust, rugged, sturdy **7** healthy, in shape **8** vigorous **9** energetic, in the pink, strapping **10** able-bodied, robustious **12** in fine fettle

Hale, Edward Everett
author of: 21 The Man Without a Country

Hale, George Ellery
field: 9 astronomy
initiated: 20 Mt Palomar Observatory
invented: 17 spectroheliograph

Halevy, Ludovic
author of: 17 The Abbe Constantin

Haley, Alex
author of: 5 Roots

Haley, Jack
born: 8 Boston MA
roles: 6 Tin Man **13** The Wizard of Oz

half 4 part, some **6** all but, barely, fairly, feebly, halved, in part, meager, partly, rather, scanty, skimpy, slight, weakly **7** divided, faintly, limited, partial, portion, section **8** fraction, middling, moderate, passable, passably, slightly **9** deficient, imperfect, partially, tolerable, tolerably **10** fractional, inadequate, incomplete, moderately, relatively **12** fifty percent, inadequately, insufficient, pretty nearly **13** after a fashion, comparatively **14** insufficiently

half-asleep 6 drowsy, groggy, unwary **7** out-of-it, unaware **8** sluggish **9** not-with-it, oblivious

half-hearted 4 cold, cool, tame **5** blase, faint **7** languid, passive **8** listless, lukewarm **9** apathetic, lethargic **10** ambivalent, irresolute, lackluster, phlegmatic, spiritless, unaspiring **11** indifferent, perfunctory **13** lackadaisical **14** unenthusiastic

half homer 15 Biblical measure

half-moon 3 arc, bow **4** arch **5** curve **8** crescent

halfway 6 almost, in part, medial, medium, middle, midway, nearly, partly, rather **7** midmost **8** somewhat **9** partially, to a degree **10** middlemost, moderately **11** equidistant, in the middle **12** intermediate, pretty nearly, to some extent **13** in some measure **18** between two extremes

half-wit 4 dolt, dope, fool **5** dummy, dunce, idiot, moron, ninny **6** dimwit, nitwit **7** dullard **8** dumb-dumb, imbecile, numskull **9** blockhead, numbskull, simpleton **10** nincompoop **15** mental defective, mental deficient

half-witted 4 dumb **5** silly **6** stupid **7** asinine, foolish, idiotic, moronic **9** dimwitted, imbecilic, senseless **11** lamebrained **12** feeble-minded, simple-minded

Halirrhothius
father: 8 Poseidon
mother: 6 Euryte
raped: 7 Alcippe
killed by: 4 Ares

Halitherses
origin: 6 Ithaca
form: 4 seer

hall 5 entry, foyer, lobby **6** arcade **7** chamber, gallery, hallway, passage **8** anteroom, club room, corridor, entrance **9** vestibule **10** auditorium, dining hall, passageway **11** antechamber, banquet hall, concert hall, waiting room **12** amphitheater, assembly room, meeting place **13** reception room

Hall, Diane
real name of: 11 Diane Keaton

Hall, James
field: 7 geology **9** chemistry
nationality: 7 British
founded: 12 geochemistry **19** experimental geology

Hall, James Norman
author of: 17 Mutiny on the Bounty
co-author: 15 Charles Nordhoff

Hallel 6 praise **16** liturgical prayer

Haller, Albrecht von
field: 7 biology
nationality: 5 Swiss
founded: 15 modern neurology

Haller, Harry
character in: 11 Steppenwolf
author: 5 Hesse

Halley, Edmund
field: 9 astronomy
nationality: 7 British
discovered: 12 Halley's Comet

hallmark 4 sign **5** badge, stamp **6** device, emblem, symbol **14** characteristic

Hall of Fame ***see box, p. 426***

halloo 3 cry **4** call, hail, yell **5** shout **6** cry out, holler

hallow 5 bless **7** respect **8** dedicate, sanctify, venerate **10** consecrate

hallowed 4 holy **6** sacred **7** blessed, honored **9** beatified, dedicated **10** sacrosanct, sanctified **11** consecrated

hallucination 5 dream **6** mirage, vision **7** chimera, fantasy, figment **8** delusion, illusion **9** nightmare **10** aberration, apparition **14** phantasmagoria

hallway 4 hall **7** passage **8** corridor, entryway **10** passageway

halo 6 aurora, corona, luster, nimbus **7** aureole, dignity, majesty **8** grandeur, holiness, radiance, sanctity, splendor **9** solemnity, sublimity **11** ring of light **12** chromosphere, luminousness, magnificence, resplendence **13** spiritual aura **15** illustriousness

Haloa
event: 8 festival
origin: 5 Greek
honoring: 7 Demeter **8** Dionysus **10** Persephone

Hals, Franz
born: 7 Antwerp, Holland
artwork: 9 Gypsy Girl **10** Hille Bobbe (The Witch of Haarlem) **13** The Jolly Toper **14** Jacobus Zaffius **15** The Merry Company **19** The Laughing Cavalier **22** Portrait of a Standing Man **24** The Regents of the Almshouse **26** Yonker Ramp and his Sweetheart **28** The Regentesses of the Almshouse **33** The Banquet of the St George Civic Guard

Halsey, William F
served in: 3 WWI **4** WWII

Hall of Fame
author: **3** Poe **5** Paine, Stowe **6** Bryant, Cooper, Holmes, Irving, Lanier, Lowell, Motley **7** Clemens, Emerson, Parkman, Thoreau, Whitman **8** Bancroft, Whittier **9** Hawthorne
aviation: **3** Six **4** Bell, Byrd, Lear, Luke, Post, Ryan **5** Beech, Eaker, Glenn, LeMay, Piper, Reeve **6** Arnold, Boeing, Cessna, Fokker, Hughes, Levier, Rogers, Spaatz, Sperry, Towers, Trippe, Wright, Yeager **7** Chanute, Earhart, Goddard, Langley, Shepherd, Twining **8** Mitchell, Northrup, Sikorsky **9** Armstrong, Chennault, Lindberg, Mcdonnell **12** Rickenbacker
baseball: **3** Ott **4** Bell, Cobb, Dean, Ford, Foxx, Hoyt, Kell, Mack, Mays, Mize, Rice, Ruth, Ward, Wynn **5** Aaron, Anson, Baker, Banks, Berra, Carey, Duffy, Faber, Gomez, Grove, Hafey, Irvin, Kelly, Lemon, Lloyd, Paige, Reese, Rusie, Terry, Vance, Wheat, Young **6** Alston, Barrow, Bender, Cuyler, Dickey, Feller, Frisch, Galvin, Gehrig, Gibson, Goslin, Grimes, Haines, Herman, Hooper, Hunter, Kaline, Keeler, Kelley, Koufax, Lajoie, Mantle, Musial, Schalk, Sewell, Sisler, Snider, Tinker, Wagner, Wilson, Youngs **7** Averill, Appling, Beckley, Hubbell, Jackson, Leonard, McCovey, Nichols, O'Rourke, Pennock, Roberts, Stengel, Traynor, Vaughan, Waddell, Wallace, Wilhelm **8** Bancroft, Boudreau, Clemente, Comiskey, DiMaggio, Drysdale, Jennings, McCarthy, Radbourn, Robinson, Thompson, Williams **9** Alexander, Delahanty, Greenberg, Mathewson **10** Campanella, Maranville
basketball: **4** Gola, Page, Reed, West **5** Cousy, Fulks, Greer, Hyatt, Lucas, Mikan **6** Barlow, Baylor, Cooper, Foster, Hanson, Holman, Pettit, Philip, Ramsey, Roosma, Sedran, Wooden **7** Beckman, Bradley, Johnson, Kurland, Pollard, Russell, Schmidt, Sharman **8** Borgmann, Endacott, Lapchick, Schommer **9** Robertson, Steinmetz, Vandivier **11** Chamberlain, Debusschere
business: **4** Ford, Kroc, Land, Luce, Vail **5** Beech, Deere, Heinz **6** Batten, Carrier, Cooper, Disney, du Pont, Edison, Hilton, Lowell, Mellon, Morgan, Penney, Schwab **7** Bechtel, Merrill, Peabody, Proctor, Whitney **8** Carnegie, Eastman, Franklin **9** Baekeland, Kettering, McCormick **10** Vanderbilt **11** Rockefeller **12** Westinghouse
football: **3** Mix, Ray **4** Bell, Carr, Ford, Hein, Huff, Hunt, Lane, Lary, Mara, Otto, Owen **5** Baugh, Berry, Brown, Clark, Davis, Fears, Green, Gregg, Groza, Guyon, Halas, Henry, Jones, Layne, Lilly, Lyman, Moore, Musso, Neale, Olsen, Perry, Pihos, Ringo, Starr **6** Atkins, Badgro, Blanda, Butkus, Connor, Dudley, Ewbank, Gatski, George, Graham, Grange, Healey, Herver, Hewitt, Hinkle, Hirsch, Hutson, Kinard, Langer, Lanier, Matson, McAfee, Motley, Namath, Nevers, Parker, Reeves, Rooney, Sayers, Strong, Taylor, Thorpe, Tittle, Trippi, Turner, Unitas, Upshaw, Walker, Willis, Wilson **7** Alworth, Battles, Bidwell, Canadeo, Donovan, Edwards, Gillman, Gifford, Hubbard, Lambeau, Lavelli, Leemans, Luckman, McNally, Millner, Schmidt, Trafton, Tunnell **8** Adderley, Bednarik, Driscoll, Fortmann, Kiesling, Lombardi, Marshall, Mitchell, Nagurski, Nitschke, Stautner, Stydahar, Van Buren, Warfield **9** Conzelman, Jurgensen, Marchetti, McElhenny, Michalske, Nomellini, Tarkenton **10** Robustelle, Waterfield **11** Chamberlain, Van Brocklin **12** Christiansen **13** Wohciechowicz
golf: **4** Berg, Ford, Hope, Wood **5** Boros, Brady, Burke, Dutra, Evans, Hagen, Hogan, Jones, Shute, Smith, Snead **6** Armour, Barnes, Casper, Cooper, Diegel, Dudley, Ghezzi, Harper, Little, McLeod, Nelson, Ouimet, Palmer, Picard, Runyan, Travis **7** Demaret, Guldahl, Harbert, Littler, Mangrum, Revolta, Sarazen, Travers **8** Anderson, Harrison, Zaharias **9** De Vicenzo, Hutchinson, McDermott **10** Middlecoff **11** Cruickshank
scientist: **4** Gray **5** Gibbs, Henry, Maury **6** Carver **7** Agassiz, Audubon, Burbank, Newcomb **8** Mitchell **9** Michelson
theater: **4** Drew, Kerr **5** Brook, Hecht, Kelly, Simon **6** Prince **7** Dunnock, Youmans **8** Kingsley, Lansbury, Meredith, Sondheim **9** MacArthur **11** Bloomgarden

rank: **12** fleet admiral
battle: **9** Leyte Gulf **11** Philippines **14** Solomon Islands

halt **3** end **4** balk, curb, foil, quit, rest, rout, stay, stem, stop, wait **5** abate, block, brake, break, cease, check, close, crush, delay, pause, quash, quell, stall, tarry **6** bridle, cut off, defeat, draw up, hamper, hinder, impede, linger, pull up, recess, rein in, scotch, subdue, thwart, wind up **7** heave to, inhibit, prevent, put down, repress, respite, squelch, suspend, time out **8** break off, breather, choke off, don't move, hang fire, interval, knock off, leave off, overturn, prohibit, restrain, restrict, shut down, suppress, vanquish **9** cessation, frustrate, interlude, interrupt, overthrow, terminate **10** call it a day, extinguish, shut up shop, standstill, suspension **11** come to a halt, come to a stop, discontinue, hold in check, termination **12** intermission, interruption, throttle down **13** spike one's guns **14** breathing spell, discontinuance

halting **6** ending **7** curbing **8** episodic, hesitant, stopping **9** faltering, stumbling **10** calling off, discursive, suspending **11** restraining, terminating **13** discontinuous **14** calling a halt to, putting a stop to

halting place
Spanish: **6** posada

halutz **7** pioneer **26** person who emigrates to Israel

halve **6** bisect **9** cut in half **10** split in two **13** divide equally

Ham
character in: **16** David Copperfield
author: **7** Dickens

Ham
father: **4** Noah
brother: **4** Shem **7** Japheth
son: **3** Put **4** Cush **6** Canaan **7** Misraim
descendant of: **6** Hamite

Hamadryad
form: **5** dryad
spirit of: **4** tree

Haman
served: **9** Ahasuerus

Hamill, Mark
born: **9** Oakland CA

roles: **8** Star Wars **13** Luke Skywalker **15** Return of the Jedi **20** The Empire Strikes Back

Hamilton
capital of: **7** Bermuda

Hamilton, Charles
character in: **15** Gone With the Wind
author: **8** Mitchell

Hamilton, Iain
composer of: **6** Aurora **7** Alastor **8** Sinfonia **9** Pharsalia **11** The Bermudas **18** Threnos In Time of War **20** The Royal Hunt of the Sun **21** The Catiline Conspiracy

Hamilton, Margaret
real name: **23** Margaret Hamilton Meserve
born: **11** Cleveland OH
roles: **4** Cora **13** The Wizard of Oz **23** The Wicked Witch of the West

Hamito-Semitic
language also known as: **11** Afro-Asiatic
branch: **6** Berber, Chadic **7** Semitic **8** Cushitic, Egyptian

hamlet **4** burg **7** village **8** hick town, tank town **10** crossroads **11** whistle stop **12** one-horse town, small village **13** jerkwater town

Hamlet
author: **18** William Shakespeare
character: **7** Horatio, Laertes, Ophelia **8** Claudius, Gertrude, Polonius, The Ghost **11** Rosencrantz **12** Guildenstern
skull: **6** Yorick
castle: **8** Elsinore
setting: **7** Denmark
director: **15** Laurence Olivier
cast: **11** Basil Sydney, Felix Aylmer, Jean Simmons **12** Eileen Herlie **15** Laurence Olivier
Oscar for: **5** actor (Olivier) **7** picture

Hamlet, The
author: **15** William Faulkner
character: **4** Eula, Jody **6** Labove **8** Ab Snopes **9** V K Ratliff **10** Flem Snopes, Mink Snopes, Will Varner **11** Isaac Snopes **12** Henry Armstid

Hamlin, Vincent T
creator/artist of: **8** Alley Oop

hammer **3** hit, tap **4** bang, form, make, nail **5** drive, forge, knock, pound, punch, shape, whack **6** pummel, rammer, strike **7** beat out, fashion
type: **4** claw, jack, tack **5** gavel, steam **6** mallet, sledge **8** ballpeen **10** pile driver **12** upholsterers

Hammer, Mike
detective created by: **14** Mickey Spillane

hammered **6** banged, beaten, shaped **7** knocked, pounded, whipped, wrought **8** battered, repeated **10** terrorized

Hammett, Dashiell
author of: **10** Red Harvest, The Thin Man **11** The Glass Key **12** The Dain Curse **16** The Maltese Falcon
character: **8** Sam Spade **11** Miles Archer, Nick Charles, Nora Charles **13** Continental Op

hamper **3** gag **4** balk, curb, stem **5** block, check, stall **6** fetter, hinder, hog-tie, hold up, impede, muzzle, retard, thwart **7** inhibit, prevent, shackle **8** encumber, handicap, obstruct, restrain, restrict **9** frustrate **13** interfere with

Hampton, Hope
nickname: **22** The Duchess of Park Avenue
born: **14** Philadelphia PA
roles: **8** Star Dust **13** Lawful Larceny, The Road to Reno **16** The Price of a Party

hamstring **6** impair, muscle, tendon **7** cripple, disable **8** handicap **10** debilitate

Hamsun, Knut
author of: **3** Pan **6** August, Hunger **8** Victoria **9** Mysteries, Vagabonds **16** Children of the Age **18** The Growth of the Soil

Hananiah *see* **8** Shadrach

hand, hands **3** aid, man, paw **4** care, fist, give, help, hold, lift, mitt, palm, pass **5** guide, power, reach **6** assist, charge, convey, helper, menial, script, worker **7** command, control, custody, deliver, keeping, laborer, ovation, present, support, workman **8** auspices, dominion, employee, guidance, handyman, hired man, longhand, meat-hook **9** assistant, associate, authority, hired hand **10** assistance, domination, management, minister to, penmanship, possession, turn over to, workingman **11** calligraphy, furnish with, handwriting, supervision **12** jurisdiction **13** member of a crew **15** burst of applause, manual extremity, round of applause

handbag **3** bag **4** grip **5** purse **6** clutch, valise **7** satchel **8** moneybag, reticule **10** pocketbook, portmanteau

handbill **5** flier **6** notice **7** leaflet **8** bulletin, circular **12** announcement **13** advertisement

handbook **5** bible **6** manual **9** guidebook **13** reference book

hand by hand
Spanish: **9** mano a mano

handcart **4** cart **6** barrow **8** pushcart **10** handbarrow **11** wheelbarrow

handcuffs **5** cuffs, irons **6** chains **7** fetters **8** manacles, shackles **9** bracelets

hand down **4** will **5** leave **6** hand on, pass on **8** bequeath

Handel, George Frederick (Georg Friedrich)
born: **5** Halle **7** Germany
composer of: **4** Nero, Saul **5** Serse, Silla, Siroe, Teseo **6** Admeto, Alcina, Almira, Esther, Flavio, Jeptha, Joseph, Ottone, Samson, Semele, Xerxes **7** Amadigi, Athalia, Deborah, Lotario, Messiah, Rinaldo, Rodrigo, Solomon, Tolomeo **8** Atalanta, Berenice, Hercules, Scipione, Theodora **9** Agrippina, Radamisto, Rodelinda, Tamerlano **10** Alessandro, Belshazzar, Floridante, Water Music **12** Giulio Cesare, Il Pastor Fido, Muzio Scevola **13** Israel in Egypt, Riccardo Primo **14** Acis and Galatea, Fireworks Music **15** Alexander's Feast, Judas Maccabaeus **16** Hornpipe Concerto **19** Julius Caesar in Egypt, Ode for St Cecilia's Day **22** The Royal Fireworks Music **23** Hallelujah Organ Concerto, The Harmonious Blacksmith **24** The Triumph of Time and Truth

handful **7** minimum, modicum **10** scattering, smattering, sprinkling, thimbleful, tiny amount **11** scant amount, small number **13** small quantity

Handful of Dust, A
author: **11** Evelyn Waugh

handgun **3** rod **5** piece, rifle **6** pistol, weapon **7** firearm, shotgun **8** revolver **9** automatic, twenty-two **12** shooting iron **20** Saturday night special

handicap **4** curb **5** limit **6** burden, defect, hamper, hinder, impede, retard, thwart **7** barrier, inhibit, repress, shackle **8** deafness, drawback, encumber, hold back, lameness, obstacle, restrain, restrict, suppress **9** blindness, detriment **10** difficulty, impediment, inhibition, limitation **11** encumbrance, restriction, shortcoming **12** disadvantage **13** inconvenience **14** stumbling block

handicapped **7** limited **8** burdened, disabled, held back, hindered, impaired, retarded **10** encumbered, restrained, restricted **13** disadvantaged

handicrafts
god of: **10** Hephaestus, Hephaistos

handicraftsman **7** artisan **10** handworker **12** handicrafter

handiness **7** utility **8** deftness **9** dexterity **10** adroitness, usefulness **11** convenience **12** availability **13** accessibility

hand in glove **5** as one **10** side by side **13** close together

handle **3** paw, ply, run, tag, use **4** feel, grip, hilt, hold, knob, name, poke, pull, sell, work **5** carry, grasp, guide, knead, pilot, pinch, shaft, shank, steer, swing, touch, treat **6** caress, deal in, employ, finger, fondle, manage, market, pick up, stroke **7** care for, command, conduct, control, massage, moniker, operate, paw over, trade in, utilize **8** cognomen, deal with, maneuver **9** traffic in **10** manipulate, take care of **11** appellation, merchandise **12** offer for sale **13** bring into play

Handley Cross
author: **18** Robert Smith Surtees

handout **4** alms, dole **7** freebie **19** something for nothing

hand out **4** give **5** grant **6** bestow, confer, donate **7** dole out, mete out, present **8** dispense **9** apportion **10** contribute, distribute

hand over **4** cede **5** grant, yield **6** give up, tender **7** abandon, release **8** transfer **9** deliver up, surrender **10** relinquish

handsome **4** fair **5** ample, bonny, noble **6** benign, comely, lovely, pretty **7** elegant, liberal, sightly, sizable, stately **8** abundant, generous, gracious, imposing, merciful, princely, splendid, stunning, tasteful **9** beauteous, beautiful, bountiful, exquisite, unselfish **10** attractive, benevolent, bighearted, impressive, sufficient, well-formed **11** fine-looking, good-looking, magnanimous **12** considerable, easy to look at, humanitarian **13** compassionate, easy on the eyes **16** well-proportioned

handy **4** deft, near, nigh **5** adept, on tap **6** adroit, at hand, clever, expert, on call, on hand, useful, wieldy **7** capable, helpful, skilled **8** skillful **9** available, competent, dexterous, easy to use, efficient, practical **10** accessible, convenient, manageable, obtainable, proficient **11** at one's elbow, close at hand, in readiness, ready to hand, serviceable **12** accomplished **14** nimble-fingered **15** within easy reach **16** easily accessible **17** at one's beck and call

hang **3** bow, sag **4** drop, gist, rest **5** affix, hinge, knack, lie in, lower, lynch, point, trail **6** append, attach, dangle, depend **7** incline, meaning, suspend, thought **8** lean over, let droop, repose in, string up, turn upon **9** be pendant, be pendent **11** be dependent, be subject to, bend forward, swing freely **12** be contingent, bend downward **13** revolve around **15** die on the gallows, fasten from above **16** execute by hanging, send to the gallows

hangdog **6** abject **7** ashamed **8** defeated, degraded, hopeless, resigned, wretched **9** miserable **10** browbeaten, chapfallen, humiliated, shamefaced **11** crestfallen, embarrassed, intimidated **13** guilty-looking

hang down **3** sag **5** droop

hanger-on **7** admirer, groupie **8** follower **9** sycophant

hanging object
Japanese: **8** kakemono

hang loosely **3** bag, sag **5** droop

hangout **3** den **5** haunt

hang out **3** mix **4** live **5** dwell **6** hobnob, loiter, mingle, reside **7** consort **9** associate, be friends, pal around, run around **10** fraternize, hang around **11** keep company

hanker after **4** want **5** covet, crave, fancy **6** desire **7** long for, pine for **8** aspire to, yearn for **9** lust after **11** have a yen for, have an eye on, hunger after, thirst after

hankering **3** yen **4** itch, urge **6** aching, desire, hunger, pining, thirst **7** craving, longing **8** yearning

Hanna-Barbera
creators of: **8** Yogi Bear **14** The Flintstones

Hannah
husband: **7** Elkanah
son: **6** Samuel

Hanoi
capital of: **7** Vietnam **12** North Vietnam
river: **3** Red **4** Yuan **7** Song Koi
delta: **6** Tonkin
airport: **6** Gia Lam

Hans Brinker
author: **5** (Mary Elizabeth Mapes) Dodge
character: **4** Raff **5** Gleck, Hilda **6** Gretel **7** Boekman, Mevrouw

Hansel and Gretel
author: **13** Grimm Brothers (Jakob and Wilhelm)
opera by: **11** Humperdinck
character: **5** Witch

Hans Kristian
character in: **16** Giants of the Earth
author: **7** Rolvaag

Hanson, Howard
born: **7** Wahoo NE
composer of: **5** Sacra (symphony No 5) **6** Nordic (symphony No 1) **7** Requiem (symphony No 4) **8** Romantic (symphony No 2) **10** Merry-Mount

Hap *see* **4** Apis

haphazard **6** casual, chance, fitful, random **7** aimless, chaotic **8** careless, on-and-off, slapdash, sporadic **9** arbitrary, hit-or-miss **10** accidental, disordered, disorderly, fortuitous, undesigned, undirected, unthinking **11** purposeless, unorganized **12** disorganized, unmethodical, unsystematic **14** indiscriminate, unpremeditated **15** catch-as-catch-can

Hapi *see* **4** Apis, Nile

hapless **5** lousy **6** cursed, jinxed, no-good, rotten, woeful **7** forlorn, unhappy, unlucky **8** accursed, hopeless, ill-fated, luckless, wretched **9** miserable **10** ill-starred **11** star-crossed, unfortunate

happen **5** arise, ensue, occur **6** appear, befall, betide, crop up, result **7** turn out **8** become of, spring up **9** be borne by, be the case, come about, eventuate, take place, transpire **10** be one's fate, come to pass **11** be endured by **12** be suffered by **13** be one's fortune, fall to one's lot, present itself

happening 4 case **5** event **6** advent, affair, matter **7** episode **8** accident, incident, occasion **9** adventure, incidence **10** experience, occurrence, proceeding **11** vicissitude **12** circumstance, happenstance **20** just one of those things

happenstance 4 luck **6** chance **8** accident, fortuity

happiness 3 joy **4** glee **5** bliss, cheer, mirth **6** gaiety **7** comfort, content, delight, ecstasy, elation, jollity, rapture **8** blessing, felicity, gladness, pleasure **9** beatitude, enjoyment, merriment, rejoicing, transport **10** cheeriness, exuberance, exultation, jubilation **11** blessedness, contentment, high spirits **12** cheerfulness, satisfaction **13** gratification **16** lightheartedness, sense of well-being

happy 3 fit, gay **4** glad, meet **5** lucky **6** elated, joyful, joyous, timely **7** content, fitting, gleeful, pleased, tickled **8** blissful, cheerful, cheering, ecstatic, exultant, jubilant, pleasant, pleasing **9** agreeable, contented, delighted, exuberant, favorable, fortunate, gratified, opportune, overjoyed, rapturous, rhapsodic **10** auspicious, convenient, delightful, felicitous, gratifying, propitious, seasonable **11** exhilarated, tickled pink, transported **12** advantageous **13** in high spirits **15** in seventh heaven

Happy Days
character: 6 Arnold, Fonzie **10** Ralph Malph **11** Potsie Weber **12** Chachi Arcola **14** Pinky Tuscadero **15** Chuck Cunningham **16** Alfred Delvecchio, Arthur Fonzarelli, Howard Cunningham, Joanie Cunningham, Leather Tuscadero, Marion Cunningham, Richie Cunningham
cast: 8 Roz Kelly **9** Donny Most, Erin Moran, Pat Morita, Ron Howard, Scott Baio, Tom Bosley **10** Al Molinaro, Marion Ross, Suzi Quatro **12** Henry Winkler **13** Anson Williams, Gavan O'Herlihy **15** Randolph Roberts

happy-go-lucky 6 blithe **7** buoyant, flighty, relaxed **8** carefree, careless, feckless, heedless, skittish **9** easygoing, unworried **10** insouciant, nonchalant, optimistic, untroubled **11** free-and-easy, unconcerned **12** devil-may-care, light-hearted **13** irresponsible **14** scatterbrained **23** without a worry in the world

harangue 6 speech, tirade **7** lecture, oration **8** diatribe, scolding **9** contumely, sermonize **12** denunciation, vituperation

Harare
capital of: 8 Zimbabwe

harass 3 cow, irk, vex **4** bait, ride **5** annoy, beset, bully, harry, hound, tease, worry **6** attack, badger, bother, heckle, hector, pester, plague **7** assault, bedevil, besiege, disturb, torment **8** browbeat, distress, irritate **9** persecute **10** discommode, exasperate, intimidate **14** raid frequently

harbinger 4 clue, omen **5** token **6** herald, symbol **7** portent **8** signaler **9** announcer, first sign, precursor **10** forerunner, indication, proclaimer

Harbonna 6 eunuch

harbor 3 bay **4** cove, dock, feel, goal, hide, hold, keep, pier, port, quay **5** basin, haven, house, inlet, lodge, wharf **6** asylum, billet, foster, lagoon, refuge, retain, shield, take in **7** care for, cling to, conceal, nurture, protect, quarter, retreat, shelter **8** hideaway, keep safe, maintain, muse over, terminus **9** brood over, sanctuary **11** concealment, destination, hiding place **12** give refuge to **13** bear in the mind, terminal point **18** protected anchorage

harbors
god of: 8 Portunus
goddess of: 6 Matutu

Harcorates *see* **5** Horus

hard *see box*

hard-and-fast 3 set **6** strict **7** binding **8** exacting, rigorous **9** mandatory, unbending **10** compelling, compulsory, inflexible, obligatory, undeniable, unyielding **11** irrevocable, unalterable, unremitting **12** indisputable **13** incontestable **14** uncompromising

Hardcastle family
characters in: 18 She Stoops to Conquer
author: 9 Goldsmith

hard drinker 3 sot **4** lush, soak, wino **5** drunk, rummy,

hard 3 sad **4** cold, firm, mean, ugly **5** cruel, eager, harsh, heavy, rigid, rough, solid, stern, stiff, stony, tight, tough **6** bitter, brutal, fierce, firmly, keenly, knotty, severe, steely, strict, strong, sullen, thorny, unkind **7** angrily, arduous, callous, closely, complex, cryptic, eagerly, earnest, harmful, heavily, hostile, hurtful, inhuman, intense, onerous, sharply, solidly, tightly, to heart, vicious, violent, willing, zealous **8** animated, baffling, critical, diligent, exacting, fiercely, forceful, forcibly, hardened, intently, involved, pitiless, powerful, puzzling, rocklike, ruthless, severely, spirited, spiteful, steadily, strongly, stubborn, untiring, venomous, vigorous **9** arduously, assiduous, bellicose, confusing, difficult, earnestly, energetic, furiously, Herculean, insulting, intensely, intricate, laborious, malicious, merciless, painfully, rancorous, seriously, strenuous, stringent, unbending, unpliable, unsparing, violently, wearisome **10** burdensome, diligently, forcefully, formidable, impervious, implacable, inexorable, inflexible, lamentable, melancholy, oppressive, perplexing, persistent, powerfully, relentless, resolutely, rigorously, tormenting, unbearable, unflagging, unfriendly, unpleasant, untiringly, unyielding, vigorously, vindictive **11** acrimonious, agonizingly, assiduously, belligerent, bewildering, complicated, distressing, emotionally, hardhearted, industrious, insensitive, intolerable, laboriously, persevering, troublesome, unceasingly, unmalleable, unrelenting, unremitting, unsparingly **12** antagonistic, cantankerous, determinedly, disagreeable, enterprising, impenetrable, persistently, relentlessly, thick-skinned, unfathomable, unflaggingly **13** conscientious, disheartening, distressfully, energetically, indefatigable, industriously, with much anger **14** uncompromising, with much sorrow **15** conscientiously **16** with all one's might **18** with strong feelings souse, toper **6** barfly, boozer **7** guzzler, imbiber, tippler **8** drunkard **9** alcoholic **11** dipsomaniac **14** problem drinker **16** two-fisted drinker

harden **3** dry, gel, set **4** cake, fire, firm **5** adapt, adjust, blunt, enure, inure, steel **6** anneal, freeze, season, temper **7** calcify, callous, congeal, fortify, petrify, stiffen, thicken, toughen **8** accustom, solidify **9** fossilize, make tough, reinforce **10** discipline, invigorate, strengthen **11** crystallize, turn to stone **12** restrengthen **13** make unfeeling

hard feelings **5** anger **6** grudge, hatred, rancor **7** ill will **8** acrimony **9** animosity, hostility **10** antagonism, bitterness **12** spitefulness

hardheaded **4** cool **5** balky **6** astute, mulish, poised, shrewd **7** willful **8** contrary, sensible, stubborn **9** immovable, objective, obstinate, pigheaded, practical, pragmatic, realistic, unbending, unfeeling **10** coolheaded, impersonal, inflexible, refractory, self-willed, unyielding **11** down-to-earth, intractable, tough-minded, unemotional, unflappable **14** self-controlled

hardhearted **4** cold, hard, mean **5** cruel, stony **6** brutal **7** callous, inhuman **8** pitiless, ruthless, uncaring **9** heartless, merciless, unfeeling, unpitying, unsparing **11** coldblooded, indifferent, insensitive, remorseless, unforgiving **12** cruelhearted, thick-skinned **13** unsympathetic

hardihood **4** grit **5** pluck, spunk **6** mettle **7** courage **8** strength **9** endurance, fortitude **10** resolution **12** resoluteness

Harding, Warren Gamaliel *see box*

hardly **4** just, only **6** barely, rarely **7** faintly, in no way **8** not often, not quite, scarcely **9** almost not, by no means **10** in no manner, uncommonly **12** certainly not, infrequently **13** not by any means **15** not by a great deal

hardnosed **4** hard **5** harsh, rigid, stern, tough **6** severe, shrewd, strict **8** critical, hardline, exacting, stubborn **9** demanding, unbending, unsparing **10** hardheaded, inflexible, no-nonsense, unyielding **11** calculating, intractable **12** unsentimental **14** uncompromising

Hardouin-Mansart, Jules
architect of: **8** Orangery (Versailles) **12** Chateau du Val (St Germain-en-Laye), Grand Trianon (Versailles), Place Vendome (Paris) **15** Chateau de Clagny (Versailles) **16** Galerie des Glaces (Hall of Mirrors at Versailles), Les Invalides (Church of the Dome, Paris)

hard-pressed **7** harried, put-upon **9** embattled **10** overworked

hardship **3** woe **4** load **5** agony, grief **6** burden, misery, ordeal, sorrow **7** problem, travail, trouble **8** handicap **9** adversity, privation, suffering **10** affliction, difficulty, misfortune **11** cross to bear, encumbrance, tribulation, unhappiness **12** wretchedness

hard sledding **8** tough job **10** difficulty, tough going, uphill work **11** arduousness **13** laboriousness

hard times **4** bust **5** slump **8** bad times **9** recession **10** depression

Hard Times
author: **11** Studs Terkel

Hard Times
author: **14** Charles Dickens
character: **9** Sissy Jupe **10** Mrs Sparsit **11** Mr Boun-

---

Harding, Warren Gamaliel
presidential rank: **11** twenty-ninth
party: **10** Republican
state represented: **2** OH
defeated: **3** (James Middleton) Cox, (William Wesley) Cox **4** (Eugene Victor) Debs **7** (Aaron Sherman) Watkins **8** (Robert Charles) Macauley **11** (Parley Parker) Christensen
vice president: **8** (Calvin) Coolidge
cabinet:
state: **6** (Charles Evans) Hughes
treasury: **6** (Andrew William) Mellon
war: **5** (John Wingate) Weeks
attorney general: **9** (Harry Micajah) Daugherty
navy: **5** (Edwin) Denby
postmaster general: **3** (Harry Stewart) New **4** (Hubert) Work, (William Harrison) Hays
interior: **4** (Albert Bacon) Fall, (Hubert) Work
agriculture: **7** (Henry Cantwell) Wallace
commerce: **6** (Herbert Clark) Hoover
labor: **5** (James John) Davis
born: **9** Corsica OH (now Blooming Grove)
died: **2** CA (while in office) **12** San Francisco
buried: **8** Marion OH
education:
College: **11** Ohio Central
religion: **7** Baptist
interests: **5** poker
played musical instrument: **6** cornet **7** helicon
political career: **8** US Senate **15** Ohio State Senate
lieutenant governor of: **4** Ohio
civilian career: **9** publisher **13** schoolteacher **15** newspaper editor **17** insurance salesman
notable events of lifetime/term:
Act: **21** Fordney-McCumber Tariff
peace treaty with: **7** Austria, Germany, Hungary
scandal: **10** Teapot Dome (oil)
Treaty: **9** Five-Power, Nine-Power **16** Four-Power Pacific
father: **11** George Tryon
mother: **6** Phoebe (Elizabeth Dickerson)
stepmother: **4** Mary (Alice Severns) **6** Eudora (Kelley Luvisi)
siblings: **11** George Tryon **12** Mary Clarissa **14** Charity Malvina, Phoebe Caroline **15** Abigail Victoria **16** Charles Alexander, Eleanor Priscilla
wife: **8** Florence (Kling DeWolfe)
children:
illegitimate daughter: **21** Elizabeth Ann Christian (by mistress Nan Britton)

derby **12** Tom Gradgrind **14** James Harthouse **15** Louisa Gradgrind, Thomas Gradgrind **16** Stephen Blackpool

hard to catch **4** foxy, wily **6** crafty, shifty, tricky **7** elusive, evasive **8** slippery

hard to grasp **7** elusive **8** baffling, puzzling, slippery **9** difficult **10** perplexing **16** incomprehensible

hard to manage **6** unruly **7** froward, willful **8** perverse, stubborn **9** difficult, fractious, obstinate **10** inflexible, refractory, unyielding **11** intractable **12** obstreperous, unmanageable

hard to please **5** fussy, picky **7** exigent, finicky **8** critical **10** fastidious, meticulous, particular

hard to understand **7** complex **9** difficult, intricate **10** perplexing **11** bewildering, complicated

Hardwick, Elizabeth
author of: **11** Simple Truth **12** A View of My Own **15** Sleepless Nights **20** Seduction and Betrayal

Hardwicke, Sir Cedric
born: **3** Lye **7** England
roles: **14** On Borrowed Time **21** Livingstone and Stanley **36** A Connecticut Yankee in King Arthur's Court

hardwood **4** wood **8** leadwood
kind: **3** ash, elm, oak **4** teak **5** beech, birch, maple **6** cherry, linden, walnut **7** hickory **8** mahogany, rosewood, sycamore

hardworking **8** diligent, sedulous **9** assiduous **11** industrious, persevering **12** enterprising **13** conscientious

hardy **3** fit **4** hale **5** tough **6** hearty, mighty, robust, rugged, strong, sturdy **7** healthy **8** stalwart, vigorous **9** strapping **10** able-bodied **12** in fine fettle **13** physically fit **15** in good condition

Hardy, Oliver
partner: **10** Stan Laurel
born: **8** Harlem GA
roles: **8** Pardon Us **9** Saps at Sea **10** Way Out West

Hardy, Thomas
author of: **10** The Dynasts **14** Jude the Obscure **20** The Return of the Native **21** Tess of the D'Urbervilles **22** Far from the Madding Crowd, The Mayor of Casterbridge
mythical county: **6** Wessex

hare
constellation of: **5** Lepus
group of: **4** down, husk

harebrained **5** silly, wacko, wacky **7** asinine, flighty, foolish **8** skittish **9** dimwitted, senseless **10** half-witted **11** empty-headed **12** simple-minded **13** rattlebrained **14** featherbrained, scatterbrained

Haredale, Reuben
character in: **12** Barnaby Rudge
author: **7** Dickens

harem **5** serai **6** purdah, serail, senana, zenana **8** love nest, seraglio

Hargreaves, James
nationality: **7** English
inventor of: **13** spinning jenny

Harker, Jonathan
character in: **7** Dracula
author: **6** Stoker

harlot **3** pro **4** bawd, doxy, jade, pros, slut, tart **5** whore **6** chippy, wanton **7** jezebel, trollop **8** call girl, mistress, strumpet **9** courtesan, kept woman **10** prostitute **11** fallen woman **12** painted woman, scarlet woman, streetwalker

Harlow, Jean
real name: **16** Harlean Carpenter
nickname: **15** Blonde Bombshell
born: **12** Kansas City MO
roles: **7** Red Dust **8** Riffraff, Saratoga **9** Bombshell, China Seas **11** Hell's Angels, Libeled Lady **13** Dinner at Eight

harm **3** ill, mar, sin **4** evil, hurt, maim, pain, ruin, vice **5** abuse, agony, havoc, spoil, wound, wrong **6** damage, debase, deface, ill-use, impair, injure, injury, malice, misuse, trauma **7** blemish, cripple, degrade, scourge **8** aggrieve, calamity, hardship, iniquity, maltreat, mischief, villainy **9** adversity, detriment, disfigure, suffering, undermine **10** defacement, immorality, impairment, misfortune, sinfulness, wickedness **11** destruction, devastation, malevolence **12** do violence to **13** deterioration, maliciousness

harmful **3** bad **7** adverse, baneful, hurtful, ruinous **8** damaging **9** dangerous, injurious, unhealthy **10** pernicious **11** deleterious, destructive, detrimental, unhealthful, unwholesome **17** counterproductive

harmless **4** mild, safe **6** benign, gentle **7** sinless **8** innocent, nontoxic **9** blameless, guiltless, incorrupt, innocuous, peaceable **10** not hurtful **11** inoffensive **12** not dangerous **15** unobjectionable

harmlessness **6** safety **9** innocence **10** gentleness **11** nontoxicity **12** nonvirulence **13** innocuousness **15** inoffensiveness

Harmon, Young John
character in: **15** Our Mutual Friend
author: **7** Dickens

Harmonia
father: **4** Ares
mother: **9** Aphrodite
husband: **6** Cadmus
daughter: **3** Ino

Harmonides *see* **9** Phereclus

harmonious **5** sweet **6** dulcet **7** amiable, cordial, unified **8** amicable, friendly, in accord, matching **9** agreeable, congenial, in harmony, melodious **10** compatible, consistent, euphonious, likeminded **11** coordinated, harmonizing, in agreement, mellifluous, sympathetic **12** synchronized **13** sweet-sounding **17** agreeably combined

harmonize **3** fit **4** jibe, mesh **5** agree, blend, chime, tally **6** accord, adjust, attune **7** conform **8** be in tune **9** reconcile **10** complement, correspond, go together **13** sing in harmony

harmony **5** amity, order, peace, unity **6** accord **7** balance, concord **8** matching, symmetry, sympathy **9** agreement, unanimity **10** conformity, fellowship, friendship, proportion **11** amicability, cooperation, correlation, parallelism **12** congeniality, coordination, mutual regard **13** compatibility, mutual fitness **14** likemindedness **15** organic totality **17** good understanding **19** harmonious relations, pleasing consistency **21** concurrence in opinions

Harmony
goddess of: **9** Concordia

harness **4** curb, rein, tugs, yoke **5** lines, reins, rig up **6** bridle, collar, employ, halter, muzzle, straps, tackle, traces **7** exploit, hitch up, utilize **8** restrain **9** caparison, trappings **12** put in harness, render useful **13** control and use, turn to account **14** make productive **22** direct to a useful purpose

Harold
author: **18** Edward Bulwer-Lytton

Harper, Joe
character in: **9** Tom Sawyer
author: **5** Twain

Harphlyce
father: **8** Clymenus
husband: **7** Alastor
vocation: **8** huntress
violated by: **8** Clymenus
killed by: **8** Clymenus **9** shepherds

Harpina
father: **6** Asopus
son: **8** Oenomaus

harp on **7** dwell on **9** reiterate **18** repeat persistently

Harpy
form: **7** monster
head of: **5** woman
body of: **4** bird
father: **7** Thaumas
mother: **7** Electra
names: **5** Aello **7** Celaeno, Ocypete, Podarge

harridan **3** hag **5** crone, shrew, witch **6** virago **8** battle-ax, old crone **12** mean old woman

harried **5** upset **7** worried **8** harassed, troubled **10** distraught

Harris, Joel Chandler
author of: **10** Uncle Remus (His Songs and Sayings)

Harris, Julie
real name: **14** Julia Ann Harris
born: **18** Grosse Pointe Park MI
roles: **6** Harper **10** East of Eden, I Am a Camera **11** The Haunting **14** A Shot in the Dark, The Hiding Place **19** The Last of Mrs Lincoln **21** The Member of the Wedding **22** Requiem for a Heavyweight **27** And Miss Reardon Drinks a Little

Harris, Richard
born: **7** Ireland **8** Limerick
roles: **7** Camelot **8** Cromwell **15** A Man Called Horse **16** The Molly Maguires, This Sporting Life **17** Mutiny on the Bounty, The Guns of Navarone **20** The Cassandra Crossing **26** The Return of a Man Called Horse

Harris, Roy
composer of: **16** Folksong Symphony **17** American Portraits **27** When Johnny Comes Marching Home (overture)

Harrison, Benjamin ***see box***

Harrison, Lou
born: **10** Portland OR
composer of: **8** Rapunzel, Solstice **13** Changing World **15** Four Strict Songs, Johnny Appleseed **17** The Perilous Chapel **19** Almanac of the Seasons **22** At the Tomb of Charles Ives

Harrison, Peter
architect of: **11** Brick Market (Newport RI), King's Chapel (Boston) **14** Redwood Library (Newport RI), Touro Synagogue (Newport RI)

Harrison, Rex
real name: **21** Reginald Carey Harrison
nickname: **8** Sexy Rexy
wife: **10** Kay Kendall **11** Lilli Palmer **13** Rachel Roberts
born: **6** Huyton **7** England
roles: **9** Cleopatra **10** My Fair Lady (Oscar) **12** Blithe Spirit **14** Doctor Dolittle **16** The Foxes of Harrow **17** Unfaithfully Yours **18** The Ghost and Mrs Muir **20** Anna and the King of Siam

Harrison, Wallace K
architect of: **13** Lincoln Center (NYC) **14** Socony Building (NYC) **17** Rockefeller Center (NYC) **22** Metropoli-

Harrison, Benjamin
nickname: **3** Ben **9** Little Ben
presidential rank: **11** twenty-third
party: **10** Republican
state represented: **2** IN
defeated: **4** (Clinton Bowen) Fisk **6** (James Langdon) Curtis **7** (Robert Hall) Cowdrey **8** (Albert) Redstone, (Alson Jenness) Streeter, (Belva Ann Bennett) Lockwood **9** (Grover) Cleveland
vice president: **6** (Levi Parsons) Morton
cabinet:
state: **6** (James Gillespie) Blaine, (John Watson) Foster
treasury: **6** (Charles) Foster, (William) Windom
war: **6** (Stephen Benton) Elkins **7** (Redfield) Proctor
attorney general: **6** (William Henry Harrison) Miller
navy: **5** (Benjamin Franklin) Tracy
postmaster general: **9** (John) Wanamaker
interior: **5** (John Willock) Noble
agriculture: **4** (Jeremiah McLain) Rusk
born: **11** North Bend OH
died/buried: **14** Indianapolis IN
education:
prep school: **14** Farmer's College
University: **21** Miami University of Ohio
later studied: **3** law
religion: **12** Presbyterian
interests: **7** fishing, hunting **8** swimming
author: **17** This Country of Ours **20** Views of An Ex-President
political career: **8** US Senate
city attorney: **12** Indianapolis
reporter of: **19** Indiana supreme court
secretary of: **31** Republican state central committee
civilian career: **6** lawyer **12** law professor
military service: **8** Civil War **16** brigadier general
notable events of lifetime/term:
Act: **16** Dependent Pension, Sherman Anti-Trust **21** Sherman Silver Purchase
Tariff: **8** McKinley
father: **9** John Scott
mother: **9** Elizabeth (Ramsey Irwin)
siblings: **8** Mary Jane **9** John Irwin, John Scott **10** Anna Symmes, James Irwin **12** James Findlay **13** Carter Bassett **14** Archibald Irwin
half sisters: **9** Elizabeth **13** Sarah Lucretia
wife: **4** Mary (Scott Lord Dimmick) **8** Caroline (Lavinia Scott)
children: **9** Elizabeth, Mary Scott **15** Russell Benjamin

tan Opera House (NYC) **25** United Nations Headquarters (NYC) **34** Nelson A Rockefeller Empire State Plaza (Albany NY), ALCOA Building (Pittsburgh, with Max Abramovitz)

Harrison, William Henry
see box

harrowing **7** fearful, painful **8** alarming, chilling **9** traumatic, upsetting **10** disturbing, terrifying, tormenting **11** distressing, frightening **13** bloodcurdling

harry **3** irk, vex **4** bait, gall, raid, ride, sack **5** annoy, beset, bully, haunt, hound, tease, worry **6** badger, bother, harass, heckle, hector, pester, plague **7** disturb, pillage, plunder, torment, trouble **8** distract, distress, irritate **9** terrorize **10** exasperate, intimidate **16** attack repeatedly

harsh **4** hard, mean **5** cruel, raspy, rough, sharp, stern **6** bitter, brutal, hoarse, severe, shrill, unkind **7** abusive, caustic, glaring, grating, jarring, rasping, raucous, squawky **8** piercing, pitiless, ruthless, scratchy, strident, ungentle **9** Draconian, heartless, merciless, too bright, unmusical, unsparing **10** discordant, overbright, unpleasant, vindictive **11** cacophonous, hardhearted **12** uncharitable, unharmonious

harshness **5** rigor **7** cruelty, discord **9** brutality, cacophony, raspiness, roughness, sternness, stridency **10** dissonance, shrillness, unkindness **12** ungentleness **13** heartlessness **14** unpleasantness **15** hardheartedness

Hart, Johnny
creator/artist of: **2** B C **13** The Wizard of Id

Harrison, William Henry
nickname: **6** Old Tip **22** The Washington of the West
presidential rank: **5** ninth
party: **4** Whig
state represented: **2** OH
defeated: **6** (James G) Birney **8** (Martin) Van Buren
vice president: **5** (John) Tyler
cabinet:
state: **7** (Daniel) Webster
treasury: **5** (Thomas) Ewing
war: **4** (John) Bell
attorney general: **10** (John Jordan) Crittenden
navy: **6** (George Edmund) Badger
postmaster general: **7** (Francis) Granger
born: **2** VA **17** Charles City County **18** Berkeley plantation
died: **12** Washington DC
buried: **11** North Bend OH
education: **16** privately tutored (at home)
College: **13** Hampden-Sydney (did not graduate)
later studied: **8** medicine
religion: **12** Episcopalian
political career: **8** US Senate **11** state Senate **24** US House of Representatives
governor of: **16** Indiana Territory
minister: **8** Columbia
civilian career: **6** farmer **7** soldier
military service: **6** US Army **12** major general **19** War of Eighteen Twelve
battle: **6** (the) Thames **8** Lake Erie **10** Tippecanoe
notable events of lifetime/term: **24** Land Act of Eighteen Hundred
campaign slogan: **21** Tippecanoe and Tyler too
treaty of: **10** Greenville
father: **8** Benjamin
mother: **9** Elizabeth (Bassett)
siblings: **3** Ann **4** Lucy **5** Sarah **8** Benjamin **9** Elizabeth **13** Carter Bassett
wife: **4** Anna (Tuthill Symmes)
children: **8** Benjamin **9** John Scott **10** Mary Symmes **11** Anna Tuthill **12** James Findlay, William Henry **13** Carter Bassett, Lucy Singleton **16** Elizabeth Bassett, John Cleves Symmes

Hart, Moss
author of: **15** Once in a Lifetime **20** You Can't Take It with You (with George S Kaufman) **21** The Man Who Came to Dinner (with George S Kaufman)

Harte, Bret
author of: **20** The Luck of Roaring Camp **22** The Outcasts of Poker Flat

Hartford
hockey team: **7** Whalers

Harthouse, James
character in: **9** Hard Times
author: **7** Dickens

Hartley, Vivian Mary
real name of: **11** Vivien Leigh

harum-scarum **5** giddy **6** wildly **7** erratic, flighty, foolish **8** careless, confused **9** aimlessly, haphazard, impetuous, impulsive, unplanned, unsettled **10** bewildered, recklessly, unreliable **11** haphazardly, harebrained, impulsively **12** absent-minded, capriciously, disorganized, inconsistent, undependable **13** rattlebrained **14** featherbrained, scatterbrained

harvest **3** cut, mow **4** crop, gain, pick, reap **5** amass, fruit, pluck, yield **6** gather, haying, mowing, output, result, return, reward **7** benefit, collect, cutting, picking, produce, product, reaping **8** fruition, gleaning, proceeds **9** aftermath, amassment, gathering, outgrowth **10** accumulate, collection, harvesting **12** accumulation **13** season's growth

harvest time **4** fall **6** autumn **8** maturity **12** Indian summer

Harvey
director: **11** Henry Koster
based on play by: **9** Mary Chase
cast: **8** Peggy Dow **12** James Stewart (Elwood P Dowd) **13** Cecil Kellaway, Josephine Hull
Oscar for: **17** supporting actress (Hull)

Harvey, Laurence
real name: **19** Larushka Misch Skikne
wife: **16** Margaret Leighton
born: **9** Lithuania, Yomishkis
roles: **7** Darling **12** Life at the Top, Room at the Top **14** Of Human Bondage, Summer and Smoke **16** Butterfield Eight **17** Walk on the Wild Side

Harvey, William
field: **7** anatomy

nationality: **7** British
discovered: **18** circulation of blood

Hasen, Irwin
creator/artist of: **5** Dondi **9** Goldbergs **11** Wonder Woman **12** Green Lantern

hash out **6** review **7** discuss **8** consider, talk over

hasp **4** lock **5** catch, clasp, latch **7** closure **8** fastener

Hassam, (Frederick) Childe
born: **12** Dorchester MA
artwork: **13** Southwest Wind **14** Summer Sunlight, Washington Arch **15** Against the Light **23** Boston Commons at Twilight

hassle **3** bug, row, vex **5** annoy, fight, harry, hound, scrap, set-to **6** badger, battle, bother, harass, tussle **7** contest, dispute, quarrel **8** argument, conflict, squabble, struggle **9** persecute

hassock **4** boss, pess, seat, tuft, weed **5** bunch, chair, group, trush **6** buffet, plants, tuffet **7** ottoman, tussock **9** footstool, vegetable

hasta la vista **6** good-by, so long **7** goodbye **12** until I see you **16** until we meet again

hasta manana **13** until tomorrow **14** see you tomorrow

haste **4** rush **5** hurry, speed **8** celerity, dispatch, rapidity, rashness **9** fleetness, quickness, swiftness **10** expedition, speediness, undue speed **11** hurriedness **12** recklessness **13** careless hurry, impetuousness, impulsiveness, precipitation

hasten **3** fly, run **4** bolt, dart, dash, flit, jump, race, rush **5** egg on, hurry, impel, speed, whisk **6** hustle, incite, scurry, sprint, urge on **7** advance, drive on, hurry on, hurry up, promote, quicken, scamper, scuttle, speed up **8** expedite, make time **10** accelerate, lose no time **11** go full blast, precipitate, push forward **12** step on the gas **13** go on the double **14** step right along **15** go like lightning, make short work of, work against time **20** go hell-bent for leather

hastily **4** fast **5** apace **6** pronto, rashly **7** quickly **8** promptly, speedily **9** hurriedly, like a shot, posthaste, summarily **10** carelessly, heedlessly, recklessly, too quickly **11** impetuously, impulsively, on the double **12** lickety-split, straightaway **13** precipitately, thoughtlessly **18** hell-bent for leather **20** like greased lightning, on the spur of the moment

Hastings, Thomas *see* **17** Carrere, John Merven

hasty **4** fast, rash **5** brief, fleet, quick, rapid, swift **6** abrupt, prompt, rushed, speedy **7** cursory, hurried, passing **8** fleeting, headlong, heedless, reckless **9** impetuous, impulsive, momentary **10** breathless **11** precipitate, superficial, unduly quick **12** quick as a wink **19** without deliberation

hat
French: **7** chapeau

hatch **4** plan, plot **5** frame **6** cook up, create, design, devise, evolve, invent, make up **7** concoct, dream up, fashion, produce, think up **8** conceive, contrive **9** construct, fabricate, formulate, improvise, originate **10** bring forth **11** give birth to, manufacture

hatchlings **5** brood, young **6** chicks **9** offspring

hate **5** abhor, dread, venom **6** animus, detest, enmity, hatred, loathe, malice, rancor **7** be sorry, despise, dislike, wince at **8** acrimony, aversion, be sick of, distaste, execrate, loathing **9** abominate, animosity, antipathy, be tired of, disliking, hostility, not care to **10** abhorrence, be averse to, feel sick at, recoil from, repugnance, resentment, shrink from **11** abomination, be hostile to, be reluctant, be unwilling, detestation, malevolence, wish to avoid **12** be repelled by **14** have no taste for, hold in contempt, revengefulness, vindictiveness **16** bear malice toward, have no stomach for **17** feel disinclined to, not have the heart to **19** regard as distasteful

hateful **4** evil, foul, mean, ugly, vile **5** nasty **6** odious, sinful, wicked **7** heinous **8** infamous, scornful **9** abhorrent, atrocious, loathsome, monstrous, obnoxious, offensive, repellent, repugnant, revolting, sickening **10** abominable, deplorable, despicable, detestable, disdainful, disgusting, forbidding, full of hate, irritating, unbearable, unpleasant, villainous **11** distasteful, intolerable, unendurable **12** contemptible, contemptuous, insufferable **13** objectionable

Hathor
origin: **8** Egyptian
goddess of: **3** joy **4** love
symbol: **4** ears, head **5** horns
patron of: **5** dance, music
personifies: **3** sky

Hat on the Bed, The
author: **9** John O'Hara

hatred **4** hate **5** venom **6** animus, enmity, malice, rancor **7** disgust, dislike, ill will **8** acrimony, aversion, bad blood, distaste, loathing **9** animosity, antipathy, hostility, revulsion **10** abhorrence, antagonism, bitterness, repugnance, resentment **11** abomination, detestation, malevolence **14** revengefulness, vindictiveness

haughtiness **4** airs **5** pride **7** conceit, hauteur **8** snobbery **9** arrogance **10** snootiness **13** condescension **14** disdainfulness, high-handedness **16** superciliousness

haughty **5** aloof **6** lordly, snooty, uppish, uppity **7** high-hat, stuck-up **8** arrogant, scornful, snobbish **9** conceited, officious **10** disdainful, high-handed, hoity-toity **11** highfalutin, overbearing, overly proud, patronizing, swell-headed **12** contemptuous **13** condescending, high and mighty

haul **3** bag, lug, tow, tug **4** cart, drag, draw, gain, jerk, move, pull, swag, take, tote, yank **5** booty, bring, carry, catch, fetch, heave, truck, yield **6** convey, profit, remove, reward, spoils, wrench **7** capture, takings **9** transport

haunches **4** buns, rear, rump, seat **5** nates **7** rear end **8** buttocks **9** fundament, posterior **12** hindquarters

haunt **3** vex **5** beset, worry **6** live in, obsess, plague, prey on **7** disturb, terrify, torment, trouble, weigh on **8** distress, frequent, frighten **9** hang out at, preoccupy, terrorize **10** hang around, hover about, loiter near, visit often **11** beat a path to **12** linger around

haunts **3** den **4** cave, hole, lair, nest **6** burrow **7** hangout **8** hideaway **9** waterhole **10** rendezvous **12** meeting place **14** gathering place **15** stamping grounds

Hauptmann, Gerhart
author of: **10** Before Dawn, The Weavers

haute couture **11** high fashion

haute cuisine **11** fine cooking **14** gourmet cooking

hauteur **5** swank **7** conceit, disdain **8** snobbery **9** arrogance, loftiness **10** snootiness **11** haughtiness **12** affectedness, snobbishness **13** condescension **14** disdainfulness, high-handedness **16** superciliousness **19** patronizing attitude

haut monde **5** elite **10** blue bloods, upper class, upper crust **11** aristocracy, high society **14** creme de la creme

Havana
capital of: **4** Cuba
gulf: **6** Mexico
landmark: **15** Cabaret Parisien **16** Castillo del Morro **17** Castillode la Punta, Jose Marti Monument **18** Castillo de la Atares, Castillo de la Fuerza, Garcia Lorca Theater **19** Maximo Gomez Monument **21** Latinamericano Stadium **22** Academy of Science of Cuba
river: **10** (Rio) Almendares
Spanish: **8** La Habana

Havasupai, Supai
location: **7** Arizona **11** Grand Canyon
related to: **7** Yavapai **8** Hualapai

have **3** buy, eat, get, own, use **4** bear, fool, gain, gull, hold, host, keep, make, must **5** beget, carry, cheat, drink, enjoy, force, grasp, ought, smoke, trick **6** accept, affirm, compel, harbor, obtain, outwit, permit, retain, suffer **7** achieve, acquire, defraud, exhibit, possess, realize, receive, swindle **8** comprise, maintain, manifest, outsmart, perceive, tolerate **9** encompass, encounter, partake of, recognize, victimize **10** comprehend, experience, understand

have a fancy for **4** want **5** covet, crave **6** desire **7** long for, wish for **8** yearn for **11** hanker after, have a yen for

have a go at **3** try **6** hazard, tackle **7** attempt **8** give a try **9** undertake **10** give a whirl **12** take a crack at, take a whack at

have a good opinion of **5** favor **6** admire, revere **7** approve, respect **9** believe in **10** appreciate

have a hand in **7** advance, forward **9** influence **10** take part in **12** contribute to **13** be conducive to, participate in **14** help bring about

have an eye on **4** want **5** covet, crave, fancy **6** desire **7** long for, pine for **8** aspire to, yearn for **9** lust after **11** have a yen for

have a yen for **4** want **5** covet, crave **6** desire **7** long for, wish for **8** yearn for **9** lust after **11** hanker after **13** have a fancy for

have bearing on **5** apply, refer **6** relate **7** concern, pertain **9** appertain, touch upon **13** be pertinent to, have respect to

have done with **4** drop, junk, shed **7** abandon, discard **9** dispose of **10** relinquish **12** dispense with

have faith in **5** trust **6** rely on **9** believe in **16** have confidence in

have guests **8** play host **9** entertain **10** give a party **13** keep open house **16** offer hospitality

Have Gun Will Travel
character: **6** Hey Boy **7** Hey Girl, Paladin
cast: **6** Lisa Lu **7** Kam Tong **12** Richard Boone
setting: **12** San Francisco **13** Hotel Carleton

have in mind **4** mean, want, wish **6** desire, intend **10** think about

haven **4** port **5** cover **6** asylum,

Hawaii
abbreviation: **2** HI
nickname: **5** Aloha **15** Sandwich Islands **20** Paradise of the Pacific
capital/largest city: **8** Honolulu
others: **3** Ewa **4** Aiea, Hana, Hilo, Laie, Paia **5** Kapaa, Kapaa, Lihue, Maili **6** Kailua, Kekaha **7** Kahului, Kaneohe, Lanikae, Wahiawa, Waianae, Wailuku
college: **9** Chaminade, Hawaii Loa **12** Brigham Young **13** Hawaii Pacific
explorer: **4** Cook **7** Gaetano
feature:
district: **7** Lahaina
national park: **9** Haleakala **15** Hawaii Volcanoes
people: **9** Hiram Fong **10** Polynesian **11** Sanford Dole **12** Daniel Inouye
island name: **4** Kure **9** Kahoolawe
big isle: **6** Hawaii
friendly isle: **7** Molokai
garden isle: **5** Kauai
gathering place: **4** Oahu
house of the sun: **9** Haleakala
mystery isle: **6** Niihau
pineapple isle: **5** Lanai
valley isle: **4** Maui
lake: **5** Waiau
land rank: **12** forty-seventh
mountain: **3** Kea, Loa **5** Kaala **6** Kohala, Kohala, Koolau **7** Kamakou, Waianae **8** Maunaloa **9** Lanaihale
highest point: **8** Maunakea
physical feature:
bay: **5** Pohue **6** Halawa, Kiholo, Mamala **7** Kamohio, Kaneohe, Waiagua **8** Kawaihae, Maunalua
beach: **7** Waikiki
canyon: **6** Waimea
channel: **3** Aua **5** Kaiwi **6** Kalohi **7** Pailolo
crater: **7** Kilauea **9** Punchbowl
desert: **3** Kau
harbor: **5** Pearl
promontory: **11** Diamond Head
valley: **3** Iao **5** Manoa
volcano: **7** Kilauea **8** Maunakea, Maunaloa **9** Haleakala
state admission: **8** Fiftieth
state bird: **4** nene **13** Hawaiian goose
state flower: **5** lehua **11** red hibiscus **15** scarlet hibiscus
state motto: **44** The Life of the Land is Perpetuated in Righteousness
state song: **11** Hawaii Ponoi **12** Our Own Hawaii
state tree: **5** kukui **9** candlenut

harbor, refuge **7** hideout, retreat, shelter **8** hideaway **9** sanctuary

have no hope 6 give up **7** despair **11** be desperate

have plenty 6 abound, be rich **8** flourish, overflow **10** be numerous, have enough **11** be plentiful **14** be well supplied **18** have more than enough

have the body
Latin: 12 habeas corpus
legal writ guards against: 19 illegal imprisonment

have too few 4 lack, want **7** be scant **9** fall short **13** be deficient in, have a dearth of **14** have a paucity of **15** be in short supply, have a scarcity of, not have enough of

having life 5 alive, vital **6** living, viable **7** animate

having the means 3 fit **4** able **6** fitted **7** capable, equal to **8** adequate **9** qualified **12** being solvent **20** having the wherewithal

Havisham, Miss
character in: 17 Great Expectations
author: 7 Dickens

havoc 4 ruin **5** chaos **8** calamity, disaster, disorder, upheaval **9** cataclysm, ruination **11** catastrophe, destruction, devastation **12** wrack and ruin **16** widespread damage

Hawaii ***see box, p. 435***

Hawaii
author: 13 James Michener

Hawaiian swimmer 14 Duke Kahanamoku

Hawaii Five-O
character: 4 Kono **5** Wo Fat **8** Ben Kokua **11** Chin Ho Kelly **13** Danny Williams **14** Steve McGarrett
cast: 4 Zulu **7** Kam Fong **8** Jack Lord **11** Khigh Dhiegh **12** Al Harrington **14** James MacArthur

hawk 4 bird, sell, vend **6** falcon, peddle **8** militant **9** accipiter, warmonger
young: 4 eyas
group of: 4 cast

Hawk, Sir Mulberry
character in: 16 Nicholas Nickleby
author: 7 Dickens

Hawkes, John
author of: 10 Second Skin **11** The Cannibal, The Lime Twig **12** The Beetle Leg **15** The Blood Oranges

Hawkeye State
nickname of: 4 Iowa

Hawkins, Jim
character in: 14 Treasure Island
author: 9 Stevenson

Hawkline Monster, The
author: 16 Richard Brautigan

Hawks, Howard
director of: 8 Red River, Rio Bravo, Scarface **11** The Big Sleep **12** Sergeant York **13** His Girl Friday **14** Bringing Up Baby **16** To Have and Have Not, Twentieth Century

Hawn, Goldie
husband: 12 Gus Trinkonis
born: 12 Washington DC
roles: 7 Laugh-In, Shampoo **8** Foul Play **12** Cactus Flower **15** Private Benjamin **18** Butterflies Are Free

hawser 4 line, rope **5** cable **7** mooring

hawthorn 9 Crataegus
varieties: 5 water, yeddo **6** Indian **7** English

Hawthorne, Nathaniel
author of: 13 The Marble Faun **14** Twice-told Tales **16** The Scarlet Letter **20** Mosses from an Old Manse **24** The House of the Seven Gables

Haydee
character in: 21 The Count of Monte Cristo
author: 5 Dumas (pere)

Haydn, Franz Joseph ***see box***

Hayes, Elvin
nickname: 4 Big E
sport: 10 basketball
team: 8 San Diego **14** Houston Rockets

Hayes, Helen
real name: 15 Helen Hayes Brown
nickname: 29 First Lady of the American Theater
son: 14 James MacArthur
roles: 7 Airport **9** Anastasia **22** The Sin of Madelon Claudet (Oscar)

Hayes, Rutherford B (Birchard) ***see box***

hayseed 4 hick, rube **5** yokel **6** rustic **7** bumpkin, peasant **10** clodhopper

Hayward, Susan
real name: 14 Edythe Marrener
husband: 10 Jess Barker
born: 10 Brooklyn NY
roles: 11 I Want to Live (Oscar) **14** I'll Cry Tomorrow, My Foolish Heart **18** With a Song in My Heart **23** Smash Up The Story of a Woman

Hayworth, Rita
real name: 22 Margarita Carmen Cansino
husband: 7 Aly Khan **10** Dick Haymes **11** Orson Welles
born: 10 Brooklyn NY
roles: 5 Gilda **9** Cover Girl **14** Separate Tables **17** Miss Sadie Thompson, You'll Never Get Rich

hazan 18 cantor of a synagogue

Haydn, Franz Joseph
born: 6 Rohrau **7** Austria
composer of: 7 The Bird, The Joke **10** Gypsy Rondo, The Seasons **11** The Creation **12** Emperor's Hymn, Wild Band Mass **13** The Apothecary **14** Lord Nelson Mass, Theresienmesse **15** Mass in Time of War **16** Il Mondo della Luna, Mariazellermesse **17** The World of the Moon **38** The Seven Last Words of Our Savior on the Cross
***quartet:* 3** Sun **4** Bird, Frog, Lark, Tost **5** Dream, Razor, Witch **6** Fifths, Maiden **7** Emperor, Erdoedy, Russian, Sunrise, The Bell, The Hunt **8** Farmyard, Horseman, The Jokes **9** The Donkey **14** The House on Fire, The Row in Vienna
***symphony:* 4** Fire **5** Paris **6** Le Midi, Le Soir, Loudon, Merkur, Oxford, The Hen **7** Evening, Le Matin, Mercury, Morning, Salomon, The Bear, The Hunt **8** Abschied, Alleluia, Drum Roll, Farewell, Military, Mourning, Surprise, The Clock, The Queen, The Storm **9** Children's, Christmas **10** La Passione, La Tempesta, The Miracle, The Passion **11** The Imperial **12** Der Philosoph, Maria Theresa, The Afternoon **13** Auf dem Anstand **14** The Philosopher **15** The Schoolmaster, Trauersymphonie, With the Horn Call **17** At the Hunting Place **18** Mit dem Hornersignal

Hayes, Rutherford B (Birchard)
nickname: **8** Rud Hayes
presidential rank: **10** nineteenth
party: **10** Republican
state represented: **2** OH
defeated: **5** (Green Clay) Smith **6** (James B) Walker, (Peter) Cooper, (Samuel Jones) Tilden
vice president: **7** (William Almon) Wheeler
cabinet:
state: **6** (William Maxwell) Evarts
treasury: **7** (John) Sherman
war: **6** (Alexander) Ramsey **7** (George Washington) McCrary
attorney general: **6** (Charles) Devens
navy: **4** (Nathan) Goff (Jr) **8** (Richard Wigginton) Thompson
postmaster general: **3** (David McKendree) Key **7** (Horace) Maynard
interior: **6** (Carl) Schurz
born: **10** Delaware OH
died/buried: **9** Fremont OH
education:
preparatory school: **4** Webb
College: **6** Kenyon
Law School: **7** Harvard
religion: **9** Methodist
political career: **24** US House of Representatives
city solicitor of: **10** Cincinnati
governor of: **4** Ohio
civilian career: **6** farmer, lawyer
military service: **6** US Army **8** Civil War **12** Ohio infantry **18** brevet major general
notable events of lifetime/term: **10** Depression (of 1873) **15** railroad strikes (of 1877) **18** civil service reform **24** specie payments resumption
Act: **26** Bland-Allison Silver Purchase
father: **10** Rutherford
mother: **6** Sophia (Birchard)
siblings: **7** Lorenzo **11** Sarah Sophia **13** Fanny Arabella
wife: **4** Lucy (Ware Webb)
children: **5** Fanny **9** James Webb (renamed Webb Cook) **11** George Crook **12** Manning Force, Scott Russell **14** Joseph Thompson, Sardis Birchard (renamed Birchard Austin) **15** Rutherford Platt

hazard **3** bet **4** dare, luck, risk **5** fluke, guess, offer, peril, stake, wager **6** chance, danger, expose, gamble, menace, mishap, submit, threat **7** advance, daresay, imperil, pitfall, presume, proffer, suppose, venture **8** accident, chance it, endanger, jeopardy, theorize, threaten, throw out **9** mischance, speculate, tempt fate, volunteer **10** conjecture, jeopardize, misfortune **11** coincidence, hypothesize, imperilment, take a chance, trust to luck **12** endangerment, happenstance, stroke of luck

Hazard of New Fortunes, A
author: **18** William Dean Howells

hazardous **4** iffy **5** risky, shaky **6** chancy, unsafe, unsure **7** dubious, unsound **8** doubtful, insecure, perilous, unstable **9** dangerous, uncertain **10** precarious, unreliable **11** speculative, threatening **13** untrustworthy

haze **3** fog **4** daze, film, mist, pall, veil **5** cloak, cloud, smoke, vapor **6** mantle, muddle, screen **9** fogginess **12** befuddlement, bewilderment **16** state of confusion

hazel **3** nut **4** tree **5** brown, shrub, tawny **8** brownish **14** yellowish-brown
varieties: **4** tree **5** Chile, witch **6** winter **7** Chinese, Turkish **8** American, European, Japanese **11** spike winter **12** Chinese witch **13** Japanese witch **15** buttercup winter

Hazel
character: **12** George Baxter, Harold Baxter **13** Dorothy Baxter
cast: **9** Don DeFore **12** Shirley Booth, Whitney Blake **13** Bobby Buntrock
creator: **6** Ted Key

hazelnut **7** Corylus
varieties: **6** beaked **7** Chinese, Turkish **8** American, European, Japanese

Hazlitt, William
author of: **17** The Spirit of the Age **32** The Characters of Shakespeare's Plays

hazy **3** dim **5** dusky, faint, filmy, foggy, misty, murky, smoky, vague **6** bleary, blurry, cloudy, smoggy, veiled **7** bleared, general, muddled, obscure, unclear **8** confused, nebulous, overcast **9** ambiguous, uncertain **10** ill-defined, indefinite

head ***see box, p. 438***

head
contains: **4** eyes **5** brain, mouth, skull **9** braincase **10** optic nerve **12** ocular muscle **13** cranial cavity, lacrimal organ, orbital cavity **14** buccaval cavity

headache **5** trial **6** strain, stress **7** problem, trouble **8** migraine, nuisance **10** affliction, difficulty **13** inconvenience, pain in the neck

headdress **3** cap, hat **6** bonnet **7** chapeau **12** headcovering

headland **4** bank, crag **5** bluff, cliff **8** palisade **9** precipice **10** promontory

headlong **6** abrupt **8** abruptly, heedless, pell-mell, reckless **9** headfirst, impetuous **10** heedlessly, recklessly **11** impetuously, precipitate, precipitous **13** head over heels, precipitously

Headlong Hall
author: **17** Thomas Love Peacock

headman **5** chief **6** leader **7** foreman **8** alderman, princeps **9** commander **10** councilman, supervisor **14** public official, superintendent

head-on **6** direct **7** frontal **10** face-to-face

headshrinker **6** shrink **7** analyst **12** psychiatrist **13** psychoanalyst

headstrong **4** rash **6** dogged, mulish, unruly **7** defiant, froward, willful **8** contrary, obdurate, reckless, stubborn **9** hotheaded, imprudent, impulsive, obstinate, pigheaded

head **2** go, IQ **3** aim, CEO, end, hie, tip, top **4** acme, apex, bent, boss, czar, font, fore, gift, king, lead, main, mind, peak, rise, rule, turn, well **5** begin, brain, chief, crest, crown, drive, first, front, guide, pilot, prime, queen, ruler, start, steer **6** climax, crisis, direct, genius, govern, launch, leader, manage, origin, ruling, source, spring, summit, talent, vertex, zenith **7** ability, admiral, captain, command, conduct, control, foreman, general, go first, highest, leading, make for, manager, marshal, monarch, precede, premier, primary, proceed, ranking, supreme, topmost **8** aptitude, be head of, big wheel, capacity, chairman, dictator, director, dominant, foremost, fountain, fruition, headmost, initiate, judgment, managing, pinnacle, start off, superior, suzerain, upper end **9** acuteness, beginning, commander, commodore, extremity, forefront, front rank, governing, intellect, introduce, mentality, paramount, potentate, president, principal, sovereign, supervise, uppermost **10** administer, be master of, birthplace, cleverness, commandant, commanding, conclusion, first place, gray matter, inaugurate, lead the way, move toward, perception, preeminent, supervisor, wellspring **11** be at the helm, controlling, culmination, discernment, forward part, highest rank, officiate at, preside over, superintend, take the lead, termination **12** apprehension, field marshal, fountainhead, guiding light, place of honor, take charge of, take the reins, turning point, utmost extent **13** administrator, go at the head of, most prominent, prime minister, understanding **14** chief executive, highest ranking, superintendent **15** be in the vanguard, make a beeline for, quickness of mind **16** commander-in-chief, direct one's course, inevitable result **17** commanding general, have authority over **18** be in the driver's seat, chairman of the board, go in the direction of **21** chief executive officer

10 bullheaded, incautious, refractory **11** intractable **12** incorrigible, recalcitrant, ungovernable, unmanageable **14** uncontrollable **22** bent on having one's own way

heady **4** hard **6** potent, strong **8** alluring, exciting, inviting, stirring, tempting **9** seductive, thrilling **10** high-octane **11** high-voltage, tantalizing **12** exhilarating, intoxicating

heal **4** cure, knit, mend **5** right, salve, treat **6** heal up, remedy, settle, soothe **7** compose, get well, improve, recover, rectify, relieve **8** heal over, make well **9** alleviate, make whole, reconcile **10** conciliate, convalesce, recuperate **11** set to rights **14** make harmonious, return to health **20** restore good relations

healed **4** knit **5** cured **6** mended **7** got well **8** relieved

healing **6** curing **7** mending **8** knitting, soothing **9** emollient, improving, restoring **10** making well **11** restorative **13** strengthening
god of: **6** Apollo **7** Phoebus, Pythius **9** Asclepius, Musagetes **11** Aesculapius
goddess of: **4** Iaso

health **5** vigor **7** fitness, stamina **8** strength, vitality **9** hardihood, hardiness, well-being **10** robustness **16** general condition **17** physical condition
goddess of: **6** Hygeia

healthful **7** healthy **8** hygienic, salutary **9** wholesome **10** beneficial, nourishing, nutritious, salubrious **12** healthgiving, invigorating

healthiness **6** health **9** good shape, soundness **10** good health, robustness **12** salutariness **13** good condition, healthfulness, wholesomeness **14** salubriousness

healthy **3** fit **4** hale **5** hardy, sound **6** hearty, robust, strong, sturdy **8** vigorous **9** in the pink **10** able-bodied **12** in fine fettle **18** sound of mind and limb

heap **3** gob, lot **4** fill, gobs, hunk, load, lots, lump, mass, mess, pack, pile, slew **5** amass, award, batch, bunch, flood, group, mound, ocean, slews, stack, store, world **6** accord, assign, bundle, deluge, engulf, gather, jumble, load up, oceans, oodles, pile up, plenty, worlds **7** barrels, cluster, collect, mete out, present **8** good deal, inundate, pour upon **9** abundance, gathering, great deal, multitude, profusion **10** assemblage, collection, shower upon **11** aggregation, concentrate **12** accumulation **13** agglomeration

heap up **5** amass **6** pile up **7** stack up **10** accumulate

hear **4** heed **5** admit, favor, grant, judge, learn **6** attend, be told, gather, look on **7** approve, concede, examine, find out, receive, witness **8** accede to, appear at, discover, hear tell, hold with, listen to **9** acquiesce, ascertain, hearken to **10** understand **11** acknowledge

hear!
French: **4** oyez
cry used by: **10** court crier
preceded: **12** proclamation

hearing **5** probe, sound **6** review **7** council, earshot, inquiry **8** audience **9** interview **10** conference **11** examination, questioning **12** consultation **13** interrogation, investigation

hearken to **4** heed, mark, mind **6** attend **8** listen to **11** take to heart **14** pay attention to

Hearns, Thomas
nickname: **6** Hitman
sport: **6** boxing
class: **12** middleweight, welterweight

hearsay **4** talk **5** rumor **6** gossip, report **8** idle talk **9** grapevine **11** scuttlebutt

heart **3** hub, nub **4** base, core, crux, guts, love, meat, mood, pith, root, soul **5** humor, pluck, spunk, valor **6** center, daring, desire, kernel, middle, nature, source, spirit **7** bravery, charity, courage, emotion, essence, nucleus, stomach **8** audacity, backbone, boldness, clemency, feelings, firmness, fondness, gameness, interior, main part, sympathy **9** affection, fortitude, gallantry, inner part, rudiments, sentiment, tolerance **10** brass tacks, compassion, enthusiasm, essentials, foundation, gentleness, indulgence, manfulness, principles, resolution, tenderness, true nature **11** busiest part, central part, disposition, forgiveness, nitty-gritty, temperament **12** fearlessness, fundamentals, quintessence, resoluteness **13** audaciousness
part: **5** aorta, valve **6** atrium **7** chamber **9** ventricle
pumps: **5** blood

heartache **3** woe **4** pain

5 grief 6 misery, sorrow 7 anguish, sadness, torment, trouble 8 distress 9 suffering 11 tribulation, unhappiness

heartbreaker 4 vamp 5 flirt, tease 8 coquette

Heartbreak House
author: 17 George Bernard Shaw

hearten 4 abet 5 cheer 6 assure, solace 7 animate, cheer up, comfort, console, enliven, gladden 8 brighten, embolden, energize, inspirit, reassure 9 encourage 10 invigorate

heartening 7 hopeful 9 favorable 10 auspicious, reassuring 11 encouraging

heartfelt 4 deep, full 5 total 6 ardent, devout, entire, honest 7 earnest, fervent, genuine, intense, sincere 8 complete, profound, thorough 10 keenly felt 12 all-inclusive, wholehearted

hearth 4 home 5 abode, house 8 fireside 9 fireplace, household 10 family life 12 family circle 13 chimney corner
goddess of: 4 Caca 5 Salus, Vesta 6 Hestia

Heart Is a Lonely Hunter, The
author: 15 Carson McCullers
character: 8 Mr Singer 9 Mick Kelly 10 Dr Copeland, Jake Blount 11 Biff Brannon

heartless 4 cold, mean 5 cruel 6 brutal, savage, unkind 7 callous, inhuman, unmoved 8 pitiless, ruthless, uncaring 9 unfeeling, unpitying, unstirred 10 unmerciful 11 coldhearted, cold-blooded, hardhearted, insensitive 12 cruelhearted, unresponsive 13 unsympathetic

Heart of Darkness
author: 12 Joseph Conrad
character: 5 Kurtz 7 Marlowe

Heart of Dixie
nickname of: 7 Alabama

Heart of Juliet Jones, The
creator: 9 Stan Drake
character: 3 Eve

Heart of Midlothian, The
author: 14 Sir Walter Scott

Heart of the Matter, The
author: 12 Graham Greene
character: 5 Yusef 6 Wilson 7 Mrs Rolt 9 Mrs Scobie 11 Major Scobie

heart-stopper 5 belle 6 beauty 7 charmer, stunner 8 knockout 10 good-looker 13 beautiful girl 14 beautiful woman

hearty 4 hale, warm, well 5 ample, hardy, sound 6 lively, robust, strong 7 cordial, genuine, healthy, profuse, sincere, zestful 8 complete, effusive, generous, thorough, vigorous 9 heartfelt, unbounded 10 unreserved 12 enthusiastic, unrestrained, wholehearted 13 physically fit

hearty appetite
French: 10 bon appetit

Heaslop, Ronald
character in: 15 A Passage to India
author: 7 Forster

heat 3 fry 4 bake, boil, cook, sear, stew, warm, zeal 5 ardor, broil, roast, steam 6 braise, climax, fervor, height, simmer, stress, thrill, warmth, warm up 7 hotness, make hot, passion, rapture, swelter 8 fervency, hot spell, warmness 9 eagerness, intensity, transport 10 enthusiasm, excitement 12 bring to a boil

heated 3 hot 5 angry, fiery, irate 6 bitter, fierce, raging, stormy 7 excited, fervent, furious, intense, violent 8 frenzied, inflamed, vehement 9 emotional 10 infuriated, passionate 11 impassioned, tempestuous

heated discussion 7 dispute 8 argument 10 war of words 11 controversy 12 disagreement

heath 5 Erica
varieties: 4 Tree 5 Berry, Besom, Irish, Otago, Spike 6 Dorset, Scotch, Spring 7 Cornish, Fringed, Spanish, Twisted 9 Cranberry 11 Cross-leaved

Heathcliff
character in: 16 Wuthering Heights
author: 6 Bronte

heathen 3 goy 4 boor 5 pagan 6 savage 7 atheist, gentile, infidel 8 agnostic, idolator 9 barbarian, ignoramus 10 polytheist, troglodyte, unbeliever 11 non-believer 17 uncivilized native

heather 7 Calluna
varieties: 3 Bog, Red 4 Bell, Snow 5 Beach, False, White 6 French, Golden, Scotch 8 Corsican, Mountain 9 Christmas 11 White winter 13 Mediterranean 18 Everblooming French

Heat of the Day, The
author: 14 Elizabeth Bowen

heat up 3 fan 4 goad, warm, whet 6 arouse 7 enhance, sharpen 8 increase 9 aggravate, intensify 10 strengthen

heave 3 peg, pry, sob 4 arch, blow, cast, emit, fire, hurl, lift, moan, pant, puff, puke, toss 5 boost, bulge, chuck, eject, fling, groan, hoist, lever, pitch, raise, retch, sling, surge, swell, throw, vomit 6 dilate, drag up, draw up, exhale, expand, haul up, launch, let fly, propel, pull up, tilt up, yank up 7 elevate 8 thrust up 9 discharge, palpitate 11 regurgitate

heaven, Heaven, the Heavens 3 wow 4 Zion 5 bliss, glory, mercy, space 6 my oh my, utopia 7 delight, ecstasy, Elysium, my stars, nirvana, Olympus, rapture 8 boy oh boy, goodness, land sake, paradise, Valhalla 9 afterlife, dreamland, next world, Shangri-la 10 afterworld, Beulah Land, life beyond, outer space, perfection, sheer bliss 11 enchantment, the Holy City, world beyond, world to come 12 eternal bliss, good gracious, New Jerusalem, the City of God, the firmament 13 Abraham's bosom, Elysian fields, seventh heaven 14 heavens to Betsy, our eternal home 15 life everlasting, our Father's house, the heavenly city 16 goodness gracious, Isle of the Blessed, supreme happiness, the abode of saints, the Celestial City, the vault of heaven 17 complete happiness, the wild blue yonder 18 Island of the Blessed, the celestial sphere, the heavenly kingdom, the kingdom of Heaven 19 the celestial expanse 21 the happy hunting ground
god of: 2 An 3 Anu 4 Jove, Zeus 7 Jupiter

Heaven Can Wait (1943)
director: 13 Ernst Lubitsch
cast: 9 Don Ameche 11 Gene Tierney 12 Marjorie Main 13 Charles Coburn

Heaven Can Wait (1978)
director: 9 Buck Henry 12 Warren Beatty
cast: 10 Dyan Cannon, Jack Warden 12 Warren Beatty 13 Julie Christie
remake of: 17 Here Comes Mr Jordan

heavenly 6 divine 7 angelic, blessed, saintly, sublime 8 beatific, blissful

Heavens and Earth
author: **19** Stephen Vincent Benet

Heaven's My Destination
author: **14** Thornton Wilder

heavy ***see box***

heavy-handed **5** harsh **6** clumsy **7** awkward **8** bungling **9** graceless, maladroit **10** blundering, oppressive, ungraceful

heavyhearted **3** sad **4** glum **6** dismal, gloomy, morose **7** doleful, forlorn, joyless, unhappy **8** dejected, downcast **9** cheerless, depressed, sorrowful **10** despondent, melancholy **11** downhearted **14** down in the dumps, down in the mouth

Hebe
goddess of: **5** youth **6** spring
father: **4** Zeus
mother: **4** Hera
brother: **4** Ares
husband: **8** Hercules
handmaiden to: **4** gods
corresponds to: **8** Juventas

Heber
wife: **4** Jael

Hebrew alphabet
or: **5** aleph
b/v: **4** beth
g: **5** gimel
d: **6** daleth
h: **2** he **5** cheth
v/w: **3** vav
z: **5** zayin
y/j/i: **3** yod
k/kh: **4** kaph
l: **5** lamed
m: **3** men
n: **3** nun
`: **4** ayin
p/f: **2** pe
k: **4** koph
r: **4** resh
sh/s: **4** shin
s: **3** sin **4** sadi **6** samekh
t: **3** tav **4** teth

Hebrew Judge **4** Ehud, Elon, Jair, Tola **5** Abdon, Ibzan **6** Gideon, Samson, Samuel **7** Deborah, Othniel, Shamgar **8** Jephthah

Hebrew months
first: **4** Ahib, Nisn **6** Ehanim, Tishri
second: **3** Bul, Civ **4** Iyar **7** Heshvan
third: **5** Sivan **6** Kislev
fourth: **5** Tebet **6** Tammuz, Tebeth
fifth: **2** Ab **7** Shelbat
sixth: **4** Adar, Elul **6** Veadar
seventh: **4** Abib **5** Nisan **6** Tishri **7** Ethanim
eighth: **3** Zif **4** Iyer **11** Marcheshvan
ninth: **5** Sivan **7** Chislev
tenth: **6** Tabeth, Tammuz
eleventh: **2** Ab **6** Shebat
twelfth: **4** Adar, Elul

Hecabe *see* **6** Hecuba

Hecaleius
epithet of: **4** Zeus

he carved it
Latin: **8** sculpsit

Hecate
also: **6** Hekate
goddess of: **5** earth, Hades
associated with: **6** hounds **7** sorcery **10** crossroads
corresponds to: **5** Brimo

Hecatonchires
also: **9** Centimani
form: **5** giant
names: **5** Gyges **6** Cottus **8** Briareus
father: **6** Uranus
mother: **4** Gaea
number of heads: **5** fifty
number of arms: **10** one hundred

heckle **3** boo **4** bait, hiss, hoot, mock, ride, twit **5** annoy, bully, chivy, harry, hound, taunt **6** badger, harass, harrow, hector, jeer at, molest, needle **7** provoke **9** shout down

hectare
abbreviation of: **2** ha

hectic **3** mad **4** wild **6** stormy **7** chaotic, frantic, furious **8** feverish, frenetic, frenzied, headlong **9** breakneck, turbulent **10** tumultuous

hectoliter
abbreviation of: **2** hl

hectometer
abbreviation of: **2** hm

hector **4** bait, ride **5** bully, harry, hound, tease, worry **6** badger, harass, needle, plague **7** torment

Hector
father: **5** Priam
mother: **6** Hecuba
brother: **5** Paris
sister: **9** Cassandra
wife: **10** Andromache
son: **8** Astyanax
hero of: **9** Trojan War
killed by: **8** Achilles

Hecuba
also: **5** Maera **6** Hecabe
father: **5** Atlas
husband: **5** Priam **8** Tegeates
son: **5** Paris **6** Hector **7** Helenus, Polites, Troilus **9** Deiphobus, Polydorus
daughter: **6** Creusa **7** Laodice **8** Polyxena **9** Cassandra
changed into: **3** dog **5** bitch
hound of: **7** Icarius

Hecuba
author: **9** Euripides
character: **8** Odysseus, Polyxena **9** Agamemnon, Polydorus **10** Polymestor

Hedda Gabler
author: **11** Henrik Ibsen
character: **10** Judge Brack **11** Hedda Tesman, Thea Elvsted **12** George Tesman **13** Eilert Lovberg **17** Miss Juliana Tesman

heder **12** Jewish school

heavy **3** big, fat, sad **4** deep, dull, full, hard, lazy, slow **5** broad, bulky, dense, grave, gross, harsh, hefty, large, obese, plump, rough, stout, thick **6** clumsy, coarse, deadly, dreary, fierce, gloomy, leaden, pained, portly, raging, rugged, savage, solemn, strong, sturdy, torpid, woeful **7** awesome, complex, copious, doleful, forlorn, furious, intense, joyless, languid, lumpish, massive, notable, onerous, profuse, roaring, ruinous, serious, tearful, tedious, violent, weighty **8** abundant, agonized, burdened, crushing, cumbrous, damaging, dejected, desolate, downcast, forceful, grieving, grievous, imposing, lifeless, listless, mournful, pedantic, profound, seething, sluggish, stricken, tiresome, unwieldy **9** apathetic, cheerless, corpulent, depressed, difficult, excessive, extensive, harrowing, important, injurious, laborious, lethargic, lumbering, miserable, momentous, ponderous, rampaging, sorrowful, turbulent, wearisome **10** burdensome, calamitous, cumbersome, distressed, full of care, immoderate, impressive, inordinate, melancholy, monotonous, noteworthy, oppressive, overweight, pernicious, phlegmatic, unbearable, unstinting **11** crestfallen, deleterious, destructive, detrimental, distressing, extravagant, intemperate, intolerable, significant, tempestuous, unendurable, unrelenting, unremitting **12** considerable, disconsolate, hard to endure, overwhelming, unrestrained **13** consequential, grief-stricken, of great import **16** laden with sorrows **18** of great consequence

hedge **3** hem **4** duck, edge, ring, wall **5** bound, dodge, evade, fence, guard, hem in, limit **6** border, margin, shut in, waffle **7** barrier, enclose, mark off, outline **8** encircle, hedgerow, surround **9** be evasive, delineate, demarcate, insurance, pussyfoot, temporize **10** equivocate, protection **11** delineation, row of bushes **12** compensation **13** circumference, fence of shrubs **14** beg the question, counterbalance **17** beat around the bush

he died
Latin: **5** obiit

he does not pursue
Latin: **14** non prosequitur

hedonist **8** Sybarite **9** debauchee, libertine **10** dissipater, profligate, sensualist, voluptuary **14** pleasure seeker

hedonistic **7** sensual **9** epicurean, libertine, sybaritic **10** voluptuous **11** intemperate **13** self-indulgent **15** pleasure-seeking

he drew this
Latin: **10** delineavit

Hedrick, Zelma Kathryn
real name of: **14** Kathryn Grayson

heed **4** care, mind, obey **5** bow to, pains, study **6** concur, follow, hold to, notice, regard **7** defer to, observe, perusal, respect, yield to **8** accede to, consider, listen to, prudence, scrutiny, submit to **9** attention, be ruled by, give ear to **10** bear in mind comply with, precaution, take note of **11** carefulness, examination, heedfulness, mindfulness, observation, take to heart **12** take notice of **13** attentiveness **14** fastidiousness, meticulousness, pay attention to, scrupulousness **17** conscientiousness

heedful **4** wary **5** alert, aware, cagey, chary **7** alive to, careful, mindful, prudent **8** cautious, discreet, vigilant, watchful **9** attentive, concerned, conscious

heedless **3** lax **4** rash **5** slack **6** remiss, unwary **7** foolish, unaware, witless **8** careless, mindless, reckless, uncaring **9** foolhardy, frivolous, impetuous, imprudent, negligent, oblivious, unheeding, unmindful **10** incautious, neglectful, unthinking, unwatchful **11** harebrained, improvident, inattentive, thoughtless, unconcerned, unobservant, unobserving **12** happy-go-lucky **14** scatterbrained

heedlessly **5** blind **6** rashly **8** headlong **9** foolishly, witlessly **10** carelessly, mindlessly, recklessly **11** frivolously, impetuously, impulsively, negligently, unmindfully **12** neglectfully, unthinkingly **13** inattentively, thoughtlessly, unconcernedly **15** inconsiderately, uncooperatively

heedlessness **8** rashness **9** unconcern **10** negligence **11** inattention, unawareness **12** carelessness, indiscretion, mindlessness, recklessness **13** unmindfulness **15** thoughtlessness **16** irresponsibility

heel **3** cad, cur, end, rat **4** list, rind, tilt **5** churl, crust, louse **6** rotter **7** bounder, caitiff, dastard

he engraved it
Latin: **8** sculpsit

Heep, Uriah
character in: **16** David Copperfield
author: **7** Dickens

he flourished
Latin: **7** floruit

hefty **3** big **5** beefy, bulky, burly, heavy, husky, large, stout **6** brawny, hearty, mighty, robust, rugged, strong, sturdy **7** hulking, massive, sizable, weighty, well-fed **8** muscular, powerful, stalwart, thickset **9** corpulent, strapping **11** substantial

Hegeleos
father: **8** Tyrsenus

Hegemone
origin: **8** Athenian
member of: **6** Graces

hegemony **7** control **9** authority, dominance, influence, supremacy

Heggen, Thomas
author of: **9** Mr Roberts

hegira **6** exodus, flight **7** journey

Heh *see* **6** Ogdoad

he himself said it
Latin: **9** ipse dixit

Heidrun
origin: **12** Scandinavian
form: **4** goat
yields: **4** mead
feeds warriors in: **8** Valhalla

height **4** acme, apex, hill, peak, rise **5** bluff, cliff, crest, knoll, limit, mound, tower **6** apogee, heyday, summit, zenith **7** hilltop, maximum, plateau **8** altitude, eminence, highland, highness, mountain, palisade, pinnacle, tallness, ultimate **9** elevation, extremity, flowering, high point, loftiness, supremacy **10** perfection, promontory **11** culmination **12** consummation, upward extent, utmost degree, vantage point

heighten **5** raise **7** elevate **8** increase **9** aggravate, intensify

heil **4** hail

Heimberger, Eddie Albert
real name of: **11** Eddie Albert

Heimdall
origin: **12** Scandinavian
god of: **4** dawn **5** light
number of mothers: **4** nine
guards: **7** bifrost **13** rainbow bridge
killed by: **4** Loki
noted for: **7** hearing **8** eyesight

Heine, Heinrich
author of: **9** Atta Troll **11** Book of Songs **19** Germany A Winter's Tale

Heinlein, Robert
author of: **10** Double Star **16** Starship Troopers **20** The Green Hills of Earth **22** Stranger in a Strange Land **23** The Moon Is a Harsh Mistress

heinous **4** evil, foul, vile **5** gross, nasty **6** grisly, horrid, odious, sinful, wicked **7** beastly, ghastly, hideous, inhuman, vicious **8** infamous, shocking, terrible **9** abhorrent, atrocious, loathsome, monstrous, nefarious, offensive, repugnant, repulsive, revolting, sickening **10** abominable, deplorable, despicable, detestable, disgusting, iniquitous, outrageous, scandalous, villainous **11** disgraceful, distasteful **12** contemptible **13** objectionable, reprehensible

heinousness **4** evil **7** outrage **8** atrocity, baseness, enormity, foulness, savagery, vileness, villainy **9** barbarity, depravity, malignity **10** inhumanity **13** loathsomeness, monstrousness **14** outrageousness

heir, heiress **7** legatee **9** inheritor **10** inheritrix **11** beneficiary, inheritress **12** heir apparent **15** heir presumptive

Heiress, The
director: **12** William Wyler
based on novel by: **10** Henry James

entitled: **16** Washington Square
cast: **13** Miriam Hopkins **15** Montgomery Clift, Ralph Richardson **17** Olivia de Havilland
score: **12** Aaron Copland
Oscar for: **7** actress (de Havilland)

Hekate *see* **6** Hecate

Hel
origin: **12** Scandinavian
goddess of: **5** death
rules: **8** Niflheim
father: **4** Loki
mother: **9** Angerboda, Angrbodha, Angurboda
brother: **6** Fenrir, Fenris **11** Iormungandr, Jormungandr **14** Midgard Serpent
color of body: **4** blue **5** flesh
home of: **4** dead

Helen
father: **4** Zeus
mother: **4** Leda
brother: **6** Castor, Pollux
sister: **8** Timandra **12** Clytemnestra
husband: **8** Menelaus
abducted by: **5** Paris
carried off to: **4** Troy
abduction caused: **9** Trojan War

Helena
character in: **20** All's Well That Ends Well **21** A Midsummer Night's Dream
author: **11** Shakespeare

Helenor
mentioned in: **6** Aeneid
position: **6** prince
home: **5** Lydia
accompanied: **6** Aeneas

Heliadae
sons of: **6** Helius, Rhodes

helicopter
invented by: **8** Sikorsky

Heliopolis
city of: **2** On

Helios
origin: **5** Greek
god of: **3** sun
father: **8** Hyperion
mother: **4** Thia
children: **5** Circe **6** Aeetes **8** Phaethon
corresponds to: **3** Sol

heliotrope **12** Heliotropium
varieties: **6** garden, winter, yellow **7** seaside

helium
chemical symbol: **2** He

hell, Hell **5** agony, grief, Hades **6** misery, the pit **7** Abaddon, anguish, despair, Gehenna, inferno, remorse, torment **8** Appolyons, hell fire, the abyss **9** martyrdom, perdition, suffering **10** lake of fire **12** hopelessness, wretchedness **13** bottomless pit, Satan's kingdom, the lower world, the underworld **14** place of the lost, the Devil's house, the nether world, the shades below **15** everlasting fire, home of lost souls, infernal regions **16** abode of the damned

Helle
father: **7** Athamas
mother: **7** Nephele
stepmother: **3** Ino
brother: **7** Phrixus
death by: **8** drowning

Hellen
king of: **8** Thessaly
father: **9** Deucalion
mother: **6** Pyrrha
wife: **6** Orseis
son: **5** Dorus **6** Aeolus, Xuthus
ancestor of: **8** Hellenes

Hellenic Republic *see* **6** Greece

Heller, Joseph
author of: **10** Good as Gold **14** Catch-Twenty-Two **17** Something Happened

hellion **5** devil, rogue, scamp **9** scoundrel **13** mischief-maker

hellish **4** foul, vile **5** awful **6** brutal **7** hateful **8** accursed, damnable, dreadful, horrible, infernal **9** atrocious, revolting **10** abominable, disgusting

Hellman, Lillian
author of: **5** Maybe **10** Pentimento **13** Scoundrel Time **14** The Little Foxes, Toys in the Attic **15** Watch on the Rhine **16** The Children's Hour **17** An Unfinished Woman **22** Another Part of the Forest

hello
French: **7** bonjour
German: **8** guten tag
Spanish: **10** buenos dias
Italian: **4** ciao **10** buon giorno
Latin: **5** salve

Hello-Central
character in: **36** A Connecticut Yankee in King Arthur's Court
author: **5** Twain

help ***see box***

helper **3** aid **4** aide **5** angel **6** backer, deputy, patron, second **7** adjunct, partner, servant **8** adjutant, advocate, champion, confrere, coworker, employee, retainer **9** assistant, associate, auxiliary, colleague, man Friday, right hand, supporter **10** accomplice, aide-de-camp, apprentice, benefactor, girl Friday **11** confederate, helping hand, subordinate **12** collaborator, right-hand man **13** good samaritan **14** fairy godmother

helpful **4** fine, good, kind, nice **6** usable, useful **8** obliging, splendid, valuable **9** excellent, favorable, practical **10** beneficial, profitable, supportive **11** considerate, cooperative, serviceable **12** advantageous, constructive **13** accommodating

helping hand **3** aid **4** aide, hand **5** boost **6** assist, hand up, helper, succor **7** abettor, support **9** assistant **10** assistance

helplessness **8** weakness **9** impotence, inability, infirmity **10** dependence, feebleness, ineptitude **12** incapability, incompetence, inefficiency **13** powerlessness, vulnerability

help **3** aid **4** back, balm, calm, care, crew, cure, ease, gift, lift, save **5** allay, emend, force, guide, hands, salve, serve, staff **6** advice, advise, assist, give to, menial, relief, remedy, rescue, soothe, succor, uphold **7** advance, backing, console, correct, endorse, further, helpers, improve, nurture, promote, rectify, relieve, servant, service, stand by, support, welfare, workers, workmen **8** advocate, befriend, champion, domestic, factotum, farmhand, guidance, laborers, maintain, mitigate, retainer, retrieve, side with **9** alleviate, chip in for, employees, encourage, extricate, lend a hand, make whole, promotion, put at ease, underling, workhands, work force **10** ameliorate, apprentice, assistance, assistants, bring round, corrective, friendship, go to bat for, hired hands, kind regard, minister to, preventive, protection, stick up for **11** advancement, benevolence, cooperation, endorsement, furtherance, good offices, helping hand, make healthy, restorative **12** bring through, contribute to, contribution, hired helpers, intercede for **13** collaboration, cooperate with, encouragement, take the part of

Helsinki
capital of: **7** Finland

hem **3** box, rim **4** bind, brim, edge, welt **5** bound, brink, skirt, verge **6** border, edging, fringe, impede, margin, turn up **7** confine, enclose, stammer, stutter, turning **8** compress, encircle, restrain, surround

he made it
Latin: **5** fecit

Hemera
father: **6** Erebus
mother: **3** Nyx
corresponds to: **3** Eos

Hemerasia
epithet of: **7** Artemis
means: **13** she who soothes

hem in **4** best **5** fence **7** besiege, confine, enclose **8** encircle, surround

Hemingway, Ernest
author of: **9** In Our Time **14** A Moveable Feast **15** A Farewell to Arms, The Sun Also Rises **16** To Have and Have Not **18** Islands in the Stream, The Old Man and the Sea **19** For Whom the Bell Tolls **21** The Snows of Kilimanjaro **34** The Short Happy Life of Francis Macomber

hemiptera
class: **8** hexapoda
phylum: **10** arthropoda
group: **3** bug

Hemithea
father: **6** Cycnus
mother: **7** Proclea
sister: **5** Tenes
pursued by: **8** Achilles
swallowed up by: **5** earth

hemlock **5** Tsuga **15** Conium maculatum
varieties: **5** Dwarf, Water **6** Canada, Ground, Poison **7** Siebold, Spotted, Western **8** Carolina, Japanese, Mountain

hemp **14** Cannabis sativa
varieties: **3** Bog **5** Cuban, Sisal **6** Deccan, Indian, Manila **7** African **8** Deckaner **9** Bowstring, Mauritius **10** New Zealand **13** Colorado River **15** Ceylon bowstring, Indian bowstring **16** African bowstring

hen
young: **6** pullet

Henchard, Michael
character in: **22** The Mayor of Casterbridge
author: **5** Hardy

henchman **4** goon, thug **6** flunky, lackey, minion, stooge, yes-man **7** gorilla **8** hanger-on, hireling, retainer **9** attendant, bodyguard **10** hatchet man, lieutenant **12** right-hand man, strong-arm man

Henderson, Marge
creator/artist of: **10** Little Lulu

Henioche
epithet of: **4** Hera
means: **10** charioteer

henna **3** dye **5** rinse **6** auburn, russet **8** cinnamon **11** rust-colored **12** reddish-brown **13** copper-colored

henpecked **4** meek **5** timid **6** docile **8** obedient **10** browbeaten, submissive, wife-ridden **11** unassertive

Henry, Frederic
character in: **15** A Farewell to Arms
author: **9** Hemingway

Henry Esmond
author: **16** William Thackeray
character: **5** Frank **7** Beatrix **9** Lord Mohun **10** Father Holt **11** James Stuart **12** Rachel Esmond **13** Francis Esmond

Henry IV
author: **18** William Shakespeare
character: **7** Hotspur **11** Prince Henry, Thomas Percy **14** Edmund Mortimer, Sir Walter Blunt **15** John of Lancaster, Mistress Quickly, Sir John Falstaff **18** Earl of Westmoreland, King Henry the Fourth

Henry V
author: **18** William Shakespeare
character: **7** Dauphin, Montjoy **15** Charles the Sixth (King of France) **17** Princess Katharine
director: **15** Laurence Olivier
cast: **11** Leslie Banks **12** Robert Newton **13** Renee Asherson **15** Laurence Olivier

Henry VI
author: **18** William Shakespeare
character: **6** Edward (Prince of Wales) **7** Charles (Dauphin of France), Eleanor, Louis XI (King of France) **8** Lady Bona, Lady Grey **9** Joan of Arc **10** Lord Talbot **11** Bolingbroke **12** John Beaufort, Lord Clifford, Lord Hastings **13** Henry Beaufort, Joan La Pucelle **15** Margaret of Anjou, Margery Jourdain **16** Bastard of Orleans, Cardinal Beaufort
duke: **4** York (Richard Plantagenet) **7** Bedford, Suffolk **8** Somerset **10** Gloucester
earl: **7** Suffolk, Warwick **9** Salisbury
Richard Plantagenet's son: **6** Edmund, Edward, George **7** Richard

Henry VIII
author: **18** William Shakespeare
character: **7** Cranmer **8** Gardiner **10** Anne Boleyn **12** Thomas Wolsey **14** Queen Katharine, Thomas Cromwell **16** Cardinal Campeius
duke: **7** Norfolk, Suffolk **10** Buckingham

Henze, Hans Werner
born: **7** Germany **10** Westphalia
composer of: **6** Ariosi, Ondine **8** King Stag **10** El Cimarron **11** Konig Hirsch **12** The Bassarids, The Young Lord **14** Being Beauteous **15** The Runaway Slave **17** Boulevard Solitude **18** Der Prinz von Homburg, The Raft of the Medusa **19** Elegy for Young Lovers **48** The Long and Weary Journey to the Flat of Natasha Ungeheur

Heorot
great hall in: **7** Beowulf
author: **7** unknown

he painted it
Latin: **6** pinxit

Hepburn, Audrey
real name: **19** Audrey Hepburn-Ruston
husband: **9** Mel Ferrer
born: **7** Belgium **8** Brussels
roles: **6** Ondine **7** Charade, Sabrina **9** Bloodline, Funny Face **10** My Fair Lady **11** War and Peace **12** Roman Holiday (Oscar), The Nun's Story **13** Green Mansions, Wait Until Dark **18** Love in the Afternoon **19** Breakfast at Tiffany's

Hepburn, Katharine
co-star: **12** Spencer Tracy
born: **10** Hartford CT
roles: **7** Desk Set, Holiday **8** Adam's Rib **10** Alice Adams, Pat and Mike, Summertime **12** Morning Glory (Oscar), On Golden Pond (Oscar), The Rainmaker **14** Woman of the Year **15** The African Queen, The Lion in Winter (Oscar) **18** Suddenly Last Summer **20** The Philadelphia Story

23 Guess Who's Coming to Dinner (Oscar) 24 Long Day's Journey into Night

Hephaestus
also: 10 Hephaistos
father: 4 Zeus
mother: 4 Hera
god of: 4 fire 11 handicrafts 12 metalworking
vocation: 5 smith
wife: 9 Aphrodite
corresponds to: 6 Vulcan

Hephaistos *see* 10 Hephaestus

Hephzibah
husband: 8 Hezekiah
son: 8 Manasseh

Hepzibah *see* 9 Hephzibah

Hera
also: 4 Here
origin: 5 Greek
queen of: 6 Heaven
father: 6 Cronos, Cronus, Kronos
mother: 4 Rhea
brother: 4 Zeus
husband: 4 Zeus
son: 4 Ares
daughter: 9 Eilithyia 10 Hephaestus
birthplace: 5 Samos
festival: 7 Daedala
counterfeit: 7 Nephele
corresponds to: 4 Juno
epithet: 6 Anthea, Bunaea 8 Henioche 9 Prodromia

Heracles *see* 8 Hercules

Heracles, Children of
author: 9 Euripides
character: 6 Hyllus, Iolaus 7 Alcmene, Macaria 8 Demophon 10 Eurystheus

Heracles, Madness of
author: 9 Euripides
character: 4 Hera 5 Lycus 6 Megara 7 Theseus 8 Heracles 10 Amphitryon

Heraclid
descendant of: 8 Hercules

Heraclidae
children of: 8 Hercules

Heraea
origin: 5 Greek
form: 8 festival

Herakles *see* 8 Hercules

herald 4 clue, omen, sign 5 crier, envoy, token, usher 6 augury, inform, report, reveal, symbol 7 courier, divulge, portent, presage, publish, usher in, warning 8 announce, forecast, foregoer, foretell, proclaim 9 advertise, harbinger, indicator, make known, messenger, precursor, prefigure, publicize 10 forerunner, indication, proclaimer 11 bruit abroad, communicate, give voice to, predecessor 13 give tidings of

heraldic emblem 4 arms 5 crest 8 blazonry, insignia 10 coat of arms

heraldry ***see box***

herb 4 drug 5 plant, spice 6 annual, physic 7 herbage, perfume 8 aromatic, biennial, medicine 9 flavoring, perennial, seasoning, succulent
kind: 3 bay, rue 4 corn, dill, hemp, mint, rose, sage 5 anise, basil, curry, chili, grass, onion, peony, thyme, wheat 6 catnip, celery, chives, clover, fennel, garlic, pepper, sesame 7 boneset, caraway, ginseng, lavender, mustard, oregano, parsley 8 camomile, licorice, rosemary, tarragon 9 buttercup, marijuana, spearmint 10 peppermint 11 wintergreen

Herbert, George
author of: 9 The Temple

Herbert, Victor
born: 6 Dublin 7 Ireland
composer of: 14 Babes in Toyland, Hero and Leander 15 Naughty Marietta

herbivorous 10 vegetarian 11 plant-eating 14 noncarnivorous

Herceius
epithet of: 4 Zeus
means: 14 of the courtyard

herculean, Herculean 4 hard 5 burly, hefty, tough 6 brawny, mighty, robust, rugged, strong, sturdy 7 arduous, onerous 8 muscular, powerful, toilsome, wearying 9 difficult, fatiguing, laborious, strapping, strenuous 10 burdensome, exhausting, formidable, prodigious 12 backbreaking

Hercules
also: 7 Alcides 8 Heracles, Herakles 9 Carnopian
father: 4 Zeus
mother: 7 Alcmene
cousin: 10 Eurystheus
wife: 4 Hebe 6 Megara 8 Deianira
son: 5 Lamus 6 Hyllus 8 Telephus 11 Therimachus
daughter: 7 Macaria
teacher: 6 Chiron
gift: 8 strength
performed: 6 labors
number of labors: 6 twelve
epithet: 7 Charops 8 Buphagus 9 Ipoctonus
corresponds to: 6 Sancus 10 Semo Sancus

Hercyna
form: 5 nymph

heraldry
also called: 4 arms 10 coat of arms
black: 5 sable
blue: 5 azure
bottom: 4 base
center: 5 fesse
coat of arms of cities/countries/colleges: 14 impersonal arms
coat of arms on shield/crest/helmet/motto: 19 armorial achievement
colors: 8 tincture
concerns family's: 8 heritage 9 genealogy
described as: 9 blazoning
divided diagonally: 7 per bend
divided vertically and horizontally: 9 quartered
for holding shield: 10 supporters
fur: 4 vair 6 ermine
gold/yellow: 2 or
green: 4 vert
helmet top: 5 crest
horizontal band: 4 fess
intrafamily distinctions: 12 differencing
daughter: 7 lozenge
eldest son: 5 label
younger son: 7 cadency
left part: 8 sinister
main figure: 6 charge 8 ordinary 14 heraldic device
metal: 2 or 6 argent
motto in: 6 scroll
orange: 5 tenne
placed on lord's: 6 banner, shield 8 garments 14 horse trappings
portrayed as: 6 emblem, symbol
purple: 7 purpure
red: 5 gules
red-purple: 8 sanguine
right part: 6 dexter
shield: 10 escutcheon
sunshade: 8 mantling
held by: 6 wreath
made of: 4 silk
surface/background: 5 field
top: 5 chief
two or more colors: 16 lines of partition
vertical band: 4 pale
when worn by followers: 5 badge 6 livery
white/silver: 6 argent

location: 8 fountain
playmate: 10 Persephone

herd 3 lot, mob 4 army, band, body, gang, goad, host, lead, mass, pack, spur 5 array, bunch, crowd, drive, drove, flock, force, group, guide, horde, party, press, rally, swarm, tribe, troop 6 gather, huddle, legion, muster, number, throng 7 cluster, collect, company, convene, round up 8 assemble, assembly, conclave 9 gathering, multitude 10 assemblage, collection 11 convocation 12 congregation

Herds
god of: 8 Silvanus, Sylvanus

herdsman 6 cowboy, driver, drover 7 cowpoke 8 shepherd

Herdsman
constellation of: 6 Bootes

herd together 5 flock, group 6 gather 7 cluster, collect 10 congregate 12 band together

Here *see* 4 Hera

hereafter 5 limbo 6 heaven 8 paradise 9 afterlife, from now on, next world, Purgatory 10 afterworld, future life, henceforth, life beyond, ultimately 11 in the future, world to come 12 at a later date, at a later time, henceforward, subsequently 14 life after death 15 heavenly kingdom

here and there 6 around 11 at intervals 18 in this place and that
Latin: 6 passim

Here Comes Mr Jordan
director: 13 Alexander Hall
cast: 11 Claude Rains, Evelyn Keyes, Rita Johnson 16 Robert Montgomery
remade as: 13 Heaven Can Wait

hereditary 6 inborn, inbred 7 genetic 9 ancestral, heritable, inherited 10 congenital, handed-down 11 established, inheritable, traditional

here lies
Latin: 8 hic jacet

heresy 7 dissent, fallacy 8 apostasy 10 dissension, heterodoxy, iconoclasm, irreligion 11 unorthodoxy 13 nonconformity 15 unsound doctrine

heretic 7 skeptic 8 apostate, recreant, recusant, renegade 9 dissenter 10 backslider 11 freethinker, misbeliever 12 deviationist 13 nonconformist

heretical 7 radical 9 dissident 10 unorthodox 12 iconoclastic 13 nonconforming, nonconformist 14 unconventional

heretofore
French: 8 ci-devant

Hereward the Wake
author: 15 Charles Kingsley

Hergesheimer, Joseph
author of: 8 Java Head 19 The Three Black Pennys

heritage 6 estate, legacy 7 portion 9 patrimony, tradition 10 birthright 11 inheritance 16 family possession

Hermaphroditus
father: 6 Hermes
mother: 9 Aphrodite
loved by: 8 Salmacis
joined with: 8 Salmacis
became: 8 bisexual

Hermes
origin: 5 Greek
occupation: 6 herald
messenger of: 4 gods
father: 4 Zeus
mother: 4 Maia
son: 3 Pan 6 Prylis 7 Daphnis 14 Hermaphroditus
birthplace: 7 Arcadia
god of: 4 luck 5 roads, sleep 6 dreams, wealth 7 cunning, thieves 8 commerce 9 fertility, invention, merchants
invented: 4 lyre
sandals had: 5 wings
epithet: 6 Dolius 8 Agoraeus 9 Spelaites 10 Criophorus 11 Argiphontes 12 Argeiphontes, Psychopompus
corresponds to: 5 Thoth 7 Mercury

hermetic 6 mystic, occult 7 obscure 8 abstruse, airtight, esoteric, mystical 9 recondite

Hermia
character in: 21 A Midsummer Night's Dream
author: 11 Shakespeare

hermine, L'
author: 11 Jean Anouilh

Hermione
character in: 14 The Winter's Tale
author: 11 Shakespeare

Hermione
father: 8 Menelaus
mother: 5 Helen
husband: 7 Orestes
son: 9 Tisamenus

hermit 7 eremite, recluse 8 cenobite, monastic, solitary 9 anchorite 11 desert saint 14 solitudinarian 16 religious recluse

hermitage 5 abbey 6 friary, priory 7 convent, retreat 8 cloister 9 monastery

Hermod
origin: 12 Scandinavian
father: 4 Odin 5 Othin
race: 4 Asar 5 Aesir
negotiates return of: 5 Baldr 6 Balder, Baldur

hero, heroine 4 idol, star 7 gallant 8 brave man, champion, great man, male lead, male star, noble man 9 daredevil, daring man, main actor 10 adventurer, leading man 11 protagonist, valorous man 12 man of courage, man of the hour 13 chivalrous man, popular figure 15 fearless fighter, idealized person, intrepid warrior, legendary person

Hero
character in: 19 Much Ado About Nothing
author: 11 Shakespeare

Hero
vocation: 9 priestess
priestess of: 9 Aphrodite
lover: 7 Leander
death by: 7 suicide 8 drowning

Herod Antipas
father: 13 Herod the great
mother: 8 Malthace
grandfather: 9 Antipater
wife: 8 Herodias
half brother: 6 Philip
beheaded: 14 John the Baptist

Herodias
husband: 6 Philip 12 Herod Antipas
daughter: 6 Salome

Herodotus
called: 15 Father of History
wrote history of: 11 Persian Wars

Herod Philip
daughter: 6 Salome

heroic 4 bold, epic 5 brave, grand, noble 6 daring 7 classic, exalted, gallant, Homeric, valiant 8 elevated, fearless, highbrow, inflated, intrepid, mythical, resolute, valorous 9 bombastic, dauntless, dignified, grandiose, high-flown, legendary, undaunted 10 chivalrous, courageous 11 exaggerated, extravagant, lionhearted, pretentious, unflinching 12 mythological, ostentatious, stouthearted

heroic act 4 feat 7 exploit 9 brave deed

heroism **5** valor **6** daring **7** bravery, courage, prowess **8** boldness, chivalry, nobility **9** fortitude, gallantry **11** intrepidity **12** fearlessness **13** dauntlessness **14** courageousness **15** lionheartedness

Herophilus
field: **7** anatomy
nationality: **5** Greek
experimented with: **15** post-mortem exams

Heros
author: **8** Menander

herpetophobia
fear of: **8** reptiles

Herrenvolk **10** master race

Herrick, Robert
author of: **10** Hesperides **20** Corinna's Going A Maying **26** Gather ye rosebuds while ye may

Herriman, George
creator/artist of: **8** Krazy Kat

Herschel, William
field: **9** astronomy
nationality: **7** British
discovered: **6** Uranus

Herse
father: **7** Cecrops
sister: **8** Aglauros, Aglaurus, Agraulos
lover: **6** Hermes
son: **5** Ceryx **8** Cephalus

Hersey, John
author of: **7** The Wall **9** Hiroshima **13** A Bell for Adano, The Conspiracy **22** My Petition for More Space

Hertz, Heinrich
field: **7** physics
nationality: **6** German
discovered: **13** electric waves **18** wireless telegraphy
named for him: **13** hertzian waves

Herzog
author: **10** Saul Bellow

he sculptured it
Latin: **8** sculpsit

Hesiod
author of: **8** Theogony **12** Works and Days

Hesione
father: **8** Laomedon
husband: **7** Telamon
son: **6** Teucer
rescued by: **8** Hercules

hesitancy **10** indecision, reluctance, unsureness **11** uncertainty, vacillation **12** irresolution

hesitant **5** loath **6** unsure **7** halting **8** doubtful, wavering **9** diffident, faltering, reluctant, tentative, uncertain, undecided **10** hesitating, indecisive, irresolute **11** half-hearted, hanging back, vacillating **15** shilly-shallying **17** lacking confidence, sitting on the fence

hesitate **4** balk, halt **5** delay, pause, shy at, waver **6** falter **7** scruple, stick at **8** be unsure, hang back **9** stickle at, vacillate **10** dillydally, shrink from, think twice **11** be reluctant, be uncertain, be undecided, be unwilling, stop briefly **12** be irresolute, shilly-shally **16** straddle the fence

hesitating **8** doubtful, hesitant **10** indecisive, irresolute, on the fence

he speaks
Latin: **8** loquitur

Hesperia
also: **5** Italy **16** Iberian Peninsula

Hesperides
author: **13** Robert Herrick

Hesperides
form: **6** nymphs
guarded: **12** golden apples
guarded with: **5** Ladon **6** dragon
names: **5** Aegle **6** Hestia **7** Erythea, Hespera **8** Arethusa **9** Hespereia, Hesperusa
islands of the: **7** blessed
form of: **6** heaven

Hesperis
mother: **8** Hesperus
mother of: **10** Hesperides

Hess, Victor Francis
field: **7** physics
discovered: **10** cosmic rays
awarded: **10** Nobel Prize

Hesse, Hermann
author of: **6** Demian **9** Rosshalde **10** Siddhartha **11** Steppenwolf **12** Magister Ludi **14** Peter Camenzind **15** Beneath the Wheel **16** Death and the Lover, Journey to the East, The Glass Bead Game

Hesselberg, Melvyn Edouard
real name of: **13** Melvyn Douglas

hessionite
species: **6** garnet

Hestia
origin: **5** Greek
goddess of the: **6** hearth
father: **6** Cronos, Cronus, Kronos
mother: **4** Rhea
corresponds to: **5** Vesta

Heston, Charlton
real name: **13** Charles Carter
born: **10** Evanston IL
roles: **5** El Cid, Moses **6** Ben-Hur (Oscar) **15** Planet of the Apes **18** The Ten Commandments **21** The Agony and the Ecstasy **22** The Greatest Show on Earth

Heterodontosaurus
type: **8** dinosaur **10** ornithopod
location: **6** Africa
period: **8** Triassic

heterogeneous **5** mixed **6** motley, unlike, varied **7** diverse, jumbled **8** assorted **9** composite, disparate, divergent, unrelated **10** dissimilar, variegated **11** diversified **13** miscellaneous

hew **2** ax **3** cut, lop **4** chop, form, hack, mold **5** carve, model, prune, sever, shape **6** chisel, cut out, devise **7** cut down, fashion, whittle **8** chop down **9** sculpture

He Who Gets Slapped
author: **14** Leonid Andreyev

he wrote it
Latin: **8** scripsit

hex **4** harm, jinx, sign **5** curse, spell, witch **6** hoodoo, voodoo, whammy **7** bewitch, evil eye, ill wind, possess **8** sorcerer **9** sorceress **11** malediction

Hexateuch **27** first six books of Old Testament
see also: **7** Books of **12** Old Testament

heyday **4** acme **5** bloom, crest, flush, prime, vigor **6** zenith **9** flowering, salad days

Heyerdahl, Thor
author of: **7** Kon-Tiki **16** The Ra Expeditions

Hezekiah
father: **4** Ahaz
wife: **9** Hephzibah
means: **18** Jehovah strengthens

Hi and Lois
creator: **9** Dik Browne **10** Mort Walker
character:
brother: **12** Beetle Bailey
children: **3** Dot **4** Chip **5** Ditto **6** Trixie
dog: **4** Dawg
friend: **7** Thirsty

hiatus **3** gap **4** void **5** blank, break, lapse, space **6** lacuna, vacuum **7** interim **8** interval **10** disruption **12** interruption

Hiawatha, The Song of
author: **24** Henry Wadsworth Longfellow

character: 5 Nahma 7 Kwasind, Nokomis, Wenonah 8 Mondamin 9 Chibiabos, Minnehaha 11 Mudjekeewis 12 Pau-Puk-Keewis, Pearl-Feather

hibernate 5 sleep 6 retire 8 withdraw 13 become dormant

hibernating 6 asleep 7 dormant 8 inactive, sleeping 9 quiescent

Hibernia *see* 7 Ireland

hibiscus
varieties: 7 Chinese 8 Hawaiian, Japanese

Hicetaon
father: 8 Laomedon
brother: 5 Priam

hic jacet 8 here lies

hickory 5 Carya
varieties: 4 Pale, Sand 5 Broom, Swamp, Water 6 Pignut 7 Chinese 8 Mountain, Shagbark 9 Mockernut, Shellbark 10 White-heart 12 Small-fruited

Hicks, Edward
born: 11 Attleboro PA
artwork: 19 The Peaceable Kingdom

Hidatsa (Minitari, Gros Ventre)
language family: 6 Siouan
location: 7 Montana 11 North Dakota
related to: 6 Mandan 7 Arikara

hidden away 6 buried, cached 7 stashed 8 closeted, pocketed, secluded, secreted 9 concealed 10 out of sight 11 stashed away 12 inaccessible, undiscovered

hidden meaning 6 enigma, puzzle, riddle, secret 7 mystery

hidden motive
French: 13 arriere pensee

hide 4 mask, pelt, skin, veil 5 cache, cloak, cloud, cover 6 lie low, screen, shroud 7 conceal, curtain, leather, obscure, repress, seclude, secrete 8 disguise, suppress

hideaway 7 hideout, retreat 11 hiding place, secret place

hideous 4 grim, ugly, vile 5 awful 6 horrid, odious 7 ghastly, macabre 8 dreadful, gruesome, horrible, shocking 9 abhorrent, appalling, frightful, grotesque, loathsome, monstrous, repellent, repugnant, repulsive, revolting, sickening 10 abominable, detestable, disgusting, horrendous

hiding place 5 cache 8 hideaway 9 hidey hole 10 repository 11 secret place

Hieronimo
character in: 17 The Spanish Tragedy
author: 3 Kyd

hier wird Deutsch gesprochen 18 German is spoken here

Higgins, Henry
character in: 9 Pygmalion 10 My Fair Lady
author: 4 Shaw

Higgs
character in: 7 Erewhon
author: 6 Butler

high 3 gay, top 4 main, tall 5 aloft, chief, far up, grand, great, jolly, lofty, merry, noble, prime, sharp, undue, way up 6 alpine, august, elated, jovial, joyful, joyous, shrill 7 capital, eminent, exalted, excited, extreme, gleeful, leading, notable, playful, primary, serious, soaring, soprano 8 cheerful, elevated, exultant, foremost, imposing, jubilant, mirthful, peerless, piercing, strident, superior, towering, uncurbed 9 ascendant, excellent, excessive, exuberant, important, overjoyed, principal, prominent, unbridled, uppermost 10 exorbitant, immoderate, inordinate, preeminent 11 cloud-capped, exaggerated, exhilarated, extravagant, high-pitched, illustrious, intemperate, predominant, significant, sky-scraping 12 earsplitting, high-reaching, lighthearted, unreasonable, unrestrained 13 consequential, distinguished

high-and-mighty 5 lofty 6 lordly 7 haughty 8 arrogant 9 imperious 11 overbearing

highborn 5 noble 8 highbred, wellborn 9 patrician 10 of high rank, upper-class 12 aristocratic, of high degree, silk-stocking 13 of gentle blood

highbred 5 noble, regal 6 lordly 7 refined 8 highborn, wellborn 9 patrician 11 aristocracy, blue-blooded

highbrow 4 snob 5 brain 7 bookish, Brahmin, egghead, elitist, erudite, scholar, thinker 8 cultured, mandarin, snobbish 9 scholarly 10 cultivated, double-dome, mastermind 12 intellectual 13 knowledgeable

highest good
Latin: 11 summum bonum

highest point
Latin: 11 ne plus ultra

high fashion
French: 12 haute couture

high-flown 4 wild 5 lofty, proud 6 absurd, florid, lordly, turgid, unreal 7 flowery, orotund, pompous 8 elevated, fabulous, inflated 9 bombastic, excessive, fantastic, grandiose 10 flamboyant, immoderate, inordinate, outrageous 11 exaggerated, extravagant, highfalutin, pretentious, sententious 12 magniloquent, preposterous, presumptuous, unreasonable, unrestrained 13 grandiloquent, self-important

High-German
language family: 12 Indo-European
branch: 8 Germanic
group: 15 Western Germanic
subgroup: 11 German-Dutch
division: 6 German 7 Yiddish

high-hat 5 aloof 6 formal, la-di-da, snooty 7 haughty 8 snobbish 12 supercilious

highjinks, hijinks 6 antics, capers, pranks, stunts 11 shenanigans 12 monkeyshines

highland, Highlands 4 rise 7 heights, plateau, uplands 8 headland 9 tableland 10 promontory 11 hill country 17 mountainous region
refers especially to: 8 Scotland

highlight 4 peak 6 accent, climax, stress 7 feature, point up 9 emphasize, high point, underline 10 accentuate, focal point, make bright

highly qualified 3 fit 4 able 7 trained 8 eligible, prepared, skillful 9 practiced 10 proficient 11 experienced 12 accomplished

highly regarded 6 prized 7 admired, revered 8 esteemed 9 respected, treasured 13 well thought of

highly valued 4 dear 5 loved 6 adored 7 beloved, revered 8 esteemed, precious 9 cherished, treasured

highly visible 7 glaring, obvious 8 distinct 9 prominent 11 conspicuous, outstanding

high-minded 4 fair, just 5 lofty, moral, noble 6 honest, worthy 7 ethical, sincere, upright 8 truthful, virtuous 9 exemplary, honorable, reputable, righteous, uncorrupt **10** chivalrous, idealistic, principled, scrupulous **13** conscientious, square-dealing

High Noon
director: 13 Fred Zinnemann
cast: 10 Gary Cooper (Will Kane), Grace Kelly **12** Lloyd Bridges **14** Thomas Mitchell
score: 14 Dimitri Tiomkin
Oscar for: 5 actor (Cooper)

high old time 4 ball, lark **5** fling, revel, spree **8** escapade

high-pitched 5 acute, sharp **6** shrill **7** clarion, squeaky **8** piercing

high place 4 hill, peak, rise **5** bluff, cliff, knoll, ridge **6** height, summit, upland **7** hillock, hummock, plateau **8** eminence, mountain **9** elevation **10** prominence, promontory

high point, highest point 3 cap, top **4** acme, apex, peak **5** crest, crown **6** apogee, climax, height, heyday, summit, tiptop, vertex, zenith **8** eminence, pinnacle **9** flowering **10** prominence **11** culmination

high position 4 note **8** eminence, high rank, standing **9** supremacy **10** ascendancy, importance, notability, prominence **11** distinction, preeminence

high-powered 7 driving, dynamic **8** forceful **9** ambitious, assertive, energetic, go-getting **10** aggressive **11** hard-driving

high praise 5 kudos, paean **6** eulogy **7** hosanna, plaudit **8** encomium **9** laudation, panegyric **11** acclamation

high-priced 4 dear, high **6** costly, pricey **9** expensive **10** exorbitant, overpriced **11** extravagant

high-principled 5 moral, noble **6** chaste, honest, worthy **7** ethical, upright **9** honorable, reputable **10** idealistic **11** responsible, trustworthy **13** conscientious

high quality 5 merit **7** quality **9** greatness **10** excellence, perfection **11** distinction, superiority

high-ranking 3 top **5** grand, great, lofty, regal, royal **6** august **7** eminent, exalted, supreme **8** elevated, esteemed, imposing **9** important, paramount, venerable **10** preeminent **11** illustrious **13** distinguished

High Sierra
director: 10 Raoul Walsh
cast: 9 Ida Lupino **10** Alan Curtis, Joan Leslie **13** Arthur Kennedy **14** Humphrey Bogart (Mad Dog Earle)
remade as: 17 Colorado Territory **19** I Died a Thousand Times

high society 5 elite **9** haut monde, top drawer **11** aristocracy **14** creme de la creme
French: 9 haut monde

High Society
director: 14 Charles Walters
cast: 10 Bing Crosby, Grace Kelly **11** Celeste Holm **12** Frank Sinatra, Louis Calhern **14** Louis Armstrong
score: 10 Cole Porter
remake of: 20 The Philadelphia Story
song: 8 True Love **10** Did You Evah? **16** You're Sensational

high-speed 4 fast **5** quick, rapid, swift **6** speedy **7** express

high-spirited 5 vital **6** lively **8** animated **9** exuberant, vivacious **12** effervescent, enthusiastic

high spirits 5 vigor **6** gaiety **7** delight, elation **8** gladness, vitality, vivacity **9** animation **10** enthusiasm, exaltation, excitement, joyousness, liveliness **12** exhilaration **16** lightheartedness

high-strung 4 edgy **5** jumpy, moody, tense **6** uneasy **7** jittery, nervous, uptight **8** neurotic, restless, skittish **9** emotional, excitable, impatient, wrought-up **10** hysterical **13** oversensitive, temperamental **14** easily agitated, hypersensitive

High Tor
author: 15 Maxwell Anderson

highway 7 freeway, parkway, thruway **8** hard road, highroad, main road, speedway, turnpike **9** paved road **10** expressway, interstate, main artery **12** four-lane road, thoroughfare
British: 9 coach road, royal road **12** King's highway **13** Queen's highway

highwayman 5 crook, thief **6** bandit, outlaw, robber **7** brigand, footpad

hike 4 rise, roam, rove, trek, walk **5** leg it, march, raise, tramp **6** draw up, hoof it, jerk up, pull up, ramble, trudge, wander **7** hitch up, raise up **8** addition, increase **9** expansion **10** escalation **12** augmentation **13** journey on foot **14** go by shank's mare

Hilaira
vocation: 9 priestess
priestess of: 7 Artemis
father: 9 Leucippus
abducted by: 6 Castor

hilarious 3 gay **5** jolly, merry, noisy **6** jocund, jovial, joyful, joyous, lively **7** comical, gleeful, riotous **8** jubilant, mirthful **9** exuberant, laughable, very funny **10** boisterous, hysterical, rollicking, uproarious, vociferous **11** exhilarated **12** high-spirited **13** highly amusing **14** laugh-provoking

hilarity 3 fun, gig, joy **4** glee, riot **5** laugh, mirth, noisy **6** comedy, gaiety, giggle, levity **7** chortle, chuckle, jollity **8** hysteria, laughter **9** amusement, funniness, joviality, jubilance, merriment **10** exuberance **12** exhilaration, humorousness **14** uproariousness

Hilbert, David
field: 8 geometry **11** mathematics
nationality: 6 German
formulated: 12 modern axioms

Hilda Lessways
author: 13 Arnold Bennett

hill 4 bank, dune, heap, pile, ramp, rise **5** bluff, butte, cliff, climb, grade, knoll, mound, mount, slope **6** height **7** hillock, hilltop, hummock, incline, upgrade **8** eminence, foothill, highland, hillside **9** acclivity, declivity, downgrade, elevation **10** prominence, promontory

Hill, Arthur
born: 6 Canada **7** Melfort **12** Saskatchewan
roles: 13 All the Way Home **15** The Ugly American **17** Look Homeward Angel **25** Who's Afraid of Virginia Woolf?

Hill, George Roy
director of: 8 The Sting (Oscar) **23** The World According to Garp **29** Butch Cassidy and the Sundance Kid

Hiller, Arthur
director of: 25 The Americanization of Emily

hillock 4 hill, rise **5** knoll, mound **7** hummock **8** eminence

Hill Street Blues
character: 5 LaRue, Renko **9** Bobby Hill, Jablonski, Joe

Coffey, Lucy Bates **10** Fay Furillo, Mick Belker, Washington **11** (Lt) Norman Buntz **12** Howard Hunter, (Captain) Frank Furillo **13** Henry Goldblum **14** Joyce Davenport
cast: **8** Joe Spano **10** Bruce Weitz, Ed Marinaro, Kiel Martin **11** Betty Thomas, Charles Haid, Dennis Franz **12** Robert Prosky **13** James B Sikking, Michael Warren, Veronica Hamel **14** Taurean Blacque **15** Daniel J Travanti

Hilton, James
author of: **11** Lost Horizon **14** Good-Bye Mr Chips

Himeros
origin: **5** Greek
god of: **12** erotic desire
associated with: **4** Eros

Hind *see* **5** India

Hind and the Panther, The
author: **10** John Dryden

Hindarfjall *see* **8** Hindfell

Hindemith, Paul
born: **5** Hanau **7** Germany
composer of: **8** The Demon **9** Cardillac **10** Heriodiade **12** Ludus Tonalis, Neues vom Tage, News of the Day **13** Sancta Susanna **14** Cupid and Psyche, Mathis Der Maler **15** In Praise of Music **17** Murder Hope of Women **18** Die Harmonie der Welt, Nobilissima Visione **19** The Four Temperaments **23** Morder Hoffnung der Frauen

hinder **3** bar **4** curb, foil, stay, stop **5** block, check, delay, deter, spike, stall **6** arrest, detain, fetter, hamper, hobble, hog-tie, hold up, impede, retard, stifle, stymie, thwart **7** inhibit **8** encumber, handicap, hold back, obstruct, restrain, slow down **9** frustrate, hamstring **13** interfere with

Hindfell
also: **11** Hindarfjall
origin: **12** Scandinavian
mountain slept on by: **8** Brynhild

Hindi
language family: **12** Indo-European
branch: **11** Indo-Iranian
group: **5** Indic
official language of: **5** India

hindmost **4** last, rear **7** tail end **12** farthest back

hindpart **4** tail **6** far end **7** rear end **8** backside, buttocks, haunches **9** afterpart, posterior

hindquarters **4** rear, rump **7** rear end, tail end **8** back legs, backside, buttocks, haunches **9** posterior

hindrance **3** bar **4** clog, curb, snag **5** catch **6** fetter **7** barrier, shackle **8** blockade, blockage, handicap, obstacle **9** barricade, restraint, retardant **10** constraint, difficulty, impediment, limitation **11** encumbrance, obstruction, restriction **12** interference **14** stumbling block

hinge **4** hang, rest, turn **5** pivot, swing **6** depend **7** be due to **9** arise from **10** result from **11** be subject to, emanate from **13** revolve around

hint **3** bit, jot, tip **4** clue, idea, iota **5** grain, imply, pinch, tinge, touch, trace, whiff **6** little, notion, tip off **7** inkling, pointer, signify, soupcon, suggest, whisper **8** allusion, indicate, innuendo, intimate **9** insinuate, suspicion **10** impression, indication, intimation, smattering, suggestion **11** implication, indirection, insinuation **12** flea in the ear, slight amount **13** word to the wise

hinted **7** implied, oblique **8** implicit, indirect **9** suggested

hinterland **6** sticks **7** boonies, country **8** interior, midlands **9** backwater, backwoods, boondocks, rural area **11** countryside

Hiordis
also: **7** Hjordis
origin: **12** Scandinavian
mentioned in: **8** Volsunga
husband: **7** Sigmund
son: **6** Sigurd

Hippalectryon
form: **7** monster
head and forelegs of: **5** horse
legs, tail and body of: **4** cock

Hippocampus
form: **7** monster
body of: **5** horse
tail of: **4** fish

Hippocrene
form: **6** spring
location: **12** Mount Helicon

Hippocurius
epithet of: **8** Poseidon
means: **12** horse tending

Hippodamas
daugher: **8** Perimele
drowned: **8** Perimele

hippodrome **5** arena **6** circus **7** stadium **8** coliseum

Hippogriff
form: **7** monster
combined: **5** horse **7** griffin

Hippolochus
father: **11** Bellerophon
son: **7** Glaucus

Hippolyta *see* **9** Hippolyte

Hippolyte
also: **7** Antiope **9** Hippolyta
queen of: **7** Amazons
husband: **7** Theseus
son: **10** Hippolytus
Hercules stole her: **6** girdle

Hippolytus
author: **9** Euripides
character: **7** Artemis, Phaedra, Theseus **9** Aphrodite

Hippolytus
father: **7** Theseus
mother: **9** Hippolyta
stepmother: **7** Phaedra
loved by: **7** Phaedra
killed by: **8** Poseidon

Hippomedon
member of: **18** Seven against Thebes

Hippomenes
suitor of: **8** Atalanta
son: **13** Parthenopaeus

Hipponous
vocation: **7** warrior
home: **4** Troy
daughter: **8** Periboea
killed by: **8** Achilles

Hippothous
king of: **7** Arcadia
father: **8** Poseidon
mother: **5** Alope

hire **3** fee, get, let, pay **4** cost, gain, rent **5** lease, wages **6** charge, employ, engage, income, obtain, profit, retain, reward, salary, secure, take on **7** appoint, charter, payment, procure, stipend **8** earnings, receipts **9** emolument **10** recompense **12** compensation, remuneration

hireling **4** goon, thug **6** flunky, lackey, menial, minion, stooge **7** gorilla **8** henchman, retainer **9** strong-arm **10** hatchet man

Hiroshima
author: **10** John Hersey

hirsute **5** bushy, downy, hairy, nappy, wooly **6** shaggy, woolly **7** bearded, bristly, prickly, unshorn **8** bristled, unshaven **9** whiskered **11** bewhiskered

His Girl Friday
director: **11** Howard Hawks
cast: **9** Cary Grant **12** Gene Lockhart, Ralph Bellamy **15** Rosalind Russell

remake of: **12** The Front Page

Hispania *see* **5** Spain

hiss **3** boo **4** mock, razz **6** deride, heckle, hoot at, jeer at, revile **7** catcall, scoff at, sneer at **9** shout down **10** Bronx cheer **16** give the raspberry

histology
study of: **6** tissue

historian
American: **4** Webb **5** Adams **6** Brooks, De Voto, Durant, Fisher, Miller, Nevins, Sparks, Turner **7** Morison, Parkman, Taussig **8** Bancroft, Channing, Prescott, Robinson **10** Hofstadter
British: **4** Bede (the Venerable) **6** Gibbon, Turner **7** Toynbee **8** Macaulay **9** Trevelyan
Chinese: **10** Ssu-ma Ch'ien, Ssu-Ma Kuang
French: **5** Bayle, Blanc, Bloch, Taine **7** Braudel **8** Mabillon, Michelet, Voltaire **11** Tocqueville
German: **5** Ranke **7** Mommsen **8** Spengler **10** Burckhardt, Treitschke
Greek: **8** Polybius **9** Herodotus **10** Thucydides
Islamic: **8** al Tabari **10** Ibn Khaldun
Italian: **4** Polo, Vico **5** Croce **11** Machiavelli **12** Guicciardini
Latin: **4** Livy **7** Sallust, Tacitus
Scottish: **7** Carlyle

historic **5** famed **7** notable **8** renowned **9** memorable, well-known **10** celebrated **11** outstanding

historical **4** past, real, true **6** actual, bygone, former **7** ancient, factual **8** attested, recorded **9** authentic **10** chronicled, documented

historical period **3** age, era **4** date, time **5** epoch, stage

history **4** epic, saga, tale **5** story **6** annals, change, growth, record, resume, review **7** account, the past **8** old times **9** chronicle, days of old, narration, narrative, portrayal, tradition, yesterday **10** bygone days, days of yore, olden times, the old days, yesteryear **11** bygone times, development, former times, local events, major events, world events **12** actual events **13** an unusual past, human progress **14** military action, national events, recapitulation **15** political change

History of Colonel Jacque, The
author: **11** Daniel Defoe

History of Henry VII
author: **12** Francis Bacon

History of Mr Polly, The
author: **7** H G Wells
character: **6** Miriam **8** Uncle Jim **13** The Plump Woman

History of the English-Speaking Peoples, A
author: **17** Winston S Churchill

His Toy, His Dream, His Rest
author: **12** John Berryman

histrionics **4** fuss **6** acting, tirade **7** bluster, bombast **8** outburst **9** dramatics, hamminess, staginess, theatrics **10** dramaturgy, playacting **11** performance, rodomontade **13** melodramatics, temper tantrum, theatricality **16** ranting and raving

hit *see box*

hit **3** bat, jab, lob, rap, tap **4** bang, bash, beat, belt, blow, boon, bump, butt, clip, club, coup, cuff, damn, drub, find, flog, hurt, move, pelt, poke, slam, slap, slug, sock, stir, swat **5** abash, baste, clout, crack, crush, flail, knock, paste, pound, punch, reach, rouse, smack, smash, smite, thump, touch, upset, whack **6** affect, arouse, assail, attack, attain, batter, cudgel, effect, impact, incite, pommel, revile, strike, thrash, thwack, wallop, winner **7** achieve, assault, censure, clobber, condemn, execute, godsend, impress, inflame, provoke, quicken, realize, shatter, success, triumph, trounce, victory **8** arrive at, bang into, blessing, bring off, denounce, lambaste, overcome, reproach **9** criticize, deal a blow, devastate, lash out at, overwhelm, sensation, smash into **11** collide with, connect with, deal a stroke, strike out at **12** go straight to **13** make a bull's-eye, send to the mark **14** popular success, strike together **16** mount an offensive

hit back **7** counter, get even, pay back **9** fight back, retaliate **10** strike back

hitch **3** tie, tug **4** curb, draw, halt, haul, hike, jerk, knot, loop, pull, snag, stop, yank, yoke **5** catch, check, clamp, delay, raise, tying **6** attach, couple, fasten, mishap, secure, tether **7** bracket, connect, harness, joining, mistake, problem, trouble **8** coupling, handicap, make fast, obstacle **9** attaching, fastening, hindrance, mischance, restraint **10** connection, difficulty, impediment, limitation **11** restriction **12** complication, interruption, loop together, put in harness **14** stumbling block

Hitchcock, Alfred
director of: **6** Frenzy, Marnie, Psycho **7** Rebecca, Vertigo **8** Lifeboat, The Birds **9** Notorious, Suspicion **10** Family Plot, Rear Window, Spellbound **13** To Catch a Thief **14** Dial M for Murder, Shadow of a Doubt **15** The Lady Vanishes **16** North by Northwest **17** Strangers on a Train **18** The Thirty-Nine Steps **19** The Trouble with Harry **20** Foreign Correspondent

hither **2** on **4** here, near **5** close **6** closer, nearby, nearer, onward **7** close by, forward **8** over here **11** to this place **12** to the speaker

hitherto **6** ere now, hereto **7** thus far, till now, up to now **8** until now **10** before this, heretofore

Hitler, Adolf
author of: **9** Mein Kampf

hit man **6** killer, slayer **8** assassin, hired gun, murderer **11** executioner **12** exterminator

Hitman
nickname of: **12** Thomas Hearns

hit-or-miss **3** lax **6** casual, fitful **7** aimless, cursory **8** slapdash **9** haphazard **10** incomplete **11** purposeless, superficial, unorganized **12** unsystematic **15** catch-as-catch-can

hive **3** hub **5** heart **6** center, colony **7** cluster **9** busy place **11** swarm of bees

Hjordis *see* **7** Hiordis

Hliod *see* **4** Liod

H M S Pinafore
subtitle: **23** The Lass That Loved a Sailor
operetta by: **18** Gilbert and Sullivan
character: **11** Dick Deadeye **14** Ralph Rackstraw **15** Captain Corcoran, Little Buttercup, Sir Joseph Porter **17** Josephine Corcoran

Hoagland, Edward
author of: **15** African Calliope **17** The Tugman's Passage

hoar **3** old **4** aged, rime **5** frost, moldy, mushy, passe, stale, white **6** old hat **7** ancient, antique, elderly, grayish **8** grizzled **9** out of date

hoard **4** fund, heap, mass, pile **5** amass, buy up, cache, lay up, store **6** save up, supply **7** acquire, collect, lay away, reserve **8** quantity **9** amassment, gathering, stockpile, store away **10** accumulate, collection **12** accumulation

hoarse **5** gruff, harsh, husky, raspy, rough **6** croaky **7** cracked, rasping, raucous, throaty **8** gravelly, guttural, scratchy

hoary **3** old **4** aged, gray, hoar **5** dated, passe, white **6** grayed, old hat **7** ancient, antique, grizzly **8** grizzled, whitened **9** out-of-date **11** gray with age **12** white with age

hoax **3** gyp **4** bilk, dupe, fake, fool, gull, yarn **5** bluff, cheat, cozen, fraud, prank, spoof, trick **6** canard, delude, humbug, take in **7** deceive, defraud, fiction, mislead, swindle **8** hoodwink **9** bamboozle, chicanery, deception, fish story, victimize **10** hocus-pocus

Hoban, James
architect of: **13** The White House, Great Hotel (Washington, DC)

Hobbes, Thomas
author of: **9** Leviathan

Hobbit, The
part of: **14** Lord of the Rings
author: **10** J R R Tolkien

hobble **4** bind, gimp, halt, limp **5** block, check, cramp **6** fetter, hamper, hinder, hogtie, impede, lumber, stymie, thwart, toddle **7** inhibit, manacle, shackle, shamble, shuffle, stagger, stumble **8** encumber, handicap, hold back, lame gait, obstruct, restrain, restrict **9** constrain, frustrate, hamstring **10** uneven gait, walk lamely **13** interfere with

hobby **7** pastime, pursuit **8** sideline **9** amusement, avocation, diversion **10** relaxation **13** entertainment **14** divertissement

hobbyhorse **5** hobby **7** pastime **8** interest, toy horse **9** diversion **10** enthusiasm **11** distraction **12** rocking horse

hobgoblin **3** imp **5** bogey **6** goblin **7** bugaboo

hobnob **3** mix **4** club **6** mingle **7** consort, hang out **9** associate, rub elbows **10** fraternize

hobo **3** beg, bum **5** stiff, tramp **6** beggar, cadger, loafer **7** drifter, migrant, moocher, vagrant **8** derelict, vagabond, wanderer **9** scrounger **11** beachcomber

hoc est **6** this is

Ho Chi Minh City
formerly: **6** Saigon
river: **6** Saigon
delta: **6** Mekong
former capital of: **9** Indochina **11** Cochin China **12** South Vietnam

hockey
athlete: **8** Bobby Orr, Brad Park **9** Bobby Hull, Ken Dryden, Mike Bossy **10** Doug Harvey, Eddie Shore, Ed Giacomin, Gordie Howe, Guy Lafleur, Rod Gilbert, Stan Mikita **11** Bobby Clarke, Denis Potvin, Howie Morenz, Jean Ratelle **12** Emile Francis, Jean Beliveau, Marcel Dionne, Phil Esposito, Wayne Gretzky **13** Bernard Parent, Bryan Trottier, Jacques Plante, Larry Robinson **14** Alex Delvecchio, Maurice Richard **15** Bernie Geoffrion **18** Yvan Serge Courneyer

hockey team ***see box***

hockey team
Boston: **6** Bruins
Buffalo: **6** Sabres
Calgary: **6** Flames
Chicago: **10** Black Hawks
Detroit: **8** Red Wings
Edmonton: **6** Oilers
Hartford: **7** Whalers
Los Angeles: **5** Kings
Minnesota: **10** North Stars
Montreal: **9** Canadiens
New Jersey: **6** Devils
New York: **7** Rangers **9** Islanders
Philadelphia: **6** Flyers
Pittsburgh: **8** Penguins
Quebec: **9** Nordiques
St Louis: **5** Blues
Toronto: **10** Maple Leafs
Vancouver: **7** Canucks
Washington: **8** Capitals
Winnepeg: **4** Jets

hocus-pocus **4** bosh, bull, hoax, sham **5** chant, charm, cheat, magic, spell **6** bunkum, deceit, fakery, humbug **7** con game, hogwash, rubbish, swindle **8** delusion, flimflam, tommyrot, trickery **9** deception, moonshine, poppycock **10** dishonesty, flapdoodle, hanky-panky, magic spell, magic words, mumbo jumbo, subterfuge **11** bewitchment, incantation, legerdemain, magic tricks **12** fiddle-faddle, magic formula **13** sleight of hand **14** confidence game **16** prestidigitation, stuff and nonsense

Hoder
also: **5** Hodur
origin: **12** Scandinavian
brother: **5** Baldr **6** Balder, Baldur
father: **4** Odin **5** Othin
killed: **5** Baldr **6** Balder, Baldur

hodgepodge, hotchpotch **3** mix **4** hash, mess **6** jumble, medley, muddle **7** melange, mixture **8** mishmash **9** composite, confusion, patchwork, potpourri **10** miscellany **14** conglomeration

Hodur *see* **5** Hoder

Hoenir
origin: **12** Scandinavian
race: **5** Vanir
created: **3** Ask **5** Embla

Hoff, Jacobus Hendricus van't
field: **9** chemistry
nationality: **5** Dutch
researched: **7** gas laws **10** carbon atom **14** thermodynamics
awarded: **10** Nobel Prize

Hoffman, Dustin
born: **12** Los Angeles CA
roles: **5** Lenny **6** Ishtar **7** Tootsie **8** Papillon **10** Ratso Rizzo **11** The Graduate **12** Little Big Man **14** Kramer vs Kramer (Oscar), Midnight Cowboy **19** All the President's Men

Hofmann, Hans
born: **7** Germany **11** Weissenberg
artwork: **6** Spring **7** The Gate **13** Effervescence **14** Fantasia in Blue, Magenta and Blue **16** Sanctum Sanctorum

Hofstadter, Richard
author of: **14** The Age of Reform

hog **3** pig, sow **4** arch, boar, trim **5** broom, sheep, swine **6** gorger, porker **7** baconer, glutton, take all **9** razorback **10** locomotive

Hogan, Paul
country: **9** Australia
roles: **10** Mick Dundee **15** Crocodile Dundee

Hogan's Heroes
character: **7** (Peter) Newkirk **8** Lt Carter **10** Sgt (Hans) Schultz **11** Louis LeBeau **14** Col Robert Hogan **15** Col Wilhelm Klink
cast: **8** Bob Crane **10** John Banner, Larry Hovis **11** Robert Clary **13** Richard Dawson **15** Werner Klemperer

Hogarth, William
born: **6** London **7** England
artwork: **12** Captain Coram **14** A Rake's Progress **15** Marriage a la Mode, The Beggar's Opera **16** A Harlot's Progress **19** Garrick as Richard III

hogshead **3** keg, tun, vat **4** butt, cask, drum **6** barrel

hogwash **3** rot **4** bull, bunk **5** hokum, hooey, stuff **6** bunkum, drivel, hot air, humbug **7** baloney, blather, spinach, twaddle **8** claptrap, nonsense, tommyrot **9** poppycock **10** applesauce **11** foolishness **13** horsefeathers **16** stuff and nonsense

hoi polloi **6** rabble, the mob **7** the herd **8** canaille, populace, riffraff, the crowd, the plebs **9** the masses, the proles, the vulgar **10** commonalty **12** the multitude **14** the lower orders, the proletariat, the rank and file **15** the common people, the lower classes, the working class

hoist **4** lift **5** heave, raise, run up **6** bear up, pull up, take up, uplift **7** elevate, raise up, upraise **9** bear aloft

Hokan
language family: **17** Hokan-Coahuiltecan
subgroup: **4** Pomo, Seri, Yana **5** Karok, Washo, Yuman **7** Chontal, Chumash, Esselen, Jicaque **8** Subtiaba **9** Chimariko **14** Shasta-Achomawi
tribe: **8** Achomawi

Hokan-Coahuiltecan
language branch: **5** Hokan **12** Coahuiltecan **17** Subtiaba-Tlappanec

Hokusai, Katsushika
born: **3** Edo **5** Japan, Tokyo
artwork: **5** Crabs, Manga **10** Waterfalls **11** Chushingura **25** Thirty-six Views of Mount Fuji

Holabird, William
partner: **11** Martin Roche
architect of: **12** Gage Building **13** Cable Building, Crerar Library (City Hall, Chicago) **14** Tacoma Building **15** McClurg Building **17** Marquette Building

Holbein, Hans (the Elder)
born: **7** Germany **8** Augsburg
son: **11** Hans Holbein (the Younger)
artwork: **11** St Sebastian **14** Fountain of Life **18** Kaisheim Altarpiece **31** Presentation of Christ in the Temple

Holbein, Hans (the Younger)
born: **7** Germany **8** Augsburg
father: **11** Hans Holbein (the Elder)
artwork: **7** Erasmus **9** Henry VIII **11** Jane Seymour **12** Dance of Death **13** The Dead Christ

hold ***see box***

hold a candle to **5** equal, match **6** be up to **7** compare **8** approach **10** be as good as **11** come close to, compete with **12** be comparable **14** bear comparison

hold against **6** resent **8** begrudge

hold back **3** lag **4** curb, deny, keep, slow **5** check, dally, limit, stall **6** arrest, bridle, falter, refuse **7** contain, inhibit, keep out, reserve, retrain **8** hesitate, keep back, maintain, restrain, withhold **9** constrain

hold close **3** hug **5** clasp **6** cuddle, harbor **7** cherish, embrace, snuggle

Holden, William
real name: **23** William Franklin Beedle Jr
nickname: **4** Bill
born: **9** O'Fallon IL
roles: **6** Picnic **7** Network, Sabrina **9** Golden Boy **13** Born Yesterday **14** The Country Girl **15** Stalag Seventeen (Oscar), Sunset Boulevard **23** The Bridge on the River Kwai

hold fast **4** fuse, hold **5** cling, stick **6** adhere

hold firmly **4** grip **5** clasp, grasp **6** clench, clinch, clutch **10** grab hold of

hold forth **7** expound **9** discourse, expatiate

hold in abeyance **5** table **6** recess, shelve **7** suspend **8** lay aside, postpone

hold in bondage **7** control, enchain, enslave, entrall **8** dominate **9** subjugate **12** make a slave of

hold **4** bear, bind, bond, curb, deem, grip, halt, have, hilt, keep, knob, lock, prop, rule, stay, sway, take, urge **5** block, brace, carry, check, clasp, cling, count, defer, grasp, guard, limit, offer, power, shaft, shore, stall, stand, stick, strap, think, unite, watch **6** adhere, affirm, assert, assume, cleave, clinch, clutch, deduct, detain, direct, enfold, handle, hinder, hold up, join in, manage, occupy, reckon, regard, retain, submit, take in, tender, thwart, uphold **7** advance, believe, carry on, command, conduct, confine, contain, control, declare, embrace, enclose, enforce, execute, hold off, include, inhibit, mastery, possess, present, presume, prevent, profess, propose, protect, repress, reserve, support, suppose, surmise, suspend, toehold, venture **8** advocate, conceive, conclude, consider, engage in, foothold, handhold, hold back, hold down, leverage, maintain, obligate, postpone, purchase, put forth, restrain, restrict, set aside, suppress, withhold **9** advantage, anchorage, authority, be in force, dominance, forestall, frustrate, influence, keep valid, ownership, stay fixed, stick fast **10** ascendancy, attachment, desist from, domination, possession, put forward, understand **11** accommodate, preside over

holdings 6 assets **8** property **10** securities **11** commodities

hold in high regard 5 honor, prize, value **6** admire, esteem, revere **7** cherish, respect **8** look up to, treasure, venerate **10** rate highly, set store by **13** think highly of **18** attach importance to

hold one's own 4 cope **6** manage **7** contend **11** be a match for **20** maintain one's position **22** keep one's head above water

hold rapt 5 charm **7** beguile, bewitch, enchant **8** enthrall, entrance **9** captivate, enrapture, fascinate, spellbind, transport

hold to 4 bind **8** obligate

hold together 4 bind, fuse, glue, hold, join **5** cling, stick, unite **6** cement, cohere **7** combine **11** consolidate

holdup 3 rob **4** bear, halt, stay, stop **5** delay, heist, steal, theft **6** hijack, retain, uphold **7** robbery, stickup, support, sustain **8** stoppage **9** hindrance **12** interruption

hold up 4 prop, slow **5** block, brace, check, delay **6** bear up, detain, endure, hinder, impede, manage **7** bolster, present, stand up, support, sustain **8** keep back, obstruct **13** rob at gunpoint

hold up under 4 bear **6** endure, manage **8** tolerate

hold warmly 3 hug **5** clasp **6** cuddle **7** embrace, snuggle

hole 3 den, gap, pit **4** brig, cage, cave, flaw, keep, lair, rent, slit, slot **5** break, crack, fault, shaft **6** breach, burrow, cavern, cavity, crater, defect, dugout, lockup, pocket, prison, tunnel **7** dungeon, fallacy, opening, orifice, slammer **8** aperture, dark cell, puncture **9** concavity, open space **10** depression, excavation **11** discrepancy, hollow place, indentation, perforation **13** inconsistency

Holgrave, Mr
character in: 24 The House of the Seven Gables
author: 9 Hawthorne

holiday ***see box***

holiday 3 gay **4** fete, gala **6** cheery, fiesta, joyful, joyous, junket, outing **7** festive, holy day, jubilee **8** cheerful, feast day, festival, vacation **11** celebrating, celebration, merrymaking
American: 6 Easter **8** Arbor Day, Labor Day **9** Christmas (Dec 25), Halloween (Oct 31) **10** Father's Day, Good Friday, Mother's Day **11** Columbus Day, Election Day, Memorial Day, New Year's Day (Jan 1), Veterans' Day (Nov 11) **12** Children's Day, Thanksgiving **15** Independence Day (July 4), St Valentine's Day (Feb 14) **23** National Grandparents' Day
***birthday:* 8** Lincoln's **11** Robert E Lee's (Jan 19), Washington's **17** Martin Luther King's (Jan 15)
***Hawaiian:* 13** Kamehameha Day (June 11)
British: 8 Hogmanay (Dec 31) **9** Boxing Day (Dec 26) **11** Harvest Home **12** Guy Fawkes Day (Nov 5), Twelfth Night (Jan 5) **14** Queen's Birthday (June) **15** Commonwealth Day (May 24), Mothering Sunday **19** Feast of Saint Swithin (July 15)
Canadian: 11 Victoria Day **14** Queen's Birthday, Remembrance Day
Chinese: 7 New Year **15** Lantern Festival **17** Confucius' Birthday (Sept 28) **18** Dragon Boat Festival
French: 11 Bastille Day (May 14)
German: 11 Oktoberfest
Greek: 7 Genesia **11** Feast of Pots
Indian: 4 Holi **6** Basant, Diwali (New Year) **17** Hindu fire festival **22** Mahatma Gandhi's Birthday (Oct 2)
Irish: 16 Saint Patrick's Day (March 17)
Italian: 13 Liberation Day (April 25)
Japanese: 11 Hina-Matsuri **12** Children's Day (May 5), Feast of Dolls (March 3) **15** Constitution Day (May 3) **17** Girls' Doll Festival
Jewish: 5 Purim **6** Sukkot **7** Shavuot, Sukkoth **8** Hanukkah, Passover **9** Yom Kippur **12** Rosh Hashanah **20** Hamishah Assar B'Shevat, The New Year of the Trees **21** Feast of the Tabernacles
Korean: 6 Ch'usok
Latin American: 12 Day of the Race
Moslem: 7 Mouloud **8** Id-al-Adha, Id-al-Fitr **12** Maulid-an-Nabi **14** month of Ramadan
religious: 6 Advent **7** Lady Day (Mar 25) **8** Epiphany, Shabuoth **9** Candlemas, Mardi Gras, Martinmas (Nov 11), Pentecost **10** Whitsunday **11** All Souls' Day (Nov 2) **12** Ascension Day, Ash Wednesday, Feast of Weeks **13** Shrove Tuesday, Trinity Sunday **15** Annunciation Day (Mar 25) **16** Feast of All Saints **20** Feast of Corpus Christi **23** Day of Our Lady of Guadalupe (Dec 12) **27** Purification of the Virgin Mary **30** Feast of the Immaculate Conception (Dec 8)
Roman: 7 Feralia **10** Saturnalia
Scottish: 8 Hogmanay **12** Candlemas Day **19** Festival of the Virgin
South American: 21 Simon Bolivar's Birthday (July 24)
Sri Lankan: 5 Wesak
Soviet Union: 6 May Day (May 1) **14** Lenin's Birthday (April 22) **39** Day of the Great October Socialist Revolution (Nov 7)
Swedish: 13 Santa Lucia Day (Dec 13)
Thailand: 11 Visakha Puja

holiness 8 sanctity **9** godliness **10** sacredness **11** blessedness, saintliness

Holland *see* **11** Netherlands

Holle
origin: 8 Germanic
goddess of: 4 moon
corresponds to: 7 Berchta, Perchta
form: 5 witch

holler 4 bark, roar, yell **5** gripe, shout **6** bellow, cry out, grouse **8** complain **9** hue and cry

Holliday, Judy
real name: 11 Judith Tuvim
born: 9 New York NY
roles: 8 Adam's Rib **13** Born Yesterday (Oscar) **15** Bells Are Ringing

Hollinshed, Raphael
author of: 37 Chronicles of

England Scotland and Ireland

hollow **3** dip, low, rut **4** cave, dale, deep, dell, dent, dull, glen, hole, sink, vain, vale, void **5** ditch, empty, false, muted **6** cavern, cavity, crater, dig out, dimple, furrow, futile, groove, pocket, sunken, vacant, vacuum, valley **7** channel, concave, useless **8** crevasse, empty out, excavate, gouge out, indented, not solid, nugatory, rumbling, scoop out, specious, unfilled **9** cavernous, concavity, deceptive, depressed, fruitless, pointless, valueless, worthless **10** depression, profitless, sepulchral, unavailing, unresonant **11** indentation, meaningless, nonresonant **12** unprofitable **13** curving inward, disappointing, reverberating **14** expressionless, unsatisfactory **15** inconsequential

Holloway, Stanley
born: **6** London **7** England
roles: **10** My Fair Lady **15** Alfred Doolittle **18** The Lavender Hill Mob

Hollow Men
author: **7** T S Eliot

hollowness **4** void **6** vacuum **7** vacancy **9** emptiness

hollow out **4** bore **5** drill **6** dig out **8** carve out, gouge out, scoop out **9** chisel out **13** tunnel through

holly **4** Ilex
varieties: **3** box, sea **4** dune **5** Cuban, Dutch, dwarf, false, Furin, Kashi, swamp, Tsuru **6** desert, horned, Oregon, Sarvis, Soyogo, summer **7** African, Chinese, English, Georgia, Madeira **8** American, European, hedgehog, Japanese, Kurogane, mountain **9** box-leaved, Highclere, miniature, moonlight, porcupine, Singapore **10** Costa Rican, luster-leaf, West Indian **11** large-leaved, Puerto Rican, screw-leaved **12** Canary Island, gold hedgehog, myrtle-leaved, smooth-leaved **14** silver hedgehog

hollyhock **6** mallow **7** Antwerp, figleaf **8** biennial **9** ficifolia, Malvaceae **10** alcea rosea

Hollywood's Mermaid
nickname of: **14** Esther Williams

Hollywood Squares
host: **12** John Davidson **13** Peter Marshall
regular: **8** Wally Cox **10** Joan Rivers **13** Charley Weaver, Shadoe Stevens

Holmes, Oliver Wendell
author of: **12** Old Ironsides **30** The Autocrat of the Breakfast Table

Holmes, Sherlock
address: **11** (221B) Baker Street
appears in: **13** The Sign of Four **14** The Naval Treaty **15** A Study in Scarlet, The Speckled Band **16** Scandal in Bohemia, The Blue Carbuncle, The Copper Beeches **18** The Red-Headed League, The Solitary Cyclist **22** Hound of the Baskervilles
assistants: **21** Baker Street Irregulars
author: **16** (Sir) Arthur Conan Doyle
brother: **7** Mycroft
foe: **17** Professor Moriarty
hat: **11** deerstalker
hobby: **6** violin
housekeeper / landlady: **9** Mrs Hudson
keeps tobacco in: **7** slipper **14** Turkish slipper
police: **17** Inspector Lestrade
sidekick: **12** Dr John Watson
vice: **7** cocaine **17** hypodermic syringe **20** seven-per-cent solution

Holmwood, Arthur
character in: **7** Dracula
author: **6** Stoker

holocaust **4** ruin **5** havoc **6** ravage **7** bonfire, carnage, inferno, killing **8** butchery, genocide, massacre **10** deadly fire, mass murder **11** devastation **12** annihilation **13** conflagration

Holofernes
character in: **16** Love's Labour's Lost
author: **11** Shakespeare

Holofernes
general of: **14** Nebuchadnezzar
killed by: **6** Judith

Holst, Gustav Theodore
born: **7** England **10** Cheltenham
composer of: **7** Savitri **10** Egdon Heath, Ode to Death, The Planets **11** Hammersmith **12** St Paul's Suite **13** Fugal Concerto **14** The Hymn of Jesus, The Perfect Fool **16** Somerset Rhapsody **17** The Cloud Messenger **19** Hymns from the Rig-Veda

holy **4** pure **5** godly, moral, pious **6** adored, devout, divine, sacred, solemn **7** angelic, blessed, from God, revered, saintly, sinless **8** faithful, hallowed, heavenly, reverent, virtuous **9** from above, guileless, religious, righteous, spiritual, undefiled, unspotted, unstained, unworldly, venerated, worshiped **10** heaven-sent, immaculate, inviolable, sacrosanct, sanctified, worshipped **11** consecrated, pure in heart, uncorrupted
Latin: **7** sanctus

Holy Ark
Hebrew: **10** Aron Kodesh

holy of holies
Latin: **16** sanctum sanctorum

Holy one *see* **5** Jesus

Holy Spirit, Holy Ghost
9 Paraclete **13** presence of God **23** third person of the Trinity
Latin: **15** Spiritus Sanctus
Greek: **12** Hagion Pneuma

holy war
Arabic: **5** jehad, jihad

Holy Willie's Prayer
author: **11** Robert Burns

Homadus
form: **7** centaur
killed by: **8** Hercules

homage **5** honor **6** esteem, praise, regard **7** respect, tribute, worship **8** devotion **9** adoration, adulation, deference, obeisance, reverence **10** exaltation, veneration **13** glorification

Homagyrius
epithet of: **4** Zeus
means: **9** assembler

hombre **3** man

home **5** abode, haunt, haven, house **6** asylum, cradle, refuge **7** habitat, hangout **8** domicile, dwelling, hospital **9** orphanage, poorhouse, residence **10** habitation, native land, sanatorium **11** institution **12** fountainhead **13** dwelling place, home sweet home **14** stamping ground **16** place of residence **18** natural environment **25** place where one hangs one's hat

Home Burial
author: **11** Robert Frost

homegrown **5** local **6** native **8** domestic **10** indigenous

Home Is the Sailor
author: **10** Jorge Amado

homelike **4** cozy **5** comfy, homey **6** simple **8** cheerful, domestic, familiar, informal, inviting **11** comfortable

homely **4** cozy, drab, snug **5** comfy, homey, plain **6** modest, rustic, simple **7** artless, natural **8** everyday, familiar, homelike, homespun, ordinary, uncomely **9** graceless **10** ill-favored, provincial, unaffected, unassuming, ungraceful, unhandsome **11** comfortable **12** plain-looking, unattractive **13** unpretentious

homer **15** Biblical measure

Homer
author of: **5** Iliad **7** Odyssey

Homer, Winslow
born: **8** Boston MA
artwork: **9** High Cliff **10** Breezing Up, Eight Bells **11** Marine Coast, Northeaster, The Life Line **13** The Fog Warning, The Gulf Stream **21** Inside the Bar Tynemouth, Prisoners from the Front

home rule **8** autonomy **11** sovereignty **12** independence **14** self-government

homespun **5** plain **6** folksy, homely, modest, native, simple **7** artless, natural **8** down-home, homemade **9** hand-woven **10** hand-loomed, unaffected **11** hand-crafted, hand-wrought **13** unpretentious

homey **4** cozy **6** casual, folksy **8** down-home, homelike, homespun, informal **15** unsophisticated

homicide **6** killer, murder, slayer **7** slaying **8** foul play, murderer, regicide, vaticide **9** bloodshed, man killer, manslayer, matricide, parricide, patricide, uxoricide **10** fratricide **11** infanticide **12** manslaughter

homiletic **7** preachy **8** didactic **10** moralizing

homily **6** sermon **7** lecture **10** preachment **11** exhortation

homogeneous **4** akin, pure **7** kindred, similar, uniform, unmixed **8** all alike, constant, of a piece **9** identical, unvarying **10** consistent **13** of the same kind, unadulterated

homology **7** analogy **8** likeness, relation **10** similarity **12** relationship **14** correspondence

Honduras ***see box***

hone **4** long, moan, pine, tool, whet **5** stroke, strope, whine, yearn **6** hanker, grumble, mutter, sharpen **9** whetstone

Honegger, Arthur
born: **5** Havre **6** France
nationality: **5** Swiss
member of: **6** Les Six, The Six
composer of: **5** Rugby **6** Judith **7** L'Aiglon **8** Antigone **9** The Eaglet **10** Le Roi David **13** Pastorale d'ete **18** Jeanne d'Arc au Bucher, Liturgical Symphony **19** Pacific Two-Thirty-One

honest **4** fair, just, open, real, true **5** blunt, frank, legal, plain, solid, valid **6** candid, decent, lawful, proper, square **7** artless, ethical, genuine, sincere, upright **8** bona fide, clear-cut, faithful, innocent, reliable, straight, true-blue, truthful, virtuous **9** authentic, blameless, guileless, honorable, ingenuous, reputable, righteous **10** aboveboard, dependable, forthright, law-abiding, legitimate, on the level, principled, reasonable, scrupulous, unaffected, unreserved **11** plainspoken, trustworthy, undisguised **12** on the up-and-up, tried and true **13** conscientious, fair and square **15** straightforward, unsophisticated **16** as good as one's word, straight-shooting **17** open and aboveboard

honesty **4** word **5** honor **7** probity **8** fairness, good name, morality, scruples, veracity **9** innocence, integrity, rectitude, sincerity **10** principles **11** just dealing, uprightness **12** faithfulness,

Honduras
name means: **6** depths
capital/largest city: **11** Tegucigalpa
others: **4** Tela, Yoro **5** Copan, Danli, Lapaz **6** Roatan **7** Gracias, La Ceiba **8** Trujillo, Yuscaran **9** Choluteca, Juticalpa **10** El Progreso **11** Comayaguela **12** Puerto Cortes, San Pedro Sula
measure: **4** vara **5** milla **6** mecate **7** cajuela
monetary unit: **4** peso **7** centavo, lempira
island: **3** Bay **5** Bahia, Utila **6** Roatan **7** Bonacca, Guanaja
lake: **5** Criba, Yojoa **6** Brewer
mountain: **4** Pija **6** Agalta **7** Celaque **9** Esperanza
highest point: **8** Las Minas
river: **4** Coco, Sico, Ulua **5** Aguan, Lempa, Negro, Tinto, Wanks **6** Patuca, Sulaco **7** Olancho, Paulaya, Segovia **8** Guiavope, Santiago **9** Choluteca **10** Chamelecon
sea: **7** Pacific **8** Atlantic **9** Caribbean
physical feature:
coast: **5** North **8** Mosquito **10** Costa Norte
gulf: **7** Fonseca **8** Honduras
port: **7** Laceiba **8** Trujillo
people: **4** Maya, Paya, Sumo, Ulva **5** Carib, Lenca, Pipil **6** Tauira **7** Jicaque, mestizo, Miskito **8** Mosquito
discoverer: **8** Columbus
farmer: **9** campesino
language: **7** English, Spanish
religion: **13** Roman Catholic
place:
ruins: **5** Copan **8** Tenampua
feature:
bird: **9** zenzontle
dance: **5** sique **7** mascaro
estate: **10** latifundia
farm: **6** milpas **10** minifundia
musical instrument: **7** caramba, marimba
tree: **8** cockspur
food:
beans: **8** frijoles
beef dish: **6** tapado
corn: **5** maize
stuffed corn cake: **10** naca tamale
tripe stew: **8** mondongo

reputability, truthfulness **13** guiltlessness, square dealing **15** trustworthiness **16** incorruptibility, straight shooting

honeybee
classification: 6 social
live in: 4 hive **6** colony
headed by: 5 queen
male: 5 drone
laborer: 6 worker
food-gatherer: 7 forager
gather: 6 nectar, pollen
produce: 5 honey
queen's food: 10 royal jelly

honeyed 4 kind **5** sweet **6** sugary **7** cloying, fawning **10** flattering, saccharine **12** ingratiating **13** complimentary

honeyed words 4 line **7** blarney **8** cajolery, flattery, soft soap **9** sweet talk

Honey in the Horn
author: 7 H L Davis

Honeymooners, The
character: 8 Ed Norton **12** Alice Kramden, Ralph Kramden, Trixie Norton
cast: 8 Jane Kean **9** Art Carney **12** Sheila MacRae **13** Audrey Meadows, Jackie Gleason, Joyce Randolph
Ralph's job: 9 bus driver
Ed's job: 5 sewer
lodge: 8 Raccoons

honor 3 pay **4** cash, fame, laud, note, take **5** adore, exalt, extol, favor, glory, grant, leave, power, right, truth, value **6** accept, admire, credit, esteem, homage, praise, redeem, regard, renown, repute, revere, virtue **7** acclaim, commend, decency, dignify, glorify, honesty, liberty, probity, respect, tribute, worship **8** eminence, fairness, good name, goodness, justness, look up to, make good, pleasure, prestige, sanction, venerate, veracity **9** adoration, celebrity, constancy, deference, greatness, integrity, principle, privilege, rectitude, reverence, sincerity **10** admiration, compliment, exaltation, good report, importance, notability, permission, prominence, veneration **11** acknowledge, approbation, distinction, pay homage to, recognition, think much of, uprightness **12** commendation, faithfulness, high standing, pay tribute to, truthfulness **13** authorization, bow down before, glorification, have regard for, honorableness, make payment on **14** high-mindedness, scrupulousness **15** illustriousness, trustworthiness **17** a feather in one's cap, conscientiousness

honeysuckle 8 Lonicera **19** Aquilegia canadensis, Justicia californica **24** Rhododendron prinophyllum
varieties: 3 fly **4** bush, cape **5** coral, giant, grape, hairy, swamp **6** desert, French, purple, yellow **7** Arizona, Jamaica, trumpet **8** Himalaya, Japanese, swamp fly, Tatarian **9** chaparral, Tartarian **10** yellow cape **11** European fly **12** giant Burmese, long-flowered, South African **13** Hall's Japanese

Honeythunder, Mr
character in: 22 The Mystery of Edwin Drood
author: 7 Dickens

Hong Kong ***see box***

Hong Kong
name means: 13 incense harbor **14** fragrant harbor
capital: 8 Victoria
largest city:
section: **7** Kowloon **8** Hong Kong, Victoria
others: 4 Tai O **5** Tai Po **8** Aberdeen, Pingshan, Yuenlong **9** Shataukok **10** Sheungshui
division: 7 Kowloon **8** Hong Kong **14** New Territories
government: 18 British crown colony
head of state: 14 British monarch **15** governor general
island: 5 Lamma **6** Lan Tao, Lantau, Middle, Poi Toi **8** Hong Kong **9** Ap Lei Chau **11** Stonecutter
mountain: 6 Castle **8** Victoria
highest point: 9 Tai Mo Shan
river: 5 Pearl **6** Canton **8** Sham Chun
sea: 10 South China
physical feature:
bay: **4** Mirs **6** Quarry **7** Kowloon, Repulse **9** Deep Water
harbor: **4** Tolo **8** Aberdeen, Hong Kong, Victoria
peak: **8** Victoria
peninsula: **7** Kowloon
people: 5 Hakka, Haklo, Punti, Tanka **7** British, Chinese **8** American, Japanese **9** Cantonese **10** Portuguese
language: 7 Chinese, English **9** Cantonese
religion: 5 Hindu, Islam **6** Taoism **8** Buddhism **12** Christianity
feature:
airport: **6** Kai Tak
clothing: **6** samfoo **9** cheongsam
houseboat: **6** sampan
rock: **5** Amahs **6** Sha Tin
temple: **18** Ten Thousand Buddhas

Honiara
capital of: 14 Solomon Islands

honi soit qui mal y pense 31 shamed be the one who thinks evil of it
motto of: 16 Order of the Garter

honk 4 toot **5** blare, blast **7** trumpet

honky-tonk 4 dive **7** gin mill **9** roadhouse, nightclub

honor ***see box***

honorable 4 good **5** noble, title **6** decent, honest, lordly, square **7** upright **9** elevated, reputable, respected **10** creditable **11** distinctive, illustrious, respectable, trustworthy **12** considerable **13** distinguished

hood 4 cowl, lout, punk **5** bully, rowdy, scarf, tough **6** vandal **7** hoodlum, ruffian **8** hooligan **9** barbarian, roughneck **10** delinquent **12** headcovering

Hood, Raymond
architect of: 11 RCA Building (Rockefeller Center) **17** Daily News Building (NYC) **18** McGraw-Hill Building (NYC) **22** Chicago Tribune Building **24** American Radiator Building
style: 13 International

hoodlum 4 hood, punk, thug **5** crook, rowdy, tough **6** gunman **7** bruiser, gorilla, mobster, ruffian **8** criminal, gangster, hooligan, plug-ugly **9** desperado, strong arm **10** delinquent

hoodwink **3** gyp **4** dupe, fool, gull, hoax, rook **5** cheat, cozen, trick **7** deceive, defraud, mislead, swindle **8** inveigle **9** bamboozle, victimize

hook **3** arc, bag, bow, nab, net **4** arch, bend, bill, curl, gaff, grab, loop, take, trap, wind **5** angle, catch, crook, curve, elbow, fluke, hitch, latch, seize, snare **6** buckle, collar, fasten, peavey, secure **7** capture, crampon, ensnare, grapnel, grapple, pothook **8** crescent, make fast **9** horseshoe

Hooke, Robert
field: **7** physics **9** astronomy
nationality: **7** British
discovered: **9** Orion star **15** Jupiter rotation **20** moon's center of gravity **21** earth's center of gravity
invented: **10** microscope
named for him: **15** law of elasticity

hooked **8** addicted **9** compelled, obsessive **10** compulsive, habituated **14** uncontrollable

hooked cross
German: **10** Hakenkreuz

hook up **4** ally, dock, join **5** hinge **6** couple, link up **7** connect **8** assemble **10** articulate **11** fit together **14** fasten together

hooligan **4** hood, lout, punk **5** bully, rowdy, tough **6** vandal **7** hoodlum, ruffian **9** barbarian, roughneck **10** delinquent

hoopla **4** hype **8** ballyhoo **9** promotion, publicity **10** hullabaloo, propaganda **11** advertising **15** public relations

Hoosier Schoolmaster, The
author: **15** Edward Eggleston

Hoosier State
nickname of: **7** Indiana

hoot **3** boo, din **4** bawl, blow, hiss, honk, howl, jeer, moan, mock, razz, roar, wail, yelp, yowl **5** shout, sneer, taunt, whoop **6** bellow, chorus, cry out, deride, outcry, racket, scream, shriek, shrill, tumult, uproar **7** catcall, cry down, scoff at, screech, sing out, sneer at, snicker, ululate, wailing, whistle **8** proclaim, shouting **9** caterwaul, commotion, raspberry, screaming, snicker at **10** Bronx cheer, screeching

Hoover, Herbert Clark
nickname: **13** Great Engineer **14** Great Secretary **17** Great Humanitarian **18** Great Public Servant
presidential rank: **11** thirty-first
party: **10** Republican
state represented: **2** CA
defeated: **5** (Alfred Emanuel) Smith **6** (George William) Norris, (Norman) Thomas, (William Frederick) Varney, (William Zebulon) Foster **8** (Verne L) Reynolds
vice president: **6** (Charles) Curtis
cabinet:
state: **7** (Henry Lewis) Stimson
treasury: **5** (Ogden Livingston) Mills **6** (Andrew William) Mellon
war: **4** (James William) Good **6** (Patrick Jay) Hurley
attorney general: **8** (William DeWitt) Mitchell
navy: **5** (Charles Francis) Adams
postmaster general: **5** (Walter Folger) Brown
interior: **6** (Ray Lyman) Wilbur
agriculture: **4** (Arthur Mastick) Hyde
commerce: **6** (Robert Patterson) Lamont, (Roy Dikeman) Chapin
labor: **4** (William Nuckles) Doak **5** (James John) Davis
born: **12** West Branch IA
died: **13** New York City NY
buried: **12** West Branch IA
education:
University: **8** Stanford
religion: **5** Quaker **16** Society of Friends
interests: **7** fishing
vacation spot: **10** Camp Hoover **11** Rapidan Camp **22** Shenandoah National Park
author: **7** Memoirs **11** On Growing Up **14** An American Epic **16** Years of Adventure **18** Principles of Mining, The Great Depression **20** America's First Crusade **21** American Individualism, The Challenge to Liberty **24** The Ordeal of Woodrow Wilson **25** The Problems of Lasting Peace **26** The Cabinet and the Presidency **28** Addresses Upon the American Road **51** The State Papers and Other Public Writings of Herbert Hoover
political career: **19** US Food Administrator
head of: **23** American Relief Committee **28** Commission for Relief in Belgium
director: **38** General Relief and Reconstruction of Europe
member/chairman: **22** Supreme Economic Council
secretary of: **8** Commerce
chairman of: **17** Hoover Commissions
civilian career: **6** author **14** mining engineer **18** consulting engineer
notable events of lifetime/term: **15** Great Depression
conference: **11** London Naval
crash of: **11** stock market
independence for: **11** Philippines
Tariff: **11** Hawley-Smoot
father: **10** Jesse Clark
mother: **6** Huldah (Randall Minthorn)
siblings: **3** May **13** Theodore Jesse
wife: **3** Lou (Henry)
children: **10** Allan Henry **12** Herbert Clark
first lady:
vice president of: **10** Girl Scouts

hop **3** bob **4** ball, jump, leap, prom, romp, skip, step, trip **5** bound, caper, dance, frisk, mixer, vault **6** bounce, gambol, prance, soiree, spring **7** Humulus
varieties: **4** Wild **5** False **6** Common **8** European, Japanese

hope **3** yen **4** help, wish **5** crave, dream, faith, fancy, trust **6** aspire, belief, chance, desire, expect, hunger, rescue, yen for **7** believe, count on, craving, dream of, longing, long for **8** ambition, daydream, feel sure, optimism, prospect, reckon on, reliance, yearn for, yearning **9** assurance, hankering, have faith, hunger for, salvation, take heart **10** anticipate, aspiration, assumption, be bent upon, confidence, conviction, expectancy **11** be confident, contemplate, expectation, have an eye to, possibility, presumption, reassurance, saving grace **12** anticipation, be optimistic, heart's desire **13** encouragement, have a fancy for, look forward to **14** have a hankering **17** great expectations **18** have one's heart set on **19** look on the bright side

Hope, Anthony
real name: 21 Sir Anthony Hope Hawkins
author of: 15 Rupert of Hentzau **18** The Prisoner of Zenda

Hope, Bob
real name: 16 Leslie Townes Hope
co-star: 10 Bing Crosby **13** Dorothy Lamour
born: 6 Eltham **7** England
roles:
Road to: **3** Rio **4** Bali **6** Utopia **7** Morocco **8** Hong Kong, Zanzibar **9** Singapore

hopeful 7 assured, in hopes **8** cheering, sanguine, trusting **9** confident, expectant, favorable, fortunate, promising **10** auspicious, heartening, of good omen, optimistic, propitious, reassuring **11** encouraging **12** anticipative

hopeless 3 sad **4** lost, vain **6** abject, futile **7** forlorn, useless **8** dejected, downcast **9** depressed, incurable, pointless **10** beyond help, despairing, despondent, impossible, melancholy, past remedy **11** downhearted, heartbroken, irreparable, irrevocable, pessimistic, sick at heart **12** beyond recall, disconsolate, heavyhearted, irredeemable, irreversible **13** grief-stricken, irretrievable **14** down in the mouth, sorrow-stricken

hopelessness 7 despair **8** futility **9** pessimism **11** uselessness

Hopi (Hopitu, Moki)
language family: 10 Shoshonean
location: 7 Arizona
adapted culture of: 6 Pueblo
ceremony: 10 snake dance

Hopkins, Anthony
born: 5 Wales **10** Port Talbot
roles: 10 Audrey Rose **11** A Doll's House **12** Young Winston **14** The Elephant Man **15** The Lion in Winter

Hoples
father: 3 Ion

Hopper, Edward
born: 7 Nyack NY
artwork: 10 Nighthawks **18** Early Sunday Morning, House by the Railroad **19** Second Story Sunlight **20** Sunlight in a Cafeteria **21** Lighthouse at Two Lights

Horae
also: 4 Hour
goddesses of: 5 decay **6** growth **7** seasons **11** social order
names: 4 Dice, Dike **5** Irene **7** Eunomia

Horatii
form: 7 triplets **8** brothers
sister: 7 Horatia
champions of: 4 Rome
fought: 8 Curiatii

Horatio
character in: 6 Hamlet
author: 11 Shakespeare

Horatio
character in: 17 The Spanish Tragedy
author: 3 Kyd

Horatius
origin: 5 Roman
defended: 6 bridge
over: **5** Tiber
against: **9** Etruscans

Horcus
origin: 5 Greek
god of: 5 oaths

horde 3 mob **4** band, gang, host, pack **5** bunch, crowd, crush, drove, party, swarm, tribe, troop **6** legion, throng **7** company **8** assembly **9** gathering, multitude **10** assemblage **12** congregation

Horgan, Paul
author of: 10 Whitewater **13** Lamy of Santa Fe **18** The Thin Mountain Air

horizon 4 area **5** field, range, realm, scope, vista, world **6** bounds, domain, sphere **7** compass, expanse, outlook, purview, stretch **8** frontier, prospect **11** perspective

horizontal 4 even, flat **5** flush, level, plane, plumb, prone **6** supine **8** parallel (to something) **9** lying down, prostrate, reclining, recumbent **14** flat on one's back

horizontal support 3 tie **4** beam **5** brace, joist **6** girder, header, lintel **8** crossbar

hormone 5 auxin **6** cortin **7** estrone, insulin, steroid **8** endocrin, estrogen, galactin, lactogen, secretin **9** adrenalin, cortisone **12** progesterone, testosterone

horn 4 tusk **5** cornu, point, spike **6** antler **11** excrescence
brass instrument: 4 oboe, tuba **5** bugle **6** cornet **7** bassoon, trumpet **8** alto horn, baritone, clarinet, trombone **9** euphonium, saxophone **10** French horn, mellophone, sousaphone **11** English horn

Horn of Africa *see* **7** Somalia

Hornung, Paul
nickname: 9 Golden Boy
sport: 8 football
position: 6 runner **11** placekicker
team: 15 Green Bay Packers

horny 4 hard **5** tough **7** callous **8** callused, hardened **12** thick-skinned **14** pachydermatous

horologe 5 clock **9** timepiece **11** chronometer

horrendous 4 gory **5** awful **6** horrid **7** ghastly, hideous **8** dreadful, horrible, shocking, terrible **9** appalling, frightful, repellent, repulsive, revolting **10** horrifying

horrible 3 bad **4** foul, rank, vile **5** awful, nasty **6** grisly, horrid, odious **7** ghastly, hideous **8** dreadful, gruesome, shocking, terrible, unsavory **9** abhorrent, appalling, atrocious, frightful, harrowing, loathsome, monstrous, obnoxious, repellent, repulsive, revolting, sickening **10** abominable, despicable, detestable, disgusting, forbidding, nauseating, unbearable, unpleasant **11** disquieting, distasteful, unspeakable **12** disagreeable, insufferable

horrid 3 bad **4** foul, grim, ugly **5** awful, nasty, rough **6** bratty, horror, shaggy, wicked **7** fearful, hideous **8** dreadful, gruesome, horrible, shocking, terrible **9** bristling, frightful, offensive, revolting, vexatious **10** abominable, detestable, unpleasant **11** troublesome **12** disagreeable

horrific 4 dire **5** awful **7** fearful, ghastly **8** dreadful, horrible, shocking, terrible **9** appalling

horrified 6 aghast **8** appalled

9 petrified, terrified **10** frightened **13** thunderstruck **14** terror-stricken

horrify **5** daunt, repel, shock **6** appall, dismay, revolt, sicken **7** disgust, petrify, terrify **8** affright, disquiet, frighten, nauseate **10** disconcert, dishearten **11** make one sick **15** make one turn pale **18** make one's flesh creep **22** make one's hair stand on end

horrifying **5** awful, dread **8** alarming, dreadful **10** terrifying **11** frightening, hair-raising

horror **3** woe **4** fear **5** alarm, crime, dread, panic **6** dismay, hatred, misery, terror **7** anguish, cruelty, disgust, dislike, outrage, torment **8** atrocity, aversion, distaste, distress, hardship, loathing **9** antipathy, awfulness, privation, repulsion, revulsion, suffering **10** abhorrence, affliction, discomfort, inhumanity, repugnance **11** abomination, detestation, hideousness, trepidation **12** apprehension, terribleness, wretchedness

horror-struck **6** aghast **7** fearful **8** appalled **9** horrified, terrified **10** frightened **13** scared to death

hors de combat **8** disabled **13** out of the fight

hors d'oeuvre **3** dip **6** canape, relish, tidbit **9** antipasto, appetizer **10** finger food

horse *see box, p. 460*

horseback riding
athlete: **11** Frank Chapot **17** William Steinkraus

horse collar **3** zip **4** zero **5** aught, zilch **6** cipher, naught **8** goose egg

Horse Knows the Way, The
author: **9** John O'Hara

horseman **5** groom, rider **6** hussar, jockey, lancer, ostler **7** cossack, dragoon, hostler, trainer, trooper **9** postilion, stableboy, stableman **10** cavalryman, equestrian, roughrider **11** horse marine, stable owner **12** equestrienne, horse breeder, horse soldier, stable keeper **14** cavalry soldier, horseback rider, mounted trooper

horseplay **6** pranks **7** foolery **9** cutting up **10** buffoonery, tomfoolery **13** fooling around, horsing around

horse racing
jockey: **8** Del Insko **11** Bill Hartack, Eddie Arcaro **12** Angel Cordero, Bill Haughton, Laffit Pincay, Steve Cauthen **13** Johnny Longden, Stanley Dancer **15** Willie Shoemaker
god of: **6** Consus

Horseshoe Robinson
author: **12** John P Kennedy

horse soldier **6** hussar, lancer **7** dragoon, trooper **8** cavalier, horseman **10** cavalryman

horse trooper **6** hussar, lancer **7** dragoon, Mountie **8** cavalier, horseman **10** cavalryman **12** horse soldier **14** mounted soldier **16** mounted policeman

Horton, Edward Everett
sidekick of: **11** Fred Astaire
born: **10** Brooklyn NY
roles: **15** Cinderella Jones, Her Primitive Man **18** Springtime for Henry

Horus
origin: **8** Egyptian
god of: **3** sun
Greek name: **10** Harcorates
symbol: **6** falcon
mother: **4** Isis
father: **6** Osiris
enemy: **3** Set **4** Seth

hosannas **4** yeas **5** kudos **6** bravos, cheers, paeans **7** acclaim, hurrahs, huzzahs, yippees **8** applause **10** hallelujas **11** halleluiahs

hose **5** socks **7** hosiery **9** stockings

Hosea
father: **5** Beeri

hosiery **3** sox **4** hose **5** socks **6** nylons, tights **7** leotard **9** stockings

hospitable **4** open, warm **6** genial **7** cordial **8** amenable, amicable, friendly, gracious, sociable, tolerant **9** agreeable, convivial, receptive, welcoming **10** accessible, gregarious, neighborly, openhanded, open-minded, responsive **12** approachable

hospital **4** home **6** asylum, clinic **7** sick bay **8** pavilion, rest home **9** infirmary **10** polyclinic, sanatorium **11** nursing home **13** medical center
French: **9** hotel Dieu

hospital, private
French: **13** maison de sante

hospitality **5** cheer **6** warmth **7** welcome **8** openness **9** geniality **10** cordiality, heartiness, kindliness **11** amicability, sociability **12** congeniality, conviviality, friendliness **13** Gemutlichkeit **14** hospitableness, neighborliness **15** warmheartedness
god of: **6** Sancus **10** Dius Fidius, Semo Sancus

host, hostess **3** lot, mob **4** army, band, body, crew, gang, mess **5** array, crowd, drove, group, horde, party, swarm, troop **6** legion, throng **7** company, maitre d', meeting **8** conclave, congress, hosteler, hotelier, landlord, welcomer **9** gathering, innkeeper, multitude **10** confluence, convention, headwaiter, party giver, proprietor **11** convocation, hotel keeper **12** congregation, head waitress, hotel manager, proprietress, receptionist **17** restaurant manager **18** master of ceremonies **20** mistress of ceremonies

hostage **7** captive **8** prisoner

Hostage, The
author: **12** Brendan Behan

hostel **3** inn **4** hall **5** hotel, lodge **7** hospice, lodging, shelter **8** hospital, hostelry

hostile **3** icy **4** cold, mean, ugly **5** angry, at war, enemy, testy **6** at odds, at outs, bitter, chilly, cranky, malign, touchy, unkind **7** opposed, vicious, warring **8** battling, clashing, contrary, fighting, opposing, snappish, spiteful, venomous **9** bellicose, bristling, dissident, malicious, malignant, truculent **10** contending, ill-natured, malevolent, on bad terms, unfriendly **11** belligerent, contentious, disagreeing, ill-disposed, quarrelsome **12** antagonistic, cantankerous, disagreeable, disputatious, incompatible **13** argumentative, at loggerheads, unsympathetic

hostile act **4** raid **6** strike, threat **7** assault, offense **8** act of war, invasion **9** hostility, incursion **10** aggression

hostile nation **5** enemy **7** invader

hostility **3** war **4** duel, feud, fray, hate **5** anger, clash, fight, venom **6** battle, combat, enmity, fracas, hatred, malice, rancor, spleen **7** contest, dispute, ill will, scuffle, warfare, warring **8** act of war, argument, battling, conflict, fighting **9** animosity, antipathy, bickering **10** antagonism, bitterness, contention, dissidence, opposition, state of war **11** altercation, malevolence, vi-

horse 4 colt, foal, hack, jade, mare, plug, pony, sire, stud **5** bronc, filly, mount, pacer, pinto, steed **6** bronco, dobbin, equine **7** cavalry, charger, cow pony, gelding, hackney, hussars, lancers, mustang, palfrey, trotter **8** cossacks, dragoons, galloper, stallion, troopers, yearling **9** broodmare, racehorse **10** cavalrymen, draft horse **12** horse cavalry, horse marines, quarter horse, thoroughbred **13** horse soldiers, mounted troops **15** mounted troopers, mounted warriors

Achilles': 7 Xanthus
Alexander the Great's: 10 Bucephalus
anatomy: 4 hock, hoof, loin, mane, tail **5** croup, flank, shank **6** cannon, gaskin, haunch, stifle **7** coronet, crupper, fetlock, gambrel, nostril, pastern, withers **11** throatlatch
Australian: 5 dingo, myall **8** warragal, warrigal, yarraman
breed: 6 Morgan, Nubian, Tarpan **7** Arabian, Belgian, mustang **8** Galloway, Shetland **9** Appaloosa, Percheron **10** Clydesdale, Lippizaner **12** Narragansett, Standardbred, Thoroughbred **15** Tennessee-Walker
Caligula's: 9 Incitatus (made a senator)
castrated: 7 gelding
color: 3 bay, dun **4** gray, pied, roan, zain **5** morel, pinto **6** calico, dapple, sorrel **7** piebald **8** chestnut, palomino, schimmel (gray)
combining form: 4 eque, equi **5** hippo
Dick Turpin's: 9 Black Bess
Don Quixote's: 9 Rosinante
family: 7 Equidae **9** Miohippus, Orohippus
female: 3 dam **4** mare **5** filly
French: 6 cheval
gear: 3 bit **4** rein, tack **6** saddle **7** blinder, harness, snaffle **9** surcingle **11** saddlecloth
Gen Custer's: 8 Comanche
Gen Grant's: 10 Cincinnati
Gen Robert E Lee's: 9 Traveller
Gen Sherman's: 6 Rienzi
genus: 5 equus
Gulliver's Travels: 9 Houyhnhnm
kind: 3 cob **4** race **6** bronco, hunter, jumper **7** charger, mustang, palfrey, quarter, trotter **8** destrier
legendary: 6 Trojan
Lone Ranger's: 6 Silver
male: 4 colt **8** stallion
measure: 4 hand
Mohammed's: 7 Alborak
movie/story: 6 Flicka **8** Champion **11** Black Beauty **14** National Velvet **16** The Black Stallion
Napoleon's: 7 Morengo
Orlando's: 11 Vegliantino
pace: 4 lope, trot **5** amble **6** canter, gallop
pair of: 4 span, team **6** tandem
race: 5 derby, plate **6** exacta **7** pick six **8** claiming, handicap **9** allowance **11** daily double, sweepstakes **12** steeplechase, weight-for-age
***Triple Crown:* 7** Belmont **9** Preakness **13** Kentucky Derby
riding show: 8 gymkhana
Rinaldo's: 6 Bayard
Roy Rogers': 7 Trigger
Sigurd's: 5 Grani
small: 4 pony
Stonewall Jackson's: 12 Little Sorrel
Tom Mix's: 4 Tony
three: 6 randem, troika **7** unicorn
Wellington's (at Waterloo): 10 Copenhagen
wild: 5 fuzzy **6** bramby, kumrah, outlaw, tarpan **7** jughead **8** bangtail, fuzztail, warragal, warrigal
Will Rogers': 8 Soapsuds **10** Bootlegger
winged: 7 Pegasus
young: 4 colt, foal **5** filly **8** yearling

ciousness **12** belligerence, contrariness, disagreement **14** unfriendliness, vindictiveness

hot 3 new, top **4** good, late, live, near, warm **5** fiery, fresh, nippy, sharp **6** ardent, baking, biting, fervid, fierce, heated, hectic, latest, molten, raging, recent, red-hot, stormy, sultry, torrid **7** boiling, burning, earnest, excited, furious, intense, melting, peppery, piquant, popular, pungent, searing, violent **8** agitated, animated, broiling, feverish, frenzied, roasting, scalding, sizzling, steaming, vehement, very warm **9** emotional, excellent, scorching, simmering, very close, wrought-up **10** attractive, blistering, passionate, smoldering, successful, sweltering **11** electrified, fast-selling, most popular, radioactive, sought after, tempestuous **12** incandescent **14** fast and furious, highly seasoned, in close pursuit

hot air **7** bombast **8** rhetoric **9** hyperbole **12** exaggeration **13** overstatement

hotel **3** inn **5** lodge, motel **6** hostel **7** hospice, lodging **8** hostelry, motor inn

Hotel, The
author: **14** Elizabeth Bowen

hotel de ville **9** a city hall
literally: **16** mansion of the city

hotel Dieu **9** a hospital **12** mansion of God

Hotel New Hampshire, The
author: **10** John Irving

hothouse **6** tender **7** fragile, nursery **8** delicate **10** glasshouse, greenhouse **12** conservatory **13** over-protected

hot temper **4** fire **5** anger **6** pepper **8** acrimony **9** short fuse

hot-tempered **7** peppery **9** emotional, excitable **13** easily ruffled, quick-tempered

hot water **3** jam **4** mess **6** pickle **7** trouble **10** difficulty **11** predicament

Houghston, Walter
real name of: **12** Walter Huston

hound **3** dog, fan, nag, nut, pup **4** bait, buff, hunt, mutt, tail **5** annoy, chase, doggy, freak, harry, lover, pooch, puppy, stalk, track, trail, whelp, worry **6** addict, badger, canine, follow, harass, hector, keep at, needle, pester, pursue **7** bedevil, poochie **9** keep after **10** aficionado, hunting dog **11** afficionado
dog breed: **6** beagle, borzoi, saluki **7** basenji, harrier, whippet **9** dachshund, greyhound **10** bloodhound, otter hound **11** Afghan hound, basset hound, Ibizan hound **12** pharaoh hound **14** Irish wolfhound **15** English foxhound **16** American foxhound **17** Norwegian elkhound, Scottish deerhound **18** Rhodesian ridgeback **20** black and tan coonhound
group of: **3** cry **4** mute, pack

Hound of the Baskervilles, The
author: **19** Sir Arthur Conan Doyle
character: **8** Dr Watson **14** Sherlock Holmes **19** Sir Henry Baskerville

hour **3** day **4** span, time **5** space **6** period **8** interval
abbreviation: **2** hr

Hour *see* **5** Horae

house, House **4** clan, firm, hall, home, keep, line, shop **5** abode, board, lodge, put up, store **6** billet, church, family, garage, harbor, strain, temple **7** Commons, company, concern, contain, council, descent, dynasty, lineage, quarter, shelter, theater **8** ancestry, assembly, audience, building, business, congress, domicile, dwelling **9** ancestors, household, residence **10** auditorium, family tree, habitation, hippodrome, opera house, spectators **11** accommodate, concert hall, corporation, legislature, noble family, partnership, royal family **12** business firm, lower chamber, meeting place, organization **13** dwelling place, establishment
god of: **8** Silvanus, Sylvanus

housebreaker **5** thief **6** robber **7** burglar **8** pilferer **9** purloiner **10** cat burglar **14** second-story man

housebreaking **5** theft **7** break-in, robbery **8** burglary, stealing **12** burglarizing **19** breaking and entering

House Divided, A
author: **9** Pearl Buck

House for Mr Biswas, A
author: **9** V S Naipaul

household **4** home **5** house **6** family, hearth **8** of a house **9** for a house **10** for a family, for home use **12** family circle
goddess of: **6** Brigit

household help **4** cook, maid **7** footman, steward **8** domestic, gardener, handyman, houseboy **9** charwoman, chauffeur, domestics, majordomo, nursemaid **11** housekeeper

household of three
French: **12** menage a trois

House in Paris, The
author: **14** Elizabeth Bowen

House Made of Dawn
author: **13** N Scott Momaday

House of Atreus, The
author: **9** Aeschylus
character: **7** Electra, Orestes **9** Aegisthus, Agamemnon, Cassandra **12** Clytemnestra

house of health
French: **13** maison de sante

House of Mirth, The
author: **12** Edith Wharton
character: **8** Lily Bart, Mr Selden **9** Gus Trenor **10** Judy Trenor, Mr Rosedale, Percy Gryce **12** Bertha Dorset, George Dorset

House of the Seven Gables, The
author: **18** Nathaniel Hawthorne
character: **10** Mr Holgrave **14** Phoebe Pyncheon **16** Clifford Pyncheon **20** Judge Jaffrey Pyncheon, Miss Hepzibah Pyncheon

house of worship **6** chapel, church, mosque, temple **8** basilica **9** cathedral, synagogue **10** house of God, Lord's house, tabernacle

housewife **4** wife **9** homemaker **11** housekeeper

housing **4** case, home **5** abode, house **6** casing, jacket, sheath, shield **7** lodging, shelter **8** covering, domicile, dwelling, envelope, lodgment, quarters **9** enclosure, residence **10** habitation **14** accommodations

Housman, A E
author of: **14** A Shropshire Lad

Houston
baseball team: **6** Astros
basketball team: **7** Rockets
canal: **11** Houston Ship
channel: **12** Buffalo Bayou
football team: **6** Oilers **8** Gamblers
landmark: **4** NASA **12** Alley Theater **14** Jesse James Hall **22** Manned Spacecraft Center **29** San Jacinto Battlefield Monument
battleship: **5** Texas
named after: **10** Sam Houston
planned by: **7** A C Allen, J K Allen
stadium: **9** Astrodome
street: **15** Old Spanish Trail
university: **4** Rice **12** Texas Medical **13** Texas Southern

Houston, Sam
position: **9** US Senator
governor of: **5** Texas **9** Tennessee
president of: **15** Republic of Texas
served in: **9** Creek Wars **15** Texas Revolution
battle: **10** San Jacinto
defeated: **9** Santa Anna

Houyhnhnms
fictional people in: **16** Gulliver's Travels
author: **5** Swift

hovel **3** hut **4** dump, hole **5** cabin, shack **6** shanty

hover **4** flit, hang **5** float, haunt, pause, poise, waver **6** attend, falter, seesaw **7** flitter, flutter **9** fluctuate, hang about, vacillate

Hovhaness, Alan
born: **12** Somerville MA
composer of: **10** Magnificat

how
Latin: **7** quo modo

Howard, Ron
born: **2** OK **6** Duncan
roles: **4** Opie **9** Happy Days **16** American Graffiti, Richie Cunningham **19** The Andy Griffith Show
director of: **6** Cocoon, Gung Ho, Splash, Willow

Howard, Sidney
author of: **13** The Silver Cord **22** They Knew What They Wanted

Howard, Trevor
born: **7** England **12** Cliftonville
roles: **6** The Key **13** Ryan's Daughter, Sons and Lovers **14** Brief Encounter **23** The Invincible Mr Disraeli

Howard's End
author: **9** E M Forster
character: **9** Jacky Bast **10** Paul Wilcox, Ruth Wilcox **11** Henry Wilcox, Leonard Bast **13** Charles Wilcox, Helen Schlegel **16** Margaret Schlegel, Theobald Schlegel

how are you
German: **8** wie geht's **9** wie geht es

Howe, Elias
nationality: **8** American
invented: **13** sewing machine

Howells, William Dean
author of: **12** Indian Summer **15** A Modern Instance **20** A Hazard of New Fortunes, The Rise of Silas Lapham

How Green Was My Valley
author: **16** Richard Llewellyn
director: **8** John Ford
character: **6** Marged **7** Bronwen **10** Beth Morgan **11** Iestyn Evans **12** Gwilym Morgan
Morgan children: **4** Davy, Huur, Ivor, Owen **5** Ianto **6** Gwilym **8** Angharad
cast: **7** Anna Lee **9** John Loder **11** Donald Crisp **12** Maureen O'Hara **13** Roddy McDowall, Walter Pidgeon
Oscar for: **7** picture **8** director **15** supporting actor (Crisp)

howl **3** bay, cry **4** bark, hoot, roar, wail, yell, yelp, yowl **5** groan, shout, whine **6** bellow, clamor, cry out, outcry, scream, shriek, uproar **7** ululate

howler **4** goof **5** error **6** booboo **7** blooper, blunder, mistake

How To Win Friends and Influence People
author: **12** Dale Carnegie

hoyden **3** imp **4** brat, chit **6** tomboy

Hoyle, Fred
field: **9** astronomy
nationality: **7** British
developed: **17** steady-state theory

Hoyt, Rosemary
character in: **16** Tender Is the Night
author: **10** Fitzgerald

Hreidmar
origin: **12** Scandinavian
mentioned in: **8** Volsunga
son: **5** Otter, Regin **6** Fafnir
killed by: **6** Fafnir

Hsitsang *see* **5** Tibet

Hualapai
language family: **5** Yuman
location: **7** Arizona
related to: **7** Yavapai **9** Havasupai

hub **3** nub **4** axis, core **5** focus, heart, pivot **6** center, middle **10** focal point

Hubble, Edwin Powell
field: **9** astronomy
studied: **15** galactic nebulae
named for him: **14** Hubble constant

hubbub **3** din **4** fuss, stir, to-do **5** noise **6** babble, bedlam, bustle, clamor, pother, racket, ruckus, tumult, uproar **7** ferment, turmoil **8** disorder **9** agitation, commotion, confusion, hue and cry **10** hullabaloo, hurly-burly **11** disturbance, pandemonium **12** perturbation

Hubert
creator: **11** Dick Wingert

huckleberry **9** Vaccinium **11** Gaylussacia
varieties: **2** He **3** Box, Red **4** Blue, Shot **5** Black, Dwarf, Hairy, Squaw, Sugar **6** Garden **8** Thin-leaf **9** Evergreen **10** California, Little-leaf

Huckleberry Finn (The Adventures of)
author: **9** Mark Twain
character: **3** Jim **9** Tom Sawyer **12** Widow Douglas **13** Judge Thatcher

huckster **5** adman **6** badger, hawker, kidder, seller, vendor **7** haggler, peddler

Hud
director: **10** Martin Ritt
cast: **10** John Ashley, Paul Newman **12** Patricia Neal **13** Melvyn Douglas **14** Brandon de Wilde
Oscar for: **7** actress (Neal) **15** supporting actor (Douglas)

huddle **4** heap, herd, mass, mess **5** bunch, crowd, group **6** cuddle, curl up, jumble, medley, muddle, nestle, throng **7** cluster, collect, meeting, snuggle **8** converge, disarray, disorder **9** confusion, gathering **10** conference, discussion, hodge-podge **12** think session

Hudibras
author: **12** Samuel Butler
character: **6** Ralpho **8** Crowders **9** Sidrophel

Hudson, Rock
real name: **12** Roy Scherer Jr
co-star: **8** Doris Day
born: **10** Winnetka IL
roles: **5** Giant **10** Pillow Talk **15** A Farewell to Arms, McMillan and Wife **20** Magnificent Obsession

Hudson, W H
author of: **13** Green Mansions, The Purple Land **17** Far Away and Long Ago

hue **4** cast, tint, tone **5** color, shade, tinge **8** tincture **10** coloration

hue and cry **4** call, howl, roar, yell, yowl **5** alarm, alert, shout, storm **6** bellow, clamor, hubbub, outcry, shriek, uproar **7** thunder **10** cry of alarm, hullabaloo

huff **3** pet **4** fury, rage, snit **7** bad mood, dudgeon, outrage **8** ill humor, vexation **9** annoyance, petulance **10** fit of anger, fit of pique, resentment

huffy **4** curt, hurt **5** angry, cross, irate, moody, sulky, surly, testy **6** cranky, grumpy, moping, morose, shirty, sullen, touchy **7** in a snit, peevish, waspish, wounded **8** churlish, offended, petulant, snappish **9** glowering, in a lather, in a pucker, irritable, querulous, rancorous, resentful, sensitive **10** ill-humored, out of sorts **11** disgruntled, quarrelsome, thin-skinned **12** discontented **14** easily offended, hard to live with, hypersensitive

hug **4** hold **5** clasp **6** clutch, cuddle, nestle **7** cling to, embrace, snuggle, squeeze **9** hold close, hover near **11** keep close to **13** cling together, follow closely **15** parallel closely, press to the bosom

huge **4** vast **5** giant, great, jumbo **6** mighty **7** immense, mammoth, massive, titanic **8** colossal, enormous, gigantic, imposing **9** cyclopean, extensive, herculean, leviathan, monstrous **10** gargantuan, monumental, prodigious, staggering, stupendous **11** elephantine, extravagant, spectacular **12** overwhelming **14** Brobdingnagian

hugeness **4** bulk **8** enormity, vastness **9** great size, immensity, largeness, magnitude **11** massiveness

Huggins, Charles Brenton
field: **10** physiology
researched: **6** cancer **12** chemotherapy
awarded: **10** Nobel Prize

Hughes, Langston
author of: **9** The Big Sea **12** One-Way Ticket **13** The Weary Blues **19** Shakespeare in Harlem **20** The Panther and the Lash

Hughes, Richard
author of: **18** A High Wind in Jamaica

Hughes, Thomas
author of: **19** Tom Brown's Schooldays

Hugh the Drover
opera by: **15** Vaughan Williams
character: **4** Mary **12** The Constable **14** John the Butcher

Hugin
origin: **12** Scandinavian
form: **5** raven
owned by: **4** Odin **5** Othin
personifies: **7** thought
duty: **10** newsbearer
other raven: **5** Munin

Hugo, Victor
author of: **13** Les Miserables **16** Notre Dame de Paris **23** The Hunchback of Notre Dame
character: **9** Esmeralda, Quasimodo

hulk **4** ship **5** giant, wreck **8** behemoth

hulking **3** big **5** bulky, heavy, husky **7** massive **8** powerful, unwieldy **9** oversized, ponderous **10** cumbersome

hull **3** pod **4** case, husk, peel, rind, skin **5** shell, shuck **7** coating **8** carapace **9** epidermis, tegmentum **10** integument

Hull, Isaac
served in: **19** War of Eighteen-Twelve
sunk ship: **9** Guerriere (British)
commander of ship: **12** Constitution

hullabaloo **3** din **4** stir **5** babel **6** bedlam, clamor, hubbub, ruckus, tumult, uproar **9** confusion **11** pandemonium
Yiddish: **7** tzimmes

hum **4** buzz, purr, whir **5** croon, drone, thrum **6** be busy, bustle, intone, murmur, thrive **7** buzzing, droning, purring, vibrate **8** be active, whirring **9** vibration **10** faint sound **13** be in full swing

human **3** man **5** of man, of men **6** gentle, humane, kindly, mortal, person **7** hominid, like man, manlike **8** merciful, personal **10** anthropoid, individual **11** Homo sapiens, sympathetic

Human Comedy, The
author: **14** Honore de Balzac, William Saroyan

Human Condition, The
author: **12** Hannah Arendt

humane **4** kind **5** human **6** kindly, tender **7** pitying **8** merciful **9** unselfish **10** benevolent, bighearted, charitable, goodwilled **11** magnanimous, sympathetic, warmhearted **12** humanitarian **13** compassionate, philanthropic

humaneness **8** kindness, sympathy **10** compassion, gentleness, kindliness **11** benevolence **12** mercifulness **15** warmheartedness

Human Factor, The
author: **12** Graham Greene

humanitarian **4** kind **6** humane **8** generous **10** altruistic, benevolent, charitable **11** kindhearted **12** large-hearted **13** compassionate, philanthropic **14** philanthropist

humanity **3** man **4** love **5** mercy **6** people **7** charity, mankind, mortals **8** goodwill, kindness, sympathy **9** humankind, humanness, mortality **10** compassion, gentleness, humaneness, kindliness, tenderness **11** benevolence, Homo sapiens, human beings, human nature, magnanimity **12** the human race **13** brotherly love, fellow feeling **15** warmheartedness **16** fraternal feeling

humanum est errare **12** to err is human

Humbert Humbert
character in: **6** Lolita
author: **7** Nabokov

humble **3** low **4** meek, poor **5** abase, abash, crush, lower, lowly, plain, shame **6** common, debase, demean, demure, gentle, modest, shabby, simple, subdue **7** chasten, conquer, degrade, mortify, obscure, put down **8** bring low, derogate, disgrace, dishonor, inferior, ordinary, plebeian, pull down, wretched **9** bring down, embarrass, humiliate, make lowly, miserable **10** inglorious, low-ranking, make humble, obsequious, put to shame, respectful, unassuming **11** deferential, subservient, unimportant, unpresuming **12** self-effacing, take down a peg **13** insignificant, unpretentious **14** unostentatious **15** inconsequential, undistinguished

humbled **5** cowed **7** abashed, debased, subdued **9** conquered, disgraced **10** brought low, humiliated

Humboldt, Alexander von
nationality: **6** German
originator of: **7** ecology **10** geophysics

Humboldt's Gift
author: **10** Saul Bellow

humbug **3** fib, gyp, lie **4** bull, bunk, dupe, fake, fool, gull, hoax, liar, lies, sham **5** cheat, cozen, dodge, faker, fraud, hokum, lying, quack, spoof, trick **6** bunkum, con man, deceit, fibber, phooey, take in **7** beguile, blather, cheater, deceive, falsify, fiction, forgery, mislead, rubbish, sharper, swindle **8** artifice, claptrap, flimflam, flummery, hoodwink, impostor, nonsense, perjurer, pretense, swindler, trickery **9** bamboozle, charlatan, deception, fabricate, falsehood, hypocrisy, hypocrite, imposture, mendacity, poppycock, trickster **10** balderdash, hocus-pocus, mountebank, pretension **11** counterfeit, make-believe **12** equivocation, misrepresent **13** confidence man, double-dealing, falsification **15** pretentiousness

humdinger **4** lulu **5** dandy, doozy **6** beauty, hummer, marvel **8** Jim dandy, superior **10** ripsnorter **12** lollapalooza **13** extraordinary

humdrum **4** blah, dull, dumb, flat **5** banal, trite **6** boring, common, dreary **7** insipid, mundane, routine, tedious, trivial **8** everyday, lifeless, mediocre, ordinary, tiresome, wearying **9** hackneyed, unvarying, wearisome **10** monotonous, pedestrian, uneventful, unexciting, uninspired **11** commonplace, indifferent, uninspiring **12** conventional, run-of-the-mill **13** unexceptional, uninteresting

humerus
bone of: **8** upper arm

humid **4** damp, dank **5** moist, muggy, soppy **6** clammy, steamy, sticky, sultry

humidity **4** smog **8** dampness, moisture **9** mugginess **10** stickiness

humiliate **5** abash, crush, shame **6** debase, humble, subdue **7** chagrin, chasten, degrade, mortify, put down **8** belittle, bring low, disgrace, dishonor **9** discomfit, embarrass **11** make ashamed **13** bring down a peg

humiliated **7** abashed, crushed, debased, humbled **8** degraded **9** chagrined, disgraced, mortified

humiliation **5** shame **7** chagrin **8** disgrace, dishonor **9** abasement **10** debasement **11** degradation **12** discomfiture **13** embarrassment, mortification

humility **7** modesty, shyness **8** meekness, timidity **9** lowliness **10** demureness, diffidence, humbleness **11** bashfulness **13** self-abasement **17** unpretentiousness

hummock **4** hill, rise **5** knoll, mound **7** hillock, tussock

Humologumena **17** New Testament books

humor **3** wit **4** baby, gags, mood, puns **5** farce, jests, jokes, spoil **6** cajole, comedy, joking, pamper, parody, satire, soothe, suffer, temper, whimsy **7** appease, flatter, foolery, fooling, indulge, jesting, mollify, placate, spirits, waggery **8** drollery, give in to, jocosity, low humor, nonsense, raillery, ridicule, tolerate, travesty, wordplay **9** burlesque, funniness, low comedy, put up with, slapstick, wittiness **10** buffoonery, caricature, comicality, comply with, high comedy, jocoseness, jocularity, tomfoolery, wisecracks, witticisms **11** broad comedy, disposition, foolishness, frame of mind, go along with **12** monkeyshines **13** ludicrousness **14** ridiculousness

humorist **3** wag, wit **4** card **5** comic **8** comedian

humorous **5** comic, droll, funny, witty **6** jocose **7** amusing, comical, jocular, waggish **8** farcical, mirthful, sportive **9** facetious, laughable, ludicrous, satirical, whimsical **10** ridiculous **11** nonsensical, rib-tickling **13** sidesplitting

hump **4** arch, bend, bump, knob, lift, lump, rise **5** bulge, hunch, knurl, mound, put up, tense **8** swelling **9** convexity **10** projection, prominence **11** excrescence

Humperdinck, Engelbert
born: **4** Bonn **7** Germany
composer of: **10** The Miracle **15** Hansel and Gretel

Humphry Clinker
author: **19** Tobias George Smollet
character: **10** Mr Dennison **12** Jerry Melford, Lydia Melford **14** George Dennison, Matthew Bramble **15** Winifred Jenkins **18** Miss Tabitha Bramble **26** Lieutenant Obadiah Lismahago

Humpty Dumpty
character in: **22** Through the Looking Glass
author: **7** Carroll

hunch **4** arch, bend, clue, hump, idea **5** tense **7** feeling, glimmer, inkling **8** good idea **9** intuition, suspicion **10** foreboding **11** premonition **12** presentiment

Hunchback of Notre Dame, The
author: **10** Victor Hugo
character: **9** Esmeralda, Gringoire, Quasimodo **12** Claude Frollo **20** Phoebus de Chateaupers

hunched **4** bent **7** crooked, slumped, stooped **9** contorted

hundredweight
abbreviation: **3** cwt

Hungary ***see box***

hunger **3** yen **4** itch, love, lust, want, wish **5** crave, greed **6** desire, famine, hanker, liking, relish, thirst **7** burn for, craving, itch for, long for, pant for **8** appetite, fondness, voracity, yearn for, yearning **9** hankering, lust after **10** greediness, starvation **11** have a yen for, thirst after **12** malnutrition, ravenousness

hungry **5** eager **6** greedy **7** starved **8** ravenous, starving **9** voracious

hunk **3** gob, wad **4** clod, glob, lump, mass **5** block, chunk, piece **6** gobbet **7** portion **8** quantity

hunt **4** seek **5** chase, probe, shoot, stalk, trace, track, trail **6** course, follow, pursue **7** explore, go after, look for **8** coursing, drive out **9** ferret out, search for, try to find **11** go in quest of, inquire into **14** riding to hounds **20** leave no stone unturned

Hunt, Richard Morris
architect of: **8** Biltmore (Asheville NC) **11** Marble House (Newport RI), The Breakers (Newport RI) **12** Lenox Library (NYC) **14** Studio Building (NYC) **19** National Observatory (Washington DC) **22** William Vanderbilt House (NYC) **23** Metropolitan Museum of Art (NYC)

hunter
constellation of: **5** Orion
French: **8** chasseur

Hunter, Jim
nickname: **7** Catfish
sport: **8** baseball
position: **7** pitcher
team: **14** New York Yankees **16** Oakland Athletics

Hunter, Kim
real name: **8** Jane Cole
born: **9** Detroit MI
roles: **16** Stairway to Heaven, The Seventh Victim **21** A Streetcar Named Desire

Hunters
goddess of: **11** Britomartis

Hunting
god of: **7** Verbius
goddess of: **5** Diana **7** Artemis

Hunting Dogs
constellation of: **13** Canes Venatici

hurdle **4** jump, leap, snag, wall **5** bound, clear, fence, hedge, vault **6** hazard **7** barrier **8** obstacle, surmount **9** hindrance, roadblock **10** difficulty, impediment, spring over **11** obstruction **12** interference **14** stumbling block

hurl **4** cast, toss **5** chuck, fling, heave, pitch, sling, throw **6** launch, let fly, propel **7** fire off, project **9** discharge

hurly-burly **4** stir **5** furor **6** action, bustle, hubbub, hustle, uproar **8** activity **9** commotion **10** hullabaloo

hurrah, hurray **4** fine, good **5** bravo, cheer, great, huzza **6** huzzah, salute **7** acclaim, hosanna **9** excellent, halleluia, wonderful **10** exaltation, hallelujah

Hungary
capital/largest city: 8 Budapest
others: 4 Gyor, Pecs **5** Harta **6** Mohacs, Sopron, Szeged **7** Komarom, Miskolc, Szentes **8** Dubrecen, Kaposuar, Szegedin **9** Kecskemet **10** Albertirsa **11** Nagykanizsa, Szombathely
measure: 3 ako **4** hold, yoke **5** itcze, marok, metze **7** huvelyk
monetary unit: 4 gara **5** balas, krone, pengo **6** filler, forint, gulden, korona, ongara, ungara
weight: 7 vamfont **8** vammazsa
island: 8 Margaret
lake: 5 Ferto **7** Balaton, Velence **9** Blatensee **10** Neusiedler, Plattensee
mountain: 4 Alps, Bukk **5** Matra, Tatra **6** Bakony, Mecsek, Vertes **7** Cserhat, Gerecse **8** Borzsony, Zempleni **9** Korishegy **10** Carpathian
highest point: 5 Kekes
river: 3 Mur, Sio **4** Duna, Raab, Raba, Sajo, Zala **5** Bodva, Drava, Drave, Ipoly, Kapos, Koros, Maros, Tarna, Tisza **6** Danube, Henrad, Poprad, Szamos, Theiss, Zagyva **7** Vistula **8** Berretyo
physical feature:
***canal:* 3** Sio **6** Sarviz
***forest:* 6** Bakony
***plain:* 6** Puszta
***port:* 5** Fiume
people: 3 Hun **4** Serb **5** Croat, Gypsy **6** Cigany, Magyar, Slovak, Ugrian
***composer:* 5** Lehar, Liszt **6** Bartok, Kodaly
***national hero:* 5** Arpad
***playwright:* 6** Molnar
language: 6 German, Magyar, Slovak **8** Croatian **9** Hungarian **10** Finno-Ugric
religion: 8 Lutheran **9** Calvinism **13** Roman Catholic **16** Eastern Orthodoxy
place:
***church:* 32** Gothic Coronation Church of Matthias
***ruins:* 8** Aquincum
***square:* 6** Heroes
***tomb:* 14** Turbe of Gul Baba **16** Father of the Roses
feature:
***dance:* 3** kos **7** czardas **10** varsoviana
***dog:* 4** puli
***musical instrument:* 8** taragata **9** czimbalom
food:
***dish:* 6** gulyas **7** goulash **15** chicken paprikas
***pastry:* 4** rete **5** torte
***wine:* 5** Tokay **10** Bulls Blood

hurricane 7 cyclone, monsoon, tempest, typhoon **9** windstorm

Hurricane, The
director: 8 John Ford
cast: 7 Jon Hall **9** Mary Astor **12** C Aubrey Smith **13** Dorothy Lamour, Raymond Massey
setting: 9 Manikoora

hurried 4 fast **5** hasty **6** hectic, rushed, speedy **7** cursory, frantic **8** careless, feverish, frenetic, headlong, slapdash, slipshod **9** breakneck, haphazard, impulsive **11** precipitate, superficial

hurry 3 ado, zip **4** bolt, dart, dash, fuss, goad, prod, rush, stew, whiz **5** egg on, haste, speed **6** flurry, hasten, hustle, push on, scurry, tumult, urge on **7** drive on, flutter, press on, scuttle, speed up, turmoil **8** make time, move fast, pressure, scramble, step on it **9** commotion, go quickly, make haste, step along **10** accelerate, get a move on, get hopping, lose no time, make tracks **11** come quickly, get cracking, go like a shot, go like sixty **12** step on the gas **13** go like the wind **14** cover the ground **15** hustle and bustle

hurt ***see box, p. 466***

Hurt, John
born: 7 England **22** Chesterfield Derbyshire
roles: 5 Alien **8** Partners **14** The Elephant Man **15** Midnight Express

Hurt, William
roles: 8 Body Heat **9** Gorky Park **10** Eyewitness **11** The Big Chill **13** Broadcast News **20** Kiss of the Spider Woman, Children of a Lesser God

hurtful 5 cruel **6** deadly **7** abusive, baleful, harmful **8** crushing, improper, stinging, wounding **9** injurious

hurtle 3 fly, hie, run, zip **4** bolt, dart, dash, race, rush, tear, whiz **5** bound, lunge, scoot, shoot, speed, spurt, whisk **6** charge, gallop, plunge, scurry **7** scamper, scuttle **11** go like a shot **13** go like the wind **14** go lickety-split

husband 3 man **4** keep, mate, save **5** amass, groom, hoard, hubby, store **6** old man, retain, save up, spouse **7** consort **8** conserve, maintain, preserve, set aside **10** accumulate, bridegroom, married man

husbandry 7 farming **9** geoponics **11** agriculture, crop-raising **12** conservation
god of: 9 Aristaeus

hush 4 calm **5** quell, quiet, shush, still **6** shut up, soothe **7** be quiet, be still, keep mum, mollify, silence **8** be silent, pipe down, quietude **9** quiet down, quietness, stillness **10** knock it off **11** tranquility **12** peacefulness, tranquillity

hushed 4 calm **5** quiet, still **6** calmed, gentle, lulled, silent **7** allayed, quieted, soothed, stifled **8** pacified, silenced, tranquil **12** tranquilized **13** tranquillized

hush money 5 bribe **6** payoff, payola **7** tribute **9** blackmail, extortion

huskiness 5 brawn **9** beefiness **10** hoarseness, robustness, ruggedness, sturdiness **11** muscularity

husky 3 big **5** beefy, burly, gruff, harsh, hefty, plump, rough, solid, stout, thick **6** brawny, coarse, hoarse, robust, stocky, strong, sturdy **7** cracked, grating, rasping, raucous, throaty **8** athletic, croaking, guttural, muscular, powerful, thickset **9** strapping **10** overweight **12** strong as an ox **15** broad-shouldered

hurt **3** cut, mar **4** ache, balk, burn, foil, harm, lame, maim, mark, maul, pain, pang, scar **5** agony, block, check, grief, limit, lower, pique, smart, spike, sting, stung **6** aching, bruise, damage, deface, dismay, grieve, hamper, hinder, impair, impede, injure, lessen, mangle, marked, miffed, misery, morose, narrow, offend, oppose, pained, piqued, reduce, retard, thwart, weaken **7** agonize, bruised, chagrin, cripple, crushed, damaged, disable, exclude, inhibit, injured, mangled, painful, scarred, scratch, torment, torture, trouble, wounded **8** aggrieve, crippled, decrease, dejected, diminish, disabled, dismayed, distress, encumber, hold back, minimize, mutilate, obstruct, offended, preclude, restrain, smarting, soreness, wretched **9** aggrieved, annoyance, chagrined, dejection, disfigure, forestall, frustrate, heartsick, indignant, miserable, mortified, mutilated, resentful, scratched, suffering **10** discomfort, distressed, heartbreak, melancholy, resentment **11** aggravation, crestfallen, heartbroken **12** disheartened, wretchedness **13** cut to the quick, embarrassment, mortification

hussar **8** cavalier, horseman **10** cavalryman **12** horse soldier, horse trooper **14** mounted soldier

hussy **4** bawd, jade, minx, tart **5** wench, whore **6** harlot, wanton **7** baggage, trollop **8** strumpet **9** brash girl, lewd woman, saucy miss **10** adulteress, loose woman, prostitute **11** brazen woman, fallen woman **12** scarlet woman **17** woman of easy virtue

hustle **3** ado, fly **4** bolt, dart, dash, fuss, prod, push, rush, stir, toss **5** elbow, hurry, nudge, scoot, shove, throw **6** bounce, bustle, flurry, hasten, hubbub, jostle, scurry, tumult **7** flutter, scuttle, speed up, turmoil **8** make time, scramble, shoulder, step on it **9** commotion, make haste, step along **10** lose no time **11** hurry-scurry, move quickly **12** be aggressive

hustler **4** doer **6** con man, dynamo, hooker **8** go-getter, livewire, swindler **10** prostitute **12** streetwalker

Hustler, The
director: **12** Robert Rossen
cast: **10** Paul Newman **11** Piper Laurie **12** George C Scott **13** Jackie Gleason (Minnesota Fats)

Huston, John
director of: **8** Key Largo **10** The Misfits **11** Moulin Rouge **12** Prizzi's Honor **13** Asphalt Jungle **15** The African Queen **16** The Maltese Falcon **19** The Night of the Iguana **27** The Treasure of the Sierra Madre (Oscar)
father: **12** Walter Huston
wife: **11** Evelyn Keyes
born: **8** Nevada MO
roles: **9** Chinatown **11** Winter Kills

Huston, Walter
real name: **15** Walter Houghston
son: **10** John Huston
born: **6** Canada **7** Toronto
roles: **9** Dodsworth **18** All That Money Can Buy **27** The Treasure of the Sierra Madre

hut **4** shed **5** cabin, hutch, shack **6** lean-to, shanty **7** cottage, shelter

hutch **3** pen, sty **4** cage, coop, cote, crib, shed **5** stall **9** enclosure

Hutchinson, A S M
author of: **13** If Winter Comes

Hutton, Betty
real name: **18** Betty June Thornburg
born: **13** Battle Creek MI
roles: **15** Annie Get Your Gun **19** Greatest Show on Earth

Hutton, James
field: **7** geology
nationality: **8** Scottish
founder of: **7** geology

Hutton, Timothy
father: **9** Jim Hutton
roles: **4** Taps **6** Daniel **14** Ordinary People **22** The Falcon and the Snowman

Huxley, Aldous
author of: **11** Crome Yellow **13** Brave New World **17** Point Counter Point

Huxley, Julian
field: **7** biology
nationality: **7** British
promoted theory of: **9** evolution

Huygens, Christiaan
nationality: **5** Dutch
invented: **13** pendulum clock
discovered: **12** Saturn's rings
formulated: **17** wave theory of light

hyacinth **10** Hyacinthus **20** Hyacinthus orientalis
varieties: **4** musk, pine, star, wild, wood **5** Dutch, grape, Roman, water **6** common, garden, meadow, nutmeg, starry, summer, Tassel **7** feather, peacock **11** common grape

Hyacinthus
father: **7** Amyclas
daughter: **7** Orthaea
loved by: **6** Apollo **8** Zephyrus
killed by: **5** quoit **6** discus
from his blood sprang: **6** flower
petals marked: **4** AI-AI
means: **4** alas

Hyades
also: **5** Hyads **10** Palilicium
form: **6** nymphs
father: **5** Atlas **7** Oceanus
mother: **6** Tethys **7** Pleione
sisters: **8** Pleiades
nurtured: **8** Dionysus
placed among: **5** stars

Hyads *see* **6** Hyades

hybrid **5** cross **7** amalgam, mixture **9** composite, half-breed **10** crossbreed

hybridize **5** cross **14** cross-fertilize, cross-pollinate

Hydra
form: **12** water serpent
number of heads: **4** nine
killed by: **8** Hercules

hydrangea
varieties: **4** Wild **6** French, Peegee **8** Climbing

hydrogen
chemical symbol: **1** H

hydrophobia **6** rabies
fear of: **5** water

Hygeia
father: **9** Asclepius
goddess of: **6** health
corresponds to: **5** Salus

hygienic **4** pure **5** clean **7** aseptic, healthy, sterile **8** germ-free, harmless, salutary, sanitary **9** healthful, wholesome **10** salubrious, unpolluted **11** disease-free, disinfected, uninjurious **12** prophylactic **14** uncontaminated

Hylaeus
form: **7** centaur
born on: **5** cloud

Hylas
father: **9** Thiodamas
mother: **8** Menodice
companion of: **8** Hercules

Hyllus
father: **8** Hercules
mother: **6** Melite **8** Deianira
wife: **4** Iole
son: **9** Cleodaeus
grandson: **7** Temenus
built: **11** funeral pyre
for: **8** Hercules

Hymen
also: **9** Hymenaeus
god of: **8** marriage
holds: **5** torch
corresponds to: **8** Talassio

Hymenaeus *see* **5** Hymen

hymenoptera
class: **8** hexapoda
phylum: **10** arthropoda
group: **3** ant, bee **4** wasp **6** chacid, sawfly **12** ichneumon fly

hymn **5** paean, psalm **6** anthem **12** song of praise **14** devotional song **17** song in praise of God

Hymn to Proserpine
author: **24** Algernon Charles Swinburne

Hypatia
author: **15** Charles Kingsley

hyperbole **8** metaphor **11** enlargement **12** exaggeration **13** magnification, overstatement **14** figure of speech

hyperbolize **6** overdo **7** amplify, magnify, stretch **9** embroider, overstate **10** exaggerate

hyperborean **6** arctic **8** freezing, northern **13** septentrional

Hyperborean
inhabitant of: **8** Paradise

Hyperenor
mentioned in: **5** Iliad
brother: **9** Euphorbus, Polydamas
member of: **6** Sparti
killed by: **8** Menelaus

Hyperion
also: **6** Helios
form: **5** Titan
father: **6** Uranus
mother: **4** Gaea
sister: **5** Theia
son: **6** Helios
daughter: **3** Eos **6** Selene
corresponds to: **6** Apollo

Hyperion
author: **9** John Keats **24** Henry Wadsworth Longfellow

Hypermnestra
member of: **8** Danaides
husband: **7** Lynceus
son: **4** Abas

hypersensitive **6** touchy **9** emotional **13** temperamental

Hypnos
also: **6** Hypnus
god of: **5** sleep
father: **6** Erebus
mother: **3** Nyx
brother: **8** Thanatos
corresponds to: **6** Somnus

hypnotic **9** soporific **11** mesmerizing **12** spellbinding

hypnotize **7** control **9** mesmerize, spellbind

Hypnus *see* **6** Hypnos

hypocrisy **6** deceit, fakery **7** falsity **9** duplicity, mendacity, phoniness **10** dishonesty **11** dissembling, insincerity **12** two-facedness

hypocrite **5** phony **8** deceiver **9** pretender **10** dissembler

Hypocrite **15** whited sepulcher

hypocritical **5** false, phony **7** feigned **8** feigning, two-faced **9** deceitful, deceptive, dishonest, insincere, truthless **11** counterfeit

hyporchema
form: **9** choral ode
origin: **5** Greek
honored: **6** Apollo **8** Dionysus

hypothalamus
regulates: **15** body temperature
located in: **5** brain

hypothesis **6** theory, thesis **7** premise, theorem **8** proposal **9** assertion, postulate **10** assumption, conclusion, conjecture **11** explanation, guesstimate, presumption, proposition, speculation, supposition

hypothesize **5** infer **6** assume **7** imagine, presume, suppose **8** theorize **9** postulate, speculate **10** conjecture

hypothetical **7** assumed, dubious **8** possible, supposed **9** imaginary, uncertain **10** contingent, postulated **11** conditional, conjectural, presumptive, speculative, theoretical **12** questionable **13** suppositional

Hypselosaurus
type: **8** dinosaur, sauropod
location: **6** France **8** Mongolia
period: **10** Cretaceous

Hypseus
king of: **7** Lapiths
father: **6** Peneus
mother: **6** Creusa
daughter: **6** Cyrene **8** Themisto **9** Astyagyia

Hypsilophodon
type: **8** dinosaur **10** ornithopod
location: **7** England
period: **10** Cretaceous

Hyrie
transformed into: **4** swan

Hyrmina
grandfather: **8** Endymion
son: **5** Actor

Hyrnetho
father: **7** Temenus
grandfather: **12** Aristomachus
husband: **10** Deiphontes

Hyrtius
allied with: **7** Trojans

hyssop **8** Hyssopus **18** Hyssopus officialis
varieties: **5** anise, giant, water **9** blue giant **10** nettleleaf **11** fennel giant, purple giant, yellow giant **12** Mexican giant **13** fragrant giant, wrinkled giant

Hyssop **13** Biblical plant

hysteria **3** fit **5** panic **6** frenzy **8** delirium

hysterical **5** crazy, droll **6** absurd, crazed, raving **7** amusing, comical **8** farcical, frenzied, worked-up **9** laughable, ludicrous, wrought-up **10** distracted, distraught, ridiculous, uproarious **11** carried away, overwrought, wildly funny **13** beside oneself, out of one's wits **14** uncontrollable

hysterics **3** fit **12** emotionalism

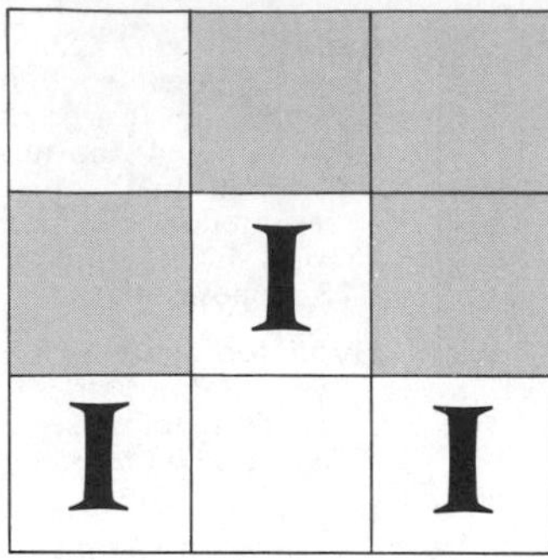

I, Claudius
author: 12 Robert Graves
story of: 36 Tiberius Claudius Drusus Nero Germanicus (Emperor of Rome)

I, the Jury
author: 14 Mickey Spillane

Iache
form: 5 nymph
companion of: 10 Persephone

I Am a Fugitive from a Chain Gang
director: 11 Mervyn LeRoy
cast: 8 Paul Muni 11 Helen Vinson 13 Glenda Farrell, Preston Foster

Iambe
occupation: 11 storyteller
storyteller for: 7 Demeter

I am unwilling to contend
Latin: 14 nolo contendere

Iamus
father: 6 Apollo
mother: 6 Evadne
became: 7 prophet

Ianthe
husband: 5 Iphis

Iapetus
member of: 6 Titans
father: 6 Uranus
mother: 4 Gaea
wife: 6 Themis
son: 5 Atlas 9 Menoetius 10 Epimetheus, Prometheus

Iapyx
father: 8 Daedalus

Iardanus
king of: 5 Lydia
daughter: 7 Omphale

Iasion
founder of: 7 Trojans
twin brother: 8 Dardanus

Iaso
goddess of: 7 healing
father: 9 Asclepius

Iasus
father: 8 Lycurgus
daughter: 8 Atalanta
abandoned: 8 Atalanta

Ibanez, Vicente Blasco
author of: 30 The Four Horsemen of the Apocalypse

Iberian Peninsula
also: 8 Hesperia

Ibsen, Henrik
author of: 6 Ghosts 8 Peer Gynt 11 A Doll's House, Hedda Gabler, Rosmersholm, The Wild Duck 16 The Master Builder 18 An Enemy of the People, John Gabriel Borkman

Iceland
other name: 15 Lydveldid Island
capital/largest city: 9 Reykjavik
others: 3 Hof 6 Geysir 7 Akranes, Husavik 8 Akureyri, Keflavik, Kopasker 9 Kopavogur 10 Hveragerdi, Isafjordur 12 Siglufjordur 13 Hafnarfjordur, Neskaupstadur, Seydisfjordur
government:
general assembly: 7 Althing
measure: 3 set 4 alin 5 almud 6 almenn, ferfet, pattur 7 fathmur, fermila, oltunna
monetary unit: 5 aurar, eyrir, krona
weight: 4 pund 5 pound, tunna 6 smjors
island: 7 Heimaey, Surtsey, Westman
lake: 6 Myvatn 10 Thorisvatn 14 Thingvallavatn
mountain: 5 Jokul 10 Orafajokul
volcano: 4 Laki 5 Askja, Hekla, Katla 7 Surtsey
highest point: 17 Hvannadalshnjukur
river: 5 Hvita 7 Fnjoska, Thjorsa 15 Jokulsa a Fjollum
sea: 9 Greenland 13 North Atlantic
physical feature:
fjord: 4 Eyja
geyser: 5 gryla 6 geysir 11 Great Gusher
glacier: 6 Jokull 11 Orafajokull, Vatnajokull
plain: 15 Skeidharasandur
waterfall: 8 Godafoss, Gullfoss 9 Dettifoss
people: 6 Celtic, Viking 8 Norseman 9 Norwegian
first settler: 8 Arnarson
hero: 4 Bele, Eric, Leif 10 Sigurdsson
language: 5 Norse 9 Icelandic
religion: 19 Evangelical Lutheran
place:
national shrine: 11 Thingvellir
feature:
airport: 9 Kopavogur
bird: 4 gull 6 falcon 9 gyrfalcon
literary genre: 4 saga
wrestling: 5 glima
food:
dish: 4 skyr, svio 7 bloomor 8 harofisk

Ibzan **11** Hebrew judge

I came, I saw, I conquered
Latin: **12** veni vidi vici
author: **12** Julius Caesar

Icarius
son: **8** Perilaus
daughter: **7** Erigone **8** Penelope
hospitable to: **8** Dionysus
hound dog: **5** Maera

Icarus
father: **8** Daedalus
built: **5** wings
flew too near: **3** sun
death by: **8** drowning

ice **3** gem **4** berg, floe, gems, rime **5** chill, frost, glace **6** freeze, icicle, jewels **7** crystal, dessert, glacier, jewelry, sherbet **8** diamonds **11** refrigerant, refrigerate

ice-cold **3** icy **4** cold **5** gelid, polar **6** arctic, bitter, frigid, frosty, wintry **7** chilled, frosted, glacial, subzero **8** chilling, freezing, Siberian, unheated, unwarmed **9** stonecold, supercold **11** hyperborean, supercooled **12** bone-chilling

ice cream **7** dessert, sherbet

Iceland ***see box***

Icelus
origin: **5** Greek
god of: **6** dreams
assumed shapes of: **7** animals
epithet: **8** Phobetor
corresponds to: **8** Morpheus

Iceman
nickname of: **12** George Gervin

Iceman Cometh, The
author: **12** Eugene O'Neill

Ice Palace
author: **10** Edna Ferber

ice skating
athlete: **9** Janet Lynn, John Curry **10** Carol Heiss, Dick Button, Eric Heiden, Sonja Henie **11** Sheila Young **12** Peggy Fleming **13** Dorothy Hamill, Scott Hamilton **14** Linda Fratianne

ich dien **6** I serve
motto of: **13** Prince of Wales

I Ching **30** ancient Chinese book of divination

ichor
form: **5** fluid
in veins of: **4** gods

Ichthyocentaur
form: **8** creature
location: **3** sea
head/torso: **5** human
legs: **5** horse
tail: **4** fish

iciness **4** cold **5** chill **9** frigidity **10** chilliness, frostiness, wintriness **12** slipperiness

ici on parle francais
18 French is spoken here
19 here one speaks French

icky **5** gluey, gooey, gross, gucky, gummy, mushy, nasty, tacky, weepy **6** sticky, syrupy, viscid **7** maudlin, viscous **8** bathetic **9** glutinous, offensive, repulsive, revolting **10** disgusting **12** mucilaginous

icon, ikon **4** idol **5** image **6** effigy, figure, statue **7** picture **8** likeness **11** sacred image

iconoclast **5** rebel **7** radical, upstart **9** dissenter **13** nonconformist, revolutionary

icy **3** raw **4** cold, cool **5** aloof, gelid **6** arctic, chilly, frigid, frosty, frozen, glazed, sleety, wintry **7** distant, glacial, haughty, hostile **8** chilling, freezing, slippery **9** impassive **10** forbidding, unfriendly **11** coldhearted, unemotional

Ida
form: **5** nymph
watched over: **4** Zeus

Idaea
form: **5** nymph
domain: **8** Mount Ida
husband: **7** Phineus **9** Scamander
son: **6** Teucer

Idaho ***see box***

Idas
father: **8** Aphareus
mother: **5** Arene
brother: **7** Lynceus
wife: **8** Marpessa
daughter: **9** Cleopatra

idea **4** clue, hint, view **6** belief, notion **7** concept, feeling, inkling, insight, opinion, outlook, thought **8** approach, proposal, solution **9** sentiment **10** conception, conclusion, conviction, impression, indication, intimation, suggestion **12** apperception, appreciation **13** approximation, mental picture, understanding **14** interpretation, recommendation

ideal **3** aim **4** hero, idol

Idaho
abbreviation: **2** ID **3** Ida
nickname: **3** Gem
capital/largest city: **5** Boise
others: **4** Buhl **5** Malad, Nampa **6** Moscow **7** Orofino, Rexburg **8** Caldwell, Lewiston **9** Pocatello, Twin Falls **10** Idaho Falls **11** Coeur d'Alene
college: **17** Northwest Nazarene
explorer: **13** Lewis and Clark
feature: **9** Sun Valley **17** Continental Divide
dam: **5** Oxbow **8** Brownlee
national monument: **16** Craters of the Moon
tribe: **5** Banak, Shake **6** Cayuse, Paiute, Spokan **7** Bannock, Kutenai, Spokane **8** Kalispel, Nez Perce, Sahaptin, Shoshone, Shoshoni **9** Shoshonee **11** Coeur d'Alene
people: **9** Ezra Pound, Sacagawea **11** Chief Joseph **17** William Edgar Borah
lake: **4** Bear **5** Grey's **6** Priest **11** Coeur d'Alene, Pend Oreille **22** American Falls Reservoir
land rank: **10** thirteenth
mountain: **4** Ryan **5** Rocky **6** Rhodes, Taylor, Tetons **7** Cabinet **8** Bannocks, Big Baldy, Bluenose, Sawtooth **9** Wasatches **10** Clearwater **11** Beaverheads, Bitterroots **13** Selkirk Ranges
highest point: **5** Borah
physical feature:
falls: **5** Moyie **8** Shoshone **9** Upper Mesa
springs: **4** Soda **6** Hooper **7** Lavahot
river: **4** Bear **5** Boise, Snake, St Joe **6** Locksa, Salmon **7** Payette, Spokane **8** Kootenai **11** Coeur d'Alene, Pend Oreille
state admission: **10** forty-third
state bird: **16** mountain bluebird
state flower: **7** syringa
state motto: **13** It Is Perpetual **16** Let It Be Perpetual
state song: **15** Here We Have Idaho
state tree: **16** western white pine

5 dream, model 7 epitome, optimal, pattern, perfect 8 exemplar, last word, paradigm, standard, ultimate 9 archetype, criterion, excellent, exemplary, faultless, matchless, objective 10 impeccable 11 inspiration

idealism 8 optimism 9 meliorism 10 utopianism 11 romanticism

idealist 7 dreamer, utopian 8 romantic 9 Pollyanna, stargazer, visionary 11 romanticist 13 perfectionist

idealized 6 dreamy 7 utopian, wishful 8 fanciful, illusory, romantic 10 optimistic 11 pie-in-the-sky, unrealistic 13 insubstantial

idea man 7 advisor 8 inventor 9 innovator 10 consultant 12 entrepreneur

idee fixe 9 fixed idea
music: 14 recurring motif

idem 24 the same as previously given 28 the same as previously mentioned

identical 4 twin 7 uniform 8 self-same, very same 9 duplicate 15 interchangeable 17 indistinguishable

identification 5 badge, label 8 passport 9 detection 10 connection, revelation 11 affiliation, association, credentials, pinpointing, recognition 12 confirmation, verification 13 ascertainment

identify 4 know 5 place 6 verify 7 combine, pick out, specify 9 associate, designate, determine, recognize, single out 11 distinguish

identifying device 4 logo, mark, sign 5 badge 6 emblem, ensign, symbol 8 insignia, logotype

identity 4 name, self 6 accord 7 harmony, oneness, rapport 9 unanimity 11 delineation, duplication, personality 13 individuality 15 differentiation, distinctiveness

ideology 5 dogma, ethos 6 ideals, theory 7 program 8 doctrine 9 rationale 10 principles

Ides of March, The
author: 14 Thornton Wilder

id est 6 that is
abbreviation: 2 ie

idiocy 5 folly 6 lunacy 7 fatuity, inanity, madness, suicide 8 insanity 9 absurdity, asininity, cretinism, mongolism, stupidity 11 foolishness 13 foolhardiness, senselessness

idiom 5 argot, lingo, slang 6 brogue, jargon, patois, phrase, speech 7 dialect 8 language, localism, parlance 10 vernacular 13 colloquialism

idiomatic 6 common 8 informal, ordinary 10 vernacular 14 conversational

idiosyncrasy 5 quirk 6 oddity 7 anomaly 9 mannerism 11 distinction, peculiarity 12 eccentricity

idiot 3 ass 4 boob, dolt, dope, fool, jerk 5 cluck, dummy, dunce, moron, ninny 6 cretin, dimwit, nitwit 7 halfwit 8 dumbbell, numskull 9 blockhead, numbskull, simpleton 10 nincompoop

Idiot, The
author: 16 Fyodor Dostoevsky
character: 7 Myshkin 11 Mme Epanchin 14 Aglaya Epanchin, Parfen Rogozhin 16 Natasya Filipovna 19 Ganya Ardalionovitch 22 Prince Lef Nicolaievitch

idiotic 5 crazy, dopey, nutty 6 absurd, addled, stupid 7 asinine, doltish, foolish, moronic 9 foolhardy, imbecilic, senseless 10 half-witted, irrational, ridiculous 12 feebleminded 13 rattlebrained

I direct
Latin: 6 dirigo
motto of: 5 Maine

idle 4 laze, lazy, loaf, vain 5 empty, inert, petty, vapid, waste, while 6 drowsy, fallow, futile, otiose, putter, torpid, unused 7 aimless, fritter, jobless, languid, trivial, useless, wait out 8 baseless, bootless, fool away, inactive, indolent, listless, slothful, sluggish, trifling 9 at leisure, enervated, fruitless, lethargic, out of work, pointless, somnolent, valueless, worthless 10 not working, unemployed, unoccupied 11 unimportant 12 unproductive 15 unsubstantiated

idleness 5 sloth 7 inertia 8 laziness, lethargy 9 indolence 10 inactivity 11 joblessness, languidness 12 sluggishness, unemployment
French: 8 flanerie

idler 3 bum 6 loafer 7 drifter, vagrant 10 ne'er-do-well
French: 7 flaneur

idol 4 hero, icon 5 relic 6 effigy, statue 7 darling 8 artifact 10 simulacrum, golden calf 11 graven image, inspiration

idolatry 5 mania 7 madness, passion, worship 8 devotion 9 adoration, obsession 10 veneration 11 idolization, infatuation 12 image worship 13 preoccupation

idolization 7 worship 9 adulation, reverence 10 exaltation, veneration

idolize 5 adore, deify, honor, prize 6 admire, revere 7 worship 8 treasure, venerate 9 reverence 11 apotheosize

Idomeneo, re di Creta
also: 20 Idomeneus King of Crete
opera by: 6 Mozart
character: 4 Ilia 7 Electra 8 Idamante, Poseidon

Idomeneus
king of: 5 Crete
father: 9 Deucalion

I don't know what
French: 12 je ne sais quoi

Idothea
form: 5 nymph
father: 7 Proteus

I Dream of Jeannie
character: 7 Jeannie 9 Dr Bellows 10 (Captain) Tony Nelson 11 Gen Peterson, (Captain) Roger Healey 13 Amanda Bellows
cast: 9 Bill Daily 11 Barbara Eden, Hayden Rorke, Larry Hagman 13 Barton MacLane, Emmaline Henry
Tony's job: 9 astronaut

Idun, Iduna
also: 5 Ithun 6 Ithunn
origin: 12 Scandinavian
goddess of: 6 spring
husband: 5 Brage, Bragi
kept: 11 youth apples

idyllic 6 rustic, sylvan 7 bucolic 8 arcadian, pastoral, peaceful, romantic 9 unspoiled

Idylls of the King, The
author: 18 Alfred Lord Tennyson
based on story of: 10 King Arthur

Ierne *see* 7 Ireland

if 2 an 6 though 7 whether 8 although, provided 9 condition, supposing 10 even though 11 stipulation, supposition

iffy 4 moot 5 risky 6 chancy, unsure 7 dubious, erratic 8 arguable, doubtful 9 debatable, uncertain, undecided, unsettled, whimsical 10 capricious, disputable, unresolved 11 conjectural, speculative 12 questionable 13 problematical, unpredictable

Ifriqiyah *see* **7** Tunisia

If Winter Comes
author: **13** A S M Hutchinson

if you please
French: **12** s'il vous plait

Iggdrasil *see* **9** Yggdrasil

ignitable **8** burnable **9** flammable **10** combustive, incendiary **11** combustible, inflammable **13** conflagrative

ignite **4** burn, fire **5** blaze, flame, light **6** blow up, kindle **7** explode, inflame **8** take fire, touch off **9** catch fire, set fire to, set on fire **11** catch on fire

ignoble **3** low **4** base, foul, mean, vile **6** craven **7** debased, heinous **8** cowardly, degraded, depraved, indecent, infamous, inferior, shameful, unworthy **9** dastardly, nefarious **10** degenerate, despicable **11** disgraceful **12** contemptible, dishonorable **13** discreditable, pusillanimous **14** unconscionable

ignominious **3** low **5** sorry **6** abject **8** grievous, shameful, wretched **9** degrading **10** despicable, inglorious, unbearable **11** disgraceful, humiliating **12** dishonorable, disreputable **13** discreditable

ignominy **5** shame **6** infamy **8** contempt, disgrace, dishonor **11** degradation, humiliation

ignoramus **4** fool **5** dunce **6** nitwit **7** low-brow **8** numskull **9** numbskull, simpleton **10** illiterate **11** know-nothing

ignorance **9** confusion **10** illiteracy **11** unawareness **12** backwardness **13** obliviousness, unfamiliarity **15** unenlightenment

ignorant **4** dumb **5** naive **6** stupid **7** asinine, blind to, fatuous, shallow, unaware **8** innocent, untaught **9** in the dark, unknowing, unlearned, untrained, untutored, unworldly **10** illiterate, uneducated, uninformed, unlettered, unschooled **11** insensitive, uncognizant **12** unperceptive **13** irresponsible, unenlightened, unintelligent **15** unknowledgeable

ignore **4** omit, skip, snub **5** scorn **6** eschew, slight **7** neglect **8** overlook, pass over **9** disregard

Igraine
character in: **16** Arthurian romance
son: **6** Arthur

Iguanodon
type: **8** dinosaur **10** ornithopod
means: **11** iguana tooth
found by: **13** Gideon Mantell
location: **6** Africa, Europe, Sussex **7** Belgium, England
period: **10** Cretaceous
characteristic: **10** duck-billed

ikebana
Japanese: **21** art of arranging flowers

Ile de France *see* **9** Mauritius

Ilha Formosa *see* **6** Taiwan

Iliad, The
author: **5** Homer
character: **5** Paris, Priam **6** Hector **8** Achilles, Menelaus **9** Agamemnon, Patroclus **11** Helen of Troy
subject: **9** Trojan War

Iliniwek *see* **8** Illinois

Ilion
Greek name for: **11** ancient Troy

Ilione
father: **5** Priam
mother: **6** Hecuba
husband: **11** Polymnestor
son: **8** Deipylus
raised: **9** Polydorus

Ilioneus
mentioned in: **6** Aeneid
home: **4** Troy
vocation: **7** warrior
fled: **4** Troy
fled with: **6** Aeneas
killed by: **8** Peneleus

Ilithyia *see* **10** Eileithyia

Ilium
Latin name for: **11** ancient Troy

ill, ills **3** woe **4** evil, foul, harm, sick, vile **5** abuse, cross, no way, surly, trial **6** ailing, damage, hardly, injury, laid up, malady, malice, nowise, plague, poorly, sickly, sorrow, unkind, unwell, wicked **7** ailment, cruelty, disease, failing, harmful, invalid, not well, ominous, outrage, peevish, trouble, unlucky, unsound **8** diseased, mischief, scarcely, sinister, vengeful **9** afflicted, complaint, infirmity, malicious, unhealthy **10** affliction, disturbing, foreboding, indisposed, misfortune, wickedness **11** abomination, acrimonious, malefaction, threatening, unfavorable **12** inauspicious, unpropitious **15** under the weather

ill-advised **4** dumb, rash **5** hasty, silly **6** myopic, stupid, unwise **7** foolish **9** foolhardy, ill-judged, impolitic, imprudent, misguided, senseless **10** indiscreet, unthinking **11** injudicious **12** shortsighted **13** ill-considered, irresponsible

ill-at-ease **3** shy **4** edgy **6** on edge, uneasy **7** abashed, fidgety, nervous **8** bothered, troubled **9** disturbed, nonplused, perturbed **10** disquieted, nonplussed **11** discomfited, discomposed, embarrassed **12** disconcerted **13** self-conscious, uncomfortable **15** discountenanced

ill-boding **4** dire **7** ominous **9** ill-omened **11** apocalyptic **12** inauspicious

ill-bred **4** rude **5** crude **7** boorish, uncivil, uncouth **8** churlish, impolite **10** unmannerly **11** ill-mannered **12** discourteous

ill-defined **3** dim **4** hazy **5** faint, murky **6** blurry **7** blurred, clouded, shadowy **8** nebulous, obscured **10** indistinct

illegal **5** wrong **6** banned **7** illicit **8** criminal, not legal, outlawed, unlawful **9** felonious, forbidden **10** actionable, prohibited, proscribed **12** illegitimate, unauthorized, unsanctioned **13** against the law

illegible **7** unclear **8** obscured **9** scribbled **10** unreadable **14** indecipherable, undecipherable, unintelligible

illegitimate **7** bastard, illegal, illicit, lawless, natural **8** baseborn, improper, unlawful **10** prohibited **11** misbegotten, unwarranted **12** unauthorized, unsanctioned

ill-fated **6** doomed, jinxed **7** hapless, unlucky **8** blighted, luckless **9** ill-omened **10** ill-starred

ill-favored **4** ugly **5** plain **6** homely **8** unlovely **9** repulsive, unsightly **12** disagreeable, unattractive

ill-fortune **6** mishap **7** bad luck **8** calamity, disaster, hardship **9** adversity **10** misfortune **11** catastrophe

ill health **6** malady **7** ailment, disease, illness **8** sickness **9** infirmity

ill-humored **5** sulky, testy **6** crabby, grumpy, sullen **7** grouchy **10** in a bad mood, unfriendly, unsociable

illiberal **5** petty, small **6** biased, narrow **7** bigoted **9** hidebound **10** brassbound, intolerant, prejudiced, ungenerous **11** opinionated, small-minded **12** narrow-minded, shortsighted

illicit **7** illegal, lawless **8** criminal, improper, not legal, unlawful **9** felonious **10** prohibited **11** black-market, clandestine **12** illegitimate, not permitted, unauthorized **13** against the law, impermissible **15** under-the-counter

Illinois ***see box***

Illinois (Iliniwek)
language family: **9** Algonkian **10** Algonquian
tribe: **6** Peoria **7** Cahokia, Tamaroa **9** Kaskaskia, Moingwena **10** Michigamea
location: **4** Iowa, Ohio **7** Indiana **8** Illinois, Michigan, Missouri **9** Wisconsin
built: **12** Cahokia Mound
murdered: **7** Pontiac
related to: **5** Miami **6** Ojibwa **7** Ojibway

illiterate **7** witless **8** childish, ignorant, unversed **9** unlearned, untutored **10** amateurish, incoherent, uneducated, uninformed, unlettered, unreliable, unschooled **11** not educated, uninitiated, unscholarly **12** uninstructed **13** unenlightened, ungrammatical **15** unknowledgeable

ill-made **6** shoddy **7** awkward **8** deformed, inferior **9** makeshift, malformed **10** jerry-built, jury-rigged **15** misproportioned

ill-mannered **4** rude **5** crude **6** coarse **7** boorish, ill-bred, loutish, uncivil **8** impolite **9** offensive, ungallant **10** ill-behaved, ungracious **12** discourteous **13** disrespectful

ill-natured **4** sour **5** cross, nasty, surly **6** bitter, cranky, malign **7** caustic, grouchy, peevish **8** captious, churlish, spiteful, venomous **9** crotchety, irascible, irritable, malignant, rancorous, splenetic **10** ill-humored, unfriendly **11** acrimonious, contentious, quarrelsome **12** antagonistic, cantankerous

illness **6** malady **7** ailment, disease **8** disorder, sickness **9** complaint, ill health, infirmity **10** affliction, disability, poor health **11** malfunction **13** indisposition

illness recovery
god of: **11** Telesphorus

illogical **4** wild **5** crazy, dopey, nutty, silly, wacky **6** absurd, far-out, screwy **7** asinine, offbeat, unsound **9** erroneous, senseless **10** fallacious, irrational, off-the-wall, ridiculous **11** incongruent, incongruous, nonsensical, unreasoning **12** inconsistent, preposterous, unreasonable **13** contradictory

ill-omened **4** dire **7** adverse, ominous **9** ill-boding **11** apocalyptic, unfavorable **12** inauspicious, unpropitious

ill-smelling **4** foul, high, olid, rank **5** fetid, fusty **6** putrid, rancid, smelly, stinky, strong **7** reeking **8** stinking **10** malodorous

ill-starred **4** dire **5** fatal **6** tragic **7** adverse **8** ill-fated **10** calamitous, disastrous **11** unfortunate **12** catastrophic, inauspicious

ill-suited **5** inapt **8** mismated, unsuited **9** misjoined, unfitting **10** ill-adapted, ill-matched, malapropos, mismatched, unbecoming, unsuitable **11** incongruous, unbefitting, uncongenial **12** incompatible, inconsistent **13** inappropriate

ill-tempered **4** mean, rude, sour **5** angry, cross, harsh, nasty, testy **6** bitter, cranky, shirty **7** acerbic, furious, grouchy, peevish, waspish **8** choleric, churlish, petulant **9** crotchety, irascible, irritable **10** bad-natured, ill-humored, ill-natured, in a bad mood, unpleasant **11** acrimonious **12** cantankerous

ill-treatment **4** harm **5** abuse **6** ill-use, injury, misuse **7** cruelty **13** mortification

illuminate **5** edify, light **7** clarify, enhance, explain, light up **8** brighten, illumine, instruct, spell out **9** elucidate, enlighten, exemplify, irradiate, make clear **12** throw light on **13** cast light upon

Illinois
abbreviation: **2** IL **3** Ill
nickname: **4** Tall **6** Sucker **7** Prairie **13** Land of Lincoln
capital: **11** Springfield
largest city: **7** Chicago
others: **4** Pana **5** Alton, Cairo, Elgin, Flora, Olney, Pekin **6** Albion, Berwyn, Canton, Herrin, Joliet, Peoria, Skokie **7** Batavia, Decatur, Genesco, Mendota, Nokomis **8** Evanston, Rockford, Waukegan **9** Centralia **10** Barrington **11** Bloomington
college: **4** Knox **5** Barat **6** Aurora, DePaul, Eureka, Loyola, Olivet, Quincy, Shimer **7** Bradley, Chicago, Wheaton **8** Millikin **9** Augustana **12** Northwestern **16** Illinois Wesleyan **23** Illinois Institute of Tech
explorer: **6** Joliet **7** Jolliet **9** Marquette
feature: **10** stockyards
airport: **5** O'Hare
museum: **18** Science and Industry
seaway: **10** St Lawrence
trail: **7** Lincoln
tribe: **3** Fox **4** Sauk **9** Kaskaskia
people: **9** Black Hawk, Jack Benny **10** Jane Addams, Walt Disney **12** Carl Sandburg **15** Ernest Hemingway **18** Engineer Casey Jones **20** William Jennings Bryan
lake: **3** Fox **5** Grass **7** Calumet **8** Michigan, Pistakee
land rank: **12** twenty-fourth
mountain: **6** Ozarks
highest point: **12** Charles Mound
physical feature:
hills: **7** Shawnee
president: **14** Abraham Lincoln
river: **4** Ohio, Rock **5** Spoon **6** Wabash **7** Chicago, Elkhorn **8** Big Muddy, Illinois, Mackinaw, Sangamon **9** Kaskaskia **10** Des Plaines **11** Mississippi
state admission: **11** twenty-first
state bird: **8** cardinal
state flower: **6** violet
state motto: **29** State Sovereignty—National Union
state song: **8** Illinois
state tree: **7** burl oak **8** white oak

illuminated **3** lit **5** lit up **6** bright **7** lighted **9** clarified, decorated, illumined **10** brightened, elucidated, irradiated

illumination **6** lights, wisdom **7** insight **8** lighting **9** education, knowledge **10** illumining, lighting up, perception, revelation **11** edification, information, instruction, irradiation **13** comprehension, enlightenment

Illuminations, Les
author: **13** Arthur Rimbaud

illumined **3** lit **7** lighted **8** luminous **11** illuminated

ill-use **4** harm, hurt **5** abuse **6** injure, misuse **7** assault, cruelty, harming **8** maltreat, mistreat **10** bodily harm **12** maltreatment, mistreatment

illusion **5** error, fancy **6** mirage, vagary, vision **7** caprice, chimera, fallacy **8** delusion, phantasm **9** deception, false idea, misbelief, semblance, unreality **10** apparition, false image, hocus-pocus, humbuggery, impression **11** false belief **13** hallucination, misconception, misimpression **15** misapprehension

illusive **5** false **6** unreal **7** phantom, seeming **8** apparent, chimeric, fanciful, fantastic, illusory **9** deceptive **10** ostensible **11** illusionary

illusory **4** sham **5** false **6** unreal **7** seeming **8** apparent, delusive, fanciful, illusive, spurious **9** deceptive, erroneous, imaginary **10** fallacious, misleading, ostensible **11** counterfeit, unrealistic **13** hallucinatory

illustrate **4** show **6** define **7** clarify, explain, picture, point up, portray **8** decorate, ornament **9** bring home, delineate, elucidate, emphasize, make clear, represent **10** illuminate **11** demonstrate **12** pictorialize, throw light on **16** make intelligible

illustration **5** image, plate **6** figure **7** drawing, example, picture **8** instance, specimen **9** portrayal **10** photograph **14** representation **15** exemplification

illustrious **5** famed, great **6** famous **7** eminent, honored **8** glorious, lustrous, peerless, renowned, splendid **9** acclaimed, brilliant, exemplary, matchless, prominent **10** celebrated **11** magnificent **13** distinguished

illustriousness **8** grandeur **9** greatness **11** distinction **12** magnificence

ill will **4** gall **5** anger, spite **6** animus, enmity, hatred, malice, rancor, spleen **7** dislike **8** acrimony, aversion, bad blood, loathing **9** animosity, antipathy, hostility **10** abhorrence, antagonism, bitterness, contention **11** malevolence **12** hard feelings, spitefulness

ill wind **7** bad luck **8** bad break, hard luck **9** adversity, mischance **10** misfortune

Illyrius
father: **6** Cadmus

Ilmarinen
origin: **7** Finnish
form: **10** blacksmith
hero in: **8** Kalevala
forged: **5** Sampo
Sampo's owner: **5** Louhi

I Love Lucy
character: **9** Fred Mertz **10** Ethel Mertz **11** Little Ricky, Lucy Ricardo **12** Ricky Ricardo
cast: **9** Desi Arnaz **11** Lucille Ball, Vivian Vance **14** William Frawley
Ricky's club: **7** Babaloo **9** Tropicana

Il Penseroso
author: **10** John Milton
companion piece: **8** L'Allegro

image **4** copy, icon, idea, idol **6** double, effigy, fetish, figure, memory, simile, statue, symbol, visage **7** concept, picture, replica **8** likeness, metaphor, portrait **9** depiction, duplicate, facsimile, mirroring, semblance **10** photograph, reflection, simulacrum **11** countenance, delineation, incarnation **12** recollection, reproduction **13** mental picture **14** figure of speech, representation

imaginable **8** feasible **9** thinkable **11** conceivable

imaginary **4** sham **5** fancy, phony **6** made-up, unreal **7** fancied, fiction, figment **8** delusion, fabulous, fanciful, illusion, illusory, invented, mythical, romantic **9** fantastic, figmental, legendary **10** factitious, fictitious **11** counterfeit, make-believe

imagination **5** fancy **7** cunning, thought **9** ingenuity, invention **10** astuteness, creativity, enterprise **12** creativeness **13** inventiveness **14** thoughtfulness **15** creative thought, resourcefulness

imaginative **6** clever **7** unusual **8** creative, inspired, original **9** ingenious, inventive **10** innovative **11** resourceful **12** enterprising **16** off the beaten path, out of the ordinary

imagine **5** fancy, guess, infer, judge **6** assume, gather **7** believe, dream up, picture, presume, pretend, project, suppose, surmise, suspect **8** conceive, envisage, envision **9** fantasize, visualize **10** conjecture

imbecile **3** ass **4** dolt, dope, fool, jerk **5** dummy, dunce, idiot, moron, ninny **6** nitwit **7** dingbat **8** dumbbell **9** blockhead, simpleton **10** nincompoop

imbecilic **4** dumb **5** inane, silly **6** absurd, stupid **7** asinine, foolish **8** careless, mindless **11** thoughtless

imbecility **6** idiocy **8** dullness, dumbness **9** asininity, stupidity, thickness **16** simplemindedness

imbibe **4** swig, tope **5** drink, quaff **6** guzzle, ingest, tipple **7** consume, partake, swallow **8** chugalug, toss down, wash down

imbiber **4** wino **5** drunk, toper **7** drinker, tippler **8** consumer, drunkard, ingester

Imbrius
mentioned in: **5** Iliad
father: **6** Mentor
killed by: **6** Teucer

imbroglio **3** row **4** fray **5** brawl, broil, clash, fight, melee, scrap **6** fracas, ruckus, rumpus, uproar **7** scuffle **8** argument **9** confusion **11** altercation, embroilment **12** entanglement **13** embarrassment

imbue **4** fill, fire, tint **5** bathe, color, endow, steep, tinge **6** arouse, infuse **7** animate, impress, ingrain, inspire, instill, pervade, suffuse **8** permeate, tincture **9** inculcate

Imhotep
father: **4** Ptah
mother: **7** Sekhmet
position: **6** scribe, vizier, writer **9** architect, physician
architect of pyramid: **8** Sakkarah

imitate **3** ape **4** copy, mime **5** mimic **6** mirror, parody, parrot **7** emulate, pass for **8** look like, simulate **9** duplicate, represent **10** caricature **11** counterfeit, impersonate

imitation **4** fake, mock, sham **5** aping, phony **6** ersatz, parody **7** man-made, mimicry, takeoff **8** travesty **9** burlesque, facsimile, semblance, simulated, synthetic **10** adaptation, artificial, caricature, impression, similarity, simulation **11** counterfeit, duplication, make-believe **12** reproduction **13** impersonation **14** representation

Imitation of Christ, The
author: **13** Thomas a Kempis

immaculate **4** pure **5** clean, ideal **6** chaste, intact, virgin **7** perfect, saintly, sinless **8** flawless, innocent, spotless, unsoiled, virginal, virtuous **9** faultless, guiltless, shipshape, stainless, unstained, unsullied **11** spic and span, untarnished **13** above reproach, unimpeachable **14** irreproachable **15** unexceptionable

immanent **6** inborn, inbred, innate **7** natural **8** inherent **9** ingrained, intrinsic **10** congenital, deep-rooted, deep-seated, indigenous, indwelling **11** instinctive, instinctual

Immanuel **7** Messiah **11** Jesus Christ
means: **9** God with us

immaterial **7** ghostly, shadowy, trivial **8** bodiless, ethereal, mystical, noumenal, spectral, trifling, unbodied **9** spiritual, unearthly **10** evanescent, extraneous, impalpable, intangible, irrelevant, of no moment **11** disembodied, incorporeal, not relevant, unimportant **12** extramundane, extrasensory **13** insignificant, insubstantial, unsubstantial **14** of no importance **15** inconsequential, of little account

immature **5** green, young **6** callow, unripe **7** babyish, kiddish, puerile **8** childish, juvenile, unformed, youthful **9** embryonic, half-grown, infantile, not mature, pubescent **10** unfinished, unmellowed **11** out of season, rudimentary, undeveloped **16** wet behind the ears

immeasurable **7** endless, immense **8** infinite **9** boundless, limitless, unbounded, unlimited **10** fathomless **11** illimitable, inestimable, measureless, never-ending **12** incalculable, interminable, unfathomable **13** inexhaustible

immediate **4** near, next, nigh **5** close, hasty, local, swift **6** abrupt, nearby, prompt, recent, speedy, sudden **7** express, instant, nearest **8** adjacent, punctual **9** proximate, undelayed **10** contiguous **13** instantaneous

immediately **3** now **9** instantly, right away **10** this minute **12** without delay
French: **11** tout de suite

immemorial **5** olden **7** ageless, ancient **8** dateless, hallowed, timeless **9** ancestral, legendary, venerable **11** time-honored **12** long-standing, mythological **15** long-established

immense **4** huge, vast **5** great **7** mammoth, massive **8** colossal, enormous, gigantic **9** extensive, monstrous **10** prodigious, stupendous, tremendous **11** measureless **14** Brobdingnagian

immensity **8** enormity, hugeness, vastness **9** largeness **12** enormousness

immerse **3** dip **4** duck, dunk, sink, soak **5** bathe, douse, lower, steep **6** absorb, drench, engage, occupy, plunge **7** engross **8** submerge

immerse briefly **3** dip **4** dunk

immersion **7** bathing, dunking **8** drowning **10** absorption, submersion **11** engrossment, involvement, submergence **13** concentration, preoccupation

immigrant **5** alien **7** migrant, settler **8** colonist, newcomer **9** foreigner, nonnative

immigrate **6** move to, settle **7** migrate **8** colonize

imminent **4** near **7** looming **8** menacing, perilous **9** immediate, impending **10** near at hand **11** approaching, close at hand, threatening

immobile **4** fast **5** fixed, quiet, rigid, stiff, still **6** at rest, laid up, rooted, secure, stable, static **7** riveted **9** immovable, not moving, quiescent, steadfast **10** motionless, stationary, stock-still **11** unbudgeable **13** incapacitated

immobilize **3** fix, set **4** stud **6** disarm, freeze, splint **7** disable **8** paralyze, transfix **12** incapacitate

immoderate **5** undue **7** extreme **8** whopping **9** excessive, unbridled **10** exorbitant, gargantuan, inordinate, prodigious **11** extravagant, intemperate, uncalled-for **12** unreasonable, unrestrained **14** unconscionable

immoderation **6** excess **10** debauchery **11** dissipation, prodigality, unrestraint **12** extravagance, intemperance, recklessness **13** excessiveness **14** prodigiousness

immodest **4** lewd, vain **5** gross, loose **6** brazen, coarse, risque, wanton **7** pompous **8** boastful, braggart, indecent, inflated, unchaste **9** bombastic, conceited, shameless **10** indecorous, indelicate, peacockish, suggestive **11** exaggerated, pretentious **12** self-centered

immoral **4** evil, lewd **5** dirty, wrong **6** sinful, wicked **7** corrupt, heinous, obscene, raunchy, vicious **8** depraved, indecent, infamous, prurient **9** debauched, dissolute, nefarious, salacious, unethical **10** dissipated, iniquitous, licentious, profligate **12** pornographic, unprincipled

Immoralist, The
author: **9** Andre Gide

immorality **3** sin **4** evil **9** decadence, depravity, indecency, obscenity, prurience **10** corruption, debasement, degeneracy, sinfulness **13** salaciousness

immortal **3** god **6** divine **7** abiding, eternal, undying **8** enduring **9** deathless **11** everlasting **12** imperishable

Immortals **6** giants, greats, titans **7** the gods **8** demigods **13** all-time greats
Greek/Roman: **8** pantheon

immovable **3** icy, set **4** cold, fast **5** fixed **6** dogged, secure, steely, stolid **7** adamant, settled **8** detached, fastened, immobile, obdurate, resolute, stubborn **9** heartless, impassive, unfeeling **10** inexorable, inflexible, stationary, unbendable **11** coldhearted, unbudgeable **12** unchangeable **13** unimpressible, unsympathetic **16** unimpressionable

immune **4** free, safe **5** clear **6** exempt **9** protected, resistant **12** invulnerable **13** unsusceptible

immunity **7** freedom **9** exemption **10** resistance **16** unsusceptibility

immure **3** hem, pen **4** cage, coop, jail, wall **6** entomb, intern, wall in, wall up **7** confine, enclose, seclude **8** cloister, imprison **11** incarcerate

immutability **9** endurance, stability **14** changelessness

immutable **4** firm **5** fixed,

solid **6** stable **7** lasting **8** constant, enduring **9** permanent, unaltered, unvarying **10** changeless, inflexible, unchanging **11** unalterable **12** unchangeable, unmodifiable **14** intransmutable **16** incontrovertible

Imogen
character in: 9 Cymbeline
author: 11 Shakespeare

imp 3 elf **4** brat **5** demon, devil, gnome, pixie, scamp **6** goblin, hoyden, rascal, sprite, urchin **7** upstart **9** hobgoblin **10** evil spirit, leprechaun

impact 4 jolt **5** brunt, crash, force, shock, smash **6** burden, effect, thrust **7** contact **9** collision, influence **10** concussion **11** implication **12** repercussion

impair 3 mar **4** harm, hurt **6** damage, hinder, injure, lessen, reduce, weaken, worsen **7** cripple, subvert, vitiate **8** decrease, enervate, enfeeble, undercut **10** debilitate **11** detract from

impaired 6 broken, faulty, flawed **7** damaged **9** defective, deficient, imperfect

impairment 4 flaw, harm **5** fault **6** damage, defect, injury, malady **7** ailment, illness **8** debility, disorder, handicap, sickness, weakness **9** detriment, hindrance, infirmity **10** disability, impediment, inadequacy **12** debilitation

impale 3 fix, pin **4** tack **5** affix, stick **8** transfix **10** run through

impart 4 give, lend, tell **5** grant, offer, share **6** accord, afford, pass on, relate, render, report, reveal **7** confide, consign, deliver, divulge, mention **8** bestow on, confer on, disclose, dispense **9** make known **10** contribute **11** communicate

impartial 4 fair, just **7** neutral **8** detached, unbiased **9** equitable, objective **10** evenhanded, fair-minded, open-minded **11** nonpartisan **12** unprejudiced **13** disinterested, dispassionate

impartiality 7 justice **8** equality, fair play, fairness **10** detachment, neutrality **11** objectivity

impasse 4 snag **7** dead end, dilemma **8** cul-de-sac, deadlock, quandary, standoff **9** stalemate **10** blind alley, bottleneck, standstill **11** predicament

impassioned 5 eager, fiery **6** ardent, heated **7** earnest, excited, fervent, intense, rousing, zealous **8** animated, forceful, inspired, stirring

impassive 4 calm, cool **5** aloof, stony **6** sedate, stolid **7** stoical, unmoved **8** reserved **9** apathetic, untouched **10** impervious, insensible, phlegmatic **11** emotionless, indifferent, inscrutable, unemotional, unperturbed **13** dispassionate, imperturbable, unimpressible **16** unimpressionable

impassiveness 8 coldness **9** aloofness, stolidity **12** indifference **15** emotionlessness

impassivity 6 apathy **8** coolness, stoicism **9** aloofness, stolidity **10** dispassion **15** emotionlessness **16** imperturbability

impatient 4 edgy **5** fussy, hasty, itchy, rabid, tense, testy **6** ardent, touchy **7** annoyed, anxious, brusque, hurried, nervous, peevish, restive **8** agitated, feverish, restless **9** excitable, irascible, irritable, irritated **10** high-strung, intolerant, passionate **12** enthusiastic

impeach 4 slur **6** accuse, assail, attack, charge, impugn, indict **7** arraign, slander **8** badmouth, belittle, question **9** challenge, discredit, disparage, inculpate **11** incriminate **16** call into question

impeccable 7 perfect **8** flawless **9** blameless, excellent, faultless **10** immaculate **11** unblemished **12** irreprovable, unassailable **13** unimpeachable **14** irreproachable **15** unexceptionable

impecunious 4 poor **5** broke, needy **6** hard-up **7** pinched **8** bankrupt, indigent **9** destitute, insolvent, penniless **10** down-and-out, straitened **12** impoverished **15** poverty-stricken

impede 5 block, check, delay, deter, stall **6** arrest, halter, hamper, hinder, retard, stymie, thwart **7** disrupt, inhibit **8** hold back, obstruct, slow down **9** frustrate, interrupt, sidetrack **13** interfere with

impediment 4 flaw **5** block, delay **6** defect **7** barrier **8** blockage, drawback, handicap, obstacle **9** deformity, hindrance **10** detraction **11** obstruction **12** interference **14** stumbling block

impedimenta 4 gear **7** baggage **9** equipment **13** accoutrements, paraphernalia

impel 4 goad, prod, push, spur, urge **5** drive, force **6** compel, incite, induce, prompt **7** require **8** motivate **9** constrain, stimulate **11** necessitate

impend 4 brew, hang, loom **5** hover, lower **6** menace **8** approach, draw near, overhang, threaten

impending 4 near **6** coming **7** brewing, looming **8** imminent, menacing, oncoming **9** immediate **11** approaching, forthcoming, threatening

impenetrable 5 dense, solid, thick **6** sealed **7** elusive, obscure **8** puzzling **9** insoluble **10** impassable, impervious, insensible, intangible, inviolable, mysterious, unpalpable **11** inscrutable, unenterable **12** inaccessible, inexplicable, invulnerable, unfathomable **16** incomprehensible

impenitent 4 lost **6** inured **7** callous, defiant **8** hardened, obdurate **9** unashamed **10** uncontrite **11** remorseless, unrepentant, unrepenting **12** incorrigible, unapologetic **13** irreclaimable

imperative 6 urgent **7** crucial, needful **8** critical, pressing **9** essential, mandatory, necessary, requisite **10** compulsory, obligatory **11** unavoidable

imperceptible 5 minor, scant, small **6** hidden, minute, slight, subtle **7** minimal **8** academic **10** indistinct **12** undetectable, unnoticeable **13** infinitesimal, insignificant, unappreciable, unperceivable **14** inconsiderable

imperceptive 5 blind **9** unfeeling **11** insensitive, unobservant **12** inpercipient, unperceptive **13** unsympathetic

imperfect 6 faulty, flawed **8** deformed, fallible, impaired **9** blemished, defective

imperfection 4 flaw **5** fault **6** defect **7** blemish **8** weakness **9** deformity **10** faultiness, impairment, inadequacy **11** fallibility, shortcoming **13** insufficiency **14** incompleteness

imperial 5 bossy **6** feudal, lordly **8** despotic **9** arbitrary, imperious **10** autocratic, high-handed, peremptory, repressive, tyrannical **11** dictatorial, domineering, magisterial, overbearing **13** authoritarian

Imperial Presidency, The
author: **20** Arthur M Schlesinger Jr

imperil **4** risk **6** chance, expose, gamble, hazard **8** endanger **10** compromise, jeopardize **13** put in jeopardy

imperious **5** bossy, lofty **6** lordly **7** haughty **8** arrogant, despotic, imperial **10** autocratic, commanding, peremptory, tyrannical **11** dictatorial, domineering, overbearing **13** high-and-mighty

imperiousness **9** arrogance, loftiness **11** haughtiness

imperishable **6** stable **7** durable, lasting **14** indestructible

imperium **4** rule **5** realm **6** domain, empire **8** dominion **11** sovereignty

impermanent **7** passing **8** fleeting, fugitive, not fixed, unstable **9** ephemeral, temporary, transient **10** evanescent, transitory, unenduring

impermeable **5** dense, solid, tight **6** opaque **9** nonporous **10** impervious, waterproof

impersonal **4** dead **6** remote **7** general, inhuman, neutral **8** detached, lifeless, soulless **9** impartial, impassive, inanimate, inorganic, objective **10** spiritless **11** perfunctory **13** disinterested, dispassionate

impersonate **3** ape **4** copy, mime **5** mimic **6** pose as **7** imitate, portray **9** personify, represent **11** pretend to be **12** masquerade as

impertinence **4** sass **5** cheek, sauce **7** affront **8** audacity, boldness, rudeness **9** freshness, impudence, insolence, sauciness **10** cheekiness, disrespect, effrontery, incivility **11** irrelevance **17** disrespectfulness, inappropriateness

impertinent **4** rude **5** fresh, surly **6** brassy, brazen, smarty **7** uncivil **8** arrogant, impudent, insolent **9** extrinsic, insulting, unrelated **10** extraneous, immaterial, irrelevant, not germane, peremptory, unmannerly **11** unimportant **12** discourteous, presumptuous **13** disrespectful, inappropriate **14** beside the point

imperturbability **5** poise **6** aplomb **8** calmness, coolness **9** composure, sangfroid **10** equanimity, steadiness **11** self-control, tranquility **12** tranquillity **14** presence of mind, self-possession

imperturbable **4** calm, cool **6** sedate, serene **8** composed **9** collected, impassive, unanxious, unfazable, unruffled **10** impervious **11** levelheaded, undisturbed, unexcitable, unflappable, unflustered **13** dispassionate, unsusceptible

impervious **6** closed **8** immune to **11** impermeable **12** impenetrable, inaccessible, invulnerable **14** unapproachable

impetuosity **8** rashness **11** spontaneity, unrestraint **12** recklessness **13** impulsiveness **14** capriciousness

impetuous **4** rash **5** hasty **6** abrupt, stormy **7** rampant, violent **8** forcible, headlong, vehement **9** impulsive **10** capricious, inexorable, relentless, unexpected **11** precipitate **14** unpremeditated

impetus **4** prod, push, spur **5** boost, drive, force, start **6** motive **7** impulse **8** momentum, stimulus **9** impulsion, incentive **10** motivation, propulsion **11** moving force, stimulation

impiety **9** blasphemy, sacrilege **10** disrespect, irreligion **11** irreverence, ungodliness

impinge **7** intrude, obtrude, violate **8** encroach, infringe, trespass **10** transgress

impious **7** godless, immoral, profane, ungodly **8** apostate, renegade **9** perverted **10** iniquitous, irreverent **11** blasphemous, irreligious **12** iconoclastic, sacrilegious **13** disrespectful

impiousness **7** impiety **9** blasphemy, sacrilege **10** disrespect **11** irreverence, ungodliness

impish **5** elfin **7** implike, puckish, roguish **8** prankish, rascally, sportive **11** mischievous

implacable **10** inexorable, inflexible, relentless, unamenable **11** intractable, unrelenting **12** unappeasable, unpacifiable **14** irreconcilable, uncompromising

implant **3** fix, set, sow **4** root **5** embed, graft, imbed, inlay, teach **6** infuse, insert **7** impress, instill **8** entrench **9** establish, inculcate **10** impregnate

implausible **8** doubtful, unlikely **9** illogical, senseless **10** far-fetched, improbable, incredible, outrageous, ridiculous **12** preposterous, unbelievable, unreasonable **13** inconceivable

implement **4** tool **5** begin, enact, piece, start **6** device **7** achieve, article, fulfill, realize, utensil **8** activate, carry out **9** apparatus, appliance, equipment, materials **10** accomplish, bring about, instrument **11** set in motion **13** put into effect

implicate **7** connect, embroil, ensnare, involve **8** entangle **9** associate, inculpate **11** incriminate

implication **6** effect **7** outcome **8** innuendo, overtone **9** inference **10** connection, intimation, suggestion **11** association, connotation, consequence, insinuation, involvement **12** entanglement, ramification, significance

implicit **5** total **6** hinted, innate **7** certain, implied, staunch **8** absolute, complete, inferred, inherent, profound, resolute **9** deducible, steadfast, suggested **10** understood, unreserved, unshakable **13** unquestioning

implied **5** tacit **7** oblique **8** indirect **9** implicity, indicated

implode **11** burst inward **17** compress violently

implore **3** beg **4** urge **6** obtest **7** beseech, entreat **9** importune, plead with **10** supplicate

imply **4** hint, mean **6** denote **7** bespeak, betoken, connote, presume, signify, suggest **8** evidence, indicate, intimate **9** insinuate **10** presuppose

impolite **4** rude **7** ill-bred, uncivil **9** impolitic, unfitting, ungenteel, unrefined **10** undecorous, unmannerly **12** discourteous **13** disrespectful, inconsiderate

impoliteness **8** rudeness **10** bad manners, incivility **11** boorishness, discourtesy

import **6** burden, moment, thrust **7** meaning **9** overtones **10** importance **11** connotation, implication **12** ramification, significance

importance **4** rank **5** value, worth **6** esteem, import, moment, repute, weight **7** stature **8** eminence, position **9** influence, relevance **11** consequence, seriousness, weightiness **12** significance **13** essentialness, momentousness

Importance of Being Earnest, The
author: **10** Oscar Wilde
character: **12** Cecily Cardew,

Jack Worthing, Letitia Prism **16** Gwendolen Fairfax **17** Algernon Moncrieff (Algy) **20** Lady Augusta Bracknell **21** Reverend Canon Chasuble

important **5** great, major **7** leading, notable, seminal, serious, weighty **8** creative, esteemed, foremost, original **9** momentous, prominent **10** imperative, meaningful, preeminent, remarkable **11** distinctive, influential, significant **13** consequential

imported **5** alien **6** exotic **7** foreign **9** not native

importunate **7** begging **8** pleading **9** imploring **10** entreating, persistent **11** troublesome **12** supplicating

importune **3** beg, sue **4** pray **5** plead **6** adjure, exhort **7** beseech, entreat, implore **8** appeal to, petition **10** supplicate

importunity **4** plea **6** appeal **7** request **8** entreaty, petition **12** supplication

impose **3** set **4** levy **5** apply, enact, foist, force, lay on **6** peddle, slap on **7** command, dictate, inflict, palm off, place on **9** establish, institute, introduce, prescribe **10** thrust upon

impose upon **5** annoy **6** bother, ill-use **8** ill-treat, maltreat, mistreat **15** take advantage of

imposing **5** grand, lofty **7** massive, stately **8** majestic, striking, towering **10** commanding, impressive, monumental **11** outstanding **12** awe-inspiring

imposition **5** abuse **6** burden, ill use **8** foisting **10** obligation **15** taking advantage

impossible **8** stubborn **9** insoluble **10** unbearable, unsolvable, unyielding **11** intolerable, intractable, not possible **12** insufferable, intransigent, unachievable, unanswerable, unattainable, unimaginable, unmanageable **13** inconceivable **16** out of the question

impost **3** fee, tax **4** duty, fine, toll **6** charge, excise, tariff **10** assessment

impostor **4** sham **5** cheat, duper, fraud, phony, quack **6** con man **7** bluffer, shammer **8** deceiver **9** charlatan, defrauder, pretender, trickster **10** dissembler, mountebank **11** counterfeit, flimflam man, masquerader, pettifogger **12** impersonator

imposture **4** fake, hoax, play, ruse, sham **5** cheat, fraud, trick **6** deceit, humbug **7** forgery, swindle **8** artifice, delusion, pretense, quackery **9** deception, falsehood, imitation **10** pretension **11** charlatanry, counterfeit, fraudulence **12** charlatanism **13** impersonation, mountebankery

impotence **8** weakness **9** paralysis **10** disability, incapacity, inefficacy **12** helplessness **13** powerlessness **14** ineffectuality **15** ineffectiveness

impotent **4** weak **5** frail **6** feeble **7** hapless **8** disabled, feckless, helpless **9** paralyzed, powerless **11** ineffective

impound **3** pen **4** cage **5** pen in, seize **6** coop up, encage, lock up, shut in **7** confine **13** hold in custody

impoverish **4** bust, ruin **5** break, drain **6** beggar, pauper, reduce **7** deplete, exhaust **8** bankrupt, make poor **9** pauperize **18** send to the poorhouse

impoverished **4** poor **6** abject, barren, bereft, effete, used up **7** drained, sterile, wanting, worn out **8** depleted, indigent, wiped out **9** destitute, exhausted **10** down-and-out, pauperized **11** impecunious **12** unproductive, without means

impractical **6** sloppy, unwise **8** careless, quixotic, romantic **10** loose-ended, starry-eyed **11** unrealistic **12** disorganized **13** helter-skelter, unintelligent

imprecation **5** curse **8** anathema **11** malediction

impregnable **6** mighty, potent, strong, sturdy **8** powerful **10** invincible **12** invulnerable, unassailable, unattackable **13** unconquerable

impregnate **3** wet **4** soak **5** steep **6** dampen, drench, imbrue, infuse **7** moisten, suffuse **8** fructify, inundate, permeate, saturate **9** fecundate, fertilize **10** inseminate

impresario **7** manager, sponsor **8** director **9** conductor, organizer **12** entrepreneur

impress **4** grab, move, stir, sway **5** reach, touch **6** affect, excite, sink in, strike **8** bedazzle **9** electrify, influence, overpower, overwhelm

impression **4** idea, mark, mold, view **5** hunch, stamp, trace, track **6** belief, effect, impact, notion **7** contour, feeling, impress, imprint, opinion, outline, surmise **9** influence, reception, sensation **10** conviction **11** indentation **13** understanding

impressionable **8** gullible, passible, sentient **9** affective, receptive **10** vulnerable **11** suggestible

impressive **5** grand **6** august, moving **8** exciting, imposing, majestic, striking **9** memorable, thrilling **11** magnificent, outstanding **12** awe-inspiring, overpowering, soul-stirring **13** unforgettable

imprimis **15** in the first place

imprint **3** fix **4** etch, mark, sign **5** infix, press, stamp, title **6** indent **7** engrave, impress **8** inscribe **9** engraving **10** depression, impression **11** indentation

imprison **3** pen **4** jail **6** coop up, engage, entomb, immure, lock up **7** confine, fence in, impound, shackle **8** restrain **9** constrain **11** hold captive, incarcerate

improbable **8** doubtful, unlikely **9** illogical **11** implausible **12** unreasonable **13** unforeseeable

improbable solution in a play's plot
Latin: **13** deus ex machina

impromptu **6** sudden **7** offhand **9** impulsive, makeshift, on the spot **10** improvised, off the cuff, unexpected, unprepared **11** spontaneous, unrehearsed **14** extemporaneous, unpremeditated, without warning **15** spur-of-the-moment **16** extemporaneously, on a moment's notice **19** off the top of one's head

improper **4** lewd **5** inapt, unfit **8** indecent, off-color, unseemly **9** ill-suited, irregular **10** indecorous, malapropos, out of place, suggestive, unbecoming, unsuitable **12** inharmonious **13** inappropriate, unconformable
French: **5** outre

impropriety **5** gaffe **7** blunder, faux pas **9** gaucherie, indecorum, vulgarity **10** bad manners **11** boorishness **12** impoliteness, indiscretion

improve **4** help **5** rally **6** better, enrich, repair **7** correct, develop, enhance **9** cultivate **10** ameliorate, recuperate

improvement **4** gain **6** reform, repair **7** advance, upswing

8 additive, progress 9 amendment 10 betterment, emendation, refinement 11 advancement, enhancement, reclamation 12 amelioration 14 reconstruction

improvidence 10 imprudence 11 prodigality 12 extravagance, wastefulness 13 shiftlessness 16 shortsightedness

improvident 6 lavish 8 prodigal, reckless, wasteful 9 imprudent, negligent, unthrifty 10 thriftless 11 extravagant, spendthrift 12 shortsighted 14 unparsimonious

improvise 5 ad-lib 6 make up, wing it 11 extemporize

improvised 5 ad-lib 7 devised, offhand 8 invented 9 concocted, contrived, dreamed-up, extempore, hatched-up, impromptu, makeshift 10 off-the-cuff, originated, unprepared 11 extemporary, spontaneous, unrehearsed 12 extemporized 14 extemporaneous, unpremeditated 15 improvisational, spur-of-the-moment

imprudent 4 rash 5 crazy, dopey 6 unwise 7 foolish 8 heedless, mindless, untoward 9 foolhardy 10 ill-advised, incautious, indiscreet, unthinking 11 inadvisable, injudicious, thoughtless 13 ill-considered

impudence
Yiddish: 7 chutzpa 8 chutzpah

impudent 4 bold, rude 5 brash, fresh, nervy, saucy 6 brazen, cheeky 7 forward, upstart 8 impolite, insolent 9 bumptious, shameless 11 impertinent, smart-alecky, wiseacreish 12 discourteous 13 disrespectful

impugn 4 deny 5 knock, libel 6 assail, attack, berate, negate, oppose 7 asperse, slander 8 denounce, question 9 challenge, criticize 10 contradict 14 call in question, cast aspersions 16 call into question

impugnment 7 slander 10 aspersions

impulse 4 bent, goad, push, spur, urge, whim 5 drive, fancy, force 6 desire, motive, notion, thrust, whimsy 7 caprice, impetus, whimsey 8 instinct, momentum, movement, stimulus, stirring 9 incentive 10 incitement, motivation 11 inclination, inspiration, instigation

impulsive 4 rash 7 driving, offhand 8 forceful, forcible, notional 9 impelling, impetuous, impromptu, unplanned, whimsical 10 capricious, incautious, propellant, propelling 11 involuntary, spontaneous 12 devil-may-care 13 unpredictable 14 extemporaneous, unpremeditated 15 spur-of-the-moment

impulsiveness 8 rashness 11 impetuosity, spontaneity, unrestraint 12 recklessness, whimsicality 14 capriciousness

impunity 8 immunity 9 clearance, exemption, privilege 10 absolution 11 prerogative 12 dispensation

impure 4 foul, lewd 5 dirty 6 coarse, filthy, smutty 7 debased, defiled, immoral, lustful, noisome, noxious, obscene, sullied, tainted, unclean 8 degraded, devalued, immodest, improper, indecent, polluted, prurient, unchaste, vitiated 9 lecherous, salacious, unrefined 10 indecorous, indelicate, libidinous, licentious 11 adulterated, depreciated, unwholesome 12 contaminated

impurity 5 alloy, dross, filth, taint 8 foulness 9 dirtiness, pollutant, pollution 10 adulterant, corruption, defilement 11 contaminant, taintedness, uncleanness 12 adulteration 13 contamination, foreign matter 15 unwholesomeness

imputation 6 charge 10 accusation, allegation, ascription 11 attribution

impute 5 refer 6 assign, charge, credit, relate 7 ascribe 9 attribute

inability 10 inaptitude, incapacity, ineptitude 12 helplessness, incapability, incompetence 13 maladroitness, powerlessness

in absence
Latin: 10 in absentia

in absentia 9 in absence

inaccessible 9 not at hand 11 unreachable 12 unattainable, unobtainable 14 unapproachable

in accord 9 agreeable, approving, in harmony, of one mind 10 concurring, consenting 11 in agreement
French: 9 en rapport

inaccuracy 4 goof, slip 5 error, fault, wrong 6 boo-boo 7 blunder, erratum, fallacy, mistake 9 unclarity 10 faultiness 11 imprecision, inexactness 13 incorrectness, unreliability 14 fallaciousness

inaccurate 3 off 5 false, wrong 6 faulty 7 inexact 8 mistaken 9 erroneous, imprecise, incorrect, off target 10 fallacious, unreliable 11 not on target, off the track 13 wide of the mark

Inachus
god of: 6 rivers
king of: 5 Argos
father: 7 Oceanus
mother: 6 Tethys
wife: 5 Melia
son: 9 Aegialeus, Phoroneus
daughter: 2 Io

inaction 8 abeyance, deferral, dormancy, dullness, idleness 9 cessation, indolence 10 inactivity, quiescence, somnolence, suspension 11 complacency

inactive 4 dull, idle, lazy 5 inert, quiet, still 6 low-key, otiose, static, torpid, unused 7 dormant, languid 8 indolent, slothful, sluggish 9 do-nothing, easygoing, leisurely, sedentary, somnolent 10 on the shelf 11 inoperative 12 out of service

inactivity 4 rest 5 quiet 6 disuse 7 inertia 8 dormancy, idleness, inaction 9 stillness 10 quiescence

in actuality
Latin: 6 in esse

in addition 3 and, too 4 also, more, plus, then 5 above, added, again, extra 6 as well, beyond 7 besides, further 8 moreover 10 additional 12 additionally, supplemental

inadequacy 4 lack 7 failing 10 deficiency, impairment 11 shortcoming 13 insufficiency

inadequate 5 inept, short, unfit 6 meager, scanty, too raw 7 lacking, not up to, wanting 8 below par, unfitted 9 deficient, imperfect, incapable 11 incompetent, unqualified 12 insufficient

inadmissible 10 disallowed, extraneous 11 intolerable 12 not permitted, unacceptable 14 nonpermissible

in advance 6 before, in time, sooner 7 earlier 9 before now 10 beforehand 11 ahead of time 13 before the fact

inadvertent 7 unmeant 10 accidental, fortuitous, unintended, unthinking 11 involuntary 13 unintentional 14 unpremeditated

inadvisable 5 risky 6 chancy, unwise 9 impolitic, imprudent

10 ill-advised **11** inexpedient, injudicious, inopportune

in aeternum 7 forever

in agreement
French: 9 en rapport

inalienable 6 sacred **8** absolute, defended, inherent **9** protected **10** inviolable, sacrosanct **12** unassailable **13** unforfeitable, unimpeachable

in all
Latin: 6 in toto

in all places 10 every place, everywhere, far and near, far and wide

in a low voice
Latin: 9 sotto voce

inamorata 4 lady, love **5** lover **7** beloved, darling **8** ladylove, mistress, paramour, truelove **10** sweetheart

inane 4 dumb **5** dopey, empty, silly, vapid **6** absurd, jejune, stupid **7** asinine, fatuous, foolish, idiotic, insipid, shallow, vacuous **9** pointless, senseless **10** ridiculous, unthinking **11** meaningless, nonsensical **13** unintelligent

inanimate 4 cold, dead, dull **5** inert **6** asleep, stolid **8** lifeless, soulless **9** inorganic, insensate, nonliving, senseless, unfeeling **10** insensible, insentient **11** unconscious

inanity 6 drivel **7** hogwash, vacuity **8** nonsense, vapidity **9** absurdity, asininity, silliness **11** foolishness **13** pointlessness, senselessness **14** ridiculousness

Inanna
origin: 8 Sumerian
goddess of: 3 war **4** love
sister: 10 Ereshkigal
realm: 6 heaven
corresponds to: 6 Ishtar **7** Astarte, Mylitta **9** Ashtoreth

in any case 6 anyhow, anyway **9** at any rate **10** in any event

in any event 6 anyhow, anyway **9** at any rate, in any case

inapplicable 5 unfit **6** not apt **8** unsuited **10** inapposite, irrelevant, not germane, unsuitable **12** incompatible, not pertinent **13** inappropriate

inappropriate 5 inapt **8** ill-timed, improper, unsuited **9** unfitting **10** indecorous, in bad taste, out of place, unbecoming, unsuitable **11** incongruous **12** incompatible, infelicitous
French: 10 mal a propos

inapt 8 improper, unseemly, unsuited **9** ill-suited, incorrect, unfitting **11** incongruous **13** inappropriate

inaptness 9 inability, ineptness **10** clumsiness, inaptitude, ineptitude **12** incompetence **13** maladroitness **14** unskillfulness

in arrears 4 late **7** overdue **10** delinquent

inarticulate 4 dumb, mute **7** babbled, blurred, garbled, mumbled **8** confused, wordless **9** paralyzed **10** incoherent, indistinct, speechless, tongue-tied **12** inexpressive **14** unintelligible **15** uncommunicative

inartistic 9 graceless, inelegant, tasteless **10** ungraceful **11** unaesthetic **12** unattractive

in a series
French: 7 en suite

in a set
French: 7 en suite

in attendance 4 here **7** present, serving **9** appearing, caring for, on the spot, waiting on **12** accompanying, looking after, taking care of

inattention 6 apathy **10** negligence **12** carelessness **14** lack of interest **16** absentmindedness, unresponsiveness

inattentive 7 unaware **8** careless, heedless **9** forgetful, negligent, unmindful **10** distracted **11** daydreaming, thoughtless, unobservant **12** absentminded

inaugurate 5 set up, start **6** induct, launch **7** instate, kick off, usher in **8** initiate **9** institute, undertake **10** embark upon **11** set in action

inauguration 5 start **9** beginning, induction **10** dedication **11** origination **12** commencement

inaugurator 6 author, father **7** creator, founder, starter **9** initiator, organizer **10** originator, prime mover

inauspicious 7 unlucky **9** ill-chosen, ill-omened **10** badly timed, disastrous **11** unfavorable, unfortunate, unpromising **12** infelicitous, unpropitious

in a vacuum
Latin: 7 in vacuo

in bad faith
Latin: 8 mala fide

in being
Latin: 6 in esse

in blazing crime
Latin: 18 in flagrante delicto

inborn 5 basic **6** inbred, innate, native **7** natural **8** inherent **9** inherited, intrinsic, intuitive **10** congenital **11** fundamental, instinctive **14** constitutional

inbred 6 inborn, innate, primal **7** natural **8** inherent **9** ingrained, inherited, intrinsic, intuitive **10** congenital, deep-rooted, deep-seated, hereditary, indwelling **11** instinctive, instinctual **12** deeply rooted **14** constitutional

Inca
language family: 7 Quechua
location: 4 Peru **5** Chili **7** Bolivia, Ecuador **9** Argentina **12** South America
leader: 7 Huascar **8** Topa Inca **9** Atahualpa, Pachacuti **10** Manco Capac **11** Huayna Capac
conquered by: 7 Pizarro
ruins: 11 Machu Picchu, Sacsahuaman, Tambo Machay

incalculable 7 dubious **8** infinite **9** countless, uncertain **11** inestimable, innumerable, measureless, uncountable **12** immeasurable, incomputable **13** unforeseeable, unpredictable

incandesce 4 burn, glow **5** flare, flash

incandescent 7 dynamic, glowing, radiant **8** electric, galvanic, magnetic, white-hot **9** brilliant **11** high-powered **12** electrifying **13** scintillating

incantation 3 hex **4** jinx **5** chant, charm, magic, spell **6** voodoo **7** sorcery **8** wizardry **10** black magic, hocus-pocus, invocation, mumbo-jumbo, necromancy, witchcraft **11** abracadabra, conjuration

incapable 5 inept, unfit **6** unable **8** helpless, impotent, inferior **9** powerless, unskilled, untrained **10** inadequate **11** incompetent, ineffective, inefficient, unqualified

incapacitate 4 maim, undo **5** lay up **7** cripple, disable **8** enfeeble, handicap, paralyze, sideline **9** make unfit **10** disqualify **13** make powerless **14** put out of action **15** render incapable

incapacitated 6 laid up **8** crippled, disabled, disarmed, helpless, stricken **9** hamstrung, paralyzed, sidelined **10** on the shelf, prostrated **11** immobilized, out of action **12** hors de combat **14** flat on one's back

incapacity **7** illness **8** sickness **9** crippling **10** deficiency, disability **12** incapability

incarcerate **3** pen **4** jail **6** commit, coop up, immure, intern, lock up **7** confine, impound **8** imprison, restrain

incarceration **9** detention **10** commitment, internment **11** confinement, durance vile **12** imprisonment **18** institutionalizing

incarnate **8** embodied, manifest **9** personify **10** actualized, in the flesh **11** objectified, personified

Incarnations
author: **16** Robert Penn Warren

incautious **4** rash **5** brash **6** unwary **8** careless, heedless, reckless **9** hotheaded, impetuous, imprudent, impulsive, overhasty **10** headstrong, indiscreet, unthinking **11** injudicious, thoughtless

incendiary **8** agitator, arsonist **12** inflammatory

incense **5** anger **6** burn up, enrage, madden **7** inflame, provoke **9** infuriate, make angry **13** make indignant
spice: **6** stacte

incensed **3** mad **5** angry, irate **6** fuming, raging **7** enraged, furious **8** burned up, inflamed, outraged, provoked **9** affronted, indignant **10** infuriated

incentive **4** lure, spur **6** come-on, motive **8** stimulus **10** enticement, inducement, motivation **11** inspiration **13** encouragement

inception **5** birth, debut, onset, start **6** origin, outset **7** arrival **9** beginning **12** commencement, inauguration

incessant **8** constant, unbroken, unending **9** ceaseless, continual, perpetual, unceasing **10** continuous, persistent **11** everlasting, unrelenting, unremitting **12** interminable **13** uninterrupted

inch
abbreviation: **2** in

In Chancery
author: **14** John Galsworthy
part of trilogy: **11** Forsyte Saga

inchoate **7** budding, nascent **8** formless, unformed, unshaped **9** amorphous, beginning, embryonic, incipient, shapeless **10** commencing, disjointed, uncohesive **11** unorganized **12** disconnected

incidence **4** rate **5** range, scope **6** extent **8** occasion **9** frequency, happening **10** commonness, occurrence, phenomenon **11** routineness

incident **5** clash, event, scene **6** affair **7** episode, related **8** occasion **9** happening **10** incidental, occurrence **11** contretemps, disturbance

incidental **5** minor **9** accessory, secondary **10** extraneous, unexpected **11** subordinate, unlooked-for

incidentally **7** apropos, by the by **8** by the way **9** in passing **14** speaking of that **15** parenthetically **21** while we're on the subject

incidentals **6** extras **8** minutiae **10** minor items **11** accessories, odds and ends **13** appurtenances

incinerate **4** burn **7** consume, cremate **9** carbonize **13** reduce to ashes

incineration **6** firing **7** burning, flaming **8** ignition, kindling **9** cremation **10** combustion **13** carbonization

incinerator **4** oven **6** burner **7** furnace

incipient **7** budding, nascent **8** inchoate **9** beginning, embryonic, fledgling, promising **10** developing, half-formed **11** rudimentary

in circulation **4** rife **6** abroad, around **7** at large **9** all around **11** going around **12** spread around **14** around and about **15** making the rounds

incise **4** etch **5** carve **7** cut into, engrave

incision **3** cut **4** scar, gash, nick, slit **5** cleft, notch, score, slash, slice, wound **6** furrow

incisive **4** curt, keen **5** acute, brisk, crisp, sharp **6** biting, shrewd **7** cutting, express, mordant, precise, probing, summary **8** analytic, piercing **9** trenchant, well-aimed **10** perceptive **11** intelligent, penetrating

incite **4** goad, prod, stir **5** drive, egg on, impel, rouse **6** arouse, excite, fire up, foment, induce, prompt, stir up, urge on **7** actuate, agitate, inflame, provoke **8** activate **9** instigate, stimulate

incitement **6** urging **7** arousal, driving, goading **8** egging on, exciting, firing up, stirring **9** agitating, fomenting, inflaming, prompting, provoking **10** activation, stirring up **11** provocation, stimulation

incivility **8** rudeness **9** barbarism, impudence, indecorum, surliness, vulgarity **10** bad manners, coarseness, disrespect **11** boorishness, discourtesy, misbehavior, uncouthness **12** impoliteness, tactlessness **14** unpleasantness

inclement **3** raw **4** foul **5** harsh, nasty, rough **6** bitter, severe, stormy **7** violent **11** tempestuous

inclination **3** bow, dip, nod **4** bend, bent, hill, rake, rise **5** grade, pitch, slant, slope **6** liking **7** bending, leaning, sloping **8** fondness, lowering, penchant, tendency **9** acclivity, inclining, proneness **10** preference, proclivity, propensity **11** disposition **12** predilection **14** predisposition

incline **3** bow **4** bend, cant, hill, lean, like, rake, seem, tend, tilt, wont **5** be apt, enjoy, pitch, slant, slope **6** prefer **7** decline **8** be likely, gradient **9** acclivity **10** lean toward **11** bend forward, have a mind to

inclined **3** apt **5** prove **6** liable, likely **7** given to **10** disposed to **11** predisposed

incline downward **3** dip, sag **4** sink **5** droop, slant, slope

inclined to delay **4** slow **5** tardy **6** remiss **8** dawdling, dilatory, sluggish **9** reluctant **12** foot-dragging **13** dillydallying **15** procrastinating

include **5** cover **6** enfold, entail, take in **7** contain, embrace, involve, subsume **8** comprise **9** encompass **10** comprehend **11** incorporate

inclusive **7** general, overall **8** sweeping, taking in **9** embracing, including **10** comprising, encircling **11** surrounding **12** encyclopedic **13** comprehending, comprehensive, incorporating **15** all-encompassing

incognito **7** unknown, unnamed **8** nameless **9** concealed, disguised, protected **10** in disguise, uncredited, undercover, unrevealed **11** undisclosed **12** unidentified **14** unacknowledged, unrecognizable

incognizant **6** obtuse **7** unaware **8** ignorant, unseeing **9** unknowing **13** unconscious of **15** uncomprehending

incoherent **7** muddled, unclear **8** confused, rambling **9** illogical **10** disjointed, irrational **11** bewildering, nonsensical **12** inconsistent **14** unintelligible

In Cold Blood
author: **12** Truman Capote
director: **13** Richard Brooks
cast: **11** Paul Stewart, Robert Blake, Scott Wilson **12** John Forsythe

income **5** means, wages **6** salary **7** revenue **8** earnings **9** emolument **10** livelihood

income, annual
French: **5** rente

incomparable **8** peerless **9** matchless, unequaled, unrivaled **10** inimitable **11** superlative **12** transcendent **13** beyond compare **14** unapproachable

incompatible **6** at odds **7** jarring **8** clashing, contrary, unsuited **10** at variance, discordant, mismatched **11** disagreeing, incongruous, uncongenial **12** antagonistic, inconsistent, inharmonious **13** contradictory, inappropriate

incompatibility **6** strife **7** discord **8** friction, variance **9** disaccord, wrangling **10** antagonism **11** being at odds, discordance **13** lack of harmony

incompetency **9** inability, unfitness **10** ineptitude **11** lack of skill **12** inefficiency **15** ineffectiveness

incompetent **5** inept, unfit **8** inexpert **9** incapable, unskilled, untrained **11** ineffective, ineffectual, inefficient, unqualified **14** lacking ability

incomplete **6** broken **7** partial, wanting **9** defective, deficient **10** unfinished **11** fragmentary

incompleteness **8** omission **10** deficiency **11** shortcoming **15** unfinished state

incomprehensible **7** obscure **8** abstruse, baffling **9** confusing **10** befuddling **11** bewildering, inscrutable, ungraspable **12** impenetrable, unfathomable **14** unintelligible **19** beyond comprehension, beyond understanding

incomprehension **10** bafflement, puzzlement **12** bewilderment **19** failure to understand

inconceivable **7** strange **8** unlikely **10** improbable, incredible **11** unthinkable **12** beyond belief, unbelievable, unimaginable **14** highly unlikely

in conclusion
French: **5** enfin

inconclusive **4** open **9** unsettled **10** indecisive, indefinite, unresolved, up in the air **11** not definite **12** unconvincing, undetermined **13** indeterminate

incongruity **8** variance **9** disparity **10** aberration, disharmony, divergence **11** abnormality, discrepancy **13** dissimilarity, inconsistency, unsuitability **17** inappropriateness

incongruous **3** odd **6** far-out **8** contrary **10** at variance, discrepant, out of place, outlandish, unsuitable **11** conflicting, disagreeing **12** incompatible, inconsistent, out of keeping **13** contradictory, inappropriate **14** irreconcilable

inconsequential **5** petty **6** slight **7** trivial **8** nugatory, picayune, piddling, trifling **9** valueless **10** negligible, of no moment **11** meaningless, unimportant **13** insignificant **15** of no consequence

inconsiderable **5** light, minor, petty, small **6** little, modest, paltry, slight **7** minimal, trivial **8** picayune, trifling **9** no big deal **10** negligible **11** unimportant **13** insignificant, no great shakes **15** inconsequential

inconsiderate **4** rash, rude **6** remiss, unkind **7** uncivil **8** careless, impolite, tactless, uncaring **9** negligent **10** ungracious, unthinking **11** insensitive, thoughtless **12** disregardful, uncharitable

inconsistency **8** variance **9** disparity **10** difference, divergence **11** discrepancy, incongruity **12** disagreement **13** dissimilarity

inconsistent **6** fickle **7** erratic, wayward **8** contrary, notional, unstable, variable **9** changeful, dissonant **10** changeable, discrepant, inconstant, irresolute **11** inaccordant, incongruous, inconsonant, vacillating **12** incompatible, inharmonious **13** contradictory, unpredictable **14** irreconcilable

inconsolable **7** crushed **8** dejected, desolate, wretched **9** miserable **10** despondent **12** disconsolate **13** brokenhearted

inconsonant **10** discordant **12** out of keeping, unharmonious

inconspicuous **3** dim **5** faint, muted **6** modest **9** unnoticed **10** unapparent, unassuming **11** unobtrusive **12** not egregious, unnoticeable **14** unostentatious

inconstancy **10** fickleness, infidelity **11** instability **14** capriciousness, changeableness, unfaithfulness

inconstant **6** fickle, untrue **7** erratic **8** cavalier, disloyal, unstable **9** mercurial **10** capricious, changeable, unfaithful **11** interrupted, uncommitted, undedicated, unsteadfast

incontinence **8** rashness **12** recklessness **13** lack of control **16** irresponsibility

incontinent **8** unchaste **12** unrestrained

incontrovertibility **8** sureness **9** certainty **12** absoluteness, definiteness **13** undeniability **14** irrefutability, conclusiveness **15** indisputability **16** incontestability **17** unquestionability

incontrovertible **9** apodictic **10** unarguable, undeniable **11** established, irrefutable **12** indisputable **14** beyond question, unquestionable

inconvenience **6** bother, put out **7** trouble **8** hardship, headache, nuisance **9** annoyance, disoblige, put one out **10** discomfort **13** be a nuisance to, pain in the neck

inconvenient **7** awkward, unhandy **8** annoying, tiresome, untimely **10** bothersome, burdensome **11** distressing, inopportune, troublesome

Incoronazione di Poppea, L'
also: **22** The Coronation of Poppaea
opera by: **10** Monteverdi
character: **4** Nero **6** Ottone **7** Ottavia

incorporate **4** fuse **6** embody, work in **7** include **10** amalgamate, assimilate **11** consolidate

incorporated **6** united **8** embodied, included **11** amalgamated, assimilated **12** consolidated

incorporeal **6** occult, unreal **7** ghostly, phantom **8** bodiless **9** spiritual, unearthly, unfleshly, unworldly **10** immaterial, intangible **11** disembodied **12** supernatural **13** insubstantial

incorrect **5** false, wrong **6** untrue **7** inexact **8** mistaken **9** erroneous **10** fallacious, inaccurate

incorrectness **5** error **9** wrongness **10** inaccuracy **12** carelessness, slovenliness

incorrigible **6** unruly **8** hardened, hard-core, hopeless **10** beyond help, delinquent **11** intractable **12** beyond saving, past changing, unmanageable **14** uncontrollable

incorrigible child
French: **14** enfant terrible

incorruptible **4** pure **6** honest **7** upright **8** reliable **9** faultless, righteous **10** unbribable **11** trustworthy **14** irreproachable

increase **3** wax **4** grow **5** add to, swell **6** enrich, expand **7** advance, augment, burgeon, enhance, enlarge **8** multiply **12** become larger

increasing **7** growing **9** enlarging, expansion, extending, extension **10** drawing out **11** enlargement **12** augmentation

incredible **6** absurd **7** amazing, awesome **10** astounding, far-fetched, remarkable **11** astonishing **12** preposterous, unbelievable, unimaginable **13** extraordinary, inconceivable

Incredible Hulk, The
character: **9** Jack McGee **11** David Banner
cast: **9** Bill Bixby **10** Jack Colvin **11** Lou Ferrigno

incredulous **7** dubious **8** doubtful **9** skeptical **10** suspicious **11** distrustful **12** disbelieving

increment **4** gain, rise **5** raise **6** growth, profit **7** benefit **8** addition, increase **9** accretion **10** supplement **11** enlargement **12** accumulation, appreciation, augmentation **13** proliferation

incriminate **5** blame **6** accuse, charge, indict

incrimination **5** blame **7** charges **10** accusation, indictment

incubate **3** set, sit **4** plot **5** breed, brood, clock, cover, hatch **6** scheme **7** develop, gestate, sit upon **8** generate

incubus **5** demon **8** bad dream **9** nightmare

inculcate **5** drill, imbue, infix, teach, train **6** impart, infuse **7** implant, impress, instill **8** instruct **9** brainwash, condition, enlighten **12** indoctrinate

inculpable **5** clear **8** innocent **9** blameless, guiltless, not guilty **10** not at fault, unblamable **14** not responsible

incur **6** arouse, assume, incite, stir up **7** acquire, bring on, involve, provoke **8** bring out, contract, fall into

incurable **8** cureless, hopeless **9** ceaseless **10** beyond cure, inveterate, relentless, unflagging **12** incorrigible, irremediable **13** dyed-in-the-wool, uncorrectable

incursion **4** push, raid **5** foray **6** attack, inroad, sortie **7** assault **8** invasion **11** advance into, impingement **12** encroachment, infiltration

indebted **5** bound **7** bounden **8** beholden, grateful, thankful **9** obligated **10** chargeable **11** accountable **15** under obligation

indebtedness **4** debt **5** debit **7** arrears **9** liability **10** balance due, obligation **11** liabilities

indecency **10** immorality **12** unseemliness **13** offensiveness, salaciousness **14** indecorousness

indecent **4** blue, lewd, rude **5** bawdy, dirty **6** filthy, smutty, vulgar **7** ignoble, ill-bred, immoral, obscene, uncivil **8** immodest, improper, prurient, unseemly **9** offensive, salacious **10** in bad taste, indecorous, indiscreet, licentious, unbecoming **11** unwholesome **12** pornographic

Indecent Obsession, An
author: **17** Colleen McCullough

indecipherable **7** cryptic **9** enigmatic, illegible **10** unreadable **11** inscrutable

indecision **5** doubt **6** acrisy **7** dilemma, swither **8** wavering **10** hesitation **11** fluctuation, vacillating, vacillation, uncertainty **12** irresolution

indecisive **4** weak **7** dubious, unclear **8** doubtful, hesitant, wavering **9** confusing, debatable, mercurial, uncertain, unsettled **10** disputable, hesitating, irresolute, wishy-washy **11** halfhearted, vacillating **12** inconclusive **13** indeterminate **17** blowing hot and cold

indecorous **5** gross **6** sinful, wicked **7** ill-bred **8** immodest, improper, low-class, unseemly **9** unfitting **10** unbecoming, unsuitable **11** blameworthy **13** inappropriate, reprehensible

indecorum **8** bad taste **9** immodesty, indecency, vulgarity **11** impropriety **12** impoliteness, unseemliness

indeed **5** truly **6** in fact, really **7** for sure, in truth **8** actually, to be sure **9** certainly, in reality, veritably **10** positively, to be honest, undeniably **11** joking apart **13** in point of fact, with certainty **14** to tell the truth **15** as a matter of fact, without question **16** strictly speaking

indefatigable **6** dogged **7** staunch **8** diligent, sedulous, tireless, untiring **9** energetic **10** persistent, unflagging, unwearying **11** persevering, unfaltering **13** inexhaustible

indefensible **8** improper, vincible **9** pregnable, untenable **10** vulnerable **11** defenseless, inexcusable, unprotected, unspeakable **12** open to attack, unpardonable **13** unjustifiable

indefinite **3** dim **5** vague **6** unsure **7** inexact, obscure, unknown **8** doubtful **9** ambiguous, amorphous, limitless, tentative, uncertain, unsettled **10** ill-defined, indecisive, indistinct, inexplicit **11** illimitable, measureless, unspecified **12** undetermined **13** indeterminate

indefiniteness **6** vagary **9** ambiguity, vagueness **10** indecision **11** uncertainty **12** equivocation

indelible **4** fast **5** fixed, vivid **7** lasting **8** deep-dyed **9** ingrained, memorable, permanent **10** unerasable **11** unremovable **12** ineradicable **13** unforgettable

indelicate **4** lewd, rude **5** broad, crude, gross **6** clumsy, coarse, risque, vulgar **7** awkward, obscene **8** immodest, improper, indecent, off-color, unseemly **9** offensive, unrefined **10** indecorous, indiscreet, suggestive, unbecoming

in demand **7** popular **9** desirable **11** sought after

indemnification **7** payment **10** recompense, reparation **12** compensation

indemnify **3** pay **5** atone, cover, repay **6** insure, secure **7** pay back, protect, rectify, requite, satisfy **8** make good **9** make right, make up for, reimburse **10** compensate, make amends, recompense, remunerate **15** make restitution

indemnity **7** redress **8** coverage, security **9** insurance, repayment **10** protection **11** restitution **12** compensation **15** indemnification

indent **5** notch, set in **6** recess **7** set back

indentation **3** bay, cut, pit **4** dent, nick **5** gouge, inset, niche, notch, score **6** cavity, furrow, pocket, recess **8** incision **9** concavity **10** depression

indented **6** hollow, sunken, zigzag **7** concave, notched **9** depressed

indenture **4** bind **8** contract **10** apprentice

indentured **5** bound **10** contracted **11** apprenticed

independence **7** freedom, liberty **8** autonomy **10** liberation **11** sovereignty **12** emancipation, self-reliance **14** self-government **17** self-determination

independent **4** free **7** solvent, well-off **8** affluent, separate, unallied, well-to-do **9** apart from, exclusive, on one's own, sovereign, uncoerced, well-fixed **10** autonomous, well-heeled **11** self-reliant, unconnected **12** unassociated, uncontrolled **13** self-directing, self-governing, unconstrained **15** individualistic, self-determining

indescribable **9** ineffable **11** beyond words, indefinable, unutterable **12** overwhelming **13** inexpressible **17** beyond description **20** beggaring description

indestructible **8** enduring **9** permanent **11** everlasting, infrangible, unbreakable **12** imperishable

indeterminate **5** vague **7** obscure, unclear **8** not clear **9** ambiguous, uncertain, undefined **10** indefinite, perplexing, unresolved **11** problematic, unspecified **12** undetermined, unstipulated

index **4** clue, mark, sign **5** proof, token **7** catalog, symptom **8** evidence, glossary, register **9** catalogue, indicator **10** indication **13** manifestation **16** alphabetical list

Index Librorum Prohibitorum **22** index of prohibited books

index of prohibited books
Latin: **25** Index Librorum Prohibitorum

India ***see box, p. 484***

Indian
constellation: **5** Indus

Indiana ***see box, p. 485***

Indiana
basketball team: **6** Pacers

Indiana
author: **10** George Sand
character: **4** Noun **7** Delmare **13** Rodolphe Brown **15** Raymon de Ramiere

Indianapolis
football team: **5** Colts

Indic
language family: **12** Indo-European
branch: **11** Indo-Iranian
subgroup: **5** Hindi, Oriya **6** Nepali, Sindhi **7** Bengali, Marathi, Pakrits, Panjabi **8** Assamese, Gujarati, Kashmiri **9** Sinhalese

indicate **4** mean, show, tell **5** imply **6** denote, evince, record, reveal **7** bespeak, point to, signify, specify, suggest **8** point out, register, stand for **9** be a sign of, designate, establish, make known, represent, symbolize

indication **4** clue, hint, mark, omen, sign **5** token **6** augury, boding, signal **7** gesture, mention, portent, presage, showing, symptom, telling, warning **8** evidence, pointing **9** foretoken **10** foreboding, indicating, intimation, signifying, suggestion **11** designation, premonition **13** demonstration, manifestation

indicative **8** symbolic **10** denotative, emblematic, evidential, expressive, indicatory, suggestive **11** connotative, designative, significant, symptomatic **13** symptomatical **14** characteristic, representative

indicator **4** clue **5** guide **7** pointer **10** indication

indict **4** cite **6** accuse, charge, have up, impute, pull up **7** arraign, bring up, impeach **9** criminate, inculpate, prosecute **11** incriminate **13** prefer charges

indifference **6** apathy **7** disdain, neglect **8** coldness, no import **9** aloofness, unconcern **10** negligence, paltriness, triviality **11** disinterest, impassivity, inattention, insouciance, nonchalance **12** carelessness, unimportance **13** impassiveness, insensibility, insensitivity **14** insignificance, lack of interest

indifferent **4** cool, fair, rote, so-so **5** aloof **6** medium, modest **7** average, unmoved **8** detached, mediocre, middling, moderate, ordinary, passable **9** apathetic, impassive, not caring, unmindful **10** impervious, insensible, insouciant, nonchalant, second-rate, uninspired **11** commonplace, perfunctory, unconcerned **12** uninterested **13** insusceptible **15** undistinguished **17** betwixt and between, neither good nor bad

indigence **4** need, want **6** penury **7** begarry, poverty **9** pauperism, privation **11** destitution, dire straits **13** pennilessness

indigenous **6** native **7** endemic **8** domestic, homebred **9** home-grown **10** aboriginal **13** autochthonous, originating in

indigent **4** poor **5** needy **6** hard-up, in need, in want **7** pinched **8** badly off **9** destitute, moneyless, penniless **12** impoverished **15** poverty-stricken

indiges
title in: **4** Rome
suggests: **11** deification
for service to: **7** country

indigestible **4** rich **13** unassimilable

indignant **3** mad **4** sore **5** angry, huffy, irate, riled **6** fuming, miffed, peeved, piqued, put off, put out **8** incensed, offended, provoked, steaming, worked up, wrathful **9** resentful, wrought up **10** displeased, infuriated **15** on one's high horse

indignation **3** ire **4** fury, huff, rage **5** pique, wrath **6** animus, choler, dismay, uproar **7** umbrage **8** vexation **9** annoyance **10** irritation, resentment **11** displeasure

indignity **4** slur **5** abuse **6** insult, slight **7** affront, offense, outrage **8** dishonor, rudeness **9** injustice **11** discourtesy, humiliation **12** mistreatment **13** slap in the face

indigo **3** dye **4** blue **8** dark blue, deep blue, navy blue **10** Indigofera
varieties: **4** wild **5** false

India

other name: 4 Hind **6** Bharat **12** Bharat Varsha
capital: 8 New Delhi
largest city: 8 Calcutta
others: 4 Agra, Gaya, Pune **5** Dacca, Poona, Surat **6** Bombay, Jaipur, Kanpur, Lahore, Madras, Madura, Mysore, Nagpur **7** Banaras **8** Kolhapur, Mandalay, Mirzapur, Shahpura, Srinagar **9** Ahmedabad, Bangalore, Hyderabad **10** Darjeeling
division: 3 Goa **5** Assam, Bihar, Jammu **6** Kerala, Orissa, Punjab, Sikkim **7** Gujarat, Haryana, Kashmir, Manipur, Tripura **8** Nagaland **9** Karnataka, Meghalaya, Rajasthan, Tamil Nadu **10** West Bengal **11** Daman and Diu, Maharashtra, Pondicherry **12** Uttar Pradesh **13** Andhra Pradesh, Madhya Pradesh **15** Himachal Pradesh
measure: 3 ady, gaz, gez, jow, lan **4** byee, coss, depa, doph, hath, koss, kunk, raik, rati, seit, taun, tola **5** bigha, covid, crosa, denda, depoh, drona, erosa, garce, hasta, krosa, parah, ratti, salay, yojan **6** adhaka, amunam, covido, cudava, dumbha, geerah, moolum, mushti, ouroub, palgat, parran, prasha, ropani, tipree, unglee, yojana **7** dhanush, gavyuti, khahoon, niranga, prastha **8** okthabah
monetary unit: 3 lac, pie **4** lakh, pice **5** abidi, rupee
weight: 3 mod, pai, vis **4** drum, hoen, kona, pala, pank, pice, ruay, tael, tali, tola, wang, yava **5** adpad, candy, hubba, maund, tical **6** karsha **8** mangelin
island: 6 Agatti, Chilka **7** Andaman, Minicoy, Nicobar **8** Amindivi **9** Laccadive **11** Lakshadweep
lake: 5 Jheel, Lonar, Wular **6** Chilka, Colair, Dhebar, Kolair **7** Kolleru, Pulicat, Pushkar, Sambahr
mountain: 8 Aravalli **9** Broad Peak, Distaghil, Himalayas, Karakoram, Nanda Devi, Rakaposhi **10** Gasherbrum, Masherbrum **11** Nanga Parbat **12** Eastern Ghats, Kanchenjunga, Western Ghats
hills: **4** Chin, Naga **5** Khasi **6** Lushai **7** Nilgiri
highest point: 12 Godwin Austen
river: 3 Son **4** Beas, Kosi, Tapi **5** Gogra, Indus, Jumna, Tapti **6** Gandak, Ganges, Jhelum, Kaveri, Kistna, Sutlej, Yamuna **7** Cauveri, Cauvery, Chambal, Damodar, Hooghly, Krishna, Narbada, Narmada **8** Godavari, Mahanadi **10** Bhagirathi **11** Brahmaputra
sea: 6 Indian **7** Arabian
physical feature:
bay: **6** Bengal
cape: **7** Comorin
desert: **4** Thar **9** Rajasthan
forest: **3** Gir
gulf: **5** Kutch **6** Cambay, Mannar
pass: **9** Karakoram
plain: **12** Indo-Gangetic
plateau: **6** Deccan **7** Shillon **11** Chota Nagpur
rains: **7** monsoon
strait: **4** Palk
swamp: **9** Sundarban **11** Rann of Kutch
valley: **13** Vale of Kashmir
people: 2 Ao **3** Gor **4** Bhil **5** Aryan **6** Badaga, Pathan **7** Sherani **9** Dravidian **10** Andamanese
caste: **3** Jat **5** Sudra **6** Rajput, Shudra **7** Brahman, Brahmin, Harijan, Maratha, Vaishya **9** Kshatriya **11** Untouchable
dynasty: **5** Gupta, Mogul **6** Maurya, Rajput **8** Marathas **14** Delhi Sultanate
god: **4** Kali, Rama, Siva **5** Durga, Laxmi, Shiva **6** Brahma, Kumara, Vishnu **7** Ganesha, Hanuman, Krishna, Lakshmi **9** Kartikeya **10** Subramanya
ruler: **5** Akbar, Asoka, Babur, Timur **7** Humayun **8** Hyder Ali, Jahangir **9** Aurangzeb, Shah Jahan **11** Rajiv Gandhi, Tippu Sultan **12** Indira Gandhi **13** Queen Victoria **15** Jawaharlal Nehru, Mohandas K (Mahatma) Gandhi **18** Chandragupta Maurya
language: 4 Urdu **5** Hindi, Oriya, Tamil **6** Sindhi, Telugu **7** Bengali, English, Kannada, Malayam, Marathi, Punjabi **8** Assamese, Gujarati, Kashmiri, Sanskrit **9** Malayalam
religion: 4 Sikh **5** Hindu, Islam, Parsi **7** Jainist, Judaism **8** Buddhism **11** Zoroastrian **12** Christianity
place:
cathedral: **10** Saint Thome
fortress: **3** Red **11** Saint George
mausoleum: **8** Taj Mahal
minaret: **9** Qutb Minar
mosque: **10** Jama Masjid
park: **6** Maidan
president's residence: **17** Rashtrapati Bhavan
railway station: **8** Victoria
shrine: **7** Raj Ghat
street: **7** Raj Path **11** Chowringhee, Marine Drive **12** Chandni Chauk **14** Connaught Place
temple: **5** Birla **6** Ellora, Golden **7** Kailasa **10** Ajanta Cave
feature:
dance: **6** nautch **7** cantico
religious text: **7** Rig Veda
shrine: **5** stupa
food:
beer: **5** apong
bread: **7** chapati
liquor: **4** soma, sura **5** shrab
tea: **5** assam

Indiana
abbreviation: **2** IN **3** Ind
nickname: **7** Hoosier
capital/largest city: **12** Indianapolis
others: **4** Gary, Peru **6** Brazil, Goshen, Hobart, Jasper, Kokomo, Marion, Muncie, Wabash **7** Elkhart, Ft Wayne, Hammond, LaPorte, Whiting **8** Columbus, Richmond **9** Lafayette, Mishawaka, South Bend, Vincennes **10** Evansville, Huntington, Logansport, Terre Haute **11** Bloomington, East Chicago **12** Connorsville, Michigan City
college: **4** Ball **6** Bethel, Butler, DePauw, Goshen, Marion, Purdue, Wabash **9** Notre Dame **10** Evansville, Valparaiso
explorer: **7** La Salle
feature: **10** New Harmony **12** Indian mounds
national memorial: **14** Lincoln boyhood
tribe: **3** Wea **5** Miami **7** Shawnee
people: **7** Hoosier **10** Cole Porter, Eugene Debs, Gus Grissom, Red Skelton **12** Wilbur Wright **15** Booth Tarkington, Theodore Dreiser **18** James Whitcomb Riley
lake: **5** Clear, James **6** Monroe **7** Manitou, Wawasee **8** Michigan **9** Mansfield **11** Maxinkuckee
land rank: **12** thirty-eighth
mountain: **13** Greensfort Top
physical feature:
cave: **9** Wyandotte
river: **4** Ohio **5** White **6** Maumee, Wabash **8** Kankakee **10** Tippecanoe, Whitewater
state admission: **10** nineteenth
state bird: **8** cardinal
state flower: **5** peony **6** zinnia
state motto: **19** Crossroads of America
state song: **28** On the Banks of the Wabash Far Away
state tree: **5** tulip **11** tulip poplar

7 bastard **8** wild blue **9** blue false **10** plains wild, white false **12** prairie false **13** fragrant false

indirect **5** vague **6** remote, zigzag **7** crooked, devious, distant, evasive, hedging, oblique, winding **8** rambling, tortuous **9** ancillary, secondary **10** circuitous, derivative, digressive, discursive, incidental, meandering, roundabout, unintended **13** unintentional

indirection **8** rambling **10** digression, meandering, zigzagging **14** circuitousness, circumlocution, roundaboutness

indiscernible **6** hidden **9** invisible **10** indistinct **12** undetectable, unnoticeable **13** imperceptible

indiscreet **6** unwise **7** foolish **8** careless, tactless, unseemly **9** foolhardy, ill-judged, impolitic, imprudent, tasteless, untactful **10** incautious **11** improvident, injudicious, thoughtless, unbefitting, uncalled-for **12** undiplomatic **13** inconsiderate, uncircumspect

indiscretion **8** rashness **10** imprudence **12** carelessness, heedlessness, recklessness, tactlessness **13** foolhardiness, insensitivity **15** thoughtlessness **16** irresponsibility

indiscriminate **6** motley, random **7** aimless, chaotic, jumbled, mongrel **8** confused, slapdash, unchoosy **9** haphazard, hit-or-miss **10** hodgepodge **11** promiscuous, unselective **12** disorganized, unsystematic **16** higgledy-piggledy, undistinguishing

in disorder **5** messy **6** blowsy, frowsy, mussed, sloppy, untidy **7** ruffled, rumpled, tousled, unkempt **8** uncombed **10** disarrayed, disheveled, disordered, disorderly **11** disarranged

indispensable **5** basic, vital **6** needed **7** crucial, needful **8** required **9** essential, mandatory, necessary, requisite **10** compulsory, imperative, obligatory **11** fundamental

indispensable condition
Latin: **10** sine qua non

indispensable element
9 basic need, essential, necessity, requisite **10** sine qua non **11** requirement

indisposed **3** ill **5** loath **6** ailing, averse, laid up, sickly, unwell **7** opposed **8** hesitant, taken ill **9** bedridden, reluctant, unwilling **10** not oneself **11** disinclined **15** under the weather

indisposition **5** upset **6** malady **7** ailment, illness **8** sickness **9** complaint, ill health

indisputable **4** sure **7** assured, certain, decided, evident, obvious **8** absolute, apparent, clear-cut, definite, positive **10** conclusive, unarguable, undeniable **11** indubitable, irrefutable **12** unassailable, unmistakable **13** incontestable **14** unquestionable **16** incontrovertible **20** beyond a shadow of doubt

indissoluble **5** fixed **7** abiding, lasting **8** constant, enduring **9** immutable, indelible, permanent, perpetual **11** everlasting **12** imperishable, ineradicable

indistinct **3** dim **4** weak **5** faint, muddy, murky, vague **6** cloudy, hidden **7** blurred, clouded, muffled, obscure, shadowy, unclear **8** confused, nebulous, puzzling **9** ambiguous, enigmatic, illegible, inaudible, uncertain **10** ill-defined, incoherent, indefinite, mysterious, out of focus **11** not distinct **13** indeterminate **14** indecipherable, unintelligible **16** incomprehensible

indistinguishable **7** obscure, unclear **9** invisible **10** indistinct, unapparent **12** unnoticeable, unobservable **13** a carbon copy of, identical with, imperceptible, inconspicuous, indiscernible

individual **6** person, unique **7** one's own, private, special, unusual **8** distinct, especial, original, personal, separate, singular, somebody, specific, uncommon **9** different, exclusive **10** particular **11** distinctive, independent **12** personalized **14** characteristic, unconventional

individuality **6** cachet **10** uniqueness **11** distinction, singularity, specialness **13** particularity **15** distinctiveness

individually **4** each **5** apart **6** apiece, singly **8** a la carte, uniquely **10** one at a time, peculiarly, personally, separately **12** respectively **13** distinctively **18** characteristically

indoctrinate **5** brief, drill, teach, train, tutor **6** infuse, school **7** educate, implant, instill **8** initiate **9** brainwash, inculcate **12** propagandize

indoctrination **5** drill **8** drilling, teaching, training **9** education, schooling **10** initiation, instilling **11** inculcation, instruction

Indo-European
language branch: **5** Greek **6** Celtic, Italic **7** Romance **8** Albanian, Armenian, Germanic **9** Anatolian, Tocharian **11** Balto-Slavic, Indo-Iranian

Indo-Iranian
language family: **12** Indo-European
ancient: **7** Avestan **8** Sanskrit **10** Old Persian
modern Iranian: **5** Indic, Tajik **6** Pashto **7** Baluchi, Kurdish, Persian
modern Indic: **4** Pali **5** Hindi, Oriya **6** Nepali, Sindhi **7** Bengali, Marathi, Panjabi **8** Assamese, Gujarati, Kashmiri **9** Sinhalese

indolence **5** sloth **7** inertia, languor, laxness **8** idleness, laziness **10** inactivity

indolent **4** lazy **5** inert, slack **7** lumpish **8** dawdling, dilatory, inactive, listless, slothful, sluggish **9** do-nothing, easygoing, lethargic, shiftless **13** lackadaisical

indomitable **6** dogged **7** doughty, staunch, valiant **8** cast-iron, fearless, intrepid, resolute, stalwart, stubborn **9** dauntless, steadfast, undaunted **10** courageous, formidable, invincible, unwavering, unyielding **11** insuperable, persevering, unflinching, unshrinking **12** invulnerable, unassailable **13** indefatigable, irrepressible, unconquerable

Indonesia ***see box***

indoors **6** at home, inside, shut in, shut up, within **10** in the house **11** sequestered

Indo-Pacific
language subgroup: **4** Kate **5** Kiwai **7** Andaman, Merauke **8** Highland, Tasmania **9** Ekari-Moni, Hollandia, Timor-Alor **10** New Britain **12** Astrolabe Bay, Bougainville **14** Vogelkop-Kamoro **16** Eastern New Guinea, Northern Salomons **17** Northern Halmahera

indorse *see* **7** endorse

In Dubious Battle
author: **13** John Steinbeck

indubitable **4** sure **7** certain **9** undoubted **10** conclusive **11** irrefutable, unequivocal **12** indisputable, unmistakable **14** unquestionable **16** incontrovertible

indubitably **6** surely **7** for sure **8** of course **9** certainly, doubtless **10** for certain **11** undoubtedly **12** without doubt **14** unquestionably, with no question

induce **3** get **4** coax, spur, sway **5** cause, impel **6** arouse, effect, incite, lead to, prompt **7** actuate, bring on, dispose, incline, inspire, produce, provoke, win over **8** activate, motivate, occasion, persuade **9** encourage, influence, instigate, prevail on **10** bring about, bring round, give rise to **11** prevail upon, set in motion

inducement **4** bait, goad, spur **5** cause **6** ground, motive, reason **8** stimulus **9** incentive **10** allurement, attraction, en-

Indonesia
other name: **9** Nusantara **12** Tanah Airkita **21** Netherlands East Indies
capital/largest city: **7** Jakarta **8** Djakarta
others: **5** Bogor, Medan **6** Malang, Manado **7** Bandung **8** Macassar, Semarang, Surabaya **9** Hollandia, Palembang, Surakarta **10** Jogjakarta, Yogyakarta **11** Banjarmasin
measure: **5** depah, depoh
monetary unit: **3** sen **6** rupiah
weight: **5** catty, ounce, thail **6** soekoe
island: **3** Aru **4** Bali, Buru, Java **5** Ambon, Ceram, Seram, Spice, Sumba, Timor **6** Bangka, Borneo, Flores, Lombok, Madura, Tidore **7** Belawan, Celebes, Morotai, Sumatra, Sumbawa, Ternate **8** Belitung, Moluccas, Sulawesi **9** Halmahera, New Guinea **10** Kalimantan **11** Lesser Sunda **12** Greater Sunda
lake: **4** Toba **5** Ranau **6** Towuti
river: **4** Hari, Musi, Solo **5** Rokan **6** Asahan, Barito, Kampar **7** Brantas, Kaptuas **9** Indrogiri, Mamberamo, Martapura
sea: **4** Java, Savu **5** Banda, Ceram, Timor **6** Flores, Indian **7** Arafura, Celebes, Molucca, Pacific **10** Philippine, South China
physical feature:
strait: **5** Sunda **7** Makasar, Malacca **8** Makassar
volcano: **6** Slamet **8** Krakatoa
people: **5** Batak, Dayak, Dyaks, Malay **6** Papuan, Toraja **7** Battaks, Chinese, Igorots **8** Acehnese, Achinese, Balinese, Javanese, Madurese, Sudanese **11** Minang Kabau
leader: **7** Suharto, Sukarno
language: **5** Tetum **6** Bahasa, Igorot **7** English, Gyarung, Malayan **8** Balinese, Chamorro, Javanese, Madurese, Sudanese **10** Indonesian, Polynesian
religion: **5** Hindu, Islam **7** animism **8** Buddhism **12** Christianity, Confucianism
place:
palace: **6** Kraton
pyramid: **5** Stupa **9** Borobudur
shrine: **6** Dagoba, Kraton
feature:
cap: **5** pitji
cloth: **5** batik
jacket: **6** kebaja
lizard: **12** Komodo dragon
scarf: **9** selendang
shadow play: **6** wajang, wayang
skirt: **4** kain **6** sarong
tree: **4** supa
food:
ceremonial dinner: **9** selamatan

ticement, incitement, persuasion, temptation **11** inspiration, instigation, provocation

induct **5** crown, draft, frock **6** enlist, invest, lead in, ordain, sign up **7** bring in, install, instate, usher in **8** enthrone, initiate, register **9** conscript, establish, introduce **10** consecrate, inaugurate

in due course **4** then **6** thence **10** eventually **11** accordingly **15** at the proper time **19** in the fullness of time

indulge **4** baby **5** favor, humor, serve, spoil, treat **6** coddle, cosset, oblige **7** appease, cater to, gratify, yield to **8** pander to **9** give way to **11** accommodate, go along with, mollycoddle

indulgence **6** excess, luxury **8** kindness, lenience, patience **9** allowance, benignity, tolerance **10** compassion, debauchery, profligacy, sufferance **11** dissipation, forbearance, forgiveness **12** extravagance, graciousness, immoderation, intemperance **13** understanding **14** permissiveness

indulgent **4** kind **6** benign, tender **7** clement, lenient, patient, sparing **8** humoring, obliging, tolerant, yielding **9** easygoing, forgiving, pampering **10** forbearing, permissive **11** complaisant, forebearing **12** conciliatory **13** understanding

industrious **4** busy **6** active **7** zealous **8** diligent, occupied, sedulous, tireless **9** assiduous, energetic **10** productive, purposeful, unflagging **11** hardworking, painstaking, persevering, unremitting **12** businesslike, enterprising **13** indefatigable

industry **2** go **4** toil, zeal **5** field, labor, trade **6** bustle, energy, hustle **8** activity, business, commerce, hard work **9** assiduity, diligence **10** enterprise **11** application, manufacture **12** perseverance, sedulousness **13** assiduousness **15** industriousness **16** indefatigability

inebriate **3** sot **4** lush, soak, wino **5** drunk, rummy, souse, toper **6** barfly, boozer **7** tippler **8** drunkard **9** alcoholic **11** dipsomaniac

inebriated **4** high **5** drunk, oiled, tight, tipsy **6** bombed, loaded, potted, stoned, tanked, zonked **7** drunken, smashed, sozzled, wrecked **8** besotted **9** befuddled, plastered **10** in one's cups **11** intoxicated **12** drunk as a lord **17** under the influence **20** three sheets to the wind

ineffable **5** ideal **6** divine, sacred **9** spiritual **10** indefinite, untellable **11** indefinable, unspeakable, unutterable **12** transcendent **13** indescribable, inexpressible **14** incommunicable, transcendental

in effect **6** active **8** a reality **9** activated, effective, operative **11** in operation

ineffective **4** vain, weak **6** futile **7** useless **8** impotent **9** fruitless, incapable, powerless, worthless **10** inadequate **11** inefficient, inoperative, not much good, of little use **12** unproductive

ineffectual **4** lame, vain, weak **5** inept **6** feeble, futile **7** hapless, useless **8** impotent **10** inadequate, not up to par, profitless, unavailing **11** incompetent, ineffective, inefficient **12** unproductive, unprofitable, unsuccessful **13** inefficacious **14** unsatisfactory

inefficient **5** inept, slack **6** futile **8** slipshod **9** pointless, unskilled **10** inadequate **11** incompetent, indifferent, ineffective, ineffectual **12** not efficient, unproductive **13** inefficacious **14** good-for-nothing

inelegance **9** crudeness, grossness, roughness, vulgarity **10** coarseness **13** tastelessness

inelegant **4** ugly **6** coarse, common **8** inferior **9** tasteless, unrefined **10** ungraceful

ineligible **5** unfit **10** unentitled, unsuitable **11** not eligible, unqualified **12** disqualified, unacceptable

ineluctable **4** sure **5** fated **7** certain **10** ineludible, inevasible, inevitable, inexorable, sure as fate, unevadable **11** inescapable, irrevocable, unavoidable, unstoppable **13** unpreventable

inept **5** empty, inane, silly, unapt **6** clumsy **7** asinine, awkward, fatuous, foolish **8** bungling **9** maladroit, pointless, senseless, unfitting, unskilled, untrained **10** out of place, unsuitable **11** incompetent, ineffective, ineffectual, inefficient, nonsensical, unqualified **13** inappropriate, inefficacious

ineptitude **9** inability **10** clumsiness, inadequacy **11** awkwardness **12** incompetence **14** ineffectuality **15** ineffectiveness

inequality **8** imparity, inequity **9** disparity, diversity, prejudice **10** difference, divergence, favoritism, unfairness, unlikeness **11** inconstancy, unequalness **12** irregularity, variableness **13** disproportion, dissimilarity, dissimilitude

inequity **4** bias **9** injustice, prejudice **10** favoritism, inequality, unfairness **14** discrimination

ineradicable **7** lasting **9** indelible, permanent **10** inerasable **12** ineffaceable **14** indestructible

inert **4** dull, numb **5** slack, still **6** leaden, static, supine, torpid **7** languid, passive **8** immobile, inactive, listless, sluggish **9** impassive, inanimate, quiescent **10** motionless, phlegmatic, stationary

inertia **6** apathy, stupor, torpor **7** languor **8** dullness, inaction, laziness, lethargy **9** indolence, inertness, lassitude, passivity, torpidity, weariness **10** inactivity, supineness **11** passiveness **12** listlessness, sluggishness

inertness **6** apathy **8** lethargy **9** passivity **10** quiescence **12** sluggishness **14** motionlessness

inescapable **4** sure **7** certain, evident **8** manifest, positive **10** inevitable **11** ineluctable, predestined, unavoidable

in esse **7** in being **11** in actuality **16** actually existing

inestimable **7** sumless **8** precious **9** priceless **10** invaluable **11** beyond price, measureless **12** immeasurable, incalculable, unmeasurable

inevitable **4** sure **5** fated **7** certain **8** destined **10** ineludible **11** ineluctable, inescapable, predestined, unavoidable **13** predetermined, unpreventable

inexact 3 off 6 faulty, sloppy 8 careless, slovenly 9 defective, imperfect, imprecise 10 inaccurate, unspecific 11 approximate

in exactly the same words Latin: 19 verbatim et literatim

inexcusable 10 unbearable 11 intolerable, unallowable 12 indefensible, unforgivable, unpardonable 13 unjustifiable

inexhaustible 7 endless 8 infinite, tireless, unending 9 boundless 13 indefatigable 15 measurelessness

in existence 5 alive 6 extant, living 8 existent, existing 9 surviving, to be found

inexorable 4 firm 5 cruel, stiff 6 dogged 7 adamant 8 obdurate, pitiless, ruthless 9 immovable, merciless, unbending 10 adamantive, determined, inflexible, relentless, unyielding 11 inescapable, intractable 12 irresistible 14 uncompromising

inexpedient 6 futile, unwise 7 useless 11 detrimental, impractical, inadvisable, injudicious, undesirable 13 not worthwhile 15 disadvantageous

inexpensive 5 cheap 8 moderate 9 low-priced 10 economical, reasonable 13 nominal-priced, popular-priced

inexpensive table wine French: 12 vin ordinaire

inexperienced 5 fresh, green, naive 6 callow 7 untried 8 inexpert, unversed 9 unfledged, unskilled, untrained, untutored 10 unfamiliar, unschooled, unseasoned 11 uninitiated, unpracticed 12 unaccustomed, unacquainted, unconversant 15 unsophisticated

inexpert 5 inept 6 clumsy, gauche 7 awkward 8 bungling 9 incapable, maladroit 10 amateurish, unpolished, unskillful 11 incompetent, ineffective, inefficient, unqualified 14 unaccomplished

inexplicable 8 abstruse, baffling, puzzling 9 insoluble 10 insolvable, mysterious, mystifying, perplexing 11 enigmatical, inscrutable 12 unfathomable 13 unaccountable, unexplainable 14 undecipherable 16 incomprehensible

inexpressive 5 blank, empty 6 vacant 14 expressionless

in extenso 12 at full length

in extremis 9 near death 11 in extremity 15 on the outer edges 19 at the uttermost limit

in extremity Latin: 10 in extremis

in fact Latin: 7 de facto

infallible 4 sure 7 assured, certain, perfect 8 flawless, inerrant, positive, reliable, surefire, unerring 9 apodictic, faultless, foolproof, unfailing 10 dependable, impeccable 11 irrefutable 13 unimpeachable 16 incontrovertible

infamous 3 low 4 base, evil, foul, vile 6 odious, sinful, sordid, wicked 7 corrupt, heinous, ignoble, immoral, knavish 8 damnable, recreant, shameful 9 abhorrent, monstrous, nefarious, notorious 10 abominable, detestable, iniquitous, of evil fame, outrageous, perfidious, profligate, scandalous, scurrilous, villainous 11 disgraceful, of ill repute, opprobrious, treacherous 12 dishonorable, disreputable

infamy 4 evil 5 odium, shame 7 scandal 8 contempt, disgrace, dishonor, ignominy, villainy 9 discredit, disesteem, disrepute, notoriety 10 corruption, opprobrium, wickedness 11 abomination 13 despicability, notoriousness

infancy 6 cradle, nonage 8 babyhood, minority 9 beginning, childhood, inception 10 immaturity

infant 3 kid 4 babe, baby 5 child 7 neonate, newborn, toddler 8 nursling, suckling

infantile 7 babyish 8 childish, juvenile 9 childlike, infantine 10 infantlike, sophomoric

infantryman 6 Zouave 7 dogface, dragoon 8 chasseur, doughboy, sorefoot 11 foot soldier

infatuated 7 charmed, smitten 8 beguiled, enamored, inflamed, obsessed 9 bewitched, enchanted, entranced 10 captivated, enraptured, enthralled, spellbound 11 carried away, intoxicated 12 having a crush

infatuation 4 rave 5 craze, crush, folly, mania 6 desire 7 passion 9 obsession, puppy love 10 enthusiasm 11 fascination, foolishness 12 passing fancy

infect 4 ruin 5 spoil, taint, touch 6 blight, damage, poison 7 afflict, corrupt 9 indispose, influence 11 contaminate

infected 6 impure, morbid, septic 7 corrupt, tainted 8 cankered, diseased, poisoned 12 contaminated

infection 6 blight 7 disease 9 contagion, virulence 11 suppuration

infectious 8 catching, epidemic, virulent 9 catchable, infective, spreading 10 compelling, contagious, inoculable 11 captivating 12 communicable, irresistible

infecund 6 barren, farrow 7 sterile 9 infertile 12 unproductive

infer 4 deem 5 glean, guess, judge, opine 6 deduce, gather, reason, reckon 7 presume, suppose, surmise 8 conclude 9 speculate 10 conjecture

inference 4 clue 10 intimation, suggestion 11 insinuation

inferior 4 poor 6 junior 8 low-grade, mediocre 9 secondary 10 low-quality, second-rate, subsidiary 11 indifferent, subordinate, subservient, substandard 12 not up to snuff

infernal 4 vile 5 awful, black, lower 6 cursed, Hadean, nether 7 heinous, hellish, Stygian, vicious 8 accursed, damnable, devilish, fiendish, horrible, terrible 9 atrocious, execrable, malicious, monstrous, nefarious, Plutonian 10 abominable, demoniacal, diabolical, flagitious, horrendous, iniquitous
also: 9 Tartarean
refers to: 10 underworld

inferno 4 hell, oven 5 abyss, Hades 6 hotbox, the pit, Tophet 7 furnace, roaster, sizzler 8 hellfire, hellhole, scorcher 9 perdition 10 lower world, underworld 11 netherworld 12 fiery furnace 13 nether regions 15 infernal regions 16 fire and brimstone, the bottomless pit

Inferno
part I of: 12 Divine Comedy
author: 14 Dante Alighieri

infertile 4 arid, bare 6 barren, effete, fallow 7 drained, sterile 8 depleted, desolate, impotent, infecund **9** exhausted, fruitless **10** unfruitful, unprolific **12** unproductive **13** nonproductive

infest **4** team **5** beset, crawl, creep, swarm **6** abound, infect, plague, ravage **7** overrun, torment **9** crawl with, swarm with

infestation **6** plague, ravage **9** lousiness, pervasion **11** overrunning **12** overswarming

in few words
Latin: **12** paucis verbis

infidel **5** pagan **6** savage **7** atheist, heathen, heretic, skeptic **8** agnostic, apostate, idolater **9** barbarian **10** unbeliever **11** nonbeliever

infidelity **6** breach **7** falsity, perfidy **8** adultery, betrayal **9** disregard, violation **10** disloyalty, infraction **12** nonadherence **13** nonobservance, transgression **14** unfaithfulness

infiltrate **4** leak, seep **5** imbue, steep **6** absorb, seep in **7** pervade **8** colonize, permeate **9** insinuate, penetrate

infinite **4** vast **5** great **7** endless, immense **8** enormous **9** boundless, limitless, unbounded, unlimited **10** tremendous, without end **11** illimitable, measureless **12** immeasurable, incalculable, interminable **13** inexhaustible **15** uncircumscribed

infinitesimal **3** wee **4** puny, tiny **6** minute **10** diminutive, negligible **11** microscopic **13** imperceptible, inappreciable, insignificant, undiscernible **14** extremely small, inconsiderable

infinity **7** forever **8** eternity **10** infinitude, perpetuity **11** endlessness, eternal time **12** sempiternity **13** boundlessness, limitlessness **14** illimitability **15** everlastingness, immeasurability, incalculability, measurelessness **16** inexhaustibility **19** incomprehensibility

Infiri
gods of: **10** underworld

infirm **3** ill **4** weak, worn **5** anile, frail, shaky **6** ailing, feeble, poorly, sickly **7** failing, fragile, unsound **8** decrepit, disabled, helpless, unstable, weakened **9** doddering, emaciated, enervated, enfeebled, powerless **11** debilitated **12** strengthless

infirmary **6** clinic **7** sick bay **8** hospital

infirmity **4** flaw **5** fault **6** defect, malady **7** ailment, failing, frailty, illness **8** debility, disorder, handicap, sickness **9** fragility, frailness **10** deficiency, disability, infirmness **11** instability **12** debilitation, imperfection, unstableness **13** indisposition, vulnerability

in flagrante delicto **14** in blazing crime **22** in the heat of the evil deed

inflame **4** fire, rile **5** craze, rouse **6** arouse, enrage, excite, heat up, ignite, incite, kindle, madden, stir up, work up **7** agitate, incense, provoke **8** enkindle **9** electrify, stimulate **10** intoxicate

inflamed **3** mad **5** angry, irate, riled **6** crazed, fuming, roused **7** aroused, enraged, excited, fired up, furious, incited **8** agitated, incensed, provoked, reddened **9** steamed up, stirred up **10** infuriated **11** intensified

inflame with love **6** enamor **9** enrapture, impassion, infatuate

inflammable **5** fiery **8** choleric, volatile **9** excitable, flammable, ignitable, impetuous, overhasty, sensitive **10** high-strung, incendiary **11** combustible, precipitate **12** inflammatory

inflammation **4** acne, fire, gout, sore **6** canker, firing **7** arousal, chafing **8** bursitis, ignition, kindling, soreness, sore spot, swelling **9** agitation **10** incitement, irritation **13** conflagration, rabblerousing
suffix: **4** itis

inflammatory **5** fiery, rabid **8** arousing, enraging, inciting, mutinous, volcanic **9** demagogic, explosive, insurgent **10** incendiary, rebellious **11** combustible, fulminating, inflammable, intemperate, provocative **13** rabble-rousing, revolutionary

inflate **5** bloat, swell **6** blow up, dilate, expand, fill up, pump up **7** distend, improve, puff out **10** appreciate **11** rise in value

inflated **5** blown, gassy, tumid, wordy **6** blew up, turgid **7** bloated, blown up, dilated, flowery, pompous, swollen, verbose **8** boastful, enlarged, expanded **9** bombastic, distended, overblown, swelled up **10** rhetorical, swelled out **11** exaggerated, pretentious

inflection **4** tone **5** tenor **6** accent **10** modulation **11** enunciation, tone of voice **12** articulation **13** pronunciation

inflexible **4** firm, hard, taut **5** fixed, rigid, solid, stiff **6** dogged, mulish **7** adamant **8** obdurate, resolute, stubborn **9** hidebound, immovable, immutable, ironbound, obstinate, pigheaded, stringent, tenacious, unbending, unplastic **10** adamantine, determined, headstrong, impervious, implacable, inexorable, unwavering, unyielding **11** hard and fast, intractable, not flexible, unmalleable **12** unchangeable **14** uncompromising

inflict **4** dump **5** lay on, wreak **6** impose, unload **7** put upon **9** visit upon **10** administer, perpetrate **11** bring to bear

inflorescence **5** bloom **6** flower **7** blossom, cluster **8** blooming **9** flowering **10** blossoming
type: **4** cyme **5** spike, umbel **6** corymb, raceme, spadix **7** panicle **9** capitulum **14** verticillaster

influence **4** hold, move, pull, stir, sway **5** clout, guide, impel, power **6** arouse, effect, incite, induce, prompt, weight **7** act upon, actuate, control, dispose, incline, inspire, mastery, potency, provoke **8** dominion, leverage, persuade, pressure, prestige **9** advantage, authority **10** ascendancy, domination, predispose

influential **6** moving, potent, strong **7** leading, weighty **8** forceful, powerful, puissant **9** effective, effectual, important, inspiring, momentous **10** activating **11** efficacious, significant **12** instrumental **13** consequential

influx **5** entry **6** inflow **7** arrival, indraft, ingress **9** flowing in, incursion, inpouring **10** converging, inundation **12** infiltration

in force **6** extant **7** en masse **8** in effect **9** effective, operative **11** in existence, in operation, operational **14** in large numbers

inform **3** rat **4** fink, tell **5** edify **6** advise, clue in, notify, snitch, squeal, tattle, tell on, tip off **7** apprise, let know **8** acquaint, denounce, forewarn, report to **9** declare to, enlighten **11** communicate, familiarize, serve notice **14** blow the whistle

inform against **5** rat on **6** betray, fink on, tell on **7** sell out **8** denounce, squeal on **11** double-cross **16** blow the whistle on

informal **4** easy **6** casual, simple **7** natural, offhand **8** familiar **9** easygoing, not formal **10** unofficial **11** spontaneous **12** come-as-you-are **13** unceremonious, unconstrained **14** unconventional

informal preliminary conference
French: **10** pourparler

informant **6** source **7** adviser, tipster **8** appriser, informer, notifier, reporter **9** announcer, spokesman **10** respondent **11** enlightener, horse's mouth, spokeswoman

information **4** data, news **5** facts, notes **6** notice, papers, report **7** account, tidings **8** briefing, bulletin, evidence, material **9** documents, knowledge, materials **10** communique **11** fact-finding **12** announcement, intelligence, notification **13** enlightenment

informed **4** told, up on, wise **5** aware, posted, talked, taught, warned **7** abreast, advised, knowing, learned, tattled **8** apprised, betrayed, educated, notified, reported, snitched, up to date **9** au courant, permeated **10** acquainted, instructed **11** enlightened, intelligent **13** knowledgeable

informer **3** rat **4** fink **5** Judas **6** canary **7** blabber, stoolie, tattler, traitor **8** betrayer, mouchard, snitcher, squealer **11** stool pigeon

Informer, The
author: **13** Liam O'Flaherty
director: **8** John Ford
cast: **10** Una O'Connor **11** Wallace Ford **12** Heather Angel **13** Margot Grahame, Preston Foster **14** Victor McLaglen
score: **10** Max Steiner
remade as: **7** Up Tight

infraction **6** breach **8** trespass **9** violation **10** peccadillo **11** lawbreaking **12** disobedience, encroachment, infringement, unobservance **13** nonobservance, transgression

infrastructure **4** base, root **5** basis **6** bottom, fabric, ground **7** bedrock, footing, support **9** framework, substrate **10** foundation, groundwork, substratum **12** substructure, underpinning **14** understructure

infrequent **3** few **4** rare **6** fitful, seldom, unique **7** unusual **8** sporadic, uncommon **9** spasmodic **10** occasional **16** few and far between

infringe **5** break **6** butt in, invade **7** disobey, impinge, infract, intrude, violate **8** encroach, overstep, trespass **10** contravene, transgress

in front **5** ahead, first **6** before **7** forward

in full possession of one's faculties
Latin: **12** compos mentis

infuriate **3** vex **4** gall, rile **5** anger, chafe **6** enrage, madden, offend **7** incense, inflame, outrage, provoke **8** irritate **9** aggravate, burn one up, make angry **10** exasperate **15** raise one's dander

infuriating **7** irksome **8** annoying, enraging **9** maddening, provoking **10** irritating **11** aggravating **12** exasperating, inflammatory

infuse **5** imbue **7** fortify, implant, inspire, instill **8** impart to, pour into **9** inculcate, insinuate, introject

in futuro **11** in the future

Inge, William
author of: **6** Picnic **7** Bus Stop **19** Come Back Little Sheba **26** The Dark at the Top of the Stairs

in general **7** as a rule, usually **10** by and large, on the whole

ingenious **4** deft **6** adroit, artful, clever, crafty, expert, shrewd **7** cunning **8** masterly, original, skillful, stunning **9** brilliant, dexterous, inventive, masterful **11** resourceful

ingenuity **5** flair, skill **7** cunning, know-how, mastery **8** aptitude, deftness, facility **9** adeptness, dexterity, expertise, sharpness **10** adroitness, astuteness, brilliance, cleverness, shrewdness **11** imagination **12** good thinking, skillfulness **13** ingeniousness, inventiveness **15** imaginativeness, quick-wittedness, resourcefulness

ingenuous **4** open **5** frank, naive **6** direct, honest **7** artless, genuine, natural, up front **8** trusting **9** guileless **10** unaffected **11** openhearted **13** simplehearted **15** straightforward, unsophisticated **16** straight-shooting

ingenuousness **7** naivete **8** openness **9** frankness **11** artlessness

ingest **3** eat **4** gulp, take **5** drink **6** absorb, devour, imbibe, take in **7** consume, swallow **8** gulp down

inglorious **3** low **4** base, evil, mean, vile **6** odious **7** corrupt, heinous, ignoble **8** depraved, flagrant, infamous, shameful, shocking **9** atrocious, degrading, nefarious **10** despicable, detestable, outrageous, scandalous **11** disgraceful, ignominious, opprobrious **12** contemptible, dishonorable

in good condition
French: **10** embonpoint

in good health **2** OK **4** fine, hale, well **6** hearty, robust, tiptop **7** healthy **8** all right, blooming, vigorous **9** full of pep, in the pink **17** full of vim and vigor

in good time **5** early **7** betimes **11** ahead of time

ingot **3** bar **5** block

ingrained **4** deep, firm **5** fixed **6** inborn, inbred, innate, rooted **8** inherent, thorough **9** confirmed, implanted, indelible, intrinsic **10** deep-rooted, deep-seated, inveterate **14** constitutional

Ingram, Blanche
character in: **8** Jane Eyre
author: **6** Bronte

ingratiating **4** oily **5** sweet **6** genial, smarmy **7** affable, amiable, cordial, fulsome, gushing, likable, lovable, winning, winsome **8** charming, engaging, friendly, gracious, magnetic, pleasing, unctuous **9** appealing, congenial **10** attractive, enchanting, obsequious, oleaginous, personable, persuasive **11** captivating, good-humored, self-serving **12** presumptuous

ingratiation **7** blarney **8** flattery **9** sweet talk **12** inveiglement **13** blandishments

ingratitude **14** ungratefulness **18** lack of appreciation

ingredient **4** part **6** aspect, factor **7** element, feature **9** component, essential, principle **11** constituent, contributor **12** integral part

Ingres, Jean-Auguste-Dominique
born: **6** France **9** Montauban
artwork: **9** Odalisque, The Source **13** Mme Moitessier **14** The Turkish Bath **15** Valpincon Bather **16** Roger and Angelica **17** The Vow of Louis XIII **21** Comtesse d'Haussonville **25** The Ambassadors of Agamemnon **26** The Vow of Louis the Thirteenth

ingress **5** entry, way in **6** access **8** entrance

inhabit **5** lodge **6** live in, occupy, people, settle, tenant **7** dwell in **8** populate, reside in

inhabitant **6** inmate, lessee, lodger, native, renter, tenant **7** boarder, citizen, denizen, dweller, settler **8** occupant, occupier, resident, villager **9** inhabiter

inhalation **4** gasp **5** sniff **6** breath **11** breathing in

inhale **5** sniff, snuff **6** suck in **7** inspire, respire **9** breathe in, inbreathe

inherent **6** inborn, inbred, innate, native **7** natural **9** essential, ingrained, intrinsic **10** deep-rooted, hereditary, inveterate **11** inalienable, inseparable **14** constitutional

inherit **3** get **6** be left, come by **7** acquire **8** come into **9** come in for **10** fall heir to

inheritance **6** devise, estate, legacy **7** bequest **8** bestowal, heritage **9** endowment, patrimony **10** bequeathal, birthright

inherited **8** came into, heirloom, unearned **10** handed down

inheritor **4** heir **7** legatee **11** beneficiary

Inherit the Wind
director: **13** Stanley Kramer
based on play by: **10** Robert E Lee **14** Jerome Lawrence
cast: **8** Dick York **9** Gene Kelly **10** Elliot Reid **11** Harry Morgan **12** Spencer Tracy (Clarence Darrow) **13** Frederic March (William Jennings Bryan) **16** Florence Eldridge

inhibit **3** bar, gag **4** curb, stop **5** block, check **6** arrest, enjoin, forbid, hinder, impede, muzzle **7** control, harness, prevent, repress, smother **8** hold back, obstruct, prohibit, restrain, restrict, suppress **9** constrain **11** hold in leash

inhibited **4** cold **6** barred, curbed, frigid **7** bridled, checked, guarded **8** hindered, reserved **9** repressed **10** controlled, obstructed, restrained **11** constrained, discouraged, held in check **12** unresponsive **14** under restraint

inhibition, inhibitions **5** check **7** reserve **8** blockage **9** misgiving, restraint, stricture **10** constraint, impediment **11** guardedness, mental block, obstruction, restriction **12** constriction **17** self-consciousness

in high spirits **2** up **3** gay **5** happy, merry **6** elated, jaunty, joyful, joyous **7** buoyant **8** carefree, ecstatic, exultant, jubilant **9** overjoyed **11** exhilarated, on cloud nine **13** up in the clouds **15** on top of the world

in hoc signo vinces **26** in this sign shalt thou conquer
motto of: **19** Constantine the Great
from vision of: **5** cross

inhospitable **4** cold, cool, rude **5** aloof **6** unkind **7** distant, hostile **8** impolite **10** unfriendly, ungracious, unobliging, unsociable **11** standoffish, uncongenial, unreceptive, unwelcoming **12** discourteous, unneighborly **13** inconsiderate **14** unapproachable **15** unaccommodating

inhuman **5** cruel **6** brutal, savage **7** brutish, satanic, vicious **8** barbaric, demoniac, fiendish, pitiless, ruthless, venomous **9** barbarous, heartless, malignant, merciless, monstrous, unfeeling **10** diabolical, malevolent **11** coldhearted, cold-blooded, hardhearted

inhumane **6** brutal, savage **7** inhuman **8** fiendish, pitiless, ruthless **9** barbarous, heartless, merciless, unfeeling, unpitying **10** unmerciful **11** cold-blooded, hardhearted **12** bloodthirsty **13** unsympathetic

inhumanity **6** sadism **7** cruelty **8** atrocity, savagery **9** barbarism, barbarity, brutality **11** brutishness, heinousness, malevolence, viciousness **12** fiendishness, ruthlessness **13** heartlessness, mercilessness **15** cold-bloodedness **16** bloodthirstiness

inhumation **6** burial **9** interment **10** entombment

inimical **5** toxic **6** at odds **7** harmful, hateful, hostile, hurtful, ruinous **8** venomous, virulent **9** dangerous, ill-willed, injurious, on the outs, poisonous, rancorous **10** unfriendly **11** acrimonious, deleterious, destructive, detrimental, ill-disposed **12** antagonistic, antipathetic, disputatious **13** at loggerheads, at sword's point

inimitable **4** rare **6** unique **7** supreme **8** peerless **9** matchless, nonpareil, unequaled, unmatched, unrivaled **10** consummate, preeminent, unexcelled **11** superlative, unsurpassed **12** incomparable, unparalleled **13** beyond compare

iniquitous **4** base, evil, vile **6** sinful, wicked **7** corrupt, debased, immoral, vicious **8** depraved, infamous **9** nefarious **10** evil-minded **12** blackhearted **13** reprehensible

iniquity **3** sin **4** evil, vice **5** wrong **6** infamy **7** knavery, outrage, roguery **8** inequity, villainy **9** depravity, evildoing, flagrancy, turpitude **10** corruption, dishonesty, immorality, miscreancy, profligacy, sinfulness, unfairness, unjustness, wickedness, wrongdoing **11** abomination **13** transgression **14** gross injustice **15** unrighteousness

in isolation
Latin: **7** in vacuo

initial **5** first **6** maiden, primal **7** opening, primary **8** germinal, original, starting **9** beginning, inaugural, incipient **10** commencing, initiatory **12** introductory

initiate **4** haze, open **5** begin, found, set up, start **6** induct, invest, launch, take in **7** bring in, install, kick off, receive, usher in **8** be opened, commence, get going, set afoot, set going **9** enter upon, establish, institute, introduce, originate **10** inaugurate, lead the way **11** break ground, get under way, take the lead **12** acquaint with **13** blaze the trail **15** familiarize with **16** lay the first stone, lay the foundation **19** start the ball rolling

initiation **5** onset, start **6** outset **7** genesis, opening **8** entrance, guidance, outbreak, starting **9** beginning, inception, induction **10** admittance, initiating, ushering in **11** inculcation **12** commencement, inauguration, introduction **14** indoctrination **15** formal admission

initiative **4** lead **8** dynamism **9** first move, first step **10** creativity, enterprise, get-up-and-go, leadership **11** originality **12** forcefulness **14** aggressiveness

in its original place
Latin: **6** in situ

inject **3** put **4** pump **5** force, imbue, infix **6** infuse, insert **7** instill, throw in **8** intromit **9** interject, introduce **11** interpolate

injection **4** hypo, shot **7** booster, vaccine **9** antitoxin, insertion **10** hypodermic **11** inoculation, vaccination **12** shot in the arm

injudicious **4** dumb, wild **5** crazy **6** stupid, unwise **7** foolish, unsound **8** heedless, reckless **9** audacious, foolhardy, hotheaded, imprudent, senseless **10** self-willed, unsuitable **11** inadvisable

injunction **4** writ **5** edict, order **7** command **10** admonition, court order

Injun Joe
character in: **9** Tom Sawyer
author: **9** Mark Twain

injure **3** mar **4** harm, hurt, lame, maim **5** abuse, spoil, stain, sting, sully, wound, wrong **6** bruise, damage, debase, deface, deform, impair, malign, mangle, misuse, offend, scathe **7** afflict, affront, blemish, violate, vitiate **8** do harm to, ill-treat, lacerate, maltreat, mutilate **9** disfigure

injured **4** hurt, lame **6** abused, harmed, maimed, marred, piqued **7** bruised, damaged, defaced, grieved, scathed, wounded, wronged **8** crippled, deformed, impaired, insulted, offended **9** afflicted, affronted, aggrieved **10** disfigured

injurious **7** abusive, adverse, harmful, hurtful, noxious, ruinous **8** damaging, inimical **9** corrosive **10** calamitous, disastrous, pernicious **11** deleterious, destructive, detrimental

injury **3** cut **4** blow, gash, harm, hurt, stab **5** abuse, wound **6** bruise, damage, lesion **7** affront, outrage, scratch **9** aspersion, contusion, indignity, injustice **10** affliction, defamation, detraction, disservice, impairment, laceration, mutilation **12** vilification

injustice **3** sin **4** bias, evil **5** wrong **6** injury **7** bigotry, offense, tyranny **8** foul play, inequity, iniquity **9** prejudice, unjust act **10** disservice, favoritism, inequality, infraction, partiality, unfairness, unjustness, wrongdoing **11** malpractice, persecution **12** encroachment, infringement, partisanship **13** transgression

in keeping **6** normal **7** natural **8** becoming **9** congruous, consonant **10** consistent **11** appropriate, in agreement **12** in compliance, in conformity

inkling **3** cue, tip **4** clue, hint, idea **6** notion **7** glimmer, whisper **8** innuendo **9** suspicion, vague idea **10** conception, glimmering, indication, intimation, suggestion **11** insinuation, supposition

inky **3** jet **4** dark **5** black, raven, sable **7** stygian **9** coal-black

inlet **3** bay **4** cove, gulf **5** bight, fiord, firth, fjord **6** harbor, strait **7** estuary, narrows **8** waterway

in line **4** even **6** in a row **7** aligned, in order **8** queued up, straight **12** under control

in loco **7** in place **16** in the proper place

in loco parentis **16** replacing a parent **19** in the place of a parent

inmate **3** con **5** felon **6** lodger, tenant **7** convict, denizen **8** prisoner, resident **10** inhabitant

in medias res **19** in the middle of things **21** in the middle of the story

in memoriam **10** in memory of **13** as a memorial to, to the memory of

In Memoriam A H H
author: **18** Alfred Lord Tennyson

in memory of
Latin: **10** in memoriam

In Memory of W B Yeats
author: **7** W H Auden

inmost **5** inner **6** inside **7** central **8** interior **9** innermost

in motion **5** afoot, astir **6** active, moving **7** on the go, working **8** under way **9** on the move, operating, operative **10** responsive

In My Father's Court
author: **19** Isaac Bashevis Singer

inn **5** hotel, lodge, motel **6** hostel, tavern **7** hospice, pension **8** hostelry **9** roadhouse **11** caravansary, public house
French: **7** auberge
Spanish: **6** posada

innards **4** guts **6** bowels, vitals **7** gizzard, insides, viscera **10** intestines **14** liver and lights

innate **6** inborn, inbred, native **7** natural **8** inherent **9** essential, ingrained, inherited, intrinsic, intuitive **10** congenital, hereditary, indigenous **11** instinctive **14** constitutional

inner **6** hidden, inside, inward, mental, middle **7** central, private, psychic **8** esoteric, interior, internal **9** concealed, emotional, spiritual, unobvious **10** more secret **12** more intimate **13** psychological

inner circle **4** core **5** bosom, heart **6** center **7** nucleus

inner city **8** core city, downtown **9** urban area **10** city limits, metropolis **11** central city **16** metropolitan area

Inner Mongolia
other name: **9** Neimenggu, Neimengku
capital: **6** Hohhot **7** Huhehot
desert: **4** Gobi
tent: **4** yurt

innermost **6** inmost, secret **7** deepest **10** deep-rooted, deep-seated **11** most private **12** most intimate, most personal

innermost part **4** core, crux, pith, soul **6** center, kernel **7** essence, nucleus

Inness, George
born: **10** Newburgh NY
artwork: **7** The Monk **14** Home of the Heron, Peace and Plenty **16** Delaware Water Gap **17** The Delaware Valley **19** The Lackawanna Valley

Innisfail *see* **7** Ireland

innkeeper **4** host **6** tapper, venter **7** padrone **8** boniface, hosteler, hotelier, landlord, publican **10** proprietor **12** maitre d'hotel, restaurateur

innocence **6** purity **7** naivete **8** chastity **9** freshness **10** clean hands, simplicity **11** artlessness, sinlessness **12** incorrup-

tion, spotlessness
13 blamelessness, guilelessness, guiltlessness, impeccability, inculpability, ingenuousness, stainlessness
14 immaculateness

innocent **3** tot **4** baby, naif, open, pure, tyro **5** clean, naive **6** chaste, honest, novice, simple **7** artless, ingenue, sinless, upright **8** harmless, pristine, spotless, virginal, virtuous **9** blameless, childlike, faultless, greenhorn, guileless, guiltless, ingenuous, innocuous, little one, stainless, uncorrupt, undefiled, unstained, unsullied, unworldly, well-meant **10** artless one, immaculate, impeccable, inculpable, tenderfoot, young child **11** inoffensive, unblemished, uncorrupted, unmalicious, unoffending **12** unsuspicious **13** meaning no harm, unimpeachable **14** above suspicion, irreproachable
15 unsophisticated
Latin: **12** integer vitae

Innocents, The
director: **11** Jack Clayton
based on story by: **10** Henry James (The Turn of the Screw)
cast: **11** Deborah Kerr, Megs Jenkins **13** Peter Wyngarde **15** Michael Redgrave
script: **12** Truman Capote **16** William Archibald

Innocents Abroad, The
author: **9** Mark Twain (Samuel Clemens)

innocuous **4** dull, mild **5** banal, empty, trite, vapid **6** barren **7** insipid **8** harmless, innocent, painless **9** pointless **11** commonplace, inoffensive, meaningless

innocuousness **6** safety **9** blandness, innocence **12** harmlessness **15** inoffensiveness

in no uncertain terms **7** clearly, plainly **9** expressly **10** definitely, distinctly **13** categorically, unequivocally

innovation **5** shift **7** novelty **8** updating **10** alteration, dernier cri, new measure, remodeling, renovation **11** institution, latest thing **12** commencement, inauguration, introduction, streamlining **13** modernization

innovator **7** deviser, planner **9** contriver **10** instigator, originator **11** inaugurator

Innu *see* **17** Montagnais-Naskapi

innuendo **4** hint **7** whisper **8** overtone **9** inference **10** imputation, intimation **11** implication, insinuation

innumerable **6** myriad **8** numerous **9** countless **10** numberless, unnumbered **12** incalculable **13** multitudinous

Ino
also: **9** Leucothea
goddess of: **3** sea
father: **6** Cadmus
mother: **8** Harmonia
sister: **5** Hgave **6** Semele **7** Autonoe
husband: **7** Athamas
son: **8** Learchus **10** Melicertes
stepson: **7** Phrixus
stepdaughter: **5** Helle
saved: **8** Odysseus
cared for infant: **8** Dionysus
changed into: **10** sea goddess

inoculate **5** imbue, shoot **6** infuse, inject, insert **7** implant, instill **8** immunize **9** inculcate, vaccinate

inoculation **4** shot **6** needle **7** booster **9** injection **10** hypodermic **11** vaccination **12** immunization

inoffensive **4** mild, safe **5** bland **7** neutral **8** harmless, innocent **9** endurable, innocuous, tolerable **10** sufferable **11** unoffending **15** unobjectionable

inoffensiveness **6** safety **9** innocence **10** neutrality **12** harmlessness **13** innocuousness

in one's debt **7** obliged **8** beholden, indebted **9** obligated **15** under obligation

in one's own person
Latin: **16** in propria persona

in one's own place
Latin: **7** suo loco

in one's own right
Latin: **7** suo jure

in one's rightful place
Latin: **7** suo loco

inoperable **6** broken **10** broken down, unworkable **11** ineffective

in operation **5** in use **7** in force, working **8** in effect **9** operating, operative

inoperative **4** dead, down **8** inactive **10** not working, out of order

inopportune **7** awkward **8** ill-timed, untimely **10** badly timed, ill-advised, unsuitable **11** troublesome, undesirable, unfavorable, unfortunate **12** inauspicious, incommodious, inconvenient, unpropitious, unseasonable **13** inappropriate **15** disadvantageous

in order **2** OK **4** neat, tidy **6** proper **7** correct, perfect **8** all right

inordinate **5** undue **6** lavish, wanton **7** extreme, profuse, surplus **8** needless, overmuch, shocking **9** excessive **10** deplorable, exorbitant, immoderate, irrational, outrageous, scandalous **11** disgraceful, extravagant, intemperate, overflowing, superfluous, uncalled-for, unnecessary **12** unreasonable, unrestrained **13** superabundant **14** supersaturated, unconscionable **16** disproportionate

inordinately **6** overly, unduly **9** extremely **11** excessively **12** immoderately, outrageously, prodigiously **13** extravagantly, intemperately, superfluously, unnecessarily

inorganic **4** dead **7** mineral **8** lifeless **9** inanimate, nonliving **10** artificial

in passing
French: **9** en passant

in perpetuum **7** forever

in petto **11** in the breast **12** not disclosed

in pieces **6** broken **7** asunder, smashed **8** in shreds, sundered **9** torn apart **13** in smithereens

in place
Latin: **6** in loco, in situ

in plain sight **7** exposed, obvious **10** in full view, noticeable **12** out in the open **17** in front of one's nose

in posse **11** potentially **13** in possibility

in possibility
Latin: **7** in posse

In Praise of Darkness
author: **15** Jorge Luis Borges

in propria persona **15** in one's own person

inquest **5** probe **7** autopsy, delving, hearing, inquiry, probing **8** necropsy **10** postmortem **11** inquisition **13** investigation

inquire **3** ask **5** probe, query, study **6** search **7** examine, explore, inspect **8** check out, look into, look over, question **9** track down **10** look deeper, scrutinize **11** investigate

inquirer **5** asker, snoop **6** seeker **7** auditor, querier, quizzer, student **8** pollster, searcher **9** catechist **10** inquisitor, questioner **12** interlocutor, interrogator, investigator

inquiry, enquiry **4** hunt, quiz **5** probe, query, quest, study **6** search, survey **7** inquest **8** analysis, question, research, scrutiny **9** interview **10** inspection **11** examination, exploration, inquisition, questioning **13** interrogation, investigation

inquisitive **4** nosy **6** prying, snoopy **8** meddling, snooping **9** inquiring, intrusive, searching **10** meddlesome, too curious **11** interfering, overcurious, questioning

in re **13** in the matter of

in reality
Latin: **7** de facto

in rem **15** against the thing
of a legal proceeding: **18** against the property

in rerum natura **19** in the nature of things

in retreat **10** backing off, retreating **11** withdrawing, backing away

in reverse **8** backward **9** backing up **22** in the opposite direction

insalubrious **7** harmful, noisome, noxious **8** inimical, virulent **9** injurious, unhealthy **10** pernicious **11** deleterious, detrimental, unhealthful, unwholesome

insane **3** mad **4** bats, daft, dumb, loco, nuts, wild, zany **5** balmy, batty, crazy, loony, manic, nutty, potty **6** absurd, crazed, raving **7** berserk, bizarre, bonkers, cracked, foolish, idiotic, lunatic, tetched, touched, unsound **8** demented, frenzied, maniacal, unhinged **9** eccentric, imbecilic, imprudent, insensate, paranoiac, psychotic, senseless **10** ridiculous, unbalanced **11** injudicious **12** mad as a hatter, off one's chump, round the bend, unreasonable **13** off one's rocker, out of one's head, out of one's mind, out of one's wits, schizophrenic **15** bats in the belfry, mad as a March hare, stark staring mad **17** nutty as a fruitcake

insanity **5** folly, mania **6** idiocy, lunacy, raving **7** madness **8** dementia, paranoia **9** aberrance, absurdity, craziness, monomania, psychosis, stupidity **10** aberration **11** derangement, foolishness, unsoundness **12** loss of reason **13** hallucination, mental illness, schizophrenia, senselessness

insatiable **8** ravenous **9** insatiate, limitless, voracious **10** bottomless, gluttonous, implacable, omnivorous **12** unappeasable, unquenchable

inscribe **3** pen **4** etch, mark, seal, sign **5** blaze, brand, carve, write **6** chisel, incise, letter, scrawl **7** engrave, impress, imprint **8** scribble **9** autograph

inscription **5** motto, title **6** legend, rubric **7** address, caption, epigram, epitaph, heading, titulus, writing **8** colophon, epigraph, graffiti **9** engraving, lettering **10** dedication

inscrutable **6** arcane, hidden, masked, veiled **7** deadpan, elusive **8** baffling, puzzling **9** concealed, enigmatic **10** mysterious, mystifying, perplexing, poker-faced, unknowable, unreadable, unrevealed **12** inexplicable, unfathomable, unsearchable **14** indecipherable, unintelligible **16** incomprehensible

In Search of Identity
author: **12** Anwar el-Sadat

insect **3** ant, bee, bug, fly **4** flea, gnat, moth, pest, wasp **5** aphid, imago **6** bedbug, beetle, cicada, earwig, hornet, mantis, mayfly, vermin **7** chigger, cricket, firefly, katydid, ladybug, termite **8** horsefly, housefly, lacewing, mosquito **9** arthropod, butterfly, cockroach, dragonfly **10** silverfish **11** grasshopper
study of: **10** entomology
young: **4** grub, pupa **5** larva, nymph **6** larvae, maggot **9** chrysalis **11** caterpillar
anatomy: **4** palp **5** cerci, notum **6** cercus, feeler, labium, labrum, ocelli, thorax **7** antenna, maxilla, ocellus **8** antennae, mandible, maxillae **9** proboscis, spiracles **10** ovipositor **11** exoskeleton

insectivore **4** mole **5** shrew **6** desman, tenrec **7** moon rat **8** alamiqui, anteater, hedgehog **9** solenodon

insecure **4** weak **5** frail, risky, shaky **6** infirm, unsafe, unsure, wobbly **7** dubious, exposed, not firm, not sure, rickety, unsound **8** critical, doubtful, in danger, perilous, unstable, unsteady **9** dangerous, diffident, hazardous, in a bad way, tottering, unassured, uncertain, under fire **10** endangered, precarious, ramshackle, unreliable, unshielded, vulnerable **11** defenseless, dilapidated, unprotected, unsheltered

insecurities **4** risk **5** peril **6** danger, hazard **7** pitfall **8** jeopardy **11** contingency

insecurity **5** doubt **9** self-doubt, shakiness **10** diffidence, unsafeness **11** dubiousness, incertitude, instability, uncertainty **12** doubtfulness, endangerment, insecureness, unsteadiness **13** vulnerability **14** precariousness **15** defenselessness, lack of assurance **16** apprehensiveness

insensate **4** cold **5** cruel **6** brutal **8** inhumane **9** heartless, unfeeling **11** unconscious

insensibility **4** coma **5** swoon **6** apathy, torpor, trance **8** blackout, dullness, lethargy, numbness, obduracy, oblivion, stoicism **9** analgesia, catalepsy **10** anesthesia, obtuseness **12** incognizance, indifference, mindlessness **13** insensitivity, unfeelingness **15** unconsciousness

insensible **4** cold **9** insensate, senseless **11** unconscious

insensitive **4** cold, dead, numb **5** blase **7** callous **8** hardened **9** apathetic, impassive, insensate, unaware of, unfeeling **10** impervious, insensible **11** indifferent, unconcerned **12** thick-skinned **15** uncompassionate

insensitiveness **8** rudeness **10** coarseness, indelicacy **12** tactlessness **13** insensibility, insensitivity **17** inconsiderateness

inseparable **8** attached **11** indivisible, unseverable **12** indissoluble

insert **3** add **5** embed, enter, imbed, infix, inlay, inset, pop in, put in, set in **6** infuse, inject, push in, tuck in **7** drive in, implant, intrude, place in, press in, slide in, stick in, stuff in, wedge in **8** thrust in **9** interject, interlard, interpose, introduce **10** put between **11** interpolate, intersperse

insertion **2** ad **5** entry, graft, inlay, inset **7** implant **11** insinuation, parenthesis **12** interjection **13** advertisement

inset **4** gore **5** embed, godet,

imbed, inlay, panel **6** insert **9** insertion

in seventh heaven **6** elated, joyful, joyous **8** ecstatic, euphoric **9** exuberant, rapturous **11** on cloud nine **13** up in the clouds

inside **2** in **5** inner **6** inmost, inward, secret **7** private **8** cliquish, esoteric, interior, internal, intimate **9** inner part, inner side, innermost **12** confidential

inside information **3** tip **10** inside dope

inside out **9** backwards **10** in disorder, topsy turvy **11** wrong side to

insides **4** guts **6** bowels, vitals **7** gizzard, innards, viscera **10** intestines

insidious **3** sly **4** foxy, wily **5** shady **6** artful, covert, crafty, sneaky, subtle, tricky **7** crooked, cunning, devious, furtive **8** guileful, slippery, sneaking, stealthy **9** concealed, deceitful, designing, disguised, secretive, underhand **10** contriving, perfidious, pernicious, undercover, undetected **11** clandestine, deleterious, treacherous, underhanded **12** disingenuous, falsehearted **13** Machiavellian, surreptitious

insight **6** acumen **9** intuition **10** perception **11** discernment, penetration **12** apprehension, perceptivity, perspicacity **13** comprehension, intuitiveness **14** perceptiveness
French: **6** apercu

insignia **3** bar **4** mark, sign, star **5** badge, medal, patch **6** emblem, stripe, symbol **7** chevron, epaulet, oak leaf **10** decoration **13** badge of office

insignificance **8** puniness **9** pettiness, smallness **10** meagerness, triviality **11** irrelevance **12** unimportance

insignificant **4** puny **5** petty, small **6** flimsy, meager, minute, paltry **7** trivial **8** niggling, not vital, nugatory, picayune, piddling, trifling **9** minuscule, worthless **10** immaterial, irrelevant, negligible, of no moment, second-rate **11** indifferent, meaningless, unimportant **12** nonessential **13** small potatoes **14** inconsiderable **15** inconsequential, of little account, of no consequence **18** not worth mentioning

insincere **5** false, lying **6** untrue **7** devious, evasive **8** guileful, two-faced, uncandid **9** deceitful, dishonest, equivocal **10** fraudulent, perfidious, untruthful **11** dissembling **12** disingenuous, hypocritical, mealymouthed **13** dissimulating, double-dealing

insincerity **4** sham **6** deceit **8** pretense, uncandor **9** deception, falseness, hypocrisy, mendacity **11** affectation, shallowness, unfrankness **12** uncandidness **13** artificiality **16** disingenuousness

insinuate **5** imply **6** inject, insert **7** asperse, let fall, suggest, wheedle, whisper **8** intimate **10** ingratiate **11** worm one's way

insinuation **4** hint **8** allusion, infusion, innuendo **9** aspersion, insertion, intrusion **10** allegation, imputation, intimation, suggestion **11** implication, penetration **12** ingratiation, interjection

insipid **4** arid, blah, drab, dull, flat, lean **5** banal, bland, empty, inane, stale, trite, vapid **6** barren, boring, jejune, stupid **7** prosaic **8** lifeless, zestless **9** pointless, savorless, tasteless, wearisome **10** monotonous, namby-pamby, wishy-washy **11** commonplace **12** unappetizing **13** characterless, uninteresting

insist **4** aver, hold, urge, warn **5** claim, vouch **6** assert, demand, exhort, repeat, stress **7** caution, command, contend, persist, protest, require **8** admonish, maintain **9** reiterate **10** asseverate **13** lay down the law **14** take a firm stand **15** stand one's ground

insistence **6** demand, urging **7** urgency **8** exigency, pressure **9** clamoring **11** persistence **12** perseverance **14** imperativeness

insistent **4** firm **7** adamant **8** emphatic, repeated, stubborn **9** assertive, demanding **10** determined, unyielding **11** unrelenting

in situ **7** in place **18** in its original place

insolence **4** gall **7** disdain, hauteur **8** audacity **9** arrogance, impudence **10** brazenness, disrespect, effrontery, incivility, lordliness **11** haughtiness, presumption **12** disobedience, impertinence, impoliteness **13** bumptiousness, imperiousness **14** unmannerliness **16** superciliousness

insolent **4** rude **5** fresh, nervy **6** brazen, cheeky **7** defiant, galling, haughty **8** arrogant, impolite, impudent **9** audacious, bumptious, insulting **10** disdainful, outrageous, unmannerly **11** impertinent, overbearing **12** contemptuous, discourteous, presumptuous, supercilious **13** disrespectful

insoluble **12** inexplicable, unanswerable **13** undissolvable, unexplainable **14** undecipherable **16** incomprehensible

insolvent **5** broke **6** ruined **8** bankrupt, wiped out **9** destitute, moneyless, penniless **10** down-and-out, out of money **11** impecunious **12** impoverished, overextended

insomnia **11** nuit blanche, pervigilium, wakefulness **12** insomnolence **13** sleeplessness

insouciant **4** airy **5** perky **6** breezy, casual, jaunty **7** buoyant, offhand **8** carefree, debonair, flippant **9** easygoing, mercurial, unruffled, sans souci, whimsical **10** capricious, nonchalant, untroubled **11** free and easy, indifferent, unconcerned **12** devil-may-care, happy-go-lucky, lighthearted

inspect **3** eye **4** scan **5** probe, study **6** peer at, peruse, review, survey **7** examine, explore, observe **8** pore over **10** scrutinize **11** contemplate, investigate, reconnoiter

inspection **4** scan **5** audit, check, probe, study **6** review, survey **7** perusal **8** checking, scrutiny **9** appraisal, oversight **11** examination

inspector **7** analyst, auditor **8** analyzer, examiner, overseer, reviewer **9** appraiser, detective **11** scrutinizer **12** investigator

Inspector-General, The
author: **12** Nikolai Gogol
character: **4** Anna, Osip **5** Maria **26** Ivan Alexandrovich Hlestakov **35** Anton Antonovich Skvoznik-Dmukhanovsky

inspiration **4** idea, spur **5** fancy, flash **6** motive **7** impulse **8** afflatus, stimulus **9** incentive, influence, prompting **10** compulsion, incitement, motivation, revelation **13** encouragement

inspire **4** fire, stir **5** cause, exalt, impel, rouse **6** arouse, excite, induce, prompt, vivify

7 animate, enliven, hearten, produce, promote, provoke, quicken 8 embolden, engender, enkindle, illumine, inspirit, motivate, occasion 9 encourage, galvanize, influence, stimulate 10 give rise to, illuminate

inspired 3 apt 5 fired, moved 6 elated 7 elegant, exalted, excited, incited, touched, well-put 8 creative, original, prompted 9 impressed, ingenious, inventive, motivated 10 encouraged, felicitous, influenced, stimulated, well-chosen 11 exhilarated, imaginative 13 well-expressed

inspiring 5 grand 6 moving 7 awesome 8 eloquent, stirring 9 affecting, brilliant 10 impressive 11 encouraging, magnificent, stimulating

inspirit 5 boost, cheer, rouse 6 buoy up, uplift 7 animate, comfort, enliven, hearten, inspire 9 encourage, give a lift

in spite of himself
French: 9 malgre lui

instability 8 wavering, weakness 9 hesitancy 10 fitfulness, hesitation, indecision, insecurity 11 flightiness, fluctuation, inconstancy, vacillation 12 irresolution, unstableness, unsteadiness 13 changeability, inconsistency, mercurialness, vulnerability 14 capriciousness, changeableness

install, instal 3 lay 4 seat 5 crown, embed, imbed, lodge, plant 6 induct, invest, locate, move in, ordain 7 arrange, emplace, instate, receive, situate, station, usher in 8 coronate, initiate, position 9 establish 10 inaugurate, set in place

installation 5 plant 6 agency 8 facility 9 formation, induction 10 foundation, initiation, ordination 11 appointment, institution, investiture 12 inauguration, military base, organization 13 establishment

installment 4 part, unit 5 issue 6 laying 7 chapter, payment, section, segment 8 division, fragment, locating

instance 4 case, time 6 sample 7 example 8 occasion, specimen 9 precedent, prototype 10 antecedent 11 case in point 12 circumstance, illustration

instant 5 flash, jiffy, quick, trice 6 abrupt, minute, moment, prompt, second, sudden 8 premixed 9 immediate, on the spot, precooked, twinkling 10 ready-to-use 11 split second 12 unhesitating

instantaneous 5 rapid, swift 6 abrupt, direct, prompt, speedy, sudden 9 immediate 13 quick as a flash

instantaneously 6 at once 7 quickly, rapidly 8 in a flash, in no time, instanter, right now 9 on the spot, right away 11 immediately 21 in the twinkling of an eye

instantly 6 at once 7 quickly 8 directly, in a flash, promptly, right now 9 instanter, on the spot 10 here and now 11 immediately 12 quick as a wink, without delay 15 instantaneously 17 without hesitation

instar
insect period between: 5 molts 7 molting

in statu quo 17 in the state in which (something is or was)

Instauratio Magna
author: 12 Francis Bacon

instead 6 in lieu, rather 10 in its place

instigate 4 goad, spur, urge 5 begin, rouse, start 6 foment, incite, kindle, prompt, stir up 7 provoke 8 initiate 9 stimulate 10 bring about 11 set in motion

instigator 6 shaper 7 inciter 9 architect, innovator 10 prime mover, ringleader

instill, instil 4 pour 5 mix in, teach 6 impart, induce 7 implant, inspire 8 engender 9 inculcate

instinct 4 gift 5 knack 6 genius, nature 7 faculty 8 aptitude, capacity, tendency 9 intuition, mother wit 10 proclivity

instinctive 6 inborn, inbred, innate, native 7 natural 8 inherent, inspired 9 automatic, impulsive, intuitive, unlearned 10 deep-seated, unacquired 11 instinctual, involuntary, spontaneous

institute 4 pass 5 begin, enact, found, set up, start 6 ordain, school 7 academy, college, society 8 commence, get going, initiate, organize 9 establish, introduce, originate, prescribe, undertake 10 constitute, foundation, inaugurate 11 association, get under way 13 put into effect 14 bring into being

institution 4 rite 5 habit, usage 6 custom, prison, ritual, school 7 academy, college, company, fixture 8 bughouse, madhouse, nuthouse, seminary 9 institute 10 convention, crazy house, foundation, university 11 association 12 organization 13 establishment

institutionalize 6 commit, detain 7 confine, put away 8 imprison 11 incarcerate

in strict confidence 7 sub rosa 9 between us, entre nous, privately 14 confidentially 15 between you and me 16 between me and thee, between ourselves

instruct 3 bid 5 brief, coach, drill, guide, order, teach, train, tutor 6 advise, direct, inform, notify, school 7 apprise, command, educate 8 acquaint 9 catechize, enlighten 12 indoctrinate

instruction 8 coaching, guidance, pedagogy, teaching, training, tutelage, tutoring 9 education 11 instructing 14 indoctrination

instructions 4 rule 5 maxim, moral, motto 6 advice, homily, lesson 7 precept 9 direction, guideline 11 explanation, information 12 prescription 13 specification 14 recommendation

instructive 8 didactic, edifying 11 educational 12 enlightening

instructor 3 don 4 guru 5 coach, guide, tutor 6 mentor 7 counsel, maestro, teacher, trainer 8 educator, lecturer 9 governess, pedagogue, preceptor, professor 10 schoolmarm 12 schoolmaster 13 schoolteacher 14 schoolmistress

instrument 4 deed, tool 5 agent, grant, means, paper 6 agency, device, gadget, medium 7 charter, machine, utensil, vehicle 8 contract 9 apparatus, appliance, equipment, expedient, implement, mechanism 11 contrivance

Instrument, The
author: 9 John O'Hara

instrumental 5 vital 6 active, useful 7 crucial, helpful 8 a means to, decisive, valuable 9 assisting, conducive, effective, effectual, essential 10 functional 12 contributory

instrumentality 5 force, means 6 agency, charge 9 influence, mediation **12** intervention

insubordinate 6 unruly **7** defiant **8** insolent, mutinous **9** fractious **10** disorderly, rebellious, refractory **11** disobedient, intractable, uncompliant **12** recalcitrant, ungovernable, unsubmissive

insubordination 6 mutiny, revolt **7** anarchy **8** sedition **9** rebellion **10** dissention, insurgence, unruliness **12** disobedience, insurrection **13** noncompliance **14** refractoriness

insubstantial 4 airy, weak **5** frail, shaky, small **6** flimsy, modest, paltry, slight, unreal **7** fragile, trivial, unsound **8** baseless, bodiless, delicate, ethereal, gossamer, piddling, trifling, unstable **9** imaginary, visionary **10** groundless, immaterial, impalpable, intangible **12** apparitional **14** inconsiderable

in succession
French: 7 en suite

insufferable 7 hateful **8** dreadful **10** abominable, detestable, disgusting, outrageous, unbearable **11** intolerable, unendurable, unspeakable **13** insupportable

insufficiency 4 lack, need, want **6** dearth **7** drought, paucity **8** scarcity, shortage **10** deficiency, inadequacy, meagerness, scantiness **11** undersupply

insufficient 6 scanty, skimpy, sparse **7** lacking, wanting **8** impotent **9** deficient, not enough **10** inadequate **11** incompetent **14** unsatisfactory

insular 5 petty **6** biased, narrow **7** bigoted, limited **8** isolated **9** illiberal, insulated, parochial **10** intolerant, prejudiced, provincial **12** narrow-minded

insulate 5 cover **6** cut off, detach, enisle, shield **7** cushion, isolate, protect, seclude **8** separate **9** segregate, sequester **10** disconnect

insult 3 cut **4** slap **5** abuse, cheek, scorn **6** deride, offend, slight **7** affront, offense, outrage **8** be rude to, belittle, rudeness **9** disparage, impudence, indignity **11** discourtesy, lese majesty

insulting 4 rude **5** nasty **7** abusive, uncivil, vicious **8** impolite, insolent **9** invidious, offensive **10** defamatory, derogatory **11** disparaging **12** discourteous **13** disrespectful

insuperable 8 crushing **9** defeating **10** impassable, impossible, invincible, unbeatable, unyielding **12** inexpugnable, overpowering, overwhelming **13** overmastering, unconquerable **14** insurmountable

insurance 6 policy **8** coverage, security, warranty **9** assurance, guarantee, indemnity

insure 6 secure **10** underwrite

insurgent 5 rebel **7** lawless **8** mutineer, mutinous, partisan, renegade, resister, revolter **9** breakaway, dissident, guerrilla **10** disorderly, rebellious **11** disobedient **13** insubordinate, revolutionary, revolutionist **15** insurrectionist

insurmountable 8 hopeless, too great **10** unbeatable **11** beyond reach, insuperable **13** unconquerable

insurrection 4 riot **6** mutiny, revolt, rising **8** outbreak, uprising **9** rebellion **10** insurgence, revolution

intact 4 safe **5** sound, whole **6** unhurt **7** perfect **8** complete, integral, unbroken, unharmed **9** undamaged, uninjured, untouched **10** in one piece, unimpaired **11** in good shape **15** without a scratch

intangible 5 vague **7** elusive, shadowy **8** abstract, ethereal, fleeting, fugitive **9** transient **10** accidental, evanescent, immaterial, impalpable **11** abstraction, untouchable **12** imponderable **13** imperceptible, insubstantial

integer 5 digit, whole **6** entity, figure, number **7** numeral **11** whole number

integer vitae 8 innocent **15** blameless in life

integral 4 full **5** basic, total, whole **6** entire, intact **7** perfect, rounded **8** complete, finished, inherent **9** component, essential, fulfilled, necessary, requisite **10** fulfilling **11** constituent, well-rounded **13** indispensable

integrate 3 mix **4** fuse **5** blend, merge, unify, unite **6** mingle **7** combine **8** intermix **10** amalgamate **11** desegregate **13** bring together

integrated 6 entire, joined, linked, united **7** blended, merged, unified, unitary **8** combined **9** composite, undivided **10** harmonized, reconciled **11** coordinated, synthesized **12** desegregated, unsegregated

integration 5 union **6** fusion, mixing **8** blending **9** combining, synthesis **11** combination **12** assimilation **13** desegregation

integrity 5 unity **6** purity, virtue **7** decency, honesty, probity **8** cohesion, morality, strength **9** character, coherence, principle, rectitude, wholeness **11** reliability, self-respect, uprightness **12** completeness

integument 4 coat, hide, husk, rind, skin **5** shell, **7** coating, cuticle, epiderm, exoderm **8** covering, envelope, membrane

integumentary system
component: 4 hair, skin **5** nails

intellect 3 wit **4** mind **5** brain, sense **6** brains, wisdom **7** thinker **9** cognition, mentality **10** perception **11** mental power, rationality **12** intellectual, intelligence **13** consciousness, understanding

intellectual 4 sage **5** brain **6** brainy, mental, pundit, savant **7** bookish, egghead, scholar, thinker **8** abstract, academic, cerebral, highbrow, longhair, mandarin, rational, studious **9** intellect, of the mind, reasoning, scholarly **10** thoughtful **11** intelligent
French: 9 bel-esprit

intelligence 4 dope, news **6** acumen, advice, brains, notice, report, wisdom **7** tidings **8** sagacity **9** intellect, knowledge **10** advisement, shrewdness **11** information **12** notification, perspicacity **13** comprehension, understanding

intelligent 4 keen, sage, wise **5** alert, canny, quick, sharp, smart **6** astute, brainy, bright, clever, shrewd **7** knowing, prudent **8** informed, sensible, thinking **9** brilliant, sagacious **10** perceptive, thoughtful **11** clearheaded, quick-witted, sharp-witted **12** well-informed **13** perspicacious

intelligentsia 7 academe **8** thinkers **10** ivory tower **13** intellectuals

intelligible 5 clear, lucid **7** evident, obvious **8** apparent, clear-cut, coherent, definite, distinct **11** unambiguous, well-defined **12** unmistakable

14 comprehensible, understandable

intemperance 10 alcoholism, insobriety 11 dissipation, drunkenness, inebriation 12 immoderation, recklessness 13 excessiveness 16 irresponsibility

intemperate 5 harsh 6 brutal, rugged, severe 7 extreme, violent 8 bibulous, uncurbed 9 dissolute, excessive, inclement 10 dissipated, gluttonous, immoderate, inordinate 11 extravagant, inabstinent, incontinent 12 unrestrained 13 overindulgent

intend 3 aim 4 mean, plan, wish 6 aspire, design, expect 7 project, propose, resolve 9 calculate, determine 10 have in mind 11 contemplate

intended 5 meant 6 fiance, future 7 engaged, fiancee, implied, willful 8 proposed, purposed 9 affianced, betrothed, bride-to-be, groom-to-be, voluntary 10 calculated, deliberate 11 intentional

intense 4 deep, keen 5 acute, sharp 6 ardent, potent, strong 7 burning, earnest, extreme, fervent, violent 8 emphatic, forceful, forcible, powerful, vehement 10 passionate 12 concentrated, considerable

intensely 4 very 5 hotly 6 deeply, keenly 7 acutely, eagerly, vividly 8 ardently, heatedly, terribly 9 extremely, fervently, seriously, violently, zealously 10 forcefully, powerfully, profoundly, vehemently, vigorously 11 excessively, exquisitely, strenuously 12 considerably, passionately 13 energetically

intensify 5 boost 6 deepen, worsen 7 magnify, quicken, sharpen 8 escalate, heighten, increase, redouble 9 aggravate, reinforce 10 accelerate, strengthen

intensifying 9 worsening 10 increasing, magnifying, redoubling, sharpening 11 aggravating, heightening, reinforcing 12 exacerbating 13 strengthening

intensity 4 zeal 5 ardor, depth, force, power, vigor 6 energy, fervor 7 emotion, passion, potency 8 severity, strength 9 magnitude, vehemence 11 earnestness 12 forcefulness

intensive 6 all-out 7 growing, radical 8 complete, sweeping, thorough 10 exhaustive, increasing 11 comprehensive 12 concentrated 13 thoroughgoing

intent 3 aim, end, set 4 bent, gist, plan 5 drift, fixed 6 burden, design, import, steady 7 earnest, intense, meaning, purport, purpose 8 absorbed, piercing, resolved 9 engrossed, insistent, intention, steadfast, substance, tenacious, unbending 10 determined, unwavering 11 preoccupied 12 concentrated, significance, undistracted 13 determination, premeditation

intention 3 aim, end 4 goal, plan 6 design, intent, object, target 7 purpose, resolve 9 objective 10 resolution 13 determination

intentional 6 willed 7 planned 8 designed, intended 9 voluntary 10 calculated, deliberate, purposeful 12 contemplated, premeditated 13 done on purpose

intently 6 deeply, raptly 9 fervently, zealously 10 absorbedly 11 attentively 12 passionately 18 without distraction 22 with undivided attention

intentness 10 absorption 11 engrossment 13 concentration

inter 4 bury 5 inurn 6 entomb, inhume 7 inearth, lay away 9 lay to rest 11 ensepulcher

interact 4 join, mesh 5 coact, unite 6 engage 7 combine, conjoin 8 dovetail 9 cooperate, interlace, intermesh, interplay, interwork 10 coordinate, interreact

inter alia 16 among other things

inter alios 17 among other persons

interbreed 3 mix 5 cross 8 intermix 10 crossbreed

intercede 5 plead 6 step in 7 mediate, speak up 9 arbitrate, interpose, intervene, offer help 12 offer support 14 put in a good word 16 lend a helping hand

intercept 3 nab 4 grab, stay, stop, take 5 catch, seize 6 ambush, arrest, cut off, detain 7 deflect, reroute

intercessor 5 agent 6 bishop, broker 8 advocate, mediator 9 go-between, middleman 12 intermediary, spokesperson

interchange 5 shift 6 switch 7 trading 8 exchange, junction, swapping, transfer 9 alternate, crossover 10 substitute 11 give and take, reciprocity

interchangeable 8 parallel, tradable 9 analogous 10 equivalent, switchable, synonymous 12 exchangeable, transposable 13 corresponding

interconnected 8 adjacent 10 contiguous, juxtaposed 12 conterminous, labyrinthine

intercourse 4 talk 5 trade 6 coitus, parley 7 pairing, traffic 8 colloquy, commerce, congress, coupling, dealings, exchange 9 communion, discourse, relations 10 connection, copulation 12 conversation 14 communications, correspondence

interdict 3 ban, bar 5 taboo 6 enjoin, forbid 7 barring, censure 8 prohibit, restrain, restrict 9 proscribe 11 forbiddance, prohibition 12 proscription

interdiction 3 ban 7 barring 11 forbiddance, prohibition 12 proscription

interest, interests 4 gain, good, part, weal 5 bonus, hobby, share, stake, touch, yield 6 absorb, affect, behalf, divert, engage, notice, profit, regard 7 attract, benefit, concern, holding, involve, pastime, portion, pursuit, service 8 dividend 9 advantage, attention, avocation, curiosity, preoccupy, suspicion 10 absorption, investment 11 engrossment 13 preoccupation

interested 6 active 7 engaged 8 diverted 9 committed, concerned 10 fascinated, responsive

interesting 7 curious 8 engaging, magnetic, pleasing, riveting, striking 9 absorbing, appealing, arresting 10 attractive, suspicious 11 fascinating, stimulating 12 entertaining

interfere 3 jar, mix 6 butt in, horn in, meddle, rush in, step in 7 counter, intrude 8 conflict 9 frustrate, intercede, interpose, intervene 11 get in the way 14 be a hindrance to, be an obstacle to, be inconsistent, stick in one's oar

interference 3 bar 6 static 8 clashing, conflict, friction, invasion, meddling 9 collision, hindrance, intrusion 12 interception, interruption, intervention

interfere with 6 hinder, impede, thwart 7 disrupt 9 interrupt

interim **7** stopgap **8** interval, meantime, temporal **9** interlude, temporary, tentative **10** pro tempore **11** provisional

interior **4** bush **5** inner **6** inmost, inside, inward **8** internal **9** backwoods, heartland, innermost, upcountry **10** hinterland

Interiors
director: **10** Woody Allen
cast: **10** E G Marshall **11** Diane Keaton **12** Marybeth Hurt **13** Geraldine Page **15** Kristin Griffith **16** Maureen Stapleton
screenplay: **10** Woody Allen

interject **5** put in **6** inject, insert, slip in **7** force in, sneak in, throw in **9** interpose, introduce **11** interpolate

interjection **2** ah, er, lo, oh, ow, um **3** aha, cry, fie, hey, huh, ugh, wow **4** ahem, alas, darn, dear, drat, egad, gosh, heck, jeez, oops, ouch, phew, rats **5** aside, golly, zowie **6** eureka, hooray, hurrah, hurray **7** gee-whiz, jeepers **9** insertion **11** ejaculation, exclamation **13** interpolation, interposition

interlace **3** mix **4** knit, link **5** braid, plait, twine, twist, weave **7** wreathe **9** alternate **10** intertwine, interweave **11** intersperse

interlaced **5** woven **6** linked, twined **7** braided, knitted, plaited, twisted **8** entwined, latticed, wreathed **9** interknit **10** interwoven **11** intertwined **12** interspersed

interlocutor **8** minstrel **9** converser, dialogist **12** interrogator **14** man in the middle

interlope **6** invade, meddle **7** intrude, obtrude **8** encroach, infringe, trespass **9** interfere

interloper **7** invader, meddler **8** intruder, outsider **10** interferer, trespasser **11** gatecrasher **15** persona non grata

interlude **5** break, event, letup, pause **6** recess **7** episode, respite **8** incident, interval **12** intermission **14** breathing spell

intermediary **6** midway, umpire **7** referee **8** bridging, mediator **9** go-between, inbetween, mediating, middleman **10** arbitrator **11** adjudicator, arbitrating

intermediate **3** mid **4** fair, mean, so-so **6** median, medium, middle, midway **7** average, halfway, mediate, midmost **8** mediocre, middling, moderate **11** intervening

interment **6** burial **7** funeral **10** entombment, inhumation

Intermezzo
director: **13** Gregory Ratoff
cast: **8** Edna Best **12** Leslie Howard **13** Cecil Kellaway, Ingrid Bergman

interminable **6** prolix **7** endless **8** infinite, unending **9** boundless, ceaseless, incessant, limitless, perpetual, unlimited **10** continuous, longwinded **11** illimitable **12** longdrawn-out

intermingle **3** mix **4** fuse **5** blend, merge, mix up, unite **6** commix **7** combine **8** emulsify, intermix **9** commingle, interfuse, interlace **10** amalgamate, homogenize, interblend **12** conglomerate

intermission **3** gap **4** halt, rest, stop **5** break, pause **6** hiatus, recess **7** interim **8** interval, stoppage **9** interlude **10** suspension

intermittent **6** fitful **8** on and off, periodic, sporadic **9** irregular, recurrent, spasmodic **10** occasional **13** discontinuous **15** on-again-off-again

intermix **3** mix **5** blend, cross, mix in **6** mingle **10** crossbreed, interbreed **11** intermingle, intersperse

intern **6** commit, detain **7** confine, impound **8** imprison, restrain

internal **5** inner, state **6** inmost **8** domestic, interior **9** executive, political, sovereign **12** governmental **14** administrative

international **9** worldwide **12** cosmopolitan

international affairs
god of: **6** Sancus **10** Dius Fidius, Semo Sancus

internment **9** detention **10** commitment, impounding **11** confinement **12** imprisonment

inter nos **16** between ourselves

interpolate **3** add **5** put in **6** inject, insert, work in **7** implant, intrude, stick in, throw in, wedge in **8** sandwich **9** insinuate, interject, interlard, interline, intervene, introduce **11** intercalate, intersperse

interpose **6** butt in, impose, inject, insert, meddle, step in **7** intrude, mediate, obtrude **9** arbitrate, insinuate, intercede, interfere, interject, interrupt, intervene, negotiate **11** come between, interpolate

interpret **3** see **4** read, take **6** accept, define, render, reword **7** clarify, explain, make out, restate, unravel **8** construe, decipher **9** elucidate, explicate, figure out, make clear, puzzle out, translate **10** account for, paraphrase, understand

interpretation **7** reading, version **8** analysis **9** rendition **10** commentary **11** explanation **12** construction

interpreter **7** analyst **9** explainer **10** translator **11** commentator

interrelated **9** companion, connected **10** compatible, correlated **13** complementary, correspondent, corresponding

interrelation **10** connection **11** association, correlation **12** relationship

interrogate **3** ask **4** test **5** grill, probe, query **7** examine **8** question **9** catechize **11** investigate **12** crossexamine **18** give the third degree

interrogation **4** quiz **5** probe, query **7** inquiry **8** grilling, querying, question, quizzing **9** catechism, inquiring **11** examination, inquisition, questioning

interrupt **4** stop **5** sever **7** cut in on, disjoin, disturb **8** break off **9** break in on, intersect, punctuate **10** disconnect **11** discontinue **13** interfere with

interrupted **6** broken, cut off, halted **7** checked, stalled, stopped **8** arrested, broke off, deferred **9** broken off, disturbed, suspended **11** broke in upon, intercepted **12** discontinued

interruption **3** gap **4** halt, rift, stop **5** break, pause **6** hiatus, lacuna **9** hindrance, interlude **11** obstruction **12** interference, intermission **13** disconnection, discontinuity

inter se **15** among themselves **17** between themselves

intersect **4** meet **5** cross **6** bisect, divide **7** overlap **8** crosscut, transect, traverse **9** cut across **10** crisscross

intersection **6** corner **8** crossing, junction **10** crossroads **11** interchange

intersperse 3 dot, mix **5** strew **6** mingle, pepper **7** bestrew, scatter, wedge in **8** disperse, intermix, sprinkle **9** broadcast, interfuse, interject, interlard, interpose **11** intercalate, interpolate

interstice 4 slit, slot **5** crack, space **7** opening, orifice **8** aperture, interval

intertwine 4 lace **5** braid, plait, twine, twist, weave **7** entwine **8** entangle **9** interlace

interval 3 gap **4** gulf, rest, rift **5** break, cleft, pause, space, spell **6** breach, hiatus, recess, season **7** interim, opening **9** interlude **10** interspace, separation **12** intermission, interruption

intervene 4 pass **6** befall, butt in, step in **7** break in, intrude, mediate **9** arbitrate, intercede, interfere, interpose, interrupt, take place **10** come to pass **11** come between

intervention 9 butting in, intrusion, mediation **10** breaking in, stepping in **11** arbitration **12** intercession, interference **13** interposition **14** intermediation

interview 4 chat, talk **6** parley **7** meeting **8** audience **10** conference, evaluation, round table **11** questioning **12** consultation, conversation

interweave 3 mix **4** fuse, join, knit, lace, link **5** blend, braid, plait, twine, twist **6** splice **7** wreathe **9** interlace, interknit **10** intertwine **11** intersperse

intestinal 5 inner **7** enteric **8** internal, visceral

intestines 4 guts **6** bowels **7** insides, viscera **8** entrails

in the air 2 up **5** above, aloft **7** skyward **8** all about, in the sky, overhead **10** everywhere **11** in the clouds

in the doghouse 9 in bad odor **10** in disfavor, in disgrace, in ill favor **11** in disrepute

in the end 6 one day **7** finally **8** sometime **10** eventually, ultimately **13** sooner or later **17** in the course of time
French: 5 enfin

in the family
French: 9 en famille

in the first place
Latin: 8 imprimis

in the future
Latin: 8 in futuro
Spanish: 6 manana

In the Heat of the Night
director: 13 Norman Jewison
cast: 8 Lee Grant **10** Rod Steiger **11** Warren Oates **13** Sidney Poitier (Virgil Tibbs)
score: 11 Quincy Jones
Oscar for: 5 actor (Steiger) **7** picture **10** screenplay

in the know 9 cognizant **11** on the inside **13** fully informed, knowledgeable **23** having inside information

in the manner of
French: 3 a la **7** a la mode

in the matter of
Latin: 4 in re

in the meantime
Latin: 9 ad interim

in the middle of things
Latin: 11 in medias res

in the midst of 5 among **7** amongst **12** surrounded by **13** in the middle of

in the nature of things
Latin: 13 in rerum natura

in the neighborhood of 6 almost, around, nearly **7** close to **9** generally, just about **10** more or less, not far from **13** approximately **15** in the vicinity of

in the place cited
Latin: 6 loc cit **10** loco citato

in the place of a parent
Latin: 14 in loco parentis

in the same manner that
Latin: 7 quo modo

in the same place
Latin: 4 ibid **6** ibidem

in the state in which
Latin: 10 in statu quo

in the style of
French: 7 a la mode

in the very act of committing the crime
Latin: 18 in flagrante delicto

in the vicinity of 4 near **6** almost, around, nearly **7** close to **9** just about **10** more or less, not far from **13** approximately **19** in the neighborhood of

in the way
French: 6 de trop

in the whole
Latin: 6 in toto

in the work cited
Latin: 5 op cit **11** opere citato

in the year of the reign
Latin: 9 anno regni

in the year of the world
Latin: 9 anno mundi

In This House of Brede
author: 11 Rumer Godden

in this sign shalt thou conquer
Latin: 16 in hoc signo vinces
motto of: 19 Constantine the Great
from vision of: **5** cross

intimacy 5 amity **6** caring, warmth **8** dearness, fondness **9** affection, closeness **10** chumminess, endearment, fraternity, lovemaking, tenderness **11** brotherhood, camaraderie, familiarity **12** friendliness

intimate 3 pal **4** chum, dear, deep, hint **5** bosom, buddy, close, crony, imply, rumor **6** allude, direct **7** guarded, private, special, suggest **8** detailed, familiar, indicate, personal, profound, thorough **9** cherished, confidant, firsthand, innermost, insinuate **12** confidential
French: 6 intime

intimately 7 closely **8** secretly, very well **9** privately **10** familiarly, personally **11** essentially **13** intrinsically **14** confidentially

intimation 4 clue, hint, sign **5** rumor **7** inkling, portent **8** allusion, innuendo **10** indication, suggestion **11** insinuation **13** veiled comment

Intimations of Immortality
author: 17 William Wordsworth

intime 4 cozy **8** intimate

in time 6 before, sooner **7** earlier **9** before now, in advance **10** beforehand, eventually **11** ahead of time **13** before the fact, sooner or later

intimidate 3 cow **5** alarm, bully, daunt, scare **6** coerce, menace, subdue **7** buffalo, terrify **8** browbeat, frighten **9** terrorize

intimidated 5 cowed, fazed **6** scared **7** crushed, daunted, subdued **10** browbeaten, frightened, terrorized

intimidation 7 tyranny **8** bullying, coercion **9** despotism **11** browbeating, terrorizing, tyrannizing **12** scare tactics

intimidator 5 bully **6** despot **7** coercer **9** oppressor, tormenter, tormentor **10** browbeater

into **2** in, to **5** among **6** inside, toward, within **7** against

intolerable **7** hateful, racking **9** abhorrent, agonizing, excessive, loathsome, torturous **10** abominable, outrageous, unbearable **11** unendurable **12** excruciating, insufferable, unreasonable **13** insupportable

intolerance **4** bias **6** racism **7** bigotry **8** weak spot **9** no stomach, prejudice **10** chauvinism, xenophobia **12** low tolerance **16** hypersensitivity, narrow-mindedness

Intolerance
director: **10** D W Griffith
cast: **8** Mae Marsh **11** Lillian Gish **12** Robert Harron **17** Constance Talmadge

intolerant **7** bigoted, hostile, jealous **9** fanatical, parochial, resentful, sectarian **10** prejudiced, xenophobic **11** mistrustful **12** chauvinistic, closed-minded, narrow-minded

intonation **4** tone **5** pitch **6** accent **8** chanting **10** modulation, inflection

intone **3** hum, say **4** song **5** chant, croon, drawl, mouth, speak, utter, voice **6** murmur, recite **8** intonate, modulate, singsong, vocalize **9** enunciate, pronounce **10** articulate

in toto **5** in all, uncut **6** entire, wholly **7** totally **8** as a whole, entirely, outright **10** completely, in the whole, unabridged **11** all together, uncondensed

intoxicant **3** gin, rum **4** beer, grog, wine **5** booze, drink **6** liquor, tipple, whisky **7** alcohol, spirits, whiskey **8** cocktail, highball **9** inebriant

intoxicated **4** high, rapt **5** drunk, oiled, tight, tipsy **6** bombed, elated, loaded, stewed, stinko, stoned, zonked **7** drunken, exalted, smashed, wrecked **9** delighted, enchanted, entranced, plastered **10** enthralled, inebriated, infatuated, in one's cups **11** exhilarated, transported

intoxicating **4** hard **5** heady **6** potent **7** elating **9** alcoholic, spiritous **11** inebriating **12** exhilarating

intoxication **3** joy **5** bliss **7** elation, rapture **8** euphoria **9** poisoning, tipsiness **10** excitement, insobriety **11** drunkenness, inebriation **12** befuddlement, stupefaction

intractable **6** mulish, ornery, unruly **7** froward, willful **8** obdurate, perverse, stubborn **9** fractious, obstinate **10** headstrong, inflexible, refractory **11** unmalleable **12** contumacious, incorrigible, ungovernable, unmanageable **14** hard to cope with, uncontrollable

intransigent **7** diehard **8** obdurate, stubborn **9** steadfast, unmovable **10** inflexible, iron-willed, unyielding **11** intractable, unbudgeable **14** uncompromising

intrepid **4** bold **5** brave **6** daring, heroic **7** doughty, valiant **8** fearless, resolute, valorous **9** audacious, dauntless **10** courageous, undismayed **11** adventurous

intrepidity **4** guts **5** spunk, valor **6** mettle **7** bravery, courage **8** backbone **9** fortitude, sangfroid **12** fearlessness **13** dauntlessness

intricacy **10** complexity **11** involvement **12** complication, entanglement **15** complicatedness

intricate **6** knotty, tricky **7** complex, devious, tangled **8** involved **9** entangled **11** complicated

intrigue **3** spy **4** fire, plot **5** amour **6** absorb, arrest, scheme **7** attract, collude, knavery, romance **8** conspire, enthrall, scheming **9** fascinate, machinate, titillate **10** conspiracy, love affair **11** machination **13** double-dealing **15** interest greatly, tickle one's fancy

intriguer **7** cheater, plotter, schemer **8** conniver, finagler **9** trickster **10** machinator, wirepuller **11** conspirator, Machiavelli, manipulator

intriguing **8** engaging, exciting **9** absorbing, beguiling **11** captivating, enthralling, fascinating, interesting

intrinsic **5** basic, per se **6** inborn, inbred, innate, native **7** natural **8** inherent **9** essential, ingrained **10** indigenous, underlying **11** fundamental

introduce **3** add **4** show, urge **5** begin, offer, put in, start **6** create, expose, import, inform, infuse, insert **7** advance, bring in, kick off, lead off, present, propose, sponsor, throw in **8** acquaint, initiate, lead into **9** establish, institute, interject, interpose, make known, originate, recommend **10** put forward **11** familiarize, interpolate

introduction **6** change **7** novelty, opening, preface, prelude **8** foreword, preamble, prologue **9** insertion, precursor **10** bringing in, conducting, innovation, ushering in **11** instituting, institution

introductory **7** initial **9** beginning, prefatory **10** initiatory, precursory **11** acquainting, preliminary **13** get-acquainted

introspection **8** brooding **10** meditation, reflection, rumination **12** deliberation, self-analysis, self-scrutiny **13** contemplation, soul-searching **15** self-examination, self-observation, self-questioning

introspective **7** pensive **10** reflective **13** contemplative, lost in thought

introversion **7** reserve **8** brooding **10** constraint, diffidence, withdrawal **13** introspection

introvert **5** loner **7** brooder, thinker **13** contemplative, private person

introverted **3** shy **5** stiff **8** reserved **9** inhibited, repressed, withdrawn **10** antisocial, restrained **13** inner-directed, introspective

intrude **4** push **6** butt in, impose, meddle, thrust **7** obtrude **8** encroach, trespass **9** interfere, interlope, interpose, intervene

intruder **10** encroacher, interferer, interloper, intervener, trespasser **11** gate-crasher

Intruder in the Dust
author: **15** William Faulkner

intrusive **4** nosy **5** pushy **6** prying, snoopy **8** in the way, invasive **9** hindering, obtrusive, officious, unwelcome **10** meddlesome **11** impertinent, interfering, interruptive

intuition **5** flash, hunch **7** insight, surmise **8** instinct **9** guesswork, telepathy **10** sixth sense **11** second sight **12** clairvoyance, precognition

intuitive **6** inborn, inbred, innate, native **7** natural, psychic **10** telepathic **11** clairvoyant, instinctive, intuitional, nonrational **12** extrasensory

Inuit *see* **6** Eskimo

inundate **4** glut **5** drown, flood, swamp **6** deluge, drench, engulf **8** load down, overcome, overflow, saturate, submerge **9** overwhelm **10** overburden, overspread

inundation **4** glut **5** flood **6** deluge **9** avalanche

in unison **5** as one **8** in chorus **9** all at once **11** all together

inure **5** adapt, steel, train **6** adjust, custom, harden, season, temper **7** toughen **8** accustom **9** acclimate, get used to, habituate **10** discipline, naturalize, strengthen **11** acclimatize, desensitize, familiarize **12** become used to **15** learn to live with **16** become hardened to

in use **8** employed **9** operating **11** functioning, operational

in vacuo **9** in a vacuum **11** in isolation

invade **5** flood, limit **6** assail, attack, engulf, infect, infest **7** assault, overrun, violate **8** permeate, restrict, strike at, trespass **9** intrude on, march into, penetrate

invader **6** raider **8** attacker, intruder, marauder **9** aggressor, assailant **10** trespasser

invalid **4** null, sick, void, weak **5** false **6** ailing, infirm, sickly, unwell **7** amputee, cripple, unsound, useless **8** disabled, not valid, nugatory, weakened **9** enfeebled, forceless, illogical, paralytic, powerless, worthless **10** dead letter, fallacious, paraplegic **11** debilitated, ineffective, inoperative, unsupported **12** unconvincing **13** incapacitated, unsupportable **14** good-for-nothing, valetudinarian

invalidate **5** annul **6** cancel, refute, repeal, weaken **7** nullify, vitiate **8** abrogate, make void, undercut **9** discredit, undermine **11** countermand

invalidation **7** voiding **9** annulment **10** abrogation **12** cancellation **13** nullification

invaluable **4** rare **6** choice **9** priceless **11** beyond price, inestimable

invariable **7** uniform **8** constant **9** immutable, unfailing, unvarying **10** changeless, consistent, unchanging, unwavering **11** unalterable, undeviating **12** unchangeable

invariably **4** ever **6** always **7** forever **9** every time, uniformly **10** all the time, constantly **11** perpetually, universally **15** in every instance **16** without exception

invasion **4** raid **5** foray **6** attack, breach, inroad, sortie **7** assault **8** trespass **9** incursion, intrusion, onslaught **10** aggression, juggernaut, usurpation **11** penetration **12** encroachment, infiltration, infringement, overstepping

Invasion of the Body Snatchers
director:
1956 version: **9** Don Siegel
1978 version: **13** Philip Kaufman
cast:
1956 version: **10** Dana Wynter, Larry Gates **11** King Donovan **13** Kevin McCarthy
1978 version: **11** Brooke Adams **12** Jeff Goldblum, Leonard Nimoy **16** Donald Sutherland

invective **4** rant **5** venom **6** insult **7** censure, railing, sarcasm **8** diatribe **9** contumely **10** execration, harsh words, revilement **11** verbal abuse **12** billingsgate, denunciation, vilification, vituperation

inveigh **4** rail, slam **5** abuse, knock, scold **6** rebuke, revile **7** censure, put down, run down, upbraid **8** belittle, denounce, harangue, reproach **9** castigate, criticize, dress down **10** vituperate

inveigh against **5** abuse **6** defame, rail at, revile **7** protest **8** denounce **9** castigate

inveigle **4** coax, lure **5** tempt, trick **6** allure, cajole, entice, rope in, seduce, suck in **7** beguile, ensnare, flatter, mislead, wheedle **8** persuade, soft-soap **9** bamboozle, sweet-talk

inveiglement **7** coaxing **8** cajolery, flattery **9** wheedling **10** enticement, persuasion **13** blandishments

invent **4** coin **6** cook up, create, devise, make up **7** concoct, develop, fashion, think up, trump up **8** conceive, contrive **9** conjure up, fabricate, formulate, originate **10** come up with **11** put together

invented **6** fabled, made up **8** fabulous, fanciful, mythical **9** fantastic, imaginary, legendary **10** apocryphal, fictitious

Inventing America
author: **10** Garry Wills

invention **3** lie **4** fake, sham **6** design, device, gadget **7** fiction, forgery, machine **8** creation, trumpery **9** apparatus, discovery, fertility, implement, ingenuity, inventing **10** concoction, creativity, production **11** contraption, contrivance, development, fabrication, imagination, originality, origination **13** dissimulation, inventiveness, prevarication **15** resourcefulness

invention
god of: **6** Hermes

inventive **6** bright, clever **9** ingenious **11** resourceful

inventiveness **9** ingenuity **10** cleverness, creativity **11** imagination, orgininality **15** imaginativeness

inventor **5** maker **6** author **7** creator, deviser **8** engineer, producer, tinkerer **9** architect, generator, innovator **10** discoverer, originator
of air brake: **12** Westinghouse
of automobile: **7** Daimler
of barometer: **10** Torricelli
of camera: **7** Eastman
of cotton gin: **7** Whitney
of cylinder lock: **4** Yale
of dynamite: **5** Nobel
of elevator: **4** Otis
of gyrocompass: **6** Sperry
of helicopter: **8** Sikorsky
of linotype: **12** Mergenthaler
of machine gun: **7** Gatling
of movable type: **9** Gutenberg
of phonograph, incandescent lamp, mimeograph, dictating machine, fluoroscope: **6** Edison
of photography: **6** Niepce, Talbot **8** Daguerre
of reaper: **9** McCormick
of radio: **7** Marconi
of revolver: **4** Colt
of rocket engine: **7** Goddard
of sewing machine: **4** Howe
of sleeping car: **7** Pullman
of steamboat: **6** Fulton
of steam engine: **4** Watt
of steam locomotive: **10** Stephenson
of telegraph: **5** Morse
of telephone: **4** Bell
of wireless telegraph: **7** Marconi
of vulcanized rubber: **8** Goodyear

inventory **4** roll **5** goods, index, stock **6** roster, supply **7** catalog **8** register, schedule **9** stock list **10** accounting **11** merchandise, stock-taking

inverse **8** backward, contrary, converse, indirect, inverted, opposite, reversed **11** back to front, bottom-to-top, right-to-left

inversion **7** turning **8** reversal **9** ectropion, turnabout **10** transposal **12** resupination **13** transposition

inverted **7** inverse **8** bottom up **10** upside-down

invest **4** fill, garb, give **5** adorn, allot, array, color, cover, dress, endow, imbue **6** clothe, devote, enable, enrich, infuse, supply **7** appoint, license **8** set aside **9** apportion

investigate **4** sift **5** probe, query, study **6** survey **7** analyze, dissect, explore, inspect **8** ask about, look into, pore over, question, research **9** anatomize, delve into **10** scrutinize

investigation **5** probe, study **6** review, search, survey **7** anatomy, inquiry **8** analysis, research, scrutiny **10** dissection, inspection **11** fact-finding

investigator **6** shamus **7** analyst, gumshoe **8** examiner, inquirer, observer **9** detective **10** private eye, researcher

investment **4** ante, risk **5** share, stake **7** venture **8** offering

inveterate **6** inured **7** adamant, chronic, diehard **8** constant, habitual, hardened **9** confirmed, incurable, ingrained, recurrent, steadfast **10** continuous, deep-rooted, deep-seated **11** established **12** long-standing, unregenerate **15** unreconstructed

invidious **7** vicious **8** spiteful **9** insulting, malicious, offensive, rancorous, resentful, slighting **10** malevolent

invigorate **4** stir **5** brace, cheer, liven, pep up, renew, rouse, zip up **6** jazz up, vivify **7** animate, enliven, fortify, refresh, restore **8** energize, vitalize **9** stimulate **10** exhilarate, rejuvenate, strengthen

invigorated **6** braced **7** revived **8** animated, restored, vivified **9** energized, full of pep, quickened, refreshed **10** stimulated **11** rejuvenated **12** strengthened **17** full of vim and vigor

invigorating **7** bracing **9** animating, healthful **10** energizing, enlivening, quickening, refreshing, vitalizing **11** restorative, stimulating **12** rejuvenating **13** strengthening

invincible **10** unbeatable **11** impregnable, indomitable, insuperable **12** invulnerable, undefeatable **13** irrepressible, unconquerable **14** insurmountable

in vino veritas **18** in wine there is truth

inviolable **4** holy, pure **6** chaste, divine, sacred, secret **7** blessed **8** hallowed **9** dedicated, inviolate, undefiled **10** sacrosanct **11** consecrated, impregnable, trustworthy **12** impenetrable, invulnerable, unassailable **13** incorruptible

inviolate **4** pure **6** intact, sacred, secret **8** hallowed **9** unaltered, unchanged, undefiled, unstained **10** inviolable, sacrosanct

invisible **6** covert, hidden, unseen, veiled **7** obscure **9** concealed, unseeable **10** unapparent **13** imperceptible, undiscernible

Invisible Man, The
author: **7** H G Wells
character: **4** Hall **6** Dr Kemp, Marvel **7** Griffin **11** Colonel Ayde

invitation **3** bid **4** call, lure **5** offer **7** bidding, summons **8** open door **9** challenge **10** allurement, enticement, inducement, temptation **12** solicitation

invite **3** bid **4** call, lure, urge **5** tempt **6** entice, induce **7** attract, solicit, welcome **9** encourage

inviting **4** warm **8** alluring, charming, engaging, enticing, magnetic, tempting **9** appealing, welcoming **10** attractive, intriguing

invocation **4** plea **6** appeal, orison, prayer **8** petition **9** summoning **12** supplication

in vogue **2** in **6** modish **7** a la mode, current, in style, stylish **9** in fashion **11** fashionable **12** le dernier cri

invoke **3** beg, use **5** apply **6** ask for, employ **7** beseech, conjure, entreat, implore, pray for **8** call upon, petition, resort to **9** appeal for, call forth, implement, importune, introduce **10** supplicate

involuntary **6** forced, reflex **7** coerced **8** unchosen, unwilled **9** automatic, reluctant, unwilling **10** compulsory **11** inadvertent, instinctive, spontaneous, unconscious **13** unintentional **15** against one's will

involve **5** imply, mix up **6** commit, engage, entail, wrap up **7** contain, embroil, include **8** comprise, depend on, entangle **9** implicate, preoccupy

involved **7** complex, engaged, mixed up, wound up **8** absorbed, immersed **9** committed, elaborate, embroiled, engrossed, entangled, intricate, wrapped up **10** implicated **11** complicated, preoccupied

involve deeply **5** mix up **6** absorb, commit, wrap up **7** embroil, engross, immerse **8** entangle **9** implicate, preoccupy

invulnerable **10** formidable, invincible, unbeatable **11** impregnable, indomitable, insuperable **12** imperishable, inexpugnable, unassailable, undefeatable **13** unconquerable, undestroyable

inward, inwards **5** inner **6** mental, toward **7** going in, ingoing, private **8** incoming, interior, inwardly, personal **9** spiritual, the inside **10** interiorly

in what way
Latin: **7** quo modo

in which case **4** then, when **6** thence **9** whereupon **11** accordingly **12** at which point

In Which We Serve
director: **9** David Lean **10** Noel Coward
script: **10** Noel Coward
cast: **9** John Mills **10** Noel Coward **12** Bernard Miles, Celia Johnson

in wine there is truth
Latin: **13** in vino veritas

Io
father: **7** Inachus
husband: **9** Telegonus
loved by: **4** Zeus
son: **7** Epaphus
changed into: **6** heifer
color of heifer: **5** white
guarded by: **5** Argus
pursecuted by: **6** gadfly
sent by: **4** Hera
corresponds to: **4** Isis

Iobates
king of: **5** Lycia
son-in-law: **7** Proteus
commissioned to kill: **11** Bellerophon

Iodama
priestess of: **6** Athena

iodine
chemical symbol: **1** I

Iolanthe
author: **9** W S Gilbert

Iolaus
father: **8** Iphicles

mother: **10** Automedusa
uncle: **8** Hercules
companion: **8** Hercules
charioteer of: **8** Hercules

Iole
father: **7** Eurytus
loved by: **8** Heracles
husband: **6** Hyllus

Ion
author: **9** Euripides
character: **6** Apollo, Athene, Crensa, Xuthus

Iormungandr *see* **11** Jormungandr

iota **3** bit, jot **4** atom, spot, whit **5** shred, spark, speck **7** smidgin **8** particle **9** scintilla **11** faint degree, small amount **15** tiniest quantity

IOU **4** chit, debt, note **10** obligation **12** promise to pay **14** promissory note

Iowa *see box*

Iowa, Ioway
language family: **6** Siouan
location: **4** Iowa
related to: **3** Oto **8** Missouri

Ioxus
father: **10** Melanippus
grandfather: **7** Theseus
grandmother: **8** Perigune

Iphicles
father: **10** Amphitryon
mother: **7** Alcmene
half-brother: **8** Hercules
son: **6** Iolaus

Iphidamas
father: **7** Antenor
mother: **6** Theano
killed by: **9** Agamemnon

Iphigenia
father: **9** Agamemnon
mother: **12** Clytemnestra
brother: **7** Orestes
sister: **7** Electra **12** Chrysothemis
saved by: **7** Artemis

Iphigenia in Aulis
author: **9** Euripides
character: **8** Achilles, Menelaus **9** Agamemnon **12** Clytemnestra

Iphigenia in Tauris
author: **9** Euripides
character: **5** Thoas **6** Athena **7** Orestes, Pylades

Iowa
abbreviation: **2** IA
nickname: **7** Hawkeye
capital/largest city: **9** Des Moines
others: **4** Ames **5** Amana, Mason, Perry **6** Algona, Keokuk, Le Mars, Marion, Newton **7** Anamosa, Clinton, Dubuque, Ft Dodge, Ottumwa **8** Waterloo **9** Davenport, Ft Madison, Marquette, Mason City, Sioux City **10** Burlington, Cedar Falls, West Branch **11** Cedar Rapids **12** Marshalltown **13** Council Bluffs
college: **3** Coe **5** Corot, Drake, Loras **7** Cornell, Parsons **8** Grinnell, Wartburg **12** Iowa Wesleyan
explorer: **6** Joliet **7** Jolliet **9** Marquette **13** Lewis and Clark
feature: **13** Amana Colonies **17** first apple orchard
church: **11** Little Brown
national historical site: **13** Herbert Hoover
national monument: **12** Effigy Mounds
state fair: **4** Iowa
tribe: **3** Fox **4** Sauc **5** Ioway, Omaha **9** Muscoutin, Winnebago
people: **7** Hawkeye **9** Grant Wood **10** John L Lewis **11** Billy Sunday **15** Buffalo Bill Cody, Charles Ringling
lake: **5** Clear, Storm **6** Spirit **7** Rathbun **11** East Okoboji, West Okoboji
land rank: **11** twenty-fifth
president: **13** Herbert Hoover
river: **4** Iowa **5** Cedar, Floyd, Skunk **8** Big Sioux, Missouri **9** Des Moines **11** Mississippi, Nishnabotna **12** Wapsipinicon
state admission: **11** twenty-ninth
state bird: **16** eastern goldfinch
state flower: **8** wild rose
state motto: **45** Our Liberties We Prize and Our Rights We Will Maintain
state song: **13** The Song of Iowa
state tree: **3** oak

Iphigenie en Aulide
also: **16** Iphigenia in Aulis
opera by: **5** Gluck
character: **7** Artemis, Calchas **8** Achilles **9** Agamemnon **12** Clytemnestra

Iphigenie en Tauride
also: **17** Iphigenia in Tauris
opera by: **5** Gluck
character: **5** Diana, Thoas (King of Scythia) **7** Orestes, Pylades **9** the Furies

Iphitus
father: **7** Eurytus
sister: **4** Iole

Ipoctonus
epithet of: **8** Hercules
means: **10** worm-killer

ipse dixit **15** he himself said it **21** assertion without proof

ipsissima verba **8** verbatim **12** the very words

ipso facto **15** by the fact itself **24** by the very nature of the deed

ipso jure **14** by the law itself **16** by operation of law

Iraklion
capital of: **5** Crete

Iran *see box*

Iraq *see box*

irascibility **8** acerbity **9** bad temper, crossness, testiness **10** crabbiness, crankiness **11** peevishness, waspishness **12** irritability **16** cantankerousness

irascible **5** cross, testy **6** cranky, grumpy, ornery, touchy **7** grouchy, peevish, waspish **8** choleric **9** irritable, splenetic **10** ill-humored **11** bad-tempered, hot-tempered, intractable **12** cantankerous

irate **3** mad **5** angry, livid, rabid, riled, vexed **6** galled **7** angered, annoyed, enraged, furious **8** burned up **9** indignant, irritated **10** infuriated

ire **4** fury, rage **5** anger, wrath **6** choler **7** outrage, umbrage **8** vexation **10** resentment **11** indignation

Ireland *see box, p. 506*

Ireland forever
Gaelic: **11** Erin go bragh

I Remember Mama
director: **13** George Stevens
based on play by: **13** John Van Druten

Irish Mythology
cats: **8** Kilkenny
fairies: **4** Side
god of love/beauty/youth: **7** Angus Og
god of poetry/eloquence: **4** Ogma
god of sea: **8** Manannan
gods: **14** Tuatha De Danann
hero: **10** Cuchulainn
invaders/ancestors: **9** Milesians
king: **4** Bres **5** Ronan **9** Conchobar **10** Matholwych
king of gods: **4** Finn **5** Fionn
pirate/demon: **8** Fomorian
sea goddess: **3** Ler, Lir
spirit: **4** Puca **5** Pooka
corresponds to British: **4** Puck

some, irritating, nettlesome **11** troublesome

iron
chemical symbol: **2** Fe

Iron Age
period of: **4** time
followed age of: **6** Bronze

ironclad **5** fixed **6** strict **9** immutable, permanent **10** inexorable, inflexible, rigoristic, unchanging **11** irrevocable, unalterable **12** irreversible, unchangeable, unmodifiable

Iron Horse
nickname of: **9** Lou Gehrig

ironic, ironical **3** odd **5** funny, weird **6** biting **7** abusive, caustic, curious, cutting, mocking, strange **8** derisive, sardonic, sneering, stinging **9** facetious, insincere, pretended, sarcastic **10** surprising, unexpected **11** implausible, incongruous **12** inconsistent **13** contradictory

irons **5** bonds **6** chains **7** fetters, presses, smooths **8** manacles, shackles **9** golf clubs, handcuffs **10** restraints

Ironside
character: **7** (Det Sgt) Ed Brown **10** Mark Sanger **11** Fran Belding **12** Eve Whitfield **14** Robert Ironside
cast: **11** Don Galloway, Don Mitchell, Raymond Burr **13** Elizabeth Baur **15** Barbara Anderson

irony **7** mockery, sarcasm **9** absurdity **11** incongruity, indirection **12** contrariness **13** facetiousness **14** implausibility

Iroquoian
tribe: **6** Cayuga, Mohawk, Oneida, Seneca **8** Cherokee, Iroquois, Onandaga **9** Tuscarora **12** Kaniengehaga

Iroquois
language family: **9** Iroquoian
tribe: **6** Cayuga, Mohawk, Oneida, Seneca **8** Onondaga **9** Tuscarora
location: **6** Canada **7** New York **11** Connecticut **13** Massachusetts
leader: **11** Cornplanter, Joseph Brant
formed: **10** Six Nations **19** League of the Iroquois
supernatural force: **6** Orenda
prophet: **10** Ganiodaiyo

Irra
origin: **8** Akkadian
god of: **10** pestilence

irrational **6** absurd **7** foolish, unsound **8** baseless **9** illogical, unfounded **10** ill-advised, unthinking **11** nonsensical, unreasoning **12** unreasonable

irreclaimable **4** lost **6** wicked **7** corrupt, debased **9** abandoned, reprobate **12** disreputable, irredeemable, irreformable **16** beyond redemption

irreconcilable **7** opposed **12** incompatible, inconsistent, intransigent, unadjustable, unappeasable, unbridgeable

irreformable **6** wicked **7** corrupt **9** abandoned, reprobate, shameless **11** unrepentant **12** disreputable **13** irreclaimable

irrefutable **10** undeniable **12** indisputable, not refutable **13** proof positive **14** unquestionable **16** incontrovertible

irrefutably **6** surely **10** definitely, positively, undeniably **12** conclusively, indisputably **13** incontestably **14** unquestionably **16** incontrovertibly

irregular **3** odd **5** bumpy, queer, rough **6** broken, uneven **7** crooked, unusual **8** aberrant, abnormal, improper, peculiar, singular **9** anomalous, desultory, eccentric, haphazard, not smooth, out of line, unaligned, unfitting **10** indecorous, unexpected, unsuitable **12** asymmetrical, unmethodical, unsystematic **13** inappropriate, nonconforming **14** unconventional **16** uncharacteristic

irregularity **7** anomaly **9** asymmetry, deviation **10** aberration, divergence, unevenness **11** abnormality, peculiarity **12** constipation, eccentricity

irrelevant **5** inapt **7** foreign, off base **9** unfitting, unrelated **10** extraneous, immaterial, malapropos, not apropos, not germane **11** impertinent, unconnected **12** nonpertinent **14** beside the point

irreligion **7** atheism **8** apostasy, unbelief **9** disbelief **11** godlessness

irreligious **6** unholy **7** godless, impious, profane, ungodly **8** agnostic **9** atheistic **10** irreverent **11** unbelieving **12** not religious, sacrilegious

irremediable **8** hopeless **9** incurable **11** irreparable **12** beyond remedy

irreparable **9** unfixable **10** remediless **12** irremediable, irreversible **13** beyond redress, uncompensable, uncorrectable

irreplaceable **6** unique **9** essential **13** indispensable

irrepressible **7** vibrant **8** bubbling, galvanic, undamped **9** ebullient **10** boisterous, full of life **11** tempestuous **12** unquenchable **13** unsquelchable **14** uncontrollable, unrestrainable

irreproachable **8** flawless **9** blameless, faultless, stainless, unspotted **10** impeccable, inculpable **11** unblemished **12** above reproof, without fault **13** unimpeachable

irresistible **8** alluring, enticing **9** beckoning, seductive **10** enchanting, superhuman **11** tantalizing **12** overpowering, overwhelming

irresolute **4** weak **6** fickle, unsure **8** doubtful, hesitant, unsteady, wavering **9** faltering, uncertain, undecided, unsettled **10** changeable, hesitating, indecisive, unresolved **11** vacillating

irresolution **5** doubt **9** hesitancy **10** hesitation, indecision

irresponsibility **8** rashness **10** immaturity, imprudence

11 foolishness 12 carelessness, heedlessness, indifference, indiscretion, recklessness 13 unreliability 15 thoughtlessness, undependability
17 untrustworthiness

irresponsible 4 rash 7 foolish 8 careless, immature, reckless 9 imprudent, overhasty 10 capricious, incautious, unreliable 11 harebrained, indifferent, injudicious, thoughtless 12 undependable 13 ill-considered, untrustworthy 14 not responsible, scatterbrained

irresponsible person
French: 14 enfant terrible

irreverence 7 impiety 9 blasphemy, sacrilege
10 irreligion

irreverent 5 saucy 6 brazen 7 impious, profane 8 critical, impudent, sneering 9 debunking, shameless, skeptical, slighting 11 blasphemous, disparaging, irreligious 12 nose-thumbing 13 disrespectful

irrevocable 5 final 10 conclusive 11 unalterable 12 irreversible, unchangeable

irritability 6 spleen 8 acerbity, edginess 9 crossness, huffiness, petulance, testiness 10 crabbiness, crankiness, impatience 11 fretfulness, peevishness, short temper, waspishness
12 irascibility

irritable 5 testy 6 grumpy, touchy 7 fretful, grouchy, peevish, pettish, waspish 8 snappish 9 impatient, irascible 10 ill-humored 11 easily vexed, ill-tempered

irritate 3 irk, vex 5 anger, annoy, chafe, peeve 6 nettle, worsen 7 inflame, provoke 8 make sore 9 aggravate, make angry 10 exasperate

irritated 3 mad, raw 4 sore 5 cross, irked, irate, testy, vexed 6 chafed, crabby, galled, miffed, peeved, piqued, put out 7 annoyed, burning, nettled, peevish 8 burned up, choleric, incensed, inflamed, provoked 9 impatient, irascible 10 aggravated
11 exasperated

irritating 5 acrid, harsh, rough 7 caustic, chafing, galling, irksome, rasping 8 abrasive, annoying 9 provoking, vexatious 10 bothersome
11 infuriating, troublesome
12 exasperating

irritation 6 bother 7 chafing 8 distress, vexation 9 annoyance 10 discomfort
11 irksomeness

irruption 4 raid 5 break, foray 6 inroad 7 upsurge 8 bursting, invasion 9 incursion, intrusion

Irus *see* 7 Arnaeus

Irving, John
author of: 20 The Hotel New Hampshire 23 The World According to Garp

Irving, Washington
author of: 10 Salmagundi 12 Rip Van Winkle 13 The Sketch Book 23 The Legend of Sleepy Hollow

Isaac
father: 7 Abraham
mother: 5 Sarah
brother: 7 Ishmael
wife: 7 Rebekah
son: 4 Esau 5 Jacob
birthplace: 5 Gerar
burial place: 9 Machpelah
blessed: 5 Jacob
sacrificed at: 6 Moriah

Isaac of York
character in: 7 Ivanhoe
author: 5 Scott

Isabella
character in: 17 Measure for Measure
author: 11 Shakespeare

Isaiah
means: 12 Jehovah saves
father: 4 Amoz
son: 11 Shearzashub
18 Maharshalalhashbaz

Iscariot *see* 5 Judas

Ischepolis
father: 9 Alcathous

Ischys
killed because of: 10 infidelity
loved: 7 Coronis
Coronis loved by: 6 Apollo

Isenstein
origin: 12 Scandinavian
home of: 8 Brunhild
location: 8 Isenland

I serve
German: 7 ich dien
motto of: 13 Prince of Wales

Iseult, Isolde
character in: 16 Arthurian romance

I shall rise again
Latin: 8 resurgam

Ishbosheth
father: 4 Saul
killed by: 6 Baanah, Rechab
burial place: 6 Hebron

Isherwood, Christopher
author of: 13 Berlin Stories 17 Down There on a Visit
character: 11 Sally Bowles

Ishmael
character in: 8 Moby Dick
author: 8 Melville

Ishmael
father: 7 Abraham
mother: 5 Hagar
means: 11 God will hear
brother: 5 Isaac
son: 5 Kedar 7 Kedemah
descendant of: 10 Ishmaelite

Ishtar
also: 7 Mylitta
origin: 8 Assyrian
10 Babylonian
goddess of: 3 war 4 love
queen of: 6 heaven
corresponds to: 6 Inanna
7 Astarte 9 Ashtoreth

Ishum
origin: 8 Akkadian
god of: 4 fire
companion: 4 Irra

Isis
origin: 8 Egyptian
goddess of: 9 fertility
hieroglyphic symbol: 6 throne
husband: 6 Osiris
brother: 6 Osiris
son: 5 Horus
father: 3 Geb, Keb
mother: 3 Nut
horns of: 3 cow
headdress: 9 solar disk
corresponds to: 2 Io

Iskowitz, B Edward Israel
real name of: 11 Eddie Cantor

Islam
adherent: 4 Sufi 5 Shiah 6 Moslem, Muslim, Shiite, Wahabi 7 Sunnite 8 Islamite 9 Mussulman
10 Mohammedan
crusade: 5 Jahad, Jihad
deity: 5 Allah
flight from Mecca: 6 hegira
founder / prophet: 8 Mohammed, Muhammad
holy city: 5 Mecca 6 Medina
other names: 9 Moslemism
13 Mohammedanism
pilgrimage to Mecca: 4 hadj
priest: 4 imam
scripture: 5 Koran

Islamabad
capital of: 8 Pakistan

Islamic 6 Moslem, Muslim
10 Mohammedan

island 4 isle 5 atoll, haven, islet, oasis 6 refuge 7 enclave, retreat, shelter 9 sanctuary

Islands of the Blessed *see* 10 Hesperides

isle, islet 3 ait, cay, key
4 holm 5 islet 6 island

Isle of Cloves *see* 8 Tanzania

Isle of Spice *see* 7 Grenada

Isleta (Tuei)
language family: **6** Pueblo, Tanoan
location: **9** New Mexico, Rio Grande

Ismene
father: **7** Oedipus
mother: **7** Jocasta
uncle: **5** Creon
sister: **8** Antigone
brother: **9** Polynices

isn't that so?
French: **9** n'est-ce pas?
German: **9** nicht wahr?

isolate **6** banish, detach **7** seclude **8** insulate, separate, set apart **9** segregate, sequester **10** disconnect, place apart, quarantine

isolated **4** lone, solo **5** alone, apart **6** cut off, lonely, remote, unique **7** insular, removed **8** detached, secluded, set apart, solitary **9** separated, unrelated **10** segregated **11** out-of-the-way, quarantined, sequestered

isolation **7** privacy **8** solitude **9** aloneness, apartness, hermitism, seclusion **10** desolation, detachment, insularity, insulation, quarantine, separation **11** confinement, segregation **12** separateness

isoptera
class: **8** hexapoda
phylum: **10** arthropoda
group: **7** termite **8** white ant

Ispahan
also: **7** Isfahan **8** Aspadana
location: **4** Iran
capital of: **6** Persia
river: **8** Zayandeh

I Speak for Thaddeus Stevens
author: **15** Elsic Singmaster

I Spy
character: **13** Kelly Robinson **14** Alexander Scott
cast: **9** Bill Cosby **10** Robert Culp
Kelly's cover: **9** tennis pro

Israel
former name: **5** Jacob
means: **12** soldier of God
wrestled with: **5** angel

Israel ***see box***

Israel, tribes of **3** Dan, Gad **4** Levi **5** Asher, Judah **6** Joseph, Reuben, Simeon **7** Zebulun **8** Benjamin, Issachar, Naphtali

Israel-born
Hebrew: **5** sabra

Israelite **3** Jew **6** Hebrew, Jewish, Semite **7** Judaist **8** Hebraist
descended from: **5** Jacob

Israel

other name: **4** Zion **6** Canaan, Yishuv **9** Palestine **12** Promised Land

capital: **9** Jerusalem

largest city: **12** Tel Aviv-Jaffa

others: **4** Acre, Elat, Gaza **5** Eilat, Elath, Haifa, Holon, Jaffa, Jenin **6** Ashdod, Bat Yam, Dimona, Hebron, Nablus **7** Netanya, Rehovot, Tel Aviv **8** Nazareth, Ramallah, Ramat Gan **9** Beersheba, Bene Beraq, Bethlehem, Giv'atayim **10** Pitah Tiqwa **14** Rishon le Ziyyon

school: **6** Hebrew **14** Technion-Israel **26** Weizmann Institute of Science

division: **5** Judea, Negev, Sinai **7** Galilee **8** West Bank **9** Gaza Strip **12** Golan Heights

government:
legislature: **7** Knesset

measure: **3** cab, car, hin, kab, kor **4** bath, ezba, omer, reed **5** cubit, donum, dunam, ephah, ganeh, homer, kaneh

monetary unit: **3** mil **5** agora, agura, pound, pruta **6** agorot, shekel

lake: **5** Huleh **7** Dead Sea **8** Kinneret, Tiberias **12** Sea of Galilee

mountain: **4** Nafh, Sagi **5** Harif, Ramon, Tabor **6** Atzmon, Carmel, Hatira

highest point: **5** Meron **6** Meiron

river: **4** Qarn **5** Faria, Malik, Sareq **6** Hadera, Jordan, Kishon, Qishon, Sarida, Yarkon, Yarmuk **7** Lakhish

sea: **3** Red **4** Dead **7** Galilee **13** Mediterranean

physical feature:
bay: **5** Haifa
desert: **5** Negev, Sinai
gulf: **5** Aqaba
plain: **5** Judea **6** Sharon **7** Zebulun **9** Esdraelon

people: **3** Jew **4** Arab **5** Druze **10** Circassian
ancient: **6** Hebrew
immigrant: **4** olim
Jew born in Israel: **5** sabra
leader: **4** Eban, Meir **5** Begin, Dayan, Herzl, Peres, Rabin **6** Ben-Zvi, Eshkol **7** Sharett **8** Weizmann **9** Ben-Gurion

language: **6** Arabic, French, Hebrew **7** English

religion: **5** Baha'i, Islam **7** Judaism **12** Christianity

place:
church: **13** Holy Sepulcher
gates to Old Jerusalem: **3** New **4** Dung, Zion **5** Jaffa **6** Herod's **8** Damascus **10** St Stephen's
mosque: **13** Dome of the Rock
mount: **4** Zion **6** Olives, Scopus
shrine: **3** Bab **4** Book **11** Wailing Wall, Western Wall **18** Garden of Gethsemane
site of Last Supper: **9** Upper Room
tomb: **9** Sanhedrin **10** King David's
way of sorrows: **11** Via Dolorosa

feature: **14** Dead Sea Scrolls
collective village: **7** kibbutz **9** kibbutzim
cooperative village: **6** moshav **8** moshavim
dance: **4** hora
movement: **7** Zionism
tree: **5** judas
wave of immigration: **5** aliya **6** aliyot

food:
dish: **4** pita **6** hummus **7** falafel

king: **4** Ahab, Elah, Jehu, Omri, Saul **5** David, Hosea, Nadab, Zimri

Issachar
father: **5** Jacob
mother: **4** Leah
brother: **3** Dan, Gad **4** Levi **5** Asher, Judah **6** Joseph, Reuben, Simeon **7** Zebulun **8** Benjamin, Naphtali
sister: **5** Dinah
descendant of: **11** Issacharite

Is Sex Necessary?
author: **7** E B White **12** James Thurber

issuance **8** emission **9** allotment, discharge, emanation **12** dispensation, distribution

issue **4** gush, rise, stem **5** allot, arise, ensue, erupt, go out, heirs, spout, yield **6** emerge, follow, number, result, spring **7** dispute, emanate, flow out, give out, outcome, outflow, pass out, problem, proceed, product, progeny **8** children, dispense, drainage, eruption, granting, heritors, issuance, question **9** circulate, discharge, effluence, grow out of, offspring, posterity, pour forth **10** distribute, outpouring **11** consequence, descendants, publication **12** dispensation, distributing

Istanbul
area: **7** Beyoglu **8** Stamboul
capital of: **6** Turkey
formerly: **9** Byzantium **14** Constantinople
landmark: **10** Hippodrome **11** Hagia Sophia **12** Galata Bridge **14** Bosporus Bridge **26** Palais de la Culture d'Istanbul
mosque: **3** New **8** Mihrimah **9** Yeni Camii **11** Suleymaniye

Italy
also: **8** Hesperia
capital/largest city: **4** Roma, Rome
others: **4** Pisa **5** Genoa, Milan, Padua, Turin, Udine **6** Amalfi, Ancona, Assisi, Naples, Rimini, Savona, Venice, Verona **7** Bologna, Bolzano, Brescia, Catania, Messina, Palermo, Ravenna, Taranto, Trieste **8** Florence
division: **6** Apulia, Latium, Marche, Molise, Umbria, Veneto **7** Abruzzi, Liguria, Tuscany **8** Calabria, Campania, Lombardy, Piedmont **10** Basilicata **12** Valle d'Agosta **13** Emilia-Romagna **17** Trentino-Alto Adige **19** Friuli-Venezia Giulia
independent enclave: **9** San Marino **11** Vatican City
measure: **3** pie **4** orna **5** palma, palmo, punto, salma, stero **6** barile, miglie, moggio, rubbio, tomolo **7** braccio, secchio **8** giornata, quadrato
monetary unit: **4** lira, lire, tara **5** grano, paolo, soldo **6** danaro, denaro, ducato **7** testone **8** zecchino **9** centesini
weight: **5** carat, libra, oncia, pound **6** denaro, libbra
island: **4** Elba **5** Capri, Egadi, Eolie **6** Ischia, Istria, Linosa, Lipari, Sicily, Ustica **7** Aeolian, Trieste, Vulcano **8** Lampione, Sardinia **9** Borromean, Lampedusa, Stromboli **10** Isola Bella **11** Pantelleria
lake: **4** Como, Iseo, Nemi **5** Garda **6** Albano, Lesina, Lugano, Varano **7** Bolsena, Perugia **8** Maggiore **9** Bracciano, Trasimeno
mountain: **4** Alps, Etna, Visa **5** Amaro, Blanc, Corno, Somma **6** Cimone, Ortles **9** Apennines, Dolomites, Maritimes **11** Gennargentu **12** Gran Paradiso **16** Abruzzi Apennines
Alps: **6** Apuane, Carnic, Julian, Otztal **7** Bernina **8** Ligurian **9** Lepontine
volcano: **7** Vulcano **8** Vesuvius **9** Stromboli
highest point: **4** Rosa
river: **2** Po **4** Adda, Agri, Arno, Liri, Nera, Reno, Sele, Taro **5** Adige, Crati, Mannu, Oglio, Parma, Piave, Salso, Stura, Tiber, Tirso **6** Aniene, Belice, Isonzo, Mincio, Ofanto, Panaro, Rapido, Sangro, Simeto, Tanaro, Tevere, Ticino **7** Biferno, Bradano, Chienti, Metauro, Montone, Ombrone, Pescara, Rubicon, Secchia, Trebbia **8** Volturno
sea: **6** Ionian **8** Adriatic, Ligurian **10** Tyrrhenian **13** Mediterranean
physical feature:
bay: **6** Naples
channel: **5** Malta
grotto: **4** Blue
gulf: **5** Gaeta, Genoa **6** Venice **7** Salerno, Taranto **11** Manfredonia
hills of Rome: **7** Caelian, Viminal **8** Aventine, Palatine, Quirinal **9** Esquiline **10** Capitoline
lagoon: **6** Venice
pass: **5** Resia **6** Maloja **7** Bernina, Brenner, Simplon **9** Mont Cenis **13** Saint Gotthard **17** Great Saint Bernard
resort: **14** Italian Riviera
strait: **6** Sicily **7** Messina, Otranto **9** Bonifacio
people: **7** Italian
ancient: **5** Latin, Remus **6** Sabine **7** Lombard, plebian, Romulus **8** Etruscan **9** patrician
architect: **5** Nervi, Ponti, Salvi **6** Vasari **7** Alberti, Guarini, Juvarra, Vignola **8** Ammanati, Bramante, Palladio **9** Borromini, De Sanctis **12** Brunelleschi, Michelangelo
artist: **5** Balla, Carra **6** Batoni, Gaulli, Guardi, Titian **7** Bellini, Chirico, Cimabue, Cortona, Da Vinci, Raphael, Tiepolo, Uccello **8** Carracci, Mantegna, Masaccio, Severini **9** Benvenuti, Canoletto, Giorgione **10** Botticelli, Caravaggio, Modigliani, Tintoretto **11** Buoninsegna, Fra Angelico **12** Michelangelo **13** Giotto Bondone **14** della Francesca
composer: **5** Verdi **7** Bellini, Cavalli, Corelli, Puccini, Rossini, Vivaldi **8** Mascagni, Piccinni **9** Donizetti, Scarlatti **10** Monteverdi, Palestrina **11** Leoncavallo

museum: **13** Topkapi Palace **14** Archaeological **20** Turkish and Islamic Art
rulers: **4** Rome **6** Athens, Darius, Rhodes, Sparta **8** Persians, Suleiman **9** Macedonia **11** Latin Empire **12** Ottoman Turks **15** Byzantine Empire, Turkish Republic **19** Constantine the Great
sea: **5** Black **7** Marmara **8** Bosporus **10** Golden Horn

isthmus **4** neck, spit **5** point, strip **6** narrow, strait, tongue **7** narrows
name: **4** Suez **6** Panama **7** Corinth

Isus
father: **5** Priam
killed by: **9** Agamemnon

I sustain the wings
Latin: **12** sustineo alas
motto of: **10** US Air Force

Italiano, Anna Maria Louise
real name of: **12** Anne Bancroft

Italic
language family: **12** Indo European
branch: **5** Latin, Oscan **7** Umbrian

Italy *see box*

itch **3** yen **4** ache, long, pine **5** crave, crawl, creep, yearn **6** desire, hanker, hunger, thirst, tickle **7** craving, prickle **8** appetite, have a yen, pruritis, tingling, yearning **9** hankering

it does not follow
Latin: **11** non sequitur

item **4** unit **5** entry, piece, point, story, thing **6** detail, matter, notice, report **7** ac-

emperor: **4** Nero, Otho **5** Galba, Nerva, Titus **6** Trajan **7** Hadrian **8** Caligula, Claudius, Commodus, Domitian, Octavian, Tiberius **9** Caracalla, Vespasian, Vitellius **10** Diocletian **11** Constantine **13** Antoninus Dius **14** Caesar Augustus, Marcus Aurelius
film director: **6** de Sica **7** Fellini **8** Visconti **9** Antonioni **10** Bertolucci, Rossellini, Wertmuller, Zeffirelli
god: **4** Juno, Mars **5** Ceres, Diana, Janus, Lares, Venus **6** Apollo, Vulcan **7** Bacchus, Jupiter, Minerva, Neptune, Penates **8** Quirinus
Italian author: **4** Levi **5** Bembo, Bruno, Pulci, Tasso **6** Artino, Vasari **7** Ariosto, Bassani, Deledda, Moravia **8** Bandello, Petrarch **9** Boccaccio, D'Annunzio, Sannazaro **10** Cavalcanti, Guinicelli, Metastasio, Pirandello, Straparola **11** Castiglione, Machiavelli **12** Guicciardini, Michelangelo **14** Dante Alighieri
Latin author: **4** Cato, Livy, Ovid **5** Pliny, Varro **6** Cicero, Gallus, Horace, Seneca, Vergil, Virgil **7** Donatus, Juvenal, Martial, Plautus, Sallust, Tacitus, Terence **8** Boethius, Catullus, Lucilius, St Jerome **9** St Ambrose, Suetonius **11** St Augustine
ruler: **4** Moro **6** Cavour, Enrico **7** Mazzini **9** Mussolini **10** Berlinguer **14** Victor Emmanuel **15** Alcide de Gasperi
ruler/military leader: **5** Sulla **6** Brutus, Pompey, Seneca **7** Crassus, Lepidus **8** Gracchus **10** Mark Antony **12** Gaius Marious, Julius Caesar **15** Cassius Longinus, Scipio Africanus **18** Tarquinius Superbus
ruling family of city-state: **4** Este **6** Medici, Sforza **8** Visconti
sculptor: **6** Canova, Marini, Pisano **7** Bernini, Bologna, Cellini **8** Antelami, Boccioni, Ghiberti **9** Donatello, Sansovino **10** Giacometti, Pollaiuolo, Verrocchio **11** Della Robbia **12** Michelangelo
wife: **7** Poppaea **9** Agrippina, Messalina **13** Livia Drusilla
language: **5** Ladin, Latin **6** French, German **7** Italian, Slovene **8** Friulian **9** Sardinian
religion: **13** Roman Catholic
place:
arch: **11** Constantine
baths: **9** Caracalla
bridge: **5** Sighs **12** Ponte Vecchio
cathedral/church: **5** Siena **7** St Mark's, Vatican **8** San Marco, St Peter's **13** Sistine Chapel
fountain: **5** Trevi
museum: **5** Duomo **6** Uffizi **8** Bargello, National **10** Capitoline **11** Pitti Palace, Villa Giulia **16** Gallerio Borghese
opera house: **7** La Scala
palace: **5** Doges
road: **9** Appian Way
ruins: **5** Forum **7** Capitol, Pompeii **8** Pantheon **9** Catacombs, Colosseum **11** Herculaneum **13** Circus Maximus
steps: **7** Spanish
tower: **18** Leaning Tower of Pisa
feature:
unification movement: **12** Risorgimento
food:
cheese: **6** romano **7** fontina, ricotta **8** parmesan
dish: **5** pizza **6** scampi **7** gnocchi, lasagna, lasagne, polenta, ravioli, risotto **9** antipasti, antipasto **17** chicken cacciatora, cacciatore
ice cream: **6** gelato **7** spumoni
meat: **6** salami **9** pepperoni **10** mortadella, prosciutto
soup: **8** caciucco **10** minestrone
wine: **7** Chianti

count, article, feature, subject **8** dispatch, notation **9** paragraph **10** particular **11** news article

itemization **4** list **7** listing **11** enumeration

itemize **6** detail **7** specify **8** spell out **9** enumerate

items of business **4** list **6** agenda, docket **7** program **8** schedule

iterate **6** repeat **7** restate **9** reiterate

It Girl
nickname of: **8** Clara Bow

it grows as it goes
Latin: **12** crescit eundo
motto of: **9** New Mexico

It Happened One Night
director: **10** Frank Capra
cast: **8** Alan Hale, Ward Bond **10** Clark Gable **11** Roscoe Karns **14** Walter Connolly **16** Claudette Colbert
Oscar for: **5** actor (Gable) **7** actress (Colbert), picture **8** director
remade as: **16** Eve Knew Her Apples **20** You Can't Run Away from It

I think therefore I am
Latin: **13** cogito ergo sum
said by: **9** Descartes

Ithomatas *see* **4** Zeus

Ithun, Ithunn *see* **4** Idun

itinerant **5** nomad, rover **6** roamer, roving **7** migrant, nomadic, roaming, vagrant **8** vagabond, wanderer, wayfarer **9** footloose, transient, traveling, wandering, wayfaring **11** peripatetic

itinerary **3** log **5** diary, route **6** course **7** account, circuit, day book, journal **8** schedule **9** timetable **10** travel plan

it is not clear; it is not evident
Latin: **9** non liquet

it is not lawful; it is not permitted
Latin: **8** non licet

it is sweet to do nothing
Italian: **14** dolce far niente

Itonia
epithet of: **6** Athena

It's a Gift
director: **13** Norman Z McLeod
cast: **8** W C Fields **9** Baby LeRoy, Tommy Bupp **10** T Roy Barnes **13** Charles Sellon, Morgan Wallace **14** Kathleen Howard
remake of: **17** It's the Old Army Game

It's a Wonderful Life
director: **10** Frank Capra
cast: **9** Donna Reed **11** Beulah Bondi **12** Henry Travers, James Stewart **13** Gloria Grahame **15** Lionel Barrymore
remade as: **22** It Happened One Christmas

itsy-bitsy **3** wee **4** tiny **5** dwarf, pygmy, small, teeny **6** bantam, little, minute, petite **9** miniature, miniscule **10** diminutive, teeny-weeny **11** microscopic, pocket-sized

It Takes a Thief
character: **8** Noah Bain **12** Alister Mundy, Wallie Powers **14** Alexander Mundy
cast: **11** Edward Binns, Fred Astaire **12** Robert Wagner **13** Malachi Throne

Itylus
father: **6** Zethus
mother: **5** Aedon
killed by: **5** Aedon

Itys
father: **6** Tereus
mother: **6** Procne
killed by: **6** Procne
to revenge: **9** Philomela

Itza
language family: **6** Toltec
location: **6** Mexico **7** Chichen, Yucatan **14** Central America

Iulus *see* **8** Ascanius

Ivanhoe
author: **14** Sir Walter Scott
character: **7** Rebecca **8** Guilbert **9** Robin Hood **10** Lady Rowena **11** Isaac of York **12** King Richard I **14** Cedric the Saxon, Sir Brian de Bois **16** Wilfred of Ivanhoe **19** King Richard the First

Ivanhoe, Burle Icle
real name of: **8** Burl Ives

I've Got a Secret
host: **10** Bill Cullen, Garry Moore, Steve Allen

Ives, Burl
real name: **16** Burle Icle Ivanhoe
nickname: **17** Wayfaring Stranger
born: **6** Hunt IL
roles: **8** Big Daddy **10** East of Eden **13** The Big Country **14** Our Man in Havana **16** Cat on a Hot Tin Roof **18** Desire Under the Elms

Ives, Charles
born: **9** Danbury CT
composer of: **11** Putnam's Camp **13** Concord Sonata **19** Washington's Birthday **20** Central Park in the Dark **21** The Unanswered Question **23** Three Places in New England

Ivory Coast
capital/largest city: **7** Abidjan
new capital: **12** Yamoussoukro
others: **3** Man **4** Divo **5** Daloa, Tabou **6** Adzobe, Bonoua, Bouake, Danane, Gagnoa **7** Korhogo, Odienne, Seguela **8** Dimbokro **9** Agboville, Bondoukou, Sassandra **10** Abengourou **11** Grand Bassam **14** Ferkessedougou
monetary unit: **5** franc **7** centime
highest point: **5** Nimba
river: **3** Bia **5** Comoe, Komoe **7** Bandama, Cavally **9** Sassandra
ocean: **8** Atlantic
physical feature:
cape: **6** Palmas
gulf: **6** Guinea
lagoon: **3** Aby **5** Ebrie
wind: **9** harmattan
people: **3** Abe, Dan, Kru, Kwa **4** Akan, Bete, Dida, Guro, Koua, Lobi, Wobe **5** Abron, Abure, Attie, Baule, Guere, Mande, Mossi **6** Baoule, Lagoon, Senufo, Senufu **7** Dan Guro, Kroumen, Malinke, Voltaic **10** Anyi-Baoule **11** Lobi-Kulango **12** Agnis-Ashanti
language: **4** Akan **6** Dioula, French
religion: **5** Islam **7** animism **13** Roman Catholic
place:
canal: **5** Vridi
dam: **7** Bandama
game reserve: **9** Sassandra
feature: **7** kola nut

Ivory Coast *see* **11** Sierra Leone

ivory-towered **6** remote **8** academic, romantic **11** conjectural, impractical, theoretical, unrealistic **12** hypothetical

ivy **6** Cissus, Hedera **15** Kalmia latifolia
varieties: **3** fan, red **4** baby, tree **5** grape, Irish, Nepal,

water **6** aralia, Baltic, Boston, canary, devil's, German, ground, marine, parlor, poison, spider, switch **7** colchis, English, Italian, Madeira, Mexican, parsley, Persian, Swedish **8** Algerian, American, coliseum, fragrant, Japanese, red-flame **9** bird's-foot, ghost-tree, heart-leaf **10** five-leaved, Kenilworth, variegated **12** Hagenburger's **13** Solomon Island **14** miniature grape **15** Gloire-de-Marengo

Ivy League colleges **4** Yale **5** Brown **7** Cornell, Harvard **8** Columbia **9** Dartmouth, Princeton **12** Pennsylvania (Penn)

I Want to Live!
director: **10** Robert Wise
cast: **12** Simon Oakland, Susan Hayward (Barbara Graham) **13** Theodore Bikel **15** Virginia Vincent
score: **12** Johnny Mandel
Oscar for: **7** actress (Hayward)

I will defend
Latin: **6** tuebor

IWW **8** Wobblies **10** labor union **27** Industrial Workers of the World
leader: **4** Debs **6** DeLeon **7** Haywood
members: **6** miners **9** lumbermen **16** migratory workers

Ixion
king of: **8** Lapithae
wife: **3** Dia
son: **9** Pirithous
children: **8** centaurs
loved: **4** Hera
punished by: **4** Zeus
bound to: **5** wheel

Iyar **17** second Hebrew month

Iynx
father: **3** Pan
mother: **4** Echo

Izmir
formerly: **6** Smyrna
location: **6** Turkey **9** Aegean Sea **11** Gulf of Izmir
settle by: **7** Ionians **8** Aeolians
ruled by: **13** Ottoman Empire

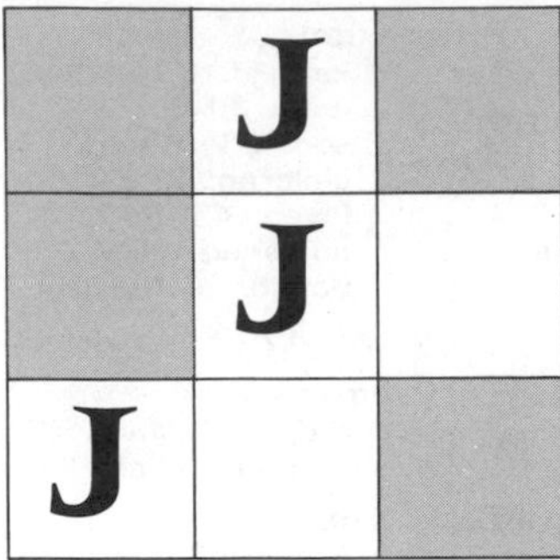

ja **3** yes

jab **3** cut, dig, hit, rap, tap **4** belt, blow, bump, clip, goad, lick, pelt, plug, poke, poke, prod, sock, stab, swat **5** elbow, nudge, paste, swing **6** strike, stroke

Jabal
father: **6** Lamech
mother: **4** Adah
brother: **5** Jubal

jabber **3** gab, gas **4** blab **5** clack, prate **6** babble, cackle, drivel, gibber, gossip, hot air, patter, ramble, rattle, raving **7** blabber, blather, chatter, gushing, maunder, palaver, prating, prattle, ranting, twaddle, twattle **8** chitchat, idle talk, nonsense, talk idly **9** gibberish **10** maundering **14** chitter-chatter

jack **4** flag **5** knave **6** ensign

Jack, Esther
character in: **16** The Web and the Rock **18** You Can't Go Home Again
author: **5** Wolfe

jackass **3** ass **4** fool, mule **5** burro, dummy, idiot **6** donkey

Jack Benny Show, The
cast: **8** Mel Blanc **9** Dennis Day, Don Wilson **11** Frank Nelson **13** Artie Auerbach, Eddie (Rochester) Anderson **14** Mary Livingston
Jack's car: **7** Maxwell
Jack played: **6** violin

jacket **4** case, coat **5** cover **6** blazer, casing, folder, sheath **7** wrapper **8** envelope, mackinaw, wrapping **9** container, enclosure, short coat, sport coat **10** dinner coat **11** windbreaker

Jack Sheppard
author: **16** William Ainsworth

Jackson, Andrew ***see box***

Jackson, Anne
husband: **10** Eli Wallach
born: **10** Millvale PA
roles: **3** Luv **10** The Typists

Jackson, Charles
author of: **14** The Lost Weekend

Jackson, Glenda
born: **7** England **10** Birkenhead
roles: **10** Elizabeth R **11** Women in Love (Oscar) **13** A Touch of Class (Oscar) **14** The Music Lovers **16** Mary Queen of Scots **18** Sunday Bloody Sunday

Jackson, Jesse Louis
party: **10** Democratic
born: **12** Greenville SC
education: **20** University of Illinois **26** Chicago Theological Seminary **49** North Carolina Agricultural and Technical State College
religion: **7** Baptist
political career: **17** Democratic primary
civilian career: **4** SCLC **9** PUSH Excel **13** Operation PUSH **20** Operation Breadbasket **24** National Rainbow Coalition **37** Southern Christian Leadership Conference
father: **17** Noah Louis Robinson
mother: **10** Helen Burns
stepfather: **12** Charles Henry (Jackson)
wife: **22** Jacqueline Lavinia Brown
children: **7** Santita **10** Jesse Louis **11** Yusef DuBois **14** Jonathan Luther **17** Jacqueline Lavinia

Jackson, Reggie
nickname: **13** Mister October
sport: **8** baseball
position: **8** outfield
known for: **7** hitting
team: **9** Oakland A's **14** New York Yankees **16** Los Angeles Angels

Jackson, Shirley
author of: **10** The Lottery **28** We Have Always Lived in the Castle

Jackson, Stonewall (Thomas)
served in: **8** Civil War **10** Mexican War
side: **11** Confederate
battle: **7** Bull Run **8** Antietam, Richmond **9** Seven Days **14** Fredericksburg **16** Chancellorsville, Shenandoah Valley

Jacksonville
football team: **5** Bulls

Jacob
father: **5** Isaac
mother: **7** Rebekah
brother: **4** Esau
wives: **4** Leah **6** Rachel
concubines: **5** Bilah **6** Zilpah
son: **3** Dan, Gad **4** Levi **5** Asher, Judah **6** Joseph, Reuben, Simeon **7** Zebulun **8** Benjamin, Issachar, Naphtali
daughter: **5** Dinah
dream of: **6** ladder
wrestled with: **5** angel
name changed to: **6** Israel
burial place: **9** Machpelah

Jacob, Francois
field: **7** biology
nationality: **6** French
discovered: **3** RNA
awarded: **10** Nobel Prize

Jacobs, Amos Muzyad
real name of: **11** Danny Thomas

jade
species: **7** jadeite **8** nephrite
source: **5** Burma, China **6** Mexico **7** Mogaung **10** New Zealand **12** United States

jaded **5** blase, bored, sated, spent, stale, tired, weary

Jackson, Andrew
nickname: **10** Old Hickory
presidential rank: **7** seventh
party: **10** Democratic
state represented: **2** TN **9** Tennessee
defeated: **4** (Henry) Clay **5** (John Quincy) Adams
vice president: **7** (John Caldwell) Calhoun **8** (Martin) Van Buren
cabinet:
state: **6** (Louis) McLane **7** (John) Forsyth **8** (Martin) Van Buren **10** (Edward) Livingston
treasury: **5** (William John) Duane **6** (Louis) McLane, (Samuel Dulucenna) Ingham **8** (Levi) Woodbury
war: **4** (Lewis) Cass **5** (John Henry) Eaton
attorney general: **5** (Roger Brooke) Taney **6** (Benjamin Franklin) Butler **7** (John McPherson) Berrien
navy: **6** (John) Branch **8** (Levi) Woodbury **9** (Mahlon) Dickerson
postmaster general: **5** (William Taylor) Barry **7** (Amos) Kendall
born: **8** Waxhaw SC
died/buried: **11** Nashville TN
education:
college: **4** none
studied: **3** law
admitted to: **3** bar
religion: **12** Presbyterian
political career: **8** US Senate **24** US House of Representatives
judge: **22** Tennessee Superior Court
civilian career: **6** lawyer
military service: **12** major general **16** brigadier general
defeated: **6** Creeks **9** Cherokees
captured: **9** Pensacola
military governor of: **7** Florida
notable events of lifetime/term:
battle: **5** Alamo **10** New Orleans
fought: **5** duels
scandal/wife suspected of: **6** bigamy
war: **8** Creek War **13** Revolutionary **16** First Seminole War **19** War of Eighteen Twelve
father: **6** Andrew
mother: **9** Elizabeth (Hutchinson)
siblings: **4** Hugh **6** Robert
wife: **6** Rachel (Donelson Robards)
children:
adopted: **11** wife's nephew **15** Andrew Jackson Jr

6 cloyed, dulled, fagged **7** glutted, satiate, spoiled, wearied, worn-out **8** dog-tired, fatigued, overused, satiated, shopworn, tired out **9** exhausted, played out, surfeited **11** overwearied **12** overindulged

jadeite
variety: **4** jade

Jael
husband: **5** Heber
killed: **11** Sisera

jagged **5** jaggy, rough, spiny **6** barbed, broken, craggy, nicked, ridged, rugged, snaggy, spiked, thorny, uneven, zigzag **7** angular, bristly, cragged, notched, pointed, spinous, studded **8** indented, serrated **9** irregular, knifelike **10** crenulated, saw-toothed **12** sharp-toothed

Jaggers, Mr
character in: **17** Great Expectations
author: **7** Dickens

jaguar **3** cat **5** tiger **6** feline **7** panther **8** uturuncu

jail **3** bag, can, jug, nab, pen **4** book, brig, bust, cell, keep, stir **5** clink, pinch, pound, run in, seize **6** arrest, collar, cooler, lockup, prison, take in **7** arraign, bring in, capture, confine, dungeon, slammer **8** bastille, big house, hoosegow, imprison, stockade **9** apprehend, black hole, calaboose, guardroom, workhouse **10** guardhouse **11** incarcerate, reformatory **12** halfway house, penitentiary, reform school, station house **13** hold in custody, police station **14** detention house **16** penal institution **17** house of correction

jailbird **3** con **5** felon **7** convict **8** prisoner

jailer **5** guard, screw **6** gaoler, keeper, warden **7** turnkey **9** custodian

Jair **11** Hebrew judge

Jakarta, Djakarta
capital of: **9** Indonesia

Jake's Thing
author: **12** Kingsley Amis

jalopy **3** car **4** auto, heap **5** motor **6** wheels **7** flivver, machine, vehicle **8** motorcar **9** tin lizzie **10** automobile

jam **3** fix, mob, ram, sea **4** army, cram, herd, host, mess, pack, push, stop **5** block, cease, crowd, crush, drove, flock, horde, pinch, press, shove, stall, stick, stuff, swarm, tie-up, wedge **6** arrest, edge in, pickle, plight, scrape, strait, throng, thrust, work in, worm in **7** congest, dilemma, foist in, force in, squeeze, suspend, trouble **8** hot water, obstruct, quandary, sandwich **9** interrupt, multitude, overcrowd **11** malfunction, predicament **13** agglomeration

Jamaica ***see box, p. 516***

jamboree **2** do **4** bash, gala **5** party, revel, spree **6** fiesta, frolic **7** blowout, jubilee, shindig **8** carnival, carousal, festival **9** festivity **11** celebration
French: **4** fete **13** fete champetre

James **7** apostle
also called: **12** James the Less
father: **7** Zebedee **8** Alphaeus
brother: **4** John, Levi **5** Judas
disciple of: **5** Jesus
killed by: **12** Herod Agrippa
with John called: **13** sons of thunder

James, Henry
author of: **11** Daisy Miller, The American **13** The Bostonians, The Golden Bowl **14** Roderick Hudson, The Ambassadors **15** The Aspern Papers **16** Washington Square **17** The Turn of the Screw, The Wings of the Dove **18** The Portrait of a Lady **19** Princess Casamassima

Jamaica
name means: **18** land of wood and water
capital/largest city: **8** Kingston
others: **6** May Pen **8** Ocho Rios **9** Morant Bay, Port Maria, Port Royal **10** Mandeville, Montego Bay **11** Port Antonio, Spanish Town **12** Saint Ann's Bay, Savanna-la-Mar
head of state: **14** British monarch **15** governor general
monetary unit: **7** quattie
island: **4** Navy **15** Greater Antilles
mountain: **8** Sir John's
highest point: **4** Blue
river: **5** Black, Cobre, Great, Minho, White **9** Rio Grande
sea: **8** Atlantic **9** Caribbean
physical feature: **13** Portland Bight
area: **14** Cockpit Country
bay: **4** Buff, Hope, Long **6** Morant **9** Discovery **10** Black River, Bluefield's, Old Harbour
point: **6** Galina **8** Portland **9** North East, North West, South East **11** North Negril, South Negril
people: **7** African, Chinese **10** East Indian
ancient: **6** Arawak **7** Ciboney
discoverer: **8** Columbus
leader: **5** Seaga **6** Garvey, Manley **10** Bustamente
language: **6** Creole **7** English
religion: **7** Baptist **8** Anglican **9** Methodist **11** Church of God, Rastafarian **13** Roman Catholic
place:
beach: **11** Doctor's Cave
botanical garden: **4** Hope
racetrack: **12** Caymanas Park
feature:
evil spirits: **7** duppies
guerrilla fighters: **7** Maroons
tree: **4** poui **5** cedar, ceiba, mahoe, saman **6** cassia, guango **7** logwood **8** mahogany **9** casuarina, poinciana **10** silkcotton **11** lignum vitae
witch doctor: **8** obeah man
food:
coffee: **12** Blue Mountain
drink: **3** rum **4** jake **8** tia maria
fruit: **5** guava, mango **6** pawpaw
spicy soup: **9** pepper pot

James, P D
author of: **12** Cover Her Face **13** Innocent Blood **15** Unnatural Causes **21** Shroud for a Nightingale **22** Death of an Expert Witness
character: **13** Adam Dalgliesh

James the Less *see* **5** James

jammed **4** full **5** stuck **6** filled, loaded, massed, packed, rammed, wedged **7** blocked, crammed, crowded, crushed, pressed, stuffed **8** overfull, squeezed **10** obstructed, sandwiched **11** overcrowded

Janacek, Leos
born: **8** Hukvaldy **14** Czechoslovakia
composer of: **5** Mladi, Youth **6** Jenufa **9** In the Mist **10** Taras Bulba **13** Katya Kabanova **14** Glagolitic Mass **17** On an Overgrown Path **18** The Makropoulus Case **21** From the House of the Dead, The Cunning Little Vixen **24** The Diary of One Who Vanished, The Excursions of Mr Broucek

Jane
character in: **6** Tarzan
author: **9** Burroughs

Jane Eyre
author: **15** Charlotte Bronte
character: **5** Mason **7** Mrs Reed **10** Grace Poole, Mary Rivers, Mrs Fairfax **11** Adele Varens, Bertha Mason, Diana Rivers **12** Bessie Leaven, St John Rivers **13** Blanche Ingram **15** Edward Rochester
school: **6** Lowood
house: **10** Thornfield
director: **15** Robert Stevenson
cast: **11** Orson Welles **12** Joan Fontaine **14** Margaret O'Brien

jangle **3** din, jar **4** ring **5** annoy, chime, clang, clank, clash, crash, upset **6** jingle, racket, rattle **7** clangor, clatter, grate on **8** irritate **9** cacophony **11** reverberate **13** reverberation **14** tintinnabulate

janitor **5** super **6** porter **8** handyman **9** caretaker, custodian, janitress **11** cleaning man **12** cleaning lady **13** cleaning woman **14** maintenance man, superintendent

Janssen, David
real name: **16** David Harold Meyer
born: **9** Naponee NE
roles: **6** Harry O **11** The Fugitive **14** Richard Diamond **15** Dr Richard Kimble

January
event: **15** Inauguration Day (every 4 years)
flower: **8** snowdrop **9** carnation
French: **7** Janvier
gem: **6** garnet
German: **6** Januar
holiday: **8** Epiphany (6) **11** New Year's Day (1) **12** Twelfth Night (5)
Italian: **7** Gennaio
number of days: **9** thirty-one
origin of name: **5** Janus
Roman god of: **5** doors **8** doorways **10** beginnings
place in year:
Gregorian: **5** first
Julian/Roman: **8** eleventh
Spanish: **5** Enero
Zodiac sign: **8** Aquarius **9** Capricorn

Janus
origin: **5** Roman
god of: **8** doorways **9** rising sun **10** beginnings, setting sun

Japan ***see box***

Japanese
independent language of: **5** Japan **13** Ryukyu Islands

jape **4** gibe, joke **5** antic, caper, prank **7** mockery

Japheth
father: **4** Noah
brother: **3** Ham **4** Shem

Jaques
character in: **11** As You Like It
author: **11** Shakespeare

Japan

other name: **5** Nihon **6** Nippon
name means: **18** Land of the Rising Sun
capital/largest city: **3** Edo **5** Tokyo
others: **4** Kobe, Naha **5** Kyoto, Osaka **6** Nagoya, Sendai **7** Fukuoka, Niigata, Sapporo **8** Kanazawa, Kawasaki, Nagasaki, Yokohama **9** Hiroshima, Kagoshima **10** Kitakyushu
school: **4** Chuo, Keio **5** Hosei, Kyoto, Nihon, Tokyo **6** Sophia, Waseda **7** Fukuoka **8** Doshisha
head of state: **7** emperor
measure: **2** go **3** boo, cho, djo, fun, inc, ken, kin, kon, rin, shi, sho, sun, tan **4** hiro, isse, kati, koku, niyo, shoo **5** carat, catty, issho, ittan, momme, picul, shaku **6** kwamme **8** hiyakkin **9** hiyak-hiro **11** komma-ichida, kujira-shaku
monetary unit: **2** bu **3** mon, rin, rio, sen, shu, yen **4** cash, mibu, oban **5** koban, obang, tempo **6** cobang, ichebu, ichibu, itzebu, kobang **7** itzeboo, itziboo
weight: **2** mo **3** fun, kon, rin **4** kati, kwan **5** carat, catty, momme **8** hiyakkin
island: **3** Iki, Izu, Oki, Tsu **4** Oita, Sado, Yaku **5** Amami, Awaji, Bonin, Hondo, Kuril, Rebun, Sikok **6** Honshu, Kiushu, Kyushu, Loochu, Marcus, Riukiu, Tanega, Tyukyu **7** Cipango, Hachijo, Iwo Jima, Okinawa, Rishiri, Shikoko, Shikoku, Volcano **8** Hokkaido, Miyajima, Okigunto, Okushiri, Tsushima, Yakujima
lake: **4** Biwa, Suwa, Toya **6** Towada **8** Kutchawa, Shikotsu
mountain: **3** Uso, Zao **5** Asahi, Asama, Hondo, Yesso **6** Asosan, Enasan, Hiuchi, Kiusiu, Yariga **7** Hakusan, Kujusan, Tokachi **8** Fujiyama **9** Japan Alps
highest point: **4** Fuji **7** Fujisan
river: **4** Tone, Yalu **8** Ishikari, Tonegawa **11** Shinano-gawa
sea: **3** Suo **5** Japan **6** Inland **7** Amakusa, Okhotsk, Pacific **8** Tsushima
physical feature:
bay: **3** Ise **4** Miku, Tosa, Yedo **5** Amort, Mutsu, Osaka, Otaru, Tokyo **6** Ariake, Atsumi, Sendai, Suruga, Toyama, Wakasa **7** Uchiura
cape: **3** Iro, Oki, Oma, Toi **4** Daio, Esan, Jizo, Mela, Mino, Noma, Nomo, Sada, Sawa, Shio, Soya, Suzu **5** Erimo, Kyoga, Rurui **6** Todoga **7** Shiriya **8** Ashizuri, Shakotan **12** Muroto Nojima
channel: **3** Kii **5** Bungo
current: **5** Japan **7** Okhotsk **8** Kuro Shio
divine wind: **8** kamikaze
gulf: **6** Sagami
plain: **4** Nobi **5** Kanto
strait: **4** Soya **5** Korea, Osumi **6** Nemuro, Tanega, Tokara **7** Tsugaru **8** Tsushima **9** La Perouse
people: **3** Eta **6** Korean **8** Japanese, Okinawan **10** Buramkumin
ancient: **4** Ainu **5** Jomon, Yayoi
artist: **4** Okyo **5** Buson, Jocho, Korin, Taiga, Unkei **6** Buncho, Eitoku, Kenzan, Koetsu, Reisai, Sesshu, Sesson, Shubun **7** Baiitsu, Choshun, Foujita, Gyokudo, Hokusai, Josetsu, Sanraku, Sharaku, Sotatsu, Utamaro **8** Harunobu, Kiyonaga, Motonobu **9** Hiroshige, Mitsunobu
author: **5** Basho **7** Abe Kobo **8** Mori Ogai **11** Ueda Akinari **12** Ihara Saikaku, Mishima Yukio, Sakyo Komatsu **13** Natsume Soseki, Zeami Motokiyo **14** Shimazaki Toson, Tsubouchi Shoyo **15** Motoori Norinaga, Murasaki Shikibu **16** Fujiwara Nokisaki, Kawabata Yasunari **17** Tanizaki Junichiro **19** Chikamatsu Monzaemon
dynasty: **5** Meiji, Taira **6** Yamato **8** Fujiwara, Minamoto
leader: **4** Hojo **5** Kammu, Meiji **6** Go-Toba, Ieyasu **7** Akihito, Go-Daigo **8** Hirohito, Nobunaga, Yoritomo **9** Hideyoshi, Yoshimasa **10** Tojo Hideki, Yoshimitsu **11** Hara Takashi, Ito Hirobumi **12** Tanaka Kakuei **13** Konoe Fumimaro, Shotoku Taishi **14** Yoshida Shigeru **15** Ashikaga Takauji **18** Matsukata Mayayoshi
legendary ruler: **5** Jimmu, Jingo **7** Izanagi
shogunate: **8** Ashikaga, Kamakura, Tokugawa
language: **8** Japanese
alphabet/characters: **4** kana **5** kanji **8** hiragana, katakana
dialect: **5** Kanto
religion: **6** Tendai **7** Shingon **8** Buddhism **9** Shintoism **12** Confucianism
place:
castle: **4** Nijo
hall: **5** Hoodo **7** Phoenix **12** Golden Buddha
mausoleum: **4** Ojin **7** Nintoku
palace: **7** Akasaka, Katsura
shrine: **5** Heian **11** Itsukushima **16** Grand Shrine of Ise
temple: **6** Kotoku **7** Byodoin, Horyuji, Ryoanji, Senso-ji, Todaiji **8** Enkakuji, Kenchoji, Kofukuji **9** Kinkakuji **13** Asakusa Kannon
feature:
abacus: **7** soroban
bed: **5** futon
clothing: **6** kimono
festival: **13** Cherry Blossom

(*continued*)

Japan (*continued*)
firm: **4** Sony **5** Honda **6** Mitsui, Nissan, Toyota, Yasuda **7** Iwasaki **8** Sumitomo **10** Mitsubishi
flower arranging: **7** ikebana
painting style: **4** kano, tosa **5** nanga, nisee, onnae, rarae, rimpa, shijo **6** chinso, otokoe, sesshu, ukiyoe **7** konpeki, nihonga, yamatoe
paper folding art: **7** origami
poem: **4** waka **5** haiku, tanka
puppet theater: **7** bunraku
rush floor covering: **6** tatami
sport: **4** judo **6** karate **13** sumo wrestling
statue: **8** Daibutsu **11** Great Buddha
tea ceremony: **7** chanoyu
theater: **2** no **3** noh **6** kabuki
the way of the warrior/code of honor: **7** bushido
tree: **6** bonsai
wood block print: **6** ukiyoe
food:
beverage: **4** sake **8** green tea
dish: **5** sushi **7** sashimi, tempura **8** sukiyaki, teriyaki, yakitori
noodle: **4** soba

jar **3** din, jug, pot, urn **4** bong, bray, buzz, daze, faze, jolt, rock, stir, stun **5** blare, blast, brawl, clang, clank, crash, crock, flask, floor, quake, shake, shock, throw, upset **6** beaker, bottle, impact, jangle, jiggle, joggle, racket, rattle, vessel **7** agitate, astound, clangor, clatter, confuse, disturb, fluster, perturb, shake up, startle, stupefy, trouble, upheave, vibrate **8** befuddle, bewilder, bleating, canister, clashing, convulse, decanter, demijohn, disquiet, distract, unsettle **9** agitation, cacophony, container **10** concussion, discompose, disconcert, receptacle **11** discordance
Spanish: **4** olla

jargon **4** bosh, bull, bunk, cant **5** argot, fudge, hooey, idiom, lingo, prate, usage **6** babble, brogue, drivel, patois, pidgin, piffle **7** baloney, blabber, blather, dialect, fustian, hogwash, prattle, rubbish, twaddle **8** folderol, malarkey, nonsense, parlance, tommyrot, verbiage **9** gibberish, moonshine, poppycock, rigmarole **10** balderdash, flapdoodle, hocus-pocus, rigamarole, vernacular, vocabulary **11** abracadabra, jabberwocky, phraseology, shibboleths **12** gobbledygook, lingua franca **14** grandiloquence

Jarley, Mrs
character in: **19** The Old Curiosity Shop
author: **7** Dickens

Jarndyce, John
character in: **10** Bleak House
author: **7** Dickens

jarring **4** rude **5** harsh, rough **6** jangly **7** grating, jolting, rasping, shaking **8** clashing, grinding, jangling, rattling, strident **9** dissonant, wrenching **10** discordant **12** nerveracking **13** nerve-wracking

Jarry, Alfred
author of: **7** King Ubu **11** Ubu in Chains **13** Ubu the Cuckold

jasmine **8** Jasminum
varieties: **4** blue, cape, rock, star **5** crape, night, royal

Java
other name: **5** Djawa
capital/largest city: **7** Jakarta **8** Djakarta
others: **5** Bogor, Dessa **6** Kediri, Malang **7** Bandung, Batavia **8** Semarang, Surabaja, Surabaya **9** Surakarta **11** Djokjakarta **13** Pelabuhanratu
government: **17** island of Indonesia
measure: **3** kan **4** paal, rand **5** palen
weight: **4** amat, pond, tali **5** pound **6** soekel
island: **4** Bali **5** Sunda **6** Lombok, Madura
mountain: **4** Amat, Gede **5** Lawoe, Murjo, Prahu **6** Raoeng, Slamet **8** Soembing
highest point: **6** Semuru **7** Semeroe
river: **4** Solo **7** Brantas
sea: **4** Java **6** Indian **7** Pacific
physical feature:
plateau: **4** Ijen
strait: **5** Sunda
people: **5** Krama, Kromo **6** Kalang **8** Javanese, Madurese **9** Sundanese
dynasty: **7** Mataram **9** Majapahit, Srivijaya
language: **4** Kavi, Kawi **5** Malay **6** Sassak **8** Balinese, Madurese, Sudanese **16** Bahasa Indonesian
religion: **5** Hindu, Islam **7** animism **8** Buddhism
place:
temple: **6** Chandi, Thandi **9** Borobudur, Prambanan
feature:
cloth: **3** kat **5** batik, kapok
dance: **7** seri mpi
dancer: **6** bedoyo
fishing boat: **4** prau
ornamental dagger: **4** kris
puppet play: **6** wajang, wayang
food:
fruit: **6** durian, lomboy, nangca **7** gondang

6 orange, yellow **7** Arabian, Chilean, Italian, Spanish **8** Carolina, cinnamon, Japanese, Paraguay, pinwheel, primrose, windmill **9** angelwing **10** Catalonian, Madagascar **11** Confederate

Jason
leader of: 9 Argonauts
father: 5 Aeson
mother: 8 Alcimede, Polymede
half-brother: 6 Pelias
son: 5 Thoas **6** Euneus, Pheres **7** Medeius **8** Mermerus, Tisander **9** Alcimenes, Thessalus
daughter: 7 Eriopis
teacher: 6 Chiron **7** centaur, Cheiron
retrieved: 12 Golden Fleece
ship: 4 Argo
loved by: 5 Medea
loved: 6 Glauce

Jasper, John
character in: 22 The Mystery of Edwin Drood
author: 7 Dickens

jaundiced 5 blase, bored **6** bitter **7** cynical, envious, hostile, jealous **8** covetous, doubting, satiated **9** green-eyed, resentful, skeptical **10** embittered, suspicious **11** mistrustful

jaunt 4 spin, tour, trip **6** airing, flight, junket, outing, ramble, stroll **9** adventure, excursion, promenade, short trip **10** expedition

jaunty 4 airy, neat, trim **5** natty, perky **6** blithe, bouncy, breezy, dapper, lively, sporty, spruce **7** buoyant **8** carefree, debonair **9** sprightly, vivacious **12** lighthearted, high-stepping, high-spirited

Java ***see box***

javelin 4 dart **5** lance, shaft, spear **10** projectile

jaw 3 gab, rap **4** chat, chin, talk **7** jawbone, palaver **8** chitchat, converse, mandible **10** chew the fat, chew the rag **11** confabulate

Jaws
author: 13 Peter Benchley
director: 15 Steven Spielberg
cast: 10 Robert Shaw **11** Roy Scheider **12** Lorraine Gary **15** Richard Dreyfuss
score: 12 John Williams
Oscar for: 5 score

Jayhawker State
nickname of: 6 Kansas

jazz musician 8 Art Tatum **10** Miles Davis **11** Lester Young **12** Benny Goodman, John Coltrane **13** Charlie Parker, Duke Ellington **14** Dizzy Gillespie, Louis Armstrong, Ornette Coleman

jealous 4 wary **7** anxious, envious, mindful **8** covetous, grudging, watchful **9** concerned, green-eyed, regardful, resentful **10** possessive, protective, suspicious **11** mistrustful, mistrusting **12** apprehensive

jealousy 4 envy **8** distrust, jaundice, mistrust **9** suspicion **10** resentment **12** covetousness **14** possessiveness **16** green-eyed monster
color: 5 green

Jebus
city captured by: 5 David
renamed: 9 Jerusalem
inhabitant: 8 Jebusite

jeer 3 boo, bug, dig, rap **4** barb, hiss, hoot, mock, razz, slam, slur **5** abuse, flout, hound, knock, scoff, scorn, sneer, taunt, whoop **6** deride, harass, heckle, hector, insult, revile **7** catcall, laugh at, mockery, obloquy **8** derision, ridicule, scoffing **9** aspersion, contumely, poke fun at, whistle at

Jeffers, Robinson
author of: 5 Medea, Tamar **6** Cawdor **8** Solstice **9** Dear Judas **12** Roan Stallion **14** Thurso's Landing **18** The Women at Point Sur **21** The Tower Beyond Tragedy

Jefferson, Arthur Stanley
real name of: 10 Stan Laurel

Jefferson, Thomas ***see box***

Jeffersons, The
character: 8 Florence **9** Tom Willis **11** Helen Willis **12** Harry Bentley **15** George Jefferson, Lionel Jefferson, Louise Jefferson, Ralph the Doorman **20** Jenny Willis Jefferson
cast: 9 Mike Evans **10** Da-

Jefferson, Thomas
nickname: 16 Sage of Monticello
presidential rank: 5 third
party: 20 Democratic-Republican
state represented: 2 VA
defeated: 5 (John) Adams **8** (Charles Cotesworth) Pinckney
vice president: 4 (Aaron) Burr **7** (George) Clinton
cabinet:
***state:* 7** (James) Madison
***treasury:* 6** (Samuel) Dexter **8** (Albert) Gallatin
***war:* 8** (Henry) Dearborn
***attorney general:* 6** (Caesar Augustus) Rodney **7** (Levi) Lincoln **12** (John) Breckenridge
***navy:* 5** (Robert) Smith
born: 2 VA **14** Shadwell estate **15** Goochland (Albemarle) County
died/buried: 10 Monticello
education: 14 William and Mary
interests: 6 violin **7** writing **11** agriculture **12** architecture
favorite foods: 10 French food **11** French wines
vacation: 12 Poplar Forest
author: 25 Declaration of Independence, Notes on the State of Virginia **39** A Summary View of the Rights of British America
political career: 8 governor **16** House of Burgesses **19** Virginia legislature **25** Declaration of Independence, Second Continental Congress
***secretary of:* 5** state
***minister to:* 6** France
civilian career: 6 farmer, lawyer
notable events of lifetime/term:
***expedition:* 13** Lewis and Clark
***prohibition of:* 19** importation of slaves
***purchase:* 9** Louisiana
father: 5 Peter
mother: 4 Jane (Randolph)
siblings: 4 Jane, Lucy, Mary **6** Martha **8** Randolph **9** Anna Scott, Elizabeth **10** Peter Field
wife: 6 Martha (Wayles Skelton)
children: 4 Mary **6** Martha

mon Evans, Marla Gibbs, Roxie Roker **11** Ned Wertimer **12** Paul Benedict **13** Franklin Cover, Isabel Sanford **14** Sherman Hemsley **15** Berlinda Tolbert
George's business: 11 dry cleaning
spinoff from: 14 All in the Family

Jeffreys, Harold
field: 7 physics **9** astronomy
nationality: 7 British
explained: 7 weather
studied: 10 Earth's core **11** solar system

Jeffries, James Jackson
nickname: 14 The Boilermaker
sport: 6 boxing
class: 11 heavyweight

jehad, jihad 6 strife **7** holy war **8** struggle

Jehioada
father: 7 Paseach
son: 7 Benaiah
means: 12 Jehovah knows

Jehoshaphat
father: 3 Asa **6** Ahitub, Nimshi, Parnah
mother: 8 Jehorani
means: 13 Jehovah judges

Jehova 3 god **5** diety

Jehu
father: 6 Hanani **11** Jehoshaphat

jejune 4 dull **5** banal, inane, stale, trite, vapid **7** humdrum, insipid, puerile **8** ordinary **9** hackneyed **10** pedestrian, unexciting, unoriginal, wishy-washy **11** commonplace **12** conventional **13** uninteresting

jell 3 gel, jam, set **4** clot, firm **5** jelly **7** congeal, thicken **9** coagulate **10** gelatinize

Jellyby, Mrs
character in: 10 Bleak House
author: 7 Dickens

jellyfish 5 hydra, polyp, softy **6** coward, medusa, nettle **7** sunfish **8** weakling **10** ctenophore, pantywaist **11** milquetoast, mollycoddle **12** coelenterate, invertebrate, siphonophore **18** Portuguese man-of-war

je ne sais quoi 13 I don't know what **18** indefinable quality

Jenkins, Richard Walter, Jr
real name of: 13 Richard Burton

Jenner, Bruce
sport: 13 track and field
known for: 9 decathlon
won: 8 Olympics

Jenner, Edward
nationality: 7 British
discovered: 11 vaccination **19** smallpox inoculation

Jenney, William Le Baron
architect of: 21 Home Insurance Building (Chicago)

jeopardize 4 risk **6** expose, hazard **7** imperil **8** endanger **10** compromise **11** put into danger

jeopardy 4 risk **5** peril **6** danger, hazard **8** exposure, unsafety **9** liability **10** insecurity **11** imperilment **12** endangerment **13** vulnerability **14** precariousness

Jephthah 11 Hebrew judge
father: 6 Gilead

Jeremiah
father: 7 Hilkiah **10** Habazaniah
daughter: 7 Mamutal
grandson: 7 Jehohaz
friend, scribe: 6 Baruch

jerk 3 ass, tic, tug **4** dope, dupe, fool, pull, snap, yank **5** dummy, dunce, idiot, klutz, pluck, shake, spasm, start, twist **6** quiver, reflex, thrust, twitch, wrench **7** tremble **8** convulse **9** trembling

jerky 4 beef, meat **5** jolty, jumpy **6** choppy, elboic, jouncy **7** biltong, charqui, fidgety, twitchy **9** dried beef, spasmodic, twitching

Jeroboam
father: 5 Joash, Nebat
successor: 9 Zachariah

jerry-built 4 weak **5** frail, run-up, shaky, tacky **6** faulty, flimsy, shoddy, sleazy **7** rickety, unsound **8** gimcrack, slipshod, thrown-up, unstable **9** cheap-jack, defective **10** ramshackle **13** unsubstantial **14** thrown-together

jersey 3 cow **5** maillot, shirt **6** tricot **7** sweater **8** camisole, guernsey, pullover **10** undershirt

Jersey Joe
nickname of: 10 Joe Walcott

Jerubbaal *see* **6** Gideon

Jerusalem
author: 12 William Blake

Jerusalem
former name: 5 Jebus
pool of: 6 Siloam **8** Bethesda

Jerusalem
Arabic: 14 Bayt al-Muqaddas
capital of: 6 Israel
Hebrew: 12 Yerushalayim
hills: 7 Judaean
landmark: 6 al-Aqsa **11** Wailing Wall, Western Wall **12** Israel Museum **13** Dome of the Rock **14** Dead Sea Scrolls **15** Shrine of the Book **17** Rockefeller Museum **24** Church of the Holy Sepulcher
mount: 6 Olives, Scopus
river: 6 Kidron
ruler: 5 Arabs, David, Herod **6** Persia, Romans **7** British, Saladin, Seljuks, Solomon **8** Ayyubids, Fatimids, Ptolemy I **9** Crusaders, Maccabees, Mamelukes **10** Canaanites **12** Antiochus III **13** Pontius Pilate **15** Byzantine Empire **17** Alexander the Great, Antiochus the Third
street: 11 Via Dolorosa

Jerusalem Delivered
author: 13 Torquato Tasso

Jervis, Mrs
character in: 6 Pamela
author: 10 Richardson

jessamine 8 Jasminum
varieties: 3 day **5** night, poet's **6** orange, yellow **12** willow-leaved **13** night-blooming **14** Carolina yellow

Jesse
father: 4 Obed
grandfather: 4 Boaz
grandmother: 4 Ruth
great-grandfather: 5 Rahab
son: 5 David, Eliab **7** Shammah **8** Abinadab

jest 3 gag, pun **4** fool, game, gibe, jape, joke, josh, quip **5** act up, crack, laugh, prank, tease, trick **6** banter, bon mot **9** wisecrack, witticism **10** crack jokes, pleasantry **11** horse around

jester 3 wag, wit **4** card, fool, mime, zany **5** clown, comic, joker, mimer, mimic **6** madcap, mummer **7** buffoon **8** comedian, funnyman, humorist, quipster **9** harlequin **10** motley fool **11** merry-andrew, pantomimist, punchinello

jesting 6 joking **7** teasing **8** sportive **9** bantering, unserious **12** wisecracking

Jesus
also called: 7 Holy One, Messiah **8** Nazarene, Son of God **9** the Christ **12** Man of Sorrows **13** Prince of Peace **14** Savior Anointed
mother: 4 Mary
stepfather: 6 Joseph
birthplace: 9 Bethlehem
lived in: 8 Nazareth
death place: 9 Jerusalem
buried by: 17 Joseph of Arimathea
disciples: 4 John, Jude

5 James, Peter, Simon **6** Andrew, Philip, Thomas **7** Matthew **12** James the Less **13** Judas Iscariot **20** Bartholomew Nathanael
secret follower: 9 Nicodemus
famous discourse: 16 Sermon on the Mount

jet 4 gush **5** flush, issue, shoot, spout, spray, spurt, surge, swash **6** effuse, nozzle, rush up, squirt, stream **7** sparger, sprayer, Spritze, syringe **8** atomizer, fountain, shoot out, Spritzer **9** discharge, sprinkler

Jethro
daughter: 8 Zipporah
son-in-law: 5 Moses

Jetsons, The
character: 5 Astro **10** Jane Jetson, Judy Jetson **11** Elroy Jetson **12** George Jetson **13** Cosmo G Spacely
voices: 8 Mel Blanc **10** Daws Butler, Don Messick, Janet Waldo **13** George O'Hanlon **14** Penny Singleton

jettison 4 dump **5** eject, scrap **6** unload **7** cast off, discard **8** throw out **9** discharge, eliminate, pitch over, throw over **13** toss overboard

jetty 4 dike, dock, mole, pier, quay, slip **5** black, ebony, groin, levee, raven, sable, wharf **6** bridge **7** sea wall **8** buttress **10** breakwater

jeu de mots 3 pun **11** play on words

jeu d'esprit 9 witticism **17** witty literary work
literally: 12 play of spirit

jeune fille 4 girl **9** young girl **13** unmarried girl

jeunesse doree 11 gilded youth, golden youth

Jeven 3 God

Jew 6 Essene, Hebrew, Judean, Semite **7** Edomite, Judaist, Moabite **8** Hebraist, Sephardi **9** Israelite

jewel 3 ace, gem, pip **4** bead, dear, find, ring, whiz **5** honey, pearl, prize, stone, tiara **6** bangle, bauble, brooch, locket, winner **7** earring, pendant, trinket **8** bracelet, knockout, necklace, ornament, pure gold, treasure **9** humdinger, lavaliere **10** topnotcher **11** crackerjack, masterpiece

jewelry 4 gems, gold **6** silver **7** bangles, gewgaws, regalia **8** trinkets **10** adornments **14** precious stones

Jewett, Sarah Orne
author of: 26 The Country of the Pointed Firs

Jewish 6 Hebrew, Judaic **7** Hebraic, Semitic
bread: 5 matzo **6** matzoh **7** challah
candelabrum: 7 menorah
ceremonial robe: 5 kitel
***color:* 5** white
coming of age: 10 bar mitzvah, bat mitzvah
dietary laws: 7 kashrut **8** kashruth
group: 8 Hadassah **9** B'nai B'rith
holy day/festival: 5 Purim, seder **6** Sukkot **7** Shavuot **8** Chanukah, Hanukkah, Passover **9** Yom Kippur **12** Rosh Hashanah
law/scripture: 5 Torah **6** Gemara, Talmud, Tanach **7** Mishnah
liturgical prayer: 6 Yigdal **8** Kol Nidre
***recited on eve of:* 9** Yom Kippur
marriage canopy: 6 chupah
prayerbook: 6 mahzor, siddur **7** machzor
quarter: 6 ghetto, mellah
school: 5 heder **6** cheder
skullcap: 5 kipah **8** yarmulka
service to commemorate the dead: 6 Yizkor
synagogue: 4 shul **5** schul
toast: 8 mazel tov

Jewkes, Mrs
character in: 6 Pamela
author: 10 Richardson

Jew of Malta, The
author: 18 Christopher Marlowe
character: 7 Abigail, Barabas **8** Ithamore **15** Governor of Malta

Jezebel
director: 12 William Wyler
cast: 10 Bette Davis, Fay Bainter, Henry Fonda **11** Donald Crisp, George Brent **15** Margaret Lindsay
Oscar for: 7 actress (Davis) **17** supporting actress (Bainter)

Jezebel
father: 7 Ethbaal
husband: 4 Ahab
daughter: 8 Athaliah
opposed: 6 Elijah
killed: 6 Naboth
father-in-law: 4 Omri

jib 3 arm, shy **4** balk, boom, sail, tack **5** demur, gigue, stick **6** recoil **7** scruple

Jibaro *see* **6** Jivaro

jibe 2 go **3** fit **4** mesh, tack **5** agree, fit in, match, shift, tally **6** accord, concur, square **7** conform **8** coincide, dovetail **9** harmonize **10** correspond, go together **11** fit together

jiffy 4 jiff **5** flash, shake, trice **6** minute, moment, second **7** half a mo, instant **9** twinkling **10** nanosecond **11** microsecond, millisecond, split second

jigger 4 dram, shot **5** glass **6** device, doodad, gadget, object **7** bicycle, gimmick, measure **9** doohickey, shot glass **10** boneshaker **11** contraption, thingumabob

jiggle 4 jerk **5** shake **6** bounce, fidget, joggle, jostle, twitch, wiggle **7** agitate, wriggle

jihad *see* **5** jehad

jilt 5 leave **6** betray, desert **7** forsake, let down **12** break off with **17** break an engagement

Jim
character in: 15 (The Adventures of) Huckleberry Finn
author: 5 Twain

jimmy 3 bar, pry **5** force, lever **7** crowbar

jingle 4 ring **5** clang, clank, clink, ditty **6** jangle, tinkle **7** clatter, ringing **8** doggerel, facetiae, limerick **10** catchy poem, catchy song **12** product theme **13** reverberation **14** commercial tune **16** tintinnabulation

Jingle, Alfred
character in: 14 Pickwick Papers
author: 7 Dickens

jingoism 10 chauvinism, flag-waving, patriotics **11** nationalism **14** overpatriotism, spread-eagleism **15** superpatriotism **16** ultranationalism

jinn 3 imp **5** afrit, demon, genie, jinni **6** afreet, spirit **8** jinniyeh

jinx 3 hex **5** curse **6** plague, whammy **7** bugaboo, bugbear, evil eye, ill wind, nemesis **9** evil spell
French: 9 bete noire

jitterbug 5 dance, lindy **8** lindy hop **12** boogie-woogie

jitters 6 shakes **7** anxiety, fidgets, jim-jams, shivers, willies **9** jumpiness, quivering, shakiness, tenseness, the creeps, whim-whams **10** uneasiness **11** butterflies, fidgetiness, nervousness **12** skittishness **13** heebie-jeebies **16** screaming-meemies

jittery **5** jumpy **6** uneasy **7** anxious, nervous

Jivaro, Shuara, Jibaro
tribe: **6** Achual, Antipa **8** Aguaruna, Huambiza
location: **4** Peru **7** Ecuador **12** South America
noted for: **7** tsantsa (shrunken heads)

Joab
mother: **7** Zeruiah
brother: **6** Asahel **7** Abishai
commanded: **10** David's army
killed: **5** Abner, Amasa **7** Absalom
killed by: **7** Benaiah
conspired to overthrow: **5** David

Joad family
characters in: **16** The Grapes of Wrath
members: **2** Ma, Pa **3** Tom **4** Noah **6** Connie **12** Rose of Sharon
author: **9** Steinbeck

Joakim
wife: **7** Susanna

Joash
means: **15** Jehovah is strong
father: **4** Ahab **7** Ahaziah, Jehohaz
son: **6** Gideon, Shelah **7** Amaziah
succeeded: **8** Athaliah

job **3** lot **4** care, duty, part, role, spot, task, work **5** chore, craft, field, place, quota, share, stint, trade, trust **6** affair, career, charge, errand, living, metier, office, output **7** calling, concern, mission, opening, portion, product, pursuit **8** activity, business, capacity, contract, exercise, function, position, province, vocation **9** allotment, piecework, situation **10** assignment, commission, engagement, enterprise, livelihood, occupation, profession **11** achievement, appointment, performance, undertaking **14** accomplishment, responsibility

Job
father: **8** Issachar
friend: **5** Elihu **6** Bildad, Zophar **7** Eliphaz

job holder **6** worker **8** employee, hireling

job seeker **7** hopeful **8** aspirant **9** applicant, candidate

Jocasta
also: **8** Epicaste
queen of: **6** Thebes
father: **9** Menoeceus
brother: **5** Creon
husband: **5** Laius **7** Oedipus
son: **7** Oedipus **8** Eteocles **9** Polynices
daughter: **6** Ismene **8** Antigone
death by: **7** hanging, suicide

Jochebed
father: **4** Levi
husband: **5** Amram
nephew: **5** Amram
son: **5** Aaron, Moses

jockey **5** Baeza **6** Arcaro, Pincay **7** Cauthen, Cordero, Cruguet, Hartack **8** McCarron, McHargue, Turcotte **9** Shoemaker, Velasquez

jocose **3** fun **4** arch **5** comic, droll, funny, jolly, merry, witty **6** joking, jovial **7** amusing, comical, jesting, jocular, playful, roguish, teasing, waggish **8** humorous, mirthful, prankish, sportive **9** facetious

jocular **3** gay **5** droll, funny, jolly, merry, witty **6** jocose, jocund, joking, jovial **7** amusing, jesting, playful, roguish, rompish, waggish **8** humorous, mirthful, prankish, sportive **9** facetious **10** frolicsome **12** entertaining, lighthearted

jocund **5** jolly, merry **6** breezy, cheery, elated, jovial, lively **8** cheerful, debonair, pleasant **9** easygoing **10** untroubled **12** happy-go-lucky, lighthearted

Joel
means: **12** Jehovah is God
father: **4** Nebo **6** Samuel **7** Azariah, Pedaiah, Pethuel
brother: **6** Nathan

Joe Palooka
creator: **9** Ham Fisher **11** Tony DiPreta
character:
children: **3** Joe **5** Buddy **7** Joannie
friend: **9** Little Max **10** Jerry Leemy
manager: **11** Knobby Walsh
valet: **6** Smokey
wife: **8** Anne Howe
profession: **5** boxer

jog **3** bob, jar, tug **4** jerk, pull, rock, stir, trot, yank **5** nudge, shake, twist **6** bounce, jiggle, jostle, jounce, prompt, twitch, wrench **7** actuate, animate **8** activate, energize **9** stimulate

jogger **4** memo **6** layboy, runner **7** trotter **8** reminder **10** memorandum

Johannesburg
airport: **8** Jan Smuts
area: **4** Rand **9** Transvaal
capital of: **11** South Africa
landmark: **13** Carlton Centre **14** Africana Museum **16** Union Observatory **17** Zoological Gardens **20** Melrose Bird Sanctuary
township: **6** Soweto **7** Lenasia **10** Nancefield
university: **13** Rand Afrikaans, Witwatersrand

John
father: **7** Zebedee
brother: **5** James
son: **5** Peter
called, with brother: **9** Boanerges **13** sons of thunder
pertaining to John or his writings: **9** Johannine

John Brown's Body
author: **19** Stephen Vincent Benet

John Gabriel Borkman
author: **11** Henrik Ibsen

John Mark *see* **4** Mark

Johnny Belinda
director: **13** Jean Negulesco
cast: **8** Lew Ayres **9** Jane Wyman **15** Charles Bickford
Oscar for: **7** actress (Wyman)

Johnny Cash Show, The
cast: **9** Jim Varney **10** Howard Mann **11** Carl Perkins, Steve Martin **14** June Carter Cash, Tennessee Three **15** Statler Brothers **32** Mother Maybelle and the Carter Family

Johnny-come-lately **8** newcomer **9** latecomer **10** new arrival **11** late arrival

Johnny U
nickname of: **12** Johnny Unitas

Johns, Glynis
born: **8** Pretoria **11** South Africa
roles: **11** Mary Poppins **13** The Sundowners **17** A Little Night Music **26** Around the World in Eighty Days

Johns, Jasper
born: **9** Augusta GA
artwork: **4** Flag **6** Studio, Target **8** Watchman **10** Fool's House **12** Device Circle **13** Painted Bronze (Beer Cans) **14** The Barber's Tree **19** Target with Four Faces **22** Target with Plaster Casts

Johnson, Andrew
see box

Johnson, Earvin
nickname: **5** Magic
sport: **10** basketball
position: **5** guard
team: **16** Los Angeles Lakers

Johnson, Andrew
presidential rank: 11 seventeenth
party: 8 Democrat
state represented: 2 TN
defeated: 5 no one
***succeeded upon death of:* 7** Lincoln
vice president: 4 none
cabinet:
***state:* 6** (William Henry) Seward
***treasury:* 9** (Hugh) McCulloch
***war:* 7** (Edwin McMasters) Stanton **9** (John McAllister) Schofield
***attorney general:* 5** (James) Speed **6** (William Maxwell) Evarts **8** (Henry) Stanbery
***navy:* 6** (Gideon) Welles
***postmaster general:* 7** (Alexander Williams) Randall **8** (William) Dennison
***interior:* 5** (John Palmer) Usher **6** (James) Harlan **8** (Orville Hickman) Browning
born: 9 Raleigh NC
died: 16 Carter's Station TN
buried: 13 Greeneville TN
education: 9 no college **12** self-educated
political career: 8 US Senate **13** vice president **22** House of Representatives
***only president to be:* 9** impeached (1868)
***found:* 9** not guilty
***mayor of:* 11** Greeneville (TN)
***governor of:* 9** Tennessee
civilian career: 6 tailor
military service: 8 Civil War **12** US Volunteers **16** brigadier general
***military governor of:* 9** Tennessee
notable events of lifetime/term: 14 Reconstruction
***Purchase:* 6** Alaska
father: 5 Jacob
mother: 4 Mary (McDonough)
***stepfather:* 15** Turner Dougherty
sibling: 7 William
wife: 5 Eliza (McCardle)
children: 4 Mary **6** Andrew, Martha, Robert **7** Charles

Johnson, Jack (John Arthur)
nickname: 11 Little Artha **14** Galveston Giant
sport: 6 boxing
class: 11 heavyweight

Johnson, Lyndon Baines
see box, p. 524

Johnson, Philip Cortelyou
architect of: 10 Glass House (New Canaan CT), Wiley House (New Canaan CT) **12** Hodgson House (New Canaan CT) **13** Pennzoil Place (Houston TX) **14** Bolssonas House (New Canaan CT) **16** Amon Carter Museum (Ft Worth TX) **17** Sheldon Art Gallery (Lincoln NE) **18** A T and T Headquarters (NYC), Kline Science Center (Yale) **19** New York State Theater (Lincoln Center)

Johnson, Samuel
author of: 8 Rasselas, The Idler **18** The Lives of the Poets **22** The Vanity of Human Wishes **30** Dictionary of the English Language

Johnson, Walter
nickname: 8 Big Train
sport: 8 baseball
position: 7 pitcher
team: 18 Washington Senators

John the Baptist
father: 9 Zechariah
mother: 9 Elizabeth
descendant of: 5 Aaron
precurser of: 5 Jesus **10** the Messiah

joie de vivre 11 joy of living **19** delight in being alive

join 3 hug, mix **4** abut, ally, band, bind, fuse, glue, link, meet, pool **5** affix, brush, chain, enter, graze, marry, merge, paste, reach, skirt, stick, touch, unify, unite **6** adjoin, attach, bridge, cement, cohere, couple, fasten, scrape, solder, splice **7** combine, connect, verge on **8** border on, enlist in, enroll in, federate, hold fast **9** associate, cooperate, syndicate **10** amalgamate, fraternize **11** confederate, consolidate **12** conglomerate

joined 3 met, wed **4** tied **5** bound, fused, glued, mated, yoked **6** allied, bonded, linked, merged, paired, seamed, united, welded **7** coupled, married, related, spliced **8** attached, cemented, combined, enlisted, fastened **9** bracketed, connected **10** associated, hand-in-hand, integrated **11** hand-in-glove

join forces 4 ally **5** merge, unite **6** league, team up **7** combine **8** coalesce **9** affiliate, cooperate **11** consolidate **12** band together

joint 4 hock, knee, knot, link **5** elbow, hinge, nexus **6** allied, common, mutual, shared, united **7** knuckle, unified **8** combined, communal, coupling, junction, juncture **9** associate, community, conjoined, corporate, unanimous **10** associated, collective, connection, hand-in-hand, like-minded **11** coalitional, conjunctive, cooperative **12** articulation, consolidated **13** collaborative
kind:
***ball and socket:* 3** hip **8** shoulder
***fused:* 5** skull **11** base of spine
***hinged:* 4** knee **5** elbow
***unfused:* 3** hip, jaw **4** knee **5** elbow **8** shoulder

joint action 7 concert **8** teamwork **11** cooperating, cooperation, give-and-take **13** collaboration, participation

joint effort 7 concert **8** teamwork **11** cooperation **13** collaboration

jointly 8 arm in arm, in common, in unison, mutually, together, unitedly **10** conjointly, hand-in-hand, side by side **12** collectively **13** in association, in conjunction

join together 3 wed **4** fuse, weld **5** marry, unify, unite **6** solder **9** integrate **10** amalgamate **11** consolidate, incorporate

Johnson, Lyndon Baines
nickname: **3** LBJ **15** Landslide Lyndon
presidential rank: **11** thirty-sixth
party: **10** Democratic
state represented: **2** TX
succeeded upon death of: **7** Kennedy
defeated: **4** (Earle Harold) Munn, (Eric) Hass **6** (John) Kasper **7** (Clifton) DeBerry **9** (Barry Morris) Goldwater
vice president: **4** none (first term) **8** (Hubert Horatio) Humphrey
cabinet:
state: **4** (David Dean) Rusk
treasury: **4** (Joseph William) Barr **6** (Clarence Douglas) Dillon, (Henry Hamill) Fowler
defense: **8** (Clark McAdams) Clifford, (Robert Strange) McNamara
attorney general: **5** (William Ramsey) Clark **7** (Robert Francis) Kennedy **10** (Nicholas deBelleville) Katzenbach
postmaster general: **6** (Lawrence Francis) O'Brien, (William Marvin) Watson **9** (John Austin) Gronouski
interior: **5** (Stewart Lee) Udall
agriculture: **7** (Orville Lothrop) Freeman
commerce: **5** (Cyrus Rowlett) Smith **6** (John Thomas) Connor, (Luther Hartwell) Hodges **10** (Alexander Buel) Trowbridge
labor: **5** (William Willard) Wirtz
HEW: **5** (Wilbur Joseph) Cohen **7** (John William) Gardner **10** (Anthony Joseph) Celebrezze
HUD: **4** (Robert Colwell) Wood **6** (Robert Clifton) Weaver
transportation: **4** (Alan Stevenson) Boyd
born: **11** (near) Stonewall TX
died/buried: **13** (near) Johnson City TX
education:
teachers' college: **19** Southwest Texas State
law school: **10** Georgetown
religion: **17** Disciples of Christ
vacation spot: **8** LBJ Ranch
author: **15** The Vantage Point
political career: **8** US Senate **13** vice president **24** US House of Representatives
civilian career: **7** teacher
military service: **6** US Navy **10** World War II **11** World War Two
notable events of lifetime/term: **9** race riots **12** Great Society
act: **11** Civil Rights **12** Voting Rights **19** Economic Opportunity
assassination of: **14** Robert F Kennedy **18** Martin Luther King Jr
capture of: **6** Pueblo
Pueblo captured by: **10** North Korea
treaty: **23** Nuclear Non-Proliferation
war: **7** Vietnam **11** Arab-Israeli
father: **7** Sam Ealy
mother: **7** Rebekah (Baines)
siblings: **10** Sam Houston **12** Lucia Huffman **13** Josefa Hermine, Rebekah Luruth
wife: **7** Claudia (Alta Taylor)
nickname: **8** Lady Bird
children: **9** Lynda Bird **10** Luci Baines
First Lady:
responsible for: **24** Highway Beautification Act
author: **16** A White House Diary

6 solder **9** integrate **10** amalgamate **11** consolidate, incorporate

join up **6** enlist, enroll, sign up **9** volunteer

joist **4** beam **5** brace **6** timber **7** support

joke **3** gag, pun, wit **4** butt, dupe, fool, gibe, goof, gull, jape, jest, josh, lark, mock, quip **5** antic, caper, cinch, clown, farce, prank, put-on, roast, tease, trick **6** banter, bon mot, deride, frolic, gambol, gibe at, jeer at, parody, satire, take in, target, trifle, whimsy **7** buffoon, bumpkin, chortle, lampoon, laugh at, nothing, scoff at, smile at, snicker **8** anecdote, badinage, pooh-pooh, pushover, repartee, ridicule, town fool, travesty **9** burlesque, diversion, horseplay, simpleton, wisecrack, witticism **10** pleasantry **11** horse around, monkeyshine **13** facetiousness, laughingstock

joker **3** wag, wit **4** snag, trap, zany **5** catch, clown, hitch, mimic, rider, snare, trick **6** jester, madcap **7** codicil, pitfall, punster **8** addendum, comedian, funnyman, humorist **10** subterfuge, supplement **11** wisecracker
French: **7** farceur

jokester **3** wag **5** comic, cutup, joker **8** comedian **9** prankster

Joliba *see* **5** Niger

Joliot-Curie, Frederic
field: **9** chemistry
nationality: **6** French
discovered: **23** artificial radioisotopes
awarded: **10** Nobel Prize
wife: **16** Irene Joliot-Curie

Joliot-Curie, Irene
field: **7** physics
nationality: **6** French
discovered: **23** artificial radioisotopes
awarded: **10** Nobel Prize
husband: **14** Frederic Joliot
father: **11** Pierre Curie
mother: **10** Marie Curie

jollity **3** fun **4** glee, play, romp **5** cheer, mirth, revel, sport **6** frolic, gaiety **7** revelry, whoopee **8** hilarity **9** amusement, festivity, jocundity, joviality, merriment, pleasure **10** jocularity **11** merrymaking **12** conviviality

jolly **3** gay **5** droll, funny, happy, merry **6** jocund, jovial **7** gleeful, jocular, playful **8** cheerful, mirthful, sportive

9 fun-loving 10 delightful, rollicking 12 high-spirited

jolt 3 bob, jar, jog 4 bump, jerk, jump, stun 5 lurch, quake, shake, shock, start, throw, upset 6 bobble, bounce, jiggle, joggle, jostle, jounce, quiver, trauma, twitch 7 disturb, perturb, setback, shake up, shaking, startle 8 convulse, reversal 9 agitation, take aback 11 thunderbolt

Joltin' Joe
nickname of: 11 Joe DiMaggio

Jonah
father: 7 Amittai
swallowed by: 9 large fish
preached in: 7 Nineveh
hometown: 10 Gathhepher

Jonathan
means: 11 Jehovah gave
father: 4 Jada, Saul 6 Joiada, Kereah 8 Abiathar
friend: 5 David
son: 9 Meribkaal 12 Mephibosheth

Jonathan Livingston Seagull
author: 11 Richard Bach

Jonathan Wild
author: 13 Henry Fielding

Jones, Carolyn
born: 10 Amarillo TX
roles: 8 Morticia 15 The Addams Family

Jones, Inigo
architect of: 11 Queen's House (Greenwich) 14 Banqueting Hall (Whitehall Palace, London)
restoration: 16 St Paul's Cathedral

Jones, James
author of: 7 Whistle 14 The Thin Red Line 15 Some Came Running 18 From Here to Eternity

Jones, James Earl
born: 11 Arkabutla MS
roles: 6 The Man 7 Othello 8 Star Wars 15 The Emperor Jones 17 The Great White Hope
voice of: 10 Darth Vader

Jones, John Paul
served in: 11 Russian navy 16 Revolutionary War 21 British merchant marine
commander of ship: 6 Ranger 10 Providence 15 Bonhomme Richard
defeated ship: 7 Serapis
saying: 23 "I have not yet begun to fight"

Jones, Shirley
husband: 11 Jack Cassidy, Marty Ingels
born: 10 Smithton PA
roles: 8 Carousel, Oklahoma 11 Elmer Gantry, The Music Man 18 The Partridge Family

Jong, Erica
author of: 5 Fanny 12 Fear of Flying 18 At the Edge of the Body 20 How to Save Your Own Life

jonquil 4 bulb, lily 8 daffodil 9 narcissus

Jonson, Ben
author of: 6 The Fox 7 Sejanus, Volpone 11 A Tale of a Tub 12 The Alchemist 15 Bartholomew Fair 18 Every Man in His Humo(u)r 21 Every Man out of His Humo(u)r 23 Epicene or the Silent Woman

Jordan *see box*

Jordan, Robert
character in: 19 For Whom the Bell Tolls
author: 9 Hemingway

Jormungandr
also: 10 Jormungand 11 Iormungandr 14 Midgard Serpent
origin: 12 Scandinavian
form: 7 serpent
father: 4 Loki
mother: 9 Angerboda, Angrbodha, Angurboda
brother: 6 Fenrir, Fenris
sister: 3 Hel
wrapped around: 5 world
killed by: 4 Thor
death place: 6 Vigrid
killed: 4 Thor

Jo's Boys
author: 15 Louisa May Alcott

Jordan
other name: 24 Hashemite Kingdom of Jordan
capital/largest city: 5 Amman
ancient name: 12 Philadelphia
others: 4 Krak, Ma'an, Salt 5 Agaba, Ariha, Irbid, Jenin, Karak, Kerak, Sarga, Zarga, Zerke 6 Bethel, Hebron, Jarash, Jerash, Madaba, Nablus, Ramtha 7 Al-Agaba, Bethany, El-Kerak, El Zerga, Jericho, Kirmoab, Nabulus, Samaria 8 Al-Khalil, Ram Allah 9 Bethlehem, Jerusalem
school: 7 yarmouk
division: 8 East Bank, West Bank 11 Transjordan
ancient state: 4 Edom, Moab 5 Ammon, Judah 6 Gilead
head of state: 4 king
monetary unit: 4 fils 5 dinar
mountain: 3 Hor 4 Nebo 5 Bukka, Dabab 6 Ataiba, Gilead, Mubrak
highest point: 9 Jabal Ramm, Jebel Ramm
river: 6 Jordan, Yarmuk 11 Nahr-az-Zarga
sea: 3 Red 4 Dead 7 Galilee 13 Mediterranean
physical feature:
desert: 6 Syria
gulf: 5 Aqaba
plateau: 11 Transjordan
valley: 4 Ghor 9 Great Rift
wind: 7 Khamsin
people: 4 Arab, Kurd 7 Bedouin, Checher 8 Armenian, Assyrian 10 Circassian 11 Palestinian
ancient: 8 Armonite 9 Nabataean
ruler: 5 Talal 6 Faisal, Greeks, Romans 7 Hussein 8 Abdullah, Selucidas 9 Crusaders 10 Ibn Hussein, Nabataeans 12 Ottoman Turks 18 Abdullah Ibn Hussein
tribe: 5 Qaysi 6 Yamani
language: 6 Arabic
religion: 5 Islam 13 Greek Orthodox
place:
canal: 8 East Gher
ruins: 5 Ajlun, Petra 6 Jarash 7 Al Karak
feature:
headdress: 8 kaffiyeh
village headman: 7 mukhtar
village square: 5 sahah
food:
dessert: 7 baklava
pastry: 7 katayif

Joseph
father: **4** Bani **5** Aseph, Jacob **10** Mattathias
mother: **6** Rachel
brother: **3** Dan, Gad **4** Levi **5** Asher, Judah **6** Reuben, Simeon **7** Zebulun **8** Benjamin, Issachar, Naphtali
wife: **4** Mary **7** Asenath
stepson: **5** Jesus
also called: **20** Barsabbas of Arimathea **21** Barsabbas of Arimathaea
buried: **5** Jesus
slave of: **8** Potiphar

Joseph Andrews
author: **13** Henry Fielding
character: **5** Fanny **9** Lady Booby **11** Mrs Slipslop, Parson Adams, Peter Pounce **13** Pamela Andrews

josh **3** guy, kid, rag, rib **4** dish, haze, jape, jest, jive, joke, quiz, razz, ride, twit **5** chaff, jolly, put on, roast, tease **6** banter, needle **8** ridicule

Joshua
means: **18** Jehovah is salvation
father: **3** Nun
succeeded: **5** Moses
captured: **7** Jericho, Lachish
hid spies: **5** Rahab

Josiah
means: **12** Jehovah heals
father: **9** Zephaniah
succeeded: **4** Amon

jostle **3** jab **4** bump, butt, poke, prod, push **5** crowd, elbow, shove **7** collide **8** shoulder **10** hit against, run against **12** knock against

jot **3** bit, dot **4** list, mite, note, snip, whit **5** enter, speck, trace **6** record, trifle **7** modicum, one iota, put down, set down, smidgen, snippet **8** flyspeck, particle, register, scribble, take down **9** scintilla

Jotham
son: **4** Ahaz

Jo the crossing sweeper
character in: **10** Bleak House
author: **7** Dickens

jotting **4** memo, note **6** doodle **8** scribble **10** memorandum, scribbling

Jotun
origin: **12** Scandinavian
form: **5** giant
conflicts with: **4** gods
enemy: **4** Asar **5** Aesir

Jotunheim
origin: **12** Scandinavian
realm of: **6** giants

Joukahainen
origin: **7** Finnish
form: **8** magician
location: **7** Lapland
tried to kill: **11** Vainamoinen

Joule, James Prescott
field: **7** physics
nationality: **7** British
established law of: **20** conservation of energy
named for him: **10** unit of work

jounce **3** bob **6** bounce **7** rebound **8** ricochet

Jourdain, Monsieur
character in: **21** The Bourgeois Gentleman **22** Le Bourgeois Gentilhomme
author: **7** Moliere

Jourdan, Louis
real name: **11** Louis Gendre
born: **6** France **9** Marseille
roles: **4** Gigi **6** Can Can **9** Octopussy **15** The Paradine Case **23** Three Coins in the Fountain **24** Letter from an Unknown Woman

journal **3** log **5** album, daily, diary, paper, sheet **6** annual, ledger, memoir, record, weekly **7** almanac, daybook, gazette, history, logbook, monthly, tabloid **8** calendar, magazine, notebook, register, yearbook **9** chronicle, newspaper, quarterly, scrapbook **10** chronology, confession, memorandum, memory book, periodical, record book **11** account book, daily record, publication **13** autobiography

journalist **6** author, editor, writer **7** byliner, diarist, newsman **8** reporter **9** columnist, newswoman **12** newspaperman **13** correspondent **14** newspaperwoman

Journal of the Plague Year, A
author: **11** Daniel Defoe

journey **3** fly, way **4** roam, rove, sail, tour, trek, trip, wend **5** jaunt, quest, route, tramp **6** course, cruise, flight, junket, outing, ramble, roving, travel, voyage, wander **7** circuit, meander, odyssey, passage, transit **8** divagate, navigate, sightsee, vagabond **9** excursion, itinerary, take a trip, wandering **10** divagation, expedition, pilgrimage **11** peregrinate **13** peregrination

Journey Into Fear
author: **10** Eric Ambler

journey's end **4** goal **9** objective **11** destination

Journey to the End of the Night
author: **20** Louis-Ferdinand Celine

joust **4** tilt **5** combat, jostle **7** contend, contest, tourney **8** run a tilt **10** contention, tournament

Jove *see* **7** Jupiter

jovial **3** gay **5** jolly, merry, sunny **6** blithe, cheery, hearty, jocose, jocund **7** buoyant, gleeful, jocular, playful, zestful **8** cheerful, humorous, laughing, mirthful, sportive **9** convivial, fun-loving, hilarious **10** delightful, frolicsome, rollicking

joviality **3** fun **4** glee **5** cheer, gaity, mirth **7** delight, jollity, revelry **8** buoyancy **9** jocundity, merriment **10** joyfulness, liveliness **11** high spirits

jowl **3** jaw **5** cheek, chops **6** muzzle **8** mandible

joy **3** gem **4** glee **5** jewel, pride, prize **6** gaiety **7** delight, ecstasy, elation, rapture **8** gladness, pleasure, treasure **9** enjoyment, happiness **10** excitement, exultation, jubilation **11** contentment, delectation **12** cheerfulness, exhilaration, satisfaction
goddess of: **6** Hathor

Joyce, James
author of: **7** Ulysses **9** Dubliners **13** Finnegan's Wake **31** A Portrait of the Artist as a Young Man

joyful **4** glad, rosy **5** happy **6** bright, elated **7** blessed, pleased **8** cheerful, ecstatic, exultant, gladsome, jubilant, pleasing **9** delighted, full of joy, overjoyed **10** delightful, enraptured, gratifying, heartening **11** pleasurable, transported **12** heartwarming

joyless **3** sad **4** glum, grim **5** black **6** dismal, gloomy, morbid, woeful **7** doleful, forlorn, unhappy **8** dejected, desolate, dolorous, downcast, mournful **9** cheerless, depressed, sorrowful, woebegone **10** despondent, in the dumps, lugubrious, melancholy **11** downhearted, pessimistic **12** disconsolate, heavyhearted **14** down in the mouth

joy of living
French: **11** joie de vivre

Joy of Sex, The
author: **11** Alex Comfort

joyous **3** gay **4** glad **5** happy, merry **7** festive, gleeful **8** cheerful, gladsome, mirthful **9** rapturous, wonderful **10** delightful, gratifying, heartening **11** pleasurable **12** heartwarming, lighthearted

joyousness **4** glee **8** gladness **9** happiness, merriment **10** blitheness, exuberance **11** high spirits **16** lightheartedness

Jubal
father: **6** Lamech
mother: **4** Adah
brother: **5** Jabal

jubilant **3** gay **4** glad **5** happy, jolly, merry **6** blithe, cheery, elated, enrapt, joyful, joyous **7** buoyant, charmed, gleeful, pleased, radiant, smiling **8** cheerful, ecstatic, exultant, gladsome, laughing, mirthful **9** delighted, delirious, exuberant, gladdened, gratified, overjoyed, rapturous, rejoicing, rhapsodic **10** blithesome, captivated, enraptured **11** exhilarated, intoxicated, tickled pink **12** happy as a lark, lighthearted **13** in high spirits

jubilation **5** bliss **9** rejoicing **11** celebration **12** exhilaration

jubilee **2** do **4** bash, fete, gala **5** blast, party **6** frolic, revels **7** blowout, holiday, revelry, shindig **8** festival, wingding **9** festivity **10** jubilation, observance **11** anniversary, celebration, merrymaking **12** conviviality **13** commemoration

Juda
father: **6** Joanna, Joseph **8** Haneniah

Judah
father: **5** Jacob
mother: **4** Leah
brother: **3** Dan, Gad **4** Levi **5** Asher, Judah **6** Joseph, Reuben, Simeon **8** Benjamin, Issachar, Naphtali
sister: **5** Dinah
wife: **5** Shuah
son: **2** Er **4** Onan **5** Perez, Zerah **6** Baruch, Shelah
daughter-in-law: **5** Tamar
last king of: **8** Zedekiah
descendant of: **8** Judahite

Judah, tribes of *see* **14** Israel, tribes of

Judas
brother: **5** James
also called: **8** Thaddeus
disciple of: **5** Jesus

Judas Iscariot **8** betrayer
disciple of: **5** Jesus
betrayed: **5** Jesus
replaced by: **8** Matthias

Jude **7** apostle
brother: **5** James

Jude the Obscure
author: **11** Thomas Hardy
character: **10** Jude Fawley **12** Arabella Donn, Sue Bridehead **14** Drusilla Fawley **16** Little Father Time **17** Richard Phillotson

judge **3** try **4** deem, find, hear, rank, rate **5** fancy, gauge, guess, infer, juror, value, weigh **6** assess, assume, censor, critic, decide, deduce, expert, reckon, regard, review, rule on, settle, size up, umpire **7** adjudge, analyze, arbiter, believe, conduct, discern, imagine, justice, referee, resolve, suppose, surmise **8** appraise, assessor, conclude, consider, estimate, official, reviewer **9** appraiser, arbitrate, ascertain, authority, determine, evaluator, moderator **10** adjudicate, arbitrator, conjecture, magistrate **11** adjudicator, connoisseur, distinguish **12** pass sentence

judgment, judgement **4** view **5** sense, taste **6** acumen, belief, decree, ruling **7** finding, opinion, verdict **8** decision, estimate, sentence **9** appraisal, deduction, valuation **10** assessment, conclusion, conviction, discretion, perception, persuasion, shrewdness **11** arbitration, discernment, percipience **14** discrimination, perceptiveness

Judgment at Nuremberg
director: **13** Stanley Kramer
cast: **11** Judy Garland **12** Spencer Tracy **13** Burt Lancaster **14** Richard Widmark, William Shatner **15** Marlene Dietrich, Montgomery Clift **16** Maximilian Schell
Oscar for: **5** actor (Schell)

Judgment Day **8** doomsday **13** end of the world **14** day of reckoning **15** the Last Judgment

Judgment Day
author: **13** James T Farrell

Judgment of Paris *see* **5** Paris

judicial **5** legal **8** imposing, juristic, majestic, official **9** magistral **11** magisterial **13** distinguished

judiciary **5** bench, court **11** court system

judicious **4** just, sage, wise **5** acute, sober, sound **6** astute, shrewd **7** knowing, politic, prudent, tactful **8** sensible **9** sagacious **10** diplomatic, discerning, percipient, reasonable, reflective, thoughtful **11** levelheaded **13** perspicacious **14** discriminating

judiciousness **4** tact **6** acumen, wisdom **8** prudence, sagacity **9** good sense **10** discretion **11** discernment, percipience **12** perspicacity **14** discrimination

Judique, Mrs Tanis
character in: **7** Babbitt
author: **5** Lewis

Judith
husband: **4** Esau
killed: **10** Holofernes

Judith Paris
author: **11** Hugh Walpole

jug **3** jar, urn **4** ewer **5** crock, stein **6** bottle, carafe, flagon, vessel **7** pitcher, tankard **8** decanter, demijohn **9** container

juggle **4** redo **5** alter **6** modify **7** falsify **8** disguise, fool with **9** keep aloft **10** manipulate, meddle with, reorganize, tamper with, tinker with **12** misrepresent

juggler **5** cheat **6** jester **8** conjuror, deceiver, jongleur, magician, shuffler **15** prestidigitator

Juice
nickname of: **9** O J Simpson

juicy **3** wet **4** lush, racy **5** fluid, lurid, moist, pulpy, runny, sappy, spicy, vivid **6** fluent, liquid, risque, watery **7** flowing, graphic **8** colorful, dripping, exciting, luscious **9** succulent, thrilling **10** intriguing **11** captivating, fascinating, picturesque, provocative, sensational, tantalizing

Jules and Jim
director: **16** Francois Truffaut
cast: **10** Henri Serre **11** Marie Dubois, Oskar Werner **12** Jeanne Moreau

Julia
character in: **20** Two Gentlemen of Verona
author: **11** Shakespeare

Julia
character: **10** Corey Baker, Eddie Edson, Julia Baker **11** Hannah Yarby **14** Earl J Waggedorn, Marie Waggedorn **15** Dr Morton Chegley
cast: **10** Lloyd Nolan, Marc Copage **11** Betty Beaird, Michael Link **12** Eddie Quillan, Lurene Tuttle, Paul Winfield **14** Diahann Carroll

Julia
director: **13** Fred Zinnemann
based on story by: **14** Lillian Hellman (Pentimento)
cast: **9** Jane Fonda (Lillian

Hellman) **11** Hal Holbrook **12** Jason Robards (Dashiell Hammett) **15** Vanessa Redgrave (Julia) **16** Maximilian Schell
Oscar for: 12 screenwriter **15** supporting actor (Robards) **17** supporting actress (Redgrave)

Julius Caesar
author: 18 William Shakespeare
character: 6 Brutus (Marcus Brutus), Portia **7** Cassius (Gaius Cassius) **9** Calpurnia **10** Mark Antony (Marcus Antonius)
director: 17 Joseph L Mankiewicz
cast: 10 James Mason **11** Deborah Kerr, Greer Garson, John Gielgud **12** Edmond O'Brien, Louis Calhern, Marlon Brando

July
flower: 8 larkspur **9** water lily
French: 7 Juillet
holiday: 11 Bastille Day (14), Dominion Day (1) **15** Independence Day (4) **16** Saint Swithin's Day (15)
gem: 4 ruby
German: 4 Juli
Italian: 6 Luglio
number of days: 9 thirty-one
origin of name: 12 Julius Caesar
place in year:
***Gregorian:* 7** seventh
***Roman:* 5** fifth
Spanish: 5 Julio
Zodiac sign: 3 Leo **6** Cancer

jumble 3 mix **4** heap, mess, olio, stew **5** bunch, chaos, mix up, pitch, snarl **6** ball up, medley, muddle, pile up, tangle, tumble **7** clutter, farrago, melange, mixture, scatter **8** disarray, mishmash **9** aggregate, confusion, patchwork, potpourri **10** hodgepodge, miscellany, salmagundi **11** gallimaufry **12** accumulation **14** conglomeration

jumbled 5 messy **7** chaotic, mixed up, snarled, tangled **8** confused **9** cluttered, illogical **10** disjointed, incoherent **11** disarranged **12** disconnected, disorganized

jumbo 4 huge, vast **5** giant **6** mighty **7** immense, mammoth, titanic **8** colossal, enormous, gigantic, towering **9** cyclopean, monstrous, oversized **10** monumental, stupendous **11** elephantine, mountainous

jump 3 hop **4** buck, leap, pass, skip **5** boost, bound, pitch, start, surge, vault, wince **6** ambush, attack, blench, bounce, flinch, gambol, go over, hurdle, prance, recoil, spring, switch, upturn, zoom up **7** advance, barrier, digress, maunder, overrun, upsurge **8** fall upon, obstacle **9** barricade, increment, skyrocket **10** impediment **11** obstruction **12** augmentation

jumper 4 frog, sled, toad **5** dress, horse, shirt, smock **6** blouse, hopper, jacket, leaper **7** overall **8** coverall, kangaroo

jump for joy 5 exult **7** rejoice

jumpy 5 nervy, shaky **6** goosey, uneasy **7** alarmed, anxious, fidgety, fretful, jittery, nervous, panicky, twitchy, uptight **8** aflutter, agitated, fluttery, skittish **9** trembling, twitching **10** frightened **12** apprehensive

junction 6 linkup **7** conflux, joining **10** confluence, crossroads **11** concurrence, convergence, interchange **12** intersection

juncture 4 pass, seam **5** joint **6** crisis, linkup, moment **7** closure, joining, meeting **8** interval, occasion **10** confluence, connection **11** convergence, point in time **12** intersection **13** critical point

June ***see box***

jungle 4 bush, wild **5** woods **10** rain forest, wilderness **11** undergrowth **12** swampy forest, virgin forest

Jungle, The
author: 13 Upton Sinclair
character: 3 Ona **5** Jonas **6** Marija **8** Elzbieta **12** Jurgis Rudkus **13** Antanas Rudkus
criticism of: 19 meat-packing industry

Jungle Books, The
author: 14 Rudyard Kipling
character: 3 Kaa **5** Akela, Baloo, Hathi **6** Buldeo, Messau, Mowgli **8** Bagheera **9** Shere Khan **11** Gray Brother

Jungle Jim
creator: 11 Alex Raymond
character: 4 Joan, Kolu

junior 5 later, lower, minor, newer **6** lesser **7** younger **8** inferior **9** secondary **11** subordinate

June
characteristic: 8 weddings
event: 12 Midsummer Day (24), Midsummer Eve (23) **14** summer solstice (21)
flower: 4 rose
French: 4 Juin
gem: 5 pearl **9** moonstone **11** alexandrite
German: 4 Juni
holiday: 7 Flag Day (14) **10** Father's Day (third Sunday) **13** Kamehameha Day (11) **22** Jefferson Davis' birthday (3)
Italian: 6 Giugno
number of days: 6 thirty
origin of name: 4 Juno (Roman goddess) **6** Junius (Roman clan) **8** juniores (youths)
place in year:
***Gregorian:* 5** sixth
***Roman:* 6** fourth
saying: 24 What is so rare as a day in June
Spanish: 5 Junio
Zodiac sign: 6 Cancer, Gemini

juniper 9 Juniperus
varieties: 4 ashe, plum **5** Greek, Irish, shore **6** common, ground, needle, Polish, Sierra, Syrian **7** African, incense, prickly, Sargent **8** creeping, drooping, mountain, red-berry, Waukegan **9** alligator, blue-spire, Himalayan, prostrate **10** California **11** cherrystone **12** Canary Island, sweet-fruited **13** Rocky Mountain

junk 4 dump **5** scrap, trash, waste **6** debris, litter, refuse **7** clutter, discard, garbage, rubbish, rummage **8** castoffs, oddments, throw out **9** dispose of, throw away **11** odds and ends

junket 4 tour, trip **7** journey **9** excursion

Juno
origin: 5 Roman
queen of: 6 heaven
father: 6 Saturn
brother: 7 Jupiter
husband: 7 Jupiter
son: 4 Mars
protectress of: 5 women **8** marriage
epithet: 6 Lucina, Moneta **7** Curitis, Pronuba, Sospita
festival: 10 Matronalia
corresponds to: 4 Hera, Here

Juno and the Paycock
author: **10** Sean O'Casey

junta **5** cabal **7** council **9** committee **18** military government

Jupe, Sissy
character in: **9** Hard Times
author: **7** Dickens

Jupiter
also: **4** Jove
god of: **5** light **7** heavens, weather **9** lightning **11** thunderbolt
epithet: **5** Ultor **7** Elicius, Pluvius
corresponds to: **4** Zeus

Jupiter
position: **5** fifth
satellite: **2** Io **6** Europa **8** Amalthea, Callisto, Ganymede
characteristic: **7** red spot

Jurassic period
dinosaur from: **10** Diplodocus **11** Apatosaurus, Stegosaurus **12** Brontosaurus, Camarasaurus, Camptosaurus, Ceratosaurus, Megalosaurus **13** Brachiosaurus, Compsognathus, Ornitholestes

Jurgen
author: **17** James Branch Cabell

Jurgens, Curt
also: **11** Curd Jurgens
born: **6** Munich **7** Germany
roles: **12** The Blue Angel **16** The Spy Who Loved Me

jurisdiction **3** say **4** area, beat, rule, sway, zone **5** field, range, reach, scope **6** bounds, domain, sphere **7** circuit, command, compass, control, quarter **8** district, dominion, hegemony, latitude, precinct, province **9** authority, bailiwick **10** legal right **11** prerogative

jurist **5** judge **6** lawyer **7** counsel, justice **8** advocate, attorney **9** barrister, counselor, solicitor **10** magistrate **12** legal adviser **13** attorney-at-law

jury **5** panel, peers **6** assize, twelve **9** committee, makeshift, veniremen

jury-rigged **9** improvised, makeshift, temporary

jus **3** law **5** right

jus civile **8** civil law

jus gentium **12** law of nations

jus naturale **11** law of nature

jus sanguinis **12** right of blood
(law) citizenship of child is same as: **7** parents

jus soli **11** right of land, right of soil
(law) citizenship of child based on place of: **5** birth

just **3** but, due **4** fair, firm, good, only, sane **5** fully, moral, quite, solid, sound **6** at most, barely, decent, hardly, honest, lately, merely, proper, simply, strong, worthy **7** condign, ethical, exactly, fitting, logical, merited, only now, upright **8** adequate, balanced, deserved, entirely, narrowly, recently, scarcely, sensible, suitable, unbiased **9** befitting, blameless, equitable, honorable, impartial, justified, objective, perfectly, precisely, reputable, righteous, unbigoted, uncorrupt **10** aboveboard, absolutely, acceptable, completely, evenhanded, fair-minded, high-minded, no more than, nothing but, not long ago, principled, reasonable, scrupulous, upstanding **11** appropriate, justifiable, trustworthy, well-founded **12** conscionable, open to reason, unprejudiced, well-grounded **13** conscientious, disinterested, dispassionate

just about **6** almost, around, barely, nearly **7** close to **10** not far from **12** on the point of **13** approximately

Just Above My Head
author: **12** James Baldwin

just a moment ago
French: **11** tout a l'heure

justice **5** honor, right, truth **6** amends, equity, the law, virtue **7** honesty, payment, penalty, probity, redress **8** fair play, fairness, goodness, legality **9** atonement, integrity, rightness **10** correction, lawfulness, legitimacy, reparation **11** just desserts, proper cause, uprightness **12** chastisement, compensation, equitability, remuneration, satisfaction **13** due punishment, equitableness, justification, righteousness **17** constitutionality
god of: **7** Forsete, Forseti
goddess of: **4** Dice, Dike **6** Astrea **7** Astraea

Justice
author: **14** John Galsworthy

Justice Clement
character in: **19** Every Man in His Humour
author: **6** Jonson

justice to all
Latin: **15** justitia omnibus
motto of: **18** District of Columbia

justifiable **9** excusable **10** defensible **11** explanatory, extenuating, supportable

justification **5** alibi **6** excuse **7** apology, defense, pretext, support **8** sanction **10** accounting, adjustment, validation **11** explanation, vindication **12** confirmation **13** rectification **14** reconciliation

justification for existence
French: **11** raison d'etre

justify **6** back up, defend, excuse, uphold **7** bear out, confirm, explain, support, sustain, warrant **8** sanction, validate **9** vindicate **10** account for, prove right

justitia omnibus **12** justice to all
motto of: **18** District of Columbia

just now
French: **11** tout a l'heure

just the same **6** anyhow, anyway **12** nevertheless

just the thing **7** apropos **8** suitable **11** appropriate **12** exactly right

Justus *see* **5** Titus

jut **5** bulge **6** beetle, extend **7** poke out, project **8** overhang, protrude, shoot out, stand out, stick out **13** thrust forward

jute **19** Corchorus capsularis
varieties: **5** Bimli, China, Tossa, white **7** bastard **10** Bimlipatum

Juturna
form: **5** nymph
goddess of: **5** lakes **7** streams
father: **6** Daunus
brother: **6** Turnus
loved by: **7** Jupiter

juvenile **5** child, minor, young, youth **6** boyish, callow, infant, junior **7** girlish **8** childish, immature, teenager, youthful **9** childlike, pubescent, stripling, youngster **10** adolescent, sophomoric **15** unsophisticated

Juventas
protectress of: **14** military age men

juxtaposed **6** next to **8** adjacent, touching **9** proximate **10** contiguous, side by side **12** conterminous

juxtaposition **5** touch **7** balance, contact **8** contrast, nearness **9** adjacency, proximity **10** apposition, contiguity

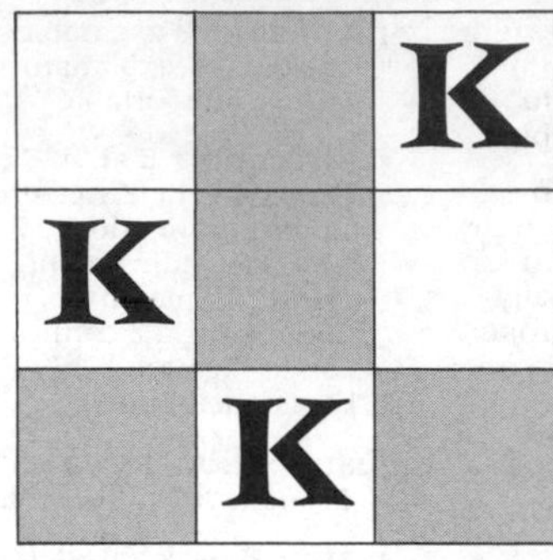

K
character in: **9** The Castle
author: **5** Kafka

Ka
origin: **8** Egyptian
form: **6** spirit
trait: **11** immortality

kabob **5** cabab, cabob, kabab, kebab, kebob **7** shaslik **8** shashlik **9** shashlick

Kabul
capital of: **11** Afghanistan

Kafka, Franz
author of: **7** Amerika **8** The Trial **9** The Castle **16** The Metamorphosis

kahlua
type: **6** brandy
origin: **6** Mexico
flavor: **6** coffee
with rum: **10** Black Maria
with tequila: **9** Brave Bull
with vodka: **12** Black Russian

Kahn, Albert
architect of: **15** River Rouge Plant **17** Highland Park Plant **20** Athletic Club Building (Detroit) **21** General Motors Building (Detroit)

Kahn, Louis Isadore
architect of: **16** Kimbell Art Museum (Ft Worth TX) **23** Yale Center for British Art **24** Yale University Art Gallery **28** Phillips Exeter Academy Library (NH) **31** Richards Medical Research Building (U of PA) **33** Salk Institute for Biological Studies (La Jolla CA)

Kahn, Madeline
born: **8** Boston MA
roles: **9** Paper Moon **10** What's Up Doc? **14** Blazing Saddles **17** Young Frankenstein

kaiser **5** ruler **7** emperor, Wilhelm **8** autocrat

kakemono **6** scroll **13** hanging object

kale **16** Brassica oleracea (Acephala Group)
varieties: **3** sea **4** Ruvo, tall, tree **6** Indian, Scotch **7** cabbage, Chinese, Italian, kitchen **8** Siberian **9** flowering, Tronchuda **10** decorative, ornamental, Portuguese **13** dwarf Siberian **16** ornamental-leaved

kaleidoscopic **6** mobile, motley **7** protean **8** shifting, unstable, variable **9** checkered **10** changeable, variegated **11** fluctuating, many colored, rainbowlike, vacillating **12** ever-changing

Kaleva **8** folk hero
origin: **7** Finnish **8** Estonian

Kalevala
origin: **7** Finnish
form: **4** epic

Kali
also: **3** Uma **5** Durga **7** Parvati
husband: **4** Siva **5** Shiva
festival: **6** dewali
goddess of: **5** death **7** disease

Kalidasa
author of: **9** Meghaduta, Sakuntala **10** Shakuntala **14** Cloud Messenger

Kalimantan *see* **6** Borneo

Kalki
author: **9** Gore Vidal

Kampala
capital of: **6** Uganda

Kampuchea *see* **8** Cambodia

Kandinsky, Wassily (Vasily)
born: **6** Moscow, Russia
artwork: **7** Striped **8** Twilight **10** Black Lines **11** Impressions **12** Blue Mountain (no 84), Compositions, Violet Orange **13** Black Relation **14** Improvisations **15** Capricious Forms **17** Bavarian Mountains, The Street in Murnau **23** Painting with White Border

Kanga
character in: **13** Winnie the Pooh
author: **5** Milne

kangaroo
young: **4** joey
group of: **3** mob **5** troop

Kaniengehaga *see* **6** Mohawk

Kansas ***see box***

Kansas City
baseball team: **6** Royals
basketball team: **5** Kings
football team: **6** Chiefs
landmark: **12** Union Station **22** Nelson-Atkins Art Gallery
river: **6** Kansas **8** Missouri

Kant, Immanuel
author of: **20** Critique of Pure Reason

Kantor, MacKinlay
author of: **13** Andersonville

Karloff, Boris
real name: **17** William Henry Pratt
born: **7** Dulwich, England
roles: **12** Frankenstein

karma **3** act **4** aura, deed, duty, fate, rite **5** force, power **6** action, kismet, spirit **7** destiny **9** vibration

Kasdan, Lawrence
director of: **11** The Big Chill

Kashmiri
language family: **12** Indo-European
branch: **11** Indo-Iranian
group: **5** Indic
spoken in: **5** (northern) India

kashruth, kashrut **7** fitness **17** Jewish dietary laws

Kansas
abbreviation: **2** KS **4** Kans
nickname: **5** Wheat **9** Jayhawker, Sunflower **15** Garden of the West
capital: **6** Topeka
largest city: **7** Wichita
others: **4** Hays, Iola **5** Colby, Dodge **6** Salina **7** Abilene, Chanute, Emporia, Liberal **8** Atchison, Lawrence **9** Great Bend **10** Belleville, Hutchinson, Kansas City **11** Coffeeville, Leavenworth **12** Junction City
college: **5** Baker, Tabor **7** Bethany **8** Sterling, Washburn
explorer: **8** Coronado
feature: **16** Eisenhower Center
fort: **5** Riley, Scott
Indian training school: **16** Haskell Institute
penitentiary: **11** Leavenworth
reservoir: **11** Tuttle Creek
tribe: **3** Kaw **4** Pani **5** Kansa, Kiowa, Osage **6** Pawnee **7** Arapaho, Wichita **8** Cheyenne, Comanche, Kickapoo
people: **7** Jayhawk **11** Damon Runyon **13** Amelia Earhart, Karl Menninger **14** Walter Chrysler **15** Edgar Lee Masters
lake: **6** Cheney, Kerwin, Neosho **7** Milford
land rank: **10** fourteenth
mountain:
highest point: **9** Sunflower
physical feature:
plains: **5** Great, Osage
president: **17** Dwight D Eisenhower
river: **3** Kaw **6** Kansas **8** Arkansas, Cimarron, Missouri **9** Smoky Hill **10** Republican
state admission: **12** thirty-fourth
state bird: **17** western meadowlark
state flower: **9** sunflower
state motto: **29** To the Stars Through Difficulties
state song: **14** Home on the Range
state tree: **10** cottonwood

Katczinsky, Stanislaus (Kat)
character in: **25** All Quiet on the Western Front
author: **8** Remarque

Kate Fennigate
author: **15** Booth Tarkington

Katharina
character in: **19** The Taming of the Shrew
author: **11** Shakespeare

Katmandu, Kathmandu
capital of: **5** Nepal

Katzenjammer Kids
also: **17** Captain and the Kids
creator: **12** Rudolph Dirks
character: **4** Hans **5** Fritz, Momma **10** der Captain **12** der Inspector

Kaufman, George S
author of:
with Edna Ferber: **9** Stage Door **13** Dinner at Eight **14** The Royal Family
with Moss Hart: **15** Once in a Lifetime **20** You Can't Take It with You **21** The Man Who Came to Dinner

Kay (Sir Kay)
character in: **16** Arthurian romance
foster brother: **6** Arthur

Kaye, Danny
real name: **19** David Daniel Kaminski
born: **10** Brooklyn NY
roles: **19** The Inspector General **21** Hans Christian Andersen **26** The Secret Life of Walter Mitty

Kaye, M M
author of: **9** Trade Wind **12** Death in Kenya **15** Death in Zanzibar, Shadow of the Moon, The Far Pavilions

Kazan, Elia
director of: **10** East of Eden, Viva Zapata **15** On the Waterfront (Oscar) **18** Splendor in the Grass **19** Gentleman's Agreement (Oscar) **20** A Tree Grows in Brooklyn **21** A Streetcar Named Desire

Kazantzakis, Nikos
author of: **13** Zorba the Greek **14** Freedom or Death, The Greek Passion **25** The Last Temptation of Christ

kazoo **5** bazoo, zarah **6** hewgag **11** eunuch flute
French: **8** mirliton

Keach, Stacy
real name: **18** Walter Stacy Keach Jr
born: **10** Savannah GA
roles: **3** Doc **6** Luther **10** Mike Hammer **24** Twinkle Twinkle Killer Kane

Kearny, Stephen Watts
served in: **10** California, Mexican War
commander of: **13** Army of the West
occupied: **9** New Mexico
battle: **10** San Gabriel, San Pasqual

Keaton, Buster
real name: **19** Joseph Francis Keaton
born: **7** Piqua KS
roles: **6** Go West **7** College **10** The General **12** The Cameraman

Keaton, Diane
real name: **9** Diane Hall
born: **12** Los Angeles CA
roles: **4** Reds **7** Sleeper **8** Baby Boom **9** Annie Hall (Oscar) **12** Shoot the Moon, The Godfather **13** The Good Mother **14** Play It Again Sam **19** Looking for Mr Goodbar **20** The Little Drummer Girl

Keats, John
author of: **5** Lamia **8** Endymion, Hyperion, Isabella **11** Ode to Autumn, Ode to Psyche **14** Ode on Indolence **15** Ode on Melancholy, The Eve of St Agnes **16** Ode on a Grecian Urn **17** Ode to a Nightingale **20** La Belle Dame Sans Merci **31** On First Looking into Chapman's Homer

Keb *see* **3** Geb

Kedar *see* **7** Kedemah

Kedemah
also called: **5** Kedar
father: **7** Ishmael
mother: **5** Hagar
descendant of: **8** Kedarite

Keel (of Argo)
constellation of: **6** Carina

Keel, Howard
real name: **17** Harry Clifford Leek
costar: **14** Kathryn Grayson
born: **11** Gillespie IL
roles: **6** Dallas, Kismet **8** Showboat **10** Kiss Me

Kate **13** Clayton Farlow **15** Annie Get Your Gun **27** Seven Brides for Seven Brothers

Keeler, Ruby
husband: 8 Al Jolson
costar: 10 Dick Powell
born: 6 Canada **7** Halifax
roles: 15 Footlight Parade **17** Forty-Second Street **32** Gold Diggers of Nineteen Thirty Three

keel over 5 faint, swoon, upset **7** capsize, tip over **8** collapse, fall down, fall flat, flip over, overturn, turn over **10** turn turtle

keen 4 avid, fine **5** acute, alert, eager, sharp **6** ardent, astute, clever, fervid, fierce, shrewd **7** earnest, excited, fervent, intense, zealous **8** incisive **9** impatient, paper thin, razorlike **10** discerning **11** finely honed, impassioned, penetrating, quick-witted **12** enthusiastic **13** perspicacious **14** discriminating

keen-eyed 5 alert **8** vigilant, watchful **9** attentive, eagle-eyed, observant, sharp-eyed, wide-awake

keen-minded 5 acute, sharp, smart **6** astute, clever, shrewd **10** perceptive **11** penetrating

keenness 4 zeal, zest **5** ardor **6** acumen, fervor **7** passion **9** acuteness, eagerness, sharpness **10** astuteness, cleverness, enthusiasm, excitement, shrewdness **11** discernment **12** anticipation, intelligence, perspicacity

keen-sighted 4 sage, wise **5** acute, sharp **6** astute, shrewd **8** piercing **9** eagle-eyed, judicious, sagacious, sharp-eyed **10** discerning **11** intelligent, penetrating **12** clear-sighted, sharp-sighted **13** perspicacious

keep 3 bar **4** clog, fort, have, heap, hold, mind, pile, stay **5** abide, block, carry, cramp, delay, deter, guard, honor, lay in, place, stack, stall, stand, stick, stock, store, tie up, tower **6** arrest, castle, detain, donjon, endure, hamper, hinder, hobble, hold up, impede, living, pay for, remain, retain, retard **7** care for, carry on, citadel, deposit, furnish, inhibit, observe, possess, prevent, shackle, support, sustain **8** conserve, continue, encumber, fortress, hang on to, hold back, maintain, obstruct, preserve, restrain **9** celebrate, constrain, hamstring, persevere, persist in, ritualize, safeguard, solemnize, watch over **10** accumulate, daily bread, livelihood, provide for, stronghold, sustenance **11** commemorate, maintenance, memorialize, subsistence **12** room and board **13** fortification

keep an eye on 5 watch **7** oversee **9** chaperone, look after, watch over

keep apart 7 isolate **8** separate **9** segregate

keep at bay 7 beat off, fend off, ward off **8** stave off

keep back 5 check, delay **6** detain, hold up, retain **8** withhold

keep busy 3 use **6** employ, engage, occupy **7** utilize

keep clear of 4 shun **5** avoid, dodge, elude, evade, skirt **6** escape

keep company 4 date **5** court **7** consort, hang out **8** go around, go steady **9** accompany, associate **10** fraternize, go together

keeper 5 guard, nurse **6** duenna, escort, jailer, sentry, warden **7** curator **8** chaperon, guardian, retainer, sentinel, wet nurse **9** attendant, bodyguard, caretaker, chaperone, custodian, governess, nursemaid, protecter, protector **11** conservator, nurserymaid **13** guardian angel

keep in mind 8 consider, remember **10** think about

keep mum 13 button one's lip

keep off 7 fend off, stay off, ward off **8** stave off

keep one's counsel 12 remain silent **13** button one's lip

keep open 8 hold open **16** leave unscheduled

keep out 6 reject **8** prohibit **9** blackball, blacklist

keep out of sight 4 hide **5** cover **6** lay low, lie low **7** conceal, cover up, secrete **10** camouflage

keep private 4 hide **7** conceal, reserve **8** withhold

keepsake 5 relic, token **6** emblem, memory, symbol **7** memento **8** memorial, reminder, souvenir **11** remembrance **18** token of remembrance

keep secret 4 hide **6** hush up **7** conceal, cover up **8** suppress, withhold

keep silent 10 remain dumb **15** not breathe a word

keep steady 5 poise **7** balance **9** stabilize

keep to 5 cling, stick **6** adhere, be true, cleave, hold to **7** be loyal, stand by **8** maintain

keg 3 tub, tun, vat **4** butt, cask, drum, tank **6** barrel **7** rundlet **8** hogshead, puncheon **9** container, kilderkin

Kellerman, Sally
born: 11 Long Beach CA
roles: 4 MASH **15** Hot Lips Houlihan

Kelly, Gene
real name: 17 Eugene Curran Kelly
born: 12 Pittsburgh PA
roles: 7 Pal Joey **9** Brigadoon, On the Town **13** Anchors Aweigh **15** Singin' in the Rain **17** An American in Paris **18** The Three Musketeers

Kelly, Grace
husband: 21 Prince Rainier Grimaldi
nickname: 11 Ice Princess
born: 14 Philadelphia PA
roles: 7 Mogambo **8** High Noon **10** Rear Window **11** High Society **13** To Catch a Thief **14** Dial M for Murder, The Country Girl (Oscar)

Kelly, Walt
creator/artist of: 4 Pogo

kelp 3 ash **4** agar, alga, leag **5** varec, varic, wrack **7** seaweed
source of: 4 soda **6** iodine **9** potassium

Kelpie
origin: 8 Scottish
form: 5 horse **6** spirit
habitat: 4 lake **5** river
causes: 8 drowning
warns of: 8 drowning

Kelvin
abbreviation: 1 K

Kelvin, William Thomson
field: 7 physics **11** mathematics
nationality: 7 British
worked on: 4 heat **11** electricity
invented: 12 electrometer, galvanometer **13** tide predictor
named for him: 22 Kelvin temperature scale

Kempis, Thomas a
author of: 20 The Imitation of Christ

Kenaz
father: **7** Eliphaz
son: **5** Caleb **7** Othniel

Keneally, Thomas
author of: **12** Confederates **14** Schindler's List

Kenilworth
author: **14** Sir Walter Scott
character: **6** Alasco, Dudley (Earl of Leicester) **10** Amy Robsart **12** Wayland Smith **13** Richard Varney **14** Queen Elizabeth **15** Flibbertigibbet **16** Edmund Tressilian

Kennedy, Arthur
real name: **17** John Arthur Kennedy
born: **11** Worcester MA
roles: **6** Becket **9** All My Sons **11** Peyton Place **12** Blind Victory **16** Death of a Salesman

Kennedy, Frank
character in: **15** Gone With the Wind
author: **8** Mitchell

Kennedy, John Fitzgerald
see box

Kennicott, Dr Will and Carol
characters in: **10** Main Street
author: **5** Lewis

Kentucky ***see box, p. 534***

Kenya ***see box, p. 535***

Kepler, Johannes
nationality: **6** German
invented: **14** convex eyepiece **21** astronomical telescope
formulated:
three laws of planetary motion (Kepler's Laws): **10** law of areas **11** harmonic law **24** elliptical orbit of planets
author of: **14** Astronomia nova, Harmonice mundi **16** Rudolphine Tables **23** Mysterium cosmographicum **30** Epitome astronomiae Copernicanae

Ker
form: **6** spirit
associated with: **5** death
corresponds to: **6** Furies

kerchief **5** cloth, scarf **7** muffler **8** babushka, neckwear **9** headpiece, neckcloth **11** neckerchief **12** handkerchief

Keres
origin: **5** Greek
spirits of: **4** evil **5** death **6** old age **7** disease

Keres-Siouan
language branch: **5** Keres **7** Caddoan **9** Iroquoian **11** Siouan-Yuchi

kernel **3** nub, nut, pip, pit **4** core, germ, gist, pith, seed **5** grain, stone **6** center, marrow **7** nucleus **12** quintessence

Kerouac, Jack
author of: **6** Big Sur **9** On the Road **13** The Dharma Bums **16** Lonesome Traveler

Kerr, Deborah
real name: **22** Deborah Jane Kerr-Trimmer
born: **8** Scotland **11** Helensburgh
roles: **11** Edward My Son, The King and I **12** The Hucksters **13** The Sundowners **14** Separate Tables, The Chalk Garden **18** From Here to Eternity **19** The Night of

---

Kennedy, John Fitzgerald
nickname: **3** JFK **4** Jack
presidential rank: **11** thirty-fifth
party: **10** Democratic
state represented: **2** MA
defeated: **5** (Richard Milhous) Nixon
vice president: **7** (Lyndon Baines) Johnson
cabinet:
state: **4** (David Dean) Rusk
treasury: **6** (Clarence Douglas) Dillon
defense: **8** (Robert Strange) McNamara
attorney general: **7** (Robert Francis) Kennedy
postmaster general: **3** (James Edward) Day **9** (John Austin) Gronouski
interior: **5** (Stewart Lee) Udall
agriculture: **7** (Orville Lothrop) Freeman
commerce: **6** (Luther Hartwell) Hodges
labor: **5** (William Willard) Wirtz **8** (Arthur J) Goldberg
HEW: **8** (Abraham Alexander) Ribicoff **10** (Anthony Joseph) Celebrezze
born: **11** Brookline MA
died: **8** Dallas TX
died by: **13** assassination
assassinated by: **6** (Lee Harvey) Oswald
buried: **25** Arlington National Cemetery
education:
prep school: **6** Choate
University: **7** Harvard **9** Princeton **23** London School of Economics
religion: **13** Roman Catholic
interests: **7** sailing **8** football **13** touch football
vacation spot: **9** Cape Cod MA **13** Hyannis Port MA
author: **15** Strategy of Peace, Why England Slept **17** Profiles in Courage (Pulitzer Prize)
political career: **9** US Senator **24** US House of Representatives
civilian career: **17** newspaper reporter
military service: **6** US Navy **10** lieutenant **11** World War Two
commander of: **6** PT boat
notable events of lifetime/term: **9** Bay of Pigs **10** Berlin Wall, Peace Corps **18** Cuban missile crisis
march: **11** Civil Rights
treaty: **14** Nuclear Test-Ban
quote: **17** Ich bin ein Berliner (I am a Berliner) **35** We stand today on the edge of a New Frontier **61** Ask not what your country can do for you ask what you can do for your country
father: **13** Joseph Patrick
mother: **4** Rose (Fitzgerald)
siblings: **4** Jean **6** Eunice, Joseph **8** Kathleen, Patricia, Rosemary **11** Edward Moore **13** Robert Francis
wife: **10** Jacqueline (Lee Bouvier)
nickname: **6** Jackie
second marriage to: **7** Onassis
children: **14** John Fitzgerald, Patrick Bouvier (died in infancy) **15** Caroline Bouvier

Kentucky
abbreviation: **2** KY
nickname: **9** Bluegrass **11** Corncracker
capital: **9** Frankfort
largest city: **10** Louisville
others: **5** Berea **6** Corbin, Hazard **7** Ashland, Glasgow, Newport, Paducah, Shively **8** Danville **9** Covington, Henderson, Lexington, Owensboro **12** Bowling Green, Hopkinsville, Madisonville
college: **5** Berea **6** Centre **7** Ashbury, Brescia **8** Ursuline **12** Transylvania
explorer: **11** Daniel Boone
feature: **7** Obelisk
birthplace: **14** Abraham Lincoln
fort: **4** Knox
national park: **11** Mammoth Cave
race: **13** Kentucky Derby
racetrack: **14** Churchill Downs
trail: **10** Wilderness
tribe: **7** Shawnee **8** Cherokee, Iroquois
people: **11** corncracker, John M Harlan **13** Louis Brandeis **16** Frederick M Vinson, Robert Penn Warren
lake: **8** Kentucky **10** Cumberland
land rank: **13** thirty-seventh
mountain: **4** Pine **10** Cumberland
highest point: **5** Black **8** Big Black
physical feature:
basin: **9** Bluegrass
cave: **7** Mammoth
gap: **10** Cumberland
plain: **7** Coastal
plateau: **10** Cumberland
president: **14** Abraham Lincoln
Confederate president: **14** Jefferson Davis
river: **3** Dix **4** Ohio, Salt **5** Green **6** Barren **7** Licking **8** Big Sandy, Kentucky **9** Tennessee **10** Cumberland **11** Mississippi
state admission: **9** fifteenth
state bird: **8** cardinal
state flower: **9** goldenrod
state motto: **26** United We Stand Divided We Fall
state song: **17** My Old Kentucky Home
state tree: **10** coffee tree **11** tulip poplar **12** yellow poplar

the Iguana **20** Heaven Knows Mr Allison

Kesey, Ken
author of: **21** Sometimes a Great Notion **25** One Flew Over the Cuckoo's Nest

Ketcham, Hank
creator/artist of: **15** Dennis the Menace

kettle **3** pan, pot, tub, vat **6** boiler, teapot, tureen **8** cauldron, crucible, saucepan

Ketubim **8** writings **11** Hagiographa

Keturah
husband: **7** Abraham

key **3** cue, fit **4** clue, gear, mode, suit **5** adapt, light, point, scale **6** adjust, answer, direct, opener **7** address, finding, meaning, pointer **8** indicant, solution, tonality **9** indicator **10** exposition, indication, resolution **11** elucidation, explanation, explication, translation **14** interpretation

Key, Ted
creator/artist of: **5** Hazel

keyboard instrument **5** organ, piano **6** spinet **8** psaltery, virginal **9** harmonium **10** clavichord, pianoforte **11** harpsichord

keyed up **5** tense **7** excited, nervous **8** volatile **9** emotional, explosive

key element **9** essential, vital part **18** primary constituent **20** indispensable element

Key Largo
director: **10** John Huston
based on story by: **15** Maxwell Anderson
cast: **12** Claire Trevor, Lauren Bacall **14** Humphrey Bogart **15** Edward G Robinson, Lionel Barrymore
Oscar for: **17** supporting actress (Trevor)

Keynes, John Maynard
author of: **44** The General Theory of Employment Interest and Money

keynote **3** nub **4** core, gist, pith **5** heart, theme **6** marrow **7** essence, nucleus, pattern **8** main idea, quiddity **9** substance **11** nitty-gritty, salient idea **12** central point

keystone **4** base, crux, root **5** basis **8** gravamen, linchpin **9** principle **10** foundation, mainspring

Keystone State
nickname of: **12** Pennsylvania

Key to Rebecca, The
author: **10** Ken Follett

Khachaturian, Aram Ilich
born: **6** Tiflis **7** (Soviet) Georgia
composer of: **6** Gayane **9** Spartacus **12** Song of Stalin

khaki **5** cloth **6** fabric **7** uniform **9** olive-drab **14** yellowish-brown

khan, kahn **3** inn **4** lord **5** chief, ruler **6** prince **7** emperor **9** chieftain, sovereign **11** caravansary
famous: **4** Yuan **6** Kublai **7** Genghis **8** Ghenghis

Khartoum
capital of: **5** Sudan

Khartvelian
language family: **9** Caucasian
includes: **8** Georgian

Khayyam, Omar
author of: **11** The Rubaiyat

Khnum
origin: **8** Egyptian
form: **3** ram
created: **6** humans
used: **4** clay

Khoisan
language spoken by: **3** San **7** Bushmen **9** Khoikhoin **10** Hottentots
includes: **5** Hatsa **7** Sandawe
distinguishing sound: **5** click

kibitzer **3** pry **5** prier, snoop **6** butt-in **7** meddler, snooper, watcher **8** busybody **9** buttinsky

kick **3** fun, hit, out, pep, vim **4** beef, boot, dash, fret, fume, fuss, life, punt, snap, tang, zest **5** eject, force, gripe, growl, power, punch, verve, vigor **6** flavor, grouch, grouse,

Kenya
capital/largest city: 7 Nairobi
others: 5 Nyeri, Thika, Wajir 6 Kisumu, Kitale, Lodwar, Moyale, Nakuru, Webuye 7 Eldoret, Kericho, Malindi, Mandera, Mombasa, Nanyuki 9 Lokitaung
measure: 4 wari
monetary unit: 4 cent 5 pound 8 shilling
island: 5 Manda, Patta
lake: 6 Magadi, Nakuru, Natron, Rudolf 7 Turkana 8 Naivasha, Victoria
mountain: 5 Elgon, Kulai, Nyira, Nyiru 6 Matian 7 Logonot 8 Aberdare
highest point: 5 Kenya 6 Kinyaa 9 Kirinyaga
river: 3 Lak 4 Athi, Dawa, Kuja, Tana 5 Nzoia 6 Galana 8 Turkwell
sea: 6 Indian
physical feature:
bay: 7 Formosa
desert: 6 Chalbi
escarpment: 3 Mau
gulf: 9 Kavirondo
highlands: 5 Kenya, Kisii, Luyla 7 Kericho
plain: 4 Kano
plateau: 5 Nandi, Yatta 6 Elgeyo
valley: 9 Great Rift
people: 3 Luo 4 Arab, Meru 5 Bantu, Elgey, Galla, Kamba, Kisii, Luhya, Masai, Nandi, Tugen 6 Kikuyu, Ogaden, Somali 7 Baluhya, Hamitic, Hilotic, Kipsigi, Swahili, Turkana 8 Kalenjin, Marakwet
god: 4 Ngai
leader: 5 Mboya 12 Jomo Kenyatta 13 Daniel Arap Moi
language: 3 Luo 5 Bantu, Luhya, Masai 6 Kikuyu 7 English, Swahili 8 Guyerati 10 Hindustani
religion: 5 Islam 7 animism 8 Anglican 13 Roman Catholic
place:
archeological excavation: 11 Gamble's Cave
mosque: 5 Khoja
museum: 9 Fort Jesus
national park/wildlife preserve: 4 Meru 5 Nyeri, Tsavo 6 Arusha 7 Manyara, Nairobi, Samburu 8 Aberdare, Amboseli 10 Lake Nakuru, Mount Kenya, Rift Valley
ruins: 4 Gedi
feature:
garment: 5 kanga 7 kitenge
round house: 6 shamba
secret organization: 6 Mau Mau
tree: 6 ayieke, baobab
food:
fish: 7 tilapia
wine: 5 tembo

object, recoil, remove, return, strike, stroke, thrill 7 boot out, cast out, grumble, fly back, protest, rebound, sparkle, turn out 8 backlash, complain, jump back, piquancy, pleasure, pungency, reaction, throw out, vitality 9 amusement, animation, complaint, enjoyment, find fault, grievance, intensity, make a fuss, objection 10 excitement, spring back 11 give the gate, remonstrate, send packing, show the door 12 protestation 13 gratification, remonstration

Kickapoo
language family: 9 Algonkian 10 Algonquian
location: 5 Texas 6 Kansas, Mexico 9 Chihuahua, Wisconsin
related to: 3 Fox, Sac 4 Sauk

kickback 3 cut 5 bribe, graft, share 6 boodle, payoff, payola 9 hush money 10 commission, percentage, protection, recompense 12 compensation, remuneration 15 protection money

kick downstairs 4 bust 6 demote 7 degrade

kickoff 5 start 7 opening 9 beginning, inception, launching 12 inauguration

kick out 4 oust 5 eject, evict, expel 8 throw out 9 discharge

kicks 3 fun 7 thrills 8 pleasure 10 excitement 11 stimulation

kick upstairs 5 boost 7 advance, elevate, promote

Kicva
origin: 5 Welsh
husband: 7 Pryderi

kid 3 rag, rib, tot 4 baby, fool, gull, jest, joke, josh, mock, ride, tyke 5 bluff, child, cozen, harry, put on, tease, trick, youth 6 delude, infant, moppet, plague, shaver, squirt 7 beguile, deceive, laugh at, mislead 8 goat hide, goatskin, hoodwink, juvenile, ridicule, teenager, yearling 9 bamboozle, billy goat, little one, make fun of, nanny goat, offspring, young goat, youngster 10 adolescent 11 goat leather, young person 12 little shaver

Kid, The
nickname of: 11 Ted Williams

kid around 5 clown, cut up 10 fool around, play around 11 clown around

Kidder, Margot
born: 6 Canada 11 Yellow Knife
roles: 7 Sisters 8 Lois Lane, Superman 14 Some Kind of Hero 19 The Amityville Horror

Kiddush 6 prayer 8 blessing 14 sanctification

kidnap 5 seize, steal 6 abduct, hijack, snatch 7 bear off, capture, impress, skyjack 8 bear away, carry off, shanghai 10 run off with 11 make off with 13 hold for ransom

Kidnapped
author: 20 Robert Louis Stevenson
character: 9 Alan Breck 10 Rankeillor 12 David Balfour 15 Ebenezer Balfour

Kigali
capital of: 6 Rwanda

Kiley, Richard
born: 9 Chicago IL
roles: 7 Redhead 13 Man of La Mancha 16 Advise and Consent

Kilkenny Cats
origin: 5 Irish
form: 4 cats
number: 3 two
left after fight: 5 tails

kill 4 beat, do in, halt, hang, ruin, slay, stay **5** break, check, drown, erase, lynch, quell, shoot, waste **6** behead, defeat, murder, poison, rub out, stifle **7** bump off, butcher, cut down, destroy, execute, garrote, silence, smother, squelch, wipe out **8** blow away, dispatch, get rid of, knock off, massacre, strangle, string up **9** dismember, finish off, shoot down, slaughter, suffocate **10** asphyxiate, decapitate, disembowel, extinguish, guillotine, put a stop to, put an end to, put to death **11** assassinate, burn to death, electrocute, exterminate **13** mortally wound

killer 6 hit man, slayer **7** butcher **8** assassin, murderer **11** executioner **12** exterminator

Killers, The
director: 13 Robert Siodmak
based on story by: 15 Ernest Hemingway
cast: 10 Ava Gardner **12** Edmond O'Brien **13** Burt Lancaster

killer whale 4 orca **7** grampus **11** Orcinus orca

killing 4 coup **5** fatal **6** big hit, deadly, lethal, mortal, murder **7** bonanza, cleanup, deathly, hanging, slaying, success, suicide **8** butchery, fatality, homicide, lynching, massacre, regicide, shooting, smash hit, stabbing, windfall **9** bloodshed, execution, garroting, martyrdom, matricide, murderous, patricide, poisoning, slaughter, uxoricide **10** cleaning up, decimation, fratricide, immolation, impalement, sororicide, strangling **11** crucifixion, devastating, elimination, infanticide **12** annihilation, death-dealing, decapitation, excruciating, guillotining, manslaughter, master stroke, stroke of luck, violent death **13** electrocution, extermination, strangulation **17** capital punishment

Killing Fields
director: 11 Roland Joffe
based on article by: 15 Sydney Schanberg (The Death and Life of Dith Pran)
cast: 10 Haing S Ngor **12** Sam Waterston
Oscar for: 15 supporting actor (Ngor)

Killing Time
author: 12 Thomas Berger

killjoy 6 grouch **8** grumbler, sourball, sourpuss **9** Cassandra, gloomy Gus, worrywart **10** complainer, malcontent, spoilsport, wet blanket **11** crapehanger, party-pooper

kill time 4 idle **6** dawdle **9** waste time **10** fool around

Kilmer, Joyce
author of: 5 Trees

kiln 3 ost **4** bake, burn, fire, oast, oven **5** drier, glaze, stove, tiler **7** furnace **8** calciner, limekiln **9** oasthouse

kiloliter
abbreviation: 2 kL

kilometer
abbreviation: 2 km

Kilwich
origin: 5 Welsh
form: 6 prince
performed: 6 labors
number of labors: 4 five
married: 5 Olwen

Kim
author: 14 Rudyard Kipling
character: 9 Mahbub Ali **11** Tibetan Lama **12** Kimball O'Hara **16** Colonel Creighton **22** Hurree Chunder Mookerjee

kin 4 akin, clan, kith, race **5** folks, tribe **6** family, people **7** kinfolk, kinsmen, related **8** clansmen, kinfolks **9** next of kin, relations, relatives, tribesmen **10** kith and kin **11** connections, consanguine, distaff side, spindle side **13** flesh and blood **14** kissing cousins

kind 3 ilk **4** cast, make, mold, sort, type **5** brand, breed, caste, civil, class, genre, genus, style **6** benign, gentle, kidney, kindly, nature, polite, strain, tender **7** amiable, cordial, variety **8** amicable, friendly, generous, gracious, merciful, obliging **9** courteous **10** bighearted, charitable, neighborly, thoughtful **11** considerate, description, designation, good-hearted, good-humored, good-natured, softhearted, sympathetic, warmhearted, well-meaning **12** affectionate, well-disposed **13** accommodating, compassionate, tenderhearted, understanding
French: 6 gentil

kindhearted 4 good, warm **6** benign, gentle, humane, kindly, loving **7** helpful **8** amicable, generous, gracious, merciful **10** altruistic, charitable, thoughtful **11** considerate, good-hearted, good-natured, softhearted, sympathetic, warmhearted, well-meaning **12** affectionate, humanitarian **13** accommodating, compassionate, philanthropic, tenderhearted, understanding

kindheartedness 5 mercy **8** altruism, goodness, goodwill, humanity, sympathy **10** compassion, humaneness, tenderness **11** benefaction, benevolence, magnanimity **12** graciousness, philanthropy **13** consideration, understanding, unselfishness **14** charitableness **15** humanitarianism

kindle 4 fire, goad, prod, stir, urge, whet **5** awake, light, rouse, waken **6** arouse, excite, foment, ignite, incite, induce, stir up **7** agitate, animate, inflame, inspire, provoke, quicken, sharpen **8** enkindle **9** call forth, intensify, set fire to, set on fire, stimulate **10** invigorate

kindling 4 fuel **5** brush, paper, twigs **6** firing, tinder **7** burning, flaming **8** firewood, igniting, ignition, lighting, shavings **9** brushwood **10** combustion, enkindling

kindly 4 good, warm **6** benign, gentle, gently, humane, tender, warmly **7** amiable, amiably, civilly, cordial, devoted, patient **8** amicable, amicably, benignly, friendly, generous, gracious, humanely, merciful, tenderly **9** cordially, courteous **10** benevolent, bighearted, charitable, charitably, generously, graciously, mercifully, neighborly **11** considerate, good-humored, good-natured, magnanimous, softhearted, sympathetic, warmhearted, well-meaning **12** affectionate, benevolently, bigheartedly, humanitarian **13** compassionate, considerately, good-humoredly, good-naturedly, magnanimously, philanthropic, softheartedly, tenderhearted, understanding, warmheartedly, well-meaningly **14** affectionately, well-manneredly **15** compassionately, sympathetically, tenderheartedly, understandingly **17** philanthropically

kindness 3 aid **4** gift, help **5** favor, grace, mercy **6** bounty **7** charity **8** good deed, good turn, goodness, goodwill, humanity, patience, sympathy **9** tolerance **10** act of grace, assistance, compassion, generosity, humaneness, kind office, toleration **11** benefaction, beneficence, benevolence, magnanimity **12** act of charity, graciousness, philanthropy **13** consideration, understanding, unselfishness

14 charitableness
15 humanitarianism

Kind of Anger, A
author: 10 Eric Ambler

kindred 4 akin, like 5 alike 6 allied, united 7 related, similar 8 agreeing, familial, matching 9 accordant, analogous, congenial, simpatico 10 harmonious, resembling 11 consanguine, sympathetic 13 corresponding

kine 4 cows, oxen 6 cattle 9 livestock

kinfolk 3 kin 6 family 7 kinsmen 9 relations, relatives 10 kith and kin

king 3 HRH 5 liege, ruler 7 monarch 8 suzerain 9 potentate, protector, sovereign 10 His Majesty 11 crowned head, royal person, the anointed 18 defender of the faith
Latin: 3 rex

king/emperor/dynasty ***see box***

King, Frank
creator/artist of: 13 Gasoline Alley

King, Stephen
author of: 2 It 4 Cujo 6 Carrie, Misery 9 Christine, Salem's Lot, The Stand 10 Night Shift, The Shining 11 Firestarter, Pet Sematary, The Dead Zone 12 Skeleton Crew, The Dark Tower 16 Different Seasons, The Tommyknockers

King and I, The
director: 10 Walter Lang
cast: 10 Rita Moreno, Yul Brynner 11 Deborah Kerr 12 Martin Benson
score: 21 Rodgers and Hammerstein
remake of: 20 Anna and the King of Siam
song: 12 Shall We Dance? 16 Getting to Know You, Hello Young Lovers 18 Something Wonderful

King Arthur
opera by: 7 Purcell
character: 6 Merlin, Osmond, Oswald 8 Emmeline, Philadel 14 Duke of Cornwall

kingdom 4 land 5 duchy, field, realm, state 6 domain, empire, nation, sphere 7 country, dukedom 8 dominion, monarchy 9 territory 12 principality

King John
author: 18 William Shakespeare
character: 6 Elinor 9 Constance 11 Prince Henry 13 Hubert de Burgh 15 Blanch of Castile, Lewis the Dauphin 16 Arthur of Bretagne, Cardinal Pandulph, William Longsword, William Mareshall 19 Philip Faulconbridge, Robert Faulconbridge

King Kong
director: 13 Merian C Cooper 17 Ernest B Schoedsack
cast: 7 Fay Wray 10 Bruce Cabot 11 James Flavin 12 Noble Johnson 15 Robert Armstrong
setting (final scene): 19 Empire State Building
score: 10 Max Steiner

King Lear
author: 18 William Shakespeare
character: 5 Edgar, Regan 6 Edmund 7 Goneril 8 Cordelia 10 Earl of Kent 12 Duke of Albany, King of

king/emperor/dynasty
of Afghanistan: 8 Barakzai
of Albania: 3 Zog 9 Ahmet Zogu
of Algeria: 3 bey, dey 6 disawa 8 Jugurtha 9 bevlerbay, Masinissa
of Austria: 7 Charles, Francis 9 Ferdinand, Habsburgs 10 Franz Josef
of Bahrain: 9 al-Khalifa
of Belgium: 7 Leopold 8 Baudouin
of China: 3 Han, Sui 4 Chou, Ch'in, Ming, Sung, T'ang 5 Ch'ing, Shang 6 Manchu
of Crete: 5 Minos
of Denmark 4 Hans, Knud 6 Canute 8 Frederik 9 Christian 10 Gorm the Old 15 Harold Bluetooth
of Egypt: 5 Khufu, Menes, Zoser 6 Farouk, Khafre, Ptulol, Ramses 7 Saladin 8 Horemheb, Menkaure 9 Akhenaten, Amenemhet, Amenhotep 10 Mentuhotep 11 Tutankhamen
of England: 3 Hal 4 Cnut, John, Lear 5 Henry, James 6 Alfred, Arthur, Canute, Edmund, Edward, Egbert, George, Harold 7 Charles, Richard, Stephen, William 9 Cymbeline 18 Richard Coeur de Lion 19 Richard the Lionheart 21 Richard the Lionhearted
of France: 5 Henri, Louis 6 Clovis, Philip 7 Charles 8 Napoleon 9 Hugh Capet 11 Charlemagne 13 Louis Philippe 14 Henry of Navarre
of Germany: 6 Kaiser 7 Wilhelm 9 Frederick 10 Barbarossa
of Greece: 5 Creon 6 Atreus 7 Theseus 8 Menelaus 10 Agammemnon 11 Constantine
of India: 5 Akbar, Asoka, Babur, Gupta, Mogul, Timur 6 Maurya, Rajput 7 Humayun 8 Hyder Ali, Jahangir, Marathas 9 Aurangzeb, Shah Jahan 11 Tippu Sultan 14 Delhi Sultanate 18 Chandragupta Maurya
of Iran: 5 Abbas, Cyrus, Qajar 6 Darius, Xerxes 7 Arsacid, Pahlavi, Safavid 8 Parthian, Seleucid 9 Sassanian 10 Achaemenid 15 Shah Reza Pahlavi
of Iraq: 6 Faisal, Sargon 7 Hussein 9 Hammurabi 13 Harun al-Rashid 14 Nebuchadnezzar
of Ireland: 9 Brian Boru
of Italy/Rome: 4 Nero, Otho 5 Galba, Nerva, Titus 6 Trajan 7 Hadrian 8 Caligula, Claudius, Commodus, Domitian, Octavian, Tiberius 9 Caracalla, Vespasian, Vitellius 10 Diocletian 11 Constantine 13 Antoninus Dius 14 Caesar Augustus, Marcus Aurelius, Victor Emmanuel
of Japan: 5 Jimmu, Jingo, Meiji, Taira 6 Yamato 7 Akihito, Izanagi 8 Ashikaga, Fujiwara, Hirohito, Kamakura, Minamoto, Tokugawa
of Java: 7 Mataram 9 Majapahit, Srivijaya
of Jordan: 5 Talal 6 Faisal 7 Hussein 8 Abdullah, Selucidas 10 Ibn Hussein, Nabataeans

(*continued*)

king / emperor / dynasty *(continued)*
of Korea: **2** Yi **4** Choe **5** Ki-tse, Koryo **6** Chi-tsi, Chi-tzu, Tangun
of Kuwait: **5** Ahmad, Sabah, Salem **7** Mubarak **12** Jaber al-Ahmed, Sabah al-Salim **15** Abdullah al-Salim
of Liechtenstein: **7** Florian **13** Francis Joseph **16** von Liechtenstein
of Luxembourg: **8** Sigefroi, Wencelas **12** Jean l'Aveugle **21** House of Nassau-Weilburg
of Madagascar: **6** Merina
of Malawi: **6** Maravi
of Maldives: **4** Didi
of Mexico: **10** Maximilian
of Monaco: **5** Louis **6** Albert, Honore **7** Antoine, Charles, Rainier **9** Florestan
of Mongolia: **8** Jahangir, Jehangir **10** Kublai Khan, Tsendenbal **11** Genghis Khan
of Morocco: **7** Alawite, Almohad **9** Almoravid
of Nepal: **8** Mahendra **9** Tribhuwan **10** Birenda Bir **12** Bikram Sha Dev **17** Prithwi Narayan Sha
of the Netherlands: **7** William
of Nigeria: **3** Ife, Nok, Oyo **5** Benin **6** Fulani **10** Kanem-Borno
of Norway: **4** Olaf, Olav **5** Olave, Oscar **6** Haakon, Harold, Magnus, Sverre
of Peru: **7** Huascar **9** Atahualpa **10** Manco Capac
of Poland: **5** Piast **7** Casimir, Jagello **8** Augustus
of Portugal: **6** Manuel, Philip, Sancho **7** Alfonso **9** Ferdinand, Sebastian **23** Prince Henry the Navigator
of Qatar: **18** Ahmad bin Ali al-Thani **22** Khalifa bin Hamad al-Thani
of Rumania: **5** Carol **7** Michael
of Russia: **4** Ivan, Paul **5** Peter **6** Alexis **7** Michael **8** Nicholas **9** Alexander **12** Boris Godunov
of Sardinia: **12** Charles Felix **13** Charles Albert **14** Victor Emmanuel
of Saudi Arabia: **4** Fahd, Saud **6** Faisal, Khalid **7** Ibn Saud **9** Abdul Aziz
of Scotland: **5** David, James **6** Duncan **7** Kenneth, Macbeth, Malcolm, Stuarts, William **9** Alexander **14** Robert the Bruce **19** Bonnie Prince Charlie
of Sicily: **4** Eryx **5** Bomba, Henry, Peter, Roger **7** Charles, Cocalus, Leontes **9** Ferdinand, Frederick
of Spain: **6** Pelayo, Philip, Ramiro, Sancho, Witiza **7** Alfonso, Almohad, Charles, Umayyad **8** al-Mansur, Reccared, Roderick **9** Almoravid, Ferdinand, Leovigild **10** Juan Carlos **11** Abd al-Rahman, Reccosvinth
of Swaziland: **3** Kbe **5** Nyama **6** Mswati, Sozisa **7** Sobhuza
of Sweden: **4** Vosa, Wasa **5** Oscar **6** Gustav **8** Gustavus **10** Carl Gustav **12** Gustav Adolph **13** Charles Gustav **22** Jean Baptiste Bernadotte
of Syria: **5** Rezin **6** Faisal, Hazael **8** Benhadad **9** Antiochus
of Thailand: **4** Rama **7** Chakkri, Mongkut **10** Chao Phraya **12** Prahjadhipok **13** Chulalongkorn **17** Bhumibol Adulyadej
of Tongo: **11** George Tupou **14** Taufaahau Tupou
of Tunisia: **6** Hafsid **7** Fatimid **8** Aghlabid, Almohade **10** Husseinite
of Turkey: **8** Mausolus
of Uganda: **6** Mutesa, Mwanga **8** Kabarega
of Upper Volta: **4** Naba **5** Mogho
of Zimbabwe: **9** Lobengula, Mzilikaze

France **14** Duke of Cornwall **16** Earl of Gloucester

kingly **5** grand, noble, regal, royal **6** august, lordly, mighty **7** queenly, stately **8** absolute, despotic, glorious, kinglike, imperial, majestic, princely, splendid **9** imperious, monarchal, patrician, sovereign **10** autocratic, commanding, tyrannical **11** magnificent **12** awe-inspiring

Kingman, Dave
nickname: **4** Kong
sport: **8** baseball
position: **8** outfield **9** first base
team: **11** Chicago Cubs, New York Mets **14** New York Yankees, San Diego Padres **16** California Angels **18** San Francisco Giants

king of gods **4** Amen, Amon, Finn, Zeus **5** Ammon, Enlil, Fionn, Wotan **6** Marduk **8** Merodach **12** Baal Merodach **13** Fionn MacCumal

King of Hearts
character in: **28** Alice's Adventures in Wonderland
author: **7** Carroll

King of Righteousness
11 Melchizedek

Kingsley, Ben
roles: **6** Gandhi (Oscar) **8** Betrayal

Kingsley, Charles
author of: **7** Hypatia **10** Alton Locke **11** Westward Ho! **14** The Water Babies **15** Hereward the Wake

King Solomon's Mines
author: **13** H Rider Haggard
character: **5** Twala **6** Gagool, Umbopa **14** Sir Henry Curtis **15** Allan Quatermain, Captain John Good

King's Row
author: **14** Henry Bellamann
director: **7** Sam Wood
cast: **10** Betty Field **11** Ann Sheridan, Claude Rains **12** Ronald Reagan **13** Charles Coburn **14** Judith Anderson, Robert Cummings
score: **21** Erich Wolfgard Korngold
character: **11** Drake McHugh, Elise Sandor **13** Randy Monaghan **14** Cassandra Tower, Parris Mitchell

Kingston
capital of: **7** Jamaica

Kingu
origin: **8** Akkadian
father: **4** Apsu
mother: **6** Tiamet
blood used by: **2** Ea **6** Marduk **8** Merodach **12** Baal Merodach
blood used for: **8** creation

kink **4** coil, flaw, knot, pang **5** cramp, crick, crimp, frizz, gnarl, hitch, quirk, snarl, spasm, twist **6** defect, foible, glitch, oddity, tangle, twinge, vagary **7** crinkle, frizzle **8** crotchet **9** queerness, stiffness, weirdness **10** difficulty **11** peculiarity, singularity **12** charley horse, complication, eccentricity, freakishness, idiosyncrasy, imperfection

kinky **3** odd **4** sick, wiry **5** kooky, queer **6** frizzy, matted, quirky, twisty **7** bizarre, deviant, frizzly, knotted, strange, tangled, twisted, unusual **8** aberrant, abnormal, crinkled, freakish, frizzled, peculiar, perverse **9** eccentric, unnatural **10** unorthodox **13** idiosyncratic

Kinshasa
capital of: **5** Zaire

kinsman **3** sib, son **4** aunt, heir **5** child, uncle **6** cousin, father, mother, parent, sister **7** brother **8** daughter, landsman, relation, relative **9** offspring **10** countryman **11** grandfather, grandmother **13** blood relation, blood relative

Kiowa
language family: **6** Tanoan
location: **6** Plains **7** Montana **8** Colorado, Oklahoma
allied with: **7** Arapaho **8** Comanche **11** Kiowa Apache
deity: **5** Taime

Kiowa Apache
language family: **12** Shapwailutan
location: **6** Plains

Kipling, Rudyard
author of: **3** Kim **8** Gunga Din, Mandalay **11** Danny Deaver **12** The Seven Seas **13** Just So Stories, The Jungle Book **18** Barrack-Room Ballads, Captains Courageous

Kipps
author: **7** H G Wells

Kirchhoff, Gustav Robert
field: **7** physics
nationality: **6** German
discovered: **6** cesium **8** rubidium
developed: **12** spectroscope
named for him: **19** electric circuit laws

Kirchner, Ernst Ludwig
born: **7** Germany **13** Aschaffenburg
artwork: **11** Street Scene **12** Street Berlin **13** Moonlit Winter **21** Self-portrait with Model

Kiribati
other name: **14** Gilbert Islands
capital/largest city: **6** Tarawa
others: **5** Betio **7** Bairiki, Bonriki **9** Bikenibeu
school: **12** South Pacific
monetary unit: **4** cent **6** dollar
island: **5** Flint, Ocean **6** Banaba, Canton, Malden, Tarawa **7** Abemama, Fanning, Gilbert, Marakei, Nonouti, Phoenix, Vostock **8** Caroline, Starbuck **9** Christmas, Enderbury, Tabiteuea **10** Butaritari, Equatorial, Washington **12** Northern Line, Southern Line
sea: **7** Pacific
people: **8** Banabans **10** Polynesian **11** Micronesian
language: **6** Samoan **7** English **10** Gilbertese
religion: **5** Baha'i **8** Anglican **9** Methodist **11** Church of God **13** Roman Catholic **19** Seventh Day Adventist

kirsch, kirschwasser
type: **6** brandy **7** liqueur
origin: **6** France **7** Germany **11** Switzerland
flavor: **6** cherry
with gin: **7** Florida **10** Lady Finger
with vodka: **12** Volga Boatman

kismet **3** end, lot **4** doom, fate **5** moira **7** destiny, fortune, portion **8** God's will **10** Providence **11** will of Allah **12** circumstance **13** inevitability **14** predestination

kiss **4** buss, neck **6** smooch, salute **8** osculate

Kiss for Cinderella, A
author: **12** James M Barrie

kit **3** rig **4** gear **5** tools **6** outfit, tackle, things **7** devices **8** supplies, utensils **9** equipment, trappings **10** implements, provisions **11** furnishings, impediments, instruments, necessaries **13** accoutrements, paraphernalia

Kitasato, Shibasaburo
field: **12** bacteriology
nationality: **8** Japanese
isolated: **7** anthrax, tetanus **9** dysentery **13** bubonic plague
developed: **19** diphtheria antitoxin

kitchen **6** bakery, cocina, galley **7** cuisine **8** cookroom, scullery **9** bakehouse, cookhouse

Kitchener, Horatio Herbert
also: **18** first Earl Kitchener
nationality: **7** British
served in: **7** Boer War **15** South African War
battle: **8** Khartoum, Omdurman
governor of: **8** the Sudan
commander in chief of: **5** India **12** Egyptian army
consul general of: **5** Egypt

kitel **20** Jewish ceremonial robe
color: **5** white

Kitely
character in: **19** Every Man in His Humour
author: **6** Jonson

kittenish **3** coy **7** playful **10** coquettish

Klamath
language family: **8** Penutian
location: **6** Oregon **10** California
related to: **5** Modoc **6** Cayuse, Molala

Klee, Paul
born: **11** Switzerland **14** Munchenbuchsee
artwork: **9** Locksmith **11** Ad Parnassum **18** Barbarian Sacrifice, Demon above the Ships **20** The Twittering Machine **22** Revolution of the Viaduct **23** Dance-Play of the Red Skirts **24** Dance Monster to my Soft Song **35** The Vocal Fabric of the Singer Rosa Silber

Kleist, Heinrich von
author of: **11** Penthesilea **14** The Marquise of O **16** The Broken Pitcher **18** The Prince of Homburg

Kline, Kevin
roles: **11** The Big Chill **13** Sophie's Choice **17** Pirates of Penzance

Klugman, Jack
born: **14** Philadelphia PA
roles: **6** Quincy **12** Oscar Madison, The Odd Couple

klutz **5** dummy **9** blockhead **11** satchelfoot **13** fumblefingers

klutzy **4** dumb **6** clumsy, stupid **7** awkward **9** graceless

knack **4** bent, gift, turn **5** flair, forte, skill **6** genius, talent **7** ability, faculty, finesse **8** aptitude, capacity, facility **9** dexterity, expertise, ingenuity, quickness, readiness **10** adroitness, capability, cleverness, competence, efficiency, propensity **11** inclination, proficiency **13** dexterousness

knave **3** cad, cur, dog, rat **5** phony, rogue, scamp **6** con man, rascal, rotter, varlet, wretch **7** bounder, culprit **8** scalawag, swindler **9** charlatan, con artist, reprobate, scoundrel **10** blackguard **11** rapscallion **14** good for nothing

knee breeches **8** breeches, jodhpurs, knickers **9** plus fours

kneel **3** bow **6** curtsy, kowtow, salaam **7** bow down **9** genuflect **13** make obeisance **16** prostrate oneself

knell **4** peal, ring, toll **5** chime, sound **6** stroke **7** pealing, ringing, tolling

Knickerbocker Holiday
author: **15** Maxwell Anderson

knickknack, nicknack **3** toy **6** bauble, gewgaw, trifle **7** bibelot, trinket **8** frippery, gimcrack **9** bagatelle, bric-a-brac, plaything **11** thingamajig

knife **3** cut **4** dirk, shiv, stab **5** blade, slash, wound **6** cutter, pierce **7** cut down, cutlery **8** cut apart, lacerate, mutilate
type: **3** pen **4** jack **5** bowie, bread, putty, table **6** dagger, paring, pocket **7** butcher, carving, hunting, machete, palette, pruning, scalpel **8** skinning, stiletto, surgical **11** switchblade

knight **4** hero **7** fighter, gallant, paladin, soldier, Templar, warrior **8** cavalier, champion, defender, guardian, horseman, Lancelot **9** gentleman, man-at-arms, protecter, protector **10** equestrian, vindicator

Knight
character in: **18** The Canterbury Tales
author: **7** Chaucer

Knightley, George
character in: **4** Emma
author: **6** Austen

Knights, The
author: **12** Aristophanes
character: **5** Demus **6** Nicias **11** Demosthenes **20** Cleon the Paphlagonian

knit **3** tat **4** ally, bind, draw, join, knot, link **5** braid, plait, twist, unify, unite, weave **6** attach, crease, fasten, furrow, stitch **7** connect, crochet, wrinkle **10** intertwine, interweave **12** draw together

knob **3** nub **4** bulb, bump, grip, hold, hump, knot, knur, lump, node, snag **5** bulge, gnarl, knurl, latch, lever, swell **6** handle, nubbin **8** handhold, swelling, tubercle **9** convexity **10** projection, prominence, protrusion **12** protuberance, protuberancy

knock **3** bat, hit, pat, rap, tap **4** bang, beat, belt, blow, bomb, bump, clip, cuff, dash, kick, lick, push, slam, slap, sock, swat, thud **5** abuse, cavil, clout, crack, crash, decry, pound, punch, smack, smash, smite, thump, whack **6** batter, carp at, defeat, hammer, jostle, murder, peck at, pummel, strike, stroke, thwack, wallop **7** censure, condemn, failure, setback **8** belittle, lambaste **9** criticism, criticize, deprecate, disparage, reprehend **12** condemnation, faultfinding, reprehension

knock down **4** deck, down, drop, fell **5** floor **7** flatten **8** bowl over, discount **9** take apart **11** disassemble

knock off balance **6** rattle **7** shake up **8** unsettle **9** take aback **11** disorganize

knockout **2** KO **4** doll **5** beaut, Venus **6** beauty, eyeful **7** stunner

knock out of shape **4** maul **5** crush **6** batter, beat up, mangle

knoll **4** hill, rise **5** mound

knot **3** bun **4** bump, frog, heap, hump, loop, lump, mass, pack, pile, star, tuft **5** braid, bunch, clump, group, hitch, knurl, plait, twist **6** bundle, circle **7** cat's-paw, chignon, cluster, epaulet, rosette **8** ornament **9** gathering **10** assemblage, collection, intertwist **13** interlacement
type: **3** bow, top **4** flat, slip **5** slide **6** double, single, square **7** running **8** hangman's, overhand, shoulder, surgeon's **9** half-hitch **11** figure-eight, midshipman's

Knots Landing
character: **9** Abby Ewing, Gary Ewing **10** Greg Sumner **11** Valene Ewing **12** Mac Mackenzie **14** Karen Mackenzie, Paige Forrester
cast: **10** Donna Mills, Joan Van Ark **11** Julie Harris, Kevin Dobson, Michelle Lee **13** William Devane **14** Douglas Sheehan, Ted Shackelford **17** Nicolette Sheridan

knotty **4** hard **5** bumpy, rough, tough **6** coarse, flawed, knobby, knurly, rugged, snaggy, thorny, tricky, uneven **7** complex, gnarled, knurled, nodular **8** baffling, involved, puzzling, ticklish, unsmooth **9** blemished, difficult, intricate **10** perplexing **11** complicated, troublesome **12** rough-grained **13** coarse-grained, problematical

know **3** see **6** be sure, be wise, notice **7** be smart, discern, make out, realize **8** identify, perceive **9** apprehend, be assured, be aware of, be certain, be close to, get wise to, recognize **10** be informed, be positive, understand **11** be confident, be sagacious, be thick with, distinguish, feel certain, have down pat, have no doubt **12** discriminate, have down cold, have the ear of **13** be cognizant of, be intelligent, have knowledge, rub elbows with **14** be familiar with

knowable **9** thinkable **11** conceivable, discernible, perceivable **14** understandable

Knowell, Edward
character in: **19** Every Man in His Humour
author: **6** Jonson

know for sure **9** be certain **10** be positive

know-how **3** art **4** bent, gift **5** craft, flair, knack, savvy, skill **6** talent **7** ability, mastery **8** aptitude, capacity, deftness **9** adeptness, expertise, knowledge, technique **10** adroitness, capability, competence, experience, expertness **11** proficiency **12** skillfulness **15** professionalism
French: **11** savoir-faire

knowing **4** deep, wise **5** aware, canny, sharp, smart, sound **6** astute, brainy, bright, clever, shrewd **7** erudite, fraught, learned, sapient **8** academic, educated, eloquent, highbrow, literary, profound, schooled, sensible **9** conscious, judicious, revealing, sagacious **10** discerning, expressive, meaningful, perceptive, percipient, scholastic, widely read **11** enlightened, intelligent, significant **12** intellectual, well-informed **13** comprehending, knowledgeable, perspicacious, philosophical, sophisticated, understanding

knowing how to live
French: 11 savoir-vivre

knowing just what to do
French: 11 savoir-faire

know-it-all 5 brash **13** overconfident

knowledge 3 ken, tip **4** data, hint, news **5** sense **6** memory, notice, report, wisdom **7** inkling, mention, tidings **8** learning **9** awareness, education, erudition, schooling, statement **10** cognizance, intimation, perception **11** cultivation, declaration, familiarity, information, realization, recognition, revelation, scholarship **12** announcement, book learning, intelligence, notification **13** communication, comprehension, consciousness, enlightenment, pronouncement
god of: 4 Odin **5** Othin

knowledgeable 3 hip **8** at home in, versed in **12** familiar with, well-informed **14** acquainted with, conversant with
French: 9 au courant

knowledge of the world
French: 11 savoir-vivre

known 5 noted, plain **6** common, famous, patent **7** evident, obvious, popular **8** apparent, definite, distinct, familiar, manifest, palpable **9** notorious, prominent **10** celebrated, recognized **11** self-evident

know thyself
Greek: 13 gnothi seauton

knuckle under 5 yield **6** give in, submit **7** bow down **9** surrender **10** capitulate

knurled 5 bumpy, lumpy **6** gnarly, knobby, knotty, knurly, nubbly, ridged **7** bulging, gnarled, knotted, nodular

Koch, Robert
field: 12 bacteriology
nationality: 6 German
isolated: 2 TB **12** tuberculosis
awarded: 10 Nobel Prize

Kodaly, Zoltan
born: 7 Hungary **9** Kecskemet
composer of: 9 Hary Janos **11** Czinka Panna, Missa Brevis, Szekely Fono **14** Budavari Te Deum **15** Dances of Galanta **17** Dances of Marosszek, Peacock Variations, Psalmus Hungaricus **28** The Spinning Room of the Szekelys

Koestler, Arthur
author of: 14 Darkness at Noon **15** The Sleepwalkers

Kojak
character: 5 (Det) Rizzo **7** (Det) Stavros **9** (Lt) Theo Kojak **10** (Det) Saperstein **11** Frank McNeil **12** (Lt) Bobby Crocker
cast: 9 Dan Frazer **10** Vince Conti **11** Kevin Dobson, Mark Russell **12** Telly Savalas **13** George Savalas (Demosthenes)
trademark: 8 lollipop
phrase: 14 Who loves ya baby?

Kollwitz, Kathe
real name: 12 Kathe Schmidt
born: 10 Konigsberg **11** East Prussia
artwork: 3 War **5** Death, Pieta **11** Proletariat **13** Weavers' Revolt (Weaver's Rebellion) **14** Mother and Child, The Peasants' War **18** Death Seizing a Woman

Kol Nidre 4 vows **8** promises **22** Jewish liturgical prayer
recited on eve of: 9 Yom Kippur

Kong
nickname of: 11 Dave Kingman

Kon-Tiki
author: 13 Thor Heyerdahl

kook 3 nut **5** crazy, flake, loony, wacko **6** cuckoo, weirdo **7** dingbat **8** crackpot **9** ding-a-ling, eccentric, fruitcake, harebrain, screwball **10** crackbrain

Korah
father: 4 Esau **6** Hebron **7** Eliphaz
conspired with: 6 Abiram, Dathan
rebelled against: 5 Aaron, Moses

Korea ***see box, p. 542***

Koridethianus 16 Greek unical codex

Korman, Harvey
born: 9 Chicago IL
roles: 11 High Anxiety **13** Danny Kaye Show **14** Blazing Saddles **16** Carol Burnett Show

Kornberg, Arthur
field: 12 biochemistry
sythesized: 3 DNA, RNA **15** ribonucleic acid **20** deoxyribonucleic acid
awarded: 10 Nobel Prize

kosher 5 right **6** proper **7** ethical **10** aboveboard **12** on the up and up

Kosinski, Jerzy
author of: 5 Steps **7** Cockpit **9** Blind Date **10** Being There **11** Passion Play **12** The Devil Tree **14** The Painted Bird

Kowalski, Stanley
character in: 21 A Streetcar Named Desire
author: 8 Williams

kowtow 4 bend, fawn **5** cower, stoop, toady **6** bow low, cringe, curtsy, grovel, salaam **7** truckle **8** bootlick, butter up, softsoap **9** genuflect **11** apple-polish **12** bow and scrape **16** prostrate oneself

kowtowing 7 fawning, servile **8** toadying **9** groveling **10** obsequious

Kraken
origin: 9 Norwegian
form: 7 monster
habitat: 3 sea
caused: 10 whirlpools

Kramer, Stanley
director of: 10 On the Beach **11** Ship of Fools **14** Inherit the Wind, The Defiant Ones **19** Judgment at Nuremberg

Kramer vs Kramer
director: 12 Robert Benton
based on novel by: 11 Avery Corman
cast: 10 Howard Duff **11** Justin Henry, Meryl Streep **13** Dustin Hoffman, Jane Alexander
Oscar for: 5 actor (Hoffman) **7** picture **8** director **10** screenplay **17** supporting actress (Streep)

Krantz, Judith
author of: 8 Scruples **13** Princess Daisy **16** I'll Take Manhattan, Mistral's Daughter

Krazy Kat
creator: 14 George Herriman
character:
***cop:* 12** Offissa B Pupp
***mouse:* 6** Ignatz
prop: 5 brick
place: 4 jail **14** Coconino County **24** Kelly's Exclusive Brick Yard

Krebs, Hans Adolf
field: 9 chemistry
nationality: 6 German
discovered: 15 citric acid cycle
awarded: 10 Nobel Prize

Korea
other name: 6 Choson 17 land of morning calm
capital:
North Korea: 9 Pyongyang
South Korea: 5 Seoul
largest city: 5 Seoul
others: 5 Masan, Mokpo, Pusan, Sinpo, Suwon, Taegu, Wonju 6 Chonju, Inchon, Kangso, Kunsan, Taejon, Wonsan 7 Hanyang, Hungnam, Kaesong, Kangson, Kwangju 8 Chongjin, Chunchon, Kimchaek
school: 5 Busan 6 Yonsei 7 Hanyang 8 Kim Chaek, Kyung Hee 9 Kim II Sung
division:
ancient: 5 Silla 6 Choson 7 Koguryo, Paekche
monetary unit: 3 woh, won 4 chun, hwan, kwan
weight: 3 won
island: 4 Chin, Koje 5 Cheju, Sinmi 6 Anmyon, Huksan, Namhae 7 Tokchok 8 Quelpart 10 Paengnyong
mountain: 4 Wang 5 Chiri, Halla 6 Kwanmo, Sobaek 7 Diamond, Kyebang, Nangnim, Taebaek 8 Chang-pai, Hamgyong, Myohyang 9 Paektu-san 10 Kumgang-san
highest point: 6 Paektu 9 Paektu-san
river: 3 Han, Kin, Kum, Kun, Nam 4 Lobk, Yalu 5 Amnok, Imjin, Tumen 6 Namhan, Pukhan, Somjin, Soyang, Yesong 7 Naktong, Taedong 8 Changjin, Youngsan 9 Chongchon
sea: 5 Japan 6 Yellow 9 East China
physical feature:
bay: 5 Korea 6 Yongil 7 Kanghwa, Kyonggi 9 Tongjoson
cape: 4 Musu
point: 7 Changgi 8 Changsan
strait: 5 Korea
valley: 7 Naktong
people: 6 Korean
artist: 8 Chong Son 10 Kimtlong-do
dynasty: 2 Yi 4 Choe 5 Koryo
leader: 6 Sejong 8 Yi Sung-gy 9 Kim II Sung 11 Chun Doo Hwan, Syngman Rhee 12 Park Chung Hee
legendary leader: 5 Ki-tse 6 Chi-tse, Chi-tzu, Tangun
poet: 10 Hwang Chini
language: 6 Korean
alphabet: 6 hangul
religion: 6 Taoism 7 animism 8 Buddhism 9 Chondogyo 12 Christianity, Confucianism
place:
palace: 8 Kyongbok
temple: 7 Haein-sa 17 Hall of Eternal Life
tomb: 14 Dancing Figures
feature:
clothing: 5 chima
game: 3 yut 5 akoan 6 ho-hpai 7 kol-ye-si 9 ryong-hpai, sang-ryouk 10 ke-pouk-hpai, sin-syo-tyen 12 tjak-matchi-ki 15 kko-ri-pouk-tchi-ki
martial art: 9 tae-kwon-do
musical instrument: 6 chaing 7 kayagum, komungo
porcelain: 7 Celadon
porch: 4 maru
pottery: 8 pun-chong
food:
bean curd: 4 tubu
hot pickle: 6 kimchi
meat-filled dumpling: 5 mandu
noodle: 5 kuksu

Kreisler, Fritz
born: 6 Vienna 7 Austria
composer of: 7 Allegro 10 Praeludium 15 Caprice Viennois 16 Tambourin Chinois

Kreutzer, Rodolphe
born: 6 France 10 Versailles
composer of: 16 Etudes ou Caprices

Kreutzer Sonata, The
author: 10 Leo Tolstoy
character: 13 Mme Pozdnishef, Trukhashevsky 16 Vasyla Pozdnishef

Krieg 3 war

Kriemhild
origin: 8 Germanic
mentioned in: 14 Nibelungenlied
brother: 7 Gunther
husband: 9 Siegfried
slew: 5 Hagan 7 Gunther
avenged: 6 murder 9 Siegfried
corresponds to: 6 Gudrun, Kudrun 7 Guthrun

Kristin Lavransdatter
author: 12 Sigrid Undset

Kronos *see* 6 Cronus

Krook
character in: 10 Bleak House
author: 7 Dickens

Kropp, Albert
character in: 25 All Quiet on the Western Front
author: 8 Remarque

krypton
chemical symbol: 2 Kr

Kuala Lumpur
capital of: 8 Malaysia

Kubla Khan
author: 15 Samuel Coleridge

Kubrick, Stanley
director of: 6 Lolita 9 Spartacus 11 Barry Lyndon 12 Paths of Glory 13 Dr Strangelove (or How I Learned to Stop Worrying and Love the Bomb) 16 A Clockwork Orange 30 Two Thousand and One A Space Odyssey

kudo, kudos 4 fame 5 award, glory, honor, prize 6 esteem, praise, renown, repute 7 acclaim, plaudit 8 citation, prestige 9 celebrity, laudation 10 admiration, decoration 12 commendation 14 celebratedness

Kudrun *see* 6 Gudrun

Kukla, Fran & Ollie
hostess: 11 Fran Allison
puppet: 5 Kukla, Ollie (Oliver J Dragon) 8 Mercedes 9 Cecil Bill 10 Col Crackie 11 Beulah Witch 12 Olivia

Dragon **13** Delores Dragon **14** Fletcher Rabbit **18** Mme Ophelia Oglepuss

Kulla
origin: 8 Egyptian, Sumerian
world of: 4 dead
god of: 6 bricks

Kullervo
origin: 7 Finnish
mentioned in: 8 Kalevala
form: 5 slave
death: 7 suicide

kummel
origin: 7 Germany
flavor: 7 caraway

kumquat 10 Fortunella
varieties: 4 oval **5** round **6** Marumi, Nagami **16** Australian desert

Kung Fu
character: 8 Master Po **9** Master Kan **14** Kwai Chang Caine
cast: 8 Keye Luke **9** Philip Ahn **11** Radames Pera **14** David Carradine
Caine raised in: 13 Shaolin Temple

kunzite
species: 9 spodumene

Kupka, Frank (Frantisek)
born: 6 Opocno **7** Bohemia **14** Czechoslovakia
artwork: 12 Black Accents, The Cathedral **16** Etude pour la Fugue **17** Fugue in Red and Blue **23** Fugue in Two Colors Amorpha **25** Philosophical Architecture

Kuprin, Aleksandr
author of: 7 The Duel **10** Yama the Pit

Kurosawa, Akira
director of: 3 Ran **8** Rashomon **12** Seven Samurai

Kurtz
character in: 15 Heart of Darkness
author: 6 Conrad

Kuwait ***see box***

Kwa
language family: 16 Niger-Kordofanian
group: 10 Niger-Congo
includes: 3 Ewe, Ibo, Twi **4** Bini, Nupe, Togo **6** Yoruba **7** Dahomey

Kwakiutl
language family: 8 Wakashan
location: 6 Canada **15** British Columbia, Vancouver Island **20** Queen Charlotte Island
related to: 6 Nootka **10** Bellabella
noted for: 10 totem poles **15** Cannibal Society, wooden sculpture
called: 14 potlatch people

Kyd, Thomas
author of: 17 The Spanish Tragedy

Kyrie eleison 13 Lord have mercy

Kuwait
name means: 9 small fort
capital/largest city: 10 Kuwait City
others: 6 Ahmadi **7** Hawalli **8** Abdullah, al-Jahrah, Fahaheel, Shuwaykh **9** al-Shuayba **12** Mena al Ahmadi, Mina Abd Allah, Mina al-Ahmadi
head of state: 4 emir
monetary unit: 4 fils **5** dinar
island: 5 Warba **7** Bubiyan, Failaka
physical feature:
***bay:* 6** Kuwait **12** Khor Abdullah
***duststorm:* 4** kaus
***gulf:* 7** Persian
***oasis:* 6** Jahrah
people: 4 Arab **5** Iraqi, Saudi **6** Indian **7** Bedouin **8** Egyptian **9** Pakistani **11** Palestinian
***ruling family:* 5** Sabah
***sheikh (Sabah family):* 5** Ahmad, Salem **7** Mubarak **12** Jaber al-Ahmed, Sabah al-Salim **15** Abdullah al-Salim
religion: 5 Islam

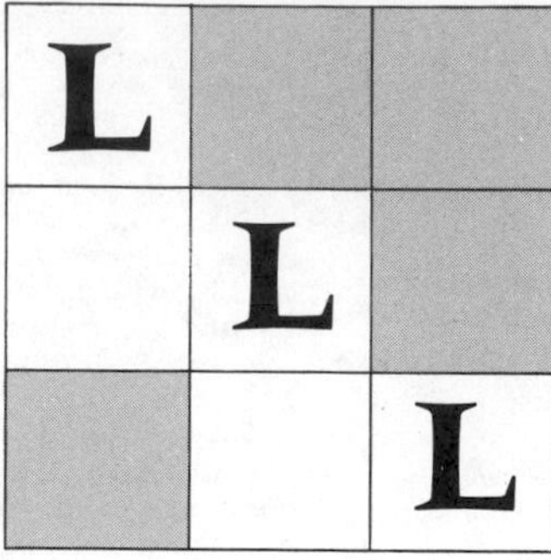

Laban
father: 7 Bethuel
grandfather: 5 Nahor
daughter: 4 Leah 6 Rachel
sister: 7 Rebekah
son-in-law: 5 Jacob

Labdacus
king of: 6 Thebes
father: 9 Polydorus
mother: 7 Nycteis
grandfather: 7 Nycteus
brother: 5 Lycus
son: 5 Laius
grandson: 7 Oedipus

label 3 tag 4 mark, name, note, seal, sign, slip 5 brand, stamp, tally, title 6 define, docket, ticket 7 earmark, mark off, sticker 8 classify, describe 9 designate 10 denominate, put a mark on 11 appellation, designation, inscription 12 characterize 13 specification 14 classification, identification 16 characterization

labor, labour 4 plod, toil, work 5 slave, sweat 6 drudge, effort, suffer 7 agonize, travail, workers, workmen 8 drudgery, exertion, laborers, manpower, plodding, plug away, struggle, struggle 9 employees, grind away, work force 10 birth pangs, childbirth, menial work, smart under 11 birth throes, manual labor, parturition 12 accouchement, be affected by, be burdened by, be troubled by 13 be the victim of 14 employ one's time, work like a slave

labored 5 heavy, stiff 6 clumsy, forced, wooden 7 awkward, cramped, halting, studied 8 drawnout, overdone, strained 9 contrived, difficult, laborious, maladroit, ponderous, unnatural 13 self-conscious, unspontaneous

laborer 4 hand 6 coolie, drudge, menial, toiler, worker 7 plodder, workman 8 handyman, hired man, hireling, workhand 9 hired hand 10 roustabout, wage earner, workingman 11 proletarian 12 manual worker 16 blue-collar worker

laborious 4 hard 6 brutal, severe, uphill 7 arduous, irksome, labored, onerous, wearing 8 rigorous, tiresome, toilsome, wearying 9 demanding, difficult, effortful, fatiguing, herculean, strenuous, wearisome 10 burdensome, oppressive, struggling 11 troublesome

laboriously 4 hard 9 arduously 14 with difficulty 15 with great effort

laboriousness 5 trial 8 tough job 10 difficulty, rough going, uphill work 11 arduousness 12 hard sledding 15 troublesomeness

labor omnia vincit 15 work conquers all
motto of: 8 Oklahoma

Labors of Hercules *see* 8 Hercules

labyrinth 3 web 4 knot, maze 5 snarl 6 jungle, morass, riddle, tangle 7 complex, network 9 intricacy, mare's nest 10 complexity, perplexity, wilderness 11 convolution

Labyrinth
form: 4 maze
location: 5 Crete
built by: 8 Daedalus
housed: 8 Minotaur

Lacaille, Nicholas Louis de
field: 9 astronomy
nationality: 6 French
mapped: 14 constellations

lace 3 tie 4 beat, bind, cane, dope, lash, whip 5 braid, cinch, close, flail, spank, spike, strap, tie up, truss 6 dope up, fasten, flavor, infuse, punish, secure, switch, tether, thrash 7 fortify, spice up, suffuse, tighten 8 chastise, make fast, make taut 10 strengthen 11 add liquor to 12 add spirits to, draw together, give a beating

Lacedaemon
father: 4 Zeus
mother: 8 Taygete
wife: 6 Sparta
son: 7 Amyclas
daughter: 8 Eurydice
founder of: 6 Sparta

lacerate 3 cut, rip 4 gash, hurt, pain, scar, stab, tear 5 lance, sever, slash, slice, wound 6 deface 7 agonize, scratch, torment, torture 8 distress, give pain, puncture 10 excruciate 11 inflict pain

lacerating 5 acute 6 fierce, severe 7 cutting, extreme, intense, violent 12 excruciating

laceration 3 cut, rip 4 tear 5 wound 10 mutilation

Lachaise, Gaston
born: 5 Paris 6 France
artwork: 12 Standing Nude 13 Standing Woman 14 Floating Figure

Lachesis
form: 4 Fate
holds: 12 thread of life
determines: 6 length 7 destiny

lachrymose 3 sad 5 teary, weepy 6 crying 7 maudlin, tearful, weeping 8 mournful 10 melancholy

lack 4 miss, need, want 6 dearth 7 absence 8 omission, scarcity, shortage 9 be missing, be short of, depletion, neediness, privation, scantness 10 deficiency, exhaustion 11 deprivation, fall short of 12 be inadequate 13 be caught short, be deficient in **14** be found wanting, be insufficient

lackadaisical **4** idle **7** languid, loafing **8** lifeless, listless, mindless **9** apathetic, lethargic, unexcited **10** inanimated, phlegmatic, spiritless, unaspiring, uninspired **11** indifferent, languishing, unambitious, unconcerned, unexcitable, unmotivated **12** uninterested **13** dillydallying

lackey **4** page **5** slave, toady, usher, valet **6** butler, flunky, helper, menial, minion, squire, waiter **7** servant, steward **8** employee, follower, hanger-on, hireling, inferior, retainer **9** assistant, attendant, cupbearer, mercenary, underling

lacking **7** needing, wanting **9** deficient **10** inadequate **12** falling short, insufficient
French: **6** manque

lackluster **4** blah, dead, drab, dull **5** bland, muted **6** boring, dreary, leaden, pallid, somber **7** humdrum, nothing, prosaic, subdued **8** lifeless, mediocre, ordinary **9** colorless **10** lusterless **11** commonplace **12** run-of-the-mill **13** uninteresting

lack of conviction **5** doubt **8** question **9** misgiving **10** hesitation, indecision **11** uncertainty

lack of faith **5** doubt **7** atheism **8** distrust, mistrust **9** disbelief, suspicion

lack of feeling **6** apathy **8** coldness, numbness **11** impassivity **15** emotionlessness, hardheartedness, passionlessness

lack of interest **5** ennui **6** apathy **7** boredom **9** unconcern **12** indifference

lack of respect **8** contempt, rudeness **9** disregard **10** disrespect **11** discourtesy, irreverence **12** impoliteness

lack of skill **9** inability **10** clumsiness, ineptitude **11** awkwardness **12** incompetency

Laclos, Pierre Choderlos de
author of: **22** Les Liaisons Dangereuses

Lacombe, Lucien
director: **10** Louis Malle
cast: **12** Pierre Blaise **13** Aurore Clement **16** Holger Lowenadler

laconic **4** curt **5** blunt, brief, pithy, short, terse **7** compact, concise, pointed, summary **8** succinct **9** condensed **10** to the point **12** concentrated **14** sparing of words

lacquer **4** coat **5** glaze **7** coating, shellac, varnish

lacrimoso
music: **7** tearful

lacrosse
Indian name: **9** bagataway
circle around goal: **6** crease
players/team: **3** ten
position: **6** goalie **9** attackman **10** defenseman, midfielder
term: **6** riding **8** clearing

lacuna **3** gap, pit **4** gulf, hole, void **5** blank, break, crack, ditch, pause, space **6** breach, cavity, hiatus **7** caesura, fissure, interim, opening, vacancy **8** interval, omission **10** interstice, suspension **12** interruption **13** discontinuity

lacustrine **7** aquatic **11** lake-growing **12** lake-dwelling

lacy **4** fine **5** filmy, gauzy, meshy, netty, sheer, webby **6** barred, frilly, netted, porous, webbed **7** gridded, netlike **8** cobwebby, delicate, filigree, gossamer, lacelike, retiform **9** filigreed **10** diaphanous, reticulate **11** latticelike, transparent

lad **3** boy, kid **5** sprig, youth **6** shaver, sprout **8** juvenile, young man **9** schoolboy, stripling, young chap, youngster **11** young fellow

Ladd, Alan
son: **5** David **6** Alan Jr
co-star: **12** Veronica Lake
born: **12** Hot Springs AR
roles: **5** Shane **13** The Blue Dahlia **14** The Great Gatsby, This Gun for Hire

ladies' man **4** beau, stud **5** spark **7** playboy **8** cavalier, gay blade

La Dolce Vita
director: **15** Federico Fellini
cast: **9** Lex Barker, Nadia Gray **10** Anouk Aimee **11** Anita Ekberg **19** Marcello Mastroianni

Ladon
form: **6** dragon
father: **6** Typhon
mother: **7** Echidna
number of heads: **7** hundred
guarded: **6** garden
garden owned by: **10** Hesperides
killed by: **8** Hercules

ladrone **5** thief **6** bandit, outlaw

lady **4** wife **5** woman **6** female, matron, spouse **7** duchess, peeress **8** baroness, countess **10** aristocrat, noblewoman **11** gentlewoman, marchioness, viscountess, woman of rank **13** well-bred woman
German: **4** frau
Italian: **5** donna
Spanish/Portuguese: **4** dona

Lady Chatterley's Lover
author: **10** D H Lawrence
character: **7** Mellors **19** Constance Chatterley

Lady Eve, The
director: **14** Preston Sturges
cast: **10** Henry Fonda **13** Charles Coburn **14** Eugene Pallette **15** Barbara Stanwyck, William Demarest

Lady for a Day
director: **10** Frank Capra
based on story by: **11** Damon Runyon
cast: **9** Guy Kibbee, May Robson **13** Warren William
remade as: **19** Pocketful of Miracles

Lady from Dubuque, The
author: **11** Edward Albee

Lady from the Sea, The
author: **11** Henrik Ibsen

Lady in Chair
constellation of: **10** Cassiopeia

ladylike **5** civil **6** modest, polite, proper **7** courtly, elegant, genteel, refined **8** cultured, decorous, mannerly, polished, well-bred **9** courteous, dignified **10** cultivated **11** respectable **12** well-mannered **13** well brought up

Lady of the Camellias, The
see **7** Camille

Lady of the Lake, The
author: **14** Sir Walter Scott
character: **9** Allan Bane **11** Roderick Dhu **12** Ellen Douglas **13** Malcolm Graeme **14** James Fitz-James, James of Douglas

Lady Oracle
author: **14** Margaret Atwood

lady's maid
French: **14** femme de chambre

Lady's Not for Burning, The
author: **14** Christopher Fry

lady's-slipper, Lady-slipper
11 Cypripedium **13** Paphiopedilum, Phragmipedium
varieties: **4** pink **5** showy **8** mountain, ram's-head **9** two-leaved **10** small

white **11** large yellow, small yellow

Lady Vanishes, The
director: 15 Alfred Hitchcock
cast: 9 Paul Lukas **13** Dame May Whitty **15** Michael Redgrave **16** Margaret Lockwood

Lady Windermere's Fan
author: 10 Oscar Wilde
character: 10 Mrs Erlynne **14** Lord Darlington, Lord Windermere **18** Lord Augustus Lorton

Laelaps
form: 5 hound
borrowed from: 8 Cephalus
borrowed by: 10 Amphitryon

Laertes
son: 8 Odysseus

Laertes
character in: 6 Hamlet
author: 11 Shakespeare

Laertiades
epithet of: 8 Odysseus
means: 12 son of Laertes

Laestrygones
form: 6 giants
characteristic: 9 cannibals

La Farge, John
born: 9 New York NY
artwork: 14 Maua Our Boatman **17** The Muse of Painting **18** Red and White Peonies

La Fayette, Comtesse de
author of: 19 La Princesse de Cleves

Lafayette, Marquis de
also: 38 Marie Joseph Paul Yves Roch Gilbert du Motier
nationality: 6 French
served in: 14 July Revolution **16** French Revolution **18** American Revolution
battle: 8 Yorktown **10** Brandywine

Lafcadio's Adventures (The Vatican Swindle)
author: 9 Andre Gide

La Fontaine, Jean de
author of: 6 Fables

lag 4 drag, halt, inch, limp, snag **5** dally, delay, hitch, tarry, trail **6** be idle, be late, be slow, dawdle, falter, hold up, linger, loiter, trudge **7** be tardy, setback, slacken, stagger **8** be behind, hang back, slowdown **9** be overdue, inch along **10** drag behind, slackening **11** slowing down **12** bide one's time, take one's time **13** falling behind, procrastinate

laggard 4 mope, poke, slow, slug **5** idler, snail, tardy **6** loafer, remiss **7** dallier, dawdler, lounger **8** lingerer, loiterer, potterer, putterer, slowfoot, slowpoke, sluggard, sluggish **9** do-nothing, straggler **12** dilly-dallier **13** stick-in-the-mud

lagniappe, lagnappe 3 tip **4** gift, perk **5** bonus, favor, prize **7** largess, memento, present **8** gratuity, largesse **9** pourboire

Lagos
former capital of: 7 Nigeria

Lahr, Bert
real name: 14 Irving Lahrheim
born: 9 New York NY
roles: 12 Cowardly Lion **13** The Wizard of Oz

laic 3 lay **5** civil **6** laical **7** amateur, popular, profane, secular, worldly **8** temporal **11** nonclerical, nonpastoral **12** secularistic **13** inexperienced **15** nonprofessional **17** nonecclesiastical

lair 3 den, lie, mew **4** hole, nest **5** cover, haunt **6** burrow, cavern, covert **7** hideout, retreat **8** hideaway **9** sanctuary **12** resting place

laissez-faire, laisser-faire 8 hands off **9** let them be, unconcern **12** indifference **14** let-alone policy, live and let live **15** noninterference, nonintervention

laissez-passer 4 pass **6** permit **11** allow to pass

Laius
king of: 6 Thebes
father: 8 Labdacus
great-grandfather: 6 Cadmus
wife: 7 Jocasta
son: 7 Oedipus
killed by: 7 Oedipus

Lajeunesse, Gabriel
character in: 10 Evangeline
author: 10 Longfellow

lake ***see box***

Lake, Harriette
real name of: 10 Ann Sothern

Lake, Veronica
real name: 29 Constance Frances Marie Ockelman
co-star: 8 Alan Ladd
born: 10 Brooklyn NY
roles: 13 The Blue Dahlia **14** I Married a Witch, This Gun for Hire **16** Sullivan's Travels

Lake Isle of Innisfree, The
author: 7 W B Yeats

Lakes
goddess of: 7 Juturna

L'Allegro
author: 10 John Milton
companion piece: 11 Il Penseroso

Lalo, (Victor Antoine) Edouard
born: 5 Lille **6** France
composer of: 7 Namouna **8** Le Roi d'Ys **11** The King of Ys **15** Spanish Symphony **18** Symphonie Espagnole

Lamar, Ruby
character in: 9 Sanctuary
author: 8 Faulkner

Lamarck, Jean B
field: 7 biology
forerunner of theory of: 9 evolution
author of: 21 Philosophie Zoologique

La Mare, Walter de
author of: 16 Memoirs of a Midget

Lamarr, Hedy
real name: 21 Hedwig Eva Maria Kiesler
born: 6 Vienna **7** Austria
roles: 7 Ecstasy **16** Samson and Delilah

Lamas, Fernando
wife: 10 Arlene Dahl **14** Esther Williams
born: 9 Argentina **11** Buenos Aires
roles: 13 The Merry Widow **16** Dangerous When Wet **23** The Girl Who Had Everything

Lamb, Charles
author of: 12 Essays of Elia **13** Dream Children **25** A Dissertation upon Roast Pig **31** Specimens of English Dramatic Poets

lambaste 4 beat, drub, lick, pelt, whip **5** scold, smear **6** berate, defeat, pummel, rebuke, subdue, thrash, wallop **7** bawl out, censure, chew out, clobber, cuss out, shellac, trounce **8** bludgeon, denounce, vanquish **9** castigate, dress down, light into, overwhelm, reprimand

lambent 6 bright **7** radiant, shining **8** luminous, lustrous **10** flickering, shimmering

Lambeosaurus
type: 8 dinosaur **10** ornithopod
location: 6 Canada
period: 10 Cretaceous

Lambert, Constant
born: 6 London **7** England
composer of: 9 Horoscope, Rio Grande **14** Romeo and Juliet **17** Music for Orches-

lake

of Afghanistan: 7 Helmand **13** Hamud-i-Helmand
of Albania: 4 Ulze **5** Matia, Ohrid **6** Prespa **7** Ochrida, Scutari, Shkoder **8** Ohridsko
of Algeria: 5 Hodna **6** Sabkha **7** Cherqui, Fedjadj, Meirhir **10** Azzel Matti, Meherrhane
of Andorra: 11 Engolasters
of Argentina: 6 Viedma **7** Cardiel, Fagnano, Musters **11** Buenos Aires, Mar Chiquita, Nahuel Huapi
of Armenia: 3 Van **5** Sevan, Urmia **8** Urumiyah
of Australia: 4 Eyre **5** Carey, Cowan, Frome, Moore, Wells **6** Austin, Barlee, Bulloo, Dundas, Harris, Mackay **7** Amadeus, Blanche, Everard, Torrens **8** Carnegie, Gairdner **9** MacDonald **10** Yammayamma **14** Disappointment
of Austria: 6 Almsee **7** Fertoto, Mondsee **8** Bodensee, Traunsee **9** Constance **10** Neusiedler
of Benin: 5 Aheme **6** Nokoue
of Bolivia: 5 Poopo **7** Allagas, Coipasa, Rogagua **8** Titicaca **10** Desaguader
of Botswana: 3 Dow, Xau **5** Ngami
of Brazil: 4 Aima, Feia **5** Mirim **13** Logo dos Platos
of Burma: 4 Inle
of Burundi: 7 Rugwero **8** Tshohoha **10** Tanganyika
of Cambodia/Kampuchea: 8 Tonle Sap
of Cameroon: 4 Chad
of Canada: 4 Cree, Erie, Gras, Seul **5** Garry, Huron, Rainy **6** Louise, St John **7** Abitibi, Dubawnt, Nipigon, Ontario, Testlin **8** Kootenay, Manitoba, Okanagan, Reindeer, Superior, Winnipeg **9** Athabaska, Great Bear, Nipissing **10** Great Slave, Mistassini **12** Winnipegosis
of Central African Republic: 4 Assa
of Chad: 4 Chad
of Chile: 5 Ranco **6** Yelcho **7** Puyehue, Rupanco **8** Cochrane **10** General Paz, Llanquihue **11** Buenos Aires
of China: 3 Tai **4** Chao, Na-mu **5** Kaoyu, Oling, Telli **6** Bamtso, Bornor, Ebinor, Erhhai, Khanka, Lopnor, Namtso, Poyang **7** Chaling, Hungtse, Karanor, Kokonor **8** Hulunnor, Montcalm, Taroktso, Tellinor, Tienchih, Tsinghai, Tungting
of Colombia: 4 Tota
of the Congo: 5 Mweru, Tumba **6** Albert, Nyanza, Upemba **7** Leopold **11** Stanley Pool
of Costa Rica: 6 Arenal
of Denmark 6 Arreso
of Djibouti: 4 Abbe **5** Assal
of Dominican Republic: 10 Enriquillo
of Egypt: 4 Edku, Idku **5** Qarun **6** Maryut, Moeris, Nasser **7** Manzala **8** Burullus, Mareotis
of El Salvador: 5 Guiha, Guija **8** Ilopango **10** Coatepeque
of England: 8 Grasmere **9** Ennerdale, Ullswater, Wastwater **10** Buttermere, Windermere **12** Derwentwater **13** Coniston Water
of Estonia: 5 Pskov **6** Peipus **9** Vortsjarv
of Ethiopia: 3 Abe **4** Tana **5** Abaya, Shola, Tanna, Tsana, Tzana, Zeway **6** Dambea, Dembea, Rudolf **8** Blue Nile, Stefanie
of Finland: 3 Juo, Muo **4** Kemi, Kiui, Nasi, Oulu, Puru, Pyha, Simo **5** Enara, Enare, Hauki, Inari, Kalla, Lappa, Lesti, Puula, Saima **6** Ladoya, Lentua, Saimaa, Sounne, Syvari **7** Koitere, Nilakka **8** Pielinen **9** Kallavesi, Pielavesi
of France: 6 Annecy, Cazaux, Geneva
of Gabon Republic: 7 Anengue, Azinguo
of Germany, East: 6 Muritz
of Germany, West: 9 Constance **11** Inner Alster, Outer Alster
of Ghana: 5 Volta **8** Bosumtwi
of Greece: 5 Karla, Volve **6** Copais, Kopais, Prespa, Voweis **8** Ioannina, Koroneia, Vistonis **9** Trichonis, Vegoritis
of Grenada: 10 Grand Etang
of Guatemala: 5 Dulce, Guija, Peten **6** Izabal **7** Atitlan **9** Amatitlan, Peten Itza
of Haiti: 8 Saumatre
of Honduras: 5 Criba, Yojoa **6** Brewer
of Hungary: 5 Ferto **7** Balaton, Velence **9** Blatensee **10** Neusiedler, Plattensee
of Iceland: 6 Myvatn **10** Thorisvatn **14** Thingvallavatn
of India: 5 Jheel, Lonar, Wular **6** Chilka, Colair, Dhebar, Kolair **7** Kolleru, Pulicat, Pushkar, Sambahr
of Indonesia: 4 Toba **5** Ranau **6** Towuti
of Iran: 5 Niris, Tasht, Tuzlu, Urmia **6** Sahweh, Sistan **7** Maharlu **8** Nemekser, Urumiyeh
of Iraq: 6 al-Milh **7** Sanniya **8** al-Hammar
of Ireland: 3 Doo, Key, Ree, Tay **4** Conn, Derg, Erne, Mask **5** Allen, Barra, Carra, Gowna, Leane, Lough, Neagh **6** Boderg, Cooter, Corrib, Ennell **7** Dromore, Gougane, Oughter, Sheelin **9** Killarney
of Israel: 5 Huleh **7** Dead Sea **8** Kinneret, Tiberias **12** Sea of Galilee
of Italy: 4 Como, Iseo, Nemi **5** Garda **6** Albano, Lesina, Lugano, Varano **7** Bolsena, Perugia **8** Maggiore **9** Bracciano, Trasimeno

(*continued*)

lake (*continued*)
of Japan: **4** Biwa, Suwa, Toya **6** Towada **8** Kutchawa, Shikotsu
of Kenya: **6** Magadi, Nakuru, Natron, Rudolf **7** Turkana **8** Naivasha, Victoria
of Lebanon: **5** Quran **6** Qirawn
of Lithuania: **5** Dysna
of Luxembourg: **8** Haut Sure
of Madagascar: **5** Itasy **7** Alaotra, Kinkony
of Malawi: **5** Nyasa **6** Chilwa, Malawi
of Mali: **2** Do **4** Debo **5** Garou **7** Korarou **9** Faguibine
of Mexico: **7** Chapala, Texcoco **9** Patzcuaro
of Mongolia: **3** Uvs **5** Har Us **6** Bor Nor **7** Ghirgis, Ubsa Nor **8** Airik Nor, Durga Nor, Hobsogol, Khara Usu **9** Khubsugul, Khukhu-Nur **10** Khirgis Nor
of Montenegro: **7** Scutari, Shkoder
of Mozambique: **5** Nyasa **6** Chuali, Nyassa **8** Nhavarre
of Nauru: **11** Buada Lagoon
of the Netherlands: **7** Haarlem **10** Ijsselmeer **11** Grevelingen, Hazinguliet
of New Zealand: **3** Ada **4** Gunn, Ohau **5** Hawea, Taupo **6** Pukaki, Pupuke, Te Anau, Tekapo, Wanaka **7** Brunner, Diamond, Kanieri, Okareka, Rotorua **8** Okataina, Paradise, Rotoaira, Wakatipi **9** Manapouri
of Nicaragua: **7** Managua **9** Nicaragua
of Niger: **4** Chad
of Nigeria: **4** Chad
of the Nile: **4** Tana **5** Kyoga, Tsana **6** Albert, Edward, Nasser **8** Victoria
of Norway: **4** Alte **5** Ister, Mjosa, Snasa **6** Femund **7** Rostavn, Tunnsjo
of Panama: **5** Gatun
of Paraguay: **4** Vera, Ypoa **8** Ypacarai
of Peru: **8** Titicaca
of Poland: **5** Goplo, Mamry **8** Niegocin, Sniardwy **13** Stettin Lagoon
of Puerto Rico: **5** Loiza **6** Carite **8** Dos Bocas **9** Caonillas, Guatajaca
of Rumania: **5** Sinoe **6** Snagov
of Russia: **3** Seg **4** Aral, Azof, Kola, Neva, Sego, Topo, Vigo **5** Byelo, Chany, Elton, Erara, Ilmen, Lacha, Onega, Pskov, Vozhe **6** Baikal, Ladoga, Peipus, Selety, Taymyr, Tengiz, Zaysan **8** Balkhash **10** Caspian Sea
of Rwanda: **4** Kivu **5** Ihema **6** Bufera, Bulera, Mohasi **7** Rugwero, Ruhnodo **8** Mugesera, Tshohoha
of Sardinia: **6** Omodeo
of Scotland: **3** Awe, Dee, Lin, Tay **4** Earn, Fyne, Gair, Gare, Linn, Ness, Oich, Ryan, Sloy **5** Duich, Leven, Lochy, Lough, Morar, Maree, Nevis **6** Laggan, Linnhe, Lomond **7** Katrine, Rannoch, St Marys
of Senegal: **6** Guiers
of Sicily: **7** Pergusa **8** Camarina
of Spain: **4** Lago **9** Albrifera
of the Sudan: **2** No **4** Chad, Toad **6** Nasser
of Sweden: **4** Ster **5** Asnen, Malar, Silja, Vaner **6** Vanern, Vatter, Wennen **7** Hielmar, Malaren, Vattern **8** Dalalven **9** Hjalmaren
of Switzerland: **3** Uri, Zug **4** Biel, Thon, Thun **5** Ageri, Leman, Morat **6** Bienne, Brienz, Geneva, Lugano, Sarnen, Wallen, Zurich **7** Hallwil, Lucerne, Lungern **8** Maggiore, Vierwald **9** Bielersee, Constance, Neuchatel, Sarnersee, Thunersee
of Syria: **5** Merom **7** Djeboid **8** Tiberias
of Tanzania: **5** Eyasi, Nyasa, Rukwa **6** Malawi, Natron, Nyassa **7** Manyara **8** Victoria **10** Tanganyika
of Thailand: **9** Nong Lahan
of Tibet: **3** Aru, Bam, Bum, Nam **4** Mema, Tosu **5** Jagok, Tabia **6** Dagtse, Garhur, Kashun, Nam Iso, Seling, Tangra, Yamdok **7** Kyaring, Terinam, Tsaring, Zilling **8** Jiggitai **9** Tengrinor **11** Manasarowar
of Tunisia: **6** Achkel, Djerid **7** Bizerte
of Turkey: **3** Tuz, Van **7** Egridir **8** Beysehir
of Uganda: **5** Kioga, Kyoga **6** Albert, Edward, George **8** Victoria
of the United States: **4** Erie, Mead **5** Huron, Tahoe **6** Cayuga, Finger, George, Itasca, Oneida, Seneca **7** Iliamma, Ontario **8** Michigan, Superior **9** Champlain, Great Salt, Salton Sea, Teshekpuk, Winnebago **10** Okeechobee **11** Yellowstone **13** Pontchartrain, Wallenpaupack, Winnipesaukee **14** Lake of the Woods
of Uruguay: **5** Merin, Mirim **18** Embalse del Rio Negro
of Venezuela: **9** Maracaibo, Tacarigua
of Wales: **4** Bala **6** Vyrnwy
of Yugoslavia: **4** Bled **5** Ohrid **6** Prespa **7** Ochrida, Scutari
of Zaire: **4** Kivu **5** Mweru, Tumba **6** Albert, Edward, Upemba **9** Mai-Ndombe **10** Tanganyika
of Zambia: **5** Mweru **6** Kariba **9** Bangweulu **10** Tanganyika
of Zimbabwe: **4** Kyle **6** Kariba

tra **27** Summer's Last Will and Testament

lame **4** game, halt, weak **5** sorry **6** clumsy, feeble, flimsy, infirm, maimed **7** failing, halting, hobbled, limping, unsound, wanting **8** crippled, deformed, disabled **9** deficient, faltering **10** inadequate **11** ineffectual **12** insufficient, unconvincing, unpersuasive **14** unsatisfactory

lamebrain **3** ass, sap **4** fool **5** booby, dunce, idiot, moron, ninny **6** dimwit, nitwit **7** fathead, half-wit **8** bonehead, dumb-dumb, imbecile, lunkhead, numskull **9** blockhead, numbskull **10** dunderhead, nincompoop **11** chowderhead

lamebrained **4** dumb **6** stupid **7** asinine, foolish, idiotic, moronic **8** crackpot **9** dimwitted, imbecilic **10** half-witted **12** feeble-minded, simple-minded

Lamech
father: **9** Methusael **10** Methuselah
wives: **4** Adah **6** Zillah
son: **5** Jabal, Jubal **9** Tubalcain
daughter: **6** Naamah

lament **3** cry, sob **4** moan, wail, weep **5** dirge, mourn **6** bewail, outcry, plaint, regret **7** deplore, keening, requiem, whimper **8** mourning **9** death song **11** condole with, lamentation **12** funeral music **13** complain about **14** express pity for, show concern for, sympathize with **15** commiserate with

lamentable **4** dire **6** woeful **7** piteous **8** dreadful, grievous, pathetic, pitiable, shameful, terrible, wretched **9** miserable **10** deplorable **11** distressing, regrettable, unfortunate **13** disheartening, heartbreaking

Lamia
author: **9** John Keats

Lamia
form: **7** monster
characteristic: **12** bloodsucking

La Motta, Jake (Jacob)
nickname: **9** Bronx Bull
sport: **6** boxing
class: **12** middleweight
movie biography: **10** Raging Bull

Lamour, Dorothy
real name: **23** Mary Leta Dorothy Kaumeyer
trademark: **6** sarong
co-star: **7** Bob Hope **10** Bing Crosby
born: **12** New Orleans LA
roles:
Road to: **3** Rio **4** Bali **6** Utopia **7** Morocco **8** Hong Kong, Zanzibar **9** Singapore

L'Amour, Louis
author of: **5** Hondo, Lando **7** Sackett, Shalako **8** Conagher **10** Key-Lock Man, Rivers West **14** The Californios, The Daybreakers **15** Westward the Tide **16** How the West Was Won, Over on the Dry Side **21** The Man from Broken Hills, To the Far Blue Mountains

lamp **4** bulb **5** light, torch **6** beacon **7** blinker, lantern **9** headlight, spotlight **10** chandelier, floodlight, klieg light, night light **11** searchlight **12** ceiling light, reading light **14** ceiling fixture
invented by:
arc: **6** Staite
incandescent: **6** Edison
incandescent frosted: **6** Pipkin
incandescent gas: **8** Langmuir
Kleig: **7** Kleigel
mercury vapor: **6** Hewitt
miner's safety: **4** Davy
neon: **6** Claude

Lampedusa, Giuseppe di
author of: **10** The Leopard

Lampetia
father: **6** Helius
mother: **6** Neaera

lampoon **5** farce, put-on, spoof, squib **6** parody, satire, send up **7** mockery, takeoff **8** diatribe, ridicule, satirize, travesty **9** broadside, burlesque **10** caricature, pasquinade **11** make light of

Lamus
father: **8** Hercules
mother: **7** Omphale
attacked: **5** ships

Lamy of Santa Fe
author: **10** Paul Horgan

lanai **7** veranda

Lancaster, Burt
real name: **22** Burton Stephen Lancaster
born: **9** New York NY
roles: **5** Moses **9** All My Sons, Local Hero **11** Elmer Gantry (Oscar) **12** Atlantic City, The Rainmaker **13** The Rose Tattoo **14** Seven Days in May **16** Sorry Wrong Number **17** Birdman of Alcatraz **18** From Here to Eternity **19** Come Back Little Sheba, Sweet Smell of Success

lance **4** gaff, pike **5** shaft, spear **7** assegai, halberd, harpoon, javelin

Lancelot, Launcelot
character in: **16** Arthurian romance
lover: **9** Guinevere
home: **10** Joyous Gard

lancer **8** cavalier, horseman **10** cavalryman **12** horse soldier, horse trooper **14** mounted soldier

Lanchester, Elsa
real name: **17** Elizabeth Sullivan
husband: **15** Charles Laughton
born: **7** England **8** Lewisham
roles: **15** Come to the Stable **22** The Bride of Frankenstein **24** Witness for the Prosecution **25** The Private Life of Henry VIII **31** The Private Life of Henry the Eighth

land **3** get, lea, nab, net **4** area, dirt, dock, gain, grab, lawn, loam, moor, park, soil, take, ward, zone **5** acres, catch, earth, grass, green, humus, light, put in, realm, seize, shire, snare, state, tie up, tract **6** alight, anchor, canton, clinch, colony, county, debark, domain, empire, fields, ground, meadow, nation, parish, realty, region, secure **7** acreage, capture, country, descend, dry land, grounds, kingdom, pasture, section, set down, subsoil, terrain, win over **8** come down, district, dominion, farmland, homeland, location, mainland, make land, make port, precinct, property, province, republic, vicinity **9** cornfield, disembark, grassland, lay anchor, lay hold of, lead one to, reach land, territory **10** bring one to, carry one to, come to land, drop anchor, fatherland, motherland, native land, native soil, real estate, settle down, settlement, terra firma, wheat field **11** countryside, put into port **12** commonwealth, put into shore, real property, village green **13** the old country

Landau, Lev Davidovitch
field: **7** physics
nationality: **7** Russian
discovered: **12** liquid helium **14** ferromagnetism
awarded: **10** Nobel Prize

landed property **5** manor **6** estate **8** compound **12** countryplace

land force **4** army **6** legion, troops **7** legions **8** infantry, soldiers, soldiery **9** artillery

Landless, Neville and Helena
characters in: **22** The Mystery of Edwin Drood
author: **7** Dickens

landlord **5** owner **6** holder, squire **8** landlady **9** landowner, possessor **10** freeholder, landholder, proprietor **13** property owner **14** lord of the manor

landmark **8** keystone, monument, signpost **9** benchmark, guidepost, highlight, high point, milestone, watershed **11** cornerstone **12** turning point **16** historic building

Landmarks
god of: **8** Terminus

Land of Enchantment
nickname of: **9** New Mexico

Land of Lincoln
nickname of: **8** Illinois

Land of Opportunity
nickname of: **8** Arkansas

Land of Sky-blue Waters
nickname of: **9** Minnesota

Land of Steady Habits
nickname of: **11** Connecticut

Land of Ten Thousand Lakes
nickname of: **9** Minnesota

Land of the Dakotas
nickname of: **11** North Dakota

Land of the Midnight Sun
nickname of: **6** Alaska

Landon, Michael
real name: **20** Eugene Maurice Orowitz
born: **13** Forest Hills NY
roles: **7** Bonanza **15** Highway to Heaven **19** Little Joe Cartwright **20** I Was a Teenage Werewolf **23** Little House on the Prairie

landscape **4** view **5** scene, sight, vista **6** aspect **7** scenery **8** panorama, prospect **9** spectacle **10** rural scene, scenic view **14** natural scenery

landscape architect **7** Le Notre, Olmsted

landsman **10** countryman **13** fellow citizen

Landsteiner, Karl
field: **8** medicine **9** pathology
distinguished: **10** blood types
identified: **8** RH factor
awarded: **10** Nobel Prize

lane **3** way **4** pass, path, road **5** alley, byway, drive, route, track, trail **6** access, avenue, bypath, course **7** passage, roadway **8** alleyway, approach, footpath **10** passageway

Lang, Walter
director of: **7** Desk Set **11** The King and I

Lange, Jessica
born: **9** Cloquet MN
roles: **7** Country, Frances, Tootsie **8** King Kong **11** All That Jazz **16** Crimes of the Heart **26** The Postman Always Rings Twice

Langella, Frank
born: **9** Bayonne NJ
roles: **7** Dracula **23** The Diary of a Mad Housewife

Langhanke, Lucille Vasconcellos
real name of: **9** Mary Astor

Langland, William
author of: **12** Piers Plowman

Langmuir, Irving
field: **9** chemistry
invented: **15** atomic blowtorch **17** gas-tungsten lights
awarded: **10** Nobel Prize

language ***see box***

language, artificial
of James Cooke Brown: **6** Loglan
of Hans Freudenthal: **6** Lincos **13** Lingua Cosmica
of Alexander Gode: **11** Interlingua
of C K Ogden: **12** Basic English
of J M Schleyer: **7** Volapuk
of Jean Francois Sudre: **8** Solresol
of L L Zamehof: **9** Esperanto

language, extinct **6** Dacian, Hattic, Lycian, Lydian, Palaic **7** Cornish, Elamite, Hittite, Hurrian **8** Etruscan, Illyrian, Phrygian, Sumerian, Thracian, Urartian **9** Dalmatian **15** Cuneiform Luwian **18** Hieroglyphic Luwian

languid **4** dull, slow, weak **5** faint, heavy, inert, shaky, spent, weary **6** feeble, infirm, leaden, sickly, supine, torpid **7** rickety, unsound, worn-out **8** drooping, fatigued, inactive, lifeless, listless, sluggish, unstable **9** apathetic, declining, doddering, enervated, exhausted, inanimate, lethargic, trembling, unhealthy **10** indisposed, spiritless **11** debilitated **12** on the decline **13** lackadaisical

languidness **6** apathy, torpor **7** inertia **8** lethargy **12** listlessness, sluggishness **13** indisposition

languish **3** ebb **4** fade, fail, flag, wane, wilt **5** covet, droop, faint **6** desire, hunger, sicken, thirst, wither **7** dwindle, long for, pine for, sigh for **8** diminish, give away, take sick, yearn for **9** become ill, break down, hanker for, hunger for, thirst for, waste away **10** go downhill **11** deteriorate, have a yen for, hunger after **12** be desirous of **13** go into decline

Languish, Lydia
character in: **9** The Rivals
author: **8** Sheridan

languor **5** ennui **6** torpor **7** inertia **8** dullness, hebetude, lethargy **9** indolence, lassitude, torpidity, weariness **10** dispassion, dreaminess **11** languidness, leisureness **12** lifelessness, listlessness, sluggishness

lank **4** bony, lean, limp, thin **5** gaunt, spare **6** skinny, slight **7** angular, scrawny **8** straight

lanky **4** bony, lean **5** gaunt, gawky, rangy, spare, weedy **6** skinny **7** angular, scrawny **8** gangling, rawboned **11** tall and thin

La Nouvelle Heloise
author: **10** J J Rousseau

Lansbury, Angela
born: **6** London **7** England
roles: **4** Mame **8** Gaslight **10** JB Fletcher **11** Sweeney Todd **14** Murder She Wrote **15** Jessica Fletcher **22** The Manchurian Candidate

Laocoon
vocation: **6** priest
father: **5** Capys
brother: **8** Anchises
son: **10** Thymbraeus
warned: **7** Trojans
warned of: **11** Trojan horse
killed by: **8** serpents

Laodamas
father: **8** Eteocles
defended: **6** Thebes
killed: **9** Aegialeus
killed by: **8** Alcmaeon

Laodamia
father: **7** Acastus **11** Bellerophon
mother: **9** Astydamia
husband: **11** Protesilaus
lover: **4** Zeus
son: **8** Sarpedon

Laodice
father: **5** Priam
mother: **6** Hecuba

language **4** cant, jive **5** argot, idiom, lingo, prose, slang, words **6** jargon, patois, speech, tongue **7** cursing, cussing, dialect, diction, wording **8** parlance, rhetoric, swearing, verbiage **9** discourse, elocution, profanity **10** expression, use of words, vernacular, vocabulary **11** imprecation, phraseology, profane talk **12** mother tongue, native tongue **13** colloquialism **14** public speaking, self-expression **16** manner of speaking, mode of expression **17** oral communication, reading and writing, verbal intercourse

of Afghanistan: **4** Dari **5** Farsi **6** Afghan, Pashto, Pushtu **7** Balochi, Baluchi, Persian
of Albania: **3** Geg **4** Cham, Gheg, Hish, Tosk **5** Greek **8** Albanian
of Algeria: **6** Arabic, Berber, French, Zenata **7** Senhaja
of Andorra: **6** French **7** Catalan, Spanish
of Angola: **5** Bantu **8** Kimbundu, Oumbundu **9** Ovimbundu **10** Portuguese
of Antigua and Barbuda: **7** English
of Argentina: **7** Spanish
of Armenia: **7** Russian **8** Armenian
of Australia: **6** Yabber **7** English **9** aborigine (dialects)
of Austria: **5** Czech **6** German, Magyar **8** Croatian **9** Slovenian
of the Bahamas: **6** Creole **7** English
of Bahrain: **4** Urdu **5** Farsi **6** Arabic **7** English, Persian
of Bangladesh: **6** Bihari **7** Bengali, English
of Barbados: **7** English
of Belgium: **5** Dutch **6** French, German **7** Flemish
of Benin: **3** Fon **5** Dendi **6** Bariba, French, Fulani, Yoruba
of Bermuda: **7** English
of Bhutan: **5** Hindi, Lhoke **7** Tibetan **8** Dzongkha, Nepalese
of Bolivia: **6** Aymara **7** Quechua, Spanish
of Borneo: **5** Malay **7** Chinese, English
of Botswana: **5** Bantu, Click **6** Tswana **7** English, Khoisan **8** Setswana
of Brazil: **10** Portuguese
of Brunei: **4** Iban **5** Malay **7** Chinese, English
of Bulgaria: **9** Bulgarian
of Burma: **3** Lai **4** Chin, Kuki, Pegu, Shan **5** Karen **6** Kachin **7** Burmese
of Burundi: **6** French **7** Kirundi, Swahili
of Cambodia/Kampuchea: **8** Tonle Sap
of Cameroon: **4** Bulu **5** Bantu, Bassa, Hausa **6** Douala, Ewondo, French, Fulani **7** English **8** Bamileke, Fulfulde
of Canada: **6** Eskimo, French **7** English
of Canary Islands: **7** Spanish
of Cape Verde: **7** Crioulo **10** Portuguese **13** Verdean Creole
of Central African Republic: **5** Sango, Zande **6** French
of Chad: **4** Sara **5** Turku **6** Arabic, French
of Chile: **7** Spanish
of China: **7** Chinese **8** Mandarin, Shanghai **9** Cantonese
of Colombia: **7** Spanish
of Comoros: **6** Arabic, French **7** Swahili **8** Malagasy
of Congo: **4** Susu **5** Bantu, Fiote **6** French, Kituba **7** Bangala, Lingala
of Costa Rica: **7** Spanish
of Crete: **5** Greek **6** Minoan **7** Linear A, Linear B
of Cuba: **7** Spanish
of Cyprus: **5** Greek **7** Turkish **8** Armenian
of Czechoslovakia: **5** Czech **6** German, Magyar, Slovak **7** Russian **9** Hungarian
of Denmark: **4** Odan **6** Danish **8** Faeroese **11** Greenlander
of Djibouti: **4** Afar **6** Arabic, French, Somali
of Dominican Republic: **6** French **7** English, Spanish
of Ecuador: **6** Jibaro **7** Quechua, Spanish
of Egypt: **6** Arabic, Coptic, French **7** English
of El Salvador: **7** Spanish
of England: **7** English
of Equatorial Guinea: **4** Bubi, Fang **6** pidgin **7** Spanish
of Estonia: **5** Tartu **10** Finno-Ugric
of Ethiopia: **3** Giz **4** Afar, Agow, Geez, Saho **5** Geeze, Ghese, Smali, Tigre **6** Arabic, Harari **7** Amharic, English, Italian, Russian **8** Gallinya, Irob-Saho, Tigrinya
of Fiji: **5** Hindi **6** Fijian **7** English
of Finland: **4** Avar, Lapp **5** Karen, Ugric, Vogul **6** Magyar, Ostyak, Tarast **7** Finnish, Olonets, Samoyed, Swedish **8** Estonian **10** Olenetsian
of France: **6** French
of Gabon Republic: **6** French
of the Gambia: **4** Fula **5** Wolof **6** Fulani **7** English, Malinke **8** Mandingo
of Germany: **6** German **10** High German **11** Hochdeutsch
of Ghana: **2** Ga **3** Ewe, Gur, Kwa, Twi **5** Fanti, Hausa **7** Dagomba, English
of Gibraltar: **7** English, Spanish
of Greece: **5** Greek

(*continued*)

language (*continued*)
of Greenland: **6** Danish, Eskimo **11** Greenlandic
of Grenada: **7** English
of Guatemala: **6** Quiche **7** Spanish
of Guinea: **5** Fulbe, Mande **6** Arabic, French, Fulani **7** English
of Guinea-Bissau: **5** Fulah **7** Balante, Crioulo **8** Mandingo **10** Portuguese **21** Cape Verde-Guinea Creole
of Guyana: **5** Hindi **7** English
of Haiti: **6** Creole, French, patois
of Honduras: **7** English, Spanish
of Hong Kong: **7** Chinese, English **9** Cantonese
of Hungary: **6** German, Magyar, Slovak **8** Croatian **9** Hungarian **10** Finno-Ugric
of Iceland: **5** Norse **9** Icelandic
of India: **4** Urdu **5** Hindi, Oriya, Tamil **6** Sindhi, Telugu **7** Bengali, English, Kannada, Malayam, Marathi, Punjabi **8** Assamese, Gujarati, Kashmiri, Sanskrit **9** Malayalam
of Indonesia: **5** Tetum **6** Bahasa, Igorot **7** English, Gyarung, Malayan **8** Balinese, Chamorro, Javanese, Madurese, Sudanese **10** Indonesian, Polynesian
of Iran: **4** Luri, Zend **5** Farsi, Turki **6** Arabic **7** Baluchi, Kurdish, Persian **8** Armenian **11** Azerbaijani
of Iraq: **5** Farsi **6** Arabic **7** Kurdish, Persian, Turkish
of Ireland: **5** Irish **6** Gaelic **7** English
of Israel: **6** Arabic, French, Hebrew **7** English
of Italy: **5** Ladin, Latin **6** French, German **7** Italian, Slovene **8** Friulian **9** Sardinian
of Ivory Coast: **4** Akan **6** Dioula, French
of Jamaica: **6** Creole **7** English
of Japan: **5** Kanto **8** Japanese
of Java: **4** Kavi, Kawi **5** Malay **6** Sassak **8** Balinese, Madurese, Sudanese **16** Bahasa Indonesian
of Jordan: **6** Arabic
of Kenya: **3** Luo **5** Bantu, Luhya, Masai **6** Kikuyu **7** English, Swahili **8** Buyerati **10** Hindustani
of Kiribati: **6** Samoan **7** English **10** Gilbertese
of Korea: **6** Korean
of Kuwait: **6** Arabic
of Laos: **3** Lao, Man, Meo **6** French **7** English
of Latvia: **7** Lettish
of Lebanon: **6** Arabic, French, Syriac **7** English, Turkish **8** Armenian
of Lesotho: **5** Sotho **7** English, Sesotho
of Liberia: **3** Kru, Kwa **5** Mande **7** English
of Libya: **6** Arabic, Berber **7** English, Italian
of Liechtenstein: **6** German **10** Alemannish
of Lithuania: **5** Zmudz **6** Baltic **10** Lithuanian
of Luxembourg: **6** French, German **7** English **13** Letzeburgesch
of Macao: **7** Chinese, English **9** Cantonese **10** Portuguese
of Madagascar/Malagasy Republic: **6** French **8** Malagasy, Malgache
of Malawi: **3** Yao **4** Cewa **5** Bantu, Ngoni, Tonga **6** Nyanja **7** English, Tumbuka **8** Chichewa **10** Chitumbuka
of Malaysia: **4** Bugi, Dyak **5** Malay, Tamil **6** Battok, Rejang **7** Chinese, English, Lampong, Niasese **8** Achinese, Javanese, Makassar **14** Bahasa Malaysia
of Maldives: **6** Arabic, Divehi
of Mali: **5** Dogon, Dyula, Feulh, Mande, Marka **6** Berber, French, Fulani **7** Bambara, Malinke, Senoufo, Songhai
of Malta: **7** English, Italian, Maltese
of Mauritania: **4** Fula **5** Wolof **6** Arabic, French **7** Phoolor, Tukulor **8** Fulfulde, Mandingo **9** Sarakolle **10** Hassaniyya
of Mauritius: **4** Urdu **5** Hindi, Tamil **6** Creole, French **7** English
of Mexico: **5** Mayan, Otomi **6** Mixtec **7** Mazahua, Mazatec, Nahuatl, Spanish, Totonac, Zapotec **8** Tarascan
of Monaco: **6** French **7** English, Italian **10** Monegasque
of Mongolia: **6** Kazakh **16** Khalkha Mongolian
of Montenegro: **13** Serbo-Croatian
of Morocco: **6** Arabic, Berber, French **7** Spanish
of Mozambique: **3** Yao **5** Makua **6** Nyanji, Thonga **7** Swahili **10** Portuguese
of Namibia: **5** Bantu **6** German **7** English, Khoisan **9** Afrikaans
of Nauru: **7** English, Nauruan
of Nepal: **6** Nepali, Newari **7** English
of the Netherlands: **5** Dutch **7** English, Frisian
of New Guinea: **4** Motu **7** English **16** Melanesian Pidgin
of New Zealand: **5** Maori **7** English
of Nicaragua: **7** English, Spanish
of Niger: **5** Hausa, Mande **6** Djerma, French, Fulani, Tuareg **8** Mandingo, Tamashek
of Nigeria: **3** Ibo **4** Efik, Igbo **5** Hausa **6** Yoruba **7** English
of Norway: **4** Lapp **5** Norse **6** Bokmal **7** Nynorsk, Riksmal **8** Landsmal, Samnorsk **9** Landsmaal, Norwegian
of Oman: **4** Urdu **5** Hindi **6** Arabic **7** Baluchi

of Pakistan: 4 Urdu **6** Pushtu, Sindhi **7** Baluchi, Bengali, English, Punjabi
of Panama: 7 English, Spanish
of Paraguay: 6 German **7** Guarani, Spanish
of Peru: 6 Aymara **7** English, Quechua, Spanish
of the Philippines: 4 Moro **5** Bicol, Bikol **6** Ibanag **7** Cebuano, English, Ilocano, Spanish, Tagalog, Visayan **8** Filipino **9** Pampangan, Philipino **10** Samar-Leyte **13** Bamboo-English **14** Panay-Hiligayon
of Poland: 6 Kaszub, Polish **10** Pomeranian
of Polynesia: 4 Niue, Uvea **5** Maori **6** Samoan, Tongan **7** Austral, Tagalog, Tokelau **8** Hawaiian, Tahitian **9** Marquesan, Tuamatuan **10** Mangarevan
of Portugal: 10 Portuguese
of Qatar: 6 Arabic
of Rumania: 6 French, Magyar **7** Russian **8** Romanian, Rumanian **9** Hungarian
of Russia: 5 Evenk, Tatar, Uzbek **6** Buriat, Kalmyk, Kazakh **7** Finnish, Kirghiz, Latvian, Russian, Tadzhik, Turkmen **8** Armenian, Estonian, Georgian, Ossetian **9** Moldavian, Ukrainian **10** Lithuanian **11** Belorussian
of Rwanda: 6 French **7** Swahili **11** Kinyarwanda
of Samoa: 6 Samoan **7** English
of San Marino: 7 Italian
of Sao Tome and Principe: 10 Portuguese
of Sardinia: 7 Italian
of Saudi Arabia: 6 Arabic
of Scotland: 4 Erse **6** Celtic, Gaelic, Keltic, Lallan **7** English, Lalland
of Senegal: 5 Wolof **6** French
of the Seychelles: 6 Creole, French **7** English
of Sierra Leone: 4 Krio **5** Limba, Mende, Mendi, Temne **6** Creole **7** English
of Singapore: 5 Malay, Tamil **7** Chinese, English **8** Mandarin
of the Solomon Islands: 7 English **13** Pidgin English **16** Melanesian Pidgin
of Somalia: 6 Arabic, Somali **7** English, Italian
of South Africa: 4 Taal, Zulu **5** Bantu, Hindi, Nguni, Sotho, Swazi, Tamil, Venda, Xhosa **6** Telegu, Thonga **7** English, Khoisan, Ndebele, Sesotho **8** Bujarati, Fanakalo **9** Afrikaans **13** Kitchen-Kaffir
of Spain: 6 Basque **7** Catalan, Spanish **8** Balearic, Galician **9** Castilian, Valencian
of Sri Lanka: 4 Pali **5** Tamil **7** English **9** Sinhalese
of Sudan: 2 Ga **3** Efe, Ewe, Ibo, Kru, Vak, Vei **4** Efik, Mole, Tshi **6** Arabic, Nubian, Yoruba **7** English **8** Mandango, Mandingo **9** Ta Bedawie
of Suriname: 5 Carib, Dutch, Hindi **6** Arawak **7** English **8** Javanese, Taki-Taki **10** Hindustani **11** Sranan Tongo **12** Sranang Tongo
of Swaziland: 5 Ngumi **7** English, Siswati **9** Afrikaans **10** Portuguese
of Sweden: 4 Lapp **7** Swedish
of Switzerland: 5 Ladin **6** French, German **7** Italian **8** Romansch **14** Switzerdeutsch
of Syria: 6 Arabic, French, Syriac **7** Aramaic, English, Kurdish, Turkish **8** Armenian
of Taiwan: 4 Amon, Amoy **5** Hakka, Kuo Yu **6** Minnan **9** Taiwanese **15** Mandarin Chinese
of Tanzania: 5 Bantu **6** Arabic **7** English, Khoisan, Nilotic, Swahili **8** Cushitic, Gujarati
of Thailand: 3 Lao, Tai **4** Ahom, Shan, Thai **5** Kadai **7** Bangkok, English **9** Krung Thep **12** Chinese Malay
of Tibet: 5 Balti **6** Ladkhi **7** Bhutani, Bodskad **8** Sanskrit **9** Bhutanese
of Togo: 3 Ana, Ewe, Twi **4** Mina **5** Hausa **6** French, Kabrai, Kabrie **7** Bassari, Dagomba, Quatchi **8** Kotokoli, Lotocoli
of Tonga: 6 Tongan **7** English
of Trinidad and Tobago: 6 French **7** Chinese, English, Spanish **10** Portuguese **12** French Patois
of Tunisia: 6 Arabic, Berber, French
of Turkey: 6 Arabic **7** Kurdish, Turkish
of Tuvalu: 6 Samoan **7** English **8** Tuvaluan **10** Polynesian
of Uganda: 5 Ateso, Ganda **7** English, Luganda, Swahili
of United Arab Emirates: 5 Farsi **6** Arabic **7** English, Persian
of Upper Volta: 4 Bobo, Lobi, More, Samo **5** Dyula, Mande, Mossi **6** French
of Uruguay: 7 Italian, Spanish
of Vanuatu: 6 French **7** Bislama, English **16** Melanesian Pidgin
of Venezuela: 4 Pume **7** Spanish
of Vietnam: 3 Yue **4** Cham **5** Khmer, Rhade **6** French **7** Chinese, English **9** Cantonese **10** Vietnamese
of Wales: 5 Welsh **6** Celtic, Cymric, Keltic, Kymric **7** Cymraeg, English
of Western Sahara: 16 Hassaniyya Arabic
of Western Samoa: 6 Samoan **7** English
of Yemen: 6 Arabic
of Yugoslavia: 7 Bosnian, Slovene **8** Albanian, Croatian **9** Hungarian, Slovenian **10** Macedonian **11** Montenegrin **13** Herzegovinian, Serbo-Croatian
of Zaire: 5 Bantu **6** French **7** Chiluba, Kikongo, Lingala, Swahili **8** Sudanese, Tshiluba
of Zambia: 4 Lozi **5** Bemba, Lunda, Tonga **6** Luvale, Nyanja **7** English **9** Afrikaans
of Zimbabwe: 3 Ila **5** Bantu, Shona **7** English, Ndebele

husband: **8** Helicaon
son: **6** Pereus **7** Munitus

Laodocus
father: **6** Apollo
mother: **6** Phthia
killed by: **7** Aetolus

Laomedon
king of: **4** Troy
father: **4** Ilus
wife: **6** Strymo
son: **5** Priam **6** Lampus **7** Clytius **8** Hicetaon, Tithonus
daughter: **7** Hesione **8** Themiste

Laos *see box*

Laothoe
concubine of: **5** Priam
son: **6** Lycaon **9** Polydorus

Lao-tzu
author of: **10** Tao Te Ching

lap **3** sip **4** lick, wash **5** awash, drink, plash, slosh **6** babble, bubble, gurgle, lick up, murmur, ripple, splash, tongue

La Paz
administrative capital of: **7** Bolivia

Laphria
epithet of: **7** Artemis

Laphystius
epithet of: **4** Zeus

lapis lazuli
species: **8** lazurite
source: **10** Badakhshan **11** Afghanistan

Laplace, Pierre S
field: **7** physics **9** astronomy
nationality: **6** French
hypothesis of: **18** nebular solar system

lapse **3** gap, sag **4** drop, fall, flaw, go by, loss, sink, slip, stop, wane **5** boner, break, cease, droop, error, fault, pause, slump **6** breach, elapse, expire, hiatus, laxity, pass by, period, recede, recess, run out, slip by, wither, worsen **7** blunder, decline, descent, failing, failure, faux pas, interim, passage, relapse, respite, subside **8** collapse, downfall, elapsing, interval, omission, slip away **9** backslide, disregard, interlude, oversight, slump down, terminate **10** degenerate, falling off, forfeiture, infraction, negligence, peccadillo, regression **11** backsliding, delinquency, dereliction, deteriorate, shortcoming **12** degeneration, intermission, interruption, lose validity **13** deterioration, process of time, slight mistake **14** become obsolete, fall into disuse

lapsus linguae **16** a slip of the tongue

Laputa
fictional land in: **16** Gulliver's Travels
author: **5** Swift

lar *see* **5** lares

Lara
character in: **9** Dr Zhivago
author: **9** Pasternak

Laraia, Carol Maria
real name of: **13** Carol Lawrence

Laramie
character: **6** Jonesy **9** Mort Corey **10** Jess Harper **11** Andy Sherman, Daisy Cooper, Slim Sherman **12** Mike Williams
cast: **9** John Smith **12** Dennis Holmes, Robert Fuller **13** Stuart Randall **14** Spring Byington **15** Bobby Crawford Jr, Hoagy Carmichael

larceny **5** fraud, theft **7** bilking, forgery, looting, robbery, sacking **8** burglary, cheating, fleecing, stealing **9** extortion, pilferage, pilfering, swindling **10** absconding, peculation, plagiarism, purloining **11** defalcation, depredation **12** embezzlement, grand larceny, petit larceny, petty larceny, safecracking **13** appropriation, housebreaking **16** misappropriation

larder **5** cuddy **6** pantry, spence **7** buttery **8** food room **9** stillroom, storeroom **10** supply room **11** storage room

Lardner, Ring
author of: **11** The Love Nest, You Know Me Al **12** Treat Em Rough **16** Gullible's Travels

Larentalia
origin: **5** Roman
event: **8** festival

lares
form: **7** spirits
watched over: **5** house **6** hearth **9** community **10** crossroads
single member: **3** lar
companions: **7** penates
correspond to: **8** Dioscuri

large **3** big, fat **4** high, huge, vast, wide **5** ample, broad, grand, great, heavy, hulky, obese, plump, roomy **6** goodly, mighty, portly, rotund **7** copious, immense, liberal, massive, sizable **8** colossal, enormous, gigantic, imposing, man-sized, outsized, spacious, sweeping, towering **9** boundless, capacious, expansive, extensive, giantlike, kingsized, limitless, monstrous, overgrown, ponderous, strapping, unlimited, unstinted **10** exorbitant, gargantuan, stupendous **11** extravagant, far-reaching, magnificent, substantial **12** considerable **13** comprehensive **14** Brobdingnagian

Laos
other name: **7** Lan Xang **23** land of a million elephants
capital/largest city: **9** Viengchan, Vientiane
others: **4** Nape **5** Pakse, Xieng **6** Paklay **7** Thakhek **11** Savannakhet, Xiang Khoang **12** Luang Prabang **14** Louangphrabang
school: **12** Sisavangvong
measure: **3** bak
monetary unit: **2** at **3** att, kip
mountain: **3** Lai, Loi, San **4** Copi, Khat **5** Atwat **6** Khoung, Tiubia **15** Annam Cordillera
highest point: **3** Bia **7** Phou Bia
river: **3** Noi **4** Done **5** Khong **6** Mekong, Sebang
physical feature:
plain: **4** Jars
plateau: **8** Bolovens
people: **2** Lu **3** Kha, Lao, Man, Meo, Tai, Yao, Yun **4** Miao, Thai **5** Hmong **8** Lao Teung **10** Phoutheung
leader: **7** Fa Ngoun **13** Souphanouvong **14** Souligna Vongsa, Souvanna Phouma
language: **3** Lao, Man, Meo **6** French **7** English
religion: **7** animism **8** Buddhism **17** Theravada Buddhism
feature:
Buddhist priest: **5** bonze
Communist guerrilla group: **9** Pathet Lao
musical instrument: **5** khene
temple: **3** wat
trail: **9** Ho Chi Minh

large-hearted **8** generous **10** altruistic, benevolent, charitable **12** humanitarian **13** philanthropic

largely **6** mainly, mostly, widely **7** chiefly, greatly **9** generally, primarily **10** on the whole **11** extensively, principally **12** considerably **13** predominantly, substantially **14** for the most part, to a great extent

largeness **7** bigness **8** enormity, hugeness **9** amplitude, greatness, immensity **11** massiveness **12** enormousness

large-scale **3** big **4** huge, vast, wide **5** broad, great **6** all-out, mighty **8** colossal, far-flung, gigantic **9** extensive, monstrous **10** gargantuan, stupendous, tremendous **11** far-reaching, wide-ranging **15** all-encompassing

largess, largesse **3** aid **4** boon, gift, help **5** favor, mercy **6** bounty, reward **7** charity, payment **8** bestowal, donation, gratuity, kindness, offering **9** benignity **10** assistance, generosity **11** benefaction, benevolence **12** philanthropy, remuneration

large store **8** emporium **11** supermarket **15** department store

largo
music: **4** slow **14** dignified tempo

lark **3** gag **4** game, jape, romp, whim **5** antic, caper, fling, prank, spree, trick **6** frolic, gambol **7** caprice **8** escapade **11** high old time **12** sportiveness
group of: **10** exaltation

larkspur **9** Consolida **10** Delphinium
varieties: **4** Tall **5** Dwarf **6** Rocket

La Rochefoucauld, Francois
author of: **6** Maxims **7** Maximes

larva
insect stage after: **3** egg
insect stage before: **4** pupa
legless: **6** maggot

larvae
form: **6** ghosts
characteristic: **9** malignant

lascivious **4** foul, lewd **5** bawdy, dirty, gross, lurid **6** coarse, filthy, impure, ribald, sordid, vulgar, wanton **7** immoral, lustful, obscene, ruttish, squalid **8** depraved, immodest, improper, indecent, prurient **9** lecherous, salacious, shameless **10** indelicate, licentious, unblushing **11** dirty-minded, unwholesome

lash **3** fix, hit, tie **4** beat, bind, blow, flog, moor, rope, whip **5** brace, curse, flail, hitch, knock, leash, pound, scold, smack, strap, thong, tie up, truss **6** attach, berate, buffet, fasten, hammer, pinion, revile, secure, strike, stroke, tether, thrash, whip up **7** lecture, scourge, upbraid **8** lambaste, make fast **9** castigate, horsewhip **10** take to task, tongue-lash **11** rail against **13** cat-o'-nine-tails

Lash, Joseph P
author of: **18** Eleanor and Franklin

lashed together **4** tied **5** bound **6** tied up **7** secured, trussed **8** fastened

lash out at **5** fly at **6** assail, attack, strike **8** fall upon

Las Palmas
capital of: **13** Canary Islands

lass **4** girl, maid, miss **5** wench **6** damsel, female, lassie, lovely, maiden, pretty, virgin **7** colleen **10** schoolgirl, young woman

Lasser, Louise
father: **8** S J Lasser
husband: **10** Woody Allen
born: **9** New York NY
roles: **22** Mary Hartman Mary Hartman

lassie **4** girl, lass, maid **6** maiden **7** colleen **10** young woman

Lassie
character: **5** Timmy **9** Doc Weaver **10** Jeff Miller, Paul Martin, Ruth Martin **11** Corey Stuart, Ellen Miller **12** Gramps Miller **17** Sylvester (Porky) Brockway
cast: **10** Jan Clayton, Jon Provost, Jon Shepodd, Robert Bray **11** Arthur Space, Tommy Rettig **12** Donald Keeler, June Lockhart **14** Cloris Leachman, George Chandler **15** George Cleveland

lassitude **5** ennui **6** apathy, torpor **7** boredom, fatigue, inertia, languor, malaise **8** debility, doldrums, dullness, lethargy, weakness **9** faintness, indolence, tiredness, torpidity, weariness **10** droopiness, drowsiness, enervation, exhaustion, feebleness, supineness **11** languidness, prostration **12** indifference, lack of energy, listlessness, sluggishness

lasso **4** lash, rope **5** catch, noose, reata, riata, thong **6** lariat

last **3** end **4** go on, keep, live, stay, wear **5** abide, after, exist, final, stand **6** behind, ending, endure, extend, finale, finish, hold on, hold up, remain, utmost **7** carry on, closing, extreme, finally, hold out, outlive, outwear, persist, stand up, subsist, survive, tailing **8** at the end, continue, doomsday, farthest, final one, furthest, hindmost, hold good, in back of, maintain, rearmost, terminal, terminus, trailing, ultimate **9** in the rear, persevere **10** Armageddon, concluding, conclusion, conclusive, eventually, terminally, ultimately **11** crack of doom, crucial time **12** in conclusion, tagging along **13** Day of Judgment
French: **7** dernier

Last Analysis, The
author: **10** Saul Bellow

Last Days of Pompeii, The
author: **18** Edward Bulwer-Lytton
character: **4** Ione **5** Nydia **7** Arbaces, Glaucus **9** Apaecides

Last Frontier
nickname of: **6** Alaska

lasting **4** firm **5** fixed, solid **7** abiding, chronic, durable, eternal **8** constant, enduring, immortal, lifelong, long-term **9** incessant, lingering, long-lived, permanent, perpetual, steadfast, unceasing **10** continuing, deep-rooted, deep-seated, perdurable, persistent, protracted **11** established, never-ending **12** indissoluble **14** indestructible, of long duration **17** firmly established

Last Lion, The
author: **17** William Manchester

lastly **6** at last **7** finally, to sum up **8** after all, in the end **10** on the whole **12** in conclusion **19** all things considered **33** taking everything into consideration

Last of the Barons, The
author: **18** Edward Bulwer-Lytton

Last of the Mohicans, The
author: **19** James Fenimore Cooper
character: **5** Magua, Uncas **9** Cora Munro **10** Alice Munro **11** Natty Bumppo

12 Chingachgook 18 Major Duncan Heyward

last part 3 end 6 ending, finale, finish 8 third act 10 denouement 12 final chapter

Last Picture Show, The
director: 16 Peter Bogdanovich
based on story by: 13 Larry McMurtry
cast: 10 Ben Johnson 11 Jeff Bridges 12 Ellen Burstyn 13 Eileen Brennan 14 Cloris Leachman, Cybill Shepherd, Timothy Bottoms
Oscar for: 15 supporting actor (Johnson) 17 supporting actress (Leachman)

Last Puritan, The
author: 15 George Santayana

La Strada
director: 15 Federico Fellini
cast: 11 Aldo Silvana 12 Anthony Quinn 15 Giulietta Masina, Richard Basehart
score: 8 Nino Rota
Oscar for: 11 foreign film

last resort
French: 8 pis aller

last resource
French: 8 pis aller

Last Tango in Paris
director: 18 Bernardo Bertolucci
cast: 12 Marlon Brando 14 Maria Schneider

Last Things
author: 6 C P Snow

Last Valley, The
author: 11 A B Guthrie Jr

Last Waltz, The
director: 14 Martin Scorsese
cast: 7 The Band 8 Bob Dylan 9 Neil Young 10 The Staples 11 Eric Clapton, Muddy Waters, Neil Diamond, Van Morrison 12 Joni Mitchell 13 Emmylou Harris

latch 3 bar 4 bolt, clip, hasp, hook, lock, loop, shut, snap 5 catch, clamp, close 6 buckle, button, clinch, fasten, secure 8 make fast 9 fastening

late 3 new 4 dead, gone, slow 5 fresh, tardy 6 held up, put off, recent 7 delayed, newborn, overdue, tardily 8 departed, detained, dilatory, passed on 9 after time, postponed 10 behindhand, behind time, dilatorily, unpunctual 16 recently deceased

late arrival 7 laggard 8 lateness, newcomer 9 immigrant, latecomer, tardiness 16 Johnny-come-lately

Late George Apley, The
author: 10 J P Marquand

lately 6 of late 7 just now 8 latterly, recently, right now 9 currently, presently, yesterday 10 not long ago 13 a short time ago

Late Mattia Pascal, The
author: 15 Luigi Pirandello

latency 8 abeyance, deferral, dormancy, inaction 10 quiescence, suspension

Late Night with David Letterman
feature: 11 Ask Mr Melman 15 Stupid Pet Tricks 18 Brush with Greatness, Stupid People Tricks
bandleader: 10 Paul Shafer
city: 7 New York

latent 6 covert, hidden 7 abeyant, dormant, lurking, passive 8 inactive, sleeping 9 concealed, potential, quiescent, suspended, unaroused, unexposed 10 in abeyance, intangible, unapparent, unrealized 11 not manifest, undeveloped, unexpressed 13 inconspicuous

later 4 next 5 since 6 behind, in time, mature 7 ensuing, tardily 8 in a while, in sequel 9 afterward, following, presently, thereupon 10 consequent, more recent, most recent, subsequent, succeeding, successive, thereafter 11 after a while, consecutive 12 subsequently, successively, toward the end

lateral 4 side 5 sided 7 flanked, oblique, sloping 8 edgeways, edgewise, flanking, sidelong, sideward, sideways, sidewise, skirting, slanting

latest cry
French: 10 dernier cri

latest fashion
French: 10 dernier cri

latest word
French: 10 dernier cri

lather 4 foam, head, scum, soap, suds 5 froth, spume, sweat 6 soap up 8 make foam, soapsuds 9 make froth 11 shaving foam

Latin
language family: 12 Indo-European
branch: 6 Italic
group: 7 Romance
subgroup: 6 French 7 Catalan, Italian, Romansh, Spanish 8 Romanian 9 Provencal 10 Portuguese 13 Rhaeto-Romanic

Latinus
king of: 6 Latium
father: 6 Faunus
mother: 6 Marica
wife: 5 Amata
daughter: 7 Lavinia

latitude 5 range, scope, sweep 6 leeway, margin 7 license 8 free play 9 amplitude, elbowroom, full swing 10 indulgence, liberality 11 opportunity, unrestraint 12 independence 15 freedom of action, freedom of choice 16 unrestrictedness

Latona *see* 4 Leto

La Tour, Georges de
born: 3 Vic 6 France 8 Lorraine
artwork: 7 Peasant 10 The New Born 12 Peasant's Wife, The Card Cheat 15 St Peter Penitent 16 The Fortune Teller 18 The Denial of St Peter 23 The Education of the Virgin 31 St Sebastian Tended by the Holy Women

Latrobe, Benjamin Henry
architect of: 9 US Capitol 15 Sedgeley Mansion (PA) 18 Baltimore Cathedral 22 Philadelphia Waterworks
style: 12 Greek Revival, Neoclassical 13 Gothic Revival

latter 3 end 4 last 5 final, later 6 ending, latest, modern 7 ensuing 8 terminal 10 most recent, subsequent, succeeding, successive 13 last-mentioned 15 second-mentioned

lattice 4 fret, grid 5 frame, grate 6 grille, screen 7 framing, grating, network, trellis, webwork 8 fretwork, openwork 9 framework, reticulum 11 trelliswork 12 reticulation

Latvia ***see box***

laud 5 extol, honor 6 praise 7 acclaim, commend, glorify

laudable 5 model, noble 8 sterling 9 admirable, estimable, excellent, exemplary 10 creditable 11 commendable, meritorious 12 praiseworthy 13 unimpeachable 17 deserving of esteem 18 worthy of admiration

laudation 6 praise 7 acclaim 8 applause, approval 11 approbation 12 commendation

laudatory 8 admiring, honoring, praising 9 adulatory, approving, extolling, favorable 10 eulogistic, eulogizing, flattering, glorifying 11 acclamatory, approbatory, celebratory, encomiastic, panegyrical

Latvia
other name: **30** Latvian Soviet Socialist Republic
capital/largest city: **4** Riga
others: **5** Cesis, Libau **6** Dvinsk, Libava, Tukums **7** Jelgava, Jurmala, Liepaja, Rezekne **8** Dunaberg, Dunaburg, Valmiera **9** Ventspils **10** Daugavpils
government: **23** Soviet Socialist Republic
measure: **3** let **4** stof **5** stoff, verst **6** arshin, kulmet **7** verchoc, verchok **8** krouchka, pourvete **9** deciatine, lofstelle, pourvette **10** tonnseteel
monetary unit: **3** lat **4** latu **6** rublis, santim **7** kapeika, santima
weight: **9** liespfund
lake: **7** Aluksne
river: **4** Ogre **5** Gauja, Venta **6** Salaca **7** Daugava, Lielupe **12** Western Dvina
sea: **6** Baltic
physical feature:
cape: **8** Domesnes
gulf: **4** Riga
strait: **4** Irbe
people: **3** Kur, Liv **4** Balt, Cour, Lett **7** Latgale, Latvian, Russian, Zemgale
former ruler: **15** Teutonic Knights
language: **7** Lettish
religion: **8** Lutheran **13** Roman Catholic

12 commendatory **13** complimentary

Laudianus **16** Greek unical codex

laugh **4** glee, ha-ha, ho-ho, howl, roar **5** mirth **6** cackle, giggle, guffaw, titter **7** break up, chortle, chuckle, snicker, snigger **10** bellylaugh, horselaugh **12** express mirth **14** roll in the aisle, split one's sides

laughable **5** comic, dopey, droll, funny, inane, merry, silly, witty **6** absurd, stupid **7** amusing, asinine, comical, foolish, risible **8** farcical, tickling **9** diverting, grotesque, hilarious, ludicrous **10** outlandish, outrageous, ridiculous **11** rib-tickling **12** preposterous **13** sidesplitting

Laugh-In, Rowan & Martin's
regular: **8** Dan Rowan **9** Gary Owens, Judy Carne, Ruth Buzzi **10** Dick Martin, Goldie Hawn, Larry Hovis, Lily Tomlin **11** Arte Johnson, Henry Gibson **12** Jo Anne Worley **13** Eileen Brennan
saying: **10** Sock it to me **15** Here come de judge, You bet your bippy **24** Beautiful downtown Burbank **31** Look that up in your Funk and Wagnalls

laughingstock **3** ass **4** butt, dupe, fool, joke **8** fair game **11** figure of fun

laugh off **6** deride **7** dismiss, put down **8** belittle, ridicule **9** disparage

laughter **3** joy **4** glee **5** mirth **6** gaiety **7** jollity, revelry **8** hilarity **9** joviality, merriment **11** merrymaking **12** convivial-ity, exhilaration

Laughton, Charles
wife: **14** Elsa Lanchester
born: **7** England **11** Scarborough
roles: **9** Rembrandt **10** Jamaica Inn **13** Les Miserables **15** Ruggles of Red Gap, The Paradine Case **16** Advise and Consent **17** Mutiny on the Bounty **23** Barretts of Wimpole Street, The Hunchback of Notre Dame **24** Witness for the Prosecution **25** The Private Life of Henry VIII (Oscar)

launch **4** fire, hurl **5** begin, eject, float, found, impel, shoot, start, throw **6** let fly, propel, unveil **7** fire off, project, send off **8** catapult, initiate, premiere, put to sea **9** cast forth, discharge, establish, institute, introduce, set afloat **10** embark upon, inaugurate, set forth on **11** set in motion, venture upon **13** thrust forward **15** set into the water

launder **4** soak, wash **5** clean, rinse, scour, scrub **7** cleanse, wash out **11** wash and iron

Launfal
knight of: **10** roundtable

Laura
director: **13** Otto Preminger
cast: **11** Clifton Webb, Dana Andrews, Gene Tierney **12** Vincent Price **14** Judith Anderson

laurel **6** Kalmia, Laurus **13** Laurus nobilis **14** Ficus benjamina **15** Cordia alliodora
varieties: **3** bog, pig **4** pale **5** black, dwarf, great, sheep **6** Alpine, cherry, ground, Indian, purple, Sierra, spurge, tropic **7** Chinese, English, red-twig, weeping, western **8** American, drooping, Himalaya, Japanese, mountain, Portugal **9** Tasmanian **10** Australian, California, variegated **11** Alexandrian

Laurel, Stan
real name: **22** Arthur Stanley Jefferson
partner: **11** Oliver Hardy
born: **7** England **9** Ulverston
roles: **8** Pardon Us **9** Saps at Sea **10** Way Out West

laurels **4** fame **5** award, glory, honor, kudos, prize **6** credit, praise, renown, reward **7** acclaim, tribute **8** accolade, applause, citation **9** celebrity **10** decoration, popularity **11** acclamation, distinction, recognition **12** commendation **15** illustriousness

Laurie
also: **16** Theodore Laurence
character in: **11** Little Women
author: **6** Alcott

laus Deo **11** praise to God **13** praise be to God

Lautreamont, Comte de
author of: **19** Les Chants de Maldoror

lavation **7** bathing, washing **8** ablution, cleaning **9** cleansing

lavender **4** herb, mint **5** aspic, behen, lilac, spick, spike **6** purple **7** inkroot **8** amethyst, stichado **9** lavendula
represents: **6** purity
uses: **6** sachet **7** perfume **8** medicine **9** cosmetics

laver **11** footed basin

Laverne and Shirley
character: **12** Frank De Fazio **13** Carmine Ragusa, Lenny Kolowski, Mrs Edna Babish, Shirley Feeney **14** Laverne De Fazio **15** Andrew (Squiggy) Squiggman
cast: **10** Eddie Mekka, Phil

Foster **12** Betty Garrett, David L Lander **13** Cindy Williams, Michael McKean, Penny Marshall
girls worked in: 12 Shotz Brewery
theme song: 23 Making Our Dreams Come True
spinoff from: 9 Happy Days

Lavinia
father: 7 Latinus
mother: 5 Amata
husband: 6 Aeneas

lavish 4 free, lush, wild **5** plush, waste **6** shower **7** copious, opulent, pour out, profuse **8** abundant, effusive, generous, prodigal, squander **9** bounteous, bountiful, dissipate, excessive, exuberant, impetuous, luxuriant, plenteous, plentiful, sumptuous, unsparing **10** immoderate, munificent, profligate, unstinting **11** extravagant, fritter away, intemperate, overindulge, overliberal, spend freely **12** give overmuch, greathearted, overwhelming, unrestrained, without limit

lavishness 6 bounty **8** lushness, opulence **9** profusion **10** luxuriance **11** munificence, prodigality **12** extravagance, immoderation **13** bountifulness, plenteousness, sumptuousness

Lavoisier, Antoine
field: 9 chemistry
nationality: 6 French
founder: 15 modern chemistry
named: 6 oxygen **8** hydrogen

law 3 act **4** bill, code, fuzz, rule, writ **5** axiom, bylaw, canon, dogma, edict, model, truth **6** decree, police **7** justice, mandate, precept, statute, theorem **8** absolute, legality, standard **9** criterion, enactment, gendarmes, legal form, ordinance, postulate, principle **10** civil peace, convention, due process, invariable, regulation **11** commandment, formulation, fundamental, orderliness, working rule **13** jurisprudence, standing order **14** generalization, rules of conduct **15** legal profession
Latin: 3 jus
goddess of: 4 Maat

law-abiding 6 honest **7** upright **9** honorable **10** aboveboard, principled

lawbreaker 3 con **4** hood, thug **5** crook, felon **6** outlaw **7** convict, culprit **8** criminal, jailbird, offender, scofflaw **9** miscreant, wrongdoer **10** delinquent, malefactor, recidivist **11** perpetrator **12** transgressor

lawful 3 due **5** legal, licit **6** proper, titled **7** allowed, granted **8** rightful **9** legalized, statutory, warranted **10** authorized, legitimate, prescribed **11** legitimized, permissible **15** legally entitled **16** legally permitted

lawless 6 unruly, wanton **7** chaotic, defiant, illegal, riotous, wayward **8** anarchic, mutinous, unlawful, wide open **9** insurgent, out of hand, unbridled **10** disorderly, licentious, rebellious, refractory, ungoverned **11** disobedient, lawbreaking, terroristic **12** disorganized, freewheeling, illegitimate, noncompliant, unrestrained **13** insubordinate, transgressive **14** uncontrollable

lawlessness 5 chaos **7** anarchy **8** disorder

lawn 4 park, turf, yard **5** glade, grass, sward **7** grounds, terrace **10** grassy plot, green field, greensward, meadowland **12** grassy ground

law of a place
Latin: 7 lex loci

Law of Moses 5 Torah **10** Pentateuch **15** Ten Commandments

law of nations
Latin: 10 jus gentium

law of nature
Latin: 11 jus naturale

Lawrence, Carol
real name: 16 Carol Maria Laraia
husband: 12 Robert Goulet
born: 13 Melrose Park IL
roles: 5 Maria **13** West Side Story

Lawrence, D H
author of: 10 The Rainbow **11** Women in Love **13** Sons and Lovers **20** Lady Chatterley's Lover

Lawrence, Ernest Orlando
field: 7 physics
invented: 9 cyclotron
awarded: 10 Nobel Prize

Lawrence, Gertrude
real name: 29 Alexandra Dagmar Lawrence Klasen
born: 6 London **7** England
roles: 9 Pygmalion **11** The King and I **17** The Glass Menagerie

Lawrence, T E
also: 16 Lawrence of Arabia
served in: 3 WWI **10** Arab Revolt
advisor to: 6 Faisal **12** Husayn Ibn Ali
fought against: 5 Turks **8** Ottomans
author of: 20 Seven Pillars of Wisdom

Lawrence of Arabia
director: 9 David Lean
cast: 10 Jose Ferrer, Omar Sharif **11** Claude Rains, Jack Hawkins, Peter O'Toole (T E Lawrence) **12** Alec Guinness, Anthony Quinn **13** Arthur Kennedy, Anthony Quayle
Oscar for: 7 picture **8** director **14** cinematography

Lawrence Welk Show, The
champagne lady: 8 Alice Lon **11** Norma Zimmer
cast: 7 Aladdin **11** Larry Hooper, Myron Floren **12** Bobby Burgess **13** Barbara Boylan, Lennon Sisters
Welk played: 9 accordion

lawyer 6 jurist, legist **7** counsel, shyster **8** advocate, attorney **9** barrister, counselor, solicitor **10** mouthpiece, prosecutor **11** pettifogger **12** legal advisor **14** special pleader **15** ambulance chaser

lax 4 hazy, limp, weak **5** agape, loose, slack, vague **6** casual, flabby, floppy, remiss **7** cryptic, flaccid, inexact, lenient, not firm, relaxed **8** careless, derelict, drooping, heedless, nebulous, slipshod, uncaring, yielding **9** confusing, imprecise, negligent, oblivious, undutiful, unheeding, unmindful **10** ill-defined, incoherent, neglectful, permissive **11** hanging open, indifferent, thoughtless, unconcerned **12** loose-muscled, unstructured **13** irresponsible **15** unconscientious

laxness 7 neglect **9** looseness, slackness **10** negligence **11** imprecision **12** carelessness, indifference

Laxness, Halldor Kiljan
author of: 12 Iceland's Bell **14** The Atom Station **17** Independent People **25** The Great Weaver from Kashmir

lay 3 air, bet, put, set **4** bear, fell, fine, form, give, laic, lend, levy, make, plan, poem, raze, rest, seat, song, tune **5** align, allot, apply, ditty, exact, floor, hatch, level, offer, place, stage, wager **6** assess, assign, ballad, charge, demand, depict, devise, gamble, ground, hazard, impose, impute, laical, layout, locate, melody, repose, strain **7** amateur, arrange, concoct, contour, deposit, dispose, forward, present, produce, profane, proffer, refrain, secular, set down, situate, station **8** allocate, assemble, beat down, give odds, inexpert, organize, oviposit, position **9** attribute, elucidate, enunciate, formulate, knock down, knock over, prostrate, roundelay, situation **10** cause to lie, topography **11** arrangement, disposition, nonclerical, orientation, put together **12** conformation **13** configuration, inexperienced, nonspecialist **14** partly informed, unprofessional **15** nonprofessional **17** nonecclesiastical

lay at the door of **6** assign **7** ascribe **8** charge to **9** attribute

lay bare **4** bare, show **6** expose, reveal, unmask, unveil, unwrap **7** divulge, exhibit, publish, uncover **8** disclose **9** broadcast, make known **10** make public **11** communicate

lay down arms **5** yield **6** give up **7** succumb **8** cry quits **9** surrender **10** capitulate **11** come to terms, sue for peace **13** declare a truce **17** acknowledge defeat

layer **3** bed, lap, ply **4** coat, fold, leaf, seam, slab, tier, zone **5** level, plate, scale, sheet, stage, story **6** lamina **7** stratum **9** thickness

layman **4** laic **6** sister **7** amateur, brother **8** outsider **9** churchman **10** catechumen **11** churchwoman, communicant, parishioner **15** nonprofessional **16** member of the flock

layoff **4** fire **6** firing, idling, ouster, the axe **7** dismiss, release, sacking, the boot, the gate, the sack **8** pink slip, shutdown **9** closedown, discharge, dismissal, hard times, the bounce **10** cashiering, depression, the heave-ho **11** furloughing, termination **12** unemployment **13** disemployment, walking papers **20** discharge temporarily

lay off **7** dismiss, forfeit, release, set free **8** get rid of, liberate **9** discharge, terminate **11** give the gate, send packing

Lay of the Last Minstrel, The
author: **14** Sir Walter Scott
character: **8** Margaret, The Dwarf **13** Lady Buccleuch, Lord Cranstoun **17** Master of Buccleuch **19** Ghost of Michael Scott **21** Sir William of Deloraine

lay on **6** bestow, confer, supply **7** present, provide

lay open **4** open **6** expose, open up **7** clarify **9** make plain **18** make understandable

layout **4** form, plan **5** chart, draft, dummy, model, motif, spend **6** design, expend, pay out, sketch, spread **7** diagram, drawing, fork out, outline, pattern **8** disburse, shell out **9** blueprint, delineate, placement, spread out, structure **11** arrangement, composition

lay waste **4** ruin **5** level, wreck **6** ravage **7** despoil, destroy, wipe out **8** demolish, desolate **9** devastate, eradicate **10** annihilate, obliterate

Lazarus **6** beggar
means: **8** God helps
sister: **4** Mary **6** Martha
hometown: **7** Bethany
resurrected by: **5** Jesus

Lazarus
author: **14** Leonid Andreyev

Lazarus, Mell
creator/artist: **5** Momma **9** Miss Peach

lazurite
variety: **11** lapis lazuli

lazy **3** lax **4** idle, slow **5** inert, slack **6** drowsy, sleepy, torpid **7** laggard, languid **8** inactive, indolent, listless, slothful, sluggish **9** apathetic, easygoing, lethargic, shiftless **10** languorous, slow-moving **13** unindustrious **15** unwilling to work

lazy person **5** drone, idler **6** loafer **14** good-for-nothing

Leach, Archibald Alexander
real name of: **9** Cary Grant

Leachman, Cloris
born: **11** Des Moines IA
roles: **7** Phyllis **11** High Anxiety **12** Kiss Me Deadly **17** Young Frankenstein **18** Mary Tyler Moore Show, The Last Picture Show

lead **2** go **3** aim, top **4** clue, draw, edge, have, head, hero, hint, live, lure, pass **5** charm, excel, guide, model, outdo, pilot, steer, tempt **6** allure, convey, direct, entice, extend, induce, manage, margin, pursue, seduce **7** advance, attract, bring on, command, conduct, control, example, go first, incline, issue in, marshal, pioneer, precede, proceed, produce, stretch, surpass, undergo **8** domineer, go before, guidance, moderate, outstrip, persuade, priority, result in, shepherd, star part **9** advantage, come first, direction, go through, headliner, influence, plurality, rank first **10** branch into, experience, first place, indication, precedence, precedency, set the pace, show the way, tend toward **11** antecedence, be in advance, leading role, preside over, protagonist

lead
chemical symbol: **2** Pb

lead astray **4** dupe, lure **6** delude **7** beguile, deceive, ensnare, mislead **19** lead up the garden path

leaden **4** dark, dull, glum, gray **5** inert, murky **6** dreary, gloomy, numbed, somber, torpid **7** grayish, languid **8** burdened, careworn, darkened, deadened, listless, sluggish, unwieldy **9** depressed, inanimate **10** cumbersome, hard to move

leader **4** boss, guru, head **5** chief, guide, mogul **6** bigwig, honcho, master, mentor, tycoon **7** captain, foreman, kingpin, magnate, manager, pioneer, prophet **8** director, superior **9** chieftain, commander, conductor, godfather, pacemaker, patriarch **10** forerunner, pacesetter, pathfinder, supervisor **11** frontrunner, torchbearer, trailblazer

leadership **4** helm, lead, sway **5** reins, wheel **7** command, primacy **8** charisma, guidance, headship, hegemony **9** captaincy, supremacy **10** domination, mastership **11** managership, preeminence, stewardship **12** directorship, governorship, guardianship, self-reliance **13** ability to lead, self-assurance **14** administration **15** managerial skill, superintendency **17** authoritativeness

leading **3** top **4** head, main **5** basic, chief, first, great, prime **6** ruling **7** advance, guiding, initial, leadoff, notable, primary, ranking, stellar, supreme, topmost **8** advanced, dominant, foremost **9** directing, essential, governing, nonpareil, paramount, principal, prominent, sovereign, unrivaled **10** motivating, preeminent, underlying **11** controlling, outstanding, pacesetting **12** unchallenged, unparalleled **13** most important **14** quintessential **15** most influential, most significant

lead on **4** goad **5** egg on **6** entice **7** mislead, support **9** encourage **19** lead up the garden path

lead the way 4 lead, show, take **5** guide **6** escort **7** conduct

leaf 4 flip, foil, page, skim **5** blade, bract, folio, frond, green, inset, petal, sheet, thumb **6** browse, glance, insert, needle **7** foliole, lamella, leaflet **9** cotyledon, extension, turn green **10** lamination **12** sheet of metal

leaflet 2 ad **4** bill **5** flier, flyer, tract **6** folder, notice **7** booklet, handout **8** brochure, bulletin, circular, handbill, pamphlet **9** broadside, throwaway **10** broadsheet **12** announcement **13** advertisement

league 4 ally, band **5** cabal, group, guild, merge, union **6** cartel **7** combine, compact, company, network, society **8** alliance **9** coalition **10** conspiracy, federation, fraternity, join forces **11** association, confederacy, confederate, consolidate, cooperative, partnership **13** collaboration, confederation, confraternity

Leah
means: 7 wild cow
father: 5 Laban
husband: 5 Jacob
sister: 6 Rachel
slave: 6 Zilpah
son: 4 Levi **5** Judah **6** Reuben, Simeon **7** Zebulun **8** Issachar
daughter: 5 Dinah
burial place: 9 Machpelah

leak 3 ebb, rip **4** blab, gash, hole, ooze, rent, rift, seep, vent **5** break, chink, cleft, crack, drain, exude, fault, spill **6** breach, efflux, escape, filter, let out, reveal, take in **7** confide, crevice, divulge, dribble, fissure, let slip, opening, outflow, rupture, seepage **8** aperture, disclose, draining, give away, puncture **9** discharge, percolate **10** interstice, make public **11** be permeable, perforation **12** admit leakage **16** let enter or escape

leakage 5 issue **7** outflow, seepage **9** discharge

Leakey, Louis S Bazett
field: 12 anthropology
discovered: 8 early man
worked at: 8 Tanzania **12** Olduvai Gorge
wife: 4 Mary
son: 7 Richard

lean 3 aim, bow, tip **4** bend, cant, lank, list, poor, rely, rest, slim, tend, thin, tilt **5** gaunt, lanky, lurch, scant, slant, slope, small, spare, weedy **6** barren, depend, meager, modest, nonfat, prefer, scanty, skinny, sparse, svelte **7** angular, count on, incline, recline, scraggy, scrawny, slender, spindly, trust in, willowy **8** exiguous, rawboned, resort to, skeletal **9** emaciated **10** inadequate, set store by **11** be partial to, have faith in, prop oneself **12** insufficient, seek solace in **14** rest one's weight, support oneself

Lean, David
director of: 10 Summertime **11** Oliver Twist **13** Doctor Zhivago, Ryan's Daughter **15** A Passage to India **16** Lawrence of Arabia (Oscar) **17** Great Expectations **23** The Bridge on the River Kwai (Oscar)

Leander
loved: 4 Hero
swam nightly: 10 Hellespont
death by: 8 drowning

leaning 4 bent, turn **5** slant **7** relying **8** affinity, tendency **9** proneness **10** dependence, partiality, preference, proclivity, propensity **11** inclination **14** predisposition

leap 3 hop **4** jete, jump, romp, rush, skip **5** bound, caper, frisk, vault **6** bounce, cavort, frolic, gambol, hasten, hurtle, prance, spring **7** hop over **8** jump over **9** bound over, saltation **10** hurtle over, jump across, spring over

Learchus
father: 7 Athamas
mother: 3 Ino
killed by: 7 Athamas

learn 3 con **4** hear **6** detect, master, pick up **7** find out, uncover, unearth **8** discover, memorize **9** ascertain, determine, ferret out **10** become able **12** find out about

learned 4 deep, wise **7** erudite **8** cultured, educated, informed, lettered, literate, profound, schooled, well-read **9** scholarly **10** cultivated **12** accomplished, intellectual, well-educated **13** knowledgeable

Learned, Michael
roles: 5 Nurse **10** The Waltons

learner 4 tyro **5** pupil **6** novice, rookie **7** draftee, recruit, scholar, student, trainee **8** beginner, disciple, enlistee, follower, freshman, neophyte **9** fledgling, greenhorn, novitiate, proselyte, schoolboy **10** apprentice, schoolgirl, tenderfoot **11** schoolchild

learning 5 study **6** wisdom **7** culture **8** teaching **9** education, erudition, knowledge, schooling **11** cultivation, edification, information, instruction, scholarship **13** comprehension, enlightenment, understanding

Learning
god of: 5 Thoth

leash 4 curb, lead, line, rein, ruin **5** strap, thong **6** bridle, choker, fasten, hold in, stifle, string, tether **7** contain, control, harness **8** restrain, suppress

Leather-Stocking Tales
author: 19 James Fenimore Cooper
includes: 10 The Prairie **11** The Pioneers **13** The Deerslayer, The Pathfinder **20** The Last of the Mohicans
hero of: 7 Hawkeye **10** Pathfinder, The Trapper **11** Natty Bumppo **13** The Deerslayer **15** Leather-stocking **16** Le Longue Carabine

leave 2 go **3** fly **4** cede, exit, flee, keep, quit, will **5** allot, be off, cause, endow, forgo, going, split, waive, yield **6** assign, bug out, commit, decamp, depart, desert, eschew, forego, give up, legate, move on, recess, resign, retain, set out **7** abandon, abscond, bequest, consent, consign, deposit, entrust, forsake, holiday, let stay, liberty, parting, produce, push off, release, respite, retreat, sustain, take off, time off **8** approval, bequeath, farewell, furlough, generate, give over, maintain, result in, sanction, shove off, vacation **9** allowance, apportion, departure, hotfoot it, let remain, surrender, tolerance **10** concession, depart from, embark from, go away from, indulgence, permission, relinquish, retire from, sabbatical, sufferance, withdrawal **11** bid farewell, endorsement **13** absent oneself, understanding

leave a ship 4 land **6** debark **8** go ashore **9** disembark **11** abandon ship

leave behind 6 desert, vacate **7** abandon, discard, forsake **8** evacuate **9** cast aside **10** relinquish **11** outdistance

leave cold 4 bore **12** leave unmoved **15** leave unaffected

Leave It To Beaver
character: **11** June Cleaver, Ward Cleaver **12** Eddie Haskell, Wally Cleaver **13** Beaver (Theodore) Cleaver
cast: **7** Tony Dow **9** Ken Osmond **12** Hugh Beaumont, Jerry Mathers **18** Barbara Billingsley

leave off **3** end **4** halt, quit, stop **5** cease **6** desist, finish **7** suspend **8** conclude **11** discontinue, refrain from

leave out **4** drop, omit **6** except, reject **7** exclude

Leaves of Grass
author: **11** Walt Whitman

leave suddenly **3** fly **4** flee **6** cut out, decamp, run off **7** abscond, make off, run away, rush off, take off **11** take a powder **15** be off and running

leave-taking **4** exit **5** adieu **7** good-bye, leaving, parting, send-off **8** au revoir, farewell **9** departure **10** withdrawal

leave undone **4** quit **6** give up **7** abandon, forsake, neglect **8** give up on

Lebanon ***see box***

Le Bel, Joseph Achille
field: **9** chemistry
nationality: **6** French
founded: **15** stereochemistry

Le Bourgeois Gentilhomme
author: **7** Moliere
character: **7** Cleonte, Dorante **9** M Jourdain **16** Monsieur Jourdain

Le Carre, John
real name: **13** David Cornwell
author of: **11** A Perfect Spy **13** Smiley's People **18** The Looking Glass War **19** A Small Town in Germany **20** The Little Drummer Girl **21** The Honorable Schoolboy **22** Tinker Tailor Soldier Spy **26** The Spy Who Came in from the Cold

lechayim, lehayim **6** to life

Lecheates
epithet of: **4** Zeus
means: **10** in childbed

lecherous **4** lewd **5** randy **6** carnal **7** goatish, lustful, ruttish **8** prurient **9** salacious, satyrlike **10** lascivious, libidinous, licentious, lubricious

lechery **4** lust **8** lewdness **9** carnality, prurience **10** satyriasis **11** lustfulness, nymphomania **13** salaciousness **14** lasciviousness

Le Cid
author: **9** Corneille
composer: **13** Jules Massenet

Leconte de Lisle, Charles
author of: **14** Poemes Antiques, Poemes Barbares

Le Corbusier
real name: **23** Charles Edouard Jeanneret
architect of: **10** La Tourette (monastery) **15** Notre Dame du Haut (Ronchamp France) **16** Unite d'Habitation (Marseilles)
planned city of: **10** Chandigarh (capital of the Punjab)
style: **6** Purism **12** New Brutalism

lecture **4** talk **5** chide, scold, speak **6** homily, preach, rail at, rebuke, sermon, speech **7** address, censure, chiding, expound, oration, reading, reproof, reprove, upbraid, warning **8** admonish, call down, harangue, moralize, reproach **9** discourse, hold forth, reprimand, sermonize, talking-to **10** preachment, take to task **12** chastisement, disquisition, remonstrance

lecture hall **9** classroom

Lebanon
ancient name: **9** Phoenicia
capital/largest city: **6** Beirut **8** Beyrouth
others: **3** Sur **4** Arca, Tyre **5** Ehden, Halba, Hamat, Sahle, Saida, Sayda, Sidon, Sofar, Zahla, Zahle **6** Byblos, Ghazir, Juniye, Tibnin **7** Baalbek, Batroun, Bsherri, Rachaya, Tripoli, Zgharta **8** Djezzine, El Hermel, Hasbaiya, Merjuyun **9** Broummana, Marjayoun **10** Beited Dine, Heliopolis
ancient city: **8** Carthage
school: **4** Arab **8** American, Lebanese **11** Saint Joseph
division:
ancient: **4** Tyre **5** Arwad, Sidon **6** Byblos, Jubayl
monetary unit: **5** livre, pound **7** piastre
lake: **5** Quran **6** Qirawn
mountain: **4** Mzar **5** Aruba **6** Hermon **7** Lebanon, Sannine **8** Kadischa, Kenisseh **9** Kennisseh **10** al-Mukammal **11** Anti-Lebanon
highest point: **7** es Sauda **13** Qurnat al-Sawda
river: **3** Dog, Joz **5** Barid, Kebir, Lycos **6** Auwali, Barada, Damour, Litani **7** Hasbani, Leontes, Orontes **8** Kasemieh
sea: **13** Mediterranean
physical feature:
cape: **10** Pigeon Rock **11** Ras esh Shiqa **12** Qadisha Gorge
plain: **4** Bika **5** Bekaa
valley: **5** Beqaa **6** al-Biqa **9** Great Rift
wind: **7** khamsin
people: **4** Arab **11** Palestinian
ancient: **9** Canaanite **10** Phoenician
leader: **6** Bashir, Sarkis **7** Chamoun **8** Franjieh **9** al-Din Maan **11** Amin Gemayel **13** Bashir Gemayel
poet: **11** Kahil Gibran
rulers: **5** Arabs **6** French, Greeks, Romans **8** Hittites, Ottomans, Persians **9** Assyrians, Crusaders, Egyptians, Mamelukes **11** Babylonians
language: **6** Arabic, French, Syriac **7** English, Turkish **8** Armenian
religion: **5** Druse, Druze, Islam **8** Maronite, Melchite **10** Protestant **11** Monophysite **12** Christianity **13** Greek Catholic **14** Greek Orthodoxy **17** Armenian Orthodoxy
place:
dam: **5** Qarun
ruins: **7** Baalbek **15** Temple of Bacchus, Temple of Jupiter
feature:
Christian group: **10** Phalangist
dance: **6** dabkeh, dabkey
tree: **5** cedar
food:
dish: **6** kibbeh **8** tabouleh
drink: **4** arak **6** arrack

10 auditorium 12 amphitheater, assembly hall

lecturelike 7 donnish, preachy 8 academic, didactic, pedantic 9 homiletic 10 moralizing

Leda
father: 8 Thestius
husband: 9 Tyndareus
lover: 4 swan, Zeus
son: 6 Castor, Pollux 8 Dioscuri 10 Polydeuces
daughter: 5 Helen 6 Phoebe 8 Philonoe, Timandra 12 Clytemnestra

Leda and the Swan
author: 7 W B Yeats

ledge 4 sill, step 5 ridge, shelf 6 mantel, offset 8 foothold, shoulder 10 projection 11 mantelpiece, mantelshelf, outcropping

Lee, Annie
character in: 10 Enoch Arden
author: 8 Tennyson

Lee, Henry
nickname: 15 Light Horse Harry
served in: 16 Revolutionary War
member of: 10 US Congress 19 Continental Congress
governor of: 8 Virginia
suppressed: 16 Whiskey Rebellion
son: 7 Robert E

Lee, Robert E
father: 5 Henry 15 Light Horse Harry
born: 11 Stratford VA 18 Westmoreland County
wife: 21 Mary Ann Randolph Custis
served in: 8 Civil War 10 Mexican War
commander of: 22 Army of Northern Virginia
suppressed raid of: 9 John Brown
suppressed raid on: 12 Harper's Ferry
battle: 7 Bull Run 8 Antietam 10 Gettysburg 14 Fredericksburg 16 Chancellorsville, Seven Days' Battles
surrendered at: 20 Appomattox Court House
president of: 17 Washington College

leek 18 Allium ampeloprasum
varieties: 4 lily, rose, sand, wild 5 lady's 6 meadow

leer 4 ogle 5 fleer, smirk 6 goggle

leery 4 wary 5 cagey, chary 6 unsure 7 guarded 8 cautious, doubtful, hesitant 9 skeptical, undecided 10 suspicious 11 circumspect, distrustful, mistrustful

Leeuwenhoek, Anton van
field: 10 microscopy
father of: 12 microbiology
discovered: 13 red blood cells

leeway 4 play 5 scope, slack 6 margin 7 cushion, headway, reserve 8 headroom, latitude 9 allowance, clearance, elbowroom, extra time, tolerance 11 flexibility 13 room for choice 14 margin for error 15 maneuverability

LeFarge, Christopher Grant
architect of: 19 Roman Catholic Chapel (West Point)

left behind 7 vacated 8 deserted, forsaken, forsook 9 abandoned, discarded, evacuated 12 relinquished

leftover 6 excess, legacy, unused 7 overage, residue, surplus, uneaten 8 leavings, oddments, residual, survivor 9 carry-over, remainder, remaining

left-wing 7 leftist, liberal, radical 9 socialist 11 progressive

left-winger 7 leftist, liberal, radical 9 socialist 11 progressive

Lefty
nickname of: 12 Steve Carlton

leg 3 gam, lap, pin 4 limb, part, post, prop 5 brace, femur, shank, stage, stump, tibia 6 column, fibula, member, pillar 7 portion, section, segment, stretch, support, upright

legacy 4 gift 6 devise, estate 7 bequest, vestige 8 heirloom, heritage, leftover, survivor 9 carry-over, throwback, tradition 10 birthright, hand-me-down 11 inheritance

legal 4 fair 5 licit, of law, valid 6 kosher, lawful 7 cricket 8 forensic, judicial, juristic, rightful 9 courtroom, juridical 10 legitimate, sanctioned 11 permissible 12 adjudicatory, within bounds 14 constitutional 15 jurisprudential

legal advisor 6 lawyer 7 counsel 8 advocate, attorney 9 barrister, counselor, solicitor 13 attorney-at-law 14 counselor-at-law

legal form 4 writ 8 document 10 instrument

legality 8 validity 9 licitness 10 lawfulness, legitimacy 17 constitutionality

legalization 8 sanction 9 enactment 10 permission, validation 13 authorization 14 legitimization

legalize 5 enact 6 permit 8 sanction, validate 9 authorize 10 legitimize

legal residence 4 home 8 domicile, dwelling

legal tender 4 cash 5 money 8 currency

legate 5 agent, envoy 6 deputy 8 emissary 14 representative

legatee 4 heir 9 inheritor 11 beneficiary

legation 7 embassy, mission 8 ministry 9 consulate 10 delegation 11 chancellery

legend 3 key 4 edda, lore, myth, saga, tale 5 fable, motto, story, title 7 caption, fiction, proverb 8 folklore 11 inscription

legendary 5 famed 6 fabled, famous, mythic 7 storied 8 fabulous, fanciful, mythical 9 imaginary 10 apocryphal, celebrated, fictitious, proverbial

Legend of Good Women, The
author: 15 Geoffrey Chaucer
character: 4 Dido 5 Medea 6 Thisbe 7 Alceste, Ariadne, Lucrece, Phyllis 9 Cleopatra, Hypsipyle, Philomela 12 Hypermnestra

Legend of Sleepy Hollow, The
author: 16 Washington Irving
character: 12 Brom Van Brunt (Brom Bones), Ichabod Crane 16 Katrina Van Tassel

Leger, Fernand
born: 6 France 8 Argentan
artwork: 8 Bargeman 10 Adam and Eve, The Wedding, Three Women 11 The Builders, The Cyclists, The Mechanic, The Stairway 14 The Great Parade 15 Le Grand Dejeuner 16 Contrasting Forms, Nudes in the Forest 21 Butterflies and Flowers

legerdemain 7 cunning 8 deftness, jugglery, juggling, trickery 9 deception 10 adroitness, artfulness 11 maneuvering 13 sleight of hand 16 prestidigitation

legible 4 neat 5 clear, plain 7 visible 8 clear-cut, distinct, readable 12 decipherable

14 comprehensible, understandable

legion **3** mob, sea **4** army, host, mass **5** corps, drove, horde, spate, swarm **6** myriad, throng, troops **7** brigade **8** division **9** multitude

leg irons **5** bonds, irons **6** chains **7** fetters **8** shackles

legislation **3** act **4** bill **6** ruling **7** measure, statute **9** amendment, enactment, lawmaking, ordinance

legislator **7** senator **8** alderman, delegate, lawgiver, lawmaker **10** councilman **11** assemblyman, congressman **13** congresswoman **14** representative **15** parliamentarian

legislature **4** diet **5** house **6** senate **7** chamber, council **8** assembly, congress **10** parliament

legitimacy **8** legality, validity **10** lawfulness **11** correctness, genuineness **12** authenticity, rightfulness **15** appropriateness

legitimate **4** fair, just, true **5** legal, licit, sound, valid **6** lawful, proper **7** correct, genuine, logical, tenable **8** rightful **9** authentic, justified, plausible **10** believable, reasonable **11** appropriate, well-founded

leg-pull **4** hoax **9** deception **13** practical joke

Legree, Simon
character in: **14** Uncle Tom's Cabin
author: **5** Stowe

LeGuin, Ursula K
author of: **13** Lathe of Heaven **14** Rocannon's World **15** The Dispossessed **16** Always Coming Home **21** The Left Hand of Darkness

Lehar, Franz (Ferencz)
born: **7** Komarno (then Hungary, now Czechoslovakia)
composer of: **9** Gipsy Love **13** The Merry Widow **20** The Count of Luxembourg

Lehmbruck, Wilhelm
born: **7** Germany **9** Meiderich
artwork: **11** Rising Youth **12** Man Flung Down, Praying Woman, Seating Youth **13** Kneeling Woman, Standing Woman, Standing Youth

Leigh, Janet
husband: **10** Tony Curtis
daughter: **14** Jamie Lee Curtis
born: **8** Merced CA
roles: **6** Psycho, The Fog **10** The Vikings **11** Little Women, Touch of Evil

Leigh, Vivien
real name: **17** Vivian Mary Hartley
husband: **15** Laurence Olivier
born: **5** India **10** Darjeeling
roles: **11** Ship of Fools **12** Anna Karenina **13** Blanche du Bois, Scarlett O'Hara **14** Waterloo Bridge **15** Gone With the Wind (Oscar) **17** That Hamilton Woman **21** A Streetcar Named Desire (Oscar), Roman Spring of Mrs Stone

Leighton, Margaret
husband: **12** Max Reinhardt **14** Laurence Harvey, Michael Wilding
born: **7** England **10** Barnt Green **14** Worcestershire
roles: **12** The Go-Between **13** The Winslow Boy **14** Separate Tables **19** The Night of the Iguana

leisure **4** ease, rest **6** recess, repose **7** holiday, respite, time off **8** free time, vacation **9** diversion, idle hours, spare time **10** recreation, relaxation

leisurely **4** idle, slow **6** casual, slowly **7** languid, relaxed, restful **9** unhurried **10** slow-moving **11** lingeringly, unhurriedly **12** without haste **13** lackadaisical

Lemminkainen
origin: **7** Finnish
mentioned in: **8** Kalevala
role: **4** hero

Lemmon, Jack
real name: **18** Jack Uhler Lemmon III
wife: **11** Felicia Farr
born: **8** Boston MA
roles: **7** Missing **10** April Fools **12** Save the Tiger (Oscar), The Apartment, The Great Race, The Odd Couple **13** China Syndrome, Mister Roberts, Some Like It Hot **18** Days of Wine and Roses, Under the Yum-Yum Tree **19** How to Murder Your Wife

lemon **11** Citrus limon
varieties: **4** wild **5** dwarf, giant, Meyer, water **6** garden, wonder **9** wild water **12** Chinese dwarf **14** American wonder

Lemuralia
origin: **5** Roman
event: **8** festival
to exorcise: **6** ghosts

lemures
form: **6** ghosts
characteristic: **10** maleficent **11** troublesome

Lenaea
origin: **8** Athenian
event: **8** festival

lend **4** give, loan **6** impart, invest, supply **7** advance, furnish **10** contribute

lend a hand **3** aid **6** assist **7** help out

lend assistance **3** aid **4** abet, help **6** succor **7** relieve **16** give a helping hand

lend one's name to **7** endorse, support **9** recommend

length **3** run **4** span, term, time **5** piece, range, reach **6** extent, period **7** compass, measure, portion, section, segment, stretch **8** distance, duration, end to end **9** longitude, magnitude **11** elapsed time, measurement

lengthen **3** pad **5** add to **6** expand, extend, let out, pad out **7** augment, drag out, draw out, fill out, prolong, spin out, stretch **8** elongate, flesh out, increase, protract **9** attenuate, string out

lengthened **8** drawn out, extended **9** augmented, elongated, prolonged, stretched **10** attenuated, grew longer

lengthening **8** full form **9** extending, extension **10** elongation, stretching **11** extenuation, protraction **12** prolongation

lengthy **5** windy, wordy **6** padded, prolix **7** endless **8** drawn out, extended, overlong, rambling **9** elongated, extensive, garrulous, long-drawn, prolonged **10** digressive, discursive, long-winded, protracted **12** interminable

leniency **5** mercy **7** charity **8** clemency **9** tolerance **10** compassion **11** forbearance, magnanimity **12** mercifulness **13** forgivingness

lenient **4** kind, mild, soft **6** gentle **7** clement, liberal, patient, sparing **8** merciful, moderate, tolerant **9** easygoing, forgiving, indulgent **10** benevolent, charitable, forbearing, permissive **11** kindhearted, soft-hearted, sympathetic **13** compassionate, tenderhearted

Lenni-Lenape *see* **8** Delaware

Lenny
director: **8** Bob Fosse

cast: **8** Jan Miner **11** Stanley Beck **13** Dustin Hoffman (Lenny Bruce) **14** Valerie Perrine (Honey Harlowe)

Le Notre, Andre
landscape architect of: **6** Clagny **9** Tuileries **10** Versailles **12** Saint Germain **13** Fontainebleau **22** Chateau de Vaux-le-Vicomte

lens
invented by:
achromatic: **7** Dollond
bifocal: **8** Franklin
fused bifocal: **6** Borsch

Lenya, Lotte
real name: **16** Karoline Blamauer
husband: **9** Kurt Weill
born: **7** Austria, Hitzing
roles: **5** Jenny **18** From Russia with Love, The Seven Deadly Sins, The Threepenny Opera

Leo
symbol: **4** lion
planet: **3** Sun
rules: **7** romance **10** creativity
born: **4** July **6** August

Leonard, Elmore
author of: **4** Swag **5** Glitz, Stick **6** Hombre **7** La Brava **9** Cat Chaser, Gold Coast, Gunsights, The Hunted **10** Mr Majestyk **12** The Big Bounce **14** Fifty-Two Pick-Up, Valdez Is Coming **16** Double Dutch Treat, The Bounty Hunters **18** Forty Lashes Less One

Leonardo da Vinci
born: **5** Italy, Vinci
artwork: **8** Mona Lisa **13** The Last Supper **15** The Annunciation **19** The Battle of Anghiari **21** The Adoration of the Magi

Leonato
character in: **19** Much Ado About Nothing
author: **11** Shakespeare

Leoncavallo, Ruggiero
born: **5** Italy **6** Naples
composer of: **8** Serafita **9** Pagliacci

Leontes
character in: **14** The Winter's Tale
author: **11** Shakespeare

Leonteus
leader of: **6** Greeks
leader at: **4** Troy
suitor of: **5** Helen

leopard **3** cat **7** panther **10** spotted cat
group of: **4** leap

Leos
occupation: **6** herald
father: **7** Orpheus
sacrificed: **9** daughters

Leo the Lip
nickname of: **11** Leo Durocher

lepidoptera
class: **8** hexapoda
phylum: **10** arthropoda
group: **4** moth **9** butterfly

leprechaun **3** elf, imp **5** dwarf, gnome **6** sprite **12** little person

Ler
also: **3** Lir
origin: **5** Irish
personifies: **3** sea
son: **8** Manannan
corresponds to: **4** Llyr

Lesage, Alain
author of: **7** Gil Blas **8** Turcaret

Lescaze, William
architect of: **18** Borg-Warner Building (Chicago) **38** Philadelphia Savings Fund Society Building

Lescot, Pierre
architect of: **10** Cour Carree **20** Fontaine des Innocents
rebuilding of: **6** Louvre

Lesotho ***see box***

less **6** barely, little **7** smaller **8** meagerly, slighter **10** not as great **11** more limited

lessen **3** ebb **4** ease, sink, thin, wane **5** abate, lower **6** dilute, reduce, shrink **7** abridge, decline, dwindle, lighten, slacken, subside **8** contract, decrease, diminish, mitigate, wind down **9** alleviate **10** depreciate

lessening **6** waning **8** decrease, dilution **9** abatement, deduction, dwindling, reduction, shrinkage **10** diminution, lightening, mitigation, shortening, slackening **11** abridgement, alleviation, contraction, diminishing, slacking off **12** abbreviation, condensation, depreciation

lesser **4** less **5** minor **7** humbler, smaller **8** inferior, slighter **9** secondary **11** secondarily

Lesser Dionysia
also: **13** Rural Dionysia
event: **8** festival
origin: **6** Attica

Lessing, Doris
author of: **8** Shikasta **16** The Four-Gated City **17** The Golden Notebook **20** The Sirian Experiments **21** The Children of Violence **37** Marriages Between Zones Three Four and Five **42** The Making of the Representative for Planet Eight

lesson **5** class, drill, guide, model, moral, study **6** caveat, notice, rebuke **7** caution, example, message, reading, segment, warning **8** exemplar, exercise, homework **9** deterrent **10** admonition, advisement, assignment, punishment, recitation, Scrip-

Lesotho
other name: **10** Basutoland
capital/largest city: **6** Maseru
others: **4** Roma **5** Joels **6** Leribe, Morija **7** Quthing, Sekakes **8** Mafeteng, Matsieng **9** Marakabei, Qachas Nek, Semonkong **10** Butha Buthe, Mokhotlong, Thaba Bosiu **11** Mohales Hoek **12** Sehlabathebe, Teyateyaneng
head of state: **4** king
monetary unit: **4** cent, rand
mountain: **6** Maloti, Maluti **7** Central **8** Injasuti, Machache **10** Ben Macdhui **11** Drakensberg, Thaba Putsoa
highest point: **16** Thabana Ntlenyana
river: **5** Senqu **6** Orange, Tugela **7** Caledon **9** Makhaleng
physical feature:
gorge: **5** Oxbow
people: **4** Zulu **5** Bantu, Tembu **6** Basuto **7** Basotho
leader: **7** Moshesh **9** Mosheshwe **10** Moshoeshoe **14** Leabua Jonathan
language: **5** Sotho **7** English, Sesotho
religion: **7** animism **13** Roman Catholic **18** Lesotho Evangelical
feature:
blanket: **4** kobo
house: **8** rondavel
water project: **11** Malibamatso

tures **11** instruction **12** remonstrance

Lestrade, Inspector
character in: 14 (The Adventures of) Sherlock Holmes
author: 10 Conan Doyle

Le Sueur, Lucille Fay
real name of: 12 Joan Crawford

let 4 make, rent **5** admit, allow, cause, grant, lease, leave **6** enable, permit, sublet, suffer **7** approve, charter, concede, empower, endorse, hire out, license, warrant **8** sanction, sublease, tolerate **9** authorize

let down 4 drop **5** lower **6** betray **8** push down **10** disappoint **11** disillusion

letdown 3 rue **4** balk, blow **6** fizzle, regret **7** chagrin, setback **8** comedown **10** anticlimax, bafflement, bitter pill, dashed hope, discontent **11** frustration **12** blighted hope, discomfiture **13** mortification **14** disappointment, disenchantment, disgruntlement **15** disillusionment, dissatisfaction

let fall 4 drop **5** let go **7** release

let fly 4 cast, hurl **5** eject, fling, heave, sling, throw **6** launch, propel

let go 3 axe, can **4** fire, free, lose, oust, sack **6** bounce, give up

lethal 5 fatal, toxic **6** deadly, mortal **7** baneful, killing **8** venomous, virulent **9** dangerous, malignant, poisonous **11** destructive **13** mortally toxic

lethargic 4 dull, idle, lazy **5** inert **6** drowsy, sleepy, torpid **7** languid, passive **8** comatose, indolent, listless, slothful, sluggish **9** apathetic, enervated, somnolent, soporific **10** dispirited, lackluster, unspirited **11** debilitated, indifferent

lethargy 5 sloth **6** apathy, stupor, torpor **7** inertia, languor **8** dullness, laziness **9** indolence, lassitude, torpidity **10** drowsiness, inactivity **12** indifference, listlessness, slothfulness, sluggishness

Lethe
form: 5 river
location: 5 Hades
caused: 13 forgetfulness

let in 5 admit **7** receive **12** allow to enter

let loose 4 free **5** let go **6** let fly **7** release, set free, unleash **8** give vent, liberate **12** give free rein

Leto
also: 6 Latona
form: 7 goddess
father: 5 Coeus
mother: 6 Phoebe
son: 6 Apollo
daughter: 7 Artemis

let off 5 let go **6** acquit, excuse, exempt **7** release, set free **8** liberate **9** discharge

let slip 6 betray, expose, reveal **7** divulge, uncover **8** blurt out, disclose, give away

Let's Make a Deal
host: 9 Monty Hall
announcer: 10 Jay Stewart

letter 4 note **7** epistle, message, missive **8** dispatch, document **9** substance **10** billet-doux

Letter, The
director: 12 William Wyler
based on story by: 15 Somerset Maugham
cast: 10 Bette Davis **14** Frieda Inescort **15** Gale Sondergaard, Herbert Marshall, James Stephenson
setting: 6 Malaya

letter ordering imprisonment
French: 14 lettre de cachet
carried seal of: 4 king **9** sovereign

letters 8 learning **9** erudition **10** literature **13** belles lettres

Letters from the Underground
author: 16 Fyodor Dostoevsky

Letter to Three Wives, A
director: 17 Joseph L Mankiewicz
cast: 10 Ann Sothern **11** Jeanne Crain, Jeffrey Lynn, Kirk Douglas, Paul Douglas **12** Linda Darnell, Thelma Ritter
Oscar for: 6 script **8** director

let the buyer beware
Latin: 12 caveat emptor

let the people rule
Latin: 13 regnat populus
motto of: 8 Arkansas

let there be light
Latin: 7 fiat lux

lettre de cachet 26 letter ordering imprisonment **28** letter under the sovereign's seal

lettuce 7 Lactuca
varieties: 3 cos **5** chalk, frog's, lamb's, water **6** Boston, garden, miner's **7** iceberg, prickly, romaine **8** escarole **9** asparagus **11** common lamb's

letup 4 lull **5** pause **6** relief **7** respite **8** decrease, interval, slowdown, stopping, surcease, vacation **9** abatement, cessation, interlude, lessening, remission **10** slackening **11** retardation

Let Us Now Praise Famous Men
author: 9 James Agee

Let us therefore be joyful
Latin: 15 Gaudeamus igitur

Leucaeus
epithet of: 4 Zeus
means: 16 of the white poplar

Leuce
form: 5 nymph
changed into: 6 poplar
color of poplar: 5 white

Leucippe
father: 6 Minyas **7** Thestor
mother: 10 Orchomenus
son: 8 Teuthras

Leucippides
refers to: 6 Phoebe **7** Hilaira

Leucippus
father: 8 Perieres
mother: 10 Gorgophone
brother: 8 Aphareus
fathered: 11 Leucippides
daughter: 6 Phoebe **7** Arsinoe, Hilaira
pursued: 6 Daphne
***disguised as:* 4** girl
killed by: 6 nymphs

Leucophryne
epithet of: 7 Artemis

Leucothea *see* **3** Ino

Leucus
mentioned in: 5 Iliad
companion of: 8 Odysseus
usurped throne of: 9 Idomeneus
killed by: 8 Antiphus

Le Vau, Louis
architect of: 6 Louvre **10** Versailles **12** Hotel Lambert **22** Chateau de Vaux-le-Vicomte **24** College des Quatres Nations

levee 3 dam **4** bank, dike, pier, quay, wall **5** ditch, jetty, ridge, wharf **6** durbar **9** reception **10** embankment

level 3 aim, bed **4** even, flat, rank, raze, tied, vein, zone **5** align, floor, flush, grade, layer, plane, point, stage, story, wreck **6** direct, height, lay low, reduce, smooth, topple **7** aligned, even out, flatten, landing, on a line, station, stratum, uniform **8** equalize, make even, position, tear down, together **9** devastate, elevation, knock down **10** consistent, horizontal, on a par with, unwrinkled **11** achievement, neck and neck **12** on an even keel

level-headed 4 sage **5** sound **6** poised, stable, steady **7** prudent **8** balanced, cautious, composed, sensible **9** collected, judicious, practical, unruffled **10** cool-headed, dependable, thoughtful **11** circumspect **12** even-tempered **13** dispassionate **14** self-controlled

levelheadedness 6 aplomb **9** good sense, soundness, stability **10** equanimity **11** common sense **13** judiciousness

Levene, Sam
real name: 12 Samuel Levine
born: 6 Russia
roles: 12 Guys and Dolls **13** Nathan Detroit **15** The Sunshine Boys

lever 3 bar, pry **5** jimmy, raise **7** crowbar

Lever, Charles
author of: 14 Charles O'Malley

Leverrier, Urbain Jean Joseph
field: 9 astronomy
nationality: 6 French
co-discovered: 7 Neptune
worked with: 14 John Couch Adams

Levi
father: 5 Jacob **6** Melchi, Symeon
mother: 4 Leah
son: 6 Kohath, Merari **7** Gershom
brother: 3 Dan, Gad **5** Asher, Judah **6** Joseph, Reuben, Simeon **7** Zebulun **8** Benjamin, Issachar, Naphtali
sister: 5 Dinah
violated: 5 Dinah
also called: 7 Matthew
descendant of: 6 Levite

Leviathan 6 dragon **10** sea monster
means: 13 spirally bound
represents: 14 terrible powers

Leviathan
author: 12 Thomas Hobbes

Levin, Ira
author of: 13 Rosemary's Baby

Levin, Konstantin
character in: 12 Anna Karenina
author: 7 Tolstoy

Levi-Strauss, Claude
method: 13 structuralism
author of: 13 Mythologiques, The Savage Mind **16** Tristes Tropiques **22** Structural Anthropology **29** Elementary Structures of Kinship

Levitch, Joseph
real name of: 10 Jerry Lewis

levity 3 fun **5** mirth **6** joking, whimsy **8** hilarity, trifling **9** flippancy, frivolity, lightness, silliness **10** jocularity, pleasantry, triviality **11** flightiness, foolishness **16** lightheartedness

levy 3 fee, tax **4** duty, make, toll, wage **5** draft, exact, start **6** assess, call up, charge, demand, enlist, excise, impose, muster, pursue, tariff **7** carry on, collect **9** calling up, conscript, prosecute **10** assessment, imposition **12** conscription

Levy, Marion
real name of: 15 Paulette Goddard

Lew Archer, Private Detective
author: 13 Ross MacDonald

lewd 5 bawdy **6** ribald, risque, vulgar, wanton **7** goatish, immoral, lustful, obscene **8** indecent, prurient **9** lecherous, libertine, salacious **10** lascivious, libidinous, licentious, lubricious **11** Rabelaisian **12** pornographic

Lewis, C S
author of: 10 Perelandra **13** Prince Caspian, The Last Battle **14** Surprised by Joy, The Silver Chair, Til We Have Faces **17** The Horse and His Boy **18** The Magician's Nephew **19** The Screwtape Letters **20** Out of the Silent Planet **21** The Chronicles of Narnia **25** The Voyage of the Dawn Treader **29** The Lion the Witch and the Wardrobe

Lewis, Jerry
real name: 13 Joseph Levitch
partner: 10 Dean Martin
born: 8 Newark NJ
roles: 8 The Caddy **10** The Bellboy, The Sad Sack **11** Cinderfella **12** The Geisha Boy **16** Artists and Models **17** The Nutty Professor **20** The Disorderly Orderly

Lewis, Sinclair
author of: 7 Babbitt **9** Dodsworth **10** Arrowsmith, Main Street **11** Elmer Gantry **14** Cass Timberlane

lexicon 5 gloss, index **8** code book, glossary, synonymy, wordbook, wordlist **9** thesaurus, wordstock **10** dictionary, vocabulary **11** concordance, onomasticon

lex loci 11 law of a place

lex non scripta 9 common law **12** unwritten law

lex scripta 10 statute law, written law

Leyden, Lucas (Lukas) van
born: 6 Leiden, Leyden **14** The Netherlands
artwork: 12 Last Judgment **14** The Card Players, The Game of Chess **26** Mohammed and the Murdered Monk

Lhasa, Lassa
capital of: 5 Tibet

liability 4 debt, drag, duty, onus **5** debit, minus **6** arrear, burden **8** drawback, handicap, obstacle **9** hindrance **10** impediment, obligation **11** encumbrance, shortcoming **12** disadvantage, indebtedness **13** inconvenience **14** responsibility, stumbling block

liable 3 apt **4** open **5** prone **6** likely **7** exposed, ripe for, subject **8** disposed, inclined **9** obligated, sensitive **10** answerable, chargeable, vulnerable **11** accountable, responsible, susceptible

liaison 4 bond, link **5** amour, union **7** contact **8** alliance, intrigue, mediator **9** adventure, dalliance, go-between **10** connection, flirtation, love affair **11** association, cooperation, interchange **12** coordination, entanglement **13** communication

liar 6 fibber **8** perjurer **9** falsifier **10** fabricator **11** storyteller **12** prevaricator

libation 4 wine **5** drink, water **6** liquid **8** ambrosia, beverage, offering, potation **9** sacrifice

Libation Bearers, The *see* **10** Choephoroe

libel 4 slur **5** smear **6** defame, malign, revile, vilify **7** asperse, blacken, calumny, obloquy, slander **8** derogate **9** aspersion, discredit, disparage **10** calumniate, defamation **12** vilification

Libeled Lady
director: 10 Jack Conway
cast: 8 Myrna Loy **10** Jean Harlow **12** Spencer Tracy **13** William Powell **14** Walter Connolly
remade as: 9 Easy to Wed

Libera
origin: 7 Italian
goddess of: 4 wine **9** fertility, vineyards

husband: 5 Liber
corresponds to: 10 Persephone

liberal 5 ample, broad 6 casual, lavish 7 leftist, lenient 8 abundant, advanced, flexible, generous, handsome, left-wing, prodigal, reformer, tolerant, unbiased 9 bounteous, bountiful, impartial, not strict, plenteous, reformist, unbigoted, unsparing 10 fair-minded, forbearing, left-winger, munificent, not literal, openhanded, open-minded, unrigorous, unstinting 11 broad-minded, enlightened, extravagant, libertarian, magnanimous, progressive 12 freethinking, humanitarian, open to reason, unprejudiced 14 latitudinarian

Liberalia
origin: 5 Roman
event: 8 festival

liberality 10 generosity 11 benevolence, munificence 12 philanthropy 13 bountifulness 14 openhandedness

liberate 5 let go 6 let out, redeem, rescue, spring 7 absolve, deliver, manumit, release, set free 8 let loose 9 discharge, disengage, extricate, unshackle 10 emancipate 11 disencumber

liberated 5 freed, let go 7 rescued, set free 8 let loose, released 10 discharged, extricated 11 emancipated

liberation 6 escape, rescue 7 freedom, freeing, release 8 delivery 9 letting go, releasing 11 manumission 12 emancipation

Liberia *see box*

Libertas
origin: 5 Roman
personifies: 7 liberty

liberte egalite fraternite 25 liberty equality fraternity
motto of: 16 French Revolution

liberties 6 misuse 7 license 9 violation 10 distortion 11 familiarity, impropriety 13 falsification

libertine 4 goat, lewd, rake, roue 5 loose, satyr 6 lecher, wanton 7 immoral, lustful, seducer 8 unchaste 9 debauchee, dissolute, lecherous, reprobate, womanizer 10 immoralist, lascivious, libidinous, licentious, profligate, sensualist, voluptuary

liberty 5 leave, right 7 freedom, license 8 autonomy, delivery, free time, furlough, sanction, vacation 9 privilege 10 liberation, permission, shore leave 11 citizenship, manumission 12 carte blanche, dispensation, emancipation, independence 15 enfranchisement 17 self-determination

liberty equality fraternity
French: 24 liberte egalite fraternite
motto of: 16 French Revolution

Libra
symbol: 6 scales 7 balance
planet: 5 Venus
rules: 8 marriage
born: 7 October 9 September

Libreville
capital of: 13 Gabon Republic

Libya *see box, p. 568*

lice
variety: 4 bird, crab 5 human, pubic, spiny 7 chewing, sucking 8 barklice, booklice 9 guinea pig 13 mammal chewing

license 3 let 4 pass, visa 5 allow, grant, leave, right 6 enable, laxity, permit 7 anarchy, approve, certify, charter, empower, endorse, freedom, liberty, warrant 8 accredit, audacity, disorder, latitude, passport, sanction, temerity 9 admission, allowance, authorize, franchise, looseness, privilege, slackness 10 brazenness, commission, debauchery, unruliness 11 certificate, free passage, lawlessness, libertinism, presumption, safe-conduct 12 carte blanche, dispensation, recklessness

licentious 4 lewd 5 dirty, loose 6 amoral, sleazy, wanton 7 brutish, goatish, immoral, lawless, lustful, raunchy, ruttish 8 depraved, prodigal 9 abandoned, debauched, dissolute, excessive, lecherous, libertine, salacious 10 dissipated, lascivious, libidinous, lubricious, profligate, ungoverned 11 promiscuous 12 unprincipled, unrestrained, unscrupulous 13 irresponsible, unconstrained

licentiousness 7 abandon 8 lewdness 10 immorality, wantonness

licit 5 legal, legit, valid 6 kosher, lawful 9 allowable, statutory 10 acceptable, admissible, authorized, legitimate, sanctioned 11 permissible 12 authorizable, sanctionable 14 constitutional

lick 3 bit, dab, hit, jot, lap 4 beat, blow, drub, fire, hint, iota, rout, slap, snip, sock,

---

Liberia
capital/largest city: 8 Monrovia
others: 4 Sino 5 Gribo, Rebbo 6 Bopora, Gbanga, Harper, Kakata 7 Bgarnga, Kolahun, Nanakru, Tappita, Vonjama 8 Buchanan, Garraway, Marshall, Nanakaru, Sass Town 9 Grand Cess, River Cess, Roysville 10 Careysburg, Greenville, Sanoquelli 11 Robertsport 12 Sanniquellie
school: 7 Liberia 10 Cuttington 15 Our Lady of Fatima 16 Booker Washington
religious school/secret society: 4 poro 5 sande
measure: 4 kuba
monetary unit: 4 cent 6 dollar
mountain: 3 Uni 4 Bong, Putu 5 Niete, Nimba 9 Bomi Hills
highest point: 6 Wutivi
river: 4 Cess, Lofa, Mano 5 Duobe, Lotta, Manna, Morro, Sinoe 6 Cestos, Douobe 7 Cavalla, Cavally 8 San Pedro 9 Saint John, Saint Paul, Sehnkwehn
sea: 8 Atlantic
physical feature:
wind: 9 harmattan
people: 2 Gi 3 Gio, Kra, Kru, Kwa, Vai, Vei 4 Gola, Kroo, Krou, Loma, Mano, Toma 5 Bassa, Gibbi, Gissi, Grebo 6 Gbande, Kpelle, Kpuesi, Krooby, Kruman 7 Krooboy, Krooman 8 Mandingo 15 Americo-Liberian
leader: 3 Doe 6 Tubman 7 Roberts, Tolbert
language: 3 Kru, Kwa 5 Mande 7 English
religion: 5 Islam 7 animism 10 Protestant 12 Christianity
feature:
clothing: 5 lappa
rubber plantation: 9 Firestone

Libya
capital/largest city: **7** Tripoli
summer capital: **8** Benghazi
others: **4** Homs, Marj, Surt **5** Beida, Darna, Derna, Khums, Kufra, Sebha, Sidri, Zawia **6** Garian, Murzuq, Tobruk **7** Es Sidar, Gharyan, Misrata **8** Ajdabiya, Misurata, Rashanuf **12** Marsa el Brega
school: **7** Alfateh **9** Garyounis
division: **6** Fezzan **9** Cyrenaica **12** Tripolitania
measure: **3** dra, pik, saa **4** kele **5** bozze, donum, jabia, teman, uckia **6** barile, gorraf, misura **7** mattaro, termino **8** kharouba
weight: **4** kele **6** gorraf **8** kharouba
monetary unit: **5** dinar
mountain: **5** Green **13** Jabal al Akhdar, Tibesti Massif
highest point: **9** Bette Peak
sea: **13** Mediterranean
physical feature:
desert: **6** Libyan, Sahara **9** Calanscio
gulf: **5** Bomba, Sidra, Sirte
oasis: **4** Ghat **5** Kufra, Sebha **7** Tazerbo **8** Al-Kufrah, Ghudamis
plain: **6** al Marj, Gefara **7** Jaffara
plateau: **12** Gebel Nefuisa, Jabal Nafusah
wind: **6** ghibli
people: **4** Arab, Tebu **6** Berber, Tuareg **7** Gaetuli **8** Getulans, Harratin
leader: **6** Battus **7** Jalloud, Qadhafi **8** Aegyptus **9** al-Qaddafi, Karamanli **13** Idris al-Senusi
religious leader: **8** al-Senusi
ruler: **4** Rome **5** Italy **6** Greece **9** Phoenicia **12** Ottoman Turks
language: **6** Arabic, Berber **7** English, Italian
alphabet: **8** tifinagh
religion: **5** Islam
feature: **14** Tropic of Cancer
clothing: **5** lanaf **9** barracano
festival: **3** Mez **7** Fantasi
Islamic law: **6** sharia
leader: **6** sheikh
ruins: **11** Leptis Magna
food:
dish: **5** bazin **8** couscous
red pepper: **6** filfil

suck, whip **5** crack, punch, sally, shred, spank, speck, taste, touch, trace **6** defeat, ignite, kindle, master, sample, stroke, subdue, thrash, tongue, wallop **7** clobber, conquer, modicum, smidgen, trounce **8** outmatch, overcome, particle, vanquish **9** overpower, overthrow, scintilla, subjugate **10** smattering **12** denunciation

Licymnius
father: **9** Electryon
mother: **5** Midea
wife: **8** Perimede
son: **5** Melas **6** Oeonus **7** Argeius
nephew: **8** Hercules

lid **3** cap, top **4** cork, curb, plug **5** cover, limit **7** ceiling, maximum, stopper, stopple **9** operculum, restraint

lie **3** fib **4** loll, rest, stay **5** abide, exist, range, story **6** belong, deceit, extend, inhere, lounge, obtain, remain, repose, sprawl **7** falsify, fiction, perjury, recline, romance, untruth **8** misstate, tall tale **9** deception, embellish, embroider, fabricate, falsehood, invention **10** equivocate **11** fabrication, prevaricate **12** equivocation **13** falsification, prevarication **17** misrepresentation

Liechtenstein ***see box***

lie down **6** retire **7** go to bed, recline **8** take a nap **11** take a snooze **15** catch forty winks

life **4** path, soul, zest **5** being, human, plant, story, verve, vigor **6** animal, career, course, energy, memoir, person, spirit **8** creature, duration, life span, lifetime, lifework, organism, survival, vitality, vivacity **9** animation, biography, existence, life story, longevity **11** subsistence **13** autobiography
French: **3** vie

Life at the Dakota
author: **17** Stephen Birmingham

Life Before Man
author: **14** Margaret Atwood

Lifeboat
director: **15** Alfred Hitchcock
cast: **10** John Hodiak **12** Mary Anderson **13** William Bendix **16** Tallulah Bankhead

life-giving **5** vital **9** vivifying **12** invigorating

lifeless **4** dead, dull, flat, late **5** inert, stiff, vapid **6** boring, hollow, static, torpid, wooden **7** defunct **8** deceased, departed, inactive, lifeless, sluggish **9** colorless, inanimate **10** lackluster, spiritless

Liechtenstein
capital/largest city: **5** Vaduz
others: **4** Haag **6** Balzer, Eschen, Iradug, Schaan **7** Balzers, Bendern, Nendeln, Planken, Triesen **12** Schellenberg
division:
ancient province: **6** Rhaeti **7** Rhaetia
government:
legislature: **7** Landtag
monetary unit: **6** rappen **7** franken
mountain: **4** Alps **8** Naafkopf, Rhatikon **12** Three Sisters
highest point: **15** Vorder-Grauspitz
river: **5** Rhine
physical feature:
valley: **6** Lavena, Samina
people: **8** Alemanni
leader: **7** Florian **15** Francis Joseph II **16** von Liechtenstein
language: **6** German **10** Alemannish
religion: **13** Roman Catholic
place:
castle: **9** Gutemburg, Gutenberg
feature:
legendary dwarf: **10** wildmannli
wine: **7** Vaduzer

lifelessness **5** death **7** inertia **8** dullness, limpness, vapidity **9** blandness **10** flaccidity, inactivity **13** colorlessness

Life of Dante
author: **17** Giovanni Boccaccio

Life of Emile Zola
director: **15** William Dieterle
cast: **8** Paul Muni **11** Donald Crisp **12** Gloria Holden **15** Gale Sondergaard **17** Joseph Schildkraut (Dreyfus)
Oscar for: **7** picture

Life of Man, The
author: **14** Leonid Andreyev

Life of Riley, The
character: **4** Babs **6** Dangle, Junior **8** Peg Riley **9** Jim Gillis **10** Cunningham, Digby (Digger) O'Dell **11** Waldo Binney **13** Chester A Riley **14** Honeybee Gillis
cast: **9** John Brown, Lanny Rees, Sid Tomack **10** Tom D'Andrea **12** Emory Parnell, Wesley Morgan **13** Gloria Winters, Jackie Gleason, Lugene Sanders, Robert Sweeney, William Bendix **14** Gloria Blondell, Rosemary DeCamp **16** Douglas Dumbrille, Marjorie Reynolds, Sterling Holloway

Life of Samuel Johnson, The
author: **12** James Boswell

life of the party **7** show-off **9** extrovert **13** exhibitionist **17** hail-fellow-well-met

Life on the Mississippi
author: **9** Mark Twain

life span **4** life **8** lifetime **14** life expectancy

Life Studies
author: **12** Robert Lowell

Life With Father
author: **13** Clarence Day Jr
director: **13** Michael Curtiz
cast: **9** ZaSu Pitts **10** Irene Dunne **11** Edmund Gwenn **13** William Powell **15** Elizabeth Taylor
setting: **11** New York City

lifework **6** career **7** calling **8** vocation **10** livelihood, occupation, profession

lift **4** high, palm, pick, rear, rise, soar, take **5** boost, climb, exalt, filch, heave, hoist, pinch, raise, steal, swipe **6** ascend, ascent, banish, cancel, pilfer, pirate, pocket, remove, revoke, snatch, thieve, uplift, vanish **7** elation, elevate, purloin, raise up, raising, rescind, scatter, upraise **8** disperse **9** disappear, dissipate, float away **10** ascendance, move upward, plagiarize, put an end to **11** appropriate, countermand, inspiration, make off with, reassurance **12** give a boost to, shot in the arm **13** encouragement, enheartenment

ligament
holds: **5** bones

Ligeia
author: **13** Edgar Allan Poe
character: **19** Lady Rowena Trevanion

Ligeti, Gyorgy
composer of: **7** Lontano **11** Atmospheres **13** Ramifications

light ***see box***

light-colored **4** pale **5** beige, blond **6** blonde, flaxen, pastel **7** neutral, whitish **9** yellowish

light-complexioned **4** fair, pale **12** white-skinned

lighten **4** buoy, ease, lift **5** abate, allay, blaze, elate, flare, flash, gleam, shine **6** buoy up, lessen, reduce, revive, temper, unload, uplift **7** assuage, enliven, gladden, inspire, light up, relieve **8** brighten, mitigate, moderate, unburden **9** alleviate, coruscate, disburden, irradiate **10** illuminate, make bright **11** become light, disencumber, make lighter, scintillate

light-filled **5** sunny **6** bright **7** well-lit **11** illuminated

lighthearted **3** gay **4** airy, glad **5** jolly, merry, sunny **6** blithe, cheery, joyful, joyous, lively **7** buoyant, cheered, chipper **8** carefree, cheerful, sanguine **9** sprightly **10** insouciant, untroubled **11** free and easy **12** effervescent

lightheartedness **3** joy **4** glee **5** mirth **8** gladness **9** happiness, merriment **10** blitheness, exuberance, joyfulness, joyousness **11** high spirits

Light in August
author: **15** William Faulkner
character: **8** Doc Hines, Joe Brown **9** Lena Grove, McEachern **10** Byron Bunch **12** Joanna Burden, Joe Christmas

lightless **4** dark **5** black, murky **7** stygian **9** unlighted **13** unilluminated

lightly **6** airily, easily, gently, nimbly, softly, thinly, weakly **7** blandly, faintly, quickly, readily, swiftly, timidly **8** blithely, facilely, gingerly, meagerly, slightly, sparsely **9** buoyantly, sparingly **10** carelessly, flippantly, hesitantly, moderately **11** frivolously, slightingly **13** indifferently, thoughtlessly, unconcernedly, without effort **14** without concern

light **3** gay **4** airy, beam, easy, fair, fall, find, fire, glow, lamp, land, pale, puny, side, soft, stop **5** aglow, angle, blaze, blond, faint, flame, funny, glare, guide, happy, jolly, match, model, perch, petty, put on, roost, shine, slant, small, spare, spark, sunny, torch **6** alight, aspect, beacon, blithe, bright, candle, chance, frugal, gentle, get off, ignite, jaunty, kindle, luster, meager, paltry, scanty, settle, simple, slight, turn on **7** amusing, buoyant, chipper, clarify, come off, descend, get down, gleeful, insight, lantern, lighten, lighter, lucifer, not dark, not rich, paragon, radiant, radiate, sparkle, sunbeam, trivial **8** approach, attitude, bleached, blondish, brighten, carefree, cheerful, come upon, discover, dismount, ethereal, exemplar, gossamer, graceful, illumine, jubilant, luminous, meet with, moderate, moonbeam, not heavy, paradigm, radiance, sportive, step down, switch on, trifling, untaxing **9** brilliant, catch fire, direction, encounter, frivolous, irradiate, light-hued, set fire to, sprightly, stumble on, sylphlike, viewpoint **10** abstemious, brightness, brilliance, burdenless, come across, come to rest, effortless, effulgence, floodlight, happen upon, illuminate, light-toned, luminosity, manageable, restricted, set burning, weightless **11** conflagrate, elucidation, illuminated, information, make radiant, superficial, undemanding, underweight **15** inconsequential
god of: **6** Apollo **7** Mithras, Phoebus, Pythius **8** Heimdall **9** Musagetes
Latin: **3** lux
measurement: **7** candela **11** candlepower

lightness **8** airiness, radiance **10** brightness, fluffiness, luminosity **12** illumination, luminousness

lightning rod
invented by: **8** Franklin

light of day **8** daylight, sunlight, sunshine

light sleep **3** nap **4** doze **6** catnap, snooze **10** forty winks

light wind **4** waft **6** breeze, zephyr **10** gentle wind **11** breath of air

Lightwood, Mortimer
character in: **15** Our Mutual Friend
author: **7** Dickens

lignum vitae **10** wood of life
tree species: **8** Guaiacum

Ligure **8** gemstone

likable, likeable **4** nice **6** genial **7** amiable, lovable, winsome **8** charming, engaging, loveable, pleasant, pleasing **9** agreeable, appealing, simpatico **10** attractive **11** complaisant, sympathetic

like **4** akin, care, dote, same, wish **5** enjoy, equal, fancy, favor, savor **6** admire, allied, choose, esteem, relish **7** approve, cognate, endorse, matched, related, similar, support, uniform **8** be fond of, parallel, selfsame, think fit **9** analogous, congruent, have a mind, identical **10** comparable, equivalent, homologous, resembling **11** be partial to, much the same **12** feel inclined, have a crush on, take a shine to **13** corresponding, find agreeable **14** take pleasure in

Like a Bulwark
author: **13** Marianne Moore

likelihood **8** prospect **10** good chance **11** possibility, probability **12** potentiality

likely **3** apt, fit **4** able **6** liable, proper **8** credible, destined, inclined, probable, probably, rational, reliable, suitable **9** befitting, plausible, promising, qualified **10** believable, presumably, reasonable **11** appropriate, verisimilar **16** in all probability

like-mindedness **6** accord **7** concord, harmony, rapport **8** affinity **9** agreement **12** congeniality **13** compatibility

likeness **5** image, model, study **6** effigy **7** analogy, picture, replica **8** affinity, portrait **9** agreement, depiction, facsimile, portrayal, rendition, semblance **10** similarity, similitude **11** delineation, resemblance **14** correspondence, representation

likes **9** favorites **10** prejudices **11** preferences **12** inclinations, partialities

likewise **3** and, eke, too **4** also **5** ditto **6** as well **7** besides, equally, the same **8** moreover **9** similarity **10** in addition

liking **4** bent **5** fancy, taste **7** leaning **8** affinity, appetite, fondness, penchant, soft spot, weakness **9** affection **10** partiality, preference, proclivity, propensity **11** inclination **12** predilection

Li'l Abner
creator: **6** Al Capp
character: **5** Pappy **7** Wolf Gal **10** Joe Btfsplk, Mammy Yokum, Marryin' Sam **11** Adam Lazonga, Hairless Joe **12** Tobacco Rhoda **13** Joanie Phoanie **14** Daisy Mae Scragg, Evil-Eye Fleegle, Stupefyin' Jones **15** Fearless Fosdick, Henry Cabbage Cod, Lonesome Polecat, Moonbeam McSwine **16** General Bullmoose, Sir Cecil Cesspool **17** Sen Jack S Phogbound **18** J Roaringham Fatback **21** Appassionata von Climax
brewery: **23** Big Barnsmell's Skonk Works
event: **15** Sadie Hawkins Day
juice: **16** Kickapoo Joy Juice
kingdom: **14** Lower Slobbovia
mountain: **11** Onnecessary
people: **7** Schmoos **8** Kingmies
place: **8** Dogpatch
railroad: **11** West Po'k Chop
ruler: **14** King Nogoodnick

lilac **7** Syringa
varieties: **4** late, vine, wild **6** common, Indian, summer **7** Chinese, cut-leaf, Persian **9** Himalayan, Hungarian **12** Japanese tree **16** Catalina mountain

Lili
director: **14** Charles Walters
cast: **9** Mel Ferrer **11** Leslie Caron, Zsa Zsa Gabor **16** Jean-Pierre Aumont

Lilies of the Field
director: **11** Ralph Nelson
cast: **8** Lisa Mann **10** Lilia Skala **13** Sidney Poitier
Oscar for: **5** actor (Poitier)

Liliom
author: **12** Ferenc Molnar

lillet
type: **8** aperitif
origin: **6** France
flavor: **6** orange
color: **3** red **5** white

Lilliput
fictional land in: **16** Gulliver's Travels
author: **5** Swift

lilliputian **3** wee **4** tiny **5** dwarf, short, small, teeny, weeny **6** little, midget, minute, petite **9** miniature **10** diminutive, teeny-weeny **11** pocket-sized

Lilongwe
capital of: **6** Malawi

lily ***see box***

lily-livered **6** afraid, craven, scared, yellow **7** chicken, fearful, gutless **8** cowardly **9** dastardly **12** fainthearted **13** pusillanimous, yellow-bellied **14** chicken-hearted, chicken-livered **22** showing the white feather

lily-white **4** good, pure **6** biased, decent, proper, racist **7** bigoted, upright **8** all-white, innocent, virtuous **9** blameless, exclusive, exemplary, faultless, guiltless, honorable, righteous **10** impeccable, inculpable, prejudiced, segregated, upstanding **11** uncorrupted **12** unintegrated **13** unimpeachable **14** discriminatory, irreproachable

Lima
capital of: **4** Peru
foothills of: **5** Andes
founder: **7** Pizarro
nickname: **11** city of kings
ocean: **7** Pacific
port: **6** Callao
river: **5** Rimac
square: **12** Plaza de Armas

limb **3** arm, gam, leg, pin **4** part, spur, twig, wing **5** bough, shoot, sprig **6** branch, member **9** appendage, extension, outgrowth **10** projection, prosthesis

limber **5** agile, lithe, relax **6** loosen, pliant, supple **7** bending, elastic, lissome, pliable **8** flexible **9** lithesome, malleable

lime **18** Citrus aurantifolia
varieties: **3** key **4** wild **7** Mexican, Persian, Rangpur, Spanish **8** Mandarin **10** West Indian **14** Australian wild **15** Australian round **16** Australian desert, Australian finger

lily 6 Lilium
varieties: 3 Alp, cow, day, pig **4** Arum, bell, boat, corn, fawn, fire, flax, herb, palm, pine, pond, rain, roan, rock, sand, Sego, star, toad, wood **5** adobe, Aztec, blood, bugle, calla, coast, cobra, crane, Cuban, fairy, globe, glory, Gray's, Ifafa, lemon, magic, natal, queen, regal, royal, showy, snake, spear, swamp, sword, tiger, torch, trout, water, wheel **6** Alpine, Amazon, Canada, Crinum, desert, Easter, eureka, ginger, hidden, Kaffir, Marhan, meadow, one-day, orange, Oregon, shasta, Sierra, spider, sunset, tartar, turban, voodoo, yellow, Zephyr **7** African, Bermuda, chamise, checker, garland, leopard, madonna, Nankeen, panther, redwood, thimble, toad-cup, triplet, trumpet, western **8** Atamasco, Barbados, bluebead, Carolina, climbing, Columbia, flamingo, gloriosa, Guernsey, Humboldt, Jacobean, Japanese, long's red, Mariposa, Martagon, Michigan, mountain, paradise, Peruvian, plantain, Siberian, Solomon's, St Bruno's, St James's, turk's cap **9** alligator, avalanche, butterfly, caucasian, celestial, chaparral, checkered, Eucharist, Kamchatka, naked-lady, orange-cup, pineapple, pinewoods, pot-of-gold, red ginger, red spider, St Joseph's **10** belladonna, blackberry, blue funnel, fairy water, giant water, globe spear, gold-banded, Josephine's, orange-bell, pink Easter, pygmy water, royal water, small tiger, St Bernard's, Washington, white water, wild yellow, yellow-bell, yellow pond **11** African corn, Amazon water, blue African, candlestick, dwarf ginger, golden-rayed, milk-and-wine, Palmer spear, Scarborough, southern red, yellow water **12** African blood, Chinese white, golden spider, prickly water, resurrection, speckled wood, white trumpet **13** Bermuda Easter, cape blue water, Chinese sacred, Egyptian water, fragrant water, India red water, lavender globe, magnolia water, minor Turk's-cap, perfumed fairy, pink porcelain, scarlet ginger, showy Japanese, tuberous water, wild orange-red **14** Chinese-lantern, lesser Turk's cap, little Turk's-cap, Santa Cruz water, yellow Turk's-cap **15** Australian water, backhouse hybrid, golden hurricane, scarlet Turk's-cap **16** American Turk's cap, Bellingham hybrid, Cape Cod pink water, fragrant plantain, Japanese Turk's-cap, western orange-cup **17** midsummer plantain **18** European white water, seersucker plantain **20** narrow-leaved plantain

Limenia
epithet of: 9 Aphrodite
means: 11 of the harbor

limit 3 end **4** curb **8** boundary, end point, restrain, ultimate **13** breaking point

limitation 4 curb **5** quota **8** boundary, decrease **9** lessening, reduction, restraint **10** shortening **11** abridgement, restriction, shortcoming **13** qualification, specification

limited 5 fixed **6** finite, narrow **7** bounded, cramped, defined, minimal, special **8** confined **9** delimited, specified **10** controlled, restrained, restricted **13** circumscribed

limitless 7 endless, eternal, unbound **8** infinite, unending **9** boundless, unlimited **11** measureless **12** immeasurable

limits 3 rim, top **4** curb, edge **5** bound, check, quota **6** border, define, fringe, margin, narrow **7** ceiling, confine, delimit, inhibit, maximum, qualify **8** confines, frontier, restrain, restrict **9** perimeter, periphery, prescribe, restraint **10** boundaries **11** limitations **12** restrictions

limn 4 draw **6** sketch **7** picture **9** delineate

Limnaea
epithet of: 7 Artemis
means: 9 of the lake

Limnoria
member of: 7 Nereids

Limon
father: 8 Tegeates
mother: 5 Maera
brother: 8 Scephrus
killed: 8 Scephrus

limp 3 lax **4** gimp, halt, soft, weak **5** crawl, loose, skulk, slack **6** droopy, falter, flabby, floppy, hobble **7** flaccid **8** drooping, lameness, yielding **9** dead tired, enervated, exhausted

limpid 4 pure **5** clear, lucid **8** clear-cut, pellucid, vitreous **11** crystalline, perspicuous, translucent, transparent, unambiguous **15** straightforward

Lincoln, Abraham ***see box, p. 572***

Lind, James
field: 8 medicine
nationality: 8 Scottish
eliminated: 6 scurvy

Lindbergh, Anne Morrow
author of: 14 Gift from the Sea **15** Bring Me a Unicorn **16** North to the Orient **19** War Within and Without

linden 5 Tilia
varieties: 6 Indoor **7** Crimean **8** American, Japanese **9** Mongolian **10** Manchurian **11** Large-leaved **13** Pendent silver **19** Small-leaved European

lindy 5 dance **8** lindy hop **9** jitterbug

line, lines 4 card, cord, dash, draw, file, idea, mark, note, part, race, rank, rope, rule, tier, word **5** align, array, breed, cable, craft, front, house, model, queue, range, score, slash, stock, trade **6** belief, border, column, crease, family, furrow, letter, method, metier, policy, report, scheme, series, stance, strain, strand, streak, stripe, system, thread **7** calling, circuit, conduit, contour, cordage, example, lineage, marshal, outline, pattern, purpose, pursuit, queue up, routine, towline, wrinkle **8** ancestry, business, dialogue, doctrine, fishline, ideology, inscribe, position, postcard, trenches, vanguard, vocation **9** conductor, crow's foot, direction, frontline, genealogy, intention, principle **10** barricades, convention, firing line, livelihood, long stroke, occupation, procession, profession, underscore **11** demarcation

lineage 4 line **5** blood, stock **7** descent **8** ancestry, heredity, pedigree **9** genealogy, parentage **10** derivation, extraction

linen
fabric: 6 canvas, damask **7** butcher, cambric **8** birdseye **9** huckaback
plant: 4 flax

Lincoln, Abraham
nickname: **9** Honest Abe **20** Illinois Rail Splitter
presidential rank: **9** sixteenth
party: **4** Whig **10** Republican
state represented: **2** IL
defeated: **4** (John) Bell **7** (John Charles) Fremont, (Stephen Arnold) Douglas **9** (George Brinton) McClellan **12** (John Cabell) Breckinridge
vice president: **6** (Hannibal) Hamlin **7** (Andrew) Johnson
cabinet:
state: **6** (William Henry) Seward
treasury: **5** (Salmon Portland) Chase **9** (Hugh) McCulloch, (William Pitt) Fessenden
war: **7** (Edwin McMasters) Stanton, (Simon) Cameron
attorney general: **5** (Edward) Bates, (James) Speed
navy: **6** (Gideon) Welles
postmaster general: **5** (Montgomery) Blair **8** (William) Dennison
interior: **5** (Caleb Blood) Smith, (John Palmer) Usher
born: **2** KY **8** log cabin **11** Larue County **17** Sinking Spring farm
died: **12** Washington DC, Fords Theater
died by: **13** assassination
assassinated by: **15** John Wilkes Booth
buried: **13** Springfield IL
education:
educated by: **4** self
studied: **3** law
interests: **7** theater
received patent for: **25** adjustable buoyant chambers (for lifting boats)
political career: **16** state legislature **24** US House of Representatives
civilian career: **6** lawyer **8** surveyor **10** postmaster
military service:
War: **9** Black Hawk
US Army: **7** private
captain of company of: **10** volunteers
notable events of lifetime/term: **8** Civil War **24** Emancipation Proclamation
Act: **9** Homestead, Income Tax, Judiciary **12** Conscription
debates: **14** Lincoln-Douglas
speech: **17** Gettysburg Address
father: **6** Thomas
mother: **5** Nancy (Hanks)
stepmother: **5** Sarah (Bush Johnston)
siblings: **5** Sarah **6** Thomas
stepbrother: **4** John
stepsister: **7** Matilda **9** Elizabeth
wife: **4** Mary (Ann Todd)
children: **6** Thomas **10** Robert Todd **11** Edward Baker **14** William Wallace

finest from: **7** Belgium, Ireland
processing term: **6** shives, sliver **7** carding, hackled, retting **8** beetling, breaking, rippling, spinning **9** scutching

line of march **4** path **5** route, track **11** parade route

line of reasoning **4** case **7** premise **8** argument **10** hypothesis

line up **4** book **5** align **6** engage, even up **7** arrange, procure, program, queue up **8** schedule **9** form a line, put in a row **10** arrange for

line-up **5** slate **6** roster **8** schedule

linger **3** lag **4** idle, last, stay, wait **5** dally, delay, tarry, trail **6** dawdle, hang on, loiter, remain **7** persist, survive **9** die slowly **10** dillydally, hang around

lingering **4** slow **7** abiding, chronic, delayed, lagging, lasting, staying, waiting **8** dawdling, delaying, dragging, drawn out, dwelling, enduring, hovering, tarrying **9** loitering, remaining **10** protracted, sauntering **15** procrastinating

lingo **4** cant, talk **5** argot, idiom, slang **6** jargon, patois, tongue **7** dialect **8** language, parlance **10** vernacular

linguist **8** polyglot **10** grammarian, translator **11** etymologist, interpreter, philologist, phonetician, phonologist, semanticist **12** morphologist **13** lexicographer

liniment **4** balm **5** salve **7** unguent **8** ointment **9** emollient

link **3** tie **4** bind, bond, fuse, loop, ring **5** group, joint, tie in, unite **6** couple, relate, splice **7** bracket, combine, conjoin, connect, involve, liaison **8** junction, relation **9** associate, implicate **10** connection, connective **11** association **12** interconnect, relationship

linkage **3** tie **4** bond **6** hookup **10** connection **11** affiliation, association, correlation

link up **4** dock, join **6** couple, hook up **7** connect **9** affiliate **14** fasten together

Linnaeus, Carolus
field: **6** botany
nationality: **7** Swedish
developed: **8** taxonomy **18** nomenclature system

linotype
invented by: **12** Mergenthaler

Linton, Edgar
character in: **16** Wuthering Heights
author: **6** Bronte

Linus
vocation: **4** poet **8** musician
father: **6** Apollo
mother: **8** Psamathe
inventor of: **6** melody, rhythm
identified with: **5** crops **9** withering **10** harvesting
student: **8** Hercules
killed by: **8** Hercules

Liod
also: **4** Ljod **5** Hliod
origin: **12** Scandinavian
mentioned in: **8** Volsunga
husband: **7** Volsung
daughter: **5** Signy
son: **7** Sigmund

lion **3** cat **6** cougar **7** wildcat **9** celebrity **12** man of the hour **15** king of the jungle
group of: **5** pride
constellation of: **3** Leo

lionhearted **4** bold **5** brave

6 heroic **7** valiant **8** fearless, intrepid, stalwart, unafraid, valorous **9** audacious, dauntless **10** courageous **11** indomitable **12** stouthearted

Lion in Winter, The
director: **13** Anthony Harvey
cast: **10** Jane Merrow **11** Peter O'Toole (Henry II) **13** Timothy Dalton **14** Anthony Hopkins **16** Katharine Hepburn (Eleanor of Aquitaine)
Oscar for: **7** actress (Hepburn)

lionize **5** deify, exalt **6** admire, praise, revere **7** acclaim, adulate, ennoble, flatter, glorify **8** enshrine, eulogize **9** celebrate, glamorize **10** aggrandize **11** immortalize

lion's share **4** bulk, most **8** majority **9** major part **11** greater part **13** preponderance

lip **3** lap, rim **4** brim, edge, kiss, lick, wash **5** apron, mouth, spout, utter **6** labial, labium, margin **8** backtalk, labellum **9** insincere **10** embouchure, mouthpiece **11** superficial

Lipchitz, Jacques
real name: **17** Chaim Yakob Lipchiz
born: **9** Lithuania **11** Druskieniki **12** Druskininkai
artwork: **4** Head **6** Bather, Figure **7** Harpist **9** Sacrifice **10** Prometheus **11** Benediction, Joie de Vivre **12** Peace on Earth **14** Man with a Guitar **15** Acrobats on a Ball, Man with Mandolin, Song of the Vowels **17** Notre Dame de Liesse, Sailor with a Guitar **19** Pierrot with Clarinet, Return of the Prodigal **24** Virgin of the Inverted Heart

Lipmann, Fritz Albert
field: **12** biochemistry
discovered: **9** Coenzyme A
awarded: **10** Nobel Prize

Lippi, Filippino
born: **5** Italy, Prato
father: **15** Fra Filippo Lippi
artwork: **20** The Vision of St Bernard **24** The Life of St Thomas Aquinas **26** The Lives of Sts Philip and John

Lippi, Fra Filippo
born: **5** Italy **8** Florence
son: **9** Filippino
artwork: **15** Madonna and Child, The Feast of Herod **19** The Tarquinia Madonna **21** Coronation of the Virgin **25** The Madonna Adoring Her Child

liqueur **3** ale **4** beer, grog **5** booze, drink, hooch **7** alcohol, potable, spirits **8** beverage, potation **9** aqua vitae, drinkable, inebriant, moonshine **10** intoxicant
almond: **8** amaretto
anise: **8** absinthe
apple: **8** calvados
apricot: **10** abricotine
caraway: **6** kummel **7** aquavit
chocolate: **12** creme de cacao
citrus: **10** goldwasser, liquor d'or
coffee: **6** Kahlua
grape: **6** Metaxa
herb: **6** pernod **7** raspail **10** vielle cure **11** fiori alpini
honey: **8** Drambuie
medicinal: **11** Benedictine
mint: **13** creme de menthe
orange: **6** strega **7** curacao **9** cointreau **12** Grand Marnier
raspberry: **9** framboise

liquid **5** drink, fluid **6** melted, molten, thawed **7** potable **8** beverage, solution

liquidate **3** hit, pay **4** kill **5** clear, erase, waste **6** cancel, murder, pay off, rub out, settle, wind up **7** abolish, break up, destroy, wipe out **8** close out, conclude, demolish **9** discharge, dispose of, eradicate, put to rest, terminate **10** account for, do away with **11** assassinate

liquor **3** gin, rum, rye **5** booze, broth, hooch, juice, sauce, vodka **6** brandy, liquid, Scotch **7** bourbon, extract, spirits, whiskey **9** drippings **10** inebriants **11** intoxicants
measure: **4** pint, pony, shot **5** fifth, quart **6** jigger, magnum

Lir *see* **3** Ler

Lisbon
capital of: **8** Portugal
landmark:
castle: **11** Saint George
monastery: **9** Jeronimos
square: **10** Black Horse
tower: **5** Belem
Moorish name: **7** Lixbuna
ocean: **8** Atlantic
Portuguese: **6** Lisboa
river: **5** Tagus
Roman name: **14** Felicitas Julia
rulers: **5** Moors **6** French, Romans **7** British, Germans, Spanish **11** Phoenicians

lissome **5** agile, lithe, quick **6** limber, lively, nimble, pliant, supple **7** slender **8** flexible, graceful **9** lithesome, sprightly **11** light-footed

list **3** tip **4** bend, heel, lean, roll, tilt **5** index, slant, slate, slope, table **6** careen, muster, record, roster **7** catalog, incline, leaning **8** register, schedule, tabulate **9** catalogue, inventory

listen **4** hark, hear, heed, list **6** attend **7** give ear, hearken **8** give heed, listen in, overhear **9** be all ears, bend an ear, eavesdrop **10** take notice **12** pay attention

listener **3** ear **6** hearer **7** auditor **10** overhearer **12** eavesdropper

Lister, Joseph
field: **7** surgeon **8** medicine
nationality: **7** British
pioneer of: **17** antiseptic surgery

listless **4** down, dull, lazy **6** dreamy, drowsy, leaden, mopish, torpid **7** languid **8** inactive, indolent, lifeless, sluggish **9** apathetic, enervated, lethargic, soporific **10** phlegmatic, spiritless **11** indifferent, unconcerned **12** uninterested **13** lackadaisical

Liston, Charles
nickname: **5** Sonny
sport: **6** boxing
class: **11** heavyweight

Liszt, Franz (Ferencz)
born: **7** Hungary, Raiding
composer of: **5** Dante (symphony), Faust (symphony) **8** Christus **9** Psalm XIII **10** Nuages gris **13** Psalm Thirteen **17** Years of Pilgrimage **18** Annees de Pelerinage **19** Hungarian Rhapsodies **22** The Legend of St Elizabeth

Litae
daughters of: **4** Zeus
personify: **6** prayer

litany **4** list **7** account, catalog, recital **9** catalogue, narration, rendition **10** recitation, repetition **11** description, enumeration

lit de justice **32** formal sessions of French parliament
literally: **12** bed of justice

literacy **7** culture **8** learning **9** erudition **11** edification, eruditeness, learnedness, scholarship **12** intelligence **13** enlightenment

literal **4** real, true **5** exact **6** actual, direct, honest, strict **7** correct, factual, precise, prosaic **8** accurate, faithful, reliable, truthful, verbatim **9** authentic **10** ad litteram, dependable, meticulous, scrupulous, undisputed

11 trustworthy, undeviating, word-for-word 12 matter-of-fact 13 authoritative, conscientious, unimaginative, unimpeachable

literary 6 poetic 7 bookish, of books 8 artistic, lettered, literate 12 intellectual

literate 7 learned 8 cultured, educated, lettered, literary, schooled, well-read 12 well-informed 13 knowledgeable

literati 9 highbrows 12 connoisseurs 13 intellectuals 14 intelligentsia

literature 4 lore 5 books, works 6 papers, theses 7 letters 8 classics, writings 9 treatises 11 scholarship 12 publications 13 belles lettres, dissertations

lithe 5 agile 6 limber, nimble, pliant, supple 7 lissome, pliable 8 bendable, flexible, graceful

Lithgow, John
roles: 9 Footloose 17 Terms of Endearment 21 Harry and the Hendersons 23 The World According to Garp

lithium
chemical symbol: 2 Li

Lithuania ***see box***

litigation 4 suit 7 contest, dispute, lawsuit 10 contention, day in court 11 controversy, disputation, legal action, prosecution

litter 3 bed 4 heap, junk, lair, mess, nest, pile 5 issue, strew, trash, young 6 debris, jumble, pallet, refuse 7 bedding, clutter, kittens, progeny, puppies, rubbish, scatter 8 leavings 9 offspring, stretcher

little 3 bit, dot, jot, wee 4 dash, drop, hint, iota, mean, mild, tiny, whit 5 brief, crumb, elfin, faint, fleet, hasty, never, petty, pinch, pygmy, quick, scant, short, small, speck, trace 6 bantam, hardly, meager, minute, narrow, paltry, petite, rarely, seldom, skimpy, slight, trifle 7 minimum, modicum, not much, passing, stunted, trivial 8 dwarfish, fragment, inferior, mediocre, not at all, not often, particle, piddling, pittance, scarcely, slightly, somewhat, trifling, unworthy 9 by no means, deficient, hardly any, itsy-bitsy, itty-bitty, miniature, momentary, pint-sized, third-rate, worthless 10 diminutive, inflexible, negligible, short-lived, suggestion, undersized 11 commonplace, Lilliputian, microscopic, of no account, opinionated, pocket-sized, scarcely any, small amount, unimportant 12 insufficient, run-of-the-mill, short-sighted 13 infinitesimal, insignificant, next to nothing

Little Annie Rooney
creator: 14 Darrell McClure

Little Artha
nickname of: 11 Jack Johnson

Little Big Man
author: 12 Thomas Berger
director: 10 Arthur Penn
cast: 11 Faye Dunaway 12 Martin Balsam 13 Dustin Hoffman (Jack Crabb) 14 Chief Dan George 15 Richard Mulligan

Lithuania
other name: 5 Litva 7 Lietuva 33 Lithuanian Soviet Socialist Republic
capital/largest city: 5 Vilna 6 Kaunas 7 Vilnius
others: 4 Balt, Lett 5 Aesti, Kouno, Memel 6 Kovnac 7 Jelgava, Palanga, Telsiai 8 Ignalina, Kapsukas, Klaipeda, Siauliai 9 Panevezys 10 Elektrenai
government: 21 republic of Soviet Union
monetary unit: 3 lit 5 marka 6 centas 7 ostmark, skatiku 8 auksinas
lake: 5 Dysna
mountain: 15 Samogitian Hills
highest point: 9 Juozapine
river: 5 Neman, Neris, Rusne 6 Dubysa, Nieman, Viliya 7 Nemunas, Nevezis, Nevezys 8 Pregolya
sea: 6 Baltic
physical feature:
lagoon: 8 Courland, Kuronian
people: 4 Balt, Lett 5 Zhmud 6 Jewish, Litvak, Polish 7 Aistian, Russian, Yatvyag 10 Lithuanian, Samogitian 11 Belorussian
language: 5 Zmudz 6 Baltic 10 Lithuanian
religion: 8 Lutheran 13 Roman Catholic

little by little
French: 7 peu a peu
Spanish: 9 poco a poco

Little Caesar
director: 11 Mervyn LeRoy
cast: 13 Glenda Farrell 15 Edward G Robinson (Caesar Enrico Bandello) 18 Douglas Fairbanks Jr

Little Daedala
origin: 7 Boeotia
event: 8 festival
honoring: 4 Hera, Zeus

Little Dorrit
author: 14 Charles Dickens
character: 3 Amy (Little Dorrit), Tip 4 Rugg 5 Casby, Fanny, Flora, Gowan 6 Affery, Merdle, Pancks, Rigaud (Blandois) 7 Meagles 8 Mr F's Aunt 9 Mrs Merdle 10 Flintwinch 13 Arthur Clennam, William Dorrit 16 Monsieur Blandois, Young John Chivery

Little Drummer Girl, The
author: 11 John Le Carre

Little Emily, Little Em'ly
character in: 16 David Copperfield
author: 7 Dickens

Little Fox
constellation of: 9 Vulpecula

Little Foxes, The
author: 14 Lillian Hellman
character: 13 Regina Giddens
director: 12 William Wyler
cast: 10 Bette Davis (Regina) 12 Teresa Wright 14 Richard Carlson 15 Herbert Marshall
prequel: 22 Another Part of the Forest

Little Gidding
author: 7 T S Eliot

Little Girls
author: 14 Elizabeth Bowen

Little House on the Prairie
author: 18 Laura Ingalls Wilder
character: 6 Albert 7 Dr Baker 8 Rev Alden 9 Mr Edwards 10 Andy Garvey, Lars Hanson, Nels Oleson 11 Adam Kendall, Alice Garvey, Mary Ingalls 12 Grace Ingalls, Laura Ingalls, Nellie Oleson, Willie Oleson 13 Carrie Ingalls, Harriet Oleson 14 Charles Ingalls, Eva Beadle Simms, Jonathan Garvey 15 Caroline Ingalls
cast: 10 Dabbs Greer, Kevin Hagen 11 Karl Swenson, Merlin Olsen, Richard Bull 12 Hersha Parady, Karen Grassle, Victor French 13 Alison Arngrim, Linwood Boomer, Michael Landon

14 Melissa Gilbert 15 Jonathon Gilbert, Sidney Greenbush, Wendy Turnbeaugh 16 Brenda Turnbeaugh, Charlotte Gilbert, Lindsay Greenbush 17 Katherine McGregor, Matthew Laborteaux, Patrick Laborteaux 18 Melissa Sue Anderson
setting: 6 Winoka 9 Minnesota, Plum Creek 11 Walnut Grove

Little John
character in: 9 Robin Hood

Little King, The
creator: 10 Otto Soglow
technique: 9 pantomine

little-known 6 unsung 7 obscure, unnoted 10 unrenowned

Little Learning, A
author: 11 Evelyn Waugh

Little Lord Fauntleroy
author: 15 Frances H Burnett

Little Lulu
creator: 14 Marge Henderson

Little Match Girl, The
author: 21 Hans Christian Andersen

Little Men
author: 15 Louisa May Alcott

Little Mermaid, The
author: 21 Hans Christian Andersen

Little Minister, The
author: 12 James M Barrie

Little Mo
nickname of: 15 Maureen Connolly

Little Nemo in Slumberland
creator: 11 Winsor McCay
character: 6 Dr Pill 8 cannibal, princess
clown: 4 Flip
dog: 6 Blutch

little one 3 tot 4 babe, baby, tyke 5 child 6 infant, wee one 7 toddler

Little Orphan Annie
creator: 10 Harold Gray
character:
foster father: 13 Daddy Warbucks
dog: 5 Sandy
saying: 13 Leapin' Lizards

Little Prince, The
author: 21 Antoine de Saint-Exupery

Little Rhody
nickname of: 11 Rhode Island

Little Tramp
nickname of: 14 Charlie Chaplin

Little Women
author: 15 Louisa May Alcott
character: 6 Laurie (Theodore Lawrence), Marmee 10 John Brooke 14 Professor Bhaer
March sisters: 2 Jo 3 Amy, Meg 4 Beth
director:
1933 version: 11 George Cukor
1949 version: 11 Mervyn LeRoy
cast (1933): 9 Paul Lukas 10 Frances Dee, Jean Parker 11 Joan Bennett 16 Katharine Hepburn (Jo)
cast (1949): 9 Mary Astor 10 Janet Leigh 11 June Allyson 12 Peter Lawford 14 Margaret O'Brien 15 Elizabeth Taylor

liturgical 6 ritual 10 ceremonial 11 ceremonious, sacramental

liturgy 4 mass, rite 6 ritual 7 service, worship 8 ceremony, services 9 communion, sacrament

lituus
form: 5 staff
shape: 7 crooked

Lityerses
father: 9 King Midas
held: 15 reaping contests
killed: 6 losers

livable, liveable 4 cozy, snug 5 comfy, homey 8 bearable, passable, pleasant, suitable 9 agreeable, endurable, enjoyable, habitable, tolerable 10 acceptable, convenient, gratifying, satisfying, worthwhile 11 comfortable

live 2 be 3 hot 4 bunk, feed, stay 5 abide, afire, aglow, alive, dwell, exist, fiery, lodge, quick, stand, vital 6 ablaze, active, aflame, alight, at hand, billet, bodily, endure, hold on, living, obtain, occupy, red-hot, remain, reside, settle, thrive 7 animate, at issue, be alive, blazing, breathe, burning, current, flaming, fleshly, going on, ignited, persist, prevail, subsist, survive 8 existent, flourish, get ahead, get along, have life, increase, multiply, physical, pressing, take root, up-to-date, white-hot 9 breathing, corporeal 10 draw breath

live and keep well
Latin: 11 vive valeque

Live and Let Die
author: 10 Ian Fleming

live dissolutely 7 carouse, debauch 9 dissipate 11 overindulge

livelihood 3 job 5 trade 6 career, living, metier 7 calling, support, venture 8 business, position, vocation 9 situation 10 enterprise, line of work, occupation, profession, sustenance 11 maintenance, subsistence, undertaking

liveliness 3 pep, zip 5 vigor 7 agility 8 alacrity, vitality, vivacity 9 animation, briskness, eagerness 10 ebullience, nimbleness 13 sprightliness

lively 5 alert, brisk, eager, peppy, perky, vivid 6 active, ardent, bouncy 7 buoyant, excited, fervent, intense 8 animated, spirited, vigorous 9 energetic, excitable, sprightly, vivacious 12 enthusiastic

liven 4 buoy 5 cheer, elate, pep up 6 perk up, vivify 7 animate, delight, enliven, fortify, gladden, hearten, punch up, quicken 8 brighten, embolden, energize, inspirit 10 exhilarate, invigorate, strengthen

liver
stores: 8 glycogen
color: 3 red 5 brown
produces: 4 bile 10 blood cells

Livermore Larruper
nickname of: 7 Max Baer

livery 4 garb, suit 5 dress 6 attire 7 costume, raiment, regalia, uniform 8 clothing 9 vestments

Lives of a Bengal Lancer
director: 13 Henry Hathaway
cast: 10 Gary Cooper 12 Franchot Tone 14 Sir Guy Standing 15 Richard Cromwell

Lives of the Poets, The
author: 13 Samuel Johnson

live through 4 know 7 survive, undergo 9 go through 10 experience

livid 3 mad 5 angry, irate, riled, vexed 6 fuming, galled, purple, raging 7 bruised, enraged, furious 8 contused, incensed, inflamed, outraged, provoked, wrathful 9 indignant, steamed up, ticked off 10 discolored, infuriated 11 exasperated

living 3 job 4 life, live, work 5 alive, being, quick, trade 6 active, bodily, career, extant, income 7 animate, calling, fleshly, going on, organic, venture 8 business, embodied, enduring, existent, existing, material, up-to-date, vocation 9 animation, breathing, corporeal, existence, incarnate, lifestyle, operative, permanent, remaining, surviving, way of life **10** employment, enterprise, having life, in the flesh, line of work, livelihood, occupation, persisting, prevailing, profession, subsisting, sustenance **11** maintenance, subsistence **13** drawing breath

living being **8** creature, organism

living conditions **10** atmosphere **11** environment **13** circumstances

living picture
French: **13** tableau vivant

living quarters **4** home **5** abode, house **6** billet **7** housing, lodging, shelter **8** domicile, dwelling, quarters **9** apartment, residence **10** habitation **13** dwelling place

Livy
also: **11** Titus Livius
author of: **13** Ab urbe condita **26** From the Foundation of the City

lizard **3** dab, eft, uma **4** adda, gila, newt, seps, tegu **5** agama, anole, anoli, gecko, idler, shrink **6** aguana, dragon, iguana, komodo, moloch **7** lounger, monitor, reptile, saurian **8** dinosaur, lacerata, scorpion **9** alligator, blindworm, chameleon, crocodile, galliwasp **10** chuckwalla, glass snake, horned toad, salamander **11** gila monster **12** Komodo dragon
characteristic: **6** scales **7** molting **9** oviparous **11** cold-blooded **12** regeneration
constellation of: **7** Lacerta

Ljod *see* **4** Liod

llama **6** alpaca, kechua, mammal, vicuna **7** guanaco **8** ungulate **13** Peruvian sheep

Llewellyn, Richard
author of: **19** How Green Was My Valley

Llew Llaw Gyffes
origin: **5** Welsh
father: **7** Gwydion
mother: **9** Arianhrod
wife: **10** Blodenwedd
curses bestowed by: **9** Arianhrod

Lloyd
origin: **5** Welsh
form: **8** magician
cast spells upon: **7** Pryderi

Lloyd, Harold
born: **10** Burchard NE
roles: **9** Feet First **10** Safety Last **11** The Freshman **13** The Kid Brother

Llud
also: **4** Ludd, Nudd
origin: **5** Welsh
king of: **7** Britain
rid kingdom of: **6** plague
famous for: **10** generosity

Llyr
origin: **5** Welsh
son: **10** Manawyddan
corresponds to: **3** Ler, Lir

load **3** try, vex **4** care, fill, haul, heap, lade, pack, pile **5** cargo, crush, stack, stuff, worry **6** burden, hamper, hinder, lading, misery, strain, weight **7** afflict, carload, freight, oppress, trouble **8** capacity, contents, encumber, handicap, pressure, shipload, shipment **9** overwhelm, planeload, truckload, wagonload, weigh down **10** affliction, deadweight, depression, misfortune, oppression **11** encumbrance

loads **4** lots, much **5** heaps, piles, scads **6** oodles, plenty **14** more than enough

loaf **4** idle, loll **5** dally **6** be lazy **7** goof off **8** kill time, malinger **9** do nothing, goldbrick, laze about, waste time **10** take it easy **12** lounge around

loafer **3** bum **4** shoe **5** idler **6** no-good **7** laggard, shirker, sponger, wastrel **8** deadbeat, loiterer, sluggard **9** goldbrick, lazybones **10** lazy person, malingerer, ne'er-do-well **11** couch potato **12** lounge lizard **15** drugstore cowboy
French: **7** flaneur

loan **4** lend **5** allow **6** credit **7** advance, lending **8** mortgage **9** advancing

loath **4** loth **6** averse **7** against, counter, hostile, opposed **8** inimical **9** reluctant, resisting, unwilling **10** indisposed, set against **11** disinclined

loathe **4** hate **5** abhor, scorn **6** detest, eschew **7** deplore, despise, disdain, dislike **9** abominate **10** blench from, flinch from, recoil from, shrink from **11** keep clear of, shy away from **12** draw back from **14** be unable to bear, find disgusting, view with horror **16** have no stomach for

loathing **4** hate **5** odium **6** hatred **7** disgust, dislike **8** aversion, distaste **9** antipathy, repulsion, revulsion **10** abhorrence, repugnance **11** abomination, detestation

loathsome **4** foul, mean, rank, vile **5** nasty **6** odious **7** hateful **9** abhorrent, invidious, obnoxious, offensive, repugnant, repulsive, revolting, sickening **10** abominable, despicable, detestable, disgusting, nauseating, unbearable **11** distasteful

lobby **5** foyer **8** anteroom, politick **9** vestibule **11** antechamber, pull strings, waiting room **12** entrance hall

local **6** narrow, native, nearby **7** insular, limited **8** citywide, confined, regional **9** adjoining, homegrown, parochial, sectional **10** provincial **11** territorial **12** neighborhood **13** circumscribed

locale **4** area, site, spot, zone **6** region **7** quarter, section, setting **8** locality, location, precinct, province, vicinity **12** neighborhood

locality **4** area, site, spot, zone **5** place **6** locale, region **7** quarter, section **8** district, location, precinct, province, vicinity **9** territory **12** neighborhood

locate **3** fix, put **4** find, live, post, seat, stay **5** dwell, place **6** detect, move to, reside, settle **7** deposit, discern, hit upon, set down, situate, station, uncover, unearth **8** come upon, meet with, pinpoint **9** establish, ferret out, light upon, search out, stumble on, track down **10** settle down **12** put down roots

location **4** site, spot **5** place **6** locale **8** district, position **9** situation **11** whereabouts **12** neighborhood

Lochinvar
character in: **7** Marmion
author: **5** Scott

lock **3** bar, dam, pen **4** bang, bolt, cage, coil, curl, grab, grip, hank, hold, hook, jail, join, link, tuft **5** catch, clamp, clasp, grasp, latch, seize, skein, tress, unite **6** clinch, coop up, fasten, lock up, secure, shut in **7** confine, embrace, entwine, grapple, impound, padlock, ringlet **8** dock gate, imprison **9** canal gate, fastening, floodgate, interlink **10** intertwine, sluice gate **11** incarcerate

lock, cylinder
invented by: **4** Yale

Lockhart, Gene
daughter: **12** June Lockhart
granddaughter: **11** Ann Lockhart
born: **6** Canada, London **7** Ontario
roles: **12** Madame Bovary

16 Death of a Salesman
19 The Inspector General
20 Abe Lincoln in Illinois

lock horns **4** feud, tiff **5** argue, brawl, clash, fight **7** dispute, quarrel, wrangle **8** squabble **9** altercate

Lockit
character in: **12** Beggar's Opera
author: **3** Gay

lockup **3** jug, pen **4** jail, stir **5** clink, pokey **6** cooler, prison **7** slammer **8** big house, hoosegow **11** reformatory **12** penitentiary

lock up **3** pen **4** cage, jail **6** coop up, secure **7** confine, impound **8** imprison, restrain, restrict **11** incarcerate

Lockyer, Joseph Norman
field: **9** astronomy
nationality: **7** British
discovered: **6** helium

loco citato **15** in the place cited
abbreviation: **6** loc cit

locomotive
invented by:
electric: **4** Vail
experimental: **6** Fenton, Hedley **10** Stephenson, Trevithick
first US: **6** Cooper
practical: **10** Stephenson

Locrian Ajax *see* **4** Ajax

Locrus
king of: **8** Locrians

locust **7** Robinia
varieties: **4** moss **5** black, honey, mossy, swamp, sweet, water **6** clammy, yellow **7** African, bristly **8** shipmast **10** West Indian **13** Allegheny moss, South American

locution **4** term **5** idiom, trope, usage **6** phrase, saying **7** wording **8** idiolect, phrasing **9** set phrase, utterance, verbalism **10** expression **11** phraseology, regionalism **12** turn of phrase **14** figure of speech

lode **3** bed **4** seam **7** deposit

lodge **3** bed, hut **4** camp, file, room, stay **5** cabin, catch, hotel, house, motel, put up **6** billet, harbor, resort, submit **7** cottage, quarter, shelter, sojourn **8** register

lodging **4** room **8** quarters **13** accommodation

Lofn
origin: **12** Scandinavian
goddess of: **18** forbidden marriages
permission given by: **4** Odin **5** Othin

loft **3** lob **5** attic, pop up **6** belfry, garret **7** balcony, gallery, hit high, mansard **8** top floor **9** attic room, throw high **10** clerestory

loftiness **5** pride **9** arrogance **11** haughtiness **13** imperiousness **16** superciliousness

Lofting, Hugh
author of: **11** Dr Doolittle

lofty **4** cold, high, tall **5** aloof, grand, great, noble, proud **6** lordly, mighty, remote, snooty **7** distant, eminent, exalted, haughty, leading, soaring, stately, stuck-up, sublime **8** arrogant, elevated, glorious, imposing, insolent, majestic, puffed-up, scornful, snobbish, superior, towering **9** conceited, dignified, imperious, important **10** disdainful, hoity-toity, preeminent **11** high ranking, illustrious, patronizing **12** high-reaching **13** condescending, distinguished, high-and-mighty, self-important

lofty bearing **7** dignity, majesty **10** augustness **11** stateliness

log **5** block, diary, stump **6** docket, lumber, record, timber **7** account, daybook, journal, logbook **8** calendar, schedule

loges **5** boxes **7** balcony **9** mezzanine

loggia **5** lanai, porch **6** arcade, piazza **7** balcony, gallery

Logi
origin: **12** Scandinavian
form: **3** man
personifies: **4** fire
defeated: **4** Loki

logic **5** sense **6** reason **7** cogency **8** analysis, argument **9** coherence, deduction, good sense, induction **10** dialectics

logical **5** clear, sound, valid **6** cogent, likely **7** germane **8** coherent, rational, relevant, sensible **9** deducible, pertinent, plausible **10** analytical, consistent, most likely, reasonable **11** enlightened, intelligent **13** well-organized

logos **4** word **5** ratio **6** saying, speech **7** thought **9** discourse, reckoning **10** proportion

logy **4** dull **5** inert, tired, weary **6** drowsy, groggy, sleepy, torpid **8** comatose, lifeless, listless, sluggish **9** enervated, inanimate, lethargic **10** phlegmatic **12** hebetudinous

Lohengrin
opera by: **6** Wagner
character: **4** Elsa **6** Ortrud **9** Gottfried (Duke of Brabant) **25** Count Frederick of Telramund

Lohengrin
origin: **8** Germanic
knight of: **9** Holy Grail
father: **8** Parsifal, Parzival

loiter **4** idle, laze, loaf, loll, lurk **5** dally, skulk, slink, tarry **6** dawdle **10** dillydally, hang around **11** hover around **12** shilly-shally

Loki
origin: **12** Scandinavian
mentioned in: **9** Lokasenna
god of: **4** fire
son: **6** Fenrir, Fenris
daughter: **3** Hel
fathered: **10** Jormungand **11** Iormungandr, Jormungandr **14** Midgard Serpent
mother of his children: **9** Angerboda, Angrbodha, Angurboda
caused death of: **5** Baldr **6** Balder, Baldur
form: **5** giant
extorted treasure from: **7** Andvari
function: **4** evil **6** strife

Lolita
author: **15** Vladimir Nabokov
character: **14** Humbert Humbert
director: **14** Stanley Kubrick
based on novel by: **15** Vladimir Nabokov
cast: **7** Sue Lyon (Lolita) **10** James Mason (Humbert Humbert) **12** Peter Sellers **14** Shelley Winters

loll **3** sag **4** drag, drop, flap, flop, idle, lean, loaf **5** droop, relax, slump **6** dangle, dawdle, lounge, repose, slouch, sprawl **7** goof off, recline **8** flop over, languish

Lollobrigida, Gina
born: **5** Italy **7** Subiaco
roles: **7** Trapeze **14** Anne of Brooklyn, The Wayward Wife **15** Solomon and Sheba **20** Buona Sera Mrs Campbell **27** The World's Most Beautiful Woman

Loman, Willy
character in: **16** Death of a Salesman
author: **6** Miller

Lombard, Carole
real name: **15** Jane Alice Peters
husband: **10** Clark Gable
born: **11** Fort Wayne IN
roles: **12** My Man Godfrey **13** Nothing Sacred, To Be

Or Not To Be **16** Twentieth Century

Lome
capital of: **4** Togo

London ***see box***

London, Jack
author of: **9** White Fang **10** The Sea Wolf **16** The Call of the Wild

lone **4** only, sole **5** alone **6** single, unique **8** isolated, singular, solitary, unpaired **9** unabetted **10** individual, unattended, unescorted **13** companionless, unaccompanied

loneliness **9** isolation, seclusion **12** lonesomeness, solitariness **14** friendlessness

Loneliness of the Long Distance Runner, The
director: **14** Tony Richardson
cast: **11** Avis Bunnage, Peter Madden **12** Tom Courtenay **15** Michael Redgrave

lonely **6** remote **7** forlorn **8** deserted, desolate, forsaken, hermitic, isolated, lonesome, secluded, solitary, unsocial **9** by oneself, reclusive, withdrawn **10** friendless, unattended **11** uninhabited, unpopulated **12** unfrequented **13** companionless, unaccompanied

Lone Ranger, The
character: **5** Tonto
cast: **8** John Hart **12** Clayton Moore **14** Jay Silverheels
horse: **5** Scout **6** Silver
Lone Ranger used: **13** silver bullets
theme: **19** William Tell Overture

lonesome **5** alone, aloof **6** lonely **7** forlorn, insular **8** desolate, detached, forsaken **9** alienated, withdrawn **10** friendless, unfriended **13** companionless

Lone Star State
nickname of: **5** Texas

long **4** hope, lust, pine, sigh, want, wish **5** covet, crave, yearn **6** aspire, hanker, hunger, thirst **7** lengthy, spun out **8** drawn-out, extended, have a yen, in length, unending **9** elongated, extensive, prolonged **10** be bent on, protracted **11** far-reaching, have a desire **12** from end to end, interminable, outstretched

Long, Crawford Williamson
field: **8** medicine
first used: **5** ether

Longaville
character in: **16** Love's Labour's Lost
author: **11** Shakespeare

Long Day's Journey into Night
author: **12** Eugene O'Neill
director: **11** Sidney Lumet
cast: **13** Dean Stockwell **14** Jason Robards Jr **15** Ralph Richardson **16** Katharine Hepburn

Longest Day, The
director: **10** Ken Annakin **12** Andrew Marton, Bernard Wicki
cast: **9** John Wayne, Mel Ferrer **10** Henry Fonda, Red Buttons, Robert Ryan, Rod Steiger **12** Peter Lawford
setting: **8** Normandy (Allied invasion)

Longevity
goddess of: **11** Anna Perenna

long-faced **4** glum **6** dismal, gloomy **7** doleful, unhappy **8** dejected, mournful **10** lugubrious **14** down in the mouth

Longfellow, Henry Wadsworth
author of: **8** Hyperion, (The Song of) Hiawatha **10** Evangeline **15** Paul Revere's Ride **18** Tales of a Wayside Inn **21** The Wreck of the Hesperus **27** The Courtship of Miles Standish

longing **3** yen **4** wish **6** ardent, pining, thirst **7** craving, wishful **8** desirous, yearning **9** hankering, hungering **10** aspiration **11** languishing

long-lasting **7** chronic, lengthy, tedious **8** enduring, extended **9** prolonged **10** continuing, protracted

long live
French: **4** vive

long past **3** old **5** olden **6** gone by, of yore **7** ancient, long ago **8** long gone

long-standing **4** long **5** hardy, hoary **6** rooted **7** abiding, ancient, chronic, durable, lasting **8** enduring, habitual, hallowed, unfading **9** confirmed, continual, long-lived, perennial, perpetual, venerable **10** continuous, deep-rooted, deep-seated, inveterate, persistent, persisting **11** long-lasting, time-honored **15** long-established

Longstreet, James
served in: **8** Civil War
side: **11** Confederate
battle: **7** Bull Run **10** Gettysburg **11** Chickamauga **14** Fredericksburg **18** Wilderness Campaign
after war joined: **11** Republicans
US minister to: **6** Turkey

Long Voyage Home, The
director: **8** John Ford
based on play by: **12** Eugene O'Neill
cast: **9** Ian Hunter, John Wayne **13** Wilfrid Lawson **14** Thomas Mitchell **15** Barry Fitzgerald

---

London
airport: **7** Gatwick **8** Heathrow, Stansted
architect: **4** Wren
area: **4** Soho **6** Camden **7** Brixton, Chelsea, Holborn, Pimlico **8** Vauxhall **9** Bayswater, Belgravia, Islington, Southwark **10** Bloomsbury, Kensington, Paddington, Shoreditch **11** Notting Hill, St John's Wood **13** Knightsbridge
capital of: **7** England **12** Great Britain **13** United Kingdom
landmark: **6** Big Ben **8** Hyde Park **9** Whitehall, Wimbledon **11** Regent's Park, Saint James's, Tate Gallery, Tower Bridge **12** Covent Garden, London Bridge **13** British Museum, Tower of London **14** British Library, Speaker's Corner **15** National Gallery, Trafalgar Square **16** Buckingham Palace, Piccadilly Circus, Westminster Abbey **17** Kensington Gardens, Royal Festival Hall, Westminster Palace **18** Houses of Parliament **19** Saint Paul's Cathedral **23** Victoria and Albert Museum
police: **7** bobbies
established by: **13** Sir Robert Peel
prime minister's residence: **16** Ten Downing Street
river: **6** Thames
Roman name: **9** Londinium
subway: **11** Underground

long-wearing **5** tough **6** strong, sturdy **7** durable, lasting **8** enduring **11** substantial

long-winded **5** wordy **6** prolix **7** lengthy, tedious, verbose **8** rambling **9** garrulous **10** digressive, discursive

long-windedness **8** rambling **9** garrulity, prolixity, verbosity, wordiness **14** discursiveness

Lonnrot, Elias
author of: **8** Kalevala

look **3** air, see **4** cast, face, gape, gaze, mien, ogle, peek, peep, scan, seem, show, view **5** front, glare, guise, sight, stare, study, watch **6** appear, behold, glance, regard, survey **7** bearing, examine, exhibit, glimpse **8** demeanor, manifest, once-over, presence, scrutiny **10** appearance, be directed, cut a figure, expression, scrutinize **11** contemplate, countenance, observation

look after **4** help **6** assist, defend **7** help out, protect **10** minister to **11** watch out for **17** take under one's wing

look askance at **7** condemn **8** object to **9** frown upon **10** disapprove **14** discountenance **15** take exception to **16** find unacceptable, view with disfavor

look at **3** see **4** view **6** behold, notice, regard **7** examine, inspect, witness **10** scrutinize

Look Back in Anger
director: **14** Tony Richardson
based on play by: **11** John Osborne
cast: **7** Mary Ure **10** Edith Evans **11** Claire Bloom **13** Richard Burton **15** Donald Pleasance

look down on **7** despise, disdain **9** frown upon, patronize **10** condescend **13** put on airs with **14** hold in contempt

looker-on **6** viewer **7** watcher, witness **8** beholder, observer, onlooker **9** bystander, spectator

look for **4** seek **5** await **6** expect, pursue **7** hunt for **9** search for **10** anticipate

look for the woman
French: **15** cherchez la femme

look forward to **5** await **6** expect **7** long for, wait for **9** pin hope on **10** anticipate **17** count the days until

Look Homeward, Angel
author: **11** Thomas Wolfe
character: **7** Ben Gant **9** Eliza Gant **10** Eugene Gant, Laura James, Oliver Gant **15** Margaret Leonard

Looking Backward
author: **13** Edward Bellamy

look in the eye **4** defy, face **5** brave **8** confront **9** challenge

look into **5** probe **7** examine, explore **10** scrutinize **11** inquire into, investigate

lookout **4** heed **5** guard, scout, vigil **6** patrol, sentry **7** spotter **8** observer, sentinel, watchdog, watchman **9** alertness, attention, awareness, readiness, vigilance **10** precaution **11** guardedness, mindfulness, watchkeeper **12** surveillance, watchfulness

look out **4** mind **6** beware **8** take care, watch out **9** be careful, be on guard **11** take warning **12** be on the alert

look over **4** scan, skim **5** judge **6** assess, peruse, survey **7** dip into **8** appraise, evaluate **13** browse through, glance through

look through **4** scan, skim **6** browse, peruse **7** dip into **8** look over **9** check over **13** glance through

look toward **7** count on **10** anticipate **13** look forward to

look upon **3** see **4** view **6** behold, gaze at, look at **7** observe, stare at

look upon as **4** deem, hold **5** count, judge, think **6** regard, view as **7** account, believe **8** consider, take to be

look up to **5** honor **6** admire, esteem, revere **7** respect **8** venerate

loom **4** hulk, rise, soar **5** tower **6** appear, ascend, emerge **8** stand out **9** take shape

loom, power
invented by: **10** Cartwright

loop **3** eye **4** bend, coil, curl, furl, ring, roll, turn **5** braid, curve, noose, plait, twirl, twist, whorl **6** circle, eyelet, spiral **7** opening, ringlet **8** aperture, encircle, loophole **10** wind around **11** convolution, curve around

Loos, Anita
author of: **22** Gentlemen Prefer Blondes

loose **4** fast, free, lewd, undo, wild **5** freed, let go, slack, untie, vague **6** freely, loosen, unbind, undone, untied, wanton **7** immoral, inexact, loosely, release, set free, slacken, unbound, uncaged, unchain, unleash, unloose, unyoked **8** careless, heedless, liberate, not tight, rakehell, unbridle, unchaste, unfasten, unjoined, untether **9** abandoned, debauched, dissolute, imprecise, liberated, libertine, unbridled, unchained, unleashed, unmanacle, unshackle **10** dissipated, inaccurate, licentious, not binding, profligate, unattached, unexacting, unfastened, unfettered, unhandcuff, untethered **11** not fastened, unconnected **12** unimprisoned **13** unconstrained

loose-fitting **4** limp **5** baggy, loose, slack **6** draped, droopy **7** sagging **9** overlarge, oversized

loosely connected **5** jerky **6** fitful **8** episodic, rambling **9** spasmodic, wandering **10** digressive, discursive, meandering

loosen **3** lax **4** ease, free, undo **5** break, relax, untie **6** limber, unbend, unbind **7** release, relieve, slacken, unchain, unscrew **8** liberate, unbuckle, unfasten, work free **10** emancipate

looseness **8** fastness, lewdness, wildness **9** slackness, vagueness **10** debauchery, immorality, inaccuracy, profligacy, wantonness **11** dissipation, dissolution, imprecision **12** carelessness, heedlessness, inexactitude **14** licentiousness

loot **3** rob **4** haul, raid, sack, swag, take **5** booty, prize, strip **6** boodle, fleece, pilfer, ravage, spoils **7** pillage, plunder, ransack **11** stolen goods

looter **5** thief **6** robber, vandal **7** brigand **8** pillager **9** despoiler, plunderer

lop **3** cut **4** chip, chop, crop, dock, flop, sned, snip, trim **5** droop, prune, sever **6** cut off, deduct, detach, remove, slouch **7** cut back **8** amputate, truncate

Lopez, Nancy
sport: **4** golf
husband: **9** Ray Knight
plays: **8** baseball

lopsided **4** awry **5** askew **6** aslant, tipped, uneven **7** crooked, leaning, listing, slanted, tilting, unequal **8** cockeyed, inclined, slanting **9** irregular **10** asymmetric, off-balance, unbalanced **15** dis-

proportional
16 disproportionate

loquacious 5 gabby, talky, windy, wordy **6** blabby, chatty, prolix **7** prating, verbose, voluble **8** babbling, chattery **9** garrulous, prattling, talkative **10** chattering, long-winded

loquitur 8 he speaks **9** she speaks

lord 4 king **5** chief, crown, ruler **6** leader, master **7** monarch **8** overlord, seignior, superior **9** commander, landowner, sovereign **10** landholder, proprietor
Japanese: 6 daimyo
Turkish: 3 beg, bey

Lord
Latin: 7 Dominus

Lord be with you, the
Latin: 15 Dominus vobiscum

Lord have mercy
Greek: 12 Kyrie eleison

Lord Jim
author: 12 Joseph Conrad
character: 5 Stein **6** Marlow **9** Dain Waris **14** Gentleman Brown

lordliness 7 disdain **8** contempt **9** arrogance, insolence, loftiness **11** haughtiness **13** imperiousness **16** superciliousness

lordly 4 cold **5** aloof, bossy, grand, lofty, noble, proud, regal **6** august, remote, snooty **7** distant, elegant, eminent, exalted, haughty, stately, stuck-up **8** arrogant, despotic, imposing, majestic, princely, puffed-up, scornful, snobbish **9** conceited, dignified, imperious, sumptuous **10** disdainful, hoity-toity, tyrannical **11** dictatorial, domineering, magisterial, magnificent, patronizing **13** condescending, high-and-mighty, self-important

Lord of the Flies
author: 14 William Golding

Lord of the Rings, The
author: 10 J R R Tolkien

Lord Raingo
author: 13 Arnold Bennett

Lord Weary's Castle
author: 12 Robert Lowell

lore 7 beliefs, legends **10** traditions

Lorelei
also: 7 Lurelei
origin: 8 Germanic
form: 5 nymph
dwelling place: 5 cliff, Rhine
lured: 7 boatmen
caused shipwrecks by: 7 singing

Loren, Sophia
real name: 14 Sofia Scicolone
husband: 10 Carlo Ponti
born: 4 Rome **5** Italy
roles: 5 El Cid **8** Two Women (Oscar) **9** Arabesque, Houseboat **13** Man of La Mancha **14** The Black Orchid **18** Desire Under the Elms **20** Marriage Italian Style **21** A Countess from Hong Kong, The Pride and the Passion

Lorentz, Hendrik Anton
field: 7 physics
nationality: 5 Dutch
discovered: 17 special relativity
named for him: 21 Lorentz transformation **34** Lorentz-Fitzgerald Length Contraction
awarded: 10 Nobel Prize

Loring, Eugene
choreographer of: 11 Billy the Kid

Lorna Doone
author: 11 R D Blackmore
character: 8 John Ridd **9** Tom Faggus **11** Carver Doone **13** Sir Ensor Doone **14** Jeremy Stickles **15** Reuben Huckaback

Lorre, Peter
real name: 16 Laszlo Lowenstein
born: 7 Hungary **9** Rosenberg
roles: 1 M **7** Mad Love **10** Casablanca, The Verdict **12** The Big Circus **14** Three Strangers **16** The Maltese Falcon **18** Crime and Punishment, The Mask of Dimitrios

Lorry, Jarvis
character in: 16 A Tale of Two Cities
author: 7 Dickens

Los Angeles ***see box***

lose 4 fail, miss **6** forget, ignore, mislay **7** confuse, forfeit **8** misplace **9** fail to win, stray from **10** be the loser, fail to heed **11** be thrown off **12** be defeated in, be deprived of, suffer loss of, take a licking

lose control 5 break, crack **7** crack up **9** fall apart **10** go to pieces **15** go off the deep end

lose faith 6 give up **7** despair **9** lose heart **10** have no hope **18** become disenchanted

lose force 3 die **7** run down **9** lose power

lose heart 6 give up **7** despair **17** become discouraged

lose one's cool 12 fly into a rage **13** become enraged, throw a tantrum **14** lose one's temper **15** fly off the handle

loser 4 flop **7** failure **8** de-

Los Angeles
airport: 3 LAX **7** Burbank **23** Los Angeles International
area: 5 Watts **6** Bel Air, Downey, Venice **7** Anaheim, Compton, Norwalk **8** Mar Vista, Pasadena, Torrance, Westwood **9** Brentwood, Hollywood, Inglewood, Long Beach **10** Culver City **11** Century City, Garden Grove, Palos Verdes, Santa Monica **12** Beverly Hills, Marina del Rey **16** Pacific Palisades
***San Fernando Valley:* 6** Encino **7** Tarzana, Van Nuys, Ventura **10** Northridge **11** Sherman Oaks
baseball team: 7 Dodgers
basketball team: 6 Lakers **8** Clippers
football team: 4 Rams **7** Express, Raiders
hockey team: 5 Kings
landmark: 5 Forum **10** Disneyland **11** Civic Center, Getty Museum, Watts Towers **12** Griffith Park **13** Farmers' Market, Hollywood Bowl, Hollywood Park, La Brea Tar Pits, Magic Mountain **15** Knott's Berry Farm **16** Bonaventure Hotel **17** Norton Simon Museum **22** Grauman's Chinese Theater **23** Griffith Park Observatory
mountains: 10 San Gabriel **11** Santa Monica
nickname: 15 City of the Angels
street: 4 Vine **10** Rodeo Drive **12** Olvera Street **15** Mulholland Drive **16** Van Nuys Boulevard **17** Wilshire Boulevard **18** Hollywood Boulevard **20** Santa Monica Boulevard
university: 3 USC **4** UCLA **7** Caltech **10** Pepperdine **17** Occidental College **31** California Institute of Technology

feated **9** conquered **10** vanquished

lose track of **4** lose **9** let escape **11** lose sight of

lose vigor **4** flag **5** droop **6** sicken, weaken, wither **7** decline

Losing Battles
author: **11** Eudora Welty

loss **4** ruin **5** wreck **6** defeat, losing **7** licking, removal, undoing **8** overturn, riddance, wrecking **9** abolition, mislaying, privation **10** amount lost, demolition, extinction, forfeiture, misplacing, number lost **11** bereavement, deprivation, destruction, dissolution, eradication, expenditure, extirpation

loss of life **5** death **8** fatality **9** mortality

lost **5** stray **6** absent, astray, killed, ruined, wasted **7** lacking, mislaid, missing, misused, strayed, wrecked **8** absorbed, murdered, perished, vanished, wiped out **9** abolished, destroyed, engrossed, misplaced, off-course **10** demolished, eradicated, extirpated, gone astray, misapplied, squandered **11** annihilated, misdirected, obliterated, preoccupied **12** exterminated

Lost Honor of Katharina Blum, The
author: **12** Heinrich Boll

Lost Horizon
author: **11** James Hilton
character: **10** Hugh Conway, Rutherford **12** Henry Barnard, Miss Brinklow **14** Father Perrault **20** Captain Mallison Chang
director: **10** Frank Capra
cast: **5** Margo **8** H B Warner, Sam Jaffe **9** Jane Wyatt **10** John Howard **12** Isabel Jewell, Ronald Colman **14** Thomas Mitchell **19** Edward Everett Horton
setting: **5** Tibet

Lost Illusions
author: **14** Honore de Balzac

Lost in America
director: **12** Albert Brooks
cast: **12** Albert Brooks, Julie Hagerty

Lost in Space
character: **5** Robot **7** Don West **12** Judy Robinson, Will Robinson **13** Penny Robinson **14** Dr Zachary Smith **15** Maureen Robinson **16** Prof John Robinson
cast: **9** Billy Mumy **11** Guy Williams, Mark Goddard **12** June Lockhart, Marta Kristen **14** Jonathan Harris **16** Angela Cartwright
ship: **9** Jupiter II

Lost in the Funhouse
author: **9** John Barth

Lost in the Stars
author: **15** Maxwell Anderson

lost in thought **7** pensive **8** absorbed **9** engrossed, wrapped up **13** contemplative, in a brown study, introspective

Lost Lady, A
author: **11** Willa Cather

Lost Ones, The
author: **13** Samuel Beckett

Lost Patrol, The
director: **8** John Ford
cast: **8** Alan Hale **11** Wallace Ford **12** Boris Karloff **14** Victor McLaglen
score: **10** Max Steiner

Lost Weekend, The
author: **14** Charles Jackson
director: **11** Billy Wilder
cast: **9** Jane Wyman, Mary Young **10** Frank Falen, Ray Milland **11** Philip Terry **12** Doris Dowling **13** Howard da Silva
Oscar for: **5** actor (Milland) **7** picture **8** director **10** screenplay

lot **4** fate, lots, many, much, plot **5** field, patch, quota, share, straw, tract **6** oceans, oodles, ration **7** counter, measure **8** beaucoup, property **9** allotment, allowance, great deal

Lot
grandfather: **5** Terah
father: **5** Haran
uncle: **7** Abraham
son: **5** Ammon
hometown: **5** Sodom
rescued by: **6** angels
fled to: **4** Zoar

lothario **3** rip **4** rake, roue, wolf **5** lover, Romeo, sheik **6** lecher **7** Don Juan, seducer, swinger **8** Casanova, loverboy **9** debauchee, debaucher, libertine, womanizer **10** ladykiller, profligate, sensualist **11** philanderer, skirt-chaser

Lothario
character in: **15** The Fair Penitent
author: **4** Rowe

Loti, Piere
author of: **18** An Iceland Fisherman

lotion **4** balm, wash **5** salve **6** liquid **7** unction, unguent **8** cosmetic, liniment, ointment, solution **9** demulcent, emollient, freshener, skin cream **10** after-shave, astringent **11** conditioner, embrocation, moisturizer

Lotis
form: **5** nymph
changed into: **4** tree **5** lotus

lotophagi
means: **11** lotus-eaters

lots **4** much **5** heaps, loads, plots, scads **10** quantities

lotus **7** Nelumbo **13** Nymphaea lotus
varieties: **4** blue **5** water, white **6** sacred **8** American, Egyptian **10** East Indian

lotus-eaters **9** lotophagi

loud **5** gaudy, noisy, showy, vivid **6** bright, flashy, garish **7** blatant, booming, intense, splashy **8** colorful, sonorous **9** clamorous, deafening **10** resounding, stentorian, thundering, vociferous **11** ear-piercing, loudmouthed **12** earsplitting, ostentatious

loud sound **4** bang, boom, clap, honk, howl, peal, roar, slam, toot **5** blare, blast, burst, crash **6** bellow, report, scream, shriek **7** clatter, thunder **9** explosion **10** detonation

Lou Grant
character: **6** Animal **8** Joe Rossi **10** Art Donovan **11** Charlie Hume **12** Billie Newman **15** Margaret Pynchon
cast: **10** Jack Bannon, Mason Adams **11** Edward Asner, Linda Kelsey **12** Robert Walden **13** Nancy Marchand **14** Darryl Anderson
paper: **17** Los Angeles Tribune
spinoff of: **18** Mary Tyler Moore Show

Louhi
origin: **7** Finnish
form: **9** sorceress
mistress of: **7** Pohjola
defeated by: **11** Vainamoinen
enemy of: **5** Finns

Louis, Joe
real name: **14** Joe Louis Barrow
nickname: **11** Brown Bomber
sport: **6** boxing
class: **11** heavyweight

Louis, Morris
born: **11** Baltimore MD
artwork: **4** Veil **5** Signa **7** Stripes **8** Unfurled **15** Mountains and Sea

Louise
opera by: **11** Charpentier
character: **6** Julian

Louisiana
abbreviation: **2** LA
nickname: **5** Bayou, Sugar **6** Creole **7** Pelican
capital: **10** Baton Rouge
largest city: **10** New Orleans
others: **5** Houma **6** Bunkie, Gretna, Kenner, Minden, Monroe, Ruston **7** Bastrop **8** Bogalusa **9** Lafayette, Opelousas **10** Alexandria, Shreveport **11** Lake Charles
college: **3** LSU **6** Loyola, Tulane **7** Dillard, Newcomb **9** Grambling
explorer: **7** La Salle **9** Iberville **13** Pierre Lemoyne
feature:
area: **5** bayou **13** French Quarter
festival: **9** Mardi Gras
music: **4** jazz
stadium: **9** Sugar Bowl
street: **7** Bourbon
tribe: **4** Adai, Ioni, Rees, Waco **5** Caddo, Haini, Washa **6** Eyeish, Pawnee **7** Andarko, Arikara, Atakapa **8** Ovachita **9** Bayogoula, Nachitoch
people: **5** Cajun **6** Creole **7** Acadian, pelican **8** Huey Long **14** Lillian Hellman, Louis Armstrong
island: **5** Avery
lake: **3** Iat **4** Iatt **5** Caddo, Clear, Cross, Larto, White **6** Borgne, Saline **8** Darbonne, Maurepas **9** Bistineau, Calcasieu, Catahoula **10** False River **13** Pontchartrain
land rank: **11** thirty-first
mountain:
highest point: **8** Driskill
physical feature: **15** Head of the Passes **17** coastal marshlands
delta: **11** Mississippi
gulf: **6** Mexico
salt domes: **11** Five Islands
river: **3** Red **5** Amite, Bayou, Pearl **6** Tensas **8** Ouachita **11** Mississippi
state admission: **10** eighteenth
state bird: **19** eastern brown pelican
state flower: **8** magnolia
state motto: **5** Union **7** Justice **10** Confidence
state song: **15** Give Me Louisiana **16** You Are My Sunshine
state tree: **11** bald cypress

Louisiana Lightning
nickname of: **9** Ron Guidry

lounge **4** flop, idle, laze, loaf, loll, rest, sofa **5** couch, dally, divan, lobby, relax, sleep, slump **6** dawdle, daybed, repose, slouch, sprawl **7** recline, slumber **8** kill time, languish **9** davenport, do nothing, lie around, vestibule **10** dillydally, stretch out, take it easy

lourd
music: **5** heavy

Lourenco Marques
capital of: **10** Mozambique

louse **3** cad, rat **4** heel **5** churl, knave **6** rascal, rotter, vermin **8** parasite **9** scoundrel

louse up **3** mar **4** goof, muff, ruin **5** botch, spoil **6** bungle, foul up, mess up **7** butcher, do badly, screw up **9** mismanage **11** make a mess of

lousiness **9** nastiness **10** crumminess, horridness, rottenness **11** inferiority, infestation **13** despicability, unsuitability **14** unpleasantness

lousy **3** bad **4** mean **5** awful, nasty **6** crummy, rotten, shabby, unkind **7** hateful, vicious **8** dreadful, inferior, infested, terrible **9** unethical, worthless **10** pediculous, second-rate, unpleasant **12** contemptible

lout **3** ape, oaf **4** boor, clod **5** booby, churl, clown, dummy, dunce, klutz, yokel **6** lummox, rustic **7** bumpkin, dullard

loutish **4** rude **5** crude **6** coarse, gauche, oafish, vulgar **7** boorish, uncouth **9** unrefined **10** unpolished **11** peasantlike

lovable, loveable **4** cute **5** sweet **6** cuddly, lovely, taking **7** darling, winning, winsome **8** adorable, charming, engaging, fetching **9** endearing **10** enchanting **11** captivating

Lovberg, Eilert
character in: **11** Hedda Gabler
author: **5** Ibsen

love **3** man **4** beau, bent, dear, girl, mind, turn **5** adore, amity, amour, angel, ardor, enjoy, fancy, flame, honey, lover, savor, taste, woman **6** admire, bask in, choice, esteem, fellow, relish **7** beloved, charity, cherish, concord, darling, dearest, emotion, leaning, passion, rapture, revel in, sweetie **8** affinity, be fond of, devotion, fondness, goodwill, hold dear, loved one, mistress, paramour, penchant, precious, sympathy, treasure, truelove, weakness **9** adoration, affection, boyfriend, delight in, inamorata, rejoice in, sentiment **10** admiration, appreciate, attachment, cordiality, friendship, girlfriend, partiality, proclivity, solicitude, sweetheart, sweetie pie, tenderness **11** amorousness, benevolence, brotherhood, inclination, infatuation **12** be enamored of, congeniality, predilection
god of: **4** Amor, Eros **5** Cupid **7** Angus Og
goddess of: **5** Freia, Freya **6** Hathor, Inanna, Ishtar **7** Mylitta **9** Aphrodite

Love, the Magician
also: **11** El Amor Brujo
ballet by: **5** Falla

love affair **5** amour **7** liaison, romance **14** affaire de coeur

Love Boat, The
character: **3** Ace **10** (Cruise Director) Julie McCoy **11** (Dr) Adam Bricker, (Purser Burl) Gopher Smith **14** (Captain) Merrill Stubing **15** (Bartender) Isaac Washington
cast: **8** Ted Lange **10** Fred Grandy **11** Lauren Tewes **12** Bernie Kopell, Gavin MacLeod
ship: **15** Pacific Princess

love child **7** bastard **12** natural child **17** illegitimate child

love conquers all
Latin: **15** omnia vincit amor

loved one **4** love, wife

5 lover 6 fiance, spouse 7 beloved, dearest, fiancee, husband 9 boyfriend 10 girlfriend, sweetheart 12 family member

Love for Three Oranges, The
opera by: 9 Prokofiev

Love in the Afternoon
director: 11 Billy Wilder
cast: 10 Gary Cooper 13 Audrey Hepburn 16 Maurice Chevalier
setting: 5 Paris

Lovelace, Richard
author of: 18 To Althea from Prison 23 To Lucasta Going to the Wars

loveliness 6 beauty 9 good looks 11 pulchritude 14 attractiveness

lovely 4 cute, fine, good 5 sweet 6 comely 7 elegant, lovable, winning, winsome 8 adorable, alluring, charming, engaging, fetching, handsome, pleasant, pleasing 9 agreeable, beautiful, endearing, enjoyable, exquisite 10 attractive, delightful, enchanting 11 captivating, fascinating 12 irresistible

Love Machine, The
author: 16 Jacqueline Susann

Love Me Tonight
director: 15 Rouben Mamoulian
cast: 8 Myrna Loy 14 Charlie Ruggles 16 Maurice Chevalier 17 Jeanette MacDonald
score: 14 Rodgers and Hart
song: 4 Mimi 5 Lover 14 Isn't It Romantic

love of country
Latin: 11 amor patriae

Love of One's Neighbor
author: 14 Leonid Andreyev

lover 3 fan, man, nut 4 beau, buff, dear, girl, love 5 freak, honey, swain, woman, wooer 6 fellow, suitor 7 admirer, beloved, darling, devotee, fanatic, sweetie 8 follower, loved one, lover boy, mistress, paramour, truelove 9 boyfriend, inamorata 10 aficionado, enthusiast, girlfriend, sweetheart 11 afficionado
French: 6 bon ami 9 bonne amie
Italian: 8 cicisbeo

Lovers and Other Strangers
director: 8 Cy Howard
cast: 8 Gig Young 9 Anne Meara, Bea Arthur 11 Anne Jackson 13 Bonnie Bedelia, Harry Guardino 14 Cloris Leachman, Michael Brandon 17 Richard Castellano

love seat 4 sofa 5 couch 6 settee 13 courting chair

lovesick 7 amorous 8 yearning 10 moonstruck

Love's Labour's Lost
author: 18 William Shakespeare
character: 4 Dull 5 Maria 7 Berowne, Costard, Dumaine 8 Rosaline 9 Ferdinand, Katherine 10 Holofernes, Jaquenetta, Longaville 16 Princess of France 18 Don Adriano de Armado

Love Song of J Alfred Prufrock, The
author: 7 T S Eliot

Love Story
author: 10 Erich Segal

Love-wit
character in: 12 The Alchemist
author: 6 Jonson

loving 4 fond, kind, warm 6 ardent, caring, doting, erotic, tender 7 amatory, amorous, devoted 8 enamored, friendly 10 benevolent, passionate, solicitous 11 sympathetic, warmhearted 12 affectionate

loving word 9 sweet talk 10 endearment 12 sweet nothing

low 4 base, blue, deep, down, evil, glum, mean, soft, vile 5 awful, cruel, dirty, dumpy, faint, gross, lower, lowly, muted, prone, quiet, short, small, squat 6 brutal, coarse, common, cruddy, crummy, feeble, gentle, gloomy, humble, hushed, little, paltry, scurvy, softly, sordid, stubby, stumpy, sunken, vulgar, wicked 7 coastal, concave, corrupt, doleful, heinous, muffled, obscene, quietly, snubbed, squalid, subdued, unhappy 8 cowardly, degraded, dejected, depraved, downcast, inferior, low-lying, low-slung, mediocre, murmured, sawed-off, soothing, terrible, trifling, undersea, unworthy 9 dastardly, depressed, lethargic, nefarious, prostrate, repugnant, repulsive, submarine, submerged, truncated, unethical, whispered 10 abominable, despicable, despondent, dispirited, melancholy, outrageous, scandalous 11 ignominious, scoundrelly, underground, unimportant 12 contemptible, disheartened, dishonorable 14 down in the mouth

lowbred 6 coarse, common, vulgar 7 lowbrow, peasant 10 lower-class, uncultured

low-down 4 base, mean 5 dirty 10 despicable 12 contemptible 13 reprehensible

Lowell, James Russell
author of: 12 The Cathedral 15 The Biglow Papers 16 A Fable for Critics 21 The Vision of Sir Launfal

Lowell, Robert
author of: 8 Day by Day 9 Skunk Hour 10 The Dolphin 11 Life Studies 15 For the Union Dead 16 Lord Weary's Castle

Lowenstein, Laszlo
real name of: 10 Peter Lorre

lower 3 cut, dim 4 damp, drop, duck, mute, pare, sink, sulk 5 frown, glare, pared, prune, scowl 6 deduct, glower, lop off, muffle, reduce, soften, subdue 7 curtail, depress, immerse, let down, put down, reduced, repress, shorten 8 decrease, diminish, grow dark, lessened, make less, pare down, pull down, submerge, take down, tone down 9 curtailed, decreased, make lower, pared down 10 abbreviate, diminished

lower-case letter 9 minuscule 11 small letter

lower-class 4 poor 6 common 7 lowbred, lowbrow, peasant 9 unrefined 10 blue-collar 12 working-class

lower classes 6 proles, rabble 8 canaille, riffraff 9 hoi polloi, peasantry 11 proletariat 13 the common herd, working people 16 the great unwashed

lower depths 4 pits, scum 5 dregs 6 rabble 8 canaille, riffraff 14 scum of the earth

Lower Depths, The
also called: 11 At the Bottom 14 A Night's Lodging
author: 10 Maxim Gorky

lower in rank 4 bust 6 demote 7 degrade

lower in spirits 6 deject, sadden 7 depress 8 dispirit 10 dishearten

low-key 4 soft 5 loose, muted 6 gentle, subtle 7 muffled, relaxed, subdued 8 laid-back, softened, soft-sell 9 modulated, toned-down 10 low-pitched, restrained 11 low-pressure, understated, unobtrusive 14 unostentatious

lowliness **8** baseness **9** obscurity **10** humbleness

lowly **3** low **6** humble, modest, simple, softly **7** ignoble, lowborn, lowbred, obscure **8** baseborn, plebeian **10** unassuming **11** proletarian **13** unpretentious

low-minded **4** lewd, vile **5** crude, gross **6** coarse, smutty, vulgar **7** obscene, uncouth **9** obnoxious, offensive **11** disgraceful **12** contemptible

low point, lowest point **4** base, foot, zero **5** depth, nadir, worst **6** bottom **7** perigee **10** rock bottom

low-priced **5** cheap, token **6** budget, modest **7** bargain, cut-rate, low-cost, nominal, reduced **8** closeout, moderate **9** dirt-cheap **10** discounted, economical, marked-down, reasonable **11** inexpensive **15** bargain-basement

low-ranking **5** minor, petty **11** subordinate, unimportant

low-spirited **3** low, sad **4** blue, down, glum **6** gloomy, morose, woeful **7** doleful, forlorn, unhappy **8** dejected, desolate, downcast **9** depressed, heartsore, sorrowful, woebegone **10** despondent, dispirited, melancholy **11** crestfallen, discouraged, downhearted **12** disconsolate, disheartened **14** down-in-the-mouth

low spirits **4** funk **5** gloom **6** dismay, sorrow **7** despair **8** dejected **9** pessimism **10** depression, desolation, melancholy, moroseness **11** despondency **12** hopelessness **14** discouragement **15** downheartedness

Loxias
epithet of: **6** Apollo
means: **9** ambiguous

Loy, Myrna
real name: **13** Myrna Williams
co-star: **13** William Powell
born: **13** Raidersburg MT
roles: **10** The Thin Man **11** Nora Charles **17** Cheaper by the Dozen **22** The Best Years of Our Lives

loyal **4** firm, true **6** trusty **7** devoted, dutiful, staunch **8** constant, faithful, reliable, resolute, true-blue **9** steadfast **10** dependable, scrupulous, unswerving, unwavering **11** trustworthy **12** tried and true

loyalist **4** tory **12** conservative

Loyalties
author: **14** John Galsworthy

loyalty **6** fealty **8** devotion, fidelity, firmness **9** adherence, constancy **10** allegiance **11** reliability, staunchness **12** faithfulness **13** dependability, steadfastness **15** trustworthiness

lozenge **4** drop, pill **6** tablet, troche **8** pastille **9** cough drop

Luanda
capital of: **6** Angola

Lubitsch, Ernst
director of: **9** Ninotchka **13** Heaven Can Wait, To Be or Not To Be

Lucas, Charlotte
character in: **17** Pride and Prejudice
author: **6** Austen

Lucentio
character in: **19** The Taming of the Shrew
author: **11** Shakespeare

Lucerne
German: **6** Luzern
river: **5** Reuss
landmark: **9** Hofkirche **11** Am Rhyn House **15** Mariahilf Church

Lucia di Lammermoor
opera by: **9** Donizetti
based on novel by: **14** Sir Walter Scott
called: **20** The Bride of Lammermoor

Luciana
character in: **17** The Comedy of Errors
author: **11** Shakespeare

Luciani, Albino **13** Pope John Paul I **20** Pope John Paul the First

lucid **5** clear **6** bright, direct, normal **7** certain, precise, radiant, shining **8** accurate, apposite, dazzling, luminous, lustrous, pellucid, positive, rational, specific **9** brilliant, sparkling **10** articulate, perceptive, responsive, to the point **11** clearheaded, crystalline, illuminated, resplendent, transparent **12** crystal clear, intelligible **13** clear thinking, scintillating, well-organized **14** comprehensible, understandable **15** straightforward

Lucifer
means: **5** Satan **11** fallen angel, light bearer

Lucina
origin: **5** Roman
goddess of: **10** childbirth
corresponds to: **4** Juno **8** Ilithyia **10** Eileithyia

Lucio
character in: **17** Measure for Measure
author: **11** Shakespeare

luck **3** lot **4** fate **5** karma **6** chance, kismet **7** destiny, fortune, success, triumph, victory **8** accident, fortuity, good luck, Lady Luck **11** good fortune, piece of luck **12** happenstance
god of: **12** Bonus Eventus

lucky **4** good **5** happy **6** in luck, timely **7** blessed, favored **9** favorable, fortunate, opportune, promising **10** auspicious, beneficial, felicitous, of good omen, propitious **12** providential

Lucky Jim
author: **12** Kingsley Amis

lucky piece **5** charm **6** amulet **8** talisman **10** lucky charm

lucrative **7** gainful **8** fruitful **10** beneficial, high-income, high-paying, profitable **11** moneymaking **12** remunerative

Lucretia
husband: **26** Lucius Tarquinius Collatinus
raped by: **16** Sextus Tarquinius
death by: **7** suicide

Lucretius
author of: **13** De rerum natura **19** On the nature of things

Lucullan **4** rich **6** lavish **7** gourmet **9** epicurean, luxurious

Lucy Show, The
also: **9** Here's Lucy
character: **9** Kim Carter **10** Lucy Carter **11** Craig Carter **12** Harry Conners, Vivian Bagley **13** Mary Jane Lewis, Sherman Bagley **14** Lucy Carmichael **15** Chris Carmichael, Harrison Cheever, Jerry Carmichael, Theodore J Mooney **18** Harrison Otis Carter
cast: **9** Ralph Hart **10** Candy Moore, Dick Martin, Gale Gordon, Lucie Arnaz, Roy Roberts **11** Desi Arnaz Jr, Lucille Ball, Vivian Vance **12** Jimmy Garrett **13** Mary Jane Croft

Ludd *see* **4** Llud

ludicrous **4** wild **5** comic, crazy, funny **6** absurd, far-out **7** amusing, comical **8** farcical **9** laughable **10** outlandish, ridiculous **11** nonsensical **12** preposterous

Ludlum, Robert
author of: **15** The Matlock Paper **17** The Bourne Identity, The Parsifal Mosaic, The Road to Gandolfo **18** The Osterman Weekend **19** The Gemini Contenders **20** The Rhinemann Exchange **23** The Chancellor Manuscript, The Scarlatti Inheritance

Luftwaffe **9** air weapon **18** German Nazi air force

lug **3** tow, tug **4** bear, drag, draw, haul, pull, tote **5** carry, heave **9** transport

Lug
origin: **5** Irish
habitat: **5** solar

luggage **4** bags, gear **6** trunks **7** baggage, effects, valises **9** suitcases **13** accouterments

Luggnagg
fictional land in: **16** Gulliver's Travels
author: **5** Swift

Lugnasad
origin: **5** Irish
feast date: **11** August first

Lugosi, Bela
real name: **10** Bela Blasko
born: **5** Lugos **7** Hungary
roles: **7** Dracula **21** Murders in the Rue Morgue

lugubrious **4** dour, glum **6** gloomy, morose, rueful, somber, woeful **7** doleful, elegiac **8** dolorous, downcast, funereal, mournful **9** miserable, sorrowful, woebegone **10** depressing, melancholy

Lukas, George
director of: **8** Star Wars **16** American Graffiti

Luke
birthplace: **7** Antioch
companion: **4** Paul
wrote: **6** Gospel

lukewarm **4** cool, mild, warm **5** aloof, tepid **8** detached, uncaring **9** apathetic, temperate **11** halfhearted, indifferent, perfunctory, unconcerned **12** uninterested **13** lackadaisical **14** unenthusiastic **15** body-temperature, room-temperature

lull **3** gap **4** calm, ease, halt, hush **5** break, pause, quell, quiet, still **6** hiatus, lacuna, pacify, recess, soothe, subdue **7** assuage, caesura, compose, mollify, respite **8** breather, calmness **9** interlude **12** brief silence, interruption

Lully, Jean-Baptiste
born: **5** Italy **8** Florence
composer of: **4** Atys, Isis **6** Persee, Psyche, Roland, Thesee **7** Alceste, Phaeton **10** Le Sicilien, Proserpine **11** Bellerophon **13** Acis et Galatee, Amadis de Gaule, L'Amour medecin **14** Acis and Galatea, Armide et Renaud, Le mariage force **16** Cadmus et Hermione **17** Achille et Polyxene, Cadmus and Hermione **19** Achilles and Polyxene **20** Les Amants magnifiques **22** Le Bourgeois Gentilhomme, Monsieur de Pourceaugnac

lulu **3** pip **5** dandy, doozy **8** Jim Dandy **9** allowance, humdinger, wonderful **10** remarkable

lumber **3** log **4** plod, wood **5** barge, clump, stamp **6** boards, planks, trudge, waddle **7** shamble, shuffle **8** flounder **9** fell trees

Lumber State
nickname of: **5** Maine

Lumet, Sidney
director of: **7** Network, Serpico **13** The Pawnbroker **14** Twelve Angry Men **15** Dog Day Afternoon **24** Long Day's Journey Into Night

luminary **3** VIP **5** light, wheel **6** bigwig **7** big shot, notable **8** somebody **9** celebrity, dignitary, personage **10** luminosity **11** illuminator

luminescent **5** aglow **7** glowing **8** gleaming, luminous **9** twinkling **10** flickering, glimmering, glistening, shimmering **11** fluorescent **14** phosphorescent

luminosity **4** glow **5** gleam, sheen, shine **6** luster **8** radiance **10** brightness, brilliance

luminous **6** bright **7** glowing, radiant, shining **8** lustrous **9** brilliant **10** irradiated **11** illuminated, luminescent **15** reflecting light

lump **3** gob, mix **4** bump, cake, clod, fuse, heap, hunk, knob, knot, mass, node, pile, pool **5** amass, batch, blend, bunch, chunk, clump, group, knurl, merge, tumor, unite **6** gather, growth, nodule **7** collect, combine, compile **8** assemble, swelling **9** aggregate **10** protrusion, tumescence **11** excrescence **12** protuberance

lumpish **4** dull, slow **5** bulky, dumpy, heavy, lumpy **6** clumsy **7** awkward **8** cloddish, ungainly, unwieldy **9** corpulent **10** cumbersome, overweight

Lumpkin, Tony
character in: **18** She Stoops to Conquer
author: **9** Goldsmith

lump together **4** fuse, pool **7** combine **10** amalgamate **11** consolidate, incorporate

Luna
personifies: **4** moon

lunacy **5** folly, mania **6** idiocy **7** madness **8** dementia, insanity **9** absurdity, asininity, craziness, silliness, stupidity **10** imbecility, imprudence, insaneness **11** foolishness **13** foolhardiness, senselessness

lunatic **3** mad, nut **4** daft, loco **5** batty, crazy, loony, nutty, potty **6** cuckoo, insane, madman, maniac, screwy **7** bonkers, cracked, touched **8** crackers, demented, demoniac, deranged, maniacal, unhinged **9** psychotic, senseless **10** irrational, psychopath, reasonless, unbalanced **11** crazy person, mentally ill, not all there **12** crackbrained, insane person, psychopathic, round the bend **13** off one's rocker, of unsound mind, out of one's mind

lunch
French: **8** dejeuner

luncheonette **4** cafe **5** diner **7** beanery **8** snack bar **9** hash house, lunchroom **10** coffee shop **11** eating house **12** lunch counter, sandwich shop

lunchroom **4** cafe **5** diner, grill **8** snack bar **9** cafeteria **12** luncheonette

lunge **3** cut, jab **4** dash, dive, pass, rush, stab **5** hit at, lurch, swing, swipe **6** attack, charge, plunge, pounce, thrust **7** set upon **8** fall upon, strike at **9** make a pass

lunkhead **3** ass **4** dope, fool **5** booby, dunce, idiot, moron, ninny **6** dimwit, nitwit **7** fathead, halfwit **8** bonehead, dumb-dumb, imbecile, numskull **9** blockhead, lamebrain, numbskull **10** dunderhead, nincompoop **11** chowderhead

Lunt, Alfred
wife: **12** Lynn Fontanne
born: **11** Milwaukee WI
roles: **12** The Guardsman **13** The Ragged Edge

Lupercalia
origin: **5** Roman
event: **8** festival

honoring: **6** Faunus **8** Lupercus
to procure: **9** fertility

Lupercus
origin: **5** Roman
god of: **9** fertility
corresponds to: **3** Pan **6** Faunus

Lupino, Ida
husband: **10** Howard Duff **12** Collier Young, Louis Hayward
born: **6** London **7** England
roles: **8** Devotion **10** The Hard Way **12** Junior Bonner, Women's Prison **13** Escape Me Never **15** Strange Intruder **17** On Dangerous Ground **18** The Light That Failed, While the City Sleeps

lurch **4** cant, keel, list, reel, roll, sway, tilt, toss **5** lunge, pitch, slant **6** careen, plunge, swerve, teeter, totter **7** incline, stagger, stumble

lure **4** bait, coax, trap **5** bribe, decoy, snare, tempt **6** allure, cajole, come-on, entice, induce, seduce **7** attract, beguile **8** cajolery, persuade **9** fascinate, tantalize **10** allurement, attraction, enticement, inducement, temptation **11** drawing card **12** blandishment

Lurelei *see* **7** Lorelei

lurid **4** gory, grim **5** eerie, fiery, vivid **6** bloody **7** carmine, flaming, ghastly, glaring, glowing, graphic, scarlet, shining **8** dramatic, rubicund, sanguine, shocking **9** appalling, bright-red **11** sensational **12** melodramatic **13** bloodcurdling

lurk **4** hide **5** prowl, skulk, slink, sneak **9** lie in wait

Lusaka
capital of: **6** Zambia

luscious **5** tasty **6** savory **7** scented **8** aromatic, fragrant, perfumed **9** delicious, flavorful, succulent, toothsome **10** appetizing, delectable **13** mouthwatering

lush **4** posh, rich **5** dense, fancy, grand **6** ornate **7** elegant, profuse **8** abundant, prolific, splendid **9** elaborate, luxuriant, luxurious, sumptuous **11** flourishing, magnificent

Lusia
epithet of: **7** Demeter
means: **6** bather

lust **5** covet, crave **6** be lewd **7** craving, lechery, passion **8** lewdness **9** carnality, hunger for, sexuality **10** satyriasis **14** lasciviousness, libidinousness

lust after **4** want **5** covet, crave **6** desire **11** have a yen for, have an eye on, hunger after, thirst after

luster **4** fame, glow **5** gleam, glory, gloss, honor, merit, sheen, shine **6** dazzle **7** burnish, glimmer, glitter, sparkle **8** prestige, radiance **9** radiation **10** brightness, brilliance, luminosity, notability, refulgence **11** distinction **12** luminousness, resplendence **15** illustriousness

lusterless **3** dim, wan **4** dead, drab, dull, flat **5** faded, matte, muted **7** prosaic **9** colorless, tarnished

Lust for Life
author: **11** Irving Stone
director: **16** Vincente Minnelli
based on story by: **11** Irving Stone
cast: **11** James Donald, Kirk Douglas (Vincent Van Gogh), Pamela Brown **12** Anthony Quinn (Gaugin)
Oscar for: **15** supporting actor (Quinn)

lustful **4** lewd **6** carnal **8** prurient **9** lecherous, salacious **10** lascivious, libidinous

lustrous **6** bright, glossy **7** glowing, radiant, shining **8** dazzling, gleaming, luminous, polished **9** burnished, effulgent **10** glistening **11** coruscating, illuminated **12** incandescent

lusty **4** hale **5** husky, sound **6** brawny, hearty, robust, rugged, sturdy, virile **7** healthy **8** vigorous **9** exuberant, strapping **10** full of life **11** uninhibited **12** unrestrained, wholehearted **13** irrepressible

Luther, Martin
born: **7** Germany **8** Eisleben
author: **16** Ninety-Five Theses **27** On the Freedom of a Christian Man **46** Address to the Christian Nobility of the German Nation **51** A Prelude Concerning the Babylonian Captivity of the Church
excommunicated by: **8** Pope Leo X **15** Pope Leo the Tenth
summoned before: **11** Diet of Worms
founded: **11** Lutheranism, Reformation **13** Protestantism

lux **5** light

Luxembourg ***see box***

Luxembourg
other name: **9** Luxemburg **13** Lucilinburhuc
name means: **10** little fort
capital/largest city: **10** Luxembourg
others: **4** Hamm **5** Roodt, Wiltz **6** Mersch, Remich **7** Kopstal, Lintgen, Petange, Redange, Vianden **8** Capellen, Clervaux, Diekirch, Frisange **9** Dudelange **10** Echternach, Ettelbruck, Hesperange, Larochette **11** Differdange, Wormeldange **12** Grevenmacher, Troisvierges, Wasserbillig **14** Esch-sur-Alzette
division: **6** Esleck **7** Bon Pays, Gutland, Oesling
measure: **5** fuder
monetary unit: **5** franc **7** centime
lake: **8** Haut Sure
mountain: **8** Ardennes
highest point: **8** Huldange **9** Burgplatz **11** Wemperhardt
river: **3** Our **4** Sure, Syre **5** Alert, Clerf, Eisch, Mosel, Sauer, Wiltz **6** Chiers **7** Alzette, Moselle **8** Petrusse **11** Ernz Blanche
physical feature:
plateau: **4** Bock **8** Ardennes, Lorraine
valley: **7** Moselle
people: **6** French, German **12** Luxembourger
ruler: **8** Sigefroi, Wencelas **12** Jean l'Aveugle **21** House of Nassau-Weilburg
saint: **10** Willibrord
language: **6** French, German **7** English **13** Letzeburgesch
religion: **13** Roman Catholic
food:
pastry: **20** les pensees brouillees

luxuriant **4** lush, rank **5** dense, fancy, grand **6** florid, ornate **7** elegant, flowery, profuse, teeming **8** abundant, splendid **9** elaborate, exuberant, luxurious, overgrown, sumptuous **10** flamboyant **11** extravagant, flourishing, magnificent

luxuriate **4** bask **6** relish **7** delight **8** wallow in **9** indulge in

luxurious **4** rich **5** grand **6** costly, effete **7** elegant, wealthy **8** decadent, pampered **9** enjoyable, expensive, indulgent, sumptuous **10** gratifying **11** comfortable, pleasurable

luxuriousness **4** ease **6** luxury **7** comfort **8** richness **10** costliness **13** sumptuousness

luxury **5** bliss **6** heaven, riches, wealth **7** delight **8** paradise, pleasure **9** enjoyment **10** high living, indulgence **12** extravagance, nonessential, nonnecessity, satisfaction **13** gratification

LXX *see* **15** Septuagint

Lyaeus
epithet of: **8** Dionysus
means: **8** loosener

Lycaeus
epithet of: **4** Zeus
means: **7** wolfish

Lycaon
king of: **7** Arcadia
father: **8** Pelasgus
son: **8** Maenalus, Tegeates
tested: **4** Zeus
turned into: **4** wolf

Lycidas
author: **10** John Milton
elegy for: **10** Edward King

Lycomedes
king of: **6** Scyrus
daughter: **8** Deidamia
pushed over cliff: **7** Theseus

Lycon
mentioned in: **5** Iliad
vocation: **7** warrior
home: **4** Troy
killed by: **8** Peneleus

Lycophron
origin: **5** Greek
father: **9** Periander
exiled to: **7** Corcyra
killed by: **10** Corcyreans
committed: **6** murder
went to: **4** Troy
killed by: **6** Hector

Lycotherses
king of: **7** Illyria
wife: **5** Agave
killed by: **5** Agave

Lycurgas
king of: **6** Edones, Thrace
son: **5** Dryas
persecuted: **8** Dionysus
killed: **5** Dryas

Lycus
king of: **6** Thebes **7** Cilicia
father: **7** Pandion **9** Chthonius
mother: **5** Pylia
brother: **7** Nycteus
wife: **5** Dirce
niece: **7** Antiope
son: **5** Lycus
succeeded: **8** Sarpedon
killed by: **6** Zethus **7** Amphion **12** Antiope's sons

Lygodesma
epithet of: **7** Artemis
means: **11** willow-bound

lying down **5** in bed, prone **6** supine **7** napping, resting **8** snoozing **9** reclining, recumbent **10** taking a nap **13** taking a snooze

Lyle, Albert Walter
nickname: **6** Sparky
sport: **8** baseball
position: **7** pitcher
team: **12** Boston Red Sox **14** New York Yankees
author of: **11** The Bronx Zoo

Lyly, John
author of: **20** Euphues and His England **22** Euphues the Anatomy of Wit

lynch **4** hang **6** gibbet **8** string up

Lynde, Paul
born: **13** Mount Vernon OH
roles: **12** Bye Bye Birdie **16** Hollywood Squares **17** Beach Blanket Bingo **18** Under the Yum-Yum Tree

Lyngi
origin: **12** Scandinavian
mentioned in: **8** Volsunga
rival of: **7** Sigmund
sought: **7** Hiordis, Hjordis
killed: **7** Sigmund
killed by: **6** Sigurd

lynx **3** cat **6** bobcat **7** wildcat

Lyonnesse
place in: **16** Arthurian romance
birthplace of: **8** Tristram

Lyre
constellation of: **4** Lyra

lyric, lyrical **6** poetic **7** lilting, melodic, musical, singing, tuneful **8** songlike **9** melodious **10** euphonious **11** mellifluent, mellifluous **13** sweet-sounding

Lyrical Ballads
author: **17** William Wordsworth **21** Samuel Taylor Coleridge

lyrics **4** poem **5** words

Lyrus
father: **8** Anchises
mother: **9** Aphrodite

Lysander
character in: **21** A Midsummer Night's Dream
author: **11** Shakespeare

Lysippe
father: **7** Proetus
mother: **5** Antia

Lysistrata
author: **12** Aristophanes
character: **7** Lampito **8** Cinesias, Cleonice, Myrrhine **10** Magistrate **14** Old Men of Athens (Chorus)

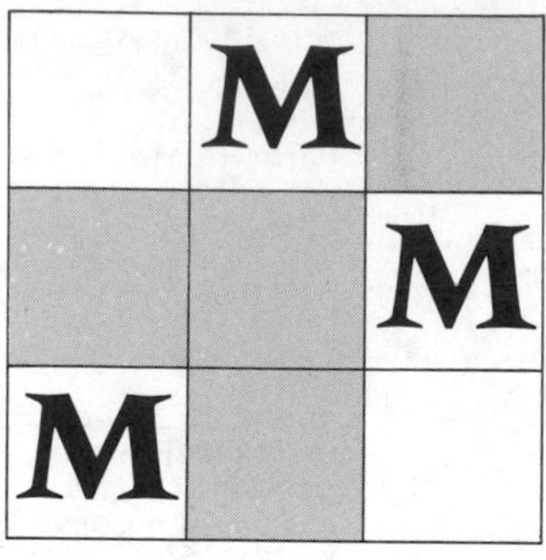

M
director: **9** Fritz Lang
cast: **10** Peter Lorre **11** Inge Landgut **12** Ellen Widmann **15** Gustav Grundgens
setting: **6** Berlin

Maat
origin: **8** Egyptian
goddess of: **3** law **13** righteousness
symbol: **7** feather

Mabinogian
origin: **5** Welsh
tales of: **7** romance

macabre **4** grim **5** eerie, weird **6** grisly, horrid **7** ghastly, ghostly **8** dreadful, gruesome, horrible, horrific **9** frightful, ghostlike, unearthly **11** frightening

Macao ***see box***

Macareus
father: **6** Aeolus
mother: **7** Encrete
sister: **6** Canace

MacArthur, Douglas
served in: **3** WWI **4** WWII **9** Korean War, World War I **10** World War II **11** World War One, World War Two
commander of: **15** Rainbow (42nd) Division **19** United Nations forces **24** US army forces in the Pacific
rank: **15** five-star general **16** army chief of staff
battle: **5** Luzon, Pusan **6** Inchon **9** New Guinea **11** Leyte Island, Philippines **14** Bismark Islands, Solomon Islands **15** Bataan Peninsula **16** Admiralty Islands, Corregidor Island
accepted surrender of: **5** Japan
surrender occurred aboard: **8** Missouri
chairman of: **13** Remington Rand
author of: **13** Reminiscences
smoked: **11** corncob pipe
saying: **12** "I shall return"

Macbeth
author: **18** William Shakespeare
character: **6** Banquo, Duncan (King of Scotland) **7** MacDuff, Malcolm **11** Lady Macbeth **12** Three Witches
director: **13** Roman Polanski
cast: **8** Jon Finch **10** Martin Shaw **13** Nicholas Selby **14** Francesca Annis

Maccabees
title of: **5** Judas
patriarch: **10** Mattathias
means: **8** hammerer

Macao
other name: **5** Ao-men, Macau
government: **19** territory of Portugal
head of government: **27** governor appointed by Portugal
monetary unit: **3** avo **6** pataca, pataco
island: **5** Taipa **7** Coloane
highest point: **5** Hag-Sa
river: **5** Pearl **6** Canton
sea: **10** South China
physical feature:
estuary: **9** Chu Chiang
peninsula: **5** Macao
people: **6** Macaon **7** Chinese **10** Portuguese
language: **7** Chinese, English **9** Cantonese **10** Portuguese
religion: **6** Taoism **8** Buddhism **13** Roman Catholic
place:
street: **11** Praia Grande
feature:
houseboat: **6** sampan

MacDonald, John D
author of: **11** Condominium **13** A Flash of Green **15** The Executioners
character: **11** Travis McGee

MacDonald, Ross
real name: **13** Kenneth Millar
author of: **8** The Chill **10** Black Money **13** The Blue Hammer **14** The Goodbye Look **16** Archer in Jeopardy **25** Lew Archer Private Detective

MacDowell, Edward Alexander
born: **9** New York NY
composer of: **9** Sea Pieces **11** To a Wild Rose **13** Fireside Tales **15** Poems after Heine **16** Hamlet and Ophelia, New England Idylls, Woodland Sketches **17** Idylls after Goethe

MacDuff
character in: **7** Macbeth
author: **11** Shakespeare

mace
origin: **9** Indonesia
from same tree as: **6** nutmeg
tree: **17** Myristica fragrans
use: **4** fish **7** seafood **9** cherry pie, pound cake **16** chicken fricassee

macerate **4** fade, mash, pulp, soak **5** souse, steep **6** shrink, soften, squash, wither **7** decline, liquefy, shrivel **8** dissolve, emaciate, fluidize, permeate, saturate **9** liquidize, waste away **10** lose weight

MacGraw, Ali
real name: **12** Alice MacGraw
husband: **8** Bob Evans **12** Steve McQueen
born: **12** Pound Ridge NY
roles: **7** Dynasty **9** Love Story **10** The Getaway

13 The Winds of War
15 Goodbye Columbus

Machaerus
killed: 11 Neoptolemus

Machaon
father: 9 Asclepius
brother: 10 Podalirius
wife: 8 Anticlea
son: 8 Alexanor, Gorgasus 10 Nicomachus
vocation: 9 physician
served in: 9 Trojan War

Macheath, Captain
character in: 12 Beggar's Opera
author: 3 Gay

ma chere 6 my dear

Machiavelli, Niccolo
author of: 9 The Prince 11 The Art of War 16 Discourses on Livy

Machiavellian 6 amoral, crafty 7 cunning, devious 8 scheming 9 deceitful, designing 10 perfidious 11 self-serving, treacherous, underhanded 12 falsehearted, unscrupulous

machination 4 plot, rule, ruse 5 dodge 6 design, device, scheme 8 artifice, intrigue, maneuver 9 stratagem 10 conspiracy 11 contrivance

machine 3 set 4 army, body, camp, club, gang, pool, ring 5 corps, crowd, force, group, setup, trust, union 6 device, system 7 combine, coterie, faction, society 9 apparatus, appliance, machinery, mechanism, structure 11 association 12 organization 13 establishment

machine gun
invented by: 7 Gatling
improved by: 5 Maxim 9 Hotchkiss

machinery 4 gear 5 setup, tools 6 agency, makeup, system, tackle, wheels 9 apparatus, mechanism, resources, structure 12 contrivances, organization

macho 5 he-man, manly 6 strong, virile

Machpelah
location: 6 Hebron
burial place of: 4 Leah 5 Isaac, Jacob, Sarah 7 Abraham, Rebekah

Macilente
character in: 22 Every Man out of His Humour
author: 6 Jonson

MacInnes, Helen
author of: 13 North from Rome 14 Above Suspicion 16 Decision at Delphi 17 The Venetian Affair 21 The Salzburg Connection

macintosh, mackintosh 7 slicker 8 raincoat 10 waterproof

Mack, Connie
real name: 30 Cornelius Alexander McGillicuddy
sport: 8 baseball
position: 7 manager
team: 21 Philadelphia Athletics

MacKellar
character in: 21 The Master of Ballantrae
author: 9 Stevenson

mackerel
young: 5 spike 6 tinker 7 blinker

mackinaw 4 coat 6 jacket 8 overcoat

MacLaine, Shirley
real name: 19 Shirley MacLean Beaty
brother: 12 Warren Beatty
born: 10 Richmond VA
roles: 6 Can Can 10 Being There 11 Irma La Douce 12 Sweet Charity, The Apartment 15 Some Came Running, The Turning Point, Two for the Seesaw 16 The Children's Hour 17 Terms of Endearment (Oscar) 19 The Trouble with Harry 20 The Bliss of Mrs Blossom

MacMurray, Fred
wife: 9 June Haver
born: 10 Kankakee IL
roles: 11 My Three Sons 12 The Apartment 14 Above Suspicion, The Caine Mutiny 15 Double Indemnity 20 The Miracle of the Bells

Macro-Chibchan
language branch: 6 Paezan 8 Chibchan

macrocosm 6 cosmos, nature 7 heavens 8 creation, universe 9 firmament

Macro-Ge
language family: 11 Ge-Pano-Carib
group: 2 Ge 6 Bororo, Caraja

Macro-Panoan
language family: 11 Ge-Pano-Carib
group: 6 Panoan 10 Guaycuruan

mad 4 avid, daft, loco, nuts, wild 5 angry, balmy, crazy, irate, nutty 6 ardent, crazed, cuckoo, fuming, insane, miffed, screwy, ticked 7 cracked, enraged, excited, fanatic, furious, in a huff, lunatic, riled up, teed off, touched 8 crackers, demented, deranged, frenzied, incensed, maniacal, provoked, unhinged, up in arms, worked up, wrathful 9 devoted to, non compos, seeing red, ticked off, wrought up 10 distracted, distraught, infatuated, infuriated, in love with, irrational, unbalanced 11 boiling over, exasperated, impassioned, not all there 12 enthusiastic, round the bend 13 beside oneself, in high dudgeon, not quite right, off one's rocker, out of one's mind

Madagascar *see box, p. 590*

madam, madame 3 Mrs 4 dame, lady 6 matron 7 dowager 8 mistress
German: 4 Frau
Spanish: 6 senora
Italian: 7 signora
Spanish/Portuguese: 4 dona
Italian: 5 donna

Madame Bovary
author: 15 Gustave Flaubert
character: 10 Emma Bovary, Leon Dupuis 13 Charles Bovary 17 Rodolphe Boulanger

Madame Butterfly
also: 15 Madama Butterfly
opera by: 7 Puccini
character: 5 Bonze 6 Suzuki 9 Cho-Cho-San, Cio-Cio-San, Sharpless 14 Prince Yamadori 19 Lieutenant Pinkerton

mad as a hatter 3 mad 4 daft, nuts 5 crazy, nutty 6 insane 7 cracked, touched 8 demented, deranged, unhinged 10 unbalanced 13 off one's rocker, out of one's head 14 off one's trolley 15 mad as a March hare 17 nutty as a fruitcake

mad as a March hare 3 mad 4 daft, nuts 5 crazy, nutty 6 insane 7 cracked, touched 8 demented, deranged, unhinged 10 unbalanced 12 mad as a hatter 13 out of one's head 14 off one's trolley 17 nutty as a fruitcake

madcap 4 rash, wild, zany 5 brash, clown, giddy, joker 6 unruly 7 erratic, flighty, foolish 8 reckless 9 hotheaded, impetuous, impulsive, senseless 10 incautious 11 impractical, thoughtless 12 unconsidered 13 inconsiderate, undisciplined

madden 3 vex 4 gall 5 anger, craze, pique, upset 6 enrage, frenzy 7 derange, incense, inflame, outrage, provoke, tor-

Madagascar
other name: 16 Malagasy Republic
capital/largest city: 10 Tananarive 12 Antananarivo
others: 6 Tulear 7 Majanga, Nossibe, Toliary 8 Manakara, Tamatave 9 Faradofay, Mananjory, Toamasina 10 Antsirabe 11 Antsiranana, Diego-Suarez, Fort Dauphin
measure: 7 gantang
monetary unit: 5 franc 7 centime
island: 6 Barren, Radama 7 Nossi-Be 11 Sainte-Marie 12 Chesterfield
lake: 5 Itasy 7 Alaotra, Kinkony
mountain: 4 Boby 9 Ankaratra 12 High Plateaus, Tsiafajavona 17 Tsaratanana Massif
highest point: 11 Maromokotro
river: 5 Ikopa, Mania, Sofia 7 Mangoky, Mangoro, Onilahy 8 Ivoloina, Manambao, Mananara 9 Betsiboka, Manambolo 10 Manarandra 11 Tsiribihina
ocean: 6 Indian
physical feature:
bay: 6 Radama 8 Antongil 9 Mahajamba 10 Sahamalaza
cape: 5 Amber 10 Saint-Andre 11 Sainte-Marie 14 Saint-Sebastien
channel: 10 Mozambique
lagoon: 9 pangalane
plateau: 9 Ankaizina
people: 4 Arab, Bara, Hova 5 Malay 6 Merina, Tanala 7 African 8 Betsileo, Mahafaly, Malagasy, Sakalava 9 Antaimoro, Antaisaka, Antandroy, Tsimihety 10 Indonesian, Polynesian 13 Betsimisaraka
dynasty: 6 Merina
leader: 9 Ratsiraka, Tsiranana 11 Ranamantsoa
language: 6 French 8 Malagasy, Malgache
religion: 5 Islam 7 animism 10 Protestant 13 Roman Catholic
place:
market: 4 Zoma
royal estate: 4 Rova
feature:
animal: 4 zebu 5 lemur 6 foussa
musical instrument: 11 jego vaotavo
proverb: 8 hainteny
shawl: 5 lamba
food:
vegetable: 7 brettes

ment, unhinge 9 aggravate, infuriate, unbalance 10 exasperate

made 5 built 6 formed 7 created 8 composed, produced 9 assembled, developed 10 fabricated 11 constructed 12 manufactured

madeira
type: 4 wine 6 brandy 7 liqueur 8 aperitif
origin: 7 Madeira

Madeira Islands
capital: 7 Funchal
city: 5 Monte
island: 6 Grande 7 Dezerte, Madeira 8 Desertas 9 Selvagens 10 Porto Santo
ocean: 8 Atlantic
owned by: 8 Portugal
stone aqueduct: 7 levadas
wine: 4 Bual 5 Tinta, Tinto 6 Canary, Gomera 7 Malmsey, Marsala, Sercial 8 Verdelho

Mademoiselle de Maupin
author: 16 Theophile Gautier

Mademoiselle Fifi
author: 15 Guy de Maupassant

made-up 5 false 7 assumed, created 8 fanciful, invented 9 fictional, imaginary, pretended, thought-up 10 fictitious 11 make-believe, theoretical 12 hypothetical

Mad Hatter
character in: 28 Alice's Adventures in Wonderland
author: 7 Carroll

madhouse 6 asylum, bedlam, uproar 7 turmoil 8 loony bin, nuthouse

Madinat al-Shaab
capital of: 10 South Yemen

Madison, James ***see box***

madman 3 nut 5 loony 6 maniac 7 lunatic 8 demoniac 9 psychotic 10 psychopath 11 crazy person

Mad Max
director: 12 George Miller
cast: 9 Mel Gibson
sequel: 14 The Road Warrior 17 Beyond Thunderdome (with Tina Turner)

madness 6 lunacy, oddity 8 delusion, dementia, illusion, insanity 9 craziness 11 derangement

madre 6 mother

Madrid
area: 9 Salamanca 19 Ciudad Universitaria
capital of: 5 Spain
landmark: 14 National Palace 18 Biblioteca Nacional
bull ring: 22 Plaza de Toros Monumental
cathedral: 8 Almudena 9 San Isidro
Moorish fortress: 6 Majrit
museum: 5 Prado
mountain: 18 Sierra de Guadaramma
river: 10 Manzanares
square: 10 Plaza Mayor 11 Plaza del Sol 13 Plaza de Espana
street: 13 Paseo del Prado

Madwoman of Chaillot
author: 13 Jean Giraudoux

Mael
origin: 5 Irish
father: 5 Ronan
killed by: 5 Ronan

maelstrom 4 eddy 5 shoot, swirl 6 bedlam, rapids, tumult, uproar, vortex 7 riptide, torrent 8 disorder, madhouse, undertow, upheaval 9 confusion, whirlpool 10 white water 11 pandemonium

maenad, menad 5 lenae 7 bacchae, bassara 8 clodones, thyiades 9 bacchante 10 mimallones
companion of: 7 Bacchus 8 Dionysus

Maenalus
father: 6 Lycaon

Maeon
survived ambush of: 6 Tydeus

Maeterlinck, Maurice
author of: 8 The Blind 11 The Blue Bird, The Intruder 19 Pelleas and Melisande

Madison, James
nickname: **23** Father of the Constitution
presidential rank: **6** fourth
party: **20** Democratic-Republican
state represented: **2** VA
defeated: **7** (DeWitt) Clinton **8** (Charles Cotesworth) Pinckney
vice president: **5** (Elbridge) Gerry **7** (George) Clinton
cabinet:
state: **5** (Robert) Smith **6** (James) Monroe
treasury: **6** (Alexander James) Dallas **8** (Abraham Alfonse Albert) Gallatin, (George Washington) Campbell, (William Harris) Crawford
war: **6** (James) Monroe, (William) Eustis **8** (William Harris) Crawford **9** (John) Armstrong
attorney general: **4** (Richard) Rush **6** (Caesar Augustus) Rodney **7** (William) Pinkney
navy: **5** (William) Jones **8** (Paul) Hamilton **13** (Benjamin Williams) Crowninshield
born: **12** Port Conway VA **16** King George County
died/buried: **2** VA **12** Orange County **16** Montpelier estate
education:
tutored at home by: **15** Rev Thomas Martin
school: **15** Donald Robertson
college of: **9** New Jersey (now Princeton University)
religion: **12** Episcopalian
interests: **3** law **11** agriculture **14** natural history
author: **16** Federalist Papers (with Hamilton and Jay) **24** Memorial and Remonstrances **29** Journal of the Federal Convention
political career: **24** US House of Representatives **25** Second Continental Congress
secretary of: **5** state
signed: **12** Constitution
civilian career: **6** farmer **7** planter
military service:
colonel of: **19** Orange County militia
notable events of lifetime/term: **19** War of Eighteen Twelve
battle of: **10** New Orleans
treaty of: **5** Ghent
Washington DC burned by: **7** British
father: **5** James
mother: **7** Eleanor (Rose Conway)
siblings: **5** Sarah **6** Reuben **7** Ambrose, Catlett, Francis, William **9** Elizabeth **11** Nelly Conway **13** Frances Taylor
wife: **8** Dorothea (Payne Todd)
nickname: **6** Dolley
first lady:
saved: **11** state papers **25** George Washington's portrait

ma foi **6** my word, really **7** my faith

magazine **6** weekly **7** arsenal, journal, monthly **9** quarterly **10** periodical, powder room **13** military depot, munitions room

Magdalene *see* **4** Mary

magenta **6** maroon **7** carmine, crimson, fuchsia **9** vermilion **12** purplish rose **13** reddish purple

Maggie
character in: **16** Cat on a Hot Tin Roof
author: **8** Williams

Maggie: A Girl of the Streets
author: **12** Stephen Crane

maggot **4** grub, worm **5** larva **8** mealworm

Magi
also called: **7** Wisemen **11** astrologers
followed: **15** Star of Bethlehem
visited: **5** Jesus
gifts: **4** gold **5** myrrh **12** frankincense
singular: **5** magus

magic **4** lure **5** charm, spell **6** hoodoo, voodoo **7** sorcery **8** charisma, jugglery, witchery, wizardry **9** occultism, voodooism **10** allurement, black magic, demonology, divination, hocus-pocus, witchcraft **11** captivation, conjuration, enchantment, fascination, legerdemain, the black art **12** entrancement **13** sleight of hand **16** prestidigitation
god of: **5** Thoth

Magic
nickname of: **13** Earvin Johnson

Magic Flute, The
also: **14** Die Zauberflote
opera: **6** Mozart
character: **6** Pamina, Tamino **8** Papagena, Papageno, Sarastro **10** Monostatos **12** Queen of Night

magician **5** magus **6** shaman, wizard **7** juggler, warlock **8** conjurer, sorcerer **9** alchemist **11** illusionist, medicine man, necromancer, witch doctor **12** escape artist **15** prestidigitator

Magic Mountain, The
author: **10** Thomas Mann
character: **6** Naphta **7** Clavdia **11** Hans Castorp, Settembrini **15** Joachim Ziemssen

magisterial **9** imperious **10** autocratic, peremptory **11** dictatorial, domineering, overbearing **13** condescending

Magister Ludi: The Glass Bead Game
author: **12** Hermann Hesse

magistrate **2** JP **5** judge **7** prefect **17** justice of the peace

magna cum laude **15** with great praise

Magna Graecia **27** ancient Greek colonies in Italy

Magna Mater **3** Ops **4** Rhea **6** Cybele

Magnani, Anna
nickname: **10** Nannerella
roles: **8** Open City **13** The Rose Tattoo (Oscar) **15** The Fugitive Kind **21** Secret of Santa Vittoria

magnanimous **7** liberal **8** generous, princely **9** forgiving, unselfish **10** altruistic, beneficent, charitable **12** largehearted **13** philanthropic

magnate **3** VIP **5** giant, mogul, nabob **6** big gun, bigwig, leader, tycoon **7** big shot, notable **8** big wheel, great man **9** celebrity **13** empire builder, industrialist

magnesium
chemical symbol: **2** Mg

magnetic **8** alluring, charming, inviting **9** of a magnet, seductive **10** attractive, enchanting, entrancing, persuasive **11** captivating, charismatic, fascinating **12** irresistible

magnetism **4** lure **5** charm **6** allure **8** charisma **9** mesmerism, seduction **10** allurement, attraction, enticement **11** captivation, enchantment, fascination

magnification **5** honor **7** worship **9** adoration, blowing up, expansion, inflation, reverence **11** acclamation, enlargement, idolization **12** exaggeration **13** amplification, glorification, overstatement

magnificence **4** pomp **5** glory, state **6** luxury **7** glitter, majesty, royalty **8** grandeur, richness, splendor **10** brilliance **13** sumptuousness

magnificent **4** fine **5** grand, noble **6** august, superb **7** elegant, exalted, stately, sublime **8** glorious, imposing, majestic, splendid **9** brilliant, exquisite, wonderful **10** commanding, impressive **11** resplendent **12** transcendent **13** extraordinary

Magnificent Ambersons, The
director: **11** Orson Welles
based on novel by: **15** Booth Tarkington
cast: **7** Tim Holt **10** Anne Baxter **12** Joseph Cotten **14** Agnes Moorehead **15** Dolores Costello

Magnificent Obsession, The
author: **13** Lloyd C Douglas

Magnificent Seven, The
director: **11** John Sturges
cast: **10** Brad Dexter, Eli Wallach, Yul Brynner **11** James Coburn **12** Robert Vaughn, Steve McQueen **13** Horst Buchholz **14** Charles Bronson
setting: **6** Mexico
score: **14** Elmer Bernstein
remake of: **12** Seven Samurai
sequel: **16** Return of the Seven **20** Magnificent Seven Ride

magnify **4** laud **5** adore, boost, exalt, extol **6** blow up, double, expand, praise, puff up, revere **7** acclaim, amplify, enlarge, glorify, greaten, inflate, stretch, worship **8** heighten, maximize, overrate **9** embroider, overstate, reverence **10** exaggerate

magniloquence **7** bombast, fustian **8** euphuism, tumidity **9** pomposity, turgidity **10** orotundity **11** fanfaronade, grandiosity **14** grandiloquence **15** pretentiousness

magniloquent **5** tumid, windy, wordy **6** turgid **7** pompous, verbose **8** inflated **9** bombastic **13** grandiloquent

magnitude **4** bulk, fame, mass, size **6** extent, renown, repute, volume **7** bigness, expanse, measure **8** eminence, enormity, hugeness, vastness

magnolia
varieties: **4** ashe, star **6** saucer **7** Chinese **8** southern, umbrella **11** great-leaved

Magnum, P. I.
character: **2** TC **4** Rick **7** Higgins **12** Thomas Magnum
cast: **10** Tom Selleck **12** Roger E Mosley **13** John Hillerman
setting: **6** Hawaii

Magog
father: **7** Japheth

Magritte, Rene Francois Ghislain
born: **7** Belgium **8** Lessines
artwork: **14** La Belle Captive, The False Mirror, The Key of Dreams **15** Memory of a Voyage **18** L'Empire des Lumieres (The Empire of Light), The Menaced Assassin

Magua
character in: **20** The Last of the Mohicans
author: **6** Cooper

Magus *see* **4** Magi

Magwitch, Abel
character in: **17** Great Expectations
author: **7** Dickens

Magyar **9** Hungarian

Mahican *see* **7** Mohican

Mahler, Gustav
born: **7** Austria, Bohemia
composer of: **12** Resurrection (symphony No 2) **15** Das Klagendelied **16** Songs of a Wayfarer **17** Das Lied von der Erde, Kindertotenlieder, The Song of the Earth **19** Des Knaben Wunderhorn **28** Lieder eines fahrenden Gesellen

mahogany **4** tree, wood **5** brown **8** hardwood **9** Swietenia **12** reddish-brown
varieties: **3** red **5** swamp, white **7** African, big-leaf, Florida, Senegal, Spanish **8** Honduras, mountain **9** Nyasaland, Venezulan **10** West Indian

Mahon, Christopher
character in: **27** The Playboy of the Western World
author: **5** Synge

mahzor, machzor **16** Jewish prayer book

Maia
member of: **8** Pleiades
place in group: **6** eldest
father: **5** Atlas
mother: **7** Pleione
son: **6** Hermes

maid **6** tweeny **7** servant **8** domestic **9** hired girl, housemaid, lady's maid, nursemaid **10** parlor maid **11** maidservant **12** upstairs maid **13** female servant
French: **6** au pair

maiden, maidenly **4** girl, lass, maid, miss **5** chick, first **6** chaste, damsel, lassie, virgin **7** colleen, girlish, ingenue, initial, untried **8** original, virginal, youthful **9** inaugural, soubrette, unmarried **10** demoiselle, initiatory **12** introductory

Maid Marian
beloved of: **9** Robin Hood

maidservant **4** amah, ayah, char, lass, maid **5** bonne **6** au pair, tweeny **7** abigail **8** charlady, domestic **9** hired girl, lady's maid, tirewoman **10** handmaiden, parlormaid

Maidu
language family: **8** Penutian
location: **10** California
noted for: **8** basketry

mail **4** arms, post **5** armor **6** get out **7** airmail, harness, letters, panoply **8** dispatch, packages **9** postcards **10** send by mail, send by post, suit of mail **11** surface mail **12** mail delivery, put in the mail **13** postal service **14** defensive armor, drop in a mailbox **17** post-office service

Mailer, Norman
author of: **15** An American Dream **16** Armies of the Night **18** The Naked and the Dead **19** The Executioner's Song

Maillol, Aristide
born: **6** France **13** Banyuls-sur-mer

artwork: **5** Night, Torso **7** Le Desir (Desire) **11** Ile de France **12** Young Cyclist **14** Action in Chains, The Three Nymphs **16** The Mediterranean (Seated Woman) **17** Monument to Cezanne, Monument to Debussy **18** Venus with a Necklace

maim **3** cut, rip **4** gash, lame, maul, rend, tear **5** slash, wound **6** deface, hobble, injure, mangle, savage **7** cripple, disable **8** lacerate, mutilate **9** disfigure, dismember, hamstring **12** incapacitate

main **4** head **5** chief, prime, vital **6** urgent **7** capital, central, crucial, leading, primary, special, supreme **8** critical, foremost, pressing **9** essential, important, necessary, paramount, principal, requisite **10** particular, preeminent **11** outstanding, predominant **13** consequential, indispensable

Main, Marjorie
real name: **13** Mary Tomlinson
partner: **12** Wallace Beery **13** Percy Kilbride
born: **7** Acton IN
roles: **7** Dead End **8** Ma Kettle

Maine ***see box***

mainly **6** mostly **7** chiefly **8** above all **9** in the main, most of all, primarily **10** on the whole **11** principally **13** predominantly **14** for the most part, in great measure **16** first and foremost

main point **3** nut **4** core, crux, gist, meat **5** basis, heart, theme **6** kernel **7** essence **10** brass tacks **11** nitty-gritty **15** sum and substance

mainspring **5** agent, cause **6** motive **9** incentive **10** motivation

mainstay **4** prop **6** anchor, pillar **7** bulwark **8** backbone, buttress **16** pillar of strength

Main Street
author: **13** Sinclair Lewis
character: **14** Carol Kennicott **15** Dr Will Kennicott

maintain **4** aver, avow, hold, keep **5** claim, state, swear **6** affirm, allege, assert, defend, insist, keep up, uphold **7** care for, contend, declare, finance, profess, stand by, support, sustain **8** conserve, continue, preserve **9** keep alive, keep going **10** provide for, take care of

maintenance **4** keep **6** living, repair, upkeep **7** keeping, support **10** livelihood, protection, sustenance **11** safekeeping, subsistence, sustainment **12** conservation, preservation, safeguarding

Main-Travelled Road
author: **13** Hamlin Garland

maison de sante **10** sanitarium **13** house of health

maize **4** corn, milo **5** grain **6** cereal, silage, yellow **7** zea mays **10** Indian corn

majestic, majestical **5** grand, lofty, noble, regal, royal **6** august, famous, superb **7** elegant, eminent, stately, sublime **8** esteemed, glorious, imperial, imposing, princely, renowned, splendid **10** impressive **11** illustrious, magnificent **13** distinguished

majesty **4** pomp **5** glory **6** luster **7** dignity **8** elegance, eminence, grandeur, mobility, splendor **9** elevation, loftiness, solemnity, sublimity **10** augustness **11** distinction, stateliness **12** gloriousness, magnificence **14** impressiveness

major **4** main **5** chief, prime, vital **6** larger, urgent **7** capital, crucial, greater, leading, primary, ranking, serious, supreme **8** critical, foremost, pressing **9** essential, important, necessary, paramount, principal, requisite **10** preeminent **11** outstanding, predominant, significant **13** consequential, indispensable

Major Barbara
director: **13** Gabriel Pascal
based on play by: **17** George Bernard Shaw
cast: **11** Deborah Kerr, Rex Harrison, Wendy Hiller **12** Robert Morley, Robert Newton **14** Sybil Thorndike

majority **4** bulk, mass **8** best part, legal age, maturity **9** adulthood, seniority, woman-

---

Maine
abbreviation: **2** ME
nickname: **6** Lumber **8** Pine Tree **10** Wonderland
capital: **7** Augusta
largest city: **8** Portland
others: **4** Bath, Saco **5** Hiram, Orono **6** Auburn, Bangor **7** Kittery **8** Boothbay, Lewiston, Ogunquit **9** Bar Harbor, Biddeford, Brunswick, Skowhegan **10** Waterville **11** Millinocket, Presque Isle
college: **5** Bates, Colby **7** Bowdoin
explorer: **6** Cabots **8** Norsemen
feature: **8** lobsters **19** West Quoddy Headlight
beach: **10** Old Orchard
national park: **6** Acadia
waterway: **18** Allagash Wilderness
tribe: **6** Abnaki **7** Wewenoc
people: **10** downeaster **11** Dorothea Dix **19** Edna St Vincent Millay **24** Henry Wadsworth Longfellow
island: **4** Orrs **8** Mt Desert **10** Campobello
lake: **5** Sebec, Wyman **6** Sebago **8** Rangeley, Schoodic **9** Flagstaff, Moosehead **10** Chesuncook
land rank: **11** thirty ninth
mountain: **5** Kineo, White **7** Bigelow **8** Cadillac
highest point: **8** Katahdin
physical feature:
bay: **5** Casco **9** Penobscot **12** Merrymeeting **13** Passamaquoddy
sand dunes: **13** Desert of Maine
river: **4** Saco **6** St John **7** St Croix **8** Allagash, Kennebec **9** Aroostook, Kennebago, Penobscot **12** Androscoggin
state admission: **11** twenty third
state bird: **9** chickadee
state fish: **16** land-locked salmon
state flower: **7** thistle **8** pine cone **22** white pine cone and tassel
state motto: **7** I Direct
state song: **16** State of Maine Song
state tree: **16** eastern white pine

hood **10** lion's share **13** preponderance

major key (in music) **German: 3** dur

Major prophets *see* **8** prophets

majuscule 7 capital **11** large letter **13** capital letter **15** upper-case letter

make 3 fix **4** form, kind, mark, meet, pass **5** beget, brand, build, catch, cause, enact, erect, force, frame, impel, press, reach, shape, speak, utter **6** attain, compel, create, devise, draw up, effect, foment, makeup, oblige, render **7** appoint, compose, deliver, dragoon, fashion, produce, require **8** arrive at, assemble, engender **9** cause to be, constrain, construct, establish, fabricate, formation, legislate, pronounce, structure **10** bring about, fashioning **11** composition, manufacture

make a bet 3 bet **4** risk **5** stake, wager **6** chance, gamble, hazard, plunge **7** venture

make a clean breast of 7 confess, lay bare, own up to **8** blurt out **14** come clean about

make a dash 3 fly, run **4** flee **6** escape **7** get away **8** make a run **10** make a break, take flight **12** make a getaway

make a deal 5 agree **6** settle **10** compromise **11** come to terms, meet halfway **14** strike a bargain

make advances 8 approach, come on to, sound out **11** proposition **13** make overtures, put the moves on

make a fuss over 6 dote on **7** protest **8** crow over

make again 4 copy **6** remake, repeat **9** duplicate **11** reconstruct

make a getaway 4 bolt, flee, skip **6** escape **7** get away, make off, run away **8** make a run, slip away **9** break free, cut and run, make a dash **10** break loose, fly the coop, take flight

make a gift of 4 give **6** donate **7** present **8** bequeath **10** contribute

make allowance for 6 excuse, pardon **7** forgive, indulge **8** bear with, pass over

make amends 5 atone **6** make up, square **7** expiate **9** do penance **10** compensate

make a mess of 3 mar **4** goof, muff, ruin **5** botch, spoil **6** bungle, foul up, mess up **7** butcher, do badly, louse up, screw up **9** mismanage

make a mistake 3 err **4** goof **6** mess up, slip up **12** miscalculate

make an effort 3 try **5** essay **6** strive, work at **7** attempt **8** endeavor

make appear 5 evoke **6** elicit **7** produce **9** conjure up **10** bring forth

make a racket 3 cry **4** howl, yell **5** shout **6** bellow, clamor, holler, scream **7** bluster **8** make a din **10** vociferate **12** raise a rumpus

make a stab at 3 try **5** essay, guess **6** reckon, take on **7** attempt, surmise, venture **8** estimate, give a try **9** undertake **10** conjecture **11** approximate **12** take a crack at, take a fling at

make a stand 9 stand fast **13** refuse to yield **17** fight to the last man

make a statement 6 remark **7** clarify, comment, discuss, explain, expound **9** elucidate, talk about

make aware 4 tell **5** edify **6** advise, inform, notify, reveal **7** apprise **8** acquaint, disclose **9** divulge to, enlighten, introduce **11** familiarize **16** bring to (one's) attention

make away with 3 eat **4** kill, take **5** spend, steal **6** kidnap, murder **7** abolish, consume, destroy **8** carry off, embezzle, get rid of **9** dissipate

make-believe 4 fake, sham **5** false, phony **6** made-up, make-up, unreal **7** assumed, charade, fantasy, feigned, fiction **8** creation, imagined, invented, pretense, spurious **9** fantastic, imaginary, invention, pretended, simulated **10** artificial, fictitious **11** counterfeit, fabrication **13** falsification

make certain of 6 assure, clinch, ensure **8** be sure of **10** make sure of

make damp 5 bedew **6** dampen **7** moisten **8** sprinkle

make dark 3 dim **6** darken **7** blacken, obscure

make different 4 vary **5** alter, amend **6** change, modify, mutate **7** convert, remodel **9** transform, transmute **12** metamorphose

make distinctive 8 set apart **9** single out **11** distinguish **12** characterize **13** differentiate

make easy 4 ease **6** smooth **7** explain, lighten **8** simplify **10** clear a path, facilitate

make eligible 5 allow **6** permit **7** entitle, qualify **9** authorize

make evident 4 show **5** prove **6** reveal **7** exhibit **8** manifest **9** establish, make clear, make plain **11** demonstrate

make fast 3 fix **4** moor **5** affix, tie up **6** attach, fasten, secure **7** connect

make feeble 6 weaken **7** wear out **8** enervate **10** debilitate, devitalize

make furious 5 anger **6** enrage, madden **7** incense, inflame **9** infuriate

make giddy 5 dizzy **12** make unsteady **15** make lightheaded

make good 5 repay **6** arrive, make it **7** fulfill, succeed **11** reach the top **15** make restitution

make happy 5 amuse, cheer **6** please **7** delight, gratify **9** entertain

make haste slowly **Latin: 12** festina lente

make hostile 5 repel **6** offend **7** provoke **8** alienate **10** antagonize

make ill 5 repel **6** infect, revolt, sicken **7** afflict, disgust, repulse **8** disagree, distress, make sick, nauseate **9** discomfit **14** turn the stomach

make ill at ease 5 upset **6** rattle **7** fluster **8** distress **9** discomfit, embarrass **10** disconcert

make impure 4 foul, soil **5** dirty, spoil, taint **6** befoul, blight, defile, infect, poison **7** corrupt, pollute **10** adulterate **11** contaminate

make inroads 6 invade **7** impinge, intrude **8** encroach, infringe, trespass **9** penetrate

make known 4 tell **6** advise, impart, inform, notify, report, reveal, unveil **7** apprise, divulge, lay bare, publish, uncover **8** disclose **9** broadcast **10** give notice, make public **11** communicate

make less forceful 6 soften,

weaken **9** undermine **10** devitalize, emasculate

make light of 8 belittle, minimize, pooh-pooh, sneeze at **9** deprecate, disparage, underrate **10** depreciate, undervalue **13** underestimate

make merry 5 revel **7** carouse, roister **9** celebrate, have a ball **15** paint the town red

make much of 5 honor **6** praise **7** acclaim, applaud, commend, flatter **8** fuss over

make nervous 5 annoy, upset **7** agitate, disturb, perturb, trouble, unnerve **10** disconcert

make off with 5 steal **6** abduct, kidnap, snatch **7** bear off **8** carry off **10** run off with **11** get away with

make one's blood boil 5 anger **6** enrage, madden **7** incense, inflame **9** infuriate

make one's eyes pop 4 stun **5** shock **6** dazzle **7** stagger, startle **8** astonish **9** electrify **11** flabbergast

make out 3 see **4** espy **6** behold, descry, detect, fill in, notice **7** discern, observe, pick out **8** get along, perceive, write out **12** catch sight of

make plain 7 clarify, clear up, explain, lay open **9** elucidate, explicate, make clear **10** illuminate **11** disentangle, shed light on **12** bring to light

make possible for 5 allow **6** enable, permit **7** empower, qualify **10** capacitate

make public 3 air **4** tell, vent **5** print, utter, voice **6** expose, inform, reveal, spread **7** declare, display, divulge, exhibit, express, give out, publish **8** announce, disclose, proclaim, televise **9** broadcast, circulate, publicize

maker, Maker 3 god **4** poet **5** smith **6** author, forger **7** builder, creator, founder **8** declarer, inventor, producer **9** architect, generator **10** originator **12** manufacturer

make ready 5 prime **7** arrange, forearm, prepare

make reparation for 5 atone, repay **6** pay for **10** compensate, recompense, remunerate

make restitution 5 repay **7** pay back **9** reimburse **10** compensate, recompense

make right 3 fix **5** amend, emend **6** remedy, repair **7** correct, improve, rectify

make self-conscious 5 abash **6** rattle **7** chagrin, fluster **9** discomfit, embarrass **10** disconcert

makeshift 6 make-do **7** standby, stopgap **8** slapdash **9** alternate, expedient, temporary, tentative **10** substitute **11** provisional

make sick 6 revolt **7** disgust **8** nauseate

make smaller 6 lessen, reduce, shrink, take in **8** decrease, diminish

make sure 5 cinch **6** assure, clinch, decide, ensure, secure, settle **9** ascertain **11** double-check

make thinner 4 thin **6** dilute **9** water down **10** adulterate

make tracks 2 go **4** scat, shoo **5** be off, leave, scram **6** beat it, cut out, depart, go away **8** withdraw **10** hit the road

make uncomfortable 3 try **7** agitate, perturb **8** disquiet, distress **9** discomfit, embarrass **10** discompose

make uneasy 7 disturb, perturb, trouble, unnerve **8** disquiet, distress **9** discomfit, embarrass **10** discomfort, discompose, disconcert

make uniform 4 even **5** equal **6** smooth **7** balance **8** equalize **10** straighten

makeup 5 frame **9** character, cosmetics, framework, structure **11** composition, personality **12** constitution, organization

make up 4 form **5** cover **6** invent **7** arrange, concoct **8** assemble **9** improvise, reconcile **10** compensate, constitute **11** put together

make up for 5 atone **7** expiate **8** make good **10** make amends **13** compensate for

make up one's mind 6 decide **7** resolve **9** determine

make use of 3 use **5** apply **6** employ, engage, occupy **7** exploit, utilize **8** keep busy, put to use **13** turn to account

make weary 4 do in, poop, tire **7** exhaust, wear out **8** enervate

makeweight 6 weight **7** ballast

make well 4 cure, heal

make wider 5 widen **6** dilate, expand **7** broaden, stretch **9** spread out

make worse 6 worsen **8** heighten, increase **9** aggravate, intensify **10** exacerbate

making excuses 8 alibiing **9** defending **10** justifying **11** apologizing

Making of the President, The (series)
author: 14 Theodore H White

Making of the Representative for Planet 8
author: 12 Doris Lessing

making the rounds 5 about **6** abroad **11** circulating, going around **13** going the route, in circulation

Malabo
capital of: 16 Equatorial Guinea

Malachi
means: 11 my messenger
identified with: 4 Ezra **8** Mordecai, Nehemiah **10** Zerubbabel

maladroit 5 inept **6** clumsy, gauche **7** awkward, unhandy **8** bumbling, bungling, tactless **9** impolitic, unskilled **10** blundering, left-handed, ungraceful, unskillful **12** undiplomatic

maladroitness 9 gaucherie, inability **10** clumsiness, ineptitude **11** awkwardness, unhandiness **12** incompetence

malady 7 ailment, disease, illness **8** disorder, sickness **9** affection, complaint, infirmity **10** affliction, disability **13** indisposition, unhealthiness

mala fide 10 in bad faith, not genuine

malaise 4 pang **5** throb **6** twinge **7** anxiety **8** disquiet **9** lassitude **10** uneasiness, discomfort **11** nervousness **12** discomposure

Malamud, Bernard
author of: 8 The Fixer **9** God's Grace **10** The Natural, The Tenants **11** Dubin's Lives **12** The Assistant

Malaprop, Mrs
character in: 9 The Rivals
author: 8 Sheridan

malapropos 13 inappropriate **15** inappropriately

Malawi ***see box, p. 596***

Malaysia ***see box, p. 597***

Malcolm
character in: 7 Macbeth
author: 11 Shakespeare

malcontent 4 glum, sour **5** rebel **6** grouch, grumpy, morose, sullen, uneasy **7** grouchy, growler, repiner, restive **8** de-

Malawi
other name: 9 Nyasaland
capital: 8 Lilongwe
largest city: 8 Blantyre
others: 4 Bana 5 Dedza, Limbe, Mzuzu, Zomba 6 Kasese, Mzimba, Salima 7 Chipoka, Chiromo, Deep Bay, Karonga, Katumbi 8 Chikwawa, Chilumbe, Kota Kota, Nkata Bay 9 Monkey Bay 10 Port Herald 12 Fort Johnston, Livingstonia
monetary unit: 6 kwacha 7 tambala
lake: 5 Nyasa 6 Chilwa, Malawi
mountain: 11 Livingstone
highest point: 6 Mlanje 7 Mulanje
river: 3 Bua 5 Shire 7 Dwangwa 11 South Rukuru
physical feature:
highlands: 5 Shire
plateau: 5 Nyika
valley: 5 Shire 9 Great Rift
people: 3 Yao 4 Sena 5 Bantu, Lomwe, Ngoni 6 Cheiva, Maravi, Ngonde, Nyanja 7 Tumbuka
dynasty: 6 Maravi
explorer: 16 David Livingstone
leader: 5 Banda
language: 3 Yao 4 Cewa 5 Bantu, Ngoni, Tonga 6 Nyanja 7 English, Tumbuka 8 Chichewa 10 Chitumbuka
religion: 5 Islam 7 animism 10 Protestant 12 Presbyterian 13 Roman Catholic
feature:
village: 5 mudzi

jected, downcast, grumbler, restless 9 insurgent, irritable 10 complainer, despondent 11 faultfinder 12 discontented, dissatisfied, faultfinding, hard to please

mal de mer 11 seasickness

Malden, Karl
real name: 16 Mladen Sekulovich
born: 6 Gary IL
roles: 6 Patton 8 Baby Doll 15 On the Waterfront 21 A Streetcar Named Desire 24 The Streets of San Francisco

Maldives *see box*

male 3 boy, man, ram 4 bull 5 manly, youth 6 tomcat 7 manlike, rooster 8 stallion 9 billy goat, masculine

Male
capital of: 8 Maldives

male bird 4 cock 5 drake 6 gander 7 rooster

maledict 4 damn 5 curse 8 denounce 9 proscribe 12 anathematize

malediction 5 curse 8 anathema, diatribe 9 damnation, evil spell 10 execration 11 fulmination, imprecation 12 denunciation, proscription

malefactor 5 felon, knave, rogue 6 sinner 7 culprit 8 criminal, evil-doer, offender 9 miscreant, scoundrel, wrongdoer 10 malfeasant

male hairdresser
French: 8 coiffeur

malentendu 7 mistake 16 misunderstanding

male power
god of: 7 Priapus

Malevich, Kasimir Severinovich
born: 4 Kiev 6 Russia
artwork: 11 Black Square 15 The Knife Grinder 18 Eight Red Rectangles 19 Woman with Water Pails 34 Suprematist Composition White on White

malevolence 4 evil, hate 5 spite 6 enmity, grudge, hatred, malice, rancor, spleen 7 despite, ill will 9 hostility, malignity 10 antagonism, malignance, malignancy 12 spitefulness 13 maliciousness

malevolent 5 surly 6 malign, sullen 7 baleful, vicious 8 sinister, spiteful, venomous 9 invidious, malicious, malignant, rancorous, resentful 10 ill-natured, pernicious, revengeful 11 acrimonious, ill-disposed 14 ill-intentioned

malfeasance 5 crime 8 misdeeds 10 misconduct, wrongdoing

malformation 9 deformity 10 aberration, distortion 11 abnormality, monstrosity, peculiarity 12 grotesquerie, irregularity 13 disfigurement

malformed 7 twisted 8 deformed 9 contorted, distorted, grotesque, irregular, misshapen

malfunction 6 glitch, malady 7 problem 9 complaint

malgre lui 16 in spite of himself

Mali *see box, p. 598*

malice 4 hate 5 spite, venom 6 enmity, grudge, hatred, rancor 7 ill will 8 acrimony 9 animosity, malignity 10 antagonism, bitterness, evil intent, resentment 11 malevolence 12 spitefulness

malice aforethought
legal term: 51 planning to commit a crime without just cause or provocation

malicious 7 baleful, harmful, hateful, vicious 8 spiteful 9 invidious, malignant, rancorous, resentful 10 malevolent, revengeful, vindictive 11 acrimonious, ill-disposed

malign 3 bad 4 evil 5 abuse, black 6 defame, revile, vilify 7 baneful, harmful, hateful, noxious, ominous, put down, run down, slander 8 backbite, bad mouth, belittle, derogate, menacing, sinister 9 denigrate, deprecate, disparage, injurious, malicious, malignant 10 malevolent, pernicious, speak ill of 11 deleterious, detrimental, threatening 14 inveigh against

malignancy 5 spite, tumor 6 cancer, malice, rancor 7 ill will, sarcoma 8 acrimony, neoplasm, toxicity 9 carcinoma, hostility, virulence 10 bitterness 11 malevolence, viciousness 12 hard feelings, spitefulness, vengefulness 13 poisonousness

malignant 4 evil 5 fatal, toxic 6 bitter, deadly 7 hateful, hostile, vicious 8 fiendish, spiteful, venomous, virulent 9 invidious, malicious, poisonous, rancorous, resentful 10 diabolical, evil-minded, malevolent, pernicious, revengeful, vindictive 11 acrimonious, ill-disposed

malignant spirit 3 imp 5 demon, devil 7 gremlin

malignity 4 evil 5 spite, venom 6 animus, rancor,

Malaysia
capital/largest city: 11 Kuala Lumpur
others: 4 Ipoh, Sibu **5** Anson, Davao, Telok **6** Iloilo, Johore, Kupang, Manado, Penang, Pinang **7** Bintulu, Kuantan, Kuching, Melalap **8** Port Weld, Sandakan **10** Georgetown, Kota Baharu **11** Johor Baharu, Port Dickson **12** Kota Kinabulu **14** Port Swettenham
division: 5 Sabah **6** Malaya **7** Malacca, Sarawak
head of state:
***supreme head of state:* 18** yang di-pertuan agong
measure: 3 pau, tun **4** para, pipe, tael, wang **5** parah **6** chupak, parrah **7** gantang
monetary unit: 3 sen, tra **4** taro, trah **7** ringgit, tampang
weight: 4 chee, mace, tael, wang **7** tampang
island: 6 Banggi, Borneo, Labuan, Penang, Pinang, Tioman **7** Pangkor, Sebatik **8** Langkawi **10** Perhentian **11** Balambangan
mountain: 4 Bulu, Hose, Iban, Iran, Main, Mulu, Niut, Raja **5** Murjo, Niapa, Ophir **6** Blumut, Kapuas, Leuser, Slamet **7** Binaija, Brassey, Crocker **8** Rindjani **11** Gunong Korbu, Gunong Tahan
highest point: 8 Kinabalu
river: 5 Klang, Kutai, Perak **6** Barito, Pahang, Rajang, Rejang **7** Sarawak **12** Kinabatangan
sea: 4 Sulu **7** Celebes **10** South China
physical feature:
***bay:* 5** Labuk
***cape:* 5** Sirik
***highlands:* 7** Cameron
***passage:* 6** Sibutu
***peninsula:* 5** Malay
***point:* 13** Tanjong Gelang
***strait:* 6** Johore **7** Balabac, Malacca
people: 4 Iban **5** Dayak, Malay **6** Indian **7** Chinese, Kadazan **9** Pakistani, Sri Lankan **10** Bangladesh, Indonesian
language: 4 Bugi, Dyak **5** Malay, Tamil **6** Battok, Rejang **7** Chinese, English, Lampong, Niasese **8** Achinese, Javanese, Makassar **14** Bahasa Malaysia
***alphabet:* 5** tagal
religion: 5 Hindu, Islam **6** Taoism **7** animism **8** Buddhism **12** Christianity, Confucianism
place:
***mosque:* 8** National
feature:
***cap:* 7** songkok
***cloth:* 4** tapa **5** batik
***clothing:* 4** baju, malo, sari **5** badju, pareu **6** cabaya, kebaya, sam-foo, sarong **9** cheongsam
***dance:* 4** haka, hula **5** joget
***game:* 9** sepakraga
***hamlet:* 7** kampong
***parish:* 5** mukim
***rice paddy:* 4** padi
***scarf:* 9** selendang
***self-defense:* 5** silat
***shadow play:* 6** menora
***spirit:* 5** hantu
food:
***drink:* 4** kava
***fruit:* 6** durian **8** rambutan **10** mangosteen

Maldives
capital/largest city: 4 Male
government:
***legislature:* 6** Majlis
monetary unit: 5 laree, rupee
island: 3 Ari, Gan **4** Addu, Male **5** Rasdu **6** Felidu, Hulele, Mulaku **7** Malcolm, Minicoy, Nilandu **8** Maldives, Suvadiva **9** Fadiffolu, Wilingili **10** Haddummati, Kolumadulu **11** Tiladummati **13** Ihavandiffulu, Miladummadulu **16** North Malosmadulu, South Malosmadulu
sea: 6 Indian **7** Arabian **9** Laccadive
physical feature:
***channel:* 4** Wadu **7** Kardiva **8** Veimandu **10** Equatorial **11** Eight Degree **17** One and a Half Degree
people: 4 Arab **6** Indian **9** Sinhalese **10** Singhalese
***ruling family/sultans:* 4** Didi
language: 6 Arabic, Divehi
religion: 5 Islam
feature:
***coconut fiber:* 4** coir
***dried coconut:* 5** copra

spleen **7** ill will **8** acrimony **9** animosity **12** hard feelings, spitefulness, venomousness

malinger 4 loaf **5** dodge, evade, shirk, slack **7** goof off **9** goldbrick

mall 4 yard **5** court, plaza **6** arcade, circus, piazza, square **8** cloister **9** colonnade, esplanade, promenade **10** quadrangle **12** parade ground

Mallarme, Stephane
author of: 8 Herodias **18** L'Apres Midi d'un faune **19** The Afternoon of a Faun

Malle, Louis
director of: 10 Pretty Baby **12** Atlantic City **13** Lacombe Lucien **16** Murmur of the Heart

malleable 6 docile, pliant **7** ductile, plastic, pliable **8** flexible, moldable, workable **9** adaptable, compliant, teachable, tractable **10** governable, manageable **12** easily shaped **13** easily wrought **14** impressionable

mallet
type: 6 rubber, wooden **12** plastic-faced

mallophaga
class: 8 hexapoda
phylum: 10 arthropoda
group: 8 bird lice **10** biting lice

malnutrition 10 emaciation, starvation **16** undernourishment

malodorous 4 rank **5** acrid, fetid, musty **6** putrid, smelly

Mali
other name: **11** French Sudan **12** French Soudan **16** Sudanese Republic
capital/largest city: **6** Bamako
others: **3** Gao **5** Kayes, Mopti, Segou **6** Djenne **7** Sikasso **8** Taoudeni, Timbuktu **10** Tombouctou
division: **5** Sahel **7** Azaouad
monetary unit: **5** franc **7** centime
lake: **2** Do **4** Debo **5** Garou **7** Korarou **9** Faguibine
mountain: **4** Mina **6** Iforas **7** Manding
highest point: **12** Hombori Tondo
river: **4** Bani **5** Bagoe, Bakoy, Diaka, Niger **6** Bafing, Bakoye, Baoule, Faleme **7** Azaouak, Senegal
physical feature:
desert: **6** Sahara **8** Chech Erg **10** Sekkane Erg **13** Haricha Hamada
plateau: **14** Adrar des Iforas
valley: **5** Niger **7** Tilemsi
people: **3** Bwa **4** Fula, Kyan, Moor, Peul **5** Dogon, Dyula, Fulbe, Marka **6** Berber, Dognon, Fulani, Senufo, Tuareg **7** Bambara, Fellata, Malinke, Miniaka, Songhai, Soninke **8** Khasonke, Mandingo, Senoulfo
leader: **4** Umar **5** Keita **6** Traore **9** Mansa Musa
language: **5** Dogon, Dyula, Feulh, Mande, Marka **6** Berber, French, Fulani **7** Bambara, Malinke, Senoufo, Songhai
religion: **5** Islam **7** animism
place:
ruins: **8** Terhazza
feature:
empire: **4** Mali **5** Ghana **7** Bambara, Songhai

7 noisome, reeking **8** stinking **12** foul-smelling

Malone, Dorothy
real name: **20** Dorothy Eloise Maloney
husband: **15** Jacques Bergerac
born: **9** Chicago IL
roles: **11** Peyton Place **14** Too Much Too Soon **16** Written on the Wind

Malory, Sir Thomas
author of: **14** Le Morte d'Arthur

Malpighi, Marcello
field: **10** physiology
nationality: **7** Italian
founded: **18** microscopic anatomy

malpractice **10** negligence

Malraux, Andre
author of: **8** Man's Fate **11** Anti-Memoirs, Days of Wrath, The Royal Way **13** The Conquerors **18** The Voices of Silence

Malta *see box*

Maltese Falcon, The
author: **15** Dashiell Hammett
director: **10** John Huston
cast: **9** Mary Astor (Bridget O'Shaughnessy) **10** Peter Lorre (Joel Cairo) **12** Elisha Cook Jr (Wilmer), Gladys George **14** Humphrey Bogart (Sam Spade) **17** Sydney Greenstreet (the Fat Man)
character: **6** Wilmer **8** Sam Spade **9** Joel Cairo **11** Miles Archer **12** Casper Gutman, Floyd Thursby **18** Brigid O'Shaughnessy
remade as: **13** Satan Met a Lady

malt liquor **3** ale **4** beer, bock, brew **5** stout **6** porter

maltreat **4** harm, hurt **5** abuse **6** ill-use, injure **8** mistreat

maltreatment **5** abuse **6** ill-use, injury **7** assault, cruelty **10** bodily harm, oppression **11** manhandling, molestation, persecution **12** mistreatment

Malvolio
character in: **12** Twelfth Night
author: **11** Shakespeare

Mama
character: **4** Nels **6** Dagmar, Katrin, TR Ryan **9** Aunt Jenny **10** (Papa) Lars Hansen **11** (Mama) Marta Hansen
cast: **8** Iris Mann **9** Peggy Wood, Ruth Gates **11** Judson Laire, Robin Morgan **12** Rosemary Rice **13** Dick Van Patten, Kevin Coughlin
dog: **6** Willie
based on book: **16** Mama's Bank Account
setting: **12** San Francisco
theme: **12** Holverg Suite **13** The Last Spring

Mamers *see* **4** Mars

mamma, mama **2** ma **3** mam, mom, mum **4** wife **5** madre, mammy, mater, mommy,

Malta
capital: **8** Valletta
largest city: **6** Sliema
others: **5** Marfa, Mdina, Mgarr, Mosta, Nadut, Paola, Rabat **6** Zejtun **7** Senglea, Zeibrun **8** Cospicua, Floriana, Mellieha, Victoria **10** Birkirkara, Birzebbuga, Vittoriosa
measure: **4** rotl **5** artal, canna, parto, ratel, salma **6** kantar **7** caffiso
monetary unit: **4** cent **5** grain, grano, pound
island: **4** Gozo **5** Malta **6** Comino, Filfla **7** Filfola **9** Cominotto **10** Comminotto
highest point: **12** Dingli Cliffs
sea: **13** Mediterranean
physical feature:
bay: **7** St Paul's **8** Mellieha **10** Marsaxlokk
channel: **11** North Comino, South Comino
harbor: **5** Grand **10** Marsamxett
people: **7** Maltese
leader: **7** Mintoff **9** Buttigieo **18** Parisot de La Valette
ruler: **5** Arabs **6** Romans **7** British **8** Napoleon **10** Byzantines **11** Hospitalers, Phoenicians **13** Carthaginians **15** Holy Roman Empire, Knights of St John
language: **7** English, Italian, Maltese
religion: **13** Roman Catholic
feature:
gondola boat: **7** dghaisa

mummy, mumsy, woman **6** mother, parent

mammal ***see box***

mammon, Mammon **4** gain, gold **5** money **6** profit, riches, wealth **9** affluence **11** possessions **13** material goods, the god of money

Mammon, Sir Epicure
character in: **12** The Alchemist
author: **6** Jonson

mammoth **4** huge **5** great **6** mighty **7** immense, massive **8** colossal, enormous, gigantic, whopping **9** cyclopean, herculean, monstrous, ponderous, very large **10** gargantuan, monumental, prodigious, stupendous, tremendous **11** elephantine, mountainous

Mammy
character in: **15** Gone With the Wind
author: **8** Mitchell

Mamoulian, Rouben
director of: **13** Love Me Tonight, Silk Stockings **14** Queen Christina, The Mark of Zorro

mammal
bat (chiroptera): **4** tomb **5** fruit, naked, smoky **7** mastiff, vampire **9** fisherman, horseshoe, leaf-nosed, sac-winged, slit-faced, thumbless **10** disk-winged, free-tailed, moustached **11** funnel-eared, hollow-faced, mouse-tailed **12** false vampire, sheath-tailed, sucker-footed, yellow-winged **14** vespertilionid **21** New Zealand short-tailed
carnivore: **3** cat, dog, fox **4** bear, lion, lynx, mink, puma, wolf **5** civet, dingo, fossa, hyena, otter, panda, skunk, tayra, tiger **6** badger, bobcat, coyote, ferret, grison, hyaena, jackal, jaguar, marten, olingo, weasel **7** polecat, raccoon **8** aardwolf, kinkajou, mongoose, suricate **9** wolverine **10** cacomistle, coatimundi
cetacea: **4** gray **5** pilot, right, whale **6** beluga, killer **7** dolphin, rorqual **8** humpback, narwhale, porpoise **10** sperm whale **11** beaked whale **16** bottle-nosed whale
edentata: **5** sloth **8** anteater **9** armadillo, tree sloth
egg-laying: **7** echidna **13** spiny anteater **18** duck-billed platypus
even-toed ungulate: **2** ox **3** elk, hog, pig **4** deer, goat, oxen **5** bison, camel, llama, moose, okapi, sheep **6** alpaca, cattle, duiker, vicuna **7** buffalo, caribou, gazelle, giraffe, guanaco, muntjak, peccary **8** antelope **9** mouse deer **10** chevrotain **12** hippopotamus
hyracoidea: **5** hyrax
insect-eating: **4** mole **5** shrew **6** desman, tenrec **7** gymnure, moon rat **8** hedgehog **9** shrew-mole, solenodon **10** golden mole, otter shrew, water shrew **13** elephant shrew
lagomorpha: **4** hare, pika **6** rabbit
marsupials/pouched: **5** koala **6** cuscus, numbat, possum, wombat **7** opossum, wallaby **8** kangaroo **9** bandicoot, phalanger **14** Tasmanian devil
odd-toed ungulate: **3** ass **5** horse, kiang, tapir, zebra **6** onager, quagga **10** rhinoceros
pinnipedia: **4** seal **6** walrus **7** sea lion
primate: **5** lemur, loris, potto **6** avahis, aye-aye, baboon, galago, gibbon, indris, monkey, people **7** gorilla, tamarin, tarsier **8** marmoset, simpoona **9** orangutan, tree shrew **10** chimpanzee
proboscidea: **8** elephant
rodent: **4** cavy, vole **5** coypu, gundi, hutia, mouse **6** agouti, beaver, coruro, gerbil, gopher, jerboa, nutria **7** blesmol, cane rat, hamster, lemming, mole-rat, rock rat **8** capybara, chipmunk, dormouse, sewellel, spiny rat, squirrel, tucu-tuco, viscacha **9** chozchori, false paca, pacaranas, porcupine, woodchuck **10** chinchilla, prairie dog, springhare **11** kangaroo rat, pocket mouse, viscacha rat **13** kangaroo mouse **16** Speke's pectinator
sirenia: **6** dugong, sea cow **7** manatee
tubulidentata: **8** aardvark

Mamurius
copied: **6** Ancile

man **3** boy, guy, one **4** chap, gent, hand, male, soul **5** equip, hubby, human, staff **6** anyone, attend, butler, fellow, fit out, helper, outfit, people, person, spouse, waiter, worker **7** footman, husband, laborer, mankind, someone, subject, workman **8** employee, garrison, handyman, henchman, humanity, liegeman, somebody **9** assistant, gentleman, hired hand, humankind **11** Homo sapiens
Spanish: **6** hombre

Man, first **4** Adam **12** Alalcomeneus
Nordic: **3** Ask

Man, Woman and Child
author: **10** Erich Segal

man-about-town **5** blade **7** playboy **8** cavalier, gay blade **12** boulevardier

manacle, manacles **3** ply, run, use **4** cope, fare, head, rule, work **5** bonds, get on, guide, irons, order, pilot, shift, steer, wield **6** chains, direct, fetter, govern, handle, make go **7** command, conduct, control, operate, oversee, shackle, succeed, survive, work out **8** cope with, deal with, dominate, get along, handcuff, maneuver, shackles **9** bracelets, handcuffs, look after, supervise, watch over **10** accomplish, administer, bring about, manipulate, put in irons, take care of **11** be at the helm, hand-fetters, preside over, put in chains, superintend **12** have charge of, hold the reins

manage **4** care, rule **6** bosses, charge, wheels **7** bigwigs, command, conduct, control, dealing, running, tactics **8** big shots, guidance, handling, ordering, planning, strategy, top brass **9** direction, directors, operation **10** conducting, executives, overseeing, regulation **11** generalship, negotiation, supervision, supervisors, transaction **12** manipulation, organization **14** administration, administrators **15** superintendence

manageable **4** easy **6** docile, pliant, wieldy **8** amenable, flexible **9** compliant, tractable **10** governable, submissive **12** controllable

management **4** boss, head **5** agent, chief **7** foreman, planner **8** overseer **9** budgeteer, majordomo, organizer, tactician **10** impresario, negotiator, supervisor **11** manipulator **13** administrator **14** superintendent

manager **4** boss, head **5** agent, chief **7** foreman, planner **8** overseer **9** budgeteer, majordomo, organizer, tactician **10** impresario, negotiator, supervisor **11** manipulator **13** administrator **14** superintendent

managerial **9** executive **10** management **11** supervisory **14** administrative, organizational

Managua
capital of: **9** Nicaragua

Manala *see* **7** Tuonela

Manama
capital of: **7** Bahrain

manana **6** future **8** tomorrow **11** in the future

Man and Superman
author: **17** George Bernard Shaw

Manannan
origin: **5** Irish
god of: **3** sea
father: **3** Ler, Lir

Manassa Mauler
nickname of: **11** Jack Dempsey

Manasseh
father: **6** Joseph
mother: **7** Asenath
great uncle: **4** Esau
grandfather: **5** Jacob
descendant of: **9** Manassite

man-at-arms **7** fighter, soldier, warrior **9** combatant **10** cavalryman

Manawyddan
origin: **5** Welsh
father: **4** Llyr
sister: **7** Branwen
brother: **4** Bran **9** Evnissyen
wife: **8** Rhiannon
rescued: **7** Pryderi

Manchester, William
author of: **11** The Last Lion **14** American Caesar **15** Goodbye Darkness

Manchuria ***see box***

Mandalay
found in: **18** Barrack-Room Ballads
author: **14** Rudyard Kipling

mandamus
legal term: **48** writ from a superior court commanding that a thing be done
literally: **9** we command

Mandan
language family: **6** Siouan

Manchuria
also: **7** Manchow
city: **5** Aigun, Hulan, Kirin, Peian, Penki **6** Anshan, Antung, Dairen, Fu-Shun, Hailar, Harbin, Hokang, Mukden, Penchi, Yenchi **7** Hulutao, Ikuliho, Ssuping, Tantung **8** Chinchao, Paicheng, Shenyang **9** Changchun, Chiamussu, Manchouli, Miuchwang **10** Port Arthur **11** Chichihaerh, Mutanchiang
peninsula: **8** Liaotung
province: **5** Jehol, Jilin, Kirin **8** Liaoning **12** Heilongjiang, Heilungkiang
river: **4** Amur, Liao, Yalu **5** Argun, Mutan, Nonni, Tumen **6** Ussuri **7** Sungari
tribe: **5** Tungu **6** Manchu, Mongol

location: **11** North Dakota
ceremony: **5** Okipa

Mandarins, The
author: **16** Simone de Beauvoir

Mandasuchus
type: **8** dinosaur
period: **8** Triassic

mandate **5** edict, order **6** behest, charge, decree **7** bidding, command, dictate **8** approval, sanction **9** authority, direction, directive **10** commission, dependency **11** instruction, requisition **12** protectorate **13** authorization

mandatory **7** binding, exigent, needful **8** required **9** called for, essential, necessary, requisite **10** compulsory, imperative, obligatory, peremptory

Mande
language family: **16** Niger-Kordofanian
group: **10** Niger-Congo
includes: **3** Vai **5** Mende **7** Bambara, Malinke

Mandelbaum Gate, The
author: **11** Muriel Spark

Manderly
house in: **7** Rebecca
author: **9** Du Maurier

mandible **3** jaw **4** beak, bill, jowl **7** maxilla **8** lower jaw
part: **4** mala **5** angle, molar, ramus **6** corpus

Mandrake the Magician
creator: **7** Lee Falk **9** Phil Davis
character: **5** Narda **6** Lothar

Manes
spirits or souls of: **4** dead

Manet, Edouard
born: **5** Paris **6** France
artwork: **7** Olympia **8** The Fifer **9** Emile Zola **10** Argenteuil **12** The Guitarist **19** Le Dejeuner sur l'Herbe (Luncheon on the Grass) **25** The Bar at the Folies-Bergeres **31** Execution of the Emperor Maximilian

Manette, Dr and Lucie
characters in: **16** A Tale of Two Cities
author: **7** Dickens

maneuver **4** move, plot, ploy **5** dodge, guide, pilot, steer, trick **6** deploy, device, gambit, scheme, tactic **7** finagle **8** artifice, contrive, intrigue **9** stratagem **10** manipulate **11** contrivance, machination, pull strings

Man for All Seasons, A
director: **13** Fred Zinnemann
based on play by: **10** Robert Bolt
cast: **9** Leo McKern **10** Robert Shaw **11** Orson Welles, Wendy Hiller **12** Paul Scofield (Sir Thomas More), Susannah York **14** Nigel Davenport **15** Vanessa Redgrave
Oscar for: **5** actor (Scofield) **7** picture **8** director

Manfred
author: **21** George Gordon Lord Byron

man Friday **4** aide **8** adjutant, employee **9** assistant **10** aide de camp **12** right-hand man

Man from St Petersburg, The
author: **10** Ken Follett

Man from UNCLE, The
character: **9** Mr Waverly **12** Napoleon Solo **13** Illya Kuryakin
cast: **11** Leo G Carroll **12** Robert Vaughn **13** David McCallum
foe: **6** THRUSH

manful **5** brave **8** resolute **10** courageous

manganese
chemical symbol: **2** Mn

mangle **3** cut **4** harm, hurt, lame, maim, maul, ruin, tear **5** crush, press, slash **6** damage, impair, injure **7** flatten **8** lacerate, mutilate **9** disfigure

manhandle **4** maul **5** abuse **6** batter **7** rough up **8** maltreat, mistreat **9** pull about, push about **10** knock about, slap around

Manhattan
director: **10** Woody Allen
cast: **9** Anne Byrne **10** Woody Allen **11** Diane Keaton, Meryl Streep **13** Michael Murphy **15** Mariel Hemingway

Manhattan Transfer
author: **13** John Dos Passos

manhood **5** prime **8** legal age, machismo, majority, maleness, maturity, virility **9** adulthood, manliness, mature age **10** manfulness **11** masculinity

mania **4** rage **5** craze **6** frenzy, lunacy, raving **7** craving, madness, passion **8** delirium, delusion, dementia, fixation, hysteria, insanity **9** monomania, obsession **10** aberration, compulsion, enthusiasm, fanaticism **11** fascination, infatuation

maniac **3** ass, nut **4** fool **5** loony **6** cuckoo, madman, nitwit **7** half-wit, lunatic **9** psychotic, screwball, simpleton **10** crackbrain, psychopath

manic **2** up **4** high **7** excited, frantic, hyped up **8** agitated, frenzied, worked up **9** wrought up **10** freaked out, switched on **11** hyperactive

manifest **4** bare, open, show **5** clear, frank, plain **6** candid, evince, expose, patent, reveal, unveil **7** display, divulge, evident, exhibit, express, obvious, uncover, visible **8** apparent, disclose, evidence, indicate, palpable **9** make known **10** noticeable **11** demonstrate, make visible, self-evident, transparent, unconcealed, undisguised

manifestation **4** show **7** display, example, symptom **8** evidence, instance **10** exhibition, expression, indication, revelation **12** illustration, presentation, proclamation, public notice **13** demonstration

manifesto **4** bull **5** edict, ukase **6** notice **9** broadside, statement **10** communique, encyclical **11** declaration **12** announcement, annunciation, notification, proclamation, public notice **13** position paper, pronouncement **14** pronunciamento

manifold **4** many **6** myriad, varied **7** complex, diverse **8** multiple, numerous **9** many-sided, multiform **10** variegated **11** diversified, innumerable **12** multifarious **13** multitudinous

Manila
capital of: **11** Philippines
former name: **8** Maynilad
island: **5** Luzon
landmark: **9** Rizal Park **16** San Agustin Church
river: **5** Pasig
section: **10** Quezon City
university: **10** Santo Tomas

Man in the Gray Flannel Suit, The
author: **11** Sloan Wilson

manipulate **3** pat, ply, use **4** feel, work **5** drive, pinch, wield **6** employ, finger, handle, manage, stroke **7** control, deceive, defraud, massage, operate, squeeze

Manitoba ***see box***

Mankiewicz, Joseph L
director of: **6** Sleuth **9** Cleopatra **11** All About Eve (Oscar) **12** Guys and Dolls, Julius Caesar **18** The Ghost and Mrs Muir **19** A Letter to Three Wives (Oscar)

mankind **3** man **6** people **7** mortals, persons, society **8** humanity **9** humankind **11** Homo sapiens

manlike **5** macho, manly **6** virile **8** hominoid **9** masculine

manly **4** bold, male **5** brave, hardy, husky, noble **6** brawny, daring, heroic, manful, plucky, robust, strong, sturdy, virile **7** gallant, staunch, valiant **8** athletic, fearless, malelike, muscular, powerful, resolute, stalwart, vigorous **9** masculine, strapping **10** chivalrous, courageous **11** gentlemanly, indomitable, self-reliant **12** stouthearted
Spanish: **5** macho

man-made **4** mock, sham **6** formed **7** crafted, created **8** produced **9** fashioned, ready-made, simulated, synthetic **10** artificial, fabricated, factitious, originated **11** constructed, handcrafted **12** manufactured

Mann, Delbert
director of: **5** Marty (Oscar) **14** Separate Tables

Mann, Thomas
author of: **12** Buddenbrooks **13** Death in Venice, Doctor Faustus **16** The Magic Mountain

manna, Manna **4** boon **5** award **6** reward **7** bonanza **16** divine sustenance

mannequin **4** form **5** dummy, model **6** figure

manner **3** air, way **4** form, kind, make, mode, mold, race, rank, sort, type **5** brand, breed, caste, genre, grade, guise, habit, stamp, style **6** aspect, custom, method, strain **7** bearing, conduct, fashion, species, variety **8** behavior, carriage, category, demeanor,

Manitoba
bay: **6** Hudson
capital: **8** Winnipeg
city: **6** Carman, The Pas **7** Brandon, Caribou, Dauphin, Selkirk **8** Flin Flon, Lynn Lake, Wabowden, Winnipeg **9** Churchill, Killarney, Sherridon, Swan River **10** St Boniface **11** Norway House, York Factory **16** Portage La Prairie
flower: **11** windflower **13** prairie crocus
Indian tribe: **4** Cree **6** Eskimo, Ojibwa **8** Chippewa **10** Assiniboin
lake: **4** God's, Swan **5** Cedar, Moose **6** Island **7** Dauphin, Red Deer **8** Manitoba, Reindeer, St Martin, Waterhen, Winnipeg **9** Granville
mountain: **4** Hart **5** Baldy
name means: **16** lake of the prairies **18** Great Spirit's strait **19** Great Spirit's narrows
nickname: **15** Prairie Province **16** Keystone Province
province of: **6** Canada
river: **3** Red **4** Seal, Swan **5** Hayes **6** Nelson, Roseau, Souris **7** Pembina **8** Winnipeg **9** Churchill **11** Assiniboine **12** Saskatchewan
university: **7** Brandon **10** St Boniface

practice, presence **9** character **10** appearance, deportment **14** classification

mannered **6** formal **7** stilted, studied **8** affected **9** contrived, unnatural **10** artificial **11** ceremonious

mannerism **4** airs, pose **5** habit **8** pretense **10** pretension **11** affectation, singularity **12** eccentricity, idiosyncrasy

mannerly **5** civil **6** polite **7** courtly, gallant, genteel, refined **8** well-bred **9** courteous **10** chivalrous **11** gentlemanly, well-behaved

manner of living
Latin: **12** modus vivendi

manner of looking at the world
German: **14** Weltanschauung

manner of speaking **7** diction **9** elocution **10** intonation **13** pronunciation

manners **6** polish **7** decorum **8** behavior, breeding, courtesy **9** amenities, deference, etiquette, gallantry, gentility, politesse, propriety **10** deportment, politeness, refinement **11** courtliness

Mannix
character: **9** Joe Mannix, Peggy Fair **10** (Lt) Adam Tobias **13** Lou Wickersham
cast: **10** Gail Fisher, Robert Reed **11** Mike Connors **16** Joseph Campanella

Mannon family
members: **4** Ezra, Orin **7** Lavinia **9** Christine
characters in: **22** Mourning Becomes Electra
author: **6** O'Neill

Manoah
son: **6** Samson

mano a mano **5** alone **8** conflict **13** confrontation, in a small group
literally: **10** hand to hand

Man of a Thousand Faces
nickname of: **9** Lon Chaney

Man of Nazareth
author: **14** Anthony Burgess

Man of Property, The
author: **14** John Galsworthy

Man of Sorrows *see* **5** Jesus

Manolin
character in: **18** The Old Man and the Sea
author: **9** Hemingway

Manon Lescaut
author: **11** Abbe Prevost

Manor, The
author: **19** Isaac Bashevis Singer

manor house **6** estate, manoir **7** chateau, mansion **11** stately home

manpower **4** help **5** brawn, labor **9** work force, employees

manque **6** failed, missed **7** lacking **11** fallen short, unfulfilled

Mansart, Francois
architect of: **14** Chateau de Berny **18** Hotel de la Vrilliere **33** Church of Sainte Marie de la Visitation
feature: **11** mansard roof

manservant **5** groom, valet **6** butler **7** footman **8** factotum **9** chauffeur

Man's Fate
author: **12** Andre Malraux

Mansfield, Jayne
real name: **14** Vera Jane Palmer
husband: **14** Mickey Hargitay
born: **10** Bryn Mawr PA
roles: **15** Hell on Frisco Bay **26** Will Success Spoil Rock Hunter

Mansfield, Katherine
author of: **5** Bliss **12** The Dove's Nest **14** The Garden Party

Mansfield Park
author: **10** Jane Austen
character: **5** Yates **8** Mrs Grant **9** Mrs Norris, Rushworth **10** Fanny Price **11** Lady Bertram **12** Mary Crawford **13** Henry Crawford **16** Sir Thomas Bertram
Bertram children: **3** Tom **5** Julia, Maria **6** Edmund

mansion **5** manor, villa **6** castle, estate, palace **7** chateau **10** manor house

manslaughter **6** murder **7** killing **8** homicide

manta **3** ray **4** cape **5** cloak, shawl **9** devilfish

Mantegna, Andrea
born: **5** Italy **14** Isola di Carturo
artwork: **9** Parnassus **16** Camera degli Sposi (Bridal Chamber) **18** The Triumph of Caesar, The Triumph of Virtue **20** Madonna della Vittoria

Man That Corrupted Hadleyburg, The
author: **9** Mark Twain

Mantius
father: **8** Melampus
son: **6** Clitus

mantle **4** cape, film, mask, pall, veil **5** cloak, cloud, cover, scarf, tunic **6** canopy, screen, shroud **7** blanket, curtain, wrapper **8** covering, envelope, mantilla

Mantle, Mickey (Charles)
sport: **8** baseball
position: **8** outfield
team: **14** New York Yankees

manual **6** primer **8** handbook, physical, textbook, workbook **9** guidebook **10** done by hand **12** hand-operated, nonautomatic **15** instruction book

manual skill **8** deftness **9** dexterity, handiness **10** adroitness **12** coordination

manufacture **4** form, make, mold **5** build, frame **6** cook up, create, devise, invent, make up **7** concoct, fashion, produce, think up, trump up **8** assemble **9** construct, fabricate **11** mass-produce, put together

manufacturing **8** devising **9** inventing, producing **10** industrial **11** fabricating, nonagrarian

manumission **7** freeing **10** liberation **11** setting free **12** emancipation

manumit **4** free **7** set free **8** liberate **10** emancipate

manure **4** dung **5** feces **6** ordure **7** compost, excreta **8** dressing **10** fertilizer

manuscript **6** script **10** typescript **14** shooting script **15** written document

Manvah
son: **6** Samson

Man Who Came to Dinner, The
director: **15** William Keighley
based on play by: **8** Moss Hart **14** George S Kaufman
cast: **10** Bette Davis **11** Ann Sheridan, Billie Burke **12** Monty Woolley **13** Richard Travis

Man Who Fell to Earth, The
director: **12** Nicholas Roeg
cast: **7** Rip Torn **9** Buck Henry **10** Candy Clark, David Bowie

Man Who Shot Liberty Valence, The
director: **8** John Ford
cast: **9** John Wayne, Lee Marvin, Vera Miles **12** Edmund O'Brien, James Stewart

Man Who Was Thursday, The
author: **12** G K Chesterton

Man Without a Country, The
author: **17** Edward Everett Hale
character: **11** Philip Nolan

many **4** a lot, lots **5** a heap, heaps, piles **6** divers, dozens, myriad, scores, sundry **7** numbers, several, various **8** numerous **9** countless **10** a profusion, numberless **11** an abundance, innumerable **13** multitudinous

manzanita **14** Arctostaphylos
varieties: **4** dune, Ione, Otay **5** hairy, hoary, Morro, Parry, Pecho **6** island, Sonoma, woolly **7** Mexican, Pajarro, pine-mat **8** big-berry, Del Norte, Eastwood, Mariposa, Monterey, shagbark, Stanford **9** Fort Bragg, green-leaf, heart-leaf, little Sur, white-leaf **10** serpentine, silver-leaf **11** brittle-leaf, pink-bracted

map **4** plan, plot **5** chart, graph, ready **6** design, devise, lay out **7** arrange, diagram, prepare, project **8** contrive, organize **9** elevation **10** make a map of, projection **14** representation **18** topographical chart

maple **4** Acer
varieties: **3** red **4** Amur, hard, rock, soft, vine **5** black, chalk, field, hedge, Nikko, river, sugar, swamp, white **6** Balkan, canyon, Norway, Oregon, parlor, sierra, silver, Triden **7** bigleaf, Florida, Persian, scarlet, striped **8** big-tooth, Drummond, full-moon, Hawthorn, Hornbeam, Japanese, mountain, Shantung, Sycamore, Tatarian **9** ash-leaved, eagle-claw, flowering, paperbark, Schwedler, Tartarian **11** Montpellier **12** Pennsylvania **13** Rocky Mountain, Southern sugar **18** Rocky Mountain sugar

map out **3** map **5** chart, draft **6** devise, lay out **7** diagram, outline **8** block out **9** delineate, formulate

Maputo
capital of: **10** Mozambique

mar **4** hurt, maim, mark, nick, ruin, scar **5** botch, spoil, stain, taint **6** blight, damage, deface, defile, impair **7** blemish, destroy, scratch **8** diminish, mutilate **9** disfigure

Marabar Caves
setting in: **15** A Passage to India
author: **7** Forster

Maranatha
means: **9** O Lord come

maraschino
type: **7** liqueur
origin: **5** Italy
flavor: **6** cherry
color: **3** red **5** white

Marathi
language family: **12** Indo-European
branch: **11** Indo-Iranian
group: **5** Indic
spoken in: **5** (northern) India

Marathonian bull *see* **10** Cretan bull

marauder **6** looter, pirate, ranger **7** corsair, ravager, spoiler **8** pillager **9** buccaneer, despoiler, guerrilla, plunderer, privateer **10** depradator, freebooter

marble **3** jet **4** vein **5** agate **6** basalt, blotch, mottle, streak **7** calcite **8** dolomite **9** limestone **10** serpentine, travertine **12** anthraconite
quarry: **7** Carrara

Marble Faun, The
author: **18** Nathaniel Hawthorne
character: **5** Hilda **6** Kenyon, Miriam **9** Donatello

marbles
type: **3** mib, taw **4** aggy, duck, immy, migg **5** agate, monny, scrap **6** commie, glassy, hoodle, marine **7** cat's eye, rainbow, shooter **9** carnelian **16** peppermint stripe
term: **3** hit **4** shot **6** edgers, ringer **7** bowling, for fair, histing, lagging, lag line, lofting **8** circling, for keeps, hunching **9** pitch line **10** roundsters **11** knuckle down **13** knuckling down

Marc, Franz
born: **6** Munich **7** Germany
artwork: **10** Blue Horses **12** Yellow Horses **13** Fighting Forms

Marceline
character in: **19** The Marriage of Figaro
author: **12** Beaumarchais

march **2** go **4** hike, rise, step, trek, walk **5** tramp **6** file by, growth, parade **7** advance, proceed **8** progress **9** group walk **10** go directly, procession, walk in step **11** advancement, development, progression **12** martial music

March
event: **8** Passover **9** Mardi Gras **11** Ides of March (15) **12** Ash Wednesday **13** vernal equinox (21)
flower: **7** jonquil **8** daffodil
French: **4** Mars
gem: **10** aquamarine, bloodstone
German: **4** Marz
holiday: **6** Easter **12** St Joseph's Day (19) **13** St Patrick's Day (17)
Italian: **5** Marzo
number of days: **9** thirty-one
origin of name: **4** Mars
Roman god of: **3** war
place in year:
Gregorian: **5** third
Roman: **5** first
saying: **20** Beware the Ides of March **40** March comes in like a lion and goes out like a lamb
Spanish: **6** Marcha
Zodiac sign: **5** Aries **6** Pisces

March, Fredric
real name: **29** Ernest Frederick McIntyre Bickel
born: **8** Racine WI
roles: **11** A Star Is Born **12** Anna Karenina, The Buccaneer **13** Les Miserables **14** Anthony Adverse, Inherit the Wind, Mary of Scotland, Seven Days in May **16** Death of a Salesman **17** Alexander the Great, Dr Jekyll and Mr Hyde (Oscar), The Desperate Hours **18** Death Takes a Holiday **19** The Affairs of Cellini **22** The Best Years of Our Lives (Oscar) **23** Barretts of Wimpole Street

Marchen **8** folk tale **9** fairy tale

Marcheshvan **17** eighth Hebrew month

March family
members: **2** Jo **3** Amy, Meg **4** Beth **6** Marmee
characters in: **11** Little Women
author: **6** Alcott

March Hare
character in: **28** Alice's Adventures in Wonderland
author: **7** Carroll

Marchmain family
characters in: **19** Brideshead Revisited
author: **5** Waugh

Marciano, Rocky
real name: **23** Rocco Francis Marchegiano
nickname: **19** Brockton Blockbuster
sport: **6** boxing
class: **11** heavyweight

Marconi, Guglielmo
nationality: **7** Italian
nickname: **16** father of wireless
invented/discovered: **5** radio **12** radio signals **16** magnetic detector **30** wireless high frequency telegraph
shared (1919): **20** Nobel Prize for physics

Marcus Welby MD
character: **11** (Dr) Steven Kiley **13** Consuelo Lopez
cast: **11** James Brolin, Robert Young **12** Elena Verdugo

Mardi (and a Voyage Thither)
author: **14** Herman Melville
character: **4** Alma, Jarl, Mohi, Taji **5** Media, Samoa, Yoomy **6** Yillah **7** Annatoo **10** Babbalanja, Braidbeard **11** Queen Hautia

Mardi Gras **7** holiday **8** carnival, festival, jamboree **10** fat Tuesday

Marduk
also: **8** Merodach **12** Baal Merodach
origin: **10** Babylonian
chief of: **4** gods

mare **3** sea **9** brood-mare **11** female horse

mare nostrum **6** our sea
ancient Roman name for: **13** Mediterranean

mares of Diomedes *see* **8** Diomedes

margin **3** hem, rim **4** edge, side **5** bound, skirt, verge **6** border, fringe, leeway **7** confine **8** boundary **9** allowance, extra room, safeguard

marginal **9** on the edge **11** in the margin **12** barely useful

mariage de convenance **21** marriage of convenience

Marica
also: **9** Dea Marica
origin: **5** Roman
goddess of: **7** marshes

marigold **7** Tagetes
varieties: **3** big, bur, fig, pot **4** cape, corn, wild **5** Aztec, fetid, field, marsh, water **6** desert, French, signet **7** African **12** sweet-scented

marijuana, marihuana **3** boo, kif, pot, tea **4** hash, hemp, herb, weed **5** bhang, dagga, ganja, grass, joint **6** moocah, reefer **7** hashish **8** cannabis, locoweed, mary jane

Marin, John Cheri (3rd)
born: **12** Rutherford NJ
artwork: **8** Sea Piece **12** Maine Islands **13** Tunk Mountains **16** Beach Flint Island **19** Movement Fifth Avenue **21** Seaside Interpretation **26** Camden Mountain across the Bay

marine **3** sea **5** naval **7** aquatic, oceanic, of ships, pelagic **8** maritime, nautical, of the sea, seagoing **9** salt-water, seafaring **10** oceangoing **13** oceanographic

mariner **3** gob, tar **4** salt **5** pilot **6** sailor, sea dog, seaman **7** boatman **8** deck hand, helmsman, seafarer **9** navigator, yachtsman **10** bluejacket **12** seafaring man **16** able-bodied seaman

Marion, Francis
nickname: **8** Swamp Fox
served in: **16** Revolutionary War
type of warfare: **9** guerrilla
area fought in: **13** South Carolina
battle: **12** Eutaw Springs

marionette **6** puppet **10** fantoccino

Maris
companion of: **8** Sarpedon

marital **6** wedded, wifely **7** married, nuptial, spousal **8** conjugal **9** connubial, husbandly **10** of marriage **11** matrimonial

maritime **5** naval **6** marine **7** aquatic, coastal, oceanic, of ships **8** nautical, of the sea, seagoing **9** seafaring

marjoram
botanical name: **8** Majorana, O vulgare, Origanum **16** M hortensis moench
origin: **4** Asia **13** Mediterranean
family: **4** mint
symbol of: **5** honor **9** happiness
charm against: **10** witchcraft
used as: **12** air sweetener
use: **4** eggs, fish, meat **5** salad **8** stuffing **9** vegetable

Marjorie Morningstar
author: **10** Herman Wouk

mark **3** cut, mar, pit **4** dent, goal, harm, heed, line, mind, nick, note, pock, rate, scar, show, sign, spot **5** badge, brand, grade, judge, label, notch, point, proof, score, stain, stamp, token, track **6** attend, bruise, deface, denote, emblem, evince, injure, intent, rating, regard, reveal, streak, symbol, target, typify **7** betoken, blemish, correct, imprint, measure, scratch, signify, suggest, symptom, write in, write on **8** bull's-eye, colophon, disclose, evidence, hallmark, indicate, manifest, point out, standard, stand for **9** be a sign of, criterion, designate, disfigure, objective, symbolize, yardstick **10** impression, indication, touchstone **11** distinguish **12** characterize **13** differentiate

Mark
also: **8** John Mark
mother: **4** Mary
cousin: **8** Barnabas
wrote: **11** Gospel

Mark (King Mark)
character in: **16** Arthurian romance

Mark Antony
also: **14** Marcus Antonius
character in: **12** Julius Caesar
author: **11** Shakespeare

mark down **4** note **5** enter, lower **6** record, reduce **7** put down **9** write down

marked **5** clear, great, noted, plain **6** dotted, scored, severe, showed, spotty, tabbed, tagged, traced **7** branded, labeled, pointed, specked, spotted, stained, tracked **8** destined, speckled, striking, targeted **9** indicated, prominent **10** emphasized, identified, made note of, noticeable, remarkable, singled out **11** conspicuous, distinctive, outstanding **12** considerable **13** distinguished

marker **3** IOU, peg, run, tab **4** chip, flag, sign **5** score **6** etcher, scorer, tablet, ticket **7** counter **8** bookmark, memorial, monument, recorder

market **4** hawk, sell, vend **5** stand **6** bourse, peddle, retail **7** grocery **9** dispose of **10** curb market, meat market **11** butcher shop, grocer's shop, marketplace

marketplace **4** mart **5** agora, arena, plaza **6** bazaar, market, square **8** exchange

Mark of Zorro, The
director: **15** Rouben Mamoulian

cast: 11 Tyrone Power 12 Linda Darnell 13 Basil Rathbone 15 Gale Sondergaard
score: 12 Alfred Newman

mark out 8 describe 9 delineate

marksman 8 dead shot, good shot, sure shot 9 crack shot 12 sharpshooter

marksmanship 3 aim 5 skill 8 accuracy 13 sharpshooting

Marley's Ghost
character in: 15 A Christmas Carol
author: 7 Dickens

Marlow
character in: 7 Lord Jim
author: 6 Conrad

Marlowe
character in: 15 Heart of Darkness
author: 6 Conrad

Marlowe, Christopher
author of: 8 Edward II 13 Doctor Faustus, The Jew of Malta 14 Hero and Leander 15 Edward the Second 19 Tamburlaine the Great

Marmax
suitor of: 10 Hippodamia
murdered by: 8 Oenomaus

Marmee
character in: 11 Little Women
author: 6 Alcott

Marmion
author: 14 Sir Walter Scott
character: 11 Lord Marmion 13 Ralph de Wilton 14 Clare Fitz-Clare 16 Archibald Douglas 19 Constance de Beverley

Marnie
director: 15 Alfred Hitchcock
cast: 10 Diane Baker 11 Sean Connery, Tippi Hedren

maroon 4 plum, wine 6 desert, strand 7 abandon, forsake, magenta 8 cast away, jettison 9 put ashore 10 cast ashore, terra cotta 11 brownish-red, leave behind 15 leave high and dry

Marpessa
origin: 5 Greek
father: 6 Euenos
loved by: 4 Idas 6 Apollo
chose: 4 Idas

Marple, Miss Jane
detective created by: 14 Agatha Christie

Marquand, J P
author of: 13 Wickford Point 18 The Late George Apley
character: 6 Mr Moto

marquee 4 tent 6 awning, canopy 8 marquise

marred 6 ruined 7 damaged, injured, spoiled 8 impaired 9 blemished, destroyed 10 disfigured

Marrener, Edythe
real name of: 12 Susan Hayward

marriage 7 wedding, wedlock 8 nuptials 9 matrimony
god of: 4 Frey 5 Freyr, Hymen 9 Hymenaeus
goddess of: 3 Fri 5 Frigg, Frija 6 Frigga, Tellus

Marriage a la Mode
author: 10 John Dryden

marriage broker
Yiddish: 8 shadchan 9 schatchen

marriage of convenience
French: 19 mariage de convenance

Marriage of Figaro, The
also: 15 Le Nozze di Figaro
opera: 6 Mozart
character: 7 Susanna 8 Countess 9 Cherubino, Dr Bartolo 10 Marcellina 13 Count Almaviva

Marriage of Figaro, The
author: 12 Beaumarchais
character: 6 Figaro 7 Suzanne 8 Cherubin 9 Marceline 10 Dr Bartholo 13 Count Almaviva 16 Countess Almaviva

Marriages Between Zones Three, Four and Five
author: 12 Doris Lessing

married 3 wed 5 mated 6 joined, united, wedded 7 hitched, marital 8 combined, espoused 9 connubial 11 matrimonial, tied the knot

married woman
German: 4 frau

marry 3 wed 7 espouse, make one 10 get spliced, tie the knot 13 join in wedlock 14 join in marriage, lead to the altar, take in marriage

Marryat, Frederick
author of: 11 Peter Simple 16 Mr Midshipman Easy

Mars
also: 6 Mamers, Mavors
origin: 5 Roman
god of: 3 war
mother: 4 Juno
wife: 5 Nerio
epithet: 5 Ultor 8 Gradivus
corresponds to: 4 Ares

Mars
position: 6 fourth
nickname: 9 Red Planet
satellite: 6 Deimos, Phobos

Marseillaise 20 French national anthem

marsh 3 bog, fen 5 swamp 6 morass, slough 7 bottoms, wetland 8 quagmire 9 everglade, marshland, quicksand

Marsh, Dame Ngaio
author of: 9 Dead Water 12 Final Curtain 13 Death at the Bar 14 Enter a Murderer 19 Singing in the Shrouds
character: 10 Troy Alleyn 14 Roderick Alleyn

Marsh, Reginald
born: 5 Paris 6 France
artwork: 9 The Bowery 10 Pip and Flip 14 Why Not Use the El? 16 Tattoo and Haircut 17 Twenty-Cent Haircut

marshal 5 align, array, chief, group, order 6 deploy, draw up, gather, leader, line up, muster 7 arrange, collect, manager, sheriff 8 assemble, director, marechal, mobilize, organize 9 fire chief 10 law officer, supervisor 11 police chief 12 chief officer, field marshal 13 generalissimo

Marshall, George C
served in: 3 WWI 4 WWII 9 Korean War, World War I 10 World War II 11 World War One, World War Two
rank: 12 chief of staff 16 general of the army
author of: 12 Marshall Plan
secretary of: 5 state 7 defense
winner of: 15 Nobel Peace Prize (1953)

Marshall, Penny
husband: 9 Rob Reiner
born: 7 Bronx NY
roles: 5 Myrna 12 The Odd Couple 14 Laverne DeFazio 17 Laverne and Shirley
director: 3 Big

marshy 3 wet 4 miry 5 boggy, fenny, muddy 6 swampy 7 paludal, paludic 11 waterlogged

marsupial 5 koala 6 numbat, possum, wombat 7 cuscuse, opossum, wallaby 8 kangaroo 9 bandicoot, phalanger 14 Tasmanian devil

Marsyas
form: 5 satyr
played: 5 flute

mart 4 show 6 market 8 exchange **9** trade fair, trade show **10** exposition

Martha
sister: **4** Mary
brother: **7** Lazarus
hometown: **7** Bethany

martial **7** hostile, Spartan, warlike **8** militant, military **9** bellicose, combative, soldierly **10** pugnacious **11** belligerent, contentious

Martian Chronicles, The
author: **11** Ray Bradbury

Martin, Dean
real name: **16** Dino Paul Crocetti
partner: **10** Jerry Lewis
born: **14** Steubenville OH
roles: **8** Matt Helm, Rio Bravo, The Caddy **9** The Stooge **10** Living It Up **12** Four for Texas, Sailor Beware **14** Toys in the Attic **15** Some Came Running **16** Artists and Models

Martin, Mary
son: **11** Larry Hagman
born: **13** Weatherford TX
roles: **6** I Do I Do **8** Peter Pan **12** Sound of Music, South Pacific

Martin, Steve
born: **6** Waco TX
roles: **7** The Jerk **17** Pennies From Heaven, Saturday Night Live **19** The Man with Two Brains **20** Dead Men Don't Wear Plaid **26** Planes Trains and Automobiles

Martin Chuzzlewit
author: **14** Charles Dickens
character: **5** Mercy **7** Charity **8** Tom Pinch **9** Pecksniff, Ruth Pinch, Sarah Gamp **10** Mark Tapley, Mary Graham **15** Jonas Chuzzlewit **17** Anthony Chuzzlewit

martinet **6** despot, tyrant **8** dictator **10** hard master, taskmaster **11** drillmaster, Simon Legree **12** little Caesar **13** authoritarian, drill-sergeant

Marty
director: **11** Delbert Mann
cast: **10** Betsy Blair **11** Joe De Santis **14** Ernest Borgnine **15** Esther Minciotti
Oscar for: **5** actor (Borgnine) **7** picture
script: **14** Paddy Chayefsky

martyr **5** saint **8** sufferer

martyrdom **5** agony **6** ordeal **7** anguish, torment, torture **9** bitter cup, suffering **10** affliction **11** cup of sorrow **13** crown of thorns

marvel **4** gape **6** be awed, rarity, wonder **7** miracle **8** be amazed **9** spectacle **10** phenomenon

Marvell, Andrew
author of: **9** The Garden **16** To His Coy Mistress

marvelous, marvellous **4** A-one, fine **5** grand, great, super **6** divine, lovely, superb **7** amazing **8** colossal, fabulous, heavenly, smashing, splendid **9** fantastic, first-rate, wonderful **10** phenomenal, remarkable, stupendous **11** astonishing, magnificent, outstanding, sensational **13** extraordinary

marvelous to relate
Latin: **13** mirabile dictu

Marwood, Mrs
character in: **16** The Way of the World
author: **8** Congreve

Marx, Bernard
character in: **13** Brave New World
author: **6** Huxley

Marx, Karl
author of: **10** Das Kapital **18** Communist Manifesto (with Friedrich Engels)

Marx Brothers **5** Chico (Leonard), Gummo (Milton), Harpo (Adolph, Arthur) Zeppo (Herbert) **7** Groucho (Julius)
costar: **14** Margaret Dumont
born: **9** New York NY
roles: **8** Coconuts, Duck Soup **11** The Big Store **13** Horse Feathers **14** A Day at the Races, Animal Crackers, Monkey Business **16** A Night at the Opera
Groucho's TV show: **14** You Bet Your Life

Mary **6** Virgin **7** Madonna **8** Holy Mary **9** Magdalene, of Cleopas **10** Virgin Mary **11** Mother of God, Regina Coeli **13** Queen of Heaven **15** Mother of Sorrows **17** Mother of the Church
mother: **4** Anna, Anne
husband: **6** Joseph **7** Alpheus, Cleopas
son: **4** Jude, Mark **5** Jesus, Moses, Simon **12** James the Less
sister: **6** Martha
brother: **7** Lazarus **8** Barnabas
cousin: **9** Elizabeth
hometown: **8** Nazareth
visitor: **7** Gabriel
flower: **4** lily **8** marigold

Mary
author: **10** Sholem Asch

Maryland ***see box***

Mary Poppins
director: **15** Robert Stevenson
based on story by: **9** P L Travers
cast: **6** Ed Wynn **11** Dick Van Dyke (Bert), Glynis Johns **12** Julie Andrews **14** David Tomlinson **16** Hermione Baddeley
score: **13** Robert Sherman **14** Richard Sherman
Oscar for: **4** song **5** score **7** actress (Andrews) **13** visual effects
song: **14** Chim-chim-cheree

Mary Queen of Scots
director: **14** Charles Jarrott
cast: **12** Trevor Howard **13** Glenda Jackson (Elizabeth I), Timothy Dalton **14** Nigel Davenport **15** Patrick McGoohan, Vanessa Redgrave (Mary of Scotland)

Mary Tyler Moore Show, The
character: **8** Lou Grant **9** Ted Baxter **12** Gordon (Gordy) Howard, Mary Richards, Sue Ann Nivens **13** Bess Lindstrom **14** Marie Slaughter **15** Murray Slaughter **16** Phyllis Lindstrom, Rhoda Morgenstern **23** Georgette Franklin Baxter
cast: **8** John Amos **9** Ted Knight **10** Betty White **11** Edward Asner **12** Gavin MacLeod, Georgia Engel **13** Joyce Bulifant, Lisa Gerritsen, Valerie Harper **14** Cloris Leachman
setting: **11** Minneapolis

Mary Worth
creator: **8** Carey Orr **9** Dale Allen **10** Dale Connor **13** Allen Saunders
character: **4** Bill, Slim

Masaccio
real name: **26** Tommaso di Ser Giovanni di Mone
born: **5** Italy **27** Castel San Giovanni di Valdarno
artwork: **14** The Holy Trinity **15** The Tribute Money **24** The Expulsion from Paradise

Mascagni, Pietro
born: **5** Italy **7** Leghorn
composer of: **4** Iris **6** Nerone **7** Isabeau **10** Le Maschere **11** L'Amico Fritz **14** Il Piccolo Marat **19** Cavalleria Rusticana

masculine **4** bold, male **5** brave, hardy, husky, macho, manly **6** brawny, daring, manful, plucky, robust, strong, sturdy, virile **7** staunch, valiant **8** athletic, fearless, forceful, intrepid, muscular,

Maryland
abbreviation: 2 MD
nickname: 4 Free **7** Cockade **12** Old Line State
capital: 9 Annapolis
largest city: 9 Baltimore
others: 5 Essex **6** Easton, Laurel, Towson **8** Aberdeen, Bethesda, Pocomoke **9** Frederick, Ocean City, Rockville **10** Cumberland, Hagerstown, Pikesville **11** Catonsville, College Park
college: 4 Hood **7** Goucher, St John's **10** Washington **11** Towson State **12** Johns Hopkins **21** Annapolis Naval Academy
feature:
fort: **7** McHenry
national battlesite: **8** Antietam
presidential retreat: **9** Camp David
race: **9** Preakness **12** Steeplechase
racetrack: **5** Bowie **6** Butler, Laurel **7** Pimlico
tribe: 5 Conoy **9** Nanticoke
people: 6 Wesort **8** Terrapin **10** Spiro Agnew **11** crawthumper **14** Sargent Shriver **15** Francis Scott Key
explorer: **7** Calvert
lake: 8 Patapsco **9** Deep Creek, Loch Raven, Pretty Boy **10** Rocky Gorge **11** Triadelphia
land rank: 11 forty second
mountain: 4 Dans **8** Piedmont **9** Blue Ridge **11** Appalachian
highest point: **8** Backbone
physical feature:
bay: **10** Chesapeake
sea: **8** Atlantic
swamp: **7** Pocoson
valley: **5** Great **10** Hagerstown
river: 3 Elk **7** Chester, Potomac **8** Choptank, Patapsco, Patuxent, Pocomoke **11** Susquehanna
state admission: 7 seventh
state bird: 15 Baltimore oriole
state fish: 11 striped bass
state flower: 14 black-eyed Susan
state motto: 22 Manly Deeds Womanly Words **43** Thou Hast Crowned Us With the Shield of Thy Good Will
state song: 18 Maryland My Maryland
state tree: 8 white oak

powerful, resolute, vigorous **9** strapping **10** courageous **11** indomitable, self-reliant **12** stouthearted

Masefield, John
author of: 7 Cargoes **8** Sea Fever **16** Salt Water Ballads

Maseru
capital of: 7 Lesotho

mash 4 mush **5** crush, paste, puree, smash **6** squash **8** mishmash **9** pulverize

M*A*S*H
character: 10 (Capt) BJ Hunnicut, (Lt Col) Henry Blake, (Maj) Frank Burns **12** (Corp) Radar O'Reilly **13** Father (John) Mulcahy, (Capt Benjamin Franklin) Hawkeye Pierce, (Col) Sherman Potter **14** (Corp) Maxwell Klinger **15** (Maj Margaret) Hot Lips Houlihan **19** (Capt John) Trapper John McIntyre **24** (Maj) Charles Emerson Winchester
cast: 8 Alan Alda **9** Jamie Farr **11** Harry Morgan, Loretta Swit, Mike Farrell, Wayne Rogers **12** Gary Burghoff **13** Larry Linville **15** McLean Stevenson **16** David Ogden Stiers **18** William Christopher
war: 6 Korean
MASH stands for: 26 Mobile Army Surgical Hospital
tent: 5 Swamp
theme: 17 Suicide Is Painless

M*A*S*H
director: 12 Robert Altman
cast: 10 Jo Ann Pflug **11** Elliot Gould (Trapper John McIntyre), Tom Skerritt (B J Hunnicut) **12** Gary Burghoff (Radar O'Reilly), Robert Duvall (Frank Burns) **14** Sally Kellerman (Margaret Hot Lips Houlihan) **16** Donald Sutherland (Hawkeye Pierce)

masjid 6 mosque

mask 4 hide, veil **5** blind, cloak, cover **6** domino, screen, shroud **7** conceal, cover-up, curtain, obscure **8** disguise **9** face guard, false face **10** camouflage, keep secret

Mask
director: 16 Peter Bogdanovich
cast: 4 Cher **10** Eric Stoltz (Rocky Dennis), Sam Elliott

masked 9 concealed, covered up, disguised **10** in disguise, masquerade

Masked Ball, A
also: 17 Un Ballo in Maschera
opera by: 5 Verdi
character:
first version: **9** Count Horn **10** King Gustav **12** Count Ribbing
second version: **3** Sam, Tom **13** Count Riccardo

masking 6 hiding **7** veiling **8** covering **9** eclipsing, obscuring **10** concealing, covering up

Mason, Bertha
character in: 8 Jane Eyre
author: 6 Bronte

Mason, James
wife: 6 Pamela
born: 7 England **12** Huddersfield
roles: 6 Lolita **7** Lord Jim **9** Bloodline **10** Georgy Girl **13** Heaven Can Wait **14** Humbert Humbert, Murder by Decree, The Seventh Veil **15** Prisoner of Zenda **16** North by Northwest **17** The Boys from Brazil

Mason, Marsha
husband: 9 Neil Simon
born: 9 St Louis MO
roles: 10 Chapter Two **11** Blume in Love **14** The Goodbye Girl **15** Max Dugan Returns **17** Cinderella Liberty

Masque of the Red Death, The
author: 13 Edgar Allan Poe

masquerade 4 mask, ruse, veil **5** cloak, cover, guise, trick **6** masque, pose as, screen, shroud **7** cover-up, pretext **8** artifice, pretense **9** bal masque **10** camouflage, masked ball, subterfuge **11** impersonate **12** harlequinade

Masquerade Party
host: 9 Bert Parks **10** Bud

Collier **11** Peter Donald **12** Eddie Bracken, Robert Q Lewis **14** Douglas Edwards

mass, Mass **3** jam, lot, mob **4** body, bulk, cake, clot, heap, host, hunk, knot, lump, pack, pile **5** amass, batch, block, bunch, chunk, clump, corps, crowd, crush, group, horde, press, stack, troop **6** bundle, gather, matter, throng, weight **7** collect, pyramid **8** assemble, best part, main body, majority, material **9** aggregate, Eucharist, gathering, plurality **10** accumulate, assemblage, assortment, collection, concretion, congregate, cumulation, lion's share **11** aggregation, consolidate, greater part **12** accumulation, congregation **13** Holy Communion, holy sacrament, preponderance **14** conglomeration

Massachusetts ***see box***

Massachusetts
abbreviation: **2** MA **4** Mass
nickname: **3** Bay **7** Puritan **9** Baked Bean, Old Colony
capital/largest city: **6** Boston
others: **4** Ayer, Lynn, Otis **5** Athol, Barre, Lenox, Salem **6** Agawam, Dedham, Groton, Nahant, Natick, Revere, Saugus, Woburn **7** Belmont, Beverly, Concord, Danvers, Everett, Holyoke, Ipswich, Medford, Peabody, Taunton, Waltham **8** Brockton, Chicopee, Cohasset, Plymouth, Scituate, Yarmouth **9** Arlington, Attleboro, Braintree, Brookline, Cambridge, Lexbridge, Lexington, Worcester **10** Gloucester, New Bedford, Pittsfield **11** Springfield **12** Provincetown, Williamstown
college: **3** MIT **5** Clark, Curry, Smith, Tufts **6** Babson **7** Amherst, Harvard, Simmons, Wheaton **8** Brandeis, Williams **9** Hampshire, Holy Cross, Merrimack, Radcliffe, Wellesley **11** Springfield **12** Mount Holyoke, Northeastern **13** Boston College
feature: **10** Walden Pond **12** Plymouth Rock
national seashore: **7** Cape Cod
village: **13** Old Sturbridge
tribe: **6** Nauset **8** Pocomtuc **10** Wampanoags
people: **8** Pilgrims **9** Amy Lowell, Elias Howe **10** Cyrus Field, Eli Whitney **11** Clara Barton, John Hancock, Samuel Adams, Samuel Morse **12** Henry Thoreau, Robert Lowell, Winslow Homer **13** James Whistler, Joseph Kennedy, Robert Kennedy **14** Emily Dickinson **15** Henry Cabot Lodge **16** Benjamin Franklin, Edward "Ted" Kennedy **17** Ralph Waldo Emerson **18** Bartholomew Gosnold, James Russell Lowell, Nathanial Hawthorne **19** Oliver Wendell Holmes, William Cullen Bryant **21** John Greenleaf Whittier
explorer: **8** Norsemen
island: **5** Duke's **9** Nantucket **13** Chappaquidick **15** Martha's Vineyard
lake: **5** Onota **7** Quabbin, Rohunta, Webster **8** Long Pond **11** Watuppa Pond **16** Assawompsett Pond **17** Chaubunagungamaug
land rank: **10** forty-fifth
mountain: **3** Tom **6** Brodie, Potter **7** Alander, Everett, Taconic **10** Berkshires
highest point: **8** Greylock
physical feature:
bay: **8** Buzzard's
cape: **3** Ann, Cod
sea: **8** Atlantic
president: **9** John Adams **14** Calvin Coolidge **15** John Quincy Adams **21** John Fitzgerald Kennedy
river: **6** Nashua **7** Charles, Concord, Quaboag, Taunton **8** Chicopee **9** Deerfield, Merrimack **10** Blackstone, Housatonic **11** Connecticut
state admission: **11** thirty-sixth
state bird: **9** chickadee
state flower: **9** mayflower **15** trailing arbutus
state motto: **37** With the Sword She Seeks Peace Under Liberty **45** By the Sword We Seek Peace But Peace Only Under Liberty
state song: **22** All Hail to Massachusetts
state tree: **11** American elm

massacre **7** butcher, carnage **8** butchery, decimate **9** bloodbath, slaughter **10** mass murder **12** bloodletting

massage **3** rub **4** flex **5** chafe, knead **6** finger, handle, stroke **7** rubbing, rub down, stretch **8** kneading, stroking **10** manipulate **12** manipulation

Massasoit *see* **10** Wampanoags

Massenet, Jules Emile Frederic
born: **6** France **9** St Etienne
composer of: **5** Le Cid, Manon, Thais **7** Werther **9** Herodiade **11** David Rizzio **12** Don Quichotte **13** Le Roi de Lahore **21** Le Jongleur de Notre-Dame

masses **6** plebes, proles, rabble, the mob **7** the many **8** the crowd **9** hoi polloi, plebeians **11** the populace, the riffraff **12** the multitude **13** the common herd **14** the proletariat, the rank and file **15** the common people, the lower classes, the working class **16** the great unwashed

Masset *see* **10** Skidegatta

massive **4** huge, vast **5** ample, bulky, great, heavy, hefty, massy, solid **7** hulking, immense, mammoth, titanic, weighty **8** colossal, enormous, gigantic, imposing, towering, whopping **9** cyclopean, extensive, monstrous, ponderous **10** gargantuan, impressive, monumental, stupendous **11** elephantine, substantial

massiveness **4** bulk, size **8** enormity, hugeness, vastness **9** amplitude, bulkiness, greatness, immensity, largeness, magnitude

mast **4** main, nuts, pole, post, spar **5** spirit, staff, stick, stuff **6** acorns, pillar **9** beechnuts, chestnuts
type: **4** fore, main **6** jigger, mizzen
support: **4** bibb

master **3** ace **4** able, A-one, best, boss, curb, deft, head, lord, main, tame, whiz **5** check, chief, crack, grasp, owner, prime, ruler **6** bridle, choice, expert, genius, gifted, govern, leader, manage, subdue, wizard **7** conquer, control, excel at, head man, manager, primary, skilled, skipper, supreme **8** director, dominate, finished, governor, masterly, overcome, overlord, overseer, regulate, suppress, talented, virtuoso **9** authority, conqueror, craftsman, first-rate, paramount, practiced, principal **10** controller, proficient, supervisor **12** get the hang of, ship's captain

Master Builder, The
author: **11** Henrik Ibsen

master craftsman **7** artisan **12** masterworker **13** skilled worker

masterful **4** able, deft **5** bossy **6** expert, superb **7** dynamic, skilled **8** finished, forceful, masterly, resolute, skillful, virtuoso **9** excellent **10** commanding **11** domineering, self-reliant **12** accomplished, strong-willed **13** authoritarian, self-confident

masterfulness **6** genius **10** capability, competence, excellence **11** proficiency

Master Melvin
nickname of: **6** Mel Ott

mastermind **4** plan, sage **6** direct, expert, genius, master, pundit, wizard **7** old hand, planner **8** conceive, director, engineer, organize, virtuoso **9** authority, initiator, organizer **10** specialist **11** moving force

Master of Ballantrae, The
author: **20** Robert Louis Stevenson
character: **4** Chew **5** Teach **9** MacKellar **11** Henry Durrie, James Durrie **12** Alison Graeme, Francis Burke, Secundra Dass

master of the family
Latin: **13** paterfamilias

masterpiece **5** jewel, prize **7** classic, paragon **8** monument, treasure **9** nonpareil **10** brainchild **11** chef d'oeuvre, ne plus ultra, prizewinner

Masterpiece Theater
host: **13** Alistair Cooke

master race
German: **10** Herrenvolk

Masters, Edgar Lee
author of: **19** Spoon River Anthology

Mastersingers of Nuremberg, The
also: **27** Die Meistersinger von Nurnberg
opera by: **6** Wagner
character: **9** Eva Pogner, Hans Sachs **10** Beckmesser **18** Walther von Stolzing

mastery **4** rule, sway **5** grasp **7** ability, command, control **8** deftness, whip hand **9** dominance, supremacy, upper hand **10** adroitness, attainment, domination, leadership **11** achievement, acquirement, proficiency, superiority **14** accomplishment

masticate **4** chew, gnaw **5** champ, munch **6** nibble

Mastroianni, Marcello
born: **5** Italy **11** Fontana Liri
roles: **13** Eight and a Half **7** La Notte **11** La Dolce Vita, The Stranger, White Nights **19** Divorce Italian Style

mat **3** dim, pad, rug **4** dead, dull, flat **5** doily, muted **6** carpet, matrix, tangle **7** bedding, bolster, coaster, cushion, support **8** entangle **10** lackluster, lusterless
Japanese: **6** tatami

Mata Hari
real name: **21** Gertrud Margarete Zelle
worked as: **3** spy **6** dancer
worked for: **7** Germans
executed by: **6** French

match **3** fit **4** game, join, mate, meet, pair, peer, suit, twin, yoke **5** adapt, agree, equal, event, unite **6** couple, double, oppose **7** be alike, be equal, combine, connect, contend, contest, vie with **8** parallel **9** companion, duplicate, harmonize **10** correspond, equivalent, tournament **11** competition, counterpart

matched **5** equal **8** of a piece **9** identical **11** coordinated

matching **4** twin **5** equal **6** paired **10** equivalent **11** harmonizing **13** corresponding

matchless **4** rare **7** supreme **8** crowning, foremost, peerless, sterling, superior **9** exemplary, first rate, priceless, paramount, unequaled, unmatched, unrivaled **10** invaluable, preeminent, unbeatable, unexcelled **11** inestimable, superlative, unsurpassed **12** incomparable, unparalleled

matchmaker
Yiddish: **8** shadchan **9** schatchen

mate **3** pal **4** chum, twin, wife **5** buddy, crony, hubby, match **6** couple, friend, spouse **7** cohabit, comrade, consort, husband, pair off, partner **8** copulate, coworker, sidekick **9** associate, colleague, companion, duplicate **10** better half, equivalent **11** confederate, counterpart **12** fellow worker, ship's officer

materfamilias **15** mother of a family

material **5** stuff **6** matter **8** elements **9** substance **12** constituents

materialism **5** greed **12** covetousness **15** acquisitiveness

materialistic **6** greedy **8** covetous, grasping **11** acquisitive, unspiritual

materiality **9** existence **11** tangibility

materialization **5** ghost, shade **6** coming, wraith **7** phantom, specter **9** emergence **10** apparition, appearance **13** manifestation

materialize **4** loom, rise, show **5** bob up, issue, pop up **6** appear, crop up, emerge, turn up **9** come forth **10** burst forth **11** come to light, spring forth **12** come into view

materially **7** vitally **8** palpably, tangibly **9** in the main, seriously **10** monetarily **11** corporeally, essentially, financially, in substance **12** considerably, emphatically **13** significantly, substantially **14** for the most part

material possessions **6** assets, estate, wealth **7** fortune **8** property **10** belongings **12** worldly goods

material proof **8** evidence **13** documentation

materials **4** data **5** cloth, facts, notes, tools **6** stocks, stores, timber **7** fabrics, figures **8** concrete, dry goods, supplies, textiles **9** citations, equipment, machinery, yard goods **10** essentials, piece goods, quotations, references **11** impressions **12** observations **15** bricks and mortar

materiel **4** gear **6** stores **8** supplies **9** equipment, materials **10** provisions **16** military supplies

Mater Matuta *see* **6** Matuta

maternal **4** fond **6** doting **8** motherly **9** of a mother, shielding **10** motherlike, protective, sheltering

maternity **5** labor **8** delivery **9** pregnancy **10** childbirth, motherhood **11** parturition **12** accouchement, childbearing

Mater Turrita *see* **6** Cybele

mathematical, mathematic **5** exact, rigid **6** strict **7** precise **8** accurate, rigorous, unerring **10** meticulous, scientific, scrupulous **11** punctilious, well-defined **13** computational

mathematician
American: **5** Aiken **6** Wiener
British: **6** Newton **7** Babbage
French: **6** Fermat **9** D'Alembert, Descartes
German: **5** Frege, Gauss **6** Bessel **7** Hilbert
Greek: **6** Euclid, Thales **11** Anaximander
Norwegian: **4** Abel
Swiss: **5** Euler **9** Bernoulli

Mathewson, Christy
nickname: **5** Matty **6** Big Six
sport: **8** baseball
position: **7** pitcher
team: **13** New York Giants

Matholwych
king of: **7** Ireland
wife: **7** Branwen

matinee **9** early show **16** early performance **20** afternoon performance

Mating Season, The
author: **11** P G Wodehouse

Matisse, Henri Emile Benoit
born: **6** France **16** Chateau Cambresis (Le Cateau)
artwork: **5** Dance, Music **8** The Slave **10** Odalisques **11** Joie de Vivre **12** Harmony in Red, La Serpentine **13** Head with Tiara, The Open Window **15** Bathers by a River, Memory of Oceanie, Woman with the Hat **16** Heads of Jeannette **19** Torso with Arms Raised **20** Goldfish and Sculpture

Matralia
origin: **5** Roman
event: **8** festival

matriarch **7** dowager **10** female head, grande dame **11** female ruler **12** female leader **13** materfamilias

matriculate **4** join **5** enter **6** enlist, enroll, sign up **7** check in **8** register

matriculation **9** signing up **10** enrollment **12** registration

matrimonial **6** bridal, wedded, wifely **7** marital, married, nuptial, spousal **8** conjugal, hymeneal **9** affianced, connubial, husbandly **11** epithalamic

matrimony **7** wedlock **8** marriage **11** holy wedlock

matrix **3** die **4** cast, form, mold **5** frame, punch, stamp

matron **4** dame **5** madam **7** dowager **8** forelady, mistress, overseer **9** forewoman **10** directress **11** housekeeper **12** married woman **14** superintendent

Matronalia
origin: **5** Roman
event: **8** festival

matter **3** fix **4** gist, snag, text **5** count, drift, event, sense, stuff, theme, thing, topic **6** affair, crisis, import, moment, object, scrape, strait, thesis **7** content, dilemma, episode, essence, purport, signify, subject, trouble **8** argument, business, elements, exigency, material, obstacle, quandary **9** adventure, emergency, happening, situation, substance **10** difference, difficulty, experience, impediment, importance, occurrence, perplexity, proceeding **11** carry weight, consequence, predicament, transaction **12** circumstance, significance

matter-of-course **5** usual **6** common **7** routine **8** everyday, ordinary, standard **9** customary **11** commonplace, established

matter-of-fact **4** real **5** blunt, frank **6** candid, direct **7** factual, literal, mundane, natural, prosaic **8** ordinary, sensible **9** outspoken, practical, pragmatic, realistic **10** hardheaded, no-nonsense, unaffected, uninspired, unromantic **11** commonplace, common-sense, down-to-earth, straight-out **13** unimaginative, unsentimental **15** straightforward

matter-of-factness **10** detachment **11** impassivity **12** practicality **13** impassiveness **17** unimaginativeness

Matter of Time, A
author: **12** Jessamyn West

Matthau, Walter
real name: **13** Walter Matthow **23** Walter Matuschanskavasky
born: **9** New York NY
roles: **5** Kotch **8** A New Leaf **10** Plaza Suite **11** Pete n Tillie **12** Bad News Bears, Ensign Pulver, Oscar Madison, The Front Page, The Odd Couple **15** California Suite, The Sunshine Boys **16** The Fortune Cookie **22** A Guide for the Married Man

Matthew **7** apostle
father: **7** Alpheus
also called: **4** Levi
wrote: **6** Gospel

Matthiessen, Peter
author of: **10** Sand Rivers **14** The Snow Leopard

maturation **6** growth **8** fruition, ripening **9** growing up

mature **4** ripe **5** adult, bloom, grown, manly, of age, ready, ripen **6** flower, grow up, mellow, nubile, virile **7** blossom, develop, grown-up, matured, womanly **8** finished, maturate, seasoned **9** come of age, completed, full-blown, full-grown, perfected, practiced **10** middle-aged **11** become adult, experienced, full-fledged, in one's prime **12** marriageable

Mature, Victor
born: **12** Louisville KY
roles: **7** The Robe **11** After the Fox, Kiss of Death **12** Cry of the City, One Million BC **16** Samson and Delilah **19** Androcles and the Lion

matured **3** big **4** aged, ripe **5** adult, grown **6** formed **7** ripened **8** flowered, mellowed, seasoned **9** blossomed, developed, full-blown, full-grown **11** full-fledged

maturity **7** manhood **8** legal age, majority, practice, ripeness **9** adulthood, composure, full bloom, readiness, seasoning, womanhood **10** completion, experience, full growth, maturation, matureness, perfection **11** culmination, fulfillment **12** age of consent

Matuschanskavasky, Walter
real name of: **13** Walter Matthau

Matuta
origin: **5** Roman
goddess of: **3** sea **4** dawn **7** harbors **10** childbirth
called: **11** Mater Matuta

Maud
author: **18** Alfred Lord Tennyson

Maude
character: **5** Carol **7** Phillip **10** Henry Evans **12** Florida Evans, Maude Findlay, Mrs Naugatuck **13** Walter Findlay **14** Dr Arthur Harmon **20** Vivian Cavender Harmon
cast: **8** Bill Macy, John Amos **10** Conrad Bain **11** Esther Rolle **13** Brian Morrison, Rue McClanahan **14** Beatrice Arthur, Kraig Metzinger **15** Adrienne Barbeau **16** Hermione Baddeley

spinoff from: **14** All in the Family
spinoff: **9** Good Times

maudlin **5** gushy, mushy, teary **6** slushy **7** gushing, mawkish, tearful **8** bathetic **9** emotional **10** lachrymose **11** sentimental **13** overemotional

maudlinism **6** bathos **11** mawkishness **14** sentimentalism, sentimentality

Maugham, W Somerset
author of: **9** The Circle **10** Our Betters **11** Cakes and Ale **12** Miss Thompson **13** The Razor's Edge **14** Of Human Bondage **15** The Constant Wife **18** The Moon and Sixpence **21** Lady Frederick Ashenden

maul **4** beat **5** stomp **6** batter, beat up, bruise, mangle, pummel, thrash **7** rough up **9** manhandle **10** knock about

Mauldin, Bill
creator/artist of: **7** Up Front **12** Willie and Joe

maunder **4** loaf **5** drift, run on, stray **6** babble, dawdle, gabble, gibber, ramble, wander **7** blather, meander, prattle, saunter **8** flounder, ramble on, straggle **9** go on and on, hem and haw **10** dillydally

maundering **7** diffuse **8** rambling **9** wandering **10** digressive, disjointed, roundabout **14** drift, run on, stray **6** babble, dawdle, gabble, gibber, ramble, wander **7** blather, meander, prattle, saunter **8** flounder; ramble on, straggle **9** go on and on, hem and haw **10** dillydally

Maupassant, Guy de
author of: **6** Belami **9** Ball of Fat, Mont-Oriol **11** A Woman's Life, The Necklace **12** Ball of Tallow **16** Mademoiselle Fifi

Mauriac, Francois
author of: **8** Genitrix **10** The Egoists **12** Viper's Tangle **15** A Kiss to the Leper, The Desert of Love **20** A Woman of the Pharisees

Mauritania ***see box***

Mauritius ***see box***

mausoleum **10** family tomb **11** stately tomb **18** sepulchral monument

mauve **4** plum, puce **5** lilac **6** violet **8** lavender **11** light purple **12** bluish purple

maverick **5** loner **8** yearling **9** dissenter, dissident, eccentric **11** independent **13** individualist, noncomformist

Maverick
character: **12** Bart Maverick, Bret Maverick **13** Brent Maverick **16** Samantha Crawford **24** Cousin Beauregard Maverick
cast: **9** Jack Kelly **10** Roger Moore **11** James Garner **13** Diane Brewster, Robert Colbert

Mavors *see* **4** Mars

maw **4** craw, crop, jaws **5** mouth **6** gullet, muzzle, throat

mawkish **5** gushy, mushy, teary **7** maudlin, tearful **9** emotional, nostalgic, schmaltzy **10** lachrymose **11** sentimental **15** oversentimental

mawkishness **4** mush **5** slush **6** bathos **9** mushiness, soppiness **10** maudlinism, slushiness **14** sentimentalism, sentimentality

maxim **3** saw **4** rule **5** adage, axiom, motto **6** old saw, saying, truism **7** proverb **8** aphorism, apothegm **9** platitude

---

Mauritius
other name: **11** Ile de France
capital/largest city: **9** Port Louis
others: **6** Reduit **8** Curepipe **9** Mahebourg **13** Quartre Bornes **19** Grande Riviere Sud-Est
head of state: **14** British monarch **15** governor general
monetary unit: **4** cent **5** rupee
island: **3** Est **4** Flat **5** Ambre, Cerf's, Morne, Round **7** Agalega, Serpent **9** Mauritius, Rodrigues, Rodriguez, St Brandon **12** Gunner's Quoin **15** Cargados Carajos
highest point: **27** Piton de la Petite Riviere Noire
sea: **6** Indian
people: **6** Creole, French, Indian **7** African, Chinese **8** European **13** Indo-Mauritian
leader: **8** Jugnauth **9** Ramgoolam
ruler: **5** Dutch **6** French **7** English
language: **4** Urdu **5** Hindi, Tamil **6** Creole, French

Mauritania
capital/largest city: **10** Nouakchott
others: **4** Atar **5** Kaedi, Rosso **6** Fderik **7** Akjoujt **10** Nouadhibou
division: **5** Sahel **7** Chemama
monetary unit: **5** khoum **7** ouguiya
highest point: **11** Kediat Idjil
river: **7** Senegal
sea: **8** Atlantic
physical feature:
desert: **6** Sahara
valley: **7** Chemama **12** Senegal River
people: **4** Arab, Fula, Moor **5** Black, Fulbe, Wolof **6** Bafour, Berber, Fulani **7** African, Soninke, Tukulor **8** Sarakole **9** Sarakolle **10** Toucouleur **12** Halphoolaren
leader: **4** Luly **5** Salek **6** Daddah **8** Haidalla
ruler: **6** France **9** Almoravid **14** Kingdom of Ghana
language: **4** Fula **5** Wolof **6** Arabic, French **7** Phoolor, Tukulor **8** Fulfulde, Mandingo **9** Sarakolle, Hassaniya
religion: **5** Islam
place:
mosque: **5** Grand
feature:
beehive hut: **4** ruga
priest-teacher: **8** marabout
waterskin: **6** guerba
food:
dish: **7** meshuri
tea: **5** attay

Maximes
author: **23** Francois La Rochefoucauld

Maxims of the Law
author: **12** Francis Bacon

maximum **3** top **4** most **6** utmost **7** highest, largest, maximal, optimum, supreme **8** foremost, greatest **9** paramount **11** unsurpassed

May
characteristic: **7** Maypole **13** queen of the May
flower: **8** hawthorn **15** lily of the valley
French: **3** Mai
gem: **7** emerald
German: **3** Mai
holiday: **6** May Day (1) **10** Mother's Day (2nd Sunday) **11** Memorial Day (last Monday) **14** Armed Forces Day (3rd Saturday)
Italian: **6** Maggio
number of days: **9** thirty-one
origin of name: **4** Maia
Roman goddess of: **6** spring
place in year:
Gregorian: **5** fifth
Roman: **5** third
saying: **27** April showers bring May flowers
Spanish: **4** Mayo
Zodiac sign: **6** Gemini, Taurus

May, Elaine
real name: **12** Elaine Berlin
partner: **11** Mike Nichols
born: **14** Philadelphia PA
roles: **8** A New Leaf **15** California Suite
director of: **16** The Heartbreak Kid
writer/director of: **8** A New Leaf

Maya
city: **4** Coba **5** Tulum, Uxmal **6** Akumal, Cuello, Izamal **8** Calakmul, Palenque **11** Chichen Itza
conqueror: **8** Alvarado
day: **5** uayeb
language family: **5** Mayan **10** Maya-Quiche
location: **5** Tikal **6** Belize, Mexico **7** Chiapas, Mayapan, Tabasco, Yucatan **8** Honduras **9** Guatemala **11** Chichen Itza **14** Central America
month: **5** uinal **6** uninal
noted for: **9** astronomy **12** architecture **19** hieroglyphic writing
rain god: **4** Chac **5** Chaac **7** Chac Mol **8** Chac Mool
ruins: **9** Yaxchilan **20** Temple of Inscriptions
underworld: **7** Xibalba
year: **4** haab

maybe **6** mayhap **7** perhaps **8** feasibly, possibly **9** perchance **10** God willing, imaginably **11** conceivably **12** peradventure

Maybe
author: **14** Lillian Hellman

Mayberry RFD
character: **5** Alice **7** Aunt Bee **8** Sam Jones **9** Mike Jones **10** Goober Pyle **11** Emmett Clark **13** Howard Sprague, Millie Swanson
cast: **8** Ken Berry **10** Jack Dodson **11** Buddy Foster, Paul Hartman **13** Alice Ghostley, Arlene Golonka, Frances Bavier, George Lindsey

mayfly
varieties: **5** small **6** stream **9** burrowing

mayhem **4** maim **6** felony **7** battery, cripple **8** mutilate, violence **9** crippling, dismember **10** mutilation **13** disfigurement

may he rest in peace
Latin: **16** requiescat in pace

may it do good
Latin: **6** prosit

Maylie, Mrs and Rose
characters in: **11** Oliver Twist
author: **7** Dickens

Mayo, Virginia
real name: **13** Virginia Jones
husband: **12** Michael O'Shea
born: **9** St Louis MO
roles: **17** The West Point Story **22** The Best Years of Our Lives **26** The Secret Life of Walter Mitty

Mayor of Casterbridge, The
author: **11** Thomas Hardy
character: **13** Donald Farfrae, Richard Newson **14** Lucetta Le Sueur **15** Michael Henchard **19** Elizabeth Jane Newson, Susan Henchard-Newson

Mays, Willie
nickname: **9** Say Hey Kid
sport: **8** baseball
position: **11** center field
team: **11** New York Mets **13** New York Giants **18** San Francisco Giants

may she live forever
Latin: **12** esto perpetua
motto of: **5** Idaho

may she rest in peace
Latin: **16** requiescat in pace

maze **5** snarl **6** jungle, tangle **7** complex, meander, network **9** labyrinth **11** convolution

mazel tov **8** good luck

Mbabane
capital of: **9** Swaziland

McCambridge, Mercedes
real name: **32** Carlotta Mercedes Agnes McCambridge
born: **8** Joliet IL
roles: **5** Giant **8** Cimarron **11** Touch of Evil **14** All the King's Men **15** A Farewell to Arms **18** Suddenly Last Summer

McCarey, Leo
director of: **8** Duck Soup **10** Going My Way (Oscar) **13** The Awful Truth (Oscar) **15** Ruggles of Red Gap **17** The Bells of St Mary's

McCarthy, Mary
author of: **8** The Group

McCay, Winsor
creator/artist of: **23** Little Nemo in Slumberland

McClellan, George B
nickname: **25** Little Mac the Young Napoleon
served in: **8** Civil War **10** Mexican War
side: **5** Union
commander of: **16** Army of the Potomac
battle: **8** Antietam **18** Peninsular campaign
governor of: **9** New Jersey

McCloud
character: **10** Sam McCloud **13** Chris Coughlin, (Sgt) Joe Broadhurst **14** Peter B Clifford
cast: **8** JD Cannon **11** Terry Carter **12** Dennis Weaver, Diana Muldaur

McClure, Darrell
creator/artist of: **17** Little Annie Rooney

McCrea, Joel
wife: **10** Frances Dee
born: **12** Los Angeles CA
roles: **11** Buffalo Bill **14** Palm Beach Story **16** Sullivan's Travels, The Great Man's Lady **17** Reaching for the Sun, The More the Merrier **20** Foreign Correspondent

McCreary, Fainy (Mac)
character in: **3** USA
author: **9** Dos Passos

McCullers, Carson
author of: **17** The Mortgaged Heart **18** Member of the Wedding **21** The Ballad of the Sad Cafe **23** Reflections

in a Golden Eye, The Heart Is a Lonely Hunter

McCullough, Colleen
author of: 13 The Thornbirds **19** An Indecent Obsession

McCutcheon, George Barr
author of: 9 Graustark

McEvoy, JP
creator/artist of: 10 Dixie Dugan

McFee, William
author of: 15 Casuals of the Sea

McGillicuddy, Cornelius Alexander
real name of: 10 Connie Mack

McGinley, Phyllis
author of: 12 Three Decades **15** A Pocketful of Wry **24** The Horse Who Lived Upstairs

McHale's Navy
character: 7 Christy **9** Willy Moss **11** Fuji Kobiaji, Happy Haines **12** Harrison (Tinker) Bell, Lester Gruber **13** Virgil Farrell, (Ensign) Charles Parker, (Lt Cdr) Quinton McHale **14** (Lt) Elroy Carpenter **18** (Capt) Wallace B Binghamton
cast: 8 Joe Flynn **9** Tim Conway **10** Billy Sands, Gary Vinson, John Wright, Yoshio Yoda **11** Bob Hastings, Edson Stroll **12** Gavin MacLeod **14** Carl Ballantine, Ernest Borgnine

McKenna, Siobhan
born: 7 Belfast, Ireland
roles: 11 King of Kings **13** Doctor Zhivago **14** Of Human Bondage **24** Playboy of the Western World

McKim, Charles M
architect of: 27 Lutheran Church of the Redeemer (Houston)

McKim, Mead, and White
partners: 13 Stanford White **18** Charles Follen McKim **21** William Rutherford Mead
architects of: 11 Century Club **14** University Club, Washington Arch **17** Vanderbilt Mansion **18** Columbia University (NYC) **19** Boston Public Library, Pennsylvania Station (NYC), (first) Madison Square Garden (NYC) **21** New York Herald Building, Pierpont Morgan Library (NYC) **31** Madison Square Presbyterian Church
style: 7 Shingle **18** Italian Renaissance

McKinley, William
nickname: 13 Major McKinley
presidential rank: 11 twenty-fifth
party: 10 Republican
state represented: 2 OH
defeated: 4 (Eugene Victor) Debs **5** (Seth Hockett) Ellis, (William Jennings) Bryan **6** (John McCauley) Palmer, (Wharton) Barker **7** (Charles Eugene) Bentley, (John Granville) Woolley, (Jonah Fitz Randolph) Leonard **8** (Charles Horatio) Matchett, (Joseph Francis) Malloney, (Joshua) Levering
vice president: 6 (Garret Augustus) Hobart **9** (Theodore) Roosevelt
cabinet:
***state:* 3** (John Milton) Hay, (William Rufus) Day **7** (John) Sherman
***treasury:* 4** (Lyman Judson) Gage
***war:* 4** (Elihu) Root **5** (Russell Alexander) Alger
***attorney general:* 4** (Philander Chase) Knox **6** (John William) Griggs **7** (Joseph) McKenna
***navy:* 4** (John Davis) Long
***postmaster general:* 4** (James Albert) Gary **5** (Charles Emory) Smith
***interior:* 5** (Cornelius Newton) Bliss **9** (Ethan Allen) Hitchcock
***agriculture:* 6** (James) Wilson
born: 7 Niles OH
died: 9 Buffalo NY
***died by:* 13** assassination
buried: 8 Canton OH
education:
***college:* 10** Allegheny
***law school:* 6** Albany
religion: 9 Methodist
author: 37 The Tariff in the Days of Henry Clay and Since
political career: 24 US House of Representatives
***governor of:* 4** Ohio
civilian career: 6 lawyer
military service: 7 captain **8** Civil War **11** brevet major
notable events of lifetime/term:
***Act:* 13** Dingley Tariff
***Peace Conference:* 5** Hague
***Treaty of:* 5** Paris
***war with:* 5** Spain
father: 7 William
mother: 5 Nancy (Campbell Allison)
siblings: 4 Anna, Mary **5** Abner, Helen, James **10** Abbie Celia **12** David Allison **14** Sarah Elizabeth
wife: 3 Ida (Saxton)
children: 3 Ida **9** Katherine

McManus, George
creator/artist of: 12 The Newlyweds **16** Bringing Up Father

McMath, Virginia Katherine
real name of: 12 Ginger Rogers

McMeekan, Wayne
real name of: 10 David Wayne

McMillan, Edwin Mattison
field: 7 physics **9** chemistry
developed: 16 synchrocyclotron
awarded: 10 Nobel Prize

McMillan and Wife
character: 7 Mildred **13** Sally McMillan **14** (Sgt) Charles Enright **15** (Commissioner) Stewart McMillan
cast: 10 John Schuck, Rock Hudson **11** Nancy Walker **15** Susan Saint James

McMurtry, Larry
author of: 10 Texasville **12** Lonesome Dove **14** Horseman Pass By **18** The Last Picture Show

McPhee, John
author of: 16 In Suspect Terrain **20** Coming into the

Country **23** The Curve of Binding Energy **26** Encounters with the Archdruid

McQueen, Steve
real name: 21 Terrence Steven McQueen
wife: 10 Ali MacGraw
born: 8 Slater MO **14** Indianapolis IN
roles: 7 Bullitt, The Blob **8** Papillon **14** The Great Escape, The Sand Pebbles **16** The Cincinnati Kid **17** Thomas Crown Affair, Wanted Dead or Alive **19** The Magnificent Seven

McTeague
author: 11 Frank Norris

mea culpa 7 my fault **14** through my fault

Mead, Margaret
author of: 14 My Earlier Years **16** Blackberry Winter **18** Coming of Age in Samoa **20** Growing Up in New Guinea **42** Sex and Temperament in Three Primitive Societies
husband: 14 Gregory Bateson

Meade, Dr and Mrs
characters in: 15 Gone With the Wind
author: 8 Mitchell

Meade, George Gordon
served in: 8 Civil War **10** Mexican War
side: 5 Union
battle: 7 Bull Run **8** Antietam **10** Gettysburg **13** South Mountain **14** Fredericksburg **16** Chancellorsville **18** Peninsular campaign
commander of: 16 Army of the Potomac

meadow 3 lea **4** mead, park **5** field, green **6** forage **7** herbage, pasture, savanna **9** grassland, pasturage

meager 4 bare, lean, slim, thin **5** scant, short, spare, token **6** little, paltry, scanty, scarce, skimpy, slight, sparse **7** scrimpy, slender, stinted, wanting **9** deficient **10** inadequate **12** insufficient **13** insubstantial

meagerness 8 sparsity **9** smallness **10** inadequacy, measliness, scantiness, skimpiness, sparseness **13** insufficiency **14** insignificance

Meagles
character in: 12 Little Dorrit
author: 7 Dickens

meal 4 bran, chow, diet, eats, fare, food, grub, menu **5** feast, flour, grits **6** farina, groats, repast, spread **7** banquet, cooking, cuisine, oatmeal **8** cornmeal, victuals **10** bill of fare **11** nourishment, refreshment

mealymouthed 6 unsure **7** devious **8** hesitant **9** deceptive, insincere

mean *see box*

meander 4 loop, rove, wind **5** snake, stray, twist **6** circle, ramble, spiral, wander, zigzag **8** undulate **9** convolute, corkscrew

meandering 7 devious, sinuous, turning, winding **8** indirect, rambling, tortuous, twisting **9** wandering **10** circuitous, roundabout, serpentine

meaning 3 aim, end **4** gist, goal, hint, meat, pith, plan, view **5** drift, force, point, sense, value, worth **6** burden, design, intent, object, scheme, thrust, upshot **7** content, essence, pointer, purport, purpose **9** intention, substance **10** denotation, indication, intimation, suggestion **11** implication **12** significance **15** sum and substance

meaningful 4 deep **5** meaty, pithy **6** useful **7** pointed, serious **8** eloquent, explicit, pregnant **9** designing, important **10** expressive, gratifying, portentous, purposeful, suggestive, worthwhile **11** significant, substantial **13** consequential

meaningless 5 trite **6** absurd, paltry, stupid **7** aimless, fatuous, foolish, idiotic, shallow, trivial, useless **8** baffling, piddling, puzzling **9** enigmatic, facetious, frivolous, illegible, senseless, valueless, worthless **10** incoherent, mystifying, perplexing **11** bewildering, inscrutable, nonsensical, purposeless, unessential, unimportant **12** impenetrable, inexplicable, inexpressive, preposterous **13** insignificant, unsubstantial **14** undecipherable

Mean Joe
nickname of: 9 Joe Greene

means 3 way **4** jack, mode **5** bread, dough, funds, money **6** avenue, course, income, method, resort, riches, wealth **7** capital, dollars, measure, process, revenue **8** property **9** affluence, long green, resources, substance **11** alternative, wherewithal

mean-spirited 3 low **4** base, poor, vile **5** cheap, nasty, petty, small, snide, sorry, tight, venal **6** abject, measly, paltry, scurvy, shabby, sordid, stingy **7** ignoble, miserly, selfish, vicious **8** tightwad, wretched **9** miserable, penurious **10** ungenerous **12** parsimonious

Mean Streets
director: 14 Martin Scorsese
cast: 11 Amy Robinson, David Proval **12** Harvey Keitel, Robert DeNiro

meantime 7 interim **8** interval **9** meanwhile

meanwhile 8 meantime **12** concurrently, in the interim **13** at the same time **14** simultaneously

measurable 10 assessable, computable, mensurable, reckonable **11** appraisable **12** determinable

---

mean 3 low, par, say **4** base, evil, norm, plan, poor, rude, rule, vile, want, wish **5** aim at, cheap, close, cruel, imply, nasty, petty, small, tight, venal **6** denote, flimsy, greedy, hint at, intend, malign, medium, menial, normal, paltry, sleazy, sordid, stingy, tell off, trashy, unfair **7** average, balance, betoken, dream of, drive at, express, hoggish, inhuman, miserly, point to, propose, purpose, regular, resolve, selfish, signify, squalid, suggest, think of, trivial, vicious **8** aspire to, gimcrack, grasping, indicate, inferior, inhumane, intimate, low-grade, picayune, piddling, pitiless, rubbishy, say truly, shameful, standard, stand for, trifling, uncaring, wretched **9** illiberal, low-paying, malicious, mercenary, merciless, miserable, niggardly, penurious, symbolize, unfeeling **10** avaricious, compromise, despicable, have in mind, have in view, jerry-built, low-ranking, malevolent, pinchpenny, second-rate, ungenerous, villainous **11** closefisted, commonplace, disgraceful, happy medium, hardhearted, self-seeking, small-minded, tightfisted, unimportant **12** contemptible, disagreeable, dishonorable **13** insignificant, unsympathetic **15** inconsequential

measure **3** act, law **4** bill, plan, rule, size, step, time **5** bound, clock, gauge, judge, limit, means, plumb, quota, range, scale, scope, share, sound, value **6** amount, assess, course, degree, design, extent, method, resort, scheme, survey **7** portion, project **8** appraise, evaluate, proposal, quantity **9** allotment, allowance, enactment, procedure, restraint, yardstick **10** limitation, moderation, proceeding, temperance

measure, unit of *see box, p. 616*

measured **5** equal, exact **6** steady **7** precise, regular, studied, uniform **8** verified **10** calculated, deliberate **11** cold-blooded, intentional, well-planned **12** premeditated **13** predetermined

Measure for Measure
author: **18** William Shakespeare
character: **5** Lucio **6** Angelo, Juliet **7** Claudio, Escalus, Mariana **8** Isabella **9** Vincentio

measureless **7** endless **8** infinite **9** boundless, unlimited **12** immeasurable

measurement *see box, p. 618*

measure out **6** ration **7** dole out, mete out **9** apportion

meat **3** nut **4** core, fare, food, gist, grub **5** heart, point **6** kernel **7** edibles, essence, nucleus **8** victuals **9** provender, substance **10** provisions, sustenance **11** comestibles, nourishment

Mechaneus
epithet of: **4** Zeus
means: **9** contriver

mechanic **6** joiner **7** artisan **9** automatic, craftsman, machinist **11** uninspired **12** grease monkey

mechanical **4** cold **7** routine **9** automatic, unfeeling **10** impersonal, self-acting, unthinking **11** instinctive, involuntary, machinelike, perfunctory, unconscious **13** machine-driven

mechanism **4** tool **5** motor, works **7** machine, utensil **9** apparatus, appliance, implement, machinery **10** instrument **11** contrivance

Meda
husband: **9** Idomeneus
lover: **6** Leucus

medal **5** award, honor, prize **6** laurel, reward, ribbon, trophy **8** citation **9** medallion **10** decoration

Medawar, Peter Brian
field: **7** biology
nationality: **7** British
discovered: **23** acquired immune tolerance
awarded: **10** Nobel Prize

meddle **5** mix in **6** butt in, horn in, kibitz **7** intrude, pry into **9** interfere, interlope, intervene **10** tamper with

meddler **3** pry **5** snoop **7** Paul Pry **8** busybody **10** interferer, Nosy Parker

meddlesome **4** nosy **5** pushy **6** prying, snoopy **7** pushing **8** meddling, snooping **9** intrusive, obtrusive, officious **11** impertinent, interfering **12** presumptuous

Medea
author: **9** Euripides
character: **5** Creon, Jason **6** Aegeus, Glauce

Medea
form: **9** sorceress
father: **6** Aeetes
mother: **5** Idyia
aunt: **5** Circe
brother: **8** Apsyrtus
sister: **9** Chalciope
lover: **5** Jason
son: **6** Medeus, Pheres **8** Mermerus, Tisander **9** Alcimenes, Thessalus
killed: **7** her sons
escaped to: **6** Athens

Medeus
father: **6** Aegeus
mother: **5** Medea

media **5** press, radio **9** magazines **10** billboards, journalism, newspapers, television **11** journalists
singular: **6** medium

medial **4** mean **6** median **7** average

median **3** mid, par **4** mean, norm **5** mesne **6** center, medial, medium, middle **7** average, central, halfway **8** middling, midpoint, moderate **12** intermediate

mediate **6** pacify, step in, umpire **7** referee **8** moderate **9** arbitrate, intercede, interpose, intervene, negotiate, reconcile **10** conciliate, propitiate

mediation **6** parley **10** adjustment, compromise, discussion **11** arbitration, give-and-take, negotiation, peacemaking **12** conciliation, intercession, intervention, pacification **14** reconciliation

mediator **6** umpire **7** referee **9** go-between, moderator **10** arbitrator, negotiator, peacemaker, reconciler **12** intermediary

medical **7** healing **8** curative, remedial, salutary, sanative **9** medicinal **10** medicative **11** restorative, therapeutic

medical abbreviation *see box, p. 618*

Medical Center
character: **9** (Dr) Joe Gannon **11** Nurse Wilcox, (Dr) Paul Lochner **13** Nurse Chambers **14** Nurse Courtland, (Dr) Jeanne Bartlett
cast: **9** James Daly **11** Chad Everett, Chris Hutson **12** Audrey Totter, Jayne Meadows **14** Corinne Camacho

medical practitioner **6** doctor, medico **9** physician

medication **4** balm **5** tonic **6** elixir, remedy **7** nostrum, panacea **8** medicine **10** medicament, palliative **11** restorative

Medici, Giovanni de' **8** Pope Leo X **15** Pope Leo the Tenth

Medici, Giulio **14** Pope Clement VII **21** Pope Clement the Seventh

medicine **4** balm, drug, pill **5** salve, tonic **6** remedy **7** nostrum **10** healing art, medication **11** restorative **12** therapeutics **13** materia medica
god of: **9** Asclepius **11** Aesculapius

medieval **8** Dark Ages **10** antiquated, Middle-Ages **12** old-fashioned **14** pre-Renaissance

mediocre **4** so-so **5** petty **6** common, meager, medium, normal, paltry, slight **7** average **8** inferior, ordinary, passable, trifling **9** tolerable **10** negligible, pedestrian, second-rate **11** commonplace, indifferent, unimportant **12** run-of-the-mill **13** inappreciable, insignificant **14** fair-to-middling, inconsiderable **15** inconsequential, undistinguished

mediocrity **8** poorness **9** pettiness **10** low-quality, meagerness, paltriness, triviality **11** inferiority **12** indifference, ordinariness, unimportance **14** insignificance **15** commonplaceness

meditate **4** muse, plan **5** aim at, study, think **6** devise, ponder **7** concoct, dream of, propose, reflect **8** cogitate,

measure, unit of

of Afghanistan: 3 paw, sir **5** jerib, karoh **6** khurds **7** kharwar
of Algeria: 3 pik **5** rebis, tarri **6** termin
of Argentina: 4 sino **5** legua **6** cuadra, lastre **7** manzana
of Australia: 4 arna, naut, saum
of Austria: 4 fass, fuss, joch, mass, muth, yoke **5** halbe, linie, meile, metze, pfiff, punkt **6** achtel, becher, leipoa, seidel **7** klafter, viertel **8** dreiling **12** futtermassel
of Belgium: 3 vat **4** aune, pied **5** carat **6** perche **8** boisseau
of Bolivia: 6 league **7** celemin
of Borneo: 7 gantang
of Brazil: 2 pe **4** moio, sack, vara **5** braca, legoa, milha, tonel **6** canada, cuarto, quarto, tarefa **7** garrafa **8** alqueire
of Bulgaria: 3 oka, oke **5** krine, lekhe, likhe
of Burma: 2 ly **3** dha, gon, mau, sao, tao, tat **4** byee, phan, seit, taun, that **5** shita, thuoc **6** lamany, palgat **7** chaivai **8** okthabah
of Canada: 3 ton **5** minot, perch, point **6** arpent **7** chainon
of the Canary Islands: 8 fanegada
of Chile: 4 vara **5** legua, linea **6** cuadra **7** fanega
of China: 3 cho, fan, fen, pau, tou, tun, yan, yin **4** chek, chih, fang, kish, papa, quei, shih, teke, tsan, tsun **5** catty, chang, ching, sheng, shing **6** chupak, gungli, kungho, kungmu, tching **7** kungfen, kungyin **8** kungchih, kungshih **9** kungching
of Colombia: 4 vara **7** azumbre, celemin
of Costa Rica: 4 vara **5** cafiz, cahiz **6** fanega, tercia **7** cajuela, cantaro, manzana **10** caballeria
of Cuba: 4 vara **5** bocoy, cocoy, tarea **6** cordel, fanega **10** caballeria
of Czechoslovakia: 3 lan **4** mira **5** korec, liket, stopa **6** merice, strych
of Denmark: 3 ell, fod, mil, pot **4** alen **5** album, anker, kande, linje, paegl **7** landmil, oltonde, ortonde, skieppe, viertel **8** fjerding **9** ottingkar **10** korntonde
of the Dominican Republic: 3 ona **5** tarea **6** fanega
of Ecuador: 5 libra **6** cuadra, fanega
of Egypt: 3 apt, dra, hen, rob **4** arab, dira, draa, khet, nief, ocha, roub, theb, wudu **5** abdat, ardab, cubit, farde, fedan, keleh, kerat, kilah, sahme **6** artaba, aurure, baladi, kantar, keddah, robhah, schene **7** choryos, daribah, malouah, roubouh, toumnah **8** kassabah, kharouba **10** diramimari, diribaladi
of El Salvador: 4 vara **5** cafiz, cahiz **6** fanega **7** batella, botella, cantara, manzana
of England: 3 cut, ell, lea, pin, rod, ton, tun, vat **4** acre, bind, butt, comb, coom, cran, foot, gill, goad, hand, hank, heer, hide, inch, last, line, mile, nail, pace, palm, peck, pint, pipe, pole, pool, rood, rope, sack, seam, span, trug, typp, wist, yard, yoke **5** bodge, chain, cubit, digit, float, floor, fluid, hutch, jugum, minim, ounce, perch, point, prime, quart, skein, stack, truss **6** barrel, bovate, bushel, cranne, fathom, firkin, gallon, hobbet, hobbit, league, manent, oxgang, pottle, runlet, square, strike, sulung, thread, tierce **7** auchlet, furlong, kenning, quarter, rundlet, seamile, spindle, tertian, virgate **8** carucate, chaldron, hogshead, landyard, puncheon, quadrant, standard
of Estonia: 3 tun **4** elle, liin, sund, toll, toop **5** verst **6** sagene, versta **7** kulimet **8** tonnland
of Ethiopia: 3 tat **4** cubi, kuba **5** derah, messe **6** cabaho, sinjer, sinzer, tanica **7** entelam, farsakh, farsang, ghebeta
of Finland: 5 kannu, verst **6** fathom, kannor **8** ottinger, skalpund, tunnland
of France: 3 pot, sac **4** aune, mine, pied, velt **5** arpen, carat, ligne, minot, pinte, point, pouce, velte **6** arpent, hemine, league, quarte, setier
of Greece: 3 pik **4** bema, piki, pous **5** baril, chous, cubit, diote, doron, maris, pekhe, podos, pygon, xylon **6** acaena, bacile, barile, cotula, dichas, gramme, hemina, koilon, lichas, milion, orgyia, palame, pechys, schene, xestes **7** bacvhel, chenica, choenix, cyathos, diaulos, metreta, stadium, stremma **8** condylos, daktylos, dekapode, dolichos, medimnos, medimnys, metretes, palaiste, plethron, plethrum, stathmos **9** hemiekton, oxybaphon
of Guatemala: 4 vara **6** cuarta, tercia **7** cajuela, manzana **10** caballeria
of Guinea: 7 jacktan
of Honduras: 4 vara **5** milla **6** mecate **7** cajuela
of Hungary: 3 ako **4** hold, yoke **5** itcze, marok, metze **7** huvelyk
of Iceland: 3 set **4** alin **5** almud **6** almenn, ferfet, pottur **7** fathmur, fermila, oltunna
of India: 3 ady, gaz, gez, jow, lan **4** byee, coss, depa, doph, hath, koss, kunk, raik, rati, seit, taun, tola **5** bigha, covid, crosa, danda, depoh, drona, erosa, garce, hasta, krosa, parah, ratti, salay, yojan **6** adhaka, amunam, covido, cudava, cumbha, geerah, moolum, mushti, ouroub, palgat, parran, prasha, ropani, tipree, unglee, yojana **7** dhanush, gavyuti, khahoon, niranga, prastha **8** okthabah
of Indonesia: 5 depah, depoh
of Iran: 3 gaz, zar, zer **4** cane **5** gareh, kafiz, makuk, qasab **6** charac, chebel, ghalva **7** capicha, chenica, farsakh, mansion, mishara **8** parasang, piamaneh, stathmos
of Ireland: 4 mile **6** bandle **8** crannock
of Israel: 3 cab, car, hin, kab, kor **4** bath, ezba, omer, reed **5** cubit, donum, dunam, ephah, ganeh, homer, kaneh

of Italy: **3** pie **4** orna **5** palma, palmo, punto, salma, stero **6** barile, miglie, moggio, rubbio, tomolo **7** braccio, secchio **8** giornata, quadrato
of Japan: **2** go **3** boo, cho, djo, fun, inc, ken, kin, kon, rin, shi, sho, sun, tan **4** hiro, isse, kati, koku, niyo, shoo **5** carat, catty, issho, ittan, momme, picul, shaku **6** kwamme **8** hiyakkin **9** hiyak-hiro **11** komma-ichida, kujira-shaku
of Java: **3** kan **4** paal, rand **5** palen
of Kenya: **4** wari
of Laos: **3** bak
of Latvia: **3** let **4** stof **5** stoff, verst **6** arshin, kulmet **7** verchoc, verchok **8** krouchka, pourvete **9** deciatine, lofstelle, pourvette **10** tonnseteel
of Liberia: **4** kuba
of Libya: **3** dra, pik, saa **4** kele **5** bozze, donum, jabia, teman, uckia **6** barile, gorrah, misura **7** mattaro, termino **8** kharouba
of Luxembourg: **5** fuder
of Madagascar: **7** gantang
of Malaysia: **3** pau, tun **4** para, pipe, tael, wang **5** parah **6** chupak, parrah **7** gantang
of Malta: **4** rotl **5** artal, canna, parto, ratel, salma **6** kantar **7** caffiso
of Mexico: **3** bag, pie **4** alma, onza, vara **5** almud, baril, carga, jarra, labor, legua, libra, linea, marco, sitio **6** adarme, almude, arroba, carega, fanega, ochaua, terceo **7** pulgada, quintal **9** cuarteron, cuartillo **10** caballeria
of Morocco: **4** kala, muhd, rotl, saah, sahh, uebà **5** artal, cadee, gerbe, ratel **6** covado, dirhem, fanega, izenbi, kintar, tangin, tomini **8** quintral
of the Netherlands: **2** el **3** aam, ahm, ell, kan, vat **4** duim, mijl, rood, rope **5** anker, roede, wisse **6** bunder, legger, maatje, mutsje, streep **7** schepel **8** mimgelen, steekkan
of Nicaragua: **4** vara **5** cahiz **6** suerte **7** cajuela, manzana **10** cabelleria
of Norway: **3** fot, mal **4** alen **5** kande **6** fathom **7** skieppe **9** korntonde
of Panama: **7** celemin
of Paraguay: **3** pie **4** lino, lira, lire, vara **5** legua **6** cuadra, fanega
of Peru: **4** topo **5** galon **7** celemin **8** fanegada
of the Philippines: **4** loan **5** braza, catty, cavan, chupa, fardo, ganta, picul, punto **6** apatan, balita, lachsa, quinon **7** quilate **8** chinanta
of Poland: **3** cal **4** mila, pret **5** morga, sazen, vloka, wloka **6** cwierc, cwierk, kwarta, lokiec **7** garniec **9** kwarterka
of Portugal: **2** pe **4** bota, moio, vara **5** almud, fanga, geira, linha, milha **6** almude, covado **7** alquier, ferrado, selamin **8** alqueire
of Puerto Rico: **6** cuerda **10** cabelleria
of Rumania: **7** faltche
of Russia: **3** fut, lof **4** duim, fass, loof, pood, quar, stof **5** duime, foute, korec, korek, ligne, osmin, pajak, stoff, stoof, vedro, verst **6** charka, liniya, osmina, paletz, sagene, stekar, tchast, tsarki, versta, verste **7** archine, arsheen, botchka, chkalik, garnetz, verchoc, verchok **8** boutylka, chetvert, krouchka, kroushka **9** chetverik **10** dessiatine **11** polugarnetz
of Scotland: **3** cop **4** boll, cran, fall, mile, peck, pint, rood, rope, span **5** crane, lippy **6** audlet, davach, firlot, lippie, noggin **7** chalder, choppin **8** mutchkin, stimpart, stimpert **9** particate, shaftment, shathmont
of Sicily: **5** salma **7** caffiso
of Sierra Leone: **4** load **6** kettle
of Somalia: **3** top **4** caba **5** chela, darat, tabla **6** cubito **8** parsalah
of South Africa: **4** vara
of Spain: **3** pie **4** codo, dedo, paso, vara **5** braza, cahiz, carga, legua, medio, palmo, sesma **6** cordel, cuarta, fanega, racion, yugada **7** azumbre, celemin, estadel, pulgada **8** fanegada
of Sri Lanka: **4** para, seer **5** parah **6** amunam, parrah
of Sudan: **2** ud
of Suriname: **7** ketting
of Sweden: **3** aln, fot, ref, tum **4** alar, amar, famn, kapp, last, stop **5** carat, foder, kanna, linje, nymil, spann **6** fathom, jumfru **7** oxhuvud, tunland **8** fjarding, koltunna, tunnland
of Switzerland: **3** imi, pot **4** aune, fuss, muid, pied, zoll **5** lieue, linie, maass, pouce, staab, toise **6** perche, strich **7** klafter, viertel **9** quarteron **10** holzlafter **11** holzklafter
of Syria: **5** makuk **6** garava
of Thailand: **2** wa **3** can, ken, niv, rai, sat, sok, wah **4** cohi, keup, niou, tang **5** kwien, leeng, sesti, vouah **6** kabiet, kanahn **7** chaimeu **8** changawn **9** anukabiet
of Tunisia: **3** saa **4** saah **5** cafiz **6** mettar **8** milerole
of Turkey: **3** dra, oka, pik **4** draa, khat, kile, zira **5** berri, kileh, zirai **6** arshin, chinik, fortin, halebi **7** nocktat
of Uruguay: **4** vara **6** cuadra, suerte
of Venezuela: **5** galon, milla **6** fanega **7** estadel
of Vietnam: **4** gang, phan, thon
of Wales: **5** cover **7** cantred, crannoc, listred
of Yugoslavia: **3** oka, rif **4** akov, ralo **5** donum, khvat, lanaz, plaze, stopa **6** motyka, ralico **9** danoranja

measurement **4** area, mass, size **5** depth, width **6** extent, height, length, volume, weight **7** breadth, content, gauging **8** capacity, plumbing, sounding **9** amplitude, appraisal, dimension, magnitude, measuring, reckoning, surveying **10** assessment, estimation, evaluation **11** mensuration
Biblical: **4** omer **5** cubit, ephah **6** shekel
champagne: **6** magnum **8** jeroboam, rehoboam **9** balthazar **10** methuselah, salmanazar **14** Nebuchadnezzar
cloth: **4** bolt
cotton: **4** bale
electricity: **3** ohm **4** volt, watt **5** joule **6** ampere **10** horsepower
energy: **3** BTU **5** joule **7** calorie **11** kilocalorie **18** British thermal unit
firewood: **4** cord
force: **4** dyne **6** newton **7** poundal
gold/jewelry: **5** carat, karat, point
Greek: **4** mina **5** cubit **6** obolos, talent **7** drachma, stadion
gun: **5** gauge **7** caliber
light: **7** candela **11** candlepower
liquor/spirits: **4** pint, pony, shot **5** fifth, quart **6** jigger, magnum
metric system: **5** liter, meter **9** deciliter, decimeter, dekaliter, dekameter, kiloliter, kilometer, nanometer **10** centiliter, centimeter, cubic meter, hectoliter, hectometer, milliliter, millimeter **11** square meter **14** cubic dekameter **15** cubic centimeter, cubic millimeter, square decimeter, square dekameter, square kilometer **16** square centimeter, square hectometer, square millimeter
metric weight: **3** ton **4** gram **5** tonne **7** quintal **8** dekagram, kilogram **9** centigram, hectogram, microgram, milligram
paper: **4** ream **5** quire
pressure: **6** pascal **10** atmosphere
Roman: **2** as **5** cubit, libra **6** pondus **7** stadium
sound: **7** decibel
temperature: **6** degree, Kelvin **7** Celsius **10** Fahrenheit
time: **3** day **4** hour, week, year **5** month, score **6** decade, minute, second **7** century **10** millennium, nanosecond **11** microsecond, millisecond
typography: **2** em, en **4** pica **5** point
unit: **3** cup, rod **4** acre, dram, foot, gill, inch, link, mile, peck, pint, yard **5** chain, minim, ounce, quart **6** barrel, bushel, circle, degree, fathom, gallon **7** furlong, hectare **8** angstrom, hogshead, teaspoon **9** cubic foot, cubic inch, cubic yard, square rod **10** fluid ounce, right angle, square foot, square inch, square mile, square yard, tablespoon **25** international nautical mile
weight: **3** ton **4** dram **5** grain, ounce, pound **7** scruple **8** short ton **9** ounce troy, pound troy **11** pennyweight **13** hundredweight

medical abbreviation
a c: **11** before meals
ad lib: **8** as needed **9** as desired
agit: **5** shake
aq: **5** water
b i d: **9** twice a day
cap: **4** take **7** capsule
coch: **8** spoonful
dil: **6** dilute **8** dissolve
fldxt: **12** fluid extract
ft: **4** make
ft mist: **12** make a mixture
ft pulv: **11** make a powder
gr: **5** grain
gt: **4** drop
gtt: **5** drops
h s: **9** at bedtime
in d: **5** daily
lot: **6** lotion
mod praesc: **21** in the manner prescribed
O: **4** pint
O D: **8** right eye
O S: **7** left eye
O U: **9** in each eye
ol: **3** oil
p c: **9** after food **10** after meals
p o: **7** by mouth
p r n: **25** as circumstances may require
pil: **3** pill
pulv: **6** powder
q i d: **14** four times daily
rep: **6** repeat
s o s: **11** if necessary
ss: **7** one half
tab: **6** tablet
t i d: **15** three times daily
ut dict: **10** as directed

consider, contrive, mull over, ruminate **9** dwell upon **10** deliberate **11** contemplate

meditation **4** yoga **5** study **6** musing, poring **7** mulling, reverie, thought **8** brooding **9** discourse, pondering **10** cogitation, reflection, rumination **12** deliberation **13** consideration, contemplation

Mediterranean
called by ancient Romans: **11** mare nostrum
coast: **7** Riviera
gulf: **5** Lions, Sidra, Tunis **7** Antalya, Catania, Taranto **8** Hammamet **9** Iskenderon
island: **4** Elba **5** Capri, Corfu, Crete, Ibiza, Malta **6** Cyprus, Euboea, Lesbos, Rhodes, Sicily **7** Corsica, Majorca, Minorca **8** Balearic, Sardinia
resort: **4** Nice **5** Capri **6** Cannes **7** Riviera **9** Cote d'Azur **10** Costa Brava
river into: **2** Po **4** Ebro, Nile **5** Rhone
sea: **5** Black **6** Aegean, Ionian **8** Adriatric, Ligurian **10** Tyrrhenian
strait: **8** Bosporus **9** Bosphorus, Gibraltar **11** Dardanelles
wind: **7** mistral, sirocco

medium **3** way **4** form, mean, mode, tool **5** means, organ **6** agency, avenue, common, milieu, normal **7** average, balance, channel, diviner, psychic, setting, vehicle **8** middling, moderate, ordinary **9** go-between, middle way, mid-course **10** atmosphere, compromise, golden mean, instrument, moderation **11** clairvoyant, environment, happy medium **12** crystal-gazer, intermediary, intermediate, middle ground, spiritualist, surroundings **13** fortuneteller **15** instrumentality

medley **4** hash, mess, olio **6** jumble, mosaic **7** farrago, melange, mixture **8** mishmash, pastiche **9** patchwork, potpourri **10** assortment, hodgepodge, miscellany **11** gallimaufry

Medon
mentioned in: **5** Iliad **7** Odyssey
father: **6** Oileus
mother: **5** Rhene
position: **6** herald
friend of: **8** Penelope
killed by: **6** Aeneas

medulla
part of: **5** brain
controls: **6** glands **7** muscles

Medusa
form: **6** Gorgon
father: **7** Phorcys
mother: **4** Ceto
sisters: **6** Graiae
loved by: **8** Poseidon
children: **7** Pegasus **8** Chrysaor
sight of her caused people to turn to: **5** stone
killed by: **7** Perseus

meek **4** mild **6** docile, gentle, humble, modest **8** lamblike, retiring, tolerant, yielding **9** compliant, spineless, tractable, weak-kneed **10** spiritless, submissive, unassuming **11** acquiescent, complaisant, deferential, unassertive, unresisting **13** long-suffering, tenderhearted, unpretentious

meekness **7** pliancy, shyness **8** docility, humility **9** passivity **10** diffidence, humbleness **11** bashfulness **13** nonresistance **14** self-effacement

meet **3** apt, fit **4** abut, face, good, heed, obey **5** cross, equal, greet, match, rally, right **6** adjoin, answer, border, follow, gather, muster, proper, seemly **7** abide by, collect, convene, execute, fitting, fulfill, observe, perform, respect, run into, satisfy, welcome **8** assemble, becoming, bump into, confront, converge, decorous, opposite, relevant, suitable **9** agreeable, allowable, befitting, congruous, discharge, encounter, intersect, permitted, pertinent **10** admissable, comply with, congregate, felicitous **11** acknowledge, appropriate, permissible **12** come together

meet eye to eye **4** face **8** confront, face up to **11** meet vis-a-vis

meet halfway **6** settle **9** make a deal **10** compromise **11** come to terms **14** strike a bargain **18** split the difference

meet head on **4** face **5** crash **6** oppose **7** collide, crack up **8** confront, face up to **9** challenge, encounter

meeting **4** date **5** group, tryst **6** caucus **7** council **8** assembly, conclave, congress **9** encounter, gathering **10** conference, convention, engagement, rendezvous **11** assignation, convocation, get-together **12** introduction, presentation **13** confrontation

Meeting at Telgte
author: **11** Gunter Grass

meeting of the minds
7 concert, concord, harmony **9** agreement **11** concordance **13** understanding

meeting place **5** mecca **10** focal point, rendezvous

Meet Me in St Louis
director: **16** Vincente Minnelli
cast: **8** Leon Ames, Tom Drake **9** Mary Astor **11** Judy Garland **12** June Lockhart, Marjorie Main **13** Lucille Bremer **14** Margaret O'Brien
song: **11** Trolley Song **14** The Boy Next Door **33** Have Yourself a Merry Little Christmas

Meet the Press
moderator: **9** Ned Brooks **10** Bill Monroe **11** Edwin Newman **14** Lawrence Spivak, Martha Rountree

meet with **4** meet **6** endure **7** undergo **8** come upon **9** encounter **10** come across, experience

Mefitis
also: **8** Mephitis
prevented: **5** winds
kind of winds: **7** harmful

Megaera
member of: **6** Furies

Megalosaurus
type: **8** dinosaur
means: **11** great lizard
found by: **15** William Buckland
period: **8** Jurassic

Megamede
husband: **12** King Thespius
number of daughters: **5** fifty

Megapenthes
father: **7** Proetus **8** Menelaus
mother: **10** Stheneboea

Megara
father: **5** Creon
husband: **8** Hercules
son: **11** Therimachus

Mehuman **6** eunuch

Meilichius
epithet of: **4** Zeus
means: **8** gracious

Mein Kampf
author: **11** Adolf Hitler
means: **7** my fight **8** my battle

Meitner, Lise
field: **7** physics
nationality: **8** Austrian
contributed to: **21** atomic bomb development
discovered: **12** protactinium **16** fission of uranium

Melaenis
epithet of: **9** Aphrodite
means: **5** black

Melampus
father: **8** Amythaon
mother: **7** Idomene
brother: **4** Bias
wife: **7** Lysippe
son: **4** Abas **7** Mantius **10** Antiphates
vocation: **4** seer **6** healer

melancholia **7** despair **10** depression, desolation, melancholy **11** despondency

melancholy **4** blue, glum **5** blues, dumps, gloom, moody **6** dismal, dreary, gloomy, mopish, morose, somber **7** despair, doleful, forlorn, joyless, unhappy **8** dejected, desolate, doldrums, dolorous, downcast, funereal, mournful **9** cheerless, dejection, depressed, heartsick, moodiness, plaintive **10** calamitous, depressing, depression, despondent, dispirited, gloominess, low spirits **11** despondency, discouraged, downhearted, forlornness, languishing, melancholia, sick at heart, unfortunate **12** disconsolate, heavyhearted **14** down in the dumps, down in the mouth **16** disconsolateness
French: **6** triste **9** tristesse

melange **3** mix **6** jumble, medley **7** mixture **8** compound, mishmash, pastiche **9** pasticcio, patchwork, potpourri **10** assemblage, assortment, hodgepodge, miscellany **11** gallimaufry

Melanion
suitor of: **8** Atalanta

Melanippe
form: **4** foal
foal born to: **6** Euippe
transformed into: **4** Arne, girl
father: **4** Ares
queen of: **7** Amazons

Melanosaurus
type: **8** dinosaur
period: **8** Triassic

Melanthius
goatherd for: **8** Odysseus

Melantho
handmaiden for: **8** Penelope

Melas
father: **7** Phrixus
mother: **10** Chalciiope
brother: **5** Argus **8** Phrontis **10** Cytissorus

Melbourne
bay: **7** Hobson's **11** Port Phillip
landmark: **20** Flemington Racecourse
river: **5** Yarra **6** Plenty **9** Mary Creek, Patterson **11** Maribyrnong **12** Diamond Creek **13** Kororoit Creek **14** Dandenong Creek, Gardiner's Creek **16** Moonee Ponds Creek
state: **8** Victoria
university: **6** Monash **7** La Trobe

Melchizedek
means: **19** king of righteousness
hometown: **5** Salem
contemporary: **7** Abraham

meld **3** mix **4** fuse, join **5** blend, merge, unite **6** jumble, mingle **7** combine **8** coalesce, intermix, scramble **9** commingle **10** amalgamate, intertwine, interweave **11** consolidate, incorporate, intermingle

Meleager
father: **4** Ares **6** Oeneus
mother: **7** Althaea
uncle: **9** Plexippus
slew: **14** Calydonian boar
loved: **8** Atalanta
killed: **15** mother's brothers
sisters: **11** Meleagrides

Meleagrides
sisters of: **8** Meleager
transformed into: **10** guinea hens
transformed by: **7** Artemis

melee **3** row **4** fray, riot **5** brawl, scrap, set-to **6** fracas, rumpus, tussle **7** scuffle **8** disorder, dogfight **9** commotion, fistfight **10** free-for-all **11** altercation, pandemonium

Melete
member of: **5** Muses
personifies: **10** meditation

Melia
form: **5** nymph
born from: **5** blood
blood of: **6** Uranus

Meliad
form: **5** nymph
nymph of: **6** flocks **10** fruit trees

Meliae
nymphs of: **5** Melic

Meliboea
form: **6** maiden

Melicertes
father: **7** Athamas
mother: **3** Ino
changed into: **8** Palaemon

Melie
form: **5** nymph
son: **6** Amycus

Melissa
sister: **8** Amaethea
nourished: **4** Zeus

mellifluous **4** soft **5** sweet **6** dulcet, mellow, smooth **7** musical **8** resonant **9** full-toned, melodious **10** euphonious, harmonious, sweet-toned **13** sweet-sounding

Mellors
character in: **20** Lady Chatterley's Lover
author: **8** Lawrence

mellow **4** rich, ripe, soft **5** drunk, sweet **6** mature, season, soften **7** matured, relaxed **8** luscious, tolerant **9** delicious **10** full-bodied **11** sympathetic **12** full-flavored **13** compassionate, understanding

mellowness **8** full body, fullness, maturity, richness, ripeness, softness **9** tolerance **10** compassion, smoothness **12** lusciousness, pleasantness

melodic **5** lyric **7** tuneful

melodious **4** rich, soft **5** clear, lyric, sweet **6** dulcet, mellow, smooth **7** melodic, musical, ringing, tuneful **8** resonant **9** full-toned **10** euphonious, sweet-toned **11** mellifluent, mellifluous

melodrama **9** theatrics **12** emotionalism **13** theatricality

melodramatic **5** corny, hammy, hokey, stagy **7** maudlin, mawkish **8** cornball, frenzied **10** flamboyant, histrionic **11** exaggerated, overwrought, sensational, sentimental, spectacular **13** overemotional

melody **3** air **4** aria, song, tune **5** ditty, theme **6** ballad, strain, timbre **7** concord, euphony **10** musicality **11** tunefulness **12** mellifluence **13** melodiousness **14** harmoniousness **15** mellifluousness

melon
varieties: **4** pear **5** mango, snake, stink **6** casaba, citron, Dudaim, netted, nutmeg, orange, winter **7** Persian, serpent **8** honeydew **10** cantaloupe, preserving, watermelon **11** pomegranate **16** Oriental pickling, Queen Anne's pocket **17** Chinese preserving

Melpomene
member of: **5** Muses
personifies: **7** tragedy

melt **4** fade, fuse, pass, thaw **5** blend, merge, shade, touch **6** affect, disarm, dispel, soften, vanish **7** appease, dwindle, liquefy, mollify, scatter **8** dissolve **9** disappear, dissipate, evaporate, waste away **10** arouse pity, conciliate, propitiate

melt away **5** dry up **8** vaporize **9** evaporate

Melus
father: **7** Cinyras
mother: **6** Cyprus
changed into: **9** apple tree

Melville, Herman
author of: **4** Omoo **5** Mardi, Typee **7** Redburn **8** Moby Dick **9** Billy Budd **12** Benito Cereno **16** The Confidence Man **20** Bartleby the Scrivener

Melville, Julia
character in: **9** The Rivals
author: **8** Sheridan

Melvin and Howard
director: **13** Jonathan Demme
cast: **9** Paul LeMat **12** Jason Robards **15** Mary Steenburgen
Oscar for: **6** script **17** supporting actress (Steenburgen)

member **3** arm, leg, toe **4** foot, hand, limb, part, tail, wing **5** bough, digit, organ, piece, shoot **6** branch, finger, pinion **7** element, portion, section, segment **8** fragment **9** appendage, component, extremity **10** ingredient **11** constituent

member
of the bar: **4** beak **7** counsel **8** advocate, attorney **9** barrister, counselor **10** mouthpiece **12** legal advisor **13** attorney-at-law
of a crew: **4** hand, mate **6** ensign, ganger, gunner, purser, yeoman **7** bowsman, oarsman, steward, swabbie **8** cabin boy, coxswain, deckhand, helmsman **9** first mate, navigator
of faculty: **3** don, PhD **4** prof **5** tutor **6** doctor, master **7** teacher **8** lecturer **9** professor **10** instructor
of family: **3** son **4** aunt **5** niece, uncle **6** cousin, father, mother, nephew, sister **7** brother **8** daughter, grandson **11** grandfather,

grandmother
13 granddaughter
of legislature: 4 whip 6 deputy 7 senator, speaker 8 delegate, lawmaker
10 legislator, politician
11 congressman 12 congresswoman
14 representative
of religious order: 3 nun
4 dame, monk 5 Clare, friar, priest 6 father, hermit, Jesuit, sister 7 Alexian, ascetic, brother, Cluniac, Templar
8 Capuchin, cenobite, minister, Trappist 9 Carmelite, Dominican 10 Carthusian, Cistercian, Franciscan
11 Augustinian, Benedictine
14 mother superior

Member of the Wedding, The
author: 15 Carson McCullers
character: 6 Jarvis 11 Janice Evans 13 Frankie Addams, John Henry West 16 Honey Camden Brown 18 Berenice Sadie Brown

membership 4 club 6 league, roster 7 company, society
9 community, personnel
10 connection, fellowship, fraternity 11 affiliation, association, brotherhood

membrane 3 web 4 film, skin
6 lining, sheath 7 coating
8 envelope, pellicle 9 thin sheet 10 integument

memento 5 favor, relic, token
6 record, trophy 8 keepsake, memorial, reminder, souvenir
11 memorabilia, remembrance 12 remembrancer
13 commemoration

memento mori 23 remember that thou must die 31 object serving as a reminder of death

Memnon
origin: 8 Oriental 9 Ethiopian
father: 8 Tithonus
mother: 3 Eos 4 Dawn
brother: 8 Emathion
companions: 10 Memnonides
fought with: 7 Trojans
killed by: 8 Achilles

Memnonides *see* 6 Memnon

memo
French: 11 aide memoire

memoir 4 life 5 diary 7 journal 9 biography, life story
10 adventures 11 confessions, experiences, reflections 13 autobiography, recollections, reminiscences

Memoirs of a Dutiful Daughter
author: 16 Simone de Beauvoir

memorabilia 6 papers 7 records 8 archives 9 documents

memorable 6 famous 7 eminent, notable, salient 8 historic, stirring, striking
9 important, momentous, prominent, red-letter 10 celebrated, impressive, noteworthy, remarkable 11 illustrious, outstanding, significant 13 distinguished, extraordinary, unforgettable

memorandum 4 memo, note
5 brief 6 agenda, minute, record 7 jotting 8 reminder
11 brief report, list of items

memorial 6 homage 7 tribute
8 monument 10 monumental
11 testimonial
13 commemorative

memorialization 11 celebration 13 commemoration

memorialize 4 mark 5 honor
9 celebrate 11 commemorate, pay homage to 12 pay tribute to

memory 4 fame, mark, name, note 5 glory, honor, token
6 esteem, recall, regard, renown, repute 7 memento, respect 8 eminence, keepsake, memorial, prestige, reminder, souvenir 10 estimation, reputation 11 distinction, remembering, remembrance, testimonial 12 recollection, remembrancer, reminiscence
13 commemoration
goddess of: 9 Mnemosyne

Memphis
football team: 9 Showboats

menace 3 cow 4 risk 5 bully, daunt, peril 6 danger, hazard, threat 7 imperil, pitfall, portend, presage, terrify 8 browbeat, endanger, forebode, jeopardy, threaten 9 terrorize
10 intimidate, jeopardize 11 be a hazard to, imperilment
12 endangerment

menacing 7 hostile 9 dangerous 11 belligerent, threatening, treacherous
12 antagonistic

Menaechmi
author: 7 Plautus

menage a trois 9 threesome
16 household of three

Menander
author of: 5 Heros 13 Perikeiromene 14 The Arbitration, The Misanthrope
16 The Rape of the Lock

Men at Arms
author: 11 Evelyn Waugh

Mencken, H L
author of: 10 Prejudices
19 The American Language
editor of: 10 The Mercury
11 The Smart Set

mend 3 fix 4 cure, darn, heal, knit 5 amend, emend, patch
6 better, reform, remedy, repair, revise 7 correct, improve, rectify, restore, retouch, touch up 8 overhaul, renovate
9 meliorate 10 ameliorate
11 recondition

mendacious 5 false, lying
8 spurious 9 deceptive 10 misleading, untruthful

mendacity 5 fraud, lying 6 deceit 7 falsity, perfidy 9 chicanery, deception, duplicity, falsehood, hypocrisy 10 dishonesty 11 insincerity
13 double-dealing, falsification, prevarication 14 untruthfulness 17 misrepresentation

Mendel, Gregor Johann
field: 6 botany
nationality: 8 Austrian
discovered: 14 laws of heredity
founded: 8 genetics

Mendeleyev (Mendeleev), Dimitri Ivanovich
field: 9 chemistry
nationality: 7 Russian
devised: 11 periodic law
13 periodic table

Mendelssohn, (Jakob Ludwig) Felix
born: 7 Germany, Hamburg
composer of: 6 Elijah, St Paul 7 Athalie, Italian (symphony No 4), Lorelei, Ruy Blas 8 Antigone, Scottish (symphony No 3) 11 Reformation (symphony No 5), The Hebrides 12 Hymn of Praise (symphony No 2)
17 Songs without Words
21 A Midsummer Night's Dream

mendicant 6 beggar 10 almsseeker, panhandler

Mending Wall
author: 11 Robert Frost

Menelaus
king of: 6 Sparta
father: 6 Atreus
mother: 6 Aerope
brother: 9 Agamemnon
wife: 5 Helen
son: 11 Megapenthes, Nicostratus
daughter: 8 Hermione

mene mene tekel upharsin
30 numbered numbered weighed divided
foretells destruction of: 10 Belshazzar

from Biblical book of: 6 Daniel

Menestheus
regent of: 5 Athens
rejected by: 5 Helen
assisted: 8 Menelaus

Menesthius
father: 9 Areithous
fought with: 6 Greeks
killed by: 5 Paris

menhaden 4 pogy 5 pogie 6 bunker 7 alewife, bugfish, ellfish, fatback, herring, oldwife, sardine 8 bonyfish, hardhead, ladyfish 10 mossbunker

menial 3 low 4 mean 5 drone, lowly, slave, toady 6 abject, drudge, flunky, helper, humble, lackey 7 fawning, ignoble, servant, servile, slavish 8 cringing, employee 9 degrading, groveling, sycophant, truckling, underling 10 apprentice, obsequious 11 bootlicking, subordinate, subservient, sycophantic

menial labor 4 toil 5 grind 8 drudgery

Menjou, Adolphe
born: 12 Pittsburgh PA
roles: 9 Golden Boy, Pollyanna 11 A Star Is Born 12 The Front Page 13 A Woman of Paris 15 A Farewell to Arms, State of the Union 16 Little Miss Marker 18 A Bill of Divorcement

meno
music: 4 less

Menodice
form: 5 nymph
son: 5 Hylas

Menoeceus
descendant of: 6 Sparti
father: 5 Creon
son: 5 Creon
daughter: 7 Jocasta
death by: 7 suicide

Menoetes
occupation: 7 cowherd

Menoetius
member of: 6 Titans 9 Argonauts
father: 7 Iapetus
mother: 7 Clymene
brother: 5 Atlas 10 Epimetheus, Prometheus
son: 9 Patroclus

Menominee, Menomini, Menomonie
language family: 9 Algonkian 10 Algonquian
location: 4 Ohio 7 Indiana 8 Illinois, Michigan 9 Wisconsin

menorah 11 candelabrum, candlestick 12 candleholder
number of candles: 5 seven

Menotti, Gian-Carlo
born: 5 Italy 10 Cadigliano
composer of: 9 The Consul, The Medium 12 The Island God, The Telephone 19 Amelia Goes to the Ball 24 Amahl and the Night Visitors

mens sana in corpore sano 22 a sound mind in a sound body

mental 5 crazy, nutty 6 insane, psycho 7 cracked, lunatic, psychic 8 abstract, cerebral, neurotic, rational 9 disturbed, in the mind, of the mind, psychotic 10 disordered, subjective, unbalanced 11 intelligent, mentally ill 12 intellectual, metaphysical 13 psychological

mental application 9 diligence 10 absorption, intentness 11 deep thought, engrossment, fixed regard 13 concentration 14 close attention

mental disorder 5 quirk 6 lunacy, oddity 7 madness 8 delusion, insanity, neurosis 9 craziness, psychosis 10 aberration 11 abnormality, derangement, mental lapse, peculiarity, strangeness 12 eccentricity, idiosyncrasy 13 schizophrenia 15 manic depression

mental hospital 6 asylum 8 madhouse 11 institution

mental institution 6 asylum 8 madhouse 12 insane asylum

mentality 4 mind 6 acumen, brains, wisdom 8 judgment, sagacity 9 intellect 10 gray matter, perception 11 discernment 12 intelligence, perspicacity

mental lapse 5 quirk 6 lunacy, oddity 7 madness 8 rambling, straying 9 wandering 10 aberration 11 derangement, peculiarity 12 eccentricity 13 forgetfulness

mentally incapable
Latin: 15 non compos mentis

mentally sound
Latin: 12 compos mentis

Mentes
origin: 7 Taphian
rank: 7 captain

mention 3 say 4 cite, hint, name, tell 5 imply, state 6 hint at, notice, remark, report, tell of 7 comment, divulge, inkling, narrate, observe, recount, refer to, specify 8 allude to, allusion, disclose, intimate 9 insinuate, make known, reference, statement, touch upon, utterance 10 advisement, indication, suggestion 11 designation, insinuation, observation 12 acquaintance, announcement, notification 13 communication, enlightenment, specification

mentor 4 guru 5 guide, tutor 6 master 7 adviser, monitor, proctor, teacher 9 counselor, preceptor, professor 10 instructor

Mentor
advisor of: 8 Odysseus
educated: 10 Telemachus

Mephibosheth
father: 4 Saul 8 Jonathan
also called: 9 Meribbaal
grandfather: 4 Saul
son: 5 Micha

Mephistopheles
character in: 5 Faust
author: 6 Goethe

Mephitis *see* 7 Mefitis

mer 3 sea

Merab
father: 4 Saul
sister: 6 Michal
brother-in-law: 5 David

mercantile 5 trade 8 business 10 commercial 16 buying-and-selling

mercantilism 5 trade 8 business, commerce, exchange 13 commercialism

Mercedes
character in: 21 The Count of Monte Cristo
author: 5 Dumas (pere)

mercenary 5 venal 6 for pay, greedy 7 for gain, selfish 8 covetous, grasping, hireling, monetary 10 avaricious 11 acquisitive, paid soldier 12 hired soldier

merchandise 4 sell 5 goods, stock, trade, wares 6 deal in, market 7 effects, staples 8 huckster 9 advertise, publicize, traffic in 10 belongings, buy and sell, distribute 11 commodities 12 stock in trade

merchant 6 broker, dealer, hawker, jobber, monger, trader, vendor 7 peddler 8 chandler, retailer, salesman 9 purchaser, tradesman 10 saleswoman, shopkeeper, wholesaler 11 storekeeper, tradeswoman

Merchant of Venice, The
author: **18** William Shakespeare
character: **6** Portia **7** Antonio, Jessica, Lorenzo, Nerissa, Shylock **8** Bassanio, Gratiano

merci **8** thank you

merci beaucoup **16** thank you very much

merciful **4** kind **6** benign, humane, tender **7** clement, feeling, lenient, pitying, sparing **8** gracious **9** forgiving **10** beneficent **11** kindhearted, softhearted, sympathetic **13** compassionate, understanding

mercifulness **8** clemency, kindness, leniency, sympathy **9** benignity **10** compassion, humaneness **11** beneficence, forgiveness **13** understanding

merciless **4** fell **5** cruel, harsh **6** fierce, severe **7** callous, inhuman **8** inhumane, pitiless, ruthless **9** ferocious, heartless, unpitying, unsparing **10** relentless, unmerciful **11** coldblooded, hardhearted, remorseless, unrelenting

Mercouri, Melina
husband: **11** Jules Dassin
born: **6** Athens, Greece
roles: **7** Topkapi **10** Gaily Gaily **13** Never on Sunday **15** Once Is Not Enough

mercurial **6** fickle, lively, mobile **7** erratic, flighty, kinetic, protean **8** electric, spirited, unstable, variable, volatile **9** impetuous, impulsive **10** capricious, changeable, inconstant **11** fluctuating **13** irrepressible, unpredictable

mercury
chemical symbol: **2** Hg

Mercury
origin: **5** Roman
messenger of: **4** gods
god of: **7** science, thieves **8** commerce **9** eloquence
corresponds to: **6** Hermes, Ogmios

Mercutio
character in: **14** Romeo and Juliet
author: **11** Shakespeare

mercy **4** pity **5** grace **6** lenity **7** charity **8** blessing, clemency, humanity, kindness, lenience, leniency, sympathy **9** good thing, tolerance **10** compassion, humaneness, lucky break **11** benevolence, forbearance, forgiveness, piece of luck **13** commiseration, fellow feeling **15** softheartedness **17** tenderheartedness
Latin: **12** misericordia

Mercy seat *see* **16** Ark of the Covenant

Merdle
character in: **12** Little Dorrit
author: **7** Dickens

mere **4** bald, bare, sole **5** plain, scant, sheer, utter **6** common, paltry **7** mundane **8** nugatory, ordinary, trifling **10** negligible, uneventful **11** commonplace, unmitigated **13** insignificant, unappreciable **14** inconsiderable

mere **6** mother

Meredith, Burgess
wife: **15** Paulette Goddard
born: **11** Cleveland OH
roles: **5** Magic, Rocky **6** Batman (the Penguin) **7** Madame X **8** Foul Play **12** Hurry Sundown, Of Mice and Men **15** Magnificent Doll, Such Good Friends **16** Advise and Consent

Meredith, George
author of: **9** The Egoist **10** Modern Love **14** Evan Harrington **16** Beauchamp's Career **19** Diana of the Crossways **25** The Ordeal of Richard Feverel

merely **3** but **4** just, only **5** quite **6** barely, in part, purely, simply, solely **7** utterly **8** scarcely, wholly **10** absolutely

meretricious **4** mock, sham **5** bogus, false, phony **6** pseudo, shoddy, tawdry **8** delusive, specious, spurious **9** deceptive **10** fraudulent, misleading **11** counterfeit

merge **4** fuse, join, weld **5** blend, unify, unite **6** link up **7** combine **8** coalesce, converge, intermix **9** associate, become one, integrate, interfuse, interlock **10** amalgamate, synthesize **11** confederate, consolidate **12** band together, interconnect

mergence **3** mix **5** blend **7** merging, mixture **8** mingling **10** concoction **11** combination

Mergenthaler, Ottmar
nationality: **8** American
invented: **8** linotype

merger **5** union **7** wedding **8** marriage **9** coalition **12** amalgamation **13** confederation, consolidation

Meribbaal *see* **12** Mephibosheth

meridian **3** tip, top **4** acme, apex, brow, peak **5** crest, crown, point, ridge **6** apogee, climax, summit, vertex, zenith **7** heights **8** pinnacle **11** culmination

Merimee, Prosper
author of: **6** Carmen **7** Colomba

Meriones
mentioned in: **5** Iliad
vocation: **6** archer
father: **5** Molus

merit **4** earn, rate **5** value, worth **6** credit, desert, invite, prompt, talent, virtue **7** ability, benefit, deserve, quality, stature, warrant **8** efficacy **9** advantage **10** be worthy of, excellence, worthiness **11** distinction **12** be entitled to, have a right to **13** justification

merited **3** due **5** rated **6** earned **8** deserved, rightful

meritorious **4** fine **6** worthy **8** laudable **9** admirable, estimable, excellent, exemplary **10** creditable, noteworthy **11** commendable, exceptional **12** praiseworthy

Mermaid Tycoon
nickname of: **14** Esther Williams

Merman, Ethel
real name: **20** Ethel Agnes Zimmermann
husband: **14** Ernest Borgnine
born: **9** Astoria NY
autobiography: **6** Merman
roles: **11** Call Me Madam **12** Anything Goes, Panama Hattie **15** Annie Get Your Gun **16** Stage Door Canteen **21** Alexander's Ragtime Band

Mermerus
father: **5** Jason
mother: **5** Medea

Merodach *see* **6** Marduk

Merope
member of: **8** Pleiades
father: **5** Atlas **8** Oenopion
husband: **7** Polybus **8** Sisyphus **11** Cresphontes, Polyphontes
son: **7** Aepytus
raped by: **5** Orion
raised: **7** Oedipus

merrily **5** gaily **6** gladly **7** briskly, happily, lightly, lustick, quickly **8** blithely, jocundly, jovially, joyfully, joyously **9** festively, gleefully **10** cheerfully, laughingly, mirthfully **11** hilariously, vivaciously **14** lightheartedly

Merrimac *see* **9** Pennacook

merriment **3** fun **4** glee **5** cheer, mirth **6** frolic, gaiety, hoopla, levity **7** good fun, jollity, revelry, whoopee **8** hilarity, laughter **9** amusement, festivity, good humor, jocundity, joviality **10** jocularity, jubilation, liveliness, skylarking **11** celebration, gleefulness, good spirits, merrymaking **12** conviviality, exhilaration, sportiveness **16** lightheartedness

Merriweather, Mrs
character in: **15** Gone With the Wind
author: **8** Mitchell

merry **3** gay **5** happy, jolly **6** blithe, cheery, jocund, jovial, joyous, lively **7** festive, gleeful, jocular **8** animated, carefree, cheerful, gladsome, laughing, mirthful, partying, reveling, sportive **9** convivial, fun-loving, sprightly, vivacious **10** frolicsome, rollicking, skylarking **12** high-spirited, lighthearted

merrymaking **5** sport **6** frolic, gaiety, hoopla, revels **7** jollity, revelry, whoopee **8** carousal **9** festivity, fun-making, high jinks, merriment, rejoicing, whoop-de-do **10** saturnalia **11** bacchanalia, celebration, festivities **12** conviviality

Merry Wives of Windsor, The
author: **18** William Shakespeare
character: **4** Ford, Page **5** Caius **6** Doctor, Fenton **7** Slender **8** Anne Page **12** Mistress Ford, Mistress Page **15** Mistress Quickly, Sir John Falstaff

mesa **4** hill, peak **5** bench, butte, table **7** plateau, terrace **9** cartouche, tableland

Mescalero
language family: **6** Apache
location: **6** Mexico **9** New Mexico
related to: **5** Lipan **10** Chiricahua

Meserve, Margaret Hamilton
real name of: **16** Margaret Hamilton

Meservey, Robert Preston
real name of: **13** Robert Preston

mesh **3** fib, net, web **4** grid, jibe **5** agree, sieve, tally **6** engage, enmesh, grille, plexus, screen **7** connect, engaged, netting, network, webbing, webwork **8** dovetail, interact, lacework, meshwork, openwork **9** grillwork, interlock, intermesh **10** coordinate, correspond, interweave, wickerwork **11** fit together, latticework **12** reticulation

Meshach
former name: **7** Mishael
companion: **6** Daniel
friend: **8** Abednego, Shadrach

Mesmer, Franz (Friedrich) Anton
nationality: **6** German
developed: **8** hypnosis

mesmerize **5** charm **7** bewitch **8** enthrall, entrance **9** fascinate, hypnotize, magnetize, spellbind, transport

Mesopotamian mythology
god of agriculture/earth: **5** Dagan
corresponds to Phoenician: **5** Dagon

Mesquakie *see* **3** Fox

mess **3** fix **4** hash, stew **5** mix-up, pinch **6** crisis, jumble, litter, muddle, pickle, plight, scrape, strait **7** clutter, dilemma, trouble **8** disarray, disorder, hot water, mess hall, mishmash, quandary **9** cafeteria, confusion, imbroglio, refectory, situation **10** commissary, difficulty, dining hall, dining room, hodgepodge **11** predicament **14** conglomeration

message **4** news, note, word **5** moral, point, theme **6** letter, notice, report **7** meaning, missive, purport, tidings **8** bulletin, dispatch **9** statement **10** communique, memorandum **12** intelligence **13** communication

mess around with **4** test **6** try out **8** fool with, play with **10** tinker with **14** experiment with

Messene
husband: **8** Polycaon

messenger **5** envoy **6** bearer, runner **7** carrier, courier **8** delegate, emissary **9** deliverer, go-between **11** delivery boy, delivery man **12** intermediary

messenger of gods **4** Iris **6** Hermes **7** Mercury

Messiaen, Olivier Eugene Prosper Charles
born: **6** France **7** Avignon
composer of: **11** Exotic Birds, Turangalila **13** Chronochromie **20** Le Nativite du Seigneur **22** Quartet for the End of Time **27** Vingt Regards sur l'Enfant Jesus **33** Et exspecto resurrectionem mortuorum **41** Transfiguration de Notre Seigneur Jesus Christ

Messiah
means: **11** anointed one
see also: **10** Jesus

Messick, Dale
creator/artist of: **19** Brenda Starr Reporter

messiness **5** chaos, mix-up, upset **6** jumble **7** clutter **8** disarray, disorder, scramble, shambles **9** confusion **10** disharmony, sloppiness, untidiness **12** dishevelment **14** disarrangement **15** disorganization

mess up **3** mar **4** goof, muff, ruin **5** botch, spoil **6** bungle, foul up, jumble **7** blunder, butcher, disturb, do badly, louse up, screw up **9** mismanage **10** disarrange **11** disorganize, make a mess of, make an error **12** make a mistake

messy **4** ugly **6** blowsy, frowsy, grubby, sloppy, tricky, untidy **7** awkward, chaotic, jumbled, tangled, unkempt **8** confused, littered **9** cluttered, difficult **10** bedraggled, disheveled, disordered, slatternly, topsy-turvy, unenviable, unpleasant **11** disarranged **12** embarrassing, inextricable **13** uncomfortable

Mesthles
commander of army of: **5** Maeon

mesto
music: **8** mournful

Mestor
father: **7** Perseus
mother: **9** Andromeda
daughter: **9** Hippothoe

Metabus
daughter: **7** Camilla

metal ***see box***

Metalious, Grace
author of: **11** Peyton Place

metalworking
god of: **6** Vulcan **10** Hephaestus, Hephaistos

metamorphose **6** change, mutate **7** convert **9** transform **11** transfigure

Metamorphoses
author: **4** Ovid

metamorphosis **8** mutation **10** alteration, conversion **11** permutation **12** change of form, modification **13** radical change, transmutation **14** transformation **15** series of changes, startling change, transfiguration **18** transmogrification

metal
alloy: **5** brass **6** bronze, nickel, pewter, solder
bar: **3** gad **4** risp **5** ingot
bolt: **5** rivet
box: **8** canister
casting: **3** peg
classification: **5** light, noble **6** alkali, common **7** coinage **8** platinum, precious **9** rare earth **10** low-melting, refractory, transition **11** high-melting **14** semiconductors
clippings: **7** scissel
coarse: **5** matte
corrosion: **4** rust
crude: **3** ore **4** slug
cymbals: **3** tal
deposit: **4** lode, vein
design: **7** chasing
disk or plate: **4** shim **5** medal, paten **6** platen, sequin
eyelet: **7** grommet
filings: **5** lemel
god of: **6** Vulcan **10** Hephaestus
heaviest: **6** osmium
kind: **3** tin **4** gold, iron, lead, zinc **6** barium, cerium, cesium, copper, erbium, nickel, osmium, radium, silver, sodium **7** arsenic, bismuth, calcium, holmium, iridium, lithium, rhodium, silicon, terbium, thulium **8** actinium, aluminum, antimony, europium, lutetium, platinum, rubidium, samarium, selenium, titanium, tungsten **9** beryllium, magnesium, palladium, potassium, ruthenium, strontium **10** molybdenum, phosphorus
layer: **7** plating
leaf: **4** foil
lightest: **7** lithium
liquid: **7** mercury
mass: **3** pid **5** ingot **7** bullion
piece: **4** jack, slug
refuse: **4** slag **5** dross
shaper: **5** swage
suit: **4** mail **5** armor **6** armour
thread: **4** lame, wire
trademark: **5** monel
ware: **4** tole **6** Revere
worker: **5** smith **6** forger, welder **7** armorer, riveter **8** armourer **9** goldsmith, ironsmith **10** blacksmith **11** coppersmith, silversmith **12** metallurgist

Metamorphosis, The
author: **10** Franz Kafka

Metanira
husband: **6** Celeus
son: **4** Abas **9** Demophoon **11** Triptolemus

metaphor **5** image, trope **6** simile **7** analogy **8** metonymy, parallel **11** equivalence **14** figure of speech, representation

metaphysical **5** basic, lofty, vague **6** far-out **7** eternal **8** abstract, abstruse, esoteric, mystical, ultimate **9** essential, high-flown, recondite, universal **10** impalpable, intangible, jesuitical, oversubtle **11** existential, fundamental, ontological, speculative **12** cosmological, intellectual, unanswerable **13** philosophical **15** epistemological

Metaphysics
author: **9** Aristotle

metaxa
type: **6** brandy **7** liqueur
origin: **6** Greece

mete, mete out **5** allot **6** assign, divide **7** deal out, dole out **8** allocate, disburse, dispense **9** apportion, parcel out **10** administer, distribute, measure out

meteoric **4** fast **5** fiery, rapid, swift **6** speedy, sudden **7** blazing, flaming, instant **8** flashing, unabated **10** inexorable **11** ineluctable, unstoppable

meter
abbreviation: **1** m

Meter
epithet of: **6** Athena
means: **6** mother

method **3** way **4** form, mode, plan, tack **5** means, order, style, usage **6** course, design, manner, scheme, system **7** fashion, formula, process, program, purpose, routine **8** approach, efficacy **9** procedure, technique, viability **13** modus operandi

methodical, methodic **4** neat, tidy **5** exact **7** careful, logical, orderly, precise, regular, uniform **10** analytical, deliberate, meticulous, systematic **12** businesslike **13** well-regulated

methodization **5** order **11** arrangement **12** organization **14** categorization, classification **15** systematization

methodize **5** order **7** arrange **8** classify, organize **11** systematize

Methuselah
father: **5** Enoch
son: **6** Lamech
years lived: **23** nine hundred and sixty nine
known as: **9** oldest man

meticulous **4** nice **5** exact, fussy **7** finical, finicky, precise **8** exacting, sedulous **10** fastidious, particular, scrupulous **11** painstaking, punctilious **13** conscientious, perfectionist

meticulousness **4** care **5** pains **12** sedulousness, thoroughness **14** fastidiousness, scrupulousness **17** conscientiousness

metier **3** job **4** area, line, work **5** craft, field, forte, trade **7** calling, pursuit **8** activity, business, lifework, province, vocation **9** specialty **10** employment, livelihood, occupation, profession

meting out **8** alloting **9** bestowing, doling out **10** allocating, conferring, consigning, dealing out, dispensing **11** designating **12** apportioning, distributing, measuring out

Metioche
father: **5** Orion
sister: **7** Menippe

Metion
father: **10** Erechtheus
mother: **9** Praxithea
brother: **7** Cecrops

Metis
member of: **6** Titans
father: **7** Oceanus
mother: **6** Tethys
consort of: **4** Zeus
daughter: **6** Athena

Metiscus
charioteer of: **6** Turnus

metrical narrative
French: **5** roman

Metropolis
director: **9** Fritz Lang
cast: **10** Alfred Abel **12** Brigitte Helm

metropolitan area **4** city **8** core city, downtown, environs **9** inner city, precincts, urban area **10** city limits, metropolis **11** central city **16** business district

mettle **3** vim **4** grit, guts **5** nerve, pluck, spunk, valor, vigor **6** spirit **7** bravery, courage, heroism **8** audacity, backbone, boldness, gameness, temerity **9** derring-do, fortitude, gallantry, manliness **10** enthusiasm, resolution **11** intrepidity **12** fearlessness **13** determination

mettlesome **4** bold, edgy **5** brave, fiery **6** ardent, plucky, spunky **7** gingery, peppery **8** restless, skittish, spirited **9** excitable, impatient **10** courageous, high-strung **12** high-spirited

Mexica *see* **5** Aztec

Mexico ***see box***

Mexico City
Aztec name: **12** Tenochtitlan
capital of: **6** Mexico
landmark: **13** Mercado Merced **15** Chapultepec Park **19** Basilica of Guadalupe
bull ring: **11** Plaza Mexico
floating gardens: **10** Xochimilco
pyramids: **11** Teotihuacan
square: **6** Zocalo **22** Plaza de las Tres Culturas
street: **16** Paseo de la Reforma

Meyer, David Harold
real name of: **12** David Janssen

Meyerbeer, Giacomo
real name: **17** Jacob Liebmann Beer
born: **6** Berlin **7** Germany
composer of: **7** Dinorah **10** Le Prophete, The African, The Prophet **12** Les Huguenots, The Huguenots, The North Star **14** Robert le Diable, Robert the Devil

Mezentius
king of: **7** Etruria
noted for: **7** cruelty
son: **6** Lausus
killed by: **6** Aeneas

mezza voce
music: **9** half voice **10** half volume

mezzo
music: **4** half

Miami
bay: **8** Biscayne
county: **4** Dade
developer: **7** Flagler
football team: **8** Dolphins
museum: **4** Lowe **12** Villa Viscaya
ocean: **8** Atlantic
people: **5** Cuban **8** Hispanic
section: **7** Hialeah **10** Bal Harbour **11** Coral Gables

---

Mexico
other name: **8** New Spain
capital/largest city: **10** Mexico City
others: **4** Leon **5** La Paz, Taxco **6** Cancun, Celaya, Merida, Oaxaca, Puebla, Toluca **7** Durango, Guaymas, Tampico, Tijuana, Torreon **8** Acapulco, Culiacan, Ensenada, Irapuato, Mazatlan, Mexicali, Saltillo, Veracruz **9** Chihuahua, Matamoras, Monterrey, Queretaro, Salamanca, Zacatecas **10** Hermosillo **11** Guadalajara, Nuevo Laredo **12** Ciudad Juarez, Villahermosa **13** Coatzacoalcos, Piedras Negras, San Luis Potosi **14** Puerto Vallarta **15** Netzahualcoyotl
ancient city: **4** Tula **7** Texcoco **8** Tlacopan **10** Monte Alban **11** Teotihuacan **12** Tenochtitlan **13** Tula de Allende
division: **6** Colima, Oaxaca, Puebla, Sonora **7** Chiapas, Durango, Hidalgo, Jalisco, Sinaloa, Tabasco, Yucatan **8** Campeche, Coahuila, Tlaxcala, Veracruz **9** Chihuahua, Michoacan, Nuevo Leon, Zacatecas **13** San Luis Potosi **14** Baja California
measure: **3** bag, pie **4** alma, onza, vara **5** almud, baril, carga, jarra, labor, legua, libra, linea, marco, sitio **6** adarme, almude, arroba, carega, fanega, ochaua, terceo **7** pulgada, quintal **9** cuarteron, cuartillo **10** caballeria
monetary unit: **4** onza, peso **5** adobe, claco, tlaco **6** azteca, cuarto, dinero **7** centavo, piaster
weight: **3** bag **4** onza **5** libra, marco **6** arroba, tercio **7** quintal
island: **6** Carmen, Cedros **7** San Jose, Tiburon **8** Cerralvo **10** Tres Marias **13** Espiritu Santo **14** Santa Magdelena, Santa Margarita **15** Angel de la Guarda
lake: **7** Chapala, Texcoco **9** Patzcuaro
mountain: **6** Colima, Tacana, Toluca **9** Paricutin **11** Ixtacihuatl, Sierra Madre **12** Popocatepetl **14** Sierra Zacateca **16** Chiapas Highlands **24** Transverse Volcanic Sierra
highest point: **7** Orizaba **12** Citlaltepetl
river: **4** Mayo **5** Yaqui **6** Balsas, Fuerte, Grande, Panuco **8** Colorado, Grijalva **10** Papaloapan, Usumacinta **13** Bravo del Norte, Coatzacoalcos, Lerma-Santiago
sea: **7** Pacific **8** Atlantic **9** Caribbean
physical feature:
bay: **8** Campeche **9** Olas Atlas
cape: **10** Corrientes
desert: **6** Sonora
gulf: **6** Mexico **8** Campeche **10** California **11** Tehuantepec
isthmus: **11** Tehuantepec
peninsula: **7** Yucatan **14** Baja California
plain: **7** Tabasco
plateau: **7** Mexican
valley: **7** Chiapas
people: **6** Indian **7** mestizo, Spanish
architect: **7** O'Gorman

stadium: **10** Orange Bowl
tropical garden: **9** Fairchild
university: **5** Barry **8** St Thomas
zoo: **11** Crandon Park

Miami (Twightwee)
language family: **9** Algonkian **10** Algonquian
tribe: **3** Wea **5** Miami **10** Piankashaw
location: **4** Ohio **7** Indiana **8** Illinois, Michigan **9** Wisconsin
leader: **12** Little Turtle
allied with: **6** Peoria

Miami Vice
character: **4** Gina **5** Trudy **8** (Capt) Castillo **13** Riccardo Tubbs, Sonny Crockett
cast: **10** Don Johnson **11** Olivia Brown **15** Saundra Santiago **16** Edward James Olmos **20** Phillip Michael Thomas

Micah Clarke
author: **19** Sir Arthur Conan Doyle

Micawber, Mr
character in: **16** David Copperfield
author: **7** Dickens

Micha
father: **9** Meribbaal **12** Mephibosheth
grandfather: **8** Jonathan
great-grandfather: **4** Saul

Michael
author: **17** William Wordsworth

Michael
means: **12** Who is like God
father: **8** Izrahiah **11** Jehoshaphat
son: **4** Omri **8** Zabadiah
also: **9** archangel

Michel
father: **4** Saul
husband: **5** David, Palti
sister: **5** Merab

Michelangelo di Buonarotti (Simoni)
architect of: **11** Campidoglio (Capitoline Hill) **12** Medici Chapel (Florence) **13** Farnese Palace **21** Palazzo Medici-Riccardi (Florence) **22** Palazzo dei Conservatori (Capitoline Hill) **24** Convent of San Marco Library
born: **5** Italy **7** Caprese
patron: **12** Pope Julius II **14** Lorenzo d'Medici **19** Pope Julius the Second **21** Lorenzo the Magnificent
artwork: **5** David, Moses, Pieta **6** Brutus, Slaves **7** Bacchus **9** The Victor **10** Holy Family **12** Madonna Pitti **15** The Last Judgment **18** Conversion of St Paul **20** Madonna Seated on a Step, Sistine Chapel Ceiling **21** The Flight of the Lapites, The Martyrdom of St Peter

Michelozzo
architect of: **21** Palazzo Medici-Riccardi (Florence) **24** Convent of San Marco Library

Michelson, Albert A
field: **7** physics

artist: **6** Orozco, Rivera, Tamayo **9** Siqueiros
composer: **6** Chavez
emperor: **10** Maximilian
explorer: **6** Cortes, Cortez **7** Cordoba **8** Alvarado, Grijalva
god: **6** Tlaloc **12** Quetzalcoatl **14** Huitzilopochtl
leader: **3** Gil **4** Diaz **5** Lopez, Rubio, Villa **6** Calles, Huerta, Juarez, Madero, Valdes, Zapata **7** Obregon **8** Carranza, Iturbide, Portillo, Santa Ana **9** Diaz Ordaz, Montezuma, Rodriguez **13** Madrid Hurtado
revolutionary/priest: **13** Morelos y Pavon **16** Hidalgo y Costilla
soldier/explorer: **12** conquistador
viceroy: **7** Mendoza
writer: **3** Paz **5** Nervo, Reyes, Yanez **6** Azuela, Guzman, Najera **7** Fuentes
language: **5** Mayan, Otomi **6** Mixtec **7** Mazahua, Mazatec, Nahuatl, Spanish, Totonac, Zapotec **8** Tarascan
religion: **13** Roman Catholic
place:
cathedral: **10** Assumption
center of Mexico City: **6** Zocalo **21** Plaza de la Constitucion
floating gardens: **10** Xochimilco
museum: **28** Shrine of the Virgin of Guadalupe
park: **7** Alameda **11** Chapultepec
ruins: **5** Mitla, Uxmal **8** Palenque **10** Monte Alban **11** Chichen Itza, Teotihuacan **20** Temple of Quetzalcoatl
street: **13** Avenida Juarez **16** Paseo de la Reforma
temple/pyramid: **7** Cholula **8** Castillo
feature:
Christmas tradition: **6** pinata
coffee plantation: **5** finca
empire: **4** Maya **5** Aztec, Olmec **6** Mixtec, Toltec **7** Zapotec
large estate: **8** hacienda
musician: **8** mariachi
small farm/commune: **6** ejidos
sport: **7** jai alai **12** bullfighting
tree: **9** sapodilla **11** chicozapote
food:
corn cake: **8** tortilla
dish: **4** mole, taco **5** huevo, pollo **6** tamale **7** burrito, chorizo, taquito, tostada **8** empanada **9** enchilada, guacamole, sopadilla **10** chili verde, quesadilla **11** chimichanga **12** chili relleno
drink: **6** pulque **7** tequila

established: **12** speed of light **15** velocity of Earth
awarded: **10** Nobel Prize

Michener, James A
author of: **5** Space **6** Alaska, Hawaii, Iberia, Legacy, Poland **8** Caravans, Sayonara **9** The Source **10** Centennial, Chesapeake **11** The Covenant, The Drifters **16** The Fires of Spring **18** The Bridges at Toko-ri **22** Tales of the South Pacific

Mickey Mouse
creator: **10** Walt Disney
character: **5** Morty **6** Ferdie **11** Minnie Mouse
cow: **10** Clarabelle

Micklewhite, Maurice Joseph
real name of: **12** Michael Caine

Micmac
language family: **9** Algonkian **10** Algonquian
location: **6** Canada **10** Nova Scotia **12** Newfoundland, New Brunswick **14** Gaspe Peninsula **16** Cape Breton Island **18** Prince Edward Island

Michigan
abbreviation: **2** MI **4** Mich
nickname: **4** Lake **9** Wolverine **10** Automobile **15** Water Wonderland **16** Winter Wonderland
capital: **7** Lansing
largest city: **7** Detroit
others: **4** Caro, Troy **5** Flint, Niles, Wayne **6** Adrien, Alpena, Bad Axe, Monroe, Owosso, Warren, Wassar **7** Bay City, Holland, Jackson, Livonia, Midland, Pontiac, Saginaw, Trenton, Wyoming **8** Ann Arbor, Cadillac, Dearborn, Escanaba, Ironwood, Manistee, Muskegon, Petoskey, Royal Oak **9** Cheboygan, Hillsdale, Kalamazoo, Marquette, Port Huron, Roseville, Wyandotte **10** Birmingham, River Rouge **11** Battle Creek, Grand Rapids **12** Benton Harbor, Traverse City **13** Sault Ste Marie, St Clair Shores
college: **4** Alma, Hope **5** Wayne **6** Adrian, Albion, Calvin, Olivet, Owosso **7** Detroit, Oakland **9** Hillsdale, Kalamazoo, Marygrove
feature:
bridge: **8** Mackinac
canal: **3** Soo **12** Sault St Marie
festival: **12** Holland Tulip
national park: **10** Isle Royale
village: **10** Greenfield
tribe: **6** Ojibwa, Ottawa **8** Chippewa **10** Potawatomi
people: **9** Henry Ford, wolverine **11** Bruce Catton, Edgar A Guest, Julie Harris, Ralph Bunche, Ring Lardner **16** Charles Lindburgh
explorer: **6** Joliet **7** La Salle, Nicolet **9** Marquette **12** Etienne Brule, Sault St Marie
island: **8** Mackinaw
lake: **4** Burt, Erie **5** Clear, Huron, Round, Torch **6** Austin, Devils, Moline **7** Bawbees, St Clair **8** Houghton, Michigan, Superior
land rank: **11** twenty-third
mountain: **6** Copper **7** Gogebic **9** Menominee, Porcupine
highest point: **12** Mount Curwood
physical feature:
bay: **7** Saginaw, Thunder **8** Keweenaw, Sturgeon
straits: **8** Mackinac
president: **10** Gerald Ford
river: **4** Cass **5** Grand, Huron **6** Raisin **7** Detroit, Saginaw, St Clair, St Mary's **8** Escanaba, Muskegon **9** Menominee
state admission: **11** twenty-sixth
state bird: **5** robin
state fish: **5** trout
state flower: **12** apple blossom
state motto: **11** I Will Defend **39** If You Seek a Pleasant Peninsula Look About You
state song: **18** Michigan My Michigan
state tree: **16** eastern white pine

microbe **4** germ **5** virus **6** gamete, zygote **8** bacillus, parasite **9** bacterium **10** spirochete **13** microorganism, streptococcus **14** staphylococcus

microbiologist
American: **7** Waksman **9** Baltimore
Dutch: **11** (van) Leeuwenhoek

Micronesia
part of: **7** Oceania
island: **3** Nui **4** Guam, Rota, Truk, Wake **5** Makin, Nauru, Wotho **6** Bikini, Ellice, Majuro, Ponape **7** Gilbert, Mariana **8** Caroline, Kiribati, Marshall

microorganism **3** bug **4** germ **5** virus **7** microbe **8** bacillus, pathogen **9** bacterium

microphobia
fear of: **12** small objects

microscope
invented by:
compound: **7** Janssen
electronic: **5** Knoll, Ruska
field ion: **7** Mueller
single lens model improved by: **11** (van) Leeuwenhoek
first observed: **8** protozoa **13** red blood cells **19** single-celled animals

microscopic, microscopical **4** tiny **5** teeny **6** atomic, minute **9** invisible **10** diminutive, very little **13** imperceptible, infinitesimal

microscopy
founder: **11** Robert Hooke **13** Jan Swammerdam **16** Marcello Malpighi **19** Anton van Leeuwenhoek

Midas
king of: **7** Phrygia
father: **7** Gordius
gift: **11** golden touch
gift from: **7** Silenus
ears changed to those of: **3** ass
changed by: **6** Apollo

midday **4** noon **7** noonday **8** meridian, noontide, noontime

middle **3** act, gut, hub, mid **4** core, main **5** belly, heart, midst, waist **6** center, course, medial, median, midway, throes **7** central, halfway, midmost, midriff, nucleus, process, stomach **8** midpoint **9** heartland **10** midsection **12** intermediate

Middle Ages
French: **8** moyen age

middle-class **4** mass **8** ordinary **9** bourgeois **10** mainstream, middlebrow

middle Europe
German: **12** Mitteleuropa

middle ground **4** mean **7** balance **8** midpoint **11** equilibrium **12** common ground

Middle Kingdom *see* **5** China

middleman **5** agent **6** broker, dealer, jobber **7** liaison **8** mediator **9** go-between **10** wholesaler **11** distributor, intercessor **12** entrepreneur, intermediary

Middlemarch
author: **11** George Eliot
character: **5** Celia **12** Will Ladislaw **13** Rosamond Viney **14** Dorothea Brooke, Edward Casaubon, Tertius Lydgate **15** Sir James Chettam

middlemost **4** mean **5** inner **6** inmost, median **7** central, midmost **8** interior

middle-of-the-road **8** moderate **10** mainstream

middle-of-the-roader **8** moderate **12** mainstreamer

middle way
Latin: **8** via media

middling **4** fair, so-so **6** medium **7** average, fairish, minimal **8** mediocre, moderate, ordinary, passable **9** tolerable **10** pretty good, second-rate **11** indifferent **12** run-of-the-mill, unremarkable

Midea *see* **9** Licymnius

Midgard
also: **10** Mithgarthr
origin: **12** Scandinavian
means: **10** abode of man
located between: **8** Niflheim **10** Muspelheim
connected to Asgard by: **7** bifrost **13** rainbow bridge
formed from brow of: **4** Ymir

Midgard Serpent *see* **11** Jormungandr

midget **4** doll, runt **5** dwarf, pygmy **6** peewee, puppet, shrimp, squirt **7** manikin **8** half-pint, munchkin, small fry, Tom Thumb **9** pipsqueak **10** fingerling, homunculus **11** hop-o'-my-thumb, lilliputian

Midian
father: **7** Abraham
mother: **7** Keturah
descendant of: **9** Midianite

midlands **8** interior **10** hinterland **13** central region

midmost **5** inner **6** inmost, middle **7** central, pivotal **8** interior **10** middlemost

Midnight Cowboy
director: **15** John Schlesinger
cast: **9** Jon Voight **11** John McGiver, Sylvia Miles **13** Brenda Vaccaro, Dustin Hoffman (Ratso Rizzo)
Oscar for: **7** picture

Midnight Express
director: **10** Alan Parker
cast: **8** John Hurt **9** Bo Hopkins, Brad Davis (Billy Hayes) **10** Randy Quaid **12** Irene Miracle
setting: **13** Turkish prison
score: **14** Giorgio Moroder
Oscar for: **5** score **6** script

midori
type: **7** liqueur
origin: **5** Japan
flavor: **5** melon

midpoint **4** core, mean **5** focus **6** center, middle **15** point of no return

midriff **3** gut **4** guts **5** belly, tummy **6** paunch **7** abdomen, stomach **9** diaphragm **10** midsection **11** breadbasket

midst **3** eye, hub **4** core **5** bosom, heart, thick **6** center, depths, middle **7** nucleus **8** interior

Midsummer Night's Dream, A
author: **18** William Shakespeare
character: **4** Puck (Robin Goodfellow) **6** Bottom, Helena, Hermia, Oberon **7** Theseus, Titania **8** Lysander **9** Demetrius, Hippolyta

midterm **4** exam, test **6** review **11** examination

midwife
French: **11** accoucheuse

mien **3** air **4** look **5** guise, style **6** aspect, manner, visage **7** bearing, feature **8** attitude, behavior, carriage, demeanor, presence **9** semblance **10** appearance, deportment, expression **11** countenance

Mies van der Rohe, Ludwig
architect of: **14** German Pavilion (1929 International Exposition, Barcelona), Lake Shore Drive (apartment towers, Chicago), Tugendhat House (Brno Czechoslovakia) **15** National Gallery (West Berlin), Seagram Building (NYC)
style: **13** International
principle: **10** less is more

miff **3** irk, vex **4** rile **5** anger, annoy, chafe, pique **6** nettle, offend, rankle **7** affront, provoke **8** irritate **9** put one off **10** exasperate **11** make one sore **14** rub the wrong way **15** raise one's dander

Mifune, Toshiro
born: **5** China **8** Tsingtao
roles: **6** Midway, Shogun **8** Rashomon **12** Seven Samurai **13** Throne of Blood

Miggs, Miss
character in: **12** Barnaby Rudge
author: **7** Dickens

might **3** may **5** brawn, clout, force, power, vigor **6** energy, muscle **7** potency, prowess **8** strength **9** influence, lustihood, puissance, toughness **10** capability, competence, durability, robustness, sturdiness **11** capableness **12** forcefulness

mighty **4** able, bold, huge, vast, very **5** brave, hardy, husky, lusty, stout, truly **6** brawny, manful, potent, really, robust, strong, sturdy **7** immense, massive, titanic, valiant **8** colossal, enormous, forceful, gigantic, imposing, majestic, powerful, puissant, stalwart, towering, valorous, vigorous **9** monstrous, strapping **10** courageous, gargantuan, invincible, monolithic, monumental, prodigious, stupendous **11** elephantine, exceedingly, indomitable, of great size **12** overpowering, particularly **13** exceptionally **14** Brobdingnagian

Migonitis
epithet of: **9** Aphrodite
means: **6** uniter

migrate **4** move, trek **6** travel **7** journey **8** emigrate, relocate, resettle **9** immigrate

migration **4** trek **6** exodus, flight, moving **7** passage **8** diaspora, movement

mikado **5** ruler **7** emperor, monarch **9** sovereign **15** Japanese emperor

Mikado, The
subtitle: **15** The Town of Titipu
operetta by: **18** Gilbert and Sullivan
character: **4** Ko-Ko **6** Peep-Bo, Yum-Yum **7** Katisha, Pooh-Bah **8** Nanki-Poo, Pish-Tush **9** Pitti-Sing

Mikkelsen, Dahl
also: **3** Mik
creator/artist of: **8** Ferd'nand

mikrophobia
fear of: **5** germs

mikvah **35** public establishment for ritual bathing
used by: **12** Orthodox Jews

mild **4** calm, easy, soft, warm **5** balmy, bland **6** docile, gentle, placid, serene, smooth **7** pacific, summery **8** delicate, moderate, not sharp, pleasant, soothing, tranquil **9** easygoing, emollient, not severe, not strong, temperate **10** forbearing, not extreme, springlike **11** complaisant, uninjurious **12** good-tempered

mildew **4** mold **6** blight, fungus

mildewed **5** fusty, moldy **10** discolored

mildness **8** calmness, delicacy, serenity, softness **9** placidity **10** gentleness, good temper

Mildred Pierce
director: **13** Michael Curtiz
based on novel by: **10** James M Cain
cast: **8** Ann Blyth, Eve Arden **10** Jack Carson **12** Bruce Bennett, Joan Crawford, Zachary Scott
Oscar for: **7** actress (Crawford)

mild-tempered **7** equable, patient **9** easygoing **11** good-natured, unflappable

mile
abbreviation: **2** mi

Miles, Sarah
brother: **11** Christopher
husband: **10** Robert Bolt
born: **7** England **11** Ingatestone
roles: **6** Blow-Up **10** The Servant **11** The Hireling **13** Ryan's Daughter **16** Lady Caroline Lamb

miles gloriosus **15** boastful soldier

Miles Gloriosus
author: **7** Plautus

Milesian
origin: **5** Irish
invaders from: **5** Spain
invaded: **7** Ireland
defeated: **14** Tuatha De Danann
ancestors of: **5** Irish

milestone **7** jubilee **8** milepost, signpost **10** road marker **11** anniversary **12** red-letter day, turning point

Milestone, Lewis
director of: **12** Of Mice and Men, The Front Page **13** A Walk in the Sun **17** Mutiny on the Bounty **25** All Quiet on the Western Front (Oscar)

Milestones
author: **13** Arnold Bennett

Miletus
father: **6** Apollo
mother: **4** Aria
son: **6** Caunus
daughter: **6** Byblis

milieu **5** scene **7** culture, element, setting **8** ambience, backdrop **10** background **11** environment, mise-en-scene **12** surroundings

militant **7** defiant, extreme, martial, warlike, warring **8** fighting, military **9** assertive, bellicose, combatant, combative **10** aggressive, pugnacious **11** belligerent, contentious **12** disputatious, paramilitary, warmongering **14** uncompromising

military **4** army **5** armed, crisp **6** strict, troops **7** martial, militia, Spartan, warlike **8** generals, soldiers **9** combative, defensive, regulated, soldierly, warmaking **10** regimented **11** armed forces, belligerent, soldierlike

military force **4** army, navy **6** legion, troops **7** legions, militia **8** military, regiment, soldiers, soldiery **9** battalion **11** fighting men **13** fighting force

military machine **4** army **6** legion, troops **11** armed forces **13** fighting force

military rank abbreviation *see box*

military storehouse **6** armory **7** arsenal **8** magazine **9** arms depot **13** ordnance depot **14** ammunition dump

military stores **7** arsenal, weapons **8** ordnance **9** munitions **10** ammunition

military unit **4** army, crew, unit **5** corps, force, squad **6** legion, outfit **7** brigade, company **8** regiment, squadron **9** battalion, task force **10** contingent, detachment

milksop **4** baby, wimp **5** mouse, pansy, sissy, softy **6** coward **7** crybaby, nebbish **8** mama's boy, poltroon, weakling **9** fraidy-cat **10** namby-pamby, pantywaist, scaredy-cat, weak sister **11** milquetoast, mollycoddle

military rank abbreviation
admiral: **3** adm
brigadier general: **2** bg **7** brig gen
captain: **3** cpt **4** capt
chief petty officer: **3** CPO
colonel: **3** col
commander: **5** comdr
corporal: **3** cpl
ensign: **3** ens
general: **3** gen
lieutenant: **2** lt **5** lieut
lieutenant colonel: **3** ltc **5** lt col
lieutenant general: **5** lt gen **8** lieut gen
major: **3** maj
master sergeant: **4** msgt
private: **3** pvt
private first class: **3** pfc
sergeant: **3** sgt
sergeant first class: **3** sfc
sergeant major: **4** smaj **6** sgt maj
specialist: **4** spec

mill **4** roam, teem **5** crush, grind, shape, swarm, works **6** finish, groove **7** factory, meander **8** converge **9** granulate, pulverize

Mill, John Stuart
author of: **9** On Liberty **14** Utilitarianism **20** The Subjection of Women **28** Principles of Political Economy

Millais, Sir John Everett
born: **7** England **12** Southhampton
artwork: **7** Bubbles **9** Blind Girl **12** Autumn Leaves, Chill October **13** My First Sermon **18** Lorenzo and Isabella **25** Christ in the Carpenter's Shop **36** Young Men of Benjamin Seizing Their Brides

Millament, Mrs
character in: **16** The Way of the World
author: **8** Congreve

Milland, Ray
real name: **21** Reginald Truscott-Jones
born: **5** Neath, Wales
roles: **9** Beau Geste **11** Blonde Crazy **14** Dial M for Murder, The Lost Weekend (Oscar) **22** Bulldog Drummond Escapes

Millar, Kenneth
real name of: **13** Ross MacDonald

Millay, Edna St Vincent
author of: **11** Second April **13** The Harp Weaver **19** Make Bright the Arrows **20** A Few Figs from Thistles

Mille, Agnes de
choreographer of: **5** Rodeo **15** Fall River Legend

millennium **13** thousand years **9** age of gold **21** one-thousandth anniversary

Miller
character in: **18** The Canterbury Tales
author: **7** Chaucer

Miller, Ann
real name: **17** Lucille Ann Collier
autobiography: **15** Miller's High Life
born: **9** Chireno TX
roles: **9** On the Town, Stage Door **10** Hit the Deck, Kiss Me Kate **11** Sugar Babies **16** The Kissing Bandit

Miller, Arthur
wife: **13** Marilyn Monroe
author of: **8** The Price **11** The Crucible **12** After the Fall **16** Death of a Salesman **18** A View from the Bridge

Miller, Henry
author of: **5** Nexus, Sexus **6** Plexus **14** Tropic of Cancer **17** Tropic of Capricorn **18** The Rosy Crucifixion **21** The Colossus of Maroussi

Milles, Carl
real name: **23** Wilhelm Carl Emil Anderson
born: **5** Lagga **6** Sweden
artwork: **5** Diana, Jonah **6** Europa **12** Man and Nature, Playing Bears **13** Peace Monument **15** Orpheus Fountain **18** Meeting of the Waters, Saltsjobaden Church (bronze doors)

millet **16** Panicum miliaceum
varieties: **3** hog **5** pearl, Sanwa **6** finger, Indian **7** African, foxtail, Italian **8** barnyard, browntop, Japanese **16** Japanese barnyard

Millet, Jean-Francois
born: **6** France, Gruchy
artwork: **5** Sower **7** Angelus **11** The Gleaners, The Winnower **14** Potato Planters, The Man with a Hoe **23** Oedipus Taken from the Tree

Millett, Kate
author of: **6** Flying **14** Sexual Politics

milligram
abbreviation: **2** mg

milliliter
abbreviation: **2** mL

millimeter
abbreviation: **2** mm

Millionaire, The
character: **14** Michael Anthony
cast: **12** Marvin Miller

Mill on the Floss, The
author: **11** George Eliot
character: **8** Bob Jakin, Mrs Glegg **9** Lucy Deane, Mrs Pullet **11** Philip Wakem, Tom Tulliver **12** Stephen Guest **14** Maggie Tulliver

Mills, Hayley
real name: **15** Rose Vivian Mills
father: **4** John
sister: **6** Juliet
husband: **11** Ray Boulting
born: **6** London **7** England
roles: **8** Tiger Bay **9** Pollyanna **11** Summer Magic **13** The Parent Trap **14** The Chalk Garden **15** The Moon-Spinners **19** In Search of Castaways **20** The Trouble with Angels

Mills, John
daughter: **6** Hayley, Juliet
born: **7** England **10** Felixstowe
roles: **12** Tunes of Glory **13** Ryan's Daughter **14** The Chalk Garden **17** Great Expectations **19** Swiss Family Robinson

Mills, Robert
architect of: **10** Post Office (Washington DC) **12** Patent Office (Washington DC) **14** Circular Church (Charleston) **15** Unitarian Church (Philadelphia) **16** Treasury Building (Washington DC) **18** Washington Monument **25** Sansom Street Baptist Church (Philadelphia) **29** Egyptian Revival Monument Church (Richmond VA)
style: **12** Greek Revival

millstream **3** run **4** race **5** brook, canal, creek, river **6** branch

Milne, A A
author of: **13** Winnie-the-Pooh **20** The House at Pooh Corner
character: **3** Roo **4** Pooh **5** Kanga **6** Eeyore, Piglet, Tigger **16** Christopher Robin

Milosz, Czeslaw
author of: **11** Native Realm, The Usurpers **13** Bells in Winter **14** Seizure of Power, The Captive Mind

milquetoast **4** wimp **7** milksop, nebbish **11** mollycoddle

Milton
author: **12** William Blake

Milton, George
character in: **12** Of Mice and Men
author: **9** Steinbeck

Milton, John
author of: **7** Lycidas **8** L'Allegro **11** Il Penseroso **12** Areopagitica, Paradise Lost **15** Samson Agonistes **16** Paradise Regained **29** On the Morning of Christ's Nativity

Milton Berle Show, The
host: **11** Milton Berle
regulars: **10** Fatso Marco **11** Arnold Stang, Jack Collins, Milton Frome, Ruth Gilbert **12** Irving Benson **13** Bobby Sherwood
announcer: **8** Sid Stone **11** Jimmy Nelson **13** Jack Lescoulie
orchestra: **8** Alan Roth, Billy May **11** Victor Young
theme: **7** Near You
Milton Berle's nickname: **12** Mr Television
sponsor: **5** Buick **6** Texaco

Milwaukee
baseball team: **7** Brewers
basketball team: **5** Bucks
Indian name: **16** Mahn-a-waukee Seepe
lake: **8** Michigan
river: **9** Milwaukee, Menomonee, **12** Kinnickinnic
university: **9** Marquette

mimic **3** ape **4** aper, copy, echo, mime **6** mirror, parrot **7** copycat, copyist, feigner, imitate, take off **8** imitator, simulate **9** reproduce **10** burlesquer **11** counterfeit, impersonate **13** impressionist

Mimir
origin: **12** Scandinavian
god of: **3** sea
decapitated by: **5** Vanir
head sent to: **4** Odin **5** Othin
oracle for: **4** Asar **5** Aesir

mimosa **14** Acacia dealbata **18** Albizia Julibrissin
varieties: **5** Texas **6** golden **7** prairie **8** Egyptian

mince **4** dice, pose **5** grate, shred **6** refine, soften **7** posture, qualify **8** chop fine, hold back, mitigate, moderate, palliate **9** gloss over, put on airs, whitewash **12** attitudinize **14** affect delicacy, affect primness **15** give oneself airs **16** affect daintiness, soften one's speech **18** cut into small pieces **19** be mealymouthed about **20** cut into tiny particles

mince words **5** dodge, hedge, stall **10** equivocate **11** be ambiguous **13** avoid the issue **17** beat around the bush

mind **4** hate, heed, note, obey, tend, will, wits **5** abhor, bow to, brain, focus, sense, watch **6** brains, choice, detest, eschew, follow, intent, liking, memory, notice, notion, reason, recall, regard, resent, sanity **7** dislike, marbles, observe, opinion, outlook, thought **8** adhere to, attend to, be wary of, judgment, object to, reaction, response, submit to, take care, thinking **9** attention, awareness, be careful, cognition, faculties, intellect, intention, look after, sentiment **10** be cautious, comply with, conception, conclusion, gray matter, impression, perception, propensity, recoil from, reflection, shrink from, take care of **11** acquiesce to, be wary about, inclination, percipience, point of view, rationality, remembrance **12** apprehension, disapprove of, intelligence, recollection, reminiscence, take charge of, take notice of **13** be conscious of, comprehension, concentration, consciousness, consideration, contemplation, look askance at, preoccupation, ratiocination, retrospection, understanding **14** pay attention to
German: **5** Geist

mindful **4** wary **5** aware **7** alert to, alive to, careful, heedful **8** cautious, sensible, watchful **9** cognizant, conscious, observant, regardful **10** absorbed in, open-eyed to, thoughtful **11** attentive to, engrossed in, taken up with **12** occupied with **15** preoccupied with

mindfulness **9** alertness, awareness **10** perception **12** acquaintance **13** attentiveness, consciousness, understanding

mindless **6** insane, obtuse, stupid **7** asinine, doltish, idiotic, unaware, witless **8** careless, heedless **9** apathetic, cretinous, imbecilic, oblivious, unattuned, unheeding **10** neglectful, regardless, sophomoric, unthinking **11** inattentive, indifferent, nonsensical, thoughtless, unobservant, unreasoning **12** disregardful, simple-minded **13** inconsiderate, unintelligent **14** indiscriminate

mine **3** pit **4** fund **5** cache, hoard, shaft, stock, store **6** dig for, quarry, supply, tunnel, wealth **7** extract, reserve **8** dig under, excavate, treasure **9** abundance, booby-trap **10** excavation **12** accumulation

Mineo, Sal
real name: **14** Salvatore Mineo
born: **7** Bronx NY
roles: **5** Giant, Tonka **6** Exodus **18** Rebel Without a Cause, Who Killed Teddy Bear?

mineral ***see box***

Minerva
origin: **5** Roman
goddess of: **3** war **4** arts **6** wisdom **11** handicrafts
corresponds to: **6** Athena

mingle **3** mix **4** fuse, join **5** blend, merge, unite **6** hobnob **7** combine, consort **8** coalesce, intermix **9** associate, circulate, commingle, interfuse, interlard, socialize **10** amalgamate, fraternize, intertwine, interweave **11** intermingle, intersperse **12** rub shoulders

miniature **3** wee **4** tiny **5** elfin, pygmy **6** bantam, little, petite **9** minuscule **10** diminutive, pocket-size, small-scale **11** Lilliputian, microcosmic, microscopic

minim
abbreviation: **3** min

minimal **5** token **7** minimum, nominal **13** least possible, unappreciable

minimize **5** dwarf **6** reduce, shrink **8** belittle, mitigate **9** underrate **10** depreciate, undervalue

minimum **4** base **5** basic, least **7** modicum **8** smallest

minister **4** abbe, tend **5** padre, rabbi, serve, vicar **6** answer, cleric, father, oblige, parson, pastor, priest **7** care for, cater to **8** attend to, chaplain, pander to, preacher, reverend **9** clergyman, secretary **10** evangelist, revivalist, take care of **11** accommodate **12** ecclesiastic **13** cabinet member

ministerial **6** cleric **8** churchly, clerical, pastoral, priestly **14** ecclesiastical

ministration **3** aid **4** care **6** charge **7** comfort **9** attention **10** protection **11** supervision

Ministry of Fear, The
author: **12** Graham Greene

Minitari *see* **7** Hidatsa

Minnehaha
character in: **8** Hiawatha
author: **10** Longfellow

Minnelli, Liza
father: **8** Vincente
mother: **11** Judy Garland
born: **12** Los Angeles CA
roles: **6** Arthur **7** Cabaret (Oscar) **14** New York New York **16** The Sterile Cuckoo **17** Flora the Red Menace

Minnelli, Vincente
director of: **4** Gigi (Oscar) **9** Brigadoon **11** Lust for Life **15** Bells Are Ringing, Meet Me in St Louis **16** Father of the Bride **17** An American in Paris

Minnesota ***see box***

Minni *see* **7** Armenia

minor **5** child, light, petty, small, youth **6** infant, lesser, paltry, slight **7** trivial **8** nugatory, picayune, piddling, teenager, trifling **9** secondary, youngster **10** adolescent **11** subordinate, unimportant **13** insignificant **14** inconsiderable **15** inconsequential

mineral **3** jet, ore **4** coal, gold, iron, mica, opal, spar, talc **5** beryl, topaz **6** augite, barite, blende, cerine, copper, galena, garnet, iolite, pinite, rutile, sandix, silver, sphene, spinel, sulfur **7** amesite, apatite, azurite, biotite, bornite, calcite, citrine, coesite, crystal, cuprite, cyanite, element, gahnite, helvite, jadeite, kernite, kunzite, niobite, olivine, prasine, zeolite, zircon **8** asbestos, borocite, chlorite, cinnabar, corundum, dolomite, epsomite, fayalite, feldspar, fluorite, graphite, hematite, lazulite, siderite, sodalite, stibnite, triplite, wellsite **9** aragonite, argentite, carnelian, celestite, cerussite, danburite, fosterite, kaolinite, lawsonite, magnetite, malachite, muscovite, petroleum, phenakite, scapolite, tridymite, turquoise, wulfenite **10** calaverite, chalcedony, orthoclase, pyrrhotite, sphalerite, tourmaline, wolfachite **11** alexandrite, chrysoberyl, melanterite **12** brazilianite, chalcopyrite, fincalconite, fluorapatite **13** rhodochrosite

Minnesota
abbreviation: **2** MN **4** Minn
nickname: **6** Gopher **9** North Star **19** Land of Sky-blue Waters **22** Land of Ten Thousand Lakes
capital: **6** St Paul
largest city: **11** Minneapolis
others: **3** Ada, Ely **4** Mora **5** Edina **6** Austin, Duluth, Newulm, Winona **7** Babbitt, Bemidji, Fosston, Hibbing, Mankato, Red Wing, St Cloud **8** Brainerd, Moorhead **9** Albertlea, Blue Earth, Richfield, Rochester, Roseville **10** Minnetonka, Robinsdale **11** Bloomington, St Louis Park **14** Brooklyn Center **18** International Falls
college: **6** Bethel, St Olaf, Winona **7** Bemidji, Hamline **8** Adolphus, Augsburg, Carleton, St Thomas **10** Macalester
feature:
monument: **10** Paul Bunyan
national monument: **9** Pipestone **12** Grand Portage
national park: **9** Voyageurs'
Norse artifact: **19** Kensington Rune Stone
tribe: **5** Sioux **6** Dakota, Ojibwa, Santee **8** Chippewa **9** Menominee
people: **11** Judy Garland **12** Mayo brothers **13** Harold Stassen, Lauris Norstad, Sinclair Lewis **16** F Scott Fitzgerald
explorer: **8** Hennepin, Norsemen, Radisson **9** Greysolon **12** Groseilliers **19** Sieur Duluth of du Lhut
lakes: **3** Red **5** Leech, Rainy **6** Itasca **7** Bemidji **8** Superior **9** Mille Lacs **10** Minnewaska **14** Lake of the Woods, Winnibigoshish
land rank: **7** twelfth
mountain: **6** Cuyuna, Mesabi **7** Misquah **9** Vermilion
highest point: **5** Eagle
physical feature: **6** Big Bog **14** Northwest Angle
falls: **9** Minnehaha
river: **3** Red **5** Rainy **6** Pigeon **7** St Croix, St Louis **9** Des Moines, Minnesota **10** St Lawrence **11** Mississippi
state admission: **12** thirty-second
state bird: **10** common loon
state fish: **7** walleye
state flower: **14** moccasin flower **24** pink and white lady's slipper
state motto: **17** The Star of the North
state song: **13** Hail Minnesota
state tree: **13** Norway red pine
baseball team: **5** Twins
football team: **7** Vikings
hockey team: **10** North Stars

minority **4** less **5** youth **6** lesser, nonage **7** boyhood, infancy **8** girlhood **9** childhood, juniority **10** immaturity **11** adolescence

minor-league **4** punk **5** dinky, seedy, tacky **6** cheesy, common, lesser, shabby **8** inferior, small-fry **9** secondary, small-time **10** bush-league, second-rate **13** insignificant

Minos
king of: **5** Crete
father: **4** Zeus
mother: **6** Europa
brother: **8** Sarpedon **12** Rhadamanthys
wife: **8** Pasiphae
daughter: **7** Ariadne, Phaedra
ordered: **9** Labryinth
became: **5** judge
in: **5** Hades

Minotaur
form: **7** monster
combined: **3** man **4** bull
father: **10** Cretan bull
mother: **8** Pasiphae
home: **9** Labyrinth
ate flesh of: **6** humans
killed by: **7** Theseus

minstrel **4** bard, poet **6** dancer, end man, lyrist, player, singer **8** comedian, songster **9** blackface, poetaster, serenader, versifier **10** troubadour **11** entertainer **12** interlocutor, vaudevillian **15** song-and-dance man

mint
varieties: **3** dog, red **4** wood **5** apple, field, lemon, stone, water **6** coyote, dotted, orange, Scotch **7** Meehan's **8** bergamot, Corsican, creeping, Japanese, mountain **9** pineapple
flavor: **7** menthol **9** spearmint **10** peppermint
liqueur: **13** creme de menthe
botanical name: **6** Mentha **8** Labiatae, M spicata **9** M piperita
origin: **13** Mediterranean
related herb: **7** oregano **8** marjoram, rosemary
symbol of: **11** hospitality
mythical nymph: **6** Mintha
beloved of: **5** Pluto
Mintha trod underfoot by: **10** Persephone
cure for: **7** hiccups
antidote for: **16** sea serpent stings
use: **4** lamb **5** salad **6** fruits

Minthe
form: **5** nymph
changed into: **9** mint plant
changed by: **10** Persephone

minuscule **3** wee **4** tiny **5** small **6** minute **10** teeny-weeny **11** small letter **13** infinitesimal **15** lower-case letter

minute **3** wee **4** fine, puny, tiny, wink **5** close, exact, flash, jiffy, petty, scant, shake, teeny, trice **6** breath, little, moment, petite, second, slight, strict **7** careful, instant, minikin, precise **8** detailed, itemized, trifling **9** miniature, twinkling **10** a short time, diminutive, exhaustive, meticulous, negligible, scrupulous **11** Lilliputian, microscopic **12** sixty seconds **13** conscientious, imperceptible, inappreciable, infinitesimal, insignificant **14** extremely small, inconsiderable
abbreviation: **3** min

minute portion **3** bit, sip **4** bite **5** crumb, grain, scrap, shred, speck **6** morsel, sliver **7** swallow **8** fragment, mouthful, particle

minutiae **6** trivia **7** trifles **8** niceties **10** bagatelles, pedantries, subtleties **11** odds and ends, particulars **12** minor details, trivialities **15** particularities

minx **4** jade, slut **5** hussy, huzzy, wench **7** baggage **10** prostitute

Minyades
daughters of: **6** Minyas

Miolnir
hammer of: **4** Thor

mir **5** peace, world **21** Russian village commune

mirabile dictu **12** strange to say **17** marvelous to relate

miracle **4** omen, sign **6** marvel,

wonder **7** mystery, portent, prodigy **9** divine act, sensation, spectacle **10** phenomenon **11** masterpiece

Miracle of Morgan's Creek, The
director: **14** Preston Sturges
cast: **9** Diana Lynn **11** Betty Hutton **12** Brian Donlevy, Eddie Bracken **15** William Demarest

Miracle on 34th Street
director: **12** George Seaton
based on story by: **15** Valentine Davies
cast: **9** John Payne **11** Edmund Gwenn (Kris Kringle), Natalie Wood **12** Gene Lockhart, Maureen O'Hara, Thelma Ritter
Oscar for: **12** screenwriter **15** supporting actor (Gwenn)

Miracle Worker, The
director: **10** Arthur Penn
cast: **9** Patty Duke (Helen Keller) **10** Victor Jory **11** Inga Swenson **12** Anne Bancroft (Anne Sullivan)
Oscar for: **7** actress (Bancroft) **17** supporting actress (Duke)

miraculous **6** divine **7** amazing, magical **9** marvelous, visionary, wonderful **10** incredible, mysterious, phenomenal, prodigious, remarkable **11** astonishing, astounding, exceptional, spectacular, supernormal **13** extraordinary, preternatural, wonderworking **14** thaumaturgical

miraculous food **5** manna

Miraculous writing
also: **4** mene **5** perez, tekel **8** upharsin
means: **7** divided, weighed **8** numbered
interpreted by: **6** Daniel

mirage **5** fancy **7** fantasy **8** delusion, illusion, phantasm **9** unreality **12** will-o'-the-wisp **13** hallucinations, misconception **14** castle in the air **15** optical illusion

Miranda
character in: **10** The Tempest
author: **11** Shakespeare

Miranda, Carmen
real name: **26** Maria do Carmo Miranda da Cunha
nickname: **18** Brazilian Bombshell
born: **8** Portugal **16** Marco de Canavezes
roles: **10** Copacabana **14** That Night in Rio **15** Weekend in Havana **16** Down Argentine Way **22** Springtime in the Rockies

mire **3** bog, fen, mud **4** cake, muck, ooze, soil **5** marsh, muddy, slime, slush, smear **6** enmesh, sludge **7** begrime, bog down, ensnare, spatter **8** besmirch, entangle, quagmire

Miriam
father: **5** Amram
mother: **8** Jochebed
brother: **5** Aaron, Moses

Miro, Joan
born: **5** Spain **8** Montroig **9** Barcelona
artwork: **9** Help Spain, The Reaper **13** Dutch Interior **14** Constellations **16** Catalan Landscape **19** Dog Barking at the Moon **20** Still Life with Old Shoe **26** Woman and Bird in the Moonlight

mirror **4** copy, show **5** glass, image, model **7** epitome, example, paragon, reflect **8** exemplar, manifest, paradigm, standard **10** reflection **11** cheval glass **12** looking glass

mirth **4** glee **6** gaiety, levity **7** jollity **8** drollery, hilarity, laughter **9** amusement, festivity, happiness, jocundity, joviality, merriment **10** jocularity **11** good spirits, merrymaking, playfulness **12** cheerfulness

mirthful **3** gay **4** glad **5** happy, jolly, merry **6** blithe, jocose, jovial, joyful, joyous **7** gleeful, jocular, risible

mirthless **3** sad **4** dour, glum **6** gloomy, morose **7** joyless, unhappy **8** dejected **9** cheerless, sorrowful **10** in the dumps, melancholy **14** down in the mouth

miry **3** wet **4** oozy **5** boggy, mucky, muddy, slimy, slushy, soggy **6** claggy, swampy **7** sloughy

misadventure **3** ill **4** slip **6** mishap **7** debacle, failure, reverse, setback **8** bad break, calamity, casualty, disaster **9** adversity, mischance **10** infelicity, misfortune **11** catastrophe, contretemps

misanthrope **5** cynic **7** skeptic **9** pessimist **10** misogynist

Misanthrope, Le
author: **7** Moliere
character: **7** Alceste, Arsinoe, Eliante **8** Celimene, Philinte

misanthropic **4** cold **5** surly **6** morose **7** cynical, distant **10** antisocial, unfriendly, unsociable **11** distrustful **12** discourteous, inhospitable, unneighborly, unpersonable, unresponsive **14** unapproachable **15** unaccommodating

misapplication **5** abuse **6** misuse **11** improper use **13** misemployment

misapply **5** abuse **6** misuse **9** misemploy **13** use improperly

misapprehension **5** mixup **7** mistake **11** misjudgment **13** misconception **14** miscalculation **15** false impression, misconstruction **16** misunderstanding **17** misinterpretation

misappropriate **4** bilk **5** abuse, cheat, mulct, steal **6** misuse **7** defraud, purloin, swindle **8** embezzle, misapply, peculate **9** defalcate, misemploy

misappropriation **6** misuse, taking **11** defalcation **12** embezzlement

misbehave **5** act up **7** disobey, do wrong **10** transgress **15** get into mischief

misbehavior **5** lapse **7** misdeed, offense **8** acting up, trespass **9** impudence **10** bad conduct, bad manners, disrespect, misconduct **11** delinquency, dereliction, impropriety, misdemeanor **12** indiscretion **13** transgression **16** obstreperousness, unmanageableness

misbelief **8** delusion, illusion **13** misconception

miscalculate **3** err **8** misjudge **10** guess wrong **11** misestimate

miscalculation **5** error **10** inaccuracy **13** misestimation

miscarriage **4** slip **5** botch **6** fizzle **7** default, failing, failure, misfire, undoing, washout **8** casualty, collapse

miscarry **4** fail **5** abort, botch **6** fizzle, go awry **9** terminate **12** come to naught

miscellanea **8** analects **9** anthology, gleanings, scrapbook **10** collection, miscellany, selections **11** collectanea

miscellaneous **5** mixed **6** divers, motley, sundry, varied **7** diverse, mingled, various **8** assorted, manifold **9** different **11** diversified **13** heterogeneous

miscellaneous collection
Latin/pseudo Latin: **14** omnium-gatherum

miscellany **5** blend **6** jumble, medley **7** melange, mixture, variety **8** analects, extracts, mishmash, pastiche **9** anthology, gleanings, potpourri

10 assortment, collection, hodgepodge, salmagundi, selections **11** collectanea, compilation, gallimaufry, miscellanea **14** conglomeration, omnium-gatherum

mischance **6** ill lot, mishap **7** bad luck, ill luck, ill wind **8** accident **9** adversity **10** infelicity, misfortune **12** misadventure

mischief **4** evil **5** wrong **6** injury, malice **7** devilry, knavery, roguery **8** deviltry, foul play, plotting, scheming, villainy **9** depravity, devilment, rascality **10** orneriness, wrongdoing **11** naughtiness, playfulness, roguishness, shenanigans, willfulness **12** prankishness, sportiveness **14** capriciousness

mischief-maker **3** imp **5** demon, devil, scamp **7** gremlin, hellion **9** scoundrel **10** hellraiser

mischievous **3** sly **5** elfin **6** elfish, impish, malign, vexing, wicked **7** harmful, naughty, noxious, playful, roguish, teasing, vicious, waggish **8** annoying, devilish, prankish, spiteful, sportive **9** injurious, malicious, malignant, uninvited **10** frolicsome, gratuitous, pernicious **11** deleterious, destructive, detrimental, uncalled for **12** exacerbating

misconceive **3** err **4** lose, miss **8** misjudge **12** misinterpret **13** misunderstand

misconception **5** error **8** delusion **11** misjudgment **13** erroneous idea **14** misinformation **15** misapprehension, misconstruction **16** misunderstanding **17** misinterpretation, misrepresentation

misconduct **7** misdeed, misstep **10** misprision, peccadillo, wrongdoing **11** delinquency, dereliction, impropriety, malefaction, malfeasance, misbehavior, misdemeanor **13** transgression

misconstrue **7** distort, mistake **8** misjudge **9** misreckon, misrender **12** misapprehend, miscalculate, misinterpret, mistranslate **13** misunderstand

miscreant **3** bum **4** heel **5** knave, scamp **6** bad egg, rascal, sinner, wretch **7** villain **8** evildoer, lost soul, scalawag **9** reprobate, scoundrel **10** blackguard, black sheep, malefactor

misdeed **3** sin **4** slip **5** crime, lapse, wrong **6** felony **7** faux pas, offense, outrage **8** atrocity, trespass **9** violation **10** misconduct, peccadillo **11** malfeasance, misbehavior, misdemeanor **12** indiscretion, infringement **13** transgression

misdemeanor **3** sin **5** crime, fault **7** offense, misdeed **8** disorder **10** peccadillo **11** misbehavior **13** transgression

misdoer **5** crook **8** criminal **9** miscreant, wrongdoer **10** delinquent

mise en scene **6** milieu **7** setting **8** ambience **10** atmosphere, background **11** environment **12** stage setting, surroundings

misemployment **6** misuse **14** misapplication

Misenus
father: **6** Aeolus

miser **5** piker **7** hoarder, niggard, Scrooge, skimper **8** tightwad **9** skinflint **10** cheapskate, pinchpenny **12** pennypincher, stingy person

Miser, The
also: **6** L'Avare
author: **7** Moliere
character: **5** Elise **6** Valere **7** Anselme, Cleante, Mariane **8** Harpagon

miserable **3** sad **4** mean **5** inept, needy, sorry **6** abject, scurvy, shabby, sordid, woeful **7** abysmal, crushed, doleful, forlorn, grieved, hapless, unhappy **8** beggarly, degraded, dejected, desolate, dolorous, feckless, inferior, mournful, pathetic, pitiable, rubbishy, very poor, wretched **9** appalling, atrocious, cheerless, depressed, desperate, heartsick, sorrowful, woebegone **10** chapfallen, deplorable, despicable, despondent, heavy-laden, lamentable, second-rate, unbearable **11** crestfallen, heartbroken, unfortunate **12** contemptible, disconsolate, impoverished **13** brokenhearted **14** down in the mouth

Miserables, Les
author: **10** Victor Hugo
character: **6** Javert **7** Cosette, Fantine **10** Thenardier **11** Jean Valjean **15** Father Madeleine, Marius Pontmercy **17** Eponine Thenardier

misericordia **5** mercy **10** compassion

miserliness **6** penury **9** frugality, parsimony **10** stinginess **13** niggardliness, penny-pinching **15** tight-fistedness

miserly **4** mean, near **5** cheap, tight **6** frugal, greedy, meager, stingy **7** selfish **8** grasping, grudging, pinching **9** illiberal, niggardly, penurious, scrimping **10** avaricious, ungenerous **11** closefisted, closehanded, tight-fisted **12** parsimonious **13** penny-pinching

misery **3** woe **4** blow **5** agony, curse, grief, trial **6** ordeal, regret, sorrow **7** anguish, bad deal, bad news, chagrin, despair, sadness, torment, trouble **8** bad scene, calamity, disaster, distress, exaction, hardship **9** dejection, heartache, privation, suffering **10** affliction, bitter pill, depression, desolation, melancholy, misfortune **11** catastrophe, despondency, tribulation **12** wretchedness

Misfits, The
director: **10** John Huston
based on story by: **12** Arthur Miller
cast: **10** Clark Gable, Eli Wallach **12** Thelma Ritter **13** Marilyn Monroe **15** Montgomery Clift

misfortune **4** blow, loss **6** misery, mishap **7** bad luck, reverse, setback, tragedy, trouble **8** calamity, casualty, disaster, downfall, hard luck, hardship **9** adversity, hard times, ruination **10** affliction, ill fortune **11** catastrophe, tribulation **12** misadventure

misgiving, misgivings **4** fear **5** alarm, doubt, dread, qualm, worry **7** anxiety, dubiety **8** disquiet, mistrust **9** suspicion **10** foreboding, skepticism **11** dubiousness, uncertainty **12** apprehension, doubtfulness, presentiment, reservations **14** second thoughts

misguided **5** at sea **6** adrift, faulty, misled, unwise **7** in error **8** mistaken **9** erroneous, imprudent, led astray, off course **10** ill-advised, indiscreet, misadvised **11** injudicious, misdirected, misinformed

Mishael *see* **7** Meshach

mishap **4** slip, snag **5** botch **6** fiasco, slipup **7** reverse, setback **8** casualty, disaster **9** mischance **10** difficulty, misfortune **11** miscarriage **12** misadventure

mishmash **3** mix **4** hash, stew **5** salad **6** jumble, medley, muddle **7** melange **8** mixed bag, pastiche, scramble **9** patchwork **10** assemblage, crazy quilt, hodgepodge, miscellany, salmagundi **14** conglomeration, omnium-gatherum

misinform 7 deceive, mislead **8** misguide **9** misdirect **10** lead astray **12** misrepresent

misinterpret 11 misconstrue **12** misapprehend **13** misunderstand

misinterpretation 13 misconception **16** misunderstanding **17** misrepresentation

misjudge 3 err **7** mistake **10** exaggerate, understate **11** misconceive, misconstrue **12** misapprehend, miscalculate, misinterpret, overestimate **13** misunderstand, underestimate

mislay 4 lose, miss **8** displace, misplace

mislead 4 dupe, fool, gull **6** betray, delude, entice, seduce, take in **7** beguile, deceive **8** hoodwink, inveigle, misguide **9** bamboozle, misdirect, misinform, play false, victimize **10** lead astray **11** double-cross, string along

misleading 6 luring **8** deluding **9** deceiving **10** misguiding **11** hoodwinking

mismanage 3 mar **4** flub, muff, ruin **5** botch, spoil **6** bollix, bungle, foul up, mess up **7** louse up, screw up **9** mishandle **11** make a hash of, make a mess of

misnomer 8 misusage, solecism **9** barbarism, misnaming **11** malapropism

misogynic 7 cynical **11** woman-hating **12** misanthropic

misogynist 5 cynic **10** woman-hater **11** misanthrope

misplace 4 lose **5** abuse **6** mislay **11** lose track of

misreckon 8 misjudge **10** guess wrong, miscompute **11** misestimate **12** miscalculate

misrepresent 7 falsify, mislead **8** disguise

misrepresentation 7 mockery **8** altering, travesty, twisting **9** burlesque, doctoring **10** caricature, distortion, falsifying **12** adulteration, exaggeration, misstatement **13** falsification

miss 4 blow, girl, lack, lady, lass, lose, loss, maid, muff, skip, slip, want **5** avert, avoid, error, forgo, let go, woman **6** bypass, damsel, escape, forego, lassie, maiden, miscue, pass by **7** blunder, colleen, default, failure, fly wide, let pass, let slip, long for, mistake, neglect, old maid, overrun, pine for **8** leave out, omission, overlook, pass over, senorita, slip up on, spinster, yearn for **9** disregard, fall short, false step, gloss over, go without, overshoot, oversight, surrender, young lady **10** demoiselle, schoolgirl **12** be absent from **13** feel the loss of, mademoiselle

missal 10 prayer book

missed
French: 6 manque

misshapen 7 twisted **8** deformed **9** contorted, distorted

missile 4 ball, dart **5** arrow, lance, shaft, shell, spear, stone **6** bullet, rocket **7** harpoon, javelin **10** projectile

missing 4 AWOL, gone, lost **6** absent **7** lacking, left out, not here **8** avoiding, skipping **10** longing for, not present **11** overlooking, yearning for **12** disregarding

Missing
director: 22 Constantine Costa-Gavras
cast: 8 John Shea **10** Jack Lemmon **11** Sissy Spacek **13** Melanie Mayron

Missing Persons and Other Essays
author: 12 Heinrich Boll

mission 3 end, job **4** task **5** quest **6** charge **7** calling, mandate, pursuit **8** legation, ministry **9** objective **10** assignment, commission, delegation, enterprise **11** raison d'etre, undertaking

Mission
tribe: 7 Chumash, Juaneno, Luiseno **8** Diegueno **9** Costanoan **10** Gabrielino **11** Fernandario
location: 10 California

Mississippi
abbreviation: 2 MS **4** Miss
nickname: 5 Bayou **6** Mudcat **8** Magnolia
capital/largest city: 7 Jackson
others: 6 Biloxi, Helena, Laurel, Tupelo, Winona **7** Belzoni, Corinth, Grenada, Natchez **8** Bogalusa, Columbus, Gulfport, Meridian **9** Kosciusko, Vicksburg **10** Clarksdale, Pascagoula **11** Hattiesburg **13** Pass Christian
college: 4 Rust **6** Alcorn **7** Jackson **8** Belhaven, Millsaps, Tougaloo **11** Mississippi **12** Blue Mountain, William Carey
feature: 12 Natchez Trace
***national military park:* 9** Vicksburg
***national seashore:* 11** Gulf Islands
tribe: 3 Sac **5** Tious **6** Biloxi, Mandan, Tunica **7** Choctaw, Natchez, Tonikan **8** Chicksaw
people: 11 Eudora Welty **15** William Faulkner **17** Tennessee Williams
***explorer:* 6** DeSoto, Joliet **9** Iberville, Marquette
island: 3 Cat **4** Horn, Ship **9** Petit Bois
lake: 4 Enid **6** Sardis **7** Barnett, Grenada **8** Pickwick **9** Arkabutla, Okatibbee
land rank: 12 thirty-second
highest point: 7 Woodall
physical feature:
***delta:* 10** Yazoo Basin
***hills:* 8** Fall Line **9** Tennessee **11** Loess Bluffs
***prairie:* 5** Black **7** Jackson
***sound:* 11** Mississippi
river: 4 Leaf **5** Pearl, Yazoo **8** Big Black **9** Tombigbee, Yalobusha **10** Homochitto, Pascagoula **11** Mississippi **12** Tallahatchie
state admission: 9 twentieth
state bird: 11 mockingbird
state flower: 8 magnolia
state motto: 14 By Valor and Arms
state song: 13 Go Mississippi
state tree: 8 magnolia

Mission: Impossible
character: **5** Casey, Paris **10** Rollin Hand **11** Dana Lambert, James Phelps **12** Daniel Briggs **13** Barney Collier **14** Cinnamon Carter, Willie Armitage
cast: **10** Greg Morris, Peter Lupus, Steven Hill **11** Barbara Bain, Peter Graves **12** Leonard Nimoy, Martin Landau **14** Lynda Day George **15** Lesley Ann Warren

Mississippi ***see box***

missive **4** note **6** billet, letter **7** epistle, message **13** communication **14** correspondence

Miss Julie
author: **16** August Strindberg

Miss Lonelyhearts
author: **13** Nathanael West

Missouri ***see box***

Miss Peach
creator: **11** Mell Lazarus
character: **3** Ira **6** Arthur, Lester, Marcia **8** Francine
place: **9** Kamp Kelly **11** Kelly School

misspend **5** waste **8** squander **9** dissipate, throw away **11** fritter away

misspent **6** wasted **8** depraved **9** debauched, dissolute, idled away **10** misapplied, profitless, squandered, thrown away

misstate **5** alter **6** bollix, garble **7** confuse, distort, falsify, pervert **8** misquote **9** misreport **12** misrepresent

misstatement **3** fib, lie **4** tale **5** error **7** falsity, untruth **9** falsehood **13** prevarication **17** misrepresentation

misstep **3** sin **4** goof, slip, vice **5** boner, error, fault, gaffe, lapse **6** boo-boo, defect, foul-up **7** blooper, faux pas, offense, screw-up **11** delinquency, dereliction, shortcoming **12** indiscretion **13** transgression

miss the mark **4** fail **9** fall short **11** come up short

miss the point **7** mistake **11** fail to catch, misconceive **12** misapprehend **13** misunderstand

mist **3** fog **4** haze, murk, smog **5** steam, vapor **7** drizzle

mistake **4** slip **5** boner, error, gaffe, mix-up **6** slipup **7** blooper, blunder, confuse, faux pas, misstep **8** confound, misjudge **9** misreckon, oversight **11** misconstrue, misidentify **12** misapprehend, miscalculate, misinterpret **13** misunderstand **14** miscalculation
French: **10** malentendu

mistaken **5** at sea, false, wrong **6** faulty, untrue **7** at fault, in error, unsound **8** deceived **9** erroneous, illogical, incorrect, off course, unfounded **10** fallacious, groundless, inaccurate, ungrounded **11** unjustified

Mister
Yiddish: **3** Reb

Mister Roberts
author: **12** Thomas Heggen
director: **8** John Ford **11** Mervyn LeRoy
cast: **8** Ward Bond **10** Henry Fonda, Jack Lemmon (Ensign Pulver) **11** Betsy Palmer, James Cagney **13** William Powell
Oscar for: **15** supporting actor (Lemmon)

Mister Saturday Night
nickname of: **13** Jackie Gleason

mistreat **4** harm **5** abuse, bully, hound, wrong **6** harass, ill-use, injure, misuse, molest **7** assault, oppress, outrage, pervert, torment, violate **8** ill-treat, maltreat **9** brutalize, manhandle, mishandle, persecute

mistreatment **5** abuse **6** ill-use, injury **7** assault, cruelty, harming **10** bodily harm, oppression **11** manhandling, molestation, persecution **12** maltreatment

mistress **3** Mrs **4** doxy, lady, Miss **5** lover, Madam **6** matron **8** ladylove, paramour **9** concubine, headwoman, housewife, inamorata, kept

---

Missouri
abbreviation: **2** MO
nickname: **5** Ozark **6** Show-Me **7** Bullion **15** Mother of the West
capital: **13** Jefferson City
largest city: **7** St Louis
others: **5** Eldon, Hayti, Lamar, Macon, Rolla **6** Butler, Joplin, Mexico **7** Bethany, Bolivar, Cameron, Clayton, Lebanon, Moberly, Sedalia **8** Berkeley, Columbia, Hannibal, Kirkwood, Sikeston, St Joseph **10** Bonne Terre, Kansas City **11** Springfield, Warrensburg **12** Independence **13** Cape Girardeau, Webster Groves
college: **5** Avila, Drury **6** Tarkio **7** Lincoln, St Louis, Webster **8** Stephens **10** Washington **11** Westminster
feature:
dam: **5** Osage
tribe: **3** Fox, Sac **4** Sauk **5** Osage **7** Shawnee **8** Cherokee, Missouri
people: **7** TS Eliot **9** Mark Twain **10** Jesse James **11** Omar Bradley **12** Helen Traubel, Sara Teasdale **13** John J Pershing, Marianne Moore, Samuel Clemens **15** Reinhold Niebuhr **22** George Washington Carver
explorer: **6** Joliet **7** La Salle **9** Marquette
lake: **7** Norfolk **9** Tablerock, Taneycomo **10** Bull Shoals **14** Kaysinger Bluff **15** Lake of the Ozarks
land rank: **10** nineteenth
mountain: **6** Ozarks **10** St Francois
highest point: **8** Taumsauk
physical feature: **8** Bootheel **9** Big Spring
plains: **4** Till **5** Osage
plateau: **5** Ozark
president: **12** Harry S Truman
river: **4** Salt **5** Grand, Osage, White **6** Platte **7** Current, Meramec **8** Big Muddy, Chariton, Missouri **9** Des Moines, Gasconade, St Francis **11** Mississippi
state admission: **12** twenty-fourth
state bird: **8** bluebird
state flower: **8** hawthorn
state motto: **41** The Welfare of the People Shall Be the Supreme Law
state song: **13** Missouri Waltz
state tree: **7** dogwood

woman **10** chatelaine, girlfriend, sweetheart

mistrust 5 doubt, qualm **7** anxiety, dubiety, suspect **8** distrust, question, wariness **9** challenge, chariness, leeriness, misgiving, suspicion **10** disbelieve, skepticism

misty 4 dewy, hazy **5** filmy, foggy, murky **6** cloudy, opaque, steamy **8** nebulous, overcast, vaporous **10** indistinct

misunderstand 7 confuse, misread, mistake **8** misjudge **9** misreckon **11** misconceive, misconstrue **12** misapprehend, miscalculate, misinterpret, miss the point

misunderstanding 4 rift, spat **5** set-to **7** discord, dispute, quarrel, wrangle **8** conflict, squabble **10** difference, dissension, misreading **11** altercation, contretemps, misjudgment **12** disagreement **13** misconception **15** false impression, misapprehension **16** miscomprehension **17** misinterpretation
French: 10 malentendu

misuse 4 harm, hurt **5** abuse, waste, wrong **6** debase, injure **7** corrupt, exploit, outrage, pervert, profane **8** ill-treat, maltreat, misapply, mistreat, wrong use **9** misemploy **10** corruption, perversion, prostitute **11** desecration, profanation, squandering **12** ill treatment, maltreatment, mistreatment, prostitution **13** misemployment **14** misapplication **15** take advantage of

Mitchell, Billy (William Lendrum)
advocate of: 8 air power
court-martialed for: 15 insubordination
served in: 3 WWI
rank: 16 brigadier general
commander of: 15 US army air forces

Mitchell, Margaret
author of: 15 Gone With the Wind

Mitchell, Silas Weir
author of: 9 Hugh Wynne (Free Quaker) **11** Roland Blake

Mitchell, Thomas
born: 11 Elizabeth NJ
roles: 7 Our Town **8** Doc Boone **9** The Outlaw **10** Stagecoach **11** Gerald O'Hara, Lost Horizon **15** Gone With the Wind **19** Only Angels Have Wings

Mitchell, William
real name of: 10 Peter Finch

Mitchum, Robert
born: 12 Bridgeport CT
roles: 6 Midway **10** Winds of War **11** Thunder Road **13** Ryan's Daughter, The Longest Day, The Sundowners **15** The Story of G I Joe **16** Farewell My Lovely **20** Heaven Knows Mr Allison

mite 3 bit, jot **4** atom, iota, whit **5** scrap, speck **6** spider **7** smidgen **8** arachnid, particle

Mitford, Jessica
author of: 21 The American Way of Death **22** Kind and Usual Punishment

Mitford, Nancy
author of: 14 Noblesse Oblige **16** The Pursuit of Love **18** Love in a Cold Climate

Mithgarthr *see* **7** Midgard

Mithraeum
temple of: 7 Mithras

Mithras
origin: 7 Persian
god of: 5 light, truth
corresponds to: 3 Sol

mitigate 4 ease **5** allay, blunt **6** lessen, reduce, soften, soothe, temper, weaken **7** assuage, lighten, mollify, placate, relieve **8** diminish, moderate, palliate **9** alleviate, extenuate **10** ameliorate

mitigating 6 easing **8** allaying, blunting, reducing **9** assuaging, lessening, relieving, softening, tempering **10** lightening, moderating, palliating, palliative **11** diminishing, extenuating **12** ameliorating

Mitrephorus
epithet of: 8 Dionysus
means: 15 headband-bearing

Mitteleuropa 12 middle Europe

mitzvah, mitsvah 8 good deed **11** commandment

mix 3 add **4** beat, club, fold, fuse, join, stir, whip **5** admix, alloy, blend, merge, put in, unite **6** commix, fusion, hobnob, mingle **7** combine, consort, include, mixture **8** assembly, coalesce, compound, intermix, mingling **9** associate, commingle, interfuse, interlard, introduce, socialize **10** amalgamate, fraternize, intertwine, interweave **11** incorporate, intermingle, intersperse, put together

mixed 4 coed **5** fused **6** hybrid, motley **7** alloyed, blended, inmixed, mingled, mongrel, not pure **8** combined **9** composite, uncertain **10** ambivalent, indecisive, interwoven, variegated **11** adulterated, diversified, half and half, put together **12** conglomerate, inconclusive **13** heterogeneous, male-and-female, miscellaneous

mixed-up 6 addled **7** chaotic, jumbled, muddled, tangled **8** confused, rambling **9** befuddled, illogical, nonplused, perplexed **10** bewildered, disjointed, incoherent, irrational, nonplussed **12** disconnected, disorganized **13** disharmonious, heterogeneous

Mixtec
tribe: 7 Zapotec

mixture 3 mix **4** hash, stew **5** alloy, blend, union **6** fusion, jumble, medley **7** amalgam, melange **8** compound, mishmash, pastiche **9** admixture, composite, potpourri **10** commixture, hodgepodge, salmagundi **11** association, combination **12** adulteration, amalgamation, intermixture

mixup 4 mess, riot **5** fight, melee **6** fracas, muddle, tangle **7** mistake **8** disorder **9** confusion, imbroglio **11** misjudgment **14** miscalculation **16** miscomprehension, misunderstanding

mix up 5 addle **6** mess up, muddle **7** confuse, nonplus, perplex **8** befuddle, bewilder **10** disarrange

Mneme
member of: 5 Muses
personifies: 6 memory

Mnemosyne
origin: 5 Greek
member of: 6 Titans
goddess of: 6 memory
father: 6 Uranus
mother: 4 Gaea
daughters: 5 Muses

Moabite god 7 Chemosh

moan 3 sob **4** keen, wail **5** groan **6** bemoan, bewail, lament, plaint **7** grumble **11** lamentation

moan over 5 mourn **6** bemoan, bewail, lament **7** cry over **8** weep over **10** grieve over

moat 4 foss **5** ditch, fosse, graff **6** gutter, rundel, trench

mob 4 gang, herd **5** crowd, crush, horde, Mafia, swarm **6** masses, rabble, throng

7 flock to 8 assembly, populace, surround 9 gathering, hoi polloi, multitude, plebeians, syndicate 10 converge on 11 proletariat, rank and file 14 organized crime

mobile 6 active, motile 7 kinetic, movable, nomadic 8 portable, rootless 9 footloose, traveling, wandering 10 ambulatory, locomotive

mobilize 6 call up, muster, summon 7 marshal 8 activate, organize 10 call to arms 11 put in motion

mobster 4 hood 6 hitman 7 hoodlum, Mafioso 8 gangster 10 gang member

Moby Dick
author: 14 Herman Melville
character: 4 Ahab 5 Stubb 7 Ishmael 8 Fedallah, Queequeg, Starbuck

mock 3 ape 4 copy 5 belie, mimic, scorn, spurn, taunt 6 deride, insult, jeer at, parody, revile, show up 7 imitate, laugh at, let down, profane, scoff at, sneer at 8 ridicule 9 burlesque, frustrate, make fun of, poke fun at 10 caricature, disappoint, make game of 11 make sport of

mockery 4 joke, sham 5 farce, scorn 7 jeering, mimicry, sarcasm 8 derision, raillery, ridicule, scoffing, travesty 9 burlesque, contumely 10 disrespect, ridiculing 13 laughingstock

Mock Turtle
character in: 28 Alice's Adventures in Wonderland
author: 7 Carroll

mode 3 cut, fad, way 4 form, rage, rule 5 craze, means, style, taste, trend, vogue 6 course, custom, manner, method, system 7 fashion, process 8 approach, practice 9 condition, procedure, technique 10 appearance

model 4 cast, copy, form, mold, show, type 5 build, dummy, ideal, shape, sport, style 6 design, mirror, mockup 7 display, example, fashion, outline, paragon, pattern, perfect, replica, subject, variety, version 8 exemplar, paradigm, peerless, standard 9 archetype, criterion, exemplary, facsimile, mannequin, prototype, simulated 10 simulacrum 14 representation, representative

model on 6 base on 7 found on 10 derive from

mode of operating
Latin: 2 mo 13 modus operandi

moderate 4 calm, cool, curb, fair, hush, mild, tame 5 abate, chair, sober 6 direct, gentle, lessen, manage, medium, modest, soften, subdue, temper 7 average, careful, conduct, control, oversee 8 diminish, measured, mediocre, middling, ordinary, passable, rational, regulate, restrain, tone down 9 judicious, peaceable, temperate, unruffled 10 not violent, reasonable 11 inexpensive, preside over 12 mainstreamer, medium-priced

moderation 7 abating, economy 8 allaying 9 abatement, frugality, lessening, remission, restraint 10 continence, diminution, mitigation, palliation, relaxation, temperance 11 alleviation, forbearance, self-control 12 moderateness 13 temperateness 14 abstemiousness 19 avoidance of extremes

moderator 8 chairman, mediator 10 chairwoman, negotiator

modern 3 new 6 modish, recent 7 current, in vogue 8 up-to-date 10 present-day 11 fashionable, streamlined 12 contemporary 15 contemporaneous 16 twentieth-century

Modern Comedy, A
author: 14 John Galsworthy

modernistic 6 modern 7 moderne 10 new-fangled 12 contemporary

modernity 5 vogue 7 fashion, new look, novelty, the rage 8 last word 14 newfangledness 15 contemporaneity 16 new fashionedness

modernize 4 redo 5 renew 6 do over, revamp, update 7 restore 8 redesign, renovate 9 refurbish 10 regenerate, rejuvenate, streamline 11 recondition 13 bring up to date 16 move with the times

modern times 5 today 8 nowadays 10 the present 13 the here and now

Modern Times
director: 14 Charles Chaplin
cast: 12 Henry Bergman 14 Charlie Chaplin, Chester Conklin 15 Paulette Goddard 19 Stanley "Tiny" Sandford

modest 3 coy, shy 4 meek, prim 5 plain, quiet, timid 6 demure, humble, proper, simple 7 bashful, limited, nominal, prudish, unshowy 8 blushing, discreet, moderate, reserved, timorous 9 diffident, shrinking 10 unassuming 11 circumspect, constrained, inexpensive, puritanical, strait-laced, unassertive, unobtrusive 12 medium-priced, not excessive, self-effacing, unpretending 13 unpretentious 14 unostentatious

modesty 7 coyness, prudery, reserve, shyness 8 humility, plainess, timidity 9 propriety, restraint, reticence 10 constraint, demureness, diffidence, humbleness, simplicity 11 bashfulness, naturalness 12 timorousness 14 reasonableness, self-effacement 15 inexpensiveness

modicum 3 bit, dab, jot 4 atom, dash, drop, inch, iota, mite, whit 5 crumb, grain, pinch, scrap, speck, tinge, touch 6 morsel, sliver, snatch, trifle 7 handful, minimum, smidgen 8 fraction, fragment, particle 9 little bit 10 sprinkling 11 small amount 13 small quantity

modification 6 change 8 revision 9 variation 10 adjustment, alteration, conversion, emendation, regulation 14 transformation 15 differentiation

modify 4 redo, vary 5 adapt, alter, limit, lower, remit 6 adjust, change, narrow, reduce, remold, revise, rework, soften, temper 7 control, convert, qualify, remodel, reshape 8 moderate, modulate, restrain, restrict, tone down 9 condition, refashion, transform, transmute 10 reorganize 12 transmogrify

Modigliani, Amedeo
born: 5 Italy 7 Leghorn, Livorno
artwork: 10 Seated Nude 13 Reclining Nude, Yellow Sweater 15 Jeanne Hebuterne

modish 2 in 3 now 4 chic 5 natty, nifty, sharp, smart, today 6 dapper, snazzy, spiffy, trendy, with it 7 a la mode, current, faddish, in style, in vogue, stylish, voguish 9 high-style 11 fashionable 13 up-to-the-minute

Modoc
language family: 12 Shapwailutan
division: 10 Lutuamnian
location: 6 Oregon 10 California

leader: 14 Chief Kintpuash (Captain Jack)
related to: 7 Klamath

Modred
character in: 16 Arthurian romance

Mod Squad, The
character: 9 Linc Hayes, (Capt) Adam Greer 11 Julie Barnes, Pete Cochran
cast: 11 Michael Cole, Peggy Lipton, Tige Andrews 19 Clarence Williams III

modulate 4 pass 5 lower 6 accord, attune, change, reduce, soften, temper 8 moderate, progress, regulate, tone down, turn down 9 harmonize

modulation 4 tone 5 pitch 6 accent 9 reduction 10 expression, regulation, transition

modus operandi 15 mode of operating
abbreviation: 2 mo

modus vivendi 14 manner of living

Moerae *see* 5 Fates

Mogadishu, Mogadiscio
capital of: 7 Somalia

mogul 3 VIP 4 czar, lord 5 baron, power, wheel 6 bigwig, tycoon 7 big shot, magnate, notable 8 big wheel 9 personage, potentate

Mohammed *see box*

Mohammedan 4 Sufi 6 Moslem, Muslim, Shiite 7 Islamic, Moorish, Sunnite 10 Mahometan, Muhammadan, Muhammedan

Mohave, Mojave
language family: 5 Yuman
location: 7 Arizona 10 California

Mohawk (Kaniengehaga)
language family: 9 Iroquoian
location: 6 Canada, Quebec 7 New York 11 Lake Ontario
leader: 8 Hiawatha 11 Joseph Brant
member of: 19 League of the Iroquois

Mohegan, Mohican, Mahican
language family: 9 Algonkian 10 Algonquian
location: 7 New York 9 Wisconsin 11 Connecticut 12 Hudson Valley
leader: 5 Occom, Uncas 12 Chingachgook
allied with: 6 Pequot
with Delaware: 11 Loup Indians, Wolf Indians

Mohammed
also: 7 Mahomet, Prophet 8 Muhammad
born: 5 Mecca
clan: 6 Hashim
daughter: 6 Fatima
deity: 5 Allah
died: 6 Medina
father: 8 Abdallah, Abdullah
father-in-law: 7 Abu Bakr, Abubekr
flight: 4 hadj 6 hegira, hejira
follower: 6 Moslem, Muslim, Wahbi 10 Mohammedan
grandfather: 13 Abd al-Muttalib
horse: 5 Buraq 7 Alborrak
mother: 5 Amina
religion: 5 Islam
shrine: 5 Kaaba
son: 7 Ibrahim
adopted: 3 Ali
successor: 4 imam 5 calif 6 caliph 7 Abu Bakr
tribe: 7 Koreish, Quraysh
uncle: 5 Abbas 8 Abu Talib
wife: 5 Aisha 6 Ayesha, Safiya 7 Khadija 8 Khadidja, Kadijah

subject of novel: 20 The Last of the Mohicans
author: 19 James Fenimore Cooper

Moira
personifies: 4 fate

Moirai *see* 5 Fates

moist 3 wet 4 damp, dank, dewy 5 humid, misty, muggy, rainy 6 clammy, drippy, watery 7 aqueous, drizzly, tearful, wettish, wet-eyed 8 dripping, vaporous 10 lachrymose

moisten 3 dew, wet 4 damp, hose, mist, soak 5 spray, water 6 dampen, douche, splash, sponge 8 humidify, irrigate, saturate, vaporize 10 moisturize

moisture 3 dew, wet 4 damp, mist 5 sweat, vapor 7 drizzle, exudate, wetness 8 dampness, dankness, humidity 9 moistness, mugginess 10 wateriness 11 evaporation 12 perspiration

Mojave *see* 6 Mohave

Moki *see* 4 Hopi

mold 3 cut, die, ilk 4 cast, form, kind, line, make, rust, sort, turn, type 5 brand, frame, knead, model, shape, stamp, train 6 blight, create, figure, fungus, kidney, lichen, matrix, mildew, render, sculpt, shaper 7 contour, convert, develop, fashion, outline, pattern, quality, remodel 9 character, construct, formation, structure, transform, transmute

moldy 5 fusty, hoary, musty, stale 7 spoiled 8 blighted, mildewed

Molech *see* 6 Moloch

molecular biology
study of: 9 molecules

molest 3 irk, vex 4 fret, harm, hurt 5 abuse, annoy, beset, harry, worry 6 attack, bother, harass, hector, injure, pester, plague 7 assault, disturb, torment, trouble 8 distress, ill-treat, irritate, maltreat

Moliere (Jean-Baptise Poquelin)
author of: 6 Scapin 8 Tartuffe, The Miser 10 Amphitryon 13 Le Misanthrope 17 The School for Wives 19 The Imaginary Invalid 20 The School for Husbands 22 Le Bourgeois Gentilhomme

Molione
son: 7 Cteatus, Eurytus

Moll Flanders
author: 11 Daniel Defoe
character: 5 Robin 6 Jemmy E 10 Sea Captain

mollification 8 soothing 9 placation 11 appeasement, assuagement 12 conciliation

mollify 4 calm, curb, dull, ease, lull 5 abate, allay, blunt, check, quell, quiet, still 6 lessen, pacify, reduce, soften, soothe, temper 7 appease, assuage, lighten, placate 8 decrease, mitigate, moderate, palliate, tone down 10 conciliate

mollusk 4 clam, slug 5 conch, cowry, murex, snail, squid, whelk 6 chiton, cockle, cowrie, limpet, mussel, oyster, teredo, triton 7 abalone, bivalve, geoduck, octopus, scallop 8 argonaut, nautilus, shipworm 9 shellfish 10 cuttlefish, nudibranch, periwinkle

Molly
author: 13 Samuel Beckett

mollycoddle 3 pet 4 baby, wimp 5 sissy, spoil 6 cosset, coward, pamper 7 cater to, crybaby, indulge, milksop 8 give in to, mama's boy, weakling **9** cream puff **11** milquetoast, overindulge

Molnar, Ferenc
author of: 6 Liliom **7** The Swan **12** The Guardsman

Moloch 3 god **5** diety
also: 6 Molech
worshiped by: 9 Ammonites

Molorchus
form: 7 peasant

Molossus
father: 11 Neoptolemus
mother: 10 Andromache

molt 4 cast, shed, slip **6** change, slough **7** castoff, discard, ecdysis **8** exuviate

molten 6 melted, red-hot **7** fusible, igneous, smelted **8** magmatic **9** liquefied

molto
music: 4 very

Molus
father: 4 Ares
mother: 8 Demonice
son: 8 Meriones

Moly
form: 4 herb
given to: 8 Odysseus
given by: 6 Hermes
to counteract spells of: 5 Circe

Momaday, N Scott
author of: 18 The House Made of Dawn **21** The Way to Rainy Mountain

moment 5 flash, jiffy, trice, value, worth **6** import, minute, second, weight **7** concern, gravity, instant **8** interest, juncture **9** twinkling **10** importance **11** consequence, weightiness **12** significance

momentary 5 brief, hasty, quick, short **6** sudden **7** instant, passing **8** flashing, fleeting, fugitive, imminent **9** ephemeral, immediate, temporary, transient **10** short-lived, transitory **13** instantaneous

momentous 5 grave **7** crucial, fateful, salient, serious, weighty **8** critical, decisive, eventful **9** essential, important, ponderous **11** far-reaching, influential, significant, substantial **12** earthshaking **13** consequential

momentous occurrence
5 event **8** occasion **9** milestone **12** red-letter day, turning point

momentum 2 go **4** dash, push **5** drive, force, speed, vigor **6** energy, moment, thrust **7** headway, impetus, impulse **8** velocity **10** propulsion

Mommsen, Theodor
author of: 16 The History of Rome

Momus
also: 5 Momos
god of: 7 censure **8** ridicule

Monaco ***see box***

Monaco-Ville
capital of: 6 Monaco

monarch 3 HRH **4** czar, doge, emir, khan, king, rani, shah **5** rajah, ruler, queen **6** kaiser, prince **7** czarina, emperor, empress, majesty, pharaoh **8** kaiserin, princess **9** chieftain, potentate

monarchical 9 czaristic **10** autocratic **11** dictatorial

monastery 5 abbey **6** friary, priory **7** convent, nunnery, retreat **8** cloister

monastic 7 ascetic, monkish, recluse **8** celibate, hermitic, secluded, solitary **9** cloistral, reclusive, unworldly **10** cloistered, hermitlike **11** sequestered **13** contemplative

mon cher 6 my dear

Moncrieff, Algernon (Algy)
character in: 27 The Importance of Being Earnest
author: 5 Wilde

Mond, Mustapha
character in: 13 Brave New World
author: 6 Huxley

Monday
French: 5 lundi
German: 6 montag
heavenly body: 4 moon
Italian: 6 lunedi
means: 12 day of the moon
Spanish: 5 lunes

Mondrian, Piet
real name: 23 Pieter Cornelis Mondriaan
born: 10 Amersfoort **14** The Netherlands
artwork: 5 Trees **10** The Red Tree **12** Ocean and Pier **17** Evening Landscapes **18** Landscape with a Mill **20** Broadway Boogie-Woogie **29** Composition in Red Yellow and Blue

Monet, Claude Oscar
born: 5 Paris **6** France
artwork: 7 Poplars **9** Haystacks, The Thames **11** Water Lilies **14** Rouen Cathedral **16** Women in the Garden **17** Impression Sunrise **18** Mornings on the Seine **21** The Bridge at Argenteuil

Moneta
epithet of: 4 Juno
means: 7 advisor

monetary 6 fiscal **9** budgetary,

Monaco
capital: 11 Monaco-Ville
largest city: 10 Monte Carlo
others: 9 Fontville
division: 9 Fontville **10** Monte Carlo **11** La Condamine, Monaco-Ville
head of government: 15 minister of state
head of state: 6 prince
monetary unit: 5 franc **7** centime
river: 7 Vesubie
sea: 13 Mediterranean
physical feature: 9 Cote d'Azur
people: 6 French **7** Italian **10** Monegasque
***oceanographer:* 15** Jacques Cousteau
***prince:* 5** Louis **6** Albert, Honore **7** Antoine, Charles, Rainier **9** Florestan
***princess:* 10** Grace Kelly
***ruler:* 4** Rome **5** Genoa **6** Greece **8** Grimaldi, Saracens **9** Phoenicia
language: 6 French **7** English, Italian **10** Monegasque
religion: 13 Roman Catholic
place:
***beach:* 8** Larvotto
***casino:* 10** Monte Carlo
***gardens:* 6** Exotic
***museum:* 12** Oceanography
***park:* 18** Princess Antoinette
feature:
***auto race:* 15** Monaco Grand Prix

financial, pecuniary, sumptuary

money **4** cash, coin **5** bread, bucks, dough, funds **6** assets, riches, specie, wealth **7** capital, coinage, payment, revenue, scratch **8** currency, hard cash, proceeds **9** affluence, long green **10** collateral, greenbacks **11** wherewithal

money-carrier
French: **12** porte-monnaie

moneyed, monied **4** rich **5** flush, swell **6** flashy, loaded **7** elegant, opulent, solvent, wealthy **8** affluent **10** prosperous

money-grubbing **5** venal **6** greedy **8** covetous, grasping **9** mercenary **10** avaricious

money lender **6** banker, lender, usurer **7** lombard, shylock **9** loanshark **10** pawnbroker

money saved **7** nest egg, savings **10** investment

money spent **6** outlay **7** payment **8** expenses **11** expenditure

Mongolia ***see box***

Mongolian
language family: **6** Altaic
group: **6** Buryat **7** Khalkha

Mongoose, The
nickname of: **11** Archie Moore

mongrel **3** cur **4** mutt **5** mixed **6** hybrid **7** bastard **8** offshoot **9** anomalous, crossbred **10** crossbreed

moniker **3** tag **4** name **5** label, title **6** eponym, handle **7** epithet, surname **8** cognomen, nickname, taxonomy **9** sobriquet **11** appellation, designation **12** denomination

monitor **2** TV **4** tend **5** guide, teach **6** censor, direct, pickup, police, screen, sensor **7** oversee, proctor, scanner **8** overseer, watchdog **9** supervise **14** disciplinarian

monk **4** abbe **5** abbot, friar **6** hermit **7** brother, holy man, recluse **8** cenobite, monastic **9** anchorite
French: **5** frere

Monk, The
author: **19** Matthew Gregory Lewis

Monkees, The
cast/musician: **9** Davy Jones, Peter Tork **10** David Jones **11** Micky Dolenz, Mike Nesmith

Mongolia
other name: **13** Outer Mongolia
capital/largest city: **9** Ulan Bator
others: **5** Kobdo **6** Darhan **10** Choibalsan, Sukhe Bator, Tsetserlik, Uliassutai
ancient capital: **9** Karakoram
government:
legislature: **17** People's Great Hural **18** People's Great Khural
monetary unit: **5** mongo, mungo **6** tugrik **7** tughrik
weight: **3** lan
lake: **3** Uvs **5** Har Us **6** Bor Nor **7** Ghirgis, Ubsa Nor **8** Airik Nor, Durga Nor, Hobsogol, Khara Usu **9** Khubsugul, Khukhu-Nur **10** Khirgis Nor
mountain: **4** Cast, Orog **5** Altai **6** Kentei, Sevrej **7** Ich Ovoo, Khangai, Khentei **8** Tannu-Ola **9** Edrengijn **10** Cagaan Bogd **11** Munky Sardyk **14** Hangayn-Hentiyn, Monch Chajrchan
highest point: **10** Tabun Bogdo
river: **3** Tes **4** Egin, Onon, Tuul, Uldz **5** Kobdo, Tesin **6** Orkhon **7** Kerulen, Selenga, Selenge **8** Dzabkhan, Dzavchan
physical feature:
desert: **4** Gobi **5** Ordos, Shamo
plateau: **8** Mongolia
region: **10** Great Lakes
people: **5** Oirat, Tungu **6** Buryat, Darbet, Khoton, Mongol **7** Kazakhs, Khalkha **8** Tuvinian **9** Dariganga
leader: **8** Jahangir, Jehangir **10** Kublai Khan, Tsendenbal **11** Genghis Khan
ruler: **4** Huns **5** Ching **6** Manchu **7** Kirghiz, Uighurs **8** Hsiung-nu
spiritual/secular ruler: **12** Living Buddha **21** Jebtsun Damba Khutu Khtu
language: **6** Kazakh **16** Khalkha Mongolian
religion: **7** Lamaism **9** Shamanism **15** Tibetan Buddhism
place:
monastery: **6** Gandun
feature:
felt tent: **4** yurt
nomadic herder: **4** arat
food:
fermented mare's milk: **5** airag

monkey **3** ape, ass, toy **4** butt, dupe, fool, jerk **5** clown, jimmy **6** baboon, fiddle, meddle, simian, tamper, tinker, trifle **7** buffoon, primate **13** laughingstock
group of: **5** troop
god: **7** Hanuman
kind: **3** owl **4** saki, titi **5** aotus, lemur **6** baboon, guenon, howler, langur, rhesus, spider **7** colobus, Goeldi's, guereza, macaque, tamarin, tarsier, uakaris **8** capuchin, mandrill, marmoset, squirrel, talapoin **11** douroucouli

monkey business **6** capers **9** highjinks **11** shenanigans

monkeyshines **6** antics, capers, pranks **7** hijinks **10** buffoonery, tomfoolery **11** foolishness

Monks (Edward Leeford)
character in: **11** Oliver Twist
author: **7** Dickens

monocle **4** quiz **5** glass **7** lorgnon **8** eyeglass

Monoclonius
type: **8** dinosaur **10** ceratopsid
location: **12** North America
characteristic: **6** horned

Monod, Jacques
field: **7** biology
nationality: **6** French
researched: **3** RNA **8** genetics
awarded: **10** Nobel Prize

monograph **8** tractate, treatise **9** discourse **12** disquisition, dissertation

monolith **5** stone **6** column, menhir, pillar, statue **7** obelisk **8** memorial, monument

monologue, monolog
6 screed, sermon, speech **7** address, lecture, oration **9** discourse, soliloquy
11 expatiation **12** disquisition

monopolize **3** own **6** absorb, corner, manage, take up
7 consume, control, preempt
8 arrogate, dominate, regulate, take over **9** cartelize
11 appropriate

monopoly **4** bloc **5** trust **6** cartel, corner **7** combine, control
8 dominion **9** copyright, ownership, syndicate **10** consortium, domination
11 sovereignty **12** jurisdiction
14 proprietorship

monotonous **3** dry **4** dull, flat
5 banal **6** boring, dreary, jejune, stodgy, torpid **7** droning, humdrum, insipid, mundane, prosaic, routine, tedious
8 plodding, singsong, tiresome, toneless, unvaried **9** colorless, soporific, wearisome **10** pedestrian **11** repetitious, somniferous **13** uninteresting

monotony **3** rut **5** ennui **6** tedium **7** boredom, humdrum
8 dullness, flatness, prosaism, sameness **9** iteration **10** dreariness, redundancy, uniformity
11 reiteration, tediousness
13 wearisomeness
14 predictability

Monroe, Earl
nickname: **12** Earl the Pearl
sport: **10** basketball
position: **5** guard
team: **16** Baltimore Bullets
21 New York Knickerbockers

Monroe, James ***see box***

Monroe, Marilyn
real name: **23** Norma Jean Mortenson Baker
husband: **11** Joe DiMaggio
12 Arthur Miller
born: **12** Los Angeles CA
roles: **7** Bus Stop, Niagara
10 The Misfits **13** Some Like It Hot **16** The Seven-Year Itch **22** Gentlemen Prefer Blondes, How To Marry a Millionaire **23** The Prince and the Showgirl

Monrovia
capital of: **7** Liberia

monseigneur **6** my lord

monsieur **2** Mr **3** sir **6** mister, my lord

Monsieur Beaucaire
author: **15** Booth Tarkington

Monsignor Quixote
author: **12** Graham Greene

Monroe, James
presidential rank: **5** fifth
party: **20** Democratic-Republican
state represented: **2** VA
defeated: **4** (Rufus) King **5** (John Quincy) Adams
vice president: **8** (Daniel D) Tompkins
cabinet:
state: **5** (John Quincy) Adams
treasury: **8** (William Harris) Crawford
war: **7** (John Caldwell) Calhoun
attorney general: **4** (Richard) Rush, (William) Wirt
navy: **8** (Samuel Lewis) Southard, (Smith) Thompson
13 (Benjamin Williams) Crowninshield
born: **2** VA **18** Westmoreland County
died: **13** New York City NY
buried: **10** Richmond VA
education: **14** William and Mary (did not graduate)
religion: **12** Episcopalian
author: **67** A View of the Conduct of the Executive in the Foreign Affairs of the United States
political career: **8** US Senate
governor of: **8** Virginia
minister: **5** Spain **6** France **12** Great Britain
secretary of: **3** war **5** state
civilian career: **6** lawyer
military service: **5** major **7** captain **10** lieutenant **16** Revolutionary War **17** lieutenant colonel
wounded in Battle of: **7** Trenton
notable events of lifetime/term: **5** Panic (of 1819)
14 Monroe Doctrine
Agreement: **9** Rush-Bagot
Compromise: **8** Missouri
war: **8** Seminole
father: **6** Spence
mother: **9** Elizabeth (Jones)
siblings: **6** Andrew, Spence **9** Elizabeth **11** Joseph Jones
wife: **9** Elizabeth (Kortright)
nickname: **5** Eliza
children: **11** Maria Hester **14** Eliza Kortright

monster **4** Fury **5** beast, brute, demon, devil, fiend, freak, ghoul, giant, golem, harpy, hydra, satyr, titan **6** dragon, gorgon, marvel, oddity, savage, threat, wonder, wretch, zombie **7** anomaly, caitiff, centaur, chimera, deviant, incubus, mammoth, mermaid, vampire, variant, villain **8** bogeyman, colossus, gargoyle, succubus, werewolf **9** barbarian, curiosity, cutthroat, scoundrel **10** blackguard, phenomenon **11** abnormality, miscreation **12** Frankenstein, lusus naturae

monstrosity **5** freak **7** monster

monstrous **4** bald, evil, huge
5 cruel, giant **6** grisly, mighty, odious **7** ghastly, harried, heinous, hideous, hulking, immense, mammoth, obscene, obvious, satanic, titanic, vicious **8** colossal, enormous, fiendish, flagrant, gigantic, gruesome, horrible, outright, shocking **9** atrocious, egregious, nefarious, revolting
10 diabolical, gargantuan, outrageous, prodigious, scandalous, stupendous, tremendous, villainous **14** Brobdingnagian

monstrousness **8** baseness, enormity, evilness, vileness, villainy **9** barbarity, depravity, malignity **10** inhumanity, wickedness **11** heinousness, viciousness **13** atrociousness, offensiveness **14** outrageousness

Montagnais-Naskapi (Innu)
language family: **9** Algonkian **10** Algonquian
tribe: **8** Nascapee **9** Mistassin
10 Bersiamite, Montagnais
11 Papinachois
location: **5** Maine **6** Canada, Quebec **17** Maritime Provinces
occupation: **7** hunters **10** fur traders

Montague family
characters in: **14** Romeo and Juliet
author: **11** Shakespeare

Montaigne, Michel de
author of: **6** Essais, Essays

Montalban, Ricardo
born: **6** Mexico **10** Mexico City
roles: **4** Khan **8** Mr Roarke **9** The Colbys **13** Fantasy Island **24** Star Trek II The Wrath of Khan

Montalvo, Garcia de
author of: **12** Amadis of Gaul

Montana *see box*

Montana, Bob
creator/artist of: **6** Archie

Montand, Yves
real name: **7** Ivo Livi
wife: **14** Simone Signoret
born: **5** Italy **14** Monsummano Alto
roles: **1** Z **12** Let's Make Love **14** Is Paris Burning?

montani semper liberi
28 mountaineers are always free men
motto of: **12** West Virginia

Montcalm, Louis Joseph
also: **17** Marquis de Montcalm
nationality: **6** French
served in: **18** French and Indian War
battle: **6** Oswego, Quebec (siege) **8** Carillon **11** Ticonderoga **16** Fort William Henry
killed in battle at: **6** Quebec **15** Plains of Abraham

mont-de-piete **10** pawnbroker
literally: **10** bank of pity

Montenegro *see box*

Monteverdi, Claudio
born: **5** Italy **7** Cremona
composer of: **5** Adone, Orfeo **7** Arianna **14** La Favola d'Orfeo **17** The Fable of Orpheus **21** The Coronation of Poppea **22** L'incoronazione di Poppea **24** Il Ritorno d'Ulisse in patria **34** Il Combattimento di Tancredi e Clorinda

Montevideo
capital of: **7** Uruguay

Montana
abbreviation: **2** MT **4** Mont
nickname: **6** Big Sky **7** Bonanza, Stubtoe **8** Mountain, Treasure
capital: **6** Helena
largest city: **8** Billings
others: **4** Kipp **5** Butte, Haure, Havre, Malta **6** Hardin **7** Bozeman, Chinook, Choteau, Glasgow, Roundup **8** Anaconda, Forsythe, Missoula **9** Kalispell **10** Great Falls
college: **7** Carroll **10** Great Falls **13** Rocky Mountain
feature: **17** Continental Divide
cemetery: **6** Custer
national park: **7** Glacier **11** Yellowstone
tribe: **4** Cree, Crow, Hohe **5** Sioux **6** Atsima, Atsina, Salish **7** Arapaho, Bannock, Kutenai, Siksika **8** Cheyenne, Chippewa, Flatfoot, Flathead, Shoshone **9** Blackfeet **11** Assiniboine
people: **8** Myrna Loy **9** Will James **10** Gary Cooper **14** Charles Russell **15** Jeannette Rankin
explorer: **13** Lewis and Clark **16** Pierre Jean de Smet
lake: **5** Tiber **6** Hebgen **8** Flathead, Fort Peck, Medicine **10** Yellowtail **11** Canyon Ferry, Hungry Horse
land rank: **6** fourth
mountain: **4** Ajax **5** Baldy, Cowan, Crazy, Lewis **6** Sphinx, Torrey **7** Bighorn, Big Belt, Hilgard, Purcell, Rockies, Trapper **8** Absaroka, Gallatin, Pentagon, Snowshoe
highest point: **11** Granite Peak
physical feature: **10** Great Falls
river: **3** Sun **4** Milk **5** Clark, Teton **6** Marias, Powder, Tongue, Willow **7** Madison, Shields **8** Columbia, Kootenai, Missouri **9** Blackfoot **10** Bitterroot **11** Musselshell, Yellowstone
state admission: **10** forty-first
state bird: **17** western meadowlark
state fish: **26** black-spotted cutthroat trout
state flower: **10** bitterroot
state motto: **13** Gold and Silver
state song: **7** Montana
state tree: **13** Ponderosa pine

Montenegro
name means: **13** black mountain
other name: **4** Zeta **8** Crna Gora
capital: **7** Cetinje **8** Titograd **9** Podgorica
cities: **3** Bar **5** Kotor, Tivat **6** Niksic, Ulcinj **8** Antivari, Dulcigno, Ivangrad, Pljevlja **10** Hercegnovi **11** Sveti Stefan
division:
Roman province: **7** Illyria
government: **20** republic of Yugoslavia
monetary unit: **4** para **6** florin **7** perpera
lake: **7** Scutari, Shkoder
mountain: **8** Durmitor **11** Dinaric Alps
river: **3** Lim **4** Diva, Tara, Zeta **6** Moraca **7** Ceotina
sea: **8** Adriatic
physical feature:
gulf: **5** Kotor
people: **4** Serb, Slav **11** Montenegrin
former ruler (Orthodox bishop): **7** vladike **8** vladlika
language: **13** Serbo-Croatian
religion: **16** Serbian Orthodoxy

Montgomery, Bernard Law *see box*

Montgomery, Robert
real name: **17** Henry Montgomery Jr
daughter: **9** Elizabeth
born: **8** Beacon NY
roles: **11** The Big House **13** Night Must Fall **17** Here Comes Mr Jordan

month
abbreviation: **2** mo

Month in the Country, A
author: **12** Ivan Turgenev

months, Hebrew *see box*

Mont-Oriol
author: **15** Guy de Maupassant

Montreal *see box*

Montresor
character in: **20** The Cask of Amontillado
author: **3** Poe

Mont Saint Michel and Chartres
author: **10** Henry Adams

Montgomery, Bernard Law
also: **27** (first) Viscount Montgomery of Alamein
author of: **7** Memoirs **17** A History of Warfare
battle: **9** El Alamein
chief: **19** British general staff
commander of: **17** British Eighth Army **32** British occupation forces in Germany
commando raid: **6** Dieppe
deputy supreme commander: **4** NATO
Eighth Army called: **10** Desert Rats
evacuation of: **7** Dunkirk
fought against: **6** Rommel **11** Africa Corps, Afrika Korps
invasion: **6** Sicily **8** Normandy
member: **12** House of Lords
nationality: **7** British
nickname: **5** Monty
served in: **3** WWI **4** WWII

months, Hebrew
first: **4** Ahib, Nisn **6** Ehanim, Tishri
second: **3** Bul, Civ **4** Iyar **7** Heshvan
third: **5** Sivan **6** Kislev
fourth: **5** Tebet **6** Tammuz, Tebeth
fifth: **2** Ab **7** Shelbat
sixth: **4** Adar, Elul **6** Veadar
seventh: **4** Abib **5** Nisan **6** Tishri **7** Ethanim
eighth: **3** Zif **4** Iyar **11** Marcheshvan
ninth: **5** Sivan **7** Chislev
tenth: **6** Tebeth, Tammuz
eleventh: **2** Ab **6** Shabat
twelfth: **4** Adar, Elul

Monty
nickname of: **15** Montgomery Clift **17** (General) Bernard Montgomery

monument **4** slab **5** token **6** shrine **7** memento, obelisk, witness **8** cenotaph, memorial, monolith, reminder **9** testament, tombstone **10** gravestone **11** remembrance, testimonial **13** commemoration

Montreal
airport: **6** Dorval **8** St Hubert **12** Cartierville
baseball team: **5** Expos
founder: **11** Maisonneuve
hill: **10** Mount Royal
hockey team: **9** Canadiens
island: **5** Jesus **6** Bizard, Perrot **8** Montreal **9** des Soeurs **14** de Boucherville
lake: **7** St Louis
landmark: **12** Place des Arts **13** Molson Stadium **16** Chateau de Ramezay **17** Church of Notre Dame, St Sulpice Seminary **21** Man and His World Exhibit
original name: **10** Ville-Marie
province: **6** Quebec
river: **6** Ottawa **10** St Lawrence **11** des Prairies **14** des Milles Isles
subway: **5** Metro
university: **6** McGill

monumental **4** huge **5** fatal, heavy **7** awesome, classic, epochal, immense, lasting, massive **8** colossal, decisive, enduring, gigantic, historic, immortal, statuary **9** cyclopean, egregious, memorable **10** horrendous, monolithic, shattering, stupendous **11** inestimable **12** catastrophic **13** unprecedented

mooch **3** beg, bum **5** cadge **6** hustle, sponge **7** solicit **8** freeload

mood **5** blues, dumps, humor **6** spirit, temper **7** feeling **8** doldrums, vexation **9** condition **10** depression, gloominess, melancholy **11** disposition, melancholia, temperament **14** predisposition **16** hypersensitivity

moody **4** mean **5** sulky, surly, testy **6** crabby, dismal, fickle, gloomy, mopish, morbid, morose, sullen **7** erratic, flighty, peevish, unhappy **8** brooding, dejected, notional, variable, volatile **9** impetuous, impulsive, irascible, irritable, mercurial, saturnine, whimsical **10** capricious, changeable, despondent, inconstant, lugubrious, melancholy **11** pessimistic **12** inconsistent **13** temperamental, unpredictable

Mookerjee, Hurree Chunder
character in: **3** Kim
author: **7** Kipling

moon **4** gape, lamp, luna, roam **5** dream, month, stare **6** dawdle, wander **8** daydream **9** satellite
god of: **3** Sin **5** Nanna **6** Meztli
goddess of: **4** Luna **5** Diana, Holle, Tanit **6** Hecate, Hekate, Phoebe, Selena, Selene, Tanith **7** Artemis, Astarte, Cynthia
full: **9** plenilune
new: **5** prime
waning: **7** waiand

Moon and Sixpence, The
author: **16** W Somerset Maugham

moonless **4** dark **5** black, murky **7** stygian **9** lightless, unlighted **13** unilluminated

Moonlighting
character: **11** Maddie Hayes **12** Agnes Dipesto, David Addison
cast: **11** Bruce Willis **13** Allyce Beasley **14** Cybill Shepherd
detective agency: **8** Blue Moon

Moon Mullins
creator: **12** Frank Willard
character: **4** Kayo **5** Mamie **9** Mushmouth **11** Uncle Willie **15** Lady Plushbottom, Lord Plushbottom **16** Moonshine Mullins

Moon of the Caribbees, The
author: **12** Eugene O'Neill

moonshine **5** hokum **6** bunkum, humbug **7** bootleg **8** clockade, homebrew, malarky, nonsense **10** balderdash, bathtub gin **11** mountain dew

moonstone
species: **8** feldspar
source: **5** Burma, Mogok

Moonstone, The
author: **13** Wilkie Collins
character: **7** Dr Candy **12** Lady Verinder, Sergeant Cuff **13** Franklin Blake **14** John Herncastle, Rachel Verinder **15** Rosanna Spearman **16** Godfrey Ablewhite

moor **3** fen **4** dock, down, fell, lash, wold **5** affix, berth, chain, heath, marsh, tie up **6** anchor, attach, fasten, secure, steppe, tether, tundra, upland **7** savanna, tie down **8** make fast **9** wasteland

Moore, Archie
nickname: **11** The Mongoose

real name: 18 Archibald Lee Wright
sport: 6 boxing
class: 16 light-heavyweight

Moore, Clement C
author of: 23 A Visit from Saint Nicholas

Moore, Dick
creator/artist of: 13 Gasoline Alley

Moore, Dudley
nickname: 12 Cuddly Dudley
wife: 11 Suzy Kendall, Tuesday Weld
born: 5 Essex 7 England 8 Dagenham
roles: 3 Ten 6 Arthur 8 Lovesick, Six Weeks 9 Bedazzled 13 Micki and Maude 16 Arthur on the Rocks 17 Like Father Like Son
plays: 5 piano

Moore, George
author of: 12 Esther Waters 15 Hail and Farewell

Moore, Henry
born: 7 England 10 Castleford
artwork: 4 Mask 8 Two Forms 9 North Wind 10 Bird Basket 11 Family Group, Head of a Girl 12 Locking Piece 13 Nuclear Energy 15 Reclining Figure 20 Four-Piece Composition

Moore, Marianne
author of: 12 Like a Bulwark, Nevertheless, O To Be a Dragon, Tell Me Tell Me

Moore, Mary Tyler
husband: 11 Grant Tinker
born: 10 Brooklyn NY
roles: 4 Mary 12 Mary Richards 14 Ordinary People 18 The Dick Van Dyke Show 21 The Mary Tyler Moore Show

Moore, Mrs
character in: 15 A Passage to India
author: 7 Forster

Moore, Roger
born: 6 London 7 England
roles: 8 The Saint 12 Simon Templar
as James Bond: 9 Moonraker, Octopussy 13 Live and Let Die 16 The Spy Who Loved Me 22 The Man with the Golden Gun

Moorehead, Agnes
born: 9 Clinton MA
roles: 6 Endora 9 Bewitched 11 Citizen Kane 13 Johnny Belinda 15 Dear Dead Delilah 20 Magnificent Obsession 23 The Magnificent Ambersons

mooring 4 hook, line, rope 5 cable, chain 6 anchor, hawser

moot 4 open 7 eristic 8 arguable, disputed 9 debatable, undecided, unsettled 10 disputable, unresolved 11 conjectural 12 questionable 13 controversial, problematical 14 controvertible

mope 4 fret, pine, pout, sulk 5 brood, worry 6 grieve, grouse, lament, repine 7 grumble 8 languish

Mopsus
occupation: 4 seer
mother: 5 Manto
grandfather: 8 Tiresias
member of: 9 Argonauts
founded: 6 oracle
location: 6 Mallus 7 Cilicia
cofounder: 11 Amphilochus
epithet: 9 Ampycides

moral 3 tag 4 fair, just, pure 5 adage, maxim, motto, noble, right 6 honest, lesson, proper, saying 7 epigram, ethical, message, proverb, saintly 8 aphorism, didactic, personal, virtuous 9 estimable, homiletic, honorable, preaching 10 aboveboard, high-minded, principled 11 meritorious, sermonizing, tendentious 12 conscionable

moral code 6 ethics 9 integrity, standards 10 principles

morale 4 mood 6 spirit, temper 10 confidence, resolution 11 disposition
French: 13 esprit de corps

morality 5 honor 6 ethics, habits, tastes, virtue 7 modesty, probity 8 fairness, goodness 9 integrity, rectitude 10 chasteness 11 uprightness 13 righteousness

moralize 6 preach 7 lecture

moralizing 7 preachy 8 didactic 9 homiletic

morally corrupt 6 effete 8 decadent, depraved 10 degenerate

moral sense 9 integrity 10 conscience

morass 3 bog, fen 4 mire 5 marsh, swamp 6 slough 8 quagmire, wetlands 9 quicksand

morbid 3 sad 4 dour, glum, grim 5 moody 6 gloomy, morose, somber 8 brooding 9 depressed, saturnine 10 despondent, lugubrious 11 melancholic, pessimistic, unwholesome

morbid condition 6 malady 7 ailment, disease, illness 8 sickness 9 infirmity

Morcerf, Comte de (Fernand)
character in: 21 The Count of Monte Cristo
author: 5 Dumas (pere)

mordant 6 biting, bitter 7 acerbic, caustic, cutting, waspish 8 incisive, piercing, scathing, scornful, stinging, venomous, virulent 9 acidulous, malicious, sarcastic, trenchant 11 acrimonious

Mordecai
cousin: 6 Esther
served: 15 Ahasuerus Xerxes
enemy: 5 Haman

more 5 added, extra, other, spare 6 longer 7 further, reserve 10 additional 12 additionally, supplemental 13 supplementary

More, Thomas
author of: 6 Utopia

Moreau, Frederic
character in: 21 A Sentimental Education
author: 8 Flaubert

Moreau, Gustave
born: 5 Paris 6 France
artwork: 7 Orpheus 13 Dance of Salome (Salome Dancing), The Apparition 16 Hesiod and the Muse 18 The Poet and the Siren 19 Oedipus and the Sphinx 27 Diomedes Devoured by His Horses

Morehouse, J Ward
character in: 3 USA
author: 9 Dos Passos

Morel, Paul
character in: 13 Sons and Lovers
author: 8 Lawrence

Moreno, Rita
real name: 20 Rosita Dolores Alverio
born: 7 Humacao 10 Puerto Rico
roles: 13 Pagan Love Song, The Deerslayer, West Side Story 15 Singin' in the Rain

more or less 5 about 6 around 8 somewhat 9 generally, just about 13 approximately

moreover 3 too 4 also 7 besides, further 11 furthermore 12 more than that

mores 4 code 5 ethos, forms, rules 6 usages 7 customs, rituals 9 etiquette, practices, standards 10 traditions

11 conventions, observances, proprieties

more than enough **5** ample **6** excess, plenty **7** copious, profuse **8** plethora **9** abundance, amplitude, bountiful, excessive, profusion **10** oversupply

Morgan, Daniel
served in: **16** Revolutionary War
commander of: **8** riflemen **13** sharpshooters
battle: **7** Cowpens **8** Saratoga **12** Bemis Heights, Freeman's Farm
helped suppress: **16** Whiskey Rebellion

Morgan, Thomas Hunt
founder of: **8** genetics
awarded: **10** Nobel Prize

Morgan, William De
author of: **11** Joseph Vance

Morgan family
characters in: **19** How Green Was My Valley
members: **4** Beth, Davy, Huur, Ivor, Owen **5** Ianto **6** Gwilym **8** Angharad
author: **9** Llewellyn

morganite
color: **4** pink **5** peach

Morgan le Fay
character in: **16** Arthurian romance

Moriae Encomium (In Praise of Folly)
author: **7** Erasmus

Moriarty, Professor
character in: **14** (The Adventures of) Sherlock Holmes
author: **10** Conan Doyle

moribund **5** dying **6** doomed, waning **10** stagnating

Morier, James
author of: **18** Hajji Baba of Ispahan

morituri te salutamus **28** we who are about to die salute thee
said by: **15** Roman gladiators
said to: **13** Roman emperors

Mork & Mindy
character: **4** Mork **6** Eugene **10** Cora Hudson **13** Mindy McConnel **17** Frederick McConnel
cast: **9** Pam Dawber **11** Conrad Janis **13** Elizabeth Kerr, Robin Williams **14** Jeffrey Jacquet
Mork's planet: **3** Ork
phrase: **8** nanu nanu
spinoff from: **9** Happy Days

Morland, Catherine
character in: **15** Northanger Abbey
author: **6** Austen

Morley, Robert
born: **6** Semley **7** England
roles: **5** Melba **10** Oscar Wilde **11** Beau Brummel, Edward My Son **12** Major Barbara **15** Marie Antoinette, The African Queen **21** The Man Who Came to Dinner

Mormon State
nickname of: **4** Utah

morning **4** dawn **5** early, sunup **7** sunrise **8** daybreak, daylight, forenoon **9** matutinal

morning-glory **7** Ipomoea **10** Calystegia **11** Convolvulus
varieties: **3** red **4** wild **5** beach, dwarf **6** Ceylon, common, silver, woolly, yellow **9** Brazilian **16** Imperial Japanese

Morocco ***see box***

moron **3** ass, nut, oaf, sap **4** boob, dolt, dope, fool **5** dummy, dunce, idiot, loony, ninny **6** dimwit, nitwit **7** halfwit, jackass **8** bonehead, dumbbell, dumbhead, imbecile,

Morocco
other name: **7** Barbary **8** Maroquin **9** Al Maghrib **13** Maghrib el Aksa **19** Mauretania Tingitana
capital: **5** Rabat **6** Rabbat
largest city: **10** Casablanca
others: **3** Fes, Fez, Sla **4** Ifni, Safi, Sale, Sali, Taza **5** Ceuta, Oujda, Porte, Saffi **6** Agadir, Meknes, Semara, Tetuan **7** Elarish, Kenitra, Larache, Mazagan, Mililla, Mogador, Tangier, Tetouan **8** Kouribga, Tinerhir **9** Marrakech, Marrakesh **10** Youssoufia **11** Port-Lyautey
division:
disputed territory: **13** Western Sahara
head of state: **4** king
measure: **4** kala, muhd, rotl, saah, sahh, ueba **5** artal, cadee, gerbe, ratel **6** covado, dirhem, fanega, izenbi, kintar, tangin, tomini **8** quintral
monetary unit: **4** flue, okia, rial **5** floos, franc, okieh, ounce **6** dirham, miskal **8** mouzouna
weight: **4** rotl **5** artel, ratel **6** dirhem, kintar **7** quintal
island: **7** Madeira
mountain: **3** Rif **4** Bani **5** Abyla, Atlas, Sarro **8** Tidiguin **9** Anti-Atlas, High Atlas, Jebel-Musa **11** Middle Atlas
highest point: **12** Jebel Toubkal **13** Djebel Toubkal
river: **3** Dra, Ziz **4** Sous **5** Sebou **6** Gheris **7** Tensift **8** Moulouya **9** Oum er Rbia
sea: **8** Atlantic **13** Mediterranean
physical feature:
cape: **3** Nun, Sim **4** Juby, Noun, Rhir **6** Cantin
desert: **6** Sahara
oasis: **8** Tafilelt
plain: **5** Rharb
strait: **9** Gibraltar
valley: **7** Ouergha
wind: **5** leste **7** charqui
people: **4** Arab, Moor **6** Berber, French **7** Spanish
dynasty: **7** Alawite, Almohad **9** Almoravid
leader: **5** Idris **7** Lyautey **8** Hassan II **9** Abd el-Krim
philosopher: **8** Averroes
language: **6** Arabic, Berber, French **7** Spanish
religion: **5** Islam
place:
ruins: **9** Volubilis
feature:
clothing: **4** haik **7** jellaba
hat: **3** fez
Islamic holy war: **5** jehad, jihad
shanty town: **10** bidonville
food:
dish: **8** couscous

numskull **9** blockhead, numbskull, simpleton **10** muttonhead, nincompoop

Moroni
capital of: 7 Comoros

Moros
mother: 3 Nyx
personifies: 4 fate

morose 3 low, sad **4** blue, dour, glum, sour **5** cross, moody, sulky, surly, testy **6** cranky, gloomy, grumpy, mopish, solemn, sullen **7** waspish **8** churlish, downcast, mournful **9** depressed, irascible, saturnine **10** despondent, melancholy **11** crestfallen

moroseness 5 gloom **8** glumness **9** pessimism, sulkiness, surliness **10** sullenness

Morpheus
god of: 6 dreams
father: 6 Hypnos

morphology
study of: 9 structure

Morris, Dinah
character in: 8 Adam Bede
author: 5 Eliot

Morris, Willie
author of: 5 Yazoo **10** Good Old Boy **15** North Toward Home

Morris, Wright
author of: 8 Will's Boy **10** Plain's Song **13** Field of Vision, My Uncle Dudley

Morrison, Jeanette Helen
real name of: 10 Janet Leigh

Morrison, Marion Michael
real name of: 9 John Wayne

Morrison, Toni
real name: 19 Chloe Anthony Wofford
author of: 4 Sula **7** Beloved, Tar Baby **12** The Bluest Eye **13** Song of Solomon

Morrow, Vic
born: 7 Bronx NY
roles: 6 Combat **8** Cimarron **14** God's Little Acre **15** The Twilight Zone **18** Portrait of a Mobster **19** The Blackboard Jungle

Mors
personifies: 5 death

Morse, Samuel F B
nationality: 8 American
invented: 9 Morse code **17** electric telegraph **24** electromagnetic telegraph

morsel 3 bit, nip, sip **4** bite, drop, iota, whit **5** crumb, grain, piece, scrap, snack, speck, taste, touch, trace **6** dollop, nibble, sliver, tidbit **7** modicum, segment, swallow **8** fraction, fragment, mouthful, particle **9** scintilla

mortal 4 deep, type **5** fatal, grave, human **6** deadly, lethal, living, person, severe **7** earthly, extreme, intense, mundane **8** creature, enormous, fleeting, temporal **9** character, corporeal, ephemeral **10** individual, transitory **12** unimaginable

mortality 7 carnage **8** fatality **9** bloodshed, ephemeral, slaughter **10** transience **11** evanescence **12** impermanence **13** extermination **14** transitoriness

mortar 6 cannon, cement, vessel **7** plaster **8** adhesive

Morte d'Arthur, Le
author: 12 Thomas Malory

Mortgaged Heart, The
author: 15 Carson McCullers

mortification 3 rot **5** decay, shame **7** chagrin, penance **8** ignominy **11** humiliation **12** putrefaction **13** embarrassment

mortified 6 rotted **7** abashed, ashamed, debased **8** dismayed, festered, tortured **9** chagrined, putrefied **11** discomfited, embarrassed

mortify 3 rot **4** deny, fast **5** abash, decay, shame **6** appall, fester **7** chagrin, horrify, putrefy **9** discomfit, embarrass **10** discipline, disconcert

Mosaic law 10 Pentateuch **15** Ten Commandments

Mosan
language family: 14 Algonkian-Mosan
subgroup: 6 Nootka **8** Chemakum, Kwakiutl, Quileute, Salishan, Wakashan **9** Chemakuan

Moscow
airport: 12 Sheremetyevo
canal: 11 Moscow-Volga
capital of: 4 USSR **6** Russia **11** Soviet Union
hills: 5 Lenin
landmark: 7 Kremlin **9** Gorky Park, Red Square **12** Lenin Library **13** Izmailovo Park, Sokolniki Park **14** Bolshoi Theater **16** Moscow Art Theater **21** Luzhniki Sports Complex
museum: 6 Armory **7** Pushkin **10** Historical **16** Tretyakov Gallery **28** Central Museum of the Soviet Army
river: 5 Setun, Volga, Yauza **6** Moscow
Russian: 6 Moskva

Moses
father: 5 Amram
mother: 8 Jochebed
sister: 6 Miriam
brother: 5 Aaron
wife: 8 Zipporah
son: 7 Eliezar, Gershom
father-in-law: 6 Jethro
received: 15 Ten Commandments
patriarch of: 10 Israelites
saw: 11 burning bush
successor: 6 Joshua
pertaining to: 6 Mosaic

Moses, Grandma
real name: 17 Anna Mary Robertson, Mary Anne Robertson
born: 11 Greenwich NY
artwork: 23 Out for the Christmas Trees

mosey 4 poke **5** amble **6** stroll **7** saunter, shuffle

Moslem 4 Moor **5** Islam **6** Muslim, Shiite **7** Islamic **10** Mohammadan

mosque 6 temple
Arabic: 6 masjid, musjid

Mosquito Coast, The
author: 11 Paul Theroux

Mosquito State
nickname of: 9 New Jersey

moss
varieties: 4 ball, club, gold, rose **5** broom, bunch, coral, ditch, fairy, Irish, spike, water **6** Scotch, spring **7** cushion, haircap, peacock, Spanish **8** floating, fountain, Japanese, mat spike **9** dwarf club, flowering **10** little club, pincushion **11** basket spike, meadow spike, shining club **12** treelet spike **13** Douglas's spike **15** Willdenow's spike

Mossbauer, Rudolph Ludwig
field: 7 physics
nationality: 6 German
discovered: 15 Mossbauer effect **28** recoil-free gamma ray absorption
awarded: 10 Nobel Prize

Mosses from an Old Manse
author: 18 Nathaniel Hawthorne

most 4 best, very **6** degree **7** maximum **9** extremely

most distant point 5 limit, reach **8** boundary **9** extremity

Mostel, Zero
real name: 16 Samuel Joel Mostel
born: 10 Brooklyn NY
roles: 8 The Front **10** Rhinoceros **11** The Enforcer **12** The Producers **15** Du

Barry Was a Lady **16** Fiddler on the Roof **17** Panic in the Streets

most important **3** key, top **4** head, main **5** chief **7** central, highest, leading **8** cardinal, dominant, foremost, greatest **9** paramount, principal, uppermost **10** preeminent **11** outstanding, predominant

mostly **6** mainly **7** as a rule, chiefly, greatly, largely **8** above all **9** generally, primarily, specially **10** especially **11** principally **12** particularly **13** predominantly

most prominent **7** leading **8** dominant **10** preeminent **11** outstanding

most successful **6** banner, record **7** winning **10** triumphant **11** outstanding

mote **3** dot **4** iota **5** speck **8** particle **9** scintilla

moth
varieties: **4** hawk, luna, tent **5** ghost, gypsy, plume, royal, swift, yucca **6** hornet, lappet, miller, urania **7** clothes, emperor, flannel, hook tip, leopard, tussock **8** army worm, forester, imperial, polka dot **9** carpenter, clearwing **10** forest tent **11** pseudosphex **12** African peach **13** American tiger, giant Hercules **14** tropical sphinx **15** Chinese silkworm, glover's silkworm **20** striped morning sphinx

moth-eaten **5** holey **6** old-hat **7** worn-out **8** outmoded **10** antiquated, threadbare **11** dilapidated

mother **3** mom, mum **4** bear, mama, mind, mums, rear, tend **5** beget, breed, mater, momma, mommy, mummy, nurse, raise **6** origin, source **7** care for, indulge, nurture, old lady, produce, protect **8** conceive, stimulus **10** wellspring **11** inspiration
French: **4** mere
Spanish: **5** madre
of wind: **3** Eos
of stars: **3** Eos
of gods: **5** Nammu

mother country **8** homeland **10** fatherland, native land, native soil, old country **13** native country

Mother Goose in Prose
author: **14** Lyman Frank Baum

motherly **4** kind **6** gentle, loving, tender **7** devoted **8** maternal, parental **9** indulgent **10** protective, sheltering

mother of a family
Latin: **13** materfamilias

Mother of the West
nickname of: **8** Missouri

mother's helper
French: **6** au pair

motif **4** form, idea **5** shape, style, theme, topic **6** design, figure, thread **7** pattern, refrain, subject **9** treatment

motion **3** cue, nod **4** flow, flux, move, sign, stir **5** drift **6** action, beckon, signal, stream **7** gesture, kinesis, passage, request **8** mobility, movement, progress **10** indication, suggestion **11** gesticulate, proposition **13** gesticulation **14** recommendation

motionless **4** calm, dead, idle **5** fixed, inert, still **6** at rest, frozen, stable, static **8** immobile, inactive, lifeless, tranquil, unmoving **9** immovable, quiescent **10** stationary, transfixed **11** immobilized **12** unresponsive

motion picture **3** pic **4** cine, film, show **5** flick, movie **6** cinema, talkie **8** flickers **10** photodrama **11** picture show **13** moving picture

motivate **4** goad, move, stir **5** egg on, impel **6** arouse, induce, prompt, stir up, turn on **7** actuate, provoke **8** activate, persuade **9** influence, stimulate

motivation **5** cause **6** reason **7** impetus, impulse **9** causation, impulsion **11** provocation

motive **3** aim, end **4** goal, spur **5** cause **6** design, object, reason **7** grounds, purpose **8** occasion, stimulus, thinking **9** incentive, intention, prompting, rationale **10** enticement, incitement, inducement **11** inspiration, instigation, provocation

motley **4** pied **5** mixed, tabby **6** hybrid, sundry, unlike, varied **7** dappled, piebald, watered **8** assorted, brindled, speckled **9** checkered, composite, different, disparate, divergent, harlequin, patchwork **10** dissimilar, iridescent, polychrome, variegated **11** diversified, incongruous, varicolored **12** multicolored **13** heterogeneous, kaleidoscopic, miscellaneous

motor **3** car **4** auto, ride, tour **5** drive, pilot, wheel **6** engine, turbine **7** machine **8** efferent **10** automobile

motorcar **4** auto, heap **6** jalopy, wheels **7** flivver, machine, vehicle **9** tin lizzie **10** automobile

motor vehicle **3** bus, car, van **4** auto, heap, limo **5** motor, truck, wagon **6** jalopy, pickup, wheels **7** flivver, hardtop, machine, omnibus, town car, vehicle **8** limosine **9** tin lizzie **10** automobile **11** convertible

mottled **4** pied **5** tabby **7** blotchy, flecked, piebald, specked **8** brindled, speckled, stippled **10** iridescent, multicolor, variegated **11** varicolored **12** parti-colored **13** kaleidoscopic, polychromatic

motto **3** saw **4** rule **5** adage, axiom, maxim **6** byword, dictum, saying, slogan, truism **7** epigram, precept, proverb **8** aphorism **9** catchword, principle, watchword

moue **4** pout **7** grimace

Moulin Rouge
director: **10** John Huston
cast: **10** Jose Ferrer (Toulouse-Lautrec) **11** Suzanne Flon, Zsa Zsa Gabor **12** Eric Pohlmann
setting: **5** Paris **10** Montmartre

mound **4** bump, dune, heap, hill, pile, rick **5** knoll, mogul, ridge, stack **7** bulwark, hillock, hummock, rampart **9** earthwork **10** embankment **12** entrenchment

Mound Builders
location: **15** Ohio River Valley **22** Mississippi River Valley
known for: **13** earthen mounds

mount **3** fit, fix, rig, set, wax **4** go up, grow, pony, rise, soar **5** affix, camel, climb, equip, frame, horse, scale, steed, surge, swell **6** ascend, fit out, outfit, set off **7** augment, charger, climb up, get over, get upon, install, set into **8** elephant, increase, multiply, straddle **9** intensify

mountain ***see box, p. 650***

Mountain
constellation of: **5** Mensa

mountaineers are always free men
Latin: **19** montani semper liberi
motto of: **12** West Virginia

mountain **3** alp **4** peak **5** bluff, butte, range, ridge **6** height, massif **7** volcano **8** eminence, highland **9** elevation

of **Afghanistan:** **3** Koh **5** Safeo **6** Chagai, Pamirs **7** Nowshak **8** Koh-i-Baba, Safed Koh, Sulaiman **9** Himalayas, Hindu Kush, Istoro Nal **11** Khwaja Amran, Paropamisus

of **Albania:** **5** Shala **6** Pindus **8** Koritnjk **10** Mount Korab **12** Albanian Alps

of **Algeria:** **5** Aissa, Atlas, Aures, Dahra, Tahat **6** Chelia **7** Ahaggar, Kabylia, Mouydir **8** Djurjura **9** Djurdjura, Tell Atlas **12** Saharan Atlas

of **Andorra:** **6** d'Etats **8** l'Estanyo **8** Pyrenees **10** Cataperdis **11** Como Pedrosa

of **Angola:** **4** Moco **5** Chela **6** Loviti **16** Humpata Highlands

of **Antigua and Barbuda:** **9** Boggy Peak

of **Argentina:** **4** Toro **5** Andes, Chato, Laudo, Potro **6** Conico, Pissis, Rincon **8** Famatina, Murallon, Olivares, Tronador, Zapaleri **9** Aconcagua, Tupungato **10** Cordillera **13** Ojos del Salado **15** Cerro Mercedario, Sierra de Cordoba

of **Armenia:** **6** Ararat, Taurus **8** Karabekh **7** Aladagh **12** Mount Aragats

of **Australia:** **3** Ise **4** Blue, Olga, Ossa, Zeil **5** Bruce, Snowy **6** Cradle, Doreen, Garnet, Gawler, Magnet, Morgan **7** Bongong, Gregory **8** Augustus, Brockman, Cuthbert, Herbert, Jusgrave, Mulligan, Surprise **9** Murchison, Kosciusko, Woodroffe **14** Australian Alps **15** New England Range **18** Great Dividing Range

of **Austria:** **4** Alps **6** Tirols, Tyrols, Stubai **8** Eisenerz, Rhatikon **9** Dolomites, Kitzbuhel **10** Hohe Tauern **13** Grossglockner **14** Silvretta Group

of **Bangladesh:** **10** Keokradong **15** Chittagong Hills

of **Barbados:** **6** Chalky **7** Hillaby

of **Belgium:** **8** Ardennes **16** Signal de Botrange

of **Benin:** **7** Atakora

of **Bhutan:** **5** Black **9** Himalayas **10** Chomo Lhari, Kula Kangri

of **Bolivia:** **4** Jara **5** Andes, Cusco, Cuzco **6** Sajama, Sorata, Sunsas **7** Illampu **8** Ancohuma, Illimani, Mururata, Sansimon, Santiago, Zapaleri **12** Eastern Range, Western Range **18** Cordillera Oriental **20** Cordillera Occidental

of **Borneo:** **4** Iran, Raja **5** Saran **6** Kapuas, Muller, Nijaan, Tebang **8** Kinabalu, Kinibalu, Schwaner

of **Brazil:** **3** Mar **5** Geral, Organ, Piaui **6** Acarai, Gurupi, Parima, Urucum **7** Amambai, Carajas, Gradaus, Neblina, Oragaos, Roraima **8** Bandeira, Itatiaia, Roncador, Tombador **9** Pacaraima, Sugar Loaf **10** Tumuc-Humac

of **Brunei:** **6** Teraja **9** Ulu Tutong **10** Pagon Priok

of **Bulgaria:** **3** Kom **5** Botev, Pirin, Sapka **6** Balkan, Musala, Sredna **7** Vikhren **8** Musallah **11** Rila-Rhodope

of **Burma:** **4** Chin, Naga, Pegu, Popa **5** Dawna **6** Arakan, Kachin, Lushai, Patkai **7** Karenni **8** Nattaung, Peguyoma, Saramati, Victoria **10** Tenasserim **11** Hkakabo Razi, Manipur Hill **12** Tanen Taunggi

of **Burundi:** **8** Nyarwana **9** Nyamisana

of **Cambodia:** **3** Pan **7** Dangrek, Dong Rek **8** Cardamom, Elephant **10** Phnom Aoral, Phnom Aural

of **Cameroon:** **5** Mbabo **7** Bambuto, Kapsiki, Mandara **8** Batandji, Cameroon **9** Atlantika

of **Canada:** **5** Coast, Logan, Royal **6** Robson, Skeena **7** Cariboo, Cascade, Purcell, Rockies, Selkirk, Stelias, St Elias **8** Columbia, Hazelton, Monashee **9** Mackenzie, Notre Dame, Tremblant **10** Laurentian, Richardson, Shickshock **14** Jacques Cartier

of **Canary Islands:** **5** Teide, Teyde **6** La Cruz **8** El Cumbre, Tenerife

of **Cape Verde:** **4** Cano, Fogo **10** Pico de Cano

of **Central African Republic:** **5** Karre, Tinga **6** Mongos **9** Dar Challa **11** Kayagangiri

of **Chad:** **7** Tibesti, Touside **9** Emi Koussi

of **Chile:** **4** Maca, Toro **5** Chato, Maipo, Maipu, Paine, Potro, Pular, Torre, Yogan **6** Apiwan, Burney, Conico, Jervis, Poquis, Rincon **7** Chaltel, Copiapo, Fitzroy, Palpana, Velluda **8** Cochrane, Tronador, Yanteles **9** Tupungato **13** Ojos del Salado

of **Colombia:** **5** Abibe, Andes, Baudo, Chita, Cocuy, Huila, Pasto **6** Ayapel, Perija, Purace, Tolima, Tunahi **7** Chamusa, del Ruiz **8** Oriengal **10** Santa Marta **14** Cristobal Colon **17** Central Cordillera, Eastern Cordillera, Western Cordillera

of **Costa Rica:** **4** Poas **5** Barba, Irazu **6** Blanco **7** Central, Gongora **9** Talamanca, Turrialba **10** Guanacaste **14** Chirripo Grande

of **Crete:** **3** Ida **5** Dikte, Phino **6** Juktas **7** Lasithi, Madaras **8** Leuka Ori, Theodore, Thriphte **9** Psiloriti

of **Cuba:** **6** Copper **7** Cristal, Maestra, Organos **8** Camaguey, Trinidad, Turquino **9** Las Villas **11** Pinar del rio **12** Guaniguanico **14** Sancti-Spiritus

of **Czechoslovakia:** **3** Ore **5** Grant, Tatra **6** Sumava **7** Gerlach, Sudeten **8** Krkonose **9** High Tatra **10** Carpathian **11** Gerlachovka

of **Denmark:** **12** Ejer Bavnehoj, Yding Skovhoj **14** Himmelbjaerget

of **Djibouti:** **5** Gouda **9** Moussa Ali

of **Dominican Republic:** **4** Tina **5** Gallo, Neiba **6** Duarte **7** Baoruco, Central **8** Bahoruco, Oriental **13** Septentrional

of **Ecuador:** **5** Andes **6** Condor, Sangay **7** Cayambe **8** Antisana, Cotopaxi **9** Cotacachi, Pichincha **10** Chimborazo

of **Egypt:** **5** Sinai, Uekia **6** Gharib **8** Katerina **9** Katherina **13** Shayib al-Banat

of El Salvador: **6** Izalco **8** Santa Ana
of England: **5** Black **7** Pennine, Snowdon **8** Cambrian, Cumbrian **11** Scafell Pike
of Equatorial Guinea: **5** Mitra **11** Santa Isabel
of Ethiopia: **4** Amba, Batu, Guge, Guna, Talo **5** Ahmar, Choke **9** Rasdashan, Ras Deshen
of Finland: **6** Haltia **7** Laltiva **10** Saari Selka **11** Haldetsokka
of France: **4** Alps, Jura **5** Blanc, Pelat **6** Vosges **8** Ardennes, Pyrenees **9** Mont Blanc **10** French Alps **11** Pic Montcalm
of Gabon Republic: **5** Mpele **7** Chaillu, Cristal, Mikongo **8** Balaquri, Birougou, Iboundji
of Germany: **3** Ore **4** Harz **8** Feldberg **9** Zugspitze **10** Erzgebirge **11** Black Forest, Fichtelberg **12** Bavarian Alps
of Ghana: **8** Afadjato **12** Akwapim Hills
of Gibraltar: **6** Misery
of Greece: **3** Ida **4** Idhi, Oeta, Oite, Ossa **5** Athos **6** Ithome, Peleon, Pelion, Pindus **7** Grammos, Helicon, Olympus, Rhodope **8** Hymettos, Smolikas, Targetos, Taygetus **9** Parnassus **10** Hagion Oros, Lycabettus, Pentelicus
of Greenland: **5** Forel, Payer **7** Khardyu **8** Peterman **9** Gunnbjorn **15** Petermannsbjerg **16** Gunnbjornsfjaeld
of Guatemala: **4** Agua, Mico **5** Fuego, Madre **6** Pacaya, Tacana **7** Atitlan, Toliman **8** La Candon, Las Minas, Tajumuko **9** Tajamulco **10** Acatenango, Santa Maria **12** Cuchumatanes
of Guinea: **4** Loma **5** Nimba **6** Tamgue **11** Fouta Djalon
of Guyana: **5** Amuku, Ariwa, Kamoa **6** Akarai, Kanuku **7** Caburai **9** Pacaraima
of Haiti: **4** Nord **5** Cahos **6** Macaya, Noires **7** Lahotte, Laselle **8** Troudeau
of Honduras: **4** Pija **6** Agalta **7** Celaque **8** Las Minas **9** Esperanza **25** Central American Cordillera
of Hong Kong: **6** Castle **8** Victoria **9** Tai Mo Shan
of Hungary: **4** Alps, Bukk **5** Kekes, Matra, Tatra, Vetes **6** Bakony, Mecsek **7** Cserhat, Gerecse **8** Borzsony, Zempleni **9** Korishegy **10** Carpathian
of Iceland: **4** Laki **5** Askja, Hekla, Jokul, Katla **7** Surtsey **10** Orafajokul **16** Hvannadalshnukur
of India: **8** Aravalli **9** Broad Peak, Distaghil, Himalayas, Karakoram, Nanda Devi, Rakaposhi **10** Gasherbrum, Masherbrum **11** Nanga Parbat **12** Eastern Ghats, Godwin Austen, Kanchenjunga, Western Ghats
of Iran: **6** Elburz, Zagros **8** Demavend
of Iraq: **6** Qalate, Zagros **7** Halgurd, Qaarade **9** Kurdistan
of Ireland: **5** Galty **6** Croagh, Mourne **7** Errigal, Muckish, Patrick, Wicklow **8** Comeragh **10** Benna Beola, Twelve Bens, Twelve Pins **13** Carrantuohill, Knockmealdown **19** Macgillycuddy's Reeks
of Israel: **4** Nafh, Sagi **5** Harif, Meron, Ramon, Tabor **6** Atzmon, Carmel, Hatira, Meiron
of Italy: **4** Alps, Etna, Rosa, Viso **5** Amaro, Blanc, Corno, Somma **6** Cimone, Ortles **7** Vulcano **8** Vesuvius **9** Apennines, Dolomites, Maritimes, Stromboli **10** Apuane Alps, Carnic Alps, Julian Alps, Otztal Alps **11** Bernina Alps, Gennargentu **12** Gran Paradiso, Ligurian Alps **13** Lepontine Alps **16** Abruzzi Apennines
of Jamaica: **4** Blue **8** Sir Johns
of Japan: **3** Uso, Zao **4** Fuji **5** Asahi, Asama, Hondo, Yesso **6** Asosan, Enasan, Hiuchi, Kiusiu, Yariga **7** Fujisan, Hakusan, Kujusan, Tokachi **8** Fujiyama **9** Japan Alps
of Java: **4** Amat, Gede **5** Lawoe, Murjo, Prahu **6** Raoeng, Semuru, Slamet **7** Semeroe **8** Soembing
of Jordan: **9** Jabal Ramm, Jebel Ramm
of Kenya: **5** Elgon, Kenya, Kulai, Nyira, Nyiru **6** Kinyaa, Matian **7** Logonot **8** Aberdare **9** Kirinyaga
of Korea: **4** Wang **5** Chiri, Halla **6** Kwanmo, Paektu, Sobaek **7** Diamond, Kyebang, Nangnim, Taebaek **8** Chang-pai, Hamgyong, Myohyang **9** Paektu-san **10** Kumgang-san
of Laos: **3** Bia, Lai, Loi, San **4** Copi, Khat **5** Atwat **6** Khoung, Tiubia **7** Phou Bia **15** Annam Cordillera
of Lebanon: **4** Mzar **5** Aruba **6** Hermon **7** es Sauda, Lebanon, Sannine **8** Kadischa, Kenisseh **9** Kennisseh **10** al-Mukammal **11** Anti-Lebanon **13** Qurnat al-Sawda
of Lesotho: **6** Maloti, Maluti **7** Central **8** Injasuti, Machache **10** Ben Macdhui **11** Drakensberg, Thaba Putsoa **16** Thabana Ntlenyana
of Liberia: **3** Uni **4** Bong, Putu **5** Niete, Nimba **6** Wutivi **9** Bomi Hills
of Libya: **5** Green **9** Bette Peak **13** Jabal al Akhdar, Tibesti Massif
of Liechtenstein: **4** Alps **8** Naafkopf, Rhatikon **12** Three Sisters **15** Vorder-Grauspitz
of Lithuania: **9** Juozapine **15** Samogitian Hills
of Luxembourg: **8** Ardennes, Huldange **9** Burgplatz **11** Wemperhardt
of Madagascar: **4** Boby **9** Ankaratra **11** Maromokotro **12** High Plateaus, Tsiafajavona **17** Tsaratanana Massif
of Malawi: **6** Mlanje **7** Mulanje **11** Livingstone
of Malaysia: **4** Bulu, Hose, Iban, Iran, Main, Mulu, Niut, Raja **5** Murjo, Niapa, Ophir **6** Blumut, Kapuas, Leuser, Slamet **7** Binaija, Brassey, Crocker **8** Kinabalu, Rindjani **11** Gunong Korbu, Gunong Tahan
of Mali: **4** Mina **6** Iforas **7** Manding **12** Hombori Tondo
of Mexico: **6** Colima, Tacana, Toluca **7** Orizaba **9** Paricutin **11** Ixtacihuatl, Sierra Madre

(*continued*)

mountain (*continued*)
12 Citlaltepetl, Popocatepetl **14** Sierra Zacateca **16** Chiapas Highlands **24** Transverse Volcanic Sierra
of Mongolia: 4 Cast, Orog **5** Altai **6** Kentei, Sevrej **7** Ich Ovoo, Khangai, Khentei **8** Tannu-Ola **9** Edrengijn **10** Cagaan Bogd, Tabun Bogdo **11** Munky Sardyk **14** Hangayn-Hentiyn, Monch Chajrchan
of Montenegro: 8 Durmitor **11** Dinaric Alps
of Morocco: 3 Rif **4** Bani **5** Abyla, Atlas, Sarro **8** Tidiguin **9** Anti-Atlas, High Atlas, Jebel-Musa **11** Middle Atlas **12** Jebel Toubkal **13** Djebel Toubkal
of Mozambique: 5 Binga **7** Lebombo
of Namibia: 9 Brandberg **14** Khomas Highland, Koakoveld Hills
of Nepal: 6 Cho Oyu, Churia, Makalu **7** Everest, Lhotse I, Manaslu, Siwalik **8** Lhotse II **9** Annapurna, Himalayas **10** Dhaulagiri, Gosainthan, Himalchuli **11** Ganesh Himal **12** Kanchenjunga **14** Mahabharat Lekh
of New Guinea: 4 Snow **6** Orange **7** Bismark, Wilhelm **8** Victoria **9** Carstensz **10** Puncak Jaya **11** Owen Stanley **12** Albert Edward
of New Zealand: 4 Cook, Eden, Flat, Owen **5** Allen, Chope, Lyall, Mitre, Ohope, Otari, Young **6** Egmont, Stokes, Tasman **7** Aorangi, Cameron, Coronet, Ernslaw, Huiarau, Pihanga, Ruahine, Ruapehu, Tauhera, Tutamee, Tyndall **8** Aspiring, Richmond, Tauranga **9** Messenger, Murchison, Ngauruhoe, Raukumara, Tongariro **11** Remarkables **12** Southern Alps
of Nicaragua: 4 Leon **5** Negro, Viejo **6** Madera, Telica **7** Managua, Mogoton, Saslaya **9** Momotombo
of Niger: 7 Bagzane, Greboun **9** Air Massif
of Norway: 5 Sogne **6** Kjolen **7** Numedal **8** Blodfjel, Snohetta, Telemark, Ustetind **9** Harteigen, Jotunheim, Langfjell, Ramnanosi **10** Dovrefjell, Galdhoepig, Glitretind, Vibmesnosi **11** Myrdalfjell **12** Galdhopiggen **13** Glittertinden **14** Aardangerjokul, Hallingskarvet, Skagastolstind
of Oman: 4 Qara **5** Green, Hafit, Harim, Nakhl, Tayin **6** al-Sham **8** el-Akhdar **11** Jabal Akhdar **13** Green Mountain
of Pakistan: 3 Pab, Pub **4** Salt **6** Makran **7** Kirthar **8** Himalaya, Safed Koh, Sulaiman **9** Hindu Kush, Karakoram, Tirich Mir **11** Makran Coast **12** Godwin Austin **13** Central Makran **14** Takht-i-Sulaiman
of Panama: 4 Baru, Maje **5** Chico, Gandi **6** Darien **7** Columan, San Blas, Veragua **8** Chiriqui, Santiago, Tabasara **10** Costa Rican **14** Serrania de Sapo **15** Aspave Highlands **17** Cordillera Central
of Peru: 5 Andes **7** El Misti, Huamina **8** Coropuna **9** Huascaran
of Philippines: 3 Apo, Iba **4** Mayo, Taal **5** Albay, Askja, Hibok, Mayon, Pulog **6** Pagsan **7** Banahao, Canlaon
of Poland: 4 Rysy **5** Tatra **6** Beskid **7** Pieniny, Sudeten **9** Beshchady, High Tatra, Holy Cross **10** Carpathian
of Portugal: 4 Acor, Lapa **5** Gerez, Marao, Mousa **6** Bornes, Peneda **7** Larouco **8** Caramulo **9** Caldeirao, Monchique **11** Pico da Serra **14** Serra da Estrela
of Puerto Rico: 4 Toro **5** Cayey, Punta **6** Yunque **8** Guilarte, Luquilla **10** Torrecilla **17** Cordillera Central
of Rumania: 5 Banat, Bihor, Negoi **6** Codrul, Rodnei **7** Apuseni, Balkans, Caliman, Fagaras **8** Pietrosu **9** Moldavian **10** Carpathian, Moldoveanu **17** Transylvanian Alps
of Russia: 5 Altai, Lenin, Sayan, Urals **6** Anadyr, Elbrus, Koryak, Pamirs, Pobedy **7** Belukha, Crimean, Khibiny, Stanovi, Zhiguli **8** Caucasus, Dzhughur, Stanavoi, Tien Shan **9** Communism, Kopet Dagh, Narodnaya, Pamir-Alai, Yablonovy **10** Carpathian **11** Sikhote-Alin, Verkhoyansk
of Rwanda: 7 Mitumba, Virunga **8** Muhavura **9** Karisimbi
of Samoa: 4 Fito, Vaea **5** Alava **6** Savaii **7** Matafao **8** Silisili **9** Rainmaker
of San Marino: 6 Titano **9** Apennines
of Sardinia: 4 Rasu **5** Ferry, Linas **7** Gallura, Limbara **8** Marghine, Serpeddi, Vittoria **11** Gennargentu
of Saudi Arabia: 5 Razih **6** Tuwayq **10** Jebal Sawda
of Scotland: 5 Attow, Ochil **6** Sidlaw **7** Cheviot **8** Ben Nevis, Grampian **9** Ben Lomond, Highlands, Trossachs
of Senegal: 6 Gounou **12** Fouta Djallon
of Sicily: 4 Erei, Etna, Moro, Sori **5** Aetna, Atlas, Erici, Hybla, Iblei, Ibrei **7** Nebrodi, Vulcano **9** Apennines, Le Madonie, Stromboli **10** Peloritani
of Sierra Leone: 4 Loma **9** Bintimani **10** Tingi Hills

Mountain State
nickname of: 7 Montana **12** West Virginia

Mountbatten, Louis
also: 27 first Earl Mountbatten of Burma
nationality: 7 British
position: 12 first sea lord
supreme allied commander of: 13 Southeast Asia
chief of: 25 British combined operations
viceroy of: 5 India
served in: 3 WWI **4** WWII
directed invasion of: 10 Madagascar
recaptured: 5 Burma

mountebank 5 cheat, fraud, phony, quack **6** con man,

of Sikkim: **7** Dongkya, Donkhya **9** Himalayas, Singalili **10** Darjeeling **12** Kanchenjunga
of Singapore: **6** Mandai **7** Panjang **10** Bukit Timah
of the Solomon Islands: **5** Balbi **11** Popomanasiu
of Somalia: **5** Guban **7** Surud Ad **11** Migiurtinia, Ogo Highland
of South Africa: **3** Aux, Kop **5** Table **7** Kathkin **8** Injasuti **9** Stormberg **10** Devil's Peak, Sneeuwberg **11** Drakensberg **12** Giant's Castle **13** Witwatersrand **14** Mont-aux-Sources **15** Great Escarpment
of Spain: **4** Gata **5** Aneto, Rouch, Teide **6** Cuenca, Estats, Europa, Gredos, Magina, Morena, Nethou, Nevada, Teleno, Toledo **7** Alcaraz, Banuelo, Catalan, Cerredo, Demanda, Iberian, La Sagra, Moncayo, Perdido **8** Almanzor, Asturias, Galician, Maladeta, Monegros, Montseny, Mulhacen, Penalara, Pyrenees **10** Albarracin, Cantabrian, Guadarrama, Torrecilla
of Sri Lanka: **5** Pedro **7** Sri Pada **9** Adams Peak **14** Pidurutalagala
of Sudan: **4** Nuba **6** Red Sea **7** Imatong, Kinyeti **9** Dongotona **10** Jabal Marra, Jebel Marra **18** Ethiopian Highlands
of Surinam: **4** Emma **6** Kayser, Oranje **10** Julianatop, Tumuc-Humac, Wilhelmina **13** Eilert's Il Haan, Van Ach Van Wyck **15** Guiana Highlands
of Swaziland: **7** Emlembe **8** Highveld **11** Drakensberg
of Sweden: **4** Sarv **5** Ammar, Kebne **6** Helags, Kjolen, Ovniks, Sarjek **7** Kjollen **10** Kebnekaise
of Switzerland: **3** Dom **4** Alps, Jura, Rigi, Rosa, Todi **5** Adula, Blanc, Cenis, Eiger, Genis, Karpf, Righi **6** Linard, Pizela, Sentis **7** Bernina, Beverin, Grimsel, Pilatus, Rotondo **8** Balmhorn, Jungfrau **9** Weisshorn **10** Diablerets, Matterhorn, St Gotthard, Wetterhorn **11** Burgenstock **12** Dufourspitze **13** Rheinwaldhorn **14** Finsteraarhorn
of Syria: **6** Carmel, Hermon **7** Alawite, Libanus **10** Nusairiyya **11** Anti-Lebanon
of Taiwan: **5** Tatun **6** Tzukao, Yu Shan **7** Taitung **8** Morrison **10** Sinkao Shan **11** Hsin-Kao Shan **15** Chungyang Shanmo
of Tanzania: **4** Kibo, Mero **8** Usambara **11** Kilimanjaro
of Thailand: **5** Dawna, Khieo **6** Phanom **8** Dang Raek, Inthanon, Kao Prawa, Maelamun **9** Khao Luang **11** Bilauktaung, Doi Inthanon
of Tibet: **5** Kamet, Sajum **6** Kailas, Kunlun **7** Bandala, Everest **9** Himalayas, Karakoram
of Togo: **4** Togo **7** Atakora, Baumann, Koronga
of Tunisia: **5** Atlas **6** Chambi, Mrhila **7** Tebessa **8** High Tell, Zaghouan **12** Northern Tell **18** Dorsale Tunnisienne
of Turkey: **2** Ak **3** Ala **4** Alai, Dagh, Kara **5** Hasan, Hinis, Honaz, Murat, Murit **6** Ala Dag, Ararat, Bingol, Bolgar, Pontic, Suphan, Taurus **7** Aladagh, Erciyas **8** Karacali **10** Kackar Dagi
of Uganda: **4** Oboa **5** Elgon **7** Virunga **9** Mufumbiro, Ruwenzori **10** Margherita **18** Mountains of the Moon
of United States: **4** Hood **5** Coast, Green, Kenai, Ozark, Rocky, White **6** Alaska, Brooks, DeLong, Elbert, Helena, Mesabi, Pocono, Shasta **7** Cascade, Chugach, Foraker, Harvard, Kilauea, Massive, Olympic, Olympus, Rainier, St Elias, Whitney **8** Catskill, Davidson, Endicott, Katahdin, Mauna Loa, McKinley, Mitchell, Ouachita, St Helens, Wrangell **9** Allegheny, Blue Ridge, Kuskokwim, North Peak, Pike's Peak **10** Black Hills, Blanca Peak, Grand Teton, Washington, Williamson **11** Appalachian, Santa Monica **12** Sierra Nevada **14** Berkshire Hills
of Upper Volta: **4** Tema **8** Nakourou **10** Tenakourou, Tenekourou
of Uruguay: **6** Animas **10** Grand Hills **14** Cuchilla Grande **15** Mirador Nacional
of Vanuatu: **6** Lopevi **11** Tabwemasana
of Venezuela: **3** Pao **4** Pava, Yair **5** Andes, Duida, Icutu **6** Concha, Cuneva, Merida, Parima, Sierra, Yumari **7** Bolivar, Imutaca, Masaiti, Roraima **8** Gurupira **9** Pacaraima **10** Auyan-Tepui **11** Turimiquire **18** Cordillera del Norte
of Vietnam: **6** Badinh, Badink **7** Nindhoa, Ninhhoa **8** Fansipan, Knontran, Ngoklinh, Ngoklink, Tchepone, Tclepore **18** Annamese Cordillera
of Wales: **6** Berwyn **7** Snowdon **8** Cambrian **9** Prescelly **13** Brecon Beacons
of Western Samoa: **4** Fito, Vaea **13** Mauga Silisili
of Yemen: **6** Shuayb, Thamir **7** Djehaff
of Yugoslavia: **5** Karst **6** Balkan **7** Rhodope, Triglav **8** Crna Gora, Durmitor **9** Sar-Pindus **10** Carnic Alps, Julian Alps, Karawanken **11** Dinaric Alps **13** Slovenian Alps **20** Northern Albanian Alps
of Zaire: **7** Crystal, Mitumba, Virunga **9** Ruwenzori **10** Margherita, Nyaragongo **18** Mountains of the Moon
of Zambia: **8** Muchinga **12** Mafinga Hills
of Zimbabwe: **5** Vumba **6** Manica **7** Inyanga **9** Inyangani **11** Chimanimani, Matopo Hills

humbug **7** hustler, sharper **8** huckster, operator, swindler **9** charlatan, con artist **11** quacksalver

mounted soldier **6** hussar, lancer **7** dragoon **8** cavalier, horseman **10** cavalryman

mourn **3** cry, rue, sob **4** keen, pine, wail, weep **6** bemoan, bewail, grieve, lament, regret, sorrow **7** deplore, despair **8** languish, weep over

mournful **3** sad **5** black, sorry, weepy **6** dismal, rueful, somber, triste, woeful **7** doleful, joyless, unhappy **8** dejected, dirgeful, dolorous, funereal, grevious, saddened **9** depressed, plaintive, sorrowful **10** depressing, dispirited, lamentable, lugubrious, melancholy **11** distressing, melancholic **12** heavy hearted

mourning **3** woe **5** black, crape, dolor, grief, weeds **6** sorrow **7** anguish, despair **8** grieving **9** lamenting, sorrowing **11** bereavement, lamentation

Mourning Becomes Electra
author: **12** Eugene O'Neill
character: **4** Seth **10** Hazel Niles, Peter Niles **16** Captain Adam Brant
Mannon family: **4** Ezra, Orin **7** Lavinia **9** Christine

mourning period
Hebrew: **6** shibah, shivah

mouser **3** cat **4** puss **5** kitty, pussy **6** feline **8** pussycat

Mousetrap, The
author: **14** Agatha Christie

mousseline **6** muslin

mousy **3** shy **4** drab, dull **5** timid, wimpy **7** bashful, fearful **8** timorous **9** colorless, unnoticed, withdrawn **11** unobtrusive **13** inconspicuous

mouth **3** bay, say **4** bell, jaws, lips **5** inlet, speak, voice **6** outlet, portal **7** declare, estuary, opening **8** aperture, propound **9** pronounce

mouthful **3** dab **4** bite **5** taste **6** morsel, nibble

mouthpiece **4** reed **6** lawyer **7** counsel **8** advocate, attorney **9** counselor

mouth-watering **8** inviting, tempting **9** appealing **10** appetizing **11** tantalizing

movable, moveable **4** free **5** loose **6** mobile, motile, moving **8** portable **10** changeable

movables **4** gear **5** goods **7** baggage, effects, luggage **9** equipment **10** belongings **11** impedimenta, possessions **13** accoutrements, paraphernalia

move **2** go **3** act, ask, get **4** bear, deed, fire, lead, pass, ploy, step, stir, sway, turn, urge **5** begin, budge, carry, cause, drive, impel, plead, rouse, shift, touch **6** action, affect, arouse, attack, convey, excite, exhort, incite, induce, motion, prompt, strike, stroke, switch **7** advance, budging, gesture, go ahead, impress, inspire, measure, operate, proceed, propose, provoke, request, suggest **8** function, interest, locomote, maneuver, motivate, persuade, relocate, start off, stirring, transfer, transmit **9** impassion, influence, recommend, stimulate, transport, transpose **10** transplant **11** opportunity

move downward **3** dip **4** dive, drop, fall, sink **6** plunge, tumble **7** decline, descend, plummet **8** decrease

movement **4** part **5** drive, steps, works **6** action, effort, motion **7** crusade, measure, program, section **8** activity, division, gestures, maneuver, progress, stirring **9** agitation, execution, mechanism, operation **10** locomotion **11** undertaking

move out **5** leave **6** depart, vacate **8** evacuate

move quickly **3** fly, run **4** bolt, dash, race, rush, tear **5** hurry **6** hasten, sprint

move sideways **4** edge **5** sidle **8** sidestep

move slyly **4** edge, lurk **5** sidle, skulk, slink, sneak, steal

move up **5** boost, climb, heave, hoist, raise, scale **6** ascend, uplift **7** advance, elevate, promote, upraise

move upward **4** rise, soar **5** climb, mount **6** ascend **7** take off

movie **4** film, show **5** flick **6** cinema **7** feature, picture, showing **9** screening
invented by:
machine: **7** Jenkins
panoramic: **6** Waller
projector: **6** Edison
talking: **14** Warner Brothers

moving **5** motor **6** mobile, motile **8** exciting, poignant, spurring, stirring, touching **9** affecting, inspiring **10** impressive, locomotive, motivating **11** interacting, stimulating

moving about **5** astir **6** active **7** on the go

Moving Target, A
author: **14** William Golding

Mowgli
character in: **14** The Jungle Books
author: **7** Kipling

moxie **4** grit, guts, sand **5** nerve, pluck, spunk **6** mettle, spirit **7** courage, stamina **8** audacity, backbone **9** hardihood,

Mozambique
capital/largest city: **6** Maputo **15** Lourenco Marques
others: **4** Tete **5** Beira, Pemba, Zumbo **6** Chemba, Nacala, Pafuri, Sofala **7** Nampula **8** Mutarara **9** Inhambane, Quelimane **11** Porto Amelia
school: **15** Eduardo Mondlane
monetary unit: **6** escudo **7** centavo, metical
island: **6** Inhaca **7** Angoche **8** Bazanuto **9** Benguerua
lake: **5** Nyasa **6** Chuali, Nyassa **8** Nhavarre
mountain: **7** Lebombo
highlands: **6** Namuli **9** Gorongosa
highest point: **5** Binga
river: **4** Buzi, Save **5** Lurio, Msalu **6** Rovuma, Ruvuma **7** Ligonha, Limpopo, Lugenda, Messaio, Zambezi **8** Changane
ocean: **6** Indian
physical feature:
cape: **7** Delgado
channel: **10** Mozambique
people: **3** Yao **5** Bantu, Chopi, Lomue, Lomwe, Macua, Makua, Ngoni, Nguni, Shona **6** Maravi, Thouga **7** Maconde, Makonde **10** Portuguese
explorer: **11** Vasco de Gama
leader: **8** Chissano **9** Dos Santos **12** Samora Machel **15** Eduardo Mondlane
language: **3** Yao **5** Makua **6** Nyanji, Thonga **7** Swahili **10** Portuguese
religion: **5** Islam **7** animism **13** Roman Catholic
place:
game reserve: **8** Marromeu **9** Gorongosa, Gorongoza **18** Maputo Elephant Park
reservoir: **11** Cabora Bassa
feature:
bride price: **6** lobolo

toughness **10** pluckiness **13** dauntlessness

moyen age **10** Middle Ages

Mozambique ***see box***

Mozart, Wolfgang Amadeus ***see box***

Mr, Mister
Russian: **8** gospodin
French: **8** monsieur
Yiddish: **3** Reb

Mr B
character in: **6** Pamela
author: **10** Richardson

Mr Basketball
nickname of: **8** Bob Cousy

Mr Britling Sees It Through
author: **7** H G Wells

Mr Cub
nickname of: **10** Ernie Banks

Mr Deeds Goes to Town
director: **10** Frank Capra
cast: **10** Gary Cooper (Longfellow Deeds), Jean Arthur **14** George Bancroft

Mr Ed
character: **9** Carol Post **10** Kay Addison, Wilbur Post **12** Roger Addison **14** Gordon Kirkwood, Winnie Kirkwood
cast: **8** Leon Ames **9** Alan Young **11** Connie Hines, Edna Skinner **12** Larry Keating **18** Florence MacMichael
Mr Ed was: **12** talking horse

Mr Flood's Party
author: **22** Edwin Arlington Robinson

Mr Midnight
nickname of: **10** Steve Allen

Mr Peepers
character: **9** Mrs Gurney **11** Marge Weskit, Mr Remington **12** Harvey Weskit **14** Nancy Remington **15** Robinson Peepers **20** Superintendent Bascom
cast: **8** Wally Cox **9** Gage Clark **11** Ernest Truex, Marion Lorne, Tony Randall **14** Patricia Benoit **16** Georgiann Johnson
Mr Peepers taught: **7** science
school: **13** Jefferson High

Mr Sammler's Planet
author: **10** Saul Bellow

Mrs Dalloway
author: **13** Virginia Woolf
character: **10** Miss Kilman, Peter Walsh, Sally Seton **15** Richard Dalloway **16** Clarissa Dalloway **17** Elizabeth Dalloway

Mrs Miniver
director: **12** William Wyler
cast: **11** Greer Garson **12** Teresa Wright **13** Dame May Whitty, Walter Pidgeon
Oscar for: **7** actress (Garson), picture **8** director **17** supporting actress (Wright)

Mr Smith Goes to Washington
director: **10** Frank Capra
cast: **9** Guy Kibbee **10** Jean Arthur **11** Claude Rains **12** Edward Arnold, James Stewart **14** Thomas Mitchell

Mrs Parkington
author: **14** Louis Bromfield

Mrs Stevens Hears the Mermaids Singing
author: **9** May Sarton

Mrs Warren's Profession
author: **17** George Bernard Shaw

Mr Television
nickname of: **11** Milton Berle

much **3** far **4** a lot, lots **5** about, ample, heaps, loads, often **6** almost, indeed, nearly, overly, rather, scores **7** copious, greatly **8** abundant, good deal, plenty of, quantity, somewhat, striking **9** decidedly, important, plenteous, plentiful, regularly **10** frequently, impressive, noteworthy, oftentimes, satisfying, sufficient, worthwhile **11** appreciable, exceedingly, excessively, sufficiency **12** considerable **13** approximately, consequential

Much Ado About Nothing
author: **18** William Shakespeare
character: **4** Hero **7** Claudio, Don John, Leonato **8** Beatrice, Benedick, Dogberry, Don Pedro

much in little
Latin: **13** multum in parvo

much loved **4** dear **7** beloved, darling, dearest **8** precious **9** cherished, treasured

mucilage **3** gum **4** glue **5** paste **6** cement **8** adhesive

mucilaginous **5** gluey, gummy, gunky **6** gloppy, sticky **8** adhesive

muck **3** mud **4** dirt, dung, gunk, mire, ooze, slop **5** filth, slime **6** sewage, sludge **7** compost, garbage

muck up **4** soil **5** dirty, muddy **7** pollute

mud **4** dirt, muck, soil, wire

Mudcat State
nickname of: **11** Mississippi

muddied **5** dirty, grimy **6** grubby, soiled **7** stained **8** begrimed, confused

muddle **3** fog **4** blow, daze, haze, mess, muff, ruin **5** botch, chaos, mix up, spoil, throw **6** boggle, bungle, fumble, goof up, jumble, mess up, pother, rattle **7** blunder, clutter, confuse, nonplus, stupefy **8** bewilder, confound, disarray, disorder **13** disconcertion **14** disarrangement

muddlebrained **5** inept **7** witless **8** confused **11** lamebrained

muddled **5** fuzzy **7** bemused **8** confused **10** bewildered

Mozart, Wolfgang Amadeus
born: **7** Austria **8** Salzburg
composer of: **4** Linz (symphony No 36) **5** Paris (symphony No 31) **6** Prague (symphony No 38) **7** Don Juan, Haffner (symphony No 35), Jupiter (symphony No 41), Requiem, Turkish (concerto) **8** Idomeneo **9** Credo Mass, Mitridate **10** Lucio Silla **11** Don Giovanni, Hunt Quartet, Il Re Pastore, Sparrow Mass **12** A Musical Joke, Cosi Fan Tutte (So Do They All or Women Are Like That), Haydn Quartet, Spatzenmesse **13** The Magic Flute, Trumpet Sonata, Turkish Sonata **14** Coronation Mass, Stadler Quintet, Die Zauberflote **15** Haffner Serenade, La Finta Semplice, Prussian Quartet **16** Dissonant Quartet, La Clemenza di Tito, Posthorn Serenade, Serenata Notturna **17** A Little Night Music **18** Jeunehomme Concerto, La Finta Giardiniera, The Clemency of Titus **19** Bastien und Bastienne, The Marriage of Figaro **20** Eine Kleine Nachtmusik, The Pretender Gardener **21** Der Schauspieldirektor, Ein Musikalischer Spass **22** The Pretending Simpleton **25** Die Entfuhrung aus dem Serail **27** The Abduction from the Seraglio

muddy **4** dull **5** dirty, grimy, vague **6** filthy, grubby **7** obscure **8** begrimed, confused

muff **5** botch, spoil **6** bungle **10** handwarmer

muffle **3** gag **4** dull, hush, mask, mute, veil, wrap **5** cloak, cover, quell, quiet, still **6** dampen, deaden, shroud, soften, stifle, swathe **7** conceal, enclose, envelop, silence, swaddle

muffled **3** low **4** dull, soft **5** faint, muted **6** dulled, feeble, hushed, veiled **7** cloaked, covered, quelled, quieted, stilled, subdued, swathed, wrapped **8** deadened, shrouded, silenced, softened, swaddled **9** concealed, enveloped, inaudible **10** indistinct, suppressed

mug **3** cup **4** face, puss, toby **5** stein, stoup **6** beaker, flagon, goblet, kisser, visage **7** chalice, tankard, toby jug, tumbler **11** countenance

mugger **8** assailer, attacker **9** assailant, assaulter

mugginess **4** damp **8** dampness, dankness, humidity **9** humidness **10** sultriness **14** oppressiveness

muggy **5** close, humid **6** clammy, steamy, sticky, stuffy, sultry, sweaty **8** steaming, vaporous **10** oppressive, sweltering

Muisca *see* **7** Chibcha

mulberry **5** Morus
varieties: **3** red **4** Aino **5** black, paper, white **6** French, Indian **7** Russian **8** American, silkworm

Mulciber
epithet of: **6** Vulcan
means: **6** melter

mulct **4** bilk **6** extort **7** defraud, swindle

mule **3** ass **5** burro **6** donkey **7** jackass
group of: **4** span

mulish **5** balky **6** ornery **8** perverse, stubborn **9** fractious, obstinate **10** refractory **11** intractable **12** recalcitrant

Mulius
wife: **7** Agamede
father-in-law: **6** Augeas
position: **8** spearman
killed by: **6** Nestor

mull, mull over **5** study, weigh **6** ponder **8** consider, meditate, pore over, ruminate **10** deliberate

Muller
character in: **25** All Quiet on the Western Front
author: **8** Remarque

Muller, Hermann Joseph
field: **8** genetics
researched: **5** X-rays **8** mutation
awarded: **10** Nobel Prize

Muller, Paul
field: **9** chemistry
nationality: **5** Swiss
established: **16** DDT as insecticide
awarded: **10** Nobel Prize

Mulligan, Buck
character in: **7** Ulysses
author: **5** Joyce

multicolored **10** variegated

multifarious **4** many **5** mixed **6** divers, motley, sundry, varied **7** diverse, protean, several, various **8** manifold, numerous **9** different, multiplex **10** variegated **11** diversified **13** heterogeneous, miscellaneous

multiple **4** many **7** various **8** manifold

multiply **5** add to, beget, breed, raise **6** extend, spread **7** augment, enhance, enlarge, magnify **8** generate, heighten, increase **9** intensify, procreate, propagate, reproduce **11** proliferate

multitude **3** mob **4** army, herd, host, mass, pack, slew **5** array, crowd, crush, drove, flock, flood, horde, troop **6** legion, myriad, scores, throng **7** conflux

multum in parvo **12** much in little **23** a great deal in a small space

mum **4** mute **5** quiet, still, tacit **6** silent **8** taciturn, wordless **9** secretive **12** close-mouthed **15** uncommunicative

mumble **5** growl, grunt, mouth **6** murmur, mutter, rumble **7** stammer **9** hem and haw

mumbo jumbo **3** rot **4** blah, bosh, cant, tosh **5** bilge, hokum, hooey, tripe **6** hot air, humbug **7** baloney **8** flummery **9** gibberish, sophistry **10** double talk, hocus pocus **11** doublespeak, jabberwocky, obfuscation **12** fiddle-faddle, gobbledygook, obscurantism

Mummy, The
director: **10** Karl Freund
cast: **10** Zita Johann **12** Boris Karloff, David Manners **16** Bramwell Fletcher

munch **4** chew, gnaw **5** champ, chomp, crush, grind **9** masticate

Munch, Edvard
born: **5** Loten **6** Norway **10** Hedemarken
artwork: **6** The Cry **7** Puberty, The Kiss **9** The Scream **11** Dance of Life **12** Frieze of Life **21** Death in the Sick Chamber

Munchkins
characters in: **13** The Wizard of Oz
author: **4** Baum

mundane **5** petty **7** earthly, humdrum, prosaic, routine, worldly **8** day-to-day, everyday, ordinary **9** practical **10** pedestrian **11** commonplace, down-to-earth, terrestrial

Muni, Paul
real name: **16** Muni Weisenfreund
born: **7** Austria, Lemberg (now Lvov USSR)
roles: **6** Juarez **8** Scarface **10** The Valiant **12** The Good Earth **14** Clarence Darrow, Inherit the Wind **15** The Last Angry Man **18** The Life of Emile Zola **22** The Story of Louis Pasteur (Oscar) **26** I Am a Fugitive from a Chain Gang

municipal **4** city **5** civic **6** public **9** community **14** administrative

municipality **4** city, town **6** parish **7** village **8** township **9** bailiwick

munificence **6** bounty **7** charity **8** largesse **9** patronage **10** generosity, liberality **11** benefaction, beneficence, benevolence **12** philanthropy **13** bounteousness, bountifulness **14** charitableness **15** humanitarianism

munificent **4** free **6** kindly, lavish **7** liberal, profuse **8** generous, princely **9** bounteous, bountiful **10** altruistic, beneficent, benevolent, charitable, freehanded, open-handed **11** extravagant, magnanimous **12** eleemosynary, humanitarian **13** philanthropic

Munin
origin: **12** Scandinavian
form: **5** raven
owned by: **4** Odin **5** Othin
personifies: **6** memory
duty: **10** newsbearer
other raven: **5** Hugin

Munitus
father: **6** Acamas
mother: **7** Laodice

Munsters, The
character: **11** Lily Munster **12** Eddie (Edward Wolfgang) Munster **13** Herman Munster **14** Grandpa Munster, Marilyn Munster
cast: **7** Al Lewis **9** Pat Priest **10** Fred Gwynne **11** Beverly Owen **12** Butch Patrick **13** Yvonne DeCarlo

Muppet Show, The
character: **4** Rolf **5** Gonzo **6** Animal, Beaker **7** Scooter **9** Miss Piggy **10** Fozzie Bear **13** Kermit the Frog (Kermie)

Murasaki, Lady
author of: **14** The Tale of Genji

murder **4** kill, slay **5** abuse, waste **6** mangle, misuse **7** butcher, corrupt, cut down, killing **8** homicide, knock off **9** agonizing, slaughter **10** bastardize, formidable, impossible, oppressive, unbearable **11** assassinate, intolerable **12** manslaughter **13** assassination, very difficult **14** commit homicide, use incorrectly

Murder, She Wrote
character: **15** Jessica (JB) Fletcher
cast: **14** Angela Lansbury
setting: **9** Cabot Cove

murderer **4** Cain **6** killer, slayer **7** butcher **8** assassin, Barabbas, homicide **9** cutthroat

Murder in the Cathedral
author: **7** T S Eliot

Murder of Roger Ackroyd, The
author: **14** Agatha Christie

Murder on the Orient Express
author: **14** Agatha Christie

murderous **4** gory **5** cruel, rough **6** bloody, brutal, deadly, savage, trying **7** killing **9** dangerous, difficult, ferocious **11** devastating **12** bloodthirsty, disaggreeable

Murdoch, Iris
author of: **7** The Bell **11** Under the Net **12** A Severed Head, The Sea the Sea **14** The Black Prince **15** Nuns and Soldiers **17** The Good Apprentice, The Nice and the Good **20** The Philosopher's Pupil **24** The Book and The Brotherhood **30** The Sacred and Profane Love Machine

Murdstone, Mr
character in: **16** David Copperfield
author: **7** Dickens

Murillo, Bartolome (Bartolomeo) Esteban
born: **5** Spain **7** Seville
artwork: **13** Angels' Kitchen **14** Death of St Clare **15** The Two Trinities **17** Vision of St Anthony **23** The Immaculate Conception **24** Dream of the Roman Patrician

murk **3** fog **4** haze, mist **5** gloom **6** miasma **8** darkness

murky **3** dim **4** dark, gray, hazy **5** dusky, foggy, misty **6** cloudy, dismal, dreary, gloomy, somber **7** obscure, sunless **8** lowering, overcast, vaporous **9** cheerless

murmur **3** hum **4** buzz, purl, purr, sigh **5** drone, sough, swish **6** lament, mumble, mutter, rumble, rustle **7** grumble, lapping, whimper, whisper **8** low sound, susurrus **9** complaint, undertone

murophobia
fear of: **4** mice

Murphy, Eddie
roles: **3** Raw **13** Trading Places **14** The Golden Child **15** Coming to America, Forty-Eight Hours **16** Beverly Hills Cop **17** Saturday Night Live **19** Beverly Hills Cop Two

Murray, Bill
roles: **7** Stripes **9** Meatballs **10** Caddyshack **12** Ghostbusters **13** The Razor's Edge **17** Saturday Night Live **27** Not Ready for Prime Time Players

Murray, Don
wife: **9** Hope Lange
born: **11** Hollywood CA
roles: **7** Bus Stop **13** A Hatful of Rain **16** The Bachelor Party, The Hoodlum Priest

Murray, Jeanne
real name of: **13** Jean Stapleton

Murray, Mina
character in: **7** Dracula
author: **6** Stoker

Musaeus
occupation: **4** poet, seer

Musagetes *see* **6** Apollo

Muscat, Masqat
capital of: **4** Oman

muscle ***see box***

muscular **3** fit **5** burly, husky, tough **6** brawny, sinewy, strong **8** athletic, powerful **9** strapping

muscular contraction
5 cramp, crick, spasm **6** stitch **12** charley horse

muscle **4** grit, thew **5** bicep, brawn, force, might, power, sinew, vigor **6** energy, flexor, tendon **7** potency, prowess, stamina **8** virility **9** puissance **10** sturdiness **16** muscular strength
kind: **4** limb **5** axial **6** smooth **7** dynamic, flexors, special, striped **8** postural, striated **9** abductors, extensors, voluntary **11** involuntary
fuel: **4** food
action: **4** pull
specific: **6** rectus **7** deltoid, oblique **8** omohyoid **9** abdominal, abdominis, sartorius **10** pectoralis **11** intercostal, sternohyoid **13** biceps brachii, rectus femoris **14** vastus medialis **15** brachioradialis, vastus lateralis **16** serratus anterior, tensor fascia lata **17** quadriceps femoris **18** transverse thoracic **19** sternocleidomastoid **20** transversus abdominis
supplementary structure: **6** sheath **10** deep fascia, retinacula **14** synovial bursae, synovial sheath

musculoskeletal system
component: **4** bone **6** muscle, tendon **8** ligament

muse **4** mull **6** ponder, review **7** reflect **8** cogitate, consider, meditate, ruminate **9** speculate **10** deliberate **11** contemplate

Musee des Beaux Arts
author: **7** W H Auden

Muses
also: **7** the Nine **8** Pierides **10** Castalides
form: **9** goddesses
names: **4** Clio **5** Aoede, Erato, Mneme **6** Melete, Thalia, Urania **7** Euterpe **8** Calliope **9** Melpomene **10** Polyhymnia **11** Terpsichore
father: **4** Zeus
mother: **9** Mnemosyne
corresponds to: **7** Camenae

Musgrave, Thea
born: **8** Scotland **9** Edinburgh
composer of: **11** The Decision **16** The Five Ages of

Man **17** Beauty and the Beast, The Voice of Ariadne

mush **5** slush **6** drivel **8** porridge **14** sentimentalism, sentimentality

mushiness **5** slush **6** bathos **10** sponginess **11** mawkishness **14** sentimentalism, sentimentality

mushroom **4** grow **5** burst, fungi **6** blow up, expand, fungus, spread, sprout **7** burgeon, explode, shoot up **8** flourish, increase, spring up **9** toadstool **11** proliferate
part: **3** cap **4** veil **5** gills, stalk, tubes, volva **6** button, hyphae, spores **7** annulus, basidia **10** rhizomorph
non-poisonous: **5** field, honey, morel, table **6** oyster **7** inky cap, parasol **8** puffball, shiitake **9** fairy-ring, morchella, shaggy cap, stinkhorn **10** champignon **11** chanterelle **12** edible bolete, slippery jack **16** old man of the woods
poisonous: **7** amanita **8** death cap, sickener **9** fly agaric **12** jack-o-lantern **13** devil's boletus **15** destroying angel
study of: **8** mycology

mushy **4** soft **5** foggy, misty, pappy, pulpy, vague **6** cloudy, quaggy, spongy **7** maudlin, mawkish, squashy, squishy **8** effusive, romantic, squelchy **10** lovey-dovey **11** sentimental, tear-jerking **12** affectionate

Musial, Stan
nickname: **10** Stan the Man
sport: **8** baseball
team: **16** St Louis Cardinals

music **4** song, tune **5** score **6** melody **7** euphony, harmony **8** lyricism **10** minstrelsy **11** tunefulness **13** melodiousness
god of: **5** Brage, Bragi **6** Apollo **7** Phoebus, Pythius **9** Musagetes

musical **5** lyric, sweet **6** dulcet **7** lilting, lyrical, melodic, tuneful **9** melodious **10** euphonious, harmonious **11** mellifluent

musical instrument ***see box***

musical terms ***see box***

musician **4** bard **5** piper **6** artist, player, singer, violer **7** bandman, cellist, drummer, pianist, twanger **8** minstrel, organist, virtuoso **9** performer, trumpeter, violinist **11** saxophonist

Music Man, The
director: **13** Morton Da Costa
cast: **12** Buddy Hackett, Shirley Jones (Marian the librarian) **13** Robert Preston (Professor Harold Hill) **15** Hermione Gingold
setting: **9** River City
score: **15** Meredith Willson
song: **15** Till There Was You **19** Seventy-six Trombones

music school **12** conservatory
French: **13** conservatoire

musing **6** absent, dreamy **7** mulling **8** absorbed **9** pondering **10** meditating, meditative, reflecting, reflective

musical terms
agitated: **7** agitato
all players/singers together: **5** tutti
becoming quicker: **11** accelerando
continue without a break: **5** segue
disconnected/each note separate: **8** staccato
end: **4** fine
expressively: **10** espressivo
abbreviation: **4** espr
fast: **6** veloce **7** allegro
gentle: **5** soave
gently: **9** doucement
getting slower: **10** allargando
getting weaker and slower: **7** calando
gradually getting louder: **9** crescendo
abbreviation: **5** cresc
gradually getting softer: **10** diminuendo **11** decrescendo
abbreviation: **3** dim **4** decr
gradually slowing: **11** rallentando
abbreviation: **4** rall
half: **5** mezzo
half voice/half volume: **9** mezza voce
heavy: **5** lourd
in an undertone/in a low voice: **9** sotto voce
leisurely: **6** comodo
less: **4** meno
light: **8** leggiero
little: **4** poco
lively: **3** vif
loud: **5** forte
abbreviation: **1** f
moderately slow and even: **7** andante
more: **3** piu
mournful: **5** mesto

musical instrument **3** lur, sax, saz **4** bass, bell, drum, fife, gong, harp, horn, lute, lyre, oboe, outi, pipe, tuba, viol **5** argul, banjo, bugle, cello, cobza, flute, kazoo, organ, piano, guena, rabob, sansa, shawm, sheng, sitar, viola **6** bagana, chimes, cornet, cymbal, fiddle, guitar, spinet, treble, violin, zither **7** bagpipe, bassoon, cittern, clavier, kithara, marimba, panpipe, pibcorn, piccolo, samisen, strings, tambura, theorbo, timpani, trumpet, ukulele **8** autoharp, bass drum, calliope, clarinet, dulcimer, Jew's harp, mandolin, psaltery, recorder, talharpa, triangle, trombone, virginal **9** accordion, balalaika, castanets, harmonica, harmonium, krummhorn, rommelpot, saxophone, snare drum, xylophone **10** bongo drums, clavichord, concertina, flugelhorn, French horn, kettledrum, sousaphone, tambourine, vibraphone **11** English horn, harpsichord **12** jouhikantele
classification: **4** horn, reed, wind **5** brass **6** string **8** keyboard, woodwind **10** electronic, percussion

musjid **6** mosque

Muskogean, Muskhogean
tribe: **4** Cree **7** Alabama, Alibamu, Choctaw, Natchez **8** Seminole **9** Chickasaw

Muslim *see* **6** Moslem

muslin
French: **10** mousseline

muss **4** mess **6** foul up, jumble, ruffle, rumple, tangle, tousle **7** crumple, disturb **8** dishevel, disorder **9** bedraggle **10** disarrange

mussed **5** messy **6** frowzy, untidy **7** ruffled, rumpled, tou-

not too much: **9** non troppo
plucked instead of bowed: **9** pizzicato
abbreviation: **4** pizz
quick / vivacious: **6** vivace
repeat from beginning: **6** da capo
abbreviation: **2** D C
shaking and quavering / rapid alternation of notes: **5** trill
silent: **4** tace
singing / songlike / flowing: **9** cantabile
sliding: **9** glissando
slow: **5** lento **6** adagio
slow dignified tempo: **5** largo
slow down: **5** cedez
smooth / connected: **6** legato
soft: **5** piano
abbreviation: **1** p
solemn / serious: **5** grave
sorrowful: **7** dolente
strict time: **10** tempo gusto
sudden accent: **9** sforzando
abbreviation: **2** sf
sweetly: **5** dolce
tearful: **9** lacrimoso
tenderly: **10** affettuoso
trembling vibrating effect / rapid reiteration of a single pitch: **7** tremolo
very: **5** molto
very loud: **10** fortissimo
abbreviation: **2** ff
very soft: **10** pianissimo
abbreviation: **2** pp
with fire: **8** con fuoco
with spirit / vigor: **7** con brio
with style / taste: **8** con gusto
with the mute: **10** con sordino

sled, unkempt **8** uncombed **10** disarrayed, disheveled, disordered, disorderly **11** disarranged

Mussorgsky (Moussorgsky), Modest Petrovich
born: **5** Pskov **6** Russia
member of: **7** The Five
composer of: **7** Sunless **10** The Nursery **12** Boris Godunov **13** Khovanshchina **19** Night on Bald Mountain **21** Songs and Dances of Death **22** Pictures at an Exhibition

mustard
botanical name: **5** B alba **6** B hirta, B nigra **7** B juncea **8** Brassica
also called: **7** sinapis
origin: **4** Asia **5** China
use: **6** hotdog, sauces **7** egg roll **9** hamburger **13** salad dressing

muster **4** call **5** amass, raise, rally **6** gather, line up, summon **7** collect, company, convene, convoke, marshal, meeting, round up, turnout **8** assemble, assembly, mobilize **9** convocate, gathering **10** assemblage, confluence, congregate, inspection **11** aggregation **12** accumulation **13** agglomeration

musty **3** old **4** damp, dank, worn **5** banal, dirty, dusty, moldy, stale, tired, trite **6** frousy, frouzy, frowsy, frowzy, old hat, stuffy **7** worn-out **8** familiar, mildewed **9** hackneyed **10** antiquated, threadbare **11** commonplace

mutable **6** fickle **7** pliable **8** flexible, variable **9** adaptable, alterable, mercurial, versatile **10** adjustable, changeable, inconstant, modifiable, permutable **11** convertible, metamorphic **13** transformable

mutate **4** turn **5** alter **6** change **7** convert **9** transform

mutation **6** change **7** anomaly **9** deviation, variation **10** alteration **12** modification **13** metamorphosis **14** transformation **15** transfiguration **18** transmogrification

mutatis mutandis **30** necessary changes having been made

mute **3** mum **4** dumb **5** quiet, tacit **6** silent **8** aphasiac, nonvocal, reserved, reticent **9** unsounded, unuttered, voiceless **10** speechless **12** inarticulate, noncommittal, unpronounced **13** unarticulated **15** uncommunicative

muted **3** dim, low **4** dull, soft, weak **5** quiet **6** dulled, feeble **7** muffled **8** deadened, softened **10** indistinct, lackluster

mutilate **4** lame, maim **6** cut off, deform, excise, mangle **7** butcher, cripple **8** amputate, lacerate, truncate **9** disfigure, dismember

mutineer **5** rebel **9** dissident, insurgent **10** malcontent **15** insurrectionist

mutinous **6** unruly **10** dissenting, rebellious **13** revolutionary

Mutinus
origin: **5** Roman **7** Italian
god of: **9** fertility
fertility in: **8** marriage
corresponds to: **7** Priapus

mutiny **4** coup **5** rebel **6** revolt, rise up **8** takeover, upheaval, uprising **9** overthrow, rebellion **10** insurgency **12** insurrection

Mutiny on the Bounty
author: **15** Charles Nordhoff, James Norman Hall
character: **6** Tehani **9** Roger Byam **12** William Bligh (Captain Bligh) **13** George Stewart **17** Fletcher Christian
director: **10** Frank Lloyd
cast: **10** Clark Gable (Fletcher Christian) **12** Eddie Quillan, Franchot Tone **13** Herbert Mundin **15** Charles Laughton (Captain Bligh)
Oscar for: **7** picture

mutt **3** cur, dog, pup **5** puppy **7** mongrel

Mutt and Jeff
creator: **7** Al Smith **9** Bud Fisher
character: **5** A Mutt **6** Cicero **7** Mrs Mutt

mutter **4** carp **5** gripe, growl, grunt **6** grouch, grouse, kvetch, mumble, murmur, rumble **7** grumble, whisper **8** complain

mutual **5** joint **6** common, shared **7** related **8** communal, returned **10** coincident, reciprocal **11** correlative, interactive **12** interchanged, reciprocated **15** interchangeable

mutual understanding **6** accord **9** agreement

muzzle **3** gag **4** bind, curb **5** check, quiet, still **6** bridle, rein in, stifle **7** harness, silence **8** strangle, suppress, throttle

My Antonia
author: **11** Willa Cather
character: **9** Jim Burden **15** Antonia Shimerda

My Darling Clementine
director: **8** John Ford
cast: **7** Tim Holt **8** Ward Bond **10** Henry Fonda (Wyatt Earp) **12** Linda Darnell, Victor Mature (Doc Holliday) **13** Walter Brennan

my dear
French: **7** ma chere, mon cher

My Fair Lady
director: **11** George Cukor

based on play by: **17** George Bernard Shaw (Pygmalion)
cast: **11** Rex Harrison (Professor Henry Higgins) **13** Audrey Hepburn (Eliza Doolittle) **15** Stanley Holloway **16** Wilfrid Hyde-White
score: **14** Lerner and Loewe
Oscar for: **7** picture
song: **14** The Rain in Spain **24** I Could Have Danced All Night

my faith
French: **5** ma foi

my fault
Latin: **8** mea culpa

My Favorite Martian
character: **8** Tim O'Hara **11** Uncle Martin **15** Mrs Lorelei Brown
cast: **9** Bill Bixby **10** Ray Walston **13** Pamela Britton

Mygdon
king of: **8** Bebryces
killed by: **8** Hercules

Myles
king of: **7** Laconia
invented: **9** grain mill

Mylitta *see* **6** Ishtar

My Little Margie
character: **7** Charlie **9** Mrs Odetts **11** Mr Honeywell **13** Freddie Wilson **14** Margie Albright, Vernon Albright **15** Roberta Townsend
cast: **9** Don Hayden, Gale Storm **10** Willie Best **12** Clarence Kolb **13** Hillary Brooke **14** Charles Farrell **15** Gertrude Hoffman

my lord
French: **8** monsieur **11** monseigneur
Italian: **9** monsignor **10** monsignore

My Man Godfrey
director: **13** Gregory La Cava
cast: **10** Alice Brady, Mischa Auer **11** Gail Patrick **13** Carole Lombard, William Powell

Mynes
king of: **9** Lyrnessus
wife: **7** Briseis
killed by: **8** Achilles

myriad **6** untold **7** endless **8** infinite, manifold **9** boundless, countless, limitless, uncounted **11** innumerable, measureless **12** immeasurable, incalculable **13** multitudinous

Myrina
husband: **8** Dardanus

myrmidon **6** cohort **8** follower, henchman

Myrmidons
people of: **6** Aegina **8** Thessaly
created by: **4** Zeus
created from: **4** ants
characteristic: **7** warlike
leader: **6** Peleus **8** Achilles

Myrrha
also: **6** Smyrna
father: **11** King Cinyras
loved: **7** Cinyras
crime: **6** incest
son: **6** Adonis
changed into: **6** myrtle **9** myrrh tree

Myrtilus
charioteer of: **8** Oenomaus

myrtle **6** Myrtus **10** Vinca minor **14** Myrtus communis **18** Cyrilla racemiflora **23** Umbellularia californica
varieties: **3** bog, gum, sea, wax **4** cape, Jew's, sand **5** crape, crepe, downy, dwarf, Greek, honey, scent **6** German, Oregon, Polish, willow **7** box sand, classic, running, Swedish **10** Western tea **11** candleberry, Queen's crape, sand-verbena **13** Allegheny sand, bracelet honey, California wax **16** Australian willow

Mysia
epithet of: **7** Demeter

mysophobia
fear of: **4** dirt

Mysteries of Paris, The
author: **9** Eugene Sue

Mysteries of Udolpho, The
author: **15** Mrs Ann Radcliffe

mysterious **4** dark **6** cloudy, covert, hidden, secret **7** cryptic, obscure, strange, unknown **8** baffling, puzzling **9** enigmatic, secretive **10** perplexing, sphinxlike, undercover **11** clandestine, inscrutable **12** impenetrable, inexplicable, supernatural, unfathomable **13** surreptitious **14** undecipherable

Mysterious Stranger, The
author: **9** Mark Twain

mystery **6** enigma, occult, puzzle, riddle, secret **7** problem, secrecy **9** conundrum, obscurity, symbolism, vagueness **11** ambivalence, elusiveness **12** ineffability, quizzicality **13** ineffableness, mystification

Mystery of Edwin Drood, The *see* **10** Edwin Drood

mystical, mystic **5** inner **6** hidden, occult **7** cryptic, obscure **8** abstruse, esoteric, ethereal, symbolic **9** enigmatic, secretive **10** cabalistic, symbolical, unknowable **11** inscrutable, nonrational **12** metaphysical, otherworldly **14** transcendental

mystification **9** confusion **10** bafflement, perplexity, puzzlement **12** bewilderment

mystify **4** fool **5** elude **6** baffle, puzzle **7** confuse, deceive, mislead, perplex **8** bewilder, confound **9** bamboozle

myth **3** fib, lie **4** tale, yarn **5** error, fable, story **6** canard, legend **7** fantasy, fiction, hearsay, parable **8** allegory, delusion, illusion, tall tale **9** fairy tale, falsehood **10** shibboleth **13** prevarication

mythical, mythic **6** fabled, unreal **8** illusory **9** imaginary, legendary, pretended **10** conjured-up, fabricated, fantasized, fictitious **13** unsubstantial

mythological, mythologic **6** unreal **8** fabulous, illusory, imagined **9** fantastic, imaginary, legendary, unfactual **10** fictitious

My Three Sons
character: **11** Chip Douglas, Mike Douglas **12** Steve Douglas **13** Robbie Douglas **18** Katie Miller Douglas, Uncle Charley O'Casey **20** Ernie Thompson Douglas, Michael Francis (Bub) O'Casey
cast: **8** Don Grady, Tina Cole **12** Tim Considine **13** Fred MacMurray **14** William Frawley **15** Barry Livingston, William Demarest **17** Stanley Livingston
dog: **5** Tramp

my word
French: **5** ma foi

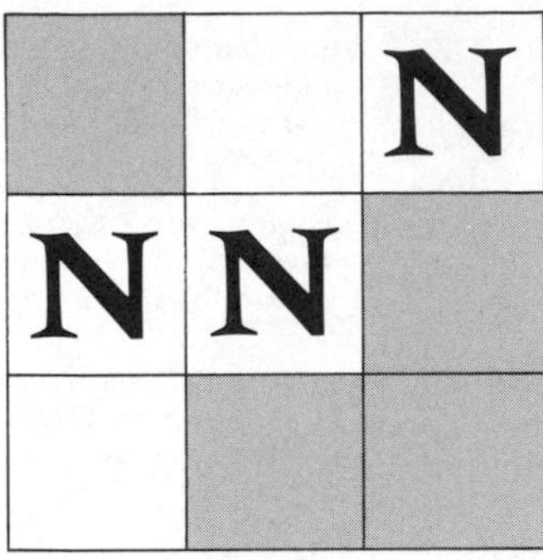

nab **4** bust, grab, nail, snag **5** catch, pinch, seize, snare **6** arrest, collar, detain, haul in, pick up, pull in, snatch **7** capture **9** apprehend

nabob **4** lord **5** mogul, nawab **6** deputy, tycoon **7** magnate **8** governor **9** plutocrat **10** capitalist **11** billionaire, millionaire

Nabokov, Vladimir
author of: **3** Ada **6** Lolita **8** Pale Fire

Nabonidus
son: **10** Belshazzar

Nadab
father: **5** Aaron **6** Gibeon **7** Shammai **8** Jeroboam
mother: **8** Elisheba
brother: **5** Abihu **7** Eleazar, Ithamar

nadir **4** base, zero **5** floor **6** apogee, bottom **7** nothing **8** low point **10** rock bottom **11** lowest point

Nadja
author: **11** Andre Breton

nag **4** fury, goad, harp **5** annoy, devil, harpy, scold, shrew, vixen **6** badger, bicker, harass, hassle, heckle, hector, nettle, peck at, pester, pick at, pick on, plague, rail at, tartar, virago **7** bedevil, upbraid **8** battle-ax, irritate **9** importune, termagant, Xanthippe

Nahua *see* **5** Aztec

Nahuatl *see* **10** Uto-Aztecan

Naiad
form: **5** nymph
location: **5** water

nail **3** fix, pin **4** claw **5** talon **6** fasten, hammer, secure
part: **3** bed **4** root

Naipaul, V S
author of: **10** Guerrillas **15** A Bend in the River **17** A House for Mr Biswas **19** The Return of Eva Peron, The Suffrage of Elvira

Nairobi
capital of: **5** Kenya

naive **4** open **5** green, plain **6** candid, simple, unwary, unwise **7** artless, foolish, natural, unjaded **8** gullible, immature, innocent **9** childlike, credulous, guileless, ingenuous, unspoiled, unworldly **10** unaffected, unassuming **11** susceptible **12** unsuspecting, unsuspicious **15** unsophisticated

naivete, naivete **6** candor **7** modesty **8** openness **9** credulity, frankness, greenness, innocence, sincerity **10** callowness, simplicity **11** artlessness, foolishness, naturalness **12** childishness, inexperience **13** ingenuousness **14** unaffectedness **16** simplemindedness

naked **4** bald, bare, nude, pure **5** bared, frank, plain, sheer **6** patent, simple, unclad **7** blatant, exposed **8** disrobed, laid bare, manifest, palpable, undraped, wide-open **9** in the buff, unclothed, uncovered, undressed **11** perceptible, unappareled, unqualified, unvarnished **15** in the altogether

Naked and the Dead, The
author: **12** Norman Mailer

Naked City
character: **5** Libby **9** (Det) Adam Flint **10** (Det Lt) Dan Muldoon, (Lt) Mike Parker **11** (Det) Jim Halloran, (Ptlm/Sgt) Frank Arcaro **13** Janet Halloran
cast: **9** Paul Burke **11** Nancy Malone **12** John McIntire **13** Harry Bellaver, Horace McMahon, Suzanne Storrs **15** James Franciscus
setting: **11** New York City
theme: **19** Somewhere in the Night

Namath, Joe (Joseph William)
nickname: **11** Broadway Joe
sport: **8** football
position: **11** quarterback
team: **11** New York Jets

namby-pamby **3** coy **4** dull, prim, weak **5** banal, inane, vapid **6** prissy **7** insipid, mincing, sapless **9** colorless, innocuous, simpering **10** indecisive, wishy-washy **13** characterless

name **3** tag **4** call, term **5** label, title **6** choose, ordain, select **7** appoint, baptize, epithet, specify **8** christen, cognomen, delegate, deputize, nominate, taxonomy **9** authorize, designate, signature, sobriquet **10** commission **11** appellation, designation **12** denomination, nomenclature

nameless **5** minor **7** obscure, unknown, unnamed **8** untitled **9** anonymous, unheard-of, unhonored **12** undesignated

namely
Latin: **3** viz **9** videlicet

Name of the Game
character: **8** Andy Hill **9** Joe Sample, Ross Craig **10** Dan Farrell, Jeff Dillon **11** Glenn Howard **12** Peggy Maxwell
cast: **9** Ben Murphy, Gene Barry **10** Mark Miller **11** Cliff Potter, Robert Stack **13** Tony Franciosa **15** Susan Saint James
business: **8** magazine **10** publishing

Name of the Rose, The
author: **10** Umberto Eco

Name That Tune
host: **9** Red Benson **10** Bill Cullen **12** George de Witt
orchestra: **11** Harry Salter

Namibia ***see box, p. 662***

Nammu
origin: **8** Sumerian

Namibia
other name: **15** South West Africa
capital/largest city: **8** Windhoek
others: **6** Tsumeb **8** Luderitz **9** Walvis Bay **10** Oranjemund, Swakopmund **12** Keetmanshoop
monetary unit: **4** cent, rand
mountain: **14** Khomas Highland, Koakoveld Hills
highest point: **9** Brandberg
river: **4** Fish **6** Cunene, Orange **7** Zambezi **8** Okavango
sea: **8** Atlantic
physical feature:
bay: **6** Walvis
desert: **5** Namib **8** Kalahari
region: **12** Caprivi Strip
people: **4** Nama **5** Bantu **6** Damara, Herero, Ovambo, Tswara **7** Bushman, colored **8** Okavango **9** Hottentot
language: **5** Bantu **6** German **7** English, Khoisan **9** Afrikaans
religion: **7** animism **8** Lutheran
feature:
homeland: **9** bantustan

mother of: **4** gods
personifies: **3** sea

Namtar
origin: **8** Akkadian, Sumerian
form: **5** demon
personifies: **5** death

Nana
author: **9** Emile Zola

Nana (Nurse)
character in: **8** Peter Pan
author: **6** Barrie

Nancy
character in: **11** Oliver Twist
author: **7** Dickens

Nancy
creator: **15** Ernie Bushmiller
character: **6** Sluggo **10** Aunt Fritzi

Nanna
origin: **12** Scandinavian
husband: **5** Baldr **6** Balder, Baldur
habitat: **4** moon

Nannerella
nickname of: **11** Anna Magnani

nanometer
abbreviation: **2** nm

Naoise
origin: **5** Irish
wife: **7** Deirdre
uncle: **9** Conchobar
killed by: **9** Conchobar
father: **6** Usnach, Usnech

Naomi
husband: **9** Elimelech
daughter-in-law: **4** Ruth
son: **6** Mahlon **7** Chilion

nap **3** nod **4** doze, rest **6** catnap, drowse, siesta, snooze **7** doze off, drop off, goof off, shut-eye, slumber **8** drift off **10** forty winks

Napaeae
form: **6** nymphs
location: **4** dell

napery **5** doily **6** linens, napkin **10** tablecloth

Naphtali
father: **5** Jacob
mother: **6** Bilkah
brother: **3** Dan, Gad **4** Levi **5** Asher, Judah **6** Joseph, Reuben, Simeon **7** Zebulun **8** Benjamin, Issachar
sister: **5** Dinah
descendant of: **10** Naphtalite

Napoleon Bonaparte *see box*

Napoleon of Notting Hill, The
author: **12** G K Chesterton

Narcaeus
father: **8** Dionysus
mother: **7** Physcoa

narcissism **6** egoism, vanity **7** conceit **8** self-love **11** egocentrism **16** self-centeredness

narcissist **6** egoist **7** egotist **11** egocentrist **12** self-absorbed, self-admiring

narcissistic **4** smug, vain **6** vanity **7** conceit, selfish **8** egotistic, puffed-up **9** conceited **10** egocentric, egoistical **11** egomaniacal, egotistical

narcissus
varieties: **5** poet's **6** poetaz **7** leedsii, trumpet **10** paperwhite, polyanthus **16** primrose peerless

Narcissus
father: **8** Cephisus
mother: **8** Leiriope
loved: **7** himself
loved by: **4** Echo
punished by: **9** Aphrodite
changed into: **6** flower

narcotic **4** drug **6** opiate **8** medicine, sedative **9** soporific **10** medicament, medication, painkiller **12** tranquilizer **14** pharmaceutical

Narragansett
language family: **9** Algonkian **10** Algonquian
location: **11** Connecticut, Rhode Island
related to: **7** Niantic
involved in: **9** Pequot War **14** King Philip's War **15** Great Swamp Fight

narrate **6** detail, recite, relate, render, repeat, retell **7** portray, recount **8** describe, set forth **9** chronicle **10** tell a story **15** give an account of

narration **7** recital, telling **8** relating, speaking **9** voiceover **10** recitation, recounting **11** chronicling, description **12** storytelling

narrative **4** tale **5** story **6** report **7** account, recital **8** dialogue, episodic **9** anecdotal, chronicle, statement **10** historical **12** storytelling

Narrative of Arthur Gordon Pym, The
author: **13** Edgar Allan Poe

Napoleon Bonaparte
also: **9** Napoleon I **18** Emperor of the French
battle: **3** Ulm **5** Eylau **6** Lutzen, Moscow, Toulon (siege), Wagram **7** Bautzen, Dresden, Leipzig, Marengo, Mondovi **8** Borodino, Waterloo **9** Friedland **10** Austerlitz **13** Aspern-Essling, Jena-Auerstadt, Peninsular War **22** War of the Fifth Coalition
born: **7** Corsica
exile to: **4** Elba **11** Saint Helena
fought against: **7** Kutuzov **10** von Blucher, Wellington **14** Barclay de Tolly
French fleet destroyed at: **9** Trafalgar
destroyed by: **6** Nelson
laws: **14** Napoleonic Code
marshal/general under: **3** Ney **5** Murat **7** Massena **10** Bernadotte
position: **7** emperor **11** first consul **13** consul for life
tomb: **5** Paris **9** Invalides
wife: **9** Josephine **20** Marie-Louise of Austria

narrow **3** set **4** fine, slim **5** close, scant, small, tight **6** biased, scanty **7** bigoted, cramped, pinched, shallow, slender, tapered **8** confined, dogmatic, isolated, squeezed **9** hidebound, illiberal, parochial **10** attenuated, compressed, intolerant, provincial, restricted **11** constricted, incapacious, opinionated, reactionary **12** conservative

narrowing **5** taper **8** tapering **9** squeezing **11** compressing **12** constricting

narrow-minded **5** petty **7** bigoted, prudish **8** one-sided **9** hidebound, parochial, unworldly **10** provincial **11** opinionated, reactionary, straitlaced **12** conservative **15** unsophisticated

narrow-mindedness **4** bias **7** bigotry **9** prejudice **10** unfairness **11** intolerance

narrows **4** neck, pass **5** canal **6** ravine, strait **7** channel, isthmus, passage

Nasca *see* **5** Nazca

Nascimento, Edson Arantes do
real name of: **4** Pele

Nash, Ogden
author of: **6** Versus **9** Hard Lines **20** The Private Dining Room **21** I'm a Stranger Here Myself

Nashville
director: **12** Robert Altman
cast: **10** Karen Black, Lily Tomlin **11** Henry Gibson **12** Ronee Blakley **13** Barbara Harris, Michael Murphy **14** Keith Carradine **16** Geraldine Chaplin
Oscar for: **4** song
song: **6** I'm Easy

Nassau
capital of: **7** Bahamas

nasty **4** foul, mean, vile **5** awful **6** odious **7** beastly, hateful, vicious **8** horrible **9** repellent, revolting **10** abominable, disgusting, nauseating, unpleasant **11** distasteful **12** disagreeable

Natchez
language family: **10** Muskhogean
tribe: **6** Avoyel, Taensa
location: **11** Mississippi **13** South Carolina
allied with: **7** Choctaw
practiced: **14** head flattening

nates **4** buns, rear, rump, seat **7** rear end **8** buttocks, haunches **9** fundament, posterior **12** hindquarters

Nathan
father: **5** Attai
served: **5** David **7** Solomon

Nathanael *see* **5** Jesus **8** Apostles **11** Bartholomew

nation **4** host, race **5** realm, state, tribe **6** empire, people **7** country, kingdom **8** republic **9** community **11** sovereignty **12** commonwealth

national park ***see box***

National Velvet
director: **13** Clarence Brown
cast: **10** Anne Revere **11** Donald Crisp **12** Mickey Rooney **14** Angela Lansbury **15** Elizabeth Taylor
Oscar for: **17** supporting actress (Revere)
sequel: **19** International Velvet

native **4** home **5** basic, local, natal **6** inborn, inbred, innate, savage **7** citizen, endemic, natural **8** domestic, inherent, national, paternal **9** aborigine, elemental, homegrown, ingrained, inherited, intrinsic, primitive **10** congenital, countryman, hereditary, indigenous **11** instinctive **12** countrywoman **13** autochthonous

native country **7** country **8** homeland **10** fatherland **13** mother country

native-grown **5** local **8** domestic **9** homegrown **10** indigenous

native land **8** homeland **10** birthplace, fatherland, native soil **13** mother country, native country

native of Israel
Hebrew: **5** sabra

native soil **8** homeland **10** fatherland, native land **13** mother country, native country

Native Son
author: **13** Richard Wright

natty **4** chic, neat, posh, tidy, trim **5** smart **6** dapper, jaunty, snappy, spruce **7** dashing, modish, stylish **11** fashionable

Natty Bumppo
also: **7** Hawkeye **10** Pathfinder, The Trapper **13** The Deerslayer **15** Leatherstocking **16** Le Longue Carabine
character in: **23** The Leatherstocking Tales
friend: **5** Uncas **12** Chingachgook
author: **6** Cooper

national park
Alaska: **13** Mount McKinley
Arizona: **11** Grand Canyon **15** Petrified Forest
Arkansas: **10** Hot Springs
California: **7** Redwood, Sequoia **8** Yosemite **11** Kings Canyon **14** Channel Islands, Lassen Volcanic
Canada: **4** Yoho **5** Banff, Fundy **6** Jasper, Kluane **8** Kootenay **9** Auyuittuq **13** Waterton Lakes
Colorado: **5** Estes **9** Mesa Verde **13** Rocky Mountain
Florida: **10** Everglades
Hawaii: **9** Haleakala **15** Hawaii Volcanoes
Kentucky: **11** Mammoth Cave
Maine: **6** Acadia
Michigan: **10** Isle Royale
Minnesota: **9** Voyageurs
Montana: **7** Glacier **11** Yellowstone
New Mexico: **15** Carlsbad Caverns
North Carolina: **19** Great Smoky Mountains (with Tennessee)
North Dakota: **17** Theodore Roosevelt
Oklahoma: **6** Platte
Oregon: **10** Crater Lake
South Dakota: **8** Badlands, Wind Cave
Tennessee: **6** Shiloh **13** Cumberland Gap **19** Great Smoky Mountains (with North Carolina)
Texas: **7** Big Bend **18** Guadalupe Mountains
Utah: **4** Zion **6** Arches **11** Bryce Canyon, Canyonlands, Capital Reef
Virginia: **10** Shenandoah **26** Colonial National Historical
Washington: **7** Olympic **12** Mount Rainier **13** North Cascades
Wyoming: **10** Grand Teton **11** Yellowstone

natural **5** plain **6** inborn, native, normal **7** earthly, genuine, regular **8** God-given, inherent **9** essential, intuitive, unstudied **10** unaffected, unmannered **11** instinctive, spontaneous, terrestrial **13** unpretentious **14** characteristic **15** straightforward

Natural, The
director: **13** Barry Levinson
based on story by: **14** Bernard Malamud
cast: **10** Glenn Close **12** Robert Duvall **13** Robert Redford

natural child **7** bastard **9** love child **17** illegitimate child

natural gift **5** flair **6** talent **7** ability, faculty **8** aptitude **9** attribute, endowment

natural habitat **5** range **6** domain, milieu **7** element **9** territory **11** environment

naturalize **5** adapt, adopt **6** adjust **8** accustom **9** acclimate **11** domesticate, familiarize

naturalness **4** ease **9** sincerity **10** simplicity **11** artlessness, genuineness **12** unconstraint **14** unaffectedness

nature **4** bent, kind, mood, sort, type **5** birth, earth, globe, humor, stamp, style, trait **6** cosmos, spirit **7** essence, feature, variety **8** category, creation, instinct, property, universe **9** character **11** disposition, peculiarity **12** constitution **13** particularity **14** characteristic
goddess of: **6** Cybele **9** Dindymene **10** Berecyntia

Nature
author: **17** Ralph Waldo Emerson

naught **3** nil **4** zero **5** nihil, zilch **6** cipher **7** nothing, useless **9** worthless

naughty **3** bad **4** blue **5** bawdy, dirty **6** ribald, risque, vulgar **7** wayward, willful **8** devilish, off-color, perverse **9** fractious, obstinate **11** disobedient, misbehaving, mischievous **12** pornographic, recalcitrant, unmanageable **13** disrespectful

Naum
son: **4** Amos

Nauru ***see box***

nausea **7** disgust, heaving **8** contempt, loathing, retching, sickness, vomiting **9** repulsion, revulsion **10** queasiness **11** airsickness, biliousness, car sickness, seasickness **12** upset stomach **14** motion sickness, travel sickness

Nauru
other name: **14** Pleasant Island
capital: **13** Yaren District
cities: **3** Boe, Ewa **4** Aiwo, Ijuw **5** Baiti, Buada, Nibok, Uaboe, Yaren **6** Anabar, Anetan, Meneng **7** Anibare **10** Denigomodu
monetary unit: **4** cent **6** dollar
lake: **11** Buada Lagoon
sea: **7** Pacific
physical feature:
bay: **7** Anibare
lagoon: **5** Buada
point: **4** Anna **6** Meneng
people: **7** Chinese **10** Melanesian, Polynesiàn **11** Micronesian
explorer: **9** John Fearn
language: **7** English, Nauruan
religion: **10** Protestant **13** Roman Catholic
feature: **9** phosphate

Nausea
author: **14** Jean-Paul Sartre

nauseate **5** repel, upset **6** offend, revolt, sicken **7** disgust, repulse **8** make sick **15** turn one's stomach

nauseated **3** ill **4** sick **5** upset **6** queasy **8** repelled, revolted **9** disgusted

nauseating **9** offensive, repellent, repulsive, revolting, sickening **10** disgusting

nauseous **4** sick **5** upset **6** queasy **9** abhorrent, nauseated, offensive, repellent, repulsive, revolting, sickening, upsetting **10** disgusting, nauseating **12** unappetizing

Nausicaa
father: **8** Alcinous
position: **8** princess
aided: **8** Odysseus

Nausithous
father: **8** Poseidon
mother: **8** Periboea
occupation: **8** helmsman
employer: **7** Theseus
became: **4** king
realm: **8** Phaeacia

Nautes
advisor to: **6** Aeneas

nautical **5** naval **6** marine **7** aquatic, boating, oceanic **8** maritime, of the sea, seagoing, yachting

nautical mile
abbreviation: **3** nmi

Nautilus
submarine in: **32** Twenty Thousand Leagues Under the Sea
author: **5** Verne

Navajo, Navaho (Dine)
language family: **10** Athapascan, Athapaskan
location: **4** Utah **7** Arizona **9** New Mexico
noted for: **7** weaving **14** silversmithing
dwelling: **5** hogan

navigate **3** fly **4** ride, sail, ship **5** cross, steer **6** cruise, voyage **8** maneuver, sail over **11** plot a course **12** chart a course

navigation **7** boating, sailing **8** cruising, piloting, voyaging **9** traveling **10** seamanship
god of: **5** Niord, Njord

Navigators Islands *see* **12** Western Samoa

navy **5** fleet **6** armada, convoy **8** flotilla, warships

navy-blue **6** indigo **8** dark blue, deep blue

nay **4** also, deny, vote **5** never **6** denial, refuse **7** against, but also, refusal **8** negative

Nazarene *see* **5** Jesus

Nazarene, The
author: **10** Sholem Asch

Nazca, Nasca
location: **4** Peru **12** South America
noted for: **8** ceramics, textiles **10** Nazca lines (sketches on plain)

Nazi air force
German: **9** Luftwaffe

Nazi swastika
German: **10** Hakenkreuz

N'Djamena
capital of: **4** Chad

Neaera
mentioned in: **7** Odyssey
form: **5** nymph
father: **6** Pereus
cousin: **9** King Aleus
husband: **9** King Aleus
son: **7** Cepheus
daughter: **4** Auge **6** Evadne **8** Lampetia

Neal, Patricia
husband: **9** Roald Dahl
born: **9** Packard KY
roles: **3** Hud (Oscar) **15** A Face in the Crowd, The Fountainhead **18** The Subject Was Roses

near **4** nigh **5** about, close **6** all but, almost **7** close by, close to, looming **8** approach, come up to, imminent, next door **9** alongside, close with, impending **10** hereabouts **11** approaching, practically, proximately, threatening **13** approximately

nearby **5** close, handy **6** at hand **7** close by **8** next door **9** adjoining **10** accessible, hereabouts

near death
Latin: **10** in extremis

near home **5** close **7** close by **10** hereabouts

nearly **4** nigh **5** about **6** all but, almost **7** close to, roughly **11** practically **13** approximately

nearly equal **5** close **7** similar **10** nip-and-tuck **11** approaching

nearly even **5** close **10** head to head, nip-and-tuck **11** neck and neck

nearness **8** intimacy, vicinity **9** adjacency, closeness, handiness, immediacy, proximity **10** contiguity **11** propinquity **12** availability, neighborhood **13** accessibility, approximation

neat **4** tidy **5** clean, great **6** groovy **7** concise, correct, orderly **8** accurate, exciting, original, straight, striking, succinct **9** competent, dexterous, efficient, ingenious, organized, purposive, shipshape **10** controlled, immaculate, methodical, systematic **11** imaginative, intelligent, uncluttered

neatness **5** order **8** tidiness **11** orderliness **12** organization

Nebraska ***see box***

Nebraska
abbreviation: **2** NE **4** Nebr
nickname: **4** Beef **8** Antelope **10** Blackwater, Cornhusker **12** Treeplanter's
capital: **7** Lincoln
largest city: **5** Omaha
others: **5** Cozad **6** Gering **7** Kearney **8** Beatrice, Hastings **9** Broken Bow **11** Grand Island, North Platte, Scottsbluff
college: **4** Dana **5** Doane **8** Duchesne, Hastings **9** Creighton **15** Midland Lutheran
feature: **8** Boys' Town
national monument: **11** Scott's Bluff **15** Agate Fossil Beds
tribe: **3** Oto **4** Otoe **5** Kiowa, Omaha, Ponca, Sioux **6** Pawnee
people: **10** Henry Fonda **11** Fred Astaire, Roscoe Pound
lake: **7** Merritt, Sherman, Swanson **10** McConaughy **13** Lewis and Clark
land rank: **9** fifteenth
physical feature: **8** Badlands
hills: **4** Sand **5** Drift, Loess
plains: **5** Great
river: **4** Loup **5** Logan **6** Dismal, Nemaha, Platte **7** Big Blue, Elkhorn **8** Missouri, Niobrara **10** Little Blue, Republican **12** Harlan County
state admission: **13** thirty-seventh
state bird: **17** western meadowlark
state flower: **9** goldenrod
state motto: **20** Equality Before the Law
state song: **17** Beautiful Nebraska
state tree: **3** elm **10** cottonwood

nebris
skin of: **4** fawn

Nebrophonus *see* **5** Thoon

Nebuchadnezzar
father: **12** Nabopolassar
son: **12** Evilmerodach

nebula **4** Crab, Ring, Veil **5** Great **6** Lagoon **7** Rosette **9** Horsehead

nebulous **3** dim **4** dark, hazy **5** murky, vague **6** cloudy **7** obscure, unclear **8** confused **9** ambiguous, uncertain **10** impalpable, indefinite, indistinct, intangible **13** indeterminate

necessarily **8** perforce **9** naturally **10** inevitably, inexorably **11** accordingly **12** compulsorily **13** automatically, axiomatically, unqualifiedly **16** incontrovertibly

necessary **6** needed, urgent, wanted **7** crucial, desired, exigent, fitting, needful **8** required **9** called for, essential, requisite **10** compulsory, imperative, obligatory **13** indispensable

necessary changes having been made
Latin: **15** mutatis mutandis

necessitate **5** cause, force, impel **6** compel, demand, oblige **7** call for, enforce, require **9** constrain, prescribe

necessitation **5** cause, force **6** demand, duress **8** coercion, pressure **10** compulsion, constraint, obligation **11** enforcement, requirement

necessity, necessities
4 must, need **6** demand, needed **7** urgency **8** exigency, pressure **9** essential, requisite **10** sine qua non **11** requirement **13** indispensable
Latin: **10** sine qua non

neck **3** pet **4** kiss, nape, pass **6** caress, cervix, cuddle, fondle, smooth, strait **7** channel, isthmus, make out **9** narrowing

neckerchief **5** scarf **8** bandanna, kerchief

necklace **3** tie **5** beads, chain, noose **6** choker, collar, locket, pearls, string **7** jewelry, pendant **8** ornament **9** lavaliere

necktie **3** bow **4** band **5** ascot, black, scarf **6** cravat, string **7** Windsor **10** four in hand **11** half Windsor **12** hangman's rope

necromancer **5** hexer, magus, witch **6** wizard **7** charmer, warlock **8** conjurer, exorcist, magician, sorcerer **9** enchanter, occultist, voodooist **10** soothsayer **13** black magician, thaumaturgist

necromancy **5** magic, spell **7** sorcery **8** black art **10** witchcraft **11** enchantment, foretelling

necrophobia
fear of: **5** death **10** dead bodies

necropolis **8** cemetery **9** graveyard **12** burial ground **13** burying ground

Nectar
drink of: **4** gods
gives: **4** life

Neda
form: **5** nymph, river
location: **11** mountaintop

need **4** lack, want, wish **5** crave, exact **6** demand, penury **7** call for, longing, poverty, require, straits **8** distress, exigency, yearn for **9** essential, extremity, indigence, necessity, requisite **10** bankruptcy, insolvency **11** desideratum, destitution, necessitate, requirement **13** impecuniosity, pennilessness

needed **5** vital **7** crucial **9** essential, necessary, requisite **13** indispensable

needful **7** wishful **8** required **9** essential, necessary, requisite **10** imperative **13** indispensable

needle **3** vex **4** josh, leaf, ride, twit **5** annoy, chaff, harry, taunt, tease **6** badger, harass, hector **7** torment **9** indicator

needle-shaped **5** sharp **6** peaked, spiked **7** pointed **8** piercing **10** bodkin-like

needless **7** useless **9** excessive, pointless, redundant **10** gratuitous, pleonastic, unavailing **11** dispensable, purposeless, superfluous, uncalled-for, unessential, unnecessary **12** overabundant

needlework **6** sewing **7** basting, brocade, darning, tacking, tatting **8** applique, knitting, quilting **9** stitching **10** embroidery **11** cross stitch, needle point

needy **4** poor **5** broke **6** hard-up, in want **8** indigent, strapped **9** destitute, moneyless, penniless **10** down-and-out **12** impoverished **15** poverty-stricken

ne'er-do-well **3** bum **5** idler, loser **6** loafer, no-good **7** goof-off, sad sack, wastrel **8** layabout **9** do-nothing, no-account **10** black sheep **14** good-for-nothing

nefarious **3** bad, low **4** base, evil, foul, vile **6** odious, wicked **7** beastly, ghastly, heinous, hellish, ungodly, vicious **8** depraved, devilish, infamous, infernal, shameful **9** atrocious, execrable **10** abominable, despicable, detestable, iniquitous, scandalous, villainous **11** disgraceful, opprobrious, unspeakable **12** dishonorable **13** unmentionable

Nefertem
origin: **8** Egyptian
personifies: **5** lotus
true identity: **4** Ptah

negate **4** deny, veto, void **5** quash, quell, rebut **6** defeat, disown, refute, repeal, revoke, squash **7** blot out, destroy, disavow, gainsay, nullify, retract, reverse, squelch, wipe out **8** abrogate, disallow, disclaim, set aside, vanquish **9** overthrow, overwhelm, repudiate **10** contradict, invalidate

negating **7** denying, voiding **8** refuting, revoking **9** reversing **10** cancelling, nullifying **11** disallowing **12** invalidating, setting aside **13** contradicting

negation **6** denial **7** counter **8** reversal **9** rejection **10** abrogation, disclaimer, refutation **11** confutation, repudiation **12** invalidation **13** contradiction, nullification

negative **4** blue, dark **5** bleak **6** at odds, gloomy **7** dubious, opposed **8** contrary, doubtful, downbeat, inimical, opposing, refusing **9** declining, demurring, dissident, jaundiced, objecting, rejecting, reluctant, skeptical, unwilling **10** dissenting, fatalistic **11** disagreeing, pessimistic **12** antagonistic, disapproving **13** uncooperative **14** unenthusiastic

neglect **4** fail, omit **5** let go, shirk **6** forget, ignore, laxity, pass by, pass up, slight **7** abandon, default, laxness, let pass, let ride, let slip **8** be remiss, idleness, let slide, omission, overlook, pass over, shake off **9** disregard, oversight, passivity, slackness **10** inaccuracy, negligence, remissness **11** dereliction, inattention, inexactness **12** carelessness, fecklessness, indifference, slovenliness **13** noncompliance, unfulfillment **14** nonpreparation **16** underachievement

neglected **7** dropped, ignored, omitted, shirked, unkempt **8** forsaken, untended **9** abandoned, cast aside, forgotten **10** overlooked, uncared for **11** disregarded

neglectful **4** lazy **5** slack **6** remiss, untrue **8** careless, derelict, heedless **9** forgetful, negligent, oblivious, unheeding, unmindful **10** inconstant, thriftless, unfaithful, unthinking, unwatchful **11** improvident, inattentive, indifferent, respectless, thoughtless, unobservant **12** devil-may-care, disregardant, disregardful, happy-go-lucky **15** procrastinating

negligee, neglige **4** robe **6** kimono **7** wrapper **8** bathrobe, peignoir **9** housecoat **12** dressing gown

negligence **6** laxity **7** neglect **11** disregarded **12** carelessness

negligent **3** lax **5** slack **6** remiss, untidy **8** careless, heedless, slovenly **9** forgetful, unheeding, unmindful **10** neglectful, unthinking, unwatchful **11** inattentive, indifferent, thoughtless, unobservant **13** inconsiderate

negligible **5** minor, petty, small **6** minute, paltry, slight **7** trivial **8** piddling, trifling **11** unimportant **13** insignificant **15** inconsequential

negotiate **4** cash, make, pass **6** barter, cash in, convey, dicker, haggle, handle, manage, redeem, settle **7** arrange, consign, deliver, discuss, get over **8** contract, cope with, deal with, hand over, make over, pass over, sign over, transact, transfer, transmit, turn over **10** bargain for **11** come to terms, meet halfway

negotiation **4** deal **6** treaty **8** argument, haggling **9** dickering **10** bargaining **11** arbitration, arrangement **12** compromising

negotiator **7** arbiter **8** mediator **9** go-between **10** arbitrator **12** intermediary

Negrette, Lolita Dolores
real name of: **13** Dolores Del Rio

Nehemiah
father: **5** Azbuk **14** Hachaliah

neigh **5** hinny **6** nicker, whinny

neighbor **4** abut, meet **5** touch **6** adjoin, be near, border, friend **7** conjoin **8** borderer, border on **9** associate **12** acquaintance

neighborhood **4** area, part, side, ward **5** place, range **6** locale, parish, region, sphere **7** quarter, section **8** confines, district, environs, precinct, purlieus, vicinity **9** community

neighboring **4** near, next **5** close **6** at hand, nearby **7** close by **8** abutting, adjacent **9** adjoining, bordering **10** contiguous **11** surrounding **12** circumjacent

neighborly **4** kind **5** civil **6** chummy, kindly, polite **7** affable, amiable, cordial, helpful **8** amicable, friendly, gracious, obliging **9** courteous **10** hospitable **11** considerate, warmhearted **12** well-disposed

Neighbors
author: **12** Thomas Berger

Neith
origin: **8** Egyptian
personifies: **10** femininity
son: **2** Ra
corresponds to: **6** Athena

Nekhbet
origin: **8** Egyptian
form: **7** vulture
guardian of: **5** Egypt **10** Upper Egypt

Neleus
king of: **5** Pylos, Pylus
father: **8** Poseidon
mother: **4** Tyro
twin brother: **6** Pelias
wife: **7** Chloris
son: **6** Nestor **12** Periclymenus
daughter: **4** Pero
refused purification to: **8** Hercules
killed by: **8** Hercules

Nelides
epithet of: **6** Nestor

Nelson, Harriet Hilliard
real name: **14** Peggy Lou Snyder
husband: **5** Ozzie
son: **4** Rick **5** David
born: **11** Des Moines IA
roles: **30** The Adventures of Ozzie and Harriet

Nelson, Horatio
also: **14** Viscount Nelson
nationality: **7** British
battle: **9** Trafalgar **11** Bay of Abukir **15** Battle of the Nile **16** Cape Saint Vincent **18** Battle of Copenhagen
defeated: **5** Danes **6** French **7** Spanish
flagship: **7** Victory
killed at: **9** Trafalgar
lover: **16** Emma Lady Hamilton

Nelson, Ozzie
real name: **18** Oswald George Nelson
wife: **15** Harriet Hilliard
son: **4** Rick **5** David
born: **12** Jersey City NJ
roles: **30** The Adventures of Ozzie and Harriet

Nemean
epithet of: **4** Zeus

Nemean lion
strangled by: **8** Hercules

nemesis **4** ruin **5** match, rival **7** avenger, justice, revenge, undoing **8** downfall, punisher, Waterloo **9** overthrow, vengeance **10** punishment **11** destruction, retaliation, retribution **16** instrument of fate

Nemesis *see* **8** Adrastea

nemine contradicente **11** unanimously **18** no one contradicting

nemine dissentiente **11** unanimously **15** no one dissenting

Nemo
character in: **10** Bleak House
author: **7** Dickens

Nemo, Captain
character in: **32** Twenty Thousand Leagues Under the Sea
author: **5** Verne

neologism, neology **7** coinage **9** nonce word

neon
chemical symbol: **2** Ne

neonate **4** baby **6** infant **7** newborn

neophyte **4** tyro **5** pupil **6** novice, rookie **7** convert, entrant, learner, recruit, student, trainee **8** beginner, disciple, newcomer **9** greenhorn, novitiate, proselyte **10** apprentice, tenderfoot **11** probationer

neoplasm **5** tumor **6** cancer, growth **7** sarcoma **9** carcinoma **10** malignancy **14** carcinosarcoma

Nepal ***see box***

Nepali
language family: **12** Indo-European
branch: **11** Indo-Iranian
group: **5** Indic
spoken in: **5** Nepal

nepenthe **4** drug **5** drink, opium **6** heroin, opiate **7** hashish **8** narcotic

Nephele
counterfeit of: **4** Hera
formed by: **4** Zeus
husband: **7** Athamas
children: **8** centaurs
son: **7** Phrixus
daughter: **5** Helle

nephrite
variety: **4** jade

ne plus ultra **4** acme **12** highest point

Neptune
origin: **5** Roman

Nepal
other name: **9** Shangri-La
capital/largest city: **8** Katmandu **9** Kathmandu
others: **5** Patan, Patna **6** Gurkha **7** Birganj **8** Bhadgaon, Lalitpur **9** Bhaktapur **10** Biratnagar
university: **9** Tribhuvan
division: **5** Terai **13** High Himalayas
monetary unit: **4** anna, pice **5** mohar, paisa, rupee
mountain: **6** Cho Oyu, Churia, Lhotse, Makalu **7** Manaslu, Siwalik **9** Annapurna, Himalayas **10** Dhaulagiri, Gosainthan, Himalchuli **11** Ganesh Himal **12** Kanchenjunga **14** Mahabharat hekh
highest point: **9** Mt Everest
river: **4** Kali, Kosi, Mugu, Seti **5** Babai, Bheri, Rapti, Sarda, Tamur **6** Gandak **7** Karnali **8** Narayani
physical feature:
plain: **5** Terai
valley: **5** Nepal **8** Katmandu
people: **3** Rai **4** Aoul **5** Bhote, Limbu, Magar, Murmi, Newar, Tharu **6** Bhutia, Gurkha, Gurung, Nepali, Sherpa, Tamang **7** Kiranti, Tibetan **8** Gorkhali, Nepalese
birthplace of: **6** Buddha **13** Gautama Buddha **17** Siddhartha Gautama
king: **8** Mahendra **9** Tribhuwan **18** Prithwi Narayan Shah **23** Birenda Bir Bikram Shah Dev
ruler: **4** Rana **5** Malla **6** Rajput
language: **6** Nepali, Newari
religion: **8** Buddhism, Hinduism
place:
dam: **6** Gandak
shrine: **9** Swayambhu **10** Gorakhnath
feature:
animal: **3** dzo, yak **7** dzopkyo
arch: **6** Juddha
god/goddess: **5** Indra **6** Kumari
legend: **4** Yeti **17** abominable snowman
soldiers: **6** Gurkha

god of: 3 sea
corresponds to: 8 Poseidon

Neptune
position: 6 eighth
satellite: 6 Nereid, Triton
color: 5 green

Nereid
form: 5 nymph
location: 3 sea
father: 6 Nereus

Nereus
god of: 3 sea
father: 6 Pontus
mother: 4 Gaea
father of: 7 Nereids
number of Nereids: 5 fifty
son: 7 Nerites

Nergal
origin: 8 Akkadian
ruler of: 4 dead
consort of: 10 Ereshkigal

Nerissa
character in: 19 The Merchant of Venice
author: 11 Shakespeare

Nerites
father: 6 Nereus
mother: 5 Doris
transformed into: 6 mussel
transformed by: 9 Aphrodite

neritic 7 aquatic, coastal 8 offshore

Nero
name: 18 Nero Claudius Caesar
emperor of: 4 Rome
mother: 9 Agrippina
father: 19 Domitius Ahenobarbus
stepfather: 8 Claudius
tutor: 6 Seneca
son: 11 Britannicus
wife: 7 Octavia 13 Poppaea Sabina

nerve 4 dash, gall, grit, guts, sass 5 brass, cheek, crust, pluck, spunk, valor 6 mettle, spirit 7 bravery, courage 8 backbone, boldness, coolness, gameness, strength, tenacity 9 arrogance, assurance, derring-do, endurance, flippancy, fortitude, gallantry, hardihood, hardiness, impudence, insolence, sauciness 10 assumption, brazenness, confidence, effrontery, steadiness 11 intrepidity, presumption 12 fearlessness, impertinence, resoluteness 13 determination 16 stoutheartedness

nerveless 4 calm, dead, weak 5 brave, frail, inert 6 feeble, flabby 7 flaccid 8 cowardly 9 powerless 10 courageous 12 fainthearted

nervous 4 wild 5 jumpy, shaky, tense 6 touchy, uneasy 7 alarmed, anxious, excited, fearful, fidgety, jittery, peevish, ruffled 8 feverish, neurotic, skittish, startled, timorous, unstrung 9 delirious, disturbed, excitable, impatient, irritable, sensitive, trembling, tremulous, unsettled 10 highstrung, hysterical 12 apprehensive

nervousness 6 tremor 7 anxiety, flutter, shaking, tension 8 hysteria, timidity 9 agitation, quivering, the creeps, the shakes, trembling, twitching 10 the fidgets, touchiness 11 disturbance, fidgetiness, stage fright 12 apprehension, excitability, irascibility, irritability, perturbation, timorousness 16 hypersensitivity

nervous system
component: 4 ears, eyes 5 brain, taste, touch 7 ganglia 8 nerve end 10 nerve fiber, spinal cord

nervy 4 bold, firm, rude 5 brash, gutty, gutsy, sassy 6 brassy, brazen, cheeky, gritty, plucky, strong 7 assured, nervous 10 courageous, determined 12 stouthearted

Nesbitt, Cathleen
born: 7 England 8 Cheshire
roles: 10 My Fair Lady 18 Upstairs Downstairs 23 Three Coins in the Fountain

Nessus
form: 7 centaur
shot by: 8 Hercules
caused death of: 8 Hercules

n'est-ce pas? 10 isn't that so?

nestle 3 lie, pet 4 live, snug, stay 5 clasp, dwell, lodge 6 bundle, caress, coddle, cosset, cuddle, enfold, fondle, huddle, nuzzle, occupy, remain, settle 7 embrace, inhabit, lie snug, snuggle 8 lie close 10 settle down

Nest of Gentlefolk
author: 23 Ivan Sergeyevich Turgenev

Nest of Simple Folk, A
author: 12 Sean O'Faolain

Nestor
origin: 5 Greek
attributes: 6 oldest, wisest
father: 6 Neleus
son: 10 Thasymedes 11 Pisistratus
epithet: 7 Nelides

net 3 web 4 earn, gain, grab, grid, grip, mesh, snag, take, trap 5 catch, clasp, grate, seize, snare 6 clutch, enmesh, gather, grille, obtain, pick up, screen, snap up, take in 7 acquire, bring in, capture, collect, ensnare, grating, lattice 8 entangle, gather in, gridiron, meshwork 9 apprehend, grillwork, lay hold of, screening 10 accumulate 11 latticework
constellation of: 9 Reticulum

nether 5 basal, below, lower, under 6 bottom, lowest 8 downward, inferior 9 subjacent 10 bottommost

Netherlands ***see box***

Netherlands East Indies
see 9 Indonesia

netherworld 4 hell 5 Hades 10 underworld 14 infernal region

nettle 3 vex 4 bait, gall, miff, rile 5 annoy, beset, chafe, harry, pique, sting 6 bother, harass, ruffle 7 perturb, prickle, provoke 8 irritate 9 displease 10 exasperate

nettle 6 Urtica
varieties: 4 dead, dumb, hemp, rock 5 false, flame, hedge, horse, Roman 6 spurge 7 painted 8 stinging 9 white dead 11 spotted dead 12 western horse

network 3 web 4 grid, mesh, trap 5 grate, group, snare 6 grille, scheme, system 7 complex, netting, station

Network
director: 11 Sidney Lumet
based on story by: 14 Paddy Chayefsky
cast: 9 Ned Beatty 10 Peter Finch, Wesley Addy 11 Faye Dunaway 12 Robert Duvall 13 William Holden 16 Beatrice Straight
Oscar for: 5 actor (Finch) 7 actress (Dunaway) 17 supporting actress (Straight)

neuroptera
class: 8 hexapoda
phylum: 10 arthropoda
group: 7 ant lion, fishfly 8 alderfly, lacewing, snakefly

neurotic 4 sick 7 anxious, intense, nervous 8 abnormal, unstable 9 disturbed, obsessive, unhealthy 10 distraught, immoderate 11 overwrought

neuter 5 fixed 6 barren, fallow, gelded, spayed 7 asexual, sexless, sterile 8 impotent 9 infertile

Neutra, Richard J
architect of: 15 Mathematics Park (Princeton) 16 Lovell Heath House (Los Angeles

Netherlands

other name: **7** Holland **12** Low Countries
capital/largest city: **9** Amsterdam
others: **3** Urk **5** Delft, Lisse **6** Almelo, Arnhem, Leiden, Velsen **7** Haarlem, Helmond, Hengelo, Limburg, Tilberg, Tilburg, Utrecht **8** Aalsmeer, Enschede, Ijmuiden, Nijmegen, The Hague **9** Apeldoorn, Dordrecht, Eindhoven, Groningen, Rotterdam **12** Scheveningen
division: **6** Twente **7** Drenthe, Limburg, Utrecht, Zeeland **9** Friesland, Groningen **10** Gelderland, Overijssel **12** North Brabant, North Holland, South Holland **19** Netherlands Antilles
government:
legislature: **4** Raad **11** Eerste Kamer, Tweede Kamer
head of state: **5** queen
measure: **2** el **3** aam, ahm, ell, kan, vat **4** duim, mijl, rood, rope **5** anker, roede, wisse **6** bunder, legger, maatje, mutsje, streep **7** schepel **8** mimgelen, steekkan
monetary unit: **4** doit, oord, raps **5** crown, daler, rider, ryder **6** florin, gulden, stiver, suskin **7** daalder, ducaton, escalan, escalin, guilder, stooter, stuiver **8** albertin, ducatoon **9** dubbeltje **12** rijksdaalder **13** albertustaler
weight: **3** ons **4** last, pond **5** bahar **6** korrel **7** wichtje
island: **5** Texel **7** Ameland, Frisian **8** Antilles, Vlieland
lake: **7** Haarlem **10** Ijsselmeer **11** Grevelingen, Havingvliet
highest point: **11** Vaalserberg
river: **3** Eem, Lek **4** Leck, Maas, Waal, Ysel **5** Donge, Hunse, Meuse, Rhine, Schie, Yssel **6** Dintel, Dommel, Ijssel, Kromme **7** Scheldt
sea: **5** North
physical feature:
canal: **6** Oranje **7** Juliana, Merwede **8** Drentsch, North Sea **10** Wilhelmina **11** New Waterway
former bay: **9** Zuider Zee
port: **9** Europoort
people: **5** Dutch **7** Frisian **9** Hollander **10** Surinamese **12** Netherlander **13** South Moluccan
artist: **4** Eyck, Hals **5** Appel, Bosch **7** Van Gogh, Vermeer **8** Mondrian, Ruisdael **9** Rembrandt
author: **6** Vondel **7** Erasmus, Grotius, Spinoza **8** Vestdijk **9** Anne Frank
explorer: **6** Tasman
king: **7** William
queen: **7** Beatrix, Juliana **10** Wilhelmina
ruler: **5** Spain **13** House of Orange **15** Holy Roman Empire
scientist: **7** Huygens **11** Leeuwenhoek
language: **5** Dutch **7** English, Frisian
religion: **13** Dutch Reformed, Protestantism **16** Roman Catholicism
place:
airport: **8** Schiphol
bird sanctuary: **9** Waddenzee
miniature town: **9** Madurodam
museum: **9** Frans Hals, Stedelijk **11** Mauritshuis, Rijksmuseum **14** Vincent Van Gogh **19** Boymans-van Beuningen
seat of government: **7** Den Haag **8** The Hague **11** 'sGravenhage
tower: **14** Schreierstoren
feature:
cheese market: **9** kaasmarkt
earth mounds: **6** terpen
flower: **5** tulip
flower parade: **12** Bloemencorso
pottery: **5** Delft
reclaimed land: **6** polder
wooden shoes: **7** klompen
food:
cheese: **4** Edam **5** Gouda **6** Leyden **7** cottage
dish: **10** nasi goreng, rijsttafel
drink: **3** gin **8** anisette, schnapps
pea soup: **10** erwtensoep

CA) **17** von Sternberg House (Northridge CA) **22** Orange County Courthouse (Santa Ana CA)

neutral **4** mean **5** aloof **6** medium, middle, normal, remote **7** average **8** pacifist, peaceful, unbiased **9** impartial, in-between, peaceable, withdrawn **10** achromatic, indefinite, of two minds, unaffected, uninvolved **11** half-and-half, indifferent, nonpartisan, unconcerned **12** fence sitting, intermediate, noncombatant **13** disinterested, dispassionate **14** nonbelligerent, noninterfering **16** nonparticipating **18** noninterventionist

neutralize **4** halt, stop **5** annul, block, check **6** cancel, defeat, impede, negate, offset, stymie **7** balance, disable, nullify, prevent **8** overcome, suppress **9** frustrate, overpower

Nevada
abbreviation: **2** NV **3** Nev
nickname: **6** Silver **9** Sagebrush
capital: **10** Carson City
largest city: **8** Las Vegas
others: **3** Ely, Nye **4** Elko, Reno **6** Fallon, Nellis, Sparks, Storey, Washoe **7** Boulder, Gerlach **9** Hawthorne, Henderson **11** Weed Heights **12** Virginia City
explorer: **7** Fremont **13** Jedediah Smith
feature: **12** Comstock Lode
dam: **5** Davis **6** Hoover
hot springs: **4** Tule **9** Punch Bowl, Steam Boat
national monument: **11** Death Valley
tribe: **5** Modoc, Washo **6** Digger, Mohave, Paiute **7** Klamath **8** Achomawi, Atsugewi, Shoshone
lake: **4** Mead, Ruby **5** Tahoe, Weber **6** Mohave, Walker **7** Pyramid **8** Lahontan, Rye Patch **9** Wild Horse
land rank: **7** seventh
mountain: **4** East, Pine, Ruby **5** White **7** Rockies, Toiyabe, Wasatch **13** Sierra Nevadas
highest point: **12** Boundary Peak
physical feature: **7** geysers **10** hot springs
basin: **5** Great
cave: **6** Gypsum
desert: **7** Sonoran
plateau: **8** Columbia
river: **5** Reese **6** Carson, Walker **7** Truckee **8** Colorado, Humboldt
state admission: **11** thirty-sixth
state bird: **7** sagehen **16** mountain bluebird
state flower: **9** sagebrush
state motto: **16** All for Our Country
state song: **15** Home Means Nevada
state tree: **9** pinon pine **15** single-leaf pinon

10 counteract **12** counterpoise, incapacitate **14** counterbalance

neutralizer **7** blocker **9** nullifier **12** counteractor, counteragent **15** counterbalancer

Neuvillette, Christian de
character in: **16** Cyrano de Bergerac
author: **7** Rostand

Nevada ***see box***

never **4** ne'er **7** not ever **8** at no time, not at all

never-ending **6** steady **7** abiding, eternal, lasting, nonstop **8** constant, enduring, immortal, infinite, repeated, unbroken **9** ceaseless, continual, incessant, perennial, perpetual, recurring, unceasing **10** continuous, persistent, relentless **11** everlasting, unremitting **12** interminable, undiminished **13** uninterrupted

never-failing **4** firm, sure **6** proven, trusty **7** abiding **8** enduring, reliable **9** steadfast **10** dependable **11** trustworthy, undeviating, unfaltering **12** unhesitating, tried-and-true

nevermore **6** no more **10** never again

Never on Sunday
director: **11** Jules Dassin
cast: **11** Jules Dassin, Titos Vandis **14** Georges Foundas, Melina Mercouri
setting: **6** Greece

nevertheless **3** but, yet **6** anyhow, anyway, even so, though **7** however **8** after all, although **10** contrarily, in any event, regardless **12** contrariwise **15** notwithstanding

Neville, Constance
character in: **18** She Stoops to Conquer
author: **9** Goldsmith

new **4** late **5** fixed, fresh, green, novel **6** modern, reborn, recent, remote, unused **7** altered, changed, current, just out, rebuilt, resumed, untried **8** original, reopened, repaired, restored, up-to-date **9** recreated, refreshed, remodeled, renovated, uncharted, unessayed, untouched **10** revivified, unexplored, unfamiliar, ungathered, unseasoned, unventured **11** regenerated, uncollected, unexercised **12** unaccustomed **13** reconstructed, reinvigorated

New Atlantis
author: **12** Francis Bacon

New Brunswick ***see box***

New Centurions, The
author: **14** Joseph Wambaugh

newcomer **4** tyro **5** alien **6** novice **7** entrant **8** intruder, neophyte, outsider, stranger **9** foreigner, immigrant, outlander **10** interloper, trespasser

Newcomes, The
author: **25** William Makepeace Thackeray

New Deal Agency **3** AAA, CCC, CWA, FCA, FHA, FSA, NRA, NYA, PWA, REA, SEC, SSB, TVA, WPA **4** FCIC, FDIC, FERA, HOLC, NLRD, USHA

New Brunswick
abbreviation: **2** NB
bay: **5** Fundy, Maces **7** Shepody **9** Chignecto, Miramichi **13** Passamaquoddy
channel: **5** Minas **10** Grand Manan
city: **7** Moncton **8** Bathurst **9** Riverview **10** Edmundston, Saint John **11** Fredericton
island: **4** Deer **6** Miscou **7** Machias **10** Campobello, Grand Manan
known as: **16** Atlantic province, maritime province
lake: **5** Grand **8** Oromocto **12** Magaguadavic **14** Chiputneticook
people: **5** Irish **6** French **7** Acadian, English **8** American, Scottish **9** Algonkian **10** Anglo Saxon
religion: **6** Canaan **7** Baptist **8** Anglican **10** Protestant **12** Presbyterian, United Church **13** Roman Catholic
river: **5** Cains, Green **6** Renous, Salmon **7** Tobique **8** Kedgwick, Nashwak, Oromocto **9** Miramichi, Patapedia, Saint John **10** Nepisiguit, Richibucto, Saint Croix **11** Petitcodiac, Restigouche, Upsalguitch **12** Kennebecasis

New Delhi
capital of: 5 India
designed by: 7 Lutyens
earlier city: 5 Dilli 8 Dhillika, Din Panah, Kilookai 9 Firozabad 11 Tughlukabad 12 Indraprastha 13 Shah Jahanabad
invader: 5 Timur 6 Abdali 7 British, Rohilas 8 Marathas 9 Nadir Shah
landmark: 7 Red Fort 9 India Gate, Qutb Minar 10 Iron Pillar, Jama Masjid 12 Humayun's Tomb 14 Connaught Place 15 Rajghat Memorial 17 Rashtrapati Bhavan (Presidential Palace) 23 Jantar Mantar Observatory 30 Gandhi National Museum and Library
river: 6 Yamuna
street: 7 Raj Path (Kingsway)
university: 15 Jawaharlal Nehru

New England *see box*

newfangled 5 novel 6 modern, modish 7 stylish

new-fashioned 6 modern, modish 7 stylish 8 up-to-date

Newfoundland
abbreviation: 4 Nfld
capital: 10 Saint Johns
city: 19 Happy Valley Goose Bay
lake: 7 Jeddore, Melville 8 Meelpaeg 10 Michikamau
mountain: 9 Long Range
river: 5 Eagle 6 Fraser, Gander 8 Exploits, Naskaupi 9 Churchill
section: 8 Labrador

New Granada *see* 8 Colombia

New Guinea *see box*

New Hampshire *see box, p. 672*

Newhart
character: 4 Dick 6 Joanna 7 Michael 9 Stephanie
cast: 9 Mary Frann 10 Bob Newhart, Julia Duffy 12 Peter Scolari

New England
capital: 6 Boston 7 Augusta, Concord 8 Hartford 10 Montpelier, Providence
city: 4 Lynn 5 Barre 6 Bangor, Lowell, Nashua 7 Hyannis, Rutland, Warwick 8 Brockton, Cranston, Lawrence, Lewiston, New Haven, Portland, Stamford 9 Cambridge, Fall River, New London, Pawtucket, Waterbury, Worcester 10 Bridgeport, Burlington, Manchester, Pittsfield, Portsmouth, Woonsocket 11 Brattleboro, Springfield
football team: 8 Patriots
Indians: 6 Abnaki, Pequot 7 Mahican, Mohegan, Niantic, Nipmuck, Wangunk 8 Algonkin, Iroquois 9 Algonquin, Pennacook 10 Quinnipiac 12 Narragansett
lake: 6 Sebago, Tiogue 7 Sunapee 9 Champlain, Moosehead 10 Candlewood 11 Pemaduncook 13 Winnipesaukee
mountain: 5 Green, White 8 Greylock, Katahdin 9 Berkshire, Mansfield 10 Washington 11 Appalachian
river: 5 Otter 6 Thames 7 Charles 8 Kennebec, Pawtucket, Winooski 9 Merrimack, Missiquoi, Naugatuck, Pawcatuck, Penobscot, Saint John 10 Housatonic, Providence, Quinnipiac 11 Connecticut 12 Androscoggin
state: 5 Maine 7 Vermont 11 Connecticut, Rhode Island 12 New Hampshire 13 Massachusetts

New Guinea
other name: 14 Papua New Guinea
capital/largest city: 11 Port Moresby
others: 3 Lae, Wau 4 Daru 5 Soron, Wewak 6 Aitape, Kikori, Medang, Rabaul 7 Gorolka, Kitbadi
division:
eastern half of island: 9 Indonesia, Irian Jaya
western half of island: 14 Papua New Guinea
government: 22 constitutional monarchy
head of state: 14 British monarch 15 governor-general
monetary unit: 4 kina, toea
island: 3 Aru 4 Aroe, Buka 5 Arroe, Ceram, Japen, Jobie, Manus 6 Cretin, Mussau, Ninigo, Waigeu 7 Sainson, Solomon 8 Bismarck, Kiriwina, Schouten, Woodlark 9 Admiralty, Trobriant 10 Louisiande, New Britain, New Ireland 12 Bougainville 14 D'Entrecasteaux
mountain: 4 Snow 6 Orange 8 Bismarck, Victoria 9 Carstensz 11 Owen Stanley 12 Albert Edward
highest point:
Irian Jaya: 9 Carstensz 10 Puncak Jaya
Papua New Guinea: 7 Wilhelm
river: 3 Fly 4 Hamu, Hany, Ramu 5 Degul, Sepik 6 Kikori, Purari 7 Amberno, Markham
sea: 5 Ceram, Coral, Sepik 6 Indian 7 Arafura, Pacific, Solomon 8 Bismarck
physical feature:
bay: 3 Oro 5 Milne 8 Geelvink
gulf: 4 Huon 5 Papua
strait: 6 Torres, Vitiaz
people: 5 Pygmy 6 Papuan 7 Negrito 10 Melanesian
explorer: 15 Jorge de Menesses
ruler: 7 Germany 9 Australia 12 Great Britain
language: 4 Motu 7 English 16 Melanesian Pidjin
religion: 7 animism 10 Protestant 13 Roman Catholic
feature:
bird: 7 mudlark 9 cassowary
food:
dried coconut meat: 5 copra

Newhart, Bob
born: 9 Chicago IL
roles: 7 Newhart 10 Cold Turkey 17 The Bob Newhart Show

New Hebrides *see* 7 Vanuatu

New Jersey *see box, p. 672*

New Hampshire

abbreviation: 2 NH
nickname: 7 Granite
capital: 7 Concord
largest city: 10 Manchester
others: 5 Dover, Keene **6** Berlin, Durham, Exeter, Nashua **7** Hanover, Laconia **8** Sandwich **9** Claremont, Rochester **10** Portsmouth **12** Bretton Woods
college: 5 Keene **6** Rivier **9** Dartmouth, St Anselms **10** New England
feature: 14 Great Stone Face
notch: **7** Kinsman, Pinkham **8** Crawford **9** Franconia
tribe: 6 Abnaki **9** Pennacook
people: 11 Robert Frost **12** Daniel French **13** Daniel Webster, Horace Greeley, Mary Baker Eddy
explorer: **9** Champlain **16** Captain John Smith
island: 4 Star **5** White **6** Shoals **7** Lunging
lake: 5 Squam **7** Ossipee, Sunapee, Umbagog **8** Newfound **10** Winnisquam **13** Winnipesaukee
land rank: 11 forty-fourth
mountain: 5 Flume, White **6** Moriah, Paugus **7** Waumbek **8** Chocorua, Sandwich **9** Franconia, Monadnock **11** Profile Peak **12** Presidential
highest point: **10** Washington
physical feature:
bay: **5** Great
president: 14 Franklin Pierce
river: 4 Saco **6** Israel **7** Bellamy **8** Souhegan **9** Merrimack **10** Piscataqua **11** Connecticut, Salmon Falls **12** Androscoggin
state admission: 5 ninth
state bird: 11 purple finch
state flower: 11 purple lilac
state motto: 13 Live Free Or Die
state song: 15 Old New Hampshire **26** New Hampshire My New Hampshire
state tree: 10 paper birch, white birch

New Jersey

abbreviation: 2 NJ
nickname: 6 Garden **8** Mosquito
capital: 7 Trenton
largest city: 6 Newark
others: 4 Lodi **5** Ewing, Ft Lee **6** Camden, Dumont, Haddon, Kearny, Linden, Nutley, Orange, Rahway, Totowa **7** Bayonne, Cape May, Clifton, Hoboken, Hohokus, Keyport, Madison, Matawan, Netcong, Oradell, Paramus, Passaic, Raritan, Teaneck, Tenafly, Wyckoff **8** Carteret, Cranford, Freehold, Garfield, Hillside, Metuchen, Paterson, Secaucus, Watchung **9** Bridgeton, Elizabeth, Englewood, Hawthorne, Irvington, Maplewood, Montclair, Ocean City, Princeton **10** Asbury Park, Belleville, Ft Monmouth, Hackensack, Jersey City, Livingston, Long Branch, Morristown, Perth Amboy **11** Bergenfield **12** Atlantic City, Collingswood, New Brunswick
colleges: 4 Drew **6** Upsala **7** Rutgers **8** Caldwell, Monmouth, St Peter's **9** Princeton, Seton Hall **10** Bloomfield **18** Fairleigh-Dickinson
feature: 9 Boardwalk **16** Delaware Water Gap
tribe: 8 Delaware **11** Lenni-Lanape
people: 9 Aaron Burr **11** Joyce Kilmer, Paul Robeson **12** Stephen Crane, Thomas Edison **13** James Lawrence **19** James Fenimore Cooper
explorer: **6** Hudson **9** Verrazano
lake: 6 Mohawk **9** Greenwood, Hopatcong
land rank: 10 forty-sixth
mountain: 8 Piedmont **10** Kittatinny **13** First Watchung **14** Second Watchung
highest point: **9** High Point
physical feature: 9 Palisades, Sandy Hook
bay: **8** Delaware
cape: **3** May
sea: **8** Atlantic
president: 15 Grover Cleveland
river: 4 Toms **6** Dennis, Haynes, Hudson, Mantua, Ramapo **7** Mullica, Passaic, Raritan **8** Cohansey, Delaware, Tuckahoe **10** Hackensack
state admission: 5 third
state bird: 16 eastern goldfinch
state flower: 6 violet
state motto: 20 Liberty and Prosperity
state tree: 6 red oak
basketball team: 4 Nets
football team: 8 Generals
hockey team: 6 Devils

New Mexico
abbreviation: **2** NM **4** N Mex
nickname: **8** Sunshine **17** Land of Enchantment
capital: **7** Santa Fe
largest city: **11** Albuquerque
others: **3** Jal **4** Taos **5** Aztec, Belen, Hobbs, Raton **6** Clovis, Deming, Gallup, Grants **7** Artesia, Bananea, Roswell, Socorro, Torreon **8** Carlsbad **9** Las Cruces, Los Alamos **10** Alamogordo **13** Piedras Negras
college: **7** Sante Fe **11** Albuquerque
feature: **11** Four Corners
dam: **5** Butte **8** Elephant
labs: **6** Sandia **17** Los Alamos National
national monument: **10** Aztec Ruins, White Sands **11** Chaco Canyon **17** Gila Cliff Dwelling
national park: **15** Carlsbad Caverns
observatory: **14** Sacramento Peak
tribe: **3** Sia **4** Hano, Piro, Tano, Taos, Tewa, Tiwa, Zuni **5** Acoma, Jemez, Kares, Manso, Pecos, Tiqua, Tonoa **6** Apache, Isleta, Laguna, Navaho, Navajo, Pueblo **7** Anasazi, Picuris **8** Santa Ana **9** Mescalero **12** Santo Domingo
people: **9** Kit Carson, Peter Hurd **11** Bill Mauldin
explorer: **5** Onate **6** de Niza, de Vaca **8** Coronado
lake: **6** El Vado, Navajo, Sumner **7** Conchas **8** McMillan **10** Alamogordo **13** Elephant Butte
land rank: **5** fifth
mountain: **5** Jemez **6** Sandia **7** Manzano, Mimbres, Rockies, Truchas **8** Mogollon **9** Guadalupe, San Andres **10** Nacimiento, Sacramento **11** Mount Taylor **15** Sangre de Christo
highest point: **11** Wheeler Peak
physical feature:
basin: **8** Tularosa
desert: **15** Jornada de Muerto
plains: **5** Great
river: **3** Ute **4** Gila **5** Pecos **7** San Jose, San Juan **8** Canadian **9** Rio Grande
state admission: **12** forty-seventh
state bird: **10** roadrunner
state fish: **14** cutthroat trout
state flower: **5** yucca
state motto: **15** It Grows as It Goes
state song: **14** O Fair New Mexico **16** Asi es Nuevo Mexico
state tree: **5** pinon **8** tarantah **15** velvet ash pinyon

Newley, Anthony
wife: **11** Joan Collins
born: **6** London **7** England
roles: **11** Oliver Twist **25** Stop the World I Want to Get Off **41** The Roar of the Greasepaint The Smell of the Crowd

newly **4** anew **6** afresh, lately, of late **7** freshly, just now **8** recently

newly rich person
French: **12** nouveau riche

Newlywed Game, The
host: **10** Bob Eubanks
executive producer: **11** Chuck Barris

Newlyweds, The
creator: **13** George McManus
character: **12** Baby Snookums

Newman, Barnett
born: **9** New York NY
artwork: **7** Abraham, The Wild **8** Onement I **18** Stations of the Cross **19** Vir Heroicus Sublimis

Newman, Christopher
character in: **11** The American
author: **5** James

Newman, John Henry (Cardinal)
author of: **18** Apologia pro Vita Sua

Newman, Paul
wife: **14** Joanne Woodward
born: **11** Cleveland OH
roles: **3** Hud **6** Harper, Picnic **8** The Sting **10** The Hustler, The Verdict **12** Cool Hand Luke **15** Absence of Malice, The Color of Money **16** Cat on a Hot Tin Roof, The Left-Handed Gun, The Long Hot Summer, The Silver Chalice **29** Butch Cassidy and the Sundance Kid

New Mexico ***see box***

New Orleans
basketball team: Jazz
event: **9** Mardi Gras, Sugar Bowl **25** International Jazz Festival
football team: **6** Saints
landmark: **7** Cabildo **9** Old Square, Superdome **10** Vieux Carre **12** Pirate's Alley **13** French Quarter
noted for: **4** jazz
people: **5** Cajun **6** Creole **7** Acadian
river: **11** Mississippi
street: **5** Royal **7** Bourbon
university: **6** Loyola, Tulane

news **4** dirt, dope, talk, word **5** flash, libel, piece, rumor, story **6** babble, expose, gossip, report **7** account, article, chatter, hearsay, lowdown, mention, message, release, scandal, slander, tidings **8** bulletin, dispatch, exposure **9** statement **10** communique, disclosure, divulgence, revelation **11** information **12** announcement, intelligence

news account **4** item **5** story **6** report **7** release **8** bulletin, dispatch **10** communique

newsmonger **6** gossip **8** busybody, reporter

News of the Day
also: **12** Neues vom Tage
opera by: **9** Hindemith
character: **5** Laura **7** Eduoard

Newsome, Chadwick
character in: **14** The Ambassadors
author: **5** James

New Spain *see* **6** Mexico

newspaper **3** rag **5** daily, paper, sheet **6** herald, weekly **7** courant, gazette, journal, tabloid, tribune **10** periodical **11** publication

New Testament
books of: **4** Acts, John, Jude, Luke, Mark **5** James, Peter, Titus **6** Romans **7** Hebrews, Matthew, Timothy **8** Philemon **9** Ephesians, Galatians **10** Colossians, Revelation **11** Corinthians, Philippians **13** Thessalonians
books: **12** Humologumena

Newton, Isaac
field: **11** mathematics
nationality: **7** British

New York
abbreviation: 2 NY
nickname: 6 Empire **9** Excelsior
capital: 6 Albany
largest city: 7 New York
others: 3 Rye **4** Rome, Troy **5** Ilion, Islip, Nyack, Olean, Owego, Utica **6** Attica, Auburn, Cohoes, Elmira, Goshen, Ithaca, Oneida, Oswego, Tappan **7** Ardsley, Babylon, Batavia, Buffalo, Congers, Endwell, Geneseo, Hewlett, Mahopac, Merrick, Messena, Mineola, Montauk, Oneonta, Pennyan, Suffern, Syosset, Wantagh, Yaphank, Yonkers **8** Bethpage, Catskill, Endicott, Herkimer, Kingston, Ossining, Pottsdam, Saratoga, Tuckahoe **9** Rochester, Scarsdale **10** Binghamton, Bronxville, Mamaroneck **11** Cooperstown, New Rochelle, Schenectady, White Plains **12** Poughkeepsie
college: 4 Bard, CUNY, Iona, Pace, SUNY **5** Finch, Keuka **6** Hobart, Hunter, Vassar **7** Adelphi, Barnard, Colgate, Cornell, Fordham, St John's **8** Columbia, Skidmore, Syracuse **9** Juilliard, Rochester, West Point **13** Sarah Lawrence **30** Rensselaer Polytechnic Institute
feature:
***building:* 11** Empire State
***hall of fame:* 8** baseball
***park:* 7** Central
***prison:* 6** Attica **8** SingSing
***square:* 5** Times **6** Herald
***statue:* 7** Liberty
***street/avenue:* 4** Park, Wall **5** Fifth **7** Madison **8** Broadway
***tomb:* 6** Grant's
tribe: 4 Erie **6** Cayuga, Mohawk, Oneida, Seneca **7** Mohican, Montauk **8** Iroquois, Onondaga **9** Manhattan, people: **7** John Jay **8** Walloons **9** Jonas Salk **10** Henry James **11** Rockefeller, Walt Whitman **12** Eugene O'Neill **13** DeWitt Clinton, John Burroughs **14** Herman Melville **15** Peter Stuyvesant **16** Eleanor Roosevelt, Washington Irving **17** Fiorello La Guardia
***explorer:* 6** Hudson **9** Champlain, Verrazano **16** Dutch West India Co
island: 4 Fire, Long **5** Ellis **6** Staten **7** Bedloe's, Fisher's, Liberty, Shelter, Welfare **8** Thousand **9** Governors, Manhattan
lake: 4 Erie **6** Cayuga, Finger, George, Oneida, Otisco, Otsego, Owasco, Placid, Seneca **7** Conesus, Ontario, Saranac, Schroon **8** Saratoga **9** Champlain
land rank: 9 thirtieth
mountain: 4 Bear **5** Slide **7** Taconic **9** Catskills **11** Adirondacks
***highest point:* 5** Marcy
physical feature:
***bay:* 7** Jamaica, Peconic **8** Moriches
***canal:* 4** Erie **7** Gowanus
***falls:* 7** Niagara
***valley:* 6** Mohawk
president: 14 Martin Van Buren **14** Teddy Roosevelt **15** Millard Fillmore **17** Theodore Roosevelt **23** Franklin Delano Roosevelt
river: 4 East **5** Black, Tioga **6** Harlem, Hoosic, Hudson, Mohawk, Oswego **7** Ausable, Genesee, Niagara **10** St Lawrence **11** Susquehanna
state bird: 8 bluebird
state fish: 10 brook trout
state flower: 4 rose
state motto: 9 Excelsior (Ever upward, Still higher)
state tree: 10 sugar maple

discovered laws of: 6 motion **7** gravity **8** calculus
discovered: 13 color spectrum **15** binomial theorem **16** method of fluxions
invented: 21 infinitesimal calculus

New York ***see box***

New York City ***see box***

New Zealand ***see box, p. 676***

next-door 8 adjacent **9** adjoining **10** connecting, contiguous, juxtaposed, side-by-side, **12** conterminous

next to 6 beside **8** abutting, adjacent **9** adjoining, bordering **10** contiguous, juxtaposed **12** conterminous

next world, the 6 Heaven **8** eternity, paradise **12** the hereafter **14** the world to come

Nez Perce (Numipu)
language family: 10 Shahaptian
location: 5 Idaho **6** Oregon **10** Washington
leader: 11 Chief Joseph

Niamey
capital of: 5 Niger

nib 3 end, tip, top **4** apex, peak **5** point **6** height, tiptop, vertex **7** extreme **8** pinnacle **9** extremity

nibble 3 nip **4** bite, chew, gnaw, peck **5** crumb, munch, speck, taste **6** crunch, morsel, peck at, tidbit **8** fragment, particle

Nibelung, ring of
origin: 8 Germanic
mentioned in: 14 Nibelungenlied
stolen by: 8 Alberich

Nibelungenlied
origin: 8 Germanic
form: 4 epic

New York City
airport: **3** JFK **6** Newark **9** La Guardia **12** John F Kennedy
area: **4** Soho **6** Harlem **7** Chelsea, Midtown, Tribeca **9** Chinatown, Manhattan **10** Stuyvesant **11** Brownsville, Little Italy **13** Spanish Harlem **16** Greenwich Village **17** Bedford-Stuyvesant
baseball team: **4** Mets **7** Yankees
basketball team: **6** Knicks **14** Knickerbockers
borough: **5** Bronx **6** Queens **8** Brooklyn, Richmond **9** Manhattan
early governor: **10** Stuyvesant
football team: **4** Jets **6** Giants
former name: **12** New Amsterdam
hockey team: **7** Rangers **9** Islanders
island: **4** City, Long **5** Ellis, Ward's **6** Riker's, Staten **7** Liberty **8** Randall's **9** Governor's, Manhattan, Roosevelt
landmark: **5** Macy's **8** Bronx Zoo **11** Battery Park, Central Park, Penn Station, Shea Stadium, Times Square **12** Carnegie Hall **13** Gracie Mansion, Lincoln Center, Port Authority, Trinity Church, United Nations, Yankee Stadium **14** Waldorf-Astoria **15** NY Public Library, NY Stock Exchange, Seagram Building, Statue of Liberty **16** Bellevue Hospital, Chrysler Building, World Trade Center **17** Hayden Planetarium, Rockefeller Center, Woolworth Building **18** Radio City Music Hall **19** Empire State Building, Grand Central Station, Madison Square Garden, St Patrick's Cathedral **22** Metropolitan Opera House **26** Sloan-Kettering Cancer Center **29** Cathedral of Saint John the Divine
mayor: **4** Koch **6** Walker **9** La Guardia
museum: **6** Jewish **7** Whitney **9** Cloisters **10** Guggenheim **12** Cooper-Hewitt, Metropolitan **15** Frick Collection **17** Museum of Modern Art (MOMA) **30** American Museum of Natural History
river: **4** East **6** Harlem, Hudson
street: **6** Bowery **8** Broadway **9** Lexington **10** Park Avenue, Wall Street **11** Central Park, Fifth Avenue, Sutton Place **13** Madison Avenue **17** Forty-Second Street
university: **3** NYU **6** Queens **7** Barnard, Fordham, Yeshiva **8** Brooklyn, Columbia **13** Hunter College **22** Juilliard School of Music **23** City University of New York

date written: **17** thirteenth century
related to: **8** Volsunga
author: **7** unknown
character: **5** Etzel (Attila), Hagen **6** Gernot **7** Gunther **8** Brunhild, Dankwart, Giselher **9** Kriemhild, Siegfried

Nibelungs, Niblungs
origin: **8** Germanic, Teutonic
followers of: **9** Siegfried
race: **6** dwarfs
possessed: **8** treasure
captured by: **9** Siegfried
family of: **7** Gunther

Nicaragua *see box, p. 677*

nice **4** deft, fine, good, kind **5** dandy, exact, fussy, great, swell **6** divine, genial, lovely, proper, seemly, strict, subtle **7** amiable, amusing, careful, cordial, correct, finicky, genteel, likable, precise, refined, winning **8** accurate, charming, cheerful, delicate, friendly, gracious, jim-dandy, ladylike, pleasant, pleasing, rigorous, skillful, unerring, virtuous, well-bred **9** agreeable, congenial, excellent, fantastic, marvelous, sensitive, wonderful **10** attractive, delightful, enchanting, entrancing, fastidious, methodical, meticulous, scrupulous **11** interesting, painstaking, pleasurable, punctilious, respectable, sympathetic, warmhearted **13** compassionate, understanding, well brought up **17** overconscientious

Nice and the Good, The
author: **11** Iris Murdoch

nicely **6** neatly **7** exactly, fussily, happily **9** carefully, precisely **10** accurately, critically, pleasantly, unerringly **11** faultlessly, fortunately, opportunely **12** attractively, fastidiously

nicety **4** care, tact **5** flair, grace **6** acumen, polish **7** culture, finesse, insight **8** accuracy, delicacy, elegance, subtlety **9** attention, exactness, precision **10** refinement **11** cultivation, penetration, preciseness, sensitivity **12** perspicacity, subtle detail, tastefulness **13** elaborateness, particularity **14** discrimination, fastidiousness, meticulousness

niche **4** cove, nook, slot **5** berth, trade **6** alcove, cavity, corner, cranny, dugout, hollow, metier, recess **7** calling **8** position, vocation **9** cubbyhole **10** depression, pigeonhole **11** proper place **13** hole in the wall

Nicholas Nickleby
author: **14** Charles Dickens
character: **5** Smike **11** Arthur Gride, Newman Noggs **12** Kate Nickleby, Madeline Bray **13** Lord Verisopht, Ralph Nickleby **14** Frank Cheeryble **15** Sir Mulberry Hawk, Vincent Crummles, Wackford Squeers **17** Cheeryble Brothers

Nichols, Mike
director of: **7** Catch-22 **11** The Graduate (Oscar) **15** Carnal Knowledge **25** Who's Afraid of Virginia Woolf?

Nicholson, Ben
born: **6** Denham **7** England
artwork: **9** Fireworks **11** White Relief **12** Tuscan Relief **13** Painted Relief **14** At the Chat Botte

Nicholson, Jack
born: **9** Neptune NJ
roles: **8** Ironweed **9** Chinatown, Easy Rider **10** The Shining **12** Prizzi's Honor, The Passenger **13** The Last Detail **14** Five Easy Pieces **15** Carnal Knowledge **17** Terms of Endearment **20** The Witches of Eastwick **22** The King of Marvin Gardens **25** One Flew Over the Cuckoo's Nest (Oscar) **26** The Postman Always Rings Twice

nicht wahr? **10** isn't that so?

Nicippe
father: **6** Pelops
son: **10** Eurystheus

nick **3** cut, jag, mar **4** chip, dent, gash, mark, scar **5** cleft, gouge, notch, score, wound **6** damage, deface, indent, injure, injury **7** marking, scarify, scoring, scratch **8** incision, lacerate **10** depression **11** indentation

nickel
chemical symbol: **2** Ni

New Zealand
other name: **8** Aotearoa **12** Nieuw Zeeland **23** Land of the Long White Cloud
capital: **10** Wellington
largest city: **8** Auckland
others: **5** Leuin, Oreti, Otaki, Taupo **6** Clutha, Foxton, Oamaru, Picton, Timaru **7** Dunedin, Manu Kau, Raetihi, Rotorua **8** Hamilton, Kawakawa, Touranga **9** Lyttelton **10** Queenstown **12** Christchurch, Invercargill, Port Chalmers **13** Port Nicholson **14** Napier-Hastings **15** Palmerston North
school: **5** Otago **6** Massey **7** Waikato **8** Auckland, Victoria **10** Canterbury
division: **11** North Island, South Island
head of state: **14** British monarch **15** governor general
monetary unit: **4** cent **6** dollar
island: **4** Cook, Niue, Otea **5** North, South **6** Bounty, Chatam, Snares **7** Stewart, Tokelau **8** Auckland, Campbell, Kermadec, Puketutu **9** Antipodes **10** Resolution, Three Kings **12** Great Barrier
lake: **3** Ada **4** Gunn, Ohau **5** Hawea, Taupo **6** Pukaki, Pupuke, Te Anau, Tekapo, Wanaka **7** Brunner, Diamond, Kanieri, Okareka, Rotorua **8** Okataina, Paradise, Rotoaira, Wakatipu **9** Manapouri
mountain: **4** Eden, Flat, Owen **5** Allen, Chope, Lyall, Mitre, Ohope, Otari, Young **6** Egmont, Stokes, Tasman **7** Cameron, Coronet, Ernslaw, Huiarau, Pihanga, Ruahine, Ruapehu, Tauhera, Tutamoe, Tyndall **8** Aspiring, Richmond, Tauranga **9** Messenger, Murchison, Ngauruhoe, Raukumara, Tongariro **11** Remarkables **12** Southern Alps
highest point: **4** Cook **7** Aorangi
river: **4** Avon **5** Mokau, Waipa **6** Clutha, Rakaia, Tamaki, Waihou, Wairau, Wairoa **7** Waikato, Waitaki **8** Clarence, Manawatu, Wanganui **10** Rangitikei
sea: **6** Tasman **12** South Pacific
physical feature:
bay: **4** Ohua **5** Evans, Hawke, Lyall **6** Awarua, Cloudy, Golden, Plenty, Tasman **7** Fitzroy, Pegasus, Poverty **8** Halfmoon, Rangaunu
bight: **7** Karamea **10** Canterbury **13** North Taranaki, South Taranaki
cape: **4** East, West **5** North **6** Egmont **8** Farewell, Foulwind, Palliser **9** Southwest
channel: **8** Colville
falls: **10** Sutherland
glacier: **3** Fox **6** Tasman **11** Franz Joseph
gulf: **7** Hauraki
harbor: **7** Kaipara, Manukau **9** Waitemata
peninsula: **5** Mahia, Otago
plains: **10** Canterbury
sound: **8** Doubtful
strait: **4** Cook **7** Foveaux
people: **3** Ati **5** Arawa, Dutch, Maori **7** British, Ringatu **10** Polynesian
author: **5** Frame **9** Mansfield **10** Ngaio Marsh **12** Ashton-Warner
explorer: **4** Cook **6** Tasman
mountain climber: **7** Hillary
language: **5** Maori **7** English
religion: **8** Anglican **9** Methodist **10** Protestant **12** Presbyterian **13** Roman Catholic
place:
national park: **9** Fiordland, Fjordland, Tongariro
feature:
animal: **7** tuatara
bird: **3** kea, tui **4** kiwi, weka **6** takahe **7** apteryx **8** bellbird
tree: **4** rimu, tawa **5** kauri, matai **6** totara
food:
fish: **4** mako
fruit: **4** kiwi **9** tamarillo **17** Chinese gooseberry

Nickel Mountain
author: **11** John Gardner

nickname **6** handle **7** agnomen, epithet, moniker, pet name **8** baby name, cognomen **9** pseudonym, sobriquet **10** diminutive **11** appellation, designation

Nicomachean Ethics
author: **9** Aristotle

Nidhogg
origin: **12** Scandinavian
form: **7** serpent
domain: **8** Niflheim
gnaws on lowest root of: **9** Iggdrasil, Yggdrasil

Nielsen, Carl August
born: **6** Odense **7** Denmark
composer of: **9** Maskarade **12** Saul and David **16** Inextinguishable (symphony No 4)

Nietzsche, Friedrich
author of: **14** The Will to Power **17** Beyond Good and Evil, The Birth of Tragedy **20** Thus Spake Zarathustra

Niflheim
origin: **12** Scandinavian
ruler of: **3** Hel
purpose: **10** punish dead
climate: **3** fog **4** cold

nifty **4** chic, fine, neat, posh **5** natty, smart **6** clever, dapper **7** dashing, stylish **8** splendid **10** attractive **11** fashionable

Niger ***see box***

Nicaragua
capital/largest city: 7 Managua
others: 4 Leon, Rama **6** Masaya **7** Corinto, Granada **8** Jinotega **9** Matagalpa **10** Bluefields, Chinandega
division: 13 Mosquito Coast
measure: 4 vara **5** cahiz **6** suerte **7** cajuela, manzana **10** cabelleria
monetary unit: 4 peso **7** centavo, cordoba
weight: 3 bag **4** caha, caja **8** tonelada
island: 7 Ometepe
lake: 7 Managua **9** Nicaragua
mountain: 4 Leon **5** Negro, Viejo **6** Madera, Telica **7** Managua, Saslaya **9** Momotombo
highest point: 7 Mogoton
river: 4 Coco, Tuma **5** Wanks **6** Grande, Poteca **7** San Juan **8** Tipitapa **9** Escondido
sea: 7 Pacific **9** Caribbean
physical feature:
***gulf:* 7** Fonseca
people: 4 Mico, Mixe, Rama, Smoo, Ulva **5** Cukra, Diria, Lenca, Sambo, Toaca **6** Mangue **7** mestizo, Miskito **8** Mosquito **9** Matagalpa
***author:* 5** Dario
***explorer:* 6** Davila **7** Cordoba **8** Columbus
***group:* 10** Sandinista
***leader:* 6** Somoza, Walker, Zelaya **7** Nicardo
language: 7 English, Spanish
religion: 13 Roman Catholic
place:
***cathedral:* 12** Metropolitan
feature:
***dance:* 5** sones **10** zapateados, zarabandas
food:
***beans:* 8** frijoles
***dish:* 10** naca tamale
***drink:* 5** tiste **9** pinolillo
***fruit:* 6** zapote

Niger
other name: 6 Joliba, Kworra, Ramtil
capital/largest city: 6 Niamey
others: 5 Goure **6** Agadex, Agadez, Maradi, Tahoua, Zinder
division:
***region:* 3** Air **5** Arlit, Sahel
monetary unit: 5 franc **7** centime
lake: 4 Chad
mountain: 7 Bagzane **9** Air Massif
highest point: 7 Greboun
river: 5 Niger **6** Dillia
physical feature:
***desert:* 6** Sahara
***oasis:* 6** Kaouar
***plateau:* 5** Djado **6** Tegama **7** Tchigai **8** Mengueni **11** Adar Doutchi, Djerma Ganda
people: 4 Daza, Idjo, Idyo, Idzo, Peul, Teda **5** Hausa, Warri **6** Djerma, Fulani, Kanuri, Songha, Toubou, Tuareg **13** Djerma-Songhai
***conqueror:* 13** Usman Dan Fodio
***leader:* 5** Diori **8** Kountche
language: 5 Hausa, Mande **6** Djerma, French, Fulani, Tuareg **8** Mandingo, Tamashek
religion: 5 Islam **7** animism **12** Christianity
place:
***ruins:* 6** Agadez
feature:
***cavalry:* 5** Dosso
***empire:* 4** Mali **6** Fulani **7** Songhai **10** Kanem-Borno
***tree:* 6** acacia, baobab

Nigeria ***see box, p. 678***

niggard 4 mean **5** cheap, miser, tight **6** stingy **7** miserly **8** scrimper **9** skinflint **10** ungenerous **12** parsimonious

niggardliness 6 penury **8** meanness **9** closeness, parsimony **10** stinginess **11** miserliness **13** penny-pinching **15** tight-fistedness

niggardly 4 mean, poor **5** cheap, close, sorry, tight **6** flimsy, frugal, meager, measly, paltry, saving, scanty, shabby, stingy, tawdry **7** miserly, scrubby, sparing, thrifty **8** beggarly, grubbing, grudging, stinting, wretched **9** illiberal, mercenary, miserable, penurious **10** hardfisted, second-rate, ungenerous **11** closefisted **12** contemptible, insufficient, parsimonious

Nigger of the Narcissus, The
author: 12 Joseph Conrad
character: 5 Baker **6** Donkin **9** James Wait **12** Old Singleton

niggling 5 fussy, minor, petty, small **7** finicky **8** caviling, nugatory, picayune, piddling, trifling **9** quibbling **10** negligible, nit-picking **12** pettifogging **13** insignificant **15** inconsequential

nigh 4 near **5** close, handy **6** almost, at hand, nearly **7** close by **8** adjacent **9** bordering **11** neighboring, practically

night 4 dark, dusk **7** bedtime, evening, sundown **8** darkness, eventide **9** murkiness, obscurity **13** tenebrousness
goddess of: 3 Nox

nightclub
French: 5 boite **11** boite de nuit

nightfall 4 dark, dusk **6** sunset **7** evening, sundown **8** darkness, eventide, gloaming, moonrise, twilight
French: 10 crepuscule

Night Gallery
host: 10 Rod Serling

nightingale
group of: 5 watch

Nightline
host: 9 Ted Koppel

nightly 4 dark **7** evening, obscure **9** nocturnal **11** nocturnally

nightmare 7 incubus **8** bad dream, succubus **13** hallucination

Nigeria
capital/largest city: **5** Lagos
new capital: **5** Abuja
others: **3** Aba, Ado, Ede, Isa, Iwo, Jos, Oyo **4** Bida, Bidi, Buea, Kano, Offa, Yola **5** Benin, Bonny, Enugu, Warri, Zaria **6** Burutu, Ibadan, Ilesha, Ilorin, Kachia, Kaduna, Kadunc, Kokoto, Mushin, Takoba **7** Calabar, Onitsha, Oshogbo **8** Abeokuta **9** Maiduguri, Ogbomosho **12** Port Harcourt
division: **3** Air, Isa, Oyo **4** Kano, Nupe, Ondo **5** Asben, Benin, Bornu, Ijebu, Ogoja, Warri **6** Biafra, Degema, Owerri, Sokoto **7** Adamawa
monetary unit: **4** kobo **5** naira
lake: **4** Chad
highest point: **7** Dimlang
river: **3** Oli **4** Gana, Yobe **5** Benin, Benue, Cross, Niger **6** Kaduna, Sokoto **7** Calabar, Gongola **8** Komadugu **9** Sambreiro
sea: **8** Atlantic
physical feature:
bight: **5** Benin, Bonny **6** Biafra
delta: **5** Niger
gulf: **6** Guinea
plains: **5** Bornu **9** Hausaland
plateau: **3** Jos, Udi **6** Bauchi
port: **5** Lagos **7** Calabar **8** Harcourt
people: **3** Abo, Aro, Djo, Ebo, Edo, Ibo, Ijo, Tiv, Vai **4** Beni, Bini, Eboe, Efik, Egba, Ejam, Ekoi, Idyo, Igbo, Ijaw, Nupe **5** Angas, Benin, Gwari, Hausa **6** Chamba, Fulani, Ibibio, Kanuri, Yoruba **11** Hausa-Fulani
author: **6** Achebe
British colonial ruler: **6** Goldie, Lugard
kingdom: **3** Ife, Nok, Oyo **5** Benin **6** Fulani **10** Kanem-Borno
leader: **5** Gowon **6** Balewa, Ojukwu, Schick **7** Awolowo, Azikine, Azikiwe, Shagari **8** Obasanjo **13** Usman dan Fodio
language: **3** Ibo **4** Efik, Igbo **5** Hausa **6** Yoruba **7** English
religion: **5** Islam **7** animism **12** Christianity
place:
dam: **6** Kainji
mosque: **4** Kano
walled city: **4** Kano
feature:
dress: **4** riga **7** agbados
tree: **5** abura, afara **6** obeche **10** terminalia

Nile
boat: **5** baris **6** cangia, nuggar, sandal **7** felucca, gaiassa **8** dahabeah
cities: **3** Qus **4** Abri, Argo, Idfu, Isna, Juba, Qina **5** Aswan, Asyut, Cairo, Kokka, Kusti, Luxor, Meroe, Minya, Rejaf, Saite, Tanis, Tanta **6** Atbara, Faiyum **7** Malakel, Mansura, Rosetta **8** Khartoum, Omdurman, Rusayris **9** Was Madani **10** Alexandria
dam: **6** Sannar **9** Aswan High, White Nile
desert bordering: **6** Libyan, Nubian **7** Arabian
falls: **5** Ripon **8** Kabalega **9** Murchison
feature: **6** Sphinx
pyramid: **4** Giza
temple: **8** Ramses II **9** Abu Simbel **11** Deir el-Bahri, Medinet Habu
flows into: **13** Mediterranean
flows through: **5** Egypt, Kenya, Sudan, Zaire **6** Rwanda, Uganda **7** Burundi **8** Ethiopia, Tanzania
island: **4** Roda **6** Philae
lake: **4** Tana **5** Kyoga, Tsana **6** Albert, Edward, Nasser **8** Victoria
other name: **4** Hapi **20** The Father of the Rivers
people: **3** Jur, Luo, Lwo, Nuo, Suk **4** Bari, Beja, Golo, Luoh, Madi **5** Nilot **7** Shilluk
plain: **6** Gezira
plant: **4** sudd **5** lotus
starting point: **5** Tsana **8** Victoria
swamp: **4** Sudd
tributary: **4** Arab **5** Rahad, Sobat **6** Atbara, Ghazai, Kagera **7** Rosetta **8** Blue Nile, Damietta **9** Bahr Jebel, White Nile

Night of the Iguana, The
director: **10** John Huston
based on play by: **17** Tennessee Williams
cast: **7** Sue Lyon **8** Skip Ward **10** Ava Gardner **11** Deborah Kerr **13** Richard Burton
setting: **6** Mexico

nightshade **16** Solanum dulcamara
varieties: **4** ball **5** black **6** common, deadly, sticky **7** Malabar **8** stinking **9** melon-leaf, poisonous, soda-apple **10** enchanter's

Nights of Cabiria
director: **15** Federico Fellini
cast: **13** Amedeo Nazzari **14** Francois Perier **15** Giulietta Masina
remade as: **12** Sweet Charity

nightstick **3** rod **4** mace, wand **5** baton, staff **6** cudgel **7** scepter **8** bludgeon **9** billy club, truncheon **10** shillelagh

nighttime **4** late **5** night **9** late-night, nighttide, nocturnal

Night to Remember, A
director: **8** Roy Baker
based on story by: **10** Walter Lord
cast: **9** Jill Dixon **11** Kenneth More **13** David McCallum **16** Laurence Naismith
setting: **7** Titanic

nihil **7** nothing

nihilism **5** chaos **6** anomie **7** license **9** amorality, anarchism, emptiness, terrorism **10** alienation, iconoclasm, radicalism, skepticism **11** agnosticism, lawlessness, nothingness **12** nonexistence **16** irresponsibility

nihilist **5** rebel **9** anarchist, terrorist **13** revolutionary

Nihon *see* **5** Japan

Nike
origin: **5** Greek
goddess of: **7** victory
father: **11** Titan Pallas
mother: **4** Styx

brother: 5 Zelos
corresponds to: 6 Athena 8 Victoria

nil 4 none, null, zero 6 cipher, naught 7 nothing, nullity 11 nonexistent

Nile *see box, p. 678*

Niles, Hazel and Peter
characters in: 22 Mourning Becomes Electra
author: 6 O'Neill

nil nisi bonum 21 nothing unless it is good

nil sine numine 27 nothing without the divine will
motto of: 8 Colorado

nimble 4 deft, spry 5 agile, fleet, light, quick, rapid, ready, swift 6 active, expert, lively, prompt, speedy, supple 8 animated, skillful, spirited 9 dexterous, mercurial, sprightly 10 proficient

nimbleness 7 agility 8 alacrity, spryness 9 dexterity, quickness 10 limberness, suppleness

nimble-witted 5 droll, witty 6 clever 11 resourceful

nimbus 4 aura, disk, halo 5 cloud, vapor 7 aureole 8 radiance

Nimitz, Chester
served in: 3 WWI 4 WWII
commander of: 12 Pacific fleet
rank: 12 fleet (five-star) admiral 22 chief of naval operations
battle: 6 Midway 9 Leyte Gulf 13 Philippine Sea

Nimoy, Leonard
born: 8 Boston MA
roles: 7 Mr Spock 8 Star Trek 17 Mission Impossible 21 Star Trek: The Voyage Home 22 Star Trek: The Wrath of Khan 25 Star Trek: The Search for Spock

Nimrod
father: 4 Cush
grandfather: 3 Ham
great grandfather: 4 Noah
founded: 5 Calah, Resen 7 Nineveh 8 Rehoboth

nincompoop 4 boob, dolt, dope, fool, jerk 5 dummy, dunce, idiot, klutz, moron, ninny 6 dimwit, lummox, nitwit 7 half-wit, jackass 8 bonehead, dummkopf, imbecile, lunkhead, numskull 9 blockhead, dumb bunny, harebrain, numbskull, simpleton 10 dunderhead, dunderpate, muddlehead, noodlehead 11 knucklehead, rattlebrain 12 featherbrain, scatterbrain

Nine, the *see* 5 Muses

Nineteen Eighty-Four
author: 12 George Orwell
character: 5 Julia 6 O'Brien 11 Charrington 12 Winston Smith

1919
author: 13 John Dos Passos

Ninety-Five Theses
author: 12 Martin Luther

Nineveh
founder: 6 Nimrod

Nine worthies
mentioned in: 16 medieval romances
three each of: 4 Jews 6 Pagans 10 Christians
names: 5 David 6 Arthur, Hector, Joshua 11 Charlemagne 12 Julius Caesar 15 Judas Maccabaeus 17 Alexander the Great 18 Godefroy de Bouillon

Ningal
origin: 8 Sumerian
son: 3 Utu
consort of: 5 Nanna

Ninib *see* 7 Ninurta

Ninlil
origin: 8 Sumerian
goddess of: 3 air

ninny 3 ass, sap 4 fool, simp 5 booby, dunce, idiot, moron 6 dimwit, nitwit 7 fathead, half-wit 8 bonehead, dumbdumb, imbecile, lunkhead, numskull 9 blockhead, dumb bunny, lamebrain, numbskull 10 dunderhead, nincompoop 11 chowderhead

Ninotchka
director: 13 Ernst Lubitsch
cast: 9 Ina Claire 10 Bela Lugosi, Greta Garbo 13 Melvyn Douglas
setting: 5 Paris
remade as: 13 Silk Stockings

Ninurta
also: 5 Ninib
origin: 8 Sumerian 10 Babylonian
type of god: 4 hero
personifies: 4 wind 9 south wind
father: 5 Enlil
avenger of: 5 Enlil

Ninus
wife: 9 Semiramis
founder of: 7 Nineveh

Niobe
father: 8 Tantalus
mother: 5 Dione
brother: 6 Pelops
husband: 7 Amphion
children: 9 seven sons 14 seven daughters
children called: 6 Niobid
taunted: 4 Leto
children killed by: 6 Apollo 7 Artemis
changed into: 5 stone
changed by: 4 Zeus

Niord
also: 5 Njord
origin: 12 Scandinavian
god of: 4 wind 10 navigation, prosperity
king of: 5 Vanir
son: 4 Frey 5 Freyr
daughter: 5 Freia, Freya

nip 3 cut, lop 4 bite, clip, crop, dock, grab, grip, ruin, snag, snap, snip 5 blast, check, chill, clamp, clasp, crack, crush, frost, grasp, pinch, quash, seize, sever, shear, snare, tweak 6 benumb, clutch, cut off, freeze, pierce, snatch, sunder, thwart 7 curtail, destroy, shorten, squeeze 8 compress, cut short, demolish 9 frustrate 10 abbreviate

nip-and-tuck 5 close

nip in the bud 7 prevent 8 preclude 9 forestall, frustrate

Nipper, Susan
character in: 12 Dombey and Son
author: 7 Dickens

Nippon *see* 5 Japan

nippy 3 raw 5 brisk, chill, crisp, sharp 6 biting, chilly 7 cutting

Nisn 16 first Hebrew month

nit-pick 4 carp, pick 5 cavil 9 criticize

nitrate 4 salt 5 ester 6 sodium 9 potassium 10 fertilizer

nitrogen
chemical symbol: 1 N

nitty-gritty 4 core, crux, gist, meat, pith 5 heart 7 essence 9 substance

nitwit 3 ass 4 clod, dolt, fool 5 booby, dummy, dunce, idiot, klutz, moron, ninny 7 fathead, pinhead 8 bonehead, dumbdumb, imbecile, lunkhead, meathead, numskull, peabrain 9 birdbrain, blockhead, lamebrain, numbskull 10 dunderhead, nincompoop, noodlehead 11 chowderhead

Niven, David
real name: 21 James David Graham Niven
autobiography: 16 The Moon's a Balloon 21 Bring on the Empty Horses
born: 8 Scotland 10 Kirriemuir
roles: 11 Phileas Fogg 12 Casino Royale, My Man Godfrey 14 The Pink Panther,

Nixon, Richard Milhous
presidential rank: **13** thirty-seventh
party: **10** Republican
state represented: **2** NY
defeated: **7** (George Corley) Wallace **8** (Hubert Horatio) Humphrey
vice president: **4** (Gerald Rudolph) Ford **5** (Spiro Theodore) Agnew
cabinet:
state: **6** (William Pierce) Rogers **9** (Henry A) Kissinger
treasury: **5** (William E) Simon **6** (George P) Shultz **7** (David Matthew) Kennedy **8** (John Bowden) Connally
defense: **5** (Melvin Robert) Laird **10** (Elliot L) Richardson **11** (James R) Schlesinger
attorney general: **5** (William B) Saxbe **8** (John Newton) Mitchell **10** (Elliot L) Richardson **11** (Richard G) Kleindienst
postmaster general: **6** (Winton Malcolm) Blount
interior: **6** (Rogers Clark Ballard) Morton, (Walter Joseph) Hinkel
agriculture: **4** (Earl Lauer) Butz **6** (Clifford Morris) Hardin
commerce: **4** (Frederick B) Dent **5** (Maurice Hubert) Stans
labor: **6** (George Pratt) Shultz **7** (James Day) Hodgson, (Peter J) Brennan
HEW: **5** (Robert Hutchinson) Finch **10** (Caspar W) Weinberger, (Elliot Lee) Richardson
HUD: **4** (James T) Lynn **6** (George Wilcken) Romney
transportation: **5** (John Anthony) Volpe **8** (Claude S) Brinegar
born: **2** CA **10** Yorba Linda
education:
college: **8** Whittier
law school: **14** Duke University
religion: **6** Quaker **16** Society of Friends
interests: **8** football
vacation spot: **11** Key Biscayne (FL), San Clemente (CA)
dog: **8** Checkers **11** King Timahoe
author: **9** Six Crises **10** The Real War **27** RN: The Memoirs of Richard Nixon
political career: **8** US Senate **13** Vice President **24** US House of Representatives
civilian career: **6** lawyer
military service: **6** US Navy **10** lieutenant, World War II
notable events of lifetime/term:
Calley court martialed for: **13** Mylai Massacre
court martial of: **6** Calley
creation of: **10** Bangladesh
crisis: **3** oil **6** energy
embargo on: **3** oil
first men on: **4** moon
incident: **11** Wounded Knee
pardon of Nixon by: **4** Ford
publication of: **14** Pentagon Papers
resignation of: **5** Agnew, Nixon
scandal: **9** Watergate
student deaths at: **9** Kent State
treaty: **10** Seabed Arms **32** Nonproliferation of Nuclear Weapons
trip to: **5** China
war: **7** Vietnam **10** Middle East **12** East Pakistan
quotes: **31** A respectable Republican cloth coat **35** You won't have Nixon to kick around any more
father: **14** Francis Anthony
mother: **6** Hannah (Milhous)
siblings: **11** Arthur Burdg **12** Harold Samuel **13** Edward Calvert, Francis Donald
wife: **8** (Thelma Catherine) Patricia (Ryan)
nickname: **3** Pat
children: **5** Julie **8** Patricia
Julie married: **15** David Eisenhower
Patricia married: **9** Edward Cox
Patricia's nickname: **6** Tricia

Separate Tables (Oscar) **16** Stairway to Heaven, Wuthering Heights **18** The Prisoner of Zenda **26** Around the World in Eighty Days

Nix
origin: **8** Germanic
form: **6** spirit
habitat: **5** water

Nixon, Richard Milhous ***see box***

Njord *see* **5** Niord

no **3** nay, nix, not **4** none, veto

Noah
father: **6** Lamech
grandfather: **10** Methuselah
son: **3** Ham **4** Shem **7** Japheth
grandson: **3** Put **4** Cush **6** Canaan **7** Misraim
great grandson: **6** Nimrod
built: **3** ark

collected: **7** animals
survived: **5** flood
pertaining to: **8** Noachian

Noah's Ark
made of: **10** gopherwood

nob **4** peer, toff **5** swell **9** patrician **10** aristocrat

Nobel, Alfred
nationality: **7** Swedish
invented: **8** dynamite
originated: **10** Nobel Prize

Nobel Prizes ***see box, p. 682***

nobility **5** elite, lords **7** dignity, majesty, peerage, primacy, royalty **8** breeding, eminence, grandeur, high rank, prestige, splendor **9** gentility, grandness, greatness, loftiness, sublimity, supremacy **10** blue bloods, mightiness, patricians, patriciate, upper crust **11** aristocracy, distinction, exaltedness, preeminence, stateliness, superiority **12** magnificence

nobility obliges
French: **14** noblesse oblige

noble **3** don **4** high, just, lord, peer **5** famed, grand, great, lofty, moral, regal, royal **6** famous, gentle, honest, knight, lordly, squire, superb, worthy **7** awesome, courtly, eminent, ethical, exalted, grandee, stately, sublime, supreme, upright **8** baronial, cavalier, elevated, glorious, handsome, highborn, imperial, imposing, lordlike, majestic, princely, renowned, selfless, splendid, superior, virtuous **9** chevalier, dignified, estimable, excellent, exemplary, gentleman, honorable, patrician, personage, reputable **10** aristocrat, impressive, preeminent **11** magnanimous, magnificent, meritorious, pureblooded, trustworthy **12** aristocratic, thoroughbred **13** distinguished, incorruptible
French: **6** gentil

Noble House
author: **12** James Clavell

nobleman **4** lord, peer **7** grandee **9** patrician **10** aristocrat

noblesse oblige **15** nobility obliges

noblewoman **4** dame, lady, rani **5** begum, queen **6** milady **7** czarina, duchess, empress, peeress, sultana **8** baroness, contessa, countess, maharani, princess **11** marchioness

Nobody Knows My Name
author: **12** James Baldwin

nocturnal **4** dark **5** night **7** nightly, obscure **8** darkling **9** nighttime

Nocturne
author: **15** Frank Swinnerton

nod **3** bob **4** doze, hail, show, sign **5** agree, greet, lapse, let up **6** assent, beckon, concur, drowse, motion, reveal, salute, signal **7** consent, drop off, fall off, gesture, signify **9** recognize

node **3** bud **4** bump, burl, hump, knob, knot, lump **5** bulge, joint **6** button **8** swelling **10** prominence, tumescence **11** excrescence **12** protuberance

Nodosaurus
type: **8** dinosaur **10** ornithopod
location: **12** North America

nodule **3** sac, wen **4** bump, cyst, knob, knot, lump, stud **5** bulge **6** growth **8** swelling **9** outgrowth **10** projection, prominence, protrusion, tumescence **11** excrescence **12** protuberance

noel, Noel **4** yule **5** carol **8** yuletide **9** Christmas **13** Christmastide

Noemon
mentioned in: **7** Odyssey
supplied: **4** ship
supplied ship to: **10** Telemachus

No Exit
author: **14** Jean-Paul Sartre

noggin **3** cup, mug **4** bean, head, pate **5** gourd **6** noodle

Noggs, Newman
character in: **16** Nicholas Nickleby
author: **7** Dickens

Noguchi, Hideyo
field: **12** bacteriology
nationality: **8** Japanese
isolated: **8** syphilis

noise **3** ado, din **4** bang, blab, boom, echo, pass, roar, stir, wail **5** babel, blare, blast, bruit, rumor, sound, voice **6** bedlam, clamor, hubbub, racket, repeat, report, rumble, tumult, uproar **7** barrage, bluster, clatter, thunder **8** brawling, gabbling, rumbling, shouting **9** cacophony, cannonade, circulate, commotion, discharge **10** dissonance, hullabaloo **11** pandemonium **12** caterwauling, vociferation **13** reverberation

noiseless **5** quiet, still, tacit **6** hushed, silent **9** soundless, voiceless

noisemaker **4** bell, horn **5** siren **6** rattle **7** clacker, clapper, snapper, whistle

noisome **4** foul, rank **5** acrid, fetid, toxic **6** putrid, rotten, smelly **7** baneful, harmful, hurtful, noxious, reeking **8** mephitic, stinking **9** injurious, offensive, poisonous, unhealthy **10** malodorous, nauseating, pernicious **11** deleterious, detrimental **12** evil-smelling

noisy **4** loud **5** alive **6** lively, raging, shrill, stormy **7** blaring, blatant, furious, grating, jarring, rackety **8** animated, piercing, strident **9** clamorous, deafening, dissonant, turbulent **10** boisterous, clangorous, discordant, rampageous, resounding, thundering, thunderous, tumultuous, uproarious **11** cacophonous, tempestuous **12** earsplitting

Nolan, George Brendan
real name of: **11** George Brent

Nolan, Lloyd
born: **14** San Francisco CA
roles: **22** Lieutenant Colonel Queeg **26** The Caine Mutiny Court Martial

Nolde, Emil
real name: **10** Emil Hansen
born: **5** Nolde **7** Germany
artwork: **7** Prophet **10** Papua Youth **11** Tropical Sun **12** The Magicians, The Pentecost **13** The Last Supper, Three Russians **14** Doubting Thomas **20** Life of Maria Aegyptica **22** Christ Among the Children, Christ and the Adulteress

nolens volens **10** willy-nilly **19** whether willing or not

noli me tangere **10** touch me not

nolle prosequi **14** do not prosecute **19** be unwilling to pursue

nolo contendere **21** I am unwilling to contend

no longer able to fight
French: **12** hors de combat

no longer in existence **4** dead, gone, lost **7** defunct, died out, extinct **8** vanished

Nolte, Nick
born: **7** Omaha NE
roles: **5** Weeds **7** The Deep **10** Cannery Row **14** Rich Man Poor Man **15** Forty-Eight Hours **16** North Dallas Forty

Nobel Prizes

Literature:

1901: **20** Rene F A Sully-Prudhomme
1902: **14** Theodor Mommsen
1903: **20** Bjornstjerne Bjornson
1904: **13** Jose Echegaray **15** Frederic Mistral
1905: **17** Henryk Sienkiewicz
1906: **14** Giosue Carducci
1907: **14** Rudyard Kipling
1908: **13** Rudolf C Eucken
1909: **13** Selma Lagerlof
1910: **12** Paul von Heyse
1911: **18** Maurice Maeterlinck
1912: **16** Gerhart Hauptmann
1913: **21** Sir Rabindranath Tagore
1915: **13** Romain Rolland
1916: **19** Verner von Heidenstam
1917: **11** K A Gjellerup **17** Henrik Pontoppidan
1919: **15** Carl F G Spitteler
1920: **10** Knut Hamsun
1921: **13** Anatole France
1922: **25** Jacinto Benavente y Martinez
1923: **18** William Butler Yeats
1924: **17** Wladyslaw S Reymont
1925: **17** George Bernard Shaw
1926: **13** Grazia Deledda
1927: **12** Henri Bergson
1928: **12** Sigrid Undset
1929: **10** Thomas Mann
1930: **13** Sinclair Lewis
1931: **14** Erik A Karlfeldt
1932: **14** John Galsworthy
1933: **10** Ivan A Bunin
1934: **15** Luigi Pirandello
1936: **12** Eugene O'Neill
1937: **17** Roger Martin du Gard
1938: **10** Pearl S Buck
1939: **15** Frans E Sillanpaa
1944: **15** Johannes V Jensen
1945: **15** Gabriela Mistral
1946: **12** Hermann Hesse
1947: **9** Andre Gide
1948: **7** T S Eliot
1949: **15** William Faulkner
1950: **15** Bertrand Russell (Earl Russell)
1951: **14** Par F Lagerkvist
1952: **15** Francois Mauriac
1953: **21** Sir Winston L S Churchill
1954: **15** Ernest Hemingway
1955: **15** Halldor K Laxness
1956: **16** Juan Ramon Jimenez
1957: **11** Albert Camus
1958: **15** Boris L Pasternak
1959: **18** Salvatore Quasimodo
1960: **14** Saint-John Perse
1961: **9** Ivo Andric
1962: **13** John Steinbeck
1963: **13** George Seferis
1964: **14** Jean Paul Sartre
1965: **17** Mikhail A Sholokhov
1966: **10** Nelly Sachs **17** Samuel Joseph (Shmuel Y) Agnon
1967: **19** Miguel Angel Asturias
1968: **16** Yasunari Kawabata
1969: **13** Samuel Beckett
1970: **22** Aleksandr I Solzhenitsyn
1971: **11** Pablo Neruda
1972: **12** Heinrich Boll
1973: **12** Patrick White
1974: **13** Eyvind Johnson **14** Harry Martinson
1975: **14** Eugenio Montale
1976: **10** Saul Bellow
1977: **17** Vicente Aleixandre
1978: **19** Isaac Bashevis Singer
1979: **14** Odysseus Elytis
1980: **13** Czeslaw Milosz
1981: **12** Elias Canetti
1982: **20** Gabriel Garcia Marquez
1983: **14** William Golding
1984: **15** Jaroslav Seifert
1985: **11** Claude Simon
1986: **11** Wole Soyinka
1987: **13** Joseph Brodsky
1988: **13** Naguib Mahfouz

Physiology/Medicine:

1901: **15** Emil A von Behring
1902: **13** Sir Ronald Ross
1903: **12** Niels R Finsen
1904: **11** Ivan P Pavlov
1905: **10** Robert Koch
1906: **12** Camillo Golgi **19** Santiago Ramon y Cajal
1907: **16** Charles L A Laveran
1908: **11** Paul Ehrlich **15** Elie Metchnikoff
1909: **11** Emil T Kocher
1910: **14** Albrecht Kossel
1911: **16** Allvar Gullstrand
1912: **12** Alexis Carrel
1913: **14** Charles R Richet
1914: **12** Robert Barany
1919: **11** Jules Bordet
1920: **12** Shack A S Krogh
1922: **12** Otto Meyerhof **14** Archibald V Hill
1923: **13** John J R Macleod **20** Sir Frederick G Banting
1924: **15** Willem Einthoven
1926: **15** Johannes Fibiger
1927: **19** Julius Wagner-Jauregg
1928: **16** Charles J H Nicolle
1929: **17** Christiaan Eijkman **20** Sir Frederick G Hopkins
1930: **15** Karl Landsteiner
1931: **12** Otto H Warburg
1932: **12** Edgar D Adrian **21** Sir Charles Sherrington
1933: **13** Thomas H Morgan
1934: **12** George R Minot **14** George H Whipple, William P Murphy
1935: **11** Hans Spemann
1936: **9** Otto Loewi **13** Sir Henry H Dale
1937: **31** Albert Szent-Gyorgyi von Nagyrapolt
1938: **16** Corneille Heymans
1939: **13** Gerhard Domagk
1943: **9** Henrik Dam **12** Edward A Doisy
1944: **14** Herbert S Gasser, Joseph Erlanger
1945: **11** Ernst B Chain **16** Sir Howard W Florey **19** Sir Alexander Fleming
1946: **14** Hermann J Muller
1947: **9** Carl F Cori **10** Gerty T Cori **16** Bernardo A Houssay
1948: **11** Paul H Muller
1949: **11** Walter R Hess **21** Antonio C de A F Egas Moniz
1950: **12** Philip S Hench **14** Edward C Kendall **16** Tadeus Reichstein
1951: **10** Max Theiler
1952: **14** Selman A Waksman
1953: **13** Fritz A Lipmann, Sir Hans A Krebs
1954: **11** John F Enders **13** Thomas H Weller **17** Frederick C Robbins
1955: **14** Axel H T Theorell
1956: **13** Andre Cournand **15** Werner Forssmann **20** Dickenson W Richards Jr
1957: **11** Daniel Bovet
1958: **12** Edward L Tatum **13** George W Beadle **15** Joshua Lederberg
1959: **11** Severo Ochoa **14** Arthur Kornberg
1960: **13** Peter B Medawar **15** Sir Frank M Burnet

Nobel Prizes
1961: **14** Georg von Bekesy
1962: **12** James D Watson **14** Francis H C Crick **16** Maurice H F Wilkins
1963: **16** Alan Lloyd Hodgkin **18** Sir John Carew Eccles **20** Andrew Fielding Huxley
1964: **11** Feodor Lynen **12** Konrad E Bloch
1965: **10** Andre Lwoff **12** Jacques Monod **13** Francois Jacob
1966: **17** Francis Peyton Rous **21** Charles Brenton Huggins
1967: **10** George Wald **12** Ragnar Granit **20** Haldan Keffer Hartline
1968: **13** Robert W Holley **14** H Gobind Khorana **18** Marshall W Nirenberg
1969: **11** Max Delbruck **14** Alfred D Hershey, Salvador E Luria
1970: **11** Ulf von Euler **13** Julius Axelrod **14** Sir Bernard Katz
1971: **17** Earl W Sutherland Jr
1972: **13** Rodney R Porter **14** Gerald M Edelman
1973: **12** Konrad Lorenz **13** Karl von Frisch **17** Nikolaas Tinbergen
1974: **12** Albert Claude **15** Christian de Duve **16** George EmilPalade
1975: **12** Howard M Temin **14** David Baltimore, Renato Dulbecco
1976: **15** Baruch S Blumberg **22** Daniel Carleton Gajdusek
1977: **13** Andrew Schally, Rosalyn S Yalow **14** Roger Guillemin
1978: **11** Werner Arber **13** Daniel Nathans, Hamilton Smith
1979: **13** Allan M Cormack **17** Godfrey Hounsfield
1980: **11** Jean Dausset **12** George D Snell **15** Baruj Benacerraf
1981: **11** David H Hubel **12** Roger W Sperry **14** Torsten N Wiesel
1982: **9** John R Vane **15** Bengt Samuelsson **17** Sune Karl Bergstrom
1983: **17** Barbara McClintock
1984: **11** Niels K Jerne **13** Cesar Milstein **16** Georges J F Koehler
1985: **13** Michael S Brown **16** Joseph L Goldstein
1986: **12** Stanley Cohen **18** Rita Levi-Montalcini
1987: **14** Susumu Tonegawa
1988: **10** James Black **14** Gertrude B Elion **16** George H Hitchings

Chemistry:
1901: **16** Jacobus H van't Hoff
1902: **11** Emil Fischer
1903: **16** Svante A Arrhenius
1904: **16** Sir William Ramsay
1905: **17** J F W Adolf von Baeyer
1906: **12** Henri Moissan
1907: **13** Eduard Buchner
1908: **19** Sir Ernest Rutherford
1909: **14** Wilhelm Ostwald
1910: **11** Otto Wallach
1911: **11** Marie S Curie
1912: **12** Paul Sabatier **14** Victor Grignard
1913: **12** Alfred Werner
1914: **17** Theodore W Richards
1915: **18** Richard Willstatter
1918: **10** Fritz Haber
1920: **13** Walther Nernst
1921: **14** Frederick Soddy
1922: **13** Francis W Aston
1923: **10** Fritz Pregl
1925: **16** Richard Zsigmondy
1926: **15** Theodor Svedberg
1927: **15** Heinrich Wieland
1928: **12** Adolf Windaus
1929: **15** Sir Arthur Harden **19** Hans von Euler-Chelpin
1930: **11** Hans Fischer
1931: **9** Carl Bosch **16** Friedrich Bergius
1932: **14** Irving Langmuir
1934: **11** Harold C Urey
1935: **16** Irene Joliot-Curie **19** Frederic Joliot-Curie
1936: **12** Peter J W Debye
1937: **10** Paul Karrer **17** Sir Walter N Haworth
1938: **11** Richard Kuhn
1939: **14** Adolf Butenandt, Leopold Ruzicka
1943: **14** Georg von Hevesy
1944: **8** Otto Hahn
1945: **16** Artturi I Virtanen
1946: **12** James B Sumner **13** John H Northrop **15** Wendell M Stanley
1947: **17** Sir Robert Robinson
1948: **12** Arne Tiselius
1949: **15** William F Giauque
1950: **9** Kurt Alder, Otto Diels
1951: **13** Glenn T Seaborg **14** Edwin M McMillan
1952: **14** Archer J P Martin, Richard L M Synge
1953: **17** Hermann Staudinger
1954: **13** Linus C Pauling
1955: **17** Vincent du Vigneaud
1956: **15** Nikolai N Semenov **20** Sir Cyril N Hinshelwood
1957: **17** Sir Alexander R Todd (Baron Todd)
1958: **15** Frederick Sanger
1959: **17** Jaroslav Heyrovsky
1960: **13** Willard F Libby
1961: **12** Melvin Calvin
1962: **10** Max F Perutz **12** John C Kendrew
1963: **11** Giulio Natta, Karl Ziegler
1964: **26** Dorothy Mary Crowfoot Hodgkin
1965: **19** Robert Burns Woodward
1966: **15** Robert S Mulliken
1967: **12** Manfred Eigen **15** Sir George Porter **27** Ronald George Wreyford Norrish
1968: **11** Lars Onsager
1969: **9** Odd Hassel **13** Derek H R Barton
1970: **18** Luis Federico Leloir
1971: **15** Gerhard Herzberg
1972: **13** Stanford Moore **18** Christian B Anfinsen, William Howard Stein
1973: **16** Ernst Otto Fischer **17** Geoffrey Wilkinson
1974: **10** Paul J Flory
1975: **14** John W Cornforth, Vladimir Prelog
1976: **16** William N Lipscomb
1977: **13** Ilya Prigogine
1978: **13** Peter Mitchell
1979: **11** Georg Wittig **13** Herbert C Brown
1980: **8** Paul Berg **13** Walter Gilbert **15** Frederick Sanger
1981: **12** Kenichi Fukui **13** Roald Hoffmann
1982: **9** Aaron Klug
1983: **10** Henry Taube
1984: **21** Robert Bruce Merrifield
1985: **11** Jerome Karle **16** Herbert A Hauptman
1986: **8** Yuan T Lee

Nobel Prizes (*continued*)
12 John C Polanyi
16 Dudley Herschbach
1987: **11** Donald J Cram
16 Charles J Pederson
1988: **11** Robert Huber
13 Hartmut Michel
17 Johann Deisenhofer

Physics:
1901: **16** Wilhelm K Roentgen
1902: **12** Pieter Zeeman **15** Hendrik A Lorentz
1903: **11** Marie S Curie, Pierre Curie **15** A Henri Becquerel
1904: **11** John W Strutt (Lord Rayleigh)
1905: **13** Philipp Lenard
1906: **16** Sir Joseph Thomson
1907: **16** Albert A Michelson
1908: **15** Gabriel Lippmann
1909: **10** Karl F Braun **16** Guglielmo Marconi
1910: **20** Johannes D van der Waals
1911: **11** Wilhelm Wien
1912: **10** Nils G Dalen
1913: **20** Heike Kamerlingh Onnes
1914: **10** Max von Laue
1915: **16** Sir William H Bragg, Sir William L Bragg
1917: **14** Charles B Barkla
1918: **9** Max Planck
1919: **13** Johannes Stark
1920: **17** Charles E Guillaume
1921: **14** Albert Einstein
1922: **10** Nils H D Bohr
1923: **15** Robert A Millikan
1924: **14** Karl M G Siegbahn
1925: **11** Gustav Hertz, James Franck
1926: **11** Jean B Perrin
1927: **14** Arthur H Compton **15** Charles T R Wilson
1928: **18** Sir Owen W Richardson
1929: **15** Louis V de Broglie
1930: **23** Sir Chandrasekhara V Raman
1932: **16** Werner Heisenberg
1933: **11** Paul A M Dirac **16** Erwin Schrodinger
1935: **16** Sir James Chadwick
1936: **11** Victor F Hess **13** Carl D Anderson
1937: **16** Clinton J Davisson **17** Sir George P Thomson
1938: **11** Enrico Fermi
1939: **15** Ernest O Lawrence
1943: **9** Otto Stern
1944: **11** Isidor I Rabi
1945: **13** Wolfgang Pauli
1946: **14** Percy W Bridgman
1947: **18** Sir Edward V Appleton
1948: **17** Patrick M S Blackett
1949: **12** Hideki Yukawa
1950: **12** Cecil F Powell
1951: **14** Ernest T S Walton **17** Sir John D Cockcroft
1952: **10** Felix Bloch **14** Edward M Purcell
1953: **12** Frits Zernike
1954: **7** Max Born **12** Walther Bothe
1955: **13** Polykarp Kusch, Willis E Lamb Jr
1956: **11** John Bardeen **15** Walter H Brattain **16** William B Shockley
1957: **11** Tsung Dao Lee **12** Chen Ning Yang
1958: **9** Igor Y Tamm **10** Ilya M Frank **15** Pavel A Cherenkov
1959: **11** Emilio Segre **15** Owen Chamberlain
1960: **13** Donald A Glaser
1961: **16** Robert Hofstadter, Rudolf L Mossbauer
1962: **10** Lev D Landau
1963: **11** J Hans Jensen **16** Eugene Paul Wigner **18** Maria Goeppert Mayer
1964: **17** Charles Hard Townes **25** Nikolai Gennadiyevich Basov **30** Aleksandr Mikhailovich Prokhorov
1965: **18** Shinichiro Tomonaga **22** Julian Seymour Schwinger, Richard Phillips Feynman
1966: **13** Alfred Kastler
1967: **17** Hans Albrecht Bethe
1968: **12** Luis W Alvarez
1969: **14** Murray Gell-Mann
1970: **12** Hannes Alfven **15** Louis Eugene Neel
1971: **11** Dennis Gabor
1972: **11** John Bardeen, Leon N Cooper **20** John Robert Schreiffer
1973: **8** Leo Esaki **11** Ivar Giaever **15** Brian D Josephson
1974: **12** Antony Hewish **13** Sir Martin Ryle
1975: **8** Aage Bohr **13** Ben R Mottelson **15** L James Rainwater
1976: **12** Samuel C C Ting **13** Burton Richter
1977: **13** John H Van Vleck, Sir Nevill Mott **15** Philip W Anderson
1978: **12** Arno A Penzias, Peter Kapitza (Pyotr Kapitsa) **13** Robert W Wilson
1979: **10** Abdus Salam **14** Sheldon Glashow, Steven Weinberg
1980: **9** Val L Fitch **12** James W Cronin
1981: **12** Kai M Siegbahn **14** Arthur Schawlow **19** Nicolaas Bloembergen
1982: **14** Kenneth G Wilson
1983: **14** William A Fowler **25** Subrahmanyan Chandrasekhar
1984: **11** Carlo Rubbia **15** Simon van der Meer
1985: **16** Klaus von Klitzing
1986: **10** Ernst Ruska, Gerd Binner **14** Heinrich Rohrer
1987: **12** K Alex Mueller **13** J Georg Bednorz
1988: **13** Leon M Lederman **14** Melvin Schwartz **15** Jack Steinberger

Peace:
1901: **13** Frederic Passy **15** Jean Henri Dunant
1902: **12** Elie Ducommun **18** Charles Albert Gobat
1903: **17** Sir William R Cremer
1904: **27** Institute of International Law
1905: **24** Baroness Bertha von Suttner
1906: **17** Theodore Roosevelt
1907: **12** Louis Renault **14** Ernesto T Moneta
1908: **12** Fredrik Bajer **14** Klas P Arnoldson
1909: **16** Auguste Beernaert **35** Paul H Balluat d'Estournelles de Constant
1910: **24** International Peace Bureau
1911: **12** Alfred H Fried **13** Tobias M C Asser
1912: **9** Elihu Root
1913: **15** Henri La Fontaine
1917: **30** International Red Cross Committee
1919: **13** Woodrow Wilson
1920: **13** Leon Bourgeois
1921: **15** Christian L Lange **19** Karl Hjalmar Branting
1922: **14** Fridtjof Nansen
1925: **13** Charles G

(*continued*)

Nobel Prizes *(continued)* Dawes **26** Sir Joseph Austen Chamberlain
1926: **14** Aristide Briand **16** Gustav Stresemann
1927: **12** Ludwig Quidde **17** Ferdinand E Buisson
1929: **13** Frank B Kellogg
1930: **15** (Lars Olof Jonathan) Nathan Soderblom
1931: **10** Jane Addams **20** Nicholas Murray Butler
1933: **15** Sir Norman Angell
1934: **15** Arthur Henderson
1935: **16** Carl von Ossietzky
1936: **19** Carlos Saavedra Lamas
1937: **13** E A Robert Cecil (Viscount Cecil)
1938: **36** Nansen International Office for Refugees
1944: **30** International Red Cross Committee
1945: **11** Cordell Hull
1946: **9** John R Mott **11** Emily G Balch
1947: **21** Friends Service Council **31** American Friends Service Committee
1949: **11** John Boyd Orr (Baron Orr)
1950: **12** Ralph J Bunche
1951: **11** Leon Jouhaux
1952: **16** Albert Schweitzer
1953: **15** George C Marshall
1954: **51** Office of the United Nations High Commissioner for Refugees
1957: **14** Lester B Pearson
1958: **28** Rev Dominique Georges Henri Pire
1959: **16** Philip J Noel-Baker
1960: **14** Albert J Luthuli
1961: **15** Dag Hammarskjold
1962: **13** Linus C Pauling
1963: **25** League of Red Cross Societies **30** International Red Cross Committee
1964: **18** Martin Luther King Jr
1965: **26** United Nations Children's Fund (UNICEF)
1968: **10** Rene Cassin
1969: **30** International Labor Organization (ILO)
1970: **14** Norman E Borlaug
1971: **11** Willy Brandt
1973: **8** Le Duc Tho **15** Henry A Kissinger
1974: **10** Eisaku Sato **12** Sean MacBride
1975: **15** Andrei D Sakharov
1976: **13** Betty Williams **15** Mairead Corrigan
1977: **20** Amnesty International
1978: **10** Anwar Sadat **13** Menachem Begin
1979: **12** Mother Teresa
1980: **19** Adolfo Perez Esquivel
1981: **51** Office of the United Nations High Commissioner for Refugees
1982: **10** Alva Myrdal **19** Alfonso Garcia Robles
1983: **10** Lech Walesa
1984: **17** Bishop Desmond Tutu
1985: **51** International Physicians for the Prevention of Nuclear War
1986: **10** Elie Wiesel
1987: **17** Oscar Arias Sanchez
1988: **31** United Nations peacekeeping troops
Economics:
1969: **12** Jan Tinbergen, Ragnar Frisch
1970: **14** Paul A Samuelson
1971: **13** Simon S Kuznets
1972: **13** Kenneth J Arrow, Sir John R Hicks
1973: **15** Wassily Leontief
1974: **12** Gunnar Myrdal **18** Friedrich A von Hayek
1975: **17** Tjalling C Koopmans **18** Leonid V Kantorovich
1976: **14** Milton Friedman
1977: **11** Bertil Ohlin, James E Meade
1978: **13** Herbert A Simon
1979: **14** Sir Arthur Lewis **15** Theodore Schultz
1980: **14** Lawrence R Klein
1981: **10** James Tobin
1982: **14** George J Stigler
1983: **12** Gerard Debreu
1984: **15** Sir Richard Stone
1985: **16** Franco Modigliani
1986: **19** James McGill Buchanan
1987: **12** Robert M Solow
1988: **13** Maurice Allais

nomad **4** hobo **5** gypsy, mover, rover, stray, tramp **6** roamer **7** migrant, rambler, refugee, runaway, strayer, vagrant **8** bohemian, emigrant, migrator, renegade, traveler, vagabond, wanderer **9** immigrant, itinerant, straggler

nomadic **6** roving **7** migrant, roaming, vagrant **8** drifting, vagabond **9** footloose, itinerant, migratory, strolling, traveling, wandering **11** peripatetic **13** peregrinating

nom de guerre **5** alias **7** war name **9** pseudonym **11** assumed name

nom de plume **5** alias **7** pen name **9** false name, pseudonym **11** assumed name, writing name

nomenclature **5** lingo, terms **6** jargon, naming **8** language, taxonomy **10** nomination, vocabulary **11** appellation, designation, phraseology, terminology

Nomia
form: **5** nymph
blinded: **7** Daphnis

nominal **3** low **5** cheap, small **6** puppet **7** minimum, titular **8** baseless, moderate, official, so-called **9** pretended, professed, purported, suggested **10** groundless, ostensible, reasonable **11** inexpensive, theoretical **13** insignificant, unsubstantial

nominate **3** tag **4** call, name, pick, term **5** elect, label, style **6** choose, invest, select **7** elevate, install, propose, suggest **9** authorize, recommend

nomination **8** election **9** accession, selection **10** suggestion **11** appointment, designation, investiture **12** inauguration, installation

nominee **7** hopeful **8** aspirant, eligible **9** applicant, candidate **10** competitor, contestant **11** possibility

nonadjustable **5** fixed, rigid **9** immovable **10** inflexible **11** unalterable **12** nonadaptable

nonalcoholic **4** soft **15** nonintoxicating

No Name
author: **13** Wilkie Collins

No Name in the Street
author: **12** James Baldwin

nonappearance **7** absence **11** absenteeism

nonattendance **3** cut **7** absence, truancy **11** absenteeism

nonbeliever **5** cynic, pagan **7** atheist, doubter, heathen, infidel, skeptic **8** agnostic, apostate **10** backslider, empiricist, questioner, unbeliever **11** disbeliever, freethinker **14** doubting Thomas

nonbinding **8** optional **9** voluntary **12** unimperative **13** discretionary

nonchalance **9** composure, unconcern **13** offhandedness **French: 11** insouciance

nonchalant **3** lax **4** cool, idle, lazy **5** blase, slack **6** casual **7** languid, offhand, unmoved **8** careless, heedless, indolent, listless **9** apathetic, collected, easygoing, lethargic, unexcited, unheeding, unmindful, unruffled, unstirred, withdrawn **10** insensible, insouciant, phlegmatic, unaffected **11** indifferent, unconcerned, unemotional **12** uninterested **13** dispassionate, imperturbable

noncombatant **7** neutral **8** civilian

noncommittal **3** mum **4** cool, mute, safe, wary **5** vague **7** careful, evasive, guarded, neutral, politic, prudent **8** cautious, discreet, reserved **9** ambiguous, equivocal, tentative **10** indecisive, indefinite, unspeaking **11** circumspect, temporizing

noncompliance **6** breach **7** failure, neglect **9** disregard **10** resistance **11** dereliction **12** disobedience, stubbornness **13** fractiousness, individuality **14** rebelliousness **15** insubordination

noncompliant **6** unruly **7** defiant, froward, naughty, wayward **8** contrary, mutinous, perverse, stubborn **9** differing, dissident, fractious, objecting, obstinate, resistant, resistive, undutiful **10** disorderly, dissenting, rebellious, refractory, unorthodox, unyielding **11** disagreeing, disobedient, intractable **12** iconoclastic, recalcitrant, ungovernable, unmanageable, unsubmissive **13** insubordinate **14** unconventional

non compos mentis **14** not of sound mind **17** mentally incapable

nonconfirming **7** denying **8** negating, refuting **9** rejecting **10** disavowing **11** disclaiming, repudiating

nonconformist **3** nut **4** beat, card **5** freak, hippy, loner, rebel **6** oddity, weirdo **7** heretic, oddball, radical **8** bohemian, crackpot, deserter, maverick, original, reformer, renegade, vagabond **9** character, dissenter, dissident, eccentric, exception, insurgent, protester, screwball **10** dissenting, iconoclast, rebellious, schismatic **13** individualist, revolutionary

nonconformity **5** quirk **6** oddity **7** anomaly **9** deviation, rebellion **10** aberration, divergence, resistance **11** abnormality, peculiarity **12** disobedience, eccentricity, idiosyncrasy, irregularity **13** individualism, individuality **14** rebelliousness

noncongenial **6** unlike **8** opposite **9** different, disparate, ill-suited, unrelated **10** dissimilar **11** disagreeing **12** disagreeable, incompatible **13** unsympathetic

nondescript **5** usual, vague **8** ordinary **9** amorphous, colorless **11** stereotyped **12** unimpressive **13** characterless, undistinctive, unexceptional **15** undistinguished

nonentity **4** zero **6** cipher, nobody **7** nothing, no-count, nullity **8** small-fry, unperson **10** mediocrity

nonessential **6** luxury, trivia **7** trivial **9** extrinsic, secondary, trimmings **10** accidental, extraneous, incidental, irrelevant, peripheral, subsidiary **11** dispensable, impertinent, unconnected, unessential, unimportant, unnecessary **12** disallowable **13** inappropriate, insignificant **14** inconsiderable **15** inconsequential

nonexclusive **4** open **6** public, shared **7** divided **12** unrestricted

nonexistence **4** lack, void **7** absence **8** oblivion **11** nothingness

nonexistent **4** gone **5** short **6** absent **7** lacking, missing, wanting **11** unavailable **12** insufficient

nonindulgence **7** refusal **8** eschewal, forgoing **9** avoidance, eschewing **10** abstaining, abstention, refraining **11** forbearance **16** nonparticipation

nonirritating **4** calm **5** bland **6** benign **7** calming **8** soothing, tranquil **9** temperate

non licet **13** it is not lawful **16** it is not permitted

non liquet **12** it is not clear **14** it is not evident

nonmaterialistic **9** spiritual **10** idealistic **12** intellectual

nonmember **5** guest **7** outcast, visitor **8** outsider

nonnatural **7** manmade **9** synthetic **10** artificial, fabricated, factitious **12** manufactured

nonobservance **6** breach **7** failure, neglect **9** disregard **11** dereliction **13** noncompliance

non obstante **15** notwithstanding

no-nonsense **4** grim, hard **5** grave, harsh, rigid, sober, stern **6** ardent, intent, severe, solemn, strict **7** earnest, serious **8** critical, diligent, exacting, resolute **9** committed, dedicated, demanding, hard-nosed, practical, pragmatic, unbending, unsparing **10** determined, hard headed, purposeful, sobersided **12** businesslike

nonpareil **5** elite, ideal, model, super **6** symbol, unique **7** epitome, paragon, pattern, supreme **8** exemplar **9** unequaled, unmatched, unrivaled **10** apotheosis **11** exceptional, unsurpassed **13** extraordinary **14** representative **French: 11** ne plus ultra **14** creme de la creme

nonparticipation **7** refusal **8** eschewal, forgoing **9** avoidance, eschewing **10** abstaining, abstention, refraining, sitting out **11** forbearance

nonpartisan **4** fair, just **8** unbiased, unswayed **9** equitable, impartial, objective, unbigoted **10** impersonal, uninvolved **12** freethinking, unaffiliated, unimplicated, uninfluenced, unprejudiced **13** disinterested

nonpermissible **9** forbidden **10** disallowed **11** intolerable **12** inadmissible, unacceptable

nonplus **4** balk, faze, foil, halt, stop **5** abash, stump, upset **6** baffle, bother, dismay, muddle, puzzle, stymie **7** astound, confuse, disturb, mystify, perplex **8** astonish, bewilder, confound, deadlock **9** dumbfound, embarrass **10** disconcert **11** flabbergast **14** discountenance

nonplussed, nonplused **5** at sea, fazed **7** at a loss, baffled, floored, mixed-up, muddled, puzzled, stumped **8** confused **9** befuddled, mystified, unsettled **10** bewildered, confounded **12** disconcerted

nonpoisonous **4** safe **8** nontoxic **11** nonvenomous, nonvirulent

non possumus **8** we cannot

nonpresence **3** cut **7** absence, truancy **11** absenteeism

nonprofessional **3** lay **4** laic **7** dabbler
French: **7** amateur **10** dilettante

non prosequitur **15** he does not pursue

non repetatur **11** do not repeat

nonresident **7** tourist, visitor **9** transient **11** out-of-towner

nonresistance **6** assent **7** pliancy **8** docility, giving in, meekness, yielding **9** deference, obedience, passivity **10** compliance, conforming, conformity, pliability, submission **12** acquiescence, complaisance

nonresistant **4** meek **6** docile, pliant **7** passive, pliable **8** deferent, obedient, yielding **9** compliant **10** conforming, submissive **11** acquiescent, complaisant, deferential

nonscholarly **8** untaught **9** unlearned **10** uneducated, unlettered, unpedantic, unschooled

nonsectarian **10** ecumenical **11** interchurch **16** undenominational **17** nondenominational **19** interdenominational

nonsense **3** rot **4** bosh, bunk **5** folly, trash **6** antics, babble, drivel, joking, piffle **7** baloney, blather, bombast, chatter, fooling, garbage, hogwash, inanity, prattle, rubbish, trifles, twaddle **8** claptrap, flummery **9** absurdity, frivolity, gibberish, high jinks, horseplay, moonshine, silliness, stupidity **10** balderdash, flapdoodle, tomfoolery, triviality **11** foolishness, shenanigans **12** childishness, extravagance **13** facetiousness, ludicrousness, senselessness **14** ridiculousness **15** meaninglessness

nonsensical **4** wild **5** crazy, funny, inane, silly **6** absurd, stupid **7** asinine, comical, foolish **8** farcical **9** facetious, laughable, ludicrous **10** irrational, ridiculous

non sequitur **15** it does not follow

nonspecialized **11** generalized

nonspecific **4** hazy **5** vague **7** general, inexact **9** imprecise, uncertain **10** indefinite, undetailed **11** approximate, generalized

nonspiritual **7** earthly, profane, secular, worldly **8** material, temporal **13** materialistic

nonstop **7** endless, express **8** constant, unbroken **9** incessant **10** continuous, unrelieved **11** unremitting **12** interminable

nonstudious **9** unlearned **10** uneducated, unlettered, unpedantic, unschooled

nontaxable **9** sheltered **10** deductible

nontechnical **6** simple **8** academic **13** uncomplicated

nontypical **7** unusual **8** abnormal, uncommon **9** anomalous, irregular **16** unrepresentative

nonuniform **5** mixed **6** unlike **7** altered, changed, erratic, unalike **8** changing, variable **9** deviating, different, irregular, multiform **10** dissimilar **11** fluctuating, nonstandard **12** inconsistent

nonvital **9** accessory, extrinsic **10** disposable, expendable, incidental **11** dispensable, superfluous, unessential, unimportant, unnecessary

nonvocational **8** academic

nonvolitional **6** reflex **8** unwilled **9** automatic **11** instinctive, involuntary, spontaneous **12** uncontrolled

noodle **4** bean, head, pate **5** gourd, pasta **6** noggin **8** practice **9** improvise

nook **3** den **4** cove, lair **5** haven, niche **6** alcove, cavity, corner, cranny, dugout, recess, refuge **7** retreat, shelter **8** hideaway **9** cubbyhole **10** depression **11** hiding place

noon **6** midday, zenith **8** high noon, meridian

no one contradicting
Latin: **19** nemine contradicente

no one dissenting
Latin: **18** nemine dissentiente

noose **3** tie **4** bond, hang, loop **5** catch, hitch, lasso, snare **6** choker, entrap, halter, lariat, tether

Nootka
language family: **8** Wakashan
tribe: **5** Makah **6** Hoiath, Ozette **7** Ahosath, Nitinat **8** Machlath, Otsosath, Tokwaath **9** Ihatisath, Mowachath, Nochalath, Qayokwath, Tsishaath, Yoloilath **10** Hishkwiath, Hochoqtlis, Manohisath, Tlaokwiath **11** Chiqtlisath, Hopachasath, Qiltsamaath
location: **10** Washington **15** Vancouver Island
leader: **8** Maquinna **10** Wikaninish
related to: **5** Makah
noted for: **7** whaling

Nordhoff, Charles
author of: **17** Mutiny on the Bounty (with James Norman Hall)

Nordic Mythology *see* **21** Scandinavian Mythology

Norge *see* **6** Norway

norm **3** par **4** rule, type **5** gauge, model **7** average, measure, pattern **8** standard **9** barometer, criterion, yardstick **12** measuring rod

norm, the norm **7** the mean, the rule **9** the median **10** the average **14** the common thing

normal **3** fit, par **4** sane **5** sound, usual **6** steady **7** average, healthy, natural, regular, typical, uniform **8** constant, expected, mediocre, middling, ordinary, rational, reliable, standard **9** incessant, steadfast, unceasing **10** conforming, consistent, continuous, dependable, reasonable, unchanging **11** conformable, right-minded, unremitting **12** conventional **13** uninterrupted **14** representative

Normandy, Normandie
beach: **4** Gold, Juno, Utah **5** Omaha, Sword
borders: **7** Picardy **8** Brittany **14** English Channel
church/shrine: **12** Saint Etienne **15** Mont Saint Michel
city: **4** Caen **5** Rouen **7** Le Havre **9** Cherbourg
event: **4** D Day **17** Operation Overlord
region of: **6** France
river: **5** Seine

Norma Rae
director: **10** Martin Ritt
cast: **9** Pat Hingle **10** Ron Liebman, Sally Field **11** Beau Bridges
Oscar for: **4** song **7** actress (Field)
song: **16** It Goes Like It Goes

Norn
origin: **12** Scandinavian
form: **6** virgin **7** goddess
personifies: **4** fate
original Norn: **5** Urdar
the three: **3** Urd **5** Skuld **8** Verdandi
known as: **12** weird sisters

Norris, Frank
author of: **6** The Pit **8** McTeague **10** The Octopus

Norse Mythology *see* **21** Scandinavian Mythology

north **5** polar, upper **6** arctic

North America ***see box***

Northanger Abbey
author: **10** Jane Austen
character: **8** Mrs Allen **10** John Thorpe **12** James Morland **14** Isabella Thorpe **16** Catherine Morland
Tilney family: **5** Henry **7** Captain, Eleanor, General

North by Northwest
director: **15** Alfred Hitchcock
cast: **9** Cary Grant **10** James Mason **11** Leo G Carroll **12** Martin Landau **13** Eva Marie Saint **17** Jessie Royce Landis
setting (climax): **13** Mount Rushmore
score: **15** Bernard Herrmann

North Carolina ***see box***

North Dakota ***see box, p. 690***

North Dallas Forty
director: **11** Ted Kotcheff
based on story by: **9** Peter Gent
cast: **8** Mac Davis **9** Nick Nolte **11** Dayle Haddon **14** Charles Durning

Northern Crown
constellation of: **14** Corona Borealis

Northern Rhodesia *see* **6** Zambia

North Korea *see* **5** Korea

North Star State
nickname of: **9** Minnesota

North Toward Home
author: **12** Willie Morris

North Vietnam *see* **7** Vietnam

Northwest Passage
director: **9** King Vidor
author: **14** Kenneth Roberts
cast: **10** Ruth Hussey **11** Robert Young **12** Spencer Tracy **13** Walter Brennan

Northwest Territory ***see box, p. 690***

North wind
associated with: **6** Boreas

Norton, Thomas
author of: **8** Gorboduc (with Thomas Sackville)

Norway ***see box, p. 691***

Norwegian Mythology *see* **21** Scandinavian Mythology

nose
sense of: **5** smell
part: **7** nostril **14** olfactory patch

nosegay **4** posy **7** bouquet **10** tussy-mussy

nosiness **6** prying **9** curiosity **15** inquisitiveness

nostalgia **6** pining, regret **7** remorse **11** languishing, remembrance **12** homesickness **13** regretfulness

Nostradamus
name: **7** Michael **17** Michelde Notredame
occupation: **7** prophet **9** physician **10** astrologer **13** metaphysicist
wrote: **9** Centuries

Nostromo
author: **12** Joseph Conrad

nostrum **4** balm, cure, dose, drug **5** draft **6** elixir, physic, potion, remedy **7** cure-all, formula, panacea **8** medicine **9** treatment **10** medicament **12** prescription

nosy, nosey **6** prying, snoopy **7** all ears, curious **8** snooping **9** intrusive **11** inquisitive, overcurious **13** eavesdropping

nota bene **8** note well **10** take notice

notability **4** fame **6** import, moment, renown **8** eminence **9** celebrity **10** importance, prominence **11** consequence, distinction, preeminence **12** significance

notable **3** VIP **4** name **5** famed, wheel **6** biggie, bigwig, famous, marked **7** eminent, salient **8** luminary, renowned, striking **9** celebrity, dignitary, personage, prominent, reputable **10** celebrated, pronounced, remarkable **11** conspicuous, outstanding, personality **13** distinguished

notably **7** visibly **8** markedly **10** distinctly, strikingly **11** prominently **12** unmistakably **13** conspicuously, outstandingly

not alike **8** distinct **9** different, differing, disparate, divergent **10** dissimilar **11** contrasting

---

North America
nation: **4** Cuba **5** Haiti **6** Belize, Canada, Mexico, Panama **7** Bahamas, Jamaica **8** Barbados, Honduras **9** Costa Rica, Guatemala, Nicaragua **10** El Salvador, Puerto Rico, Saint Lucia **12** Saint Vincent, United States **17** Dominican Republic, Trinidad and Tobago **28** Saint Vincent and the Grenadines
desert: **7** Sonoran
island: **4** Long **6** Baffin, Cayman, Kodiak **7** Antigua, Bermuda, Iceland **8** Aleutian, Catalina, Thousand **9** Antilles, Greenland, Nantucket, Vancouver **10** Cape Breton **12** Newfoundland, Prince Edward **14** Queen Charlotte
ocean/sea/bay: **6** Arctic, Baffin, Bering, Hudson, Mexico **7** Chukchi, Lincoln, Pacific **8** Amundsen, Atlantic, Beaufort, Labrador **9** Caribbean, Greenland **10** California, Chesapeake, St Lawrence
river: **3** Red **4** Ohio **5** Peace, Snake, Yukon **6** Hudson **8** Arkansas, Colorado, Columbia, Missouri **9** Churchill, Mackenzie, Rio Grande **10** St Lawrence **11** Mississippi **12** Saskatchewan
lake: **4** Erie **5** Huron **7** Ontario **8** Michigan, Superior, Winnipeg **9** Great Bear, Nicaragua **10** Great Lakes, Great Slave
mountain range: **5** Ozark, Rocky **6** Alaska **7** Cascade **9** Blue Ridge **10** Laurentian **11** Appalachian, Sierra Madre **12** Sierra Nevada
highest point: **13** Mount McKinley
lowest point: **11** Death Valley
city: **4** Nome **5** Miami **6** Boston, Dallas, Denver, Havana, Ottawa, Quebec **7** Atlanta, Calgary, Chicago, Detroit, Houston, Memphis, New York, Phoenix, Seattle, Toronto **8** Montreal, Portland, San Diego **9** Anchorage, Milwaukee, Reykjavik, Vancouver **10** Kansas City, Los Angeles, Mexico City, New Orleans, Washington **11** Philadelphia, San Antonio, San Francisco
mineral: **3** oil, tin **4** coal, gold, lead, salt, zinc **6** cobalt, copper, nickel, quartz, silver **7** iron ore, mercury, sulphur, uranium **8** aluminum, antimony, asbestos, chromium, platinum, titanium, tungsten **9** magnesium, manganese, petroleum **10** molybdenum, natural gas

North Carolina
abbreviation: **2** NC **4** N Car
nickname: **7** Tar Heel **8** Old North **10** Turpentine
capital: **7** Raleigh
largest city: **9** Charlotte
others: **4** Bath **6** Durham, Lenoir, Shelby, Wilson **7** Edenton, Hickory, Kinston, New Bern, Roxboro, Tarboro **8** Gastonia **9** Albemarle, Asheville, Goldsboro, Henderson, Kitty Hawk, Lumberton **10** Chapel Hill, Greensboro, Greenville, Kannapolis, Wilmington **11** Statesville, Thomasville, Williamston **12** Fayetteville, Jacksonville, Winston-Salem
college: **4** Duke, Elon **7** Catawba **8** Davidson **10** Wake Forest
feature:
battle site: **18** Guilford Courthouse
national park: **19** Great Smoky Mountains (with Tennessee)
national seashore: **11** Cape Lookout **12** Cape Hatteras
tribe: **3** Eno **5** Coree **6** Cheraw **7** Buffalo, Moratok, Pamlico **8** Chowanoc, Hatteras **9** Tuscarora
people: **6** O Henry (William Sidney Porter) **7** tarheel **11** Billy Graham, Thomas Wolfe **13** Dolley (Dolly) Madison, Edward R Murrow **14** Richard Gatling
explorer: **6** de Soto **8** de Ayllon **9** Verrazano
island: **7** Roanoke
lake: **6** Norman, Phelps **7** Fontana **8** Waccamaw **12** Mattamuskeet
land rank: **12** twenty-eighth
mountain: **5** Black, Unaka **6** Harris **9** Blue Ridge **10** Great Smoky **13** Clingman's Dome
highest point: **8** Mitchell
physical feature: **10** Outer Banks **11** French Broad **15** Little Tennessee
cape: **4** Fear **7** Lookout **8** Hatteras
plateau: **8** Piedmont
sea: **8** Atlantic
sound: **4** Core **5** Bogue **7** Croatan, Pamlico
swamp: **6** Dismal
president: **9** James Polk **13** Andrew Johnson
river: **3** Haw, Tar **4** Fear **5** Neuse **6** Chowan, Lumber, Peedee, Yadkin **7** Roanoke, Wateree
state admission: **7** twelfth
state bird: **8** cardinal
state fish: **11** channel bass
state flower: **7** dogwood **9** goldenrod
state motto: **20** To Be Rather Than To Seem
state song: **16** The Old North State
state tree: **4** pine
state dance: **4** shag

notation **5** entry **10** memorandum

not bright **3** dim **4** dark, dull **5** dense, dusky, murky **6** cloudy, stupid **7** clouded **8** obscured **13** unilluminated

notch **3** cut **4** dent, mark, nick **5** grade, level, score **6** degree **7** scoring, scratch **11** indentation

not disclosed
Italian: **7** in petto

note **4** bill, fame, line, mark **5** bread, draft, enter, green, money, write **6** regard, renown **7** epistle, jot down, lettuce, message, missive, put down, scratch, set down, voucher **8** currency, dispatch, eminence, mark down, perceive **9** bank draft, celebrity, greenback **10** communique, importance, memorandum, prominence, reputation **11** certificate, consequence, distinction

notebook **3** log **5** diary **6** record **7** journal **9** looseleaf
French: **6** cahier

noted **6** famous **7** eminent **8** renowned **9** prominent, reputable **10** celebrated, remarkable **11** illustrious, outstanding **13** distinguished

Notes from the Underground
author: **16** Fyodor Dostoevsky

note well
Latin: **8** nota bene

noteworthy **7** unusual **8** singular **9** important **10** remarkable **11** outstanding, significant, substantial **12** considerable **13** distinguished, exceptionable

not far from **4** near **6** all but, almost, nearly **7** close to **8** not quite **13** approximately

not genuine **4** fake, sham **5** bogus, false, phony **6** ersatz, unreal **7** feigned **8** spurious **9** imitation, insincere, pretended, synthetic **10** artificial, fraudulent **11** counterfeit **12** hypocritical
Latin: **8** mala fide

not germane **9** extrinsic, unrelated **10** extraneous, immaterial, irrelevant **11** incongruous, inconsonant, unconnected **12** incompatible, nonessential **13** inappropriate

not guilty **5** clear **8** innocent **9** blameless **10** inculpable, unblamable

nothing **3** air, nix, zip **4** none, zero **5** stuff, trash, zilch **6** bauble, bubble, cipher, gewgaw, naught, trifle, trivia **7** duck egg, nullity, rubbish, trinket **8** goose egg **9** bagatelle, obscurity **14** insignificance **16** inconsequentials
Latin: **5** nihil

nothing is created from nothing
Latin: **16** ex nihilo nihil fit

nothingness **4** void **5** death **8** oblivion **9** emptiness **10** triviality **12** nonexistence **14** insignificance

Nothing Sacred
director: **14** William Wellman
cast: **13** Carole Lombard, Frederic March **14** Walter Connolly
score: **11** Oscar Levant
remade as: **10** Living It Up
script: **8** Ben Hecht

nothing unless it is good
Latin: **12** nil nisi bonum

nothing without the divine will
Latin: **13** nil sine numine
motto of: **8** Colorado

notice **3** eye, see **4** dope, heed, info, mark **5** goods **6** poster, rating, regard, review, take in **7** leaflet, mention, observe, warning **8** brochure, circular, critique, handbill, pamphlet

North Dakota
abbreviation: **2** ND **4** N Dak
nickname: **5** Sioux **11** Flickertail **16** Land of the Dakotas
capital: **8** Bismarck
largest city: **5** Fargo
others: **5** Minot **9** Bottineau, Jamestown, Williston **10** Grand Forks
college: **4** Mary **9** Jamestown
feature:
dam: **4** Oahe **8** Garrison
garden: **18** International Peace
national park: **17** Theodore Roosevelt
tribe: **5** Sioux **6** Mandan **7** Arikara, Hidatsa **8** Chippewa
people: **12** Eric Sevareid
explorer: **6** Carver **8** Thompson, Varennes **13** Lewis and Clark
lake: **5** Stump **6** Devils **9** Sakakawea
land rank: **11** seventeenth
mountain: **6** Turtle **8** Killdeer **10** Black Butte
highest point: **10** White Butte
physical feature:
basin: **9** Williston
plain: **8** The Slope
valley: **8** Red River
river: **3** Red **4** Park, Rush **5** Cedar, Goose, Heart, James, Knife, Mouse **6** Souris **7** Deslacs, Pembina **8** Missouri, Cheyenne, Wild Rice **9** Otter Tail **10** Cannonball **11** Yellowstone **12** Boise de Sioux **14** Little Missouri **18** Red River of the North
state admission: **8** fortieth **11** thirty-ninth (with South Dakota)
state bird: **17** western meadowlark
state fish: **12** northern pike
state flower: **15** wild prairie rose
state motto: **45** Liberty and Union Now and Forever One and Inseparable
state song: **15** North Dakota Hymn
state tree: **11** American elm

9 appraisal, attention, knowledge, statement **10** advisement, cognizance, disclosure **11** declaration, information **12** announcement, intelligence **13** advertisement, communication, specification

noticeable **5** clear, plain **7** evident, obvious **8** definite, distinct, manifest, palpable, striking **10** observable **11** appreciable, conspicuous, perceivable, perceptible **12** unmistakable

notification **4** news, word **6** advice, report **7** message, release **8** bulletin, dispatch **9** statement **10** communique **11** information **12** announcement, intelligence **13** communication

notify **4** tell, warn **6** advise, inform **7** apprise, let know **8** acquaint, send word **9** enlighten

not indigenous **5** alien **6** exotic **7** foreign **8** imported **9** nonnative **10** extraneous **11** naturalized

notion **4** idea, view, whim **5** fancy, humor, quirk **6** belief, vagary, whimsy **7** caprice, conceit, concept, opinion **8** crotchet **9** suspicion **10** conception, intimation **12** eccentricity

not native **5** alien **6** exotic **7** foreign **8** imported **10** extraneous **11** naturalized

not of sound mind
Latin: **15** non compos mentis

not ordinary **4** rare **6** exotic, unique **7** bizarre, foreign, strange, unusual **8** peculiar, singular, uncommon **9** anomalous, different, fantastic **11** distinctive, outstanding **14** unconventional

notoriety **4** blot **5** shame, stain **6** infamy, stigma **7** scandal **8** disgrace, dishonor, ignominy **9** discredit, disrepute **11** degradation

notorious **6** arrant **7** blatant, glaring **8** infamous, renowned **9** egregious **10** celebrated, outrageous **11** outstanding

Notorious
director: **15** Alfred Hitchcock
cast: **9** Cary Grant **11** Claude Rains **12** Louis Calhern **13** Ingrid Bergman

not pertinent **9** unrelated **10** extraneous, immaterial, irrelevant **11** incongruous, unconnected **13** inappropriate

not quite **6** all but, almost, nearly

not required **8** elective, optional **9** voluntary

not too seriously
Latin: **13** cum grano salis

Notus
origin: **5** Greek
personifies: **9** south wind

not wanted
French: **6** de trop

notwithstanding
Latin: **11** non obstante

not working **4** dead **8** inactive **10** unemployed **11** inoperative **12** unresponsive

Nouakchott
capital of: **10** Mauritania

nourish **4** feed **5** nurse **6** suckle **7** nurture, sustain

nourishing **4** rich **6** hearty **7** healthy **9** fostering, nurturing, wholesome **10** nutritious, sustaining **11** maintaining

Northwest Territory
abbreviation: **3** NWT
borders: **7** Alberta **8** Manitoba **9** Baffin Bay, Hudson Bay **11** Arctic Ocean, Beaufort Sea, Labrador Sea **12** Saskatchewan **15** British Columbia
city: **6** Inuvik **8** Hay River **9** Fort Smith **11** Yellowknife **12** Frobisher Bay
country: **6** Canada
island: **5** Banks, Devon **6** Baffin **7** Melville **8** Bathurst, Somerset, Victoria **9** Ellesmere **11** King William **13** Prince of Wales, Prince Patrick **14** Queen Elizabeth
mineral: **3** oil **4** gold, lead, zinc **6** silver **8** tungsten **9** petroleum
mountain: **21** Mount Sir James Mac Brien
native: **5** Inuit **6** Eskimo
territory: **8** Franklin, Keewatin **9** Mackenzie

Norway
other name: **5** Norge **20** Land of the Midnight Sun
capital: **4** Oslo **11** Christiania
largest city: **4** Oslo
others: **3** Gol, Nes **4** Bodo, Moss, Odda, Rena, Voss **5** Bjort, Floro, Hamar, Molde, Skien, Skjak, Vadso **6** Bergen, Horton, Larvik, Narvik, Tromso **7** Alesund, Arendal, Drammen, Harstad, Sandnes **8** Aalesund, Kirkenes **9** Stavanger, Trondheim **10** Hammerfest **12** Kristiansand
division: **3** Amt **4** Oslo **5** Fylke, Troms **6** Bergen, Opland, Tromso **7** Finmark, Hedmark, Ostfold **8** Letemark, Nordland, Rogaland, Vestfold **9** Ostlandet
former: **11** Kalmar Union
province called: **6** fylker
government:
legislature: **8** Storting
head of state: **4** king
measure: **3** fot, mal **4** alen **5** kande **6** fathom **7** skieppe **9** korntonde
monetary unit: **3** ore **5** krone
weight: **3** lod **4** mark, pund **10** bismerpund
island: **4** Vega **5** Bomlo, Donna, Froya, Hitra, Hopen, Senja, Smola, Soroy **6** Alsten, Averoy, Bouvet, Hinnoy, Karmoy, Kvaloy, Solund, Vannoy **7** Gurskoy, Lofoten, Mageroy, Seiland **8** Jan Mayen, Svalbard
lake: **4** Alte **5** Ister, Mjosa, Snasa **6** Femund **7** Rostavn, Tunnsjo
mountain: **5** Sogne **6** Kjolen **7** Numedal **8** Blodfjel, Snohetta, Telemark, Ustetind **9** Harteigen, Jotunheim, Langfjell, Ramnanosi **10** Dovrefjell, Galdhoepig, Glitretind, Vibmesnosi **11** Myrdalfjell **14** Aardangerjokul, Hallingskarvet, Skagastolstind
highest point: **12** Galdhopiggen **13** Glittertinden
river: **3** Ena **4** Alta, Klar, Otra, Rana, Tana, Teno **5** Bardu, Begna, Glama, Lagen, Orkla, Otter, Rauma, Reisa **6** Glomma, Lougen, Namsen, Pasvik
sea: **5** North **6** Arctic **7** Barents **8** Atlantic **9** Norwegian, Skagerrak
physical feature:
cape: **4** Naze **7** Nordkyn **8** Nordkapp **9** Lindesnes
fjord: **4** Oslo **5** Sogne
glacier: **12** Jostedalsbre
inlet: **2** Is **3** Kob, Ran **4** Alst, Ands, Bokn, Nord, Ofot, Salt, Sunn, Tyri, Vest **5** fiord, fjord, Folda, Lakse, Sogne **6** Bjorna, Hadsel **7** Hortens **9** Trondheim
plateau: **5** Doure, Dovre, Fjeld **9** Hardanger
people: **4** Lapp **5** Samme **6** Nordic, Viking
artist: **5** Munch
author: **5** Ibsen **6** Hamsun, Undset **7** Holberg **8** Bjornson **9** Wergeland
composer: **5** Grieg **7** Sinding **8** Svendsen
explorer: **4** Eric, Leif, Mohn, Sars **6** Nansen **8** Amundsen
explorer/statesman: **6** Nansen **8** Amundsen **9** Heyerdahl
king: **4** Olaf, Olav **5** Olave, Oscar **6** Haakon, Harold, Magnus, Sverre
Nazi collaborator: **8** Quisling
Norse god/goddess: **3** Sif, Tyr **4** Frey, Idun, Loki, Odin, Thor **5** Bragi, Freya, Hoder, Woden **6** Balder, Eostre, Frigga, Hermod
sculptor: **8** Vigeland
language: **4** Lapp **5** Norse **6** Bokmal **7** Nynorsk, Riksmal **8** Landsmal, Samnorsk **9** Landsmaal, Norwegian
religion: **19** Evangelical Lutheran **22** National Church of Norway
place:
castle: **8** Akershus
cathedral: **7** Nidaras
museum: **7** Kon Tiki **10** Viking Ship **15** Polar Expedition
park: **7** Frogner
former colony: **7** Vinland
feature:
dance: **6** gangar **7** halling **8** springar **9** spingleik
literature form: **4** edda, saga
food:
bread: **8** flat brod
cheese: **3** Ost **7** gjetost **9** gammelost, Jarlsberg
drink: **7** aquavit

12 invigorating **13** strengthening

nourishment **4** chow, eats, food, grub, meat **5** bread **6** viands **8** victuals **9** nutriment, nutrition **10** sustenance **11** comestibles

nouveau riche **9** newly rich (person)

Novak, Kim
real name: **19** Marilyn Pauline Novak
born: **9** Chicago IL
roles: **6** Picnic **7** Pal Joey, Vertigo **14** Of Human Bondage **17** Bell Book and Candle **20** The Jeanne Eagels Story **22** The Man with the Golden Arm **31** Amorous Adventures of Moll Flanders

Nova Scotia *see box, p. 692*

Nova Scotia
borders: **10** Bay of Fundy **12** New Brunswick **13** Atlantic Ocean **16** Gulf of St Lawrence **20** Northumberland Strait
city: **5** Truro **6** Sydney **7** Amherst, Halifax **8** Glace Bay, Yarmouth **9** Dartmouth **10** New Glasgow
country: **6** Canada
island: **10** Cape Breton
means: **11** New Scotland
mineral: **3** oil **4** lead, salt, sand, zinc **6** barite, gravel, gypsum, silver **9** celestite, petroleum **10** natural gas
mountain: **5** North **8** Cobequid
part of: **12** Appalachians **17** Maritime Provinces **18** Atlantic Provinces
river: **4** Avon **5** Clyde **6** LaHave, Medway, Mersey **7** St Mary's **12** Shubenacadie

novel **3** new **6** unique **7** unusual **8** original, singular, uncommon **9** different **10** innovative, unorthodox **14** unconventional
French: **5** roman

novelty **5** token **6** bauble, change, gewgaw **7** memento, newness, trinket **8** gimcrack, souvenir, surprise **9** bagatelle, variation **10** innovation, knickknack, uniqueness **11** originality

November *see box*

novice **4** tyro **5** pupil **7** amateur, learner, student **8** beginner, disciple, newcomer **9** greenhorn **10** apprentice, tenderfoot

Novum Organum
author: **12** Francis Bacon

novus ordo seclorum **24** a new order of the ages is born
author: **6** Vergil, Virgil
work: **8** Eclogues
motto of: **11** US Great Seal

Now, Voyager
director: **12** Irving Rapper
cast: **10** Bette Davis **11** Claude Rains, Janis Wilson, Paul Henreid **12** Gladys Cooper
score: **10** Max Steiner

now and then **8** on-and-off, periodic, sometime, sporadic **9** irregular, sometimes, temporary **10** infrequent, occasional **11** irregularly **12** infrequently, occasionally, periodically, sporadically

Now Playing at Canterbury
author: **14** Vance Bourjaily

Nox
goddess of: **5** night

noxious **4** foul **6** deadly, lethal, putrid **7** baneful, beastly, harmful, hurtful, noisome **8** damaging, virulent **9** injurious, loathsome, poisonous, revolting **10** abominable, disgusting, pernicious, putrescent **11** deleterious **12** foul-smelling

nth degree **5** limit **6** utmost **7** extreme

nuance **5** shade, touch **6** nicety **7** finesse **8** delicacy, fineness, keenness, subtlety **9** sharpness, variation **10** modulation, refinement **11** discernment

nub **4** core, crux, gist, hump, knob, knot, lump, node **5** bulge, heart **6** kernel **7** essence **8** swelling **10** projection, prominence, tumescence **11** nitty-gritty **12** protuberance

nubbin **3** ear **4** corn, lump, stub **5** bulge, fruit, piece, stump **10** diminutive

Nubbles, Kit
character in: **19** The Old Curiosity Shop
author: **7** Dickens

nubbly **5** lumpy, rough **6** coarse, knobby, pebbly

nucleus **3** nub **4** core, pith, seed **5** heart **6** center, kernel

Nudd *see* **4** Llud

nude **3** raw **4** bare **5** bared, naked **6** unclad **7** exposed **8** in the raw, stripped **9** unadorned, unarrayed, unclothed, uncovered, undressed
French: **9** au naturel

nudge **3** jab, jog, nod **4** bump, jolt, poke, prod, push **5** elbow, press, punch, shove, touch **6** jostle, motion, signal **8** indicate

nugatory **4** idle **5** empty **6** hollow, otiose, paltry **7** trivial, useless **8** piddling, trifling **9** meritless, valueless, worthless **10** profitless **11** ineffectual **12** functionless **15** inconsequential

nugget **4** hunk, lump **5** chunk, piece

nuisance **4** bore, fret, hurt, pain, pest **5** curse, thorn, worry **6** blight, bother, burden, plague **7** scourge, torment, trouble **8** handicap, vexation **9** annoyance, grievance **10** affliction, irritation, misfortune, pestilence **11** aggravation, botheration **13** inconvenience

Nuk
capital of: **9** Greenland

Nukualofa
capital of: **5** Tonga

null **2** NG **4** void **6** no good **7** invalid **9** valueless, worthless **10** immaterial **11** inoperative, nonexistent, unimportant **13** insignificant

nullification **6** repeal **7** voiding **8** recision **9** abolition, annulment **10** abrogation, rescinding **11** abolishment **12** cancellation, invalidation

nullify **4** veto, void **5** annul **6** cancel, repeal, revoke **7** abolish, rescind, retract **8** abrogate, make void, override, set aside **10** invalidate

nullity **6** cipher, naught **7** nothing **9** nonentity

Numanus
brother-in-law: **6** Turnus

numb **4** dead **6** frozen **8** dead-

November
event: **11** Election Day
flower: **13** chrysanthemum
French: **8** Novembre
gem: **5** topaz
German: **8** November
holiday: **11** All Souls' Day (2), Veterans Day (11) **12** All Saints' Day (1), Guy Fawkes Day (5), Thanksgiving (4th Thursday)
Italian: **8** Novembre
number of days: **6** thirty
origin of name: **5** novem (Latin meaning nine)
place in year:
Gregorian: **8** eleventh
Roman: **5** ninth
Spanish: **9** Noviembre
Zodiac sign: **7** Scorpio **11** Sagittarius

ened **9** insensate, unfeeling **10** insensible, narcotized **12** anesthetized

number **3** mob, sum, tot **4** army, bevy, book, herd, host, mass, part **5** array, bunch, count, crowd, digit, group, issue, swarm, tally, total **6** amount, cipher, figure, reckon, scores, symbol **7** chapter, company, compute, edition, foliate, integer, numeral, passage, section **8** division, estimate, magazine, numerate, paginate, quantity **9** abundance, aggregate, calculate, character, enumerate, multitude, paragraph, quarterly **10** assemblage, quantities **13** preponderance

numbered numbered weighed divided
Aramaic: **21** mene mene tekel upharsin
foretells destruction of: **10** Belshazzar
Biblical book of: **6** Daniel

numberless **6** myriad **7** copious, umpteen **8** unending, zillions **9** countless, plenteous, unbounded, uncounted **11** illimitable, uncountable **12** immeasurable **13** multitudinous

numbness **8** deadness **11** insentience

numeral **5** digit **6** cipher, figure, letter, number, symbol **7** integer **9** character

numerate **3** add **5** count, tally, total **6** number, reckon **7** compute, tick off **9** calculate

numerophobia
fear of: **7** numbers

numerous **4** many **6** myriad **7** copious, profuse **8** abundant **9** plentiful **13** multitudinous

Numidia *see* **7** Algeria

Numipu *see* **8** Nez Perce

Numitor
king of: **9** Alba Longa
father: **5** Proca
brother: **7** Amulius
daughter: **10** Rhea Silvia
grandson: **5** Remus **7** Romulus

numskull, numbskull **3** sap **4** dolt, dope, fool, jerk **5** dummy, dunce, idiot, klutz, ninny **6** dimwit, nitwit **7** dullard, half-wit **8** bonehead, dummkopf, imbecile, lunkhead, silly ass **9** blockhead, simpleton **10** dunderhead, muttonhead, nincompoop, noodlehead **11** chowderhead, knucklehead **12** scatterbrain

Nun *see* **4** Nunu

nuncio **5** envoy **6** legate **8** diplomat, minister **9** messenger **10** ambassador **11** papallegate **14** representative

nunnery **5** abbey, order **6** priory **7** cenacle, convent **8** cloister **9** hermitage, monastery **10** sisterhood

Nun's Story, The
director: **12** Fred Zinneman
based on story by: **12** Kathryn Hulme
cast: **10** Dean Jagger, Edith Evans, Peter Finch **13** Audrey Hepburn, Peggy Ashcroft **15** Colleen Dewhurst

Nunu
also: **3** Nun
origin: **8** Egyptian
god of: **5** ocean
personifies: **5** chaos

nuptial **7** marital **8** conjugal, hymeneal **9** connubial **11** matrimonial

nuptials **7** wedding **8** marriage **9** espousals, hymeneals **12** matrimonials

Nurmi, Paavo
nickname: **13** The Flying Finn
sport: **5** track
won: **8** Olympics

nurse **4** feed **5** nanny, treat **6** attend, doctor, foster, harbor, remedy, sister, succor, suckle **7** care for, nourish, nurture, promote **8** attend to, guardian **9** attendant, cultivate, encourage, governess
Hindi/Indian: **4** ayah

nursery **6** hotbed **9** incubator, preschool **10** greenhouse, schoolroom **12** conservatory, kindergarten

nurture **4** feed, mess, rear, tend **5** breed, raise, teach, train, tutor **6** foster, school **7** bring up, develop, educate, nourish, prepare, sustain, victual **8** instruct, maintain **9** cultivate, provision **10** discipline, strengthen

Nusantara *see* **9** Indonesia

Nusku
origin: **8** Sumerian **10** Babylonian
visier of: **5** Enlil

nut **3** fan, pit **4** buff, seed **5** freak, idiot, loony, stone **6** madman, maniac, zealot **7** devotee, fanatic, lunatic, oddball **8** crackpot **9** eccentric, screwball **10** aficionado, enthusiast, psychopath **11** afficionado

Nut
origin: **8** Egyptian
goddess of: **3** sky

nut-brown **5** tawny **6** auburn, brunet **8** brunette, cinnamon

Nutcracker, The
also: **13** Shchelkunchik
ballet by: **11** Tchaikovsky
based on fairy tale by: **11** E T A Hoffmann
contains: **17** Waltz of the Flowers **24** Dance of the Sugar-Plum Fairy

nutmeg
botanical name: **17** Myristica fragrans
from same plant as: **4** mace
origin: **9** Indonesia
use: **5** punch **6** eggnog **8** desserts **10** vegetables **11** baked dishes

Nutmeg State
nickname of: **11** Connecticut

nutriment **4** chow, eats, fare, feed, food, meat, mess **5** board **6** fodder, forage **7** aliment, edibles **8** eatables, victuals **9** foodstuff, groceries, provender **10** provisions, sustenance **11** nourishment, subsistence

nutrition **4** chow, feed, food, grub **6** fodder, forage, silage **7** edibles, rations **8** eatables **9** groceries, pasturage, provender **10** foodstuffs, provisions, sustenance **11** nourishment, subsistence

nutritious **9** wholesome **10** nourishing, sustaining

nuts **3** mad **4** bats, daft **5** balmy, crazy, dotty, loony, potty, wacko, wacky **6** insane **7** bananas, bonkers, cracked, touched **8** demented, deranged, unhinged **10** unbalanced

nutty **3** mad **4** daft **5** balmy, crazy, dippy, dotty, goofy, inane, loony, silly, wacko, wacky **6** cuckoo, insane, screwy, weirdo **7** bonkers, cracked, foolish, lunatic, meshuga, touched **8** bughouse, demented **9** senseless **10** addlepated, squirrelly **11** harebrained **12** crackbrained

nuzzle **3** pat, pet **4** buss, kiss **5** smack **6** caress, coddle, cosset, cuddle, fondle, nestle **7** embrace, snuggle

Nyasaland *see* **6** Malawi

Nycteus
father: 9 Chthonios
brother: 5 Lycus
daughter: 7 Antiope, Nycteis

Nyctimus
father: 6 Lycaon

nyctophobia
fear of: 8 darkness **14** the dark of night

nymph 5 belle, dryad, naiad, sylph **6** beauty **7** charmer

Nymphaea
epithet of: 9 Aphrodite
means: 6 bridal

Nyx
form: 7 goddess
personifies: 5 night
originated from: 5 Chaos
children: 3 Ker **4** Eris **5** Fates, Geras, Momus, Moros, Oizys **6** Aether, Hemera, Hypnos, Somnus **7** Nemesis, Oneiroi **8** Thanatos

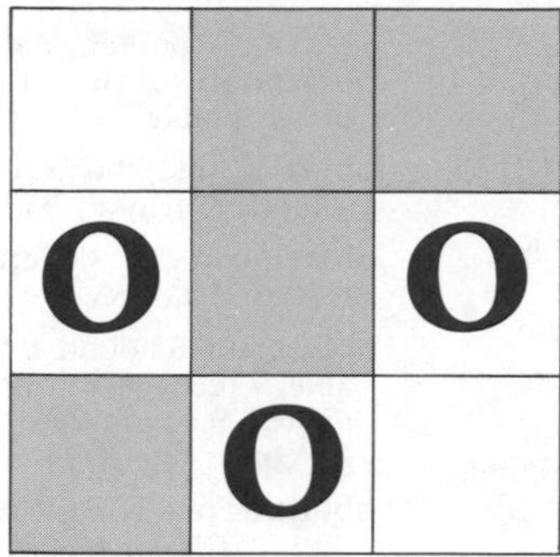

oaf 3 sap **4** boob, boor, clod, dolt, dope, fool, jerk, lout **5** booby, dummy, dunce, idiot, klutz, moron, ninny **6** lummox, nitwit **7** dullard, halfwit **8** bonehead, imbecile, numskull **9** blockhead, ignoramus, numbskull, simpleton **10** dunderhead, nincompoop

oafish 4 rude **5** crude **6** coarse, gauche, vulgar **7** boorish, doltish, loutish, uncouth **9** unrefined **10** unpolished

oak ***see box***

Oak, Gabriel
character in: 22 Far From the Madding Crowd
author: 5 Hardy

Oakie, Jack
real name: 19 Lewis Delaney Offield
born: 9 Sedalia (Sadalia) MO
roles: 16 The Great Dictator **17** Alice in Wonderland

Oakland
baseball team: 2 As **9** Athletics
football team: 8 Invaders

oar 3 row **4** pole **5** blade, rower, scull **6** paddle, propel **9** propeller
blade: 4 palm, peel
fulcrum: 5 thole **7** oarlock, rowlock
part: 4 loom **5** shaft **6** collar

oarsman 5 pilot, rower **6** bowman **7** mariner, sculler **8** helmsman **9** gondolier, propeller

oasis 5 haven **6** asylum, harbor, refuge **7** retreat, sanctum, shelter **9** green spot, sanctuary, water hole **11** fertile area **13** watering place

oast 4 kiln, oven

oat, oats 5 Avena **11** Avena sativa
varieties: 3 sea **4** wild **6** potato **8** animated **9** Tartarian **11** slender wild

Oates, Joyce Carol
author of: 4 Them **9** Childwold **10** Bellefleur, Wonderland **11** Unholy Loves, Wheel of Love **15** Son of the Morning **18** A Bloodsmoor Romance **19** Do With Me What You Will

oath 3 vow **5** curse **6** avowal, pledge **8** cuss word, swearing **9** affidavit, blasphemy, expletive, obscenity, profanity **10** adjuration, deposition **11** affirmation, attestation, declaration, imprecation, malediction

oaths
god of: 6 Horcus, Sancus **10** Dius Fidius, Semo Sancus

oatmeal 6 cereal **7** pottage **8** drammock, porridge

Obadiah 4 Obad **7** prophet **12** minor prophet
father: 4 Azel **6** Jehiel **8** Izrahiah, Shemaiah
son: 8 Ishmaiah
predicted fall of: 4 Edom

Obata, Gyo
architect of: 20 Dallas-Ft Worth Airport **25** National Air and Space Museum (Smithsonian Institute)

obdurate 5 cruel, harsh **6** mulish **7** adamant, callous, unmoved, willful **8** hardened, pitiless, stubborn, uncaring **9** immovable, merciless, obstinate, pigheaded, unfeeling, unpitying, unsparing, untouched **10** bullheaded, headstrong, inflexible, unmerciful, unyielding **11** cold-blooded, hardhearted, intractable **12** ungovernable, unmanageable **13** unsympathetic **14** uncontrollable **15** uncompassionate

oak 7 Quercus
varieties: 3 bur, cow, pin, red, she **4** bear, blue, cork, deer, Holm, jack, live, maul, post, silk **5** black, Emory, holly, scrub, ubame, water, white **6** basket, Belote, canyon, Ceylon, Daimyo, gambel, gander, Havard, Indian, island, Kermes, Konara, laurel, Oregon, poison, possum, Turkey, Turner, valley, willow, yellow **7** Ballota, Bartram, Belloot, Catesby, Durmast, English, Georgia, Italian, Kellogg, leather, Lebanon, overcup, scarlet, shingle, Spanish, tanbark, truffle, western **8** Arkansas, bluejack, chestnut, McDonald, mossy-cup, shinnery, Texas red **9** blackjack, Engelmann, flowering, Jerusalem, Mongolian, pubescent, swamp post **10** Chinquapin, Darlington, ring-cupped, Spanish red, swamp white **11** huckleberry, Japanese red, northern pin, northern red, Shumard's red **12** interior live, laurel-leaved, rock chestnut, southern live, yellow-barked **13** dwarf chestnut, oriental white, swamp chestnut **14** Austrian turkey, California live, yellow chestnut **15** California black, California field, California scrub, California white **16** high-ground willow **17** Japanese evergreen **18** Rocky Mountain scrub

obedience **8** docility, yielding **9** deference, ductility, obeisance **10** accordance, allegiance, compliance, subjection, submission **11** conformance, dutifulness, willingness **12** acquiescence, subservience, tractability **14** conformability, submissiveness

obedient **5** loyal **6** docile **7** devoted, dutiful **8** amenable, faithful, obeisant, yielding **9** compliant, tractable **10** governable, law-abiding, respectful, submissive **11** acquiescent, deferential, subservient

obeisance **3** bow **5** honor **6** curtsy, esteem, fealty, homage, regard **7** loyalty, respect **8** courtesy, fidelity, humility, kneeling **9** deference, obedience, reverence **10** allegiance, humbleness, subjection, submission, veneration **11** prostration **12** genuflection **13** self-abasement

obelisk **5** pylon, shaft, tower **6** column, dagger, needle, pillar **8** memorial, monolith, monument

Oberon
character in: **21** A Midsummer Night's Dream
author: **11** Shakespeare

Oberon
opera by: **5** Weber
character: **5** Reiza
setting: **18** court of Charlemagne **21** court of Haroun al Rashid

Oberon, Merle
real name: **26** Estelle Merle O'Brien Thompson
husband: **14** Alexander Korda
born: **8** Tasmania
roles: **5** Hotel **7** Desiree **15** A Song to Remember **16** Wuthering Heights **19** The Scarlet Pimpernel **25** The Private Life of Henry VIII **30** The Private Life of Henry the Eighth

obese **3** fat **5** gross, heavy, plump, porky, pudgy, stout, tubby **6** chubby, fleshy, portly, rotund **7** paunchy **9** corpulent **10** overweight, potbellied

obesity **3** fat **7** fatness, liposis **8** adiposis, enormity **9** heaviness, plumpness, stoutness **10** corpulence, overweight

obey **4** heed, mind **5** bow to, serve **6** assent, concur **7** abide by, observe, respect, yield to **8** accede to, submit to **9** acquiesce, conform to, succumb to **10** comply with, toe the line **12** follow orders

obfuscate **4** blur **5** befog **6** garble, mess up, muddle **7** becloud, confuse, distort, fluster, obscure, stupefy **8** confound, scramble **10** complicate

obfuscation **8** flummery **9** confusion **10** doubletalk, mumbo jumbo

obi **4** sash **5** obeah **6** girdle

obiit **6** he died **7** she died

obiter dictum **9** diversion **10** digression, divagation, side remark

object **3** aim, end, use **4** body, butt, dupe, form, gist, goal, pith, prey **5** abhor, basis, cause, knock, point, sense, thing **6** balk at, carp at, design, device, dingus, gadget, intent, loathe, motive, oppose, quarry, reason, target, victim **7** article, cavil at, condemn, dislike, essence, frown on, meaning, mission, protest, purpose, subject **8** be averse, cynosure, denounce **9** abominate, criticize, doohickey, incentive, intention, objective, principle, recipient, substance **10** inducement, phenomenon **11** contrivance, explanation, thingamabob, thingamajig **12** be at odds with, disapprove of, significance **13** find fault with, take exception **18** remonstrate against

objection **4** beef, kick **5** cavil **7** protest **8** demurral, rebuttal **9** challenge, complaint, criticism, exception **10** dissension, opposition **11** disapproval, reservation **12** disagreement **13** contradiction **14** disapprobation, opposing reason **15** counter argument

objectionable **4** foul, vile **5** nasty **6** odious **8** unseemly **9** abhorrent, loathsome, obnoxious, offensive, revolting **10** abominable, despicable, disgusting, unbearable, unpleasant **11** displeasing, distasteful, intolerable, unendurable **12** disagreeable, unacceptable **13** inappropriate

objective **3** aim, end **4** fair, goal, just, mark, real **6** actual, design, intent, target **7** mission, purpose **8** detached, unbiased, unswayed **9** impartial, intention, uncolored **10** impersonal, open-minded **11** destination **12** uninfluenced, unprejudiced **13** disinterested, dispassionate

objectivity **8** fairness **10** detachment, neutrality **12** impartiality

object to **7** condemn, dislike **9** frown upon **12** disapprove of **14** discountenance **15** take exception to **16** find unacceptable

objet d'art **5** bijou, curio **7** bibelot, trinket **9** art object

oblation **4** gift **8** offering **9** offertory **10** collection

obligated **5** bound **6** forced, liable **7** pledged **8** beholden, indebted **9** committed **11** constrained

obligation **4** bond, care, debt, duty, oath, onus, word **6** charge, pledge **7** compact, promise **8** contract, guaranty, warranty **9** agreement, guarantee, liability **10** a favor owed, commitment, constraint **12** indebtedness **13** answerability, understanding **14** accountability, responsibility

obligatory **7** binding **8** coercive, enforced, required **9** mandatory, necessary, requisite **10** compulsory, imperative, peremptory **11** unavoidable

oblige **3** aid **4** bind, help, make **5** favor, force, impel, serve **6** assist, coerce, compel **7** require, support **8** obligate **9** constrain **11** accommodate, do a favor for, necessitate **13** do a service for, to be duty bound

obliged **5** bound **7** favored, pleased **8** assisted, beholden, indebted, required, thankful **9** compelled **12** accommodated

obliging **4** kind **6** polite **7** amiable, helpful **8** cheerful, friendly, gracious **9** agreeable, courteous **10** solicitous **11** complaisant, considerate, cooperative, good-natured, sympathetic **12** well-disposed **13** accommodating

oblique **3** sly **4** awry **5** askew **6** aslant, covert, hinted, masked, tilted, veiled **7** cloaked, devious, furtive, implied, slanted, sloping **8** allusive, diagonal, inclined, indirect, slanting, sneaking **9** suggested, underhand

obliterate **4** raze **5** erase, level **6** cancel, delete, efface, remove, rub out **7** abolish, blot out, destroy, expunge, wipe out **9** eradicate, write over **10** annihilate, strike over

obliteration **8** deletion **9** abolition, expunging, wiping out **11** blotting out, destruction, eradication **12** annihilation

oblivion **5** limbo **7** the void **9** blankness, disregard, obscurity, unconcern **11** blotting out, nothingness **12** nonexistence **13** forgetfulness, insensibility, obliviousness **14** insignificance **15** unconsciousness

oblivious **8** careless **9** forgetful, unaware of, unmindful **10** heedless of, insensible **11** inattentive, unconcerned, unobservant **12** disregardful, undiscerning **13** unconscious of

Oblonsky, Prince Stepan
character in: **12** Anna Karenina
author: **7** Tolstoy

obloquy **5** abuse, odium, shame **6** infamy, rebuke **7** calumny, censure, railing **8** contempt, disfavor, disgrace, ignominy, reviling **9** discredit, invective **10** defamation, opprobrium, scurrility **11** degradation, humiliation, verbal abuse **12** billingsgate, condemnation, denunciation, dressing-down, vilification

obnoxious **4** foul, vile **5** nasty **6** odious **7** hateful **8** unseemly **9** abhorrent, loathsome, offensive, repellent, repugnant, revolting **10** abominable, despicable, detestable, disgusting, nauseating, unbearable, unpleasant **11** displeasing, intolerable, unendurable **12** disagreeable, insufferable **13** inappropriate, objectionable

oboe family
instruments: **5** shawm **6** curtal, pommer, racket **7** bassoon, bombard, curtall, hautboy **8** crumhorn, schalmey, tenoroon **10** Cor Anglais, oboe d'Amore **11** English horn, heckelphone, sarusophone **12** oboe da caccia, sarrusophone **13** contra bassoon, double bassoon

O'Brian, Hugh
real name: **11** Hugh J Krampe
born: **11** Rochester NY
roles: **9** Wyatt Earp **27** The Life and Legend of Wyatt Earp

O'Brien, Edna
author of: **5** Night **11** A Pagan Place **13** The Lonely Girl **14** The Country Girl **20** August Is a Wicked Month **24** Girls in Their Married Bliss

O'Brien, Margaret
real name: **18** Angela Maxine O'Brien
born: **12** Los Angeles CA
roles: **8** Jane Eyre **11** Little Women **15** Meet Me in St Louis **24** Our Vines Have Tender Grapes

O'Brien, Pat
real name: **26** William Joseph Patrick O'Brien
born: **11** Milwaukee WI
roles: **12** Hildy Johnson, The Front Page **13** Some Like It Hot, The Last Hurrah **20** Angels with Dirty Faces **22** Knute Rockne All American
autobiography: **12** Wind on My Back

obscene **4** blue, foul, lewd **5** dirty **6** filthy, smutty, vulgar **8** indecent, prurient **9** salacious **10** lascivious, lubricious **12** pornographic, scatological **16** morally offensive

obscenity **8** cuss word, lewdness **9** dirtiness, indecency, profanity, prurience, swear word, taboo word, vulgarity **10** filthiness, smuttiness **11** pornography **13** salaciousness **14** four-letter word, lasciviousness

obscuration **7** eclipse, masking, veiling **8** cloaking, clouding, covering **9** darkening, shadowing **10** concealing **11** concealment

obscure **3** dim, fog **4** blur, dark, hide, mask, veil **5** bedim, befog, block, cloak, cloud, cover, dingy, dusky, faint, murky, vague **6** cloudy, darken, hidden, muddle, screen, shadow, shroud, somber, unsung **7** becloud, conceal, confuse, cryptic, curtain, eclipse, shadowy, unclear, unknown, unnoted **8** befuddle, confused, disguise, nameless, puzzling **9** confusing, enigmatic, forgotten, lightless, obfuscate, uncertain, unheard of, unlighted **10** indefinite, indistinct, overshadow, perplexing, unrenowned **11** indefinable, inscrutable, little known, out-of-the-way, unimportant **12** unfathomable **13** inconspicuous, insignificant, unilluminated **15** inconsequential

obscurity **3** fog **4** mist **5** cloud, shade **6** shadow **7** dimness, mystery, opacity, privacy **8** darkness **9** ambiguity, seclusion, vagueness **10** cloudiness

obsequies **5** rites **6** burial **7** funeral **15** memorial service

obsequious **6** menial **7** fawning, servile, slavish **8** cowering, cringing, toadying **9** kowtowing, truckling **11** bootlicking, deferential, subservient, sycophantic **12** ingratiating, mealy-mouthed **14** apple-polishing

observance **4** rite **6** custom, regard, ritual **7** heeding, keeping, obeying **8** ceremony, practice **9** adherence, attending, attention, following, formality, solemnity **10** ceremonial, compliance **11** celebration, observation **13** commemoration **15** memorialization

observant **5** alert, awake, aware **7** careful, heedful, mindful **8** vigilant, watchful **9** attentive, conscious, regardful, wide-awake **10** perceptive **12** on the lookout

observation **4** heed, idea, view **5** probe **6** eyeing, notice, remark, search, seeing, survey, theory **7** comment, finding, opinion, viewing **8** interest, judgment, scrutiny, spotting, watching **9** assertion, attention, beholding, detection, diagnosis, discovery, glimpsing, observing, statement **10** cognizance, commentary, inspection, reflection **11** description, examination, heedfulness **12** surveillance, watchfulness **13** pronouncement **20** first-hand information

observatory **5** tower **7** lookout **9** satellite **11** planetarium
name: **4** Hale, Lick **6** Yerkes **7** Palomar, Whipple **8** Kitt Peak, Mt Wilson **11** Las Campanas, Mount Wilson **12** Big Bear Solar **14** Royal Greenwich

observe **3** eye, say, see **4** espy, heed, keep, mark, note, obey, ogle, spot, view **5** honor, opine, state, watch **6** assert, behold, detect, follow, notice, peer at, regard, remark, size up, survey **7** abide by, comment, declare, defer to, execute, fulfill, glimpse, inspect, make out, mention, perform, reflect, respect, stare at **8** adhere to, announce, carry out, discover, perceive, sanctify, theorize **9** celebrate, recognize, solemnize **10** be guided by, comply with, consecrate **11** acknowledge, acquiesce to, commemorate, take stock of **12** catch sight of **14** pay attention to

observer **6** viewer **7** watcher **8** onlooker **12** investigator

obsessed **5** beset **7** haunted **8** hung up on, maniacal **9** dominated, possessed **10** controlled **15** having a fixation

obsession **5** craze, mania, quirk **6** phobia **8** fixation **9** fixed idea, monomania **11** infatuation **13** preoccupation **16** overwhelming fear **18** neurotic conviction

obsolescent **8** dying out **9** declining **11** on the way out **12** disappearing **16** becoming obsolete **17** becoming out-of-date

obsolete **3** out **5** dated, passe **6** bygone **7** antique, archaic, extinct **8** outdated, out of use, outmoded **9** out-of-date **10** antiquated **12** old-fashioned, out of fashion

obstacle **3** bar **4** curb, snag **5** block, catch, check **6** hurdle **7** barrier, problem **8** blockade, stoppage **9** barricade, hindrance, roadblock **10** difficulty, impediment, limitation **11** obstruction, restriction **12** interference **14** stumbling block

obstetrician
French: **10** accoucheur

obstinacy **8** rigidity **10** mulishness, resistance **11** willfulness **12** stubbornness **13** inflexibility, intransigence, pigheadedness

obstinate **6** dogged, mulish **7** staunch, willful **8** obdurate, resolute, stubborn **9** pigheaded, steadfast, tenacious, unbending **10** headstrong, inflexible, refractory, self-willed, unyielding **11** intractable **12** recalcitrant, ungovernable, unmanageable **14** uncontrollable **20** unreasonably stubborn

obstreperous **4** loud **5** noisy **6** unruly **8** perverse **9** clamorous, rampaging **10** boisterous, disorderly, refractory, roistering, uproarious, vociferous **11** disobedient **12** uncontrolled, ungovernable, unmanageable, unrestrained **14** uncontrollable

obstruct **3** bar **4** curb, halt, hide, mask, stop **5** block, check, cloak, close, cover, dam up, debar, delay, limit, stall **6** arrest, hinder, hobble, impede, plug up, retard, shroud, stifle, thwart **7** eclipse, inhibit, shut off **8** blockade, choke off, close off, restrict, suppress, throttle **9** barricade, frustrate **18** bring to a standstill

obstruction **3** bar **4** curb, snag, stop **5** block, check, hitch **6** hurdle **7** barrier **8** blockage, obstacle, stoppage **9** barricade, hindrance **10** bottleneck, impediment **11** encumbrance

obtain **3** get **4** earn, gain, hold, take **5** exist, glean, stand **6** attain, come by, gather, pick up, secure **7** achieve, acquire, prevail, procure, receive **9** get hold of **14** get one's hands on **16** gain possession of

obtainment **11** achievement, acquirement, acquisition, procurement

obtrude **5** eject, expel, force **6** butt in, impose, meddle, thrust **7** presume, project **9** interfere

obtrusive **4** nosy **5** brash **6** prying, snoopy **7** bulging, forward, salient **8** familiar, meddling **9** intruding, intrusive, prominent **10** aggressive, jutting out, meddlesome, projecting, protruding **11** conspicuous, impertinent, interfering, outstanding, protuberant, sticking out, trespassing **12** interrupting, presumptuous

obtuse **4** dull, slow **5** blunt, dense, thick **6** simple, stupid **7** blunted **8** ignorant, not sharp **9** unpointed **10** insensible, not pointed, slow-witted **11** insensitive, unsharpened **12** imperceptive, thick-skinned **15** uncomprehending

obtuseness **8** dullness **9** denseness, ignorance, stupidity **13** insensitivity **14** slow-wittedness **15** thick-headedness **16** lack of perception, simplemindedness **19** lack of comprehension

obverse **4** face **5** front **10** complement **11** counterpart
of coin: **4** head

obviate **5** avert, avoid, parry **6** divert, remove **7** fend off, prevent, ward off **8** preclude, stave off **9** forestall, sidetrack, turn aside **10** circumvent, do away with **11** nip in the bud

obvious **5** clear, plain **6** patent **7** evident, glaring, visible **8** apparent, distinct, manifest, palpable, striking, unhidden, unmasked, unveiled **10** undeniable **11** conspicuous, discernible, perceptible, self-evident, unconcealed, undisguised **12** in plain sight, unmistakable **24** plain as the nose on your face

O'Casey, Sean
author of: **10** Purple Dust **12** The Green Crow **17** Juno and the Paycock **18** The Shadow of a Gunman **20** The Plough and the Stars

occasion **4** base, time **5** basis, cause, event **6** advent, affair, chance, elicit, ground, lead to, motive, prompt, reason **7** episode, grounds, inspire, opening, provoke, venture **8** incident, instance **9** adventure, happening, rationale, situation **10** bring about, experience, motivation, occurrence **11** celebration, explanation, opportunity, provocation **12** circumstance, special event, suitable time **13** justification, opportune time **14** convenient time, important event, particular time

occasional **4** rare **6** fitful, random **8** sporadic, uncommon **9** irregular, recurring, scattered, spasmodic, uncertain **10** incidental, infrequent, now and then, unreliable **12** intermittent

occasionally **6** rarely, seldom **7** at times **8** fitfully **9** sometimes **10** now and then **11** irregularly **12** infrequently, once in a while, periodically, sporadically **14** from time to time, intermittently **15** every now and then, once in a blue moon

occidental **7** Western **8** American, European **9** Hesperian, Westerner

occlude **4** clog, plug **5** block, choke, close **6** shut up, stop up **7** congest, shut off, stopper **8** choke off, obstruct **9** barricade, constrict **11** strangulate

occult **4** dark **5** magic **6** arcane, hidden, mystic, secret, veiled **7** obscure, private **8** esoteric, mystical, shrouded **9** concealed **10** cabalistic, mysterious, unrevealed **11** undisclosed **12** supernatural

occupancy **3** use **6** tenure **7** tenancy **8** lodgment **9** enjoyment, habitancy **10** engagement, habitation, occupation, possession **11** inhabitancy

occupant **5** owner **6** lessee, lodger, native, renter, roomer, tenant **7** dweller, settler **8** colonist, occupier, resident **9** addressee **10** inhabitant **11** householder

occupation **3** job **4** line, work **5** craft, forte, trade **6** career, living, metier, sphere **7** calling, control, pursuit, seizure **8** activity, business, capacity, conquest, lifework, vocation **9** specialty **10** employment, line of work, livelihood, possession, profession, subjection **11** foreign rule, subjugation **14** specialization **15** military control **18** military occupation

occupied **5** in use **6** amused, took up, used up **7** dwelt in, engaged, lived in, overran, overrun, taken up **8** absorbed, tenanted **9** concerned, conquered, inhabited, resided in **12** had control of, held in thrall **13** was situated in **16** took possession of

occupy **3** use **4** be in, be on, busy, fill, hold **5** amuse, sit in **6** absorb, employ, engage, fill up, room in, take up **7** concern, conquer, dwell in, engross, enslave, inhabit, lodge in, overrun, pervade, possess **8** permeate, reside in, saturate **9** entertain, subjugate **10** monopolize **11** have control **12** be situated in, hold in thrall **14** be the tenants of **16** take possession of

occur **3** hit **4** rise **5** arise, ensue **6** appear, befall, crop up, emerge, happen, result, strike, turn up **7** be found, come off, develop **8** spring up **9** come about, eventuate, take place, transpire **10** come to pass **11** materialize **13** cross one's mind, enter one's mind

occurrence **5** event **6** affair **7** episode, venture **8** business, incident, instance, occasion **9** adventure, emergence, happening, situation, unfolding **10** appearance, experience, proceeding **11** development, transaction **12** circumstance **13** manifestation **15** materialization

ocean **3** sea **4** deep, main, pond **5** flood, water **7** big pond, high sea **9** briny deep
- **god of:** **3** Nun **4** Nanu **7** Neptune, Oceanus **8** Poseidon

Oceania, Oceanica **9** Melanesia, Polynesia **10** Micronesia **11** Australia
- **ocean:** **12** South Pacific
- **island:** **4** Cook, Guam, Fiji, Maui, Niue, Wake **5** Aunuu, Bonin, Kauai, Lanai, Tonga **6** Bikini, Futuna, Hawaii, Marcus, Midway, Rurutu, Tahiti, Tubuai, Tuvalu, Wallis **7** Gambier, Gilbert, Iwo Jima, Leeward, Mariana, Molokai, Phoenix, Solomon, Tokelau, Tuamotu, Tutuila, Vanuatu, Volcano **8** Aitutaki, Bismarck, Bora-Bora, Johnston, Kiribati, Marshall, Pitcairn, Windward **9** Australia, Christmas, Marquesas, Trobriand **10** New Zealand **12** New Caledonia, Western Samoa **14** Papua New Guinea **15** French Polynesia

oceanic **6** marine **7** aquatic, pelagic **8** seagoing **9** thalassic

Oceanid
- **form:** **5** nymph
- **location:** **3** sea
- **father:** **7** Oceanus
- **mother:** **6** Tethys

Oceanus
- **member of:** **6** Titans
- **father:** **6** Uranus
- **mother:** **4** Gaea
- **consort of:** **6** Tethys
- **father of:** **8** Oceanids **9** river gods
- **son:** **7** Proteus
- **daughter:** **5** Doris, Persa **7** Philyra
- **form:** **6** stream

ocelot **3** cat **7** wildcat

Ochimus
- **king of:** **6** Rhodes
- **father:** **6** Helius
- **wife:** **9** Hegetoria
- **daughter:** **7** Cydippe

ochlophobia
- **fear of:** **6** crowds

Ockelman, Constance Frances Marie
- **real name of:** **12** Veronica Lake

Ocnus
- **origin:** **6** Tuscan
- **father:** **8** river god
- **mother:** **5** Manto
- **founded:** **6** Mantua
- **personifies:** **16** unavailing effort

O'Connor, Carroll
- **born:** **7** Bronx NY
- **roles:** **12** Archie Bunker, Archie's Place **14** All in the Family
- **restaurant:** **12** The Ginger Man

O'Connor, Donald
- **born:** **9** Chicago IL
- **roles:** **9** Beau Geste **15** Singin' in the Rain **18** Tom Sawyer Detective **21** Francis the Talking Mule

O'Connor, Flannery
- **author of:** **9** Wise Blood **15** The Habit of Being **17** Mystery and Manners **20** A Good Man Is Hard to Find, The Violent Bear It Away

Ocrisia
- **position:** **5** slave
- **slave to:** **7** Tarquin **8** Tanaquil
- **son:** **14** Servius Tullius

Octavia
- **brother:** **8** Augustus
- **husband:** **4** Nero **10** Mark Antony
- **grandson:** **8** Caligula

October
- **flower:** **6** cosmos **9** calendula
- **French:** **7** Octobre
- **gem:** **4** opal **10** tourmaline
- **German:** **7** Oktober
- **holiday:** **9** Halloween (31), Yom Kippur **11** Columbus Day (12) **12** Rosh Hashanah **16** United Nations Day (24)
- **Italian:** **7** Ottobre
- **number of days:** **9** thirty-one
- **origin of name:** **4** octo (Latin meaning eight)
- **place in year:**
  - ***Gregorian:*** **5** tenth
  - ***Roman:*** **6** eighth
- **Spanish:** **7** Octubre
- **Zodiac sign:** **5** Libra **7** Scorpio

October Light
- **author:** **11** John Gardner

Octopus, The
- **author:** **11** Frank Norris

odd **4** rare **5** extra, funny, queer, spare, weird **6** casual, far-out, quaint, single, sundry, unique **7** bizarre, curious, not even, strange, surplus, unusual, various **8** freakish, leftover, peculiar, periodic, singular, sporadic, uncommon **9** irregular, remaining, spasmodic, unmatched **10** occasional, outlandish **13** miscellaneous **15** being one of a pair **16** out of the ordinary **17** not divisible by two

oddball **3** nut **4** kook **5** freak **6** weirdo **8** crackpot, original **9** character, eccentric, screwball **10** one-of-a-kind

Odd Couple, The
- **character:** **3** Roy **5** Myrna, Roger, Speed **6** Miriam, Murray, Vinnie **10** Felix Unger **11** Gloria Unger **12** Cecily Pigeon, Oscar Madison **14** Blanche Madison **15** Gwendolyn Pigeon, (Dr) Nancy Cunningham
- **cast:** **10** Al Molinaro, Archie Hahn **11** Brett Somers, Carol Shelly, Jack Klugman, Larry Gelman, Monica Evans, Tony Randall **12** Garry Walberg, Janice Hansen, Ryan McDonald **13** Elinor Donahue, Joan Hotchkiss, Penny Marshall
- **setting:** **11** New York City
- **Felix's job:** **12** photographer
- **Oscar's job:** **12** sportswriter

based on play by: 9 Neil Simon

Odd Couple, The
director: 8 Gene Saks
based on play by: 9 Neil Simon
cast: 10 Jack Lemmon (Felix Unger) 11 Herb Edelman, John Fiedler 13 Walter Matthau (Oscar Madison)

oddity 5 freak, sight 6 marvel, rarity, wonder 9 curiosity, queerness 10 phenomenon, uniqueness 11 abnormality, bizarreness, peculiarity, singularity, strangeness, unusualness 12 eccentricity, freakishness 13 individuality, unnaturalness 14 outlandishness
Latin: 8 rara avis

oddly amusing 5 droll, kooky 9 laughable, whimsical 10 ridiculous

odd person 3 nut 4 kook 5 flake, freak 6 looney, weirdo 7 oddball 8 crackpot 9 character, eccentric, screwball

odds and ends 4 olio 6 scraps 8 remnants 9 leftovers 10 hodgepodge, miscellany 11 this and that 13 bits and pieces 18 miscellaneous items

ode 4 epic, hymn, poem 5 lyric, paean, psalm, verse 6 ballad 8 canticle
type: 8 Horatian, Pindaric

Ode on a Grecian Urn
author: 9 John Keats

Ode on Indolence
author: 9 John Keats

Ode on Melancholy
author: 9 John Keats

Ode to a Nightingale
author: 9 John Keats

Ode to Autumn
author: 9 John Keats

Ode to Duty
author: 17 William Wordsworth

Ode to Psyche
author: 9 John Keats

Ode to the West Wind
author: 18 Percy Bysshe Shelley

Odets, Clifford
author of: 9 Golden Boy 12 Awake and Sing 14 The Country Girl 15 Waiting for Lefty 17 The Flowering Peach

Odin *see box*

odious 4 evil, foul, vile 5 hated, nasty 6 rotten 7 hateful, heinous, hideous 8 infamous 9 invidious, loathsome, monstrous, obnoxious, offensive, repugnant, repulsive, revolting, sickening 10 abominable, despicable, detestable, disgusting, nauseating, unbearable 11 intolerable, unendurable 12 contemptible 13 objectionable

odium 5 shame 6 hatred, infamy 7 disgust 8 contempt, disfavor, disgrace, dishonor, ignominy 9 antipathy, discredit, disesteem, disrepute 10 abhorrence, disrespect, opprobrium, repugnance 11 detestation, disapproval 14 disapprobation

odonata
class: 8 hexapoda
phylum: 10 arthropoda
group: 9 damselfly, dragonfly

odor 4 aura 5 aroma, scent, smell, stink 6 flavor, stench 7 bouquet, essence, perfume 9 effluvium, fragrance 10 atmosphere

odoriferous 4 rank 5 acrid, fetid 6 putrid, smelly 7 noisome, odorous, pungent, reeking, scented 8 aromatic, fragrant, perfumed, stinking 10 malodorous

odorous 4 rank 5 acrid, fetid 6 smelly 7 noisome, pungent, reeking, scented 8 aromatic, fragrant, perfumed, stinking

Odysseus
also: 7 Ulysses
king of: 6 Ithaca
father: 7 Laertes
mother: 8 Anticlea
hero of: 5 Iliad 7 Odyssey
wife: 8 Penelope 9 Callidice
son: 9 Telegonus 10 Polypoetes, Telemachus 11 Polyporthis
seduced by: 5 Circe
killed by: 9 Telegonus
epithet: 10 Laertiades

Odin
also: 5 Othin
brother: 2 Ve 4 Vili
children: 4 Hodr, Thor 5 Baldr 6 Balder, Baldur
corresponds to: 5 Wotan
counterpart: 5 Wotan
court: 8 Valhalla
father: 3 Bor
god of: 3 war 6 poetry, wisdom 9 knowledge
grandson: 7 Volsung
home: 9 Gladsheim
horse: 8 Sleipnir
magic ring: 8 Draupnir
origin: 12 Scandinavian
raven: 5 Hugin, Munin
remaining eye: 3 sun
ruler of: 5 Aexir
spear: 7 Gungnir
throne: 10 Hlidskjalf
wife: 3 Fri 5 Frigg, Frija 6 Frigga
wolf: 4 Geri 5 Freki

Odyssey
author: 5 Homer
character: 4 Zeus 5 Arete, Circe, Helen 6 Athene, Nestor, Scylla, Sirens 7 Calypso, Cyclops 8 Alcinous, Menelaus, Nausicaa, Odysseus, Penelope, Poseidon, Tiresias 9 Charybdis 10 Telemachus 11 Lotus-eaters

Oedipus
king of: 6 Thebes
father: 5 Laius
mother: 7 Jocasta
foster father: 7 Polybus
foster mother: 6 Merope 8 Periboea
wife: 7 Jocasta
son: 8 Eteocles 9 Polynices
daughter: 6 Ismene 8 Antigone
killed: 5 Laius
defeated: 6 Sphinx

Oedipus at Colonus
author: 9 Sophocles
character: 5 Creon 6 Elders, Ismene 7 Theseus 8 Antigone 9 Polynices

Oedipus Rex (Oedipus Tyrannus)
author: 9 Sophocles
character: 5 Creon, Laius 7 Jocasta 8 Tiresias

oeil-de-boeuf 16 small round window
literally: 8 bull's eye

Oeneus
king of: 7 Calydon
wife: 7 Althaea
son: 8 Meleager

Oenomaus
king of: 4 Elis, Pisa
father: 4 Ares
mother: 7 Sterope
daughter: 10 Hippodamia
murdered: 6 Marmax

Oenone
form: 5 nymph
father: 6 Cebren
husband: 5 Paris

Oenopion
king of: 5 Chios
father: 8 Dionysus
mother: 7 Ariadne
daughter: 6 Merope
blinded: 5 Orion

Oersted, Hans Christian
field: 7 physics
nationality: 6 Danish

founded: **16** electromagnetism
isolated: **16** metallic aluminum
named for him: **11** oersted unit

oeuvre **4** work **5** works **13** artist's output

O'Faolain, Sean
author of: **15** The Heat of the Sun **17** A Nest of Simple Folk **22** Midsummer Night's Madness

of a piece **5** alike, equal **7** matched, the same **8** all in one **9** analogous, identical **10** equivalent, homogenous, synonymous **13** evenly matched, one and the same

of bad character **5** shady **8** unsavory **11** of ill repute **12** disreputable, unprincipled

off **2** by **3** bad, far, ill, odd **4** afar, away, down, from, kill, poor, stop **5** amiss, apart, aside, crazy, wrong **6** absent, begone, lessen, remote **7** distant, further, in error, stopped, tainted **8** abnormal, canceled, inferior, mistaken **9** imperfect

offal **4** junk, slag **5** dregs, trash, waste **6** debris, refuse **7** carcass, carrion, garbage, grounds, remains, residue, rubbish **8** leavings

off base **5** amiss, wrong **8** improper, mistaken **10** out of order, unsuitable **13** inappropriate

offbeat **3** odd **7** strange **8** peculiar **9** different, eccentric **14** unconventional

off-center **6** askew **7** strange **9** eccentric **10** imbalanced, nonaligned, unbalanced **12** unreasonable **14** unconventional

off-color **4** blue, lewd, racy, sexy **5** bawdy, dirty, salty, spicy **6** earthy, risque, smutty, wicked **7** naughty, obscene, raunchy **8** improper, indecent, scabrous **9** offensive **10** indelicate, indiscreet, suggestive

off duty **8** inactive **9** at leisure **10** unoccupied **13** on one's own time

Offenbach, Jacques
born: **7** Cologne, Germany
composer of: **13** La Belle Helene **15** Tales of Hoffmann, La Vie Parisienne **22** Orpheus in the Underworld

offend **3** err, sin, vex **4** fret, gall, miff, rile **5** anger, annoy, chafe, lapse, pique, wound **6** insult, madden, nettle, rankle **7** affront, disgust, incense, inflame **8** irritate **9** aggravate, displease, misbehave **10** antagonize, disgruntle, exasperate, transgress **13** fall from grace

offender **5** crook, felon **6** sinner **7** culprit **8** criminal, violator **9** wrong doer **10** malefactor, trespasser

offense **3** sin **4** gibe, harm, slap, slip, snub, twit **5** abuse, crime, lapse, taunt **6** attack, charge, felony, insult **7** affront, assault, misdeed, outrage, umbrage **8** atrocity, enormity, evil deed, rudeness **9** impudence, indignity, insolence, offensive, violation **10** aggression, disrespect, infraction, peccadillo, wickedness **11** delinquency, humiliation, malfeasance, misdemeanor, shortcoming **13** embarrassment, transgression **15** breach of conduct

offensive **4** foul, rank, rude, ugly **5** nasty, onset **6** attack, horrid **7** abusive, assault, hideous, offense, uncivil **8** charging, impudent, insolent, storming **9** abhorrent, assailing, attacking, insulting, loathsome, obnoxious, onslaught, repugnant, repulsive, revolting, sickening, ungallant **10** abominable, aggression, aggressive, assaulting, bombarding, detestable, disgusting, nauseating, unmannerly, unpleasant **11** belligerent, distasteful, intolerable **12** disagreeable, embarrassing, insufferable **13** disrespectful, objectionable

offensiveness **8** rudeness **9** impudence, insolence, nastiness **10** disrespect, horridness, incivility **13** repulsiveness **14** unpleasantness **15** distastefulness

offer **3** bid **5** put up **6** bestow, extend, render, submit, tender **7** advance, hold out, present, proffer, propose, suggest **8** bestow on, offering, overture, proposal, propound, put forth **9** be willing, volunteer **10** invitation, put forward, submission, suggestion **11** make a motion, proposition **12** bring forward **14** put on the market **19** place at one's disposal

offer hospitality **4** host **7** welcome **8** play host **9** entertain **10** give a party, have guests **13** keep open house

offering **3** bid **4** alms, gift **5** goods, wares **6** course **7** charity, present, tribute **8** anathema, bestowal, donation, oblation **9** sacrifice **11** beneficence **12** contribution
to God: **6** corban **7** deodate
to household deities: **4** bali

offertory **4** gift **8** oblation, offering **10** collection

offhand, offhanded **5** ad-lib, hasty **6** casual, chance, random **7** relaxed **8** careless, cavalier, heedless **9** facetious, haphazard, impromptu, unplanned, unstudied **10** improvised, nonchalant, off-the-cuff, unprepared **11** spontaneous, thoughtless, unconcerned, unrehearsed **12** off-the-record **14** extemporaneous, unpremeditated

office **3** job **4** post, role **8** capacity, function, position **10** commission, occupation **11** appointment

officer **3** cop **4** head **7** manager **8** director, gendarme, governor **9** constable, detective, executive, patrolman, policeman, president, secretary, treasurer **10** bureaucrat **12** commissioner **13** administrator, vice-president

officers **8** managers **10** executives, management **14** administration

Officers and Gentlemen
author: **11** Evelyn Waugh

offices **4** duty, help, task **5** favor, trust **6** charge **7** service **8** function, province **10** assistance

office seeker **7** hopeful, nominee **8** aspirant **9** candidate

office worker **5** clerk, steno **6** typist **9** file clerk, secretary **10** bookkeeper, keypuncher **13** data processor **14** clerical worker

official **5** agent **6** formal, vested **7** manager, officer **8** approved, chairman, director, licensed **9** authentic, certified, dignitary, executive, warranted **10** accredited, authorized, sanctioned, supervisor **11** functionary **13** administrator, authoritative **14** administrative **18** administrative head

official communication **5** edict, order, ukase **6** report **7** release **8** bulletin **10** communique **12** proclamation

officialdom **10** government **11** authorities, bureaucracy **14** administration

official paper **4** writ **5** order **8** document **10** instrument

officiate **3** run **4** head, lead **5** chair, emcee **6** direct, handle, manage **7** oversee, preside **8** moderate, regulate **9** supervise **10** administer **11** superintend **12** be in charge of

officious **6** prying **7** pompous **8** meddling **9** intrusive, kibitzing, obtrusive **10** high-handed, meddlesome **11** domineering, interfering, overbearing, patronizing **13** high and mighty, self-assertive, self-important **16** poking one's nose in

Offield, Lewis Delaney
real name of: **9** Jack Oakie

offset **6** redeem **7** balance, nullify **8** equalize, knock out **9** cancel out, make up for **10** counteract, neutralize **11** countervail **13** compensate for, counterweight **14** counterbalance

offshoot **4** limb **5** scion, shoot **6** branch **7** adjunct **9** aftermath, by-product, outgrowth **10** descendant

offspring **3** fry **4** heir, seed **5** brood, child, issue, scion, spawn, young **6** family, litter **7** progeny **8** children, increase **9** posterity **10** descendant, succession **11** descendants

off the mark **5** amiss **6** afield, astray **9** off target **16** off the right track

off-the-record **5** privy **6** secret **7** private **11** undisclosed **12** confidential **16** not to be disclosed **17** not for publication

off the top of one's head **5** ad-lib **7** offhand **9** extempore, impromptu **10** improvised, unprepared **11** extemporary, unrehearsed **14** extemporaneous, unpremeditated

of good quality **4** good **6** worthy **8** superior **9** excellent **10** creditable

of high rank **5** noble, regal, royal **6** lordly, titled **7** courtly **11** blue-blooded **12** aristocratic

Of Human Bondage
author: **16** W Somerset Maugham
director: **12** John Cromwell
character: **5** Weeks **7** Hayward **11** Louisa Carey, Philip Carey **12** Sally Athelny, William Carey **13** Mildred Rogers, Miss Wilkinson, Thorpe Athelny
cast: **10** Bette Davis, Frances Dee, Kay Johnson **12** Leslie Howard

of its own kind
Latin: **10** sui generis

Of Mice and Men
author: **13** John Steinbeck
director: **14** Lewis Milestone
character: **4** Slim **5** Candy **6** Crooks, Curley **11** Lennie Small **12** George Milton
cast: **10** Betty Field **11** Lon Chaney Jr (Lenny) **15** Burgess Meredith, Charles Bickford
score: **12** Aaron Copland

of one's own right
Latin: **8** sui juris

of poor quality **5** junky **6** flimsy, shoddy, sleazy, trashy **8** inferior **11** substandard

of secondary importance **8** nonvital **9** accessory, extrinsic **10** incidental **11** dispensable, unnecessary **12** nonessential

often **3** oft **4** much **7** usually **8** commonly, ofttimes **9** generally, regularly **10** constantly, frequently, habitually, oftentimes, repeatedly **11** continually, customarily, over and over, recurrently **12** periodically, time and again

of the dead say nothing but good
Latin: **21** de mortuis nil nisi bonum

of the faith
Latin: **6** de fide

of their own kind
Latin: **10** sui generis

of the old school **5** passe **8** outdated, outmoded **9** out-of-date **12** conservative, old-fashioned **18** establishmentarian

Of Time and the River
author: **11** Thomas Wolfe
character: **10** Eugene Gant

oft-repeated **5** trite **7** popular **8** constant, familiar, frequent, habitual, well-worn **9** continual, recurring, well-known **10** persistent **11** widely-known

of what good
Latin: **7** cui bono

Ogdoad
also: **3** Heh
origin: **8** Egyptian
number of gods: **5** eight

ogle **3** eye **6** gape at, gawk at, goggle, leer at **7** stare at **8** goggle at **10** give the eye, scrutinize **15** give the once-over, stare at greedily **16** cast sheep's eyes at, gaze at with desire

Ogma
origin: **5** Irish
god of: **6** poetry **9** eloquence
inventor of: **12** Ogham letters

Ogmios
origin: **6** Gaelic
god of: **9** eloquence
corresponds to: **7** Mercury

ogre, ogress **5** brute, demon, fiend, ghoul, harpy **6** despot, tyrant **7** bugbear, monster **8** bogeyman, dictator, martinet **11** slave driver

Ogygia
island of: **7** Calypso

Ogygus
king of: **7** Boeotia
father: **8** Poseidon

O'Hara, John
author of: **7** Pal Joey **11** A Rage to Live **13** The Instrument **14** From the Terrace, The Hat on the Bed **16** Butterfield Eight **17** Ten North Frederick **19** The Horse Knows the Way **20** Appointment in Samarra

O'Hara, Maureen
real name: **18** Maureen Fitzsimmons
nickname: **18** Queen of Technicolor
born: **7** Ireland **8** Milltown
roles: **10** Lady Godiva **11** The Quiet Man **13** North to Alaska, The Parent Trap **16** The Foxes of Harrow **19** How Green Was My Valley **20** Hunchback of Notre Dame **27** Miracle on Thirty-fourth Street

O'Hara, Scarlett
character in: **15** Gone With the Wind
family: **6** Gerald **7** Carreen, Suellen
author: **8** Mitchell

O Henry
real name: **19** William Sidney Porter
author of: **11** The Last Leaf **16** Cabbages and Kings, The Gift of the Magi **18** The Cop and the Anthem **19** The Ransom of Red Chief

Ohio ***see box***

Ohm, Georg Simon
field: **7** physics
nationality: **6** German
discovered: **20** electrical resistance
named for him: **7** ohm unit

oil **4** balm, lard **5** cream, salve **6** anoint, grease, pomade **7** unguent **8** liniment, ointment **9** lubricant, lubricate, melted fat, petroleum **12** melted grease
type: **4** corn, fuel, hair

Ohio
abbreviation: 2 OH
nickname: 7 Buckeye
capital: 8 Columbus
largest city: 9 Cleveland
others: 3 Ada **4** Kent, Lima **5** Akron, Berea, Cadiz, Niles, Parma, Piqua, Xenia **6** Athens, Canton, Dayton, Elyria, Lorain, Marion, Newark, Tiffin, Toledo, Warren **7** Ashland, Findlay, Fremont, Norwood, Wooster **8** Alliance, Bluffton, Fostoria, Lakewood, Marietta, Sandusky **9** Ashtabula, Kettering, Lancaster, Massillon, Struthers, Vermilion, Willowick **10** Cincinnati, Huntington, Portsmouth, Rocky River, Willoughby, Youngstown, Zanesville **11** Painesville, Springfield **12** Steubenville
college: 4 Kent **5** Akron, Hiram, Miami **6** Dayton, Kenyon, Xavier **7** Antioch, Oberlin, Wooster **8** Defiance, Dennison, Marietta, Ursuline **10** Wittenberg **11** Case Western **12** Bowling Green, Ohio Wesleyan
feature:
hall of fame: **11** Pro Football
race: **12** Soap Box Derby
tribe: 4 Erie **7** Wyandot **13** Mound Builders
people: 7 buckeye, Cy Young **8** Zane Grey **10** Clark Gable, T Hart Crane **11** Annie Oakley, Lillian Gish **12** James Thurber, Lowell Thomas, Norman Thomas **13** Neil Armstrong, Orville Wright, Thomas A Edison **14** Barney Oldfield, Clarence Darrow **15** William T Sherman **16** Sherwood Anderson **18** Norman Vincent Peale
explorer: **7** La Salle
lake: 4 Erie **5** Grand **6** Berlin, Dillon, Hoover, Indian **8** Delaware **13** Mosquito Creek
land rank: 35 thirty-fifth
mountain:
highest point: **12** Campbell Hill
physical feature:
caverns: **4** Ohio, Zane **6** Seneca
spring: **8** Blue Hole
president: 13 Ulysses S Grant **14** James A Garfield, Warren G Harding **15** William McKinley **16** Rutherford B Hayes **17** William Howard Taft **20** William Henry Harrison
river: 5 Grand, Miami **6** Maumee, Scioto, Wabash **7** Hocking **8** Cuyahoga, Sandusky **9** Muskingum, Tennessee **10** Cumberland **11** Monongahela
state admission: 11 seventeenth
state bird: 8 cardinal
state flower: 16 scarlet carnation
state motto: 27 With God All Things Are Possible
state song: 13 Beautiful Ohio
state tree: 7 buckeye

5 crude, motor, olive, whale **7** cooking, mineral **9** safflower, vegetable

Oilean Ajax *see* **4** Ajax

Oileus
king of: 6 Locris
member of: 9 Argonauts
father: 10 Hodoedocus
mother: 9 Agrianome
son: 5 Medon **13** Ajax the Lesser

oily 5 fatty, lardy, slick **6** greasy, smarmy **7** buttery, fawning, servile **8** slippery, slithery, toadying, unctuous **9** groveling, sebaceous **10** lubricious, oleaginous **11** bootlicking, subservient **12** ingratiating

ointment 4 balm **5** salve **6** lotion, pomade **7** pomatum, unguent **8** liniment **9** emollient, spikenard

Oizys
mother: 3 Nyx
personifies: 4 pain

Ojibwa, Ojibway *see* **8** Chippawa

OK 4 fine, good **7** approve, endorse **8** all right, approval **9** authorize **11** endorsement **13** authorization
French: 7 d'accord

O'Keeffe, Georgia
born: 12 Sun Prairie WI
artwork: 7 Stables **9** Black Iris **14** Patio with Cloud **15** Lake George Barns **22** Light Coming on the Plains **26** Black Flower and Blue Larkspur

Oklahoma ***see box, p. 704***

Oklahoma!
director: 13 Fred Zinnemann
cast: 10 Rod Steiger **11** Eddie Albert **12** Gordon MacRae, Shirley Jones **13** Gloria Grahame, James Whitmore **18** Charlotte Greenwood
score: 21 Rodgers and Hammerstein
song: 23 People Will Say We're in Love **24** Surrey with the Fringe on Top

Olbers, Heinrich Wilhelm Matthaus
field: 9 astronomy
nationality: 6 German
discovered: 5 Vesta **6** comets, Pellas **9** asteroids

old 4 aged, used **5** hoary, of age **6** beat-up, bygone, of yore **7** ancient, antique, archaic, elderly, outworn, rundown, vintage, wornout **8** battered, decrepit, familiar, grizzled, much-used, obsolete, outdated, timeworn **9** crumbling, hackneyed, out-of-date, venerable, weathered **10** antiquated, broken-down, grayheaded, ramshackle, tumbledown **11** dilapidated, from the past, gray with age, obsolescent, time-honored, traditional **12** deteriorated, old-fashioned, white with age **13** weather-beaten **14** of long standing **15** long established

Old Aches and Pains
nickname of: 11 Luke Appling

old age 6 dotage **7** ripe age **8** maturity, senility **11** advanced age **15** second childhood

Old and the Young, The
author: 15 Luigi Pirandello

Old Bay State
nickname of: 13 Massachusetts

Old Bulgarian
also: 15 Old Church Slavic
language family: 12 Indo-European
group: 11 Balto-Slavic
status: 7 archaic
used in: 14 Orthodox church

Old Chinook
nickname of: 10 Washington

Oklahoma
abbreviation: **2** OK **4** Okla
nickname: **6** Boomer, Sooner
capital/largest city: **12** Oklahoma City
others: **3** Ada **4** Alva, Enid, Hugo **5** Altus, Miami, Ponca, Tulsa **6** Duncan, El Reno, Guymon, Idabel, Lawton **7** Ardmore, Guthrie, Sapulpa, Shawnee **8** Anadarko, Fort Sill, Muskogee **9** Blackwell, Claremore, McAlester **10** Stillwater **12** Bartlesville
college: **5** Tulsa **6** Norman **7** Cameron **8** Langston, Phillips **10** Stillwater **11** Oral Roberts **12** Oklahoma City **15** Bethany Nazarene **17** American Christian
feature:
hall of fame: **14** American Indian
national park: **6** Platte
tribe: **3** Kaw, Oto **4** Iowa, Loup, Otoe, Waco **5** Caddo, Kansa, Osage, Ponca **6** Apache, Ottawa, Pawnee, Quapaw **7** Shawnee, Wichita **8** Arapahoe, Tawakoni
Five Civilized Tribes: **5** Creek **7** Choctaw **8** Cherokee, Seminole **9** Chickasaw
people: **4** Okie **6** sooner **9** Jim Thorpe **10** Will Rogers **12** Mickey Mantle **14** Maria Tallchief
explorer: **8** Coronado
lake: **5** Atoka, Grand, Hulah **6** Texoma, Wister **7** Eufaula, Heyburn, Oologah **8** Keystone **9** Pensacola, Tenkiller **10** Fort Gibson **11** Thunderbird **12** Markham Ferry **17** Lake O' The Cherokees
land rank: **10** eighteenth
mountain: **6** Ozarks **8** Ouachita
highest point: **9** Black Mesa
physical feature: **9** Panhandle
plains: **5** Great
river: **3** Red **5** Grand **6** Little, Neosho **7** Washita **8** Arkansas, Canadian, Cimarron **9** Verdigris **15** Muddy Boggy Creek
state admission: **10** forty-sixth
state bird: **23** scissor-tailed flycatcher
state fish: **9** white bass
state flower: **9** mistletoe
state motto: **22** Labor Conquers All Things
state song: **8** Oklahoma
state tree: **6** redbud

Old Colony State
nickname of: **13** Massachusetts

Old Curiosity Shop, The
author: **14** Charles Dickens
character: **5** Quilp **9** Fred Trent, Mrs Jarley **10** Kit Nubbles, Sally Brass **11** Grandfather **12** Sampson Brass **13** Dick Swiveller **15** Little Nell Trent **18** The Single Gentleman

Old Dominion
nickname of: **8** Virginia

olden **4** past **6** bygone, former, of yore **7** ancient, long-ago **8** departed

Oldest Man **10** Methuselah

old-fashioned **5** corny, dated, passe **7** antique, archaic **8** obsolete, outdated, outmoded **9** out-of-date **10** antiquated, out of style **11** obsolescent, traditional **12** long-standing, out of fashion **13** unfashionable **14** behind the times

Old-Fashioned Girl, An
author: **15** Louisa May Alcott

Old Franklin State
nickname of: **9** Tennessee

old hand **3** pro **6** expert, master **8** virtuoso **9** authority **12** professional

old hat **5** passe, stale **6** demode **7** archaic, outworn **8** obsolete, outdated, outmoded **9** out-of-date **10** antiquated, superseded **11** obsolescent **12** old-fashioned **13** unfashionable **14** behind the times

old-line **11** established, traditional **12** conservative

Old Line State
nickname of: **8** Maryland

Old Love
author: **19** Isaac Bashevis Singer

Old Maid, The
author: **12** Edith Wharton

Old Man and the Sea, The
author: **15** Ernest Hemingway
character: **7** Manolin **8** Santiago

Old Mortality
author: **14** Sir Walter Scott
character: **5** Edith **11** Henry Morton **12** Basil Olifant, Lord Evandale **19** John Balfour of Burley **21** Lady Margaret Bellenden **27** Colonel Grahame of Claverhouse

Old Mortality
author: **19** Katherine Anne Porter

Old North
nickname of: **13** North Carolina

Old Patagonian Express, The
author: **11** Paul Theroux

old saw **5** adage, maxim **6** cliche, saying, truism **7** bromide, proverb **9** old saying **10** expression **11** old chestnut

oldster **5** elder **6** codger, old man **7** ancient **8** old woman **13** senior citizen

Old Testament
first five books: **10** Pentateuch
first six books: **9** Hexateuch
first seven books: **10** Heptateuch
books of: **3** Job **4** Amos, Ezra, Joel, Ruth **5** Hosea, Jonah, Kings, Micah, Nahum, Songs, Tobit **6** Baruch, Daniel, Esther, Exodus, Haggai, Isaiah, Joshua, Judges, Judith, Psalms, Samuel, Sirach, Wisdom **7** Ezekiel, Genesis, Malachi, Numbers, Obadiah **8** Habakkuk, Jeremiah, Macabees, Nehemiah, Proverbs **9** Leviticus, Zechariah, Zephaniah **10** Chronicles **11** Deuteronomy **12** Ecclesiastes **13** Song of Solomon **14** Ecclesiasticus

Oldtown Folks
author: **19** Harriet Beecher Stowe

Old Wives' Tale, The
author: **13** Arnold Bennett

old-world **6** formal **7** courtly, gallant, old-line **8** European, orthodox **10** ceremonial, chivalrous, prescribed **11** ceremonious, continental, established, traditional **12** conservative, conventional, old-fashioned

Ole
character in: **16** Giants of the Earth
author: **7** Rolvaag

Olen
occupation: **4** poet
location: **5** Lycia

Olenska, Ellen
character in: **17** The Age of Innocence
author: **7** Wharton

oleoresin **3** gum **5** anime, apiol, elemi **6** balsam **7** solvent **10** turpentine

olio **4** stew **6** jumble, medley **7** melange, mixture **8** mishmash **9** potpourri **10** assortment, collection, hodgepodge, hotchpotch, miscellany

olive **12** Olea europaea
varieties: **3** tea **4** wild **5** black, false, holly, sweet **6** common, desert, spurge **7** Russian **8** American, fragrant **11** Californian

olive-drab **5** khaki **13** greenish-brown

Oliver
character in: **11** As You Like It
author: **11** Shakespeare

Oliver!
director: **9** Carol Reed
based on story by: **14** Charles Dickens (Oliver Twist)
cast: **8** Jack Wild, Ron Moody (Fagin) **10** Mark Lester (Oliver), Oliver Reed **11** Shani Wallis
Oscar for: **7** picture **8** director
remake of: **11** Oliver Twist
song: **16** Consider Yourself, Food Glorious Food **17** As Long As He Needs Me

Oliver Twist
author: **14** Charles Dickens
character: **5** Fagin, Monks (Edward Leeford), Nancy **6** Bumble **9** Bill Sikes, Mrs Maylie **10** Mr Brownlow, Rose Maylie
director: **9** David Lean
cast: **8** Kay Walsh **12** Alec Guinness (Fagin), Robert Newton **13** Anthony Newley (Artful Dodger) **16** Francis L Sullivan, John Howard Davies
remade as: **7** Oliver!

Olivia
character in: **12** Twelfth Night
author: **11** Shakespeare

Olivier, Sir Laurence
born: **7** Dorking, England
wife: **11** Vivien Leigh **13** Joan Plowright
roles: **6** Becket, Hamlet (Oscar), Henry V, Sleuth **7** Rebecca **11** Marathon Man **16** Wuthering Heights **17** Pride and Prejudice, The Boys from Brazil, The Devil's Disciple **19** Shoes of the Fisherman **23** The Prince and the Showgirl

olivine
variety: **7** peridot

olla **3** jar, pot **10** earthen pot

Olmsted, Frederick Law
landscape architect of: **11** Central Park (NYC, with Calvert Vaux) **12** Prospect Park (Brooklyn NY) **13** Fairmount Park (Philadelphia) **14** Biltmore Estate (Asheville NC), Mount Royal Park (Montreal)

Olsen, Merlin (Jay)
sport: **8** football
team: **14** Los Angeles Rams
TV roles: **12** Father Murphy **15** Highway to Heaven **23** Little House on the Prairie

Olsson, Ann-Margret
real name of: **10** Ann-Margret

O Lucky Man
director: **15** Lindsay Anderson
cast: **9** Alan Price **13** Rachel Roberts **15** Malcolm McDowell, Ralph Richardson
score: **9** Alan Price

Olwen
origin: **5** Welsh
form: **8** princess
father: **16** Yspadaden Penkawr

Olympic Games ***see box***

Omaha
language family: **6** Siouan **7** Dhegiha
location: **4** Iowa **8** Nebraska, Oklahoma

Oman ***see box, p. 706***

omega **3** end **4** last **5** final **6** ending **8** terminus
opposite: **5** alpha

omen **4** sign **5** token **6** augury, herald **7** auspice, portent, presage, warning **9** foretaste, harbinger, precursor **10** foreboding, indication

Omet **15** Biblical measure

ominous **7** unlucky **8** menacing, minatory, monitory, sinister **9** dismaying, ill-omened **10** foreboding, ill-starred, portentous **11** disquieting, threatening, unfavorable, unpromising **12** inauspicious, unpropitious

Olympic games
site:
1896: **6** Athens
1900: **5** Paris
1904: **7** St Louis
1906: **6** Athens
1908: **6** London
1912: **9** Stockholm
1920: **7** Antwerp
1924: **5** Paris **8** Chamonix
1928: **8** St Moritz **9** Amsterdam
1932: **10** Lake Placid, Los Angeles
1936: **6** Berlin **21** Garmisch-Partenkirchen
1948: **6** London **8** St Moritz
1952: **4** Oslo **8** Helsinki
1956: **9** Melbourne **15** Cortina d'Ampezzo
1960: **5** Tokyo **11** Squaw Valley
1968: **8** Grenoble **10** Mexico City
1972: **6** Munich **7** Sapporo
1976: **8** Montreal **9** Innsbruck
1980: **6** Moscow **10** Lake Placid
1984: **8** Sarajevo **10** Los Angeles
1988: **5** Seoul **7** Calgary

omission **3** gap **4** hole **7** neglect **9** exception, exclusion, oversight **10** leaving out, negligence **11** delinquency, elimination **12** noninclusion **13** neglected item **16** something omitted

omit **3** cut **4** drop, fail, jump, miss, shun, skip **5** avoid, elide **6** bypass, delete, except, forget, ignore, slight **7** excerpt, exclude, let slip, neglect **8** leave out, overlook, pass over, preclude, set aside **11** forget about

omnia vincit amor **15** love conquers all

Omnibus
host: **13** Alistair Cooke

omnipotent **6** mighty **7** supreme **8** almighty, powerful, puissant **11** all-powerful

omniscient **7** all-wise, su-

Oman
other name: **13** Muscat and Oman
capital: **6** Masqat, Muscat
largest city: **5** Matra **6** Matrah
others: **3** Sur **4** Fida **5** Dubai, Nazwa, Nigwa, Sohar, Wazit **6** Khasab, Marbat, Murbat, Suwaih, Tinouf **7** Khabura, Salalah **8** Ashkhara
government: **9** Sultanate
head of state/government: **6** sultan
monetary unit: **3** gaj, gaz **4** rial **5** baiza, ghazi **7** mahmudi
island: **6** Masera, Masira **7** Masirah **10** Kuria Muria
mountain: **4** Qara **5** Hafit, Harim, Nakhl, Tayin **8** el-Akhdar **11** Jabal Akhdar **13** Green Mountain
highest point: **6** al-Sham
sea: **6** Indian **7** Arabian
physical feature:
cape: **7** Madraka **9** Ras Al Hadd **13** Ras Dharbat 'Ali
gulf: **4** Oman
peninsula: **7** Arabian **8** Musandam
plain: **6** Dhofar **7** Batinah
strait: **6** Hormuz
people: **4** Arab
ruler: **12** Qabus Bin Said **13** Said Bin Taimur
language: **4** Urdu **5** Hindi **6** Arabic **7** Baluchi
religion: **5** Islam

preme **8** infinite **9** all-seeing **10** all-knowing, preeminent

omnium gatherum **23** miscellaneous collection

omnivorous **7** hoggish **8** edacious, ravenous **9** crapulous, rapacious, voracious **10** gluttonous, polyphagic, predacious **12** pantophagous

Omoo
author: **14** Herman Melville
character: **10** Captain Bob **15** Doctor Long Ghost

Omphale
queen of: **5** Lydia
father: **8** Iardanus
husband: **6** Tmolus
son: **5** Lamus
served by: **8** Hercules

Omri
father: **6** Becher **7** Michael
son: **4** Ahab
daughter-in-law: **7** Jezebel

on **2** at **4** atop, near, over, upon **5** about, above, ahead, along, anent **7** against, forward, planned **8** abutting, adjacent, attached, intended, touching **9** occurring **10** concerning, juxtaposed

On
father: **6** Peleth
city of: **10** Heliopolis

on-and-off **6** spotty **8** episodic **9** irregular, spasmodic, temporary **10** now-and-then, occasional

On Beginning and Perishing
author: **9** Aristotle

once **7** ages ago, long ago, one time **8** formerly, hitherto, years ago **9** at one time **10** heretofore, previously **11** a single time, for the nonce, in times past, some time ago **12** in the old days, some time back **13** once upon a time, on one occasion

once-in-a-lifetime **6** unique **7** special **8** singular **11** one-time-only

once more **4** anew **5** again **9** once again, over again **11** one more timc

on cloud nine **6** elated, joyful, joyous **8** ecstatic, euphoric **9** exuberant, rapturous **15** in seventh heaven

oncoming **5** close **7** looming, nearing **8** imminent **9** advancing, impending, onrushing **11** approaching, bearing down

on course **8** on target **15** on the right track

Ondine
author: **13** Jean Giraudoux

one **2** an **3** you **4** a man, lone, only, sole **5** a body, a soul, whole **6** a thing, entire, single, unique **7** a person, someone **8** complete, singular, solitary, somebody **10** individual, unrepeated

One, Two, Three
director: **11** Billy Wilder
cast: **11** James Cagney **12** Pamela Tiffin **13** Arlene Francis, Horst Buchholz
setting: **10** West Berlin
score: **11** Andre Previn

O'Neal, Ryan
real name: **16** Patrick Ryan O'Neal
born: **12** Los Angeles CA
daughter: **10** Tatum O'Neal
roles: **9** Love Story, Paper Moon **10** What's Up Doc **11** Barry Lyndon, Peyton Place **16** Rodney Harrington

O'Neal, Tatum
born: **12** Los Angeles CA
father: **9** Ryan O'Neal
roles: **9** Paper Moon **12** Bad News Bears **14** Little Darlings **19** International Velvet
husband: **11** John McEnroe

one and the same **5** equal **7** matched **9** identical

one by one **6** singly **10** one at a time, separately, single file **12** individually

One Day at a Time
character: **9** Ann Romano **11** Julie Cooper **13** Barbara Cooper **15** Dwayne Schneider
cast: **14** Bonnie Franklin **15** Pat Harrington Jr **17** Mackenzie Phillips, Valerie Bertinelli

One Day in the Life of Ivan Denisovich
author: **23** Aleksandr Solzhenitsyn Jr

One Fat Englishman
author: **12** Kingsley Amis

One Flew Over the Cuckoo's Nest
director: **11** Milos Forman
based on story by: **8** Ken Kesey
cast: **13** Jack Nicholson **14** Louise Fletcher, Michael Beryman **15** William Redfield
Oscar for: **5** actor (Nicholson) **7** actress (Fletcher), picture **8** director **10** screenplay

One Hour with You
director: **11** George Cukor **13** Ernst Lubitsch
cast: **14** Genevieve Tobin **16** Maurice Chevalier **17** Jeanette MacDonald
remake of: **17** The Marriage Circle
song: **14** What Would You Do

one-hundred percent
5 sheer, total, utter, whole **7** supreme **8** absolute, complete **10** consummate **17** through-and-through

O'Neill, Eugene
author of: **8** The Straw **11** The Hairy Ape **12** Ah

Wilderness, Anna Christie **13** Marco Millions **14** Glencairn Cycle **15** The Emperor Jones, The Iceman Cometh **16** Beyond the Horizon, Strange Interlude, The Great God Brown **18** Desire Under the Elms **20** The Moon of the Caribees **22** A Moon for the Misbegotten, All God's Chillun Got Wings, Mourning Becomes Electra **24** Long Day's Journey into Night

Oneiros
also: 6 Oniros
origin: 5 Greek
god of: 6 dreams

oneness 5 union, unity **7** concord, harmony **8** entirety, identity, sameness, totality **9** agreement, aloneness, integrity, wholeness **10** uniformity, uniqueness **11** singularity **12** completeness **13** individuality

one-of-a-kind 4 rare **6** unique **7** strange, unusual **8** original **9** eccentric

onerous 5 heavy **6** taxing **7** arduous, painful, weighty **8** crushing, grievous **9** demanding, wearisome **10** burdensome, exhausting, oppressive **11** distressing **12** hard to endure

one thing in return for another
Latin: 10 quid pro quo

one-time 3 old **4** past **5** early, prior **6** former, recent **7** earlier, quondam **8** previous **9** erstwhile
French: 8 ci-devant

one voice 4 solo **6** unison **7** concert

one who has a fixed income
French: 7 rentier

On First Looking Into Chapman's Homer
author: 9 John Keats

on foot
French: 5 a pied

ongoing 7 endless, lasting **8** enduring, unbroken, unending **10** continuing, proceeding **11** never-ending, unremitting **13** uninterrupted

On Golden Pond
director: 10 Mark Rydell
based on play by: 14 Ernest Thompson
cast: 9 Jane Fonda **10** Doug McKeon, Henry Fonda (Norman Thayer Jr) **16** Katharine Hepburn
setting: 5 Maine
Oscar for: 5 actor (Fonda) **7** actress (Hepburn)

on guard 4 wary **5** alert **7** careful, heedful **8** cautious, vigilant, watchful

on hand 5 handy, on tap **6** at hand **9** available **10** accessible, convenient **14** at one's disposal

on horseback
French: 7 a cheval

onion 6 Allium **10** Allium cepa
varieties: 3 red, sea, top **4** leek, tree, wild **5** green, gypsy, pearl, swamp, Welsh, white **6** German, potato, yellow **7** Bermuda, Danvers, nodding, prairie, shallot, Spanish **8** climbing, Egyptian, false sea, scallion, Valencia **9** Catawissa, ever-ready, flowering, two-bladed **10** multiplier, red-skinned **16** Japanese bunching
origin: 9 Asia Minor
called by Robert Louis Stevenson: 14 rose among roots

Onion Field, The
author: 14 Joseph Wambaugh

Oniros *see* **7** Oneiros

On Liberty
author: 14 John Stuart Mill

onlooker 5 gazer, ogler **6** viewer **7** watcher, witness **8** beholder, kibitzer, observer **9** bystander, spectator **10** eyewitness, rubberneck

only 4 just, lone, sole **5** alone **6** barely, merely, purely, simply, single, singly, solely, unique **7** at least **8** by itself, singular, solitary **9** by oneself, exclusive, unmatched **10** individual, no more than, nothing but, one and only, unrepeated **11** exclusively **12** individually, unparalleled

on one's uppers 5 broke **9** destitute **10** down and out

On Plants
author: 9 Aristotle

On Revolution
author: 12 Hannah Arendt

onrush 4 flow, flux, gush, tide, wave **5** flood, onset, storm, surge **6** attack, charge, deluge, spring, stream **7** assault, cascade, current, torrent **9** avalanche

onset 4 push, raid **5** birth, sally, start **6** attack, charge, onrush, outset, thrust **7** assault, genesis, infancy, offense **8** founding, invasion, outbreak, storming **9** beginning, inception, incursion, offensive, onslaught **10** incipience, initiation **12** commencement, inauguration

onslaught 4 coup, push, raid **5** blitz, foray, onset, sally **6** attack, charge, putsch, thrust **7** assault, offense **8** invasion **9** incursion, offensive **10** aggression, blitzkrieg

on tap 5 handy **6** at hand, on hand **9** available **10** accessible, convenient

Ontario
bay: 6 Hudson
canal: 5 Trent **6** Rideau
capital: 7 Toronto
city: 3 Emo **4** Galt **6** London, Ottawa **7** Windsor **8** Hamilton, Kingston **9** Kitchener
explored by: 5 French **6** British
industry: 6 mining **11** agriculture **13** manufacturing
lake: 6 Simcoe
province of: 6 Canada
river: 6 Ottawa, Thames **7** Niagara **10** St Lawrence
settled by: 9 Loyalists
university: 4 York **5** Brock, Trent **8** McMaster

on the alert 4 wary **7** careful, mindful, on guard **8** cautious, watchful **9** wide awake **12** on the lookout

On the Beach
author: 10 Nevil Shute
director: 13 Stanley Kramer
cast: 10 Ava Gardner **11** Fred Astaire, Gregory Peck **13** Donna Anderson **14** Anthony Perkins

on the contrary
French: 11 au contraire

on the dot 7 exactly **8** promptly **9** on the nose, precisely **10** punctually

on the face
Latin: 7 ex facie

on the go 4 busy **6** active, mobile **8** in motion **9** energetic, on the move **13** indefatigable

On the Heavens
author: 9 Aristotle

On the Morning of Christ's Nativity
author: 10 John Milton

on the move 5 astir **6** active, mobile **7** on the go **8** in motion

on the nose 5 exact **7** exactly, precise **8** accurate, on target **9** precisely **10** accurately, on the money

on the outer edges
Latin: **10** in extremis

on the right track **8** on course, on target

On the Soul
author: **9** Aristotle

On the Town
director: **9** Gene Kelly **12** Stanley Donen
cast: **9** Ann Miller, Gene Kelly, Vera-Ellen **12** Betty Garrett, Frank Sinatra
setting: **11** New York City
score: **11** Adolph Green, Betty Comden **16** Leonard Bernstein
song: **14** New York New York

On the Waterfront
director: **9** Elia Kazan
cast: **8** Lee J Cobb **10** Karl Malden, Pat Henning, Rod Steiger **12** Leif Erickson, Marlon Brando **13** Eva Marie Saint
Oscar for: **5** actor (Brando) **7** picture **8** director **10** screenplay **17** supporting actress (Saint)

on the whole **9** in general **10** by and large **27** considering the circumstances

onto **4** atop, upon **5** aware, privy **6** aboard

onus **4** duty, load **5** cross **6** burden, strain, weight **9** liability **10** obligation **11** encumbrance **13** burden of proof **14** responsibility

onus probandi **13** burden of proof

onward, onwards **5** ahead, along **7** forward, ongoing **9** advancing, frontward **11** moving ahead, progressive
French: **7** en avant, en route

On Wings of Eagles
author: **10** Ken Follett

oodles **4** gobs, lots, many **5** heaps, loads, scads **6** plenty

ooze **4** drip, leak, mire, muck, seep, silt **5** bleed, drain, exude, slime, sweat **6** filter, sludge **7** dribble, leakage, seepage, soft mud, trickle **8** alluvium **9** discharge, exudation, percolate, secretion, transpire

oozing **5** leaky, weepy **6** sweaty **7** exuding, seepage, seeping **8** bleeding, sweating

opal
color: **3** red **5** black, white **6** orange **11** transparent
source: **6** Mexico **9** Australia **14** Lightning Ridge
variety: **8** fire opal

opalescent **5** milky **6** pearly **8** irisated, luminous **10** iridescent

opaque **4** dark, dull, hazy **5** muddy, murky **7** clouded, muddied, obscure, unclear **8** abstruse **9** difficult **12** impenetrable, unfathomable **14** nontranslucent, nontransparent, unintelligible **16** incomprehensible

opaqueness **7** opacity **8** dullness **9** denseness, muddiness, murkiness, obscurity **10** cloudiness **11** unclearness **15** impenetrability **17** unintelligibility **19** incomprehensibility

open **4** ajar, fair, just, wide **5** agape, begin, clear, crack, found, frank, plain, unbar **6** candid, create, direct, expand, gaping, honest, launch, unfold, unlock, unseal, unshut **7** artless, exposed, lay open, natural, not shut, sincere, unblock, unclose, yawning **8** commence, extended, outgoing, unbiased, unclosed, unfasten, unfenced, unfolded, unlocked, unsealed **9** available, coverless, establish, expansive, impartial, institute, not closed, objective, originate, receptive, unbigoted, unbounded, uncovered, uncrowded, undertake, welcoming **10** accessible, forthright, impersonal, inaugurate, responsive, unenclosed, unfastened **11** extroverted, uncluttered, uninhabited **12** permit access, unobstructed, unprejudiced **13** disinterested, doing business **15** straightforward

open-air **7** outdoor, outside **10** unconfined
Italian: **8** al fresco

open and aboveboard **6** candid, honest **7** ethical **10** forthright **12** on the up and up **15** straightforward

Open Boat, The
author: **12** Stephen Crane

Open City
director: **17** Roberto Rossellini
cast: **11** Aldo Fabrizi, Anna Magnani **16** Marcello Pagliero
setting: **4** Rome

open-eyed **5** alert, awake, aware **7** heedful, mindful **8** vigilant, watchful, wide-eyed **9** attentive, wide-awake

open-handed **6** lavish **7** liberal **8** generous, prodigal **9** bounteous, bountiful **10** altruistic, beneficent, benevolent, ungrudging, unstinting **11** magnanimous

openhandedness **10** generosity, liberality **11** benevolence, generousity, munificence **12** extravagance

openhearted **7** artless, sincere **8** trusting **9** ingenuous

opening **3** gap, job **4** gash, hole, rent, rift, slit, slot, spot, tear, vent **5** break, chink, cleft, crack, place, space, start **6** breach, chance **7** fissure, kickoff, preface, prelude, send-off, vacancy **8** aperture, occasion, overture, position **9** beginning, first part, launching, situation **10** initiation **11** opportunity, possibility **12** commencement, inauguration, installation, introduction

openly **6** freely **7** frankly **8** directly, honestly, publicly **9** obviously

open-minded **4** fair **7** liberal **8** amenable, flexible, tolerant, unbiased **9** adaptable, impartial, objective, receptive **10** responsive, undogmatic **11** broad-minded **12** unprejudiced **13** disinterested, nonjudgmental

openmouthed **4** agog, awed **5** agape **6** aghast, amazed **8** wide-eyed **9** awestruck, bewitched, marveling, staggered, stupefied, surprised **10** astonished, confounded **10** dumbstruck, enthralled, spellbound **11** dumbfounded **12** wonderstruck **13** flabbergasted, thunderstruck

openness **6** candor **7** honesty **8** daylight **9** frankness, sincerity **11** artlessness **13** guilelessness **14** forthrightness **19** straightforwardness

open sanction **8** free hand, free rein **13** full authority
French: **12** catre blanche

open the eyes of **8** disabuse **11** set straight

open to choice **8** elective, optional **9** voluntary

openwork **3** net **4** lace **6** eyelet **7** lattice, Madeira, tracery **8** filigree

opera **5** score **7** musical **8** libretto **11** composition
by Bizet: **6** Carmen
by Delibes: **5** Lakme
by Gounod: **5** Faust
by Leoncavallo: **10** I Pagliacci
by Mozart: **8** Idomeneo **10** Magic Flute **11** Don Giovanni **12** Cosi fan tutte **16** Marriage of Figaro
by Offenbach: **15** Tales of Hoffmann
by Ponchielli: **10** La Gioconda
by Puccini: **5** Tosca **8** La Boheme **12** Manon Lescaut **15** Madame Butterfly
by Rossini: **8** Tancredi **11** William Tell **15** The Barber of Seville
by Smetana: **13** The Bartered Bride
by Strauss: **6** Salome **7** Elektra **15** Ariadne auf Naxos **16** Der Rosenkavalier
by Tchaikovsky: **12** Eugene Onegin
by Verdi: **4** Aida **6** Otello **8** Falstaff **9** Rigoletto **10** La Traviata **11** Il Trovatore
by Wagner: **8** Parsifal **9** Lohengrin **10** Tannhauser **16** Tristan and Isolde **17** The Flying Dutchman **21** The Ring of the Nibelungs
comic: **5** buffa **7** comique
glass: **9** lorgnette
hat: **5** crush, gibus
house: **3** Met **6** Sydney **7** La Scala **12** Covent Garden, Metropolitan
singer: **4** bass, diva **5** buffa, buffo, tenor **7** soprano **10** coloratura, prima donna
singular: **4** opus
solo: **4** aria
text: **8** libretto

operate **2** go **3** run **4** go in, work **6** behave, manage, open up **7** oversee, perform **8** function **11** superintend **14** perform surgery **18** perform an operation

operating **6** active **7** working **8** in motion **9** operative **10** responsive

operation **5** force **6** action, agency, effect **7** conduct, pursuit, running, surgery, working **8** activity, exertion **9** influence, procedure **10** management, overseeing **11** exploratory, performance, supervision **15** instrumentality, superintendence

operative **3** spy **4** dick **5** agent, in use **6** acting, active, shamus, worker **7** in force, working **8** in effect, in motion, workable **9** activated, detective, effective, effectual, operating **10** functional, private eye, responsive **11** efficacious, secret agent

operator **4** doer, user **5** agent, pilot **6** driver, worker **7** manager **9** performer

opere citato **14** in the work cited
abbreviation: **5** op cit

Ophelia
character in: **6** Hamlet
author: **11** Shakespeare

Opheltes
also: **10** Archemorus

ophidiophobia
fear of: **6** snakes

Ophion
form: **7** serpent
created from: **9** north wind
created by: **8** Eurynome

Ophir
father: **6** Joktan
source of: **4** gold

opiate **4** dope **6** downer **7** anodyne **8** hypnotic, narcotic, nepenthe, sedative **9** analgesic, calmative, soporific, stupefier **10** depressant, painkiller, palliative **12** somnifacient, stupefacient, tranquilizer

opine **3** say **4** deem **5** allow, guess, offer, state, think **6** assume, reckon **7** believe, imagine, presume, suggest, surmise **8** conclude, consider, estimate **9** speculate, volunteer **10** conjecture, have a hunch

opinion **4** idea, view **6** belief, notion, theory **7** surmise **8** estimate, judgment, thinking **9** sentiment, suspicion **10** assessment, assumption, conception, conclusion, conjecture, conviction, estimation, evaluation, impression, persuasion **11** speculation

opinionated **8** dogmatic, obdurate, stubborn **9** obstinate, pigheaded, unbending **10** bullheaded, headstrong, inflexible, unyielding **12** closed-minded **14** uncompromising

O Pioneers!
author: **11** Willa Cather

Opis
companion of: **7** Artemis

Opobalsammum **12** Biblical tree

Oppenheimer, Julius Robert
field: **7** physics
directed development of: **10** atomic bomb
location: **9** Los Alamos, New Mexico
chaired: **3** AEC **22** Atomic Energy Commission

Opper, Frederick
creator/artist of: **13** Happy Hooligan **17** Alphonse and Gaston, And Her Name Was Maud

opponent **3** foe **5** enemy, rival **8** resister **9** adversary, assailant, contender, disputant **10** antagonist, challenger, competitor, opposition

opportune **3** apt **5** happy, lucky **6** proper, timely **7** fitting **8** suitable **9** expedient, favorable, fortunate, well-timed **10** auspicious, convenient, felicitous, profitable, propitious, seasonable **11** appropriate **12** advantageous

opportunity **4** time, turn **5** means **6** chance, moment **7** opening **8** occasion **9** situation **10** good chance **11** contingency

oppose **4** buck, defy **5** fight **6** battle, combat, resist, thwart **7** contest **8** obstruct **9** withstand **12** be set against, speak against

opposed **3** con **4** anti **6** averse, pitted **7** adverse, against, counter, hostile **8** contrary, disputed, objected, resisted **9** contested, countered **10** confronted, contrasted, reciprocal **12** contradicted

opposer **5** rival **8** opponent **9** adversary **10** antagonist, competitor

opposite **5** other **6** facing **7** adverse, counter, reverse **8** contrary, converse, opposing **9** differing **11** conflicting **12** antagonistic, antithetical **13** contradictory, counteractive

opposite number **5** equal **8** parallel **10** equivalent **11** correlative, counterpart

opposition **3** foe **5** enemy, rival **6** enmity **8** aversion, defiance, opponent **9** adversary, contender, hostility, other side, rejection **10** antagonism, antagonist, competitor, negativism, resistance **11** contrariety, disapproval **12** disagreement

oppress **3** tax, try, vex **4** pain **5** abuse, worry **6** burden, deject, grieve, sadden, sorrow **7** depress, trouble **8** cast down, dispirit, maltreat **9** despotize, persecute, tyrannize, weigh down **10** discourage, dishearten

oppressed **7** crushed **9** exploited **10** tyrannized **11** downtrodden, subservient

oppressive **5** cruel, harsh **6** brutal, severe, trying, vexing **7** onerous, painful, wearing **8** despotic, grievous, pressing **9** worrisome **10** burdensome, depressing, repressive, tyrannical, unbearable **11** distressing, hardhearted, troublesome **12** discouraging **13** uncomfortable

oppressor **6** despot, tyrant **8** autocrat, dictator

opprobrious **4** base **6** wicked **7** abusive, corrupt, damning **8** infamous, reviling, shameful, shocking **9** malicious, maligning, nefarious, vilifying, vitriolic **10** censorious, deplorable, despicable, malevolent, outrageous, scandalous, scurrilous, unbecoming **11** acrimonious, disgraceful, fulminating **12** condemnatory, denunciatory, dishonorable, disreputable, faultfinding **13** hypercritical, objectionable, reprehensible

opprobrium **5** shame **6** infamy **8** disgrace, dishonor **9** disrepute **12** denunciation

Ops
origin: **5** Roman
goddess of: **6** plenty
husband: **6** Saturn
son: **7** Jupiter
called: **10** Magna Mater
corresponds to: **4** Rhea **6** Cybele **9** Dindymene **10** Berecyntia

opt **4** pick, take **5** elect, fix on, go for **6** choose, prefer, select **7** vote for **8** decide on, settle on

opt for **4** pick, take **5** adopt **6** choose, select, take up **7** embrace, espouse, fix upon, pick out **8** decide on, settle on

optimism **10** confidence **11** hopefulness **12** cheerfulness, sanguineness **13** bright outlook, encouragement

optimistic **6** bright **7** hopeful, roseate **8** buoyed up, cheerful, sanguine **9** confident, favorable, heartened, promising **10** auspicious, encouraged, heartening, propitious **11** encouraging, rose-colored **12** enthusiastic

Optimist's Daughter, The
author: **11** Eudora Welty

optimum **4** acme, A-one, best, peak **5** crest, ideal, prime **6** choice, height, select, zenith **7** capital, perfect, supreme **8** flawless **9** faultless, first-rate **10** perfection, unexcelled **11** superlative **12** quintessence

option **4** will **5** voice **6** choice, liking **8** decision, election, free will, pleasure **9** franchise, privilege, selection **10** discretion, partiality, preference **11** alternative **12** predilection

optional **4** open **8** elective, unforced **9** allowable, open-ended, voluntary **10** volitional **11** not required **12** discretional **13** discretionary, nonobligatory

opulence **6** bounty, plenty, riches, wealth **7** fortune **8** elegance, luxuries, richness **9** abundance, affluence, amplitude, profusion **10** cornucopia, lavishness, plentitude, prosperity **11** copiousness, great wealth **13** sumptuousness

opus **4** work **5** piece **6** effort **7** attempt, product **8** creation **9** handiwork, invention **10** brainchild, production **11** composition

oracle, Oracle **4** sage, seer **5** augur, sibyl **6** wizard **7** adviser, diviner, prophet **9** predictor, Scripture **10** forecaster, soothsayer **11** clairvoyant

oral **5** vocal **6** spoken, verbal, voiced **7** uttered **8** ingested **9** swallowed **10** of the mouth, verbalized **11** articulated, using speech
Latin: **8** viva voce

orange
varieties: **4** king, mock, sour, wild **5** blood, hardy, natal, navel, Osage, sweet **6** bitter, common, Panama, Temple **7** Florida, Mexican, Satsuma, Seville, Spanish **8** Bergamot, Mandarin, Otaheite, Valencia **9** Tachibana, vegetable **10** Chinese box, trifoliate **13** African cherry, Mediterranean **15** Jamaica mandarin **17** house-blooming mock
liqueur: **7** Curacao

orangutan, orang-outang **3** ape **4** mias **5** satyr **6** primate **10** anthropoid
characteristic: **8** arboreal **11** herbivorous
native land: **6** Borneo **7** Sumatra
species: **13** Pongo pygmaeus

ora pro nobis **9** pray for us

orate **6** recite, speak **7** declaim **11** make a speech

oration **4** talk **5** spiel **6** eulogy, sermon, speech **7** address, lecture, recital **9** discourse, monologue, panegyric **10** peroration **11** declamation **12** disquisition, formal speech

orator **6** talker **7** speaker **8** lecturer, preacher **9** declaimer **10** sermonizer **11** rhetorician, speechmaker, spellbinder **12** elocutionist **13** public speaker

oratory **6** speech **7** bombast **8** delivery, rhetoric **9** elocution, eloquence, preaching **11** declamation **12** speechifying, speechmaking **14** grandiloquence

orb **4** ball, moon **5** globe **6** sphere **7** globule **8** spheroid

orbit **3** way **4** path **5** cycle, route, track **6** circle, course **7** channel, circuit, pathway **10** trajectory **13** revolve around **14** circumnavigate

orchards
god of: **9** Vertumnus

orchestra **3** pit **4** band **6** stalls **7** parquet **8** ensemble, parterre **12** Philharmonic

orchestrate **5** adapt, score **7** arrange, compose

orchestration **5** score **10** adaptation **11** arrangement **12** organization

orchid ***see box***

Orcus
god of: **10** underworld
punishes: **7** perjury
corresponds to: **3** Dis **5** Hades, Pluto **8** Dis Pater

ordain **4** name, rule, will **5** elect, enact, frock **6** decree, invest **7** adjudge, appoint, command, dictate **8** delegate, deputize, instruct **9** determine,

orchid
varieties: **3** bat, bee, fen, fly, nun, nut **4** baby, blue, dove, moth, nun's, rein, swan **5** black, chain, cigar, cobra, coral, giant, jewel, pansy, Salep, showy, snowy, spice, tiger, water, widow **6** bamboo, bottle, cradle, dollar, Easter, helmet, mirror, monkey, pigeon, ragged, sawfly, shower, spider, stream, virgin **7** Alaskan, cow-horn, fringed, hooker's, jumping, peacock, rainbow, rosebud, scarlet, soldier **8** bee-swarm, Cooktown, cranefly, fried-egg, gold-lace, green-fly, hyacinth, nun's-hood, poor-man's, Savannah, scorpion, white nun, windmill, woodland **9** blunt-leaf, butterfly, chocolate, Christmas, clamshell, green rein, green swan, white rein **10** buttonhole, five-leaved, golden swan, hay-scented, late spider, leafy white, Sierra rein, slender bog **11** cockle-shell, crested rein, dancing-doll, dancing-lady, early spider, golden chain, green-winged, one-leaf rein, pink slipper, purple-spire, rattlesnake, round-leaved **12** green fringed, pink scorpion, purple-hooded, Southern rein, tall white bog, white fringed **13** crested yellow, golden fringed, green woodland, Northern green, ragged fringed, yellow fringed **14** crested fringed, large butterfly, little club-spur, white butterfly **15** lesser butterfly, lily-of-the-valley **16** downy rattlesnake, Florida butterfly, Northern small bog, purple fringeless, small round-leaved, white-flowered bog **18** large purple fringed, leafy Northern green, small purple fringed, Southern small white **19** lesser purple fringed **20** greater purple fringed

legislate, prescribe, pronounce **10** commission, consecrate

ordeal **4** care, pain **5** agony, grief, trial, worry **6** burden, misery, sorrow, strain, stress **7** anguish, concern, torment, tragedy, trouble **8** calamity, distress, pressure, vexation **9** heartache, nightmare, suffering **10** affliction, oppression **11** tribulation, unhappiness **12** wretchedness **16** trying experience

Ordeal of Richard Feverel, The
author: **14** George Meredith

order **3** bid, law **4** body, book, calm, club, fiat, form, kind, rank, rule, sort, type **5** breed, caste, class, grade, group, guild, house, lodge, quiet, ukase **6** adjure, ask for, charge, decree, degree, demand, dictum, direct, engage, enjoin, family, status, stripe, system **7** agree to, bidding, caliber, call for, command, company, control, dictate, harmony, pattern, quality, request, reserve, silence, society, species, station **8** alliance, category, division, grouping, instruct, neatness, position, purchase, sorority, standing, tidiness **9** framework, structure, ultimatum **10** discipline, federation, fraternity, imperative, sisterhood, tabulation **11** arrangement, association, brotherhood, commandment, confederacy, designation, instruction, tranquility **12** codification, organization, peacefulness, tranquillity **13** pronouncement **14** categorization, classification

ordered **4** bade, neat, trim **7** regular, uniform **8** arranged **9** shipshape **10** systematic

orderliness **8** neatness, tidiness **10** discipline **12** organization

orderly **4** neat, tidy **5** civil, quiet **6** proper, spruce **8** peaceful **9** organized, peaceable, shipshape, tractable **10** classified, controlled, methodical, restrained, systematic **11** disciplined, uncluttered, well-behaved

ordinance **3** act, law **4** bull, fiat, rule, writ **5** canon, edict, order **6** decree, dictum, ruling **7** command, mandate, statute **9** enactment **10** regulation **11** commandment

ordinarily **7** as a rule, usually **8** commonly, normally **9** generally, regularly, routinely **10** habitually **11** customarily **12** on the average **14** conventionally

ordinary **4** dull, so-so **5** usual **6** common, normal **7** average, humdrum, routine, trivial, typical **8** everyday, familiar, habitual, mediocre, standard **9** customary **10** pedestrian, uninspired **11** commonplace, indifferent, stereotyped, traditional, unimportant **12** conventional, run-of-the-mill, unimpressive **13** insignificant, unexceptional, unimaginative, uninteresting **15** inconsequential, undistinguished

Ordinary People
director: **13** Robert Redford
author: **11** Judith Guest
cast: **10** Judd Hirsch **13** Timothy Hutton **14** Mary Tyler Moore **16** Donald Sutherland
Oscar for: **7** picture **8** director **12** screenwriter **15** supporting actor (Hutton)

ordinary wine
French: **12** vin ordinaire

ordnance **4** arms **6** cannon **9** armaments, artillery, munitions

ordnance depot **6** armory **7** arsenal **18** military storehouse

ore **3** tin **4** gold, iron, lead, paco, rock, zinc **5** metal **6** bronze, copper, galena, sulfur **7** halvans, mineral **8** aluminum, cinnabar, hematite **9** melachite
byproduct: **6** gangue
deposit: **3** bed **4** lode, mine, vein **7** bonanza
layer: **4** seam **5** stope
trough: **6** strake
worthless: **4** slag **5** dross, matte

Oread
form: **5** nymph
location: **8** mountain
companion of: **7** Artemis

oregano
name means: **16** joy of the mountain
botanical name: **8** O vulgare, Origanum
also: **6** organy, origan **8** marjoram **9** pizza herb **11** Mexican sage, winter sweet
origin: **13** Mediterranean
family: **4** mint
cure for: **11** indigestion **14** loss of appetite
first aid for: **12** spider stings **14** scorpion stings
use: **5** pizza **6** broths **8** stuffing **12** tomato dishes **13** Italian dishes

Oregon ***see box, p. 712***

Oregon Trail, The
author: **14** Francis Parkman

Oresteia
author: **9** Aeschylus
trilogy includes: **9** Agamemnon, Eumenides **10** Choephoroe

Oregon
abbreviation: **2** OR **4** Oreg
nickname: **6** Beaver, Sunset **7** Webfoot **13** Sawdust Empire
capital: **5** Salem
largest city: **8** Portland
others: **5** Nyssa **6** Albany, Eugene **7** Ashland, Astoria, Medford **8** Portland, Roseburg **9** Corvallis, Pendleton **10** Grant's Pass, Willamette **12** Klamath Falls
college: **4** Reed **7** Pacific **8** Linfield, Portland **10** Willamette **13** Lewis and Clark
feature:
fort: **5** Boise **6** Casper **7** Kearney, Laramie
national park: **10** Crater Lake
tribe: **4** Coos **5** Alsea, Kusan, Modoc, Wasco, Yanan, Yunca **6** Cayuse, Chetco, Chinoo, Kuitsh, Molala, Siletz, Tenino, Umpqua **7** Bannock, Clatsop, Klamath, Sastean, Shastan, Takelma, Walpapi, Yaquina **8** Clackama, Klikitat, Nez Perce, Sahaptin, Umatilla **9** Kalapuyan, Tillamook **10** Kalapooian, Wallawalla
people: **10** Wayne Morse **12** Linus Pauling **15** Phyllis McGinley
explorer: **13** Lewis and Clark
lake: **5** Abert, Waldo **6** Harney, McNary **7** John Day, Klamath, Malheur
deepest in US: **6** Crater
land rank: **5** tenth
mountain: **6** Mazama, Tacoma, Walker, Wilson **7** Elkhorn, Grizzly, Jackass, Rainier, Tidbits, Wallowa **8** Cascades **9** Blue Coast, Marys Peak **10** Strawberry
highest point: **4** Hood
physical feature:
bay: **4** Coos
caves: **11** Marble Halls
wind: **7** Chinook
river: **5** Rogue, Snake **6** Imnaha, Owyhee, Powder, Umpqua **7** Blitzen, John Day, Klamath, Silvie's **8** Columbia **9** Deschutes **10** Willamette
state admission: **11** thirty-third
state bird: **17** western meadowlark
state fish: **13** chinook salmon
state flower: **7** mahonia **11** Oregon grape
state motto: **8** The Union
state song: **14** Oregon My Oregon
state tree: **10** Douglas fir

Orestes
author: **9** Euripides
character: **5** Helen **6** Apollo, Furies **7** Electra, Pylades **8** Menelaus

Orestes
father: **9** Agamemnon
mother: **12** Clytemnestra
sister: **7** Electra **9** Iphigenia
wife: **8** Hermione
son: **9** Tisamenus
killed: **9** Aegisthus **12** Clytemnestra
pursued by: **6** Furies

Orfeo, L'
also: **17** The Story of Orpheus
opera by: **10** Monteverdi

Orfeo ed Euridice
also: **18** Orpheus and Eurydice
opera by: **5** Gluck
character: **4** Amor, Zeus **6** Furies

Orff, Carl
born: **6** Munich **7** Germany
composer of: **7** Der Mond, The Moon **8** Antigone, Die Kluge **9** Schulwerk **10** Prometheus **13** Carmina Burana, The Clever Girl **14** Catulli Carmina **16** Oedipus der Tyrann, Oedipus the Tyrant

organ **6** agency **7** journal, vehicle **9** harmonium **10** hurdy-gurdy, instrument **11** publication

organic **5** alive, quick **6** living **7** animate, natural, ordered, planned, unified **8** designed, physical **9** patterned **10** anatomical, harmonious, methodical, systematic **12** nonsynthetic **13** physiological **14** constitutional

organism **4** cell **5** plant, whole **6** animal, entity, system **7** complex, network, society **8** creature **9** bacterium **10** federation **11** association, corporation, institution, living thing **13** microorganism

organization **4** club, firm, sect **5** corps, group, order, party, union **6** design, league, making, outfit **7** company, forming, harmony, pattern, society **8** alliance, assembly, business, grouping, ordering **9** arranging, formation **10** federation, fellowship, fraternity **11** arrangement, association, composition, corporation, formulation, structuring **12** constitution, coordination **13** establishment, incorporation

organizational **10** managerial **13** developmental **14** administrative

organize **4** file, form, tidy **5** found, group, index, order, set up **6** codify, create, neaten, tidy up **7** arrange, catalog, develop **8** classify, tabulate **9** establish, formulate, originate **10** categorize, coordinate **11** make orderly, systematize

organized **4** neat, tidy **7** logical, orderly **8** coherent **10** methodical, systematic

orgiastic **4** wild **6** wanton **7** drunken, riotous **9** abandoned, debauched, Dionysian, dissolute, libertine **10** dissipated, licentious **12** bacchanalian, unrestrained **13** overindulgent, undisciplined

orgy **7** debauch, wassail **8** carousal **9** bacchanal **10** saturnalia **11** bacchanalia

orient, the Orient **3** fix, set **4** Asia, find **6** locate, relate, square **7** situate **8** accustom **9** acclimate, reconcile **10** the Far East **11** Eastern Asia, familiarize

oriental **4** Arab, fine, Thai, Turk **5** Asian **6** bright, Indian, Korean **7** Asiatic, Chinese, Eastern, Iranian, shining **8** Japanese, lustrous, precious, superior **10** Vietnamese
animal: **4** zebu **5** rasse
building: **6** pagoda
dish: **5** pilau, pilaw **6** pilaff
drum: **6** tomtom
food fish: **3** tai
garment: **3** aba **6** sarong
inn: **4** Khan **5** serai **6** imaret **11** caravansary

laborer: **6** coolie
market: **3** suk, sug **4** souk **6** bazaar
nurse: **4** amah, ayah
prince: **4** amir, haja
sail: **6** lateen
sash: **3** obi
shrub: **3** tea **5** henna **8** oleander
wagon: **5** araba
weight: **2** mo **4** rotl, tael **5** catty, liang **6** cantar

orientation **8** location **9** alignment, direction, situation **10** adjustment **11** acclimation **15** acclimatization, familiarization

orifice **3** gap, pit **4** hole, slit, slot, vent **5** cleft, inlet, mouth **6** cavity, cranny, hollow, lacuna, pocket, socket **7** crevice, fissure, opening, passage **8** alveolus, aperture, entrance

origin **4** base, line, race, rise, root **5** agent, basis, birth, breed, cause, house, stock **6** author, family, father, ground, growth, mother, reason, source, spring, strain **7** creator, descent, genesis, lineage, taproot **8** ancestry, nativity, producer **9** beginning, emergence, evolution, generator, inception, parentage, principle **10** derivation, extraction, foundation **12** commencement, fountainhead

Origin, The
author: **11** Irving Stone

original **3** new **4** bold **5** basic, basis, first, fresh, novel **6** daring, primal, unique **7** example, initial, pattern, primary, seminal, strange, unusual **8** atypical, creative, earliest, germinal, primeval, singular, uncommon **9** different, essential, first copy, formative, inaugural, ingenious, inventive, prototype **10** aboriginal, newfangled, primordial, underlying, unfamiliar, unorthodox **11** fundamental, imaginative **12** introductory **13** extraordinary **14** unconventional

Original Amateur Hour, The
host: **7** Ted Mack

originality **6** daring **7** newness, novelty **8** boldness **9** freshness, ingenuity **10** cleverness, creativity, uniqueness **11** imagination, singularity, unorthodoxy **13** individuality, inventiveness **17** unconventionality

originally **7** at first, by birth **8** uniquely **9** initially, unusually **10** creatively **11** differently, inventively **13** imaginatively

originate **4** come, flow, rise, stem **5** arise, begin, draft, found, issue, start **6** create, crop up, derive, design, devise, emerge, evolve, father, invent, sprout **7** develop, emanate, proceed **8** commence, conceive, envision, initiate, organize, spring up **9** establish, fabricate, formulate, germinate **10** inaugurate

origination **5** birth **7** genesis **9** inception, invention **10** conception, initiation **11** germination **12** commencement **13** establishment

Origin of Species, The
author: **13** Charles Darwin

Origins of Totalitarianism, The
author: **12** Hannah Arendt

Orion
form: **5** giant
vocation: **6** hunter
pursued: **8** Pleiades
killed by: **7** Artemis
became: **13** constellation

Orithyia
father: **10** Erechtheus
mother: **9** Praxithea
abducted by: **6** Boreas
son: **5** Zetes **6** Calais
daughter: **6** Chione **9** Cleopatra

Oriya
language family: **12** Indo-European
branch: **11** Indo-Iranian
group: **5** Indic
spoken in: **5** (northern) India

Orkney Islands
county seat: **8** Kirkwall
country: **8** Scotland
firth: **8** Pentland
island: **3** Hay **6** Rousay, Sanday **7** Westray **8** Stronsay **14** South Ronaldsay
largest city: **6** Pomona

Orlando
author: **13** Virginia Woolf
character: **5** Sasha **14** Nicholas Greene **28** Archduchess Harriet of Roumania, Marmaduke Bonthrop Shelmerdine

Orlando
character in: **11** As You Like It
author: **11** Shakespeare

Orlando Furioso
author: **7** Ariosto
character: **6** Rogero **7** Rinaldo **8** Agramant, Angelica, Rodomont **9** Bradamant **11** Charlemagne

Orley Farm
author: **15** Anthony Trollope

ormolu **5** alloy, brass, paste **6** bronze **7** gilding **8** ornament
imitation of: **4** gold
used to decorate: **5** clock **9** furniture

ornament **4** deck, gild, trim **5** adorn **6** bedeck, enrich, finery, frills **7** festoon, furbish, garnish **8** beautify, decorate, furbelow, trick out, trimming **9** accessory, adornment, embellish **10** decoration, enrichment **11** elaboration **13** embellishment **14** beautification

ornamental **4** gilt **5** fancy **6** chichi, rococo **10** decorative
ball: **4** bead **6** pompom
button: **4** stud
grass: **4** neti
loop: **5** picot
metal: **5** niello

ornamentation **7** garnish **8** trimming **9** adornment **10** decoration **13** embellishment

ornate **5** fancy, showy **6** flashy, florid, lavish, rococo **7** adorned, baroque, flowery **9** decorated, elaborate, sumptuous **10** flamboyant **11** embellished, pretentious **12** ostentatious

ornery **4** curt, mean **5** surly, testy **6** crabby, grumpy, shirty **7** grouchy, peevish, waspish **8** snappish **9** dyspeptic, irascible, irritable **10** ill-natured **11** ill-tempered, quarrelsome **12** cantankerous

Orneus
father: **10** Erechtheus
brother: **6** Metion **7** Cecrops
son: **6** Peteos

Ornitholestes
type: **8** dinosaur
period: **8** Jurassic

Ornithomimus
type: **8** dinosaur
period: **10** Cretaceous

ornithophobia
fear of: **5** birds

ornithopod
type of: **8** dinosaur
member: **9** Iguanodon **10** Edmontonia, Nodosaurus **11** Anatosaurus, Polacanthus, Saurolophus, Scolosaurus, Stegosaurus **12** Ankylosaurus, Camptosaurus, Lambeosaurus, Pisanosaurus **13** Acanthopholis, Corythosaurus, Hypsilophodon, Palaeoscincus **14** Thescelosaurus

15 Parasaurolophus, Procheneosaurus
17 Heterodontosaurus

Ornytus *see* 7 Teuthis

orotund 4 full, rich 5 clear 6 strong 7 pompous, ringing, vibrant 8 resonant, sonorous 9 bombastic 10 resounding, rhetorical, stentorian
Latin: 10 ore rotundo

Orowitz, Eugene Maurice
real name of: 13 Michael Landon

oro y plata 13 gold and silver
motto of: 7 Montana

Orozco, Jose Clemente
born: 6 Mexico 7 Jalisco (Zapotlan) 12 Ciudad Guzman
artwork: 5 Grief 9 Catharsis 11 Omniscience 12 House of Tears 16 National Allegory, Social Revolution 18 Hidalgo and Castillo

Orphans of the Storm
director: 10 D W Griffith
cast: 11 Dorothy Gish, Lillian Gish 17 Joseph Schildkraut

Orpheus
vocation: 4 poet 8 musician
mother: 8 Calliope
wife: 8 Eurydice
member of: 9 Argonauts
went into: 5 Hades
killed by: 7 Maenads

Orpheus in the Underworld
also: 15 Orphee aux Enfers
operetta by: 9 Offenbach

Orsino
character in: 12 Twelfth Night
author: 11 Shakespeare

ort 3 bit 5 crumb, dregs, scrap 6 morsel, refuse, trifle 7 remnant 8 leavings, leftover

Orthaea
father: 10 Hyacinthus

Orthia
epithet of: 7 Artemis
means: 7 upright

orthodox 5 fixed, pious, usual 6 devout, narrow 7 limited, regular, routine 8 accepted, approved, official, ordinary, standard 9 customary, religious 11 commonplace, conformable, established, traditional 12 conventional 13 authoritative, circumscribed

orthoptera
class: 8 hexapoda
phylum: 10 arthropoda
group: 4 leaf 5 stick 6 locust, mantid 7 cricket 9 cockroach 11 grasshopper

Orwell, George
real name: 15 Eric Arthur Blair
author of: 4 1984 10 Animal Farm 18 Nineteen Eighty Four 29 Politics and the English Language

oryx 5 beisa 6 pickax 7 gazelle, gemsbok 8 antelope, leucoryx

Osage (Wazhazhe)
language family: 6 Siouan
location: 6 Kansas 8 Arkansas, Missouri, Oklahoma

Oscan
language family: 12 Indo-European
branch: 6 Italic

Oschophoria
origin: 8 Athenian
event: 8 festival
honoring: 7 vintage 8 Dionysus

oscillate 4 vary 5 pulse, swing, waver 6 change, seesaw 7 librate, pulsate, vibrate 8 hesitate 9 alternate, come and go, fluctuate, hem and haw, vacillate 10 ebb and flow, equivocate 12 shilly-shally 16 move back and forth

O'Shaughnessy, Brigid
character in: 16 The Maltese Falcon
author: 7 Hammett

osier 3 rod 4 wand 5 salix, withe 6 willow 7 dogwood, wilgers 9 twigwithy
species: 14 Salix viminalis
use: 6 wicker 8 basketry

Osiris
origin: 8 Egyptian
god of: 4 dead, Nile
judge of: 4 dead
king of: 4 dead
wife: 4 Isis
sister: 4 Isis
son: 5 Horus
brother: 3 Set 4 Seth 5 Horus
killed by: 3 Set 4 Seth

Oskar Matzerath
character in: 7 Tin Drum
author: 5 Grass

Oslo
capital of: 6 Norway
former name: 11 Christiania
landmark: 8 Storting (Parliament) 11 Royal Palace
mountain: 12 Holmenkollen
park: 7 Frogner
peninsula: 8 Akershus
street: 14 Karl Johansgate

Osmond, Gilbert
character in: 18 The Portrait of a Lady
author: 5 James

Ossian
character in: 12 Gaelic poetry

ossify 6 harden 7 stiffen 9 fossilize

ossuary 8 boneyard 10 depository, receptacle

ostensible 6 avowed 7 alleged, assumed, feigned, implied, nominal, outward, seeming, surface, titular, visible 8 apparent, declared, illusory, manifest, specious 9 pretended, professed 10 presumable 11 perceivable

ostentation 4 airs, dash, fuss, pomp, ritz, show 5 glitz, gloss, swank 6 splash 7 display, glitter 8 flourish, pretense 9 pageantry, pomposity, showiness, spectacle
French: 7 etalage

ostentatious 4 loud 5 gaudy, showy 6 flashy, florid, garish 7 pompous 8 affected, immodest, overdone 9 grandiose, obtrusive 10 flamboyant, showing off 11 conspicuous, exaggerated, pretentious 15 flaunting wealth

Osterreich *see* 7 Austria

ostracize 3 cut 4 oust, shun, snub 5 avoid, expel 6 banish, disown, reject 7 exclude, shut out 9 blackball, blacklist

Ostwald, Wilhelm
field: 9 chemistry
nationality: 6 German
founded: 17 physical chemistry

O'Sullivan, Maureen
born: 5 Boyle 7 Ireland 15 County Roscommon
daughter: 9 Mia Farrow
roles: 4 Jane (Tarzan movies) 16 David Copperfield 17 Pride and Prejudice 19 Hannah and her Sisters

Otello
also: 7 Othello
opera by: 5 Verdi 7 Rossini

O tempora! O mores! 14 O times! O customs!

Othello
director: 11 Stuart Burge
author: 18 William Shakespeare
character: 4 Iago 6 Cassio, Emilia 9 Desdemona
cast: 11 Frank Finlay, Joyce Redman, Maggie Smith 15 Laurence Olivier

other 4 more 5 added, extra, spare 6 unlike 7 further, reverse 8 contrary, opposite 9 alternate, auxiliary, different, remaining 10 additional, contrasted, dissimilar 11 contrasting 13 contradictory, supplementary 14 differentiated

Other Gods
author: 9 Pearl Buck

Other Side of Midnight, The
author: 13 Sidney Sheldon

other than 3 but 4 save 6 except, saving 7 barring, besides 9 excepting, excluding

otherwise 5 if not 6 or else 9 inversely 10 contrarily 11 differently 12 contrariwise

otherworldly 7 sublime 8 heavenly 9 celestial 14 transcendental

Othin *see* 4 Odin

Othniel 11 Hebrew judge
father: 5 Kenaz
brother: 5 Caleb
wife: 6 Achsah

O times! O customs!
Latin: 14 O tempora! O mores!

Otionia
father: 10 Erechtheus
sister: 10 Protogonia
death by: 9 sacrifice
for victory of: 9 Athenians
over: 11 Eleusinians

otiose 4 idle, lazy 6 futile 7 laggard, resting, useless, worn-out 8 abortive, impotent, inactive, indolent, listless, slothful, sluggish 9 fruitless, lethargic, powerless, somnolent 10 unavailing 11 incompetent, ineffective, inoperative, unrewarding 12 unproductive

Otomi
tribe: 7 Capotec

O'Toole, Peter
born: 7 Ireland 9 Connemara
roles: 6 Becket 7 Creator, Lord Jim 13 Man of La Mancha 14 Goodbye Mr Chips, My Favorite Year, The Last Emperor 15 The Lion in Winter 16 Lawrence of Arabia, What's New Pussycat 18 How to Steal a Millon

O'Trigger, Sir Lucius
character in: 9 The Rivals
author: 8 Sheridan

Ott, Mel
nickname: 9 Boy Wonder 12 Master Melvin
sport: 8 baseball
position: 8 outfield
team: 13 New York Giants

Ottawa
capital of: 6 Canada
early name: 6 Bytown
falls: 6 Rideau 9 Chaudiere
landmark: 18 National Arts Centre 19 Dominion Observatory, Parliament Buildings
river: 6 Ottawa, Rideau 8 Gatineau
university: 8 Carleton

Ottawa
language family: 9 Algonkian 10 Algonquian
location: 4 Ohio 6 Canada, Kansas 7 Ontario 12 Lake Michigan
leader: 7 Pontiac

Otter
origin: 12 Scandinavian
mentioned in: 8 Volsunga
form: 5 otter
father: 8 Hreidmar
killed by: 4 Loki

ottoman, Ottoman 4 seat, Turk 5 couch, divan, stool 7 sultane, Turkish 9 footstool
color: 3 red 9 vermilion
governor: 3 bey, dey 5 pasha
ruler: 5 Osman 8 Suleiman
standard: 4 ale

Otus
form: 5 giant
member of: 7 Aloidae
father: 8 Poseidon
mother: 9 Iphimedia
brother: 9 Ephialtes

Ouagadougou
capital of: 10 Upper Volta 11 Burkina Faso

oui 3 yes

ounce
abbreviation of: 2 oz

ounce troy
abbreviation of: 3 oz t

Our Bill
creator: 14 Harry Haenigsen
character: 6 Walter

Our Crowd
author: 17 Stephen Birmingham

Our Miss Brooks
character: 8 Mrs Davis 12 Connie Brooks, Walter Denton 13 Osgood Conklin, Philip Boynton 14 Harriet Conklin
cast: 8 Eve Arden 10 Dick Crenna, Gale Gordon, Jane Morgan 14 Gloria McMillan, Robert Rockwell
Miss Brooks taught: 7 English
school: 11 Madison High

Our Mutual Friend
author: 14 Charles Dickens
character: 4 Wegg 5 Venus 6 Boffin 11 Bella Wilfer 17 Mortimer Lightwood, Young John Harmon (Handford, Rokesmith)

our sea
Latin: 11 mare nostrum
ancient Roman name for: 13 Mediterranean

Our Town
author: 14 Thornton Wilder
character: 12 Simon Stimson
Gibbs family: 2 Dr 3 Mrs 6 George 7 Rebecca
Webb family: 2 Mr 3 Mrs 5 Emily, Wally
director: 7 Sam Wood
cast: 10 Fay Bainter 11 Martha Scott 13 William Holden

oust 4 fire, sack 5 eject, evict, expel 6 banish, bounce, put out, remove, unseat 7 boot out, cashier, cast out, dismiss, kick out 8 throw out 9 discharge, give the ax 11 give the gate, send packing

ouster 6 firing 7 removal, sacking 8 bouncing, ejection, eviction 9 discharge, dismissal, expelling, expulsion, overthrow 10 banishment, cashiering 11 dislodgment, drumming out, throwing out 13 dispossession

out 2 ex 4 away 5 aloud, eject, forth, not in, passe 6 absent, begone, excuse, public 7 outside 8 exterior, external, revealed 9 in society, in the open, published 10 extinguish

out-and-out 4 pure, sure 5 sheer, total, utter 6 arrant 7 perfect 8 absolute, complete, hardened, outright, positive, thorough 9 confirmed, downright, unlimited 10 inveterate 11 straight out, unequivocal, unmitigated, unqualified 12 unregenerate, unrestricted 13 dyed-in-the-wool, thoroughgoing, unadulterated, unconditional 14 unquestionable

outbrazen 4 dare, defy, face 8 confront 9 challenge, stand up to

outbreak 5 burst 7 display 8 epidemic, eruption, invasion, outburst 9 explosion 10 outpouring 13 demonstration

outbuilding 4 barn, shed 5 privy 6 garage, stable 7 latrine 8 outhouse, woodshed

outburst 5 blast, burst 7 display, thunder 8 eruption, outbreak 9 explosion 10 outpouring 11 fulmination 13 demonstration

outcast 5 exile, rover 6 ousted, outlaw, pariah, roamer 7 refugee, runaway 8 banished, castaway, deportee, derelict, expelled, fugitive, rejected, vagabond 9 discarded 10 expatriate

Outcast of the Islands, The
author: 12 Joseph Conrad

Outcault, R F
creator/artist of: **11** Buster Brown **12** The Yellow Kid

outcome **3** end **5** fruit, issue **6** effect, payoff, result, upshot **9** aftermath, outgrowth **11** aftereffect, consequence

outcry **3** cry **4** howl, roar, yell, yelp, yowl **5** noise, shout, whoop **6** bellow, clamor, hubbub, scream, shriek, uproar **7** clangor, protest, screech **9** commotion, complaint, crying out, hue and cry, objection **10** cry of alarm, hullabaloo **12** caterwauling, remonstrance

outdated **5** passe **7** antique **8** outmoded **9** out-of-date **10** antiquated **12** old-fashioned

outdo **3** top **4** beat, best **5** excel, worst **6** better, defeat, exceed, outfox, outwit **7** eclipse, outplay, outrank, surpass **8** outclass, outshine, outstrip, overcome **9** transcend

outdoor festival
French: **13** fete champetre

outdoor market **5** agora **6** bazaar **10** flea market **11** marketplace

outer **6** distal, remote **7** extreme, farther, outside, outward, without **8** exterior, external, outlying **9** outermost **10** farther out, peripheral

outer edge **3** lip, rim, tip **5** bound **6** margin **8** boundary **9** extremity

Outer Mongolia
also: **24** Mongolian People's Republic
border: **5** China **6** Russia **11** Soviet Union
capital: **4** Urga **5** Kulun **9** Ulan Bator
currency: **5** mongo **6** tugrik
desert: **4** Gobi **5** Shamo
language: **7** Khalka
mountain range: **5** Altai, Altay **7** Khangai

outermost **5** outer **6** utmost **7** extreme, outside, outward, surface **8** exterior, external **11** farthest out, most distant, superficial

outfit **3** fit, rig **4** gear **5** array, dress, equip, getup, habit, rig up **6** clothe, supply **7** appoint, costume, furnish **8** accouter, ensemble, wardrobe **9** equipment, provision, trappings **13** accoutrements, paraphernalia

outflow **5** issue **7** leakage, seepage **8** drainage **9** discharge

outgo **4** beat, cost, exit, pass **5** excel, issue, outdo **6** efflux, egress, outlay, outlet **7** outflow, surpass **8** outstrip **9** departure **11** expenditure

outgoing **4** warm **6** genial, social **7** amiable, cordial, exiting, leaving **8** friendly, going out, outbound, sociable **9** convivial, departing **10** gregarious **11** extroverted, sympathetic, warmhearted

outgoing person **9** extrovert **17** hail-fellow-well-met

outgrowth **3** end **4** knob, knot, node **5** bulge, fruit, issue, shoot **6** result, sequel, sprout, upshot **7** product **8** offshoot **9** aftermath **10** conclusion, projection **11** aftereffect, consequence, culmination, excrescence, outcropping **12** protuberance

outing **4** hike, ride, spin, tour, trip, walk **5** drive, jaunt, tramp **6** airing, junket, ramble **7** holiday **9** excursion **10** expedition

outlander **5** alien, exile **6** emigre **7** invader, settler **8** intruder, newcomer, stranger, wanderer **9** Auslander, barbarian, foreigner, immigrant **10** tramontane **12** ultramontane

outlandish **3** odd **5** kooky, queer, weird **6** far-out **7** bizarre, curious, strange, unusual **8** freakish, peculiar **9** eccentric, fantastic, grotesque, unheard-of **10** incredible, outrageous, ridiculous **12** preposterous, unbelievable, unimaginable, unparalleled **13** inconceivable **14** unconventional

outlast **6** endure, hold on, keep on, remain, stay on **7** carry on, hold out, outstay, outwear, perdure, persist, prevail, survive **8** continue

outlaw **3** ban, bar **4** deny, stop **5** felon **6** bandit, forbid, pariah **7** exclude, outcast **8** criminal, disallow, fugitive, prohibit, suppress **9** desperado, interdict, miscreant, proscribe **10** highwayman

outlay **3** fee **4** cost **5** outgo, price **6** charge **7** expense, payment **8** spending **11** amount spent, expenditure **12** disbursement

outlet **3** way **4** door, duct, exit, gate, path, vent **5** means **6** avenue, egress, escape, portal **7** channel, conduit, gateway, opening, passage

outline **4** plot **5** brief, trace **6** digest, limits, resume, review **7** contour, diagram, profile, summary, tracing **8** abstract, synopsis **9** blueprint, delineate, lineation, perimeter, periphery, sketch out **10** abridgment, silhouette **11** delineation **12** condensation
French: **6** apercu

outlook **4** view **5** scene, sight, vista **6** aspect, chance **7** picture, promise **8** attitude, forecast, panorama, prospect **9** spectacle, viewpoint **10** assumption **11** expectation, frame of mind, perspective, point of view, presumption, probability **12** anticipation

outlying **5** outer, rural **6** far-off, remote **7** distant, exurban **8** exterior, suburban **10** peripheral

outmoded **5** corny, dated, passe, tired **6** demode, old hat **7** antique, archaic, vintage **8** obsolete, old-timey, outdated **9** out-of-date **10** antiquated **12** old-fashioned, out-of-fashion **14** behind the times
French: **6** demode

Out of Africa
director: **13** Sydney Pollack
cast: **11** Meryl Streep (Baroness Karen Blixen, Isak Dinesen) **13** Robert Redford (Denys Finch Hatton) **19** Klaus Maria Brandauer (Baron Bror von Blixen)

out of bed **2** up **5** astir **9** up and at 'em **10** on one's feet, up and about **12** rise and shine

out-of-date **5** dated, passe **8** outmoded **10** antiquated **12** old-fashioned
French: **6** demode

out of doors **3** out **5** forth **6** abroad **7** outside **8** alfresco **12** in the open air

out-of-fashion **5** passe **8** obsolete, outmoded **9** out-of-date **12** old-fashioned
French: **6** demode

out of hand **4** wild **5** rowdy **6** unruly **10** disorderly **12** obstreperous, out of control, unmanageable, unrestrained **14** uncontrollable

out of keeping **8** atypical, peculiar, unseemly **9** anomalous, irregular **11** incongruous **12** inconsistent **13** inappropriate

out of kilter **4** awry **5** askew **6** uneven **7** crooked, oblique

out of line **6** unruly **9** excessive **10** exorbitant **12** presumptuous, unreasonable

out of many one
Latin: **13** e pluribus unum
motto of: **12** United States

out of one's head **3** mad **4** daft, nuts **5** crazy, nutty **6** insane **7** cracked, touched **8** demented, deranged, unhinged **10** unbalanced **12** mad as a hatter, off his rocker **15** mad as a March hare **17** nutty as a fruitcake

out of operation **4** dead, down **8** inactive **10** not working, out of order **11** inoperative

out of order **5** amiss **6** faulty **10** not working **11** inoperative, uncalled-for **13** inappropriate

out of place **3** odd **8** unseemly **10** unsuitable **11** incongruous, inconsonant **13** inappropriate

out of shape **4** bent **5** unfit **6** flabby, warped **7** crooked **8** deformed **9** distorted, untrained

out of sorts **5** cross, huffy, testy **6** crabby, cranky, touchy **7** bearish, grouchy, peevish **8** petulant, snappish **9** crotchety, irritable **10** ill-humored **11** ill-tempered **12** cantankerous **13** short-tempered

out of the books of
Latin: **8** ex libris

out of the fight
French: **12** hors de combat

out of the ordinary **4** rare **6** unique **7** notable, unusual **8** singular, uncommon **10** phenomenal, remarkable **11** exceptional **13** extraordinary

Out of the Past
director: **15** Jacques Tourneur
based on novel by: **13** Geoffrey Homes (Daniel Mainwaring) (Build My Gallows High)
cast: **9** Jane Greer **11** Kirk Douglas, Richard Webb **13** Rhonda Fleming, Robert Mitchum

out of touch **7** mixed-up **8** unstable **11** disoriented **12** out of contact **13** incommunicado

out-of-towner **7** tourist, visitor **9** sojourner, transient **11** nonresident

outpace **4** pass **5** outdo **6** exceed, outrun **8** outstrip

outpouring **6** deluge **7** barrage, gushing, outflow **8** effusion

output **4** crop, gain, take **5** yield **6** profit **7** harvest, produce, product, reaping, turnout **8** gleaning, proceeds **9** gathering **10** production **11** achievement **12** productivity **14** accomplishment

outrage **4** evil, gall, rile **5** anger, shock, wrong **6** arouse, enrage, insult, madden, offend, ruffle **7** affront, incense, provoke, steam up **8** atrocity, disquiet, enormity, iniquity **9** barbarity, indignity, infuriate **10** discompose, disrespect, exasperate, gross crime, scandalize **11** desecration, monstrosity, profanation **13** barbarousness, get one's back up, make one see red, slap in the face, transgression **17** make one's blood boil

outraged **3** mad **5** angry, irate, riled **6** fuming, raging **7** enraged, furious **8** incensed, inflamed, offended **9** affronted, indignant **10** displeased, infuriated

outrageous **4** base, foul, rank, rude, vile **5** gross **6** brutal, odious, wicked **7** abusive, extreme, galling, heinous, immense, inhuman **8** enormous, flagrant, inhumane, insolent, scornful, shocking **9** atrocious, barbarous, excessive, insulting, maddening, monstrous, nefarious, offensive, shameless **10** despicable, exorbitant, horrifying, immoderate, iniquitous, scandalous **11** disgraceful, infuriating, unspeakable, unwarranted **12** contemptible, contemptuous, exasperating, preposterous, unreasonable **13** disrespectful, reprehensible **14** unconscionable

outrageousness **8** enormity **9** immensity **10** wickedness **13** atrociousness, monstrousness, offensiveness **16** preposterousness

outre **8** improper

outreach **6** exceed **7** surpass

outright **4** full **5** sheer, total, utter **6** at once, entire, openly **7** utterly, visibly **8** absolute, complete, entirely, patently, promptly, thorough **9** downright, forthwith, instantly, on the spot, out-and-out **10** absolutely, altogether, completely, manifestly, thoroughly, unreserved **11** immediately, unmitigated, unqualified **12** demonstrably, undiminished **13** thoroughgoing, unconditional

outrival **3** dim **5** excel, outdo **6** exceed **7** eclipse, surpass **8** outshine **9** transcend **10** overshadow, tower above

outrush **4** gust **8** overflow

outset **4** dawn **5** birth, start **7** dawning **9** beginning, departure, threshold **12** commencement

outshine **3** dim **5** excel, outdo **6** exceed **7** eclipse, surpass **9** transcend **10** overshadow

outside **4** case, face, skin **5** alien, faint, outer **6** facade, remote, sheath, slight **7** coating, distant, foreign, obscure, outdoor, outward, strange, surface **8** covering, exterior, external, outdoors **9** nonnative, outer side, outermost **10** extraneous, out-of-doors, unfamiliar

outsider **5** alien **7** outcast **8** onlooker, stranger **9** bystander, foreigner, nonmember **14** nonparticipant

outskirts **3** rim **4** edge **6** limits, verges **7** borders, fringes, margins, suburbs **8** environs **9** periphery, precincts **10** perimeters **11** extremities

outspoken **5** blunt, frank **6** candid, direct, honest **7** artless **9** guileless, ingenuous, unsparing **10** forthright, unreserved **11** opinionated, plainspoken **13** undissembling **15** straightforward, undissimulating

outspread **5** broad **6** opened, spread **7** laid out **8** expanded, extended, unfolded, unfurled, unrolled **9** spread out, stretched **12** outstretched

outstanding **3** due **5** famed, great, owing **6** famous, unpaid **7** eminent, notable, payable **8** foremost, renowned, striking **9** best known, exemplary, in arrears, marvelous, memorable, prominent, unsettled **10** celebrated, noteworthy, phenomenal, remarkable **11** exceptional, magnificent, uncollected **13** distinguished, extraordinary, unforgettable

outstrip **4** pass **6** exceed, outrun **7** outpace, surpass **11** leave behind

outward **5** outer **7** evident, outside, surface, visible **8** apparent, exterior, external, manifest **10** observable, ostensible **11** perceivable, perceptible, superficial

outward appearance 4 mien **6** aspect, facade, manner **7** bearing **8** demeanor, exterior

Outward Bound
author: 10 Sutton Vane

outwardly 7 clearly, visibly **9** evidently, seemingly **10** apparently, manifestly, ostensibly **13** on the face of it **16** to all appearances

outwards 3 out **4** away

outweigh 6 exceed **7** eclipse, surpass **8** override **9** rise above **10** overshadow **11** predominate, prevail over **13** be heavier than, weigh more than

outwit 4 dupe, foil, fool, trap **5** trick **6** baffle, outfox, take in, thwart **7** ensnare **8** outsmart **9** get around **10** circumvent **11** outmaneuver

outworn 5 dated, passe **6** bygone **7** defunct, disused, extinct **8** obsolete, rejected **9** abandoned, discarded, forgotten, out-of-date **10** antiquated, superseded **12** old-fashioned **13** unfashionable

ouzo
type: 7 liqueur
origin: 6 Greece
flavor: 5 anise
substitute for: 8 absinthe

oval 5 ovate, ovoid **6** curved, ovular **7** obovate, oviform, rounded **9** egg-shaped **10** elliptical **11** ellipsoidal

ovation 6 cheers, homage, hurrah, hurray, huzzah **7** acclaim, fanfare, tribute **8** applause, cheering **9** adulation **11** acclamation

oven 3 umu **4** kiln, oast **5** baker, range, stove **6** hearth **7** broiler, chamber, kitchen, roaster
clay: 7 tandoor
fork: 7 fruggan, fruggin
mop: 6 scovel

over 3 too **4** also, anew, done, else, gone, past **5** above, again, ended, extra, often **6** afresh, bygone, lapsed, no more, to boot **7** at an end, elapsed, expired, settled, surplus **8** finished, in excess, once more, too great **9** completed, concluded, excessive, remaining **10** additional, all through, in addition, passed away, repeatedly, terminated **11** a second time, superfluous

overabundance 4 glut **6** excess **7** surfeit, surplus **8** plethora **9** abundance, profusion **10** oversupply **11** superfluity **14** superabundance **15** supersaturation **21** embarrassment of riches
French: 19 embarras de richesses

over again 4 anew **5** again **7** all over **8** once more **9** once again

overall 5 total **6** entire **7** general **8** complete, long-term, sweeping **9** extensive, long-range, panoramic **10** exhaustive, widespread **12** all-embracing, all-inclusive **13** comprehensive, thoroughgoing

over-and-above 5 added, extra **7** added on, besides **10** additional, in addition **13** supplementary

overawe 6 dazzle **9** overpower, overwhelm **10** intimidate

overbalance 5 upset **6** topple **8** outweigh

overbearing 5 cocky **6** lordly, snooty **7** haughty, high-hat, pompous, stuck-up **8** arrogant, despotic, egoistic **9** conceited, imperious, know-it-all **10** autocratic, disdainful, egoistical, high-handed, tyrannical **11** dictatorial, domineering, egotistical **13** high-and-mighty, self-assertive, self-important

overburden 3 tax **4** load, task, tire **5** whelm **7** exhaust, wear out **8** encumber, overwork, surcharge **9** overwhelm

overcast 4 dark, dull, gray, hazy **5** foggy, misty, murky **6** cloudy, dreary, gloomy, leaden **7** sunless **8** lowering **11** overclouded, threatening

overcharge 3 gyp, pad **4** rook, skin, soak **5** bleed, cheat, gouge, stick, sting, usury **6** extort, fleece **7** exploit **10** exaggerate

overcoat 3 mac **5** parka **6** duster, poncho, raglan, tabard, ulster **7** oilskin, paletot, topcoat **8** burberry, mackinaw **9** greatcoat, inverness, pea jacket **10** mackintosh, trenchcoat **12** chesterfield, Prince Albert

Overcoat, The
author: 12 Nikolai Gogol
character: 9 Petrovich **26** A Certain Important Personage **28** Akakii Akakiievich Bashmachkin

overcome 4 beat, best, lick **5** crush, quell **6** defeat, master, subdue **7** conquer, put down, survive, win over **8** suppress, surmount, vanquish **9** overpower, overthrow, overwhelm, transcend **11** prevail over, triumph over **14** get the better of

overconfident 5 brash **6** cheeky **8** arrogant, cocksure, egoistic, immodest, impudent **9** conceited **10** egoistical **11** egotistical, self-assured **12** presumptuous

overcrowd 3 jam **4** cram, fill, pack **5** stuff **7** congest

overcrowded 6 filled, jammed, packed **7** crammed, stuffed **9** congested, jampacked

overdecorated 5 gaudy, showy **6** flashy, garish **9** unsightly **12** ostentatious

overdelicacy 11 genteelness, prudishness **12** priggishness **14** overrefinement

overdo 4 gild **6** expand **7** amplify, ham it up, magnify, overact **8** overplay **9** embroider, overstate **10** do to excess, exaggerate **11** carry too far, hyperbolize **12** lay it on thick **13** stretch a point

overdue 4 late, slow **5** tardy **7** belated, delayed, past due **8** dilatory **10** behindhand, behind time, unpunctual **11** long delayed

overdue debt 7 arrears **10** balance due **18** balance outstanding

overflow 4 glut **5** flood **6** excess **7** run over, surplus **8** flow over, inundate, plethora, slop over **9** overspill, profusion **10** overspread, oversupply **11** copiousness, superfluity **13** overabundance **14** superabundance

overflowing 4 full **5** flush **7** replete, swamped **8** abundant, flooding **9** abounding, inundated **11** running over

overgarment 4 cape, coat, robe **5** cloak, habit, parka, shawl, smock **6** blazer, blouse, duster, jacket, kimono, mantle, poncho **7** sweater, topcoat, wrapper **8** cardigan, raincoat **9** gaberdine, housecoat

overgrown 4 rank **5** giant **7** blown-up **8** colossal, enlarged, forested, gigantic **9** luxuriant, oversized

overhang 3 jut **4** eave **5** bulge, drape, eaves, jetty **6** beetle, impend, sadden, shelve **7** project, suspend **8** protrude, threaten **9** projection

overhaul 4 beat, pass **5** catch **6** revamp **7** rebuild, remodel, restore, service **8** overtake, renovate **11** catch up with, recondition, reconstruct

overhead **3** nut **4** atop, roof **5** above, aloft, on top, upper **6** upward **7** ceiling, topmost, up above **8** superior **9** overlying, uppermost **11** overhanging

overindulge **4** baby **5** spoil, stuff **6** overdo, pamper, pig out **7** carouse, overeat **9** dissipate **11** mollycoddle

overjoyed **6** elated, joyous **8** ecstatic, euphoric, exultant, jubilant, thrilled **9** delighted, enchanted, exuberant, gratified **10** enraptured, enthralled **11** carried away, tickled pink, transported **12** happy as a lark

overlay **4** coat **5** cover, layer **6** carpet, veneer **7** blanket, coating **8** covering **11** superimpose

overload **3** tax **4** glut **5** flood, whelm **6** deluge, excess **7** burnout, surfeit **8** encumber **9** innundate, surcharge

overlook **4** miss, omit, skip **6** excuse, forget, give on, ignore, pass up, slight, survey, wink at **7** blink at, command, forgive, let ride, neglect **8** leave out, look over, pass over, shrug off **9** disregard, look out on **10** tower above **11** forget about, have a view of, leave undone

overlord **4** czar, tsar **7** emperor, monarch **8** autocrat **12** supreme ruler **13** absolute ruler

overly **3** too **4** very **6** highly, unduly **7** acutely, too much **8** overmuch, severely, to a fault, unfairly **9** extremely, intensely **10** needlessly **11** exceedingly, excessively **12** exorbitantly, immoderately, inordinately, unreasonably **18** disproportionately

overly trusting **5** naive **8** gullible **9** credulous **12** unsuspicious

overmodest **3** coy **4** prim **7** prudish **8** priggish **11** puritanical

overmuch **3** too **6** excess **7** surplus **8** plethora **9** profusion

overpass **4** span **6** bridge **9** crossover

overpower **4** beat, best, move, sway **5** crush, quell, worst **6** defeat, master, subdue **7** conquer **8** overcome, vanquish **9** influence, overwhelm

overpowering **6** mighty, strong **8** crushing **10** astounding **12** overwhelming

overpraise **4** line **7** blarney, fawning **8** flattery **11** fulsomeness

overpriced **6** costly **7** too high **9** expensive **10** exorbitant

overproud **4** vain **8** arrogant, egoistic **9** conceited **10** egoistical **11** egotistical, swell-headed **13** self-important

overrate **9** overprize, overvalue **10** overesteem, overpraise **12** overestimate **13** make too much of

overrefined **7** genteel, prudish **8** priggish **12** overdelicate

override **5** crush, quash **7** reverse **8** set aside **10** commission **11** countermand

overrule **4** deny, veto **5** annul, eject, repel, waive **6** cancel, refuse, reject, revoke **7** dismiss, nullify, outvote **8** disallow, outweigh, override, overturn, preclude, set aside, throw out **9** repudiate **10** invalidate **11** countermand

overrun **4** loot, raid, sack **5** choke **6** deluge, engulf, infest, invade **7** despoil, pillage, plunder, surplus **8** inundate, overgrow, pour in on, rove over **9** overwhelm, surge over, swarm over

overseas, oversea **5** alien **6** abroad, exotic **7** foreign **8** external **11** ultramarine **12** transoceanic **14** in foreign lands

oversee **3** run **4** boss, rule **5** guide, pilot, see to, steer, watch **6** direct, govern, handle, manage **7** carry on, command **8** attend to, overlook, regulate **9** supervise **10** administer **11** keep an eye on, preside over, superintend **12** have charge of

overseeing **7** bossing, guiding, running **8** guidance, handling, managing **10** leadership, management **11** attending to, supervising, supervision **13** administering **14** administrating, administration, superintending **15** superintendence

overseer **4** boss, head **5** chief **7** captain, foreman, manager **8** director, governor **10** supervisor, taskmaster **11** slave driver **13** administrator **14** superintendent

overshadow **3** fog **4** hide, mask, veil **5** cover, dwarf, shade **6** darken, screen, shroud **7** conceal, eclipse, obscure **8** outshine **9** tower over

overshadowing **7** eclipse, masking, shading, veiling **8** cloaking **9** darkening, eclipsing, obscuring **10** concealing, surpassing **11** concealment, obscuration **12** towering over

overshoe **3** gum **4** boot **6** arctic, gaiter, galosh, patten, rubber **7** galoshe

overshoot **4** pass **6** exceed, go over **8** go beyond

oversight **6** laxity, slight **7** blunder, mistake, neglect **8** omission **9** disregard **10** negligence **11** inattention **12** carelessness, heedlessness, inadvertence **13** careless error **14** neglectfulness **15** thoughtlessness

oversized **4** huge, vast **7** immense, mammoth **8** colossal, enormous, gigantic **10** monumental **14** Brobdingnagian

overspending **12** extravagance, throwing away

overspread **3** fog **4** coat, fill, pave **5** bathe, cloud, cover, paint, plate, smear **6** clothe, infest **7** blanket, diffuse, overlay, overrun, pervade, suffuse **8** disperse **9** whitewash

overstate **6** overdo, play up **7** enlarge, inflate, lay it on, magnify, stretch, touch up **8** increase, overdraw, oversell **9** embellish, embroider, enlarge on, overpaint **10** exaggerate, overstress **15** spread it on thick

overstep **6** exceed **7** violate **10** transgress

oversupply **4** glut **6** excess **7** surfeit, surplus, too much **8** plethora **11** undue amount **13** overabundance **14** superabundance

overt **4** open **5** plain **6** public **7** evident, obvious, visible **8** apparent, manifest, palpable, revealed **10** easily seen, noticeable, observable, ostensible **11** perceivable, perceptible, unconcealed, undisguised

overtake **4** go by, pass **5** catch, reach **6** befall, gain on **7** run down **8** approach, overhaul **11** catch up with

overtax **4** tire **5** abuse, hoist **6** burden, exceed, strain, stress **7** exhaust **8** overload, overwork **9** misemploy **10** overburden

over the hill **3** old **4** aged **5** aging **7** elderly **11** past the peak **13** past one's prime

overthrow **4** undo **5** crush **6** defeat, mutiny, topple

7 abolish, undoing 8 downfall, overcome, overturn, toppling 9 abolition, bring down, overpower, rebellion 10 do away with, revolution

overtire 3 fag 4 bush, do in, poop 5 drain 7 exhaust, fatigue, wear out 8 enervate

overtone 3 hue 4 hint 5 drift 8 coloring, innuendo 10 intimation, suggestion 11 connotation, implication, insinuation

overtrustful 8 gullible 9 credulous 12 unsuspecting, unsuspicious 13 unquestioning

overture 3 bid 6 motion, signal, tender 7 advance, gesture, preface, prelude 8 approach, foreword, offering, preamble, prologue, proposal 9 beginning 10 invitation, suggestion 11 opening move, proposition 12 introduction

overturn 4 beat, oust 5 crush, upend, upset 6 defeat, depose, thrash, topple 7 capsize, conquer, turn out 8 overcome, push over, vanquish 9 knock down, knock over, overpower, overthrow, overwhelm 14 turn topsy-turvy, turn upside down

overturning
French: 14 bouleversement

overweening 5 bossy, cocky, pushy 6 brassy 7 haughty, pompous 8 arrogant, egoistic 9 bigheaded, imperious 10 disdainful, egoistical, highhanded, immoderate 11 domineering, egotistical, overbearing, patronizing 12 presumptuous 13 high-and-mighty, overconfident, self-important

overweight 3 fat 5 dumpy, fatty, gross, hefty, obese, piggy, plump, pudgy, stout, tubby 6 chubby, chunky, fleshy, portly, rotund 7 fattish, well-fed 8 roly-poly 9 corpulent 10 potbellied, well-padded 11 beer-bellied, overstuffed 15 well-upholstered

overwhelm 4 beat, bury 5 crush, quash, quell, swamp 6 defeat, engulf 7 conquer, overrun, stagger 8 bowl over, confound, inundate, overcome, vanquish 9 devastate, overpower, overthrow, subjugate

overwhelming 8 crushing 10 staggering 11 astonishing, devastating 12 overpowering

overwork 3 tax 4 task, tire, toil 5 labor 6 burden, strain 7 exhaust, overtax, wear out 9 misemploy 10 overburden

overwrought 4 wild 5 riled 6 touchy, uneasy 7 excited, nervous, ruffled 8 agitated, frenzied, inflamed, wild-eyed, worked up 9 perturbed, wrought up 10 distracted, high-strung 11 carried away, overexcited

Ovid
author of: 6 Amores 7 Tristia 8 Heroides 11 Ars Amatoria 12 The Art of Love 13 Metamorphoses

ovule 3 egg, nit 4 germ, ovum 6 embryo 7 seedlet

ovum 3 egg 4 cell, germ, seed 5 spore 6 gamete 8 oosphere

owe 8 be in debt 11 be obligated 12 be beholden to, be indebted to

owed 3 due 5 owing 6 unpaid 9 in arrears 11 outstanding

Owen Marshall, Counselor at Law
character: 11 Jess Brandon 12 Frieda Krause 15 Melissa Marshall
cast: 9 Lee Majors 10 Arthur Hill 11 Joan Darling 17 Christine Matchett

owing 3 due 4 owed 6 unpaid 9 in arrears 11 outstanding

own 4 avow, have, hold, keep, tell 5 admit, allow, grant, yield 6 assent, concur, retain 7 concede, possess, private 8 disclose, maintain, personal 9 acquiesce, confess to, consent to, recognize 10 individual, particular 11 acknowledge

owner 6 holder, master 7 partner 8 landlady, landlord, mistress 9 copartner, landowner, possessor 10 landholder, proprietor 11 householder, titleholder 12 proprietress

own up to 5 admit 6 accept 7 confess 8 blurt out 9 recognize 11 acknowledge 14 come clean about

ox 3 oaf 4 bull, clod, musk, urus, zebu 5 aiver, beast, bison, gayal, steer 6 auroch, bantin, bovine 7 banteng, buffalo 10 clodhopper
Cambodian: 7 Kouprey, Kouproh
Celebesian: 3 goa, noa 4 anoa
extinct: 4 urus 7 aurochs
family: 7 bovidae
genus: 3 bos
horned: 4 reem
hornless: 4 moil
Indian: 4 gaur
Paul Bunyan's: 4 Babe
color: 4 blue
stall: 4 crib
team: 4 yoke
Tibetan: 3 yak
wild: 3 ure 4 anoa
young: 4 stot 5 stirk

Ox-Bow Incident, The
author: 21 Walter Van Tilburg Clark
character: 5 Canby, Croft 6 Davies, Gerald, Martin, Tetley 9 Gil Carter
director: 14 William Wellman
cast: 10 Henry Fonda 11 Dana Andrews 12 Anthony Quinn 13 William Blythe 14 Mary Beth Hughes

oxen
group of: 4 yoke

oxide 8 compound
afterburn: 4 calx
calcium: 4 calx, lime
cobalt: 6 zaffer, zaffre
element: 6 oxygen
iron: 4 rust 8 hematite, limonite 9 colcothar, magnetite
make by heat: 7 calcine
sodium: 4 soda
zinc: 6 cadmia

oxidize 4 burn, char, rust 7 corrode

Oxyderces
epithet of: 6 Athena
means: 10 bright-eyed

oxygen
chemical symbol: 1 O

Oxylus
origin: 8 Aetolian
punishment: 5 exile
chosen leader of: 10 Heraclidae
led invasion of: 12 Peloponnesus

oyez 4 hear 6 attend
cry used by: 10 court crier
preceded: 12 proclamation

Ozark Jubilee
host: 8 Red Foley 10 Webb Pierce
theme: 12 Sugarfoot Rag

Ozark State
nickname of: 8 Missouri

Ozick, Cynthia
author of: 10 Levitation 17 The Cannibal Galaxy 21 The Messiah of Stockholm

Ozzie and Harriet, The Adventures of
cast: 11 David Nelson, Ozzie Nelson, Ricky (Eric) Nelson 13 Harriet Nelson

pa **3** dad, paw, pop **4** papa **5** daddy **6** father
mate: **2** ma

pace **4** clip, flow, gait, rate, step, walk **5** amble, speed, tread **6** motion, stride, stroll **7** saunter **8** momentum, slow gait, velocity

Pacelli, Eugenio Maria Giuseppe Giovanni **11** Pope Pius XII

pachyderm **5** hippo, rhino **8** elephant, ungulate **10** rhinoceros **12** hippopotamus
characteristic: **4** tusk **5** ivory, trunk **12** thick-skinned
prehistoric: **7** mammoth **8** mastodon

pachydermatous **4** hard **5** horny, tough **7** callous **8** callused, hardened, leathery **12** thick-skinned **13** elephant-hided

pacific **4** calm **5** quiet, still **6** gentle, placid, serene, smooth **7** halcyon, restful **8** dovelike, peaceful, tranquil **9** pacifying, peaceable, reposeful, unruffled **10** harmonious, untroubled **11** inoffensive, undisturbed **12** conciliatory

pacification **8** soothing **11** appeasement, peacemaking **12** conciliation, nonagression **14** reconciliation

pacify **4** calm **5** allay, quiet **6** soothe **7** appease, assuage, compose, mollify, placate **9** reconcile **10** conciliate, propitiate

Pacino, Al
real name: **13** Alberto Pacino
born: **9** New York NY
roles: **7** Serpico **8** Scarface **12** Author Author, The Godfather **15** Dog Day Afternoon, Michael Corleone **16** And Justice for All

pack **3** box, jam, kit, lot, mob, set, tie **4** bevy, bind, cram, fill, heap, herd, load, mass **5** batch, bunch, clump, covey, crowd, drove, flock, group, horde, stuff, swarm, truss **6** bundle, gaggle, gather, packet, parcel, passel, throng **7** cluster, package **8** assemble **9** container, multitude **10** assortment, collection, miscellany **12** accumulation

package **3** box, kit **4** case, pack, wrap **6** bundle, carton, encase, packet, parcel, wrap up **9** container, wrappings

packed **4** full **6** filled, jammed, loaded, massed, rammed, wedged **7** crammed, crowded, crushed, pressed, stuffed **8** overfull, squeezed **10** sandwiched **11** overcrowded

packet **3** bag, box **4** bale, pack, roll **5** pouch, sheaf **6** bundle, parcel, quiver **7** package

pack closely **4** cram, pack **5** press, stuff **7** compact **8** compress

pact **4** bond **6** treaty **7** compact **8** alliance, contract, covenant **9** agreement, concordat **10** convention **11** concordance **13** understanding

pad **3** mat **4** fill **5** stuff **6** blow up, fatten, tablet **7** bolster, cushion, inflate, protect, puff out **8** mattress, notebook **9** upholster **10** cushioning, stretch out

padding **6** filler, lining **7** filling, packing, surfeit, surplus, wadding **8** stuffing, verbiage, wrapping **9** prolixity, verbosity, wordiness **10** redundancy **11** verboseness **12** extravagance **14** superabundance

Paderewski, Ignace (Ignacy Jan)
born: **6** Poland **9** Kurilowka
composer of: **5** Manru **9** Minuet in G

pad out **5** add to **6** expand, extend **7** amplify, augment, enlarge, stretch **8** elongate, increase, lengthen

padre **6** cleric, father, priest **8** chaplain **9** clergyman

paean **6** anthem, eulogy **7** hosanna **9** laudation, panegyric **10** hallelujah **11** acclamation **12** hymn of praise
form: **4** hymn, song
characteristic: **6** joyful **12** thanksgiving

Paeon
form: **3** god
position: **9** physician
served gods of: **7** Olympia
corresponds to: **6** Apollo

Paeonia
epithet of: **6** Athena
means: **6** healer

Paezan
language family: **13** Macro-Chibchan
group: **4** Paez **5** Choco **6** Warrau **8** Colorado

pagan **7** atheist, heathen, infidel **8** idolator **9** barbarian **10** heathenish, idolatrous, polytheist, unbeliever **11** nonbeliever **12** polytheistic

Paganini, Niccolo
born: **5** Genoa, Italy
played: **6** violin
composer of: **19** The Carnival of Venice

page **3** boy, lad **4** beep, call, girl, leaf **5** folio, groom, sheet, youth **6** knight, number, summon **7** callboy, contact **8** announce **9** attendant, messenger **10** apprentice, manservant
blank: **7** flyleaf
left-hand: **5** verso
right-hand: **5** recto

Page, Geraldine
born: **12** Kirksville MO
husband: **7** Rip Torn

roles: **5** Hondo **9** Interiors **11** Pete-n-Tillie **14** Summer and Smoke **16** A Trip to Bountiful (Oscar), Sweet Bird of Youth

Page and Mistress Page
characters in: **22** The Merry Wives of Windsor
author: **11** Shakespeare

pageant **4** pomp, rite, show **6** parade, ritual **7** display **8** ceremony **9** spectacle **10** exhibition, procession **12** extravaganza

pageantry **4** pomp, rite, show **5** drama, flair **6** ritual, splash **7** display, glitter, pageant **8** ceremony, grandeur, splendor **9** showiness, spectacle, theatrics **10** flashiness **11** ostentation **12** extravagance, magnificence

Paget, James
field: **7** surgery **8** medicine
nationality: **7** British
founder of: **9** pathology

Pagliacci, I
also: **9** The Clowns
opera by: **11** Leoncavallo
character: **5** Canio, Nedda, Tonio **6** Silvio

Pagnol, Marcel
author of: **5** Cesar, Fanny **6** Marius, Topaze

Pago Pago
capital of: **13** American Samoa

Paige, Leroy
nickname: **7** Satchel
sport: **8** baseball
position: **7** pitcher

pain **3** vex, woe **4** ache, gall, hell, hurt, pang, rile **5** agony, annoy, chafe, grief, pinch, pique, smart, sting, throb, worry **6** aching, grieve, harass, misery, ordeal, sadden, sorrow, stitch, twinge **7** agonize, anguish, disturb, hurting, malaise, sadness, torment, torture, trouble **8** distress, smarting, soreness **9** displease, heartache, suffering **10** affliction, discomfort, exasperate, heartbreak **11** unhappiness **12** wretchedness

Paine, Thomas
author of: **9** The Crisis **11** Common Sense **14** The Rights of Man

painful **3** sad **4** dire **5** sharp **6** aching, dismal, dreary, trying **7** arduous, hurtful, racking **8** grievous, grueling, pathetic, piercing, smarting, stinging, very sore **9** agonizing, difficult, sorrowful, throbbing, torturous **10** afflictive, disturbing, lamentable, unpleasant **11** disquieting, distasteful, distressful, distressing **12** disagreeable, excruciating

pain in the neck **4** bane **6** bother **7** torment **8** headache, nuisance **9** annoyance **10** affliction

painstaking **5** fussy **7** careful, earnest, finicky, precise **8** diligent, exacting, thorough **9** assiduous, energetic, strenuous **10** meticulous, scrupulous **11** industrious, persevering, punctilious **13** conscientious, thoroughgoing

paint **4** coat, daub, draw, limn, swab, tint **5** adorn, brush, color, cover, horse, rouge, shade, stain **6** depict, enamel, makeup, opaque, sketch **7** pigment, portray, stipple, touch up **8** cosmetic, decorate, describe, variegate **9** delineate, represent

Painted Bird, The
author: **13** Jerzy Kosinski

painter **6** artist, drawer **8** sketcher **9** old master **10** delineator **11** illustrator, landscapist, miniaturist **13** watercolorist

Painter, Painter's Easel
constellation of: **6** Pictor

painting **3** art, oil **5** draft, mural, piece **6** canvas, design, tablet **7** cartoon, daubing, drawing, graphic, picture, tableau **8** panorama, portrait, seascape **9** depiction, landscape, still life **10** cerography, watercolor **11** perspective **12** illustration
colloidal: **7** tempera
method: **9** encaustic
on plaster: **5** secco **6** fresco
one-color: **8** monotint **10** monochrome
opaque: **7** gouache
religious: **5** Pieta
style: **5** genre
tool: **5** brush, easel, knife **6** canvas, roller, sponge **7** palette **8** spraygun

pair **3** duo **4** dyad, mate, span, team, yoke **5** brace, match, unite **6** couple **7** combine, doublet, match up, pair off, twosome

pair off **10** go two by two **11** form couples

Paiute
language family: **10** Shoshonean
tribe: **12** Mono-Paviosto, Snake Indians **13** Digger Indians **14** Northern Paiute, Southern Paiute
location: **4** Utah **5** Idaho **6** Nevada, Oregon **7** Arizona **10** California

Pakistan ***see box***

Pakula, Alan
director of: **19** All the President's Men

pal **4** chum, mate, pard **5** buddy, crony **6** cohort, friend **7** comrade, partner **8** alter ego, intimate, sidekick **9** associate, colleague, companion, confidant **10** accomplice, bosom buddy **13** boon companion

palace **5** villa **6** castle **7** chateau, mansion **8** hacienda
French: **6** palais
Italian: **7** palazzo

Palaeoscincus
type: **8** dinosaur **10** ornithopod
location: **12** North America
period: **10** Cretaceous

palais **6** palace **17** municipal building **18** government building

Palamedes
lieutenant of: **9** Agamemnon

pal around **7** consort, hang out **9** associate, be friends, run around **10** fraternize

palatable **5** tasty **6** savory **8** pleasant **9** agreeable, toothsome **10** appetizing

palatial **4** posh, rich **5** grand, noble, plush, regal, ritzy, showy **6** swanky **7** elegant, opulent, stately **8** imposing, splendid **9** grandiose, luxurious, sumptuous **10** monumental **11** magnificent

palaver **3** gab **4** chat, talk **5** prate **6** confer, gossip, parley **7** consult, discuss, prattle **8** chitchat, idle talk **10** chew the fat, chew the rag, conference, discussion

palazzo **6** palace

pale **3** pen, wan **4** fold, post **5** ashen, close, light, pasty, stake, white **6** anemic, blanch, paling, pallid, picket, sallow, whiten **7** closure, confine, deathly, ghastly, upright, whitish **8** bleached, palisade **9** bloodless, colorless, deathlike, enclosure, ghostlike **10** ash-colored, cadaverous, light-toned

Pale Horse, Pale Rider
author: **19** Katherine Anne Porter

paleness **6** pallor **7** wanness **8** dullness **9** whiteness **13** colorlessness

Pakistan
name means: 13 Land of the Holy, Land of the Pure
capital: 9 Islamabad
largest city: 7 Karachi
others: 3 Dir, Sui **4** Mari, Sidi **5** Dacca, Qasim, Ralat **6** Chalna, Khulna, Lahore, Multan, Quetta **7** Larkana, Sialkot **8** Jamalpur, Lyallpur, Peshawar, Sargodha **9** Hyderabad **10** Gujranwala, Rawalpindi
school: 9 U of Punjab **10** U of Karachi **12** U of Hyderabad **16** Allama Iqbal Open U **22** Pakistan U of Agriculture **39** Pakistan Institute of International Affairs
division: 3 Dir **4** Sind, Swat **5** Hunza, Kalat **6** Bengal, Kharan, Punjab **7** Chitral **8** Khairpur, Peshawar **10** Bahawalpur, Waziristan **11** Baluchistan
empire: **5** Gupta, Mogul **6** Kushan, Maurya **7** British, Magadha
seceded state: **10** Bangladesh
monetary unit: 4 anna, pice **5** paisa, rupee
weight: 4 seer, tola **5** maund
mountain: 3 Pab, Pub **4** Salt **6** Makran **7** Kirthar **8** Himalaya, Safed Koh, Sulaiman **9** Hindu Kush, Karakoram **11** Makran Coast **13** Central Makran **14** Takht-i-Sulaiman
highest point: 9 Tirich Mir **12** Godwin Austin
river: 3 Nal **4** Bado, Beas, Ravi, Swat, Zhob **5** Dasht, Indus, Kabul **6** Chenab, Ganges, Jamuna, Jhelum, Kundar, Porali, Sutlej **7** Jamunna
sea: 7 Arabian
physical feature:
bay: **8** Soymiani
canal: **4** Nara **5** Rohri
cape: **5** Fasta, Jaddi **6** Jiwani
delta: **6** Ganges **11** Char-Manpura
desert: **4** Sind, Thal, Thar
mountain pass: **5** Bolan **6** Khyber
plateau: **11** Baluchistan
valley: **5** Kohat
people: 5 Sindi, Wazir **6** Afridi, Bengal, Mahsud, Pathan, Sindhi **7** Baluchi, Brahuis, Puktuns, Punjabi, Sherani **8** Khattack, Pushtuns, Shinwari, Yusefazi **11** Mohammedzai
leader: **6** Jinnah **7** Aly Khan **8** Ayub Khan, Zia Ul-Haq **9** Ali Bhutto, Yahya Khan **13** Benazir Bhutto, Mujibur Rahman **15** Mahmud of Ghaznbi
poet: **5** Igbal, Iqbal
language: 4 Urdu **6** Pushtu, Sindhi **7** Baluchi, Bengali, English, Punjabi
religion: 5 Hindu, Islam **8** Buddhism **12** Christianity
place:
dam: **6** Mangla **7** Tarbela
gardens: **8** Shalamar
mosque: **8** Badshahi
tomb: **15** Emperor Jahangir
feature:
clothing: **5** kurta, pugri, qamis **6** jinnah **7** dupatta, shalwar **8** sherwani **9** churidars
food:
bread: **8** chappati
dish: **5** kebab, pilaf **6** qormas, salans, sautes **10** vermicelli
yogurt: **4** dahi

paleontology
study of: 18 correlation of parts
founder: 13 Georges Cuvier

Palermo
capital of: 6 Sicily

Pales
origin: 5 Roman
protector of: 6 flocks **9** shepherds
festival: 7 Parilia

Palestine *see* **6** Israel

Palestrina, Giovanni Pierluigi da
born: 5 Italy **10** Palestrina
composer of: 11 Stabat Mater **18** Missa Papae Marcelli

Paley, Grace
author of: 26 The Little Disturbances of Man **30** Enormous Changes at the Last Minute

Palici
origin: 5 Roman
form: 4 gods **5** twins
gods of: 14 sulphur springs

Palilicium *see* **6** Hyades

paling 4 pale, rail **5** fence, stake **6** picket

Palinurus
steersman of: 6 Aeneas

palisade 5 close, fence **7** bulwark, rampart **8** stockade **9** enclosure

palisades 4 crag **5** ledge **6** bluffs, cliffs **10** escarpment, promontory

pall 4 cloy, haze, sate **5** gloom, weary **6** shadow, sicken **7** dimness, satiate **8** darkness **10** become dull, be tiresome, depression, desolation, melancholy, moroseness, oppression

Palladio, Andrea
real name: 26 Andrea di Pietro della Gondola
architect of: 12 Villa Rotunda (Vicenza Italy) **14** Teatro Olimpico (Vicenza) **19** Church of Il Redentore (Venice) **26** Church of San Giorgio Maggiore (Venice)
style: 9 Palladian

Pallas *see* **6** Athena

Pallas Athena *see* **6** Athena

pallet 3 bed, cot **4** bunk, tick **5** berth **8** mattress, platform

palliate 4 calm, curb, ease, hush, lull, tame **5** abate, allay, check, quiet, sooth, still **6** lessen, modify, reduce, soften, subdue, temper **7** assuage, comfort, cushion, lighten, relieve **8** decrease, diminish, minimize, mitigate, moderate **9** alleviate **10** ameliorate

palliative 4 balm **6** solace **7** anodyne, comfort **10** comforting

pallid 3 wan **4** ashy, blah, dull, pale **5** ashen, bland, pasty, vapid, waxen **6** boring, chalky, peaked, sallow **7** ghostly, humdrum, insipid, tedious **8** blanched, lifeless **9** bloodless, colorless **10** monotonous **13** anemic looking, unimaginative, uninteresting

pallor 7 wanness **8** paleness

9 pastiness, whiteness
10 ashen color, pallidness
11 ghostliness 13 bloodlessness, colorlessness

palm ***see box***

Palm Beach Story, The
director: 14 Preston Sturges
cast: 9 Mary Astor 10 Joel McCrea, Rudy Vallee 15 William Demarest 16 Claudette Colbert

Palmer, Arnold
sport: 4 golf
noted for: 10 Arnie's Army

Palmer, Lilli
real name: 17 Lillie Marie (Maria Lilli) Peiser
born: 5 Posen 7 Germany
husband: 11 Rex Harrison 14 Carlos Thompson
roles: 11 Body and Soul
autobiography: 22 Change Lobsters and Dance

Palmer, Vera Jane
real name of: 14 Jayne Mansfield

Palmetto State
nickname of: 13 South Carolina

Palm Sunday
author: 12 Kurt Vonnegut

palmy 4 rosy 5 balmy, sunny 6 golden 7 booming, halcyon 8 blooming, pleasant, thriving 9 agreeable, bounteous, congenial 10 prosperous, successful 11 flourishing, pleasurable

Palmyra
Biblical name: 6 Tadmor

palpable 5 clear, plain 7 evident, obvious, tactile, visible 8 apparent, definite, distinct, feelable, manifest, tangible 9 touchable 10 noticeable 11 discernible, perceivable, perceptible 12 recognizable, unmistakable

palpitate 4 beat 5 pound, shake, throb 6 quaver, quiver, shiver 7 flutter, tremble, vibrate 9 go pit-a-pat

palsied 7 quaking, shaking, spastic 9 trembling

palm
varieties: 3 Fan, Ita, Key, Nut, Oil, Wax 4 Cane, Date, Doom, Doub, Doum, Fern, Hair, Hemp, King, Lady, Nipa, Nypa, Rock, Sago, Step, Tala, Wine 5 Areca, Areng, Assai, Betel, Black, Bread, Broom, Curly, Grass, Honey, Inaga, Ivory, Jelly, Latan, Manac, Nikau, Peach, Queen, Royal, Snake, Spine, Sugar, Syrup, Toddy, Yatay, Zombi 6 Bamboo, Barbel, Barrel, Bottle, Cherry, Cohune, Coyoli, Gebang, Gomuti, Gru-gru, Hesper, Kentia, Licuri, Manila, Mazari, Needle, Nibung, Parlor, Pignut, Raffia, Rattan, Ruffle, Sagisi, Sentry, Silver, Thatch, Thread, Yellow 7 Arikury, Cabbage, Calappa, Coconut, Coquito, Feather, Fiji fan, Funeral, Jaggery, Leopard, Mexican, Moriche, Overtop, Palmyra, Prickly, Spindle, Talipot, Weddell 8 Betel nut, Carnauba, Cucurite, Dwarf fan, Fishtail, Good luck, Ivory-nut, Mangrove, Pandanus, Peaberry, Princess, Roebelin, Umbrella, Wild date, Windmill 9 Alexander, Alexandra, Butterfly, Christmas, Desert fan, Gippsland, Guadalupe, Hurricane, India date, Macarthur, Ouricouri, Panama-hat, Petticoat, Piccabeen, Porcupine, Pygmy date, Silver saw, Solitaire, Spiny-club, Traveler's 10 African oil, Black-fiber, Canary date, Chinese fan, Cuban belly, Cuban royal, Everglades, Franceschi, Saw cabbage, Sealing-wax, Thatch-leaf, Washington 11 American oil, Chilean wine, European fan, Gingerbread, Mexican blue, Morass royal, Senegal date, Slender lady, Woolly butia 12 Caribee royal, Egyptian doum, Florida royal, Miniature fan, Walking-stick 13 Australian fan, Australian ivy, Australian nut, Belmore sentry, Feather-duster, Florida silver, Florida thatch, Forster sentry, Golden feather, Miniature date, San Jose hesper 14 Common princess, East Indian wine, Puerto Rican hat, Tufted fishtail, Yellow princess 15 Burmese fishtail, Chinese fountain, Chinese windmill, Yellow butterfly 16 Hispaniolan royal, Northern bangalow, Puerto Rican royal 17 Australian cabbage, Clustered fishtail, Mexican Washington, Piccabeen bangalow 18 South American royal

palsy-walsy 5 close, palsy, thick 6 chummy 8 friendly, intimate 10 buddy-buddy 14 thick as thieves

paltriness 10 triviality 12 unimportance 14 insignificance 18 inconsequentiality

paltry 4 poor, puny 5 petty, sorry 6 measly, shabby 7 scrubby, trivial 8 inferior, picayune, piddling, trifling, wretched 11 unimportant 13 insignificant, of little value 14 inconsiderable 15 inconsequential

Pama-Nyungan
language spoken by: 10 aborigines
spoken in: 9 Australia

Pamela
author: 16 Samuel Richardson
character: 3 Mr B 9 Mrs Jervis, Mrs Jewkes 10 Lady Davers 13 Pamela Andrews

pamper 5 humor, spoil 6 coddle, cosset 7 cater to, indulge 8 give in to 11 mollycoddle

pampered 7 coddled, humored 8 indulged 9 catered-to, cossetted

pamphlet 5 tract 6 folder 7 booklet, leaflet 8 brochure, bulletin, circular 9 monograph, throwaway

pan 3 boo, map, mug, pot 4 face, hiss 6 kisser 8 ridicule, saucepot 9 criticize

Pan
also: 7 Sinoeis
origin: 5 Greek
form combined: 3 man 4 goat
god of: 6 flocks 7 forests 8 pastures 9 shepherds
father: 4 Zeus 6 Hermes
loved: 4 Echo 5 Pitys 6 Syrinx
invented: 5 pipes 6 syrinx
corresponds to: 6 Faunus

panacea 6 elixir 7 cure-all, nostrum 13 universal cure

panache 4 dash, tuft 5 flair, plume, style, verve 11 flamboyance

Panama ***see box***

Panama City
capital of: 6 Panama

pancake 4 blin 5 blini, crepe, kisra, latke, lefse 6 blintz, makeup 7 fritter, hotcake 8 flapjack, slapjack 11 griddlecake 12 silver dollar
day: 13 Shrove Tuesday

Panama
capital/largest city: **10** Panama City
others: **4** Daid **5** Ancon, Colon **6** Azuero, Balboa, Gamboa **8** Dos Bocas, Penonome, Santiago **9** Cristobal **10** Portobello
division: **5** Cocle, Colon **6** Darien, Panama **7** Herrera **8** Chiriqui, Veraguas **9** Los Santos **12** Bocas del Toro
measure: **7** celemin
monetary unit: **4** cent **6** balboa **10** centesimos
island: **5** Coiba, Pearl **6** Cebaco, Multas, Taboga **7** San Blas **10** Isla Del Rey **12** Bocas del Toro, Juan Gallegos **13** Barro Colorado
lake: **5** Gatun
mountain: **4** Baru, Maje **5** Chico, Gandi **6** Darien **7** Columan, San Blas, Veragua **8** Santiago, Tabasara **10** Costa Rican **14** Serrania de Sapo **15** Aspave Highlands **17** Cordillera Central
highest point: **8** Chiriqui
river: **5** Chepo, Sambu, Tuira **6** Bayano, Panugo **7** Chagres
sea: **7** Pacific **9** Caribbean
physical feature:
bay: **5** Limon **6** Panama
dam: **5** Gatun
gulf: **6** Darien, Panama, Parita **7** Montijo, San Blas **8** Chiriqui **9** Mosquitos, San Miguel
isthmus: **6** Darien, Panama **7** San Blas
lagoon: **8** Chiriqui
peninsula: **6** Azuero **8** Valjente
people: **4** Cuna **5** Choco **6** Guaymi **7** mestizo
canal builder: **7** Lesseps
explorer: **6** Balboa **8** Bastidas, Columbus
leader: **4** Royo **5** Arias **7** Herrera **8** Guerrero **9** Espriella **12** Simon Bolivar
poet: **4** Miro **5** Korsi, Sinan
language: **7** English, Spanish
religion: **13** Roman Catholic
place:
church: **7** San Jose **15** Virgen del Carmen
plaza: **13** Independencia
ruins: **9** Old Panama
feature:
clothing: **7** montuno, pollera
dance: **4** caja **7** pujador **9** tamborito
tree: **4** yaya **5** maria, quira **6** alfaje, cativo
food:
meat: **6** tazajo
soup: **8** sancocho

Pancks
character in: **12** Little Dorrit
author: **7** Dickens

pancreas
produces: **7** insulin

Pandareus
father: **6** Lycaon, Merops
daughter: **5** Aedon **6** Merope **9** Cleothera
wounded: **8** Menelaus
stole: **9** golden dog
turned to: **5** stone
killed by: **8** Diomedes

Pandarus
character in: **18** Troilus and Cressida, Troilus and Criseyde
author: **7** Chaucer **11** Shakespeare

Pandarus
son: **7** Alcanor
companion of: **6** Aeneas

pandemic **4** rife **7** rampant **8** epidemic **10** prevailing, widespread **21** dangerously contagious

pandemonium **3** din **5** chaos **6** bedlam, clamor, hubbub, racket, rumpus, tumult, uproar **7** turmoil **8** disorder **9** commotion **10** hullabaloo **11** disturbance

Pandemos
epithet of: **9** Aphrodite

pander, panderer **4** mack, pimp **5** cadet **7** hustler **8** procurer **9** maquereau, souteneur **12** flesh-peddler

Pandion the Younger
king of: **6** Athens
later reigned in: **6** Megara

Pandora
form: **10** first woman
created by: **10** Hephaestus
presented to: **10** Epimetheus
daughter: **6** Pyrrha
given by gods: **3** box
box contained: **4** hope **5** evils

Pandrosos
position: **9** priestess
first priestess of: **6** Athena
father: **7** Cecrops
mother: **8** Agraulos

panegyric **6** eulogy, homage, praise **7** tribute **8** citation, encomium, good word **9** extolment, laudation **10** compliment **11** testimonial **12** commendation

panegyrize **4** laud **5** extol **6** praise **8** eulogize

panel **4** jury, pane **5** board, group, piece **6** insert **7** divider **8** bulkhead **9** committee, partition **10** round table **11** compartment, expert group, select group **13** advisory group

pang **4** ache, pain **5** agony, pinch, smart, stick, sting, throb **6** stitch, twinge **7** anguish **8** distress **9** suffering **10** discomfort

Pangloss
character in: **7** Candide
author: **8** Voltaire

pang of conscience **5** demur, qualm **6** unease **7** remorse, scruple **9** misgiving **10** uneasiness **11** compunction

panhandle **3** beg, bum **5** cadge, mooch **6** hustle **7** solicit **9** importune

Panhandle State
nickname of: **12** West Virginia

Panhellenius
epithet of: **4** Zeus
means: **14** god of all Greeks

panic **5** alarm, dread, go ape, scare **6** fright, horror, terror **7** anxiety **8** affright, hysteria **9** cold sweat, confusion, fall apart **10** go to pieces **11** nervousness, trepidation **12** apprehension, perturbation **13** consternation

panicky **6** scared **7** alarmed, anxious **9** terrified **10** frightened **13** panic-stricken, scared to death **14** terror-stricken

panic-stricken **6** afraid, scared **7** alarmed, anxious, fearful, panicky **9** terrified

13 scared to death 14 terror-stricken

Panjabi
language family: 12 Indo-European
branch: 11 Indo-Iranian
group: 5 Indic
spoken in: 5 (northern) India

Pankrits
language family: 12 Indo-European
branch: 11 Indo-Iranian
form of: 5 Indic
followed use of: 8 Sanskrit

pannier 3 bag 4 hoop 6 basket, dossel, pantry 7 corbeil, drapery 9 framework, overskirt
literally: 11 breadbasket

Panomphaeus *see* 4 Zeus

Panopeus
father: 6 Phocus
mother: 7 Asteria
twin brother: 6 Crisus

Panoptes
epithet of: 5 Argus
means: 7 all eyes

panorama 5 scene, vista 6 survey 7 diorama, picture, scenery, tableau 8 long view, overview, prospect 10 scenic view 11 perspective 12 bird's-eye view

panoramic 3 ide 7 overall 8 bird's-eye, extended, sweeping 9 extensive 10 far-ranging 11 far-reaching 12 all-embracing, all-inclusive 15 all-encompassing

pansy 5 Viola
varieties: 4 Wild 5 Field 6 Garden, Orchid 8 Japanese 9 Miniature 11 Monkey-faced 12 European wild

pant 4 blow, gasp, huff, puff 6 wheeze

pant after 4 seek 5 covet, crave 6 desire, pursue 7 hope for, long for, lust for, wish for 8 yearn for 9 hanker for, hunger for, lust after 11 thirst after, have a yen for 14 set one's heart on

Pantagruel *see* 22 Gargantua and Pantagruel

panther 3 cat 6 cougar 7 leopard

Panthous
priest of: 6 Apollo
counselor of: 5 Priam
father: 6 Othrys
son: 9 Euphorbus, Hyperenor, Polydamas

Pantomime Quiz
host: 10 Mike Stokey 15 Pat Harrington Jr

pantry 5 ambry, store 6 closet, galley, larder 7 butlery, buttery, pannier, spicery 8 cupboard, scullery

pants 5 jeans 6 denims, shorts, slacks 7 drawers, panties 8 breeches, britches, knickers, trousers 9 bluejeans, dungarees 10 underpants 11 undershorts 12 underdrawers

pantywaist 4 wimp 5 sissy, softy 7 crybaby, milksop 8 mama's boy, weakling 10 namby-pamby, sissy-pants, weak sister 11 Milquetoast, mollycoddle 13 sissy-britches

Panurge
character in: 22 Gargantua and Pantagruel
author: 8 Rabelais

Panza, Sancho
character in: 10 Don Quixote
author: 9 Cervantes

pap 3 rot 4 bosh, junk, mash, mush, pulp, tosh 5 gruel, paste 6 cereal, drivel, Pablum, trivia 7 rubbish, twaddle 8 soft food 10 balderdash, flapdoodle, triviality

papa 2 pa 3 dad, doc, paw, pop 5 daddy, poppy 6 father, priest 9 Hemingway
mate: 4 mama

Papa Bear
nickname of: 11 George Halas

Papago
language family: 5 Piman 10 Uto-Aztecan
location: 6 Mexico 7 Arizona
related to: 4 Pima

papal 9 apostolic, of the pope 10 pontifical

Papaleo, Anthony
real name of: 16 Anthony Franciosa

paper 4 bond, deed, news, opus, pulp, work 5 daily, draft, essay, stock, theme 6 record, report, tissue, weekly 7 article, gazette, journal, monthly, tabloid, writing 8 document, gift wrap 9 cardboard, chronicle, newspaper, newsprint, onionskin 10 instrument, manuscript, paperboard, periodical, stationery, typescript 11 certificate, composition, publication

Paper Chase, The
character: 10 James T Hart, Willis Bell 13 Asheley Brooks 14 Elizabeth Logan, Jonathan Brooks 15 Franklin Ford III 19 Thomas Craig Anderson 29 Professor Charles W Kingsfield Jr
cast: 10 James Keane 11 Robert Ginty 12 Deka Beaudine, John Houseman 13 James Stephens, Jonathan Segal 14 Francine Tacker, Tom Fitzsimmons
subject: 9 law school
Kingsfield's specialty: 11 contract law

paper measure 4 ream 5 quire

Paper Moon
director: 16 Peter Bogdanovich
cast: 9 Ryan O'Neal 10 Tatum O'Neal 12 Madeline Kahn (Trixie Delight) 13 John Hillerman
Oscar for: 17 supporting actress (O'Neal)

Paphian *see* 9 Aphrodite

Paphos
also: 6 Paphus
father: 9 Pygmalion
mother: 7 Galatea

Paphus *see* 6 Paphos

Papua New Guinea
formerly: 16 British New Guinea
capital: 11 Port Moresby
town: 3 Thu, Lae 4 Ioma 6 Kikori, Madang
province of: 9 Indonesia
province: 9 West Irian
monetary unit: 4 kina
island: 6 Misima 10 New Britain
archipelago: 8 Bismarck
lake: 6 Murray
river: 3 Fly 4 Ramu
sea: 5 Coral 7 Solomon
strait: 6 Torres
people: 4 Hula, Kate 5 Kiwai, Kwoma 6 Banaro 7 Arapesh 10 Melanesian
language: 7 English

papyrus 4 pith, reed 5 paper, sedge 6 scroll 7 bulrush 8 document 10 manuscript
accordion pleated: 6 orihon
genus: 7 Cyperus
origin: 5 Egypt 9 Nile delta 10 Nile valley
use: 3 mat 4 rope, shoe, sail 5 paper

par 5 level, usual 6 normal, parity 7 average, balance, the norm 8 equality, evenness, identity, sameness, standard 9 stability 11 equilibrium, equivalency 12 equal footing 13 identicalness

parable 4 myth, tale 5 fable, story 6 homily, legend 8 allegory, apologue, folk tale **9** folk story **12** morality tale

Paracelsus
author: **14** Robert Browning

parade **4** line, pomp, show **5** array, march, strut, train, vaunt **6** column, defile, flaunt, review, string **7** caravan, cortege, display, show off **8** vaunting **9** cavalcade, flaunting, march past, motorcade, pageantry, put on airs, spectacle **10** exposition, grandstand, procession **11** progression **13** demonstration

paradigm **5** ideal, model **6** matrix, sample **7** example, paragon, pattern **8** exemplar, original, standard **9** archetype, criterion, prototype, yardstick

paradise **3** joy **4** Eden **5** bliss **6** heaven, utopia **7** delight, ecstasy, nirvana, rapture **8** pleasure **9** enjoyment, happiness, Shangri-la, transport **11** happy valley **12** Garden of Eden, satisfaction **13** gratification, seventh heaven **15** Land of Cockaigne

Paradise **5** Annwn **6** Annfwn

Paradise
also: **9** Paradisio
part three of: **12** Divine Comedy
author: **14** Dante Alighieri

Paradise Lost
author: **10** John Milton
character: **3** Eve, God **4** Adam **5** Satan **6** Christ **7** Lucifer

Paradise of the Pacific
nickname of: **6** Hawaii

Paradise Regained
author: **10** John Milton

paradisiacal **7** elysian, sublime **8** blissful, empyreal, empyrean, ethereal, heavenly **9** celestial, unearthly **12** otherworldly

paradox **5** poser **6** enigma, oddity, puzzle, riddle **7** anomaly **11** incongruity **13** inconsistency

paradoxical **9** ambiguous, enigmatic, equivocal **13** contradictory

paragon **4** norm **5** ideal, model **6** symbol **7** example, pattern **8** exemplar, paradigm, standard **9** archetype, criterion, prototype, yardstick **10** apotheosis

Paraguay ***see box***

parallel **4** akin, like, same, twin **5** alike, equal, match **6** follow **7** abreast, analogy, be alike, similar **8** analogue, likeness, relation **9** alongside, analogous, corollary, duplicate **10** collateral, comparable, comparison, concurrent, connection, equivalent, similarity **11** coextensive, coincidence, comparative, compare with, correlation, correlative, counterpart, equidistant, resemblance **12** correspond to **13** corresponding **14** correspondence

parallelism **8** affinity, likeness, sameness **9** agreement **10** comparison, similarity, similitude **11** resemblance **14** correspondence

parallelogram **5** rhomb **6** square **7** diamond, rhombus **8** rhomboid **9** rectangle **11** plane figure **13** quadrilateral

paralyze **4** stun **6** benumb, deaden, disarm, freeze,

Paraguay
capital/largest city: **8** Asuncion
others: **3** Ita **4** Rica, Yuty **5** Belen, Luque, Pilar, Villa **7** Caacupe **8** Trinidad **9** Paraguari **10** Concepcion, Villarrica **11** Encarnacion **26** Puerto Presidente Stroessner
division: **6** Guaira, Itapua, Olimpo **7** Caazapa **8** Boqueron **10** Concepcion
measure: **3** pie **4** lino, lira, lire, vara **5** legua **6** cuadra, fanega
monetary unit: **4** peso **7** guarani, centimo
weight: **7** quintal
island:
floating island: **8** camalote
lake: **4** Vera, Ypoa **8** Ypacarai
river: **3** Apa **5** Guazu, Negro, Plata, Verde, Ypane **6** Acaray, Parana **7** Aguaray, Confuso **8** Paraguay **9** Aquidaban, Pilcomayo, Tebicuary, Tibiquare **10** Monte Lindo **14** Riacho Gonzales **15** Riacho Mosquitos
physical feature:
falls: **6** Guaira
plains: **5** Chaco
plateau: **6** Parana
people: **6** Abipon, Moskoi **7** Guarani, mestizo **8** Guayaqui
artist: **7** Bestard
author: **3** Pla **4** Baez **6** Alcala, Bastos, Correa, O'Leary **7** Cervera **8** Casaccia
composer: **8** Asuncion
leader: **5** Lopez **7** Francia **10** Stroessner **16** Antequera y Castro
sculptor: **8** Guggiari
language: **6** German **7** Guarani, Spanish
religion: **9** Mennonite **13** Roman Catholic
place:
church: **10** Villarrica **11** Incarnation
dam: **6** Itaipu
memorial: **16** Pantheon of Heroes
museum: **5** Godoi
palace: **10** Government
feature:
animal: **4** puma **5** tapir **6** iguana, jaguar **7** peccary
bird: **6** toucan
clothing: **5** fajas, typoi **6** poncho **7** rebozos **9** bombachas **10** alpargatas
communes: **11** reducciones
dance: **7** Sante Fe **15** Paraguayan polka
fish: **7** piranha
lace: **7** nanduti
music: **8** quarania
townspeople: **9** comuneros
tree: **5** ceiba **7** lapacho **9** quebracho
food:
bread: **5** chipa, mbeyu
dish: **12** sopa paraguay
tea: **9** yerba mate
vegetable: **8** mandioca

weaken **7** cripple, destroy, disable, petrify, stupefy, wipe out **8** demolish, enfeeble **10** debilitate, immobilize, neutralize **12** incapacitate

Paramaribo
capital of: 8 Suriname

paramount 4 main **5** chief **6** utmost **7** capital, highest, leading, premier, supreme **8** cardinal, dominant, foremost, greatest, peerless, superior **9** essential, principal, unmatched **10** preeminent **11** outstanding, predominant **12** incomparable, preponderant, transcendent

paramour 3 man **4** doxy **5** lover, Romeo **6** gigolo **7** Don Juan **8** Casanova, fancy man, lothario, lover boy, mistress **9** boyfriend, concubine, courtesan, inamorata, inamorato, kept woman **10** girl friend, lady friend, sugar daddy

paranoid 4 wary **7** deluded **9** paranoiac **11** distrustful **14** oversuspicious

parapet 7 bulwark, rampart **8** abutment, palisade **9** barricade, earthwork **10** battlement, breastwork

paraphernalia 3 rig **4** gear **5** stuff **6** outfit, tackle, things **7** effects, harness, regalia **8** fittings, material, supplies, utensils **9** apparatus, equipment, trappings **10** belongings, implements, properties, provisions **11** accessories, furnishings **13** accoutrements

paraphrase 5 recap **6** rehash, reword **7** restate **8** rephrase **12** recapitulate

Parasaurolophus
type: 8 dinosaur **10** ornithopod
location: 6 Canada
period: 10 Cretaceous

parasite 5 leech **6** beggar, cadger, loafer **7** moocher, shirker, slacker, sponger **8** deadbeat **9** goldbrick, scrounger **10** freeloader **11** bloodsucker
inside host: 12 endoparasite
outside host: 12 ectoparasite

parasol 5 shade **6** shadow **7** roundel **8** sunshade, umbrella
mushroom: 7 lepiota

par avion 5 by air

parboil 4 boil **5** scald **6** blanch **7** precook

Parca
origin: 5 Roman
member of: 6 Parcae
goddess of: 7 destiny **10** childbirth

Parcae *see* **5** Fates

parcel 3 lot **4** bale, pack, part, plot **5** allot, piece, tract **6** bundle, divide, packet **7** carve up, deal out, dole out, package, portion, section, segment, split up **8** allocate, dispense, disperse, division, fraction, fragment, property **9** allotment, allowance, apportion, partition **10** distribute **11** piece of land

parceling out 9 allotment, doling out, meting out **10** allocation, assignment, dealing out **12** distribution **13** apportionment

parcel out 5 allot **7** dole out, give out, mete out **8** allocate, dispense, divide up **9** apportion **10** distribute, portion out

parch 4 bake, burn, char, sear **5** dry up, singe **6** dry out, scorch, sun-dry, wither **7** blister, shrivel **9** dehydrate, dessicate, evaporate

parched 3 dry **4** arid **6** barren **8** withered **9** shriveled **10** dehydrated, desiccated

parchment 6 scroll, vellum **7** papyrus **8** goatskin **9** sheepskin

pardon 5 grace, mercy **6** excuse, wink at **7** absolve, amnesty, blink at, forbear, forgive, indulge, release, set free **8** overlook, reprieve, shrug off **9** discharge, disregard, exculpate, exonerate, remission, vindicate **10** absolution, indulgence **11** deliverance, exculpation, forbearance, forgiveness **12** grant amnesty **16** forgive and forget

Pardoner
character in: 18 The Canterbury Tales
author: 7 Chaucer

pare 3 cut, lop **4** clip, crop, dock, hull, husk, peel, skin, trim **5** lower, prune, shave, shear, shell, shuck, slash, strip **6** lessen, reduce, shrink **7** curtail, cut back **8** decrease, diminish **11** decorticate

pare down 3 cut **4** trim **5** shave **6** reduce **7** abridge, curtail, cut down, shorten **8** condense, cut short, diminish **10** abbreviate

parent 3 dam **4** sire **5** model **6** father, mother **7** creator **8** ancestor, begetter, exemplar, original, producer **9** precursor, prototype **10** antecedent, forerunner, originator, procreator, progenitor **11** predecessor

parentage 5 birth, roots, stock **6** family, origin, strain **7** descent, lineage **8** ancestry, forbears, heredity, pedigree **9** ancestors, genealogy **10** background, derivation, extraction, family tree **11** antecedents

Parentalia
origin: 5 Roman
event: 8 festival

parenthetical 5 aside **6** braced, casual **8** inserted **9** bracketed **10** extraneous, immaterial, incidental, interposed, irrelevant **11** impertinent, intervening, superfluous

par excellence 8 superior **10** preeminent

parfait d'amour
type: 7 liqueur
flavor: 7 violets
color: 6 purple

Paria
form: 5 nymph
loved by: 5 Minos
children: 7 Chryses **9** Eurymedon, Nephalion, Philolaus

pariah 5 exile, rover, stray **6** outlaw, roamer **7** outcast **8** vagabond, wanderer **10** expatriate **11** undesirable, untouchable

paring 4 chip, snip **5** scrap, shred, slice **6** sliver **7** cutting, peeling, shaving **8** fragment

pari passu 6 fairly **7** equably **10** side by side **13** equal progress **17** without partiality

Paris ***see box***

Paris
character in: 14 Romeo and Juliet
author: 11 Shakespeare

Paris
postion: 6 prince
father: 5 Priam
mother: 6 Hecuba
brother: 6 Hector **9** Polydorus
sister: 9 Cassandra
wife: 6 Oenone
abducted: 5 Helen
judgment of: 14 apple of discord
awarded apple to: 9 Aphrodite
killed by: 11 Philoctetes

parish 4 fold **5** flock, shire **6** canton, county **7** diocese, section **8** brethren, district, precinct, province **9** community, pastorate **10** department **11** archdiocese **12** congregation, neighborhood

parity 7 balance **8** equality,

Paris
airport: **4** Orly **9** Le Bourget **15** Charles de Gaulle
area: **5** Passy **6** Clichy, Marais, Ternes, Wagram **7** Auteuil **8** Chaillot, Gobelins, Left Bank, St Honore **9** Les Halles, Right Bank, St Germain **10** Montmartre, Rive Droite, Rive Gauche, Val de Grace **11** Ile de la Cite **12** Hotel de Ville, Latin Quarter, Montparnasse
capital of: **6** France
city planner: **9** Haussmann
island: **10** Ile St Louis **11** Ile de la Cite
landmark: **8** Pantheon **9** Notre Dame **10** Paris Opera, Sacre Coeur **11** Eiffel Tower, La Madeleine, Palais Royal **12** Elysee Palace, Hotel de Ville, Place Vendome **13** Arc de Triomphe, Palais Bourbon **14** Bois de Boulogne, Place de l'Etoile, Pompidou Center, Sainte Chapelle, Tomb of Napoleon **15** Bois de Vincennes **16** Luxembourg Palace **17** Hotel des Invalides, Place de la Bastille, Place de la Concorde **18** Jardin des Tuileries **20** Place Charles de Gaulle
nickname: **11** city of light
river: **5** Seine
street: **9** Haussmann, Invalides **10** Grand Armee **11** Saint Michel **12** Montparnasse, Saint Germain **13** Champs Elysees **15** Charles de Gaulle
subway: **5** Metro
university: **8** Sorbonne

sameness **10** coequality, uniformity **11** equivalence, equivalency **14** correspondence

park **4** lawn **5** field, green, grove, woods **6** common, meadow, square **7** grounds, reserve **8** parkland, preserve, woodland **9** grassland, sanctuary **10** public park, quadrangle

Parker, Dorothy
author of: **9** Big Blonde **10** Enough Rope **13** Death and Taxes **18** After Such Pleasures **19** Laments for the Living

Parkman, Francis
author of: **30** France and England in North America

parkway **6** avenue **9** boulevard **12** thoroughfare

parlance **4** talk **5** idiom, lingo **6** speech **16** manner of speaking

Parlement of Fowles, The
author: **15** Geoffrey Chaucer

parley **4** talk **6** confab, powwow, summit **7** council, meeting, palaver **8** conclave **9** discourse, mediation, peace talk **10** conference, discussion **11** arbitration, negotiation **12** conversation

parliament **4** diet **5** court, house, junta **6** fan-tan, senate, sevens **7** cabinet, council **8** assembly, congress **9** high court **11** legislature **12** three estates
Communist: **6** Soviet **9** politburo, presidium
estate: **12** House of Lords **14** House of Commons
Germanic: **9** Bundesrat, Bundestag, Bolksraad **11** Volkshammer
Greek: **5** Boule
Icelandic: **7** Althing
Israeli: **7** Knesset **8** Knesseth
Scandinavian: **7** Lagting, Riksdag **8** Lagthing, Storting **9** Odelsting, Storthing
Spanish: **6** Cortes

parlor **5** salon **6** saloon **8** best room **9** front room **10** living room **11** drawing room, sitting room

Parnopius
epithet of: **6** Apollo
means: **9** locust god

parochial **5** local, petty, small **6** church, little, narrow, parish **7** insular, limited **8** regional **9** hidebound, illiberal, religious, sectional, small-town **10** provincial, restricted **11** countrified **12** narrow-minded

parodos
from Greek drama: **9** choral ode

parody **5** mimic **6** satire **7** lampoon, takeoff **8** satirize, travesty **9** burlesque, take off on **10** caricature

Parolles
character in: **20** All's Well That Ends Well
author: **11** Shakespeare

paroxysm **3** fit **5** spasm, spell **7** seizure **10** convulsion

parrot **3** ape **4** bird, echo, lory **5** macaw, mimer, mimic **6** chorus, monkey **7** copycat, imitate **8** cockatoo, imitator, parakeet **9** reiterate

parry **4** duck, shun **5** avert, avoid, dodge, elude, repel **7** beat off, fend off, repulse, ward off **8** sidestep, stave off **10** circumvent, fight shy of

Parsifal
opera by: **6** Wagner
character: **6** Kundry **8** Amfortas, Klingsor **9** Gurnemanz

Parsifal Mosaic, The
author: **12** Robert Ludlum

parsimonious **5** close, tight **6** frugal, saving, stingy **7** miserly, sparing, thrifty **9** niggardly, penurious **10** economical, ungenerous **11** closefisted, tightfisted **13** money-grubbing, penny-pinching

parsimony **6** thrift **7** economy **8** meanness **10** stinginess **13** niggardliness **15** tightfistedness

parsley **19** Petroselinum crispum
varieties: **5** Horse **7** Chinese, Italian **12** Turnip-rooted
related herb: **4** dill **5** cumin **6** fennel
garland worn by: **8** Hercules
gives speed to: **6** horses
use in: **11** fines herbes **12** bouquet garni

parson **5** clerk, padre **6** cleric, divine, father, pastor, priest, rector **7** dominie **8** minister, preacher, reverend, shepherd, sky pilot **9** clergyman
French: **4** abbe, cure

parsonage **5** glebe, manse **7** deanery, rectory, Vatican **8** vicarage **9** pastorate

part **2** go **3** bit, job **4** care, chip, duty, hunk, item, open, rend, role, slit, task, tear, unit **5** break, chore, crumb, guise, leave, piece, place, scrap, sever, shard, share, sherd, shred, slice, split **6** branch, charge, cleave, depart, detach, detail, divide, go away, member, morsel, region, sector, set out, sliver, sunder **7** concern, cutting, disjoin, element, portion, push off, section, segment, snippet **8** break off, business, capacity, disguise, disunite, division, fraction, fragment, function, separate, set forth, start out **9** character, component, disengage, go one's way **10** assignment, break apart, department, disconnect, get up and go, ingredient, mosey along, say good-bye **11** be on one's way, call it quits, constituent, subdivision

partake **5** enjoy, savor, share **6** join in, sample **7** share in **8** engage in **11** participate

part from **5** leave **9** break with **12** separate from

Parthenia
epithet of: **6** Athena
means: **6** virgin

Parthenius *see* **9** Plexippus

Parthenopaeus
father: **10** Hippomenes
mother: **8** Atalanta
member of: **18** Seven against Thebes

Parthenope
form: **5** siren

Parthenos
means: **6** virgin

partial **6** biased, unfair, unjust **7** limited, slanted **8** one-sided, partisan **9** factional **10** fractional, incomplete, interested, prejudiced, subjective, unbalanced, unfinished **11** fragmentary, inequitable, predisposed, uncompleted **12** inconclusive, prepossessed

partiality **4** bent, bias, love, tilt **5** fancy, slant, taste **6** choice, liking **7** leaning **8** affinity, fondness, penchant, tendency, weakness **9** prejudice **10** attraction, favoritism, preference, proclivity, propensity **11** inclination **12** one-sidedness, partisanship, predilection **14** predisposition

partially **6** in part, partly **7** partway **8** somewhat **9** piecemeal **12** fractionally, incompletely

participant **4** ally **5** party **6** cohort, fellow, helper, member, player, sharer, worker **7** partner **8** confrere, partaker **9** accessory, associate, colleague, performer **10** accomplice **11** contributor, shareholder **12** collaborator, participator

participate **5** share **6** join in **7** partake, perform **8** engage in, take part **9** play a part

particle **3** bit, jot **4** atom, iota, mite, snip, whit **5** crumb, grain, scrap, shred, speck, trace **6** morsel, tittle, trifle **7** granule, modicum, smidgen, snippet **9** scintilla

parti-colored **4** pied **5** plaid **6** motley **7** checked, dappled, mottled **8** colorful **9** checkered **10** variegated **11** many-colored **12** multicolored

particular **4** sole **5** exact, fixed, fussy, picky **6** single, strict **7** express, finicky, special **8** concrete, critical, definite, detailed, distinct, especial, exacting, explicit, itemized, personal, separate, specific **9** demanding **10** fastidious, individual, meticulous, scrupulous **11** painstaking, persnickety, punctilious, well-defined **12** hard to please

particularize **6** detail **7** itemize, specify **9** enumerate

particularly **6** mainly **7** notably **8** markedly **9** eminently, expressly, specially, supremely, unusually **10** definitely, distinctly, especially, explicitly, strikingly **11** principally, prominently **13** exceptionally **15** extraordinarily

particulars **5** facts, items **6** events **7** details **9** specifics **13** circumstances

parti pris **15** position decided **20** preconceived attitude

partisan **3** fan **4** ally **6** backer, biased, rooter, zealot **7** booster, devotee, partial, slanted **8** adherent, advocate, champion, follower, one-sided, upholder **9** guerrilla, insurgent, irregular, jayhawker, supporter **10** bushwacker, enthusiast, prejudiced, subjective, unbalanced **11** sympathizer

partition **4** wall **5** allot, fence, panel **6** assign, divide, screen **7** barrier, deal out, divider, mete out, parting, split up **8** allocate, bulkhead, dispense, disperse, dividing, division, separate **9** allotment, apportion, parcel out, separator, severance, splitting, subdivide **10** allocation, assignment, distribute, separation **11** demarcation, segregation **12** distribution, dividing wall **13** apportionment

partly **6** in part **7** part way **8** somewhat **9** not wholly, partially, to a degree **10** relatively **12** fractionally, incompletely **13** after a fashion, comparatively

partly open **4** ajar **5** agape **6** gaping **7** cracked **8** half-open, unclosed **9** squinting **10** half-closed

partner **3** aid, pal **4** ally, chum, mate, wife **5** aider, buddy **6** fellow, friend, helper, sharer, spouse **7** comrade, co-owner, husband **8** confrere, helpmate, partaker, sidekick, teammate **9** accessory, assistant, associate, colleague, companion, co-partner **10** accomplice, better half, joint owner **11** confederate, participant **12** collaborator

Partners, The
author: **16** Louis Auchincloss

Parton, Dolly
roles: **10** Nine to Five, Rhinestone **30** The Best Little Whorehouse in Texas

partridge
group of: **5** covey

Partridge
character in: **8** Tom Jones
author: **8** Fielding

Partridge Family, The
character: **13** Reuben Kinkaid **14** Danny Partridge, Keith Partridge, Tracy Partridge **15** Connie Partridge, Laurie Partridge **20** Christopher Partridge
cast: **8** Susan Dey **11** David Madden **12** Brian Forster, David Cassidy, Shirley Jones **13** Danny Bonaduce, Suzanne Crough **14** Jeremy Gelbwaks
song: **14** I Think I Love You

Parts of Animals
author: **9** Aristotle

parturition **5** birth **8** delivery **10** childbirth **11** giving birth **12** childbearing

party **2** do **4** band, bash, body, crew, fete, gang, team, unit, wing **5** corps, force, group, squad **6** affair, at-home, league, soiree **7** accused, blowout, company, coterie, faction **8** alliance, claimant, conclave, litigant, wingding **9** appellant, coalition, defendant, festivity, gathering, plaintiff, reception **10** contestant, federation, petitioner, respondent **11** celebration, confederacy, get-together, participant, paticipator, perpetrator

party-pooper **4** drag **10** spoilsport, wet blanket

parvenu **4** snob **6** nobody **7** upstart **8** arrivist, mushroom **9** arriviste **12** nouveau riche

Pascal, Blaise
nationality: **6** French
invented: **7** syringe **13** adding machine **14** hydraulic press
author of: **7** Pensees **19** Lettres provinciales **20** Essay pour les coniques

Pascin, Julius
real name: **6** Pincas

born: 5 Vidin 8 Bulgaria
artwork: 6 Femmes 12 Les Deux Amies 17 Ginette et Mireille

Pasiphae
father: 6 Helios
mother: 7 Perseis
husband: 5 Minos
daughter: 7 Ariadne, Phaedra 9 Acacallis
became enamored of: 10 Cretan bull
mother of: 8 Minotaur

Pasithea
member of: 6 Graces

Pasolini, Pier Paolo
director of: 13 Arabian Nights

pass 2 go 3 cap, die, end, gap, hit, top, use, way 4 best, busy, fill, flow, give, go by, go on, hand, kick, lane, meet, toss 5 canal, exact, excel, gorge, gulch, leave, outdo, route, spend, throw, trail 6 accept, affirm, avenue, be over, canyon, convey, course, decree, depart, devote, elapse, employ, engage, exceed, expend, expire, finish, go away, go past, occupy, ordain, permit, pickle, plight, ratify, ravine, slip by, strait, take up, vanish 7 achieve, advance, approve, channel, confirm, consume, deliver, die away, eclipse, freebie, glide by, go ahead, let have, narrows, pathway, present, proceed, qualify, satisfy, slide by, surpass 8 blow over, dissolve, exigency, fade away, furlough, go beyond, go onward, hand over, juncture, legalize, melt away, outshine, outstrip, pass away, peter out, progress, quandary, sanction, transfer, transmit, turn over 9 authorize, disappear, evaporate, extremity, hand along, legislate, situation, terminate 10 accomplish, difficulty, free ticket, get through, move onward, overshadow, passageway 11 predicament, proposition 12 complication, run its course, solicitation, stand the test 13 authorization 15 amorous overture
French: 13 laissez passer

passable 4 fair, open, so-so 5 clear 6 not bad 8 adequate, fordable, mediocre, middling 9 allowable, crossable, navigable, tolerable 10 acceptable, admissible, pretty good 11 presentable, respectable, traversable 12 unobstructed

passage 3 way 4 hall, pass, path, road, tour, trek, trip 5 aisle, canal, piece, route, verse 6 access, clause, column, course, junket, tunnel, voyage 7 channel, chapter, hallway, journey, passing, portion, section, transit 8 approach, approval, corridor, movement, sanction, sentence 9 enactment, excursion, paragraph, selection, ship's fare 10 acceptance, expedition, ordainment 11 affirmation, endorsement, legislation, progression 12 confirmation, legalization, ratification 13 authorization

passage out 4 exit 6 egress, outlet

Passages
author: 10 Gail Sheehy

Passage to India, A
author: 9 E M Forster
character: 6 Dr Aziz 8 Mrs Moore 12 Adela Quested 13 Cecil Fielding, Ronald Heaslop 16 Professor Godbole
setting: 11 Chandrapore 12 Marabar Caves
director: 9 David Lean
cast: 9 Judy Davis 12 Alec Guinness 13 Peggy Ashcroft 15 Victor Bannerjee
Oscar for: 17 supporting actress (Ashcroft)

passageway 4 exit, hall, lane, path, walk 5 aisle 6 access, arcade, tunnel 7 doorway, gangway, gateway, hallway, passage 8 corridor, entrance, entryway, sidewalk 12 companionway

pass away 3 die 6 depart, expire, pass on, perish 7 decease 8 pass over 13 go to one's glory 14 give up the ghost

pass by 4 go by, pass 5 lapse 6 elapse, roll by, slip by 7 glide by, slide by 8 slip away

passe 4 past 5 faded, hoary, stale 6 demode, lapsed, quaint 7 ancient, antique, archaic, disused, outworn, retired 8 obsolete, outdated, outmoded 9 out-of-date 10 antiquated 11 prehistoric 12 antediluvian, old-fashioned, out of fashion 13 superannuated

passenger 4 fare 5 rider 8 commuter, stowaway, traveler, wayfarer

Passepartout
character in: 26 Around the World in Eighty Days
author: 5 Verne

pas seul
ballet: 9 solo dance
literally: 8 solo step

passim 12 here and there, repeated item

passing 5 brief, death, dying 6 demise, fickle 7 decease, passage 8 adequate, fleeting 9 enactment, ephemeral, momentary, temporary, transient 10 evanescent, expiration, not failing, short-lived, transitory 11 impermanent, legislating

passing the bounds of propriety
French: 5 outre

passion 4 fire, idol, love, lust, rage, urge 5 ardor, craze, fancy, flame, gusto, heart, mania 6 desire, fervor, hunger, thirst, warmth 7 beloved, craving, ecstasy, emotion, feeling, rapture 8 loved one 9 carnality, eagerness, inamorata, intensity, obsession, sentiment, transport, vehemence 10 carnal love, enthusiasm 11 amorousness, earnestness, infatuation

passionate 3 hot 4 sexy 5 fiery 6 ardent, carnal, erotic, fervid, fierce, heated, loving, raging 7 amorous, earnest, excited, feeling, fervent, furious, intense, lustful 8 desirous, ecstatic, inflamed, sensuous, vehement 9 emotional, heartfelt, wrought-up 11 tempestuous 12 enthusiastic, intoxicating

passionfruit
type: 7 liqueur
origin: 6 Hawaii
flavor: 5 peach

passionless 4 calm, cold 6 placid, serene 7 passive 8 tranquil 9 apathetic, unfeeling 10 spiritless 11 emotionless, indifferent, unemotional

Passion Play
author: 13 Jerzy Kosinski

passive 5 inert 6 docile 7 dormant, patient, pliable 8 enduring, inactive, lifeless, listless, resigned, yielding 9 apathetic, compliant, impassive, quiescent, tractable 10 spiritless, submissive 11 acquiescent, unassertive, unresisting 12 nonresistant

passiveness 6 apathy 7 inertia 8 docility 10 quiescence 11 resignation 12 acquiescence, lifelessness 14 submissiveness 16 unresponsiveness

passivity 6 apathy 7 inertia 8 docility, meekness 11 resignation 12 complaisance, lifelessness 13 nonresistance 14 submissiveness

pass muster 2 do 5 serve 6 answer 8 be enough 10 be

adequate **12** be sufficient **14** be satisfactory

pass on **3** die **6** depart, expire **7** decease **8** pass away **13** go to one's glory **14** give up the ghost, leave this world **15** breathe one's last

pass over **6** ignore, slight **7** neglect **8** overlook **10** brush aside

pass up **4** miss **6** ignore, refuse

password **3** key **4** word **6** byword, slogan **7** keyword, tessera **9** catchword, watchword **10** open sesame, secret word, shibboleth **11** countersign, passe-parole

Password
host: **11** Allen Ludden

past **2** by **4** gone **5** ended, prior **6** beyond, bygone, former, gone by **7** ancient, earlier, elapsed, expired, history, long ago, through **8** departed, finished, previous **9** antiquity, days of old **10** days gone by, days of yore, historical, olden times, passed away, yesteryear **11** dead and gone, former times, times gone by **12** ancient times

pasta **4** orzo, ziti **6** elbows, shells **7** gnocchi, lasagna, pastina, ravioli, rotelli **8** ditalini, linguini, macaroni, rigatoni, tortelli **9** canelloni, cavatelli, fettucine, manicotti, spaghetti **10** tortellini, vermicelli
ingredient: **3** egg **5** flour

past due **4** late **5** tardy **7** belated, overdue **9** in arrears **10** behindhand

paste **3** gum, hit **4** glue, seal, sock **5** affix, punch, stick **6** attach, cement **7** stickum **8** adhesive, mucilage

pastel **3** dim **4** pale, soft **5** chalk, faded, faint, light, muted **6** crayon **9** washed-out **13** coloring stick **14** coloring pencil

Pasternak, Boris
author of: **9** Dr Zhivago

Pasteur, Louis
field: **9** chemistry
nationality: **6** French
originated: **14** anti-rabies shot, pasteurization
founded: **12** microbiology
disproved: **21** spontaneous generation

pastime **3** fun **4** game, play **5** hobby, sport **9** amusement, avocation, diversion **10** relaxation **11** distraction **13** entertainment **14** divertissement

pastis
type: **7** liqueur
flavor: **8** licorice
substitute for: **8** absinthe

past one's prime **3** old **4** aged **5** aging **7** elderly **9** venerable **11** over the hill **12** in one's dotage

pastor **4** cure, dean **5** padre, vicar **6** cleric, father, parson, priest, rector **8** chaplain, minister, preacher **9** clergyman

pastoral **5** rural **6** rustic **7** bucolic, idyllic **8** arcadian, clerical, priestly **9** episcopal **10** sacerdotal **11** ministerial **14** ecclesiastical

Pastoral Symphony, The
author: **9** Andre Gide

pastorate **6** clergy **8** ministry, the cloth **10** priesthood

pastures
god of: **3** Pan **6** Dumuzi

pasty **3** wan **4** ashy, gray, pale **5** ashen, gluey, gooey, gummy, white **6** anemic, chalky, doughy, pallid, peaked, sallow, sticky **7** deathly, starchy **9** bloodless, colorless, ghostlike, glutinous, like paste **12** mucilaginous

pat **3** apt, dab, hit, pet, rap, tap **4** cake, daub, easy, glib, slap **5** exact, ideal, ready, slick, thump **6** caress, facile, fondle, simple, smooth, stroke, thwack **7** apropos, fitting, perfect, precise, reliant **8** flippant, suitable **9** contrived, pertinent, rehearsed

patch **3** fix, lot **4** area, darn, mend, plot, spot, zone **5** field, sew up, tract **6** garden, repair, stitch **7** expanse, stretch **8** clearing, insignia **9** reinforce **13** reinforcement

patchwork **4** hash, mess **6** jumble, medley, muddle, tangle **7** grab bag, melange, mixture **8** mishmash, mixed bag, pastiche, scramble **9** confusion, potpourri **10** hodgepodge, miscellany, salmagundi **11** gallimaufry **14** conglomeration, omniumgatherum

pate **3** pie **4** brow, head **5** brain, crown, paste, pastry, patty, skull **6** noddle, noggin, noodle **9** meat paste

patella
bone of: **7** kneecap

patent **4** bald, bold, open, rank **5** clear, gross, overt, plain **6** permit **7** decided, evident, express, glaring, license, obvious **8** apparent, distinct, flagrant, manifest, palpable, registry, striking **9** copyright, downright, prominent **10** pronounced, unreserved **11** conspicuous, copyrighted, indubitable, self-evident, trademarked, transparent, unconcealed, undisguised **12** unmistakable **15** nonprescription

paterfamilias **6** father **17** father of the family, master of the family **20** master of the household

paternal **4** kind **6** tender **8** fatherly, parental, vigilant, watchful **9** concerned, indulgent **10** benevolent, fatherlike, interested, solicitous **11** patriarchal

Pater Patriae **18** father of his country

path **3** way **4** lane, plan, road, walk **5** byway, means, orbit, route, track, trail **6** access, bypath, course **7** pathway, process, walkway **8** approach, footpath

pathetic **3** sad **6** moving, rueful, woeful **7** doleful, piteous, pitiful **8** dolorous, grievous, pitiable, poignant, touching, wretched **9** affecting, miserable, plaintive, sorrowful **10** deplorable, lamentable, to be pitied **11** distressing

Pathfinder, The
author: **19** James Fenimore Cooper
character: **9** Arrowhead, Dew-of-June **10** Charles Cap **11** Mabel Dunham, Natty Bumppo **12** Chingachgook **13** Jasper Western **14** Sergeant Dunham **18** Lieutenant Davy Muir

Pathfinders, The
author: **10** Gail Sheehy

pathogen **3** bug **4** germ **5** virus **7** microbe **8** bacillus **9** bacterium **13** microorganism

pathophobia
fear of: **7** disease

pathos **3** woe **5** agony **6** misery **7** anguish, feeling, sadness **8** distress **9** heartache, poignancy, sentiment **10** desolation **12** pitiableness **13** plaintiveness

Paths of Glory
director: **14** Stanley Kubrick
cast: **11** Kirk Douglas, Ralph Meeker **13** Adolphe Menjou

pathway **4** lane, path, road **5** alley, route, track **6** course **7** passage, walkway **8** footpath **10** passageway

patience **5** poise **7** stamina **8** industry, tenacity **9** composure, diligence, fortitude, restraint, tolerance **10** equanimity, resolution, sufferance **11** application, forbearance, longanimity, persistence, self-control **12** perseverance, tirelessness

Patience
author: **9** W S Gilbert

patient **4** case **6** dogged, serene **8** composed, diligent, enduring, resolute, tireless **9** dauntless, tenacious, undaunted **10** determined, forbearing, persistent, sick person, unflagging, unswerving, unwavering **11** industrious, persevering, unfaltering, unperturbed **13** indefatigable, long-suffering, uncomplaining

patio **4** deck **5** lanai, porch **6** piazza **7** terrace, veranda

patois **5** argot, idiom, lingo **6** jargon **7** dialect **10** vernacular

Paton, Alan
author of: **19** Too Late the Phalarope **20** Cry the Beloved Country **24** Ah but Your Land Is Beautiful

pat on the back **6** praise **7** plaudit **10** compliment **12** commendation

patriarch **5** elder, ruler **6** father, leader, old man **8** male head **9** chieftain **13** paterfamilias

patrician **4** lord, peer **5** noble **6** lordly **7** genteel, stately **8** highborn, imposing, nobleman, princely, well-bred **9** blueblood, dignified, gentleman **10** aristocrat, upper-class **12** aristocratic, silk-stocking

patrimony **3** lot **5** dower, share **6** devise, estate, legacy **7** portion **8** bestowal, heritage, jointure **9** endowment **10** bequeathal, birthright **11** inheritance **12** hereditament

patriotism
Latin: **11** amor patriae

Patroclus
father: **9** Menoetius
mother: **8** Periapis
friend: **8** Achilles
killed by: **6** Hector

patrol **5** guard, scout, watch **6** ranger, sentry, warden **7** protect **8** sentinel **9** safeguard, walk a beat, watchman, watch over **10** stand watch

patron **5** angel, buyer **6** backer, client, friend, helper **7** habitue, shopper, sponsor, visitor **8** advocate, attender, champion, customer, defender, financer, promoter, upholder **9** protector, spectator, supporter **10** benefactor, encourager, frequenter, well-wisher **11** sympathizer **12** benefactress **14** philanthropist

patronage **3** aid **4** help **5** favor, plums, trade **6** buying, custom, spoils **7** backing, charity, clients, dealing, support **8** advocacy, auspices, business, commerce **9** clientele, customers, fosterage **10** assistance, friendship, pork barrel, protection, purchasing **11** benefaction, sponsorship **12** philanthropy **13** encouragement

patronize **5** humor **6** shop at **7** buy from **8** deal with, frequent **9** trade with **10** condescend

patsy **4** dupe, pawn, tool **7** cat's-paw, fall guy

patter **3** pad, pat, rap, tap **4** beat, drum **5** pound, thrum **6** tattoo **7** rat-a-tat, spatter, tapping **8** drumming, sprinkle

pattern **4** copy, form, mold, plan **5** draft, guide, ideal, mimic, model, motif, shape **6** design, follow, sample **7** emulate, example, fashion, imitate, paragon **8** exemplar, original, paradigm, parallel, simulate, specimen, standard **9** archetype, criterion, duplicate, prototype **10** apotheosis, stereotype **12** illustration

Patton
director: **17** Franklin Schaffner
cast: **10** Karl Malden (Omar Bradley) **12** George C Scott (George Patton), Stephen Young **13** Michael Strong
Oscar for: **5** actor (Scott), story **7** picture **8** director **10** screenplay (Francis Ford Coppola and Edmund H North)

Patton, George S
nickname: **15** Old Blood and Guts
served in: **3** WWI **4** WWII **11** World War One, World War Two
commander of: **9** Third Army
invasion of: **8** Normandy **11** North Africa
capture of: **6** Sicily
battle: **5** Bulge
wore: **21** ivory-handled revolvers
memoirs: **12** War As I Knew It

Patty Duke Show, The
character: **7** Richard **8** Ross Lane **9** Cathy Lane, Patty Lane **10** Martin Lane **14** Natalie Masters
cast: **9** Jean Byron, Patty Duke **10** Paul O'Keefe **14** Eddie Applegate **16** William Schallert

paucis verbis **10** by few words, in few words **12** with few words

paucity **4** lack **6** dearth **7** fewness, poverty **8** exiguity, poorness, puniness, scarcity, shortage, sparsity, thinness **10** deficiency, meagerness, scantiness, scarceness **13** insufficiency

Paul
former name: **4** Saul
hometown: **6** Tarsus
teacher: **8** Gamaliel
companion: **5** Silas **7** Timothy **8** Barnabas, John Mark **9** Trophimus
cities visited: **4** Rome **5** Derbe, Perga, Troas **6** Lystra, Paphos **7** Antioch, Corinth, Ephesus, Iconium, Miletus, Salamis **8** Caesarea, Damascus, Neapolis, Philippi **9** Macedonia **12** Thessalonica
conversion place: **14** road to Damascus
wrote: **8** epistles

Paul Bunyan
author: **12** James Stevens
character: **9** Shanty Boy **10** Hels Helson **11** King Bourbon **12** Sourdough Sam **13** Babe the Blue Ox **14** Hot Biscuit Slim **16** Johnny Inkslinger

Pauli, Wolfgang
field: **7** physics
researched: **13** quantum theory
established: **14** Pauli principle **18** exclusion principle
awarded: **10** Nobel Prize

Paulina
character in: **14** The Winter's Tale
author: **11** Shakespeare

Pauling, Linus Carl
field: **12** biochemistry
worked on: **8** proteins **18** molecular structure
advocated: **8** Vitamin C
awarded: **10** Nobel Prize
awarded for: **5** peace **9** chemistry

paunch **3** gut, pot **5** belly, tummy **7** abdomen, stomach **8** potbelly **9** bay window, beer belly, spare tire **10** midsection **11** breadbasket, corporation

pauper **6** beggar **7** almsman **8** bankrupt, indigent **9** insolvent, mendicant **10** poor person, starveling **11** charity case **12** down-and-outer

pause **3** gap **4** halt, rest, stop, wait **5** break, cease, delay, let up **6** hiatus **7** interim, time out **8** break off, hesitate, interval **9** cessation, interlude **10** deliberate, suspension **12** intermission, interruption

pave **3** tar **4** face **6** cement **7** asphalt, surface **8** black top **9** resurface **10** macadamize

pavement **4** slab **5** brick **6** cement, hearth, street, tarmac **7** asphalt, cobbles, macadam **8** concrete, driveway, flagging, sidewalk **9** flagstone

pavilion **4** tent, ward, wing **5** arbor, kiosk **6** gazebo **7** pergola **9** bandshell **11** summerhouse

Pavlov, Ivan Petrovich
nationality: **7** Russian
researched: **9** digestion
studied: **20** behavior conditioning **21** Pavlovian conditioning
awarded: **10** Nobel Prize

paw **2** pa **3** dad, pop, toe **4** feel, foot, grab, hand, maul, mitt, papa **5** daddy, flail, touch **6** caress, clutch, father, handle, scrape, strike **7** rough up **8** forefoot **9** mishandle
mate: **3** maw

pawn **4** bond, dupe, hock, tool **5** agent, patsy **6** flunky, lackey, pledge, puppet **7** cat's paw **8** borrow on, creature, guaranty, henchman, hireling, security **9** assurance, guarantee, underling **10** instrument **12** raise money on **14** give as security

pawnbroker
French: **11** mont-de-piete

Pawnbroker, The
director: **11** Sidney Lumet
cast: **10** Rod Steiger (Sol Nazerman) **11** Brock Peters **12** Jaime Sanchez **19** Geraldine Fitzgerald
setting: **6** Harlem

Pawnee (Chahiksichhiks)
language family: **7** Caddoan
location: **5** Texas **8** Nebraska, Oklahoma **9** New Mexico
related to: **7** Arikara
god: **6** Tirawa

Pawtuxet
location: **13** Massachusetts
leader: **7** Squanto

Pax
origin: **5** Roman
goddess of: **5** peace
corresponds to: **5** Irene

pax vobiscum **14** peace be with you

pay **3** fee **4** foot, give, meet **5** grant, honor, remit, repay, serve, wages, yield **6** ante up, chip in, extend, income, profit, render, return, salary, settle **7** benefit, bring in, cough up, payment, present, proffer, stipend **8** be useful, earnings, paycheck, shell out **9** bear fruit, liquidate, reimburse **10** come across, compensate, make good on, recompense **12** compensation **13** reimbursement

payable **3** due **4** owed **5** owing **6** mature, unpaid **8** to be paid **9** in arrears, spendable **10** demandable, expendable, receivable **11** outstanding

pay attention **4** heed, note **6** attend, notice **7** observe

Payaya
language family: **12** Coahuiltecan
location: **5** Texas

pay back **5** repay **7** counter, get even **9** reimburse, retaliate **10** recompense, remunerate **15** make restitution

pay for **6** redeem **7** expiate **8** atone for **9** answer for, suffer for **10** compensate, recompense, remunerate **13** make amends for **17** make reparation for

pay heed **6** notice **8** consider **11** concentrate **12** pay attention **13** put one's mind to

pay homage **5** defer, honor **7** acclaim **10** pay tribute

paying back **9** repayment **11** getting even **12** making good on **13** reimbursement

paymaster **6** bursar, purser **7** cashier **10** cashkeeper

payment **3** fee, pay **4** debt **6** outlay, paying, salary **7** premium **8** defrayal, spending **9** allowance, discharge **10** recompense, remittance, settlement **11** expenditure, installment, liquidation **12** compensation, contribution, disbursement, remuneration **13** reimbursement

pay no heed to **4** defy **6** ignore, slight **7** disobey, neglect, violate **8** overlook, pass over **9** disregard **10** brush aside, infringe on **14** shut one's eyes to **16** pay no attention to **17** transgress against

payoff **3** end **4** soap **5** bribe, graft **6** climax, crunch, finale, finish, grease, payola, result, upshot, windup **7** outcome **8** clincher **9** hush money **10** bottom line, conclusion, denouement, protection, resolution **11** culmination

pay off **5** bribe **6** buy off, suborn **13** grease the palm

payola **5** bribe, graft **6** grease, payoff

pay out **5** spend **6** expend, lay out **7** fork out **8** allocate, disburse, dispense, shell out **10** distribute

pay suit **3** woo **5** court **8** pay court

Payton, Walter
nickname: **9** Sweetness
sport: **8** football
position: **11** running back
team: **12** Chicago Bears

pay tribute to **4** laud, tout **5** boost, toast **6** praise, salute **7** applaud, commend **8** eulogize **10** compliment **16** sing the praises of

Payuga
tribe: **4** Agaz **6** Magach **7** Cadigue, Payagua, Sarigue, Siacuas, Tacumbu
location: **8** Paraguay **12** South America

pea **5** Pisum **12** Pisum sativum
varieties: **4** Flat, Love, Snow, Wild **5** Beach, Caley, Chick, Congo, Coral, Field, Glory, Green, Heart, Heath, Hoary, No-eye, Rough, Sugar, Sweet **6** Angola, Canada, Desert, Garden, Marble, Pigeon, Rosary, Scurfy, Winged, Winter **7** Catjang, Darling, English, Rabbit's, Seaside **8** Earthnut, Egyptian, Princess, Shamrock **9** Asparagus, Black-eyed, Butterfly, Chaparral, Jerusalem, Partridge, Perennial **10** Australian, Singletary, Wild winter **11** Everlasting, Sturt desert, Two-flowered, Winter sweet **12** Edible-podded **14** Austrian winter **15** Australian flame

peace **4** calm, ease **5** amity, truce **6** accord, repose **7** concord, content, entente, harmony **8** serenity **9** agreement, armistice, composure, placidity **12** pacification, tranquillity **14** reconciliation
god of: **4** Frey **5** Freyr
goddess of: **3** Pax **9** Concordia
Hebrew: **6** shalom
Russian: **3** mir

Peace
author: **12** Aristophanes

peace be with you
Latin: **11** pax vobiscum

peaceful **4** calm **5** quiet, still **6** placid, serene, silent **7** pacific, restful **8** amicable, friendly, tranquil **9** agreeable, peaceable, peacetime **10** harmonious, nonviolent, nonwarring, pacifistic, untroubled **11** undisturbed

peacefulness **4** calm **7** concord, harmony **8** calmness, serenity **9** placidity **11** tranquility

peacemaker **8** diplomat, mediator, placater **9** go-between **10** ambassador, arbitrator, negotiator **11** adjudicator, conciliator, pacificator, peacekeeper, peacemonger **12** intermediary

peacemaking **9** pacifying, placating, placatory **11** reconciling **12** conciliating, conciliatory, pacification

peace offering **6** amends **11** appeasement **12** conciliation

peace of mind **8** security, serenity **11** tranquility **16** freedom from worry

peace to you
Hebrew: **14** shalom aleichem

peach **13** Prunus persica
varieties: **4** Muir, Peak, Sims, Vine, Wild **5** Gaume, Hiley, Pavie **6** Carmen, Crosby, Desert, Foster, J H Hale, Lovell, Orejon, Paloro, Peento, Salwey **7** Dixigem, Dixired, Elberta, Persian, Quadong **8** Champion, Crawford, Isabella, Redhaven, Russelet **9** Alexander, Freestone, Halehaven, Rochester, Southland **10** Clingstonc, Goldeneast, Heath Cling, Summer Snow **12** Chinese Cling, Iron Mountain, Mountain Rose, Oldmixon Free **13** Golden Jubilee, Oldmixon Cling, Phillips Cling **14** Belle of Georgia
peach-like: **7** apricot **9** nectarine

Peach State
nickname of: **7** Georgia

Peachum, Polly
character in: **12** Beggar's Opera
author: **3** Gay

peachy **4** fine, keen **5** dandy, super, swell **9** excellent, marvelous, wonderful

peacock
group of: **6** muster

Peacock
constellation of: **4** Pavo

Peacock, Thomas Love
author of: **12** Headlong Hall **14** Crotchet Castle, Nightmare Abbey

Peacock Spring, The
author: **11** Rumer Godden

peak **3** tip, top **4** acme, apex **5** crest, crown, flood, prime **6** apogee, climax, summit, zenith **8** pinnacle **9** culminate **11** culmination

peaked **3** ill, wan **4** lean, pale, thin, weak **5** ashen, drawn, gaunt, spare, spiked, spiny, white **6** ailing, infirm, pallid, pointy, sallow, sickly, skinny, spiked **7** haggard, pinched, pointed, scrawny, tapered, wizened **9** emaciated, shriveled **11** debilitated

peal **3** din **4** boom, clap, ring, roar, roll, toll **5** blare, blast, clang, crack, crash, knell **6** rumble **7** clangor, resound, ringing **10** resounding **11** reverberate **13** reverberation **14** tintinnabulate **16** tintinnabulation

Peale, Charles Willson
born: **17** Queen Anne County MD
son: **9** Raphaelle, Rembrandt **12** Titian Ramsay
artwork: **26** The Exhumation of the Mastodon
portrait: **8** Franklin **9** Jefferson, John Adams **10** Washington

Peale, Raphaelle
born: **13** Bucks County PA
father: **14** Charles Willson
brother: **9** Rembrandt **12** Titian Ramsay
artwork: **12** After the Bath

Peale, Rembrandt
born: **13** Bucks County PA
father: **14** Charles Willson
brother: **9** Raphaelle **12** Titian Ramsay
artwork: **15** The Court of Death
portrait: **9** Jefferson **10** Washington

peal of bells **7** clangor, ringing **16** tintinnabulation

peanut **3** pod, tot **4** puny, seed **5** petty, small **6** goober, legume, measly, paltry **8** earthpea **9** little one
species: **15** Arachis hypogaea

Peanuts
creator: **13** Charles Schulz
character: **4** Lucy **5** Linus **6** Marcie, Snoopy **9** Schroeder **12** Charlie Brown **15** Peppermint Patty
Halloween figure: **12** Great Pumpkin
Snoopy's plane: **12** Sopwith Camel
Snoopy's foe: **8** Red Baron
saying: **9** Good Grief

pear **5** Pyrus **13** Pyrus communis
varieties: **4** Bosc, Sand **5** Anjou, Asian, Blind, Melon, Smith **6** Balsam, Burrel, Butter, Comice, Common, Garber, Garlic, Orient, Seckel, Warden **7** Chinese, Kieffer, Prickly, Vinegar **8** Bartlett, Japanese, Oriental **9** Alligator, Evergreen, Muscadine **10** Beurre Bosc, Brandywine, Chaumontel **11** Birch-leaved, Bon Chretien, Paper-spined, Winter Nelis **12** Beurre d'Anjou, Easter Beurre, Sacred garlic, Willow-leaved **13** Flemish Beauty, Waite Bergamot **15** Doyenne du Comice **18** Duchesse d'Angouleme

pearl
grows in: **6** oyster
genus: **8** Pinctada
source: **6** Red Sea **9** Caribbean **11** Persian Gulf **12** South Pacific **16** Gulf of California
composed of: **5** nacre **9** aragonite **10** conchiolin **13** mother-of-pearl
quality: **6** luster **11** iridescence
color: **4** blue, rose **5** black, brown, cream, green, white **6** yellow
shape: **5** round **7** baroque
type: **8** cultured, Oriental (saltwater) **9** simulated **10** freshwater

Pearl-Fishers, The
also: **19** Les Pecheurs de Perles
opera by: **5** Bizet
setting: **6** Ceylon

Pearl of the Antilles *see* **4** Cuba

peasant **4** boor, esne, peon, serf **5** churl, knave, yokel **6** farmer, rustic, worker **7** laborer, lowlife, villein **10** countryman, dirt farmer
Arabic: **6** fellah
Indian: **4** ryot **5** kisan **6** raiyat
Irish: **4** kern
Russian: **5** kulak **6** muzhik
Scottish: **6** cotter

peasantlike **5** crude, rough **6** coarse, oafish, rustic, vulgar **7** boorish, loutish, uncouth **9** unrefined **10** unpolished

peccadillo **4** slip **5** lapse **6** booboo **7** blunder, faux pas, misdeed, misstep **8** petty sin, trespass **9** false move, wrong step **10** misconduct, wrongdoing **11** misdemeanor **13** transgression

peck **3** pat, rap, tap **4** buss, gobs, lots, mess **5** a slew, batch, bunch, heaps, scads, smack, snack, stack, thump **6** nibble, oodles, pick at, strike, stroke, worlds **8** light jab **9** abundance, light kiss **11** eight quarts
abbreviation of: **2** pk

Peck, Gregory
real name: **17** Eldred Gregory Peck
born: **9** La Jolla CA
roles: **8** Moby Dick **10** On the Beach, Spellbound **11** The Yearling **12** Duel in the Sun, Roman Holiday **15** The Paradine Case **16** Twelve O'Clock High **17** The Boys from Brazil, The Guns of Navarone **18** To Kill a Mockingbird (Oscar) **19** Gentleman's Agreement, The Keys of the Kingdom **21** The Snows of Kilimanjaro **26** The Man in the Gray Flannel Suit
autobiography: **12** An Actor's Life

Peckinpah, Sam
director of: **9** Straw Dogs **12** The Wild Bunch

Pecksniff
character in: **16** Martin Chuzzlewit
author: **7** Dickens

peculiar **3** odd **5** queer, weird **6** far-out, quaint, unique **7** bizarre, curious, erratic, private, special, strange, typical, unusual **8** abnormal, distinct, freakish, personal, singular, specific **9** eccentric, exclusive, whimsical **10** capricious, individual, outlandish, particular **11** distinctive **13** idiosyncratic **14** characteristic, distinguishing, representative, unconventional

peculiarity **4** mark **5** badge, stamp, trait **6** oddity **7** feature, quality **8** odd trait **9** attribute, queerness, weirdness **10** erraticism, uniqueness **11** abnormality, bizarreness, distinction, singularity, strangeness **12** eccentricity, freakishness, idiosyncrasy **13** particularity, unnaturalness **14** characteristic **21** distinguishing quality

pecuniary **6** fiscal **8** economic, monetary **9** budgetary, financial

pedagogic **7** bookish, donnish **8** academic, didactic, pedantic, tutorial **9** scholarly **11** educational **12** professorial **13** instructional

pedagogue, pedagog **5** tutor **7** teacher **8** academic, educator **9** professor **10** instructor, schoolmarm **12** educationist, schoolmaster **13** schoolteacher **14** schoolmistress

pedant **6** purist **8** bookworm **9** dogmatist **13** methodologist

pedantic **5** fussy **7** bookish, finicky, pompous, stilted **8** academic, didactic, dogmatic **10** nitpicking, scholastic **11** doctrinaire, punctilious **13** hairsplitting **14** overparticular

Pedasus
mentioned in: **5** Iliad
twin brother: **7** Aesepus
killed by: **8** Euryalus

peddle **4** hawk, sell, vend **6** retail **7** deal out **8** dispense

Peder Victorious
character in: **16** Giants of the Earth
author: **7** Rolvaag

pedestal **4** base, foot **6** bottom, plinth **10** foundation

pedestrian **6** walker **7** mundane, prosaic, tedious, trekker **8** mediocre, ordinary, stroller **9** itinerant **10** ambulatory, for walking, unexciting **11** commonplace, peripatetic, unimportant **12** foot-traveler, run-of-the-mill **13** insignificant, perambulating, perambulatory, unimaginative **15** inconsequential

pedigree **4** line **6** family, strain **7** descent, lineage **8** ancestry **9** bloodline, parentage **10** derivation, extraction, family tree **13** line of descent

peek **3** pry **4** peep, peer **5** watch **6** glance **7** glimpse

peel **4** bark, hull, husk, pare, rind, skin, tear, zest **5** flake, scale, shuck, spade, strip **6** remove **7** undress **11** decorticate

peel off **6** remove **7** veer off **8** strip off

peep **4** peek, peer, skim, word **5** cheep, chirp, tweet **6** emerge, glance, murmur, mutter, squeak **7** chirrup, glimpse, peeping, peer out, twitter, whimper, whisper **9** come forth, quick look

peeper **3** eye **4** frog **6** voyeur **10** peeping Tom

peer **4** gape, gaze, look, lord, peek, peep **5** equal, noble, stare **6** appear, emerge, squint **7** compeer **8** nobleman **9** blue blood, gentleman, patrician **10** aristocrat

peerage **8** nobility **10** blue bloods, patricians **11** aristocracy

Peer Gynt
author: **11** Henrik Ibsen
character: **3** Ase **7** Solveig **12** The Great Boyg **16** The Button Moulder

peerless **7** supreme **8** flawless **9** faultless, matchless, unequaled, unmatched, unrivaled **10** consummate, inimitable, preeminent, surpassing, unexcelled **11** superlative, unsurpassed **12** incomparable, transcendent

peeve **3** bug, eat, irk, vex **4** fret, gall, rile **5** annoy, chafe, eat at, frost, gripe **6** gnaw at, nettle **7** dislike, perturb, provoke **8** irritate, vexation **9** aggravate, annoyance, complaint, grievance **10** exasperate, irritation **11** aggravation, provocation **12** exasperation, give one a pain **13** pain in the neck **14** thorn in the side

peevish **4** mean **5** cross, huffy, sulky, surly, testy **6** crabby, cranky, grumpy **7** grouchy, pettish **8** churlish, petulant, snappish **9** fractious, irritable, querulous, splenetic **10** ill-humored, ill-natured **11** bad-tempered, ill-tempered, quarrelsome **12** cantankerous

peewee **4** tiny **5** dwarf, small, teeny **6** little, midget, minute **9** itsy-bitsy, itty-bitty, minuscule **10** diminutive, teeny-weeny **11** Lilliputian

Pee Wee
nickname of: **11** Harold Reese

peg **3** pin **4** nail **5** cleat, dowel, spike, thole **6** skewer, toggle **8** fastener, tholepin

Pegae
form: **6** spring
spring of: **6** Dryope

Pegasus
form: **5** horse
characteristic: **6** winged
mother: **6** Medusa
ridden by: **11** Bellerophon

Peggotty, Clara
character in: **16** David Copperfield
author: **7** Dickens

Pei, I M (Ieoh Ming)
architect of: **12** East Building (National Gallery of Art), L'Enfant Plaza (Washington DC) **14** East-West Center (U of Hawaii), Mile High Center (Denver) **15** Place Ville Marie (Montreal) **16** John

Hancock Tower (Boston) **18** Everson Museum of Art (Syracuse NY) **22** Kips Bay Plaza Apartments (NYC) **36** National Center for Atmospheric Research (Boulder CO)

peignoir **4** gown **6** kimono **8** negligee **9** nightgown **12** dressing gown

Peiser, Lillie Marie
real name of: **11** Lilli Palmer

pejorative **7** mocking **8** debasing, negative, scornful **9** degrading, demeaning, slighting **10** belittling, derogatory, detracting, disdainful, ridiculing, unpleasant **11** deprecatory, disparaging, downgrading **12** contemptuous, depreciatory, disapproving **15** uncomplimentary

Peking
also: **7** Beijing
means: **15** northern capital
capital of: **5** China
landmark: **9** Bell Tower, Drum Tower, Ming Tombs **10** Pei-hai Park **12** Palace Museum **13** Forbidden City **14** Hall of Classics, Temple of Heaven **15** Marco Polo Bridge **17** Temple of Confucius **18** Old Legation Quarter **19** Temple of Agriculture **20** Great Hall of the People, Hall of Supreme Harmony **21** Mausoleum of Mao Tse-tung **22** Palace of Heavenly Purity **26** Monument to the People's Heroes **32** Revolutionary and Historical Museum
mountain: **7** Taihang
river: **3** Hai **7** Ch'ao-pai **8** Yungting
square: **9** T'ien-an Men
university: **8** Tsinghua
walled city: **5** Inner, Outer, Tatar **7** Chinese

pelagic **6** marine **7** aquatic, oceanic **9** thalassic **11** sea-dwelling

Pelagon
mentioned in: **5** Iliad
ally of: **8** Sarpedon

Pelasgus
also: **9** Corynetes
son: **6** Lycaon **7** Temenus
first: **3** man
founder of: **10** Pelasgians

Pele
real name: **24** Edson Arantes do Nascimento
sport: **6** soccer
team: **13** New York Cosmos
nationality: **9** Brazilian

Pelegon
mentioned in: **5** Iliad
god of: **5** river
mother: **8** Periboea
son: **11** Asteropaeus

Peleus
king of: **6** Phthia **9** Myrmidons
father: **6** Aeacus
mother: **6** Endeis
brother: **7** Telamon
half-brother: **6** Phocus
wife: **6** Thetis **8** Antigone
son: **8** Achilles
daughter: **8** Polydora

pelf **4** gain **5** booty, lucre, money **6** mammon, riches, spoils

Pelias
father: **8** Poseidon
mother: **4** Tyro
twin brother: **6** Neleus
wife: **8** Anaxibia
son: **7** Acastus
nephew: **5** Jason

Pelican State
nickname of: **9** Louisiana

Pelides
descendant of: **6** Peleus

pelisse **4** cape, coat **5** cloak **6** mantle

Pelleas (King Pelleas)
character in: **16** Arthurian romance
daughter: **6** Elaine

Pelleas and Melisande
also: **18** Pelleas et Melisande
opera by: **7** Debussy
character: **6** Golaud, Yniold
author: **18** Maurice Maeterlinck

pellet **3** pea **4** ball, bead, drop, pill **5** pearl, stone **6** marble, pebble, sphere **7** globule

pell-mell **6** rashly **7** hastily **8** slapdash **9** hurriedly, posthaste **10** at half cock, carelessly, heedlessly, recklessly **11** hurry-scurry, impetuously, imprudently **12** incautiously **13** helter-skelter, precipitately, thoughtlessly

pellucid **5** clear, lucid **10** articulate **11** crystalline, translucent, transparent **12** intelligible **14** understandable

Pelopia
father: **8** Thyestes
raped by: **8** Thyestes
son: **9** Aegisthus

Pelops
father: **8** Tantalus
sister: **5** Niobe
son: **6** Atreus, Sciron **7** Letreus **8** Pittheus, Thyestes **9** Alcathous **10** Chrysippus
daughter: **7** Nicippe **8** Lysidice **9** Astydamia
resurrected by: **6** Hermes

pelt **3** fur, hit, rap **4** belt, coat, hide, skin, sock **5** pound, punch, whack **6** batter, buffet, fleece, pepper, pummel, strike, thrash, thwack **7** clobber

Pemphredo
member of: **6** Graeae, Graiae

pen **3** sty **4** cage, coop, crib, fold **5** draft, hutch, pound, quill, stall, write **6** corral, pencil, scrawl **7** compose, paddock **8** compound, scribble, stockade **9** ballpoint, enclosure

penal **7** of jails **8** punitive **9** punishing **10** corrective, penalizing **11** castigatory, retributive **12** disciplinary

penalty **4** fine **7** forfeit **8** handicap **9** suffering **10** assessment, forfeiture, infliction, punishment **11** retribution **12** disadvantage

penance **9** atonement, expiation, hair shirt, penitence **10** contrition, repentance **12** propitiation **13** mortification

Penates
protectors of: **4** home
companions: **5** lares

penchant **4** bent, bias, gift, turn **5** fancy, flair, knack, taste **6** liking, relish **7** leaning **8** affinity, fondness, tendency **9** prejudice, proneness, readiness **10** attraction, partiality, preference, proclivity, propensity **11** disposition, inclination **12** predilection **14** predisposition

pendant **3** fob **6** locket **15** hanging ornament

Pendennis
author: **25** William Makepeace Thackeray
character: **9** Laura Bell **10** Henry Foker **12** Blanche Amory **13** Emily Costigan **14** Helen Pendennis, Major Pendennis **15** Arthur Pendennis

pendent, pendant **7** hanging, jutting, pensile **8** dangling, swinging **9** extending, pendulous, suspended **10** projecting, protruding **11** overhanging, protuberant

pendente lite **16** during litigation **19** with a lawsuit pending

pending **8** imminent **9** undecided, unsettled **10** in suspense, unfinished, unresolved, up in the air **11** in the offing **12** undetermined

pendulous 7 hanging, pendent, pensile, sagging **8** dangling, drooping, swinging **9** suspended

pendulum
invented by: 7 Galileo

Penelope
father: 7 Icarius
mother: 8 Periboea
husband: 8 Odysseus **9** Telegonus
son: 6 Ifalus **10** Telemachus **11** Polyporthis
fended off: 7 suitors

penetrate 3 get **4** bore **5** catch, enter, prick **6** decode, fathom, invade, pierce, seep in **7** cut into, discern, pervade, unravel **8** decipher, perceive, permeate, puncture, saturate, traverse **9** figure out, perforate **10** comprehend, cut through, impregnate, infiltrate, see through, understand **11** pass through

penetrating 4 keen **5** acrid, alert, alive, aware, harsh, heady, sharp, smart **6** astute, biting, clever, shrewd, strong **7** caustic, pungent, reeking **8** piercing, redolent, stinging **9** pervading, pervasive, trenchant **10** discerning, perceptive, percipient, permeating, saturating, thoughtful **11** intelligent, sharp-witted **13** perspicacious

penetration 5 foray, grasp **6** access, boring **7** insight, passage **8** infusion, invasion, keenness, piercing **9** intrusion, quickness, sharpness **10** astuteness, cleverness, perception, puncturing, shrewdness **11** discernment, perforation **12** intelligence, perspicacity

Peneus
god of: 5 river
river: 6 Peneus
son: 7 Hypseus
daughter: 6 Daphne

Penguin Island
author: 13 Anatole France

peninsula 4 cape **5** point **8** headland **10** promontory

Peninsular State
nickname of: 7 Florida

penitence 6 regret, sorrow **7** penance, remorse **9** atonement, attrition, expiation **10** contrition, repentance **11** compunction, humiliation

penitent 5 sorry **6** rueful **7** atoning, devotee, pilgrim **8** contrite **9** regretful, repentant **10** remorseful

penitentiary 3 pen **4** jail, stir **5** joint **6** prison **7** slammer **8** big house

Penn, Arthur
director of: 12 Little Big Man **14** Bonnie and Clyde **16** The Miracle Worker

Penn, Sean
wife: 7 Madonna
roles: 7 Bad Boys **15** Shanghai Express **22** The Falcon and the Snowman **24** Fast Times at Ridgemont High

Pennacook (Merrimac)
language family: 9 Algonkian **10** Algonquian
location: 5 Maine **6** Quebec **7** New York, Vermont **10** New England **12** New Hampshire **13** Massachusetts
leader: 11 Wannalancet **12** Passaconaway
related to: 6 Abnaki

pen name
French: 10 nom de plume

pennant 4 flag, jack **6** banner, burgee, colors, ensign, pennon **7** bunting **8** ensignia, standard, streamer **9** banderole, oriflamme

penniless 4 poor **5** broke, needy **6** busted, ruined **8** bankrupt, indigent, strapped, wiped out **9** destitute, flat broke, insolvent, moneyless **10** down-and-out, pauperized **12** impoverished **15** poverty-stricken

pennon 4 flag, jack **6** banner, colors, ensign **7** pennant **8** standard, streamer

Pennsylvania *see box*

penny 3 sum **4** cent **5** cheap, pence **6** copper, stiver **7** trivial

penny-pinching 5 close, tight **6** stingy **7** miserly **8** grudging **9** niggardly, penurious **10** ungenerous **11** tight-fisted **12** parsimonious

Penny Serenade
director: 13 George Stevens
cast: 9 Cary Grant **10** Irene Dunne **11** Beulah Bondi **13** Edgar Buchanan

pennyweight
abbreviation of: 3 dwt

Penobscot
language family: 9 Algonkian **10** Algonquian
location: 5 Maine **13** Old Town Island
members of: 17 Abnaki Confederacy

Penrod
author: 15 Booth Tarkington
sequel: 12 Penrod and Sam **13** Penrod Jashber
character: 6 Herman, Verman **9** Sarah Crim **11** Rupe Collins **13** Marjorie Jones **15** Penrod Schofield
***dog:* 4** Duke

pensee 7 thought **10** reflection

Pensees
author: 12 Blaise Pascal

pension 5 grant **6** income, retire **7** annuity, stipend, subsidy **9** allowance **13** boardinghouse **14** retirement fund

pensive 3 sad **5** grave **6** dreamy, musing, solemn, somber **7** serious, wistful **8** dreaming **10** meditative, melancholy, reflective **11** daydreaming **13** contemplative, introspective **15** sadly thoughtful

Pentateuch 10 Law of Moses **28** first five books of Old Testament
see also: 7 books of **12** Old Testament

Penthesilea
queen of: 7 Amazons
father: 4 Ares
mother: 6 Otrere
sister: 9 Hippolyta
killed by: 8 Achilles

Pentheus
king of: 6 Thebes
father: 6 Echion
mother: 5 Agave
grandfather: 6 Cadmus

pent-up 7 boxed-up, checked, stifled **8** hedged-in, held back, penned-in, penned-up, reined in, stored-up **9** bottled-up, repressed **10** restrained, suppressed

penurious 5 close **6** frugal, stingy **7** miserly, sparing **8** stinting **9** niggardly **12** parsimonious **13** penny-pinching

penury 4 need, want **7** poverty **9** indigence, privation **10** bankruptcy, insolvency **11** destitution **14** impoverishment

Penutian
language branch: 4 Coos **5** Huave, Maidu, Mayan, Miwok **6** Wintun, Yokuts **7** Chinook, Klamath, Takelma, Totonac **8** Sahaptin **9** Mixe-Zoque, Tsimshian
tribe: 5 Maidu **7** Klamath

peon 4 pawn, serf **5** slave **6** drudge, menial, worker **7** footman, laborer, orderly, peasant, servant

peony 7 Paeonia
varieties: 4 Tree **7** Chinese,

Pennsylvania
abbreviation: 2 PA **5** Penna
nickname: 8 Keystone
capital: 10 Harrisburg
largest city: 12 Philadelphia
others: 4 Erie, Etna, Plum, York **5** Avoca, Baden **6** Beaver, Bethel, Butler, Easton, Emmaus, Radnor, Ridley, Sharon **7** Altoona, Baldwin, Bristol, Chester, Ephrata, Hanover, Hershey, Lebanon, Reading **8** Abington, Braddock, Bradford, Bryn Mawr, Carlisle, Clairton, Harrison, Hazelton, Monessen, Scranton, Shamokin **9** Aliquippa, Allentown, Bethlehem, Charleroi, Haverford, Jeannette, Johnstown, Lancaster, Meadville, Mill Creek, Newcastle, Swissvale, Uniontown, Whitehall **10** Carbondale, Gettysburg, McKeesport, Norristown, Pittsburgh **11** Springfield, Wilkes Barre **12** State College, Williamsport
college: 3 PSU **4** Penn, Pitt **5** Gratz, Thiel **6** Drexel, Lehigh, Temple **7** Juniata, LaSalle, Ursinus **8** Alliance, Bryn Mawr, Bucknell, Duquesne, Lycoming **9** Dickinson, Lafayette, Penn State, St Josephs, Villanova **10** Pittsburgh, Swarthmore **12** Carnegie Tech **17** Pennsylvania State
feature:
battle site: **10** Gettysburg
bell: **7** Liberty
hall: **12** Independence
historical site: **11** Valley Forge
tribe: 6 Seneca **7** Shawnee **8** Delaware **11** Lenni-Lanape **13** Susquehannock
people: 5 Amish, Dutch **10** Stan Musial **11** Andrew Wyeth, Ethel Waters, Mary Cassatt, Stuart Davis **12** Andrew Mellon, Anthony Wayne, Margaret Mead, Martha Graham, Samuel Barber, Thomas Eakins **13** Clifford Odets, Gertrude Stein **14** George S Kaufman **15** Maxwell Anderson **19** Stephen Vincent Benet
explorer: **5** Brule **6** Hudson **11** Hendrickson
lake: 4 Erie **7** Harveys **8** Conneaut **10** Pymatuning **13** Wallenpaupack
land rank: 11 thirty-third
mountain: 5 South **6** Pocono **11** Alleghenies
highest point: **5** Davis
physical feature:
peninsula: **11** Presque Isle
valley: **5** Great
president: 13 James Buchanan
river: 4 Ohio **6** Lehigh **7** Clarion, Genesee, Juniata, Licking, Towanda **8** Caldwell, Delaware, Schrader **9** Allegheny **10** Schuylkill **11** Monongahela, Susquehanna
state admission: 6 second
state bird: 12 ruffed grouse
state fish: 10 brook trout
state flower: 14 mountain laurel
state motto: 28 Virtue Liberty and Independence
state tree: 7 hemlock

Tibetan **8** Majorcan **11** Chinese tree **12** Common garden

people 3 kin **5** folks **6** family, humans, the mob **7** kinfolk, mankind, mortals, the herd **8** citizens, humanity, populace, the crowd **9** ancestors, citizenry, commoners, humankind, relatives, the masses, the public, the rabble **10** population **11** homo sapiens, human beings, individuals, inhabitants, John Q Public, men and women, the millions

People Are Funny
host: 13 Art Linkletter

pep 3 vim, zip **4** dash, life, snap **5** gusto, verve, vigor **6** energy, ginger, spirit **8** vitality, vivacity **9** animation **10** enthusiasm, get-up-and-go, liveliness

Pepe Le Moko
director: 14 Julien Duvivier
cast: 9 Jean Gabin **13** Gabriel Gabrio, Mireille Balin
remade as: 6 Casbah **7** Algiers

peperomia
varieties: 3 Ivy **6** Prayer, Vining **7** Ivy-leaf, Leather, Rededge **8** Coin-leaf, Platinum **9** Flowering **10** Silver-edge, Silver-leaf, Watermelon **11** Green-ripple **13** Emerald-ripple, Little fantasy

Pepita
character in: 21 The Bridge of San Luis Rey
author: 6 Wilder

Peppard, George
born: 9 Detroit MI
wife: 15 Elizabeth Ashley
roles: 6 Tobruk **7** Banacek **8** The A-Team **16** The Carpetbaggers **19** Breakfast at Tiffany's

pepper 3 dot **6** shower, strafe **7** bombard **8** sprinkle **9** condiment, vegetable

pepper, peppercorn
botanical name: 5 Piper **7** P nigrum **8** Capsicum **10** Piperaceae **11** C frutescens
color: 3 red **5** black, green, white
origin: 5 India **6** Brazil, Ceylon **7** Malabar, Sarawak, Sumatra **8** Alleppey, Pandjang, Sri Lanka **11** Tellicherry
varieties: 3 Red **4** Baby, Bell, Bird, Cone, Long, Wild **5** Betle, Black, Chili, Cubeb, Green, Japan, Sweet, White **6** Cherry **7** Cayenne, Celebes, Cluster, Tabasco **8** Capsicum **9** Mild water **10** Australian, Red cluster **12** Mountain long, Tabasco-sauce
French: 6 poivre
German: 7 pfeffer
Italian: 4 pepe
Latin: 5 piper
Persian: 5 biber **6** pilpil
Spanish: 8 pimienta
Swedish: 6 peppar
Sanskrit: 7 pippali

peppermint 6 Mentha
varieties: 4 Gray **5** Black, River, White **6** Silver, Sydney **9** Blackbutt **10** Robertson's **11** Broad-leaved **15** Mount Wellington **17** Narrow-leaved black **19** Nichol's willow-leaved

peppermint schnapps
type: 7 liqueur
flavor: 4 mint

peppery 3 hot **5** fiery, sharp, spicy **7** burning, piquant, pungent **14** highly seasoned

peppy 4 spry **5** brisk, perky **6** active, bouncy, frisky, lively, snappy **7** dynamic **8** animated, spirited, vigorous **9** energetic, full of pep, sparkling, sprightly, vivacious **12** enthusiastic

pep up **4** fire **6** excite, vivify, wake up **7** animate, enliven, quicken **8** vitalize

Pepys, Samuel
author of: **10** Pepys' Diary

Pepys' Diary
author: **11** Samuel Pepys

Pequot
language family: **9** Algonkian **10** Algonquian
location: **11** Connecticut, Rhode Island

perambulate **4** pace, tour, walk **5** amble, mosey **6** ramble, stroll **7** meander, saunter **9** promenade

perceivable **7** visible **8** apparent, distinct **10** detectable, noticeable, observable **11** discernible, perceptible **13** ascertainable

perceive **3** get, see **4** feel, hear, know, note **5** grasp, savvy, sense, smell, taste **6** deduce, detect, gather, notice **7** discern, make out, observe, realize **8** conclude, discover **9** apprehend, be aware of, recognize **10** comprehend, understand **11** distinguish

perceptible **5** clear, plain **7** evident, notable, obvious, visible **8** apparent, distinct, manifest, palpable, tangible, unhidden **9** prominent **10** detectable, noticeable, observable **11** conspicuous, discernible, perceivable, unconcealed, well-defined **12** discoverable, unmistakable **13** ascertainable

perception **5** grasp, sense **7** faculty **8** judgment **9** awareness, detection **10** cognizance, conception **11** discernment, recognition **12** apprehension **13** comprehension, consciousness, understanding **14** discrimination

perceptive **4** keen **5** acute, aware, quick, sharp **6** astute, shrewd **8** sensible **9** sensitive **10** discerning, insightful, responsive **11** intelligent, penetrating, quick-witted **13** understanding

perch **3** sit **4** land, rest, seat **5** eyrie, light, roost **6** alight, settle

Perchta
also: **7** Berchta
origin: **8** Germanic
goddess of: **5** death **9** fertility
corresponds to: **5** Holle

Percival, Perceval
character in: **16** Arthurian romance

percolate **4** boil, brew **6** bubble, seethe

percussion instrument **4** gong **5** anvil, bells, tabor **6** chimes, rattle **7** celesta, cymbals, marimba, taboret, timpani **8** bass drum, side drum, triangle **9** castanets, dulcitone, snare drum, tenor drum, typophone, xylophone **10** kettledrum, tambourine **12** Glockenspiel, tubular bells

Percy, Walker
author of: **8** Lancelot **12** The Moviegoer **14** Love in the Ruins **15** The Second Coming **16** The Last Gentleman

Perdita
character in: **14** The Winter's Tale
author: **11** Shakespeare

perdition **4** Hell, ruin **8** hellfire **9** damnation, ruination **11** destruction **12** condemnation

Perdix
also: **9** Polycaste
brother: **8** Daedalus
son: **5** Talus
changed into: **9** partridge

pere **6** father, senior

Pere Goriot
author: **14** Honore de Balzac
character: **15** Monsieur Vautrin **17** Eugene de Rastignac, Madame de Beauseant **18** Victorine Taillefer **26** Countess Anastasie de Restaud, Baroness Delphine de Nucingen

peregrination **4** trip **5** jaunt, sally **6** hiking, junket, roving, travel **7** journey, roaming **8** rambling, trekking **9** excursion, wandering **10** expedition

Peregrine Pickle
author: **14** Tobias Smollett

Pereira, William
architect of: **13** Cape Canaveral **20** Transamerica Building (San Francisco)

Perelman, S J
author of: **10** Eastward Ha **15** One Touch of Venus (with Ogden Nash and Kurt Weill) **16** The Road to Miltown **18** Strictly from Hunger **24** Under the Spreading Atrophy

peremptory **5** final **6** biased, lordly **8** absolute, decisive, dogmatic **9** assertive, imperious **10** aggressive, high-handed, imperative, obligatory, undeniable **11** dictatorial, domineering, irrevocable, opinionated, overbearing, unavoidable, unequivocal **12** closed-minded, irreversible **13** authoritative **14** unquestionable **16** incontrovertible

perennial **5** fixed **7** durable, lasting, undying **8** constant, enduring, timeless **9** ceaseless, continual, immutable, incessant, long-lived, permanent, perpetual, unceasing, unfailing **10** changeless, continuous, persistent, unchanging **11** everlasting, long-lasting, unremitting **12** imperishable **14** indestructible

Pereus
father: **6** Elatus
mother: **7** Laodice

Perez, Manuel Benitez
nickname: **10** El Cordobes

perfect **4** pure, true **5** exact, ideal, whole **6** effect, entire, evolve, strict **7** achieve, develop, fulfill, precise, realize, sublime, supreme **8** absolute, accurate, complete, faithful, finished, flawless, peerless, thorough, unbroken, unerring **9** blameless, faultless, matchless, undamaged, unequaled, unrivaled, untainted **10** accomplish, consummate, immaculate, impeccable, scrupulous, unimpaired **11** superlative, unblemished, unmitigated, unqualified

perfection **6** purity **9** achieving, evolution, exactness, precision, sublimity **10** completion, excellence, ideal state **11** development, fulfillment, perfectness, realization, superiority **12** accurateness, consummation, flawlessness **13** faultlessness, impeccability **14** accomplishment

perfectly **5** fully, quite **6** purely, wholly **7** totally, utterly **8** entirely, superbly **9** downright, supremely **10** absolutely, altogether, completely, flawlessly, impeccably, infinitely, positively, thoroughly **11** faultlessly, wonderfully **12** consummately, preeminently, to perfection, without fault **13** without defect **14** to the nth degree, without blemish

perfidious **5** false, lying **6** shifty, sneaky **7** corrupt **8** cheating, disloyal, two-faced **9** deceitful, dishonest, faithless **10** traitorous, treasonous, unfaithful, untruthful **11** treacherous, treasonable

12 dishonorable, undependable, unscrupulous 13 double-dealing, untrustworthy

perfidy 6 deceit 7 treason 8 bad faith, betrayal 9 falseness, recreancy, treachery, two-timing 10 disloyalty, infidelity 11 double-cross, inconstancy 13 breach of faith, deceitfulness, double-dealing, faithlessness 14 unfaithfulness

perforate 4 bore, gash, hole, slit, stab 5 drill, prick, punch, slash, split, stick 6 pierce 8 puncture 9 lancinate, penetrate

perform 2 do 3 act 4 meet, play 5 enact 6 attain, depict, effect, finish, render, troupe 7 achieve, execute, fulfill, portray, present, pull off, realize 8 carry out, knock off 9 discharge, dispose of, polish off, represent 10 accomplish, bring about, consummate, perpetrate, take part in

performance 4 play, show 5 doing, opera 6 ballet 7 concert, conduct, recital 8 ceremony, dispatch, exercise 9 acquittal, discharge, execution, rendering, spectacle 10 attainment, completion, exhibition, performing, production 11 achievement, fulfillment, realization, transaction 12 consummation, effectuation, perpetration, presentation 13 entertainment 14 accomplishment

perfume 4 odor 5 aroma, scent, smell 7 bouquet, cologne, essence, extract, sweeten 9 aromatize, fragrance

perfumed 7 odorous, scented 8 aromatic, fragrant 11 odoriferous 12 sweet-scented 13 sweet-smelling

perfunctory 3 lax 5 hasty 6 casual 7 cursory, offhand, routine 8 careless, listless, lukewarm 9 apathetic, negligent 10 mechanical, spiritless, unthinking 11 halfhearted, inattentive, indifferent, passionless, superficial, unconcerned 13 disinterested

Pergamus
father: 11 Neoptolemus
mother: 10 Andromache

pergola 5 arbor, bower 6 ramada 7 balcony, trellis

Per Hanea
character in: 16 Giants of the Earth
author: 7 Rolvaag

perhaps 5 maybe 6 mayhap 8 peut-etre, possibly 9 perchance 10 God willing, imaginably 11 conceivably 12 peradventure

Perialla
form: 9 priestess
priestess of: 6 Delphi

Periapis
also: 8 Periopis
father: 6 Pheres
son: 9 Patrocles

Periboea
father: 9 Alcathous, Hipponous
husband: 6 Oeneus 7 Polybus
son: 6 Tydeus 7 Olenias, Pelegon 14 Telamonian Ajax
foster son: 7 Oedipus

Perichole, La
character in: 21 The Bridge of San Luis Rey
author: 6 Wilder

Pericles, Prince of Tyre
author: 18 William Shakespeare
character: 5 Cleon 6 Marina, Thaisa 7 Dionyza 9 Antiochus 10 Lysimachus

Periclymenus
father: 6 Neleus 8 Poseidon
grandfather: 8 Poseidon
gift: 13 shape-changing
killed by: 8 Hercules

periderm 4 bark 8 covering 9 sheathing

peridot
species: 7 olivine
source: 5 Burma, Mogok 8 Zebirget
color: 11 yellow-green

perigee 5 depth, nadir 8 low point

Perikeiromene (The Rape of the Ringlets)
author: 8 Menander

peril 4 risk 6 danger, hazard, menace, threat 7 pitfall 8 jeopardy, unsafety 10 insecurity 11 uncertainty 13 cause for alarm, vulnerability

Perilaus
father: 7 Icarius
cousin: 12 Clytemnestra

perilous 5 risky, shaky 6 chancy, unsafe, unsure 7 ominous 8 insecure, slippery, ticklish 9 dangerous, hazardous, uncertain 10 precarious, vulnerable 11 threatening, venturesome

Perimedes
mentioned in: 7 Odyssey
companion of: 8 Odysseus
father: 10 Eurystheus

Perimele
father: 10 Hippodamas
ravished by: 8 Achelous
changed into: 6 island

perimeter 4 edge 6 border, bounds, margin 8 confines 9 periphery 10 borderline 13 circumference

period 3 age, end, eon, era 4 halt, stop, term, time 5 close, epoch, limit 6 finale, finish, season 7 curtain 8 duration, interval 9 cessation, interlude
French: 6 siecle

periodic, periodical 6 cyclic 7 regular, routine 8 frequent, repeated, seasonal 9 recurrent, recurring 12 intermittent

periodical 5 daily, paper 6 annual, review, weekly 7 journal, monthly 8 bulletin, magazine 9 newspaper, quarterly 10 newsletter 11 publication 12 newsmagazine

periodically 5 often 9 regularly, routinely 10 frequently, repeatedly 12 occasionally

Periopis *see* 8 Periapis

peripatetic 6 roving 7 migrant, nomadic, roaming, walking 8 rambling, tramping 9 itinerant, migratory, traveling, wandering 10 ambulating, ambulatory 12 Aristotelian, gallivanting 13 peregrinating

Periphas
mentioned in: 5 Iliad
king of: 6 Attica
father: 6 Epytus
vocation: 6 herald 7 warrior
changed into: 5 eagle
changed by: 4 Zeus

periphery 4 edge 5 bound 6 border 7 fringes 8 boundary 9 outskirts, perimeter 13 circumference

Periphetes
form: 5 giant
father: 7 Copreus
ally of: 7 Trojans
killed by: 7 Theseus

perish 3 die 5 decay 6 expire, vanish 7 crumble 8 pass away 9 disappear 10 come to ruin, wither away 11 be destroyed

perishable 8 fleeting, unstable 9 ephemeral 10 evanescent, short-lived, transitory 12 decomposable

perished 4 dead, died 7 expired 8 lifeless 10 passed away

periwinkle 5 Vinca 12 Catharanthus
varieties: 4 Rose 6 Common, Lesser 7 Greater 10 Madagascar

perjury **13** false swearing **14** lying under oath **20** giving false testimony

Perker
character in: **14** Pickwick Papers
author: **7** Dickens

Perkins, Anthony
born: **9** New York NY
roles: **6** Psycho **11** Norman Bates **14** Catch Twenty-Two **17** Look Homeward Angel **18** Desire Under the Elms, Friendly Persuasion

perk up **4** lift **5** cheer, rally, renew **6** buoy up, lift up, revive **7** animate, enliven, gladden **8** brighten, vitalize **9** stimulate **10** rejuvenate

perky **3** gay **4** pert **5** alert, brisk, happy, saucy, sunny **6** jaunty, lively **7** smiling **8** animated, cheerful, spirited **9** sprightly, vivacious **11** free and easy **12** full of spirit, lighthearted

permanent **3** set **4** perm, wave **6** stable **7** abiding, durable, endless, eternal, lasting, undying **8** constant, enduring, immortal, infinite, unending, unfading **9** deathless, immutable, long-lived, perpetual, unfailing **10** changeless, unyielding **11** everlasting, long-lasting, never-ending, unalterable **12** imperishable

permeate **4** fill **5** imbue **6** infuse **7** pervade **8** saturate **9** penetrate **11** pass through, seep through, soak through

per mensem **10** by the month

permissible **5** legal, licit **6** lawful **7** allowed, granted **8** licensed **9** allowable, permitted, tolerated **10** admissible, authorized, legitimate, sanctioned **12** unprohibited

permission **5** grant, leave **6** assent, permit **7** consent, license **8** approval, sanction **9** agreement, allowance **10** compliance, concession, indulgence **11** approbation, endorsement **12** acquiescence, dispensation **13** authorization

permissive **3** lax **7** lenient **8** allowing, granting, tolerant **9** assenting, easygoing, indulgent **10** consenting, forbearing, permitting **11** acquiescent **13** unprohibitive **14** unproscriptive

permit **2** OK **3** let **5** allow **6** endure, suffer **7** agree to, approve, condone, endorse, let pass, license, warrant **8** bear with, sanction, tolerate **9** authority, authorize, consent to, put up with **11** give leave to **12** give assent to **13** authorization
French: **13** laissez passer

permit to leave **4** free **5** let go **6** excuse **7** dismiss, release, set free **8** liberate **9** allow to go, discharge, send forth

pernicious **5** fatal, toxic **6** deadly, lethal, mortal **7** baneful, harmful, noxious, serious **8** damaging, venomous **9** dangerous, injurious, malignant, poisonous **10** disastrous **11** deleterious, destructive, detrimental

pernod
type: **8** aperitif
flavor: **5** anise
substitute for: **8** absinthe
with gin: **7** Dubarry
with orange juice: **9** Tiger Tail
with rum: **8** Shanghai
with rye: **3** TNT

Pero
father: **6** Neleus
mother: **7** Chloris
husband: **4** Bias

peroration **6** sermon, speech, tirade **7** address, lecture, oration **8** diatribe, harangue, jeremiad **9** discourse, philippic **10** filibuster **11** declamation, exhortation

perpendicular **4** sine **5** erect, plumb, sheer, steep **7** upright **8** vertical **10** right angle

perpetrate **2** do **5** enact **6** commit, pursue **7** execute, inflict, perform, pull off **8** carry out, transact

perpetration **5** doing **9** committal **10** commission, committing, performing **11** carrying out, performance

perpetrator **9** performer **11** participant

perpetual **7** abiding, endless, eternal, lasting **8** constant, enduring, repeated, unending **9** ceaseless, continual, incessant, permanent, sustained, unceasing **10** continuous **11** everlasting, never ending, unremitting **12** interminable **13** inexhaustible, uninterrupted

perpetuate **4** save **7** sustain **8** continue, maintain, make last, preserve **10** eternalize **11** immortalize, memorialize

perpetuity **7** all time, forever **8** eternity, infinity **9** end of time **10** permanence **11** endlessness **12** perpetuation, timelessness **13** perdurability, perennialness

perplex **5** mix up, stump **6** baffle, boggle, muddle, puzzle, rattle **7** confuse, mystify, nonplus **8** befuddle, bewilder, confound **9** dumbfound

perplexed **7** anxious, amazed, baffled, bemused, muddled, puzzled **8** confused, doubtful, involved **9** befuddled, intricate, mystified **10** astonished, bewildered, nonplussed

perplexing **4** hard, mazy **6** thorny **7** complex **10** mysterious
riddle: **9** conundrum

perplexity **9** confusion **10** bafflement, puzzlement **12** bewilderment **13** mystification

perquisite **3** due **4** gift, perk **5** right **6** reward **7** benefit, present **9** advantage, emolument, privilege **10** honorarium, inducement, recompense **13** fringe benefit

Perrine, Valerie
born: **11** Galveston TX
roles: **5** Lenny **8** Superman **18** Slaughterhouse Five

Perry, Matthew Calbraith
served in: **10** Mexican War **19** War of Eighteen Twelve
rank: **9** commodore
helped establish: **7** Liberia
commander of: **17** US African Squadron
gained treaty with: **5** Japan

Perry, Oliver Hazard
nickname: **14** Hero of Lake Erie
served in: **13** Tripolitan War **19** War of Eighteen-Twelve
battle: **8** Lake Erie
commander of ship: **7** Niagara **8** Lawrence
defeated: **7** British
saying: **31** We have met the enemy and they are ours

Perry, William
nickname: **12** Refrigerator
sport: **8** football
team: **12** Chicago Bears

Perry Como Show, The
regulars: **8** Don Adams **9** Jack Duffy, Paul Lynde **10** Pierre Olaf **11** Kaye Ballard **12** Sandy Stewart **14** Fontane Sisters **17** Ray Charles Singers **18** Louis Da Pron Dancers **19** Peter Gennaro Dancers
announcer: **9** Dick Stark, Ed Herlihy **11** Frank Gallop, Martin Block **12** Durward Kirby
orchestra: **13** Mitchell Ayres
theme: **16** Dream Along with Me

Perry Mason
character: **6** Lt Drum **7** Lt

Tragg **9** Paul Drake **10** Lt Anderson **11** Della Street **14** Hamilton Burger
cast: 9 Wesley Lau **10** Ray Collins **11** Barbara Hale, Raymond Burr **13** William Hopper, William Talman **15** Richard Anderson

Persa
father: 7 Oceanus
mother: 6 Tethys

persecute 3 vex **4** bait **5** abuse, annoy, bully, harry, hound **6** badger, harass, harrow, hector, plague **7** oppress, torment **8** maltreat **9** tyrannize, victimize

Persephone
also: 4 Cora, Kore **10** Perserpina, Proserpine
queen of: 5 Hades
father: 4 Zeus
mother: 7 Demeter
husband: 5 Hades
abducted by: 5 Pluto
ate seeds of: 11 pomegranate
epithet: 11 Carpophorus
corresponds to: 5 Brimo **6** Libera **8** Despoena

Perseus
father: 4 Zeus
mother: 5 Danae
grandfather: 8 Acrisius
wife: 9 Andromeda
son: 6 Mestor, Perses **7** Alcaeus, Heleius **9** Electryon, Sthenelus
daughter: 10 Gorgophone
saved: 9 Andromeda
killed: 6 Gorgon, Medusa

perseverance 8 tenacity **10** doggedness, resolution **11** persistence **12** resoluteness **13** determination, steadfastness

persevere 6 hang on, keep on **7** persist **8** keep at it, plug away, work hard **9** not give up, stick to it **10** be resolute, be resolved, hammer away **11** be obstinate, be steadfast, hang in there

persevering 6 dogged **8** constant, diligent, resolute, sedulous **9** keeping on, steadfast, tenacious **10** determined, persistent, unflagging **11** hardworking, industrious, unremitting

Pershing, John J
nickname: 9 Black Jack
served in: 3 WWI **11** Philippines, World War One **18** Spanish-American War
commander of: 21 Mexican border campaign
trained: 27 American Expeditionary Forces
battle: 10 Kettle Hill **11** San Juan Hill
fought against: 5 Moros **11** Pancho Villa
rank: 16 brigadier general **18** general of the armies
memoirs: 26 My Experiences in the World War
***won:* 13** Pulitzer Prize (for history)

Persia *see* **4** Iran

Persian Mythology
god of light/truth: 7 Mithras

Persians, The
author: 9 Aeschylus
character: 6 Atossa, Xerxes **13** Ghost of Darius

persist 4 go on, last, stay **6** endure, hang on, hold on, remain **7** hold out, survive **8** continue, keep at it, not yield **9** not give up, persevere, stand fast, stick to it **10** be resolute **11** be obstinate, be tenacious, hang in there, never say die

persistence 8 tenacity **9** diligence **11** application **12** perseverance **13** determination

persistent 6 dogged **7** abiding, endless, eternal, lasting **8** constant, enduring, obdurate, resolute, stubborn **9** continual, incessant, obstinate, perpetual, steadfast, sustained, tenacious, unceasing, unfailing **10** continuous, determined, persisting, relentless, unshakable, unswerving **11** persevering, unrelenting, unremitting **12** interminable **13** inexhaustible

Perske, Betty Joan
real name of: 12 Lauren Bacall

persnickety 5 fussy **6** choosy **7** finical, finicky **8** picayune **10** fastidious, fuddy-duddy, meticulous, nitpicking, particular, pernickety **11** overprecise, punctilious **13** overdemanding

person 4 body, soul **5** being, human **6** mortal **8** creature **9** earthling **10** human being, individual, living body, living soul

persona 5 being **6** facade **9** character

personable 4 warm **7** affable, amiable, cordial, likable, tactful **8** amicable, charming, friendly, outgoing, pleasant, sociable **9** agreeable **10** attractive, diplomatic **11** complaisant, sympathetic **12** well-disposed, well-mannered

Personae
author: 9 Ezra Pound

personage 3 VIP **5** nabob **6** bigwig **7** big name, big shot, notable **8** big wheel, luminary, somebody **9** celebrity, dignitary **11** heavyweight **12** leading light, public figure **13** high-muck-a-muck

persona grata 16 acceptable person **34** acceptable diplomatic representative

personal 3 own **5** privy **6** bodily, inward, secret **7** private, special **8** intimate, physical **9** corporeal, exclusive **10** individual, particular, subjective **12** confidential

Personal Anthology, A
author: 15 Jorge Luis Borges

personality 5 charm **6** makeup, nature **8** charisma, identity **9** magnetism **10** affability, amiability **11** disposition, temperament **12** friendliness **13** agreeableness, individuality **15** distinctiveness

persona non grata 15 unwelcome person **18** unacceptable person **33** unwelcome diplomatic representative

personification of ***see box, p. 744***

personify 6 embody **7** express **9** exemplify, incarnate, represent, symbolize **11** externalize, incorporate, personalize **12** characterize

personnel 4 crew **5** staff **7** members, workers **8** manpower **9** employees, work force **10** associates

Person to Person
host: 13 Edward R Murrow **18** Charles Collingwood

perspective 4 view **5** scape, scene, vista **7** outlook **8** overview, prospect **9** broad view, viewpoint **12** bird's-eye view

perspicacious 4 keen **5** acute, alert, awake, sharp **6** astute, shrewd **9** clear-eyed, sagacious **10** discerning, perceptive **11** clearheaded, keen-sighted, penetrating, sharp-witted **12** clear-sighted

perspicacity 6 acumen **8** keenness, sagacity **9** acuteness, alertness, sharpness **10** astuteness, perception, shrewdness **11** discernment **14** discrimination

persuadable 7 willing **8** amenable, obliging **9** malleable, tractable **10** open-minded **16** open to suggestion

persuade 3 get **4** coax, lure, move, sway **5** tempt **6** cajole, entice, induce, prompt

Personification of
aging: **4** Elli
air: **4** Amen, Amon **5** Ammon **6** Aether
astronomy: **6** Urania
breath: **4** Amen, Amon **5** Ammon
chaos: **4** Nunu
choral song: **11** Terpsichore
comedy: **6** Thalia
confusion: **5** Chaos
conscience: **5** Aidos
courage: **5** Arete **6** Virtus
dance: **8** Polymnia **10** Polyhymnia **11** Terpsichore
death: **4** Mors **6** Namtar **8** Thanatos
desert: **3** Set **4** Seth
desire: **6** Pothos
divine punishment: **3** Ate **7** Nemesis
east wind: **5** Eurus **9** Volturnus
echo: **4** Echo
emulation: **5** Zelos
familial affection: **6** Pietas
fate: **4** Norn **5** Moira, Moras
fear: **6** Deimos
femininity: **5** Neith
fire: **4** Logi
force: **3** Bia
good faith: **5** Fides
grain blight: **7** Robigus
heaven: **6** Uranus
hostile nature: **8** Fomorian
idyllic poetry: **6** Thalia
liberty: **8** Libertas
longing: **6** Pothos
lotus: **8** Nefertem
meditation: **6** Melete
memory: **5** Mneme, Munin
moon: **4** Luna
nature: **7** Eriking
night: **3** Nox
north wind: **6** Boreas
order: **7** Eunomia
pain: **5** Oizys
past: **3** Urd
peace: **5** Irene
prayer: **5** Litae
present: **8** Verdandi
punishment: **5** Poena, Poine
recklessness: **3** Ate
revenge: **5** Poena, Poine
Roman nation: **8** Quirinus
sacred music: **8** Polymnia **10** Polyhymnia
sea: **3** Ler, Lir **5** Nammu **6** Pontus **8** Thalassa
sky: **6** Aether, Hathor
soul: **6** Psyche
southeast wind: **5** Eurus **9** Volturnus
south wind: **5** Notus **7** Ninurta
strength: **6** Cratus
sun: **3** Sol
thought: **5** Hugin
tragedy: **9** Melpomene
truth: **7** Alethia
unavailing effort: **5** Ocnus
wealth: **6** Plutus
west wind: **8** Favonius, Zephyrus
wind: **7** Ninurta
zeal: **5** Zelos

7 wheedle, win over **8** convince, inveigle, motivate, talk into **9** influence

Persuasion
author: **10** Jane Austen
character: **7** Mrs Clay **8** Mrs Croft **11** Lady Russell **12** Admiral Croft **25** Captain Frederick Wentworth
Elliot family: **4** Anne **7** William **9** Elizabeth, Sir Walter
Musgrove family: **4** Mary **6** Louisa **7** Charles **9** Henrietta

persuasive **6** cogent **7** coaxing, logical, winning **8** alluring, credible, forceful, inviting **9** effective, plausible, seductive **10** believable, compelling, convincing **11** influential

pert **4** flip, spry **5** alert, brash, brisk, fresh, nervy, perky, quick, saucy **6** brassy, brazen, cheeky, lively, nimble **7** chipper **8** flippant, impolite, impudent, insolent **9** audacious, energetic, insulting, sprightly, wide-awake **11** impertinent, smart-alecky **12** discourteous

pertain **2** be **5** apply, touch **6** befall, belong, relate **7** concern, connect

pertinacious **6** dogged **8** stubborn **9** obstinate, tenacious **10** persistent, unyielding **11** persevering

pertinacity **9** obstinacy **10** mulishness **11** persistence, willfulness **12** contrariness, obdurateness, perverseness, stubbornness **13** determination, inflexibility, intransigence, pigheadedness **14** bullheadedness, intractability

pertinence **9** relevance **11** germaneness **12** appositeness **13** applicability

pertinent **3** apt **4** meet **7** apropos, fitting, germane, related **8** apposite, material, relevant, suitable **9** befitting, concerned, congruent, connected **10** applicable, consistent, to the point
Latin: **5** ad rem

perturb **5** upset, worry **6** bother **7** disturb, fluster, trouble **8** disquiet, distress **10** discompose, disconcert

perturbation **5** alarm, upset, worry **6** dismay **7** anxiety, concern, turmoil **8** distress **9** agitation, commotion **10** excitement **11** disquietude, trepidation **12** apprehension, discomposure **13** consternation

perturbed **5** upset **7** annoyed, worried **8** agitated, troubled **9** disturbed **12** disconcerted

perturbing **6** vexing **7** irksome **8** annoying **9** vexatious **10** bothersome, irritating, unsettling **11** disquieting, distressing, troublesome **13** disconcerting

Peru ***see box***

Perugino, Pietro
real name: **14** Pietro Vannucci
also called: **10** Il Perugino **14** Pier della Pieve
born: **5** Italy **15** Citta della Pieve
artwork: **24** The Crucifixion with Saints **26** Delivery of the Keys to St Peter **27** The Giving of the Keys to St Peter **32** Apparition of the Virgin to St Bernard, Christ Delivering the Keys to St Peter

perusal **5** study **6** review **7** reading **8** scanning, scrutiny **10** inspection, run-through **11** examination, look-through **12** scrutinizing **13** contemplation

peruse **3** con **4** read, scan **5** study **6** search, survey **7** examine, inspect **10** scrutinize

pervade **4** fill **5** imbue **6** infuse **7** suffuse **8** permeate, saturate **9** penetrate **13** spread through **17** diffuse throughout

pervasive **4** rife **7** rampant **8** dominant **9** prevalent **10** ubiquitous **11** omnipresent, predominant

perverse **5** balky **6** dogged, mulish, ornery **7** wayward, willful **8** contrary, obdurate, stubborn **9** obstinate, pigheaded **10** hardheaded, headstrong, inflexible, rebellious

Peru

capital/largest city: **4** Lima
Inca capital: **5** Cuzco

others: **3** Ica **4** Puno **5** Cuzco, Paita, Pisco, Tacna **6** Callao, Talara **7** Huanuco, Iquitos **8** Arequipa, Castilla, Chiclayo, Chimbote, Mollendo, Pucallpa, Trujillo **9** Cajamarca **10** Yurimaguas

school: **8** Trujillo **20** National U of San Marcos

division: **3** Ica **4** Lima, Puno **5** Cusco, Cuzco, Junin, Piura, Tacna **6** Ancash, Loreto, Tumbes
Inca empire: **13** Tahuantinsuyo

measure: **4** topo **5** galon **7** celemin

monetary unit: **3** sol **5** libra **6** dinero, reseta **7** centavo

weight: **5** libra **7** quintal

island: **6** Chinca **7** Chincha

lake: **8** Titicaca

mountain: **5** Andes **7** El Misti, Huamina **8** Coropuna

highest point: **9** Huascaran

river: **3** Ene, Ica, Ilo **4** Napo, Napu **5** Piura, Rimac **6** Amazon, Oroton, Pampas, Yaguas, Yavari **7** Curaray, Mantaro, Maranon, Pastaza, Tapiche, Ucayali **8** Apurimac, Huallaga, Urubamba **11** Madre de Dios, Paucartambo

sea: **7** Pacific

physical feature:
current: **6** el nino
desert: **5** Nazca **7** Atacama, Sechura
drizzling rain: **8** ilovizna
fog: **5** garua
gulf: **9** Guayaquil
plateau: **7** Tablazo

people: **4** Ande, Boro, Cana, Inca, Inka, Lama, Pano, Peba, Piro, Yutu **5** Campa, Carib, Chana, Colan, Colla, Jwaro, Moche, Nasca, Senci, Yagua, Yunca **6** Atalan, Aymara, Canchi, Chanca, Chanka, Chimer, Cholos, Cocama, Jibaro, Kechua, Omagua, Quiche, Quolla, Setibo, Sipibo **7** Changos, Chincha, Chuncho, Mestizo, Mochica **8** Amahuaca, Criollos, Mayoruma, Quechuia **9** Callawaya **10** Tiahuanaca, Tiatinagua **11** Chumpivilca
artist: **4** Lazo **7** Montero, Sabogal, Szyszlo **8** Codesido
author: **4** Vega **5** Palma, Prada **8** Caviedes **10** Mariategui
explorer: **7** Pizarro
Inca leader: **7** Huascar **9** Atahualpa **10** Manco Capac
leader: **5** Balta, Pardo, Prado, Torre **7** Bolivar **8** Castilla **9** Santa Cruz **13** Belaunde Terry **15** Leguiay y Salcedo, Morales Bermudez

language: **6** Aymara **7** English, Quechua, Spanish

religion: **13** Roman Catholic

place:
bullring: **11** Plaza de Acho
center of Lima: **12** Plaza de Armas
church: **10** La Compania
open market/street: **9** Calle Real
ruins: **5** Huaco **8** Chan-Chan **9** Cajamarca **11** Machu-Picchu **22** Fortress of Sacsayhuaman

feature:
animal: **5** llama **6** alpaca, vicuna **7** guanaco
commune: **6** ayllus
dance: **5** cueca, kaswa **6** cachua
farmers: **10** campesinos
priest: **6** villac
slums: **9** barriadas
tree: **8** cinchona

food:
dish: **3** aji, cuy **7** ceviche **10** anticuchos
drink: **5** pisco **6** chicha **11** aguardiente

11 disobedient, intractable, wrongheaded

perversion **9** depravity **10** corruption, degeneracy, immorality **11** dissipation, dissolution

pervert **4** warp **5** abuse **6** debase, misuse **7** contort, corrupt, degrade, deprave, distort, falsify, subvert **8** misapply **9** desecrate **12** misrepresent

perverted **5** false **6** faulty, untrue, warped **7** corrupt, debased, deviant, twisted, unsound **8** aberrant, abnormal, degraded, depraved **9** contorted, distorted, erroneous, imperfect, unnatural **10** fallacious, unbalanced **12** misconceived, misconstrued **13** misunderstood

Peschkowsky, Michael Igor
real name of: **11** Mike Nichols

pesky **7** chafing, galling, irksome **8** annoying **9** maddening, obnoxious, offensive, vexatious **10** bothersome, disturbing, nettlesome **11** aggravating, distasteful, infuriating, pestiferous, troublesome **12** disagreeable, exasperating **13** objectionable

pessimism **5** gloom **7** despair **10** gloominess **12** hopelessness **13** gloomy outlook **14** discouragement **15** downheartedness

pessimist **7** kill-joy **8** sourpuss **9** Cassandra, defeatist, gloomy Gus **10** spoilsport, wet blanket **11** crepehanger **13** prophet of doom

pessimistic **6** gloomy **8** hopeless **10** despairing, dispirited **11** discouraged, downhearted

pest **4** bane **5** curse **6** blight, bother **7** scourge **8** nuisance, vexation **9** annoyance **10** irritation **13** pain in the neck

pester **3** irk, nag, vex **4** bait, fret **5** annoy, harry, taunt, worry **6** badger, bother, harass, hector, nettle, plague **7** disturb, provoke, torment, trouble **8** irritate

pesticide **3** DDT **7** biocide **8** fumigant **9** fungicide, germacide, vermicide **11** insecticide
user: **12** exterminator

pestilence **6** blight, plague **7** disease **8** epidemic
god of: **4** Irra

pet **3** pat **4** baby, dear **6** caress, choice, fondle, stroke **7** beloved, darling, dearest, favored **8** favorite **9** cherished, preferred **10** sweetheart **14** apple of one's eye

pet activity **5** hobby **7** passion **8** interest **10** enthusiasm, hobbyhorse

Peter **7** apostle
means: **4** rock
also called: **5** Simon **6** Cephas
father: **4** John **5** Jonas
brother: **6** Andrew
birthplace: **9** Bethsaida
hometown: **9** Capernaum
disciple of: **5** Jesus
companion: **4** John **5** James
rebuked: **7** Ananias **8** Sapphira
secretary: **8** Silvanus
pertaining to: **7** Petrine

Peter and the Wolf
composed by: **9** Prokofiev

Peter Grimes
opera by: **7** Britten
character: **11** Ellen Orford

Peter Heering, Cherry Heering
type: **6** brandy **7** liqueur
origin: **7** Denmark
flavor: **6** cherry
color: **3** red

Peter Ibbetson
author: **15** George Du Maurier

peter out **3** ebb **7** decline, dwindle, fall off, give out **8** diminish

Peter Pan
author: **11** James Barrie
character: **9** Nurse Nana **10** Tinker Bell **11** Captain Hook **12** Wendy Darling

Peter Quince at the Clavier
author: **14** Wallace Stevens

Peters, Jane Alice
real name of: **13** Carole Lombard

petiole **4** stem **5** spine, stalk, stipe **8** peduncle **9** leafstalk

petite **3** wee **4** tiny **5** small **6** little **9** miniature **10** diminutive

petition **3** ask, beg, sue **4** plea, pray, seek, suit, urge **5** press **6** appeal, invoke, orison, prayer **7** apply to, beseech, entreat **8** appeal to, call upon, entreaty, proposal **9** imploring, plead with, request of **10** invocation, supplicate **11** application, beseechment, requisition **12** solicitation, supplication

petitioner **6** suitor **8** claimant **9** solicitor, suppliant **10** supplicant

pet name **8** nickname **9** sobriquet **10** diminutive, endearment

pet phrase **5** maxim, motto **6** saying, slogan **9** catchword

Petre (Lord)
character in: **16** The Rape of the Lock
author: **4** Pope

petrified **4** hard **5** dense, solid, stony **6** frozen **8** hardened, rocklike **9** paralyzed **10** solidified **11** hard as a rock, scared stiff **13** turned to stone

Petrified Forest, The
director: **10** Archie Mayo
based on play by: **14** Robert Sherwood
cast: **9** Dick Foran **10** Bette Davis **12** Leslie Howard **14** Humphrey Bogart (Duke Mantee)
setting: **7** Arizona

Petronius
author of: **9** Satyricon

Petruchio
character in: **19** The Taming of the Shrew
author: **11** Shakespeare

Petticoat Junction
character: **10** Floyd Smoot, Sam Drucker **11** Homer Bedloe, Kate Bradley **12** Charlie Pratt, Dr Janet Craig, Steve Elliott, Wendell Gibbs **14** Betty Jo Bradley, Uncle Joe Carson **15** Billie Jo Bradley, Bobbie Jo Bradley
cast: **9** Frank Cady, Linda Kaye, Mike Minor, Rufe Davis **10** Pat Woodell **11** Charles Lane **12** Bea Benaderet, Byron Foulger, June Lockhart, Lori Saunders **13** Edgar Buchanan, Gunilla Hutton, Jeannine Riley **14** Meredith MacRae, Smiley Burnette
setting: **11** Hooterville **14** Shady Rest Hotel
train: **10** Cannonball

petto **5** chest **6** breast

petty **4** mean **5** minor, small **6** flimsy, paltry, shabby, slight **7** ignoble, trivial **8** niggling, picayune, piddling, trifling **10** ungenerous **11** small-minded, unimportant **12** narrow-minded **13** insignificant **14** inconsiderable **15** inconsequential

petulance **9** poutiness, sulkiness **11** fretfulness, peevishness **12** irritability

petulant **4** sour **5** cross, gruff, huffy, sulky, surly, testy **6** grumpy, sullen, tetchy, touchy **7** bearish, crabbed, fretful, grouchy, peevish, pettish, uncivil **8** snappish **9** crotchety, fractious, irascible, irritable **10** ill-natured, out of sorts, ungracious **11** complaining, contentious, ill-tempered, quarrelsome, thin-skinned **12** cantankerous, faultfinding

Petulia
director: **13** Richard Lester
cast: **10** Arthur Hill, Pippa Scott **12** George C Scott, Joseph Cotten **13** Julie Christie, Shirley Knight **18** Richard Chamberlain
setting: **12** San Francisco

petunia
varieties: **4** Wild **7** Mexican, Seaside **10** Large white **12** Common garden **14** Violet-flowered

peu a peu **14** little by little

peu de chose **14** trifling matter **17** unimportant matter

pew **4** seat **5** bench **6** settle

Peychaud Bitters
type: **8** aperitif
origin: **10** New Orleans

Peyton Place
author: **14** Grace Metalious
character: **9** Rita Jacks (Harrington) **10** Hannah Cord, Steven Cord **12** Matthew Swain **13** Betty Anderson (Harrington Cord Harrington), Elliott Carson, Julie Anderson **14** Dr Michael Rossi, Dr Robert Morton, George Anderson **16** Allison Mackenzie (Harrington), Leslie Harrington, Norman Harrington, Rodney Harrington **18** Constance Mackenzie (Carson)
cast (television): **8** Ed Nelson **9** Kent Smith, Mia Farrow, Ryan O'Neal **10** Tim O'Connor **11** Kasey Rogers, Paul Langton, Ruth Warrick **12** Henry Beckman, James Douglas **13** Dorothy Malone **14** Barbara Parkins, Patricia Morrow, Warner Anderson **19** Christopher Connelly
director (movie): **10** Mark Robson
cast (movie): **9** Hope Lange **10** Lana Turner, Lloyd Nolan **13** Arthur Kennedy
score: **11** Franz Waxman

Phaeax
father: **8** Poseidon
mother: **7** Corcyra
ancestor of: **10** Phaeacians

Phaedo
author: **5** Plato

Phaedra
father: **5** Minos
mother: **8** Pasiphae

sister: **7** Ariadne
husband: **7** Theseus
son: **6** Acamas **8** Demophon
stepson: **10** Hippolytus
loved: **10** Hippolytus
death by: **7** hanging, suicide

Phaenna
origin: **5** Greek **7** Spartan
member of: **6** Graces

Phaethon
father: **6** Helios
mother: **7** Clymene

phalanx **6** column, parade **9** formation **13** ranks and files

Phallus
image of: **9** male organ
symbol of: **9** fertility
carried in: **6** comedy **9** festivals
associated with: **3** Pan **6** Hermes **7** Demeter **8** Dionysus

phantasm **5** ghost, shade, spook **6** mirage, spirit, vision **7** fantasy, figment, incubus, phantom, specter **8** delusion, illusion, succubus **10** apparition

Phantasus
origin: **5** Greek
god of: **6** dreams

phantom **5** dream, ghost **6** mirage, spirit, vision, wraith **7** chimera, specter **8** illusion, phantasm **10** apparition **13** hallucination

Phantom, The
creator: **7** Lee Falk **8** Ray Moore
nickname: **16** The Ghost Who Walks
mask: **5** black
costume: **6** purple

Phantom of the Opera, The
director:
1925 version: **12** Rupert Julian
1943 version: **11** Arthur Lubin
cast:
1925 version: **9** Lon Chaney **11** Mary Philbin, Norman Kerry
1943 version: **10** Hume Cronyn, Jane Farrar, Nelson Eddy **11** Claude Rains **12** Edgar Barrier **13** Susanna Foster
setting: **10** Paris Opera

Phaon
occupation: **7** boatman
location: **8** Mitylene
given: **5** youth **6** beauty
given by: **9** Aphrodite

pharos **5** light **6** beacon, signal **7** seamark **10** lighthouse, watchtower

phase **4** side, step, view **5** angle, facet, guise, level, slant, stage **6** aspect, degree, period **7** feature **8** attitude, juncture **9** condition, viewpoint **10** appearance **11** development **12** circumstance

pheasant
group of: **4** nest, nide

Phedre, Phaedra
author: **6** Racine
character: **6** Aricia **7** Theseus **10** Hippolytus

Phegeus
king of: **7** Psophis
son: **5** Axion **7** Temenus
daughter: **7** Arsinoe
purified: **8** Alcmaeon
ordered death of: **8** Alcmaeon

Phenix *see* **7** Phoenix

phenomenal **5** super **6** unique **7** amazing, unusual **8** singular, superior, uncommon **9** fantastic, marvelous, unheard-of **10** incredible, miraculous, prodigious, remarkable, stupendous, surpassing **11** astonishing, exceptional, outstanding, sensational, spectacular **12** overwhelming, unparalleled **13** extraordinary, unprecedented

phenomenon **5** thing **6** marvel, rarity, wonder **7** episode, miracle **8** incident, occasion **9** actuality, curiosity, exception, happening, nonpareil, sensation **10** fact of life, occurrence, proceeding **11** contingency

Phereclus
also: **10** Harmonides
father: **6** Tecton
built: **5** ships

Pheres
king of: **6** Pherae
father: **8** Cretheus
mother: **4** Tyro
son: **7** Admetus, Idomene
daughter: **8** Periapis

Pheriphetes
epithet: **9** Corynetes

phial **4** vial **6** bottle, vessel **9** container

Phidias
born: **6** Athens, Greece
artwork: **4** Zeus **6** Amazon **13** Lemnian Athene (Athena Lemnia) **15** Apollo Parnopios, Athena Parthenos, Athena Promachos

Philadelphia
baseball team: **8** Phillies
basketball team: **13** Seventy-sixers
bay: **8** Delaware
football team: **5** Stars **6** Eagles
founded/planned by: **4** Penn
hockey team: **6** Flyers
landmark: **6** US Mint **8** City Hall **11** Liberty Bell **12** Christ Church, Congress Hall **13** Franklin Field, Roosevelt Park **14** Betsy Ross House, Carpenter's Hall **15** Gloria Dei Church, Veterans Stadium **16** Independence Hall
means: **19** city of brotherly love
museum: **5** Rodin **15** Fels Planetarium **16** Barnes Foundation **17** Franklin Institute
river: **8** Delaware **10** Schuylkill
university: **4** Penn **6** Drexel, Temple **9** Jefferson, St Joseph's **22** Curtis Institute of Music

Philadelphia Story, The
director: **11** George Cukor
based on play by: **11** Philip Barry
cast: **9** Cary Grant **10** Ruth Hussey **12** James Stewart **16** Katharine Hepburn
Oscar for: **5** actor (Stewart)
remade as: **11** High Society

Philammon
father: **6** Apollo
mother: **6** Chione
half-brother: **9** Autolycus
son: **8** Thamyris
vocation: **8** musician

philanderer **3** rip **4** rake, wolf **5** flirt **6** lecher, tomcat, wanton **7** dallier, Don Juan, gallant, swinger, trifler **8** lothario, lover boy, rakehell **9** adulterer, libertine, womanizer **10** ladykiller **11** woman-chaser

philanthropic, philanthropical **7** liberal **8** generous **9** bounteous **10** almsgiving, beneficent, benevolent, charitable, munificent **11** magnanimous **12** eleemosynary, humanitarian

philanthropist **5** donor, giver **8** do-gooder **9** almsgiver **11** contributor **12** humanitarian **13** Good Samaritan

philanthropy **6** bounty **7** charity **8** goodness **10** almsgiving, generosity, liberality **11** beneficence, benevolence, munificence **13** unselfishness **14** charitableness, openhandedness **15** humanitarianism **16** largeheartedness **18** public-spiritedness

Philaster
author: **30** Francis Beaumont and John Fletcher

Philemon
friend: **4** Paul

Philippines

named for: 15 Philip II of Spain

capital/largest city: 6 Manila

others: 3 Iba **4** Agoa, Bogo, Cebu, Debu, Naga, Palo **5** Albay, Davao, Gapan, Iriga, Lanao, Laoag, Pasay, Vigan **6** Aparri, Baguio, Cavite, Ilagan, Iloilo, Tarlac **7** Bacolod, Basilan, Calapan, Dagupan, Legaspi **8** Batangas, Caloocan, Cotabato, Tacloban **9** Zamboanga **10** Cabanutuan, Dumaguette, Quezon City

school: 10 Santo Tomas **14** Ateneo de Manila

division: 4 Abra, Cebu **5** Aklan, Albay, Bohol, Capiz, Davao, Lanao, Leyte, Rizal, Samar **6** Agusan, Bataan, Cavite, Iloilo, Laguna, Quezon, Tarlac **7** Isabela, Lepanto, Surigao

measure: 4 loan **5** braza, catty, cavan, chupa, fardo, ganta, picul, punto **6** apatan, balita, lachsa, quinon **7** quilate **8** chinanta

monetary unit: 4 peso **6** conant, peseta **7** centavo

weight: 5 catty, picul **6** lachsa **7** quilate **8** chinanta

island: 4 Cebu, Cuyo, Jolo, Poro, Sulu **5** Batan, Bohol, Leyte, Luzon, Panay, Samar, Ticao **6** Culion, Lubang, Negros **7** Babuyan, Batanes, Bisayan, Masbate, Mindoro, Palawan, Paragua, Polillo, Visoyan **8** Mindanao **10** Corregidor, Marinduque

lake: 4 Taal **5** Lanao

mountain: 3 Iba **4** Mayo, Taal **5** Albay, Askja, Hibok, Mayon, Pulog **6** Pagsan **7** Banahao, Canlaon

highest point: 3 Apo

river: 4 Abra, Agno **5** Magat, Pasig **6** Agusan, Laoang **7** Cagayan **8** Mindanao, Pampanga

sea: 4 Sulu **5** Samar **7** Celebes, Pacific, Visayan **10** Philippine, South China

physical feature:

bay: **6** Manila

falls: **9** Pagsanjan **14** Maria Christina

gulf: **4** Moro **5** Albay, Davao, Leyte, Ragay **8** Lingayen

hot springs: **8** Los Banos

national park: **12** Mayon Volcano

ocean trench: **8** Mindanao

peninsula: **6** Bataan

storm: **6** bagyos **7** monsoon, typhoon

people: 3 Ati, Eta, Ita, Tao **4** Aeta, Ifil, Moro, Sulu, Tino **5** Abaca, Aripa, Batak, Batan, Bicol, Bikol, Busao, Lutao, Mundo, Sinay, Tagal, Vicol, Yakan **6** Apayao, Baluga, Bilaan, Biscol, Bontoc, Bontok, Busaos, Ibanag, Ibilao, Ifugao, Igalot, Igorot, Illano, Isinai, Lutayo, Manabo, Manobo, Montes, Sambal, Tagala, Timaua, Timawa, Zambal **7** Bagoboo, Bisoyan, Cagayan, Ilocano, Itanega, Malanoa, Mangyan, Naboloi, Negrito, Tagalog, Tirurai, Visayan **8** Arupaata, Babaylan, Bukidono, Filipino, Igorotte, Manguian, Pampanga **9** Arupaatta, Dulangane, Macajambo, Pampangao, Tinguiane **10** Magindanao, Pangasinan **11** Calalangane

author: **5** Rizal

explorer: **7** Legazpe **8** Magellan **10** Villalobos

leader: **6** Aquino, Marcos, Osmena, Quezon **9** Aguinaldo, Bonifacio, Macapagal, Magsaysay **11** Roxas y Acuna

language: 4 Moro **5** Bicol, Bikol **6** Ibanag **7** Cebuano, English, Ilocano, Spanish, Tagalog, Visayan **8** Filipino, Pilipino **9** Pampangan **10** Samar-Leyte **13** Bamboo-English **14** Panay-Hiligayon

religion: 7 animism **9** Aglipayan **10** Protestant **13** Roman Catholic **15** Iglesia ni Kristo **21** Philippine Independent

place:

church: **14** Saint Augustine

esplanade: **6** Luneta

fort: **4** Cota, Gota, Kota **5** Lotta **10** Corregidor

president's palace: **10** Malacanang

street: **7** Escolta

walled city: **10** Intramuros

feature:

animal: **7** carabao, tamarau, tarsier **9** mouse deer

bird: **7** creeper

clothing: **4** saya **6** camisa **10** balintawak **12** mestiza terno **13** barong tagalog

dance: **9** tinikling

drama: **8** moro-moro

guerrilla fighter: **3** huk

musicians: **12** musikongbuho

naval base: **6** Cavite

song: **8** kundiman

village: **8** barangay

food:

dish: **3** poi **4** baha, sabu, taro **5** balut

drink: **4** beno, vino **5** bubud **6** tampoy **7** pangasi

slave: **8** Onesimus
wife: **6** Baucis
entertained: **4** Hera, Zeus
became: **12** temple priest

Philip
hometown: **9** Bethsaida
disciple of: **5** Jesus

Philippines ***see box***

philistine **5** yahoo **6** savage **7** Babbitt, lowbrow, prosaic **8** ignorant **9** barbarian, bourgeois, unrefined, untutored **10** conformist, uncultured, uneducated, uninformed, unlettered **11** commonplace **12** conventional, uncultivated **13** unenlightened **15** conventionalist **16** anti-intellectual

Philistine city **4** Gath

Philius
epithet of: **4** Zeus
means: **8** friendly

Phillotson, Richard
character in: **14** Jude the Obscure
author: **5** Hardy

Philoctetes
author: **9** Sophocles
character: **8** Heracles, Odysseus **11** Neoptolemus
inherits arms of: **8** Hercules
father: **5** Poeas, Poias
killed: **5** Paris

philodendron
varieties: **5** Dubia, giant **6** common **7** cut-leaf, red-leaf **8** blushing **9** black-gold, heart-leaf, horsehead, spade-leaf, split-leaf **10** fiddle-leaf, variegated, velvet-leaf **11** leather-leaf

Philoetius
cowherd of: **8** Odysseus

Philomela
position: **8** princess
realm: **6** Athens
father: **7** Pandion
sister: **6** Procne
brother-in-law: **6** Tereus
raped by: **6** Tereus
transformed into: **7** swallow **11** nightingale

Philomelides
king of: **6** Lesbos
defeated by: **8** Odysseus

Philonome *see* **9** Phylonome

philosopher/theologian ***see box***

Philosopher's Pupil, The
author: **11** Iris Murdoch

philosophic, philosophical **4** calm **5** quiet, stoic **6** serene **7** erudite, learned, logical, patient, stoical **8** abstract, composed, rational, resigned, tranquil **9** impassive, judicious, sagacious, unexcited, unruffled **10** complacent, fatalistic, reasonable, theorizing, thoughtful **11** imperturbed, theoretical, unemotional **14** self-restrained

philosophy **4** calm, view **5** ideas, logic **6** reason **7** beliefs, opinion, thought **8** doctrine, fatalism, patience, serenity, stoicism, thinking **9** basic idea, composure, esthetics, principle, reasoning, restraint, viewpoint **10** conception, theorizing **11** complacency, convictions, forbearance, impassivity, metaphysics, rationalism, resignation
means: **12** love of wisdom
branch: **6** ethics **8** ontology **10** aesthetics **11** metaphysics **12** epistemology
term: **8** noumenon **9** causality, dialectic, solipsism
school of: **7** Sophism **8** idealism, Milesian, Stoicism **9** Epicurean, pantheism, Platonism **10** empiricism, pragmatism, Skepticism **11** rationalism **12** Aristotelian, neoplatonism **13** Phenomenology, scholasticism **14** existentialism **17** logical positivism

Phil Silvers Show, The
character: **6** Fender **7** Col Hall, Henshaw **8** Doberman **9** Sgt Ritzik **12** Sgt Joan Hogan **13** Rocco Barbella, Sgt Ernie Bilko
cast: **8** Joe E Ross, Paul Ford **10** Alan Melvin, Herbie Faye **13** Harvey Lembeck **15** Elisabeth Fraser, Maurice Gosfield

---

philosopher/theologian **4** sage **6** savant **7** thinker, wise man **8** logician, reasoner **9** theorizer **11** rationalist, truth seeker **12** dialectician **13** metaphysician
Alsatian: **10** Schweitzer
American: **4** Eddy **5** Dewey, James, Royce, Smith, Young **6** Mather, Peirce **7** Edwards, Niebuhr, Russell, Tillich **8** Williams **9** McPherson **14** Elijah Muhammad
Austrian: **12** Wittgenstein
British: **3** Fox **4** Hume, Inge, Knox, More, Owen **5** Bacon, Burke, Locke, Moore **6** Biddle, Cotton, Hobbes, Huxley, Newman, Wesley **7** Bentham, Bradley, Carlyle, Cranmer, Russell, Spencer **8** Berkeley, Wycliffe **9** Whitehead **13** Thomas a Becket **14** William of Occam
Chinese: **6** Lao-tzu **9** Confucius
Christian: **6** Calvin, Luther, Origen, St Paul **7** Abelard **8** St Anselm **9** St Patrick **10** Duns Scotus, St Benedict **11** St Augustine **14** William of Occam **15** St Thomas Aquinas **16** St Albertus Magnus
Czech: **3** Hus
Danish: **11** Kierkegaard
Dutch: **7** Erasmus, Spinoza
El Salvadorian: **9** Masferrer
French: **5** Comte **6** Calvin, Pascal, Sartre **7** Abelard, Bergson, Diderot **8** Maritain, Rousseau, Voltaire **9** Descartes, Levy-Bruhl, Montaigne **11** Montesquieu
German: **4** Kant, Marx **5** Buber, Hegel **6** Boehme, Fichte, Herder, Luther **7** Husserl, Jaspers, Leibniz **9** Heidegger, Nietzsche, Schelling **10** Muhlenberg **11** Melanchthon **12** Schopenhauer **13** Thomas a Kempis **14** Schleiermacher
Greek: **5** Plato **6** St Paul, Thales **8** Socrates **9** Aristotle **10** Anaxagoras, Anaximenes, Heraclitus, Parmenides, Pythagoras **11** Anaximander
Indian: **6** Buddha **16** Siddharta Gautama
Islamic: **7** al Kindi **8** al-Farabi, Averroes, Avicenna **9** al Ghazali **10** Ibn Khaldun
Italian: **5** Bruno **7** Aquinas, Mazzini **10** St Benedict, Zeno of Elea **17** St Francis of Assisi
Japanese: **6** Suzuki
Jewish: **7** Spinoza **10** Maimonides
Latin: **8** Plotinus **11** St Augustine
Spanish: **8** Averroes **10** Maimonides **13** Ortega y Gasset **16** Ignatius of Loyola
Swedish: **10** Swedenborg
Swiss: **7** Zwingli

setting: 6 Kansas 10 Fort Baxter

Philyra
father: 7 Oceanus
mother: 6 Tethys
mother of: 6 Chiron
changed into: 10 linden tree

Phlegethon
also: 14 Pyriphlegethon
form: 5 river
location: 10 underworld

phlegmatic 4 calm, cool, dull 6 serene 7 languid, passive, stoical 8 listless, sluggish, tranquil 9 apathetic, impassive, lethargic, unfeeling 10 nonchalant, spiritless 11 indifferent, insensitive, unconcerned, unemotional, unexcitable 12 unresponsive 13 imperturbable, unimpassioned 15 undemonstrative

Phlegyas
king of: 8 Lapithae
condemned: 6 Apollo

Phlias
father: 8 Dionysus
member of: 9 Argonauts

phlox
varieties: 4 blue, fall, moss, sand, star 6 annual, smooth 7 prickly 8 creeping, drummond, mountain, trailing 9 perennial, sword-leaf, thick-leaf 15 summer perennial

Phnom-Penh
airport: 10 Pochentong
also: 8 Pnom Penh
capital of: 8 Cambodia 9 Kampuchea
pagoda: 12 Preah Morokot
river: 6 Mekong 8 Tonle Sap

Phobetor
epithet of: 6 Icelus
means: 9 terrifier

phobia *see box*

Phobos
also: 6 Phobus
father: 4 Ares

Phocus
father: 6 Aeacus 8 Ornytion
mother: 8 Psamathe
half-brother: 6 Peleus 7 Telamon
wife: 7 Antiope
killed by: 7 Telamon
burial place: 8 Tithorea

Phoebe
member of: 6 Titans
father: 6 Uranus
mother: 4 Gaea
sister: 6 Themis
daughter: 4 Leto 7 Asteria
identified with: 4 moon
corresponds to: 5 Diana 7 Artemis

Phoebus *see* 6 Apollo

Phoenicia *see* 7 Lebanon

Phoenician Mythology
god of agriculture/earth: 5 Dagon
corresponds to Mesopotamian: 5 Dagan
bird: 6 Phenix 7 Phoenix 8 Phoeonix
goddess of fertility/reproduction: 7 Astarte

Phoenissae (The Phoenician Maidens)
author: 9 Euripides
character: 5 Creon 7 Jocasta, Oedipus 8 Adrastus, Antigone, Eteocles, Tiresias 9 Polynices 10 Menoikieus

Phoenix
basketball team: 4 Suns
capital of: 7 Arizona
event: 5 rodeo
feature: 10 Papago Park 22 Desert Botanical Gardens
football team: 9 Wranglers
river: 4 Salt

Phoenix, Phoeonix
also: 6 Phenix
origin: 10 Phoenician
form: 4 bird
gift: 11 immortality
king of: 9 Dolopians
father: 7 Amyntor
mother: 8 Cleobule
brother: 6 Cadmus
sister: 6 Europa
foster son: 8 Achilles
ancestor of: 11 Phoenicians

Pholus
form: 7 centaur
guarded: 4 wine
wine a gift from: 8 Dionysus

phonograph 4 hi-fi 5 phono 6 stereo 8 Victrola 9 turntable 10 gramophone 12 record player

phonophobia
fear of: 13 speaking aloud

phony, phoney 4 fake, hoax, mock, sham 5 bogus, false, fraud, trick 6 forged, pseudo, unreal, untrue 7 forgery 8 specious, spurious 9 decep-

phobia 5 dread 6 horror, terror 7 bugaboo, bugbear 8 aversion, loathing 12 apprehension 16 unreasonable fear 19 overwhelming anxiety
fear of animals: 9 zoophobia
fear of birds: 13 ornithophobia
fear of blushing: 13 erythrophobia
fear of bridges: 13 gephyrophobia
fear of cats: 10 gatophobia 12 aelurophobia, ailurophobia
fear of closed/confined spaces: 14 claustrophobia
fear of crowds: 11 ochlophobia
fear of darkness/the dark of night: 11 nyctophobia
fear of death: 13 thanatophobia
fear of death/dead bodies: 11 necrophobia
fear of dirt: 10 mysophobia
fear of disease: 11 pathophobia
fear of fire: 10 pyrophobia
fear of flowers: 11 anthophobia
fear of flying: 10 aerophobia
fear of germs: 11 mikrophobia
fear of hair: 12 trichophobia
fear of heights: 10 acrophobia
fear of insanity: 13 dementophobia
fear of lightning: 11 astraphobia
fear of men: 11 androphobia
fear of mice: 10 murophobia
fear of numbers: 12 numerophobia
fear of open spaces: 11 agoraphobia
fear of pain: 10 algophobia
fear of people: 12 anthrophobia
fear of reptiles: 13 herpetophobia
fear of snakes: 13 ophidiophobia
fear of speaking aloud: 11 phonophobia
fear of spiders: 13 arachnophobia
fear of strangers: 10 xenophobia
fear of thunder: 12 brontophobia
fear of the number thirteen: 17 triskaidekaphobia
fear of vehicles/driving: 11 amaxophobia
fear of water: 10 aquaphobia 11 hydrophobia
fear of women: 10 gynophobia

tive, imitation, pretended, synthetic **10** artificial, fraudulent, not genuine **11** counterfeit, make-believe, unauthentic

Phorbas
son of: **8** Lapithes
dispelled: **6** plague
plague of: **8** serpents
leader of: **4** Troy
allies of: **9** Phygians
killed by: **4** Ajax
form: **5** boxer
killed: **8** pilgrims
killed by: **6** Apollo

Phorcids
father: **7** Phorcys
mother: **4** Ceto

Phorcys
god of: **3** sea
sister: **4** Ceto
children: **5** Ladon **6** Graiae **7** Echidna, Gorgons **8** Phorcids
harbor in: **6** Ithaca

Phormio
author: **7** Terence

phosphorus
chemical symbol: **1** P

photograph **3** pic **4** film, snap **5** image, print, shoot, still **6** candid, glossy **7** mugshot, picture, tintype **8** likeness, portrait, snapshot **12** daguerrotype
bath: **5** fixer, toner **7** reducer **9** developer
book: **5** album

photographer
American: **4** Haas, Hine, Penn, Riis, Rose, Tice **5** (Ansel) Adams, Annan, Arbus, Brady, Evans, Hawes, Lange, Lynes, Smith, White **6** Avedon, Coburn, Eakins, Man Ray, Strand, Turner, Weston **7** Burrows, Eastman, Gardner, Jackson, Watkins **8** Bogardus, Davidson, Steichen **9** Muybridge, O'Sullivan, Rothstein, Stieglitz **10** Cunningham, Southworth **11** Bourke-White, Eisenstaedt, Turberville **13** Watson-Schutze
British: **5** Evans, Frith **6** Bailey, Beaton, Fenton, Mayall, Talbot **7** Cameron **8** Brewster, Robinson **9** Rejlander **10** MacPherson
French: **5** Marey, Nadar **6** Baldus, DuCamp, Le Secq, Newton, Niepce **7** Lumiere **8** Daguerre **12** Sabatier-Blot **14** Cartier-Bresson
German: **4** Hoch **5** Ernst **7** Hausman **8** Stelzner **13** Renger-Patzsch
Hungarian: **7** Kertesz **10** Moholy-Nagy
Japanese: **4** Ikko
Scottish: **4** Hill **7** Adamson
Spanish: **7** Picabia

photostat **4** copy **7** replica **9** duplicate, facsimile **12** reproduction

phrase **3** put, say **4** word **5** couch, idiom, maxim, state, utter, voice, words **6** cliche, dictum, impart, remark, saying, truism **7** declare, express, proverb **8** aphorism, banality, locution **9** enunciate, find words, platitude, utterance, verbalize, word group **10** articulate, expression **11** communicate

phraseology **5** style **7** diction, wording **13** choice of words **18** manner of expression

Phrixus
father: **7** Athamas
mother: **7** Nephele
stepmother: **3** Ino
sister: **5** Helle
wife: **9** Chalciope
son: **5** Argus, Melas **8** Phrontis **10** Cytissorus

Phrontis
father: **7** Phrixus
mother: **9** Chalciope
brother: **5** Argus, Melus **10** Cytissorus
husband: **8** Panthous

Phthia
mentioned in: **5** Iliad
concubine of: **7** Amyntor
seduced by: **7** Phoenix
son: **5** Dorus **8** Laodocus **10** Polypoetes

Phyleus
king of: **6** Ephyra
father: **6** Auglas
wife: **8** Timandra
children: **5** Meges **10** Astyocheia

Phyllis
father: **8** Phylleus
husband: **8** Demophon
loved: **6** Acamas

Phylomache
son: **7** Acastus
daughter: **8** Alcestis

Phylonome
also: **9** Philonome
husband: **6** Cycnus
stepson: **5** Tenes

physical **4** real **5** human, solid **6** actual, animal, bodily, carnal, living **7** fleshly, natural, sensual **8** apparent, concrete, corporal, existent, existing, external, material, palpable, tangible **9** corporeal, essential, of the body **11** substantive

physical checkup **4** exam **8** physical **11** examination **19** physical examination

physical condition **5** shape **7** fitness, stamina **12** constitution

physical disorder **6** malady **7** ailment, disease, illness **8** sickness **9** ill health, infirmity

physical training **3** gym **6** sports **8** exercise **9** athletics, shaping up **10** gymnastics, working out **12** conditioning

physician **2** GP, MD **3** doc **5** medic **6** doctor, medico **7** surgeon **8** sawbones **10** specialist **11** medicine man, pill peddler **13** medical doctor
Alsatian: **10** Schweitzer
American: **4** Long, Rush, Salk **5** Sabin **6** Dooley, Gorgas **7** Huggins, Whipple **8** Williams **9** Blackwell **11** Landsteiner
British: **5** Paget **6** Adrian, Harvey, Jenner, Lister
Canadian: **4** Best **7** Banting
Dutch: **7** Eijkman
French: **7** Charcot
German: **6** Mesmer **7** Fechner, Virchow **10** Blumenbach
Greek: **10** Herophilus **11** Hippocrates **12** Erasistratus
Italian: **8** Malpighi
Russian: **6** Pavlov
Scottish: **4** Lind
South African: **7** Barnard

Physician to Olympian gods **5** Paeon **6** Apollo

physicist
American: **4** Hess, Rabi **5** Bethe, Gamow, Pauli, Yalow **6** Bekesy, Teller, Townes, Watson **7** Richter, Seaborg **8** Einstein, Lawrence, Van Allen **9** Michelson **11** Chamberlain, Oppenheimer
Austrian: **7** Doppler, Meitner
British: **4** Born **5** Bragg, Hooke, Joule **6** Kelvin **7** Gilbert, Thomson **8** Chadwick, Rayleigh **9** Cockcroft **10** Rutherford
Danish: **4** Bohr **7** Oersted
Dutch: **6** Zeeman **7** Lorentz
French: **6** Ampere **7** Broglie, Coulomb, Fresnel **8** Foucault **9** Becquerel **11** Joliot-Curie
German: **3** Ohm **5** Hertz, Stark **6** Planck **7** Rontgen, Wegener **8** Humboldt, Roentgen **9** Kirchhoff, Mossbauer **10** Fahrenheit, Fraunhofer
Indian: **5** Raman
Irish: **7** Tyndall **10** Fitzgerald
Italian: **5** Fermi

Russian: **6** Landau **8** Cerenkov, Sakharov
Scottish: **7** Rankine

Physics
author: **9** Aristotle

physiognomy **4** face **5** shape **6** facade, visage **7** contour, outline, profile **8** features **10** silhouette **11** countenance

physiology
founder: **13** William Harvey
study of: **8** function
study of nervous sytem: **15** neurophysiology

Phytalus
hospitable to: **7** Demeter
given: **7** fig tree

Phyteus
epithet of: **6** Apollo

pianissimo
music: **8** very soft
abbreviation: **2** pp

pianist **4** Hess **5** Liszt, Watts **6** Busoni, Chopin, Gilels, Serkin **7** Cliburn, Hofmann, Richter **8** Backhaus, Horowitz, Schnabel, Schumann, Thalberg, von Bulow **9** Barenboim, Casadesus, Gieseking **10** Gottschalk, Rubinstein **12** Rachmaninoff

piano
invented by: **10** Cristofori
player piano: **9** Fourneaux

piano
music: **4** soft
abbreviation: **1** p

piazza **5** patio, porch **6** square **7** gallery, portico, veranda

Piazzi, Giuseppe
field: **9** astronomy
nationality: **7** Italian
discovered: **5** Ceres
catalogued: **5** stars

picaresque **6** daring **7** raffish, roguish, waggish **8** devilish, prankish, rascally, scampish **9** foolhardy **10** roistering **13** adventuresome **14** mischief-loving

Picasso, Pablo
born: **5** Spain **6** Malaga
artwork: **4** Dove **6** Guitar, Jester **7** Ma Jolie, Rooster, She-Goat **8** Guernica **9** Bull's Head, Notre Dame **11** Seated Woman, Woman Diving **12** Head of a Woman **13** Seated Bathers **14** Minotauromachy, Mother and Child, Women of Algiers **15** Ambroise Vollard, Man Holding a Lamb, The Charnel-House, The Large Profile, The Three Dancers **16** Nude in an Armchair **17** Girl Before a Mirror, The Glass of Absinth, The Three Musicians **20** Still Life with a Candle **22** Les Demoiselles d'Avignon **23** Portrait of Gertrude Stein

picayune, picayunish **5** dinky, petty, small **6** flimsy, little, measly, paltry, slight **7** trivial **8** niggling, nugatory, piddling, trifling **11** unimportant **13** insignificant **14** inconsiderable **15** inconsequential

Piccini, Nicola (Piccinni, Niccola)
born: **4** Bari **5** Italy
composer of: **5** Didon **6** Roland **11** The Good Girl **15** La buona figliola **18** Iphigenie en Tauride

pick **3** cut **4** crop **5** cream, elect, elite, pluck, prize **6** choice, choose, detach, flower, gather, opt for, select **7** collect, fix upon, harvest, pull off, pull out, the best **9** single out **10** decide upon, favored one, preference, settle upon

picket **4** pale, post **5** fence, go out, guard, hem in, pen in, stake, watch **6** corral, paling, patrol, sentry, shut in, strike, tether, wall in **7** boycott, enclose, hedge in, lookout, striker, upright, walk out **8** blockade, palisade, restrain, restrict, sentinel **9** blockader, boycotter, protester, restraint, stanchion

picketing **5** march **7** protest **8** marching, on strike, striking **10** protesting **12** protest march **13** demonstrating, demonstration

Pickett, George E
served in: **8** Civil War **10** Mexican War
side: **11** Confederate
battle: **10** Gettysburg
famous for: **6** charge

Pickford, Mary
real name: **15** Gladys Mary Smith
nickname: **18** America's Sweetheart
born: **6** Canada **7** Toronto
husband: **16** Douglas Fairbanks **18** Charles Buddy Rogers
roles: **4** Rags **8** Coquette (Oscar) **9** Pollyanna **19** The Taming of the Shrew **21** The Poor Little Rich Girl **23** Rebecca of Sunnybrook Farm
home: **8** Pickfair
memoirs: **17** Sunshine and Shadow
formed: **13** United Artists
partners: **10** D W Griffith **14** Charlie Chaplin **16** Douglas Fairbanks

pickings **4** loot **5** booty **6** scraps, spoils **7** plunder, takings **9** leftovers

pickle **3** fix, jam **4** corn, dill, mess, sour **6** crisis, plight, scrape **7** dilemma, gherkin, mustard **8** cucumber, hot water, quandary **9** emergency, extremity, tight spot **10** difficulty, kosher dill, pretty pass **11** predicament **14** bread-and-butter

pickled **5** drunk **6** soused **8** powdered

pick on **5** annoy, bully **6** harass, jibe at **7** torment **8** browbeat

pick out **3** see **4** espy **6** choose, descry, detect, notice, select **7** discern, make out **8** perceive **12** catch sight of

pickup **4** rise **5** boost, truck **7** advance **9** impromptu **11** improvement **12** acceleration

pick up **3** buy, get **6** gather, lift up, look up, obtain, secure **7** acquire, develop, improve, procure **8** contract, retrieve **9** cultivate, get better

Pickwick Papers
author: **14** Charles Dickens
character: **6** Perker, Tupman, Wardle, Winkle **9** Sam Weller, Snodgrass **10** Mrs Bardell **11** Emily Wardle **12** Alfred Jingle, Rachel Wardle **13** Arabella Allen

picky **5** fussy **6** choosy **7** finicky **10** fastidious, particular **11** persnickety **14** discriminating

Picrochole
character in: **22** Gargantua and Pantagruel
author: **8** Rabelais

picture **3** see **4** copy, draw, film **5** fancy, flick, image, model, movie, paint, photo, study **6** cinema, depict, double, mirror, sketch **7** believe, drawing, essence, etching, feature, imagine, paragon, portray, tintype **8** envision, likeness, painting, snapshot **9** delineate, duplicate, facsimile, portrayal, represent **10** call to mind, carbon copy, conceive of, dead ringer, embodiment, illustrate, photograph **11** delineation **12** illustration, see in the mind **13** daguerreotype, motion picture, moving picture, spitting image **14** representation **15** exemplification, personification

Picture of Dorian Gray, The
author: **10** Oscar Wilde
character: **9** James Vane, Sibyl Vane **13** Basil Hallward **15** Lord Henry Wotton

picturesque **6** exotic, quaint **7** unusual **8** artistic, charming, colorful, striking **9** beautiful, pictorial **10** attractive **11** distinctive, imaginative, interesting

Picumnus
also: **8** Pilumnus
origin: **5** Roman
god of: **9** fertility **11** agriculture

Picus
origin: **5** Roman **7** Italian
god of: **11** agriculture
father: **6** Saturn
associated with: **10** woodpecker
loved by: **5** Circe
changed into: **10** woodpecker
son: **6** Faunus

piddling **4** puny **5** petty, small **6** flimsy, little, measly, modest, paltry, skimpy, slight **7** trivial **8** picayune, trifling **9** niggardly **11** unimportant **13** insignificant **15** inconsequential

pie **4** tart **6** pastry, quiche **7** cobbler, dessert **8** turnover
liner: **5** crust, shell
top: **7** lattice **8** meringue

piebald **6** motley **7** dappled, flecked, mottled, spotted **8** many-hued, speckled **10** variegated **11** many-colored, varicolored **12** multicolored, parti-colored

piece **3** bit, cut, fix, pat **4** blob, case, hunk, item, lump, mend, part, play, unit, work **5** chunk, drama, essay, patch, scrap, shard, share, shred, slice, story, study, thing **6** amount, entity, length, member, paring, repair, review, sample, sketch, sliver, swatch **7** article, cutting, example, patch up, portion, restore, section, segment **8** creation, division, fraction, fragment, instance, quantity, specimen **9** component, selection **11** composition

piece de resistance **13** principal dish **14** principal event

piece goods **5** cloth, goods **6** fabric **8** dry goods, material **9** yard goods

piecemeal **9** gradually **10** fragmented, one at a time **14** little by little

piece of the action **3** cut, fee **5** piece **7** portion, rake-off **10** commission, percentage

pied **6** motley **7** checked, dappled, mottled, piebald **8** colorful **9** checkered **10** variegated **11** many-colored **12** parti-colored

pied-a-terre **17** temporary dwelling
literally: **12** foot on ground

Pied Piper of Hamlin, The
author: **14** Robert Browning

Pielus
father: **11** Neoptolemus
mother: **10** Andromache

pier **4** anta, dock, mole, quay, slip **5** jetty, levee, wharf **6** pillar **7** landing, support **10** breakwater

pierce **3** cut **4** hurt, pain, stab **5** drill, lance, prick, spear, spike, stick, sting, wound **6** grieve, impale **7** affront **8** distress, puncture **9** penetrate, perforate **10** cut through, run through

Pierce, Franklin ***see box***

piercing **3** raw **4** keen, loud **5** angry, cruel, sharp **6** biting, bitter, fierce, shrill **7** caustic, cutting, furious, grating, hurtful, intense, painful, probing **8** strident **9** agonizing, deafening, searching, shrieking, torturous **10** screeching **11** penetrating **12** earsplitting, excruciating **13** ear-shattering

Pierian
pertains to: **5** Muses

Pierian Spring
form: **8** fountain

Pierides *see* **5** Muses

Pierce, Franklin
nickname: **29** Young Hickory of the Granite Hills
presidential rank: **10** fourteenth
party: **8** Democrat
state represented: **2** NH
defeated: **4** (John Parker) Hale **5** (Winfield) Scott
vice president: **4** (William Rufus Devane) King (died in office)
cabinet:
state: **5** (William Learned) Marcy
treasury: **7** (James) Guthrie
war: **5** (Jefferson) Davis
attorney general: **7** (Caleb) Cushing
navy: **6** (James Cochran) Dobbin
postmaster general: **8** (James) Campbell
interior: **10** (Robert) McClelland
born: **14** Hillsborough (Hillsboro) NH
died/buried: **9** Concord NH
education:
Academy: **7** Hancock **11** Francestown
College: **7** Bowdoin
studied: **3** law
religion: **12** Episcopalian
political career: **8** US Senate **16** state legislature **24** US House of Representatives
civilian career: **6** lawyer
military service: **6** US Army **10** Mexican War **16** brigadier general
notable events of lifetime/term:
Act: **6** Tariff (of 1857)
bill: **14** Kansas-Nebraska
civil war in: **6** Kansas
first US: **10** World's Fair
Manifesto: **6** Ostend
Purchase: **7** Gadsden
treaty of: **8** Kanagawa
father: **8** Benjamin
mother: **4** Anna (Kendrick)
siblings: **5** Henry, Nancy **7** Charles, Harriet **9** Charlotte **12** John Sullivan **16** Benjamin Kendrick
half sister: **9** Elizabeth
wife: **4** Jane (Means Appleton)
children: **8** Benjamin, Franklin **11** Frank Robert

Piero della Francesca (Piero dei Franceschi)
born: **5** Italy **16** Borgo San Sepolcro
artwork: **12** Duke of Urbino **15** The Resurrection **18** Federigo and His Wife **19** St John the Evangelist **20** Flagellation of Christ **23** The Compassionate Madonna, The Legend of the True Cross, The Old Age and Death of Adam **24** The History of the True Cross **45** The Madonna and Saints with Frederigo da Montefeltro

Pierre
author: **14** Herman Melville

Piers Plowman
author: **15** William Langland

Pietas
personifies: **17** familial affection

piety **7** loyalty, respect **8** devotion, humility **9** godliness, piousness, reverence **10** devoutness **11** dutifulness, religiosity **13** religiousness

pig **3** hog **5** piggy, porky, swine **6** porker **7** glutton, guzzler **8** gourmand **9** chowhound **11** gormandizer
male: **4** boar
female: **3** sow
young: **5** shoat **6** piglet **11** suckling pig

pigeon
young: **5** squab **8** squeaker

pigeonhole **4** rank, rate, type **5** brand, cubby, group, label, niche **8** category, classify **9** cubbyhole **10** categorize **11** compartment

pigheaded **6** dogged, mulish **7** willful **8** contrary, obdurate, perverse, stubborn **9** insistent, obstinate, unbending **10** bullheaded, inflexible, refractory, unyielding **11** opinionated, wrongheaded

Piglet
character in: **13** Winnie-the-Pooh
author: **5** Milne

pigment **3** dye **4** tint **5** color **8** coloring, dyestuff **14** coloring matter

pigmentation **5** color **9** skin color **10** coloration

pigtail **5** braid, plait, queue **8** ponytail

pike **4** bill **5** lance, spear, spike **6** poleax **7** assegai, freeway, halberd, harpoon, highway, javelin, parkway, thruway **8** autobahn, hard road, speedway, toll road, turnpike **10** expressway, interstate, throughway **12** superhighway
British: **12** King's Highway **13** Queen's highway
German: **8** autobahn

piker **5** miser **7** niggard, trifler **8** tightwad **9** skinflint **10** cheapskate, pinchpenny **12** penny pincher

Pilar
character in: **19** For Whom the Bell Tolls
author: **9** Hemingway

pilaster **4** pier **6** column, pillar **7** support, upright **8** baluster

pile **3** nap **4** heap, mass, pier, post, shag, warp **5** amass, batch, fluff, grain, hoard, mound, plush, stack, store **6** fleece, gather, piling, pillar **7** collect, pyramid, support, surface, upright **8** assemble, quantity **9** abundance, amassment, profusion, stanchion **10** accumulate, assortment, collection, foundation **11** agglomerate, aggregation, fibrousness **12** accumulation

pile up **4** bank, heap **5** amass, hoard, mound, stack **7** collect **10** accumulate

pile-up **3** jam, mob **4** mass **5** snarl **8** crowding, gridlock **10** bottleneck, congestion **11** obstruction **12** overcrowding

pilfer **3** cop, rob **4** hook, lift **5** boost, filch, heist, pinch, steal, swipe **6** finger, pirate, snitch, thieve **7** purloin **8** shoplift **10** plagiarize

pilferer **5** thief **6** robber **7** burglar **10** shoplifter, sneak thief

pilgrim, Pilgrim **4** haji **5** exile, hadji **6** palmer **7** pioneer, Puritan, settler **8** newcomer, traveler, wanderer, wayfarer **9** foreigner
father: **5** Alden
founder: **10** Separatist
interpreter: **7** Squanto
leader: **8** Standish
protector: **7** Templar
ship: **9** Mayflower, Speedwell

Pilgrim, Billy
character in: **18** Slaughterhouse Five
author: **8** Vonnegut

pilgrimage **4** hadj, trek **6** ramble, roving, voyage **7** journey, roaming, sojourn **8** long trip **9** excursion, wandering **13** peregrination

Pilgrim's Progress, The
author: **10** John Bunyan
character: **7** Despair, Hopeful **8** Apollyon, Faithful **9** Christian, Ignorance **10** Evangelist **14** Worldly Wiseman

pill **3** rob **4** ball, pell **5** bolus **6** bullet, pellet, tablet, pilule **7** capsule **8** medicine **9** cigarette

pillage **3** rob **4** loot, raid, sack **5** booty, rifle, strip **6** fleece, maraud, piracy, ravage, spoils **7** despoil, looting, plunder, robbery **9** filchings **10** plundering

pillager **6** looter, vandal **7** brigand **9** despoiler, plunderer

pillar **3** VIP **4** pile, post, rock **5** shaft, wheel **6** column, piling **7** obelisk, support, upright **8** champion, mainstay, pilaster, somebody **9** colonnade, stanchion

Pillars of Society, The
author: **11** Henrik Ibsen

pillow **3** pad **7** bolster, cushion **8** headrest

pilot **4** lead **5** flyer, guide, steer **6** airman, direct, escort, fly-boy, handle, leader, manage **7** aviator, birdman, conduct, control **8** aeronaut, coxswain, helmsman, navigate, wheelman **9** accompany, sky jockey, steersman

Pilot, The
author: **19** James Fenimore Cooper

Pima (Aatam, Pima Alto)
language family: **10** Uto-Aztekan
location: **7** Arizona
related to: **6** Papago
descendants of: **7** Hohokam

Pima Alto *see* **4** Pima

Piman
tribe: **6** Papago

pin **4** bind, clip, tine **5** affix, badge, clasp, dowel, medal, prong **6** brooch, fasten, pinion, secure, skewer **8** hold down, hold fast, restrain **10** decoration
type: **3** hat **4** push **5** stick, thole **6** breast, common, diaper, safety **8** straight

pincer **4** claw **5** chela

pinch **3** bit, cop, jam, jot, nab, nip **4** bust, crib, grab, iota, lift, mite, pain, snip, spot **5** catch, cramp, crimp, crush, filch, run in, speck, steal, swipe, trace, trial, tweak **6** arrest, clutch, collar, crisis, misery, ordeal, pickle, plight, snatch, snitch, strait, tittle

7 capture, purloin, squeeze, tighten 8 compress, exigency, hardship 9 apprehend, emergency 10 affliction, difficulty, discomfort 11 predicament

Pinch, Tom
character in: 16 Martin Chuzzlewit
author: 7 Dickens

pinch hitter 5 proxy 7 stand-in 9 alternate 10 substitute

pinchpenny 5 miser 6 frugal, stingy 7 niggard, prudent, thrifty
Dickensian: 7 Scrooge

Pindar
author of: 4 Odes 8 Epinicea

pine 3 die, ebb 4 flag, long, sigh, wilt 5 covet, crave, droop, yearn 6 desire, expire, hanker, weaken, wither 7 decline, dwindle, pant for 8 languish 9 hunger for, waste away 11 have a yen for, thirst after 12 fail in health

pine *see box*

Pine Tree State
nickname of: 5 Maine

pin hope on 6 bank on 7 count on, long for, wish for 8 aspire to, yearn for 10 anticipate

pink 8 Dianthus
varieties: 3 Sea 4 fire, moss, pine, rose, wild 5 cameo, clove, dairy, grass, marsh, swamp 6 button, ground, indian, Kirtle, maiden 7 cheddar, cottage, cushion, Mullein, rainbow 8 Childing, Deptford, election 11 clusterhead 13 fringed indian, spottle kirtle 16 California indian

pinnacle 3 cap, top 4 acme, apex, peak 5 crest, crown, spire, tower 6 belfry, height, summit, tiptop, vertex, zenith 7 steeple 9 bell tower, campanile

pinochle
also known as: 7 binocle, pinocle 8 penuchle
derived from: 7 bezique
points/game: 11 one thousand

pinpoint 3 dot, jot 4 iota, spot 5 speck 6 detail 8 home in on, localize, zero in on 12 characterize

pint
abbreviation of: 2 pt

pinxit 11 he painted it 12 she painted it

pioneer 5 found, start 6 create, father, herald, invent, leader 7 develop, founder 8 colonist, discover, explorer 9 be a leader, developer, establish, harbinger, innovator, precursor 10 antecedent, forerunner, lead the way, pathfinder, show the way 11 establisher, predecessor, trailblazer 12 first settler, frontiersman 13 blaze the trail 14 early immigrant, founding father
Hebrew: 6 halutz 7 chalutz

Pioneers, The
author: 19 James Fenimore Cooper
character: 10 Indian John 11 Judge Temple, Natty Bumppo 13 Oliver Edwards 14 Hiram Doolittle 15 Elizabeth Temple

pious 4 holy 5 godly 6 devout, divine 7 sainted, saintly 8 faithful, reverent, unctuous 9 dedicated, insincere, pietistic, religious, spiritual 10 worshipful 11 reverential 12 hypocritical 13 rationalizing, sanctimonious, self-righteous 14 holier-than-thou

Pip
character in: 17 Great Expectations
author: 7 Dickens

pipe 4 duct, main, peep, sing, tube 5 cheep, chirp, trill, tweet 6 warble 7 conduit, twitter, whistle 8 conveyor 9 conductor 10 play a flute 12 play a bagpipe

Pippa Passes
author: 14 Robert Browning

piquant 3 hot 4 acid, racy 5 peppy, salty, sharp, spicy, tangy, zesty 6 biting, bitter, bright, clever, lively, savory 7 mordant, peppery, pungent, rousing 8 animated, incisive, piercing, spirited, stinging, vigorous 9 sparkling, trenchant 11 interesting, provacative, stimulating 13 scintillating 14 highly seasoned, strong-flavored

pique 3 ire, irk, vex 4 gall, goad, miff, snit, spur, stir 5 annoy, peeve, rouse, spite 6 arouse, excite, grudge, kindle, malice, nettle, offend 7 affront, incense, perturb, provoke, quicken, umbrage 8 disquiet, irritate, vexation 9 annoyance, displease, stimulate 10 discomfort, exasperate, irritation, resentment 11 displeasure, humiliation, ill feelings, indignation 12 exasperation, hurt feelings 13 embarrassment, mortification, put one's back up 14 vindictiveness

piqued 5 angry, riled, vexed 6 galled, miffed, peeved 7 annoyed, aroused, excited, kindled, nettled, stirred 9 affronted, irritated 10 displeased, stimulated

---

pine 5 Pinus
varieties: 3 air, nut, red 4 blue, chir, gray, hoop, Huon, Imou, Jack 5 beach, cedar, Cuban, Emodi, giant, house, Kauri, pitch, Scots, screw, scrub, shore, slash, stone, sugar, white 6 Aleppo, Apache, Bhutan, Bishop, celery, Dammar, digger, ground, Jersey, Korean, limber, Mallee, Norway, Parana, Pinyon, Scotch, spruce, Torrey, Totara, yellow 7 Amboina, Benguet, big-cone, Chilean, Chinese, cluster, Cypress, Formosa, Georgia, Gerard's, hickory, jointed, long-tag, poverty, prickly, prince's, running, Soledad 8 Austrian, Buddhist, cow's-tail, knob-cone, lace-bark, Loblolly, longleaf, mahogany, Monterey, mountain, Nepal nut, old-field, princess, umbrella 9 Brazilian, Calabrian, Chilghoza, Jerusalem, lodgepole, Oyster Bay, shortleaf, white-bark 10 Australian, Bunya-bunya, dwarf stone, Macedonian, Moreton Bay, red cypress, Swiss stone, Tenasserim 11 African fern, bristlecone, common screw, Japanese red, Parry pinyon, Port Jackson, thatch screw, twisted-leaf, Veitch screw 12 black cypress, Canary Island, Chinese water, eastern white, frankincense, Italian stone, Mexican stone, Mexican white, two-leaved nut, western white 13 dwarf Siberian, Japanese black, Japanese white, Mexican yellow, New Caledonian, Norfolk Island, Swiss mountain, table mountain 14 Himalayan white, Rottnest Island, southern yellow 15 Mueller's cypress 16 Japanese umbrella, single-leaf pinyon 18 Rough-barked Mexican 19 Rocky Mountain yellow

Pirandello, Luigi
author of: 17 The Old and the Young **18** Tonight We Improvise **19** The Late Mattia Pascal **31** Six Characters in Search of an Author

pirate 3 rob **5** steal **6** raider, robber, sea dog **7** brigand, corsair, plunder **8** marauder **9** buccaneer, privateer **10** freebooter
flag: 9 blackjack **10** Jolly Roger
name: 4 Kidd **6** Morgan **7** Lafitte **10** Blackbeard

Pirate Coast *see* **18** United Arab Emirates

Pirates of Penzance, The
author: 9 W S Gilbert
comic opera by: 18 Gilbert and Sullivan
character: 4 Kate, Ruth **5** Edith, Mabel **6** Isabel **8** Frederic, Sergeant **10** Pirate King **14** General Stanley

Pirithous
prince of: 8 Lapithae
father: 4 Zeus
mother: 3 Dia
son: 10 Polypoetes
friend of: 7 Theseus

Pirous
led allies of: 6 Thrace

pis aller 10 last resort **12** last resource

Pisan Cantos
author: 9 Ezra Pound

Pisander
rank: 7 captain
member of: 9 Myrmidons

Pisanio
character in: 9 Cymbeline
author: 11 Shakespeare

Pisanosaurus
type: 8 dinosaur **10** ornithopod
location: 12 South America
period: 8 Triassic

Pisces
symbol: 4 fish
planet: 7 Jupiter, Neptune
rules: 7 secrets
born: 13 February-March

Pisistratidae
sons of: 11 Pisistratus
names: 7 Hippias **10** Hipparchus

Pisistratus
tyrant of: 6 Athens
father: 11 Hippocrates
son: 7 Hippias **10** Hipparchus

Pissarro, Camille
born: 8 St Thomas **16** Danish West Indies
artwork: 8 Red Roofs **15** Morning Sunlight **21** Lower Norwood Snow Scene **28** Peasant Woman with a Wheelbarrow

pistol (revolver)
invented by: 4 Colt

pit 3 dip, nut **4** dent, hole, nick, pock, scar, seed **5** gouge, gully, match, notch, stone **6** cavity, crater, dimple, furrow, hollow, indent, kernel, oppose, trough **7** scratch **8** contrast, pockmark **9** concavity, juxtapose **10** depression, set against **11** indentation

Pit, The
author: 11 Frank Norris

Pitana
form: 5 nymph
daughter: 6 Evadne

Pit and the Pendulum, The
author: 13 Edgar Allan Poe

pitch 3 bob, dip, fix, lob, set, shy, top **4** apex, cant, cast, fall, fire, hurl, jerk, jolt, peak, rock, tone, toss **5** angle, chuck, crown, erect, fling, grade, heave, level, lurch, place, plant, point, raise, set up, shake, slant, sling, slope, sound, throw **6** degree, height, let fly, locate, plunge, propel, settle, summit, topple, tumble, zenith **7** bobbing, incline, rocking, station **8** delivery, harmonic, lurching, pinnacle, undulate **9** declivity, establish, oscillate **10** undulation **11** oscillation **12** fall headlong
speed of: 9 vibration

pitcher 3 jar, jug **4** ewer **6** carafe **8** decanter **9** container **10** spitballer
and catcher: 7 battery
award: 7 Cy Young
brother duo: 4 Dean **5** Perry **6** Niekro
Hall of Famer: 4 Ford, Wynn **6** Koufax **8** Drysdale
left-hander: 8 southpaw
relief staff: 7 bullpen
reliever: 7 fireman

pitch in 5 begin **7** share in **8** take part **9** cooperate, get to work, join hands **10** act jointly, contribute, get started **11** collaborate, participate **12** make an effort, pull together, work together

pitch into 5 fly at **6** assail, have at **7** assault, set upon

piteous 3 sad **6** moving, woeful **7** pitiful **8** pathetic, pitiable, poignant, touching **9** affecting **10** deplorable **11** distressing **12** heart-rending **13** heartbreaking

pitfall 4 risk, trap **5** peril, snare **6** ambush, danger, hazard **7** springe **8** quagmire **9** booby trap, quicksand **14** stumbling block

pith 4 core, gist, meat **5** heart, point **7** essence, meaning **12** significance

pithy 5 terse **6** cogent **7** concise **8** forceful, succinct **9** effective, trenchant **10** expressive, meaningful, to the point **12** concentrated

pitiful 3 sad **4** poor **5** sorry **6** abject, measly, moving, paltry, shabby **7** doleful, forlorn, piteous **8** dreadful, god-awful, mournful, pathetic, pitiable, poignant, touching, wretched **9** miserable, plaintive, worthless **10** abominable, despicable, lamentable **11** distressing **12** arousing pity, contemptible, heartrending

pitiless 5 cruel **6** brutal **7** inhuman, unmoved **8** ruthless, uncaring **9** heartless, merciless, unpitying, unsparing, untouched **10** implacable, relentless, unmerciful **11** cold-blooded, hardhearted, indifferent, insensitive, unrelenting

pittance 4 mite **5** crumb **6** little, trifle **7** minimum, modicum, smidgen

Pittheus
father: 6 Pelops
mother: 10 Hippodamia
brother: 7 Troezen
daughter: 6 Aethra

Pittsburgh
baseball team: 7 Pirates
feature: 14 Fort Pitt Museum **15** Buhl Planetarium
football team: 8 Steelers
formerly: 8 Fort Pitt **12** Fort Duquesne
hockey team: 8 Penguins
noted for: 5 steel
river: 4 Ohio **9** Allegheny **11** Monongahela
university: 8 Duquesne **14** Carnegie-Mellon

Pittypat, Aunt
character in: 15 Gone With the Wind
author: 8 Mitchell

pituitary
located in: 5 brain
known as: 11 master gland

pity 5 mercy, shame **6** lament, lenity, regret **7** charity, feel for, weep for **8** bleed for, clemency, humanity, leniency, sad thing, sympathy **10** compassion, condolence, indulgence, kindliness, tenderness **11** crying shame, forbearance, magnanimity **12** feel sorry for **13** commiseration

Pityocamptes
epithet of: **5** Sinis
means: **10** pine-bender

Pitys
form: **5** nymph
loved by: **3** Pan
changed into: **8** pine tree

piu
music: **4** more

pivot **4** axis, axle, hang, rely, spin, turn **5** focus, hinge, twirl, wheel, whirl **6** center, circle, depend, rotate, swivel **7** fulcrum, hinge on, revolve **9** pirouette

pivotal **5** vital **7** crucial **8** critical, decisive **9** climactic **11** determining

pivotal point **4** axis **12** turning point **13** crucial moment

pixy **3** elf **5** fairy **6** sprite **10** leprechaun

pizzicato
music: **21** plucked instead of bowed
abbreviation: **4** pizz

placable **7** lenient **8** flexible, tolerant, yielding **9** indulgent, relenting **10** appeasable, forbearing **12** reconcilable

placard **4** bill, sign **6** notice, poster **8** bulletin **13** advertisement

placate **4** calm, lull **5** quiet **6** pacify, soothe **7** appease, assuage, mollify, win over **9** alleviate **10** conciliate, propitiate

placatory **9** appeasing, pacifying **10** mollifying **12** conciliatory **13** accommodative

place **3** fix, job, put, set **4** area, city, digs, duty, farm, firm, home, land, plot, post, rank, rest, shop, site, spot, town, zone **5** abode, affix, array, berth, house, lodge, niche, plant, point, ranch, space, stand, state, store, venue **6** assign, attach, county, harbor, invest, locale, locate, office, region, settle **7** appoint, borough, company, concern, country, deposit, install, quarter, shelter, situate, station, village **8** building, business, classify, district, domicile, dwelling, ensconce, find hire, function, identify, locality, location, lodgings, position, premises, property, province, quarters, remember, standing, township, vicinity **9** recognize, residence, situation, territory **10** commission, get a job for, habitation **11** appointment, find work for, whereabouts **12** neighborhood **13** establishment
Latin: **4** situ

Place in the Sun, A
director: **13** George Stevens
based on novel by: **15** Theodore Dreiser (An American Tragedy)
cast: **14** Keefe Brasselle, Shelley Winters **15** Elizabeth Taylor, Montgomery Clift
Oscar for: **5** score **9** direction **10** screenplay

placement **8** grouping, location **10** assignment, employment **11** arrangement, disposition, positioning

place of residence **4** home **5** abode, house **7** address, lodging **8** domicile, dwelling **9** residence **10** habitation **14** living quarters

place to stand on
Greek: **6** pou sto

place upright **5** erect, raise **7** stand up

placid **4** calm, mild **5** quiet **6** gentle, poised, serene, smooth **7** pacific, restful **8** composed, peaceful, tranquil **9** collected, unexcited, unruffled **10** untroubled **11** undisturbed, unexcitable **13** imperturbable, self-possessed **15** undemonstrative

plague **3** irk, vex, woe **4** bane, evil, fret, gall, pain, pest **5** agony, chafe, curse, harry, haunt, peeve, worry **6** badger, blight, bother, burden, cancer, harass, misery, nettle **7** afflict, disturb, perturb, scourge, torment, trouble **8** aggrieve, calamity, disquiet, distress, hardship, pandemic **9** embarrass, persecute, suffering **10** affliction, Black Death, pestilence, visitation
French: **5** peste

Plague, The
author: **11** Albert Camus
character: **7** Rambert **10** Jean Tarrou **11** Joseph Grand **14** Father Paneloux, Raymond Cottard **15** Dr Bernard R Rieux

Plague Dogs, The
author: **12** Richard Adams

plain **4** bald, bare, open **5** blunt, clear, frank, naked, vivid **6** candid, common, direct, homely, honest, modest, simple **7** average, glaring, legible, obscure, obvious, plateau, prairie, sincere, visible **8** apparent, clear-cut, distinct, everyday, explicit, manifest, ordinary, palpable, specific, straight, striking, uncomely, unlovely **9** grassland, outspoken, prominent, tableland, unadorned, undiluted **10** forthright, pronounced, unaffected, unassuming, unhandsome, unreserved, well-marked **11** commonplace, conspicuous, discernible, not striking, open country, outstanding, plain-spoken, unambiguous, undecorated, undisguised, unequivocal, ungarnished, unvarnished, well-defined **12** matter-of-fact, not beautiful, unattractive, unmistakable, unornamented **13** unembellished, unpretentious, without frills **14** comprehensible, understandable **15** straightforward, undistinguished

Plain Dealer, The
author: **16** William Wycherley

plainly **6** baldly, openly, simply **7** bluntly, clearly, frankly, visibly, vividly **8** candidly, directly, honestly, markedly, modestly **9** doubtless, obviously **10** apparently, definitely, distinctly, explicitly, manifestly, ordinarily, positively, strikingly, undeniably **11** beyond doubt, discernibly, prominently, undoubtedly **12** unaffectedly, unassumingly, unmistakably, without doubt **13** conspicuously, unambiguously, unequivocably **14** comprehensibly, unquestionably

plainness **10** homeliness, simplicity **12** ordinariness

plainspoken **4** open **5** bluff, blunt, frank, plain **6** candid, direct, honest **7** genuine, sincere **8** explicit, straight **9** open-faced, outspoken, unsparing **10** above board, forthright, point-blank **11** straight-out **15** straightforward

plaint **3** cry, sob **4** beef, moan, wail **5** gripe **6** charge, grouse, grudge, lament, regret, squawk **7** grumble, reproof **8** reproach **9** complaint, grievance, objection **10** accusation, resentment **12** remonstrance

plaintive **3** sad **6** rueful **7** doleful, moaning, piteous, pitiful, tearful **8** dolorous, grievous, mournful, pathetic, wretched **9** lamenting, sorrowful, woebegone **10** lugubrious, melancholy **12** heartrending

plait **5** braid, queue, twine, twist, weave **7** pigtail **10** intertwine

plan **3** aim, map, way **4** form, idea, plot **5** frame, shape

6 design, devise, intend, lay out, map out, method, scheme, sketch 7 diagram, outline, prepare, program, project, propose, purpose 8 block out, conceive, contrive, organize, proposal, strategy, think out 9 blueprint, fabricate, procedure, stratagem 10 conception, suggestion 11 proposition
French: 8 demarche

Planchet
character in: 18 The Three Musketeers
author: 5 Dumas (pere)

Planck, Max
field: 7 physics
nationality: 6 German
developed: 13 quantum theory 15 Planck's constant
awarded: 10 Nobel Prize

Planctae
form: 5 rocks
characteristic: 8 shifting

plane 3 jet 4 bird, flat 5 level, plumb 6 degree, status 7 regular, station 8 aircraft, airplane, position, standing 9 condition, elevation
type: 4 jack 5 block

planet, planets 13 celestial body
first: 7 Mercury
second: 5 Venus
third: 5 Earth
satellite: 4 Moon
fourth: 4 Mars
satellite: 6 Deimos, Phobos
nickname: 9 Red Planet
fifth: 7 Jupiter
satellite: 2 Io 6 Europa 8 Amalthea, Callisto, Ganymede
characteristic: 7 red spot
sixth: 6 Saturn
satellite: 4 Rhea 5 Dione, Janus, Mimas, Titan 6 Phoebe, Tethys 7 Iapetus 8 Hyperion 9 Enceladus
characteristic: 5 rings
seventh: 6 Uranus
satellite: 5 Ariel 6 Oberon 7 Miranda, Titania, Umbriel
color: 9 blue-green
characteristic: 5 rings
eighth: 7 Neptune
satellite: 6 Nereid, Triton
color: 5 green
ninth: 5 Pluto
satellite: 6 Charon
asteroid/minor planet/planetoid: 4 Eros, Juno 5 Ceres, Vesta 6 Chiron, Hermes, Icarus, Pallas 7 Astraea, Hidalgo

planetary 6 astral 7 earthly 9 celestial 11 terrestrial 12 astronomical

Planet of the Apes
director: 18 Franklin J Schaffner
based on novel by: 12 Pierre Boulle
cast: 9 Kim Hunter 12 Maurice Evans 13 Roddy McDowall 14 Charlton Heston
script: 10 Rod Serling

plank 4 deal, deck, slab 5 board, shole, stone 8 platform

planned 7 devised, schemed 8 designed, expected, foreseen, intended, prepared 9 mapped out, organized, projected, rehearsed 10 calculated, purposeful, thought out 11 intentional, prearranged, prepared for 12 premeditated

planner 6 author, framer 7 creator, deviser 8 arranger, designer 9 architect, organizer

plant 4 bush, herb, mill, moss, shop, slip, tree, vine, weed, wort, yard 5 algae, flora, fungi, grass, set in, shrub, works 6 flower, foster, infuse, set out 7 factory, foundry, herbage, implant, inspire, instill, scatter, sow seed 8 business, engender, seedling 9 broadcast, cultivate, establish, inculcate, propagate, vegetable 10 transplant, vegetation 13 establishment, sow the seeds of 14 put in the ground

plaster 4 coat, daub, sand 5 grout, smear 6 bedaub, gypsum, lather, stucco 7 overlay, spackle
mixture of: 4 lime 5 water 6 gypsum

plastered 5 drunk 6 coated, daubed, soused 7 covered, crocked, smeared, swacked 8 mortared, polluted, stuccoed 10 inebriated 11 intoxicated

plastic 4 soft 6 pliant, supple 7 ductile, elastic, pliable 8 flexible, formable, moldable, shapable, yielding 9 malleable, tractable

Platanistius
epithet of: 6 Apollo
means: 22 god of the plane-tree grove

plate 4 dish 6 saucer 7 helping, platter, portion, serving 10 platterful 11 serving dish

plateau 4 mesa 5 table 6 upland 8 highland 9 tableland

Plateosaurus
type: 8 dinosaur, sauropod
location: 6 Europe 7 Germany
period: 8 Triassic

platform 4 dais, goal, plan 5 creed, plank, stage, stand 6 podium, policy, pulpit, tenets 7 program, rostrum

Plath, Sylvia
author of: 5 Ariel 10 The Bell Jar

platinum
chemical symbol: 2 Pt

platitude 3 saw 6 cliche, old saw, truism 7 bromide 8 banality, chestnut 11 commonplace

platitudinous 5 banal, corny, stale, tired, trite, vapid 6 jejune 8 bromidic, ordinary 9 hackneyed 10 pedestrian, unexciting, unoriginal 12 cliche-ridden, conventional 13 unimaginative

Plato
author of: 4 Laws 5 Crito 6 Phaedo 7 Apology, Gorgias, Sophist, Timaeus 8 Philebus, Republic 9 Symposium 10 Parmenides

platoon 4 band, body, crew, team, unit 5 corps, force, group 10 detachment

platter 4 dish, disk, lanx 6 salver 7 record 8 trencher 9 recording

plaudit, plaudits 4 rave 5 cheer, kudos 6 hurrah, huzzah, praise 7 acclaim, bouquet, ovation 8 applause, approval, cheering 10 compliment, hallelujah 11 approbation 12 commendation

plauditory 8 admiring, praising 9 extolling, laudatory, praiseful 12 commendatory 13 complimentary

plausible 5 sound, valid 6 likely 7 logical, tenable 8 credible, feasible, possible, probable, rational, sensible 10 acceptable, believable, convincing, persuasive, reasonable 11 conceivable, justifiable

Plautus
author of: 7 Stichus 8 Mercator 9 Amphitruo, Menaechmi, Pseudolus 10 Amphitryon 14 Miles Gloriosus

play 3 act, fun, toy 4 jest, lark, romp, room, show 5 antic, caper, drama, enact, farce, frisk, revel, space, sport, sweep, swing 6 act out, cavort, comedy, frolic, gambol, leeway, trifle 7 disport, have fun, pageant, perform, skylark, tragedy, vie with 8 pleasure, take part 9 amusement, diversion, elbowroom, enjoyment, make merry, melodrama, perform on, personify, represent, spectacle **10** recreation **11** impersonate, merrymaking

playboy 4 rake, wolf **5** Romeo, sheik **6** lecher **7** Don Juan, swinger **8** Casanova, hedonist, Lothario, party boy **9** jet-setter, ladies' man, partygoer, womanizer **10** lady-killer, profligate **14** pleasure seeker **15** good-time Charlie

Playboy of the Western World, The
author: 19 John Millington Synge
character: 8 Old Mahon **9** Widow Quin **10** Shawn Keogh **16** Christopher Mahon, Margaret Flaherty (Pegeen)

play down 9 underplay **11** deemphasize

played out 4 beat **5** all in, spent, weary **6** bushed, done in, pooped **7** drained, wearied, worn out **8** depleted, dog tired, fatigued, tired out, unreeled **9** dead tired, exhausted

player 4 jock, mime **5** actor **6** mummer **7** actress, athlete, trouper **8** gamester, opponent, thespian **9** adversary, contender, performer **10** antagonist, competitor, contestant, team member **11** entertainer, participant

play false 4 dupe **5** trick **6** betray **7** deceive, two-time **10** be disloyal **12** be unfaithful **13** be treacherous

playfellow 3 pal **4** chum **5** buddy **6** friend **8** playmate

playful 6 frisky, impish, lively **7** amusing, coltish, jesting, waggish **8** humorous, mirthful, prankish, sportive **9** fun-loving, sprightly **10** capricious, frolicsome, rollicking **12** lighthearted
French: 8 espiegle

playful trick
French: 11 espieglerie

play host 4 host **9** entertain **10** give a party, have guests **13** keep open house

playing field 4 bowl **5** arena **7** diamond, stadium **8** gridiron **10** playground **12** amphitheater

playing piece 3 man **4** disk **5** piece **7** counter

play in water 3 dip **4** swim **6** dabble, paddle, splash

play Judas 6 betray **7** sell out, two-time **9** play false **11** double-cross

playmate 3 pal **4** chum **5** buddy **6** friend **10** playfellow

play of spirit
French: 10 jeu d'esprit

play on words
French: 9 jeu de mots

plaything 3 toy **4** dupe **5** patsy, sport **6** bauble, trifle **9** diversion

play truant 3 cut **4** skip **8** be absent **9** play hooky

play with 5 bandy **7** torment, toy with **11** have fun with

playwright 6 author, writer **9** dramatist, scenarist **10** dramatizer, dramaturge, librettist, play doctor **12** dramatic poet, dramaturgist, scriptwriter **13** melodramatist

plea 4 suit **5** alibi **6** appeal, excuse, prayer **7** apology, begging, defense, pretext, request **8** argument, entreaty, petition **10** adjuration, beseeching **11** explanation, extenuation, vindication **12** solicitation, supplication **13** justification

plead 3 ask, beg **6** adjure, enjoin **7** beseech, entreat, implore, request, solicit **8** appeal to, petition **9** importune **10** supplicate

pleader 6 beggar **8** advocate, defender, implorer **9** apologist, beseecher **10** importuner, supplicant

plead with 3 beg **4** pray **6** adjure **7** beseech, implore **10** supplicate

Pleasance, Donald
born: 7 England, Worksop
roles: 12 The Caretaker **14** The Great Escape **16** You Only Live Twice **17** The Eagle Has Landed **24** The Greatest Story Ever Told

pleasant 4 fine, good, mild, nice, soft, warm **6** genial, gentle, lovely, polite **7** affable, amiable, cordial, likable, tactful **8** amicable, charming, cheerful, friendly, inviting, pleasing, sociable **9** agreeable, congenial, enjoyable **10** attractive, felicitous, gratifying, gregarious, satisfying **11** goodhumored, good-natured, pleasurable **13** companionable

Pleasant Island *see* **5** Nauru

pleasantry 4 jape, jest, joke, quip **5** sally **6** bon mot **8** greeting **9** wisecrack, witticism **10** salutation

pleasant-tasting 4 mild **5** sweet, tasty **6** savory **8** luscious **9** delicious, palatable, succulent **10** appetizing, delectable **11** scrumptious **13** mouth-watering

please 3 opt **4** like, suit, want, will, wish **5** amuse, charm, elate, elect **6** choose, desire, divert, prefer, thrill, tickle **7** content, delight, gladden, gratify, satisfy **8** enthrall, entrance **9** enrapture, entertain, fascinate, make happy **10** be inclined **14** give pleasure to
French: 12 s'il vous plait
German: 5 bitte
Spanish: 8 por favor

pleased 4 glad **5** happy, proud **6** elated **8** thrilled **9** delighted, gratified

please reply
French: 4 rsvp **20** repondez s'il vous plait

pleasing 6 genial, polite **7** affable, amiable, amusing, likable, winning **8** charming, cheerful, friendly, inviting, mannerly **9** agreeable, congenial, diverting, enjoyable **10** attractive, delightful, gladdening, gratifying, satisfying **11** captivating, fascinating, good-humored, good-natured, pleasurable **12** entertaining, well-mannered

pleasing inactivity
Italian: 14 dolce far niente

pleasurable 8 pleasing **9** agreeable, enjoyable **10** delightful

pleasure 3 fun, joy **4** like, will, wish **5** bliss, cheer, mirth **6** choice, desire, gaiety, option **7** delight, elation, rapture **9** amusement, diversion, enjoyment, festivity, happiness, merriment, selection **10** exultation, jubilation, preference, recreation **11** high spirits, inclination **13** entertainment, gratification **15** beer and skittles **16** lightheartedness
goddess of: 8 Voluptas

pleasure-giving 7 amusing **8** pleasing **9** agreeable, enjoyable **10** delightful **11** pleasurable **12** entertaining

Pleasure of His Company, The
author: 19 Cornelia Otis Skinner

pleasure trip 4 tour **5** jaunt **6** outing **8** vacation **9** excursion

pleat 4 fold **5** crimp, frill **6** crease

pleated 6 fluted, folded **7** creased, crimped **10** corrugated

plebeian **3** low **4** base, mean **5** banal **6** coarse, common, vulgar **7** lowborn, lowbrow, popular **8** commoner, everyman, low-class, ordinary **9** bourgeois, common man, unrefined **10** average man, uncultured **11** bourgeoisie, commonplace, proletarian **12** uncultivated

plebs **5** demos **6** masses **7** commons **8** populace **9** commoners, hoi polloi, plebeians **11** bourgeoisie **12** common people

plecoptera
class: **8** hexapoda
phylum: **10** arthropoda
group: **8** stone fly

pledge **3** vow **4** bail, bond, oath, pact, pawn, word **5** swear, troth **6** assert, avowal, surety **7** compact, promise, warrant **8** contract, covenant, guaranty, security, warranty **9** agreement, assurance, guarantee **10** adjuration, collateral

Pleiades
father: **5** Atlas
mother: **7** Pleione
half-sisters: **6** Hyades
names: **4** Maia **6** Merope **7** Alcyone, Celaeno, Electra, Sterope, Taygete
number of daughters: **5** seven

plenary **4** full **6** entire **7** perfect **8** absolute, complete

plenitude **4** glut, heap, mass **5** flood **6** bounty, plenty, wealth **7** quality, surfeit, surplus **8** fullness, plethora, totality **9** abundance, amplitude, profusion, repletion, wholeness **10** cornucopia, entireness, quantities **11** ample supply, copiousness, full measure, sufficiency **12** completeness **14** more than enough

plenteous **6** lavish **7** copious, profuse **8** abundant **9** bountiful, plentiful

plentiful **4** lush **5** ample, large **6** lavish **7** copious, liberal, profuse **8** abundant, generous, infinite, prolific **9** abounding, bounteous, bountiful, plenteous, unsparing, unstinted **11** overflowing **13** inexhaustible

plenty **4** gobs, lots, slew **5** scads **6** luxury, oceans, oodles, riches, wealth, worlds **8** opulence **9** abundance, affluence, good times, great deal, plenitude, profusion, well-being **10** prosperity **11** ample amount, good fortune, sufficiency **12** a full measure
goddess of: **3** Ops

plethora **4** glut **5** flood **6** excess, wealth **7** overage, surfeit, surplus **8** fullness **9** abundance, amplitude, plenitude, profusion **10** oversupply, redundancy, surplusage **11** superfluity **13** overabundance **14** more than enough, superabundance

Plexippus
also: **10** Parthenius
father: **7** Phineus **8** Thestius
brother: **7** Pandion
sister: **7** Althaea
nephew: **8** Meleager
killed by: **8** Meleager

pliable **5** lithe **6** limber, pliant, supple **7** elastic, plastic, springy, willing **8** flexible, yielding **9** adaptable, compliant, receptive, resilient, tractable **10** manageable, responsive, submissive **11** acquiescent **13** accommodating **14** easily bendable, impressionable

pliancy **8** docility, meekness, yielding **9** passivity **10** compliance, pliability, submission, suppleness **11** flexibility **12** complaisance

pliant **4** meek **6** supple **7** pliable **8** flexible, yielding **9** compliant **10** submissive **11** deferential

pliers
type: **10** fixed-joint **11** combination, needle-nosed, side-cutting **17** offset combination

plight **3** fix, jam **5** pinch, state, trial **6** crisis, muddle, pickle, scrape **7** dilemma, impasse, straits, trouble **8** distress, exigency **9** condition, emergency, extremity, situation **10** difficulty **11** predicament, tribulation, vicissitude **12** circumstance

Plisthenes
brother/half-brother: **8** Menelaus **9** Agamemnon
father: **6** Atreus
mother: **6** Cleola
sister/half-sister: **8** Anaxibia
sister-in-law: **12** Clytemnestra
uncle: **8** Thyestes

plod **4** drag, grub, moil, plug, slog, toil **5** grind, sweat, tramp **6** drudge, lumber, trudge, waddle **7** peg away, shuffle **8** struggle **9** persevere

plodding **4** dull **6** clumsy **8** trudging **9** laborious **10** pedestrian

plot **3** lot, map **4** area, draw, mark, plan, tale, yarn **5** chart, draft, field, patch, space, story, tract **6** action, design, scheme, sketch **7** collude, compute, diagram, outline, section **8** clearing, conspire, contrive, evil plan, intrigue, maneuver **9** blueprint, calculate, determine, incidents, narrative, story line, stratagem **10** conspiracy, secret plan **11** machination

plotting **4** wily **6** artful, crafty **7** cunning **8** scheming **9** conniving, designing **10** intriguing

Plough and the Stars, The
author: **10** Sean O'Casey

plover
group of: **4** wing **12** congregation

plow, plough **3** cut, dig **4** push, till, work **5** break, dig up, drive, forge, press, shove, spade **6** furrow, harrow, loosen, plunge, turn up **7** break up **8** bulldoze **9** cultivate
invented by:
cast iron: **7** Ransome
disc: **5** Hardy

plowable **6** arable **7** friable **8** farmable, tillable **10** cultivable

Plowright, Joan
born: **5** Brigg **7** England
husband: **15** Laurence Olivier
roles: **13** A Taste of Honey **15** The Entertainers

ploy **4** game, ruse, wile **5** trick **6** design, gambit, scheme, tactic **7** gimmick **8** artifice, maneuver, strategy **9** stratagem **10** subterfuge

pluck **4** draw, grab, grit, guts, jerk, pick, sand, yank **5** spunk, valor **6** daring, mettle, pull at, snatch, spirit, uproot **7** bravery, courage, pull off, pull out, resolve **8** boldness, temerity, tenacity **9** extirpate, fortitude **10** doggedness, resolution **11** persistence **12** perseverance **13** determination

pluck out **7** extract, pick out, pull out

plucky **4** bold, game **5** brave, gutsy **6** daring, spunky **7** doughty, valiant **8** fearless, intrepid, spirited, unafraid, valorous **9** audacious, dauntless, undaunted **10** courageous, mettlesome **11** lionhearted, unflinching **12** stouthearted

plug **4** bung, cork **5** close, stuff **6** fill up, stanch, stop up **7** shut off, stopper, stopple

plug up **3** dam **4** clog, plug **5** block, choke, dam up, stuff **6** stop up **7** congest **8** obstruct

plum
varieties: **3** hog **4** Coco, date, Duhr, gage, Java, sand, sloe, wild **5** beach, black, goose, Islay, Jaman, Lansa, Moxie, nanny, Natal, shore, Simon **6** August, Batoko, Canada, Cheney, cherry, common, Damson, ground, Indian, Jambul, Kaffir, Kelsey, Lomboy, Pigeon, Sapote, Sierra, Sisson **7** apricot, Burbank, Cheston, Jambosa, Malabar, Orleans, Pacific, Spanish, Wickson **8** American, Assyrian, Burdekin, European, Hortulan, Jambolan, Japanese, Oklahoma, Prunello, Victoria **9** Allegheny, Chickasaw, Governor's, greengage, marmalade, Myrobalan, wild-goose **10** Madagascar **13** Queensland hog

plumb **4** lead, test, true **5** gauge, level, probe, sheer, sound **6** fathom **7** examine, measure, plummet **8** plumb bob, straight, vertical **9** penetrate

plume **3** pen **4** down **5** egret, pique, preen, pride, prize, quill **7** feather
military: **7** panache

Plumed Serpent, The
author: **10** D H Lawrence

Plummer, Christopher
real name: **28** Arthur Christopher Orme Plummer
born: **6** Canada **7** Toronto
wife: **11** Tammy Grimes **12** Elaine Taylor
roles: **14** Murder by Decree **15** The Sound of Music **18** Baron Georg von Trapp **20** The Man Who Would Be King **25** The Return of the Pink Panther

plummet **4** dive, fall **6** plunge, tumble **8** nosedive **12** fall headlong

plump **4** drop, firm, flop, plop, sink **5** blunt, buxom, obese, plunk, pudgy, solid, spill, stout **6** abrupt, chubby, direct, fleshy, portly, rotund, sprawl, stocky, tumble **7** rounded **8** collapse, outright **9** corpulent

plumpness
French: **10** embonpoint

plunder **3** rob **4** haul, loot, raid, sack, swag, take **5** booty, rifle, prize, strip **6** fleece, maraud, pilfer, ravage, spoils **7** despoil, pillage, ransack, takings **9** filchings **10** pilferings

plunderer **6** looter, vandal **7** brigand **8** pillager **9** despoiler

plunge **3** dip, fly, run **4** bolt, cast, dart, dash, dive, drop, duck, fall, jerk, roll, jump, leap, push, reel, rock, rush, sink, sway, tear, toss **5** douse, drive, heave, lunge, lurch, pitch, press, shoot, speed, surge, swarm, whisk **6** charge, hasten, hurtle, hustle, scurry, sprint, streak, thrust, tumble **7** descend, immerse, scuttle **8** scramble, submerge, submerse **12** fall headlong

plunk **4** pick, thud **5** pluck, plumb, strum, twang **6** dollar **7** exactly **8** squarely **9** precisely

plurality **4** bulk, most **8** majority **13** preponderance

plus **5** added, extra, other, spare **6** useful **7** helpful **9** auxiliary, desirable **10** additional, beneficial **12** advantageous, supplemental **13** supplementary

plush **4** lush, posh, rich **5** fancy, grand, ritzy, swank, thick **6** classy, deluxe, lavish, snazzy, swanky **7** elegant, opulent **8** palatial **9** luxurious, sumptuous **11** extravagant

plushy **4** soft **5** cushy, swank **7** opulent, velvety **9** luxurious, sumptuous

Plutarch
author of: **13** Parallel Lives

Plutarch's Lives
author: **8** Plutarch

Pluto
also: **5** Hades
god of: **10** underworld
corresponds to: **3** Dis **5** Orcus **8** Dis Pater

Pluto
position: **5** ninth
satellite: **6** Charon

plutocrat **5** mogul **6** fat cat, tycoon **9** financier **10** capitalist

plutonic **7** abyssal, igneous **9** cimmerian, intrusive, vulcanian

plutonium
chemical symbol: **2** Pu

Plutus
author: **12** Aristophanes
character: **5** Cario **9** Chremylus **11** Blepsidemus
god of: **6** wealth

Plutus
personifies: **6** wealth
father: **6** Iasion
mother: **7** Demeter

Pluvius
epithet of: **7** Jupiter

ply **3** fly, run **4** leaf, sail, work **5** layer, offer, plait, plate, press, sheet, slice, twist, wield **6** employ, follow, handle, lamina, pursue, sheath, strand, supply **7** besiege, carry on, labor at, operate, stratum, utilize **8** exercise, navigate, practice, put to use, urge upon **9** thickness **10** manipulate

poach **3** rob **4** cook **5** shirr, steal **6** plunge, simmer **7** trample **8** encroach, trespass

pocket **3** bag, get, pit **4** gain, lode, sack, vein **5** pouch, purse, pygmy, small, steal, strip, usurp **6** attain, bantam, cavity, come by, hollow, little, obtain, pilfer, strain, streak **7** chamber, compact, handbag, placket, receive **8** arrogate, envelope, portable **9** miniature **10** diminutive, receptacle **11** appropriate, compartment

Pocket, Herbert
character in: **17** Great Expectations
author: **7** Dickens

pocketbook **3** bag **5** pouch, purse **6** clutch, wallet **7** handbag, satchel **8** moneybag, notecase **9** coin purse **10** money purse **11** shoulder bag
French: **12** porte-monnaie

pocket flask **5** flask **6** bottle **7** canteen

pocket-sized **3** wee **4** tiny **5** dwarf, pygmy, small **6** bantam, little, midget, minute, petite **7** compact **9** miniature **10** diminutive, vest-pocket

poco
music: **6** little

Pocock, Mamie
character in: **14** The Ambassadors
author: **5** James

pod **4** case, hull, husk **5** shell **6** jacket, sheath **8** pericarp, seed case **10** seed vessel

Podarces
mentioned in: **5** Iliad
father: **8** Iphiclus
brother: **11** Protesilaus
commanded: **8** Pythians

Podes
home: **4** Troy
occupation: **7** warrior
killed by: **8** Menelaus

Podgorica
capital of: **10** Montenegro

podium **4** dais, foot, wall **5** stipe **7** lectern **8** pedestal, platform **9** footstalk

Poe, Edgar Allan
author of: **6** Ligeia **7** Israfel, To Helen **8** The Bells, The Raven **10** Annabel Lee, The Gold Bug **18** The Purloined Letter **20** The Cask of Amontillado, The Pit and the Pendulum **22** The Masque of the Red Death **24** The Fall of the House of Usher, The Murders in the Rue Morgue **29** The Narrative of Arthur Gordon Pym

Poeas
also: **5** Poias
lit: **11** funeral pyre
pyre of: **8** Hercules
son: **11** Philoctetes

poem **3** lay, ode **4** epic, song **5** elegy, idyll, lyric, rhyme, verse **6** ballad, jingle, sonnet **8** doggerel, limerick, madrigal

Poema del Cid *see* **6** The Cid

Poems Chiefly in the Scottish Dialect
author: **11** Robert Burns

Poena
also: **5** Poine
personifies: **7** revenge **10** punishment

poet **4** bard **5** maker **6** lyrist, rhymer, singer **7** reciter **8** lyricist, minstrel, verseman **9** balladeer, balladist, poetaster, rhymester, sonneteer, versifier **10** improviser, librettist, songwriter

poetaster **4** bard, poet **6** rhymer, writer **8** poetizer, rimester **9** rhymester, versifier

poetic, poetical **5** lyric **7** lilting, lyrical, melodic, musical **8** metrical, rhythmic, songlike **9** melodious **11** imaginative

Poetics
author: **9** Aristotle

poetizer **4** bard, poet **6** rhymer, writer **8** rhymster **9** poetaster, versifier

poetry **5** poesy, rhyme, verse **13** versification
god of: **4** Odin, Ogma **5** Brage, Bragi, Othin **6** Apollo **7** Phoebus, Pythius **9** Musagetes

Pogo
creator: **9** Walt Kelly
character: **9** Porkypine, Wiley Catt **10** Boll Weevil **12** PT Bridgeport **13** Deacon Mushrat, Mole MacCarony
alligator: **6** Albert
fox: **11** Seminole Sam
frog: **15** Moonshine Sonata
hound: **18** Beauregard Bugleboy
possum: **4** Pogo
skunk: **16** Ma'm'selle Hepzibah
snake: **7** Snavely
sorcerer: **10** Howland Owl
turtle/pirate captain: **14** Churchy La Femme
place: **15** Okefenokee Swamp

Pohjola
origin: **7** Finnish
identified with: **7** Lapland
location: **12** North Finland

poignant **3** sad **5** sharp **6** biting, moving, rueful, woeful **7** cutting, doleful, piquant, piteous, pitiful, pungent, tearful **8** grievous, pathetic, piercing, pitiable, touching **9** affecting, sorrowful, trenchant **10** lamentable **11** distressing, penetrating **12** heartrending

Poine *see* **5** Poena

point **3** aim, end, hit, nib, run, tip, use **4** apex, bend, bode, core, game, gist, goal, item, mark, meat, pike, pith, spur, time, turn, unit **5** argue, cause, guide, heart, imply, level, limit, place, prong, prove, score, sense, slant, spike, stage, steer, tally, train, value **6** aspect, basket, degree, detail, direct, hint at, kernel, marrow, moment, number, object, reason **7** essence, feature, instant, portend, presage, purpose, quality, signify, suggest, testify **8** indicate, intimate, juncture, main idea, manifest, offshoot, position, sharp end **9** condition, extension, intention, objective, outgrowth **10** foreshadow, particular, projection, prominence, promontory **11** demonstrate **12** protuberance

point-blank **5** blunt **6** direct **10** forthright **11** plainspoken

Point Counter Point
author: **12** Aldous Huxley

point d'appui **4** prop, stay **24** point of battle line support

pointed **5** acute, blunt, sharp **6** biting, direct, peaked, pointy **7** cutting, fitting, hinting, telling **8** accurate, incisive, piercing **9** aciculate, acuminate, cuspidate, pertinent, trenchant **10** emphasized, forthright **11** appropriate, conspicuous, insinuating, penetrating

pointer **3** arm, tip **4** hand, hint **5** arrow, guide, stick **6** needle **7** caution, warning **9** indicator **10** admonition, advisement, suggestion **13** piece of advice **14** recommendation
dog breed: **16** German wirehaired **17** German shorthaired **25** wirehaired pointing griffon

pointless **4** dull **5** blunt **6** absurd, futile, obtuse, stupid **7** aimless, invalid, rounded, unedged, useless **8** bootless, worn down **9** fruitless, illogical, senseless, unpointed, worthless **10** irrational, irrelevant, ridiculous, unavailing **11** ineffectual, meaningless, purposeless, unsharpened **12** inapplicable, preposterous, unproductive, unprofitable, unreasonable

point of view **4** side **5** angle, slant **6** aspect **7** outlook **8** attitude **9** viewpoint **10** standpoint **11** frame of mind, perspective

point the way **5** guide, pilot, usher **6** direct **8** indicate, navigate **14** give directions

point to **5** argue, imply **6** denote **7** express **8** indicate

point up **6** stress **9** emphasize, underline **10** accentuate, underscore

Poirot, Hercule
detective created by: **14** Agatha Christie
nationality: **7** Belgian
famed for: **10** moustaches
phrase: **15** little grey cells
played by: **12** Peter Sellers

poise **4** calm **5** raise **6** aplomb **7** balance, elevate **8** presence **9** assurance, composure, hold aloft, sangfroid **10** equanimity **11** savoir faire, self-command, self-control **13** self-assurance **14** presence of mind, self-confidence **15** be in equilibrium

poised **7** assured **8** composed **9** confident **10** controlled **11** self-assured **13** self-possessed

poison **4** bane, evil, harm **5** curse, taint, toxin, venom **6** cancer, canker, debase, defile, impair, infect, plague, weaken **7** corrode, corrupt, degrade, disease, outrage, pollute **8** enormity, make sick **9** malignity **10** adulterate, corruption, debilitate, malignancy, pestilence **11** abomination, contaminate

poisonous **5** fatal, toxic **6** deadly, lethal, mortal **7** baneful, noxious **8** venomous, virulent **10** pernicious **11** deleterious **12** pestilential

Poitier, Sidney
born: **7** Miami FL
wife: **13** Joanna Shimkus
roles: **11** Virgil Tibbs **12** A Patch of Blue, For Love of

Ivy, Porgy and Bess **13** To Sir with Love **14** The Defiant Ones **15** A Raisin in the Sun **16** Lilies of the Field (Oscar) **17** They Call Me Mr Tibbs **19** In the Heat of the Night, The Blackboard Jungle, Uptown Saturday Night **23** Guess Who's Coming to Dinner?

Pokanoket *see* **10** Wampanoags

poke **3** dig, hit, jab **4** butt, drag, gore, idle, jolt, prod, push, stab **5** crawl, dally, delay, mosey, nudge, punch, stick, thump **6** dawdle, fiddle, potter, thrust **7** meander, saunter, shamble, shuffle **8** hang back **10** dillydally **12** shilly-shally

poker
derived from: **5** as nas, gilet **6** brelan **7** primero **11** brouillotte
cards/hand: **4** five **5** seven
bets: **4** ante **5** chips
hand: **4** pair **5** flush **8** straight, two pairs **9** full house **10** royal flush **11** four of a kind **12** three of a kind **13** straight flush
term: **4** call, fold **5** check, raise **6** ante up **7** reraise
variation: **4** draw, stud **5** jacks **8** jackpots **12** five-card draw **13** seven-card stud

poky, pokey **4** dull, jail, slow **5** dowdy, small **6** dreary, shabby, stodgy, stuffy **7** cramped **8** confined, dawdling, dilatory, frumpish **9** puttering **10** monotonous
creature: **5** sloth, snail **6** turtle **8** slowpoke, tortoise

Polacanthus
type: **8** dinosaur **10** ornithopod

Poland ***see box, p. 764***

Polanski, Roman
director of: **4** Tess **7** Macbeth **9** Chinatown **13** Rosemary's Baby

polar **3** icy **6** arctic, frigid, wintry **7** glacial, ice-cold **8** freezing **9** antarctic **11** nothernmost **12** southernmost

pole **3** rod **4** mast, spar **5** shaft, staff, stick **6** tongue **9** pikestaff
flax holder: **7** distaff
pertaining to: **5** nodal
sacred: **7** Asherah
Scottish: **5** caber
tribal: **5** totem
vehicular: **4** neap

Polias, Poliatas
epithet of: **6** Athena

police, police officer **4** cops, dick, fuzz, tidy **5** clean, guard **6** neaten, patrol, tidy up **7** clean up, control, marshal, officer, protect, sheriff **8** bluecoat, flatfoot, gendarme, regulate, spruce up, troopers **9** gendarmes, men in blue, patrolmen **10** traffic cop **11** arm of the law, keep in order **12** constabulary, cop on the beat
French: **8** gendarme
Italian: **11** carabiniere

Police Woman
character: **9** (Det) Joe Styles, (Lt) Paul Marsh **11** (Det) Pete Royster, (Lt) Bill Crowley **12** (Sgt Suzanne) Pepper Martin
cast: **9** Ed Bernard **11** Val Bisoglio **12** Earl Holliman **14** Angie Dickinson, Charles Dierkop

policy **3** way **4** plan, rule **5** habit, style **6** custom, design, method, scheme, system **7** program, routine, tactics **8** behavior, platform, practice, strategy **9** principle, procedure

Polieus
epithet of: **4** Zeus
means: **5** urban

polish **3** oil, wax **4** buff, sand **5** class, emend, glaze, gloss, grace, rouge, rub up, shine **6** pumice, refine, smooth **7** burnish, correct, culture, enhance, finesse, improve, perfect, sauvity, touch up, varnish **8** abrasive, courtesy, elegance, round out, urbanity **9** gentility, politesse, sandpaper **10** politeness, refinement **11** cultivation, good manners

polished **4** able, deft, fine, oily **5** oiled, suave, waxed **6** buffed, expert, glassy, glazed, glossy, polite, rubbed, sanded, shined, urbane **7** capable, elegant, genteel, refined, skilled **8** cultured, finished, mannerly, masterly, skillful, smoothed **9** brilliant, burnished, courteous, masterful, practiced, varnished **10** cultivated, proficient **11** experienced **12** accomplished

polish off **6** finish **8** complete, get rid of **9** dispose of

polite **4** high **5** civil, elite **6** proper **7** courtly, elegant, gallant, genteel, refined **8** cultured, mannerly, polished, well-bred **9** civilized, courteous, diffident, patrician **10** cultivated, respectful **11** ceremonious, fashionable, gentlemanly, well-behaved **12** well-mannered

politeness **7** decorum **8** courtesy **9** gentility, propriety **10** refinement **11** good manners

Polites
character in: **7** Odyssey
brother: **5** Paris **6** Hector
companion: **8** Odysseus
father: **5** Priam
mother: **6** Hecuba
sister: **9** Cassandra
transformed by: **5** Aeaea, Circe
transformed into: **3** hog, pig **5** swine

politic **4** wily, wise **5** chary, suave **6** artful, astute, shrewd, subtle **7** mindful, prudent, tactful **8** cautious, discreet, scheming **9** designing, expedient, judicious, opportune **10** contriving, diplomatic **11** calculating, circumspect, machinating **13** Machiavellian

political party **3** GOP **4** Tory, Whig **5** Labor **7** faction **9** Communist, Greenback, Socialist **10** Democratic, Republican **11** Know-Nothing

political refugee **2** DP **5** exile **6** emigre **10** expatriate **15** displaced person

politician **8** politico **9** incumbent, statesman **10** campaigner, legislator **12** officeholder, office seeker **13** public servant

politics **10** government, statecraft **11** party policy **13** statesmanship **14** affairs of state

Politics
author: **9** Aristotle

Politic Would-Be, Lord and Lady
characters in: **7** Volpone
author: **6** Jonson

Poliuchus
epithet of: **6** Athena
means: **14** city-protecting

Polixenes
character in: **14** The Winter's Tale
author: **11** Shakespeare

Polk, James Knox ***see box, p. 765***

polka **5** dance **10** round dance **13** Bohemian dance

poll **4** head, vote **5** count, tally **6** census, survey, voting **7** canvass, figures, returns **8** register, sampling **9** interview, nose count **10** count noses, voting list **11** voting place

Pollack, Sydney
director of: **11** Out of Africa (Oscar) **12** The Way We

Poland
other name: 6 Polska **17** the land of the plain
capital/largest city: 6 Warsaw
medieval capital: **6** Cracow, Krakow
others: 3 Lwo **4** Kodz, Kolo, Lida, Lodz, Lvov, Lyck, Nysa, Oels, Pila **5** Brest, Bytom, Chelm, Dukla, Narev, Opole, Posen, Radom, Sroda, Torun, Vilna **6** Danzig, Elblag, Gdansk, Gdynia, Gnesen, Grodno, Kalisz, Kielce, Kracow, Lublin, Poznan, Tarnow, Zabrze **7** Beuthen, Breslau, Chorzow, Garocin, Gliwice, Litousk, Litovsk, Lyublin, Oleztyn, Stettin, Wroclaw **8** Frombork, Gleiwitz, Katowice, Lidzbark, Liegnitz, Oswiecim, Przemysl, Szczecin, Tarnopol **9** Auschwitz, Bialogard, Bialystok, Bydgoszcz, Sosnowiec, Szczezecin, Walbrzych **11** Czestochowa
school: 6 Warsaw **12** Jagiellonian
division: 7 Galicia, Silesia **8** Podlesia, Volhynia **9** Lithuania, Pomerania
measure: 3 cal **4** mila, pret **5** morga, sazen, vloka, wloka **6** cwierc, cwierk, kwarta, lokiec **7** garniec **9** kwarterka
monetary unit: 4 abia **5** dalar, ducat, grosz, marka, zloty **6** fennig, groszy, gulden, halerz, korona **8** groschen
weight: 3 lut **4** funt **6** kamian **7** skrupul
island: 5 Wolin
lake: 5 Goplo, Mamry **8** Niegocin, Sniardwy **13** Stettin Lagoon
mountain: 5 Tatra **6** Beskid **7** Pieniny, Sudeten **9** Beshchady, High Tatra, Holy Cross **10** Carpathian
highest point: 4 Rysy
river: 3 Bug, San **4** Alle, Brda, Gwda, Lyna, Nysa, Oder, Styr **5** Biala, Drana, Dwina, Narev, Narew, Notec, Podra, Seret, Warta, Wista **6** Neisse, Niemen, Nyeman, Pilica, Pripet, Prosna, Styrpa, Wieprz **7** Nemunas, Vistula, Wistoka **8** Dniester
sea: 6 Baltic
physical feature:
forest: **10** Bialowieza
gulf: **6** Danzig, Gdansk
lagoon: **7** Stettin **12** Frischeshaff
plain: **7** Silesia
plateau: **6** Lublin
people: 4 Pole, Slav **5** Mazur **8** Silesian
astronomer: **10** Copernicus
author: **7** Reymont **8** Zeromski **10** Mickiewicz, Wyspianski **11** Sienkiewicz
composer: **6** Chopin **10** Paderewski
dynasty: **5** Piast **7** Jagello
king: **7** Casimir **8** Augustus
leader: **5** Kania **6** Gierek **7** Gomulka, Mieszko **8** Boleslaw **9** Pilsudski, Stanislaw **10** Jaruzelski, Kosciuszko, Lech Walesa
pope: **10** John Paul II **20** Cardinal Carol Wojtyla
queen: **7** Jadwiga
language: 6 Kaszub, Polish **10** Pomeranian
religion: 13 Roman Catholic
place:
castle: **5** Wawel
church: **6** St John **10** Panna Maria
monastery: **9** Jasna Gora
monument: **17** Heroes of the Ghetto
national park: **5** Ojcow **10** Bialowieza
palace: **7** Casimir
feature:
folk dance: **5** polka **7** mazurka **9** krakowiak, polonaise
union: **10** Solidarity
food:
dish: **5** bigos **7** kolduny
drink: **5** vodka **7** Krupnik
sausage: **8** kielbasa
soup: **7** barszca

Were **15** Absence of Malice **23** They Shoot Horses Don't They?

Pollock, Jackson
born: 6 Cody WY
artwork: 5 Scent **9** Blue Poles **10** The She-Wolf **11** Convergence **12** Autumn Rhythm **13** Eyes in the Heat **17** Easter and the Totem **20** Guardians of the Secret

pollutant 5 fumes, smoke, waste **7** exhaust **8** emission, impurity

pollute 4 foul, soil **5** dirty, sully **6** befoul, debase, defile **7** deprave, profane **9** desecrate **10** adulterate, make filthy **11** contaminate

polluted 4 foul **5** dirty, drunk **6** impure, soiled **7** corrupt, profane, smashed, unclean **9** poisonous **12** contaminated

Polk, James Knox
presidential rank: 8 eleventh
party: 8 Democrat
state represented: 2 TN
defeated: 4 (Henry) Clay **6** (James Gillespie) Birney
vice president: 6 (George Mifflin) Dallas
cabinet:
***state:* 8** (James) Buchanan
***treasury:* 6** (Robert John) Walker
***war:* 5** (William Learned) Marcy
***attorney general:* 5** (John Young) Mason **6** (Isaac) Toucey **8** (Nathan) Clifford
***navy:* 5** (John Young) Mason **8** (George) Bancroft
***postmaster general:* 7** (Cave) Johnson
born: 2 NC **17** Mecklenburg County
died/buried: 2 TN **9** Nashville
education: 11 prep schools **16** tutored privately
***University:* 13** North Carolina
religion: 9 Methodist
political career: 16 state legislature **17** Speaker of the House **24** US House of Representatives
***governor of:* 9** Tennessee
civilian career: 6 lawyer
notable events of lifetime/term:
***boundary dispute:* 9** Northwest
***discovery in California of:* 4** gold
***Proviso:* 6** Wilmot
***treaty of:* 16** Guadalupe Hidalgo
***war:* 7** Mexican
father: 6 Samuel
mother: 4 Jane
siblings: 7 John Lee **9** Jane Maria, Naomi Tate **10** Lydia Eliza **12** Marshall Tate, Samuel Wilson **14** William Hawkins **15** Franklin Ezekiel, Ophelia Clarissa
wife: 5 Sarah (Childress)
children: 4 none

pollution 7 fouling, soiling **8** defiling, dirtying, foulness, impurity **9** befouling, pollutant **11** uncleanness **12** adulteration **13** contaminating, contamination

Pollux *see* **15** Castor and Pollux

Pollyanna
director: 10 David Swift
based on story by: 13 Eleanor Porter
cast: 9 Jane Wyman **10** Karl Malden **11** Hayley Mills, Richard Egan

polo
equipment: 6 mallet
period of play: 7 chukker
championship: 10 Camacho Cup **13** Coronation Cup **16** Cup of the Americas

Polonius
character in: 6 Hamlet
author: 11 Shakespeare

Polska *see* **6** Poland

poltergeist 5 ghost **6** spirit
literally: 10 noise-ghost
manifestation: 5 knock, noise, prank

Poltergeist
director: 10 Tobe Hooper
cast: 12 Craig T Nelson **14** Jobeth Williams **16** Beatrice Straight
co-writer/producer: 15 Steven Spielberg

poltroon 6 coward, craven **7** caitiff, chicken, dastard **11** yellow-belly

Polybates
member of: 8 Gigantes

Polycaste *see* **6** Perdix

Polydora
father: 6 Peleus
mother: 8 Antigone
husband: 5 Borus
son: 10 Menestheus

Polydorus
mentioned in: 5 Iliad
father: 5 Priam **10** Hippomedon
mother: 6 Hecuba
killed by: 10 Polymestor **11** Polymnestor
avenged by: 6 Hecuba
member of: 7 Epigoni
***descendant of:* 18** Seven against Thebes

polygon 9 multangle **11** plane figure
eight-sided: 7 octagon
equal angled: 6 isogon
five-sided: 8 pentagon
four-sided: 6 square **7** rhombus **8** tetragon **9** rectangle, trapezoid
nine-sided: 7 nonagon
seven-sided: 8 heptagon
six-sided: 7 hexagon
ten-sided: 7 decagon
three-sided: 8 triangle
twelve-sided: 9 dodecagon

Polyhymnia
also: 8 Polymnia
member of: 5 Muses
personifies: 5 dance **11** sacred music
mother: 9 Mnemosyne

Polyidus
revived: 7 Glaucus

Polymastus
epithet of: 7 Artemis
means: 12 many-breasted

polymer 5 dimer, nylon **6** hydrol **7** hexamer **8** oligomer

Polymnestor
king of: 6 Thrace
killed: 9 Polydorus

Polymnia *see* **10** Polyhymnia

Polyneices *see* **9** Polynices

Polynesia ***see box, p. 766***

Polynices
also: 10 Polyneices
father: 7 Oedipus
mother: 7 Jocasta
uncle: 5 Creon
brother: 7 Oedipus **8** Eteocles
sister: 6 Ismene **8** Antigone
killed by: 8 Eteocles

polyp 5 coral, hydra, tumor **6** growth, isopod **7** octopod **10** sea anemone

Polypemon *see* **10** Procrustes

Polyphemus
form: 7 Cyclops **12** one-eyed giant
father: 6 Elatus **8** Poseidon
mother: 6 Thoosa
joined: 9 Argonauts
killed: 4 Acis
blinded by: 8 Odysseus
loved: 7 Galatea

Polyphides
king of: 6 Sicyon
vocation: 4 seer
protected: 8 Menelaus **9** Agamemnon

Polyphontes
brother: 11 Cresphontes
killed: 11 Cresphontes

polyphony 7 organum **8** faburden **11** fauxbourdon **12** counterpoint

Polynesia
name means: **11** many islands
cities: **4** Apia **7** Papeete **8** Auckland, Pago Pago **9** Nukualofa
island: **4** Cook, Line **5** Samoa, Tonga **6** Easter, Ellice, Hawaii, Midway, Tahiti, Tubuai, Tuvalu **7** Austral, Maupiti, Phoenix, Society, Tokelau, Tuamotu **8** Pitcairn **9** Marquesas **10** New Zealand **15** French Polynesia
sea: **7** Pacific
people: **3** Ati **5** Maori **6** Kanaka, Nivean, Samoan, Tongan **9** Nesogaean **10** Polynesian
explorer: **4** Cook **6** Tasman, Wallis **8** Magellan **9** Roggeveen **12** Bougainville
language: **4** Niue, Uvea **5** Maori **6** Samoan, Tongan **7** Austral, Tagalog, Tokelau **8** Hawaiian, Tahitian **9** Marquesan, Tuamatuan **10** Mangarevan
religion: **12** Christianity
place:
legendary origin: **8** Hawaiiki
feature:
chief: **5** matai
clothing: **5** pareu **6** sarong **8** lavalava
dance: **4** hula, siva
dwelling: **4** fale
family social unit: **4** aiga
priest: **7** kahunas
supernatural power: **4** mana
food:
dish: **3** kai, poi **4** taro **8** palusami
drink: **3** ava **4** kava, kawa

Polypoetes
king of: **10** Thesprotia
father: **6** Apollo **8** Odysseus **9** Pirithous
mother: **6** Phthia **9** Callidice **10** Hippodamia
leader of: **6** Greeks

Polyporthis
father: **8** Odysseus
mother: **8** Penelope

polysaccharide **6** insulin, starch **7** dextrin **8** galactin, lichenin **9** cellulose **12** carbohydrate

Polytechnus
wife: **5** Aedon

Polyxena
father: **5** Priam
mother: **6** Hecuba
loved by: **8** Achilles

Polyxenus
grandfather: **6** Augeas

Polyxo
advisor to: **9** Hypsipyle

Pomaria *see* **7** Algeria

Pomerania
capital: **7** Stettin
city: **5** Thorn, Torun **6** Anklam
country: **6** Poland **7** Germany
island: **5** Rugen **6** Usedom
province: **7** Pomorze

pommel, pummel **4** beat, hilt, horn, knob, pake **6** finial, strike **9** saddlebow

Pomona
origin: **5** Roman
goddess of: **10** fruit trees

pomp **4** show **5** front, glory, style **7** display **8** ceremony, flourish, grandeur, splendor **9** pageantry, showiness, solemnity, spectacle **10** brilliance **11** affectation, grandiosity, ostentation, pompousness **12** magnificence **14** stately display **15** pretentiousness

pompous **4** vain **5** proud **6** lordly, uppish **7** haughty **8** affected, arrogant, mannered, overdone, puffed-up, snobbish **9** conceited, egotistic, grandiose, imperious **10** blustering, swaggering **11** overbearing, patronizing, pretentious **12** ostentatious, presumptuous, supercilious, vainglorious **13** condescending, high and mighty, self-important

Ponchielli, Amilcare
born: **5** Italy **7** Cremona
composer of: **10** La Gioconda **15** Dance of the Hours

poncho **4** cape **5** cloak, shawl **6** mantle, serape

pond **4** pool, tarn **5** basin **6** lagoon **9** small lake, water hole

ponder **4** muse **5** study **6** wonder **7** examine, reflect **8** cogitate, consider, mull over, ruminate **9** brood over, cerebrate, reflect on, speculate, think over **10** deliberate, meditate on, puzzle over **11** contemplate

ponderous **3** big **4** dull **5** bulky, heavy, hefty, large, wordy **6** boring, bovine, dreary **7** awkward, droning, hulking, labored, lumpish, massive, tedious, weighty **8** cumbrous, enormous, sluggish, unlively, unwieldy **9** corpulent, graceless, lumbering, wearisome **10** burdensome, cumbersome, long-winded, lusterless, monotonous, unexciting, ungraceful **11** heavy-handed

pontiff **4** pope **6** bishop, priest **8** pontifex

pontifical **7** pompous **8** churchly, clerical, dogmatic, priestly **9** apostolic, episcopal, imperious **11** opinionated, overbearing, patronizing, pretentious **13** authoritarian, condescending **14** ecclesiastical

Pontus
personifies: **3** sea
father: **2** Ge
son: **6** Nereus **7** Phorcys

pony **3** nag **4** crib, trot **5** glass, horse, pinto **7** mustang **9** racehorse
breed: **6** Exmoor **8** Shetland

pooh-pooh **5** knock **7** disdain, put down, run down, sneer at **8** belittle **9** disparage

Pooka *see* **4** Puca

pool **3** pot **4** ally, bank, lake, mere, pond, tarn **5** group, kitty, merge, share, union, unite **6** puddle, splash, stakes **7** combine **8** alliance, fishpond, millpool **9** coalition **10** amalgamate, collective **11** association, consolidate, cooperative **13** confederation

Poole, Grace
character in: **8** Jane Eyre
author: **6** Bronte

poop **3** fag **4** bush, deck, do in, tire **7** exhaust, fatigue, wear out **8** enervate

pooped **4** beat **5** all in, spent, tired, weary **6** bushed, done in **7** drained, wearied, worn out **8** fatigued, tired out **9** dead tired, exhausted, played out

poor **3** sad **4** bare, dead, vain, worn **5** broke, empty, needy, sorry **6** barren, fallow, faulty, futile, hard up, in need, in want, meager, paltry, wasted **7** forlorn, sterile, unhappy, unlucky, wanting **8** badly off, bankrupt, beggarly, depleted, desolate, devoid of, grieving, indigent, inferior, pathetic, pitiable, strapped, unworthy, wretched **9** defective, deficient, destitute, exhausted, fruitless, imperfect, infertile, insolvent, in straits, miserable, moneyless, penniless, unfertile, worthless **10** distressed, inadequate, pauperized **11** impecunious, unfortunate **12** impoverished, uncultivable, unproductive, unprofitable **15** poverty-stricken

Poor People
author: **16** Fyodor Dostoevsky

Poor Richard's Almanac
author: **16** Benjamin Franklin

Poor White
author: **16** Sherwood Anderson

pop **4** bang, boom, come, shot, snap, soda **5** arise, blast, burst, crack **6** appear, report **7** explode **8** detonate **9** discharge, explosion, soft drink **10** detonation

pope ***see box***

Pope, Alexander
author of: **10** The Dunciad **12** An Essay on Man **15** Eloisa to Abelard **16** The Rape of the Lock **18** An Essay on Criticism **20** Epistle to Dr Arbuthnot

Pope, John Russell
architect of: **17** Jefferson Memorial **20** National Gallery of Art **23** Temple of the Scottish Rite **24** National Archives Building

Popeye
character in: **9** Sanctuary
author: **8** Faulkner

popinjay **3** fop **4** beau **5** dandy **7** coxcomb

poplar **7** Populus **22** Liriodendron tulipifera
varieties: **4** gray **5** black, downy, tulip, white **6** balsam, Eugene, yellow **8** Carolina, Lombardy, necklace **10** Queensland **12** Chinese white, silver-leaved **13** Western balsam

poppy **7** Papaver
varieties: **3** sea **4** blue, bush, corn, snow, tree, wind, wood **5** field, opium, plume, satin, tulip, water, Welsh **6** arctic, desert, horned **7** Asiatic, flaming, Iceland, Mexican, prickly, Shirley, Western **8** Flanders, harebell, Matilija, oriental **9** Celandine **10** California, island tree **12** Mexican tulip **13** yellow Chinese **14** California tree
drug: **5** opium **6** heroin **8** morphine

poppycock **3** rot **4** bosh, bunk, jive, tosh **5** froth, fudge, hooey, stuff, trash **6** drivel, humbug **7** baloney, blabber, blather, eyewash, fustian, garbage, hogwash, inanity, prattle, rubbish, twaddle **8** falderal, flummery, nonsense, tommyrot, wish-wash **9** absurdity, gibberish, moonshine, rigmarole **10** applesauce, balderdash, flapdoodle, hocus-pocus, mumbo-jumbo, rigamarole **11** abracadabra, jabberwocky **12** fiddlefaddle, gobbledygook

poppy seed
botanical name: **7** Papaver **11** P somniferum (sleep-bearing poppy)
color: **4** blue **5** white
origin: **4** Asia **6** Europe
guards against: **9** creditors
use: **5** bread, cakes, rolls **6** sweets **10** vegetables **11** butter sauce

populace **4** folk **6** people, public **7** society **9** citizenry, community **10** population

popular **5** cheap, civic, civil, stock **6** famous, public, social **7** admired, current, general, in favor **8** accepted, approved, communal, familiar, favorite, in demand, national, orthodox **9** community, preferred, prevalent, well-known, well-liked **10** affordable, celebrated,

pope **3** Leo **4** John, Paul, Pius **5** Peter, Urban **6** Adrian, Eugene, Julius, Martin, Sixtus **7** Clement, Gregory **8** Benedict, Innocent, John Paul, Nicholas **9** Alexander, Callistus
also: **12** Bishop of Rome **13** Vicar of Christ **14** Primate of Italy, Supreme Pontiff **16** Archbishop of Rome **18** Metropolitan of Rome, Patriarch of the West **25** Servant of the Servants of God
office: **6** Papacy **7** Holy See **11** Seat of Peter
elected by: **18** College of Cardinals
elected in: **8** conclave
signal that election is concluded: **10** white smoke
resides: **4** Rome **10** the Vatican **11** Vatican City
former residence: **13** Lateran Palace
summer residence: **14** Castel Gondolfo
papal land holding: **9** patrimony **21** patrimony of Saint Peter
first pope: **10** Saint Peter
pope who crowned Charlemagne: **6** Leo III
pope who excommunicated Luther: **4** Leo X
pope who authorized Michelangelo to paint Sistine Chapel: **8** Julius II
"September Pope": **9** John Paul I
real name of pope:
Alexander VI: **15** Rodrigo de Borgia
Callistus III: **15** Alfonso de Borgia
Clement VII: **14** Giulio de' Medici
John XXIII: **22** Angelo Giuseppe Roncalli
John Paul I: **13** Albino Luciani
John Paul II: **12** Karol Wojtyla **18** Archbishop of Krakow
Leo X: **16** Giovanni de' Medici
Pius XI: **12** Achille Ratti
Pius XII: **35** Eugenio Maria Giuseppe Giovanni Pacelli
popes of Avignon papacy: **6** Urban V **8** Clement V, John XXII **9** Clement VI, Gregory XI, Nicholas V **10** Innocent VI **11** Benedict XII
popes during Great Western Schism:
Avignon: **10** Clement VII **12** Benedict XIII
Pisa: **9** John XXIII **10** Alexander V
Rome: **7** Urban VI **10** Boniface IX, Gregory XII **11** Innocent VII
papal bull/encylical: **11** Unam sanctam **12** Humanae vitae, Rerum novarum, Vox in excelso **13** Pacem in terris **15** Mater et magistra **19** Populorum progressio **22** Sacerdotalis caelibatus

democratic **11** established, fashionable, inexpensive, of the people, sought-after

popularity **4** fame, note **5** favor, glory, kudos, vogue **6** esteem, regard, renown, repute **7** acclaim, fashion **8** approval **9** celebrity, notoriety **10** acceptance, admiration, notability, reputation **11** acclamation

popular opinion
Latin: **9** vox populi

popular whim **3** fad **4** rage **5** craze, mania **7** passion **11** infatuation

populate **6** occupy, people, settle **7** inhabit

populated **5** urban **7** peopled, settled **8** citified, occupied **9** inhabited

population **4** folk **6** people, public **8** citizens, populace **9** citizenry, habitancy, residents **11** body politic, commonality, inhabitants

populous **5** dense **6** jammed **7** crowded, peopled, teeming **8** swarming, thronged

porcelain **5** china **11** ceramic ware

porch **4** stoa **5** lanai, plaza, stoop **7** balcony, narthex, portico, veranda **8** solarium, verandah **9** colonnade, vestibule

pore **4** hole, read, scan **5** probe, study **6** outlet, peruse, ponder, review, search, survey **7** dig into, examine, explore, inspect, orifice **8** aperture, consider **9** delve into

Porfiry
character in: **18** Crime and Punishment
author: **10** Dostoevsky

Porgy
author: **13** DuBose Heyward

Porgy and Bess
opera by: **14** George Gershwin
character: **4** Bess **5** Porgy **11** Sportin' Life

pornographic **4** blue, lewd **5** bawdy, dirty, gross **6** coarse, filthy, smutty, vulgar **7** obscene **8** indecent, off-color, prurient **9** salacious **10** lascivious, licentious

porous **4** lacy **6** spongy **7** riddled **8** cellular, pervious **9** absorbent, permeable, sievelike **10** penetrable **11** honeycombed

Porphyrion
member of: **8** Gigantes

porpoise **4** leap **5** whale **6** palach, puffer, seahog **7** cowfish, dolphin, surface **8** cetacean
genus: **8** Phocaena **9** Delphinus

porridge **4** pobs, samp **5** atole, brose, brout, gruel **6** cereal **7** crowdie, oatmeal, polenta **8** flummery

Porrima *see* **9** Antevorta

porringer **4** bowl, dish **6** vessel **9** container **10** receptacle

port **4** dock, pier, quay **5** haven, wharf **6** harbor, refuge **7** dry dock, landing, mooring, seaport, shelter **9** anchorage, harborage **11** destination

port
type: **4** wine **6** brandy
origin: **8** Portugal
variety: **4** ruby **5** tawny **7** vintage
with brandy: **9** Betsy Ross
with vermouth: **10** Broken Spur

portable **5** handy, light, small **6** bantam, pocket **7** compact, folding, movable **8** cartable, haulable, liftable **9** ready-to-go **10** convenient, conveyable, manageable, vest-pocket **11** pocket-sized

portal, portals **4** adit, arch, door, gate **5** entry **6** wicket **7** doorway, gateway, portico **8** approach, entrance **9** threshold, vestibule **10** portcullis **11** entranceway

Port-au-Prince
capital of: **5** Haiti

porte-monnaie **5** purse **10** pocketbook **12** money-carrier

portend **4** bode **5** augur **6** denote, herald, warn of **7** bespeak, betoken, point to, predict, presage, signify, suggest **8** forebode, forecast, foretell, forewarn, prophesy **9** foretoken, prefigure **10** foreshadow

portent **4** omen, sign **5** token **6** augury, boding, threat **7** presage, warning **9** harbinger **10** foreboding **11** forewarning

portentous **6** superb **7** amazing, fateful, ominous, pompous **8** alarming, menacing **9** bombastic, grandiose, prophetic **10** foreboding, incredible, prodigious, remarkable, stupendous, surprising **11** astonishing, exceptional, frightening, pretentious, significant, superlative, threatening **12** inauspicious, intimidating, unpropitious

porter **4** brew **5** stout **6** bearer, coolie, redcap, skycap **7** carrier **8** conveyer **9** conductor

Porter, Katherine Anne
author of: **11** Ship of Fools **12** Old Mortality **14** Flowering Judas **15** The Leaning Tower **18** Pale Horse Pale Rider

Porter, William Sidney
real name of: **6** O Henry

portfolio **4** case, file **5** album **6** binder, folder **7** dossier **8** envelope **9** scrapbook **10** securities

Porthos
character in: **18** The Three Musketeers
author: **5** Dumas (pere)

Portia
character in: **12** Julius Caesar **19** The Merchant of Venice
author: **11** Shakespeare

portico **4** stoa **5** lanai **6** piazza **7** balcony, veranda, walkway

portion **3** cut, lot, sum **4** dole, doom, fate, luck, part **5** carve, cut up, moira, piece, sever, share, slice, split **6** amount, divide, kismet, parcel, ration, sector **7** break up, deal out, destiny, fortune, helping, measure, section, segment, serving **8** allocate, disperse, division, fraction, fragment, quantity, separate **9** allotment, allowance, demarcate, partition **10** allocation, distribute, percentage

portion out **5** allot **6** ration **7** dole out, mete out, prorate **8** allocate, dispense, divide up **9** apportion, parcel out **10** distribute, measure out

Portland
basketball team: **12** Trailblazers
football team: **8** Breakers
river: **8** Columbia **10** Willamette
university: **4** Reed

Port Louis
capital of: **9** Mauritius

portly **3** big, fat **4** full **5** beefy, burly, heavy, large, obese, plump, pudgy, round, stout, tubby **6** brawny, chubby, fleshy, rotund, stocky **9** corpulent

Portman, John
architect of: **15** Peachtree Center (Atlanta)

portmanteau **3** bag **4** grip **5** cloak **6** mantle, valise **8** suitcase **9** gladstone

Port Moresby
capital of: **9** New Guinea

Portnoy's Complaint
author: **10** Philip Roth

Port of Spain
capital of: **17** Trinidad and Tobago

Porto-Novo
capital of: **5** Benin

portrait **5** cameo **6** sketch **7** drawing, picture **8** likeness, painting, vignette **9** depiction **10** impression, photograph **11** description

Portrait of a Lady, The
author: **10** Henry James
character: **11** Madame Merle, Pansy Osmond **12** Isabel Archer **13** Gilbert Osmond, Lord Warburton, Ralph Touchett **14** Caspar Goodwood **18** Henrietta Stackpole

Portrait of the Artist as a Young Man
author: **10** James Joyce
character: **4** Emma **12** Simon Dedalus **14** Stephen Dedalus

portray **3** ape **4** draw, play **5** carve, enact, mimic, model, paint **6** depict, detail, figure, pose as, sketch **7** imitate, narrate, picture **8** describe, set forth, simulate **9** delineate, represent, sculpture **10** illustrate, photograph **11** impersonate **12** characterize

portrayal **7** picture **8** portrait **9** picturing **11** delineation, description **14** representation **16** characterization

ports
god of: **8** Portunus

Portugal ***see box, p. 770***

Portuguese Guinea *see* **12** Guinea-Bissau

Portuguese West Africa
see **6** Angola

Portunus
origin: **5** Roman
god of: **5** ports **7** harbors

posada **3** inn **12** halting place

pose **3** air, set **4** cast, mien **5** group, order, state, style **6** line up, stance, submit **7** advance, arrange, bearing, bring up, posture, present, propose, show off, suggest **8** attitude, carriage, position, propound, set forth, throw out **9** mannerism, postulate **10** put forward

Poseidon
also: **9** Asphalius
origin: **5** Greek
god of: **3** sea
caused: **11** earthquakes
father: **6** Cronos
mother: **4** Rhea
brother: **4** Zeus
wife: **10** Amphitrite
lover: **2** Ge **6** Aethra, Medusa, Thoosa **7** Demeter
child: **5** Arion **6** Triton **7** Antaeus, Pegasus, Theseus **8** Chrysaor **10** Polyphemus
symbol: **5** horse **7** trident
epithet: **11** Ennosigaeus, Hippocurius **12** Prosclystius
corresponds to: **7** Neptune

poser **5** facer **6** puzzle **7** problem **8** examiner, stickler

posh **4** chic **5** fancy, ritzy, smart, swell **6** chi-chi, classy, deluxe, lavish, swanky **7** elegant, opulent, refined, stylish **9** high-class, luxurious **11** extravagant

position **3** fix, job, put, set **4** duty, pose, post, role, site **5** array, caste, class, locus, lodge, order, place, stand, state **6** career, charge, ground, locate, office, plight, stance, status **7** arrange, deposit, opinion, outlook, posture, situate, station, vantage **8** attitude, capacity, eminence, function, locality, location, prestige, standing **9** condition, elevation, establish, placement, situation, viewpoint **10** assignment, commission, importance, notability, prominence **11** appointment, consequence, disposition, distinction, frame of mind, point of view

position decided upon
French: **9** parti pris

positive **4** firm, good, real, sure **5** total **6** narrow, useful **7** assured, certain, gainful, helpful **8** absolute, cocksure, complete, decisive, definite, dogmatic, explicit, obdurate, salutary **9** assertive, confident, convinced, effective, immovable, practical, satisfied, veritable **10** applicable, autocratic, beneficial, conclusive, definitive, optimistic, undisputed, undoubting **11** affirmative, cooperative, dead certain, dictatorial, irrefutable, opinionated, overbearing, practicable, progressive, self-assured, serviceable, unequivocal, unqualified **12** confirmatory, constructive, contributory, unchangeable **13** corroborative, thoroughgoing **16** incontrovertible

positively **9** assuredly, certainly, decidedly, literally **10** absolutely, definitely **11** confidently, indubitably **12** emphatically, indisputably, unmistakably, without doubt **13** affirmatively, categorically, unqualifiedly **14** beyond question, unhesitatingly, unquestionably

possess **3** own **4** grab, have, hold **5** boast, enjoy **6** absorb, fixate, obsess, occupy **7** acquire, bedevil, bewitch, command, conquer, consume, control, enchant, overrun **8** dominate, dominate, maintain, take over, vanquish **9** fascinate, hypnotize, influence, mesmerize

Possessed, The
author: **16** Fyodor Dostoevsky
character: **5** Marya, Pyotr **6** Shatov **7** Nikolay **16** Varvara Stavrogin **17** Stepan Verhovensky

possession **4** hold **5** asset, poise, title **6** effect, owning **7** command, control, control, custody, tenancy **8** calmness, coolness, dominion, province, resource **9** belonging, composure, occupancy, ownership, placidity, sangfroid, territory **10** equanimity, even temper, occupation, possessing **11** equilibrium, self-control **12** accoutrement, protectorate

possibility **4** hope, odds, risk **6** chance, gamble, hazard **7** promise **8** prospect **9** prospects **10** likelihood **11** contingency, eventuality, feasibility, probability, workability **12** potentiality **14** practicability

possible **8** credible, feasible, workable **9** potential, thinkable **10** achievable, admissible, attainable, cognizable, compatible, contingent, imaginable, manageable, obtainable, reasonable **11** conceivable, performable, practicable **12** hypothetical

possibly **5** at all, maybe **6** mayhap **7** could be, perhaps **8** in any way, normally **9** at the most, perchance **10** by any means, God willing **11** conceivably

post **2** PX **3** fix, job, put, set **4** base, beat, camp, pale, part, pile, pole, role, seat, send, spot, work **5** brace, house, lodge, place, put up, round, shaft, stake **6** advise, column, inform, locate, notify, office, picket, report, settle, splint, tack up **7** apprise, declare, install, mission, publish, quarter, routine, situate, station, support, upright **8** acquaint, announce, capacity, disclose, exchange, fasten up, function, instruct, mainstay, position, proclaim **9** advertise, broad-

Portugal
capital/largest city: 6 Lisbon
others: 4 Beja, Faro, Ovar **5** Braga, Evora, Olhao, Porto, Viseu **6** Aveiro, Guarda, Leiria, Oporto, Sintra **7** Algarve, Amadora, Bragama, Cascoes, Coimbra, Covilha, Estoril, Funchal, Granada, Setubal **8** Barreiro, Portimao **9** Lusitania **10** Portalegre **14** Vila Nova de Gaia
Roman city: **10** Portus Cale
school: 5 Minho **6** Aveiro, Lisbon, Oporto **7** Coimbra
division: 3 Goa **4** Tejo, Tete **5** Beira, Evora, Macao, Minho, Timor **6** Azores, Loanda **7** Algarve, Madeira **8** Alemteho, Rebatejo **9** Cape Verde **10** Mozambique **11** Estremadura
Roman district: **9** Lusitania
measure: 2 pe **4** bota, moio, vara **5** almud, fanga, geira, linha, milha **6** almude, covado **7** alquier, ferrado, selamin **8** alqueire
monetary unit: 3 avo, rei **4** peca, real **5** conto, crown, dobra, indio, justo, rupia **6** escudo, macuta, octave, pataca, testad, tostao, vintem **7** angalar, centavo, crusado, miereis, testone **8** equipaga, johannes
weight: 4 onca, once **5** libra, marco **6** arroba **7** arratel **9** excropulo
island: 6 Azores **7** Madeira **8** Terceira
mountain: 4 Acor, Lapa **5** Gerez, Marao, Mousa **6** Bornes, Peneda **7** Larouco **8** Caramulo **9** Caldeirao, Monchique **14** Serra da Estrela
highest point: 11 Pico da Serra
river: 3 Sor, Tua **4** Lima, Mino, Mira, Sado, Seda, Tago, Tajo, Tejo, Vara **5** Douro, Duero, Legoa, Micha, Minho, Sabar, Tagus, Vouga, Zatas **6** Cavado, Chanca, Quarto, Tamega, Zezere **7** Mondego, Selamin, Sorraia **8** Quadiana, Tonelada
ocean: 8 Atlantic
physical feature:
bay: **7** Setubal
cape: **4** Roca **7** Mondego **8** Espichel **9** St Vincent
peninsula: **7** Iberian
port: **4** Faro **6** Aveiro, Lisbon, Oporto **7** Leixoes
people: 4 Celt, Moor **7** Iberian **10** Portuguese
artist: **7** Pereira **9** Goncalves **13** Soares dos Reis
author: **5** Dinis **6** Camoes, Vieiva **7** Garrett, Vicente **9** Deus-Ramos
explorer: **3** Cam, Cao **4** Dias, Diaz **6** Cabral, Da Gama **7** Almeida **8** Magellan **11** Albuquerque **23** Prince Henry the Navigator
king: **6** Manuel, Philip, Sancho **7** Alfonso **9** Ferdinand, Sebastian
leader: **5** Eanes **6** Dombal, Soares **7** Caetano, Carmona, Salazar, Spinola
queen: **5** Maria **9** Elizabeth
language: 10 Portuguese
religion: 13 Roman Catholic
place:
church: **5** Jesus **6** Christ **11** Os Jeronimos, Sao Lourenco **12** Old Cathedral **13** Santa Engracia **16** Sao Vicente de Fora
city square: **15** Praca do Comercio
dam: **6** Belver, Idanha **13** Castelo do Bode
fortress-church: **12** Leco do Bailio
monastery: **8** Alcobaca **12** Ilieronymites **20** Santa Maria da Victoira
monument: **11** Discoveries
museum: **13** Soares dos Reis
palace: **6** Cintra
shrine: **6** Fatima
colony: 5 Macad, Macao
former colony: **3** Goa **5** Timor **6** Angola **7** Sao Tome **8** Principe, St Thomas **9** Cape Verde **10** Mozambique **12** Guinea Bissau
feature:
song: **4** fado
food:
dish: **8** bacalhau, bucellas **10** calcavella **11** carcavellos
sausage: **8** linguica
wine: **4** port **7** madeira

cast, circulate, enlighten, establish, make known, situation **10** assignment, settlement

postdate 6 follow **7** succeed **9** come after

poster 4 bill, sign **6** notice **7** placard **8** bulletin **13** advertisement

posterior 3 bum, can **4** back, butt, prat, rear, rump, seat, tail, tush **5** fanny, stern, tushy **6** behind, bottom, caudal, dorsal, hinder **7** keister **8** backside, buttocks, derriere, hindmost, rearward **9** aftermost

Posterior Analytics
author: 9 Aristotle

posterity 5 heirs, issue, young **6** family **7** descent, history, lineage, progeny **8** children **9** offspring **10** succession, successors **11** descendants

post hoc, ergo propter hoc **29** after this therefore because of it
describes: **14** logical fallacy

Posthumus, Leonatus
character in: **9** Cymbeline
author: **11** Shakespeare

Postman Always Rings Twice, The
director: **10** Tay Garnett
based on story by: **10** James M Cain
cast: **10** Hume Cronym, Lana Turner **12** John Garfield **13** Cecil Kellaway

postpone **4** stay **5** defer, delay, table, waive **6** put off, remand, shelve **7** adjourn, lay over, reserve, suspend

postponement **4** stay **5** delay **6** recess **7** tabling **8** abeyance, deferral **9** deferment, extension **10** suspension

postscript **2** ps **5** rider **7** codicil **8** addendum **10** attachment

postulate **5** axiom, guess **6** assume, hazard, submit, theory **7** premise, presume, propose, surmise, theorem **8** put forth, theorize **9** speculate **10** assumption, conjecture, hypothesis, presuppose **11** hypothesize, presumption

posture **3** air, set **4** case, mien, mood, pose, post, tone **5** phase, place, shape, state, tenor **6** aspect, stance, status **7** bearing, contour, station **8** attitude, carriage, position, standing **9** condition, situation **11** predicament **12** circumstance

Postvorta
form: **5** nymph
member of: **7** Camenae
knowledge of: **4** past

posy **5** bloom, motto **6** flower, phrase **7** blossom, bouquet, corsage, garland, nosegay

pot **3** pan **4** ruin **5** crock, kitty **6** vessel **9** container, marijuana **11** rack and ruin
Spanish: **4** olla

potable **3** ale **5** clean, drink, water **6** liquor **8** beverage, quencher **9** drinkable

potage **4** soup **9** thick soup

potassium
chemical symbol: **1** K

potato **16** Solanum tuberosum
varieties: **3** air, yam **4** duck, swan, wild, Zulu **5** Idaho, Irish, Maine, rural, swamp, sweet, white **6** Russet **7** Burbank, epicure, prairie, Telinga
dish: **4** chip **5** baked, salad **6** mashed **8** au gratin **9** lyonnaise, scalloped **11** french fries **12** baked stuffed

Potawatomi
language family: **9** Algonkian **10** Algonquian
location: **4** Ohio **6** Kansas **7** Indiana **8** Illinois, Michigan, Oklahoma **9** Wisconsin
leader: **7** Pontiac
united with: **6** Ojibwa, Ottawa **7** Ojibway

Potemkin
director: **17** Sergei Eisenstein
cast: **14** Vladimir Barsky **16** Alexander Antonov **17** Grigori Alexandrov
famous segment: **11** Odessa Steps

potency **3** vis **5** force, power **6** energy **8** efficacy, strength, virility, vitality

potent **5** solid, tough **6** mighty, strong **7** dynamic **8** forceful, forcible, powerful, vigorous **9** effective, operative **10** compelling, convincing, formidable, impressive, persuasive **11** efficacious, influential **12** overpowering

potentate **4** lord **5** chief, mogul, ruler **6** prince, satrap, sultan **7** emperor, monarch **8** overlord, suzerain **9** chieftain, sovereign

potential **6** covert, hidden, latent **7** dormant, lurking, passive **8** implicit, possible **9** concealed, quiescent, unexerted **10** unapparent, unrealized **11** conceivable, undisclosed, unexpressed

potentiality **7** ability **10** capability **13** possibilities

potentially
Latin: **7** in posse

pother **3** ado **4** fuss, stir, to-do **6** bustle, flurry, hustle, tumult **8** activity **9** agitation, commotion

Pothos
companion of: **9** Aphrodite
personifies: **6** desire **7** longing

potion **4** brew, dram **5** draft, tonic **6** elixir **7** mixture, philter **8** libation, potation **10** concoction

Pot of Gold, The
author: **7** Plautus

Potok, Chaim
author of: **9** The Chosen **10** Wanderings **15** The Book of Lights

potpourri **4** hash, mess, olio, stew **6** jumble, medley, mosaic, motley **7** farrago, goulash, melange, mixture **8** mishmash, pastiche **9** patchwork **10** hodgepodge, miscellany, salmagundi **11** gallimaufry, olla podrida

pottage **4** soup, stew **6** brewis **8** porridge

Potter, Beatrix
author of: **11** (The Tale of) Peter Rabbit **21** The Tailor of Gloucester

Potter, Muff
character in: **9** Tom Sawyer
author: **5** Twain

potter's field **8** boneyard, cemetery **9** graveyard **12** burial ground **13** burying ground

pottery **5** china **8** clayware, crockery **11** ceramic ware, earthenware

pouch **3** bag, kit, sac **4** sack **5** purse **6** pocket, wallet **7** handbag, satchel **8** carryall, ditty bag, reticule, rucksack **9** container **10** pocketbook, receptacle

Poulenc, Francis
born: **5** Paris **6** France
member of: **6** Les Six, The Six
composer of: **9** Les Biches **13** The Carmelites **22** Dialogues des Carmelites

poultice **7** plaster **8** dressing **10** medicament

poultry **3** hen **4** cock, duck, fowl, swan **5** capon, geese, goose, quail **6** grouse, layers, pigeon, turkey **7** chicken, peacock, rooster **8** pheasant **9** partridge **10** guinea fowl
breed: **6** Ancona, Bantam **7** Cornish, Dorking, Leghorn **9** Wyandotte **12** Plymouth Rock **14** Rhode Island Red
disease: **3** pip **4** roup, tick
farm: **7** hennery
house: **4** coop

pounce **4** jump, leap **5** fly at, swoop **6** ambush, dash at, jump at, plunge, snatch, spring **8** downrush, fall upon, surprise

Pounce, Peter
character in: **13** Joseph Andrews
author: **8** Fielding

pound **4** bang, beat, drub, drum, maul **5** clomp, clout, crush, grind, march, paste, smack, stomp, throb, thump,

tramp **6** batter, bruise, cudgel, hammer, pummel, strike, thrash, thwack, wallop **7** clobber, crumble, pulsate, thunder, trounce **8** lambaste **9** fustigate, palpitate, pulverize **13** sixteen ounces
abbreviation: **2** lb

Pound, Ezra
author of: **6** Cantos **8** Personae **11** Exultations, Pisan Cantos

pound troy
abbreviation: **3** lb t

pour **3** tap **4** drip, drop, flow, gush, ooze, rain, seep, slop **5** drain, flood, issue, spill, spout **6** decant, deluge, drench, effuse, squirt, stream **7** cascade, draw off, dribble, lade out **15** rain cats and dogs **16** come down in sheets **17** come down in buckets

pourboire **3** tip **8** gratuity
literally: **11** for drinking

pourparler **29** informal preliminary conference
literally: **10** for talking

Poussin, Nicholas
born: **6** France **10** Les Andelys
artwork: **10** The Seasons **14** Birth of Bacchus, St John on Patmos **17** Bacchanalian Revel **18** The Burial of Phocion **19** The Poet's Inspiration **20** The Arcadian Shepherds **23** Landscape with Polyphemus, The Holy Family on the Steps **27** The Adoration of the Golden Calf

pou sto **14** place to stand on, where I may stand **16** base of operations

pout **4** crab, fret, fume, mope, sulk **5** brood, frown, lower, scowl **6** glower
French: **4** moue

poverty **4** lack, need, want **6** dearth, penury **7** beggary, deficit, paucity **8** scarcity, shortage **9** indigence, neediness, pauperism, privation **10** bankruptcy, deficiency, insolvency, meagerness, mendicancy **11** destitution **13** insufficiency, pennilessness **14** impoverishment

poverty-stricken **4** poor **5** broke, needy **8** indigent **9** destitute, penniless **10** down and out

powder **4** dust, talc **5** emery **6** pollen, talcum **7** crumble **9** pulverize
antiseptic: **6** formin **7** aristol
applier: **4** puff
cookery: **4** soda
cosmetic: **5** blush, rouge **7** compact
poisonous: **5** robin

powder-blue **5** azure **6** pastel **7** sky-blue **8** pale-blue **9** light-blue, robin's egg

powdery **5** dusty, mealy **6** chalky, floury, grated, ground, milled **7** crushed, pestled **8** shredded **10** comminuted, pulverized, triturated

Powell, Dick
real name: **14** Richard E Powell
born: **14** Mountain View AR
wife: **11** June Allyson **12** Joan Blondell
costar: **10** Ruby Keeler
roles: **7** Mrs Mike **8** Cornered **12** Johnny O'Clock **13** Murder My Sweet **15** Footlight Parade **17** Forty-second Street **32** Gold Diggers of Nineteen Thirty-three

Powell, Jane
real name: **12** Suzanne Burce
born: **10** Portland OR
roles: **5** Irene **12** Royal Wedding **13** A Date with Judy **27** Seven Brides for Seven Brothers

Powell, John
nickname: **4** Boog
sport: **8** baseball
team: **16** Baltimore Orioles

Powell, Michael
codirector: **17** Emeric Pressburger
director of: **11** The Red Shoes **14** Black Narcissus **16** Stairway to Heaven

Powell, SR
creator/artist of: **22** Sheena Queen of the Jungle

Powell, William
born: **12** Pittsburgh PA
wife: **13** Carole Lombard
costar: **8** Myrna Loy
roles: **10** Philo Vance, The Thin Man **11** Nick Charles **12** My Man Godfrey **13** Mister Roberts **14** Life with Father **16** The Great Ziegfeld **22** How to Marry a Millionaire

power **4** gift, sway **5** brawn, force, might, right, ruler, skill, vigor **6** energy, genius, muscle, status, talent **7** faculty, license, operate, potency, quality **8** activate, aptitude, capacity, energize, iron grip, pressure, prestige, property, strength, vitality **9** attribute, authority, endowment, influence, puissance **10** capability, competence
Latin: **3** vis

Power, Tyrone
born: **12** Cincinnati OH
wife: **9** Annabella **14** Linda Christian
roles: **10** Jesse James **12** Blood and Sand **13** The Razor's Edge **14** Nightmare Alley, The Mark of Zorro **15** The Sun Also Rises **18** Captain from Castile

Power and the Glory, The
author: **12** Graham Greene

powerful **5** hardy, husky, stout **6** brawny, cogent, mighty, moving, potent, robust, sturdy **7** intense, rousing **8** athletic, emphatic, exciting, forceful, incisive, muscular, stalwart, vigorous **9** effective, energetic, herculean, strapping **10** able-bodied, commanding, invincible

powerhouse **9** strongman **10** power plant **15** generating plant

powerless **4** weak **6** feeble, infirm **7** unarmed **8** crippled, disabled, feckless, helpless, impotent **9** incapable, pregnable, prostrate **10** impuissant, vulnerable, weaponless **11** debilitated, defenseless, immobilized **13** incapacitated

powerlessness **8** debility, weakness **9** impotence, inability, infirmity **10** enervation, feebleness, inadequacy, incapacity **12** helplessness, incapability, inefficiency **13** vulnerability

Power Politics
author: **14** Margaret Atwood

powers that be **9** higher-ups **10** government **11** authorities **13** establishment **14** administration

Powhatan
language family: **9** Algonkian **10** Algonquian
tribe: **11** Confederacy
location: **8** Atlantic, Maryland, Virginia
leader: **8** Powhatan **11** Opechancano **13** Wahunsonacock
member: **10** Pocahontas

powwow **4** meet, talk **5** forum **6** caucus, confer, huddle, parley **7** consult, convene, council, discuss, meeting, palaver **8** assembly, colloquy, conclave, congress **9** discourse, interview **10** colloquium, conference, convention, discussion, round table **12** consultation

Poyser, Martin
character in: 8 Adam Bede
author: 5 Eliot

practicable 6 doable, viable **8** feasible, possible, workable **9** practical **10** achievable, attainable, functional

practical 4 able **5** solid, sound **6** expert, useful, versed **7** skilled, trained, veteran, working **8** seasoned, sensible, skillful **9** efficient, judicious, practiced, pragmatic, qualified, realistic **10** functional, hardheaded, instructed, proficient, systematic, unromantic **11** down-to-earth, experienced, pragmatical, serviceable, utilitarian **12** accomplished, businesslike, matter-of-fact **13** unsentimental

practical joke 4 jape **5** caper, prank, stunt, trick

practically 6 all but, almost, nearly **8** actually, in effect **9** basically, in the main, just about, virtually **11** essentially **13** fundamentally, substantially

practice 2 do **3** use, way **4** deed, mode, play, rule, ruse, ways, wont **5** apply, dodge, drill, habit, train, trick, usage **6** action, custom, device, effect, follow, manner, method, pursue, ritual, work at **7** conduct, fashion, perform, process, qualify, routine, utilize **8** carry out, engage in, exercise, live up to, maneuver, rehearse, tendency, training **9** execution, operation, perform in, procedure, rehearsal, seasoning, set to work, turn to use **10** discipline, observance, prepare for, repetition **11** application, be engaged in, performance, preparation

practiced 4 able, fine **5** adept **6** adroit, expert **7** capable, drilled, pursued, skilled, trained **8** masterly, polished, seasoned, skillful, worked at **9** competent, engaged in, masterful, qualified, rehearsed **10** cultivated, proficient **11** experienced, prepared for **12** accomplished

practice sorcery 5 charm **7** bewitch, conjure, enchant **9** work magic **10** cast a spell

Practicing History
author: 15 Barbara W Tuchman

practitioner 6 doctor **7** dentist **9** performer **12** professional

pragmatic 5 sober **8** sensible **9** hard-nosed, practical, realistic **10** hardheaded, hard-boiled **11** down-to-earth, utilitarian **12** businesslike, matter-of-fact, unidealistic **13** materialistic, unsentimental

Praia
capital of: 9 Cape Verde

prairie 3 bay **5** llano, pampa, plain **6** camass, meadow, steppe **7** quamash **9** grassland
apple: 9 breadroot
berry: 9 trampillo
chicken: 6 grouse
dog: 6 gopher, marmot
schooner: 12 covered wagon
state: 8 Illinois
wolf: 6 coyote

Prairie, The
author: 19 James Fenimore Cooper
character: 4 Inez **9** Dr Battius, Ellen Wade, Hard-Heart, Paul Hover **10** Esther Bush **11** Abiram White, Ishmael Bush, Natty Bumppo **16** Captain Middleton

Prairie State
nickname of: 8 Illinois

praise 4 laud, tout **5** cheer, exalt, extol, honor **6** esteem, eulogy, hurrah, regard, revere **7** acclaim, applaud, approve, build up, commend, glorify, plaudit, respect, root for, tribute, worship **8** accolade, applause, approval, encomium, eulogize, venerate **9** adoration, celebrate, good words, laudation, panegyric **10** admiration, compliment, panegyrize **11** approbation, compliments, testimonial **12** appreciation, commendation, congratulate **14** congratulation
Hebrew: 6 hallel

praise be to God
Latin: 7 laus Deo

praiseful 8 praising **9** extolling, laudatory **10** plauditory **12** commendatory **13** complimentary

praiseworthiness 5 merit **10** excellence **12** admirability, desirability **14** commendability

praiseworthy 4 fine **6** worthy **8** laudable **9** admirable, estimable, excellent, exemplary **11** commendable, meritorious

pram, praam, prahm 4 boat **5** buggy **6** vessel **7** rowboat **8** carriage, stroller **12** perambulator

prance 4 jump, leap, romp, skip **5** bound, caper, dance, frisk, strut, vault **6** bounce, cavort, frolic, gambol, spring **7** swagger

prank 4 joke, lark **5** antic, caper, spoof, stunt, trick **6** gambol **8** escapade, mischief **9** horseplay **10** shenanigan, tomfoolery

prate 3 gab, yak **4** blab, brag, chat, crow, talk **5** boast **6** babble, gabble, jabber **7** blabber, chatter, prattle, twaddle, twattle

Prathet Thai *see* **8** Thailand

Pratt, William Henry
real name of: 12 Boris Karloff

prattle 3 gab, yak **4** blab **5** prate **6** babble, gabble, hot air, jabber **7** blather, chatter, twaddle **8** cackling, chitchat, gabbling **9** gibbering, jabbering

Pravda 16 Russian newspaper
literally: 5 truth

Praxithea
husband: 10 Erechtheus
daughters: 8 Orithyia **10** Protogonia

pray 3 beg, bid, sue **4** urge **5** cry to, plead **7** beseech, entreat, implore, request, solicit **8** call upon, invocate, petition **9** importune **10** supplicate

prayer 6 litany, orison, praise **7** worship **9** adoration **12** thanksgiving **13** glorification

prayerful 4 holy **5** godly, pious **6** devout, solemn **8** reverent **9** pietistic, religious, spiritual **10** worshipful **11** reverential

prayers 4 hope, plea, suit **5** dream **6** appeal **7** request **8** entreaty, petition **10** aspiration, invocation **11** beseechment **12** solicitation, supplication

prayer service 9 devotions **13** prayer meeting **14** worship service

pray for us
Latin: 11 ora pro nobis

pray to 3 beg **5** plead **7** address, entreat, worship **8** call upon, petition, venerate **10** supplicate

preach 4 urge **6** advise, exhort **7** counsel, declare, expound, profess **8** admonish, advocate, homilize, proclaim, stand for **9** discourse, hold forth, preachify, prescribe, pronounce, propagate, sermonize **10** evangelize, promulgate

preacher 5 vicar **6** curate, parson, pastor **8** chaplain, homilist, minister, reverend, sky pilot **9** churchman, clergyman **10** evangelist, prebendary, sermonizer **12** ecclesiastic **13** man of the cloth

preachy **8** didactic, pedantic **10** moralistic, moralizing

prearranged **7** planned **10** calculated, deliberate, purposeful **11** intentional **12** premeditated

pre-Cambrian **5** Azoic **6** Eozoic **7** primary **10** Archeozoic **11** Proterozoic

precarious **5** risky, shaky **6** chancy, unsafe **7** dubious **8** alarming, critical, doubtful, insecure, perilous, sinister, ticklish, unstable, unsteady **9** hazardous, uncertain **10** touch-and-go, unreliable, vulnerable **12** questionable, uncontrolled, undependable **13** problematical

precaution **4** care **7** caution, defense **8** prudence, security, wariness **9** foresight, provision, safeguard **10** protection **11** carefulness, forethought, heedfulness **12** anticipation **14** circumspection

precede **8** antecede, antedate, go before **9** go ahead of **10** come before

precedence, precedency **8** priority **10** importance, preference, prevalence **11** antecedence, preeminence **12** predominance, preexistence

precedent **5** model **7** example, pattern **8** standard **9** criterion, guideline

preceding **5** prior **6** former **7** earlier **8** anterior, previous **9** aforesaid, foregoing **10** antecedent, first-named, precursory **11** preexistent, preliminary **14** abovementioned, aforementioned, firstmentioned

precept **3** law **4** bull, code, rule **5** axiom, canon, edict, maxim, motto, tenet, truth, ukase **6** byword, decree, dictum **7** dictate, mandate, statute **8** standard, teaching **9** ordinance, principle, yardstick **10** regulation **11** commandment, declaration

preceptor **5** coach, tutor **6** mentor **7** advisor, teacher **8** director **9** admonitor, counselor, principal **10** headmaster **12** headmistress

precincts **7** suburbs **8** environs **9** districts, outskirts **10** boundaries **12** subdivisions **15** surrounding area

precious **4** dear, rare **5** fussy, sweet **6** adored, choice, costly, dainty, prissy, prized, valued **7** beloved, darling, finical, finicky, lovable **8** adorable, affected, uncommon, valuable **9** cherished, expensive, exquisite, priceless, treasured **10** fastidious, high-priced, invaluable, meticulous, particular **11** beyond price, inestimable, overrefined, pretentious

Precious Bane
author: **8** Mary Webb

precipice **4** crag **5** bluff, cliff, ledge **8** headland, palisade **9** cliff edge, declivity **10** escarpment

precipitate **4** cast, hurl, rash, spur **5** drive, fling, hasty, throw **6** abrupt, hasten, launch, let fly, propel, rushed, speedy, thrust **7** advance, bring on, hurried, quicken, speed up **8** catapult, expedite, headlong, reckless **9** discharge, foolhardy, impetuous, imprudent, impulsive **10** accelerate, incautious **11** thoughtless

precipitation **4** hail, rain, rush, snow **5** haste, sleet **8** rainfall, rashness **9** hastiness **11** impetuously

precipitous **5** hasty, sharp, sheer, steep **6** abrupt **9** impetuous

precis **5** brief **6** apercu, digest, resume, sketch **7** epitome, outline, rundown, summary **8** abstract, synopsis **10** abridgment, compendium **12** condensation **14** recapitulation

precise **4** true **5** exact, fussy, rigid **6** strict **7** careful, express, finicky, literal **8** accurate, clear-cut, definite, distinct, explicit, incisive, specific **9** unbending **10** fastidious, inflexible, meticulous, particular, to the point **11** painstaking, unequivocal

precision **5** rigor **8** accuracy, fidelity **9** attention, exactness **11** factualness, preciseness **12** authenticity, truthfulness **14** meticulousness

preclude **3** bar, dam **4** balk, curb, foil, stop **5** avert, avoid, block, check, debar, deter **6** arrest, hamper, hinder, thwart **7** head off, inhibit, prevent **8** stave off **9** forestall, frustrate **11** nip in the bud

preclusion **9** exclusion, restraint **10** prevention

precocious **3** apt **5** quick, smart **6** bright, clever, gifted, mature **8** advanced **9** brilliant

preconception **4** bias **6** notion **9** fixed idea, prejudice **11** prejudgment, presumption **14** predisposition

precursor **4** mark, omen, sign **5** token, usher **6** herald **7** portent, symptom, warning **8** vanguard **9** harbinger, messenger **10** antecedent, forerunner **11** predecessor

precursory **5** prior **8** anterior, previous **9** precedent **10** antecedent **11** preexistent

predaceous, predacious **9** predatory, rapacious **10** meat-eating **11** carnivorous, flesh-eating

predate **7** precede **8** antecede, antedate, go before

predatory **8** thievish **9** larcenous, marauding, pillaging, piratical, rapacious, raptorial, vulturine **10** plunderous, predacious

predecessor **7** forbear **8** ancestor, forebear, foregoer **10** antecedent, forefather, forerunner

predestination **4** fate **6** kismet **7** destiny, fortune **8** God's will **10** providence **13** inevitability, preordination **16** predetermination

predetermined **5** fated **7** decided, planned **8** destined **10** calculated, deliberate, preplanned **11** intentional, prearranged, predestined **12** foreordained, premeditated

predicament **3** fix, jam **4** bind, mess **5** pinch **6** corner, crisis, pickle, plight, scrape, strait **7** dilemma, trouble **8** hot water, quandary **9** imbroglio, sad plight **10** difficulty, perplexity

predicate **4** base, real, rest, true **5** found, imply **6** affirm, assert **7** commend, connote, declare **8** proclaim

predict **4** omen **5** augur **6** divine **7** betoken, foresee, presage **8** envision, forecast, foretell, prophesy **10** anticipate **13** prognosticate

prediction **6** augury **7** portent **8** forecast, prophecy **10** divination **11** declaration, foretelling, soothsaying **12** announcement, anticipation, proclamation **13** crystal gazing **15** prognostication

predilection **4** bent, bias, love **5** fancy, favor, taste **6** desire, hunger, liking, relish **7** leaning **8** appetite, fondness, penchant, tendency **9** prejudice, proneness **10** attraction, partiality, preference, proclivity, propensity **11** inclination **13** prepossession **14** predisposition

predispose **4** bias, lure, sway, urge **5** tempt **6** entice, induce, prompt, seduce **7** dispose, incline, win over **8** persuade **9** encourage, influence, prejudice

predisposed **3** apt **5** given, prone **8** inclined

predisposition **7** leaning **8** tendency **11** inclination

predominance **7** command, control **8** currency **9** dominance, supremacy **10** ascendancy, importance, prevalence **11** preeminence, superiority **12** universality

predominant **4** main **5** chief, major **6** potent, ruling, strong **7** leading, supreme **8** dominant, forceful, powerful, reigning, vigorous **9** ascendant, important, paramount, sovereign **11** controlling, influential **13** authoritative

predominate **4** lead **7** prevail **8** dominate

predominating **5** chief **6** ruling **8** dominant, superior **9** principal **10** commanding, prevailing **11** controlling, predominant **13** authoritative

preeminence **9** greatness, supremacy **10** ascendancy, importance, leadership, notability, prominence **11** distinction, superiority **12** predominance

preeminent **4** best **5** famed **6** famous **7** eminent, honored, supreme **8** dominant, foremost, greatest, peerless, renowned, superior **9** matchless, paramount, unequaled, unrivaled **10** celebrated, consummate **11** illustrious, predominant, unsurpassed **12** incomparable, second to none, unparalleled **13** distinguished
French: **13** par excellence

preempt **4** take **5** seize, usurp **8** arrogate, take over **10** commandeer, confiscate **11** appropriate, expropriate

preen **3** pin **4** perk, trim **5** adorn, dress, groom, plume, pride, primp, prink **6** brooch, smooth
wings: **4** whet

preexistent **5** prior **8** anterior, previous **9** precedent **10** antecedent, precursory

preface **4** open **5** begin, proem, start **6** launch **7** prelude **8** commence, foreword, initiate, lead into, overture, preamble, prologue **9** introduce **12** introduction

prefer **3** opt **4** file **5** adopt, elect, exalt, fancy, favor, lodge, offer **6** select, take to, tender **7** dignify, elevate, ennoble, fix upon, pick out, present, proffer, promote **8** graduate, set forth **9** single out

preference **4** bent, bias, pick **5** fancy **6** liking, option **7** leaning **8** favoring, priority **9** advantage, prejudice, proneness, selection, supremacy **10** ascendancy, partiality, precedence, proclivity, propensity **11** first choice, inclination **12** predilection **13** predomination **14** predisposition
French: **4** gout

prefigure **4** hint, type **6** shadow, typify **7** foresee, imagine, presage, suggest **9** adumbrate **10** foreshadow

pregnant **4** full, rich **6** fecund, filled, gravid **7** copious, fertile, fraught, replete, seminal, teeming, weighty **8** forceful, fruitful, prolific **9** abounding, expecting, gestating, important, luxuriant, momentous, plenteous, potential, with child, with young **10** impressive, life-giving, meaningful, parturient, productive, suggestive **11** having a baby, proliferous, provocative, significant **12** fructiferous, in a family way
French: **8** enceinte

prehistoric **3** old **7** ancient **10** immemorial
continent: **8** Atlantis
epoch: **6** Eocene **7** Miocene **8** Pliocene **9** Oligocene, Paleocene **11** Pleistocene
era: **8** Cenozoic, Mesozoic **9** Paleozoic **10** Archeozoic **11** Proterozoic
implement: **4** celt **6** eolith
period: **7** Neogene, Permian **8** Cambrian, Devonian, Jurassic, Silurian, Triassic **9** Paleogene **10** Cretaceous, Ordovician, Quaternary
reptile: **8** dinosaur

prehistoric era **6** Ice Age **8** Cenozoic, Jurassic, Mesozoic, Triassic **9** Paleozoic **10** Cenomanian, Cretaceous **11** Precambrian **15** Upper Cretaceous **16** Pleistocene Epoch

prehistoric man *see* **8** early man

prejudice **3** ill, mar **4** bias, harm, hurt, loss, sway **5** slant, spoil, taint **6** damage, impair, infect, injure, injury, poison **7** bigotry **8** jaundice **9** detriment **10** favoritism, impairment, partiality, predispose, unfairness **11** contaminate, intolerance, prejudgment **12** disadvantage, one-sidedness, predilection **13** preconception **14** discrimination, predisposition

prejudiced **6** biased, unfair, unjust **7** bigoted, slanted **9** arbitrary **10** intolerant **11** close-minded, opinionated **12** narrow-minded

prejudicial **3** bad **6** biased **7** harmful, hurtful **8** damaging, inimical, sinister **9** injurious **11** deleterious, detrimental

prelate **5** abbot **6** bishop, cleric **9** churchman, clergyman **12** ecclesiastic

preliminary **9** prelusive, prelusory **10** initiatory, precursory, prefactory **11** preparative, preparatory **12** introductory

prelude **7** opening, preface **8** overture, preamble, prologue **9** beginning **11** preliminary, preparation **12** introduction

Prelude, The
author: **17** William Wordsworth

premature **3** raw **5** green, hasty **6** callow, unripe **7** too soon, unready **8** abortive, ill-timed, immature, previous, too early, untimely **9** embryonic, overhasty, unfledged, unhatched, vestigial **10** incomplete, unprepared **11** inopportune, precipitate, rudimentary, undeveloped **12** unseasonable

premeditated **7** planned, plotted, studied, willful **8** intended **9** conscious, contrived, voluntary **10** calculated, considered, deliberate, predevised, purposeful **11** in cold blood, intentional, prearranged, predesigned **13** predetermined **22** with malice aforethought

premeditation **4** plan **6** design **7** purpose **11** calculation, forethought, preplanning **12** deliberation

premier **3** bet **4** head **5** chief, first **6** oldest **7** leading, supreme **8** earliest, foremost **9** principal **13** prime minister

Preminger, Otto
director of: **5** Laura **11** Carmen Jones **16** Anatomy of a Murder

premise **6** theory **8** argument **9** postulate, principle **10** assumption, hypothesis **11** presumption, proposition, supposition **14** presupposition

premises **4** site **8** environs, property, vicinity **9** precincts

premium **4** gain, gift **5** award, bonus, prize **6** bounty, return, reward **7** benefit, payment **8** priority **9** high value, incentive **10** great stock, recompense, reparation **11** overpayment **12** appreciation, compensation, inflated rate, remuneration **13** consideration, encouragement

premonition **4** omen, sign **5** hunch, token **6** augury **7** auspice, feeling, inkling, portent, presage **9** foretoken **10** foreboding, indication, prediction **11** forewarning **12** presentiment

Prendergast, Maurice Brazil
born: **6** Canada **7** St John's **12** Newfoundland
artwork: **6** Dieppe **8** Seashore **11** Picnic Grove **12** The Promenade **16** Ponte della Paglia **17** Along the Boulevard, Four Girls in Meadow **24** Umbrellas in the Rain Venice

Prentice, John
creator/artist of: **8** Rip Kirby

preoccupation **9** immersion, obsession **10** absorption, detachment, dreaminess, employment **11** abstraction, involvement **16** absent-mindedness

preoccupied **6** absent, dreamy **8** absorbed, immersed, involved, obsessed **9** engrossed, wrapped up **10** abstracted, distracted **12** absent-minded

preoccupy **6** absorb, arrest, obsess, take up, wrap up **7** engross, immerse **9** fascinate

preparation **8** prudence, readying **9** foresight, preparing, provision, safeguard **10** precaution **11** expectation, forethought **12** anticipation

preparations **5** plans **7** elixirs **8** guidance, measures, mixtures, training, tutelage **9** dressings, educaiton, seasoning, tinctures **11** concoctions, confections **12** arrangements **13** preliminaries, prepared foods, prescriptions **14** qualifications

prepare **3** fix **5** adapt, prime, ready **7** arrange, be ready, provide **8** get ready **9** make ready, rearrange, take steps

prepared **4** done **5** fixed, ready **6** cooked, primed **7** planned **8** arranged, finished **9** made ready, rehearsed **11** provided for

prepayment **6** credit **7** advance **9** allowance **11** downpayment

preponderance, preponderancy **4** bulk, glut, mass **6** excess **7** surfeit, surplus **8** majority, plethora **9** dominance, plurality, profusion **10** domination, lion's share, oversupply, prevalence, redundance **12** predominance **14** superabundance

preponderant **3** key **4** main **5** chief, first, major, prime **7** highest, leading, primary, supreme **8** dominant, foremost, greatest **9** paramount, principal, uppermost **10** prevailing **11** outstanding, predominant

prepossessing **4** nice **7** winsome **8** alluring, charming, engaging, inviting, pleasant, striking **9** beguiling **10** attractive, bewitching, enchanting, entrancing, personable **11** captivating, fascinating, tantalizing

preposterous **5** inane, outre, silly **6** absurd, stupid **7** asinine, bizarre, fatuous, foolish, idiotic **9** imbecilic, laughable, ludicrous **10** irrational, outrageous, ridiculous **11** nonsensical, unthinkable **12** unreasonable

prerequisite **4** need **6** demand **8** demanded, exigency, required **9** called for, condition, de rigueur, essential, mandatory, necessary, necessity, postulate, requisite **10** imperative, sine qua non **11** requirement, stipulation **13** indispensable, qualification

prerogative **3** due **5** claim, grant, right **6** choice, option **7** freedom, liberty, license, warrant **9** advantage, exemption, franchise, privilege **10** birthright

presage **4** bode, omen, osse, sign **5** augur, token **6** augury, herald **7** betoken, portend, portent, predict **8** forecast, foreshow, foretell, indicate **9** foresight **10** foreboding, foreshadow, indication, prediction, prescience, prognostic **11** premonition **12** presentiment

presbyter **5** elder **13** church officer

prescience **7** presage **9** foresight, prevision **13** foreknowledge

prescribe **3** fix, set **4** rule, urge **5** enact, order **6** assign, decree, demand, direct, enjoin, impose, ordain, settle **7** appoint, command, dictate, require, specify **8** advocate, proclaim **9** authorize, establish, institute, legislate, recommend, stipulate

prescribed **3** set **5** fixed **6** thetic **9** formulary

prescript **3** law **4** rule **5** order **7** precept, statute **10** regulation

prescriptive **7** binding **8** demanded, dictated, didactic, required **9** customary, mandatory, requisite **10** compulsory, imperative, obligatory

presence **3** air **4** life, look, mien **5** being, curse, favor, ghost, group, midst **6** aspect, entity, figure, manner, shadow, spirit, vision, wraith **7** bearing, company, eidolon, phantom, specter **8** carriage, charisma, demeanor, features, phantasm, revenant, vitality **9** character, existence **10** apparition, attendance, deportment, expression, lineaments **11** reification, subsistence **12** neighborhood **13** manifestation

presence of mind **6** aplomb **8** calmness, coolness **9** composure, sangfroid **10** equanimity, steadiness **14** self-possession **16** imperturbability

present **2** in **3** fee, now, tip **4** alms, aver, boon, cite, gift, give, here, near, nigh, read, show, tell **5** about, award, frame, grant, offer, state, today **6** accord, allege, assert, at hand, bestow, bounty, call up, chip in, coeval, confer, donate, hand in, impart, legacy, nearby, on hand, recite, relate, render, rooted, submit, summon, supply, tender, turn in **7** advance, bequest, bring on, current, declare, deliver, display, dole out, exhibit, expound, give out, instant, largess, mete out, not away, produce, profess, proffer, propose, provide, recount, vicinal **8** donation, embedded, existent, existing, give away, give over, gratuity, hand over, nowadays, oblation, offering, propound, put forth **9** apprise of, attending, draw forth, endowment, ensconced, hold forth, immediate, implanted, in the room, introduce, make known, not absent, on-the-spot, prevalent, pronounce, surrender, the moment, unremoved **10** asseverate, come up with, contribute, here and now, liberality, perquisite, put forward **11** benefaction, communicate **12** accounted for, bring forward, contemporary, in attendance

presentable 4 chic, so-so **6** decent, modish, not bad, proper **7** stylish **8** becoming, passable, suitable **9** tolerable **10** acceptable, good enough **11** appropriate, fashionable, fit to be seen, respectable

presentation 3 fee, tip **4** boon, gift, show **5** favor, grant, offer **6** bounty **7** advance, display, exhibit, largess, present, proffer **8** bestowal, exposure, gratuity, oblation, offering, overture, proposal **9** unfolding **10** appearance, compliment, disclosure, exhibition, exposition, liberality, production, proffering, submission, unfoldment **11** benefaction, performance, proposition **13** demonstration

Present at the Creation
author: 11 Dean Acheson

presentiment 7 feeling **10** foreboding **11** forewarning, premonition **12** apprehension

presently 3 now **4** anon, soon **7** shortly **8** directly, in a while, this week, this year **9** at present, currently, forthwith **10** any time now, before long, pretty soon **11** after a while, at the moment **12** in a short time
French: 11 tout a l'heure

preservation 6 saving **7** defense **9** salvation **10** protection **11** maintenance, safekeeping **12** conservation, safeguarding

preservative 4 salt **5** brine, spice **8** marinade **12** formaldehyde

preserve, preserves 3 can, dry, jam **4** corn, cure, park, salt, save, seal **5** guard, haven, jelly, nurse, put up, smoke, sweet **6** comfit, defend, embalm, foster, freeze, pickle, refuge, season, secure, shield **7** care for, compote, mummify, protect, reserve, shelter **8** conserve, insulate, keep safe, maintain, marinate **9** dehydrate, keep sound, marmalade, safeguard, sanctuary, sweetmeat, watch over **10** confection, keep intact, perpetuate **11** refrigerate, reservation

preside 4 boss, host, rule **5** chair, watch **6** direct, govern, manage **7** command, conduct, control, hostess, oversee **8** chairman, overlook, regulate **9** keep order, supervise **10** administer **11** superintend **12** administrate, take the chair

president, President 4 head **5** ruler **8** chairman **12** chief officer, chief of state, first citizen **14** chief executive **16** commander in chief, executive officer, head of government

president of US ***see box***

President's Analyst, The
director: 16 Theodore J Flicker
cast: 8 Will Geer **11** James Coburn **12** Severn Darden **16** Godfrey Cambridge

preside over 5 chair, guide **6** direct, govern, manage **7** conduct **8** dominate **9** supervise **10** administer **11** superintend

press 2 TV **3** beg, bug, dun, hit, hug, jam, mob, pet, tap, tax **4** army, body, cram, duty, heap, herd, host, iron, mash, mill, pack, prod, push, rush **5** beset, bunch, clasp, crowd, crush, drove, exact, flick, force, horde, hound, hurry, media, plead, radio, set on, steam, stuff, surge, swarm **6** appeal, bother, burden, caress, compel, duress, enjoin, exhort, extort, fondle, gather, huddle, legion, mangle, push in, reduce, smooth, strain, stress, throng **7** cluster, collect, depress, embrace, entreat, flatten, implore, newsmen, oppress, snuggle, squeeze, trouble **8** assemble, bear down, bear upon, calender, compress, condense, hot-press, insist on, pressure, printing, push down **9** annoyance, be hard put, constrain, constrict, final form, force down, force

president of US
first: 16 George Washington
second: 9 John Adams
third: 15 Thomas Jefferson
fourth: 12 James Madison
fifth: 11 James Monroe
sixth: 15 John Quincy Adams
seventh: 13 Andrew Jackson
eighth: 14 Martin Van Buren
ninth: 20 William Henry Harrison
tenth: 9 John Tyler
eleventh: 10 James K Polk
twelfth: 13 Zachary Taylor
thirteenth: 15 Millard Fillmore
fourteenth: 14 Franklin Pierce
fifteenth: 13 James Buchanan
sixteenth: 14 Abraham Lincoln
seventeenth: 13 Andrew Johnson
eighteenth: 13 Ulysses S Grant
nineteenth: 16 Rutherford B Hayes
twentieth: 14 James A Garfield
twenty-first: 17 Chester Alan Arthur
twenty-second: 15 Grover Cleveland
twenty-third: 16 Benjamin Harrison
twenty-fourth: 15 Grover Cleveland
twenty-fifth: 15 William McKinley
twenty-sixth: 17 Theodore Roosevelt
twenty-seventh: 17 William Howard Taft
twenty-eighth: 13 Woodrow Wilson
twenty-ninth: 14 Warren G Harding
thirtieth: 14 Calvin Coolidge
thirty-first: 13 Herbert Hoover
thirty-second: 18 Franklin D Roosevelt
thirty-third: 12 Harry S Truman
thirty-fourth: 17 Dwight D Eisenhower
thirty-fifth: 12 John F Kennedy
thirty-sixth: 14 Lyndon B Johnson
thirty-seventh: 13 Richard M Nixon
thirty-eighth: 11 Gerald R Ford
thirty-ninth: 11 (James E) Jimmy Carter (Jr)
fortieth: 12 Ronald Reagan
forty-first: 10 George Bush

from, importune, multitude, reporters **10** compulsion, congregate, newspapers, obligation, supplicate, television, thrust down **11** journalists, periodicals, publication **12** bear down upon, broadcasting, come together, news services, newspapermen **14** Fourth Estate

Pressburger, Emeric *see* **13** Michael Powell

press down **7** compact, depress **8** push down

press forward **5** drive **6** push on **7** advance **10** forge ahead

press home **6** stress **9** emphasize, underline **10** accentuate, underscore

pressing **5** vital **6** crying, needed, urgent **7** crucial, exigent, needful **8** critical **9** clamoring, demanding, essential, important, insistent, necessary **10** imperative **11** importunate **13** indispensable

pressing necessity **6** crisis **7** urgency **8** exigency **9** emergency

press on **9** move ahead, persevere **10** accelerate, forge ahead **11** move forward

pressure **4** bias, care, load, need, pull, sway, want **5** force, hurry, pinch, power, press, trial **6** burden, demand, strain, stress, weight **7** anxiety, density, gravity, potency, squeeze, straits, tension, trouble, urgency **8** coercion, distress, exigency, interest **9** adversity, grievance, heaviness, influence, necessity **10** affliction, compaction, compulsion, difficulty, oppression

pressure measurement **6** pascal **10** atmosphere

prestige **4** fame, mark, note **5** glory, honor **6** esteem, import, regard, renown, report, repute **7** account, respect **8** eminence **9** authority, celebrity **10** importance, notability, prominence, reputation **11** consequence, distinction, preeminence **12** significance

prestigious **5** famed **6** famous **7** eminent, honored, notable **8** esteemed, renowned **9** acclaimed, important, prominent, reputable, respected, well-known **10** celebrated **11** illustrious, outstanding **13** distinguished

Preston, Robert
real name: **21** Robert Preston Meservey
born: **17** Newton Highlands MA
roles: **4** Mame **9** Semi-Tough **11** The Music Man **12** Junior Bonner **14** Victor Victoria **16** How the West Was Won

presumable **6** likely **8** apparent, probable **10** ostensible

presumably **6** likely **8** probably **9** assumably, doubtless **10** apparently, ostensibly **13** presumptively **14** unquestionably **15** in all likelihood **16** in all probability

presume **4** dare **5** fancy, guess, posit **6** assume, deduce, gather, have it, impose, take it **7** believe, imagine, suppose, surmise, suspect, venture **8** be so bold, conceive, make bold, make free **9** postulate, take leave **11** hypothesize, rely too much, think likely **12** take a liberty

presumed **7** assumed, deduced, posited **8** believed, imagined, supposed, surmised **9** suspected **10** postulated **13** took advantage **15** taken for granted

presumption **3** lip **4** gall **5** brass, cheek, guess, nerve, pride **6** belief, daring **7** egotism, premise, surmise **8** audacity, boldness, chutzpah, rudeness **9** arrogance, flippancy, impudence, insolence, postulate **10** assumption, conjecture, effrontery **11** forwardness, haughtiness, prejudgment, speculation, supposition **12** impertinence **13** preconception **14** presupposition

presumptuous **4** bold **5** brash, cocky, fresh, lofty, nervy, proud **6** brassy, brazen, daring, lordly **7** forward, haughty, pompous **8** arrogant, assuming, snobbish **9** audacious, imperious, shameless **10** disdainful **11** dictatorial, domineering, overbearing, patronizing **12** contemptuous, overfamiliar **13** overconfident

presuppose **6** assume **7** presume, suppose **9** speculate **10** conjecture **11** hypothesize

presupposed **7** assumed **8** presumed, supposed **10** speculated **11** conjectured

presupposition **7** premise **10** assumption **11** postulation, presumption

pretend **4** fake, sham **5** claim, fancy, feign, mimic, put on **6** affect, assume **7** imagine, imitate, playact, purport, suppose **8** simulate **9** dissemble **10** masquerade **11** counterfeit, dissimulate, impersonate, make believe

pretended
French: **9** soi-disant

pretender **5** faker, fraud, phony **8** claimant, imposter

pretense **4** airs, fake, hoax, mask, sham, show **5** cloak, cover, feint, guile, trick, vaunt **6** deceit **7** bluster, bombast, display, pretext **8** boasting, bragging, disguise, trickery **9** deception, false show, imposture, invention, pomposity **10** camouflage, pretension, showing off, subterfuge **11** affectation, counterfeit, fabrication, fanfaronade, make-believe, ostentation **12** affectedness

pretension **4** airs, pomp, show **5** claim, right, title **7** bombast, display **8** ambition, pretense, snobbery **9** hypocrisy, pomposity, showiness **10** aspiration, showing off **11** affectation, ostentation **13** grandioseness **14** self-importance **16** ostentatiousness

pretentious **4** airy, smug **5** gaudy, lofty, showy, stagy **6** flashy, florid, garish, ornate, tawdry **7** blown-up, fatuous, pompous, stuck-up **8** affected, assuming, boastful, inflated, overdone, pedantic, puffed-up, snobbish **9** bombastic, flaunting, insincere, presuming, unnatural **10** hoity-toity, theatrical **11** exaggerated, extravagant, overbearing **12** ostentatious, self-praising **13** high-and-mighty, self-important

pretentiousness **4** cant **6** humbug **9** hypocrisy **11** insincerity **17** sanctimoniousness

preternatural **5** eerie, weird **6** arcane, occult **7** bizarre, strange, uncanny **8** esoteric, mystical **9** unearthly, unworldly **10** miraculous, mysterious, superhuman **11** hypernormal, preterhuman, supernormal **12** extramundane, metaphysical, supernatural, supranatural **14** transcendental

pretext **5** basis, bluff, feint **6** excuse, ground **8** pretense **9** semblance **10** pretension, subterfuge **11** vindication

pretty **4** fair **5** bonny **6** comely, dainty, fairly, goodly, lovely, rather **7** shapely, sightly, well-set **8** alluring, charming, delicate, engaging, fetching, graceful, handsome, some-

Princess Casamassima
author: **10** Henry James

Princess Daisy
author: **12** Judith Krantz

Princesse de Cleves, La
author: **14** Mme de LaFayette

Princess Flavia
character in: **15** Prisoner of Zenda
author: **4** Hope

Prince Valiant
creator: **12** Harold Foster
character: **5** Ilene **9** Prince Arn **10** King Arthur
wife: **5** Aleta
nickname: **3** Val

principal **4** dean, fund, main, star **5** basic, chief, first, money, prime **6** master **7** capital, leading, primary, supreme **8** cardinal, dominant, foremost, greatest, superior, ultimate **9** essential, paramount, preceptor, prominent **10** capital sum, headmaster, leading man, preeminent **11** fundamental, predominant, protagonist **13** most important

principal constituent **4** base **12** chief feature **14** main ingredient

principal dish of a meal
French: **17** piece de resistance

principal event
French: **17** piece de resistance

principality **5** angel **9** princedom **14** celestial being, heavenly spirit

principally **6** mainly, mostly **7** chiefly, largely **8** above all **9** basically, primarily **10** especially **12** particularly **13** fundamentally, predominantly **14** for the most part **16** first and foremost

principe **6** prince

principle **3** law **4** code, fact, rule, view **5** axiom, basis, canon, credo, creed, dogma, honor, maxim, tenet, truth **6** belief, dictum, ethics, morals, theory, virtue **7** element, formula, honesty, precept, probity, scruple, theorem **8** attitude, doctrine, goodness, morality, position, rudiment, scruples, teaching **9** direction, integrity, rectitude, standards **10** assumption, regulation **11** fundamental, proposition, uprightness

principled **6** honest **7** upright **9** honorable **10** aboveboard, forthright

Pringle, John
real name of: **11** John Gilbert

prink **4** deck, fuss **5** adorn, preen, primp **6** spruce

print **3** die **4** copy, text, type **5** issue, plate, press, stamp, write **7** compose, edition, engrave, etching, gravure, impress, picture, publish, woodcut **10** lithograph, silkscreen **11** letterpress

printing press
invented by:
rotary: **3** Hoe
web: **7** Bullock

prior **6** former **7** earlier **8** anterior, previous **9** aforesaid, erstwhile, foregoing, prefatory **10** antecedent, precursory **11** going before, preexistent, preexisting, preparatory **14** aforementioned

Prior Analytics
author: **9** Aristotle

Prioress
character in: **18** The Canterbury Tales
author: **7** Chaucer

priority **7** urgency **9** immediacy, seniority **10** ascendancy, precedence, precedency, preference **11** antecedence, preeminence, superiority

priory **5** abbey **6** friary **7** convent, nunnery **8** cloister **9** hermitage, monastery

Prism, Letitia
character in: **27** The Importance of Being Earnest
author: **5** Wilde

prison **3** can, jug, pen **4** brig, gaol, jail, stir, tank **5** clink, joint, pokey, tower **6** cooler **7** dungeon, slammer **8** bastille, big house **9** calaboose, jailhouse

Prisoner of Zenda
author: **11** Anthony Hope
character: **14** Princess Flavia **17** Lady Rose Burlesdon, Rudolph Rassendyll **18** Antoinette de Mauban, Fritz von Tarlenhein **21** Michael Duke of Strelsau **22** Rudolph King of Ruritania
director: **12** John Cromwell
cast: **9** Mary Astor **10** David Niven **12** C Aubrey Smith, Ronald Colman (Rudolf Rassendyll) **16** Madeleine Carroll **18** Douglas Fairbanks Jr (Rupert of Hentzau)
setting: **9** Ruritania

prissy **4** prim **5** fussy **6** proper, stuffy **7** finicky, prudish **8** overnice **9** sissified **10** effeminate **11** strait-laced

Prissy
character in: **15** Gone With the Wind
author: **8** Mitchell

pristine **4** pure **8** unmarred, virginal **9** undefiled, unspoiled, unsullied, untouched **10** unpolluted **11** untarnished **14** uncontaminated

Pritchett, V S
author of: **11** Midnight Oil **16** Collected Stories, The Spanish Temper **19** On the Edge of the Cliff

privacy **6** secret **7** privity, retreat, secrecy **8** security, solitude **9** integrity, isolation, seclusion **10** retirement, withdrawal **11** privateness **12** dissociation, solitariness **13** sequestration

private **4** dark **5** fixed, privy **6** buried, closed, covert, hidden, lonely, remote, secret **7** cryptic, express, limited, obscure, special **8** confined, desolate, esoteric, hush-hush, isolated, lonesome, personal, secluded, solitary **9** concealed, exclusive, inviolate, invisible, nonpublic, not public, reclusive **10** classified, indistinct, mysterious, restricted, undercover, under wraps, unofficial, unrevealed **11** clandestine, nonofficial, sequestered, underground, undisclosed **12** confidential, off-the-record, unfrequented

privateer **6** pirate **7** brigand, corsair **9** buccaneer

private eye **4** dick **6** shamus **7** gumshoe **9** detective **12** investigator

Private Life of Henry VIII, The
director: **14** Alexander Korda
cast: **11** Merle Oberon, Robert Donat **12** Binnie Barnes **14** Elsa Lanchester (Anne of Cleves) **15** Charles Laughton (Henry VIII)

Private Life of the Master Race, The
author: **13** Bertold Brecht

Private Lives
author: **10** Noel Coward
character: **10** Elyot Chase, Sibyl Chase **12** Amanda Prynne, Victor Prynne

Private Lives of Elizabeth and Essex, The
director: **13** Michael Curtiz
cast: **10** Bette Davis (Elizabeth I), Errol Flynn (Essex) **11** Donald Crisp **12** Vincent Price **13** Nanette Fabray **17** Olivia de Havilland

also known as: 17 Elizabeth the Queen

privately 7 sub rosa 8 in secret, secretly 9 between us, entre nous, in private 12 in confidence 14 confidentially 15 between you and me 16 between ourselves 17 behind closed doors

privation 4 lack, need, want 5 pinch 6 misery, penury 7 beggary, poverty, straits 8 distress, exigency, hardship 9 indigence, neediness, pauperism 10 bankruptcy, mendicancy 11 destitution 14 impoverishment 15 impecuniousness

privilege 3 due 4 boon 5 allow, favor, grant, honor, power, right, title 6 patent, permit 7 benefit, charter, empower, entitle, freedom, liberty, license 8 pleasure 9 advantage, authority, franchise 10 birthright 11 entitlement, prerogative 12 prerequisite

privileged 4 free 6 exempt, immune 7 allowed, excused, granted, limited, special 8 entitled, licensed 9 empowered, not liable, permitted, warranted 10 authorized, sanctioned 13 unaccountable

prize 3 cup, gem, pip 4 like, lulu 5 award, catch, crown, dandy, honey, honor, jewel, medal, peach, pearl, value 6 admire, esteem, honors, regard, reward, ribbon, trophy 7 cherish, diamond, guerdon, honored, laurels, premium, respect, winning 8 accolade, champion, citation, hold dear, look up to, pure gold, treasure 9 humdinger, medallion 10 appreciate, blue ribbon, decoration, set store by 11 crackerjack, masterpiece

prized 4 dear 8 esteemed, precious 9 cherished, treasured

prizefight 2 go 4 bout 5 match 6 boxing 7 contest 10 fisticuffs

prizefighter 3 pug 5 boxer 7 slugger 8 pugilist 9 flyweight 11 heavyweight, lightweight 12 bantamweight, middleweight, welterweight 13 featherweight 16 light heavyweight

pro 3 for 5 forth 6 before, expert, master 8 favoring 9 authority 11 affirmative
opposite: 3 con 7 amateur

probability 4 odds 6 chance 10 likelihood

probable 6 likely 7 logical, seeming, tenable 8 apparent, assuring, credible, expected, possible, presumed, supposed 9 plausible, promising, thinkable 10 believable, in the cards, ostensible, presumable, reasonable 11 conceivable, encouraging, presumptive

probably 6 likely 10 most likely, presumably, supposedly 11 as like as not 15 in all likelihood

probe 4 hunt, quiz, seek, test 5 query, study, trial 6 pursue, review, search, survey 7 examine, fish for, inquest, inquire, inquiry, inspect, pry into, rummage 8 analysis, look into, question, research 9 penetrate 10 inspection, scrutinize 11 examination, exploration, interrogate, investigate 13 investigation

probity 5 honor 6 virtue 7 decency, honesty 8 goodness, morality 9 character, integrity, principle 11 uprightness 12 straightness 13 righteousness 14 high-mindedness 15 trustworthiness 16 incorruptibility

problem 5 poser, query 6 puzzle, riddle, unruly 8 question, stubborn 9 conundrum, difficult 10 difficulty 11 intractable 12 disagreement, hard to manage, incorrigible, unmanageable

problematic 7 dubious, unknown 8 doubtful, puzzling 9 difficult, enigmatic, uncertain, unsettled, worrisome 10 perplexing 11 paradoxical, troublesome 12 questionable, undetermined

pro bono publico 16 for the public good

proboscis 4 beak, nose 5 snoot, snout, trunk 6 siphon, sucker, syphon 7 rostrum
monkey: 4 kaha 5 kahua

procedure 2 MO 3 way 4 mode 6 course, manner, method 7 process, routine 8 approach, strategy 9 technique 11 methodology 13 modus operandi

proceed 2 go 3 act 4 come, flow, go on, grow, move, stem, work 5 arise, begin, ensue, issue, start 6 derive, follow, move on, push on, result, set out, spring 7 advance, carry on, emanate, go ahead, operate, press on, succeed 8 be caused, commence, continue, function, progress, take rise 9 be derived, go forward, move ahead, originate, undertake

proceedings 4 case, suit 5 cause, trial 6 doings, events, report 7 account, actions, affairs, lawsuit, matters, minutes, records, returns 8 activity, archives, goings on 9 incidents, memoranda 10 happenings, litigation, operations 11 occurrences 12 transactions

proceeds 3 net 4 gain, gate, pelf, take 5 gross, lucre, money, yield 6 assets, income, profit, reward 7 returns, revenue 8 earnings, pickings, receipts, winnings 9 box office

process 3 can, dry 4 fill, flow, flux, mode, plan, ship, step, writ 5 alter, candy, smoke, treat, usage 6 change, course, freeze, handle, manner, method, motion, policy, scheme, system 7 convert, measure, passage, prepare, project, summons 8 deal with, function, movement, practice, preserve, progress, subpoena 9 dehydrate, dispose of, freeze-dry, procedure, transform, unfolding 10 court order, proceeding

procession 4 file, line, rank 5 array, march, train 6 column, course, parade 7 caravan, cortege, pageant, passage 8 progress, sequence 9 cavalcade, motorcade 10 succession 11 progression

Procheneosaurus
type: 8 dinosaur 10 ornithopod
location: 6 Canada
period: 10 Cretaceous

proclaim 3 cry 4 tell 5 blare, state, voice 6 affirm, assert, blazon, herald, report, reveal 7 call out, declare, divulge, give out, profess, publish, release, sing out, trumpet 8 announce, disclose, set forth 9 advertise, broadcast, circulate, enunciate, hawk about, make known, publicize 10 make public, promulgate

proclamation 5 edict, ukase 6 decree 12 announcement 13 pronouncement

Proclea
husband: 6 Cycnus
son: 5 Tenes

Procles
twin of: 11 Eurysthenes

proclivity 3 yen 4 bent, bias 5 taste 6 desire, liking 7 impulse, leaning 8 affinity, appetite, penchant, soft spot, tendency 9 affection, prejudice, proneness **10** partiality, propensity **11** disposition, inclination **12** predilection **14** predisposition

Procne
sister: 9 Philomela
husband: 6 Tereus
changed into: 7 swallow

procrastinate 3 lag **5** dally, defer, delay, stall, tarry **6** dawdle, linger, loiter **7** adjourn **8** hang back, hesitate, hold back, kill time, postpone, put on ice **9** temporize, waste time **10** be dilatory, dillydally **11** play for time **12** drag one's feet

procrastinating 4 slow **5** tardy **6** remiss **8** dilatory **9** reluctant **12** foot-dragging **13** dillydallying

procreate 3 get **4** bear, sire **5** beget, breed, spawn **6** create, father, mother **7** produce **8** conceive, engender, generate, multiply **9** propagate, reproduce **10** bring forth **11** give birth to, proliferate

procreation
god of: 7 Priapus

procreator 4 sire **6** father **8** begetter

Procris
father: 8 Thespius **10** Erechtheus
husband: 8 Cephalus

Procrustes
also: 8 Damastes **9** Polypemon
robber who: 6 maimed
killed by: 7 Theseus

procure 3 buy, get, win **4** earn, gain, take **5** evoke, seize **6** attain, come by, effect, elicit, gather, incite, induce, obtain, pick up, secure **7** achieve, acquire, receive **8** contrive, purchase **10** accumulate, bring about, commandeer, lay hands on **11** appropriate

procurement 4 gain **7** seizure **8** purchase **10** attainment, purchasing **11** achievement, acquirement, acquisition **12** accumulation **13** appropriation

prod 3 jab, nag **4** flog, goad, lash, move, poke, push, spur, stir, urge, whip **5** egg on, impel, prick, rouse, shove, speed **6** excite, exhort, incite, needle, prompt, propel, stir up **7** actuate, animate, provoke, quicken **8** motivate, pressure **9** encourage, instigate, stimulate

prodigal 4 lush **5** ample **6** lavish, myriad, wanton **7** copious, profuse, replete, spender, teeming, wastrel **8** abundant, generous, numerous, reckless, swarming, wasteful **9** abounding, bounteous, bountiful, countless, excessive, exuberant, impetuous, luxuriant, plentiful, unthrifty **10** exorbitant, gluttonous, immoderate, inordinate, numberless, profligate, squanderer, thriftless **11** dissipating, extravagant, improvident, innumerable, intemperate, overliberal, precipitate, spendthrift **13** multitudinous

prodigality 10 imprudence, lavishness **12** extravagance, improvidence, overspending, wastefulness

prodigious 3 big **4** huge, rare, vast **5** grand, great, large **6** mighty, unique **7** amazing, immense **8** colossal, enormous, gigantic, renowned, singular, striking, terrific, uncommon, unwonted, wondrous **9** marvelous, monstrous, startling, wonderful **10** astounding, impressive, miraculous, monumental, noteworthy, remarkable, stupendous, surprising, tremendous **11** astonishing, exceptional, far-reaching, uncustomary, unthinkable **12** dumbfounding, overwhelming, unimaginable **13** extraordinary, inconceivable, unprecedented

prodigiously 10 enormously, incredibly, remarkably **12** inordinately, tremendously **13** astonishingly, exceptionally, extravagantly, outstandingly, spectacularly **14** overwhelmingly

prodigiousness 6 rarity **8** enormity, hugeness, vastness **10** uniqueness **11** singularity **12** extravagance

prodigy 4 whiz **6** expert, genius, marvel, master, rarity, wizard, wonder **7** stunner, whiz kid **8** rara avis **9** sensation **10** mastermind, phenomenon, wunderkind **11** wonder child

Prodromia
epithet of: 4 Hera
means: 7 pioneer

produce 4 bear, form, give, make, show **5** beget, bloom, cause, found, frame, hatch, set up, shape, yield **6** adduce, afford, create, devise, effect, evince, evolve, flower, fruits, greens, invent, reveal, sprout, supply, unmask, unveil **7** achieve, advance, bring in, compose, concoct, develop, display, divulge, exhibit, fashion, furnish, present, provide, staples, turn out, uncover **8** bring off, bring out, conceive, disclose, discover, generate, manifest, set forth **9** bear fruit, construct, fabricate, institute, make plain, originate, procreate, put on view, show forth **10** accomplish, bring about, come up with, effectuate, foodstuffs, give life to, give rise to, put in force, vegetables **11** bring to pass, give birth to, manufacture, materialize **14** bring into being

Producers, The
director: 9 Mel Brooks
cast: 9 Dick Shawn **10** Gene Wilder, Zero Mostel **11** Kenneth Mars

production 4 film, play, show **5** drama, movie **6** cinema, circus, making **7** display, exhibit, musical, showing **8** building, carnival, creation **9** execution, formation, producing, stage show **10** appearance, disclosure, revelation **11** fabrication, fulfillment, manufacture, origination, performance **12** construction, effectuation, introduction, presentation **13** demonstration, entertainment, manifestation, manufacturing, motion picture **15** materialization

productive 4 busy, rich **6** active, fecund, paying, useful **7** causing, copious, dynamic, fertile, gainful, teeming **8** creating, creative, fruitful, prolific, valuable, vigorous, yielding **9** effectual, luxuriant, plenteous, plentiful, producing **10** invaluable, profitable, worthwhile **11** efficacious, moneymaking, proliferous **12** contributing, fructiferous, remunerative

Proetus
father: 4 Abas
mother: 6 Aglaia
twin brother: 8 Acrisius
wife: 5 Antia **10** Stheneboea
son: 11 Megapenthes
daughter: 7 Iphinoe, Lysippe **10** Iphianassa
invented: 6 shield
enemy: 8 Acrisius

profanation 9 sacrilege **10** defilement **11** desecration

profane 3 lay **4** evil, foul, lewd, mock, vile **5** abuse, bawdy, crude, nasty, scorn, waste **6** coarse, debase, filthy, ill-use, impure, misuse, offend, revile, ribald, sinful, unholy, vulgar, wicked **7** abusive, earthly, godless, impious, obscene, outrage, pervert, pollute, satanic, secular, ungodly, violate, worldly **8** agnostic, diabolic, off-color, temporal, unchaste, undevout, unseemly **9** atheistic, blaspheme, desecrate, hellbound, heretical, misemploy, shameless, unsaintly **10** irreverent, prostitute **11** blasphemous, contaminate, irreligious, terrestrial, unbelieving **12** nonreligious, sacrilegious

profanity **5** filth, oaths **7** cursing, cussing, impiety **8** swearing **9** blasphemy, obscenity, scatology **10** dirty words, execration, expletives, scurrility, swearwords **11** irreverence, obscenities, ungodliness **12** billingsgate **15** four-letter words

profess **3** act, own, say **4** aver, avow, fake, sham, tell **5** admit, claim, feign, offer, put on, state, vouch **6** affirm, allege, assert, assume, depose **7** advance, certify, confess, confirm, contend, declare, embrace, pretend, purport **8** announce, lay claim, maintain, practice, proclaim, propound, simulate **9** believe in, dissemble, enunciate, hold forth **10** asseverate, put forward **11** acknowledge, counterfeit, dissimulate

professed **6** avowed **7** alleged **8** admitted **9** confessed, purported **12** acknowledged, self-declared **14** self-proclaimed

profession **3** job, law, vow **4** line, post, word, work **5** claim, craft, field, trade, troth **6** avowal, career, metier, office, pledge, plight, sphere **7** calling, promise, pursuit, service **8** averment, business, endeavor, industry, medicine, position, practice, teaching, vocation **9** assertion, assurance, guarantee, situation, specialty, statement, testimony **10** allegation, confession, deposition, employment, line of work, occupation, walk of life **11** affirmation, attestation, declaration, undertaking, word of honor **12** announcement, confirmation **13** pronouncement **15** acknowledgement

professional **4** paid **5** adept **6** expert **9** authority, competent, practiced **10** specialist **11** experienced

professionalism **5** savvy, skill **7** know-how **9** expertise **10** expertness

professor **3** don **6** regent **7** adjoint, teacher **8** lecturer **10** instructor
retired: **8** emeritus

Professor, The
author: **15** Charlotte Bronte

professorial **6** teachy **7** bookish, donnish, preachy **8** academic, didactic, pedantic, teachery **11** pedagoguish **13** schoolmarmish **15** schoolmasterish **16** schoolteacherish

Professor's House, The
author: **11** Willa Cather

proffer **5** offer **6** extend, tender **7** advance, hold out, present

proficiency **5** knack, skill **6** acumen **7** ability, know-how **8** aptitude, capacity, deftness, facility **9** adeptness, dexterity, expertise, handiness **10** adroitness, capability, competence **13** qualification **14** accomplishment

proficient **3** apt **4** able, deft, good **5** adept, handy, quick, ready, sharp **6** adroit, clever, expert, gifted **7** capable, skilled, trained **8** masterly, polished, skillful, talented **9** competent, dexterous, effective, efficient, masterful, practiced, qualified, versatile **11** experienced **12** accomplished, professional

profile **4** form, side, tale **5** shape **6** figure, sketch **7** contour, drawing, outline, picture, skyline **8** half face, portrait, side view, vignette **9** biography **10** lineaments, silhouette **11** delineation **13** configuration

Profiles in Courage
author: **12** John F Kennedy

profit **3** pay, use **4** boon, earn, gain, good, help **5** avail, favor, money, serve, value **6** income, return **7** account, benefit, revenue, service, utility, utilize **8** earnings, interest, proceeds, receipts **9** advantage, make money **11** advancement

profitable **6** paying, useful **7** gainful **8** fruitful, salutary, valuable **9** favorable, lucrative, rewarding **10** beneficial, invaluable, productive, well-paying, worthwhile **11** moneymaking, serviceable **12** advantageous, remunerative

profitmaking **8** business **11** moneymaking **13** noncharitable

profits **4** gate, take **5** gains, yield **6** assets, income **7** returns, revenue **8** earnings, receipts

profligacy **10** lavishness **11** dissipation, dissolution, prodigality, unrestraint **12** extravagance, immoderation, improvidence, recklessness, wastefulness **13** excessiveness

profligate **4** evil, fast, rake, roue, wild **5** loose, satyr **6** erotic, lavish, sinful, sinner, wanton, wicked **7** corrupt, immoral, pervert, satyric, wastrel **8** degraded, depraved, prodigal, reckless, wasteful **9** abandoned, debauched, debauchee, dissolute, libertine, reprobate, sybaritic, unbridled, unthrifty, wrongdoer **10** degenerate, dissipated, dissipater, iniquitous, lascivious, licentious **11** extravagant, improvident, promiscuous, spendthrift **12** unprincipled, unrestrained

pro forma **15** according to form, as a matter of form

profound **4** deep, keen, sage, wise **5** acute, sober, utter **6** abject, hearty, moving, severe **7** decided, erudite, extreme, intense, knowing, learned, radical, serious, sincere **8** complete, educated, informed, piercing, positive, thorough **9** heartfelt, out-and-out, recondite, sagacious, scholarly **10** all-knowing, consummate, deep-seated, omniscient, pronounced, reflective, thoughtful **11** enlightened, far-reaching, penetrating **12** intellectual, soul-stirring **13** comprehensive, knowledgeable, philosophical, thoroughgoing

profundity **5** abyss, depth **6** wisdom **8** deepness, sagacity, sapience **9** erudition **11** learnedness, penetration **12** abstractness, abstruseness, profoundness **13** reconditeness, sagaciousness **16** impenetrableness

profuse **4** rich **5** ample, wordy **6** lavish, prolix **7** copious, diffuse, verbose **8** abundant, generous, prodigal, rambling, wasteful **9** bounteous, bountiful, excessive, garrulous, unthrifty **10** digressive, discursive, immoderate, inordinate, long-winded, loquacious, munificent **11** extravagant, improvident, intemperate, spendthrift

profuseness **9** abundance, diffusion, profusion, prolixity, verbosity, wordiness **10** lavishness **11** copiousness, diffuseness

profusion **4** glut **5** waste **6** excess **7** surfeit, surplus **8** plethora **9** abundance, multitude **10** oversupply **11** superfluity **12** extravagance, multiplicity

progenitor **8** ancestor, forebear **10** forefather

progeny **3** kin, son **4** clan, heir, line, race, seed **5** blood, breed, child, heirs, issue, scion, stock, young **6** family **7** kindred, lineage **8** children, offshoot **9** offspring, posterity **10** descendant

prognosticate **7** predict, presage **8** forecast, foretell, prophesy **9** foretoken

prognostication **6** augury **8** forecast, prophecy **10** divination, prediction

prognosticator **4** seer **5** augur **7** prophet **9** predictor **10** forecaster

program **4** bill, book, card, list, plan, show **5** slate **6** agenda, design, docket, expect, intend, line up, notice, series, sketch **7** arrange, outline **8** bulletin, calendar, playbill, register, schedule, syllabus **9** timetable **10** curriculum, production, prospectus **12** presentation

progress **4** gain, grow, rise **5** climb, get on, mount, ripen **6** action, course, grow up, growth, mature, stride **7** advance, develop, headway, improve, proceed, process, success **8** get ahead, increase, movement **9** get better, go forward, move ahead, promotion, unfolding **10** betterment, enrichment, gain ground **11** achievement, advancement, development, enhancement, furtherance, improvement, make headway, make strides

progression **3** run **5** chain, climb, order **6** ascent, course, series, strain, string **7** advance **8** progress, sequence **10** succession **11** advancement, continuance, furtherance **12** continuation **14** continuousness **15** consecutiveness

progressive **7** dynamic, gradual, liberal, ongoing **8** activist, advanced, populist, up-to-date **9** advancing, enlarging, reformist, spreading, traveling **10** ameliorist **11** incremental **12** enterprising

prohibit **3** ban, bar **4** curb, deny, stay, stop, veto **5** block, check, delay, limit **6** enjoin, forbid, hamper, hinder, impede, negate **7** inhibit, obviate, prevent, repress **8** disallow, obstruct, preclude, restrain, restrict, suppress, withhold **9** proscribe

prohibited
German: **8** verboten

prohibition **3** ban **4** veto **5** edict **7** embargo, sanction **10** temperance **11** forbiddance **12** interdiction

prohibitive, prohibitory **9** enjoining, hindering **10** forbidding, inhibitive, injunction, preventative, repressive **11** disallowing, obstructive, restraining, restrictive, suppressive **12** inadmissible, unacceptable **13** disqualifying **15** circumscriptive

project **3** aim, job **4** cast, emit, fire, goal, plan, send, task, work **5** draft, eject, expel, fling, frame, shoot, throw **6** beetle, design, devise, extend, hurtle, invent, jut out, launch, map out, propel, scheme **7** concoct, outline, propose **8** activity, ambition, bend over, contrive, forecast, overhang, protrude, stand out, stick out, throw out, transmit **9** calculate, discharge, ejaculate, intention, objective, plan ahead **10** assignment **11** extrapolate, undertaking **12** predetermine

projected **6** hurled **7** hurtled, planned **8** extended, forecast, launched, overhung, proposed, stood out, stuck out **9** mapped out, propelled, protruded **10** catapulted **11** conjectural

projectile **4** dart **5** arrow, spear **6** rocket **7** javelin, missile

projecting part **3** arm, ell, leg **4** eave, limb, tail **6** branch, feeler, member **7** antenna **8** tentacle **9** appendage

projection **4** brow, bump, eave **5** bulge, guess, jetty, jutty, ledge, ridge, shelf **8** estimate, forecast, overhang **9** extension, extrusion **10** estimation, prediction, prospectus, protrusion **11** guesstimate **12** protuberance **13** approximation, extrapolation

Prokofiev, Serge
born: **6** Russia **9** Sontsovka
composer of: **6** Lt Kije **10** Cinderella, The Gambler **11** War and Peace **13** Scythian Suite, The Fiery Angel **14** Lieutenant Kije, Romeo and Juliet, The Prodigal Son **15** Alexander Nevsky, Peter and the Wolf **17** Classical Symphony **22** The Love for Three Oranges **57** Cantata for the Twentieth Anniversary of the October Revolution

proletarian **6** worker **7** laborer **10** working man

proletariat **5** plebs **6** rabble, the mob **7** populus **8** canaille, laborers, populace **9** commonage, commoners, hoi polloi, the masses **10** commonalty **11** lower orders, rank and file, wage earners **12** lower classes, vulgus mobile, working class **15** the common people **16** the great unwashed

proliferate **4** teem **5** breed, hatch, spawn, swarm **8** increase, multiply **9** procreate, propagate, pullulate **10** regenerate **11** overproduce

prolific **4** lush **6** fecund **7** copious, fertile, profuse **8** abundant, breeding, creative, fruitful, yielding **9** luxuriant **11** germinative, multiplying, procreative, progenitive, proliferous, propagating **12** reproductive

prolix **5** wordy **7** verbose **10** long-winded

prolixity **9** verbosity, wordiness **11** profuseness **14** long-windedness

prologue **7** opening, preface, prelude **8** foreword, overture, preamble **9** beginning **12** introduction

prolong **5** delay **6** extend, retard **7** drag out, draw out, spin out, stretch, sustain **8** continue, elongate, lengthen, maintain, protract **9** attenuate **10** perpetuate

prolongation **5** delay **9** extending, extension **10** drawing out **11** attenuation, dragging out, lengthening, protraction, retardation **12** perpetuation **13** streching out

prolonged **7** lengthy **8** drawn-out, extended **9** continued, long-lived **10** continuing, lengthened, persistent, protracted **11** long-lasting

prom **3** hop **4** ball **5** dance **9** cotillion, promenade

Promachorma
epithet of: **6** Athena
means: **25** protectress of the anchorage

Promachus
member of: **7** Epigoni
leader of: **9** Boeotians
epithet of: **6** Athena
means: **8** defender **9** protector

promenade **3** hop **4** ball, prom, walk **5** dance **6** soiree, stroll **9** cotillion

Prometheus
member of: **6** Titans
father: **7** Iapetus
mother: **6** Themis **7** Clymene
brother: **5** Atlas **10** Epimetheus
son: **9** Deucalion
created mankind from: **4** clay
stole: **4** fire
punished by: **4** Zeus
chained to: **4** rock
released by: **8** Hercules

Prometheus Bound
author: **9** Aeschylus
character: **2** Io **3** Bia **6** Hermes, Kratos **7** Oceanus **10** Hephaestus

Prometheus Unbound
author: **18** Percy Bysshe Shelley
character: **4** Asia, Ione **5** Earth **7** Jupiter, Mercury, Panthea **8** Hercules **9** Demogoron

prominence **3** tor **4** bump, dune, fame, hill, hump, knob, lump, mark, mesa, name, node, peak, rise, spur **5** bluff, bulge, cliff, crest, honor, jetty, jutty, knoll, knurl, might, mound **6** credit, height, renown, rising, summit, weight **7** dignity, hillock, majesty, process **8** eminence, grandeur, mountain, nobility, outshoot, overhang, pinnacle, prestige, salience, splendor, swelling **9** celebrity, convexity, elevation, extension, extrusion, greatness, influence, notoriety, precipice **10** brilliance, importance, notability, popularity, projection, promontory, protrusion, reputation, tumescence **11** distinction, excrescence, excurvature, preeminence, superiority **12** protuberance, significance

prominent **6** convex, famous **7** bulging, eminent, evident, glaring, honored, jutting, leading, notable, obvious, salient, staring, swollen **8** apparent, definite, excurved, extended, renowned, striking, swelling **9** arresting, important, respected, well-known **10** celebrated, easily seen, jutting out, noticeable, preeminent, projecting, pronounced, protruding, protrusive, remarkable **11** conspicuous, discernible, illustrious, outstanding, prestigious, protuberant **12** recognizable **13** distinguished

promiscuous **3** lax **4** fast, lewd, wild **5** loose, mixed **6** casual, impure, medley, motley, rakish, wanton **7** aimless, chaotic, diverse, immoral, jumbled, mingled, mixed-up, satyric **8** careless, confused, immodest, sweeping, unchaste **9** composite, desultory, dissolute, haphazard, perplexed, scrambled, wholesale **10** commingled, disordered, disorderly, dissipated, intermixed, lascivious, licentious, uncritical, undirected, unvirtuous, variegated **11** disarranged, incontinent, indifferent, intemperate, unselective **12** disorganized, of easy virtue, undiscerning **13** helter-skelter, heterogeneous, miscellaneous **14** indiscriminate

promise **3** vow **4** aver, avow, oath, word **5** agree, augur, imply, swear, troth, vouch **6** assure, avowal, hint of, parole, pledge, plight **7** be bound, betoken, suggest, warrant **8** covenant, indicate, warranty **9** agreement, assurance, guarantee, potential, undertake **11** declaration, stipulation, swear an oath, word of honor

Promised Land **6** Canaan
nickname of: **10** California **6** Israel

Promises
author: **16** Robert Penn Warren

promising **4** rosy **5** happy, lucky **6** bright, rising **7** hopeful **8** assuring, cheerful, cheering **9** advancing, favorable, fortunate, looking up **10** auspicious, of good omen, optimistic, propitious, reassuring **11** encouraging, inspiriting, up-and-coming

promissory note **3** IOU **4** bond, chit **6** pledge **7** promise **9** agreement **10** obligation **11** certificate

promontory **4** cape, hill, ness, spur **5** bluff, cliff, jetty, jutty, point **6** height **8** headland, overhang **9** peninsula, precipice **10** embankment, projection

promote **3** aid **4** abet, ease, help, plug, push **5** raise **6** assist, foster, prefer, refine **7** advance, develop, elevate, enhance, forward, further, support, upgrade, work for **8** advocate, expedite, graduate **9** advertise, cultivate, encourage, publicize

promoter **6** backer **8** advocate, champion **9** proponent, supporter

promotion **4** hype **5** raise **7** advance, fanfare, puffery **8** ballyhoo, boosting, progress **9** elevation, publicity, upgrading **10** preferment **11** advancement, advertising, furtherance **12** promulgation **13** advertisement, encouragement

promotive **7** helpful **9** conducive **10** beneficial **12** contributive, contributory, instrumental

prompt **3** cue **4** goad, keen, move, prod, push, spur, stir **5** alert, alive, cause, drive, eager, force, impel, press, quick, ready, sharp **6** active, assist, bright, excite, incite, induce, intent, lively, on time, propel, remind, thrust, timely **7** actuate, animate, dispose, help out, incline, inspire, instant, on guard, provoke, zealous **8** activate, inspirit, motivate, occasion, open-eyed, persuade, punctual, vigilant, watchful **9** attentive, determine, efficient, immediate, influence, instigate, observant, open-eared, stimulate, wide-awake **10** on one's toes **12** jog the memory, unhesitating **13** instantaneous

prompting **6** cueing, urging **7** goading **8** egging on **10** motivation **11** exhortation

promptly **3** pat **4** anon, soon, tite **6** pronto **7** quickly, swiftly **10** punctually **11** immediately

promptness **5** haste **8** alacrity, celerity, dispatch **9** quickness, readiness, swiftness **11** punctuality **15** expeditiousness

promulgate **6** foster **7** explain, expound, present, promote, sponsor **8** instruct, set forth **9** elucidate, enunciate, interpret **11** communicate

promulgation **9** fostering, promotion **11** circulation, instruction, sponsorship **12** distribution, presentation, transmission **13** communication **14** interpretation

Pronaus
epithet of: **6** Athena
means: **12** of the pronaos
pronaos: **15** before the temple

prone **3** apt **4** flat **5** level **6** liable, likely **7** subject, tending **8** disposed, face-down, inclined **9** prostrate, reclining, recumbent **10** accustomed, habituated, horizontal **11** predisposed, susceptible

proneness **4** bent, bias, turn **7** leaning **8** penchant, tendency **9** prejudice **10** proclivity, propensity **11** inclination

12 predilection
14 predisposition

prong **4** barb, hook, horn, spur, tine **5** point, spike, tooth **6** branch **10** projection

Pronoea
epithet of: **6** Athena
means: **11** forethought

pronoun **2** he, it, me, my, us, we, ye **3** all, any, few, her, his, one, she, thy, who, you **4** hers, mine, ours, some, thee, them, they, that, this, thou, what, whom **5** no one, their, these, thine, those, which, whose, yours **6** anyone, itself, myself, nobody **7** anybody, herself, himself, nothing, someone, whoever **8** somebody, whomever **9** everybody, something, whosoever **10** everything, themselves
French: **2** il, je, tu **3** lui, mes, moi **4** elle, vous
German: **2** er, es, du **3** ich, mir, sie **4** mein, mich
Italian: **2** io, me, mi, ti, tu, vi **3** cio, lei, lui, mio, tei, voi **4** egli, ella, essa, esse, essi, loro
Spanish: **2** el, la, lo, me, mi, tu, yo **4** ella, ello, suyo, tuyo **5** usted

pronounce **3** say **4** emit, form, rule **5** frame, judge, orate, sound, speak, state, utter, voice **6** decree **7** declare, enounce **8** announce, proclaim, vocalize **9** enunciate **10** articulate

pronounced **4** bold **5** broad, clear, plain, vivid **6** patent **7** decided, evident, obvious, visible **8** apparent, clear-cut, definite, distinct, manifest, positive, unhidden **9** arresting **10** noticeable **11** conspicuous, outstanding, undisguised, well-defined **12** recognizable, unmistakable **14** unquestionable

pronouncement **6** decree **11** declaration **12** announcement, proclamation

pronto **3** now **4** asap, fast, stat **5** quick **7** quickly **8** promptly **11** immediately

Pronuba
epithet of: **4** Juno

pronunciamento **5** edict **12** proclamation **13** pronouncement

pronunciation **6** accent **10** inflection **11** enunciation **12** articulation **16** manner of speaking

proof **4** test **5** essay, proof, sheet, trial **6** galley, ordeal **8** scrutiny, weighing **9** probation **10** assessment **11** attestation, examination **12** confirmation, ratification, verification **13** certification, corroboration, documentation **14** substantiation

proofreader's mark **3** cap, rom **4** dele, ital, stet **5** caret, space

prop **3** set **4** lean, rest, stay **5** brace, stand **6** hold up, pillar **7** bolster, shore up, support **8** buttress, mainstay, shoulder, underpin **9** stanchion, supporter, sustainer **13** reinforcement
French: **11** point d'appui

propaganda **6** hoopla **8** ballyhoo **9** party line, promotion, publicity **10** persuasion **11** advertising

propagandist **6** zealot **8** activist, exponent **9** apologist, proponent, publicist **12** spokesperson

propagate **3** air, sow **4** bear, tell **5** beget, breed, hatch, issue, rumor, spawn, spray **6** blazon, herald, impart, notify, preach, purvey, repeat, report, spread **7** bestrew, give out, implant, instill, publish, scatter, trumpet **8** disperse, engender, generate, increase, multiply, proclaim, put forth **9** broadcast, circulate, enunciate, give birth, inculcate, make known, procreate, publicize, reproduce

propagation **6** laying, siring **7** bearing **8** breeding, hatching, issuance, spawning, yielding **9** begetting, diffusion, gestation, pregnancy, spreading **10** dispersion, generation **11** circulation, engendering, giving birth, procreation, publication **12** distribution, reproduction, transmission **13** dissemination

pro patria **14** for one's country

propel **4** cast, goad, hurl, poke, prod, push, send, toss **5** drive, eject, force, heave, impel, pitch, shoot, shove, sling, start **6** launch, thrust **7** project **8** catapult **9** discharge **11** precipitate, set in motion

propeller, screw
invented by: **7** Stevens **8** Ericsson

propensity **4** bent, bias, turn **5** fancy, favor, taste **6** liking **7** leaning **8** affinity, penchant, pleasure, sympathy, tendency, weakness **9** prejudice **10** attraction, partiality, preference, proclivity **11** disposition, inclination **12** predilection **14** predisposition

proper **3** apt, fit, own **4** meet, nice, true **5** per se, right **6** decent, marked, modest, polite, seemly **7** apropos, correct, express, fitting, germane, precise, typical **8** assigned, becoming, decorous, orthodox, peculiar, relevant, specific, suitable **9** befitting, courteous, pertinent **10** acceptable, applicable, individual, particular, respective **11** appropriate, conformable, distinctive **12** conventional **14** characteristic, distinguishing, representative
French: **11** comme il faut

properly **5** aptly, right **7** exactly **8** decently, politely, suitably **9** correctly, perfectly, precisely **10** acceptably, accurately, decorously, tastefully **12** without error **13** appropriately **14** conventionally

property **4** hold, land, mark **5** acres, badge, funds, goods, means, point, stock, title, trait **6** aspect, assets, estate, moneys, realty, wealth **7** acreage, capital, earmark, effects, estates, feature, grounds, quality **8** chattels, holdings, treasure **9** attribute, ownership, resources, territory **10** belongings, real estate **11** investments, peculiarity, possessions, singularity **12** appointments, idiosyncrasy **13** individuality, particularity **14** characteristic, proprietorship

prophecy **6** augury **7** portent **8** forecast **10** divination, prediction, revelation **15** prognostication
god of: **6** Apollo **7** Phoebus, Pythius **9** Musagetes

prophesy **4** warn **5** augur **6** divine **7** forbode, foresee, portend, predict, presage **8** forecast, foretell, forewarn, soothsay **9** apprehend, premonish **13** prognosticate

prophet **4** seer **5** augur, guide, sibyl **6** oracle **7** diviner, palmist, seeress **8** preacher, sorcerer **9** Cassandra, divinator, geomancer, predictor, sorceress **10** evangelist, forecaster, foreteller, prophesier, prophetess, soothsayer **11** clairvoyant, intercessor, interpreter **12** crystal gazer **13** fortuneteller **14** prognosticator

Prophet, major **6** Baruch, Daniel, Elijah, Isaiah **7** Ezekiel **8** Jeremiah

Prophet, minor **3** Gad **4** Amos, Joel **5** Hosea, Jonah, Micah, Nahum **6** Haggai, Nathan **7** Malachi, Obadiah **8** Habakkuk **9** Zechariah, Zephaniah

Prophetess **4** Anna **6** Miriam **7** Deborah

prophetic, prophetical **5** vatic **6** mantic **7** fateful, ominous **8** oracular **10** portentous, predictive, presageful

Prophetic Books
author: **12** William Blake

Prophet of famine **11** Agabus

prophylactic **8** hygienic **10** preventive **13** contraceptive

propinquity **7** kinship **8** affinity, nearness, vicinity **9** closeness, proximity **10** similarity

propitiate **4** calm **5** allay **6** pacify, soothe **7** appease, assuage, mollify, placate **10** conciliate **11** accommodate

propitiation **8** soothing **11** appeasement **12** conciliation, pacification

propitious **3** fit **5** bonny, happy, lucky **6** benign, golden **8** suitable **9** agreeable, favorable, fortunate, opportune, promising, well-timed **10** auspicious, beneficial, felicitous **12** advantageous, providential

Propoetides
form: **7** maidens
home: **6** Cypria
changed into: **5** stone
angered: **9** Aphrodite
denied her: **8** divinity

proponent **6** backer, friend, patron, votary **7** booster **8** advocate, champion, defender, endorser, espouser, exponent, partisan, upholder **9** apologist, spokesman, supporter **10** enthusiast, vindicator **14** representative

proportion **5** ratio **7** balance, harmony **8** evenness, symmetry **9** agreement **11** consistency, correlation, perspective **12** distribution, relationship **14** commensuration, correspondence

proportionate **5** equal **8** balanced **10** comparable, equivalent **12** commensurate **13** commensurable, corresponding

proportions **3** fit, lot **4** area, bulk, form, gear, mass, part, size, span **5** adapt, gauge, grade, match, order, poise, quota, range, ratio, scope, shape, share, width **6** amount, degree, equate, extent, spread, volume **7** balance, breadth, conform, correct, expanse, measure, portion, rectify, segment **8** capacity, division, equalize, fraction, graduate, modulate, regulate **9** amplitude, apportion, greatness, harmonize, magnitude **10** dimensions **12** measurements

proposal **3** bid **4** idea, plan, plot, suit **5** draft, offer **6** appeal, course, design, motion, scheme, sketch, theory **7** outline, proffer, program, project **8** overture, prospect **9** stratagem **10** conception, invitation, nomination, prospectus, resolution, suggestion **11** proposition **12** presentation **14** recommendation

propose **3** aim, woo **4** hope, mean, plan, plot **6** aspire, design, expect, intend, scheme, submit, tender **7** advance, present, proffer, purpose, suggest, venture **8** affiance, propound, put forth, set about, set forth **9** determine, have a mind, introduce, recommend, undertake **10** come up with, have in mind, have in view, put forward **11** contemplate **14** pop the question **21** offer for consideration

proposition **4** deal, pass, plan **5** issue, offer, point, topic **6** matter, scheme **7** advance, bargain, solicit, subject **8** contract, proposal, question **9** agreement, assurance, guarantee **10** resolution, suggestion **11** make a pass at, negotiation, stipulation, undertaking **14** recommendation

propound **4** pose **5** boost **6** assert **7** advance, profess, propose **8** put forth, set forth

proprieties **7** decorum, manners **8** protocol **9** amenities, etiquette **10** civilities **11** conventions

proprietor **5** owner **6** holder, master **7** manager **8** landlord **9** landowner, possessor **10** landholder **11** titleholder **12** proprietress

propriety **7** aptness, decorum, dignity, fitness **8** courtesy **9** etiquette, formality, rightness **10** seemliness **11** correctness, good manners, savoir faire **12** becomingness, decorousness, good behavior, suitableness **13** applicability **14** respectability **15** appropriateness

propulsion **6** launch, thrust **9** launching **10** propelling

prop up **5** brace **7** bolster, support **8** buttress

prorate **6** divide **9** apportion **10** distribute

Prorsa *see* **9** Antevorta

prosaic **3** dry **4** blah, dull, flat **5** prosy, stale, trite, vapid, wordy **6** common, jejune **7** humdrum, tedious **8** ordinary, plebeian, tiresome **9** hackneyed **10** monotonous, pedestrian, spiritless, unpoetical **12** matter-of-fact **13** platitudinous, unimaginative, uninteresting

Prosclystius
epithet of: **8** Poseidon
means: **7** flooder

proscribe **3** ban **4** damn **5** curse, exile **6** banish, forbid, outlaw **7** boycott, censure, condemn **8** denounce, prohibit **9** interdict, repudiate **10** disapprove **12** anathematize **13** excommunicate

proscription **3** ban **7** barring, censure **8** anathema **9** interdict **11** forbiddance, prohibition **12** condemnation, denunciation, interdiction **15** excommunication

prose **3** dry **4** dull **5** novel **7** fiction, quality, tedious, writing **8** sequence **9** discourse **10** expression **11** commonplace **13** unimaginative

prosecute **3** sue, try **4** wage **6** direct, go with, handle, indict, manage, pursue **7** arraign, carry on, conduct, execute, go to law, perform, prolong, stick to, sustain **8** continue, deal with, follow up, maintain **9** discharge, persist in **10** administer, put on trial, see through **11** take to court **12** bring to trial **14** bring to justice

prosecution **4** suit **6** action **7** conduct, pursuit **11** performance **14** administration

Proserpina *see* **10** Persephone

prosit **11** may it do good
used as: **5** toast

prospect, prospects **4** hope, plan, seek, view **5** scene, vista **6** aspect, design, search, vision **7** chances, explore, go after, look for, outlook, picture, promise, scenery **8** ambition, panorama, proposal

9 candidate, foretaste, intention, landscape, work a mine **10** expectancy, likelihood **11** expectation, possibility, probability **12** anticipation **13** contemplation

prospective 4 to be **6** coming, future, in view, likely, to come **7** looming **8** destined, eventual, expected, foreseen, hoped-for, intended, possible **9** about to be, impending, in the wind, looked-for, potential, promising **10** in prospect **11** approaching, forthcoming, threatening

prosper 4 gain **5** get on **6** flower, thrive **7** advance, succeed **8** fare well, flourish, fructify, get ahead, grow rich, increase, make good, progress **9** bear fruit **15** make one's fortune

prosperity 4 ease, gain **6** luxury, plenty, profit, wealth **7** advance, success, welfare **8** good luck, progress **9** abundance, advantage, affluence, blessings, golden age, good times, palmy days, run of luck, well-being **11** advancement, good fortune
 god of: 4 Frey **5** Freyr, Niord, Njord **12** Bonus Eventus
 goddess of: 5 Salus

Prospero
 character in: 10 The Tempest
 author: 11 Shakespeare

prosperous 4 fair, good, rich, rosy **5** happy, lucky, sunny **6** bright, golden, timely **7** hopeful, moneyed, opulent, smiling, wealthy, well-off **8** affluent, cheering, pleasing, thriving, well-to-do **9** favorable, fortunate, opportune, promising **10** auspicious, heartening, of good omen, propitious, reassuring, successful **11** comfortable, encouraging, flourishing **12** on easy street

Pross, Miss
 character in: 16 A Tale of Two Cities
 author: 7 Dickens

prostitute 4 bawd, jade, slut, tart **5** abuse, hussy, lower, spoil, whore **6** chippy, debase, defile, demean, floozy, harlot, hooker, misuse **7** cheapen, corrupt, debauch, degrade, hustler, pervert, profane, sell out, trollop **8** call girl, misapply, strumpet **9** courtesan, desecrate, misdirect, misemploy **12** streetwalker **14** lady of the night

prostrate 4 deck, flat **5** abase, floor, prone, spent **6** fagged, kowtow **7** bow down, flatten, laid out, worn out **8** bowed low, overcome **9** bone weary, crouching, dead tired, exhausted, kneel down, lying flat, overthrow, recumbent **10** beseeching, horizontal **11** on one's knees **12** on bended knee, stretched out, supplicating **13** lying face down **15** fall to one's knees

prostration 3 bow, woe **5** grief **6** misery, sorrow **7** anguish, despair **8** distress, kneeling, weakness **9** abasement, dejection, heartache, impotence, lowliness, paralysis, weariness **10** depression, desolation, enervation, exhaustion, subjection, submission **11** desperation, despondency **12** genuflection, helplessness, wretchedness **13** depth of misery

prosy 4 dull, flat **5** banal, inane **6** stupid **7** humdrum, prosaic, tedious **9** wearisome **11** commonplace **13** uninteresting

protagonist 4 diva, hero, lead, star **7** heroine **9** headliner, principal, superstar, title role **10** leading man, prima donna **11** leading lady **12** danseur noble, jeune premier **13** jeune premiere, main character **14** prima ballerina **16** central character

protect 4 hide, keep, save, tend, veil **5** cover, guard **6** defend, harbor, screen, secure, shield **7** care for, shelter, sustain **8** conserve, maintain, preserve **9** look after, safeguard, watch over **10** take care of

protected 4 safe **5** saved **6** immune, secure **7** guarded, secured **8** anchored, defended, shielded **9** sheltered **10** inviolable **12** invulnerable

protection 3 aid **4** care, keep, wall **5** cover, fence, guard, haven, shade **6** asylum, buffer, charge, harbor, refuge, safety, saving, screen, shield **7** barrier, custody, defense, shelter, support **8** guarding, immunity, preserve, security **9** preserver, safeguard, sanctuary **10** assistance **11** safekeeping **12** championship, conservation, guardianship, preservation

protective 7 careful, heedful **8** fatherly, guarding, maternal, motherly, paternal, sisterly, vigilant, watchful **9** avuncular, brotherly, defensive, shielding **10** preventive, sheltering, solicitous **11** safekeeping **12** big-brotherly, safeguarding

protective covering 4 coat, hust, mail **5** armor, shell **6** shield **7** coating, plating **8** carapace **10** coat of mail **11** suit of armor **12** armor plating

protectorate 6 colony **7** mandate **8** province, dominion **9** satellite, territory **10** dependency, possession, settlement

protege 4 ward **5** pupil **6** charge **7** student, trainee **9** dependent

pro tempore 9 temporary **11** temporarily **15** for the time being

Protesilaus
 father: 8 Iphiclus
 brother: 8 Podarces
 wife: 8 Laodamia

protest 3 vow **4** aver, avow, beef, deny, kick **5** gripe, march, offer, sit-in, speak, state **6** affirm, allege, assert, assure, attest, avouch, cry out, insist, object, oppose, strike **7** boycott, contend, declare, dispute, dissent, hold out, profess, testify **8** announce, complain, demurral, disagree, maintain, propound, put forth, set forth **9** enunciate, objection, picketing, pronounce **10** asseverate, contradict, controvert, disapprove, disclaimer, dissidence, opposition, put forward, resistance **11** beg to differ, deprecation **12** disaffection, disagreement, remonstrance, renunciation **13** contradiction, demonstration, remonstration, take exception **14** discountenance

Protestant 5 Amish **6** Mormon, Quaker, Shaker **7** Baptist, Puritan **8** Anglican, Huguenot, Lutheran **9** Adventist, Calvinist, Methodist, Unitarian **12** Episcopalian, Presbyterian **17** Congregationalist **18** Christian Scientist

protest meeting 5 rally **13** demonstration

Proteus
 character in: 20 Two Gentlemen of Verona
 author: 11 Shakespeare

Proteus
 god of: 3 sea
 king of: 5 Egypt
 father: 7 Oceanus
 mother: 6 Tethys
 wife: 8 Psamathe
 son: 12 Theoclymenus
 daughter: 7 Theonoe

gift: **8** prophesy **12** form-changing **13** shape-changing

Prothoenor
leader of: **9** Boeotians

Protoceratops
type: **8** dinosaur **10** ceratopsid
period: **10** Cretaceous
location: **8** Mongolia **10** Gobi Desert
characteristic: **6** horned **7** armored

protocol **5** usage **7** customs, decorum, manners **8** good form **9** amenities, etiquette, formality, standards **11** conventions, proprieties **14** code of behavior, court etiquette, diplomatic code **17** dictates of society

Protogonia
father: **10** Erechtheus
mother: **9** Praxithea
sister: **7** Otionia

prototypal **5** model **7** classic **9** exemplary **10** archetypal, definitive **12** prototypical

prototype **5** model **7** example **8** original **9** archetype

protozoan **4** cell **5** ameba, cilia **6** amoeba **7** euglena **8** flagella, protista **9** eukaryote, pseudopod **10** paramecium, plasmodium **11** microscopic, unicellular **17** nonphotosynthetic

protract **6** extend, keep up **7** drag out, draw out, prolong, spin out **8** lengthen **9** keep going **10** stretch out

protracted **4** long **7** lengthy **8** drawn-out, extended **9** continued, long-lived, prolonged **10** lengthened, persistent **11** long-lasting

protraction **4** stay **7** lasting **9** extension **10** continuing, drawing out **11** continuance, dragging out, persistence **12** perseverance, prolongation

protrude **5** belly, bulge, swell **6** jut out **7** project **8** stand out, stick out **11** push forward

protrusion **4** bump, hump **6** hernia **8** swelling **9** extension **10** projection **12** prolongation, protuberance

protuberance **3** bow **4** bump, hump, knob, knot, lump, node, weal, welt **5** bulge, gnarl, ridge **6** rising **8** swelling **9** convexity, elevation, roundness **10** projection, prominence **11** excrescence, excurvature

protura
class: **8** hexapoda
phylum: **10** arthropoda
characteristic: **5** small **6** minute **7** eyeless **8** wingless

proud **4** fine, smug, vain **5** aloof, cocky, grand, great, happy, lofty, noble **6** august, lordly, snooty, snotty, strict, uppish, uppity **7** bloated, exalted, haughty, high-hat, pleased, pompous, revered, stately, storied, stuck-up, swollen **8** affected, arrogant, assuming, boastful, braggart, bragging, elevated, euphoric, glorious, inflated, insolent, majestic, prideful, puffed up, reserved, snobbish **9** admirable, cherished, conceited, contented, delighted, dignified, flaunting, gratified, honorable, imperious, know-it-all, satisfied, venerable **10** complacent, disdainful, high-minded, intolerant, principled, scrupulous **11** egotistical, independent, magnificent, overbearing, patronizing, punctilious **12** contemptuous, self-praising, supercilious, vainglorious **13** condescending, distinguished, high-and-mighty, self-important, self-satisfied **14** self-respecting, self-sufficient

Proudie, Dr
character in: **16** Barchester Towers
author: **8** Trollope

Proust, Marcel
author of: **23** Remembrance of Things Past **24** A la Recherche du Temps Perdu

prove **3** try **4** test **5** check, end up, probe **6** affirm, attest, result, try out, uphold, verify, wind up **7** analyze, bear out, certify, confirm, examine, justify, support, sustain, warrant, witness **8** document, evidence, look into, make good, manifest, result in, validate **9** ascertain, establish, eventuate, testify to **11** corroborate, demonstrate **12** authenticate, substantiate

proved **5** known **6** proven, upheld **8** affirmed, attested, borne out, verified **9** certified, confirmed, supported, sustained, warranted, witnessed **10** documented **11** established **12** corroborated, demonstrable **13** authenticated, substantiated

prove false **5** belie **6** refute, reject **7** explode **8** disprove **9** discredit **10** invalidate

proven **5** known **6** proved, upheld **8** accepted, affirmed, attested, borne out, verified **9** certified, confirmed, supported, sustained, warranted, witnessed **10** documented, verifiable **11** established **12** corroborated, demonstrable **13** authenticated, substantiated

provender **3** hay **4** chow, corn, eats, feed, food, grub, oats **5** grain **6** fodder, forage, ration, viands **7** nurture **10** provisions **11** subsistence

proverb **3** mot, saw **5** adage, axiom, maxim, moral, motto **6** byword, cliche, dictum, saying, truism **7** bromide, epigram, precept **8** aphorism, apothegm **9** platitude **11** commonplace **13** accepted truth, popular saying

prove wrong **5** belie **6** expose, refute **7** explode **8** disprove **9** discredit

provide **3** arm, fit, pay **4** give, plan **5** allow, award, cater, equip, grant, offer, state, yield **6** accord, afford, bestow, confer, donate, impart, outfit, render, save up, submit, supply, tender **7** arrange, deliver, furnish, prepare, present, produce, require, specify **8** dispense, get ready **9** make plans, postulate, stipulate **10** accumulate, contribute

provide for **7** care for **8** attend to, wait upon **9** look after **10** minister to, take care of

providence **8** prudence **9** foresight, husbandry, provision **11** forethought **14** circumspection, farsightedness, forehandedness

provident **4** wary **5** chary, ready **6** frugal, saving **7** careful, prudent, thrifty **8** cautious, discreet, equipped, vigilant **9** farseeing, judicious **10** discerning, economical, farsighted, forehanded, foreseeing, thoughtful **11** circumspect, foresighted, precautious **12** parsimonious, well-prepared

province **3** job **4** area, duty, part, role, zone **5** field, place, state **6** canton, charge, county, domain, office, region, sphere **7** section, station **8** business, capacity, function **9** authority, bailiwick, territory **10** assignment, department **11** subdivision **12** jurisdiction **13** scope of duties **14** arrondissement, responsibility

provincial **4** rude **5** crude, gawky, local, rough, rural **6** clumsy, gauche, homely, narrow, oafish, rustic **7** awkward, boorish, bucolic, country, hayseed, insular, loutish **8** cloddish, clownish, downhome, homespun, regional, yokelish **9** backwoods, parochial, small-town, unrefined **10** unpolished **11** clodhopping, countrified, territorial **15** unsophisticated

provision **6** giving **8** donation **9** endowment, providing, supplying **10** furnishing

provisional **6** acting, pro tem **7** interim **9** surrogate, temporary, tentative **10** substitute **11** conditional **12** probationary **15** for the time being

provisions **4** feed, food, term **6** clause, fodder, forage, stores, string, viands **7** article, commons, edibles, proviso **8** eatables, supplies, victuals **9** condition, groceries, provender, readiness, requisite **10** limitation, obligation, precaution, sustenance **11** arrangement, comestibles, forethought, preparation, requirement, reservation, restriction, stipulation, wherewithal **12** anticipation, modification **13** qualification **14** forehandedness, prearrangement

proviso **5** rider **6** clause, string **8** addition **9** amendment, condition **10** limitation **11** requirement, restriction, stipulation **12** modification **13** qualification

provocation **4** goad, spur **5** cause, pique **6** insult, slight **7** affront, offense **8** prodding, stimulus, vexation **9** actuation, annoyance **10** excitation, incitement, irritation, motivation **11** aggravation, fomentation, instigation, stimulation **12** perturbation

provocative **4** sexy **6** vexing **7** irksome **8** alluring, annoying, arousing, exciting, inviting, tempting **9** beguiling, provoking, ravishing, seductive, thrilling, vexatious **10** attractive, bewitching, enchanting, entrancing, intriguing, irritating **11** aggravating, captivating, fascinating, stimulating, tantalizing **12** intoxicating, irresistible

provoke **3** irk, vex **4** fire, gall, move, rile, stir **5** anger, annoy, cause, chafe, evoke, grate, impel, pique, rouse **6** arouse, awaken, compel, create, effect, elicit, enrage, excite, foment, incite, induce, kindle, madden, prompt, put out, stir up **7** actuate, agitate, animate, bring on, incense, inflame, inspire, outrage, produce, quicken **8** generate, get to one, irritate, motivate **9** aggravate, call forth, establish, galvanize, infuriate, instigate, stimulate **10** bring about, exasperate, give rise to **11** get one's goat, put in motion **15** try one's patience **16** get under one's skin

prow **3** bow **4** stem **5** front **10** forward end

prowess **4** grit, guts **5** knack, might, nerve, power, skill, spunk, valor, vigor **6** daring, genius, mettle, spirit, talent **7** ability, bravery, courage, faculty, heroism, know-how, stamina **8** aptitude, boldness, strength **9** adeptness, derring-do, endurance, fortitude, gallantry, hardihood **10** competence, expertness **11** intrepidity, proficiency **12** fearlessness, skillfulness **13** dauntlessness **14** accomplishment

prowl **4** hunt, lurk, roam **5** creep, range, skulk, slink, snack, stalk, steal **6** ramble **8** scavenge

prowler **7** burglar **10** peeping Tom **16** suspicious person

proximate **4** near **5** close **6** beside, nearby, next to **8** adjacent, imminent, next-door **11** forthcoming

proximity **7** presence **8** locality, nearness, vicinity **9** closeness **10** contiguity **11** propinquity **12** togetherness

proxy **3** sub **4** vote **5** agent **6** ballot, deputy **7** stand-in **9** alternate **10** substitute

prude **4** prig **6** modest **7** puritan **9** hypocrite **10** goody-goody **13** prim and proper

prudence **4** care, tact **6** thrift, wisdom **7** caution, economy **9** austerity, foresight, frugality, parsimony **10** discretion, precaution **11** calculation, thriftiness **14** thoughtfulness

prudent **4** sage, sane, wary, wise **5** chary **6** frugal, saving, shrewd **7** careful, guarded, heedful, politic, sapient, sparing, thrifty **8** cautious, discreet, prepared, rational, sensible, vigilant **9** expedient, judicious, provident, sagacious, wideawake **10** discerning, economical, farsighted, prudential, reflecting, thoughtful **11** circumspect, considerate, foresighted, levelheaded, precautious, well-advised **13** self-possessed

Prud'hon, Pierre-Paul
born: **5** Cluny **6** France
artwork: **14** Venus and Adonis **15** The Rape of Psyche **16** Empress Josephine **33** Crime Pursued by Vengeance and Justice **38** Justice and Divine Vengeance Pursuing Crime

prudish **3** shy **4** prim, smug **5** timid **6** demure, modest, prissy, queasy, stuffy **7** finical, mincing, precise, stilted **8** pedantic, priggish, skittish, starched **9** squeamish, Victorian **10** fastidious, old-maidish, overmodest, particular **11** punctilious, puritanical, straitlaced **13** sanctimonious, self-righteous

prudishness **8** primness **10** prissiness, puritanism **11** overmodesty **12** overdelicacy, priggishness **14** overrefinement

prudish phrase **9** euphemism **10** bowdlerism

prune **3** cut, lop **4** clip, crop, pull, snip, thin, trim **5** shear **6** reduce **7** abridge, clarify, curtail, shorten, thin out **8** condense, simplify **10** abbreviate

prunelle
type: **7** liqueur
origin: **6** France
flavor: **4** plum

pruning **6** digest **8** clipping, snipping, synopsis, trimming **10** shortening **11** abridgement, cutting back, cut-down form **12** abbreviation, condensation

prurient **4** lewd, sexy **6** carnal **7** fleshy, goatish, immoral, lustful, obscene, priapic, satyric **9** lecherous, salacious **10** hot-blooded, lascivious, libidinous, licentious, lubricious, passionate **12** concupiscent

pry **4** butt, nose, peek, peer, poke, tear, work, worm **5** break, crack, delve, force, jimmy, lever, mix in, prize, probe, smoke, sniff, snoop, wrest, wring **6** butt in, ferret, horn in, meddle, search, winkle, wrench **7** explore, extract, inquire, intrude, squeeze **9** interfere, intervene **15** stick one's nose in

Pryderi
origin: **5** Welsh
father: **5** Pwyll
mother: **8** Rhiannon
stolen by: **5** Gwawl
wife: **5** Kicva

prying **4** busy, nosy **7** peering, raising, seeking **8** levering, snooping **9** searching **10** intrusive, meddling **11** inquisitive

Prylis
father: **6** Hermes

Prynne, Hester
character in: **16** The Scarlet Letter
author: **9** Hawthorne

Pryor, Richard
born: **8** Peoria IL
roles: **6** The Wiz **9** Stir Crazy **12** Silver Streak **17** Lady Sings the Blues **19** Uptown Saturday Night

Prytanis
ally of: **8** Sarpedon
killed by: **8** Odysseus

psalm **3** ode **4** hymn, poem, song **5** canon, chant, verse **6** praise **7** cantata, glorify, introit **8** canticle

Psalter **12** Book of Psalms

Psamathe
member of: **6** Nereid
form: **8** princess
husband: **7** Proteus
son: **5** Linus **6** Phocus **12** Theoclymenus
daughter: **7** Theonoe

pseudo **4** fake, mock, sham **5** bogus, false, phony **6** forged **7** feigned **8** spurious **9** pretended, simulated, soi-disant **10** fictitious, fraudulent, self-styled **11** counterfeit, make-believe **13** self-described

pseudonym **5** alias **6** anonym **7** pen name **8** cognomen, nickname **9** false name, sobriquet, stage name **11** assumed name **16** professional name
French: **10** nom de plume **11** nom de guerre **12** nom de theatre

pseudonymic **7** assumed **10** fictitious **12** pseudonymous

pseudonymous **7** assumed **10** fictitious **11** pseudonymic

Psittacosaurus
type: **8** dinosaur **10** ceratopsid
period: **10** Cretaceous

psocoptera
class: **8** hexapoda
phylum: **10** arthropoda
group: **8** booklice

psyche **2** id **3** ego **4** mind, self, soul **5** anima **6** bowels, make up, spirit **8** superego **10** penetralia **11** personality, unconscious **12** subconscious

Psyche
personifies: **4** soul
loved by: **4** Eros **5** Cupid
daughter: **8** Voluptas

psychic **5** augur **6** medium, mental, mystic, occult, voyant **7** diviner, prophet, voyante **8** cerebral **9** paragnost, sensitive, spiritual **10** soothsayer, telepathic **11** clairvoyant, telekinetic, telepathist **12** extrasensory, intellectual, spiritualist, supernatural, supersensory **13** preternatural

Psycho
director: **15** Alfred Hitchcock
cast: **9** John Gavin, Vera Miles **10** Janet Leigh **12** Martin Balsam **14** Anthony Perkins
score: **15** Bernard Herrmann

psychoanalysis **7** therapy **8** analysis **14** physchotherapy

psychoanalyst **6** shrink **7** analyst **12** headshrinker

psychologist / psychiatrist
American: **4** Hall, Hull **5** Dewey, James, Lewin **6** Harlow, Horney, Miller, Rogers, Terman, Tolman, Watson, Witmer **7** Cattell, Chomsky, Erikson, Goddard, Guthrie, Johnson, Masters, Skinner **8** Brothers, Wechsler **9** Thorndike **10** Westheimer
Austrian: **5** Adler, Freud, Reich
British: **5** Ellis **7** Eysenck **9** Titchener
French: **5** Binet
German: **5** Wundt **6** Koffka, Kohler **7** Fechner **9** Helmholtz, Kraepelin **10** Ebbinghaus, Wertheimer **11** Krafft-Ebing
Russian: **6** Pavlov
Swiss: **4** Jung **6** Piaget

psychology ***see box***

psychopomp
conductor of spirits to: **5** Hades **10** otherworld
epithet: **12** psychopompus
epithet of: **6** Charon, Hermes

psychosis **8** dementia, insanity, neurosis, paranoia **9** paranomia, unreality **10** pathomania **12** hallucinosis **13** schizophrenia **14** mental disorder

psychotherapy **7** therapy **8** analysis **14** psychoanalysis

psychotic **3** mad, nut **4** kook, loon **5** crazy, kooky, loony, nutty **6** insane, madman, maniac **7** lunatic **8** demented, deranged **9** disturbed **10** psychopath **12** insane person, psychopathic **15** non compos mentis

---

psychology **4** head, mind **6** makeup **7** feeling **8** attitude **15** mental processes
problem / illness: **6** phobia **7** obesity, smoking **8** hysteria, neuroses, paranoia, schizoid **9** drug abuse, obsession, psychoses **10** alcoholism, compulsion, depression **11** sociopathic **13** schizophrenia **14** sexual deviance **15** anxiety reaction **17** passive-aggressive
term: **2** id **3** ego **6** libido **7** empathy **8** neuroses, superego **9** catatonic, cognition, psychoses **10** inhibition, repression **11** behaviorism, unconscious **12** conditioning, transference **13** actualization, Rorschach test **14** identification, Oedipus complex **19** operant conditioning **20** behavior modification
type: **6** social **7** Gestalt **8** abnormal, clinical **9** cognitive **10** industrial **11** educational **12** experimental **13** developmental, physiological, psychometrics, psychophysics

---

Ptah
origin: **8** Egyptian
diety of: **17** universal creation
worshiped at: **7** Memphis

Pterelaus
descendant of: **8** Poseidon
mother: **9** Hippothoe
daughter: **8** Comaetho

Ptolemy
author of: **8** Almagest **9** Geography

Ptous
father: **7** Athamas
mother: **8** Themisto

pub **3** bar, inn **5** local **6** bistro, saloon, lounge, tavern **7** barroom, ginmill, rummery, rumshop, taproom **8** alehouse, grogshop, pothouse **9** roadhouse, speakeasy **10** beer parlor **11** public house

pubescent **7** teenage **8** immature, juvenile **10** adolescent

public ***see box***

publication **4** book, news **5** is-

public **3** mob **4** folk, open **5** civic, civil, frank, overt, plain, state, trade **6** buyers, common, in view, masses, nation, patent, people, shared, social **7** evident, exposed, general, in sight, obvious, outward, patrons, popular, society, visible **8** apparent, audience, communal, divulged, everyone, manifest, national, passable, populace, revealed, societal, unbarred, unfenced **9** available, citizenry, clientele, community, disclosed, followers, following, free to all, hoi polloi, multitude, notorious, political, statewide, unabashed, unashamed, unbounded, used by all **10** accessible, attendance, nationwide, not private, observable, population, purchasers, recognized, supporters, unenclosed **11** body politic, bourgeoisie, commonality, conspicuous, countrywide, discernible, perceivable, proletariat, rank and file, unconcealed, undisguised **12** acknowledged, constituency, unobstructed, unrestricted **14** community-owned

sue, paper **6** digest, report **7** edition, gazette, journal, tabloid **8** bulletin, magazine, pamphlet **9** broadcast, newspaper **10** periodical **11** circulation, information **12** announcement, notification

public disturbance **4** riot **6** fracas, ruckus, uproar **7** turmoil **9** commotion

public house **3** bar, pub **5** local **6** saloon, tavern **7** gin mill, taproom **8** alehouse **9** roadhouse

publicity **4** hype, plug, puff **5** blurb, flack **7** build-up, puffery, write-up **8** ballyhoo, currency **9** attention, notoriety, promotion **10** propaganda, publicness **11** advertising, circulation, information **12** promulgation, public notice, salesmanship

publicize **4** hype, plug, puff, push, sell **6** herald **7** acclaim, promote **8** announce, ballyhoo, emblazon, proclaim **9** advertise, broadcast, make known, propagate **10** make public, promulgate **11** circularize **12** propagandize

publicly
Latin: **11** coram populo

public matter
Latin: **10** res publica

public notice **5** edict, ukase **6** decree **8** bulletin **9** manifesto **12** proclamation **13** pronouncement **14** pronunciamento
French: **7** affiche

public speaking **7** oratory **9** lecturing **12** speechmaking

public-spirited **8** generous **10** altruistic, benevolent **12** humanitarian

publish **3** air **4** tell, vent **5** issue, print, utter **6** herald, impart, put out, spread **7** declare, diffuse, divulge, give out, placard, promote, release, trumpet **8** announce, bring out, disclose, proclaim **9** advertise, broadcast, circulate, make known, propagate, publicize **10** make public, promulgate, put to press **11** communicate, disseminate

Puca
also: **5** Pooka
origin: **5** Irish
form: **6** spirit
corresponds to: **4** Puck

Puccini, Giacomo
born: **5** Italy, Lucca
composer of: **5** Tosca **8** La Boheme, Turandot **12** Manon Lescaut **14** Madam Butterfly **15** Madama Butterfly **18** La Fanciulla del West **22** The Girl of the Golden West

puce **3** red **7** dark red **13** purplish-brown

Puck
also: **15** Robin Goodfellow
character in: **21** A Midsummer Night's Dream
author: **11** Shakespeare
form: **6** spirit
characteristic: **11** mischievous
corresponds to: **4** Puca **5** Pooka

pucker **4** fold, tuck **5** pinch, pleat, purse **6** crease, gather, ruffle, rumple, shrink **7** crinkle, crumble, squeeze, wrinkle **8** compress, contract **12** draw together

puckered **6** pursed, rucked, tucked **7** creased, crinkly, pinched, pleated **8** crinkled, gathered, wrinkled **10** compressed, corrugated

puckish **5** elfin **6** impish **7** playful **8** annoying **9** whimsical **11** mischievous

pudding **5** jello **6** junket **7** custard, dessert, tapioca **8** pandowdy **9** charlotte, yorkshire **14** floating island

pudgy, podgy **3** fat **5** buxom, dumpy, obese, plump, squat, stout, tubby **6** chubby, chunky, fleshy, rotund, stocky, stubby **7** paunchy **8** roly-poly, thickset

Pueblo (Cliff Dwellers)
language family: **4** Tewa, Zuni **6** Queres, Tanoan **10** Shoshonean
tribe: **4** Hopi, Tiwa, Towa, Tuei **5** Acoma, Kiowa **6** Isleta
location: **4** Utah **7** Arizona **8** Colorado **9** New Mexico
noted for: **5** adobe **12** architecture
spirit: **7** Kachina **8** Katchina

puerile **3** raw **5** green, inane, petty, silly, vapid **6** callow, simple **7** babyish, foolish, trivial **8** childish, immature, juvenile, piddling **9** childlike, frivolous, infantile, senseless, worthless **10** irrational, ridiculous, sophomoric **11** harebrained, nonsensical

Puerto Rico ***see box, p. 794***

puff **3** bow **4** blow, draw, emit, gasp, hump, node, pant, plug, suck, wisp **5** bloat, blurb, bulge, heave, smoke, swell, whiff **6** blow up, breath, dilate, exhale, expand, extend, flurry, inhale, rising, wheeze **7** bluster, bombast, distend, inflate, puffery, stretch **8** ballyhoo, be winded, dilation, encomium, flattery, flummery, swelling **9** convexity, discharge, elevation, euphemism, extension, inflation, panegyric, publicity, sales talk **10** be inflated, distention, exhalation, overpraise, protrusion, tuberosity **11** be distended, breathe hard, excrescence, excurvature **12** exaggeration, inflammation, protuberance, protuberancy **13** overlaudation **16** overcommendation **17** misrepresentation

puffed **5** baggy **7** bulbous, swollen **9** ballooned

puffed up **4** vain **5** proud, puffy **7** swollen **8** inflated **9** conceited **11** swell-headed **12** vainglorious **13** self-important

puffery **4** hype **7** big talk, blus-

Puerto Rico
name means: 8 rich port
other name: 9 Borinquen **15** San Juan Bautista
capital/largest city: 7 San Juan
others: 5 Cayey, Coamo, Lares, Ponce **6** Caguas, Dorado, Manati, Utuado **7** Arecibo, Bayamon, Fajardo, Guanica, Guayama, Humacao **8** Adjuntas, Cabo Rojo, Mayaguez **9** Aquadilla **11** Santa Isabel
government: 32 self-governing commonwealth of the U S
measure: 6 cuerda **10** caballeria
island: 4 Mona **7** Culebra, Vieques **13** Caja de Muertos **15** Greater Antilles
lake: 5 Loiza **6** Carite **8** Dos Bocas **9** Caonillas, Guatajaca
mountain: 4 Toro **5** Cayey **6** Yunque **8** Guilarte, Luquilla **10** Torrecilla **17** Cordillera Central
highest point: 5 Punta
river: 5 Camuy, Canas, Loiza, Yauco **6** Anasco, Manati, Tanama **7** Arecibo, Fajardo, La Plata **9** Caonillas
sea: 8 Atlantic **9** Caribbean
physical feature:
bay: **5** Sucia **6** Rincon **8** Boqueron **9** Aquadilla **14** Phosphorescent
sound: **7** Vieques
people: 6 gibaro **10** borinqueno
explorer: **8** Columbus **11** Ponce de Leon
leader: **10** Munoz Marin
language: 7 English, Spanish
religion: 10 Protestant **13** Roman Catholic
place:
area of San Juan: **7** Hato Rey **10** Rio Piedras
beach: **7** Condado
cathedral: **15** San Juan Bautista
fortress: **7** El Morro **11** San Jeronimo **12** San Cristobal
governor's residence: **11** La Fortaleza
museum: **14** El Museo de Ponce
reservoir: **5** Loiza
tomb: **11** Ponce de Leon
feature:
bird: **4** rola **7** yeguita
festival: **6** Casals
housing development: **14** urbanizaciones
song: **9** aguinaldo
strolling musicians: **9** parrandas
tree: **4** mora **5** yafua, yaray **8** emajagua, guayrote **10** guaranguao
food:
dish: **4** sama, sisi **9** moreillas **11** lechon asado
drink: **3** rum **10** anis-golila

ter, bombast **9** hyperbole **11** braggadocio

puff out 5 bloat, bulge, swell **6** billow, expand **7** balloon, distend, enlarge, inflate

puffy 3 fat **5** round **6** fleshy **7** bloated, bulging, swollen **8** enlarged, expanded, inflamed, inflated, puffed up **9** corpulent, distended

pugilist 3 pug **5** boxer **7** battler, bruiser, fighter **12** prizefighter

pugnacious 7 defiant, hostile, warlike **8** menacing, militant **9** bellicose, combative, fractious **10** aggressive, unfriendly **11** belligerent, contentious, quarrelsome, threatening **12** antagonistic, disputatious **13** argumentative

pugnacity 9 hostility **10** antagonism **12** belligerence **13** combativeness **14** aggressiveness, fighting spirit **15** contentiousness

puissance 5 force, might, power **6** energy **7** potency, prowess **8** strength

pulchritude 6 beauty **8** fairness **9** bonniness, good looks **10** comeliness, loveliness, prettiness **12** gorgeousness, handsomeness **13** beauteousness, exquisiteness **14** attractiveness, personableness

pulchritudinous 4 fair, fine **5** bonny **6** comely, lovely, pretty **8** gorgeous, handsome **9** beauteous, beautiful, ravishing **10** attractive **11** good-looking

Pulitzer
author: 10 W A Swanberg

Pulitzer Prize
originator: 14 Joseph Pulitzer
administered by: 18 Columbia University
awarded for: 4 play **5** drama, music, novel **6** poetry **7** cartoon, feature, fiction, letters **9** biography, criticism, editorial, reporting **10** commentary, journalism, literature, nonfiction **11** photography **13** autobiography

pull 2 go **3** lug, rip, tow, tug **4** drag, draw, grab, haul, jerk, lure, move, rend, rive, tear, yank **5** drive, sever, shake, split, trawl, troll, twist, wrest, wring **6** allure, appeal, detach, dig out, entice, remove, sprain, strain, uproot, wrench **7** attract, draw out, extract, gravity, stretch, weed out **8** withdraw **9** extirpate, influence, magnetism, take in tow **10** allurement, attraction, enticement **11** fascination **14** attractiveness

pull apart 3 rip, tug **4** drag, rend, tear **6** detach, wrench **7** extract **8** separate **9** criticize, disengage **10** disconnect

pull away 5 wrest **7** remove **8** drawback, withdraw

pull back 7 back off, retreat **8** fall back, withdraw

Pullman, George Mortimer
nationality: 8 American
developed: 9 (railroad) dining car **11** (railroad) sleeping car

pull off 4 pull **6** commit, effect **7** execute, perform **8** carry out **10** perpetuate **13** participate in

pull on 3 don **5** put on **7** get into

pull one's leg 3 kid **4** fool, hoax **5** tease, trick **7** deceive **9** make fun of

pull out 5 leave **7** draw out, extract **8** withdraw

pull over, pullover 4 cite, stop **5** shirt **6** arrest, jersey, slip on, ticket, t-shirt **7** maillot, sweater **8** slip over

pull together 4 join **5** unite

7 pitch in, share in **8** take part **9** cooperate, join hands **10** act jointly, join forces **11** collaborate, participate

pull to pieces 5 shred **6** tear up **7** destroy **9** tear apart

pull up 4 halt, rein, stop, weed **5** check, hoist **6** arrest, uplift, uproot **7** extract, reprove

pulp 4 curd, mash, mush, pith **5** crush, flesh, paste, puree, slush, smash **6** squash, tissue **7** journal **8** magazine **9** masticate

pulsate 4 beat, tick, wave **5** pound, pulse, shake, throb, thump, waver **6** quaver, quiver, shiver **7** flutter, shudder, tremble, vibrate **8** undulate **9** alternate, come and go, oscillate, palpitate **10** ebb and flow **11** reverberate

pulse 4 beat **5** throb, thump **6** quiver, rhythm, stroke **7** cadence, pulsate, shudder, tremble, vibrate **9** oscillate, palpitate, pulsation, vibration **10** recurrence, undulation **11** oscillation, palpitation

pulverize 4 mash, mill **5** crumb, crush, grind, mince, pound **6** powder **7** atomize, crumble **9** comminate, granulate, triturate **12** reduce to dust

pulverized 6 ground, milled **7** crumbed, crushed, pounded **8** atomized, crumbled, crunched, powdered **10** granulated **12** ground to dust

pummel 4 beat, maul **5** pound **6** batter, thrash **7** trounce

pump 4 quiz, shoe, well **5** grill **7** inflate, slipper **8** question **9** draw water

Pump
constellation of: 6 Antlia

Pump House Gang, The
author: 8 Tom Wolfe

pumpkin 5 fruit, gourd, melon **6** squash **9** vegetable **12** jack o'lantern

pun
French: 9 jeu de mots

punch 3 box, hit, jab **4** beat, blow, chop, clip, conk, cuff, pelt, plug, poke, slam, sock, swat **5** baste, clout, knock, paste, pound, smite, thump, whack **6** pummel, strike, stroke, thrust, thwack, wallop **7** clobber **8** haymaker **10** roundhouse

punchy 3 fat **5** dazed **6** stubby **8** confused, forceful **9** befuddled

punctilious 5 exact, fussy, picky, rigid **6** proper, strict **7** correct, finicky, precise **8** exacting, rigorous **9** demanding **10** meticulous, particular, scrupulous **11** painstaking

punctual 5 early, quick, ready **6** on time, prompt, steady, timely **7** instant, not late, regular **8** constant, on the dot **9** immediate, well-timed **10** in good time, seasonable **11** expeditious **13** instantaneous

punctuate 4 lace **5** break **6** pepper **7** scatter **8** separate, sprinkle **9** interrupt **11** intersperse

punctuation mark 4 dash **5** colon, comma, pause, point, slash **6** accent, ending, hyphen, parens, period, quotes **7** bracket **8** ellipsis **9** semicolon **10** apostrophe **11** parenthesis **12** question mark **13** quotation mark **16** exclamation point

puncture 3 cut **4** bite, hole, nick, pink **5** break, prick, stick, sting, wound **6** pierce **7** deflate, let down, opening, rupture **9** knock down, shoot down **10** depreciate **11** perforation

pundit 4 guru, sage **5** guide **6** critic, expert, master, mentor, savant, wizard **7** thinker **9** authority **13** learned person

pungent 3 hot **4** acid, keen, racy, sour, tart **5** acrid, acute, nippy, salty, sharp, smart, spicy, tangy, tasty, witty **6** biting, bitter, clever, savory, snappy, strong **7** acetous, caustic, cutting, mordent, peppery, piquant, pointed **8** incisive, piercing, poignant, smarting, stinging, stirring, vinegary, wounding **9** brilliant, flavorful, invidious, palatable, sarcastic, sparkling, trenchant **10** astringent, flavorsome, keen-witted **11** acrimonious, penetrating, provocative, stimulating, tantalizing **12** sharp-tasting **13** scintillating, sharp-smelling **14** highly flavored, highly seasoned

punish 4 beat, fine, flog, whip **6** avenge, rebuke **7** chasten, correct, reprove **8** admonish, chastise, imprison, penalize, sentence **9** castigate, dress down, retaliate **10** discipline, take to task **11** get even with, take revenge **14** bring to account **15** take vengeance on

punishing 5 harsh, penal **6** brutal, severe **7** abusive **8** scolding **9** torturing **10** chastizing, tormenting **11** castigating

punishment 4 fine **5** price **7** damages, deserts, flaying, forfeit, hanging, payment, penalty, penance, redress **8** flogging, punition, spanking, whipping **10** chastening, correction, crucifying, discipline, reparation **11** castigation, retribution **12** chastisement, penalization

punk 4 hood, lout, poor **5** bully, lousy, rowdy, tough **6** crummy, rotten **7** hoodlum, ruffian **8** hooligan **9** barbarian, roughneck **10** delinquent

Punt *see* **7** Somalia

Puntarvolo
character in: 22 Every Man Out of His Humour
author: 6 Jonson

punt e mes
type: 8 aperitif
origin: 5 Italy
flavor: 6 orange
color: 12 reddish-brown

puny 4 poor, thin, tiny, weak **5** frail, light, petty, runty, small **6** bantam, feeble, flimsy, infirm, little, meager, measly, paltry, sickly, slight, weakly **7** fragile, shallow, tenuous, trivial **8** delicate, impotent, picayune, piddling, runtlike, sawed-off, trifling **9** emaciated, miniature, mite-sized, pint-sized, worthless **10** diminutive, inadequate, picayunish, undersized **11** unimportant **12** insufficient **13** insignificant **14** inconsiderable, underdeveloped

pupa 3 egg **5** larva, nymph **6** cocoon **7** wiggler **9** chrysalis **14** transformation

pupil 4 coed, tyro **6** novice **7** learner, scholar, student, trainee **8** beginner, disciple, initiate **9** schoolboy **10** apprentice, schoolgirl **11** probationer **13** undergraduate

puppet 3 toy **4** doll, dupe, pawn, tool **6** flunky, lackey **7** cat's paw, manikin, servant **8** creature, henchman, hireling **9** jackstraw, lay figure, underling **10** figurehead, instrument, man of straw, marionette **11** subordinate

puppy 3 dog, pet, pup **6** canine

Purcell, Henry
born: 6 London **7** England
composer of: 9 Fantasias

10 Bell Anthem, Dioclesian, King Arthur (The British Worthy), The Tempest 12 Golden Sonata 13 Dido and Aeneas 14 The Indian Queen

purchase 3 buy 4 edge, hold 6 buying, pay for, pick up 7 footing, support, toehold 8 foothold, leverage 9 advantage, influence 11 acquirement, acquisition

pure 4 full, mere, neat, true 5 basic, clean, fresh, moral, sheer, stark, utter, whole 6 chaste, decent, entire, higher, virgin 7 angelic, ethical, perfect, sincere, sinless, sterile, unmixed, upright 8 absolute, abstract, complete, flawless, germfree, innocent, positive, purebred, sanitary, spotless, straight, thorough, unmarred, virginal, virtuous 9 blameless, downright, faultless, guileless, guiltless, healthful, inviolate, out-and-out, pedigreed, righteous, unalloyed, undefiled, unmingled, unspoiled, unsullied, untainted, wholesome 10 antiseptic, immaculate, inviolable, sterilized, uninfected, unmodified, unpolluted 11 conjectural, disinfected, fundamental, pure-blooded, speculative, theoretical, unblemished, uncorrupted, unqualified, untarnished 12 full-strength, hypothetical, thoroughbred 13 unadulterated, unimpeachable 14 above suspicion, uncontaminated

puree 4 bisk, pulp, soup 5 paste 6 bisque

purely 4 only 5 fully 6 merely, simply, solely, wholly 7 cleanly, morally, piously, totally 8 chastely, devoutly, entirely, worthily 9 admirably 10 absolutely, completely, flawlessly, in all honor, innocently, virginally, virtuously 11 essentially, faultlessly 13 incorruptibly

Purgatory, Purgatorio
part II of: 12 Divine Comedy
author: 14 Dante Alighieri

purge 4 kill, oust 5 crush, expel 6 banish, emetic, pardon, physic, purify, remove, uproot 7 clean up, cleanse, cleanup, clyster, dismiss, expiate, purging, rout out, shake up 8 aperient, atone for, clean out, get rid of, laxative, sweep out, wash away 9 cathartic, discharge, eliminate, eradicate, liquidate, purgation, purgative 10 do away with 11 exterminate 12 obtain pardon (from), purification 15 obtain remission (from) 16 obtain absolution (from) 17 obtain forgiveness

purification 7 baptism 9 cleansing 13 sterilization

purify 4 boil 5 clear 6 filter 7 clarify, distill 8 make pure, sanitize 9 disinfect, sterilize 10 chlorinate, pasteurize 13 decontaminate

Puritani, I
also: 11 The Puritans
opera by: 7 Bellini
character: 14 Oliver Cromwell, Queen Henrietta 16 Lord Arthur Talbot

puritanical 4 prim 5 rigid, stiff 6 narrow, prissy, severe, strict, stuffy 7 ascetic, austere, bigoted, prudish, puritan, stilted 8 dogmatic, priggish 9 bluenosed, fanatical 11 stiff-necked, straitlaced 13 sanctimonious

Puritan State
nickname of: 13 Massachusetts

purity 5 honor, piety 6 virtue 7 clarity, decency, honesty, modesty 8 chastity, fineness, holiness, lucidity, morality, pureness, sanctity 9 cleanness, clearness, innocence, integrity, limpidity, plainness, rectitude, virginity 10 brilliance, chasteness, directness, excellence, immaculacy, simplicity, temperance, uniformity 11 cleanliness, homogeneity, saintliness, uprightness 12 virtuousness 13 guilelessness, guiltlessness 14 immaculateness 15 clear conscience 16 incorruptibility

purlieu 4 area 5 haunt, limit 6 border, locale, region, resort 7 district, environ 8 outskirt 11 surrounding 12 neighborhood

purloin 3 rob 5 steal 6 pilfer 11 appropriate, make off with

Purloined Letter, The
author: 13 Edgar Allan Poe

purloiner 5 thief 6 robber 7 burglar 8 pilferer

purple 4 plum, puce, racy 5 color, grape, lilac, lurid, mauve, royal 6 florid, orchid, turgid, violet 7 crimson, flowery, furious, fushia, magenta 8 amethyst, burgundy, imperial, lavender 9 gastropod

Purple Land *see* 7 Uruguay

Purple Rose of Cairo, The
director: 10 Woody Allen
cast: 9 Mia Farrow 11 Danny Aiello, Jeff Daniels

purport 3 aim, end 4 gist 5 claim, drift, point, sense, tenor, trend 6 allege, burden, design, import, intent, object, reason 7 bearing, meaning, profess, purpose 9 intention, objective, rationale, substance 11 implication 12 significance 13 signification

purpose 3 aim 4 goal, hope, mean, plan, will, wish 5 elect, point, sense 6 aspire, choose, decide, design, desire, intend, intent, motive, object, reason, scheme, target 7 drive at, meaning, mission, persist, project, propose, resolve, think to 8 ambition, conclude, endeavor, function, proposal, set about 9 determine, intention, objective, persevere, rationale, undertake 10 aspiration, motivation, resolution 11 contemplate, disposition, expectation, fixed intent, have a mind to, raison d'etre 13 commit oneself, determination

purposeful 7 decided, studied 8 resolute, resolved 9 committed, conscious 10 calculated, considered, deliberate, determined 11 intentional 12 premeditated, strong-willed

purposefulness 7 purpose, resolve 10 resolution 11 decidedness 12 decisiveness, resoluteness 13 determination

purposeless 6 random 7 aimless, useless 8 needless, plotless 9 desultory, driftless, haphazard, irregular, senseless, unplanned 11 meaningless 12 functionless, undetermined, unprofitable

purposely 8 by design 9 advisedly, expressly, knowingly, on purpose, willfully, wittingly 10 designedly, with intent 11 consciously, voluntarily 12 calculatedly, deliberately 13 intentionally

purse 3 bag 4 fold, fund, knit 5 award, bunch, pinch, pleat, pouch, prize, stake 6 clutch, coffer, gather, pucker, wallet 7 handbag, sporran, wrinkle

8 contract, moneybag, proceeds, treasury, winnings 10 pocketbook 11 shoulder bag
French: 12 porte-monnaie

purser 6 bursar 7 cashier 9 paymaster 10 cashkeeper

pursue 4 seek 5 aim at, chase, track, trail 6 aim for, follow, try for 7 be after, carry on, go after, perform 8 aspire to, engage in, labor for, run after 9 race after, strive for 10 chase after, push toward

pursuer 5 pupil 6 seeker 7 devotee, student 8 disciple, follower, searcher 10 aficionado

pursuit 4 hunt 5 chase 6 search 7 pastime 8 activity 9 following 10 occupation

purvey 3 get 4 give, hand 5 cater, equip, yield 6 obtain, outfit, supply 7 deliver, furnish, procure, provide

purveyor 4 pimp 6 seller 8 procurer, provider, supplier

purview 3 ken 4 area 5 field, range, reach, realm, savvy, scope, sweep 6 domain, extent 7 compass, horizon, outlook 8 dominion, overview 9 territory, viewpoint 10 commission, experience 11 mental grasp 13 comprehension, understanding 14 responsibility

push 2 go 3 dun, ram 4 butt, goad, jolt, move, plug, prod, spur, sway, urge, work, worm 5 boost, drive, egg on, elbow, fight, foray, force, forge, harry, hound, impel, nudge, press, rouse, shove, stick, stuff, vigor, wedge 6 arouse, badger, coerce, compel, energy, exhort, harass, heckle, hustle, incite, induce, inroad, jostle, plunge, prompt, propel, thrust, wiggle 7 advance, animate, buffalo, inspire, promote, provoke, squeeze 8 ambition, browbeat, motivate, persuade, shoulder, struggle, vitality 9 advertise, constrain, encourage, importune, incursion, instigate, make known, publicize, stimulate, strong-arm 10 get-up-and-go 11 make one's way, prevail upon, vim and vigor 12 force one's way, propagandize 13 determination

pushcart 5 wagon 6 barrow 8 handcart 10 handbarrow 11 wheelbarrow

push forward 4 goad, prod, spur 5 drive, impel, press 9 urge along

Pushkin, Alexander (Aleksandr)
author of: 12 Boris Godunov, Eugene Onegin 16 The Queen of Spades 17 The Bronze Horseman 19 The Captain's Daughter

push through 6 hasten 7 advance, forward 8 dispatch, expedite 10 accelerate, facilitate

pushy 8 forceful 9 assertive, insistent 10 aggressive 11 domineering 12 strong-willed 13 self-assertive

pusillanimous 7 fearful 8 cowardly, timorous 10 spiritless 11 lily-livered 12 apprehensive, fainthearted, mean-spirited

pusillanimousness 8 timidity 9 cowardice 12 yellow streak 13 yellow feather 16 faint-heartedness 18 chickenheartedness

puss 3 cat, mug, pan 4 face 5 kitty 6 feline, kisser, kitten

pussyfoot 5 dodge, evade, hedge, sneak 6 tiptoe, weasel 8 sidestep 13 evade the issue 14 beg the question 15 walk on eggshells 16 straddle the fence

put 3 fix, lay, set 4 cast, pose, rest, word 5 bring, drive, force, heave, offer, pitch, place, state, throw 6 assign, employ, impute, phrase, submit 7 ascribe, deposit, express, present, propose 8 position 9 attribute, enunciate 10 articulate

put a damper on 4 cool, dull 7 depress, squelch 10 discourage, dishearten

put an edge on 4 hone, whet 6 excite 7 sharpen 9 stimulate

put an end to 4 halt, stop 5 annul, quash 6 cancel, finish, repeal, revoke 7 abolish, blot out, rescind, squelch, wipe out 8 abrogate, demolish, dispatch, stamp out 9 eliminate, eradicate, finish off 10 discourage, do away with, put a stop to 12 write finis to

put aside 5 table 6 forget 7 discard, lay away 10 relinquish

put away 3 eat 4 down, stow 5 stash 6 commit 7 confine, consume 9 drink down

put back 4 rout 5 delay 6 defeat, demote, impair, reject, return 7 replace, restore 9 reinstate

put down 4 note, post 5 crush, enter, knock, quash, quell 6 dispel, enlist, record, subdue 7 deposit, disdain, sneer at, squelch 8 belittle, derogate, laugh off, pooh-pooh, suppress 9 denigrate, disparage, humiliate, write down 10 depreciate

put forth 5 offer 6 extend, put out 7 proffer, send out

put forward 4 pose 6 assert 7 advance, profess, propose 8 propound

put in irons 5 chain 6 fetter 7 manacle, shackle 8 handcuff

put in motion 4 move 5 begin, start 6 arouse, launch 8 activate, carry out, commence, initiate 9 instigate, undertake

put in order 5 array 6 neaten, tidy up 7 arrange 8 organize 10 straighten

put in plain sight 4 show 6 set out 7 display, exhibit

put in shackles 6 fetter, hobble 7 enchain, enslave, manacle 8 handcuff, imprison

put into circulation 4 move 5 issue, print 7 publish 10 pass around

put into effect 6 effect 7 achieve, enforce, execute, fulfill, realize 8 carry out, complete 10 accomplish, administer, consummate, effectuate, perpetrate 12 carry through

put into words 5 voice 7 express 8 describe 9 verbalize 10 articulate 11 communicate

Putnam, Abbie
character in: 18 Desire Under the Elms
author: 6 O'Neill

put off 5 delay, repel, stall 6 offend, rebuff, recess 7 adjourn, repulse, set sail, suspend 8 hold back, launched, offended, postpone, rebuffed, repelled, repulsed 9 interrupt 11 discontinue 13 procrastinate

put off guard 4 lull 6 disarm 10 make unwary

put on 3 don 5 affix 6 attach 7 dress in, get into, stick on 8 fasten to

put-on 8 pretense 11 affectation

put on guard 4 warn 5 alert 6 advise, tip off 7 caution 8 forewarn 9 make ready 10 precaution

put out 3 irk 5 annoy, issue

6 quench, retire 7 produce, publish 8 irritate 9 strike out 10 extinguish 11 manufacture 13 leave the shore

put out of order 5 mix up, upset 6 jumble, mess up, muddle 7 confuse, scatter 8 disarray, disorder, displace, put askew, scramble 10 disarrange 11 disorganize

putrefaction 3 rot 5 decay 7 rotting 8 spoilage, spoiling 10 rottenness 12 decompostion

putrefy 3 rot 4 turn 5 decay, spoil, taint 6 molder 8 putresce, stagnate 9 decompose 10 biodegrade 11 deteriorate 12 disintegrate

putrescent 4 foul, rank 5 fetid 6 smelly 7 rotting 8 decaying, spoiling, stinking 9 offensive 10 malodorous, putrefying 11 decomposing

putrid 3 bad 4 foul, rank 5 fetid 6 rancid, rotten, spoiled 7 tainted 8 decaying, polluted, purulent, stinking 9 putrefied 10 putrescent 11 decomposing 12 contaminated, putrefactive

putridity 5 decay, filth, taint 8 foulness, impurity 9 dirtiness, pollution, purulence, rancidity 10 rottenness 11 putrescence, uncleanness 13 contamination, decomposition

putsch 6 revolt 8 uprising

putter 4 fool, idle, laze, loaf, loll 5 dally, drift 6 dawdle, diddle, fiddle, loiter, lounge, piddle, potter, tinker 8 golf club, lallygag 10 dillydally

put to death 4 do in, hang, kill, slay 5 slain 6 done in, hanged, killed, murder, poison, rub out 7 bump off, butcher, execute 8 dispatch, executed, massacre, murdered, poisoned, strangle 9 bumped off, butchered, finish off, massacred, strangled, suffocate 11 assassinate, electrocute, exterminate 12 assassinated, electrocuted, exterminated

put to flight 4 rout, shoo 5 chase 6 dispel 7 cast out, scatter 8 drive off, send away 11 send packing

put together 4 join 5 unite 7 combine 8 assemble

put to shame 6 ashame 7 chagrin, mortify 9 discomfit, embarrass, humiliate

put to sleep 4 lull 5 quiet 6 sedate 8 knock out 9 narcotize 11 anesthetize

put to use 3 use 5 apply 6 employ, engage, occupy 7 exploit, utilize 9 make use of

put under a spell 5 charm 7 bewitch, enchant 8 entrance 9 fascinate, mesmerize, spellbind

put up 3 can 4 hang 5 erect, house, lodge, raise, store 6 billet 7 shelter 8 preserve 11 accommodate 14 furnish room for

put up with 4 bear, take 5 abide, brave, brook, stand 6 endure, suffer 7 stomach, sustain, undergo 8 stand for, submit to, tolerate 9 withstand 11 countenance

Puvis de Chavannes, Pierre Cecile
born: 5 Lyons 6 France
artwork: 6 Summer 13 Shepherd's Song 14 Ludus pro patria 16 The Poor Fisherman 17 Life of St Genevieve, The Inspiring Muses 21 Science Arts and Letters

Puyallop
language family: 8 Salishan, Wakashan 9 Algonkian 10 Algonquian
location: 10 Washington

Puzo, Mario
author of: 12 The Godfather

puzzle 4 foil, mull 5 brood, stump 6 baffle, enigma, outwit, ponder, riddle, wonder 7 confuse, dilemma, mystery, mystify, nonplus, perplex, problem 8 bewilder, confound, hoodwink 9 conundrum 10 bafflement, difficulty, perplexity 12 bewilderment, complication 13 mystification

puzzled 6 amazed 7 baffled 8 befogged, confused, troubled 9 astounded, befuddled, mystified, perplexed 10 bewildered, confounded, nonplussed

puzzling 7 elusive 8 baffling 9 confusing, enigmatic 10 mysterious, mystifying, perplexing 11 bewildering, confounding, enigmatical 12 unfathomable 16 hard to understand, incomprehensible

Pwyll
origin: 5 Welsh
form: 6 prince
steals: 8 Rhiannon
wife: 8 Rhiannon
son: 7 Pryderi

Pyanepsia
origin: 5 Greek 8 Athenian
event: 8 festival
honoring: 6 Apollo 7 harvest

Pygmalion
author: 17 George Bernard Shaw
character: 12 Henry Higgins 14 Eliza Doolittle
basis for: 10 My Fair Lady
director: 14 Anthony Asquith
cast: 11 Wendy Hiller (Eliza Doolittle) 12 Leslie Howard (Professor Henry Higgins) 13 Wilfrid Lawson

Pygmalion
king of: 6 Cyprus
avocation: 8 sculptor
statue named: 7 Galatea
loved: 7 Galatea
statue changed to: 5 woman
wife: 7 Galatea
daughter: 6 Paphos 8 Metharme

pygmy 3 elf, toy, wee 4 mite, runt, tiny 5 dwarf, elfin, short, small 6 bantam, midget, peewee, shrimp 7 manikin 8 dwarfish, half-pint, Tom Thumb 9 miniature, pipsqueak 10 diminutive, homunculus, undersized 11 Lilliputian

Pylades
father: 9 Strophius
mother: 8 Anaxibia
cousin: 7 Orestes
wife: 7 Electra
son: 5 Medon 9 Strophius
friend: 7 Orestes

Pylaemenes
king of: 13 Paphlagonians
killed by: 8 Menelaus

Pylaeus
mentioned in: 5 Iliad
rank: 7 captain

Pylas
king of: 6 Megara
uncle: 4 Bias
gave throne to: 17 Pandion the Younger

Pyncheon family
character in: 24 The House of the Seven Gables
members: 6 Phoebe 8 Clifford, Hepzibah 12 Judge Jaffrey
author: 9 Hawthorne

Pynchon, Thomas
author of: 1 V 15 Gravity's Rainbow 23 The Crying of Lot Forty-Nine

Pyongyang
capital of: 10 North Korea

Pyramus
form: 5 youth
location: 7 Babylon
loved: 6 Thisbe
died at tomb of: 5 Ninus

Pyrigenes
epithet of: 8 Dionysus
means: 10 born of fire

Pyriphlegethon *see* **10** Phlegethon

pyromaniac 7 firebug **8** arsonist **10** incendiary **11** firestarter

Pyronia
epithet of: 7 Artemis
means: 11 fire goddess

pyrope
species: 6 garnet
color: 3 red

pyrophobia
fear of: 4 fire

pyrotechnics 9 fireworks **16** brilliant display **19** dazzling performance

Pyrrha
father: 10 Epimetheus
mother: 7 Pandora
husband: 9 Deucalion

Pythia
priestess of: 6 Apollo
location: 6 Delphi
delivered: 7 oracles

Pythias
friend: 5 Damon

Pythius *see* **6** Apollo

Python *see* **8** Delphyne

Qatar
capital/largest city: **4** Doha **7** al-Dawha
others: **3** Juh **5** Wagra **6** Dukhan, Umm-Bab **7** al-Khawr, Musayid, Umm Said **11** Al Jamaliyah
government: **7** emirate
head of state/government: **4** emir
monetary unit: **5** riyal **6** dirham
highest point: **13** Aba al-Bawl Hill
physical feature:
bay: **5** Salwa
cape: **5** Rakan **6** Laffan **8** Ushayriq **9** al-Matbakh
gulf: **7** Bahrain, Persian
people: **4** Arab **6** Pushtu, Yemeni **7** Baluchi, Iranian **9** Pakistani
rulers: **12** Great Britain, Ottoman Turks
sheik/sheikh: **18** Ahmad bin Ali al-Thani **22** Khalifa bin Hamad al-Thani
language: **6** Arabic
religion: **5** Islam
sect: **7** Wahhabi

quack **4** fake, sham **5** phony **6** pseudo **9** charlatan, pretender **10** fake doctor, fraudulent **11** counterfeit, quacksalver **15** medical impostor

quackery **5** bluff, guile **6** deceit **7** cunning **9** deception, duplicity **12** charlatanism

quaff **4** down, gulp, swig **5** drink, lap up, swill **6** guzzle, imbibe, tipple **7** swallow, toss off **8** belt down, chug-a-lug **9** knock back **11** drink deeply

quagmire **3** bog, fen, fix, jam **4** mess, mire, ooze, quag, sump **5** marsh, pinch, swamp **6** crisis, morass, muddle, pickle, plight, scrape, slough, sludge, strait **7** dilemma **8** hot water, quandary **9** imbroglio, intricacy, quicksand **10** difficulty, perplexity **11** Gordian knot, involvement, predicament **12** entanglement

quail **3** shy **5** cower, quake, shake **6** blanch, flinch, recoil, shrink **7** run away, shudder, tremble **8** fight shy, turn tail **9** lose heart **10** be cowardly, lose spirit, take fright **11** lose courage **12** have cold feet **16** shake in one's boots **17** shiver in one's shoes, show a yellow streak

quail
group of: **4** bevy **5** covey

quaint **3** odd **4** rare **5** droll, queer **6** unique **7** antique, bizarre, curious, strange, unusual **8** charming, fanciful, old-timey, original, peculiar, singular, uncommon **9** eccentric, whimsical **10** antiquated, outlandish **11** out-of-the-way, picturesque **12** old-fashioned **13** extraordinary **14** unconventional

quake **4** wave **5** quail, shake, spasm, throb **6** blanch, quaver, quiver, ripple, shiver, thrill, tremor **7** shudder, tremble **9** trembling **10** earthquake **18** seismic disturbance

qualification **4** gift **5** forte, skill **6** talent **7** ability, faculty, fitness, proviso **8** aptitude, bona fide, capacity, property, standard **9** attribute, condition, endowment, exception, exemption, objection, postulate, provision, requisite **10** capability, competency, credential, limitation **11** achievement, arrangement, eligibility, requirement, reservation, restriction, stipulation **12** escape clause, modification, prerequisite, suitableness **13** certification **14** accomplishment

qualified **3** fit **4** able, meet **5** adept, equal **6** expert, fitted, suited, versed **7** capable, guarded, hedging, knowing, limited, skilled, trained **8** eligible, equipped, licensed, reserved, skillful, talented **9** ambiguous, certified, competent, efficient, equivocal, practiced **10** authorized, indefinite, proficient, restricted **11** conditional, efficacious, experienced, provisional **12** accomplished

qualify **3** fit **4** ease **5** abate, adapt, alter, endow, equip, limit, ready, train **6** adjust, enable, ground, modify, narrow, permit, reduce, soften, temper **7** assuage, certify, empower, entitle, license, make fit, prepare **8** describe, diminish, mitigate, moderate, restrain, restrict, sanction **9** authorize, condition, give power, measure up **10** be accepted, be eligible, commission, legitimate **11** accommodate **12** characterize, circumscribe, make eligible

qualifying **9** tempering **10** mitigating **11** eligibility, extenuating, preparatory

quality **4** mark, rank **5** blood, class, grade, merit, trait, value, worth **6** aspect, family, nature **7** caliber, dignity, faculty, feature **8** capacity, eminence, position, property, standing **9** attribute, character **11** disposition, distinction, high station, temperament **12** constitution, social status **13** qualification **14** characteristic

Quality Street
author: **12** James M Barrie

qualm **4** turn **6** nausea **7** scruple, vertigo **9** faintness, giddiness, misgiving **10** dizzy spell, hesitation, queasiness, reluctance, uneasiness **11** compunction, reservation, sick feeling **13** indisposition, unwillingness **14** disinclination **18** twinge of conscience

quandary **3** fix, jam **4** mire **5** pinch **6** crisis, morass, pickle, plight, scrape, strait **7** dilemma, impasse **8** hot water, quagmire **9** imbroglio **10** difficulty **11** involvement, predicament **12** entanglement, kettle of fish

quantities **4** lots, much **5** heaps, loads **7** amounts

quantity **3** sum **4** area, bulk, dose, mass, size **5** quota, share **6** amount, dosage, extent, length, number, volume **7** expanse, measure, portion **8** vastness **9** abundance, aggregate, allotment, amplitude, extension, greatness, magnitude, multitude **10** proportion **11** measurement **13** apportionment

quarantine **7** confine, isolate **9** isolation, segregate, sequester **13** sequestration **15** cordon sanitaire **18** medical segregation

Quare Fellow, The
author: **12** Brendan Behan

quarrel **3** jar, nag, row **4** carp, feud, fuss, spat, tiff **5** argue, brawl, cavil, clash, fight, scrap **6** bicker, differ, strife **7** contend, discord, dispute, dissent, fall out, wrangle **8** argument, be at odds, conflict, squabble **9** altercate, bickering, complaint, find fault, have words, objection **10** contention, difference, dissension, dissidence, falling out **11** controversy **12** disagreement **13** breach of peace, contradiction, misunderstand **14** apple of discord **15** be at loggerheads **16** bone of contention, misunderstanding

quarreling **6** strife **7** discord **8** clashing, conflict, disunity, friction **9** bickering, disputing, scrapping, wrangling **10** contention, dissension, dissidence, squabbling **11** discordance **12** disagreement

quarrelsome **7** peevish **8** captious, churlish, contrary, militant, petulant **9** bellicose, combative, fractious, irascible, querulous, truculent **10** pugnacious **11** belligerent, contentious **12** antagonistic, cantankerous, disagreeable, disputatious **13** argumentative

quarry **3** bed, dig, pit **4** game, lode, mine, prey **5** catch, stone **6** source, victim **8** excavate

quart
abbreviation: **2** qt

quarter, quarters **4** area, part, pity, post, side, spot, zone **5** board, house, lodge, mercy, place, put up, realm, rooms **6** billet, domain, fourth, locale, region, sphere **7** housing, install, lodging, shelter, station, terrain **8** clemency, district, humanity, leniency, locality, location, lodgings, position, precinct, province, sympathy **9** percent, direction, one-fourth, situation, territory **10** compassion, fourth part, indulgence, quadrisect **11** place to live, place to stay, three months **13** quarter dollar, specific place **14** accommodations **15** twenty-five cents

quarterstaff **4** pole **5** staff **6** cudgel

quartz
varieties: **4** sard **5** agate, topaz **8** amethyst **9** carnelian, tiger's-eye **11** rock crystal

quash **4** ruin, stop, undo, void **5** annul, crush, erase, quell, smash, wreck **6** cancel, delete, dispel, efface, quench, recall, revoke, squash, subdue, vacate **7** blot out, destroy, expunge, nullify, put down, repress, rescind, retract, reverse, squelch **8** abrogate, dissolve, override, overrule, overturn, set aside, suppress **9** devastate, eradicate, extirpate, overthrow, overwhelm, repudiate, strike out **10** annihilate, extinguish, invalidate, obliterate, put an end to **11** countermand, exterminate

quasi **4** near, part, semi **6** almost, ersatz **7** halfway, seeming, virtual **8** apparent, somewhat, so-called **9** imitation, synthetic **10** resembling

Quasimodo
character in: **23** The Hunchback of Notre Dame
author: **4** Hugo

Quatermain, Allan
character in: **17** King Solomon's Mines
author: **7** Haggard

quaver **4** beat, sway, wave **5** quake, shake, throb, trill, waver **6** falter, quiver, shiver, teeter, totter, tremor, wobble, writhe **7** pulsate, shudder, tremble, tremolo, vibrate, vibrato, wriggle **9** oscillate, trembling, vibration **14** tremulous shake

quay **4** dock, mole, pier **5** basin, jetty, levee, wharf **6** marina **7** landing **10** waterfront

queasy **5** giddy, upset **6** uneasy **7** bilious, sickish **8** nauseous, qualmish, troubled **9** nauseated, sickening, uncertain **10** nauseating **13** uncomfortable **16** sick to the stomach

Quebec
borders: **7** Ontario **8** Labrador **9** Hudson Bay **12** Newfoundland, United States **13** Atlantic Ocean **16** Gulf of St Lawrence
cape: **5** Gaspe
city: **6** Quebec **8** Montreal **10** Chicoutimi, Sherbrooke **13** Trois Rivieres
highest point: **18** Mont Jacques Cartier
hockey team: **9** Canadiens, Nordiques
island: **9** Anticosti
lake: **5** Gouin **9** Bienville, Eau Claire, Saint Jean **10** Mistassini **11** Manicouagan
mineral: **4** gold, zinc **6** copper **7** iron ore **8** asbestos **9** limestone
mountain: **5** Otish **10** Laurentian, Shickshock **11** Appalachian **12** Monteregians
province of: **6** Canada

Quechua
tribe: **4** Inca

Quedens, Eunice
real name of: **8** Eve Arden

queen **5** ranee **7** czarina, empress **8** princess **13** female monarch
French: **5** reine
German: **7** Konigin
Latin: **6** regina
Spanish: **5** reina

queen/empress/princess
of Egypt: **9** Cleopatra, Nefertari, Nefertiti **10** Hatshepsut, Hetepheres
of England: **3** Mab **4** Anne, Bess, Jane, Mary **7** Eleanor **8** Boadicea, Victoria **9** Catherine, Charlotte, Elizabeth, Guinevere **10** Bloody Mary, Elizabeth I **11** Elizabeth II, Jane Seymour

of France: **7** Eugenie **9** Josephine **11** Marie Louise **14** Marie de Medicis **15** Marie Antoinette
of Italy/Rome: **7** Poppaea **9** Agrippina, Messalina **13** Livia Drusilla
of Monaco: **8** Caroline **9** Stephanie **10** Grace Kelly
of the Netherlands: **7** Beatrix, Juliana **10** Wilhelmina
of Poland: **7** Jadwiga
of Portugal: **5** Maria **9** Elizabeth
of Russia: **9** Alexandra, Catherine **17** Catherine the Great
of Scotland: **4** Mary **13** Saint Margaret **16** Mary Queen of Scots
of Spain: **8** Isabella **16** Elizabeth Farnese
of Sweden: **9** Christina
of Syria: **7** Zenobia

Queen Christina
director: **15** Rouben Mamoulian
cast: **8** Ian Keith **10** Greta Garbo, Lewis Stone **11** John Gilbert **12** C Aubrey Smith

Queen Mab
author: **18** Percy Bysshe Shelley

Queen of Amazons **9** Hippolyta, Hippolyte

Queen of Hearts
character in: **28** Alice's Adventures in Wonderland
author: **7** Carroll

Queen of Heaven **4** Hera, Mary **6** Ishtar **7** Mylitta

Queen of Spades, The
also: **12** Pikovaya Dama
opera by: **11** Tchaikovsky
character: **4** Lisa **6** Herman **8** Countess

Queen of Spades, The
author: **16** Alexander Pushkin

Queen of Technicolor
nickname of: **12** Maureen O'Hara

Queen of the Surf
nickname of: **14** Esther Williams

Queen's Necklace, The
author: **14** Alexandre Dumas (pere)
character: **5** Oliva **13** Count de Charny **15** Cardinal de Rohan, Count Cagliostro, Marie Antoinette **16** Andree de Taverney **18** Philippe de Taverney **21** Jeanne de la Motte Valois

Queequeg
character in: **8** Moby Dick
author: **8** Melville

queer **3** odd **4** daft, harm, hurt, rare, ruin **5** crazy, dizzy, droll, faint, fishy, funny, giddy, shady, spoil, weird, woozy, wreck **6** absurd, damage, exotic, impair, injure, quaint, qualmy, queasy, thwart, unique **7** bizarre, comical, curious, disrupt, erratic, reeling, strange, touched, unusual **8** abnormal, bohemian, doubtful, fanciful, freakish, original, peculiar, uncommon, unhinged **9** eccentric, fantastic, grotesque, irregular, laughable, ludicrous, unnatural **10** capricious, compromise, farfetched, irrational, outlandish, remarkable, ridiculous, suspicious, unbalanced, unexampled, unorthodox **11** astonishing, exceptional, light-headed, out of the way, slightly ill, vertiginous **12** preposterous, questionable, unparalleled **13** extraordinary, nonconforming, unprecedented **14** unconventional
French: **5** outre

quell **4** calm, dull, ease, hush, lull, rout, ruin, stay, stem **5** abate, allay, blunt, crush, quash, quiet, still, worst, wreck **6** becalm, deaden, defeat, pacify, quench, reduce, soften, soothe, subdue **7** appease, assuage, compose, conquer, destroy, mollify, put down, scatter, silence, squelch **8** beat down, disperse, mitigate, overcome, palliate, stamp out, suppress, vanquish **9** alleviate, overpower, overthrow, overwhelm, subjugate **10** extinguish **11** tranquilize

quench **4** cool, sate **5** allay, crush, douse, quell, slake **6** dampen, put out, stifle **7** appease, blow out, put down, satiate, satisfy, smother **8** stamp out, suppress **10** annihilate, extinguish

Quentin Durward
author: **14** Sir Walter Scott
character: **8** Isabelle **9** Le Balafre **10** Jacqueline **11** King Louis XI **12** Lady Hameline **13** Ludovic Lesley **15** Countess of Croye **16** William de la Marck **18** Hayraddin Maugrabin **20** King Louis the Eleventh **21** Charles Duke of Burgundy **23** Count Philip de Crevecoeur

querulous **4** sour **5** cross, fussy, testy, whiny **6** cranky, touchy **7** crabbed, finical, finicky, fretful, grouchy, peevish, pettish, waspish, whining **8** captious, exacting, petulant, shrewish **9** difficult, grumbling, irascible, irritable, long-faced, obstinate, resentful, splenetic **10** nettlesome **11** complaining, quarrelsome **12** disagreeable, discontented, disputatious, dissatisfied, faultfinding

query **3** ask **4** quiz **5** doubt, issue, quest **6** demand, impugn, search **7** dispute, examine, impeach, inquest, inquiry, inspect, problem, request, suspect **8** distrust, look into, mistrust, question, sound out **9** catechize, challenge, inquire of **10** controvert **11** examination, inquisition, interrogate, investigate, make inquiry **13** interrogation, investigation

quest **4** hunt, seek **6** pursue, search, voyage **7** crusade, journey, mission, pursuit, seeking **9** adventure **10** enterprise, pilgrimage **11** exploration

Quested, Adela
character in: **15** A Passage to India
author: **7** Forster

Quest for Fire
director: **17** Jean-Jacques Annaud
cast: **10** Ron Perlman **12** Rae Dawn Chong **13** Everett McGill

question **3** ask, rub **4** pump, quiz, test **5** doubt, drill, grill, issue, query **6** impugn, matter, motion, oppose **7** dispute, dubiety, examine, problem, subject, suspect **8** distrust, look into, mistrust, proposal, sound out **9** catechize, challenge, inquire of, misgiving, moot point, objection **10** difficulty, disbelieve **11** controversy, interrogate, investigate, proposition, uncertainty **12** cross-examine **13** consideration

questionable **4** moot **5** fishy, shady **6** unsure **7** dubious, in doubt, suspect **8** arguable, doubtful, puzzling, unproven **9** ambiguous, confusing, debatable, enigmatic, equivocal, in dispute, uncertain, undecided **10** apocryphal, disputable, indefinite, mysterious, mystifying, perplexing, suspicious **12** hypothetical **13** controversial, problematical

queue **3** row **4** file, line, rank **5** chain, train **6** column, string

quibble **3** nag **4** carp, spar **5** argue, cavil, dodge, fence, fudge, shift **6** bicker, haggle, hassle, nicety, niggle, waffle **7** evasion, nitpick, shuffle **8** artifice, pretense, squabble, subtlety, white lie **9** be evasive, duplicity **10** equivocate, pick a fight, subterfuge **11** distraction **12** equivocation

13 dodge the issue, prevarication

Quiche
language family: 5 Mayan
location: 9 Guatemala **12** South America **14** Central America

quick 3 apt **4** able, deft, fast, keen, spry **5** acute, adept, agile, alert, brief, brisk, eager, fiery, fleet, hasty, rapid, sharp, smart, swift, testy **6** abrupt, active, adroit, astute, brainy, bright, clever, expert, facile, flying, frisky, lively, nimble, prompt, shrewd, speedy, sudden, touchy, winged **7** hurried, peppery, waspish **8** animated, choleric, headlong, petulant, skillful, snappish, spirited, vigilant, vigorous **9** dexterous, energetic, excitable, impatient, impetuous, impulsive, irascible, irritable, sagacious, splenetic, sprightly, vivacious, whirlwind, wide-awake **10** discerning, high-strung, hot-blooded **11** accelerated, expeditious, hot-tempered, intelligent, lightfooted, penetrating, precipitate **12** nimble-footed **13** perspicacious, temperamental

quicken 4 fire, goad, move, rush, spur, stir, urge **5** drive, egg on, hurry, impel, pique, press, rouse, speed **6** affect, arouse, excite, hasten, hustle, incite, kindle, propel, revive, vivify **7** actuate, advance, animate, enliven, further, hurry on, inspire, provoke, refresh, sharpen **8** activate, dispatch, energize, enkindle, expedite, inspirit, vitalize **9** galvanize, instigate, stimulate **10** accelerate, invigorate **11** precipitate

quick glance
French: 9 coup d'oeil

quickly 4 anon, fast, soon **6** keenly, presto, pronto **7** briefly, hastily, rapidly, swiftly **8** promptly, speedily **9** instantly **11** immediately **12** lickety-split

Quickly, Mistress
character in: 22 The Merry Wives of Windsor
author: 11 Shakespeare

quickness 5 haste, speed **6** acuity **8** alacrity, celerity, keenness, rapidity **9** acuteness, alertness, dexterity, sharpness **10** cleverness, nimbleness, promptness **15** expeditiousness

quick-tempered 5 cross, testy **6** cranky, shirty, touchy **7** grouchy, peevish, waspish **8** choleric, churlish, shrewish, snappish **9** emotional, excitable, irascible, irritable **10** ill-humored **11** bad-tempered, hot-tempered, quarrelsome **12** cantankerous **13** temperamental

quick-witted 4 keen **5** acute, alert, aware, quick, ready, sharp, smart, witty **6** astute, bright, clever, shrewd **8** incisive **9** brilliant, wide-awake **10** discerning, perceptive **11** clear-headed, intelligent, penetrating **13** perspicacious

quid pro quo 4 swap **5** trade **8** exchange **9** tit for tat **21** something for something

¿quien sabe 8 who knows?

quiescence 7 latency **8** dormancy, inaction **10** inactivity

quiescent 6 latent **7** dormant **8** inactive **10** in abeyance

quiet ***see box***

quietly 5 coyly **6** calmly, humbly, meekly, mildly, mutely, softly, tamely **8** demurely, modestly, placidly, serenely, silently **9** bashfully, inaudibly, patiently **10** composedly, moderately, peacefully, tranquilly **11** collectedly, contentedly, diffidently, noiselessly, pacifically, soundlessly, temperately, unexcitedly **12** speechlessly, unassumingly, unboastfully **13** unobtrusively, unperturbedly **15** dispassionately, unpretentiously, without ceremony **16** unostentatiously **17** undemonstratively

Quiet Man, The
director: 8 John Ford
author: 13 Liam O'Flaherty
cast: 9 John Wayne **12** Maureen O'Hara **14** Mildred Natwick, Victor McLaglen **15** Barry Fitzgerald
setting: 7 Ireland
score: 11 Victor Young
Oscar for: 8 director

quietness 5 peace, quiet **7** silence **8** softness **9** stillness **12** peacefulness

quietude 4 calm, rest **6** repose **8** easiness **9** composure

Quigley, Jane
real name of: 13 Jane Alexander

quill 3 pen **4** fold, hair, pick, seta, stem, tube **5** pluck, plume, spike, spine, spool **6** bobbin, needle **7** bristle, feather, spindle **9** toothpick

Quilp
character in: 19 The Old Curiosity Shop
author: 7 Dickens

quilt 5 cover **6** spread **7** blanket **8** coverlet **9** bedspread, comforter

Quin, Widow
character in: 24 Playboy of the Western World
author: 5 Synge

Quincy, M. E.
character: 3 Lee **5** Danny, (Sgt) Brill **11** Sam Fujiyama, (Dr) Robert Astin **12** (Lt) Frank Monahan

quiet 3 low, mum **4** calm, curb, dull, ease, hush, lull, meek, mild, mute, rest, soft, stay, stop **5** abate, allay, blunt, check, fixed, inert, peace, plain, quell, still **6** arrest, at rest, deaden, docile, dozing, gentle, humble, hushed, lessen, mellow, modest, muffle, pacify, placid, repose, sedate, serene, settle, silent, simple, soften, soothe, stable, steady, stifle, subdue, weaken **7** assuage, clement, comfort, compose, dormant, halcyon, mollify, not busy, pacific, passive, patient, relieve, restful, silence, smother, subdued, suspend, unmoved **8** becalmed, calmness, comatose, composed, decrease, immobile, inactive, mitigate, moderate, muteness, not rough, not showy, palliate, peaceful, quietude, reserved, reticent, retiring, serenity, sleeping, stagnant, taciturn, tranquil **9** alleviate, collected, contented, easygoing, immovable, lethargic, make quiet, noiseless, not bright, peaceable, placidity, quietness, set at ease, soundless, stillness, temperate, terminate, unruffled, voiceless **10** coolheaded, gentleness, motionless, phlegmatic, put a stop to, relaxation, slumbering, speechless, stationary, stock-still, unassuming, untroubled **11** discontinue, tranquility, tranquilize, undisturbed, unexcitable, unobtrusive, unperturbed **12** bring to an end, even-tempered, inarticulate, peacefulness, tranquillity **13** at a standstill, dispassionate, imperturbable, noiselessness, soundlessness, unimpassioned, unpretentious **14** unostentatious, unpresumptuous **15** uncommunicative, undemonstrative

cast: **9** Robert Ito **10** John S Ragin **11** Jack Klugman, Joseph Roman, Val Bisoglio **12** Garry Walberg **13** Lynette Mettey
setting: **10** Los Angeles **11** Danny's Place

Quinn, Anthony
born: **6** Mexico **9** Chihuahua
wife: **16** Katherine DeMille
roles: **8** La Strada **10** Viva Zapata **11** Lust for Life **13** Zorba the Greek **17** The Guns of Navarone **22** Requiem for a Heavyweight, The Shoes of the Fisherman
autobiography: **14** The Original Sin

Quintana and Friends
author: **16** John Gregory Dunne

quintessence **4** core, gist, pith, soul **5** heart **6** elixir, marrow, nature **7** essence **8** exemplar, quiddity, sum total **9** substance **10** embodiment **12** distillation **15** personification, sum and substance

quip **3** gag, pun **4** barb, gibe, jape, jeer, jest, joke **5** crack, sally, spoof, taunt **6** banter, retort **7** epigram, putdown, riposte, sarcasm **8** badinage, raillery, repartee, wordplay **9** wisecrack, witticism
French: **6** bon mot **14** double entendre

Quirinus
origin: **5** Roman
god of: **3** war
personifies: **11** Roman nation
identified with: **7** Romulus

quirk **4** kink, turn, whim **6** fetish, foible, oddity, vagary, whimsy **7** caprice **8** crotchet, odd fancy **9** mannerism **10** aberration **11** abnormality, affectation, peculiarity, sudden twist **12** eccentricity, idiosyncrasy

quisling **6** puppet **7** traitor **12** collaborator **16** collaborationist

quit **3** end, rid **4** free, stop **5** cease, clear, forgo, leave, let go, waive, yield **6** depart, desist, disown, exempt, forego, give up, reject, resign, retire **7** abandon, disavow, drop out, forsake, take off **8** abdicate, absolved, forswear, renounce, withdraw **9** acquitted, foreswear, leave a job, surrender, terminate **10** discharged, exculpated, exonerated, relinquish **11** discontinue

quite **4** very **5** fully, truly **6** highly, hugely, indeed, in fact, in toto, really, surely, vastly, verily, wholly **7** exactly, in truth, totally, utterly **8** actually, entirely, outright **9** assuredly, certainly, extremely, in reality, out-and-out, perfectly, precisely, unusually, veritably **10** absolutely, altogether, completely, enormously, positively, remarkably, throughout **11** exceedingly, excessively **12** considerably **13** exceptionally

Quito
capital of: **7** Ecuador

quiver **3** tic **4** jerk, jolt, jump, pant **5** quake, shake, spasm, throb **6** quaver, shiver, totter, tremor, twitch, wobble **7** flicker, flutter, pulsate, seizure, shudder, tremble, vibrate, wriggle **8** convulse **9** fluctuate, oscillate, palpitate, pulsation, quivering, twitching, vibration **10** convulsion **11** palpitation

Quiverful, Mr
character in: **16** Barchester Towers
author: **8** Trollope

quivering **7** shaking **9** agitating, quavering, shimmying, shivering, trembling, vibrating **10** flittering, fluttering, shuddering, twittering **11** palpitating

qui vive? **12** who goes there?

quixotic **4** wild **6** absurd, dreamy, madcap, poetic **7** utopian **8** fanciful, romantic **9** fantastic, impulsive, visionary, whimsical **10** chimerical, idealistic, ridiculous, starry-eyed **11** impractical, ineffective, sentimental, unrealistic **12** preposterous **13** inefficacious

quiz **3** ask, rib **4** exam, joke, mock, pump, test **5** prank, query, taunt, tease **6** banter **7** examine, inquest, inquiry **8** question, ridicule, sound out **9** catechism, eccentric, inquire of **11** examination, inquisition, interrogate, investigate, questioning **12** cross-examine **13** interrogation, investigation **16** cross-examination

Quiz Kids
host: **8** Joe Kelly **14** Clifton Fadiman

quizzical **3** coy **4** arch **6** joking **7** baffled, curious, mocking, puzzled, teasing **8** derisive, impudent, insolent **9** bantering, inquiring, perplexed, searching **11** inquisitive, questioning

quoad hoc **12** as much as this, to this extent

quod erat demonstrandum **17** which was to be shown **24** which was to be demonstrated
abbreviation: **3** QED

quod erat faciendum **16** which was to be done

quod vide **8** which see
abbreviation: **2** qv

quo jure? **11** by what right?

quo modo **3** how **9** in what way **19** in the same manner that

quondam **4** erst, late, once, past **6** bygone, former **8** formerly, sometime **9** erstwhile

quota **4** part **5** share **6** ration **7** measure, minimum, portion **8** quantity **9** allotment **10** allocation, assignment, percentage, proportion **12** distribution **13** apportionment

quotation **5** quote **7** cutting, excerpt, extract, passage **8** citation, clipping **9** reference, selection **12** illustration

quote **4** cite, name **6** adduce, recall, repeat, retell **7** excerpt, extract, refer to **8** instance **9** exemplify, recollect, reproduce **10** paraphrase

quoted passage **7** excerpt, extract **9** quotation

quotidian **5** daily **6** common **8** everyday, ordinary **11** commonplace

Quo Vadis?
author: **17** Henryk Sienkiewicz
character: **4** Nero **5** Chilo, Lygia, Peter **8** Vinitius **9** Petronius, Tigellius
director: **11** Mervyn LeRoy
cast: **7** Leo Genn **11** Deborah Kerr **12** Peter Ustinov, Robert Taylor
setting: **11** ancient Rome

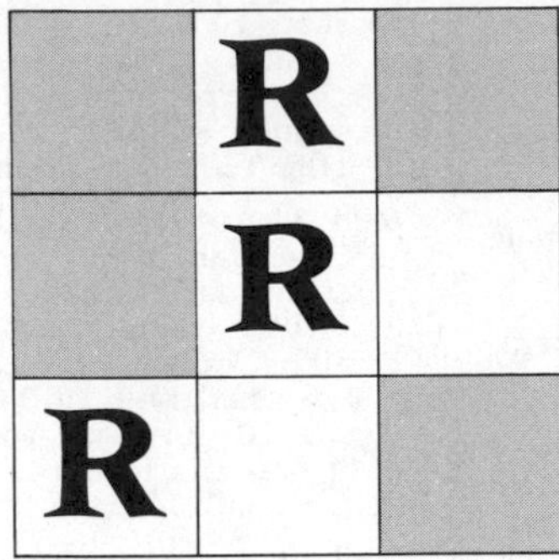

Ra
also: **2** Re
origin: **5** Greek **10** Heliopolis
god of: **3** sun
also worshipped by:
9 Egyptians

Rabat, Rabbat
capital of: **7** Morocco

rabbi **6** master, rabbin **7** scholar, teacher **9** clergyman **15** spiritual leader

rabbinical, rabbinic **8** clerical

rabbit **4** cony, hare, jack, lure **5** bunny, coney, lapin **6** novice, rodent **8** beginner **10** cottontail, pacesetter

Rabbit Is Rich
author: **10** John Updike

Rabbit Redux
author: **10** John Updike

rabble **3** mob **5** swarm **7** the herd **8** populace, riffraff **9** commoners, hoi polloi, the masses **11** proletariat, rank and file **12** lower classes **15** disorderly crowd **16** the great unwashed
French: **8** canaille
German:
17 Lumpenproletariat

Rabelais, Francois
author of: **22** Gargantua and Pantagruel

rabid **4** wild **6** ardent, crazed, raging **7** berserk, fervent, frantic, violent, zealous **8** deranged, frenzied, maniacal, wild-eyed **9** fanatical **11** hydrophobic **17** foaming at the mouth

race **3** fly, run **4** dart, dash, heat, rush **5** hurry **6** hasten, hustle **7** contest, operate **8** campaign **11** competition

racecourse **4** turf **5** track **6** course **9** racetrack

Rachel
father: **5** Laban
husband: **5** Jacob
sister: **4** Leah
son: **6** Joseph **8** Benjamin
slave: **6** Bilhah

Rachmaninov (Rachmaninoff, Rakhmaninov), Sergei
born: **6** Russia **8** Novgorod
composer of: **15** Symphonic Dances **16** The Isle of the Dead **19** Second Piano Concerto **26** Rhapsody on a Theme by (of) Paganini

Racine, Jean Baptiste
author of: **6** Phedre **7** Athalie **8** Berenice **10** Andromache **11** Britannicus

racism **7** bigotry **8** color bar **9** color line **10** race hatred, racial bias **11** segregation **15** racial prejudice **20** racial discrimination

rack **4** buck, gait, hurt, neck, pace, pain, path **5** agony, cloud, exert, frame, raise, track, trail, worry, wreck, wring **6** canter, holder, strain **7** afflict, agonize, draw off, oppress, stretch, torment, torture **8** distress **9** suffering **10** destruction, excruciate, iron maiden

racked **4** torn **5** paced **6** framed, pained, traced, walked **7** annoyed, tracked, trotted, wronged, worried **8** cantered, suffered, tortured **9** afflicted, anguished, destroyed, oppressed, tormented **10** persecuted

racket **3** din **4** game, line, roar, stir **5** babel **6** clamor, hubbub, rumpus, tumult, uproar **7** clangor, clatter, turmoil **8** business, shouting **9** commotion, loud noise **10** hullabaloo, hurly-burly, occupation, turbulence **11** disturbance, pandemonium **12** caterwauling, vociferation

racketeer **4** hood **5** crook **6** bagman, bandit, extort **7** hoodlum, mafioso, mobster **8** criminal, gangster **12** extortionist

racking **7** painful **9** agonizing, torturous **10** tormenting, unbearable **11** intolerable, unendurable **12** excruciating, insufferable

raconteur **8** fabulist, narrator, romancer **10** anecdotist **11** storyteller **13** teller of tales **14** spinner of yarns

racy **4** keen **5** bawdy, crude, heady, lurid, zesty **6** erotic, lively, ribald, risque, smutty, vulgar **7** buoyant, glowing, obscene, zestful **8** animated, exciting, immodest, indecent, off-color, prurient, spirited, vigorous **9** energetic, fast-paced, salacious, sparkling **10** suggestive **11** stimulating **12** exhilarating, pornographic

radar
invented by: **4** Watt **6** Watson

Radcliffe, Mrs Ann
author of: **10** The Italian **21** The Mysteries of Udolpho

raddle **3** rod **4** reed, scar, twig **5** fence, hedge, rouge, stick, weave **6** branch, ruddle **8** hematite, red ocher, red ochre **10** interweave

radiance, radiancy **3** joy **5** gleam, gleem, sheen **6** dazzle, luster **7** glitter, rapture, sparkle **8** lambency, splendor **9** animation, happiness **10** brightness, brilliance, brilliancy, effulgence, luminosity, refulgence **11** coruscation, iridescence **12** luminousness, resplendence **13** incandescence
god of: **5** Baldr **6** Balder, Baldur

radiant **5** aglow, happy, sunny **6** bright, elated, joyous **7** beaming, glowing, pleased, shining **8** blissful, dazzling, ecstatic, flashing, gladsome, gleaming, luminous, lustrous **9** brilliant, delighted, effulgent, overjoyed, rapturous, refulgent, sparkling **10** glittering **12** incandescent **13** scintillating

radiate **4** beam, pour, shed **5** carry **6** spread **7** diffuse, diverge, give off, give out, scatter **8** disperse, emit heat, transmit **9** branch out, circulate, emit light, spread out **11** disseminate

radical **4** rash **5** basic, rebel **6** severe **7** drastic, extreme **8** left-wing, militant **9** extremist, firebrand **10** immoderate, inordinate **11** freethinker, fundamental, precipitate **13** revolutionary **22** antiestablishmentarian

radio
invented by: **7** Donovan, Fleming, Marconi **8** De Forest, Nicolson **9** Armstrong, Fessenden **12** Alexanderson

radium
chemical symbol: **2** Ra

radon
chemical symbol: **2** Rn

raffish **3** low **4** fast, wild **5** cheap, rowdy, showy **6** common, flashy, rakish, tawdry, vulgar **7** boorish **8** rakehell **9** worthless **10** dissipated **12** devil-may-care, disreputable

raft **3** lot **4** mass **5** barge, float **6** plenty **7** carrier, pontoon **8** flatboat, platform, quantity **9** abundance, multitude

Raft, George
real name: **11** George Ranft
born: **9** New York NY
roles: **8** Scarface **11** Johnny Angel **12** Guido Rinaldo **13** Some Like It Hot

rag **3** kid, rib **4** scap, song, tune, twit **5** cloth, taunt, taunt, tease **6** harass **7** torment **8** magazine **9** newspaper **11** ragtime tune **14** worn-out garment

ragamuffin **3** bum **4** hobo, waif **5** gamin, tramp **6** beggar, gamine, hoyden, sloven, urchin, wretch **7** vagrant **8** derelict, vagabond **9** itinerant, ragpicker **10** panhandler, street arab **11** guttersnipe **14** tatterdemalion

rage **3** fad, ire **4** boil, fume, fury, mode, rant, rave, roar **5** craze, furor, mania, pique, storm, vogue, wrath **6** blow up, choler, frenzy, seethe, spleen, temper **7** explode, fashion, ferment, flare up, madness, passion, rampage, umbrage **8** paroxysm, the thing **9** animosity, fulminate, raise cain, throw a fit, vehemence **10** bitterness, excitement, irritation, resentment, the "in" thing **11** displeasure, high dudgeon, indignation, the last word **12** current style, le dernier cri, perturbation, violent anger **13** temper tantrum **14** the latest thing **15** fly off the handle, froth at the mouth

Rage of Angels
author: **13** Sidney Sheldon

ragged **4** rent, torn, worn **5** seedy, tacky **6** beat up, frayed, shabby, shaggy, shoddy **7** patched, run down, worn-out **8** battered, shredded, strained, tattered **9** overtaxed **10** aggravated, threadbare, worn to rags **11** exacerbated

ragging **5** chaff **6** banter **7** kidding, ribbing, teasing **8** chaffing, needling, raillery, taunting, twitting

raging **3** mad **4** wild **5** angry, livid, rabid, rough **6** fierce, raving, stormy **7** fervent, frantic, furious, rampant, violent **8** frenzied, incensed, storming **9** turbulent **10** blustering, ferocious, infuriated **11** tempestuous

Raging Bull
director: **14** Martin Scorsese
cast: **8** Joe Pesci **12** Frank Vincent, Robert De Niro (Jake La Motta) **13** Cathy Moriarty
Oscar for: **5** actor (De Niro)

Ragnarok
also: **15** Gotterdammerung **17** Twilight of the Gods
origin: **12** Scandinavian
event: **11** final battle
battlefield: **6** Vigrid

ragout **4** hash, stew **7** borscht, goulash **9** fricassee

Ragtime
author: **10** E L Doctorow

Rahab
hometown: **7** Jericho
husband: **6** Solmon
hid: **12** Joshua's spies

raid **4** bust **5** foray, onset, sally, storm **6** attack, inroad, invade, razzia, sortie **7** assault, roundup **8** invasion **10** pounce upon **14** surprise attack

Raiders of the Lost Ark
director: **15** Steven Spielberg
cast: **10** Karen Allen, Wolf Kahler **11** Paul Freeman **12** Harrison Ford
sequel: **30** Indiana Jones and the Temple of Doom

rail **3** bar **4** rage, rant **5** scold, fence, train **6** blow up, scream, take on **7** barrier, carry on, declaim, inveigh, railing, railway, the cars **8** banister, railroad **9** fulminate **10** vituperate, vociferate **11** rant and rave **14** foam at the mouth

rail at **5** scold **6** berate **7** chew out **9** castigate **14** inveigh against

railing **3** bar **5** fence, grate, rails **6** fender **7** barrier, parapet, support **8** banister **9** enclosing **10** balustrade

raillery **5** chaff, sport **6** banter, japing, joking, satire **7** fooling, jesting, joshing, kidding, ragging, razzing, ribbing, teasing **8** badinage, chaffing, roasting, twitting **10** lampoonery, persiflage, pleasantry

railroad sleeping car
French: **8** wagon-lit

railroad station **5** depot **8** terminal, terminus

railway **4** tube **5** track, train **6** cogway, subway **7** cogroad, trolley **8** elevated, monorail, railroad **9** streetcar

raiment **4** duds, togs **5** dress **6** attire **7** apparel, clothes, costume, threads **8** clothing, garments **11** habiliments

rain, rains **4** down, drop, mist, pour **5** spate **6** deluge, lavish, shower, squall **7** drizzle, monsoon, torrent **8** downpour, drencher, plethora, rainfall, send down, sprinkle **9** hurricane, rainstorm **10** cloudburst **13** precipitation, thundershower **15** rain cats and dogs **16** come down in sheets **17** come down in buckets
god of: **4** Thor

Rainbow
goddess of: **4** Iris

Rainbow, The
author: **10** D H Lawrence
character: **10** Anna Lensky **11** Lydia Lensky, Tom Brangwen **12** Will Brangwen **14** Ursula Brangwen **15** Anton Skrebensky

Rainbow Bridge *see* **7** bifrost

raincoat **3** mac **4** mack **6** poncho, ulster **7** oilskin, slicker **8** burberry **9** tarpaulin **10** mackintosh, trenchcoat, waterproof

rainless **3** dry **4** arid, sere **10** desertlike

Rains, Claude
born: **6** London **7** England
wife: **11** Isabel Jeans
roles: **9** Notorious **10** Casablanca, Now Voyager **13** Mr Skeffington **14** Anthony Adverse **15** The Invisible Man **16** Lawrence of Arabia **17** Here Comes Mr Jordan **20** The Phantom of the Opera **23** Mr Smith Goes to Washington **24** The Adventures of Robin Hood

rain shower **6** shower **7** drizzle **8** sprinkle **12** thunderstorm

rainstorm **6** deluge, shower **8** downfall, downpour **10** cloudburst **12** thunderstorm

rainy **3** wet **4** damp **7** drizzly, showery **11** pouring rain **18** raining cats and dogs

raise **3** end **4** grow, hike, lift, rear, spur, urge **5** amass, boost, breed, build, erect, nurse, pique, put up, rouse, set up, spark **6** arouse, awaken, excite, foster, hike up, jack up, kindle, obtain, stir up **7** advance, bring in, bring up, canvass, collect, develop, elevate, inflame, inflate, inspire, nurture, procure, produce, sharpen, solicit **8** increase, summon up **9** construct, cultivate, elevation, promotion, stimulate, terminate **10** make higher, put forward **11** advancement

raise aloft **5** boost, hoist **6** lift up, uplift **7** elevate, upraise

raised **4** bred, grew **5** anted, built, grown **6** anteed, convex, jacked, lifted, reared, roused **7** aroused, erected, exalted, hoisted, honored, incited **8** elevated, embossed, leavened, mustered **9** brought up, collected **10** cultivated **11** resurrected

Raisin in the Sun, A
director: **12** Daniel Petrie
based on play by: **17** Lorraine Hansberry
cast: **7** Ruby Dee **9** Ivan Dixon **10** Diana Sands **13** Claudia McNeil, Sidney Poitier
setting: **7** Chicago

rake **4** comb, goat, roue **5** rogue, satyr, scour, sport **6** lecher, pepper, rascal **7** Don Juan, playboy, ransack, seducer, swinger **8** Casanova, Lothario, enfilade, prodigal, rakehell **9** debauchee, libertine, womanizer **10** immoralist, profligate, sensualist, voluptuary

rake-off **3** cut, fee **5** piece **10** percentage **16** piece of the action

Rake's Progress, The
opera by: **10** Stravinsky
character: **10** Ann Trulove, Nick Shadow **11** Baba the Turk, Mother Goose, Tom Rakewell

rakish **4** airy **6** breezy, dapper, jaunty, sporty **7** dashing, gallant, immoral, lustful **8** cavalier, debonair, depraved, sporting **9** bumptious, debauched, dissolute, lecherous, libertine **10** dissipated, lascivious, profligate, sauntering, swaggering

rally **4** meet, rush **5** score, unite **6** caucus, gather, muster, pick up, powwow, revive **7** catch up, collect, get well, improve, recruit, reunite, revival **8** assemble, assembly, recovery **9** come round, gathering, get better, reconvene **10** assemblage, convalesce, convention, reassemble, recuperate **11** convocation, improvement, mass meeting, pull through, restoration **12** call together, congregation, recuperation **13** convalescence

ram **3** hit, jam **4** beat, bump, butt, dash, goat, slam **5** crash, drive, force, smash **6** batter, hammer, hurtle, strike, thrust **7** run into

Ram
constellation of: **5** Aries

ramble **3** gad **4** hike, roam, rove, wind **5** amble, drift, range, snake, twist **6** stroll, wander, zigzag **7** meander, saunter, traipse **8** gad about, idle walk **9** gallivant **11** perambulate, peregrinate

rambling **6** prolix, uneven **7** diffuse **10** circuitous, digressive, discursive, disjointed

rambunctious **4** wild **5** noisy, rowdy **6** active, unruly **7** raucous, untamed, violent **9** irascible **10** boisterous, pugnacious **11** quarrelsome **14** uncontrollable

Rameau, Jean-Philippe
born: **5** Dijon **6** France
composer of: **6** Platee **8** Dardanus **13** Les Fetes d'Hebe **14** Castor et Pollux **15** Castor and Pollux **16** Les Indes Galantes, The Indigo Suitors **17** Hippolyte et Aricie **20** La Princesse de Navarre

ramification **3** arm **4** part, spur **5** prong **6** branch **8** division, offshoot **9** branching, outgrowth **10** divergence, separation **11** consequence, subdivision

rampage **4** rage **5** storm **7** run amok, run riot

rampant **4** rife **5** erect **6** raging **8** epidemic, pandemic **9** prevalent, unchecked, universal **10** on hind legs, standing up, widespread **12** ungovernable, unrestrained **14** uncontrollable

rampart **7** barrier, bastion, bulwark, parapet **9** barricade, earthwork **10** breastwork **13** defensive wall, fortification **14** protective wall

Ramsay, William
field: **9** chemistry
nationality: **7** British
discovered: **4** neon **5** argon (in air) **6** helium **7** krypton
awarded: **10** Nobel Prize

ramshackle **5** shaky **6** flimsy, shabby **7** rickety, run-down **8** decrepit, unstable, unsteady **9** crumbling, tottering **10** tumbledown **11** dilapidated **13** deteriorating

Ramtil *see* **5** Niger

Ran
origin: **12** Scandinavian
goddess of: **3** sea
husband: **5** Aegir

ranch **4** farm **5** range **6** grange, spread **7** acreage, station **8** hacienda **10** plantation

rancher **6** cowboy, farmer, gaucho **7** cowhand, cowpoke **8** herdsman, sheepman, stockman **9** cattleman **10** cowpuncher

rancid **3** old **4** foul, gamy, high, rank **6** putrid, strong **8** mephitic, stinking **10** malodorous

rancor **4** hate **5** spite **6** animus, enmity, hatred, malice, spleen **7** ill will **8** acrimony **9** animosity, antipathy, hostility **10** antagonism, bitterness, ill feeling, resentment **11** malevolence **12** spitefulness

rancorous **5** nasty **6** bitter **7** hostile **8** churlish, spiteful, vengeful, venomous **9** splenetic **10** ill-natured **11** acrimonious **12** antagonistic

Rand, Ayn
author of: **13** Atlas Shrugged **15** The Fountainhead **17** Romantic Manifesto

Randall, Tony
real name: **16** Leonard Rosenberg
born: **7** Tulsa OK
roles: **9** Mr Peepers **10** Felix Unger, Pillow Talk **12** Harvey Weskit, The Odd Couple **13** The Mating Game **20** The Seven Faces of Dr Lao

random **5** stray **6** casual, chance **7** aimless, offhand **9** haphazard, hit-or-miss, unplanned **10** accidental, fortuitous, occasional, undesigned, unexpected, unintended **12** adventitious **13** unintentional **14** unpremeditated

Ranft, George
real name of: **10** George Raft

range **3** run **4** roam, rove **5** field, gamut, limit, orbit, reach, ridge, scope **6** bounds, domain, extend, massif, plains, radius, sierra, sphere, wander **7** explore, pasture, purview, stretch, variety **8** province **9** selection **11** grazing land **16** chain of mountains

Rangoon
capital of: **5** Burma
former name: **5** Dagon **6** Yangon
founder: **10** Alaungpaya
landmark: **10** Sule Pagoda **15** Shwe Dagon Pagoda
name means: **11** end of strife
river: **7** Rangoon
square: **12** Independence

rangy **4** tall **5** broad, lanky **9** expansive, extensive

rank **3** row **4** bald, file, foul, line, lush, rate, sort, tall, type, wild **5** class, crass, dense, grade, gross, level, nasty, order, sheer, stale, stand, total, utter **6** arrant, coarse, column, estate, filthy, jungly, lavish, rancid, status **7** come out, echelon, glaring, profuse, quality, rampart **8** absolute, complete, flagrant, position, standing, tropical **9** atrocious, be classed, come first, downright, have place, luxuriant, monstrous, overgrown **10** outrageous, scurrilous **11** highgrowing, ill smelling, unmitigated **12** overabundant **14** classification, social standing, strong smelling

rank and file **6** troops **17** enlisted personnel, general membership

Rankine, William John Macquorn
field: **7** physics
nationality: **8** Scottish
devised: **12** Rankine Cycle, Rankine Scale **26** Fahrenheit temperature scale
author of: **22** Manual of the Steam Engine

rankle **4** gall, rile **5** chafe, gripe, pique **6** fester **8** irritate **10** not sit well

ransack **3** gut **4** comb, loot, raid, rake, sack **5** rifle, scour, strip **6** ravage, search **7** despoil, pillage, plunder **8** lay waste **9** devastate, vandalize **14** rummage through, turn upside down

ransom **3** buy **4** free, save **5** atone, price **6** redeem, rescue **7** deliver, expiate, reclaim, recover, release **8** liberate, retrieve **10** liberation, redemption

Ransom, John Crowe
member of: **12** the Fugitives
author of: **14** I'll Take My Stand **16** Captain Carpenter **30** Bells for John Whiteside's Daughter

rant **4** fume, rage, rave, yell **5** orate, scold, spout, storm **6** bellow **7** bluster, bombast, bravado, explode **8** harangue **11** declamation **12** exaggeration

rap **3** jaw, pan, tap **4** bang, chat, drum, talk **5** blame, knock, roast, speak, thump **6** dump on **7** clobber **8** converse **9** criticize **10** come down on **11** communicate **14** responsibility, shoot the breeze

rapacious **6** greedy **7** looting, wolfish **8** covetous, grasping, ravenous, thievish **9** marauding, mercenary, pillaging, predatory, voracious **10** avaricious, insatiable, plundering, ransacking

rapacity **5** greed **7** avarice **10** greediness **12** covetousness, graspingness **13** mercenariness

Rape of Lucrece
author: **18** William Shakespeare
character: **7** Tarquin **9** Collatine

Rape of the Lock, The
author: **13** Alexander Pope
character: **5** Ariel **7** Belinda, Umbriel **9** Lord Petre **10** Thalestris

Raphael **9** archangel

Raphael
real name: **14** Raffaello Santi **15** Raffaello Sanzio
born: **5** Italy **6** Urbino
artwork: **7** Disputa **8** Julius II **10** Entombment **14** Sistine Madonna **17** The School of Athens, The Virgin and Child **18** Madonna di Casa Tempi, The Transfiguration **19** The Triumph of Galatea **21** Baldassare Castiglione **22** The Marriage of the Virgin **24** The Expulsion of Heliodorus **28** The Madonna and Child with St John (La Belle Jardiniere)
architect of: **11** Villa Madama (Rome) **16** Pandolfini Palace (Florence) **22** Vidoni-Caffarelli Palace (Rome)

rapid **4** fast **5** brisk, fleet, hasty, quick, swift **6** active, flying, prompt, speedy **7** express, hurried, instant, rushing **8** agitated, feverish **9** galloping, unchecked **11** accelerated, expeditious, precipitate

rapidity **5** haste, speed **8** celerity, velocity **9** fleetness, quickness, swiftness **10** promptness

rapidly **4** fast **5** apace **7** briskly, hastily, quickly, swiftly **8** pell-mell, speedily **9** hurriedly, like a shot, overnight **10** in high gear **11** at full speed **13** expeditiously, helter-skelter

rapids **5** chute **7** current **10** white water

rapport **3** tie **4** link **10** connection, fellowship **11** affiliation, camaraderie **12** relationship **13** understanding **17** interrelationship

rapprochement **6** accord **7** detente, entente **9** agreement **10** adjustment, compromise, settlement **11** appeasement, arrangement **12** conciliation, pacification **13** accommodation, harmonization, reconcilement, understanding **14** reconciliation **16** mutual concession

rapscallion **5** knave, rogue, scamp **6** rascal **7** low-life, villain **8** scalawag **9** scoundrel **10** blackguard, ne'er-do-well, rascallion **14** good-for-nothing

rapt **6** dreamy, enrapt, intent **7** bemused, charmed **8** absorbed, ecstatic **9** attentive, bewitched, delighted, enchanted, engrossed, entranced, rapturous **10** captivated, enraptured, enthralled, fascinated, interested, moonstruck, spellbound **11** transported

rapture **3** joy **5** bliss **6** thrill **7** delight, ecstasy, elation **8** euphoria, felicity **9** beatitude

rapturous **4** rapt **8** beatific, blissful, ecstatic **9** entralled **10** enraptured

rare **3** few **6** scarce, unique **7** unusual **8** uncommon **10** hard to find, infrequent **11** exceptional, seldom found **16** few and far between

rarefied **4** thin **6** dilute, purify, rarify, reduce, refine, subtle **7** inflate **8** diminish **9** attenuate, extenuate

rarely **6** hardly, seldom **8** not often **10** hardly ever, uncommonly **12** infrequently, scarcely ever **15** once in a blue moon, on rare occasions **17** once in a great while

raring **4** agog, avid, keen **5** eager **8** desirous **9** impatient **12** enthusiastic

rarity **6** oddity **7** anomaly **8** scarcity **11** unusualness **12** uncommonness **14** remarkableness

rascal **3** cad, imp **4** rake **5** devil, knave, rogue, scamp **7** villain **8** rakehell, scalawag **9** prankster, reprobate, scoundrel, trickster **10** blackguard, delinquent **11** rapscallion

rash **5** brash, hasty **6** abrupt **7** foolish **8** careless, headlong, heedless, reckless **9** foolhardy, impetuous, imprudent, impulsive, premature, unadvised, unchecked **10** incautious, indiscreet, ungoverned, unthinking **11** adventurous, harebrained, injudicious, precipitate, thoughtless **12** devil-may-care, uncontrolled **13** irresponsible

rashness **8** audacity, boldness **9** riskiness **12** heedlessness, indiscretion, recklessness **13** foolhardiness, impulsiveness **15** precipitousness, thoughtlessness

Rashomon
author: **18** Ryunosuke Akutagawa
director: **13** Akira Kurosawa

Raskolnikov
character in: **18** Crime and Punishment
author: **10** Dostoevsky

rasp **3** irk, nag, rub, vex **4** fiie **5** chafe, grate, worry **6** abrade, scrape, wheeze **7** grating, scraper, scratch **8** abrasive, irritate **9** huskiness **10** hoarseness

raspberry **11** Rubus idaeus
varieties: **3** red **4** hill **5** black, dwarf **6** Mysore, purple **8** European **9** flowering, Mauritius **11** American red **13** Rocky Mountain **15** Purple-flowering **22** Rocky Mountain flowering
brandy: **9** Framboise

rasping **5** harsh, raspy, rough **6** hoarse **7** chafing, grating, nagging **8** abrading, scraping, worrying **9** offensive **10** irritating

Rasselas
author: **13** Samuel Johnson
character: **5** Imlac **6** Pekuah **7** Nekayah
Rasselas's title: **17** Prince of Abyssinia

Rassendyll, Rudolph
character in: **15** Prisoner of Zenda
author: **4** Hope

rat **3** cad, cur **4** fink, heel **5** churl, knave, louse **6** betray, rascal, rotter, squeal, vermin **7** bounder, villain **8** informer, inform on **9** scoundrel **10** blackguard **11** stool pigeon

rate **3** fee **4** cost, deem, dues, levy, pace, rank, toll **5** class, count, price, speed, tempo **6** charge, figure, look on, regard, tariff **7** expense, measure **8** classify **10** assessment

rate highly **5** prize, value **6** admire, esteem **7** cherish, respect **8** treasure

Rathbone, Basil
real name: **25** Philip St John Basil Rathbone
born: **11** South Africa **12** Johannesburg
roles: **6** Tybalt **7** Karenin **10** Dawn Patrol **11** Mr Murdstone **12** Anna Karenina **14** Romeo and Juliet, Sherlock Holmes, The Mark of Zorro **16** A Tale of Two Cities, David Copperfield **20** The Last Days of Pompeii **24** The Adventures of Robin Hood **25** Thc Hound of the Baskervilles

rather **4** a bit, very **5** quite **6** fairly, kind of, pretty, sort of **8** slightly, somewhat **10** moderately, more or less, relatively **13** comparatively

ratification **2** OK **4** okay **7** consent **8** approval, sanction **10** validation **11** affirmation, endorsement **12** confirmation **13** authorization, corroboration **14** seal of approval

ratify **2** OK **4** okay **6** affirm, uphold **7** agree to, approve, certify, confirm, endorse, support **8** accede to, make good, sanction, validate **9** authorize, consent to, make valid **11** acknowledge **12** authenticate

rating **4** mark, rank **5** class, grade, ratio, value **6** degree, rebuke, sailor, seaman **7** ranking **8** standing **9** appraisal **10** assessment, evaluation, percentage **14** classification

ratio **8** equation **10** proportion **11** arrangement **12** distribution **13** apportionment, fixed relation **15** proportionality **17** interrelationship **20** proportional relation

ration, rations **3** due **4** dole, food **5** allot **6** stores **7** measure, mete out **8** allocate **9** allotment, apportion, food share, provender, provision **10** provisions **13** apportionment

rational **4** sage, sane, wise **5** lucid, solid, sound **6** normal **7** logical **8** all there, balanced, credible, feasible **9** advisable, judicious, plausible, sagacious **10** reasonable **11** clearheaded, responsible **12** compos mentis **13** perspicacious **15** in one's right mind

rationale **5** basis, logic **6** excuse, reason **7** grounds **9** reasoning **10** key concept, philosophy **11** explanation, foundations **16** underlying reason

rationalize **6** excuse **7** explain, justify **8** palliate **9** whitewash **10** account for **11** explain away **13** put a gloss upon **14** make excuses for **16** make allowance for

rattan, ratan **4** cane, lash, palm, whip **5** thong **6** switch, wicker

Ratti, Achille **10** Pope Pius XI

rattle **3** gab, jar **4** faze **5** clang, clank, clink, prate, shake, throw, upset **6** bounce, flurry, jangle **7** agitate, blather, chatter, clatter, confuse, disturb, fluster, maunder, nonplus, perturb **8** bewilder, clacking, distract **9** discomfit **10** discompose, disconcert **11** roll loosely

rattlebrained **4** dumb **5** silly **6** stupid **7** asinine, doltish, foolish, idiotic, moronic, witless **9** brainless, imbecilic **10** fool-headed, half-witted **11** harebrained, lamebrained

rattled **5** fazed, upset **7** annoyed **9** disturbed, flustered, perturbed, thrown off **10** distracted **11** discomposed **12** disconcerted

rattle on **3** gab **4** blab **5** prate, run on **6** babble, gabble

7 blabber, chatter, prattle **16** run off at the mouth

ratty 4 poor, worn **5** angry, cross, nasty, testy **6** cranky, shabby, touchy **7** tangled, unkempt **8** wretched **9** irascible, motheaten **11** dilapidated

raucous 4 loud **5** harsh, raspy, rough **6** hoarse, shrill **7** blaring, grating, jarring **8** grinding, jangling, piercing, strident **9** dissonant **10** discordant, stertorous **11** cacophonous **12** earsplitting, inharmonious

raunchy 4 lewd **5** dirty, gross **6** coarse, smutty, vulgar **8** offcolor

Rauschenberg, Robert
born: 12 Port Arthur TX
artwork: 3 Bed **5** Barge **7** Jammers **8** Monogram **11** Retroactive

ravage 3 gut **4** loot, raid, rape, raze, ruin, sack **5** strip, waste, wreck **6** maraud **7** despoil, destroy, overrun, pillage, plunder, ransack, shatter **8** demolish, desolate, lay waste, spoliate **9** devastate **10** lay in ruins

rave 3 wax **4** fume, go on, gush, rage, rant **5** be mad, kudos, storm **6** babble, bubble, ramble **7** be angry, bluster, carry on, explode, flare up, run amok, sputter, thunder **8** flattery **9** be furious, expatiate, go on and on, good press, laudatory **10** effervesce, high praise, rhapsodize **11** blow one's top, compliments

ravel 4 undo **6** unknit **7** unravel, untwine, untwist

Ravel, Maurice
born: 6 France **7** Ciboure
composer of: 6 Bolero **7** La Valse, Mirrors **8** Jeux d'eau **9** Fountains **11** Mother Goose, Sheherazade **14** Daphnis et Chloe **15** Gaspard de la Nuit, L'Heure Espagnole **17** Rapsodie Espagnole, The Tomb of Couperin **20** Pavane for a Dead Infant **21** Don Quichotte a Dulcinee **22** L'Enfant et les Sortileges, Pavane for a Dead Princess **27** Pavane pour une infante defunte, Valses nobles et sentimentales

raven 3 jet **4** crow, dark, inky, rook **5** black, ebony, sable **6** devour **9** coal-black

Raven, The
author: 13 Edgar Allan Poe

ravenous 6 greedy, hungry **7** piggish, starved **8** covetous, famished, grasping, ravening, starving **9** insatiate, predatory, rapacious, voracious **10** avaricious, gluttonous, insatiable

Ravenshoe
author: 13 Henry Kingsley

ravine 3 gap **4** pass, rift, wadi **5** abyss, break, chasm, cleft, crack, gorge, gulch, gully, split **6** arroyo, breach, canyon, clough, divide, valley **7** fissure **8** crevasse

raving 3 mad **4** wild **6** insane **7** ranting **8** frenzied **9** delirious

ravish 4 rape **5** abuse, charm, cheer **6** defile, snatch, tickle **7** delight, enchant, gladden, outrage, overjoy, violate **8** deflower, enthrall, entrance, knock out **9** captivate, enrapture, fascinate, transport

ravishing 8 alluring, charming, gorgeous, smashing, splendid, striking **9** beautiful **10** bewitching, delightful, enchanting, entrancing **11** captivating, fascinating, sensational

raw 4 bare, cold, damp, rare **5** basic, bleak, crude, frank, fresh, green, harsh, plain, rough, young **6** biting, bitter, brutal, callow, chilly, rookie, unripe **7** cutting, natural, nipping, numbing, unbaked, untried **8** blustery, freezing, ignorant, immature, inexpert, piercing, pinching, uncooked, untaught, untested **9** inclement, underdone, undrilled, unfledged, unrefined, unskilled, untrained, windswept **10** amateurish, unprepared, unseasoned **11** not finished, undercooked, undeveloped, unexercised, uninitiated, unpracticed, unprocessed, unvarnished **13** inexperienced, undisciplined, unembellished **15** not manufactured

rawboned 4 lean **5** gaunt, lanky, spare **7** angular

Rawdon, Captain
character in: 10 Bleak House
author: 7 Dickens

Rawhide
character: 5 Mushy **8** Gil Favor, Ian Cabot, Wishbone **9** Jim Quince, Pete Nolan **10** Rowdy Yates **11** Joe Scarlett, Solomon King **13** Clay Forrester **14** Hey Soos Patines
cast: 10 Sheb Wooley **11** Charles Gray, David Watson, Eric Fleming, Robert Cabal, Rocky Shahan, Steve Raines **12** James Murdock, Paul Brinegar **13** Clint Eastwood **16** Raymond St Jacques

Rawlings, Marjorie Kinnan
author of: 11 The Yearling

rawness 3 nip **4** bite **5** chill **8** rudeness **9** crudeness, greenness, roughness, sharpness, vulgarity **10** chilliness **12** inexperience

ray 3 arm **4** beam, fish, line **5** gleam, light, shaft, shine, skate, trace **6** branch, streak, stream, stripe **7** radiate **8** particle, plowfish, radiance **9** emanation, radiation

Ray, Man
born: 14 Philadelphia PA
artwork: 4 Gift (Le Cadeau) **7** Manikin **9** The Lovers **13** Observing Time **45** The Rope Dancer Accompanies Herself with Her Shadows

Rayleigh, John William Strutt
field: 7 physics
nationality: 7 British
discovered: 5 argon
awarded: 10 Nobel Prize

rayon
invented by: 4 Swan

raze 4 fell, ruin **5** level, smash, wreck **6** reduce, remove, topple **7** destroy, flatten, wipe out **8** demolish, pull down, tear down **9** break down, dismantle, knock down **10** obliterate

razor
invented by: 6 Schick **8** Gillette

Razorback State
nickname of: 8 Arkansas

Re *see* **2** Ra

reach 3 get, hit **4** find, go to, grab, make, move **5** climb, enter, get to, grasp, seize, touch **6** attain, clutch, come to, extend, grab at, land at, secure, spread **7** contact, stretch **8** amount to, approach, arrive at **9** get hold of, set foot in **10** get as far as, outstretch, stretch out

reachable 6 at hand **8** possible **10** accessible, achievable, attainable, obtainable, procurable

reach the top 6 arrive **7** prosper, succeed **8** make good **13** hit the big time

react 4 work **6** answer, behave, resist, return **7** respond **11** reverberate

reaction **5** reply **6** answer, reflex **8** backlash, response **11** restoration **13** counteraction **14** chemical change **17** counterrevolution, right-wing comeback

reactionary **7** diehard **8** mossback, rightist **9** right-wing **10** regressive **11** right-winger **12** reversionary **17** ultraconservative **20** counterrevolutionary

react to **5** reply **6** answer **7** respond **11** acknowledge

read **2** go **3** say **4** note, scan, show **5** study, utter **6** adduce, peruse, recite **7** analyze, deliver, discern, explain, present **8** construe, decipher, indicate, perceive, pore over **9** apprehend, interpret, translate **10** comprehend, glance over, understand **11** extrapolate

Read, Piers Paul
author of: **5** Alive **9** Polonaise **10** Monk Dawson, The Junkers, The Upstart **18** Professor's Daughter

Reade, Charles
author of: **13** Peg Woffington **23** The Cloister and the Hearth

readily **6** at once, easily, freely, pronto **7** quickly **8** in no time, promptly, smoothly, speedily **9** expressly, hands down, instantly, willingly **10** graciously **11** immediately, straightway **12** effortlessly, ungrudgingly

readiness **8** alacrity, dispatch **9** alertness **10** promptness **12** preparedness

Reading on the Statute of Uses
author: **12** Francis Bacon

read the riot act **5** chide, scold **6** berate, rebuke **7** censure, chasten, correct, lecture, reprove **8** admonish **9** dress down, reprimand **10** take to task

ready **3** apt, fit, set **4** deft, keen, ripe, up to **5** acute, alert, eager, equip, handy, on tap, prone, sharp **6** adroit, all set, artful, astute, at hand, bright, clever, expert, facile, fit out, liable, mature, on hand, primed, prompt, shrewd, speedy **7** cunning, equal to, prepare, present, tending, willing **8** disposed, inclined, masterly, punctual, skillful **9** attentive, dexterous, fitted out, furnished, ingenious, in harness, versatile, wide-awake **10** accessible, discerning, perceptive, put in order **11** acquisitive, expeditious, predisposed, quick-witted, resourceful, serviceable

ready for use **5** handy, on tap **6** at hand, on hand **9** available **10** accessible, convenient **11** at one's elbow **14** at one's disposal

ready-made **10** off-the-rack **11** ready-to-wear, store-bought **17** store manufactured

ready money **4** cash **8** currency **10** cash on hand

ready to go **5** peppy **9** full of pep **10** raring to go **17** full of vim and vigor **24** bright-eyed and bushy-tailed

Reagan, Ronald Wilson *see box, p. 812*

real **4** pure, true **5** solid, valid **6** actual, honest **7** certain, factual, genuine, sincere **8** absolute, bona fide, positive, rightful, tangible, truthful **9** authentic, unalloyed, unfeigned, veracious, veritable **10** legitimate, unaffected **11** not affected, substantial, substantive, unvarnished **12** well-grounded **13** unadulterated **14** unquestionable

realistic **4** real **7** genuine, graphic, natural, precise **8** faithful, lifelike, truthful **9** authentic, depictive, objective, pragmatic **10** true-to-life **11** descriptive, down-to-earth **12** naturalistic **16** representational

reality **4** fact **5** truth **6** verity **9** actuality **11** materiality, tangibility **12** corporeality **14** substantiality **17** physical existence

realization **7** success **8** grasping **10** attainment, perception **11** achievement, culmination, fulfillment **12** appreciation, consummation **13** comprehension, understanding **14** accomplishment

realize **2** do **3** get, net **4** gain **5** clear, grasp **6** absorb, attain, fathom, gather, profit **7** achieve, acquire, cognize, discern, execute, fulfill, imagine, make out, perform, produce **8** carry out, complete, conceive, make good, perceive **9** actualize, apprehend, discharge, make money, penetrate, recognize **10** accomplish, appreciate, bring about, comprehend, consummate, effectuate, understand **11** bring to pass **12** carry through

realized **3** got **6** gained, netted, proved, proven **7** cleared, grasped, made out, saw into **8** absorbed, accepted, effected, executed, existing, fathomed, gathered, imagined, made good, profited **9** completed, conceived, discerned, fulfilled, perceived, performed **10** actualized, penetrated, recognized, understood **11** appreciated, apprehended, consummated, established **12** accomplished, comprehended

really **5** truly **6** indeed, in fact, surely, verily **8** actually **9** certainly, genuinely, literally, veritably **10** absolutely, positively, truthfully **13** categorically **14** unquestionably

realm **4** land **5** field, orbit, state **6** domain, empire, nation, region, sphere **7** country, demesne, kingdom **8** dominion, monarchy, province **11** royal domain

real McCoy, the **4** real **7** genuine **9** authentic **12** the real thing

reap **3** get, win **4** earn, gain **5** glean, score **6** derive, gather, obtain, profit, secure, take in **7** acquire, bring in, harvest, procure, realize

rear **3** aft, end **4** back, heel **5** after, nurse, raise, stern, train **6** dorsal, foster **7** bring up, care for, cherish, develop, educate, nurture, postern, tail end **8** back part, hind part, hindmost **9** aftermost, after part, at the back, cultivate, in the back, posterior

Rear Window
director: **15** Alfred Hitchcock
based on story by: **15** Cornell Woolrich
cast: **10** Grace Kelly **11** Raymond Burr **12** James Stewart, Thelma Ritter, Wendell Corey

Rea Silvia
also: **4** Ilia **10** Rhea Silvia
form: **12** vestal virgin
lover: **4** Mars
son: **5** Remus **7** Romulus

reason **3** wit **4** head **5** cause, logic, sense, solve **6** acumen, brains, figure, motive, sanity **7** grounds, insight **8** lucidity, occasion **9** awareness, faculties, intellect, normality, rationale, reasoning **10** perception **11** common sense, discernment, exhortation, explanation, penetration, rationality **12** apprehension, intelligence, perspicacity, think through **13** argumentation, comprehension, justification, mental bal-

Reagan, Ronald Wilson
nickname: **5** Dutch **6** Ronnie
presidential rank: **8** fortieth
party:
current: **10** Republican
former: **10** Democratic
state represented: **2** CA
defeated: **6** (James Earl) Carter (Jr) **7** (Walter Frederick "Fritz") Mondale **8** (John Bayard) Anderson
vice president: **4** (George Herbert Walker) Bush
cabinet:
state: **4** (Alexander M) Haig (Jr) **6** (George P) Shultz
treasury: **5** (Donald T) Regan
defense: **10** (Caspar W) Weinberger
attorney general: **5** (William French) Smith
interior: **4** (James) Watt **5** (William P) Clark
agriculture: **5** (John R) Block
commerce: **8** (Malcolm) Baldrige
labor: **7** (Raymond J) Donovan
health and human services: **7** (Margaret M) Heckler **9** (Richard S) Schweiker
education: **4** (Terrel H) Bell
HUD: **6** (Samuel R) Pierce (Jr)
transportation: **4** (Elizabeth H) Dole **5** (Andrew L) Lewis (Jr)
energy: **5** (Donald P) Hodel **7** (James B) Edwards
born: **9** Tampico IL
education:
College: **6** Eureka
religion: **17** Disciples of Christ
interests: **2** TV **5** track **6** movies **8** football **9** chops wood **10** basketball, jelly beans **13** weightlifting **15** horseback riding
vacation spot: **14** Rancho del Cielo (Santa Barbara CA)
dog: **5** Lucky
author: **18** Where Is the Rest of Me?
political career:
governor of: **10** California
civilian career: **5** actor **17** radio sportscaster
host: **15** Death Valley Days **22** General Electric Theater
president of: **17** Screen Actors Guild
roles: **8** King's Row **10** Brother Rat **13** John Loves Mary, The Hasty Heart **15** Bedtime for Bonzo **19** The Voice of the Turtle **20** Cattle Queen of Montana **21** The Girl from Jones Beach **22** Knute Rockne All American
military service: **6** US Army **7** captain **10** World War II
notable events of lifetime/term:
approval of: **10** MX missiles
assassination attempt on: **6** Reagan **14** Pope John Paul II
attempted assassination on Reagan by: **15** John W Hinckley Jr
bombing of: **5** Libya
hostages freed in: **4** Iran
invasion of: **7** Grenada
marines sent to: **7** Lebanon
nuclear disaster at: **9** Chernobyl
Russians shot down: **14** Korean airliner
scandal: **8** Irangate
father: **10** John Edward
nickname: **4** Jack
mother: **5** Nelle (Wilson)
siblings: **4** (John) Neil
wife: **4** Jane (Wyman) **5** Nancy (Davis)
Nancy Davis born: **18** Anne Frances Robbins
children: **6** Ronald **7** Maureen, Michael (adopted) **8** Patricia
Patricia also actress known as: **10** Patti Davis
first lady:
program: **9** Drug abuse, Just Say No **12** Alcohol abuse **18** Foster Grandparents

ance, understanding **15** clearheadedness

reasonable **4** fair, just, sage, sane, wise **5** sound **6** likely, proper **7** fitting, knowing, lenient, logical, natural, patient, prudent **8** credible, moderate, possible, probable, rational, sensible, suitable, thinking **9** equitable, impartial, judicious, objective, plausible, temperate, tolerable **10** admissible, coolheaded, legitimate, not extreme, reflective, thoughtful **11** circumspect, intelligent, justifiable, levelheaded, not unlikely, of good sense, predictable, well-founded **12** not excessive, well-grounded **13** understanding **14** understandable **15** of sound judgment

reasonableness **5** logic **6** sanity, wisdom **8** fairness, prudence **9** good sense **10** moderation **11** credibility, objectivity, rationality **12** good judgment, impartiality, intelligence **13** judiciousness **14** circumspection, thoughtfulness **15** clearheadedness

reasonably **6** almost, fairly **8** passably, somewhat **10** moderately, more or less **13** approximately

reasoning **5** basis, logic **6** ground **7** thought **8** analysis, argument, thinking **9** deduction, inference, rationale **10** cogitation, reflection **11** penetration **13** ratiocination **14** interpretation

reason out **8** mull over **10** deliberate **12** think through

reassure **5** cheer **6** buoy up, uplift **7** bolster, comfort **8** inspirit **9** encourage **13** inspire hope in

reassured **6** buoyed **9** bolstered, comforted, heartened **10** emboldened, encouraged, inspirited

reassuring **7** hopeful **10** auspicious, comforting, heartening **11** encouraging

Reb **2** Mr **5** Rabbi **6** Mister

rebate **6** refund **8** discount **9** abatement

Rebecca
author: **15** Daphne du Maurier
character: **10** Jack Favell, Mrs Danvers (Danny) **12** Frank Crawley **13** Colonel Julyan, Maxim de Winter
house: **9** Manderley
director: **15** Alfred Hitchcock
cast: **10** Nigel Bruce **12** Joan Fontaine **13** George Sanders **14** Judith Anderson (Mrs Danvers) **15** Laurence Olivier (Maxim de Winter)
Oscar for: **7** picture

Rebecca
character in: **7** Ivanhoe
author: **5** Scott

Rebecca *see* **7** Rebekah

Rebecca of Sunnybrook Farm
author: **17** Kate Douglas Wiggin
character: **4** Cobb **8** Adam Ladd **11** Aunt Miranda **14** Rebecca Randall **15** Emma Jane Perkins

Rebekah
also: **7** Rebecca
father: **7** Bethuel
husband: **5** Isaac
brother: **5** Laban
son: **4** Esau **5** Isaac, Jacob

rebel **3** shy **4** riot **5** avoid, quail, react, wince **6** flinch, mutiny, recoil, revolt, rise up, shrink **7** seceder, traitor, upstart **8** deserter, maverick, resister, turncoat **9** anarchist, dissenter, insurgent **10** iconoclast, malcontent, separatist **12** secessionist **13** nonconformist, revolutionary, revolutionist **15** insurrectionist

rebellion **6** mutiny, putsch, revolt **8** defiance, sedition, upheaval, uprising **9** coup d'etat **10** insurgency, revolution **12** insurrection

rebellious **6** unruly **7** defiant **8** contrary, mutinous, up in arms **9** alienated, fractious, insurgent, seditious, truculent, turbulent **10** disorderly, pugnacious, refractory **11** disobedient, intractable, quarrelsome **12** contumacious, recalcitrant, ungovernable, unmanageable **13** insubordinate, revolutionary **14** uncontrollable **15** insurrectionary

rebelliousness **8** defiance **9** rebellion **12** disobedience

Rebel Without a Cause
director: **11** Nicholas Ray
cast: **8** Sal Mineo **9** James Dean, Jim Backus **11** Natalie Wood

Rebirth
god of: **4** Gwyn

rebound **3** bob **6** bounce, recoil, re-echo **7** flounce **8** recovery, ricochet **10** spring back

rebounding **7** rubbery, springy **9** resilient **11** ricocheting **12** bouncing back

rebuff **4** deny, snub **5** check, repel, spurn **6** ignore, put off, refuse, reject, slight **7** decline, put-down, refusal, repulse **8** turn down **9** disregard, rejection **10** putting off **12** cold shoulder **13** slap in the face **15** keep at a distance

rebuke **5** blame, chide, scold, score **6** berate **7** censure, chew out, chiding, lecture, reproof, reprove, upbraid **8** admonish, berating, call down, reproach, reproval, scolding **9** dress down, reprimand **10** admonition, chewing out, take to task, upbraiding **11** castigation, disapproval **12** admonishment, dressing down, remonstrance, reprehension, take down a peg **13** find fault with, tongue-lashing **15** remonstrate with

rebuttal **5** reply **6** answer, denial, retort **7** defense, riposte **8** disproof, negation, response **9** disproval, rejoinder **10** refutation **11** confutation **12** counterreply, disagreement, surrejoinder **13** contradiction **15** counterargument

recalcitrant **5** balky **6** mulish, unruly **7** willful **8** contrary, stubborn **9** obstinate, pigheaded, unwilling **10** bullheaded, headstrong, refractory **11** disobedient, intractable **12** unsubmissive

recall **5** place **6** memory, revive **8** call back, remember **9** reanimate, recognize, recollect **10** reactivate, remobilize **11** reinstitute, remembrance **12** recollection **17** ability to remember

recant **4** deny **5** unsay **6** abjure, disown, recall, renege, repeal, revoke **7** disavow, rescind, retract **8** disclaim, forswear, renounce, take back, withdraw **9** foreswear, repudiate **10** apostatize **12** eat one's words **14** change one's mind

recantation **6** denial **9** disavowal **10** refutation, retraction, revocation **11** repudiation **12** renunciation

recapitulate **5** recap, sum up **6** relate, repeat, reword **7** recount, restate **8** rephrase **9** epitomize, reiterate, summarize **15** repeat in essence

recapture **6** retake **7** reprise **15** experience again

recede **3** ebb **5** abate **6** back up, go back, retire **7** regress, retreat, subside **10** retrogress

receipt **7** arrival, release, voucher **9** admission, discharge, receiving, reception **10** acceptance, admittance, possession, recipience **11** acquisition, transferral

receipts **3** pay **4** gain, gate, take **5** share, split, wages **6** income, recipe, return **7** formula, payment, profits, returns, revenue **8** earnings, proceeds **9** emolument **10** net profits **12** remuneration **13** reimbursement

receive **3** get **4** meet **5** admit, greet, put up **6** accept, come by, obtain, regard, secure, suffer, take in **7** acquire, adjudge, approve, be given, react to, sustain, undergo, welcome **8** meet with, submit to **9** encounter, entertain **10** experience **11** accommodate

receive willingly **6** accept **10** take gladly **16** accept with thanks **18** accept with open arms

receive with favor **6** praise **7** approve **10** appreciate

receive with open arms **6** invite **7** embrace, welcome **13** accept eagerly **19** roll out the red carpet

recent **3** new **4** late **5** fresh, novel **6** modern **8** up-to-date **9** latter-day **12** contemporary **13** up-to-the-minute

receptacle **3** bag, bin, box, can, jar **4** file, tray **6** basket, bottle, hamper, holder, hopper, vessel **7** carrier **8** receiver **9** container **10** depository, repository **11** compartment

reception **2** do **4** fete **5** party **6** affair, soiree **7** welcome **8** greeting **11** recognition **15** social gathering

receptive **8** amenable, friendly **10** accessible, hospitable, interested, open-minded, responsive **11** susceptible **12** approachable **17** favorably disposed

recess **3** bay, gap **4** bend, cell, cove, fold, gulf, lull, nook, pass, rest, slot **5** break, cleft, gorge, inlet, letup, niche, pause **6** alcove, corner, harbor, hiatus, hollow **7** holiday, interim, respite, time out **8** interval, vacation **9** interlude **10** pigeonhole **11** coffee break, indentation **12** intermission **14** breathing spell

recessed **4** sunk **6** paused, sunken **7** delayed **8** deferred, extended, indented **9** adjourned, dissolved, postponed, prolonged, withdrawn **10** terminated
church wall: **5** ambry
wall: **6** alcove

recesses **6** depths **10** inmost part, penetralia

recession **10** depression **11** recessional **16** economic downturn

recherche **4** rare **5** prize **6** choice, exotic, scarce, select, unique **7** special, unusual **8** original, superior, uncommon, valuable **9** different, priceless **10** one of a kind **11** exceptional

recipe **2** Rx **4** cure, rule **5** axiom **6** elixir, remedy **7** formula, receipt **12** instructions, prescription

recipient **4** heir **5** donee, taker **6** getter **7** legatee **8** accepter, acquirer, obtainer, receiver **9** presentee **11** beneficiary

reciprocal **6** common, linked, mutual, shared **8** returned **9** bilateral, exchanged, one for one **10** equivalent **11** give-and-take **12** interchanged, interrelated **13** complementary, corresponding, given in return **14** interdependent **15** interchangeable

reciprocate **4** feel **6** return **7** requite, respond **9** retaliate **10** make return **11** act likewise, give and take, interchange **12** give in return **19** return the compliment

reciprocity **8** exchange **11** give and take, interchange

recital **4** talk **6** report **7** concert, telling **8** delivery, reciting **9** discourse, narration, narrative, rendition **10** recitation **11** description, particulars, performance **12** dissertation, oral exercise **13** public reading **14** graphic account, recapitulation

recite **4** tell **5** quote, speak **6** relate, repeat **7** declaim, deliver, narrate, perform, recount **10** say by heart **11** communicate

reckless **4** rash, wild **5** giddy, hasty **6** daring, fickle, madcap, unwary **7** flighty, foolish, unaware **8** careless, cavalier, heedless, mindless, unsteady, volatile **9** daredevil, desperate, foolhardy, imprudent, impulsive, negligent, oblivious, unheeding, unmindful **10** incautious, indiscreet, insensible, neglectful, regardless, unthinking, unwatchful **11** harebrained, inattentive, precipitate, thoughtless, unconcerned **12** devil-may-care, unsolicitous **13** inconsiderate, irresponsible, uncircumspect **14** scatterbrained

recklessly **4** fast **5** blind **6** rashly, wildly **7** hastily **8** headlong **9** headfirst **10** carelessly, heedlessly **11** audaciously, desperately, impetuously, impulsively **12** unmindfully **13** irresponsibly, unconcernedly

recklessness **7** abandon **8** rashness **9** disregard, unconcern **10** imprudence, profligacy **11** impetuosity **12** heedlessness, immoderation **13** foolhardiness **15** thoughtlessness **16** irresponsibility

reckon **3** add **4** bank, cope, deal, deem, plan, rank, rate **5** add up, class, count, fancy, guess, judge, tally, think, total, value **6** assess, decide, esteem, expect, figure, handle, regard **7** account, adjudge, balance, bargain, compute, imagine, presume, suppose, surmise **8** appraise, consider, estimate **9** calculate, determine, speculate

reckoning **3** tab **4** bill, doom **5** count, tally, total **6** adding, charge **7** account **8** estimate, judgment **9** appraisal, summation **10** estimation, evaluation **11** calculation, computation **13** final judgment **19** settling of an account

reclaim **6** reform, rescue **7** correct, recover, rectify, restore

recline **4** lean, loll, rest **6** lounge, repose, sprawl **7** lie back, lie down **12** take one's ease

reclining **7** lolling, resting **8** lounging, reposing **9** lying down, recumbent

recluse **3** nun **4** monk **5** crank, loner **6** hermit, hidden, secret **7** ascetic, eremite, erratic, oddball **8** cenobite, crackpot **9** eccentric **10** cloistered **11** sequestered **13** nonconformist

recognition **6** notice **9** discovery **10** acceptance, validation **13** comprehension, understanding **14** acknowledgment, identification **19** diplomatic relations

recognizable **5** clear, plain **8** distinct **10** detectable **11** discernable, perceivable, perceptible **12** identifiable, intelligible **13** ascertainable **14** comprehensible, understandable **15** distinguishable

recognizance **4** bond **6** pledge **10** obligation **11** recognition **15** acknowledgement

recognize **3** see **4** know, spot **5** admit, place, sight **7** discern, make out, pick out, realize, respect, yield to **8** identify, submit to **9** be aware of, concede to **10** appreciate, comprehend, understand **11** acknowledge **14** give the floor to

recognized **5** known **8** accepted, admitted, approved, familiar, realized **9** customary **10** accredited **11** traditional **12** acknowledged, conventional

recoil **4** fail, kick **5** blink, cower, demur, quail, shirk, start, wince **6** blench, cringe, falter, flinch, revolt **7** fly back, rebound, retreat **8** draw back, hang back, jump back **9** bound back **10** shrink back, spring back

recoil at **4** hate **5** abhor **6** detest, eschew, loathe **7** despise **9** abominate, shudder at **10** shrink from **12** be revolted by **14** view with horror **18** feel aversion toward

recoiling **7** wincing **9** flinching **10** rebounding **11** drawing back **13** shrinking back, springing back

recollect **5** place **6** recall **8** remember **10** call to mind

recollection **4** mind **6** memoir, memory, recall, record **11** remembrance **12** reminiscence **13** retrospection
French: **8** souvenir

recommend **4** urge **5** favor, order **6** advise **7** counsel, endorse, propose, suggest **8** advocate, vouch for **9** encourage, prescribe **10** put forward **11** speak well of

recommendable **9** advisable, favorable **10** worthwhile

recommendation **4** plug **6** behest, praise **8** approval, good word **9** reference **11** endorsement **12** commendation

recompense **3** pay **5** repay **6** return, reward **7** payment **9** reimburse, repayment **10** compensate, remunerate, reparation **12** compensation, remuneration **15** indemnification

reconcile **5** fix up **6** adjust, make up, resign, settle, square **7** correct, patch up, rectify, reunite, win over **8** persuade **9** harmonize **10** conciliate, propitiate **11** set straight

reconcile oneself **6** submit **9** acquiesce **13** resign oneself

reconciliation **8** fixing up, making up, settling, squaring **10** adjustment, correction, patching up, rectifying **11** resignation, winning over **12** conciliation **13** justification, rectification **15** setting straight

recondite **4** deep **6** arcane, hidden **7** obscure **8** abstruse, esoteric **9** concealed **10** mysterious **16** incomprehensible

reconnaissance **6** survey **7** viewing **8** scouting, scrutiny **10** inspection **11** exploration, observation **12** surveillance **13** investigation **14** reconnoitering

reconnoiter **4** look **5** probe, scout **6** patrol, picket, survey **7** examine **8** remember, traverse

reconsider **5** amend **6** modify, ponder, review, revise **7** correct, rethink, sleep on **8** mull over, reassess **9** reexamine, think over **10** reevaluate **13** think better of **15** think twice about

reconstitute **7** restore **9** recompose **10** add water to **11** reconstruct

reconstruct **7** rebuild **8** make over, recreate **10** reassemble **11** reestablish **12** reconstitute

record **3** log **4** copy, file, list, memo, note, post, show, tape **5** admit, enter **6** annals, career, docket, enroll, report **7** account, archive, catalog, conduct, history, jot down, jotting, journal **8** document, indicate, register, take down **9** chronicle, introduce, write down **10** adventures, background, memorandum, transcribe **11** experiences, make an entry, performance, proceedings **12** unbeaten mark **14** top performance
French: **11** compte rendu

record
invented by: **4** Bell **6** Edison **7** Tainter **8** Berliner **10** Goldenmark

recount **4** tell **6** detail, recite, relate **7** explain, narrate **8** describe **9** count over

recoup **5** atone **6** redeem, regain **7** recover, replace **8** make good, retrieve **9** make up for, reacquire **13** make amends for

recourse **6** choice, option, resort **11** alternative, other choice

recover **4** heal, mend **5** rally **6** offset, pick up, recoup, redeem, regain, retake, revive **7** balance, get back, get well, improve, reclaim, restore, win back **8** make good, retrieve, revivify **9** make up for, reacquire, recapture, reconquer, repossess **10** come around, compensate, convalesce, recuperate, rejuvenate **11** pull through, resuscitate

recovery **4** cure **5** rally **6** recoup, rescue, upturn **7** revival, salvage **8** comeback **9** retrieval **10** betterment, regainment **11** improvement, reclamation, reformation, restoration **12** recuperation **13** business cycle, convalescence

recreancy **8** apostasy **9** cowardice, desertion **10** cravenness, disloyalty, infidelity **13** faithlessness, pusillanimity **14** unfaithfulness

recreant **6** coward, craven, yellow **8** apostate, cowardly, deserter, disloyal, renegade **9** undutiful **10** unfaithful **11** lily-livered **12** dishonorable **13** pusillanimous, yellow-bellied

recreation **4** play **5** hobby, sport **7** pastime **9** amusement, avocation, diversion **10** relaxation **13** entertainment **15** leisure activity

recrimination **5** blame **6** charge **10** accusation **13** countercharge

recruit **4** hire **5** raise, renew **6** employ, enlist, enroll, muster, novice, recoup, revive, rookie **7** draftee, provide, recover, restore **8** beginner, newcomer **9** conscript **10** recuperate

rectangle **3** box **6** oblong, square **7** polygon **10** quadrangle **13** parallelogram, quadrilateral

rectangular **4** long **6** square **7** boxlike **11** right-angled **12** quadrangular **13** quadrilateral

rectification **6** fixing, reform **7** redress **8** righting, squaring **9** remedying, repairing **10** adjustment, correction, regulation **12** setting right **15** putting straight, putting to rights **16** straightening out

rectify **3** fix **4** cure, mend **5** amend, emend, focus, right **6** adjust, attune, reform, remedy, repair, revise, square **7** correct, redress **8** put right, regulate, set right **9** make right **10** straighten

rectitude **5** honor **7** decency, probity **8** morality **9** integrity, principle **11** uprightness **12** virtuousness **13** righteousness **14** high-mindedness **15** trustworthiness **16** incorruptibility **17** irreproachability

rector **6** cleric, parson, pastor, priest **8** minister, preacher **9** churchman, clergyman **12** ecclesiastic

recumbent **4** flat **5** prone **6** supine **7** leaning **8** couchant **9** lying down, prostrate, reclining **10** horizontal **12** stretched out

recuperate **4** heal, mend **7** get well, improve, recover **8** come back **9** get better **10** come around, convalesce **11** be on the mend, pull through **14** return to health **16** regain one's health

recuperation **8** recovery **11** restoration **13** convalescence

recuperative **11** restorative **15** health-restoring

recur **6** repeat, resume, return **7** persist **8** come back, continue, reappear **9** come again **10** occur again

recurrence **5** cycle, round **6** repeat, return **7** relapse, renewal, reprise, routine **8** iterance, rotation **10** continuity, repetition **11** periodicity **12** reappearance

recurrent **7** regular **8** frequent, periodic **9** recurring, repeating **10** repetitive **11** reappearing **12** intermittent **14** appearing again

red **4** pink, rose, rosy, ruby, wine **5** aglow, coral, flame, ruddy **6** auburn, cherry, florid, maroon **7** burning, crimson, flaming, flushed, glowing, scarlet **8** blooming, blushing, cardinal, inflamed, reddened, rubicund **9** rubescent, vermilion **12** blood-colored

Red and the Black, The (Le Rouge et le Noir)
author: **8** Stendhal
character: **6** Fouque **8** M de Renal **11** Julien Sorel **16** Mathilde de la Mole

Red Badge of Courage, The
author: **12** Stephen Crane
character: **6** Wilson **10** Jim Conklin **12** Henry Fleming

red-blooded **5** lusty, peppy, vital **6** ardent, robust, strong, sturdy **7** dynamic, intense **8** forceful, powerful, spirited, vigorous **9** energetic **10** hot-blooded, passionate

Red Branch
origin: **5** Irish
warriors of: **9** Conchobar

Redburn
author: **14** Herman Melville

red-cheeked **4** rosy **5** ruddy **6** robust **8** blushing **12** apple-cheeked

Red Cross Knight
character in: **15** The Faerie Queene
author: **7** Spenser

redden **4** burn, glow **5** blush, color, flame, flush **9** go crimson **12** become florid

reddish **4** rosy, ruby **5** ruddy, rufus **6** flushy, rufous **7** roseate **8** rubicund

reddish-brown **4** rust **5** henna **6** auburn, copper, russet, sienna **8** chestnut, cinnamon

Red Earth People *see* **3** Fox

redeem **4** keep, save **5** cover **6** defray, ransom, recoup, reform, regain, rescue, settle **7** buy back, convert, fulfill, reclaim, recover, satisfy **8** atone for, make good, retrieve **9** discharge, make up for, repossess **10** evangelize, repurchase

redeemed **5** saved **7** claimed, rescued **8** made good, ransomed, reformed **9** atoned for, delivered, fulfilled, recovered **10** carried out, regenerate **11** repossessed

redemption **6** excuse, pardon, ransom, reform, rescue **7** salvage **8** recovery **9** amendment, atonement, exemption, expiation, salvation **10** conversion **11** deliverance, reformation

Redford, Robert
real name: **20** Charles Robert Redford
born: **13** Santa Monica CA
roles: **8** The Sting **10** The Natural **11** Legal Eagles **12** The Candidate, The Way We Were **13** Downhill Racer **14** The Great Gatsby **15** Jeremiah Johnson **17** Barefoot in the Park **19** All the President's Men **20** Three Days of the Condor **29** Butch Cassidy and the Sundance Kid
director: **14** Ordinary People (Oscar)

Redgrave, Lynn
born: **6** London **7** England
father: **18** Sir Michael Redgrave
sister: **15** Vanessa Redgrave
roles: **10** Georgy Girl **14** The Happy Hooker

Redgrave, Sir Michael
born: **7** Bristol, England
daughter: **4** Lynn **7** Vanessa
roles: **11** Dan Peggotty **15** The Lady Vanishes **16** David Copperfield **22** Mourning Becomes Electra **27** The Importance of Being Earnest

Redgrave, Vanessa
born: **6** London **7** England
father: **18** Sir Michael Redgrave
sister: **12** Lynn Redgrave
husband: **14** Tony Richardson
roles: **5** Julia, Yanks **6** Agatha, Blow-Up, Morgan **7** Camelot, Isadora **9** Guinevere **16** Mary Queen of Scots **17** The Lady from the Sea

red-hot **5** aglow, fiery **6** heated, raging **7** blazing, burning, glowing, intense **12** all-consuming

red-letter **5** happy, lucky **6** banner **10** auspicious, felicitous

redness **4** glow **5** blush, flush **8** rosiness **9** ruddiness **10** floridness

redolence **5** aroma, savor **7** bouquet **9** fragrance, good smell **12** pleasant odor

redolent **5** balmy, spicy **6** savory, smelly **7** mindful, odorous, reeking, scented **8** aromatic, fragrant, perfumed, stinking **9** evocative, odiferous **10** expressive, indicative, suggestive **11** odoriferous, reminiscent **13** sweet-smelling

Redon, Odilon
born: **6** France **8** Bordeaux
artwork: **10** In the Dream, The Cyclops **11** Le Vieil Ange **13** Flowers of Evil **15** Violette Heymann

redouble **7** augment, magnify **8** heighten, multiply **9** intensify

redoubtable **7** awesome **8** alarming, imposing **10** formidable **11** illustrious **12** awe-inspiring

redound **4** lead, tend **5** cause, surge **6** abound **7** conduce, incline **8** overflow **10** contribute **11** reverberate

redress **4** ease **5** amend, right **6** amends, reform, relief, remedy **7** correct, payment, rectify, relieve **8** easement, set right **9** make up for **10** recompense, reparation **11** restitution **12** compensation, satisfaction **13** compensate for, rectification **15** indemnification **18** make retribution for

Red River
director: **11** Howard Hawks
cast: **9** Joanne Dru, John Wayne **11** John Ireland **13** Walter Brennan **15** Montgomery Clift

Red Rover, The
author: **19** James Fenimore Cooper

Reds
director: **12** Warren Beatty
cast: **11** Diane Keaton

(Louise Bryant), Paul Sorvino **12** Warren Beatty (John Reed) **13** Jack Nicholson, Jerzy Kosinski **14** Edward Herrmann **16** Maureen Stapleton
Oscar for: 8 director **17** supporting actress (Stapleton)

Red Shoes, The
author: 21 Hans Christian Andersen
director: 13 Michael Powell **17** Emeric Pressburger
cast: 12 Marius Goring, Moira Shearer **13** Anton Walbrook **14** Robert Helpmann

Red Skelton Show, The
character: 8 Gertrude **10** Heathcliff **13** Mean Widdle Kid **14** San Fernando Red, Sheriff Deadeye, Willie Lump-Lump **16** Bolivar Shagnasty **17** Cauliflower McPugg **18** Clem Kadiddlehopper **20** Freddie the Freeloader
saying: 7 I dood it
closing line: 8 God bless

Red Sky at Morning
author: 15 Richard Bradford

reduce 3 cut **4** bust, curb, diet, dull, ease, thin **5** abate, blunt, break, check, force, lower, slash, water **6** damage, demote, dilute, lessen, retard, soften, temper, weaken **7** assuage, atrophy, cripple, cut down, leave in **8** diminish, discount, enfeeble, mark down, minimize, mitigate, moderate, modulate, slim down, slow down, tone down, trim down **9** bring down, checkmate, undermine **10** debilitate, devitalize, slenderize **11** lower in rank **12** incapacitate

reduced form 6 digest **7** summary **9** short form **11** abridgement, contraction **12** abbreviation, condensation

reduce speed 4 slow **5** brake **6** rein in **8** slow down **10** decelerate

reduce to nothing 5 erase **7** abolish, destroy, wipe out **8** lay waste **9** eradicate, liquidate **10** annihilate **11** exterminate

reductio ad absurdum
22 reduction to an absurdity

reduction 3 cut **5** break **8** decrease, discount **9** abatement, lessening **10** concession **11** abridgement, subtraction

reduction to an absurdity
Latin: 18 reductio ad absurdum

redundancy 6 excess **7** surplus **8** verbiage **9** tautology **10** repetition **11** diffuseness, superfluity **13** overabundance **14** circumlocution, repetitiveness

redundant 5 extra **6** excess **7** surplus **10** pleonastic **11** dispensable, inessential, overflowing, repetitious, superfluous, unnecessary **12** tautological **13** superabundant

redwood 19 Adenanthera pavonina, Sequoia sempervirens
varieties: 4 dawn **5** coast, giant **7** Madeira

reed
varieties: 3 bur **4** vine **5** Burma, giant **6** common **14** Mauritania vine

reed 9 six cubits

Reed, Sir Carol
director of: 6 Oliver (Oscar) **11** The Third Man

Reed, Walter S
field: 12 bacteriology
discovered cause of: 11 yellow fever

reef 3 bar **4** bank, flat, spit **5** shelf, shoal **7** sandbar, shallow

reek 4 fume **5** smell, smoke, steam, stink **6** stench **7** give off **9** effluvium, emanation

reel 4 rock, roll, spin, sway **5** lurch, pitch, swirl, waver, whirl **6** rotate, teeter, totter, wobble **7** revolve, stagger, stumble

reeling 5 dizzy, giddy, shaky **6** whirly **8** spinning, unsteady **10** staggering **11** vertiginous

Reese, Harold
nickname: 6 Pee Wee
sport: 8 baseball
position: 9 shortstop
team: 15 Brooklyn Dodgers

Reeve
character in: 18 The Canterbury Tales
author: 7 Chaucer

Reeve, Christopher
born: 9 New York NY
roles: 8 Superman **9** Deathtrap **13** The Bostonians **15** Somewhere in Time

refer 2 go **4** cite, send, turn **6** advert, allude, direct, submit **7** consult, deliver, mention **8** hand over, transfer, transmit **9** pass along

referee 5 judge **6** decree, settle, umpire **7** arbiter, mediate **8** judgment, mediator, moderate **9** arbitrate, determine, intercede, intervene, moderator, pronounce **10** adjudicate, arbitrator **11** adjudicator, intercessor **12** intermediary

reference 4 hint **7** inkling, mention **8** allusion, good word, innuendo **10** deposition, intimation, suggestion **11** affirmation, credentials, endorsement, implication, testimonial **13** certification **14** recommendation

reference book 5 atlas, bible **6** manual **9** guidebook **10** dictionary **12** encyclopedia

refine 6 filter, purify, strain **7** cleanse, develop, improve, perfect, process **9** cultivate

refined 5 clean, suave **6** gentle, polite, urbane **7** courtly, elegant, genteel **8** cleansed, cultured, delicate, finished, graceful, ladylike, mannerly, polished, purified, well-bred **9** civilized, clarified, courteous **10** cultivated, fastidious **11** gentlemanly **14** discriminating

refinement 5 grace **6** finish, nicety, polish, step up **7** advance, culture, dignity, finesse, suavity **8** breeding, civility, cleaning, courtesy, delicacy, elegance, fineness, revision, urbanity **9** amendment, cleansing, gentility, propriety **10** betterment, filtration, gentleness, politeness **11** advancement, cultivation, development, discernment, enhancement, good manners, improvement, progression, savoir faire, step forward **12** amelioration, distillation, graciousness, purification, tastefulness **13** courteousness, rectification **14** discrimination, fastidiousness

refitting 8 adapting **10** adaptation, remodeling **11** reequipping, resupplying

reflect 4 cast, copy, muse, show, undo **5** image, study, think, throw **6** betray, evince, expose, mirror, ponder, reason, return, reveal **7** condemn, display, exhibit, express, imitate, present, rebound, uncover **8** cogitate, consider, disclose, give back, indicate, manifest, meditate, mull over, register, ruminate, send back, set forth **9** bring upon, cerebrate, dwell upon, represent, reproduce, speculate, throw back, undermine **10** deliberate **11** concentrate, contemplate, demonstrate

reflection 4 blot, idea, slur, view **5** image, study **6** insult, musing, notion **7** opinion, re-

proof, thought **8** reproach, thinking **9** attention, pondering, sentiment **10** cogitation, conviction, derogation, impression, imputation, meditation, rumination **11** cerebration, insinuation, mirror image, pensiveness **12** deliberation **13** concentration, consideration, disparagement
French: 6 pensee

reflective 7 pensive **8** thinking **9** judicious, pondering **10** meditative, ruminative, thoughtful **11** speculative **13** contemplative

Reflex
author: 11 Dick Francis

reform 4 mend **5** amend, atone, emend **6** better, remedy, repair, repent, revise **7** convert, correct, improve, rebuild, rectify, remodel, restore **8** progress **9** amendment **10** correction **12** mend one's ways, rehabilitate **13** rectification **16** set straight again, turn over a new leaf

reformation 6 change, reform **9** amendment, reforming **10** alteration, conversion **11** improvement **12** modification **14** reorganization

refractory 5 balky **6** mulish, unruly **7** restive, wayward, willful **8** contrary, stubborn **9** fractious, obstinate, pigheaded **10** rebellious **11** disobedient, intractable **12** unmanageable

refrain 5 avoid, forgo **6** desist, eschew, forego, refuse, resist **7** abstain, forbear, hold off **8** leave off, renounce **11** curb oneself, keep oneself **12** stay one's hand **15** restrain oneself

refrain from 5 avoid, forgo **6** desist, eschew, forego **7** abstain, forbear **8** leave off, renounce

refresh 3 jog **4** prod **5** brace, renew, rouse **6** arouse, awaken, prompt, revive, stir up, vivify **7** cool off, freshen, quicken, recruit, restore **8** activate, energize, recreate **9** reanimate, stimulate **10** invigorate, rejuvenate, strengthen

refreshed 7 revived **8** animated, restored, vivified **9** enlivened, freshened **11** invigorated

refreshing 7 bracing **11** revivifying **12** invigorating **13** strengthening **15** thirst-quenching

refreshment 4 bite, eats **5** drink, snack **6** bracer **7** potable **8** beverage, cocktail, pick-me-up, potation **9** appetizer, drinkable, refresher **10** recreation, relaxation **11** hors d'oeuvre, nourishment, restoration, restorative **12** food and drink, invigoration, rejuvenation **14** reinvigoration, thirst quencher

refrigerate 4 cool **5** chill **6** freeze **7** congeal **8** keep cold, keep cool, put on ice **9** keep on ice

Refrigerator, The
nickname of: 12 William Perry

refuge 4 home **5** haven **6** asylum, harbor, resort **7** hideout, retreat, shelter **8** safehold **9** anchorage, harborage, sanctuary **10** protection **12** port in a storm **14** help in distress, place of shelter

refugee 2 DP **5** exile **6** bolter, eloper, emigre **7** escapee, evacuee, runaway **8** emigrant, fugitive **9** absconder **10** expatriate **15** displaced person

refulgent 6 bright, lucent **7** glowing, lambent, radiant, shining **8** luminous, relucent **9** brilliant

refund 5 remit, repay **6** rebate, return **7** pay back **9** reimburse, repayment **10** recompense, remittance, remunerate **12** amount repaid **13** give back money, reimbursement **18** make restitution for **19** make compensation for

refurbish 4 mend, redo **5** clean, fix up, renew **6** repair, tidy up **7** freshen, improve, remodel, restore **8** overhaul, renovate, spruce up **11** recondition

refusal 2 no **3** nay **4** veto **6** denial **7** regrets **8** turndown **9** declining, rejection **10** nonconsent **11** declination, disapproval **13** nonacceptance, noncompliance, unwillingness

refuse 2 no **4** deny, junk, veto **5** spurn, trash, waste **6** forbid, litter, reject **7** decline, garbage, rubbish, say no to **8** disallow, prohibit, turn down, withhold

refuse pile 4 dump **6** midden **11** rubbish heap

refuse to submit 4 defy **5** rebel **6** resist **7** disobey, hold out, violate **10** transgress **12** fail to comply

refutation 4 veto **6** denial **7** counter **8** negation, rebuttal **9** disavowal **11** confutation, repudiation **12** invalidation **13** contradiction

refutatory 8 contrary, opposing **10** discrepant **11** conflicting, disagreeing **12** antithetical, inconsistent **13** contradictory **14** countervailing, irreconcilable

refute 4 deny **5** rebut **6** answer **7** confute, counter **8** disprove **9** challenge **10** contradict, invalidate **12** give the lie to

regain 6 recoup, redeem, retake **7** get back, reclaim, recover, win back **8** gain anew, get again, retrieve **9** recapture, repossess

regal 5 grand, noble, proud, royal **6** august, kingly, lordly **7** queenly, stately **8** imposing, kinglike, majestic, princely, splendid **9** queenlike **10** princelike **11** magnificent **13** splendiferous

regale 3 ply **4** fete **5** amuse, feast **6** divert, please **7** banquet, delight, lionize **8** enthrall **9** entertain **10** serve nobly **11** wine and dine **15** feed sumptuously

Regan
character in: 8 King Lear
author: 11 Shakespeare

regard 3 eye, see **4** care, heed, hold, mind, note, rate, scan, view **5** judge, point, think, value, watch **6** accept, admire, aspect, behold, detail, esteem, follow, gaze at, look at, matter, notice, reckon, survey, take in **7** account, believe, concern, put down, respect, set down, subject, thought **8** consider, estimate, listen to, look upon, look up to, note well, relation **9** attention, hearken to, reference **10** admiration, connection, estimation, meditation, reflection, scrutinize **11** contemplate, observation, think well of **12** appreciation **13** cast the eyes on, consideration, think highly of **14** pay attention to

regardful 5 civil **6** polite **7** mindful **8** reverent **9** courteous, observant **10** respectful **11** deferential, reverential

regard highly 6 admire, esteem **7** respect **10** appreciate

regarding 4 in re **5** about, anent **7** apropos **10** concerning, respecting

regardless 6 anyhow, anyway **10** for all that **11** nonetheless **12** nevertheless **15** notwithstanding **19** in spite of everything

regard with repugnance **4** hate **5** abhor **6** detest, loathe **7** despise **8** execrate **9** abominate, can't stand, shudder at **10** recoil from, shrink from **11** can't stomach **12** be revolted by **13** be nauseated by, find repulsive **18** feel aversion toward

regard with suspicion **5** doubt **7** suspect **8** distrust, mistrust, question

regenerate **5** renew **6** redeem, reform, revive, uplift **7** restore **8** inspirit, reawaken, retrieve, revivify **9** enlighten, resurrect **10** rejuvenate **11** resuscitate **12** generate anew **13** give new life to, make a new man of

regent **4** king **5** queen, ruler **8** governor **9** protecter, protector

regime **4** rule **5** power, reign **7** command, control, dynasty **8** dominion **9** direction **10** government, leadership, management **12** jurisdiction **14** administration

regimen **4** diet, rule **6** system **10** government

regimentation **5** order, rigor **6** method, system **7** control, regimen **9** orthodoxy **10** discipline, regulation, uniformity **12** rigorousness **13** methodization **19** doctrinaire approach

Regiment of Women
author: **12** Thomas Berger

Regin
origin: **12** Scandinavian
mentioned in: **8** Volsunga
brother: **6** Fafnir
raised: **6** Sigurd

region **4** area, land, zone **5** field, range, realm, space, tract **6** domain, sphere **7** country, expanse **8** district, locality, province, vicinity **9** territory **12** neighborhood

regional **5** areal, local, zonal **7** dialect **10** locational, provincial **11** territorial **12** geographical

register **3** log **4** dial, mark, roll, show **5** diary, gauge, meter, range, scale **6** betray, enlist, enroll, heater, ledger, record, sign up **7** betoken, check in, compass, counter, daybook, exhibit, express, logbook, point to, portray, set down **8** disclose, heat duct, heat vent, indicate, manifest, note down, radiator, recorder, registry, take down **9** indicator, write down **10** calculator, heat outlet, hot-air vent, record book **12** put in writing

Regius **16** Greek unical codex

regnat populus **16** let the people rule
motto of: **8** Arkansas

regress **3** ebb **4** back, exit, fall **6** go back, recede, return, revert **7** relapse, retreat, reverse **8** fall back, pass back, withdraw **9** backslide **10** lose ground, retrogress **11** deteriorate **12** move backward

regressive **8** backward **9** declining, worsening **10** retrograde **13** retrogressive

regret **3** rue, woe **4** moan **5** grief, mourn, qualm **6** bemoan, bewail, lament, repent, sorrow, twinge **7** anguish, apology, deplore, eat crow, remorse, scruple **8** be rueful, grieve at, weep over **9** apologies, grievance, heartache, rue the day **10** be sorry for, contrition, repentance, ruefulness **11** be ashamed of, compunction, lamentation, reservation **12** be remorseful, eat humble pie, eat one's words, self-reproach **13** feel sorrow for, regretfulness, second thought **14** disappointment, feel remorse for, remorsefulness **15** dissatisfaction **16** feel distress over, pang of conscience, self-condemnation

regretful **6** rueful **8** contrite **9** sorrowful **10** apologetic, remorseful **15** self-reproachful

regrettable **6** woeful **7** unhappy **8** grievous, pitiable **10** calamitous, deplorable, lamentable **11** unfortunate

regular **3** set **4** even, fine, real **5** daily, fixed, plain, usual **6** common, normal, proper, smooth, steady, trusty **7** classic, correct, genuine, habitue, natural, typical, uniform **8** absolute, accepted, complete, constant, everyday, faithful, familiar, frequent, habitual, loyalist, ordinary, orthodox, periodic, stalwart, standard, thorough, true blue **9** customary, recurrent, recurring, unvarying **10** consistent, dependable, invariable, periodical, unchanging **11** commonplace, down-to-earth, established, old reliable, symmetrical, undeviating **12** well-balanced **16** well-proportioned

regulate **3** fix **5** guide **6** adjust, direct, govern, handle, manage **7** balance, control, monitor, oversee, rectify **8** moderate, modulate, organize **9** supervise **10** regularize **11** superintend

regulation **4** rule **5** edict, order **6** decree **7** command, control, dictate, statute **8** handling **9** adjusting, direction, ordinance **10** adjustment **11** commandment **13** standing order

regulator **5** guide **7** manager **8** director, governor, overseer **9** moderator, modulator **10** adjustment, supervisor **14** superintendent **15** adjusting device

regurgitate **4** barf **5** vomit **7** throw up **8** disgorge

rehabilitate **3** fix **4** save **6** redeem, remake **7** restore, salvage **8** make over, readjust, renovate **9** reeducate, refurbish, reinstate **11** recondition, reconstruct, resocialize, set straight **13** straighten out **16** restore to society

rehash **6** repeat, retell, reword **7** restate **8** rephrase **9** iteration, rechauffe

rehearsal **5** drill, recap **6** tryout **7** hearing, reading, test run **8** audition, exercise, practice, trial run **9** polishing **10** perfecting, repetition, run-through **11** preparation, reiteration, walk-through **14** recapitulation

rehearse **5** drill, ready, train **6** go over, polish, recite, relate, repeat, retell **7** narrate, prepare, recount **8** practice **9** reiterate **10** run through **13** read one's lines **14** give a recital of, study one's lines

Rehoboam
father: **7** Solomon
mother: **6** Naamah
son: **6** Abijah

Rehoboth
founder: **6** Nimrod

Reich, Charles
author of: **20** The Greening of America

Reichsfuhrer **11** Reich leader
chief of: **8** SS troops

reign **4** rule **6** govern, regime, regnum, tenure **7** command **8** dominion, hold sway, regnancy, tutelage **9** dominance, influence **10** government, incumbency **11** sovereignty, supervision **12** wear the crown **13** hold authority **14** have royal power, sit on the throne **15** occupy the throne **17** exercise authority **19** exercise sovereignty
Hindu: **3** raj

reign over **4** rule **6** govern **7** command, control **8** dominate

reimburse **5** pay up, remit, repay **6** rebate, refund **7** pay back **8** square up **9** indemnify **10** compensate, recompense, remunerate **15** make restitution

reimbursement **6** refund **9** indemnity, repayment **12** compensation, remuneration

rein, reins **4** curb, hold **5** check, limit, watch **6** bridle **7** control, harness **8** hold back, restrict, suppress **9** restraint **11** keep an eye on

Reiner, Carl
born: **7** Bronx NY
son: **9** Rob Reiner
roles: **15** Your Show of Shows **21** It's a Mad Mad Mad Mad World
created: **15** Dick Van Dyke Show
director: **5** Oh God **7** The Jerk **8** The Comic **11** Where's Poppa?
novel: **13** Enter Laughing

Reiner, Rob
father: **10** Carl Reiner
roles: **8** Meathead **10** Mike Stivik **14** All in the Family

reinforce **4** prop **5** steel **7** bolster, brace up, fortify, support **8** buttress **10** strengthen **12** make stronger

reinforcement **4** stay **5** brace, strut **7** bracing, support **10** assistance **11** buttressing **13** strengthening

reinstate **5** renew **6** revive **7** readmit, restore **11** reestablish, reinstitute, reintroduce

reinstatement **7** renewal, revival **11** restoration **13** reinstitution **14** reintroduction **15** reestablishment

reintroduce **6** revive **8** recreate **9** reinstate **11** reestablish, reinstitute

reintroduction **7** revival **10** recreation **11** restoration **13** reinstatement **15** reestablishment

reiterate **5** resay **6** hammer, rehash, repeat, retell, reword, stress **7** iterate, reprise, restate **8** rephrase **11** pound away at **12** recapitulate **13** go over and over

reject **4** deny **5** repel, spurn **6** rebuff, refuse **7** castoff, decline, discard, disdain, dismiss, flotsam, repulse, say no to **8** castaway, disallow, shrug off, turn down, turn from **9** repudiate

rejected **6** denied, dumped, jilted **7** cast off, outcast, refused, spurned, unloved **8** disowned, forsaken, lovelorn **9** abandoned, discarded, disproved **10** unaccepted, repudiated **11** invalidated

rejection **6** rebuff **7** disdain, refusal **8** scorning, spurning **9** declining, dismissal, rebuffing, rejecting, ruling out

rejoice **5** exult, glory, revel **6** be glad **7** be happy, delight **8** be elated, jubilate **9** be pleased, celebrate, make merry **10** exhilarate, sing for joy **11** be delighted, be overjoyed **13** be transported

rejoice in **5** eat up, enjoy, savor **6** relish **7** revel in **9** delight in **13** be pleased with, get a kick out of **14** take pleasure in

rejoicing **5** mirth **6** gaiety **7** delight, ecstasy, elation, jollity, jubilee, revelry, triumph **8** cheering, gladness, pleasure, reveling **9** festivity, good cheer, happiness, jubilance, merriment **10** exultation, joyfulness, jubilation, liveliness **11** celebration, merrymaking

rejoin **6** answer, retort **7** respond

rejoinder **5** reply **6** answer, retort, return **7** riposte **8** backtalk, comeback, rebuttal, repartee, response **10** refutation **11** surrebuttal **12** counterblast, remonstrance, surrejoinder **13** countercharge **16** counterstatement

rejuvenate **6** revive **7** restore **8** revivify **9** reanimate **10** revitalize **12** reinvigorate **14** put new life into **17** make youthful again

relapse **4** fall **5** lapse **6** revert, worsen **7** decline, regress, reverse **8** fall back, sink back, slip back, turn back **9** backslide, reversion, worsening **10** degenerate, recurrence, regression, retrogress **11** backsliding, falling back **13** deterioration, retrogression **15** return to illness, turn for the worse

relate **3** say **4** link, tell **5** apply, refer, speak, state, utter **6** attach, belong, convey, detail, impart, recite, report, reveal **7** concern, connect, divulge, narrate, pertain, recount **8** describe, disclose **9** appertain, associate, feel close, make known **10** be relevant **11** communicate, have rapport **12** be responsive, interact well, recapitulate **13** be sympathetic, have reference, particularize **15** feel empathy with, give an account of

related **3** kin **4** akin, said, told **7** kindred, recited **8** narrated, reported **9** recounted **15** of the same family

related by blood **3** kin **4** akin **7** kindred **14** consanguineous, of the same stock **21** having a common ancestor

relation **3** kin, tie **4** bond, link **5** tie-in **6** regard, report **7** account, bearing, concern, kinsman, recital, telling, version **8** relative **9** narrating, narration, narrative, reference, relevance, retelling **10** connection, pertinence, recitation **11** affiliation, application, association, correlation, description **13** applicability, communication **17** interrelationship

relationship **3** kin **5** blood, union **6** affair **7** kindred, kinship, liaison, sibship, society **8** affinity, alliance **10** connection **11** affiliation, association, correlation **13** consanguinity

relative **3** kin **4** clan, kith **5** blood, folks, tribe **6** allied, cousin, family, people **7** cognate, germane, kinfolk, kinsman, related **8** relation, relevant **9** connected, dependent, kinswoman, pertinent, referable **10** affiliated, applicable, associated, comparable, connection, connective, correlated, kith and kin, pertaining, relational, respective **11** appropriate, comparative, correlative, not absolute **12** interrelated **13** flesh and blood **14** interconnected

relax **4** bend, calm, ease, idle, laze, loaf, rest **5** let up, slack **6** be idle, be lazy, ease up, loosen, soften, soothe, unbend, unwind **7** cool off, holiday, make lax, slacken **8** decrease, loosen up, vacation **9** lie around **10** take it easy **12** enjoy oneself **13** make less tense **14** make less severe, make less strict

relaxation **3** fun **5** games, hobby, sport **6** repose **7** bending, leisure, pastime **8** pleasure **9** abatement, amusement, avocation, diversion, enjoyment, loosening, remission **10** recreation, slackening **11** refreshment **12** rest from work **13** entertainment

relaxed **3** lax **4** calm, cool,

easy, slow, soft **5** loose, slack **6** at ease, casual, gentle, remiss **7** flaccid, lenient **8** informal, laid back, unstrict **9** easygoing, leisurely, negligent, nerveless, unnervous **10** unstrained **11** free and easy, thoughtless
French: **6** degage

relaxed manner **4** ease **5** poise **6** aplomb **9** composure **10** confidence **11** naturalness **12** unconstraint **14** unaffectedness

relay **3** leg **4** race, tour **5** shift **6** length **8** transfer, transmit **9** conductor, regulator, satellite **10** retransmit
cylinder: **5** baton
part: **8** armature, receiver **11** transmitter **13** electromagnet
race: **6** medley **10** track event

release **4** free **5** let go, loose, untie **6** detach, let out, unbind **7** freeing, present, relieve, set free, unloose **8** liberate, set loose, unfasten **9** circulate, discharge, disengage, dismissal, extricate, letting go, releasing **10** distribute, liberating, liberation **11** circulation, communicate, extrication, publication, setting free **12** distribution, emancipation, set at liberty, setting loose

relegate **3** bar **5** eject, expel **6** assign, banish, charge, commit, demote, reject **7** cast out, consign, discard, dismiss, exclude, keep out, shut out **8** delegate **9** ostracize

relent **4** bend, melt **5** let up, relax, yield **6** give in, soften, unbend, weaken **7** give way **8** have pity **10** be merciful, capitulate, come around **11** give quarter, grow lenient **12** become milder **14** grow less severe

relentless **4** hard **5** harsh, rigid, stern, stiff **6** severe **7** adamant **8** pitiless, rigorous, ruthless **9** merciless **10** implacable, inexorable, inflexible, unyielding **11** remorseless, undeviating, unrelenting **14** uncompromising

relevance **7** aptness, fitness, meaning **9** propriety **10** pertinence **11** materiality, relatedness, suitability **12** significance **13** applicability **15** appropriateness

relevant **3** apt, fit **6** allied, suited, tied in **7** apropos, bearing, cognate, fitting, germane, related **8** apposite, material, suitable **9** connected, intrinsic, pertinent, referring **10** applicable, associated, concerning, to the point **11** appropriate, significant **12** on the subject, to the purpose

reliable **4** true **5** solid, sound **6** trusty **8** faithful **9** unfailing **10** dependable **11** responsible, trustworthy **12** tried and true **13** conscientious

reliance **5** faith, trust **6** belief, credit **8** credence **9** assurance **10** confidence, dependence

relic **5** scrap, token, trace **7** antique, memento, records, remnant, vestige **8** artifact, fragment, heirloom, keepsake, reminder, souvenir **11** remembrance

relief **4** balm, cure, dole, rest **5** break, cheer **6** remedy **7** anodyne, elation, panacea, respite, welfare **8** antidote, easement, lenitive **9** abatement, reduction **10** mitigation, palliation, palliative **11** alleviation, assuagement, peace of mind **12** amelioration **13** encouragement **16** public assistance **17** welfare assistance
Italian: **7** rilievo

relieve **3** aid **4** calm, ease, free, help, mark **5** abate, allay, cheer, spell **6** assist, let out, pacify, remove, set off, solace, soothe, subdue, succor, temper **7** appease, assuage, break up, comfort, console, lighten, mollify, release, replace, support, take out **8** contrast, mitigate, palliate, reassure **9** alleviate, encourage, interrupt, punctuate **12** free from fear

relieved **5** freed **6** calmed, exempt **7** cheered, excused, solaced **8** consoled **9** comforted, reassured **10** encouraged

Religio Medici
author: **15** Sir Thomas Browne

religion **4** cult, sect **5** canon, creed, dogma, faith, piety **6** belief, church, homage **7** worship **8** devotion, theology **9** adoration, godliness, reverence **10** devoutness, persuasion, veneration **11** affiliation, belief in God **12** belief in gods, denomination, spirituality **13** system of faith **15** system of worship

religionist **8** believer **16** God-fearing person

religiosity **5** piety **8** devotion **10** fanaticism **15** religious fervor

religious **3** nun **4** holy, monk **5** exact, friar, godly, rigid **6** ardent, devout, divine, priest, sacred **7** devoted, staunch **8** constant, faithful, unerring **9** spiritual, steadfast **10** devotional, fastidious, God-fearing, meticulous, scrupulous, unswerving **11** punctilious, theological, undeviating **12** wholehearted **13** conscientious **14** denominational **15** spiritual-minded

religious belief **5** canon, credo, creed, dogma, tenet **8** doctrine

religious fervor **5** piety **7** ecstasy **8** holiness **9** godliness **10** devoutness **12** religiousity, spirituality

religious group **4** sect **12** denomination

religious orders
Christian: **6** Jesuit **7** Cluniac, Templar **8** Capuchin, Theatine, Trappist, Ursuline **9** Carmelite, Dominican **10** Carthusian, Cistercian, Franciscan **11** Augustinian, Benedictine, Camaldolite **16** Sisters of Charity **20** Order of the Visitation
non-Christian: **4** Sufi **7** Jainism **8** Dasanami

relinquish **4** cede, deny, drop, quit, shed **5** forgo, leave, let go, waive, yield **6** forego, give up, resign, vacate **7** abandon, cast off, discard, dismiss, forbear, forsake, release **8** abdicate, break off, disclaim, hand over, lay aside, put aside, renounce, sign away **9** deliver up, repudiate, surrender

relinquishable **9** forgoable **10** expendable, foregoable **11** dispensable **12** renounceable

relinquished **5** ceded, let go **6** gave up **7** forgone, given up, yielded **8** cast away, foregone, forsaken **9** abandoned, given away, renounced **10** left behind

relinquishment **7** cession **8** giving up, yielding **9** letting go, rejection, surrender **10** abnegation **11** repudiation **12** renunciation

relish **3** dig **4** like, love, tang, want, wish, zest **5** enjoy, fancy, gusto, savor, spice, taste **6** accent, desire, dote on, flavor, liking, palate **7** delight, longing, stomach **8** appetite, fondness, groove on, penchant, piquancy, pleasure **9** condiment, delight in, enjoyment, hankering, rejoice in **10** appreciate, ebullience, en-

thusiasm, exuberance, partiality, propensity **11** luxuriate in **12** appreciation, be crazy about, predilection, satisfaction **13** gratification
type: **4** beef, corn **5** sweet **7** chutney **6** pickle, tomato **10** chili sauce, piccalilli **11** horseradish

reluctance **10** hesitation **13** unwillingness **14** disinclination

reluctant **3** shy **4** slow **5** loath **6** averse **7** laggard **8** hesitant **9** diffident, unwilling **10** indisposed **11** disinclined

rely **3** bet **4** bank, lean, rest **5** count, swear, trust **6** credit, depend, reckon **7** believe **10** feel sure of **11** be dependent **12** give credence

remain **4** go on, last, stay, wait **5** abide, stand **6** be left, endure, hang on, hold up, linger **7** not move, not stir, persist, prevail, stay put, subsist, survive **8** continue, stand pat **10** be left over, stay behind

remainder **4** rest **5** waste **6** excess, refuse **7** balance, overage, remains, remnant, residue, surplus, wastage **8** leavings, residual, residuum **9** leftovers, scourings **10** surplusage **11** superfluity

remains **4** body **5** stiff **6** corpse, scraps **7** cadaver **8** dead body **9** leftovers

remark **3** say, see **4** espy, mark, mind, note, view, word **6** behold, look at, notice, regard, survey **7** comment, mention, observe, pay heed **8** perceive **9** attention **10** commentary, give heed to, make note of, reflection, take note of **11** contemplate, observation **12** fix the mind on, say in passing, take notice of **13** consideration **14** pay attention to

remarkable **6** signal **7** notable, unusual **8** singular, striking **9** memorable **10** impressive, noteworthy, phenomenal **11** conspicuous, exceptional, outstanding **13** distinguished, extraordinary, unforgettable

Remarque, Erich Maria
author of: **25** All Quiet on the Western Front

Rembrandt (Harmensz) van Rijn
born: **6** Leiden, Leyden **14** The Netherlands
artwork: **6** Balaam **9** Bathsheba **13** The Night Watch (The Sortie of the Company of Captain Banning Cocq) **14** The Jewish Bride **15** Old Woman Reading, The Bridal Couple **19** The Blinding of Samson **20** Christ Healing the Sick **21** The Stoning of St Stephen **22** Man with the Golden Helmet, Self-Portrait with Saskia, The Descent from the Cross **24** The Anatomy Lesson of Dr Tulp, The Syndics of the Cloth Hall **36** Aristotle Contemplating the Bust of Homer

remedial **7** healing, helpful, mending **8** curative, salutary, sanative **10** beneficial, corrective **11** meliorative, reformative, restorative, therapeutic **12** advantageous, correctional, prophylactic

remedy **3** aid, fix **4** calm, cure, ease, heal, help, mend **5** amend, emend, right **6** relief, repair, soothe **7** assuage, correct, cure-all, improve, mollify, nostrum, panacea, rectify, redress, relieve, restore **8** make easy, medicine, mitigate, palliate, regulate, set right **9** alleviate, make sound, treatment **10** ameliorate, assistance, corrective, make better, medicament, medication, preventive **13** rectification **15** restore to health

remember **3** tip **6** recall, reward **9** not forget, recognize, recollect **10** appreciate, bear in mind, call to mind, have in mind, keep in mind, take care of, take note of **11** bring to mind **12** bear in memory

remember that thou must die
Latin: **11** memento mori

remembrance **5** favor, relic, token **6** memory, recall **7** memento **8** keepsake, memorial, reminder, souvenir **9** nostalgia **11** recognition, remembering **12** recognizance, recollection, reminiscence **13** commemoration

Remembrance of Things Past
author: **12** Marcel Proust

Remembrance Rock
author: **12** Carl Sandburg

Remick, Lee
born: **8** Quincy MA
roles: **16** Anatomy of a Murder, The Long Hot Summer **18** Days of Wine and Roses

remind **9** put in mind, suggest to **11** bring back to, bring to mind, put in memory **16** awaken memories of

reminder of death
Latin: **11** memento mori

Remington, Frederic Sackrider
born: **8** Canton NY
artwork: **12** Bronco Buster **23** Roping Horses in the Corral **32** Cavalry Charge on the Southern Plains

reminisce **4** mull, muse **6** ponder **7** reflect **8** hark back, look back, remember **9** recollect, think back **12** tell old tales **16** exchange memories, swap remembrances

reminiscent **9** nostalgic, remindful, similar to **11** analogous to, remembering **12** recollecting **13** retrospective

remiss **3** lax **4** idle, lazy, slow **5** loose, slack **6** sloppy **7** laggard, loafing **8** careless, derelict, dilatory, inactive, indolent, slipshod, slothful, uncaring **9** do-nothing, forgetful, negligent, oblivious, shiftless, undutiful, unmindful **10** delinquent, neglectful, unthinking, unwatchful **11** inattentive, indifferent, thoughtless

remission **4** cure **5** lapse, pause **6** hiatus, pardon **7** respite, retreat **8** decrease **9** abatement, acquittal, cessation, reduction, shrinkage **10** absolution, diminution, hesitation, moderation, modulation, subsidence **11** exoneration, forgiveness, vindication

remit **3** pay **4** free, send, ship **5** clear, let go, relax, slack **6** excuse, let out, pardon, reduce **7** absolve, forgive, forward, release, set free, slacken **8** decrease, diminish, dispatch, liberate, make good, moderate, overlook, pass over, transmit **9** discharge, reimburse **10** compensate **11** put to rights **13** send in payment

remnant **3** bit **5** piece, relic, scrap, shred, token, trace **7** discard, remains, residue, vestige **8** fragment, leavings, leftover, monument, residuum, survival **9** remainder **11** odds and ends

remodel **4** redo **5** adapt, alter, fix up **6** change, modify **7** convert, reshape **8** overhaul, renovate **9** refashion, transform **11** recondition

remodeling **6** change **10** alteration, conversion **12** modification **13** transmutation **14** transformation

remonstrance **6** rebuke **7** censure **8** reproach, scolding **9** criticism, reprimand **10** admonition

remonstrate **5** argue, chide,

demur, scold **6** differ, object, rebuke **7** censure, chasten, contend, dispute, dissent, protest, reprove, upbraid **8** admonish, complain, reproach **9** criticize **10** take to task **11** expostulate **13** call to account

remorse **3** rue **4** pang **5** grief, guilt, qualm **6** regret, sorrow **7** anguish **9** penitence **10** contrition, repentance, ruefulness **11** compunction, lamentation, self-reproof **12** self-reproach **13** regretfulness **14** second thoughts

remorseful **8** contrite, penitent **9** chastened, regretful, repentant, sorrowful **10** apologetic **13** grief-stricken **18** conscience-stricken

remote **3** far **4** slim **5** alien, alone, aloof, faint, quiet **6** exotic, far-off, lonely, meager, slight **7** distant, dubious, faraway, foreign, removed, strange **8** detached, doubtful, isolated, secluded, separate, set apart, solitary, unlikely **9** withdrawn **10** far-removed, segregated **11** God-forsaken, implausible, out of the way, sequestered, standoffish

removal **6** moving, ouster **7** doffing **8** deletion, ejection **9** discharge, dismissal, expulsion, taking off, taking out **10** amputation, carting off, cutting away, dislodging, evacuation, lopping off **11** carrying off, chopping off, elimination, transferral **12** cancellation, displacement **14** transportation **15** transplantation

remove **4** doff, drop, fire, move, oust, quit **5** eject, erase, expel, leave, shift **6** cancel, change, cut off, delete, depart, go away, lop off, retire, unseat, vacate **7** blot out, boot out, cart off, chop off, cut away, dismiss, extract, kick out, retreat, take off, take out, wipe out **8** amputate, carry off, dislodge, displace, evacuate, get rid of, sweep out, take away, transfer, withdraw **9** discharge, eliminate, take leave, transport **10** make an exit, transplant

removed **3** off **4** away, took **5** alone, aloof, apart **6** remote **7** distant, faraway **8** abstract, detached, isolated, reticent, secluded **9** alienated, separate, unrelated, withdrawn **10** segregated, unsociable **11** interspaced, standoffish

remove from office **4** oust **6** depose, unseat **9** discharge

remunerate **3** pay **5** award, grant, repay **6** reward **7** requite, satisfy **9** indemnify, reimburse, vouchsafe **10** compensate, recompense **15** make restitution

remuneration **7** payment **9** repayment **10** recompense, reparation **12** compensation **13** reimbursement **15** indemnification

Remus
father: **4** Mars
mother: **4** Ilia **9** Rea Silvia **10** Rhea Silvia
twin brother: **7** Romulus
raised by: **7** she-wolf

renaissance **7** rebirth, renewal, revival **10** rekindling, renascence, resurgence **11** reawakening, reemergence, restoration **12** regeneration, rejuvenation, resurrection, risorgimento **14** revitalization, revivification **15** reestablishment

rend **3** cut, rip **4** hurt, pain, rive, sear, tear **5** break, crack, sever, split, wound **6** cleave, divide, pierce, sunder **7** afflict, rupture, shatter **8** dissever, fracture, lacerate, polarize, splinter **12** disintegrate, fall to pieces **15** break into pieces

render **2** do **4** cede, give, make, play **5** allot, grant, remit, yield **6** accord, donate, give up, supply, tender **7** deal out, dole out, execute, hand out, pay back, perform, present, requite **8** construe, dispense, fork over, hand over, pay as due, shell out, turn over **9** cause to be, interpret, surrender, translate **10** relinquish **12** give in return, make requital **13** cause to become, make available, make payment of

render impotent **6** defuse, weaken **7** disable, unnerve **8** paralyze **9** undermine **10** devitalize, emasculate

render inoperable **6** damage, impair **7** cripple, disable **12** incapacitate

render null and void **4** void **5** annul **6** cancel, repeal, revoke **7** abolish, nullify, rescind, retract, reverse **8** abrogate, dissolve **10** invalidate

rendezvous **4** date **5** focus, haunt, mecca, tryst **6** gather, muster **7** retreat **8** assemble **9** encounter, tete-a-tete **10** engagement, focal point **11** appointment, assignation, get together **12** meeting place, watering hole **14** gathering place, stamping ground **15** agreement to meet **17** meet by appointment **18** prearranged meeting

rendition **7** edition, reading, version **9** depiction, portrayal, rendering **11** arrangement, performance, translation **14** interpretation

rend the air **3** cry **4** bawl, howl, wail **6** clamor, scream, shriek, squeal **7** screech **9** caterwaul

Renee Mauperin
author: **24** Edmond and Jules de Goncourt

renegade **5** rebel **6** outlaw **7** heretic, runaway, slacker, traitor **8** apostate, betrayer, defector, deserter, forsaker, fugitive, mutineer, mutinous, quisling, recreant, turncoat **9** dissenter, insurgent **10** backslider, traitorous, treasonist, unfaithful

renege **7** back out, fink out, pull out **8** back down, fall back, withdraw **9** repudiate, weasel out **11** get cold feet **12** turn one's back **13** break a promise, break one's word **16** go back on one's word

renew **4** save **6** extend, pick up, redeem, resume, retain, revive **7** prolong, refresh, restore, salvage **8** continue, maintain **9** make sound, reinstate, sign again **10** begin again, offer again, regenerate, rejuvenate, revitalize **11** reestablish, take up again **12** reinvigorate **16** put back into shape

renewal **7** revival **9** extension **10** redemption **11** restoration **12** regeneration **13** reinstatement **14** revitalization

Renoir, Pierre-Auguste
born: **6** France **7** Limoges
artwork: **4** Lise **6** La Loge **10** The Bathers **12** Margot Berard, The Umbrellas **14** La Grenouillere **19** Le Moulin de la Galette **28** Mme Charpentier and Her Children, The Luncheon of the Boating Party

renounce **4** cede, deny, quit **5** forgo, waive **6** abjure, disown, eschew, forego, give up, recant, reject, resign **7** abandon, cast off, disavow, discard, dismiss **8** abdicate, abnegate, abrogate, disclaim, forswear, lay aside, part with, put aside, turn from, write off **9** cast aside, foreswear, repudiate

10 relinquish **13** give up claim to **15** wash one's hands of

renovate 3 fix **4** mend **6** remake, repair, revamp **7** improve, remodel, restore **8** make over **9** modernize, refurbish **10** redecorate

renown 4 fame, mark, note **6** repute, status **7** acclaim **8** eminence **9** celebrity, notoriety **10** popularity, prominence, reputation **11** distinction

renowned 5 famed, noted **6** famous **7** eminent, notable, popular **9** acclaimed, prominent, well-known **10** celebrated, noteworthy **11** outstanding **13** distinguished

rent 3 fee, gap, let, rip **4** dues, gash, hire, hole, rift, slit, tear **5** break, chasm, chink, cleft, crack, lease, split **6** breach, hiatus, rental, schism, tatter, wrench **7** charter, fissure, opening, payment, rent out, rupture **8** cleavage, crevasse, division, fracture **11** buy the use of **12** sell the use of

rente 6 income **7** revenue **12** annual income

rentier 21 one who has a fixed income

renunciation 6 denial **7** refusal **8** forgoing, spurning **9** disavowal, eschewing, foregoing, rejection, repulsion **10** abjuration, renouncing **11** abandonment, disclaiming, forswearing, repudiation **12** foreswearing **14** relinquishment

Renwick, James, Jr
architect of: 8 Main Hall (Vassar College) **11** Grace Church (NYC) **15** Corcoran Gallery (now Renwick Gallery, Washington, DC) **19** St Patrick's Cathedral (NYC) **22** Smithsonian Institution (Washington DC)
style: 13 Gothic Revival

reopen 7 restart **9** begin anew, reconvene, start anew **10** recommence, reinitiate **11** reestablish, reinstitute **12** reinaugurate

repair 2 go **3** fix **4** mend, move **5** amend, emend, patch, renew, shape, state **6** fixing, remedy, remove, retire **7** correct, mending, patch up, rebuild, rectify, redress, restore **8** make good, overhaul, patching, set right, withdraw **9** condition, make up for, refurbish, repairing **10** rebuilding **11** recondition **12** refurbishing **14** reconditioning

reparation 6 amends, return **7** damages, redress **8** requital **9** quittance **10** recompense **11** restitution **12** compensation, satisfaction **13** peace offering

repartee 6 banter, bon mot **7** riposte **8** badinage, chit chat, word play **10** persiflage, witty reply **11** witty retort **12** pleasantries **14** snappy comeback

repast 4 food, meal **5** board, feast, snack, table **6** spread **7** banquet **8** victuals **9** provision **11** nourishment, refreshment

repay 5 match **6** refund, return, reward **7** pay back, requite **9** get back at, indemnify, pay in kind, reimburse **10** recompense, remunerate **11** get even with, reciprocate **12** make requital **14** give in exchange, make a return for **15** make restitution, make retribution **19** return the compliment

repayment 10 paying back, recompense **12** compensation **13** reimbursement **17** making restitution

repeal 4 void **5** annul **6** cancel, revoke **7** abolish, nullify, rescind, voiding **8** abrogate, set aside **9** abolition, annulment **10** abrogation, invalidate, revocation **11** termination **12** cancellation, invalidation **13** nullification **18** declare null and void

repeat 4 echo, redo, tell **5** mimic, quote, rerun **6** pass on, recite, relate, retell **7** imitate, recount, restate, retread, say over **8** say again **9** duplicate, reiterate, reproduce **10** repetition **11** duplication, reiteration **12** perform again

repeated exercises 4 rote **5** drill **8** practice, training

repel 4 foil, rout **5** check **6** dispel, offend, oppose, put off, rebuff, resist, revolt, sicken **7** deflect, disgust, fend off, forfend, hold off, keep off, keep out, repulse, scatter, turn off, ward off **8** alienate, beat back, disperse, nauseate, push back, stave off, throw off **9** chase away, drive away, drive back, force back, frustrate, keep at bay, withstand

repellent 5 proof **9** abhorrent, loathsome, offensive, repelling, repugnant, repulsive, resisting, revolting, sickening **10** disgusting, nauseating **11** distasteful, impermeable

repent 3 rue **6** bemoan, bewail, lament, regret, repine **7** deplore **8** mea culpa, weep over **9** be ashamed **10** be contrite, be penitent **11** be regretful, feel remorse

repentance 5 grief, guilt **6** regret, sorrow **7** remorse **9** penitence **10** contrition **11** compunction **12** self-reproach **16** self-condemnation **17** pangs of conscience

repercussion 4 echo **6** effect, result **8** backlash, reaction **10** concussion, side effect **11** aftereffect, consequence **13** reverberation **15** boomerang effect

repetition 6 repeat **9** iteration, retelling **11** reiteration, restatement **14** recapitulation

repetitious 5 wordy **6** prolix **8** repeated **9** redundant **10** repetitive

Repin, Ilya Efimovich
born: 6 Russia **8** Chugeyev
artwork: 15 The Volga Boatmen **18** Zaporozhye Cossacks **19** They Did Not Expect Him **26** Ivan the Terrible Kills His Son

replace 5 spell **6** return **7** put back, restore, succeed **8** supplant **9** supersede

replaceable 10 disposable, expendable **11** dispensable

replenish 5 renew **6** refill, reload **7** refresh, reorder, replace, restock, restore

replenished 7 renewed **8** refilled, replaced, restored **9** restocked

replenishment 7 renewal **9** refilling **10** restocking **11** replacement, restoration

replete 4 full **5** sated **6** gorged, loaded **7** crammed, fraught, stuffed, teeming **8** brimming, satiated **9** abounding, jam-packed, surfeited **11** well-stocked

repletion 4 glut **6** excess **7** surfeit, surplus **9** abundance, plenitude, profusion, satiation **11** sufficiency

replica 4 copy **5** model **6** double **8** likeness **9** duplicate, facsimile, imitation **12** reproduction

reply 5 react **6** answer, rejoin, retort **7** counter, respond **8** reaction, response **9** rejoinder **14** acknowledgment

reply if you please
French: 4 rsvp **20** repondez s'il vous plait

reply to 6 answer **7** counter, react to **8** retort to **9** respond to **11** acknowledge

repondez s'il vous plait
11 please reply **16** reply if you please
abbreviation: 4 rsvp

report 4 bang, boom, note, talk, tell, word **5** crack, noise, rumor, sound, state, story **6** appear, detail, expose, gossip, recite, record, relate, reveal, show up, tell on **7** account, article, check in, divulge, hearsay, message, missive, recount, summary, version, write-up **8** announce, denounce, describe, disclose, dispatch, relation **9** discharge, narration **10** communique, detonation, memorandum **11** communicate, description, information
French: 11 compte rendu

reporter 7 newshen, newsman **8** newshawk **9** anchorman, announcer, columnist, newshound, newswoman **10** journalist, newscaster **11** commentator **12** newspaperman **13** correspondent **14** newspaperwoman

repose 3 lie **4** calm, ease, rest **5** quiet, relax **6** be calm, settle **7** leisure, recline, respite **8** quietude **10** inactivity, quiescence, relaxation **11** tranquility **12** peacefulness, tranquillity

repository 5 depot **8** magazine **9** warehouse **10** storehouse

reprehend 5 decry **7** censure, condemn, reprove **8** denounce, reproach **9** criticize **10** disapprove

reprehensible 3 bad **4** base, evil, foul, vile **6** guilty, wicked **7** heinous, ignoble **8** blamable, culpable, infamous, shameful, unworthy **9** nefarious **10** censurable, despicable, villainous **11** blameworthy, condemnable, disgraceful, inexcusable, opprobrious **12** unpardonable **13** objectionable, unjustifiable

reprehension 6 rebuke **7** censure, reproof **8** reproach **9** criticism **11** disapproval **12** condemnation, denunciation **14** disapprobation

represent 2 be **4** mean, show **5** enact, equal, state **6** denote, depict, pose as, sketch, typify **7** betoken, express, outline, picture, portray, present, serve as **8** appear as, describe, indicate, stand for **9** delineate, designate, symbolize **10** illustrate **11** emblematize, impersonate **12** characterize

representation 5 image **6** effigy, emblem, symbol **7** epitome, essence, picture **8** likeness **9** depiction, portrayal **10** embodiment **12** illustration **15** exemplification **16** characterization

representative 2 MP **3** rep **5** agent, envoy, proxy **6** deputy, varied **7** deputed, elected, proctor, typical **8** balanced, delegate, elective, emissary, symbolic **9** delegated, exemplary, spokesman, surrogate, typifying **10** delegatory, democratic, denotative, emblematic, legislator, mouthpiece, republican, substitute, symbolical **11** assemblyman, congressman, delineative, descriptive **12** exemplifying, illustrative **13** assemblywoman, congresswoman **14** characteristic, cross-sectional

repress 4 curb, hide, mask, veil **5** box up, check, cloak, cover, crush, pen up, quash, quell **6** hold in, muffle, shut up, squash, stifle, subdue **7** conceal, control, inhibit, put down, silence, smother, squelch **8** bottle up, hold back, keep down, restrain, strangle, suppress

repression 8 muffling **9** holding in, restraint, retention **10** inhibition, throttling **11** concealment, holding back, suppression

reprieve 4 lull, stay **5** delay, pause **6** pardon, parole **7** amnesty, respite **8** breather **9** remission **10** moratorium, suspension **11** adjournment **12** postponement **14** breathing spell

reprimand 4 trim **5** chide, scold **6** berate, rail at, rebuff, rebuke, revile **7** censure, chew out, chiding, lecture, obloquy, tell off, upbraid **8** admonish, berating, chastise, denounce, reproach, reproval, scolding, take down, trimming **9** castigate, criticism, criticize, disparage, dispraise, dress down, reprehend, reprobate **10** admonition, chewing out, opprobrium, take to task, upbraiding **11** castigation **12** admonishment, denunciation, dressing down, remonstrance **13** disparagement **16** rap on the knuckles

reprisal 7 redress, revenge **8** requital **9** tit for tat, vengeance **11** counterblow, retaliation, retribution **13** counterattack **16** counteroffensive
Latin: 10 quid pro quo

reproach 4 blot, slur, spot **5** blame, chide, scold, shame, stain, taint **6** charge, insult, malign, rail at, rebuke, revile, stigma, tirade, vilify **7** asperse, blemish, censure, condemn, offense, reproof, reprove, scandal, tarnish, upbraid **8** admonish, denounce, diatribe, disgrace, dishonor, scolding **9** castigate, criticism, criticize, discredit, disparage, indignity, reprimand **10** stigmatize, take to task, tongue-lash, upbraiding **11** degradation, humiliation **12** remonstrance **13** call to account, embarrassment

reprobate 3 bad, low **4** base, evil, rake, roue, vile **5** scamp **6** pariah, rascal, rotter, sinner, wanton, wicked **7** corrupt, outcast **8** castaway, depraved, derelict, evildoer, prodigal, rakehell **9** abandoned, dissolute, miscreant, shameless, wrongdoer **10** black sheep, degenerate, immoralist, profligate, voluptuary **11** rapscallion, untouchable **12** incorrigible, transgressor, wicked person

reproduce 4 copy, redo, sire **5** beget, breed, match, spawn **6** mirror, repeat, re-echo **7** imitate, reflect **8** generate, multiply **9** duplicate, procreate, propagate, replicate, represent **11** counterfeit, proliferate

reproduction 4 copy **7** replica **8** breeding, likeness **9** duplicate, facsimile, imitation **10** carbon copy, generation, simulation **11** procreation, propagation **13** progeneration, proliferation **14** multiplication, representation
goddess of: 7 Astarte

reproductive system
component: 5 penis **6** testes, uterus, vagina **7** ovaries

reproof 5 blame **6** rebuke **7** censure, chiding **8** reproach, scolding **9** criticism, reprimand **10** admonition **12** condemnation, dressing-down, remonstrance

reprovable 7 at fault **8** blamable, culpable **10** censurable **11** blameworthy **12** reproachable

reprove 5 chide, scold **6** rebuke **7** censure, chasten **8** admonish, reproach **9** castigate, reprimand

reptile **3** asp, eft **4** newt, teju **5** agama, anole, gecko, skink, snake, viper **6** dragon, iguana, lizard, mugger, turtle **7** crawler, creeper, serpent, tuatara **8** basilisk, dinosaur, groveler, terrapin, tortoise **9** alligator, chameleon, crocodile, pterosaur **10** salamander, vertebrate **11** Gila monster, pterodactyl

republic **9** democracy
Latin: **10** res publica

Republic
author: **5** Plato

Republican Party
also called: **3** GOP **13** Grand Old Party
president belonging to: **4** Bush, Ford, Taft **5** Grant, Hayes, Nixon **6** Arthur, Hoover, Reagan **7** Harding, Lincoln, (Andrew) Johnson **8** Coolidge, Garfield, Harrison, McKinley **9** (Theodore) Roosevelt **10** Eisenhower
symbol: **8** elephant

Republic of China *see* **6** Taiwan

repudiate **4** deny, void **5** annul **6** cancel, desert, disown, reject, repeal, revoke **7** abandon, abolish, cast off, disavow, discard, forsake, nullify, protest, rescind, retract, reverse **8** abrogate, disclaim, dissolve, renounce

repudiation **6** denial **9** disavowal, rejection **10** abrogation, disclaimer, retraction

repugnance **4** hate **5** odium **6** hatred **7** disgust **8** aversion, loathing **9** antipathy, revulsion **10** abhorrence **11** abomination, detestation

repugnant **4** foul, vile **5** nasty **6** odious **7** adverse, counter, hateful, opposed **8** contrary, unsavory **9** abhorrent, loathsome, obnoxious, offensive, repellent, repulsive, revolting, sickening **10** abominable, detestable, disgusting, nauseating, unpleasant **11** distasteful, uncongenial, undesirable, unpalatable **12** antipathetic, disagreeable, insufferable, unacceptable, unappetizing **13** objectionable

repulse **4** shun **5** avoid, repel, spurn **6** ignore, rebuff, refuse, reject **7** refusal **8** shunning, spurning **9** rejection

repulsion **6** hatred **7** disgust, dislike **8** aversion, distaste, loathing **9** antipathy **10** abhorrence, repugnance **11** abomination, detestation **13** indisposition **14** disinclination

repulsive **4** vile **5** nasty **6** odious **7** hateful **9** abhorrent, loathsome, obnoxious, offensive, repellent, repugnant, revolting **10** abominable, detestable, disgusting, nauseating **11** distasteful **12** disagreeable **13** objectionable

repulsiveness **8** ugliness **13** loathsomeness, offensiveness **14** disgustingness, unpleasantness **16** disagreeableness

reputable **7** honored **8** esteemed, reliable **9** respected **10** creditable **11** respectable, trustworthy

reputation **4** name **7** stature **8** standing

repute **3** say **4** deem, fame, hold, view **5** judge, think **6** esteem, reckon, regard, renown **7** account, believe, suppose **8** consider, estimate, standing **9** celebrity, notoriety **10** prominence **14** respectability

request **3** ask **4** seek **6** ask for, bid for, desire, sue for **7** call for, entreat, solicit **8** petition **9** importune **11** application **12** solicitation

requiem **5** dirge **6** lament **8** threnody

requiescat in pace **11** rest in peace **16** may he rest in peace **17** may she rest in peace

require **3** bid **4** lack, miss, need, want **5** crave, imply, order **6** charge, compel, desire, direct, enjoin, entail, oblige **7** command, dictate **9** constrain **11** necessitate

required **6** forced, needed **7** obliged **9** compelled, essential, necessary **10** compulsory, imperative, obligatory

requirement **4** must **8** standard **9** criterion, essential, guideline, requisite **12** prerequisite **13** specification
Latin: **10** sine qua non **11** desideratum

requisite **4** must, need **6** needed **8** required **9** essential, mandatory, necessary, necessity **10** compulsory, imperative, obligatory **11** requirement **12** prerequisite **13** indispensable
Latin: **10** sine qua non **11** desideratum

requisition **4** form **7** request **11** application

requital **7** redress **9** repayment **11** retaliation **12** compensation **15** indemnification

rescind **4** void **5** annul, quash **6** cancel, recall, repeal, revoke **7** abolish, discard, nullify, retract, reverse **8** abrogate, dissolve, override, overrule **10** invalidate **11** countermand **12** counterorder

rescinding **6** recall **7** voiding **8** recision **9** abolition **10** abrogation, retraction, revocation **11** abolishment, dissolution **12** cancellation, invalidation **13** nullification

rescue **4** save **6** ransom, saving **7** deliver, freeing, recover, release, salvage **8** liberate, recovery **9** extricate **10** liberation **11** deliverance, extrication

research **5** probe, study **7** delving, inquiry **8** analysis, scrutiny **10** inspection **11** examination, exploration, fact-finding, investigate, scholarship **13** investigation

resemblance **7** analogy **8** affinity, likeness, parallel **10** congruence, similarity, similitude **14** correspondence

resemble **5** favor **6** be like **8** be akin to, look like, parallel **9** take after

Resen
founder: **6** Nimrod

resent **7** dislike

resentful **5** angry **6** bitter **7** annoyed **8** grudging, offended, provoked **10** displeased **12** dissatisfied

resentfulness **5** anger, spite **10** bitterness **15** dissatisfaction

resentment **3** ire **4** huff **5** anger, pique, spite **6** animus, malice, rancor **7** dudgeon, ill will, offense, umbrage **8** acerbity, acrimony, asperity, jealousy, soreness, sourness **9** animosity, crossness **10** bitterness, irritation **11** displeasure, indignation **12** irritability, vengefulness **14** vindictiveness

reservation **4** date **5** doubt **7** booking, proviso, scruple, strings **8** preserve **9** condition, hesitancy, provision **10** encampment, reluctance, settlement **11** appointment, compunction, stipulation, uncertainty **12** installation **13** accommodation, establishment, qualification **14** prearrangement

reserve **4** book, hold, keep, save **5** amass, delay, extra, hoard, lay up, spare, stock, table **6** backup, engage, retain, shelve, unused **7** husband, nest egg, savings **8** conserve, keep back, postpone, preserve, salt away, schedule, withhold **9** aloofness, reticence, stockpile **10** additional, prearrange

reserved **5** aloof, taken **6** booked, formal **7** distant, engaged **8** bespoken, retained, reticent, strained, unsocial **9** inhibited, spoken for **10** restrained, unsociable **11** ceremonious, constrained, standoffish **12** unresponsive **15** uncommunicative, undemonstrative

reservoir **4** fund, pool, tank, well **5** basin, fount, hoard, stock, store **6** supply **7** backlog, cistern **8** millpond **9** container, stockpile **10** depository, receptacle, repository **12** accumulation

res gestae **5** deeds **10** things done **15** accomplishments

reshape **4** redo **5** adapt, alter, block **6** change, modify, reform, remold, rework **7** convert, reframe, remodel **9** refashion, transform

reside **3** lie **4** live, rest, room **5** dwell, exist, lodge **6** belong, occupy **7** inhabit, sojourn **8** domicile

residence **3** pad **4** digs, flat, home, room, stay **5** abode, house, place **7** address, lodging, sojourn **8** domicile, dwelling, quarters **9** apartment, homestead, household **10** habitation
French: **10** pied a terre

resident **5** local **6** lodger, tenant **7** citizen, denizen, dweller **8** occupant, townsman **9** sojourner **10** inhabitant **11** housekeeper

residual **5** extra **7** abiding, lasting, surplus **8** enduring, leftover **9** lingering, remaining **10** continuing **13** supplementary

residue **4** rest **5** dregs **6** scraps **7** balance, remains, remnant **8** leavings **9** remainder
Latin: **8** residuum

resign **4** quit **5** leave **6** give up, submit **8** abdicate, disclaim, renounce **9** reconcile **10** relinquish

resignation **8** fatalism, patience, quitting, stoicism **9** departure **10** equanimity, retirement, submission, withdrawal **11** passiveness **12** acquiescence **13** nonresistance **14** submissiveness

resign oneself **5** yield **6** submit **9** acquiesce

resilience **6** recoil **7** rebound **8** buoyancy **10** elasticity **11** flexibility **12** adaptability **13** changeability, nonuniformity **16** lightheartedness

resilient **5** hardy **6** supple **7** buoyant, elastic, rubbery, springy **8** flexible **9** adaptable, expansive, resistant, tenacious **10** rebounding, responsive **13** irrepressible

resist **4** balk, foil, stem, stop **5** fight, repel **6** baffle, combat, oppose, refuse, reject, thwart **7** contest, counter, weather **8** beat back, turn down **9** frustrate, withstand **10** counteract

resistance **6** mutiny, rebuff **7** refusal **8** defiance, struggle **9** obstinacy, rebellion, rejection **10** contention, insurgency, opposition **11** obstruction **12** insurrection **13** intransigence, noncompliance, recalcitrance

resolute **5** stern **6** dogged, steady **7** earnest, staunch, zealous **8** decisive, diligent, intrepid, stubborn, untiring, vigorous **9** assiduous, obstinate, purposive, steadfast, tenacious, unbending **10** deliberate, determined, inflexible, persistent, relentless, unflagging, unswerving, unwavering, unyielding **11** industrious, persevering, undeviating, unfaltering, unflinching **12** pertinacious, strong-minded, strong-willed **13** indefatigable **14** uncompromising

resoluteness **7** purpose, resolve **8** decision, tenacity **11** decidedness, persistence **12** decisiveness, perseverance **13** determination, steadfastness **14** purposefulness

resolution **3** aim **4** goal, plan, zeal **6** design, energy, intent, mettle, motion, object, spirit **7** promise, purpose, resolve **8** ambition, proposal, solution, tenacity **9** constancy, intention, objective, resolving, stability **10** resilience, steadiness **11** earnestness, persistence **12** perseverance, resoluteness **13** determination, steadfastness **14** aggressiveness **16** indefatigability

resolve **4** plan **6** answer, decide, design, intend, set out, settle, vote on **7** adjudge, clear up, explain, purpose **8** decision **9** determine, elucidate **10** commitment, resolution **12** resoluteness **13** determination **14** make up one's mind

resonant **4** full, rich **7** booming, orotund, ringing, vibrant **8** sonorous **9** bellowing **10** resounding, stentorian, thunderous **11** reverberant

resort **3** use **4** hope **5** apply, avail **6** chance, employ, take up **7** utilize **8** exercise, recourse **9** expedient

resound **4** echo, peal, ring **5** clang **6** re-echo **7** vibrate **11** reverberate **14** tintinnabulate

resounding **7** echoing, ringing **9** re-echoing **10** thundering, thunderous **13** reverberating

resource **8** recourse **9** expedient **11** wherewithal

resourceful **4** able **5** ready, sharp, smart **6** adroit, artful, bright, shrewd **7** capable, cunning **8** creative, original, skillful, talented **9** competent, effectual, ingenious, inventive **10** innovative, proficient **11** imaginative **12** enterprising

resourcefulness **9** ingenuity **10** creativity, enterprise **13** inventiveness

resources **5** funds, means, money **6** assets, income **7** capital, effects, revenue **10** belongings, collateral **11** possessions, wherewithal

respect **5** honor, point, sense **6** detail, esteem, matter, notice, praise, regard **7** bearing, feature, viewing **8** approval, courtesy, relation **9** affection, attention, deference, laudation, reference, relevance, reverence **10** admiration, connection, particular, veneration **11** point of view, recognition **12** appreciation, circumstance **13** consideration

respectability **7** decency, decorum **9** gentility, propriety **11** correctness, genteelness

respectable **4** fair **5** ample, civil, noble **6** decent, honest, polite, proper, worthy **7** correct, courtly, passing, refined, upright **8** becoming, decorous, moderate, polished **9** admirable, dignified, estimable, honorable, reputable **10** aboveboard, admissible, sufficient **11** presentable **12** considerable, praiseworthy, satisfactory

respected **6** valued, worthy **7** admired, honored, revered **8** esteemed **9** admirable, venerated

respectful **5** civil **6** formal, genial, polite **7** amiable, winning **8** admiring, decorous, gracious, mannerly, obliging, reverent **9** attentive, courteous, regardful **10** personable, solicitous **11** ceremonious, deferential, reverential **13** accommodating

respects **4** heed, obey **5** honor, prize, value **6** admire, esteem, fealty, follow, regard, revere **7** abide by, cherish, defer to, observe, regards, tribute **8** adhere to, consider, venerate **9** greetings **10** appreciate, understand **11** acknowledge, compliments **12** remembrances **13** consideration

Respighi, Ottorino
born: **5** Italy **7** Bologna
composer of: **8** La Fiamma, The Birds **14** The Pines of Rome **18** The Fountains of Rome **19** La Boutique Fantasque, The Fantastic Toyshop **27** Ancient Airs and Dances for Lute

respiration **9** breathing

respiratory system
component: **4** lung, nose **6** larynx **7** pharynx, trachea **8** voice box, windpipe **9** bronchius, diaphragm
action: **9** breathing

respire **7** breathe

respite **4** lull **5** break, delay, letup, pause **6** recess **8** reprieve **9** extension **12** intermission

resplendence **6** dazzle, luster **7** glitter **8** lambency, radiance **10** brilliance, luminosity, refulgence **12** circumstance, magnificence

resplendent **6** bright **7** beaming, blazing, glowing, lambent, radiant **8** dazzling, gleaming, luminous, lustrous, splendid **9** brilliant, refulgent, sparkling **10** glittering **11** coruscating

respond **5** react, reply **6** answer, rejoin **7** speak up **9** recognize **11** acknowledge

respond to **6** answer **7** act upon, react to, reply to **8** thank for **11** acknowledge

response **5** reply **6** answer, retort, return **7** riposte **8** comeback, feedback, reaction, rebuttal **9** rejoinder **10** impression **13** countercharge **14** acknowledgment **16** counterstatement

responsibility **4** duty, task **5** blame, order, trust **6** burden, charge **8** function **9** liability **10** obligation **11** culpability, reliability **13** answerability, dependability **14** accountability **15** trustworthiness

responsible **5** adult, of age **6** guilty, liable, mature **7** at fault, capable **8** culpable, reliable **9** demanding, executive, important **10** answerable, creditable, dependable **11** accountable, challenging, trustworthy **13** conscientious **14** administrative

responsive **5** alive, awake, sharp **8** reactive **9** receptive, sensitive **11** retaliative, retaliatory, susceptible, sympathetic **13** compassionate, understanding **14** impressionable

responsiveness **6** action **7** concern **8** interest **9** attention, awareness **11** sensitivity **13** understanding

res publica **8** republic, the state **12** commonwealth, public matter

rest **2** be **3** end, lay, lie, nap, set **4** base, ease, halt, hang, keep, laze, lean, loaf, loll, lull, prop, rely, stay, stop **5** break, death, exist, hinge, let up, pause, peace, place, quiet, relax, sleep, stand **6** demise, depend, holder, lounge, others, recess, remain, repose, reside, scraps, snooze, trivet **7** balance, be based, be found, be quiet, decease, deposit, holiday, leisure, lie down, recline, remains, remnant, residue, respite, set down, slumber, support **8** breather, platform, vacation **9** cessation, departure, leftovers, remainder, stillness **10** complement, quiet spell, relaxation, standstill, suspension **11** hibernation, take time out **12** intermission, interruption **13** take a breather
Spanish: **6** siesta
Latin: **8** residuum

restaurant **5** diner **6** eatery **7** beanery, tearoom **9** cafeteria, chop house, grillroom, hashhouse, lunchroom **11** coffeehouse **12** luncheonette
French: **4** cafe **6** bistro **9** brasserie
German: **11** rathskeller

restful **4** calm **5** quiet **6** placid, serene **7** pacific, relaxed **8** peaceful, soothing, tranquil **10** unagitated **11** comfortable, undisturbed

restfulness **4** ease **5** quiet **6** repose **8** serenity, softness **10** relaxation **11** tranquility **12** tranquillity

rest in peace
Latin: **16** requiescat in pace

restitution **6** amends **7** redress, replevy **8** replevin, requital, restoral **9** atonement, indemnity, repayment **10** recompense, reparation **11** restoration **12** compensation, remuneration, satisfaction **13** reimbursement, reinstatement **15** indemnification

restive **5** balky **6** mulish, ornery, unruly **7** fidgety, wayward, willful **8** contrary, stubborn **9** fractious, pigheaded **10** rebellious, refractory **11** disobedient, intractable **12** recalcitrant, unmanageable

restless **5** awake, jumpy **6** fitful, uneasy **7** anxious, fidgety, fretful, jittery, nervous, on the go, unquiet, wakeful, worried **8** agitated **9** excitable, impatient, incessant, insomniac, on the move, sleepless, transient, unsettled **10** disquieted, high-strung **11** hyperactive **13** uncomfortable

restoration **7** revival **8** recovery **12** recuperation **13** convalescence, reinstatement **14** rehabilitation, reintroduction, reinvigoration **15** reestablishment

restorative **5** tonic **6** elixir **7** bracing, healing **8** curative **10** beneficial, energizing, fortifying **11** revivifying **12** invigorating, revitalizing **13** strengthening

restore **3** fix **4** cure, dose, heal, mend **5** rally, renew, treat **6** do over, recoup, remedy, repair, rescue, return, revive **7** convert, get back, patch up, put back, rebuild, reclaim, recover, refresh, remodel, retouch, touch up **8** energize, give back, make over, make well, medicate, renovate, retrieve, revivify, recreate **9** reanimate, refurbish, reinstall, reinstate, stimulate **10** exhilarate, revitalize, strengthen **11** recondition, reconstruct, reestablish, reinstitute, resuscitate **12** rehabilitate, reinvigorate

restored **4** kept **5** saved **7** revived **8** replaced **9** conserved, pressured **11** replenished **13** rehabilitated

restrain **3** gag **4** bind, curb,

hold, stop **5** check, leash, limit **6** arrest, bridle, fetter, muzzle, pinion, temper, tether **7** chasten, contain, curtail, harness, inhibit, prevent, shackle, trammel **8** handicap, hold back, restrict, suppress, withhold

restrained **4** cool **5** aloof **6** curbed **7** checked, distant **8** held back, reined in, reserved **10** controlled, unfriendly

restraint **4** curb **5** check **7** control **10** limitation

restrict **4** curb, hold **5** check, cramp, crimp, hem in, limit **6** hamper, impede, narrow, thwart **7** confine, inhibit, prevent, squelch **8** hold back, obstruct, straiten, suppress **9** constrain, frustrate **12** circumscribe

restricted **7** cramped, limited **8** confined, hampered, held back **9** exclusive **10** suppressed **13** circumscribed

restriction **4** rule **7** control, curbing, proviso **9** condition, provision **10** limitation, regulation **11** requirement, reservation, stipulation **13** consideration, qualification

restrictive **8** limiting **9** confining, exclusive **12** constraining

result **4** stem **5** arise, end up, ensue, fruit, issue, owe to **6** derive, effect, happen, pan out, report, sequel, spring, upshot, wind up **7** finding, opinion, outcome, product, turn out, verdict **8** decision, judgment, reaction, solution **9** aftermath, culminate, eventuate, originate, outgrowth **10** resolution **11** aftereffect, consequence, development, eventuality **13** determination

resume **2** CV **3** bio **4** go on **5** brief **6** digest **7** epitome, proceed, summary **8** abstract, continue, reembark, synopsis **9** biography, summation **10** abridgment, recommence **11** reestablish **12** condensation
Latin: **15** curriculum vitae
French: **6** precis

resumption **11** recommenced, restoration **12** continuation

resurgam **15** I shall rise again

resurgence **6** return **7** rebirth, renewal, revival **10** renascence **11** reemergence, renaissance **12** rejuvenation **13** recrudescence

retailer **5** store **6** dealer, seller, trader **8** merchant, provider, supplier **9** tradesman **10** wholesaler **11** distributor, storekeeper, tradeswoman **12** merchandiser
French: **9** vivandier **10** vivandiere

retain **4** hold, keep **5** grasp **6** absorb, recall **7** possess **8** hang on to, hold on to, maintain, memorize, remember **9** recollect

retainer **7** servant **8** employee **9** attendant

retainership **4** hire **6** employ **7** service **10** employment

retaliate **5** repay **6** avenge, pay off, return **7** counter, pay back, requite, revenge **11** reciprocate

retaliation **6** talion **7** deserts, revenge **8** reprisal, requital **9** vengeance **10** recompense **11** comeuppance, eye for an eye, interchange, just deserts, lex talionis, retribution **12** compensation **13** reciprocation **14** tooth for a tooth

retard **4** clog, drag **5** block, brake, check, delay **6** arrest, baffle, detain, fetter, hamper, hinder, hold up, impede, slow up **7** draw out, inhibit, prevent, prolong, slacken **8** hold back, obstruct, slow down **10** decelerate

retarded **4** dull, slow **6** simple **7** idiotic, moronic, unsound **8** backward, disabled **9** imbecilic, mongoloid, subnormal **10** slow-witted **11** handicapped **12** simpleminded

reticent **3** shy **5** quiet **6** closed, silent **7** subdued **8** reserved, retiring, taciturn **9** diffident, withdrawn **10** restrained **11** tight-lipped **12** close-mouthed **15** uncommunicative

retinue **5** court, staff, suite, train **6** convoy **9** courtiers, employees, entourage, followers, following, personnel, retainers **10** associates, attendance, attendants

retire **6** depart, go away, remove, resign, resort, secede, turn in **7** drop out, retreat **8** abdicate, flake out, withdraw

retired
French: **8** ci-devant

retiring **3** shy **4** meek **5** quiet, timid **6** demure, humble, modest **7** bashful **8** reserved, reticent, sheepish, timorous, unsocial **9** diffident, shrinking, withdrawn **10** unassuming **11** unassertive **12** self-effacing **13** inconspicuous, unpretentious **15** uncommunicative

retort **3** say **4** quip **5** rebut, reply **6** answer, rejoin, return **7** counter, respond, riposte **8** fire back, rebuttal **9** rejoinder

retract **4** deny **6** abjure, disown, draw in, recall, recant, recede, recoil, reel in, repeal, revoke **7** disavow, rescind, retreat, reverse **8** abnegate, abrogate, disclaim, draw back, forswear, peel back, pull back, renounce, take back, withdraw **9** foreswear, repudiate

retraction **6** recall **8** recision **9** disavowal **10** disclaimer, refutation, withdrawal

retreat **2** go **3** den **4** bolt, flee, port **5** haunt, haven, leave **6** asylum, depart, escape, flight, harbor, recoil, refuge, resort, retire, shrink **7** abscond, getaway, privacy, sanctum, shelter, shy away **8** back away, draw back, fall back, hideaway, move back, solitude, turn tail, withdraw **9** departure, isolation, reclusion, sanctuary, seclusion **10** evacuation, immurement, retirement, withdrawal **11** hibernation, rustication

retrench **5** slash **6** reduce, scrape, scrimp **7** curtail, cut back, cut down **8** conserve, cut costs **9** economize **15** tighten one's belt

retribution **6** amends, return, reward **7** justice, penalty, redress, revenge **8** reprisal, requital **9** vengeance **10** punishment, recompense, reparation **11** just deserts, restitution, retaliation, vindication **12** satisfaction **13** reciprocation, recrimination

retrieve **4** snag **5** fetch **6** ransom, recoup, redeem, regain, rescue **7** get back, reclaim, recover, salvage **9** recapture, repossess

retriever
dog breed: **5** Irish **6** golden, Gordon **7** English **8** Labrador **10** flat-coated **11** curly-coated **13** Chesapeake Bay

retrograde **5** worse **6** worsen **7** inverse, retreat, reverse **8** backward **10** regressive **13** retrogressive

retrogress **6** worsen **9** backslide

retrogression **7** decline, setback **9** worsening **11** backsliding

retrogressive **8** backward **9** declining, worsening **11** backsliding

retrospect **6** review **9** flashback, hindsight **11** remembrance **12** afterthought, reminiscence **15** reconsideration

return **3** net **4** earn, gain **5** gross, recur, repay, yield **6** advent, come to, go back, income, profit, render, reseat, reward **7** arrival, benefit, produce, provide, put back, requite, restore, revenue **8** announce, come back, earnings, give back, hand down, interest, proceeds, reappear, recovery, restoral, send back **9** advantage, reinstall, reinstate, retrieval, reversion **10** homecoming, recurrence **11** reciprocate, reestablish, restoration **12** compensation, reappearance **13** reinstatement **15** reestablishment

Return, The
author: **14** Walter de la Mare

Return of the Native
author: **11** Thomas Hardy
character: **11** Diggory Venn, Eustacia Vye **12** Damon Wildeve **13** Clym Yeobright **17** Thomasin Yeobright

Return to Thebes
author: **10** Allan Drury

Reuben
father: **5** Jacob
mother: **4** Leah
brother: **3** Dan, Gad **4** Levi **5** Asher, Judah **6** Joseph, Simeon **7** Zebulun **8** Benjamin, Issachar, Naphtali
sister: **5** Dinah
descendant of: **9** Reubenite

reunite **5** rewed **7** remarry **9** reconcile

reveal **4** bare, show **6** betray, expose, impart, let out, unfold, unmask, unveil **7** display, divulge, exhibit, give out, lay bare, publish, uncover, unearth **8** disclose, evidence, manifest, point out

revealed **4** open **5** clear, known **7** evident, obvious **8** manifest

revel **4** romp **5** caper, enjoy **6** bask in, frolic, gambol, relish **7** carouse, delight, indulge, rejoice, roister, skylark **8** wallow in **9** celebrate

revelation **6** expose, vision **7** shocker **8** exposure, prophecy **9** admission, bombshell, discovery, eyeopener, unveiling **10** apocalypse, confession, disclosure, divulgence **11** divulgation, divulgement

revelatory **10** expressive **11** informative **13** communicative

reveler **6** barfly, ranter, player **7** drinker **8** bacchant, carouser, drunkard **9** roisterer, rollicker, skylarker **10** merrymaker

revelry **5** spree **7** jollity **8** carnival, carousal, festival, jamboree **9** high jinks, merriment, rejoicing **10** exultation, roistering **11** celebrating, celebration, merrymaking **12** conviviality **13** jollification **14** boisterousness
god of: **5** Comus

revenge **5** repay **7** pay back, requite **8** reprisal, requital **9** repayment, retaliate, vengeance, vindicate **10** recompense **11** eye for an eye, reciprocate, retaliation, retribution **12** satisfaction

revenue **3** pay **4** take **5** gains, wages, yield **6** income, profit, return, salary **7** annuity, pension, subsidy **8** earnings, interest, pickings, proceeds, receipts **9** allowance, emolument **12** compensation, remuneration

revenue, annual
French: **5** rente

reverberate **4** boom, echo, ring **5** carry **6** rumble **7** resound, thunder, vibrate

reverberation **4** boom, echo **6** rumble **7** ringing, thunder **8** rumbling **9** vibration **10** resounding, thundering

revere **5** honor **6** esteem **7** defer to, respect **8** venerate

revered **6** adored **7** admired, honored **9** estimable, respected, venerated, worshiped **10** worshipped

reverence **3** awe **4** fear **5** honor, piety **6** esteem, homage, regard **7** respect, worship **8** devotion **9** adoration, deference **10** admiration, devoutness, observance, veneration **11** prostration, religiosity **12** genuflection

reverent **4** pure **5** pious **6** devout, humble, solemn **7** adoring, awesome, devoted **8** faithful **9** religious, spiritual **10** respectful, worshipful

reverential **4** awed **10** respectful, worshipful **11** deferential

reverie **5** dream, fancy **6** musing **7** fantasy **8** daydream **9** dreamland, quixotism **10** brown study, meditation **12** extravagance **13** woolgathering **14** fantasticality

reverse **4** back, rear, tail, undo, void **5** annul, upend, upset **6** cancel, change, defeat, invert, mishap, negate, recall, recant, repeal, revoke, unmake, upturn **7** counter, failure, nullify, rescind, retract, setback, trouble **8** abrogate, backward, contrary, converse, hardship, inverted, opposite, override, overrule, set aside, turn over, withdraw **9** adversity, mischance, posterior, transpose **10** antithesis, invalidate, misfortune **11** countermand, counterpart, frustration **14** disappointment

revert **5** lapse **6** go back, repeat, return **7** regress, relapse **9** backslide **10** recidivate, retrogress

review **4** show **5** study, sum up **6** notice, parade, rehash, survey **7** analyze, journal, retrace, run over **8** critique, evaluate, hash over, magazine, reassess, report on, scrutiny **9** criticism, criticize, reexamine, reiterate, summarize **10** commentary, evaluation, exhibition, exposition, procession, reconsider, reevaluate, reflection, scrutinize **11** examination **12** presentation, reassessment, recapitulate, reevaluation **13** demonstration, retrospection **14** recapitulation **15** reconsideration
French: **11** compte rendu

revile **4** slur **5** abuse, curse, scold, scorn **6** berate, defame, deride, malign, rebuke, vilify **7** bawl out, chew out, slander, upbraid **8** belittle, denounce, execrate, reproach, sail into **9** blaspheme, castigate, denigrate, disparage **10** vituperate

reviler **6** critic, curser **8** vilifier **9** backbiter, slanderer **10** blasphemer

revise **4** edit, redo **5** alter, amend, emend, fix up **6** change, doctor, modify, recast, redact, revamp, review, update **7** correct, rectify, rewrite **8** emendate, overhaul

revision **6** change **7** edition **9** amendment, recension **10** alteration, correction, emendation **11** improvement **12** modification

revival **7** renewal **11** restoration **13** reinstatement, reinstitution, resuscitation

revive **5** dig up, renew **6** drag up, repeat **7** freshen, refresh, restage **8** reawaken **9** reanimate, reproduce, resurrect **11** resuscitate

revived **7** renewed **8** animated, repeated, restaged **9** enlivened, freshened, refreshed **10** reanimated, reawakened, reproduced **11** invigorated, resurrected **12** resuscitated

revocation **6** repeal **8** recision **9** abolition, annulment **10** abrogation, retraction **11** abolishment, elimination, repudiation **12** cancellation **13** nullification

revoke **4** void **5** annul, erase, quash **6** abjure, cancel, negate, recall, repeal, vacate **7** abolish, dismiss, expunge, nullify, rescind, retract, reverse **8** abrogate, call back, disallow, disclaim, override, overrule, renounce, set aside, take back, withdraw **9** repudiate **10** invalidate **11** countermand

revolt **4** coup, rise **5** rebel, repel, shock **6** appall, mutiny, offend, rise up, sicken **7** disgust, dissent, horrify, repulse **8** disorder, distress, nauseate, sedition, uprising **9** rebellion **10** insurgency, opposition, **12** factiousness, insurrection
German: **6** Putsch

revolting **4** foul, grim, vile **5** nasty **6** horrid, odious **7** hateful, noisome, noxious **8** dreadful, horrible, horrific, shocking, stinking **9** abhorrent, appalling, frightful, invidious, loathsome, obnoxious, offensive, repellent, repugnant, repulsive, sickening **10** abominable, disgusting, malodorous, nauseating **11** distasteful **12** disagreeable **13** objectionable

Revolt of the Angels, The
author: **13** Anatole France

revolution **6** mutiny, revolt, rising **8** circling, gyration, rotation, uprising **9** rebellion **12** insurrection **14** circumrotation, circumvolution
French: **4** coup **9** coup d'etat
German: **6** Putsch

revolutionary **7** radical **8** mutinous **9** extremist, insurgent, seditious **10** dissenting, rebellious, subversive **13** superadvanced, unprecedented **15** insurrectionary

revolve **4** spin, turn **5** twist, wheel **6** circle, gyrate, rotate **12** circumrotate

revolver **3** gat, gun, rod **4** colt **6** pistol, weapon **7** firearm, handgun, rotator, sidearm **10** six-shooter **20** Saturday night special

revulsion **8** aversion, distaste, loathing **10** abhorrence, repugnance **11** detestation

reward **3** due **5** bonus, prize, repay, wages **6** bounty **7** deserts, guerdon, payment, premium, requite **9** reckoning **10** compensate, recompense, remunerate **12** compensation, remuneration **13** consideration
Latin: **10** quid pro quo

rewarding **8** pleasant, valuable **9** enjoyable **10** delightful, gratifying, satisfying **11** pleasurable

rework **4** redo **5** adapt, alter **6** modify **7** remodel, reshape **9** refashion, transform

rex **4** king

Reykjavik
capital of: **7** Iceland

Reynolds, Burt
born: **10** Waycross GA
wife: **9** Judy Carne **12** Loni Anderson
roles: **6** Shamus **9** Dan August, Semi-Tough **11** Deliverance **14** The Longest Yard **18** Smokey and the Bandit

Reynolds, Debbie
real name: **19** Mary Frances Reynolds
born: **8** El Paso TX
husband: **11** Eddie Fisher
roles: **13** The Singing Nun, The Tender Trap **15** Singin' in the Rain **19** Tammy and the Bachelor **23** The Unsinkable Molly Brown

Reynolds, Sir Joshua
born: **7** England **8** Plympton
artwork: **14** Lord Heathfield, Miss Jane Bowles **15** Commodore Keppel **18** Mrs Francis Beckford **21** Mrs Abington as Miss Prue **25** Mrs Siddons as the Tragic Muse **38** Lady Sarah Bunbury Sacrificing to the Graces

Rhadamanthus, Rhadamanthys
father: **4** Zeus
mother: **6** Europa
brother: **5** Minos **6** Aeacus **8** Sarpedon
became a judge in: **5** Hades

rhapsodic **6** elated **7** beaming, excited **8** blissful, ecstatic, thrilled **9** delirious, overjoyed, rapturous **11** exhilarated, transported

Rhea
member of: **6** Titans
father: **6** Uranus
mother: **4** Gaea
brother: **6** Cronos, Cronus, Kronos
husband: **6** Cronos, Cronus, Kronos
son: **4** Zeus **5** Hades **8** Poseidon
daughter: **4** Hera **6** Hestia **7** Demeter
called: **10** Magna Mater
corresponds to: **3** Ops **6** Cybele **9** Dindymene **10** Berecyntia
epithet: **6** Antaea

Rhea Silvia *see* **9** Rea Silvia

Rhene
mistress of: **6** Oileus
son: **5** Medon

Rhesus
owned: **6** horses
horses captured by: **8** Diomedes, Odysseus

rhetoric **4** bunk, wind **5** hokum, hooey **6** bunkum, hot air **7** fustian, oratory **8** euphuism **9** discourse, elocution, eloquence, hyperbole **10** hocus-pocus **11** flamboyance **13** magniloquence **14** grandiloquence

Rhetoric
author: **9** Aristotle

rhetorical **5** showy, windy **6** florid, ornate, purple, verbal **7** aureate, flowery **8** eloquent, inflated **9** bombastic, grandiose, highflown, stylistic **10** decorative, discursive, euphuistic, expressive, flamboyant, linguistic, oratorical, ornamental **11** disputative, embellished, extravagant **12** disputatious, elocutionary, magniloquent **13** argumentative, grandiloquent

Rhiannon
origin: **5** Welsh
husband: **5** Pwyll **10** Manawyddan
son: **7** Pryderi
accused of devouring: **7** Pryderi

Rhigmus
origin: **8** Thracian
ally of: **7** Trojans
killed by: **8** Achilles

rhinoceros
group of: **5** crash

Rhoda
character: **8** Gary Levy **9** Joe Gerard **12** Benny Goodwin **14** Ida Morgenstern, Sally Gallagher **17** Brenda Morgenstern, Martin Morgenstern **22** Rhoda Morgenstern Gerard
cast: **9** Anne Meara, David Groh, Ron Silver **11** Julie Kavner, Nancy Walker **12** Harold J Gould, Ray Buktenica **13** Valerie Harper

Rhode Island
abbreviation: 2 RI
nickname: 11 Little Rhody
capital/largest city: 10 Providence
others: 7 Bristol, Newport 8 Cranston, Kingston, Westerly 9 Pawtucket, Wakefield 10 Woonsocket
college: 5 Brown 6 Bryant 8 Pembroke 10 Barrington, Providence 11 Salve Regina 13 Mount St Joseph, Roger Williams 15 Johnson and Wales, Naval War College
feature: 7 Newport
tribe: 7 Niantic 9 Wampanoag 12 Narragansett
people: 8 Puritans 12 George M Cohan 13 Gilbert Stuart, Matthew C Perry, Roger Williams 15 Ambrose Burnside, Nathanael Greene 17 Oliver Hazard Perry
island: 5 Block, Rhode 8 Prudence 9 Aquidneck, Conanicut
lake: 8 Scituate
pond: 7 Wordens 8 Stafford, Watchaug
land rank: 8 fiftieth
mountain: 10 Durfee Hill
highest point: 12 Jerimoth Hill
physical feature:
bay: 12 Narragansett
sea: 8 Atlantic
sound: 11 Block Island
river: 7 Seekonk 8 Pawtuxet 9 Pawcatuck, Pawtucket, Potowomut 10 Blackstone, Providence
state admission: 10 thirteenth
state bird: 14 Rhode Island Red
state flower: 6 violet
state motto: 4 Hope
state song: 11 Rhode Island
state tree: 8 red maple

Rhodesia *see* 8 Zimbabwe

rhodium
chemical symbol: 2 Rh

rhododendron
varieties: 4 tree 5 Bluet 6 Indian, Yunnan 7 catawba, fringed, Lapland, silvery, Smirnow 8 Carolina, Chapman's, Fortune's, Fujiyama, piedmont 9 Caucasian, honey-bell, West Coast 11 leather-leaf 12 willow-leaved

rhodolite
species: 6 garnet

Rhodope
companion of: 7 Artemis
skill: 7 hunting

Rhodopis
also: 7 Rhodope
form: 9 courtesan
origin: 5 Greek 8 Thracian
slave in: 5 Egypt
lost: 7 slipper
slipper found by: 12 Psammetichus
husband: 12 Psammetichus

Rhodus
father: 8 Poseidon
mother: 9 Aphrodite

Rhoeo
father: 9 Staphylus
mother: 12 Chrysothemis
seduced by: 6 Apollo

Rhoetus
member of: 8 Gigantes

rhubarb 5 Rheum 16 Rheum rhabarbarum
varieties: 4 wild 5 monk's 6 garden, Sikkim 7 spinach 8 mountain

rhyme 3 pun 4 poem, rune, song 5 chime, clink, meter, poesy, verse 6 jingle, poetry, rhythm 7 measure, poetize, versify 8 assonate, doggerel 10 consonance 12 alliteration
game: 6 crambo

rhymer, rhymester 4 bard, poet 6 writer 8 minstrel, poetizer 9 poetaster, versifier 10 troubadour

Rhys, Jean
author of: 7 Quartet 15 Voyage in the Dark, Wide Sargasso Sea

rhythm 4 beat, lilt, time 5 meter, pulse, swing, throb 6 accent, number, stress 7 cadence, measure 8 emphasis, movement 9 pulsation 10 recurrence 11 fluctuation, syncopation 12 accentuation

riant 3 gay 4 airy 5 jolly, merry 6 blithe, bright, jocund, jovial 7 smiling 8 cheerful, laughing, mirthful

ribald 4 lewd, racy, rude 5 bawdy, crude, gross 6 coarse, earthy, rakish, risque, vulgar, wanton 7 raffish, uncouth 8 improper, indecent, off-color, prurient, shocking 9 salacious, unrefined 10 lascivious, libidinous, licentious, suggestive

ribbon 3 bow, ray 4 band, sash 5 award, braid, prize, reins, strip 6 cordon, riband 7 binding, rosette 8 memorial, streamer 10 decoration

rice 5 Oryza 11 Oryza sativa
varieties: 4 wild 6 Indian, pampas 8 mountain 9 Tennessee 10 annual wild
dish: 5 grits, pilaf 7 pudding, risotto 8 porridge 9 jambalaya
liquor: 4 sake

Rice, Elmer
author of: 11 Street Scene 16 The Adding Machine

Riceyman Steps
author: 13 Arnold Bennett

rich 4 dark, deep, fine, lush 5 flush, heavy, loamy, sweet, vivid 6 bright, costly, fecund, lavish, mellow 7 fertile, filling, intense, moneyed, opulent, wealthy, well-off 8 abundant, affluent, fruitful, in clover, precious, prodigal, resonant, sonorous, splendid, valuable, well-to-do 9 abounding, estimable, expensive, luxuriant, luxurious, priceless, sumptuous 10 euphonious, productive, propertied, prosperous 11 mellifluous 12 on easy street

Rich, Adrienne
author of: 18 Diving into the Wreck

Richard, Maurice
nickname: 6 Rocket
sport: 6 hockey
position: 7 forward
team: 17 Montreal Canadiens

Richard Cory
author: 22 Edwin Arlington Robinson

Richard Diamond, Private Detective
character: 3 Sam 6 Lt Kile 9 Lt McGough 10 Karen Wells
cast: 10 Russ Conway 11 Barbara Bain, Regis Toomey 12 David Janssen 13 Roxanne Brooks 14 Mary Tyler Moore
viewers saw only Sam's: 4 legs

Richard II
author: 18 William Shakespeare
character: 11 John of Gaunt 13 Edmund Langley,

Thomas Mowbray **16** Henry Bolingbroke **20** Earl of Northumberland
Duke of: **4** York **7** Aumerle, Norfolk **8** Hereford **9** Lancaster

Richard III
author: **18** William Shakespeare
character: **6** George **7** Richard **8** Edward IV, Lady Anne **10** Henry Tudor (Earl of Richmond) **11** Lord Stanley **12** Lord Hastings **13** Queen Margaret **14** Queen Elizabeth **15** Edward the Fourth **17** Sir William Catesby **19** Edward Prince of Wales
Duke of: **4** York **8** Clarence **10** Buckingham, Gloucester

Richardson, Henry Hobson
architect of: **9** Sever Hall (Harvard) **11** Grace Church (West Medford MA) **13** Trinity Church (Boston) **23** State Asylum for the Insane (Buffalo NY) **27** Marshall Field Wholesale Store (Chicago)

Richardson, Samuel
author of: **6** Pamela (or Virtue Rewarded) **8** Clarissa (Harlowe) **19** Sir Charles Grandison

Richardson, Sir Ralph
born: **7** England **10** Cheltenham
roles: **6** Exodus **10** Oscar Wilde, Richard III, The Heiress **11** A Doll's House **12** Anna Karenina **13** Doctor Zhivago **15** Richard the Third **20** Little Lord Fauntleroy **24** Long Day's Journey into Night **26** Greystoke The Legend of Tarzan

Richardson, Tony
director of: **8** Tom Jones (Oscar) **15** Look Back in Anger **36** The Loneliness of the Long Distance Runner

riches **4** pelf **5** lucre, means **6** assets, mammon, wealth **7** fortune **8** opulence, treasure **9** resources **10** prosperity **11** possessions

richness **6** wealth **8** fullness, lushness, opulence **9** amplitude, intensity **10** lavishness, mellowness **12** completeness **13** luxuriousness

Richter, Charles Francis
field: **10** geophysics, seismology
developed: **12** Richter scale **24** measurement of earthquakes

rickety **4** weak **5** frail, shaky **6** feeble, flimsy, infirm, wasted, weakly, wobbly **7** fragile **8** decrepit, unsteady, withered **9** tottering **10** brokendown, tumbledown **11** debilitated, dilapidated, weakjointed **12** deteriorated

rid **4** free **5** clear, purge **6** remove **8** disabuse, liberate, unburden **9** disburden, eliminate **11** disencumber

Ridd, John
character in: **10** Lorna Doone
author: **9** Blackmore

riddance **6** ouster, relief **7** freeing, removal **8** ejection **9** clearance, expulsion **11** deliverance, dislodgment

riddle **5** poser, rebus **6** enigma, puzzle, secret **7** mystery, problem, puzzler, stumper **9** conundrum

ride **4** move **5** annoy, carry, drive, harry, hound **6** badger, handle, harass, hector, manage, needle, travel **7** control, journey, support **8** progress **9** transport

rider **5** affix **6** suffix **7** adjunct, codicil **8** addendum, addition, appendix **9** amendment, appendage **10** attachment, supplement

Riders to the Sea
author: **19** John Millington Synge

ridge **3** bar, rib, rim **4** bank, fret, hill, hump, rise, wale, weal, welt **5** bluff, crest, crimp, knoll, mound, spine **6** ripple **7** crinkle, hillock, wrinkle **10** promontory **11** corrugation

ridicule **3** guy, rib **4** gibe, jeer, josh, mock, razz, ride, twit **5** mimic, scorn, taunt, tease **6** deride, gibe at, parody **7** lampoon, laugh at, mockery, ribbing, sarcasm, scoff at, sneer at, snicker, teasing **8** belittle, derision, sneering, travesty **9** aspersion, burlesque, disparage, humiliate, make fun of, poke fun at **10** caricature, derogation, lampoonery **13** disparagement
god of: **5** Momos, Momus

ridiculous **3** odd **5** crazy, droll, funny, inane, nutty, queer, silly **6** absurd, screwy **7** amusing, asinine, bizarre, comical, fatuous, foolish, idiotic **8** farcical **9** fantastic, frivolous, grotesque, laughable, ludicrous, screwball, senseless **10** hysterical, incredible, irrational, outlandish **11** astonishing, nonsensical **12** preposterous, unreasonable

Rienzi
author: **18** Edward Bulwer-Lytton

Riesling, Paul
character in: **7** Babbitt
author: **5** Lewis

rife **5** close, dense, solid, thick **6** common, packed **7** crowded, general, studded, teeming **8** epidemic, pandemic, populous, swarming **9** chock-full, extensive, plumbfull, prevalent, universal **10** prevailing, widespread **11** predominant

riffraff **3** mob **4** herd, scum **5** crowd, dregs, trash **6** masses, proles, rabble, vermin **9** peasantry **10** commonalty **11** proletariat
French: **8** canaille

rifle **3** rob **4** loot, sack **6** ravage **7** despoil, pillage, plunder, ransack **8** spoliate **10** burglarize

rifle, repeating
invented by: **7** Spencer

Rifleman, The
character: **10** Lou Mallory, Mark McCain **11** Lucas McCain **14** Miss Milly Scott **20** Marshal Micah Torrance
cast: **7** Paul Fix **10** Joan Taylor **12** Chuck Connors **13** Patricia Blair **14** Johnny Crawford
setting: **9** New Mexico, North Fork

rift **3** cut, gap **4** gash, gulf, rent, slit **5** abyss, break, chasm, chink, cleft, crack, fault, gorge, gulch, gully, split **6** breach, cranny, ravine **7** breakup, crevice, fissure, quarrel, rupture **8** aperture, crevasse, division, fracture **12** disagreement **16** misunderstanding

rig **4** gear **5** equip **6** fit out, outfit **8** carriage **9** apparatus, equipment, machinery

Rigaud
character in: **12** Little Dorrit
author: **7** Dickens

Rigg, Diana
born: **7** England **9** Doncaster
roles: **6** Helena **8** Emma Peel **10** Bleak House **11** Lady Dedlock, The Avengers **12** Julius Caesar **21** A Midsummer Night's Dream **26** On Her Majesty's Secret Service

right **2** OK **3** due **4** deed, fair, good, just, meet, nice, real, sane, true, well **5** amend, emend, exact, grant, honor, ideal, legal, licit, moral, power, solve, sound, valid **6** actual, at once, decent, honest, lawful, morals, normal, proper, remedy, seemly, square, virtue **7** certain, correct, ethical, exactly, factual, fitting, freedom, genuine, liberty, license, perfect, precise, probity, redress, regular, standup, warrant **8** accurate, becoming, clear-cut, definite, directly, goodness, morality, promptly, properly, rational, sanction, straight, suitable, suitably, truthful, virtuous **9** allowable, authentic, authority, correctly, desirable, equitable, exemplary, favorable, favorably, honorable, integrity, nobleness, opportune, ownership, perfectly, precisely, presently, privilege, propriety, rectitude, veracious, veridical, vindicate **10** aboveboard, accurately, admissible, completely, convenient, infallible, legitimate, permission, preferable, reasonable, recompense, scrupulous, undisputed, unmistaken **11** inheritance, immediately, irrefutable, prerogative, punctilious **12** advantageous, jurisdiction, satisfactory **13** appropriately, authorization, incontestable, justification, unimpeachable **14** proprietorship, satisfactorily, unquestionable
Latin: **3** jus

right beside **6** next to **8** abutting, adjacent, touching

righteous **4** fair, good, holy, just **5** godly, moral, pious **6** chaste, devout, honest **7** ethical **8** elevated, innocent, reverent, virtuous **9** blameless, equitable, honorable, incorrupt, religious, spiritual, unsullied

righteousness
goddess of: **4** Maat

righteous person
Hebrew: **6** zaddik

rightful **3** due **4** just, true **5** legal, valid **6** lawful, proper **7** allowed, condign, correct, fitting, merited **8** deserved **9** deserving, equitable **10** authorized, designated, legitimate, prescribed, sanctioned **11** appropriate, inalienable **14** constitutional

right hand **4** aide, ally **6** helper **7** partner **8** adjutant **9** assistant
French: **10** aide-de-camp

right of blood
Latin: **12** jus sanguinis

right of soil/land
Latin: **7** jus soli

Right People, The
author: **17** Stephen Birmingham

right side up **7** upright **10** on one's feet

Right Stuff, The
director: **13** Philip Kaufman
author: **8** Tom Wolfe
cast: **8** Ed Harris **10** Sam Shepard
Oscar for: **5** score

right-wing **7** old-line **10** nonliberal **11** reactionary **12** conservative **14** nonprogressive

right-winger **8** rightist **11** reactionary **12** conservative

rigid **3** set **4** firm, hard, taut **5** fixed, harsh, sharp, stern, stiff, tense **6** formal, severe, strict, strong, wooden **7** austere **8** exacting, obdurate, rigorous, stubborn, unpliant **9** inelastic, stringent, unbending **10** inflexible, unyielding **11** puritanical, unrelenting **14** uncompromising

Rigoletto
opera by: **5** Verdi
character: **5** Gilda **9** Maddalena **11** Sparafucile **12** Duke of Mantua **15** Countess Ceprano **16** Count of Monterone

rigorous **5** exact, harsh, stern, tough **6** severe, strict, trying **7** austere, correct, precise **8** accurate, exacting **9** demanding, stringent **10** meticulous, scrupulous **11** challenging, punctilious

rig out **4** garb **5** array, dress **6** attire, clothe

rile **3** irk, vex **4** gall, miff, roil **5** anger, annoy, chafe, gripe, peeve, pique **6** bother, enrage, nettle, offend, plague **7** incense, inflame, provoke **8** irritate **9** aggravate, infuriate

Riley, James Whitcomb
author of: **18** Little Orphant Annie **25** When the Frost Is on the Punkin

rilievo **6** relief

Rilke, Rainer Maria
author of: **11** Book of Hours **12** Duino Elegies, Life and Songs **13** Divine Elegies **16** Sonnets to Orpheus **19** Letters to a Young Poet

rill **5** brook, cleft, creek **6** furrow, groove, runnel, stream **7** channel, rivulet **9** streamlet

rim **3** lip **4** edge, side **5** brink, ledge, verge **6** border, margin **9** outer edge

Rima
character in: **13** Green Mansions
author: **6** Hudson

Rimbaud, Arthur
author of: **12** Le Bateau Ivre **13** A Season in Hell **14** The Drunken Boat **16** Les Illuminations **17** Sonnet of the Vowels

rime **3** ice **4** hoar **5** chink, cleft, crack, crust, frost **7** crevice, fissure **9** hoarfrost

Rime of the Ancient Mariner, The
author: **21** Samuel Taylor Coleridge
character: **6** Hermit **9** Albatross **12** Wedding Guest **14** Ancient Mariner

Rimsky-Korsakov, Nikolai (Nicholas)
born: **6** Russia **8** Novgorod
member of: **7** The Five
composer of: **5** Mlada, Sadko **6** Kitezh **10** Night in May, Snow Maiden, Tzar Saltan **11** Sheherazade **12** Christmas Eve, Scheherezade **16** Spanish Capriccio **17** Capriccio Espagnol, The Golden Cockerel **21** Russian Easter Overture **29** Russian Easter Festival Overture

rind **4** bark, hull, husk, peel, skin **5** crust, shell **6** cortex, fringe **7** epicarp, surface **8** exterior
pork: **9** crackling

ring **4** aura, band, bloc, buzz, call, echo, gang, hoop, loop, peal, toll, tone **5** cabal, chime, clang, knell, party, sound **6** cartel, circle, cordon, herald, jangle, jingle, league, signal, strike, summon, tinkle **7** besiege, circuit, combine, enclose, quality, resound, seal off, vibrate **8** announce, blockade, encircle, proclaim, striking, surround **9** broadcast, encompass, perimeter, resonance, syndicate, ting-a-ling, vibration **10** federation **11** reverberate **12** circumscribe **13** circumference, reverberation **14** tintinnabulate **16** tintinnabulation

Ring and the Book, The
author: **14** Robert Browning

Ring des Nibelungen, Der
also: **12** The Ring Cycle **20** The Ring of the Nibelung(s)
opera by: **6** Wagner
part one: **12** Das Rheingold, The Rhine Gold
part two: **10** Die Walkure **11** The Valkyrie
part three: **9** Siegfried
part four: **15** Gotterdammerung **17** Twilight of the Gods
character: **4** Erda, Mime **5** Freia, Hagen, Wotan **6** Fafner, Fasolt **7** Gunther, Gutrune, Hunding **8** Alberich, Siegmund **9** Siegfried, Sieglinde, Valkyries **10** Brunnhilde

ring down the curtain **3** end **4** halt **6** finish **8** conclude **9** terminate

ringleader **5** chief **6** master **10** mastermind

ringlet **4** curl **6** circle

ring-shaped **5** round **8** circular

Rin Tin Tin, The Adventures of
character: **5** Rusty, (Cpl) Boone **9** (Sgt) Biff O'Hara **10** (Lt) Rip Masters
cast: **8** Lee Aaker **9** Joe Sawyer **10** James Brown, Rand Brooks

Rio Bravo
director: **11** Howard Hawks
cast: **8** Ward Bond **9** John Wayne **10** Dean Martin **11** Ricky Nelson **13** Walter Brennan **14** Angie Dickinson

Rio de Janeiro *see box*

riot **4** rage **5** act up, arise, melee, rebel **6** fracas, mutiny, resist, revolt, rumpus, strife, tumult, uproar **7** rampage, run amok, trouble, turmoil **8** disorder, outburst, uprising, violence **9** commotion, confusion, rebellion **10** Donnybrook, turbulence **11** lawlessness, pandemonium **12** insurrection

rioting **6** tumult, uproar **7** turmoil **8** disorder, outbreak, violence **9** commotion **11** disturbance

riotous **4** loud, wild **5** arroar, noisy, randy **6** stormy, unruly, wanton **7** bacchic, rampant, violent **8** bacchian **9** debauched, dissolute, insurgent, plentiful, tumultuous, turbulent **10** boisterous, dissipated, licentious, rebellious **11** intemperate, overcopious **12** unrestrained **13** superabundant **15** insurrectionary
party: **4** orgy

Rio de Janeiro
airport: **6** Galeao
architect: **5** Costa, Reidy **8** Niemeyer
area: **4** Caju, Lapa **6** Catete, Gamboa, Gloria, Grajau, Tijuca **7** Catumbi, Ipanema **8** Botafogo **10** Copacabana, Vila Isabel **12** Sao Cristovao
bay: **8** Botafogo, Jurujuba **9** Guanabara
bridge: **11** Costa e Silva
celebration: **8** Carnival **9** Mardi Gras
discovered by: **6** Coelho
former capital of: **6** Brazil
island: **10** Governador
lake: **16** Rodrigo de Freitas
landmark: **10** Candelaria **14** Mount Corcovado **15** Maracana Stadium **17** Sugarloaf Mountain: ***statue of:*** **17** Christ the Redeemer
means: **14** river of January
ocean: **8** Atlantic
people: **8** Cariocas
replaced as capital by: **8** Brasilia
slums: **7** favelas
suburb: **7** Niteroi

rip **3** cut, gap **4** rend, rent, rift, rive, slit, tear **5** burst, sever, shred, slash, split **6** cleave **7** fissure, rupture **8** cleavage, cut apart, fracture, incision, tear open **10** laceration

ripe **3** due, fit **4** come **5** ideal, ready **6** mature, mellow, primed, timely **7** perfect **8** complete, finished, seasoned **9** maturated **10** consummate **12** accomplished

ripen **3** age **4** grow **5** bloom, fruit **6** flower, mature, mellow **7** develop

Rip Kirby
creator: **11** Alex Raymond **12** John Prentice

Ripley, Robert L
author of: **14** Believe It or Not

Rip Van Winkle
author: **16** Washington Irving

rise **4** bank, defy, dune, face, gain, go up, grow, hill, lift, meet, soar **5** climb, get up, knoll, march, mount, rebel, ridge, spire, stand, surge, swell, tower **6** ascend, growth, mutiny, resist, revolt, rocket, strike, thrive **7** advance, balloon, burgeon, disobey, elevate, headway, improve, prosper, stand up, succeed, upswing **8** addition, flourish, increase, progress **9** expansion, extension **10** embankment **11** advancement, enlargement

Rise and Fall of the Third Reich, The
author: **14** William L Shirer

Rise of Silas Lapham, The
author: **18** William Dean Howells
character: **5** Irene **8** Mr Rogers, Penelope, Tom Corey **9** Mrs Lapham

risible **4** rich **5** comic, droll, funny, merry, silly, witty **6** absurd, jocose, jovial **7** amusing, comical, jocular **8** farcical, humorous, mirthful **9** facetious, laughable, ludicrous, whimsical **10** ridiculous **11** nonsensical

rising sun
god of: **5** Janus

risk **4** dare **5** peril **6** chance, danger, gamble, hazard **7** imperil, venture **8** endanger, jeopardy **9** speculate **10** jeopardize **11** imperilment, speculation, uncertainty **12** endangerment

risky **6** chancy, daring, unsafe **8** insecure, perilous, ticklish **9** dangerous, daredevil, haphazard, hazardous, hit or miss, uncertain **10** precarious **11** adventurous, unprotected, venturesome

risque **4** blue, lewd, racy **5** bawdy, dirty, gross, spicy **6** coarse, daring, ribald, smutty, vulgar **7** immoral, obscene **8** immodest, improper, indecent, off-color **9** offensive, salacious **10** indecorous, indelicate, lascivious, licentious, suggestive **12** pornographic

rite **6** ritual **7** liturgy, service **8** ceremony **9** formality, solemnity **10** ceremonial, observance

rite of passage **6** ritual **7** baptism **8** ceremony, marriage **10** bar mitzvah, bat mitzvah, initiation **11** christening **12** confirmation

Rites of Passage
author: **14** William Golding

Ritt, Martin
director of: **3** Hud **7** Sounder **8** Norma Rae,

The Front **26** The Spy Who Came in From the Cold

Ritter, John
born: 9 Burbank CA
father: 9 Tex Ritter
roles: 9 Hooperman **11** Americathon, Jack Tripper **13** Three's Company **14** Captain Avenger

Ritter, Thelma
born: 10 Brooklyn NY
roles: 10 Pillow Talk, Rear Window, The Misfits **11** All About Eve **15** The Mating Season **17** Birdman of Alcatraz **18** With a Song in My Heart **19** A Letter to Three Wives, Pickup on South Street **21** The Proud and the Profane **27** Miracle on Thirty-Fourth Street

ritual 4 rite **7** service **8** ceremony **10** observance

ritual bathing place
Jewish Orthodox: 6 mikvah

ritualistic 6 formal, solemn **10** ceremonial **11** ceremonious

ritualize 7 observe **9** celebrate, solemnize **13** ceremonialize

ritzy 4 chic, posh, tony **5** sharp, swank **6** classy, snazzy, spiffy **7** elegant, stylish **9** high-class, high-toned, luxurious, sumptuous

rival 3 foe **5** enemy, equal, excel, fight, match, outdo, touch **6** strive **7** eclipse, surpass **8** approach, opponent, opposing, outshine **9** adversary, competing, contender, disputant **10** antagonist, competitor, contending, contestant

Rivals, The
author: 23 Richard Brinsley Sheridan
character: 8 Bob Acres **9** Faulkland **11** Mrs Malaprop **13** Julia Melville, Lydia Languish **17** Sir Lucius O'Trigger **18** Sir Anthony Absolute **19** Captain Jack Absolute (Ensign Beverley)

rive 4 rend **5** crack, split **6** cleave, detach, divide, sunder **7** shatter **8** fracture

riven 4 rent, torn **5** split **7** cleaved, cracked **8** sundered **9** fractured, shattered

River, The
director: 10 Jean Renoir
based on novel by: 11 Rumer Godden
cast: 5 Radha **13** Adrienne Corri, Arthur Shields, Nora Swinburne **15** Patricia Walters
setting: 5 India **6** Bengal

Rivera, Diego
born: 6 Mexico **10** Guanajuato
artwork: 5 Sleep **8** Creation **11** Mother Earth **14** The Fecund Earth **15** Detroit Industry **18** Man at the Crossroads **21** Carnival of Mexican Life **23** Life in Pre-Hispanic Mexico

river mouth 5 delta, firth **7** estuary

rivers
god of: 6 Peneus, Simois **7** Inachus

Rivers, Reba
character in: 9 Sanctuary
author: 8 Faulkner

rivet 3 fix, pin **6** absorb, clinch, engage, fasten, occupy **7** engross **8** fastener **9** fascinate

Rivieres du Sud *see* **6** Guinea

rivulet 3 run **4** rill **5** brook, creek **6** stream **9** streamlet

Riyadh
capital of: 11 Saudi Arabia

Rizzuto, Phil
nickname: 7 Scooter
position: 9 shortstop
sport: 8 baseball
team: 14 New York Yankees

road 3 way **4** lane, path **5** byway, route, trail **6** avenue, street **7** freeway, highway, parkway **8** turnpike **9** boulevard **10** expressway, throughway **12** thoroughfare

Road Not Taken, The
author: 11 Robert Frost

roads
god of: 6 Hermes

road safety
god of: 6 Sancus **10** Semo Sancus

Road to Gandolfo, The
author: 12 Robert Ludlum

roam 3 gad **4** rove **5** drift, jaunt, prowl, range, stray, tramp **6** ramble, stroll, travel, wander **7** meander, traipse **8** divagate **9** gallivant **11** peregrinate

roan 5 horse **7** grayish, reddish, tannish **8** blackish, brownish

Roan Stallion
author: 15 Robinson Jeffers

roar 3 bay, cry, din **4** bawl, boom, howl, roll, yell **5** blare, growl, grunt, noise, shout, snort **6** bellow, clamor, guffaw, outcry, racket, rumble, scream, shriek **7** bluster, resound, thunder **8** outburst **10** vociferate

roast 3 pan **4** bake **6** berate **7** scourge **8** barbecue **9** criticize

rob 4 bilk, lift, loot, raid, sack, skin **5** cheat, filch, heist, rifle, seize, steal **6** burgle, fleece, forage, hold up, pilfer, thieve **7** despoil, pillage, plunder, purloin, ransack, stick up, swindle **8** carry off, embezzle **9** bamboozle **10** burglarize **11** appropriate

Robards, Jason
born: 9 Chicago IL
wife: 12 Lauren Bacall
roles: 5 Julia **7** Isadora **9** Dick Diver **10** Ben Bradlee **11** Jamie Tyrone **12** Hour of the Gun **15** A Thousand Clowns, Dashiell Hammett, Melvin and Howard, The Disenchanted **16** Tender Is the Night **19** All the President's Men **24** Long Day's Journey into Night

Robbe-Grillet, Alain
author of: 8 Jealousy **9** The Voyeur **10** The Erasers **14** In the Labyrinth **19** Last Year at Marienbad

robber, Robber 4 yegg **5** crook, thief **6** bandit, con man, outlaw, pirate, raider **7** brigand, burglar, forager, rustler, sharper **8** Barabbas, marauder, swindler **9** buccaneer, despoiler, embezzler, larcenist, plunderer **10** highwayman, pickpocket

Robbins, Harold
author of: 8 The Betsy **13** The Inheritors **14** Dreams Die First, The Adventurers **16** The Carpetbaggers **17** The Dream Merchants **18** Never Love a Stranger **20** A Stone for Danny Fisher **21** Seventy-Nine Park Avenue

Robbins, Jerome
choreographer of: 8 Les Noces **9** Fancy Free, Interplay
director of: 13 West Side Story (with Robert Wise, Oscar)

robe 4 gown **5** dress, habit, smock **6** duster **7** costume, garment **8** bathrobe, vestment **9** housecoat
French: 8 negligee
Japanese: 6 kimono

Robe, The
author: 13 Lloyd C Douglas

robe-de-chambre 12 dressing-gown

Robert Kennedy and His Times
author: **20** Arthur M Schlesinger Jr

Roberts, Kenneth
author of: **16** Northwest Passage

Roberts, Rachel
born: **5** Wales **8** Llanelly
husband: **11** Rex Harrison
roles: **8** Foul Play **10** Oh Lucky Man **16** This Sporting Life **24** Murder on the Orient Express **29** Saturday Night and Sunday Morning

Robertson, Cliff
real name: **23** Clifford Parker Robertson
born: **9** La Jolla CA
wife: **11** Dina Merrill
roles: **5** PT-109 **6** Charly (Oscar) **9** Obsession **11** Falcon Crest

Robertson, Oscar
nickname: **7** The Big O
sport: **10** basketball
position: **5** guard
team: **14** Milwaukee Bucks **16** Cincinnati Royals

Robeson, Paul
born: **11** Princeton NJ
roles: **7** Othello **8** Show Boat **11** Brutus Jones **15** The Emperor Jones **17** King Solomon's Mines **22** All God's Chillun Got Wings

Robigo
goddess of: **5** grain

Robigus
spirit of: **9** red mildew **11** grain blight

Robin, Christopher
character in: **13** Winnie-the-Pooh
author: **5** Milne

Robin Hood's Adventures
author: **7** unknown
character: **9** Friar Tuck **10** Little John **11** Will Scarlet **14** Band of Merry Men **18** Sir Richard of the Lea **19** Sheriff of Nottingham

robin's-egg-blue **4** aqua **5** azure **7** sky-blue **8** cerulean **9** light blue **10** aquamarine, powder-blue

Robinson, Edward G
real name: **18** Emmanuel Goldenberg
born: **7** Romania **9** Bucharest
roles: **8** Key Largo **12** Little Caesar, Rico Bandello **13** Scarlet Street **15** Double Indemnity, Flesh and Fantasy **16** House of Strangers **19** The Woman in the Window **20** A Dispatch from Reuters **21** Dr Ehrlich's Magic Bullet

Robinson, Edwin Arlington
author of: **6** Merlin **8** Amaranth, Tristram **10** King Jasper **11** Richard Cory **12** Captain Craig **13** Miniver Cheevy, Mr Flood's Party

Robinson, Jackie
sport: **8** baseball
team: **15** Brooklyn Dodgers
first black in: **12** major leagues

Robinson, Sugar Ray
real name: **19** Walker Smith Robinson
sport. **6** boxing
class: **12** middleweight, welterweight

Robinson Crusoe
author: **11** Daniel Defoe
character: **6** Friday

Rob Roy
author: **14** Sir Walter Scott
character: **11** Diana Vernon **18** Sir Frederick Vernon **23** Rob Roy MacGregor Campbell
Osbaldistone family: **5** Frank **7** William **9** Rashleigh **13** Sir Hildebrand

robust **3** fit **4** firm, hale, well, wiry **5** hardy, husky, lusty, sound, stout, tough **6** active, brawny, hearty, mighty, potent, rugged, sinewy, strong, sturdy, virile **7** healthy, staunch **8** athletic, forceful, muscular, powerful, stalwart, vigorous **9** energetic, healthful, strapping, wholesome **10** able-bodied **12** in fine fettle
French: **8** puissant

robustness **5** vigor **8** strength **10** good health, ruggedness, sturdiness **11** healthiness

Roche, Kevin
architect of: **13** Oakland Museum (CA) **14** Fine Arts Center (U of MA), Ford Foundation (NYC) **17** Knights of Columbus (New Haven CT) **21** One United Nations Plaza (NYC) **24** Union Carbide Headquarters (Danbury CT) **31** Power Center for the Performing Arts (U of Michigan)

Rochester
football team: **8** Panthers

Rochester, Edward
character in: **8** Jane Eyre
author: **6** Bronte

rock **3** bob, jar **4** crag, reef, roll, stun, sway, toss **5** cliff, flint, pitch, quake, shake, stone, swing, upset **6** gravel, marble, pebble, totter, wobble **7** agitate, bobbing, boulder, disturb, shaking **8** convulse, flounder, undulate, wobbling **9** limestone, oscillate, tottering **10** convulsion, undulation

Rock & Rye
type: **7** liqueur
flavor: **6** citrus
ingredient: **3** rye **9** rock candy

rock crystal
species: **6** quartz
color: **9** colorless

Rocket
nickname of: **14** Maurice Richard

rocket engine
invented by: **7** Goddard

Rockford Files, The
character: **10** John Cooper **11** Angel Martin, Jim Rockford **12** (Det) Dennis Becker **13** Beth Davenport, (Joseph) Rocky Rockford
cast: **9** Bo Hopkins, Joe Santos, Noah Beery **11** James Garner **14** Stuart Margolin **15** Gretchen Corbett

rock of Tarik *see* **9** Gibraltar

Rockwell, Norman
born: **9** New York NY
artwork:
covers: **19** Saturday Evening Post
mural: **15** Freedom of Speech

Rocky
director: **13** John G Avildsen
cast: **9** Burt Young **10** Talia Shire **11** Thayer David **12** Carl Weathers **15** Burgess Meredith **17** Sylvester Stallone (Rocky Balboa, the Italian Stallion)
setting: **12** Philadelphia
Oscar for: **7** editing, picture **8** director
sequel: **7** Rocky II, Rocky IV **8** Rocky III, Rocky Two **9** Rocky Four **10** Rocky Three

rod **4** cane, lash, mace, pale, pole, wand, whip **5** baton, birch, crook, staff, stake, stick **6** cudgel, rattan, switch **7** penalty, scepter, scourge **8** caduceus **9** stanchion **10** alpenstock, punishment **11** retribution **12** swagger stick
abbreviation: **2** rd

rod, Aaron's *see* **9** Aaron's rod

rodent **4** cavy, vole **5** coypu, gundi, hutia, mouse **6** agouti, beaver, cururo, gerbil, gopher, jerboa, nutria **7** blesmol, cane rat, hamster, lemming, mole-rat, rock rat **8** capybara, chipmunk, dormouse, pacarana, sewellel, spiny rat, squirrel, tucu-tuco, viscacha **9** chozchori, false paca, porcupine, woodchuck **10** chinchilla, prairie dog, springhare **11** kangaroo rat, pocket mouse, viscacha rat **13** kangaroo mouse **16** Speke's pectinator

Roderick Hudson
author: **10** Henry James

Roderick Random
author: **14** Tobias Smollett
character: **5** Strap **8** Narcissa **10** Tom Bowling **12** Miss Williams

Rodin, (Francois) Auguste Rene
born: **5** Paris **6** France
artwork: **7** The Kiss **10** Head of Iris, The Thinker, Victor Hugo, Walking Man **14** John the Baptist, The Age of Bronze, The Gates of Hell **16** Monument to Balzac **19** The Burghers of Calais **23** The Man with the Broken Nose

rodomontade **4** rant **5** boast **6** hot air **7** blather, bluster, bombast, fustian **8** bragging, folderol, nonsense, rhetoric **10** balderdash, doubletalk **11** braggadocio **12** boastfulness

roe **3** doe, elk, hen **4** buck, deer, eggs, fawn, fish, hart, hind, milt **5** spawn, sperm **6** caviar **8** fish eggs
of lobster: **5** coral

Roentgen, Rontgen, Wilhelm Konrad
field: **7** physics
nationality: **6** German
discovered: **5** X-rays
awarded: **10** Nobel Prize

Roethke, Theodore
author of: **9** Open House, The Waking **11** The Far Field **15** Straw for the Fire, Words for the Wind

Rogers, Ginger
real name: **23** Virginia Katherine McMath
born: **14** Independence MO
husband: **8** Lew Ayres **15** Jacques Bergerac, William Marshall
partner: **11** Fred Astaire
roles: **6** Top Hat **9** Stage Door **10** Hello Dolly, Kitty Foyle (Oscar) **12** Shall We Dance? **14** The Gay Divorcee **15** Flying Down to Rio, Tom Dick and Harry **17** Forty-Second Street **19** The Major and the Minor **21** The Barkleys of Broadway **30** The Story of Vernon and Irene Castle

Rogers, James Gamble
architect of: **22** Northwestern University (Chicago) **33** Columbia-Presbyterian Medical Center (NYC)

Rogers, Roy
real name: **11** Leonard Slye
born: **12** Cincinnati OH
wife: **9** Dale Evans
sidekick: **10** Gabby Hayes
singing group: **17** Sons of the Pioneers
horse: **7** Trigger
roles: **10** Apache Rose **11** Song of Texas **12** My Pal Trigger **13** Song of Arizona, Son of Paleface **17** Heart of the Rockies, Under Western Stars **18** Billy the Kid Returns **19** Tumbling Tumbleweeds **20** The Yellow Rose of Texas **22** Springtime in the Sierras

rogue **3** cur **5** devil, fraud, knave, scamp **6** bad man, rascal, rotter, varlet, wretch **7** bounder, hellion, villain **8** deceiver, evildoer, scalawag **9** miscreant, reprobate, scoundrel **10** blackguard, malefactor, mountebank, scapegrace **11** rapscallion **13** mischief-maker **14** good-for-nothing **15** snake in the grass

Rogue Herries
author: **11** Hugh Walpole

roguish **3** sly **4** arch **5** saucy **8** devilish, rascally **11** mischievous

Rohe, Vera-Ellen
real name of: **9** Vera-Ellen

roil **3** irk, vex **4** mill, rile, stir **5** annoy, muddy **6** ruffle, seethe **7** agitate, disturb, perturb, provoke, turmoil **8** irritate **9** aggravate **10** exasperate

role **3** job **4** duty, part, pose, post, task, work **5** chore, guise **7** posture, service **8** capacity, function **9** character, portrayal **10** assignment **13** impersonation **14** representation **15** personification **16** characterization
Latin: **7** persona

roll **4** boom, coil, curl, echo, flip, flow, furl, knot, list, loop, reel, roar, rock, spin, sway, toss, tube, turn, wind **5** coast, crack, lurch, pitch, sound, spool, surge, swell, swing, swirl, throw, twirl, twist, wheel, whirl **6** billow, gyrate, muster, roster, rotate, rumble, scroll, tumble **7** booming, catalog, entwine, resound, revolve, rocking, thunder, tossing, turning **8** cylinder, drumbeat, drumming, rumbling, schedule, tumbling, undulate **9** inventory **10** undulation **11** reverberate **13** reverberation **15** turn over and over

Rolland, Romain
author of: **14** Jean-Christophe **16** The Soul Enchanted

rollicking **3** gay **5** happy, jolly, merry, sunny **6** bright, hearty, jocund, jovial, joyous, lively **7** gleeful, jocular, playful, romping **8** cheerful, mirthful, spirited **9** exuberant, gamboling, sparkling, sprightly **10** frolicking, frolicsome, hysterical, rip-roaring **12** lighthearted

Rolvaag, Ole Edvart
author of: **15** Peder Victorious, Their Father's God **16** Giants in the Earth

roly-poly **3** fat **5** obese, plump, pudgy, round **6** chubby, rotund **9** corpulent

Roma
father: **7** Evander

roman **5** novel **17** metrical narrative

Roman Catholic church
council/synod: **4** Pisa **5** Basel, Trent **6** Nicaea, Vienne, Whitby **7** Ephesus, Pistoia, Sardica **9** Chalcedon, Constance **12** First Vatican **13** Fourth Lateran, Second Vatican **14** Constantinople **15** Ferrara-Florence
official Vatican yearbook: **18** Annuario Pontificio
first Christian emperor: **11** Constantine
gifts of territory/sovereignty to papacy: **15** Donation of Pepin **21** Donation of Constantine

romance **4** bosh, call, pull **5** amour, idyll, novel **6** affair, allure **7** fantasy, fiction **8** illusion **9** courtship, exoticism, fairy tale, fish story, invention, love story, melodrama, moonshine, tall story **10** attachment, concoction, flirtation, love affair **11** fabrication, fascination, imagination **12** exaggeration, relationship, self-delusion **13** flight of fancy, tender passion **16** affair of the heart

Romance language *see* **5** Latin

Romance of the Forest
author: **12** Ann Radcliffe

Romances sans paroles
author: **12** Paul Verlaine

Romancing the Stone
director: **14** Robert Zemeckis

cast: **11** Danny De Vito **14** Kathleen Turner, Michael Douglas
sequel: **17** The Jewel of the Nile

Roman Holiday
director: **12** William Wyler
cast: **11** Eddie Albert, Gregory Peck **13** Audrey Hepburn
Oscar for: **7** actress (Hepburn)

Romania *see* **7** Rumania

Roman measure **2** as **5** cubit, libra **6** pondus **7** stadium

Roman Mythology ***see box***

romantic **4** fond **5** mushy, soppy **6** ardent, dreamy, loving, tender, unreal **7** amorous, devoted, fervent, flighty, idyllic, utopian **8** enamored, fanciful, quixotic **9** fantastic, idealized, imaginary, sensitive, visionary, whimsical **10** idealistic, improbable, passionate **11** extravagant, impassioned, impractical, rhapsodical, sentimental, unrealistic, warmhearted **12** melodramatic, preposterous

Romantic Comedians, The
author: **12** Ellen Glasgow

romanticize **8** idealize **9** embroider

Romantic Manifesto
author: **7** Ayn Rand

Romany Rye, The
author: **17** George Henry Borrow

Rome, ancient ***see box, p. 841***

Rome, Roma ***see box, p. 841***

Rome Haul
author: **14** Walter D Edmonds

Romeo **4** beau **5** lover, sheik, swain, wooer **7** Don Juan, gallant **8** Casanova, cavalier, Lothario **9** boyfriend, Lochinvar
French: **8** paramour
Latin: **9** inamorato

Romeo and Juliet
author: **18** William Shakespeare
character: **5** Nurse, Paris **6** Tybalt **8** Benvolio, Mercutio **13** Friar Laurence
family: **7** Capulet **8** Montague
setting: **6** Verona

Romeo and Juliet
director:
1936 version: **11** George Cukor
1968 version: **16** Franco Zeffirelli

Roman Mythology
collective name for gods: **6** Superi
goddess of anguish: **8** Angerona
goddess of agriculture: **5** Ceres **6** Dea Dia, Vacuna **13** Acca Laurentia
Ceres corresponds to Greek: **7** Demeter
goddess of the arts: **7** Minerva
corresponds to Greek: **6** Athena
goddess of baking: **6** Fornax
goddess of chastity: **5** Fauna **7** Bona Dea
goddess of childbirth: **5** Parca **6** Lucina, Matuta, Parcae **11** Mater Matuta
goddess of the dawn: **6** Aurora, Matuta **11** Mater Matuta
Aurora corresponds to Greek: **3** Eos
goddess of destiny: **5** Parca **6** Parcae
goddess of discord: **9** Discordia
goddess of door hinges: **6** Cardea
goddess of the earth: **6** Tellus
corresponds to Greek: **4** Gaea
goddess of the family: **6** Cardea
goddess of fertility: **5** Fauna **6** Libera, Tellus **7** Bona Dea
Libera corresponds to Greek: **10** Persephone
Tellus corresponds to Greek: **4** Gaea
goddess of flowers: **5** Flora
goddess of fortune: **7** Fortuna
corresponds to Greek: **5** Tyche
goddess of fruit trees: **6** Pomona
goddess of gardens: **5** Venus
corresponds to Greek: **9** Aphrodite
goddess of grain/protectress against grain blight: **6** Robigo
goddess of harbors: **6** Matuta **11** Mater Matuta
goddess of harmony: **9** Concordia
goddess of the hearth: **4** Caca **5** Salus, Vesta
Salus corresponds to Greek: **6** Hygeia
goddess of heaven: **4** Juno
corresponds to Greek: **4** Hera
goddess of hunting: **5** Diana
corresponds to Greek: **6** Phoebe **7** Artemis
goddess of longevity: **11** Anna Perenna
goddess of love: **5** Venus
corresponds to Greek: **9** Aphrodite
goddess of marriage: **4** Juno **6** Tellus
corresponds to Greek: **4** Gaea, Hera
goddess of marshes: **6** Marica **9** Dea Marica
goddess of the moon: **5** Diana
corresponds to Greek: **6** Phoebe **7** Artemis
goddess of peace: **3** Pax **9** Concordia
Pax corresponds to Greek: **5** Irene
goddess of pleasure: **8** Voluptas
goddess of plenty: **3** Ops **10** Magna Mater
goddess of prosperity: **5** Salus
corresponds to Greek: **6** Hygeia
goddess of the sea: **6** Matuta **11** Mater Matuta
goddess of sleeping infants: **6** Cunina
goddess of the spring: **5** Venus
corresponds to Greek: **9** Aphrodite
goddess of storms: **11** Tempestates
goddess of victory: **8** Victoria
corresponds to Greek: **4** Nike
goddess of vineyards: **6** Libera
corresponds to Greek: **10** Persephone
goddess of war: **7** Bellona
corresponds to Greek: **5** Enyon
goddess of wine: **6** Libera
corresponds to Greek: **10** Persephone
goddess of wisdom: **7** Minerva
corresponds to Greek: **6** Athena

(*continued*)

Roman Mythology *(continued)*
god of agriculture: **5** Picus **6** Saturn **7** Eventus **12** Bonus Eventus
corresponds to Greek: **6** Cronos, Cronus, Kronos
god of beginnings: **5** Janus
god of boundaries: **8** Terminus
god of commerce: **7** Mercury
corresponds to Greek: **6** Hermes
god of the dead: **7** Veiovis
god of doorways: **5** Janus
god of drinking/revelry: **5** Comus
god of eloquence: **7** Mercury
corresponds to Greek: **6** Hermes
god of farm boundaries: **8** Silvanus, Sylvanus
god of fertility: **7** Mutinus, Priapus **8** Lupercus, Picumnus
god of fire/metalworking: **6** Vulcan
corresponds to Greek: **10** Hephaestus, Hephaistos
god of forest: **7** Virbius
god of gardens: **9** Vertumnus
god of good counsel: **3** Ops **6** Consus
god of grain/protector against grain blight: **7** Robigus
god of healing: **11** Aesculapius
corresponds to Greek: **9** Asclepius
god of heavens: **4** Jove **7** Jupiter
corresponds to Greek: **4** Zeus
god of herds: **8** Silvanus, Sylvanus
god of horse racing: **3** Ops **6** Consus
god of hospitality: **6** Sancus **10** Dius Fidius, Semo Sancus
god of the house: **8** Silvanus, Sylvanus
god of hunting: **7** Virbius
god of international affairs: **6** Sancus **10** Dius Fidius, Semo Sancus
god of landmarks: **8** Terminus
god of light: **6** Apollo
god of love: **4** Amor **5** Cupid
corresponds to Greek: **4** Eros
god of luck: **7** Eventus **12** Bonus Eventus
god of medicine: **11** Aesculapius
corresponds to Greek: **9** Asclepius
god of music: **6** Apollo
god of oaths: **6** Sancus **10** Dius Fidius, Semo Sancus
god of orchards: **9** Vertumnus
god of ports/harbors: **8** Portunus
god of prosperity: **7** Eventus **12** Bonus Eventus
god of the rising sun: **5** Janus
god of science: **7** Mercury
corresponds to Greek: **6** Hermes
god of sea: **7** Neptune
corresponds to Greek: **8** Poseidon
god of seasons: **9** Vertumnus
god of the setting sun: **5** Janus
god of sleep: **6** Somnus
corresponds to Greek: **6** Hypnos, Hypnus
god of springs: **4** Fons
gods of sulphur springs (twins): **6** Palici
god of the sun: **3** Sol
corresponds to Greek: **6** Helios **8** Hyperion
god of thievery: **7** Mercury
corresponds to Greek: **6** Hermes
god of thunder: **7** Taranis
god of thunderstorms: **8** Summanus
god of the Tiber: **9** Tiberinus
god of uncultivated land: **8** Silvanus, Sylvanus
god of underworld: **3** Dis **5** Orcus **8** Dis Pater
corresponds to Greek: **5** Pluto
god of war: **4** Mars **6** Mamers, Mavors **8** Quirinus
corresponds to Greek: **4** Ares
god of weather: **4** Jove **7** Jupiter
god of weddings: **8** Talassio
corresponds to Greek: **5** Hymen **9** Hymenaeus
god of the woods: **6** Faunus **8** Silvanus, Sylvanus
house spirits: **5** lares **7** penates
nymphs/deities with gift of prophecy: **7** Camenae
names: **6** Egeria **8** Carmenta **9** Antevorta, Postvorta
correspond to Greek: **5** Muses
protectress of childbirth: **8** Carmenta
protectress of cows/oxen: **6** Bubona
protector of flocks/shepherds: **5** Pales
protectress of military age men: **8** Juventas
corresponds to Greek: **4** Hebe
protectress of women: **5** Diana
corresponds to Greek: **6** Phoebe **7** Artemis
protectress of women/marriage: **4** Juno
queen of heaven: **4** Juno
corresponds to Greek: **4** Hera, Here
staff of Mercury: **8** Caduceus
troublesome ghosts: **7** lemures

based on play by: **18** William Shakespeare
cast:
1936 version: **12** Leslie Howard, Norma Shearer **13** Basil Rathbone, Edna May Oliver, John Barrymore
1968 version: **9** Milo O'Shea **11** John McEnery, Michael York **12** Olivia Hussey **14** Leonard Whiting
score: **8** Nino Rota

Romeo and Juliet
symphony by: **7** Berlioz
opera by: **6** Gounod
orchestral piece by: **11** Tchaikovsky
ballet by: **9** Prokofiev

Romney, George
born: **7** England **15** Dalton-in-Furness
artwork: **5** Circe **9** Joan of Arc **11** Mrs Robinson, Sensibility **12** Mrs Davenport, Saint Cecilia **19** Mrs Carwardine and Son **22** The Death of General Wolfe **24** The Levenson-Gower Children **26** Sir Christopher and Lady Sykes

Romola
author: **11** George Eliot
character: **5** Bardo, Tessa **10** Tito Melema **15** Baldasarre Calvo

romp **3** hop **4** skip **5** caper, cut up, frisk, sport **6** frolic, gambol **7** disport, rollick

Romulus
father: **4** Mars
mother: **4** Ilia **9** Rea Silvia **10** Rhea Silvia
twin brother: **5** Remus
raised by: **7** she-wolf **9** Faustulus **12** Acca Larentia

Rome, ancient
emperor: **4** Nero, Otho **5** Galba, Nerva, Titus **6** Trajan **7** Hadrian **8** Augustus, Caligula, Claudius, Commodus, Domitian, Tiberius **9** Caracalla, Vespasian, Vitellius **10** Diocletian **11** Constantine, Lucius Verus **13** Antoninus Pius **14** Marcus Aurelius
emperor's bodyguard: **15** Praetorian Guard
first citizen title: **8** princeps
first triumvirate: **6** Caesar, Pompey **7** Crassus
foe: **4** Gaul **5** Spain **6** Cimbri **7** Perseus, Philip V, Pyrrhus, Teutons **8** Carthage, Hannibal, Iberians, Jugurtha, Samnites, Tarentum, Umbrians **9** Etruscans, Macedonia, Seleucids **11** Latin League **12** Antiochus III **13** Achaean League, Hamilcar Barca
general: **5** Sulla **6** Brutus, Marius, Pompey **7** Crassus **8** Octavian **10** Flamininus, Mark Antony **12** Julius Caesar **14** Caesar Augustus **20** Quintus Fabius Maximus, Scipio Africanus Major, Scipio Africanus Minor
king: **12** Ancus Marcius **13** Numa Pompilius **16** Sextus Tarquinius **17** Tarquinius Priscus (Tarquin the Elder) **18** Tarquinius Superbus (Tarquin the Proud)
reformer: **8** Gracchus
republican ruler: **6** consul **7** senator, tribune **8** plebeian **9** optimates, patrician, populares **10** magistrate
Roman peace: **9** Pax Romana
second triumvirate: **6** Antony **7** Lepidus **8** Octavian (Caesar Augustus)

Rome, Roma
airport: **8** Ciampino **15** Leonardo da Vinci
area: **9** Cinecitta (Cinema City) **10** Trastevere **11** Vatican City
capital of: **5** Italy **6** Latium **11** Papal States, Roman Empire
church: **8** St Peter's **11** San Giovanni **18** Santa Maria Maggiore **19** San Paolo Fuori le Mura
Italian: **4** Roma
landmark: **5** Forum **7** Capitol **8** Pantheon **9** catacombs, Colosseum **12** Palazzo Doria **13** Circus Maximus, Lateran Palace, Sistine Chapel, Vatican Palace, Villa Borghese **14** Palazzo Corsini, Villa Farnesina **16** Baths of Caracalla, Castel Sant'Angelo, Palazzo Barberini **17** Arch of Constantine **19** Saint Peter's Basilica
legendary founders: **5** Remus **6** Aeneas **7** Romulus
nickname: **11** Eternal City
mountain: **8** Apennine
museum: **5** Doria **7** Colonna, Corsini, Vatican **8** Borghese, National **10** Capitoline
river: **5** Tiber
school: **33** Conservatorio di Musica Santa Cecilia
sea: **10** Tyrrhenian
seven hills: **7** Caelian, Viminal **8** Aventine, Palatine, Quirinal **9** Esquiline **10** Capitoline
square/piazza: **6** Popolo, Spagna **7** Colonna, Venezia **9** Quirinale **11** Campidoglio
state within: **11** Vatican City
street: **9** Appian Way, Emmanuele **11** Via del Corso **13** Corso Vittorio
subway: **13** Metropolitana

first king of: **4** Rome
founder of: **4** Rome

Romus
father: **6** Aeneas **8** Ascanius
possible founder of: **4** Rome

Ronan
origin: **5** Irish
form: **4** king
son: **4** Mael
killed: **4** Mael
killed by: **13** grandchildren

Roncalli, Angelo Giuseppe
13 Pope John XXIII **22** Pope John the Twenty-Third

Ronsard, Pierre de
author of: **17** Sonnets pour Helene
member of: **7** Pleiade

roofing **4** tile, turf **5** slate, terne **6** thatch **7** asphalt, ceiling, pantile, shingle **8** housetop

Roof of the World *see* **5** Tibet

rook **3** gyp **4** bilk, crow, dupe, gull **5** cheat, cozen, raven, trick **6** castle, fleece **7** deceive, defraud, swindle **8** chessman **9** bamboozle, victimize

rookie **4** tyro **6** novice **8** beginner **9** fledgling, greenhorn **10** apprentice, tenderfoot

Rookies, The
character: **9** Jill Danko, (Officer) Mike Danko **10** (Lt) Eddie Ryker, (Officer) Chris Owens **12** (Officer) Terry Webster, (Officer) Willie Gillis
cast: **11** Kate Jackson, Sam Melville **14** Bruce Fairbairn, Michael Ontkean **16** Gerald S O'Loughlin **18** Georg Stanford Brown

room **4** area **5** range, scope, space **6** chance, extent, leeway, margin, volume **7** chamber, cubicle, expanse, lodging **9** allowance, provision, territory **11** compartment
French: **5** salle
Spanish: **4** sala

Room at the Top
director: **11** Jack Clayton
based on novel by: **10** John Braine
cast: **12** Heather Sears **14** Laurence Harvey, Simone Signoret **16** Hermione Baddeley
Oscar for: **7** actress (Signoret)
sequel: **11** Man at the Top **12** Life at the Top

Room 222
character: **6** Bernie **9** Pete Dixon **11** Liz McIntyre **12** Alice Johnson **14** Seymour Kaufman
cast: **11** Lloyd Haynes **13** David Jolliffe **14** Denise Nicholas, Karen Valentine **18** Michael Constantine
school: **15** Walt Whitman High

roomy **3** big **4** huge, long, vast, wide **5** ample, broad, large **7** immense, lengthy, sizable **8** generous, spacious **9** boundless, capacious, expansive, ex-

Roosevelt, Franklin Delano
presidential rank: 12 thirty-second
party: 10 Democratic
state represented: 2 NY
defeated: 5 (Jacob Sechler) Coxey, (John W) Aiken, (Thomas Edmund) Dewey, (William) Lemke **6** (Alfred Mossman) Landon, (Claude A) Watson, (David Leigh) Colvin, (Herbert Clark) Hoover, (Norman) Thomas, (Roger Ward) Babson, (William David) Upshaw, (William Hope) Harvey, (William Zebulon) Foster **7** (Earl Russell) Browder, (Wendell Lewis) Willkie **8** (Edward A) Teichert, (Verne L) Reynolds
vice president: 6 (Harry S) Truman, (John Nance) Garner **7** (Henry Agard) Wallace
cabinet:
***state:* 4** (Cordell) Hull **10** (Edward Reilly) Stettinius (Jr)
***treasury:* 6** (William Hartman) Woodin **10** (Henry) Morgenthau (Jr)
***war:* 4** (George Henry) Dern **7** (Henry Lewis) Stimson **8** (Harry Hines) Woodring
***attorney general:* 6** (Francis) Biddle, (Frank) Murphy **7** (Robert Houghwoût) Jackson **8** (Homer Stille) Cummings
***navy:* 4** (Frank) Knox **6** (Charles) Edison **7** (Claude Augustus) Swanson **9** (James Vincent) Forrestal
***postmaster general:* 6** (Frank Comerford) Walker, (James Aloysius) Farley
***interior:* 5** (Harold LeClaire) Ickes
***agriculture:* 7** (Claude Raymond) Wickard, (Henry Agard) Wallace
***commerce:* 5** (Daniel Calhoun) Roper, (Jesse Holman) Jones **7** (Henry Agard) Wallace, (Henry Lloyd) Hopkins
***labor:* 7** (Frances) Perkins (Wilson)
born: 10 Hyde Park NY
died: 13 Warm Springs GA **16** Little White House
buried: 10 Hyde Park NY
education:
***prep school:* 6** Groton
***university:* 7** Harvard
***law school:* 8** Columbia
religion: 12 Episcopalian
interests: 3 art **4** polo **6** tennis, travel **7** fishing, hunting **8** shooting
vacation spot: 13 Warm Springs GA **16** Campobello Island (Canada)
dog: 4 Fala
author: 27 The Happy Warrior: Alfred E Smith
political career: 12 state senator
***assistant secretary of:* 4** Navy
***governor of:* 7** New York
civilian career: 6 lawyer **11** bank officer
notable events of lifetime/term: 4 D-Day, WWII **7** New Deal **10** atomic bomb, Depression, World War II **11** World War Two **13** United Nations **15** Atlantic Charter
***act:* 9** Lend-Lease
***attack on:* 11** Pearl Harbor
***conference:* 5** Cairo, Yalta **7** Arcadia, Crimean, Teheran
***scandal:* 11** Tammany Hall
quote: 24 A day that will live in infamy **31** Meet every day's troubles as they come **36** The only thing we have to fear is fear itself **50** This generation of Americans has a rendezvous with destiny **53** I pledge you I pledge myself to a new deal for the American people
father: 5 James
mother: 4 Sara (Delano)
siblings:
***half-brother:* 5** James
wife: 7 (Anna) Eleanor (Roosevelt)
children: 5 James **7** Elliott **11** Anna Eleanor **13** John Aspinwall **14** Franklin Delano
first lady:
***author:* 7** On My Own **13** This I Remember, This Is My Story **34** The Autobiography of Eleanor Roosevelt
***chairwoman:* 25** UN Commission on Human Rights
***codirector:* 23** Office of Civilian Defense
***member:* 35** Democratic National Campaign Committee
***newspaper column:* 5** My Day
***US delegate to:* 2** UN

tensive, unlimited
10 commodious

Rooney, Mickey
real name: 9 Joe Yule Jr
born: 10 Brooklyn NY
wife: 10 Ava Gardner **13** Martha Vickers
co-star: 11 Judy Garland
roles: 4 Puck **8** Boys' Town **9** Andy Hardy **11** Sugar Babies **13** Mickey McGuire **14** Baby Face Nelson, National Velvet, The Human Comedy **21** A Midsummer Night's Dream **30** The Adventures of Huckleberry Finn

Roosevelt, Theodore
nickname: **5** Teddy
presidential rank: **11** twenty-sixth
party: **10** Republican
state represented: **2** NY
succeeded: **8** McKinley
defeated (second term): **4** (Eugene Victor) Debs **6** (Alton Brooks) Parker, (Thomas Edward) Watson **7** (Austin) Holcomb, (Silas Comfort) Swallow **8** (Charles Hunter) Corregan
vice president: **4** none (1st term) **9** (Charles Warren) Fairbanks
cabinet:
state: **3** (John Milton) Hay **4** (Elihu) Root **5** (Robert) Bacon
treasury: **4** (Leslie Mortier) Shaw, (Lyman Judson) Gage **9** (George Bruce) Cortelyou
war: **4** (Elihu) Root, (William Howard) Taft **6** (Luke Edward) Wright
attorney general: **4** (Philander Chase) Knox **5** (William Henry) Moody **9** (Charles Joseph) Bonaparte
navy: **4** (John Davis) Long **5** (William Henry) Moody **6** (Paul) Morton **7** (Victor Howard) Metcalf **8** (Truman Handy) Newberry **9** (Charles Joseph) Bonaparte
postmaster general: **5** (Charles Emory) Smith, (George von Lengerke) Meyer, (Henry Clay) Payne, (Robert John) Wynne **9** (George Bruce) Cortelyou
interior: **8** (James Rudolph) Garfield **9** (Ethan Allen) Hitchcock
agriculture: **6** (James) Wilson
commerce and labor: **6** (Oscar Solomon) Straus **7** (Victor Howard) Metcalf **9** (George Bruce) Cortelyou
born: **13** New York City NY
died/buried: **2** NY **9** Oyster Bay **10** Long Island
education:
university: **7** Harvard
law school: **8** Columbia (did not graduate)
religion: **13** Dutch Reformed
interests: **7** hunting (African game), writing **9** exploring (South America) **14** natural history
author: **11** Rough Riders **14** Oliver Cromwell **16** Gouverneur Morris, Thomas Hart Benton **17** African Game Trails, The New Nationalism **19** The Winning of the West **20** Letters to His Children **21** America and the World War **24** The Foes of Our Own Household **25** Fear God and Take Your Own Part **27** A Booklover's Holiday in the Open, Ranch Life and the Hunting Trail, The Naval War of Eighteen-Twelve **28** Hero Tales from American History **29** Through the Brazilian Wilderness **33** Life Histories of African Game Animals
political career: **13** Vice President **15** NY State Assembly **24** US Civil Service Commission
assistant secretary: **4** Navy
governor of: **7** New York
organized party: **9** Bull Moose **11** Progressive
civilian career: **6** author **7** rancher **14** public lecturer
military service: **15** NY National Guard **18** Spanish-American War
organized cavalry regiment: **11** Rough Riders
led charge up: **11** San Juan Hill
notable events of lifetime/term: **5** Panic (of 1907) **10** Square Deal **15** Nobel Peace Prize **22** San Francisco earthquake
Act: **11** Reclamation **14** Meat Inspection **15** Hepburn Railroad, Pure Food and Drug
bureau of: **12** Corporations **28** Immigration and Naturalization
first flight by: **14** Wright Brothers
revolution: **6** Panama
treaty: **13** Hay-Pauncefote **15** Hay-Bunau-Varilla
quotes: **25** Hasten forward quickly there **28** Speak softly and carry a big stick
father: **8** Theodore
mother: **6** Martha (Bulloch)
siblings: **4** Anna **7** Corinne, Elliott
wife: **5** Alice (Hathaway Lee), Edith (Kermit Carow)
children: **6** Kermit **7** Quentin **8** Alice Lee, Theodore **10** Ethel Carow **16** Archibald Bulloch

Roosevelt, Franklin Delano *see box, p. 842*

Roosevelt, Theodore *see box*

rooster
young: **8** cockerel

root **3** fix, set **4** back, base, bind, bulb, clap, hail, nail, rise, stem **5** basis, boost, cheer, fount, radix, start, stick, tubes **6** bottom, fasten, ground, motive, origin, reason, second, source, spring **7** acclaim, applaud, bolster, cheer on, pull for, radicle, support **8** fountain, occasion, shout for **9** beginning, encourage, establish, inception, rationale **10** derivation, foundation, mainspring **11** fundamental **12** commencement, fountainhead

Root, John Wellborn
partner: **14** Daniel H Burnham
architect of: **10** The Rookery **12** Hotel Statler (Washington DC), Montauk Block **13** Hotel Tamanaco (Caracas) **17** Monadnock Build-

Roots
author: **9** Alex Haley
character: **3** Tom **4** Ames, Bell, Noah **5** Binta, Fanta, Grill, Irene, Kizzy, Lewis, Mingo, Omoro **6** Justin, Martha, Ordell **7** Fiddler, Gardner, Nyo Boto **8** Kintango, Mathilda, Mrs Moore, Tom Moore **9** Evan Brent, Missy Anne **10** Brima Cesay, Capt Davies, Carrington, Jemmy Brent, Kadi Touray, Kunta Kinte, Sam Bennett, Sister Sara **11** Mrs Reynolds, Squire James **12** John Reynolds **13** Chicken George **14** Sir Eric Russell, Stephen Bennett **15** Ol' George Johnson, Third Mate Slater **17** Dr William Reynolds
cast: **8** Burl Ives, John Amos, Ren Woods **9** Ben Vereen, Brad Davis, Moses Gunn, O J Simpson, Vic Morrow **10** Billy Hicks, Ian McShane, John Schuck, Lynne Moody, Olivia Cole, Paul Shenar, Ralph Waite, Robert Reed **11** Beverly Todd, Cicely Tyson, Doug McClure, Edward Asner, Gary Collins, Harry Rhodes, Lane Binkley, LeVar Burton, Lorne Greene, Maya Angelou, Sandy Duncan **12** Carolyn Jones, Chuck Connors, Leslie Uggams, Lloyd Bridges **13** Louis Gosset Jr, Madge Sinclair, William Watson **14** George Hamilton, Lynda Day George, Macdonald Carey **15** Lillian Randolph, Scatman Crothers, Thalmus Rasulala **16** Raymond St Jacques, Richard Roundtree **18** Georg Stanford Brown **20** Lawrence Hilton-Jacobs

ing, Palmolive Building (Chicago) **19** Rand-McNally Building

root for **5** boost **6** urge on **7** cheer on, pull for

root out **5** dig up **6** remove **7** extract, pull out, uncover, unearth **8** discover **9** extirpate, ferret out **12** bring to light

Roots ***see box***

rope **3** gad, guy, tie, tow **4** bind, cord, fast, guss, hemp, line, lure, snag, trap, wire, yarn **5** cable, catch, chord, lasso, noose, riata, shank, strap, twine **6** corral, entice, hawser, lariat, seduce, string, tether **7** bobstay, cordage, halyard, lanyard, lashing, painter **8** dragline, restrain
fiber: **5** sisal

Rosaline
character in: **16** Love's Labour's Lost
author: **11** Shakespeare

rose **4** Rosa
varieties: **3** bog, dog, sun, tea, wax **4** baby, gold, moss, musk, rock, rush, sand, wood **5** briar, brier, China, fairy, field, malva, Ophir, pygmy, swamp **6** Alpine, Burnet, copper, cotton, damask, desert, French, ground, Karroo, Lenten, mallow, Nootka, Scotch, velvet **7** baby sun, Banksia, Bourbon, cabbage, cluster, Guelder, Manetti, pasture, prairie, rambler **8** Burgundy, Champney, Cherokee, chestnut, cinnamon, climbing, Japanese, Memorial, mountain, Noisette **9** Christmas, evergreen, hybrid tea, McCartney, Polyantha, Remontant, Turkestan **10** California, Chinquapin, shaggy-rock, underwater **11** confederate, giant velvet, hairy alpine **12** green Mexican, Hawaiian wood, Seven-sisters, white Mexican **13** Himalayan musk, Hybrid Bourbon, Persian yellow, Stuart's desert **15** hybrid perpetual **16** York-and-Lancaster

Rose, Pete (Peter Edward)
nickname: **13** Charlie Hustle
sport: **8** baseball
position: **7** baseman **8** outfield
team: **14** Cincinnati Reds **20** Philadelphia Phillies

Rosedale, Mr
character in: **15** The House of Mirth
author: **7** Wharton

Rosemary's Baby
director: **13** Roman Polanski
based on novel by: **8** Ira Levin
cast: **9** Mia Farrow **10** Ruth Gordon **14** John Cassavetes, Sidney Blackmer
Oscar for: **17** supporting actress (Gordon)

Rosenberg, Stuart
director of: **12** Cool Hand Luke

Rosenbloom, Maxie
nickname: **12** Slapsie Maxie
sport: **6** boxing
class: **16** light heavyweight

Rosencrantz
character in: **6** Hamlet
author: **11** Shakespeare

Rosenkavalier, Der
also: **18** The Knight of the Rose
opera by: **7** (Richard) Strauss
character: **6** Sophie **8** Octavian **9** Baron Ochs **11** Marschallin (Princess von Werderberg)

Rose of Sharon
character in: **16** The Grapes of Wrath
author: **9** Steinbeck

Rose Tattoo, The
director: **10** Daniel Mann
based on play by: **17** Tennessee Williams
cast: **11** Anna Magnani **13** Burt Lancaster
Oscar for: **7** actress (Magnani)

rosiness **5** bloom, blush, flush **7** redness **8** pinkness

Rosmersholm
author: **11** Henrik Ibsen

Rosofsky, Barnet
real name of: **10** Barney Ross

Ross, Barney
real name: **14** Barnet Rosofsky
sport: **6** boxing
class: **12** welterweight

Ross, Herbert
director of: **14** The Goodbye Girl **15** The Turning Point

Ross, Katharine
born: **12** Los Angeles CA
aunt: **16** Katharine Hepburn
roles: **9** The Colbys **11** The Graduate **13** Stepford Wives **29** Butch Cassidy and the Sundance Kid

Rossellini, Roberto
director of: **6** Paisan **8** Open City **9** Stromboli **10** The Miracle **15** Germany Year Zero
wife: **13** Ingrid Bergman

Rossen, Robert
director of: **11** Body and Soul **14** All the King's Men

Rossetti, Dante Gabriel
author of: **17** The Blessed Damozel
born: **6** London **7** England

group: **14** Pre-Raphaelites
artwork: **12** Beata Beatrix **15** The Annunciation **17** Ecce Ancilla Domini

Rossini, Gioacchino Antonio
born: **5** Italy **6** Pesaro
composer of: **5** Moise **6** Otello **8** Tancredi **10** Le Comte Ory, Semiramide **11** William Tell **12** Mose in Egitto **13** Guillaume Tell, La Cenerentola **15** Barber of Seville **20** Il Barbiere di Siviglia **22** La Cambiale di Matrimonio

Rossner, Judith
author of: **11** Attachments **14** Ordinary People **19** Looking for Mr Goodbar

Rostand, Edmond
author of: **7** L'Aiglon **10** Chantecler **12** The Romancers **16** Cyrano de Bergerac

roster **4** list, roll **5** cadre, panel, slate **6** agenda, docket, muster, record **7** catalog, listing, posting **8** register, schedule **9** catalogue, directory

rostrum **4** dais **5** stage, stand, stump **6** podium, pulpit **7** lectern, soapbox **8** platform

rosy **4** pink **5** ruddy **6** bright, florid **7** flushed, glowing, hopeful, reddish **8** blooming, blushing, cheerful, cheering, flushing, inflamed, rubicund **9** confident, favorable, promising, reddening, rubescent **10** auspicious, felicitous, optimistic, propitious, reassuring **11** encouraging, high-colored, inspiriting **13** full of promise

Roszak, Theodore
born: **6** Poland, Poznan
artwork: **5** Raven, Surge **7** Anguish **9** Chrysalis, Scavenger, Sea Quarry **11** Sea Sentinel **12** Amorphic Form, Thorn Blossom **18** Specter of Kitty Hawk **20** The Whaler of Nantucket **27** Recollections of the Southwest

rot **3** mar **4** bosh, bull, bunk, harm, hurt, warp **5** decay, go bad, spoil, stain, taint, trash **6** damage, debase, defile, drivel, impair, infect, injure, jabber, molder, poison **7** blather, corrupt, crumble, deprave, inanity, pervert, pollute, putrefy, rubbish, twaddle **8** flummery, folderol, nonsense, putresce **9** absurdity, decompose, gibberish, moonshine, poppycock, purulence, putridity **10** balderdash, corruption, degenerate, flapdoodle **11** contaminate, deteriorate, putrescence **12** disintegrate, fiddle-faddle, gobbledygook, putrefaction **13** contamination, decomposition, deterioration **14** disintegration **16** stuff and nonsense

rotate **4** eddy, reel, roll, spin, turn **5** pivot, swirl, twirl, twist, wheel, whirl **6** change, circle, gyrate, swivel **7** revolve **9** alternate, circulate, pirouette **11** interchange

Roth, Philip
author of: **8** The Facts **15** Goodbye Columbus **16** The Anatomy Lesson, Zuckerman Unbound **17** Portnoy's Complaint

Rothko, Mark
born: **6** Dvinsk, Latvia, Russia **16** Daugavpils Latvia
artwork: **5** Light **12** Central Green, Earth and Blue **14** Four Darks in Red

rotten **3** bad **4** base, foul, rank **5** dirty, fetid, nasty, reeky, venal **6** filthy, putrid, rancid, scurvy **7** corrupt, crooked, decayed, devious, immoral, tainted, very bad, vicious **8** criminal, decaying, indecent, purulent, two-faced **9** deceitful, dishonest, dissolute, faithless, insincere, mercenary, moldering, putrefied, worm-eaten **10** decomposed, iniquitous, putrescent, scurrilous, unpleasant, villainous **11** decomposing, disgraceful, treacherous **12** contemptible, dishonorable, unforgivable, unscrupulous **13** double-dealing, untrustworthy

rotter **3** cad, cur, rat **4** heel **5** knave, louse, rogue **6** no-good, rascal **7** bounder, caitiff, villain **9** scoundrel

rotund **3** fat **5** obese, ovate, ovoid, plump, pudgy, round, stout, tubby **6** chubby, curved, fleshy, portly **7** bulbous, lumpish, rounded **8** circular, globular **9** corpulent, egg-shaped, spherical **10** potbellied **11** full-fleshed

Rouault, Georges
born: **5** Paris **6** France
artwork: **3** Mr X **5** Clown **8** Le Chahut, Miserere, Twilight **9** The Mirror **10** The Old King **11** Fleurs du mal, The Holy Face **12** Head of a Clown **13** Little Olympia **14** The Three Judges **19** Small Family of Clowns **22** Christ Mocked by Soldiers **26** Les Reincarnations du Pere Ubu **28** The Child Jesus among the Doctors

roue **3** cad, rip **4** rake, wolf **6** lecher, wanton **7** bounder, dallier, Don Juan, playboy, seducer, trifler **8** Casanova, debauche, Lothario, rakehell **9** libertine, womanizer **10** profligate **11** philanderer, skirt-chaser

rough *see box*

rough going **8** struggle **10** difficulty **11** arduousness **13** laboriousness

Roughing It
author: **9** Mark Twain
character: **12** Brigham Young, Hank Erickson **16** Slade the Terrible

rough **3** raw **4** beat, hard, rude, wild **5** bluff, blunt, bumpy, crude, cruel, draft, green, gruff, harsh, hasty, husky, quick, raspy, rocky, scaly, sharp, surly, tough, vague **6** abrupt, beat on, broken, brutal, callow, choppy, clumsy, coarse, craggy, crusty, gauche, hoarse, jagged, knotty, ragged, raging, roiled, rugged, savage, severe, stormy, thrash, turbid, uneven, vulgar **7** austere, awkward, bearish, boorish, brusque, chapped, coarsen, drastic, extreme, general, gnarled, grating, ill-bred, inexact, jarring, loutish, outline, rasping, raucous, scraggy, sketchy, stubbly, uncouth, unlevel, untamed, violent **8** agitated, churlish, rigorous, scabrous, scratchy, strident, ungentle, unsmooth **9** brutalize, difficult, ferocious, imperfect, imprecise, inelegant, irregular, manhandle, sketch out, stringent, turbulent, uncourtly, unfeeling, ungenteel, unmusical, unrefined **10** discordant, incomplete, indelicate, push around, tumultuous, unfinished, ungracious, unmannerly, unpleasant, unpolished **11** approximate, cacophonous, ill-mannered, preliminary, rudimentary, tempestuous, unluxurious **12** inharmonious **13** inconsiderate, uncomfortable, ungentlemanly

rough it **4** camp **7** camp out

roughneck **4** hood, lout, punk **5** bully, rowdy, tough **6** vandal **7** hoodlum, ruffian **8** hooligan **9** barbarian **10** delinquent

roughness **7** crudity **8** acrimony, aviation, pungency, violence **9** gruffness, harshness, vulgarity **10** coarseness, inelegance, unevenness, unkindness **11** raucousness **12** irregularity, unsmoothness, unrefinement **13** undevelopment

rough sketch **5** draft **7** cartoon, outline

rough-textured **5** harsh **6** coarse, nubbly, shaggy, tweedy **7** bristly, prickly **8** scratchy **9** bristling **10** sandpapery

round **3** fat **4** full, oval **5** cycle, obese, orbed, ovate, ovoid, plump, pudgy, stout, total, tubby, whole **6** chubby, circle, curved, entire, fluent, intact, portly, rotund, series, smooth **7** flowing, globoid, perfect, rounded **8** circular, complete, globular, resonant, sonorous, spheroid, thorough, unbroken **9** corpulent, egg-shaped, spherical, undivided **10** ball-shaped, elliptical, harmonious, pear-shaped, procession, succession **11** cylindrical, full-fleshed, mellifluent, progression

roundabout **5** wordy **6** random, zigzag **7** devious, erratic, oblique, sinuous, winding **8** indirect, rambling, tortuous, twisting **9** desultory **10** circuitous, discursive, meandering, serpentine **12** labyrinthine **14** circumlocutory

roundaboutness **9** wandering **10** digression, meandering **11** indirection **14** circuitousness, circumlocution

rounded **6** convex **7** curving **11** protuberant

rounding out **10** developing **12** augmentation **13** amplification

rounding-out **10** complement, completion, perfecting **12** consummation

rounds **4** beat **5** route, skirt, watch **7** circuit

roundup **6** muster, resume **7** meeting, summary **8** assembly **9** gathering **11** convocation

round up **6** gather, muster, summon **7** collect, convene, convoke, marshal **8** assemble **10** accumulate **12** call together

rouse **4** call, goad, move, prod, spur, stir, wake **5** arise, awake, get up, pique, rally, waken **6** awaken, excite, foment, kindle, incite, stir up, summon, turn on, wake up **7** animate, inflame, inspire, provoke, shake up **8** activate **9** galvanize, instigate, stimulate

roused **2** up **5** astir, awake **7** excited, incited, kindled, rallied, shook up **8** awakened, inflamed, inspired, out of bed, shaken up **9** stirred up **10** up and about

rousing **5** brisk, peppy **6** active, lively **8** animated, exciting, stirring, vigorous **9** awakening, inspiring **10** energizing, refreshing, remarkable **11** provocative, stimulating **12** exhilarating, intoxicating **13** extraordinary

Rousseau, Henri Julien Felix
nickname: **10** Le Douanier
born: **5** Laval **6** France
artwork: **3** War **8** The Dream **12** Child on Rocks, The Waterfall **13** The Hungry Lion **15** Carnival Evening, The Snake Charmer **16** Bouquet of Flowers, The Sleeping Gypsy **17** The Poet and his Muse

Rousseau, Jean Jacques
author of: **5** Emile **11** Confessions **17** La Nouvelle Heloise, The Social Contract

Rousseau, (Pierre Etienne) Theodore
born: **5** Paris **6** France
artwork: **7** Evening **12** After the Rain **15** Edge of the Forest, Under the Birches **18** Descent of the Cattle, Oak Trees at Apremont **19** The Marsh in the Landes **20** The Valley of Tiffauges **21** Meadow Bordered by Trees

roust **4** bust **5** rouse **6** arrest, hassle **7** capture, seizure **12** apprehension

rout **4** beat, drub, lick, ruin, trim **5** chaos, cream, crush, panic, quell, repel, worst **6** defeat, subdue, thrash **7** beating, clobber, conquer, licking, repulse, scatter **8** drive off, drubbing, lambaste, overcome, vanquish **9** chase away, drive away, overpower, overthrow **11** put to flight **15** disorganization **18** throw into confusion

route **3** run **4** beat, pass, path, road, ship, tack **5** remit, round, track **6** artery, course, detour, direct **7** circuit, highway, parkway, passage, roadway **8** dispatch, transmit, turnpike **9** boulevard, itinerary **10** throughway **12** thoroughfare

Route 66
character: **8** Linc Case **9** Tod Stiles **10** Buz Murdock
cast: **12** Glenn Corbett, Martin Milner **13** George Maharis
car: **8** Corvette

routine **4** dull **5** order, usual **6** boring, custom, method, normal, system **7** formula, regular, tedious, typical **8** habitual, ordinary, periodic, practice **9** customary, operation, technique **11** arrangement, predictable **12** conventional, run-of-the-mill **13** unexceptional

rove **4** roam **5** drift, prowl, range **6** ramble, stroll, travel, wander **7** meander, traipse **9** gallivant

roving **6** errant **7** aimless, gadding, migrant, nomadic, roaming, vagrant **8** errantry, rambling, restless **9** desultory, itinerant, traveling, uncertain, wandering **10** changeable, discursive, meandering, inconstant **11** peripatetic **14** discursiveness

row **4** file, line, rank, spat, tier, tiff **5** brawl, chain, melee, queue, range, scrap, set-to, train, words **6** column, fracas, scrape, series, string **7** echelon, quarrel, wrangle **8** argument, disorder, sequence, squabble **9** imbroglio, wrangling **10** difference, succession **11** altercation, contretemps

rowboat **3** gig **4** bark, dory **5** barge, canoe, dingy, scull, skiff **6** barque, caique, dinghy, wherry
seat: **4** taft

rowdy **6** unruly **7** lawless, raffish **9** roughneck **10** boisterous, disorderly **11** mischievous **12** obstreperous

Rowena, Lady
character in: **7** Ivanhoe
author: **5** Scott

rowing
athlete: **10** James Dietz **14** Anthony Johnson

Rowlands, Gena
real name: **23** Virginia Cathryn Rowlands
born: **9** Cambria WI
husband: **14** John Cassavetes
roles: **5** Faces **12** Opening Night **23** A Woman Under the Influence

Roxana
subtitle: **20** The Fortunate Mistress
author: **11** Daniel Defoe

royal **5** grand, regal **6** august, lavish, superb **7** stately **8** imposing, majestic, splendid **9** monarchal, sovereign **10** munificent **11** fit for a king, magnificent, resplendent

royalty **4** sway **7** command, majesty **8** dominion, hegemony, kingship, regality **9** queenship, supremacy **11** divine right, sovereignty

Royaume de Belgique *see* **7** Belgium

Roy Rogers
ingredient: **9** ginger ale, grenadine
also called: **13** Shirley Temple

Roy Rogers Show, The
regular: **8** Pat Brady **9** Dale Evans
theme: **16** Happy Trails to You
horse: **7** Trigger
dog: **6** Bullet
jeep: **10** Nellybelle
ranch: **10** Double R Bar

Ruanda *see* **6** Rwanda

rub **4** buff, swab, wipe **5** annoy, braze, catch, chafe, clean, hitch, knead, pinch, scour, scrub, smear, thing, touch, trick **6** abrade, finger, handle, polish, secret, smooth, spread, strait, stroke **7** burnish, dilemma, massage, problem, rubdown, setback, slather, trouble **8** handling, hardship, kneading, obstacle, stroking **10** difficulty, impediment, manipulate **12** manipulation

Rubaiyat of Omar Khayyam, The
author: **11** Omar Khayyam
translator: **16** Edward FitzGerald

rubber, vulcanized
invented by: **8** Goodyear

rubber plant **13** Ficus elastica
varieties: **4** baby **5** dwarf **7** Chinese **8** American, creeping, Japanese **9** mistletoe **11** small-leaved **16** broad-leaved India

rubberstamp **6** affirm **7** approve, endorse

rubber tree **10** Schefflera
varieties: **4** Para **5** India **8** Castilla **11** West African

rubbery **5** tough **6** supple **7** elastic **8** flexible **9** resilient **11** stretchable

rubbing **7** chafing **8** abrading, scraping **12** manipulation

rubbish **3** rot **4** bosh, junk **5** dross, offal, trash, waste **6** babble, debris, drivel, idiocy, jetsam, litter, refuse, rubble **7** blather, garbage, inanity, twaddle **8** folderol, nonsense **9** gibberish, rigmarole, silliness **10** balderdash, flapdoodle, rigamarole

rubbish heap **4** dump **6** midden **10** refuse pile

rubble **4** junk, rock **5** brash, chalk, stent, stone, talus, trash **6** debris, refuse **7** rubbish **8** nonsense **9** fragments **11** foolishness

rube **3** oaf **4** boor, clod, hick **5** yokel **6** rustic **7** bumpkin, hayseed, peasant **10** clodhopper

rub elbows **3** mix **4** club **6** hobnob, mingle **7** consort, hang out **9** associate **10** fraternize

Rubens, Peter Paul
born: **6** Siegen **10** Westphalia
artwork: **8** Lion Hunt **10** The Rainbow **15** The Garden of Love **17** Laocoon and his Sons **18** Battle of the Amazons **20** The Raising of the Cross **21** Landscape with Het Steen **22** The Descent from the Cross **23** Altarpiece of St Aldefonso **26** The Adoration of the Shepherds **27** Marchesa Brigida Spinola-Doria, Mystic Marriage of St Catherine **29** Rape of the Daughters of Leucippus **34** Helene Fourment with Two of her Children

rubicund **3** red **4** rosy **5** ruddy **6** florid **7** flushed, reddish

rubidium
chemical symbol: **2** Rb

rub out **4** do in, kill, slay **5** erase **6** efface, murder **7** bump off, destroy, execute, expunge **8** massacre **10** obliterate, put to death **11** assassinate, exterminate

ruby
species: **8** corundum
source: **5** Burma, India, Mogok **7** Bangkok, Kashmir **8** Sri Lanka, Thailand
kind: **4** star
color: **3** red

ruckus **3** row **4** fray, to-do **5** brawl, broil, clash, fight, melee **6** battle, fracas, rumpus, uproar **7** scuffle **9** imbroglio **10** donnybrook, free-for-all **11** embroilment

ruddy **3** red **4** rosy **6** florid **7** flushed, reddish, roseate, scarlet **8** blushing, rubicund, sanguine **11** rosy-cheeked

rude **3** raw **4** wild **5** blunt, crude, fresh, green, gross, gruff, rough, saucy, sulky, surly **6** abrupt, callow, clumsy, coarse, crusty, gauche, homely, rugged, rustic, sullen, uneven, vulgar **7** abusive, artless, awkward, boorish, brusque, brutish, ill-bred, loutish, profane, scraggy, uncivil, uncouth **8** churlish, homebred, ignorant, impolite, impudent, indecent, insolent, slapdash, untaught **9** inelegant, insulting, makeshift, primitive, roughhewn, uncourtly, ungallant, unlearned, unrefined, untrained, untutored **10** illiterate, indecorous, indelicate, peremptory, provincial, uncultured, uneducated, ungraceful, ungracious, unladylike, unmannerly, unpolished **11** bad-mannered, countrified, impertinent, uncivilized, uncourteous, undignified **12** discourteous, roughly built **13** disrespectful, inconsiderate, ungentlemanly

rudeness **9** bluntness, impudence, insolence, sauciness **10** bad manners, coarseness, disrespect, incivility **11** boorishness, discourtesy **12** impertinence, impoliteness **14** ungraciousness **17** inconsiderateness

rudimentary **5** basic **6** simple **7** initial, primary **8** immature **9** elemental, formative, imperfect, premature, primitive, vestigial **10** elementary, incomplete, prototypal **11** undeveloped

rudiments **6** basics **7** essence **8** elements **9** beginning **10** principles **12** fundamentals

Rudkus, Jurgis and Antanas
characters in: **9** The Jungle
author: **8** Sinclair

Rudolph, Paul
architect of: **16** Jewett Arts Center (Wellesley College) **24** Government Services Center (Boston) **28** School of Architecture Building (Yale)

rue **4** Ruta
varieties: **4** bush, lady, wall **5** goat's **6** common, meadow **10** tall meadow **11** early meadow **12** Alpine meadow

rue **5** mourn **6** bemoan, lament, regret, repent, repine **7** deplore

rueful **3** sad **5** sorry **6** woeful **7** doleful **8** contrite, mournful, dolorous, penitent, repining **9** depressed, plaintive, regretful, sorrowful, sorrowing **10** deplorable, lamentable, melancholy, remorseful, unpleasant

ruffian **4** hood, thug **5** brute, bully, crook, knave, rogue, rough, rowdy, tough **6** mugger **7** hoodlum, villain **8** gangster, hooligan **9** cutthroat, roisterer, roughneck, scoundrel **10** blackguard

ruffle **4** fold, muss, wave **5** frill, plait, pleat, ruche, upset **6** edging, excite, muss up, pucker, rimple, ripple, rumple **7** agitate, confuse, crinkle, disturb, flounce, perturb, roughen, trouble, wrinkle **8** dishevel, disorder, disquiet, furbelow, unsettle **9** aggravate, agitation, commotion, corrugate **10** disarrange, discompose, disconcert **11** disturbance

ruffled **5** upset, vexed **7** annoyed, frilled, nettled, pleated **8** agitated, flounced, troubled **9** nonplused, unsettled **10** nonplussed

ruffle one's feathers **3** vex **5** anger, annoy, pique **6** enrage, madden, nettle **7** incense, outrage, provoke **9** displease, infuriate

Rugg
character in: **12** Little Dorrit
author: **7** Dickens

rugged **4** hale, hard, rude, wiry, worn **5** bumpy, hardy, harsh, husky, lined, rocky, rough, stern, tough **6** brawny, coarse, craggy, jagged, ridged, robust, severe, sinewy, sturdy, taxing, trying, uneven, virile **7** arduous, cragged, onerous, scraggy, uncouth **8** athletic, furrowed, muscular, stalwart, vigorous, wrinkled **9** difficult, graceless, irregular, laborious, masculine, roughhewn, strenuous, unrefined, weathered **12** uncultivated **13** weather-beaten

Ruggles of Red Gap
director: **10** Leo McCarey
cast: **9** ZaSu Pitts **10** Mary Boland **14** Charlie Ruggles **15** Charles Laughton
remade as: **10** Fancy Pants

ruin, ruins **3** gut, pot **4** doom, fall, fell, harm, raze, seed **5** break, crush, decay, level, quash, quell, shell, spoil, upset, wreck **6** beggar, defeat, ravage, squash **7** destroy, failure, remains, shatter, undoing **8** bankrupt, demolish, downfall, lay waste, make poor, overturn, remnants, wreckage **9** breakdown, devastate, disrepair, overthrow, pauperize **10** impoverish **11** destruction, devastation, dissolution **14** disintegration

ruination **4** ruin **5** wreck **6** fiasco **7** trouble **8** disaster **9** adversity, cataclysm **11** destruction, devastation **12** misadventure

ruinous **4** dire **5** fatal **6** deadly **7** adverse, baneful **8** damaging, ravaging **10** calamitous, disastrous, pernicious **11** cataclysmic, deleterious, destructive, devastating **12** catastrophic

Ruisdael, Jacob (Jakob) van
born: **7** Haarlem **14** The Netherlands
uncle: **18** Salomon van Ruysdael
artwork: **5** Dunes **12** The Waterfall **13** View of Haarlem **14** Bentheim Castle **15** Winter Landscape **17** The Jewish Cemetery **28** View on the Amstel near Amsterdam

rule *see box*

rule out **4** omit **6** delete, except **7** exclude **9** eliminate

ruler **4** boss, czar, emir, head, khan, king, lord, shah, tsar, tzar **5** chief, judge, queen, rajah, sheik **6** dynast, leader, prince, satrap, shogun, sultan **7** arbiter, emperor, manager, measure, monarch, pharaoh, referee, viceroy **8** chairman, director, governor, suzerain **9** chieftain, commander, potentate, president, sovereign, yardstick **10** controller, supervisor **11** coordinator, crowned head, head of state, tape measure **12** straightedge **13** administrator

rules of conduct **6** ethics **9** moral code **10** principles **12** code of ethics

Rules of the Game
director: **10** Jean Renoir
cast: **10** Jean Renoir, Mila Parely, Nora Gregor **11** Marcel Dalio

ruling **6** decree **7** regnant **8** decision, dominant, reigning **9** enactment, governing, prescript **10** commanding, widespread **11** controlling, predominant **13** authoritative, predominating

ruling class **11** aristocracy **13** Establishment

Ruling Class, The
director: **10** Peter Medak
cast: **10** Arthur Lowe **11** Alastair Sim, Peter O'Toole **12** Harry Andrews

rule **3** law, run **4** find, form, head, lead, sway **5** adage, axiom, canon, guide, judge, maxim, model, order, reign **6** custom, decide, decree, direct, empire, govern, manage, method, policy, regime, settle, system **7** adjudge, command, control, declare, formula, precept, prevail, resolve, routine **8** conclude, doctrine, dominate, domineer, dominion, pass upon, practice, regnancy, regulate, standard **9** authority, criterion, determine, direction, establish, guideline, influence, ordinance, precedent, principle, pronounce, supremacy **10** adjudicate, administer, convention, domination, government, leadership, regulation, suzerainty **11** predominate, preside over, sovereignty **12** jurisdiction, prescription **14** administration
type: **5** bench **7** folding **9** steel tape
constellation of: **5** Norma

rum *see box*

Rumania *see box, p. 850*

rumble **4** bang, boom, clap, roar, roll **7** booming, resound, thunder **8** drumming **9** resonance **11** reverberate **13** reverberation

Rumford, Benjamin Thomson
invented: **10** photometer **11** calorimeter

Rumina
protectress of: **14** nursing mothers

ruminant **3** cow, elk, yak **4** deer, oxen **5** bison, camel, llama, moose, sheep **6** alpaca, cattle, vicuna **7** buffalo, giraffe, pensive **8** antelope **10** chevrotain, meditative, thoughtful **13** contemplative

ruminate **4** mull, muse **5** brood, study, think, weigh **6** ponder **7** reflect **8** cogitate, consider, meditate, mull over **9** speculate, think over **10** deliberate, think about **11** contemplate

ruminating **6** musing **7** pensive **8** thinking **10** meditating,

rum
drink: **4** Bolo, Grog **6** Mojito **7** Gauguin **8** Daiquiri, Navy Grog, Pina Fria **9** Borinquen, Hurricane **10** Pina Colada **12** Boston Cooler **13** Planter's Punch **14** Fish House Punch **15** Bacardi Cocktail **18** Barbados Rum Swizzle
ingredient: **8** molasses **9** sugar cane
origin: **10** West Indies
type: **4** dark **5** light
with apple brandy: **6** Bolero **8** Apple Pie
with apricot brandy: **11** Apricot Lady
with black coffee: **9** Black Rose
with bouillon: **6** Creole
with bourbon: **14** Artillery Punch
with brandy: **15** Quaker's Cocktail
with Cointreau: **8** Acapulco **10** Casa Blanca **11** Beachcomber **12** Blue Hawaiian
with cola: **9** Cuba Libre
with creme de cacao: **6** Panama
with curacao: **6** Mai-Tai **8** Blue Lady **12** Blue Hawaiian
with Dubonnet: **3** BVD **10** Bushranger
with Galliano: **9** Bossa Nova
with gin: **3** BVD
with guava: **8** Ocho Rios
with kahlua: **10** Black Maria
with milk: **6** Rum Cow **11** Tom-and-Jerry
with Pernod: **8** Shanghai
with sloe gin: **11** Shark's Tooth
with Tia Maria: **10** Black Maria
with vermouth: **6** Bolero **8** Apple Pie **10** Black Devil **11** Shark's Tooth

meditative, reflecting, reflective, thoughtful **11** chewing over, mulling over, speculative **13** contemplating, contemplative, introspective

rumination **5** study **6** musing **7** mulling, reverie, thought **8** brooding, thinking **9** pondering **10** cogitation, meditation, reflection **11** speculation **12** deliberation **13** consideration, contemplation **15** reconsideration

rummage **4** root **5** probe **7** examine, explore, ransack **10** disarrange, poke around **11** look through

rummy **3** sot **4** lush, soak **5** drunk, souse, toper **6** barfly, boozer **7** tippler **8** card game, drunkard **9** alcoholic **11** dipsomaniac
also known as: **3** gin, rum **4** rhum **5** romme **8** gin rummy
derived from: **8** conquien

rumor **4** talk **5** story **6** babble, gossip, report **7** hearsay, whisper **8** innuendo, intimate **9** circulate, insinuate **11** insinuation, scuttlebutt, supposition

rump **4** rear, seat **5** croup, stern **6** behind, bottom, breech, dorsum **7** rear end **8** backside, buttocks, derriere, haunches **9** posterior **12** hindquarters

Rumpelstiltskin
origin: **8** Germanic
form: **5** dwarf
spun: **4** flax
made: **4** gold

rumple **4** fold, muss **5** crimp, crush **6** crease, pucker, rimple, ruffle, tousle **7** crinkle, crumple, wrinkle **8** dishevel, disorder **9** corrugate **10** disarrange

rumpus **3** ado, row **4** fray, fuss, stir, to-do **5** brawl, melee, noise **6** affray, fracas, hubbub, pother, racket, ruckus, tumult, uproar **7** rhubarb, scuffle, tempest **8** brouhaha, upheaval **9** agitation, commotion, confusion, imbroglio **10** hullabaloo **11** disturbance, embroilment

run *see box, p. 851*

run aground **7** founder **8** collapse

runaround **4** slip **5** dodge **6** bypass **7** evasion **8** shunning, sidestep **9** avoidance **11** elusiveness, evasiveness **12** equivocation

run around **7** consort, hang out **9** associate, pal around **10** fraternize

runaway **4** pure **6** bolter **7** escapee, perfect, refugee **8** absolute, complete, deserter, fugitive **9** out-and-out, unalloyed **10** skedaddler **11** unmitigated, unqualified

run away **3** fly **4** flee **5** elope **6** decamp, escape, run off **7** abscond, make off **8** sneak off **10** fly the coop, make a break, take flight **12** make a getaway

rundown **5** brief **6** digest, precis, resume, review, sketch **7** outline, summary **8** abstract, synopsis **12** capitulation, condensation

run-down **5** frail, seedy, tacky, tired, weary **6** ailing, beat-up, feeble, shabby, sickly **7** rickety, worn out **8** fatigued, tattered **9** crumbling, exhausted **10** broken-down, tumbledown **11** dilapidated **12** deteriorated

run down **4** scan **5** knock **6** slight **7** detract, put down, run over **8** belittle, derogate, ridicule **9** denigrate, deprecate, discredit, disparage, downgrade, enumerate, underrate **10** depreciate, undervalue

run-in **5** brush, set-to **6** battle, fracas **7** scuffle **8** skirmish **9** encounter **10** engagement

run into **4** meet **8** flow into **9** encounter **10** chance upon, meet up with **11** collide with

run off **3** fly **4** flee **5** elope **6** escape **7** abscond, make off, runaway **9** steal away **10** take flight **15** head for the hills

run off at the mouth **3** gab **5** prate **6** babble, gabble **8** rattle on **11** talk too much

run off with **5** seize **6** abduct, kidnap **7** bear off **8** carry off **9** elope with **11** abscond with, make off with

run-of-the-mill **4** dull, so-so **5** banal, stock, usual **6** common, modest **7** average, humdrum, mundane, routine, typical **8** everyday, mediocre, middling, ordinary, passable, standard **10** second-rate **11** commonplace, indifferent, nondescript **12** unimpressive **13** unimaginative **15** undistinguished

runt **3** elf **4** chit **5** dwarf, pygmy **6** midget, peewee, shrimp **8** half-pint, Tom Thumb **11** Lilliputian
Latin: **10** homunculus

Rumania
other name: **7** Romania
capital/largest city: **9** Bucharest
others: **4** Aiud, Arad, Cluj, Deva, Iasi **5** Bacau, Balta, Cerna, Jassy, Neamt, Sibiu, Turnu, Yassy **6** Braila, Brasov, Brasso, Eforie, Galatz, Galeti, Lupeni, Mamaia, Oradea, Sighet **7** Bendery, Craiova, Focsani, Giurgiu, Ploesti, Severin **8** Bloiesti, Cernavti, Chisinau, Irongate, Kishenef, Satu-Mare, Temesvar **9** Constanta, Kolozsvar, Timisoara **10** Czernowitz **11** Klausenburg
school: **4** Cuza
division: **4** Alba, Iasi **5** Banat, Bihor, Jassy **6** Ardeal **7** Dobruja **8** Bucovina, Bukovina, Dobrogea, Moldavia, Walachia **9** Maramures **10** Bessarabia **12** Transylvania
Roman province: **5** Dacia
measure: **7** faltche
monetary unit: **3** ban, lei, leu, lev, ley **4** bani **5** uncia **6** triens
lake: **5** Sinoe **6** Snagov
mountain: **5** Banat, Bihor **6** Codrul, Rodnei **7** Apuseni, Balkans, Caliman, Fagaras **8** Pietrosu **9** Moldavian **10** Carpathian, Moldoveanu **17** Transylvanian Alps
highest point: **11** Moldoveanul
river: **3** Alt, Jui, Olt **4** Prut **5** Aluta, Arges, Buzdu, Moros, Mures, Oltul, Schyl, Siret, Somes, Timis, Vedea **6** Crasna, Danube **7** Argesul **8** Bistrita, Ialomita, Iniester **9** Dimbovita, Jiul Mures
sea: **5** Black
physical feature:
canal: **4** Bega
forest: **6** Snagov **7** Baneasa
gorge: **8** Iron Gate
peninsula: **6** Balkan
plain: **5** Banat **9** Moldavian, Walachian **13** Prahova Valley
plateau: **7** Dobruja
wind: **6** crivat
people: **6** Dacian **8** Romanian, Rumanian
artist: **8** Brancusi
author: **7** Ionesco
composer: **6** Enesco
leader: **6** Carol I **7** Michael **8** Ioan Cuza **9** Ceausescu **12** Gheorghiu-Dej, Ion Antonescu
language: **6** French, Magyar **7** Russian **8** Romanian, Rumanian **9** Hungarian
religion: **7** Judaism **8** Lutheran **9** Calvinism, Unitarian **10** Protestant **13** Roman Catholic **16** Rumanian Orthodox
place:
castle: **4** Bran **7** Huniady
church: **5** Golia **9** Mihaivoda **10** Cretulescu, Patriarchy **11** Curtea Veche, Stavropdeos, Trei Ierarhi
monastery: **5** Humor **6** Arbore **7** Voronet **8** Sucerita **9** Moldovita
museum: **11** Peles Castle
palace: **9** mogosoaia
park: **7** Baneasa
resort: **5** Venus **6** Eforie, Mamaia, Neptun **7** Jupiter **10** Costinesti
feature:
community gathering: **9** sezatoare
game: **4** oina
food:
dish: **6** ciorba **7** mititei, sarmala **8** mamaliga **11** imam bayildi
plum brandy: **5** tuica

run through **5** spend, waste **6** expend, pierce **7** deplete, exhaust **8** rehearse, squander

runty **5** short **6** bantam **7** dwarfed, squatty, stunted **9** pint-sized

Runyon, Damon
author of: **12** Guys and Dolls **16** Blue Plate Special

rupture **3** pop **4** part, rent, rift, snap **5** break, burst, clash, cleft, crack, split **6** breach, divide, schism, sunder **7** discord, disrupt, fissure **8** breaking, bursting, cleavage, dissever, disunion, disunite, fracture, friction, puncture **9** severance **10** dissension, falling out, separation **12** disagreement

R U R
author: **10** Karel Capek

rural **4** hick **6** rustic **7** bucolic, country **8** pastoral **10** provincial **11** countrified

rural area **6** sticks **7** boonies, country **8** farmland **9** backwater, backwoods, boondocks **10** hinterland **11** countryside

Rural Dionysia *see* **14** Lesser Dionysia

ruse **4** hoax **5** blind, dodge, feint, shift, trick **6** deceit, device, scheme **8** artifice, maneuver **9** deception, stratagem **10** subterfuge **11** contrivance, machination

rush **3** hie, run **4** dart, dash, goad, leap, push, race, spur, tear, urge, whip **5** drive, haste, hurry, press, speed, storm **6** charge, hasten, hustle, plunge, scurry, sprint, urgent **7** scamper, urgency **8** dispatch, expedite, pressure, scramble **9** emergency **10** accelerate **11** top priority

rush **6** Juncus
varieties: **3** bog **4** salt, soft, wood **5** spike **6** grassy **8** scouring **9** field wood, flowering **10** common wood, least spike **11** chair-maker's, greater wood, Japanese-mat **12** slender spike **13** dwarf scouring **14** common scouring **18** variegated scouring

Rush, Benjamin
field: **8** medicine
established first: **21** free medical dispensary
signer of: **25** Declaration of Independence

rush light **3** dip **5** torch **6** candle, tallow

run **2** be, go **3** fly, get, hie, jog, pen, ply **4** bolt, boss, cost, dart, dash, defy, flee, flow, go by, head, kind, last, meet, melt, pass, pour, push, race, roll, rush, sort, tear, tour, trip, trot, type, vary **5** bleed, bound, class, court, drift, drive, genre, glide, hurry, impel, incur, issue, leave, pilot, print, speed, spell, split, stand, surge, total, while **6** become, canter, course, decamp, direct, elapse, endure, escape, extend, gallop, hasten, hustle, invite, ladder, manage, motion, move on, outing, period, pierce, propel, scurry, series, sprint, streak, stream, thrust, vanish, voyage, wander **7** abscond, add up to, advance, bring on, compete, current, display, freedom, get past, journey, liquefy, meander, operate, oversee, passage, proceed, publish, running, scamper, stretch, take off, vamoose **8** amount to, campaign, continue, dissolve, duration, evanesce, maneuver, meet with, navigate, progress, scramble, separate, tendency **9** direction, disappear, enclosure, encounter, excursion, go quickly, lose color, penetrate, skedaddle, supervise **10** coordinate, pilgrimage **11** continuance **12** beat a retreat, continuation, perpetuation
baseball: **5** point, score, tally **17** circuit of the bases

Rushworth
character in: **13** Mansfield Park
author: **6** Austen

Ruskin, John
author of: **13** Fors Clavigera **14** Modern Painters **17** The Stones of Venice **27** The Seven Lamps of Architecture

Russell, Bertrand
author of: **19** Why I Am Not a Christian **20** Principia Mathematica (with Alfred North)

Russell, Jane
real name: **29** Ernestine Jane Geraldine Russell
born: **9** Bemidji MN
discovered by: **12** Howard Hughes
roles: **4** Waco **9** The Outlaw **13** The French Line **22** Gentlemen Prefer Blondes, The Revolt of Mamie Stover

Russell, Rosalind
born: **11** Waterbury CT
roles: **5** Gypsy **6** Picnic **8** The Women **9** Hired Wife **10** Auntie Mame **11** Sister Kenny **13** His Girl Friday **14** My Sister Eileen **22** Mourning Becomes Electra

russet **5** apple, umber **6** auburn, copper **10** terra-cotta **11** rust-colored **12** reddish-brown

Russia ***see box, p. 852***

Russian Hide-and-Seek
author: **12** Kingsley Amis

Russian village commune
3 mir

rust **3** rot **5** decay, stain **6** auburn, blight, russet **7** corrode, crumble, decline, oxidize **9** corrosion, oxidation **11** deteriorate **12** reddish-brown **13** reddish-yellow

rust-colored **5** henna **6** auburn, russet **8** cinnamon **12** reddish-brown

rustic **4** rube, rude **5** crude, plain, rough, rural, yokel **6** coarse, gauche, simple **7** awkward, boorish, bucolic, bumpkin, country, hayseed, loutish, peasant, uncouth **8** agrarian, churlish, cloddish, pastoral **9** inelegant, unrefined **10** clodhopper, countryman, provincial, uncultured, unpolished **11** countrified **13** country person **15** unsophisticated

rustle **3** rub **4** hiss, stir **5** swish, whish **6** riffle

rustler **5** thief **6** bandit, outlaw **7** brigand **9** desperado

rusty **5** moldy, stiff **6** rotten, rusted **7** reddish, tainted **8** corroded, sluggish **11** rust-colored **13** out of practice

rut **3** cut **4** mark **5** ditch, habit, score, tread **6** furrow, groove, gutter, hollow, trench, trough **7** channel, depress, dig into, pattern **8** monotony **9** deep track **10** depression **11** dull routine

Ruth
husband: **4** Boaz **6** Mahlon
son: **4** Obed
father-in-law: **9** Elimelech
mother-in-law: **5** Naomi
brother-in-law: **7** Chilion

Ruth, George Herman
nickname: **4** Babe **12** Sultan of Swat
sport: **8** baseball
position: **8** outfield
team: **14** New York Yankees

Rutherford, Dame Margaret
born: **6** London **7** England
roles: **7** The VIPs **10** Jane Marple **12** Blithe Spirit **27** The Importance of Being Earnest

Rutherford, Ernest
field: **7** physics
nationality: **7** British
discovered: **6** proton **13** atomic nucleus, beta radiation **14** alpha radiation, gamma radiation
awarded: **10** Nobel Prize

ruthless **5** cruel, harsh **6** brutal, deadly, savage **7** bestial, brutish, callous, inhuman, vicious **8** pitiless **9** barbarous, ferocious, heartless, merciless, murderous, unfeeling, unpitying, unsparing **10** relentless, sanguinary, unmerciful **11** cold-blooded, hardhearted, remorseless, unforgiving, unrelenting **12** bloodthirsty

ruthlessness **7** cruelty **9** barbarity, brutality, harshness **10** inhumanity, savageness **11** viciousness

Ruysdael, Salomon van
born: **7** Naarden **14** The Netherlands
nephew: **16** Jacob van Ruisdael
artwork: **9** River Bank **10** River Scene **14** River Landscape **18** River with Ferry Boat

Rwanda ***see box, p. 853***

Ryan, Cornelius
author of: **13** A Bridge Too Far, The Last Battle, The Longest Day

Ryan, Robert
born: **9** Chicago IL
roles: **6** Caught **8** The Set-Up **9** Billy Budd, Crossfire **12** Clash by Night, The Wild Bunch **13** Act of Vio-

Russia

other name: **4** USSR **11** Soviet Union **31** Union of Soviet Socialist Republics
capital/largest city: **6** Moscow
others: **4** Baku, Eisk, Kiev, Okha, Omsk, Poti, Riga **5** Anapa, Batum, Gorki, Gorky, Memel, Minsk, Sochi, Vilna, Yeisk **6** Batumi, Erevan, Frunze, Odessa, Rostov, Samara, Tiflis **7** Alma-Ata, Derbent, Donetsk, Kharkov, Liepaja, Petsamo, Pivonia, Saratov, Tallinn, Tbilisi, Yerevan **8** Dushanbe, Kishinev, Murmansk, Pechenga, Taganrog, Tashkent **9** Ashkhabad, Astrakhan, Balaklava, Kronstadt, Kuibyshev, Leningrad, Nikolayev, Petrograd, Ulyanovsk, Volgograd, Yaroslavl **10** Kronshtadt, Sevastopol, Stalingrad, Sverdlovsk **11** Chelyabinsk, Kaliningrad, Makhachkala, Novorossisk, Novosibirsk, Vladivostok **12** St Petersburg, Vladisvostok **14** Dnepropetrovsk
division: **6** Latvia **7** Armenia, Estonia, Georgia, Siberia, Ukraine **8** Moldavia **9** Kirghizia, Lithuania, Turkmenia **10** Azerbaijan, Belorussia, Kazakhstan, Uzbekistan **12** Tadzhikistan
former: **4** Kiev **8** Novgorod
government:
legislature: **4** Duma, Rada **7** Zemstvo
measure: **3** fut, lof **4** duim, fass, loof, pood, quar, stof **5** duime, foute, korec, korek, ligne, osmin, pajak, stoff, stoof, vedro, verst **6** charka, liniya, osmina, paletz, sagene, stekar, tchast, tsarki, versta, verste **7** archine, arsheen, botchka, chkalik, garnetz, verchoc, verchok **8** boutylka, chetvert, krouchka, kroushka **9** chetverik **10** dessiatine **11** polugarnetz
monetary unit: **5** altin, bisti, copec, denga, grosh, kopek, ruble, shaur **6** abassi, copeck, grivna, kopeck, piatak, rouble **7** poltina, valiuta **8** auksinas, deneshka, imperial, polushka **9** poltinnik **10** altininink, chervonets
weight: **3** lof, lot **4** dola, funt, lana, last, loof, loth, once, pood, poud **5** dolia
island: **5** Kuril **7** Hiiumaa, Karagin, Shantar, Vaygach, Wrangel **8** Kolguyev, Saaremaa, Sakhalin **9** Andreanof **12** Novaya Zemlya **13** Komandorskiye **14** Franz Josef Land, Novosibirskiye **15** Severnaya Zemlya
lake: **3** Seg **4** Aral, Azov, Kola, Neva, Sego, Topo, Vigo **5** Chany, Elton, Erara, Ilmen, Lacha, Onega, Pskov, Vozhe **6** Baikal, Byeloe, Ladoga, Peipus, Selety, Taymyr, Tengiz, Zaysan **8** Balkhash **10** Caspian Sea
mountain: **5** Altai, Lenin, Sayan, Urals **6** Anadyr, Elbrus, Koryak, Pamirs, Pobedy **7** Belukha, Crimean, Khibiny, Stanovi, Zhiguli **8** Caucasus, Dzhughur, Stanavoi, Tien Shan **9** Kopet Dagh, Narodnaya, Pamir-Alai, Yablonovy **10** Carpathian **11** Sikhote-Alin, Verkhoyansk
highest point: **9** Communism
river: **3** Don, Ili **4** Amur, Lena, Neva, Ural **5** Dvina, Kuban, Neman, Volga **6** Kolyma, Moskva **7** Dnieper, Pechora, Yenisei **8** Amu Darya, Dniester, Ob-Irtysh, Syr Darya **9** Indigirka
sea: **4** Aral, Azov, Kara **5** Black, Japan, White **6** Arctic, Baltic, Bering, Laptev **7** Barents, Caspian, Chukchi, Okhotsk, Pacific **12** East Siberian
physical feature:
bay: **2** Ob
gulf: **4** Azov **5** Mezen **9** Kara-Bogaz, Shelikhov
peninsula: **4** Kola **5** Yamal **6** Crimea, Taymyr **7** Chukchi, Karelia **9** Kamchatka **10** Mangyshlak
strait: **5** Tatar **6** Bering **8** Bosporus **11** Dardanelles
people: **3** Jew **4** Slav **5** Ersar, Kulak, Tatar, Uzbec **6** Kazakh, Soviet, Velika **7** Chukchi, Cossack, Kirghiz, Latvian, Russian, Tadzhik, Turkmen **8** Armenian, Estonian, Georgian, Siberian **9** Moldavian, Ukrainian **10** Lithuanian **11** Azerbaijani, Belorussian
actor: **12** Stanislavsky
author: **5** Gogol **7** Nabokov, Pushkin, Tolstoy **8** Turgenev **9** Ehrenburg, Pasternak, Sholokhov **10** Dostoevsky **12** Solzhenitsyn
composer: **6** Glinka **7** Borodin **9** Prokofiev **10** Mussorgsky, Stravinsky **11** Tchaikovsky **12** Rachmaninoff, Shostakovich **14** Rimsky-Korsakov
cosmonaut: **11** Yuri Gagarin
czar/tsar/tzar: **4** Ivan, Paul **5** Peter **6** Alexis **7** Michael **8** Nicholas **9** Alexander **12** Boris Godunov
dancer: **7** Nureyev, Pavlova **8** Danilova, Nijinsky **11** Baryshnikov
dynasty: **7** Romanov
early people: **3** Hun **4** Goth **5** Tatar **6** Khazar, Mongol, Tartar **8** Norsemen, Scythian **9** Cimmerian, Sarmatian, Varangian
empress: **9** Alexandra, Catherine
hereditary noble: **5** boyar
leader: **5** Beria, Lenin **6** Stalin, Suslov **7** Gromyko, Kosygin, Molotov, Trotsky **8** Andropov, Brezhnev, Bukharin, Bulganin, Kerensky, Malenkov, Podgorny **9** Chernenko, Gorbachev **10** Khrushchev
monk: **8** Rasputin
prince: **4** Oleg **5** Rurik **8** Vladimir
revolutionary: **10** Decembrist
ruler: **5** Tatar **6** Mongol **8** Batu Khan
scientist: **6** Pavlov **9** Mendeleev **11** Tsiolkovsky

language: **5** Evenk, Tatar, Uzbek **6** Buriat, Kalmyk, Kazakh **7** Finnish, Kirghiz, Latvian, Russian, Tadzhik, Turkmen **8** Armenian, Estonian, Georgian, Ossetian **9** Moldavian, Ukrainian **10** Lithuanian **11** Belorussian
alphabet: **8** cyrillic
religion: **5** Islam **7** Judaism **8** Buddhism, Lutheran **10** Protestant **13** Roman Catholic **15** Russian Orthodox **16** Armenian Orthodox, Georgian Orthodox
place: **7** Kremlin **9** Red Square
art gallery: **9** Tretyakov
castle: **8** Starosty
cathedral: **5** Sobor **7** Zagorsk **8** St Basils
cemetery: **11** Piskarevsky
museum: **9** Hermitage **12** Petrodvorets **18** Cathedral of St Isaac
palace: **6** Winter
park: **5** Gorky
reservoir: **5** Gorki, Volga **7** Rybinsk **9** Kuibyshev
ruins: **7** Bukhara **10** Echmiadzin **15** Gediminas Castle
street: **11** Kreshchatik **14** Nevski Prospekt
theater: **7** Bolshoi
war memorial: **11** Kurgan Slavi
feature:
collective farm: **7** kolkhoz
country house: **5** dacha
dance: **4** kolo **5** gopac, hopak, saber **6** cossac, trepak **7** cosaque, ziganka **8** kozachok **9** tzazatski
dance company: **13** Bolshoi Ballet
labor camp: **5** gulag
musical instrument: **9** balalaika
state farm: **7** sovkhoz
food:
caviar: **13** ikra zernistia
cereal: **5** kasha
sour cream: **7** smetana
dessert: **8** vareniki
dish: **4** plov **5** pirau **6** pelemo **8** osetrina, shashlyk **16** kotleta po kievski
drink: **4** kvas **5** kvass, vodka **6** chacha, kumiss
filled pastries: **8** piroshki, pirozhki
soup: **5** shchi **6** borsch

Rwanda
other name: **6** Ruanda
capital/largest city: **6** Kigali
others: **6** Biumba, Butare, Kibuye, Nyanza **7** Astrida, Gisenyi, Kibungu **8** Cyangugu **9** Ruhengeri
division:
colonial: **12** Ruanda-Urundi
monetary unit: **5** franc **7** centime
lake: **4** Kivu **5** Ihema **6** Bufera, Bulera, Mohasi **7** Rugwero, Ruhnodo **8** Mugesera, Tshohoha
mountain: **7** Mitumba, Virunga **8** Muhavura
highest point: **9** Karisimbi
river: **6** Kagera, Ruzizi **7** Akagera **8** Akanyaru **9** Luvironza **10** Nyawarongo
physical feature:
forest: **7** Nyungwe
valley: **11** Western Rift
people: **3** Twa **4** Hutu **5** Batwa, Pygmy, Tutsi **6** Bahutu, Watusi **7** Batutsi
explorer: **5** Speke **6** Gotzen
leader: **9** Kayibanda **11** Habyarimana
language: **6** French **7** Swahili **11** Kinyarwanda
religion: **7** animism **13** Roman Catholic
place:
game reserve: **6** Gabiro
park: **6** Albert, Kagera **16** Virunga Volcanoes
feature:
clothing: **5** pagne
king: **5** mwami

lence, The Longest Day **14** About Mrs Leslie, God's Little Acre **17** Bad Day at Black Rock **18** The Woman on the Beach

Ryder, Albert Pinkham
born: **12** New Bedford MA
artwork: **12** The Race Track (Death on a Pale Horse) **15** Toilers of the Sea **27** Siegfried and the Rhine Maidens

rye **6** Secale
varieties: **4** wild **5** giant **6** common **8** Aral wild, blue wild **9** Altai wild, giant wild, Volga wild **10** Canada wild **11** Chinese wild, Russian wild **12** Siberian wild, Virginia wild
type: **6** liquor **7** whiskey
origin: **7** Ireland **8** Scotland
ingredient: **10** mash grains
drink: **9** Cablegram **11** John Collins, Whiskey Sour
with Cointreau: **10** Temptation
with Pernod: **3** TNT
with vermouth: **8** Brooklyn **9** Algonquin

Saarinen, Eero
father: **5** Eliel
architect of: **11** St Louis Arch **20** Gateway to the West Arch (St Louis) **26** Trans World Airlines Terminal (NYC) **28** General Motors Technical Center (Warren MI) **39** Columbia Broadcasting Company Headquarters (NYC)
style: **13** International

Saarinen, Eliel
son: **4** Eero
architect of: **16** Cranbrook Academy (Bloomfield Hills MI) **18** Kleinhaus Music Hall (Buffalo) **19** Tanglewood Music Shed (MA) **20** Christ Lutheran Church (Minneapolis MN), First Christian Church (Columbus IN)

Saba *see* **5** Sheba

Sabaoth **6** armies

Sabbath **8** Lord's Day **9** day of rest

Sabbatical: A Romance
author: **9** John Barth

saber, sabre **3** cut **4** kill, stab **5** blade, sword, wound **6** cutlas, rapier, strike **7** cutlass, soldier **8** scimitar **10** broadsword

Sabin, Albert Bruce
field: **8** medicine
developed: **16** oral polio vaccine

sable **3** fur, jet **4** dark, inky **5** black, ebony, raven

sabotage **3** sap **6** retard **7** cripple, destroy, disable, disrupt, subvert **8** paralyze **9** undermine, vandalize **10** subversion **12** incapacitate

sabra **11** Israeli-born **14** native of Israel

Sabra
type: **7** liqueur
origin: **6** Israel
flavor: **6** orange **9** chocolate

Sac *see* **4** Sauk

saccharine **5** gooey, mushy, soppy, sweet **6** sugary, syrupy **7** candied, cloying, honeyed, maudlin, mawkish, sugared **9** offensive, oversweet, revolting, sickening **10** disgusting, nauseating **11** sentimental

sacerdotal **5** papal **8** clerical, pastoral, priestly **9** apostolic, canonical, episcopal **10** pontifical **11** ministerial **12** hierarchical **14** ecclesiastical

sack **3** bag, rob **4** loot, pack, raid **5** pouch, spoil, store, waste **6** duffel, maraud, rapine, ravage, tear up **7** despoil, pillage, plunder, ransack **8** spoliate **9** depredate, duffel bag, gunnysack, haversack, marauding **10** plundering, ravishment **11** depredation, devastation **12** despoliation

Sackbut **18** Biblical instrument

Sackville, Thomas
author of: **8** Gorboduc (with Thomas Norton)

sacrament **3** vow **4** rite **5** troth **6** pledge, plight, ritual **7** liturgy, promise, service **8** ceremony, contract, covenant **9** solemnity **10** ceremonial, obligation, observance **11** affirmation **12** ministration

sacramental **4** holy **6** ritual **7** blessed **10** ceremonial, liturgical

Sacraments, Seven **7** Baptism, Penance **9** Eucharist, Last Rites, Matrimony **10** Holy Orders **12** Confirmation **13** Holy Communion **14** Extreme Unction, Reconciliation **18** Anointing of the Sick

sacred **4** holy **6** church **7** blessed, revered **8** Biblical, hallowed, hieratic **9** religious, venerable **10** sanctified, scriptural **11** consecrated **14** ecclesiastical

Sacred and Profane Love Machine, The
author: **11** Iris Murdoch

Sacred writings **5** Bible **11** Bibliotheca

sacrifice **4** cede, loss **5** forgo, waive **6** forego, give up, homage **7** cession, forfeit, offer up **8** immolate, oblation, offering, renounce **9** surrender **10** concession, immolation, lustration, relinquish **12** renunciation **14** relinquishment

sacrilege **3** sin **7** impiety, mockery, outrage **8** iniquity **9** blasphemy, profanity, violation **10** irreligion, sinfulness, wickedness **11** desecration, impiousness, irreverence, profanation, profaneness

sacrilegious **7** impious, profane **10** irreverent **11** blasphemous, irreligious

sacrosanct **4** holy **5** godly **6** divine, solemn **8** hallowed, heavenly **9** celestial, inviolate, religious, spiritual **10** inviolable, unexamined **11** consecrated **12** unquestioned

sacrum
bone of: **11** base of spine

sad **3** low **4** blue, grim, hard, hurt **5** grave **6** dismal, solemn, taxing, tragic, trying, woeful **7** adverse, crushed, doleful, forlorn, grieved, joyless, maudlin, pitiful, serious, unhappy **8** dejected, desolate, downcast, grievous, mournful, pathetic, touching, troubled, wretched **9** cheerless, depressed, difficult, miserable, sorrowful **10** calamitous, chapfallen, despairing, despondent, dispirited, distressed, lachrymose, lament-

able, melancholy **11** crestfallen, distressing, pessimistic, troublesome, unfortunate **12** disconsolate, heartrending, heavyhearted, inconsolable **13** brokenhearted, grief-stricken, heartbreaking **14** down in the dumps, down in the mouth
French: **6** triste

Sadat, Anwar el-
president of: **5** Egypt
awarded: **15** Nobel Peace Prize
author of: **18** In Search of Identity

sadden **4** damp, dash **5** crush **6** burden, deject, grieve, sorrow, subdue **7** depress **8** aggrieve, dispirit **10** discourage, dishearten

saddle with **9** stick with **10** burden with **12** encumber with **18** make responsible for

Sade, Marquis de
author of: **7** Justine **8** Juliette

sadistic **6** brutal **7** vicious **8** fiendish, perverse **9** perverted **12** bloodthirsty

Sadness
author: **15** Donald Barthelme

sadness
French: **9** tristesse

sad poem **5** elegy **6** lament

Sad Sack
creator: **11** George Baker

Saehrimnir
origin: **12** Scandinavian
form: **4** boar
served in: **8** Valhalla
feat: **12** regeneration

safe **4** firm, sure, wary **5** sound, vault, whole **6** intact, modest, secure, stable, steady, unhurt **7** certain, guarded, prudent **8** cautious, defended, discreet, harmless, reliable, unbroken, unharmed **9** innocuous, protected, undamaged, unexposed, unscathed **10** dependable, protecting **11** circumspect, impregnable, out of danger, trustworthy, unscratched **12** conservative, invulnerable, noncommittal

safeguard **4** ward **5** armor, charm **6** amulet, buffer, defend, harbor, screen, secure, shield **7** bulwark, defense, fortify, protect, shelter **8** conserve, garrison, preserve, security, talisman **10** precaution, protection

safekeeping **4** care **6** charge **7** custody **8** security **9** husbandry **10** protection **12** conservation, guardianship, preservation

Safety Net, The
author: **12** Heinrich Boll

saffron
botanical name: **13** Crocus sativus
also called: **6** Krokus
Moorish: **6** Zafran
of all spices most: **6** costly
color: **6** orange, yellow **12** yellow-orange
used as: **8** coloring, cosmetic, medicine **9** fabric dye
origin: **5** Egypt, Syria **8** Holy Land **9** Palestine
use: **4** rice **5** bread, rolls

sag **3** bow, dip **4** drop, fail, flag, flap, flop, keel, lean, list, sink, sway, tilt, tire **5** droop, pitch, slump, weary **6** billow, plunge, settle, weaken **7** decline, descend, give way **8** diminish

saga **4** epic, myth, tale, yarn **6** legend **7** history, romance **9** adventure, chronicle, narrative
French: **11** roman-fleuve

sagacious **4** foxy, wise **5** acute, canny, sharp, smart, sound **6** astute, brainy, clever, shrewd **7** cunning, knowing, prudent, sapient, tactful **8** discreet, rational, sensible **9** judicious, practical **10** diplomatic, discerning, perceptive **11** calculating, intelligent **13** perspicacious **14** discriminating

sagacity **6** acumen, brains, smarts, wisdom **8** sapience **9** canniness, smartness **10** astuteness, braininess, cleverness, shrewdness **11** discernment **12** intelligence, perspicacity **13** judiciousness **14** discrimination

Sagan, Carl
author of: **6** Cosmos **7** Contact **16** The Dragons of Eden

Sagan, Francoise
real name: **16** Francoise Quoirez
author of: **13** A Certain Smile **15** Aimez-vous Brahms **16** Bonjour Tristesse

sage **4** guru, wise **5** sound **6** astute, pundit, savant, shrewd **7** egghead, knowing, prudent, sapient, scholar, wise man **8** mandarin, sensible **11** intelligent, philosopher
French: **6** savant
Latin: **5** magus, solon

sage **6** Salvia **12** S officinalis
varieties: **3** bog **4** baby, blue, gray, rose, sand, wood **5** black, lilac, Texas, white **6** autumn, common, desert, garden, purple, silver, yellow **7** bladder, gentian, scarlet, Spanish, thistle, Vervain **8** creeping, gray ball, mealy-cup, rose-leaf **9** Bethlehem, Jerusalem **11** Mexican bush **16** pineapple-scented
means: **6** to heal, to save
strengthens: **6** memory, wisdom **8** prudence
makes men: **8** immortal
origin: **7** Albania **10** Yugoslavia **13** Mediterranean
use: **4** pork **6** breads, cheese **7** chicken, poultry, seafood **8** stuffing

Sage of Concord
nickname of: **17** Ralph Waldo Emerson

Sagittarius
symbol: **6** archer **7** centaur
planet: **7** Jupiter
rules: **10** philosophy **15** higher education
born: **8** December, November

Sagittary
form: **7** centaur
carried: **3** bow

said **5** above, quoth **6** quoted, spoken, stated **7** related, uttered **8** repeated

Saigon
capital of: **7** Vietnam

sail **3** fly **4** boat, scud, skim, soar **5** drift, float, glide, steam **6** course, cruise, voyage **8** navigate **9** excursion

sailboat **4** saic, yawl **5** craft, ketch, sloop, yacht **6** vessel **7** sunfish **8** schooner **9** catamaran
part: **4** boom, mast **6** canvas **7** rigging **9** mainsheet

sailcloth **4** duck **6** canvas

Sailing to Byzantium
author: **7** W B Yeats

sailor **3** gob, tar **4** salt **6** sea dog, seaman **7** mariner, voyager **8** deckhand, seafarer **9** navigator, yachtsman

sailors
goddess of: **5** Brizo **11** Britomartis

Sails (of Argo)
constellation of: **4** Vela

saint **6** martyr
Buddhist: **5** arhat **11** bodhisattva
Chinese: **8** immortal
Islamic: **3** pir
lives of the saints: **8** menology **9** hagiology **11** hagiography **13** acta sanctorum
process of becoming: **12** canonization

relic box: **6** chasse
remains: **5** relic
symbol: **4** halo

Saint, Eva Marie
born: **8** Newark NJ
roles: **6** Exodus **15** On the Waterfront **16** North by Northwest

saint, patron ***see box***

Saint, The
author: **16** Antonio Fogazzaro

Saint, The
author: **15** Leslie Charteris
character: **12** Simon Templar **26** Inspector Claude Eustace Teal
cast: **10** Roger Moore

Saint Anthony's fire
6 herpes **8** ergotism, shingles **10** erysipelas

Sainte-Beuve, Charles Augustin
author of: **19** Monday Conversations

Saint Elmo's fire **5** flame, hermo **6** castor, corona, furole, helena **9** corposant **12** luminescence

Saint Esprit **9** Holy Ghost **10** Holy Spirit

Saint-Exupery, Antoine de
author of: **11** Night Flight **12** Southern Mail **15** The Little Prince **16** Wind Sand and Stars

Saint Francis
born: **6** Assisi
called: **9** Poverello

Saint-Gaudens, Augustus
born: **6** Dublin **7** Ireland
artwork: **7** Puritan **13** Mrs Henry Adams (Grief) **14** General Sherman **15** Admiral Farragut **16** President Lincoln

Saint Jack
author: **11** Paul Theroux

Saint Joan
author: **17** George Bernard Shaw

Saint John's bread **5** carob

Saint John's wort **5** amber **6** tutsan **7** ascyrum, cammock **9** androseme, hypericum, rosin-rose **10** broombrush **11** Aaron's-beard

saintliness **6** purity **8** goodness, holiness **9** beatitude, godliness **11** blessedness **12** spirituality

Saint Lucia, St Lucia
capital: **8** Castries
highest point: **5** Gimie
island group: **8** Windward **14** Lesser Antilles
language: **6** patois
location: **9** Caribbean

saint, patron
acolytes: **13** John Berchmans
actors: **8** Genesius
artists: **4** Luke
astronomers: **7** Dominic
athletes: **9** Sebastian
authors: **14** Francis de Sales
aviators: **15** Our Lady of Loreto **16** Therese of Lisieux **17** Joseph of Cupertino
bakers: **8** Nicholas **18** Elizabeth of Hungary
bankers: **7** Matthew
barbers: **5** Louis **6** Cosmas, Damian
barren women: **9** Felicitas **14** Anthony of Padua
beggars/cripples: **5** Giles
blind: **6** Odilia **7** Raphael
bodily ills: **16** Our Lady of Lourdes
boy scouts: **6** George
brides: **14** Nicholas of Myra
builders: **13** Vincent Ferrer
butchers: **4** Luke **7** Hadrian **14** Anthony of Egypt
carpenters: **6** Joseph
cancer patients: **9** Peregrine
children: **10** Santa Claus **14** Nicholas of Myra
comedians: **5** Vitus
cooks: **6** Martha **8** Lawrence
deaf: **14** Francis de Sales
dying: **6** Joseph **7** Barbara
emigrants: **14** Frances Cabrini
England: **6** George
eye sufferers: **4** Lucy
falsely accused: **15** Raymond Nonnatus
farmers: **6** George **7** Isidore
fishermen: **5** Peter **6** Andrew
foreign missions: **13** Francis Xavier **16** Therese of Lisieux
foundlings: **13** Holy Innocents
France: **5** Denis
gardeners: **6** Fiacre, Phocas **7** Adelard, Dorothy, Tryphon
heart patients: **9** John of God
hospitals: **9** John of God **12** Jude Thaddeus **16** Camillus de Lellis
housewives: **4** Anne
hunters: **6** Hubert **10** Eustachius
invalids: **4** Roch
Ireland: **7** Patrick
Italy: **7** Anthony
laborers: **5** James **7** Isidore **9** John Bosco
lawyers: **3** Ivo **4** Ives **8** Genesius **10** Thomas More
librarians: **6** Jerome
lovers: **9** Valentine
mariners: **7** Michael **19** Nicholas of Tolentino
mentally ill: **6** Dympna

saintly **4** good, holy **5** godly, moral, pious **6** devout **7** angelic, blessed, exalted, sinless, upright **8** beatific, faithful, reverent, virtuous **9** believing, religious, righteous, spiritual **10** benevolent

Saint Paul
born: **6** Tarsus
companion: **4** Luke
epistle: **5** Titus **6** Romans **7** Hebrews, Timothy **8** Philemon **9** Ephesians, Galatians **10** Colossians **11** Corinthians, Philippians **13** Thessalonians

Saint Paul's Cathedral (London)
architect: **4** Wren

Saint Peter
called: **4** Rock **5** Simon **6** Cephas
brother: **6** Andrew

Saint-Saens, (Charles) Camille
born: **5** Paris **6** France
composer of: **12** Danse Macabre **14** Samson et Dalila **16** Samson and Delilah

merchants: 14 Nicholas of Myra 15 Francis of Assisi
metalworkers: 7 Eligius
miners: 7 Barbara
mothers: 6 Monica
musicians: 7 Cecilia, Dunstan 15 Gregory the Great
Norway: 4 Olaf
nurses: 6 Agatha 7 Alexius, Raphael 9 John of God 16 Camillus de Lellis
painters: 4 Luke
philosophers: 6 Justin 21 Catherine of Alexandria
physicians: 4 Luke 6 Cosmas, Damian 7 Raphael 9 Pantaleon
pilgrims: 5 James 7 Alexius
poets: 5 David 7 Cecilia
policemen: 7 Michael
poor souls: 19 Nicholas of Tolentino
postal workers: 7 Gabriel
priests: 19 Jean-Baptiste Vianney
printers: 8 Genesius 9 John of God 16 Augustine of Hippo
prisoners: 6 Dismas 7 Barbara 13 Joseph Cafasso
rheumatism: 15 James the Greater
sailors: 4 Elmo 7 Brendan, Erasmus, Eulalia 8 Cuthbert, Nicholas 11 Christopher 13 Peter Gonzales
scholars: 6 Brigid
scientists: 6 Albert
Scotland: 6 Andrew
sculptors: 6 Claude
seamen: 14 Francis of Paolo
sick: 7 Michael 9 John of God 16 Camillus de Lellis
singers: 7 Cecilia, Gregory
skiers: 7 Bernard
shoemakers: 7 Crispin
soldiers: 6 George 7 Hadrian 8 Ignatius 9 Joan of Arc, Sebastian 13 Martin of Tours
Spain: 5 James 8 Santiago
students: 13 Thomas Aquinas 21 Catherine of Alexandria
surgeons: 6 Cosmas, Damian
tailors: 9 Homobonus
tax collectors: 7 Matthew
teachers: 15 Gregory the Great 21 Catherine of Alexandria, Jean Baptiste de la Salle
theologians: 9 Augustine 16 Alphonsus Liguori
throat sufferers: 6 Blaise
travelers: 7 Raphael 11 Christopher 14 Anthony of Padua, Nicholas of Myra
Wales: 5 David
winegrowers: 7 Vincent
workingmen: 6 Joseph
writers: 14 Francis de Sales
youth: 13 John Berchmans 15 Aloysius Gonzaga, Gabriel Possenti

18 La Jeunesse d'Hercule 20 Carnival of the Animals

Saints' lives
writer of: 12 hagiographer

Saint Vincent, St Vincent
capital: 9 Kingstown
highest point: 9 Soufriere
Indian: 5 Carib 6 Arawak
island group: 8 Windward 14 Lesser Antilles
islands: 10 Grenadines
language: 6 patois
location: 9 Caribbean
volcano: 9 Soufriere

Saint Vitus' dance 6 chorea

Saitis *see* 6 Athena

sake 3 end 4 care, gain, good 5 cause 6 behalf, object, profit, regard 7 account, benefit, concern, purpose, respect, welfare 8 interest 9 advantage 11 enhancement 13 consideration

sake
type: 4 wine 6 spirit
origin: 5 Japan
ingredient: 4 rice

Sakharov, Andrei Dimitrievich
field: 7 physics
nationality: 7 Russian
researched: 14 nuclear fission
defended: 12 civil liberty
exiled to: 5 Gorky
awarded: 10 Nobel Prize

Saki
real name: 7 H H Munro
author of: 8 Reginald 20 Beasts and Super-Beasts 21 The Chronicles of Clovis 23 The Unbearable Bassington

salaam 3 bow 6 homage 9 obeisance

Salacia
partner of: 7 Neptune

salacious 4 lewd, sexy 7 lustful, obscene 8 indecent 9 lecherous 10 lascivious, libidinous 12 pornographic

salad days 5 prime, youth 6 heyday 9 flowering

salamander 3 eft 4 newt 5 giant, siren, tiger 6 lizard, red eft 7 axolotl, urodela 8 congo eel, mudpuppy 9 amphibian, fire-eater, proteidae 10 hellbender, necturidae 14 red-spotted newt

Salamis
father: 6 Asopus
mother: 6 Metope
son: 8 Cychreus

Salammbo
author: 15 Gustave Flaubert
character: 5 Matho 8 Hamilcar, Spendius 9 Narr Havas
setting: 8 Carthage

salary 3 pay 5 wages 6 income 7 stipend 8 earnings 9 allowance, emolument 10 recompense 12 remuneration

sale 3 cut 7 bargain, selling, special 8 discount, exchange, markdown, transfer 9 reduction

Salem
home of: 11 Melchizedek

salesperson 5 agent, clerk 6 vendor 8 huckster

salient 6 arrant, marked 7 glaring, notable, obvious 8 flagrant, manifest, palpable, striking 9 egregious, important, prominent 10 noteworthy, noticeable, pronounced, protruding, remarkable 11 conspicuous, outstanding, substantial 12 considerable

Salii
also: 6 Salian
form: 7 priests
priests of: 4 Mars

guarded: 7 ancilia 13 sacred shields

saline 4 salt 5 briny, salty 8 brackish

Salinger, J D
author of: 14 Franny and Zooey 18 The Catcher in the Rye

Salisbury
capital of: 8 Zimbabwe

Salisbury, Harrison E
author of: 16 American in Russia 19 A Journey for Our Times, Black Night White Snow

Salish (Flatheads)
language family: 8 Salishan
location: 5 Idaho 6 Oregon 7 Montana 10 Washington 15 British Columbia

Salishan
tribe: 6 Salish 8 Puyallop 9 Flatheads

Salk, Jonas Edward
field: 8 medicine
developed: 12 (inactivated) polio vaccine

salle a manger 10 dining room
literally: 13 hall for eating

sallow 3 wan 4 gray, pale 5 ashen, livid 6 anemic, pallid, sickly, yellow 7 bilious 9 jaundiced, washed-out, yellowish

sallowness 6 pallor 7 wanness 8 paleness 10 sickliness 11 biliousness 13 colorlessness, yellowishness

Sallust
author of: 9 Histories 13 War of Jugurtha 20 Conspiracy of Catiline

sally 3 mot 4 flow, pour, quip, raid, trip 5 erupt, foray, surge 6 attack, banter, charge, outing, retort, sortie, spring, thrust 7 debouch, journey 8 badinage, repartee 9 excursion, wisecrack, witticism 10 expedition 13 counterattack

Salmacis
form: 5 nymph
loved: 14 Hermaphroditus
joined with: 14 Hermaphroditus
became: 13 hermaphrodite 14 bisexual person

Salmagundi
author: 16 Washington Irving

salmon 4 fish, king 5 cohoe 6 silver 7 chinook, Pacific, quinnat, sockeye, spawner 8 Atlantic, humpback
enclosure: 4 yair
female: 4 raun 6 baggit
genus: 12 Oncorhynchus
hatchling: 4 pink 6 alevin
male: 3 gib 4 buck, cock
post-spawning: 4 kelt 7 shedder
pre-spawning: 7 gilling, girling
young: 4 parr 7 essling

Salmoneus
father: 6 Aeolus
mother: 7 Enarete
brother: 8 Sisyphus
wife: 6 Sidero 8 Alcidice
daughter: 4 Tyro
struck by: 9 lightning

Salome
father: 11 Herod Philip
mother: 8 Herodias
husband: 7 Zebedee
opera by: 7 (Richard) Strauss
character: 5 Herod (the Tetrarch) 8 Herodias, Jokanaan (John the Baptist) 9 Narraboth

salon 4 hall 7 gallery 11 drawing room 13 establishment

saloon 3 bar, inn, pub 6 bistro, tavern 7 barroom, ginmill, taproom 8 alehouse 9 roadhouse, speakeasy

salt 3 wit 4 best, corn, cure, pick, save 5 brine, briny, cream, elect, humor, savor, smack, souse, spice 6 choice, flavor, pickle, saline, season, select 8 brackish, marinate, piquancy, pungency 9 seasoning 12 quintessence

Salten, Felix
author of: 5 Bambi

salt water 3 sea 5 brine, ocean

salty 4 racy 5 briny, funny, spicy, terse, witty 6 corned, ribald, risque, saline 7 pungent, zestful 8 brackish, improper

salubrious 7 bracing, healthy 9 healthful, wholesome 10 beneficial, lifegiving 11 therapeutic 12 invigorating

salubriousness 11 healthiness 13 healthfulness, wholesomeness

Salus
origin: 5 Roman
goddess of: 6 health 10 prosperity
corresponds to: 6 Hygeia

salutary 4 good 5 tonic 6 useful 7 healing, healthy 8 curative, sanitary 9 healthful, wholesome 10 beneficial, profitable 12 advantageous

salutation 3 bow 5 hello, howdy, toast 6 curtsy 7 address, welcome 8 greeting 9 reception
Hawaiian: 5 aloha
Italian: 4 ciao
Latin: 3 ave

salute 3 ave 4 hail, kiss 5 bow to, cheer, greet, honor, nod to, salvo 6 accost, homage, praise, wave to 7 address, applaud, respect, welcome 8 accolade, applause, greeting 9 laudation, reverence 11 acclamation, recognition 12 congratulate

Salvador
author: 10 Joan Didion

salvage 4 junk, save 5 scrap 6 debris, rescue 7 recover, remains, restore 8 recovery, retrieve 9 retrieval 11 reclamation 12 rehabilitate

salvation 4 rock 5 grace 6 rescue, saving 8 election, lifeline, mainstay, recovery, survival 9 retrieval 10 protection, redemption 11 deliverance, reclamation 12 preservation

salve 4 balm, calm, ease, hail 5 hello 6 lessen, lotion, pacify, reduce, soothe, temper 7 anodyne, assuage, mollify, relieve, unguent 8 dressing, liniment, mitigate, moderate, ointment 9 alleviate, emollient, greetings 11 alleviative

salver 4 bowl, dish, tray 6 waiter 7 coaster

salvia 4 herb, mint, sage 5 shrub 8 mejorana 9 artemisia

salvo 5 burst 6 volley 7 barrage, battery 8 shelling 9 cannonade, fusillade 11 bombardment

sambuca
type: 7 liqueur
origin: 5 Italy
flavor: 5 anise 10 elderberry

same 4 like, twin, very 5 alike, equal 6 on a par 7 similar, uniform 8 parallel 9 identical, unchanged 10 consistent, equivalent, invariable 13 corresponding

same as previously given
Latin: 4 idem

sameness 6 parity 8 equality, evenness, likeness, monotony 10 similarity, uniformity 11 homogeneity 14 homogenousness

Samoa ***see box***

Samoyed
language family: 6 Uralic
spoken in: 7 Siberia

sample 3 try 4 test 5 model, taste 7 dip into, examine, example, pattern, portion, segment 8 instance, paradigm,

Samoa
capital:
American Samoa: **8** Pago Pago
Western Samoa: **4** Apia
cities: **6** Utulei **7** Palauli **8** Fagatogo
division: **12** Western Samoa **13** American Samoa
monetary unit: **4** tala
island: **3** Ofu, Tau **4** Rose **5** Aunuu, Manua, Namua, Upolu **6** Manono, Nuulua, Savaii, Swains **7** Apolima, Nu-utele, Olosega, Tutuila **8** Nuusafee
mountain: **4** Vaea **5** Alava **6** Savaii **7** Matafao **9** Rainmaker
highest point: **4** Fito **8** Silisili
sea: **12** South Pacific
physical feature:
bay: **5** Afono, Leone **6** Fagasa, Falefa, Safata **7** Lafanga, Masefau, Matautu **8** Massacre, Salealua **9** Saluofata
people: **6** Samoan **10** Polynesian
explorer: **9** Roggeveen **12** Bougainville
language: **6** Samoan **7** English
religion: **6** Mormon **9** Methodist **13** Roman Catholic **15** Latter Day Saints **19** Seventh-Day Adventist **26** Congregational Christianity
feature:
bird: **3** iao **4** lulu, lupe **6** manuao, manuma, maomao **7** manuali **8** manusina, manutagi
chief: **5** matai
chief's daughter: **5** taupo
cloth: **4** para, tapa
clothing: **5** pareu **8** lavalava, puletasi
dance: **4** siva
dwelling: **4** fale
food:
drink: **3** ava

specimen **10** experience **12** cross section, illustration **14** representative **15** exemplification

Sampo
origin: **7** Finnish
stolen by: **9** Ilmarinen **11** Vainamoinen **12** Lemminkainen
stolen from: **5** Louhi

Samson **11** Hebrew judge
father: **6** Manoah
mistress/betrayer: **7** Delilah
hometown: **5** Zorah

Samson Agonistes
author: **10** John Milton

Samuel **11** Hebrew judge
father: **7** Elkanah
mother: **6** Hannah
hometown: **5** Ramah
anointed: **4** Saul **5** David

Sana, Sanaa
capital of: **10** North Yemen

San Antonio
basketball team: **5** Spurs
football team: **11** Gunslingers
landmark: **8** The Alamo **9** River Walk

sanctification **8** blessing **9** hallowing **12** consecration
Hebrew: **7** Kiddush

sanctified **4** holy **6** sacred **7** blessed **8** hallowed **11** consecrated

sanctify **5** bless, exalt **6** anoint, hallow, purify, uphold **7** absolve, beatify, cleanse **8** dedicate, enshrine, make holy **10** consecrate, legitimate, legitimize **12** legitimatize

sanctimonious **6** solemn **7** canting, pompous, preachy **8** unctuous **9** overblown, pietistic **11** pharisaical, pretentious **14** holier-than-thou

sanctimoniousness **4** cant, sham **6** humbug **9** hypocrisy **11** insincerity **15** pretentiousness

sanction **5** allow, favor, leave **6** accept, assent, permit, ratify **7** agree to, approve, consent, endorse, liberty, license, penalty, support **8** approval, coercion, pressure **9** authority, authorize **10** legitimate, permission **11** countenance, endorsement **12** commendation, confirmation, ratification **13** authorization

sanctuary **4** park **5** cover, haven **6** asylum, chapel, church, refuge, safety, shrine, temple **7** reserve, retreat, shelter **8** preserve **10** protection

Sanctuary
author: **15** William Faulkner
character: **5** Tommy **6** Popeye **9** Ruby Lamar **10** Lee Goodwin, Reba Rivers **11** Temple Drake **12** Gowan Stevens, Horace Benbow

sanctum sanctorum **12** holy of holies

sanctus **4** holy

Sancus
also: **10** Semo Sancus
origin: **5** Roman
god of: **5** oaths **10** road safety **11** hospitality **20** international affairs
corresponds to: **8** Hercules **10** Dius Fidius

sand **4** grit, guts **5** pluck, spunk **6** mettle **7** bravery, courage, resolve **8** backbone **9** fortitude **10** resolution **12** resoluteness

Sand, George
real name: **14** Aurore Dudevant
author of: **5** Lelia **7** Indiana **8** Consuelo **9** Valentine **13** Story of My Life **14** The Country Waif, The Haunted Pool **17** Fanchon the Cricket **18** Les Maitres Sonneurs **23** The Countess of Rudolstadt

sandal **4** clog, flat, shoe, zori **5** scuff, thong **6** loafer **7** slipper **8** flipflop, huarache, moccasin, overshoe **10** espadrille

sandalwood **5** Algum, Almug

sand bank **4** dune, reef **5** shelf, shoal **7** shallow

sandbar **4** bank, flat, reef, spit **5** shelf, shoal **7** shallow

Sandbox, The
author: **11** Edward Albee

Sandburg, Carl
author of: **3** Fog **7** Chicago **12** Harvest Poems **13** Smoke and Steel **14** Abraham Lincoln, The Cornhuskers **15** Remembrance Rock

Sanders, George
born: **6** Russia **12** St Petersburg
wife: **10** Benita Hume, Magda Gabor **11** Zsa Zsa Gabor
roles: **6** The Fan **7** Ivanhoe, Rebecca **8** The Saint **9** The Falcon **11** All About Eve **12** Forever Amber, The Gay Falcon **18** The Moon and Sixpence **20** Foreign Correspondent **22** The Picture of

Dorian Gray **24** The House of the Seven Gables
autobiography: 25 Memoirs of a Professional Cad

San Diego
airport: 14 Lindbergh Field
area: 7 La Jolla, Old Town **8** Coronado **9** Point Loma **10** Balboa Park, Mission Bay **13** Mission Valley **14** Gaslamp Quarter
baseball team: 6 Padres
football team: 8 Chargers
founder: 13 Junipero Serra
landmark: 11 San Diego Zoo **14** Wild Animal Park **30** Scripps Institute of Oceanography

sandpiper 3 ree **4** bird, ruff **5** reeve, stint, wader **6** common, oxbird, plover **7** fiddler, haybird, spotted, tipbird **8** graybird, sandpeep, shadbird **10** beachrobin

Sands of Iwo Jima
director: 9 Allan Dwan
cast: 8 John Agar **9** Adele Mara, John Wayne **13** Forrest Tucker

sandwich 3 sub **4** club, deli, hero **5** hogie **6** burger, hoagie, insert **7** grinder, western **8** laminate **9** interpose, submarine **10** lamination **11** combination

sane 5 lucid, sober **7** logical **8** all there, balanced, credible, rational, sensible **9** judicious, plausible, sagacious **10** farsighted, reasonable **11** clearheaded, responsible
Latin: 12 compos mentis

Sanford and Son
character: 5 Bubba **6** Melvin **10** Aunt Esther **11** Donna Harris, Fred Sanford, Grady Wilson, Rollo Larson **12** Julio Fuentes, Officer Smith (Smitty) **13** Lamont Sanford
cast: 8 Redd Foxx **9** Don Bexley **11** Hal Williams, LaWanda Page, Slappy White, Whitman Mayo **12** Demond Wilson, Lynn Hamilton **13** Gregory Sierra **15** Nathaniel Taylor

San Francisco
baseball team: 6 Giants
bay: 12 San Francisco
county: 5 Marin **8** San Mateo **12** San Francisco
football team: 11 Forty-Niners
known as: 12 City by the Bay **19** City by the Golden Gate
landmark: 8 Alcatraz **16** Golden Gate Bridge
noted for: 8 cable car **9** earthquake (1906) **26** crookedest street in the world
street/section: 6 Market **7** Lombard, Nob Hill **8** Presidio **9** Chinatown **10** Montgomery **11** Embarcadero, Russian Hill

Sangallensis 16 Greek uncial codex

sangaree, sangria
flavor: 5 fruit, spice

sangfroid 5 poise **6** aplomb **7** balance **8** coolness **9** composure **10** confidence, equanimity **11** tranquility **12** tranquillity **16** imperturbability

sanguine 3 red **4** rosy **5** happy, ruddy, sunny **6** bright, elated, florid **7** buoyant, crimson, flushed, glowing, hopeful, reddish, scarlet **8** blooming, cheerful, inflamed, rubicund **9** confident **10** optimistic **12** lighthearted

Sanhedrin 7 council

sanitarium, sanitorium
8 hospital **11** institution
French: 13 maison de sante

sanitary 5 clean **7** aseptic, healthy, sterile **8** germ-free, hygienic **9** healthful, wholesome **10** salubrious, sterilized, uninfected, unpolluted **11** disinfected **12** prophylactic

sanitorium *see* **10** sanitarium

sanity 5 sense **6** reason **8** lucidity, saneness **9** coherence, normality **11** rationality **12** sensibleness **14** reasonableness **15** clearheadedness

San Jose
capital of: 9 Costa Rica

San Juan
capital of: 10 Puerto Rico

San Juan Bautista *see* **10** Puerto Rico

San Marino *see box*

San Salvador
capital of: 10 El Salvador

sans doute 12 without doubt

Sansovino, Andrea
real name: 14 Andrea Contucci
born: 5 Italy **14** Monte San Savino
artwork: 15 Baptism of Christ **20** Virgin Child and St Anne

Sansovino, Il
real name: 11 Jacopo Tatti
born: 5 Italy **7** Caprese
artwork: 4 Mars **7** Bacchus, Logetta, Neptune **10** Old Library **15** Madonna del Parto **16** St John the Baptist

San Marino
capital/largest city: 9 San Marino
others: 10 Serravalle **13** Borgo Maggiore
division: 8 Castelli
government:
***legislature:* 22** Great and General Council
monetary unit: 4 lira, lire **9** centesimi
mountain: 9 Apennines
highest point: 6 Titano
people: 7 Italian **11** San Marinese
***founder:* 7** Marinus
language: 7 Italian
religion: 13 Roman Catholic
place: 13 Valloni Palace **17** Palazzo del Governo **19** Basilica of San Marino
***church:* 5** Pieve **9** St Francis

sans pareil 12 without equal

sans peur et sans reproche 29 without fear and without reproach

sans souci 8 carefree **11** without care

Santa Cruz de Tenerife
capital of: 13 Canary Islands

Santayana, George
author of: 14 The Last Puritan **16** The Realms of Being, The Sense of Beauty **24** Skepticism and Animal Faith

Santiago
capital of: 5 Chile

Santiago
character in: 18 The Old Man and the Sea
author: 9 Hemingway

Santo Domingo
capital of: 17 Dominican Republic

Santo Domingo *see* **5** Haiti

Sao Tome
capital of: 18 Sao Tome and Principe

Sao Tome and Principe *see box*

sap 3 rob, tax **4** ruin, wear **5** bleed, drain **6** impair, reduce, weaken **7** afflict, cripple, deplete, destroy, disable, exhaust, subvert **8** enervate, enfeeble **9** devastate, undermine **10** debilitate, devitalize

Sao Tome and Principe
capital/largest city: **7** Sao Tome
others: **8** Trindade **11** Porto Alegre **12** Santo Antonio
monetary unit: **5** dobra **6** escudo **7** centavo
highest point: **7** Sao Tome
sea: **8** Atlantic
physical feature:
bay: **11** Ana de Chaves
gulf: **6** Guinea
people: **7** African **10** Portuguese **11** Cape Verdean
explorer: **7** Escobar **8** Santarem
language: **10** Portuguese
religion: **7** animism **13** Roman Catholic **19** Seventh Day Adventist **21** Evangelical Protestant

sapient **4** wise **7** knowing **8** profound **9** sagacious **10** discerning, perceptive **11** intelligent **13** knowledgeable

sap one's energy **3** fag **4** bush, poop, tire **5** drain, weary **6** tucker, weaken **7** deplete, exhaust, fatigue, wash out **8** enervate, enfeeble **10** debilitate, devitalize

Sapphira
husband: **7** Ananias
lied to: **5** Peter

sapphire **3** gem **4** blue **5** azure, jewel **6** indigo
species: **8** corundum
source: **5** Burma, Mogok **6** Ceylon **7** Kashmir **8** Sri Lanka, Thailand **9** Australia
kind: **4** star

Sappho
author: **14** Alphonse Daudet

Sarah, Sarai
father: **5** Asher
former name: **5** Sarai
husband: **7** Abraham
son: **5** Isaac
slave: **5** Hagar
burial place: **9** Machpelah

sarcasm **3** rub **4** gibe, jeer, jest **5** irony, scorn, sneer, taunt **7** mockery **8** contempt, derision, ridicule, scoffing **13** disparagement

sarcastic **5** acerb **6** biting, bitter, ironic **7** caustic, cutting, mocking, mordant **8** derisive, piercing, sardonic, scornful, sneering, stinging, taunting **11** disparaging **12** contemptuous

sarcoma **5** tumor **6** cancer, growth **8** neoplasm **10** malignancy

sarcophagus **4** pall **6** coffin

sard
species: **6** quartz

sardine **4** bang, cram, fish, lile, lour, pack **5** crowd **7** alewife, anchovy, herring **8** pilchard

Sardinia ***see box***

Sardius **8** gemstone

sardonic **6** biting **7** caustic, cynical, jeering, mocking, mordant, satiric **8** derisive, scornful, sneering, taunting **9** sarcastic **11** disparaging **12** contemptuous

Sardonyx **8** gemstone

Sargent, John Singer
born: **5** Italy **8** Florence
artwork: **6** Madam X (Madame Gautreau) **7** El Jaleo **17** The Wyndham Sisters **20** Robert Louis Stevenson **21** Carnation Lily Lily Rose **22** Daughters of Edward D Boit **24** Oyster Gatherers of Cancale

Sargom
captured: **5** Accad
successor: **11** Sennacherib

Saron
king of: **7** Troezen

Saroyan, William
author of: **12** My Name Is Aram **14** The Human Comedy **17** The Time of Your Life **22** My Heart's in the Highlands

Sarpedon
prince of: **5** Lycia
father: **4** Zeus
mother: **6** Europa **8** Laodamia
uncle: **5** Cilix
brother: **5** Minos **12** Rhadamanthys
ally of: **4** Troy
friend: **7** Glaucus
killed by: **9** Patroclus

Sarton, May
author of: **5** Anger **11** Kinds of Love **17** Plant Dreaming Deep **20** Faithful Are the Wounds **33** Mrs Stevens Hears the Mermaids Singing

Sartor Resartus
author: **13** Thomas Carlyle

Sartre, Jean-Paul
author of: **6** Nausea, No Exit **8** The Words **17** The Roads to Freedom **19** Being and Nothingness
philosophy: **14** Existentialism
quote: **17** Hell is other people

sash **3** tie **4** band, belt **5** frame,

Sardinia
other name: **8** Sardegna
capital: **8** Cagliari
cities: **4** Bono, Bosa **5** Nuoro, Olbia **7** Alghero, Bonorva, Sassari, Thatari **8** Iglesias, Oristano **11** Porto Torres
division: **5** Nuoro **7** Arborea, Gallura, Sassari **8** Cagliari, Logudoro
government: **13** region of Italy
monetary unit: **7** carline
island: **7** Caprera **8** Tavolara **9** Maddalena
lake: **6** Omodeo
mountain: **4** Rasu **5** Ferry, Linas **7** Gallura, Limbara **8** Marghine, Serpeddi, Vittoria **11** Gennargentu
river: **5** Mannu, Tirso **6** Lascia **8** Coghinas **10** Flumendosa
sea: **13** Mediterranean
physical feature:
gulf: **6** Orosei, Palmas **7** Asinara **8** Cagliari, Oristano
plain: **7** Sassari **9** Campidano
strait: **9** Bonifacio
people:
king: **12** Charles Felix **13** Charles Albert **14** Victor Emmanuel
leader: **6** Cavour
ruler: **4** Pisa **5** Genoa, Spain **7** Austria, Vandals **9** Byzantium, Phoenicia **12** House of Savoy
language: **7** Italian
religion: **13** Roman Catholic
feature:
towers: **7** nuraghi
food:
cheese: **6** romano **8** pecorino

scarf, strip **6** casing, corset, girdle, ribbon, window **7** baldric **8** casement **9** doorframe, waistband **10** cummerbund **11** windowframe
Japanese: **3** obi
pulley weight: **5** mouse
window: **5** chess

sashay **4** move, skip **5** glide, mince **6** chasse, travel

Saskatchewan **5** river **8** province
boundary: **7** Alberta, Montana **8** Manitoba **11** North Dakota **12** Old Northwest **20** Northwest Territories
capital: **6** Regina
city: **8** Moose Jaw **9** Saskatoon **12** Prince Albert, Swift Current
country: **6** Canada
Indian: **4** Cree **9** Chipewyan **10** Assiniboin
lake: **8** Reindeer **9** Athabasca, Wollaston
mountain: **7** Cypress, Pasquia **9** Porcupine **14** Missouri Coteau
river: **9** Churchill, Frenchman
river mouth: **12** Lake Winnipeg

Sassoon, Siegfried
author of: **26** The Memoirs of a Fox-Hunting Man **26** The Memoirs of George Sherston **29** The Memoirs of an Infantry Officer

sassy **4** bark, bold, flip, rude, tree **5** brash, fresh, saucy **6** mouthy, snippy **7** forward **8** impolite, impudent, insolent **12** discourteous **13** disrespectful

Satan **6** Belial, Moloch **7** Lucifer, Old Nick **8** Apollyon, the Devil **9** Beelzebub **10** Old Scratch, the Evil One, the Tempter **11** fallen angel **12** the Foul Fiend **13** the Old Serpent **14** Mephistopheles **19** the Prince of Darkness

satanic **3** bad **4** evil, vile **5** cruel **6** wicked **7** demonic, heinous, hellish, inhuman, vicious **8** devilish, fiendish, infamous, infernal, sadistic **9** malicious, malignant **10** demoniacal, diabolical, malevolent

satchel, Satchel **3** bag **4** case, grip, sack **5** purse **6** valise **7** handbag **8** reticule, suitcase **9** carpetbag, Gladstone, schoolbag
pitcher, Hall of Famer: **5** Paige

sate **4** cloy, fill, glut **5** gorge, stuff **7** surfeit

satellite **4** moon **5** crony, toady **6** menial, puppet, vassal **7** servant **8** disciple, follower, hanger-on, parasite, retainer **9** assistant, attendant, companion, sycophant, tributary, underling

satellite state **6** colony **8** dominion **10** possession **12** protectorate

satiate **4** bore, cloy, fill, glut, jade **5** slake, stuff, weary **6** overdo, quench, sicken **7** content, disgust, gratify, suffice, surfeit **8** nauseate, overfill, saturate

Satie, Erik
born: **6** France **8** Honfleur
composer of: **6** Parade **13** Pieces froides **16** The Three Gymnasts **19** Limp Preludes for a Dog **20** Pieces en forme de poire **23** Pieces in the Shape of a Pear

satiny **4** fine **5** shiny, silky **6** smooth

satire **5** irony **6** banter, parody, send up **7** lampoon, mockery, sarcasm, takeoff **8** acrimony, derision, raillery, ridicule, travesty **9** burlesque **10** caricature, persiflage

satirical **5** comic **6** biting, bitter **7** caustic, mocking, mordant **8** derisive, humorous, ironical, sardonic, scornful, sneering **9** malicious, sarcastic

satirize **4** mock **6** parody **7** lampoon **9** burlesque **10** caricature

satisfaction **5** pride **6** amends **7** comfort, content, damages, deserts, justice, payment, redress **8** pleasure, requital **9** answering, atonement, happiness, quittance, reckoning, repayment **10** correction, recompense, remittance, settlement **11** contentment, fulfillment, restitution **12** compensation, remuneration **13** gratification, rectification, reimbursement

satisfactory **2** OK **4** okay **8** adequate, all right, passable, suitable **9** competent **10** acceptable, sufficient

satisfied **5** happy **7** content, pleased **9** gratified **10** complacent **11** comfortable

satisfy **3** pay **4** fill, meet **5** annul, clear, remit, repay, serve, slake **6** answer, assure, pacify, pay off, please, quench, remove, settle **7** appease, content, delight, fulfill, gratify, mollify, requite, suffice **8** convince, persuade, reassure **9** discharge, reimburse **10** compensate, recompense

satisfying **8** pleasant, pleasing **9** agreeable, enjoyable, rewarding **10** delightful, fulfilling, gratifying **11** pleasurable

saturate **4** fill **5** cover, douse, imbue, souse **6** drench, infuse **7** immerse, pervade, suffuse **8** permeate, submerge **10** impregnate, infiltrate

saturated **3** wet **4** full **5** drunk, soggy, soppy **6** soaked, sodden **8** bursting

Saturday
day of: **15** Biblical Sabbath
French: **6** samedi
from: **8** Saturnus
German: **7** samstag
heavenly body: **6** Saturn
Italian: **6** sabato
observance: **13** Jewish Sabbath **20** Seventh Day Adventists
Spanish: **6** sabado

Saturday Night Fever
director: **10** John Badham
cast: **11** Barry Miller **12** John Travolta **15** Karen Lynn Gorney
setting: **8** Brooklyn
score: **7** Bee Gees
sequel: **12** Staying Alive

Saturday Night Live, NBC's
regular: **10** Bill Murray, Chevy Chase, Dan Aykroyd, Jane Curtin **11** Eddie Murphy, Gilda Radner, John Belushi **13** Garrett Morris, Laraine Newman
group: **27** Not Ready For Prime Time Players
bits: **4** Bees **7** Samurai **9** Coneheads **10** Church Lady **13** Blues Brothers, Weekend Update **16** Pathological Liar **18** Rosanne Rosanna-Dana

Saturn
origin: **5** Roman
god of: **11** agriculture
consort of: **3** Ops
son: **5** Picus
corresponds to: **6** Cronos, Cronus, Kronos

Saturn
position: **5** sixth
satellite: **4** Rhea **5** Dione, Janus, Mimas, Titan **6** Phoebe, Tethys **7** Iapetus **8** Hyperion **9** Enceladus
characteristic: **5** rings

saturnalia, Saturnalia **4** orgy **5** revel, spree **7** carouse, debauch, revelry **8** carousal **9** bacchanal **10** debauchery
origin: **5** Roman
event: **8** festival

honoring: **6** Saturn **13** sowing of crops

saturnine **4** dour, glum, grim **5** grave, staid, stern, sulky **6** gloomy, moping, morose, solemn, somber, sullen **7** austere, serious **8** dejected, downcast, reserved, sardonic, taciturn **9** apathetic, cheerless, withdrawn **11** downhearted **15** uncommunicative

satyr
form: **5** deity
location: **8** woodland

Satyricon
author: **9** Petronius
character: **4** Gito **8** Ascyltus, Eumolpus **9** Encolpius **10** Trimalchio

sauce **3** dip **4** sass **5** booze, gravy **6** fillip, flavor **7** alcohol **8** dressing, pertness **9** condiment, flippancy **12** impertinence
basil: **5** pesto
fish: **4** alec
hot: **7** Tabasco
Indian: **5** curry
salty: **3** soy

saucy **4** bold, pert, rude, trim **5** brash, cocky, fresh, natty, smart **6** brazen, cheeky, jaunty, lively, spruce **7** forward **8** flippant, impolite, impudent, insolent **9** audacious, barefaced, unabashed **11** impertinent, smart-alecky **12** discourteous **13** disrespectful

Saudi Arabia ***see box***

Sauguet, Henri
born: **6** France **8** Bordeaux
composer of: **6** La Nuit **10** Les Forains, Les Mirages

Sauk, Sac
family: **9** Algonkian **10** Algonquian
tribe: **3** Fox, Sac **8** Kickapoo
location: **4** Iowa, Ohio **6** Kansas **7** Indiana **8** Illinois, Michigan, Oklahoma **9** Wisconsin
leader: **9** Blackhawk
related to: **8** Kickapoo **9** Mesquakie **11** Potawatomie
involved in: **12** Black Hawk War

Saul
king of: **4** Edom **6** Israel
father: **4** Kish
daughter: **5** Merab **6** Michal
son: **7** Abinoam **8** Jonathan **10** Ishbosheth
succeeded: **6** Samlah
anointed by: **6** Samuel
hometown: **6** Gibeah **8** Rehoboth
successor: **5** David
former name: **4** Paul

Saunders, Allen
creator/artist of: **9** Mary Worth

saunter **4** roam **5** amble, mosey, stray **6** loiter, ramble, stroll, wander **7** meander, traipse **8** straggle **9** promenade

Saurolophus
type: **8** dinosaur **10** ornithopod
location: **6** Canada **7** Alberta

sauropod
type of: **8** dinosaur
member: **9** Euhelopus **10** Diplodocus **11** Apatosaurus **12** Brontosaurus, Camarasaurus, Plateosaurus **13** Brachiosaurus, Hypselosaurus

sausage **5** frank, gigot, wurst **6** hot-dog, salami, weenie, wiener **7** baloney, bologna **8** kielbasa **9** bratwurst, pepperoni **10** liverwurst **11** frankfurter
British: **6** banger

sauve qui peut **4** rout **8** stampede **18** every man for himself **23** let him save himself who can

savage **4** boor, wild **5** brute, cruel, feral, fiend, harsh, rough, yahoo **6** animal, bloody, brutal, fierce, maniac, native, rugged, unkind **7** brutish, hoodlum, ruffian, untamed, violent **8** barbaric, hooligan, pitiless, ruthless, sadistic **9** aborigine, barbarian, barbarous, ferocious, merciless, murderous, primitive **10** aboriginal, heathenish, relentless, uncultured, unmerciful **11** uncivilized **12** uncultivated **14** undomesticated

savagery **7** cruelty **8** ferocity **9** barbarism, barbarity, brutality **10** fierceness, inhumanity **12** pitilessness, ruthlessness

savanna, savannah **5** campo, plain **9** grassland

savant **6** genius **7** scholar **13** learned person

Saudi Arabia
capital/largest city: **6** Riyadh
others: **4** Abha, Hail, Taif **5** Hofuf, Hufuf, Jedda, Jidda, Yanbu, Yenbo **6** Anaiza, Dammam, Jiddah, Jubail **7** Al-hofuf, Buraido, Dhahran **9** Ras Tanura
holy city: **5** Mecca **6** Medina
school: **5** Islam **13** King Abd al-Aziz **19** Imam Muhammad bin Saud **20** Petroleum and Minerals
division: **4** Asir, Nejd **5** Hejaz **6** El Hasa
government: **16** absolute monarchy
head of state/government: **4** king
monetary unit: **5** girsh, gursh, pound, riyal
weight: **3** oke
mountain: **6** Tuwayq
highlands: **4** Asir **5** Hejaz
highest point: **5** Razih **10** Jebal Sawda
sea: **3** Red
physical feature:
desert: **3** Red **5** Dahna, Nafud, Nefud, Nufud **6** al-Dahy, Dahana **10** Rub al Khali
gulf: **5** Aqaba **7** Persian
peninsula: **7** Arabian
plain: **6** Tihama
plateau: **4** Nejd
people: **4** Arab **7** Bedouin
king: **4** Fahd, Saud **6** Faisal, Khalid **7** Ibn Saud **9** Abdul Aziz
religious leader: **8** Mohammed, Muhammad
language: **6** Arabic
religion: **5** Islam
sect: **7** Wahhabi
place:
shrine: **5** Kaaba **10** Black Stone
feature:
annual pilgrimage: **4** hadj, hajj
clothing: **3** aba **4** agal **5** thobe **6** ghutra
kingdom: **5** Hejaz **7** Minacan, Ottoman, Sabaean **9** Himyarite
laws of Islam: **6** sharia
village school: **6** kuttab

save **3** but **4** bank, free, help, hold, keep **5** amass, guard, hoard, lay by, lay up, put by, spare, stock, store **6** defend, except, garner, heap up, redeem, rescue, shield **7** deliver, deposit, husband, protect, put away, recover, reserve, salvage **8** conserve, preserve, retrench, withhold **9** economize, safeguard **10** accumulate

save up **5** amass, hoard **7** collect, put away **8** salt away, sock away **10** accumulate **12** squirrel away

saving **5** close, tight **6** frugal, stingy **7** careful, miserly, prudent, sparing, thrifty **8** markdown, stinting **9** illiberal, niggardly, provident, redeeming, restoring **10** economical, reclaiming, redemptory, reparative **12** compensating, conservative

savings **5** hoard **7** nest egg, reserve

savior **5** freer **7** rescuer **8** champion, defender, guardian, redeemer **9** deliverer, liberator, preserver, protecter, protector, salvation **11** emancipator

Savior **5** Jesus **6** Christ **8** Redeemer **10** the Messiah **11** Jesus Christ, the Son of God **13** Prince of Peace

Savior anointed **5** Jesus

savoir-faire **4** tact **5** poise **6** aplomb, polish **7** finesse, know-how, suavity **8** presence, urbanity **9** assurance, composure **10** adroitness, discretion, smoothness **11** worldliness **12** complaisance, graciousness **14** self-possession

savoir-vivre **16** knowing how to live **19** knowledge of the world

savor **3** try **4** aura, gist, like, odor, soul, tang, zest **5** aroma, enjoy, scent, smack, smell, spice, taste, trait **6** flavor, nature, relish, sample, season, spirit **7** essence, quality **8** piquancy, property, pungency **9** character, fragrance, substance **10** appreciate, experience **11** peculiarity **13** particularity **14** characteristic

savory **5** tangy, tasty, yummy **6** honest **7** odorous, piquant, pungent **8** alluring, aromatic, charming, edifying, fragrant, luscious, tasteful **9** delicious, flavorous, palatable, reputable, toothsome **10** appetizing, attractive, delectable **11** inoffensive, respectable, scrumptious **13** mouth-watering

savory
botanical name: **8** Satureia, S montana **10** S hortensis
origin: **13** Mediterranean
varieties: **6** summer, winter
use: **4** eggs, meat **5** beans, salad **6** sauces **8** dressing **11** chicken soup

savvy **5** catch, get it **7** know-how **10** comprehend, understand **13** understanding

saw **3** cut **4** tool **5** adage, maxim, slash **6** saying **7** proverb **8** aphorism
type: **3** jig, rip **4** back, band, hack **5** miter **6** coping **7** keyhole **8** circular, crosscut

sawfly
varieties: **4** stem, wood **5** cedar **6** pergid **7** conifer **8** horntail **11** web spinning

say **2** do **4** hint, hold, read, tell, vote, word **5** bruit, claim, guess, imply, judge, mouth, rumor, speak, state, utter, voice **6** allege, assert, assume, chance, convey, phrase, reason, recite, remark, render, repeat, report, reveal, spread **7** comment, contend, declare, deliver, divulge, express, imagine, mention, perform, suggest, suppose, surmise **8** announce, disclose, intimate, maintain, rehearse, vocalize **9** circulate, franchise, insinuate, pronounce, verbalize **10** articulate, conjecture **11** communicate

Sayers, Dorothy L
author of: **9** Whose Body **12** Strong Poison **14** Have His Carcase, The Nine Tailors, Unnatural Death **15** Clouds of Witness, Five Red Herrings **16** Busman's

Scandinavian Mythology
abode of man: **7** Midgard **10** Mithgarthr
afterworld: **6** Manala **7** Tuonela
began race of giants: **4** Ymir
blacksmith/hero: **9** Ilmarinen
boar: **10** Saehrimnir
bridge of gods: **7** Bifrost
dragon: **6** Fafnir
dwarf: **5** Skuld **7** Andvari
earth is made from: **4** Ymir
elf: **4** Norn **8** Verdandi
epic: **8** Kaleva
final battle: **15** Gotterdammerung **17** Twilight of the Gods
first god: **4** Buri **7** Forsete, Forseti
first man: **3** Ask
first woman: **5** Embla
folk hero: **8** Kalevala
giant: **4** Loki **5** Jotun, Thrym **6** Thiazi, Thjazi **7** Skrymir
giantess: **3** Urd **5** Thokk **9** Angerboda, Angrbodha, Angurboda
giant's realm: **9** Jotunheim
goat: **7** Heidrun
goddesses: **7** Asynjur
goddess of death: **3** Hel
goddess of forbidden marriages: **4** Lofn
goddess of marriage: **4** Frey **5** Freyr
goddess of peace: **4** Frey **5** Freyr
goddess of prosperity: **4** Frey **5** Freyr
goddess of spring: **4** Idun **5** Iduna, Ithun **6** Ithunn
goddess of the sea: **3** Ran
god of beauty/radiance: **5** Baldr **6** Balder, Baldur
god of dawn: **8** Heimdall
god of farming: **4** Thor
god of fire: **4** Loki
god of knowledge: **4** Odin **5** Othin
corresponds to Germanic: **5** Wotan
god of justice: **7** Forseti
god of light: **8** Heimdall
god of music: **5** Bragi
god of navigation: **5** Niord, Njord
god of poetry: **4** Odin **5** Bragi, Othin
corresponds to Germanic: **5** Wotan
god of prosperity: **5** Niord, Njord

Honeymoon **19** Murder Must Advertise **30** Unpleasantness at the Bellona Club
character: 6 Bunter **11** Harriet Vane **15** Lord Peter Wimsey

Say Hey Kid
nickname of: 10 Willie Mays

saying 3 saw **5** adage, maxim, moral, motto **6** byword, dictum, truism **7** epigram, precept, proverb **8** aphorism, apothegm **10** expression

Sayonara
director: 11 Joshua Logan
author: 13 James Michener
cast: 9 Miiko Taka **10** Red Buttons **11** James Garner, Martha Scott **12** Marlon Brando, Miyoshi Umeki **16** Ricardo Montalban
score: 12 Irving Berlin
Oscar for: 15 supporting actor (Buttons) **17** supporting actress (Umeki)

scabrous 5 dirty, rough, scaly **7** immoral, leprous **8** indecent, off-color **9** salacious **10** suggestive **12** pornographic

scalding 3 hot **5** harsh **7** boiling, caustic **8** seething, steaming **9** sarcastic

scale, scales 3 key, set **4** chip, film, husk, peel, rise, rule, skin **5** crust, flake, layer, mount, order, plate, range, ratio, scour, shave, shell, weigh **6** adjust, ascend, goupen, ladder, lamina, octave, rub off, scrape, series, spread **7** balance, chip off, clamber, climb up, coating, lamella, measure **8** escalade, membrane, register, regulate, spectrum, surmount **9** continuum, gradation **10** delaminate, graduation, proportion **11** calibration, progression **14** classification

scale down 4 trim **6** reduce **7** abridge, curtail, shorten **8** compress, condense, decrease, diminish, downsize, moderate **10** abbreviate

scale insects
varieties: 3 lac, pit, wax **5** giant **6** ensign **7** armored **8** mealybug, tortoise **12** ground pearls

Scamandrius *see* **8** Astyanax

scamp 3 imp, rip **5** cut-up, knave, rogue, tease **6** rascal, rotter **7** bounder, villain **8** blighter, scalawag **9** miscreant, prankster, scoundrel **10** scapegrace **11** rapscallion **13** mischief-maker

scamper 3 fly, run, zip **4** dart, dash, flit, race, romp, rush, scud **5** frisk, hurry, scoot **6** frolic, gambol, hasten, scurry, sprint **7** scuttle **9** skedaddle **21** running about playfully

scan 4 skim **5** check, probe, scour, study, sweep **6** peruse, search, size up, survey **7** analyze, examine, explore, inspect **10** scrutinize

scandal 4 blot **5** abuse, libel, odium, shame, stain **6** expose, smirch, stigma **7** calumny, obloquy, outrage, slander **8** disgrace, dishonor, ignominy **9** aspersion, discredit, disesteem, sensation **10** debasement, detraction, opprobrium, revilement **12** vituperation **13** disparagement, embarrassment

scandalize 5 shock **6** appall, defame, insult, offend **7** horrify, outrage **10** calumniate

scandalmonger 6 gossip **8** busybody **10** talebearer, tattletale

scandalous 8 libelous, shameful, shocking **9** gossiping, offensive **10** defamatory, outrageous, scurrilous, slanderous **11** disgraceful **12** disreputable **13** reprehensible

Scandinavian
language family: 12 Indo-European
branch: 8 Germanic
group: 15 Western Germanic
language: 6 Danish **7** Swedish **9** Icelandic, Norwegian

Scandinavian Mythology *see box*

scant 3 cut **4** bare **5** limit, short, small, stint **6** in need, meager, paltry, reduce, sparse

---

god of rain: 4 Thor
god of sea: 5 Aegir, Mimir
god of thunder: 4 Thor
god of underworld: 8 Niflheim
god of victory: 3 Tyr
god of war: 4 Odin **5** Othin
corresponds to Germanic: **5** Wotan
god of wind: 5 Niord, Njord
god of wisdom: 4 Odin **5** Othin
corresponds to Germanic: **5** Wotan
hero: 11 Vainamoinen **12** Lemminkainen
home of dead: 3 Hel
king: 5 Gjuki
magician: 11 Joukahainen
magic necklace: 11 Brisingamen
misty void: 11 Ginnungagap
mountain: 11 Hindarfjall
nature spirit: 7 Eriking
oak tree: 9 Barnstock, Branstock
Odin's court/hall: 8 Valhalla
Odin's father: 3 Bor
Odin's horse: 8 Sleipnir
Odin's magic ring: 8 Draupnir
Odin's palace: 9 Gladsheim
Odin's raven: 5 Hugin, Munin
Odin's spear: 6 Gungni
Odin's throne: 10 Hlidskjalf
Odin's wolf: 4 Geri **5** Freki
race of gods: 5 Vanir
saga: 8 Vulsunga
sea monster: 6 Kraken
serpent: 7 Nidhogg **11** Jormungandr
Sigmund's sword: 4 Gram
slave: 8 Kullervo
sorceress: 5 Louhi **8** Grimhild
Thor's hammer: 7 Miolnir
Thor's servant: 7 Thialfi
tree with three roots: 9 Iggdrasil, Yggdrasil
Valkyrie: 8 Brynhild **9** Brunhilde, Sigrdrifa **11** Brunnehilde
virgin goddess: 3 Urd **4** Norn **5** Skuld, Urdar **8** Verdandi
warrior: 8 Baresark **9** Berserker
watchdog: 4 Garm
wolf monster: 6 Fenrir, Fenris

7 limited 8 exiguous, hold back 9 deficient 10 inadequate, incomplete 12 insufficient

scantiness 10 deficiency, inadequacy, meagerness, skimpiness 13 insufficiency

scanty 4 thin 5 short, small 6 meager, modest, paltry, skimpy, sparse 7 slender, stunted 9 deficient 10 inadequate, undersized 12 insufficient

scapegoat, Scapegoat 4 butt, dupe, gull 5 patsy 6 Azazel, victim 7 fall guy 11 whipping boy 13 laughingstock

scapolite
source: 5 Burma, Mogok

scapula
bone of: 13 shoulder blade

scar 3 cut, pit 4 dent, flaw, gash, hurt, mark, pock, seam 5 brand, wound 6 affect, bruise, damage, deface, defect, impair, mangle 7 blemish, scratch 8 cicatrix, lacerate, mutilate 9 disfigure, influence

scarce 4 rare 6 scanty, sparse 7 unusual, wanting 8 uncommon 9 deficient

scarcely 4 just 6 at most, barely, hardly 7 but just, faintly 8 slightly

scarcity 4 lack, want 5 stint 6 dearth, rarity 7 fewness, paucity 8 rareness, shortage, sparsity, thinness 10 deficiency, scantiness, sparseness 12 uncommonness 13 insufficiency

scare 4 turn 5 alarm, daunt, panic, shake, shock, start 6 harrow, shiver 7 horrify, jitters, startle, terrify 8 disquiet, frighten 9 terrorize 10 disconcert, dishearten, intimidate 11 nervousness, palpitation 13 consternation

scarecrow 6 effigy 8 straw man

Scarecrow
character in: 13 The Wizard of Oz
author: 4 Baum

scared 5 shaky, timid, upset 6 afraid 7 alarmed, fearful, nervous, spooked 8 startled, timorous 9 diffident, terrified, tremulous 10 frightened 12 apprehensive, fainthearted 13 panic-stricken

scarf 3 boa 4 sash, veil, wrap 5 ascot, shawl, stole 6 choker, cravat, tippet 7 foulard, muffler, overlay 8 babushka, bandanna, mantilla 11 neckerchief

Scarface
director: 11 Howard Hawks
cast: 8 Paul Muni 9 Ann Dvorak 10 George Raft 12 Boris Karloff

scarify 3 cut 6 incise, loosen 7 break up, scratch 8 lacerate 9 cultivate

Scarlatti, Alessandro
born: 6 Sicily 7 Palermo
composer of: 11 Stabat Mater 17 Mitridate Eupatore, The Triumph of Honor 18 Il Trionfo dell Onore 23 Gli equivoci nel sembiante

Scarlatti, Domenico
born: 5 Italy 6 Naples
composer of: 7 Sonatas 9 Cat's Fugue, Essercizi 18 Le Donne di Buon Umore 20 The Good-Humored Ladies 23 Ottavia risituita al trono

scarlet 3 red 6 cherry, claret 7 carmine 8 cardinal

Scarlet Letter, The
author: 18 Nathaniel Hawthorne
character: 5 Pearl 12 Hester Prynne 16 Arthur Dimmesdale 18 Roger Chillingworth

scary 3 bad 5 awful, hairy 6 creepy 7 fearful 8 alarming, menacing, shocking 9 difficult 10 disturbing, terrifying 11 frightening, goosepimply, hair-raising, threatening 12 discomfiting

scat 3 off, out 4 away, shoo 5 be off, leave, scram 6 beat it, be gone, depart, get out, go away 7 get lost, vamoose

scathing 4 keen, tart 5 sharp 6 biting, brutal, savage 7 caustic, cutting, hostile, mordant, pointed, searing 8 incisive, stinging, virulent 9 ferocious, rancorous, scorching, trenchant, vitriolic, withering 10 lacerating 11 acrimonious, excoriating

scatter 3 sow 4 cast, flee, rout 5 strew, throw 6 dispel 8 disperse, sprinkle 9 broadcast, circulate, dissipate 10 distribute 11 disseminate

scatterbrained 4 rash, wild, zany 5 crazy, dizzy, giddy, nutty, silly 6 madcap, stupid 7 flighty, foolish 8 careless, heedless, reckless, unstable, unsteady 9 foolhardy, forgetful, frivolous, imprudent 11 birdbrained, empty-headed, harebrained 12 absent-minded, muddleheaded 13 irresponsible

scattered 6 random, spotty 7 diffuse 9 irregular 10 infrequent, occasional

scattering 6 sowing 7 casting 8 strewing 9 dispersal 10 dispersing, sprinkling 12 broadcasting, distribution 13 dissemination

scavenger 6 magpie 8 salvager 9 collector

scenario 4 book, idea, plan 6 scheme 7 concept, outline, summary 8 abstract, game plan, synopsis, teleplay 10 conception, manuscript, screenplay
French: 6 precis

scene 3 act 4 fuss, part, show, site, spot, to-do, view 5 place, sight, vista 6 locale, region, survey, vision 7 display, episode, picture, scenery, setting 8 backdrop, division, locality, location, panorama, position, prospect, sequence 9 commotion, spectacle 10 background 11 whereabouts

scenery 4 sets, view 5 vista 7 terrain 9 backdrops, landscape, spectacle 11 backgrounds

Scenes from a Marriage
director: 13 Ingmar Bergman
cast: 10 Liv Ullmann 13 Bibi Andersson 15 Erland Josephson

scent 4 odor, path, wake, wind 5 aroma, smell, sniff, spoor, trace, track, trail 6 course, detect, inhale 7 bouquet, breathe, discern, essence, perfume, pursuit, suspect 9 aromatize, fragrance, get wind of, recognize 11 distinguish

scented 5 spicy 7 odorous, piquant, pungent 8 aromatic, fragrant, perfumed 9 odiferous 13 sweet-smelling

Scephrus
father: 8 Tegeates
brother: 5 Limon
killed by: 5 Limon

Schaffner, Franklin
director of: 6 Patton (Oscar) 15 Planet of the Apes

Schedius
father: 7 Iphitus
mother: 9 Hippolyte
suitor of: 5 Helen

schedule 3 fix 4 book, list, plan, roll 5 fit in, slate, table 6 agenda 7 appoint, program, put down, set down 8 calendar 9 inventory, timetable

Scheele, Karl Wilhelm
field: 9 chemistry
nationality: 7 Swedish

discovered: 6 oxygen 8 chlorine 9 glycerine

Scheider, Roy
born: 8 Orange NJ
roles: 4 Jaws 11 All That Jazz, Blue Thunder, The Seven-Ups 14 Fifty-two Pickup 19 The French Connection

Schell, Maria
real name: 15 Margarete Schell
born: 6 Vienna 7 Austria
brother: 16 Maximilian Schell
roles: 8 Cimarron, Gervaise 11 End of Desire, White Nights 13 The Last Bridge 20 The Brothers Karamazov

Schell, Maximilian
born: 6 Vienna 7 Austria
sister: 11 Maria Schell
roles: 5 Julia 13 The Young Lions 19 Judgment at Nuremberg (Oscar) 21 The Man in the Glass Booth

scheme 3 map, way 4 plan, plot, ruse 5 cabal, chart, frame, means, shift, study 6 course, design, device, devise, layout, method, policy, sketch, system 7 complot, concoct, connive, drawing, network, outline, program, project, tactics 8 conspire, contrive, grouping, intrigue, maneuver, organize, strategy 9 machinate, procedure, stratagem 10 connivance, conspiracy 11 arrangement, contrivance, delineation, disposition, machination 12 organization

scheming 3 sly 4 arch, wily 6 artful, crafty, shrewd, tricky 7 cunning 8 slippery 9 conniving, designing, insidious 10 contriving, intriguing 11 calculating 13 Machiavellian

Schiller, (Johann) Friedrich von
author of: 8 Ode to Joy 9 Don Carlos 11 Maria Stuart, William Tell 17 The Bride of Messina 18 The Maiden of Orleans

schism 5 break, split 8 division 10 separation 14 disassociation

Schlegel family
characters in: 10 Howard's End
members: 5 Helen 8 Margaret, Theobald
author: 7 Forster

schlepp 3 lug 4 cart, haul, tote 5 carry 6 convey 9 transport

Schlesinger, Arthur M, Jr
author of: 13 A Thousand Days 15 The Age of Jackson 21 The Imperial Presidency 24 Robert Kennedy and His Times

Schlesinger, John
director of: 7 Darling 14 Midnight Cowboy (Oscar) 22 The Falcon and the Snowman

Schlesinger, Leon
creator/artist of: 9 Bugs Bunny

schmaltz 4 corn 14 sentimentalism, sentimentality

Schmeling, Max (Maxmillian Adolph Otto Siegfried)
nickname: 10 Black Uhlan
sport: 6 boxing
class: 11 heavyweight

Schneider, Romy
real name: 20 Rosemarie Albach-Retty
born: 6 Vienna 7 Austria
roles: 8 The Trial 11 The Cardinal 16 Boccaccio Seventy

Schoenberg, Arnold
born: 6 Vienna 7 Austria
composer of: 9 Erwartung 11 De Profundis, Expectation, Gurrelieder 12 The Lucky Hand 13 Moses and Aaron, Ode to Napoleon 14 Verklarte Nacht 16 Die Glucklich Hand, Resplendent Night 17 Transfigured Night 19 A Survivor from Warsaw, Pelleas and Melisande 26 The Book of the Hanging Gardens

Schoenius
father: 7 Athamas
mother: 8 Themisto
wife: 7 Clymene
daughter: 8 Atalanta

scholar 4 coed, sage 5 brain, grind, pupil 6 pundit, savant 7 egghead, learner, student, studier, wise man 8 bookworm, humanist, mandarin 9 collegian, schoolboy 10 schoolgirl 11 matriculant 12 intellectual 13 undergraduate

Scholar Gypsy, The
author: 13 Matthew Arnold

scholarly 6 humane 7 erudite, learned, liberal 8 academic, educated, informed, lettered, literate, well-read 12 intellectual

scholarship 5 grant 7 stipend 8 learning 9 education, endowment, erudition 12 intelligence, thoroughness 13 enlightenment

scholastic 8 academic, pedantic 9 pedagogic 11 educational 12 professorial 13 instructional

school 3 ism 4 view 5 bunch, crowd, faith, order, style, teach, train 6 belief, lyceum, method, system, theory 7 academy, college, educate, faction, thought 8 doctrine, instruct, seminary 9 institute 10 persuasion, university 12 denomination, kindergarten

schoolbook 3 abc 4 text 5 atlas 6 manual, primer, reader 7 grammar, lessons, speller

School for Scandal, The
author: 23 Richard Brinsley Sheridan
character: 5 Maria 6 Rowley 10 Lady Teazle 13 Joseph Surface, Lady Sneerwell 14 Charles Surface, Sir Peter Teazle 16 Sir Oliver Surface

School for Wives, The
author: 7 Moliere
character: 5 Agnes 6 Horace, Oronte 7 Enrique 8 Arnolphe 9 Chrysalde

schooling 5 drill 8 drilling, training 9 education 11 instruction, preparation 14 indoctrination

schoolmaster 4 head 5 tutor 7 dominie, pedagog, scholar, teacher 9 pedagogue, principal, professor 10 headmaster, instructor 12 disciplinarian
fish: 7 snapper
genus: 8 Lutianus
species: 6 apodus

Schubert, Franz Peter
born: 6 Vienna 7 Austria
composer of: 6 Little (symphony), Tragic (symphony No 4) 8 Sad Waltz 9 Rosamunde 11 Winterreise 12 Trout Quintet 13 Mourning Waltz 17 Die Schone Mullerin 18 Unfinished Symphony (No 8) 24 Death and the Maiden Quartet, Symphony of Heavenly Length

Schulz, Charles
creator/artist of: 7 Peanuts

Schuman, William
born: 9 New York NY
composer of: 8 Undertow 9 Credendum 14 The Mighty Casey 16 American Festival 18 New England Triptych

Schumann, Robert Alexander
born: 7 Germany, Zwickau
composer of: 6 Myrten, Spring (symphony No 1) 7 Rhenish (symphony No 3) 8 Arabeske, Carnival 9 Papillons 10 Novelettes

11 Blumenstuck, Butterflies, Nachtstucke, Nightpieces, Novelletten **12** Bunte Blatter, Dichterliebe, Flower Pieces, Kinderscenen, Kreisleriana, Motley Leaves **14** Fantasiestucke **16** David's Band Dances, Symphonic Studies **18** Davidsbundlertanze **19** Frauenliebe und Leben, Scenes from Childhood **22** Carnival Jest from Vienna **23** Faschingsschwank aus Wien

Schwann, Theodor
field: **7** biology
nationality: **6** German
established: **10** cell theory

Schwarzenegger, Arnold
roles: **7** Red Heat **8** Predator **13** The Terminator **17** Conan the Barbarian, Conan the Destroyer
wife: **12** Maria Shriver

Schweitzer, Albert
field: **8** medicine
worked in: **5** Gabon **6** Africa
founded: **17** Lambarene Hospital
awarded: **15** Nobel Peace Prize

Schwitters, Kurt
born: **7** Germany **8** Hannover
artwork: **7** Merzbau
collages called: **10** Merzbilden

science **3** art **5** skill **6** method **7** finesse **8** aptitude, facility **9** technique **10** discipline **11** acquirement
god of: **7** Mercury

scintilla **3** dot **4** atom, iota **5** shred, spark, speck, trace **7** glimmer **10** smithereen

scintillate **4** joke, snap **5** amuse, charm, flash, gleam, glint, shine, spark **7** glimmer, glisten, glitter, shimmer, sparkle, twinkle **9** coruscate **10** effervesce

scintillating **5** witty **6** bright, lively **8** animated, charming, dazzling **9** brilliant, ebullient, exuberant, sparkling **10** glittering **11** stimulating **12** effervescent

scion **3** son **4** heir, seed **5** child, issue **7** heiress, progeny **8** daughter, offshoot **9** offspring, posterity, successor **10** descendant **11** progeniture

Sciron
vocation: **6** robber
killed by: **7** Theseus

Scirophoria
also: **11** Skirophoria
origin: **5** Greek
event: **8** festival
honoring: **6** Athena

scissors **5** snips **6** blades, cutter, shears **7** clipper, snipper, trimmer
French: **8** secateur

scoff **4** jeer, mock, razz **5** flout, knock, taunt **6** deride, rail at, revile **7** condemn, laugh at, put down, run down **8** belittle, ridicule

Scofield, Paul
real name: **13** David Scofield
born: **7** England **14** Hurstpierpoint
roles: **8** King Lear **13** Sir Thomas More **17** A Man for All Seasons (Oscar)

scold **3** nag **5** chide, shrew **6** berate, carp at, nagger, rail at, rebuke, virago **7** censure, reprove, upbraid **9** castigate, criticize, dress down, reprehend, reprimand, termagant **10** complainer
Yiddish: **6** kvetch

scolding **7** chiding, reproof **8** berating, rebuking **9** reprimand, talking-to **10** admonition, upbraiding **11** castigation **12** admonishment **13** tongue-lashing

Scolosaurus
type: **8** dinosaur **10** ornithopod
location: **12** North America

sconce **11** candlestick **12** candleholder

scoop **4** bail, beat **5** clean, clear, gouge, ladle, spoon **6** burrow, dig out, dipper, hollow, shovel, trowel **7** dish out, lade out, lift out **8** excavate

scoop out **3** dig **5** gouge **8** excavate

scoot **3** run **4** dash, rush **6** scurry, sprint

Scooter
nickname of: **11** Phil Rizzuto

scope **3** aim **4** area, goal, rein, room, span, vent **5** field, force, grasp, range, reach **6** bounds, effect, margin, motive, spread, vision **7** bearing, compass, freedom, liberty, purpose, stretch **8** ambition, confines, latitude **9** extension, influence, intention **10** competence **11** application, destination **13** determination

scorch **3** dry **4** char, sear **5** parch, singe **6** dry out, scathe, wither **7** blacken **8** discolor **9** dehydrate

score, scores **3** cut, mar, run, tab, win **4** bill, debt, gain, gash, goal, lots, make, mark, nick, slit **5** amass, count, facts, grade, hosts, judge, notch, point, slash, tally, truth **6** basket, charge, damage, deface, droves, groove, grudge, masses, pile up, strike, swarms, twenty **7** account, achieve, arrange, legions, reality, scratch, throngs **8** evaluate, incision, register **9** grievance **10** amount owed, difference, multitudes, obligation **11** orchestrate

scoria **4** slag **5** dross **6** cinder, refuse

scorn **5** spurn **6** ignore, rebuff, refuse, reject, slight **7** condemn, despise, disdain, mockery, repulse, sarcasm **8** contempt, derision, ridicule, scoffing, spit upon **9** arrogance, contumely, disregard, ostracize **10** look down on, opprobrium **11** haughtiness

scorned **7** derided, refused **8** despised, rebuffed, rejected, repulsed **9** disdained **10** deprecated, disparaged

scornful **6** lordly **7** cynical **8** arrogant, derisive, insolent, sardonic, scoffing, sneering **9** sarcastic **10** disdainful, ridiculing **11** disparaging **12** contemptuous, supercilious

Scorpio
symbol: **8** scorpion
planet: **4** Mars **5** Pluto
rules: **5** death **7** passion
born: **7** October **8** November

Scorpion **4** whip **7** scourge
constellation of: **8** Scorpius

Scorsese, Martin
director of: **10** After Hours, Raging Bull, Taxi Driver **11** Mean Streets **12** The Last Waltz

scotch **4** foil, kill, stop **5** crush, quash **6** thwart **7** destroy **8** confound, obstruct, sabotage, suppress **9** undermine **11** nip in the bud

scotch
type: **6** whisky **7** whiskey
origin: **8** Scotland
ingredient: **12** cereal grains
drink: **10** Scotch Mist **14** Highland Cooler
with amaretto: **9** Godfather
with cherry brandy: **12** Blood and Sand
with Drambuie: **9** Rusty Nail
with gin: **12** Barbary Coast
with vermouth: **6** Rob Roy **8** Affinity **10** Bobby Burns

Scotia
epithet of: **9** Aphrodite
means: **7** dark one

Scotland

Roman name: **9** Caledonia
capital: **9** Edinburgh
largest city: **7** Glasgow
others: **3** Ayr **4** Duns, Oban **5** Alloa, Banff, Brora, Burgh, Cupar, Ellon, Leith, Perth, Salen, Troon **6** Dundee, Girvan, Hawick **7** Airdrie, Alloway, Dunkeld, Falkirk, Frunock, Mallaig, Paisley, Renfrew **8** Aberdeen, Dumfries, Greenock, Hamilton, Kirkwall, Rothesay, Stirling **9** Clydebank, Dumbarton, Greenlock, Inverness, Kirkcaldy, Peterhead, St Andrews **10** Coatbridge, Kilmarnock, Motherwell **11** Dunfermline, Grangemouth
school: **7** Glasgow **8** Aberdeen **9** Edinburgh **12** Saint Andrew's
division: **3** Ayr **4** Bute, Fife, Ross **5** Angus, Banff, Moray, Nairn, Perth **6** Argyll, Lanark, Orkney **7** Berwick, Kinross, Lothian, Peebles, Renfrew, Selkirk, Wigtown **8** Aberdeen, Ayrshire, Cromarty, Dumfries, Roxburgh, Shetland, Stirling **9** Buteshire, Caithness, Dumbarton **10** Kincardine, Midlothian, Sutherland **11** Clackmannan, Kincudbight **12** Renfrewshire **13** Stirlingshire
kingdom: **8** Dalriada **11** Northumbria, Strathclyde
government: **13** United Kingdom
measure: **3** cop **4** boll, cran, fall, mile, peck, pint, rood, rope, span **5** crane, lippy **6** audlet, davach, firlot, lippie, noggin **7** chalder, choppin **8** mutchkin, stimpart, stimpert **9** particate, shaftment, shathmont
monetary unit: **3** ecu **4** demy, doit, lion, mark, rial, ryal **5** bodle, broad, groat, plack, rider, turne **6** bawbee, folles **7** unicorn **8** atchison, hardhead **9** halfpenny **11** bonnetpiece
weight: **4** boll, drop **5** trone **6** bushel
island: **3** Rum **4** Aran, Bute, Eigg, Fair, Inch, Iona, Jura, Lona, Muck, Mull, Rhum, Skye **5** Arran, Barra, Islay, Lewis **6** Harris, Orkney, Staffa **7** St Kilda **8** Berneray, Cumbraes, Hebrides, Shetland **9** North Uist, South Uist
lake/loch: **3** Awe, Dee, Lin, Tay **4** Earn, Fyne, Gair, Gare, Linn, Ness, Oich, Ryan, Sloy **5** Duich, Leven, Lochy, Lough, Morar, Maree, Nevis **6** Laggan, Linnhe, Lomond **7** Katrine, Rannoch, St Mary's
mountain: **4** Hope **5** Attow, Dearg, Nevis, Tinto, Wyvis **7** Cheviot, Macdhui, Merrick **8** Grampian **9** Ben Lomond, Cairngorm, Highlands, Trossachs
hills: **5** Ochil **6** Calton, Sidlaw **7** Cheviot
highest point: **8** Ben Nevis
river: **3** Ayr, Dee, Don, Esk, Tay **4** Doon, Glen, Nith, Norn, Spey **5** Afton, Annan, Clyde, Forth, Garry, North, Tweed, Ythan **6** Affric, Teviot, Tummel **7** Deveron **8** Findhorn
sea: **5** Irish, North **8** Atlantic, Hebrides
physical feature:
bay: **5** Scapa
canal: **10** Caledonian
channel: **5** Minch, North
firth: **3** Tay **4** Kyle, Lorn **5** Clyde, Forth, Lorne, Moray **6** Linnhe, Solway **7** Comarty, Dornoch **8** Pentland
glen: **8** Glen More **9** Great Glen
moor: **7** Rannoch
valley: **8** Trossach
people: **4** Gael, Pict, Scot **5** Norse
artist: **7** Raeburn
author: **5** Burns, Scott **6** Dunbar **7** Barbour, Douglas **8** Henryson **9** Stevenson **10** Conan-Doyle, MacDiarmid, Macpherson
economist: **5** Smith
historian: **7** Carlyle
inventor: **4** Bell
king: **5** David, James **6** Duncan **7** Kenneth, Macbeth, Malcolm, Stuarts, William **9** Alexander **14** Robert the Bruce
philosopher: **4** Hume
prime minister: **9** Macdonald, MacMillan **11** Douglas-Home
prince: **19** Bonnie Prince Charlie
queen: **4** Mary **13** Saint Margaret
religious leader: **8** John Knox
scientist: **7** Fleming
language: **4** Erse **6** Celtic, Gaelic, Keltic, Lallan **7** English, Lalland
religion: **12** Episcopalian, Presbyterian **13** Roman Catholic
place:
abbey: **5** Kelso **7** Melrose **8** Dryburgh, Jedburgh
castle: **8** Stirling **9** Edinburgh **11** Eilean Donan
church/kirk: **7** St Giles **11** St Cuthbert's
royal residence: **8** Balmoral
Scott's home: **10** Abbotsford
street: **7** Prince's **9** Royal Mile **11** Sauchiehall

(*continued*)

Scotland (*continued*)
feature:
bird: **3** bae, cae **4** hern, muir, smeu **6** grouse, smeuth, snabby **7** jackdaw **8** throstle **9** swinepipe
clothing: **4** kilt **6** tartan **12** Harris tweeds **13** Shetland knits **15** Fair Isle sweater
dance: **3** bob **4** reel **7** walloch **9** ecossaise **10** petronella **11** strathsprey **12** gilliecallum **13** Highland fling
game: **4** golf
monster: **6** Nessie **8** Loch Ness
musical instrument: **7** bagpipe
symbol: **7** thistle
food:
bread: **5** scone
cheese: **7** crowdie
dish: **6** haggis **12** finnan haddie **15** kippered herring
drink: **12** Scotch whisky
soup: **11** cock-a-leekie

Scott, George C
born: **6** Wise VA
wife: **14** Trish Van Devere **15** Colleen Dewhurst
roles: **4** Rage **6** Patton (Oscar, refused) **8** Jane Eyre **16** The New Centurions **18** The Day of the Dolphin

Scott, Sir Walter
author of: **6** Rob Roy **7** Ivanhoe, Marmion **8** The Abbot, Waverley **10** Kenilworth **11** The Talisman **12** Guy Mannering, Old Mortality, The Antiquary **14** Quentin Durward **16** The Lady of the Lake **20** The Bride of Lammermoor, The Heart of Midlothian **23** The Lay of the Last Minstrel

Scottish Mythology
spirit/horse: **6** kelpie

scoundrel **3** cad, cur **5** crook, knave, rogue, scamp, thief **6** rascal, rotter, varlet, weasel **7** bounder, ruffian, sharper, varmint, villain **8** scalawag, swindler, turncoat **9** miscreant, trickster **10** blackguard, copperhead, mountebank, ne'er-do-well **11** fourflusher, rapscallion **12** carpetbagger

scoundrelly **3** low **4** mean **7** debased **8** rascally **10** degenerate, despicable, villainous **12** contemptible, disreputable **13** reprehensible

Scoundrel Time
author: **14** Lillian Hellman

scour **4** buff, comb, rake, scan **5** scrub, shine **6** abrade, polish, scrape **7** burnish, cleanse, ransack, rummage **8** brighten, traverse

scourge, Scourge **3** rod **4** bane, beat, cane, flog, lash, whip **5** birch, blast, curse, flail, strap **6** punish, switch, terror, thrash **7** censure, chasten **8** chastise, scorpion, vexation **9** castigate, excoriate **10** affliction, discipline, flagellate **11** troublement **13** cat-o'-nine-tails

scout **3** spy **4** case **5** guide, pilot **6** escort, spy out, survey **7** lookout, observe **8** outrider, point man, vanguard **9** recruiter **11** reconnoiter **13** reconnoiterer

scowl **4** pout **5** frown, glare, lower **6** glower **7** grimace

scrabble **3** paw **4** claw, rake **5** climb **6** drudge, jostle, scrape, scrawl **7** clamber, grapple, scratch **8** struggle

scram **3** out **4** scat, shoo **5** be off, leave **6** beat it, begone, depart, get out, go away **7** get lost, vamoose **10** make tracks

scramble **3** run, vie **4** race, rush **5** clash, fight, mix up, scrap, upset **6** battle, combat, engage, garble, jostle, jumble, mess up, scurry, strive, tussle **7** collide, confuse, disturb, scatter, scuffle, shuffle **8** disorder, struggle, unsettle **9** scrimmage **10** disarrange, free-for-all **11** competition, disorganize

scramble up **5** climb, mount, scale **7** clamber

scrap **3** bit, dab, jot, row **4** atom, drop, iota, junk, spat **5** brawl, crumb, fight, grain, melee, speck, trace, trash **6** fracas, morsel, refuse, ruckus, sliver **7** abandon, glimmer, minimum, modicum, quarrel, snippet **8** brouhaha, fraction, fragment, jettison, molecule, particle, squabble **10** free-for-all, smattering, sprinkling

scrapbook **5** album **9** portfolio **11** memorabilia, miscellanea

scrape **3** dig **4** buff, gash, mark, rasp, save, skin **5** amass, clean, fight, glean, gouge, grate, graze, grind, plane, run-in, score, scour, scuff, stint **6** abrade, bruise, forage, gather, groove, obtain, pick up, plight, scrimp, secure, smooth, tussle **7** acquire, burnish, dilemma, procure, rub hard, scratch, scuffle, straits **8** abrasion **9** economize, tight spot **10** difficulty **11** predicament **13** confrontation

scratch **3** cut, mar, rub **4** claw, etch, gash, nick, omit, rasp **5** dig at, erase, grate, graze, grind, score **6** cancel, delete, incise, remove, rub out, scrape, scrawl, streak, strike **7** blemish, blot out, exclude, expunge, rule out **8** abrasion, cross out, lacerate, scribble, withdraw **9** eliminate **10** laceration

scratchy **5** rough **6** coarse **7** bristly, prickly **9** irritated **10** irritating

scrawl **4** draw **5** write **6** doodle **7** scratch, writing **8** scrabble, scribble, squiggle **10** penmanship **11** handwriting

scrawniness **8** lankness, leanness, slimness, thinness **10** skinniness, slightness **11** slenderness

scrawny **4** bony, lank, lean, puny **5** drawn, gaunt, lanky, runty, spare **6** sinewy, skinny, wasted **7** angular, scraggy, spindly, stunted **8** rawboned, skeletal **9** emaciated, fleshless **10** attenuated, undersized **11** underweight

screak **4** rasp **5** grate, grind **6** shriek, squeak **7** screech

scream **4** howl, loud, roar, wail, yell, yelp, yowl **5** shout, whine **6** bellow, cry out, holler, outcry, shriek, squawk, squeal **7** screech **11** lamentation

screech **3** cry **4** howl, rasp **6** screak, scream, shriek **9** caterwaul

screen **3** see, web **4** cull, mask, mesh, rate, show, sift, sort, veil, view **5** class, cloak, cover, eject, films, grade, grate, group, guard, order, shade, sieve **6** buffer, cinema, defend, filter, mantle, movies, secure, shield, shroud, sifter, size up, strain, winnow **7** arrange, conceal, curtain, defense, discard, lattice, present, preview, project, protect, secrete, shelter, shutter, weed out **8** colander, coverage, evaluate, jalousie, separate, strainer, withhold **9** eliminate, partition, safeguard **10** protection **11** concealment

screw **4** bolt, join, knot, turn, warp **5** clamp, exact, force, gnarl, rivet, twist, wrest, wring **6** adjust, attach, deform, driver, extort, fasten, garble, wrench **7** contort, distort, pervert, squeeze, tighten **8** fastener, misshape **9** propeller

screwball **3** nut **4** kook **5** flake, freak **6** looney **7** lunatic **8** crackpot **9** character, eccentric

screwdriver
type: **6** rachet **11** spiral-drive **12** Phillips-head

screwy **3** odd **4** daft **5** batty, dotty, flaky, funny, kinky, kooky, nutty, queer, wacky, weird **6** weirdo **7** oddball **8** peculiar **9** eccentric **10** unbalanced

Scriabin, Aleksandr (Scriabine, Skryabin)
born: **6** Moscow, Russia
composer of: **7** Mystery **10** Prometheus **12** Vers la flamme **13** Poem of Ecstasy, The Divine Poem, The Poem of Fire

scribble **4** tear **5** squib **6** doodle, scrawl **7** scratch **8** squiggle **9** pull apart
fiber: **4** wool
procedure: **7** carding

scribe, Scribe **3** cut **4** mark, tool **5** clerk, score **6** author, copier, penman, writer **7** copyist, teacher **8** recorder **9** archivist, scrivener, secretary **10** amanuensis, translator **12** newspaperman, stenographer **13** calligraphist
Biblical: **4** Ezra **6** Esdras
French dramatist: **8** Augustin
Palestinian: **5** sofer **6** sopher

scribe of gods **5** Thoth

scrimp **4** save **5** hoard, pinch, skimp, stint **8** begrudge **9** be sparing **12** pinch pennies

scrimping **6** frugal **7** sparing **10** economical **11** economizing **12** cheeseparing **15** pinching pennies

scrip **5** paper **8** document **11** certificate

scripsit **7** he wrote **8** she wrote

script **4** book, hand **5** lines, score **6** dialog **7** cursive **8** dialogue, libretto, longhand, scenario **10** manuscript, penmanship **11** calligraphy, chirography, handwriting

Scriptures, the **5** Bible **6** the Law, oracle **8** holy writ, the Bible, the Torah **10** the Gospels **11** The Good Book **12** New Testament, Old Testament, the Word of God **13** the Pentateuch, the Septuagint **14** sacred writings

scroll of the Torah
Hebrew: **11** Sepher Torah

Scrooge, Ebenezer
character in: **15** A Christmas Carol
author: **7** Dickens

scrub **4** swab **5** brush, scour **8** scouring **9** brushwood, scrubbing

scrubby **4** base **6** brushy **7** stunted **8** inferior **10** undersized

scrumptious **5** juicy, tasty **6** savory, tender **8** luscious, pleasant, pleasing **9** agreeable, delicious, enjoyable, flavorful, succulent, toothsome **10** appetizing, delectable, delightful, flavorsome **13** mouth-watering

scruple **3** shy **4** balk, care, halt **5** demur, pause, qualm, waver **6** blench, ethics, falter **7** anxiety, concern, refrain **8** hesitate **9** fluctuate, misgiving, principle **10** conscience, hesitation **11** compunction, fearfulness, uncertainty **12** apprehension, doubtfulness, protestation **13** squeamishness **17** conscientiousness

Scruples
author: **12** Judith Krantz

scrupulous **5** exact **6** honest **7** careful, dutiful, precise, upright **8** cautious, exacting, sedulous **9** honorable **10** deliberate, fastidious, meticulous, principled **11** painstaking, punctilious **13** conscientious

scrupulousness **4** care **5** pains **9** exactness **14** meticulousness **17** conscientiousness

scrutinize **4** scan **5** probe, study **6** peruse, search, survey **7** explore, inspect, observe **11** investigate

scrutiny **5** study, watch **7** inquiry, perusal **9** attention **10** inspection **11** examination **12** surveillance **13** investigation

scuffle **3** row **4** spar **5** brawl, clash, fight, melee, scrap **6** fracas, jostle, rumpus, tussle **8** squabble, struggle **9** commotion, imbroglio **10** donnybrook, free-for-all

sculpsit **10** he carved it **11** she carved it **12** he engraved it **13** she engraved it **14** he sculptured it **15** she sculptured it

sculptor **6** artist, carver, caster, imager, molder **7** marbler, modeler **8** chiseler, engraver
constellation: **19** Apparatus Sculptoris
French: **5** Rodin
Greek: **7** Phidias **10** Praxiteles
Irish-American: **12** Saint-Gaudens
Italian: **7** Cellini **12** Michelangelo
tool: **6** chisel, graver **7** spatula **9** ebauchoir

sculpture **3** cut **4** bust, cast, head, work **5** cameo, carve, erode, model, mould **6** chisel, relief, statue **7** carving, erosion, faience **8** intaglio, statuary **9** cloissone, medallion, statuette
medium: **4** clay **5** china, stone **6** bronze, enamel, marble **7** ceramic **9** porcelain **10** terra cotta **11** earthenware

scum **4** film, slag **5** crust, dregs, dross, trash **6** rabble, refuse **7** deposit, rubbish, surface **8** riffraff

scurrility **5** abuse **8** rudeness **9** indecency, obscenity, profanity **13** offensiveness, salaciousness

scurrilous **3** low **5** gross **6** coarse, vulgar **7** obscene **8** churlish, derisive, indecent, reviling **9** insulting, offensive, shameless **10** derogatory, detracting, indelicate, slanderous **11** disparaging, foulmouthed **12** contemptuous

scurry **3** hie **4** race, rush,

skim **5** haste, hurry, scoot, speed **6** bustle, hasten, hustle, spring **7** rushing, scamper, scuttle **8** hurrying, scooting, scramble **9** confusion, dispersal **10** scattering

scurvy **3** low **4** base, mean, vile **6** shabby **7** ignoble **9** worthless **10** despicable **12** contemptible, dishonorable

scuttle **4** sink **5** abort, hurry, scrap, speed, wreck **6** hasten, scurry **7** destroy, discard, scamper **8** dispatch, scramble

scuttlebutt **4** talk **5** rumor **6** gossip **7** hearsay, prattle, scandal **8** chitchat

Scylaceus
origin: **6** Lycian
ally of: **7** Trojans
death by: **7** stoning

Scylla
form: **5** nymph **7** monster
location: **3** sea **16** Straits of Messina **20** Whirlpool of Charybdis
father: **7** Phorcys
mother: **6** Hecate
loved by: **8** Poseidon
rival: **10** Amphitrite

Scyphius
first: **5** horse
created by: **8** Poseidon

sea **3** bay, ton **4** deep, gulf, host, lake, leap, lots, main, mass, slew, wave **5** bight, flock, flood, ocean, scads, spate, surge, swarm, swell, waves **6** legion, roller, scores, waters **7** breaker **9** abundance, multitude, profusion
French: **3** mer
god of: **5** Aegir, Memir **6** Nereus, Triton **7** Glaucus, Neptune, Phorcys, Proteus **8** Poseidon **9** Asphalius
goddess of: **3** Ino, Ran **6** Graeae, Graiae, Matuta **8** Dictynna, Menannan **9** Leucothea **10** Amphitrite

Sea, the Sea, The
author: **11** Iris Murdoch

Sea Around Us, The
author: **13** Rachel L Carson

seaboard **5** coast **9** shoreline

Seaborg, Glen Theodore
field: **7** physics
worked with: **14** actinide series **19** transuranic elements
headed: **3** AEC **22** Atomic Energy Commission
awarded: **10** Nobel Prize

seacoast **5** beach, coast, shore **7** seaside **8** littoral **9** coastland, coastline, shoreline, waterside
French: **4** cote
Italian: **4** lido **7** riviera

seafarers **5** salts **7** sailors, seadogs **8** mariners

Seagull, The
author: **12** Anton Chekhov
character: **5** Masha **6** Polina **10** Pyotr Sorin **11** Yevgeny Dorn **12** Ilya Shamraev, Irina Arkadin **13** Boris Trigorin, Nina Zaretchyn **16** Semyon Medvedenko **17** Konstantin Treplev

Seah **15** Biblical measure

Sea Hawk, The
director: **13** Michael Curtiz
cast: **10** Errol Flynn **11** Claude Rains, Donald Crisp **14** Brenda Marshall
score: **21** Erich Wolfgang Korngold

seal **2** OK **3** dam, fix **4** cork, lock, mark, plug, shut, stop **5** brand, close, stamp **6** accept, affirm, emblem, fasten, figure, ratify, secure, settle, shut up, signet, stop up, symbol, verify **7** approve, certify, confirm, endorse, imprint **8** colophon, conclude, fastener, hallmark, insignia, sanction, validate **9** determine, establish, trademark **10** impression **12** authenticate
Latin: **10** imprimatur

seal
young: **3** pup
group of: **3** pod

sea lion
young: **3** pup

seam **3** gap **4** line, lode, mark, scar, vein **5** break, chink, cleft, crack, joint, layer, notch **6** breach, furrow, incise, suture **7** crevice, fissure, joining, opening, rupture, stratum, wrinkle **8** junction, juncture **9** interface

seaman **3** gob, tar **4** hand, mate, salt **5** bosun, middy **6** lubber, merman, sailor, seadog **7** mariner **9** boatswain **10** bluejacket, midshipman

seamark **5** light **6** beacon, pharos, signal **10** lighthouse, watchtower

sea monster **6** dragon **9** Leviathan

seamstress **10** dressmaker
French: **9** midinette **10** couturiere

seamy **3** raw **4** dark **5** dirty, nasty, rough **6** coarse, sordid **7** squalid, unclean **10** unpleasant **11** unwholesome **12** disagreeable

Sea of Grass, The
author: **13** Conrad Richter

sear **4** burn, char, scar **5** blast, singe, steel **6** harden, scorch **7** blister **9** cauterize **10** caseharden

search **4** comb, drag, fish, hunt, look, seek, sift **5** check, frisk, probe, quest, rifle, scour, snoop, study **6** survey, tracer **7** dragnet, examine, explore, inquiry, inspect, pry into, pursuit, ransack, rummage **8** overhaul, scrutiny **10** inspection, scrutinize **11** examination, exploration **13** investigation

Search, The
director: **13** Fred Zinnemann
cast: **9** Ivan Jandl **13** Aline MacMahon **14** Jarmila Novotna **15** Montgomery Clift
setting: **6** Berlin

Searchers, The
director: **8** John Ford
cast: **8** Ward Bond **9** John Wayne, Vera Miles **11** Natalie Wood **13** Jeffrey Hunter

searching **4** dour, keen, nosy **5** sharp **6** prying, shrewd, snoopy **7** curious, groping **8** exacting, piercing, rigorous, thorough **9** observant, quizzical, unsparing **11** inquisitive, penetrating **13** investigative

Seascape
author: **11** Edward Albee

seashore **5** beach, coast

seasick **3** ill **5** barfy, dizzy, faint, giddy, woozy **6** queasy **8** qualmish, vomitous **9** nauseated, squeamish **11** vertiginous

seasickness
French: **8** mal de mer

seaside **5** beach, coast, shore **9** shoreline

season **3** age, dry **4** fall, lace, tame, term **5** adapt, color, drill, inure, prime, ripen, shape, spell, spice, stage, train **6** accent, autumn, finish, flavor, inform, leaven, mature, mellow, period, refine, soften, spring, summer, temper, winter **7** enhance, enliven, prepare, quarter, stretch **8** accustom, duration, heighten, interval, ornament, practice **9** condition, cultivate, embellish **10** discipline

seasoned **6** herbed, inured, salted, spiced **7** veteran **8** flavored, hardened, peppered **9** competent, qualified **10** acclimated, accustomed, habituated **11** experienced **12** familiarized

seasoning **4** dill, herb, mace, sage, salt, zest **5** aging, basil, clove, gusto, onion, spice, thyme **6** drying, garlic, ginger, nutmeg, pepper, relish **7** oregano, paprika, parsley **8** allspice, cinnamon, marjoram, practice, ripening, rosemary, training **9** condiment, flavoring **10** maturation **11** orientation, preparation **15** familiarization

Season in Hell, A
author: **13** Arthur Rimbaud

seasons
god of: **9** Vertumnus
goddess of: **4** Hour **5** Horae

seat **3** box, hub **4** axis, core, home, rump, site, sofa **5** abode, bench, chair, couch, croup, divan, fanny, heart, house, locus, place **6** behind, bottom, center, locale, settle **7** address, capital, cushion, habitat, housing, nucleus, rear end, situate **8** backside, buttocks, derriere, domicile, dwelling, haunches, location, quarters **9** posterior, residence **10** incumbency, membership **12** hindquarters

seat of justice **5** bench, court **8** tribunal **9** judiciary **10** courthouse

Seattle
baseball team: **8** Mariners
basketball team: **11** Supersonics
bay: **7** Elliott
football team: **8** Seahawks
lake: **10** Washington
landmark: **11** Space Needle
site of: **10** World's Fair
sound: **5** Puget

Sea Wolf, The
author: **10** Jack London

Sebastian
character in: **12** Twelfth Night
author: **11** Shakespeare

Seberg, Jean
born: **14** Marshalltown IA
husband: **10** Romain Gary
roles: **6** Lilith **7** Airport **9** Saint Joan **10** Breathless **16** Bonjour Tristesse

Secchi, Angelo
field: **9** astronomy
nationality: **7** Italian
classified: **5** stars

secede **4** quit **5** leave **6** resign, retire **7** forsake **8** withdraw **12** disaffiliate

secession **10** separation, withdrawal **14** disaffiliation

seclude **4** hide **6** retire **7** isolate **8** separate **9** sequester **10** dissociate

secluded **6** covert, cut off, lonely, remote, shut in **7** private **8** closeted, confined, isolated, shut away, solitary **9** reclusive, sheltered, unvisited, withdrawn **10** cloistered **11** out-of-the-way, sequestered **12** unfrequented

seclusion **5** exile **6** asylum, hiding **7** retreat **8** cloister, hideaway, solitude **9** hermitage, isolation, reclusion, sanctuary **10** quarantine, retirement, withdrawal **11** concealment **13** sequestration

second **3** aid **4** abet, back, help, wink **5** agent, favor, flash, jiffy, other, proxy, trice **6** assist, back up, deputy, fill-in, helper, minute, moment, uphold **7** advance, another, endorse, further, instant, one more, outdone, promote, stand by, stand-in, support **8** advocate, delegate, exceeded, inferior **9** alternate, assistant, attendant, encourage, surpassed, twinkling **10** additional, lieutenant, substitute, understudy **11** alternating, subordinate **14** representative
abbreviation: **1** s **3** sec

secondary **5** lower, minor, other **6** backup, lesser **7** smaller **8** inferior, mediocre, middling **9** alternate, ancillary, auxiliary, following, resultant **10** consequent, subsequent, subsidiary **11** subordinate

second childhood **6** dotage **8** senility

secondhand **4** used **8** indirect **10** derivative

second-in-command **6** deputy **8** adjutant **9** assistant **10** lieutenant **13** vice president

second-rate **3** bad **4** poor, so-so **5** cheap, tacky **6** shabby **7** average **8** everyday, inferior, mediocre, middling **9** imperfect **10** inadequate, outclassed, pedestrian **11** commonplace, substandard **15** undistinguished

Second Sex, The
author: **16** Simone de Beauvoir

second-story man **5** thief **6** robber **7** burglar **9** cracksman **10** cat burglar

second string **4** subs **5** bench **11** substitutes

second team **5** bench **11** substitutes

secrecy **6** hiding **7** mystery, privacy, private, silence, stealth **8** muteness, solitude **9** closeness, seclusion **10** covertness **11** concealment, furtiveness **13** sequestration **15** clandestineness, confidentiality, underhandedness **17** surreptitiousness **19** uncommunicativeness

secret **3** key, mum **4** dark **6** arcane, covert, enigma, hidden, mystic, occult, puzzle, recipe, unseen **7** formula, furtive, mystery, private, unknown **8** discreet, esoteric, hush-hush, secluded, stealthy **9** concealed, disguised, invisible, secretive **10** confidence, mysterious, undercover, unrevealed **11** camouflaged, clandestine, undisclosed, unpublished **12** confidential, unrevealable **13** surreptitious

Secret Agent
character: **9** John Drake
cast: **15** Patrick McGoohan
theme: **14** Secret Agent Man

secretary **4** aide, desk **5** clerk **6** scribe **7** officer **8** recorder **10** amanuensis **12** stenographer
French: **10** escritoire

secret council **8** conclave

secrete **4** hide, veil **5** cache, cloak, cover, stash **6** screen, shroud **7** conceal, curtain **8** disguise

secretive **3** mum, sly **4** mute **6** covert, silent **7** cryptic, evasive, furtive, laconic, private **8** discreet, reserved, reticent, stealthy, taciturn **9** enigmatic, withdrawn **10** mysterious **11** tight-lipped, underhanded, unrevealing **13** surreptitious **15** uncommunicative

secretiveness **7** mystery, stealth **9** reticence **11** furtiveness **14** inscrutability, mysteriousness **19** uncommunicativeness

Secret Life of Walter Mitty, The
author: **12** James Thurber

sect **4** camp, cult **7** faction **8** division **10** persuasion **11** affiliation **12** denomination

sectarian **6** narrow **7** limited **8** clannish **9** exclusive, parochial **10** provincial, restricted

section **4** area, part, side, unit, ward, zone **5** piece, range, share, slice **6** region, sample, sphere **7** chapter, cutting, measure, passage, portion, segment, terrain **8** district, division, province, specimen, vicinity **9** allotment, increment, territory **10** department, proportion **11** installment **12** neighborhood

sector **4** area, zone **7** theater **8** district

secular **3** lay **4** laic **6** carnal **7** earthly, fleshly, mundane, profane, sensual, worldly **8** material, temporal **9** nonsacred **11** nonclerical **12** nonreligious, nonspiritual **17** nonecclesiastical

secundum **11** according to

secure **3** get, set **4** bind, easy, safe, sure **5** fixed, tight **6** at ease, defend, ensure, fasten, immune, insure, obtain **7** acquire, assured, certain, protect, shelter, tie down **8** absolute, carefree, composed, defended, definite, in the bag, positive, surefire **9** confident, guarantee, protected, reassured, safeguard, sheltered **10** guaranteed **11** impregnable **12** invulnerable, unassailable, unattackable, unthreatened

securities **5** bonds, title **6** stocks **12** certificates

security **4** bond, care, hope, keep **5** faith, trust **6** guards, pledge, police, safety, surety, troops **7** defense, deposit, promise, support **8** reliance, sureness, warranty **9** assurance, certainty, guarantee **10** collateral, confidence, conviction, protection, safeguards **11** maintenance, safekeeping **12** absoluteness, decisiveness, definiteness, positiveness, preservation

sedate **4** calm, cool **5** grave, quiet, sober, staid, still **6** poised, serene, solemn, steady **7** serious, subdued **8** composed, decorous, reserved **9** collected, dignified, impassive, unexcited, unruffled **10** cool-headed **11** levelheaded **13** imperturbable **15** undemonstrative

sedateness **7** decorum, dignity, gravity, reserve **8** calmness **9** composure, soberness, solemnity **11** impassivity, seriousness

sedative **6** easing, opiate **7** anodyne, calming **8** allaying, lenitive, narcotic, relaxing, soothing **9** analgesic, assuasive, calmative, composing, mitigator, soporific **10** comforting, palliative **11** alleviative **12** tranquilizer **13** tranquilizing

sedentary **5** fixed, inert, still **6** seated **7** resting, sitting **8** inactive, unmoving **9** quiescent **10** stationary, unstirring

sedge **4** reed **5** grass **10** marsh grass

sediment **4** lees, scum, slag **5** dregs, dross, waste **6** debris, sludge **7** grounds, remains, residue **8** leavings **9** settlings

sedition **6** mutiny, revolt **7** treason **8** defiance, uprising **9** rebellion **10** disloyalty, insurgency, subversion, unruliness **11** lawlessness **12** disobedience, insurrection **14** rebelliousness, subversiveness

Sedley, Amelia and Joseph
characters in: **10** Vanity Fair
author: **9** Thackeray

seduce **4** lure, ruin **5** abuse, charm, tempt **6** allure, defile, entice, ravish **7** attract, conquer, corrupt, debauch, deprave, pervert, violate, win over **8** deflower, disgrace, dishonor, persuade **9** captivate

seducer **3** cad **4** wolf **5** letch, Romeo **7** defiler, Don Juan, playboy **8** Casanova, Lothario, lover-boy, ravisher, violater **9** corrupter, debaucher, womanizer **10** deflowerer **11** philanderer **12** heartbreaker
French: **4** roue

seductive **4** sexy **8** alluring, charming, enticing, tempting **9** beguiling, disarming **10** attractive, bewitching, come-hither, enchanting, voluptuous **11** captivating, provocative

seductress **4** vamp **5** siren **7** charmer, Jezebel, Lorelei, mantrap **9** temptress **11** adventuress, enchantress
French: **7** cocotte **11** femme fatale

sedulous **6** dogged **8** diligent, thorough **9** assiduous, steadfast **10** determined, persistent **11** industrious, painstaking, persevering **13** conscientious, indefatigable

sedulousness **4** zeal **8** industry, tenacity **9** assiduity, diligence **11** persistence **12** perseverance

see **3** dig, eye, spy, woo **4** date, espy, know, meet, mind, spot, view **5** court, grasp, sight, visit, watch **6** attend, behold, descry, escort, fathom, notice, regard, survey **7** consult, discern, glimpse, observe, picture, realize, receive, undergo, witness **8** conceive, consider, discover, envision, meditate, perceive, register, ruminate **9** accompany, apprehend, ascertain, determine, encounter, entertain, interview, recognize, visualize **10** appreciate, comprehend, experience, understand **11** contemplate, distinguish
Latin: **4** vide

see above
Latin: **9** vide supra

see after
Latin: **8** vide post

see as above, see as stated above
Latin: **11** vide ut supra

see before
Latin: **8** vide ante

see below
Latin: **9** vide infra

seed **3** pit, sow **4** germ **5** basis, grain, heirs, issue, ovule, plant, stone **6** embryo, origin, source **7** progeny **8** children **9** beginning, offspring, posterity **11** descendants

seedy **4** worn **5** dingy, faded, lousy, mangy, ratty, spent, tacky **6** scuffy, shabby **7** haggard, sickish, squalid **8** slovenly **10** threadbare **11** debilitated

see eye to eye **5** agree **6** concur **11** be of one mind

see fit **5** deign **6** choose, please

see further
Latin: **8** vide post

seek **3** try **4** hunt **5** court, essay, trace **6** demand, invite, pursue **7** attempt, examine, explore, inspect, request, solicit, venture **8** endeavor **9** undertake **10** scrutinize **11** investigate

seek out **4** find **6** pursue **7** embrace, look for, solicit

seek proof **4** test **6** try out **7** analyze, examine **8** research **10** experiment **11** investigate

seem **4** look **6** appear

seeming **7** evident, obvious, surface **8** apparent, presumed, putative, supposed **10** ostensible **11** superficial

seemly **3** due **5** right **6** decent, polite, proper **7** correct, fitting, prudent, refined **8** becoming, decorous, suitable, tasteful, well-bred **9** befitting, courteous **10** acceptable, felicitous **11** appropriate **12** conventional
French: **11** comme il faut

seep **4** drip, leak, ooze, soak **7** diffuse, dribble, suffuse, trickle **8** permeate **9** penetrate

seepage **4** ooze **5** flour, issue **7** leakage, outflow **9** discharge, dribbling, secretion, trickling

seer **4** sage **5** augur **6** medium, oracle **7** diviner, prophet, psychic **8** conjurer, sorcerer **9** sorceress, stargazer **10** astrologer, soothsayer **11** clairvoyant, necromancer 13 fortuneteller 14 prognosticator

seesaw 5 waver 6 teeter 9 alternate, fluctuate, up-and-down, vacillate 12 teeter-totter

seethe 4 boil, brew, cook, fume, rage, rant, rave, roil, stew 5 churn, storm 6 blow up, bubble, simmer 7 bluster, smolder

seething 3 mad 7 boiling 8 agitated, bubbling, frenzied 10 distraught

see through 3 get 6 detect, effect, finish 7 achieve, execute, perform 8 carry out, complete, conclude 9 catch onto, figure out, penetrate 10 comprehend, understand

Segal, Erich
author of: 9 Love Story 12 Oliver's Story 16 Man Woman and Child

Segal, George
born: 9 New York NY
roles: 11 Blume in Love, Where's Poppa? 13 A Touch of Class 18 Fun with Dick and Jane 25 Who's Afraid of Virginia Woolf?

segment 3 leg 4 part 5 cut up, piece, stage 6 cleave 7 disjoin, portion, section, split up 8 disunite, division, separate 9 increment 11 installment

segmented 5 cut up 7 split up 9 sectioned, separated

segregate 6 cut off, detach, divide 7 divorce, isolate, seclude, sort out 8 disunite, insulate, separate 9 sequester 10 disconnect, quarantine

segue
music: 21 continue without a break

seine 3 net 4 drag, fish 5 trawl 7 dragnet

seism 5 quake, shock 6 tremor 8 tremblor, upheaval 10 earthquake

seize 3 bag, nab 4 grab, read 5 catch, glean, grasp, pinch, pluck, usurp 6 arrest, clutch, collar, gather, snatch 7 capture, embrace, impound, possess, utilize 8 arrogate 9 apprehend, overpower, overwhelm 10 commandeer, comprehend, confiscate, understand 11 appropriate

seize the day
Latin: 9 carpe diem

seizure 3 fit 5 onset, spell, throe 6 access, arrest, attack, crisis, stroke, taking 7 capture, episode 8 grasping, paroxysm 9 abduction, snatching 10 convulsion, kidnapping, possession, usurpation, visitation 11 impressment 12 apprehension, confiscation 13 appropriation, commandeering

Sejanus
author: 9 Ben Jonson

Sekhmet
origin: 8 Egyptian
goddess of: 4 evil

Selden, Mr
character in: 15 The House of Mirth
author: 7 Wharton

seldom 6 rarely 8 scarcely 10 uncommonly 12 infrequently, occasionally, sporadically

select 3 tap 4 A-one, pick, posh 5 elect, elite, fancy 6 choice, choose, chosen, opt for, picked, prefer 8 four-star, superior, top-notch 9 exclusive, first-rate, preferred 10 first-class, privileged

selection 4 pick 5 range 6 choice, medley, option 7 program, variety 8 choosing, decision 9 potpourri 10 collection, miscellany, preference

selective 5 fussy, picky 6 choosy 7 careful, finicky 8 cautious 10 discerning, fastidious, meticulous, particular 14 discriminating

Selemnus
vocation: 8 shepherd
loved: 6 Argyra
changed into: 5 river
changed by: 9 Aphrodite

Selene
goddess of: 4 moon
father: 8 Hyperion
mother: 5 Theia
brother: 6 Helios
sister: 3 Eos
loved: 8 Endymion
daughter: 5 Herse 6 Pandia
corresponds to: 5 Diana 7 Artemis

self 3 ego 6 person, psyche 8 identity 10 individual 11 homogeneity, personality
inner: 5 anima 6 animus
Universal: 5 Atman

self-abnegation 7 modesty 8 humility 10 diffidence 11 bashfulness

self-absorbed 4 vain 8 egoistic 9 egotistic 10 egocentric 11 egotistical 12 narcissistic

self-absorption 6 egoism, vanity 7 conceit 11 egocentrism, selfishness 16 self-centeredness

self-admiration 6 vanity 7 conceit, egotism 8 smugness 9 immodesty, vainglory

self-assertive 4 bold 7 dynamic 8 forceful 9 ambitious, confident 10 aggressive

self-assuming 4 vain 8 arrogant, egoistic 9 conceited 10 egoistical 11 egotistical

self-assurance 6 aplomb 9 brashness 12 cocksureness
French: 9 sangfroid

self-assured 5 brash, cocky 8 cocksure 9 confident

self-centered 4 vain 8 egoistic, immodest 9 conceited, egotistic 10 egocentric 11 egotistical, swellheaded 12 narcissistic

self-centeredness 6 egoism, vanity 7 conceit 10 narcissism 11 egocentrism

self-composure 5 poise 6 aplomb 8 calmness 10 equanimity

self-confidence 5 nerve, pluck 6 mettle, spirit 8 boldness, gameness 9 cockiness 10 resolution 12 cocksureness

self-conscious 7 awkward 8 affected 9 chagrined, ill at ease, unnatural 11 discomposed, embarrassed 12 disconcerted

self-consciousness 7 modesty, reserve, shyness 8 timidity 9 abashment, hesitancy, reticence 10 constraint, demureness, diffidence 11 bashfulness, fearfulness 12 apprehension, sheepishness

self-control 5 poise 6 aplomb 8 firmness, patience, sobriety 9 composure, soberness, soundness, stability, will-power 10 temperance 11 forbearance 14 cool-headedness, unexcitability 15 levelheadedness 16 imperturbability
French: 9 sangfroid 11 savoir faire

self-critical 6 humble, modest 9 diffident 13 perfectionist

self-criticism 7 modesty 8 humility 10 diffidence 13 perfectionism

self-deception 7 fantasy 8 delusion, illusion 13 hallucination

self-declared 5 sworn 6 avowed 8 admitted 9 confessed, professed 12 acknowledged

self-denial 8 eschewal 10 abnegation, abstention, abstinence, continence

11 forbearance **12** renunciation **14** abstemiousness

self-deprecation
also: 16 self-depreciation
7 modesty **8** humility, meekness **10** humbleness

self-doubt 11 uncertainty

self-effacement 7 modesty, shyness **8** humility, meekness **10** diffidence **11** bashfulness

self-esteem 5 pride **10** confidence

self-evident 5 plain **6** patent **7** glaring, obvious **8** apparent, distinct, explicit, manifest, palpable **10** unarguable, undeniable **11** unambiguous, unequivocal **12** unmistakable **16** incontrovertible

self-explanatory 5 clear, lucid, plain **7** obvious **8** manifest **12** intelligible **15** straightforward

self-governing 4 free **9** sovereign **10** autonomous **11** independent

self-government 8 autonomy, home rule **11** sovereignty **12** independence

self-gratifying 11 intemperate

self-importance 6 egoism, vanity **8** smugness **9** arrogance, immodesty, pomposity, vainglory **11** egocentrism

self-important 4 smug, vain **7** pompous **8** egoistic, immodest **10** egocentric **11** egotistical **12** vainglorious

self-indulgence 12 extravagance, incontinence, intemperance

self-indulgent 9 libertine, sybaritic **10** hedonistic, voluptuous **11** extravagant, incontinent, intemperate

selfish 4 mean **5** tight, venal **6** greedy, stingy **7** miserly **8** covetous, egoistic grasping, grudging **9** egotistic, illiberal, mercenary, rapacious **10** avaricious, egocentric, ungenerous **11** egotistical **12** parsimonious, uncharitable

self-love 6 egoism, vanity **7** conceit, egotism **9** vainglory **10** narcissism **11** complacency, egocentrism, haughtiness **13** conceitedness **15** swellheadedness
French: 11 amour propre

self-possessed 4 calm, cool **6** poised **7** assured, courtly, refined **8** balanced, composed, polished, resolute **9** collected, confident **12** aristocratic **13** distinguished

self-possession 5 poise **6** aplomb **7** dignity **8** calmness, coolness **9** composure **10** confidence, equanimity, steadiness **16** imperturbability
French: 9 sangfroid

self-praise 6 vanity **7** conceit, egotism **8** bragging, smugness **9** arrogance, immodesty, vainglory **12** boastfulness
Italian: 11 braggadocio

self-propelling 9 automatic

self-questioning 10 uneasiness **13** soul-searching

self-reliance 8 sureness **9** assurance **12** independence

Self-Reliance
author: 17 Ralph Waldo Emerson

self-reliant 5 hardy **6** plucky **7** assured **8** resolute, spirited **10** mettlesome **11** independent **12** enterprising

self-reproachful 8 contrite **9** regretful **10** apologetic, remorseful

self-respecting 5 proud **7** upright **8** decorous **9** dignified, honorable **10** upstanding **11** circumspect **13** distinguished

self-restraint 9 willpower **10** continence **11** forbearance

self-righteous 4 smug **5** pious **7** pompous **9** insincere, pietistic **10** complacent, moralizing **11** pharisaical, pretentious **12** hypocritical, mealy-mouthed **13** sanctimonious **14** holier-than-thou

self-sacrificing 6 heroic **7** gallant **9** unselfish **10** altruistic, martyrlike

self-satisfaction 5 pride **6** vanity **8** smugness **11** complacency

self-satisfied 4 smug, vain **8** cocksure, priggish **9** overproud **10** complacent **11** egotistical **12** narcissistic, vainglorious **13** overconfident

self-secure 4 smug **7** content **9** contented **10** complacent

self-seeking 6 greedy **8** covetous

self-styled
French: 9 soi-disant

self-willed 8 obdurate, stubborn **9** obstinate, pigheaded **10** headstrong, refractory **11** intractable **12** ungovernable, unmanageable

sell 4 dump, hawk, vend **6** barter, betray, deal in, enlist, handle, market, peddle, unload **7** deceive, trade in, win over **8** convince, dispense

Selleck, Tom
roles: 8 Lassiter, Magnum PI **12** Thomas Magnum **15** High Road to China **16** Three Men and A Baby

seller 6 dealer, jobber, monger, trader, vendor **7** peddler **8** merchant, retailer, salesman **9** middleman, salesgirl, saleslady, tradesman **10** saleswoman, shopkeeper, wholesaler **11** salesperson, storekeeper

Sellers, Peter
real name: 19 Richard Henry Sellers
born: 7 England **8** Southsea
wife: 11 Britt Ekland
roles: 10 Being There **12** Casino Royale **13** Dr Strangelove, Murder by Death **14** A Shot in the Dark, The Pink Panther **16** What's New Pussycat? **17** Inspector Clouseau **18** The Mouse that Roared **21** The World of Henry Orient

Selli
priests of: 4 Zeus

sell out 6 betray **11** double-cross

semblance 3 air **4** cast, copy, look, show **5** image **6** aspect **7** bearing, replica **8** likeness, pretense **9** duplicate, facsimile **10** simulacrum **11** counterpart **12** reproduction **14** representation
French: 4 mien

Semele
also: 6 Thyone
father: 6 Cadmus
mother: 8 Harmonia
loved by: 4 Zeus
son: 8 Dionysus
sister: 3 Ino **5** Agave **7** Autonoe

seminal 7 primary **8** creative, fruitful, germinal, original **9** formative **10** generative, productive **11** germinative, originating

Seminole
language family: 9 Muskogean
tribe: 8 Cow Creek, Mikasaki
location: 6 Mexico **7** Florida, Georgia **10** Everglades
leader: 7 Osceola, Wild Cat **10** Coacoochie

Semiramis
queen of: 7 Assyria
husband: 5 Ninus
founder of: 7 Babylon

Semitic
language family: **11** Afro-Asiatic **13** Hamito-Semitic
eastern branch: **8** Akkadian, Assyrian **10** Babylonian
western branch: **4** Geez **5** Tigre **6** Arabic, Gurage, Harari, Hebrew, Minean, Sabean, Syriac **7** Amharic, Aramaic, Argobba, Moabite **8** Ethiopic, Tigrinya, Ugaritic **9** Canaanite **10** Himyaritic, Phoenician, Qatabanian
southwest branch: **6** Minean, Sabean **7** Amharic **10** Himyaritic, Qatabanian **11** North Arabic **19** South Arabic-Ethiopic

Semo Sancus *see* **6** Sancus

senatus consultum **17** Roman senate decree

send **4** cast, emit, head, hurl, lead, show, toss **5** drive, fling, guide, refer, relay, shoot, throw **6** convey, direct, launch, propel **7** conduct, deliver, forward, give off, project **8** dispatch, transmit **9** broadcast, cause to go, discharge **11** disseminate

send away **4** oust, rout, shoo **5** chase, evict

send forth **4** emit, gush **5** erupt, expel, issue, let go **7** dismiss, release **8** disgorge, dispatch **9** discharge

send off **4** post **7** forward **8** dispatch, disperse, transmit

send out **4** beam, emit **8** dispatch, transmit **9** discharge

send packing **3** axe, can **4** fire, oust, rout, sack, shoo **5** evict **6** bounce **7** cast out, dismiss

send to Coventry **3** cut **5** eject, expel **6** banish, ignore **7** cast out, exclude **9** ostracize

Seneca
language family: **9** Iroquoian
location: **7** New York **15** Canandaigua Lake
leader: **9** John Abeel, John O'Bail **11** Cornplanter
member: **19** League of the Iroquois

Senegal ***see box***

senile **6** doting, infirm **7** foolish **8** decrepit **9** doddering, senescent **13** superannuated

senior, Senior **4** head, over **5** above, chief, doyen, elder, older **6** better **7** veteran **8** superior

seniority **6** tenure **9** longevity **10** precedence
French: **4** pere

Senegal
capital/largest city: **5** Dakar
others: **5** Bakel, Matam, Thies **7** Bignona, Kaolack, Kaollak **8** Diourbel, Kedougou, Linguere, Rufisque **10** Saint-Louis, Ziguinchor **11** Richard-Toll, Tambacounda
division: **7** Sudanic **8** Sahelian **9** Casamance
empire: **4** Mali **5** Jolof **6** Tekrur
monetary unit: **5** franc **7** centime
island: **5** Goree
lake: **6** Guiers
mountain: **6** Gounou
highest point: **12** Fouta Djallon
river: **4** Sine **6** Faleme, Gambia, Saloum **7** Senegal **9** Casamance
sea: **8** Atlantic
physical feature:
desert: **5** Ferlo
peninsula: **9** Cape Verde
people: **4** Lebu, Peul, Soce **5** Diola, Dyola, Foula, Laobe, Peulh, Serer, Wolof **6** Fulani, Serere **7** Bambara, Malinke, Tukuler, Tukulor **8** Mandingo
leader: **7** Senghor
language: **5** Wolof **6** French
religion: **5** Islam **7** animism **13** Roman Catholic
feature:
musical instrument: **4** kora
tree: **6** acacia, baobab **7** juniper, oil palm **10** raffia palm

senor **2** Mr **3** don **5** title **6** mister **8** Spaniard

senora **3** Mrs **4** lady, wife **5** madam, woman **8** mistress

senorita **4** lass, miss
abbreviation: **4** srta

senorita: **6** wrasse
genus: **8** Oxyjulis
species: **11** californica

sensation **3** hit **4** stir, to-do **6** thrill, uproar **7** feeling, scandal **9** agitation, awareness, commotion, detection **10** impression, perception

sensational **5** cheap, lurid **6** superb **8** dramatic, exciting, galvanic, shocking, striking **9** emotional, excellent, thrilling **10** electrical, scandalous **11** exaggerated, exceptional, extravagant, outstanding, spectacular **12** meretricious **13** extraordinary **14** heartthrobbing

sensationalism **7** scandal **9** luridness, melodrama **13** grandstanding **15** blood and thunder **16** yellow journalism

sense **3** see, use **4** aura, espy, feel, good, mind, note **5** grasp, guess, point, sight, smell, taste, touch, value, worth **6** descry, detect, divine, reason, regard, take in, wisdom **7** benefit, discern, faculty, feeling, hearing, meaning, purpose, realize, suspect **8** efficacy, function, judgment, perceive, sagacity **9** apprehend, awareness, intuition, recognize **10** atmosphere, comprehend, definition, denotation, impression, understand **11** connotation, premonition, realization, recognition **12** appreciation, intelligence, perspicacity, practicality, presentiment **13** consciousness, signification, understanding **14** reasonableness

Sense and Sensibility
author: **10** Jane Austen
character: **10** Lucy Steele **13** Edward Ferrars, Robert Ferrars **14** Colonel Brandon, John Willoughby **16** Sir John Middleton
Dashwood family: **4** John **5** Fanny **6** Elinor **8** Marianne

senseless **4** dumb, idle, numb **5** crazy, inane, nutty, silly **6** stupid, unwise **7** aimless, foolish, stunned, useless, witless **8** comatose, deadened **9** brainless, foolhardy, illogical, insensate, pointless **10** groundless, ill-advised, insensible, irrational, ridiculous **11** harebrained, meaningless, purposeless, unconscious **12** unreasonable **13** irresponsible

sense of duty **15** moral obligation **21** sense of responsibility

sensibilities **8** feelings, sore spot, thin skin **12** Achilles' heel **14** susceptibility

sensibility 7 feeling **10** perception **11** temperament **14** responsiveness

sensible 4 just, sage, sane, wise **5** aware, plain, sound **7** evident, knowing, logical, obvious, prudent, visible **8** apparent, apprised, credible, discreet, informed, palpable, possible, rational, tangible **9** cognitive, cognizant, conscious, judicious, plausible, sagacious **10** detectable, discerning, farsighted, noticeable, perceiving, perceptive, reasonable, responsive, thoughtful **11** discernible, enlightened, intelligent, perceptible, susceptible **13** perspicacious **14** discriminating

sensitive 4 fine, keen, sore **5** acute, exact **6** tender, touchy **7** painful, precise **8** accurate, delicate, faithful, sentient **10** perceptive, responsive **11** susceptible, thin-skinned **14** impressionable

sensitiveness 8 delicacy **10** touchiness

sensual 4 lewd, sexy **6** carnal, earthy, erotic **7** fleshly, lustful **9** lecherous **10** hedonistic, licentious, voluptuous

sensualist 8 hedonist, sybarite **9** libertine **10** voluptuary

sensuous 9 delicious, exquisite **10** delightful

sententious 7 orotund, pompous, preachy, stilted **8** didactic, pedantic **9** grandiose, high-flown, pietistic **10** judgmental, moralistic **13** sanctimonious

sentient 5 aware **7** alert to, alive to, awake to, mindful **8** sensible **9** conscious

sentiment, sentiments **4** idea **5** heart **6** notion **7** emotion, feeling, opinion, romance, thought **8** attitude **9** nostalgia, viewpoint **10** tenderness **11** romanticism **12** emotionalism **15** softheartedness

sentimental 5 mushy, weepy **7** maudlin, mawkish, tearful **8** pathetic, romantic **9** emotional, nostalgic **10** lachrymose **12** melodramatic, romanticized

Sentimental Education, A
author: 15 Gustave Flaubert
character: 6 Arnoux **9** Dambreuse, Rosanette **11** Des Lauriers, Louise Roque **14** Frederic Moreau

sentimentalism 4 corn, mush **5** slush **6** bathos, pathos **8** schmaltz **9** mushiness, soppiness **10** maudlinism, slushiness **11** mawkishness

sentimentality 4 mush **5** heart **6** bathos, pathos **10** sloppiness **11** mawkishness, temperament **12** emotionalism
Yiddish: 6 kitsch

Sentimental Journey, A
author: 14 Laurence Sterne
character: 5 Maria **6** Yorick **7** La Fleur

sentinel 4 ward **5** guard, scout, watch **6** patrol, picket, ranger **7** lookout **8** guardian, watchman **9** guardsman

sentry 5 guard, watch **7** lookout, vedette, vidette **8** sentinel, watchman
greeting: 4 halt

Seoul
capital of: 10 South Korea

separate 3 cut **4** cull, fork, part, sift **5** break, crack, sever, split **6** bisect, detach, divide, ramify, remove, single, spread, sunder **7** crumble, disjoin, diverge, diverse, divorce, isolate, radiate **8** detached, discrete, distinct, disunite **9** bifurcate, break away, come apart, different, disunited, partition, segregate, subdivide **10** autonomous, disconnect, dissimilar, divaricate, individual **11** distinguish, independent

separated 6 cut off **7** severed **8** detached **10** disengaged **12** disconnected, disentangled

separate from 5 apart, leave

separately 5 apart **6** singly **7** asunder **9** severally **12** individually

Separate Tables
director: 11 Delbert Mann
based on play by: 15 Terence Rattigan
cast: 10 David Niven **11** Deborah Kerr, Wendy Hiller **12** Rita Hayworth **13** Burt Lancaster
Oscar for: 5 actor (Niven) **17** supporting actress (Hiller)

separation 3 gap **4** fork **5** break, space, split **6** breach, divide, schism **7** divider, divorce, good-bye, opening, parting, removal, sorting **8** boundary, distance, disunion, division, farewell, interval **9** branching, isolation, partition, severance **10** detachment, divergence **11** bifurcation, disjunction, segregation **12** estrangement **13** disconnection, disengagement **14** disassociation

Sepharvite god 10 Anammelech **11** Adrammelech

Sepharvites
residents of: 6 Sippar

Sepher Torah 16 scroll of the Torah
literally: 9 book of law

September
characteristic: 11 harvest moon
event: 14 aurora borealis, Northern lights **15** autumnal equinox
flower: 5 aster **12** morning glory
French: 9 Septembre
gem: 8 sapphire **12** star sapphire
German: 9 September
holiday: 8 Labor Day (1st Monday) **9** Yom Kippur **10** Michaelmas (29) **12** Rosh Hashanah **15** Grandparents' Day
Italian: 9 Settembre
number of days: 6 thirty
origin of name: 6 septum (Latin meaning seven)
place in year:
***Gregorian:* 5** ninth
***Roman:* 7** seventh
Spanish: 10 Septiembre
Zodiac sign: 5 Libra, Virgo

septentrional 6 arctic **8** northern **11** hyperborean

Septuagint
abbreviation: 3 LXX
author: 10 the Seventy

sepulcher 4 tomb **5** crypt, grave, vault **7** ossuary **8** cenotaph **9** mausoleum, reliquary **10** necropolis

sepulchral 6 hollow **7** charnel **8** funereal, mournful, tomblike **10** lugubrious

sequel 3 end **6** finish, result, upshot **7** outcome, product **8** addendum, epilogue, follow-up, offshoot **9** aftermath, corollary, outgrowth **10** conclusion, postscript **11** consequence, culmination **12** continuation
French: 10 denouement

sequence 3 run **4** flow **5** chain, cycle, order, round, train **6** course, parade, series, string **7** routine **8** schedule **9** cavalcade **10** procession, succession **11** arrangement, progression **14** successiveness **15** consecutiveness

sequester 6 banish, lock up, retire **7** confine, isolate, seclude **8** separate, withdraw **9** segregate **10** quarantine

sequestered 8 closeted, confined, isolated, secluded **9** insulated, sheltered, withdrawn **10** cloistered **11** dissociated

sequin 4 coin, disk **5** ducat **7** spangle **8** ornament
French: 9 paillette

seraglio 3 oda **5** harem, serai **6** zenana **9** gynaeceum

Seraiah
son: 4 Ezra

serape 4 cape **5** shawl **6** mantle, poncho

seraph 5 angel

seraphic 7 angelic **8** beatific, ethereal, heavenly **9** celestial

Seraphim 6 angels

Serapis
origin: 5 Greek **8** Egyptian
form: 5 deity
combination of: 4 Apis, Hapi **6** Osiris

sere 3 dry **4** arid **6** barren **7** parched, wizened **8** droughty, scorched, withered **9** shriveled, unwatered, waterless **10** dehydrated, desiccated **12** dehumidified, moistureless

Serendib *see* **8** Sri Lanka

serene 4 calm, cool, fair **5** clear, quiet, still **6** bright, limpid, placid, poised, sedate, smooth **7** halcyon **8** composed, peaceful, pellucid, tranquil **9** dignified, unruffled **10** nonchalant, unobscured, untroubled **11** undisturbed, unexcitable, unperturbed **13** unimpassioned

serenity 7 dignity **8** calmness, coolness, quietude **9** composure, placidity **10** equanimity, quiescence **11** complacence, nonchalance, tranquility **12** peacefulness, tranquillity **13** collectedness
French: 9 sangfroid

serf 6 cotter, thrall, vassal **7** bondman, peasant, villein

serfdom 4 yoke **6** thrall **7** bondage, slavery **9** servitude, thralldom, vassalage **11** enslavement, subjugation

Sergeant York
director: 11 Howard Hawks
cast: 10 Gary Cooper, Joan Leslie **12** George Tobias **13** Walter Brennan
Oscar for: 5 actor (Cooper)

Sergestus
origin: 6 Trojan
companion to: 6 Aeneas

serial 7 regular **9** continued, piecemeal, recurring **10** continuous, sequential, successive **11** consecutive, incremental

series 3 set **5** chain, cycle, group, order **6** course, number, parade, string **8** sequence **10** procession, succession **11** progression

serious 3 bad, sad **4** grim **5** grave, heavy, sober, staid **6** rueful, sedate, severe, solemn, somber **7** crucial, decided, earnest, fateful, harmful, pensive, sincere, weighty **8** alarming, critical, dejected, downcast, frowning, perilous, resolute, resolved **9** crippling, dangerous, important, momentous, saturnine **10** determined, portentous, purposeful, thoughtful **13** consequential **14** incapacitating

seriousness 7 gravity **8** severity **9** sincerity, soberness, solemnity **10** importance **11** earnestness

sermon 6 homily, rebuke, tirade **7** lecture, reproof **8** diatribe, harangue **9** preaching **10** admonition, preachment **11** exhortation

serpent, Serpent 3 asp **5** cheat, devil, rogue, Satan, snake, viper **7** reptile, traitor **8** deceiver **9** trickster
constellation of: 7 Serpens

Serpent Holder
constellation of: 9 Ophiuchus

serpentine 4 mazy **6** spiral, zigzag **7** coiling, crooked, devious, sinuous, snaking, winding **8** flexuous, tortuous, twisting **10** circuitous, convoluted, meandering, roundabout, undulating **12** labyrinthine

Serpico
director: 11 Sidney Lumet
based on story by: 9 Peter Maas
cast: 8 Al Pacino **9** Jack Kehoe **12** John Randolph
setting: 11 New York City

serrate 5 notch **6** jagged, pinked, ridged **7** dentate, grooved, notched, toothed **10** sawtoothed

serration 5 notch, ridge, teeth, tooth **8** notching, sawtooth

servant 3 man **4** cook, girl, help, maid **5** valet **6** butler, flunky, helper, lackey, menial, minion, slavey **7** footman **8** domestic, employee, factotum, henchman, hired man, retainer, scullion **9** attendant, chauffeur, hired girl, hired help, man Friday, underling **10** girl Friday **11** housekeeper

serve 2 do **3** act, aid **4** help, pass, suit, tend, work **5** avail, spend, treat **6** assist, attend, be used, do duty, oblige, supply, wait on **7** content, deliver, further, perform, present, promote, satisfy, suffice, work for **8** carry out, complete, function, hand over, minister **9** officiate **11** fill the bill

service, services 3 aid, use **4** help, mend, rite **5** avail, labor **6** adjust, agency, bureau, effort, employ, profit, repair, ritual, system **7** benefit, support, utility, waiting **8** ceremony, facility, maintain, military **9** advantage, provision, treatment **10** assistance, attendance, ceremonial, department, employment, observance, usefulness **11** celebration, convenience, maintenance **12** ministration **13** accommodation

serviceable 5 tough **6** rugged, strong, sturdy, usable, useful **7** durable, lasting **8** workable **9** effective, operative, practical **10** functional **11** utilitarian

serviceman 6 marine, sailor **7** soldier **9** repairman

servile 4 oily **6** abject, humble, menial **7** fawning, in bonds, slavish **8** cringing, scraping, toadying, unctuous **9** groveling, truckling **10** obsequious, submissive **11** bootlicking, subservient, sycophantic

serving 6 acting **7** dishful, helping, portion, waiting **8** plateful **9** assisting, attending, sufficing **11** ministering

serving counter 3 bar **6** buffet **9** sideboard

servitude 5 bonds **6** chains **7** bondage, fetters, serfdom, slavery **8** shackles **9** thralldom, vassalage **10** oppression **11** enslavement, subjugation **12** enthrallment, imprisonment

Servius Tullius
also: 7 Tullius
king of: 4 Rome
daughter: 6 Tullia
son-in-law: 7 Tarquin
killed by: 6 Tullia **7** Tarquin

sesame
also called: 10 benne seeds
botanical name: 14 Sesamum indicum
fairy tale: 10 "open sesame" **25** Ali Baba and the Forty Thieves

high in: 7 protein
former/mythical use: 3 oil 8 medicine 10 opens locks 11 lighting oil 16 discovers secrets 21 discovers secret places
use: 5 bread 6 salads 10 casseroles
use like: 8 nutmeats 11 chopped nuts

Sesame Street
character: 4 Bert, Elmo 5 Ernie, Herry, Oscar 6 Snuffy 7 Barkley, Big Bird, Muppets 8 the Count 12 Telly Monster 13 Cookie Monster 15 Mr Snuffleupagus

Sesostris
king of: 5 Egypt

session 4 bout, term 5 round, synod 6 course, period 7 meeting, quarter, sitting 8 assembly, conclave, semester 10 conference, convention

set *see box*

Set
also: 4 Seth
origin: 8 Egyptian
form: 6 animal
personifies: 6 desert
brother: 6 Osiris
killed: 6 Osiris

set about 5 begin 6 assume 9 undertake 10 surrounded

set against 8 alienate, estrange

set apart 5 allot 6 detach, divide 7 earmark, isolate 8 allocate, separate 9 apportion, segregate 11 appropriate

set aside 4 kill 5 allot, annul 6 abjure, cancel, repeal, revoke 7 abandon, abolish, call off, destroy, discard, earmark, nullify, put away, rescind, retract, reverse 8 abrogate, allocate, override, overturn 9 designate, repudiate 10 invalidate 11 discontinue

set at ease 5 cheer 6 please 7 appease, comfort, content, gratify

set at liberty 4 free 5 let go 6 parole 7 manumit, release, unchain 8 liberate, unfetter 9 unshackle 10 emancipate

setback 4 flop, loss, snag 5 hitch, slump 6 defeat, mishap, rebuff 7 failure, relapse, reverse, undoing 8 reversal 9 adversity, mischance, worsening 10 misfortune, regression 13 retrogression 14 disappointment

set down 6 record 7 deposit

set forth 2 go 5 be off, leave 6 assert, avouch, depart 7 advance 8 advocate, propound 10 sally forth

set free 5 let go, loose, untie 6 acquit, loosen, pardon, parole, unbind, uncage, unlock 7 deliver, release 8 liberate, unfetter 9 discharge, disengage, extricate 10 emancipate

Seth *see* 3 Set

Seth
means: 12 compensation
father: 4 Adam
mother: 3 Eve
son: 4 Enos

set in 5 arise, ensue, occur 6 arrive

set in motion 5 begin, start 6 launch 8 initiate 9 instigate, originate 10 inaugurate

set in order 4 rank, sort 5 align 6 line up 7 arrange, marshal 8 classify, organize 9 methodize 11 systematize

set of beliefs 5 credo, creed, dogma, ethos 6 ethnic, tenets 8 doctrine 10 philosophy, principles 11 convictions

set off 6 depart 7 explode, go forth 8 detonate, start out 10 sally forth

set on fire 4 burn 5 light 6 ignite, kindle

set out 4 pose 5 array, begin, be off, place, range 6 deploy, embark, intend 7 arrange, display 9 undertake

set right 7 correct 8 disabuse

set store by 5 prize, value 6 esteem 7 respect 8 treasure

set straight 5 edify 6 advise, inform 7 educate 8 disabuse 9 enlighten

settee 4 seat, sofa 5 bench

setting 5 scene 6 fixing, locale 7 jelling 8 aligning, ambiance, locating, location, mounting 9 adjusting, arranging, decreeing, hardening, ordaining 10 congealing, regulating, thickening 11 arrangement, determining, environment, prescribing, solidifying 12 establishing, surroundings
French: 6 milieu 11 mise-en-scene

setting sun
god of: 5 Janus

settle 3 fix, pay, sag 4 calm, drop, land, sink 5 agree, allay, clear, droop, light, lodge, perch, quiet 6 alight, choose, decide, locate, move to, pacify, people, soothe 7 arrange, clarify, clear up, compose, inhabit, rectify, resolve, satisfy, sit down, situate 8 colonize, make good, populate, take root 9 determine, discharge, establish, reconcile 11 precipitate

settled 4 sure 7 certain, decided

settlement 3 sum 4 camp, post 6 amount, colony, hamlet 7 bequest, outpost, payment, village 8 clearing, peopling 9 clearance, discharge 10 adjustment, colonizing, encampment, resolution 11 acquittance, arrangement, liquidation 12 amortization, colonization, compensation, satisfaction 14 reconciliation

settler 7 pioneer 8 colonist, squatter 9 colonizer, immigrant 11 homesteader 12 frontiersman

settle upon 6 bestow 7 consign 8 bequeath

set 3 cut, fit, fix, gel, kit, lay, put, sic 4 club, drop, firm, line, make, plop, post, rate, sink, stud, suit 5 adapt, align, array, banal, bunch, crowd, embed, fixed, group, imbed, order, place, plunk, ready, rigid, scene, stale, stiff, stock, style, trite, usual 6 adjust, assess, assign, attach, common, confer, create, decree, frozen, harden, line up, locale, locate, ordain, outfit, studio 7 arrange, bearing, complex, congeal, decided, faction, install, jellify, machine, prepare, profile, regular, release, routine, scenery, service, setting, situate, station, thicken, unleash 8 arranged, assembly, backdrop, carriage, definite, estimate, everyday, familiar, firmness, habitual, hardened, location, ornament, position, prepared, regulate, rigidity, solidify, stubborn 9 apparatus, calibrate, customary, determine, establish, hackneyed, immovable, obstinate, prescribe, represent, steadfast 10 accustomed, assortment, collection, inflexible 11 anticipated, commonplace, consolidate, established, prearranged 12 conventional
French: 6 clique 7 coterie

settlings 4 lees **5** dregs **7** deposit, grounds, remains, residue **8** leavings

set-to 4 spat **5** brush, clash, run-in **6** battle, fracas **7** dispute, quarrel, scuffle **8** argument, skirmish, squabble **10** engagement, falling out **12** disagreement **13** confrontation
French: 11 contretemps

setup 4 plan **6** scheme, system **8** practice **9** apparatus **11** arrangement **12** organization

set up 3 rig **5** erect, found **7** arrange, install **9** construct, establish, institute **10** inaugurate, prearrange

set upon 3 mug **5** beset, fly at **6** assail, attack **7** besiege, lunge at **9** pitch into

Seurat, Georges Pierre
born: 5 Paris **6** France
artwork: 9 The Chahut, The Circus, The Models, The Parade, The Uproar **10** The Bathers **12** Le Grand Jatte, The Yoked Cart **19** Une Baignade Asnieres **23** A Bathing Scene at Asnieres, The Bec du Hoc at Grandchamp **40** Sunday Afternoon on the Island of La Grand Jatte

Seuss, Dr
real name: 19 Theodore Seuss Geisel
author of: 12 If I Ran the Zoo **14** The Cat in the Hat **15** Green Eggs and Ham, Horton Hears a Who, If I Ran the Circus **19** Horton Hatches the Egg **23** Mister Brown Can Moo Can You? **26** Thidwick The Big-Hearted Moose, How the Grinch Stole Christmas

Seve
nickname of: 20 Severiano Ballesteros

Seven Against Thebes
author: 9 Aeschylus
character: 6 Ismene **8** Antigone, Eteocles **9** Polynices **11** Theban Women
seven heroes: 6 Tydeus **8** Adrastus, Capaneus **9** Polynices **10** Amphiaraus, Hippomedon **13** Parthenopaeus

Seven Beauties
director: 14 Lina Wertmuller
cast: 11 Fernando Rey **13** Shirley Stoler **17** Giancarlo Giannini

Seven Brides for Seven Brothers
director: 12 Stanley Donen
cast: 9 Tammy Rall **10** Howard Keel, Jane Powell **11** Julie Newmar (Newmeyer), Russ Tamblyn **12** Jeff Richards **14** Virginia Gibson
score: 11 Saul Chaplin **12** Johnny Mercer
choreography: 11 Michael Kidd

Seven Pillars of Wisdom
author: 10 T E Lawrence

Seven Samurai
director: 13 Akira Kurosawa
cast: 11 Yoshio Inaba **13** Toshiro Mifune **14** Takashi Shimura
remade as: 19 The Magnificent Seven

seven seas 6 Arctic, Indian **9** Antarctic **12** North Pacific, South Pacific **13** North Atlantic, South Atlantic

Seven Sisters colleges
5 Smith **6** Vassar **7** Barnard **8** Bryn Mawr **9** Radcliffe, Wellesley **12** Mount Holyoke

Seventeen
author: 15 Booth Tarkington
character: 7 Genesis **9** Miss Pratt, Mrs Baxter **10** Jane Baxter, May Parcher **21** William Sylvanus Baxter

Seventh Seal, The
director: 13 Ingmar Bergman
cast: 9 Nils Poppe **11** Max von Sydow **13** Bibi Andersson **17** Gunnar Bjornstrand

77 Sunset Strip
character: 6 J R Hale, Kookie (Gerald Lloyd Kookson III), Roscoe **7** Suzanne **11** Jeff Spencer, Rex Randolph **12** Stuart Bailey
cast: 9 Edd Byrnes **10** Louis Quinn, Roger Smith **11** Richard Long, Robert Logan **14** Jacqueline Beer **16** Efrem Zimbalist Jr
Kookie's sayings: 10 a dark seven **12** the ginchiest **13** piling up the Z's **14** lend me your comb **15** play like a pigeon **17** headache grapplers **22** keep the eyeballs rolling

seven wonders of the world 8 pyramids (Egypt) **12** Olympian Zeus (sculpted by Phidias) **15** Temple of Artemis (at Ephesus) **16** Colossus of Rhodes **22** Lighthouse at Alexandria **23** hanging gardens of Babylon (of Semiramis) **24** Mausoleum at Halicarnassus

Seven Year Itch, The
director: 11 Billy Wilder
cast: 8 Tom Ewell **10** Sonny Tufts **11** Evelyn Keyes, Victor Moore **13** Marilyn Monroe
setting: 11 New York City

sever 3 saw **4** part, rend, rive, tear **5** slice, split **6** bisect, cleave, cut off, lop off **7** disjoin, rupture, split up **8** amputate, break off, cut in two, dissolve, disunite, separate, truncate **9** dismember, terminate **10** disconnect **11** discontinue

several 3 own **4** a few, some **6** divers, single, sundry **7** certain, diverse, express, private, special **8** assorted, distinct, peculiar, personal, separate, specific **9** different, exclusive **10** individual, particular, respective **11** distinctive, independent

severe 4 cold, dour, grim, wild **5** cruel, grave, harsh, plain, rough, sober, stern, stiff **6** biting, bitter, brutal, chaste, fierce, fuming, raging, savage, sedate, simple, somber, strict, taxing **7** austere, cutting, drastic, extreme, furious, intense, painful, serious, uniform, violent **8** piercing, rigorous, ruthless, stinging, vigorous **9** dangerous, demanding, difficult, draconian, merciless, saturnine, turbulent, unadorned, unsparing **10** forbidding, restrained, tumultuous **11** distressing, undecorated, unrelenting **12** conservative

severed 6 cut off **8** detached **9** uncoupled, unhitched **10** unfastened **11** unconnected **12** disconnected

Severini, Gino
born: 5 Italy **7** Cortona
artwork: 9 Harlequin **15** The Armored Train **25** Dancer Sea and Vase of Flowers **32** Dynamic Hieroglyph of the Bal Tabarin

severity 5 rigor **7** cruelty **8** acrimony, violence **9** austerity, gruffness, harshness, sternness **10** asceticism, difficulty, strictness, stringency **11** seriousness **12** grievousness

Seville
former name: 8 Hispalis
landmark: 7 Alcazar, Giralda
plain: 9 Andalusia
river: 12 Guadalquivir
ruler: 5 Moors **6** Romans **7** Vandals **8** Abbasids, Almohads, Iberians **9** Visigoths **10** Almoravids
Spanish: 7 Sevilla

sew 3 hem **4** mend, seam,

tack **5** unite **6** fasten, ground, stitch, suture **10** run aground
loosely: 5 baste

sewage 5 waste **6** efflux, refuse **8** effluent **9** effluence

Seward, Dr
character in: 7 Dracula
author: 6 Stoker

sewing machine
invented by: 4 Howe

sex 4 Eros, love **6** coitus, gender, libido **7** coition **8** maleness **10** copulation, femaleness, femininity, generation, lovemaking **11** masculinity, procreation **12** reproduction

Sexton, Anne
author of: 15 All My Pretty Ones **22** To Bedlam and Part Way Back **23** The Awful Rowing Toward God

sexual 6 coital, erotic **7** amatory, genital, marital, sensual **8** conjugal, intimate, venereal **10** copulatory, generative, libidinous **11** procreative **12** reproductive

sexually stimulating 4 sexy **6** erotic, risque **9** salacious **10** suggestive **12** pornographic

sexy 4 lewd **5** bawdy **6** erotic **8** prurient **9** seductive **10** come-hither, coquettish, suggestive, voluptuous **11** flirtatious, provocative

Seychelles
capital/largest city: 8 Victoria
monetary unit: 4 cent **5** rupee
island: 4 Mahe **7** Aldabra, La Digue, Praslin **8** Farquhar **9** Desroches **10** Silhouette
highest point: 16 Morne Seychellois
sea: 6 Indian
people: 5 Asian **6** Creole, French, Indian **7** African, Chinese
***leader:* 4** Rene **7** Mancham
language: 6 Creole, French **7** English
religion: 8 Anglican **13** Roman Catholic

sforzando
music: 12 sudden accent

Shabbas 7 Sabbath

shabby 3 low **4** mean, poor, torn, worn **5** cheap, dirty, mangy, raggy, ratty, seedy, sorry, tatty, tight **6** frayed, meager, ragged, sordid, unfair **7** ignoble, rundown, scruffy **8** beggarly, decaying, inferior, slovenly, unworthy, wretched **9** illiberal, miserable, neglected **10** ramshackle, threadbare, tumbledown, ungenerous **11** dilapidated **12** contemptible, deteriorated, dishonorable, impoverished

shabby bar 4 dive **5** joint **7** gin mill **9** honky-tonk

shack 3 hut **5** cabin **6** lean-to, shanty

shackle 3 bar, tie **4** balk, bind, cuff, curb, foil, rein **5** block, bonds, chain, check, cramp, cuffs, deter, irons, limit, stall **6** chains, fetter, hamper, hinder, hobble, hogtie, impede, pinion, retard, secure, tether, thwart **7** inhibit, manacle, prevent **8** encumber, handcuff, restrict **9** forestall, frustrate, hamstring, handcuffs **12** circumscribe

shackled 7 chained, in irons **8** in chains, manacled **10** handcuffed

shadchan, schatchen
10 matchmaker **14** marriage broker

Shaddai 3 God

shade 3 bit, dim, hue, jot **4** atom, cast, hint, hood, iota, tint, tone, veil, whit **5** blind, color, drape, tinge, touch, trace **6** awning, canopy, darken, screen, shadow, shield **7** curtain, modicum, shadows, shutter **8** darkness, particle, semidark **9** scintilla **10** suggestion
French: 7 soupcon
form: 6 spirit
location: 5 Hades

shadow, shadows 3 bit, dog **4** blot, hint, tail **5** cloud, ghost, hound, shade, smear, stain, stalk, taint, tinge, touch, trace, track, trail **6** blight, follow, pursue, smirch, smudge, threat **7** blemish, specter, whisper **8** penumbra **10** reflection, silhouette, suggestion

Shadow of a Doubt
director: 15 Alfred Hitchcock
cast: 10 Hume Cronyn **12** Joseph Cotten, Teresa Wright **14** Macdonald Carey **16** Patricia Collinge
remade as: 16 Step Down to Terror

Shadow of the Moon
author: 6 M M Kaye

Shadows on the Rock
author: 11 Willa Cather

shadowy 3 dim **5** shady **6** gloomy, unreal **7** obscure **8** illusory **9** tenebrous **10** indistinct **13** insubstantial

Shadrach
former name: 8 Hananiah
friend: 6 Daniel
companion: 7 Meshach **8** Abednego

shady 5 fishy **7** crooked, devious, dubious, shadowy **9** dishonest, unethical **10** suspicious **11** underhanded **12** disreputable, questionable **13** untrustworthy

shady dealings 5 fraud, graft **7** bribery **10** corruption, dishonesty

shaft 3 cut, pit, ray **4** barb, beam, dart, duct, flue, gibe, hilt, stem, vent, well **5** abyss, arrow, chasm, gleam, lance, patch, pylon, quill, shank, spear, spire, stalk, tower, trunk **6** cavity, column, funnel, handle, insult, pillar, streak, stream **7** affront, chimney, conduit, minaret, obelisk, spindle, steeple **8** brickbat, monolith, pilaster **9** aspersion **10** excavation

shaggy 5 bushy, downy, fuzzy, hairy, nappy, piled, wooly **6** tufted, woolly **7** bearded, hirsute, shagged, unshorn **9** whiskered **11** bewhiskered

shah 4 king **5** ruler **7** emperor, monarch **8** autocrat **9** sovereign

Shahaptian
tribe: 6 Numipu **8** Nez Perce

Shahn, Ben
born: 6 Kaunas **9** Lithuania
artwork: 5 Epoch **8** Handball **12** Seurat's Lunch, The Physicist **16** Pacific Landscape **18** Willis Avenue Bridge **28** The Passion of Sacco and Vanzetti

shake 3 jar, jog, mix **4** jerk, jolt, move, stir, stun, sway, wave **5** elude, quake, swing, touch **6** affect, bounce, jiggle, joggle, jostle, jounce, quaver, quiver, rattle, ruffle, shimmy, shiver, slough, totter, twitch, wobble **7** agitate, disturb, flicker, flutter, perturb, quaking, shudder, stagger, startle, tremble, unnerve, vibrate **8** brandish, disquiet, distress, flourish, frighten, throw off, unsettle, unstring **9** quivering, shivering, trembling **10** discompose, flickering, fluttering

shakedown **6** extort, payoff, search, tryout **7** testing **8** thorough **9** blackmail, extortion, hush money

Shakespeare, William *see box*

shakeup **5** purge **7** cleanup **8** turnover **10** clean sweep **11** realignment **13** rearrangement, redisposition, restructuring **14** redistribution, reorganization

shake up **3** mix **4** stir **5** churn **7** agitate, disturb

shakiness **6** tremor **10** insecurity **11** instability, uncertainty **12** unsteadiness

shaky **4** weak **5** frail, jumpy **6** flimsy, unsafe, unsure, wobbly **7** dubious, fidgety, fragile, halting, jittery, nervous, teetery **8** hesitant, insecure, unstable, unsteady, wavering **9** faltering, hazardous, quivering, teetering, tottering, trembling, tremulous, uncertain, undecided **10** inconstant, irresolute, precarious, unreliable, unresolved **11** vacillating **12** undependable

shallow **5** shoal **6** frothy, slight **7** surface, trivial **8** knee-deep, skin-deep, trifling **9** frivolous **11** meaningless, superficial, unimportant **13** insubstantial **15** inconsequential

shalom **5** peace

shalom aleichem **10** peace to you

sham **3** act **4** copy, fake **5** bogus, false, feign, fraud, phony, put on, trick **6** affect, assume, forged **7** feigned, forgery, imitate, pretend **8** pretense, simulate, spurious **9** imitation, pretended, simulated, synthetic **10** artificial, fraudulent **11** counterfeit, make-believe

Shamash
origin: **8** Akkadian
god of: **3** sun

shamble, shambles **4** limp **5** hitch, lurch, stall **6** hobble **7** shuffle **8** butchery **14** slaughterhouse

shame **5** guilt, odium **6** humble, stigma **7** chagrin, mortify, remorse, scandal **8** contempt, disgrace, dishonor, ignominy **9** disrepute, embarrass, humiliate **10** debasement, disrespect **11** degradation, humiliation, self-disgust **12** unworthiness **13** embarrassment, mortification **14** disappointment

shamed be the one who thinks evil of it
Latin: **20** honi soit qui mal y pense

shamefaced **5** sorry **7** abashed, crushed, humbled, put-down **8** blushing, sheepish **9** chagrined, disgraced, mortified **10** humiliated, remorseful **11** embarrassed

shameful **3** low **4** base, mean, vile **6** odious **7** heinous, ignoble **8** shocking, unworthy **9** dastardly, degrading **10** deplorable, despicable, inglorious, iniquitous, outrageous, villainous **11** disgraceful, ignominious, opprobrious **12** contemptible, dishonorable **13** reprehensible

shameless **4** pert **5** brash, saucy **6** brazen, wanton **7** forward, immoral **8** degraded, flagrant, immodest, impudent, indecent **9** abandoned, audacious, barefaced, boldfaced, dissolute, unabashed **10** indecorous, unblushing, unreserved **11** disgraceful **12** dishonorable

shamelessness **4** gall **5** brass, cheek **8** audacity **10** brazenness, effrontery **11** forwardness, presumption

Shamgar **11** Hebrew judge

shamus **7** gumshoe **9** detective **10** private eye **12** investigator

Shane
director: **13** George Stevens
cast: **8** Alan Ladd **9** Van Heflin **10** Jean Arthur **11** Jack Palance **12** Elisha Cook Jr **13** Edgar Buchanan **14** Brandon de Wilde

Shanghai
area: **23** International Settlement
landmark: **13** Long Hua Temple **17** People's Opera House **28** Shanghai Industrial Exhibition
river: **6** Wusung **7** Huang-P'u, Yangtze

Shangri-La *see* **5** Nepal

shanty **3** hut **5** cabin, hovel, shack **6** lean-to

shape **4** form, make, mold, trim **5** array, build, frame, guide, model, order **6** create, fettle, figure, health **7** contour, develop, fashion, outline, profile **8** physique **9** condition, construct, determine **10** silhouette **12** conformation **13** configuration

shapeless **5** baggy **8** formless **9** amorphous, irregular

shapely **3** fit **4** neat, trim **6** comely, gainly **11** symmetrical

shaper **9** architect, innovator **10** instigator, prime mover

Shapley, Howard
field: **9** astronomy
studied: **6** galaxy

Shapwailutan
tribe: **5** Modoc **11** Kiowa Apache

Shardik
author: **12** Richard Adams

share **3** cut **4** dole, part **5** allot, cut up, quota, split **6** ration **7** deal out, divvy up, mete out, percent, portion **8** allocate **9** allotment, allowance, apportion **10** percentage **13** apportionment

shared **5** joint **6** common, public **7** general **8** communal **10** collective

---

Shakespeare, William
also: **10** bard of Avon **12** immortal bard
author of: **6** Hamlet, Henry V **7** Henry IV, Henry VI, Macbeth, Othello **8** King John, King Lear, Pericles (Prince of Tyre) **9** Cymbeline, Henry VIII, Richard II **10** Coriolanus, Richard III, The Tempest **11** As You Like It **12** Julius Caesar, Twelfth Night **13** Rape of Lucrece, Timon of Athens **14** Romeo and Juliet, The Winter's Tale, Venus and Adonis **15** Titus Andronicus **16** Love's Labour's Lost **17** Measure for Measure, The Comedy of Errors **18** Antony and Cleopatra, Troilus and Cressida **19** Much Ado About Nothing, The Merchant of Venice, The Taming of the Shrew **20** All's Well That Ends Well **21** A Midsummer Night's Dream **22** The Merry Wives of Windsor **23** The Two Gentlemen of Verona
birthplace: **15** Stratford-on-Avon
theater: **4** Swan **5** Globe
wife: **12** Anne Hathaway

share one's sorrow **7** condole **10** sympathize **11** commiserate

Sharif, Omar
real name: **15** Michael Shalhoub
born: **5** Egypt **10** Alexandria
roles: **3** Che **9** Dr Zhivago, Funny Girl, Funny Lady **11** Genghis Khan **12** Nick Arnstein **16** Lawrence of Arabia
expert on: **6** bridge

shark **3** ace **4** fish **5** cheat **6** expert, usurer, wizard **8** predator **9** trickster **12** extortionist

sharp *see box*

Sharp, Becky
character in: **10** Vanity Fair
author: **9** Thackeray

sharp-cornered **6** jagged **7** angular

sharp dresser **3** fop **4** dude **5** dandy **12** Beau Brummell, clotheshorse, fashion plate

sharpen **4** edge, hone, whet **5** grind, strop

sharply pointed **4** keen **5** acute **6** spiked **7** tapered **8** piercing **10** rapierlike **11** needle-nosed

sharpness **3** nip, wit **4** edge, tang **6** acuity, acumen **7** acidity, insight **8** acerbity, acridity, acrimony, keenness, pungency, saliency, tartness **9** acuteness, alertness, quickness **10** causticity, craftiness **12** perspicacity

sharp pain **4** pang, stab **5** cramp **6** twinge

sharpshooter
French: **10** tirailleur

sharp-sighted **5** acute **6** shrewd **8** piercing **9** far-seeing **10** discerning, perceptive **11** penetrating **13** perspicacious

sharp-witted **4** keen **5** acute, alert, canny, quick, smart **6** astute, brainy, clever

Shatner, William
born: **6** Canada **8** Montreal
roles: **8** Star Trek, T J Hooker **17** Captain James T Kirk

shatter **4** rive, ruin **5** break, burst, crack, crash, crush, quash, smash, split, spoil, upset, wreck **6** squash, sunder, topple **7** crumble, destroy, explode, scuttle **8** demolish, fracture, overturn, splinter **9** devastate, pulverize

shattered **6** broken, dashed **7** crushed, smashed **8** crumbled, decrepit **9** flustered **10** demolished, fragmented, splintered, tumbledown **11** crestfallen, demoralized **13** disillusioned, disintegrated

shave **3** cut, lop, mow **4** clip, crop, dock, pare, skin, snip, trim **5** brush, graze, prune, shear **6** barber, cut off, fleece, glance, scrape **7** scissor

Shaw, George Bernard
author of: **7** Candida **9** Pygmalion, Saint Joan **12** Major Barbara **13** Arms and the Man **14** Man and Superman **15** Heartbreak House **16** Back to Methuselah **17** The Devil's Disciple, The Doctor's Dilemma **18** Caesar and Cleopatra **19** Androcles and the Lion **20** Mrs Warren's Profession
member of: **13** Fabian Society

Shaw, Irwin
author of: **12** Top of the Hill **13** The Young Lions **14** Beggarman Thief, Rich Man Poor Man

Shaw, Robert
born: **7** England **12** Westhoughton
wife: **7** Mary Ure
roles: **4** Jaws **7** The Deep **8** The Sting **12** Swashbuckler **13** The Caretakers **17** A Man for All Seasons **20** Force Ten from Navarone **28** The Taking of Pelham One-Two-Three
author of: **14** The Hiding Place **21** The Man in the Glass Booth

Shawabti
origin: **8** Egyptian
form: **8** figurine
where used: **6** burial

shawl **4** wrap **5** scarf **6** mantle **7** paisley **10** fascinator
Mexican: **6** serape
Spanish: **8** mantilla

Shawnee
language family: **9** Algonkian **10** Algonquian
location: **4** Ohio **6** Kansas **8** Missouri, Oklahoma **9** Tennessee **12** Pennsylvania **13** South Carolina
leader: **8** Tecumseh **11** Tenskwatawa
related to: **8** Delaware

She
author: **13** H Rider Haggard

shear **3** cut, lop **4** clip, crop, snip, trim **5** prune, shave **6** fleece, remove **7** deprive, relieve, scissor

Shearer, Norma
real name: **17** Edith Norma Shearer
born: **6** Canada **8** Montreal
husband: **14** Irving Thalberg
roles: **8** The Women **9** A Free Soul **11** The Divorcee (Oscar) **14** Romeo and Juliet, Their Own Desire **15** Marie Antoinette **26** The Barretts of Wimpole Street

shears **5** clips, trims **6** prunes **7** pruners **8** clippers, scissors, trimmers

sheath **3** pod **4** case, coat, skin **6** casing, jacket **7** capsule, coating, wrapper **8** covering, envelope, membrane, scabbard, slipcase, wrapping **9** container **10** receptacle

sheathing **6** casing, siding **8** covering

Sheba
father: **6** Bichri, Joktan, Raamah **7** Jokshan

---

sharp **3** sly **4** acid, curt, fine, foxy, high, keen, sour, tart, wily **5** acrid, acute, alert, angry, awake, blunt, clear, cruel, edged, gruff, harsh, nippy, piked, quick, rapid, salty, sheer, spiny, steep **6** abrupt, artful, astute, barbed, biting, bitter, clever, crafty, crusty, fierce, keenly, marked, pointy, severe, shrewd, shrill, strong, sudden, thorny, tricky, unkind **7** acutely, alertly, angular, bearish, bristly, brusque, caustic, closely, crabbed, cunning, cutting, drastic, exactly, extreme, galling, intense, nipping, piquant, pointed, prickly, quickly, raucous, toothed, violent **8** abruptly, distinct, on the dot, piercing, promptly, scathing, serrated, spiteful, stinging, strident, suddenly, venomous, vertical, vigilant, vinegary **9** conniving, deceptive, excessive, on the nose, precisely, rancorous, unethical, vitriolic **10** contriving, discerning, immoderate, inordinate, perceptive, punctually **11** attentively, calculating, on the button, penetrating, precipitous **12** unprincipled, unscrupulous **13** precipitously
French: **5** juste
Spanish: **7** en punto

grandfather: **4** Cush **7** Keturah
people of: **7** Sabeans

Shebat **19** eleventh Hebrew month

she carved it
Latin: **8** sculpsit

shed **3** hut **4** cast, doff, drop, emit, molt **5** exude, hovel, shack, spill, strew, throw **6** lean-to, shanty, shower, slough, spread **7** cast off, discard, let fall, let flow, radiate, scatter **8** disperse, lose hair, toolshed **9** broadcast, discharge, tool house **10** distribute **11** disseminate, outbuilding

she died
Latin: **5** obiit

shed light on **7** clarify, explain **9** elucidate, explicate, make clear, make plain **10** illuminate

She Done Him Wrong
director: **13** Lowell Sherman
cast: **7** Mae West (Diamond Lil) **9** Cary Grant, Noah Beery **13** Gilbert Roland

shed tears **3** cry, sob **4** bawl, weep **6** boohoo **7** blubber

Sheehy, Gail
author of: **8** Passages **14** The Pathfinders

Sheeler, Charles
born: **14** Philadelphia PA
artwork: **9** Landscape, Upper Deck **11** Incantation **12** City Interior, Rolling Power **15** Bucks County Barn, River Rouge Plant **31** American Landscape Nineteen Thirty

sheen **4** glow **5** glaze, gleam, glint, gloss, shine **6** luster, patina, polish **7** burnish, glister, glitter, shimmer **8** radiance **9** shininess **10** brightness, brilliance, effulgence, glossiness, luminosity, refulgence **12** luminousness, resplendence

Sheen, Martin
real name: **12** Ramon Estevez
born: **8** Dayton OH
son: **12** Charlie Sheen **13** Emilio Estevez
roles: **8** Badlands **12** The Believers **13** Apocalypse Now **14** Catch Twenty-two **18** The Subject Was Roses **27** The Execution of Private Slovik

Sheena, Queen of the Jungle
creator: **8** SR Powell **13** W Morgan Thomas
character: **3** Bob **4** Chim

she engraved it
Latin: **8** sculpsit

sheep
breed: **5** Iraqi **6** Hirrik, Merino, Panama, Romney, Somali **7** Cheviot, Karakul, Lincoln, Suffolk, Targhee **8** Columbia, Cotswold, Tatarian **9** Montadale, Romeldale, Southdown **10** Corriedale, Dorset Down, Dorset Horn, Shropshire, Sikkim Bera **11** Rambouillet **13** Hampshire Down **15** Border Leicester
female: **3** ewe
family: **7** Bovidae
genus: **4** Ovis
group of: **5** drove, flock **6** cosset
meat: **4** lamb **6** mutton
oil from: **7** lanolin
wild: **5** urial **6** argali **7** bighorn, mouflon
young: **4** lamb **7** lambkin **8** yearling

sheepish **3** shy **4** meek **5** timid **6** docile, guilty, humble **7** abashed, ashamed, bashful, fearful, hangdog, passive, servile **8** blushing, obedient, obeisant, timorous, yielding **9** chagrined, chastened, diffident, mortified, shrinking, tractable **10** shamefaced, submissive **11** embarrassed, subservient, unassertive, unresisting

sheepishness **7** chagrin **8** docility, meekness **10** diffidence **11** bashfulness **12** tractability **13** embarrassment **14** submissiveness **15** unassertiveness

Sheep Well, The
also: **13** Fuente Ovejuna
author: **10** Lope de Vega

sheer **4** fine, pure, thin **5** bluff, filmy, gauzy, plumb, sharp, steep, total, utter **6** abrupt **7** perfect, unmixed **8** absolute, complete, gossamer, vertical **9** out and out, unalloyed, unbounded, unlimited **10** consummate, diaphanous **11** precipitous, transparent, unmitigated, unqualified **12** unrestrained **13** perpendicular, unadulterated, unconditional

sheet **3** top **4** coat, film, leaf, pane, slab **5** layer, panel, piece, plate **6** sheath, square **7** blanket, coating, overlay **8** bed sheet, covering, membrane **9** rectangle

shegetz **12** non-Jewish boy, non-Jewish man

Sheldon, Sidney
author of: **9** Bloodline **12** Rage of Angels, The Naked Face **15** If Tomorrow Comes **20** A Stranger in the Mirror **22** The Other Side of Midnight

shelf **4** bank, prop, reef, slab **5** ledge, shoal **6** mantel, mantle **7** bedrock, bracket, stratum **9** supporter **11** mantelpiece, mantlepiece

shell **3** pod **4** bomb, case, hulk, hull, husk, shot **5** pound, round, shuck **6** bullet, fire on, pepper, rocket **7** barrage, bombard, grenade, missile **8** carapace, skeleton **9** cartridge, framework **10** projectile

shellac **4** beat, drub, lick, whip **7** clobber, lacquer, trounce, varnish

Shelley, Mary Wollstonecraft
father: **13** William Godwin
husband: **18** Percy Bysshe Shelley
author of: **12** Frankenstein

Shelley, Percy Bysshe
author of: **7** Adonais, Alastor **8** Queen Mab, The Cenci **10** To a Skylark **16** A Defence of Poetry, Ode to the West Wind **17** Prometheus Unbound

shellfish **4** clam, crab **5** prawn **6** cockle, mussel, oyster, shrimp **7** abalone, lobster, mollusk, scallop **8** barnacle, crawfish, crayfish **9** trunkfish **10** crustacean **13** softshell crab
spawn: **4** spat

shell out **3** pay **6** expend **8** allocate, disburse, dispense **10** contribute

shelter **5** cover, guard, haven, house, lodge **6** asylum, defend, harbor, refuge, safety, shield, take in **7** care for, housing, lodging, protect **8** quarters, security **9** safeguard, sanctuary **10** protection

Sheltered Life
author: **12** Ellen Glasgow

shelve **5** defer, table **6** put off **7** suspend **8** lay aside, postpone, put aside, put on ice, set aside **10** pigeonhole

Shem
father: **4** Noah
brother: **3** Ham **7** Japheth
son: **8** Arphazed
descendant of: **6** Semite

shenanigans **5** sport **6** antics, capers, hijinx, pranks, stunts, tricks **8** deviltry, mischief, nonsense **9** highjinks, horseplay, silliness **10** buffoonery, tomfoolery **11** roguishness **12** monkeyshines, sportiveness **14** monkey business **15** mischievousness

she painted it
Latin: 6 pinxit

shepherd 4 herd, lead, show, tend **5** guard, guide, pilot **6** direct, escort, herder, keeper, patron, shield **7** protect, shelter **8** champion, defender, guardian, herdsman, provider **9** custodian, protector, safeguard **10** benefactor

Shepherdess and the Sweep, The
author: 21 Hans Christian Andersen

shepherds
god of: 3 Pan **6** Tammuz

sherbet 3 ade, ice **6** sorbet **7** dessert

Shere Khan
character in: 14 The Jungle Books
author: 7 Kipling

Sheridan, Ann
real name: 16 Clara Lou Sheridan
nickname: 9 Oomph Girl
born: 8 Denton TX
husband: 10 Scott McKay **11** George Brent **12** Edward Norris
roles: 8 King's Row **11** Silver River **12** Nora Prentiss **16** Wings for the Eagle **20** Angels with Dirty Faces

Sheridan, Philip H
served in: 8 Civil War **10** Indian Wars
side: 5 Union
commander of: 19 Army of the Shenandoah
rank: 22 general in chief of US army
battle: 9 Five Forks **10** Cedar Creek, Winchester **11** Chattanooga, Chickamauga, Fisher's Hill **12** Sayler's Creek **18** Wilderness Campaign

Sheridan, Richard Brinsley
author of: 9 The Critic, The Duenna, The Rivals **18** A Trip to Scarborough **19** The School for Scandal

sheriff 7 officer **9** constable

Sheriff of Nottingham
character in: 9 Robin Hood

Sherman, William Tecumseh
nickname: 4 Cump
served in: 8 Civil War **10** Mexican War
side: 5 Union
battle: 6 Shiloh **7** Atlanta, Bull Run **8** Savannah **9** Vicksburg **11** Chattanooga **15** Kenesaw Mountain
fought against: 8 Johnston
rank: 20 general in chief of army
famous for: 13 march to the sea (Georgia)
established: 29 Command and General Staff College
saying: 9 War is hell

sherry
type: 4 wine **6** brandy
origin: 5 Spain
varieties: 4 fino (dry) **7** amoroso (sweet), oloroso (medium dry)
drink: 6 Adonis, Bamboo **9** Andalusia
with gin: 11 Renaissance
with vermouth: 6 Brazil

Sherwood, Robert E
author of: 13 Idiot's Delight **15** Reunion in Vienna **18** The Petrified Forest **19** Roosevelt and Hopkins, There Shall Be No Night **20** Abe Lincoln in Illinois
screenplay: 22 The Best Years of Our Lives

she sculptured it
Latin: 8 sculpsit

she speaks
Latin: 8 loquitur

She Stoops to Conquer
author: 15 Oliver Goldsmith
character: 6 Marlow **8** Hastings **10** Sir Charles **11** Tony Lumpkin **12** Mr Hardcastle **13** Mrs Hardcastle **14** Kate Hardcastle **16** Constance Neville

she wrote (it)
Latin: 8 scripsit

shibah, shivah 14 mourning period
literally: 9 seven days

shibboleth 6 byword, saying, slogan **8** apothegm **9** catchword

Shibboleth 17 Gileadite password

shield 4 keep, star **5** aegis, badge, cover, guard, house, shade **6** buffer, button, emblem, ensign, fender, harbor, screen, secure **7** buckler, defense, protect, shelter **8** insignia, keep safe, preserve **9** medallion, protecter, protector, safeguard **10** escutcheon, protection

Shield (of Sobieski)
constellation of: 6 Scutum

shielded 6 hidden **7** guarded **9** concealed, protected, sheltered

Shields, Brooke
real name: 20 Christa Brooke Shields
born: 9 New York NY
roles: 10 Pretty Baby **11** Endless Love **13** The Blue Lagoon

shift 2 go **4** move, slip, vary, veer **5** hitch, stint **6** change, swerve, switch **7** chemise, turning, veering **8** exchange, straight, transfer **9** deviation, transpose, variation **10** alteration, assignment, reposition **11** alternating, fluctuation, interchange **12** modification
French: 8 camisole

shiftless 3 lax **4** idle, lazy **8** careless, inactive, indolent, slothful **10** ne'er-do-well **13** lackadaisical **14** good-for-nothing **15** unconscientious

shifty 4 foxy, wily **6** crafty, sneaky, tricky **7** cunning, evasive **8** scheming, slippery **9** conniving, deceitful, dishonest **10** contriving, unreliable **11** maneuvering, treacherous **13** untrustworthy

Shikasta
author: 12 Doris Lessing

shiksa 13 non-Jewish girl **14** non-Jewish woman

shillelagh 4 club **5** stick **6** cudgel **9** truncheon

shilly-shally 5 stall, waver **6** dawdle, dither, falter, seesaw **8** hesitate **9** fluctuate, hem and haw, oscillate, vacillate

shilly-shallying 8 dawdling, wavering **9** uncertain, undecided **10** indecision, indecisive, irresolute **11** vacillation

Shimazaki Toson
author of: 5 Hakai **20** The Broken Commandment

shimmer 4 beam, glow **5** blink, dance, flash, gleam, quake, shine, waver **6** quiver, shiver **7** flicker, flutter, glisten, sparkle, tremble, twinkle, vibrate **8** blinking **9** coruscate **11** scintillate **12** phosphoresce

shindig 3 hop **4** ball, bash, prom **5** dance, party **6** affair, shindy **7** blowout, revelry **9** barn dance, festivity, record hop **10** masked ball, the dansant
French: 4 fete, gala **6** soiree **9** bal masque **10** bal costume

shine 3 wax **4** beam, buff, glow **5** blink, flash, glare, gleam, glint, gloss, light, rub up, sheen **6** dazzle, luster, polish, waxing **7** buffing, burnish, flicker, glimmer, glisten, glister, glitter, radiate, shimmer, sparkle, twinkle **8** brighten, radiance **9** coruscate, irradiate, polishing **10** brightness, brilliance, burnishing, luminosity **11** scintillate **12** illumination, luminousness **13** incandescence

shininess **5** gleam, glint, gloss, sheen **6** luster, polish **7** shimmer

shining **5** aglow **6** glossy **7** glowing, radiant **8** gleaming, luminous, lustrous **9** brilliant, effulgent **11** illustrious **12** incandescent

Shining, The
author: **11** Stephen King

shiny **6** bright, glossy **7** glaring, glowing, radiant **8** gleaming, luminous, lustrous, polished **9** brilliant, burnished, effulgent, sparkling **10** glistening, glittering, shimmering **12** incandescent **13** scintillating

ship **4** crew, send **5** craft, liner, route, tramp, yacht **6** packet, tanker, vessel **7** carrier, cruiser, forward, steamer **8** dispatch **9** destroyer, freighter, steamship, transport **10** ocean liner

Ship of Fools
author: **19** Katherine Anne Porter
director: **13** Stanley Kramer
cast: **9** Jose Greco, Lee Marvin **10** Jose Ferrer **11** George Segal, Oscar Werner, Vivien Leigh **14** Simone Signoret **15** Elizabeth Ashley

shipshape **4** neat, snug, taut, tidy, trip, trim **5** tight **6** spruce **7** orderly

Shirer, William L
author of: **28** The Collapse of the Third Republic **29** The Rise and Fall of the Third Reich

shirk **4** duck, shun **5** avoid, dodge, elude, evade **6** escape, eschew, ignore **7** goof off, neglect **8** malinger, sidestep **9** goldbrick

shirker **5** piker **6** dodger, evader, loafer, rotter, truant **7** deserter, quitter, slacker **9** goldbrick **10** backslider, malingerer

Shirley Temple
ingredient: **9** ginger ale, grenadine
also called: **9** Roy Rogers

shirr **5** crimp, smock **6** gather, pucker **8** bake eggs

shirt **3** top **4** sark **5** frock, waist **6** blouse, bodice **10** underwaist

shirty **5** angry, irked, testy, vexed **7** annoyed **9** irritated **11** disgruntled

Shittimwood **12** Biblical tree

shiver **5** quake, shake **6** quaver, shimmy **7** shudder, tremble

shivers **3** bit **5** piece, shard **6** sliver **8** fragment

shivery **3** icy, raw **4** cold, cool **5** brisk, chill, crisp, nippy **6** arctic, biting, bitter, chilly, frigid, frosty, wintry **7** quaking, trembly **8** chilling **9** quivering **11** penetrating

shoal **3** bar **4** bank, flat **5** crowd, shelf **6** school **7** sand bar, shallow **8** sand bank

shock **3** jar, mat, mop **4** blow, bush, cock, crop, daze, jolt, mane, mass, pile, rick, rock, stun, turn **5** scare, shake, sheaf, stack, start, upset **6** appall, bundle, dismay, impact, offend, revolt, thatch, trauma **7** astound, disgust, disturb, horrify, outrage, perturb, stagger, startle, stupefy **8** astonish, bowl over, disquiet, distress, paralyze, surprise, unsettle **9** collision, overwhelm **10** concussion, discompose, disconcert **11** disturbance **13** consternation

shocking **4** foul **5** awful **6** grisly, horrid, odious **7** ghastly, hideous, jarring, jolting **8** gruesome, horrible, indecent, terrible, wretched **9** abhorrent, appalling, frightful, monstrous, offensive, repellent, repugnant, revolting, startling, upsetting **10** abominable, astounding, detestable, disgusting, disturbing, horrifying, outrageous, perturbing, scandalous, staggering, stupefying, surprising, unsettling **11** astonishing, disgraceful, disquieting **12** insufferable, overwhelming **13** disconcerting, reprehensible

shoddy **3** low **4** base, mean, poor **5** dirty, nasty, tacky **6** shabby, sloppy, stingy **7** lowdown, miserly **8** careless, inferior, slipshod **9** haphazard, negligent, niggardly **10** second-rate, ungenerous **11** inefficient **12** contemptible **13** inconsiderate, reprehensible

shoe
French: **9** chaussure

shoemaker **7** cobbler **9** bootmaker

Shoemaker's Holiday, The
author: **12** Thomas Dekker

Shoes of the Fisherman, The
author: **11** Morris L West

Shogun
author: **12** James Clavell

Sholokhov, Mikhail
author of: **19** And Quiet Flows the Don **21** The Virgin Soul Upturned

shoo **3** out **4** away, oust, rout, scat **5** be off, chase, leave, scram **6** beat it, be gone, depart, get out, go away **7** cast out, get lost, vamoose

shoot **3** bud, fly, hit **4** bolt, cast, dart, dash, drop, fell, fire, hurl, jump, kill, leap, nick, pelt, plug, race, rain, rush, stem, tear, toss, twig, wing **5** eject, fling, go off, hurry, shell, sling, speed, spray, sprig, spurt, sweep, throw, waste **6** charge, launch, let fly, pepper, propel, riddle, shower, spring, sprout **7** bombard, explode, pick off, tendril **8** catapult, detonate, open fire **9** discharge

Shootist, The
director: **9** Don Siegal
cast: **9** John Wayne, Ron Howard **10** Hugh O'Brien **11** Harry Morgan, Sheree North **12** James Stewart, Lauren Bacall, Richard Boone **13** John Carradine **15** Scatman Crothers

Shoot the Piano Player
director: **16** Francois Truffaut
cast: **11** Marie Dubois **12** Nicole Berger **14** Michele Mercier **15** Charles Aznavour
setting: **5** Paris

shoot up **4** rise, soar **6** rocket

shop **3** buy **4** hunt, look, mart, mill **5** plant, store, works **6** browse, market, studio **7** factory **8** emporium, purchase, workshop **9** patronize **10** windowshop **13** establishment
French: **7** atelier **8** boutique

shopkeeper **6** dealer, monger, trader, vendor **8** merchant, purveyor, retailer **9** tradesman

shopworn **5** banal, corny, faded, stale, tired, trite, vapid **6** jejune **10** threadbare

shore **4** bank, hold, land, prop **5** beach, brace, brink, coast **6** hold up, margin, strand **7** bolster, bulwark, seaside, support, sustain **8** buttress, mainstay, seaboard, seacoast, underpin **9** reinforce, riverbank, waterside **10** strengthen
Latin: **10** terra firma

shorebird **3** auk **4** rail, sora **5** snipe, stilt, wader **6** avocet, curlew, plover, puffin **7** lapwing **8** woodcock **9** guillemot, sandpiper **13** oyster catcher

shore up **4** prop **5** brace **6** prop up **7** bolster, support **8** buttress **9** reinforce

short **3** low **4** curt, lean, slim, thin **5** brief, cross, elfin, fleet, gruff, hasty, pygmy, quick, runty, scant, sharp, small, squat, terse, testy, tight **6** abrupt, bantam, little, meager, scanty, scarce, skimpy, slight, sparse, stubby **7** brusque, compact, concise, cursory, lacking, limited, not long, not tall, slender, stunted, summary, wanting **8** abridged, abruptly, dwarfish, fleeting, impolite, snappish, succinct, suddenly, unawares **9** condensed, curtailed, deficient, impatient, momentary, niggardly, pint-sized, truncated **10** by surprise, diminutive, short-lived **11** abbreviated, ill-tempered, Lilliputian, pocket-sized **12** insufficient **13** precipitously **14** without warning

shortage **4** lack, want **6** dearth **7** deficit **8** leanness, scarcity, sparsity **9** shortfall **10** deficiency, inadequacy, scantiness, sparseness **13** insufficiency

shortcoming **4** flaw **5** fault **6** defect, foible **7** blemish, failing, failure, frailty **8** drawback, handicap, weakness **10** deficiency, inadequacy **12** imperfection

shorten **3** cut **4** clip, pare, trim **5** prune, shave, shear **6** lessen, reduce **7** abridge, curtail, cut down **8** condense, contract, cut short, decrease, diminish **10** abbreviate

shortening **3** fat, oil **4** lard, oleo **6** butter, digest **7** cutting, summary **8** abstract, synopsis, trimming **9** hemming up, margarine, reduction **11** abridgement, compression, contraction, curtailment **12** abbreviation, condensation

short form **6** digest, precis **7** summary **8** abstract, synopsis **11** abridgement, contraction **12** abbreviation, condensation

Short Happy Life of Francis Macomber, The
author: **15** Ernest Hemingway

short journey **5** jaunt **6** outing **7** day trip **9** excursion

short-lived **5** brief **7** passing **8** fleeting **9** ephemeral, momentary, temporary, transient **10** evanescent, transitory, unenduring **11** impermanent **24** here today and gone tomorrow

shortly **4** anon, soon **7** by and by **8** directly, in a trice, promptly **9** forthwith, presently **10** before long **11** immediately

short narrative **5** essay, story **6** sketch **8** anecdote **10** short story

shortsighted **4** rash **6** myopic **7** foolish **8** careless, heedless, purblind, reckless, weak-eyed **9** amblyopic, imprudent **10** ill-advised, incautious, unthinking **11** improvident, injudicious, nearsighted, thoughtless **12** undiscerning **13** uncircumspect

short-tempered **4** curt **5** cross, huffy, sharp, testy **6** abrupt, cranky, crusty, grumpy, shirty, touchy **7** bearish, grouchy, peevish, waspish **8** choleric, snappish **9** irascible, irritable, splenetic **10** ill-humored, out of sorts, short-fused **11** hot-tempered, ill-tempered **12** cantankerous

Shosha
author: **19** Isaac Bashevis Singer

Shoshone (Snake)
language family: **10** Shoshonean
location: **4** Utah **5** Idaho **6** Nevada **7** Wyoming
translator: **9** Sacagawea

Shoshonean
tribe: **4** Hopi, Moki **5** Snake **6** Hopitu, Paiute **7** Bannock **8** Comanche, Shoshoni

Shostakovich, Dmitri (Dimitri)
born: **6** Russia **12** St Petersburg
composer of: **7** The Nose **9** Leningrad (symphony No 7) **11** May the First **12** The Golden Age **17** Katerina Ismailova **19** Lady Macbeth of Mzensk

shot **2** go **3** hit, try **4** dose, move, play, toss **5** balls, blast, crack, drive, essay, guess, salvo, slugs, throw **6** beat-up, archer, bowman, chance, report, ruined, shabby, stroke, volley **7** attempt, bullets, gunfire, shooter, surmise, worn-out **8** decrepit, marksman, rifleman **9** discharge, explosion, fusillade, injection **10** ammunition, conjecture, detonation **11** dilapidated, projectiles **12** falling apart, sharpshooter

shot in the arm **4** lift **5** boost **6** uplift **8** stimulus **13** encouragement

shot in the dark **5** guess **6** notion, theory **9** guesswork, suspicion **10** assumption, conjecture, hypothesis

shoulder **3** rim **4** bank, bear, brow, bump, edge, push, side, take **5** brink, carry, crest, elbow, lunge, shove, skirt, verge **6** assume, border, jostle, margin, take on, thrust, uphold **7** scapula, support, sustain **8** clavicle **9** undertake

shoulder blade **7** scapula **8** omoplate **9** bladebone

shout **3** cry **4** bawl, call, hoot, howl, roar, yell, yelp **5** burst, cheer, hollo, whoop **6** bellow, chorus, clamor, cry out, holler, hurrah, huzzah, outcry, scream, shriek **7** call out, exclaim, screech, thunder **8** outburst **9** hue and cry **10** hullabaloo

shout down **3** boo **4** hiss **6** hoot at, revile **7** catcall, condemn **8** denounce, drown out

shove **4** bump, butt, jolt, prod, push **5** boost, crowd, drive, elbow, force, impel, nudge **6** joggle, jostle, propel, thrust **8** shoulder

show *see box*

Showboat
author: **10** Edna Ferber

showcase **7** cabinet, counter, display, exhibit, vitrine

showdown **3** war **6** battle, climax, combat, crisis **7** face-off **8** clashing, conflict **9** collision, encounter **13** confrontation

shower **3** wet **4** fall, pour, rain, rush **5** flood, salvo, spray, surge **6** deluge, lavish, splash, stream, volley, wealth **7** barrage, bombard, drizzle, torrent **8** downpour, plethora, sprinkle **9** profusion **10** cloudburst, inundation **11** bombardment

showiness **7** glitter **8** splendor **9** jazziness **10** flashiness **11** ostentation **14** grandiloquence

Show-me State
nickname of: **8** Missouri

show-off **6** egoist **7** boaster, egotist, windbag **8** braggart, fanfaron, flaunter, strutter **9** extrovert, swaggerer **11** braggadocio **13** cock of the walk, exhibitionist **14** life of the party

showpiece **3** gem **5** jewel, pearl, pride, prize **6** rarity, wonder **7** classic, paragon **8** treasure **10** masterwork **11** chef d'oeuvre, masterpiece, prizewinner **17** piece de resistance

show **4** bare, bill, fair, give, lead, mark, play, pomp, pose, sham, sign **5** argue, coach, drama, endow, favor, front, grant, guide, movie, opera, prove, teach, token, tutor, usher **6** appear, attest, ballet, bestow, comedy, direct, effect, evince, expose, hint at, impart, inform, lavish, reveal, school, tender, unveil **7** bear out, bespeak, certify, conduct, confirm, display, exhibit, explain, lay bare, musical, picture, pretext, proffer, program, suggest, uncover **8** ceremony, delusion, disclose, dispense, evidence, illusion, indicate, instruct, intimate, manifest, operetta, point out, pretense, vaunting **9** establish, make clear, make known, represent, spectacle **10** appearance, disclosure, distribute, exhibition, exposition, expression, impression, indication, pretension, production, revelation **11** affectation, attestation, corroborate, counterfeit, demonstrate, performance, testimonial **12** bring to light, substantiate **13** demonstration, entertainment, manifestation, motion picture

show up **4** come **5** outdo **6** appear, arrive, attend, crop up, expose, loom up, reveal, turn up **9** be present **11** come to light, make a fool of **12** come into view **13** become visible

showy **4** loud **5** gaudy, vivid **6** flashy, florid, garish, ornate **7** pompous **8** colorful, gorgeous, imposing, splendid, striking **9** brilliant **11** magnificent, pretentious **12** ostentatious

Shqyptare, Shqiprija, Shqiperi *see* **7** Albania

shred **3** bit, ion, jot, rag **4** atom, band, hair, iota, spot, whit **5** grain, piece, scrap, speck, strip, trace **6** morsel, ribbon, sliver, tatter **7** snippet **8** fragment, molecule, particle **9** scintilla

shrew **3** hag, nag **5** harpy, scold, vixen, yenta **6** kvetch, virago **7** she-wolf **8** battle-ax, fishwife, harridan, spitfire **9** termagant, Xanthippe

shrewd **3** sly **4** foxy, keen, wily, wise **5** acute, cagey, canny, quick, sharp, slick, smart **6** artful, astute, clever, crafty, shifty, smooth, tricky **7** careful, cunning, knowing, probing, prudent **8** cautious, piercing, scheming, sensible, slippery **9** designing, farseeing, sagacious **10** contriving, discerning, farsighted, perceptive **11** calculating, circumspect, intelligent, penetrating, quick-witted, self-serving, sharp-witted **12** disingenuous **13** Machiavellian, perspicacious

shrewdness **6** acumen **7** cunning, slyness **8** foxiness, keenness, wiliness **9** acuteness, cageyness, sharpness, slickness, smartness **10** artfulness, astuteness, cleverness, craftiness, smoothness, trickiness **11** carefulness, discernment **12** slipperiness **16** disingenuousness

shriek **3** cry **4** call, hoot, howl, peal, yell, yelp **5** shout, whoop **6** cry out, holler, outcry, scream, squawk, squeak, squeal **7** screech

shrift **7** penance **9** atonement, expiation **10** confession

shrill **4** high, loud **6** piping **7** blaring, raucous **8** piercing, strident **9** clamorous **10** screeching **11** high-pitched, penetrating

shrine **5** altar **6** chapel, church, temple **7** sanctum **8** monument **9** sanctuary

shrink **3** ebb, shy **4** balk, duck, wane **5** cower, demur, dry up, quail, stick, wince **6** blench, bridle, cringe, flinch, lessen, pucker, recoil, reduce, refuse, retire **7** curtail, decline, deflate, dwindle, retreat, shorten, shrivel, shudder **8** compress, condense, contract, decrease, diminish, draw back, hang back, make less, withdraw **9** constrict **11** make smaller **12** draw together **13** become smaller

shrink from **4** hate, shun **5** abhor, evade **6** balk at, detest, eschew, loathe, resist **7** despise **8** recoil at **9** abominate, shudder at **12** be revolted by **13** find repulsive

shrinking **3** shy **5** timid **6** ebbing, waning **7** bashful **8** reticent, retiring, timorous **9** declining, dwindling **10** decreasing, shriveling **11** contraction, diminishing

shrive **6** pardon **7** absolve, forgive

shrivel **5** dry up, parch, wizen **6** pucker, scorch, shrink, wither **7** wrinkle

Shropshire Lad, A
author: **9** A E Housman

shroud **4** hide, pall, veil, wrap **5** cloak, cloud, cover, sheet **6** clothe, mantle, screen, swathe **7** blanket, conceal, envelop **8** covering **9** cerecloth, cerements **11** burial cloth **12** graveclothes, winding sheet

shrub **4** bush **5** brush **8** beverage **10** fruit drink

shrubbery **4** bush **5** brush **6** bushes, shrubs **9** brushwood **10** underbrush **11** undergrowth

Shuara *see* **6** Jivaro

shuck **4** husk, peel, shed **5** chaff, shell, strip

shudder **4** jerk, pang **5** quake, shake, spasm, throb **6** quaver, quiver, shimmy, shiver, tremor, twitch **7** flutter, tremble **8** paroxysm **9** pulsation, trembling **10** convulsion

shudder at **4** hate **5** abhor **6** detest, loathe **8** recoil at **9** abominate, can't stand **10** recoil from, shrink from

shuffle **3** mix **4** drag, gimp, limp, step **5** scuff, slide **6** clumsy, jumble, scrape **7** shamble **8** scramble **9** rearrange **10** disarrange **11** interchange

shul, schul **9** synagogue

shun **5** avoid, dodge, elude, evade, forgo **6** eschew, forego, ignore, refuse, reject **7** boycott, disdain **10** circumvent, fight shy of, shrink from **11** keep clear of, shy away from **12** have no part of, keep away from, steer clear of, turn away from

shut **3** box **4** cage, coop, draw, fold, lock, snap **5** clasp, close, drawn, latch **6** closed, closet, corral, draw to, fasten, intern, locked, lock in, secure **7** confine, drawn to, enclose, fence in, impound, latched, secured **8** cloister, closed up, fastened, imprison **9** barricade, constrain **11** incarcerate

shut down **4** halt, stop **5** cease **7** suspend **9** close down, interrupt **11** discontinue

Shute, Nevil
author of: **10** On the Beach

shut in **4** cage **5** caged, pen in **6** coop up, encage, lock up **7** confine, encaged, enclose **8** confined, cooped up, enclosed, locked up, restrain, restrict **10** restrained, restricted

shut one's eyes to **5** allow **6** ignore, wink at **8** overlook **9** connive in, disregard **11** pay no heed to **14** turn one's back on

shut out **3** bar **5** debar **6** defeat **7** exclude **8** obstruct, prohibit

shutter **5** blind, close, shade **6** screen **7** curtain

shut the door on **3** ban, bar **6** forbid, refuse, reject **7** exclude, keep out, shut out **8** prohibit

shut up **4** cage, coop, hush, lock, pent **5** close, pen in **6** immure **7** be quiet, confine, silence **8** imprison **11** incarcerate

shy **4** balk, meek, wary **5** chary, cower, dodge, leery, minus, scant, short, timid, under, wince **6** blench, demure, flinch, in need, modest, shrink, swerve **7** anxious, bashful, careful, fearful, lacking, needing, nervous, wanting **8** cautious, draw back, jump back, reserved, reticent, skittish, timorous **9** deficient, diffident, shrinking, tremulous **10** suspicious **11** distrustful **12** apprehensive **13** self-conscious

shy away from **4** duck, shun **5** avoid, dodge, spurn **6** balk at, refuse, reject **10** shrink from **12** steer clear of

Shylock
character in: **19** The Merchant of Venice
author: **11** Shakespeare

shyness **8** meekness, timidity **9** reticence **10** diffidence, insecurity **11** bashfulness **12** sheepishness, timorousness **14** self-effacement **15** unassertiveness

shyster **5** rogue **6** lawyer **8** attorney **10** mouthpiece **11** pettifogger **15** ambulance chaser

si **3** yes

Siam *see* **8** Thailand

Sibelius, Jean
born: **7** Finland **10** Tavastehus
composer of: **6** En Saga **7** Karelia, Legends, Tapiola, The Band **8** Kalevala **9** Finlandia **10** The Tempest **12** The Oceanides, Voces Intimae **14** Ride and Sunrise

Siberia, Siber **8** disfavor **10** punishment **14** undesirability
city: **4** Omsk **5** Chita, Tomsk **6** Kurgan **7** Irkutsk, Yakutsk
conqueror: **9** Timafeyev **11** Genghis Khan
continent: **4** Asia
gulf: **2** Ob
inhabitant: **4** Yaku **5** Sagai, Tatar **6** Tartar **7** Yukagir **8** prisoner **17** political prisoner
mountain range: **4** Ural **5** Altai, Altay
river: **2** Ob **3** Ket, Ili, Taz **4** Amga, Amur, Lena, Onon **5** Ishim, Tobol **6** Olekma
sea: **4** Kara **6** Laptev **7** Okhotsk

sibyl **4** seer **5** augur **6** oracle **7** diviner **9** predictor, sorceress **10** forecaster, prophetess, soothsayer **13** fortune teller **14** prognosticator

Sibyls
form: **10** prophetess
inspired by: **5** deity **6** Apollo
names: **6** Libyan **7** Cumaean **10** Erythraean
prophecies: **14** Sibylline Books

sic **2** so **4** thus

Sicilian Vespers, The
also: **20** Les Vepres Siciliennes
opera by: **5** Verdi
character: **5** Elena **6** Arrigo **7** Procida **8** Monforte

Sicily ***see box***

sick **3** ill **4** weak **5** frail, tired, weary **6** ailing, infirm, laid up, poorly, queasy, sickly, uneasy,

Sicily
other name: **7** Sicilia **9** Trinacria, Triquetra
capital/largest city: **7** Palermo
others: **3** Aci **4** Enna, Noto **6** Ragusa **7** Augusta, Catania, Marsala, Messina, Trapani **8** Syracuse **10** Montelepre
division: **4** Enna **6** Ragusa **7** Catania, Messina, Palermo, Trapani **8** Siracusa, Syracuse **9** Agrigento **13** Caltanissetta
government: **13** region of Italy
measure: **5** salma **7** caffiso
monetary unit: **5** litra, oncia, uncia **6** carlin **7** carline, oncetta
island: **5** Egadi **6** Lipari, Ustica **7** Pelagie **11** Pantelleria
lake: **7** Pergusa **8** Camarina
mountain: **4** Erei, Moro, Sori **5** Atlas, Erici, Hybla, Iblei, Ibrei **7** Nebrodi, Vulcano **9** Apennines, Le Madonie, Stromboli **10** Peloritani
highest point: **4** Etna **5** Aetna
river: **4** Acis **5** Salso, Torto **6** Belice, Simeto **7** Mazzaro, Platani
sea: **6** Ionian **10** Tyrrhenian **13** Mediterranean
physical feature:
cape: **4** Boeo, Faro **7** Lilibeo, Passaro, Passero, Pelorus
gulf: **4** Noto **7** Catania
strait: **7** Messina
wind: **7** sirocco
people: **5** Elymi, Sican, Sicel **6** Sicani, Siculi
author: **9** Lampedusa **10** Pirandello
composer: **7** Bellini
king: **4** Eryx **5** Bomba, Henry, Peter, Roger **7** Charles, Cocalus, Leontes **9** Ferdinand, Frederick
ruler: **4** Rome **5** Arabs, Goths, Spain **6** Greeks **7** Germans, Normans, Vandals, Vikings **8** Carthage, Saracens **9** Aragonese, Byzantium, Egyptians, Phoenicia **15** Holy Roman Empire
language: **7** Italian
religion: **13** Roman Catholic
place:
cathedral: **8** Monreale
resort: **4** Enna **8** Taormina
ruins: **14** Villa Imperiale **15** Temple of Concord **18** Valley of the Temples
feature:
brigands: **5** Mafia
evening stroll: **11** passeggiata

unwell **7** crushed, grieved, invalid, unsound **8** delicate, stricken, troubled, wretched **9** afflicted, bored with, disturbed, miserable, nauseated, perturbed, suffering, unhealthy **10** disquieted, distressed, indisposed **11** discomposed, heartbroken **15** under the weather

sicken **5** repel, shock, upset **6** offend, revolt **7** disgust, horrify, make ill, repulse **8** nauseate **14** turn the stomach

sickening **4** foul, vile **5** nasty **7** noisome **8** horrible, unsavory **9** abhorrent, loathsome, offensive, repellent, repugnant, repulsive, revolting **10** disgusting, nauseating **11** distasteful

sickly **3** ill, wan **4** drab, flat, lame, pale, sick, weak **5** ashen, faint, frail, silly **6** ailing, feeble, flimsy, guilty, infirm, leaden, peaked, poorly, sneaky, torpid, unwell **7** insipid, invalid, unsound **8** delicate, smirking **9** afflicted, apathetic, bloodless, simpering, unhealthy **10** cadaverous, lackluster, namby-pamby, snickering, spiritless, uninspired, wishy-washy **11** ineffective **12** unconvincing **13** self-conscious

sickness **6** malady, nausea **7** ailment, disease, illness **8** debility, disorder, vomiting **9** complaint, frailness, ill health, infirmity **10** affliction, disability, invalidism, poor health, queasiness **11** unsoundness **12** qualmishness **13** indisposition

sic passim **12** so throughout

sic semper tyrannis **19** thus always to tyrants
motto of: **8** Virginia

sic transit gloria mundi **33** thus passes away the glory of this world

Siddhartha
author: **12** Hermann Hesse
story of: **6** Buddha

siddur **16** Jewish prayer book
literally: **5** order

side **3** hem, rim **4** area, body, brim, edge, half, hand, part, sect, team, view **5** angle, bound, cause, facet, flank, group, house, light, limit, minor, party, phase, skirt, slant, stand, stock **6** allied, aspect, behalf, belief, border, circle, clique, fringe, lesser, margin, region, sector, strain **7** askance, coterie, faction, lateral, lineage, oblique, opinion, postern, quarter, related, section, segment, surface **8** alliance, attitude, boundary, division, indirect, marginal, position, skirting **9** accessory, bloodline, coalition, on one side, perimeter, periphery, secondary, territory, viewpoint **10** collateral, contingent, federation, incidental, standpoint, subsidiary **11** affiliation, association, unimportant **13** insignificant

Side
origin: **5** Irish
form: **7** fairies
owner: **14** Tuatha De Danann

sideboard **6** buffet **8** credenza

side by side **7** abreast **8** abutting, together **9** adjoining **11** cheek by jowl, in proximity
Latin: **9** pari passu

Side Effects
author: **10** Woody Allen

sidekick **3** pal **4** aide **5** buddy **6** deputy, friend **9** assistant **10** lieutenant

sideline **5** bench, hobby **8** boundary **9** avocation **14** put out of action

sidestep **4** duck **5** avert, avoid, dodge, elude, evade, skirt **6** bypass, escape **10** circumvent, fight shy of **12** steer clear of

sidestepping **7** dodging, ducking, eluding, evasion **8** skirting **9** avoidance **13** circumvention

sidewalk **4** curb **8** footpath, pavement **9** promenade

sideways, sideway **6** aslant **7** askance, lateral, oblique **8** crabwise, edgeways, edgewise, sidelong, sideward, sidewise **9** cross wise, laterally, obliquely, to the side **11** from one side

side with **5** agree **7** stand by, stick by, support **8** champion **12** take one's part

sidle **4** cant, edge, skew, veer **10** lateralize

Sidney, Sir Philip
author of: **7** Arcadia **15** Defence of Poesie, Defence of Poetry **18** Apologie for Poetrie, Astrophel and Stella

Sidney, Sylvia
real name: **11** Sophia Kosow
born: **7** Bronx NY
husband: **11** Luther Adler **12** Bennett A Cerf
roles: **4** Fury **7** Dead End **11** Street Scene **13** Les Miserables **15** Madame Butterfly **17** An American Tragedy **24** Summer Wishes Winter Dreams

Sidrophel
character in: **8** Hudibras
author: **6** Butler

siecle **3** age **6** period **7** century

Siegel, Jerry
creator/artist of: **8** Superman

Siegfried
origin: **8** Germanic
mentioned in: **14** Nibelungenlied
father: **7** Sigmund
mother: **9** Sieglinde
wife: **9** Kriemhild
killed by: **5** Hagen
same as: **6** Sigurd
killed: **6** Fafnir
won for Gunther: **10** Brunnhilde
stole: **9** Tarnkappe

Sieg Heil **13** hail to victory
salute used by: **5** Nazis

Sieglinde
origin: **8** Germanic
mentioned in: **14** Nibelungenlied
husband: **7** Sigmund
son: **9** Siegfried

Sienkiewicz, Henryk
author of: **8** Quo Vadis?

Sierra Leone ***see box, p. 892***

siesta **3** nap **4** rest **5** break, sleep **6** cat nap, snooze **10** forty winks

sieve **4** sift **6** filter, riddle, screen, sorter, strain **7** tattler **8** colander, strainer **9** separator **12** blabbermouth

sift **4** sort **5** drift, probe, study **6** filter, review, screen, search, winnow **7** analyze, inspect, scatter, sort out **8** separate **10** scrutinize **11** distinguish, investigate **12** discriminate

Siggeir
origin: **12** Scandinavian
king of: **5** Goths
wife: **5** Signy
causes death of: **7** Volsung

sigh **3** sob **4** hiss, long, moan, pine, weep **5** brood, groan, mourn, whine, yearn **6** grieve, lament, sorrow

sight **3** ken, see, spy **4** bead, espy, gaze, spot, view **5** image, scene, vista **6** behold, seeing, survey, vision **7** display, exhibit, eyeshot, glimpse, observe, pageant, scenery, viewing **8** eyesight, perceive, prospect, scrutiny **9** peepsight,

Sierra Leone
name means: **12** lion mountain
other name: **9** Gold Coast **10** Grain Coast, Ivory Coast
capital/largest city: **8** Freetown
others: **2** Bo **5** Hepel, Kissi, Lungi, Pepel **6** Bonthe, Kenema, Makeni, Shenge, Sulima
school: **6** Njaia U **9** Fourah Bay
measure: **4** load **6** kettle
monetary unit: **4** cent **5** leone
island: **4** York **6** Banana, Turtle **7** Sherbro
mountain: **4** Loma **10** Tingi Hills
highest point: **9** Bintimani
river: **3** Moa **4** Jong, Mano, Meli, Ribi, Sewa, Taia **5** Bagbe, Mongo, Morro, Rokel **6** Mabole, Rokkel, Scarcy, Waanje **13** Great Scarcies **14** Little Scarcies
sea: **8** Atlantic
physical feature:
bay: **5** Yawri **7** Sherbro
cape: **8** Shilling **11** Sierra Leone
peninsula: **7** Turners **11** Sierra Leone
wind: **9** harmattan
people: **3** Vai **4** Kono, Loko, Susu **5** Bulom, Kissi, Limba, Mende, Mendi, Temne **6** Creole, Fulani, Syrian **7** Gallina, Koranko, Kuranko, Sherbro, Yalunka **8** Lebanese, Mandingo
explorer: **6** Cintra
leader: **6** Margai **7** Stevens
language: **4** Krio **5** Limba, Mende, Mendi, Temne **6** Creole **7** English
religion: **5** Islam **7** animism **12** Christianity
place:
wharf: **10** King Jimmys
feature:
cloth: **5** garra
clothing: **5** lappa **6** caftan
secret society: **4** poro
food:
dish: **4** fufu **7** cassava
sauce: **7** palaver

sighthole, spectacle **10** appearance, visibility

sighted **3** saw **4** seen **6** seeing **8** not blind, observed

sightless **5** blind **8** unseeing **9** unsighted

sightly **4** fair **6** lovely, pretty **8** handsome, pleasing **9** appealing, beautiful **10** attractive

Sigmund
origin: **8** Germanic **12** Scandinavian
mentioned in: **8** Volsunga **14** Nibelungenlied
king of: **11** Netherlands
father: **7** Volsung
mother: **4** Liod, Ljod **5** Hliod
wife: **7** Hiordis, Hjordis **8** Borghild **9** Sieglinde
sister: **5** Signy
lover: **5** Signy
son: **6** Sigurd **9** Siegfried, Sinfiotli

sign **3** nod **4** clue, hint, mark, note, omen, wave **5** badge, brand, index, stamp, token, trait **6** emblem, ensign, figure, herald, motion, signal, symbol **7** earmark, endorse, feature, gesture, go-ahead, placard, portent, presage, symptom, warning **8** evidence, forecast, inscribe, neon sign, road sign, signpost **9** autograph, billboard, guidepost, harbinger, indicator, nameplate, trademark **10** indication, intimation, prognostic, suggestion, underwrite **11** forewarning **13** manifestation **14** characteristic

signal **3** cue, nod **4** sign **6** beckon, famous, motion, unique **7** command, eminent, gesture, guiding, honored, notable, warning **8** high sign, password, pointing, renowned, singular, striking **9** arresting, directing, direction, important, indicator, memorable, momentous, prominent, watchword **10** commanding, impressive, indicating, indication, noteworthy, one-of-a-kind, remarkable **11** conspicuous, distinctive, exceptional, illustrious, outstanding, significant **12** considerable **13** consequential, distinguished, extraordinary, unforgettable

significance **3** aim **4** note **5** drift, force, merit, sense, value, worth **6** import, intent, moment, object, virtue, weight **7** concern, gravity, meaning, portent, purpose **8** eminence, interest, priority **9** authority, direction, influence, intention, relevance **10** excellence, importance, notability, prominence **11** consequence, distinction, implication

significant **4** main **5** chief, grave, great, major, prime, vital **6** cogent, signal **7** eminent, knowing, notable, serious, telling, weighty **8** critical, distinct, eloquent, eventful, material, pregnant, symbolic **9** important, momentous, paramount, principal, prominent **10** emblematic, expressive, indicative, meaningful, noteworthy, portentous, remarkable, suggestive **11** exceptional, influential, outstanding, substantial, symptomatic **12** considerable **13** consequential, demonstrative **14** representative

signify **4** mean, omen, show, tell **5** argue, augur, imply **6** convey, denote, evince, herald, hint at, import, reveal, typify **7** bespeak, betoken, connote, declare, exhibit, express, portend, predict, presage, promise, suggest **8** announce, disclose, evidence, forebode, foretell, indicate, intimate, manifest, proclaim, set forth, stand for **9** be a sign of, designate, represent, symbolize **10** foreshadow **11** communicate, demonstrate

signing up **7** joining **9** enlisting, enrolling **10** enlistment, enrollment **11** registering **12** registration **13** matriculating, matriculation

Sign of Four, The
author: **19** Sir Arthur Conan Doyle
character: **11** Mary Morstan **12** Dr John Watson **13** Jonathan Small **14** Sherlock Holmes, Thaddeus Sholto

Signoret, Simone
real name: **32** Simone-Henriette-Charlotte Kaminker
born: **7** Germany **9** Wiesbaden
husband: **11** Yves Montand **12** Yves Allegret

roles: **10** Madame Rosa **11** Ship of Fools **12** Room at the Top (Oscar) **14** Is Paris Burning?
autobiography: **27** Nostalgia Isn't What It Used to Be

sign up **4** join **6** enlist, enroll, join up **8** register **9** volunteer **11** matriculate

Signy
origin: **12** Scandinavian
mentioned in: **8** Volsunga
father: **7** Volsung
brother: **7** Sigmund
son: **9** Sinfiotli
husband: **7** Siggeir

Sigrdrifa
also: **18** Brynhildr Sigrdrifa
origin: **9** Icelandic
mentioned in: **9** Elder Edda
member of: **9** Valkyries
disobeyed: **4** Odin **5** Othin
sleeps in circle of: **4** fire
awakened by: **6** Sigurd

Sigurd
origin: **12** Scandinavian
mentioned in: **8** Volsunga
father: **7** Sigmund
mother: **7** Hiordis, Hjordis
wife: **6** Gudrun, Kudrun **7** Guthrun
killed: **6** Fafnir
acquired treasure of: **8** Andavari
won for Gunnar: **8** Brynhild

Sigyn
origin: **12** Scandinavian
husband: **4** Loki

Sikes, Bill
character in: **11** Oliver Twist
author: **7** Dickens

Sikkim ***see box***

Sikorsky, Igor
nationality: **7** Russian **8** American
invented: **10** helicopter

Silas Marner
author: **11** George Eliot
character: **5** Eppie **11** Dunstan Cass, Godfrey Cass **13** Aaron Winthrop, Nancy Lammeter

silence **3** gag **4** calm, curb, halt, hush, kill, rout, stop **5** allay, check, crush, peace, quash, quell, quiet, still **6** banish, deaden, defeat, muffle, muzzle, repose, squash, stifle, subdue **7** conquer, nullify, put down, quieten, repress, reserve, squelch **8** choke off, dumbness, muteness, overcome, serenity, suppress, vanquish **9** lay to rest, placidity, quietness, reticence, stillness, tongue-tie **10** extinguish, placidness, put an end to, strike dumb **11** taciturnity, tranquility **12** tranquillity **13** noiselessness, secretiveness, soundlessness **14** speechlessness **16** closemouthedness **19** uncommunicativeness

Sikkim
capital/largest city: **7** Gangtok
others: **6** Dikchu, Lachen, Namchi, Rangpo, Rumtek **7** Lachung **9** Chungtang
government: **12** state of India
mountain: **7** Dongkya, Donkhya **9** Himalayas, Singalili **10** Darjeeling **12** Kanchenjunga
river: **5** Tista **6** Ranjit **9** Lachen Chu **10** Lachung Chu
physical feature:
mountain pass: **6** Natu La **7** Jelep La
storm: **7** monsoon
people: **4** Rong **5** Bhote **6** Bhotia, Bhutia, Indian, Lepcha **7** Tibetan **8** Nepalese **9** Mongoloid
king: **7** chogyal
religion: **5** Hindu **7** Lamaism **15** Tibetan Buddhism

silent **3** mum **4** calm, dumb, idle, mute **5** inert, muted, quiet, still, tacit **6** covert, hidden, hushed, placid, serene, unsaid **7** dormant, implied, muffled **8** discreet, implicit, inactive, inferred, lifeless, peaceful, reserved, reticent, taciturn, tranquil, unspoken, wordless **9** concealed, intimated, noiseless, quiescent, secretive, soundless, suggested, unsounded, unwritten **10** insinuated, mysterious, speechless, tongue-tied, undeclared, understood, unrevealed, unstirring, untalked-of **11** close-lipped, tight-lipped, unexpressed, unmentioned, unpublished, untalkative, unvocalized **12** closemouthed, unpronounced **15** uncommunicative

Silent Spring
author: **13** Rachel L Carson

Silenus
god of: **6** forest
oldest: **5** satyr
father: **3** Pan **6** Hermes
foster father of: **8** Dionysus
teacher of: **8** Dionysus
companion of: **8** Dionysus
sons: **6** Sileni

silicon
chemical symbol: **2** Si

silk
fabric: **4** crin **5** crepe, ninon, satin, surah, tulle **6** faille, pongee, sendal, tussah **7** chiffon, foulard, organza, raw silk, taffeta **8** organzie, paduasoy **10** peau de soie **12** crepe de chine
lining: **7** sarsnet **8** sarcenet
measure: **6** denier
raw silk: **5** grege **6** greige **8** marabout
source: **6** cocoon **9** silkworms
waste: **4** noil **5** floss
watered: **5** moire
yarn/thread: **4** tram **5** floss

silk-stocking **6** uptown **8** highborn, highbred, wellborn **9** patrician **10** upperclass **11** blue-blooded **12** aristocratic

Silk Stockings
director: **15** Rouben Mamoulian
cast: **10** Janis Paige, Peter Lorre **11** Cyd Charisse, Fred Astaire
setting: **5** Paris
score: **10** Cole Porter
remake of: **9** Ninotchka

silky **4** fine, soft **6** satiny, smooth **11** fine-grained

silliness **5** folly **6** drivel, idiocy **7** inanity **9** absurdity, asininity, frivolity **10** buffoonery, tomfoolery **11** foolishness **13** pointlessness **14** playing the fool, ridiculousness

Sillitoe, Alan
author of: **10** Her Victory **29** Saturday Night and Sunday Morning **36** The Loneliness of the Long-Distance Runner

silly **3** mad **4** dumb **5** crazy, giddy, inane **6** absurd, frothy, insane, stupid, unwary, unwise **7** aimless, asinine, fatuous, foolish, idiotic, shallow, witless **8** childish, farcical **9** brainless, foolhardy, frivolous, laughable, ludicrous, pointless, senseless **10** ill-advised, irrational, ridiculous **11** empty-headed, harebrained, meaningless, nonsensical, purposeless **12** muddleheaded, preposterous, simpleminded, unreasonable **13** inappropriate, irresponsible, muddlebrained, rattlebrained **14** featherbrained **15** inconsequential

Silmarillion, The
author: **10** J R R Tolkien

Silone, Ignazio
real name: **17** Secondo Tranquilli
author of: **9** Fontamara **12** Bread and Wine **26** The Story of a Humble Christian

Silvanus
also: **8** Sylvanus
god of: **5** herds, house, woods **12** farm boundary **16** uncultivated land

silver **5** coins, plate **6** argent, change **7** jewelry **8** argentum, platinum **9** argentine **10** silverware
chemical symbol: **2** Ag

Silver, Long John
character in: **14** Treasure Island
author: **9** Stevenson

Silver, Mattie
character in: **10** Ethan Frome
author: **7** Wharton

Silvers, Phil
real name: **17** Philip Silversmith
born: **10** Brooklyn NY
roles: **9** Top Banana **13** Sergeant Bilko **15** High Button Shoes **22** A Guide for the Married Man **37** A Funny Thing Happened on the Way to the Forum
autobiography: **14** The Laugh Is on Me

Silvius
father: **6** Aeneas

s'il vous plait **6** please **11** if you please

Simenon, Georges
author of: **8** The Train **12** Act of Passion **14** The Little Saint **15** Maigret's Memoirs **28** The Strange Case of Peter the Lett
character: **21** Inspector Jules Maigret

Simeon
father: **5** Jacob
mother: **4** Leah
brother: **3** Dan, Gad **4** Levi **5** Asher, Judah **6** Joseph, Reuben **7** Zebulun **8** Benjamin, Issachar, Naphtali
sister: **5** Dinah
canticle: **12** nunc dimittis
descendant of: **9** Simeonite

similar **4** akin, like, twin **5** close **6** allied **7** cognate, kindred **8** agreeing, matching, parallel **9** analogous, duplicate **10** comparable, equivalent, resembling **11** approximate, correlative, much the same, nearly alike **13** correspondent, corresponding

similarity **7** harmony, kinship, oneness **8** affinity, likeness, nearness, sameness **9** agreement, closeness, congruity, semblance **10** congruence, similitude **11** concordance, conformance, equivalence, parallelism, reciprocity, resemblance **13** comparability **14** conformability, correspondence

similarly **4** thus **5** alike **7** equally **8** likewise **11** furthermore, identically **15** correspondingly

similitude **7** analogy **8** likeness, sameness **10** similarity **11** parallelism, resemblance

simmer **4** boil, burn, foam, fume, stew **5** chafe, smart **6** bubble, burble, gurgle, seethe, sizzle

simmer down **7** cool off **8** calm down **14** collect oneself, compose oneself

Simmons, Jean
born: **6** London **7** England
husband: **13** Richard Brooks **14** Stewart Granger
roles: **4** Trio **6** Hamlet **7** Desiree, Ophelia, The Robe **9** Spartacus, Young Bess **11** Elmer Gantry **12** Guys and Dolls **14** The Happy Ending **17** Great Expectations **19** Androcles and the Lion

Simois
god of: **5** river

Simoisius
killed by: **14** Telamonian Ajax

Simon
also known as: **5** Peter
son: **13** Judas Iscariot
disciple of: **5** Jesus

Simon, Neil
author of: **10** Chapter Two, Plaza Suite **11** Biloxi Blues **12** The Odd Couple **15** The Sunshine Boys **16** Come Blow Your Horn **17** Barefoot in the Park **21** Last of the Red Hot Lovers **25** The Prisoner of Second Avenue

Simon & Simon
character: **7** AJ Simon **9** Rick Simon **12** Cecilia Simon **13** Downtown Brown
cast: **7** Tim Reid **10** Mary Carver **13** Gerald McRaney, Jameson Parker
setting: **8** San Diego

Simon Boccanegra
opera by: **5** Verdi
setting: **5** Genoa
character: **5** Maria, Paolo **6** Andrea, Fiesco, Pietro **14** Amelia Grimaldi, Gabriele Adorno

Simonov, Konstantin
author of: **13** Days and Nights

simpatico **7** likable **9** agreeable, congenial, gemutlich

simper **5** smirk **6** giggle, teehee, titter **7** snicker, snigger

simple **4** bare, dull, dumb, easy, open, slow, soft, true **5** basic, blunt, dense, frank, green, homey, naive, naked, plain, quiet, sheer, stark, thick **6** callow, candid, common, direct, honest, modest, obtuse, rustic, stupid **7** artless, foolish, natural, sincere **8** absolute, innocent, not fancy, ordinary, peaceful, straight, workaday **9** downright, elemental, guileless, ingenuous, out-and-out, unadorned, unfeigned, untrimmed, unworldly **10** elementary, manageable, not complex, unaffected, uninvolved **11** commonplace, fundamental, plainspoken, rudimentary, thick-witted, undecorated, unvarnished **12** not difficult, not elaborate, uncompounded **13** inexperienced, uncomplicated, unembellished, unpretentious **15** straightforward, unsophisticated

simple house **3** cot, hut **5** shack **6** chalet **7** cottage **8** bungalow

simpleminded **4** dull, dumb, slow **5** dense, silly, thick **6** stupid **7** asinine, fatuous, foolish, idiotic, moronic, witless **8** retarded **9** brainless, dim-witted, imbecilic **10** dull-witted, half-witted **11** empty-headed, harebrained, lame-brained **12** feeble-minded

simpleton **3** ass, oaf **4** dolt, dope, fool, hick, jerk, rube **5** booby, dummy, dunce, goose, idiot, ninny, stupe **6** donkey, rustic **7** dullard, jackass **8** dumbbell, imbecile, numskull **9** blockhead, greenhorn, ignoramus, numbskull **10** nincompoop

simplicity **6** candor, purity **7** clarity, honesty, naivete **8** easiness, openness, serenity **9** austerity, clearness, innocence, plainness, restraint, sincerity **10** directness **11** artlessness, cleanliness, naturalness, obviousness **12** truthfulness **13** guilelessness, unworldliness **19** straightforwardness

simply **7** clearly, lucidly, plainly, starkly **8** directly, modestly **9** naturally **10** explicitly **11** ingenuously **12** intelligibly, unaffectedly **15** uncomplicatedly, unpretentiously **17** straightforwardly

Simpson, O J (Orenthal James)
nickname: **5** Juice
sport: **8** football
position: **11** running back
team: **10** USC Trojans **12** Buffalo Bills **23** San Francisco Forty-Niners

simulate **3** act, ape **4** copy, fake, play, pose, sham **5** feign, mimic, put on **6** affect, assume, invent **7** imitate, playact, pretend **9** dissemble, fabricate **11** counterfeit, make believe

simulated **4** fake, sham **5** phony **6** forged **7** manmade, pretend **9** imitation, synthetic **10** artificial, fabricated **11** counterfeit, make-believe

simultaneous **6** coeval **10** coexistent, coexisting, coincident, concurrent, synchronal, synchronic **11** concomitant, synchronous **12** accompanying, contemporary **15** contemporaneous

sin **3** err **4** evil, fall, slip, vice **5** crime, error, lapse, shame, stray, wrong **6** breach, do evil, offend **7** do wrong, misdeed, offense, scandal **8** disgrace, evil deed, iniquity, trespass, villainy **9** violation **10** infraction, transgress, wrongdoing **13** transgression

Sin
origin: **8** Akkadian
god of: **4** moon

Sinaiticus **16** Greek uncial codex

Sinatra, Frank
real name: **20** Francis Albert Sinatra
nickname: **8** The Voice **11** Old Blue Eyes
born: **9** Hoboken NJ
wife: **9** Mia Farrow **10** Ava Gardner
daughter: **12** Nancy Sinatra
son: **14** Frank Sinatra Jr
leader of: **7** Rat Pack
roles: **8** Tony Rome **12** Angelo Maggio, Guys and Dolls, The Detective **14** The Joker Is Wild **17** The First Deadly Sin **18** From Here to Eternity **22** The Man with the Golden Arm

Sinbad the Sailor
character in: **27** Arabian Nights' Entertainments

since **2** as **3** ago, for, yet **4** ergo, from **5** after, hence, later **6** thence, whence **7** because, whereas **8** in as much **9** therefore **10** afterwards **11** accordingly, considering **12** subsequently
archaic: **4** sith
prefix: **3** cis
Scottish: **4** syne

sincere **4** real **5** frank **6** candid, honest **7** artless, earnest, genuine, natural, serious **8** truthful **9** authentic, guileless, heartfelt, ingenuous, unfeigned **10** forthright, unaffected **11** in good faith, undeceitful **12** wholehearted **15** straightforward

sincerely **5** truly **6** really **8** honestly **9** earnestly, genuinely, seriously **10** truthfully **14** wholeheartedly

sincerity **6** candor **7** honesty, probity **8** openness **9** frankness, good faith **11** artlessness, earnestness, genuineness, seriousness **12** truthfulness **13** guilelessness, ingenuousness **14** forthrightness, unaffectedness **16** wholeheartedness **19** straightforwardness

Sinclair, Upton
author of: **9** The Jungle, World's End **12** Dragon's Teeth
character: **9** Lanny Budd

Sindhi
language family: **12** Indo-European
branch: **11** Indo-Iranian
group: **5** Indic
spoken in: **13** Northern India

sine die **17** without fixing a day (for future action or a future meeting)
literally: **13** without the day

sine prole **14** without progeny **16** without offspring

sine qua non **15** without which not **18** something essential **22** indispensable condition

sinew, sinews **4** grit, thew **5** fiber, nerve, power, vigor **6** muscle, tendon **7** stamina **8** ligament, strength, virility, vitality **10** resilience, strengthen

sinewy **4** wiry **5** beefy, nervy, thewy, tough **6** brawny, robust, strong **7** fibrose, stringy **8** muscular, powerful, vigorous

Sinfiotli
origin: **12** Scandinavian
mentioned in: **8** Volsunga
mother: **5** Signy
father: **7** Sigmund

sinful **3** bad **4** evil, vile **5** wrong **6** errant, unholy, wicked **7** corrupt, heinous, immoral, impious, ungodly, wayward **8** criminal, depraved, shameful **9** miscreant **10** degenerate, despicable, iniquitous, profligate, villainous **11** disgraceful, irreligious, unrighteous

sing **3** hum **4** lilt, pipe **5** carol, chant, chirp, croon, trill, tweet **6** intone, warble **7** chirrup, whistle **8** melodize

Sing Along with Mitch
regulars: **10** Diana Trask **11** Mitch Miller **12** Leslie Uggams, Louise O'Brien, Sandy Stewart **13** Gloria Lambert, Sing Along Gang, Sing Along Kids

Singapore ***see box, p. 896***

singe **4** burn, char, sear **5** brand **6** scorch

singer **4** alto, bard, bass, diva, lark **5** tenor **7** crooner, soprano **8** baritone, minstrel, songbird, songster, vocalist **9** chanteuse, chantress, contralto **10** songstress, troubadour **11** nightingale **12** countertenor, mezzo-soprano

singer, female
French: **9** chanteuse

Singer, Isaac Bashevis
author of: **6** Shosha **7** Old Love **8** The Manor **9** The Estate **13** Gimpel the Fool **15** The Family Moskat **16** In My Father's Court **24** The Spinoza of Market Street

singer, professional
French, Italian: **10** cantatrice

singing group **4** trio **5** choir **6** chorus **7** quartet **8** glee club **13** choral society **17** barbershop quartet

Singin' in the Rain
director: **9** Gene Kelly **12** Stanley Donen
cast: **9** Gene Kelly, Jean Hagen **11** Cyd Charisse **13** Donald O'Connor **14** Debbie Reynolds
song: **11** Make 'em Laugh

single **3** one **4** lone, sole **5** unwed **6** maiden **7** only one **8** bachelor, singular, solitary, spinster, wifeless **9** unmarried **10** individual, spouseless **11** husbandless

single file **8** one by one **10** Indian file, one at a time **13** in a single line **16** one behind another

single-handedly **5** alone **7** unaided **9** by oneself, on one's own **10** unassisted **11** without help

single-minded **4** firm **6** dogged **7** devoted, intense,

Singapore
other name: **8** Singa Pur
name means: **13** city of the lion
capital/largest city: **9** Singapore
others: **4** Tuas **6** Changi, Jurong **7** Nee Soon **9** Paya Lebar, Woodlands **10** Bukit Timah, Queenstown **12** Bukit Panjang **15** Toa Payoh New Town
medieval town: **7** Temasek
school: **7** Nanyang **8** National **9** Singapore
monetary unit: **4** cent **6** dollar
island: **4** Ubin **5** Brani, Bukum, Pesek **7** Semakau **8** Merlimau, Southern **10** Ayer Chawan, Ayer Merbau **11** Blakang Mati, Tekong Besar **12** Tekong Kechil
mountain: **6** Mandai **7** Panjang
highest point: **10** Bukit Timah
river: **6** Jurong, Sungei **7** Kallang, Seletar **9** Singapore
sea: **6** Indian **10** South China
physical feature:
harbor: **6** Keppel **9** Serangoon
strait: **6** Johore, Pandan **8** Sembilan **9** Singapore
people: **5** Malay **6** Indian **7** Chinese **9** Malaysian, Pakistani, Sri Lankan
founder: **7** Raffles
leader: **10** Lee Kwan Yew
language: **5** Malay, Tamil **7** Chinese, English **8** Mandarin
religion: **4** Sikh **5** Hindu, Islam **6** Taoism **8** Buddhism **12** Christianity, Confucianism
place:
amusement park: **8** New World **10** Great World, Happy World
aquarium: **8** Van Kleef
cathedral: **9** St Andrews
gardens: **7** Botanic
hall: **16** Victoria Memorial
industrial park: **6** Jurong
mosque: **6** Sultan
park: **6** Farber **7** Merlion **12** Raffles Place
street: **16** Raffles Boulevard
temple: **17** One Thousand Lights
feature:
boat: **4** junk **6** sampan
clothing: **4** sari

staunch, zealous **8** resolved, tireless, untiring **9** dedicated, steadfast, tenacious **10** determined, inflexible, persistent, relentless, unswerving, unwavering **11** persevering, unflinching

singleness **12** bachelorhood, spinsterhood **14** unmarried state **17** single blessedness

single out **4** pick, take **6** choose, opt for, select **7** call out, extract, fix upon, pick out **8** decide on, set apart, settle on **11** distinguish

sing the praises of **4** hail, laud, tout **5** boost, cheer, exalt, extol, honor **6** praise **7** acclaim, applaud, approve, commend **8** eulogize **9** celebrate **10** compliment

singular **3** odd **4** rare **5** queer **6** choice, quaint, select, unique **7** bizarre, curious, strange, unusual **8** aberrant, abnormal, atypical, freakish, peculiar, peerless, superior, uncommon, unwonted **9** anomalous, different, eccentric, fantastic, marvelous, matchless, unequaled, unnatural, wonderful **10** noteworthy, outlandish, prodigious, remarkable, surpassing, unfamiliar **11** exceptional, uncustomary **12** unparalleled **13** extraordinary, unaccountable, unprecedented **14** unconventional **16** out-of-the-ordinary

Sinhalese
language family: **12** Indo-European
branch: **11** Indo-Iranian
group: **5** Indic
spoken in: **6** Ceylon **8** Sri Lanka

sinister **4** dark, dire, evil, foul, rank, vile **5** black **6** cursed, malign, wicked **7** adverse, fearful, hellish, ominous, unlucky **8** accursed, alarming, damnable, devilish, infernal, menacing, rascally **9** dismaying, insidious, malignant **10** despicable, detestable, diabolical, disturbing, malevolent, perfidious, villainous **11** disquieting, frightening, threatening, treacherous, unfavorable, unpromising **12** blackhearted, inauspicious, unpropitious **13** Machiavellian, reprehensible

sink **3** dig, dip, ebb, lay, sag, set **4** bore, bowl, bury, drop, fall, seep, slip, soak, tilt, wane **5** basin, drill, drive, droop, drown, gouge, lower, slant, slope, slump, stoop, yield **6** engulf, go down, lessen, plunge, reduce, shrink, worsen **7** decline, descend, give way, go to pot, go under, put down, regress, subside, succumb **8** diminish, excavate, languish, lavatory, scoop out, submerge, submerse, washbowl **9** hollow out, wash basin **10** degenerate, depreciate, go downhill, retrogress **11** deteriorate, go to the dogs

sinless **4** good, holy, pure **6** chaste **7** upright **8** innocent, spotless, virtuous **9** reputable, righteous

sinner **8** apostate, evildoer, offender **9** miscreant, misfeasor, reprobate, wrongdoer **10** backslider, malefactor, malfeasant, recidivist, trespasser **12** transgressor

Sinnis *see* **5** Sinis

Sinoeis *see* **3** Pan

Sinon
pretended to be: **13** Greek deserter
told Trojans of: **11** Trojan Horse

Sino-Tibetan
language branch: **7** Sinitic **12** Tibeto-Burman
includes: **4** Naga **5** Karen **7** Burmese, Chinese **8** Kuki-Chin, Mandarin

Sins, Seven **4** envy, lust **5** anger, pride, sloth **8** gluttony **12** covetousness

sinuosity **10** slinkiness **11** convolution, sinuousness **12** tortuousness

sinuous **6** curved, folded, volute, zigzag **7** bending, coiling, curving, twisted, winding **8** indirect, mazelike, rambling, tortuous, twisting **9** wandering **10** circuitous, convoluted, meandering, roundabout, serpentine, undulating **12** labyrinthine

sinuousness **9** sinuosity **10** slinkiness **11** convolution **12** tortuousness

Sinus
also: **6** Sinnis
vocation: **6** robber
daughter: **8** Perigune
killed by: **7** Theseus
epithet: **12** Pityocamptes

Siouan
tribe: **4** Crow, Iowa **5** Ioway, Omaha, Osage, Sioux **6** Dakota, Mandan **7** Hidatsa **8** Minitari, Wazhazhe **10** Assiniboin, Gros Ventre **11** Assiniboine

Sioux *see* **6** Dakota

Sioux State
nickname of: **11** North Dakota

sip **3** lap, nip, sup **4** dram, drop **5** drink, savor, taste **6** sample **7** soupcon, swallow **10** thimbleful

siphon **4** tube **5** drain **7** draw off

siphonaptera
class: **8** hexapoda
phylum: **10** arthropoda
group: **4** flea

Sippar residents **11** Sepharvites

Siqueiros, David Alfaro
born: **6** Mexico **9** Chihuahua
artwork: **12** New Democracy **13** Echo of a Scream **14** Trial of Fascism **15** Ascent of Culture, Burial of a Worker **16** Towards the Cosmos **17** Death to the Invader **18** Polyforum Siqueiros **22** March of Humanity on Earth **24** Cuauhtemoc Against the Myth

sir
French: **8** monsieur

sire **4** king, lord **5** beget, breed **6** create, father **7** creator **9** originate **10** originator, progenitor

siren, Siren **4** horn, vamp **5** alarm, nymph, witch **6** sexpot **7** charmer, whistle **8** deceiver, sea nymph **9** temptress **10** seductress **11** enchantress **13** warning signal **15** bewitching woman
French: **11** femme fatale
form: **5** nymph
location: **3** sea
lured sailors by: **7** singing

Sir Gawain and the Green Knight
author: **7** unknown
character: **10** King Arthur **22** Sir Bernlak de Hautdesert
horse: **9** Gringalet

Sirian Experiments, The
author: **12** Doris Lessing

Sisera
commander for: **5** Jabin
defeated by: **5** Barak

sissified **6** prissy **7** unmanly **8** womanish **10** effeminate

sissy **6** coward **8** weakling **9** fraidy-cat **10** scaredy-cat

sister **3** nun, kin, sib **5** nurse **6** female **7** sibling **8** feminist, relation, relative
nautically: **6** secure **10** strengthen
society: **8** sorority

Sister Carrie
author: **15** Theodore Dreiser
character: **11** G W Hurstwood **12** Carrie Meeber **13** Charles Drouet

Sister Woman
character in: **16** Cat on a Hot Tin Roof
author: **8** Williams

Sisyphean **4** hard **5** tough **6** uphill **7** arduous, onerous **8** toilsome **9** demanding, difficult, strenuous, wearisome **10** exhausting

Sisyphus
king of: **7** Corinth
father: **6** Aeolus
mother: **7** Enarete
brother: **9** Salmoneus
wife: **6** Merope
son: **5** Almus **7** Glaucus **8** Ornytion **10** Thersander
founded: **6** Ephyra **7** Corinth
rolled: **5** stone

sit **3** lie **4** loll, meet, mind, rest, rule, stay **5** abide, chair, nurse, perch, reign, roost, squat, stand, teach, watch **6** attend, endure, gather, govern, linger, remain, reside, settle, sprawl **7** baby-sit, care for, convene, preside **8** assemble, be placed, be seated, chaperon **9** have a seat, officiate **10** deliberate **11** be in session

site **4** area, post, spot, zone **5** field, locus, place, point, scene **6** ground, locale, region, sector **7** section, setting, station **8** district, locality, location, position, province **9** territory **11** whereabouts

sit in judgment **5** judge **6** decide, settle **7** adjudge, mediate **9** arbitrate, reconcile **10** adjudicate **12** bring to terms

situ **5** place

situate **3** put, set **4** post **5** build, house, lodge, place, plant, stand **6** billet, locate, settle **7** install, station **8** ensconce, position **9** construct, establish

situation **3** fix, job **4** case, duty, post, role, seat, site, spot, work **5** berth, place, state **6** locale, office, plight, status **7** dilemma, posture, station **8** capacity, function, locality, location, position, quandary **9** condition **10** assignment, livelihood **11** predicament **13** circumstances **14** state of affairs

sit upon **5** brood, cover, hatch **8** incubate

Sivan **16** third Hebrew month

Six Characters in Search of an Author
author: **15** Luigi Pirandello

six cubits **4** reed

Six Million Dollar Man
character: **11** Dr Rudy Wells, (Col) Steve Austin **12** Oscar Goldman
cast: **9** Lee Majors **13** Martin E Brooks **15** Alan Oppenheimer, Richard Anderson
spinoff: **11** Bionic Woman

Sixty Minutes
correspondent: **9** Dan Rather **10** Andy Rooney **11** Diane Sawyer, Mike Wallace, Morley Safer **13** Harry Reasoner

sizable **5** ample, broad, large, roomy **7** immense **8** spacious **9** capacious, good-sized

size **3** sum **4** area, bulk, mass, sort **5** array, grade, group, scope, total **6** amount, extent, spread, volume **7** arrange, bigness, content, expanse, stretch **8** capacity, classify, quantity, totality **9** aggregate, amplitude, greatness, largeness, magnitude **10** dimensions **11** measurement, proportions

sizzle **3** fry **4** hiss, spit **7** crackle, frizzle, hissing, sputter **8** splutter **10** sputtering

skate **3** nag, ray **4** skid, skim, slip **5** blade, coast, glide, horse, slide **6** rotter
female: **4** maid
genus: **4** Raja
mark: **4** cusp

skein **4** coil, hank, reel, yarn **5** twist **6** tangle, thread **9** filaments, twistings
members: **4** fowl **5** ducks, flock, geese **6** flyers

skeletal **4** bony, thin **5** gaunt

6 wasted 9 emaciated 10 cadaverous

skeleton 4 hulk 5 bones, frame, shell 9 framework
purpose: 7 support 8 protects 9 framework

Skelton, Red
real name: 21 Richard Bernard Skelton
born: 11 Vincennes IN
roles: 7 I Dood It 8 Ship Ahoy 12 Panama Hattie 16 Neptune's Daughter 17 The Fuller Brush Man 18 Clem Kadiddlehopper, Whistling in the Dark 20 Freddie the Freeloader

skeptic, sceptic 7 atheist, doubter, scoffer 8 agnostic 10 questioner, unbeliever 14 doubting Thomas

skeptical, sceptical 6 unsure 7 cynical, dubious 8 doubtful, doubting, scoffing 9 uncertain 11 incredulous, questioning, unbelieving, unconvinced 12 disbelieving 13 hypercritical

skepticism 5 doubt 7 dubiety 8 distrust, mistrust, unbelief 9 disbelief, suspicion 11 agnosticism, incredulity 12 doubtfulness 13 faithlessness

sketch 3 map 4 draw, plot, skit 5 chart, draft, graph, scene 6 depict, digest, precis, satire 7 drawing, lampoon, mark out, outline, picture, portray, summary, takeoff 8 abstract, rough out, synopsis, vignette 9 blueprint, burlesque, delineate, short play, summarize 11 preliminary 16 characterization

Sketch Book, The
author: 16 Washington Irving

sketchy 4 bare, hazy 5 brief, crude, light, rough, short, vague 6 meager, skimpy, slight 7 cursory, outline, shallow, slender 9 essential, rough-hewn, unrefined 10 incomplete, undetailed, unfinished, unpolished 11 preliminary, preparatory, provisional, superficial

skewed 5 slued 6 veered, warped 7 oblique, sheered, slanted, swerved, twisted 9 distorted

skewer 3 pin, rod 4 spit, stab 5 truss 6 pierce, skiver 7 impale 9 brochette 10 run through

skid 3 ski 4 drag, dray, skim, skip, sled, slip 5 coast, glide, skate, slide 6 runner, sledge 7 skitter 8 glissade, platform, sideslip

Skidbladnir
origin: 12 Scandinavian
ship of: 4 Frey 5 Freyr
feature: 11 collapsible

Skidegatta
tribe: 5 Haida

Skidmore, Owings, and Merrill
partners: 13 John Merrill Sr, Louis Skidmore 15 Nathaniel Owings
architects of: 10 Lever House (NYC) 11 AEC town site (Oak Ridge TN) 13 Banque Lambert (Brussels) 16 John Hancock Tower (Chicago) 17 Terrace Plaza Hotel (Cincinnati), US Air Force Academy (CO) 18 Mauna Kea Beach Hotel (Kamuela HI) 19 Istanbul Hilton Hotel (Turkey) 23 Beinecke Rare Book Library (Yale) 26 Chase Manhattan Bank Building (NYC) 33 American Republic Insurance Building (Des Moines IA)
world's tallest building: 10 Sears Tower (Chicago)

skiff 4 boat 6 dinghy 7 rowboat

skiing
athlete: 9 Phil Mahre 11 Bill Johnson, Cindy Nelson 13 Gustavo Thoeni, Robert Cochran 14 Marilyn Cochran, Martha Rockwell 15 Debbie Armstrong, Ingemar Stenmark, Jean Claude Killy 16 Michael Gallagher 17 Barbara Ann Cochran 20 Annemarie Proell Moser

Skikne, Larushka Misch
real name of: 14 Laurence Harvey

skill 4 gift 5 craft, knack 6 acumen, talent 7 ability, cunning, faculty, knowhow, mastery, prowess 8 artistry, capacity, deftness, facility 9 adeptness, dexterity, expertise, handiness, ingenuity 10 adroitness, cleverness, competence, experience, expertness 11 proficiency 12 skillfulness 13 inventiveness

skilled 6 adroit, expert 7 trained 8 skillful 9 competent, masterful, practiced 10 proficient 12 accomplished

skilled worker 7 artisan 9 craftsman 10 technician 15 master craftsman

skillful 3 apt 4 able, deft, keen 5 adept, handy, sharp, slick 6 adroit, clever, expert, facile, gifted 7 capable, cunning, skilled, trained, veteran 8 masterly, talented 9 competent, dexterous, ingenious, masterful, practiced, qualified 10 proficient, well-versed 11 experienced 12 accomplished, professional

skim 3 fly 4 flip, ream, sail, scan, scud, skid, skip 5 coast, float, glide, skate, sweep 6 bounce, scrape 7 dip into 8 glissade 10 glance over 11 leaf through, move lightly 12 thumb through

skimp 5 pinch, stint 6 scrimp, slight 8 be frugal, be stingy, hold back, withhold 9 economize 11 cut expenses, scrape along

Skimpole, Harold
character in: 10 Bleak House
author: 7 Dickens

skimpy 5 close, scant, small, spare, tight 6 frugal, meager, modest, scanty, slight, sparse, stingy 7 miserly, scrimpy, sparing, wanting 8 exiguous, grudging, smallish, stinting 9 illiberal, niggardly, penurious, scrimping 10 inadequate, incomplete, too thrifty 11 close fisted, tightfisted 12 insufficient, parsimonious 13 pennypinching 14 inconsiderable

skin 3 fur, pod 4 bark, case, coat, flay, hide, hull, husk, peel, pelt, rind, shell, abrade, casing, fleece, jacket, scrape, sheath, lay bare, epidermis, complexion, integument, body covering, outer coating
outer layer: 9 epidermis
contains: 3 fat 4 hair, pore, root 5 nerve 6 vessel 8 oil gland 10 sweat gland
body's largest: 5 organ
sense of: 4 cold, heat, pain 5 touch 8 pressure, tickling

skinflint 5 miser 7 hoarder, niggard, scrooge 8 tightwad 10 pinchpenny 12 penny pincher

Skinner, Cornelia Otis
author of: 23 The Pleasure of His Company (with Samuel Taylor) 24 Our Hearts Were Young and Gay (with Emily Kimbrough)

skinny 4 lank, lean, thin, wiry 5 gaunt, gawky, lanky, spare 6 slight 7 angular, scraggy, scrawny, slender, spindly 8 gangling, rawboned, shrunken, skeletal 9 emaciated

Skin of Our Teeth, The
author: 14 Thornton Wilder

skip 3 bob, cut, hop 4 flee, flit, jump, leap, miss, omit, romp, shun, trip 5 bound, caper, dodge, elude, evade **6** bounce, escape, eschew, gambol, ignore, prance, spring **7** abscond, make off, neglect **8** leap over, leave out, overlook, pass over **9** disappear, disregard, do without, play hooky, skedaddle **10** fly the coop **12** be absent from

skirmish 4 fray, tilt **5** brush, clash, joust, run-in, scrap, set-to **6** action, affray, battle, fracas, tussle **7** scuffle **8** struggle **9** encounter, firefight, scrimmage **10** engagement

skirmisher
French: 10 tirailleur

Skirnir
origin: 12 Scandinavian
servant of: 4 Frey **5** Freyr

Skirophoria *see* **11** Scirophoria

skirt 3 hem, rim **4** edge, gird, kilt, maxi, mini, ring, shun **5** avoid, evade, flank, hem in, verge **6** border, bounds, circle, dirndl, fringe, girdle, margin **7** enclose, envelop **8** boundary, encircle, go around, lie along **9** crinoline, outer area, perimeter, periphery **10** circumvent, fight shy of **12** circumscribe, detour around

skittish 3 shy **4** wary **5** chary, jumpy, leery, shaky, timid **6** fitful, unsure **7** bashful, fearful, fidgety, flighty, guarded, jittery, nervous, restive **8** cautious, restless, unstable, unsteady, volatile **9** demurring, excitable, impulsive, mercurial, reluctant **10** suspicious **11** distrustful

skittles
equipment: 4 pins **6** cheese
also called: 5 closh **6** cloddy **8** roly-poly **10** Dutch bowls
tabletop version: 15 Enfield skittles

Skrymir
also: 10 Utgardloki
origin: 12 Scandinavian
form: 5 giant
took to Jotunheim: 4 Loki, Thor **7** Thialfi

Skuld 4 Norn
origin: 12 Scandinavian
form: 5 dwarf
personifies: 6 future
developed from: 5 Urdar
companions: 3 Urd **8** Verdandi

skulduggery, skullduggery 7 knavery **8** trickery **9** chicanery, deception **10** dirty trick **12** pettifoggery

skulk 4 hide, lurk **5** cower, creep, prowl, slink, sneak **9** pussyfoot

skull
contains: 5 brain

Skull place 7 Calvary **8** Golgotha

sky 5 space **9** firmament **10** atmosphere, outer space, the heavens **12** arch of heaven
goddess of: 3 Fri, Nut **5** Frigg, Frija **6** Frigga

sky blue 5 azure **8** cerulean, pale blue **9** clear blue, light blue

Sky King
character: 5 Penny **7** Clipper
cast: 10 Kirby Grant **11** Ron Haggerty **13** Gloria Winters
ranch: 11 Flying Crown
plane: 8 Songbird

skylarking 5 sport **6** antics **7** hijinks, romping **10** frolicking

skypilot 5 padre, rabbi **6** cleric, parson, priest **8** chaplain, minister **9** clergyman

skyward 2 up **6** upward **8** to the sky **10** heavenward **12** to the heavens

slab 3 wad **4** hunk, slat **5** block, board, chunk, plank, slice, wedge **10** thick slice

slack 3 lax **4** dull, easy, free, lazy, limp, slow, soft **5** baggy, loose, quiet, relax **6** easily, flabby, freely, limply, loosen, pliant, remiss, slowly, untied **7** flaccid, let up on, loosely, not busy, not firm, not taut, offhand, relaxed, slacken **8** careless, dilatory, flexible, heedless, inactive, indolent, listless, not tight, slapdash, slipshod, slothful, sluggish **9** leisurely, lethargic, negligent, slow-paced, unmindful, untighten **10** neglectful, nonchalant, permissive, slow-moving, sluggishly, unexacting, unfastened, unthinking **11** inattentive, indifferent, thoughtless, unconcerned, undemanding

slacken 4 curb, ease, flag, free, slow **5** abate, check, let go, let up, limit, loose, relax, slack **6** arrest, go limp, lessen, loosen, reduce, retard, soften, temper, weaken **7** dwindle, inhibit, release **8** decrease, diminish, keep back, mitigate, moderate, restrain, slow down, taper off **9** untighten

slacker 5 idler **6** dodger, loafer, truant **7** dallier, dawdler, goof-off, laggard, quitter, shirker **9** do-nothing, goldbrick **10** malingerer **14** good-for-nothing, procrastinator

slag 5 dross **6** cinder, scoria **8** clinkers

slake 4 calm, cool, curb, ease, hush, sate **5** allay, quell, quiet, still **6** modify, quench, soothe, subdue, temper **7** appease, assuage, compose, gratify, mollify, relieve, satiate, satisfy **8** decrease, mitigate, moderate **9** alleviate **11** tranquilize **14** take the edge off

slake off 4 wane **5** abate **6** lessen, reduce, weaken **7** decline, subside **8** diminish, fade away, slack off

slam 3 hit **4** bang, bump, slap **5** crash, smack, smash, throw

slammer 3 jug, pen **4** jail, stir **5** clink **6** cooler, lockup, prison **8** big house, hoosegow **9** calaboose, jailhouse **12** penitentiary

Slammin' Sammy
nickname of: 8 Sam Snead

slander 4 soil **5** libel, smear, sully **6** defame, malign, revile, vilify **7** calumny **8** besmirch **9** falsehood **10** defamation, distortion **12** vilification **14** false statement **17** misrepresentation

Slaney, Mary *see* **10** Mary Decker

slang 4 cant, jive **5** argot, idiom, lingo **6** jargon **7** dialect

slant 4 bias, lean, list, rake, tilt, view **5** angle, color, pitch, slope **7** distort, incline, leaning **8** attitude **9** prejudice, viewpoint

slanted 4 awry **6** biased, tilted **7** colored, crooked, leaning, pitched, sloping **8** inclined **9** on an angle, on the bias **10** prejudiced

slanting 4 bias **5** alean, atilt **7** oblique, sloping **8** diagonal, glancing, inclined **10** distorting

slap 3 cut, hit **4** blow, clap, cuff, snub, swat **5** smack, whack **6** insult, rebuff, strike, wallop **9** rejection

slapdash 6 casual, sloppy **8** careless, slipshod, slovenly **9** haphazard

Slapsie Maxie
nickname of: 15 Maxie Rosenbloom

slash 3 cut, rip **4** drop, gash, mark, pare, rend, rent, slit, tear **5** lower, slice **6** reduce, stroke **8** decrease, lacerate, lowering **9** reduction **10** laceration

slate 4 list **6** ballot, tablet, ticket **10** blackboard, chalkboard

slattern **4** drab, slob, slut **5** bitch, frump **6** harlot, sloven **7** trollop

slatternly **6** frowsy, frumpy, sloppy, untidy **7** unkempt **8** slipshod, slovenly

slaughter **4** kill, slay **6** pogrom **7** butcher, destroy, killing, wipe out **8** decimate, massacre **9** bloodbath **10** annihilate, butchering, mass murder **11** exterminate

Slaughterhouse Five
author: **12** Kurt Vonnegut
character: **12** Billy Pilgrim
setting: **7** Dresden

Slav **4** Pole, Serb, Sorb, Wend **5** Croat, Czech **6** Bulgar, Slovak **7** Russian, Serbian, Slovene, Sorbian **8** Bohemian, Croatian, Moravian **9** Bulgarian, Ruthenian, Slavonian, Slovadian, Ukrainian

slave **4** prey, serf, toil **6** addict, drudge, menial, thrall, toiler, vassal, victim **7** chattel, plodder **8** bondsman **9** workhorse **11** bond servant

slaver **5** drool **6** drivel **7** slobber

slavery **4** toil **5** grind, labor, sweat **6** strain **7** bondage, serfdom, travail **8** drudgery, struggle **9** captivity, treadmill, vassalage **11** enslavement, impressment, subjugation **12** enthrallment

Slavic
language family: **12** Indo-European
group: **11** Balto-Slavic
subgroup: **12** Old Bulgarian **13** Eastern Slavic, Western Slavic **14** Southern Slavic **15** Old Church Slavic

slavish **5** exact **6** strict **7** literal, servile **9** imitative, slavelike **10** derivative, obsequious, submissive, unoriginal **11** subservient **13** unimaginative

slay **4** do in, kill **6** murder **7** destroy, execute **8** massacre **9** slaughter **10** annihilate

slayer **6** hit man, killer **7** butcher **8** assassin, murderer **11** executioner **12** exterminator

slaying **6** murder **7** killing **8** homicide **9** execution

sleazy **5** cheap, tacky **6** flimsy, shabby, shoddy, trashy, vulgar **7** schlock **13** insubstantial

sleek **4** oily **5** shiny, silky, slick, suave **6** glossy, satiny, smooth **7** fawning, velvety **8** lustrous, unctuous **12** ingratiating

sleep **3** nap **4** doze, rest **5** death, peace **6** repose, snooze **7** slumber
god of: **6** Hypnos, Hypnus, Somnus

sleeping **6** asleep, dozing **7** dormant, napping, resting **8** snoozing **9** quiescent, somnolent **11** hibernating **19** in the arms of Morpheus

Sleeping Beauty, The
composer: **11** Tchaikovsky

sleeping car (railroad)
invented by: **7** Pullman

sleeping infants
goddess of: **6** Cunina

sleeping place **3** bed, cot **4** bunk **5** berth **6** pallet **7** bedroom **9** dormitory **10** bedchamber

sleepless **5** alert **7** wakeful **8** restless, watchful **9** insomniac, wide awake **11** industrious

sleeplessness **8** insomnia **9** alertness, attention **11** wakefulness **12** restlessness

sleep lightly **3** nap, nod **4** doze **6** catnap, snooze **15** catch forty winks

sleepy **4** dull **5** quiet, tired, weary **6** drowsy **8** fatigued, inactive **9** exhausted

sleigh **4** dray, sled **6** cutter, sledge, troika **8** transport

Sleipnir
origin: **12** Scandinavian
horse of: **4** Odin **5** Othin
legs: **5** eight

slender **4** lean, poor, slim, thin, weak **5** faint, scant, small, spare **6** feeble, little, meager, narrow, remote, skinny, slight **7** willowy **8** delicate

Slender
character in: **22** The Merry Wives of Windsor
author: **11** Shakespeare

Sleuth
director: **17** Joseph L Mankiewicz
based on play by: **14** Anthony Shaffer
cast: **12** Michael Caine **15** Laurence Olivier

slew **3** lot, ton **4** gang, heap, load, lots, peck, pile, raft **5** batch, did in **6** killed **8** murdered **12** assassinated

Slezak, Walter
born: **6** Vienna **7** Austria
father: **9** Leo Slezak
roles: **5** Fanny **8** Lifeboat **11** Dr Coppelius

slice **3** cut **4** pare **5** carve, piece, sever, shave **6** cut off, divide **7** portion, section, segment, whittle **8** separate **9** dismember

slick **3** sly **4** coat, film, foxy, oily, scum, waxy, wily **5** sharp, shiny, sleek **6** clever, glassy, glossy, greasy, satiny, smooth, tricky **7** coating, cunning **8** slippery **10** make glossy **11** fast-talking **13** smooth-talking

slicker **8** raincoat **9** sou'wester **10** mackintosh, waterproof

slide **4** fall, pass, ramp, skid, slip, veer **5** chute, coast, glide, lapse, slope **7** slither **8** sideslip **11** diapositive **12** transparency

slide by **4** go by **5** lapse **6** elapse, roll by, slip by **7** glide by **8** slip away

slight **3** cut **4** lean, slap, slim, snub, thin, tiny **5** frail, small, spare **6** insult, little, modest, rebuff **7** fragile, limited, slender **8** moderate **10** incivility, negligible, restricted **11** unimportant **13** imperceptible, inappreciable, infinitesimal

slight amount **3** bit **4** dash, drop **5** pinch, touch, trace **6** little **7** smidgen, smidgin, soupcon **8** smidgeon **9** little bit **10** smattering

slightly **6** feebly, rarely **8** meagerly, scantily, scarcely, somewhat **10** negligibly **13** superficially **15** insignificantly

slim **4** lean, thin **5** faint, small **6** meager, remote, skinny, slight, svelte **7** distant, slender, thready, willowy **10** negligible

slime **3** mud **4** mire, muck, ooze **6** sludge

slimy **4** foul, vile **5** gummy, mucky, nasty **6** creepy, putrid, sticky **7** viscous **9** glutinous, loathsome, obnoxious, offensive, repulsive

sling **3** net **4** cast **5** fling, throw **9** slingshot **10** arm support

Slingin' Sammy
nickname of: **10** Sammy Baugh

slingshot **5** sling **8** catapult

slink **4** slip **5** creep, prowl, skulk, sneak, steal **6** tiptoe

slip **3** put **4** dock, drop, fail, fall, leak, pass, sink, skid **5** berth, error, glide, lapse, scrap, shoot, shred, slide, sneak, sprig, steal, strip **6** escape, sprout, ticket, worsen **7** blunder, chemise, cutting, decline, faux pas, receipt, sapling, voucher **9** petticoat, stripling, youngling, youngster **10** be revealed, get clear of, imprudence, underdress **12** indiscretion

slip away 4 go by **5** lapse **6** elapse, escape **7** run away, slide by **8** creep off **9** tiptoe off

slip by 4 go by, pass **5** lapse **6** elapse, pass by, roll by **7** glide by, slide by **8** slip away

slip of the tongue, a
Latin: 13 lapsus linguae

slipper 4 mule, shoe **5** scuff **6** sandal

slippery 4 foxy, oily, waxy, wily **5** slick, soapy **6** crafty, glassy, greasy, shifty, smooth, sneaky, tricky **7** devious **9** deceitful **10** contriving, unreliable **11** treacherous **13** untrustworthy

slipshod 3 lax **5** loose, messy **6** casual, sloppy, untidy **7** offhand **8** careless, slovenly **11** thoughtless

Slipslop, Mrs
character in: 13 Joseph Andrews
author: 8 Fielding

slip-up 4 flub, goof **5** botch, error, gaffe, lapse **6** boo-boo, bungle, foul-up, mess-up, miscue **7** blooper, blunder, clinker, faux pas, mistake, screw-up **9** oversight

slit 3 cut **4** gash **5** crack, slash **7** crevice, fissure **8** incision

slither 5 glide, slide **25** move with a side-to-side motion

sliver 5 crumb, shred, slice, snick **6** morsel **8** splinter

slivovitz
type: 6 brandy **7** liqueur
origin: 10 Yugoslavia
flavor: 4 plum

Sloan, John F
born: 11 Lock Haven PA
artwork: 12 McSorley's Bar **14** Wake of the Ferry **18** Hairdresser's Window **25** Backyards Greenwich Village **26** Sunday Women Drying Their Hair

slob 6 sloven **8** slattern

slobber 4 slop **5** drool **6** drivel, slaver **7** dribble, sputter **8** salivate, splutter

sloe gin
type: 7 liqueur
flavor: 9 sloe berry **15** blackthorn berry
drink: 11 Sloe Gin Fizz
with bourbon: 9 Black Hawk
with rum: 11 Shark's Tooth
with vermouth: 10 Blackthorn

slogan 5 motto **6** byword **9** battle cry, catchword, watchword

sloop 4 boat, brig, ship **5** smack **8** sailboat, schooner

slop 3 mud **4** mire, muck, ooze **5** filth, slosh, slush, spill, swash, swill, waste **6** refuse, sludge, splash **7** garbage, spatter **8** splatter

Slop, Dr
character in: 14 Tristram Shandy
author: 6 Sterne

slope 3 tip **4** bank, bend, lean, tilt **5** angle, pitch, slant **7** descent, incline **9** downgrade **11** inclination

sloping 5 alean, steep **6** aslant **7** leaning, oblique, tilting **8** diagonal, inclined, on a slant, slanting **9** slantways **11** declivitous

sloppiness 5 chaos, mix-up, upset **6** jumble **7** clutter **8** disarray, disorder, shambles **9** messiness **10** disharmony, untidiness **12** dishevelment **14** disarrangement **15** disorganization

sloppy 3 wet **5** dirty, messy, muddy **6** marshy, sloshy, slushy, sodden, soiled, swampy, untidy, watery **7** unclean **10** disorderly

sloppy person 4 slob **6** sloven

slosh 3 lap **4** drop, mire, stir **5** slush, spill, swash **6** splash **8** flounder

slot 3 gap **4** slit **5** crack, niche, notch
machine: 14 one-armed bandit

sloth 6 phlegm, torpor **7** languor **8** idleness, laziness, lethargy **9** indolence, lassitude, torpidity **12** listlessness, sluggishness **13** do-nothingness, shiftlessness

slothful 3 lax **4** idle, lazy **5** inert **6** drowsy, otiose, supine, torpid **8** indolent, listless, sluggish **9** do-nothing, lethargic, negligent, shiftless **10** sluggardly **11** unambitious

slouch 4 bend **5** droop, hunch, idler, slump, stoop **6** loafer **7** laggard, shirker, slacker **8** sluggard **9** goldbrick, lazybones

Slouching Toward Kalamazoo
author: 12 Peter DeVries

slovenly 5 dirty, dowdy, messy **6** frowzy, sloppy, untidy **7** unclean, unkempt **8** careless, slapdash, slipshod **10** disorderly, slatternly **11** indifferent, unconcerned

slow 3 dim, off **4** curb, dull, dumb, flag, late, long **5** brake, check, dense, heavy, loath, quiet **6** averse, boring, falter, hinder, hold up, impede, obtuse, retard, stupid, torpid **7** belated, delayed, laggard, lumpish, not busy, overdue, tedious, unhasty **8** backward, cautious, dawdling, dilatory, dragging, drawn out, extended, hesitant, inactive, obstruct, sluggish, tarrying **9** dim-witted, leisurely, lingering, ponderous, prolonged, reluctant, snail-like, unhurried **10** behind time, decelerate, deliberate, dull-witted, indisposed, protracted, unexciting, unpunctual **11** disinclined, halfhearted, reduce speed **12** impercipient, lose momentum, tortoiselike, unperceptive

slowdown 4 curb, flag **5** brake, delay, letup, slump **6** ease-up, falter, hinder, impede, lessen, retard, slow-up **7** decline, falloff, letdown, setback, slowing, subside **8** diminish, downturn, flagging **9** grind down **10** decelerate, slackening, stagnation **11** reduce speed, retardation **12** deceleration, drag one's feet, slow to a crawl

slow-moving 4 poky **5** pokey **6** idling **8** crawling, creeping, dawdling, sluggish **9** leisurely, snaillike **10** turtlelike **12** tortoiselike
creature: 4 slug **5** loris, sloth, snail **6** turtle **8** tortoise

slowness 6 tedium **8** dullness **9** torpidity **10** snail's pace **12** backwardness, sluggishness

slow-paced 4 easy **7** gradual, laggard **8** sluggish **9** leisurely, lethargic, unhurried **10** deliberate

slowpoke 4 slug **5** idler, snail **7** dallier, dawdler, laggard, lie-abed, plodder **8** lingerer, slugabed, tortoise **9** saunterer, straggler **11** foot-dragger **13** stick-in-the-mud

slow to learn 4 dull **5** dense, inapt **6** stupid **8** retarded **10** slow-witted

slow up 4 stem **5** delay **6** detain, hinder, impede, retard **8** slow down

slow-witted **4** dull **5** dense **7** doltish, idiotic, moronic **8** backward, retarded **9** imbecilic

sludge **3** mud **4** mire, muck, ooze, slop **5** dregs, slime, slush **8** sediment

slug **3** bat, hit **4** bash, belt, sock **5** baste, clout, pound, punch, smite, thump, whack, whale **6** batter, strike, wallop **7** clobber **8** lambaste

sluggard **4** lazy **5** drone, idler, sloth, snail **6** loafer, truant, turtle **7** dawdler, laggard **8** loiterer, slothful, slowpoke, tortoise **9** do-nothing, lazybones **11** couch potato **12** lounge lizard **13** stick-in-the-mud

sluggish **4** lazy, slow **5** inert **6** torpid **7** languid **8** inactive, indolent, lifeless, listless, slothful **9** leisurely, lethargic, soporific, unhurried **10** phlegmatic, protracted, spiritless

sluggishness **6** torpor **7** inertia **8** lethargy, slowness **9** lassitude **10** inactivity **12** listlessness

slum
Portuguese: **6** favela

slumber **3** nap **4** doze **5** sleep **6** snooze **8** vegetate **9** hibernate **10** be inactive, lie dormant

slump **3** dip, sag **4** drop, fall, slip **5** droop, lapse **6** plunge, slouch, tumble **7** decline, give way, reverse, setback **8** collapse

slur **3** cut, dig **4** mark, skip, spot **5** smear, stain, sully, taint **6** defame, ignore, insult, malign, mumble, mutter, slight **7** affront, blacken, blemish, let pass **8** mumbling, overlook, pass over **9** disregard, gloss over, muttering **11** run together

slush **4** slop **6** bathos **9** soppiness **11** mawkishness, melting snow **14** sentimentalism, sentimentality

slushiness **5** slush **10** sponginess **11** mawkishness **14** sentimentalism, sentimentality

slut **4** doxy, jade **5** bimbo, frump, hussy, tramp, wench, whore **6** floozy, harlot, sloven, wanton **7** jezebel, trollop **8** slattern, strumpet **10** prostitute

sly **4** foxy, wily **6** artful, covert, crafty, secret, shrewd, sneaky, tricky **7** cunning, furtive, playful, private **8** stealthy **9** conniving **11** dissembling, mischievous **12** confidential

Slye, Leonard
real name of: **9** Roy Rogers

slyness **5** craft **7** cunning, stealth **8** archness, foxiness, subtlety, wiliness **10** artfulness, craftiness, shrewdness, trickiness **11** furtiveness **15** underhandedness

smack **3** bit, hit, rap **4** blow, buss, clap, cuff, dash, hint, kiss, slap **5** savor, smell, smite, spank, taste, tinge, touch, trace, whack **6** buffet, flavor **7** suggest

small **4** mean, tiny, weak **5** faint, minor, petty, scant **6** feeble, lesser, little, meager, modest, narrow, petite, slight **7** bigoted, fragile, ignoble, trivial **8** not great, trifling **10** diminutive, provincial, undersized **11** of no account, opinionated, superficial, unimportant **13** insignificant **15** inconsequential

Small, Lennie
character in: **12** Of Mice and Men
author: **9** Steinbeck

small details
Latin: **8** minutiae

smaller **4** less **5** lower **6** lesser, tinier **7** dinkier, littler, pettier, reduced, shorter **8** inferior

smallest **5** least **6** lowest **7** tiniest **8** dinkiest, pettiest, shortest **9** slightest

Small House at Allington, The
author: **15** Anthony Trollope

small intestine
part of: **15** digestive system
lined with: **5** villi

small-minded **4** mean **5** petty **6** narrow **7** bigoted **9** parochial **10** prejudiced **12** mean-spirited

smallness **8** meanness, tininess **9** pettiness **10** meagerness, triviality **12** dwarfishness **14** insignificance **18** inconsequentiality

small piece **3** bit, dab **4** chip, drop, snip **5** crumb, grain, piece, pinch, scrap, shred, speck **6** dollop, morsel **7** granule, smidgen, smidgin **8** fragment, particle, smidgeon

small quantity **3** bit, dab, few **5** touch **7** smidgen, smidgin, soupcon **8** smidgeon **9** little bit

small round window
French: **11** oeil-de-boeuf

small spot **3** dab, dot **5** fleck, speck

small talk **6** banter, gossip **7** chatter, prattle **8** chitchat, idle talk, repartee **9** bavardage, prattling **12** tittle-tattle

smart **4** ache, burn, chic, hurt, keen, neat, trim **5** brash, brisk, quick, sassy, sharp, sting, wince, witty **6** astute, blench, brainy, bright, clever, flinch, modish, shrewd, suffer **7** elegant, stylish **8** feel pain, vigorous **9** be painful, energetic **10** smart-aleck **11** fashionable, intelligent

smart aleck **6** smarty **7** show-off, windbag, wiseass, wise guy **8** blowhard, braggart, saucebox, wiseacre **9** know-it-all **11** smarty-pants **12** grandstander **13** exhibitionist

smarten up **7** dress up, improve **8** beautify, spruce up

smartness **6** acumen, wisdom **8** keenness, sagacity **9** acuteness **10** astuteness, cleverness, perception, shrewdness **12** intelligence, perspicacity

smash **3** hit **4** bang, bash, beat, blow **5** break, clout, crack, crash, crush **6** batter, strike, winner **7** clobber, crack-up, destroy, shatter, success, triumph **8** accident, demolish, splinter **9** collision, sensation **12** disintegrate

smash against **4** beat, lash **5** crash, pound, smite **6** batter, buffet **7** break on

smashed **5** drunk **6** soused, wasted, zapped, zonked **7** crashed, crushed **8** squashed **9** plastered, shattered **10** inebriated **11** intoxicated **17** under the influence **20** three sheets to the wind

smashing **5** great, super **6** superb **8** fabulous, terrific **9** fantastic, marvelous, wonderful **10** stupendous **11** magnificent, sensational **13** extraordinary

smashup **5** crash, wreck **7** crackup **8** accident **9** collision **12** fender bender

smattering **3** bit, dab **4** dash, drop **5** scrap **7** smidgen, smidgin, snippet **8** smidgeon **10** sprinkling

smear **3** mar, rub **4** blur, coat, daub, soil **5** cover, lay on, libel, stain **6** blotch, injure, malign, smirch, smudge, spread, streak **7** blacken, blemish, degrade, slander, splotch, tarnish **8** besmirch, besmudge **9** denigrate **10** accusation, obliterate

smell **4** feel, nose, odor, reek **5** aroma, fetor, scent, sense, sniff, stink **6** detect, stench **7** bouquet, perfume, suspect **8** perceive **9** emanation, fragrance, get wind of

smelly **4** rank **5** fetid **6** putrid **7** noisome, odorous, reeking **8** stinking **10** malodorous

Smerdyakov
character in: **20** The Brothers Karamazov
author: **10** Dostoevsky

Smetana, Bedrich
born: **7** Bohemia **8** Litomysl **11** Leitomischl **14** Czechoslovakia
composer of: **7** Ma Vlast **9** My Country **10** From My Life **11** Czech Dances **12** The Two Widows **16** The Bartered Bride

smidgen, smidgin, smidgeon **3** bit, dab **4** mite, snip **5** crumb, pinch, scrap, shred, speck, trace **6** dollop, morsel

Smike
character in: **16** Nicholas Nickleby
author: **7** Dickens

smile **4** beam, grin **5** favor, shine, smirk **6** simper

Smiles of a Summer Night
director: **13** Ingmar Bergman
cast: **11** Eva Dahlbeck **13** Ulla Jacobsson **15** Margit Carlquist **16** Harriet Andersson
remade as: **17** A Little Night Music

Smiley's People
author: **11** John Le Carre

Smintheus
epithet of: **6** Apollo

smirch **4** blot, mark, soil, spot **5** dirty, smear, stain, sully, taint **6** blotch, damage, smudge, stigma **7** begrime, blacken, blemish, slander, tarnish **8** besmirch, besmudge, dishonor **9** discredit

smirk **4** grin, leer **5** sneer **6** simper **7** grimace

Smirke, Sir Robert
architect of: **12** King's College (U of London) **13** British Museum (London) **19** Covent Garden Theater (London)
style: **12** Greek Revival

smite **3** hit **4** swat **5** knock, smack, whack **6** enamor, strike, wallop **7** clobber

Smith, Adam
author of: **18** The Wealth of Nations

Smith, Al
creator/artist of: **11** Mutt and Jeff

Smith, Betty
author of: **20** A Tree Grows in Brooklyn

Smith, Charles Aaron
nickname: **5** Bubba
sport: **8** football
team: **14** Baltimore Colts

Smith, David
born: **8** Decatur IN
artwork: **3** Zig **4** Cubi **6** Oculus **8** Agricola, Main View, Sentinel, Star Cage **9** Australia, Royal Bird, Tank Totem **10** The Banquet **12** Detroit Queen **15** Lectern Sentinel **17** Medals for Dishonor **20** Hudson River Landscape **23** Song of an Irish Blacksmith

Smith, Gladys Mary
real name of: **12** Mary Pickford

Smith, Harriet
character in: **4** Emma
author: **6** Austen

Smith, Lillian
author: **12** Strange Fruit

Smith, Maggie
born: **6** Ilford **7** England
husband: **14** Robert Stephens
roles: **7** Othello **15** California Suite, The Pumpkin Eater **17** Travels with My Aunt **24** The Prime of Miss Jean Brodie (Oscar)

Smith, Winston
character in: **18** Nineteen Eighty-Four
author: **6** Orwell

smithereen **3** bit **4** atom **5** crumb, shard **8** fragment, particle **9** scintilla

Smithson, James
field: **9** chemistry
nationality: **7** British
discovered: **11** smithsonite **13** zinc carbonite
funded: **22** Smithsonian Institution

smitten **8** enamored **9** bewitched **10** enraptured, infatuated

smoke **4** draw, fume, pipe, puff, reek, suck **5** cigar, fumes **6** billow, inhale **7** light up, smolder **9** cigarette, have a drag

Smoke
author: **12** Ivan Turgenev
character: **5** Irina **7** Potugin **13** Tanya Shestoff **16** General Ratmiroff, Grigory Litvinoff **18** Kapitolina Shestoff

smoke screen **4** ruse **5** cover, dodge, front **6** screen **9** deception **10** camouflage, subterfuge

smoky **5** dingy, grimy, sooty **6** fuming, smudgy **7** reeking **10** smoldering

smolder **4** burn, fume, rage **5** smoke **6** seethe

Smollett, Tobias George
author of: **14** (The Expedition of) Humphry Clinker, Roderick Random **15** Peregrine Pickle

smooch **3** pet **4** buss, kiss, neck **5** smack, spoon **7** make out

smooth **4** calm, ease, easy, even, flat, glib, help, mild, open, pave **5** allay, level, silky, sleek, suave **6** facile, mellow, placid, polish, refine, serene, soften, soothe, steady **7** appease, assuage, flatten, mollify, orderly, perfect, prepare, velvety **8** civilize, composed, make even, mitigate, peaceful, pleasant **9** collected, cultivate, easygoing, make level **10** facilitate, flattering, harmonious, methodical, uneventful **11** well-ordered **12** ingratiating **13** self-possessed, well-regulated

smoothness **8** evenness, fineness, flatness **9** silkiness, sleekness

smooth the feathers **4** calm **6** pacify, soothe **7** appease, assuage, mollify, placate **10** conciliate

smooth-tongued **4** glib **5** suave **6** fluent **8** unctuous **10** flattering **11** fast-talking **12** hypocritical, ingratiating

smother **4** hide, mask, wrap **5** choke, quash, snuff **6** deaden, quench, shower **7** conceal **8** keep down, strangle, suppress, surround **9** choke back, envelop in, suffocate **10** asphyxiate, extinguish

Smothers Brothers Comedy Hour, The
regulars: **10** Don Novello, Pat Paulsen **11** Bob Einstein, Leigh French, Steve Martin, Tom Smothers **12** Betty Aberlin, Dick Smothers, John Hartford, Nino Senporty, Spencer Quinn **13** Mason Williams **14** Jennifer Warren, Sally Struthers **16** Anita Kerr Singers **17** Jimmy Joyce Singers **18** Louis DaPron Dancers

19 Marty Paich Orchestra 20 Denny Vaughn Orchestra, Ron Poindexter Dancers 21 Nelson Riddle Orchestra

smudge 4 blot, mark, soil, spot 5 dirty, smear, stain 6 smutch

smudgy 5 dirty, messy 6 filthy, grubby, smeary 7 sullied 8 befouled, unwashed 9 besmeared

smug 8 superior, virtuous 10 complacent 13 self-righteous, self-satisfied

smuggle 5 sneak 15 export illegally, import illegally

smuggled goods 10 contraband 14 illegal exports, illegal imports 18 prohibited articles

smuggler 6 runner 9 gunrunner, rumrunner 10 bootlegger 13 contrabandist

smugness 7 egotism 9 immodesty 11 superiority 12 virtuousness 16 self-satisfaction 17 self-righteousness

smut 4 dirt, porn, soot 5 filth, grime 6 smudge 9 obscenity, scatology 11 pornography

smutty 4 lewd 5 dirty, grimy, sooty 6 filthy, soiled, vulgar 7 obscene 8 indecent 12 pornographic

Smyrna *see* 6 Myrrha

Smythe, Reginald
creator/artist of: 8 Andy Capp

snack 3 eat, tea 4 bite, nosh 5 munch 6 nibble, tidbit 7 take tea 8 lap lunch, munchies, nibblies, pick-me-up, snackies 9 collation, crunchies, elevenses 10 finger food, light lunch 11 casse-croute, coffee break, light repast, refreshment

snag 3 bar, rip 4 grab, stub, tear 5 block, catch, hitch, stump 7 barrier 8 obstacle 9 hindrance 10 difficulty, impediment, projection, protrusion 11 encumbrance, obstruction 14 stumbling block

Snagsby
character in: 10 Bleak House
author: 7 Dickens

snail
French: 8 escargot

snake ***see box***

Snake *see* 8 Shoshoni

snake, poisonous 9 Coactrice

Snake, the
nickname of: 10 Ken Stabler

snake 5 sneak, viper 7 reptile, serpent, traitor 8 ophidian 9 reptilian
combining form: 4 ophi 5 ophio, ophis 6 herpes 7 herpeto
expert: 13 herpetologist
fear of: 13 herpetophobia
genus: 7 Ophidia
kind: 3 asp, boa, sea 4 file, habu, wart, whip 5 aboma, adder, cobra, coral, krait, mamba, tiger, viper 6 bongar, elapid, garter, gopher, python, taipan 7 rattler, sunbeam 8 anaconda, cerastes, moccasin, pit viper, ringhals 9 boomslang, colubrina, mole viper, puff adder 10 black mamba, bushmaster, copperhead, fer-de-lance, sidewinder 11 cottonmouth, diamond back, Gaboon viper, rattlesnake 12 slender blind 13 elephant-trunk, water moccasin 14 boa constrictor
shedding: 7 ecdysis 8 moulting
skin: 6 exuvia
snake killer: 8 mongoose

Snake Pit, The
author: 12 Sigrid Undset

snap 3 nip, pop 4 bark, bite, grab, lock, yelp 5 break, catch, cinch, clasp, click, close, crack, growl, hasty, latch, quick, snarl, spell 6 breeze, period, secure, snatch, sudden 8 careless, fastener, fracture 9 impulsive 11 thoughtless

snapdragon 11 Antirrhinum
varieties: 4 wild 5 dwarf 6 common, garden, lesser 7 spurred 8 withered

snappish 4 edgy 5 cross, huffy, surly, testy 6 crabby, cranky, shirty, touchy 7 grouchy, huffish, peevish, waspish 8 captious, petulant 9 irascible, irritable, querulous 10 ill-humored, ill-natured, out of sorts 11 hot-tempered 12 cantankerous 13 quick-tempered, short-tempered

snappy 4 fast, tony 5 hasty, quick, rapid, ritzy, sharp, smart, swank, swift, swish 6 classy, dapper, jaunty, speedy, spiffy 7 stylish 12 lickety-split

snare 3 net 4 bait, hook, lure, ruse, trap 5 catch, decoy, noose, seize, trick 6 entrap 7 capture, ensnare, pitfall 9 deception 12 entanglement

snarl 3 mat 4 bark, clog, kink, knot, mess, snap 5 chaos, growl, ravel, twist 6 hinder, impede, jumble, muddle, tangle 7 confuse, lash out 8 disorder, entangle 9 confusion

snatch 3 bit, nab 4 grab, part, pull, take 5 catch, grasp, piece, pluck, seize, wrest 7 snippet 8 fragment

Snead, Sam
nickname: 12 Slammin' Sammy
sport: 4 golf
won: 7 Masters

sneak 3 sly 4 slip 5 creep, knave, rogue, scamp, steal 6 lurker, rascal, secret, spirit 7 bounder, furtive, skulker, slinker, smuggle 8 scalawag, surprise 9 miscreant, scoundrel, secretive, underhand 11 rapscallion 13 surreptitious

sneak attack 4 raid 6 ambush 7 assault 9 ambuscade, incursion

sneak off 5 elope 6 decamp 7 abscond 9 steal away

sneaky 3 sly 4 mean 7 devious, furtive, vicious 9 malicious, secretive, underhand 10 traitorous 11 treacherous

sneer 4 jeer, leer, mock 5 scoff, scorn, smirk 6 deride, rebuff 7 disdain 8 belittle, ridicule

sneer at 5 knock, scorn 6 deride, malign 7 disdain, put down, run down 8 pooh-pooh 16 cast aspersions on

Sneerwell, Lady
character in: 19 The School for Scandal
author: 8 Sheridan

snicker 5 snort 6 cackle, giggle, simper, titter 7 snigger

snide 5 nasty 7 mocking 8 scoffing 9 malicious, sarcastic 11 insinuating 12 contemptuous

Snider, Edwin
nickname: 4 Duke
sport: 8 baseball
position: 7 fielder
team: 15 Brooklyn Dodgers

sniff 4 jeer, mock, odor 5 aroma, scoff, smell, snort, snuff, whiff 6 snivel 7 disdain, sniffle, snuffle 9 disparage

snip 3 bit, bob, cut, lop 4 brat, clip, crop, punk, snap, trim

5 clack, click, piece, prune, scrap, shear, twerp 6 sample, shrimp, swatch 7 cutting 8 fragment

snippy 4 curt, rude 5 sassy, saucy, short 6 cheeky, snotty 7 brusque 8 flippant, impudent, insolent, snippety 11 ill-mannered, impertinent, smart-alecky

snivel 3 cry 5 sniff, whine 6 boohoo 7 sniffle 8 complain

sniveler 6 coward, whiner 7 crybaby 10 complainer

snob 7 elitist 13 social climber

snobbish 4 vain 6 snooty, snotty 7 haughty, high-hat, stuck-up 8 arrogant, superior 10 disdainful 11 overbearing, patronizing, pretentious 13 condescending

Snodgrass
character in: 14 Pickwick Papers
author: 7 Dickens

snoop 3 pry 7 meddler, Paul Pry 8 busybody 10 Nosy Parker 12 eavesdropper

snoopy, Snoopy 4 nosy 6 beagle, prying 7 curious 8 meddling 10 meddlesome 11 inquisitive
brother: 5 Spike
creator: 6 Schulz
friend: 9 Woodstock
master: 12 Charlie Brown

snooze 3 nap 4 doze 5 sleep 6 cat nap, drowse, siesta 7 slumber 10 forty winks

Snopes family
characters in: 9 The Hamlet
members: 2 Ab 4 Flem, Mink 5 Isaac
author: 8 Faulkner

snort 4 blow, gasp, huff, jeer, pant, puff, rage 5 blast, grunt, scoff, sneer, storm

snout 3 neb 4 beak, bill, nose 5 snoot, spout 6 muzzle, nozzle 9 proboscis

Snow, C P (Charles Percy Snow, Lord Snow)
author of: 9 The New Men 10 Last Things, The Masters 14 A Coat of Varnish 16 Corridors of Power 20 Strangers and Brothers

Snow-Bound
author: 21 John Greenleaf Whittier

snowfall 4 firn, neve 6 flurry 8 blizzard
Scottish: 6 onding

Snow Leopard, The
author: 16 Peter Matthiessen

Snow Queen, The
author: 21 Hans Christian Andersen

Snows of Kilimanjaro, The
author: 15 Ernest Hemingway

snow-white 4 pure 5 snowy 9 lily-white, pure white 11 white as snow

Snow White
author: 15 Donald Barthelme

snowy 4 pure 5 white 7 nievous 8 pristine, spotless 9 blizzardy

snub 3 cut 5 blunt, check, scorn, short 6 ignore, rebuff, slight, stubby 7 disdain 9 retrousse 11 repudiation 12 cold shoulder 16 turn up one's nose at 19 give the cold shoulder

snuff 5 scent, smell, sniff, whiff 7 sniffle, snuffle

snuff out 5 crush 8 suppress 10 extinguish, put an end to

snug 4 cozy, neat, safe 5 close, tight 6 secure 7 compact 8 tranquil 9 sheltered, skintight 11 comfortable 12 close-fitting, tight-fitting 13 well-organized

snuggle 3 hug 4 nest 6 cuddle, curl up, enfold, nestle, nuzzle

Snyder, Peggy Lou
real name of: 21 Harriet Hilliard Nelson

so
Latin: 3 sic

soak 3 wet 4 seep 5 bathe, enter, steep 6 absorb, drench, sink in, take in, take up 7 immerse, pervade 8 permeate, saturate 9 penetrate

soaked 5 soggy 6 sodden, soused 7 sopping 8 drenched 9 saturated 11 waterlogged, wringing wet

soak up 4 blot 6 absorb, take up 8 sponge up

soak up warmth 4 bask 11 warm oneself 12 toast oneself

Soames Forsyte
character in: 14 The Forsyte Saga
author: 10 Galsworthy

Soap
character: 5 Major 6 Benson 9 Billy Tate 10 Eunice Tate 11 Chester Tate, Corrine Tate, Danny Dallas, Jessica Tate, Jodie Dallas 12 Burt Campbell 18 Mary Dallas Campbell
cast: 7 Ted Wass 9 Jimmy Baio 11 Diana Canova 12 Billy Crystal, Cathryn Damon, Jennifer Salt, Robert Mandan 14 Arthur Peterson 15 Richard Mulligan, Robert Guillaume 16 Katherine Helmond

soar 3 fly 4 rise, wing 5 climb, float, glide, mount, tower 8 take wing

soave
music: 6 gentle

sob 3 cry 4 howl, wail, weep 6 lament, plaint, snivel 7 blubber, whimper

so be it 4 amen 7 let it be 9 let it be so

sober 3 dry, sad 4 cool, drab, dull, grim, sane 5 grave, sound, staid 6 dreary, sedate, solemn, somber, steady 7 joyless, prudent, serious, subdued 8 moderate, not drunk, rational 9 judicious, realistic, sorrowful, temperate 10 abstemious 11 levelheaded 13 dispassionate

So Big
author: 10 Edna Ferber

sobriety 10 abstention, abstinence, continence, temperance 13 nonindulgence 14 abstemiousness

sobriquet 7 epithet, pet name 8 nickname 11 appellation

so-called
French: 9 soi-disant

soccer
athlete: 4 Pele 11 Johan Cruyff
players/team: 6 eleven
position: 6 goalie 7 forward 8 fullback, halfback 10 goalkeeper
championship: 8 World Cup 11 European Cup, National Cup 13 Cup Winner's Cup
violation: 5 hands 7 hacking, offside 11 obstructing
gaining control of ball: 4 trap

sociable 6 social 7 affable, cordial 8 friendly, gracious, outgoing 9 agreeable, congenial, convivial 10 gregarious, neighborly 11 extroverted 13 companionable

social 2 in 5 smart 7 stylish 8 friendly, pleasant, sociable 9 agreeable 10 gregarious, neighborly 11 cooperative, fashionable 14 interdependent

Social Contract, The
author: 19 Jean-Jacques Rousseau

social order
goddess of: 4 Hour 5 Horae

society **4** body, club **5** elite, group **6** circle, gentry, league **7** mankind **8** alliance, humanity, nobility **9** community, humankind **10** blue bloods **11** aristocracy, association, high society, social order **12** organization **14** the four hundred **16** the general public

sociologist
American: **4** Mead, Park, Ward **5** Coser, Gerth, Mills, Small, Wirth **6** Bendix, Cooley, Merton, Speier, Sumner, Thomas **7** Parsons, Sorokin **8** Eberhard **10** Lazarsfeld
British: **4** Webb **8** Hobhouse, Mannheim **12** Carr-Saunders
Danish: **6** Geiger
French: **4** Aron **5** Comte **8** Durkheim, Gurvitch **9** Friedmann
German: **5** Konig, Weber, Wiese **6** Simmel **8** Habermas, Luckmann **10** Dahrendorf, Horkheimer
Hungarian: **6** Lukacs **8** Mannheim
Israeli: **5** Buber **10** Eisenstadt
Norwegian: **6** Aubert **7** Galtung
Swedish: **8** Carlsson

sociopathic **9** alienated **10** antisocial, rebellious

sock **3** box, hit, sox **4** belt, blow, slap **5** punch, smack, smash **6** strike, wallop **7** clobber **8** knee sock **9** ankle sock **13** short stocking

sod **4** soil, turf **5** divot, earth, grass, sward **10** greensward

soda **3** pop **4** base, cola **5** tonic **6** bicarb, sodium **7** barilla, seltzer **8** beverage, root beer **9** ginger ale, soft drink **11** bicarbonate **12** sarsaparilla
ash: **6** alkali
in faro: **9** first card
maker: **4** jerk

sodden **4** dull **5** heavy, lumpy, mushy, pasty, soggy, soppy **6** doughy, soaked **7** sopping **8** besotted, drenched, dripping, listless **9** saturated **10** wet through **14** expressionless

Soddy, Frederick
field: **9** chemistry
nationality: **7** British
discovered: **8** isotopes
worked with: **13** William Ramsay **16** Ernest Rutherford
awarded: **10** Nobel Prize

sodium
chemical symbol: **2** Na

Sodom
destroyed with: **5** Admah **6** Zeboim **8** Gomorrah

sofa **5** couch, divan **6** canape, lounge, settee **8** love seat **9** davenport **12** chesterfield

Sofia
Roman name: **12** Ulpia Serdica
Byzantine name: **9** Triaditsa
capital of: **8** Bulgaria
landmark: **13** Buyuk Dzhamiya **16** Saint Sofia Church **17** Saint George Church **24** Alexander Nevsky Cathedral **32** Cyril and Methodius National Library

soft **4** easy, kind, mild, pale, weak **5** downy, faint, furry, muted, quiet, silky, sleek **6** feeble, gentle, hushed, pliant, satiny, shaded, silken, smooth, supple, tender **7** lenient, not hard, pitying, pliable, restful, subdued, velvety **8** delicate, not sharp, shadowed, tolerant, tranquil, twilight **9** malleable, not strong **10** harmonious **11** sentimental, sympathetic **12** easily molded, low intensity **13** compassionate, pleasantly low **16** easily penetrated **19** having a breathy sound **21** requiring little effort **25** incapable of great endurance

soften **5** lower **6** lessen, subdue, temper **7** cushion, mollify **8** make soft, mitigate, moderate, palliate, tone down, turn down **10** ameliorate, make softer

softhearted **4** kind, soft, warm **6** benign, gentle, humane, kindly, tender **8** generous **9** forgiving, indulgent **10** benevolent **11** considerate, kindhearted, sympathetic, warmhearted **13** compassionate, tenderhearted

softly **6** easily, gently, mildly, weakly **7** quietly

softness **8** mildness **9** downiness, silkiness **10** fluffiness, gentleness, smoothness, tenderness **11** tranquility **12** tranquillity

soft soap **7** blarney **8** cajolery, flattery **10** persuasion

sogginess **7** wetness **8** dampness **9** mushiness **10** soddenness

soggy **5** heavy, mushy, pasty, soppy **6** doughy, soaked, sodden **7** sopping **8** drenched, dripping **9** saturated

Sogliardo
character in: **22** Every Man out of His Humour
author: **6** Jonson

Soglow, Otto
creator/artist of: **13** The Little King

Sohrab and Rustum
author: **13** Matthew Arnold

soi-disant **8** so-called **9** pretended **10** self-styled **18** calling oneself thus

soigne, soignee **4** chic, neat, tidy **5** sleek, smart **6** classy, modish **7** elegant **11** well-groomed

soil **4** dirt, foul, land, loam, ruin, soot, spot **5** dirty, earth, grime, humus, muddy, smear, stain, sully **6** debase, defile, ground, region, smudge **7** blacken, country, tarnish **8** disgrace

soiled **5** dirty, grimy, messy **6** filthy, grubby, smudgy **7** muddied, sullied, unclean **8** begrimed, unwashed **9** besmeared

soiree **4** ball, prom **5** dance, party **9** cotillion, promenade

sojourn **4** stay **5** abide, pause, visit **6** stay at **7** holiday, layover **8** stay over, stopover, vacation

sojourner **6** lodger, tenant **7** pilgrim, tourist, visitor **8** traveler **9** transient, weekender **10** daytripper, vacationer

Sol
origin: **5** Roman
form: **3** god
personifies: **3** sun
corresponds to: **6** Helios **7** Mithras **8** Hyperion

sola, solus **5** alone **9** by oneself

solace **4** calm **5** cheer **6** soothe **7** assuage, comfort, console **8** reassure **10** help in need **11** consolation, reassurance **18** relief in affliction

solder **4** fuse, join, weld **5** braze, stick

soldier **2** GI **3** PFC **5** major **6** worker, zealot **7** colonel, general, private, servant, trooper, veteran, warrior **8** follower, partisan, sergeant **10** lieutenant, serviceman **11** enlisted man, military man **14** militant leader **16** brigadier general

Soldier of Orange
director: **13** Paul Verhoeven

based on novel by: **13** Erik Hazelhoff
cast: **10** Peter Faber **11** Derek De Lint, Eddy Habbema, Rutger Hauer **12** Jeroen Krabbe **15** Susan Penhaligon
setting: **14** The Netherlands

Soldier's Embrace, A
author: **14** Nadine Gordimer

soldiery **4** army **6** legion, troops **7** legions, militia **8** military, soldiers **11** fighting men

sole **4** lone, only **6** single **8** solitary **9** exclusive

solely **5** alone **6** merely, purely, singly **8** uniquely **11** exclusively **14** single-handedly

solemn **4** dark, drab, grim, holy **5** grave, sober, staid **6** formal, gloomy, sacred, sedate, somber **7** earnest, serious, sincere **8** absolute **9** dignified, religious, spiritual, steadfast **10** ceremonial, depressing, determined **11** ceremonious **12** awe-inspiring

solemnity **3** awe **7** dignity **8** ceremony **9** formality, reverence **11** seriousness **12** circumstance

solemnize **4** mark **5** honor **6** hallow **7** observe **9** celebrate **10** consecrate **11** commemorate

solicit **3** ask **4** seek **5** plead **7** entreat, request **9** appeal for, importune

solicitation **6** appeal **7** request **8** entreaty **11** importuning

solicitor **6** beggar, lawyer **7** counsel **8** salesman **10** supplicant

solicitous **4** avid, keen **5** eager **6** ardent, intent **7** anxious, intense, longing, mindful, zealous **8** desirous **9** attentive, concerned, regardful **10** thoughtful **12** enthusiastic

solicitude **4** care, zeal **5** worry **7** anxiety, avidity, concern **9** attention **10** enthusiasm, inquietude, uneasiness **11** disquietude, fearfulness, overconcern **12** apprehension

solid **4** firm, hard, pure, real **5** dense, massy, sober, sound, tough **6** rugged, stable, steady, strong, sturdy **7** durable, genuine, lasting, unmixed **8** complete, concrete, constant, rational, reliable, sensible, tangible, thorough, unbroken **9** not hollow, unalloyed, unanimous, undivided, well-built **10** continuous, dependable, solidified **11** impermeable, levelheaded, substantial, trustworthy **12** impenetrable **13** uninterrupted **15** well-constructed

solidarity **5** union, unity **7** harmony **9** closeness **11** cooperation, unification

solidify **3** fix, gel, set **4** cake, jell **6** cement, harden **7** congeal, stiffen, thicken **9** coagulate **11** crystallize **12** agglomerate

soliloquy **9** monologue **10** solo speech

Solinus
character in: **17** The Comedy of Errors
author: **11** Shakespeare

solitariness **8** solitude **9** aloneness, seclusion **13** reclusiveness

solitary **4** lone **6** hidden, lonely, remote, single **8** desolate, isolated, lonesome, secluded **9** concealed **10** cloistered **11** out-of-the-way, uninhabited **13** companionless

solitude **9** aloneness, isolation, seclusion, wasteland **10** desolation, loneliness, remoteness, wilderness

solo **5** alone **8** solitary **9** by oneself **10** unattended **12** singlehanded **13** unaccompanied
operatic: **4** aria

solo dance
ballet: **7** pas seul

Solomon
father: **5** David
mother: **9** Bathsheba
wife: **6** Naamah
son: **8** Rehoboam
brother: **5** Amnon **7** Absalom, Chileab **8** Adonijah
sister: **5** Tamar
visitor: **5** Sheba
wrote: **8** Proverbs **12** Ecclesiastes **13** Song of Solomon
built: **6** temple

Solomon Islands ***see box***

so long
Spanish: **12** hasta la vista

solution **3** key **5** blend **6** answer, cipher **7** mixture, solving **8** emulsion **9** resolving **10** resolution, suspension, unraveling **11** explanation

solve **7** resolve, unravel, work out **8** decipher, unriddle, untangle **9** figure out **10** find the key **13** find the answer

solvent **7** diluent, soluble **9** dilutable **10** dissoluble, dissolvent **11** dissolvable **16** financially sound

Solymi
origin: **9** Asia Minor
occupation: **8** warriors

Solzhenitsyn, Aleksandr
author of: **13** The Cancer Ward **14** The First Circle **19** The Gulag Archipelago 22 August Nineteen-Fourteen **31** One Day in the Life of Ivan Denisovich

Somalia ***see box, p. 908***

Solomon Islands
capital/largest city: **7** Honiara
others: **4** Auki, Bina, Gizo, Luti **5** Kieta, Munda **6** Tulagi **7** Yandina **8** Kira Kira **9** Tangarare **10** Sasamungga
division: **14** Papua New Guinea, Solomon Islands
head of state: **14** British monarch **15** governor-general
monetary unit: **4** cent **6** dollar
island: **4** Buka, Gizo, Savo **5** Ndeni, Ulawa **6** Tulagi **7** Malaita, Rennell, Solomon, Vangunu **8** Choiseul, Sikaiana, Vanikoro **9** Santa Cruz **10** New Georgia, Ontong Java **11** Guadalcanal, Santa Isabel **12** Bougainville, San Cristobal
mountain: **5** Balbi
highest point: **11** Popomanasiu
ocean: **7** Pacific, Solomon
physical feature:
gulf: **4** Huon, Kula
sound: **10** New Georgia
strait: **13** Indispensable
people: **7** Chinese **8** European **10** Melanesian, Polynesian
explorer: **14** Mendana de Neyra
leader: **9** Kenilorea
language: **7** English **13** Pidgin English **16** Melanesian pidgin
religion: **8** Anglican **13** Roman Catholic

Somalia
other name: **4** Punt **10** Somaliland **12** Horn of Africa
capital/largest city: **9** Mogadishu **10** Mogadiscio
others: **5** Burao, Merca **6** Mereka **7** Berbera, Galkayu, Kismayu **8** Belet Uen, Hargeisa **9** Chisimaio
division: **6** Hawiya **9** Mijirtein **10** Midjertein
colonial: **17** British Somaliland, Italian Somaliland
measure: **3** top **4** caba **5** chela, darat, tabla **6** cubito **8** parsalah
monetary unit: **4** besa **6** somalo **8** shilling **9** centesimi
weight: **8** parsalah
mountain: **5** Guban **11** Migiurtinia, Ogo Highland
highest point: **7** Surud Ad
river: **4** Juba **5** Daror, Nogal **9** Nugaaleed **11** Webi Shebeli **13** Webi Shabeelle
sea: **6** Indian
physical feature:
bay: **5** Negro
cape: **9** Guardafui
desert: **4** Aror
gulf: **4** Aden
plateau: **3** Ogo **4** Haud
people: **3** Sab **4** Asha **5** Galla **6** Hawiya, Isbaak, Somali **7** Danakil, Hamitic, Marehan, Samaale, Shuhali **8** Rahanwin
leader: **9** Siad Barre **12** Ali Shermarke
language: **6** Arabic, Somali **7** English, Italian
religion: **5** Islam
feature:
boat: **4** dhow
cloth: **7** banadir
clothing: **4** futa, toga **6** sarong
tree: **6** acacia, baobab **7** incense

Somaliland *see* **7** Somalia

somber **4** dark, drab, gray, grim **5** grave, sober **6** dreary, gloomy, solemn **7** serious **8** funereal, mournful, toneless **9** cheerless **10** depressing, melancholy

Sombrero Fallout
author: **16** Richard Brautigan

Some Like It Hot
director: **11** Billy Wilder
cast: **9** Joe E Brown, Pat O'Brien **10** George Raft, Jack Lemmon, Tony Curtis **13** Marilyn Monroe

Somers Islands *see* **7** Bermuda

something essential
Latin: **10** sine qua non

something for something
Latin: **10** quid pro quo

Something Happened
author: **12** Joseph Heller

sometime **4** late, once **5** later **6** former **7** quondam **8** formerly, previous **9** erstwhile **10** occasional

sometimes **7** at times **10** now and then, on occasion **12** occasionally, once in a while

somewhat **6** fairly, kind of, partly, sort of **8** passably **9** tolerably **10** moderately, more or less, reasonably **13** approximately

somnolent **4** dozy, dull **5** dopey **6** drowsy, groggy, sleepy, torpid **7** languid, nodding, out of it, yawning **8** hypnotic, sluggish **9** half-awake, lethargic, sopoforic **10** half-asleep, slumberous **11** heavy-lidded **13** semiconscious

Somnus
origin: **5** Roman
god of: **5** sleep
mother: **3** Nyx
brother: **4** Mors
corresponds to: **6** Hypnos, Hypnus

son
French: **4** fils

song **4** call, poem, tune **5** ditty, lyric, verse **6** ballad, melody, number, piping
French: **7** chanson

songbird **4** chat, lark, wren **5** robin, veery, vireo **6** canary, singer, thrush **7** warbler **11** nightingale

Song of Bernadette, The
author: **11** Franz Werfel
character: **13** Dean Peyramale **18** Sister Marie Therese **19** Bernadette Soubirous
director: **9** Henry King
cast: **8** Lee J Cobb **12** Vincent Price, William Eythe **13** Jennifer Jones **15** Charles Bickford
Oscar for: **7** actress (Jones)

Song of Hiawatha *see* **8** Hiawatha

Song of Roland, The *see* **15** Chanson de Roland

Song of Solomon
author: **12** Toni Morrison

Song of Solomon
bride: **9** Shulamite

Song of Songs, The
author: **16** Hermann Sudermann

Song of the Lark, The
author: **11** Willa Cather

Songs of Experience
author: **12** William Blake

Songs of Innocence
author: **12** William Blake

Sonnets from the Portuguese
author: **24** Elizabeth Barrett Browning

Sonnets to Orpheus
author: **16** Rainer Maria Rilke

Sonny
nickname of: **13** Charles Liston

Son of the Morning
author: **15** Joyce Carol Oates

sonorous **4** deep, rich **6** florid **7** ringing, vibrant **8** eloquent, resonant **9** full-toned, grandiose **10** flamboyant, impressive, resounding **13** reverberating

Sons and Lovers
author: **10** D H Lawrence
character: **10** Clara Dawes **11** Baxter Dawes **13** Miriam Leivers
Morel family: **4** Paul **5** Annie **6** Arthur, Walter **7** William **8** Gertrude

Sons of thunder **4** John **5** James
also: **9** Boanerges

soon **4** anon **6** pronto **7** betimes, by and by, early on, ere long, quickly, shortly **8** directly **9** any minute, forthwith, instantly, presently, right away **10** before long **12** without delay **14** in a little while

sooner 6 before, in time **7** earlier **9** before now, in advance **10** beforehand **11** ahead of time

sooner or later 6 one day **7** finally, someday **8** in the end, sometime **10** eventually, ultimately **17** in the course of time, sometime or another

Sooner State
nickname of: 8 Oklahoma

soot 4 dirt, smut **5** crock, grime **6** carbon, smudge, smutch **7** residue **9** lampblack

soothe 4 calm, ease **6** lessen, pacify **7** appease, comfort, console, mollify, placate, relieve **8** mitigate, moderate **9** alleviate **11** tranquilize

soothing 4 mild **7** calming, healing, salving **9** appeasing, consoling, emollient, pacifying, placating **10** comforting, mitigating **13** tranquilizing

soothsayer 4 seer **5** sibyl **7** diviner, prophet **10** forecaster **13** fortune-teller

soothsaying 6 augury **8** divining, prophecy **10** divination, predicting, prediction **11** foretelling, prophesying

sooty 4 inky **5** black, dingy, dirty, grimy **6** smudgy, smutty **9** coal-black

sop 3 dip, tip, wet **4** dunk, soak **5** bribe **6** absorb, drench, payoff, payola, take up **8** gratuity, saturate **9** baksheesh, become wet, hush money

Sophie's Choice
author: 13 William Styron

Sophisms
author: 9 Aristotle

sophisticate 8 civilize **11** cosmopolite, disillusion, make worldly **12** cosmopolitan

sophisticated 6 subtle **7** complex, studied, worldly **8** advanced, cultured, highbrow, mannered, precious, seasoned **9** difficult **10** artificial, cultivated **11** complicated, experienced, worldly-wise **12** cosmopolitan, intellectual

sophistry 6 deceit **7** fallacy **8** subtlety **9** casuistry, chicanery, deception **10** distortion **12** speciousness

Sophocles
author of: 4 Ajax **7** Electra, Oedipus **8** Antigone **10** Oedipus Rex, Trachiniae **11** Philoctetes **16** Oedipus at Colonus **18** The Trachinian Women

sophomoric 6 callow **7** foolish, puerile **8** childish, immature, juvenile **9** infantile **10** adolescent **12** schoolboyish

soporific 4 lazy **5** balmy, heavy **6** drowsy, sleepy **8** hypnotic, sedative, sluggish **9** lethargic, somnolent **10** slumberous **11** somniferous **12** sleep-inducer **13** sleep-inducing

soppiness 4 corn, mush **5** slush **6** bathos **7** wetness **9** mushiness **10** slushiness **11** mawkishness **14** sentimentalism, sentimentality

sopping 3 wet **5** soggy, soppy **6** soaked, sodden **8** drenched, dripping **9** saturated **10** bedraggled, soaking wet

sorcerer 5 witch **6** shaman, wizard **7** warlock **8** magician **11** medicine man

sorceress 5 siren, witch **11** enchantress

sorcery 8 witchery, wizardry **9** shamanism **10** black magic, necromancy, witchcraft **11** enchantment

Sordello
author: 14 Robert Browning

sordid 3 low **4** base, rank, vile **5** dirty, gross **6** filthy, putrid, rotten, vulgar, wicked **7** corrupt, ignoble, squalid, unclean **8** degraded, depraved **9** debauched **12** disreputable

Sordido
character in: 22 Every Man out of His Humour
author: 6 Jonson

sordino, con
music: 11 with the mute

sore 4 hurt **5** acute, angry, great, harsh, irked, sharp, upset, wound **6** aching, pained, severe, tender **7** bruised, extreme, grieved, hurting, painful **8** agonized, critical, grievous, smarting, sore spot, wounding **9** agonizing, desperate, indignant, irritated, sensitive **10** distressed, unbearable **11** distressing **12** inflammation

So Red the Rose
author: 10 Stark Young

Sorel, Julien
character in: 17 The Red and the Black
author: 8 Stendhal

sorely 5 badly **7** greatly **8** severely **9** extremely **10** critically **11** desperately

soreness 4 ache, pain **10** discomfort, irritation, tenderness

sorrel 3 bay **4** herb, roan, weed **5** brown, plant, Rumex **8** chestnut **12** reddish-brown
varieties: 3 red **4** dock, tree, wood **5** lady's, sheep **6** common, French, garden, Indian **7** redwood **8** Jamaican, mountain **10** violet wood **12** European wood

Sorrel, Hetty
character in: 8 Adam Bede
author: 5 Eliot

sorrow 3 woe **4** loss, weep **5** be sad, mourn, trial **6** grieve, lament **7** despair, sadness, travail, trouble **8** disaster, hardship **10** affliction, bad fortune, misfortune **11** catastrophe, unhappiness
French: 9 tristesse

sorrowful 3 sad **6** woeful **7** unhappy **8** affected, grieving, mournful **9** lamenting

Sorrows of Young Werther, The
author: 6 Goethe
character: 6 Albert **9** Charlotte (Lotte)

sorry 3 sad **6** woeful **7** grieved, pitiful, unhappy **8** contrite, pathetic, pitiable, wretched **9** miserable, regretful, repentant, sorrowful **10** deplorable, melancholy, remorseful, ridiculous **11** crestfallen **13** brokenhearted

sort 4 kind, list, make, sift, type **5** brand, class, grade, group, index, order **6** divide, person **7** arrange, catalog, species, variety **8** classify, organize, separate, take from **9** segregate **10** categorize, individual **11** systematize **14** classification

sortie 4 rush **5** onset **6** attack, charge **7** assault **8** storming **9** onslaught

sortilege 6 augury **7** auspice, sorcery **10** divination, witchcraft

sorting 8 dividing, grouping **9** arranging **10** organizing **11** classifying **12** categorizing

so-so 4 blah, fair **5** ho-hum **6** casual, modest **7** average, humdrum **8** adequate, bearable, mediocre, middling, ordinary, passable **9** tolerable **10** second-rate **11** commonplace, indifferent **12** run-of-the-mill **13** unexceptional **15** undistinguished

Sospita
epithet of: 4 Juno

sot 4 lush, soak **5** drunk, rummy, souse, toper **8** drunkard, rumhound **9** alcoholic, inebriate **11** dipsomaniac

Soter
epithet of: 4 Zeus
means: 6 savior

Sothern, Ann
real name: 13 Harriette Lake
born: 12 Valley City ND
husband: 10 Roger Pryor **14** Robert Sterling
roles: 6 Maisie **8** Cry Havoc **10** Lady Be Good **16** Private Secretary **19** A Letter to Three Wives

so throughout
Latin: 9 sic passim

sotto voce
music: 11 in a low voice **13** in an undertone, under the voice

sought 6 hunted **7** pursued, quested **9** attempted, looked for **10** endeavored

soul 5 being, force **6** person, spirit **7** essence **8** creature, vitality **9** inner core **10** embodiment, individual, vital force **11** inspiration **12** quintessence

soul-searching 10 discontent, insecurity, uneasiness **15** dissatisfaction, self-questioning

soul-stirring 7 rousing **8** electric, exciting, stirring **9** inspiring, thrilling **11** galvanizing

sound 3 fit **4** deep, firm, good, seem, tone, wise **5** drift, hardy, noise, range, sober, solid, tenor, utter, voice **6** intact, robust, severe, signal, stable, strong, sturdy **7** durable, earshot, healthy, lasting, perfect, solvent **8** announce, rational, reliable, sensible, thorough, unmarred **9** come off as, competent, enunciate, pronounce, undamaged, well-built **10** articulate, dependable, make a noise, reasonable, suggestion, untroubled **11** implication, penetrating, responsible, substantial **13** thoroughgoing **15** hearing distance, well-constructed

Sound and the Fury, The
author: 15 William Faulkner
character: 6 Dilsey **17** Sydney Herbert Head
***Compson family:* 5** Jason **7** Candace (Caddy), Quentin **8** Benjamin (Benjy)

Sounder
director: 10 Martin Ritt
cast: 8 Taj Mahal **10** Kevin Hooks **11** Cicely Tyson **12** Paul Winfield **13** Carmen Mathews
sequel: 13 Sounder Part II

sound measure 7 decibel

sound mind in a sound body
Latin: 21 mens sana in corpore sano

soundness of mind 6 reason, sanity **9** normality **12** mental health

Sound of Music, The
director: 10 Robert Wise
cast: 9 Peggy Wood **12** Julie Andrews (Maria Von Trapp) **13** Eleanor Parker **18** Christopher Plummer
setting: 7 Austria
score: 21 Rodgers and Hammerstein
Oscar for: 7 picture **8** director
song: 5 Maria **6** Do-Re-Mi **9** Edelweiss **16** My Favorite Things

sound out 3 ask **8** approach **15** make a proposal to, make overtures to, put out feelers to

soup
French: 6 potage

soupcon 3 bit, dab, jot, tad **4** clue, dash, drop, hint **5** pinch, shade, taint, taste, tinge, touch, trace, whiff **6** little, trifle **7** smidgen, smidgin, vestige **8** smidgeon **9** little bit, suspicion **10** smattering, sprinkling, suggestion **12** slight amount

Soupy Sales
character: 9 White Fang **10** Black Tooth **13** Herman the Flea, Hippy the Hippo, Pookie the Lion, Willie the Worm **14** Marilyn Monwolf

sour 3 bad **4** acid, dour, keen, tart, turn **5** nasty, sharp, spoil, surly, tangy, testy **6** crabby, cranky, curdle, rancid, sullen, turned **7** acerbic, bilious, crabbed, curdled, ferment, grouchy, peevish, spoiled, turn off, uncivil, waspish **8** alienate, choleric, embitter, jaundice, petulant, unsavory, vinegary **9** acidulous, clabbered, fermented, irritable, jaundiced, of-

South Africa
capital: 8 Cape Town, Pretoria **12** Bloemfontein
largest city: 12 Johannesburg
others: 3 Aus **4** Mara, Stad **6** Benoni, Bononi, Braker, Durban, Garies, Severn, Soweto, Umtata, Untata **7** Brakpan, Kokstad **8** Kaapstad, Mafeking, Modjadji **9** Germiston, Kimberley **10** East London, Oudtshoorn **11** Krugersdorp, Vereeniging **13** Port Elizabeth **16** Pietermaritzburg
school: 5 Natal **8** Capetown **13** Witwatersrand **15** Orange Free State
division: 5 Natal **8** Backveld **9** Transvaal **10** Basutoland **12** Cape Province **14** Cape of Good Hope **15** Orange Free State
***independent homelands:* 5** Venda **6** Ciskei **8** Transkei **14** Bophuthatswana
goverment:
***legislature:* 4** Raad
measure: 4 vara
monetary unit: 4 cent, pond, rand **5** pound **6** florin **7** daalder **9** krugerand
mountain: 3 Aux, Kop **5** Table **7** Kathkin **9** Stormberg **10** Devil's Peak, Sneeuwberg **11** Drakensberg **12** Giant's Castle **13** Witwatersrand **14** Mont-aux-Sources **15** Great Escarpment
highest point: 8 Injasuti
river: 3 Hex **4** Vaal **5** Nosob **6** Modder, Molopo, Orange, Tugela **7** Caledon, Kurumam, Limpopo **8** Olifants **9** Crocodile, Great Fish
sea: 6 Indian **8** Atlantic
physical feature:
***bay:* 5** Algoa, False, Table **6** Mossel, Walvis **7** Walfish **8** Richard's, Saldanha **11** Saint Helena
***cape:* 7** Agulhas **8** Good Hope
***current:* 8** Benguela
***desert:* 5** Namib **8** Kalahari
***plateau:* 6** Karroo
***region:* 8** Highveld, Zululand **9** Kaffraria **11** Great Karroo **12** Little Karroo

fensive, prejudice, repugnant **10** astringent, ill-dispose, ill-humored, unpleasant **11** bad-tempered, distasteful, ill-tempered **12** disagreeable

sourball **4** crab **5** crank, grump **6** grouch **9** hard candy **10** curmudgeon

source **4** font, head, root **5** basis, cause, fount **6** author, father, origin, rising, spring **8** begetter, fountain **9** authority, beginning, headwater **10** antecedent, derivation, foundation, prime mover, wellspring

source and origin
Latin: **11** fons et origo

Sourdough State
nickname of: **6** Alaska

sourness **7** acidity, vinegar **8** acerbity, acrimony, ill humor, pungency, tartness **9** acridness, greenness **10** bitterness

sourpuss **4** bear, crab **5** crank, grump **6** griper, grouch **7** grouser, killjoy **8** grumbler, sorehead **10** bellyacher, complainer, crosspatch, curmudgeon, spoilsport

Sousa, John Philip
born: **12** Washington DC
composer of: **9** El Capitan **14** Washington Post **25** The Stars and Stripes Forever

souse **3** dip, sot **4** duck, dunk, lush, soak **5** douse, drunk, rummy, steep, toper **6** barfly, boozer, drench, pickle **7** immerse, tippler **8** drunkard, inundate, marinate, saturate, submerge **9** alcoholic, inebriate **11** dipsomaniac

soused **5** drunk **6** dunked, potted, zapped, zonked **7** pickled, sloshed, smashed **8** immersed **9** plastered **10** inebriated **11** intoxicated **17** under the influence **20** three sheets to the wind

South Africa ***see box***

South America ***see box***

South Carolina ***see box, p. 912***

South Dakota ***see box, p. 913***

southeast wind
associated with: **5** Eurus **9** Volturnus

people: **3** San **4** Boer, Yosa, Zulu **5** Asian, Bantu, Namas, Nguni, Pondo, Sotho, Swazi, Tembu, Venda, Xhosa **6** Damara, Kaffir **7** African, British, Bushmen, English, Swahili **8** Bechuana, Coloured, Khoikhoi **9** Afrikaner, Hottentot
author: **5** Paton **7** Luthuli **8** Gordimer
civil rights advocate: **6** Gandhi
explorer: **8** Riebeeck
leader: **4** Biko **5** Botha, Malan, Smuts **6** Kruger, Rhodes **7** Hertzog, Vorster **8** Verwoerd **9** Pretorius **17** Bishop Desmond Tutu
language: **4** Taal, Zulu **5** Bantu, Hindi, Nguni, Sotho, Swazi, Tamil, Venda, Xhosa **6** Telegu, Thonga **7** English, Khoisan, Ndebele, Sesotho **8** Bujarati, Fanakalo **9** Afrikaans **13** Kitchen-Kaffir
religion: **5** Hindu, Islam **7** animism, Judaism **8** Anglican **9** Methodist **12** Episcopalian, Presbyterian **13** Dutch Reformed, Roman Catholic
place:
Cecil Rhodes' estate: **11** Groote Shuur
fort: **6** Castle
game reserve: **5** Mkuze **6** Kruger **8** Hluhluwe
hospital: **11** Groote Shuur
monument: **11** Voortrekker
museum: **8** Africana
feature:
bird: **4** taha
bride price: **6** lobolo
flower: **5** coral **6** clivia, protea **7** cowslip, fuchsia **9** phygelius **10** lachenalia
segregation: **9** apartheid
tree: **7** assagai **9** jacaranda
food:
corn: **6** mealie
drink: **9** sundowner
meat: **7** biltong **8** sosaties **9** boerewors

South America
bird: **5** macaw **7** seriema, tinamou **8** caracara
cape: **4** Horn
country: **4** Peru **5** Chile **6** Brazil, Guyana **7** Bolivia, Ecuador, Surinam, Uruguay **8** Colombia, Paraguay **9** Argentina, Venezuela **12** French Guiana
desert: **7** Atacama
explorer: **16** Francisco Pizarro **18** Pedro Alvares Cabral
hero: **12** Simon Bolivar **15** Jose de San Martin **16** Bernardo O'Higgins **18** Antonio Jose de Sucre
highest mountain: **9** Aconcagua
islands: **8** Falkland **9** Galapagos
lake: **8** Titicaca **9** Maracaibo
mountain range: **5** Andes
native: **2** Ge **3** Ona **4** Inca **5** Carib, Mayan **7** Quechua **10** Araucanian
plain: **5** llano, pampa
region: **9** Patagonia
river: **3** Apa **5** Plata **6** Amazon **7** Orinoco

Southern Comfort
type: **7** liqueur
origin: **10** New Orleans
flavor: **5** peach
base: **7** bourbon
drink: **13** Scarlett O'Hara **15** Plantation Punch
with bourbon: **14** Blended Comfort

Southern Cross
constellation of: **4** Crux

Southern Crown
constellation of: **15** Corona Australis

Southerner, The
director: **10** Jean Renoir
cast: **10** Betty Field **11** Beulah Bondi **12** Zachary Scott **13** Bunny Sunshine

Southern Fish
constellation of: **15** Piscis Austrinus

Southern Fly
constellation of: **5** Musca

Southern Rhodesia *see* **8** Zimbabwe

Southern Slavic
language family: **12** Indo-European

South Carolina
abbreviation: **2** SC
nickname: **7** Calinky **8** Palmetto
capital/largest city: **8** Columbia
others: **5** Aiken, Greer, Union **6** Belton, Camden, Cheraw, Conway, Dillon, Seneca, Sumter **7** Bamberg, Laurens, Manning **8** Beaufort, Florence, Newberry, Rock Hill, Walhalla **9** Greenwood **10** Charleston, Greenville, Orangeburg **11** Spartanburg
college: **5** Allen, Coker **6** Furman, Lander **7** Claffin, Clemson, Erskine, Wofford **8** Benedict, Bob Jones, Columbia, Winthrop **13** Francis Marion **15** Citadel Military
explorer: **6** Ayllon, Ribaut
feature:
beach: **6** Myrtle
dam: **6** Saluda
fort: **6** Sumter
gardens: **7** Cypress
tribe: **5** Pedee, Sewee **6** Cusabo, Santee, Waxhaw, Yamasi **7** Catawba, Shawnee, Sugeree, Wateree **8** Congaree
people: **11** James Byrnes **12** Althea Gibson, John C Calhoun **13** Bernard Baruch, Francis Marion **14** Dizzy Gillespie
island: **3** Sea **6** Parris **10** Hilton Head
lake: **6** Marion, Murray **7** Catawba, Wateree **8** Hartwell, Moultrie **9** Clark Hill
land rank: **8** fortieth
mountain: **5** Kings **6** Little **9** Blue Ridge, Sassafras
physical feature:
bay: **8** Carolina
plateau: **8** Piedmont
president: **13** Andrew Jackson
river: **5** Broad **6** Edisto, Pee Dee, Saluda, Santee **7** Ashepoo **8** Savannah
state admission: **6** eighth
state bird: **12** Carolina wren
state flower: **13** yellow jasmine **17** Carolina jessamine
state motto: **18** While I Breathe I Hope **26** Prepared in Mind and Resources
state song: **8** Carolina
state tree: **8** palmetto

group: **11** Balto-Slavic
branch: **6** Slavic
language: **7** Slovene **9** Bulgarian **10** Macedonian **13** Serbo-Croatian

Southern Triangle
constellation of: **18** Triangulum Australe

South Korea *see* **5** Korea

South Vietnam *see* **7** Vietnam

South West Africa *see* **7** Namibia

south wind
associated with: **5** Notus

South Wind
author: **13** Norman Douglas

South Yemen *see* **5** Yemen

souvenir **4** scar **5** relic, token **6** emblem, memory, trophy **7** memento **8** keepsake, reminder **11** remembrance

sovereign **4** czar, free, king, lord, main, tsar **5** chief, major, prime, queen, regal, royal **6** kingly, potent, prince, ruling, utmost **7** emperor, highest, leading, monarch, queenly, supreme **8** absolute, autocrat, dominant, foremost, imperial, overlord, powerful, princely, reigning **9** chieftain, governing, paramount, potentate, prepotent, principal, uppermost **10** autonomous, self-ruling **11** all-powerful, crowned head, independent, monarchical **12** supreme ruler **13** self-directing, self-governing

sovereignty **4** sway **5** crown, power **6** throne **7** command, control, freedom, primacy, scepter **8** autonomy, dominion, home rule, kingship, lordship, self-rule **9** authority, supremacy **10** ascendancy **11** paramountcy **12** independence, jurisdiction, predominance **14** self-government **17** self-determination

Soviet Union *see* **6** Russia

sow **4** cast, seed **5** lodge, plant, set in, strew **6** inject, spread **7** implant, instill, scatter **8** disperse, sprinkle **9** broadcast, establish, introduce **11** disseminate

space **3** gap, sky **4** area, part, rank, room, seat, span, spot, term, time **5** berth, blank, break, chasm, ether, field, order, place, range, reach, scope, sweep, swing, width **6** hiatus, lacuna, line up, margin, period, set out, spread **7** arrange, breadth, compass, expanse, mark out, the void **8** distance, duration, infinity, interval, latitude, omission, organize, schedule, separate **9** amplitude, emptiness, keep apart, territory **10** distribute, interspace, interstice, outer space, separation, the heavens **11** nothingness, reservation, the universe **12** interruption, the firmament **13** accommodation

Space
author: **13** James Michener

spacecraft **4** ship **6** rocket **7** orbiter, shuttle **9** satellite **10** rocketship

space flight
US mission: **6** Apollo, Gemini, Skylab **7** Mercury
US rocket: **5** Atlas, Titan **6** Saturn **8** Redstone
US space shuttle: **8** Columbia **9** Discovery **10** Challenger
Soviet mission: **5** Soyuz **6** Salyut, Vostok **7** Voskhod
Soviet astronaut:
first man in space: **11** Yuri Gagarin
first woman in space: **19** Valentina Tereshkova
first space walk by: **13** Aleksei Leonov
American astronaut: **9** John Glenn, John Young **11** Alan Shepard, Edward White, Edwin Aldrin, Frank Borman, James Lovell **12** Roger Chaffee, Wally (Walter) Schirra **13** Charles Conrad, L Gordon Cooper, Virgil Grissom **14** Scott Carpenter, Thomas Stafford
first man on moon: **13** Neil Armstrong
Challenger seven: **12** Michael Smith, Ronald McNair **13** Francis Scobee, Gregory Jarvis, Judith Resnick **14** Ellison Onizuka **16** Christa McAuliffe

Spacek, Sissy
real name: **19** Mary Elizabeth Spacek
born: **9** Quitman TX

South Dakota
abbreviation: **2** SD **4** S Dak
nickname: **6** Coyote **8** Blizzard, Sunshine
capital: **6** Pierre
largest city: **10** Sioux Falls
others: **4** Lead, Leap **5** Huron **6** Custer, Eureka, Lemmon, Miller, Winner **7** Sturgis, Webster, Yankton **8** Aberdeen, Deadwood, Sisseton **9** Brookings, Rapid City **10** Vermillion
college: **5** Huron **7** Yankton **9** Augustana **10** Mount Marty, Sioux Falls **14** Dakota Wesleyan
explorer: **8** Varennes **13** Lewis and Clark
feature: **8** Deadwood
battlefield: **11** Wounded Knee
dam: **4** Oahe
mine: **9** Homestake
monument: **13** Mount Rushmore
national park: **8** Badlands, Wind Cave
tribe: **5** Brule, Sioux **6** Dakota, Sutaio **8** Cheyenne
people: **10** Crazy Horse **11** Sitting Bull **14** George McGovern, Hubert Humphrey
lake: **4** Oahe **5** Sharp **8** Big Stone, Traverse **11** Francis Case **13** Lewis and Clark
land rank: **9** sixteenth
mountain: **4** Bear **5** Sheep, Table **6** Crook's, Moreau
highest point: **6** Harney
hills: **5** Black **7** Prairie
physical feature:
butte: **7** Thunder **9** Deer's Ears **10** Castle Rock
cave: **5** Jewel
river: **3** Bad **5** Grand, James, White **6** Moreau **8** Big Sioux, Cheyenne, Missouri **10** Vermillion
state admission: **8** fortieth **11** thirty-ninth (with North Dakota)
state bird: **18** ring-necked pheasant
state flower: **12** pasqueflower
state animal: **6** coyote
state motto: **21** Under God the People Rule
state song: **15** Hail South Dakota
state tree: **11** white spruce **16** Black Hills spruce

roles: **6** Carrie **7** Missing **8** Badlands, The River **10** Raggedy Man **16** Crimes of the Heart **18** Coal Miner's Daughter (Oscar)

spacious **4** vast, wide **5** ample, broad, large, roomy **7** immense, sizable **8** enormous **9** capacious, expansive, extensive, uncrowded **10** commodious

spaciousness **9** amplitude, largeness, roominess **13** capaciousness **14** commodiousness

Spade, Sam
character in: **16** The Maltese Falcon
author: **7** Hammett

Spain ***see box, p. 914***

span **4** arch, area, last, term, wing **5** cover, cross, range, reach, scope, spell, sweep, vault **6** bridge, endure, extent, length, period **7** archway, breadth, measure, stretch, survive, trestle **8** distance, duration, interval **9** extension, reach over, territory **10** bridge over, dimensions **11** proportions, reach across, stretch over **12** extend across

spangle **4** star **5** bedew **6** sequin **7** glisten, glitter, shimmer, twinkle **9** bugle bead, coruscate, paillette

spaniel
dog breed: **5** field **6** cocker, Sussex **7** clumber, Tibetan **10** Irish water **13** American water, English cocker, Welsh springer **15** English springer

Spanish (language, person) **7** espanol

Spanish Guinea *see* **16** Equatorial Guinea

Spanish Sahara *see* **13** Western Sahara

Spanish Tragedy, The
author: **9** Thomas Kyd
character: **7** Horatio, Lorenzo, Villupo **9** Alexandro, Balthazar, Hieronimo **10** Bel-Imperia **16** Ghost of Don Andrea

spank **3** hit, tan **4** beat, belt, blow, cane, flog, hide, lick, slap, whip, whop **5** birch, strap, whale **6** paddle, strike, switch, thrash, wallop **8** paddling **10** flagellate

spanking **4** very **5** brisk, fresh **7** beating **8** paddling, whipping **9** extremely, thrashing **10** punishment **12** chastisement

spanking new **5** fresh **6** unused **8** brand new **9** untouched

spar **4** boom, mast, pole **5** argue, fight, sprit **6** bicker **7** dispute, quarrel, wrangle **8** crossbar **10** crosspiece

spare **3** odd **4** bony, cede, free, give, keep, lank, lean, save, thin **5** amass, extra, forgo, gaunt, grant, guard, hoard, lanky, lay up, limit, pinch, rangy, scant, stint, weedy **6** acquit, afford, defend, donate, excess, exempt, forego, let off, meager, not use, pardon, scanty, shield, skimpy, skinny, slight, unused **7** forgive, haggard, husband, let go of, protect, release, relieve, reserve, scraggy, scrawny, shelter, skimp on, slender, surplus **8** conserve, hold back, leftover, liberate, part with, reprieve, set aside, skeletal, withhold **9** auxiliary, emaciated, exonerate, fleshless, safeguard, show mercy **10** additional, extraneous, relinquish, substitute, unconsumed **11** economize on, have mercy on, superfluous, unnecessary, use frugally **12** be merciful to, dispense with, supplemental **13** supernumerary, supplementary

spared **5** freed **6** exempt, immune **7** excused **8** absolved, excepted, relieved

sparing **4** near **5** close, scant **6** frugal, meager, saving, scanty, stingy **7** careful, miserly, thrifty **8** grudging, stinting **9** niggardly, penurious **10** economical, ungenerous **11** closefisted, tightfisted **12** parsimonious

spark **3** bit, jot **4** atom, beam, fire, iota, life **5** brand, ember, flash, gleam, pique, trace **6** arouse, excite, incite, spirit **7** flicker, glimmer, glitter, inspire, provoke, sparkle **8** vitality **9** animation, instigate, stimulate **10** get-up-and-go

Spain
other name: **6** Iberia **8** Hispania
capital/largest city: **6** Madrid
others: **4** Adra, Aspe, Baza, Elda, Horo, Irun, Jaen, Leon, Noya, Olot, Reus, Rota, Sama, Vigo **5** Baena, Bejar, Cadiz, Cieza, Cueta, Ecija, Eibar, Elche, Gades, Gadir, Gijon, Ibiza, Jerez, Jodar, Liego, Lorca, Oliva, Palma, Palos, Ronda, Siero, Ubeda, Xeres, Yecla, Zafra **6** Abdera, Aviles, Azuaga, Bilbao, Burgos, Coruna, Duenca, Gandia, Gerona, Getafe, Guadix, Hellin, Huelva, Huesca, Jativa, Lerida, Lucena, Malaga, Mataro, Merida, Murcia, Orense, Oviedo, Termel, Toledo, Utrera, Zamora **7** Almeria, Badajos, Cordoba, Daimiel, Granada, Jumilla, Linares, Logrono, Manresa, Segovia, Sevilla, Seville, Tarrasa, Vitoria **8** Alicante, Badalona, Figueras, Pamplona, Sabadell, Santiago, Torrente, Valencia, Zaragoza **9** Barcelona, Las Palmas, Saragossa
school: **6** Ciudad, Madrid
division: **4** Jaen, Leon, Lugo **5** Alava, Avila, Cadiz, Soria **6** Basque, Burgos, Coruna, Cuenca, Gerona, Huelva, Huesca, Lerida, Madrid, Malaga, Murcia, Orense, Oviedo, Teruel, Toledo, Zamora **7** Almeria, Caceres, Cordoba, Granada, Logrono, Navarra, Segovia, Sevilla, Vizcaya, Zadajoz **8** Albacete, Alicante, Baleares, Palencia, Valencia, Zaragoza **9** Catalonia
kingdom: **4** Leon **6** Aragon **7** Castile, Galicia, Granada, Navarre **8** Asturias **9** al-Andalus, Catalonia **12** Spanish March
government: **8** monarchy
legislature: **6** Cortes
head of state: **4** king
measure: **3** pie **4** codo, dedo, paso, vara **5** braza, cahiz, carga, legua, medio, palmo, sesma **6** cordel, cuarta, fanega, racion, yugada **7** azumbre, celemin, estadel, pulgada **8** fanegada
monetary unit: **3** cob **4** duro, peso **5** dobla **6** cuarto, dinero, escudo **7** alfonso, centimo, pistole **8** doubloon
weight: **4** onza **5** frail, libra, marco, tomin **6** arroba, dinero, dracma **7** arienzo, quilate, quintal **8** tonelada
island: **5** Ceuta, Ibiza, Iviza, Palma **6** Canary, Gomera, Hierro **7** Alboran, Majorca, Melilla, Minorca **8** Balearic, Mallorca, Tagomago, Tenerife **9** Lanzarote **13** Fuerteventura
lake: **4** lago **8** Albufera
mountain: **4** Gata **5** Aneto, Rouch **6** Cuenca, Estats, Europa, Gredos, Magina, Morena, Nethou, Nevada, Teleno, Toledo **7** Alcaraz, Banuelo, Catalan, Cerredo, Demanda, Iberian, La Sagra, Moncayo, Perdido **8** Almanzor, Asturias, Galician, Maladeta, Monegros, Montseny, Penalara, Pyrenees **10** Albarracin, Cantabrian, Guadarrama, Torrecilla
highest point: **5** Teide **8** Mulhacen
river: **3** Sil, Ter **4** Cega, Ebro, Esla, Lima, Mino, Muga, Tajo, Ulla **5** Adaja, Cinca, Douro, Duero, Genil, Jalon, Jucar, Navia, Odiel, Riaza, Segie, Tagus, Tinto, Turia **6** Alagon, Aragon, Eresma, Huerva, Jarama, Orbigo, Segura, Torote **7** Almeria, Almonte, Arlanza, Barbate, Cabriel, Gallego, Henares, Mijares, Perales **8** Duration, Guadiana **12** Guadalquivir
sea: **8** Atlantic, Balearic **13** Mediterranean
physical feature:
bay: **5** Bahia **6** Biscay
cape: **9** Trafalgar
gulf: **5** Cadiz **8** San Jorge, Valencia
peninsula: **7** Iberian
plateau: **6** meseta
strait: **9** Gibraltar
people: **5** Diego, Gente, Latin **6** Basque, Espana **7** Catalan, Espanol, Iberian **8** Galician, Gallegos, Maragato
architect: **5** Gaudi
artist: **4** Dali, Goya, Gris, Miro **6** Ribera **7** El Greco, Murillo, Picasso **8** Zurbaran **9** Velazquez

Spark, Muriel
author of: **11** Memento Mori **14** The Driver's Seat, The Only Problem **17** The Mandelbaum Gate, Territorial Rights **19** Loitering with Intent **21** A Far Cry from Kensington **24** The Prime of Miss Jean Brodie

sparkle **3** pep, pop, vim **4** dash, elan, fizz, foam, glow, life **5** be gay, brand, cheer, ember, flash, froth, gleam, glint, light, shine, verve **6** bubble, dazzle, fizzle, gaiety, spirit **7** be witty, flicker, glimmer, glisten, glitter, jollity, rejoice, shimmer, twinkle **8** radiance, vitality, vivacity **9** alertness, animation, briskness, coruscate, quickness **10** be cheerful, brilliance, ebullience, effervesce, effulgence, exuberance, liveliness, luminosity **11** be vivacious, scintillate **12** cheerfulness, exhilaration, luminousness **13** effervescence, scintillation

sparkling **5** fizzy **6** bubbly **7** fizzing, twinkly **8** bubbling, dazzling, glittery **9** twinkling **10** glistening, glittering **11** coruscating **12** effervescent **13** scintillating

Sparky Lyle
nickname of: **16** Albert Walter Lyle

sparse **3** few **4** thin **5** scant, spare **6** meager, scanty, scarce, skimpy, spotty, strewn **7** diffuse **8** exiguous, sporadic **9** dispersed, scattered, spaced-out, uncrowded **10** infrequent **16** few and far between

author: **4** Cela, Vega **5** Barea, Cueva, Rojas **6** Aleman, Alonso, Azorin, Baroja, Castro, Encina, Felipe, Ibanez, Miguel **7** Alarcon, Becquer, Cernuda, Ercilla, Gongora, Guillen, Jimenez, Machado, Unamuno **8** Montalvo, Zorrilla **9** Benavente, Cervantes, Goytisola **10** Aleixandre, Espronceda, Lope de Vega, Pardo Bazan **11** Garcia Lorca **12** Lopez de Ayala **13** Tirso de Molina **17** Calderon de la Barca
composer: **7** Albeniz **8** Granados, Victoria **13** Manuel de Falla
converted Moslem: **7** morisco
dynasty: **7** Almohad, Umayyad **9** Almoravid
explorer: **6** Balboa, Cortes **7** Pizarro **8** Columbus
Jesuit founder: **14** Ignatius Loyola
king: **6** Pelayo, Philip, Ramiro, Sancho, Witiza **7** Alfonso, Charles **8** al-Mansur, Reccared, Roderick **9** Ferdinand, Leovigild **10** Juan Carlos **11** Abd al-Rahman, Reccosvinth
leader: **4** Prim **5** Godoy **6** Franco **7** Canovas **11** Calvo Sotelo **13** Primo de Rivera **14** Suarez-Gonzalez
queen: **8** Isabella **16** Elizabeth Farnese
ruler: **4** Rome **5** Celts, Moors **6** Greece **7** Almeria, Vandals **8** Carthage **9** Phoenicia, Visigoths
scholar: **8** Averroes
warrior: **14** El Cid Campeador
language: **6** Basque **7** Catalan, Spanish **8** Balearic, Galician **9** Castilian, Valencian
religion: **7** Judaism **10** Protestant **13** Roman Catholic
place:
aqueduct: **7** Segovia
bridge: **7** Cordoba
castle: **7** Alcazar **12** Santa Barbara
cathedral bell tower: **7** Giralda
center of Madrid: **12** Puerto del Sol
church/cathedral: **4** Leon **6** Burgos, Gerona, Toledo **7** Seville **9** Barcelona, San Isidro **10** Santa Maria **14** Sagrada Familia
fountain: **6** Cibele
library: **8** Columbus
minaret: **7** Seville
mosque: **11** Great Mosque **19** Santo Cristo de la Cruz
museum: **5** Prado **15** Museo de Pinturas
palace: **7** Granada, Naranco **8** Alhambra, Escorial **9** Real Mayor
park: **6** Retiro
resort: **8** Marbella **10** Costa Brava **12** Torremolinos
shrine: **32** Saint James at Santiago de Compostela
street: **7** Ramblas **13** Paseo del Prado **16** Plaza de la Cibeles **19** Paseo de la Castellana
synagogue: **10** El Transito
theater: **6** Merida
wall paintings/caves: **8** Altamira
possession: **5** Ceuta **6** Melill
feature:
bar: **6** tascas
dance: **5** tango **8** fandango, flamenco
estate: **10** latifundia
matador's suit: **12** traje de luces
political party: **7** Falange
food:
dish: **6** cocido, paella **8** zarzuela
soup: **8** gazpacho

sparseness **7** paucity **8** sparsity, thinness **10** meagerness, scantiness

Sparsit, Mrs
character in: **9** Hard Times
author: **7** Dickens

Spartacus
director: **14** Stanley Kubrick
cast: **8** Nina Foch **9** John Gavin **10** Tony Curtis **11** Jean Simmons, Kirk Douglas **12** Peter Ustinov **15** Charles Laughton, Laurence Olivier
setting: **4** Rome
score: **9** Alex North

spartan **4** hard **5** plain, stark, stern, stiff **6** frugal, severe, simple, strict **7** ascetic, austere **8** exacting, rigorous **9** stringent **10** abstemious, inexorable, inflexible, restrained, restricted **11** disciplined, self-denying **15** self-disciplined

Sparti
occupation: **8** warriors

spasm **3** fit, tic **4** grip, jerk, pang **5** burst, cramp, crick, flash, onset, spell, spurt, start, storm, throe **6** access, attack, frenzy, twitch **7** seizure, shudder, tempest **8** eruption, paroxysm **9** explosion **10** convulsion

spasmodic **6** fitful **7** erratic, flighty **8** fleeting, periodic, sporadic **9** desultory, irregular, mercurial, transient **10** capricious, inconstant, occasional **12** intermittent **13** discontinuous

spat **4** tiff **5** argue, fight, scrap,

set-to **6** bicker, differ **7** contend, dispute, dissent, quarrel, wrangle **8** disagree, squabble **10** difference **11** altercation **12** disagreement **16** misunderstanding

spatter 4 slop, soil, spot **5** fleck, plash, spray, spurt, stain, swash **6** mottle, shower, splash **7** speckle, stipple **8** splatter, sprinkle

spawn 4 eggs, seed, teem **5** beget, breed, brood, fruit, yield **7** lay eggs, produce, product **8** engender, generate, multiply **9** offspring, propagate, reproduce **10** bring forth, give rise to **11** deposit eggs, give birth to, proliferate

speak 3 air, say **4** call, chat, deal, talk, tell **5** imply, orate, refer, shout, sound, state, treat, voice **6** advise, confer, convey, cry out, dilate, impart, mumble, murmur, mutter, preach, recite, relate, remark, report, reveal **7** bespeak, comment, consult, declaim, declare, discuss, divulge, expound, express, lecture, mention, suggest, whisper **8** announce, converse, disclose, harangue, indicate, proclaim, vocalize **9** discourse, enunciate, expatiate, hold forth, make known, pronounce, sermonize **10** articulate **11** communicate, give a speech

speakeasy 3 bar **6** saloon, tavern **7** gin mill **14** cocktail lounge

speaker 5 voice **6** orator, reader, talker **7** reciter **8** advocate, lecturer, preacher **9** declaimer, spokesman **10** discourser, monologist, mouthpiece, sermonizer **11** rhetorician, speechmaker, spokeswoman **13** valedictorian

speak highly of 4 laud **5** exalt, extol **6** praise **7** commend **8** eulogize **10** compliment **16** sing the praises of

speak ill of 4 slur **5** curse, knock, libel **6** defame, insult, malign, vilify **7** slander **8** badmouth **9** criticize, denigrate, discredit, disparage **13** find fault with **14** inveigh against

speak loudly 3 cry **4** bawl, call, hail, roar, yell **5** shout **6** bellow, clamor, cry out, halloo, holler **7** call out, speak up

speak of 7 mention, refer to **8** allude to **9** talk about, touch upon

speak to 6 talk to **7** address, lecture

speak together 3 gab, jaw, rap **4** chat, chin, talk **6** confer **7** chatter, palaver **8** chitchat, converse **10** chew the fat, chew the rag **11** communicate, confabulate

speak well of 4 laud **5** boost, extol **6** praise **7** acclaim, approve, commend, flatter, root for **8** eulogize **9** sweet talk **10** compliment, stick up for **13** speak highly of **16** sing the praises of **17** put in a good word for

spear 4 bolt, dart, gaff, gore, pike, spit, stab **5** lance, prick, shaft, spike, stick **6** impale, pierce **7** harpoon, javelin **8** puncture, transfix **9** penetrate **10** run through

spearhead 4 iron, lead **5** begin, found, start **6** launch, leader **7** creator, develop, founder, pioneer **8** begetter, conceive, initiate **9** establish, initiator, institute, originate, spokesman **10** inaugurate, instituter, prime mover **11** establisher, inaugurator, spokeswoman **12** avant-gardist

special 4 fast, good, rare **5** close, great, novel **6** ardent, proper, select, signal, unique **7** bargain, certain, devoted, endemic, feature, staunch, typical, unusual **8** distinct, especial, intimate, peculiar, personal, sale item, singular, specific, uncommon **9** headliner, high point, highlight, important, momentous, specialty, steadfast **10** attraction, individual, noteworthy, particular, remarkable **11** distinctive, exceptional, outstanding, specialized **12** extravaganza **13** distinguished, extraordinary **14** representative, unconventional **16** out of the ordinary **17** piece de resistance

specialist 4 buff **5** adept, maven **6** expert, master **9** authority **10** past master **11** connoisseur

specialization 5 focus, forte, major **6** metier **8** province **10** speciality **13** concentration

specialize 5 adapt, focus, major **6** pursue **10** narrow down **11** concentrate

specialty 4 bent, mark, turn **5** badge, focus, forte, hobby, major, stamp **6** genius, talent **7** earmark, faculty, feature, pursuit, special **8** aptitude **9** endowment, trademark **10** competence, profession **11** claim to fame, distinction

species 4 form, kind, make, sort, type **5** breed, class, genre, group, order **6** kidney, nature, stripe **7** variety **8** category, division **11** designation, subdivision **14** classification

specific 5 exact, fixed **6** minute, stated, unique **7** bounded, certain, endemic, limited, pointed, precise, special, typical **8** clear-cut, concrete, confined, definite, detailed, especial, peculiar, personal, relevant, singular, tied-down **9** intrinsic, pertinent, specified **10** individual, particular, pinned-down, restricted **11** categorical, determinate, distinctive, unequivocal **13** circumscribed **14** characteristic

specification 6 detail **7** clarity **9** condition, precision, substance **11** enumeration, itemization, requirement, stipulation **12** concreteness **13** particularity, qualification **17** particularization

specifics 4 cure, fact, item **5** datum **6** detail, physic **10** medication, particular **12** circumstance

specify 4 cite, name **5** order **6** adduce, define, denote, detail **7** call for, focus on, itemize **8** describe, indicate, set forth **9** designate, enumerate, stipulate **13** particularize

specimen 4 case, type **5** model **6** sample **7** example **8** exemplar, instance **9** prototype **14** representative **15** exemplification

specious 5 false **6** faulty, tricky, untrue **7** dubious, invalid, unsound **8** slippery, spurious **9** casuistic, deceptive, illogical, incorrect, unfounded **10** fallacious, inaccurate, misleading **11** sophistical **12** questionable **15** unsubstantiated

speck 3 bit, dot, jot, pin **4** drop, hair, iota, mark, mite, mote, spot, whit **5** fleck, grain, pinch, trace **6** shadow, trifle **7** glimmer, modicum, speckle **8** farthing, flyspeck, particle **9** scintilla

speckled 4 pied **6** dotted **7** flecked, spotted, studded **8** freckled, peppered **9** sprinkled

spectacle 5 scene, sight **6** marvel, parade, rarity, wonder **7** display, exhibit, pageant **9** curiosity, rare sight **10** exhibition, exposition, phenomenon, production **12** extravaganza, presentation **13** demonstration

spectacles **6** lenses, shades **7** glasses **8** bifocals, pince-nez **10** eyeglasses

spectacular **4** gala, rich **5** grand, showy **6** daring **7** jeweled, opulent, stately **8** dramatic, fabulous, glorious, gorgeous, splendid, striking **9** daredevil, elaborate, marvelous, spectacle, sumptuous, thrilling **10** astounding, bespangled, eye-filling, impressive, theatrical **11** ceremonious, hair-raising, magnificent, sensational **12** extravaganza, overwhelming **16** ostentatious show **19** elaborate production

spectator **3** fan **5** house **6** viewer **7** gallery, witness **8** audience, beholder, kibitzer, observer, onlooker **9** bystander, sightseer **10** aficionado, eyewitness **11** afficionado, theatergoer **12** rubbernecker

Spectator, The
author: **13** Joseph Addison, Richard Steele

specter **5** demon, ghost, ghoul, shade, spook **6** spirit, sprite, vision, wraith **7** banshee, fantasy, phantom **8** phantasm, presence, revenant **9** hobgoblin **10** apparition

spectral **4** airy **5** eerie, weird **6** creepy, spooky, unreal **7** ghastly, ghostly, phantom, shadowy, uncanny **8** ethereal, gossamer, vaporous **9** unearthly **10** chimerical, phantasmal, wraithlike **11** incorporeal **12** otherworldly, supernatural **13** insubstantial

speculate **4** muse **5** brood, dream, fancy, guess, study, think, wager **6** chance, gamble, hazard, ponder, reason, wonder **7** imagine, reflect, suppose, surmise, venture **8** cogitate, consider, meditate, ruminate, theorize **10** conjecture, deliberate, excogitate, play a hunch **11** contemplate, hypothesize, take a chance **13** play the market

speculation **4** risk **7** venture **8** gambling **9** guesswork **10** conjecture, estimation **11** supposition

speculative **4** iffy **5** dicey, risky **6** chancy **8** academic **11** conjectural, theoretical **12** experimental, hypothetical **13** suppositional

speculator **7** gambler, plunger **8** investor, operator, theorist **10** adventurer, arbitrager **11** arbitrageur

speech **4** talk **5** idiom, lingo, slang, voice **6** appeal, gossip, homily, jargon, sermon, tirade, tongue **7** address, chatter, comment, dialect, diction, lecture, oration, palaver, prattle, remarks, talking **8** chitchat, colloquy, converse, dialogue, diatribe, harangue, language, parlance, rhetoric, speaking **9** discourse, elocution, monologue, soliloquy, statement, utterance **10** discussion, expression, recitation, salutation **11** declamation, declaration, enunciation, exhortation, observation, valedictory **12** articulation, conversation, dissertation, vocalization **13** colloquialism, confabulation, pronouncement, pronunciation, verbalization

speechless **3** mum **4** dumb, mute **6** silent **7** aphonic **8** wordless **9** stupefied **10** tongue-tied

speed **3** aid, hie, run, zip **4** dart, dash, help, race, rate, rush, tear, zoom **5** boost, favor, gun it, haste, hurry, impel, speed, tempo **6** assist, barrel, gallop, hasten, hurtle, hustle, pick up, plunge, propel, scurry, step up **7** advance, further, hurry up, promote, quicken, tear off **8** alacrity, celerity, dispatch, expedite, hightail, make time, momentum, rapidity, step on it, velocity **9** bowl along, briskness, fleetness, give a lift, hastiness, make haste, move along, quickness, rapidness, swiftness **10** accelerate, expedition, get a move on, go hell-bent, lose no time, promptness, spurt ahead **11** push forward **12** acceleration **13** burn up the road

speedily **4** fast **5** apace, quick **6** pronto **7** hastily, rapidly, swiftly **8** in no time, promptly **9** post haste, right away, summarily **11** on the double **12** lickety-split

speed up **4** rush **5** hurry **6** hasten, step up **7** hop to it, quicken **8** expedite, multiply, step on it **9** encourage, intensify **10** accelerate, facilitate, get a move on **12** step on the gas

speedy **4** fast **5** brisk, early, fleet, hasty, quick, rapid, ready, swift **6** abrupt, lively, sudden **7** express, hurried, running, summary **8** headlong **9** quick-fire, rapid-fire **10** not delayed **11** precipitate

Spelaites
epithet of: **6** Hermes
means: **9** of the cave

spell **2** go **3** bit, hex **4** bout, free, lull, mean, omen, snap, term, time, tour, turn, wave **5** augur, break, charm, hitch, imply, magic, pause, round, stint, trick, while **6** allure, course, denote, herald, hoodoo, make up, period, recess, tenure, typify, voodoo **7** bespeak, betoken, connote, glamour, portend, presage, promise, purport, rapture, release, relieve, respite, signify, sorcery, stretch, suggest **8** amount to, cover for, duration, forebode, forecast, foretell, indicate, interval, stand for, witchery **9** form a word, influence, interlude, represent, symbolize **10** assignment, invocation, mumbo jumbo, open-sesame **11** abracadabra, bewitchment, enchantment, fascination, incantation, pinch-hit for, take over for **12** magic formula

spellbind **5** charm **7** bewitch, enchant **8** enthrall, entrance, intrigue, transfix **9** enrapture, fascinate, hypnotize, mesmerize, transport

spellbound **4** rapt **5** agape **7** charmed **8** wordless **9** awestruck, bewitched, enchanted, entranced, possessed **10** breathless, dumbstruck, enraptured, enthralled, fascinated, hypnotized, mesmerized, speechless, tongue-tied, transfixed **11** openmouthed, transported

Spellbound
director: **15** Alfred Hitchcock
cast: **9** John Emery **11** Gregory Peck, Leo G Carroll **13** Ingrid Bergman **14** Michael Chekhov
score: **11** Miklos Rosza
Oscar for: **5** score
dream sequences by: **12** Salvador Dali

spell out **6** define, detail **7** clarify, clear up, explain, expound, specify **8** describe **9** delineate, designate, elucidate, explicate, interpret, make plain **10** illustrate

Spemann, Hans
field: **7** zoology
nationality: **6** German
worked in: **20** embryonic development
awarded: **10** Nobel Prize

Spencer, Sir Stanley
born: **7** Cookham, England **9** Berkshire
artwork: **22** Resurrection of Soldiers, The Resurrection Cookham **31** Christ Preaching at Cookham Regatta **43** Double Nude Portrait—

the Artist and his Second Wife

spend **3** pay, use **4** dole, fill, give, pass **5** drain, empty, use up, waste **6** devote, employ, expend, invest, occupy, outlay, pay out, take up **7** burn out, consume, deplete, destroy, exhaust, fork out, scatter, wear out **8** allocate, disburse, dispense, shell out, squander **9** dissipate, while away **10** impoverish

spendable **9** available **10** expendable **13** discretionary

spend foolishly **5** waste **8** misspend, squander **9** dissipate, throw away **11** fritter away

spendthrift **6** lavish, waster **7** wastrel **8** prodigal, spend-all, wasteful **10** big spender, profligate, squanderer **11** extravagant, improvident **12** overgenerous

Spengler, Oswald
author of: **19** The Decline of the West

Spenlow, Dora
character in: **16** David Copperfield
author: **7** Dickens

Spenser, Edmund
author of: **8** Amoretti **12** Epithalamion **15** The Faerie Queene **22** The Shephearde's Calendar

spent **4** beat, done, weak **5** faint, weary **6** bushed, done in, used up **7** laid low, wearied, worn out **8** drooping, fatigued, tired out **9** enfeebled, exhausted, fagged out, played out, powerless, prostrate **11** debilitated, ready to drop **12** strengthless **14** on one's last legs

Sperry, Elmer Ambrose
invented: **11** gyrocompass **22** airplane automatic pilot

spew **5** eject, expel, heave, vomit **6** cast up **7** spit out **8** disgorge, throw out **11** regurgitate

spew up **4** spew **5** eject, expel, spout, vomit **6** cast up **7** cough up, throw up **8** disgorge **11** regurgitate

sphere **3** orb **4** area, ball, beat, pale **5** globe, orbit, range, realm, scope **6** domain **7** compass, globule **8** province, spheroid **9** bailiwick, round body, territory **10** experience

spherical **5** orbic, round **6** global, rotund **7** globate, globose, orbical **8** globular **9** orbicular **11** globe-shaped
nearly: **8** obrotund

spheroid **3** orb **4** ball **5** globe **6** sphere **7** globule

spherule **4** ball, bead, drop **6** pellet **7** droplet, globule

Sphinx
form: **7** monster
bust of: **5** woman
body of: **4** lion
father: **6** Typhon **7** Orthrus
mother: **7** Echidna **8** Chimaera
proposed: **7** riddles
location: **6** Thebes
answered by: **7** Oedipus

spice **3** zip **4** herb, kick, snap, tang, zest **5** savor **6** accent, flavor, relish, stacte **7** pizzazz **8** piquancy, pungency **9** condiment, flavoring, seasoning **10** excitement

spicule **4** barb **5** point, spine **7** prickle

spicy **3** hot **4** keen, racy **5** acute, bawdy, fiery, nippy, pithy, salty, sharp, tangy, witty, zippy **6** clever, ribald, risque, snappy, strong **7** gingery, peppery, piquant, pungent **8** aromatic, improper, incisive, indecent, off-color, piercing, redolent, spirited **9** sparkling, trenchant **10** indelicate, scandalous, suggestive **11** provocative **12** questionable **13** scintillating

spider
black widow marking: **9** hourglass
class: **9** Arachnida
combining form: **6** arachn **7** arachno
family: **7** Attidae **9** Drassidae **10** Citigradae, Pisauridae
famous: **9** Charlotte
fear of: **13** arachnophobia
kind: **4** crab, wolf **5** taint **7** jumping **8** trap-door **9** orb weaver, solpugida, tarantula **10** black widow **13** daddy longlegs
mythology: **7** Arachne
nest: **5** nidus
order: **7** Araneae
part: **4** claw, coxa **5** femur, tibia **6** tarsus **7** abdomen, mammula, patella, pedicel, scopula **9** chelicera, protarsis, spinneret **10** pedipalpus, trochanter **11** calamistrum **13** cephalothorax
study of: **10** araneology **11** arachnology
young: **11** spiderlings

Spielberg, Steven
director of: **4** Jaws **14** The Color Purple **19** Raiders of the Lost Ark **21** ET The Extra Terrestrial (in his adventures on earth) **29** Close Encounters of the Third Kind

spike **3** peg, pin **4** barb, nail, spur, tine **5** briar, point, prong, rivet, spine, stake, thorn **6** needle, skewer **7** bramble, bristle, hobnail **8** spikelet

spill **3** run **4** blab, drip, drop, dump, fall, flow, shed, slop, tell, toss **5** slosh, throw, waste **6** reveal, splash **7** let flow, pour out **8** disclose, overflow, overturn

Spillane, Mickey
real name: **13** Frank Morrison
author of: **8** I the Jury **12** Kiss Me Deadly **14** The Girl Hunters **15** The Death Dealers
character: **10** Mike Hammer

spin **4** roll, tell, turn **5** swirl, twirl, wheel, whirl **6** gyrate, invent, relate, render, rotate, unfold **7** concoct, narrate, recount, revolve **8** rotation, spinning **9** fabricate, pirouette

spinach **3** rot **4** bull, bunk **5** hokum, hooey, stuff **6** bunkum, hot air, humbug **7** baloney, blather, hogwash, potherb **8** claptrap, nonsense, tommyrot **9** poppycock, vegetable **10** applesauce **11** foolishness **16** stuff and nonsense

spinach **16** Spinacia oleracea
varieties: **4** wild **5** Cuban **6** Indian **7** Malabar **8** mountain **10** New Zealand **11** round-seeded **13** prickly-seeded

spinal column **4** back **5** spine **8** backbone

spindly **4** puny **5** frail, leggy **6** skinny **7** scraggy **8** skeletal

spine **4** barb, horn, spur **5** briar, point, prong, quill, spike, thorn **6** needle **7** bramble, bristle, prickle **8** backbone **9** vertebrae **12** spinal column

spinel
source: **5** Burma, Mogok
color: **3** red **5** mauve

spineless **4** weak **5** timid **7** fearful **8** cowardly, cowering, cringing, timorous, wavering **10** indecisive, irresolute, spiritless, weak-willed **11** lily-livered, vacillating **12** faint-hearted **13** pusillanimous **14** chickenhearted

spinelessness **8** timidity, weakness **9** cowardice **10** indecision **11** fearfulness

12 cowardliness, irresolution 13 pusillanimity

spine-tingling 7 rousing 8 exciting 9 thrilling 11 hair-raising, sensational 12 breathtaking, electrifying

spinning jenny
invented by: 10 Hargreaves

spinoff 5 issue 6 result 7 adjunct, outcome 8 offshoot 9 byproduct, outgrowth 10 descendant, side effect, supplement 11 aftereffect, consequence

spin out 4 skid 7 draw out 8 lengthen 9 attenuate

spinster 6 virgin 7 old maid 14 unmarried woman

spinsterhood 8 celibacy 9 virginity 11 old maidhood

spiral 4 coil, curl, gyre 5 helix, screw, whirl, whorl 6 coiled, curled 7 helical, ringlet, spiroid, whorled, winding 8 curlicue, twisting 9 corkscrew 11 screw-shaped

Spiral Staircase, The
director: 13 Robert Siodmak
based on story by: 14 Ethel Lina White (Some Must Watch)
cast: 9 Kent Smith 11 George Brent 13 Rhonda Fleming 14 Dorothy McGuire, Ethel Barrymore

spire 3 cap, tip 4 apex, cone, peak 5 crest, point, shaft, tower 6 belfry, summit, turret, vertex 7 minaret, obelisk, steeple 8 pinnacle 9 bell tower, campanile

spirit 3 elf 4 mind, soul, urge, will 5 fairy, ghost, ghoul, heart, shade, spook 6 animus, dybbuk, goblin, psyche, sprite, wraith 7 banshee, bugaboo, bugbear, impulse, phantom, resolve, specter 8 phantasm, presence 9 hobgoblin, intellect 10 apparition, motivation, resolution
German: 5 Geist

spirited 4 bold 5 fiery, nervy 6 frisky, lively, plucky 8 fearless, intrepid 10 courageous, mettlesome

spiritless 4 dull, limp, tame 6 abject 8 cowardly, lifeless, listless 9 apathetic, spineless 10 unanimated, world-weary 11 passionless

spirit of the time
German: 9 Zeitgeist

spirits 3 aim, vim 4 bond, elan, fire, gist, glow, grit, guts, mood, sand, tone, vein, zeal, zest 5 ardor, drive, humor, pluck, sense, spunk, tenor, valor, verve, vigor 6 daring, effect, elixir, energy, fervor, intent, liquor, mettle, morale, stripe, temper, warmth 7 alcohol, avidity, bravery, courage, essence, extract, feeling, loyalty, meaning, purport, purpose, sparkle 8 attitude, audacity, backbone, boldness, devotion, emotions, feelings, tincture, vitality, vivacity 9 animation, eagerness, fortitude, intention, sentiment, stoutness, substance 10 allegiance, attachment, enterprise, enthusiasm, liveliness 11 disposition, doughtiness, staunchness 12 fearlessness, significance 13 dauntlessness, sprightliness 16 stoutheartedness 17 alcoholic solution

spiritual 4 holy 5 godly, inner, moral, pious 6 divine, mental 7 blessed, churchy, ghostly, phantom, psychic 8 cerebral, hallowed, heavenly, platonic, priestly, spectral, supernal 9 celestial, Christian, innermost, of the soul, religious, unearthly, unfleshly, unworldly 10 devotional, immaterial, intangible, sacrosanct, sanctified 11 consecrated, incorporeal 12 metaphysical, otherworldly, supernatural 13 insubstantial, psychological 14 ecclesiastical

spirituality 5 piety 8 devotion, holiness 9 godliness, reverence 10 devoutness

spirituous 4 hard 6 strong 9 alcoholic, distilled 12 intoxicating

spit 3 bar, pop, rod 4 foam, hiss, reef, spew 5 atoll, drool, eject, fling, froth, shoal, throw 6 saliva, shower, shriek, skewer, slaver, sputum 7 dribble, scatter, slobber, spatter, spittle, sputter 8 headland, sandbank, turnspit 9 brochette, peninsula 10 promontory 11 expectorate

spite 3 irk, vex 4 gall, hate, hurt, pain 5 annoy, odium, sting, venom, wound 6 animus, enmity, grudge, harass, hatred, injure, malice, misuse, nettle, put out, rancor 7 ill will, mortify, provoke 8 bad blood, ill-treat, irritate, loathing, meanness 9 animosity, antipathy, hostility, humiliate, malignity, nastiness, vengeance 10 bitterness, resentment 11 detestation, malevolence 12 vengefulness 13 maliciousness, slap in the face 14 revengefulness, vindictiveness

spiteful 4 evil 5 nasty 6 bitter, malign, wicked 7 caustic, envious, hateful, hostile, vicious 8 grudging, vengeful, venomous 9 malicious, merciless, rancorous, resentful, sarcastic, splenetic 10 ill-natured, malevolent, vindictive 11 acrimonious, unforgiving 12 antagonistic

spitting image (the) 4 copy, mate, twin 6 double 9 duplicate 15 perfect likeness

splash 3 ado, hit 4 cast, dash, daub, soil, stir, toss, wash 5 bathe, break, fling, plash, slosh, smack, smear, stain, strew, surge, swash 6 batter, blazon, buffet, effect, impact, paddle, plunge, shower, spread, streak, strike, uproar, wallow, welter 7 bestrew, scatter, spatter, splotch 8 besmirch, discolor, disperse, splatter, sprinkle 9 bespatter, broadcast, commotion, sensation 10 spattering 11 splattering

splashy 5 jazzy, showy 6 flashy 10 glittering 11 spectacular 12 ostentatious

splatter 4 dash 6 splash 7 spatter

splay 4 awry 5 askew, broad 6 aslant, clumsy, extend, tilted, warped 7 awkward, crooked, fanlike, slanted, sloping, turn out 8 inclined, slanting 9 distorted, fan-shaped, irregular, outspread, spread out 10 stretch out

spleen 4 bile, gall 5 anger, spite, venom 6 animus, enmity, hatred, malice, rancor 7 ill will 8 acrimony, ill humor, vexation 9 animosity, bad temper, hostility 10 bitterness, resentment 11 malevolence, peevishness 12 irritability, spitefulness

splendid 4 fine, high, rare, rich 5 grand, lofty, noble, regal, royal 6 august, costly, ornate, superb 7 elegant, eminent, exalted, stately 8 dazzling, elevated, flashing, gleaming, glorious, gorgeous, imposing, majestic, palatial, peerless, terrific 9 admirable, beautiful, brilliant, effulgent, estimable, excellent, marvelous, sumptuous, wonderful 10 glittering, preeminent, remarkable, surpassing 11 exceptional, illustrious, magnificent, outstanding, resplendent, splendorous 12 transcendent 13 distinguished, splendiferous

Splendid Splinter
nickname of: **11** Ted Williams

splendor **4** fire, pomp **5** gleam, glory, light, sheen, shine **6** beauty, dazzle, luster, renown **7** burnish, glitter **8** grandeur, nobility, opulence, radiance **9** intensity, sublimity **10** augustness, brilliance, effulgence, irradiance, luminosity **11** preeminence, stateliness **12** gorgeousness, luminousness, magnificence, resplendence **13** incandescence

Splendor in the Grass
director: **9** Elia Kazan
based on story by: **11** William Inge
cast: **9** Pat Hingle **11** Natalie Wood **12** Sean Garrison, Warren Beatty **14** Audrey Christie

splenetic **5** cross, nasty, surly, testy **6** cranky, malign **7** bilious, hostile, peevish **8** choleric, spiteful, venomous **9** irascible, rancorous **11** acrimonious, ill-tempered **12** cantankerous, disagreeable

splice **3** wed **4** join, knit **5** graft, merge, plait, unite **7** connect **8** dovetail **9** interlace **10** intertwine, interweave **12** interconnect

splinter **4** chip **5** smash, split **6** needle, shiver, sliver **7** break up, crumble, explode, shatter **8** fly apart, fracture, fragment **9** pulverize **12** disintegrate

split **3** hew **4** deal, dole, dual, mete, part, rent, rift, rive, snap, tear, torn **5** allot, break, burst, cleft, crack, halve, mixed, riven, sever, share **6** bisect, breach, broken, cleave, differ, divide, ripped, schism, shiver, sunder, varied **7** be riven, cracked, diverge, divided, divorce, divvy up, fissure, give way, opening, portion, quarrel, rupture, severed, twofold **8** alienate, allocate, cleavage, disagree, dispense, disperse, dissever, disunion, disunite, division, fracture, ruptured, splinter **9** apportion, fractured, parcel out, partition, segmented, segregate, separated, set at odds, subdivide, undecided **10** alienation, ambivalent, break apart, difference, dissension, dissevered, distribute, divergence, falling out, separation, splintered **11** come between, part company, tear asunder **12** disagreement, estrangement

split off **7** deviate, diverge **8** separate **9** draw apart

split the difference **5** agree **6** settle **9** make a deal **10** compromise **11** come to terms, meet halfway **14** strike a bargain

splitting off **9** diverging **10** separating **12** drawing apart

splitting up **8** dividing **9** divorcing **10** breaking up, separating **11** subdividing **12** partitioning

splotch **4** blot, daub, mark, spot **5** smear, stain **6** blotch, smudge **13** discoloration

splurge **5** binge, spree **6** bender **8** live it up **10** indulgence, showing off **12** showy display **13** be extravagant, shoot the works **14** indulge oneself, self-indulgence **22** throw caution to the winds

splutter **4** hiss, spew, spit **5** burst, spray **6** gibber, jabber, mumble, seethe **7** bluster, slobber, spatter, sputter, stammer, stumble, stutter **9** hem and haw **11** expectorate

Spodius
epithet of: **6** Apollo
means: **10** god of ashes

spodumene
variety: **7** kunzite

spoil **3** mar, rot **4** baby, flaw, harm, mold, ruin, sour, turn **5** addle, botch, decay, go bad, humor, taint **6** blight, bungle, coddle, damage, deface, foul up, impair, injure, mess up, mildew, muddle, pamper **7** blemish, destroy, disrupt, putrefy **8** mutilate **9** decompose, disfigure **11** deteriorate, mollycoddle, overgratify, overindulge

spoiled **3** bad, off **6** putrid, rotten, ruined **7** coddled, corrupt, decayed, gone bad, went bad **8** indulged, overripe, pampered **9** putrefied **10** decomposed, frustrated **12** deteriorated **15** rotten to the core

spoiler **6** vandal **8** underdog **9** deflector

Spoilers, The
author: **8** Rex Beach

spoils **4** haul, loot, swag, take **5** booty **6** bounty, prizes, quarry **7** plunder, profits **8** benefits, comforts, pickings **9** amenities, patronage **11** perquisites **12** acquisitions

spoilsport **4** drag **10** wet blanket **11** party-pooper

spoken **4** oral, said **5** parol **6** verbal, voiced **7** uttered **9** expressed **10** pronounced **11** articulated

spokesman **5** agent, PR man, proxy **6** backer, deputy **7** speaker **8** delegate, promoter **9** middleman, proponent, supporter, surrogate **10** mouthpiece, negotiator, press agent **11** protagonist

sponge **3** bum, dry, mop, rub **4** blot, swab, wash **5** cadge, clean, leech, mooch, towel **6** borrow, live on **7** cleanse, moisten **8** freeload, impose on, scrounge **9** panhandle

sponger **5** leech **6** cadger, sponge **7** moocher **8** barnacle, borrower, deadbeat **9** scrounger **10** freeloader **11** bloodsucker

sponsor **4** back **5** angel, set up **6** backer, patron, uphold **7** finance, promote, support **8** advocate, champion, defender, financer, guardian, partisan, promoter, start out, upholder, vouch for, warranty **9** guarantee, financier, guarantor, proponent, protecter, protector, supporter **10** advertiser, stand up for, underwrite

sponsorship **5** aegis **7** support **8** advocacy, auspices **9** patronage **12** championship

spontaneity **7** freedom **11** impetuosity, naturalness **12** unconstraint **13** impulsiveness, offhandedness **18** extemporaneousness

spontaneous **4** free **5** ad lib **7** natural, offhand, willing **8** unbidden **9** automatic, extempore, impetuous, impromptu, impulsive, ingenuous, unplanned, unstudied, voluntary **10** gratuitous, improvised, off the cuff, unprompted **11** independent, instinctive, uncontrived **12** unhesitating **13** unconstrained **14** extemporaneous, unpremeditated

spoof **3** kid **4** joke, josh, twit **6** parody, satire, sendup **7** joshing, kidding, lampoon, mockery, ribbing, takeoff **8** satirize, travesty **9** burlesque, take off on **10** caricature

spook **5** alarm, bogey, ghost, haunt, scare, shade **6** goblin, shadow, spirit **7** disturb, phantom, specter, startle, terrify, unnerve **8** disquiet, frighten, unsettle **9** hobgoblin, terrorize **10** apparition, intimidate

spooky **5** eerie, jumpy, scary, weird **6** creepy **7** ghostly, nervous **8** skittish **10** mysterious

sporadic **3** few **4** rare, thin **6** fitful, meager, random, scarce, sparse, spotty **8** isolated, periodic, uncommon **9** haphazard, irregular, scattered, spasmodic **10** infrequent, now and then, occasional **11** fragmentary **12** intermittent, widely spaced **13** discontinuous **16** few and far between

sport **3** fun, toy **4** bear, butt, game, goat, jest, joke, lark, play, romp, trip **5** abuse, caper, carry, chaff, dally, frisk, hobby, mirth, revel **6** antics, cavort, frolic, gaiety, gambol, misuse, monkey, take in, trifle **7** buffoon, contest, display, disport, exhibit, gambler, jesting, jollity, kidding, mockery, rollick, show off, skylark **8** badinage, derision, fair game, flourish, hilarity, ill-treat, raillery, ridicule, scoffing, trifling **9** amusement, athletics, daredevil, diversion, festivity, joviality, make merry, play games, scapegoat **10** persiflage, pleasantry, recreation, relaxation, skylarking **11** competition, distraction, merrymaking **12** depreciation **13** entertainment, laughingstock **14** divertissement

sporting house **4** stew **5** house **6** bagnio, bordel **7** brothel **8** bordello, cathouse **10** bawdy house, fancy house, whorehouse **14** house of ill fame **16** house of ill repute **19** house of prostitution

sportive **6** blithe, frisky **7** playful **8** animated **10** frolicsome

sportsman **6** hunter **9** fisherman

Sportsman's Notebook, A
author: **12** Ivan Turgenev

sporty **6** casual, flashy, jaunty **8** informal

spot **3** dot, fix, see, spy **4** area, bind, blot, daub, espy, flaw, mark, part, seat, site, slur, soil **5** brand, fleck, grime, locus, patch, place, point, smear, space, speck, stain, sully, taint, tract **6** blotch, defect, detect, locale, locate, plight, region, sector, smirch, smudge, splash, stigma **7** blemish, dilemma, discern, light on, pick out, quarter, section, spatter, speckle, splotch, station **8** discolor, discover, disgrace, district, flyspeck, locality, location, position, premises, reproach, sprinkle **9** aspersion, discredit, recognize, situation, territory **10** difficulty, imputation **11** predicament **12** bad situation, neighborhood **13** discoloration

spotless **4** pure **5** clean, snowy **7** perfect, shining **8** flawless, gleaming, pristine, unflawed, unmarred, unsoiled **9** faultless, stainless, unspotted, unstained, unsullied, untainted **10** immaculate, impeccable **11** unblemished, untarnished **14** irreproachable **15** unexceptionable

spotted **3** saw **6** dotted, espied, soiled **7** dappled, located, mottled, stained **8** detected, speckled **9** blemished, discerned, spattered **10** discovered **13** caught sight of

spotty **6** fitful, pimply, random, uneven **7** blotchy, dappled, erratic, flecked, mottled, spotted **8** episodic, freckled, splotchy, sporadic, unsteady, variable, wavering **9** broken out, desultory, irregular, spasmodic, uncertain **10** capricious, inconstant, unreliable, variegated **11** full of spots **12** disorganized, intermittent, undependable, unmethodical, unsystematic

spouse **4** mate, wife **7** consort, husband, partner **8** helpmate **10** better half

spout **3** jet, lip **4** beak, flow, go on, gush, nose, pipe, rant, spew, tube, vent, well **5** eject, erupt, expel, exude, issue, mouth, shoot, snout, spray, spurt, surge, vomit **6** nozzle, outlet, sluice, squirt, stream, trough **7** bluster, carry on, channel, conduit, pour out **8** disgorge, fountain, harangue **9** discharge, hold forth **10** waterspout **11** pontificate **12** emit forcibly **14** speak pompously

sprawl **4** flop, lean, loll, wind **5** slump **6** branch, extend, lounge, slouch **7** gush out, meander, recline **8** languish, reach out, straggle **9** spread out **10** stretch out **11** spread-eagle

spray **4** coat, mist, posy, twig **5** bough, burst, shoot, sprig, treat, vapor **6** dampen, nozzle, shower, splash, switch, volley **7** atomize, barrage, blossom, bouquet, drizzle, moisten, nosegay, scatter, spatter, sprayer, syringe **8** atomizer, disperse, droplets, moisture, sprinkle **9** discharge, fusillade, sprinkler, vaporizer

spread **3** air, lay **4** area, cast, coat, open, pave, shed, span, vent **5** apply, bruit, cloak, cover, feast, field, issue, range, reach, scope, smear, spray, story, strew, sweep, table, tract, width **6** bedaub, be shed, blazon, extend, extent, herald, length, notice, repeat, report, unfold, unfurl, unroll **7** account, advance, article, banquet, besmear, bestrew, breadth, circuit, compass, declare, diffuse, divulge, expanse, overlay, overrun, pervade, plaster, publish, radiate, scatter, spatter, stretch, suffuse, trumpet, untwine, write-up **8** announce, coverage, disperse, distance, increase, permeate, proclaim, sprinkle **9** broadcast, circulate, diffusion, expansion, extension, make known, penetrate, pervasion, propagate, publicize, radiation, spreading, suffusion, ventilate **10** dispersion, distribute, make public, permeation, promulgate, stretch out **11** communicate, disseminate, noise abroad, proliferate **13** amplification, dissemination, proliferation

spread out **5** broad, widen **6** expand, extend **7** broaden, diffuse, enlarge, radiate, stretch **8** expanded, extended, open wide **9** dispersed, outspread, scattered **10** distribute, unhampered **11** unconfirmed **12** unrestricted **14** unconcentrated

spree **4** bout, orgy, toot **5** binge, drunk, fling, revel **6** bender **7** carouse, debauch, revelry, splurge, wassail **8** carousal **9** bacchanal **10** saturnalia

sprightliness **8** buoyancy, spryness, vivacity **9** animation, briskness **10** breeziness, liveliness **16** lightheartedness

sprightly **3** gay **4** keen, spry **5** agile, alive, brisk, jolly, merry **6** active, blithe, breezy, cheery, jaunty, jovial, lively, nimble **7** buoyant, chipper, dashing, dynamic, playful **8** animated, cheerful, spirited, sportive **9** energetic, vivacious **10** blithesome, frolicsome **12** lighthearted

spring **3** hop, jet, pop, spa **4** come, dart, flow, gush, jump, kick, leap, loom, pool, pour, rise, rush, stem, well **5** arise, baths, begin, bound, caper, ensue, fount, issue, lunge, shoot, spout, spurt, start, surge, vault **6** appear, bounce, derive, gambol, recoil,

reflex, result, sprout, stream **7** burgeon, crop out, descend, emanate, proceed, release, shoot up, start up, stretch, trigger **8** buoyancy, commence, fountain, mushroom **9** come forth, entrechat, germinate, originate, saltation, waterhole **10** break forth, burst forth, elasticity, resiliency **11** flexibility
goddess of: 4 Hebe **5** Venus

spring back 6 bounce, recoil **7** rebound **8** ricochet

spring flowers
goddess of: 6 Thallo

Springhaven
author: 11 R D Blackmore

springlike 4 mild, soft, warm **5** balmy

springs
god of: 4 Fons **6** Palici
goddess of: 4 Idun **5** Idura, Ithun **6** Ithunn

spring up 4 grow, rise **5** arise, occur, pop up **6** crop up, emerge, happen, sprout **9** originate **10** burst forth

springy 6 bouncy, spongy, supple **7** elastic **9** resilient **10** rebounding

sprinkle 4 dash, dust, rain **5** spray, strew, water **6** powder, shower, splash, spread, squirt **7** bestrew, diffuse, drizzle, moisten, scatter, spatter **8** splatter

sprinkling 4 dash, drop, hint **5** pinch, touch **7** droplet, minimum, modicum, soupcon **8** sprinkle **10** smattering

sprint 3 run **4** dart, dash, kick, race, rush, tear, whiz **5** burst, shoot, spurt, whisk **7** scamper

sprit 3 bar **4** spar **8** crossbar **10** crosspiece

sprite 3 elf **5** fairy, pixie **10** leprechaun

sprout 3 bud, wax **4** grow **5** bloom, shoot, sprig **6** come up, flower, spread, thrive **7** blossom, burgeon **8** multiply, offshoot, put forth, spring up **9** germinate, outgrowth

spruce 4 chic, neat, tidy, trim **5** kempt, natty, sharp, smart **6** dapper **7** conifer, elegant **9** evergreen, shipshape **11** well-groomed **12** spick-and-span
French: 6 soigne

spruce 5 Picea
varieties: 3 bog, cat, red **4** blue **5** black, Hondo, Sitka, snake, white, Yeddo **6** double, Norway **7** Alberta, big-cone, Finnish, hemlock **8** Colorado, Sakhalin, Siberian **9** Himalayan, tiger-tail **10** Black Hills **12** Colorado blue, Japanese bush

spry 4 deft, hale **5** agile, brisk, quick **6** active, frisky, hearty, jaunty, lively, nimble, supple **7** buoyant, chipper, playful **8** animated, spirited, sportive, vigorous **9** energetic, sprightly, vivacious **11** lightfooted

spunk 4 fire, grit, guts, salt, sand **5** heart, nerve, pluck **6** daring, ginger, mettle, pepper, spirit **7** bravery, courage **8** backbone, boldness, gumption **10** feistiness

spur 3 arm, leg **4** fork, goad, prod, whet, whip, wing **5** prick **6** branch, feeder, fillip, hasten, motive, siding **7** impetus, impulse **8** excitant, stimulus **9** boot spike, encourage, incentive, stimulant, stimulate, tributary **10** incitement, inducement **11** instigation, provocation, stimulation **13** encouragement

spurge 9 Euphorbia **11** Pachysandra
varieties: 5 caper, leafy, melon **6** ipecac, myrtle, tramp's **7** cypress, mottled, seaside, slipper **8** fiddler's, Japanese **9** Allegheny, flowering **10** Indian tree

spurious 4 fake, mock, sham **5** bogus, false, phony **6** faulty, forged, hollow **7** feigned, unsound **8** specious **9** imitation, simulated **10** fallacious, fraudulent, not genuine **11** counterfeit, make-believe, unauthentic **12** illegitimate

spurn 4 mock, snub **5** flout, repel, scorn **6** rebuff, refuse, reject, slight **7** condemn, decline, disdain, dismiss, repulse, scoff at, sneer at **8** turn down **9** cast aside, disparage, repudiate **12** coldshoulder, look down upon **16** turn up one's nose at

spur-of-the-moment 5 ad-lib **7** offhand **9** extempore, impromptu **10** improvised, unprepared **11** extemporary, spontaneous, unrehearsed **14** extemporaneous, unpremeditated

spurt 3 jet **4** dart, dash, emit, flow, gush, gust, rush, tear, whiz **5** burst, flash, issue, lunge, scoot, shoot, speed, spout, spray, surge **6** access, spring, sprint, squirt, stream **7** pour out **8** disgorge, ejection, eruption, fountain, outbreak, outburst **9** discharge, explosion, spring out **10** outpouring

spy 3 pry, see **4** find, peep, spot, view **5** scout, sight, snoop **6** behold, descry, detect, notice, shadow **7** discern, glimpse, make out, observe **8** discover, informer, Mata Hari, perceive, saboteur **9** keep watch, operative, recognize **11** reconnoiter, secret agent **12** catch sight of **13** undercover man, watch secretly **14** espionage agent, fifth columnist **16** agent provocateur **17** intelligence agent

Spy 5 Caleb

Spy, The
author: 19 James Fenimore Cooper

Spy Who Came In from the Cold, The
director: 10 Martin Ritt
based on novel by: 11 John LeCarre
cast: 11 Claire Bloom, Oskar Werner **12** Peter Van Eyck **13** Richard Burton

Spy Who Loved Me, The
author: 10 Ian Fleming
director: 12 Lewis Gilbert
cast: 10 Bernard Lee (M), Roger Moore (James Bond) **11** Barbara Bach, Curt Jurgens (Stromberg), Richard Kiel (Jaws)

squabble 3 row, war **4** spat, tiff **5** argue, brawl, clash, fight, run-in, scrap, set-to, words **6** battle, bicker, differ **7** contend, contest, dispute, quarrel, wrangle **8** argument **9** have words, lock horns **10** bandy words, contention, difference, dissension **11** altercation, controversy **12** disagreement

squadron 5 fleet **6** armada **8** flotilla **9** naval unit **10** escadrille **11** cavalry unit **12** military unit

squalid 4 foul, mean **5** dirty, nasty **6** abject, filthy, horrid, rotten, shabby, sloppy, sordid **7** decayed, reeking, run-down, unclean **8** battered, degraded, slovenly, wretched **9** miserable **10** broken-down, disheveled, ramshackle, slatternly, tumbledown **11** dilapidated **12** deteriorated

squalidness 4 dirt **5** filth **7** squalor **8** foulness, meanness, vileness **9** dirtiness **10** sordidness **11** degradation, uncleanness

squalor 4 dirt **5** filth **6** misery **7** neglect, poverty **8** foulness, meanness, ugliness **9** dinginess, dirtiness, nastiness, seediness **10** abjectness, grubbiness, sordidness **11** squalidness, uncleanness **12** wretchedness **13** uncleanliness

squander **4** blow **5** spend, waste **6** lavish, misuse **7** consume, deplete, exhaust **8** misspend **9** dissipate, throw away **10** run through **11** fritter away **14** spend like water

squanderer **6** waster **7** wastrel **8** prodigal **10** dissipater, profligate **11** spendthrift

squandering **7** wasting **8** prodigal, wasteful **9** imprudent **10** profligate **11** dissipating, extravagant, improvident, spendthrift **12** overspending, throwing away **14** frittering away **17** spending like water

square **3** box, fit **4** even, fogy, heal, hick, jerk, jibe, just, mend, park, prig **5** agree, align, blend, block, close, equal, green, match, place, plane, plaza, prude, tally **6** accord, adjust, candid, circus, cohere, common, concur, even up, fall in, honest, pay off, settle, smooth **7** arrange, balance, clear up, compose, conform, even out, flatten, mediate, patch up, rectify, resolve **8** block out, cornball, make even, quadrate, set right, settle up, truthful **9** arbitrate, discharge, equitable, harmonize, liquidate, make level, reconcile **10** clodhopper, correspond, quadrangle, straighten **11** marketplace **12** apple knocker, conservative **13** quadrilateral, stick-in-the-mud **15** straightforward
type: **1** T **3** try **11** combination

Square
character in: **8** Tom Jones
author: **8** Fielding

Square
constellation of: **5** Norma

square centimeter
abbreviation: **4** sq cm

square decimeter
abbreviation: **4** sq dm

square dekameter
abbreviation: **5** sq dam

square foot
abbreviation: **4** sq ft

square hectometer
abbreviation: **4** sq hm

square inch
abbreviation: **4** sq in

square kilometer
abbreviation: **4** sq km

square meter
abbreviation: **3** sq m

square mile
abbreviation: **4** sq mi

square millimeter
abbreviation: **4** sq mm

square rod
abbreviation: **4** sq rd

square yard
abbreviation: **4** sq yd

squash **3** jam **4** cram, mash, pulp **5** crowd, crush, level, quash, quell, smash, upset **6** dispel, squish **7** compact, destroy, flatten, put down, ram down, repress, squeeze, squelch, trample **8** compress, suppress **9** dissipate, overthrow, prostrate, undermine **10** annihilate, obliterate **11** concentrate

squash **9** Cucurbita
varieties: **4** bush **5** acorn **6** autumn, banana, summer, turban, winter **7** Hubbard, scallop **8** pattypan, zucchini **9** cocozelle, crookneck **12** Boston marrow **13** sweet dumpling **15** Canada crookneck, summer crookneck, winter crookneck

squat **5** cower, dumpy, dwell, kneel, pudgy **6** chunky, cringe, crouch, encamp, hunker, lie low, locate, move in, shrink, square, stocky, stubby, stumpy **8** thickset

squawk **5** blare, croak, gripe **6** scream, squall **7** grumble, protest, screech **8** complain

squeak **3** cry **4** peep, yelp **5** cheep, chirp, creak, grate **6** shriek, shrill, squeal **7** screech

squeal **3** cry **4** bawl, blab, fink, peep, sing, wail, yell, yelp **5** cheep, whine **6** inform, scream, shriek, shrill, squeak **7** screech

squealer **3** pig, rat **4** fink **6** canary, piglet, snitch **7** stoolie, tattler, traitor **8** informer **10** tattletale **11** stool pigeon **12** blabbermouth

squeamish **3** coy **4** prim, sick **5** fussy **6** demure, modest, proper, queasy **7** finical, finicky, mincing, prudish, sickish **8** delicate, nauseous, priggish, qualmish **9** finicking **10** fastidious **11** puritanical, straitlaced **13** sanctimonious

Squeers, Wackford
character in: **16** Nicholas Nickleby
author: **7** Dickens

squeeze **3** hug, jam, pry, ram **4** butt, cram, edge, grip, hold, pack, push **5** clasp, cramp, crowd, drive, elbow, grasp, press, shove, stuff, wedge, wrest, wring **6** clutch, coerce, compel, defile, elicit, extort, jostle, thrust, wrench **7** compact, draw out, embrace, extract, passage, pull out, tear out **8** compress, crowding, crushing, force out, pinching, press out, pressure, shoulder, withdraw **9** extricate, narrowing, stricture **10** bottleneck **11** compression, concentrate, consolidate **12** constriction

squelch **4** hush **5** abort, crush, quash, quell, quiet, smash **6** retort, squash **7** put down, riposte, silence **8** silencer, suppress

squire **4** date, take **5** court **6** attend, escort **7** consort, gallant, planter **8** cavalier, chaperon **9** accompany, attendant, boyfriend, chauffeur, companion, landowner **14** lord of the manor **16** country gentleman

Squire
character in: **18** The Canterbury Tales
author: **7** Chaucer

squirm **4** bend, jerk, toss, turn **5** pitch, shift, smart, sweat, twist, wince **6** blench, fidget, flinch, shrink, twitch, wiggle, writhe **7** agonize, contort, wriggle **8** flounder

squirt **3** jet **4** dash, gush, punk, runt **5** piker, shoot, spout, spray, spurt **6** shower, splash, stream **7** spatter **8** sprinkle **9** discharge, pipsqueak **10** besprinkle

Sri Lanka ***see box, p. 924***

SS-GB
author: **11** Len Deighton

SS troops, chief of
12 Reichsfuhrer

stab **2** go **3** cut, jab, try **4** ache, bite, gash, gore, hurt, pain, pang, pass, shot, spit **5** essay, gouge, knife, lance, lunge, prick, qualm, slash, spear, spike, stick, sting, trial, wound **6** cleave, dagger, effort, impale, pierce, shiver, stroke, thrill, thrust, twinge **7** attempt, bayonet **8** endeavor, lacerate, transfix **10** laceration, run through

stability **5** poise **6** aplomb, fixity **7** balance **8** evenness, firmness, security, solidity **9** constancy, fixedness, solidness, soundness **10** continuity, durability, permanence, stableness, steadiness, sturdiness **11** abidingness, equilibrium,

Sri Lanka
other name: **6** Ceylon **8** Serendib **9** Taprobane
capital/largest city: **7** Colombo
ancient capital: **11** Polonnaruwa **12** Anuradhapura
others: **3** Uva **5** Galle, Kandy **6** Jaffna, Mannar, Matale, Matara **7** Badulla, Kegalle, Negombo **8** Kalutara, Mankulem, Moratuwa, Puttalam **9** Ratnapura **10** Batticaloa, Mullaitivu **11** Ambalangoda, Trincomalee
division: **8** Dambulla, Sri Lanka **9** Taprobane
measure: **4** para, seer **5** parah **6** amunam, parrah
monetary unit: **4** cent **5** rupee
island: **5** Delft **6** Mannar **8** Sri Lanka
mountain: **5** Pedro **7** Sri Pada **9** Adam's Peak
highest point: **14** Pidurutalagala
river: **4** Kala **6** Deduru, Gal Ova **8** Aruvi Aru **9** Deburu Ova **11** Kelani Ganga **13** Mahaweli Ganga
sea: **6** Indian
physical feature:
bay: **6** Bengal **8** Koddiyar
falls: **8** Lazapana
gulf: **6** Mannar
peninsula: **6** Jaffna
plateau: **6** Hatton
strait: **4** Palk
people: **5** Malay, Tamil, Vedda **6** Veddah, Weddah **7** Burgher, Mahinda, Malabar **8** Eurasian **9** Cingalese, Dravidian, Sinhalese **10** Singhalese
leader: **11** Jayawardene **12** Bandaranaike
ruler: **5** Dutch **7** British, Chinese **10** Portuguese
language: **4** Pali **5** Tamil **7** English **9** Sinhalese
religion: **5** Hindu, Islam **8** Buddhism
place:
fortress: **8** Sigiriya
gardens: **8** Hakgalle **10** Peradiniya
national park: **6** Ruhuna **8** Wilpattu
temple: **5** Tooth **6** Gal Oya **7** Kelanya **8** Runaweli **9** Ruanvelli **10** Dankahlaka **12** Asokharamaya
feature:
animal: **5** loris **12** wild elephant
clothing: **4** sari **5** camba **6** sarong **7** cambaya **8** sherwani
dancer: **7** Kandyan
drama: **5** kolam **7** nadagam
festival: **8** Perahera
shrine: **6** dagoba
tree: **4** doon, hora, palu, tala **5** domba, ebony **7** talipot **8** halmilla, ironwood **9** satinwood **11** allaeanthus **12** shimohabodhi

reliability **13** steadfastness **14** changelessness **16** unchangeableness

stabilize **7** balance **8** hold firm, make firm **10** hold steady, make steady

stabilizer **7** balance, ballast **8** additive **9** equipoise, gyroscope **10** ballasting **12** airplane part **14** counterbalance

stable **4** barn, byre, even, firm, mews, safe, true **5** fixed, loyal, solid, sound **6** moored, secure, steady, sturdy **7** abiding, durable, staunch, uniform **8** anchored, constant, cowhouse, cowshed, enduring, faithful, reliable, resolute, stalwart **9** immovable, steadfast **10** dependable, persisting, stationary, unchanging, unwavering **11** established, unfaltering **12** indissoluble, unchangeable

Stabler, Ken
nickname: **8** the Snake
sport: **8** football
position: **11** quarterback
team: **13** Houston Oilers **14** Oakland Raiders

staccato
music: **12** disconnected **16** each note separate

stack **4** bank, flue, heap, load, lump, mass, pile, rick **5** amass, batch, bunch, clump, hoard, mound, sheaf **6** bundle, funnel, gather **7** chimney **8** assemble, mountain **9** amassment **10** accumulate **11** aggregation **12** accumulation

Stack, Robert
born: **12** Los Angeles CA
roles: **9** Eliot Ness **13** Name of the Game **15** The Untouchables **16** Written on the Wind **19** The High and the Mighty **24** The Bullfighter and the Lady

Stackpole, Henrietta
character in: **18** The Portrait of a Lady
author: **5** James

Stacte **5** spice

stadium **4** bowl, park **5** arena, field, stade **6** circus **8** ballpark, coliseum **9** palaestra **10** hippodrome **12** amphitheater

Stael, Madame de
author of: **7** Corinne **8** Delphine **9** On Germany **35** The Influence of Literature upon Society

staff **3** bat, man, rod **4** cane, crew, help, pole, team, tend, wand, work **5** cadre, force, group, stave, stick **6** crutch, cudgel, manage **7** retinue, scepter, service, support **8** advisors, bludgeon, flagpole **9** billy club, employees, flagstaff, personnel **10** alpenstock, assistants, shillelagh **12** walking stick

staff member **4** aide **6** worker **8** employee

stage **3** act **4** dais, play, spot, step **5** arena, drama, grade, level, phase, put on, sight, stump **6** acting, locale, period, podium, pulpit **7** perform, present, produce, rostrum, setting, show biz, soapbox, theater **8** bearings, locality, location, position, scaffold **9** dramatize, the boards

Stagecoach
director: **8** John Ford
cast: **9** John Wayne **10** Andy Devine **11** Louise Platt **12** Claire Trevor **13** John Carradine **14** George Bancroft, Thomas Mitchell
Oscar for: **15** supporting actor (Mitchell)

stagecraft **5** drama **7** theater **9** theatrics **10** dramaturgy **11** thespianism **12** dramatic arts

Stage Door
author: **10** Edna Ferber **14** George S Kaufman
director: **13** Gregory La Cava
cast: **11** Andrea Leeds, Gail Patrick **12** Ginger Rogers **13** Adolphe Menjou **16** Katharine Hepburn

stage setting
French: **11** mise en scene

stagger **3** jar **4** jolt, reel, stun, sway **5** amaze, lurch, shake, shock, waver **6** hobble, totter, wobble **7** astound, blunder, nonplus, overlap, shamble, startle, stumble, stupefy **8** astonish, bewilder, bowl over, confound, flounder, unsettle **9** alternate, dumbfound, give a turn, overwhelm, spread out **10** disconcert, knock silly, strike dumb **11** cause to reel, cause to sway, consternate, flabbergast, take in turns **12** make unsteady **15** throw off balance

staggering **7** amazing **8** shocking, stunning **9** startling **10** astounding **11** astonishing **12** breathtaking

stagnant **4** dead, dull, foul, lazy, slow **5** close, inert, quiet, slimy, stale, still **6** filthy, leaden, putrid, static, supine, torpid **7** dormant, dronish, languid, tainted **8** inactive, lifeless, listless, polluted, sluggish, standing **9** lethargic, ponderous, putrefied, quiescent **10** monotonous, motionless, not flowing, not running, stationary, unstirring, vegetative **13** uncirculating

stagnate **7** go to pot, lie idle, putrefy **8** go to seed, lie still, vegetate **10** stand still **11** cease to flow, deteriorate, stop growing **14** become inactive, become polluted, become sluggish

stagy **5** phony **8** affected, mannered **9** unnatural **10** artificial, factitious, theatrical

staid **5** grave, quiet, sober, stiff **6** decent, demure, proper, sedate, seemly, solemn, somber **7** earnest, prudish, serious, settled, subdued **8** decorous, priggish, reserved **9** dignified **10** complacent **15** undemonstrative

stain **3** dye, mar **4** blot, daub, flaw, foul, mark, ruin, slur, soil, spot, tint **5** brand, color, dirty, grime, libel, patch, shame, smear, speck, spoil, sully, taint **6** befoul, blotch, debase, defile, impair, malign, smirch, smudge, stigma, vilify **7** blacken, blemish, pigment, slander, splotch, subvert, tarnish **8** besmirch, coloring, discolor, disgrace, dishonor, dyestuff, tincture **9** denigrate, discredit, disparage, undermine **10** imputation, stigmatize **13** discoloration

stainless **5** clean, moral **6** chaste, decent **8** spotless, unsoiled **9** exemplary, unspotted, unsullied, untainted **11** unblemished

Stairway to Heaven
director: **13** Michael Powell **17** Emeric Pressburger
cast: **9** Kim Hunter **10** David Niven **12** Roger Livesey **13** Raymond Massey
original title: **21** A Matter of Life and Death

stake **3** bar, bet, peg, pot, rod **4** ante, back, grab, haul, lash, loot, moor, pale, pawn, pile, play, pole, post, prop, risk, stay, take **5** booty, brace, hitch, kitty, prize, purse, share, spike, stand, stick, treat, wager **6** chance, column, define, fasten, fetter, hazard, hold up, marker, picket, pillar, reward, secure, spoils, tether **7** delimit, finance, jackpot, mark off, mark out, outline, peg down, returns, sponsor, support, trammel, venture **8** interest, make fast, pickings, standard, winnings **9** delineate, demarcate, speculate, subsidize **10** investment, jeopardize, underwrite **11** involvement, speculation

Stalag 17
director: **11** Billy Wilder
cast: **9** Don Taylor **11** Peter Graves **12** Neville Brand **13** Harvey Lembeck, Otto Preminger, Richard Erdman, Robert Strauss, William Holden
Oscar for: **5** actor (Holden)

stale **4** dull, flat **5** banal, close, fusty, musty, trite, vapid **6** common **7** humdrum, insipid, prosaic, tedious, worn-out **8** mediocre, not fresh, ordinary, stagnant, unvaried **9** hackneyed, savorless, tasteless **10** monotonous, pedestrian, threadbare **11** commonplace **13** unimaginative, uninteresting

stalemate **3** tie **4** draw, halt **7** dead end, impasse **8** blockage, cul-de-sac, dead heat, deadlock, standoff **10** standstill

stalk **4** hunt, lurk, stem **5** haunt, march, prowl, shaft, spire, stamp, steal, stomp, strut, track, tramp, trunk **6** column, menance, stride **7** pedicel, pervade, swagger **8** hang over, threaten **9** creep up on, go through, sneak up on

stall **3** box, pen **4** cell, coop, halt, shed, shop, stop **5** block, booth, check, delay, kiosk, stand **6** arcade, arrest, hobble, impede, pull up, put off **7** bed down, confine, cubicle, disable, trammel **8** obstruct, paralyze, postpone **9** be evasive, interrupt, stop short, temporize **10** equivocate **11** compartment, play for time, stop running **12** incapacitate **13** orchestra seat

Stallone, Sylvester
born: **9** New York NY
nickname: **3** Sly
roles: **4** FIST **5** Rambo, Rocky **9** John Rambo **10** First Blood, Rhinestone **11** Rocky Balboa **18** The Lords of Flatbush

stalwart **4** bold, firm, hale **5** beefy, brave, hardy, hefty, husky, manly, sound **6** brawny, gritty, heroic, mighty, plucky, robust, rugged, spunky, stable, strong, sturdy **7** gallant, staunch, valiant **8** constant, intrepid, muscular, powerful, resolute, valorous, vigorous **9** steadfast, strapping, unbending, undaunted **10** able-bodied, courageous, persistent, unflagging, unshakable, unswerving, unwavering, unyielding **11** indomitable, lionhearted, undeviating, unfaltering, unflinching, unshrinking **12** intransigent, stouthearted, strong-willed **14** uncompromising

stamina **4** pith **5** vigor **6** energy **8** vitality **9** endurance, hardiness, stoutness **10** ruggedness, sturdiness **12** perseverance, staying power

stammer **6** falter, fumble, mumble **7** sputter, stumble, stutter **8** splutter **9** hem and haw

stamp
collecting: **9** philately
first: **10** Penny Black
issued by: **12** Great Britain
inscribed with: **8** One Penny
picture of: **13** Queen Victoria
first-day hand stamper: **6** cachet
hole measurer: **16** perforation gauge
mounting paper: **5** hinge
not perforated: **11** imperforate
paper design: **9** watermark
rolls: **4** coil
tear holes: **12** perforations
tear slit: **8** roulette
unseparated group: **5** block
used mark: **8** postmark **12** cancellation
value suspended: **11** demonetized

stamp, stamp out **2** OK **3** die, tag **4** cast, kind, make, mark, mint, mold, seal, sort, type **5** brand, breed, clump, crush, erase, genre, label, march, order, print, pound, punch, quash, smash, stalk, stomp, strut, thump, tramp **6** banish, betray, emblem, expose, matrix, nature, put out, reveal, rub out, signet, step on, strain, stride, trudge **7** abolish, blot out, display, engrave, exhibit, impress, imprint, put down, squelch, trample, variety, voucher **8** get rid of, hallmark, identify, inscribe, intaglio, manifest, suppress, typecast **9** character, eliminate, engraving, eradicate, personify, signature, trademark **10** annihilate, do away with, extinguish, imprimatur, stigmatize, validation **11** attestation, certificate, demonstrate, distinguish, endorsement, exterminate, **12** characterize, official mark, ratification **13** certification **14** authentication, characteristic, identification

stampede **4** bolt, dash, flee, race, rout, rush **5** chaos, flood, panic **6** engulf **7** overrun, retreat, scatter **8** inundate **10** take flight **11** crowd around, pandemonium **12** beat a retreat
French: **12** sauve qui peut

stanchion **4** post, prop, stay **5** brace, strut **7** support, upright

stand **2** be **3** put, set **4** draw, face, hold, last, move, rank, rear, rest, rise, stay, step, take, tent **5** abide, argue, booth, brook, erect, exist, get up, hoist, honor, kiosk, mount, place, put up, raise, shift, stall, treat **6** bear up, effort, endure, obtain, pay for, policy, remain, remove, stance, suffer, uphold **7** carry on, commend, counter, defense, endorse, finance, hold out, opinion, persist, posture, prevail, provide, stick up, stomach, support, survive, sustain, undergo, weather **8** advocate, be placed, champion, continue, pavilion, position, sanction, submit to, tolerate **9** be located, be present, be upright, persevere, put up with, sentiment, undertake, viewpoint **10** resistance, set upright **11** be permanent, countenance, disposition, point of view **13** remain in force, take a position

Stand, The
author: **11** Stephen King

standard **3** leg **4** base, flag, foot, jack, post **5** basic, canon, guide, ideal, stock, usual **6** banner, column, common, ensign, normal, pillar **7** measure, pennant, regular, support, typical, upright **8** accepted, ordinary, streamer **9** criterion, customary, guideline, principle, prototype, stanchion, universal, yardstick **10** foundation, touchstone **11** requirement **13** specification

stand behind **4** back **7** endorse, support **8** champion, vouch for **9** recommend

standby **6** backup **9** alternate, available **10** substitute, understudy **11** old reliable **12** tried-and-true

stand by **4** keep **5** cling **6** adhere, be true, defend, hold to, keep to **7** be loyal, stick by **8** cleave to, maintain **10** be constant, be faithful, stick up for

stand fast **4** hold **6** resist **8** stand pat

stand for **4** bear **5** abide, favor, stand **6** embody **7** signify **8** advocate, submit to, tolerate **9** personify, put up with, represent, symbolize

stand-in **3** sub **5** agent, proxy **6** backup, deputy, double, fill-in, second **9** alternate, assistant, surrogate **10** substitute, understudy **11** pinch hitter, replacement

standing **3** age **4** life, rank, term, time **5** erect, fixed, grade, inert, order, place, still **6** at rest, static, status, tenure **7** dormant, footing, lasting, station, upended, upright **8** duration, inactive, position, stagnant, vertical **9** immovable, permanent, perpetual, quiescent, renewable **10** continuing, importance, motionless, reputation, stationary, unstirring **11** continuance **13** perpendicular

standoff **7** impasse **8** deadlock

standoffish **4** cool **5** aloof **6** formal, remote **7** distant, haughty **8** detached, reserved, solitary, taciturn **9** reclusive, withdrawn **10** antisocial, restrained, unfriendly, unsociable **12** inaccessible, misanthropic, unresponsive **14** unapproachable **15** uncommunicative, uncompanionable

standpoint **4** side **5** angle, slant **6** aspect **9** viewpoint **11** point of view

standstill **3** end **4** halt, stop **5** pause **6** hiatus **7** dead end, impasse **8** abeyance, deadlock, dead stop, full stop **9** breakdown, cessation, stalemate **10** suspension **11** termination **14** discontinuance

stand up for **4** back **5** boost **6** defend **7** further, promote, support **8** advocate, champion

stand up to **4** defy, face **5** brave **6** resist **8** confront **9** challenge

Stant, Charlotte
character in: **13** The Golden Bowl
author: **5** James

Stan the Man
nickname of: **10** Stan Musial

Stanton, Adam
character in: **14** All the King's Men
author: **6** Warren

Stanwyck, Barbara
real name: **11** Ruby Stevens
born: **10** Brooklyn NY
husband: **8** Frank Fay **12** Robert Taylor
roles: **9** Big Valley, The Colbys **10** Ball of Fire, The Lady Eve **11** Meet John Doe **12** Stella Dallas **15** Double Indemnity **16** Sorry Wrong Number **20** Cattle Queen of Montana **22** Christmas in Connecticut

staple **3** key **4** main **5** basic, chief, major, prime, vital **6** leader **7** feature, primary, product **8** resource, vendible **9** commodity, essential, necessary **11** fundamental, raw material **13** indispensable

Stapleton, Jean
real name: **12** Jeanne Murray
born: **9** New York NY
roles: **7** Dingbat **11** Edith Bunker **14** All in the Family

Stapleton, Maureen
born: **6** Troy NY
roles: **7** Airport **9** Interiors **12** Lonelyhearts **13** The Rose Tattoo **18** A View from the Bridge

star, stars *see box*

Starbuck
character in: **8** Moby Dick
author: **8** Melville

starch **5** vigor **6** sizing **8** backbone, gumption **10** stiffening

starched **5** crisp, sized, stiff **7** starchy **9** stiffened

starchy **5** rigid, stiff **6** formal, proper **7** correct **10** meticulous

star, stars **3** god, sun, VIP **4** diva, fate, hero, idol, lead, lion, name **5** comet, excel, giant, great, omens, shine **6** bigwig, do well, galaxy, meteor, nebula, planet **7** destiny, feature, fortune, goddess, heroine, notable, soloist, starlet, succeed, top draw **8** asteroid, cynosure, eminence, immortal, luminary, mainstay, Milky Way, portents, showcase, stand out, virtuoso **9** celebrity, headliner, meteoroid, principal, satellite, top banana **10** prima donna **11** All-American, drawing card, play the lead, protagonist **12** famous person, gain approval, heavenly body **13** celestial body, constellation **14** main attraction, predestination, prima ballerina
brightest: **6** Sirius
brightness measure: **9** magnitude **10** luminosity
color: **3** red **4** blue **5** black, white **6** orange, yellow
distance measure: **6** parsec **9** light year
double star: **6** binary
exploding star: **4** nova **9** supernova
French: **6** etoile
name: **4** Mira, Ross, Vega, Wolf **5** Cygni, Deneb, Rigel, Spica **6** Altair, Luyten, Pollux **7** Antares, Canopus, Capella, Lalande, Polaris, Procyon, Regulus, Tau Ceti **8** Achernar, Arcturus, Barnard's, Lacaille, Pleiades **9** Aldebaran, Fomalhaut **10** Beta Crucis, Betelgeuse **11** Delta Cephei, Epsilon Indi, Groombridge **12** Beta Centauri **14** Epsilon Eridani
nearest: **13** Alpha Centauri
position/motion: **7** azimuth **8** parallax **11** declination
type: **5** dwarf, giant **6** pulsar **7** cluster, neutron **8** variable **9** black hole, collapsed

stare **3** eye **4** gape, gawk, gaze, ogle, peep, peer **5** glare, lower, watch **6** gaping, glower, goggle, ogling, regard **7** staring **8** once-over, scrutiny **9** fixed look **10** inspection, rubberneck

stare at **3** eye **4** ogle **5** watch **6** behold, gaze at, look at, regard **7** inspect, observe **10** scrutinize **11** contemplate

Star Is Born, A
director:
1937 version: **14** William Wellman
1954 version: **11** George Cukor
1976 version: **12** Frank Pierson
cast:
1937 version: **11** Janet Gaynor **13** Adolphe Menjou, Frederic March
1954 version: **10** Jack Carson, James Mason **11** Judy Garland **15** Charles Bickford
1976 version: **9** Gary Busey **11** Oliver Clark **15** Barbra Streisand **17** Kris Kristofferson
Oscar for:
1937 version: **5** story
song:
1954 version: **17** The Man That Got Away

stark **4** bare, bold, cold, grim, pure **5** bleak, blunt, clean, empty, fully, gross, harsh, naked, plain, plumb, quite, sheer, total, utter **6** arrant, barren, chaste, patent, severe, simple, vacant, wholly **7** austere, evident, forlorn, glaring, obvious, staring, utterly **8** absolute, complete, deserted, desolate, entirely, flagrant, forsaken, outright, palpable **9** abandoned, downright, out-and-out, unadorned, unalloyed, veritable **10** absolutely, altogether, completely, consummate **11** conspicuous, unmitigated **12** unmistakable

Stark, Johannes
field: **7** physics
nationality: **6** German
described: **11** Stark Effect **14** dispersed light
awarded: **10** Nobel Prize

Stark, Willie
character in: **14** All the King's Men
author: **6** Warren

starlet **7** actress, ingenue **9** bit player, pinup girl

Starsky and Hutch
character: **5** Hutch (Ken Hutchinson) **7** (Dave) Starsky **9** Huggy Bear **11** (Capt) Harold Dobey
cast: **9** David Soul **13** Antonio Fargas **14** Bernie Hamilton **17** Paul Michael Glaser
car: **10** Ford Torino

start **3** aid, shy **4** dawn, drop, edge, form, gush, jerk, jolt, jump, lead, leap, odds, rush, turn **5** beget, begin, birth, blink, bound, eject, erupt, evict, flush, forge, found, issue, leave, leg up, onset, rouse, set up, shoot, spasm, spurt, wince **6** blench, broach, chance, create, depart, embark, emerge, fall to, father, flinch, ignite, kindle, launch, origin, outset, pop out, propel, recoil, set off, set out, spring, take up, twitch **7** advance, backing, disturb, genesis, make off, opening, push off, scatter, set sail, support, take off, turn out, usher in **8** advocacy, commence, creation, displace, embark on, engender, generate, get going, initiate, organize, priority, set about, set going, touch off **9** advantage, beginning, establish, fabricate, first step, inception, institute, introduce, originate, propagate, undertake, venture on **10** assistance, break forth, bring about, buckle down, burst forth, give rise to, inaugurate, initiation, plunge into, sally forth, venture out **11** break ground, put in motion, set in action **12** commencement, inauguration, introduction **14** set in operation

starting point **5** onset, start **8** zero hour **9** beginning
Latin: **12** terminus a quo

startle **3** jar **4** faze **5** alarm, scare, shake, shock, upset **7** perturb, unnerve **8** disquiet, frighten, surprise, unsettle **9** give a turn **10** discompose, disconcert, intimidate

Star Trek
character: **4** Sulu **5** Uhura **6** Scotty (Engineer Montgomery Scott), (Ensign) Chekov **7** Mr Spock **10** (Captain) James T Kirk, (Yeoman) Janice Rand **12** (Dr) Leonard McCoy **15** (Nurse) Christine Chapel
cast: **11** George Takei, James Doohan **12** Leonard Nimoy, Majel Barrett, Walter Koenig **13** DeForest Kelly **14** William Shatner **15** Grace Lee Whitney, Nichelle Nichols
ship: **10** (USS) Enterprise
aliens: **8** Klingons, Romulans
Spock's planet: **6** Vulcan
pet: **7** tribble

starve **3** yen **4** burn, deny, fast, gasp, long, lust, pine **5** crave, raven, yearn **6** aspire, cut off, famish, hunger, refuse, thirst **7** deprive **8** be hungry, go hungry, languish

Star Wars
director: 11 George Lucas
cast: 10 Kenny Baker, Mark Hamill (Luke Skywalker) **12** Alec Guinness, Carrie Fisher (Princess Leia), Harrison Ford (Han Solo), Peter Cushing **14** Anthony Daniels
voice of Darth Vader: **14** James Earl Jones
score: 12 John Williams
Oscar for: 5 score
sequel: 15 Return of the Jedi **20** The Empire Strikes Back

stasimon 9 choral ode
literally: 8 standing

state 3 put **4** form, land, mind, mode, mood, pass, pomp **5** guise, offer, phase, realm, shape, stage **6** aspect, luxury, morale, nation, people, plight, recite, relate, report, ritual, status **7** comfort, country, declare, explain, expound, express, kingdom, narrate, posture, present, recount, spirits **8** attitude, ceremony, describe, dominion, monarchy, official, position, propound, republic, set forth **9** condition, elucidate, formality, full dress, high style, situation, structure **10** ceremonial, government **11** body politic, frame of mind, predicament, state of mind **12** commonwealth, constitution, governmental, principality **13** circumstances

state abbreviations *see box*

state admittance *see box*

state capitals *see box*

State Fair
author: 9 Phil Stong

state in detail 7 explain, expound **8** describe, spell out **9** explicate **16** give a full account

stateliness 7 dignity, majesty **10** augustness

stately 5 grand, lofty, noble, proud, regal, royal **6** august, formal, lordly **7** awesome, elegant, eminent **8** glorious, imperial, imposing, majestic **9** dignified, grandiose **10** ceremonial, impressive **11** magnificent

statement 3 tab **4** bill **5** check, claim, count, tally **6** avowal, charge, record, remark, report, speech **7** account, comment, invoice, mention, recital **8** relation, sentence **9** assertion, manifesto, reckoning, testimony, utterance, valuation **10** accounting, allegation, communique, exposition, profession, recitation **11** declaration, delineation, explanation, observation **12** announcement, balance sheet **13** pronouncement, specification

state abbreviations
Alabama: 2 AL **3** Ala
Alaska: 2 AK **4** Alas
Arizona: 2 AZ **4** Ariz
Arkansas: 2 AR **3** Ark
California: 2 CA **3** Cal **5** Calif
Colorado: 2 CO **4** Colo
Connecticut: 2 CT **4** Conn
Delaware: 2 DE **3** Del
Florida: 2 FL **3** Fla
Georgia: 2 GA
Hawaii: 2 HI
Idaho: 2 ID **3** Ida
Illinois: 2 IL **3** Ill
Indiana: 2 IN **3** Ind
Iowa: 2 IA
Kansas: 2 KS **4** Kans
Kentucky: 2 KY
Louisiana: 2 LA
Maine: 2 ME
Maryland: 2 MD
Massachusetts: 2 MA **4** Mass
Michigan: 2 MI **4** Mich
Minnesota: 2 MN **4** Minn
Mississippi: 2 MS **4** Miss
Missouri: 2 MO
Montana: 2 MT
Nebraska: 2 NE **4** Nebr
Nevada: 2 NV **3** Nev
New Hampshire: 2 NH
New Jersey: 2 NJ
New Mexico: 2 NM **4** N Mex
New York: 2 NY
North Carolina: 2 NC **4** N Car
North Dakota: 2 ND **4** N Dak
Ohio: 2 OH
Oklahoma: 2 OK **4** Okla
Oregon: 2 OR **4** Oreg
Pennsylvania: 2 PA **4** Penn **5** Penna
Rhode Island: 2 RI
South Carolina: 2 SC
South Dakota: 2 SD **4** S Dak
Tennessee: 2 TN **4** Tenn
Texas: 2 TX **3** Tex
Utah: 2 UT
Vermont: 2 VT
Virginia: 2 VA
Washington: 2 WA **4** Wash
West Virginia: 2 WV **3** W Va
Wisconsin: 2 WI **3** Wis
Wyoming: 2 WY **3** Wyo

state admittance
first: 8 Delaware
second: 12 Pennsylvania
third: 9 New Jersey
fourth: 7 Georgia
fifth: 11 Connecticut
sixth: 13 Massachusetts
seventh: 8 Maryland
eighth: 13 South Carolina
ninth: 12 New Hampshire
tenth: 8 Virginia
eleventh: 7 New York
twelfth: 13 North Carolina
thirteenth: 11 Rhode Island
fourteenth: 7 Vermont
fifteenth: 8 Kentucky
sixteenth: 9 Tennessee
seventeenth: 4 Ohio
eighteenth: 9 Louisiana
nineteenth: 7 Indiana
twentieth: 11 Mississippi
twenty-first: 8 Illinois
twenty-second: 7 Alabama
twenty-third: 5 Maine
twenty-fourth: 8 Missouri
twenty-fifth: 8 Arkansas
twenty-sixth: 8 Michigan
twenty-seventh: 7 Florida
twenty-eighth: 5 Texas
twenty-ninth: 4 Iowa
thirtieth: 9 Wisconsin
thirty-first: 10 California
thirty-second: 9 Minnesota
thirty-third: 6 Oregon
thirty-fourth: 6 Kansas
thirty-fifth: 12 West Virginia
thirty-sixth: 6 Nevada
thirty-seventh: 8 Nebraska
thirty-eighth: 8 Colorado
thirty-ninth/fortieth: 11 North Dakota, South Dakota
forty-first: 7 Montana
forty-second: 10 Washington
forty-third: 5 Idaho
forty-fourth: 7 Wyoming
forty-fifth: 4 Utah
forty-sixth: 8 Oklahoma
forty-seventh: 9 New Mexico
forty-eighth: 7 Arizona
forty-ninth: 6 Alaska
fiftieth: 6 Hawaii

state capitals
Alabama: 10 Montgomery
Alaska: 6 Juneau
Arizona: 7 Phoenix
Arkansas: 10 Little Rock
California: 10 Sacramento
Colorado: 6 Denver
Connecticut: 8 Hartford
Delaware: 5 Dover
Florida: 11 Tallahassee
Georgia: 7 Atlanta
Hawaii: 8 Honolulu
Idaho: 5 Boise
Illinois: 11 Springfield
Indiana: 12 Indianapolis
Iowa: 9 Des Moines
Kansas: 6 Topeka
Kentucky: 9 Frankfort
Louisiana: 10 Baton Rouge
Maine: 7 Augusta
Maryland: 9 Annapolis
Massachusetts: 6 Boston
Michigan: 7 Lansing
Minnesota: 6 St Paul
Mississippi: 7 Jackson
Missouri: 13 Jefferson City
Montana: 6 Helena
Nebraska: 7 Lincoln
Nevada: 10 Carson City
New Hampshire: 7 Concord
New Jersey: 7 Trenton
New Mexico: 7 Santa Fe
New York: 6 Albany
North Carolina: 7 Raleigh
North Dakota: 8 Bismarck
Ohio: 8 Columbus
Oklahoma: 12 Oklahoma City
Oregon: 5 Salem
Pennsylvania: 10 Harrisburg
Rhode Island: 10 Providence
South Carolina: 8 Columbia
South Dakota: 6 Pierre
Tennessee: 9 Nashville
Texas: 6 Austin
Utah: 12 Salt Lake City
Vermont: 10 Montpelier
Virginia: 8 Richmond
Washington: 7 Olympia
West Virginia: 10 Charleston
Wisconsin: 7 Madison
Wyoming: 8 Cheyenne

state of affairs 5 state **6** status **9** condition, situation **13** circumstances

State of the Union
director: 10 Frank Capra
cast: 10 Van Johnson **12** Spencer Tracy **13** Adolphe Menjou **14** Angela Lansbury **16** Katharine Hepburn

stateroom 5 cabin **8** quarters **11** compartment

statesman 8 diplomat **15** political leader

statesmanship 9 diplomacy **19** political leadership

static 5 fixed, inert, still **8** immobile, inactive, stagnant, unmoving **9** crackling, suspended **10** changeless, motionless, stationary, unchanging **12** interference

station 4 post, rank, site, spot, stop **5** caste, class, depot, grade, level, place **6** assign, degree, locate, sphere, status **7** footing, install **8** ensconce, facility, location, position, prestige, terminal, terminus **9** condition, firehouse, placement **10** dispensary, guardhouse, importance **11** emplacement, whistle-stop **12** headquarters

stationary 4 even, firm **5** fixed, inert **6** intact, moored, stable, steady **7** riveted, uniform **8** constant, immobile, standing **9** dead-still, immovable, immutable, unchanged, unvarying **10** motionless, stock-still, transfixed **11** not changing, undeviating **12** unchangeable **13** standing still

Statius
author of: 6 Silvae **10** The Thebaid **12** The Achilleid

statue 8 monument **9** sculpture **14** representation

statuesque 5 regal **7** stately **8** majestic **9** dignified

stature 4 rank, size **5** place **6** height, regard **8** eminence, position, prestige, standing, tallness **9** elevation **10** importance, prominence, reputation **11** distinction

status 4 rank **5** caste, class, grade, place, state **6** degree **7** caliber, footing, station **8** eminence, position, prestige, standing **9** condition, situation **10** estimation **11** distinction

statute 3 law **7** precept **9** prescript

statute law
Latin: 10 lex scripta

staunch, stanch 3 dam **4** firm, stem, true **5** check, loyal, solid, sound, stout **6** impede, rugged, steady, strong, sturdy **7** contain, zealous **8** constant, faithful, hold back, obstruct, resolute, stalwart **9** steadfast, well-built **10** watertight **11** substantial

stave off 7 beat off, fend off, keep off, ward off **9** keep at bay

stay 3 aim, guy, rib, rod **4** bunk, curb, foil, halt, live, pole, prop, rest, room, stem, stop **5** abide, block, brace, check, delay, dwell, lodge, quell, shore, stick, tarry, visit **6** endure, keep in, linger, rein in, remain, reside, splint, stifle, thwart **7** carry on, hold out, holiday, last out, persist, sojourn, support, ward off **8** abeyance, buttress, continue, hold back, mainstay, postpone, reprieve, restrain, standard, stopover, suppress, vacation, withhold **9** deferment, frustrate, persevere, staunchion **10** hang around, see through, suspension **12** postponement, reinforcement

stay put 4 stay **6** remain **8** stand pat

St Clare, Eva
character in: 14 Uncle Tom's Cabin
author: 5 Stowe

steadfast 4 keen, rapt **5** fixed **6** direct, intent, steady **8** resolute **9** attentive, obstinate, tenacious, undaunted **10** deep-rooted, deep-seated, inflexible, unchanging, unflagging, unwavering, unyielding **11** indomitable, persevering, unalterable, undeviating, unfaltering, unflinching **12** intransigent, single-minded, unchangeable, undistracted **14** uncompromising

steadfastness 8 tenacity **10** resolution **11** persistence **12** perseverance, resoluteness **13** determination

Steadfast Tin Soldier, The
author: 21 Hans Christian Andersen

steadiness 4 care **5** poise **6** aplomb **8** calmness, coolness, evenness, firmness **9** composure, sangfroid, stability **10** equanimity, resolution **11** carefulness, persistence, self-control, tranquility **12** resoluteness, tranquillity **13** dependability, steadfastness **14** presence of mind, self-possession **16** imperturbability

steady 4 even, firm, sure **5** sober **6** secure, stable **7** balance, careful, devoted, regular, serious, staunch **8** constant, faithful, frequent, habitual, hold fast, reliable, resolute, unending, untiring **9** ceaseless, confirmed, dedicated, immovable, incessant, stabilize, steadfast, tenacious, unceasing **10** continuing, continuous, coolheaded, deliberate, dependable, methodical, persistent, unflagging, unwavering **11** levelheaded, persevering, substantial, undeviating, unfaltering, unremitting **12** single-minded **13** conscientious

steal 3 buy, cop **4** copy, crib, flit, flow, lift, slip, take **5** creep, drift, filch, glide, pinch, skulk, slide, slink, sneak, swipe, usurp **6** borrow, elapse, escape, extort, filter, pilfer, pocket, rip off, snatch, snitch, thieve **7** bargain, defraud, diffuse, good buy, imitate, purloin, swindle **8** abstract, embezzle, good deal, liberate **10** burglarize, plagiarize **11** abscond with, appropriate, make off with **14** misappropriate

steal away 3 fly **4** bolt, flee, skip **5** elope **6** escape **7** get away, make off, slip out **8** creep off, slip away, sneak off **9** break free, tiptoe out **10** break loose, fly the coop **12** make a getaway

stealth 7 secrecy, slyness **10** covertness, sneakiness, subterfuge **11** furtiveness **12** stealthiness **13** secretiveness **15** unobtrusiveness **17** surreptitiousness

stealthy 3 sly **5** shady **6** covert, shifty, sneaky **7** devious, furtive **8** slippery, sneaking **9** secretive, underhand **11** clandestine, underhanded **12** hugger-mugger **13** surreptitious

steamboat
invented by: 6 Fulton **9** Symington

steamed up 5 angry, het up, irate **6** raging **7** enraged, furious, riled up **8** heated up, inflamed **10** infuriated **12** mad as a wet hen **14** hot and bothered **17** hot under the collar

steamer 4 boat, clam, ship **5** liner, trunk **10** paddleboat **11** side-wheeler **12** sternwheeler **13** paddle-wheeler

steel 4 dirk, foil, gird **5** blade, brace, knife, nerve, saber, sword **6** dagger, rapier **7** bayonet, cutlass, fortify, machete **8** falchion, scimitar **10** broadsword

process invented by: 8 Bessemer

Steele, Sir Richard
pseudonym: 16 Isaac Bickerstaff
author of: 9 The Tatler (with Joseph Addison) **10** The Funeral **12** The Spectator (with Joseph Addison) **13** The Lying Lover **16** The Tender Husband **18** The Conscious Lovers

steely 4 hard **5** stony **6** flinty **9** heartless, unfeeling **10** forbidding **11** cold-hearted

Steen, Jan
born: 6 Leiden, Leyden **14** The Netherlands
artwork: 7 Cabaret **11** The Egg Dance **12** Merry Company **14** Garden of the Inn **15** The Doctor's Visit, The Rhetoricians **16** The Morning Toilet **17** The Skittle Players **18** The World Topsy-Turvy, Young Woman Dressing

Steenburgen, Mary
roles: 10 Cross Creek **13** Time After Time

steep 4 brew, bury, fill, soak **5** imbue, sharp, sheer, souse **6** abrupt, drench, engulf, infuse, plunge **7** immerse, pervade, suffuse **8** marinate, saturate, submerge **10** impregnate **11** precipitous

steeple 5 spire, tower **6** belfry **9** campanile

steer 3 aim, lay, run **4** bear, head, lead, make, sail **5** coach, guide, pilot **6** direct, govern, manage **7** conduct, proceed **8** navigate **9** supervise

steer clear of 4 shun **5** avert, avoid, dodge, evade, forgo, skirt **6** escape, eschew, forego **8** sidestep **9** keep shy of **11** abstain from, refrain from **16** give a wide berth to

Steerforth
character in: 16 David Copperfield
author: 7 Dickens

Steffens, Lincoln
author of: 19 The Shame of the Cities

Stegosaurus
type: 8 dinosaur **10** ornithopod
location: 12 North America
period: 8 Jurassic
characteristic: 6 plated

Steiger, Rod
real name: 20 Rodney Stephen Steiger
born: 13 Westhampton NY
wife: 11 Claire Bloom
roles: 8 Waterloo **13** The Longest Day, The Pawnbroker, W C Fields and Me **15** On the Waterfront **19** In the Heat of the Night (Oscar)

Stein, Clarence S
architect of: 13 Temple Emanu-El (NYC)

Stein, Gertrude
author of: 10 Three Lives **13** Tender Buttons **20** The Making of Americans **27** Autobiography of Alice B Toklas
coined phrase: 14 lost generation

Steinbeck, John
author of: 8 The Pearl **10** Cannery Row, East of Eden, The Red Pony **12** Of Mice and Men, Tortilla Flat **15** In Dubious Battle **16** The Grapes of Wrath **18** Travels with Charley **24** The Winter of Our Discontent

Steinmetz, Charles P
field: 11 engineering
developed: 2 AC **18** alternating current

Stella, Frank
born: 8 Malden MA
artwork: 4 Jill **5** Itata **14** Jasper's Dilemma **15** Guadalupe Island

Stella, Joseph
born: 5 Italy **6** Naples
artwork: 8 Full Moon (Barbados) **9** Sunflower, The Bridge **14** Brooklyn Bridge **16** Pittsburgh Winter **18** New York Interpreted **28** Battle of the Lights Coney Island

Stella Dallas
director: 9 King Vidor
cast: 9 John Boles **11** Anne Shirley **12** Barbara O'Neil **15** Barbara Stanwyck

stellar 6 astral, starry **7** leading **8** starring **9** brilliant, celestial, principal **11** outstanding

stem 3 dam **4** buck, cane, come, curb, grow, halt, rise, stay, stop **5** arise, block, check, deter, ensue, issue, quell, shank, shoot, speak, spire, stalk, stall, stock, trunk **6** arrest, derive, hinder, impede, oppose, resist, result, retard, spring, stanch, thwart **7** counter, pedicel, petiole, prevent, proceed, tendril **8** hold back, obstruct, peduncle, restrain, surmount **9** leafstalk, originate, withstand

stem from 5 arise, begin, start **6** derive **9** originate

stench **4** odor, reek **5** fetor, stink **8** bad smell **9** fetidness

Stendhal (Henri Marie Beyle)
author of: **17** The Red and the Black **18** Memoirs of an Egotist **22** The Charterhouse of Parma

Stengel, Charles Dillon
nickname: **5** Casey
sport: **8** baseball
position: **7** manager
team: **11** New York Mets **14** New York Yankees **15** Brooklyn Dodgers

Stentor
vocation: **6** herald
characteristic: **10** loud-voiced
voice as loud as: **8** fifty men

step **3** act **4** clip, gait, move, pace, rank, rung, span, walk **5** notch, phase, point, riser, stage, stair, strut, track, tramp, tread **6** action, degree, hobble, period, remove, stride **7** footing, measure, process, shamble, shuffle, swagger, trample **8** footfall, foothold, maneuver, purchase **9** footprint, gradation, procedure **10** proceeding

step down **4** quit **5** leave **6** resign, retire

Stephens, James
author of: **7** Deirdre **14** The Crock of Gold **21** The Charwoman's Daughter

Stephenson, George and Robert
nationality: **7** English
developed: **15** steam locomotive

Steppenwolf
author: **12** Hermann Hesse
character: **5** Maria, Pablo **7** Hermine **11** Harry Haller

Steps
author: **13** Jerzy Kosinski

step up **4** spur **6** come up **7** quicken, speed up **8** approach, escalate, expedite, increase **9** intensify **10** accelerate

stereotype **4** type **6** cliche **7** formula **8** typecast **10** categorize, pigeonhole **13** preconception

stereotyped **5** stale, trite **9** hackneyed **11** commonplace **13** unimaginative

sterile **4** bare, pure, vain **5** empty **6** barren, fallow, futile **7** aseptic, useless **8** abortive, bootless, impotent, infecund, sanitary **9** childless, fruitless, infertile, worthless **10** antiseptic, profitless, sterilized, unavailing, unfruitful, uninfected **11** disinfected, ineffective, ineffectual, unrewarding **12** unproductive, unprofitable **13** free from germs **14** uncontaminated

sterilize **6** purify **9** autoclave, disinfect **13** decontaminate

sterling **4** pure, true **5** noble **6** silver, superb, worthy **7** genuine, perfect **8** flawless, superior **9** admirable, estimable, first-rate, honorable **10** invaluable **11** meritorious, superlative

stern **4** cold, grim, hard **5** cruel, grave, harsh, rigid, sharp, stiff **6** brutal, gloomy, severe, somber, strict, unkind **7** austere, serious **8** coercive, despotic, frowning, pitiless, rigorous, ruthless, ungentle **9** reproving, stringent, unfeeling **10** forbidding, implacable, ironfisted, ironhanded, tyrannical, unmerciful **11** admonishing, cold-blooded, reproachful **12** unreasonable **13** unsympathetic **14** unapproachable

Stern (of Argo)
constellation of: **6** Puppis

Sterne, Laurence
author of: **14** Tristram Shandy **19** A Sentimental Journey
character: **9** Uncle Toby **12** Parson Yorick, Walter Shandy

sternum
bone of: **6** breast

Sterope
also: **8** Asterope
member of: **8** Pleiades
son: **8** Oenomaus

Steve Canyon
creator: **12** Milton Caniff
character: **7** Cheetah **9** Madam Lynx **10** Doe Redwood, Miss Mizzou **11** Savannah Gay **13** Copper Calhoun **14** Herself Muldoon **17** Princess Sun Flower
wife: **6** Summer
ward/cousin: **12** Poteet Canyon
Summer's son: **13** Leighton Olson

Stevens, George
director of: **5** Giant (Oscar), Shane **8** Gunga Din **9** Swing Time **13** I Remember Mama, Penny Serenade **14** A Place in the Sun (Oscar), Woman of the Year **16** The Talk of the Town **19** The Diary of Anne Frank

Stevens, Gowan
character in: **9** Sanctuary
author: **8** Faulkner

Stevens, James
author of: **10** Paul Bunyan

Stevens, Ruby
real name of: **15** Barbara Stanwyck

Stevens, Wallace
author of: **7** The Rock **9** Harmonium **13** Sunday Morning **17** Transport to Summer **23** Peter Quince at the Clavier, The Idea of Order at Key West, The Man with the Blue Guitar

Stevenson, Robert
director of: **8** Jane Eyre **10** Back Street **11** Mary Poppins

Stevenson, Robert Louis
author of: **9** Kidnapped **13** The Black Arrow **14** Treasure Island **18** Travels with a Donkey **21** A Child's Garden of Verses, Doctor Jekyll and Mr Hyde, The Master of Ballantrae

St Evremond, Marquis
character in: **16** A Tale of Two Cities
author: **7** Dickens

stew **4** fret, fume, fuss **5** chafe, gripe, steep, tizzy, worry **6** grouse, ragout, seethe, simmer **7** agonize, fluster, flutter, grumble, mixture **10** miscellany

steward **5** agent, proxy **6** deputy, factor, waiter **7** bailiff, manager, trustee **8** executor, overseer **10** controller, supervisor **11** comptroller **13** administrator **14** representative, ship's attendant **15** flight attendant

Stewart, James
born: **9** Indiana PA
roles: **4** Rope **6** Harvey **7** Vertigo **10** Rear Window, Shenandoah **11** Elwood P Dowd **14** Cheyenne Autumn **16** Anatomy of a Murder, Destry Rides Again, The Stratton Story **17** Bell Book and Candle, It's a Wonderful Life **18** It's a Wonderful World, The Spirit of St Louis **19** The Glenn Miller Story **20** The Philadelphia Story (Oscar), You Can't Take It with You **22** The Greatest Show on Earth **23** Mr Smith Goes to Washington

Stewart, Mary
real name: **22** Florence Rainbow Stewart
author of: **11** Crystal Cave **14** The Hollow Hills **15** The Moon-Spinners **16** My Brother Michael, The Ga-

briel Hounds **18** Airs Above the Ground, The Last Enchantment

St George's
capital of: 7 Grenada

Sthenelaus
vocation: 7 warrior
killed by: 9 Patroclus

Sthenele
father: 7 Acastus
son: 9 Patroclus

Sthenelus
king of: 7 Mycenae
father: 5 Actor **7** Perseus
mother: 9 Andromeda
brother: 6 Mestor **9** Electryon
son: 10 Eurystheus
daughter: 6 Medusa **7** Alcyone
member of: 7 Epigoni
companion of: 8 Hercules

Sthenius
epithet of: 4 Zeus
means: 6 strong

Stheno
member of: 7 Gorgons

Stichius
origin: 8 Athenian
rank: 7 captain
killed by: 6 Hector

stick 3 bar, bat, cue, dig, fix, jab, pin, put, rod, set **4** balk, bind, cane, club, curb, fuse, glue, hold, join, last, mire, nail, pink, poke, pole, seal, snag, stab, stop, tack, twig, wand, weld **5** abide, affix, baton, billy, block, catch, check, fagot, leave, lodge, paste, place, plant, prick, punch, shift, snarl, spear, spike, staff, stall, stake, stand, stave, stump **6** adhere, attach, boggle, branch, burden, cement, cudgel, detain, endure, fasten, hamper, hinder, hog-tie, impede, insert, pierce, puzzle, scotch, skewer, stymie, switch, thrust, thwart **7** confuse, crosier, inhibit, perplex, shackle, trammel **8** bewilder, bludgeon, caduceus, continue, obstruct, puncture **9** checkmate, constrain, perforate, truncheon, victimize **10** immobilize, shillelagh

stick fast 4 hold **5** cling, stick **6** adhere, cleave

stickler 3 bug, nut **5** crank, poser **6** enigma, purist, puzzle, riddle, zealot **7** devotee, dilemma, fanatic, mystery, stumper **8** martinet **10** enthusiast, monomaniac

sticks 4 skis **5** bonds, glues, twigs **6** pastes, Podunk **7** adheres, boonies, catches, cements, country **8** kindling **9** backwoods, boondocks, golf clubs, provinces **10** hicksville, hinterland **11** countryside, hinterlands

stick together 4 bind, fuse, glue, hold, join **5** cling, stick, unite **6** cement, cohere

stick-to-itiveness 8 tenacity **9** endurance **10** resolution **11** persistence **12** perseverance, resoluteness **13** determination, tenaciousness

stickum 3 gum **4** glue **5** paste **6** cement **8** adhesive, mucilage **12** rubber cement

stick up for 5 boost **6** defend **7** root for **11** speak well of **17** put in a good word for

stick with 4 stay **5** abide **6** keep at **7** stand by **9** accompany, persevere

sticky 3 wet **4** damp, dank **5** gluey, gooey, gummy, humid, moist, muggy, pasty, tacky **6** clammy, clingy, steamy, sultry, viscid **7** viscous **8** adherent, adhesive, clinging, cohesive, sticking **9** glutinous, tenacious **10** gelatinous **12** mucilaginous

stiff ***see box***

stiff-necked 6 mulish **7** willful **8** contrary, obdurate, stubborn **9** obstinate, pigheaded, unbending **10** bullheaded, refractory, self-willed, unshakable, unyielding **11** intractable **12** intransigent, pertinacious

stiffness 7 tension **8** firmness, rigidity **9** aloofness, formality, tenseness, tightness **10** constraint **11** starchiness

stifle 3 gag **4** curb **5** check, choke **6** muffle, subdue **7** garrote, inhibit, repress, smother, squelch, swelter **8** keep back, restrain, strangle, suppress, throttle **9** suffocate **10** asphyxiate

stifling 3 hot **6** stuffy **7** airless **10** overheated

stigma 4 blot, flaw, mark, scar **5** brand, odium, shame, stain, taint **6** smirch, smudge **7** blemish, tarnish **8** disgrace, dishonor **11** mark of shame **12** besmirchment

stigmatize 5 brand, smear **6** debase, defame, smirch **7** villify **9** discredit, disparage

still 4 calm, hush **5** inert, quiet **6** at rest, hushed, pacify, settle, silent **7** appease, assuage, gratify, put down, repress, silence, turn off **8** immobile, overcome, restrain, suppress, unmoving **9** noiseless, soundless **10** motionless, put an end to, stationary, unstirring

stillness 4 calm, hush **5** quiet **6** repose **7** silence **8** calmness, inaction, quietude **9** composure **10** immobility, inactivity, quiescence **11** tranquility **12** tranquillity

Stillness at Appomattox, A
author: 11 Bruce Catton

stilted 4 cold, prim **5** rigid, stiff **6** forced, formal, stuffy, wooden **7** awkward, labored, pompous, starchy, studied, uptight **8** mannered, priggish, starched **9** graceless, unnatural **10** artificial **11** ceremonious, constrained

stiff 4 body, cold, cool, firm, grim, hard, high, iron, keen, prim, sore, taut **5** aloof, awful, brave, brisk, crisp, cruel, dense, fixed, gusty, harsh, heavy, rigid, sharp, smart, solid, steep, stern, tense, thick, tight, tough, undue **6** bitter, brutal, chilly, clumsy, corpse, dogged, forced, formal, raging, severe, steady, steely, strong, uneasy, viscid, wooden **7** austere, awkward, cadaver, clotted, decided, distant, drastic, extreme, fearful, intense, jellied, labored, precise, remains, settled, starchy, stately, staunch, steeled, stilted, uptight, valiant, violent, viscous **8** affected, constant, dead body, exacting, forceful, grievous, mannered, pitiless, pounding, powerful, resolute, resolved, rigorous, ruthless, spanking, stubborn, ungainly, unlimber, unshaken, vigorous **9** difficult, draconian, excessive, graceless, inelastic, inelegant, laborious, merciless, obstinate, resistant, steadfast, stringent, tenacious, unnatural **10** artificial, courageous, determined, exorbitant, formidable, gelatinous, immoderate, inflexible, inordinate, persistent, solidified, unswerving, unyielding **11** ceremonious, constrained, extravagant, indomitable, straitlaced, unfaltering, unflinching, unwarranted **12** strong-willed, unreasonable **14** uncompromising

Stilwell, Joseph W
nickname: **10** Vinegar Joe
served in: **3** WWI **4** WWII
chief of staff for: **13** Chiang Kai-shek
driven out of: **5** Burma

stimulant **5** tonic, upper **6** bracer **8** excitant **9** energizer

stimulate **3** fan **4** spur, stir, wake **5** alert, rouse **6** arouse, awaken, excite, incite, prompt, vivify **7** actuate, animate, inflame, inspire, quicken, sharpen **8** activate, enkindle, initiate, inspirit

stimulating **5** tonic **7** piquing **8** arousing, exciting, spurring, stirring, whetting **9** animating, provoking **10** energizing, refreshing **11** interesting, provocative

stimulus **4** goad, spur, whet **5** tonic **6** bracer, fillip, motive **7** impetus **8** excitant **9** activator, energizer, incentive, quickener, stimulant **10** incitement, inducement **11** provocation **13** encouragement

sting **3** cut, nip, rub, vex **4** ache, barb, bite, blow, burn, fire, gall, gnaw, goad, grip, hurt, itch, lash, move, pain, prod, rack, rasp, rile, sore, spur, stab, whip **5** anger, chafe, cross, egg on, grate, impel, pinch, pique, prick, shake, shock, smart, venom, wince, wound **6** arouse, awaken, excite, harrow, incite, insult, kindle, madden, nettle, offend, pierce, prompt, propel, stir up, tingle, twinge **7** actuate, agonize, disturb, incense, inflame, prickle, provoke, quicken, scourge, stinger, torment, torture **8** irritate, motivate, vexation **9** infuriate, instigate, penetrate **10** affliction, irritation

Sting, The
director: **13** George Roy Hill
cast: **10** Paul Newman, Ray Walston, Robert Shaw **13** Eileen Brennan, Robert Redford **14** Charles Durning
score: **11** Scott Joplin
Oscar for: **7** picture **8** director

stinginess **6** penury **9** parsimony **11** miserliness **13** niggardliness, penny-pinching **15** tight-fistedness

stinging **4** acid **5** harsh, sharp **6** biting, bitter **7** burning, caustic, cutting, pungent **8** piercing **9** sarcastic, satirical **10** astringent

stingy **4** lean, mean, thin **5** close, scant, small, tight **6** frugal, meager, modest, paltry, scanty, skimpy, sparse **7** miserly, scrimpy, slender, sparing **8** piddling, stinting **9** illiberal, niggardly, penurious **10** inadequate, ungenerous **11** closefisted, tightfisted **12** cheeseparing, insufficient, parsimonious **13** penny-pinching

stink **4** odor, reek **5** fetor **6** stench **8** bad smell **17** smell to high heaven

stint **3** job **4** curb, duty, part, save, task, term, turn **5** check, chore, limit, quota, shift **6** reduce, scrimp **8** hold back, restrain, restrict, withhold **9** constrain, cut down on, economize **10** assignment, engagement **12** circumscribe, pinch pennies

stipend **5** grant, wages **6** income, salary **7** pension **8** fixed pay **9** allowance, emolument **10** honorarium, recompense **11** scholarship **12** compensation, remuneration

stipulate **4** cite, name **5** agree, allow, grant, state **6** assure, insure, pledge **7** promise, provide, specify, warrant **8** indicate, set forth **9** designate, guarantee

stipulation **4** term **7** proviso **9** condition **10** limitation **11** requirement, restriction

stipulative **7** limited **9** qualified, tentative **10** contingent, restricted **11** conditional, provisional **16** with reservations

stir **3** act, mix **4** beat, fire, goad, jolt, move, prod, rush, spur, to-do, whip **5** blend, rouse, shake, sough, start **6** arouse, awaken, bustle, commix, excite, flurry, hasten, hustle, kindle, mingle, mixing, moving, pother, quiver, rustle, shiver, tumult, twitch, uproar, vivify, work up **7** agitate, animate, enflame, flutter, inspire, provoke, quicken, scamper **8** energize, inspirit, intermix, mingling, movement, prodding, rustling, scramble, stirring **9** agitation, commingle, commotion, electrify, stimulate **10** get a move on, step lively **11** set in motion **12** exert oneself, make an effort

Stiria
also: **8** Stiritis
epithet of: **7** Demeter

Stiritis *see* **6** Stiria

stirred up **5** riled, upset **7** aroused, excited, kindled, ruffled **8** agitated, inflamed **9** disturbed **10** stimulated

stirring **5** astir, awake **6** moving **7** rousing **8** electric, exalting, exciting, in motion, spirited **9** inspiring, thrilling **10** up and about **11** galvanizing, stimulating **12** electrifying

stir up **5** upset **6** arouse, awaken, excite, kindle, ruffle **7** agitate, disturb **9** call forth, stimulate **10** antagonize

stir vigorously **3** mix **4** beat, whip **7** agitate

stitch **3** bit, jot, sew **4** ache, iota, kink, mend, pain, pang, seam, tack **5** baste, cramp, crick, piece, scrap, shoot, shred **6** suture, tingle, twinge, twitch **7** article, garment **8** particle **9** embroider **12** charley horse

St John's
capital of: **17** Antigua and Barbuda

St Louis
baseball team: **9** Cardinals
football team: **9** Cardinals
founded by: **13** Pierre Laclede
hockey team: **5** Blues
landmark: **11** Gateway Arch
newspaper: **12** Post-Dispatch
river: **11** Mississippi
site of: **10** Exposition (1904)
university: **10** Washington

stock **4** butt, clan, form, fund, haft, herd, hold, kind, line, pull, race, root, type **5** array, basic, birth, blood, breed, broth, cache, caste, equip, goods, grasp, hoard, house, offer, shaft, store, tribe, wares **6** cattle, family, fit out, formal, handle, origin, people, shares, source, staple, strain, supply **7** appoint, capital, descent, dynasty, furnish, lineage, provide, regular, reserve, routine **8** accoutre, ancestry, bouillon, heredity, pedigree, pro forma, quantity, standard **9** forebears, genealogy, inventory, livestock, ownership, parentage, provision, reservoir, selection **10** assortment, background, extraction, family tree, investment **11** merchandise, nationality, progeniture **12** accumulation **13** capital shares

Stockhausen, Karlheinz
born: **7** Germany, Modrath
composer of: **5** Cycle, Tempi **6** Groups, Hymnen, Mantra, Zyklus **7** Anthems, Gruppen, Momente **8** Attuning, Gold Dust, Kontakte, Stimmung **9** Goldstaub, Zeitmasze **10** Procession, Prozession **12** Kontrapunkte **13** Klavierstucke **16** From

the Seven Days **17** Aus den Sieben Tagen

Stockholm
nickname: **16** Venice of the North
capital of: **6** Sweden
sea: **6** Baltic
lake: **7** Malaren
section: **8** Norrmalm **9** Sodermalm **11** Gamla Staden
landmark: **7** Skansen **8** City Hall **11** Great Church
site of: **10** Nobel Prize

stockpile **5** cache, hoard, stock, store **10** accumulate

stocky **5** dumpy, husky, pudgy, solid, squat, stout **6** blocky, chunky, stubby, stumpy, sturdy **8** thickset

Stoddard, Eleanor
character in: **3** USA
author: **9** Dos Passos

stodgy **4** dull, flat **5** dated, heavy, lumpy, passe, staid, thick **6** boring, clumsy, dreary, narrow, prolix, stuffy **7** humdrum, pompous, prosaic, serious, starchy, tedious **8** lifeless, pedantic, tiresome **9** laborious, lumbering, wearisome **10** antiquated, inflexible, monotonous **12** indigestible, old-fashioned **13** uninteresting

stoic **4** calm **8** detached, fatalist, quietist, tranquil **9** impassive, unruffled **11** philosophic **13** dispassionate, imperturbable, unimpassioned

stoicism **8** fatalism **9** fortitude **11** impassivity, tranquility **12** tranquillity **16** imperturbability

stole **3** fur **4** cape, robe, took, wrap **5** crept, orary, scarf **6** swiped **7** filched, pinched, sneaked, tiptoed **8** mantilla, pilfered, snatched, vestment **9** embezzled, purloined

stolen **3** hot **5** taken **6** swiped **7** filched, pinched **8** pilfered, snatched **9** embezzled, ill-gotten, purloined

stolid **4** dull **5** dense **6** bovine, obtuse **7** lumpish **8** sluggish **9** apathetic, impassive, lethargic **10** phlegmatic **11** insensitive, unemotional

stolidity **6** apathy **8** lethargy **9** inertness **11** impassivity **12** sluggishness

stomach **3** maw, pot **4** bear, bent, bias, craw, crop, guts, mind, take **5** abide, belly, brook, fancy, humor, stand, taste, tummy **6** desire, endure, hunger, liking, middle, paunch, relish, retain, suffer, temper, thirst **7** abdomen, gizzard, leaning, midriff, swallow **8** affinity, appetite, bear with, keenness, overlook, pass over, pleasure, potbelly, sympathy, tolerate **9** put up with **10** attraction, midsection, partiality, proclivity, propensity **11** breadbasket, countenance, disposition, inclination **12** predilection

stone **3** gem, nut, pip, pit **4** rock, seed **5** bijou, jewel **6** kernel, pebble **9** brilliant **10** throw rocks

Stone, Edward Durell
architect of: **9** US Embassy (New Delhi India) **17** Museum of Modern Art (NYC) **33** Kennedy Center for the Performing Arts (Washington DC)

Stone, Irving
author of: **9** The Origin **11** Lust for Life **12** Those Who Love **17** Sailor on Horseback, The President's Lady **19** Adversary in the House **21** The Agony and the Ecstasy

stoned to death **5** Achan

stonefly
varieties: **5** giant, green **6** spring, winter **8** perlodid **9** roachlike **11** green-winged **12** rolled-winged

stoneware **5** china **7** ceramic, pottery **8** crockery

stony **3** icy **4** cold **5** blank, bumpy, chill, rocky, rough, stern **6** coarse, craggy, flinty, frigid, jagged, marble, pebbly, rugged, severe, steely, stolid, uneven **7** austere, callous, granite, lithoid, stoical **8** concrete, deadened, gravelly, hardened, indurate, obdurate, ossified, pitiless, rocklike, soulless, uncaring **9** bloodless, heartless, merciless, petrified, unfeeling, untouched **10** adamantine, forbidding, fossilized, hard-boiled, inexorable, insensible, unaffected, unyielding **11** coldblooded, coldhearted, hardhearted, indifferent, passionless, unemotional **12** crystallized, unresponsive **13** unsympathetic **14** expressionless

stool **5** bench **7** cricket, hassock, ottoman

stool pigeon **3** rat, spy **4** fink **5** decoy, patsy **6** snitch **7** peacher, stoolie, tattler **8** informer, squealer **10** talebearer, tattletale

stoop **3** bow, sag **4** bend, fall, sink **5** deign, droop, porch, slump, steps, yield **6** resort, slouch, submit **7** concede, descend, succumb **8** doorstep **9** acquiesce **10** condescend **11** entranceway **19** round-shoulderedness

stooped **4** bent **5** bowed **7** deigned, hunched **9** contorted **12** condescended

stop **3** ban, bar, end **4** curb, fill, halt, hold, idle, plug, quit, rest, seal, stay, stem, wait **5** abide, block, brake, break, caulk, cease, check, close, depot, deter, dwell, lapse, lodge, pause, put up, spell, stall, stand, tarry, visit **6** alight, arrest, cut off, desist, draw up, expire, falter, finish, hamper, hiatus, hinder, pull up, recess, rein in, repose, run out, stanch, stop up, thwart **7** close up, halting, layover, occlude, prevent, respite, sojourn, station, suspend **8** abeyance, break off, conclude, cut short, hold back, intermit, interval, leave off, obstruct, pass away, peter out, postpone, preclude, restrain, suppress, surcease, terminal, terminus, wind down **9** cessation, frustrate, interlude, stand fast, terminate **10** desistance, drop anchor, put an end to, standstill, suspension **11** come to a halt, come to an end, destination, discontinue, prohibition, termination **12** intermission, interruption **17** come to a standstill **18** bring to a standstill

stopgap **7** stand-by **9** contrived, emergency, expedient, impromptu, makeshift, temporary, tentative **10** improvised, substitute **11** provisional
Latin: **5** ad hoc **6** pro tem

stop in **4** call **5** visit **6** drop in, look in

stop off **4** call **5** visit **6** drop in, look in, stop by

stoppage **4** halt **5** check, tieup **6** arrest **7** barrier, embargo, staying **8** blockage, checking, clogging, gridlock, obstacle **9** checkmate, hindrance, restraint, stricture **10** disruption, impediment **11** curtailment, obstruction **12** interruption

Stoppard, Tom
author of: **10** Travesties **33** Rosencrantz and Guildenstern Are Dead

stopper **3** lid **4** bung, cock, cork, plug **5** spile

Stopping by Woods on a Snowy Evening
author: **11** Robert Frost

Stop the Music
host: **9** Bert Parks
orchestra: **11** Harry Salter
vocalist: **9** June Valli **11** Jaye P Morgan, Jimmy Blaine **12** Marion Morgan **13** Betty Ann Grove, Estelle Loring

stop up **3** jam **4** clog **5** block, choke **8** obstruct

Storax **12** Biblical tree

store **3** lot **4** fund, hold, host, keep, mart, pack, pile, save, shop **5** amass, array, cache, faith, hoard, lay by, lay in, lay up, stash, stock, trust, value, wares **6** credit, esteem, gather, heap up, legion, market, plenty, regard, riches, scores, supply, volume, wealth **7** deposit, effects, husband, put away, reserve, satiety **8** emporium, lay aside, overflow, plethora, quantity, reliance, richness, salt away, sock away, stow away **9** abundance, inventory, multitude, profusion, provision, reservoir, stockpile **10** accumulate, confidence, cornucopia, dependence, estimation, exuberance, luxuriance **11** copiousness, full measure, prodigality, supermarket **12** accumulation **13** establishment

storehouse **4** bank, silo **5** depot, vault **7** arsenal, granary **8** elevator, magazine, treasury **9** stockroom, warehouse **10** depository, repository

storied **4** epic **6** fabled **8** fabulous **9** legendary

Stories and Texts for Nothing
author: **13** Samuel Beckett

storm **3** ado, row **4** blow, fume, fuss, gale, rage, rant, rave, roar, rush, stir, tear, to-do **5** burst, furor, snarl, stalk, stamp, stomp, tramp **6** assail, attack, charge, clamor, deluge, flurry, hubbub, pother, ruckus, squall, strike, tumult, uproar **7** assault, besiege, bluster, carry on, cyclone, rampage, tempest, tornado, torrent, turmoil, twister, typhoon **8** blizzard, brouhaha, downpour, eruption, fall upon, outbreak, outburst, upheaval **9** agitation, commotion, explosion, fulminate, hurricane, raise hell **10** cloudburst, hullabaloo **11** blow one's top, disturbance **12** blow one's cool, vent one's rage

storm and stress
German: **13** Sturm und Drang
name of 18th century: **16** literary movement

storms
goddess of: **11** Tempestates

storm troopers
German: **14** Sturmabteilung

stormy **4** foul, wild **5** rainy, rough, snowy, windy **6** raging, rugged **7** howling, roaring, squally, violent **8** blustery **9** inclement, turbulent **10** blustering **11** tempestuous

story **3** fib, lie **4** news, plot, tale, word, yarn **5** alibi, fable, piece **6** excuse, legend, report, sketch **7** account, article, parable, romance, tidings, version **8** allegory, anecdote, argument, dispatch, news item, white lie **9** falsehood, narrative, statement, testimony **10** allegation **11** fabrication, information **13** prevarication

Story of a Bad Boy, The
author: **19** Thomas Bailey Aldrich

Story of G I Joe, The
director: **14** William Wellman
cast: **13** Freddie Steele, Robert Mitchum **15** Burgess Meredith (Ernie Pyle)

Story of Louis Pasteur, The
director: **15** William Dieterle
cast: **8** Paul Muni (Pasteur) **11** Anita Louise **19** Josephine Hutchinson
Oscar for: **5** actor (Muni)

stout **3** big, fat, fit **4** able, bold, firm, true **5** brave, bulky, burly, hardy, heavy, hefty, husky, large, obese, plump, pudgy, round, solid, tough, tubby **6** brawny, chubby, daring, fleshy, heroic, mighty, plucky, portly, robust, rotund, rugged, spunky, steady, stocky, strong, sturdy **7** doughty, gallant, staunch, valiant **8** athletic, constant, enduring, faithful, fearless, intrepid, leathery, muscular, resolute, resolved, stalwart, thickset, untiring, valorous, vigorous **9** confident, corpulent, dauntless, steadfast, strapping **10** able-bodied, courageous, determined, inflexible, unshakable, unswerving, unwavering **11** indomitable, lionhearted, unfaltering, unflinching, unshrinking

Stout, Rex
author of: **10** Fer-de-Lance **12** Too Many Cooks **16** If Death Ever Slept
character: **5** Fritz **9** Nero Wolfe **13** Archie Goodwin

stouthearted **4** bold **5** brave, gutsy, hardy **6** heroic, plucky, spunky **7** valiant **8** fearless, intrepid, resolute, spirited, stalwart, unafraid, valorous **9** dauntless, undaunted **10** courageous **11** indomitable, lionhearted, unblenching, unflinching

stoutheartedness **4** grit, guts, sand **5** nerve, pluck, spunk, valor **6** daring, mettle **7** bravery, courage **8** boldness **12** fearlessness **13** dauntlessness

stoutness
French: **10** embonpoint

stow **3** jam, put, set **4** cram, load, pack, tuck **5** cache, crowd, place, stash, store, stuff, wedge **7** deposit, squeeze **8** ensconce, salt away

Stowe, Harriet Beecher
author of: **12** Oldtown Folks **14** Uncle Tom's Cabin

Strachey, Lytton
author of: **13** Queen Victoria **17** Elizabeth and Essex, Eminent Victorians
member of: **15** Bloomsbury Group

strafe **7** bombard **8** fire upon **10** machine-gun

straggle **4** rove **5** drift, stray **6** sprawl, wander **7** deviate, meander **8** divagate

straight **4** even, neat, tidy, true **5** clear, frank, right, solid, sound **6** candid, direct, evenly, honest, square, unbent **7** aligned, erectly, in order, orderly, upright **8** accurate, adjusted, arranged, directly, on a level, reliable, squarely, truthful, unbroken **9** ceaseless, forthwith, incessant, instantly, not curved, shipshape, sorted out, sustained, veracious **10** aboveboard, continuous, forthright, four-square, methodical, persistent, straightly, successive, unrelieved, unswerving, unwavering **11** consecutive, coordinated, immediately, trustworthy, undeviating **13** uninterrupted

straighten **4** tidy **5** align **6** adjust, neaten, unbend **7** even out **8** level out, square up **9** put in line **10** put in order, stand erect

straightening **7** tidying **9** adjusting, alignment, evening up, unbending **10** evening out **11** leveling out **13** putting in line **14** putting in order

straighten out **6** unbend **7** realign **8** redirect **10** discipline

straighten up **4** tidy **5** align,

clean, order **6** neaten, tidy up **7** arrange, stand up **8** organize

straightforward 4 open **5** blunt, frank **6** candid, direct, honest, square **7** ethical, upright **8** straight **9** guileless, honorable **10** aboveboard, creditable, forthright, scrupulous **11** plainspoken, trustworthy

straightforwardness 6 candor **7** honesty **12** truthfulness **14** forthrightness

straight from the shoulder 4 open **5** frank **6** candid, direct, openly **7** bluntly, frankly, sincere **8** candidly, directly **9** downright

straightness 7 honesty **8** evenness **10** directness **11** uprightness

strain 3 air, tax, tug **4** kind, line, pull, sift, song, sort, toil, tune, type, vein **5** blood, breed, drain, force, grain, grind, group, heave, labor, people, press, sieve, streak, stock, trait, twist **6** burden, drudge, effort, extend, family, filter, genius, injure, injury, melody, overdo, purify, refine, screen, sprain, stress, weaken, winnow, wrench **7** descent, distend, exhaust, fatigue, lineage, overtax, species, stretch, tension, tighten, try hard, variety, wear out **8** ancestry, bear down, elongate, exertion, hardship, heredity, make taut, overwork, pressure, protract, struggle, tendency **9** draw tight, make tense, overexert, parentage **10** buckle down, derivation, extraction, overburden **11** disposition, huff and puff, inclination **12** do double duty, drive oneself, exert oneself **14** predisposition, work like a horse, work like a slave

strained 5 tense **6** touchy **8** volatile **9** explosive **10** precarious

strait 7 channel, narrows, passage

straitened 5 broke, needy **6** hard-up **7** pinched **8** bankrupt, indigent, strapped, wiped-out **9** destitute, penniless, penurious **10** distressed, pauperized, restricted **11** embarrassed **12** impoverished **15** poverty-stricken

Strait Is the Gate
author: 9 Andre Gide

straitlaced 4 prim **5** rigid, stiff **6** formal, narrow, proper, severe, strict **7** austere, prudish, uptight **8** reserved **9** inhibited **11** puritanical **14** overscrupulous **15** undemonstrative

straits 3 fix **4** hole **6** pickle, plight **8** distress **9** extremity **10** difficulty **11** predicament **13** embarrassment

strand 4 bank, cord, lock, rope **5** beach, braid, coast, fiber, leave, shore, tress, twist **6** desert, ground, maroon, string, thread **8** filament, necklace, seacoast, seashore **9** component, go aground, riverside, shipwreck **10** ingredient, run aground **15** leave high and dry, leave in the lurch

stranded 5 stuck **6** ashore **7** aground, beached **8** grounded **9** foundered **11** shipwrecked **14** left high and dry, left in the lurch

strange 3 new, odd **4** lost **5** alien, queer **6** uneasy, unused **7** awkward, bizarre, curious, erratic, foreign, unknown, unusual **8** aberrant, abnormal, freakish, peculiar, singular, uncommon **9** alienated, anomalous, eccentric, estranged, fantastic, ill at ease, irregular, unnatural **10** bewildered, farfetched, out of place, outlandish, unexplored, unfamiliar **11** discomposed, disoriented, out-of-the-way **12** unaccustomed, undiscovered, unhabituated **13** extraordinary, unaccountable, uncomfortable **14** unconventional

Strange Fruit
author: 12 Lillian Smith

Strange Interlude
author: 12 Eugene O'Neill

strangeness 7 anomaly, oddness **9** queerness **10** aberration **11** abnormality, peculiarity **12** eccentricity, idiosyncrasy, irregularity, unconformity **13** nonconformity

stranger 5 alien **8** newcomer, outsider **9** auslander, foreigner, immigrant, outlander

Stranger, The
author: 11 Albert Camus

Strangers on a Train
director: 15 Alfred Hitchcock
cast: 9 Ruth Roman **11** Leo G Carroll, Marion Lorne **12** Robert Walker **13** Farley Granger **17** Patricia Hitchcock
remade as: 20 Once You Kiss a Stranger

strange to say
Latin: 13 mirabile dictu

strangle 3 gag **4** stop **5** burke, check, choke, crush, quell **6** muzzle, stifle **7** garrote, put down, repress, smother, squelch **8** choke off, snuff out, suppress, throttle **9** suffocate **10** asphyxiate, extinguish

strangulate 8 choke off, compress, strangle **9** constrict

strap 3 tie **4** band, beat, belt, bind, cord, flog, lash, whip **5** flail, leash, thong, truss **6** tether, thrash **7** scourge

strapped 8 bankrupt, wiped out **9** insolvent, penniless **12** impoverished, without funds

strapping 5 burly, hardy, husky, stout **6** brawny, robust, strong, sturdy **8** muscular, powerful, stalwart

stratagem 4 game, plan, plot, ploy, ruse, wile **5** blind, dodge, feint, trick **6** deceit, device, scheme, tactic **8** artifice, intrigue, maneuver, trickery **9** deception **10** subterfuge **11** contrivance, machination

strategic 3 key **4** wary **5** vital **6** clever **7** careful, crucial, cunning, guarded, planned, politic, prudent, turning **8** cautious, critical, decisive, military, tactical, vigilant **9** important, momentous, principal **10** calculated, deliberate, diplomatic **11** significant **13** consequential, precautionary

strategy 4 game **5** craft, wiles **6** policy, scheme **7** cunning, devices, tactics **8** artifice, art of war, game plan, plotting **9** war policy **10** artfulness, craftiness **11** grand design, machination, maneuvering **12** military plan **15** military science

stratosphere 3 sky **5** ozone **7** heavens **8** upper air **12** high altitude **14** wild blue yonder

stratum 4 band, belt, seam, zone **5** layer

Strauss, Johann (the Elder)
composer of: 13 Radetzky March

Strauss, Johann (the Younger)
composer of: 6 The Bat **13** Die Fledermaus, The Gipsy Baron **16** Der Zigeunerbaron
***waltz:* 12** Emperor Waltz **13** The Blue Danube **23** Tales from the Vienna Woods

Strauss, Joseph
composer of: 17 Music of

the Spheres **27** The Village Swallows in Austria

Strauss, Richard
born: **6** Munich **7** Germany
composer of: **6** Salome **7** Don Juan, Elektra **8** Arabella **9** Capriccio **10** Don Quixote **14** Ein Heldenleben **15** Ariadne auf Naxos **16** Der Rosenkavalier, Domestic Symphony, Till Eulenspiegel **19** Die Frau ohne Schatten **20** Die Aegyptische Helena, Thus Spake Zarathustra **21** Also Sprach Zarathustra **23** Death and Transfiguration

Stravinsky, Igor Feodorovich
born: **6** Russia **11** Oranienbaum
composer of: **4** Agon **6** Threni **7** Orpheus **8** The Flood **9** Card Party, Fireworks **10** Oedipus Rex, Petrouchka, Petruschka, Pulcinella **11** Jeu de Cartes, The Firebird **13** Dumbarton Oaks, Psalm Symphony **14** The Nightingale **15** Abraham and Isaac, The Rite of Spring **16** Requiem Canticles, The Rake's Progress **18** Le Sacre du Printemps

straw **3** hay **4** tube **5** chaff **7** pipette

strawberry **8** Fragaria
varieties: **4** mock **5** beach **6** barren, Dunlap, garden, Indian **7** sow-teat **8** Klondike, Rosacean, Virginia, woodland
liqueur: **13** creme de fraise

Straw Dogs
director: **12** Sam Peckinpah
cast: **9** T P McKenna **11** Susan George **12** Peter Vaughan **13** Dustin Hoffman

straw man **6** effigy **9** scapegoat, scarecrow

stray **4** lost, roam, rove, waif **5** drift **6** random, wander **7** digress, drifter **8** go astray, separate, set apart, straggle, straying, vagabond, wanderer **9** itinerant, misplaced, scattered, straggler **10** lost animal, lost person **11** lose one's way

straying **5** lapse **8** drifting, rambling **9** departure, deviation, wandering **10** abberation, digression, divergence

streak **3** bar, bed, fly **4** band, blot, blur, cast, dart, dash, daub, line, lode, race, rush, seam, tear, vein, whiz, zoom **5** layer, level, plane, smear, speed, strip, touch **6** blotch, hurtle, smirch, smudge, strain, stripe **7** portion, splotch, stratum

stream **3** jet, run **4** blow, file, flow, flux, gush, pour, race, rill, rush, teem, tide, waft, wave **5** brook, burst, creek, float, flood, issue, river, shoot, spate, spill, spout, spurt, surge **6** abound, branch, course, deluge, extend, feeder, onrush, sluice **7** current, flutter, freshet, rivulet, torrent **8** effusion, fountain, overflow **9** profusion, tributary **11** watercourse

streamer **4** flag **6** banner, burgee **7** pennant

streamlet **3** run **4** rill **5** brook, creek **7** rivulet

streamlined **4** racy **5** clean, sleek **7** compact **8** up-to-date **9** organized **10** futuristic, modernized, simplified **11** aerodynamic

stream of abuse **6** tirade **8** diatribe, harangue **9** contumely, invective **12** vituperation

streams
goddess of: **7** Juturna

Streep, Meryl
real name: **16** Mary Louise Streep
born: **14** Basking Ridge NJ
roles: **8** Ironweed, Silkwood **11** Out of Africa **13** Falling in Love, Sophie's Choice (Oscar), The Deer Hunter **14** Kramer vs Kramer **25** The French Lieutenant's Woman

street **3** way **4** lane, mews, road **5** alley, block, route **6** avenue **7** highway, roadway, terrace, thruway **8** turnpike **9** boulevard **10** expressway **12** thoroughfare

Streetcar Named Desire, A
author: **17** Tennessee Williams
director: **9** Elia Kazan
cast: **9** Kim Hunter (Stella Dubois Kowalski) **10** Karl Malden **11** Vivien Leigh (Blanche Dubois) **12** Marlon Brando (Stanley Kowalski)
setting: **10** New Orleans
score: **9** Alex North
Oscar for: **7** actress (Leigh) **15** supporting actor (Malden) **17** supporting actress (Hunter)

Streets of San Francisco, The
character: **9** (Det Lt) Mike Stone **10** (Inspector) Dan Robbins **11** (Inspector) Steve Keller
cast: **10** Karl Malden **12** Richard Hatch **14** Michael Douglas

strega
type: **7** liqueur
origin: **5** Italy
flavor: **6** spices **10** orange peel
with brandy: **10** Strega Flip

Streisand, Barbra
real name: **20** Barbara Joan Streisand
born: **10** Brooklyn NY
husband: **11** Elliot Gould
roles: **5** Yentl **9** Funny Girl (Oscar), Funny Lady **10** Fanny Brice, Hello Dolly, What's Up Doc? **11** A Star Is Born **12** The Main Event, The Way We Were

strength **4** beef, grit, kick, pith, sand, size **5** brawn, force, forte, might, pluck, power, sinew, spice, vigor **6** anchor, mettle, number, purity, spirit, succor, virtue **7** bravery, muscles, potency, stamina, support **8** backbone, buttress, efficacy, firmness, mainstay, security, solidity, tenacity, vitality **9** endurance, fortitude, hardiness, intensity, lustiness, puissance, stoutness, toughness, viability **10** robustness, sturdiness, sustenance **13** concentration, effectiveness **16** stoutheartedness
Latin: **3** vis

strengthen **4** prop **5** brace, renew, steel **6** harden **7** build up, enhance, fortify, improve, restore, shore up, support, sustain **8** buttress **9** reinforce

strength of character **4** grit, guts **5** pluck, spunk **6** mettle **7** resolve **8** backbone **9** fortitude **10** resolution **12** resoluteness **13** steadfastness

Strength of Fields
author: **11** James Dickey

strenuous **4** hard **5** eager **6** active, ardent, dogged, taxing, uphill **7** arduous, dynamic, earnest, intense, zealous **8** animated, diligent, sedulous, spirited, untiring, vigorous **9** assiduous, difficult, energetic, laborious, punishing **10** exhausting, on one's toes **11** hardworking, industrious, painstaking **12** enterprising **13** indefatigable

stress **4** beat, mark **5** force, value, worth **6** accent, affirm, assert, burden, moment, repeat, strain, weight **7** anxiety, concern, feature, gravity, meaning, sawdust, tension, urgency **8** emphasis, pressure **9** emphasize, necessity, underline **10** accentuate, importance, insist upon, oppression, prominence, underscore **11** consequence, seriousness **12** accentuation, significance **13** consideration

stretch **4** span, term, tire **5** cover, reach, spell, stint, tract, while, widen **6** burden, deepen, expand, extend, period, sprawl, spread, spring, strain **7** distend, draw out, expanse, fatigue, lie over, overtax, pull out **8** distance, draw taut, duration, elongate, interval, lengthen, overtask, overwork, protract, put forth, reach out, tautness, traverse **9** be elastic, draw tight, make tense, make tight, overexert **10** elasticity, exaggerate, overburden, overcharge, overstrain, push too far, resiliency **11** carry too far **12** be expandable, be extendable **14** push to the limit

stretchable **7** elastic, rubbery **8** flexible **9** resilient

stretching **9** extending, extension **10** drawing out, elongation **11** attenuation, enlargement, lengthening, protraction **12** prolongation **13** amplification

stretching out **8** outreach **9** expansion, extending, extension **10** elongation **11** attenuation, lengthening **12** prolongation

stretch out **6** expand, extend **7** amplify, augment, draw out **8** elongate, lengthen, protract

Strether
character in: **14** The Ambassadors
author: **5** James

strew **3** sow **6** litter **7** scatter **8** disperse **9** broadcast **11** disseminate

stricken **3** ill **4** hurt, sick **7** injured, smitten, wounded **8** blighted, diseased **9** afflicted, taken sick **13** incapacitated

strict **4** nice **5** exact, rigid, stern **6** severe **7** austere, perfect **8** absolute, complete, exacting, rigorous, unerring **9** stringent **10** fastidious, inflexible, meticulous, scrupulous, unyielding **13** authoritarian, conscientious **14** uncompromising

strictly required
French: **9** de rigueur

stride **4** gait, lope, pace, step **5** march, stalk **7** advance, headway **8** long step, progress **11** advancement, improvement **13** take long steps

strident **5** harsh **6** shrill **7** grating, jarring, rasping, raucous **8** clashing, grinding, jangling, piercing, twanging **9** dissonant **10** discordant, screeching **11** cacophonous, high-pitched

Striebel, John H
creator/artist of: **10** Dixie Dugan

strife **6** unrest **7** discord, trouble, turmoil, warfare **8** conflict, disquiet, fighting, struggle, upheaval, violence **10** contention, convulsion, disharmony, dissension **11** altercation, disturbance

Strife
author: **14** John Galsworthy

strike **3** bat, box, hit, run, tap **4** bang, beat, belt, bump, clap, clip, club, come, cuff, drub, find, flog, lash, make, meet, pelt, ring, slam, slap, slug, sock, toll, whip, wipe **5** chime, clout, erase, flail, knell, knock, light, pound, punch, reach, smash, smite, sound, thump, tie-up, whack, whale **6** affect, arrive, assail, attack, batter, buffet, cancel, chance, charge, cudgel, delete, effect, fold up, hammer, pommel, remove, seem to, thrash, wallop **7** achieve, arrange, assault, boycott, impress, occur to, protest, put away, ram into, run into, scourge, scratch, stumble, unearth, walk out **8** appear to, bump into, come upon, cross out, dawn upon, discover, fall upon, lambaste, pull down, take down **9** burst upon, devastate, eliminate, encounter, eradicate, knock into, take apart **10** come across, flagellate, meet head-on **11** beat against, collide with, dash against **12** labor dispute, work stoppage

strike a bargain **5** agree **6** settle **9** make a deal **10** compromise **11** come to terms, meet halfway **18** split the difference **20** reach an understanding

strike back **7** counter, get even, hit back, pay back, riposte **9** fight back, retaliate **13** counterattack

strike dumb **4** daze, stun **5** amaze, shock **7** astound, stagger, stupefy **8** astonish, dumfound **9** dumbfound, electrify **11** flabbergast

strike noisily **4** bang, beat, clap, slam **5** thump

strike out **6** delete, fan out, set off, set out **7** take out **10** sally forth

strike sharply **3** rap **4** slap **5** crack

striking **6** marked **7** notable **9** prominent **10** astounding, impressive, noteworthy, noticeable, remarkable, surprising **11** conspicuous, outstanding **13** extraordinary

Strindberg, August
author of: **9** Miss Julie, The Father **10** A Dream Play **12** The Creditors **14** The Ghost Sonata **15** The Dance of Death

string **3** row **4** cord, file, line, rope **5** chain, queue, train, twine **6** column, extend, parade, series, spread, strand, thread **7** binding, stretch **8** necklace, sequence **10** procession, succession

stringent **5** close, harsh, spare, stern, stiff, tight **6** cogent, frugal, severe, strict **7** sparing **8** exacting, forceful, rigorous **9** demanding, effectual, unbending **10** inflexible, unyielding **14** uncompromising

strip **3** rob **4** band, flay, loot, peel, raid, sack, skin, slip, tear **5** field, flake, rifle, shave **6** denude, divest, length, ravage, remove, ribbon, stripe, unwrap **7** deprive, despoil, disrobe, draw off, lay bare, measure, plunder, pull off, ransack, uncover, undrape, undress **8** airstrip, desolate, lay waste, spoliate, unclothe **9** steal from **11** disencumber

stripe **3** bar **4** band, line, tape **5** braid, strip, swath **6** ribbon, streak **7** chevron **8** insignia **9** striation

stripling **3** boy, lad **5** minor, youth **8** teenager, young man **9** schoolboy, youngster **10** adolescent

stripped **4** bare, nude **5** naked **6** peeled, unclad **7** denuded, exposed, unrobed **8** disrobed, divested **9** unclothed, uncovered, undressed

strive **3** vie **4** push **5** essay, fight, labor **6** battle, strain **7** contend, try hard **8** endeavor, struggle **9** take pains, undertake **10** do one's best **12** apply oneself, do one's utmost, exert oneself, spare no pains **15** work like a Trojan **18** move heaven and earth **20** leave no stone unturned

striving **4** toil **5** exert, labor **6** effort, strain **7** toiling, travail **8** exertion, struggle **9** straining **10** struggling

stroke **3** bat, hit, pat, pet, tap **4** blow, chop, coup, deed, feat, poke, slap, sock, swat **5** brush, chime, fluke, punch, whack **6** caress, chance, wallop **7** massage, ringing, seizure, tolling **8** accident, apoplexy, flourish, movement, sounding, striking **11** achievement, coincidence, piece of luck, transaction **15** brain hemorrhage

stroll **4** tour, turn, walk **5** amble, mosey **6** ramble, wander **7** meander, saunter **9** poke along, promenade **14** constitutional

stroller **4** pram **5** buggy **6** ambler, walker **7** rambler **8** carriage **9** itinerant, pushchair, saunterer **10** promenader **12** perambulator

strong **3** hot **4** able, bold, deep, keen, tart **5** burly, clear, close, fiery, hardy, nippy, sharp, solid, sound, stout, tangy, tough, vivid **6** ardent, biting, brawny, bright, cogent, fervid, fierce, gritty, hearty, mighty, moving, plucky, potent, robust, savory, severe, sinewy, sturdy **7** buoyant, capable, devoted, earnest, fervent, healthy, intense, piquant, pungent, skilled, violent, zealous **8** animated, athletic, definite, diligent, distinct, emphatic, faithful, forceful, muscular, powerful, puissant, sedulous, spirited, stalwart, tireless, vehement, vigorous **9** assiduous, competent, confirmed, effective, energetic, herculean, resilient, tenacious, undiluted **10** compelling, convincing, courageous, deep-seated, persistent, proficient **11** impassioned, persevering, resourceful **12** advantageous, concentrated, highly spiced, high-spirited, unmistakable **13** indefatigable, well-qualified **14** highly flavored, highly seasoned
Spanish: **5** macho

Strong
character in: **7** Erewhon
author: **6** Butler

strong-arm **3** cow **5** bully, force **6** coerce, compel **8** browbeat, threaten **10** intimidate

strong feeling **4** fear, hate, heat, love, zeal **5** anger, ardor **6** fervor, sorrow, warmth **7** despair, emotion, passion, sadness **8** jealousy **9** happiness, vehemence **12** satisfaction

stronghold **4** fort, hold, home, keep **6** bunker, center, locale, refuge **7** bastion, bulwark, citadel, rampart, redoubt **8** fastness, fortress, safehold, stockade **10** battlement, blockhouse **13** fortification

strongly committed **4** true **5** loyal **6** ardent **7** devoted, staunch, zealous **8** adhering, faithful **9** dedicated, steadfast **10** passionate, unwavering

strong point **5** forte **6** anchor **8** mainstay, strength

strong-willed **5** pushy **8** forceful, positive **9** assertive **10** aggressive **11** domineering, self-assured **13** self-assertive

Strophius
king of: **6** Phocis
reared by: **7** Orestes

structural support **3** bar **4** beam, prop, stud **5** brace, joist **6** girder, rafter, timber **7** trestle **12** underpinning

structure **4** form, plan **6** design, makeup **7** arrange, edifice, pattern **8** assemble, building, conceive, organize **9** construct, formation **11** arrangement, composition, put together **12** conformation, construction, organization **13** configuration

struggle **3** vie, war **4** duel, feud, pull, push, spar, tilt **5** argue, brawl, brush, clash, fight, grind, joust, labor, match, scrap, trial **6** action, battle, combat, differ, effort, engage, jostle, oppose, resist, strain, stress, strife, strive, tussle **7** compete, contend, contest, grapple, quarrel, scuffle **8** conflict, endeavor, exertion, long haul, skirmish, work hard **9** encounter, lock horns, take pains **10** engagement **11** altercation, cross swords **15** work like a Trojan **18** move heaven and earth **20** leave no stone unturned

strut **4** sail **6** parade, sashay **7** peacock, swagger **9** promenade

Struthiomimus
type: **8** dinosaur, theropod
known as: **15** ostrich dinosaur
period: **10** Cretaceous
characteristic: **9** toothless

Stryver
character in: **16** A Tale of Two Cities
author: **7** Dickens

Stuart, Gilbert
born: **15** North Kingston RI
artwork: **16** George Washington

Stuart, J E B
served in: **8** Civil War
side: **11** Confederate
commander of: **7** cavalry
battle: **7** Bull Run **8** Antietam **10** Gettysburg **14** Fredericksburg **16** Chancellorsville **18** Peninsular campaign

Stuart Little
author: **7** E B White

stub **3** end **4** bump, butt, dock, tail **5** crush, knock, snuff, stump **6** fag end, scrape **7** receipt, remains, tamp out, voucher **10** extinguish, torn ticket **11** counterfoil

stubble **5** beard **6** stumps **8** bristles, whiskers **9** cut stalks **16** five-o'clock shadow

stubborn **6** dogged, mulish, strong, sturdy **7** willful **8** forceful, obdurate, perverse, resolute **9** concerted, immovable, obstinate, pigheaded, resistant, tenacious, unbending, unmovable **10** bullheaded, headstrong, inflexible, persistent, purposeful, refractory, self-willed, unshakable, unyielding **11** indomitable, intractable, opinionated, uncompliant **12** hard to handle, recalcitrant, ungovernable, wholehearted

stubbornness **10** mulishness, obstinancy, resistance **11** willfulness **13** intransigence, pigheadedness

stubby **5** dumpy, pudgy, squab, squat, tubby **6** chubby, chunky, stocky, stodgy, stumpy **7** squatty **8** thickset

Stubtoe State
nickname of: **7** Montana

stuck **3** dug, put **4** held **5** bound, fixed, fused, glued, mired, poked **6** balked, curbed, jabbed, joined, nailed, pasted, pinned, placed, sealed, spiked, tacked, thrust, welded **7** adhered, affixed, boggled, impeded, planted, pricked, punched, saddled, snarled, speared, stabbed, stalled, stumped, stymied **8** attached, burdened, cemented, fastened, inserted **9** punctured **10** obstructed, perforated **11** immobilized

stuck-up **4** vain **5** cocky **6** snooty, uppish, uppity **7** haughty, high-hat **8** arrogant, snobbish **9** bigheaded, conceited **10** disdainful, egocentric, hoity-toity **11** overbearing, swellheaded **13** self-important, self-satisfied

stud **3** dot **4** beam, buck, dude, sire **5** board, rivet **6** button **7** upright **8** fastener, macho man, nailhead

student **4** coed **5** pupil **6** reader **7** analyst, learner, scholar, watcher **8** disciple, examiner, follower, observer, reviewer **9** collegian, schoolboy, spectator **10** schoolgirl **11** commentator, interpreter, matriculant **13** undergraduate

studied **8** measured **10** calculated, deliberate, purposeful **11** intentional **12** premeditated

studious **6** brainy, intent **7** bookish, earnest, erudite **8** academic, cerebral, diligent, literate, well-read **9** laborious, scholarly **10** determined, purposeful, scholastic **11** painstaking **12** intellectual

Studs Lonigan
series includes: **11** Judgment Day **12** Young Lonigan **29** The Young Manhood of Studs Lonigan
author: **13** James T Farrell

study **3** den **4** cram, read **5** grind, probe **6** office, peruse, review, search, studio, survey **7** examine, explore, inquiry, library, observe, reading **8** analysis, consider, learning, pore over, read up on, research, scrutiny **9** delve into, education **10** glance over, inspection, scrutinize **11** examination, exploration, hit the books, inquire into, instruction, investigate, read closely, reading room, scholarship **13** consideration, investigation, school oneself, search through

Study in Scarlet, A
author: **19** Sir Arthur Conan Doyle
character: **12** Dr John Watson **13** Jefferson Hope, Tobias Gregson **14** Sherlock Holmes **17** Inspector Lestrade

Study of History, A
author: **14** Arnold J Toynbee

stuff **3** act, bit, jam, pad, wad **4** best, bosh, bunk, cram, fill, gear, heap, load, pack, pile, sate, stow **5** cache, crowd, gorge, hokum, hooey, stash, store, thing, trash, wedge **6** burden, fill up, humbug, matter, staple, tackle, things, thrust, tricks, utmost **7** effects, essence, hogwash, overeat, rubbish, satiate, spinach, twaddle **8** darndest, falderal, material, nonsense **9** component, empty talk, substance **10** balderdash, belongings, gluttonize, ingredient, make a pig of **11** constituent, foolishness, overindulge, performance, possessions, raw material **12** quintessence **13** paraphernalia

stuff-and-nonsense **3** rot **4** bosh, bull, bunk **5** hokum, hooey, trash **6** bunkum, drivel, humbug **7** baloney, hogwash, spinach, twaddle **8** buncombe, claptrap, nonsense, tommyrot **9** poppycock **10** applesauce, balderdash, tomfoolery **11** foolishness **12** fiddlesticks **13** horsefeathers

stuffed **4** full **6** filled, jammed, loaded, packed, rammed, wadded **7** crammed, crushed, replete **8** overfull, satiated, squeezed **10** sandwiched

stuff in **4** cram, pack **6** devour **8** bolt down, compress, gobble up, wolf down

stuffing **5** farce **7** filling, packing, padding, wadding **8** dressing **9** forcemeat

stuffy **4** cold, smug **5** close, fusty, heavy, muggy, musty, staid **6** stodgy, sultry **7** airless, pompous **8** reserved, stagnant, stifling **9** clogged-up, congested, high-flown, stopped-up, stuffed-up **10** old-fogyish, oppressive, sweltering **11** pretentious, straitlaced, suffocating **12** supercilious, unventilated **13** ill-ventilated, self-satisfied, stale-smelling

stultify **4** balk **6** hinder, impair, impede, thwart **7** cripple, inhibit, nullify, vitiate **8** suppress **9** frustrate, hamstring **11** make useless

stumble **3** hit **4** fall, reel, roll, sway, trip **5** botch, lurch, pitch, spill **6** bungle, falter, happen, hash up, hobble, mess up, slip up, sprawl, topple, totter **7** blunder, misstep, shamble, stagger **8** flounder **10** take a spill **12** come by chance, make mistakes, pitch forward

stumble upon **4** find **7** learn of **8** come upon, discover **10** chance upon, happen upon **14** find by accident

stumbling block **3** bar, rub **4** snag **5** block, catch, hitch **6** hamper, hurdle **7** barrier, problem **8** drawback, obstacle **9** detriment, hindrance **10** difficulty, impediment **11** obstruction **12** complication, interference

stump **3** end **4** butt, foil, stub, thud **5** befog, clomp, clonk, clump, clunk, stamp, stomp, tramp **6** baffle, nubbin, stymie **7** confuse, mystify, nonplus, perplex **8** bewilder, confound, dumfound, footfall, stomping, tramping **9** bamboozle, dumbfound

stun **4** daze, numb **5** amaze, shock **7** astound, stagger, startle, stupefy **8** astonish, dumfound **9** dumbfound **11** flabbergast

stunner **4** doll **5** beaut, Venus **6** beauty, eyeful **8** knockout **9** dreamboat **10** good-looker

stunning **6** dazing, lovely **7** amazing, numbing **8** shocking, striking **9** beautiful, exquisite, startling **10** astounding, staggering, stupefying **11** astonishing, dumfounding **12** dumbfounding, electrifying **14** flabbergasting

stunt **3** act **4** curb, feat **5** abort, check, cramp, dwarf, limit, stint, trick **6** impede, number, stifle **7** curtail, delimit **8** restrain, restrict, suppress

stunted **5** dumpy, runty **6** bantam **7** dwarfed, squatty, wizened **9** pint-sized **13** foreshortened

Stunt Man, The
director: **11** Richard Rush
cast: **9** Alex Rocco **11** Peter O'Toole (Eli Cross) **13** Allen Goorwitz, Sharon Farrell **14** Barbara Hershey, Steve Railsback

stupefaction **5** shock **8** numbness, surprise **9** amazement **12** astonishment

stupefied **5** dazed **6** amazed **7** shocked, stunned **8** benumbed **10** dumbstruck, dumfounded **11** dumbfounded **13** flabbergasted, thunderstruck

stupefy **4** daze, stun **5** amaze, shock **7** astound, nonplus, stagger **8** astonish, confound, dumfound, surprise **9** dumbfound, overwhelm **11** flabbergast

stupefying **8** shocking, stunning **11** dumfounding **12** dumbfounding, electrifying, overwhelming **14** flabbergasting

stupendous **3** big **4** huge, vast **5** giant, great, jumbo **6** mighty **7** amazing, immense, mammoth, massive, titanic, unusual **8** colossal, enormous, fabulous, gigantic, imposing, stunning, terrific **9** cyclopean, herculean, marvelous, monstrous, very great, very large, wonderful **10** astounding, gargantuan, incredible, monumental, phenomenal, prodigious, remarkable, surprising, tremendous, unexpected **11** astonishing, elephantine **13** extraordinary

stupid **4** dull, dumb **5** dense, inane, inept, silly **6** absurd, oafish, obtuse, simple, unwise **7** aimless, asinine, boorish, doltish, fatuous, foolish, idiotic, moronic, witless **8** backward, childish, heedless, mistaken, reckless, tactless **9** brainless, cretinous, dimwitted, duncelike, foolhardy, ill-judged, imbecilic, imprudent, pointless, senseless **10** half-witted, ill-advised, indiscreet, irrelevant, weak-minded **11** empty-headed, meaningless, nonsensical, purposeless, thoughtless **12** absentminded, muddleheaded, preposterous, simpleminded, slow-learning, unreasonable **13** ill-considered, inappropriate, irresponsible, rattlebrained, unintelligent

stupor **4** daze **5** faint **6** apathy, torpor **7** inertia **8** blackout, lethargy, numbness **9** inertness **10** somnolence **12** stupefaction **13** insensibility

sturdy **4** able, firm **5** brave, burly, gutsy, hardy, heavy, solid, sound, stout, tough **6** daring, dogged, gritty, heroic, mighty, plucky, robust, rugged, secure, sinewy, spunky, strong **7** defiant, doughty, durable, gallant, lasting, valiant **8** enduring, fearless, forceful, intrepid, muscular, powerful, resolute, spirited, stalwart, stubborn, vigorous, well-made **9** dauntless, strapping, unabashed, undaunted, well-built **10** courageous, determined, invincible **11** indomitable, substantial, unshrinking **12** high-spirited, stouthearted **15** well-constructed

Sturges, John
director of: **14** The Great Escape **19** The Magnificent Seven

Sturges, Preston
director of: **10** The Lady Eve **16** Sullivan's Travels **17** The Palm Beach Story, Unfaithfully Yours **21** Hail the Conquering Hero **24** The Miracle of Morgan's Creek

Sturmabteilung **13** storm troopers

Sturm und Drang **22** German literary movement (18th century)
literally: **14** storm and stress

stygian **3** dim **4** dark **5** black, murky **6** dreary, gloomy, somber **7** hellish **8** funereal, infernal, starless **9** tenebrous, unlighted

style **3** fad **4** call, elan, kind, mode, name, pomp, rage, sort, type **5** charm, class, craze, favor, flair, grace, model, taste, trend, vogue **6** design, luxury, manner, polish **7** arrange, comfort, fashion, pattern **8** currency, elegance **9** affluence, designate **10** smoothness **11** savoir faire
French: **4** gout

stylish **3** hip, new **4** chic **5** natty, smart, swank **6** dapper, latest, modern, modish, with-it **7** a la mode, elegant, in vogue, voguish **8** up-to-date **9** in fashion **11** fashionable **13** sophisticated, up-to-the-minute

stymie **4** balk **5** block, check, stump **6** baffle, hinder, puzzle, thwart **7** confuse, mystify **8** confound, obstruct **9** frustrate

Stymphalides
origin: **8** Arcadian
form: **5** birds
attribute: **9** dangerous

Stymphalus
king of: **7** Arcadia
killed by: **6** Pelops
form: **4** lake
home of: **12** Stymphalides

Styracosaurus
type: **8** dinosaur **10** ceratopsid
location: **12** North America
period: **10** Cretaceous
characteristic: **6** horned

Styron, William
author of: **12** The Long March **13** Sophie's Choice **17** Lie Down in Darkness **18** Set This House on Fire **25** The Confessions of Nat Turner

Styx
form: **5** river
location: **5** Hades **10** underworld
father: **7** Oceanus
ferryman: **6** Charon

suave **6** silken, smooth, urbane **7** affable, elegant, politic **8** charming, gracious, mannerly, polished, unctuous **9** civilized **10** diplomatic, flattering **12** ingratiating **13** smooth-tongued

sub **5** below, proxy, under **6** backup, deputy, second **7** beneath, standby, stand-in **9** alternate, submarine, surrogate **10** substitute, understudy **11** pinch-hitter

subaltern **4** aide **6** helper **9** assistant **10** lieutenant **11** subordinate

subconscious **3** dim **7** dawning **9** intuitive **10** subliminal **11** instinctive

subdivide **6** divide **7** split up **8** separate **9** partition

subdivision **3** arm **4** wing **6** branch **7** chapter, section **8** offshoot **11** development **12** neighborhood

subdue **3** bow **4** calm, curb, down, drub, ease, foil, mute, rout, trim, whip **5** allay, break, check, crush, floor, quell, salve, smash, still **6** deaden, defeat, master, mellow, muffle, reduce, soften, soothe, temper, thrash **7** appease, assuage, conquer, mollify, oppress, overrun, put down, relieve, slacken, subject, trample **8** mitigate, moderate, overcome, palliate, surmount, tone down, vanquish **9** meliorate, overpower, overwhelm, quiet down, soft-pedal, subjugate **10** ameliorate **11** triumph over **12** tranquillize

subdued **4** dull **5** cowed, muted, quiet **7** abashed, crushed, humbled, muffled, quelled **8** deadened, overcame **10** humiliated, indistinct, lackluster **11** intimidated, overpowered

subduer **6** victor, winner **9** conqueror, overcomer **10** subjugator, vanquisher **11** intimidator

subject **4** bare, case, gist, open, pith, text **5** field, issue, liege, motif, prone, study, theme, topic **6** affair, expose, liable, matter, submit, thesis, vassal **7** bound by, citizen, concern, exposed, lay open **8** business, disposed, follower, obedient, question **9** dependent, subjected, substance **10** answerable, discipline, in danger of, make liable, put through, vulnerable **11** stipulatory, subordinate, subservient, susceptible

subjection **11** subjugation **12** subservience **13** regimentation, subordination

subjective **5** inner **6** biased **7** partial **8** partisan, personal **9** emotional **10** individual, prejudiced **12** nonobjective

subjoin **5** add on, affix, annex **6** append, attach, tack on

subjugate **4** tame **5** crush, quell **6** subdue **7** conquer, put down **8** dominate, suppress, vanquish **10** overmaster

subjugation **6** chains, thrall **7** bondage, slavery **9** dominance, mastering, servitude, thralldom **10** conquering, domination **11** enslavement, vanquishing

subjugator **6** master, victor **7** subduer **9** conqueror, dominator **10** vanquisher **11** slavemaster

sublimate **4** turn **5** exalt, shift **6** divert, purify **7** channel, convert, elevate, ennoble **8** redirect, transfer **9** transform, transmute **12** spiritualize

sublime **4** high **5** grand, great, lofty, noble **6** superb **7** exalted, stately **8** elevated, imposing, majestic, splendid, terrific, very good **9** estimable, excellent, marvelous, wonderful **12** awe-inspiring, praiseworthy

submarine
invented by: **7** Holland
even keel: **4** Lake
torpedo: **8** Bushnell

submerge **4** dive, sink **5** douse, drown, flood, souse **6** deluge, engulf, go down, plunge **7** go under, immerse **8** inundate, pour over, submerse

submerse **5** drown **6** engulf **7** immerse **8** inundate, submerge

submersion **7** sinking **8** drowning **9** immersion **10** inundation **11** submergence

submission **8** giving in, meekness, tameness, yielding **9** handing in, obedience, passivity, surrender, tendering **10** compliance, remittance, submitting **11** passiveness **12** acquiescence, capitulation, presentation, subservience, tractability **13** nonresistance **14** submissiveness

submissive **4** meek, mild **6** docile, humble, pliant **7** dutiful, fawning, passive, servile, slavish **8** crawling, obedient, toadying, yielding **9** compliant, malleable, tractable, truckling **10** obsequious **11** acquiescent, bootlicking, complaisant, deferential, subservient, unassertive **12** capitulating, ingratiating, nonresisting **13** accommodating

submissiveness **8** docility, meekness **9** passivity **10** compliance **11** resignation **12** complaisance, tractability

submit **3** bow **4** bend, cede **5** agree, argue, claim, defer, kneel, offer, stoop, yield **6** accede, assert, commit, comply, give in, give up, resort, tender **7** contend, hold out, present, proffer, propose, succumb, suggest **8** back down, put forth **9** acquiesce, surrender, volunteer **10** capitulate, put forward **12** knuckle under

submit an offer **3** bid **6** tender **7** proffer, propose

submit to **4** bear, take **5** abide, brave, brook, stand **6** endure, suffer **7** stomach, undergo **8** stand for, tolerate **9** put up with

subnormal **3** bad, low **5** seedy, sorry **6** crummy, dismal, shabby, sleazy, subpar **7** abysmal **8** below par, inferior, mediocre, wretched **9** defective, deficient **10** inadequate, second-rate **11** below normal, substandard **12** insufficient

subordinate **4** help **5** lower **6** junior, lackey, lesser, menial, worker **7** servant, subject **8** hireling, inferior **9** ancillary, assistant, attendant, auxiliary, dependent, of low rank, outranked, secondary, subaltern, underling **10** subsidiary **11** subservient

subordination **10** subjection **11** inferiority, subjugation **12** subservience **13** regimentation

suborn **5** bribe **6** buy off, pay off

sub rosa **8** covertly, in secret, on the sly, secretly **9** in private, privately **12** off-the-record **14** confidentially **15** behind-the-scenes **17** behind closed doors

subscribe **4** help, sign **6** assent, chip in, donate **7** consent, endorse, support **8** hold with **9** undersign **10** contribute

subsequent **4** next **7** ensuing **9** following, proximate **10** consequent, succeeding, successive

subsequently **2** so **5** after, later, since **9** afterward, following **10** succeeding **12** consequently

subservient **6** docile, menial **7** fawning, servile, slavish, subject **8** cringing, toadying **9** accessory, ancillary, auxiliary, prostrate, truckling **10** obsequious, subsidiary **11** bootlicking, subordinate, sycophantic **12** contributory, ingratiating

subside **3** ebb, sag **4** calm, drop, ease, sink, wane **5** abate, let up **6** cave in, lessen, recede, settle, shrink **7** descend, dwindle **8** decrease, diminish, level off, melt away, moderate

subsidence **5** letup **6** easing, ebbing, waning **7** calming **9** abatement, dwindling, lessening, recession, shrinking **10** decreasing, inactivity, moderation **12** diminishment

subsidiary **5** extra, lower, minor **6** branch, junior, lesser **7** adjunct **8** addition, division, inferior **9** accessory, affiliate, auxiliary, secondary **10** additional, supplement **11** subordinate **12** supplemental **13** supplementary

subsidy **3** aid **4** gift **5** award, grant **7** backing, support **9** allotment, provision **10** fellowship, grant-in-aid, honorarium, subvention **11** scholarship, sponsorship **13** appropriation, assistantship

subsist **4** live **5** exist **7** survive **9** stay alive **11** feed oneself, support life **12** make ends meet **23** keep body and soul together

subsistence **6** living, upkeep **7** support **8** survival **10** livelihood, sustenance **11** maintenance, nourishment

substance **4** body, core, germ, gist, pith, soul **5** force, heart, means, money, sense, stuff **6** burden, import, intent, marrow, matter, riches, thrust, wealth **7** element, essence, keynote, purport, reality **8** backbone, material, property, solidity **9** actuality, affluence, basic idea, main point **10** ingredient **11** connotation, constituent, corporality **12** corporeality, quintessence **13** corporealness

substandard **3** bad **4** poor **5** awful, lousy **6** crummy, shoddy **8** below par, inferior, terrible **9** imperfect **10** second-rate **11** second-class **12** below average

substantial **3** big **4** firm, full **5** ample, bulky, large, massy, solid, sound **7** massive, sizable **8** abundant **9** plenteous, plentiful **10** monumental **12** considerable

substantiate **5** prove **6** verify **7** confirm, support, sustain

11 corroborate, demonstrate **12** authenticate

substantiated 6 proved, proven **7** factual **8** verified **9** supported **11** well-founded **12** corroborated, demonstrated, well-grounded **13** authenticated

substantiation 5 proof **8** evidence **11** affirmation **12** verification **13** corroboration, demonstration, documentation **14** authentication

substitute 3 act **6** backup, change, ersatz, fill in, switch **7** standby, stand in, stopgap **8** deputize, exchange, pinch-hit, take over **9** alternate, makeshift, surrogate, temporary **10** understudy **11** alternative, pinch hitter, replacement

substitution 5 shift **6** change, switch **8** exchange, swapping **9** variation **10** alteration **11** replacement

substructure 4 base **6** ground **10** foundation, groundwork **12** underpinning

subsume 5 cover **6** assume, deduce **7** explain, include, involve **8** consider **13** subcategorize

subterfuge 4 ruse, sham, wile **5** blind, dodge, guile, shift, trick **6** scheme **7** evasion **8** artifice, intrigue, pretense, scheming **9** casuistry, chicanery, deception, duplicity, imposture, sophistry, stratagem **10** camouflage, sneakiness **11** deviousness, evasiveness, game-playing, machination, make-believe, smoke screen

subtle, subtile 3 sly **4** cagy, deft, fine, foxy, keen, wily **5** light, quick, sharp, slick **6** artful, astute, clever, crafty, expert, shifty, shrewd, tricky **7** cunning, devious, elusive, refined **8** delicate, indirect, masterly, skillful **9** deceptive, designing, ingenious, underhand **10** discerning **11** understated **13** perspicacious, sophisticated **14** discriminating

Subtle
character in: 12 The Alchemist
author: 6 Jonson

subtleties 7 nuances **10** fine points **11** refinements **12** distinctions

subtract 6 deduct, detach, lessen, reduce, remove **8** decrease, diminish, take away, withdraw

subtraction 7 removal **8** decrease **9** deduction, lessening, reduction **10** diminution, taking away, withdrawal **11** diminishing

suburbs 8 environs, vicinity **9** outskirts, periphery, precincts

sub verbo 12 under the word **15** under the heading

subversion 4 fall, ruin **6** defeat, mutiny **8** disorder, sabotage **9** overthrow, rebellion **10** corruption, disruption **11** destruction

subversive 7 traitor **8** quisling **9** insurgent, seditious **10** incendiary, traitorous, treasonous **11** seditionary **12** collaborator **13** revolutionary **14** fifth columnist **15** insurrectionary **16** collaborationist

subvert 3 mar **4** ruin, undo **5** smash, spoil, upset, wreck **6** defile, poison, ravage **7** despoil, destroy, disrupt, shatter **8** demolish, overturn **9** devastate, overthrow, undermine **11** contaminate

sub voce 21 under the specified word
literally: 13 under the voice

succeed 3 hit, win **5** avail, catch, click **6** accede, do well, follow, move up **7** inherit, prevail, prosper, replace, triumph **8** make a hit, make good, supplant, take over **9** bear fruit, strike oil

succeed at 2 do **6** attain **7** execute, fulfill, perform, realize **8** carry out **9** make a go of **10** accomplish

succeeding 5 later **6** coming, future **7** ensuing **8** oncoming **9** following, impending, posterior **10** consequent, subsequent, successive

succeed to 6 follow **7** inherit **15** ascend the throne

succes d'estime 15 critical success

success 3 hit **4** fame **5** smash **7** triumph, victory **8** conquest **9** affluence **10** ascendancy, attainment, prosperity **11** achievement, advancement, fulfillment, good fortune

successful 4 rich **6** proven **7** perfect, wealthy, well-off **8** achieved, affluent, complete, fruitful, thriving **9** effective **10** prosperous, triumphant **11** efficacious, flourishing **12** accomplished, acknowledged

successful completion 7 success, victory, winning **9** execution **10** making good **11** achievement, culmination, fulfillment, realization **12** consummation **14** accomplishment

succession 3 run **5** chain, cycle, round, train **6** course, series **8** sequence **9** accession **10** assumption, procession, stepping-up, taking over **11** inheritance, progression

successive 7 ensuing **10** continuous, succeeding **11** consecutive

successor 4 heir **5** donee **7** devisee, heiress, heritor, legatee **8** follower, parcener **9** heritress, joint heir **10** coparcener, substitute **11** beneficiary, replacement, reversioner **12** heir apparent

succinct 4 neat **5** brief, crisp, pithy, short, terse, tight **6** direct, gnomic **7** clipped, compact, concise, summary **9** condensed **10** aphoristic, to the point **12** epigrammatic

succinctness 7 brevity **9** crispness, terseness **11** compactness, conciseness **12** condensation

succor 3 aid **4** help **5** nurse **6** assist, back up, relief, shield, wait on **7** comfort, nurture, protect, relieve, support, sustain **8** befriend **10** assistance, minister to, sustenance, take care of **11** give a lift to, helping hand, lend a hand to, maintenance **13** accommodation

succulent 5 juicy **6** fleshy **9** toothsome **10** appetizing

succumb 3 die **5** yield **6** accede, expire, give in, submit **7** defer to, give way, go under **8** pass away **9** surrender **10** capitulate, comply with **12** fall victim to

such as
Latin: 2 eg **13** exempli gratia

such is life
French: 9 c'est la vie

sucker 3 sap **4** boob, butt, dupe, fool, goat, gull, jerk, mark **5** chump, patsy **6** pigeon, victim **7** cat's-paw, fall guy **8** easy mark, fair game, pushover **9** schlemiel, soft touch **11** sitting duck

Sucker State
nickname of: 8 Illinois

suck up 6 absorb, soak up **7** drink in **8** sponge up **9** swallow up

Sucre
legal capital of: **7** Bolivia

Sudan *see box*

Sudanese Republic *see* **4** Mali

sudden **4** rash **5** hasty, quick, rapid **6** abrupt, speedy **7** instant **9** immediate, impetuous **10** surprising, unexpected, unforeseen **11** precipitate, unlooked-for **13** instantaneous, unanticipated, unforeseeable

sudden development
French: **10** coup de main

suddenly **7** quickly **8** abruptly, in no time **9** all at once, instantly, on the spot **11** in an instant **12** all of a sudden, unexpectedly **13** at short notice **14** without warning **20** on the spur-of-the-moment **21** in the twinkling of an eye

sudden movement **4** dart, jolt **5** flash, spurt

sudden noise **3** pop **4** bang, clap, slam **5** burst, crash **6** report **9** explosion

Sudermann, Hermann
author of: **5** Honor **8** Dame Care **14** The Song of Songs

suds **3** ale **4** beer, brew, foam **5** draft, froth, lager **10** malt liquor

sue **3** beg **4** pray **5** plead **6** appeal **7** beseech, entreat, implore **8** petition **9** importune **10** supplicate

Sue, Eugene (Marie-Joseph)
author of: **15** The Wandering Jew **19** The Mysteries of Paris

suffer **4** ache, bear, hurt, pine **5** stand **6** endure, grieve, lament **7** agonize, despair, drop off, fall off, stomach, sustain, undergo **8** bear with, feel pain, tolerate **9** go through, put up with, withstand **10** be impaired **11** deteriorate

suffer for **6** pay for **8** atone for **9** answer for

suffering **3** woe **4** ache, care, hurt, pain, pang **5** agony, dolor, grief, throe, trial **6** misery, sorrow, twinge **7** anguish, anxiety, torment, torture, travail **8** distress, soreness **9** heartache **10** affliction, discomfort, heavy heart, irritation **11** tribulation

suffice **2** do **4** last, meet, pass **5** avail, get by, serve **6** answer, make do **7** fulfill, qualify, satisfy

sufficiency **6** enough, plenty **7** surfeit **8** adequacy **9** abundance, ampleness, profusion

sufficient **5** ample **6** enough, plenty **7** copious, minimal **8** abundant, adequate **9** plenteous, plentiful **11** up to the mark **12** satisfactory

suffocate **3** gag **5** choke **6** quench, stifle **7** garrote, smother **8** snuff out, strangle, throttle **10** asphyxiate, extinguish

suffuse **4** fill, soak **5** cover, steep **6** infuse **7** diffuse, overrun, pervade **8** overflow, permeate, saturate **9** transfuse **10** impregnate, infiltrate, overspread

Sugar State
nickname of: **9** Louisiana

sugary **5** mushy, sweet **6** syrupy **7** cloying, fulsome, gushing, honeyed, mawkish **8** cajoling, unctuous **10** flattering, saccharine

suggest **3** bid **4** move, urge **5** imply, posit **6** advise, hint at, submit **7** advance, counsel, propose **8** advocate, indicate, intimate, propound **9** give a clue, recommend **16** lead one to believe

suggested **6** hinted **7** implied, oblique **8** implicit, indirect, possible, proposed

suggestion **3** dab, tip **4** dash, hint, tint **5** grain, shade, taste,

---

Sudan
capital/largest city: **8** Khartoum
others: **3** Waw, Yei **4** Juba **5** Kosti, Meroe, Nyala, Obeid, Opari, Segon **6** Atbara, Suakin **7** Aluboyd, Elobeid, Geneina, Kassala, Malakal **8** Elfasher, Omdurman **9** al-Ubayyid, Elgeneina, Port Sudan, Wad Medani
division: **7** Jonglei **9** Upper Nile **12** Bahr el Ghazal **16** Eastern Equatoria, Western Equatoria
ancient kingdom: **4** Alwa, Funj, Kush **7** Maqurra
measure: **2** ud
monetary unit: **5** pound **8** piastres
weight: **5** habba
lake: **2** No **4** Chad, Toad **6** Nasser
mountain: **4** Nuba **7** Imatong **9** Dongotona **10** Jabal Marra, Jebel Marra **18** Ethiopian Highlands
highest point: **7** Kinyeti
river: **4** Nile **5** Sobat **6** Atbara **8** Blue Nile **9** White Nile **10** Bahr el-Arab **11** Bahr el-Jebel **12** Bahr el-Ghazal
sea: **3** Red
physical feature:
desert: **6** Libyan, Nubian
gum forest: **8** Kordofan
plain: **6** Gezira
sandstorm: **6** haboob
plateau: **8** Kordufan
swamp: **4** Sudd
people: **3** Bor, Dor, Fur **4** Arab, Bari, Beri, Bobo, Daza, Egba, Fula, Golo, Nuba, Nuer, Poul, Sere **5** Anuak, Bongo, Dinka, Fulah, Hausa, Joluo, Junje, Mosgu, Mossi, Negro, Tibbu, Volta **6** Acholi, Azande, Gurusi, Hamite, Lotuho, Makari, Nilote, Nubian, Senufo, Surhai, Tuareg **7** Balante, Baqqara, Gubayna, Jaaliin, Nilotes, Shilluk, Songhai, Songhay, Songhoi, Sourhai **8** Kababish, Mandingo, Menkiera **9** Sarakille **10** Gurmantshi, Shaiquiyya
leader: **5** Mahdi **9** al-Nimeiry **10** Mehemet Ali **22** Jaafar Mohammed al-Nemery
language: **2** Ga **3** Efe, Ewe, Ibo, Kru, Vak, Vei **4** Efik, Mole, Tshi **6** Arabic, Nubian, Yoruba **7** English **8** Mandango, Mandingo **9** Ta Bedawie
religion: **5** Islam **7** animism **12** Christianity
place:
canal: **7** Jonglei
dam: **6** Sennar **8** Roseires **10** Jebel Aulia
temple: **4** Lion
tomb: **5** Mahdi
feature:
boat: **6** murkab
food: **4** dura **5** dukhn, kisra

tinge, touch, trace **6** advice, urging **7** counsel, feeling, pointer, soupcon **9** prompting, suspicion **10** intimation, sprinkling **11** exhortation **14** recommendation

suggestive 4 lewd, racy **5** bawdy, loose **6** risque, sexual, wanton **8** allusive, improper, indecent, off-color, prurient, unseemly **9** evocative, remindful, seductive, shameless **10** expressive, indelicate, licentious **11** provocative, reminiscent, stimulating

sui generis 6 unique **12** of her own kind, of his own kind, of its own kind **14** of their own kind

sui juris 14 of one's own right **31** capable of managing one's own affairs **36** capable of assuming legal responsibility

suit 3 fit **4** duds, garb, plea, togs **5** befit, court, getup, habit, match **6** appeal, attire, become, beseem, follow, livery, oblige, outfit, please, prayer, wooing **7** apparel, begging, clothes, content, costume, delight, gladden, gratify, raiment, satisfy, uniform **8** clothing, entreaty, jell with, make glad, petition **9** addresses, agree with, conform to, courtship, do one good, overtures, tally with, trappings **10** accord with, attentions, comply with, fall in with, habiliment, lovemaking, square with **11** accommodate, go along with **12** be becoming to, blandishment, correspond to, dovetail with, solicitation, supplication **13** accoutrements, be agreeable to, harmonize with **14** be acceptable to, be convenient to **15** be appropriate to **16** be appropriate for

suitable 3 apt, fit **4** meet **5** right **6** proper, seemly, worthy **7** apropos, fitting, germane **8** adequate, becoming, relevant **9** befitting, congruous, cut out for, pertinent, qualified **10** applicable, seasonable **11** appropriate **12** commensurate

suitcase 3 bag **4** grip **6** valise **7** satchel **8** knapsack, rucksack **9** duffel bag, gladstone, two-suiter **11** portmanteau **12** overnight bag, traveling bag

suite 3 set **4** flat **5** chain, court, group, rooms, round **6** convoy, series **7** company, cortege, retinue **8** servants **9** apartment, followers, following **10** attendants **11** progression

suited 3 fit **7** adapted, attired, clothed, dressed, good for, matched **8** adjusted, agreeing, becoming **9** agreeable **11** appropriate, harmonizing

suit of armor 4 mail **5** armor **9** chain mail **10** coat of mail

suitor 4 beau, love **5** flame, lover, swain, wooer **6** fellow **7** admirer, gallant **8** young man **9** boyfriend **10** sweetheart

sulfur
chemical symbol: 1 S

sulk 4 crab, fret, fume, mope, pout **5** brood, chafe, frown, grump, scowl **6** glower, grouch **7** grumble **8** be in a pet, be miffed, be put out, be sullen, look glum **9** be in a huff **11** be resentful **12** be out of humor

sulky 6 morose, sullen **7** pouting **8** petulant

sullen 4 blue, dark, glum, grim, sore, sour **5** cross, heavy, moody, sulky, surly **6** crabby, dismal, dreary, gloomy, grumpy, morose, somber, touchy **7** crabbed, doleful, forlorn, grouchy, peevish **8** brooding, desolate, dolorous, funereal, mournful, petulant, scowling **9** cheerless, glowering, resentful, saturnine, splenetic, unamiable **10** depressing, foreboding, ill-humored, ill-natured, melancholy, out of humor, out of sorts, unsociable **11** ill-tempered **13** temperamental
French: 8 farouche

sullied 5 dirty **6** impure, soiled **7** defiled, stained, unclean **9** tarnished

Sullivan, Elizabeth
real name of: 14 Elsa Lanchester

Sullivan, John Florence
real name of: 9 Fred Allen

Sullivan, John L (Lawrence)
nickname: 15 Boston Strong Boy
sport: 6 boxing
class: 11 heavyweight
fought: 12 bareknuckled

Sullivan, Louis H
architect of: 16 Guaranty (now Prudential) Building (Buffalo NY) **18** Auditorium Building (Chicago), Wainwright Building (St Louis MO) **21** Carson Pirie Scott Store (Chicago), Stock Exchange Building (Chicago), Merchants' National Bank (Grinnell, IA), National Farmers' Bank (Owatonna, MN)
principle: 21 "form follows function"
student: 16 Frank Lloyd Wright

Sullivan, Pat
creator/artist of: 11 Felix the Cat

Sullivan's Travels
director: 14 Preston Sturges
cast: 10 Joel McCrea **12** Veronica Lake **13** Robert Warwick **15** William Demarest

sully 4 ruin, soil, spot **5** dirty, spoil, stain **6** befoul, defame, defile, smudge **7** begrime, besmear, blemish, corrupt, pollute, tarnish **8** disgrace, dishonor **10** adulterate **11** contaminate

Sully, Thomas
born: 7 England **10** Horncastle
artwork: 13 Queen Victoria **23** The Passage of the Delaware **28** Colonel Thomas Handasyd Perkins **29** Washington Crossing the Delaware

sultan 4 king **5** ruler **7** emperor, monarch **9** sovereign

sultana 5 grape **6** raisin **7** empress **11** sultan's wife

sultry 3 hot **4** sexy **5** close, humid, muggy **6** erotic, stuffy, sweaty **7** sensual **8** stifling **10** oppressive, sweltering, voluptuous **11** provocative, suffocating

sum 4 cash, coin, jack **5** bread, bucks, dough, funds, score, tally, whole **6** amount, moolah **7** lettuce, measure **8** currency, entirety, quantity, sum total, totality **9** aggregate, summation **12** entire amount **13** amount of money

sumac 4 Rhus
varieties: 5 dwarf, lemon, scrub, sugar, swamp **6** desert, laurel, poison, smooth, velvet **7** scarlet, shining, tanner's, tobacco, wing-rib **8** fragrant, lemonade, Sicilian, staghorn, Venetian **9** elm-leaved, evergreen, Virginian **11** small-leaved **12** sweet-scented

sum and substance 4 core, crux, gist, guts, meat **5** heart **7** essence **10** brass tacks **11** nitty-gritty

Sumatra
chevrotain: 4 napu
city: 5 Medan **6** Padang **9** Palembang
country: 9 Indonesia

crop: 3 tea 6 coffee, rubber
currency: 6 rupiah
empire: 9 Srivijaya
highest point: 10 Mt Kerintji
inhabitant: 5 Batak, Malay 11 Minangkabau
mountain range: 7 Barisan
river: 4 Musi, Siak 6 Asahan
squirrel shrew: 4 tana
strait: 5 Sunda 7 Malacca

Sumerian Mythology *see* 19 Babylonian Mythology

Summa Catholicae Fidei Contra Gentiles
author: 13 Thomas Aquinas

summa cum laude 17 with highest praise

Summanus
origin: 5 Roman
god of: 13 thunderstorms

summarily 6 at once 7 quickly 8 directly, promptly, speedily 9 forthwith, on the spot 11 arbitrarily, immediately, straightway 12 straightaway, with dispatch, without delay 13 at short notice, precipitately 14 unhesitatingly 20 on the spur of the moment

summarize 5 sum up 6 digest 7 abridge, outline 8 abstract, compress, condense 9 capsulize, epitomize, synopsize 10 abbreviate 11 concentrate 12 recapitulate

summary 4 curt 5 brief, hasty, rapid, short, terse, token 6 apercu, digest, precis, resume, sketch, sudden, survey 7 concise, cursory, epitome, hurried, rundown 8 abridged, abstract, analysis, succinct, syllabus, synopsis 9 breakdown, condensed 10 abridgment, peremptory 11 perfunctory 12 abbreviation, condensation, short version 13 instantaneous

Summa Theologiae
author: 13 Thomas Aquinas

summation 5 total 6 review 7 summary 8 addition 9 reckoning 19 concluding statement

Summer and Smoke
author: 17 Tennessee Williams
director: 14 Peter Glenville
cast: 9 Una Merkel 10 Rita Moreno 12 Earl Holliman 13 Geraldine Page 14 Laurence Harvey

summer fruit
goddess of: 5 Carpo

summerhouse 5 arbor, cabin, kiosk 6 cabana, gazebo, pagoda 7 cottage

Summerson, Esther
character in: 10 Bleak House
author: 7 Dickens

Summertime
director: 9 David Lean
based on story by: 14 Arthur Laurents (The Time of the Cuckoo)
cast: 10 Isa Miranda 13 Darren McGavin, Rossano Brazzi 16 Katharine Hepburn
setting: 6 Venice

summery 3 hot 4 warm 5 balmy, close, humid, muggy, sunny 6 stuffy, sultry, torrid, vernal 8 aestival, roasting, stifling, sunshiny 9 scorching, temperate 10 oppressive, summerlike

summit 3 tip, top 4 acme, apex, peak 5 crest, crown 6 apogee, climax, height, vertex, zenith 8 pinnacle 11 culmination 12 highest point 13 crowning point

summon 4 call 5 rouse 6 beckon, call on, draw on, gather, invoke, muster, strain 7 call for, call out, command, send for 8 activate, subpoena 9 call forth 12 call together 14 call into action, serve with a writ

summons 4 call 8 citation, subpoena 12 notification

summon up 4 stir 5 evoke 6 arouse, excite 7 collect, marshal, provoke 8 assemble 9 call forth, stimulate

summum bonum 9 chief good 11 highest good

sumptuous 4 dear, posh, rich 5 grand, plush, regal 6 costly, deluxe, lavish, superb 7 elegant 8 splendid 9 elaborate, expensive, luxurious 10 exorbitant, munificent 11 extravagant, magnificent, spectacular

sumptuousness 4 luxe 6 luxury 8 elegance, grandeur, richness, splendor 12 magnificence 13 expensiveness, luxuriousness

sum total 6 amount 8 totality 9 aggregate 11 final result

sum up 3 add 5 tally, total, tot up 6 reckon 7 compute, count up 9 calculate, enumerate, summarize

sun
god of: 2 Ra, Re 3 Sol, Utu 5 Horus 6 Apollo, Helios 7 Shamesh 8 Hyperion

Sun Also Rises, The
author: 15 Ernest Hemingway
character: 10 Bill Gorton, Jake Barnes, Robert Cohn 11 Pedro Romero 15 Lady Brett Ashley, Michael (Mike) Campbell

sunbathe 3 tan 4 bask 12 soak up the sun 13 catch some rays

Sunday
means: 11 day of the sun
heavenly body: 3 sun
day of: 4 rest 7 worship 8 blue laws
observance: 16 Christian Sabbath
French: 8 dimanche
Italian: 8 domenica
Spanish: 7 domingo
German: 7 sonntag

Sunday best 6 finery 8 glad rags 11 fine clothes 16 best bib and tucker

Sunday Morning
author: 14 Wallace Stevens

sunder 4 rend, rive 5 crack, sever 6 cleave, divide 8 separate 9 tear apart 10 break in two 11 break in half

sundown 4 dusk 6 sunset 7 evening 8 eventide, twilight 9 nightfall

Sundowners, The
director: 13 Fred Zinnemann
cast: 11 Deborah Kerr, Dina Merrill, Glynis Johns 12 Peter Ustinov 13 Robert Mitchum
setting: 9 Australia

sundry 4 many 5 mixed 6 divers, motley, myriad, varied 7 diverse, several, various 8 assorted, manifold, numerous 9 different 10 dissimilar 12 multifarious 13 heterogeneous, miscellaneous

sun-filled 4 fair 5 clear, sunny 6 bright, cheery 8 cheerful 9 cloudless

sunfish 5 dwarf, perch, pigmy, sunny 6 redear 7 lepomis, longear, teleost 8 bluegill, sailboat 9 blackband 10 Sacramento 11 bluespotted, centrarchid, pumpkinseed, yellowbelly

sunflower 10 Helianthus 12 Balsamorhiza
varieties: 4 ashy 5 giant, showy, stiff, swamp 6 common, desert, Oregon 7 darkeye, Mexican 8 thin-leaf 10 Maximilian 12 cucumberleaf

Sunflower State
nickname of: 6 Kansas

sunless 4 dark, dull, gray,

hazy **5** bleak, foggy, misty, murky, rainy **6** cloudy, dismal, dreary, gloomy, leaden, somber **8** overcast **9** cheerless **10** depressing

sunny **4** fair, fine **5** clear, happy, jolly, merry **6** blithe, breezy, bright, cheery, genial, jovial, joyful, joyous, sunlit **7** affable, amiable, buoyant, shining, smiling **8** cheerful, sunshiny **9** brilliant, cloudless, sparkling, unclouded **10** optimistic **12** lighthearted

sunrise **4** dawn **5** sunup **6** aurora **7** dawning **8** cockcrow, daybreak, daylight **10** break of day, crepuscule, newborn day **15** dawn's early light **16** rosy-fingered dawn

sunset **4** dusk **7** sundown **8** blue hour, eventide, gloaming, twilight **9** nightfall **10** close of day, crepuscule

Sunset Boulevard
director: **11** Billy Wilder
cast: **8** Jack Webb **9** Fred Clark **11** Hedda Hopper **12** Buster Keaton **13** Cecil B DeMille, Gloria Swanson (Norma Desmond), William Holden **16** Erich von Stroheim

Sunset State
nickname of: **6** Oregon

sunshade **3** hat **5** visor **6** awning **7** parasol, roundel **8** sombrero, umbrella **9** sunscreen

Sunshine State
nickname of: **7** Florida **9** New Mexico

sunstone
species: **8** feldspar

suntan **3** tan **5** brown **6** bronze **7** sunburn

suo jure **14** in one's own right

suo loco **14** in one's own place **19** in one's rightful place

Suomen Tasavalta *see* **7** Finland

Suomi *see* **7** Finland

sup **3** eat, sip **4** dine, feed **5** drink, feast, supra **6** absorb, supper, supply **7** consume **8** superior **10** supplement **11** superlative **13** supplementary

Supai *see* **9** Havasupai

super **4** A-one, fine **5** grand, great, prime, prize, swell **6** grade-A, superb, tip-top **7** capital **8** peerless, superior, terrific, top-notch **9** excellent, fantastic, first-rate, marvelous, matchless, non pareil, superfine, wonderful **10** first-class, tremendous, unexcelled, world-class **11** outstanding, superlative **12** incomparable **13** extraordinary

superabound **4** teem **5** swarm **6** thrive **7** burgeon **8** be rich in, flourish, overflow

superabundance **4** glut, riot **5** flood, spate **6** deluge, excess, plenty **7** surfeit, surplus **8** overdose, overflow, pleonasm, plethora **9** avalanche **10** inundation, oversupply, redundance **11** superfluity **12** extravagance **13** overabundance **14** more than enough
French: **19** embarras de richesses

superabundant **4** lush **6** lavish **7** copious, profuse, teeming **8** swarming, thriving **9** exuberant, luxuriant **10** burgeoning **11** flourishing, overflowing

superb **4** A-one, rare, rich **5** elect, grand, regal **6** choice, costly, deluxe, golden, lordly, select, tip-top **7** elegant, stately **8** gorgeous, imposing, laudable, majestic, peerless, precious, princely, splendid, top-notch, very fine **9** admirable, excellent, expensive, exquisite, first-rate, luxurious, marvelous, matchless, priceless, sumptuous, top-drawer **10** first-class **11** crackerjack, magnificent **12** breathtaking, praiseworthy **15** of the first water

Super Bowl *see box, p. 948*

supercilious **5** proud **6** lordly, snooty, uppity **7** haughty, pompous, stuck-up **8** arrogant, prideful, snobbish **10** disdainful **11** egotistical, magisterial, overbearing, patronizing **12** vainglorious **13** condescending, high-and-mighty, self-important

superciliousness **4** airs **7** hauteur **8** snobbery **9** arrogance, pomposity **10** lordliness, snootiness **11** haughtiness **12** snobbishness **14** disdainfulness

superficial **4** slim **5** faint, outer, silly, trite **6** flimsy, hollow, myopic, slight **7** cursory, minimal, nodding, partial, passing, shallow, summary, surface **8** exterior, mindless, skin-deep **9** desultory, frivolous **10** incomplete **11** empty-headed, perfunctory **12** lacking depth, narrow-minded, on the surface, shortsighted

superficiality **6** myopia **9** frivolity **11** cursoriness, shallowness **13** desultoriness **16** narrow-mindedness, shortsightedness

superfine **4** A-one **6** choice, grade-A, superb, tip-top **8** superior, top-notch **9** excellent, extra fine, first-rate **10** first-class **11** outstanding, overrefined, superlative **13** extraordinary

superfluity **3** fat **5** extra, frill **6** excess, luxury **7** greater, surfeit, surplus **8** overflow, overmuch, plethora **11** gingerbread **12** extravagance **13** embellishment **14** superabundance

superfluous **5** extra, spare **6** excess **7** surplus **8** needless **9** excessive, redundant **10** extraneous, gratuitous, pleonastic **11** inessential, unnecessary **12** nonessential, overgenerous **13** superabundant, supernumerary **14** supererogatory

superhuman **4** epic **5** great **6** divine, heroic **7** godlike, supreme **8** superior **9** herculean, unearthly **10** miraculous, omnipotent **12** otherworldly, supermundane, supernatural, supranatural, transcendent **13** preternatural

Superi
origin: **5** Roman
collective name for: **4** gods

superintend **3** run **4** boss **6** direct, govern, manage **7** oversee **9** supervise, watch over **10** administer **12** administrate, have charge of

superintendence **6** charge **7** bossing, running **9** direction, governing **10** leadership, management, overseeing **12** jurisdiction **14** administration

superintendent **4** boss, head **5** chief **6** warden **7** foreman, headman, manager, proctor, steward **8** director, guardian, overseer **9** custodian **10** supervisor

superior **4** boss, fine **5** chief **6** better, choice, deluxe, leader, lordly, senior **7** greater, haughty, notable **8** arrogant, foremost, higher-up, peerless, snobbish **9** commander, excellent, first-rate, imperious, matchless, nonpareil, unrivaled **10** inimitable, noteworthy, preeminent, supervisor **11** exceptional, illustrious, patronizing **12** incomparable, more advanced, vainglorious

Super Bowl
1967:
winner: **15** Green Bay Packers
loser: **16** Kansas City Chiefs
site: **8** Coliseum **10** Los Angeles
1968:
winner: **15** Green Bay Packers
loser: **14** Oakland Raiders
site: **5** Miami **10** Orange Bowl
1969:
winner: **11** New York Jets
loser: **14** Baltimore Colts
site: **5** Miami **10** Orange Bowl
1970:
winner: **16** Kansas City Chiefs
loser: **16** Minnesota Vikings
site: **10** New Orleans **13** Tulane Stadium
1971:
winner: **14** Baltimore Colts
loser: **13** Dallas Cowboys
site: **5** Miami **10** Orange Bowl
1972:
winner: **13** Dallas Cowboys
loser: **13** Miami Dolphins
site: **10** New Orleans **13** Tulane Stadium
1973:
winner: **13** Miami Dolphins
loser: **18** Washington Redskins
site: **8** Coliseum **10** Los Angeles
1974:
winner: **13** Miami Dolphins
loser: **16** Minnesota Vikings
site: **7** Houston **11** Rice Stadium
1975:
winner: **18** Pittsburgh Steelers
loser: **16** Minnesota Vikings
site: **10** New Orleans **13** Tulane Stadium
1976:
winner: **18** Pittsburgh Steelers
loser: **13** Dallas Cowboys
site: **5** Miami **10** Orange Bowl
1977:
winner: **14** Oakland Raiders
loser: **16** Minnesota Vikings
site: **8** Pasadena, Rose Bowl
1978:
winner: **13** Dallas Cowboys
loser: **13** Denver Broncos
site: **9** Superdome **10** New Orleans
1979:
winner: **18** Pittsburgh Steelers
loser: **13** Dallas Cowboys
site: **5** Miami **10** Orange Bowl
1980:
winner: **18** Pittsburgh Steelers
loser: **14** Los Angeles Rams
site: **8** Pasadena, Rose Bowl
1981:
winner: **14** Oakland Raiders
loser: **18** Philadelphia Eagles
site: **9** Superdome **10** New Orleans
1982:
winner: **23** San Francisco Forty-Niners
loser: **17** Cincinnati Bengals
site: **7** Pontiac **10** Silverdome
1983:
winner: **18** Washington Redskins
loser: **13** Miami Dolphins
site: **8** Pasadena, Rose Bowl
1984:
winner: **17** Los Angeles Raiders
loser: **18** Washington Redskins
site: **12** Tampa Stadium
1985:
winner: **23** San Francisco Forty-Niners
loser: **13** Miami Dolphins
site: **8** Palo Alto **15** Stanford Stadium
1986:
winner: **12** Chicago Bears
loser: **18** New England Patriots
site: **9** Superdome **10** New Orleans
1987:
winner: **13** New York Giants
loser: **13** Denver Broncos
site: **8** Pasadena, Rose Bowl
1988:
winner: **18** Washington Redskins
loser: **13** Denver Broncos
site: **8** San Diego **17** Jack Murphy Stadium
1989:
winner: **23** San Francisco Forty-Niners
loser: **17** Cincinnati Bengals
site: **5** Miami **16** Joe Robbie Stadium

13 condescending, distinguished, high-and-mighty
French: **13** par excellence

superlative **4** best **5** crack, prime **6** expert **7** supreme **8** foremost, greatest, peerless, superior **9** exquisite, first-rate, matchless, nonpareil, paramount, unequaled, unmatched, unrivaled **10** consummate, preeminent, surpassing **11** magnificent, unsurpassed **12** incomparable, transcendent, unparalleled **15** of the first water **17** of the highest order

superman
German: **10** Ubermensch

Superman
creator: **11** Jerry Siegel
character: **4** Lara **5** Jor-el, Kal-el **8** Eben Kent, Lois Lane, Sy Horton **9** Clark Kent **10** Jimmy Olsen, Martha Kent, Perry White **22** Inspector Bill Henderson **23** Professor JJ Pepperwinkle
place: **7** Krypton **10** Metropolis, Smallville **14** telephone booth
nickname: **10** Man of Steel
director: **13** Richard Donner
cast: **9** Glenn Ford, Ned Beatty **11** Gene Hackman **12** Jackie Cooper, Margot Kidder (Lois Lane), Marlon Brando **14** Valerie Perrine **16** Christopher Reeve

supernatural **6** mystic, occult **7** psychic **9** spiritual, unearthly **10** miraculous, paranormal **12** otherworldly, supranatural **13** preternatural, superphysical **14** transcendental

superpatriotism **8** jingoism **10** chauvinism **11** nationalism

supersede **7** discard, replace, succeed **8** displace, set aside, supplant

supervise **4** boss, head **5** guide **6** direct, govern, handle, manage, survey **7** conduct, control, oversee **8** regulate **9** look after, watch over **10** administer **11** preside over, superintend **12** have charge of

supervision **6** orders **7** control **8** guidance **9** direction **10** governance, government, management, regulation **12** surveillance **15** superintendence

supervisor **4** boss, head **5** chief **7** foreman, manager, steward **8** director, overseer

9 commander 13 administrator 14 superintendent

supper club 4 cafe 6 bistro 7 cabaret 9 nightclub, night spot

supplant 6 depose 7 replace 8 displace 9 supersede 14 take the place of

supple 5 lithe 6 limber, pliant 7 elastic, lissome, plastic, pliable 8 amenable, bendable, flexible, graceful, yielding 9 adaptable, compliant, malleable, tractable 10 submissive 11 acquiescent, complaisant, coordinated

supplement 5 add to, annex, extra, rider 6 extend, insert 7 adjunct, augment, codicil, section 8 addendum, addition, appendix, increase 9 added part, corollary, extension 10 attachment, complement, postscript 12 augmentation

supplementary 5 added, extra 6 backup 7 added on, reserve 8 appended, attached, expanded, extended 9 ancillary, auxiliary, enlarging, secondary 10 additional, amplifying, augmenting 11 subordinate 13 complementary

suppliant 5 asker 6 beggar, cadger, seeker, suitor 7 almsman 8 claimant 9 almswoman, appellant, beseecher, entreater, mendicant 10 petitioner, supplicant 11 supplicator

Suppliants, The
author: 9 Aeschylus
character: 6 Danaus 8 Pelasgus 19 Fifty Sons of Aegyptus 20 Fifty Maiden Daughters

Suppliants, The
author: 9 Euripides
character: 6 Aethra, Evadne 7 Theseus 8 Adrastus

supplicate 3 ask, beg 4 pray 5 plead 6 ask for 7 entreat 8 appeal to, call upon, petition

supplication 3 cry 4 plea, suit 6 appeal, orison, prayer 7 bumming, cadging, request 8 entreaty, mooching, petition 10 invocation 11 application, beseechment, imploration, imprecation, panhandling 12 solicitation

supplies 4 gear 5 goods, items 8 material 9 equipment, foodstuff, trappings 10 provisions 13 accoutrements

supply 4 fund, give 5 cache, equip, grant, quota, stock, store, yield 6 bestow, outfit, render 7 deal out, deliver, furnish, present, provide, reserve 9 providing, provision, reservoir 10 allocation, come up with, contribute, furnishing 12 provisioning

support 3 aid 4 base, bear, help, hold, keep, lift, pile, post, prop, stay 5 abide, boost, brace, brook, carry, favor, means, shore, stand 6 assist, back up, bear up, clinch, column, defend, endure, foster, hold up, pay for, pillar, ratify, second, succor, suffer, uphold, upkeep, verify 7 backing, bear out, bolster, comfort, confirm, defense, endorse, espouse, finance, further, keeping, nurture, shore up, sustain, warrant 8 abutment, accredit, advocacy, advocate, buttress, champion, espousal, maintain, pedestal, pilaster, sanction, strength, tolerate, vouch for 9 establish, guarantee, patronage, patronize, promotion, put up with, reinforce, stanchion, subsidize 10 assistance, livelihood, provide for, stand up for, stick up for, strengthen, sustenance, underwrite 11 buttressing, consolation, corroborate, countenance, furtherance, go along with, involvement, maintenance, subsistence 12 substantiate, underpinning 13 encouragement

supportable 9 endurable 10 defensible, verifiable 11 sustainable 12 demonstrable, maintainable

supporter 4 ally 6 backer, helper, patron 8 adherent, advocate, champion, defender, disciple, follower, partisan, upholder 10 benefactor, well-wisher 11 sympathizer

supposable 8 credible 9 thinkable 10 believable, imaginable 11 conceivable, perceivable

suppose 5 fancy, guess, judge, posit 6 assume, divine, gather, reckon 7 believe, imagine, presume, surmise, suspect 8 conceive, consider 9 predicate 11 hypothesize 14 take for granted

supposed 5 given 7 alleged, assumed 8 probable, putative 9 imaginary 11 conjectural, speculative, theoretical 12 hypothetical

supposition 4 idea, view 5 given, guess 6 belief, notion, theory, thesis 7 opinion, surmise 9 guesswork, postulate, suspicion 10 assumption, conjecture, hypothesis 11 predication, presumption, proposition, speculation

suppress 4 bury, curb, hide 5 check, crush, quash, quell, still 6 keep in, muffle, quench, squash, stifle, subdue 7 conceal, control, cover up, inhibit, put down, repress, silence, smother, squelch 8 hold back, keep back, overcome, restrain, restrict, snuff out, withhold 9 overpower 10 extinguish, keep secret, put an end to 11 hold in leash, keep private 12 put a damper on 13 put under wraps

suppressant 4 curb 5 brake 7 control 9 restraint

suppressed feelings 7 reserve 9 restraint 10 constraint, diffidence

supremacy 5 power 7 mastery, primacy 10 ascendancy, domination, precedence 11 omnipotence, paramountcy, preeminence, sovereignty, superiority 13 transcendency

supreme 4 tops 5 chief, first, prime 6 ruling 7 extreme, highest, leading, perfect, topmost 8 absolute, dominant, foremost, peerless 9 matchless, nonpareil, paramount, principal, sovereign, unequaled, unlimited, unmatched, unrivaled, uppermost 10 commanding, consummate, unexcelled 11 all-powerful, superlative, unqualified, unsurpassed 12 front-ranking, immeasurable, incomparable, second to none, unparalleled 13 unconditional

surcease 4 quit, rest, stop 5 abate, cease, pause 7 die away, respite 8 conclude, leave off 11 come to an end, discontinue 17 come to a standstill

surcharge 3 tax 4 levy 6 excise, impost

surcingle 4 band, belt 5 girth 6 girdle 8 cincture

sure 4 fast, firm, true 5 solid, sound 6 stable, steady 7 assured, certain 8 accurate, failsafe, faithful, flawless, positive, reliable, surefire, unerring 9 confident, convinced, unfailing 10 dependable, infallible, undoubting 11 trustworthy 12 never-failing

sure bet 4 fact 5 cinch 7 reality 9 actuality, certainty, sure thing 13 inevitability 14 inescapability

surely 7 no doubt 8 of course, to be sure 9 assuredly, certainly, doubtless **10** by all means, definitely, for certain, infallibly, positively **11** come what may, indubitably, undoubtedly, without fail **12** emphatically, without doubt **14** unquestionably

sureness **6** surety **9** assurance, certainty, certitude **10** confidence **11** assuredness **12** positiveness **13** self-assurance **14** conclusiveness, self-confidence, self-possession

sure thing **4** fact **5** cinch **7** reality, sure bet **9** actuality, certainty **13** inevitability **14** inescapability

surety **4** bail, bond **8** sureness **9** certainty, certitude, guarantee **10** confidence **12** positiveness

surface **3** top **4** coat, face, skin **5** crust, shell **6** facade, finish, veneer **7** coating, outside **8** covering, exterior **11** superficies

Surface family
characters in: **19** The School for Scandal
member: **6** Joseph **7** Charles **9** Sir Oliver
author: **8** Sheridan

surfeit **4** cloy, glut, sate **5** gorge, stuff **6** excess **7** satiate, satisfy, surplus **8** overmuch, plethora **9** plenitude, profusion, repletion, satiation **10** oversupply, surplusage **11** exorbitance, overindulge, prodigality, superfluity **12** extravagance **13** overabundance **14** more than enough, superabundance **15** supersaturation

surfeited **4** full **5** sated **6** gorged **7** glutted, replete, stuffed **8** overfull, satiated **9** satisfied

surge **4** rush, wave **5** flood, swell **7** torrent

Suriname ***see box***

Suriname
other name: **7** Surinam **11** Dutch Guiana
capital/largest city: **10** Paramaribo
others: **6** Albina **7** Totness **9** Groningen **10** Brokopondo, Onverwacht **13** Nieuw Nickerie **14** Nieuw Amsterdam
measure: **7** ketting
monetary unit: **4** cent **7** guilder
lake: **14** Van Blommestein
mountain: **4** Emma **6** Kayser, Oranje **10** Tumuc-Humac, Wilhelmina **13** Eilerts Il Haan, Van Ach Van Wyck **15** Guiana Highlands
highest point: **10** Julianatop
river: **6** Maroni **7** Surinam **8** Nickerie, Suriname **9** Coppename **10** Courantijn, Courantyne, Tapanahoni
ocean: **8** Atlantic
physical feature:
falls: **7** Kaiteur
people: **4** Boni, Bush, Trio **5** Djuka, Dutch **6** Creole, Wayana **7** African, Chinese **10** Amerindian, Boschneger, West Indian **11** Asian Indian
settler: **22** Lord Willoughby of Parham
language: **5** Carib, Dutch, Hindi **6** Arawak **7** English **8** Javanese, Taki-Taki **10** Hindustani **11** Sranan Tongo **12** Sranang Tongo
religion: **5** Hindu, Islam **10** Protestant **13** Roman Catholic
feature:
canoe: **6** corial
clothing: **4** sari **5** dhoti **6** kamisa, sarong **10** koto-missie
hat: **3** fez
hut: **5** benab
scarf: **9** selendong
tree: **4** dali, lana, mora **5** dalli, genip, icica **7** acuyari, quassia **9** bethabara
food:
drink: **7** paiwari

surliness **8** ill humor, rudeness **9** bad temper **11** discourtesy, grouchiness **12** irascibility

surly **4** rude, sour **5** cross, gruff, harsh, testy **6** abrupt, crusty, grumpy, sullen, touchy **7** bearish, crabbed, grouchy, hostile, peevish, uncivil, waspish **8** choleric, churlish, insolent, petulant, snappish, snarling **9** irascible, splenetic, unamiable **10** ill-humored, ill-natured, unfriendly **11** bad-tempered **12** discourteous

surmise **4** deem, idea **5** guess, infer, judge, opine, posit, think **6** belief, notion **7** believe, imagine, opinion, presume, suppose, suspect, thought **8** conclude, consider, theorize **9** suspicion **10** assumption, conjecture, hypothesis, presuppose **11** hypothesize, presumption, speculation, supposition **13** shot in the dark

surmount **3** top **4** best **5** clear, climb, scale, worst **6** defeat, master **7** conquer, get over **8** overcome, vanquish **11** prevail over, triumph over **14** get the better of

surpass **3** top **4** beat, best **5** excel, outdo **6** exceed, outrun **7** eclipse **8** go beyond, outclass, outshine, outstrip, override **9** rise above, transcend **10** overshadow **11** go one better, leave behind, outdistance, triumph over **12** be better than, be superior to **13** have it all over

surplus **4** glut **5** extra **6** excess **7** overage, surfeit **8** leftover, overflow, plethora, residual **10** oversupply, surplusage **11** superfluity, superfluous **14** overproduction

surprise **4** stun **5** amaze, shock **6** ambush, wonder **7** astound, nonplus, set upon, stagger, startle, stupefy **8** astonish, confound, discover, dumfound, fall upon **9** amazement, bombshell, burst in on, dumbfound, take aback **10** defy belief, pounce upon, revelation, wonderment **11** flabbergast, incredulity **12** astonishment, take unawares **13** boggle the mind **16** bolt out of the blue

surprise attack
French: **10** coup de main

surrender **4** cede **5** forgo, let go, waive, yield **6** accede, forego, give up, render, submit, vacate **7** abandon, concede, forsake **8** delivery, forgoing, give over, giving up, hand over, part with, renounce, turn over, yielding **9** deliver up, foregoing **10** capitulate, relinquish, submission **11** lay down arms **12** capitulation, renunciation **14** relinquishment **15** throw in the towel **16** show the white flag

surreptitious **6** covert, hidden, secret, veiled **7** furtive **8** hush-hush, stealthy **9** concealed, secretive **10** undercover **11** clandestine

surrogate 6 acting, deputy **7** interim, stand-in **9** temporary **10** substitute **11** provisional

surround 4 belt, ring **5** hedge, hem in **6** circle, enfold, engird, girdle, shut in **7** close in, compass, enclose, envelop, fence in, hedge in **8** encircle **9** encompass **12** circumscribe

surrounding area 7 suburbs **8** environs, vicinity **9** outskirts, precincts

surroundings 5 scene **6** milieu **7** habitat, setting **8** ambience, environs **10** atmosphere, conditions **11** environment **13** circumstances
French: 11 mise en scene

Surt
origin: 12 Scandinavian
ruler of: 10 Muspelheim

surveillance 5 vigil, watch **8** scrutiny, trailing **11** observation **13** eavesdropping

survey 4 plot, poll, scan **5** gauge, graph, plumb, probe, scout, study **6** fathom, review **7** canvass, delimit, examine, inspect, measure, observe **8** analysis, block out, consider, look over, overview **10** scrutinize **11** contemplate, reconnoiter **12** pass in review **13** investigation

survival 5 relic **6** living **7** atavism, vestige **8** hangover **9** carry-over, throwback **11** subsistence **12** continuation, keeping alive

survive 4 last **5** abide, exist **6** endure, hang on, live on **7** hold out, outlast, outlive, persist, prevail, subsist **8** be extant, continue **9** keep alive **11** live through

surviving 6 extant **7** abiding, lasting **8** enduring, existent, existing, living on **9** hanging on, outliving, to be found **10** continuing, holding out, outlasting, persistent, persisting, subsisting **11** in existence **13** living through

Susann, Jacqueline
author of: 14 The Love Machine **15** Once Is Not Enough **16** Valley of the Dolls

Susanna
husband: 6 Joakim
accused of: 8 adultery
saved by: 6 Daniel

susceptible 4 open **5** prone **7** alive to, subject **8** liable to, sensible **9** sensitive **10** disposed to, responsive, vulnerable **11** conducive to, receptive to, sensitive to, sympathetic

suspect 5 doubt, fancy, guess, judge, opine, posit, think **7** believe, imagine, presume, suppose, surmise **8** distrust, misdoubt, mistrust, question, theorize **9** speculate **10** conjecture **11** hypothesize, wonder about **14** alleged culprit, be suspicious of **19** have one's doubts about

suspend 4 halt, hang, quit, stay, stop **5** cease, check, defer, delay, sling, swing, table **6** append, arrest, dangle, put off, shelve **7** reserve **8** break off, cut short, leave off, postpone, withhold **9** interrupt, stop short **10** put an end to **11** discontinue **12** bring to a stop **18** bring to a standstill

suspenders 6 braces, straps **7** gallows, garters, hangers **8** elastics, galluses **10** supporters

suspense 7 anxiety, tension **8** edginess **9** curiosity **10** indecision **11** expectation, incertitude, uncertainty **12** anticipation **15** indetermination

suspenseful 7 anxious **8** dramatic, exciting **9** climactic, uncertain

suspension 4 stay **5** pause **6** hiatus, recess **7** tabling **8** abeyance, deferral **12** postponement **14** discontinuance

suspicion 4 idea **5** guess, hunch **6** notion **7** feeling, surmise **8** distrust, mistrust **10** conjecture, hypothesis **11** supposition

Suspicion
director: 15 Alfred Hitchcock
cast: 9 Cary Grant **10** Nigel Bruce **12** Joan Fontaine **13** Dame May Whitty **15** Cedric Hardwicke
Oscar for: 7 actress (Fontaine)

suspicious 4 wary **5** shady **7** dubious, suspect **8** doubtful, doubting, slippery **9** ambiguous **10** untrusting **11** distrustful, incredulous, mistrustful, open to doubt **12** disbelieving, questionable **13** untrustworthy

sustain 4 bear, feed, prop **5** abide, brave, brook, stand **6** bear up, endure, hold up, keep up, suffer, uphold **7** nourish, nurture, prolong, support, undergo **8** maintain, protract, tolerate, underpin **9** keep alive, withstand **10** experience **12** carry on under **14** hold out against

sustenance 4 food, gear **5** bread, means **6** living **7** aliment, support **9** provender **10** provisions **11** maintenance, nourishment, subsistence
heaven-sent: 5 manna

sustineo alas 16 I sustain the wings
motto of: 10 US Air Force

Sutherland, Donald
born: 6 Canada, St John **12** New Brunswick
roles: 4 MASH **5** Klute **13** Hawkeye Pierce **14** Eye of the Needle, Ordinary People **16** Fellini's Casanova **17** The Eagle Has Landed **26** Invasion of the Body Snatchers

Sutpen, Colonel Thomas
character in: 14 Absalom Absalom
author: 8 Faulkner

Suva
capital of: 4 Fiji

Suzanne
character in: 19 The Marriage of Figaro
author: 12 Beaumarchais

svelte 4 fine, lean, neat, slim, thin, trim **5** lithe, spare **7** elegant, lissome, shapely, slender, willowy **8** graceful **9** sylphlike

Svengali
character in: 6 Trilby
author: 9 Du Maurier

Sverige *see* **6** Sweden

swab 3 dab, mop **4** daub, lout, wipe **5** clean, cloth, patch, scrub **6** cotton, sponge **7** cleanse **8** specimen
brand name: 4 Q-tip

swagger 5 strut, sweep **6** parade, sashay, stride **7** saunter **11** swashbuckle

swaggerer 6 gascon **7** boaster, bragger **8** blowhard, braggart, strutter **11** braggadocio

swain 4 beau **6** fellow, suitor **7** admirer, gallant **8** cavalier, young man **9** boyfriend **10** sweetheart

swallow 3 bit, nip, sip **4** down, gulp, swig **5** drink, quaff, swill, taste **6** credit, devour, gobble, guzzle, hold in, imbibe, ingest, tipple **7** believe, fall for, repress **8** gulp down, hold back, keep back, mouthful, suppress, withhold

swallow up 5 drown, eat up, swamp **6** absorb, engulf **7** consume, envelop **8** inundate **9** overwhelm **10** assimilate

swallow words **6** mumble, mutter

swamp **3** bog, fen **4** fill, mire, moor, ooze, quag, sink, slew, slue **5** bayou, beset, flood, marsh, swale **6** deluge, engulf, morass, slough **7** besiege, bottoms, envelop **8** inundate, quagmire, submerge, wash over **9** everglade, marshland, overwhelm, snow under, swallow up

swamped **7** deluged, flooded, glutted, overrun **9** inundated **11** overwhelmed

Swan
constellation of: **6** Cygnus

swan
young: **6** cygnet
group of: **4** bevy

swank **4** airs **5** ritzy **6** la-di-da, snooty, swanky **9** high-class, top-drawer **11** pretensions, pretentious **12** affectations, ostentatious **15** pretentiousness **16** superciliousness

swanky **4** chic, posh, rich **5** fancy, grand, jazzy, plush, ritzy, sharp, showy, smart, swank **6** flashy, snazzy, spiffy, sporty **7** dashing, elegant, splashy, stylish **9** sumptuous **11** fashionable

Swan Lake
composer: **11** Tchaikovsky

Swanson, Gloria
real name: **25** Gloria Josephine Mae Swenson
born: **9** Chicago IL
husband: **12** Wallace Beery
roles: **13** Sadie Thompson, The Trespasser **15** Sunset Boulevard

swap **5** trade **6** barter, dicker, switch **7** bargain **8** exchange **11** give and take

sward **3** sod **4** lawn, rind, skin, turf **5** grass

swarm **4** herd, host, mass, rush, teem **5** cloud, crowd, drove, flock, horde, press, surge **6** abound, legion, myriad, stream, throng **7** cluster, overrun **8** stampede **9** multitude

swarthy **4** dark **5** dusky, swart, tawny **6** brunet **8** brunette **11** dark-skinned **12** brown-colored, brown-skinned, olive-skinned **14** dark-complected **16** dark-complexioned

swashbuckler **9** buccaneer, daredevil **10** adventurer

swashbuckling **4** bold **7** dashing **8** boasting **9** audacious, daredevil

swat **3** hit, tap **4** bash, belt, slam, slap, slug, sock **5** clout, knock, smack, smite, whack **6** buffet, strike, thwack, wallop **7** clobber

swathe **4** bind, wrap **5** cloak, cover **6** encase, enfold, enwrap **7** envelop, sheathe, swaddle

sway **4** bend, grip, hold, lead, list, move, reel, rock, roll, rule, spur, vary, wave **5** alter, clout, impel, power, reign, rouse, shift, swing, waver **6** change, domain, incite, induce, prompt, swerve, totter, waving, wobble **7** command, control, dispose, mastery, stagger, swaying **8** hesitate, iron hand, motivate, persuade, swinging, to-and-fro, undulate **9** authority, direction, encourage, fluctuate, influence, oscillate, pendulate, pulsation, stimulate, vacillate **10** domination, government, predispose, suzerainty, undulation **11** fluctuation, oscillation **12** back and forth, dictatorship, jurisdiction, manipulation

Swaziland ***see box***

swear **3** vow **4** aver, avow, cuss **5** curse, vouch **6** adjure, assert, attest, pledge **7** certify, promise, warrant **9** blaspheme **10** take an oath, utter oaths **11** bear witness

swear by **7** believe, count on **9** believe in **10** put faith in

sweat **4** ooze, toil **5** exude, worry **6** effort **7** agonize **8** drudgery, hard work, perspire **9** exudation **12** perspiration

sweaty **3** wet **6** clammy, sticky **10** perspiring

Sweden ***see box***

Swedish Punch
type: **7** liqueur
origin: **6** Sweden
base: **3** rum
with gin: **5** Biffy
with vermouth: **9** Grand Slam

Sweeney Among the Nightingales
author: **7** T S Eliot

sweep **3** arc, fly **4** dart, dash, race, rush, scud, tear, zoom **5** hurry, spell, swing, swish, swoop, whisk **6** charge, gather, scurry, stroke **7** stretch **8** distance

sweeping **5** broad **7** blanket, radical **9** extensive, out-and-out, wholesale **10** exhaustive, large-scale, widespread **11** far-reaching, wide-ranging **12** all-inclusive **13** comprehensive, thoroughgoing

sweepings **4** dirt, dust **6** refuse

sweep off one's feet **7** enchant **8** bedazzle **9** captivate, overpower, overwhelm

---

Swaziland
capital/largest city: **7** Mbabane
others: **5** Bunya, Hluti, Mpaka, Nsoko, Stegi **6** Gollel, Mhlume **7** Big Bend, Lobamba, Manzini **8** Havelock, Malkerns **9** Geodgegun, Hlatikulu, Mankaiana, Mankayana, Nhlangano, Pigg's Peak, Rocklands
government: **22** constitutional monarchy
head of state: **4** king
monetary unit: **4** rand **9** lilangeni
mountain: **8** Highveld **11** Drakensberg
highest point: **7** Emlembe
river: **5** Usutu **6** Komati, Lomati **8** Mhlatuze, Ngwavuma, Umbeluzi, Umbuluzi
physical feature:
forest: **5** Usutu
plateau: **7** Lebombo, Lubombo
people: **5** Asian, Bantu, Swazi **11** Eurafricans
king: **3** Kbe **5** Nyama **6** Mswati **7** Sobhuza
prince: **6** Sozisa
language: **5** Ngumi **7** English, Siswati **9** Afrikaans **10** Portuguese
religion: **7** animism **10** Protestant **13** Roman Catholic
feature:
bride payment: **6** lobolo
god: **14** Mkhulumngcandi
ritual dance: **7** Incwala

Sweden
other name: 7 Sverige
capital/largest city: 9 Stockholm
others: 4 Lund, Umea 5 Boden, Boras, Edane, Falun, Gavle, Lulea, Malmo, Pitea, Visby 6 Arvika, Kiruna, Orebro 7 Uppsala 8 Goteborg, Jokkmokk, Vasteras 9 Jonkoping, Linkoping, Sundsvall 10 Eskilstuna, Gottenburg, Norrkoping, Skelleftea 11 Halsingborg
school: 4 Lund 7 Uppsala 8 Goteborg 9 Stockholm
division: 3 Lan 4 Laen 5 Skane 6 Kalmar, Orebro 7 Dalarna, Gotland, Lapland 8 Alvsborg, Blekinge, Elfsborg, Gotaland, Jamtland, Malmohus, Norrland, Svealand
government: 22 constitutional monarchy
legislature: 7 Riksdag
head of state: 4 king
measure: 3 aln, fot, ref 4 alar, amar, famn, kapp, last, stop 5 carat, foder, kanna, linje, nymil, spann 6 fathom, jumfru 7 oxhuvud, tunland 8 fjarding, koltunna, tunnland
monetary unit: 3 ore 5 krona, krone 7 carolin 8 skilling 9 rigsdaler
weight: 3 ass, lod 4 last, mark, sten 5 carat 6 nylast 7 centner, lispund 8 skalpund, skeppund 9 shippound
island: 5 Oland 7 Gotland
lake: 4 Ster 5 Asnen, Malar, Silja, Vaner 6 Vanern, Vetter, Wenner 7 Hielmar, Malaren, Vattern 8 Dalalven 9 Hjalmaren
mountain: 4 Sarv 5 Ammar 6 Helags, Kjolen, Ovniks, Sarjek 7 Kjollen
highest point: 5 Kebne 10 Kebnekaise
river: 3 Dal 4 Gota, Klar, Lule, Pite, Umea 5 Indal, Kalix, Lulea, Pitea, Ranea, Torne 6 Lainio, Muonio 7 Ljusnan 8 Angerman
sea: 6 Baltic 8 Atlantic
physical feature:
canal: 4 Gota
gulf: 7 Bothnia
sound: 6 Kalmar
strait: 7 Oresund 8 Kattegat 9 Skagerrak
people: 4 Lapp 5 Norse, Swede 6 Viking
actress: 9 Liv Ullman 10 Greta Garbo 13 Ingrid Bergman
astronomer: 7 Celsius 8 Angstrom
author: 8 Lagerlof 10 Lagerkvist, Strindberg
diplomat: 12 Hammarskjold
director: 13 Ingmar Bergman 14 Arne Sucksdorff
inventor: 5 Nobel
king: 4 Vosa, Wasa 5 Oscar 6 Gustav 8 Gustavus 10 Carl Gustav 12 Gustav Adolph 13 Charles Gustav 22 Jean Baptiste Bernadotte
philosopher/scientist: 10 Swedenborg
queen: 9 Christina
scientist: 8 Linnaeus
language: 4 Lapp 7 Swedish
religion: 19 Evangelical Lutheran
place:
castle: 9 Gripsholm
center of Stockholm: 11 Gamla Staden
park: 7 Skansen 12 Millesgarden
theater: 18 Drottningholm Court
walled city: 5 Visby
food: 11 smorgasbord
cheese: 7 fontina 8 jarlberg 9 jarlsberg
dish: 10 kottbullar
drink: 5 glogg 7 aquavit

sweet 4 dear, kind, nice 5 candy, fresh 6 dulcet, mellow, smooth, sugary 7 amiable, cloying, darling, dessert, lovable, nonsalt, not salt, tuneful 8 fragrant, pleasant, pleasing 9 agreeable, melodious, sweetmeat, wholesome 10 attractive, confection, euphonious, saccharine 11 good-natured, mellifluous, silver-toned, sympathetic 12 nonfermented

Sweet Bird of Youth
director: 13 Richard Brooks
based on play by: 17 Tennessee Williams
cast: 8 Ed Begley 10 Paul Newman 13 Geraldine Page, Shirley Knight 17 Madeleine Sherwood
Oscar for: 15 supporting actor (Begley)

sweetheart 4 beau, dear, love 5 flame, honey, lover, swain 6 fiance, old man, steady, suitor 7 beloved, darling, fiancee, old lady 8 ladylove, mistress, true love 9 boyfriend, inamorata, valentine 10 girlfriend, lady friend 15 gentleman friend
French: 6 cherie

sweet life
Italian: 9 dolce vita

Sweet Mama Stringbean
nickname of: 11 Ethel Waters

sweetmeats 5 candy 6 sweets 7 bonbons 10 sugar candy 11 confections 13 confectionery

sweet-natured 5 sweet 6 benign, gentle, kindly 7 likable, lovable 8 pleasant 13 compassionate

sweetness
French: 7 douceur

sweet roll 3 bun 6 Danish 7 cruller 8 doughnut 10 coffee cake 11 cinnamon bun

sweets 5 candy 7 goodies 8 desserts 10 sugar candy, sweetmeats 11 confections 13 confectionery

sweet-scented 8 aromatic, fragrant, perfumed, redolent

sweet-smelling 5 spicy 7 scented 8 aromatic, fragrant, perfumed, redolent 9 odiferous

sweet talk 6 cajole, praise 7 blarney, flatter 8 cajolery, flattery, soft soap 10 compliment 11 endearments, loving words 13 blandishments 14 fond utterances

Sweetwater
nickname of: 16 Nathaniel Clifton

sweet words 7 blarney **8** flattery, soft soap **9** sweet talk **12** honeyed words

swell 3 fop, wax **4** A-one, fine, good, grow, okay, puff, rise, wave **5** bloat, bulge, dandy, great, heave, mount, super, surge, throb, widen **6** billow, blow up, comber, expand, extend, fatten, puff up **7** amplify, breaker, burgeon, distend, inflate, stretch, thicken **8** fabulous, heighten, increase, lengthen, splendid, terrific **9** excellent, first-rate, intensify, marvelous, spread out **10** delightful, first-class, tremendous, undulation **11** pleasurable **12** clotheshorse, fashion plate, smart dresser

swell-headed 8 egoistic, puffed up **9** conceited **10** egoistical **11** egotistical **12** vainglorious **13** self-important

swelling 4 bump, lump **5** bulge, swell **8** dilation **9** puffiness **10** distension **11** enlargement **12** protuberance

swell out 5 bloat, bulge **6** billow, expand **7** distend, inflate, puff out

swelter 3 fry **4** boil, cook **5** be hot, broil, sweat **8** languish, perspire

sweltering 3 hot **5** humid, muggy **6** sultry, torrid **7** burning **8** sweating **10** oppressive, perspiring

sweltry 3 hot **4** dank **5** humid, muggy **6** baking, clammy, steamy, sticky, sultry, torrid **7** boiling **8** broiling, roasting, sizzling, stifling **9** scorching **10** blistering **11** suffocating

Swenson, Gloria Josephine Mae
real name of: 13 Gloria Swanson

Swept Away
subtitle: 38 by an unusual destiny in the blue sea of August
director: 14 Lina Wertmuller
cast: 16 Mariangela Melato **17** Giancarlo Giannini

swerve 3 shy, yaw **4** tack, turn, veer **5** avert, dodge, sheer, shift, stray **6** careen, change **7** deviate, digress, diverge **9** turn aside

swift 4 fast **5** brisk, fleet, hasty, quick, rapid **6** abrupt, flying, prompt, speedy **8** headlong **9** immediate **11** expeditious, precipitate

Swift, Jonathan
author of: 11 A Tale of a Tub **15** A Modest Proposal **16** Battle of the Books, Gulliver's Travels
fictional places: 6 Laputa **8** Lilliput **11** Brobdingnag
character: 6 Yahoos **10** Houyhnhnms **14** Lemuel Gulliver

swiftness 5 haste, speed **8** alacrity, celerity, dispatch, rapidity **9** quickness

swill 4 mash, slop, swig **5** quaff, waste **6** guzzle, refuse, scraps, soak up, tipple **7** garbage **8** chugalug, gulp down, leavings

swimming
athlete: 9 Diana Nyad, John Naber, Mark Spitz **10** Dawn Fraser, Kim Linehan, Linda Jezek **11** Claudia Kolb, Debbie Meyer, John Hencken **12** Brian Goodell, Bruce Furniss, Greg Louganis, John Kinsella **13** Jim Montgomery, Kornelia Ender, Michael Burton, Tracy Caulkens **14** Charles Hickcox, Duke Kahanamoku, Esther Williams, Gertrude Ederle **15** Cynthia Woodhead **16** Shirley Babashoff **17** Johnny Weissmuller

Swinburne, Algernon Charles
author of: 16 Hymn to Perserpine **17** Atalanta in Calydon **18** Songs Before Sunrise

swindle 2 do **3** con, gyp **4** bilk, dupe, gull, hoax, rook **5** cheat, cozen, fraud, mulct, steal, trick **6** delude, fleece, racket, rip-off **7** con game, deceive, defraud **8** embezzle, hoodwink **9** bamboozle, defalcate **12** embezzlement **14** confidence game

swindler 3 gyp **5** cheat, crook, faker, fraud **6** con man **7** sharper **8** chiseler, deceiver **9** charlatan, embezzler **10** mountebank **12** rip-off artist

swine 3 cad, cur, rat **4** pigs **5** beast, brute **6** animal
group of: 5 drift **7** sounder

Swineherd, The
author: 21 Hans Christian Andersen

swing 4 drop, hang, loop, move, rein, rock, sway, turn **5** pivot, rally, scope, sweep, whirl **6** dangle, decide, handle, manage, rotate, seesaw, stroke, wangle **7** compass, extract, freedom, inveigh, liberty, license, listing, pull off, rocking, rolling, suspend, swaying **8** maneuver, pitching, undulate **9** determine, influence, oscillate **10** accomplish, manipulate **11** be suspended, oscillation

Swing Time
director: 13 George Stevens
cast: 9 Eric Blore **11** Fred Astaire, Victor Moore **12** Betty Furness, Ginger Rogers **14** Helen Broderick
score: 10 Jerome Kern **13** Dorothy Fields
Oscar for: 4 song
song: 12 A Fine Romance **14** Pick Yourself Up **20** The Way You Look Tonight

swirl 4 bowl, eddy, reel, roll, spin, swim, turn **5** churn, twirl, twist, wheel, whirl **6** gyrate, rotate **7** revolve

Swiss Family Robinson
director: 10 Ken Annakin
cast: 9 John Mills **10** Janet Munro **14** Dorothy McGuire, James MacArthur, Sessue Hayakawa
author: 16 Johann Rudolf Wyss
character: 13 Emily Montrose
***Robinson family:* 4** Jack **5** Fritz **6** Ernest **7** Francis

switch 3 box, rod, tan **4** cane, jerk, lash, move, whip **5** birch, lever, shift, shunt, stick, swing, trade, whisk **6** button, change, handle **8** exchange **9** sidetrack **11** alternation

Switzerland *see box*

Swiveller, Dick
character in: 19 The Old Curiosity Shop
author: 7 Dickens

swollen 5 puffy **7** bloated, bulging, swelled **8** inflated, puffed-up **9** distended

swoon 5 faint **8** collapse, keel over **13** fall prostrate **17** become unconscious

swoop 4 dive, drop, rush **5** pitch, sweep **6** plunge, pounce, spring **7** descend, plummet **8** nose-dive, swooping **9** sweep down **12** rush headlong

sword 4 epee, foil **5** blade, saber, steel **6** rapier **7** cutlass **8** scimitar **10** broadsword

sybarite 8 hedonist **10** sensualist, voluptuary

sybaritic 4 rich **6** lavish **7** sensual **9** dissolute, epicurean, luxurious **10** dissipated, hedonistic, voluptuous **12** luxury-loving, pleasure-bent **13** self-

Switzerland
capital: **4** Bern
largest city: **6** Zurich
others: **3** Zug **4** Bale, Bern, Biel, Brig, Chur, Nyon, Sion, Thun **5** Basel, Basle, Berne, Coire, Surat, Vevey **6** Geneva, Geneve, Glarus, Lugano, Sarnen, Schwyz **7** Altdorf, Fyzabad, Herisau, Locarno, Lucerne, Luzerne, Zermatt **8** Lausanne, Montreux, St Moritz **9** Neuchatel, Solothurn **10** Bellinzona, Interlaken, Winterthur **12** Schaffhausen
school: **4** Bern **5** Basel **8** Catholic, Lausanne **28** Federal Institute of Technology
division: **3** Uri, Zug **4** Bern, Chur, Nyon, Vaud **5** Aarau, Basel, Basle, Berne, Sankt, Waadt **6** Aargau, canton, Gallen, Geneva, Geneve, Glaris, Glarus, Luzern, Obwald, Schwyz, St Gall, Tessin, Ticino, Valais, Wallis, Zurich **7** Atldorf, Grisons, Lucerne, Nidwald, Thurgau **8** Fribourg, Obwalden, St Gallen **9** Appenzell, Neuchatel, Neuenberg, Solothurn **10** Graubunden **11** Unterwalden **12** Schaffhausen
measure: **3** imi, pot **4** aune, fuss, muid, pied, zoll **5** lieue, linie, maass, pouce, staab, toise **6** perche, strich **7** klafter, viertel **9** quarteron **10** holzlafter **11** holzklafter
monetary unit: **5** franc, rappe **6** hallar, rappen **7** centime, duplone **8** baetzner
weight: **4** fund **5** pfund **7** centner, quintal **12** zugthierlast
lake: **3** Uri, Zug **4** Biel, Thon, Thun **5** Ageri, Leman, Morat **6** Bienne, Brienz, Geneva, Lugano, Sarnen, Wallen, Zurich **7** Hallwil, Lucerne, Lungern **8** Maggiore, Viervald **9** Bielersee, Constance, Neuchatel, Sarnersee, Thunersee
mountain: **3** Dom **4** Alps, Jura, Rigi, Rosa, Todi **5** Adula, Blanc, Cenis, Eiger, Genis, Karpf, Righi **6** Linard, Pizela, Sentis **7** Bernina, Beverin, Grimsel, Pilatus, Rotondo **8** Balmhorn, Jungfrau **9** Weisshorn **10** Diablerets, Matterhorn, St Gotthard, Wetterhorn **11** Burgenstock **12** Dufourspitze **13** Rheinwaldhorn **14** Finsteraarhorn
mountain pass: **5** Cenis, Furka, Gemmi **6** Albula, Kinzig, Maloja, Usteri **7** Bernina, Brenner, Grimsel, Simplon, Splugen **8** Lotschen **10** St Gotthard
highest point: **12** Dufourspitze
river: **2** Po **3** Aar, Inn **4** Aare, Arve, Thur, Toss **5** Broye, Doubs, Linth, Reuss, Rhine, Rhone, Saane **6** Limmat, Maggia, Safane, Sarine, Ticino **8** Engadine, Pratigau
physical feature:
glacier: **5** Rhone
plateau: **5** Swiss
people: **5** Swiss
artist: **4** Klee
author: **5** Hesse, Spyri **6** Keller **8** Gotthelf, Rousseau **10** Durrenmatt
educational reformer: **10** Pestalozzi
hero: **4** Tell
psychologist: **4** Jung **6** Piaget
religious leader: **6** Calvin **7** Zwingli
scientist: **9** Bernoulli
language: **5** Ladin **6** French, German **7** Italian **8** Romansch **14** Switzerdeutsch
religion: **9** Calvinism **10** Protestant **13** Roman Catholic
place:
castle: **7** Chillon
fountain: **7** Jet d'Eau
playhouse: **6** Zurich
resort: **5** Arosa, Davos **6** Gstaad **7** Zermatt **8** St Moritz **9** Schwagalp **10** Interlaken
street: **14** Bahnhofstrasse
tower: **5** Clock
feature:
animal: **4** ibex **7** chamois
flower: **9** edelweiss
pageant: **9** Alpenfest
food:
cheese: **6** bagnes, sbrinz **7** Gruyere **10** Emmentaler **11** Appenzeller
dish: **5** rosti **6** fondue **8** raclette **11** grisons beef **14** bundnerfleisch
drink: **11** cheri-suisse **14** marmot-chocolat

indulgent **14** pleasure-loving **15** pleasure-seeking

Sycamire **12** Biblical tree

sycamore **8** Platanus **18** Acer pseudoplatanus
varieties: **7** eastern **8** Egyptian

Sychaeus
also: **7** Acerbas
priest of: **8** Hercules
wife: **4** Dido
brother-in-law: **9** Pygmalion
murdered by: **9** Pygmalion

sycophant **4** tool **5** slave, toady **6** fawner, flunky, jackal, lackey, puppet, stooge, yes-man **7** cat's-paw **8** hanger-on, parasite, truckler **9** flatterer **10** bootlicker **11** lickspittle, rubber stamp **13** apple-polisher

Sydney
bay: **5** Walsh **11** Rushcutter's **13** Woolloomooloo
capital of: **13** New South Wales
cove: **4** Farm
founder: **7** Phillip
harbor: **7** Darling **11** Port Jackson
island: **4** Goat **6** Garden
landmark: **10** Opera House **11** Wynyard Park **13** Har-

bour Bridge **14** Fitzroy Gardens **15** Mitchell Library **16** Australian Museum, Hyde Park Barracks, Saint James Church **18** Rushcutter's Bay Park **21** Royal Botanical Gardens
river: **10** Parramatta
university: **9** Macquarie **13** New South Wales

Syleus
position: **4** king
killed by: **8** Hercules

sylvan **5** bushy, leafy, woody **6** wooded, woodsy **8** arcadian, forested, timbered, woodland **9** luxuriant, overgrown **10** forestlike

Sylvanus *see* **8** Silvanus

Sylvia
character in: **20** Two Gentlemen of Verona
author: **11** Shakespeare

Symaethis
form: **5** nymph
location: **3** sea
mother of: **4** Aeis

symbol **4** mark, sign **5** badge, token **6** emblem, figure, signal **10** indication **14** representation **15** exemplification

symbolize **4** mean **5** imply **6** denote, embody, symbol **7** betoken, connote, express, signify **8** stand for **9** emblemize, exemplify, personify, represent, signalize **10** allegorize **11** emblematize

symmetrical **7** orderly, regular **8** balanced **9** congruent **12** well-balanced **16** well-proportioned

symmetry **4** form **5** order **7** balance, harmony **9** congruity **10** conformity, regularity **11** equilibrium, orderliness, parallelism, shapeliness **15** proportionality

sympathetic **6** benign, humane, kindly **7** feeling, pitying **8** friendly, merciful **9** agreeable, approving, benignant, sensitive **10** benevolent, comforting **11** softhearted, warmhearted **12** sympathizing, well-disposed **13** commiserative, compassionate, tenderhearted, understanding

sympathize **4** back, pity, side **5** agree, favor **7** approve, feel for, go along, support **8** sanction **9** empathize **10** appreciate, be in accord, be sorry for **11** condole with, have pity for, stand behind

sympathy **4** pity **5** amity, favor, grief **6** accord, regard, sorrow **7** concern, concert, concord, empathy, feeling, harmony, rapport, support **8** advocacy, affinity, approval, sanction **9** agreement, communion, patronage, unanimity **10** compassion, consonance, fellowship, friendship, tenderness **11** well-wishing **12** congeniality, partisanship **13** commiseration, consanguinity, fellow feeling, understanding

Symplegades
form: **5** rocks
location: **8** Bosporus **9** Euxine Sea
characteristic: **8** clashing, dark-blue

symposium **5** forum, synod **6** debate, parley, powwow **7** meeting **8** colloquy, congress **10** conference, discussion, round table **12** deliberation **15** panel discussion

Symposium
author: **5** Plato
character: **7** Agathon **8** Phaedrus, Socrates **9** Pausanias **10** Alcibiades **11** Aristodemus **12** Aristophanes

symptom **4** mark, sign **5** token **6** signal **7** earmark, warning **8** evidence, giveaway **10** indication **15** prognostication

synagogue
Yiddish: **4** shul **5** schul

synchronal **11** concomitant, synchronous **12** contemporary, simultaneous

Syria
other name: **4** Aram
capital/largest city: **8** Damascus
others: **4** Hama, Homs, Nawa **5** Busra, Calno, Derra, Emesa, Halab, Hamah, Idlib, Jerud, Raqqa **6** Aleppo, Calneh, Dumeir, Fajami, Tadmor, Ugarit **7** Antioch, Latakia, Palmyra **8** Seleucia **9** Ghabaghib
school: **6** Aleppo, Syrian **11** Arab Academy
measure: **5** makuk **6** garava
monetary unit: **4** lira **5** pound **6** talent **7** piaster
weight: **4** cola **5** artal, ratel **6** talent
lake: **5** Merom **7** Djeboid **8** Tiberias
mountain: **6** Carmel **7** Alawite, Libanus **10** Nusairiyya **11** Anti-Lebanon
highest point: **6** Hermon
river: **3** Asi **6** Balikh, Barada, Jordan, Khabur, Yarmuk **7** Orontes **9** Asi Knabur, Euphrates
sea: **13** Mediterranean
physical feature:
desert: **5** Hamad **6** Hauran, Syrian
heights: **5** Golan
people: **4** Arab, Kurd, Turk **5** Alawi, Aptal, Druse, Druze **6** Afshar, Aissor, Aushar, Avshar, Awshar **7** Amorite, Ansarie, Bedouin, Nosaris, Saracen, Shemite **8** Ansarieh, Armenian **9** Ansariyah **10** Circassian **12** Khachaturian
king: **5** Rezin **6** Faisal, Hazael **8** Benhadad **9** Antiochus
leader: **10** T E Lawrence **12** Hafiz al-Assad **16** Lawrence of Arabia
queen: **7** Zenobia
ruler: **4** Rome **5** Arabs **6** France, Greeks, Persia **7** Mongols **8** Abbasids **9** Mamelukes, Phoenicia, Seleucids **11** Seljuk Turks **12** Ottoman Turks
language: **6** Arabic, French, Syriac **7** Aramaic, English, Kurdish, Turkish **8** Armenian
religion: **5** Druze, Islam **7** Alawite **12** Christianity **13** Greek Orthodox **23** Eastern Rite Christianity
place:
dam: **5** Tabqa **9** Euphrates
ruins: **7** Palmyra
square: **7** Martyrs'
feature:
animal: **9** dromedary
clothing: **3** aba **4** abah **7** abayyah **8** kafiyyah
marketplace: **4** souk
tent: **8** bayt shar
village common: **6** maidan

synchronous **10** synchronal **11** concomitant **12** contemporary, simultaneous

syndicalist **5** rebel **9** anarchist, insurgent **13** revolutionary

syndicate **5** group, trust, union **6** cartel, league, merger **7** combine **8** alliance **9** coalition **10** consortium, federation **11** association

Synge, John Millington
author of: **14** Riders to the Sea **19** Deirdre of the Sorrows **27** The Playboy of the Western World

synod **4** diet **13** governing body **15** advisory council **21** ecclesiastical council

synonym **8** analogue **10** equivalent **11** another name

synonymous **4** like, same **5** alike, equal **7** coequal **10** equivalent

synopsis **5** brief **6** apercu, digest, precis, resume **7** epitome, outline, rundown, summary **8** abstract, argument **11** abridgement

synopsize **6** digest **7** abridge, outline **8** abstract, condense **9** summarize

Synoptist **12** Gospel writer

synthesize **3** mix **4** fuse **5** blend **7** combine **8** compound **10** amalgamate

synthetic **4** fake, sham **5** phony **6** ersatz **7** man-made **9** unnatural **10** artificial **11** counterfeit **12** manufactured

Syri **16** Greek unical codex

Syria ***see box***

Syrinx
form: **5** nymph
location: **8** mountain
transformed into: **4** reed
transformed by: **3** Pan
made into: **7** panpipe
pipes called: **6** syrinx

system **4** body, unit **5** setup **6** method, scheme, theory **7** program, regimen, routine **8** organism **9** procedure, structure **10** hypothesis **11** arrangement **12** constitution, organization **13** modus operandi **15** mode of operation

systematic **4** neat, tidy **7** ordered, orderly, planned, precise, regular **8** constant **9** organized **10** methodical **12** businesslike, systematized **13** well-organized, well-regulated

systematization **5** order **8** ordering **9** gradation **10** organizing **11** arrangement **12** categorizing, codification, organization **13** methodization **14** categorization, classification

systematize **5** order **7** arrange **8** classify, organize **9** methodize

systematized **7** ordered **8** arranged, codified **9** organized **10** classified, methodized, systematic

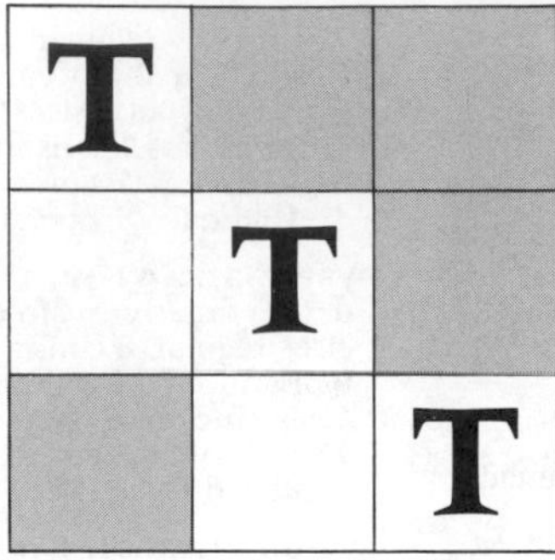

tab **3** lip **4** bill, cost, flap, loop **5** check, price, strip, tally **6** tongue **7** eyehole **10** projection

tabard **4** cape, coat **5** cloak, tunic

Tabard Inn
starting point in: **18** The Canterbury Tales

tabernacle **6** church, temple **14** house of worship

Tabeth **16** tenth Hebrew month

Tabitha
also called: **6** Dorcas
revived by: **5** Peter
hometown: **5** Joppa

table **4** fare, list, roll **5** board, chart, index **6** record, roster, shelve, spread **7** catalog **8** lay aside, postpone, put aside, register, schedule, syllabus, synopsis **9** inventory **10** tabulation

Table
constellation of: **5** Mensa

tableau **4** view **5** scene **7** pageant, picture, setting **8** grouping **9** depiction, spectacle, still life **11** arrangement, delineation **12** illustration **13** picturization

tableau vivant **13** living picture

tablespoon
abbreviation: **4** tbsp

tablet **3** pad **4** leaf **5** bolus, panel, sheet, wafer **6** pellet, plaque, troche **7** lozenge, memo pad, surface **8** flat cake, thin slab **9** tablature **10** pad of paper, writing pad

tableware **5** china **6** dishes, plates **7** cutlery **8** crockery, utensils **9** chinaware, glassware **10** dinnerware, silverware **14** cups and saucers

taboo, tabu **3** ban **4** no-no **6** banned **8** anathema, outlawed, verboten **9** forbidden, social ban **10** in bad taste, prohibited, proscribed **11** disapproved, prohibition, unthinkable **12** interdiction, proscription, religious ban, unacceptable **13** unmentionable

tabulate **4** file, list, rank, rate, sort **5** chart, grade, group, index, order, range **6** codify **7** arrange, catalog, compute, diagram, sort out **8** classify, organize **9** methodize **10** categorize, make a table **11** systematize

tace
music: **6** silent

tacit **7** assumed, implied **8** implicit, inferred, unspoken, unstated, wordless **10** undeclared, understood **11** unexpressed **15** taken for granted

taciturn **5** aloof, quiet **6** silent **7** laconic **8** reserved, reticent **9** secretive **11** tight-lipped **12** close-mouthed **15** uncommunicative

tack **3** add, peg, pin, way **4** clap, nail, slap, veer **5** affix, sheer, shift, spike, thole **6** append, attach, change, fasten, method, swerve, switch, zigzag **7** go about **8** approach, tholepin **9** short nail **12** change course **14** course of action

tackle **3** try **4** gear, lift **5** assay, begin, crane, hoist, jenny, throw, tools, winch **6** accept, assume, attack, take on, take up **7** attempt, capstan, derrick, embrace, go about, halyard, rigging **8** endeavor, engage in, material, set about, windlass **9** apparatus, enter upon, equipment, trappings, undertake **10** appliances, embark upon, implements **11** instruments **12** appointments **13** accoutrements, paraphernalia

tack on **3** add **5** annex **6** adjoin, append, attach **7** stick on, subjoin **8** fasten to

tacky **5** dowdy, gluey, gooey, gucky, gummy, messy, ratty, seedy, tatty **6** grubby, shabby, shoddy, sloppy, sticky, untidy, viscid **7** stringy, unkempt, viscous **8** adhesive, frazzled, slipshod, slovenly **10** disordered

tact **7** finesse, suavity **8** delicacy **9** diplomacy, suaveness **10** discretion **11** savoir faire, sensibility **13** consideration **14** circumspection
French: **11** savoir-faire

tactful **5** suave **6** polite, smooth, subtle **7** politic **8** decorous, delicate, discreet, mannerly **9** sensitive **10** diplomatic, thoughtful **11** considerate

tactic **3** way **4** line, plan, tack **6** method, policy, scheme **8** approach **9** stratagem **14** course of action

tactics **9** maneuvers **18** battle arrangements, military operations

tactless **4** curt, rude **5** blunt, brash, rough **6** abrupt, clumsy, gauche, stupid **7** boorish **8** impolite **9** ham-handed, impolitic, imprudent, untactful **10** blundering, indelicate, indiscreet **11** insensitive, thoughtless **12** undiplomatic **13** ill-considered, inconsiderate
French: **6** gauche

tactlessness **8** curtness **9** bluntness, gaucherie **10** abruptness, clumsiness, indelicacy **13** insensitivity, tastelessness

taedium vitae **5** ennui **12** tedium of life **22** feeling life is wearisome

Taft, William Howard ***see box***

Taft, William Howard
presidential rank: **13** twenty-seventh
party: **10** Republican
state represented: **2** OH
defeated: **4** (Eugene Victor) Debs **5** (William Jennings) Bryan **6** (Daniel Braxton) Turney, (Eugene Wilder) Chafin, (Thomas Edward) Watson, (Thomas Louis) Hisgen **8** (August) Gillhaus
vice president: **7** (James Schoolcraft) Sherman
cabinet:
state: **4** (Philander Chase) Knox
treasury: **8** (Franklin) MacVeagh
war: **7** (Henry Lewis) Stimson **9** (Jacob McGavock) Dickinson
attorney general: **10** (George Woodward) Wickersham
navy: **5** (George von Lengerke) Meyer
postmaster general: **9** (Frank Harris) Hitchcock
interior: **6** (Walter Lowrie) Fisher **9** (Richard Achilles) Ballinger
agriculture: **6** (James) Wilson
commerce and labor: **5** (Charles) Nagel
born: **12** Cincinnati OH
died: **12** Washington DC
buried: **25** Arlington National Cemetery
education:
university: **4** Yale
law school: **10** Cincinnati
religion: **9** Unitarian
interests: **4** golf
author: **22** Four Aspects of Civic Duty **23** The United States and Peace **30** Our Chief Magistrate and His Powers **33** The Anti-Trust Act and the Supreme Court **65** The Presidency: Its Duties Its Powers Its Opportunities and Its Limitation
political career: **18** US Solicitor General
judge: **19** Federal Circuit Court
president of: **21** Philippines Commission
civil governor of: **11** Philippines
secretary of: **3** War
US Supreme Court: **12** Chief Justice
civilian career:
law professor: **4** Yale
president: **22** American Bar Association
notable events of lifetime/term: **19** Postal Savings System
Act: **10** Webb-Kenyon **11** Mann-Elkinst **12** Payne-Aldrich
sinking of: **7** Titanic
father: **8** Alphonso
mother: **6** Louisa (Maria Torrey)
siblings: **5** Fanny **11** Henry Waters **12** Horace Dutton **15** Samuel Davenport
half-brothers: **11** Peter Rawson **13** Charles Phelps
wife: **5** Helen (Herron)
nickname: **6** Nellie
children: **11** Helen Herron **13** Charles Phelps **14** Robert Alphonso
first lady:
author: **24** Recollections of Full Years

tag **3** add, dog, tab **4** card, heel, mark, name, slip, stub, tail, term **5** add on, affix, annex, hound, label, title, trail **6** append, attach, attend, fasten, follow, handle, join to, marker, shadow, tack on, ticket **7** earmark, moniker, pendant **8** cognomen, identify, nickname **9** accompany, appendage, sobriquet **10** attachment **11** appellation, designation

Taggart, Dagny
character in: **13** Atlas Shrugged
author: **4** Rand

Tahiti
artist: **7** Gauguin
author: **9** Stevenson
capital: **7** Papeete
formerly: **8** Otaheite
island group: **7** Society
isthmus: **7** Taravao
ocean: **7** Pacific
volcano: **5** Roniu **7** Orohena

tail **3** dog **4** seat **5** fanny, stalk, track, trail **6** follow, shadow **7** back end, rear end **8** buttocks

tail end, tail-end **4** back, rear, rump, tail **6** caudal **7** hind end, rear end **8** backside, buttocks, last part **9** posterior

tailor **3** fit, sew **4** make, redo **5** adapt, alter, build, shape **6** change, create, design, devise, modify **7** convert, fashion, produce **8** clothier, costumer **9** construct, couturier, fabricate, transform **10** dressmaker, seamstress

taint **3** mar, rot **4** blot, flaw, ruin, soil, spot, turn **5** dirty, fault, go bad, smear, spoil, stain, sully **6** damage, debase, defect, defile, smudge, stigma **7** blemish, putrefy, tarnish **8** besmirch **12** imperfection

tainted **5** dirty **6** impure, rotten **7** spoiled, stained, unclean **9** blemished, tarnished **10** besmirched

Taipei
capital of: **6** Taiwan

Taiwan ***see box, p. 960***

take ***see box, p. 961***

take aback **5** amaze **7** astound **8** astonish, surprise **9** overwhelm

take a crack at **3** try **5** essay **6** hazard, tackle, take on **7** attempt, venture **9** have a go at, undertake **11** make a stab at **12** take a fling at, take a whack at **14** make an effort at

take advantage of **3** use **5** avail **7** exploit, utilize **10** profit from

take after **4** copy, echo **6** follow, repeat **7** imitate **8** resemble, simulate **9** duplicate, reproduce

Take a Girl Like You
author: **12** Kingsley Amis

take apart **7** destroy **8** demolish **9** dismantle, knock down **11** disassemble

take a powder **4** blow, exit **5** go out, leave, scram, split **6** cut out, depart, escape **8** withdraw

take away **5** seize **6** lessen, reduce **7** abridge, bear off, curtail, detract **8** carry off,

Taiwan
name means: **11** terraced bay
other name: **7** Formosa **11** Ilha Formosa **15** Republic of China
capital/largest city: **6** Taipei
others: **4** Suao **5** Shoka, Takao **6** Tainan **7** Chilung, Hualien, Keelong, Keelung, Taoyuan **8** Fengshan, Kaohiung, Taichung **9** Kaohsiung
school: **7** Soochow, Tunghai **14** National Taiwan
monetary unit: **4** yuan **6** dollar
island: **5** Matsu **6** Lan Hsu, Penghu, Quemoy, Taiwan **7** Hungtou, Huoshao **10** Pescadores
mountain: **5** Tatun **6** Tzukao **7** Taitung **15** Chungyang Shanmo
highest point: **6** Yu Shan **8** Morrison **10** Sinkao Shan **11** Hsin-Kao Shan
river: **5** Wuchi **6** Tachia **7** Choshui, Hualien, Tanshui
sea: **7** Pacific **9** East China **10** Philippine, South China
physical feature:
cape: **7** Olwanpi
channel: **5** Bashi
gorge: **6** Taroko
storm: **7** monsoon, typhoon
strait: **6** Taiwan **7** Formosa
people: **4** Yami **5** Hakka, Hoklo **7** Chinese, Malayan **9** Fukienese, Taiwanese **10** Indonesian, Polynesian **12** Kwangtungese
goddess: **5** Matsu
leader: **7** Koxinga **9** Sun Yat-sen **10** Yen Chia-Kan **13** Chiang Kai-shek **14** Cheng Cheng-Kung, Chiang Ching-kuo
language: **4** Amon, Amoy **5** Hakka, Kuo Yu **6** Minnan **9** Taiwanese **15** Mandarin Chinese
religion: **6** Taoism **7** animism **8** Buddhism **12** Christianity, Confucianism
place:
museum: **14** National Palace
square: **12** Presidential
feature:
festival: **5** Ghost
political party: **10** Kuomintang
food:
feast: **6** pai-pai

decrease, subtract **9** deprive of **11** make off with

take a whack at **3** try **5** essay **6** hazard, tackle **7** attempt, venture **8** give a try **9** have a go at **10** give a whirl **12** take a crack at

take back **6** abjure, recall, recant, renege **7** disavow, retract, reverse **8** forswear, withdraw

take captive **3** bag **4** snag, take, trap **5** catch, seize, snare **7** capture, ensnare **9** apprehend, lay hold of **12** take prisoner

take care **6** beware, be wary **9** be careful **10** be cautious **17** look before you leap

take care of **4** tend **6** assume **7** nurture **8** attend to, shoulder **10** minister to

take exception **5** demur **6** object, resent **11** look askance

take flight **3** fly **4** flee **6** escape, run off **7** abscond, fly away, run away, run free, take off **9** make a dash **10** fly the coop **12** make a getaway

take for granted **6** assume **10** undervalue

take heed **4** mind **6** beware **7** look out **8** take care, watch out **11** take warning

take hold **4** bite, grab, grip **5** grasp **6** clutch **7** catch on

take in stride **12** not skip a beat **13** be unperturbed

take into custody **3** bag, nab **4** book, bust, hold **5** catch, pinch, seize **6** arrest, collar, detain, secure **7** capture **9** apprehend **12** take prisoner

take into service **4** hire **6** employ, engage, retain, secure, take on

take issue **5** demur **6** differ **8** disagree **12** be at variance, stand opposed

take no notice of **6** ignore **9** disregard **11** pay no heed to **15** fail to recognize **16** pay no attention to **17** fail to acknowledge

take notice
Latin: **8** nota bene

take notice of **3** see **4** heed, mark, note **6** call on, regard **7** observe **8** call upon **9** recognize **10** get a load of **11** acknowledge **14** pay attention to

take nourishment **3** eat **4** feed **10** break bread **14** take sustenance

takeoff **5** spoof **6** parody, satire **7** lampoon **9** burlesque **10** caricature

take off **4** doff, lift **5** leave **6** decamp, depart, detach, remove **7** lift off, peel off, run away **8** strip off **14** leave the ground

take off guard **5** catch **8** surprise **14** take by surprise

take on **4** bear, hire **6** accept, assume, engage **8** shoulder **9** undertake

take one's breath away **4** daze, stun **5** shock **7** stupefy **8** astonish, dumfound **9** dumbfound, electrify **11** flabbergast **15** make one's eyes pop

take out **4** date **5** court **6** delete, escort, remove **7** extract, isolate **8** abstract, separate, take home, withdraw **9** strike out

take over **4** take **5** seize **6** assume, take on, take up **8** shoulder **10** commandeer, confiscate **11** appropriate, expropriate, gain control

take pains **6** strive **7** attempt, try hard **8** endeavor, go all out **10** do one's best **11** give one's all **12** make an effort **15** knock oneself out **16** give one's best shot

take pleasure in **4** like, love **5** adore, eat up, enjoy, fancy, savor **6** dote on, relish, relish **7** revel in **9** rejoice in **10** appreciate **13** be pleased with, get a kick out of

take possession of **5** claim **10** confiscate **11** appropriate, expropriate

take prisoner **3** bag, nab

4 book, bust **5** catch, pinch, seize **6** arrest, collar **7** capture **9** apprehend **11** take captive **15** take into custody

take sick **3** ail **6** sicken **8** collapse **9** become ill **10** be stricken

take stock of **5** audit, check **6** assess, review, survey **7** examine, inspect **8** look over **9** inventory

take sustenance **3** eat **4** feed **10** break bread **15** take nourishment

take the cake **5** excel **7** beat all, surpass **12** beat the devil, win hands down

take the edge off **6** lessen, pacify, soothe, temper **7** appease, assuage, lighten, mollify **8** tone down

take the first step **5** begin, start **6** launch, set out **8** commence, embark on, initiate **9** undertake **10** inaugurate

take the place of **7** replace **8** displace, supplant **9** supersede

take to be **4** deem, hold **5** count, judge, think **6** assume, regard, view as **7** account, believe **8** consider **10** look upon as

take to heart **4** heed, mind **6** attend **8** consider **9** hearken to **13** give thought to **14** pay attention to

take to one's heels **3** fly **4** flee **6** escape **7** get away, run away **10** fly the coop, make a break, take flight **12** make a getaway **15** head for the hills

take to task **5** chide, scold **6** accuse, berate, charge, rail at, rebuke **7** bawl out, censure, chasten, chew out, reprove, upbraid **8** admonish, chastise, reproach **9** castigate, criticize, dress down, reprimand **10** tongue-lash **11** remonstrate **13** call to account

take turns **5** share **6** rotate **9** alternate

take under one's wing **6** assist, defend **7** protect **8** befriend **9** look after

take unfair advantage of **5** abuse **6** misuse **7** exploit

take up **4** lift **6** absorb, accept, assume, occupy, pick up, resume, soak up, suck up **7** discuss, drink in **8** consider, continue, sponge up, talk over **9** cultivate, swallow up

taking a siesta **6** dozing **7** napping **8** snoozing **10** taking a nap **18** catching forty winks

takings **4** loot **5** booty **6** spoils **7** plunder **8** pickings

Talamancan
tribe: **7** Cabecar

Talaria
form: **7** sandals
owner: **6** Hermes **7** Mercury
characteristic: **6** winged

Talassio
origin: **5** Roman
form: **3** god
invoked at: **8** weddings
corresponds to: **5** Hymen **9** Hymenaeus

tale **3** fib, lie **4** epic, myth, saga, yarn **5** fable, novel, rumor, story **6** legend, report **7** account, fiction, hearsay, recital, romance, scandal, untruth **8** anecdote **9** falsehood, fish story, narration, narrative, tall story **10** short story **11** fabrication, scuttlebutt **12** tittle-tattle **13** falsification, piece of gossip **16** cock-and-bull story

talebearer **6** gossip **7** blabber, reciter, tattler **8** busybody, informer, reporter, telltale **10** newsmonger, tattletale **11** storyteller **12** blabbermouth **13** scandalmonger

talent **4** bent, gift, turn **5** flair, forte, knack, skill **6** genius **7** faculty **8** aptitude, capacity, facility, strength **9** endowment **10** capability **11** proficiency

Talent **14** Biblical weight

talented **4** able **5** adept **6** expert, gifted **7** born for, capable, endowed, skilled **8** artistic, polished **9** brilliant, competent **10** proficient **11** well-endowed **12** accomplished

Tale of a Tub, A
author: **9** Ben Jonson **13** Jonathan Swift

Tale of Genji
author: **19** Lady Murasaki Shikibu

Tale of Two Cities, A
author: **14** Charles Dickens
character: **7** Gaspard, Stryver **9** Dr Manette, Miss Pross **11** Jarvis Lorry, John Barstad **12** Lucie Manette, Sydney Carton **13** Charles Darnay, Jerry Cruncher, Madame Defarge **18** Marquis St Evremonde
director: **10** Jack Conway
cast: **12** Blanche Yurka, Isabel Jewell, Reginald Owen, Ronald Colman (Sydney Carton) **13** Basil Rathbone, Edna May Oliver **14** Elizabeth Allan
setting: **16** French Revolution

Tales Before Midnight
author: **19** Stephen Vincent Benet

Talese, Gay
author of: **14** Honor Thy Father **16** Thy Neighbor's Wife

Tales of a Fourth Grade Nothing
author: **9** Judy Blume

Tales of a Wayside Inn
author: **24** Henry Wadsworth Longfellow

Tales of Hoffmann, The
also: **18** Les Contes d'Hoffmann
opera by: **9** Offenbach

---

take **3** buy, get, lug, nab, net, see, use **4** bear, bilk, deem, draw, feel, gain, grab, grip, haul, have, heed, hire, hold, know, lead, loot, mark, mind, move, need, obey, read, rent, sack, tote, work **5** bring, brook, carry, catch, cheat, claim, clasp, filch, grasp, gross, guide, infer, lease, seize, stand, steal, use up, usher, usurp **6** accept, assume, attain, clutch, convey, deduce, deduct, demand, derive, divest, employ, endure, escort, fleece, follow, look on, obtain, pilfer, pocket, profit, regard, remove, secure, snatch, suffer **7** acquire, agree to, believe, call for, capture, conduct, consume, deliver, make out, observe, pillage, plunder, purloin, receive, require, respect, stomach, succeed, suppose, undergo **8** accede to, assent to, conceive, conclude, consider, listen to, perceive, proceeds, purchase, shoulder, submit to, subtract, take away, tolerate, transfer **9** ascertain, be ruled by, consent to, deprive of, eliminate, get hold of, interpret, lay hold of, put up with, respond to, transport, undertake **10** commandeer, comply with, comprehend, confiscate, experience, lay hands on, take effect, understand **11** appropriate, begin to work, go along with, necessitate **13** help oneself to **14** avail oneself of, misappropriate character: **6** Stella **7** Antonia, Olympia **9** Dr Miracle, Giulietta **11** E T A Hoffmann

Tales of Manhattan
author: **16** Louis Auchincloss

talisman **5** charm **6** amulet, fetish **10** lucky piece

Talisman, The
author: **14** Sir Walter Scott
character: **7** Conrade, El Hakim **10** Sir Kenneth **15** Queen Berengaria **19** Theodorick of Engaddi **20** Lady Edith Plantagenet **21** Richard the Lion-Hearted **31** Grand Master of the Knights Templars

talk **3** gab, jaw, rap, say **4** cant, chat, word **5** argot, idiom, lingo, noise, prate, rumor, slang, speak, state, utter **6** babble, bunkum, confab, confer, gossip, hot air, intone, jargon, parley, patois, powwow, preach, report, sermon, speech, take up, tirade **7** address, blarney, blather, chatter, consult, declare, deliver, dialect, discuss, express, hearsay, lecture, oration, palaver, prattle, twaddle **8** chitchat, colloquy, converse, dialogue, harangue, language, proclaim, rattle on, verbiage **9** discourse, enunciate, negotiate, pronounce, tete-a-tete, utterance **10** bandy words, conference, discussion, rap session, recitation, speak about **11** declamation, exhortation, pontificate, scuttlebutt **12** blatherskite, consultation, conversation, tittle-tattle **13** confabulation

talkative **5** gabby, talky, windy, wordy **6** babbly, chatty, prolix **7** gossipy, verbose, voluble **8** effusive **9** garrulous **10** long-winded, loquacious

talk big **4** brag, crow **5** boast, vaunt **13** puff oneself up **15** blow one's own horn **19** pat oneself on the back

talk down to **9** patronize **10** condescend

talker **6** gabber, gossip, magpie, orator **7** babbler, speaker, windbag **8** lecturer, prattler **9** chatterer, converser **10** chatterbox, mouthpiece **11** rumormonger, speechifier, speechmaker **12** blatherskite, spokesperson **13** scandalmonger **17** conversationalist

talk nonsense **6** babble, drivel, ramble

Talk of the Town, The
director: **13** George Stevens
cast: **9** Cary Grant **10** Jean Arthur **12** Ronald Colman **13** Edgar Buchanan, Glenda Farrell

talk out of **4** balk **6** thwart **8** dissuade **10** discourage

talk over **6** confer, review **7** consult, discuss, hash out

talk to **7** address, lecture, speak to **12** converse with

talk together **4** talk **6** confer **7** discuss **8** converse **9** discourse

tall **3** big **4** high **5** lanky, lofty, rangy **6** absurd **7** soaring, stringy **8** elevated, gangling, towering **10** incredible, long-limbed **11** embellished, exaggerated, implausible **12** preposterous, unbelievable **13** hard to believe, hard to swallow

tallow **3** fat, tip **5** taper **6** bougie, candle, cierge **9** rushlight

Tall State
nickname of: **8** Illinois

tall story **3** fib, lie **4** yarn **5** fable **7** fiction, untruth, whopper **9** fairy tale, falsehood, fish story, invention **11** fabrication **16** cock-and-bull story

tally **3** add, sum **4** jibe, list, mark, poll, post **5** agree, count, match, score, sum up, total **6** accord, census, concur, muster, reckon, record, square **7** catalog, compute, conform **8** coincide, mark down, register, scorepad, tabulate **9** calculate, harmonize, reckoning, scorecard **10** correspond **11** enumeration

talon **4** claw, nail, spur

Talos
form: **5** youth **7** monster
made of: **5** brass **6** bronze
made by: **10** Hephaestus
guarded: **5** Crete
destroyed by: **5** Medea
uncle: **8** Daedalus
killed by: **8** Daedalus

Talthybius
occupation: **6** herald
employer: **9** Agamemnon

Tamar
author: **15** Robinson Jeffers

Tamar
father: **5** David **7** Absalom
mother: **6** Maacah
husband: **2** Er **4** Onan **5** Judah, Uriah
brother: **5** Amnon **7** Absalom, Chileab, Solomon **8** Adonijah
son: **5** Zarah **6** Pharez
daughter: **8** Maachiah
father-in-law: **5** Judah

Tamburlaine the Great
author: **18** Christopher Marlowe
character: **6** Cosroe **7** Mycetes, Orcanes **8** Bajazeth **9** Callepine, Techelles, Zenocrate **10** Theridamas, Usumcasane

tame **4** curb, damp, dull, flat, meek, mild, rein **5** break, check, quiet, timid, train **6** boring, bridle, broken, docile, gentle, govern, manage, master, placid, pliant, serene, subdue **7** conquer, control, pliable, prosaic, repress, subdued, tedious **8** amenable, domestic, dominate, lifeless, overcome, regulate, restrain, suppress, timorous, tranquil **9** tractable **10** make docile, submissive, unexciting **11** complaisant, domesticate, unresisting **12** domesticated **13** uninteresting

tameness **8** docility **9** placidity **10** gentleness, insipidity **12** complaisance, tractability **13** domestication **14** submissiveness

Taming of the Shrew, The
author: **18** William Shakespeare
character: **6** Bianca, Gremio, Tranio **8** Baptista, Lucentio **9** Hortensio, Katharina, Petruchio, Vincentio
director: **16** Franco Zeffirelli
cast: **11** Michael York, Natasha Pyne **13** Richard Burton (Petruchio) **14** Michael Hordern **15** Elizabeth Taylor (Katharina), Vernon Dobtcheff
score: **8** Nino Rota

Tammuz
origin: **8** Sumerian
god of: **9** shepherds
Hebrew month: **6** fourth

Tam O'Shanter
author: **11** Robert Burns

Tampa Bay
football team: **7** Bandits **10** Buccaneers

tamper **3** mix **4** muck **6** butt in, fiddle, horn in, meddle, tinker **7** intrude, obtrude **9** interfere, intervene **10** fool around, mess around **12** monkey around

tamper with **5** alter **6** change, doctor **7** falsify

tan **4** roan **5** beige, brown, khaki, sandy, tawny **6** bronze, sorrel, suntan **7** bronzed

8 brownish, cinnamon, sunburnt **9** sunburned, suntanned **10** light brown **11** yellow-brown

Tanah Airkita *see* **9** Indonesia

Tananarive, Antananarivo
capital of: 10 Madagascar

Tanaquil
origin: 5 Roman
form: 5 queen
husband: 7 Tarquin **17** Tarquinius Priscus

Tandy, Jessica
born: 6 London **7** England
husband: 10 Hume Cronyn **11** Jack Hawkins
roles: 8 The Birds **10** The Gin Game **12** Forever Amber **21** A Streetcar Named Desire

tang 3 bit **4** bite, hint, odor, reek **5** aroma, punch, savor, scent, smack, smell, sting, tinge, touch, trace **6** flavor **8** acridity, piquancy, pungency, tartness **9** acridness, sharpness, spiciness **10** suggestion

Tange, Kenzo
architect of: 11 Press Center (Kofu) **16** Shizuoka Building (Tokyo) **19** Olympic Sports Stadia (Tokyo) **24** Kagawa Prefectural Offices (Takamatsu) **30** Imabara Municipal Office Building

tangibility 11 materiality, palpability **12** touchability

tangible 4 real **5** solid **6** actual **7** obvious **8** clear-cut, concrete, manifest, material, palpable, physical, positive **9** corporeal, touchable **10** verifiable **11** indubitable, substantial

tangle 3 fix, net, web **4** knot, maze, mesh, muss **5** ravel, skein, snarl, twist **6** jumble, jungle, ruffle, rumple, tousle **7** impasse, network **8** dishevel, disorder **9** labyrinth **10** disarrange

tangled 6 knotty **7** chaotic, complex, jumbled, mixed-up, snarled **11** complicated, intertwined

Tanguy, Yves
born: 5 Paris **6** France
artwork: 4 Fear **17** Mama Papa is Wounded, Untitled Landscape **18** Rose of the Four Winds **20** Slowly Toward the North **22** Four O'Clock in Summer Hope, Indefinite Divisibility **23** Multiplication of the Arcs **25** Extinction of Useless Lights

tank 3 vat **6** boiler **7** cistern **8** aquarium, fish tank **9** container, reservoir **10** armored car, receptacle **11** storage tank

Tannhauser and the Tournament of Song at Wartburg
opera by: 6 Wagner
also: 41 Tannhauser und der Sangerkrieg auf dem Wartburg
character: 5 Venus **7** Wolfram **9** Elizabeth

Tanoan
tribe: 4 Tuei **5** Kiowa **6** Isleta

tantalize 4 bait **5** charm, taunt, tease, tempt **6** entice, lead on **7** bewitch, provoke, torment **8** intrigue **9** captivate, fascinate, titillate **15** whet the appetite **18** make one's mouth water

tantalizing 7 teasing **8** inviting, tempting **9** appealing, leading on **10** intriguing **11** fascinating

Tantalus
king of: 4 Pisa **7** Phrygia
father: 8 Thyestes
wife: 12 Clytemnestra
son: 6 Pelops
daughter: 5 Niobe
punishment in Hades: 6 hunger, thirst

tantamount 4 like **5** equal **9** analogous **10** comparable, equivalent, on a par with **12** commensurate **13** commensurable

tantrum 3 fit **5** storm **7** flare-up, rampage **8** outburst, paroxysm **9** explosion **12** fit of passion **13** burst of temper, conniption fit

Tanystropheous
type: 8 dinosaur
period: 8 Triassic

Tanzania ***see box, p. 964***

Tao Te Ching
author: 6 Lao-tzu

Taotieh
origin: 7 Chinese
form: 6 animal

tap 3 pat, rap, use **4** cock, drum, peck, thud **5** spout, touch, valve **6** broach, employ, faucet, hammer, spigot, stroke, uncork, unplug **7** draw off, exploit, utilize **8** draw upon, stopcock **9** put to work, unstopper

taper 3 dip, wax **4** wick **5** light **6** candle, cierge, narrow **8** decrease **9** narrowing **10** diminution **12** come to a point

taper off 4 wane **5** abate **6** weaken **7** slacken, subside **8** decrease, diminish, fade away, slack off

tapestry 3 rug **5** arras, tapis **6** Bruges, fabric, mosaic **7** Gobelin, hanging, montage, weaving **8** Aubusson **12** wallcovering

Tapley, Mark
character in: 16 Martin Chuzzlewit
author: 7 Dickens

Tappertit, Simon
character in: 12 Barnaby Rudge
author: 7 Dickens

Taprobane *see* **8** Sri Lanka

taproom 3 bar, pub **6** lounge, saloon, tavern **8** alehouse **11** bar and grill, public house **14** cocktail lounge

Taranis
god of: 7 thunder

Taras Bulba
author: 12 Nikolai Gogol
character: 5 Ostap **6** Andrii, Yankel **26** Daughter of the Polish Waiwode

Tarascans, Tarascos
location: 6 Mexico **9** Michoacan **14** Central America
leader: 8 Zincicha **9** Tangaxoan, Tariacuri

Tarawa
capital of: 8 Kiribati

Tar Baby
author: 12 Toni Morrison

Tarchetius
king of: 9 Alba Longa

tardy 4 late, slow **5** slack **6** remiss **7** belated, languid, overdue **8** crawling, creeping, dilatory, slowpoke, sluggish **9** leisurely, not on time, reluctant, slow-paced, snail-like **10** behindhand, behind time, unpunctual **14** slow as molasses **15** procrastinating

tare 12 Biblical weed

target 3 aim, end **4** butt, dupe, goal, goat, gull, mark, plan, prey **5** patsy **6** design, intent, object, pigeon, victim **7** purpose **8** ambition **9** intention, objective **13** laughingstock

Targitaus
father: 4 Zeus
first inhabitant of: 7 Scythia

Tar Heel State
nickname of: 13 North Carolina

tariff 3 fee **4** cost, duty, fare, levy, rate, rent **5** price **6** charge, excise, impost **7** expense **8** input tax **9** excise tax, export tax **10** assessment, commission, freightage

Tarkington, Booth
author of: 6 Penrod **9** Seven-

Tanzania
other name: **12** isle of cloves
capital/largest city: **11** Dar es Salaam
new capital: **6** Dodoma
others: **4** Wete, **5** Kilwa, Lindi, Moshi, Tanga, Ujiji **6** Arusha, Kigoma, Mwadui, Mwanza, Tabora **7** Korogwe, Mtawara **8** Morogoro, Zanzibar **12** Kwasemangube, Zanzibar Town
division: **8** Zanzibar **17** union of Tanganyika
monetary unit: **4** cent **8** shilling
weight: **8** farsalah
island: **5** Mafia, Pemba **6** Latham **8** Zanzibar
lake: **5** Eyasi, Nyasa, Rukwa **6** Malawi, Natron, Nyassa **7** Manyara **8** Victoria **10** Tanganyika
mountain: **4** Kibo, Mero **8** Usambara
highest point: **11** Kilimanjaro
river: **4** Lupa, Ruvu, Wami **5** Ruaha **6** Kagera, Luwegu, Mbaesa, Rufiji, Rungwa, Ruvuma **7** Nkululu, Pangani **8** Mbenkuru **11** Mbarangandu
sea: **6** Indian
physical feature:
crater: **10** Ngorongoro
gorge: **7** Olduvai
national park: **9** Serengeti
plains: **9** Serengeti
steppe: **5** Masai **8** Iwembere
valley: **9** Great Rift
people: **2** Ha **4** Arab, Gogo, Goma, Haya, Hehe **5** Asian, Bantu, Masai **6** Arusha, Chagga, Sukuma, Wagogo, Wagoma **7** African, Makonde, Sambara, Sandawe, Shirazi, Swahili, Wabunga, Zongora **8** Nyakyusa, Nyamwezi
early man: **13** zinjanthropus
explorer: **6** Da Gama **7** Rebmann **11** Livingstone
leader: **5** Sayid **6** Karume **7** Nyerere **16** Sultan of Zanzibar
language: **5** Bantu **6** Arabic **7** English, Khoisan, Nilotic, Swahili **8** Cushitic, Gujarati
religion: **5** Islam **7** animism **12** Christianity
feature:
animal: **6** dik-dik
cattle barn: **4** byre
clothing: **4** sari **6** bui bui
fly: **6** tsetse
holiday: **8** Saba Saba
homestead: **8** manyatta
food:
dish: **5** ugali

teen **10** Alice Adams **13** Kate Fennigate **14** The Man from Home **17** Monsieur Beaucaire **19** The World Does Not Move **23** The Magnificent Ambersons

Tarleton, Stuart and Brent
characters in: **15** Gone With the Wind
author: **8** Mitchell

tarnish **3** dim **4** blot, dull, foul, soil, spot **5** dirty, erode, stain, sully, taint **6** befoul, darken, defame, defile, smirch, vilify **7** blacken, blemish, corrode, degrade, oxidize **8** besmirch, discolor, disgrace, dishonor **9** denigrate, discredit **10** lose luster, stigmatize **17** drag through the mud

tarnished **5** dirty **6** soiled **7** stained, sullied **8** oxidized **10** discolored

Tarnkappe
origin: **8** Germanic
mentioned in: **14** Nibelungenlied
form: **5** cloak
gives wearer: **8** strength **12** invisibility
stolen by: **9** Siegfried
stolen from: **8** Niblungs **9** Nibelungs

tarot
Italian: **6** naibes **7** attutti **8** tarocchi
German: **5** tarok
French: **5** tarau, tarot
cards/deck: **12** seventy-eight
division: **11** major arcana, minor arcana **12** lesser arcana **13** greater arcana
suit: **3** cup **4** coin, wand **5** baton, money, sword **6** cudgel **8** pentacle
face card: **4** king, page **5** knave, queen, valet **6** knight
major arcana: **4** Fool, Moon **5** Death **7** Justice **8** Judgment **9** Hanged Man **14** Wheel of Fortune

tarpaulin **4** tarp **6** canvas **9** dropcloth **15** waterproof cover

Tarpeia
form: **12** vestal virgin
father: **15** Spurius Tarpeius
betrayed: **4** Rome
betrayed to: **7** Sabines
killed by: **7** Sabines

Tarquin
king of: **4** Rome
origin: **8** Etruscan
also called: **17** Tarquinius Priscus **18** Tarquinius Superbus
wife: **8** Tanaquil

tarragon
botanical name: **20** Artemisia dracunculus
means: **6** dragon **12** little dragon
Arab: **7** tarkhum
French: **8** estragon
origin: **7** Siberia
used as: **8** purifier
flavor: **8** licorice
use: **4** fish **5** salad, sauce **10** mayonnaise **14** Bearnaise sauce

tarry **3** lag **4** bide, rest, stay, wait **5** abide, dally, delay, pause, stall **6** dawdle, linger, put off, remain **7** be tardy **8** hang back, postpone, stave off, take time **9** temporize **10** hang around **13** cool one's heels, procrastinate

tarsal
bone of: **5** ankle

Tarshish
father: **5** Javan **6** Bilhan

tart **3** pie **4** acid, sour **5** acerb, acrid, sharp, spicy, tangy **6** acetic, barbed, biting, bitter, crusty **7** caustic, cutting, piquant, pungent, sourish **8** vinegary **10** astringent **11** pastry shell

Tartarean *see* **8** infernal

Tartarin of Tarascon
author: **14** Alphonse Daudet

Tartarus
form: **5** abyss
below: **5** Hades
imprisoned: **6** Titans

tartness **7** acidity, sarcasm

8 acerbity 9 sharpness 11 astringency

Tartuffe
author: 7 Moliere
character: 5 Damis, Orgon 6 Dorine, Elmire, Valere 7 Cleante, Mariane 14 Madame Pernelle

Tarzan
author: 18 Edgar Rice Burroughs
character: 3 Boy 4 Jane 7 Cheetah
Tarzan also called: 15 Lord of Greystoke, Lord of the Jungle
comic strip creator: 9 Hal Foster 12 Burme Hogarth

task 3 job 4 duty, work 5 chore, labor, stint 6 charge, errand 7 mission 8 business 10 assignment 11 undertaking 14 responsibility

Task, The
author: 13 William Cowper

taskmaster 4 boss 6 despot, master, tyrant 7 foreman, headman, manager 8 director, martinet, overseer, stickler 10 supervisor 11 Simon Legree, slave driver 14 disciplinarian, superintendent

Tasmania
bay: 5 Storm 6 Oyster
capital: 6 Hobart
city: 10 Launceston
country: 9 Australia
formerly: 14 Van Diemen's Land
island: 4 Echo 6 Sorell
mountain: 4 Ossa 6 Cradle
river: 3 Esk
strait: 4 Bass

Tasso, Torquato
author of: 6 Aminta 7 Rinaldo 18 Jerusalem Delivered

taste 3 bit, nip, sip, try, yen 4 bent, bite, feel, meet, tang, test, whim 5 crumb, enjoy, fancy, savor, smack 6 desire, flavor, hunger, liking, morsel, relish, sample, thirst 7 craving, decorum, discern, forkful, insight, leaning, longing, savor of, smack of, swallow, undergo 8 appetite, delicacy, fondness, judgment, mouthful, penchant, piquancy, spoonful, yearning 9 encounter, hankering, partake of, propriety 10 experience, partiality, propensity, take a sip of 11 correctness, discernment, disposition, inclination, take a bite of 12 eat a little of, predilection 14 discrimination, drink a little of
French: 4 gout

tasteful 7 elegant, refined 8 artistic, becoming, cultured, esthetic, handsome, suitable 9 beautiful, exquisite 10 attractive, well-chosen

tasteless 3 low 4 flat, mild, rude, weak 5 bland, cheap, crass, crude, gaudy, gross, tacky 6 coarse, common, flashy, garish, ribald, watery 7 insipid, uncouth 8 improper, indecent, unseemly 9 inelegant, offensive, unrefined 10 disgusting, flavorless, indecorous, indelicate, uncultured, unesthetic, unflavored, unsuitable 11 distasteful, insensitive

tastemakers 7 leaders 10 avant-garde, innovators 12 stylesetters, trendsetters

tasty 3 hot 5 spicy, tangy, yummy 6 savory 7 piquant, zestful 8 luscious 9 delicious, flavorful, palatable, toothsome 10 appetizing, delectable, flavorsome 11 good-tasting, scrumptious 12 full-flavored, well-seasoned

Tatar, Mr
character in: 22 The Mystery of Edwin Drood
author: 7 Dickens

Tatius
also: 5 Titus
co-ruler with: 7 Romulus

Tatler, The
author: 13 Joseph Addison, Richard Steele

tattered 4 torn 6 broken, ragged, ripped, shabby, shaggy 10 disheveled 11 dilapidated

tatters 4 rags 6 shreds 7 patches

tattle 3 rat 4 blab 5 prate 6 gabble, gossip, snitch, squeal, tell on 7 blather, chatter, hearsay, prattle, twaddle 8 inform on 9 loose talk 11 mudslinging 12 tittle-tattle 13 tongue-wagging

tattletale 3 rat 4 fink 5 sneak 6 gossip, snitch 7 ratfink, stoolie, tattler 8 betrayer, busybody, informer, squealer, telltale 8 informer 10 newsmonger, talebearer 11 rumormonger, stool pigeon 12 blabbermouth, troublemaker 13 scandalmonger

Tatum, Edward Lawrie
field: 8 genetics 12 biochemistry
discovered: 19 gene characteristics
awarded: 10 Nobel Prize

taunt 3 guy, rag 4 gibe, jeer, jive, mock, slur, twit 5 scoff, sneer, tease 6 deride, harass, insult, jeer at 7 provoke, ragging, sneer at, snigger, torment 8 chaffing, derision, ridicule 9 make fun of, poke fun at, snigger at 10 harassment, make game of, tormenting 11 provocation

Taura
form: 3 cow
attribute: 6 sacred

taurobolium
rite of: 7 baptism

Taurog, Norman
director of: 6 Skippy (Oscar) 8 Boys' Town

Taurus
symbol: 4 bull
planet: 5 Venus
rules: 5 money 9 resources
born: 3 May 5 April

taut 4 neat, snug, tidy, trig, trim 5 rigid, smart, tense, tight 6 spruce 7 orderly 8 not loose, not slack 9 shipshape, unbending, unrelaxed 10 drawn tight, inflexible, nononsense 11 under strain 12 businesslike 13 well-regulated 15 well-disciplined

tavern 3 bar, pub 4 dive 6 bistro, saloon 7 barroom, gin mill, taproom 8 alehouse, drinkery, grogshop 9 beer joint, brasserie, honky-tonk, roadhouse 10 restaurant 11 public house 12 watering hole 14 cocktail lounge
French: 7 auberge
German: 8 Brauhaus

tawdry 4 loud 5 cheap, crass, gaudy, showy, tacky 6 flashy, garish, tinsel, vulgar 7 raffish 8 gimcrack 9 inelegant, obtrusive, tasteless 10 flamboyant 11 conspicuous, pretentious 12 meretricious, ostentatious

tawny 3 tan 4 fawn 5 beige, dusky, olive, sandy 6 bronze 7 swarthy 8 brownish 10 light brown 14 yellowish-brown

tax 3 sap, try 4 duty, lade, levy, load, tire, toll 5 drain, weigh 6 assess, burden, charge, custom, excise, impost, saddle, strain, tariff, weight 7 deplete, exhaust, stretch, wear out 8 exertion, overwork 10 assessment, obligation, overburden
kind: 4 city 5 sales, state 6 county, excise, income, luxury 8 property 11 inheritance 12 excess profit

Taxi
character: 9 John Burns, Tony Banta 10 Alex Rieger 11 Elaine Nardo, Latka Gravas 12 Bobby Wheeler, Louie De Palma
cast: 9 Tony Danza 10 Judd

Hirsch **11** Andy Kaufman, Danny DeVito, Jeff Conaway **12** Marilu Henner **13** Randall Carver
company: **11** Sunshine Cab

taxicab **4** hack **6** jitney **7** droshky, hackney **8** hired car, rickshaw **10** automobile **11** jinrickshaw

Taxi Driver
director: **14** Martin Scorsese
cast: **10** Peter Boyle **11** Jodie Foster **12** Albert Brooks, Harvey Keitel, Robert De Niro **13** Leonard Harris **14** Cybill Shepherd
setting: **11** New York City
score: **15** Bernard Herrmann
script: **12** Paul Schrader

taxonomy
study of: **17** structure contrast **19** structure comparison

Taygete
member of: **8** Pleiades
father: **5** Atlas
son: **10** Lacedaemon

Taylor, Elizabeth
born: **6** London **7** England
husband: **8** Mike Todd **10** John Warner **11** Eddie Fisher, Nicky Hilton **13** Richard Burton **14** Michael Wilding
roles: **5** Giant **7** Ivanhoe **9** Cleopatra **11** Little Women **12** The Sandpiper **14** A Place in the Sun, National Velvet, Raintree County **16** Butterfield Eight (Oscar), Cat on a Hot Tin Roof, Father of the Bride **18** Suddenly Last Summer **19** The Taming of the Shrew **25** Who's Afraid of Virginia Woolf (Oscar)

Taylor, Robert
real name: **22** Spangler Arlington Brugh
wife: **12** Ursula Thiess **15** Barbara Stanwyck
roles: **7** Camille, Ivanhoe **8** Quo Vadis **11** Billy the Kid **14** Waterloo Bridge **20** Magnificent Obsession

Taylor, Zachary ***see box***

Tchad *see* **4** Chad

Tchaikovsky, Peter (Piotr Ilyich Chaikovsky)
born: **6** Russia **8** Votkinsk
composer of: **7** Manfred, Mazeppa **8** Iolanthe, Pathetic (symphony No 6), Swan Lake **9** Joan of Arc **10** Nutcracker **12** Eugene Onegin, Winter Dreams **14** Italian Caprice, Romeo and Juliet, The Enchantress **16** The Queen of Spades **17** Francesca da Rimini, The Sleeping Beauty **22** Eighteen-Twelve Overture

Tchile *see* **5** Chile

tea **16** Camellia sinensis
varieties: **5** Assam, Bohea, China, green, pekoe, Yerba **6** Ceylon, Oolong, Oswego, Tisane **7** African, Arabian, cambric, crystal, Lapsang, Mexican, redroot, Spanish **8** bergamot, camomile, Earl Grey, Labrador, mountain, Paraguay, Siberian, Souchong, Woodruff **9** gunpowder, lemon balm, New Jersey, sassafras **10** Darjeeling, Philippine **11** Appalachian, Orange Pekoe **14** Irish breakfast **16** English breakfast

teach **5** coach, drill, edify, prime, tutor **6** inform, school **7** educate, implant, prepare **8** exercise, instruct **9** enlighten, inculcate **10** discipline **12** indoctrinate

Teach
character in: **21** The Master of Ballantrae
author: **9** Stevenson

teacher **3** don **5** coach, tutor **6** master, mentor **7** maestro, trainer **8** educator **9** preceptor, professor **10** instructor, schoolmarm **12** schoolmaster **13** schoolteacher **14** schoolmistress

teaching **5** dogma, tenet **6** belief **7** nurture, precept **8** doctrine, pedagogy, training, tutelage, tutoring **9** education, principle, schooling **10** conviction, philosophy **11** inculcation, instructing, instruction, preparation **14** indoctrination

tea dance
French: **10** the dansant

teal
group of: **5** ducks
color: **4** blue **5** green

team **3** rig, set **4** ally, band, crew, five, gang, join, nine, pair, side, unit, yoke **5** force, group, merge, party, squad, staff, unify, unite **6** circle, clique, couple, eleven, league, tandem **7** combine, company, coterie, faction **8** alliance, federate **9** coalition, cooperate **10** amalgamate, federation, sports team, yoked group **11** association, consolidate, get

---

Taylor, Zachary
nickname: **16** Old Rough and Ready
presidential rank: **7** twelfth
party: **4** Whig
state represented: **2** LA
defeated: **4** (Lewis) Cass **8** (Martin) Van Buren
vice president: **8** (Millard) Fillmore
cabinet:
state: **7** (John Middleton) Clayton
treasury: **8** (William Morris) Meredith
war: **8** (George Walker) Crawford
attorney general: **7** (Reverdy) Johnson
navy: **7** (William Ballard) Preston
postmaster general: **8** (Jacob) Collamer
interior: **5** (Thomas) Ewing
born: **12** Montebello VA **12** Orange County
died: **12** Washington DC
buried: **12** Louisville KY
education: **9** no college **16** privately tutored
religion: **12** Episcopalian
political career: **21** none prior to presidency
civilian career: **7** planter, soldier
military service: **6** US Army **12** major general
War: **7** Mexican **9** Black Hawk **19** War of Eighteen-Twelve **14** Second Seminole
notable events of lifetime/presidency:
treaty: **13** Clayton-Bulwer
father: **7** Richard
mother: **5** Sarah (Dabney Strother)
siblings: **6** George **7** Hancock **11** Sarah Bailey **12** Elizabeth Lee, Emily Richard **13** Joseph Pannill **21** William Dabney Strother
wife: **8** Margaret (Mackall Smith)
children: **7** Richard **9** Sarah Knox **10** Ann Mackall **13** Margaret Smith, Mary Elizabeth, Octavia Panill

together, incorporate **12** band together, join together **13** confederation

teammate **4** ally **7** partner **8** co-player, coworker **9** associate, colleague, co-partner **11** confederate **12** collaborator

team spirit **10** group pride, solidarity **13** esprit de corps

team up **4** ally **5** unite **9** cooperate **10** join forces **11** collaborate

tear **3** fly, gap, hie, rip, run **4** bolt, dart, dash, grab, hole, mist, pull, race, rend, rent, rift, rive, rush, scud, slit, snag, swim, whiz, yank **5** abuse, break, crack, fault, pluck, scoot, seize, sever, shoot, shred, speed, split, spurt, sweep, whisk **6** breach, cleave, damage, divide, gallop, hasten, hustle, injury, plunge, ravage, scurry, snatch, sprint, sunder, wrench **7** disrupt, fissure, hard use, opening, rupture, scamper, scuttle **8** disunite, teardrop, scramble, splinter **9** come apart, hotfoot it, pull apart, skedaddle **10** impairment, make tracks **11** destruction **12** pull to pieces

tear down **4** raze **5** level, smash, wreck **7** destroy, flatten **8** demolish **9** dismantle, take apart

tearful **5** teary, weepy **6** crying **7** bawling, crushed, sobbing, wailing, weeping **8** mournful **9** lamenting, sniveling **10** blubbering, lachrymose, whimpering **11** heartbroken **12** inconsolable **13** brokenhearted

tear off **5** sever **6** detach, rip off **7** pull off **8** break off, separate **10** wrench away

Teasdale, Sara
author of: **8** Love Song **11** Helen of Troy **13** Dark of the Moon **14** Flame and Shadow, Rivers to the Sea, Strange Victory

tease **3** guy, irk, nag, rag, vex **4** bait, gall, gibe, goad, haze, jeer, josh, mock, pest, rile, twit **5** annoy, chafe, harry, mimic, pique, scoff, sneer, taunt, worry **6** badger, bother, harass, hazing, heckle, hector, mocker, needle, pester, plague, teaser **7** bedevil, chafing, laugh at, needler, provoke, razzing, snigger, taunter, torment, worrier **8** derision, heckling, irritate, needling, ridicule **9** aggravate, make fun of, mimicking, persecute, tantalize, tormentor **10** harassment, tantalizer **11** persecution

teaspoon
abbreviation: **3** tsp

Teazle, Sir Peter and Lady
characters in: **19** The School for Scandal
author: **8** Sheridan

technical **5** trade **10** mechanical, vocational **11** complicated, nonacademic **13** technological

technique **3** art, way **4** form **5** craft, knack, style **6** manner, method, system **7** formula, know-how **8** approach, facility **9** procedure **10** adroitness, expertness, technology **11** proficiency **12** skillfulness

Tecmessa
father: **8** Teuthras
son: **9** Eurysaces
carried off by: **14** Telamonian Ajax

tedious **3** dry **4** drab, dull, long, slow **5** vapid **6** boring, dismal, dreary, jejune, tiring **7** humdrum, insipid, irksome, onerous, prosaic **8** drawn-out, lifeless, tiresome, wearying **9** fatiguing, laborious, wearisome **10** burdensome, exhausting, monotonous, oppressive, unexciting **13** time-consuming, unimaginative, uninteresting

tediousness **5** ennui **7** boredom **8** dullness, monotony

tedium **3** rut **5** ennui **7** boredom **8** drabness, dullness, monotony, sameness **10** dreariness **11** routineness **12** tiresomeness

tedium of life
Latin: **12** taedium vitae

teem **4** brim, gush **5** swarm **6** abound **8** be full of, overflow **9** be overrun **15** burst at the seams

teeming **4** full **7** crowded **8** swarming **9** abounding, bounteous **11** overflowing

teeny-weeny **3** wee **4** tiny **5** dwarf **6** little, minute, petite **9** miniature, minuscule **10** diminutive, pocket-size **11** lilliputian, microscopic, pocket-sized

teeter **4** reel, sway **5** lurch, waver **6** seesaw, totter, wobble **7** stagger **8** hesitate **9** vacillate

teetotaler **3** dry **9** abstainer **10** nondrinker **14** prohibitionist

Tegeates
father: **6** Lycaon

Tegucigalpa
capital of: **8** Honduras

Tegyrius
king of: **6** Thrace

Tehani
character in: **17** Mutiny on the Bounty
authors: **4** Hall **8** Nordhoff

Tehran, Teheran
capital of: **4** Iran
landmark: **10** Melaat Park **12** Marble Palace, Marmar Palace **14** Azadai Monument, Gulestan Palace, Saadabad Palace **15** Freedom Monument, Hosseineh Mosque, Shahyad Monument **23** Center for Islamic Studies
means: **9** warm place
mountain: **6** Elburz **8** Demavend
ruler: **8** Khomeini **23** Muhammad Reza Shah Pahlavi

te igitur **13** thee therefore

Teiresias *see* **8** Tiresias

Telamon
king of: **7** Salamis
member of: **9** Argonauts
father: **6** Aeacus
mother: **6** Endeis
brother: **6** Peleus
half-brother: **6** Phocus
wife: **6** Glauce **7** Eriboea
son: **4** Ajax **6** Teucer
friend: **8** Hercules

Telchines
form: **6** beings
characteristic: **9** malicious

Telegonus
father: **7** Proteus **8** Odysseus
mother: **5** Circe
wife: **2** Io **8** Penelope
killed: **8** Odysseus
killed by: **8** Hercules

telegraph
invented by: **5** Morse, Woods **6** Edison **7** Marconi

Telemachus
father: **8** Odysseus
mother: **8** Penelope
son: **7** Latinus

Telemann, Georg Philipp
born: **7** Germany **9** Magdeburg
composer of: **9** Fantasias **10** Times of Day **12** Don Quichotte **14** Die Tageszeiten, Musique de Table

Telemus
vocation: **4** seer
father: **7** Eurymus
warned: **10** Polyphemus

telepathy **3** ESP **10** sixth sense **11** second sight **12** clairvoyance **19** spirit communication, thought transference **22** extrasensory perception

Telephassa
husband: 6 Agenor

telephone
invented by: 4 Bell

Telephus
king of: 5 Mysia
father: 8 Hercules
mother: 4 Auge

telescope
invented by: 7 Galileo 10 Lippershey
astronomical: 6 Kepler

Telesphorus
god of: 15 illness recovery

telesterion
form: 8 building
purpose: 8 religion 11 celebration

television
invented by: 5 Baird 8 Zworykin 10 Farnsworth

tell 3 ask, bid, own, say, see 4 blab 5 bruit, count, order, speak, spout, state, utter, weigh, write 6 advise, babble, betray, blazon, depict, detail, direct, figure, impart, inform, number, recite, reckon, relate, report, reveal, sketch, unfold 7 apprise, command, compute, confess, declare, discern, divulge, express, find out, mention, narrate, portray, predict, publish, recount, request 8 acquaint, count off, describe, disclose, estimate, forecast, foretell, identify, instruct, perceive, register, set forth 9 apprehend, ascertain, broadcast, calculate, chronicle, enumerate, enunciate, influence, make known, pronounce, recognize 10 take effect 11 communicate, distinguish 12 discriminate 17 breathe a word about

Teller, Edward
field: 7 physics
developed: 8 atom bomb 12 hydrogen bomb

telling 5 solid, valid 6 cogent, potent 7 decided, weighty 8 decisive, definite, forceful, material, positive, powerful, striking 9 effective, effectual, important, momentous, trenchant 10 conclusive, definitive, impressive 11 efficacious, influential, significant 13 consequential

telltale 6 gossip 7 tattler 8 busybody, giveaway, informer, squealer 9 affirming, betraying, divulging, revealing, verifying 10 confirming, disclosing, newsbearer, talebearer, tattletale 11 informative 12 blabbermouth, enlightening 13 scandalmonger

Tellus
called: 10 Terra Mater
origin: 5 Roman
goddess of: 5 earth 8 marriage 9 fertility 11 agriculture
corresponds to: 4 Gaea

Telphusa
form: 5 nymph
location: 6 spring
characteristic: 7 cunning

Temenus
father: 8 Pelasgus 12 Aristomachus
brother: 11 Aristodemus, Cresphontes
reared: 4 Hera

temerity 4 gall 5 brass, cheek, nerve 8 audacity, boldness, chutzpah, rashness 9 brashness, freshness, impudence, insolence, pushiness, sauciness 10 brazenness, effrontery 11 forwardness 12 impertinence, indiscretion 13 foolhardiness, intrusiveness

Temin, Howard Martin
field: 8 genetics, oncology
discovered: 20 reverse transcriptase
awarded: 10 Nobel Prize

temper 3 ire 4 bile, calm, fury, gall, mood, rage 5 allay, anger, humor, pique, quiet, still, wrath 6 animus, anneal, choler, dander, harden, pacify, soften, soothe, spleen 7 appease, balance, compose, dudgeon, emotion, ferment, passion, toughen, umbrage 8 acrimony, bad humor, calmness, mitigate, moderate, palliate, vexation 9 annoyance, composure, huffiness 10 irritation, strengthen 11 displeasure, disposition, equilibrium, frame of mind, indignation, peevishness, tranquilize 12 churlishness, irascibility, irritability

temperament 4 bent, cast, mood, soul, tone 5 humor, tenor 6 makeup, nature, spirit, temper 7 leaning, quality 8 tendency 9 character 10 complexion 11 disposition, frame of mind, personality

temperamental 5 fiery, moody 6 fickle 7 erratic, peppery, willful 8 unstable, volatile 9 emotional, excitable, explosive, hotheaded, mercurial, sensitive, turbulent 10 capricious, headstrong, high-strung, hysterical, mettlesome, passionate, unreliable 11 tempestuous, thin-skinned 12 undependable 13 unpredictable

temperance 8 prudence, sobriety 9 restraint 10 abstention, abstinence, discretion, moderation, self-denial 11 forbearance, prohibition, self-control, teetotalism 14 abstemiousness, self-discipline

temperate 4 calm, cool, even, mild, sane, soft, warm 5 balmy, sober, sunny 6 gentle, mellow, sedate, steady 7 clement, patient, sparing 8 composed, moderate, pleasant, rational, tranquil 9 collected, easygoing, unruffled 10 coolheaded, reasonable 11 levelheaded 13 dispassionate, self-possessed, unextravagant, unimpassioned 14 self-controlled, self-restrained

temperature measurement 6 degree, Kelvin 7 Celsius 10 Fahrenheit

tempest 5 chaos, furor, storm 6 hubbub, tumult, uproar 8 brouhaha, outbreak, upheaval 9 agitation, cataclysm, commotion 10 hurly-burly, turbulence 11 disturbance

Tempest, The
author: 18 William Shakespeare
character: 5 Ariel 6 Alonso 7 Antonio, Caliban, Gonzalo, Miranda 8 Prospero 9 Ferdinand, Sebastian

Tempestates
origin: 5 Roman
goddesses of: 6 storms

tempestuous 3 hot 5 fiery 6 raging, stormy 7 excited, frantic, furious, violent 8 agitated, feverish, frenzied 9 emotional, explosive, turbulent, wrought-up 10 hysterical, passionate, tumultuous 11 impassioned, overwrought

Templar, Simon
character in: 8 The Saint
author: 9 Charteris

temple 4 fane, kirk 6 chapel, church, mosque, pagoda, priory, shrine 7 convent 8 basilica, pantheon 9 cathedral, joss house, monastery, sanctuary, synagogue 10 house of God, tabernacle 12 meetinghouse

Temple, Shirley
married name: 18 Shirley Temple Black
born: 13 Santa Monica CA
roles: 5 Heidi 10 Bright Eyes 15 Wee Willie Winkie 16 Little Miss Marker, The Little Colonel, The Littlest Rebel 18 Poor Little Rich

Girl **21** Susannah of the Mounties **23** Rebecca of Sunnybrook Farm

Temple, The
author: 13 George Herbert

Temple Beau, The
author: 13 Henry Fielding

tempo 4 clip, gait, pace, rate, time **5** meter, speed **6** pacing, stride, timing **8** momentum, velocity

tempo giusto
music: 10 strict time

temporal 3 lay **5** civil **6** mortal **7** mundane, passing, profane, secular, worldly **8** day-to-day, fleeting, fugitive **9** ephemeral, temporary, transient **10** evanescent, noneternal **11** impermanent, nonclerical **12** nonspiritual **17** nonecclesiastical

temporary, temporarily
5 brief, fleet **7** interim, passing, stopgap **8** fleeting, fugitive **9** ephemeral, momentary, provisory, transient **10** evanescent, short-lived, transitory **11** impermanent, provisional **13** flash-in-the-pan
Latin: 10 pro tempore

temporary dwelling
French: 10 pied-a-terre

temporize 5 delay, hedge, stall, tarry, waver **8** hang back, maneuver **9** hem and haw, vacillate **10** equivocate **11** play for time **12** drag one's feet, tergiversate **13** procrastinate

tempt 3 try, woo **4** bait, draw, goad, lure, pull, risk **5** charm, decoy, prick, rouse **6** allure, arouse, entice, incite, invite, seduce **7** attract, bewitch, provoke **8** appeal to, intrigue, inveigle **9** captivate, tantalize **12** put to the test **13** take one's fancy **14** fly in the face of **15** whet the appetite

temptation 4 bait, draw, lure, pull, urge **5** charm, snare, spell **8** stimulus, tempting **9** incentive, seduction **10** allurement, attraction, enticement, incitement, inducement **11** captivation, fascination, provocation

tempter 5 Satan **7** enticer, seducer **8** the Devil

temptress 4 vamp **5** Circe, flirt, siren **7** charmer, Delilah, Jezebel, Lorelei, vampire **8** coquette **9** odalisque, sorceress **10** seductress **11** enchantress, femme fatale

tempus fugit 9 time flies

Ten (10)
director: 12 Blake Edwards
cast: 7 Bo Derek **11** Dudley Moore **12** Julie Andrews

tenable 6 viable **8** arguable, rational, sensible, workable **9** excusable **10** condonable, defendable, defensible, vindicable **11** justifiable, warrantable **12** maintainable

tenacious 3 set **4** fast, firm, hard, iron **6** dogged, mulish **7** adamant, staunch **8** clinging, constant, obdurate, resolute, stalwart, stubborn **9** immovable, obstinate, pigheaded, steadfast, unbending **10** determined, inexorable, inflexible, persistent, relentless, unswerving, unwavering, unyielding **11** persevering, undeviating, unfaltering, unremitting **12** intransigent, unchangeable **14** uncompromising

tenaciousness 8 tenacity **9** endurance **10** resolution **11** persistence **12** perseverance, resoluteness **13** determination **16** stick-to-itiveness

tenacity 8 strength **9** toughness **10** resolution **11** persistence **12** cohesiveness, perseverance, resoluteness **13** determination, tenaciousness **16** stick-to-itiveness

tenant 6 lessee, lodger, renter, roomer **7** boarder, denizen, dweller **8** occupant, resident **10** inhabitant **11** householder, leaseholder, paying guest

Tenant of Wildfell Hall, The
author: 10 Anne Bronte

Tenants, The
author: 14 Bernard Malamud

Ten Commandments *see box*

Ten Commandments, The
director: 13 Cecil B DeMille
cast: 8 Nina Foch **9** John Derek **10** Anne Baxter, Debra Paget, Yul Brynner **11** Martha Scott **12** Vincent Price **13** John Carradine, Yvonne De Carlo **14** Charlton Heston (Moses), Judith Anderson **15** Cedric Hardwicke, Edward G Robinson

tend 3 aim **4** bear, head, lead, lean, mind, move **5** be apt, guide, nurse, point, watch **6** extend, foster, manage, wait on **7** care for, nurture **8** attend to, be liable, be likely **9** bid fair to, gravitate, look after, supervise, watch over **10** minister to, predispose, take care of **11** keep an eye on

Ten Commandments
also: 9 Decalogue
given to: 5 Moses
where given: 10 Mount Sinai
inscribed on: 12 stone tablets
first: 32 Thou shalt have no other Gods before me
second: 37 Thou shalt not bow down before graven images
third: 44 Thou shalt not take the name of the Lord thy God in vain
fourth: 34 Remember the Sabbath Day and keep it holy
fifth: 26 Honor thy father and thy mother
sixth: 16 Thou shalt not kill
seventh: 26 Thou shalt not commit adultery
eighth: 17 Thou shalt not steal
ninth: 46 Thou shalt not bear false witness against thy neighbor
tenth: 17 Thou shalt not covet

tendency 3 aim, set **4** bent **5** drift, drive, habit, trend **6** course **7** heading, impulse, leaning, turning **8** penchant **9** direction, proneness, readiness **10** proclivity, propensity **11** disposition, gravitation, inclination **14** predisposition

tender 3 raw **4** fond, give, good, kind, soft, sore, weak **5** frail, green, place, young **6** aching, benign, callow, caring, dainty, extend, feeble, gentle, hand in, loving, prefer, submit, weakly **7** advance, fragile, hold out, painful, present, proffer, propose, suggest, swollen **8** delicate, generous, immature, inflamed, juvenile, merciful, propound, underage, youthful **9** lay before, sensitive, volunteer **10** benevolent, put forward, thoughtful, vulnerable **11** considerate, sentimental, softhearted, sympathetic, warmhearted **12** affectionate **13** compassionate, inexperienced, understanding **14** impressionable **15** unsophisticated

tenderfoot 4 tyro **6** novice, rookie **8** beginner, neophyte **9** fledgling, greenhorn **10** apprentice

tenderhearted 4 mild **6** benign, gentle, humane **8** generous, merciful **10** altruistic, benevolent, responsive, thoughtful **11** considerate, kindhearted, softhearted, sympathetic, warmhearted **13** compassionate, understanding

tenderheartedness **4** pity **5** heart **7** empathy **8** sympathy **10** compassion

tendering **6** giving **8** offering **9** advancing, extending, proposing **10** holding out, preferring, proffering, submitting, suggesting **11** propounding **12** volunteering

Tender Is the Night
author: **16** F Scott Fitzgerald
character: **8** Abe North **9** Dick Diver **11** Nicole Diver, Tommy Barban **12** Rosemary Hoyt

tenderness **4** love **6** aching, warmth **7** rawness **8** delicacy, fondness, goodness, humanity, kindness, mildness, smarting, softness, soreness, sympathy **9** affection **10** compassion, gentleness, humaneness, kindliness, lovingness **11** beneficence, benevolence, painfulness, sensitivity **12** mercifulness **14** loving kindness

tendon
part of: **21** musculoskeletal system

tendril **4** coil, curl **5** crook, shoot, sprig, twist **6** winder **7** climber, ringlet

tenebrous **3** dim **4** dark **5** murky **6** gloomy **7** obscure, shadowy **8** darkened, obscured **13** unilluminated

Tenes
father: **6** Cycnus
mother: **7** Proclea
stepmother: **9** Phylonome
sister: **8** Hemithea

tenet **4** rule, view **5** canon, credo, creed, dogma, maxim **6** belief, thesis **7** opinion **8** doctrine, ideology, position, teaching **9** principle **10** conviction, persuasion

Tennessee ***see box***

tennis
athlete: **8** Don Budge, Jan Kodes, Rod Laver, Tom Okker **9** Bjorn Borg, Ivan Lendl, Stan Smith **10** Arthur Ashe, Bill Tilden, Jack Kramer, Maria Bueno, Pam Shriver, Roy Emerson, Steffi Graf **11** Alice Marble, Andre Agassi, Edward Dibbs, Ilie Nastase, John McEnroe, Ken Rosewall, Tracy Austin **12** Althea Gibson, Darren Cahill, Francois Durr, Jimmy Connors, John Newcombe, Mats Wilander, Roscoe Tanner, Virginia Wade **13** Dennis Ralston, Harold Solomon, Manuel Orantes, Manuel Santana, Martin Riessen, Wendy Turnbull **14** Brian Gottfried, Guillermo Vilas, Hana Mandlikova, Pancho Gonzalez, Rosemary Casals **15** Charles Pasarell, Chris Evert Lloyd, Maureen Connolly, Richard Stockton, Vitas Gerulaitis **17** Donald Schollander, Nancy Richey Gunter **18** Margaret Smith Court, Martina Navratilova **20** Helen Wills Moody Roark **21** Billie Jean Moffitt King, Evonne Goolagong Cawley

Tennyson, Alfred, Lord
author of: **4** Maud **7** Mariana, Ulysses **10** Enoch Arden, In Memoriam (A A H) **12** Locksley Hall, Morte d'Arthur **16** The Lady of Shalott **18** The Idylls of the

Tennessee
abbreviation: **2** TN **4** Tenn
nickname: **7** Big Bend **9** Volunteer **11** Old Franklin
capital: **9** Nashville
largest city: **7** Memphis
others: **5** Alcoa, Paris **6** Camden, Sparta **7** Bristol, Dickson, Pulaski **8** Franklin, Gallatin, Oak Ridge **9** Cedar Hill, Cleveland, Inglewood, Kingsport, Knoxville, Lexington **10** Greenbrier, Morristown, Old Hickory **11** Chattanooga, Clarksville, Springfield **12** Fayetteville, Murfreesboro **14** Hendersonville
college: **4** Fisk, Lane **5** Bryan, Siena **6** Bethel **7** Belmont, Lambuth, Lemoyne **8** Milligan, Tusculum **10** Vanderbilt **12** Southwestern **13** David Lipscomb **14** Meharry Medical **17** Tennessee Wesleyan
feature: **12** The Hermitage
dam: **6** Norris, Wilson **7** Douglas
fort: **5** Henry **8** Donalson, Nashboro
national park: **6** Shiloh **13** Cumberland Gap **19** Great Smoky Mountains (with North Carolina)
national parkway: **12** Natchez Trace
tribe: **7** Shawnee **8** Cherokee **9** Chickasaw
people: **7** Sequoya **8** John Bell **9** James Agee **10** Grace Moore **11** Bessie Smith, Cordell Hull **12** Davy Crockett **18** Carey Estes Kefauver **23** Alvin Cullum "Sergeant" York **32** Ernest Jennings "Tennessee Ernie" Ford
explorer: **6** Arthur, De Soto **7** Jolliet, La Salle, Needham **9** Marquette
lake: **7** Douglas **8** Barkeley, Cherokee, Reelfoot, Watts Bar **10** Center Hill **11** Chickamauga
land rank: **12** thirty-fourth
mountain: **5** Guyot **7** Lookout, Smokies **9** Blue Ridge **10** Cumberland, Great Smoky
highest point: **13** Clingman's Dome
physical feature:
basin: **9** Nashville
highlands: **11** Appalachian
plain: **7** Coastal
plateau: **10** Cumberland
president: **10** James K Polk **13** Andrew Jackson, Andrew Johnson
river: **3** Elk **4** Duck **5** Caney, Obion, Stone **6** Clinch **7** Hatchie, Holston **8** Hiwassee **9** Tennessee **10** Cumberland **11** French Broad, Mississippi **15** Little Tennessee
state admission: **9** sixteenth
state bird: **11** mockingbird
state flower: **4** flag, iris **6** maypop **13** passion flower
state motto: **16** America at Its Best **22** Agriculture and Commerce
state song: **11** My Tennessee **17** The Tennessee Waltz **19** My Homeland Tennessee **26** When It's Iris Time in Tennessee
state tree: **11** tulip poplar **12** yellow poplar

King **26** The Charge of the Light Brigade

tenor 4 gist **5** drift, sense, trend **6** course, import, intent, nature, object **7** content, essence, meaning, purport, purpose **8** argument, tendency **9** direction, intention, substance **11** connotation, implication **12** significance

tense 4 taut **5** brace, drawn, rigid, shaky, stiff, tight **6** braced, draw up, on edge, uneasy **7** anxious, excited, fearful, fidgety, jittery, nervous, restive, stiffen, uptight **8** agitated, make taut, restless, strained, timorous **9** tighten up, tremulous, wrought-up **10** high-strung, inflexible, unyielding **12** apprehensive

tension 5 dread **6** spring, strain, stress **7** anxiety, pulling, tugging **8** bad vibes, exertion, pressure, rigidity, tautness, traction **9** hostility, misgiving, stiffness, straining, tightness **10** stretching **11** fearfulness, nervousness, restiveness, trepidation **12** apprehension, elastic force, perturbation **13** bad vibrations, combativeness

tent 3 pup **4** care, hard **5** gauze, probe, tepee **6** bigtop, canvas, search, teepee, wigwam **7** shelter **8** pavilion **10** tabernacle

tentacle 3 arm **6** feeler **9** appendage

tentative 4 iffy **5** trial **6** acting **8** not final, proposed **9** ad interim, temporary, undecided, unsettled **10** contingent, indefinite, not settled **11** conditional, probational, provisional, speculative, unconfirmed **12** experimental, probationary **15** subject to change **18** under consideration

tentative procedure 4 test **5** flier, trail **6** feeler, tryout **7** venture **10** experiment **12** trial balloon

tenuous 4 slim, thin, weak **5** frail, shaky **6** flimsy, paltry, slight **7** fragile, shallow, slender **8** delicate, gossamer **9** uncertain **10** indefinite **11** halfhearted, unsupported **12** unconvincing **13** unsubstantial

tenure 4 rule, term, time **5** reign **7** tenancy **9** occupancy, retention **10** incumbency, occupation, permanency, possession **11** entitlement, job security **14** administration

tepee, teepee 4 chum, tent **5** lodge **6** wigwam **7** wickiup

tepid 4 cool, mild **7** languid, warmish **8** lukewarm, moderate **9** apathetic, impassive, temperate **10** nonchalant, phlegmatic **11** halfhearted, indifferent, unemotional **13** lackadaisical **14** unenthusiastic

tequila
type: 6 spirit
origin: 6 Mexico
made from: 5 agave **6** maguey
used with: 4 lime, salt **5** lemon
drink: 7 Chapala **8** El Diablo
with creme de cacao: 8 Toreador
with kahlua: 9 Brave Bull
with orange juice: 7 Sunrise
with Tia Maria: 9 Brave Bull
with triple sec: 9 Margarita

Terah
son: 5 Abram, Haran, Nahor

Teraphim
origin: 6 Hebrew
form: 4 idol

Ter Borch, Gerard (Terburg)
born: 6 Zwolle **14** The Netherlands
artwork: 8 Flea Hunt **10** The Concert **14** Peace of Munster **21** The Parental Admonition

Terbrugghen, Hendrick
born: 8 Deventer **14** The Netherlands
artwork: 14 The Flute Player **19** Liberation of St Peter **21** The Calling of St Matthew

terefah, trefah 9 not kosher

Tereus
prince of: 6 Thrace
father: 4 Ares
wife: 6 Procne
sister-in-law: 9 Philomela
raped: 9 Philomela
son: 4 Itys

tergal 4 back **6** dorsal

Terkel, Studs
author of: 7 Working **9** Hard Times **14** American Dreams

term, terms 3 age, dub, era, tag **4** call, cite, item, name, span, time, word **5** catch, cycle, epoch, idiom, reign, spell, stage, state, style, while **6** clause, course, detail, period, phrase, status, string **7** dynasty, footing, proviso **8** duration, interval, position, standing **9** condition, designate, provision, relations, requisite **10** expression, span of time **11** appellation, designation, requirement, stipulation **12** characterize, circumstance, prerequisite **14** administration

termagant 3 nag **4** fury **5** scold, shrew, vixen **6** ogress, virago **7** hellcat, hellion, she-wolf, tigress **8** battle-ax, fishwife, harridan, spitfire **9** Xanthippe

Termagant
character in: 21 medieval morality plays

terminal 3 end **4** last **5** depot, fatal, final, stand **6** deadly, lethal, mortal **7** station **8** terminus **10** concluding

terminate 3 end **4** stop **5** cease, close, lapse **6** expire, finish, run out, wind up **8** complete, conclude **11** come to an end, discontinue **12** bring to an end

termination 3 end **4** halt **5** close, finis, lapse **6** ending, finale, finish, windup **7** closing **8** stoppage **9** cessation **10** completion, concluding, conclusion, expiration **15** discontinuation

terminus 3 end **4** stop **5** depot, limit **6** ending **7** extreme, station **8** boundary, last stop, terminal **9** extremity **10** conclusion

Terminus
origin: 5 Roman
god of: 9 landmarks **10** boundaries

terminus ad quem 10 end to which, final limit **11** ending point

terminus a quo 9 beginning **12** end from which **13** starting point

termite
variety: 6 desert **7** dry wood **8** damp wood **10** powder-post, rotten wood **11** soldierless **12** subterranean

Terms of Endearment
director: 12 James L Brooks
based on novel by: 13 Larry McMurtry
cast: 11 Debra Winger **13** Jack Nicholson **15** Shirley MacLaine
Oscar for: 7 actress (MacLaine), picture **8** director **15** supporting actor (Nicholson)

Terpsichore
member of: 5 Muses
personifies: 7 dancing **10** choral song

Terra
goddess of: 5 Earth

Greek: 4 Gaea
mother: 5 Chaos
offspring: 6 Pontus, Titans, Uranus 7 Erinyes, Oceanus 8 Cyclopes 9 mountains 13 Hecatonchires

terrace 4 roof 5 level, patio, plane, porch 6 street 7 balcony, plateau 9 esplanade, promenade 10 embankment

Terraced Bay *see* 6 Taiwan

terra-cotta 4 clay 6 russet 8 brownish 12 reddish-brown 14 brownish-orange

terrain 4 area, zone 5 tract 6 ground, milieu, region 7 setting 8 district 9 territory 10 topography 11 countryside, environment 12 surroundings

terra incognita 11 unknown land 14 unexplored land, unknown subject 16 unknown territory

Terra Mater *see* 6 Tellus

terrapin 3 box 4 emyd, emys 6 slider, turpin, turtle 8 tortoise 11 diamond back
family: 8 Emydidae
female: 6 heifer
male: 4 bull

terrestrial 4 land 6 earth's, global, ground 7 earthly, mundane, worldly 8 riparian 10 earthbound

terrible 3 bad 4 dire, huge 5 awful, great, harsh, rough, scary 6 brutal, fierce, horrid, odious, severe, strong 7 beastly, extreme, fearful, ghastly, hateful, heinous, hideous, intense 8 alarming, dreadful, enormous, fearsome, horrible, shocking, terrific 9 appalling, excessive, harrowing, monstrous, obnoxious, offensive, repulsive, revolting, upsetting 10 disturbing, formidable, horrifying, immoderate, inordinate, terrifying, tremendous, unpleasant 11 distasteful, distressing, frightening, intolerable 12 insufferable 13 objectionable

terrier
dog breed: 3 fox 4 bull, Skye 5 Cairn, Irish, Welsh 6 border, Boston 7 Norfolk, Tibetan, wire fox 8 Airedale, Lakeland, Scottish, Sealyham 9 Kerry Blue 10 Australian, Bedlington, Manchester 13 Dandie Dinmont 17 soft-coated wheaten, Staffordshire bull, West Highland white 18 miniature schnauzer 21 American Staffordshire

terrific 3 fab 4 fine, good, huge 5 awful, great, harsh, marvy, scary, super 6 bang-up, fierce, severe, superb 7 extreme, fearful, intense, sensash 8 alarming, dreadful, enormous, fabulous, fearsome, smashing, splendid, terrible 9 excellent, excessive, fantastic, harrowing, marvelous, monstrous, upsetting, wonderful 10 disturbing, horrifying, immoderate, inordinate, remarkable, stupendous, super-duper, terrifying, tremendous 11 distressing, exceptional, frightening, sensational 13 extraordinary 14 out of this world

terrified 6 afraid, scared 7 alarmed, panicky 9 petrified 10 frightened 11 scared stiff 13 panic-stricken 14 terror-stricken 17 frightened to death

terrify 3 cow 5 abash, alarm, daunt, panic, scare, unman, upset 6 appall, dismay 7 agitate, disturb, horrify, overawe, petrify 8 disquiet, frighten 10 intimidate 17 make one's skin crawl 20 make one's blood run cold 22 make one's hair stand on end

terrifying 5 awful, dread 7 fearful 8 alarming, dreadful 9 frightful 11 frightening, hair-raising

territory 4 area, land, pale, zone 5 clime, realm, state, tract 6 bounds, colony, domain, empire, limits, locale, nation, region, sector 7 acreage, kingdom, mandate, terrain 8 confines, district, dominion, province 9 bailiwick 10 dependency 11 countryside 12 commonwealth, principality, protectorate

terror 3 awe 4 fear 5 alarm, dread, panic 6 dismay, fright, horror 7 anxiety 8 affright, disquiet 9 agitation 11 disquietude, trepidation 12 apprehension, perturbation 13 consternation 16 fear and trembling

terrorize 3 cow 5 abash, force 6 menace 7 terrify 8 browbeat, bulldoze, threaten 10 intimidate

terror-stricken 6 afraid, scared 7 alarmed, panicky 9 horrified, petrified, terrified 11 scared green, scared stiff 13 panic-stricken, scared to death

Terry and the Pirates
creator: 12 Milton Caniff
character: 7 Pat Ryan 8 Terry Lee 10 Dragon Lady

terse 4 curt, neat 5 brief, clear, crisp, pithy, short 6 abrupt 7 clipped, compact, concise, laconic, pointed, summary 8 clearcut, incisive, succinct 9 axiomatic, condensed, trenchant 10 compressed 11 unambiguous 12 epigrammatic 18 brief and to the point

terseness 7 brevity 8 curtness 9 crispness 10 abruptness 11 compactness, conciseness 12 succinctness

Tesman family
characters in: 11 Hedda Gabler
members: 5 Hedda 6 George 7 Juliana
author: 5 Ibsen

Tess (of the D'Urbervilles)
author: 11 Thomas Hardy
director: 13 Roman Polanski
cast: 8 John Bett 10 Peter Firth, Tom Chadbon 14 Rosemary Martin 15 Nastassia Kinski (Tess)

test 4 exam, quiz 5 check, final, flyer, probe, proof, prove, trial 6 dry run, feeler, try out, verify 7 analyze, confirm, examine, midterm 8 analysis, validate 9 catechism 11 corroborate, examination, investigate, questioning 12 confirmation, substantiate, verification 13 comprehensive, corroboration, investigation, questionnaire

Testament 5 Bible 7 the Book 10 Scriptures 12 New Testament, Old Testament

testament 6 legacy 7 bequest 10 settlement

tester 6 canopy 8 examiner 10 questioner

testify 4 show 5 prove, swear 6 affirm, attest, evince 7 declare, signify 8 evidence, indicate, manifest 11 bear witness, demonstrate 12 give evidence

testimonial 5 medal 6 ribbon, trophy 7 tribute 8 citation, memorial, monument 9 affidavit, reference 10 deposition 11 certificate, endorsement 12 commendation 14 recommendation

testimony 5 proof 6 avowal 7 witness 8 averment, evidence 9 affidavit, statement 10 deposition, indication, profession 11 affirmation, attestation, endorsement 12 confirmation, verification 13 certification, corroboration, demonstration, documentation, manifestation 14 acknowledgment

testy **5** cross, moody **6** crabby, cranky, crusty, filthy, grumpy, snappy, sullen, touchy **7** fretful, peevish, waspish **8** captious, caviling, choleric, churlish, perverse, petulant, snappish, snarling **9** fractious, impatient, irascible, irritable, splenetic **10** ill-humored **11** acrimonious, contentious **12** cantankerous, faultfinding, sharp-tongued **13** quick-tempered, temperamental

tete-a-tete **4** chat, talk **6** parley **9** interview **12** conversation **13** confabulation

tether **3** tie **4** cord, rein, rope **5** chain, leash **6** fasten, halter, hobble, secure

Tethys
- **member of:** **6** Titans
- **father:** **6** Uranus
- **mother:** **4** Gaea
- **husband:** **7** Oceanus
- **mother of:** **8** Oceanids **9** river gods
- **daughters:** **13** three thousand
- **foster child:** **4** Hera

Teucer
- **king of:** **4** Troy
- **father:** **7** Telamon **9** Scamander
- **mother:** **5** Idaea **7** Hesione
- **half-brother:** **9** Great Ajax **14** Telemonian Ajax
- **daughter:** **5** Batia
- **skilled in:** **7** archery
- **founded:** **7** Salamis

Teuthis
- **also:** **7** Ornytus
- **rank:** **7** general
- **wounded:** **6** Athena

Teuthras
- **mentioned in:** **5** Iliad
- **king of:** **5** Mysia **7** Phrygia
- **mother:** **8** Leucippe
- **daughter:** **8** Tecmessa
- **killed:** **4** boar
  - ***boar sacred to:*** **7** Artemis
- **killed by:** **6** Hector

Teutonic **5** Dutch **6** German, Gothic, Nordic **7** British, English **8** Germanic **12** Scandinavian
- **alphabet character:** **4** rune
- **demon:** **3** alp
- **goddess of death:** **3** Hel, Ran
- **goddess of peace:** **7** Nerthus
- **god of peace:** **6** Balder
- **god of thunder:** **4** Thor
- **god of war:** **3** Tiu, Tyr
- **god of wisdom:** **4** Odin

Teutonic Mythology *see* **17** Germanic Mythology

Texas ***see box***

text **5** motif, theme, topic, verse, words **6** manual, primer, sermon, thesis **7** content, passage, subject, wording **8** argument, sentence, textbook, workbook **9** paragraph, quotation **10** schoolbook **13** subject matter

textile **4** yarn **5** cloth, fiber **6** fabric **8** filament, material **9** yard goods **10** piece goods

texture **3** nap **4** feel, look **5** grain, touch, weave **6** makeup **7** quality, surface **8** fineness **9** character, structure **10** coarseness **11** composition

Tey, Josephine
- **real name:** **19** Elizabeth MacKintosh
- **author of:** **10** Brat Farrar **15** Miss Pym Disposes, The Singing Sands **17** The Daughter of Time **19** A Shilling for Candles
- **character:** **9** Alan Grant

Thackeray, William Makepeace
- **author of:** **9** Pendennis **10** Vanity Fair **11** Barry Lyndon, Henry Esmond, The Newcomes **13** The Virginians

Thaddeus of Arimathea
- *see* **5** Judas

Thaddeus of Warsaw
- **author:** **10** Jane Porter

Thai-Austronesian
- **language branch:** **9** Thai-Kadai **12** Austronesian
- **includes:** **5** Batak, Malay **6** Fijian, Samoan **7** Tagalog **8** Hawaiian, Javanese **15** Bahasa Indonesia
- **spoken in:** **4** Fiji, Java **5** China, Samoa **6** Hawaii, Taiwan **7** Sumatra **9** Indonesia, Polynesia **10** Madagas-

Texas
- **abbreviation:** **2** TX **3** Tex
- **nickname:** **8** Lone Star
- **capital:** **6** Austin
- **largest city:** **7** Houston
- **others:** **4** Gail, Rice, Vega, Waco **5** Bryan, Marfa, Ozona, Pampa, Tyler, Wiley **6** Baylor, Borger, Dallas, Denton, El Paso, Kileen, Laredo, Odessa, Quanah, Sonora **7** Abilene, Denison, Lubbock **8** Amarillo, Beaumont, Floydada **9** Fort Worth, Galveston **10** San Antonio **13** Corpus Christi
- **college:** **3** SMU, TCU **4** Rice **5** Lamar, Wiley **6** Austin, Baylor **7** St Mary's, Trinity **10** Texas A and M **12** Southwestern **14** Texas Christian **16** Abilene Christian **17** Southern Methodist
- **feature:**
  - ***fort:*** **5** Alamo
  - ***national park:*** **7** Big Bend **18** Guadalupe Mountains
  - ***national seashore:*** **11** Padre Island
  - ***state park:*** **10** San Jacinto
- **tribe:** **4** Adar, Waco **5** Caddo, Lipan **6** Apache, Biloxi, Jumano, Kichai, Shuman, Tejano **7** Alabama, Hasinai, Tonkawa **8** Comanche, Querecho **9** Coushatta, Karankawa
- **people:** **10** James S Hogg **12** Edward M House, Thomas C Clark **13** John B Connally, Samuel Houston **14** Chester W Nimitz, Mirabeau B Lamar, Samuel T Rayburn, Stephen F Austin, William B Travis **15** John Nance Garner, Thomas T Connally **19** Katherine Anne Porter
  - ***explorer:*** **4** Vaca **7** La Salle
- **island:** **5** Padre
- **lake:** **6** Falcon, Sabine, Texoma **7** Amistad
- **river:** **3** Red **5** Pecos **6** Brazos, Neches, Nueces, Sabine **7** Trinity **8** Colorado **9** Rio Grande **10** San Jacinto
- **land rank:** **12** second
- **physical feature:**
  - ***bay:*** **13** Corpus Christi
  - ***port:*** **7** Houston **9** Galveston **13** Corpus Christi
- **president:** **14** Lyndon B Johnson **17** Dwight D Eisenhower
  - ***Republic of Texas:*** **10** Sam Houston
- **state admission:** **12** twenty-eighth
- **state bird:** **11** mockingbird
- **state flower:** **10** bluebonnet, yellow rose
- **state motto:** **10** Friendship
- **state song:** **13** Texas Our Texas
- **state tree:** **5** pecan
- **baseball team:** **7** Rangers

Thailand
name means: **13** land of the free
other name: **4** Siam **11** Prathet Thai
capital/largest city: **6** Bankok **7** Bangkok
old capital: **8** Thonburi **9** Ayutthaya
others: **4** Ubon **5** Puket **6** Nakhon, Ranong **7** Ayudhya, Ayuthea, Lampang, Lamphur, Lopburi, Rahaeng, Singora, Songkla **8** Khonkaen, Kiangmai, Songkhla, Sukhotai, Thonburi **9** Ayutthaya, Chiangmai, Chiengmai **10** Ratchasima **11** Phitsanulok **14** Ubonratchthani
kingdom: **5** Funan **6** Khymer **8** Thonburi **9** Ayutthaya, Chiang Mai, Dvaravati, Sukhothai **12** Subarnabhumi
school: **9** Thammasat **13** Chulalongkorn
head of state: **4** king
measure: **2** wa **3** can, ken, niv, rai, sat, sok, wah **4** cohi, keup, niou, tang **5** kwien, leeng, sesti, vouah **6** kabiet, kanahn **7** chaimeu **8** changawn **9** anukabiet
monetary unit: **2** at **3** att **4** baht **5** cutty, fuang **6** pynung, salung **11** bullet money
weight: **3** bat, hap, pay, sen, sok **4** baht, haph, kati, klam **5** catty, chang, fuang, picul, pilul, tical **6** fluang, graini, salung, **7** tamlung
island: **2** Ko **3** Kut, Tao **4** Chan, Rawi **5** Chang, Lanta, Samui, Thalu **6** Libong, Phuket **7** Phangan, Terutao
lake: **9** Nong Lahan
mountain: **5** Dawna, Khieo **6** Phanom **8** Dang Raek, Kao Prawa, Maelamun **9** Khao Luang **11** Bilauktaung
highest point: **8** Inthanon **11** Doi Inthanon
river: **3** Chi, Mun, Nan, Yom **4** Ping **5** Menam **6** Mekong, Meping **7** Salween **10** Chaophraya
sea: **7** Andaman
physical feature:
gulf: **4** Siam **8** Thailand
isthmus: **3** Kra
pass: **12** Three Pagodas
peninsula: **5** Malay
plateau: **5** Korat **6** Khorat
people: **3** Lao, Mon **4** Lawa, Shan, Thai **5** Malay **6** Indian, Khymer **7** Chinese, Siamese **9** Cambodian **10** Vietnamese
king: **4** Rama **7** Chakkri, Mongkut **10** Chao Phraya **12** Prahjadhipok **13** Chulalongkorn **17** Bhumibol Adulyadej
leader: **9** Phraruang **12** Kukrit-Pramoj
language: **3** Lao, Tai **4** Ahom, Shan, Thai **5** Kadai, Malay **7** Bangkok, Chinese, English **9** Krung Thep
religion: **5** Islam **8** Buddhism **12** Christianity, Confucianism **17** Theravada Buddhism
place:
dam: **8** Bhumibol
palace: **5** Grand
ruins: **7** Ayuthia **9** Ayutthaya
street: **7** Yawarai
temple: **4** Dawn **7** Trimitr **10** Wat Phra Keo **11** Royal Chapel **13** Emerald Buddha
feature:
canal: **5** klong
clothing: **6** panung, sarong **12** saffron robes
festival: **12** Surin Round Up
houseboat: **6** sampan
temple: **3** wat
tree: **4** teak
food:
fruit: **5** camut **6** durian, litchi, pomelo **8** rambutan **10** mangosteen

car **11** Philippines **12** Easter Island

Thailand ***see box***

Thais
author: **13** Anatole France
character: **8** Athanael
composer: **8** Massenet

Thalassa
personifies: **3** sea

thalassic **6** marine **7** aquatic, deep-sea, neritic, oceanic, pelagic

Thales
field: **11** mathematics
nationality: **5** Greek
discovered: **18** geometry principles
predicted: **11** sun's eclipse

Thalestris
character in: **16** The Rape of the Lock
author: **4** Pope

Thalia
member of: **5** Muses **6** Graces
personifies: **6** comedy **13** idyllic poetry
lover: **4** Zeus
killed by: **5** Erato

Thallo
member of: **5** Horae
goddess of: **13** spring flowers

Thamyris
vocation: **4** poet **8** musician
father: **9** Philammon
mother: **7** Argiope
punished for: **9** arrogance
punished by: **5** Muses

punishment: 7 maiming 8 blinding

thanatophobia
fear of: 5 death

Thanatos
personifies: 5 death

thank 5 bless 12 be grateful to 13 be much obliged 18 express gratitude to

thankful 7 obliged 8 beholden, grateful 10 indebted to 12 appreciative, full of thanks 16 feeling gratitude 22 expressing appreciation

thankfulness 6 thanks 9 gratitude 12 appreciation, gratefulness

thankless 4 vain 7 ingrate, useless 8 bootless, caviling, critical, heedless 9 fruitless, unmindful, unwelcome 10 profitless, ungracious, ungrateful, uninviting, unpleasant, unrewarded, unthankful 11 distasteful, thoughtless, undesirable, unrewarding 12 disagreeable, faultfinding 13 inconsiderate, unappreciated 14 unacknowledged, unappreciative

thanks 5 grace 8 blessing 9 gratitude 11 benediction 12 appreciation, gratefulness

thanks be to God
Latin: 10 Deo gratias

thanksgiving 6 thanks 8 blessing

Thanksgiving
started by: 8 Bradford, Pilgrims
traditional food: 4 corn, yams 6 turkey 10 pumpkin pie 13 sweet potatoes 14 cranberry sauce
symbol: 9 ear of corn 12 horn of plenty

thank you
French: 5 merci
German: 5 danke
Spanish: 7 gracias
Italian: 6 grazie
Japanese: 4 domo

Thank You, Fog
author: 7 W H Auden

Thank You, Jeeves
author: 11 P G Wodehouse

thank you very much
French: 9 merci bien 13 merci beaucoup
German: 10 danke schon
Japanese: 11 domo arigato
Spanish: 13 muchas gracias

That Certain Feeling
author: 12 Kingsley Amis

Thatcher, Becky
character in: 9 Tom Sawyer
author: 5 Twain

Thatcher, Judge
character in: 15 (The Adventures of) Huckleberry Finn
author: 5 Twain

That Girl
character: 8 Ann Marie, Lou Marie 10 Helen Marie, Ruth Bauman 11 Jerry Bauman 12 Don Hollinger, Judy Bessemer 14 Dr Leon Bessemer
cast: 9 Lew Parker 10 Ted Bessell 11 Alice Borden, Bonnie Scott, Marlo Thomas 12 Bernie Kopell 13 Dabney Coleman 14 Carolyn Daniels, Rosemary DeCamp

that is
Latin: 2 ie 5 id est

that is to say
Latin: 3 viz 9 videlicet

that's life
French: 9 c'est la vie

thaw 4 melt, warm 5 relax 6 soften, unbend, warm up 7 liquefy, melting, thawing 8 dissolve 11 break the ice

Thea
companion of: 7 Artemis
ravished by: 6 Aeolus
changed into: 4 mare
mare named: 6 Euippe

Theale, Milly
character in: 17 The Wings of the Dove
author: 5 James

theater 4 site 5 arena, drama, house, movie, odeum, place, scene, stage 6 cinema, lyceum 7 gallery, setting 8 assembly, audience, coliseum 9 colosseum, music hall, playhouse 10 assemblage, auditorium, movie house, spectators 11 histrionics, lecture hall, theatricals 12 amphitheater, show business

theatrical 4 film 5 hammy, movie, showy, stage, stagy 6 flashy 7 fustian, show-biz, stilted 8 affected, dramatic, mannered, thespian 9 grandiose, unnatural 10 artificial, histrionic 11 exaggerated, extravagant, pretentious, spectacular 12 magniloquent, ostentatious, show-business 13 entertainment, grandiloquent 14 larger-than-life

theatrical trick
French: 13 coup de theatre

Thebaid
author: 7 Statius
character: 4 Atys 5 Creon 6 Ismene, Tydeus 7 Jocasta, Theseus 8 Antigone, Capaneus, Eteocles, Opheltes, Tiresias 9 Menoeceus, Polynices 10 Amphiaraus, Hippomedon, Melanippus

the bottle 5 booze, drink, sauce 6 liquor 7 alcohol 8 demon rum

the dansant 8 tea dance

thee therefore
Latin: 8 te igitur

theft 5 fraud 7 larceny, looting, robbery 8 burglary, filching, rustling, stealing, thievery 9 hijacking, pilfering, swindling 10 purloining 11 shoplifting 12 embezzlement
god of: 6 Hermes 7 Mercury

Theia
also: 4 Thia
member of: 6 Titans
father: 6 Uranus
mother: 4 Gaea
brother: 8 Hyperion
mother of: 8 Cercopes
son: 6 Helios
daughter: 3 Eos 6 Selene

the life of the land is maintained by righteousness
Hawaiian: 52 ua mau ke ea o ka aina i ka pono
motto of: 6 Hawaii

Them
author: 15 Joyce Carol Oates

theme 3 air 4 song, text, tune 5 essay, focus, motif, point, topic, tract 6 melody, report, review, strain, thesis 7 keynote, premise, subject 8 argument, critique, question, treatise 9 discourse, leitmotif, monograph 10 commentary 11 composition, proposition 12 dissertation

Themis
member of: 6 Titans
father: 6 Uranus
mother: 4 Gaea
sister: 6 Phoebe
consort of: 4 Zeus
husband: 7 Iapetus
mother of: 5 Fates, Horae 6 Moerae 7 Seasons
son: 10 Prometheus
personifies: 7 justice

Themiste
father: 8 Laomedon
mother: 8 Eurydice
son: 8 Anchises

Then Again, Maybe I Won't
author: 9 Judy Blume

thence 6 whence 9 from there, therefore 11 accordingly, in due course 13 from that place

the next world 6 Heaven

8 eternity, paradise 12 the hereafter 14 the world to come

the norm 7 the mean, the rule 9 the median 10 the average 14 the common thing

the Occident 7 the West 20 the western hemisphere

Theoclymenus
king of: 5 Egypt
father: 7 Proteus
mother: 8 Psamathe
vocation: 4 seer

theologian *see* 22 philosopher/theologian

theological 4 holy 6 sacred 8 Biblical, dogmatic 9 apostolic, canonical, doctrinal, religious, spiritual 10 scriptural 14 ecclesiastical

theology 5 dogma 8 divinity, doctrine, religion

Theonoe
father: 7 Proteus, Thestor

Theophane
bore: 3 ram
fleece of ram: 6 golden

theoretical 8 abstract, academic, putative 11 conjectural, postulatory, speculative 12 hypothetical, nonpractical 13 suppositional

theorize 5 infer, posit, think 6 assume 7 imagine, presume, propose, suppose, surmise 8 propound 9 formulate, postulate, predicate, speculate 10 conjecture 11 hypothecate, hypothesize

theory 3 law 4 idea, view 5 guess 6 belief, notion, thesis 7 concept, opinion, science, surmise, thought 8 doctrine, ideology, judgment 9 deduction, postulate, principle 10 conclusion, conjecture, hypothesis, persuasion, philosophy 11 presumption, speculation, supposition

therapeutic, therapeutical 7 healing 8 curative, remedial, salutary, sanative 11 restorative 12 ameliorative

Therapne
means: 12 burial ground

therapy 7 healing 9 treatment 14 rehabilitation

thereafter 5 later 9 after that, afterward 10 afterwards, from then on 11 thenceforth 12 subsequently 14 from that time on

therefore 2 so 4 ergo, thus 5 hence 11 accordingly 12 consequently, on that ground 13 for that reason, in consequence, on that account 14 for which reason

there is no disputing about tastes
Latin: 27 de gustibus non est disputandum

there it is
French: 5 voila

Therese Raquin
author: 9 Emile Zola
character: 7 Camille, Laurent

There Shall Be No Night
author: 15 Robert E Sherwood

thereupon 4 then 6 at once 7 thereon 8 directly, suddenly, upon that 9 forthwith, in a moment, upon which 11 immediately 12 straightaway, without delay

Therimachus
father: 8 Hercules
mother: 6 Megary
killed by: 8 Hercules

Theritas *see* 4 Ares

Thermasia
epithet of: 7 Demeter
means: 6 warmth

thermometer
invented by: 7 Galileo, Reaumur
mercury: 10 Fahrenheit

Thero
nurse of: 4 Ares

theropod
type of: 8 dinosaur
member: 10 Allosaurus, Antrodemus 11 Coelophysis, Gorgosaurus 13 Albertosaurus, Compsognathus, Struthiomimus, Tyrannosaurus

Theroux, Paul
author of: 9 Saint Jack 16 The Mosquito Coast 20 Riding the Iron Rooster 21 The Great Railway Bazaar 23 The Old Patagonian Express

Thersander
member of: 7 Epigoni

Thersilochus
mentioned in: 5 Iliad
killed by: 8 Achilles

Thersites
mentioned in: 5 Iliad
origin: 5 Greek
characteristics: 4 ugly 8 deformed 11 quarrelsome
accused Agamemnon of: 5 greed
accused Achilles of: 9 cowardice
fought in: 9 Trojan War
killed by: 8 Achilles

the same as 4 like 7 equal to 9 a match for 12 comparable to, equivalent to, tantamount to 16 commensurate with

thesaurus 8 synonymy 10 word finder 11 synonymicon 12 word treasury 13 synonym finder 17 synonym dictionary 18 semantic dictionary

Thescelosaurus
type: 8 dinosaur 10 ornithopod
location: 6 Canada 12 United States
period: 10 Cretaceous

These Three
director: 12 William Wyler
based on play by: 14 Lillian Hellman (The Children's Hour)
cast: 10 Alma Kruger, Joel McCrea 11 Merle Oberon 13 Miriam Hopkins 15 Bonita Granville, Catherine Doucet

These Twain
author: 13 Arnold Bennett

Theseus
king of: 6 Athens
father: 6 Aegeus 8 Poseidon
mother: 6 Aethra
wife: 7 Phaedra
consort: 9 Hippolyta
lover: 7 Ariadne
son: 6 Acamas 8 Demophon 10 Hippolytus, Melanippus
helmsman: 10 Nausithous
killed: 5 Sinis 6 Sciron 8 Minotaur 10 Cretan bull, Procrustes

thesis 5 essay, paper, tract 6 notion, theory 7 article, concept, surmise 8 argument, critique, proposal, treatise 9 discourse, monograph, postulate, term paper 10 commentary, conjecture, hypothesis 11 composition, proposition, speculation, supposition 12 disquisition, dissertation

Thesmia
epithet of: 7 Demeter
means: 12 goddess of law

Thesmophorus
epithet of: 7 Demeter
means: 8 lawgiver

Thesophoria
origin: 5 Greek
event: 8 festival

thespian 3 ham 4 star 5 actor, extra 6 co-star, player, walk-on 7 actress, ingenue, trouper 8 juvenile 9 bit-player, guest star, performer, tragedian 10 leading man 11 leading lady, stage player

Thespian Lion
attacked: 6 flocks
flock owner: 10 Amphitryon
killed by: 8 Hercules

Thespius
founded city of: **8** Thespiae
wife: **8** Megamede
daughters: **5** fifty

Thessalus
king of: **8** Thessaly
father: **5** Jason **8** Hercules
mother: **5** Medea **9** Chalciope

the state
Latin: **10** res publica

Thestius
king of: **7** Aetolia
father: **4** Ares
mother: **8** Demonice

Thestor
son: **7** Calchas
daughter: **7** Theonoe **8** Leucippe

Thetis
member of: **7** Nereids
husband: **6** Peleus
sister: **8** Eurynome
son: **8** Achilles

the very words
Latin: **14** ipsissima verba

the world over **10** every place, everywhere, far and wide, near and far **11** in all places

They Shoot Horses, Don't They?
director: **13** Sydney Pollack
cast: **8** Gig Young **9** Bruce Dern, Jane Fonda **10** Red Buttons **12** Susannah York **13** Bonnie Bedelia **15** Michael Sarrazin
Oscar for: **15** supporting actor (Young)

They Won't Forget
director: **11** Mervyn LeRoy
cast: **10** Lana Turner, Otto Kruger **11** Allyn Joslyn, Claude Rains **12** Elisha Cook Jr **13** Gloria Dickson

Thia *see* **5** Theia

Thialfi
origin: **12** Scandinavian
servant of: **4** Thor
talent: **8** fastness

Thiasos *see* **7** Thiasus

thiasus
also: **7** thiasos
group worshipping: **11** patron deity
followers of: **8** Dionysus
followers called: **6** satyrs **7** maenads

Thiazi
also: **6** Thjazi
origin: **12** Scandinavian
form: **5** giant
carried away: **4** Iden **6** apples

thick **3** big, fat **4** deep, dull, dumb, slow, wide **5** broad, bulky, close, dense, fuzzy, great, heavy, husky, piled, solid **6** chummy, heaped, hoarse, lavish, obtuse, packed, strong, stupid, viscid, wooden **7** blurred, clotted, compact, copious, crowded, decided, devoted, doltish, extreme, intense, liberal, muffled, profuse, teeming, throaty, viscous **8** abundant, familiar, friendly, generous, guttural, intimate, profound, sisterly, swarming **9** brotherly, condensed, fatheaded, glutinous, plenteous, unstinted **10** coagulated, dull-witted, gelatinous, indistinct, munificent, pronounced, slow-witted **11** inseparable, overflowing **12** concentrated, impenetrable, inarticulate

thicken **3** set **4** cake, clot, jell **5** muddy **6** darken, deepen, muddle **7** compact, congeal, jellify **8** condense **9** coagulate, intensify **10** gelatinize

thicket **4** bush, wood **5** brake, brush, copse, grove, scrub **6** bushes, covert, forest, shrubs **7** bracken **9** shrubbery **10** underbrush **11** undergrowth

thickheaded **4** dull, dumb, slow **5** blank, dense, dopey, thick **6** obtuse, stupid **8** ignorant **9** dim-witted, fatheaded **10** boneheaded, dull-witted, half-witted, slow-witted **11** blockheaded, thick-witted **12** dunderheaded, thick-skulled **13** chuckleheaded, knuckleheaded

thickset **5** bulky, close, dense, dumpy, husky, solid, squat, stout, tubby **6** chunky, packed, stocky, stubby, stumpy, sturdy **8** close-set, heavyset, roly-poly

thickskinned **4** hard **5** horny, tough **6** inured **7** callous **8** callused, hardened **9** unfeeling, unmovable **10** impervious, insensible **11** insensitive, unconcerned **13** imperturbable, unsusceptible **14** pachydermatous

thick-skulled **4** dull **5** dense **6** stupid **11** thickheaded **12** dunderheaded

thick-witted **4** dull, slow **5** dense **6** stupid **7** idiotic, moronic **9** dim-witted, imbecilic **11** thickheaded **12** dunderheaded, simple-minded

thief **5** crook **6** bandit, mugger, robber **7** burglar, filcher, rustler **8** hijacker, pilferer, swindler **9** defrauder, embezzler, holdup man, larcenist, purloiner, racketeer **10** highwayman, pickpocket, shoplifter **12** housebreaker, kleptomaniac **13** confidence man, pursesnatcher **14** second-story man

Thief of Bagdad, The
director: **9** Tim Whelan **12** Ludwig Berger **13** Michael Powell
cast: **4** Sabu **9** Rex Ingram **10** John Justin, June Duprez **11** Conrad Veidt

Thieves' Carnival
also: **15** Le Bal des Voleurs
author: **11** Jean Anouilh

thievish **3** sly **6** sneaky **7** furtive **8** stealthy, thieving **9** dishonest, larcenous, secretive, thieflike **13** light-fingered, surreptitious **14** sticky-fingered

thigh **3** ham, leg **4** hock **5** femur, flank, ilium **6** gammon
pain: **8** meralgia

Thimbu, Thimphu
capital of: **6** Bhutan

thin **4** fine, lank, lean, slim, weak **5** faint, gaunt, lanky, prune, runny, scant, sheer, spare, water **6** dilute, feeble, narrow, not fat, reduce, skinny, slight, sparse, watery **7** curtail, diluted, fragile, scrawny, slender, spindly **8** delicate, diminish, finespun **9** emaciated, water down **10** inadequate, threadlike **11** transparent **12** insufficient **13** unsubstantial

thin-blooded **3** wan **4** pale, weak **6** anemic, sickly

thing, things **3** act **4** deed, feat, gear, item **5** event, gizmo, goods, point **6** action, affair, aspect, detail, dingus, entity, gadget, matter, object, person **7** article, clothes, concern, effects, feature, thought **8** business, clothing, creature, movables **9** doohickey, equipment, happening, statement **10** belongings, human being, occurrence, particular, proceeding **11** eventuality, living being, possessions, thingamabob, thingamajig, transaction **12** circumstance **13** paraphernalia

thing already done
French: **12** fait accompli

thingamajig **5** gizmo **6** doodad, gadget **11** contraption, contrivance, thingamabob **15** whatchamacallit

thing of no value
Latin: **5** nihil

things done
Latin: **9** res gestae

think **4** deem, mean, plan **5** brood, fancy, guess, judge

6 design, expect, intend, ponder, reason, recall, reckon 7 believe, dwell on, imagine, presume, propose, purpose, reflect, suppose, surmise 8 cogitate, conceive, conclude, contrive, meditate, mull over, remember, ruminate 9 recollect, speculate 10 anticipate, deliberate, have in mind, keep in mind 11 contemplate, use one's mind, use one's wits 13 rack one's brain

thinkable 8 knowable 10 imaginable 11 conceivable, perceivable

think about 4 mull 6 debate, ponder 7 reflect 8 consider, mull over 10 deliberate

think alike 5 agree 11 be of one mind, see eye to eye

thinker 4 sage 6 savant, wizard 7 egghead, scholar 9 intellect 10 mastermind 11 mental giant, philosopher 13 metaphysician

think fit 4 deem 5 deign, stoop 7 consent 10 condescend

think highly of 5 favor, honor, value 6 admire, esteem, revere 7 approve, respect 8 look up to, venerate 10 set store by

think ill of 4 hate 5 decry 6 detest 7 condemn, deplore, despise, dislike 8 object to 9 abominate, disparage, frown upon 10 disapprove 13 look askance at 14 discountenance 15 take exception to 16 find unacceptable, view with disfavor

thinking 4 view 5 smart, stand, study 6 belief, bright 7 concept, surmise, thought 8 cultured, educated, judgment, position, rational, studious 9 brainwork, deduction, inference, reasoning 10 conclusion, cultivated, impression, meditation, meditative, reflection, reflective, rumination, thoughtful 11 intelligent, speculation 12 deliberation 13 consideration, contemplation, contemplative, philosophical, sophisticated, using one's head 15 paying attention

Thinking Reed, The
author: 15 Dame Rebecca West

think over 5 study, weigh 8 cogitate, consider, mull over 11 reflect upon 12 deliberate on

think through 5 weigh 6 ponder 7 analyze 8 appraise, consider, evaluate

think up 5 frame, hatch 6 create, invent 7 concoct, dream up 8 conceive, contrive

think well of 4 like 6 admire 8 look up to 10 appreciate

Thin Man, The
author: 15 Dashiell Hammett
character: 7 Morelli 11 Nick Charles, Nora Charles 13 Arthur Nunheim, Mimi Jorgensen 15 Herbert Macaulay 18 Christian Jorgensen
Wynant family: 5 Clyde 7 Dorothy, Gilbert
director: 11 W S Van Dyke II
cast: 4 Asta 8 Myrna Loy (Nora Charles) 13 William Powell (Nick Charles)
sequel (film): 14 Another Thin Man 15 After the Thin Man 16 Song of the Thin Man 18 The Thin Man Goes Home

Thin Mountain Air, The
author: 10 Paul Horgan

thin out 5 prune 6 dilute, reduce, weaken 7 weed out 9 water down 10 adulterate

thinskinned 5 cross, huffy, sulky, testy 6 grumpy, sullen, touchy 7 crabbed, peevish 8 petulant, snappish 9 irascible, irritable, sensitive, squeamish 11 ill-tempered, quarrelsome, susceptible 12 cantankerous 13 oversensitive 14 hypersensitive

third estate
French: 9 tiers etat

Third Man, The
director: 9 Carol Reed
based on story by: 12 Graham Greene
cast: 10 Alida Valli 11 Orson Welles (Harry Lime) 12 Joseph Cotten, Trevor Howard 16 Wilfrid Hyde-White
setting: 6 Vienna

Third Wave, The
author: 12 Alvin Toffler

thirst 3 yen 4 itch, lust, pant 5 ardor, covet, crave, yearn 6 desire, fervor, hunger, relish 7 craving, passion, stomach 8 appetite, keenness, voracity, yearning 9 hanker for, hankering 11 thirstiness

thirsty 3 dry 4 avid 5 eager 7 parched 9 thirsting

Thirteen O'Clock
author: 19 Stephen Vincent Benet

Thirty-Nine Steps, The (The 39 Steps)
author: 10 John Buchan
director: 15 Alfred Hitchcock
cast: 11 Robert Donat 13 Godfrey Tearle, Lucie Mannheim, Peggy Ashcroft 16 Madeleine Carroll

This Above All
author: 10 Eric Knight

Thisbe
loved: 7 Pyramus
location: 7 Babylon
death by: 7 suicide
death at tomb of: 5 Ninus

this is
Latin: 6 hoc est

This Is Your Life
host: 12 Ralph Edwards
announcer: 9 Bob Warren

Thisoa
form: 5 nymph
tended: 4 Zeus

thistle 7 Cirsium
varieties: 3 Oat 4 Bull, Holy, Milk, Star 5 Glove, Plume, White 6 Canada, Cotton, Golden, Scotch, Silver 7 Blessed, St Mary's 8 Fishbone, Mountain, Plumless 9 Argentine, Thornless 10 Great globe, Small globe 11 Mountain sow 14 Acanthus-leaved

Thjazi *see* 6 Thiazi

Thoas *see* 5 Thoon

Thokk
origin: 12 Scandinavian
form: 8 giantess
refused to weep for: 5 Baldr 6 Balder, Baldur
possible disguise of: 4 Loki

Thomas 7 apostle
means: 4 twin
also called: 7 Didymus, Doubter 8 Doubting

Thomas, Ambroise
born: 4 Metz 6 France
composer of: 6 Mignon

Thomas, Danny
real name: 16 Amos Muzyad Jacobs
born: 11 Deerfield MI
daughter: 11 Marlo Thomas
roles: 13 The Jazz Singer 16 Make Room for Daddy 19 I'll See You in My Dreams

Thomas, Dylan
author of: 8 Fern Hill 13 Under Milk Wood 23 A Child's Christmas in Wales

Thomas, George H
nickname: 20 The Rock of Chickamauga
served in: 8 Civil War 10 Mexican War
side: 5 Union
commander of: 19 Army of the Cumberland

battle: 9 Nashville 11 Chattanooga, Chickamauga

Thomas, Marlo
real name: 14 Margaret Thomas
born: 9 Detroit MI
father: 11 Danny Thomas
husband: 11 Phil Donahue
roles: 8 That Girl

Thomas, W Morgan
creator/artist of: 22 Sheena Queen of the Jungle

Thomas a Kempis
author of: 20 The Imitation of Christ

Thompson, Estelle Merle O'Brien
real name of: 11 Merle Oberon

Thomson, Joseph John
field: 7 physics
nationality: 7 British
discovered: 8 electron
awarded: 10 Nobel Prize

Thomson, Thomas John
born: 6 Canada 9 Claremont
artwork: 9 Spring Ice 11 The Jack Pine 12 Northern Lake 13 Northern River

Thomson, Virgil
born: 12 Kansas City MO
composer of: 9 Portraits 16 The Mother of Us All 21 Four Saints in Three Acts

thong 4 band 5 strap, strip 6 sandal 7 binding

Thoon
also: 5 Thoas 11 Nebrophonus
member of: 8 Gigantes
attacked wall of: 6 Greeks
killed by: 8 Hercules 10 Antilochus

Thor
origin: 12 Scandinavian
god of: 4 rain 7 farming, thunder
rode: 7 chariot
chariot pulled by: 5 goats
wielded: 6 hammer 7 Miolnir
father: 4 Odin 5 Othin

thorax 5 chest, trunk 6 breast, cavity 8 forebody

Thoreau, Henry David
author of: 6 Walden (Life in the Woods) 17 Civil Disobedience

thorium
chemical symbol: 2 Th

thorn 3 woe 4 bane, barb, care, gall, spur 5 cross, curse, spike, spine, sting 6 plague 7 prickle, scourge, torment, trouble 8 nuisance, vexation 9 annoyance, sore point 10 affliction, bitter pill, infliction, irritation

thorn 9 Crataegus
varieties: 3 Box 4 Lily, Pear 5 Camel, Hedge, White 6 Christ, Karroo, Mysore, Sallow, Sickle, Winter 7 Thirsty 8 Cockspur, Egyptian, Kangaroo, Quick-set 9 Jerusalem, Paper-bark 10 Washington 11 Crucifixion 13 Yellow-fruited

Thornbirds, The
author: 17 Colleen McCullough

Thornburg, Betty June
real name of: 11 Betty Hutton

Thornfield
house in: 8 Jane Eyre
author: 6 Bronte

Thornhill, Squire
character in: 19 The Vicar of Wakefield
author: 9 Goldsmith

thorn in the side 4 bane 7 torment 9 annoyance 10 irritation

thorny 4 dire, hard 5 spiny, tough 6 barbed, spiked, sticky, trying 7 arduous, brambly, complex, crucial, irksome, prickly 8 annoying, critical, involved, ticklish 9 bristling, dangerous, difficult, vexatious 10 formidable, nettlesome, perplexing 11 complicated, troublesome

thorough 4 full, pure 5 sheer, total, utter 6 entire 7 careful, perfect, uniform 8 absolute, complete, of a piece 9 downright, out-and-out 10 consistent, definitive, exhaustive, meticulous 11 painstaking, unmitigated, unqualified 12 all-embracing, all-inclusive

thoroughbred, Thoroughbred 7 unmixed 8 purebred 9 blueblood, pedigreed, racehorse 10 aristocrat 11 full-blooded, pure-blooded 12 silkstocking

thoroughfare 4 road 6 avenue, street 7 freeway, highway, parkway, roadway, thruway 8 main road, turnpike 9 boulevard, concourse 10 expressway, interstate 12 superhighway 13 through street

thoroughgoing 5 utter 6 arrant 7 extreme 8 outright 9 confirmed, notorious, out-and-out 11 undisguised, unmitigated

thoroughly 5 fully 7 totally, utterly 8 entirely 9 carefully, downright, out-and-out, perfectly, uniformly 10 absolutely, completely, throughout 11 inclusively 12 consistently, exhaustively, meticulously 13 in all respects 15 from top to bottom 17 through and through 18 from beginning to end

Thorpe, Isabella
character in: 15 Northanger Abbey
author: 6 Austen

Thorpe, Jim (James Francis)
sport: 8 football 13 track and field
won: 8 Olympics
named: 11 All-American

Thorvaldsen, Albert Bertel
born: 7 Denmark 10 Copenhagen
artwork: 4 Hope 9 Lord Byron 14 Cupid and Psyche 16 The Lion of Lucerne 22 Cupid and the Three Graces 24 Jason with the Golden Fleece

Thoth
origin: 8 Egyptian
god of: 5 magic 6 wisdom 8 learning
scribe of: 4 gods
inventor of: 6 letter 7 numbers
corresponds to: 6 Hermes
head of: 4 ibis 6 baboon

though 3 tho, yet 4 even, that 5 still 6 albeit, even if 7 granted 8 although, granting 9 admitting 12 nevertheless 15 notwithstanding

thought 3 aim, end 4 goal, idea, plan, view 5 credo, dogma, fancy, tenet 6 belief, caring, design, intent, musing, notion, object, regard, scheme 7 concept, concern, opinion, purpose, reverie, surmise 8 doctrine, judgment, kindness, thinking 9 attention, intention, objective, sentiment 10 brown study, cogitation, conception, conclusion, meditation, reflection, rumination 11 expectation, imagination, speculation, supposition 12 anticipation, deliberation 13 consideration, contemplation, introspection
French: 6 pensee

thoughtful 4 kind 6 caring, loving, musing 7 pensive, probing, serious, wistful 8 thinking 9 attentive 10 meditative, neighborly, reflective, solicitous 11 considerate, kindhearted 13 contemplative, introspective

thoughtfulness 7 probing,

thought **8** kindness, thinking **10** meditation, reflection **11** questioning **13** attentiveness, consideration, contemplation **14** solicitousness **15** kindheartedness

thoughtless **4** dumb, rash, rude **5** silly **6** stupid, unkind **7** foolish **8** careless, heedless, impolite, reckless **9** imprudent **10** ill-advised, indiscreet, neglectful, unthinking **11** harebrained, improvident, inadvertent, inattentive, insensitive **12** absent-minded, unreflecting **13** ill-considered, inconsiderate, rattlebrained **14** scatterbrained

thoughtlessness **7** neglect **8** rashness, rudeness **9** oversight, unconcern **10** imprudence, negligence, unkindness **11** inattention **12** carelessness, heedlessness, impoliteness, recklessness **13** insensitivity **15** inattentiveness **16** absentmindedness

Thousand Clowns, A
director: **7** Fred Coe
based on play by: **11** Herb Gardner
cast: **11** Barry Gordon **12** Jason Robards, Martin Balsam **13** Barbara Harris
setting: **11** New York City
Oscar for: **15** supporting actor (Balsam)

Thousand Days, A
author: **20** Arthur M Schlesinger Jr

thou too
Latin: **8** tu quoque

thrall **4** serf **5** slave **6** chains **7** bondage, serfdom, servant, slavery **9** servitude **11** enslavement, subjugation

thralldom **6** chains **7** bondage, serfdom, slavery **9** servitude **11** enslavement, subjugation

thrash **4** beat, cane, drub, flog, jerk, lash, maul, toss, whip **5** birch, flail, heave, solve, spank, strap **6** jiggle, joggle, plunge, pommel, squirm, switch, thresh, tumble, wiggle, writhe **7** flounce, resolve, scourge, trounce **8** argue out, lambaste **9** thresh out **10** flagellate

Thrasydemus
also: **11** Thrasymelus
squire of: **8** Sarpedon
killed by: **9** Patroclus

Thrasymedes
father: **6** Nestor
brother: **10** Antilochus

Thrasymelus *see* **11** Thrasydemus

threadbare **4** dull, worn **5** banal, stale, stock, tacky, trite **6** boring, frayed, jejune, ragged, shabby **7** cliched, humdrum, napless, prosaic, raveled, routine, worn-out **8** bromidic, everyday, pile-worn **9** hackneyed, well-known **11** commonplace, stereotyped **12** conventional, overfamiliar **15** the worse for wear

threads **4** duds, togs **6** attire **7** apparel, clothes, strands, strings **8** clothing, garments **9** filaments

threat **4** omen, risk **5** peril **6** danger, hazard, menace **7** ill omen, portent, warning **8** jeopardy **10** foreboding **11** commination, premonition **12** intimidation

threaten **3** cow **4** warn **6** impend, menace **7** imperil **8** endanger, forewarn, hang over **9** terrorize **10** be imminent, intimidate, jeopardize

threatening **4** grim **7** baleful, ominous, warning **8** alarming, imminent, menacing, sinister **9** ill-omened, impending **10** forbidding, foreboding **11** approaching, forewarning, terrorizing **12** inauspicious, intimidating, unpropitious

three
French: **5** trois

Three-Cornered Hat, The
author: **21** Pedro Antonio de Alarcon

Three Faces of Eve, The
director: **15** Nunnally Johnson
cast: **8** Lee J Cobb **9** Nancy Kulp **10** David Wayne **12** Vince Edwards **14** Joanne Woodward
narration by: **13** Alistair Cooke
Oscar for: **7** actress (Woodward)

Three Lives
includes: **9** Melanctha **11** The Good Anna **13** The Gentle Lena
author: **13** Gertrude Stein

Three Men in a Boat
author: **13** Jerome K Jerome

Three Musketeers, The
author: **14** Alexandre Dumas (pere)
director: **13** Richard Lester
character: **5** Athos **6** Aramis **7** Porthos **8** Planchet **9** D'Artagnan **12** Lady de Winter **17** Cardinal Richelieu **18** Constance Bonacieux
cast: **10** Oliver Reed **11** Faye Dunaway (Milady), Michael York (D'Artagnan), Raquel Welch **12** Frank Findlay **14** Charlton Heston, Christopher Lee **16** Geraldine Chaplin **18** Richard Chamberlain
sequel: **17** The Four Musketeers

Three's Company
character: **5** Larry **9** Janet Wood **10** Helen Roper **11** Chrissy Snow, Jack Tripper **12** Stanley Roper
cast: **10** John Ritter, Norman Fell **11** Joyce DeWitt **12** Audra Lindley, Richard Kline **13** Suzanne Somers

Three Sisters
director: **10** John Sichel **15** Laurence Olivier
author: **12** Anton Chekhov
character: **13** Fyodor Kuligin **14** Baron Tusenbach, Vassily Solyony **17** Alexandr Vershinin
Prozorov family: **4** Olga **5** Irina, Masha **6** Andrey **7** Natasha
cast: **9** Alan Bates **11** Derek Jacobi, Jeanne Watts **13** Joan Plowright, Louise Purnell **15** Laurence Olivier

Three Soldiers
author: **13** John Dos Passos

threnody **5** dirge, elegy **6** lament **7** requiem

threshold **4** dawn, door, edge, sill **5** brink, limen, onset, start, verge **6** portal **7** doorway, gateway, opening, prelude **8** doorsill, entrance **9** beginning, groundsel, inception **10** groundsill **11** entranceway **12** commencement **13** starting point

Thriae
form: **6** nymphs
nursed: **6** Apollo
taught: **6** Hermes

Thriambus
epithet of: **8** Dionysus

thrift **7** economy **8** prudence **9** frugality, husbandry, parsimony **10** moderation **11** sparingness, thriftiness **14** reasonableness **15** closefistedness **16** parsimoniousness

thriftiness **5** tight **6** thrift **7** economy **8** prudence **9** frugality, parsimony **13** pennypinching **15** closefistedness, tightfistedness **16** parsimoniousness

thriftless **6** lavish **8** feckless, prodigal, wasteful **11** extravagant, improvident

thrifty **6** frugal, saving, stingy **7** sparing **9** niggardly, penny-wise **10** economical **11** close-fisted, economizing, tightfisted **12** parsimonious **13** penny-pinching

thrill 4 fire, glow, kick, stir **5** flush, rouse, throb **6** arouse, excite, quiver, tickle, tingle, tremor **7** delight, impress, inspire, tremble **9** adventure, electrify, enrapture, galvanize, stimulate, transport **12** satisfaction

thrilled 4 agog **7** excited **9** delighted, overjoyed **11** transported

thrilling 7 awesome **8** engaging, exciting, riveting, stirring **9** absorbing, exquisite **10** delightful **11** fascinating, pleasurable, provocative, sensational, tantalizing, titillating **12** electrifying

thrip
variety: 6 banded **10** tube tailed **11** heterothrip, merothripid

thrive 3 wax **4** boom **5** bloom, get on **6** fatten **7** burgeon, prosper, succeed **8** flourish, get ahead, grow rich

thriving 4 busy, lush, rank, rich **7** wealthy, well-off **8** blooming, in clover, vigorous, well-to-do **9** flowering, luxuriant **10** blossoming, prospering, prosperous, succeeding, successful **11** flourishing

throat 3 maw **4** craw, gula, neck **5** gorge **6** gullet **7** chamber, jugulum, passage, pharynx
lozenge: 6 pastil
nautical: 3 jaw **4** jaws, nock
part: 6 fauces, larynx, tonsil **7** glottis, trachea
pertaining to: 5 gular
seizing: 4 knot **5** hitch **12** cuckold's knot
swelling: 6 goiter

throaty 3 dry, low **4** base, deep **5** gruff, husky, thick **6** hoarse **7** cracked, grating, rasping **8** croaking, guttural, resonant, sonorous **9** full-toned

throb 4 beat, jerk, pant **5** heave, pulse, shake **6** quiver, tremor, twitch **7** beating, flutter, pulsate, shaking, tremble, vibrate **9** palpitate, pulsation, quivering, throbbing, trembling, vibration **10** fluttering **11** oscillation, palpitation **13** reverberation

throes 5 agony, chaos, pangs **6** ordeal, spasms, tumult **7** anguish, turmoil **8** disorder, paroxysm, upheaval **9** confusion, paroxysms **10** convulsion, disruption

thrombus 4 clot **9** blood clot **11** coagulation

throng 3 jam **4** army, cram, herd, host, mass, mill, pack, rush **5** bunch, crowd, crush, flock, flood, horde, press, surge, swarm **6** deluge, gather, huddle, stream **7** cluster, collect **8** assemble, converge **9** multitude **10** assemblage, congregate

thronged 4 full **6** jammed, mobbed, packed **7** crammed, crowded, flocked, swarmed, teeming **8** swarming **9** congested, jampacked **11** overflowing

throttle 3 gag, gas **4** stop **5** block, burke, check, choke **6** stifle **7** garrote, seal off, shut off, silence, smother **8** choke off, gas pedal, strangle **9** fuel lever, fuel valve **11** strangulate

through, thru 4 done, past **5** ended **6** direct **7** express **8** finished, from A to Z, to the end **9** all the way, completed, concluded **10** terminated **12** long-distance **15** from first to last **18** from beginning to end **20** from one end to the other

through and through 5 total **6** wholly **7** totally, utterly **8** complete **10** completely, thoroughly **15** from top to bottom **18** from beginning to end **20** from one end to the other

through my fault
Latin: 8 mea culpa

throughout 7 all over **10** all the time, everywhere **11** in every part **16** all the way through **18** from beginning to end

Through the Looking Glass
sequel to: 17 Alice in Wonderland
author: 12 Lewis Carroll
character: 4 Gnat, Lion **5** Alice, Dinah **7** Red King, Unicorn **8** Red Queen **9** Red Knight, White King **10** Tweedledee, Tweedledum, White Queen **11** Black Kitten, White Kitten, White Knight **12** Humpty Dumpty

throw 3 lob, pit, put, shy **4** cast, hurl, shot, toss **5** chuck, fling, floor, heave, impel, pitch, place, put in, put on, sling **6** hurtle, launch, let fly, propel, unseat **7** project **8** delivery **9** knock down, put around

throw away 7 cast off, discard **8** get rid of

throw down 5 let go **8** drop hard, hurl down, toss down **9** fling down

throw into disorder 5 upset **7** agitate, disrupt **10** disarrange

throw off 4 emit, gush **5** exude **7** abandon, cast off, mislead **8** get rid of, shake off, shrug off **9** cast aside, discharge, give forth, pour forth

throw off the scent 7 confuse, mislead **8** confound **19** throw out a red herring

throw out 4 beam, emit, oust **5** eject, evict, expel, exude **6** banish, bounce, remove **7** discard, dismiss, toss out **8** get rid of, jettison **9** cast aside, throw away

throw overboard 4 dump **7** cast off, discard **8** jettison, toss over

throw suspicion upon
11 cast doubt on **17** bring into question

throw up 4 barf, spew **5** eject, expel, spout, vomit **6** cast up, spew up **7** cough up **8** disgorge **9** discharge **11** regurgitate

thrust 3 jab, jam, ram **4** butt, pass, poke, prod, push, raid, stab **5** boost, drive, foray, force, impel, lunge, press, sally, shove, swipe **6** attack, charge, pierce, plunge, propel, sortie, strike, stroke **7** assault, impetus, impulse, riposte **8** momentum **9** incursion **10** aggression

thrust aside 4 dump **6** shelve **7** discard **8** get rid of, throw off, throw out **9** cast aside, dispose of, throw away

thrust at 6 assail, attack **7** lunge at **8** strike at

thrust out 4 spew, spit **5** eject, expel, vomit **6** extend, propel **7** protrude

Thrym
origin: 12 Scandinavian
form: 5 giant
killed by: 4 Thor
demanded return of: 5 Freia, Freya

Thucydides
author of: 28 History of the Peloponnesian War

thud 4 bang **5** clunk, knock, smack, thump

thug 4 hood **6** bandit, gunman, hit man, killer, mugger, robber **7** hoodlum, mobster, ruffian **8** assassin, gangster, murderer **9** cutthroat

thumb 5 hitch **6** finger, handle **9** hitchhike **10** catch a ride, hitch a ride **11** flip through, leaf through

Thumbelina
author: **21** Hans Christian Andersen

thumbnail **5** brief, short **7** compact, concise

thump **3** hit, jab, rap **4** bang, beat, clip, cuff, poke, slam, slap, swat, thud **5** clout, clunk, knock, pound, punch, smack, whack **6** batter, bounce, buffet, pommel, strike, thwack **8** collapse, lambaste

thunder **4** boom, clap, echo, peal, roar, roll **5** crack, crash **6** rumble **7** explode, resound **8** rumbling **9** discharge, explosion **11** reverberate, thunderbolt, thunderclap
god of: **4** Thor **5** Donar **7** Taranis

thunderbolt **4** dart **5** flash, shaft **6** stroke

Thunderstorms, god of **8** Summanus

thunderstruck **4** agog, awed **5** agape **6** aghast, amazed **8** confused, overcome **9** astounded, awestruck, perplexed, surprised **10** astonished, bewildered **11** dumbfounded **13** flabbergasted

Thunder-ten-Tronckh
character in: **7** Candide
author: **8** Voltaire

Thurber, James
author of: **12** The New Yorker **14** Is Sex Necessary (with E B White), The Catbird Seat **16** The Owl in the Attic **18** My Life and Hard Times, The Thurber Carnival **26** The Secret Life of Walter Mitty

Thurber Carnival, The
author: **12** James Thurber

Thurio
character in: **20** Two Gentlemen of Verona
author: **11** Shakespeare

Thursday
French: **5** jeudi
from: **4** Thor
German: **10** donnerstag
heavenly body: **4** Jove **7** Jupiter
Italian: **7** giovedi
Latin: **9** Dies Jovis
observance: **12** Holy Thursday, Thanksgiving **13** Corpus Christi **14** Maundy Thursday **17** Ascension Thursday
Scandinavian: **7** torsdag
Spanish: **6** jueves

Thurso's Landing
author: **15** Robinson Jeffers

thus **2** so **4** ergo **5** hence **6** like so **8** like this **9** as follows, in this way, therefore, wherefore **11** accordingly **12** consequently, in this manner **13** for this reason
Latin: **3** sic

thus always to tyrants
Latin: **17** sic semper tyrannis
motto of: **8** Virginia

thus passes away the glory of this world
Latin: **21** sic transit gloria mundi

Thus Spake Zarathustra
also: **21** Also Sprach Zarathustra
author: **18** Friedrich Nietzsche

thwack **3** box, hit, rap **4** bang, blow, slam, slap **5** baste, clout, knock, smack, thump, whack **6** buffet, paddle, strike, wallop

Thwackum
character in: **8** Tom Jones
author: **8** Fielding

thwart **3** bar **4** balk, foil, stop **5** check, cross **6** baffle, hinder, oppose **7** inhibit, prevent, ward off **8** obstruct, stave off **9** frustrate **10** contravene

Thyestean banquet
meal of: **10** human flesh

Thyestes
author: **6** Seneca

Thyestes
father: **6** Pelops
mother: **10** Hippodamia
brother: **6** Atreus
half-brother: **10** Chrysippus
sister-in-law: **6** Aerope
son: **9** Aegisthus
daughter: **7** Pelopia

Thyiad *see* **9** bacchante

Thymbraeus
father: **7** Laocoon

thyme
botanical name: **6** Thymus **9** T vulgaris
varieties: **4** Wild **5** Basil, Lemon, Water **6** Common, Garden, Golden **7** Caraway, Spanish
symbol of: **8** activity
attracts: **4** bees
conjures: **9** fairy folk
use: **4** fish **7** poultry **8** stuffing **10** Creole food **21** New England clam chowder

Thymoetes
king of: **6** Athens
elder of: **7** Trojans

Thyone *see* **6** Semele

Thyoneus
epithet of: **8** Dionysus
means: **11** son of Thyone

Thyrsis
author: **13** Matthew Arnold

Thyrus
staff of: **8** Dionysus
tipped with: **8** pine cone
twined with: **3** ivy **5** vines

thysanoptera
class: **8** hexapoda
phylum: **10** arthropoda
group: **5** thrip

thysanura
class: **8** hexapoda
phylum: **10** arthropoda
group: **8** firebrat **10** silverfish **11** bristletail

Tia Maria
type: **6** brandy **7** liqueur
origin: **7** Jamaica
flavor: **6** coffee
with rum: **10** Black Maria
with tequila: **9** Brave Bull
with vodka: **12** Black Russian

Tiamat
origin: **8** Akkadian
consort of: **4** Apsu
children: **4** gods

tiara **4** band **5** crown, miter **6** diadem **7** coronet **8** frontlet, ornament **9** headdress

Tiaxcaltec
language family: **5** Nahua
location: **6** Mexico **14** Central America

Tiber
god of: **9** Tiberinus

Tiberinus
origin: **5** Roman
god of: **5** Tiber

Tibet ***see box***

tibia
bone of: **4** shin

tic **6** twitch **12** facial twitch **13** tic douloureux **19** trigeminal neuralgia

tick **3** dot, tap **4** beat, line, list, mark, nick, note **5** blaze, check, clack, click, enter, notch, swing, throb **6** record, slight, stroke **7** scratch, vibrate **8** mark down, register, ticktock **9** checkmark, chronicle, oscillate, pulsation, vibration

ticket **3** tag **4** card, mark, pass, slip, stub **5** label, slate **6** ballot, coupon, marker, roster **7** sticker, voucher **14** list of nominees, traffic summons
type: **4** trip **7** parking, traffic **9** admission

tickle **4** itch **5** amuse, cheer, prick, sting, throb **6** divert, please, regale, stroke, thrill, tingle, twitch **7** delight, enchant, enliven, gladden, gratify, prickle, rejoice **8** enthrall, entrance **9** captivate, fascinate, titillate **12** scratchiness **15** do one's heart good

Tibet
other name: **3** Bod **4** Bhot **5** Tobet **8** Hsitsang **10** Land of Snow **14** Roof of the World
capital: **5** Lassa, Lhasa
city: **3** Noh **5** Karak **6** Chamdo, Gartok **7** Changtu, Totling **8** Gyangtse, Jihkatse, Shigatse **9** Chiangtzu
government: **23** autonomous region of China
monetary unit: **5** tanga
lake: **3** Aru, Bam, Bun, Nam **4** Mema, Tosu **5** Jagok, Tabia **6** Dagtse, Garhur, Kashun, Nam Iso, Seling, Tangra, Yamdok **7** Kyaring, Teriman, Tsaring, Zilling **8** Jiggitai **9** Tengrinor **11** Manasarowar
mountain: **5** Kamet, Sajum **6** Kailas, Kunlun **7** Bandala **8** Himalaya **9** Karakoram
highest point: **7** Everest
river: **3** Nak, Nau, Sak **4** Song **5** Hwang, Indus **6** Mekong, Sutlej, Yellow **7** Hwang Ho, Matsang, Melsang, Salween, Tsangpo, Yangtze **11** Brahmaputra
physical feature:
plain: **4** Kham **9** Chang Tang
valley: **7** Tsangpo
people: **5** Asian, Balti, Bodpa, Drupa **6** Bhotia, Champa, Drokpa, Khamba, Khambu, Panaka, Sherpa, Tangut **7** Bhotiya, Bhutani, Gyarung, Taghlik, Tibetan **9** Mongoloid
patron god: **14** Avalokitesvara
ruler: **4** Yuan **6** Mongol **9** dalai lama **13** Songtsan Gampo
language: **5** Balti **6** Ladkhi **7** Bhutani, Bodskad **8** Sanskrit **9** Bhutanese
religion: **5** Bonko **7** Lamaism
place:
Indian border: **11** McMahon Line
palace: **7** Potalaf
temple: **7** Jokhang **10** Tashi Lumpo **11** Tashi Lhunpo
feature:
animal: **3** dzo, yak **5** kiang **7** mastiff **8** musk deer **10** giant panda
clothing: **5** chuba
dance: **4** cham **9** achelhamo
dog: **9** lhasa apso
leader: **9** dalai lama
legend: **4** yeti **17** abominable snowman
monastery: **8** lamasery
monk: **4** lama
food:
dish: **6** tsamba, tsampa
drink: **5** chang

ticklish **4** hard **5** itchy, tough **6** knotty, thorny, tickly, touchy, tricky **7** awkward, prickly **8** critical, delicate, scratchy, tingling **9** difficult, intricate, sensitive, uncertain **11** complicated

tidal basin **3** bay **5** inlet, sound **6** lagoon **7** estuary **11** arm of the sea

tidbit **3** bit **4** item **5** treat **6** morsel **8** delicacy, mouthful **9** choice bit

tide **4** flow, neap, wave **5** drift, state **7** current **8** movement, tendency, undertow **9** direction **10** ebb and flow, wax and wane **11** rise and fall

tidings **4** news, word **6** advice, notice, report **8** good word **11** declaration, information **12** announcement, intelligence, notification

tidy **4** neat, trig, trim **5** ample, array, clean **6** goodly, neaten, tidy up **7** arrange, careful, clean up, orderly, precise, regular, sizable **8** neaten up, spotless, spruce up **9** organized, regulated, shipshape **10** immaculate, methodical, meticulous, put in order, straighten, systematic **11** substantial **12** businesslike, considerable, straighten up **15** in apple-pie order

tidy up **5** clean **6** neaten **9** freshen up **10** put in order, straighten

tie **3** rod **4** ally, band, beam, belt, bind, bond, cord, draw, duty, join, knot, lash, line, link, rope, sash, yoke **5** brace, cable, cinch, limit, marry, match, truss, unite **6** attach, bow tie, clinch, couple, cravat, engage, fasten, girdle, hamper, hinder, ribbon, secure, string, tether **7** confine, connect, kinship, necktie, support **8** affinity, cincture, dead heat, make a bow, make fast, relation, restrain, restrict, tied vote **9** constrain, crossbeam, fastening **10** allegiance, connection, cummerbund, obligation **11** affiliation, come out even **12** relationship **13** connecting rod **15** divide the honors

Tiepolo, Giovanni Battista (Giambattista)
born: **5** Italy **6** Venice
artwork: **10** Kaisersaal (salon) **11** Treppenhaus (staircase) **14** The Crucifixion **16** Ronaldo and Armida **20** Madonna of Mount Carmel **21** The Communion of St Lucia, The Triumph of Aphrodite **24** St Thekla and the Pestilence **28** Apotheosis of Francesco Barbaro **28** The Worship of the Bronze Serpent

tier **3** row **4** bank, file, line, rank, step **5** layer, level, range, story **7** stratum **14** stratification

Tierney, Gene
born: **10** Brooklyn NY
husband: **11** Oleg Cassini
roles: **5** Laura **10** Belle Starr **11** Tobacco Road **13** A Bell for Adano **16** Leave Her to Heaven **18** The Ghost and Mrs Muir

tiers etat **11** third estate
in French politics: **7** commons

tie-up **3** jam **4** snag **5** block, hitch, snarl **6** slow-up **7** failure **8** blockage, gridlock, stoppage **9** breakdown **10** bottleneck, disruption **11** malfunction **13** embouteillage

tie up **3** tie **4** bind, gird, lash, rope **5** hitch, snarl, strap, truss **6** engage, fasten, hinder, impede, occupy, secure, tangle **8** entangle

tiff **4** huff, miff, rage, snit, spat **5** clash, run-in, scrap, tizzy, words **6** hassle **7** dispute, quarrel, rhubarb, wrangle **8** argument, ill humor, squabble **10** difference **11** altercation **12** disagreement **16** misunderstanding

tiger **3** cat **6** cougar, jaguar **7** fighter, wildcat
young: **5** whelp

Tiger Joy
author: **19** Stephen Vincent Benet

tiger's-eye
species: **6** quartz

Tigger
character in: **13** Winnie-the-Pooh
author: **5** Milne

tight **4** busy, firm, full, hard, high, snug, taut **5** blind, close, dense, drunk, exact, happy, harsh, lit up, rigid, scant, solid, stern, stiff, tense, tipsy, tough **6** firmly, frugal, gorged, hard-up, jammed, juiced, loaded, scarce, secure, severe, skimpy, sloppy, soused, stewed, stingy, stoned, strict, trying, zonked **7** austere, closely, compact, crammed, crowded, drunken, miserly, onerous, pickled, pie-eyed, smashed, solidly, sparing, stuffed **8** grudging, rigorous, securely, too small **9** deficient, difficult, illiberal, jam-packed, niggardly, penurious, plastered, skintight, stringent, worrisome **10** burdensome, compressed, glassy-eyed, impassable, inadequate, inebriated, inflexible, in one's cups, nip-and-tuck, nose-to-nose, tyrannical, ungenerous, unyielding **11** closefisted, constricted, dictatorial, impermeable, intoxicated, troublesome, well-matched **12** close-fitting, impenetrable, insufficient, parsimonious **13** closely fitted, feeling no pain **14** fitting closely, uncompromising **20** three sheets to the wind

tighten **5** pinch **6** anchor, fasten, narrow, secure **7** squeeze **8** contract, make fast, make taut **9** constrict **14** take up the slack

tighten one's belt **4** save **5** skimp, stint **6** scrimp **8** conserve, cut costs **9** economize **11** cut expenses **12** pinch pennies

tightfisted **5** cheap, mingy, tight **6** greedy, stingy **7** miserly **9** illiberal, niggardly, penurious **10** avaricious **11** closefisted **12** cheeseparing, parsimonious **13** penny-pinching

tightfistedness **6** penury **9** parsimony **10** stinginess **11** miserliness **13** niggardliness, penny-pinching

tight-fitting **4** snug **5** tight **8** too small **9** skintight **11** constricted **12** constricting **15** like a second skin

tight-laced **4** prim **6** prissy, stuffy **7** prudish **8** priggish **9** inhibited, repressed, Victorian **11** puritanical, standoffish, straitlaced **13** self-righteous

tight-lipped **3** mum **4** curt **5** brief, quiet, short, terse **8** discreet, reserved, reticent, taciturn **10** unsociable **11** untalkative **12** close-mouthed **15** uncommunicative

tightly packed **5** dense **6** jammed **7** compact, crammed, stuffed **10** compressed **12** concentrated

tightwad **5** miser, piker **7** niggard, Scrooge **9** lickpenny, skinflint **10** cheapskate, pinchpenny **12** moneygrubber

till **3** sow **4** even, farm, plow, seed, tray, unto up to **6** before, coffer, drawer, harrow, plough **7** as far as, develop, prepare **8** moneybox, treasury **9** cultivate **12** cash register
geological: **5** drift

tillable **6** arable **8** farmable, plowable **10** cultivable

tillage **7** farming, plowing **11** agriculture, cultivation

Till Eulenspiegel
also: **16** Tyll Eulenspiegel
origin: **8** Germanic
means: **14** practical joker

Tillie the Toiler
creator: **12** Russ Westover
character: **3** Mac **7** Mr Chase

Tilney, Henry
character in: **15** Northanger Abbey
author: **6** Austen

tilt **3** row, tip **4** cant, lean, list, rake, spar, tiff **5** brawl, fence, fight, grade, joust, pitch, slant, slope **6** affray, battle, combat, oppose **7** contest, dispute, incline, quarrel **8** argument, skirmish, squabble **9** encounter **10** tournament **11** altercation

Timaeus
author: **5** Plato

Timandra
father: **9** Tyndareus
mother: **4** Leda
brother: **6** Castor, Pollux
sister: **5** Helen **12** Clytemnestra
husband: **7** Echemus, Phyleus
son: **5** Meges
cursed by: **9** Aphrodite

timber **4** bush, logs, wood **5** copse, trees, woods **6** boards, forest, lumber **7** thicket

timberland **5** woods **6** forest, sticks **8** woodland

timbre **4** tone **5** pitch **9** resonance

time, times **3** age, day, eon, era **4** beat, days, hour, term, week, year **5** clock, cycle, epoch, event, match, month, phase, spell, stage, tempo, while, years **6** adjust, chance, decade, moment, period, rhythm, season **7** century, episode, freedom, instant, liberty, measure, stretch **8** duration, incident, interval, occasion **10** experience, generation **11** opportunity, synchronize

time flies
Latin: **11** tempus fugit

time-honored **6** common, normal **7** regular, revered **8** accepted, standard **9** customary, respected, universal

timeless **7** abiding, durable, endless, eternal, lasting, undying **8** enduring, immortal, infinite, unending **9** boundless, ceaseless, deathless, immutable, incessant, permanent, perpetual **10** continuous, persistent **11** everlasting, never-ending **12** interminable, unchangeable **13** never-stopping **14** indestructible

timely **6** prompt **8** punctual **9** opportune, well-timed **10** convenient, felicitous, seasonable **12** providential

Time Machine, The
author: **7** H G Wells
character: **4** Eloi **5** Weena **8** Morlocks **12** Time Traveler

Time of Your Life, The
author: **14** William Saroyan
director: **8** H C Potter
cast: **8** Ward Bond **11** James Cagney, Wayne Morris **12** Jeanne Cagney **13** William Bendix **17** Broderick Crawford

timepiece **5** clock, watch **8** horologe **11** chronometer

Time Remembered
author: **11** Jean Anouilh

Timerman, Jacobo
author of: **38** Prisoner Without a Name Cell Without a Number

timesaving **5** quick **6** speedy **9** efficient **11** expeditious

time without end **7** forever **8** eternity, infinity

timeworn **3** old **4** aged, worn **5** dated, hoary, passe, stale, trite **6** age-old, beat-up, old-hat, shabby **7** ancient, antique **8** battered, dog-eared, obsolete, overused **9** hackneyed, out of date, venerable, weathered **10** antiquated **12** antediluvian

timid **3** coy, shy **6** afraid, humble, modest, scared **7** bashful, fearful **8** cowardly, retiring, sheepish, timorous **9** diffident, shrinking, spineless, weak-kneed **10** unassuming **12** apprehensive, fainthearted **13** pusillanimous

timidity **7** modesty, shyness **8** cold feet, humility **9** cowardice, timidness **10** diffidence **11** bashfulness, fearfulness, trepidation **12** sheepishness, timorousness **13** spinelessness **16** faint-heartedness

timidness **7** shyness **8** meekness, timidity **10** diffidence, insecurity **11** bashfulness **12** timorousness **14** submissiveness **15** unassertiveness **16** faintheartedness

Timon of Athens
author: **18** William Shakespeare
character: **6** Lucius **7** Flavius **8** Lucullus **9** Apemantus, Ventidius **10** Alcibiades, Sempronius

Timor
capital: **4** Dili
country: **8** Portugal **9** Indonesia
islands: **5** Sunda **11** Lesser Sunda
strait: **5** Ombai

timorous **3** shy **4** meek **5** timid **6** afraid **7** anxious, bashful, fearful **8** retiring **9** shrinking **10** submissive **12** fainthearted

timorousness **7** shyness **8** cold feet, meekness, timidity **9** cowardice **11** fearfulness, trepidation **16** faintheartedness

Timothy
mother: **6** Eunice
grandmother: **4** Lois
companion: **4** Paul **8** Silvanus

tin
chemical symbol: **2** Sn

tincture **6** elixir **7** essence, extract, spirits **8** solution **11** concentrate

Tinder Box, The
author: **21** Hans Christian Andersen

Tin Drum, The
author: **11** Gunter Grass
director: **17** Volker Schlondorff
character: **14** Oskar Matzerath
cast: **10** Mario Adorf **12** David Bennent (Oskar) **13** Angela Winkler **16** Daniel Olbrychski **17** Katharina Tahlbach
Oscar for: **11** foreign film

tine **3** die, tip **4** barb, lose, tyne **5** point, prong, spike **6** bodkin, branch, perish, skewer **7** destroy, forfeit

tinge **3** dye **4** cast, dash, hint, lace, tint, tone, vein **5** color, imbue, shade, smack, stain, taste, touch, trace **6** flavor, infuse, nuance, season **7** instill, soupcon **9** suspicion

tingle **5** sting, throb **6** thrill, tickle, tremor **7** flutter, prickle **9** prickling, pulsation **11** palpitation

Tinia
origin: **8** Etruscan
chief: **3** god

Tinker, Tailor, Soldier, Spy
author: **11** John Le Carre

Tinker Bell
character in: **8** Peter Pan
author: **6** Barrie

tinkle **4** ding, peal, ping, ring **5** chime, chink, clank, clink, plink **6** jingle **9** ting-a-ling

tin lizzie **3** car **4** auto, heap **5** motor **6** jalopy, wheels **7** flivver, machine, motocar, vehicle **10** automobile **12** motor vehicle

Tin Man, Tin Woodsman
character in: **13** The Wizard of Oz
author: **4** Baum

tinsel **4** sham, show **5** gloss **6** sequin **7** glitter, spangle **8** pretense **9** gaudiness **10** camouflage, decoration, masquerade **11** affectation, false colors, make-believe, ostentation

tint **3** dye, hue **4** hint, tone, wash **5** color, frost, shade, stain, tinge, touch, trace **6** nuance **7** pigment **8** coloring, tincture **10** suggestion

Tintern Abbey
author: **17** William Wordsworth

tintinnabulate **4** peal, ring, toll **5** chime, clang, knell, sound **6** jingle, tinkle

tintinnabulation **4** gong, peal, ring, toll **5** chime, knell **6** jingle **7** clangor, pealing, ringing **8** clanging, ding-dong, jingling, tinkling **11** peal of bells

Tintoretto, Jacopo
real name: **13** Jacopo Robusti
born: **5** Italy **6** Venice
artwork: **8** Paradise **13** The Last Supper **14** The Crucifixion **16** The Road to Calvary **17** Bacchus and Ariadne **18** Apotheosis of St Roch, The Flight into Egypt **20** Susannah and the Elders **21** The Temptation of Christ **26** St Mark Frees a Christian Slave **27** The Finding of the Body of St Mark **32** The Miracle of St Mark Rescuing a Slave

tiny **3** wee **5** pygmy, runty, small, teeny **6** bantam, little, midget, minute, petite **8** dwarfish **9** itsy-bitsy, miniature, minuscule, pint-sized **10** diminutive, teeny-weeny, undersized **11** Lilliputian, microscopic, pocket-sized **12** teensy-weensy

Tiny Alice
author: **11** Edward Albee

Tiny Tim
character in: **15** A Christmas Carol
author: **7** Dickens

tip **3** cap, pat, tap, top **4** acme, apex, barb, brow, cant, clue, head, hint, hook, lean, list, peak, rake, tilt **5** crest, crown, pitch, point, prong, slant, slope, spike, upend, upset **6** advice, reward, stroke, summit, tip-off, topple, upturn, vertex, zenith **7** capsize, incline, leaning, lowdown, pointer, sharpen, tilting, tipping, warning **8** gratuity, overturn, pinnacle, slanting **9** baksheesh, lagniappe **10** admonition, inside dope, perquisite, suggestion, turn turtle **11** forewarning **13** word to the wise
French: **7** douceur

tipcart **4** cart **8** dumpcart, pushcart

Tiphys
member of: **9** Argonauts
occupation: **9** steersman

tip off **3** tip **4** warn **5** alert **6** caveat **7** caution, warning **8** forewarn **11** forewarning

tip over **5** upend, upset **7** capsize **8** flip over, keel over, overturn, turn over **10** turn turtle

Tippett, Michael Kemp
born: **6** London **7** England
composer of: **9** King Priam **13** The Knot Garden **15** A Child of Our Time **20** The Midsummer Marriage **22** The Vision of St Augustine **32** Concerto for Double String Orchestra

tipple **5** drink, quaff **6** guzzle, imbibe, liquor **8** beverage

tippler **3** sot **4** lush, soak, wino **5** drunk, rummy, souse, toper **6** bibber, boozer, sponge **7** guzzler, imbiber, swiller, tosspot **8** drunkard **9** alcoholic, inebriate **10** booze hound **11** dipsomaniac

tipsy **4** high **5** awash, blind, drunk, happy, lit-up, stiff, tight **6** juiced, loaded, sloppy, sodden, soused, stewed, stoned **7** drunken, pickled, pie-eyed, smashed **9** inebriate, plastered **10** glassy-eyed, inebriated, in one's cups **11** intoxicated **12** half seas over **13** feeling no pain **20** three sheets to the wind

tip-top **4** A-one **5** elite, super **7** supreme **8** very fine **10** consummate **11** exceptional, superlative **13** extraordinary

tirade **5** curse **6** screed **7** lecture **8** diatribe, harangue, jeremiad, scolding **9** invective, reprimand **11** castigation, fulmination **12** condemnation, denunciation, dressing-down, vilification, vituperation

tirailleur **10** skirmisher **12** sharpshooter

Tirane, Tirana
capital of: **7** Albania

tire **3** fag, irk **4** bore **5** annoy, weary **6** bother, tucker **7** disgust, exhaust, fatigue, wear out **8** be sick of **10** make sleepy **11** be fed up with **12** lose interest, lose patience

tire
invented by: **6** Dunlop **7** Thomson

tired **4** beat **5** all in, weary **6** bushed, drowsy, fagged, pooped, sleepy **7** wearied, worn out **8** dog-tired, fatigued, tuckered **9** enervated, exhausted, played out

tireless **6** steady **7** devoted, staunch **8** constant, faithful, resolute, untiring **9** steadfast, unceasing, unwearied **10** determined, unflagging, unswerving **11** hard-working, industrious, never-tiring, persevering, unfaltering, unremitting **13** indefatigable

Tiresias
also: **9** Teiresias
vocation: **7** prophet
father: **6** Everes
mother: **8** Chariclo
grandfather: **6** Udaeus
home: **6** Thebes
struck: **5** blind
character in: **7** Odyssey **10** Oedipus Rex
characteristic: **9** blind seer

tiresome **4** drab, dull, hard **6** boring, deadly, dismal, tiring, trying, vexing **7** arduous, fagging, humdrum, irksome, tedious, wearing **8** annoying, wearying **9** difficult, fatiguing, laborious, wearisome **10** bothersome, exhausting, monotonous **13** uninteresting

Tisamenus
leader of: **9** Boeotians
father: **7** Orestes
mother: **8** Hermione
vocation: **4** seer
killed by: **10** Heraclidae

Tishri **18** seventh Hebrew month

Tisiphone
member of: **6** Furies

'Tis Pity She's a Whore
author: **8** John Ford
character: **6** Donado, Florio, Putana **7** Soranzo, Vasques **8** Bergetto, Giovanni, Grimaldi **9** Annabella, Hippolita **11** Richardetto **16** Friar Bonaventura

tissue
kind: **4** bone, skin **5** nerve **6** muscle

titan **5** giant, great, mogul **7** magnate

Titan
race of: **4** gods
father: **6** Uranus
mother: **2** Ge **4** Gaea
names: **5** Coeus, Crius **6** Cronus **7** Iapetus, Oceanus **8** Hyperion
sisters: **8** Titaness
names of sisters: **4** Rhea **5** Theia **6** Phoebe, Tethys, Themis **9** Mnemosyne

Titan, The
sequel to: **12** The Financier
author: **15** Theodore Dreiser
character: **13** Peter Laughlin **15** Berenice Fleming, Stephanie Platow **16** Aileen Cowperwood **23** Frank Algernon Cowperwood

Titan, the *see* **6** Helios

Titaness *see* **5** Titan

Titania
character in: **21** A Midsummer Night's Dream
author: **11** Shakespeare

titanic **4** huge, vast **5** giant, great, stout **6** mighty, strong **7** immense, mammoth **8** colossal, enormous, gigantic, whopping **9** herculean, humongous, monstrous **10** gargantuan, monumental, prodigious, stupendous

titanium
chemical symbol: **2** Ti

Titanomachy
revolt of: **7** Iapetus

tit for tat **8** exchange **10** quid pro quo **13** an eye for an eye

Tithonus
father: **8** Laomedon
brother: **5** Priam
loved by: **3** Eos
son: **6** Memnon **8** Emathion

Titian
real name: **15** Tiziano Vecellio
born: **5** Italy **13** Pieve di Cadore
artwork: **5** Pieta **12** The Bacchanal, Tribute Money **13** Noli Me Tangere **15** Diana and Actaeon, The Rape of Europa **16** The Pesaro Madonna, The Venus of Urbino **17** Bacchus and Ariadne, The Death of Actaeon, The Girl in a Fur Wrap, The Three Ages of Man **18** Charles V at Muhlberg, The Adrian Bacchanal, The Young Englishman **19** Francis I Roi de France **20** Sacred and Profane Love **21** Venus and the Lute Player **23** The Madonna of the Cherries **24** Pope Paul III and his Nephews, The Assumption of the Virgin

titillate **5** charm, rouse, tease, tempt **6** allure, arouse, excite, seduce, tickle, turn on **7** attract, provoke **8** entrance **9** captivate, fascinate, stimulate **15** whet the appetite

titillating **8** alluring, exciting, tempting **9** seductive **10** suggestive **11** provocative

title **3** dub **4** deed, name, rank, term **5** claim, crown, grade, label, place, right **6** status, tenure **7** entitle, epithet, station **8** christen, nobility, position **9** condition, designate, ownership **10** legal right, lordly rank, noble birth, possession **11** appellation, designation **12** championship

titled **5** named, noble, regal, royal **6** called, lordly **7** courtly **8** entitled **10** designated **11** blue-blooded **12** aristocratic

Titograd
capital of: **10** Montenegro

titter **5** chirp, smirk **6** cackle, giggle, simper, teehee **7** chuckle, snicker, snigger

tittle **3** bit, dot, jot **4** atom, iota, mite **5** speck **8** particle

Tittle, Y A (Yelberton Abraham)
sport: **8** football

position: **11** quarterback
team: **13** New York Giants **14** Baltimore Colts **23** San Francisco Forty-Niners

titular **7** known as, nominal **8** so-called **10** in name only, ostensible **11** in title only

Titus
surname: **6** Justus
hometown: **7** Corinth
companion: **4** Paul

Titus *see* **6** Tatius

Titus Andronicus
author: **18** William Shakespeare
character: **5** Aaron **6** Chiron, Marcus, Tamora **7** Alarbus, Lavinia **9** Bassianus, Demetrius **10** Saturninus

Tityus
form: **5** giant
father: **4** Zeus
mother: **2** Ge **5** Elara
home: **6** Euboea
threatened: **4** Leto
killed by: **6** Apollo **7** Artemis

tizzy **4** snit **6** dither, swivet **7** dudgeon **8** tailspin
British: **8** sixpence

Tjaden
character in: **25** All Quiet on the Western Front
author: **8** Remarque

Tlepolemus
father: **8** Hercules
mother: **10** Astyocheia
wife: **6** Polyxo
son: **8** Deipylus
killed by: **8** Sarpedon

Tmolus
king of: **5** Lydia

to **2** ad, on **3** for **4** into, near, unto, upon, with **5** about, until **6** at hand, closed, toward **7** against, forward **8** together **10** concerning, included in **11** contained in
prefix: **2** ac, ad
Scottish: **3** tae

toad
group of: **4** knot

toady **4** fawn **6** fawner, flunky, stooge, yes-man **8** hanger-on, kowtow to, parasite, truckler **9** flatterer, sycophant **10** bootlicker, curry favor **11** apple-polish, lickspittle **13** apple-polisher, backscratcher

To Althea, From Prison
author: **15** Richard Lovelace

to a man **3** all **8** every one **9** one and all **10** completely **12** to the last man

To a Skylark
author: **18** Percy Bysshe Shelley

toast **3** dry **4** heat, warm **5** brown, grill, honor **6** salute, warm up **9** celebrate **10** compliment **11** commemorate **12** browned bread, clink glasses **15** drink one's health

tobacco
varieties: **4** tree, wild **6** Indian **7** jasmine, Turkish **9** broadleaf, flowering, Nicotiana **12** long-flowered **16** Nicotiana rustica, Nicotiana tabacum

Tobacco Road
author: **15** Erskine Caldwell
character: **3** Ada **4** Dude **5** Pearl **6** Bessie **8** Ellie May **9** Lov Bensey **12** Jeeter Lester

To Be or Not To Be
director: **13** Ernst Lubitsch
cast: **9** Jack Benny **11** Robert Stack **12** Lionel Atwill **13** Carole Lombard, Felix Bressart
setting: **6** Poland

Tobias
father: **5** Tobit
grandfather: **6** Tobiel
son: **8** Hycranus

Tobit
father: **6** Tobiel
son: **6** Tobias

To Catch a Thief
director: **15** Alfred Hitchcock
cast: **9** Cary Grant **10** Grace Kelly **12** John Williams **17** Jessie Royce Landis
setting: **13** French Riviera

Tocharian
language family: **12** Indo-European
spoken in: **11** Central Asia

Tocqueville, Alexis de
author of: **18** Democracy in America

tocsin **4** bell **5** alarm **7** warning

today **3** now **7** this day, this era **8** nowadays, this time **9** in this era, on this day, this epoch **10** the present **11** in this epoch, modern times **13** in modern times, the present age, the present day **15** in this day and age

Todd, Richard
real name: **27** Richard Andrew Palethorpe-Todd
born: **6** Dublin **7** Ireland
roles: **13** The Hasty Heart, The Longest Day **14** The Virgin Queen **15** A Man Called Peter

toddle **6** waddle, wobble **14** take short steps, walk unsteadily

toddler **3** tot **4** babe, baby, tyke **5** child **6** infant **9** little one

to-do **3** ado **4** fuss, stir **5** furor, noise **6** bustle, flurry, hubbub, hustle, pother, racket, ruckus, rumpus, tumult, uproar **7** turmoil **8** activity **9** agitation, commotion **10** excitement, hullabaloo, hurly-burly **11** disturbance

Toe, The
nickname of: **8** Lou Groza

to err is human
Latin: **16** errare humanum est

toff **3** nob **4** beau **5** dandy, swell **10** young blood

Toffler, Alvin
author of: **11** Future Shock **12** The Third Wave

toga **3** aba **4** garb, gown, robe **6** trabea **7** garment **12** outergarment
virilis: **9** white robe **11** manhood robe

Togo ***see box, p. 988***

togs **4** duds **6** attire, outfit **7** apparel, clothes, threads **8** clothing, garments

To Have and Have Not
director: **11** Howard Hawks
based on novel by: **15** Ernest Hemingway
cast: **12** Dolores Moran, Lauren Bacall **13** Walter Brennan **14** Humphrey Bogart **15** Hoagy Carmichael
remade as: **13** The Gunrunners **16** The Breaking Point

To His Coy Mistress
author: **13** Andrew Marvell

toil **4** grub, moil, work **5** grind, labor, pains, slave, sweat **6** drudge, effort **7** travail **8** drudgery, exertion, hardship, hard work, industry, struggle, work hard **11** application, elbow grease **12** apply oneself, exert oneself **14** work like a horse

toiler **4** peon, serf, swot **5** navvy, prole, slave **6** drudge, flunky, menial, slavey, worker **7** grubber, laborer, servant, slogger **9** workhorse **10** wage earner **11** galley slave

toilet **2** WC **3** can, loo **4** john **5** privy **7** commode, latrine **8** facility, lavatory, men's room, outhouse, rest room, washroom **10** ladies' room **11** convenience, water closet

toilet water **5** scent **7** cologne, essence, perfume **9** fragrance

toilsome **4** hard **5** tough **6** tiring, uphill **7** arduous, onerous, tedious **8** wearying **9** difficult,

Togo
other name: 14 French Togoland
capital/largest city: 4 Lome
others: 5 Badon, Kpeme **6** Anecho, Ansoho, Blitta, Klonto, Nuatja, Palime, Sokode **7** Bassari, Dopango, Pagonda **8** Atakpame, Tabligbo **10** Niamtougou
school: 5 Benin **6** Mawull
monetary unit: 5 franc **7** centime
mountain: 4 Togo **7** Atakora, Koronga
highest point: 7 Baumann
river: 3 Oti **4** Anie, Haho, Mono, Ogou
sea: 8 Atlantic
physical feature:
***bight:* 5** Benin
***gulf:* 6** Guinea
***plain:* 4** Mono
people: 3 Ana, Ewe, Twi **4** Mina **5** Hausa **6** Akposa, Kabrai **7** Bassari, Cabrais, Kabrais, Ouatchi **8** Konkomba, Kotokoli, Lotokoli
***leader:* 7** Eyadema **15** Sylvanus Olympio **16** Nicolas Grunitzky
language: 3 Ana, Ewe, Twi **4** Mina **5** Hausa **6** French, Kabrai, Kabrie **7** Bassari, Dagomba, Ouatchi **8** Kotokoli, Lotocoli
religion: 5 Islam **7** animism **12** Christianity

effortful, fatiguing, herculean, laborious, strenuous, wearisome **10** burdensome, exhausting **12** backbreaking

To Jerusalem and Back
author: 10 Saul Bellow

token 4 mark, sign **5** index, proof **6** jetton, symbol **7** for show, memento, minimal, nodding, nominal, passing **8** evidence, keepsake, reminder, souvenir, symbolic **9** vestigial **10** expression, indication **11** perfunctory, remembrance, superficial, testimonial **13** manifestation

To Kill a Mockingbird
director: 14 Robert Mulligan
based on novel by: 9 Harper Lee
cast: 9 John Megna **10** Mary Badham **11** Gregory Peck **12** Philip Alford
Oscar for: 5 actor (Peck)

Tokyo
airport: 6 Haneda
capital of: 5 Japan
district: 5 Ginza **6** Keihin **7** Chiyoda **8** Yokohama **10** Marunouchi **18** Tama New Town Project
former name: 3 Edo
island: 6 Honshu
landmark: 8 Ueno Park **11** Meiji Shrine **12** National Diet **14** Imperial Palace, Kitanomaru Park **19** Komazawa Olympic Park
means: 14 Eastern capital

Tola 11 Hebrew judge

Told in the Dog Watches
author: 12 Frank T Bullen

tolerable 4 fair, so-so **7** allowed, average **8** abidable, accepted, adequate, bearable, mediocre, middling, ordinary, passable **9** allowable, endurable, innocuous, permitted **10** acceptable, admissible, fairly good, sufferable **11** commonplace, indifferent, permissible **12** run-of-the-mill **14** fair-to-middling

tolerance 7 charity **8** fairness, goodwill, patience, sympathy **9** endurance **10** compassion, sufferance **11** forbearance **13** brotherly love, fair treatment, fellow feeling, power to endure **15** lack of prejudice

tolerant 4 easy, fair, soft **7** lenient, liberal, patient, sparing **8** moderate **9** easygoing, forgiving, indulgent, unbigoted **10** charitable, forbearing, permissive **11** broad-minded, kindhearted, softhearted, sympathetic **12** unprejudiced **13** compassionate, uncomplaining, understanding

tolerate 3 let **4** bear, take **5** abide, admit, allow, brook, stand **6** endure, permit, suffer, wink at **7** indulge, stomach, undergo **8** be easy on, be soft on, sanction, submit to **9** consent to, put up with, recognize, vouchsafe

To Let
author: 14 John Galsworthy

to life
Hebrew: 7 lehayim **8** lechayim

Tolkien, J R R
author of: 9 The Hobbit **12** Silmarillion **17** The Lord of the Rings
fictional setting: 11 Middle Earth

toll 3 fee, tax **4** duty, levy, loss **6** charge, impost, tariff **7** payment, penalty, tribute, undoing **8** exaction **9** depletion, sacrifice **10** assessment, disruption, extinction **11** destruction **12** annihilation **13** extermination

Tolstoy, Leo
author of: 11 War and Peace **12** Anna Karenina, Resurrection **17** The Kreutzer Sonata **18** Death of Ivan Ilyitch

Toltec
tribe: 4 Itza

To Lucasta, Going to the Wars
author: 15 Richard Lovelace

Tolumnius
vocation: 5 augur

tom 3 cat **6** tomcat **10** male turkey

tomato 12 Lycopersicon **24** Lycopersicon lycopersicum
varieties: 4 Husk, Pear, Tree **6** Cherry **7** Currant **10** Gooseberry, Strawberry **11** Mexican husk
soup: 8 gazpacho
sauce: 6 catsup **7** ketchup

tomb 5 crypt, grave, vault **8** monument **9** mausoleum, sepulcher **11** burial place **12** resting place **13** burial chamber

tomboy 3 meg **4** girl, romp **5** rowdy **6** female, gamine, hoiden, hoyden, tomrig **8** strumpet

Tom Brown's School Days
author: 12 Thomas Hughes

tombs
god of: 6 Anubis

tomcat 3 cat, tom **9** womanizer

To-meri *see* **5** Egypt

tomfoolery 4 play **6** antics **8** drollery, nonsense **9** high jinks, horseplay, silliness **10** goofing off, skylarking **11** foolishness **12** lollygagging, monkeyshines, prankishness **13** fooling around, messing around, playing around

Tom Jones
also: **29** The History of Tom Jones Foundling
author: **13** Henry Fielding
character: **6** Square **7** Bridget, Western **8** Mrs Honor, Thwackum **9** Mrs Miller, Partridge **11** Black George, Nightingale **12** Master Blifil **13** Lady Bellaston, Sophia Western **15** Squire Allworthy
director: **14** Tony Richardson
cast: **11** Joyce Redman **12** Albert Finney, Diane Cilento, Hugh Griffith, Susannah York **14** Dame Edith Evans
score: **11** John Addison
Oscar for: **5** score **7** picture **9** direction **10** screenplay

Tomlin, Lily
real name: **14** Mary Jean Tomlin
born: **9** Detroit MI
roles: **7** Laugh-In **8** Edith Ann **9** Ernestine, Nashville **11** The Late Show **14** Moment By Moment **27** The Incredible Shrinking Woman

Tomlinson, Mary
real name of: **12** Marjorie Main

tommyrot **3** rot **4** bosh, bull, bunk, crap, tosh **5** bilge, hokum, hooey, trash **6** bunkum, drivel, humbug **7** baloney, hogwash, spinach, rubbish, twaddle **8** buncombe, claptrap, folderol, malarkey, nonsense **9** poppycock **10** applesauce, balderdash, tomfoolery **11** foolishness **12** bullfeathers, fiddle-faddle **13** horsefeathers **16** stuff-and-nonsense

tomorrow **9** the future, the morrow **11** in the future **12** in days to come **16** the day after today **17** the next generation
Spanish: **6** manana

Tompkins, Yewell
real name of: **8** Tom Ewell

Tom Sawyer
author: **9** Mark Twain
character: **8** Huck (Huckleberry) Finn, Injun Joe **9** Aunt Polly, Joe Harper **10** Muff Potter **13** Becky Thatcher

Tom Thumb the Great
author: **13** Henry Fielding

ton
abbreviation: **1** t

tone **3** hue **4** cast, lilt, mood, note, tint **5** color, pitch, shade, sound, style, tenor, tinge **6** accent, chroma, firm up, manner, soften, spirit, stress, subdue, temper **7** cadence, quality **8** attitude, harmonic, make firm, moderate, modulate, overtone, tonality **10** inflection, intonation, make supple, modulation

Tone, Franchot
real name: **27** Stanislas Pascal Franchot Tone
born: **14** Niagara Falls NY
wife: **11** Jean Wallace **12** Joan Crawford **13** Barbara Payton **15** Dolores Dorn-Heft
roles: **10** Uncle Vanya **11** Phantom Lady **13** Three Comrades **16** Advise and Consent **17** Five Graves to Cairo, Mutiny on the Bounty **23** The Lives of a Bengal Lancer

tone up **7** make fit, shape up **9** condition **10** put in shape

Tonga *see box*

tongue **3** lap **4** flap, lick, spit **5** point, shaft **6** lingua, patois, speech **7** dialect, lingula **8** language **10** promontory, vernacular, vocabulary **13** organ of speech, power of speech, style of speech
tastes: **4** salt, sour **5** sweet **6** bitter

tongue-lash **5** scold **6** berate, rail at, rebuke **7** bawl out, chew out, reprove, upbraid **8** reproach **9** castigate, reprimand **10** take to task

tongue-lashing **6** rebuke **7** censure, chiding, reproof **8** reproach, scolding **9** reprimand **10** bawling-out, chewing-out, upbraiding **11** castigation, reprobation **12** dressing-down, remonstrance

tonic **6** bracer, pickup **7** keynote **8** pick-me-up **9** analeptic, refresher, stimulant **10** invigorant **11** restorative

tonne
abbreviation: **1** t

Tono-Bungay
author: **7** H G Wells

tonsure **3** cut **4** trim **8** bald spot **11** shaven patch

too
French: **4** trop

tool *see box, p. 990*

too little **4** lack **6** dearth, scanty, scarce **7** paucity **8** scarcity, shortage **9** deficient, not enough, scantness **10** deficiency, inadequacy, inadequate **12** insufficient **13** insufficiency

Tonga
other name: **15** Friendly Islands
capital/largest city: **9** Nukualofa
others: **3** Mua, Pea **6** Neiafu **7** Haakame, Kolonga, Kolovai **8** Fuaamotu
division: **5** Vavau **6** Haapai **9** Tongatapu
government: **8** monarchy
head of state: **4** king
monetary unit: **6** paanga, seniti
island: **3** Eua, Kao, Ono **4** Kotu **5** Tofua, Vavau **6** Haapai, Lifuke, Nomuka **7** Otu Tolu **9** Tongatapu
highest point: **3** Kao
sea: **7** Pacific
people: **10** Polynesian
explorer: **4** Cook **5** Bligh **6** Tasman
king: **11** George Tupou **14** Taufaahau Tupou
missionary: **12** Shirley Baker
queen: **6** Salote
language: **6** Tongan **7** English
religion: **9** Methodist **12** Christianity **25** Wesleyan Free Church of Tonga
feature:
fabric: **4** tapa
spiritual king: **8** tui tonga

too many
French: **6** de trop

too much **4** glut **5** flood **6** excess **7** profuse, surfeit, surplus **8** fullness, overflow, plethora **9** avalanche, excessive, profusion, repletion **10** inundation, oversupply **12** overabundant **13** overabundance **14** superabundance
French: **4** trop

Toonerville Folks
creator: **11** Fontaine Fox
character: **7** skipper **13** Aunt Eppie Hogg **15** Little Scorpions, Powerful Katrina, Suitcase Simpson **20** Mickey Himself McGuire **22** Terrible Tempered Mr Bang
rode on: **7** trolley

to one side **4** over **5** aloof, apart, aside **6** aslant **14** on the sidelines

to one's liking **7** fitting **8** pleasant, pleasing, suitable **9** agreeable **10** acceptable,

tool **4** dupe, pawn **5** agent, means **6** device, medium, puppet, stooge **7** cat's-paw, machine, utensil, vehicle **8** hireling **9** apparatus, appliance, implement, mechanism **10** instrument **11** contrivance, wherewithal **12** intermediary **15** instrumentality
carpenter's: **3** adz, awl, bit, peg, saw **4** adze, nail, rasp, vise **5** auger, brace, edger, gouge, knife, lathe, plane, ruler, screw **6** bodkin, chisel, gimlet, hammer, pliers, router, sander **7** bradawl, scraper **9** hand drill, try square **11** screwdriver
cutting/shaping: **2** ax **3** adz, axe, saw **4** adze, burr, file, froe, frow, rasp **5** burin, croze, gouge, knife, plane, razor, shave, wedge **6** chisel, sander, shears, trepan **7** hatchet, scraper **8** scissors
drilling/boring: **3** awl, bit, zax **4** pick **5** chuck, drill **6** gimlet, wimble **7** bradawl **11** countersink
farmer's: **2** ax **3** axe, hoe **4** plow, rake **5** spade **6** cradle, harrow, pickax, plough, scythe, seeder, shovel, sickle, tiller, trowel **7** hayfork **9** plowshare **10** cultivator
gripping/turning: **6** pliers, wrench **11** screwdriver
holding: **4** vise **5** clamp
measuring: **4** rule **5** gauge, level **6** square **7** caliper **8** dividers **10** micrometer
mechanic's: **3** awl, zax **4** burr, file, vise **5** bevel, lathe **6** bodkin, pliers **7** bradawl, crowbar **8** calipers **9** jackscrew **11** screwdriver **12** monkey wrench
pounding/striking: **4** maul **5** punch, wedge **6** hammer, mallet

gratifying **11** appropriate, to one's taste **12** satisfactory

toot **4** blow, honk **5** binge, blare, blast, spree **6** bender **7** trumpet **8** wingding

tooth **3** cog, nib **4** barb, cusp, fang, spur, tang, tine, tusk **5** molar, point, spike, thorn **6** canine, cuspid **7** grinder, incisor **8** bicuspid, sprocket **9** serration

toothed **6** fanged, tusked **7** dentate, notched, serrate, virgate

toothsome **6** savory **8** luscious **9** delicious, palatable **10** appetizing

Toots
character in: **12** Dombey and Son
author: **7** Dickens

top **3** cap, lid, van **4** acme, apex, best, brow, cork, fore, head, lead, peak **5** chief, cover, crest, crown, excel, front, noted, outdo, upper **6** better, exceed, famous, summit, tiptop, vertex, zenith **7** eclipse, eminent, highest, notable, put over, stopper, surpass, topmost **8** complete, foremost, greatest, outshine, outstrip, pinnacle, renowned **9** paramount, principal, put a top on, transcend, uppermost, upper part **10** celebrated, first place, overshadow, preeminent

topaz
color: **4** blue **5** brown **6** yellow
source: **5** Japan **6** Brazil, Mexico, Saxony **13** Ural Mountains **18** Cairngorm Mountains
month: **8** November

Topaze
author: **12** Marcel Pagnol

topaz quartz
species: **6** quartz
color: **4** blue, pink **5** brown, green **6** sherry

toper **3** sot **4** lush, soak **5** drunk **6** boozer **7** tippler **8** drunkard **9** alcoholic **11** dispomaniac

Top Hat
director: **12** Mark Sandrich
cast: **9** Eric Blore **11** Fred Astaire **12** Ginger Rogers **14** Helen Broderick **19** Edward Everett Horton
score: **12** Irving Berlin
song: **12** Cheek to Cheek **22** Top Hat White Tie and Tails

topic **4** text **5** theme **6** thesis **7** keynote, subject

topical **5** local **6** timely **7** current, limited **9** localized, parochial **10** particular, restricted **12** contemporary

Topkapi
director: **11** Jules Dassin
cast: **12** Peter Ustinov, Robert Morley **14** Melina Mercouri **16** Maximilian Schell
setting: **8** Istanbul
Oscar for: **15** supporting actor (Ustinov)

topknot **4** comb, tuft **5** crest **9** cockscomb, headdress, headpiece

topmost **3** top **4** head **5** chief **7** highest, leading, supreme **8** foremost **9** paramount, principal, uppermost **10** preeminent

topnotch **3** ace **4** best **5** prime **6** choice, finest, tip-top **7** supreme **8** superior, very fine **9** excellent, first-rate, nonpareil, unequaled, unrivaled **10** preeminent **11** outstanding, unsurpassed **12** incomparable, unparalleled

top of the head **4** dome, pate **5** crown **6** noggin, noodle

Topper
director: **13** Norman Z McLeod
based on novel by: **11** Thorne Smith
cast: **9** Cary Grant **11** Alan Mowbray, Billie Burke, Hedda Hopper, Roland Young **16** Constance Bennett
sequel: **13** Topper Returns **16** Topper Takes a Trip

topple **4** fall **5** crush, quash, quell, smash, upset **6** defeat, sprawl, tumble **7** abolish, shatter, tip over **8** fall over, overcome, overturn, turn over, vanquish **9** bring down, overpower, overthrow **12** pitch forward

tops **4** aces, A-one, fine **5** great, prime, super, swell **6** choice, grade-A, superb, tiptop **7** capital **8** peerless, sterling, superior, terrific, topnotch **9** excellent, first-rate, marvelous, matchless, superfine, wonderful **10** first-class, inimitable, out-of-sight, tremendous **11** outstanding, superlative **12** incomparable **13** extraordinary

top-secret **5** privy **7** private **8** eyes-only, hush-hush **12** confidential

topsoil **4** dirt, loam **5** earth

Topsy
character in: **14** Uncle Tom's Cabin
author: **5** Stowe

topsy-turvy **5** messy **6** untidy **7** chaotic **8** confused, inverted, reversed **9** confusing, inside out **10** disorderly, upside down **11** disarranged, wrong side up **12** disorganized

Torah **10** law of Moses

torch **5** brand **7** cresset **8** arsonist, flambeau **9** firebrand **9** set fire to **10** flashlight

torment **3** nag, vex **4** bane, pain, rack **5** agony, annoy, curse, worry **6** harass, harrow, misery, pester, plague **7** afflict, agonize, anguish, despair, scourge, torture, trouble **8** distress, irritate **9** annoyance, persecute, suffering **10** irritation

tormenter **5** bully, tease **6** despot, tyrant **7** coercer **9** oppressor **10** browbeater **11** intimidator

tormenting **7** painful, racking **9** agonizing, torturous **10** unbearable **11** unendurable **12** excruciating, insufferable

torn **4** rent, slit **5** split **6** ragged, ripped **8** ruptured, shredded **9** unraveled

tornado **4** wind **5** storm **6** funnel, squall, vortex **7** cyclone, twister, typhoon **8** outburst **9** hurricane, whirlwind, windstorm **10** waterspout **12** thunderstorm
belt: **7** Midwest
cloud: **4** tuba

torn apart **4** rent **6** ripped **7** asunder **8** in pieces, in shreds, shredded

toro **4** bull

Toronto
baseball team: **8** Blue Jays
bay: **6** Humber
football team: **9** Argonauts
former name: **4** York
harbor: **5** Inner
hockey team: **10** Maple Leafs
lake: **7** Ontario
landmark: **7** CN Tower **12** Ontario Place, O'Keefe Centre **13** Dufferin Grove **14** Dominion Centre **15** Roy Thompson Hall **16** Maple Leaf Stadium, St Lawrence Centre **17** Commerce Court West **18** Royal Ontario Museum **20** Nathan Phillips Square
park: **7** Chorley, Stanley, Trinity **8** Winthrow **9** Cedarvale **12** Center Island **16** Winston Churchill
street: **5** Yonge
university: **4** York

Torosaurus
type: **8** dinosaur **10** ceratopsid

torpedo **4** sink **5** wreck **7** destroy, missile, scuttle **9** explosive **10** projectile

torpedo (marine)
invented by: **6** Fulton

torpid **4** dull, lazy **5** inert **6** drowsy, sleepy **7** dormant, languid, passive **8** inactive, indolent, listless, sluggish **9** apathetic, lethargic, somnolent **10** half asleep, languorous, slow-moving, spiritless **12** slow-thinking **13** lackadaisical

torpor, torpidity **6** apathy **7** inertia, languor **8** dullness, laziness, lethargy **9** indolence, lassitude **10** drowsiness, inactivity, sleepiness, somnolence **11** languidness, passiveness **12** listlessness, sluggishness

torrent **4** gush, rain, rush **5** burst, flood, salvo **6** deluge, rapids, stream, volley **7** barrage, cascade, Niagara **8** cataract, downpour, effusion, eruption, outburst **9** discharge, heavy rain, rapid flow, waterfall **10** cloudburst, outpouring, white water

Torrey, John
field: **6** botany
developed: **16** botanical library

Torricelli, Evangelista
nationality: **7** Italian
discovered concept leading to development of: **9** barometer

torrid **3** hot **4** sexy **5** fiery **6** ardent, erotic, fervid, heated, sexual, sultry **7** amorous, boiling, burning, excited, fervent, intense, lustful **8** broiling, desirous, parching, sizzling, spirited, tropical, vehement **9** hot and dry, scorching **10** passionate, sweltering **11** hot and heavy, impassioned

torte **4** cake **7** dessert **9** layer cake

tortilla **7** tostada **8** corncake **11** Mexican cake
griddle: **5** comal

Tortilla Flat
author: **13** John Steinbeck

tortuous **4** bent **5** snaky **6** spiral, zigzag **7** crooked, devious, sinuous, turning, winding, wriggly **8** indirect, involved, twisting, wrongful **9** ambiguous **10** circuitous, convoluted, meandering, roundabout, serpentine **11** complicated **12** full of curves, hard to follow, labyrinthine

tortuousness **9** sinuosity **11** indirection, sinuousness **12** convolutions **14** circuitousness

torture **4** pain, rack **5** abuse, agony, prick, smite, trial, wring **6** harrow, ordeal **7** anguish, cruelty, torment **8** distress, maltreat, mistreat **9** brutality, suffering **10** infliction, punishment **11** tribulation **12** put to the rack

torturous **5** cruel **7** galling, irksome, painful, racking **8** annoying **9** agonizing, anguished, harrowing, miserable, tormented, torturing **10** anguishing, distressed, tormenting, unpleasant **11** distressful, distressing **12** disagreeable, excruciating

tory **8** loyalist, royalist **12** conservative

Tosca
opera by: **7** Puccini
character: **7** Scarpia **9** Angelotti **16** Mario Cavaradossi

To Sir With Love
director: **12** James Clavell
cast: **4** Lulu **10** Judy Geeson **11** Suzy Kendall **13** Sidney Poitier **16** Christian Roberts
setting: **6** London

toss **3** lob **4** cast, flip, hurl, jerk, rock, roll, sway **5** churn, fling, heave, pitch, shake, sling, throw **6** joggle, let fly, propel, tumble, wiggle, writhe **7** agitate, flounce, wriggle **8** flourish, undulate **9** oscillate

toss about **4** roil **5** bandy **6** jostle, jounce

toss back and forth **5** bandy **8** exchange

total **3** add, sum **4** full **5** add up, gross, sheer, solid, sum up, utter, whole **6** entire, figure, reckon, tote up **7** add up to, compute, perfect, total up **8** absolute, combined, complete, entirety, figure up, integral, outright, sum total, sweeping, thorough, totality **9** aggregate, calculate, downright, out-and-out, unlimited, wholesale **10** full amount, undisputed, unmodified **11** unqualified, whole amount **13** comprehensive, unconditional

totaling **8** addition, coming to **9** reckoning **10** adding up to

totalitarian **7** fascist **8** despotic **9** fascistic, tyrannous **10** autocratic, tyrannical **11** dictatorial **12** undemocratic **16** unrepresentative

totally **7** solidly, utterly **8** entirely **9** downright, out-and-out, perfectly **10** absolutely, completely, thoroughly, throughout **15** unconditionally **18** from beginning to end **20** without qualification

tote **3** lug **4** bear, cart, drag, haul, move, pack, pull **5** carry, fetch **6** convey **7** schlepp **9** transport

to the city and the world
Latin: **10** urbi et orbi
form of address used on: **10** papal bulls

to the four winds **7** all over **10** everywhere, far and wide **26** to the four corners of the world

to the letter **5** exact, right **7** correct, precise **8** accurate, explicit, specific **9** on the nose

To the Lighthouse
author: **13** Virginia Woolf
character: **4** Prue **5** James **7** Camilla **8** Mr Ramsey **9** Mr Tansley, Mrs Ramsey **11** Lily Briscoe **12** Mr Carmichael

To the North
author: **14** Elizabeth Bowen

to the point **6** direct **7** apropos, germane **8** explicit, relevant **9** pertinent **12** to the purpose

to the rear **3** aft **4** back **5** abaft **6** astern, behind **8** backward, rearward **9** backwards, sternward **10** to the stern **14** toward the stern

to the stern **6** astern, behind **8** rearward **9** sternward **10** to the stern

to the word
Latin: **8** ad verbum

to this extent
Latin: **8** quoad hoc

Toto
dog in: **13** The Wizard of Oz
author: **4** Baum

totter **4** reel, rock, sway **5** lurch, shake, waver **6** falter, teeter, waddle, wobble **7** shuffle, stagger, stumble **9** oscillate, vacillate

tottering **5** shaky **6** wobbly **7** rickety, shaking **8** insecure, topheavy, unstable, unsteady, wobbling **9** doddering, quivering, trembling **10** ramshackle, staggering

Toucan
constellation of: **6** Tucana

touch ***see box***

touched **3** mad **4** daft, felt, nuts **5** crazy, moved, nutty **6** insane, joined **7** abutted, cracked, handled **8** demented, deranged, unhinged **10** unbalanced **12** mad as a hatter **13** off one's rocker, out of one's head **14** off one's trolley **15** mad as a March hare

Touchett, Ralph
character in: **18** The Portrait of a Lady
author: **5** James

touching **3** sad **6** moving, tender **7** pitiful **8** dramatic, pathetic, poignant, stirring **9** affecting, emotional, heartfelt, saddening, sorrowful **11** distressing, sentimental **12** heartrending **13** heartbreaking

touch me not
Latin: **13** noli me tangere

Touch of Evil
director: **11** Orson Welles
cast: **10** Janet Leigh, Ray Collins **11** Joanna Moore, Orson Welles, Zsa Zsa Gabor **12** Akim Tamiroff, Dennis Weaver **13** Joseph Calleia **14** Charlton Heston
cameo: **15** Marlene Dietrich **19** Mercedes McCambridge

touch off **5** shoot **6** set off **7** explode, fire off, trigger **8** activate, detonate **9** discharge

touch on **4** pose **6** broach, submit **7** advance, bring up, mention, propose, suggest **9** introduce

touchstone **4** norm, rule **5** basis, gauge, guide, model, proof **7** example, measure, pattern **8** standard **9** benchmark, criterion, guideline, precedent, principle, yardstick

Touchstone
character in: **11** As You Like It
author: **11** Shakespeare

touch upon **7** apply to, concern, mention, refer to **8** allude to, bear upon, relate to **9** appertain

touchy **5** cross, huffy, surly, testy **6** bitter, crabby, grumpy **7** awkward, fragile, grouchy, peevish, waspish **8** captious, critical, delicate, petulant, snappish, ticklish **9** concerned, difficult, irascible, irritable, querulous, resentful, sensitive **10** precarious **11** thinskinned **12** cantankerous **13** quick-tempered

tough **4** cold, firm, hard, hood, lout, mean, punk, wily **5** bully, cagey, canny, cruel, hardy, rigid, rough, rowdy, solid, stern **6** brutal, crafty, dogged, knotty, mulish, rugged, savage, strict, strong, sturdy, thorny, trying **7** adamant, arduous, callous, complex, durable, hoodlum, inhuman, irksome, lasting, onerous, ruffian, vicious **8** baffling, barbaric, enduring, exacting, grievous, hooligan, involved, leathery, obdurate, perverse, pitiless, puzzling, ruthless, stubborn, ticklish, toilsome **9** barbarian, confusing, difficult, enigmatic, heartless, heavy-duty, intricate, laborious, obstinate, pigheaded, resistant, roughneck, strenuous, unbending, unfeeling **10** bullheaded, delinquent, exhausting, formidable, hardheaded, inflexible, perplexing, unyielding **11** bewildering, calculating, cold-blooded, complicated, hardhearted, hard-to-solve, infrangible, insensitive,

touch **3** art, bit, paw, pet, rub, use **4** abut, cite, dash, feel, fire, form, gift, hand, hint, join, meet, melt, move, note, stir, sway, tint, work **5** equal, flair, match, pinch, rival, rouse, skill, smack, speck, style, taste, thumb, tinge, trace, unite **6** adjoin, affect, arouse, border, broach, caress, excite, finger, finish, fondle, handle, hint at, manner, method, pawing, polish, sadden, soften, strike, stroke, thrill **7** concern, consume, contact, feeling, finesse, impress, inflame, inspire, mastery, mention, quality, refer to, soupcon, surface, texture, utilize **8** allude to, artistry, bear upon, come near, come up to, converge, deal with, deftness, fineness, fondling, handling, inspirit, resort to, thumbing **9** awareness, direction, electrify, fingering, influence, palpation, pertain to, suspicion, technique **10** adroitness, intimation, manipulate, perception, sprinkling, suggestion, virtuosity **11** be in contact, compare with, familiarity, guiding hand, realization **12** acquaintance, manipulation **13** communication, comprehension, understanding troublesome **12** bloodthirsty, impenetrable **13** unsympathetic **14** uncompromising

toughen **4** firm **5** inure, steel **6** firm up, harden, season, temper **7** fortify, stiffen **8** accustom **9** acclimate, habituate **10** discipline, strengthen **11** acclimatize

Toulouse-Lautrec, Henri Marie Raymond de
born: **4** Albi **6** France **8** Albigois
artwork: **7** Friends **13** The Inspection **16** At the Moulin Rouge **24** Au Salon de la Rue des Moulins **27** Jane Avril at the Jardin de Paris **29** Cirque Fernando The Equestrienne **29** In the Parlor at the Rue des Moulins **29** The English Girl at Le Star Le Havre **30** La Goulue Entering the Moulin Rouge

toupee **3** rug, wig **6** carpet, peruke **7** periwig **9** hairpiece

tour **4** trek, trip **5** jaunt, visit **6** junket, safari, travel, voyage **7** inspect, journey **8** sightsee **9** excursion, itinerary

tourist **7** pilgrim, tripper, voyager **8** traveler, vagabond, wanderer, wayfarer **9** journeyer, sightseer **10** rubberneck **12** excursionist, globetrotter

tourmaline
color: **3** red **4** blue, pink **5** green

tournament **4** game **5** event, match **7** contest, rivalry, tourney **11** competition

Tourneur, Cyril
author of: **19** The Revenger's Tragedy

tourney **4** game **5** event, match **7** contest, rivalry **10** tournament **11** competition

tousled **5** messy **6** mussed, untidy **7** rumpled, tangled, unkempt **8** mussed-up, uncombed **10** disheveled, disordered

tout **4** plug, push **5** boost, exalt, extol, vaunt **6** praise, talk up **7** acclaim, commend, glorify, promote, tipster **8** ballyhoo, eulogize, give a tip **9** advertise, brag about, celebrate, publicize, recommend **10** aggrandize, noise about

tout a fait **8** entirely
literally: **12** wholly to fact

tout a l'heure **7** just now **8** very soon **9** presently **14** just a moment ago
literally: **15** wholly to the hour

tout de suite **6** at once **11** immediately
literally: **19** wholly consecutively

tout ensemble **11** all together

tout le monde **8** everyone **9** everybody **13** the whole world

tovarich **7** comrade

tow **3** lug **4** drag, draw, haul, lift, pull **5** hoist, trail

toward the end
Latin: **5** ad fin

toward the front **5** ahead **6** before **7** forward **9** to the fore **13** in the vanguard **14** in the forefront

toward the rear **4** back **6** astern **8** backward, rearward **9** sternward

toward the stern **6** astern **8** rearward **9** sternward **10** to the stern

tower **4** keep, loom, rock, soar **5** mount, outdo, spire, surge **6** ascend, belfry, castle, column, exceed, pillar, refuge, turret **7** bulwark, eclipse, minaret, obelisk, overtop, shoot up, steeple, surpass **8** mainstay, outclass, outshine, overhang, rise high **9** bell tower, rise above, transcend **10** foundation, overshadow, skyscraper, stronghold, wellspring **12** fountainhead

towering **4** high, tall **5** lofty **6** alpine **7** soaring, sublime, supreme **8** dominant, foremost, mounting, peerless, snowclad, superior **9** ascending, matchless, paramount, principal, unequaled, unmatched, unrivaled **10** cloud-swept, preeminent, surpassing, unexcelled **11** cloud-capped, overhanging **12** incomparable, second to none, transcendent, unparalleled **13** extraordinary

Tower of London, The
author: **24** William Harrison Ainsworth

tower over **5** dwarf **7** surpass **8** dominate **9** rise above

town **4** burg, city **6** hamlet, parish **7** borough, village **9** citizenry, residents **10** settlement **11** inhabitants, townspeople **12** municipality

Town, The
author: **13** Conrad Richter

Townes, Charles Hard
field: **7** physics
invented: **5** maser
awarded: **10** Nobel Prize

town hall
German: **7** Rathaus

town house **8** row house **10** pied-a-terre **13** city residence

township **4** town **7** village **11** subdivision **12** municipality

Toxeus
father: **6** Oeneus
mother: **7** Althaea
killed by: **6** Oeneus

toxic **5** fatal **6** deadly, lethal, mortal **7** noxious **8** poisoned, venomous **9** poisonous, unhealthy **10** pernicious

toxin **4** bane **5** venom **6** poison **8** pathogen

toy **4** play, tiny **5** dally, pygmy, sport **6** bantam, bauble, fiddle, gadget, gewgaw, little, midget, trifle **7** dwarfed, for play, stunted, trinket **8** gimcrack **9** miniature, plaything, smallsize **10** diminutive, smallscale **11** Lilliputian

Toy Bulldog
nickname of: **12** Mickey Walker

Toynbee, Arnold
author of: **15** A Study of History

to your health
French: **11** a votre sante

toy with **8** play with **9** flirt with **10** trifle with **16** amuse oneself with

trace **3** bit, jot, map **4** draw, drop, find, hint, hunt, iota, mark, seek, sign **5** dig up, relic, shade, tinge, token, touch, track, trail **6** depict, flavor, trifle **7** diagram, hunt for, look for, mark out, nose out, outline, remains, uncover, unearth, vestige **8** describe, discover, draw over, evidence **9** delineate, ferret out, footprint, light upon, little bit, search for, suspicion, track down **10** come across, indication, suggestion **11** small amount

trace to **6** credit **7** ascribe **8** charge to **9** attribute

Trachiniae
author: **9** Sophocles
characters: **4** Iole **6** Hyllus, Nessus **8** Deianira, Heracles

track **3** way **4** mark, path, rail, sign, tack **5** dirty, route, scent, spoor, trace, trail **6** course, follow **9** footprint, guide rail

track and field *see box, p. 994*

tract **3** lot **4** area, plot, zone **5** essay **6** parcel, region **7** booklet, expanse, leaflet,

track and field
athlete: **7** Jim Ryun, Ray Ewry **8** Al Oerter, Lee Evans, Zola Budd **9** Bob Beamon, Carl Lewis, Henry Rono, Jim Thorpe **10** Ben Johnson, Bob Mathias, Bob Seagren, Edwin Moses, Grete Waitz, James Hines, Jesse Owens, John Carlos, Lasse Viren, Mac Wilkins, Paavo Nurmi, Peter Snell, Steve Ovett, Wyomia Tyus **11** Bill Rodgers, Bruce Jenner, Marty Liouri, David Wottle, Dick Fosbury, Doug Padilla, Emil Zatopek, Joni Huntley, Ralph Boston, Randy Matson, Tommie Smith **12** Dwight Stones, Frank Shorter, Harvey Glance, Jay Silvester, Kathy Hammond, Maren Seidler, Rafer Johnson, Sebastian Coe, Willie B White, Wilma Rudolph **13** Allan Feurbach, Arnie Robinson, Janice Merrill, Kathy McMillan, Kipchoge Keino, Rodney Milburn, Ronny Ray Smith, Rosalyn Bryant, William Toomey **14** Alberto Salazar, Francie Larrieu, Roger Bannister **15** Martha Rae Watson, Renaldo Nehemiah, Willie Davenport **16** Madeleine Manning, Mary Decker Slaney, Richard Wohlhuter, Steve Prefontaine **17** Alberto Juantoreno **18** Jackie Joyner-Kersee, Stephanie Hightower **21** Babe Didrikson Zaharias **22** Florence Griffith-Joyner

quarter, stretch **8** brochure, district, pamphlet, treatise **9** monograph, territory **12** disquisition

tractable **4** tame **6** docile **8** amenable, obedient, yielding **9** compliant, teachable, trainable **10** governable, manageable, submissive **12** controllable, easy to manage **13** easy to control

tractate **8** treatise **9** discourse, monograph **12** disquisition, dissertation

Tracy, Spencer
born: **11** Milwaukee WI
costar: **16** Katharine Hepburn
roles: **7** Desk Set **8** Adam's Rib, Boys' Town (Oscar) **10** Pat and Mike **12** San Francisco, Tortilla Flat **13** The Last Hurrah **14** Cass Timberlane, Inherit the Wind, Woman of the Year **15** State of the Union **16** Father of the Bride, Keeper of the Flame **17** Bad Day at Black Rock **18** Captains Courageous (Oscar), The Old Man and the Sea **19** Judgment at Nuremberg **23** Guess Who's Coming to Dinner

Traddles
character in: **16** David Copperfield
author: **7** Dickens

trade **3** buy **4** deal, line, shop, swap **5** craft **6** barter, buyers **7** calling, patrons, pursuit **8** business, commerce, exchange, shoppers, vocation **9** clientele, customers, patronize **10** buy and sell, do business, employment, handicraft, line of work, occupation, profession **12** transactions **13** merchandising **16** business dealings, buying and selling

trade commodity **5** goods, wares

trademark **6** emblem **7** feature **8** property **9** specialty **11** peculiarity **14** characteristic

trade off **4** swap **5** trade **6** barter **8** exchange

trader **6** dealer, monger, seller **7** drummer **8** merchant, retailer **10** shopkeeper, trafficker, wholesaler **11** salesperson, storekeeper **12** merchandiser, tradesperson **14** businessperson

tradesman **6** dealer, seller **8** merchant, retailer **9** craftsman **10** shopkeeper **11** storekeeper

Trade Wind
author: **6** M M Kaye

tradition **4** lore, myth, saga, tale **5** habit, usage **6** custom, legend **8** folklore, practice **10** convention **12** superstition

traditional **3** old **5** fixed, usual **7** typical **8** habitual, historic **9** ancestral, customary **10** accustomed, inveterate **11** established **12** acknowledged, conventional

traduce **5** abuse, libel, smear, sully **6** defame, malign, vilify **7** run down, slander **8** backbite, bad-mouth, besmirch **9** deprecate, disparage **10** calumniate

traffic **4** cars, deal **5** buses, ships, trade **6** barter, doings, planes, riders, trains, trucks **7** bootleg, contact, freight, smuggle **8** business, commerce, dealings, exchange, tourists, voyagers **9** commuters, relations, smuggling, travelers **10** buy and sell, enterprise, passengers **11** bootlegging, intercourse, pedestrians, proceedings **12** transactions, vacationists **13** excursionists

tragedy **3** woe **4** blow **5** grief **6** misery, sorrow **7** anguish, setback **8** accident, calamity, disaster, reversal, sad thing **9** heartache **10** affliction, heartbreak **11** catastrophe

tragic **3** sad **4** dire **5** awful, fatal **6** deadly, dreary, woeful **7** piteous, pitiful, ruinous, serious, unhappy **8** dramatic, dreadful, grievous, horrible, mournful, pathetic, pitiable, shocking, terrible **9** appalling, frightful **10** calamitous, deplorable, disastrous, lamentable **11** destructive, devastating, unfortunate **12** catastrophic **13** heartbreaking

trail **3** dog, tow, way **4** drag, draw, fall, flow, hunt, mark, path, poke, sign, tail **5** float, hound, scent, spoor, trace, track **6** be down, course, dangle, dawdle, follow, lessen, shrink, stream **7** dwindle, pathway, subside **8** decrease, diminish, footpath, grow weak, hand down, peter out, taper off **9** drag along, grow faint, grow small, lag behind **10** bridle path, drag behind, footprints, move slowly **11** beaten track **14** bring up the rear

trailblazers **7** leaders **8** pioneers **10** avant-garde, innovators **11** forerunners, originators, tastemakers **12** trendsetters

train **2** el **3** aim, set **4** line **5** break, chain, drill, focus, level, point, queue, sight, teach, trail, tutor **6** column, direct, escort, school, series, subway **7** caravan, cortege, educate, prepare, retinue **8** elevated, exercise, instruct, practice, rehearse, sequence **9** afterpart, appendage, entourage, followers **10** attendants, discipline, get in shape, procession, succession **11** bring to bear, domesticate, progression **12** continuation

Train, The
director: **17** John Frankenheimer
cast: **10** Albert Remy **11** Michel Simon **12** Jeanne

Moreau, Paul Scofield
13 Burt Lancaster

trained **4** able **6** expert, master **7** capable, skilled **8** schooled, seasoned **9** competent, qualified **11** experienced **12** accomplished

trainee **4** boot **5** cadet **6** rookie **7** private, rookie, student **9** greenhorn **10** apprentice

trainer **5** coach, tutor **7** teacher **16** athletic director

training **5** drill **8** coaching, drilling, practice, teaching **9** education, schooling **10** discipline **11** preparation **14** apprenticeship, indoctrination

traipse **3** gad **4** roam, walk **5** range, tramp, tread **6** stroll, trapes, wander **7** meander, saunter **8** gadabout **9** gallivant

trait **4** mark **5** quirk **7** earmark, feature, quality **8** hallmark **9** attribute, mannerism **11** peculiarity **12** idiosyncracy **14** characteristic

traitor **3** rat **5** Judas, rebel **6** ratter **7** ratfink, serpent **8** apostate, betrayer, deceiver, deserter, mutineer, quisling, renegade, turncoat **9** hypocrite **11** false friend **12** double-dealer **13** double-crosser, revolutionary **14** fifth columnist **15** snake in the grass **20** wolf in sheep's clothing

traitorous **5** false **7** corrupt **8** disloyal, renegade **9** betraying, faithless **10** perfidious, treasonous, unfaithful **11** treacherous

tramp **3** bum **4** hike, hobo, roam, rove, slog, trek, walk **5** march, prowl, stamp, stomp **6** ramble, trudge, wander **7** floater, meander, traipse, trample, vagrant **8** derelict **9** gallivant, itinerant **10** panhandler **11** perambulate, peregrinate **15** knight-of-the-road

trample **5** crush, stamp, stomp **6** squash **7** flatten, run over **14** grind under foot **15** step heavily upon

trance **4** coma, daze **5** dream, spell **6** stupor, vision **7** reverie **8** daydream, hypnosis **9** pipe dream **10** absorption, brown study **11** abstraction **12** sleepwalking **13** concentration, preoccupation, woolgathering

tranquil **4** calm, cool, mild **5** quiet, still **6** gentle, placid, serene **7** halcyon, restful **8** composed, peaceful **9** unexcited, unruffled **11** undisturbed, unperturbed **13** self-possessed

tranquility **4** calm, hush **5** peace, quiet **6** repose **7** concord, harmony **8** quietude, serenity **9** composure, placidity, stillness **11** restfulness **12** peacefulness

tranquilize **4** calm, drug, lull **5** allay, quiet, relax, still **6** becalm, pacify, sedate, settle, soothe **7** appease, assuage **9** alleviate

transact **2** do **5** exact **6** handle, manage, settle **7** achieve, carry on, conduct, execute, perform **8** carry out, exercise **9** discharge **10** accomplish, take care of **12** carry through

transaction **4** deal **6** affair **7** bargain, dealing, venture **8** exchange **9** operation **10** enterprise, settlement **11** negotiation **15** business dealing, piece of business

transcend **5** excel, outdo **6** exceed **7** eclipse, outrank, surpass **8** go beyond, outrival, outshine, outstrip, overleap, overstep, surmount **9** rise above **10** overshadow **11** outdistance

transcendence **5** merit **8** eminence **9** exceeding, greatness **10** exaltation, excellence, surpassing **11** distinction, preeminence, superiority

transcendental **5** great **6** mental **7** supreme, unusual **8** elevated, peerless, superior, uncommon **9** exceeding, intuitive, matchless, spiritual, unequaled, unrivaled **10** surpassing **11** unsurpassed **12** incomparable, metaphysical **13** extraordinary

transfer **4** cede, deed, move, send **5** bring, carry, shift **6** change, convey, moving, remove **7** consign, deeding, removal, sending **8** bringing, carrying, hand over, make over, relegate, relocate, shifting, shipment, transmit, turn over **9** conveying, transport **10** delivering, relegation, relocating, relocation **11** consignment, transmittal **12** transporting **14** transportation

transferable **8** catching **10** contagious, infectious **12** communicable **13** transmissible, transmittable

transferal **8** delivery, transfer **10** giving over **11** handing over, transmittal **12** transmission

transference **5** shift **6** change **7** passage, removal **9** transport **11** transmittal **12** dislodgement, displacement, transmission **13** transmittance

transfiguration **10** conversion **13** metamorphosis, transmutation **14** transformation

transfigure **6** change **9** transform **12** metamorphose

transfix **3** pin **4** hold, stab, stun **5** rivet, spear, spike, stick **6** absorb, impale, pierce, skewer **7** astound, bewitch, enchant, engross, fix fast, terrify **8** astonish, hold rapt, intrigue **9** captivate, fascinate, hypnotize, mesmerize, penetrate, spellbind **10** run through

transform **4** turn **5** alter **6** change, recast, remold **7** convert, remodel **8** make over **9** refurbish, transmute **11** reconstruct, transfigure **12** metamorphose, transmogrify

transformation **6** change **9** restyling **10** alteration, conversion, remodeling **13** metamorphosis, transmutation **15** transfiguration

transgress **3** err, sin **4** slip **5** break, cross, fault, lapse, wrong **6** exceed, impose, offend **7** digress, infract, violate **8** infringe, trespass

transgression **3** sin **5** crime, error, lapse, wrong **6** breach **7** misdeed, offense **8** evil deed, iniquity, trespass **9** violation **10** immorality, infraction, wrongdoing **11** lawbreaking **12** encroachment, infringement, overstepping **13** contravention

transgressor **5** felon **6** sinner **7** culprit **8** criminal, evildoer, offender, violator **9** miscreant, wrongdoer **10** lawbreaker, malefactor, trespasser

transience **7** brevity **11** evanescence **12** ephemerality, impermanence

transient **5** brief **7** passing **8** fleeting, soon past, temporal **9** ephemeral, momentary, short-term, temporary **10** evanescent, perishable, short-lived, transitory, unenduring **11** impermanent **14** passing through **24** here today and gone tomorrow

transistor
invented by: **7** Bardeen **8** Brattain, Shockley

transition **4** jump, leap **6** change **7** passage, passing **8** shifting **9** gradation, variation **10** alteration, changeover, conversion, graduation **11** progression **13** transmutation **14** transformation

transitory **5** brief **7** passing **8** fleeting, fugitive **9** ephemeral, temporary, transient **10** evanescent, not lasting, short-lived, unenduring **11** impermanent **24** here today and gone tomorrow

translate **4** turn **5** alter, apply **6** change, decode, recast, render, reword **7** clarify, convert, explain **8** decipher, rephrase, simplify, spell out **9** elucidate, interpret, make clear, transform, transmute **10** paraphrase

translucence **7** clarity **8** lucidity **10** luminosity **12** transparency **16** semi-transparency

translucent **8** pellucid **10** semiopaque, translucid **15** semitransparent

transmissible **8** catching **10** contagious, infectious **12** communicable, transferable **13** transmittable

transmission **4** note **7** message, passage, passing, sending **8** delivery, dispatch, transfer **9** broadcast **10** conveyance, forwarding, remittance **11** handing over, transmittal **12** transference, transferring **13** communication **14** transportation

transmit **4** send, ship **5** carry, issue, relay, remit **6** convey, pass on, spread **7** deliver, forward **8** dispatch, televise, transfer **9** broadcast **11** communicate, disseminate

transmittable **8** catching **10** contagious, infectious **12** communicable, transferable

transmittal **7** sending **8** delivery, transfer **10** giving over, transferal **11** handing over **12** transmission

transmutation **6** change **10** conversion **13** metamorphosis **14** transformation **15** transfiguration

transmute **5** alter **6** change **7** convert **9** transform **12** metamorphose

transparency **6** purity **7** clarity **8** lucidity **9** clearness, sheerness **11** obviousness **14** diaphanousness

transparent **4** thin **5** clear, gauzy, lucid, plain, sheer **6** glassy, limpid, patent **7** evident, obvious, visible **8** apparent, clear-cut, distinct, explicit, manifest, palpable, peekaboo, pellucid **10** diaphanous, see-through **11** perceptible, self-evident, translucent, unambiguous, unequivocal **12** crystal-clear, unmistakable

transpire **5** arise, occur **6** appear, befall, chance, crop up, evolve, happen, turn up **7** come out, leak out **9** be met with, eventuate, take place **10** be revealed, come to pass, make public **11** become known, be disclosed, come to light, show its face

transplant **5** graft, repot, shift **7** replant **8** displace, relocate, resettle, transfer **9** transport, transpose

transport **3** bus, lug **4** bear, cart, lift, move, send, ship, take, tote **5** bring, carry, charm, fetch, train, truck **6** convey, moving, remove, thrill **7** bearing, bewitch, carting, delight, deliver, enchant, freight, removal, sending, vehicle **8** airplane, carrying, delivery, dispatch, enthrall, entrance, shipment, shipping, transfer, transmit, trucking **9** captivate, cargo ship, carry away, conveying, electrify, enrapture, freighter, overpower **10** cargo plane, conveyance **12** freight train

transportation **7** cartage, haulage, portage, removal, transit **8** delivery, dispatch, movement, shipment **9** transport **10** conveyance, transferal **12** transference, transmission **13** transmittance

transported **5** moved **6** lifted **7** charmed **8** ecstatic, thrilled, uplifted **9** bewitched, entranced **10** captivated, enthralled **11** carried away, electrified **13** beside oneself

transverse **5** cross **6** across **7** athwart, oblique, transom **8** crossbar, crossing, diagonal, traverse **9** crosswise **10** crosspiece, horizontal

transversely **9** crossways, crosswise, laterally

trap **3** net, pit **4** lure, ploy, ruse, seal, stop, wile **5** catch, feint, snare, trick **6** ambush, device, enmesh, entrap, lock in **7** ensnare, pitfall, springe **8** artifice, entangle, hold back, hunt down, maneuver **9** booby trap, stratagem **11** machination **16** compartmentalize

trappings **4** garb, gear **5** array, dress **6** attire, outfit, things **7** apparel, clothes, costume, effects, raiment, vesture **8** adjuncts, clothing, fittings **9** ornaments, trimmings **10** adornments, habiliment, investment **11** decorations **13** accoutrements, paraphernalia **14** embellishments

trash **3** rot **4** bums, crap, junk, scum **5** dregs, dross, tripe, waste **6** debris, drivel, idlers, litter, refuse, rubble, tramps **7** garbage, hogwash, loafers, residue, rubbish, twaddle **8** castoffs, leavings, nonsense, riffraff **9** poppycock, sweepings **10** balderdash **11** foolishness, ne'er-do-wells, odds and ends **15** good-for-nothings, unsavory element

trashy **4** vile **5** cheap, inane, junky, tacky **6** flashy, flimsy **7** rubbish, trivial, useless **8** riffraff, trumpery, wasteful **9** worthless **13** insignificant

trauma **4** hurt **5** shock, wound **6** injury, stress

travail **4** pain, toil **5** labor, worry **6** strain, stress **7** anguish **8** delivery, distress, drudgery, exertion, hard work, hardship **9** suffering **10** birth pains, childbirth, labor pains **11** parturition **12** accouchement

travel **2** go **4** be on, move, roam, rove, sail, tour, trek, wend **5** cross, drive, range, visit **6** cruise, junket, voyage, wander **7** journey, proceed **8** pass over, progress, sightsee, traverse **9** globetrot, hitchhike, take a trip **11** pass through, press onward

traveler **5** gypsy, nomad, rover **7** drummer, migrant, pilgrim, tourist, trekker, tripper, voyager **8** vagabond, wanderer, wayfarer **9** itinerant, journeyer, sightseer **10** vacationer **12** excursionist, globetrotter

Traveller Without Luggage
author: **11** Jean Anouilh

Travels with a Donkey
author: **20** Robert Louis Stevenson
donkey: **9** Modestine

Travels with My Aunt
author: **12** Graham Greene

travel through **2** do **5** cover, cross, visit **8** traverse **9** negotiate **11** pass through

traverse **4** span **5** cross **6** bridge, travel **8** go across, move over, overpass **9** cross over, cut across, intersect, move along, negotiate, reach over **10** extend over, run through, travel over **11** move through, pass through, reach across

travesty **4** sham **5** farce, spoof **6** parody, satire **7** lampoon, mockery, takeoff **8** disgrace **9** burlesque **10** caricature, distortion, perversion **17** misrepresentation

Traviata, La
also: **9** The Misled **23** The Woman Who Was Led Astray
opera by: **5** Verdi
based on a story by: **14** Alexandre Dumas (fils)
called: **7** Camille **17** La Dame aux Camelias
character: **8** Violetta **14** Alfredo Germont

Travolta, John
born: **11** Englewood NJ
roles: **6** Carrie, Grease **10** Tony Manero **11** Urban Cowboy **12** Staying Alive **14** Moment By Moment **15** Vinnie Barbarino **17** Welcome Back Kotter **18** Saturday Night Fever

trawl **3** net **4** drag, fish, haul, line **5** seine, troll **6** dredge **7** dragnet

Treacher, Arthur
real name: **11** Arthur Veary
born: **7** England **8** Brighton
roles: **11** Mary Poppins **14** National Velvet, Thank You Jeeves **16** David Copperfield **20** Magnificent Obsession

treacherous **5** false, risky **6** tricky, unsafe, untrue **7** devious **8** disloyal, perilous, two-faced **9** dangerous, deceitful, deceptive, faithless, hazardous **10** misleading, perfidious, precarious, traitorous, treasonous, unfaithful **12** falsehearted **13** untrustworthy

treachery **5** guile **6** deceit **7** perfidy, treason **8** apostasy, betrayal, trickery **9** deception, duplicity, falseness **10** disloyalty, infidelity **11** double cross **13** breach of faith, deceitfulness, double-dealing, faithlessness **15** underhandedness **17** untrustworthiness

tread **4** gait, hike, pace, roam, rove, step, walk **5** prowl, range, stamp, stomp, tramp **6** step on, stride, stroll, trudge, walk on **7** trample **8** footfall, footstep

treason **6** mutiny, revolt **7** perfidy **8** apostasy, betrayal, sedition **9** duplicity, rebellion, treachery **10** conspiracy, disloyalty, insurgence, revolution, subversion **12** insurrection

treasonable **9** faithless, seditious **10** perfidious, subversive, traitorous **11** treacherous

treasure **3** gem **4** gold **5** hoard, jewel, prize, store, value **6** esteem, jewels, regard, revere, riches, silver **7** cherish, deposit, paragon **8** bank upon, dote upon, gold mine, hold dear **11** pride and joy **14** apple of one's eye **17** pearl of great price

treasure chest **3** box **4** case **5** chest, trunk **6** coffer

treasured **4** dear **5** loved **6** adored, valued **7** beloved **8** precious **9** cherished

Treasure Island
author: **20** Robert Louis Stevenson
character: **7** Ben Gunn **8** Smollett **9** Dr Livesey **10** Jim Hawkins **14** Long John Silver **15** Squire Trelawney
director:
1934 version: **13** Victor Fleming
1950 version: **11** Byron Haskin
based on novel by: **20** Robert Louis Stevenson
cast:
1934 version: **10** Lewis Stone **12** Jackie Cooper (Jim Hawkins), Wallace Beery (Long John Silver) **15** Lionel Barrymore
1950 version: **11** Basil Sydney **12** Robert Newton (Long John Silver) **13** Bobby Driscoll (Jim Hawkins) **16** Walter Fitzgerald

Treasure of the Sierra Madre, The
director: **10** John Huston
cast: **7** Tim Holt **12** Bruce Bennett, Walter Huston **13** Alfonso Bedoya, Barton MacLane **14** Humphrey Bogart
Oscar for: **8** director **10** screenplay **15** supporting actor (Huston)

treasurer **6** banker, bursar, purser, teller **7** auditor, cashier **9** financier **10** accountant, bookkeeper, cash-keeper, controller **16** financial officer **17** minister of finance **22** secretary of the treasury **24** Chancellor of the Exchequer

Treasure State
nickname of: **7** Montana

treasury **4** bank, safe, till **5** funds, purse, vault **6** coffer **8** money box **9** anthology, exchequer, strongbox, thesaurus **10** collection, compendium, depository, repository, storehouse **11** bank account, compilation

treasury note **4** bill **8** bank note **9** greenback **12** currency note **17** silver certificate

treat **3** joy **4** blow, coat, give **5** apply, cover, favor, grant, imbue, stand **6** attend, divert, doctor, handle, manage, remedy, spring, thrill **7** comfort, delight, discuss, patch up, take out **8** consider, deal with, look upon, medicate, pleasure, relate to **9** act toward, small gift, try to cure, try to heal **10** impregnate, minister to, speak about, write about **12** prescribe for, satisfaction **13** gratification

treat as inferior **7** disdain **9** patronize **12** condescend to **18** look down one's nose at **19** discriminate against

treatise **4** text **5** essay, study, tract **6** manual, memoir, report, thesis **8** textbook, tractate **9** discourse, monograph **12** dissertation

treatment **3** way **4** cure **6** course, remedy **7** conduct, process, regimen, therapy **8** antidote, approach, handling, treating **9** doctoring, operation, procedure **10** management, medication **11** application, medical care **12** manipulation

treaty **4** deal, pact **6** accord **7** bargain, compact, entente **8** covenant **9** concordat **13** understanding **15** formal agreement **22** international agreement

tree **3** ash, elm, fir, oak **4** bush, palm, pine, wood **5** beech, birch, chase, maple, plane, plant, scrub, staff, stake, stick **6** corner, cudgel, redbud, spruce, timber, willow **7** gallows, lineage, live oak, sapling **8** ancestry, chestnut, hardwood, mahogany, pedigree, seedling **9** ailanthus, evergreen **10** cottonwood, eucalyptus

Tree Grows in Brooklyn, A
author: **10** Betty Smith
character:
Nolan family: **5** Katie **6** Neeley **7** Francie, Johnnie
director: **9** Elia Kazan
cast: **9** James Dunn **10** Lloyd Nolan **12** Joan Blondell **14** Dorothy McGuire, Peggy Ann Garner
Oscar for: **7** special (Garner) **15** supporting actor (Dunn)

treeless **4** bald, bare **6** barren **7** denuded **8** unwooded **10** unforested

Treeplanters State
nickname of: **8** Nebraska

trek 4 hike, plod, roam, rove, sail, slog, trip **5** jaunt, march, range, tramp **6** junket, outing, travel, trudge, voyage, wander **7** journey, odyssey, passage **8** traverse **9** excursion, migration **10** expedition, pilgrimage **11** peregrinate **13** peregrination

trellis 5 arbor, bower, cross, frame, grill, trail **6** gazebo, screen **7** lattice, network, pergola **8** espalier **10** interweave **11** summerhouse

tremble 5 quail, quake, shake, waver **6** quaver, quiver, shiver **7** flutter, pulsate, shudder **9** palpitate

trembling 5 shaky **7** quaking, shaking **8** unsteady **9** doddering, quavering, quivering, shivering **10** shuddering **11** palpitating

tremblor 5 quake, seism, shock **6** tremor **8** upheaval **10** earthquake

tremendous 4 fine, huge, vast **5** giant, great, major **7** amazing, awesome, immense, mammoth, sizable, titanic, unusual **8** colossal, enormous, fabulous, gigantic, terrific, towering, uncommon **9** excellent, fantastic, first-rate, humongous, important, marvelous, monstrous, wonderful **10** formidable, gargantuan, incredible, noteworthy, stupendous **11** elephantine, exceptional **12** considerable **13** consequential, extraordinary

tremolo
music: 9 trembling, vibrating **30** rapid reiteration of a single pitch

tremor 3 jar **4** jolt **5** quake, shake, shock, spasm, throb, waver **6** quiver, shiver **7** flutter, shaking, shudder, tremble **8** paroxysm **9** pulsation, quavering, quivering, shivering, trembling, vibration **10** convulsion **11** palpitation

tremulous 5 jumpy, shaky, timid **6** wobbly **7** aquiver, excited, fearful, jittery, keyed-up, nervous, panicky, quaking **8** aflutter, agitated, atremble, hesitant, restless, wavering, worked-up **9** faltering, impatient, quivering, trembling, uncertain **10** irresolute, stimulated **13** on tenterhooks, panic-stricken

trench 3 cut, rut **4** scar **5** canal, ditch, drain, fosse, slash, slice **6** dugout, furrow, gutter, trough **7** channel, wrinkle **8** aqueduct **9** earthwork **10** depression

trenchant 4 acid, keen, tart **5** crisp **6** bitter **7** acerbic, caustic, concise, mordant, probing **8** clear-cut, distinct, incisive, scathing **9** sarcastic, scorching **10** razor-sharp **11** acrimonious, penetrating, well-defined

trend 4 bent, flow, mode **5** drift, style **7** fashion, impulse, leaning **8** movement, tendency **9** direction **10** proclivity, propensity **11** inclination

trendsetters 7 leaders **8** trendies, vanguard **10** avant-garde, innovators **11** pacesetters, tastemakers **12** advance guard, stylesetters, trailblazers

trendy 2 in **4** chic, tony **5** swank **6** modern, modish, with-it **7** current, faddish, popular, stylish, voguish **8** up-to-date **10** all the rage **11** fashionable **13** up-to-the-minute

Trenor, Gus and Judy
characters in: 15 The House of Mirth
author: 7 Wharton

Trent, Little Nell
character in: 19 The Old Curiosity Shop
author: 7 Dickens

trepidation 4 fear **5** alarm, dread, panic, worry **7** anxiety, jitters **8** cold feet, disquiet **10** uneasiness **11** butterflies, disquietude, jitteriness, nervousness **12** apprehension **13** consternation

trespass 3 sin **5** error, wrong **6** invade **7** impinge, intrude, misdeed, offense **8** encroach, infringe, iniquity, invasion **9** evildoing, intrusion, violation **10** immorality, infraction, misconduct, wrongdoing **11** delinquency, misbehavior **12** encroachment, infringement, overstepping **13** transgression, unlawful entry, wrongful entry

tress 4 curl, hair, lock, mane **5** braid, plait **6** strand **7** ringlet, wimpler **8** spitcurl

trestle 4 beam **5** board, brace, frame, table **6** timber **9** framework

trial 2 go **3** try, woe **4** care, pain, shot, test **5** agony, essay, flyer, whirl, worry **6** burden, effort, misery, ordeal, trying, tryout **7** anguish, attempt, bad luck, hearing, testing, test run, torment, trouble, venture **8** accident, distress, endeavor, hardship, vexation **9** adversity, court case, heartache, suffering **10** affliction, litigation, misfortune **11** cross to bear **12** misadventure, wretchedness

Trial, The
author: 10 Franz Kafka
character: 4 Leni **7** Joseph K **9** Titorelli **11** The Advocate

trial and error 10 experiment **13** investigation **15** experimentation **20** process of elimination

Triassic period
dinosaur from: 11 Coelophysis, Mandasuchus **12** Melanosaurus, Pisanosaurus, Plateosaurus **13** Tanystropheus **17** Heterodontosaurus

tribe *see* **11** ethnic group

Tribes of Israel *see* **6** Israel

tribulation 3 woe **4** care, pain **5** agony, grief, trial, worry **6** misery, ordeal, sorrow **7** anguish, bad luck, torment, trouble **8** distress, hardship, vexation **9** adversity, heartache, suffering **10** affliction, ill fortune, misfortune **11** unhappiness **12** wretchedness

Tribulation Wholesome
character in: 12 The Alchemist
author: 6 Jonson

tribunal 3 bar **5** bench, court, forum **6** judges **9** authority, judiciary **10** ruling body **11** judge's bench, judge's chair **14** seat of judgment

tributary 6 branch, feeder, source, stream **7** helping, subject **8** affluent **9** ancillary, auxiliary, confluent, secondary **10** subjugated, subsidiary **11** subordinate **12** contributing, contributory

tribute 3 tax **4** duty, levy, toll **5** bribe, honor, kudos **6** esteem, eulogy, excise, impost, payoff, praise, ransom **7** payment, respect **8** accolade, encomium, memorial **9** extolling, gratitude, laudation, panegyric **10** assessment, blood money, compliment, settlement **11** recognition, testimonial **12** commendation, pound of flesh **13** consideration, peace offering **14** acknowledgment

trice 3 sec **4** jiff, wink **5** blink, flash, jiffy, shake **6** minute, moment, second **7** instant **9** coup d'oeil, twinkling **11** split second

trichophobia
fear of: 4 hair

trichoptera
class: 8 hexapoda
phylum: 10 arthropoda
group: 3 fly **6** caddis

trick 3 art, gag **4** bait, dupe, feat, gift, gull, have, hoax, joke, ploy, ruse, trap, wile **5** antic, blind, bluff, caper, cheat, dodge, feint, fraud, knack, prank, put-on, skill, stunt **6** deceit, device, number, outfox, outwit, resort, secret, take in **7** deceive, gimmick, know-how, mislead, swindle **8** artifice, deftness, flimflam, hoodwink, maneuver **9** bamboozle, chicanery, deception, dexterity, imposture, sophistry, stratagem, technique **10** adroitness, hocus-pocus, manipulate, subterfuge **11** contrivance, machination, outmaneuver **13** practical joke, sleight of hand **16** prestidigitation

trickery 5 guile **6** bunkum, deceit **8** artifice, flimflam, pretense, quackery, wiliness **9** chicanery, deception, duplicity, imposture, rascality, stratagem **10** artfulness, craftiness, hocus-pocus, shiftiness **11** crookedness, deviousness **12** charlatanism, skullduggery, slipperiness **13** deceitfulness

trickiness 6 deceit **7** cunning, slyness **8** trickery **9** duplicity **10** craftiness **15** underhandedness

trickle 4 drip, leak, ooze, seep **5** exude **7** dribble, seepage **9** percolate

trickster 5 cheat, joker **6** dodger, rascal **8** deceiver, impostor, sleeveen **9** prankster

tricky 3 sly **4** foxy, wily **5** risky **6** artful, crafty, shifty, unsafe **7** cunning, devious **8** rascally, slippery, unstable **9** dangerous, deceptive, difficult, hazardous **10** touch-and-go, unreliable **11** complicated, underhanded **12** hard to handle, undependable **13** temperamental, unpredictable

trident
form: 5 spear
number of prongs: 5 three

trifle 3 bit, dab, jot, nip, toy **4** dash, drop, idle, iota, mite, play **5** crumb, dally, pinch, scrap, speck, tinge, touch, trace **6** bauble, dawdle, gewgaw, linger, little, morsel, sliver **7** modicum, nothing, trinket **8** fragment, gimcrack, kill time **9** bagatelle, plaything, waste time **10** dilly-dally, knickknack, sprinkling, triviality **11** deal lightly, small matter **12** amuse oneself, treat lightly **13** small quantity

trifler 5 flirt, idler **6** coquet **7** dabbler, dallier **8** coquette **10** dilettante

trifling 4 puny **5** petty, small, sorry, token **6** paltry, slight **7** nominal, trivial **8** beggarly, niggling, nugatory, picayune, piddling **9** worthless **10** negligible **11** unimportant **13** beneath notice, inappreciable, insignificant **14** inconsiderable **15** inconsequential

trifling circumstances
Latin: 8 minutiae

trifling matter
French: 10 peu de chose

trigger 5 shoot **6** set off **7** fire off **8** activate, detonate, touch off **9** discharge

trikerion 11 candelabrum, candlestick **12** candleholder

Trilby
author: 15 George du Maurier
character: 5 Gecko, Sandy, Taffy **8** Svengali **12** Little Billee **14** Trilby O'Ferrall

trill
music: 7 shaking, tremolo **9** quavering

trim 3 cut, fit, lop **4** clip, crop, deck, form, lean, pare, slim, thin **5** adorn, array, lithe, prune, shape, shave, shear, shift, sleek, state **6** adjust, bedeck, border, change, fettle, kilter, limber, paring, piping, supple, svelte **7** arrange, balance, bedizen, compact, cutting, fitness, furbish, garnish, lissome, pruning, shapely, slender, willowy **8** athletic, beautify, clipping, cropping, decorate, equalize, ornament, shearing, trick out, trimming **9** adornment, condition, embellish, embroider, shipshape **10** decoration, distribute **11** streamlined **13** embellishment, ornamentation

Trim, Corporal
character in: 14 Tristram Shandy
author: 6 Sterne

trimming 4 trim **5** frill **7** cutting, pruning, slicing **8** clipping **9** adornment **10** decoration, shortening, truncation **11** abridgement, contraction, curtailment **12** abbreviation **13** embellishment

Trinacria *see* **6** Sicily

Trinidad and Tobago ***see box, p. 1000***

Trinity
author: 8 Leon Uris

trinket 3 toy **5** bijou, charm, jewel **6** bauble, gewgaw, notion, trifle **8** gimcrack, ornament **9** bagatelle, plaything **10** knickknack

trip 3 bob, err **4** flip, flub, fool, muff, pull, skip, slip, tour, trek, undo **5** caper, catch, dance, fluff, foray, jaunt, outdo, throw, upset **6** bungle, cruise, frolic, gambol, junket, outfox, outing, prance, safari, set off, slip up, voyage **7** blunder, commute, confuse, flounce, journey, misstep, release, scamper, stumble **8** activate, fall over, flounder, hoodwink, throw off **9** excursion **10** disconcert, expedition, pilgrimage **11** step lightly

Triple Crown 7 Belmont **9** Preakness **13** Kentucky Derby
winner: 5 Omaha **7** Assault **8** Affirmed, Citation **9** Sir Barton, Whirlaway **10** Count Fleet, Gallant Fox, War Admiral **11** Seattle Slew, Secretariat

Triple Sec *see* **9** Cointreau

Tripoli
capital of: 5 Libya

Triptolemos, Triptolemus
favorite of: 7 Demeter
inventor of: 4 plow **5** wheel
patron of: 11 agriculture

Triquetra *see* **6** Sicily

triskaidekaphobia
fear of: 14 number thirteen

Trismegistus *see* **5** Thoth

Tristan and Isolde
also: 16 Tristan und Isolde
opera by: 6 Wagner
character: 5 Melot **8** Brangane, Kurwenal **18** King Mark of Cornwall

triste 3 sad **10** melancholy

tristesse 6 sorrow **7** sadness **10** melancholy

Tristram
author: 22 Edwin Arlington Robinson
character in: 16 Arthurian romance

Tristram Shandy
author: 14 Laurence Sterne
character: 6 Dr Slop **8** Mr Yorick **10** Toby Shandy **11** Widow Wadman **12** Corporal Trim, Walter Shandy

trite 5 banal, silly, stale **6** common **7** cliched, hum-

Trinidad and Tobago
capital/largest city: **11** Port of Spain
others: **4** Debe, Toco **5** Arima **6** Canaan, Coryal, Labrea **7** San Juan, Siparia **8** Rio Claro, Tunapuna **10** Roxborough **11** San Fernando, Scarborough **12** Princess Town, Sangre Grande **14** Charlotteville
school: **6** Fatima **7** St Mary's **11** Queen's Royal
head of state: **14** British monarch **15** governor general
monetary unit: **4** cent **6** dollar
island: **12** Chacachacare, Little Tobago **14** Bird of Paradise
lake: **5** Pitch
mountain:
hills: **7** Trinity **10** Montserrat **12** Three Sisters
highest point: **5** Aripo
river: **6** Caroni **7** Ortoire **8** Oropuche, Trinidad
sea: **8** Atlantic **9** Caribbean
physical feature:
bay: **5** Cocos, Guapo **6** Matura, Mayaro
channel: **12** Dragon's Mouth **13** Serpent's Mouth
gulf: **5** Paria
point: **5** Radix **6** Arenal, Galera **7** Chupara, Galeota **8** Columbus
people: **5** Irish **6** French, Syrian **7** African, Chinese, English, Spanish **8** European, Lebanese **10** East Indian, Portuguese, Venezuelan **11** Asian Indian **13** Latin American
explorer: **8** Columbus
leader: **8** Williams
language: **6** French **7** Chinese, English, Spanish **10** Portuguese **12** French Patois
religion: **5** Hindu, Islam **8** Anglican **10** Protestant **12** Christianity **13** Roman Catholic
place:
asphalt lake: **9** Pitch Lake
mansions: **16** Magnificent Seven
park: **18** Queen's Park Savannah
feature:
bird: **7** oilbird **8** cocorico
clothing: **4** sari **5** dhoti
dance: **6** Dragon, Shango
festival: **6** Hosein, Lights
fish: **5** guppy
music: **7** calypso, goombay
tree: **4** mora
food:
drink: **16** Angostura Bitters

drum, routine, shallow, worn-out **8** bromidic, everyday, ordinary, overdone, shopworn **9** frivolous, hackneyed **10** pedestrian, threadbare **11** commonplace, oft-repeated, stereotyped, unimportant **12** run-of-the-mill **13** platitudinous

Tritogeneia *see* **6** Athena

Triton
god of: **3** sea
father: **8** Poseidon
mother: **10** Amphitrite
shape: **6** merman
trumpet: **10** conch-shell

triumph **3** hit, win **4** best, coup **5** smash **6** subdue **7** conquer, mastery, prevail, succeed, success, surpass, victory **8** conquest, overcome, smash hit, vanquish **9** overwhelm **10** ascendancy, attainment, gain the day **11** achievement, superiority **12** come out on top, take the prize **14** accomplishment, get the better of

triumphal **5** proud **6** joyous **8** exultant **9** ascendant, rewarding **10** fulfilling, gratifying, successful, triumphant, victorious **11** spectacular

triumphant **6** elated, joyful **7** winning **8** exultant, jubilant **9** rejoicing **10** conquering, first-place, successful, victorious **11** celebrating **12** prizewinning

Triumph of Death, The
author: **17** Gabriele D'Annunzio

trivia
Latin: **8** minutiae

trivial **4** idle, puny, slim **5** banal, petty, small, trite **6** common, flimsy, little, meager, paltry, slight, two-bit **7** foolish **8** beggarly, everyday, niggling, nugatory, ordinary, picayune, piddling, trifling **9** rinky-dink, worthless **10** incidental, pedestrian **11** commonplace, meaningless, unessential, unimportant **13** inappreciable, insignificant, of little value **14** inconsiderable **15** inconsequential

triviality **5** frill **6** trifle **9** frivolity **10** paltriness **12** nonessential, unimportance **14** insignificance **18** inconsequentiality

troglodyte **5** brute **6** hermit **9** barbarian **11** cave dweller

Troilus
father: **5** Priam
mother: **6** Hecuba

Troilus and Cressida
author: **18** William Shakespeare
character: **4** Ajax **5** Priam **6** Hector **7** Ulysses **8** Achilles, Diomedes, Pandarus **9** Agamemnon

Troilus and Criseyde
author: **15** Geoffrey Chaucer
character: **8** Diomedes, Pandarus

trois **5** three

Trojan Horse
made of: **4** wood
made by: **7** Epeiosk
contained: **8** Odysseus, warriors

Trojans, The
also: **10** Les Troyens
opera by: **7** Berlioz
part one: **14** La Prise de Troie **16** The Capture of Troy
part two: **19** Les Troyens a Carthage **20** The Trojans in Carthage
character: **4** Dido **6** Aeneas, Hector

Trojan War
length: **8** ten years
combatants: **6** Greeks **7** Trojans
cause: **5** Helen, Paris **14** Apple of Discord

Trojan Women, The
author: **9** Euripides
character: **5** Helen **6** Hecuba **8** Astyanax, Menelaus, Odysseus, Polyxena **9** Agamemnon, Cassandra **10** Andromache, Talthybius **11** Neoptolemus

troll **3** imp **4** ogre **5** dwarf, gnome **6** goblin
origin: **12** Scandinavian
form: **12** supernatural
inhabits: **10** subterrain

trollop **4** doxy, slut **5** bitch, doxie, frump, hussy, trull, whore **6** floozy, harlot, wanton **7** baggage **8** slattern, strumpet **10** prostitute

Trollope, Anthony
author of: **9** Orley Farm, The Warden **15** The Way We Live Now **16** Barchester Towers, Framley Parsonage
character: **11** Phineas Finn

troop, troops **4** army, band, file, gang, herd, step, unit **5** bunch, crowd, crush, drove, flock, horde, march, press, swarm, tramp **6** parade, stride, throng, trudge **7** cavalry, company, militia **8** infantry, soldiers, soldiery, troopers **9** aggregate, gathering **10** armed force, assemblage **11** cavalry unit, fighting men, police force **12** congregation **13** military force

trop **3** too **7** too many, too much

Tropaean
epithet of: **4** Zeus
means: **14** giver of victory

Trophonius
vocation: **7** builder
father: **7** Erginus
brother: **8** Agamedes
god of: **5** earth
killed: **8** Agamedes
became: **6** oracle
oracle called: **14** Zeus Trophonius

trophy **4** palm **5** award, booty, honor, kudos, medal, prize, relic, spoil **6** wreath **7** laurels, memento **8** citation, souvenir **9** loving cup **10** blue ribbon **11** testimonial

tropical **5** muggy **6** sultry, torrid **8** stifling **10** sweltering **11** hot and humid

troppo, non
music: **10** not too much

Tros
king of: **4** Troy
father: **12** Erichthonius
mother: **8** Astyoche
wife: **10** Callirrhoe
son: **4** Ilus **8** Ganymede **9** Assaracus

trot **3** jog **9** go briskly **11** step quickly, walk smartly

troth **8** fidelity **9** betrothal **10** affiancing, engagement **12** faithfulness

Trotwood, Betsey
character in: **16** David Copperfield
author: **7** Dickens

trouble ***see box***

troubled **5** upset **7** worried **8** bothered, careworn **9** disturbed, perturbed **10** distressed **12** heavyhearted

troublemaker **6** gossip **7** inciter **8** agitator, fomenter, provoker **9** miscreant **10** incendiary, instigator **11** rumormonger, scaremonger **12** rabble-rouser **13** mischief-maker, scandalmonger **16** agent provocateur

troublesome **4** hard **5** heavy, pesky, tough **6** cursed, knotty, taxing, thorny, tiring, trying, vexing **7** arduous, irksome, onerous, tedious **8** annoying, tiresome, unwieldy **9** demanding, difficult, fatiguing, harassing, herculean, laborious, wearisome, worrisome **10** bothersome, burdensome, cumbersome, disturbing, irritating, oppressive, tormenting, unpleasant **11** disobedient, distressing **12** disagreeable, exasperating, inconvenient, uncontrolled **13** undisciplined

troublesomeness **5** trial **10** difficulty **11** arduousness **13** inconvenience, laboriousness, vexatiousness, worrisomeness **14** bothersomeness

Trouble with Harry, The
director: **15** Alfred Hitchcock
cast: **11** Edmund Gwenn **12** John Forsythe **14** Mildred Dunnock, Mildred Natwick **15** Shirley MacLaine

troubling **6** vexing **8** worrying **9** worrisome **10** bothersome, disturbing, unsettling

trough **4** duct, moat, race, tray **5** canal, ditch, flume, gorge, gully **6** furrow, hollow, ravine, trench **7** channel **8** aqueduct **10** depression

trounce **4** beat, drub, lick, trim, whip **5** cream, skunk **6** humble **7** clobber **8** vanquish **9** overpower, overwhelm **10** take care of **11** carry the day **14** get the better of

troupe **4** band, cast **5** group, troop **6** actors **7** company, players **10** performers **11** road company

trouper **5** actor **7** actress **8** thespian **9** performer **13** touring player **15** repertory player

trousers **5** jeans, pants **6** chinos, slacks **7** drawers **8** breeches, britches, jodhpurs, knickers, overalls **9** dungarees **10** pantaloons **11** bellbottoms **12** pedal pushers **14** knickerbockers

Trovatore, Il
also: **13** The Troubadour
opera by: **5** Verdi
character: **7** Azucena, Leonora, Manrico **11** Count di Luna

Troy
abducted queen: **5** Helen
archaeologist: **6** Blegen **8** Dorpfeld **10** Schliemann
defender: **5** Eneas **6** Aeneas
Greek name: **5** Ilion
hero: **6** Hector
king: **5** Priam
Latin name: **5** Ilium
modern name: **9** Hissarlik
mountain: **3** Ida
neighboring city: **6** Albany **10** Watervliet

---

trouble **3** fix, row, vex, woe **4** blow, care, fuss, heed, mess, pain, pass, snag, work **5** agony, annoy, grief, harry, labor, pains, pinch, think, trial, upset, worry **6** affect, attend, badger, bother, burden, crisis, defect, dismay, effort, grieve, harass, misery, ordeal, pester, pickle, plague, pother, put out, scrape, sorrow, strain, strait, stress, strife, unrest **7** afflict, agitate, ailment, attempt, concern, depress, dilemma, discord, disturb, ferment, ill wind, oppress, perturb, reverse, setback, torment **8** disaster, disorder, disquiet, distress, disunity, exertion, hardship, hot water, quandary, rainy day, struggle, take time, unsettle, vexation **9** adversity, agitation, annoyance, attention, breakdown, challenge, commotion, deep water, hard times, suffering **10** affliction, convulsion, difficulty, disability, discommode, discompose, disconcert, discontent, dissension, irritation, make uneasy, misfortune, opposition **11** competition, disturbance, embroilment, instability, malfunction, predicament, tribulation **12** entanglement, exert oneself **13** inconvenience, make the effort **14** discontentment **15** dissatisfaction

river: **6** Hudson
state: **7** Alabama, New York **8** Michigan
story: **5** Iliad **7** Odyssey
surrounding region: **5** Troad, Troas

Troy, Sergeant
character in: **22** Far From the Madding Crowd
author: **5** Hardy

truancy **3** cut **7** absence **11** absenteeism, nonpresence **12** playing hooky **13** nonappearance, nonattendance **14** cutting classes, skipping school

truant **4** gone **5** idler **6** absent, dodger, evader, loafer, no show **7** drifter, goof-off, missing, not here, shirker, slacker, vagrant **8** absentee, deserter, layabout **9** goldbrick **10** delinquent, malingerer, nonpresent, not present **11** boondoggler, hooky-player **12** nonattendant, playing hooky

truce **4** halt, lull, rest, stay, stop **5** break, pause **7** respite **9** armistice, cease-fire **12** interruption **14** breathing spell, discontinuance **23** suspension of hostilities

Trucial Oman, Trucial States *see* **18** United Arab Emirates

truck **3** rig, van **5** lorry **15** eighteen-wheeler
type: **5** panel **6** pickup **7** trailer **8** delivery

truckle **3** bow **4** fawn **5** court, defer, yield **6** grovel, pander, submit **7** flatter **8** bootlick, butter up, suck up to **9** shine up to **10** curry favor, take orders **11** apple-polish, fall all over **12** knuckle under **17** ingratiate oneself

truculence **8** defiance, ill humor **9** hostility, ill temper, pugnacity, surliness **10** fierceness **11** bellicosity **12** belligerence, churlishness **14** aggressiveness

truculent **4** rude, sour **5** cross, nasty, sulky, surly **6** fierce, touchy **7** defiant, hostile, peevish **8** churlish, insolent, petulant, snappish, snarling **9** bellicose **10** aggressive, ill-humored, ill-natured, pugnacious, ungracious **11** bad-tempered, belligerent, ill-tempered

Trudeau, Garry
creator/artist of: **10** Doonesbury

trudge **4** drag, limp, plod **5** clump, march, tramp **6** hobble, lumber **7** shamble

true **4** even, firm, full, just, pure, real **5** exact, legal, loyal, right, usual, valid **6** actual, lawful, normal, proper, steady, strict, trusty **7** correct, devoted, factual, genuine, literal, precise, regular, staunch, typical **8** absolute, accurate, bona fide, constant, faithful, official, positive, reliable, rightful, true-blue, truthful **9** authentic, simon-pure, steadfast **10** dependable, legitimate, unswerving, unwavering **11** trustworthy **14** unquestionable

true being **4** core, soul **6** nature, psyche, spirit **7** essence

True Grit
director: **13** Henry Hathaway
based on novel by: **13** Charles Portis
cast: **8** Kim Darby **9** John Wayne **11** Jeremy Slate **12** Glen Campbell, Robert Duvall **14** Strother Martin
Oscar for: **5** actor (Wayne)

Truffaut, Francois
director of: **11** Day for Night, Jules and Jim **19** Shoot the Piano Player, The Four Hundred Blows

truism **3** saw **5** adage, axiom **6** cliche, dictum, saying **9** platitude

truly **6** indeed, in fact, really, surely, verily **7** exactly, in truth, no doubt **8** actually, honestly, to be sure **9** assuredly, certainly, correctly, factually, genuinely, literally, precisely, sincerely **10** absolutely, accurately, definitely, faithfully, positively, truthfully, upon my word **11** beyond doubt, in actuality, indubitably, so help me God **12** indisputably **13** incontestably, unequivocally **14** beyond question, unquestionably **15** all kidding aside, without question

Truman, Harry S ***see box***

Trumbull, John
born: **9** Lebanon CT
artwork: **21** The Battle of Bunker Hill **26** The Resignation of Washington **28** The Declaration of Independence **29** The Surrender of General Burgoyne **32** The Capture of the Hessians at Trenton **38** The Surrender of Lord Cornwallis at Yorktown **46** The Death of General Montgomery in the Attack of Quebec, The Death of General Warren at the Battle of Bunker Hill

trumpery **5** showy, trash **6** deceit, trashy, trivia **7** rubbish, twaddle, useless **8** frippery, nonsense, trifling **9** deception, worthless **11** nonsensical

trumpet **4** honk, horn **5** blare, bugle **6** cornet **7** clarion **8** proclaim **10** hearing aid

Trumpet of the Swan, The
author: **7** E B White

trump up **4** fake **6** invent, make up **7** concoct, falsify **9** fabricate

truncate **3** bob, lop, nip **4** clip, crop, dock, snub, trim **5** prune **7** abridge, curtail, shorten **8** amputate, condense, cut short **10** abbreviate

truncheon **3** bat **4** club **5** baton, billy, stick **6** cudgel **8** bludgeon **9** billyclub

trunker **3** box, die **4** body, bole, dado, line, main **5** chief, pants, shaft, snout, stock, torso **6** coffer, engine, locker, shut up, thorax **7** baggage, close in

Truscott-Jones, Reginald
real name of: **10** Ray Milland

truss **3** tie **4** beam, bind, prop, stay **5** brace, hitch, shore, strap, tie up **6** bind up, fasten, girder, pinion, secure **7** confine, support **8** make fast **9** constrict, framework, stanchion **12** underpinning

trust **4** care, duty, hope **5** faith, hands **6** accept, assume, belief, charge, credit, expect, look to, rely on **7** believe, count on, custody, keeping, presume, swear by **8** credence, feel sure, reliance, sureness **9** certainty, certitude, count upon **10** anticipate, confidence, conviction, depend upon, obligation, protection **11** assuredness, contemplate, have faith in, safekeeping, subscribe to, take on faith, take stock in **12** guardianship **14** give credence to, responsibility, take for granted

trusted **6** trusty **8** reliable **9** unfailing **10** dependable **11** trustworthy

trustee **8** guardian **9** caretaker, custodian, protector

trusteeship **4** care **6** charge **7** custody **10** protection **11** safekeeping **12** guardianship

trusting **8** gullible, trustful

Truman, Harry S
nickname: **15** Give Em Hell Harry
presidential rank: **11** thirty-third
party: **10** Democratic
state represented: **8** Missouri
succeeded upon death of: **9** Roosevelt
defeated: **5** (Farrell) Dobbs, (Thomas Edmund) Dewey **6** (Claude A) Watson, (Norman) Thomas **7** (Henry Agard) Wallace **8** (Edward A) Teichert, (James Strom) Thurmond
vice president: **7** (Alben William) Barkley
cabinet:
state: **6** (James Francis) Byrnes **7** (Dean Gooderham) Acheson **8** (George Catlett) Marshall **10** (Edward Reilly) Stettinius (Jr)
treasury: **6** (Frederick Moore) Vinson, (John Wesley) Snyder **10** (Henry) Morgenthau (Jr)
war: **6** (Kenneth Claiborne) Royall **7** (Henry Lewis) Stimson **9** (Robert Porter) Patterson
defense: **6** (Robert Abercrombie) Lovett **7** (Louis Arthur) Johnson **8** (George Catlett) Marshall **9** (James Vincent) Forrestal
attorney general: **5** (Thomas Campbell) Clark **6** (Francis) Biddle **7** (James Howard) McGrath **9** (James Patrick) McGranery
navy: **9** (James Vincent) Forrestal
postmaster general: **6** (Frank Comerford) Walker **8** (Robert Emmet) Hannegan **9** (Jesse Monroe) Donaldson
interior: **4** (Julius Albert) Krug **5** (Harold LeClaire) Ickes **7** (Oscar Littleton) Chapman
agriculture: **7** (Charles Franklin) Brannan, (Claude Raymond) Wickard **8** (Clinton Presba) Anderson
commerce: **6** (Charles) Sawyer **7** (Henry Agard) Wallace **8** (William Averell) Harriman
labor: **5** (Maurice Joseph) Tobin **7** (Frances), Perkins (Wilson) **13** (Lewis Baxter) Schwellenbach
born: **2** MO **5** Lamar **8** Missouri
died: **2** MO **8** Missouri **10** Kansas City
buried: **2** MO **8** Missouri **12** Independence
education:
law school: **21** Kansas City School of Law (did not graduate)
religion: **7** Baptist
interests: **5** piano **7** history
vacation spot: **2** FL **7** Florida, Key West
author: **14** Year of Decision **19** Years of Trial and Hope
political career: **8** US Senate **13** Vice President
presiding judge of: **13** Jackson County
civilian career: **6** farmer
owned: **9** men's store **12** haberdashery
military service: **5** major **9** World War I **15** MO National Guard **18** Army Reserve colonel
notable events of lifetime/term: **4** NATO **5** V-E Day **8** Fair Deal **9** Korean War **17** iron-curtain speech **20** assassination attempt **31** North Atlantic Treaty Organization
act: **11** Taft-Hartley **12** Bretton-Woods
airlift to: **6** Berlin
conference: **7** Potsdam
dropping of first: **5** A-bomb **8** atom bomb
plan: **8** Marshall **9** Point Four
signing of: **9** UN charter
Treaty of: **12** Rio de Janeiro
trial of: **9** Alger Hiss
father: **12** John Anderson
mother: **6** Martha (Ellen Young)
siblings: **8** Mary Jane **10** John Vivian
wife: **9** Elizabeth (Virginia Wallace)
nickname: **4** Bess
children: **12** Mary Margaret

9 believing, credulous **12** unsuspicious

trustworthy **4** true **5** loyal **6** honest **7** ethical, trusted, upright **8** faithful, reliable, true-blue **9** honorable, steadfast **10** aboveboard, dependable, scrupulous **11** responsible **12** tried and true **13** incorruptible, unimpeachable **14** high-principled

trusty **7** trusted **8** reliable **9** unfailing **10** dependable **11** trustworthy

trusty companion **3** pal **5** buddy, crony **6** friend **8** intimate, sidekick **9** confidant **10** bosom buddy, confidante

truth **3** law **4** fact **5** facts **6** verity **7** reality **8** accuracy, fidelity, trueness, veracity **9** actuality, exactness, integrity **11** reliability **12** authenticity, faithfulness, truthfulness **15** proven principle, trustworthiness
Russian: **6** Pravda
also name of: **9** newspaper
god of: **7** Mithras

truth conquers all things
Latin: **18** vincit omnia veritas

truthful **4** open, true **5** exact, frank **6** candid, honest **7** artless, correct, factual, precise, sincere **8** accurate, faithful, reliable **9** authentic, guileless, veracious **10** aboveboard, meticulous, scrupulous **11** trustworthy, undeceitful, unvarnished **13** unadulterated **15** straightforward

truthfulness **6** candor **7** honesty **8** veracity

Truth or Consequences
host: **10** Jack Bailey, Steve Dunne **12** Ralph Edwards

try **2** go **3** aim, use **4** risk, seek, shot, test, turn **5** crack, essay, fling, prove, trial, whack **6** effort, sample, strain, strive, tackle **7** adjudge, attempt, venture **8** endeavor **9** have a go at, partake of, undertake **10** adjudicate, deliberate, put to a test **11** opportunity **12** have a fling at, make an effort, take a crack at

Trygon
nurse of: **9** Asclepius

trying **4** hard **5** pesky, tough **6** taxing, vexing **7** arduous, irksome, onerous, tedious **8** tiresome **9** difficult, fatiguing, harrowing, wearisome **10** bothersome, burdensome, exhausting, irritating **11** aggravating, distressing, troublesome **12** exasperating

tryout **4** test **5** trial **7** hearing **8** audition **10** experiment

try out **3** fry **6** render **7** compete **8** audition **9** give a test **11** performance

tryst **4** date **7** meeting, vis-a-vis **9** tete-a-tete **10** engagement, rendezvous **11** appointment, assignation

try the patience of **5** annoy **7** provoke **8** irritate **10** exasperate

try to equal **5** rival **7** compete, emulate

Tuatha De Danann **4** gods
origin: **5** Irish
mother: **4** Danu

tub **3** keg, kit, pot, tun, vat **4** bath, boat, butt, cask, ship, tank, tram, wash **5** barge, bathe, fatso, fatty, keeve, tramp **6** barrel, bucket, firkin, ore car, vessel **7** cistern, tankard **8** cauldron, slow boat **9** container, freighter

Tubalcain
father: **6** Lamech
mother: **6** Zillah
half-brother: **5** Jabal, Jubal
progenitor of: **12** metalworkers

tube **4** duct, hose, pipe **7** conduit **8** cylinder

tuber **3** anu, yam **4** beet, bulb, corm, eddo, root, taro **5** jalop, shoot **6** potato, turnip **8** rutabaga, swelling **11** enlargement

Tuchman, Barbara W
author of: **14** A Distant Mirror, The First Salute **15** The Guns of August, The March of Folly **17** Practicing History

tuck **3** put **4** cram **5** pleat, shove, stick, stuff **6** enwrap, gather, insert, pucker, roll up, ruffle, shroud, swathe, thrust **7** crinkle, swaddle

tucker **3** fag **4** bush, poop, tire **5** weary **7** exhaust, fatigue

tuckered out **5** all in, tired, weary **6** bushed, done in, pooped **8** fatigued **9** exhausted, fagged out

Tudor, Antony
choreographer of: **11** Lilac Garden **12** Pillar of Fire

tuebor **11** I will defend

Tuei *see* **6** Isleta

Tuesday
from: **3** Tiw
heavenly body: **4** Mars
French: **5** mardi
Italian: **7** martedi
Spanish: **6** martes
German: **8** dienstag

tuft **4** wisp **5** batch, brush, bunch, clump, crest, plume, sheaf **6** bundle, tassel **7** cluster, topknot

tug **3** lug, tow **4** drag, draw, haul, jerk, pull, yank **6** wrench **7** wrestle

tulip **6** Tulipa
varieties: **4** lady, star **5** globe **7** Turkish **9** butterfly, guinea-hen, waterlily **10** Sierra star **11** golden globe, purple globe **16** common late garden **17** common early garden

Tulkinghorn
character in: **10** Bleak House
author: **7** Dickens

Tullia
father: **14** Servius Tullius
husband: **7** Tarquin

Tullius *see* **14** Servius Tullius

Tulsa
football team: **7** Outlaws

tumble **3** mix **4** dive, drop, fall, flip, roll, toss **5** whirl **6** bounce, jumble, plunge, stir up, topple **7** descend, shuffle, stumble **9** cartwheel **10** somersault

tumbledown **5** shaky **7** rickety, run-down **8** decaying, decrepit, unstable **9** crumbling, tottering **10** broken-down, jerry-built, ramshackle **11** dilapidated, falling-down **14** disintegrating

tumbler **3** cog, dog **5** drier, glass, lever **6** goblet, vessel **7** acrobat, athlete, gymnast, juggler **12** somersaulter

tumbrel **4** cart **5** wagon **7** tipcart **8** dumpcart

tumbril
French: **7** fourgon

tumid **5** puffy **6** turgid **7** bloated, bulging, dilated, pompous, swollen **8** enlarged, expanded, inflated **9** bombastic, distended, edematous, tumescent **11** protuberant **12** magniloquent **13** grandiloquent

tummy **3** gut **5** belly **6** paunch, tum-tum **7** abdomen, midriff, stomach **9** bay window **11** breadbasket

tumor **3** wen **4** cyst, lump, wart **5** pride **6** cancer, growth **7** bombast, sarcoma **8** hematoma, neoplasm, swelling, tubercle **9** carcinoma, papilloma, pomposity **11** tumefaction

tumult **3** ado, din **6** bedlam, bustle, clamor, hubbub, racket, uproar **7** turmoil **8** disorder, upheaval **9** agitation, commotion, confusion **10** excitement, hullabaloo **11** disturbance, pandemonium

tumultuous **4** loud **5** noisy, rough, rowdy **6** stormy, unruly **7** chaotic, furious, lawless, raucous, riotous, violent **8** agitated, confused **9** clamorous, disturbed, turbulent **10** boisterous, disorderly, uproarious **11** tempestuous

tun **3** keg, tub, vat **4** butt, cast, drum **6** barrel **8** hogshead

tune **3** air **4** aria, line, song, step **5** adjust, ditty, motif, pitch, theme **6** accord, adjust, melody, number, strain, unison **7** concert, concord, harmony **9** agreement **10** conformity

tuneful **6** catchy, dulcet **7** lyrical, musical **9** melodious

tungsten
chemical symbol: **1** W

Tungusic
language family: **6** Altaic
includes: **6** Manchu

tunic **4** robe **5** cloak **6** jacket, mantle, poncho, tabard **7** garment, surcoat

Tunica
tribe: **10** Chitimacha

Tunis
capital of: **7** Tunisia

Tunisia ***see box***

Tunney, Gene
real name: **17** James Joseph Tunney
nickname: **14** Fighting Marine
sport: **6** boxing
class: **11** heavyweight

Tuonela
also: **6** Manala
origin: **7** Finnish
name of: **10** afterworld
form: **6** island
lacked: **3** sun **4** moon

Tupman
character in: **14** Pickwick Papers
author: **7** Dickens

tu quoque **7** thou too

Turandot
opera by: **7** Puccini
character: **3** Liu **4** Pang, Ping, Pong **5** Calaf, Timur **8** Turandot (Princess of China)

turbid **5** muddy, murky **6** cloudy, opaque, roiled **7** clouded, unclear **8** agitated

Tunisia
other name: **8** Carthage **9** Ifriqiyah
capital/largest city: **5** Tunis
others: **4** Beja, Sfax, Susa **5** Gabes, Gofsa **6** Djerba, Mateur, Nabeul, Remada, Sousse, Tozeur **7** Bizerte, Kairwan **8** Carthage, Jendouba, Kairouan, Monastir, Tebourba, Zaghouan **9** Grombalia **10** Ferryville
empire: **8** Carthage **13** Barbary States
school: **5** Tunis **16** Pasteur Institute
measure: **3** saa **4** saah **5** cafiz **6** mettar **8** milerole
monetary unit: **5** dinar **6** dollar **7** millime
weight: **3** saa **4** rotl **5** artal, ratel, uckia
island: **6** Djerba, Galite
lake: **6** Achkel, Djerid **7** Bizerte
mountain: **5** Atlas **6** Mrhila **7** Tebessa **8** High Tell, Zaghouan **12** Northern Tell **17** Dorsale Tunisienne
highest point: **6** Chambi
river: **8** Medjerda, Mellegue
sea: **13** Mediterranean
physical feature:
cape: **3** Bon **5** Blanc **8** Rasaddar
desert: **6** Sahara
gulf: **5** Gabes, Tunis **8** Hammamet
oasis: **5** Gabes, Gafsa, Nefta **6** Djerba, Tozeur **9** El Oudiane **13** El Hamma Djerid
plains: **5** Sahel
salt lake: **11** Chott Djerid, Shatt Djerid
valley: **8** Medjerda
wind: **5** chile **6** chilli **7** sirocco
people: **3** Jew **4** Arab **6** Berber
artist: **5** Gorgi, Turki
dynasty: **6** Hafsid **7** Fatimid **8** Aghlabid, Almohade **10** Husseinite
leader: **9** Bourguiba
language: **6** Arabic, Berber, French
religion: **5** Islam **7** Judaism **12** Christianity
place:
center of Tunis: **13** Place d'Afrique
mosque: **5** Great **7** Zitouna
museum: **5** Bardo, Kouba **6** Sousse
palace: **14** Dar Ben Abdallah
ruins: **8** Carthage
street: **14** Habib Bourguiba
feature:
cap: **7** chechia
clothing: **5** jebba **7** safasri **9** babbouche
market: **4** souk
food:
dish: **7** mesfouf **8** couscous
drink: **4** iban **5** legmi
fruit: **12** deglet en nour

9 disturbed, stirred up, unsettled

turbine
invented by: **7** Bourdin, Francis, Parsons

turbulence **4** fury **6** frenzy, hubbub, tumult, unrest, uproar **7** ferment, rioting, torrent, turmoil **8** disorder, violence **9** agitation, commotion **10** excitement, unruliness **11** disturbance

turbulent **5** rowdy **6** fierce, raging, stormy, unruly **7** chaotic, furious, riotous, violent **8** agitated, restless **9** clamorous, disturbed **10** blustering, boisterous, disorderly, tumultuous, uproarious **11** tempestuous

tureen **4** bowl, dish **9** casserole, container **10** receptacle

turf **3** sod **4** area, peat, plot, soil **5** divot, grass, haunt, sward, track **7** verdure **9** racetrack, territory **10** greensward **11** horseracing **12** neighborhood

Turgenev, Ivan
author of: **5** Smoke **9** First Love **10** Virgin Soil **14** Fathers and Sons **18** A Month in the Country **19** A Sportsman's Notebook, A Sportsman's Sketches, The Torrents of Spring

turgid **5** puffy, showy **6** florid, ornate **7** flowery, pompous, swollen **8** inflated, puffed up **9** bombastic, grandiose, overblown **10** hyperbolic **11** pretentious **12** ostentatious **13** grandiloquent

Turkey ***see box, p. 1006***

Turkic
language family: **6** Altaic
group: **5** Kazak, Nogai, Uigur, Uzbek, Yakut **7** Chuvash, Kirghiz **8** Turkoman **10** Karakalpak **11** Azerbaijani **14** Osmanli Turkish

turmeric
botanical name: **12** Curcuma longa
also called: **7** tumeric **13** Crocus indicus, Indian saffron
family: **6** ginger
color: **6** yellow
used as: **3** dye **6** amulet **8** cosmetic, medicine
origin: **4** Asia **9** Caribbean, East India
charm against: **5** ghost **10** tree spirit
use: **4** eggs, fish, pork, rice **6** relish **7** chicken, mustard, pickles **10** vegetables **11** curry powder

turmoil **4** mess **5** chaos **6** tumult, uproar **7** ferment **8** disorder **9** agitation, commotion, confusion **10** convulsion **11** disturbance, pandemonium
French: **14** bouleversement

turn **2** do, go **3** act, arc, lie, put **4** bend, coil, come, deed, flex, hang, look, loop, make, rest, ride, roll, send, shot, sour, spin, time, veer, walk, wing **5** alter, apply, crack, curve, drive, eject, fling, hinge, pivot, round, scare, shift, shock, spell, spoil, start, stint, swing, throw, twist, whack, wheel, whirl **6** action, become, chance, change, curdle, depend, direct, effort, fright, gyrate, invert, period, reside, rotate, sprain, stroll, swerve, swivel, wrench, zigzag **7** acidify, attempt, convert, deliver, execute, ferment, perform, reverse, revolve, service, winding **8** gyration, overturn, roll over, rotation, surprise **9** cause to go, deviation, discharge, transform **10** accomplish, alteration, revolution **11** fluctuation, opportunity **12** metamorphose

Turkey

capital: 6 Angora, Ankara
largest city: 8 Istanbul
others: 4 Enos, Troy, Urfa **5** Adana, Bursa, Izmir, Konya, Maras, Siirt, Sivas **6** Aintab, Edessa, Edirne, Elaziz, Marash, Samsun, Smyrna **7** Antakya, Antioch, Erzurum, Kayseri, Mersin, Scutari, Trabzon, Uskudar **8** Stamboul **9** Byzantium, Eskisehir, Gaziantep **10** Adrianople **14** Constantinople
school: 6 Aegean, Ankara **8** Istanbul
division: 4 Pera, Sert **5** Siirt, Troad **6** Angora, Eyalet, Thrace **7** Anadolu, Beyoglu, Cilicia **8** Anatolia **9** Asia Minor, Kurdistan
measure: 3 dra, oka, pik **4** draa, khat, kile, zira **5** berri, kileh, zirai **6** arshin, chinik, fortin, halebi **7** nocktat
monetary unit: 4 lira, para **5** akcha, asper, kurus, pound, rebia **6** akcheh, zequin **7** aetilik, beshlik, piaster **8** medjidie
weight: 3 oka, oke **4** aqui, dram, rotl **5** artal, cheke, kerat, obolu, ratel **6** batman, dirhem, kantar, maunch, miskal **7** drachma, quintal, yusdrum
island: 6 Cyprus, Kibris
lake: 3 Tuz, Van **7** Egridir **8** Beysehir
mountain: 2 Ak **3** Ala **4** Alai, Dagh, Kara **5** Hasan, Hinis, Honaz, Murat, Murit **6** Ala Dag, Bingol, Bolgar, Pontic, Suphan, Taurus **7** Aladagh, Erciyas **8** Karacali **10** Kackar Dagi
highest point: 6 Ararat
river: 4 Aras, Kura **5** Araks, Dicle, Firat, Gediz, Goksu, Halys, Irmak, Kizil, Mesta, Murat, Sarus **6** Araxes, Ceyhan, Seihun, Seyhan, Seylan, Tigris **7** Kurucay, Muradsu, Orontes, Sakarya **8** Granicus, Macestus, Maeander, Menderes **9** Euphrates **13** Buyukmenderes
sea: 4 Aral **5** Black **6** Aegean **7** Marmara **13** Mediterranean
physical feature:
***cape:* 4** Baba, Ince **5** Bafra **6** Anamur, Helles, Hinzir **7** Karatas, Kerempe
***gulf:* 3** Cos **5** Izmir **7** Antalya
***inlet:* 10** Golden Horn
***peninsula:* 9** Anatolian, Gallipoli
***plateau:* 9** Anatolian
***strait:* 8** Bosporus **9** Bosphorus **11** Dardanelles
people: 4 Arab, Kurd, Turk **6** Seljuk
***king:* 8** Mausolus
***leader:* 5** Inonu, Osman **6** Ecevit **7** Demirel **8** Menderes, Suleiman **12** Kemal Ataturk
***poet:* 5** Homer
language: 6 Arabic **7** Kurdish, Turkish
religion: 5 Islam **7** Judaism **12** Christianity **13** Greek Orthodox, Roman Catholic
place:
***bridge:* 6** Galata
***dam:* 9** Gokcekaya
***mosque:* 4** Blue, Yeni **8** Selimiye **11** Hagia Sophia, Sultan Ahmed
***ruins:* 4** Troy **7** Ephesus **8** Pergamum
***tomb:* 12** Kemal Ataturk
feature:
***cap:* 3** fez **6** calpac **7** calpack
***clothing:* 6** caftan, dolman, jelick **7** yashrak **8** charshaf, maharmah, shakseer
***goat hair:* 6** mohair
***grill:* 6** mangal
***harem:* 5** serai **8** seraglio
***musical instrument:* 5** canum, kanum **6** canoon, johnie, kussir, zither **8** crescent, jingling
***pipe:* 10** meerschaum
food:
***dish:* 5** halva, pilaw **10** doner kebab, shish kebab
***drink:* 4** boza, raki **5** airan, pasha, rakee **6** mastic
***pastry:* 7** baklava
***turkey:* 4** hind

turn a deaf ear to 6 ignore, slight **9** disregard

turn aside 5 avert **6** divert **7** deflect, deviate **8** turn away

turn away 5 avert **6** give up **8** alienate, estrange, send away **9** turn aside **12** turn one's back

turnback 4 fold, quit, tack **5** repel **6** defect, desert, return, revert **7** forsake, regress, relapse, repulse, retrace, retreat, reverse **9** backslide

turncoat 5 Judas **6** bolter **7** traitor **8** apostate, betrayer, defector, deserter, quisling, renegade **12** double-dealer

turn down 5 spurn **6** refuse, reject **14** lower the volume, refuse to accept

Turner, Joseph Mallord William
born: 6 London **7** England
artwork: 12 The Shipwreck, The Slave Ship, Tintern Abbey **17** Dawn After the Wreck **20** Dido Building Carthage **22** Venice S Giorgio Maggiore **24** The Sun of Venice Going to Sea **25** The Thames near Walton Bridge, Ulysses Deriding Polyphe-

mus **30** Burning of the Houses of Parliament **32** Snowstorm Hannibal Crossing the Alps **32** The Falls of the Rhine at Schaffhausen **34** The Bay of Baiae with Apollo and the Sibyl **37** Fighting Temeraire Tugged to her Last Berth **47** The Parting of Hero and Leander from the Greek of Musaeus **50** The Shipwreck Fishing Boats Endeavoring to Rescue the Crew

Turner, Kathleen
roles: **8** Body Heat **12** Prizzi's Honor **17** Romancing the Stone, The Jewel of the Nile **18** Peggy Sue Got Married

Turner, Lana
real name: **29** Julia Jean Mildred Frances Turner
nickname: **11** Sweater Girl
born: **9** Wallace ID
discovered at: **16** Schwab's Drugstore
husband: **9** Artie Shaw, Lex Barker **10** Bob Topping **12** Stephen Crane
roles: **7** Madame X **11** Peyton Place **15** By Love Possessed, Imitation of Life **26** The Postman Always Rings Twice

turning **4** bend **5** curve **7** bending, curving, winding **8** pivoting, rotating, spinning, twisting, whirling **9** revolving, swiveling

turnip **12** Brassica rapa
group: **8** Rapifera
varieties: **6** Indian **7** Italian, Swedish **8** seven-top

turn off **4** bore, exit **5** douse, leave, repel **6** revolt, sicken **7** disgust, repulse **8** alienate, turn away **9** switch off **10** deactivate

turn of phrase **5** idiom **8** locution, phrasing **10** expression **11** phraseology

Turn of the Screw, The
author: **10** Henry James
character: **5** Flora, Miles **7** Mr Quint **8** Mrs Grose **10** Miss Jessel **12** The Governess

turn on **5** start, tempt **6** allure, attack, entice, excite **7** actuate, attract **8** activate, energize, interest, switch on

turn one's stomach **6** revolt, sicken **7** disgust **8** nauseate

turnout **5** crowd **6** output, throng **8** assembly, audience **9** gathering **10** assemblage, production

turn out **4** garb, oust **5** array, dress, eject, end up, evict, exile, expel **6** appear, attend, attire, banish, clothe, evolve, fit out, invest, rig out, show up, unfold **7** cast out, come out, costume, develop, kick out **8** drive out, send away **9** switch off **11** come to light

turn over **4** flip **5** upset **6** bestow, rotate **7** deliver **8** flip-flop, give over, hand over, overturn **9** surrender **10** relinquish, somersault

turn pale **4** fade **6** blanch, whiten **7** lighten

turn tail **4** flee **7** retreat, run away **8** back away **12** beat a retreat

turn to account **7** exploit, utilize **8** profit by, put to use **9** make use of **12** capitalize on

turn topsy turvy **5** upset **7** capsize, confuse, tip over **8** flip-flop, overturn, put askew **10** disarrange, turn turtle **11** disorganize

turn turtle **5** upset **7** capsize, tip over **8** flip over, keel over, overturn, turn over **14** turn upside down

turn up **4** come **6** appear, arrive, crop up, drop in, emerge, loom up, show up **7** develop, surface **11** come to light

Turnus
father: **6** Daunus
mother: **7** Venilia
sister: **7** Juturna
sought to win: **7** Lavinia
killed by: **6** Aeneas

Turpentine State
nickname of: **13** North Carolina

turpitude **4** evil, vice **8** baseness, lewdness, vileness **9** depravity **10** corruption, debauchery, defilement, degeneracy, immorality, perversion, sinfulness, wickedness, wrongdoing **13** dissoluteness **14** licentiousness

turquoise **4** aqua **5** stone **7** mineral, sky-blue **10** aquamarine **12** greenish-blue, Prussian-blue
source: **12** United States

turret **5** tower **6** belfry, cupola, garret, gazebo, louver, terret **7** minaret, rotator, steeple **8** gunhouse, gunmount **9** belvedere, pepperbox **10** watchtower
tool: **5** lathe

turtle **3** box **4** musk, wood **6** slider **7** painted, reptile, snapper, spotted **8** slowpoke, terrapin, tortoise **10** turtledove **11** leatherback
dorsal shell: **8** carapace
nautical: **5** upset **6** pocket **7** capsize **8** overturn
order: **8** Chelonia
ventral shell: **8** plastron
young: **7** turtlet

Turveydrop
character in: **10** Bleak House
author: **7** Dickens

tussle **4** fray **5** brawl, fight, melee, scrap, set-to **6** battle, fracas **7** grapple, scuffle, wrestle **8** conflict, struggle **10** donnybrook, free-for-all **11** altercation

tussock **4** hair, tuft **5** brush, bunch, clump, grass, sedge **7** bulrush, cluster, thicket **8** feathers

tutelage **8** coaching, guidance, teaching, training, tutoring **9** direction, education, schooling **10** discipline **11** inculcation, instruction, supervision, trusteeship **12** guardianship **14** indoctrination

tutor **4** guru **5** coach, drill, teach **6** master, mentor, school **7** prepare, teacher **8** instruct **10** instructor **11** give lessons

tutorial **5** class **8** didactic, edifying **11** educational, instructive **12** prescriptive

tutti
music: **3** all **18** all players together, all singers together

Tuvalu
other name: **13** Ellice Islands, Lagoon Islands
capital: **8** Funafuti
head of state: **14** British monarch **15** governor general
monetary unit: **4** cent **6** dollar
island: **3** Nui **6** Niutao **7** Nanumea, Vaitupu **8** Funafuti **9** Nanumanga, Niulakita, Nukufetau **10** Nukulaelae
highest point: **5** Nuwak
sea: **7** Pacific
people: **6** Samoan **10** Polynesian
leader: **5** Lauti
language: **6** Samoan **7** English **8** Tuvaluan **10** Polynesian
religion: **10** Protestant **12** Tuvalu Church

Tuvim, Judith
real name of: **12** Judy Holliday

twaddle **3** rot **4** bosh, bunk **5** trash, tripe **6** babble, drivel, gabble, jabber, piffle **7** chatter, prattle, rubbish **8** claptrap, idle talk, nonsense, tommyrot **9** jabbering, silly talk **10** balderdash **16** stuff-and-nonsense

Twain, Mark
real name: **13** Samuel Clemens
author of: **9** Tom Sawyer **10** Roughing It **12** A Tramp Abroad, The Gilded Age **15** (Adventures of) Huckleberry Finn **18** The Innocents Abroad **20** Life on the Mississippi **21** The Mysterious Stranger, The Prince and the Pauper **29** The Man That Corrupted Hadleyburg **36** A Connecticut Yankee in King Arthur's Court **41** The Celebrated Jumping Frog of Calaveras County

twang **9** resonance, vibration **10** nasal sound **13** reverberation

Tweedledee
character in: **22** Through the Looking Glass
author: **7** Carroll

Tweedledum
character in: **22** Through the Looking Glass
author: **7** Carroll

tweet **4** peep **5** cheep, chirp **7** chirrup, chitter, twitter

Twelfth-Night
author: **18** William Shakespeare
character: **5** Feste, Maria, Viola (Cesario) **6** Olivia, Orsino **7** Antonio **8** Malvolio **9** Sebastian **12** Sir Toby Belch **18** Sir Andrew Aguecheek

Twelve Angry Men
director: **11** Sidney Lumet
cast: **8** Ed Begley, Lee J Cobb **10** E G Marshall, Henry Fonda, Jack Warden **11** Jack Klugman, John Fiedler **12** Martin Balsam

Twelve O'Clock High
director: **9** Henry King
cast: **10** Dean Jagger **11** Gary Merrill, Gregory Peck, Hugh Marlowe **15** Millard Mitchell
Oscar for: **15** supporting actor (Jagger)

Twentieth Century
director: **11** Howard Hawks
based on play by: **8** Ben Hecht **16** Charles MacArthur
cast: **11** Roscoe Karns **13** Carole Lombard, John Barrymore **14** Walter Connolly

Twentieth Century, The
narrator: **14** Walter Cronkite

twenty-one *see* **9** blackjack

Twenty Questions
host: **10** Bill Slater, Jay Jackson
panelist: **11** Herb Polesie **12** Bobby McGuire **13** Johnnie McPhee **14** Dickie Harrison, Florence Rinard **15** Fred Van De Venter

Twenty Thousand Leagues Under the Sea
author: **10** Jules Verne
character: **7** Conseil, Ned Land **11** Captain Nemo **22** Professor Pierre Aronnax
submarine: **8** Nautilus

Twenty Years After
author: **14** Alexandre Dumas (pere)

Twice-Told Tales
author: **18** Nathaniel Hawthorne

Twightwee *see* **5** Miami

twilight **3** ebb, eve **4** dusk **6** sunset **7** decline, evening, sundown **8** eventide, gloaming, moonrise **9** half-light, last phase, nightfall **14** edge of darkness

Twilight of the Gods **8** Ragnorak
German: **15** Gotterdammerung

Twilight Zone, The
host: **10** Rod Serling

twin **4** dual, like **5** alike **6** double, paired **7** matched, twofold **9** duplicate, identical

Twin **6** Thomas

twine **4** coil, cord, rope, wind **5** braid, cable, plait, twist, weave **6** string, thread **7** binding, entwine **9** interlace **10** intertwine

twinge **4** pain, pang, stab **5** cramp, spasm, throb **6** stitch, tingle, twitch

twinkle **4** glow **5** blaze, flare, flash, gleam, shine **7** flicker, glimmer, glisten, shimmer, sparkle **11** scintillate

Twinkleton, Miss
character in: **22** The Mystery of Edwin Drood
author: **7** Dickens

Twins
constellation of: **6** Gemini

twirl **4** spin **5** pivot, twine, wheel, whirl **6** gyrate, rotate **7** revolve **9** pirouette

twist **3** arc, way **4** bend, coil, curl, idea, kink, knot, pull, roll, spin, turn, veer, wind, wrap, yank **5** curve, pivot, ravel, slant, snake, swing, twine, whirl, wrest **6** change, method, notion, rotate, spiral, sprain, swerve, swivel, system, tangle, wrench, zigzag **7** contort, distort, entwine, meander **8** approach, rotation, surprise **9** corkscrew, interlace, treatment **10** intertwine, involution **11** convolution, development

twisted **4** bent **6** warped **7** crooked, gnarled **8** deformed **9** contorted, distorted, misshapen

twisting **7** crooked, curving, turning **9** contorted, revolving, spiraling, swiveling

twist out of shape **4** warp **6** deform **7** contort, distort

twitch **3** tic **4** jerk **5** shake, spasm, throb **6** quaver, quiver, squirm, tremor, wiggle, writhe **7** tremble **8** paroxysm **10** convulsion

twitter **4** fuss, peep, stew **5** cheep, chirp, tizzy, tweet, whirl **6** bustle, flurry, pother, uproar, warble **7** chatter, chirrup, ferment, fluster, flutter **8** chirping **10** turbulence **11** chirrupping

two-faced **5** false **7** devious **8** slippery **9** deceitful, deceptive, dishonest, insincere **10** perfidious **11** dissembling, double-faced, duplicitous, fork-tongued, treacherous, underhanded **12** dishonorable, disingenuous, falsehearted, hypocritical **13** double-dealing, untrustworthy

twofold **4** dual **6** double **7** two-part

Two Gentlemen of Verona, The
author: **18** William Shakespeare
character: **5** Julia **6** Silvia, Thurio **7** Proteus **9** Valentine **11** Duke of Milan

Two Lands, The *see* **5** Egypt

two of a kind **4** pair **5** twins **6** couple **7** doublet

two-part **4** dual, twin **6** double, paired **9** bipartite

twosome **3** duo **4** pair **5** brace **6** couple

2001: A Space Odyssey
author: **13** Arthur C Clarke
director: **14** Stanley Kubrick
character: **4** Dave **5** Steve
computer: **3** HAL

cast: **3** HAL **10** Keir Dullea **12** Gary Lockwood **16** William Sylvester
song: **20** Thus Spake Zarathustra (Richard Strauss)
sequel: **24** Two Thousand Ten: Odyssey Two

two-time **6** betray **10** be disloyal **11** double-cross **12** be unfaithful **13** be treacherous, play false with **14** break faith with

two-timing **5** false **6** tricky **7** perfidy **8** bad faith, betrayal, disloyal, trickery **9** deceiving, deception, duplicity, falseness, treachery **10** disloyalty, perfidious **11** double-cross, duplicitous, treacherous **13** breach of faith, double-dealing, faithlessness **14** double-crossing

two-wheeler **4** bike **5** cycle **7** bicycle

Two Years Before the Mast
author: **18** Richard Henry Dana Jr

Tybalt
character in: **14** Romeo and Juliet
author: **11** Shakespeare

Tyche
origin: **5** Greek
goddess of: **7** fortune
corresponds to: **7** Fortuna

tycoon **4** boss **5** mogul, nabob **6** big gun, bigwig **7** big shot, magnate **8** big wheel **9** potentate **12** entrepreneur **13** industrialist **17** captain of industry

Tydeus
father: **6** Oeneus
mother: **8** Periboea
uncle: **5** Melas **6** Agrius **9** Alcathous
son: **8** Diomedes

tyke **3** kid, tad, tot **5** child **6** shaver, squirt, wee one **9** little one

Tyler, John ***see box***

Tyler, John
presidential rank: **5** tenth
party: **4** Whig **20** Democratic-Republican
state represented: **2** VA **8** Virginia
defeated: **5** no-one
succeeded upon death of: **8** Harrison
vice president: **4** none
cabinet:
state: **6** (Abel Parker) Upshur **7** (Daniel) Webster, (John C) Calhoun
treasury: **4** (George Mortimer) Bibb **5** (Thomas) Ewing **7** (John Canfield) Spencer, (Walter) Forward
war: **4** (John) Bell **7** (John Canfield) Spencer, (William) Wilkins
attorney general: **6** (Hugh Swinton) Legare, (John) Nelson **10** (John Jordan) Crittenden
navy: **5** (John Young) Mason **6** (Abel Parker) Upshur, (George Edmund) Badger, (Thomas Walker) Gilmer
postmaster general: **7** (Francis) Granger **9** (Charles Anderson) Wickliffe
born: **2** VA **8** Greenway, Virginia **17** Charles City County
died/buried: **2** VA **8** Richmond, Virginia
education: **14** William and Mary
religion: **12** Episcopalian
vacation spot: **2** VA **7** Hampton **8** Virginia
political career: **8** US Senate **12** State Council **13** vice president **24** US House of Representatives
delegate to: **13** State Assembly
governor of: **8** Virginia
civilian career: **6** farmer, lawyer
military service: **19** War of Eighteen Twelve
notable events of lifetime/term:
act: **6** Tariff (of 1842)
annexation of: **5** Texas
treaty: **16** Webster-Ashburton
father: **4** John
mother: **4** Mary (Marott Armistead)
siblings: **7** William **8** Wat Henry **10** Maria Henry **12** Anne Contesse **14** Christina Booth **15** Martha Jefferson **18** Elizabeth Armistead
wife: **5** Julia (Gardiner) **7** Letitia (Christian)
children: **4** John, Mary **5** Alice, Julia, Pearl **6** Robert **7** Lachlan, Letitia **8** Tazewell **9** Elizabeth **12** Anne Contesse, Lyon Gardiner **13** David Gardiner, John Alexander **16** Robert FitzWalter

Tyll Eulenspiegel *see* **16** Till Eulenspiegel

Tyndall, John
field: **7** physics
nationality: **5** Irish
studied diffusion of: **5** light

Tyndareus
wife: **4** Leda
daughter: **6** Phoebe **8** Philonoe, Timandra **12** Clytemnestra

Tyndaridae *see* **15** Castor and Pollux

type **4** font, kind, race, sort **5** brand, class, genus, group, model, order, print **6** design, family, phylum, sample **7** pattern, species, variety **8** category, division, specimen, typeface **9** archetype, prototype **10** typography

type, movable
invented by: **9** Gutenberg

Typee
author: **14** Herman Melville
character: **3** Tom (Melville) **4** Toby **6** Marnoo, Mehevi **7** Fayaway **8** Kory-Kory

typewriter
invented by: **5** Soule **6** Sholes **7** Glidden

Typhoeus
form: **7** monster
father: **8** Tartarus
mother: **2** Ge
number of heads: **10** one hundred

Typhon
form: **7** monster
father: **8** Typhoeus
son: **5** Ladon

typhoon **4** gale, gust, wind **5** storm **7** cyclone, tempest, tornado, twister **9** hurricane, whirlwind

Typhoon
author: **12** Joseph Conrad

typical **5** model, stock, usual **6** normal **7** average, regular **8** ordinary, orthodox, standard **9** exemplary, in keeping **10** individual, prototypal, true to type **11** distinctive, in character **12** conventional, to be expected **14** characteristic, representative

typify **5** sum up **6** embody **7** betoken, connote, pass for **8** instance, stand for **9** epitomize, exemplify, incarnate, personify, represent **10** illustrate **12** characterize

typography measure **2** em, en **4** pica **5** point

Tyr
origin: **12** Scandinavian
god of: **7** victory
father: **4** Odin **5** Othin
mother: **3** Fri **5** Frigg, Frija **6** Frigga
killed by: **4** Garm

tyrannical **7** fascist **8** despotic **9** imperious **10** oppressive **11** dictatorial, domineering **13** authoritarian

tyrannize **7** oppress **8** domineer, overlord **10** slave drive

tyrannized **9** exploited, oppressed **11** downtrodden, subservient **12** harshly ruled

Tyrannosaurus
type: **8** dinosaur, theropod
location: **7** Montana **12** North America
period: **10** Cretaceous

tyrannous **8** despotic **9** imperious **10** iron-handed, oppressive, repressive, tyrannical

tyranny **7** cruelty, fascism **8** coercion, iron fist, iron hand, iron rule, severity **9** despotism, harshness **10** domination, oppression, repression **11** persecution **12** dictatorship **13** reign of terror **15** totalitarianism

tyrant **5** bully **6** despot **8** dictator, martinet **10** persecutor, taskmaster **11** cruel master, slave driver

Tyre
king of: **5** Hiram

tyro **6** intern, novice, rookie **7** learner, recruit, trainee **8** beginner, initiate, neophyte, newcomer **9** greenhorn **10** apprentice, tenderfoot

Tyro
father: **9** Salmoneus
loved by: **8** Cretheus, Poseidon
son: **5** Aeson **6** Nelcus, Pelias
grandson: **5** Jason **6** Nestor

Tyrrheus
occupation: **8** shepherd

Tyson, Cicely
born: **9** New York NY
roles: **5** Roots **7** Sounder **33** The Autobiography of Miss Jane Pittman

tzimmes **4** fuss **6** uproar **10** hullabaloo
literally: **4** stew **9** mixed dish

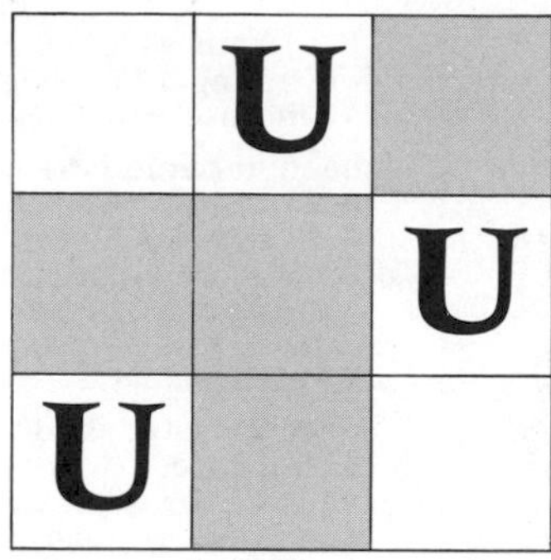

ua mau ke ea o ka aina i ka pono **43** the life of the land is maintained by righteousness
motto of: **6** Hawaii

Ubangi-Shari *see* **22** Central African Republic

Ubermensch **8** superman

ubiquitous **7** allover **9** pervading, pervasive, prevalent, universal, worldwide
10 everywhere, widespread
11 everpresent, omnipresent
12 all-pervading

ubiquitously **10** everywhere
11 extensively

ubi supra **19** where mentioned above

Ubu Roi
author: **11** Alfred Jarry

Ucalegon
counselor to: **5** Priam

Uccello, Paolo
real name: **11** Paolo di Dono
born: **5** Italy **8** Florence
artwork: **8** The Flood **12** The Night Hunt **15** Sir John Hawkwood **18** The Rout (Battle) of San Romano **20** St George and the Dragon **28** Man and Woman of Portinari Family

Udaeus
member of: **6** Sparti
grandson: **8** Tiresias

Udall, Nicholas
author of: **19** Ralph Roister Doister

Uganda ***see box, p. 1012***

ugliness **8** ill-favor **9** grossness **10** homeliness **11** hideousness, monstrosity **12** unseemliness **13** frightfulness, grotesqueness, monstrousness, repulsiveness, unsightliness **14** unpleasantness **16** unattractiveness

ugly **4** foul, mean, vile **5** nasty **6** homely, horrid, odious
7 hideous, hostile, ominous
8 dreadful, horrible, menacing, unseemly **9** abhorrent, dangerous, difficult, frightful, grotesque, monstrous, obnoxious, offensive, repellent, repugnant, repulsive, sickening, unsightly
10 abominable, disgusting, forbidding, ill-favored, portentous, unbearable, unbecoming, unpleasant **11** belligerent, evil-looking, quarrelsome, threatening, troublesome
12 cantankerous, disagreeable, inauspicious, unattractive

ugly as sin **7** hideous **9** frightful, grotesque, monstrous, repulsive

Ugly Duchess, The
author: **16** Lion Feuchtwanger

Ugly Duckling, The
author: **21** Hans Christian Andersen

Ugly Scenes, Beautiful Women
author: **8** C D B Bryan

ukase **4** fiat **5** edict, order
6 decree, dictum, ruling
7 command, mandate, statute
9 directive, manifesto, ordinance **10** injunction **12** proclamation **13** pronouncement
14 pronunciamento

Ulan Bator
capital of: **8** Mongolia

ulcer **4** sore **6** canker

Uller
also: **4** Ullr
origin: **8** Teutonic
god of: **12** winter sports
stepfather: **4** Thor

Ullmann, Liv
born: **5** Japan, Tokyo
nationality: **9** Norwegian
roles: **7** Persona **10** Face to Face **11** Forty Carats, Lost Horizon **12** The Emigrants
16 Cries and Whispers
19 Scenes from a Marriage

Ullr *see* **5** Uller

Ulman, Douglas Elton
real name of: **16** Douglas Fairbanks

ulna
bone of: **8** lower arm

ulterior **6** covert, hidden, secret **7** selfish **9** concealed
10 undivulged, unrevealed
11 self-serving, undisclosed, unexpressed **13** opportunistic

ultimate **3** end **4** acme, apex, last, peak **5** final **6** height, utmost **7** extreme, maximum, supreme **8** crowning, eventual, greatest, terminal **9** at the peak, high point, last straw, long-range, resulting **10** conclusive, definitive
French: **7** dernier

Ultor
epithet of: **7** Jupiter
means: **7** avenger

ultramodern **8** advanced, brand-new **10** avant-garde, newfangled **13** in the vanguard, up-to-the-minute

Ulysses
author: **10** James Joyce
character: **10** Molly Bloom
12 Blazes Boylan, Buck Mulligan, Leopold Bloom
14 Stephen Dedalus

Ulysses *see* **8** Odysseus

umber **5** brown **7** pigment
9 dark-brown **14** yellowish-brown

umbrage **5** pique, shade
6 leaves, shadow **7** foliage, offense, outrage **10** resentment

Umbrellas of Cherbourg, The
director: **11** Jacques Demy
cast: **10** Anne Vernon
15 Nino Castelnuovo

Uganda
capital/largest city: **7** Kampala
others: **4** Arua, Gulu, Lira **5** Atiak, Jinja, Mbale, Mengo **6** Kasese, Kiboga, Kitgum, Masaka, Moroto, Pajule, Soroti, Tororo **7** Entebbe, Kachung, Kilembe, Mbarara, Mombasa **8** Kyenjojo **11** Port Masindi
school: **8** Makerere
division: **4** Toro **6** Ankole, Busoga **7** Buganda, Bunyoro
monetary unit: **4** cent **8** shilling
island: **4** Sese
lake: **5** Kioga, Kyoga **6** Albert, Edward, George **8** Victoria
mountain: **4** Oboa **5** Elgon **7** Virunga **9** Mufumbiro, Ruwenzori **18** Mountains of the Moon
highest point: **10** Margherita
river: **4** Aswa, Kafu **5** Pager **7** Katonga **9** White Nile **10** Albert Nile **12** Victoria Nile
physical feature:
falls: **5** Owens **8** Kabalega **9** Murchison
plateau: **6** Ankole **11** East African
valley: **9** Great Rift
people: **4** Alur, Gisu, Soga, Teso **5** Ateso, Bantu, Chiga, Ganda, Langi, Lango, Nkole, Pygmy **6** Acholi, Ankole, Bagisu, Bakiga, Basoga, Batoro **7** Baganda, Banyoro, Bunyoro, Hamitic, Lugbara, Nilotic, Sudanic **9** Nyoro-Toro **10** Banyankole, Karamojong
explorer: **5** Baker, Speke **7** Stanley
king: **6** Mutesa, Mwanga **8** Kabarega
leader: **5** Obote **6** Mutesa **7** Omukama **11** Idi Amin Dada
language: **5** Ateso, Ganda **7** English, Luganda, Swahili
religion: **5** Islam **7** animism **8** Anglican **10** Protestant **13** Roman Catholic
place:
airport: **7** Entebbe
dam: **10** Owens Falls
national park: **6** Kidepo **14** Murchison Falls, Queen Elizabeth
feature:
clothing: **7** busuuti
council of chiefs: **6** lukiko
dance group: **17** Heart Beat of Africa
king: **6** kabaka
food:
drink: **6** waragi

16 Catharine Deneuve
score: **13** Michel Legrand

Umbrian
language family: **12** Indo-European
branch: **6** Italic

umpire **5** judge **7** arbiter, mediate, referee **8** mediator, moderate **9** arbitrate, go-between, moderator **10** adjudicate, arbitrator, negotiator **11** adjudicator, intercessor

Una
character in: **15** The Faerie Queene
author: **7** Spenser

unabbreviated **5** uncut **8** complete, undocked, unpruned **9** uncropped, unreduced, unsnipped, untrimmed **10** unabridged **11** uncondensed, uncurtailed, unshortened **12** uncompressed, unexpurgated

unable **5** unfit **6** cannot **8** helpless, impotent **9** incapable **10** inadequate, unequipped **11** incompetent, unqualified
to tell pitch: **8** tone deaf

unabridged **5** uncut **6** entire, intact **8** complete **10** full-length **11** uncondensed

unacceptable **8** below par, improper, unseemly, unworthy **9** deficient, out of line, unwelcome **10** disallowed, inadequate, unsuitable **11** displeasing, intolerable **12** inadmissible, not allowable, not up to snuff **13** insupportable **14** unsatisfactory **15** not up to standard

unacceptableness **8** disfavor, disgrace, ignominy **18** unsatisfactoriness

unaccommodating **4** rude **8** churlish **9** difficult, unhelpful **10** inflexible, intolerant, unyielding **11** disobliging **13** inconsiderate

unaccompanied **4** lone, solo **5** alone, apart **6** single, singly **8** isolated, lonesome, separate, solitary **9** a cappella, by oneself **10** unattended, unescorted **12** all by oneself **13** companionless

unaccountable **3** odd **4** free **5** clear, queer, weird **6** exempt, immune **7** bizarre, curious, excused, strange, unusual **8** baffling, innocent, peculiar **9** blameless, not liable, unheard-of **10** inculpable, intriguing, mysterious, surprising **11** astonishing, unexplained **12** inexplicable, unfathomable **13** extraordinary, not answerable **14** not responsible **16** incomprehensible

unaccustomed **3** new, odd **4** rare, wild **5** green, new to, novel, queer **6** quaint, unique, unused **7** amazing, bizarre, curious, foreign, not used, strange, ungiven, untried, unusual **8** original, peculiar, singular, uncommon **9** fantastic, startling, unheard-of **10** remarkable, surprising, unfamiliar, unversed in **11** astonishing, out-of-the-way, unpracticed **12** unacquainted, unhabituated, unimaginable **13** extraordinary, inexperienced **14** unfamiliar with **16** out of the ordinary

unacknowledged **9** anonymous **10** unanswered **11** disregarded **12** unidentified, unrecognized

unadorned **4** bald, bare **5** naked, plain, stark **6** simple **7** austere **11** undecorated **12** unornamented **13** unembellished **15** straightforward

unadulterated **4** pure, true **5** clear, uncut **7** genuine **9** unalloyed, untainted **14** untampered-with

unadventurous **5** chary, timid **7** careful **8** cautious, hesitant **11** circumspect

unadvisable **5** silly **6** stupid, unwise **8** unseemly **9** imprudent **11** inadvisable, inexpedient, injudicious, undesirable **15** disadvantageous

unaesthetic **9** tasteless **10** inartistic **11** insensitive **16** undiscriminating

unaffected **4** open **5** frank, naive, plain **6** candid, direct, honest, simple **7** genuine, natural, sincere, unmoved **8** innocent **9** childlike, guileless, ingenuous, unfeeling, unstirred, untouched, unworldly, wholesome **10** impervious, unbothered, unreserved **11** indifferent, insensitive, openhearted, plain-spoken, unconcerned, undesigning, undisturbed **12** unresponsive **13** unsympathetic **15** straightforward, unsophisticated

unaffectedness **4** ease **11** naturalness **12** unconstraint

unafraid **4** bold **5** brave **6** daring, heroic, plucky **7** valiant **8** fearless, intrepid, stalwart, valorous **9** audacious, daredevil, dauntless **10** courageous **11** indomitable, lionhearted, venturesome **12** stouthearted **13** adventuresome

unaggressive **3** shy **4** meek **5** timid **7** passive **8** peaceful, timorous **9** peaceable, shrinking **11** unambitious **14** unenterprising

unagitated **4** calm **6** gentle, placid, serene **8** composed, tranquil **9** collected, unexcited, unruffled **10** untroubled **11** undisturbed, unperturbed **13** self-possessed

unalloyed **4** pure **7** unmixed **11** unqualified **13** unadulterated

unalterable **5** fixed, rigid **6** stable **8** constant **9** immutable, indelible, obstinate, permanent, perennial **10** inflexible, persistent **11** irrevocable **12** indissoluble, unchangeable **13** irretrievable

unambitious **4** easy, lazy **6** humble, modest, simple **8** slothful **10** unaspiring **12** unaggressive **14** unenterprising

unamiable **4** sour **5** cross, surly, testy **6** sullen **7** grouchy, hostile, peevish **8** churlish **9** irascible **10** ill-humored, unfriendly, unpleasant, unsociable **11** bad-tempered, uncongenial **12** disagreeable

unamorous **4** cold, cool **6** frigid **8** unloving **11** passionless

unanimated **4** dull, flat, limp **5** inert, vapid **7** insipid **8** lifeless **10** insentient **11** unconscious

unanimity **6** accord **7** concord, harmony **9** agreement, consensus **11** concordance, concurrence **17** meeting of the minds

unanimous **6** allied, united **9** accordant, consonant, of one mind **10** harmonious, like-minded

unannounced **6** secret, sudden **8** surprise, withheld **10** suppressed, unheralded **11** undisclosed, unlooked for, unpublished **12** unadvertised **13** unanticipated

unanticipated **6** sudden **8** surprise **10** unexpected, unforeseen, unheralded **11** unannounced, unlooked-for, unpredicted

unappealing **10** disgusting, uninviting, unpleasant **11** displeasing **12** disagreeable, unappetizing, unattractive

unappetizing **6** horrid **7** insipid **10** bad-tasting, disgusting, uninviting **11** unpalatable **12** disagreeable

unapproachable **4** cold, cool **5** aloof **6** remote, unique **7** austere, awesome, distant, supreme **8** foremost, peerless, superior **9** matchless, nonpareil, unequaled, unrivaled **10** forbidding, inimitable, preeminent **11** beyond reach, stand-offish, unreachable **12** inaccessible, incomparable, intimidating, second to none, unattainable, unparalleled **13** beyond compare

unasked **6** wanton **8** unbidden, unsought, unwanted **9** uninvited, unwelcome **10** gratuitous **11** uncalled-for, undesirable, unrequested, unsolicited

unassertive **3** shy **5** timid **6** humble, modest **7** bashful **8** sheepish **9** diffident, shrinking

unassertiveness **7** modesty, shyness **8** docility, timidity **9** timidness **10** diffidence, humbleness **11** bashfulness **12** sheepishness

unassuming **5** muted, plain **6** homely, modest, simple **7** natural **9** easygoing **11** unassertive, unobtrusive **13** unpretentious **14** unostentatious

unattached **5** apart, split **6** single **8** detached, separate **9** separated **11** unconnected **12** disconnected

unattractive **4** dull, ugly **5** plain **6** homely **8** frumpish **11** unappealing, undesirable **12** unappetizing

unauthentic **4** fake, mock, sham **5** bogus, false, phony **6** untrue **7** dubious **8** doubtful **9** imitation, synthetic **10** fraudulent **11** counterfeit **12** questionable

unauthenticated **8** disputed **10** apocryphal, unverified **15** unsubstantiated

unauthorized **6** banned, covert **7** furtive **8** outlawed, unlawful **9** concealed, unallowed, underhand **10** prohibited, unapproved, unofficial **11** clandestine, uncertified, unpermitted, unwarranted **12** unaccredited, unsanctioned **13** under-the-table

unavailable **5** taken **6** scarce **7** lacking, married **9** not at hand **10** nonpresent **11** nonexistent

unavailing **4** idle, vain, weak **5** empty, inept **6** futile, no good **7** invalid, useless **8** bootless, impotent **9** fruitless, worthless **11** ineffective, ineffectual **12** unproductive, unsuccessful

unavoidable **4** sure **5** fated, fixed **7** certain **9** necessary, requisite **10** compulsory, imperative, inevitable, obligatory **11** inescapable **13** unpreventable **14** uncontrollable

unaware **8** heedless, ignorant, unwarned **9** in the dark, unalerted, unknowing, unmindful **10** unapprised **11** incognizant, unconscious **12** off one's guard, unacquainted, unsuspecting **13** unenlightened

unawares **8** abruptly, by chance, suddenly **9** by mistake **10** by accident, by surprise, mistakenly **11** unknowingly, unwittingly **12** accidentally, out of nowhere, unexpectedly, unthinkingly **13** inadvertently, involuntarily, unconsciously **14** without warning **15** unintentionally **16** like a thunderbolt **20** like a bolt from the blue, like a thief in the night

unbalanced **3** mad **4** daft, loco **5** batty, nutty, wacky **6** crazed, uneven, warped **7** bonkers, cracked, leaning, unequal, unglued, unsound **8** demented, deranged, lopsided, unhinged, unpoised, unstable, unsteady **9** disturbed, illogical, psychotic, unsettled **10** irrational, unadjusted **11** not all there **12** psychopathic

unbearable **11** intolerable, unendurable, unthinkable **12** inadmissible, insufferable, unacceptable **13** insupportable

unbecoming **4** ugly **6** homely, vulgar **8** improper, unfitted, unseemly, unsuited **9** offensive, tasteless, unsightly **10** indecorous, unsuitable **11** unappealing, unbefitting **12** unattractive **13** inappropriate

unbelief **5** doubt **7** dubiety **9** disbelief **10** skepticism **11** incredulity **12** doubtfulness

unbelievable **5** false **6** absurd, insane **7** amazing, asinine, idiotic **10** astounding, farfetched, incredible, irrational, remarkable, ridiculous **11** astonishing **12** preposterous, unimaginable, unreasonable **13** hard to swallow

unbeliever **7** atheist, heathen infidel, skeptic **8** apostate **10** godless one **11** disbeliever, nonbeliever

unbelieving **7** dubious **8** doubting **9** quizzical, skeptical **10** suspicious **11** distrustful, incredulous, questioning, unconvinced **12** disbelieving, nonbelieving

unbend **5** relax **6** relent, unflex **10** straighten **12** straighten up **13** straighten out

unbending **4** firm **5** rigid, stiff, tough **6** severe, strict **8** stubborn **9** obstinate **10** inflexible, stone-faced, unyielding **11** hard as nails **14** uncompromising

unbent **5** erect **7** relaxed, unbowed, upright, yielded **8** relented, straight, uncurved, unflexed **9** unstooped **12** straightened

unbiased **4** fair, just **7** liberal, neutral **8** detached, tolerant **9** impartial, unbigoted **10** fair-minded, open-minded, undogmatic **11** broad-minded **12** uninfluenced, unprejudiced **13** disinterested, dispassionate

unbigoted **8** tolerant, unbiased **10** open-minded **11** broad-minded **12** unprejudiced

unbind **4** free, undo **5** loose, untie **6** detach, loosen, ungird **7** deliver, release, undress **8** let loose, unfasten

unblamable **5** clear **8** innocent **9** blameless, guiltless, not guilty **10** inculpable, not at fault **14** not responsible

unblemished **4** pure **7** perfect **8** flawless, spotless, unmarred, unsoiled **9** unsullied **10** immaculate, unvitiated **11** white as snow **13** unadulterated **14** uncontaminated **15** clean as a whistle

unblock **4** free, open **5** unbar, unjam **6** unclog, unstop

unborn **5** fetal, later **6** coming, future, to come **7** in utero **9** embryonic **10** subsequent, succeeding **11** prospective

unbosom oneself **7** confess, confide, lay bare **15** unburden oneself

unbound **4** free **5** freed, loose **6** loosed, untied **8** detached, let loose, loosened, released **10** unconfined, unfastened **12** unrestrained

unbounded **8** absolute **9** boundless, unbridled, unlimited **12** uncontrolled, unrestrained, unrestricted **13** unconditional, unconstrained

unbreakable **5** tough **6** strong

unbroken **5** whole **6** entire, intact **7** endless **8** complete **9** ceaseless, continual, incessant, uncracked, undivided, unsmashed **10** continuous, sequential, successive, unruptured **11** consecutive, progressive, unremitting, unshattered **12** undiminished **13** uninterrupted

unbuckle **4** undo **6** loosen **7** release, unhitch, unstrap **8** uncouple, unfasten

unburden **4** free **6** reveal **7** confess, confide, relieve, unbosom **8** disclose **9** disburden **10** unencumber **11** disencumber **15** get off one's chest **18** get out of one's system

unbusinesslike **6** casual, sloppy **8** informal **11** impractical, inefficient

uncalculated **9** unplanned **10** accidental, unintended **11** inadvertent **14** unpremeditated

uncalled-for **6** wanton **7** unasked **8** needless, unneeded, unsought, unwanted **9** redundant, uninvited **10** gratuitous, unprompted **11** unjustified, unnecessary, unsolicited **12** nonessential **14** supererogatory

uncanny **5** eerie, weird **6** spooky **7** curious, strange **8** inspired **9** fantastic, intuitive, marvelous, unearthly, unheard-of, unnatural **10** incredible, mysterious, prodigious, remarkable, unexampled **11** astonishing, exceptional **12** unbelievable, unimaginable **13** extraordinary, uncomfortable

uncanonical **12** unauthorized, unscriptural

Uncas
character in: **20** The Last of the Mohicans
author: **6** Cooper

unceasing **7** endless, eternal **8** constant **9** continual, incessant, perpetual, sustained **10** continuous, persistent, without end

uncelebrated **6** unsung **7** obscure, unknown **9** anonymous **14** uncommemorated

unceremonious **4** curt, rude **5** hasty, rough **6** abrupt **7** brusque **8** informal **11** precipitate

uncertain **4** hazy **6** fitful, unsure **7** dubious, erratic, not sure, obscure, unclear **8** doubtful, hesitant, nebulous, not fixed, variable, wavering **9** debatable, undecided, unsettled **10** disputable, indefinite, indistinct, in question, irresolute, unresolved, up in the air **11** conjectural, fluctuating, not definite, speculative, unconfirmed, vacillating **12** not confident, questionable, undetermined **13** indeterminate, unpredictable

uncertainty **4** odds, risk **5** doubt **6** chance, gamble **8** quandary **9** ambiguity, confusion, hesitancy, vagueness **10** hesitation, indecision, perplexity, unsureness **11** ambivalence, vacillation **12** equivocation, irresolution, shilly-shally **14** indefiniteness

unchain **4** free **7** release, set free **8** liberate, unfetter **9** unshackle

unchangeable **5** rigid **6** stable **7** uniform **8** stubborn **9** immutable, obstinate, permanent **10** inflexible, invariable **11** unalterable **12** intransigent

unchanging **4** fast, firm **5** fixed **6** stable, static **7** abiding, durable, lasting **8** constant **9** immutable, permanent, steadfast **10** monotonous **11** everlasting **12** indissoluble

unchaperoned **10** unattended, unescorted **12** unsupervised **13** unaccompanied

uncharacteristic **8** atypical **12** out of keeping **16** unrepresentative

uncharitable **5** tight **6** stingy, unkind **7** miserly **9** illiberal, niggardly, unfeeling **10** unfriendly, ungenerous, ungracious **11** closefisted, insensitive, tightfisted **12** parsimonious **13** unsympathetic **15** uncompassionate

unchaste **4** lewd **5** loose **6** erotic, impure **7** corrupt, immoral **8** immodest **9** abandoned, debauched **10** dishonored

unchecked **4** free **5** loose **6** unruly **7** liberal, rampant **8** reinless, unreined **9** out of hand, unbridled, unmuzzled **10** unhindered **12** out of control, unrestrained, unsuppressed

uncivil **4** curt, rude **5** blunt, surly **6** abrupt, gauche **7** boorish, brusque **8** impolite **10** ungracious **11** ill-mannered **12** disagreeable, discourteous

uncivilized **4** rude **6** savage, vulgar **7** boorish, brutish, ill-bred, uncouth, untamed **8** barbaric, churlish **9** barbarous, obnoxious, ungenteel **10** uncultured, unpolished **12** uncultivated

unclad **4** bare, nude **5** naked **7** exposed, unrobed **8** disrobed, in the raw, starkers, stripped **9** in the nude, unclothed, uncovered, undressed **10** stark-naked **15** in the altogether

unclean **4** evil, foul, tref, vile **5** dirty, dusty, grimy, messy, muddy, sooty **6** filthy, impure, soiled **7** defiled, immoral, obscene, smutted, stained **8** polluted, unchaste **9** blemished **10** besmirched

unclear **3** dim **4** hazy **5** blear, faint, foggy, fuzzy, misty, vague **6** bleary, cloudy, vapory **7** clouded, obscure, shadowy **8** shrouded, vaporous **9** ambiguous, uncertain **10** indefinite, indistinct

Uncle Remus
author: **18** Joel Chandler Harris

Uncle Tom's Cabin
author: **19** Harriet Beecher Stowe
character: **5** Eliza, Topsy **10** Eva St Clare **11** Simon Legree

Uncle Vanya
author: **12** Anton Chekhov
character: **6** Marina **12** Mihail Astrov **13** Ivan Voynitsky (Uncle Vanya) **14** Marya Voynitsky **15** Sonya Andreyevna **16** Yelena Andreyevna **19** Alexandr Serebryakov

unclose **4** open **6** reveal, unclog, unfold, unshut, unstop, unwrap **7** unblock
poetic: **3** ope

unclothed **4** bare, nude **5** naked **6** unclad **7** exposed, unrobed **8** stripped **9** in the nude, uncovered, undressed

unclouded **5** clear, light, sunny **6** bright, serene **10** unobscured

uncollected **4** owed **5** owing, upset **6** shaken **8** agitated, troubled **9** disturbed, perturbed **11** discomposed, outstanding

uncolored **4** bald, bare, true **5** plain, stark **6** simple **9** unadorned **11** unvarnished **12** unelaborated **13** unembellished **15** straightforward

uncombed **5** messy **6** blowsy, frowzy, matted, mussed, untidy **7** ruffled, rumpled, snarled, tangled, tousled, unkempt **11** disarranged

uncomfortable **4** edgy **5** tense, upset **6** on edge, uneasy **7** awkward, keyed up, nervous, painful **8** confused, strained, troubled **9** ill at ease **10** bothersome, disquieted, irritating, out of place **11** discomfited, discomposed, distressful **13** on tenterhooks

uncommitted **9** unpledged **11** undedicated

uncommon **4** rare **5** novel **6** scarce, unique **7** bizarre, curious, notable, supreme, unusual **8** peculiar, peerless, superior **9** matchless, unmatched **10** infrequent, remarkable, unexcelled, unfamiliar **11** exceptional, outstanding, superlative **12** incomparable, unparalleled **13** extraordinary **14** unconventional **15** once in a lifetime **16** few and far between

uncommunicative **3** mum, shy **4** dumb, mute **5** quiet **6** silent **8** reserved, reticent, retiring, taciturn **9** secretive, withdrawn **10** speechless, tongue-tied, unsociable **11** untalkative **12** close-mouthed, inexpressive

uncomplicated **4** easy **5** clear, plain **6** simple **10** uninvolved

uncomplimentary **8** critical, derisive, negative **9** insulting **10** unadmiring **11** disparaging **12** disapproving, unflattering

uncompromising **4** firm **5** rigid, stiff **6** strict **8** exacting, hardline, obdurate **9** immovable, unbending, unvarying **10** inexorable, inflexible, scrupulous, unyielding **11** unrelenting

unconcealed **4** bald, bare, open **5** overt **6** in view **7** exposed, in sight, obvious, visible **8** apparent, manifest, revealed **9** uncovered **11** discernible, perceivable, perceptible **12** in plain sight, out in the open

unconcentrated **4** weak **7** diffuse, diluted, thinned **9** dispersed, scattered, spread out **11** watered down

unconcern **10** dispassion **11** insouciance, nonchalance **12** indifference

unconcerned **4** cold **5** aloof **6** serene **7** distant, unaware, unmoved **8** composed, uncaring **9** apathetic, oblivious, unfeeling, unmindful **10** impervious, nonchalant, uninvolved, untroubled **11** indifferent, insensitive, passionless, unperturbed **12** unresponsive **13** unsympathetic

unconditional **5** utter **6** entire **8** absolute, complete, outright **9** downright, unlimited **10** conclusive **11** categorical, unqualified **12** unrestricted **13** thoroughgoing

Unconditional Surrender
author: **11** Evelyn Waugh

unconfident **3** shy **5** timid **7** bashful **8** reticent, retiring, timorous **9** diffident, shrinking, uncertain

unconfirmed **7** dubious **8** unproved **10** unapproved, unverified **11** unvalidated **12** questionable **14** uncorroborated **15** unsubstantiated

unconformity **7** anomaly **9** deviation **10** aberration, divergence **11** abnormality, peculiarity **12** eccentricity, idiosyncrasy, irregularity **13** nonconformity

uncongenial **9** ill-suited, unamiable **10** dissimilar, unfriendly, unpleasant **12** disagreeable, incompatible **13** unsympathetic

unconnected **7** severed **8** detached, discrete, separate **9** uncoupled, unhitched, unrelated **12** disconnected

unconquerable **6** innate **9** ingrained **10** inveterate, invincible, unbeatable **12** impenetrable, invulnerable, undefeatable **14** insurmountable, unvanquishable

unconscionable **7** extreme **9** excessive **10** immoderate, inordinate, outrageous **11** inexcusable, unjustified, unwarranted **12** indefensible, preposterous, unforgivable, unpardonable, unreasonable **13** unjustifiable

unconscious 3 out **6** latent **7** in a coma, out cold **8** comatose, in a faint **9** insensate, senseless, unknowing, unmindful **10** suppressed, unrealized **11** incognizant **12** unsuspecting **14** dead to the world

unconstitutional 7 illegal **8** unlawful **12** unauthorized

unconstrained 4 bold, easy **7** natural, relaxed **8** unforced **9** abandoned **10** unaffected **11** spontaneous, uninhibited **French: 6** degage

unconstraint 4 ease **7** abandon **8** boldness, free will, openness **9** frankness **11** naturalness, spontaneity

uncontrollable 6 unruly **7** wayward **12** ungovernable, unmanageable

uncontrolled 4 free, wild **8** absolute **9** abandoned, unlimited **10** ungoverned **12** unrestrained

unconventional 3 odd **4** rare **5** crazy, kinky, nutty, queer, wacky, weird **6** far-out, quaint, unique **7** bizarre, curious, offbeat, strange, unusual **8** aberrant, atypical, bohemian, freakish, original, peculiar, singular, uncommon **9** different, eccentric, fantastic, irregular **10** newfangled, outlandish, unorthodox **11** exceptional **12** unaccustomed **13** extraordinary, idiosyncratic, nonconforming, nonconformist **15** individualistic

unconvinced 7 dubious **8** doubtful **9** skeptical, uncertain, unsettled

unconvincing 5 false, fishy **7** dubious, suspect **10** suspicious **11** implausible **12** questionable, unbelievable

uncooked
French: 9 au naturel

uncooperative 6 ornery **7** selfish **8** perverse, stubborn **9** difficult, unhelpful, unwilling **11** intractable **12** intransigent

uncoordinated 6 clumsy **7** awkward **8** ungainly **9** graceless

uncouple 4 undo **6** detach, loosen, unhook **7** release, unhitch **8** unbuckle

uncoupled 8 detached, loosened **9** separated, unhitched **10** disengaged **11** unconnected **12** disconnected

uncourageous 5 timid **8** cowardly, timorous **9** dastardly, shrinking **13** pusillanimous

uncourtly 7 ill-bred, uncivil, uncouth **9** ungallant **10** ill-behaved, ungracious, unmannerly **11** uncourteous **12** discourteous **13** ungentlemanly

uncouth 4 rude **5** crass, crude, gross, rough **6** callow, coarse **7** boorish, brutish, ill-bred, loutish, uncivil **8** barbaric, churlish, impolite **9** unrefined **10** indelicate, uncultured, unmannerly **11** ill-mannered, uncivilized **12** uncultivated

uncover 4 bare, undo **5** dig up, strip **6** denude, dig out, expose, reveal, unmask, unveil, unwrap **7** disrobe, lay bare, uncloak, undrape, undress, unearth **8** disclose, unclothe **9** make known, unsheathe **11** make visible **12** bring to light

uncovered 4 bare **5** bared, dug up, naked **7** exposed, noticed **8** detected, revealed **9** disclosed, made known **10** discovered **13** brought to view **14** brought to light

uncovering 8 exposure **9** divulging, unmasking **10** disclosure, divulgence, laying open, revelation **15** bringing to light **20** bringing out in the open

uncritical 4 dull, dumb **6** casual, obtuse, stupid **7** inexact, offhand, shallow **8** careless, ignorant, slipshod **9** imprecise, untutored **10** inaccurate, uneducated, unschooled, unthinking **11** perfunctory, superficial **12** unreflecting **16** undiscriminating

unctuous 4 oily, smug **6** smarmy **7** fawning, honeyed, servile **8** slippery, too suave **9** pietistic, too smooth **10** flattering, obsequious **11** sycophantic **12** honey-tongued, ingratiating **13** sanctimonious, self-righteous

uncultivated 3 raw **4** wild **7** uncouth **8** unfarmed, unplowed, untilled **9** unrefined **10** unimproved **11** undeveloped

uncultivated land
god of: 8 Silvanus, Sylvanus

uncultured 5 crass **6** coarse, common, vulgar **7** low-bred **9** inelegant, unrefined **10** unpolished **12** uncultivated

uncustomary 4 rare **6** unique **7** amazing, unusual **8** singular, uncommon, unwonted **9** unheard-of **10** incredible, unexpected **11** astonishing, exceptional **12** unaccustomed, unbelievable **13** extraordinary, unanticipated

undaunted 5 brave **6** gritty, heroic, plucky **7** unfazed, valiant **8** fearless, intrepid, resolute, stalwart, valorous **9** not put off **10** courageous, undismayed **11** indomitable, unflinching, unperturbed, unshrinking **12** stouthearted **13** undiscouraged

undeceive 8 disabuse **10** disenchant **11** disenthrall, disillusion **12** open one's eyes **13** break the spell **15** burst one's bubble **19** bring one down to earth **20** shatter one's illusions

undecided 4 open **5** vague **6** unsure **7** dubious, pending **8** not final, wavering **9** tentative, uncertain, unsettled **10** indecisive, indefinite, in abeyance, in a dilemma, irresolute, of two minds, open-minded, unresolved, up in the air **11** fluctuating, vacillating **12** undetermined, unformulated **16** hemming and hawing **17** blowing hot and cold **20** going around in circles

undecorated 4 bare **5** blank, plain, stark **6** simple **7** austere **9** unadorned **13** unembellished

undedicated 11 indifferent, uncommitted

undefiled 4 pure **5** clean **6** chaste, intact, virgin **7** natural **8** innocent, spotless **9** stainless, unsullied **10** unpolluted

undemanding 4 easy **6** low-key, simple **7** patient, relaxed **9** easygoing **10** submissive **12** easy to please, laissez-faire **14** live-and-let-live

undemonstrative 3 shy **4** cold **5** aloof **7** distant, stoical **8** reserved **9** impassive **11** unemotional **12** inexpressive, unresponsive **14** self-controlled

undeniable 4 sure **6** patent, proven **7** certain, obvious **8** decisive, manifest **10** conclusive **11** established, indubitable, irrefutable **12** beyond a doubt, demonstrable, indisputable **13** incontestable **14** unquestionable **16** incontrovertible

undeniably 6 surely **9** certainly **10** decisively, definitely **11** irrefutably **12** conclusively, demonstrably, indisputably **13** incontestably **14** beyond question, unquestionably **16** incontrovertibly

undependable 6 fickle **7** erratic, flighty **8** unstable, variable, wavering **10** capricious, changeable, inconstant, unreliable **13** irresponsible, unpredictable, untrustworthy

under 3 sub **5** below, lower, neath, short **7** beneath **8** inferior, less than **9** because of **11** subordinate

undercover 3 sly **6** covert, hidden, secret **7** furtive, sub rosa **8** hush-hush, stealthy **9** concealed, disguised, incognito **10** unrevealed **11** clandestine, undisclosed **12** confidential **13** surreptitious
French: 8 a couvert

undercurrent 4 aura, hint, mood **5** sense, tinge, vibes **7** quality, riptide **8** undertow **9** undertone **10** atmosphere, intimation, suggestion, vibrations **12** crosscurrent

undercut 9 discredit, undermine, undersell **10** compromise

underestimate 7 dismiss, put down **8** belittle, minimize, misjudge **9** deprecate, discredit, disparage, disregard, sell short, underrate, undersell **10** depreciate, undervalue **11** detract from **12** miscalculate

undergarment 3 bra **4** BVDs, slip **5** pants, shift, teddy **6** corset, girdle, shorts **7** chemise, panties **8** bloomers, camisole, knickers, lingerie, skivvies **9** brassiere, petticoat, union suit **12** jockey shorts

undergo 5 brave, stand **6** endure, suffer **7** sustain, weather **8** submit to **9** encounter, go through, withstand **10** experience

undergraduate 4 coed, soph **5** frosh, plebe **6** junior, senior **7** scholar, student **8** freshman **9** sophomore, undegreed **10** degreeless, nondegreed **13** underclassman, upperclassman

underground 6 buried, covert, secret **7** sub-rosa **10** undercover **11** belowground, clandestine **12** subterranean **13** surreptitious **15** below the surface

underground chamber 4 tomb **5** crypt, vault **6** cellar **8** catacomb **9** sepulcher

underhand, underhanded 6 covert, crafty, sneaky, tricky **7** corrupt, crooked, cunning, devious, evasive, furtive, illegal **8** sneaking, stealthy **9** conniving, dishonest, unethical **10** fraudulent **12** unprincipled, unscrupulous **13** surreptitious

underhandedness 5 guile **6** deceit **7** slyness **8** trickery **9** chicanery, deception, duplicity **10** sneakiness, trickiness **13** secretiveness

underline 6 accent, stress **7** dwell on, point up **9** emphasize, press home **10** accentuate, underscore **15** bring into relief

underling 4 serf **6** flunky, lackey, menial, minion, thrall, vassal **7** servant, subject **8** employee, hireling, inferior **9** attendant, hired hand **11** subordinate

underlying 5 basic **6** covert **7** beneath, radical **8** implicit **9** elemental, essential **10** subtending **11** fundamental

undermine 4 foil, ruin **5** erode **6** injure, riddle, scotch, thwart, weaken **7** cripple, destroy, subvert, torpedo **8** sabotage **9** eat away at, frustrate, hamstring **10** neutralize **11** burrow under, tunnel under

underneath 5 below, lower **6** bottom, hidden **9** disguised, subject to **14** misrepresented

undernourished 8 starving, underfed **12** malnourished

under obligation 5 bound **6** liable **7** obliged **8** beholden, indebted **9** obligated **10** answerable, in one's debt **11** accountable, responsible

underpart 4 sole **5** belly, tails **6** bottom **9** lower side, underside

underpin 4 bear **7** bolster, support **10** strengthen **12** substantiate

underpinning 4 base **5** basic **6** ground **7** support **9** essential **10** foundation, groundwork **11** fundamental **12** substructure

underplay 8 play down **11** deemphasize

underprivileged 4 poor **5** needy **6** in need **7** hapless, unlucky **8** badly-off, deprived, ill-fated, indigent **9** destitute, penniless, penurious **10** ill-starred, pauperized **11** handicapped, unfortunate **12** impoverished **13** disadvantaged **22** in adverse circumstances

underrate 6 slight **8** belittle, derogate, minimize **9** denigrate, deprecate, disparage **10** depreciate, undervalue **13** underestimate

underscore 4 mark **6** accent, deepen, play up, stress **7** feature, point up **8** heighten **9** emphasize, intensify, press home, underline **10** accentuate **15** draw attention to

underscoring 6 stress **8** emphasis **11** underlining

underside 4 back, sole **5** belly, tails **6** bottom **7** reverse **9** lower side, underpart

undersized 4 tiny **5** elfin, short, small **6** little, petite, slight **7** stunted **8** dwarfish **10** diminutive **11** lilliputian

underskirt 4 slip **7** pannier **9** crinoline, hoopskirt, petticoat

understand 3 dig, get, see **4** hear, know, read, take **5** grasp, learn **6** absorb, accept, assume, can see, fathom, gather, take it **7** be aware, discern, make out, presume, realize **8** conclude, perceive **9** apprehend, interpret, recognize **10** appreciate, comprehend, take to mean **14** sympathize with, take for granted

understandable 8 apparent **12** recognizable, unmistakable **14** comprehensible

understanding 4 pact **5** grasp **7** empathy, insight, knowing **8** sympathy, tolerant **9** agreement, awareness, intuition, knowledge, sensitive **10** cognizance, compassion, compromise, discerning, perception, perceptive, responsive **11** concordance, sensitivity, sympathetic **12** appreciation, appreciative, apprehension **13** compassionate, comprehension **17** meeting of the minds

understate 8 minimize **11** deemphasize

understated 9 minimized **10** restrained **12** conservative, deemphasized

understatement 7 litotes **10** minimizing **20** conservative estimate

understudy 3 sub **6** backup, double, fill-in, relief **7** stand-by, stand-in **9** alternate, surrogate **10** substitute **11** pinch hitter, replacement

undertake 3 try **5** begin, essay, start **6** assume, strive, tackle, take on **7** attempt **8** commence, embark on, endeavor, set about, shoulder **9** agree to do, enter upon **11** promise to do **13** get involved in

undertaking **3** job **4** task **6** effort **7** concern, project, pursuit, venture **8** endeavor **10** commitment, enterprise

Under the Greenwood Tree
author: **11** Thomas Hardy

under the influence **5** drunk **6** sodden, soused, wasted, zapped, zonked **7** smashed **8** besotted **9** plastered **10** inebriated **11** intoxicated **20** three sheets to the wind

under the weather **3** bad, ill **4** sick **6** ailing, sickly, unwell **9** unhealthy **10** indisposed

undertone **4** aura, hint, mood **5** scent, sense, tinge, trace **6** flavor, mumble, murmur, nuance **7** feeling, inkling, low tone, quality, whisper **8** coloring **10** atmosphere, intimation, suggestion **11** connotation, implication **12** subdued voice, undercurrent

undervalue **6** slight **8** belittle, derogate **9** discredit, disparage, underrate **10** depreciate **13** underestimate

underwear **3** bra **4** BVDs, slip **5** pants, teddy **6** briefs, corset, girdle, shorts **7** chemise, panties **8** bloomers, camisole, knickers, lingerie, skivvies **9** brassiere, petticoat, union suit **12** jockey shorts, smallclothes **14** unmentionables

underweight **4** bony, lank **5** gaunt, lanky **6** skinny **7** scrawny, spindly **8** skeletal, underfed **9** emaciated **12** skin-and-bones **13** hollow-cheeked **14** spindle-shanked, undernourished

underworld **4** Hell **5** Hades, limbo **6** the mob **8** mobsters, the Mafia **9** criminals, gangsters, purgatory **10** Cosa Nostra **11** shades below **12** the syndicate **13** bottomless pit, nether regions **14** organized crime **15** criminal element, infernal regions **16** abode of the damned
god of: **3** Dis **5** Hades, Orcus, Pluto **8** Dis Pater

under wraps **6** hidden, secret **9** concealed **10** suppressed, under cover

underwrite **3** aid **4** back **7** approve, endorse, finance, sponsor, support, warrant **8** invest in, sanction, validate **9** guarantee, subsidize **11** countersign

underwriter **5** angel **6** backer, patron **7** sponsor **8** investor **9** financier, guarantor

undeserving **3** bad **8** inferior, unworthy

undesirable **5** unfit **8** disliked, improper, unbidden, unsavory, unseemly, unwanted, unworthy **9** offensive, unpopular **10** unbecoming, uninviting, unsuitable, unwelcomed **11** distasteful, unbefitting, unwished-for **12** disagreeable, inadmissible, unacceptable, unattractive **13** inappropriate, objectionable **14** unsatisfactory

undetectable **12** unnoticeable, unobservable **13** imperceptible, unsubstantial

undetermined **6** chance **7** unfixed, unknown **8** unproved, unproven **9** uncertain, undecided **10** indefinite, irresolute **13** indeterminate, unascertained

undeveloped **3** raw **5** crude, green **6** callow, unripe **8** immature, inchoate, unformed **9** embryonic, half-baked **10** unfinished **11** rudimentary, unexploited **12** uncultivated

undignified **3** low **7** boorish **8** improper, shameful, unseemly, unworthy **9** degrading, inelegant, tasteless, unrefined **10** beneath one, indecorous, indelicate, in bad taste, unbecoming, unladylike, unsuitable **11** unbefitting **13** discreditable, inappropriate, ungentlemanly **18** beneath one's dignity
Latin: **8** infra dig **15** infra dignitatem

undiluted **4** neat, pure **5** sheer **7** unmixed **8** straight **11** unfortified **12** full-strength **13** unadulterated

Undine
form: **6** spirit
location: **5** water
sex: **6** female

undiscerning **11** insensitive **12** unperceptive **14** indiscriminate

undisciplined **4** wild **6** fickle, fitful **7** erratic, wayward, willful **8** unsteady, untaught **9** mercurial, untrained, untutored **10** capricious, changeable, inconstant, uneducated, unfinished, unreliable, unschooled **11** unpracticed **12** obstreperous, uncontrolled, undependable, unrestrained **13** unpredictable

undisclosed **6** hidden, secret **7** private **9** concealed **10** unrevealed **12** confidential

undisguised **4** open **5** clear, utter **7** evident, obvious **8** complete, distinct, manifest, unhidden **9** out-and-out **10** plain as day, pronounced, unreserved **11** unconcealed **12** unmistakable, wholehearted **13** thoroughgoing **24** plain as the nose on one's face

undismayed **7** uncowed **8** unafraid, unscared **9** confident, unabashed, unalarmed, undaunted **12** unfrightened **13** undiscouraged, unintimidated

undisputed **4** sure **7** certain, granted **8** accepted **9** undoubted **10** conclusive, undeniable **11** beyond doubt, indubitable, irrefutable, past dispute, uncontested **12** acknowledged, indisputable, unchallenged, unquestioned **13** a matter of fact, incontestable **14** beyond question, freely admitted, unquestionable **15** without question **16** incontrovertible

undistinguished **5** plain, usual **6** common **7** prosaic **8** everyday, mediocre, ordinary **10** pedestrian, unexciting **11** commonplace **12** run-of-the-mill, unremarkable **13** unexceptional **18** nothing to rave about

undistracted **4** calm **6** serene, stolid **7** unfazed **9** impassive, unruffled **10** untroubled **11** undisturbed

undisturbed **4** calm, cool **5** quiet **6** placid, serene, steady **7** equable, unmoved **8** composed, peaceful, tranquil **9** collected, inviolate, unexcited, unruffled, untouched **10** of solitude, unagitated, unbothered, untroubled **11** left in order, unperturbed **13** imperturbable, self-possessed, uninterrupted

undivided **5** solid, whole **6** entire, united **7** unified, unsplit **8** complete **9** of one mind, unanimous **10** not divided, unstinting **12** wholehearted

undo **3** end **4** free, open, ruin, void **5** annul, erase, loose, quash, untie **6** cancel, defeat, loosen, offset, repair, unbind, unfold, unhook, unknot, unlace, unlock, unwrap **7** destroy, nullify, rectify, reverse, subvert, unchain, unravel, wipe out **8** demolish, overturn, unbutton, unfasten **9** disengage, eliminate, make up for, undermine **10** counteract, invalidate, neutralize **11** disentangle **13** compensate for **14** counterbalance

undogmatic **7** liberal **8** flexible, tolerant **10** open-minded **11** broad-minded

undoing **4** doom, jinx, ruin **5** upset **6** defeat **7** erasure, nemesis **8** collapse, downfall, negation, reversal, weakness **9** annulment, breakdown, overthrow, ruination, thwarting, wiping out **11** cause of ruin, destruction **12** Achilles' heel, cancellation, invalidation **13** counteraction, nullification **14** neutralization

undomesticated **4** wild **5** feral **6** ferine, savage **7** untamed **8** barbaric **9** barbarous **11** uncivilized

undone **6** ruined **9** come apart, destroyed **10** incomplete, unfastened **12** not completed

undoubted **4** sure **5** utter **7** certain **8** absolute, complete, definite, positive **11** indubitable, unequivocal **12** indisputable **13** unimpeachable **14** unquestionable

undoubtedly **6** surely **7** no doubt **9** assuredly, certainly, decidedly, doubtless **10** absolutely, definitely, positively, undeniably **11** indubitably **12** beyond a doubt, unmistakably, without doubt **13** unequivocally **14** beyond question, unquestionably **15** without question

undress **5** strip **6** nudity **7** disrobe, uncover, undrape **8** disarray, unclothe **9** nakedness **10** dishabille **18** take off one's clothes

undressed **4** bare, nude **5** naked **6** unclad **7** denuded, exposed, unrobed **8** disrobed, stripped, undraped **9** unclothed, uncovered

Undset, Sigrid
author of: **6** The Axe
20 Kristin Lavransdatter, The Master of Hestviken

undue **6** unmeet **8** impolite, improper, needless, overmuch, too great, unseemly, unworthy **9** excessive, tasteless **10** ill-advised, indiscreet, in bad taste, inordinate, not fitting, unbecoming, unsuitable **11** superfluous, uncalled-for, unjustified, unnecessary, unwarranted **13** inappropriate, objectionable

undulate **4** coil **5** slink, weave **9** fluctuate **11** rise and fall

undulating **4** wavy **5** bumpy **6** uneven

undulation **7** coiling **8** slinking, twisting **10** contortion **11** convolution **16** rising and falling

undutiful **6** remiss **8** disloyal **11** disobedient

undying **6** steady **7** abiding, endless, eternal, lasting **8** constant, enduring, immortal, unending, unfading, untiring **9** continual, deathless, incessant, perennial, permanent, perpetual, unceasing **10** continuing **11** everlasting, never-ending, unfaltering, unrelenting, unremitting **12** imperishable, never-failing, undiminished **13** uninterrupted **14** indestructible

unearth **4** find, show **5** dig up **6** dig out, exhume, expose, reveal **7** display, divulge, exhibit, root out, uncover **8** disclose, discover, disinter, dredge up, excavate **9** disentomb, ferret out **10** come across, come up with **12** bring to light

unearthly **5** awful, eerie, weird **6** absurd **7** extreme, ghostly, phantom, strange, uncanny, ungodly, unusual **8** abnormal, ethereal, spectral, terrible **10** horrendous, unpleasant **11** disembodied, incorporeal, unspeakable **12** disagreeable, extramundane, supernatural **13** extraordinary, preternatural

unease **5** worry **7** tension **8** disquiet **9** misgiving **10** discomfort, uneasiness **11** disquietude **12** apprehension

uneasiness **5** dread **6** dismay **7** anxiety **9** agitation, misgiving **10** discomfort, foreboding **11** disquietude, distraction, nervousness **12** apprehension, discomfiture, discomposure, perturbation **16** apprehensiveness

uneasy **4** edgy **5** nervy, tense, upset **6** on edge, queasy, unsure **7** awkward, irksome, nervous, uptight, worried **8** strained, troubled, worrying **9** disturbed, ill at ease, perturbed, upsetting **10** bothersome, disquieted, disturbing, unpleasant **11** constrained, disquieting **12** apprehensive **13** uncomfortable

uneatable **8** inedible **11** not fit to eat

uneconomical **4** dear **6** costly **8** wasteful **9** expensive **10** exorbitant, high-priced, immoderate, overpriced **11** extravagant **12** unreasonable

uneducated **8** ignorant, untaught **9** unlearned, untrained, untutored **10** illiterate, uncultured, unlettered, unschooled **12** uncultivated, uninstructed **13** unenlightened

unelaborated **4** bald, bare **5** plain, stark **6** simple **9** essential, unadorned, uncolored **11** fundamental, unvarnished **13** unembellished **15** straightforward

unembellished **4** bald, bare **5** naked, plain, stark **7** austere **9** unadorned **11** undecorated **12** unornamented

unemotional **4** cold, cool **6** formal, remote **7** distant **8** lukewarm, reserved **9** apathetic, impassive, unfeeling **11** indifferent, passionless, unconcerned **12** unresponsive **15** undemonstrative

unemployed **4** axed, idle **5** fired **6** canned, sacked, unused **7** bounced, jobless, laid-off **8** workless **9** at leisure, at liberty, booted-out, dismissed, on the dole, on welfare, out of a job, out of work **10** discharged, unoccupied **11** pink-slipped

unencumbered **4** free **6** vacant **7** unladen **8** expedite **10** unburdened, unhindered **13** unhandicapped

unending **6** steady **7** endless, eternal, lasting **8** constant, enduring **9** continual, incessant, perennial, permanent, perpetual, unceasing **10** continuous, unwavering **11** everlasting, never-ending, unremitting **12** undiminished **13** uninterrupted

unendurable **7** racking **9** agonizing, torturous **10** tormenting, unbearable **11** intolerable **12** excruciating, insufferable

unenlightened **8** ignorant **9** in the dark, unlearned **10** uneducated, uninformed **11** uninitiated **12** uninstructed

unenterprising **4** lazy **11** unambitious **12** unaggressive

unenthusiastic **8** lukewarm **10** unspirited **11** halfhearted, indifferent **13** unimpassioned

unequal **6** biased, uneven, unfair, unjust, unlike **7** bigoted, partial **9** different, disparate, unmatched **10** dissimilar, not uniform, prejudiced **11** inequitable

unequaled **7** supreme **8** peerless **9** matchless, paramount, unmatched, unrivaled **10** consummate, unexcelled **11** ne plus ultra, unsurpassed **12** incomparable, second to none, unapproached, unparalleled **13** beyond compare **16** beyond comparison

unequivocable 4 bald **5** utter **8** outright **9** out-and-out **11** categorical, unqualified

unequivocal 5 clear, final **7** certain **8** absolute, clear-cut, decisive, definite, emphatic **11** unambiguous **12** indisputable **13** incontestable **16** incontrovertible

unequivocally 7 clearly **9** certainly, downright **10** completely, decisively, definitely, thoroughly **12** emphatically, indisputably, unmistakably **13** incontestably **14** unquestionably, wholeheartedly **16** incontrovertibly

unerring 4 sure **7** certain, precise **8** constant, faithful, reliable **9** faultless, unfailing **10** infallible, unchanging

unessential 8 nonvital **9** accessory, extrinsic **10** disposable, expendable **11** dispensable, superfluous, unimportant, unnecessary **12** nonessential

unethical 5 dirty, shady, wrong **6** shoddy, unfair **7** devious **8** unworthy **9** dishonest, underhand **10** unladylike **12** dishonorable, disreputable, questionable, unprincipled **13** ungentlemanly **14** unconscionable

uneven 4 awry, bent **5** bumpy, lumpy, rough **6** angled, coarse, craggy, curved, jagged, tilted, unfair, unjust, unlike **7** crooked, not flat, slanted, sloping, unequal **8** lopsided, not level, not plumb, onesided, unsmooth **9** different, disparate **10** dissimilar, ill-matched, unbalanced

unevenness 7 oddness **9** bumpiness, lumpiness, roughness **10** jaggedness, ruggedness **11** crookedness **12** irregularity **14** changeableness

uneventful 4 dull **5** quiet, usual **6** boring **7** average, humdrum, prosaic, routine, tedious **8** ordinary, standard, tiresome **10** monotonous **11** commonplace **12** conventional **13** insignificant, unexceptional, uninteresting

unexcelled 7 supreme **8** flawless, peerless, superior, unbeaten **9** faultless, matchless, unequaled, unmatched, unrivaled **10** consummate **11** unsurpassed **12** incomparable, second to none, transcendent, unapproached, unparalleled **13** beyond compare

unexceptional 5 usual **6** normal **7** mundane, typical **8** ordinary, standard **9** customary **12** conventional, run of the mill

unexcited 4 calm, cool **6** placid, serene **7** unmoved **8** composed, detached **9** collected, unruffled **11** undisturbed, unemotional **13** dispassionate, unimpassioned

unexciting 4 dull, flat **5** vapid **6** boring **7** insipid **10** lackluster

unexpected 6 sudden **9** startling, unplanned **10** accidental, surprising, undesigned, unforeseen, unintended **11** astonishing, unlooked-for, unpredicted **12** out of the blue **13** unanticipated, unintentional

unextinguished 5 alive **10** unquenched **12** still burning

unfaded 5 fresh **6** bright **8** undimmed **10** unwithered

unfailing 4 true **5** loyal **6** steady **7** endless **8** constant, enduring, faithful, reliable **9** continual **10** continuous, dependable, infallible, unchanging, unwavering **12** never-failing **13** inexhaustible

unfair 4 foul **5** dirty **6** biased, unjust **7** corrupt, crooked, partial, unequal **8** not right, onesided, partisan **9** dishonest, underhand, unethical **10** not cricket, prejudiced **11** inequitable **12** dishonorable, unprincipled, unreasonable, unscrupulous **14** unconscionable

unfaithful 5 false **6** faulty, untrue **7** inexact **8** disloyal, unchaste **9** deceitful, distorted, erroneous, faithless, imperfect **10** adulterous, inaccurate, inconstant, perfidious **11** not accurate, treacherous **12** falsehearted **13** untrustworthy

Unfaithfully Yours
director: 14 Preston Sturges
cast: 10 Rudy Vallee **11** Rex Harrison **12** Edgar Kennedy, Linda Darnell **15** Barbara Lawrence

unfaithfulness 7 falsity, perfidy **9** falseness, treachery **10** disloyalty, fickleness, infidelity **11** inconstancy **13** faithlessness **14** perfidiousness

unfaltering 4 firm, sure **6** steady **8** enduring, resolute **9** obstinate, steadfast, unfailing **10** dependable, persistent, unflagging, unswerving, unwavering **11** persevering, undeviating **12** never-failing, wholehearted

unfamiliar 3 new **5** novel **6** exotic, unique **7** curious, foreign, strange, unknown, unusual **9** different **10** ignorant of, unversed in **11** a stranger to, little known, out-of-the-way, unexposed to, uninitiated, unskilled in **12** not well-known, unacquainted, unconversant **13** not acquainted, unpracticed in **14** unaccustomed to **15** inexperienced in, uninformed about **18** unenlightened about

unfamiliarity 9 ignorance **11** strangeness **12** inexperience **15** lack of knowledge

unfashionable 5 dated, dowdy, passe **6** frumpy, old-hat **8** outmoded **9** out-of-date, unstylish **12** old-fashioned

unfasten 4 undo **5** unpin, untie **6** detach, unbind, unbolt, unhook, unlace, unlash, unlink, unlock **7** unclose, unhitch, unlatch, unstick **8** unbutton, uncouple

unfastened 5 apart, undid **6** undone, untied **7** severed, unlaced, unstuck **8** detached, unhooked **9** unbuckled, uncoupled, unhitched **11** unconnected **12** disconnected

unfathomable 4 deep, vast **6** arcane, remote, subtle **7** complex, extreme, obscure **8** abstract, abstruse, esoteric, profound, puzzling **9** enigmatic **10** bottomless, perplexing **16** hard to understand, incomprehensible

unfavorable 3 bad **4** poor **7** adverse, unhappy **8** unsuited, untimely **9** ill-suited **10** ill-favored, regretable **11** inopportune, regrettable, unfortunate, unpromising **12** inauspicious, inconvenient, infelicitous, unpropitious, unseasonable **15** disadvantageous

unfeasible 10 impossible, infeasible, unsuitable, unworkable **11** impractical **12** unachievable **13** impracticable

unfeeling 4 cold **5** cruel **9** heartless **11** hardhearted, insensitive **13** unsympathetic

unfeigned 4 real, true **7** genuine, sincere **10** unaffected

unfetter 4 free **7** release, set free, unchain **8** liberate **9** unshackle

unfilled **4** open **5** blank, empty **6** hollow, vacant **7** drained **9** available **10** unoccupied

unfinished **5** crude, rough **6** undone **7** lacking, sketchy, wanting **8** immature **9** deficient, imperfect, unnatural, unpainted, unrefined, unstained **10** incomplete, unexecuted, unpolished **11** uncompleted, unfulfilled, unlacquered, unvarnished

unfit **4** sick, weak **5** frail **6** infirm, not fit, sickly **7** not up to, unequal, unready, unsound, useless **8** delicate, disabled, unsuited **9** incapable, not suited, unhealthy, unskilled, untrained **10** inadequate, ineligible, not equal to, unequipped, unprepared, unsuitable **11** debilitated, ill-equipped, incompetent, ineffective, inefficient, not designed, unqualified **12** ill-contrived, not cut out for **13** inappropriate, incapacitated

unflagging **4** firm **5** fixed **6** steady **7** staunch **8** constant, enduring, resolute, tireless, unshaken, untiring **9** steadfast, tenacious, undaunted **10** determined, persistent, relentless, undrooping, unswerving, unwavering, unyielding **11** indomitable, persevering, undeviating, unfaltering, unremitting **13** indefatigable **14** uncompromising

unflappable **4** calm, cool **6** placid, serene **8** composed **9** collected **10** cool-headed **11** unexcitable **13** imperturbable, self-possessed

unflinching **4** firm, game **6** gritty, plucky, steady, strong **7** staunch **8** fearless, resolute, stalwart, unshaken **9** steadfast, tenacious, unabashed, undaunted **10** persistent, unswerving, unwavering, unyielding **11** indomitable, unfaltering, unshrinking **12** unhesitating

unfold **4** bare, show, tell **6** open up, reveal, unfurl, unroll, unveil, unwrap **7** divulge, explain, expound, lay open, open out, present, recount, uncover **8** describe, disclose, set forth **9** elucidate, explicate, make known, spread out **10** stretch out

unfolding **4** rise **5** birth, start **9** beginning, evolution, inception, unfurling **10** revelation **11** development

unforced **4** easy **5** frank **6** candid, casual **7** natural, relaxed **8** informal **9** easygoing **10** unaffected **13** unconstrained

unforeseen **6** abrupt, sudden **8** surprise **9** unplanned **10** accidental, surprising, unexpected, unintended **11** unlooked-for, unpredicted **12** out of the blue **13** unanticipated

unforeseen danger **7** pitfall **8** exigency **9** emergency **11** contingency

unforgettable **7** notable **8** eventful, exciting **9** important, memorable, thrilling **10** noteworthy **11** significant

unfortunate **5** sorry **6** cursed, jinxed, woeful **7** hapless, unblest, unhappy, unlucky **8** ill-fated, ill-timed, luckless, untimely, wretched **10** disastrous, ill-advised, ill-starred **11** inopportune, regrettable, unfavorable **12** inauspicious, infelicitous, unpropitious, unprosperous, unsuccessful

unfounded **4** idle **5** false **6** untrue **8** baseless, spurious **9** erroneous **10** fabricated, groundless

unfrequented **5** empty **6** lonely **7** remote, uncouth **8** isolated, solitary **9** unvisited **11** out-of-the-way **16** off the beaten path

unfriendly **4** cold **5** aloof **6** at odds, chilly **7** distant, haughty, hostile, warlike **8** inimical, snobbish **9** on the outs, reclusive, withdrawn **10** ungracious, unsociable **11** belligerent, contentious, quarrelsome, uncongenial **12** antagonistic, disagreeable, disputatious, inhospitable **13** at loggerheads, at sword's point, unsympathetic

unfruitful **4** vain **6** barren, fallow, futile **7** useless, worn-out **8** infecund **9** fruitless **10** unavailing **11** purposeless, unrewarding **12** impoverished, unproductive, unprofitable **14** unremunerative

unfulfilled **8** thwarted **10** frustrated, unrealized **11** unsatisfied
French: **6** manque

unfurl **4** open **6** expand, spread, unfold, unroll **7** develop, roll out **8** shake out **9** spread out

ungainly **5** stiff **6** clumsy, klutzy **7** awkward **9** lumbering, maladroit **10** ungraceful **13** uncoordinated

ungallant **4** rude **7** boorish, uncivil, uncouth **8** impolite **9** uncourtly **10** ill-behaved, ungracious, unmannerly **11** ill-mannered, uncourteous **12** discourteous **13** ungentlemanly

ungenerous **4** mean, near **5** close, cruel, petty, small, venal **6** greedy, shabby, sordid, stingy **7** miserly, selfish, sparing **8** churlish, covetous, cowardly, grudging **9** illiberal, mercenary, niggardly, penurious, rapacious **10** avaricious **11** small-minded **12** narrow-minded, parsimonious, uncharitable

ungifted **8** mediocre **9** unskilled **10** amateurish, unskillful, untalented **14** unaccomplished

unglue **6** unseal **7** peel off, unstick **9** pull apart

ungodly **4** base, vile **5** awful **6** rotten, sinful, wicked **7** corrupt, ghastly, godless, heinous, immoral, impious **8** depraved, dreadful, terrible **9** dissolute **10** degenerate, horrendous, iniquitous, outrageous, villainous **11** blasphemous **12** dishonorable, unreasonable

ungovernable **6** unruly **7** defiant, froward, naughty, wayward **8** contrary, mutinous, perverse, stubborn **9** fractious, obstinate **10** disorderly, rebellious, refractory **11** disobedient, intractable **12** noncompliant, recalcitrant, unmanageable, unsubmissive

ungraceful **5** inept **6** clumsy **7** awkward **9** inelegant

ungracious **4** rude **5** bluff, blunt, gruff, harsh, short **6** abrupt, coarse, crusty, vulgar **7** boorish, brusque, loutish, uncivil, uncouth **8** churlish, grudging, impolite **9** uncourtly, ungallant **10** ill-behaved, unladylike, unmannerly **11** bad-mannered, ill-mannered, impertinent, uncourteous **12** disagreeable, discourteous, inhospitable **13** disrespectful, ungentlemanly

unguarded **6** unwary **8** careless, tactless, too frank **9** imprudent, unmindful, unwatched **10** incautious, indiscreet, undefended **11** defenseless, unpatrolled, unprotected **12** undiplomatic, unrestrained **13** ill-considered, uncircumspect

unguent **4** balm **5** cream, salve **6** lotion **8** ointment **9** emollient

ungulate **2** ox **3** cow, gnu, hog, pig, yak **4** boar, calf, deer, goat, ibex **5** camel, daman, horse, llama, tapir **6** hoofed, vicuna **7** buffalo, caribou, giraffe, peccary **8** antelope, elephant, hooflike, ruminant **9** dromedary **10** hartebeest, rhinoceros, wildebeest **12** hippopotamus

unhampered **4** free **8** expedite **9** unimpeded **10** unconfined **12** unencumbered, unrestrained, unrestricted

unhandy **5** inept **6** clumsy, gauche, klutzy **7** awkward **8** bumbling, fumbling, inexpert, unwieldy **9** all thumbs, ham-handed, maladroit, unskilled **10** cumbersome, unskillful **11** inefficient **12** inconvenient, unmanageable **14** butterfingered

unhappiness **3** woe **5** grief **6** misery, sorrow **7** anguish, sadness **8** distress **9** heartache

unhappy **3** bad, sad **4** blue, poor **5** inapt, sorry **6** gloomy, somber, unwise **7** adverse, awkward, doleful, foolish, forlorn, hapless, joyless, unlucky **8** dejected, downcast, luckless, unseemly **9** depressed, imprudent, long-faced, sorrowful, woebegone **10** despondent, dispirited, ill-advised, melancholy, unbecoming, unsuitable **11** crestfallen, injudicious, regrettable, unbefitting, unfortunate **12** heavyhearted, infelicitous, unsuccessful **13** inappropriate **14** down in the mouth

unharmed **5** whole **6** unhurt **9** uninjured, unscathed, untouched **10** in one piece, unaffected **14** with a whole skin

unhealthy **3** bad **4** sick, weak **6** ailing, feeble, infirm, morbid, poorly, sickly, unwell **7** harmful, hurtful, invalid, not well, noxious, unsound **8** depraved, diseased, negative, perilous **9** dangerous, degrading, hazardous **10** corrupting, indisposed, morally bad **11** destructive, detrimental, undesirable, unhealthful, unwholesome **12** demoralizing, in poor health, insalubrious **13** contaminating

unheard-of **3** odd **4** rare **6** unique **7** amazing, curious, unknown, unusual **8** freakish, original, singular, uncommon **9** irregular, matchless **10** incredible, outlandish, outrageous, phenomenal, unexpected **11** exceptional **12** incomparable, preposterous, unbelievable, unparalleled, unreasonable **13** extraordinary, inconceivable, unprecedented

unheated **3** icy **4** cold **6** chilly, drafty, frosty **7** ice-cold **8** unwarmed

unheeding **7** ignored **8** mindless **12** disregarding

unhelpful **7** of no use, useless **8** in the way **9** hindering **11** disobliging **13** inconsiderate, uncooperative

unheralded **6** unsung **10** unexpected, unforeseen **11** unacclaimed, unannounced, unlooked-for **12** unproclaimed, unpublicized, unrecognized **13** unanticipated

unhesitating **5** eager, quick, ready **6** direct, prompt **9** immediate **10** unreserved **11** unflinching **12** wholehearted, without delay **13** instantaneous **18** without reservation

unhinge **6** detach **7** disrupt **8** separate, unsettle **9** disengage, dislocate, disorient, unbalance **10** disconnect **13** disarticulate

unhitch **6** detach **8** separate, uncouple, unfasten **9** disengage **10** disconnect

unhitched **8** detached **9** uncoupled **10** unfastened **12** disconnected

unholy **4** base, evil, vile **5** awful **6** rotten, sinful, wicked **7** corrupt, heinous, immoral, ungodly **8** depraved, dreadful, shocking **9** dishonest **10** horrendous, iniquitous, outrageous, villainous **12** dishonorable, unreasonable

Unholy Loves
author: **15** Joyce Carol Oates

unhurried **4** easy, slow **7** gradual **9** leisurely **10** deliberate, slow-moving

unicorn
form: **5** horse
feature: **4** horn
symbolizes: **6** purity **8** chastity
constellation of: **9** Monoceros

unidentified **5** vague **7** unknown, unnamed **8** nameless **9** anonymous, unlabeled **11** unspecified **12** undesignated, unrecognized

unification **5** union, unity **6** fusion, merger **7** uniting **8** alliance, junction **9** coalition, combining **11** coalescence, combination, confederacy **12** amalgamation **13** confederation, consolidating, consolidation, incorporation

uniform **4** even, garb **5** alike, array, at one, dress, equal, habit **6** attire, in line, in step, livery **7** apparel, costume, regalia, regular, similar, the same **8** agreeing, constant, in accord, of a piece, unvaried, vestment **9** consonant, identical, of one mind, unaltered, unvarying **10** conforming, consistent, harmonious, unchanging **11** regimentals, undeviating

uniformity **8** equality, monotony, sameness **10** consonance **11** consistency, equivalency, homogeneity **15** standardization

unify **3** wed **4** ally, fuse, join **5** blend, merge, unite **6** couple, link up **7** combine **8** coalesce, federate **10** amalgamate **11** confederate, consolidate, form into one, incorporate **12** lump together **13** bring together

unilluminated **3** dim **4** dark **5** murky, unlit **6** gloomy **7** obscure **8** darkened **9** lightless, unlighted

unimaginable **10** incredible **12** unbelievable **13** inconceivable **16** incomprehensible

unimaginative **4** dull **5** stale, stock, trite, usual, vapid **6** dreary **7** cliched, humdrum, prosaic, routine, tedious **8** everyday, mediocre, ordinary **9** hackneyed **10** pedestrian, uncreative, unexciting, uninspired, unoriginal, unromantic **11** commonplace, predictable **12** run-of-the-mill, unremarkable **13** uninteresting

unimpaired **4** good **5** clear, sound **6** intact, unhurt **8** unbroken, unharmed **9** uninjured, unscathed, unspoiled **10** undeformed

unimpassioned **4** calm, cool **6** placid, serene, stolid **7** unmoved **8** detached, unloving **9** apathetic, impassive, objective, unexcited **11** indifferent, unemotional **13** dispassionate

unimpeachable **4** pure **5** clean, solid **7** perfect **8** reliable, spotless, unmarred **9** blameless, faultless, inviolate, stainless, undefiled, untainted **10** immaculate, impeccable, inculpable, infallible **11** trustworthy, unblemished **12** unassailable **13** above reproach, totally honest **14** beyond question, irreproachable, unquestionable **15** beyond criticism, unchallengeable

unimportant **5** minor **6** lesser,

meager, paltry, slight **7** trivial **8** inferior, mediocre, not vital, nugatory, piddling, trifling **10** immaterial, irrelevant, low-ranking, negligible, of no moment, second-rate **11** subordinate **12** nonessential, not important **13** insignificant **14** inconsiderable **15** inconsequential, of no consequence

uninformed **6** unread **7** unaware **8** ignorant **9** in the dark, not with it, unadvised, unknowing, unlearned **10** uneducated, unschooled **12** unconversant, uninstructed **13** unenlightened

uninhabited **5** empty **6** vacant **8** deserted, forsaken **9** abandoned, unlived in, unpeopled, unsettled **10** unoccupied, untenanted **11** unpopulated

uninhibited **4** fast, free, open, rash **5** frank **6** candid, daring, madcap, not shy, unwary **8** careless, heedless, immodest, reckless, uncurbed, unreined **9** abandoned, impetuous, impulsive, outspoken, unbridled, unchecked, unguarded, unimpeded, unstopped **10** capricious, flamboyant, forthright, headstrong, incautious, indiscreet, unhampered, unhindered, unreserved **11** instinctive, plainspoken, spontaneous **12** free-spirited, uncontrolled, unobstructed, unrestrained, unrestricted **13** unconstrained **15** straightforward, unself-conscious

uninjured **5** whole **6** intact, unhurt **8** unharmed **9** unscathed, untouched **10** in one piece **14** with a whole skin

uninspired **4** dull **5** stale, stock, trite, vapid **7** cliched, humdrum, prosaic, unmoved **8** ordinary **9** hackneyed, unexcited, unstirred, untouched **10** pedestrian, unaffected, unexciting, unoriginal **11** commonplace, indifferent, predictable, unemotional, unimpressed **12** run-of-the-mill, uninfluenced, unstimulated **13** unimaginative, uninteresting

uninspiring **4** dull **5** bland, stale **6** boring **7** insipid, prosaic **10** lackluster **13** uninteresting

uninstructive **6** barren **9** unhelpful **10** unedifying **12** unproductive **13** uninformative

unintelligent **4** dull, dumb, slow **5** blank, dense, dopey, thick **6** obtuse, stupid **7** asinine, doltish, idiotic, moronic **8** retarded **9** cretinous, dimwitted, imbecilic **10** dull-witted, half-witted, slow-witted **11** blockheaded, thickheaded **12** simpleminded

unintelligible **8** baffling, puzzling **9** confusing, illegible, insoluble **10** incoherent, perplexing **11** meaningless **12** impenetrable, inarticulate, unfathomable **14** undecipherable **16** incomprehensible

unintentional **9** unplanned, unwitting **10** accidental, fortuitous, undesigned, unintended, unthinking **11** inadvertent, involuntary, unconscious **14** unpremeditated

uninterested **5** aloof, blase **6** remote **8** heedless, listless, uncaring **9** apathetic, incurious, unmindful **10** above it all, uninvolved **11** indifferent, unconcerned **13** unimpressible

uninteresting **3** dry **4** drab, dull **5** trite, vapid **6** boring, dreary, jejune **7** humdrum, insipid, prosaic, tedious **8** lifeless, ordinary, tiresome, unmoving **9** colorless, wearisome **10** monotonous, pedestrian, uneventful **11** uninspiring **12** unsatisfying **13** insignificant

uninterrupted **8** unbroken **9** ceaseless, continual, incessant **10** continuous **11** unremitting

uninviting **8** annoying **9** offensive **10** unalluring, unpleasant, untempting **11** displeasing, distasteful, unappealing, undesirable, unwelcoming **12** disagreeable, unappetizing, unattractive

uninvolved **4** easy **5** clear **6** simple **7** neutral, obvious, outside **8** detached **9** impartial **10** unaffected **13** disinterested, dispassionate, uncomplicated

union **5** blend, guild, unity **6** fusion, league, merger **7** amalgam, joining, mixture, oneness, uniting, wedding **8** alliance, marriage, unifying **9** synthesis **10** federation, fraternity **11** affiliation, association, combination, corporation, partnership, unification **12** amalgamation **13** confederation, consolidation
type: **5** craft, labor, trade

unique **8** by itself, peerless, singular **9** matchless, nonpareil, unequaled, unmatched, unrivaled **10** inimitable, one of a kind, surpassing, unexampled, unexcelled **11** distinctive, unsurpassed **12** incomparable, unapproached, unparalleled

unit **4** part **5** group, whole **6** entity, member **7** element, measure, package, section, segment **8** category, division, quantity **9** component **10** detachment **11** constituent, measurement **12** denomination

Unitas, Johnny
nickname: **7** Johnny U
sport: **8** football
position: **11** quarterback
team: **14** Baltimore Colts

unite **4** ally, fuse, join, pool **5** blend, merge, unify **6** couple **7** combine **8** coalesce, federate, lock arms, organize **10** amalgamate, homogenize, join forces **11** confederate, consolidate, incorporate **12** join together, lump together **13** stand together

united **3** one **5** fused **6** allied, joined, merged, pooled **7** blended, coupled, leagued, unified **8** combined **9** federated, of one mind, unanimous **10** collective **11** amalgamated, in agreement **12** consolidated, incorporated **14** joined together, lumped together

United Arab Emirates
other name: **11** Pirate Coast, Trucial Oman **13** Trucial States
capital/largest city: **8** Abu Dhabi
others: **5** Ajman, Dubai, Kalba, Tarif **6** Sharja **7** Fujaira **11** Ras al Khaima **12** Umm al Qaiwain
division: **5** Ajman, Dibai, Dubai **6** Sharja **7** Fujaira, Sharjah **8** Abu Dhabi, Fujairah **11** Ras al Khaima, Umm al Qaiwan **12** Ral al Khaimah, Umm al-Qaiwain
monetary unit: **3** fil **6** dirham
highest point: **5** Hafit
physical feature:
desert: **10** Rub al Khali
gulf: **4** Oman **7** Persian
oasis: **7** Buraimi **9** Al Buraymi
peninsula: **7** Arabian
people: **4** Arab **6** Indian **7** African, Iranian **9** Pakistani **10** South Asian
leader: **22** Zaid Bin Sultan al-Nahayan
language: **5** Farsi **6** Arabic **7** English, Persian
religion: **5** Islam

United Kingdom *see* **7** England

United States ***see box***

unity 5 peace, union **6** accord, entity, fusion, league, merger **7** concord, harmony, joining, oneness, rapport **8** alliance, goodwill **9** synthesis, unanimity, wholeness **10** federation, fellowship, friendship **11** affiliation, association, cooperation, partnership, unification **12** amalgamation, amicableness **13** compatibility, confederation, consolidation, understanding **14** like-mindedness

universal 7 general **9** worldwide **10** ubiquitous, widespread **11** omnipresent **12** affecting all, all-embracing, all-inclusive **13** international

Universal creator
Egyptian: 4 Ptah

universality 8 currency **10** prevalence **12** predominance **17** comprehensiveness

universe
god of: 6 Amen Ra, Amon Ra

university 6 campus, school **7** academy, college **11** institution
British: 6 Oxford **9** Cambridge
Cambridge: 7 Harvard
former: 9 alma mater
French: 8 Sorbonne
Hanover: 9 Dartmouth
lecturer: 9 prelector
New Haven: 4 Yale
New Jersey: 9 Princeton
New York: 8 Columbia
Providence: 5 Brown
session: 4 term **7** seminar **8** semester
Wit: 4 Lyly, Nash **5** Peele **6** Greene

unjust 6 biased, unfair, warped **7** partial **8** one-sided, partisan, wrongful **9** unmerited **10** prejudiced, unbalanced, undeserved **11** inequitable, unjustified, unwarranted

unjustifiable 11 inexcusable **12** indefensible

unjustly 7 falsely, wrongly **8** unfairly **10** wrongfully **11** dishonestly, faithlessly, inequitably **12** undeservedly

unkempt 5 messy **6** sloppy, untidy **7** rumpled, tousled **8** mussed-up, slovenly, uncombed **9** ungroomed **10** disheveled, disordered **11** disarranged

unkind 4 mean **5** nasty **7** abusive **8** uncaring **9** malicious, unfeeling **10** unfriendly, ungenerous, ungracious **11** insensitive, thoughtless **12** inhospitable, uncharitable **13** inconsiderate, unsympathetic

unknot 5 untie **7** unsnarl **8** untangle **11** disentangle

unknowable 12 inaccessible **13** inconceivable

unknown 7 obscure, unnamed **8** nameless **9** anonymous, unheard-of **10** unrenowned **12** uncelebrated, undesignated, undetermined, undiscovered, unidentified

Unknown authors
author of: 4 Edda (elder) **7** Beowulf **8** Everyman, King Horn, Stasimon **10** Cinderella **11** Poema del Cid **12** Panchatantra, Vercelli Book, Volsunga Saga **14** Gesta Romanorum, Sibylline Books **15** Chanson de Roland, The Forty Thieves, The Song of Roland **16** Grettir the Strong **17** The Nibelungenlied **20** Aucassin and Nicolette, Robin Hood's Adventures **23** The Dream of the Red Chamber, The Thousand and One Nights **26** Sir Gawain and the Green Knight **29** Collection of Ten Thousand Leaves **29** The Arabian Nights' Entertainment

unladylike 4 rude **6** coarse, common, vulgar **7** ill-bred, uncouth **8** impolite **10** unmannerly **12** discourteous

unlawful 7 illegal, illegit, illicit, lawless **8** criminal **9** forbidden **10** prohibited, unlicensed, unofficial **12** unauthorized **13** against the law **16** unconstitutional

unlawful act 5 crime **6** felony **10** wrongdoing **11** lawbreaking, malfeasance, misdemeanor

unleash 4 free **5** let go **7** release, set free **8** let loose, liberate **12** give free rein

unlettered 8 ignorant, untaught **9** unlearned, untutored **10** illiterate, uneducated, unschooled **11** unscholarly

unlighted 3 dim **4** dark **5** murky, unlit **6** gloomy **7** stygian, sunless **8** moonless **9** lightless **13** unilluminated

unlikable, unlikeable 7 hateful **9** offensive, unlovable **10** hard to like, unloveable, unpleasant **11** displeasing, unappealing **12** disagreeable

unlike 7 diverse, unalike, unequal **9** different, disparate **10** dissimilar

unlikelihood 12 doubtfulness, unlikeliness **13** improbability

unlikely 8 hopeless **10** improbable **11** unpromising **12** questionable, unbelievable, unpropitious **19** scarcely conceivable

unlikeness 8 contrast, variance **9** disparity, variation **10** difference, divergence **13** dissimilarity, dissimilitude

unlimited 4 huge, vast **5** total **7** endless, immense **8** absolute, complete, infinite **9** boundless, limitless, unbounded, unchecked **11** unqualified **12** immeasurable, totalitarian, uncontrolled, unrestrained, unrestricted **13** comprehensive, inexhaustible, unconstrained **15** all-encompassing

unload 4 dump **7** off-load **8** get rid of, unburden **9** dispose of **10** unencumber

unlooked for 6 sudden **7** unasked **8** surprise **10** unexpected, unforeseen, unheralded **11** unannounced, uncalled for, unpredicted, unsolicited **13** serendipitous, unanticipated

unlovable, unloveable 7 hateful **9** unlikable **10** hard to like, unlikeable, unpleasant **11** displeasing, unappealing **12** disagreeable

unloving 4 cold, cool **6** frigid **11** indifferent, passionless **13** unimpassioned

unlucky 6 cursed, jinxed **7** hapless, unhappy **8** ill-fated, luckless, untoward **9** ill-omened **10** ill-starred **11** star-crossed, unfortunate **12** inauspicious, misfortunate

unman 7 unnerve **8** castrate **10** discourage, emasculate

unmanageable 5 balky, bulky **6** mulish, unruly **7** awkward, unhandy, wayward, willful **8** ungainly, unwieldy **9** fractious, pigheaded **10** cumbersome, rebellious, refractory **11** disobedient, intractable, troublesome **12** incorrigible **14** uncontrollable

unmanly 5 timid **6** yellow **8** cowardly, sissyish, womanish **9** sissified, weak-kneed **10** effeminate **11** lily-livered, unmasculine, weakhearted **12** fainthearted **13** pusillanimous **14** chickenhearted

unmannerly 5 crude, gross, surly **6** coarse **7** boorish, ill-

United States

capital: 12 Washington DC

largest city: 11 New York City

others: 4 Nome **5** Miami **6** Boston, Dallas, El Paso **7** Chicago, Detroit, Houston, Memphis, Phoenix, San Jose, Seattle **8** Columbus, Honolulu, San Diego **9** Anchorage, Baltimore, Cleveland, Milwaukee **10** Los Angeles, New Orleans, San Antonio **12** Indianapolis, Jacksonville, Philadelphia, Salt Lake City, San Francisco

school: 3 MIT **4** Penn, Yale **5** Brown **6** Baylor, Drexel, Vassar **7** Amherst, Colgate, Cornell, Fordham, Harvard, Oberlin **8** Bryn Mawr, Columbia, Stanford, Wesleyan **9** Dartmouth, Princeton, Radcliffe **10** Bennington **12** Johns Hopkins, Mount Holyoke

division: 4 Iowa, Ohio, Utah **5** Idaho, Maine, Texas **6** Alaska, Hawaii, Kansas, Nevada, Oregon **7** Alabama, Arizona, Florida, Georgia, Indiana, Montana, New York, Vermont, Wyoming **8** Arkansas, Colorado, Delaware, Illinois, Kentucky, Maryland, Michigan, Missouri, Nebraska, Oklahoma, Virginia **9** Louisiana, Minnesota, New Jersey, New Mexico, Tennessee, Wisconsin **10** California, Puerto Rico, Washington **11** Connecticut, Mississippi, North Dakota, Rhode Island, South Dakota **12** New Hampshire, Pennsylvania, West Virginia **13** Massachusetts, North Carolina, South Carolina **18** District of Columbia

island: 4 Guam, Long, Maui, Oahu **5** Block, Ellis, Kauai, Lanai, Umnak **6** Hawaii, Kodiak, Niihau, Unimak, Virgin **7** Baranof, Key West, Long Key, Molokai, Nunivak, Sanibel **8** Aleutian, Hawaiian, Key Largo, Shumagin, Unalaska **9** Atka Amlia, Canal Zone, Chichagof, Kahoolawe, Nantucket, Snipe Keys **10** Islamorada, Oyster Keys, Puerto Rico, St Lawrence **11** Longboat Key **12** Santa Barbara **13** American Samoa, Marquesas Keys, Prince of Wales, Santa Catalina, Summerland Key **15** Martha's Vineyard **16** Cantout Enderbury **26** Trust Territory of the Pacific

lake: 4 Erie, Mead **5** Huron, Tahoe **6** Cayuga, Finger, George, Itasca, Oneida, Seneca **7** Iliamma, Ontario **8** Michigan, Superior **9** Champlain, Great Salt, Salton Sea, Teshekpuk, Winnebago **10** Okeechobee **11** Yellowstone **13** Pontchartrain, Wallenpaupack, Winnipesaukee **14** Lake of the Woods

mountain: 4 Hood **5** Coast, Green, Kenai, Ozark, Rocky, White **6** Alaska, Brooks, DeLong, Elbert, Helena, Mesabi, Pocono, Shasta **7** Cascade, Chugach, Foraker, Harvard, Kilauea, Massive, Olympic, Olympus, Rainier, St Elias, Whitney **8** Catskill, Davidson, Endicott, Katahdin, Mauna Loa, Mitchell, Ouachita, St Helens, Wrangell **9** Allegheny, Blue Ridge, Kuskokwim, North Peak, Pikes Peak **10** Black Hills, Blanca Peak, Grand Teton, Washington, Williamson **11** Appalachian, Santa Monica **12** Sierra Nevada **14** Berkshire Hills

highest point: 8 McKinley

river: 3 New, Red **4** Gila, Iowa, Milk, Ohio, Rock **5** Black, Cedar, Coosa, Flint, Grand, Green, James, Neuse, Osage, Pearl, Pecos, Snake, White, Yukon **6** Brazos, Hudson, Neches, Neosho, Nueces, Owybee, Pee Dee, Platte, Powder, Sabine, Salmon, Wabash **7** Alabama, Big Horn, John Day, Klamath, Potomac, Roanoke, San Juan, St Johns, Trinity **8** Arkansas, Big Black, Canadian, Cheyenne, Cimarron, Colorado, Columbia, Delaware, Humboldt, Illinois, Kentucky, Kootenay, Missouri, Niabrana, Ouachita, Savannah **9** Allegheny, Deschutes, Des Moines, Minnesota, Rio Grande, Smoky Hill, St Francis, Tennessee, Tombigbee, Wisconsin **10** Cumberland, Republican, Sacramento, San Joaquin, St Lawrence, Tallapoosa **11** Connecticut, Mississippi, North Platte, South Platte, Susquehanna, Yellowstone **12** Tallahatchie **14** Little Colorado, Little Missouri

sea: 6 Arctic, Bering **7** Pacific **8** Atlantic, Beaufort

physical feature:

bay: **5** Tampa **7** Bristol, Prudhoe **8** Biscayne, Monterey **9** Apalachee **10** Chesapeake **12** San Francisco

desert: **4** Gila **6** Mojave **7** Painted **8** Colorado, Vizcaino **9** Black Rock **11** Death Valley

falls: **7** Niagara

gulf: **6** Alaska, Mexico **10** California

plain: **5** Great

plateau: **8** Colorado, Piedmont **10** Cumberland **11** Appalachian

strait: **6** Bering **7** Florida

people:

architect: **4** Root **5** Davis **6** Upjohn, Wright **7** Burnham, Downing, Furness, Gilbert, Gropius, Latrobe **8** Bogardus, Holabird, Sullivan **9** Bullfinch, Jefferson **10** Richardson **14** Mies van der Rohe

artist: **5** Henri, Homer, Leutz, Moses, Peale, Wyeth **6** Copley, Durand, Millet, Rothko, Stuart **7** Audubon, Cassatt, O'Keeffe, Pollock, Sargent **8** Whistler

author: **3** Poe **4** Grey, Inge, Loos, Luce, West, Wouk **5** Aiken, Albee, Beach, Benet, Crane, Eliot, Frost, Guest, Harte, Hecht, James, Lewis, Oates, Odets, O'Hara, Paine, Pound, Stowe, Twain, Vidal, Welty, Wolfe, Wylie **6** Bellow, Bierce, Bryant, Cabell, Capote, Cather, Cooper, Cullen, Ferber, Holmes, Hughes, Irving, Kilmer, Lanier, London, Lowell, Mather, Millay, Miller, Norris, O'Neill, Porter, Styron, Updike, Wilder **7** Baldwin, Clemens, Costain, Dreiser, Emerson, Gallico, Hammett, Hellman, Howells, Jeffers, Kerouac, Lardner, Malamud, Nabokov, Roethke, Stevens, Thoreau, Webster, Wharton, Whitman **8** Anderson, Bradbury, Caldwell, Cummings, Faulkner, Macleish, McCarthy, Melville, Michener, Mitchell, Rawlings, Robinson, Sandburg, Schwartz, Sherwood, Sinclair, Teasdale, Whittier, Williams

(*continued*)

United States *(continued)*
9 Burroughs, Dickinson, Dos Passos, Hawthorne, Hemingway, McCullers, Steinbeck **10** Fitzgerald, Longfellow, Tarkington
composer: **4** Ives, Kern **5** Cohan, Loewe, Sousa **6** Berlin, Foster, Joplin, Lerner, Porter **7** Copland, Gilbert, Rodgers **8** Gershwin, Sullivan **9** Bernstein **11** Hammerstein
explorer: **4** Byrd, Pike **5** Boone, Cabot, Clark, Lewis, Perry **6** Hudson, Joliet **7** Jolliet **8** Columbus **9** Marquette **10** Eric the Red
leader: **3** Jay **4** Clay, King, Penn **5** Bryan, Davis, Henry, Paine **6** Revere, Sumner **7** Stevens, Webster **8** Franklin, Humphrey **9** Goldwater
military leader: **3** Lee **4** Pike **5** Clark, Gates, Grant, Meade, Tyler **6** Austin, Custer, Marion, Patton **7** Bradley, Houston, Jackson, Sherman **8** Marshall, Pershing **9** MacArthur, Roosevelt, Stillwell **10** Eisenhower, Vandenburg, Washington
president: **4** Bush, Ford, Polk, Taft **5** Adams, Grant, Hayes, Nixon, Tyler **6** Arthur, Carter, Hoover, Monroe, Pierce, Reagan, Taylor, Truman, Wilson **7** Harding, Jackson, Johnson, Kennedy, Lincoln, Madison **8** Buchanan, Coolidge, Fillmore, Garfield, Hamilton, Harrison, McKinley, Van Buren **9** Cleveland, Jefferson, Roosevelt **10** Eisenhower, Washington
sculptor: **4** Rush **6** Calder, French, Rogers **7** Borglum **9** Greenough, Remington **12** Saint-Gaudens
language: **7** English, Spanish
religion: **5** Amish **6** Mormon **7** Baptist, Judaism, Shakers **8** Lutheran **9** Methodist **10** Protestant **11** Pentacostal **12** Episcopalian, Presbyterian **13** Roman Catholic **14** Church of Christ, Congregational **15** Eastern Orthodox, Latter Day Saints **19** Seventh Day Adventist
place:
national park: **4** Zion **5** Platt **6** Acadia **7** Big Bend, Glacier, Olympic, Redwood, Sequoia **8** Wind Cave, Yosemite **9** Haleakala, Mesa Verde, Multnomah **10** Crater Lake, Everglades, Grand Teton, Hot Springs, Isle Royale, Shenandoah **11** Bryce Canyon, Canyonlands, Grand Canyon, Kings Canyon, Mammoth Cave, Yellowstone **12** Mount Rainier **13** Mount McKinley, Virgin Islands **14** Lassen Volcanic, Rocky Mountains **15** Carlsbad Caverns, Petrified Forest **19** Great Smoky Mountains
possession: **4** Guam **10** Puerto Rico **13** American Samoa, Virgin Islands **14** Mariana Islands **15** Caroline Islands, Marshall Islands
feature:
colony: **7** Roanoke **8** Plymouth **9** Jamestown **11** Rhode Island **12** New Amsterdam, New Hampshire **14** New Netherlands **16** Massachusetts Bay
festival: **9** Mardi Gras
national symbol: **9** bald eagle
tree: **7** redwood, sequoia

bred, loutish, uncivil, uncouth **8** impolite **10** ungracious, unladylike **11** ill-mannered **12** badly behaved, discourteous **13** ungentlemanly

unmarked **5** clean, clear **9** undamaged, undefaced, unnoticed **10** unobserved **11** unblemished **15** undistinguished

unmarried **4** free **5** unwed **6** maiden, single **7** old maid, widowed **8** bachelor, divorced, spinster, unwedded, virginal, wifeless **9** available, fancy free **10** spouseless, unattached **11** husbandless **21** footloose and fancy-free

unmarried girl
French: **10** jeune fille
German: **8** fraulein
Spanish: **8** senorita

Unmarried Woman, An
director: **12** Paul Mazursky
cast: **9** Alan Bates **11** Cliff Gorman **13** Jill Clayburgh, Michael Murphy

unmask **4** bare, show **6** betray, expose, reveal, unveil **7** lay open, uncover **8** disclose, discover **12** bring to light

unmasking **6** baring **8** betrayal, exposure **9** discovery, unveiling **10** disclosure, laying open, revelation, uncovering **15** bringing to light

unmatched **6** unlike **7** diverse, supreme, unequal **8** peerless, variable **9** differing, disparate, matchless, unequaled **10** dissimilar **12** second to none, unparalleled **13** beyond compare

unmerciful **4** cold, evil **5** cruel, harsh **6** brutal, severe, unkind **7** brutish, extreme, inhuman **8** inhumane, pitiless, ruthless **9** excessive, heartless, inclement, merciless, unfeeling, unpitying, unsparing **10** malevolent, relentless **11** hardhearted **14** unconscionable

unmindful **3** lax **6** remiss **7** unaware **8** careless, derelict, heedless **9** forgetful, negligent, oblivious, unheeding **11** thoughtless, unconscious

unmistakable **5** clear, plain **6** patent **7** evident, glaring, obvious **8** apparent, distinct, manifest, palpable **9** prominent **10** pronounced, undeniable **11** conspicuous, unequivocal **12** indisputable **14** unquestionable

unmistakably **7** clearly, plainly **8** palpably, patently **9** certainly, decidedly, downright, evidently, glaringly, obviously **10** definitely, distinctly, manifestly, positively, thoroughly, undeniably **11** prominently **12** indisputably **13** conspicuously, unequivocally **14** unquestionably **17** beyond all question

unmitigated **6** arrant **8** absolute, unabated, unbroken **9** downright, out-and-out **10** persistent, unrelieved **11** unqualified **12** unalleviated **13** uninterrupted

unmixed **4** neat, pure **5** sheer **6** simple **8** straight **9** unalloyed, unblended, undiluted, unmingled **13** unadulterated

unmoved **4** calm, cold, firm **5** aloof **6** dogged **7** devoted, staunch **8** resolute, resolved, uncaring, unshaken **9** dedicated, obstinate, steadfast, unfeeling, unpitying, unstirred, untouched **10** determined, inflexible, not shifted, persistent, relentless, unaffected, unswerving, unwavering **11** indifferent, unconcerned, undeviating, undisturbed, unfaltering **12** stonyhearted, uninterested, unresponsive **14** uncompromising

unmoving **4** dead, dull **5** fixed, inert, still **6** boring, serene **8** immobile **9** powerless **10** motionless, stationary **11** emotionless **13** at a standstill

unnamed **8** nameless, unsigned **9** anonymous, incognito **10** innominate, uncredited, unreported, unrevealed **11** undisclosed, unspecified **12** pseudonymous, undesignated, undiscovered, unidentified **14** unacknowledged

unnatural **4** fake **5** phony, put-on **6** forced **7** assumed, stilted, studied, unusual **8** aberrant, abnormal, affected, freakish, mannered, peculiar **9** anomalous, contrived **10** artificial, theatrical **13** self-conscious

unnecessary **5** extra **6** excess **7** surplus **8** needless, overmuch **9** auxiliary, excessive **10** expendable, gratuitous, unrequired **11** dispensable, superfluous, uncalled-for, unessential **13** supplementary

unnerve **5** daunt, scare, upset **7** agitate, unhinge **8** frighten, unsettle **10** intimidate

unnerving **5** scary **8** daunting **9** upsetting **10** enervating, unsettling **11** frightening

unnoticeable **3** dim **5** faint **6** hidden **7** obscure **9** concealed **10** indistinct, unassuming, unemphatic, unobserved **11** unobtrusive **12** undetectable **13** imperceptible, inconspicuous, insignificant, undiscernible **14** unostentatious

unnoticed **6** unfelt, unseen **7** unheard, unnoted **8** unheeded, untasted **10** not smelled, overlooked, unobserved **11** disregarded, unperceived **12** undiscovered

unobservant **4** dull **5** blind **8** unseeing **9** unmindful **11** incognizant

unobstructed **4** fair, free, open **5** clear **8** apparent **9** unimpeded **10** unhampered, unhindered **11** unprevented

unobtainable **9** hard to get **10** impossible, out of reach, out of touch **11** unavailable, unreachable **12** improcurable, inaccessible

unobtrusive **3** shy **6** humble, modest **7** bashful **8** reserved, reticent, retiring **9** diffident **10** unassuming **11** unassertive **13** inconspicuous, unpretentious **14** unostentatious

unoccupied **4** idle **5** empty **6** vacant **8** unfilled **9** abandoned, unengaged **10** untenanted **11** uninhabited

unofficial **8** informal **12** unauthorized

unorganized **5** loose **6** casual, random **7** aimless, chaotic **8** confused **9** haphazard, orderless, unordered **10** disjointed, unarranged, undirected **11** harum-scarum **12** unclassified, unsystematic **13** helter-skelter **14** unsystematized

unornamented **4** bald, bare **5** blank, naked, plain, stark **6** simple **7** austere **9** unadorned **11** undecorated **13** unembellished

unorthodox **7** erratic **9** eccentric, irregular **14** unconventional

unostentatious **3** shy **5** plain, quiet **6** humble, modest, simple **9** unadorned, unaffected **10** unassuming **11** constrained **13** inconspicuous, unpretentious **14** unpresumptuous

unpaid **3** due **4** owed **5** owing **9** in arrears **11** outstanding

unpaid debt **5** debit **7** arrears **9** liability **10** balance due, obligation **12** indebtedness

unpalatable **5** nasty **8** inedible, unsavory **9** repellent, repulsive **10** bad-tasting, unpleasant **11** displeasing, distasteful **12** disagreeable, unappetizing **13** hard to swallow

unparalleled **4** best, rare **5** alone, crack, elect **6** unique **8** gilt-edge, peerless, singular **9** matchless, superfine, unequaled, unmatched, unrivaled **10** crackajack, inimitable, unimitated **11** unsurpassed **12** unapproached **13** unprecedented **15** of the first water

unperceptive **5** blind **9** unfeeling **11** insensitive, unobservant **12** imperceptive, impercipient **13** unsympathetic

unperturbed **4** calm, cool **6** poised **8** composed, tranquil **9** collected, unexcited, unruffled **10** coolheaded, nonchalant, unagitated, undismayed, untroubled **11** levelheaded, undisturbed **13** unimpassioned

unplanned **9** impromptu **10** accidental, fortuitous, improvised, unexpected, unforeseen **11** spontaneous **12** uncalculated **13** unintentional **14** extemporaneous, unpremeditated **15** spur-of-the-moment

unpleasant **5** nasty, pesky **7** irksome, noisome **8** annoying, churlish **9** obnoxious, offensive, repugnant, repulsive, unlikable, vexatious **10** ill-humored, ill-natured **11** displeasing, distasteful **12** disagreeable, unattractive **13** objectionable

unpleasantness **8** ugliness **9** ill nature, nastiness **12** churlishness **13** obnoxiousness, offensiveness, repulsiveness **15** distastefulness **16** disagreeableness, unattractiveness

unpointed **4** dull **5** blunt **6** dulled **11** unsharpened

unpolished **3** raw **5** gawky, inept, rough **6** cloudy, clumsy **7** amateur, awkward, unwaxed **8** inexpert, unbuffed, unglazed, unshined **9** inelegant, unrefined, unskilled **10** uncultured, unfinished, unskillful **11** unburnished, unpracticed **12** uncultivated **13** inexperienced **14** unaccomplished **15** unsophisticated

unpopular **7** snubbed **8** disliked, rebuffed, rejected, slighted, unwanted **9** disdained, neglected, unwelcome **10** unaccepted **11** disapproved, undesirable **12** looked down on, unacceptable

unpopulated **5** rural **9** backwoods, unpeopled, unsettled

unprecedented **5** novel **6** unique **9** unheard-of **10** unexampled **11** exceptional **12** unparalleled **13** extraordinary **15** hitherto unknown

unpredictable **6** fitful **7** erratic **8** fanciful, unstable, variable **9** arbitrary, eccentric, impulsive, mercurial, uncertain, whimsical **10** capricious, changeable, inconstant

unprejudiced **4** fair, just **8** unbiased, unswayed **9** impartial, objective, unbigoted **10** evenhanded, fair-minded, open-minded, undogmatic **11** broad-minded **12** uninfluenced **13** disinterested

unpremeditated **5** ad-lib **9** impetuous, impromptu, impulsive, unplanned **10** accidental, improvised, unintended **11** involuntary, spontaneous **12** uncalculated, unthought-out **13** unintentional **14** extemporaneous **15** spur-of-the-moment

unprepared **5** ad-lib **7** offhand, unready **8** off guard **9** extempore, impromptu **10** flat-footed, improvised **11** spontaneous, unrehearsed **14** extemporaneous **15** spur-of-the-moment

unprepossessing **4** grim **5** seedy **10** ill-favored, ill-looking **12** unattractive

unpressed **5** baggy **6** mussed, sloppy **7** creased, rumpled **8** unironed, wrinkled **9** shapeless, uncreased

unpretentious **5** plain **6** homely, humble, modest, simple **10** unassuming, unimposing **11** unelaborate, unobtrusive **14** unostentatious

unprincipled **6** amoral **12** unscrupulous **14** conscienceless, unconscionable

unproductive **4** poor **6** barren **7** sterile, useless **8** bootless **9** infertile **10** unfruitful, unyielding **11** ineffective, ineffectual, inefficient **12** unprofitable

unprofessional **6** shoddy, sloppy **7** amateur **8** bungling, careless **9** negligent, unethical **10** amateurish **11** incompetent, inefficient, unpracticed **12** unprincipled **13** inexperienced, undisciplined, unworkmanlike **14** unbusinesslike

unprofitable **4** vain **7** useless **8** bootless **11** ineffective, ineffectual

unprogressive **7** diehard **8** backward, standpat, stubborn **9** benighted, right-wing **11** reactionary, reactionist **12** conservative **17** ultraconservative

unprolific **6** barren **7** sterile **9** infertile, unfertile **10** nonbearing **12** unproductive

unpromising **5** bleak **9** ill-omened **10** forbidding **11** unfavorable **12** inauspicious, unpropitious

unpropitious **7** adverse **8** contrary **9** unfitting **10** unsuitable **11** unfavorable **12** antagonistic, inauspicious, infelicitous

unprotected **4** open **5** naked **6** unsafe **7** exposed, unarmed **8** helpless, insecure, perilous **9** dangerous, hazardous, unguarded **10** undefended, vulnerable **11** defenseless

unproven **7** in doubt **8** arguable, doubtful **10** indefinite, in question, up in the air **11** open to doubt, unconfirmed **12** experimental, inconclusive, questionable **13** unestablished **14** open to question

unpunctual **4** late **5** tardy **7** belated **10** behindhand, behindtime

unqualified **5** total, unfit, utter **8** absolute, complete, inexpert, positive, thorough, unsuited **9** downright, out-and-out, unskilled, untrained **10** consummate, undisputed, uneducated, unprepared, unschooled **11** ill-equipped, incompetent **13** inexperienced, unconditional

unquenched **8** unslaked **11** unsatisfied **14** unextinguished

unquestionable **4** sure **5** clear, plain **6** proven **7** certain, evident, obvious, perfect **8** definite, flawless **9** blameless, errorless, faultless **10** impeccable, undeniable **11** beyond doubt, irrefutable, self-evident, unequivocal **12** indisputable, uncensurable **13** uncontestable, unimpeachable **14** irreproachable

unquestionably **6** surely **7** totally **9** certainly, doubtless **10** absolutely, completely, definitely, positively, unarguably **12** conclusively, indisputably, without doubt **13** unequivocally

unravel **4** undo **5** feaze, solve **6** unfold, unfurl, unknit **7** clear up, resolve **8** decipher, separate, untangle **9** pull apart **10** disinvolve **11** disentangle

unreachable **10** impossible, out of touch **11** out of the way, unavailable, unrealistic **12** inaccessible, unobtainable **14** unapproachable

unreal **4** airy **5** dream **6** dreamy **7** ghostly, not real, phantom, shadowy **8** ethereal, illusive, illusory, imagined, spectral **9** dreamlike, fantastic, imaginary, legendary **10** chimerical, fictitious, idealistic, intangible **11** nonexistent **13** insubstantial **16** phantasmagorical

unrealistic **4** wild **5** crazy, silly **6** absurd **7** asinine, foolish **8** crackpot, delusory, fanciful **9** illogical **10** idealistic, improbable, infeasible, starry-eyed **11** impractical **12** unreasonable

unrealized **8** thwarted **10** frustrated, incomplete **11** nonexistent, unfulfilled, unsatisfied **14** unaccomplished

unreasonable **5** undue **6** absurd, biased, mulish, unfair **7** bigoted **8** obdurate, stubborn, too great **9** excessive, fanatical, illogical, obstinate, pigheaded, senseless, unbending **10** bullheaded, exorbitant, far-fetched, headstrong, immoderate, inflexible, inordinate, irrational, prejudiced, unyielding **11** extravagant, intractable, nonsensical, opinionated, uncalled-for, unwarranted **12** closed-minded, preposterous, ungovernable, unmanageable **13** unjustifiable

unreasoning **8** careless, heedless **9** impulsive **10** irrational, unthinking **11** thoughtless **13** unintelligent

unrecognizable **9** disguised, incognito **10** in disguise **11** camouflaged **14** unidentifiable

unrecognized **6** unsung **7** cryptic, unknown **9** incognito, unnoticed

unrefined **3** raw **5** crude, rough **6** coarse, vulgar **7** boorish, low-bred **9** inelegant

unrehearsed **7** offhand **8** informal **9** extempore, impromptu, impulsive, unplanned, unstudied **10** improvised, off-the-cuff, unprepared **11** extemporary, spontaneous **14** extemporaneous, unpremeditated **15** improvisational, spur-of-the-moment **19** off the top of one's head

unrelated **6** not kin, unlike **7** foreign **8** unallied **10** dissimilar, extraneous, irrelevant, non-germane **11** unconnected **12** inapplicable, incompatible, unassociated **13** inappropriate

unrelenting **5** rigid **6** steady **7** adamant, endless **8** constant, unabated, unbroken **9** ceaseless, incessant, tenacious, unbending **10** implacable, inexorable, inflexible, relentless, unrelieved, unswerving, unwavering, unyielding **11** undeviating, unremitting **14** uncompromising

unreliable **4** fake **5** false, phony **6** fickle **8** fallible, mistaken, unstable **9** deceitful, erroneous, uncertain **10** capricious, changeable, inaccurate, inconstant **12** questionable, undependable **13** irresponsible, untrustworthy

unremarkable **5** usual **6** common **7** average **8** everyday, mediocre, ordinary **11** commonplace **12** unimpressive, unsurprising **13** insignificant, unexceptional **15** undistinguished

unremitting **6** dogged **8** constant, tireless, untiring **9** ceaseless, continual, incessant, unceasing **10** continuous, persistent **11** persevering

unrepentant **7** callous **8** hardened, obdurate, unatoned **9** unashamed **10** uncontrite, unexpiated **11** remorseless **12** incorrigible, unregenerate

unrepressed **4** free, open **7** liberal **8** effusive, outgoing **9** expansive, exuberant **11** extroverted, uninhibited **12** unrestrained

unreserved **4** full, open **5** frank **6** entire **11** unqualified **12** wholehearted

unresolved **4** moot **5** vague **7** pending **8** doubtful, unsolved **9** tentative, uncertain, undecided, unsettled **10** disputable, unanswered **11** contestable, speculative **12** questionable, undetermined **13** problematical, unascertained

unresponsive **4** cold, cool, dull, limp **5** inert **6** frigid **7** passive **8** lifeless **9** apathetic, unfeeling **11** cold-blooded, inattentive, indifferent, unemotional **13** dispassionate, unsympathetic

unresponsiveness **6** apathy **7** inertia **9** lassitude, passivity **11** inattention, passiveness **12** indifference

unrest **5** chaos **6** tumult **7** anarchy, discord, ferment, protest, turmoil **8** disorder, disquiet, upheaval **9** agitation, rebellion **10** discontent, turbulence **12** restlessness **15** dissatisfaction

unrestrained **8** uncurbed **9** abandoned, boundless, excessive, unbridled, unchecked, unlimited **10** immoderate, inordinate, unfettered, ungoverned, unhampered, unhindered, unreserved **11** extravagant, intemperate, uninhibited, unrepressed **12** uncontrolled, unrestricted, unsuppressed **13** irrepressible

unrestraint **6** excess **7** abandon **9** uncontrol **10** unruliness **12** extravagance, immoderation, recklessness **13** excessiveness, impulsiveness

unrestricted **8** absolute, complete **9** out-and-out, unbounded, unlimited **11** unqualified **12** unrestrained **13** unconditional

unrigid **3** lax **4** easy, limp, soft **5** loose **6** giving, limber, mobile, pliant, supple **7** elastic, lenient, plastic, pliable **8** flexible, informal, merciful, tolerant, yielding **9** indulgent, malleable **11** conformable

unrigorous **4** easy **5** loose, slack **6** casual, sloppy **7** inexact **8** careless, slapdash **9** imprecise

unripe **5** green **8** immature **10** unseasoned **11** undeveloped **14** underdeveloped

unrivaled **8** superior, topnotch **9** unequaled **10** undisputed **11** unsurpassed

unroll **6** reveal, uncoil, unfold, unfurl, unwind **7** display, lay open, play out **9** spread out

unruffled **4** calm, cool, even, mild **5** quiet, still **6** placid, serene, smooth **8** composed, tranquil **9** collected **10** coolheaded, nonchalant, unagitated, untroubled **11** undisturbed, unperturbed **13** self-possessed

unruly **4** wild **5** rowdy **7** restive, wayward, willful **8** contrary, perverse **9** fractious, unbridled **10** boisterous, disorderly, headstrong, refractory **11** disobedient, intractable **12** obstreperous, ungovernable, unmanageable **13** undisciplined **14** uncontrollable

unsafe **5** risky **7** exposed **8** insecure, perilous **9** dangerous, hazardous, unguarded **10** undefended, unreliable, vulnerable **11** defenseless, treacherous, unprotected **13** untrustworthy

unsatisfactory **4** poor **5** inept, unfit **8** below par, inferior, unworthy **9** deficient **10** inadequate, ineligible, unsuitable **12** inadmissible, unacceptable **13** inappropriate

unsavory **3** bad **4** flat, foul **5** nasty **7** insipid, tainted **9** tasteless **10** bad-tasting, nauseating, unpleasant **11** distasteful, unpalatable **12** disagreeable, unappetizing

unscathed **5** sound, whole **6** entire, intact, unhurt **7** perfect **8** unharmed **9** uninjured, untouched **10** unimpaired **11** unscratched **13** all in one piece

unscholarly **8** ignorant **9** unlearned **10** illiterate, uneducated, uninformed **11** ill-informed **13** unintelligent

unschooled **3** raw **5** green **6** callow **8** ignorant, untaught **9** unlearned **10** illiterate, uneducated, uninformed, unlettered, unseasoned **11** uninitiated **13** inexperienced

unscrupulous **5** sharp **6** amoral **7** crooked, devious, immoral **9** unethical **12** dishonorable, unprincipled

unseasonable **6** too hot **7** too cold, too warm **8** abnormal, untimely

unseasoned **3** raw **5** bland, green, plain **6** callow **7** untried **8** immature **13** inexperienced

unseeing **5** blind **7** unaware **9** oblivious, sightless **11** unobservant

unseemly **4** rude **5** crude, gross **6** coarse, vulgar **7** boorish, loutish **8** churlish, improper, indecent, unworthy **9** incorrect, offensive, tasteless **10** indecorous, indelicate, out of place, unbecoming, unladylike, unsuitable **11** distasteful, ill-mannered, unbefitting, undignified **12** discourteous, disreputable **13** discreditable, inappropriate, reprehensible, ungentlemanly

unselfconscious **7** artless **10** unaffected **13** unpretentious

unselfish **7** liberal **8** generous, handsome, princely, selfless **10** altruistic, benevolent, bighearted, charitable, openhanded **11** considerate, magnanimous, magnificent **12** humanitarian **13** philanthropic **15** self-sacrificing

unserviceable **7** useless **8** unusable

unsettle **5** upset **6** bother, rattle, ruffle **7** agitate, confuse, disturb, fluster, perturb, trouble, unhinge **8** bewilder, confound, disorder **9** unbalance **10** disconcert **13** throw off guard

unsettled **5** fazed **7** anxious, nervous, ruffled **8** agitated, confused, doubtful **9** disturbed, nonplused, perturbed, undecided **10** disquieted, distracted, nonplussed, up in the air **11** discomfited **12** disconcerted **16** at sixes and sevens

unshackle **4** free **7** release, set free, unchain **8** liberate, unfetter

unshakable **4** fast **6** stable **7** abiding, staunch **8** constant, enduring **9** dauntless, permanent, steadfast, unruffled **10** changeless, inflexible, unsinkable, unwavering **11** levelheaded, unflappable **13** imperturbable

unshaken **4** calm, cool **6** poised, serene, stable **7** staunch, unmoved **8** composed, constant, resolved **9** steadfast, tenacious, undaunted, unexcited, unruffled **10** controlled, determined, inflexible, relentless, unaffected, unswerving, untroubled, unwavering **11** levelheaded, undeviating, undisturbed, unemotional, unfaltering, unflinching, unperturbed **13** self-possessed **14** uncompromising

unshapely **5** baggy **9** amorphous, shapeless

unshaven **5** hairy **7** bearded, bristly, hirsute, stubbly, unkempt **9** whiskered **11** bewhiskered

unsheathe **4** bare **6** expose **7** pull out **8** withdraw

unsightly **4** ugly **6** horrid, odious **7** hideous **9** obnoxious, offensive, repellent, repulsive, revolting, sickening **11** distasteful **12** unattractive

unsigned **9** anonymous **13** bearing no name

unskilled **5** green, inept **7** untried **9** untrained **10** amateurish, apprentice **11** incompetent, unqualified **13** inexperienced

unskillful **5** inept **6** clumsy, unable **7** awkward **8** inexpert **9** incapable, maladroit, untrained **10** amateurish **11** incompetent, ineffective, unpracticed **13** inexperienced

unsmiling **3** sad **4** glum, grim **5** grave **6** dismal **7** austere, joyless, serious **9** cheerless, grim-faced

unsociable **7** haughty **9** withdrawn **10** antisocial, unfriendly, ungracious **11** introverted **14** unapproachable

unsoiled **4** pure **5** clean, fresh, white **6** chaste **8** innocent, pristine, spotless **9** unstained, unsullied **10** immaculate **11** unblemished, untarnished

unsolicited **4** free **8** unforced, unsought, unwanted **9** undesired, uninvited, unwelcome, voluntary **10** gratuitous, unasked for **11** spontaneous, unnecessary, unrequested, unwished for, volunteered

unsophisticated **4** open **5** green, naive **6** candid **7** artless, natural **8** homespun, innocent, trusting **9** ingenuous, unstudied, unworldly **10** unaffected, unassuming **11** uncontrived **13** undissembling, unpretentious **15** straightforward

unsound **3** mad, off **4** weak **5** risky, shaky, unfit, wrong **6** absurd, ailing, faulty, feeble, flawed, infirm, insane, marred, sickly, unsafe **7** foolish, invalid, rickety, tottery **8** confused, crippled, decrepit, deranged, diseased, drooping, impaired, insecure, not solid, not valid, perilous, specious, spurious, unhinged, unstable, unsteady **9** blemished, dangerous, defective, erroneous, hazardous, illogical, imperfect, incorrect, senseless, uncertain, unfounded, unhealthy, unsettled, untenable **10** disordered, fallacious, groundless, irrational, precarious, unbalanced, unreliable **11** languishing, mentally ill **12** in poor health **13** off one's rocker, unsubstantial

unsoundness **7** frailty **8** delicacy, weakness **9** fragility, frailness, shakiness **11** decrepitude, derangement, instability **12** unsteadiness

unsparing **4** full **6** giving, lavish **7** copious, liberal, profuse **8** abundant, generous **9** bountiful, plenteous, plentiful, unlimited **10** big-hearted, munificent, ungrudging, unstinting **11** extravagant, magnanimous, unqualified **13** unconditional

unspeakable **4** huge, vast **5** awful, great **6** odious **7** fearful, immense **8** enormous, shocking **9** abhorrent, frightful, loathsome, monstrous, repellent, repulsive, revolting, sickening, unheard-of **10** abominable, disgusting, incredible, nauseating, prodigious **11** astonishing, unutterable **12** overwhelming, unimaginable **13** extraordinary, inconceivable, inexpressible, undescribable

unspecified **5** vague **7** general, unnamed **9** undefined, unsettled **10** indefinite **11** unannounced, unindicated, unmentioned **12** undesignated, undetermined, unpublicized, unstipulated

unspoiled **4** open **7** artless, natural, perfect **8** pristine, spotless, trusting, unharmed, unmarred **9** preserved, undamaged, unscarred, unspotted, unstudied, unworldly **10** unaffected, unassuming, unimpaired, unpampered **11** unblemished, uncorrupted **13** unpretentious **15** unselfconscious, unsophisticated

unspoken **5** tacit **6** silent **7** implied **8** implicit **9** ineffable, not voiced, unuttered **10** understood **11** unexpressed

unspotted **5** clean **8** spotless, unsoiled **9** undefiled, unstained, unsullied **11** unblemished

unstable **4** weak **5** frail, shaky, tippy **6** fickle, fitful, flimsy, wobbly **7** erratic, fragile, rickety **8** changing, insecure, shifting, unsteady, volatile **9** emotional, mercurial, tottering **10** capricious, changeable, fly-by-night, irrational **11** fluctuating, vacillating **12** inconsistent **13** irresponsible, unpredictable, unsubstantial

unstained **5** clean **8** spotless **9** unspotted, unsullied, untainted **11** unblemished, uncorrupted

unsteady **6** fickle, wobbly **7** rickety **8** doubtful, unstable **10** unreliable **12** questionable, undependable **13** untrustworthy

unstinting **11** unqualified **12** enthusiastic, unrestrained, wholehearted

unstooped **5** erect **6** unbent **7** upright **8** straight, vertical

unstudied **4** glib **6** casual **7** artless, natural **8** informal, unforced, unversed **9** guileless, unuttered **10** unaffected **11** spontaneous **12** uncalculated

unsubmissive **6** unruly **7** defiant, froward, naughty, wayward **8** contrary, mutinous, perverse, stubborn **9** fractious, insurgent, obstinate, seditious, undutiful **10** disorderly, rebellious, refractory, unyielding **11** disobedient, intractable **12** noncompliant, recalcitrant, ungovernable, unmanageable **13** insubordinate

unsubstantial **4** airy, weak **5** filmy **6** feeble, flimsy **7** unsound **8** ethereal, fanciful, illusory **9** idealized, imaginary **10** jerrybuilt **11** lightweight **12** undetectable **13** imperceptible **17** indistinguishable

unsubstantiated **8** disputed **10** unverified **15** unauthenticated

unsuccessful **4** poor, vain **6** foiled, futile, hard up **7** baffled, hapless, unlucky, useless **8** abortive, badly off, luckless, strapped, thwarted **9** fruitless, moneyless, penniless **10** ill-starred, profitless, unavailing, unfruitful **11** ineffectual, unfortunate **12** unproductive, unprofitable, unprosperous **14** unremunerative

unsuitability **9** unfitness, wrongness **11** impropriety, uselessness **12** unseemliness **13** inconsistency **15** incompatibility, unacceptability **17** inappropriateness

unsuitable **5** inapt, unfit **7** unhappy, useless **8** improper, unseemly **9** unfitting, worthless **10** inadequate, indecorous, out of place, unbecoming, unsuitable **11** incongruous, unbefitting **12** inadmissible, incompatible, inconsistent, infelicitous, out of keeping, unacceptable **13** inappropriate

unsuited **5** inapt, wrong **9** unfitting **10** out of place **13** inappropriate

unsullied **5** clean **8** spotless, unsoiled **9** undefiled, uninjured, untainted **10** unpolluted **11** unblackened, unblemished, uncorrupted, untarnished **14** uncontaminated

unsupportable **6** faulty **9** unfounded, untenable **12** indefensible

unsure **3** shy **5** timid **7** bashful **8** hesitant, insecure, reserved **9** unassured, uncertain, undecided **11** in a quandary, unconfident, unconvinced **12** self-doubting **15** self-distrustful

unsurpassed **4** best **7** highest, supreme **8** greatest, peerless, superior **9** matchless, nonpareil, paramount, unequaled, unmatched, unrivaled **10** consummate, unexcelled **11** exceptional **12** incomparable, transcendent, unparalleled

unsuspecting **5** naive **6** unwary **7** unaware **8** gullible, off guard, trusting **9** believing, credulous **12** overtrustful, unsuspicious **13** overcredulous

unsuspicious **5** naive **8** gullible, trustful, trusting **9** credulous **12** unsuspecting **13** unquestioning

unswerving **4** firm **6** steady, strong **7** devoted, staunch **8** faithful, resolute, resolved, unshaken, untiring **9** dedicated, steadfast, undaunted **10** determined, inflexible, unflagging, unwavering, unyielding **11** undeviating, unfaltering, unflinching, unremitting **12** single-minded **14** uncompromising

unsympathetic **7** callous **8** pitiless, uncaring **9** heartless, repellent, repugnant, unfeeling, unlikable **10** hard-boiled, unlikeable, unmerciful, unpleasant **11** coldhearted, displeasing, hardhearted, indifferent, uncongenial **12** antipathetic, unattractive **15** uncompassionate

unsystematic **6** sloppy **7** chaotic, jumbled, muddled **8** confused **9** haphazard, unplanned **10** disordered, disorderly **12** disorganized, unmethodical

untainted **4** pure **5** clear **9** unsullied **11** uncorrupted **13** unadulterated

untalented **5** inept **8** mediocre, ungifted **9** unskilled **10** amateurish, unskillful **14** unaccomplished

untamed **4** wild **5** feral **6** savage **9** unsubdued **11** uncivilized **12** uncultivated

untangle **5** solve **7** clear up, unravel, unsnarl, untwist **9** extricate **11** disentangle **13** straighten out

untarnished **6** bright **7** perfect, shining **8** flawless, polished, spotless, unsoiled **9** faultless, undefiled, unstained, unsullied, untainted **10** immaculate, impeccable, undisputed, unoxidized **11** unblackened, unblemished **12** unbesmirched **13** unimpeachable

untaught **6** unread **7** natural **8** ignorant **9** untutored **10** illiterate, uneducated, unlettered, unschooled **11** spontaneous **12** uninstructed

untenable **4** weak **6** faulty, flawed **7** invalid, unsound **8** baseless, specious, spurious **9** debatable, erroneous, illogical **10** fallacious, groundless, unreliable **11** contestable **12** indefensible, questionable **13** insupportable, unjustifiable, unsustainable **14** unmaintainable

unthinkable **11** unwarranted **12** unimaginable **13** inconceivable, insupportable, unjustifiable **16** incomprehensible, out of the question

unthinking **7** witless **8** careless, heedless, mindless, tactless **9** imprudent, negligent, senseless **11** inadvertent, insensitive, thoughtless **12** undiplomatic **13** inconsiderate, uncircumspect

untidiness **5** chaos, mix-up, upset **6** jumble **7** clutter **8** disarray, disorder, scramble, shambles **9** confusion, messiness **10** sloppiness **12** dishevelment **14** disarrangement **15** disorganization

untidy **5** dowdy, messy **6** frowsy, mussed, sloppy **7** chaotic, rumpled, tousled, unkempt **8** careless, confused, littered, mussed up, slipshod, slovenly **9** cluttered **10** bedraggled, disarrayed, disheveled, disorderly, slatternly, topsy-turvy **12** unmethodical **13** helter-skelter

untie **4** free, undo **5** loose **6** loosen, unbind, unlace **7** unchain, unstrap **8** make free, unfasten **11** disentangle

untilled **6** fallow **8** unplowed **12** uncultivated

until we meet again
French: **5** adieu **8** au revoir
German: **14** auf Wiedersehen
Hawaiian: **5** aloha
Italian: **4** ciao **5** addio **11** arrivederci
Japanese: **8** sayonara
Spanish: **5** adios

untimely **5** inapt **7** unhappy **8** ill-timed, mistimed, unseemly **9** imprudent, premature, unfitting **10** ill-advised, malapropos, out of place, unbecoming, unexpected, unsuitable **11** inopportune, unbefitting, unfortunate **12** inconvenient, infelicitous **13** inappropriate

untiring **5** fresh **6** steady **7** devoted, earnest, patient, staunch, zealous **8** constant, diligent, resolute, sedulous, tireless **9** assiduous, dedicated, steadfast, tenacious, unceasing, unwearied **10** determined, persistent, relentless, unflagging **11** never tiring, persevering, unfaltering, unremitting **12** wholehearted **13** indefatigable

untold **6** myriad, secret, unsaid **7** endless, private, unknown **8** hushed up, infinite, numerous, unspoken, withheld **9** concealed, countless, limitless, unbounded, uncounted, unrelated **10** numberless, suppressed, unnumbered, unreported, unrevealed **11** innumerable, undisclosed, unexpressed, unpublished **12** immeasurable, incalculable, undetermined

Untouchables, The
character: **7** Rossman **9** Eliot Ness, Lee Hobson **10** Cam Allison, Frank Nitti **11** Enrico Rossi **14** Martin Flaherty **18** William Youngfellow
cast: **10** Jerry Paris **11** Bruce Gordon, Paul Picerni, Robert Stack, Steve London **13** Abel Fernandez, Anthony George, Nick Georgiade
narrator: **14** Walter Winchell

untouched **3** new **4** pure **5** alone **6** intact, virgin **8** pristine, unharmed **9** uninjured **10** unaffected, unmolested

untoward **5** amiss **6** unruly **7** adverse **8** contrary **9** difficult **11** unfavorable **12** inauspicious, unpropitious

untrainable **6** unruly **11** intractable, unteachable **12** ungovernable

untrained **3** raw **5** green **7** untried **9** unskilled **11** unqualified **13** inexperienced

untried **3** raw **5** green **6** callow **8** immature, untested **10** unseasoned **13** inexperienced

untroubled **4** calm **6** placid, serene **7** halcyon, relaxed **8** carefree, careless, peaceful, tranquil **9** easygoing, unworried **10** unbothered **11** free-and-easy, undisturbed, unperturbed **12** happy-go-lucky, lighthearted

untrue **4** fake, sham **5** false **6** made up **7** not true **8** disloyal, spurious, unchaste **9** dishonest, erroneous, faithless, falsified, incorrect, unfounded **10** adulterous, fallacious, fictitious, fraudulent, groundless, inaccurate, inconstant, perfidious, unfaithful, untruthful **11** promiscuous, treacherous **12** meretricious **13** double-dealing

untrustworthy **5** false **6** fickle, shifty, untrue **7** corrupt, crooked, devious **8** disloyal, fallible, slippery, two-faced **9** corrupted, deceitful, dishonest, faithless, insincere, uncertain, unethical **10** capricious, inconstant, perfidious, unfaithful, unreliable, untruthful **11** treacherous **12** dishonorable, disreputable, questionable, undependable, unprincipled, unscrupulous **13** irresponsible **15** unauthenticated

untruth **3** fib, lie **4** hoax, tale, yarn **5** fable, story **6** canard, humbug **8** flimflam **9** deception, falsehood, fish story, invention **11** fabrication **12** equivocation **13** falsification, prevarication **16** cock-and-bull story **17** misrepresentation

untruthful **5** false, lying **8** specious, spurious **9** deceptive, dishonest **10** fraudulent, mendacious

untutored **5** naive **6** native, unread **8** ignorant, untaught **10** illiterate, uneducated, unlettered, unschooled **12** uninstructed **15** unsophisticated

untypical **3** odd **4** rare **5** alien **7** bizarre, deviant, strange, unusual **8** aberrant, abnormal, atypical, uncommon **9** anomalous, irregular, unnatural **10** unfamiliar **16** unrepresentative

unused **3** new **7** strange, untried **8** left over, not given, pristine, unopened **9** remaining, untouched **10** unemployed **12** unaccustomed, unacquainted, unhabituated

unusual **4** rare **5** novel **6** unique **7** curious, offbeat, strange **8** atypical, peculiar, singular, uncommon **9** unequaled, unheard-of, unmatched, untypical **10** noteworthy, one of a kind, phenomenal, remarkable, surprising, unfamiliar **11** exceptional **12** incomparable, unparalleled **13** extraordinary, unprecedented **16** out of the ordinary

unvaried **4** even **5** fixed **6** steady **7** regular, uniform **8** all alike, constant **9** identical, unchanged **10** all the same, invariable, monotonous, unchanging **11** homogeneous, unalterable, undeviating

unvarnished **3** raw **4** bald, bare **5** blunt, crude, frank, naked, plain, stark **6** candid, direct, honest, simple **7** sincere **8** straight **9** unadorned, uncolored **10** unfinished **11** fundamental, undisguised **13** unembellished **15** straightforward **23** straight-from-the-shoulder

unvarying **4** even **6** steady **7** regular, uniform **8** constant **10** unwavering

unveil **4** bare **6** reveal **7** divulge, publish, uncloak, uncover **8** announce, disclose **9** broadcast, make known, unsheathe **12** bring to light

unveiled **5** bared **8** divulged, laid bare, revealed **9** announced, broadcast, disclosed, made known, published, uncovered **14** brought to light

unveiling **4** show **5** array **7** display, exhibit, showing **10** exhibition, exposition **13** demonstration

unverified **7** alleged, rumored **8** disputed **15** unauthenticated, unsubstantiated

unwarranted **7** illegal **8** culpable, unlawful **9** arbitrary, unfounded **10** censurable, groundless, unapproved **11** inexcusable, uncalled-for, unjustified **12** indefensible, unauthorized, unreasonable, unsanctioned

unwary **4** rash **5** hasty **7** unalert **8** careless, headlong, heedless, reckless **9** imprudent, unguarded **10** incautious, indiscreet, unwatchful **11** precipitate **12** disregardful **13** uncircumspect

unwashed **4** foul **5** dirty, grimy, muddy **6** filthy, grubby, smudgy, soiled **7** unclean **8** begrimed

unwasteful **6** frugal **7** thrifty **9** effective, effectual, efficient **10** productive

unwavering **4** firm **6** steady, strong **7** staunch **8** faithful, resolute, unshaken, untiring **9** dedicated, steadfast, tenacious **10** determined, persistent, unflagging, unswerving **11** persevering, undeviating, unfaltering, unflinching, unremitting **12** single-minded **14** uncompromising

unwelcome **7** outcast **8** excluded, rejected, unwanted **9** thankless, uninvited, unpopular **10** uncared for, unpleasant, unrequired **11** displeasing, distasteful, undesirable, unessential, unnecessary, unwished for **12** disagreeable, unacceptable

unwell **3** ill, low **4** sick **5** frail **6** ailing, infirm, laid up, poorly, queasy, sickly **7** rundown **8** delicate, qualmish **10** indisposed **11** off one's feed **15** under the weather

unwholesome **3** bad **4** evil,

foul **5** toxic **6** deadly, filthy, sinful, wicked **7** baneful, harmful, hurtful, immoral, noxious, ruinous **8** depraved, venomous **9** corrupted, dangerous, degrading, poisonous, polluting, unhealthy **10** corrupting, pernicious **11** deleterious, detrimental, undesirable, unhealthful **12** demoralizing, dishonorable, insalubrious, unnourishing **13** contaminating

unwieldy **5** bulky, heavy **6** clumsy **7** awkward, weighty **8** not handy **10** burdensome, cumbersome **12** hard to handle, incommodious, inconvenient **13** uncomfortable

unwilled **6** reflex **9** automatic **11** involuntary, unconscious **12** uncontrolled **13** nonvolitional

unwilling **5** loath **6** averse **7** against, opposed **9** demurring, reluctant, resistant **10** dissenting, indisposed, undesirous **11** disinclined **12** not in the mood, recalcitrant **14** unenthusiastic

unwillingness **8** aversion **10** opposition, reluctance, resistance **13** indisposition **14** disinclination

unwise **4** dumb **5** crazy, silly **6** stupid **7** foolish, unsound **8** reckless **9** foolhardy, imprudent, senseless **10** ill-advised **11** improvident, inadvisable, injudicious **12** shortsighted, unreasonable **13** irresponsible, unintelligent

unwitting **7** unaware, unmeant **9** unknowing, unplanned **10** accidental, undesigned, unexpected, unthinking **11** inadvertent, involuntary **12** unconsenting **13** unintentional **14** unpremeditated

unwonted **4** rare **7** unusual **8** atypical, uncommon **10** infrequent, remarkable, unexpected, unfamiliar **11** exceptional **12** unaccustomed **13** extraordinary

unworkmanlike **6** clumsy, sloppy **11** inefficient

unworldly **4** holy, pure **5** godly, green, moral, naive, pious **6** callow, devout, divine, sacred, solemn **7** ethical **8** ethereal, heavenly, innocent, trusting **9** aesthetic, celestial, religious, spiritual, unearthly **10** idealistic, immaterial, provincial **12** intellectual, metaphysical, overtrusting **13** inexperienced, philosophical **14** transcendental **15** unsophisticated

unworried **4** calm **6** serene **7** relaxed **8** carefree, composed, peaceful, tranquil **9** easygoing, unruffled **10** untroubled

unworthy **5** unfit **7** ignoble **8** improper, shameful, unseemly **9** degrading, unethical **10** unbecoming, unsuitable **11** unbefitting **12** dishonorable, disreputable, unacceptable **13** discreditable, inappropriate, objectionable

unwrap **4** open **6** loosen, unbind **7** uncover

unwrinkled **4** even, flat **6** ironed, smooth **7** unlined **8** smoothed **9** uncreased, unrumpled

unwritten **4** oral **5** tacit, vocal **7** assumed, implied **8** implicit, inferred, unstated **9** customary **10** spoken only, understood, unrecorded **11** traditional, unexpressed **12** unformulated, unregistered **13** by word of mouth

unwritten law
Latin: **13** lex non scripta

unyielding **4** firm, hard **5** rigid, stiff, stony, tough **6** wooden **8** resolute, rocklike, stubborn **9** obstinate, steadfast, unbending, unpliable **10** determined, inexorable, inflexible, persistent, unswerving, unwavering **11** undeviating **14** uncompromising

up **4** atop, lift, over, rear **5** about, above, aloft, along, aside, astir, at bat, built, close, equal, erect, raise **6** apiece, ascend, higher, lifted **7** abreast, batting, forward, promote, skyward, through **8** advanced, cheerful, increase, out of bed, overhead, standing, together, windward **9** northward **10** optimistic **11** constructed

up and about **5** afoot, astir **6** active, mobile, roused **7** walking **8** out of bed **10** ambulatory, on one's feet

up-and-down **6** fitful, seesaw, uneven **7** bobbing **8** jouncing, wavering **11** alternating, fluctuating, vacillating

upbraid **5** scold **6** berate, rebuke, revile **7** bawl out, censure, chew out, reprove **8** admonish, chastise, denounce, reproach **9** castigate, dress down, reprimand **10** tongue-lash

upbringing **7** rearing **8** breeding, training **10** background

upcoming **6** coming, nearby **7** looming, nearing, pending **8** imminent **9** impending, momentary **11** approaching, drawing nigh, forthcoming, in the offing, prospective

update **5** amend, emend, renew **6** recast, revamp, revise, rework **7** restore, touch up, upgrade **8** overhaul, renovate **9** refurbish **10** rejuvenate, reorganize, streamline

up for grabs **4** open **9** available

upgrade **5** raise, slope **6** ascent, better **7** advance, dignify, elevate, incline, inflate, promote **8** gradient

upheaval **5** flood, quake **6** blowup, tumult **7** turmoil **8** disorder, upthrust **9** cataclysm, explosion, tidal wave **10** disruption, earthquake, revolution **11** catastrophe, disturbance

uphill **4** hard **5** tough **6** rising, taxing, tiring, upward **7** arduous, onerous **8** toilsome, wearying **9** ascending, difficult, fatiguing, strenuous, wearisome **10** burdensome, enervating, exhausting **12** backbreaking

uphill work **8** struggle, tough job **10** difficulty, rough going **11** arduousness **12** hard sledding **13** laboriousness

uphold **4** bear, prop **5** brace, carry, raise, shore **6** defend, hold up, prop up **7** approve, bolster, confirm, elevate, endorse, protect, shore up, support, sustain **8** advocate, buttress, champion, maintain, preserve, underpin **9** encourage **10** stand up for, underbrace **11** acknowledge, corroborate

upholder **7** devotee **8** adherent, advocate, defender, partisan **9** supporter

up in the clouds **6** elated, joyful, joyous **8** ecstatic, euphoric **9** exuberant, rapturous **11** on cloud nine **15** in seventh heaven

Upis
goddess of: **10** childbirth

Upjohn, Richard
architect of: **13** Trinity Church (NYC)
style: **13** Gothic Revival

upkeep **4** keep **6** living **7** support **8** expenses, overhead **10** management, sustenance **11** maintenance, subsistence **12** conservation, preservation

upland **4** high, rise **5** ridge **6** height **7** plateau **8** eminence, highland **9** elevation, high place, high point **10** prominence

uplift **5** edify, raise **6** better, refine **7** advance, bracing, elevate, improve, inspire, lifting, shoring, support, upgrade **8** civilize, propping **9** cultivate, elevation **10** betterment, bolstering, enrichment, refinement **11** advancement, buttressing, cultivation, edification, enhancement, improvement **12** underpinning

uplifting **9** elevating, elevation, improving, inspiring **11** improvement **12** enlightening **13** enlightenment, inspirational

upon **2** at, on **4** atop **5** about **6** toward **7** against, thereon **9** by means of, thereupon **10** after which, thereafter

upper **3** top **4** high **5** major **6** higher, inland **7** eminent, greater, topmost **8** elevated, northern, superior **9** important

upper-case letter **7** capital **9** majuscule **13** capital letter

upper class **5** elite **6** gentry, uptown **7** (high) society **8** highborn, highbred, wellborn **9** beau monde, haut monde, high-class, patrician, top drawer **10** upper crust **11** aristocracy, blue-blooded **12** aristocratic, silk-stocking **14** creme de la creme, to the manor born **15** to the manner born

upper crust **5** elite **6** gentry **7** (high) society **9** beau monde, haut monde, top drawer **10** upper class **11** aristocracy **14** creme de la creme

upper hand **4** edge, sway **5** power **7** command, control, mastery **8** whip hand **9** advantage, authority, supremacy **10** domination **12** predominance

upper house **6** Senate **12** House of Lords

uppermost, upmost **3** top **4** main **5** chief, first, major, prime **7** highest, leading, primary, supreme, topmost **8** crowning, dominant, foremost, greatest, loftiest **9** essential, paramount, principal **10** preeminent **11** predominant **12** transcendent **13** most important

Upper Volta ***see box***

upright **3** rib **4** fair, good, just, pale, pier, pile, pole, post, prop **5** erect, moral, shaft, stake, strut **6** column, honest, picket, pillar **7** ethical, support, upended **8** reliable, standard, vertical **9** honorable, righteous, stanchion **10** aboveboard, high-minded, principled, standing-up, upstanding **11** trustworthy **12** on the up-and-up **13** perpendicular

uprightness **5** honor **7** dignity, honesty **8** morality **9** integrity **13** righteousness **15** trustworthiness

uprising **4** riot **6** mutiny, revolt **8** outbreak **9** rebellion **10** insurgence, revolution **12** insurrection

uproar **3** ado **4** stir, to-do **5** furor **6** clamor, tumult **7** turmoil **9** agitation, commotion **11** disturbance, pandemonium **16** state of confusion

uproarious **4** loud, wild **5** noisy **6** raging, stormy **7** furious, intense, riotous **9** clamorous, hilarious, turbulent, very funny **10** boisterous, disorderly, hysterical, tumultuous **11** tempestuous **13** sidesplitting

uproot **6** banish **7** abolish, cast out, destroy, root out, wipe out **8** dislodge, displace, force out **9** eliminate, extirpate **10** annihilate, do away with **11** exterminate

upset **3** ire, irk, mad, vex **4** beat **5** anger, annoy, crush, irked, messy, mix up, pique, quash, smash, upend, vexed, worry **6** bother, cancel, change, defeat, enrage, grieve, invert, jumble, muddle, mussed, rattle, thrash, untidy **7** agitate, angered, annoyed, capsize, chaotic, confuse, conquer, disturb, enraged, fluster, furious, grieved, incense, jumbled, mixed-up, perturb, reverse, tip over, trouble, trounce, unnerve, upended, worried **8** agitated, bothered, capsized, confused, demolish, disorder, distress, incensed, inverted, overcome, overturn, slovenly, troubled, turn over, unnerved, upturned, vanquish **9** discomfit, disturbed, infuriate, overpower, overthrow, overwhelm, perturbed **10** discompose, disconcert, disheveled, disordered, disorderly, disquieted, distressed, hysterical, overturned, tipped over, topple over, topsy-turvy, turned over, upside-down **11** disarranged, disorganize, overwrought, wrong side up **12** disorganized **13** make miserable **14** turn topsy-turvy

upsetting
French: **14** bouleversement

upshot **3** end **6** effect, payoff,

Upper Volta
other name: **11** Burkina Faso (Fasso)
capital/largest city: **11** Ouagadougou
others: **4** Kaya **7** Banfora **9** Koudougou **10** Ouahigouya
division: **7** Yatenga **9** Tenkodogo **11** Fada Ngourma
monetary unit: **5** franc **7** centime
mountain: **4** Tema
highest point: **8** Nakourou **10** Tenakourou, Tenekourou
river: **5** Komoe **6** Mekrou, Sourou **8** Pendjari, Red Volta **10** Black Volta, White Volta
physical feature:
plateau: **5** Sahel **7** Sikasso, Voltaic
wind: **9** harmattan
people: **4** Bobo, Lobi, Samo **5** Bella, Bissa, Dyula, Fulbe, Hausa, Mande, Marka, Mossi, Puehl **6** Fulani, Senufo, Tuareg **7** Grunshi, Voltaic, Yatenga **8** Mandingo **9** Gourounsi **15** Bunsansi Gambaga
French governor: **7** Hesling
god: **4** Wuro **5** Tenga
king: **4** Naba **5** Mogho
leader: **5** Oubri, Zerbo **7** Yameogo **8** Lamizana **9** Mogho Naba
language: **4** Bobo, Lobi, More, Samo **5** Dyula, Mande, Mossi **6** French
religion: **5** Islam **7** animism **12** Christianity
place:
game reserve: **11** Arlyand Pama
feature:
animal: **5** hyena **6** duiker, jackal **7** gazelle, warthog **10** hartebeest
tree: **4** shea **6** acacia, baobab, karite, locust

result, sequel **7** outcome **8** offshoot **9** aftermath, outgrowth **10** conclusion **11** aftereffect, consequence, culmination, eventuality **16** final development

upside down **7** chaotic **8** reversed **10** disorderly **11** topsy turvey **12** bottomside up **16** at sixes and sevens

upstairs **2** up **11** above stairs, second floor

upstanding **4** good, tall, true **5** erect, moral, on end **6** honest **7** ethical, upright **8** straight, truthful, vertical, virtuous **9** honorable, righteous **11** trustworthy **13** incorruptible, perpendicular

upstart **4** snip, snob, snub **6** nobody **7** bounder, parvenu **8** mushroom **9** conceited, newly-rich **10** adventurer **12** nouveau riche **13** self-assertive

upsurge **4** gain, push, rise **5** spurt **6** pickup, thrust, upturn **7** advance, upswing **8** increase **11** improvement

upswing **4** rise **6** pickup **7** upsurge **11** improvement, upward trend

uptight **5** tense **7** anxious, fearful, nervous, worried, wound up **8** insecure, neurotic, troubled **9** unbending **10** unyielding **12** apprehensive

up-to-date **2** in **3** new **5** today **6** modern, modish, timely, trendy, with-it **7** current, stylish **9** in fashion **12** contemporary **13** up-to-the-minute
French: **9** au courant

upturn **4** gain, push **6** thrust **7** advance, upsurge **8** increase **9** expansion **11** improvement

upward **4** high, more **5** above, aloft **7** skyward **9** ascending, uppermost

upward movement **4** rise **5** climb **6** ascent, rising, upturn **7** scaling, takeoff **8** climbing, mounting **9** ascension

upward trend **4** rise **5** boost **6** pickup **7** advance, upsurge, upswing **8** increase **11** improvement

Uralic
language branch: **7** Samoyed **10** Finno-Ugric

Urania
also: **9** Aphrodite
member of: **5** Muses
personifies: **9** astronomy

uranium
chemical symbol: **1** U

Uranus
mother: **4** Gaea
wife: **4** Gaea
father of: **6** Giants, Titans **8** Cyclopes **10** Titanesses **13** Hecatonchires
castrated by: **6** Cronos, Cronus, Kronos

Uranus
position: **7** seventh
satellite: **5** Ariel **6** Oberon **7** Miranda, Titania, Umbriel
color: **9** blue-green
characteristic: **5** rings

Urartu *see* **7** Armenia

urban **4** city, town **5** civic **8** citified **9** municipal **11** worldly-wise **12** cosmopolitan, metropolitan **13** sophisticated

urban area **4** city **9** inner city **10** metropolis **11** megalopolis **16** metropolitan area

urbane **5** civil, suave **6** polite, smooth **7** courtly, elegant, gallant, genteel, politic, refined, tactful **8** debonair, gracious, mannerly, polished, well-bred **9** civilized, courteous **10** chivalrous, cultivated, diplomatic **11** gentlemanly **12** cosmopolitan, well-mannered **13** sophisticated

urchin **3** boy, imp, lad **4** brat, waif **5** gamin, stray, whelp, youth **6** gamine, laddie **8** young pup **9** stripling, young punk, youngster **10** young rogue, young tough **11** guttersnipe

Urd **4** Norn
origin: **12** Scandinavian
form: **8** giantess
personifies: **4** past
developed from: **5** Urdar
companion: **5** Skuld **8** Verdandi

Urdar **12** original Norn
origin: **12** Scandinavian
form: **8** giantess
children: **3** Urd **5** Skuld **8** Verdandi

Urey, Harold Clayton
field: **9** chemistry
isolated: **9** deuterium
awarded: **10** Nobel prize

urge **3** yen **4** back, coax, goad, itch, poke, prod, push, spur, sway, wish **5** drive, egg on, fancy, force, press, prick, speed **6** advise, desire, exhort, hasten, hunger, motive, reason, thirst **7** beseech, counsel, craving, dictate, entreat, implore, impulse, longing, passion, push for, quicken, request, solicit, suggest **8** advocate, appeal to, argue for, champion, convince, persuade, petition, pressure, stimulus, yearning **9** hankering, importune, incentive, plead with, prescribe, prompting, recommend **10** accelerate, inducement, motivation, supplicate **11** prevail upon, provocation

urgency **4** need, urge, want **5** press **6** stress **8** exigency, pressure **9** necessity **10** importance, insistence **11** persistence **14** imperativeness **15** importunateness

urgent **5** grave **6** ardent **7** crucial, earnest, fervent, intense, serious, weighty, zealous **8** critical, pleading, pressing, required, spirited **9** demanding, essential, heartfelt, important, insistent, momentous, necessary **10** beseeching, compelling, compulsory, imperative, obligatory, passionate **12** wholehearted **13** indispensable

urge on **4** push **5** boost **7** cheer on, pull for, root for

urging **7** bidding, counsel, goading **8** egging on **9** prompting **11** exhortation

Uriah
father: **7** Shemiah
wife: **9** Bathsheba
served: **5** David

urinary system
component: **6** kidney, ureter **7** bladder, urethra
rids body of: **5** salts, waste, water **8** minerals

Uris, Leon
author of: **5** Topaz **6** Exodus **7** Trinity **9** Battle Cry **10** Armageddon

urn **3** jar, pig **4** ewer, kist, tomb, vase **5** grave, steen **6** teapot **7** samovar **9** coffeepot
botanical: **7** capsule **11** spore-bearer
in keno: **5** goose

Urn Burial
author: **15** Sir Thomas Browne

Uruguay ***see box, p. 1036***

U S A
author: **13** John Dos Passos
character: **10** Ben Compton, Mary French **11** Joe Williams **12** Margo Dowling **13** Fainy McCreary (Mac), Janey Williams **14** J Ward Morehouse **15** Charley Anderson, Eleanor Stoddard, Eveline Hutchins **18** Anne Elizabeth Trent **22** Richard Ellsworth Savage

Uruguay
other name: **10** Purple Land
capital/largest city: **10** Montevideo
others: **4** Fray, Melo **5** Minas, Rocha, Salto **6** Bentos, Rivera **7** Artigas, Colonia, Dolores, Durazno, Florida, San Jose **8** Mercedes, Paysandu, Trinidad **9** Maldonado **10** Las Piedras, Santa Lucia, Tacuarembo **12** Treinta y Tres **13** San Jose de Mayo
measure: **4** vara **6** cuadra, suerte
monetary unit: **4** peso **9** centesimo, centisimo
weight: **7** quintal
island: **5** Lobos
lake: **5** Merin, Mirim **18** Embalse del Rio Negro
mountain: **6** Animas **10** Grand Hills **14** Cuchilla Grande
highest point: **15** Mirador Nacional
river: **4** Malo **5** Mirim, Negro, Plata **6** Parana, Ulimar **7** Cuareim, Queguay, Uruguay **8** Yaguaron **9** Cebollati **10** Tacaurembo
sea: **8** Atlantic
physical feature:
estuary: **5** Plata
people: **4** Yaro **5** Swiss **6** Indian **7** Italian, mestizo, Russian, Spanish **8** Charruas
artist: **6** Figari
author: **4** Rodo **5** Reyes **6** Onetti **7** Sanchez **9** San Martin **10** Ibarbourou
leader: **5** Oribe **6** Rivera **7** Artigas **9** Lavelleja **10** Bordaberry **14** Batlle y Ordonez
language: **7** Italian, Spanish
religion: **13** Roman Catholic
place:
resort: **12** Punta del Este
square: **13** Independencia
feature:
animal: **4** puma **6** jaguar **8** capybara **9** armadillo
bird: **4** rhea **5** nandu **7** hornero, ostrich
cattle ranch: **8** estancia
cowboy: **6** gaucho
dance: **5** tango **7** milonga
festival: **8** Carnival **13** Semana Criolla
lasso: **10** boleadoras
metal straw: **8** bombilla
music: **9** candomble
musical drama: **7** tablado
ruling class: **10** Patriciado
food:
barbecue: **5** asado
dish: **7** puchero **9** churrasco **13** asado con cuero
drink: **4** mate

usable **5** handy **6** useful **9** adaptable **10** functional **11** serviceable

usage **3** use **4** care, mode **5** habit **6** custom, manner, method, system **7** control **8** good form, habitude, handling, practice **9** etiquette, operation, tradition, treatment **10** convention, employment, management **12** manipulation

use **3** aid, ply, sap **4** good, help, work **5** apply, avail, drain, exert, spend, treat, usage, value, waste, wield, worth **6** devour, employ, expend, handle, profit **7** benefit, consume, deplete, exhaust, exploit, operate, service, utilize **8** deal with, exercise, function, handling, profit by, put to use, resort to, squander **9** act toward, advantage, dissipate, enjoyment, make use of, operation, swallow up, throw away **10** employment, manipulate, run through, usefulness **11** application, convenience, fritter away, utilization **12** behave toward, capitalize on **13** make the most of **14** serviceability

used **3** old **5** eaten, spent **7** applied, treated **8** actuated, consumed, depleted, employed, occupied, operated, utilized **9** customary, exercised, exhausted, exploited, practiced **10** accustomed, habituated, secondhand **11** implemented, manipulated

used up **4** beat, shot **5** all in, spent **6** wasted **7** worn out **8** depleted, tired out **9** exhausted

useful **5** handy **7** helpful **8** valuable **9** effective, practical, rewarding **10** beneficial, convenient, functional, profitable, time-saving, worthwhile **11** serviceable, utilitarian **12** advantageous

usefulness **5** avail, value, worth **6** profit **7** benefit, purpose, utility **9** advantage **11** convenience, helpfulness, suitability **12** adaptability, practicality **13** effectiveness **14** serviceability

useless **4** vain **6** futile **7** of no use **8** bootless, unusable **9** fruitless, unhelpful, worthless **10** inadequate, profitless, unavailing **11** incompetent, ineffectual, inefficient **12** unproductive **13** impracticable, inefficacious, nonfunctional, unserviceable

uselessness **6** vanity **8** futility, idleness **9** inutility **10** inefficacy **13** fruitlessness, worthlessness

Uses of Enchantment, The
author: **15** Bruno Bettelheim

use sparingly **4** save **5** hoard, stint **6** scrimp **7** cut back, dole out **8** conserve, not waste, preserve

use to advantage **7** exploit **8** profit by **12** capitalize on **13** turn to account

use up **5** drain, spend **6** expend, finish **7** consume, deplete, exhaust **9** dissipate **10** run through

Ushant
author: **11** Conrad Aiken

usher **4** lead, show **5** guide, steer **6** attend, convoy, direct, escort, herald, launch, leader, porter, ring in, squire **7** conduct, precede, preface **8** announce, director, proclaim **9** conductor, introduce **10** doorkeeper, gatekeeper, inaugurate

Usnach
also: **6** Usnech
origin: **5** Irish
daughter: **6** Naoise

Usnech *see* **6** Usnach

USSR *see* **6** Russia

Ustinov, Peter
born: **6** London **7** England

roles: 7 Topkapi **8** Quo Vadis? **9** Billy Budd, Spartacus **12** We're No Angels

usual 5 stock, trite **6** common, normal, wonted **7** popular, regular, routine, typical **8** expected, familiar, habitual, ordinary, orthodox, standard **9** customary, hackneyed **10** accustomed, prescribed, threadbare **11** commonplace, established, oft-repeated, traditional **12** conventional, run-of-the-mill **15** well-established

usurp 4 grab **5** steal **7** preempt **8** arrogate **10** commandeer **11** appropriate **12** encroach upon, infringe upon

usurpation 6 taking **7** seizure **8** grabbing, stealing **10** arrogation, preemption **13** appropriation

Utah ***see box***

Utah
abbreviation: 2 UT
nickname: 6 Mormon **7** Beehive
capital/largest city: 12 Salt Lake City
others: 3 Roy **4** Moab, Orem **5** Delta, Heber, Kanab, Logan, Magna, Manti, Nepli, Ogden, Price, Provo **6** Beaver, Eureka, Kearns, Layton, Murray, Tooele, Vernal **7** Bingham **8** American **9** Bountiful **11** Brigham City
college: 5 Weber **11** Westminster **12** Brigham Young
feature:
bridge: **7** Rainbow
dam: **6** Hoover **10** Glen Canyon
gorge: **7** Flaming
national historic site: **11** Golden Spike
national monument: **8** Dinosaur **14** Natural Bridges
national park: **4** Zion **6** Arches **11** Bryce Canyon, Canyonlands, Capital Reef
reef: **7** Capital
tribe: 3 Ute **5** Piute, Uinta(h), Yampa **6** Navajo, Paiute **7** Gosiute **8** Paviotso, Shoshoni
people: 7 Mormons **10** Maude Adams **11** Karl G Maeser **12** Brigham Young **13** John M Browning **15** Latter-Day Saints **16** George Sutherland **19** Daniel Cowan Jackling
explorer: **9** Dominguez, Escalante
lake: 4 Mead, Swan, Utah **6** Powell, Sevier **9** Great Salt
land rank: 8 eleventh
mountain: 4 Lena, Lion, Waas **5** Cedar, Henry, Hogup, Peale, Rocky, Trail, Uinta **6** Frisco, Navajo, Swasey, Wahwah **7** Granite, Griffin, Hawkins, Pennell, Terrace, Wasatch **8** Linnaeus **9** Confusion
highest point: **9** Kings Peak
physical feature:
basin: **5** Great
canyon: **4** Echo
desert: **6** Sevier
plateau: **7** Wasatch **8** Colorado, Tavaputs
river: 4 Bear **5** Grand, Green, Weber **6** Jordan, Sevier, Virgin **7** San Juan **8** Colorado
state admission: 10 forty-fifth
state bird: 7 seagull
state flower: 8 sego lily
state motto: 8 Industry
state song: 14 Utah We Love Thee
state tree: 10 blue spruce

utensils 4 gear **5** tools **6** outfit, silver, tackle **8** flatware **9** apparatus **10** implements, silverware **11** instruments **13** paraphernalia

Utgard
origin: 12 Scandinavian
realm of: 7 Skrymir **10** Utgardloki
location: 9 Gatunheim

Utgardloki *see* **7** Skrymir

utilitarian 5 handy **6** usable, useful **8** sensible, valuable, workable **9** effective, efficient, practical, pragmatic **10** beneficial, convenient, functional, profitable **11** serviceable **12** advantageous

utility 3 aid, gas, use **4** help **5** avail, extra **6** backup **7** benefit, reserve, service **8** function **9** accessory, advantage, alternate, auxiliary, secondary, surrogate, telephone **10** additional, substitute, usefulness **11** convenience, electricity **12** availability, supplemental **13** public service **14** serviceability

utilization 3 use **10** employment **11** application **12** exploitation

utilize 3 use **6** employ **7** exploit **8** profit by, put to use, resort to **9** make use of **12** capitalize on **13** bring into play, make the most of, turn to account **14** avail oneself of, have recourse to, put into service **15** take advantage of

utmost, uttermost 4 acme, best, main, peak, tops **5** chief, first, major, prime **6** tiptop, zenith **7** capital, highest, leading, maximum, primary, supreme, the most **8** cardinal, foremost, greatest, last word, ultimate **9** paramount, principal, sovereign **10** preeminent **11** predominant

Uto-Aztecan (Nahuatl)
tribe: 4 Pima **5** Aatam, Aztec, Nahua **6** Mexica, Papago **8** Pima Alto

utopia 4 Eden **6** heaven **7** Erewhon **8** paradise **9** ideal life, Shangri-la **12** perfect bliss, perfect place **13** seventh heaven

utopian 9 visionary **10** idealistic, unfeasible, unworkable **11** unrealistic **12** otherworldly, unattainable, unrealizable **13** impracticable, insubstantial, unfulfillable

Utrillo, Maurice
born: 5 Paris **6** France
mother: 14 Suzanne Valadon
artwork: 16 The Church at Deuil, The Church of Blevy **17** Church at St Hilaire **19** La Petite Communiante **22** Sacre Coeur de Montmartre

ut supra 7 as above

utter 3 say **4** emit, pure, talk, tell, yell **5** sheer, shout, speak, state, total, voice **6** entire, mutter, reveal **7** declare, deliver, divulge, exclaim, express, perfect, whisper **8** absolute, complete, disclose, outright, proclaim, thorough, vocalize **9** downright, enunciate, out-and-out, pronounce, unchecked **10** articulate, unmodified, unrelieved **11** categorical, unequivocal, unmitigated, unqualified

utterance 4 talk, word **6** answer, remark, speech **7** opinion **9** discourse, statement **10** expression **11** declaration, exclamation **12** articulation, proclamation, vocalization **13** pronouncement, verbalization

utterly **4** just **5** fully **6** wholly **7** totally **8** entirely, outright **9** downright, extremely, perfectly **10** absolutely, completely, thoroughly **14** to the nth degree

uttermost **6** utmost **7** extreme, maximum, supreme **9** outermost, sovereign **12** extreme limit

Utu
origin: **8** Sumerian
god of: **3** sun

Uzziah
also: **7** Azariah
king of: **5** Judah
father: **7** Amaziah
son: **6** Jotham **7** Jehoram **8** Jonathan

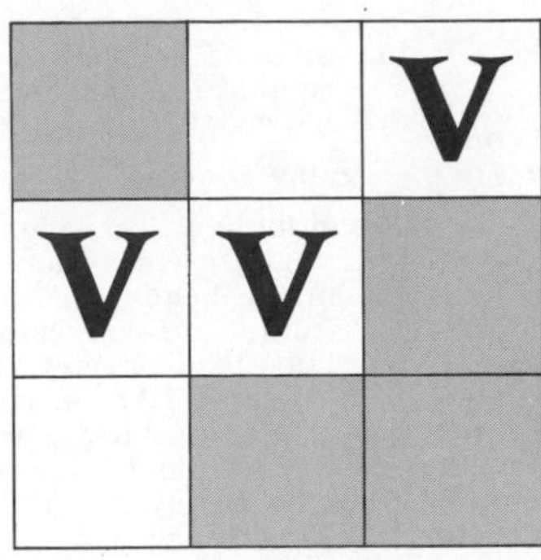

vacancy **3** gap **4** hole, void **5** abode, place **6** breach, cavity, hollow **7** crevice, fissure, housing, lodging, opening **9** emptiness, situation **10** empty space, vacantness **11** room for rent **12** house for rent

vacant **4** dull, free, idle, open **5** aloof, blank, blase, clear, empty, vapid **6** unused, wooden **7** deadpan, for rent, leisure, vacuous **8** deserted, detached, for lease, forsaken, not in use, unfilled **9** abandoned, apathetic, incurious, oblivious, poker-face, unengaged **10** tenantless, unemployed, unoccupied, untenanted **11** indifferent, unconcerned, unfurnished, uninhabited **12** unencumbered **14** expressionless **15** uncomprehending

vacate **4** quit **5** empty, leave **6** give up, resign **8** abdicate, evacuate, hand over **9** surrender **10** depart from, relinquish

vacate the throne **4** cede, flee, quit **5** yield **6** give up, resign, retire **7** abandon **8** abdicate **10** relinquish

vacation **4** rest **5** leave, R and R **6** recess **7** holiday **8** furlough, holidays **10** sabbatical **12** intermission **13** take a vacation **14** leave of absence **17** rest-and-recreation
French: **8** vacances

vacillate **4** reel, rock, roll, sway, toss **5** pitch, shift, waver **6** falter, teeter, totter, wobble **7** flutter, vibrate **8** hesitate **9** fluctuate, hem and haw, oscillate **12** shilly-shally **14** blow hot and cold

vacillating **7** swaying **8** wavering **9** diffident, uncertain, vibrating **10** hesitating, irresolute, on the fence **11** fluctuating, uncertainty **12** irresolution **15** shilly-shallying

vacillation **7** swaying **8** wavering **9** faltering, vibration **10** indecision **11** fluctuation, uncertainty **12** irresolution **15** shilly-shallying

Vacuna
origin: **6** Sabine
goddess of: **11** agriculture

vacuous **4** dull, idle, void **5** blank, empty, inane, silly **6** stupid, vacant **7** fatuous, foolish **8** indolent, unfilled **9** senseless **11** empty-headed, purposeless

Vaduz
capital of: **13** Liechtenstein

vae victis **18** woe to the vanquished

vagabond **4** hobo **5** gypsy, nomad, rover, tramp **6** roamer, roving **7** drifter, floater, migrant, nomadic, rambler, roaming, vagrant **8** bohemian, carefree, homeless, rambling, wanderer, wayfarer **9** footloose, itinerant, transient, traveling, wandering, wayfaring **10** journeying **11** beachcomber

Vagabond Lover
nickname of: **10** Rudy Vallee

vagary **4** kink, whim **5** fancy, humor, quirk **6** notion, oddity, whimsy **7** caprice, fantasy, impulse **8** crotchet, daydream **10** brainstorm, erraticism **11** peculiarity **12** eccentricity, idiosyncrasy, passing fancy

vagrant **3** bum **4** hobo **5** nomad, rover, tramp **6** beggar, loafer, roamer, roving **7** floater, migrant, nomadic, roaming **8** homeless, rambling, vagabond, wanderer **9** itinerant, transient, wandering **10** panhandler **11** peripatetic **15** knight-of-the-road

vague **4** hazy **5** fuzzy, loose **6** casual, random, unsure **7** general, unclear **8** confused, nebulous **9** imprecise, uncertain, unsettled **10** ill-defined, indefinite, inexplicit, undetailed, unspecific **11** not definite, unspecified **12** undetermined

vaguely **5** dimly **6** hazily **7** loosely **8** dreamily, slightly, vacantly **9** obscurely, sketchily **10** nebulously **11** ambiguously **12** indistinctly

vagueness **8** haziness **9** ambiguity, confusion, fuzziness **11** uncertainty **13** lack of clarity **14** indefiniteness

vain **4** idle **5** cocky, proud, silly **6** futile **7** foolish, pompous, stuck-up, useless **8** arrogant, boastful, bootless, dandyish, egoistic, nugatory, puffed-up, trifling **9** conceited, egotistic, fruitless, pointless, worthless **10** disdainful, profitless, swaggering, unavailing **11** egotistical, ineffective, ineffectual, superficial, time-wasting **12** self-admiring, supercilious, unprofitable, unsuccessful, vainglorious **13** self-important, self-satisfied

Vainamoinen
origin: **7** Finnish
hero of: **8** Kalevala
form: **8** magician
opposes: **5** Louhi **11** Joukahainen

vainglorious **5** cocky **7** haughty, pompous, stuck-up **8** affected, arrogant, boastful, bragging, insolent **9** conceited **10** egoistical, pretentious, swaggering **11** egotistical, swell-headed **12** narcissistic, supercilious **13** full of oneself, self-important

vainglory **6** vanity **7** conceit, swagger **9** cockiness **10** pretension **11** braggadocio

14 self-importance **16** overbearing pride

vale **6** good-by **8** farewell

valedictory **4** last **5** final **7** parting **8** farewell, terminal, ultimate **9** departing **10** conclusive **11** leavetaking **14** farewell speech **19** commencement address

Valentine
character in: **20** Two Gentlemen of Verona
author: **11** Shakespeare

Valentino, Rudolph
real name: **16** Rodolfo (Alfonzo Raffaele Pierre Philibert) Guglielmi
born: **5** Italy **12** Castellaneta
wife: **9** Jean Acker **14** Natasha Rambova
roles: **8** The Sheik **12** Blood and Sand **16** The Son of the Sheik **17** Monsieur Beaucaire **30** The Four Horsemen of the Apocalypse

valerian **9** Valeriana
varieties: **3** red **5** Greek **6** common **7** African **8** American **11** long-spurred

Valery, Paul
author of: **7** Cahiers, Charmes **12** The Young Fate **13** Le Jeune Parque **16** Sketch of a Serpent **20** The Graveyard by the Sea

Valhalla
origin: **8** Teutonic
hall of: **4** Odin **5** Othin

valiant **4** bold **5** brave, noble **6** daring, heroic **7** gallant **8** fearless, intrepid, knightly, resolute, stalwart, unafraid, valorous **9** audacious, dauntless, undaunted **10** chivalrous, courageous **11** lionhearted, unflinching **12** bold-spirited, great-hearted, stouthearted

valid **4** good **5** legal, licit, sound **6** lawful, proper, strong **7** fitting, genuine, logical, weighty **8** accurate, decisive, forceful, official, powerful, suitable, truthful **9** authentic, effective, legalized, realistic **10** acceptable, applicable, compelling, convincing, legitimate **11** substantial, well-founded **12** well-grounded **13** authoritative, being in effect **14** constitutional, legally binding

validate **5** enact, prove, stamp **6** ratify, verify **7** certify, confirm, sustain, warrant, witness **8** legalize, sanction **9** authorize, make legal, make valid **10** make lawful **11** corroborate, countersign **12** authenticate, make official, substantiate

validation **8** sanction **12** confirmation, legalization, ratification **13** authorization, certification

validity **5** force, logic, power, right **6** weight **7** grounds, potency **8** accuracy, legality, strength **9** authority, soundness, substance **10** legal force, legitimacy, properness **11** suitability **12** authenticity, truthfulness **13** acceptability, applicability, effectiveness **14** conclusiveness, convincingness

valise **3** bag **4** grip **7** handbag, luggage, satchel **8** suitcase **9** briefcase, Gladstone **11** portmanteau

Valjean, Jean
character in: **13** Les Miserables
author: **4** Hugo

Valkyrie
origin: **8** Teutonic
home: **8** Valhalla
attendant of: **4** Odin **5** Othin
queen: **8** Brunhild, Brynhild **10** Brunnhilde

Vallee, Rudy
real name: **17** Hubert Prior Vallee
nickname: **16** The Vagabond Lover
born: **13** Island Point VT
played: **9** saxophone
wife: **9** Jane Greer
roles: **16** The Vagabond Lover **17** The Palm Beach Story, Unfaithfully Yours **41** How to Succeed in Business Without Really Trying

Valletta
capital of: **5** Malta

valley **3** cut, dip, gap **4** dale, dell, glen, vale **5** basin, chasm, glade, gorge, gulch, gully **6** bottom, canyon, divide, hollow, ravine **8** water gap

Valley Forge
author: **15** Maxwell Anderson

Valley of Horses, The
author: **9** Jean M Auel

Valley of the Dolls
author: **16** Jacqueline Susann

valor **4** grit, guts **5** nerve, pluck, spunk **6** daring, mettle **7** bravery, courage, heroism **8** boldness, chivalry **9** fortitude, gallantry **11** intrepidity **12** fearlessness **13** dauntlessness

valorous **4** bold **5** brave, gutsy **6** heroic, plucky **7** valiant **8** fearless, intrepid, stalwart, unafraid **9** dauntless **10** courageous **11** indomitable, lionhearted **12** stouthearted

valse **5** waltz

valuable **4** dear, good **6** costly, prized, useful, valued **7** admired, helpful **8** esteemed, fruitful, precious **9** expensive, important, priceless, respected, treasured **10** beneficial, high-priced, invaluable, profitable, worthwhile **11** serviceable, significant, utilitarian **12** advantageous

valuation **9** appraisal **10** assessment, evaluation **14** estimated value

value, values **3** use **4** cost, help, rate **5** assay, count, judge, merit, price, prize, rules, weigh, worth **6** admire, amount, assess, charge, esteem, ideals, profit, reckon, revere, size up **7** beliefs, benefit, cherish, compute, customs, respect, service, utility **8** appraise, evaluate, prestige, treasure **9** advantage, appraisal, greatness, moral code, practices, standards **10** admiration, appreciate, assessment, estimation, excellence, importance, set store by, usefulness **11** conventions, market price, superiority **12** code of ethics, institutions, significance

valued **6** prized **7** revered **8** esteemed **9** cherished, respected, treasured **11** appreciated **14** highly regarded

valueless **7** trivial, useless **9** worthless **11** of no account, unimportant **13** insignificant **14** good for nothing **15** inconsequential

vamoose **3** out **4** away, scat, shoo **5** be off, leave, scram **6** beat it, begone, depart, get out, go away **7** get lost

vamp **5** siren **9** temptress **10** seductress **11** enchantress, femme fatale **12** introduction

Vamp
nickname of: **9** Theda Bara

vampire **3** bat **7** Dracula **11** bloodsucker

van **4** cart, dray, head **5** lorry, scout, truck, wagon **6** camper, picket **7** trailer **8** sentinel, vanguard **9** first line, forefront, front rank **10** avant-garde, large truck **12** advance guard, covered truck **13** front of an army **16** foremost division
french: **7** fourgon

Van, Bobby
real name: **10** Robert King
born: **9** New York NY

roles: **10** Kiss Me Kate, On Your Toes **11** No No Nanette **12** It's Only Money, The Ladies' Man **13** Small Town Girl **23** The Affairs of Dobie Gillis

van Alen, William
architect of: **16** Chrysler Building (NYC)

Van Allen, James Alfred
field: **7** physics
invented: **18** radio proximity fuse
discovered: **22** Van Allen radiation belts

Van Buren, Martin ***see box***

Vance, Vivian
real name: **11** Vivian Jones
born: **12** Cherryvale KS
roles: **9** I Love Lucy **10** Ethel Mertz

Vancouver
hockey team: **7** Canucks

vandal **6** looter, raider **7** ravager, wrecker **8** marauder, pillager, saboteur **9** barbarian, despoiler, destroyer, plunderer **10** demolisher

vandalism **6** damage **10** defacement **11** destruction **17** malicious mischief

vandalize **3** mar **5** trash, wreck **6** damage, deface **7** despoil, destroy

Vanderlyn, John
born: **10** Kingston NY
artwork: **14** Ariadne on Naxos **20** The Death of Jane McCrea **28** Marius Amid the Ruins of Carthage **31** Ariadne Asleep on the Island of Naxos

Van Dyck, Sir Anthony
born: **7** Antwerp **8** Flanders
artwork: **8** Charles I (in Hunting Dress) **11** Iconography **18** Madonna of the Rosary **19** Blessed Herman Joseph, Cardinal Bentiroglio **20** Ecstasy of St Augustine **21** Marchesa Elena Grimaldi

Van Dyke, Dick
born: **12** West Plains MO
roles: **11** Mary Poppins **12** Bye Bye Birdie **15** Dick Van Dyke Show

Vane, Sutton
author of: **12** Outward Bound

Vanessa
author: **11** Hugh Walpole

Van Gogh, Vincent
born: **12** GrootZundert **14** The Netherlands
artwork: **10** Pere Tanguy **11** Cafe at Night, L'Arlesienne **13** The Olive Grove **14** The Starry Night **15** The Potato Eaters **16** The Bridge at Arles **18** Portrait of Dr Gachet, The Chair and the Pipe **22** Cornfield with Cypresses

vanguard **3** van **7** leaders **8** forerank **9** first line, forefront, front line, front rank, spearhead **10** avant-garde, innovators, leadership, modernists **11** pacesetters, tastemakers **12** advance guard, trailblazers, trendsetters

Van Helsing, Dr
character in: **7** Dracula
author: **6** Stoker

Vanir
origin: **12** Scandinavian
race: **4** gods
conflicting with: **4** Asar **5** Aesir

vanish **3** die, end **5** cease **6** die out, expire, perish **7** die away **8** dissolve, fade away, melt away, pass away **9** disappear, evaporate, terminate **13** dematerialize **15** become invisible

vanished **4** dead, gone, lost **7** defunct, died out, extinct **11** disappeared

vanishing **8** dying out **10** extinction, fading away **11** passing away **12** disappearing **13** disappearance **15** dematerializing

vanitas vanitatum **16** vanity of vanities

vanity **4** sham **5** folly, pride **6** mirage **7** compact, conceit, egotism, falsity, inanity **8** delusion, futility, idleness, self-love **9** emptiness, powder box, vainglory, vanity bag **10** hollowness, narcissism, self-praise, vanity case **11** makeup table, mirror table, self-conceit, uselessness **13** dressing table, fruitlessness, worthlessness

---

Van Buren, Martin
nicknames: **9** The Red Fox **17** The Little Magician **18** The Careful Dutchman
presidential rank: **6** eighth
party: **8** Democrat
state represented: **7** New York
defeated: **5** (Hugh Lawson) White **6** (William Person) Mangum **7** (Daniel) Webster **8** (William Henry) Harrison
vice president: **7** (Richard Mentor) Johnson
cabinet:
state: **7** (John) Forsyth
treasury: **8** (Levi) Woodbury
war: **8** (Joel Roberts) Poinsett
attorney general: **6** (Benjamin Franklin) Butler, (Felix) Grundy, (Henry Dilworth) Gilpin
navy: **8** (James Kirke) Paulding **9** (Mahlon) Dickerson
postmaster general: **5** (John Milton) Niles **7** (Amos) Kendall
born/died/buried: **12** Kinderhook NY
education:
Academy: **10** Kinderhook
college: **4** none
studied: **3** law
religion: **13** Dutch Reformed
vacation:
toured: **6** Europe (1853-1855)
author: **64** Inquiry into the Origin and Course of Political Parties in the United States
political career: **8** US Senate **11** state Senate **13** vice president **20** state Attorney General
governor of: **7** New York
secretary of: **5** State
minister: **12** Great Britain
civilian career: lawyer
notable events of lifetime/term: **5** Panic (of 1837)
treaty: **16** Webster-Ashburton
war: **9** Aroostook
father: **7** Abraham
mother: **5** Maria (Hoes Van Alen)
siblings: **6** Derike, Hannah **7** Abraham **8** Lawrence
wife: **6** Hannah (Hoes)
children: **4** John **6** Martin **7** Abraham **13** Smith Thompson

14 self-admiration, superficiality

Vanity Fair
author: 25 William Makepeace Thackeray
character: 10 Becky Sharp **11** Miss Crawley **12** Amelia Sedley, Joseph (Jos) Sedley **13** George Osborne, Rawdon Crawley **14** Sir Pitt Crawley **20** Captain William Dobbin

vanity of vanities
Latin: 16 vanitas vanitatum

vanquish 4 beat, best, drub, lick, rout **5** crush **6** defeat, master, subdue, thrash **7** conquer **8** overcome **9** overpower, overthrow, overwhelm, subjugate **11** triumph over

vanquisher 6 master, victor, winner **7** subduer **8** champion **9** conqueror **10** subjugator

vanquishment 6 defeat **7** mastery, triumph, victory, winning **8** conquest **10** conquering, overcoming

Van Slyke, Helen
author of: 10 No Love Lost **15** A Necessary Woman, The Heart Listens **18** Always Is Not Forever

Van Tassel, Katrina
character in: 23 The Legend of Sleepy Hollow
author: 6 Irving

Vanuatu *see box*

Vanuatu
other name: 11 New Hebrides
capital/largest city: 4 Vila
others: 5 Santo **6** Forari **10** Luganville
school: 7 Malapoa
monetary unit: 5 franc **7** centime
island: 3 Api, Epi **4** Aoba, Gaua, Malo, Tana, Vate **5** Banks, Efate, Maewo, Santo, Tanna **6** Ambrym, Mabrim, Torres **8** Aneityum, Malekula **9** Erromanga, Pentecost, Vanua Lava **13** Espiritu Santo
mountain: 6 Lopevi
highest point: 11 Tabwemasana
sea: 7 Pacific
people: 8 European **10** Melanesian, Polynesian **11** Micronesian
***explorer:* 4** Cook **7** Queiros
***leader:* 4** Lini
language: 6 French **7** Bislama, English **16** Melanesian Pidgin
religion: 7 animism **8** Anglican, John Frum **10** Protestant **12** Presbyterian **13** Roman Catholic
feature:
***cult:* 5** cargo

vapid 4 dull, flat, lame, tame **5** bland, empty, stale **7** insipid **8** lifeless **9** colorless, pointless **10** flavorless, wishy-washy **11** meaningless, uninspiring **12** unsatisfying **13** characterless

vapor 3 dew, fog **4** haze, mist, smog **5** fumes, smoke, steam **6** miasma **8** moisture

vaporize 5 dry up **7** distill **8** condense, melt away **9** dissipate, evaporate

Varden, Gabriel/Dolly
character in: 12 Barnaby Rudge
author: 7 Dickens

Vargas Llosa, Mario
author of: 13 The Green House **16** The Time of the Hero **26** Conversation in the Cathedral **27** Aunt Julia and the Scriptwriter **34** Captain Pantoja and the Special Service

variable 6 fickle, fitful, uneven, unlike **7** diverse, mutable **8** changing, shifting, unstable, wavering **9** alterable, different, spasmodic, unsettled **10** capricious, changeable, inconstant, indefinite **11** fluctuating

variance 4 odds **6** change **7** dispute, quarrel **9** deviation, disparity **10** contention, difference, dissension, divergence, unlikeness **11** discrepancy, incongruity **12** disagreement, modification **13** dissimilarity, inconsistency

variant 7 altered, derived, take-off **8** modified **9** departure, different, divergent, variation **10** alteration **11** transformed **12** modification **14** transformation

variation 6 change **7** variant, variety **8** mutation, variance **9** departure, deviation, diversity **10** aberration, alteration, difference, divergency, innovation **11** discrepancy **12** disagreement, modification **13** metamorphosis **14** transformation

varicolored 6 calico, motley, tartan **7** dappled, flecked, marbled, mottled, piebald **9** multihued **10** iridescent, opalescent, variegated **11** rainbowlike, technicolor **12** multicolored, parti-colored **13** polychromatic

varied 5 mixed **6** motley, sundry **7** diverse, various **8** assorted **9** different **10** variegated **11** diversified **13** heterogeneous, miscellaneous

variegated 4 pied **6** motley **7** checked, dappled, mottled, piebald **9** checkered **12** parti-colored

variety 4 hash, kind, race, sort, type **5** brand, breed, class, genre, genus, group, stock, tribe **6** change, family, jumble, medley, motley, strain **7** melange, mixture, species **8** category, division, pastiche **9** diversity, patchwork, variation **10** assortment, collection, difference, hodgepodge, innovation, miscellany, subspecies **11** subdivision **12** denomination, multiplicity, unconformity **13** dissimilarity, heterogeneity, nonuniformity **14** classification, omnium-gatherum **15** diversification

various 3 few **4** many, some **5** other **6** divers, myriad, sundry, varied **7** diverse, several **8** assorted, manifold, numerous **9** countless, different **10** dissimilar **11** innumerable **12** multifarious **13** miscellaneous, multitudinous

varlet 3 cur **6** rascal, wretch **7** villain **9** scoundrel **10** blackguard

Varner, Will
character in: 9 The Hamlet
author: 8 Faulkner

varnish 4 gilt **5** adorn, cover, gloss, stain **6** excuse, soften **7** conceal, lacquer **8** disguise, mitigate **9** embellish, gloss over **10** smooth over

vary 4 veer **5** alter, shift **6** change, depart, differ, modify **7** deviate, dissent, diverge **8** be unlike, contrast, disagree **9** alternate, disaccord, diversify, fluctuate

vase 3 jar, jug, pot, urn **5** crock, diota **8** canister **9** container **10** jardiniere

Vashti
husband: 9 Ahasuerus
replaced by: 6 Esther

vassal 4 serf **5** helot, liege, slave **6** tenant, thrall **7** bondman, servant, subject, villein **8** retainer **9** bondslave, bondwoman, dependent **11** subordinate

vassalage **4** yoke **7** bondage, serfdom, slavery **9** servitude **11** enslavement

vast **4** huge, wide **5** great, jumbo **7** endless, immense, titanic, very big **8** colossal, enormous, far-flung, gigantic, infinite, spacious **9** boundless, capacious, extensive, limitless, monstrous, unbounded, unlimited, very large **10** monumental, prodigious, stupendous, tremendous, voluminous, widespread **11** far-reaching, measureless, significant, substantial **12** immeasurable, interminable

vastness **7** bigness **8** enormity, hugeness **9** immensity, largeness **12** enormousness

Vathek
author: **15** William Beckford

Vaticanus **16** Greek unical codex

Vaughan Williams, Ralph
born: **7** Britain **10** Down Ampney
composer of: **3** Job **8** The Wasps **9** Flos Campi **10** Antarctica (symphony No 7), **11** Old King Cole **12** A Sea Symphony **13** Hugh the Drover, On Wenlock Edge, Sir John in Love, Songs of Travel **14** Riders to the Sea, The House of Life, The Sons of Light **15** A London Symphony, The Poisoned Kiss **16** The Lark Ascending **17** A Pastoral Symphony **18** Five Tudor Portraits, Sinfonia Antarctica **19** The Pilgrim's Progress **22** Toward the Unknown Region

Vaughn, Robert
born: **9** New York NY
roles: **7** Bullitt **12** Napoleon Solo **15** The Man from UNCLE **19** The Magnificent Seven **22** The Young Philadelphians

vault **4** arch, dome, jump, leap, safe, tomb **5** bound, clear, crypt **6** arcade, cupola, hurdle, spring **7** ossuary **8** catacomb, jump over, leapfrog, leap over, wall safe **9** mausoleum, pole-vault, sepulcher, strongbox **10** arched roof, spring over, strongroom **13** arched ceiling, burial chamber

vaunt **5** strut **6** brag of, flaunt **7** exult in, show off, swagger **9** crow about, gasconade, gloat over **10** boast about

vaunted **7** exalted, praised **11** gloated over, overpraised **12** boasted about

Veary, Arthur
real name of: **14** Arthur Treacher

veer **3** yaw **4** jibe, tack, turn **5** curve, dodge, drift, shift, wheel **6** swerve, zigzag **7** go about **9** come round, turn aside **15** change direction

Vegas
character: **5** Angie **6** Binzer **8** Beatrice, Dan Tanna **10** Bernie Roth **11** (Sgt) Bella Archer
cast: **10** Tony Curtis **11** Judy Landers, Robert Urich **12** Naomi Stevens, Phyllis Davis **13** Bart Braverman

vegetable **3** pea **4** bean, beet, corn **6** carrot, greens, legume, squash, turnip **7** cabbage, lettuce, parsnip, produce, spinach **8** broccoli, eggplant, lima bean, rutabaga, zucchini **10** string bean **11** cauliflower

vegetarian **5** vegan **8** meatless **9** herbivore **11** herbivorous

vegetation **5** flora, grass, sloth, weeds **6** leaves, plants, torpor **7** foliage, herbage, languor, loafing, verdure **8** dormancy, idleness, lethargy **9** flowerage, indolence, plant life, shrubbery **10** inactivity **11** hibernation, languidness, rustication **12** sluggishness
god of: **6** Dumuzi

vehemence **4** heat, zeal **5** ardor **6** fervor, warmth **7** passion **9** intensity

vehement **3** hot **4** wild **5** eager, fiery, rabid **6** ardent, fervid, fierce, heated, stormy **7** earnest, excited, fanatic, fervent, furious, intense, violent, zealous **8** agitated, forceful, frenzied, vigorous **9** emotional, fanatical, hotheaded **10** passionate **11** impassioned, tempestuous **12** enthusiastic

vehemently **5** hotly **6** wildly **7** eagerly **8** ardently, fiercely, strongly **9** earnestly, excitedly, fervently, furiously, intensely, violently, zealously **10** vigorously **11** emotionally, fanatically **12** passionately **13** tempestuously **16** enthusiastically

vehicle **3** bus, car **4** tool **5** agent, means, organ, plane, train, truck **6** agency, device, medium **7** bicycle **9** mechanism **10** automobile, conveyance, instrument, motorcycle, rocket ship **12** intermediary **14** transportation

veil **3** dim **4** hide, mask **5** cloak, cloud, cover **6** enwrap, mantle, screen, shroud **7** blanket, conceal, curtain, envelop, obscure **8** covering **10** camouflage

veiled **3** dim **5** murky **6** draped, hidden **7** muffled **8** obscured, shrouded **9** concealed, covered up, disguised, enveloped, enwrapped **11** camouflaged

veiling **3** net **4** mesh **8** cloaking, covering **9** obscurity **10** concealing

vein **3** rib, web **4** bent, hint, line, lode, mark, mood, seam, tone **5** fleck, layer, stria, style, touch **6** furrow, manner, marble, nature, strain, streak, stripe, temper, thread **7** stratum **8** tendency **9** capillary, character **10** complexion, propensity **11** blood vessel, disposition, inclination, temperament **12** predilection **14** predisposition

Veiovis
god of: **4** dead

Velazquez (Velasquez), Diego Rodriguez de Silvay
born: **5** Spain **7** Seville
artwork: **8** Philip IV **10** Las Meninas **13** Luis de Gongora, Pope Innocent X, Venus and Cupid **14** Cardinal Borgia **17** Don Gaspar de Guzman, Isabella of Bourbon **18** Adoration of the Magi, The Tapestry Weavers **19** The Infanta Margarita, The Surrender of Breda **20** Infanta Maria Theresia **21** An Old Woman Cooking Eggs **22** Portrait of a Court Jester, Portrait of Juan de Pareja **23** The Immaculate Conception **30** Prince Balthasar Carlos at the Hunt

veloce
music: **4** fast

velocity **4** pace **5** haste, speed **8** alacrity, celerity, rapidity **9** fleetness, quickness, swiftness **10** expedition, speediness

venal **5** shady **6** greedy **7** corrupt, crooked, selfish **8** bribable, covetous, grasping **9** dishonest, mercenary, rapacious **10** avaricious **11** corruptible **12** unprincipled, unscrupulous **13** moneygrubbing

venality **7** avarice **10** corruption **11** bribe-taking **13** mercenariness, money-grubbing

vend **4** hawk, sell **5** trade **6** barter, deal in, market, peddle, retail **7** auction, trade in **8** huckster **11** merchandise

Vendetta, La
author: **14** Honore de Balzac

vendor, vender **6** dealer, hawker, monger, seller, trader **7** peddler **8** huckster, merchant, purveyor, retailer, salesman, supplier **9** tradesman **10** wholesaler **12** merchandiser **13** street peddler

veneer **4** coat, mask, show **5** front, layer **6** casing, facade, facing, jacket, sheath **7** coating, overlay, wrapper **8** covering, envelope, pretense **10** outer layer

venerable **3** old **4** aged **5** hoary **6** august **7** admired, ancient, elderly, honored, revered **8** esteemed **9** respected, venerated **11** patriarchal, white-haired

venerate **5** adore, extol, honor **6** admire, esteem, hallow, revere **7** cherish, glorify, idolize, respect, worship **8** look up to **9** reverence **11** pay homage to

venerated **4** holy **5** loved **6** adored, sacred **7** honored, revered **8** hallowed **9** respected **10** reverenced, worshipped **12** paid homage to

veneration **3** awe **5** honor **6** esteem, homage, wonder **7** respect, worship **8** devotion **9** adoration, adulation, reverence **10** admiration, exaltation **11** idolization **13** glorification

venereal **6** carnal, sexual **7** genital

Venezuela ***see box***

vengeance **7** revenge **8** avenging, reprisal, requital **11** malevolence, retaliation, retribution **12** ruthlessness **13** an eye for an eye, implacability **14** revengefulness, vindictiveness **15** a tooth for a tooth

veni, vidi, vici **19** I came I saw I conquered
author: **12** Julius Caesar

venial **5** minor **6** slight **7** trivial **9** allowable, excusable **10** defensible, forgivable, not serious, pardonable **11** justifiable, unimportant, warrantable

Venice ***see box***

Venn, Diggory
character in: **17** Return of the Native
author: **5** Hardy

venom **3** ire **4** gall, hate **5** anger, spite, toxin, virus **6** choler, enmity, grudge, hatred, malice, poison, rancor, spleen **7** ill will **8** acrimony, savagery **9** animosity, barbar-

Venezuela

name means: **12** little Venice

capital/largest city: **7** Caracas

others: **4** Aroa, Coro **6** Atures, Cumana, Merida **7** Barinas, Barines, Cabello, Guaware, Maracay, Maturin **8** Asuncion, Carupano, La Guaira, La Gyayra, Tacupita, Valencia **9** Barcelona, Maracaibo, Tacarigua **12** Barquisimeto, Puerto La Cruz, San Cristobal **13** Cuidad Bolivar, Puerto Cabello **18** Santo Tome de Guayana

division: **4** Lara **5** Apure, Sucre, Zulia **6** Aragua, Falcon, Merida **7** Barinas, Bolivar, Cojedes, Guarico, Monagas, Tachira, Yaracuy **8** Carabobo, Trujillo

measure: **5** galon **6** fanega **7** estadel

monetary unit: **4** peso **5** medio **6** fuerte **7** bolivar, centimo **8** morocota **10** venezolano

weight: **3** bag **5** libra

island: **4** Aves **7** Cubagua, Tortuga **9** La Orchila, Los Roques, Margarita **11** Los Hermanos **12** La Blanquilla

lake: **9** Maracaibo, Tacarigua

mountain: **3** Pao **4** Pava, Yair **5** Andes, Duida, Icutu **6** Concha, Cuneva, Merida, Parima, Sierra, Yumari **7** Imutaca, Masaiti, Roraima **8** Gurupira **9** Pacaraima **10** Auyan-Tepui **11** Turimiquire **18** Cordillera del Norte

highest point: **7** Bolivar

river: **3** Oro, Pao **4** Meta **5** Apure, Caura, Negro, Suata, Tigre, Unare, Zulia **6** Amazon, Arauca, Caroni, Cuyuni **7** Guanare, Guanipa, Guarico, Orinoco, Oritueo, Paragua, Suapure, Vichada, Yuruari **8** Guaviare, Manapire, Ventuari **9** Cuchivero **10** Casiquiare, Portuguesa

sea: **8** Atlantic **9** Caribbean

physical feature:
falls: **5** Angel
gulf: **5** Paria **6** Triste **9** Venezuela
highlands: **6** Guiana **7** Guayana, Segovia
plains: **6** Llanos

people: **4** Bare, Pume **5** Bello, Carib, pardo, zambo **6** Arawak, Creole, Timote **7** Charoya, Guahibo, Kaliana, mestizo, mulatto, Otomaca, Timotex **8** Caquetio, Guarauno, Matilone **11** Maquiritare
artist: **7** Marisol
author: **5** Bello **8** Gallegos **13** Diaz-Rodriguez
explorer: **8** Columbus
god: **5** Tsuma
leader: **4** Paez **5** Gomez, Leoni **6** Castro **7** Bolivar, Miranda **10** Betancourt **12** Guzman Blanco **14** Herrera Campins

language: **4** Pume **7** Spanish

religion: **5** Islam **7** Judaism **10** Protestant **13** Roman Catholic

feature:
animal: **4** puma **5** sloth **6** jaguar, ocelot **7** manatee, peccary **8** anteater, capybara **9** armadillo
cowboy: **7** llanero
dance: **6** joropo **16** diablos danzantes
folk entertainment: **10** burriquita
musical instrument: **6** cuatro **7** maracas
street performance: **8** parranda

food:
black beans: **8** caraotas
bread: **5** arepa
dish: **7** hallaca **8** cachapos, pabellon
soup/stew: **8** sancocho

Venice
art exhibition: **8** Biennale
artist: **7** Bellini, Codussi **8** Fabriano, Longhena, Mantegna, Palladio, Scamozzi, Veronese **9** Canaletto, Carpaccio, Giorgione, Sansovino **10** Tintoretto
capital of: **6** Veneto **15** Venezia province
church: **18** San Giorgio Maggiore, Santa Maria dei Frari **19** Santi Giovanni e Paolo
Italian: **7** Venezia
landmark: **6** Ca' d'Oro **9** Campanile **10** Grand Canal **11** Doge's Palace **13** Bridge of Sighs **15** Libreria Vecchia **16** Palazzo Rezzonico, Saint Mark's Church **20** Accademia di Belle Arti **21** Palazzo dei Procuratori **22** Scuola Grande di San Rocco **23** Palazzo Vendramin-Calergi
port: **8** Marghera
resort: **9** Lido Beach
sea: **8** Adriatic
small canal: **3** rii
tomb: **5** Titan
traveler: **9** Marco Polo

ity, brutality, hostility **10** bitterness, resentment **11** malevolence **12** spitefulness **13** maliciousness, rancorousness

venomous **5** cruel, fatal, toxic **6** bitter, brutal, deadly, lethal, malign, savage **7** abusive, caustic, hostile, noxious, vicious **8** spiteful, virulent **9** malicious, malignant, poisonous, rancorous, resentful **10** malevolent **11** ill-disposed **12** bloodthirsty

vent **3** air, tap **4** bare, drip, emit, flue, gush, hole, ooze, pipe **5** exude, spout, utter, voice **6** effuse, escape, faucet, let out, outlet, reveal, spigot **7** air hole, chimney, debouch, declare, divulge, express, opening, orifice, release **8** aperture, disclose, exposure, venthole **9** discharge, let escape, pour forth, utterance **10** disclosure, expression, revelation, smokestack, ventilator **11** communicate, declaration

ventilate **3** air, sow **5** voice **6** aerate, air out, report, review, spread **7** analyze, declare, discuss, dissent, divulge, examine, express **9** broadcast, circulate, comment on, criticize, oxygenate, publicize, talk about **10** bandy about **11** disseminate, noise abroad

ventilator **3** fan **4** flue **7** aerator **10** exhaust fan, smokestack **14** air conditioner

venture **2** go **3** bet, try **4** dare, risk **5** flyer, offer, wager **6** chance, gamble, hazard, plunge, submit, tender, travel **7** advance, attempt, hold out, presume, proffer, project **8** endeavor, make bold **9** adventure, risk going, strive for, undertake, volunteer **10** enterprise, put forward, take a flyer **11** speculation, uncertainty, undertaking

venturesome, adventuresome **4** bold, rash **5** risky **6** daring, tricky, unsafe, unsure **7** dubious **8** doubtful, insecure, perilous, reckless, ticklish **9** ambitious, audacious, dangerous, daredevil, energetic, foolhardy, hazardous, impetuous, impulsive, uncertain **10** aggressive, precarious **11** adventurous, speculative **12** enterprising, questionable

venturesomeness **6** daring **8** audacity, boldness **9** derring-do **11** impetuosity **12** recklessness

Venus
origin: **5** Roman **7** Italian
goddess of: **6** spring **7** gardens
son: **6** Aeneas
grandson: **5** Iulus
epithet: **7** Erycina **8** Genetrix **10** Erticordia
corresponds to: **9** Aphrodite

Venus and Adonis
author: **18** William Shakespeare

veracious **4** true **6** honest **7** sincere **8** accurate, faithful, truthful **10** scrupulous **11** punctilious

veracity **5** truth **6** candor, verity **7** honesty, probity **8** accuracy, openness **9** exactness, frankness, integrity, sincerity **10** exactitude **11** correctness **12** truthfulness **13** guilelessness, ingenuousness **14** verisimilitude

Vera-Ellen
real name: **13** Vera-Ellen Rohe
born: **12** Cincinnati OH
roles: **9** On the Town **14** White Christmas

veranda
Hawaiian: **5** lanai

verbal **4** oral, said **5** vocal **6** spoken, voiced **7** in words, of verbs, of words, uttered **9** expressed, unwritten

verbal exchange **6** dialog **8** dialogue **10** discussion **12** conversation

verbalize **5** speak, utter, voice **7** express **10** articulate **12** put into words

verbal thrust **3** dig **4** gibe, jeer **5** taunt **13** cutting remark

verbatim **5** exact **7** exactly, literal, precise **8** accurate, faithful **9** literally, literatim, precisely **10** accurately, faithfully **11** to the letter, word for word **15** chapter and verse, letter for letter
Latin: **14** ipsissima verba

verbatim et literatim **21** in exactly the same words **29** word for word and letter for letter

verbena
varieties: **4** moss, rose, sand **5** clump, lemon, shrub **7** red sand **8** pink sand **9** beach sand **10** desert sand, Mojave sand, yellow sand **12** common garden

verbiage **9** logorrhea, loquacity, prolixity, verbosity, wordiness **10** volubility **11** verboseness **12** effusiveness **14** circumlocution, grandiloquence, long-windedness

verbose **5** gabby, wordy **6** prolix **7** voluble **8** effusive **9** garrulous, talkative **10** longwinded, loquacious **13** grandiloquent **14** circumlocutory

verbosity **9** diffusion, prolixity, talkiness, wordiness **11** diffuseness **13** talkativeness **14** long-windedness

verboten **9** forbidden **10** prohibited

Verdandi **4** Norn
origin: **12** Scandinavian
form: **3** elf
personifies: **7** present
developed from: **5** Urdar
companions: **3** Urd **5** Skuld

verdant **4** lush **5** green, leafy, shady, turfy **6** grassy **7** meadowy **8** blooming, thriving **9** luxuriant **10** burgeoning, springlike **11** flourishing

Verdi, Giuseppe
born: **5** Italy **7** Busseto
composer of: **4** Aida **6** Otello **7** Macbeth, Nabucco, Othello **8** Falstaff **9** Don Carlos, Il Corsaro, Rigoletto, The Misled **10** La

Traviata **11** Il Trovatore **13** The Troubadour **14** Manzoni Requiem **15** Simon Boccanegra

verdict 6 answer, decree, ruling **7** finding, opinion **8** decision, judgment, sentence **9** valuation **10** assessment, estimation **11** arbitrament, arbitration **12** adjudication **13** determination

Vere, Captain
character in: 9 Billy Budd
author: 8 Melville

Vereen, Ben
born: 7 Miami FL
roles: 5 Roots **6** Pippin **13** Chicken George **20** Jesus Christ Superstar

verge 3 end, hem, lip, rim **4** brim, edge **5** bound, brink, ledge, limit, skirt **6** be near, border, flange, fringe, margin **7** confine, extreme **8** approach, boundary, frontier, terminus **9** threshold **11** approximate **12** be on the brink

verge upon 4 abut **5** flank **6** adjoin, border **8** be next to **10** neighbor on

Vergil, Virgil
author of: 6 Aeneid **8** Bucolics, Eclogues, Georgics

verification 5 proof **7** support **9** guarantee **10** validation **12** confirmation **13** accreditation, certification, corroboration, documentation **14** authentication, substantiation

verify 5 prove **7** certify, confirm, support, sustain, witness **8** accredit, attest to, document, validate, vouch for **9** establish, guarantee, testify to **11** corroborate **12** authenticate, substantiate

verily 4 amen **5** truly **6** really **9** certainly, yes indeed **10** positively

veritable 4 real, true **5** utter, valid **6** actual **7** genuine, literal **8** absolute, bona fide, complete, positive, true-blue **9** authentic **13** incontestable, unimpeachable **14** unquestionable **17** through-and-through

Verlaine, Paul
author of: 6 Wisdom **7** Sagesse **8** Langueur **17** Songs Without Words **19** Romances sans Paroles

Vermeer, Jan
born: 5 Delft **7** Holland
artwork: 11 View of Delft **12** The Lace Maker, The Procuress **13** Drinking Scene **14** A Street in Delft, The Head of a Girl **15** Allegory of Faith, Girl with a Red Hat **16** The Artist's Studio **18** Girl Reading a Letter, Girl with a Wine-glass **19** A Girl Asleep at a Table, A Painter in his Studio **20** A Woman Weighing Pearls **22** Maidservant Pouring Milk **23** Young Woman with a Water Jug **24** A Soldier and a Laughing Girl **31** Christ in the House of Mary and Martha

vermilion 3 red **7** scarlet **8** cinnabar **9** bright red **15** mercuric sulfide

vermin 4 ants, lice, mice, owls, rats **5** crows, fleas, foxes, pests **6** snakes, wolves **7** bedbugs, coyotes, roaches, spiders, weasels **8** termites, varmints **9** water bugs **10** centipedes, silverfish **11** birds of prey **18** pestiferous insects

Vermont ***see box***

vermouth
type: 4 wine **6** brandy **8** aperitif
origin: 5 Italy **6** France
varieties: 3 dry **5** sweet
drink: 9 Boomerang **11** Bittersweet
with bourbon: 9 Allegheny
with brandy: 3 BVD
with Dubonnet: 3 BVD
gin: 5 Bijou, Bronx, Tango **6** Caruso **7** Bermuda, Caberet, Martini **10** Bloodhound
with rum: 6 Bolero **8** Apple Pie **10** Black Devil **11** Shark's Tooth
with rye: 8 Brooklyn **9** Algonquin
with scotch: 8 Affinity **10** Bobby Burns
with sherry: 6 Bamboo, Brazil
with sloe gin: 10 Blackthorn
with vodka: 8 Kangaroo **9** Corkscrew
with whiskey: 9 Manhattan

vernacular 4 cant **5** idiom, lingo, slang **6** jargon, patois **7** dialect **8** parlance, shoptalk **9** the vulgar **12** common speech, native tongue **13** natural speech **14** informal speech, native language

vernal 3 new **5** fresh, green

Vermont
abbreviation: 2 VT
nickname: 13 Green Mountain **20** Four-Season Recreation
capital: 10 Montpelier
largest city: 10 Burlington
others: 5 Barre, Stowe **7** Grafton, Newfane, Newport, Rutland **8** St Albans, Winooski **9** Bountiful, Vergennes **10** Bennington **11** Brattleboro
college: 7 Goddard, Norwich, Trinity, Windham **8** Marlboro **10** Bennington, Middlebury, St Michaels
feature:
***covered bridge:* 5** Scott
***house:* 15** Old Constitution
***monument:* 6** Battle
people: 9 John Deere, John Dewey **10** Ethan Allen **12** Brigham Young **13** Warren R Austin **15** Stephen A Douglas
lake: 7 Caspian, Dunmore, Seymour **8** Bomoseen **9** Champlain **10** Willoughby **12** Memphremagog
land rank: 10 forty-third
mountain: 5 Green, White **7** Bromley, Hogback, Taconic **8** Prospect, Stratton
***highest point:* 9** Mansfield
physical feature:
***uplands:* 10** New England
***valley:* 9** Champlain
president: 14 Calvin Coolidge, Chester A Arthur
river: 4 West **5** Otter, White **7** Saxtons **8** Lamoille, Nulhegan, Winooski **10** Missisquoi **11** Connecticut
state admission: 10 fourteenth
state bird: 12 hermit thrush
state animal: 11 Morgan horse
state flower: 9 red clover
state motto: 15 Freedom and Unity
state song: 11 Hail Vermont
state tree: 10 sugar maple

6 spring **8** youthful **10** springlike

Verne, Jules
author of: **19** Five Weeks in a Balloon **21** From the Earth to the Moon **26** Around the World in Eighty Days **32** Twenty Thousand Leagues Under the Sea
character: **11** Captain Nemo, Phineas Fogg **12** Passepartout

Veronese, Paolo (Cagliari)
born: **5** Italy **6** Verona
artwork: **12** Book of Esther **13** The Last Supper **14** Supper at Emmaus **15** The Rape of Europa, Triumph of Venice **17** Mary with the Saints, The Finding of Moses, The Marriage at Cana, Wisdom and Strength **19** Martyrdom of St George, The Choice of Hercules **21** Esther before Ahasuerus **22** Feast at the House of Simon **24** Mars and Venus United in Love, The Feast in the House of Levi, The Temptation of St Anthony **31** Jesus and the Centurion of Capernaum **32** The Family of Darius before Alexander

Verrocchio, Andrea del
real name: **31** Andrea di Michele di Francesco Cione
born: **5** Italy **8** Florence
artwork: **5** David **15** Boy with a Dolphin **17** Christ and St Thomas **18** The Baptism of Christ **19** Bartolommeo Colleoni **23** Christ and Doubting Thomas **25** Beheading of John the Baptist

versatile **3** apt **4** able **5** handy **6** adroit, clever, expert, gifted **7** protean **8** talented **9** adaptable, all-around, ingenious, many-sided **10** proficient **11** many-skilled, resourceful **12** accomplished, multifaceted

verse **4** poem **5** meter, rhyme, stave **6** jingle, poetry, stanza **7** measure, strophe

versed **4** able **5** adept **6** expert, taught **7** erudite, learned, skilled, tutored **8** lettered, schooled, skillful, well-read **9** competent, practiced, scholarly **10** at home with, instructed, proficient **11** enlightened, experienced **12** accomplished, familiar with, well-informed **14** acquainted with, conversant with

versifier **4** bard **6** rhymer, writer **8** minstrel, poetizer, poetling, rhymster **9** poetaster, rhymester **10** rhymesmith, troubadour, versemaker, versesmith **11** versemonger **12** balladmonger

version **4** side **5** story **6** report **7** account **9** depiction, rendering **10** adaptation, paraphrase, re-creation **11** description, restatement, translation **14** interpretation

vers libre **9** free verse

vertebral column
bone of: **5** spine **8** backbone

vertex **3** cap, tip **4** apex, peak **5** crown **6** summit, zenith **8** pinnacle **12** highest point **13** crowning point

vertical **5** plumb, sheer **7** upright **12** ninety-degree **13** perpendicular

vertiginous **5** dizzy, giddy, shaky **6** whirly **7** reeling **11** lightheaded

vertigo **7** reeling **8** fainting **9** dizziness, giddiness **12** unsteadiness **15** lightheadedness

Vertigo
director: **15** Alfred Hitchcock
cast: **8** Kim Novak **12** James Stewart **16** Barbara Bel Geddes
setting: **12** San Francisco
score: **15** Bernard Herrmann

Vertumnus
also: **9** Vortumnus
origin: **5** Roman
god of: **5** fruit **7** gardens, seasons **8** orchards
wife: **6** Pomona

verve **3** vim, zip **4** dash, elan, fire, zeal **5** ardor, drive, force, gusto, punch, vigor **6** energy, fervor, relish, spirit, warmth **7** abandon, feeling, passion, rapture, sparkle **8** vitality, vivacity **9** animation, eagerness, vehemence **10** enthusiasm, liveliness

Verver, Maggie
character in: **13** The Golden Bowl
author: **5** James

very **4** bare, mere, most, much, pure **5** exact, extra, plain, quite, sheer, truly **6** deeply, highly, hugely, mighty, really, simple, vastly **7** awfully, exactly, fitting, greatly, notably, perfect, precise, totally **8** actually, entirely, markedly, specific, suitable, terribly **9** assuredly, certainly, decidedly, eminently, essential, extremely, immensely, intensely, necessary, obviously, perfectly, precisely, unusually, veritably **10** abnormally, absolutely, abundantly, completely, definitely, especially, particular, profoundly, remarkably, strikingly, thoroughly, uncommonly, undeniably **11** appropriate, exceedingly, excessively **12** emphatically, surpassingly, tremendously **13** exceptionally, significantly **14** unquestionably

very best
French: **14** creme de la creme

Very Easy Death, A
author: **16** Simone de Beauvoir

very great **4** huge **6** severe **7** extreme, intense, mammoth, titanic **8** colossal, enormous, gigantic **9** excessive, monstrous **10** gargantuan, immoderate, inordinate, prodigious **11** magnificent, spectacular **14** Brobdingnagian

very nearly **6** almost **7** close to **9** just about **10** more or less, not far from **13** approximately

very old **4** aged **6** primal **7** ancient, antique, archaic **8** primeval **10** antiquated, primordial **11** prehistoric **12** antediluvian

very soon
French: **11** tout a l'heure

vessel **3** cup, jar, jug, keg, mug, pot, tub, vat **4** boat, bowl, butt, cask, dish, duct, scow, ship, tube, vase, vein **5** barge, craft, crock, flask, glass, liner, plate, yacht **6** artery, barrel, beaker, carafe, flagon, goblet, packet, tanker, whaler **7** caldron, collier, cruiser, platter, tankard, trawler, tugboat, tumbler, utensil **8** decanter, paquebot, sailboat **9** capillary, container, ferryboat, freighter, houseboat, steamboat, steamship **10** ocean liner, receptacle

vest **3** rig **4** garb, robe **5** array, drape, dress **6** attire, clothe, enwrap, fit out, jacket, jerkin **7** apparel, deck out, doublet, envelop **8** accouter **9** waistcoat

Vesta
origin: **5** Roman
goddess of: **6** hearth
festival: **8** Vestalia
corresponds to: **4** Caca **6** Hestia

vestal **4** pure **6** chaste, maiden, simple, virgin **8** maidenly, virginal, virtuous **9** pure woman, undefiled, unmarried, unworldly **10** immaculate **15** unsophisticated

vested **5** fixed **7** settled **8** absolute, complete **9** permanent **10** guaranteed **11** established, inalienable **12** indisputable **14** unquestionable

vestibule 4 hall **5** entry, foyer, lobby **6** lounge **7** hallway, passage **8** anteroom, corridor **10** passageway **11** antechamber, entrance way, waiting room **12** entrance hall

vestige 4 sign **5** relic, token, trace **6** record **7** memento, remnant **8** evidence, souvenir

vestments 4 garb, gear **5** dress **6** livery, outfit **7** apparel, clothes, costume, raiment, regalia, uniform **8** clothing **9** trappings **13** accoutrements

vesture 4 robe **5** robes **7** apparel, clothes, garment, raiment **8** clothing, garments **9** vestments

vetch 5 Vicia
varieties: 3 cow **4** bard, bird, milk **5** crown, hairy, Sitka **6** bitter, common, kidney, purple, smooth, spring, tufted, winter **8** Narbonne **9** horseshoe, Hungarian, woolly-pod **12** large Russian

veteran 3 vet **6** expert, master **7** old hand **8** old-timer, seasoned **9** ex-soldier **10** campaigner, old soldier, war veteran **11** experienced **12** exserviceman **13** long-practiced

veto 4 deny, void **6** denial, enjoin, forbid, negate, reject **7** nullify, prevent, refusal **8** disallow, prohibit, turn down **9** rejection **10** prevention **11** disallowing, prohibition **12** disallowance **16** turn thumbs down on

vex 3 bug, irk **4** fret, gall, miff, pain, rile **5** anger, annoy, chafe, harry, pique, upset, worry **6** badger, bother, grieve, harass, hassle, nettle, pester, plague, ruffle **7** chagrin, disturb, provoke, torment, trouble **8** distress, irritate **9** displease **10** exasperate **18** ruffle one's feathers

vexation 5 pique, trial **6** hassle **7** torment **8** headache, nuisance **9** annoyance **10** affliction, harassment, irritation **11** aggravation **13** pain in the neck

vexatious 5 pesky **6** thorny, vexing **8** annoying, nettling **9** badgering, harassing, hectoring, provoking, troubling, worrisome **10** bothersome, irritating **11** disquieting, pestiferous, troublesome

vexed 5 irked, riled, testy **6** galled, miffed, piqued **7** annoyed, nettled, peevish **8** provoked **9** irritated **11** disgruntled, exasperated

viable 6 usable **8** feasible, workable **9** adaptable, practical **10** applicable **11** practicable

viaduct 4 ramp, span **8** overpass

vial 5 ampul, flask, phial **7** ampoule

via media 10 a middle way

viands 4 cate, diet, eats, fare, food **7** cuisine, edibles, vittles **8** victuals **9** provender **10** foodstuffs, provisions

vibrancy 4 fire **5** ardor **7** elation **8** vitality, vivacity **9** animation **10** enthusiasm **11** high spirits

vibrant 4 deep, loud **5** alive, eager, vital, vivid **6** ardent, bright, florid, lively **7** fervent, glowing, intense, orotund, pealing, pulsing, radiant, ringing **8** animated, bell-like, colorful, forceful, luminous, lustrous, resonant, sonorous, spirited, vehement **9** brilliant, deep-toned, energetic, quivering, thrilling, throbbing, vibrating, vivacious **10** fluttering, glittering, resounding, shimmering **11** full of vigor, resplendent, reverberant **12** electrifying, enthusiastic

vibrate 4 beat, sway **5** quake, swing, throb, waver **6** quaver, quiver, ripple, wobble **7** flutter, pulsate, tremble **8** undulate **9** oscillate, palpitate, pendulate **11** reverberate

vibration 5 quake **6** quiver, tremor **7** quaking **9** quivering, throbbing, trembling

vicar 6 cleric, parson, pastor **8** preacher **9** churchman, clergyman **12** ecclesiastic

vicarious 6 mental **7** by proxy **8** imagined, indirect **9** imaginary, surrogate **10** empathetic, fantasized, secondhand **11** at one remove, sympathetic

Vicar of Wakefield, The
author: 15 Oliver Goldsmith
character: 6 George, Olivia, Sophia **7** Deborah **10** Dr Primrose, Mr Burchill **14** Arabella Wilmot **15** Squire Thornhill **19** Sir William Thornhill

vice 4 flaw **5** fault **6** defect **7** blemish, failing, frailty **8** iniquity, weakness **9** depravity, weak point **10** corruption, debauchery, degeneracy, profligacy, wantonness, wickedness **11** shortcoming **12** imperfection **14** licentiousness

vice president
resigned: 10 Spiro Agnew **12** John C Calhoun
accused of treason: 9 Aaron Burr **17** John C Breckinridge
youngest elected: 17 John C Breckinridge
elected by Senate: 14 Richard Johnson
elected but did not serve: **11** William King
rejected nomination: **11** Frank Lowden, Silas Wright
lived longest: 15 John Nance Garner
succeeded to presidency: **9** John Tyler **10** Gerald Ford **12** Harry S Truman **13** Andrew Johnson **14** Calvin Coolidge, Chester A Arthur, Lyndon B Johnson **15** Millard Fillmore **17** Theodore Roosevelt

vice versa 9 in reverse **10** conversely **12** contrariwise **16** the other way round **18** in the opposite order

vicinity 4 area **6** region **8** environs, locality, vicinage **9** adjoining, precincts, proximity **11** environment, propinquity **12** neighborhood, surroundings

vicious 3 bad **4** base, evil, foul, mean, vile, wild **5** awful, cruel, gross, nasty, surly **6** brutal, fierce, horrid, savage, sullen, wicked **7** hateful, heinous, hellish, immoral, inhuman, untamed, violent **8** churlish, depraved, fiendish, libelous, shocking, spiteful, terrible, venomous **9** abhorrent, atrocious, barbarous, dangerous, ferocious, invidious, malicious, monstrous, nefarious, offensive, predatory, rancorous **10** abominable, defamatory, diabolical, ill-humored, ill-natured, malevolent, pernicious, slanderous, villainous, vindictive **11** acrimonious, ill-tempered, treacherous **12** bloodthirsty

viciousness 4 evil **6** malice **7** cruelty **8** ferocity, savagery, villainy, violence **9** barbarity, brutality, ill nature **10** fierceness, wickedness **11** heinousness

vicissitude 6 change **8** mutation **9** variation **10** difficulty, mutability, succession **11** fluctuation

Vicomte of Bragelonne, The
author: **14** Alexandre Dumas (pere)

victim **4** butt, dead, dupe, gull, mark, pawn, prey, tool **5** patsy **6** pigeon, quarry, sucker, target **7** injured, wounded **8** casualty, fatality, innocent **9** scapegoat

victimize **3** con **4** dupe, gull, hoax **5** bully, cheat, cozen **6** betray, delude **7** deceive, defraud **8** hoodwink **9** bamboozle

victor **6** winner **8** champion, medalist **9** conqueror **10** vanquisher **11** prizewinner

Victoria
capital of: **8** Hong Kong **10** Seychelles

Victoria
origin: **5** Roman
goddess of: **7** victory
corresponds to: **4** Nike

Victorian **4** prim, smug **6** narrow, proper, stuffy **7** insular, prudish **8** priggish **9** pietistic **10** tight-laced **11** puritanical, straitlaced **12** conventional, hypocritical **13** sanctimonious

victorious **7** winning **8** champion **10** conquering, successful, triumphant **11** vanquishing **12** championship, prizewinning

Victor Victoria
director: **12** Blake Edwards
cast: **10** Alex Karras **11** James Garner **12** Julie Andrews **13** Robert Preston **14** John Rhys-Davies **15** Lesley Ann Warren
setting: **5** Paris

victory **7** laurels, success, the palm, triumph **8** conquest, the prize **9** supremacy **10** ascendancy **11** superiority
god of: **3** Tyr
goddess of: **4** Nike **8** Victoria

Victory
author: **12** Joseph Conrad
character: **4** Lena, Wang **5** Jonas, Pedro **8** Davidson **9** Axel Heyst, Schomberg **13** Martin Ricardo

victuals **4** chow, diet, eats, fare, feed, food, grub, meat **5** meals **6** fodder, forage, repast, stores, viands **7** cooking, cuisine, edibles, rations, vittles **8** supplies **9** groceries, provender **10** foodstuffs, provisions **11** comestibles, nourishment, refreshment

Vidal, Gore
author of: **4** Burr **5** Kalki **6** Julian **8** Creation **16** Myra Breckinridge **18** Eighteen Seventy-Six, The Judgment of Paris **19** Visit to a Small Planet

Vidar
origin: **12** Scandinavian
father: **4** Odin **5** Othin
killed: **6** Fenrir, Fenris

vide **3** see

vide ante **9** see before

vide infra **8** see below

videlicet **6** namely **11** that is to say
abbreviation: **3** viz

vide post **8** see after **10** see further

vide supra **8** see above

vide ut supra **10** see as above **16** see as stated above

Vidor, King
director of: **8** The Crowd **12** Stella Dallas, The Big Parade **16** Northwest Passage

vie **4** life **5** fight **6** strive **7** compete, contend, contest **8** be a rival, struggle, tilt with **9** challenge

Vienna
airport: **9** Schwechat
area: **11** Innere Stadt
capital of: **7** Austria
early name: **4** Wena **9** Vindobono
German: **4** Wein
landmark: **7** Hofburg **10** Stadtsoper **13** Saint Stephen's **15** Albertina Museum, Belvedere Palace **16** Historical Museum, Schonbrunn Palace
river: **6** Danube
ruler: **8** Hapsburg
street: **11** Ringstrasse

Vientiane, Viengchan
capital of: **4** Laos

vi et armis **20** with force and with arms

Vietnam ***see box, p. 1050***

view **3** eye, ken, see **4** gaze, look, note, peek, peep, scan **5** judge, scene, sight, study, vista, watch **6** behold, belief, gaze at, glance, look at, notion, regard, survey, take in, theory, vision **7** diorama, examine, explore, feeling, glimpse, inspect, observe, opinion, outlook, picture, scenery, thought, witness **8** attitude, consider, glance at, judgment, panorama, perceive, pore over, prospect **9** landscape, sentiment, spectacle **10** conception, conviction, scrutinize, think about **11** contemplate, perspective

view as **4** deem, hold **5** count, judge, think **6** regard **7** account, believe **8** consider, take to be **10** look upon as

viewpoint **4** bias, side **5** angle, slant **6** aspect, belief **7** feeling, opinion **8** attitude, position **9** sentiment **10** conviction, standpoint **11** orientation, perspective **12** vantage point **16** frame of reference

view with disfavor **7** condemn, dislike **8** object to **9** frown upon **10** disapprove, think ill of **13** look askance at, regard as wrong **14** discountenance **15** take exception to

view with horror **5** abhor **6** eschew **8** sicken at **9** abominate, shudder at **10** recoil from, shrink from

vif
music: **6** lively

vigilance **4** care, heed **7** caution, concern **8** prudence **9** alertness, attention **10** precaution **11** carefulness, forethought, guardedness, heedfulness **12** cautiousness, watchfulness **14** circumspection

vigilant **4** wary **5** alert, chary **7** careful, guarded, heedful, on guard, prudent **8** cautious, watchful **9** attentive, observant, wide-awake **10** on one's toes, on the alert **11** circumspect, on one's guard **12** on the lookout, on the qui vive

vigor **3** pep, vim, zip **4** dash, elan, fire, zeal **5** ardor, drive, force, might, power, verve **6** energy, fervor, spirit **7** passion, stamina **8** haleness, strength, vitality, vivacity **9** animation, hardiness, intensity, vehemence **10** enthusiasm, liveliness, robustness **11** earnestness **12** forcefulness

vigorous **4** bold, hale **5** hardy, lusty, vital **6** active, ardent, brawny, lively, mighty, robust, strong, sturdy, virile **7** dynamic, intense, vibrant **8** forceful, muscular, powerful, spirited **9** assertive, energetic **10** aggressive

vigorously **4** hard **7** briskly, lustily **8** actively, cogently, forcibly, robustly, strongly, sturdily **9** with force **10** forcefully, powerfully **11** strenuously **13** energetically

Vigrid
origin: **12** Scandinavian
final battlefield of: **4** gods

Viking, viking **4** Dane **6** pirate **7** mariner **8** Norseman,

Vietnam
other name: **5** Annam **15** French Indochina
capital: **5** Hanoi **6** Saigon
largest city: **6** Saigon **13** Ho Chi Minh City
others: **3** Hue, Ron **4** Ngai, Vinh **5** Dalat, Hoa Da, Hoian **6** Annhon, Cholon, Danang, Hongay **7** Bacninh, Cam Ranh, Caobang, Donghoi, Hoabinh, Namdinh, Quinhon, Songoan, Tayninh, Viettri, Vinhloi **8** Binhdinh, Haiphong, Nhatrang, Panthiet, Phan Rang, Quangtri, Quangyen, Thanhhoa, Vinhlong **9** Haiphoang, Longxuyen **11** Dienbienphu
school: **3** Hue **5** Hanoi **9** Ho Chi Minh
division: **5** Annam, North, South **6** Tonkin **11** Cochin China
measure: **4** gang, phan, thon
monetary unit: **2** xu **4** dong **7** piaster
weight: **3** can, yet **4** uyen
mountain: **6** Badinh, Badink **7** Nindhoa, Ninhhoa **8** Fansipan, Knontran, Ngoolinh, Ngoolink, Tchepone, Tclepore **18** Annamese Cordillera
highest point: **8** Fan Si Pan
river: **2** Bo, Ca, Da, Lo, Ma **3** Chu, Gam, Koi, Red **4** Chay **5** Nhiha **6** Mekong **7** Dongnai
sea: **10** South China
physical feature:
delta: **6** Mekong **8** Red River
gulf: **4** Siam **6** Tonkin **7** Tonking **8** Thailand
peninsula: **11** Indochinese
people: **3** Hoa, Man, Meo, Tai, Tay **4** Cham, Kinh, Nung, Thai **5** Khmer, Malay, Muong **7** Chinese **8** Annamese, Annamite **9** Cambodian **10** montagnard, Vietnamese
leader: **5** Le Loi **8** Le Duc Tho **9** Ho Chi Minh **11** Ngo Dinh Diem, Pham Van Doug **14** Nguyen Van Thieu
language: **3** Yue **4** Cham **5** Khmer, Rhade **6** French **7** Chinese, English **9** Cantonese **10** Vietnamese
religion: **6** Cao Dai, Hoa Hao, Taoism **7** animism **8** Buddhism **12** Christianity, Confucianism **13** Roman Catholic
place:
ruins: **10** Nguyen tomb
feature:
army: **4** ARVN **5** COSVN **8** Communsi, Viet Cong, Viet Minh
clothing: **5** ao dai
new year: **3** Tet

Northman, searover **9** plunderer **12** Scandinavian
boat: **8** long ship
burial: **9** ship grave
chieftain: **4** jarl
exploration: **5** Italy, Spain **6** France, Russia **7** England, Germany, Iceland, Ireland, Vinland **9** Greenland
famous: **4** Eric **8** Eirikson, Ericsson **10** Eric the Red **11** Leif Ericson
governing council: **4** Ting **5** Thing **8** Folkmoot
legend: **4** Edda, saga
origin: **6** Norway, Sweden **7** Denmark, Finland
warrior: **7** beserk **9** berserker
writing: **4** rune

Vila
capital of: **7** Vanuatu

vile **3** bad, low **4** base, evil, foul, lewd, mean, ugly **5** awful, gross, nasty **6** coarse, filthy, odious, sinful, smutty, sordid, vulgar, wicked **7** beastly, hateful, heinous, ignoble, immoral, obscene, vicious **8** depraved, shameful, shocking, wretched **9** abhorrent, degrading, execrable, invidious, loathsome, nefarious, obnoxious, offensive, perverted, repellent, repugnant, repulsive, revolting, salacious **10** abominable, degenerate, despicable, detestable, disgusting, iniquitous, unpleasant, villainous **11** disgraceful, foulmouthed, humiliating **12** contemptible **13** objectionable

Vile Bodies
author: **11** Evelyn Waugh

vileness **4** evil **8** foulness, iniquity, villainy **9** depravity, nastiness **10** immorality, odiousness **11** degradation, heinousness, viciousness **12** wretchedness **13** offensiveness

Vili
origin: **12** Scandinavian
brother: **4** Odin **5** Othin

vilification **5** libel **7** calumny, slander **10** defamation **13** disparagement

vilifier **5** scold **6** carper, critic **7** reviler **9** backbiter

vilify **5** abuse **6** defame, revile **7** slander **8** bad-mouth, dishonor **9** criticize, disparage **14** inveigh against

vilifying **7** abusive **8** libelous **9** malignant **10** calumnious, defamatory, slanderous

villa, Villa **5** aldea, dacha **6** castle, Pancho **7** chateau, mansion **9** residence **13** country estate

village **4** burg **6** hamlet, suburb **8** hick town **9** small town **11** whistlestop **12** municipality

Village, A
author: **10** Sholem Asch

villain **3** cad, cur, rat **5** knave, louse, rogue **6** rascal, rotter, varlet **7** caitiff, stinker **8** evildoer, scalawag **9** miscreant, scoundrel **10** blackguard, malefactor **11** rapscallion **12** transgressor, wicked person **15** snake in the grass

villainous **4** base, evil, foul, vile **6** wicked **7** caddish, heinous **8** horrible, infamous **9** monstrous, nefarious **10** abominable, despicable, detestable, maleficent **12** blackguardly **13** reprehensible

villainy **4** evil **8** vilencss **9** depravity, rascality **10** wickedness **11** viciousness, maleficence

Villa-Lobos, Heitor
born: **6** Brazil **12** Rio de Janeiro
composer of: **6** Choros **20** Bachianas Brasileiras

Villefort
character in: **21** The Count of Monte Cristo
author: **5** Dumas (pere)

villein **4** carl, esne, serf **5** ceorl, churl, slave **6** drudge **7** bondman, peasant **9** bondwoman

Villette
author: **15** Charlotte Bronte

Villon, Francois
author of: **9** The Legacy **16** Le grand testament, Le petit testament
quote: **25** Mais ou sont les

neiges d'antan **31** But where are the snows of yesteryear

Villuppo
character in: 17 The Spanish Tragedy
author: 3 Kyd

vim 2 go **3** pep, zip **4** dash, fire, snap, zeal **5** ardor, drive, force, might, power, punch, verve, vigor **6** energy, fervor, spirit **7** passion, potency **8** strength, vitality, vivacity **9** animation, intensity, vehemence **10** enthusiasm, liveliness

vin 4 wine

Vincentio
character in: 17 Measure for Measure
author: 11 Shakespeare

vincit omnia veritas 16 truth conquers all **22** truth conquers all things

vindicate 4 free **5** clear **6** acquit, assert, defend, excuse, uphold **7** absolve, bear out, bolster, justify, support **8** advocate, champion, maintain **9** discharge, exculpate, exonerate **11** corroborate **12** substantiate

vindication 6 excuse **7** apology, defense **11** explanation **13** justification

vindictive 6 bitter, malign **8** avenging, punitive, spiteful, vengeful **9** malicious **10** malevolent, revengeful **11** retaliative, retaliatory, unforgiving

vinegarish 4 acid, sour, tart **5** harsh **6** acidic, biting **7** acerbic, pungent **9** acidulous **10** astringent

vin ordinaire 12 ordinary wine **20** inexpensive table wine

vintage 3 era, old **4** aged, date, fine, rare **5** epoch, great, prime, prize **6** choice, period **7** ancient, antique **8** sterling, superior **9** excellent, out-of-date, wonderful **11** outstanding **12** old-fashioned

Viola (Cesario)
character in: 12 Twelfth Night
author: 11 Shakespeare

violate 4 rape **5** abuse, break **6** defile, invade, ravish **7** disobey, outrage, profane **8** dishonor, infringe, trespass **9** blaspheme, desecrate, disregard, trample on **10** contravene, transgress **12** encroach upon

violation 5 abuse **6** breach **8** trespass **9** sacrilege **10** defilement, infraction **11** desecration, dishonoring **12** encroachment, infringement **13** contravention, nonobservance, transgression

violence 4 fury, rage **5** force, might, power **6** impact **7** outrage **8** ferocity, savagery, severity **9** brutality, intensity, onslaught **10** bestiality, fierceness **11** desecration, profanation **13** ferociousness, physical force **16** bloodthirstiness

violent 3 hot **4** wild **5** cruel, fiery **6** brutal, fierce, insane, raging, savage, severe, strong, unruly **7** berserk, furious, intense, rampant **8** maniacal, vehement **9** explosive, ferocious, hotheaded, murderous, unbridled **10** passionate **11** full of force, intractable, tempestuous **12** ungovernable **14** uncontrollable

Violent Bear It Away, The
author: 15 Flannery O'Connor

Violent Land, The
author: 10 Jorge Amado

violet 5 Viola
varieties: 3 dog, red **4** bush, pale, pine, rock, tree, wood **5** coast, cream, dame's, false, flame, green, marsh, pansy, sweet, water **6** Alaska, alpine, Canada, garden, German, horned, plains, stream **7** African, English, Mexican, Olympic, Persian, redwood, scarlet, striped, two-eyed **8** bird-foot, crowfoot, dog-tooth, florist's, hook-spur, Labrador, larkspur, Missouri, trailing **9** early blue, evergreen, ivy-leaved, marsh blue, sagebrush, tall white **10** Australian, great basin, Philippine, sweet white, western dog, woolly blue, yellow wood **11** Alpine marsh, American dog, arrow-leaved, Confederate, downy yellow, early yellow, lance-leaved, long-spurred, northern bog, strap-leaved **12** eastern water, great-spurred, kidney-leaved, northern blue, smooth yellow **13** common African, Halberd-leaved, northern downy, northern white, purple prairie, southern coast, white dog-tooth, yellow prairie **14** primrose-leaved, triangle-leaved **16** California golden, large-leaved white **17** round-leaved yellow, western sweet white **18** western round-leaved

violin family
instruments: 3 kit **5** cello, rebec, viola **7** baryton **8** bass viol, lyra viol, violetta **10** hurdy-gurdy **11** viola d'amore, violoncello **12** tromba marina, viola pomposa **13** lira da braccio **14** violino piccolo **15** hardanger fiddle

viper
group of: 4 nest

Viper's Tangle, The
author: 15 Francois Mauriac

virago 3 nag **4** fury **5** harpy, scold, shrew, vixen **6** dragon, gorgon **7** she-wolf **8** battle-ax, fishwife, harridan **9** termagant, Xanthippe

Virbius
origin: 5 Roman
god of: 6 forest **7** hunting

Virchow, Rudolf
field: 8 medicine **9** pathology
nationality: 6 German
completed formulation of: 10 cell theory

Virgil *see* **8** Vergil

virgin 4 girl, lass, maid, pure **6** chaste, damsel, maiden, unused **7** unmixed **8** pristine **9** unalloyed, undefiled, unsullied, untouched **10** unpolluted **13** unadulterated **14** uncontaminated
constellation of: 5 Virgo

Virgin *see* **4** Mary

Virginia *see box, p. 1052*

Virginian, The
author: 10 Owen Wister
character: 5 Betsy, Randy, Steve **6** Shorty **7** Trampas **9** Molly Wood **10** Judge (Henry) Garth
cast: 8 Lee J Cobb **10** Gary Clarke, James Drury, Pippa Scott, Randy Boone **11** Doug McClure **12** Roberta Shore
setting: 11 Shiloh Ranch **16** Wyoming Territory

Virginians, The
author: 25 William Makepeace Thackeray

Virgin Mary
ingredient: 11 tomato juice

Virgin Soil
author: 12 Ivan Turgenev

Virgo
symbol: 6 virgin
planet: 7 Mercury
rules: 7 service
born: 6 August **9** September

virile 4 bold **5** brave, hardy, husky, lusty, manly **6** brawny, heroic, manful, mighty, potent, robust, strong **7** valiant **8** fearless, forceful, muscular, powerful, resolute, stalwart, vigorous **9** audacious, mascu-

Virginia
abbreviation: 2 VA
nickname: 11 Old Dominion
capital: 8 Richmond
largest city: 7 Norfolk
others: 5 Galax, Luray, Salem **6** Marion **7** Bedford, Bristol, Emporia, Fairfax, Pulaski, Roanoke **8** Danville, Hopewell, Manassas, Staunton, St Albans, Tazewell, Yorktown **9** Arlington, Lexington, Lynchburg **10** Alexandria, Appomattox, Petersburg, Portsmouth, Waynesboro, Winchester **11** Newport News **12** Hampton Roads, Martinsville, Williamsburg **13** Virginia Beach **14** Fredericksburg **15** Charlottesville
college: 3 Lee **7** Hampton, Madison, Radford **8** Longwood, Richmond **10** Washington **11** Mary Baldwin, Old Dominion **13** Randolph Macon **14** Averett Hollins, Mary Washington, William and Mary
feature:
***battle site:* 7** Bull Run **8** Fair Oaks, Manassas, Richmond, Yorktown **10** Petersburg, Seven Pines, Wilderness **12** Spotsylvania **14** Fredericksburg **16** Chancellorsville
***dam:* 4** Kerr
***historical site:* 10** Monticello **11** Mount Vernon **12** Williamsburg **13** Stratford Hall
***national monument:* 26** George Washington Birthplace
***national park:* 10** Shenandoah **26** Colonial National Historical
tribe: 6 Saponi, Tutelo **7** Monacan **8** Manahoac, Meherrin, Nottaway, Pamunkey, Powhatan **9** Matchotic **10** Appomuttoc
people: 9 Henry Clay, John Rolfe, John Smith **10** Robert E Lee, Walter Reed **11** George Mason **12** John Marshall, Patrick Henry **13** Samuel Houston **14** Cyrus McCormick **15** Meriwether Lewis **17** Booker T Washington, Richard Evelyn Bird **18** Light-Horse Harry (Henry) Lee
lake: 4 Kerr **5** Smith
land rank: 11 thirty-sixth
mountain: 5 Cedar **6** Clinch, Elliot **8** Baldknob **9** Allegheny, Blueridge
***highest point:* 6** Rogers
physical feature:
***bay:* 10** Chesapeake
***bridge:* 7** Natural
***caverns:* 5** Luray
***port:* 7** Norfolk **8** Richmond **10** Portsmouth **11** Newport News
***tunnel:* 7** Natural
***valley:* 10** Shenandoah
president: 9 John Tyler **11** James Monroe **12** James Madison **13** Woodrow Wilson, Zachary Taylor **15** Thomas Jefferson **16** George Washington **20** William Henry Harrison
river: 3 Dan **4** York **5** James **7** Potomac, Rapidan, Roanoke **10** Appomattox, Shenandoah **12** Rappahannock
state admission: 5 tenth
state bird: 8 cardinal
state flower: 16 flowering dogwood
state motto: 17 Thus Ever To Tyrants
state song: 24 Carry Me Back to Old Virginia
state tree: 7 dogwood

line, masterful, strapping, undaunted **10** courageous **12** stouthearted

virtual 5 tacit **7** implied **8** implicit, indirect **9** essential, practical **11** substantial

virtually 8 in effect **9** in essence **11** essentially, in substance, practically **13** substantially **14** for the most part **23** for all practical purposes, to all intents and purposes

virtue 5 honor, value **6** purity, reward **7** benefit, decency, honesty, modesty, probity **8** chastity, goodness, morality, strength **9** advantage, good point, innocence, integrity, principle, rectitude, virginity **11** strong point, uprightness

virtuosity 7 mastery **8** artistry, wizardry **14** accomplishment

virtuoso 4 whiz **6** expert, genius, master, wizard **7** artiste, prodigy **10** master hand

virtuous 4 good, just, pure **5** moral **6** chaste, decent, modest **7** ethical, upright **8** innocent, laudable, virginal **9** continent, exemplary, honorable, righteous, unsullied **11** commendable, meritorious **12** praiseworthy **14** high-principled

virtuous person
Hebrew: 6 zaddik

Virtus
personifies: 7 courage

virtute et armis 15 by virtue and arms
motto of: 11 Mississippi

virulent 5 toxic **6** bitter, deadly, lethal, malign **7** harmful, hostile, hurtful, noxious, vicious **8** spiteful, venomous **9** injurious, malicious, poisonous, rancorous, resentful, unhealthy **10** malevolent, pernicious **11** acrimonious, deleterious

virus 3 bug **4** germ **7** microbe **13** microorganism

vis 5 force, power **8** strength

visage 3 air **4** face, look, mien **5** image **6** aspect **7** profile **8** demeanor, features **9** semblance **10** appearance **11** countenance, physiognomy

vis-a-vis 8 eye to eye, together **9** in company, privately, tete-a-tete **10** face-to-face, side by side **11** as opposed to **12** in contrast to **14** as compared with, confidentially **19** as distinguished from

viscera 4 guts **6** bowels **7** innards, insides **8** entrails **10** intestines

visceral 3 gut **5** crude **6** earthy **11** instinctive

viscous 5 gluey, gooey, gummy, slimy, tacky, thick **6** sticky, syrupy, viscid **9** glutinous

visibility 7 ceiling, clarity, horizon **10** definition, prominence **11** range of view **12** distinctness **14** perceptibility **15** conspicuousness, discernibleness

visible 4 open **5** clear, plain **6** in view, marked, patent

7 blatant, evident, glaring, in focus, in sight, obvious, pointed, salient, seeable 8 apparent, distinct, manifest, palpable, revealed 9 prominent 10 noticeable, observable, pronounced 11 conspicuous, discernible, inescapable, perceivable, perceptible, well-defined 12 unmistakable

vision 4 idea 5 dream, fancy, ghost, sight 6 notion 7 concept, fantasy, phantom, specter 8 daydream, eyesight, illusion 9 foresight 10 apparition, conception, perception, revelation 11 discernment, imagination 15 materialization

visionary 4 seer 6 dreamy, unreal, zealot 7 dreamer, fanatic, fancied, utopian 8 delusive, fanciful, idealist, illusory, romantic, theorist 9 imaginary, unfounded 10 chimerical, daydreamer, idealistic, starry-eyed 11 imaginative, impractical 13 insubstantial

Vision of Judgement, The
author: 9 Lord Byron

visit 4 call, stay 5 haunt, smite 6 affect, assail, attack, befall, call on, punish 7 afflict, assault, go to see, sojourn 8 drop in on, frequent, happen to, look in on, stay with 9 sojourn at 10 be a guest of

Visit, The
author: 19 Friedrich Durrenmatt

visitant 5 alien 7 arrival, visitor

visitor 5 guest 6 caller 7 company, tourist, tripper, voyager 8 traveler 9 journeyer, sightseer, sojourner, transient 10 house guest, vacationer

vista 4 view 5 scene 6 vision 7 outlook, picture, scenery 8 panorama, prospect 9 landscape 11 perspective

visual 5 optic 6 ocular 7 optical, seeable, visible 9 for the eye 10 noticeable, observable, ophthalmic 11 perceptible

visualize 5 fancy, image 7 dream of, foresee, imagine, picture 8 envision 10 conceive of, daydream of 16 see in the mind's eye

vital 4 life, live 5 alive, basic, chief, quick 6 lively, living, urgent, viable 7 animate, crucial, dynamic, primary, serious, vibrant 8 animated, cardinal, critical, existing, forceful, foremost, material, pressing, spirited, vigorous 9 breathing, energetic, essential, important, necessary, paramount, requisite, vivifying 11 fundamental, significant 13 indispensable

vitality 3 pep, vim, zip 4 zeal, zest 5 verve, vigor 6 energy 8 dynamism, strength, vivacity 9 animation, life force 10 ebullience, enthusiasm, exuberance, liveliness 13 animal spirits

vitalize 6 excite, vivify 7 animate, quicken 8 activate, energize 9 stimulate 10 invigorate, strengthen 11 bring to life

vital part 9 essential, necessity, requisite 10 key element, sine qua non 11 requirement

Vital Parts
author: 12 Thomas Berger

vital principle 5 blood 6 source 9 lifeblood 10 sine qua non

vitals 5 belly 6 bowels 10 intestines 11 vital organs 14 liver and lights

Vita Nuova
author: 14 Dante Alighieri

vitiate 3 mar 4 thin, undo, void 5 spoil, taint 6 blight, cancel, debase, defile, dilute, impair, infect, injure, poison, weaken 7 abolish, corrupt, pervert, pollute 8 sabotage 9 discredit, undermine 10 adulterate, depreciate, invalidate, make faulty, obliterate 11 contaminate

vitriolic 4 acid 5 acerb, nasty, sharp 6 biting 7 abusive, acerbic, caustic, cutting 8 sardonic, scathing 9 sarcastic, satirical, withering 11 acrimonious 13 hypercritical

vituperate 5 abuse 6 carp at, defame, malign, rail at, rebuke, revile, vilify 7 censure 9 castigate 10 speak ill of 14 inveigh against

vituperation 5 abuse, blame, scorn 6 insult, rebuke, tirade 7 censure, obloquy, slander 8 acrimony, scolding 9 invective 10 defamation, revilement, scurrility 11 castigation, deprecation 12 calumniation, denunciation, faultfinding, vilification 13 tongue-lashing

vituperative 5 harsh 7 abusive 8 scornful 9 insulting, maligning, vilifying 10 censorious, defamatory, scurrilous, slanderous 11 acrimonious, deprecatory

vivace
music: 5 quick 9 vivacious

vivacious 3 gay 5 jolly, merry, sunny, vital 6 active, bright, bubbly, cheery, genial, lively 7 buoyant 8 animated, bubbling, cheerful, spirited 9 convivial, ebullient, sparkling, sprightly 10 frolicsome, full of life 12 effervescent, lighthearted

vivacity 3 zip 4 dash, elan 5 gaity, verve, vigor 6 energy, spirit 8 buoyancy, vitality 9 animation 10 ebullience, liveliness 13 effervescence

Vivaldi, Antonio
born: 5 Italy 6 Venice
composer of: 10 Gloria Mass 14 L'Estro Armonico, The Four Seasons 16 Judith Triumphant 17 Juditha Triumphans, Le Quattro Stagioni 19 Harmonic Inspiration

Viva Zapata!
director: 9 Elia Kazan
cast: 10 Jean Peters 12 Anthony Quinn, Marlon Brando
Oscar for: 15 supporting actor (Quinn)
script: 13 John Steinbeck

vive 8 long live (whomever)

vive valeque 15 live and keep well

Vivian
also: 16 The Lady of the Lake
character in: 16 Arthurian romance
lover: 6 Merlin

Vivian Grey
author: 16 Benjamin Disraeli

vivid 3 gay 4 deep, loud, rich 5 clear, shiny, showy 6 bright, florid, garish, lively, moving, strong 7 glowing, graphic, intense, radiant, shining 8 colorful, definite, distinct, dramatic, emphatic, forceful, lifelike, luminous, lustrous, powerful, stirring, striking, true-life, vigorous 9 brilliant, effulgent, energetic, marvelous, memorable, pictorial, realistic 10 astounding, expressive, impressive, remarkable 11 astonishing, conspicuous, descriptive, inescapable, luminescent, picturesque, resplendent 12 unmistakable 13 extraordinary

vividness 9 intensity 10 brightness, brilliance

vivified 7 revived 8 animated, awakened 9 enlivened, quickened, vitalized 11 invigorated

vivify 6 revive, wake up 7 animate, enliven, quicken 8 vitalize 10 invigorate

vixen 4 fury 5 scold, shrew, witch 6 virago 8 fishwife, harridan, spitfire **9** female fox, termagant

Vladimir
character in: **15** Waiting for Godot
author: **7** Beckett

Vlaminck, Maurice de
born: **5** Paris **6** France
artwork: **8** Red Trees, The Storm **15** Hamlet in the Snow, Winter Landscape **17** The Bridge at Chatou **18** Picnic in the Country, Street at Marly-le-Roi **21** Landscape with Red Trees

vocabulary **4** cant **5** argot, idiom, lingo, slang, style **6** jargon, patois, speech, tongue **7** dialect, lexicon **8** language, phrasing **9** word stock **10** vernacular **11** phraseology, terminology

vocal **4** open, oral, sung **5** blunt, frank, lyric **6** candid, choral, direct, spoken, voiced **7** uttered, voluble **8** operatic **9** outspoken, vocalized **10** forthright, of the voice **11** articulated, plainspoken

vocalize **3** air, say **4** vent **5** speak, utter **7** express **9** ventilate **10** articulate **12** put into words

vocation **3** job **4** line, post, role, task **5** berth, field, stint, trade **6** career, estate, metier **7** calling, pursuit, station **8** business, lifework **9** situation **10** assignment, employment, line of work, occupation, profession

vocational **3** job **5** trade **6** career **9** technical **11** specialized **12** occupational

vociferate **4** howl, yell, yelp **5** shout, shout **6** bellow, clamor, cry out, holler, shriek, squeal **7** bluster, call out, exclaim, screech **9** ejaculate **11** make a racket **12** raise a rumpus

vociferation **3** cry **4** howl, yell, yelp **5** noise, shout **6** bellow, clamor, outcry, shriek, squeal, uproar **7** screech **11** ejaculation, exclamation

vociferous **4** loud **5** noisy, vocal **6** shrill **7** blatant **8** piercing, shouting, strident, vehement **9** clamorous, outspoken **10** boisterous, loud-voiced, uproarious **11** importunate

vodka
origin: **6** Poland, Russia
drink: **10** Moscow Mule
with amaretto: **9** Godmother
with bouillon: **8** Bullshot
with cider: **15** Brewster Special
with Cognac: **7** Cossack
with cranberry juice: **10** Cape Codder
with creme de cacao: **7** Barbara **9** Ninotchka **11** Russian Bear **12** Velvet Hammer, White Russian
with curacao: **8** Aqueduct
with Galliano: **16** Harvey Wallbanger
with gin: **15** Russian Cocktail
with kahlua or Tia Maria: **12** Black Russian
with kirsch: **12** Volga Boatman
with orange juice: **11** screwdriver
with tomato juice: **10** Bloody Mary
with vermouth: **8** Kangaroo **9** Corkscrew

Vogt, Carl Henry
real name of: **12** Louis Calhern

vogue **3** fad **4** mode, rage **5** craze, style, trend **6** custom **7** fashion **8** currency, practice, the thing **10** acceptance, popularity **11** the last word **12** popular favor **14** the latest thing **15** prevailing taste

voguish **4** chic **5** smart **6** modish **7** faddish, stylish **11** fashionable

voice **3** air, say **4** alto, bass, part, role, tone, vent, vote, will, wish **5** speak, state, tenor, utter **6** choice, desire, option, reveal, singer, speech **7** declare, divulge, express, opinion, singers, soprano **8** announce, baritone, delivery, disclose, proclaim, vocalize **9** contralto, enunciate, pronounce, ventilate **10** articulate, intonation, modulation, preference, vocal sound **11** communicate **12** articulation, mezzo-soprano **13** participation, power of speech

voiceless **3** mum **4** deaf, mute, surd **6** silent **7** anaudia, aphonic, spirate

voice of the people
Latin: **9** vox populi

void **4** bare, emit, free, null, pass **5** annul, blank, clear, drain, eject, empty, purge **6** barren, cancel, devoid, recant, repeal, revoke, vacant, vacuum **7** abolish, drained, emptied, exhaust, invalid, lacking, nullify, pour out, rescind, reverse, vacuity, wanting **8** depleted, evacuate, nugatory, renounce, throw out **9** destitute, discharge, emptiness, exhausted, repudiate **10** empty space, invalidate, not in force **11** countermand, inoperative

voidance **7** voiding **8** ejection, emission **9** discharge, expulsion

Voight, Jon
born: **9** Yonkers NY
roles: **7** Joe Buck **8** The Champ **10** Coming Home (Oscar) **11** Deliverance **13** The Odessa File **14** Catch Twenty-Two, Midnight Cowboy

voila **3** see **4** look **9** there it is

volatile **4** rash, wild **5** brash, giddy, moody **6** fickle, fitful **7** erratic, flighty, gaseous **8** eruptive, reckless, unstable, unsteady, vaporous, variable **9** explosive, frivolous, mercurial, spasmodic, unsettled **10** capricious, changeable, evaporable, inconstant, irresolute, vaporizing **12** undependable **13** temperamental, unpredictable

volition **4** will **6** choice, option **8** choosing, decision, free will **10** discretion, resolution **13** determination

volley **5** burst, salvo **6** shower **7** barrage **8** outbreak, outburst **9** broadside, discharge, fusillade **10** outpouring

Volpone (The Fox)
author: **9** Ben Jonson
character: **5** Celia, Mosca **7** Bonario, Corvino, Voltore **9** Corbaccio, Peregrine **18** Lady Politic Would-Be, Lord Politic Would-Be

Volsung
origin: **12** Scandinavian
mentioned in: **8** Volsunga
grandfather: **4** Odin **5** Othin
son: **7** Sigmund
daughter: **5** Signy

Volsunga
origin: **9** Icelandic **12** Scandinavian
form: **4** saga
time: **17** thirteenth century
subject: **8** Volsungs

Volta, Alessandro, Count
nationality: **7** Italian
invented: **15** electric battery
discovered: **10** methane gas

Voltaic
also: **3** Gur
language family: **16** Niger-Kordofanian
group: **10** Niger-Congo
includes: **5** Mossi

Voltaire, Francois
real name: **19** Francois Marie Arouet
author of: **5** Zadig, Zaire **6** Alzire, Merope **7** Candide, L'Ingenu, Mahomet **11** The Henriade **16** The Maid of

Orleans **23** Philosophical Dictionary
member of: **11** Philosophes

Volturnus
origin: **5** Roman
personifies: **4** wind **8** east wind **13** southeast wind

voluble **4** glib **5** wordy **6** chatty, fluent **7** twining **8** effusive, flippant, rotating, twisting **9** garrulous, talkative **10** loquacious

volume **4** book, bulk, heap, mass, size, tome **5** folio, sound, tract **6** amount, extent, quarto **7** measure **8** capacity, loudness, quantity, treatise, vastness **9** abundance, aggregate, magnitude, monograph **10** dimensions

voluminous **5** ample, large **7** copious, massive, sizable **8** abundant **9** extensive

Volund *see* **7** Wayland

voluntary **6** willed **8** free-will, intended, optional, unforced **10** deliberate **11** intentional, volunteered **13** discretionary, noncompulsory

volunteer **5** offer **6** extend, tender, unpaid **7** advance, present, proffer, recruit **8** enlistee **9** voluntary **10** put forward **11** step forward **12** unpaid worker **13** charity worker

Volunteer State
nickname of: **9** Tennessee

Voluptas
origin: **5** Roman
goddess of: **8** pleasure

voluptuary **4** rake, roue **7** epicure, gourmet, seducer **8** gourmand, hedonist, sybarite **9** bon vivant, debauchee, high liver, libertine, womanizer **10** gastronome, sensualist **14** pleasure seeker

voluptuous **4** soft **6** carnal, erotic, sexual, smooth, wanton **7** fleshly, lustful, sensual **8** sensuous **9** debauched, dissolute, luxurious, sybaritic **10** dissipated, hedonistic, lascivious, licentious, profligate **13** self-indulgent **14** pleasure-loving **15** pleasure-seeking

vomit **4** barf, emit, puke **5** eject, expel, heave, retch **7** bring up, throw up, upchuck **8** disgorge **9** discharge, spew forth **10** belch forth **11** regurgitate **15** toss one's cookies

Vonnegut, Kurt, Jr
author of: **8** Jailbird **9** Slapstick **10** Cat's Cradle, Palm Sunday **11** Player Piano **18** Slaughterhouse Five **20** Breakfast of Champions **22** Happy Birthday Wanda June

Von Sternberg, Josef
director of: **12** The Blue Angel

Von Sydow, Max
real name: **18** Carl Adolph von Sydow
born: **4** Lund **6** Sweden
roles: **12** The Emigrants **14** The Seventh Seal **15** The Virgin Spring **16** Wild Strawberries **24** The Greatest Story Ever Told

voracious **6** greedy **7** hoggish **8** edacious, ravenous **10** gluttonous, insatiable, omnivorous

Voragine, Jacobus de
author of: **12** Legenda Aurea (Golden Legend)

vortex **4** eddy **7** cyclone, twister **9** maelstrom, whirlpool, whirlwind

votary **3** fan **4** buff **6** zealot **7** admirer, devotee, fanatic, habitue **8** adherent, champion, disciple, follower, partisan **10** aficionado, enthusiast **11** afficionado

vote **3** say **4** poll **5** voice **6** ballot, choice, option, ticket **8** approval, decision, election, judgment, suffrage **9** franchise, selection **10** plebiscite, preference, referendum **11** cast a ballot **13** determination

vouch **4** back **6** affirm, attest, back up, uphold, verify **7** certify, confirm, endorse, support, sustain, swear to, warrant, witness **8** attest to, maintain **9** guarantee **11** corroborate **12** authenticate

voucher **4** chip, chit **5** check, proof **6** surety, ticket **7** receipt, warrant **8** warranty **9** affidavit, debenture **10** credential **11** certificate **12** verification **14** authentication

vouchsafe **4** give **5** allow, deign, favor, grant **6** bestow, convey, tender **7** concede **10** condescend

vow **4** oath, word **5** swear, troth, vouch **6** affirm, assert, assure, parole, pledge, plight, stress **7** declare, promise, resolve **8** contract **9** emphasize **11** word of honor **13** solemn promise

vox populi **14** popular opinion **16** voice of the people

voyage **4** sail **6** cruise **7** passage **8** crossing, navigate **9** ocean trip **10** sea journey

Voyage of the Beagle, The
author: **13** Charles Darwin

voyager **5** rover **7** cruiser, pilgrim, rambler, tourist **8** traveler, wayfarer **9** jet-setter, journeyer, sightseer **10** adventurer **12** excursionist, globetrotter, peregrinator **13** world traveler

Voyage to the Bottom of the Sea
character: **6** Doctor **8** Kowalsky, Stu Riley, (Cdr/Capt) Lee Crane **9** Patterson **10** (Lt Cdr) Chip Morton **11** (Chief Petty Officer) Curley Jones **12** Chief Sharkey **14** (Adm) Harriman Nelson
cast: **9** Allan Hunt, Del Monroe **10** Henry Kulky, Paul Trinka **11** Richard Bull, Terry Becker **12** David Hedison **13** Robert Dowdell **15** Richard Basehart
submarine: **7** Seaview
explorer: **7** Sea Crab
mini-sub: **10** Flying Fish

Vronsky, Count Alexei
character in: **12** Anna Karenina
author: **7** Tolstoy

Vulcan
origin: **5** Roman
god of: **4** fire **12** metalworking
epithet: **8** Mulciber
corresponds to: **10** Hephaestus, Hephaistos

vulgar **3** low **4** base, rude **5** crude, dirty, gross, rough **6** coarse, common, filthy, ribald, risque, smutty **7** boorish, ill-bred, lowbrow, obscene, uncouth **8** impolite, indecent, off-color, ordinary, plebeian **9** offensive, tasteless, unrefined **10** suggestive **11** ill-mannered, proletarian **12** pornographic, uncultivated

vulgarian **3** oaf **4** boor, lout **5** brute, yahoo **7** Babbitt **9** ignoramus **10** philistine **16** anti-intellectual

vulgarity **8** bad taste, rudeness **9** crudeness, grossness, indecency, indecorum, obscenity **10** coarseness, ill manners, indelicacy, smuttiness **11** boorishness, pornography **12** impoliteness **13** tastelessness

vulnerable **4** weak **7** exposed **8** helpless, insecure **9** sensitive, unguarded **10** easily hurt, undefended **11** defenseless, susceptible, thin-skinned, unprotected

Vye, Eustacia
character in: **17** Return of the Native
author: **5** Hardy

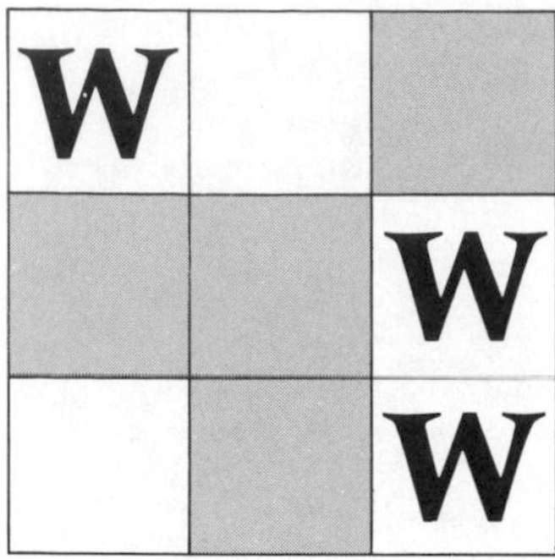

wacky, whacky **3** odd **4** nuts **5** crazy, kooky **6** cuckoo, insane, kookie **7** cracked, foolish, touched **9** eccentric, senseless **10** irrational **12** crackbrained

wad **3** bat, pad **4** cram, head, heap, lump, mass, tuft **5** money, stuff **6** bundle, riches, stop up **7** fortune **8** bankroll, plumbago

waddle **3** wag **4** sway **6** hobble, toddle, totter, wobble

wade **4** ford, plod, plow, toil, trek **5** labor **6** drudge, trudge **9** walk in mud **11** walk in water

wafer **4** chip **5** candy, flake **6** cookie **7** cracker **15** unleavened bread

waft **4** blow, puff **5** drift, float

wag **3** bob, wit **4** card, move, stir, wave **5** clown, droll, flick, joker, shake **6** jester, jiggle, switch, twitch, waggle, wiggle, wigwag **7** buffoon, farceur, flicker, flutter **8** comedian, humorist, jokester **9** oscillate **11** wisecracker **14** life of the party

wage **3** fee, pay **6** income, salary **7** carry on, conduct, payment, revenue, stipend **8** earnings, engage in, maintain, practice **9** emolument, undertake **10** recompense **12** compensation, remuneration

wage earner **6** worker **8** employee **9** job holder **12** hourly worker

wager **3** bet, pot **4** ante, pool, risk **5** fancy, guess, stake **6** assume, gamble, hazard **7** imagine, jackpot, presume, suppose, surmise, venture **8** make a bet, theorize **9** speculate **10** conjecture, take a flyer **11** speculation, try one's luck **12** tempt fortune **15** hazard an opinion

wages **3** bet, fee, pay **4** gage, hire **6** fights, reward, return, salary **7** engages, payment, stipend **8** conducts, earnings **9** emolument **10** prosecutes, recompense **12** remuneration

wage war **5** fight **6** combat **7** contend, make war **8** do battle **12** march against

waggery **5** chaff **6** banter, ridding **7** joshing, kidding, ragging, ribbing **8** chaffing, drollery, raillery, twitting
French: **8** badinage

waggish **5** droll, funny **7** comical, puckish **8** humorous

waggle **4** wave **5** wield **8** brandish

Wagner, Honus
real name: **15** John Peter Wagner
nickname: **14** Flying Dutchman
sport: **8** baseball
position: **9** shortstop
team: **17** Pittsburgh Pirates

Wagner, Richard
born: **7** Germany, Leipzig
composer of: **5** Faust **6** Rienzi **7** Die Feen **8** Parsifal **9** Lohengrin **10** Tannhauser, The Fairies **14** Siegfried Idyll **16** The Mastersingers, Tristan and Isolde, Wesendonck Lieder **17** The Flying Dutchman **20** Der Ring des Nibelungen, The Ring of the Nibelungs **27** Die Meistersinger von Nurnberg
the Ring Cycle Part 1: **12** Das Rheingold, The Rhine Gold
the Ring Cycle Part 2: **10** Die Walkure **11** The Valkyrie
the Ring Cycle Part 3: **9** Siegfried
the Ring Cycle Part 4: **15** Gotterdammerung **17** Twilight of the Gods

Wagner, Robert
born: **9** Detroit MI
wife: **11** Natalie Wood
roles: **6** Switch **10** Hart to Hart **13** It Takes a Thief, Prince Valiant, The Longest Day **24** All the Fine Young Cannibals

wagon **3** car, van **4** cart, dray, tram, wain **5** coach, lorry, tonga, truck **7** caisson **10** automobile, battleship
covered: **15** prairie schooner
maker: **10** wainwright
police: **10** Black Maria
Russian: **6** telega
sideless: **6** rolley
track: **3** rut

Wagon Train
character: **9** Bill Hawks **11** Barnaby West, Cooper Smith, Duke Shannon **14** Charlie Wooster, Major Seth Adams **15** Christopher Hale, Flint McCullough
cast: **8** Ward Bond **11** Scott Miller, Terry Wilson **12** Frank McGrath, John McIntire, Michael Burns, Robert Fuller, Robert Horton

waif **5** gamin, stray **6** gamine, urchin **7** mudlark **9** foundling **10** ragamuffin, street arab **11** guttersnipe **13** homeless child **14** tatterdemalion

wail **3** cry **4** bawl, howl, keen, moan, roar, weep, yell **5** groan, shout, whine **6** bellow, bemoan, bewail, cry out, lament, outcry, plaint **7** keening, moaning, wailing **9** caterwaul **10** rend the air **11** lamentation

waist **3** top **5** shirt **6** blouse, bodice, middle **7** midriff **9** midregion, waistband, waistline **10** middle part, midsection, shirtwaist

waistband **4** belt, sash **5** cinch **6** girdle

waistcoat **4** vest **5** benjy **6** jacket, jerkin, veskit, vestee, weskit **7** singlet
French: gilet

wait **4** halt, stay, stop **5** dally, delay, pause, tarry **6** linger, put off **7** suspend **8** postpone, stopover **9** deferment **10** suspension **11** continuance **12** postponement

wait for **6** expect **10** anticipate

Waiting for Godot
author: **13** Samuel Beckett
character: **8** Estragon, Vladimir

wait on **5** serve **6** assist, attend

waive **4** stay **5** defer, forgo, let go, table, yield **6** give up, not use, put off, shelve **7** forbear, lay over **8** disclaim, forswear, postpone, renounce **9** surrender

waiver **9** dismissal **10** abdication, disclaimer **11** abandonment **12** renunciation **14** relinquishment

Wakashan
tribe: **6** Nootka **8** Kwakiutl, Puyallup

wake **4** fire, path, stir, wash **5** rally, rouse, trail, train, vigil **6** arouse, course, excite, kindle, revive **7** enliven, provoke, quicken **8** backwash **9** galvanize, stimulate **11** resuscitate

wakeful **4** wary **5** alert, astir **7** careful, heedful **8** cautious, restless, vigilant, watchful **9** insomniac, observant, sleepless **10** unsleeping **11** circumspect

wake up **4** rise **5** arise **6** vivify **7** animate, enliven **8** vitalize **9** stimulate

Walcott, Joe
real name: **18** Arnold Raymond Cream
nickname: **9** Jersey Joe
sport: **6** boxing
class: **11** heavyweight

Walden, or Life in the Woods
author: **17** Henry David Thoreau

Wales ***see box***

Wales
other name: **5** Cymru **7** Cambria
capital: **7** Cardiff
cities: **4** Rhyl, Ross **5** Flint, Towyn **6** Amlwch, Bangor, Brecon, Sidney **7** Cwmbran, Herford, Newport, Rhondda, Swansea **8** Aberdare, Caerleon, Holyhead, Pembroke **9** Fishguard, Glamorgan **10** Caernarvon, Caerphilly, Carmarthen **11** Aberystwyth **12** Milford Haven **13** Kidderminster, Merthyr-Tydfil
division: **5** Clwyd, Dyfed, Flint, Gwent, Powys **6** Radnor **7** Denbigh, Gwynedd **8** Anglesey, Cardigan, Monmouth, Pembroke **9** Brecknoch, Glamorgan, Merioneth **10** Caernarvon, Carmarthen, Montgomery
government: **29** constituent part of Great Britain
measure: **5** cover **7** cantred, crannoc, listred
island: **4** Mona **5** Caldy **8** Anglesey, Holyhead
lake: **4** Bala **6** Vyrnwy
mountain: **6** Berwyn **8** Cambrian **9** Prescelly **13** Brecon Beacons
highest point: **7** Snowdon
river: **3** Dee, Usk, Wye **4** Alun, Taff, Tawe, Teme, Towy **5** Clwyd, Conwy, Dovey, Neath, Teifi **6** Conway, Severn, Vyrnwy
sea: **5** Irish **8** Atlantic
physical feature:
bay: **7** Swansea **8** Cardigan, Tremadoc, Tremadog
channel: **7** Bristol **9** St George's
hills: **7** Malvern
peninsula: **5** Lleyn
strait: **5** Menai
valley: **7** Rhondda
people: **4** Celt, Kelt **5** Cymry, Kymry, Welsh **7** Brython, Silures, Taffies **8** Awabokal, Cambrian **9** Siluridan
actor: **6** Burton **8** Williams
artist: **4** John
author: **3** Map **5** Jones, Lewis, Mapes, Parry **6** Machan, Thrale **9** Llewellyn **11** Dylan Thomas **14** Dafydd ap Gwylym
god: **3** Deu, Dew **4** Bran, Gwyn **5** Dylan **7** Gwydion
leader: **5** Bevan **6** Rhodri **8** Hywel Dwa **11** Cadwallader **12** Bishop Morgan **13** Owen Glendower **16** David Lloyd George **18** Llewelyn ap Gruffydd
language: **5** Welsh **6** Celtic, Cymric, Keltic, Kymric **7** Cymraeg, English
religion: **8** Anglican **9** Methodist **10** Protestant **12** Presbyterian
place:
bridge: **6** Severn
castle: **6** Conway **7** Harlech **9** Beaumaris **10** Caernarvon, Caerphilly **11** Aberystwyth
feature:
festival: **10** Eisteddfod
stories: **10** Mabinogion
food:
dish: **8** flummery

wander aimlessly **5** amble, stray **6** ramble, stroll **7** meander, saunter

Wanderer, The
author: **13** Alain Fournier

wandering **5** lapse **8** rambling, straying **9** deviation **10** aberration, digressive, discursive, maundering, meandering, roundabout **11** abnormality **12** idiosyncrasy **13** nonconformity **14** circumlocutory

Wandering Jew, The
author: **9** Eugene Sue

Wanderings
author: **10** Chaim Potok

wane **3** ebb **4** fade, sink **5** abate, droop, waste **6** ebbing, fading, lessen, weaken, wither **7** abating, decline, dwindle, subside **8** decrease, diminish, fade away **9** dwindling, lessening, recession, subsiding, weakening, withering

wangle **4** worm **5** trick **6** jockey, scheme **7** finagle, wheedle **8** engineer, intrigue, maneuver **9** machinate **10** manipulate

wanness **6** pallor **8** grayness, paleness **9** ashenness **10** sallowness, sickliness **13** colorlessness

want 4 hunt, lack, need, seek, wish **5** covet, crave, fancy **6** dearth, demand, desire, hunger, penury **7** be needy, craving, hope for, long for, paucity, pine for, poverty, require, wish for **8** scarcity, shortage, yearn for, yearning **9** indigence, necessity, pauperism, privation, requisite **10** deficiency, insolvency **11** destitution, requirement **13** impecuniosity, insufficiency, pennilessness **14** impoverishment

Wanted: Dead or Alive
character: 11 Josh Randall
cast: 12 Steve McQueen
job: 12 bounty hunter
gun: 8 Mare's Leg

wanting 5 short **6** absent **7** lacking, missing **9** defective, deficient, imperfect **10** inadequate **11** substandard **12** insufficient

wanton 4 bawd, fast, jade, lewd, rake, roue, slut, tart **5** gross, hussy, loose, satyr, whore **6** chippy, harlot, lecher **7** bestial, immoral, lustful, obscene, seducer, trollop, willful **8** careless, heedless, mindless, needless, strumpet, sybarite, unchaste **9** abandoned, adulterer, concubine, debauched, debauchee, dissolute, lecherous, libertine, malicious, senseless, womanizer **10** deliberate, fornicator, groundless, licentious, malevolent, profligate, prostitute, sensualist, unprovoked, voluptuary **11** fornicatrix, promiscuous, unjustified, whoremaster **13** inconsiderate, irresponsible

wapiti 3 elk **4** deer **11** American elk
female: 3 cow
literally: 9 white rump
male: 4 bull
species: 16 Cervus canadensis

Wapshot Chronicle
author: 11 John Cheever

war 5 clash, fight **6** attack, battle, combat, invade **7** contend **8** conflict, fighting, struggle **10** opposition **11** hostilities
god of: 4 Ares, Odin **5** Othin **8** Quirinus
goddess of: 4 Enyo **6** Athena, Athene, Inanna, Ishtar, Pallas, Saitis **7** Bellona, Mylitta **11** Tritogeneia **12** Pallas Athena **18** Alalcomenean Athena

War and Peace
author: 10 Leo Tolstoy
character: 7 Kutuzov **8** Napoleon **13** Natasha Rostov, Nikolay Rostov, Pierre Bezuhov **14** Anatole Kuragin **15** Andrey Bolkonsky **19** Ellen Kuragin Bezuhov **22** Princess Marya Bolkonsky

War and Remembrance
author: 10 Herman Wouk

warble 4 lump, purl, sing **5** carol, larva, trill, tumor, yodel **6** growth, quaver, ripple **7** twitter, vibrate, whistle

war cry 6 slogan **8** Geronimo

ward 4 zone **5** avert, block, repel **6** charge, thwart **7** beat off, fend off, prevent, quarter **8** pavilion, precinct, stave off, turn away **9** dependent, forestall
French: 7 protege

warden 5 guard **6** keeper, ranger, sentry **7** curator, manager **8** guardian, watchman **9** protector **14** superintendent

Warden, The
author: 15 Anthony Trollope

ward off 5 avert **7** prevent

wardrobe 4 togs **5** chest **6** attire, closet, outfit **7** apparel, clothes **8** clothing, garments **10** cedar chest **12** clothespress
French: 6 bureau **7** armoire, commode **10** chiffonier **11** habillement

wares 4 line **5** stock **7** staples **8** supplies **9** inventory **11** commodities, merchandise

warfare 5 fight **6** battle, combat **8** conflict, fighting **11** hostilities

Warhol, Andy
born: 14 Philadelphia PA
artwork: 9 Brillo Box, Liz Taylor **13** Marilyn Monroe **16** Campbell's Soup Can **20** Green Coca-Cola Bottles

wariness 7 caution **9** alertness, suspicion, vigilance **11** carefulness, guardedness, heedfulness **12** watchfulness **14** circumspection

warlike 7 hostile, martial, valiant **8** inimical, militant, military **9** bellicose, combative **10** unfriendly **11** belligerent, contentious, threatening
Indian: 8 Arapahoe

warlike attitude 9 hostility, pugnacity **11** bellicosity **12** belligerence, belligerency **13** combativeness **14** aggressiveness

warm 3 hot **4** cook, heat, kind, melt, thaw **5** cheer, happy, sunny, tepid, vivid **6** bright, heated, heat up, joyful, joyous, kindly, lively, loving, simmer, tender **7** affable, cordial, earnest, fervent, glowing, intense **8** animated, cheerful, friendly, gracious, outgoing, pleasant, spirited, vehement, vigorous **9** brilliant **10** passionate **11** kindhearted, sympathetic **12** affectionate, enthusiastic **13** compassionate, tenderhearted

warmhearted 4 kind **6** genial, kindly, loving **7** cordial **10** solicitous **11** sympathetic **12** affectionate **13** compassionate

warm-hued 3 red **4** rosy **5** ruddy, vivid **6** golden, orange, yellow **7** crimson, roseate, scarlet **8** blushing

warmish 5 tepid **7** cooling

warm oneself 4 bask **12** soak up warmth, toast oneself

warmth 3 joy **4** fire, heat, zeal **5** ardor, cheer, verve, vigor **6** fervor, spirit **7** hotness, passion **8** kindness, sympathy **9** animation, happiness, intensity, vehemence **10** affability, compassion, cordiality, enthusiasm, excitement, joyfulness, kindliness, liveliness, lovingness, tenderness **11** earnestness **12** cheerfulness, friendliness, graciousness **15** kindheartedness **17** tenderheartedness

warn 5 alert **6** advise, inform, notify, signal **7** apprise, caution, counsel **8** admonish

warning 4 hint, omen, sign **5** alarm, token **6** advice, notice, signal **7** portent, presage **8** apprisal **9** foretoken **10** intimation **12** notification

War of the Worlds, The
author: 7 H G Wells
invasion by: 8 Martians

war of words 7 dispute, quarrel **8** argument **11** altercation, controversy **12** disagreement

warp 4 bend, bent, bias **5** quirk, twist **6** debase, deform, infect **7** contort, corrupt, distort, leaning, mislead, pervert **8** misguide, misshape, tendency **9** prejudice, proneness **10** contortion, distortion, partiality, proclivity, propensity **11** deformation, disposition, inclination **14** predisposition

warrant 3 vow **4** aver, avow **5** swear **6** affirm, assert, assure, attest, permit, pledge **7** certify, declare, justify, license, promise **9** authorize, guarantee **10** asseverate, permission **13** authorization

warranty 6 pledge **9** agreement **11** certificate

Warren, Robert Penn
author of: 5 Flood **7** Audubon **8** Promises **10** Now and Then **12** Incarnations **14** All the King's Men **18** World Enough and Time
member of: 12 the Fugitives

warring 7 hostile **8** battling, clashing, fighting, opposing **9** combatant **10** contending **11** belligerent, conflicting, contentious

warrior 7 fighter, soldier, veteran **9** combatant, man-at-arms **10** campaigner **11** legionnaire

Warsaw
area: 11 Stare Miasto
capital of: 6 Poland
landmark: 14 Kazimierzowski **25** Palace of Culture and Science
Polish: 8 Warszawa
river: 7 Vistula
square: 5 Rynek

warship 5 Maine, U-boat **6** corvet **7** Alabama, cruiser, frigate, gunboat, Monitor **8** Bismarck, corvette, Graf Spee, ironclad, man-of-war **9** destroyer, ironsides, Merrimack, submarine **11** dreadnought, torpedo boat **12** Constitution, Old Ironsides **13** Constellation **15** aircraft carrier **16** superdreadnought
fleet: 6 armada
part: 6 turret
plating: 5 armor

wary 5 alert **7** careful, guarded, heedful, mindful, prudent, wakeful **8** cautious, discreet, vigilant, watchful **10** suspicious **11** circumspect

War Within and Without
author: 19 Anne Morrow Lindbergh

wash 3 mop, rub, wet **4** bath, lave, soak, swab, wipe **5** bathe, clean, float, flood, rinse, scour, scrub **6** drench, shower, sponge **7** cleanse, immerse, launder, laundry, moisten, mopping, shampoo **8** ablution, cleaning, inundate, irrigate, lavation, scouring **9** cleansing **10** laundering

washbasin 3 tub **4** bowl **5** laver **6** lavabo **8** lavatory

washed out 4 drab, dull, pale **5** dingy, faded, white **6** dreary, grayed **8** bleached **9** colorless

washed up, washed-up 4 lost, shot **6** bathed, broken, ruined, undone **7** done for, preened, through **8** bankrupt, done with, fatigued, finished,

Washington
abbreviation: 2 WA **4** Wash
nickname: 7 Chinook **9** Evergreen
capital: 7 Olympia
largest city: 7 Seattle
others: 4 Omak **5** Pasco **6** Renton, Tacoma, Yakima **7** Ephrata, Everett, Hoquiam, Othello, Pullman, Spokane **8** Aberdeen, Bellevue, Longview, Puyallup, Richland **9** Anacortes, Bremerton, Kennewick, Vancouver, Wenatchee **10** Bellingham, Burlington, Walla Walla **11** Port Angeles
college: 7 Gonzaga, Seattle, Whitman **9** Evergreen, Whitworth **10** Puget Sound **14** Seattle Pacific **15** Pacific Lutheran
feature:
***dam:* 10** Bonneville **11** Grand Coulee
***fort:* 5** Lewis
***national park:* 7** Olympic **12** Mount Rainier **13** North Cascades
tribe: 3 Hoh **5** Lummi, Makah, Twana **6** Cayuse, Samish, Skagit, Yakima **7** Chinook, Clallam, Clatsop, Cowlitz, Dwamish, Nooksak, Palouse, Quaitso, Sanpoil, Spokane, Squaxon, Tulalip **8** Chehalis, Chimakum, Colville, Nespelim, Nez Perce, Okanagon, Pishquow, Puyallup, Quileute, Quinault, Sahaptin, Salishan, Sinkiuse **9** Nisqually, Quinaielt, Semiahmoo, Skokomish, Swinomish **10** Senijextee, Shoalwater **11** Shahaptaine
people: 7 Seattle **10** Bing Crosby **11** Hank Ketcham **12** Elisha P Ferry **13** Marcus Whitman **15** William O Douglas **19** Isaac Ingalls Stevens
***explorer:* 4** Cook, Gray **6** Heceta **9** Vancouver **13** Lewis and Clark
lake: 4 Soap **5** Moses, Union **6** Chelan, Ozette **7** Cle Elum, Cushman, Kachess **8** Crescent, Quinault **9** Keechelus, Wenatchee **10** Washington
land rank: twentieth
mountain: 4 Blue, Jack, Tunk **5** Adams, Baker, Lemei, Logan, Moses, Sloan **6** Kettle, Quartz, Simcoe, Stuart **7** Shuksan **8** Cascades, Olympics, St Helens **11** Kettle River
***highest point:* 7** Rainier
physical feature:
***falls:* 10** Snoqualmie
***port:* 6** Tacoma **7** Everett, Seattle **10** Bellingham
***sound:* 5** Puget **7** Rosario
river: 5 Snake, White **6** Yakima **7** Spokane **8** Columbia, Quinault **9** Snohomish **10** Snoqualmie **11** Pend Oreille
state admission: 11 forty-second
state bird: 15 willow goldfinch
state fish: 14 steelhead trout
state flower: 17 coast rhododendron **19** western rhododendron
state motto: 7 By and By (Alki)
state song: 16 Washington My Home
state tree: 14 western hemlock

scrubbed **9** played out, showered

washing 6 laving **7** bathing, laundry, purging, rinsing, soaking **8** cleaning, scouring **9** ablutions, drenching, scrubbing, showering **10** laundering, shampooing

Washington (state) ***see box, p. 1059***

Washington, George ***see box***

Washington DC ***see box***

Washington Square
author: 10 Henry James

wash one's hands of
4 deny, quit **6** give up **7** abandon, decline, disavow, forsake **8** abnegate, cast away, disclaim, forswear, renounce **9** repudiate **10** relinquish

washout 6 fiasco, fizzle **7** failure, letdown **8** disaster **14** disappointment

wash out 4 fade, fail **6** bleach **7** deplete, fatigue **8** enervate, enfeeble **10** debilitate, devitalize

wasp
variety: 5 paper **6** cuckoo, ensign, hornet, potter, spider **12** yellow jacket

waspish 5 huffy, testy **6** crabby, cranky, ornery, shirty **7** bearish, fretful, peevish, pettish **8** petulant, snappish **9** crotchety, fractious, irascible, irritable, querulous **12** cantankerous

Wasps, The
author: 12 Aristophanes
character: 10 Bdelycleon, Philocleon
dog: **5** Labes

wassail 5 drink, punch, revel, toast **6** liquor, tipple **7** carouse, revelry **8** beverage, carousal

waste 3 die, ebb, rob **4** fade, loot, melt, rape, raze, ruin, sack, sink, void, wane **5** abate, crush, decay, drain, dregs, droop, empty, offal, smash, spoil, strip, trash, wreck **6** barren, burn up, debris, devour, litter, misuse, ravage, razing, refuse, scraps, steppe, tundra, weaken, wither **7** crumble, decline, deplete, despoil, destroy, dwindle, exhaust, garbage, looting, pillage, plunder, rubbish, shatter, subside **8** badlands, decrease, demolish, diminish, leavings, misapply, misspend, needless, prey upon, remnants, squander, wrecking **9** devastate, disappear, dissipate, emptiness, evaporate, excrement, leftovers, misemploy, ruination, sweepings **10** demolition, plundering, remainders, wilderness **11** destruction, devastation, dissipation, expenditure, fritter away, prodigality, squandering **12** despoliation, extravagance **14** misapplication

waste away 4 fail, rust **7** corrode, decline, eat into

wasted 5 spent **6** used-up **7** ravaged **9** emaciated, exhausted **12** unproductive

wasteful 8 prodigal **9** unthrifty **10** thriftless **11** extravagant, improvident, spendthrift, squandering **12** uneconomical

wastefulness 10 imprudence, lavishness **11** prodigality, squandering **12** extravagance, improvidence

wasteland 6 desert

Waste Land, The
author: 7 T S Eliot

waste time 5 dally **6** dawdle, loiter **10** dillydally

watch 3 eye, see **4** heed, look, mark, mind, note, ogle, save, tend **5** alert, guard, scout, stare **6** attend, be wary, gaze at, guards, look at, look on, notice, patrol, peep at, peer at, picket, regard, sentry, survey, tend to **7** be chary, care for, examine, lookout, observe, oversee, protect, stare at **8** pore over, preserve, sentinel, sentries, take heed **9** attention, patrolman, vigilance **10** observance, scrutinize **11** contemplate, observation, superintend, supervision **15** superintendence

watch fire 6 beacon
kinds: 4 bale **6** signal

watchful 4 wary **5** alert, aware, canny, chary **6** shrewd **7** careful, guarded,

Washington, George
nickname: 18 Father of His Country
presidential rank: 5 first
party: 10 Federalist
state represented: 2 VA
elected: 11 unanimously
vice president: 5 (John) Adams
cabinet:
state: **9** (Thomas) Jefferson
treasury: **8** (Alexander) Hamilton
war: **4** (Henry) Knox **7** (James) McHenry **9** (Timothy) Pickering
attorney general: **3** (Charles) Lee **8** (Edmund Jennings) Randolph, (William) Bradford
born: 2 VA **9** Wakefield **18** Westmoreland County
died/buried: 11 Mount Vernon
religion: 12 Episcopalian
interests: 7 fishing, hunting, theater **17** scientific farming
vacation: 11 Mount Vernon
author: 33 The Journal of Major George Washington
political career: 9 president **16** House of Burgesses **24** First Continental Congress **25** Second Continental Congress
signed: **12** Constitution
civilian career: 6 farmer **8** surveyor
military service:
war: **13** Revolutionary **15** French and Indian
notable events of lifetime/term: 18 American Revolution
crossed: **13** Delaware River
rebellion: **7** Whiskey
winter at: **11** Valley Forge
father: 9 Augustine
mother: 4 Mary (Ball)
siblings: 5 Betty **6** Samuel **7** Charles, Mildred **13** John Augustine
half-brother: **6** Butler **8** Lawrence **9** Augustine
half-sister: **4** Jane
wife: 6 Martha (Dandridge Custis)
children:
stepchildren: **15** John Parke Custis **17** Martha Parke Custis

Washington DC
airport: **6** Dulles **8** National
basketball team: **7** Bullets
capital of: **12** United States
designed by: **7** L'Enfant
football team: **8** Redskins
landmark: **4** Mall **7** Capitol, Ellipse **8** Pentagon **10** White House **11** National Zoo **12** Ford's Theatre, Franklin Park, Supreme Court **13** Lafayette Park, Rock Creek Park **14** Farragut Square, Reflecting Pool, Watergate Hotel **15** Lincoln Memorial, McPherson Square **16** National Archives **17** Jefferson Memorial, Library of Congress, National Arboretum **18** Washington Monument **21** Frederick Douglass Home, Robert F Kennedy Stadium **22** Smithsonian Institution **23** National Sculpture Garden **25** Arlington National Cemetery **33** Kennedy Center for the Performing Arts
museum: **5** Freer **7** Renwick **8** Corcoran **9** Hirshhorn **10** African Art **11** Smithsonian **13** Dumbarton Oaks **15** National Gallery **17** Folger Shakespeare **18** Phillips Collection **23** National Portrait Gallery
river: **7** Potomac **9** Rock Creek
street/avenue: **4** Ohio **7** New York, Potomac **12** Constitution, Independence, Pennsylvania **13** Massachusetts
university: **6** Howard **8** American, Catholic **10** Georgetown **11** George Mason **16** George Washington

heedful, mindful, prudent **8** cautious, open-eyed, vigilant **9** attentive, observant **11** circumspect

watchfulness **4** care, heed **9** attention, diligence, vigilance **13** attentiveness

watchman **5** guard, scout **6** patrol, picket, sentry **7** lookout **8** sentinel **9** patrolman

Watch on the Rhine
director: **13** Herman Shumlin
based on play by: **14** Lillian Hellman
cast: **9** Paul Lukas **10** Bette Davis **19** Geraldine Fitzgerald
Oscar for: **5** actor (Lukas)

watch over **5** guard **6** attend **7** oversee, protect **11** superintend

watchtower **6** beacon, pharos, signal **7** seamark **8** landmark **10** lighthouse

watchword **5** motto **6** byword, slogan

water **3** cut, dip, sea, wet **4** damp, lake, pond, pool, soak, tear, thin **5** douse, flood, H two O, ocean, river, souse **6** dampen, deluge, dilute, drench, lagoon, splash, stream **7** immerse, moisten **8** inundate, irrigate, sprinkle, submerge **10** adulterate
goddess of: **4** Enki

Water Carrier (Water Bearer)
constellation of: **8** Aquarius

watercolor
French: **9** aquarelle

watercourse **5** canal, river **6** strait **7** channel, conduit, narrows, passage **8** aqueduct

water down **3** cut **6** censor, dilute, weaken **7** thin out **9** expurgate **10** adulterate

watered down **4** weak **6** dilute **7** diluted **8** weakened **11** adulterated

waterfall **7** cascade, Niagara **8** cataract

waterfront **4** dock, mole, pier, quay **5** basin, jetty, levee, wharf **6** marina **7** landing

waterless **3** dry **4** arid, sere **6** barren **7** parched, thirsty **10** desertlike

Waterloo Bridge
director: **11** Mervyn LeRoy
cast: **11** Vivien Leigh **12** Lucile Watson, Robert Taylor **13** Virginia Field
remade as: **4** Gaby

Water Monster (Sea Serpent)
constellation of: **5** Hydra

water of life
Latin: **9** aqua vitae

Waters, Ethel
nickname: **19** Sweet Mama Stringbean
born: **9** Chester PA
roles: **5** Pinky **6** Beulah **21** The Member of the Wedding

Watership Down
author: **12** Richard Adams

Water Snake
constellation of: **6** Hydrus

watertight **9** nonporous **10** impervious **11** impermeable

waterway **5** canal, inlet, river, route **6** gutter, strait, strake, stream **7** channel

Water Wonderland
nickname of: **8** Michigan

watery **3** wet **4** damp, thin, weak **5** fluid, moist, teary **6** liquid, rheumy **7** aqueous, diluted, tearful, tearing **11** adulterated

Watling, Belle
character in: **15** Gone With the Wind
author: **8** Mitchell

Watt, James
nationality: **8** Scottish
developed: **11** steam engine **12** piston engine

Watteau, Jean Antoine
born: **6** France **12** Valenciennes
artwork: **6** Gilles **8** Mezzetin **9** La Finette **10** La Toilette **12** Joys of Living, L'indifferent **13** La Gamme d'Amour **16** Company in the Park, La Lecon de Musique **18** Enseigne de Gersaint, Gersaint's Signboard, La Comedie Francaise, La Concert de Famille **20** Le Dejeuner en plein air, L'assemblee dans un parc **21** Harlequin and Columbine **23** Embarquement pour Cythere, Italian and French Theater, Jupiter Surprises Antiope, Les Amusements Champetres **24** Conversation in the Open Air, The Embarkation for Cythera

wattle **6** Acacia
varieties: **5** black, broom, cedar, glory, green, hairy, oven's, Sally, swamp **6** frosty, golden, mudgee, orange, silver, sticky **7** bramble, buffalo, coastal, prickly, weeping, Wyalong **8** blueleaf, cinnamon, graceful, screw-pod, sunshine **9** red-leaved **10** golden-rain, needle-bush **11** Cootamundra, Mount Morgan, Wallangarra **12** Sydney golden **14** Peppermint-tree **16** Queensland silver

Watts, Sir George Frederic
born: **6** London **7** England
artwork: **4** Hope **14** Physical Energy **17** Paolo and Francesca **19** Anastasio degl'Onesti **45** Caractacus Led in Triumph Through the Streets of Rome **54** Alfred Inciting his Subjects to Prevent the Landing of the Danes

Waugh, Evelyn
author of: **9** Men at Arms **10** Vile Bodies **11** The Loved One **13** Black Mischief, Edmund Campion **14** A Handful of Dust, Decline and Fall **15** A Little Learning **19** Brideshead Revisited **20** Officers and Gentlemen **22** Unconditional Surrender

wave **4** coil, curl, file, flap, line, rank, rise, roll, rush, sway, tier **5** curve, flood, pulse, shake, surge, swell, swing, train, twirl, wield **6** billow, column, comber, deluge, motion, quiver, ripple, roller, signal, spiral, string **7** breaker, flutter, gesture, pulsate, tremble, vibrate, winding **8** brandish, flourish, increase, undulate, whitecap **9** advancing, oscillate, pulsation, vibration **10** salutation, undulation **11** gesticulate, heightening **13** gesticulation

wave at **4** hail **6** signal **7** gesture

wave on **6** beckon, signal **7** gesture **11** gesticulate

waver **4** flap, reel, sway, vary **5** pause, shake, swing, weave **6** careen, change, falter, quiver, totter, wobble **7** flutter, stagger, tremble **8** hesitate, undulate **9** fluctuate, vacillate **10** dillydally **12** shilly-shally

wavering **8** hesitant, waffling **9** undecided **10** hesitating, indecisive, irresolute **11** vacillating

Waverley
author: **14** Sir Walter Scott
character: **12** Flora MacIvor **14** Donald Bean Lean, Edward Waverley **15** Rose Bradwardine **16** Baron Bradwardine **17** Evan Dhu MacCombich **24** Fergus MacIvor Vich Ian Vohr **25** Prince Charles Edward Stuart

wavy **5** curly **6** coiled, curved **7** rolling, sinuous, winding **8** mazelike, rippling, tortuous **10** meandering, serpentine, undulating **11** curvilinear **12** labyrinthine

wax **4** grow **5** swell, widen **6** become, blow up, dilate, expand, extend, thrive **7** balloon, develop, enlarge, fill out, inflate, puff out **8** increase

way **3** far, off **4** area, form, lane, pass, path, road, room, wont **5** habit, means, route, space, trail, usage **6** course, custom, far off, manner, method, nature, region, system **7** conduct, passage, pathway, process **8** behavior, distance, practice, remotely, vicinity **9** direction, procedure, technique **12** neighborhood

wayfarer **8** traveler, wanderer **9** sojourner

Wayfaring Stranger
nickname of: **8** Burl Ives

way in **4** door, gate **5** entry **6** access, portal **7** doorway, gateway, ingress **8** approach, entrance

Wayland
also: **6** Volund **7** Wieland
origin: **8** European
king of: **5** elves

waylay **4** lure **5** decoy **6** ambush, assail, attack, entrap **7** assault, ensnare, set upon **8** inveigle

Wayne, Anthony
nickname: **10** Mad Anthony
served in: **10** Indian Wars **16** Revolutionary War
captured: **10** Stony Point
battle: **10** Brandywine, Germantown **13** Fallen Timbers

Wayne, David
real name: **13** Wayne McMeekan
born: **14** Traverse City MI
roles: **6** Sakini **8** Adam's Rib **12** The Front Page **13** Mister Roberts, Tonight We Sing **15** Huckleberry Finn **16** Portrait of Jennie **26** The Teahouse of the August Moon

Wayne, John
real name: **21** Marion Michael Morrison
nickname: **4** Duke
born: **11** Winterset IA
roles: **5** Hondo **6** Chisum **8** Ringo Kid, Rio Bravo, The Alamo, True Grit (Oscar) **9** McLintock, Rio Grande **10** Stagecoach **11** The Quiet Man, The Shootist **12** The Searchers **14** Rooster Cogburn, The Green Berets **16** How the West Was Won **17** The Sands of Iwo Jima **27** The Man Who Shot Liberty Valance

Way of All Flesh, The
author: **12** Samuel Butler
character: **9** Mr Overton
Pontifex family: **5** Ellen **6** Althea, Ernest, George **8** Theobald **9** Christina

Way of the World, The
author: **15** William Congreve
character: **6** Foible **7** Fainall, Witwoud **8** Mirabell, Waitwell **10** Mrs Fainall, Mrs Marwood **12** Lady Wishfort, Mrs Millamant **17** Sir Wilfull Witwoud

way of thinking **7** beliefs **9** principle **10** conviction **11** persuasions

way out **4** exit **6** egress, escape, outlet

Ways of Escape
author: **12** Graham Greene

wayward **5** balky **6** fickle, fitful, mulish, unruly **7** erratic, restive, willful **8** contrary, perverse, stubborn, variable **9** mercurial, obstinate, whimsical **10** capricious, changeable, headstrong, inconstant, rebellious, refractory, self-willed **11** disobedient, fluctuating, intractable, troublesome **12** inconsistent, incorrigible, recalcitrant, undependable, ungovernable, unmanageable **13** insubordinate

Wazhazhe *see* **5** Osage

weak **4** lame, poor, puny, soft, thin **5** faint, frail, shaky, spent **6** feeble, flimsy, unsafe, wasted, watery **7** brittle, diluted, exposed, fragile, insipid, lacking, unmanly **8** cowardly, delicate, helpless, timorous, unsteady, wide open **9** breakable, enervated, exhausted, frangible, powerless, spineless, tasteless, unguarded, untenable **10** assailable, effeminate, irresolute, namby-pamby, vulnerable, wishy-washy **11** adulterated, debilitated, defenseless, ineffective, ineffectual, inefficient, unprotected, unsupported **12** unconvincing **13** inefficacious, unsubstantial, untrustworthy **14** unsatisfactory

weaken **3** sap **4** fade, fail, flag, thin, wane **5** abate, droop, lower, unman, waste **6** dilute, expose, impair, lessen, soften **7** cripple, dwindle, exhaust, thin out **8** diminish, enervate, mitigate, moderate **9** undermine **10** devitalize, emasculate

weakened **5** frail **6** dilute, faulty, flawed, watery **7** diluted **8** delicate, disabled **9** enfeebled **10** undermined **11** adulterated, debilitated, watered down

weakling **4** twit, wimp **5** mouse, sissy **6** coward **7** chicken, milksop **9** cream puff, jellyfish **10** namby-pamby, pantywaist **11** milquetoast, mollycoddle

weak-minded **4** daft, dull **7** foolish **8** backward, mindless **10** irresolute **11** addleheaded, vacillating **12** feebleminded, muddleheaded, thick-skulled

weakness **4** bent, bias **5** fault **6** defect, hunger, thirst **7** failing, frailty, leaning, passion **8** appetite, debility, fondness, lameness, penchant, tendency **9** prejudice, proneness, shakiness **10** deficiency, feebleness, flimsiness, proclivity, propensity **11** inclination **12** debilitation, imperfection, unsteadiness **13** vulnerability **14** susceptibility **15** ineffectiveness **16** unconvincingness, unsubstantiality **17** untrustworthiness

weak point **4** flaw **5** break, crack, fault **6** defect **10** deficiency **11** shortcoming

weak position **8** handicap **12** disadvantage

weak-willed **8** hesitant, wavering **10** hesitating, indecisive, irresolute

wealth **4** fund, mine **5** goods, means, money, store **6** assets, bounty, estate, luxury, mammon, riches **7** capital, fortune **8** chattels, fullness, opulence, property, richness **9** abundance, affluence, amplitude, plenitude, profusion, resources **10** easy street, prosperity **11** copiousness **12** independence **13** luxuriousness

wealthy **4** rich **5** flush **6** loaded **7** moneyed, well-off **8** affluent, well-to-do **9** well-fixed **10** prosperous, well-heeled

weapon **3** arm **5** guard, means **6** attack, resort **7** bulwark, defense, measure, offense **8** armament, resource, security **9** offensive, safeguard **10** protection **14** countermeasure

weaponry **4** arms, guns **8** armament, materiel, ordnance

wear **3** don, tax, use **4** duds, fray, last, tire, togs, wrap **5** drain, erode, put on, shred, weary **6** abrade, attire, damage, endure, injury, shroud, slip on, swathe **7** apparel, clothes, corrode, dress in, eat away, exhaust, fatigue, frazzle, rub away, service, swaddle, utility **8** clothing, costumes, garments, overwork, wash away **9** disrepair **10** employment, overburden **11** application, consumption, utilization **12** dilapidation **13** deterioration **14** disintegration

wear away **4** rust **5** erase, erode **7** corrode, eat into

weariness
French: **5** ennui

wearing apparel **4** duds, garb, rags, togs, wear **5** dress **6** attire, finery **7** clothes, costume, raiment, regalia, threads **8** clothing, ensemble, garments, wardrobe
French: **11** habillement

wearing away **7** erosion **8** abrasion, friction, grinding, scraping **9** corrosion

wearing down **6** tiring **7** eroding, erosion **8** abrasion, friction, grinding, scraping **10** overcoming

wearisome **4** dull **6** boring, dreary, tiring, trying **7** arduous, irksome, tedious **8** annoying, tiresome, toilsome **9** fatiguing, laborious, vexatious **10** bothersome, burdensome, exhausting, irritating, monotonous, oppressive

wear out **4** tire **7** exhaust, fatigue **8** enervate, enfeeble **10** debilitate

weary **3** fag **4** beat, dull, tire **5** all in, blase, bored, fed up, jaded, spent, tired **6** boring, bushed, done in, drowsy, pooped, sleepy, tiring, tucker **7** annoyed, drained, exhaust, fatigue, humdrum, overtax, play out, routine, tedious, tire out, worn-out **8** dog tired, fatigued, overwork, tiresome **9** disgusted, exhausted, fatiguing, impatient, soporific, wearisome **10** dispirited, exhausting, monotonous, overburden **11** somniferous **12** discontented, dissatisfied

weather **3** dry, tan **4** face, rust **5** brave, clime, stand **6** bleach, season **7** climate, oxidize, toughen **8** confront, windward **9** withstand **11** temperature
god of: **4** Jove **7** Jupiter

weave **4** fuse, join, knit, lace, link, loom, meld, wind **5** blend, braid, curve, plait, snake, twist, unify, unite **6** mingle, writhe, zigzag **7** combine, entwine, meander, texture **9** interlace **10** crisscross, intertwine **11** incorporate

Weaver, Earl
nickname: **15** Earl of Baltimore
sport: **8** baseball
position: **7** manager
team: **16** Baltimore Orioles

Weaver, Dennis
born: **8** Joplin MO
roles: **7** Chester, McCloud **8** Gunsmoke **9** Gentle Ben **13** Kentucky Jones

Weaver, Sigourney
born: **12** Los Angeles CA
roles: **5** Alien **6** Aliens **10** Eyewitness **12** Ghostbusters **17** Gorillas in the Mist **26** The Year of Living Dangerously

Weavers, The
author: **16** Gerhart Hauptmann

web **3** net **4** maze, mesh, trap **5** snare **6** screen, tangle, tissue **7** complex, netting, network **8** gossamer **9** labyrinth, screening

Web and the Rock, The
author: **11** Thomas Wolfe
character: **10** Esther Jack **12** George Webber

Webb, Jack
born: **13** Santa Monica CA
wife: **11** Julie London
roles: **6** The Men **7** Dragnet **9** Joe Friday **15** Sunset Boulevard

Webber, George
character in: **16** The Web and the Rock **18** You Can't Go Home Again
author: **5** Wolfe

Webb family
characters in: **7** Our Town
member: **5** Emily, Wally
author: **6** Wilder

Weber, Karl Maria Friedrich Ernst von
born: **6** Lubeck **7** Germany
composer of: **6** Oberon **9** Euryanthe **13** Der Freischutz **20** Invitation to the Dance

Weber, Max
born: **6** Russia **9** Bialystok
artwork: **11** The Geranium **17** Chinese Restaurant **18** Adoration of the Moon

Webfoot State
nickname of: **6** Oregon

Webster
character: **6** George **7** Webster **9** Katherine
cast: **10** Alex Karras, Susan Clark **13** Emmanuel Lewis

Webster, John
author of: **13** The White

Devil **17** The Duchess of Malfi

we cannot
Latin: 11 non possumus

we command
Latin: 8 mandamus

wed 3 tie **4** bind, fuse, link, mate, meld **5** blend, hitch, marry, merge, unify, unite, weave **6** attach, commit, couple, devote, pledge, splice **7** combine, espouse, make one, win over **8** dedicate **11** incorporate

wedded 4 tied **5** bound, fused **6** joined, linked, melded, merged, united **7** blended, devoted, marital, married, pledged, unified **9** committed, connected **12** incorporated

wedding 8 marriage, nuptials

wedding anniversaries
first: 5 clock, paper
second: 5 china **6** cotton
third: 5 glass **7** crystal, leather
fourth: 4 silk **5** linen **20** electrical appliances
fifth: 4 wood **10** silverware
sixth: 4 iron, wood
seventh: 4 wool **6** copper **8** desk sets **16** pen and pencil sets
eighth: 4 lace **6** bronze, linens
ninth: 5 china **7** leather, pottery
tenth: 3 tin **8** aluminum **14** diamond jewelry
eleventh: 5 steel **11** accessories **14** fashion jewelry
twelfth: 4 silk **6** pearls **11** colored gems
thirteenth: 4 furs, lace **8** textiles
fourteenth: 5 ivory **11** gold jewelry
fifteenth: 7 crystal, watches
twentieth: 5 china **8** platinum
twenty-fifth: 6 silver **21** sterling silver jubilee
thirtieth: 5 pearl **7** diamond
thirty-fifth: 4 jade **5** coral
fortieth: 4 ruby
forty-fifth: 8 sapphire
fiftieth: 4 gold **13** golden jubilee
fifty-fifth: 7 emerald
sixtieth: 7 diamond

weddings
god of: 8 Talassio

wedge 3 jam, ram **4** cram, pack, rend, rive **5** chock, chunk, crowd, force, press, split, stuff **6** cleave **7** squeeze

wedlock 8 marriage **9** matrimony

Wednesday
Dutch: 8 woensdag
French: 8 mercredi
German: 8 mittwoch
heavenly body: 7 Mercury
Italian: 9 mercoledi
name comes from: 4 Odin **5** Woden
observance: 12 Ash Wednesday
Spanish: 9 miercoles
Swedish: 6 onsdag

wee 4 tiny **5** dwarf, scant, teeny **6** little, minute, petite, scanty **9** itty-bitty, miniature, minuscule **10** diminutive, teeny-weeny, undersized **11** Lilliputian, microscopic

weed 3 bur, hoe, nag, pot **4** burr, butt, cull, dock, hemp, rake **5** cigar, joint, vetch **6** darnel, harrow, pull up, root up, uproot **7** tobacco **8** nuisance, plantain, purslane, toadflax **9** cigarette, crabgrass, cultivate, dandelion, eliminate, extirpate, marijuana **12** mourning band

weed out 6 banish **7** abolish, discard **8** get rid of, throw out **9** eliminate

Weena
character in: 14 The Time Machine
author: 5 Wells

weeny 3 wee **4** tiny **5** frank, small, teeny **6** hotdog, little, teensy, wiener **11** frankfurter

weep 3 cry, orp, sob **4** bawl, bend, drip, leak, lerm, ooze, shed, tear, wail **5** exude, mourn **6** bewail, boohoo, lament, shower **7** blubber, lapwing, whimper **8** sweating **9** exudation
genus: 8 Vanellus

weep over 5 mourn **6** bemoan, bewail, lament

weevil
variety: 4 boll, rice

Wegener, Alfred L
field: 10 geophysics **11** meteorology
nationality: 6 German
theory of: 16 continental drift

Wegg
character in: 15 Our Mutual Friend
author: 7 Dickens

weigh 4 lift **5** count, hoist, raise, scale **6** burden, charge, ponder, regard **7** balance, compare, measure **8** consider, encumber, evaluate, ruminate **11** contemplate **12** counterbalance

weigh anchor 4 sail **7** cast off, set sail, ship out

weigh down 4 load **6** anchor, burden **7** oppress **8** encumber, obligate, overload

weight 3 tax **4** heft, load, mass **5** value **6** burden, import, saddle, strain, stress **7** ballast, concern, oppress, tonnage, urgency **8** emphasis, encumber, poundage, pressure **9** heaviness, influence, magnitude **10** importance **11** consequence **12** significance **13** consideration, ponderousness

weight, unit of *see box*

weightlessness 8 buoyancy **9** lightness **11** zero gravity

weighty 5 grave, heavy, hefty, vital **6** solemn, taxing, trying, urgent **7** arduous, crucial, earnest, massive, onerous, serious **8** critical, crushing, cumbrous, pressing **9** difficult, essential, important, ponderous **10** burdensome, cumbersome, oppressive **11** significant, substantial, troublesome **12** considerable **13** consequential

Weill, Kurt
born: 6 Dessau **7** Germany
composer of: 8 Happy End **13** Lady in the Dark **15** Down in the Valley **18** The Lindbergh Flight, The Threepenny Opera **19** Die Dreigroschenoper **31** Rise and Fall of the City of Mahagonny **32** Aufstieg und Fall der Stadt Mahagonny

Weir, Peter
director of: 7 Witness **9** Gallipoli **11** The Last Wave **26** The Year of Living Dangerously

weird 3 odd **4** wild **5** crazy, eerie, kooky, nutty, queer **6** far-out, mystic, spooky **7** bizarre, curious, ghostly, magical, strange, unusual **8** abnormal, freakish, peculiar **9** eccentric, grotesque, irregular, unearthly, unnatural **10** mysterious, outlandish, phantasmal, unortho-

weight, unit of

of Afghanistan: 3 pau, paw, ser, sir
of Algeria: 4 rotl
of Argentina: 4 last **5** grano, libra **7** quintal **8** tonelada
of Austria: 4 marc, saum, unze **5** denat, karch, pfund, stein **7** centner, pfennig **8** vierling **9** quantchen
of Belgium: 4 last **5** carat, livre, pound **6** charge **7** chariot **9** esterling
of Bolivia: 5 libra, marco
of Borneo: 4 para **6** chapah
of Brazil: 3 bag **4** onca, onza **5** libra **6** arroba, oitava **7** arratel, quilate, quintal **8** tonelada
of Bulgaria: 3 oka, oke **5** tovar
of Burma: 2 ta **3** can, mat, moo, pai, vis **4** binh, dong, kyat, ruay, viss **5** bahar, behar, candy, tical, ticul **6** abucco **7** peiktha
of Cambodia: 4 mace, tael
of Chile: 5 grano, libra **7** quintal
of China: 3 fan, fen, hao, kin, ssu, tan, yin **4** chee, chin, dong, shih, tael, tsin **5** catty, chien, picul, tchin, tsien **6** kungli **7** haikwan, kungfen, kungssu, kungtun **8** kungchin **9** candareen **10** kupingtael
of Colombia: 3 bag **4** saco **5** carga, libra **7** quilate, quintal
of Costa Rica: 3 bag **4** caja **5** libra
of Cuba: 5 libra **6** tercio
of Ecuador: 5 libra
of Egypt: 3 kat, ket, oka, oke **4** dera, heml, khar, okia, rotl **5** artal, artel, deben, kerat, minae, minas, okieh, pound, ratel, uckia **6** hamlah, kantar **7** drachma, quintal
of El Salvador: 3 bag **4** caja **5** libra
of England: 3 bag, kip, tod, ton **4** keel, last, mast, maun **5** barge, fagot, grain, maund, pound, score, stand, stone, truss **6** bushel, cental, fangot, firkin, fother, fotmal, pocket **7** quarter, quintal, sarpler
of Estonia: 4 lood, nael, puud
of Ethiopia: 3 pek **4** kasm, natr, oket, rotl **5** alada, artal, mocha, neter, ratel, wakea **6** wogiet **8** farasula **9** mutagalla
of France: 3 sol **4** gros, kilo, marc, once **5** carat, livre, pound, tonne, uckia **6** gramme, passir **7** tonneau **8** esterlin **9** esterling
of Greece: 3 mna, oka, oke **4** mina, obol **5** litra, livre, maneh, pound **6** diobol, dramme, kantar, obolos, obolus, stater, talent **7** chalcon, chalque, drachma **8** diobolon, talanton
of Guatemala: 4 caja **5** libra
of Guinea: 4 akey, piso, uzan **5** benda, seron **6** quinto **8** aguirage
of Hungary: 7 vamfont **8** vammazsa
of Iceland: 4 pund **5** pound, tunna **6** smjors
of India: 3 mod, pai, ser, vis **4** dhan, drum, hoen, kona, myat, pala, pank, pice, raik, ruay, tael, tali, tank, tola, wang, yava **5** adpad, bahar, hubba, masha, maund, tical **6** abucco, karsha **8** mangelin
of Indonesia: 5 catty, ounce, thail **6** soekoe
of Iran: 3 ser **4** dram, dung, rotl, sang, seer **5** abbas, artel, maund, pinar, ratel **6** dirhem, gandum, karwar, miscal, nakhod, nimman **7** abbassi **8** tcheirek
of Italy: 5 carat, libra, oncia, pound **6** carato, denaro, libbra, ottava
of Japan: 2 mo **3** fun, kin, kon, rin, shi **4** kati, kwan, niyo **5** carat, catty, momme, picul **6** kwamme **8** hiyakkin
of Java: 4 amat, pond, tali **5** pound **6** soekel
of Korea: 3 won
of Latvia: 9 liespfund
of Libya: 3 pik, saa **4** kele **5** teman, uckia **6** gorraf, misura **7** mattaro, termino **8** kharouba
of Malaysia: 4 chee, mace, tael, wang **7** tampang
of Mexico: 3 bag **4** onza **5** carga, libra, marco **6** adarme, arroba, ochava, tercio **7** quintal
of Mongolia: 3 lan
of Morocco: 4 rotl **5** artal, artel, gerbe, ratel **6** dirhem, kintar **7** quintal
of the Netherlands: 3 ons **4** last, lood, pond **5** bahar, grein **6** korrel **7** wichtje **8** esterlin
of Nicaragua: 3 bag **4** caha, caja **8** tonelada
of Norway: 3 lod **4** mark, pund **9** skaalpund **10** bismerpund
of Pakistan: 4 seer, tola **5** maund
of Paraguay: 7 quintal
of Peru: 5 libra **7** quintal
of the Philippines: 5 catty, fardo, picul, punto **6** lachsa **7** quilate **8** chinanta
of Poland: 3 lut **4** funt **5** uncya **6** kamian **7** centner, skrupul
of Portugal: 4 grao, onca, once **5** libra, marco **6** arroba, oitava **7** arratel, quintal **9** excropulo
of Russia: 3 lof, lot **4** dola, funt, lana, last, loof, loth, once, pood, poud **5** dolia
of Saudi Arabia: 3 oke
of Scotland: 4 boll, drop **5** trone **6** bushel
of Somalia: 8 parsalah
of Spain: 4 onza **5** frail, grano, libra, marco, tomin **6** adarme, arroba, dinero, dracma, ochava **7** arienzo, quilate, quintal **8** caracter, tonelada

(*continued*)

weight, unit of *(continued)*
of Sudan: 5 habba
of Sweden: 3 ass, lod, ort **4** last, mark, sten **5** carat **6** nylast **7** centner, lispund **8** skalpund, skeppund **9** shippound
of Switzerland: 4 fund **5** pfund **7** centner, quintal **12** zugthierlast
of Syria: 4 cola, rotl **5** artal, artel, ratel **6** talent
of Tanzania: 8 farsalah
of Thailand: 3 bat, hap, pai, pay, sen, sok **4** baht, haph, kati, klam, klom **5** catty, chang, coyan, fuang, picul, pilul, tical **6** fluang, graini, salung, sompay **7** tamlung
of Tunisia: 3 saa **4** rotl **5** artal, artel, ratel, uckia **6** kantar
of Turkey: 3 oka, oke **4** aqui, dram, kile, rotl **5** artal, artel, cheke, kerat, obolu, ratel **6** batman, dirhem, kantar, maunch, miskal **7** drachma, quintal, yusdrum
of Uruguay: 7 quintal
of Venezuela: 3 bag **5** libra
of Vietnam: 3 can, yet **4** uyen
of Yugoslavia: 3 oka **5** dramm, tovar, wagon **7** satlijk

dox **12** supernatural **14** unconventional

weirdo 3 nut **4** kook **5** flake, freak **6** looney **7** lunatic, oddball **8** crackpot, original **9** character, eccentric, screwball **10** one-of-a-kind

Weird sisters 5 Fates, Norns

Weisenfreund, Muni
real name of: 8 Paul Muni

Weismuller, Johnny
real name: 20 Peter John Weissmuller
born: 9 Windbar PA
Olympic sport: 8 swimming
Olympic gold medals: 4 five
wife: 9 Lupe Velez
roles: 6 Tarzan **9** Jungle Jim

Weiss, Peter
author of: 10 Marat/Sade **14** Vanishing Point

welcome 4 meet **5** admit, greet **6** at home, salute, wanted **7** embrace, receive, usher in, winning **8** accepted, admitted, charming, engaging, enticing, greeting, inviting, pleasant, pleasing **9** agreeable, entertain, reception **10** delightful, gratifying, salutation **11** comfortable

Weld, Tuesday
real name: 12 Susan Ker Weld
born: 9 New York NY
husband: 11 Dudley Moore
roles: 12 I Walk the Line **14** Play It as It Lays **16** The Cincinnati Kid, Wild in the Country **19** Looking for Mr Goodbar

welfare 4 good **6** health, profit, relief **7** benefit, success, the dole **9** advantage, happiness

well ***see box***

well-adjusted 6 normal, secure **8** sensible

Welland, May
character in: 17 The Age of Innocence
author: 7 Wharton

well-behaved 6 polite, sedate **8** decorous

well-being 4 ease, good, luck, weal **6** health, profit **7** benefit, comfort, fortune, success, welfare **8** felicity, good luck **9** advantage, affluence, happiness **10** prosperity

wellborn 8 highbred **9** patrician **10** upper-class **12** aristocratic, silk-stocking

Wellbred
character in: 19 Every Man in His Humour
author: 6 Jonson

well-bred 5 civil, suave **6** polite, urbane **7** elegant, gallant, genteel, refined **8** cultured, ladylike, mannerly, polished **9** civilized, courteous **10** cultivated **11** gentlemanly **13** sophisticated

well-chosen 3 apt **4** fine **5** prize **6** choice, seemly, select **7** apropos, correct, fitting, special **8** superior **9** excellent **11** appropriate

well-considered 7 careful, prudent **8** cautious **10** thoughtful **11** circumspect

well-coordinated 6 smooth **8** graceful **9** dexterous **10** effortless

well-defined 5 clear, plain **8** clear-cut, definite, distinct, palpable **10** pronounced

well-dressed 4 chic **5** natty, smart **6** dapper **11** fashionable

well-educated 7 erudite, learned **8** cultured, literate **9** scholarly **10** cultivated **13** knowledgeable

Weller, Sam
character in: 14 Pickwick Papers
author: 7 Dickens

Welles, Orson
real name: 17 George Orson Welles

well 3 jet, run **4** flow, fund, good, gush, hale, mine, ooze, pool, pour, rise **5** amply, fount, fully, issue, lucky, right, shaft, sound, spout, spurt, store, surge **6** easily, fairly, hearty, justly, kindly, nicely, proper, robust, source, spring, stream, strong, warmly **7** chipper, fitting, healthy, readily, rightly **8** famously, fountain, laudably, properly, suitably, very much, vigorous **9** agreeably, capitally, carefully, correctly, favorable, favorably, fortunate, promising, quite well **10** abundantly, acceptably, adequately, auspicious, completely, familiarly, felicitous, intimately, personally, prosperous, splendidly, successful, thoroughly **11** approvingly, commendably **12** advantageous, auspiciously, considerably, propitiously, satisfactory, successfully, sufficiently **13** substantially **14** advantageously, satisfactorily **15** sympathetically **16** enthusiastically
hole drilled in ground for: **3** gas, oil **5** water

born: **9** Kenosha WI
wife: **9** Paola Mori **12** Rita Hayworth
formed: **14** Mercury Theatre
radio show: **14** War of the Worlds
roles: **8** Jane Eyre **11** Citizen Kane, The Third Man, Touch of Evil
director of: **7** Macbeth, Othello **8** Falstaff **11** Citizen Kane, The Stranger, Touch of Evil **23** The Magnificent Ambersons

well-favored **4** fair **5** bonny **6** comely, pretty **7** sightly, winsome **8** fetching, handsome **9** beautiful **10** attractive **11** good looking

well-fed **5** hefty, plump, stout **6** portly, rotund **9** corpulent

well-fixed **4** rich **7** moneyed, wealthy **8** affluent **10** prosperous

well-founded **7** factual **9** supported **12** corroborated **13** substantiated

well-groomed **4** neat, tidy **5** natty **6** spruce **10** impeccable

well-grounded **5** valid **7** factual **8** reliable **9** supported **10** undeniable, undisputed, unshakable **11** irrefutable **12** corroborated, indisputable **13** incontestable, substantiated **16** incontrovertible

well-heeled **4** rich **7** moneyed, wealthy **8** affluent **10** in the chips, in the money, prosperous

Wellington
capital of: **10** New Zealand

Wellington, Duke of
also: **15** Arthur Wellesley
nickname: **6** Hookey **12** The Great Duke
nationality: **7** British
served in: **5** India **14** Napoleonic Wars
battle: **6** Assaye **7** Vitoria **8** Talavera, Waterloo **9** Salamanca
served as: **13** prime minister
memoirs: **20** Wellington Dispatches

well-kept **4** heat, neat, tidy **7** orderly **9** organized **10** systematic **11** disciplined, uncluttered

well-known **4** open **5** famed, noted **6** common, famous **7** big-time, eminent, evident, leading, obvious, popular **8** familiar, infamous, renowned **9** important, notorious, prominent **10** celebrated, scandalous, understood **11** established, illustrious, outstanding

well-lighted **5** lit up **6** ablaze, bright **11** illuminated

well-made **4** fine **7** perfect **8** executed, flawless **9** faultless **11** beautifully

Wellman, William
director of: **5** Wings **9** Beau Geste **11** A Star Is Born **13** Nothing Sacred **15** The Story of GI Joe **16** The Ox-Bow Incident

well-mannered **6** polite **7** genteel, refined **8** cultured, decorous, ladylike, polished **9** courteous, dignified **10** cultivated **11** gentlemanly

well-matched **5** close **10** nip-and-tuck

well-off **4** rich **5** flush **6** loaded **7** moneyed, wealthy **8** affluent **10** prosperous **11** comfortable

well-padded **5** plump, stout **6** chubby, fleshy, portly, rotund **9** corpulent

well-proportioned **7** classic, elegant, shapely **8** graceful **11** symmetrical

well-read **7** erudite, learned **8** cultured, literate **9** scholarly **10** cultivated

well-reasoned **4** wise **10** perceptive, thoughtful **11** intelligent

well-rehearsed **6** smooth **7** planned **8** prepared **9** practiced

Wells, H G (Herbert George)
author of: **5** Kipps **10** Tono-Bungay **11** Ann Veronica **14** The Time Machine **15** The Invisible Man **16** Outline of History **17** Love and Mr Lewisham, The War of the Worlds **19** The History of Mr Polly **22** The Shape of Things to Come **23** Mr Britling Sees It Through

Wells, Julia Elizabeth
real name of: **12** Julie Andrews

wellspring **4** font **6** origin, source **9** beginning **10** birthplace **12** fountainhead

well-stocked **4** full **11** overflowing

well-suited **6** proper **7** correct, fitting **8** suitable **9** congenial, congruous **10** compatible, harmonious **11** appropriate

well-to-do **4** rich **7** moneyed, wealthy **8** affluent **10** in the chips, in the money, prosperous

well up **4** boil, rise **6** bubble **7** surface

well-ventilated **4** airy **5** windy **6** breezy, drafty

well-versed **7** knowing **9** qualified **10** conversant **11** experienced **13** knowledgeable
French: **9** au courant

well-wisher **6** friend **8** advocate, champion **9** supported

Welsh Mythology
goddess: **3** Don
goddess of fire/fertility/agriculture/household/wisdom: **6** Brigit
king: **4** Bran, Llud, Ludd, Nudd
magician: **5** Lloyd
paradise: **5** Annwn **6** Annfwn
prince: **5** Pwyll **7** Kilwich
princess: **5** Olwen
romantic tales: **10** Mabinogian

welt **4** bump, lump, mark, wale, weal **6** bruise, streak, stripe **8** swelling **9** contusion

Weltanschauung **25** manner of looking at the world

Weltansicht **9** world view

welter **4** heap, mass, mess, pile, roll, toss **5** heave, storm **6** bustle, grovel, hubbub, jumble, racket, tumult, wallow, writhe **7** tempest, turmoil **9** commotion, confusion **10** hodgepodge, turbulence

Welter, Blanca Rosa
real name of: **14** Linda Christian

Weltschmerz **6** sorrow **9** world pain **20** sentimental pessimism

Welty, Eudora
author of: **12** Delta Wedding, Golden Apples **13** Losing Battles **14** The Ponder Heart **15** A Sweet Devouring **19** The Robber Bridegroom **20** The Optimist's Daughter

wench **4** doxy, girl, lass, maid, slut **5** whore **6** damsel, lassie, maiden **8** strumpet **10** prostitute

wend **4** make **5** hie to

went **3** ran **4** flew, left **5** faded, got on **6** flew by, lapsed, passed **7** elapsed, sallied **8** departed, filed off, passed by, took wing, vanished **9** proceeded, took leave **10** shuffled on, took flight **11** disappeared, forged ahead **12** sallied forth **13** pressed onward

Wentworth, Captain Frederick
character in: 10 Persuasion
author: 6 Austen

Werfel, Franz
author of: 9 Mirror Man **19** Forty Days of Musa Dagh, The Song of Bernadette

Werle, Gregers
character in: 11 The Wild Duck
author: 5 Ibsen

Werner, Oskar
real name: 24 Oskar Josef Bschliessmayer
born: 6 Vienna **7** Austria
roles: 11 Jules and Jim, Ship of Fools **17** Voyage of the Damned **22** Fahrenheit Four Fifty One, The Shoes of the Fisherman **26** The Spy Who Came in from the Cold

Wertmuller, Lina
director of: 9 Swept Away (by an unusual destiny in the blue sea of August) **13** Seven Beauties

Wescott, Glenway
author of: 14 The Grandmother, The Pilgrim Hawk **16** The Apple of the Eye **17** Apartment in Athens

Wessex
fictional place created by: 5 Hardy

West, Benjamin
born: 13 Springfield PA
artwork: 17 Death on a Pale Horse **19** Death of General Wolfe **22** Saul and the Witch of Endor

West, Dame Rebecca
real name: 28 Cicily Isabel Fairfield Andrews
author of: 8 The Judge **11** Harriet Hume **13** Birds Fall Down **15** The Thinking Reed **19** The Strange Necessity **20** The Fountain Overflows **21** The Return of the Soldier **22** Black Lamb and Grey Falcon

West, Jessamyn
author of: 11 Leafy Rivers **13** A Matter of Time **18** Except for Me and Thee **21** The Friendly Persuasion **22** The Massacre at Fall Creek

West, Mae
born: 10 Brooklyn NY
roles: 3 Sex **8** Sextette **9** I'm No Angel **10** Diamond Lil **13** Klondike Annie **14** Go West Young Man **15** Night After Night, She Done Him Wrong **16** Myra Breckinridge **17** My Little Chickadee
autobiography: 28 Goodness Had Nothing To Do With It
quote: 18 Beulah peel me a grape **22** Come up and see me sometime

West, Morris L
author of: 7 Proteus **9** Harlequin **13** The Salamander **14** The Clowns of God **15** The Tower of Babel **17** The Devil's Advocate **22** The Shoes of the Fisherman

West, Nathanael
author of: 12 A Cool Million **16** Miss Lonelyhearts **17** The Day of the Locust

Westcott, Edward Noyes
author of: 10 David Harum

Westenra, Lucy
character in: 7 Dracula
author: 6 Stoker

Western, Sophia
character in: 8 Tom Jones
author: 8 Fielding

Western Sahara ***see box***

Western Samoa ***see box***

Western Star
author: 19 Stephen Vincent Benet

Western Sahara
other name: 13 Spanish Sahara
capital: 6 Al Aiun **7** El Aaiun
city: 3 Zug **5** Daora, Smara **6** Aargub, Dakhla, Tichla **9** Asqueimat, Bir Gandus **10** Bir Enzaran **12** Guelta Zemmur
government: 33 disputed territory claimed by Morocco
river: 7 Uad Atui **8** Uad Assag **13** Saguia el Hamra
sea: 8 Atlantic
physical feature:
***cape:* 6** Barbas **7** Bojador
***desert:* 6** Sahara
***wind:* 5** leste **6** gibleh
people: 4 Arab **6** Berber
language: 16 Hassaniyya Arabic
religion: 5 Islam
feature:
political group: **14** Polisario Front

Western Samoa
other name: 17 Navigator's Islands
capital/largest city: 4 Apia
others: 6 Safotu, Sataua **7** Faleolo, Palauli, Poutasi, Tuasivi **8** Fagamalo, Falelima, Lufilufi **9** Falealupo, Mulifanua **10** Samalaeulu, Satupaitea
monetary unit: 4 sene, tala
island: 5 Upolu **6** Manono, Savaii **7** Apolima
mountain: 4 Fito, Vaea
highest point: 13 Mauga Silisili
sea: 7 Pacific
physical feature:
***bay:* 4** Asau, Salu **6** Safata **7** Lafanga, Matautu **8** Fangaloa, Salealua **9** Saluofata
***strait:* 7** Apolima
people: 6 Samoan **10** Melanesian, Polynesian
***author:* 20** Robert Louis Stevenson (Tusitala, Teller of Tales)
***explorer:* 6** Wilkes **9** Roggeveen **12** Bougainville
language: 6 Samoan **7** English
religion: 9 Methodist **10** Protestant **13** Roman Catholic **14** Congregational
place:
***observatory:* 4** Apia
***tomb:* 9** Stevenson
feature:
***chief:* 5** matai
***clothing:* 5** pareu **8** lavalava, pulctasi
***dance:* 4** siva
***daughter of chief:* 5** taupo
***house:* 4** fale
food:
***dish:* 8** palusami
***drink:* 3** ava

Westhus, Haie
character in: 25 All Quiet on the Western Front
author: 8 Remarque

West Indies ***see box***

Westinghouse, George
nationality: 8 American
invented: 8 air brake **12** railroad frog **20** railroad signal system

West Indies
11 archipelago
Associated States: **7** Antigua, Grenada, St Lucia **8** Dominica **20** St Kitts-Nevis-Anguilla
bird: **4** tody **6** mucaro
channel: **7** Jamaica **9** Old Bahama
component: **4** Cuba **5** Haiti **6** Tobago **7** Bahamas, Jamaica **8** Barbados, Trinidad **10** Hispaniola **14** Lesser Antilles **15** Greater Antilles **17** Dominican Republic
crop: **6** coffee **9** sugarcane
fish: **4** pega **5** pelon
formerly: **10** federation
fruit: **5** papaw **6** pawpaw **7** genipap
islands: **5** Turks **6** Caicos, Cayman, Virgin **7** Bahamas, Leeward **8** Windward
kale: **7** malanga
lizard: **6** arbalo
music: **7** calypso
passage: **4** Mona **8** Windward
rodent: **5** hutia
sea: **9** Caribbean
shark: **4** gata
sorcery: **3** obi **5** obeah
tree: **5** genip **6** aralie
tribesman: **5** Carib **6** Arawak **7** Ciboney
vessel: **6** droger, drogher
volcano: **5** Pelee

Westlake, Donald E
author of: **8** Bank Shot **10** The Hot Rock **13** Dancing Aztecs **15** Brothers Keepers
as Richard Stark: **9** The Hunter **10** The Seventh
as Tucker Coe: **19** Murder Among Children

Weston, Mrs
character in: **4** Emma
author: **6** Austen

Westover, Russ
creator/artist of: **15** Tillie the Toiler

West Side Story
director: **10** Robert Wise **13** Jerome Robbins
cast: **10** Rita Moreno **11** Natalie Wood, Russ Tamblyn **13** Richard Beymer **14** George Chakiris
score: **15** Stephen Sondheim **16** Leonard Bernstein
Oscar for: **7** picture **8** director **15** supporting actor (Chakiris) **17** supporting actress (Moreno)

West Virginia ***see box***

Westward Ho!
author: **15** Charles Kingsley

west wind
associated with: **8** Favonius, Zephyrus

wet **3** dip **4** damp, dank, rain, soak **5** humid, moist, rainy, soggy, steep, storm, water **6** clammy, dampen, drench, liquid, shower, soaked, sodden, splash, stormy, watery **7** immerse, moisten, showery, soaking, sopping, squishy, wetness **8** dampened, dampness, dankness, drenched, dripping, inundate, irrigate, moisture, sprinkle, submerge **9** exudation, liquified, moistness, rainstorm **10** clamminess **11** waterlogged **12** condensation **13** precipitation

wet blanket **4** drag **6** damper **10** spoilsport **11** party-pooper

wet down **5** spray **6** dampen **7** moisten **8** sprinkle

wettish **4** damp **5** moist **6** clammy

we who are about to die salute thee
Latin: **19** morituri te salutamus
said by: **15** Roman gladiators
said to: **13** Roman emperors

whack **2** go **3** box, hit, rap, try **4** bang, belt, blow, cuff, slam, slap, slug, sock, stab, turn **5** baste, clout, crack, knock, pound, punch, smack, smite, thump, trial **6** strike, wallop **7** attempt, venture **8** endeavor

whale **4** beat, cane, drub, flog, orca, whip **6** baleen, thrash **9** bastinado
constellation of: **5** Cetus
group of: **3** gam, pod

West Virginia
abbreviation: **2** WV **3** W Va
nickname: **8** Mountain **9** Panhandle
capital: **10** Charleston
largest city: **10** Huntington
others: **5** Logan **6** Elkins, Keyser, Ripley, Vienna, Weston **7** Beckley, Grafton, Spencer, Weirton **8** Fairmont, Wheeling **10** Clarksburg **11** Moundsville, Parkersburg
college: **5** Salem **7** Bethany, Concord **8** Marshall, Wheeling **9** Bluefield **10** Charleston **14** Davis and Elkins **16** Alderson Broaddus **20** West Virginia Wesleyan
feature:
historical site: **12** Harper's Ferry
national road: **10** Cumberland
tribe: **7** Moneton
people: **9** Pearl Buck **14** Arthur I Boreman **19** Walter Philip Reuther **24** Thomas "Stonewall" Jackson
explorer: **12** Morgan Morgan
island: **14** Blennerhassett
lake: **4** Lynn
land rank: **10** forty-first
mountain:
highest point: **10** Spruce Knob
physical feature:
cavern: **6** Seneca
plateau: **9** Allegheny
rock: **6** Seneca
spring: **8** Berkeley **12** White Sulphur
river: **3** Elk **4** Ohio **6** Gauley **7** Kanawha, Potomac, Tug Fork **8** Big Sandy, Guyandot **11** Monongahela
state admission: **11** Thirty-fifth
state bird: **8** cardinal
state fish: **10** brook trout
state flower: **11** great laurel **15** big rhododendron **17** great rhododendron
state motto: **25** Mountaineers Are Always Free
state song: **17** West Virginia Hills **20** This Is My West Virginia **27** West Virginia My Home Sweet Home
state tree: **10** sugar maple

whammy **3** hex **4** jinx **5** curse **7** evil eye **9** evil spell

wharf **3** key **4** dock, pier, quai, quay, slip **5** jetty **6** marina **7** landing **10** breakwater

Wharton, Edith
author of: **10** Ethan Frome, The Old Maid **15** The House of Mirth **17** The Age of Innocence **21** The Custom of the Country

Whatever Happened to Baby Jane?
director: **13** Robert Aldrich
cast: **10** Bette Davis **11** Victor Buono **12** Joan Crawford **15** Marjorie Bennett

What Every Woman Knows
author: **12** James M Barrie
character: **9** John Shand **15** Charles Venables **18** Comtesse de la Briere, Lady Sybil Tenterden
Wylie family: **5** Alick, David, James **6** Maggie

what it takes **5** skill **7** ability, mastery **9** expertise **10** capability, competence, expertness **11** proficiency **13** the right stuff

What Mrs McGillicuddy Saw!
author: **14** Agatha Christie

What Price Glory?
author: **15** Maxwell Anderson

What's Happening!!
character: **5** Rerun **6** Dwayne **7** Shirley **9** Dee Thomas, (Mama) Mrs Thomas **11** Roger (Raj) Thomas
cast: **9** Fred Berry, Mabel King **12** Ernest Thomas **13** Haywood Nelson **15** Danielle Spencer, Shirley Hemphill

What's My Line?
host: **8** John Daly
panelist: **8** Hal Block **9** Fred Allen **10** Steve Allen **11** Bennett Cerf **13** Arlene Francis **15** Louis Untermeyer **16** Dorothy Kilgallen

wheat **8** Triticum
varieties: **4** club, rice **5** durum, dwarf, India, river **6** Alaska, common, German, Polish, starch **7** English, poulard **8** hedgehog **10** one-grained, two-grained **13** Mediterranean
product: **4** bran **5** bread, flour, pasta **6** cereal **8** macaroni **9** spaghetti

Wheat State
nickname of: **6** Kansas

wheedle **4** coax, lure **5** charm **6** cajole, entice, induce **7** beguile, flatter **8** butter up, inveigle, persuade, soft soap

wheel **4** disk, drum, hoop, ring, roll, spin **5** pivot, round, swirl, twirl, whirl **6** caster, circle, gilgal, gyrate, roller, rotate, swivel **7** revolve **9** pirouette

Wheel of Fortune
host: **8** Pat Sajak
assistant: **10** Vanna White

wheels **3** car **4** auto, heap **5** motor **6** jalopy **7** flivver, vehicle **8** motorcar **9** tin lizzie **10** automobile

wheeze **4** gasp, hiss, pant, puff **7** panting, whistle

whelp **3** boy, cub, kid, lad, pup **4** brat **5** child, puppy, youth **6** urchin **9** stripling, youngster **14** whippersnapper

whence **9** from where **10** antecedent **14** from what source

Where Eagles Dare
director: **12** Brian G Hutton
based on novel by: **15** Alistair MacLean
cast: **7** Mary Ure **12** Robert Beatty **13** Clint Eastwood, Patrick Wymark, Richard Burton **14** Michael Hordern

wherefore **2** so **3** why **7** because **13** for what reason

where I may stand
Greek: **6** pou sto

where mentioned above
Latin: **8** ubi supra

whereupon **8** upon what **10** after which **14** upon which point

wherewithal **4** cash **5** funds, means **6** assets **7** capital **9** financing, resources

whet **4** edge, hone, stir **5** grind, pique, strop, tempt **6** allure, arouse, awaken, entice, excite, induce, kindle **7** animate, provoke, quicken, sharpen **9** stimulate **11** put an edge on

whether willing or not
Latin: **12** nolens volens

which see
Latin: **2** qv **8** quod vide

which was to be demonstrated
Latin: **3** QED **21** quod erat demonstrandum

which was to be done
Latin: **17** quod erat faciendum

which was to be shown
Latin: **3** QED **21** quod erat demonstrandum

whiff **4** hint, odor, puff **5** aroma, draft, scent, smell, sniff, trace **6** breath, breeze, zephyr **7** bouquet
French: **7** soupcon

Whig Party
president belonging to: **5** Tyler **6** Taylor **8** Fillmore, Harrison

while **2** as **3** yet **4** idle, till, time, when **5** until **6** during, effort, whilst **7** filling, interim, trouble, whereas **8** although, occasion

whim **4** urge **5** fancy, quirk **6** notion, vagary **7** caprice, conceit, impulse **8** crotchet **11** inspiration **12** eccentricity

whimper **3** sob **4** pule **5** whine **6** snivel **7** blubber, sniffle, sobbing **9** cry softly, sniveling **11** sob brokenly **16** whine plaintively

whimsical **5** droll **6** fickle, fitful, quaint **7** amusing, erratic, waggish **8** fanciful, notional, quixotic **9** eccentric **10** capricious, changeable, chimerical **12** inconsistent

whimsy, whimsey **4** bent, wish **5** fancy, humor, prank, quirk **6** notion, vagary **7** caprice, fantasy **8** escapade, drollery **11** make-believe

whine **3** cry, sob **4** fret, mewl, moan, wail **6** grouse, murmur, mutter, snivel **7** grumble, whimper **8** complain **9** complaint **11** gripe meekly **12** plaintive cry **14** cry plaintively

whip **3** rod **4** beat, cane, drub, flap, flog, jerk, jolt, lash, lick, maul, rout **5** birch, flick, spank, strap, thong, whisk **6** rattan, snatch, switch **7** cowhide, rawhide, scourge, trounce **8** birch rod, vanquish **9** horsewhip, toss about **10** blacksnake, flagellate **13** cat-o'-nine-tails, defeat soundly, move violently **14** beat decisively, beat into a froth

Whip **8** scorpion

whip hand **4** sway **5** power **7** control, mastery **9** advantage, authority, dominance, supremacy, upper hand **10** ascendancy, domination

whipped **5** caned, waled **6** beaten, darted, flayed, frothy, lashed, roused **7** flogged, frothed, incited, revived, spanked, subdued, swished, whisked **8** defeated, overlaid, punished, scourged, switched **9** chastised **10** vanquished

whir **3** hum **4** buzz, purr **5** drone **7** whisper

whirl **2** go **3** try **4** reel, spin, stab, turn **5** crack, fling, pivot, swirl, trial, twirl, whack, wheel **6** circle, dither, flurry, gyrate, rotate **7** attempt, revolve, turning **8** circling, gyration, pivoting, rotation, spinning, swirling, twirling, wheeling **9** feel dizzy, feel giddy, pirouette, revolving, turn round **10** dizzy round, rapid round, revolution **12** merry-go-round **17** state of excitement **18** dizzying succession

whirlpool **4** eddy **5** swirl, whirl **6** vortex **9** maelstrom **15** whirling current

whirlwind **4** rash **5** hasty, quick, rapid, short, swift **7** cyclone, tornado, twister **8** headlong **9** breakneck, impetuous, impulsive **10** waterspout

whirly **5** dizzy, giddy, shaky **7** reeling **8** spinning **11** vertiginous

whisk **3** fly, zip **4** beat, bolt, dart, dash, race, rush, tear, whip, whiz **5** bound, brush, flick, hurry, scoot, shoot, speed, spurt, sweep **6** hasten, scurry, spring, sprint
type: **4** wire **6** French **8** omelette

whiskbroom **5** brush

whiskered **5** bushy, hairy **6** shaggy **7** bearded, bristly, hirsute **8** unshaven **11** bewhiskered, mustachioed

whiskers **5** beard **7** stubble **8** bristles

whiskey, whisky **3** gin, rum, rye **4** corn, shot **5** booze, hooch, Irish, juice, vodka **6** liquor, red eye, rotgut, Scotch **7** alcohol, aquavit, blended, bourbon, spirits **8** eau-de-vie **9** aquavitae, firewater, moonshine, unblended **10** sneaky pete, usquebaugh **11** mountain dew **14** John Barleycorn, white lightning
type: **3** rye **6** Scotch **7** bourbon
drink: **8** hot toddy **14** Klondike Cooler
with beer: **11** Boilermaker
with Benedictine: **10** Frisco Sour
with Cointreau: **16** Canadian Cocktail
with vermouth: **9** Manhattan

whisper **3** hum **4** blab, buzz, hint, purr, sigh, tell **5** blurt, bruit, drone, rumor **6** gossip, murmur, mutter, reveal, rustle **7** breathe, confide, divulge, inkling **8** disclose, innuendo, intimate **9** undertone **10** suggestion **11** insinuation

whist
derived from: **8** triomphe
descendant: **6** bridge
number of players: **4** four
six tricks: **4** book

Whistle
author: **10** James Jones

Whistler, James Abbott McNeill
born: **8** Lowell MA
artwork: **6** Etudes **9** Harmonies, Nocturnes **10** Rosa Corder **12** Arrangements, The White Girl **13** Thomas Carlyle **15** Cicely Alexander, Wapping-on-Thames **24** Venetian Palaces Nocturnes **28** Arrangement in Grey and Black No 1 (The Artist's Mother) **29** Chelsea Nocturne in Blue and Green **31** Princess of the Land of the Porcelain **35** Falling Rocket Nocturne in Black and Gold **37** Cremorne Lights Nocturne in Blue and Silver

whistle-stop **5** stump **8** campaign **11** electioneer

whit **3** dab, dot, jot **4** chip, dash, drop, iota, mite, snip **5** crumb, grain, pinch, speck **6** morsel, tittle, trifle **7** modicum, smidgen **8** fragment, particle, splinter **9** scintilla

white **3** wan **4** ashy, fair, gray, pale, pure **5** ashen, blond, clean, filmy, hoary, ivory, milky, pasty, pearl, smoky, snowy **6** benign, chalky, chaste, cloudy, frosty, leaden, pallid, pearly, sallow, silver **7** ghostly, silvery **8** blanched, bleached, grizzled, harmless, innocent, spotless, virtuous **9** alabaster, bloodless, Caucasian, colorless, stainless, undefiled, unspotted, unstained, unsullied **10** cadaverous, immaculate **11** translucent, unblemished, unmalicious

White, E B (Elwyn Brooks)
author of: **11** One Man's Meat **12** Stuart Little **13** Charlotte's Web **14** Is Sex Necessary? (with James Thurber) **19** The Trumpet of the Swan
column: **13** Talk of the Town

White, Stanford *see* **17** Mead McKim and White

White, T H (Terence Hanbury)
author of: **15** The Book of Merlyn **16** The Ill-Made Knight **17** The Witch in the Wood **18** The Candle in the Wind, The Sword in the Stone **20** The Once and Future King

White Album
author: **10** Joan Didion

White Company, The
author: **19** Sir Arthur Conan Doyle

White Heat
director: **10** Raoul Walsh
cast: **11** James Cagney **12** Edmond O'Brien, Virginia Mayo **16** Margaret Wycherly

White-Jacket
author: **14** Herman Melville

whiten **4** pale **5** clean, frost **6** blanch, bleach, silver **7** lighten

whiteness **6** pallor **7** wanness **8** paleness **9** snowiness **10** sallowness **13** colorlessness

White Nights
director: **14** Taylor Hackford
cast: **12** Gregory Hines **18** Mikhail Baryshnikov
choreographer: **10** Twyla Tharp

White Rabbit
character in: **28** Alice's Adventures in Wonderland
author: **7** Carroll

whitewash **6** excuse **7** absolve, cover up, justify **8** downplay, minimize, play down **9** calcimine, exonerate, vindicate
paint made by mixing: **12** lime and water

Whitewater
author: **10** Paul Horgan

whitish **4** buff, pale **6** chalky, creamy **7** grayish

Whitman, Bert
creator/artist of: **14** The Green Hornet

Whitman, Walt
author of: **12** Song of Myself **13** Leaves of Grass **18** Oh Captain My Captain **33** When Lilacs Last in the Dooryard Bloom'd

Whitmore, James
born: **13** White Plains NY
roles: **4** Them **5** Bully **8** Oklahoma **9** Battlecry **10** Will Rogers **11** Black Like Me **12** Battleground, Harry S Truman, Tora Tora Tora **15** Command Decision, Give 'em Hell Harry **19** The Next Voice You Hear

Whitney, Eli
nationality: **8** American
invented: **9** cotton gin
pioneered use of: **14** mass production

Whittier, John Greenleaf
author of: **9** Snow-Bound **10** Maud Muller **14** The Barefoot Boy **16** Barbara Frietchie

whittle **3** cut **4** clip, pare **5** carve, shave, slash **7** curtail, shorten **8** decrease

whiz **3** fly, hum, zip **4** bolt, buzz, dart, dash, hiss, race, rush, scud, tear, whir, zoom **5** adept, drone, scoot, shark, shoot, speed, spurt, sweep, swish, whine, whisk **6** expert, genius, hasten, master, scurry, sizzle, sprint, wizard **7** prodigy, scuttle, whistle **11** crackerjack

who goes there?
French: **7** qui vive

who knows?
Spanish: **9** quien sabe

whole **4** body, bulk, full, hale, unit, well **5** sound, total, uncut **6** entire, intact, robust, system **7** essence, healthy, perfect **8** complete, ensemble, entirety, totality, unbroken, unharmed, vigorous **9** aggregate, undivided, uninjured **10** assemblage, unabridged **12** completeness, quintessence, undiminished

wholehearted **4** true **7** earnest, serious, sincere, zealous **8** complete, emphatic **9** unfeigned **10** unreserved, unstinting **12** enthusiastic

wholesome **4** hale, nice, pure, well **5** clean, fresh, hardy, moral, sound **6** decent, honest, worthy **7** chipper, dutiful, ethical, healthy, upright **8** blooming, hygienic, innocent, sanitary, vigorous, virtuous **9** exemplary, healthful, honorable, uplifting **10** nourishing, nutritious, principled **11** meritorious, responsible **12** invigorating **13** strengthening

whole world, the
French: **11** tout le monde

wholly **5** fully, quite **7** totally, utterly **8** as a whole, entirely **9** perfectly **10** altogether, completely, thoroughly
Latin: **6** in toto

whoop **3** cry **4** hoot, howl, roar, yell **5** cheer, hollo, shout **6** bellow, cry out, holler, hurrah, outcry, scream, shriek **7** screech **9** hue and cry

whopper **3** fib, lie **6** big one **7** fiction **9** falsehood, fish story, tall story **16** cock-and-bull story

whopping **4** huge **5** giant, large **8** thumping, whacking, whapping **10** incredible **13** extraordinary

whore **3** pro **4** bawd, doxy, jade, slut, tart **5** hussy, tramp **6** chippy, harlot, hooker, prosty, wanton **7** demirep, hustler, trollop **8** call girl, mistress, strumpet **9** concubine **10** prostitute **12** streetwalker
French: **9** courtesan **12** demimondaine

whorl **4** coil, curl, roll **5** helix **6** circle, spiral **9** corkscrew **11** convolution

Who's Afraid of Virginia Woolf?
author: **11** Edward Albee
director: **11** Mike Nichols
cast: **11** George Segal, Sandy Dennis **13** Richard Burton **15** Elizabeth Taylor
Oscar for: **7** actress (Taylor) **17** supporting actress (Dennis)

Who Said That?
host: **8** John Daly **11** Robert Trout **13** Walter Kiernan
panelist: **9** Bill Henry **12** Bob Considine, H V Kaltenborn, June Lockhart **14** John Mason Brown, Morey Amsterdam **17** John Cameron Swayze

Who's on First?
author: **17** William F Buckley Jr

wicked **3** bad, low **4** base, evil, foul, vile **5** acute, awful, gross, rowdy **6** cursed, fierce, impish, raging, severe, sinful **7** corrupt, extreme, fearful, galling, heinous, hellish, immoral, intense, knavish, naughty, painful, rampant, Satanic, serious, vicious **8** depraved, devilish, dreadful, fiendish, infamous, rascally, shameful **9** atrocious, malicious, monstrous, nefarious **10** abominable, bothersome, degenerate, iniquitous, malevolent, scandalous, villainous **11** disgraceful, mischievous, troublesome **12** blackhearted, dishonorable, incorrigible **13** reprehensible

wickedness **4** evil **6** infamy **8** baseness, foulness, iniquity, vileness **9** depravity, malignity **10** immorality, sinfulness **11** malevolence **13** maliciousness, nefariousness

Wicked Witch of the West
character in: **13** The Wizard of Oz
author: **4** Baum

Wickfield, Agnes
character in: **16** David Copperfield
author: **7** Dickens

Wickford Point
author: **13** John P Marquand

Wickham, Mr
character in: **17** Pride and Prejudice
author: **6** Austen

wide **4** vast **5** ample, broad, fully, great, large, roomy **7** dilated, immense **8** expanded, extended, spacious **9** boundless, capacious, distended, extensive, outspread **10** commodious, completely

wide-awake **2** up **5** alert, aware, quick **8** vigilant, watchful **9** attentive, insomniac, observant, sleepless

widely **3** far **5** broad **6** abroad **7** broadly, greatly, largely **10** by and large, far and near **11** extensively

widely known **6** common **7** popular **8** familiar **9** universal, worldwide

widen **6** expand, extend, spread **7** broaden, enlarge, stretch

widened **7** swelled, swollen **8** enlarged, expanded, extended **9** broadened, distended, stretched

wide open **4** ajar, vast **5** agape **6** gaping **7** exposed, yawning **8** extended, unfenced **9** cavernous, expansive, outspread, unbounded **12** outstretched, unobstructed

wide open spaces **7** boonies, country **9** boondocks **11** countryside, hinterlands

wide-ranging **5** broad **7** immense **8** sweeping **9** extensive, universal, unlimited **10** exhaustive **11** diversified, far-reaching **12** encyclopedic **13** comprehensive

Wide Sargasso Sea
author: **8** Jean Rhys

widespread **5** broad **9** extensive, outspread, pervasive, worldwide **10** nationwide **11** far-reaching

Widmark, Richard
born: **9** Sunrise MN
roles: **4** Coma **7** Madigan **8** The Alamo **11** Kiss of Death **12** The Long Ships **16** Halls of Montezuma, How the West Was Won **19** Judgment at Nuremberg

Widow Douglas
character in: **15** (The Adventures of) Huckleberry Finn
author: **5** Twain

wie geht's **9** how are you?

Wieland
author: **20** Charles Brockden Brown

wield **3** ply, use **4** wave **5** apply, exert, swing **6** employ, handle, manage **7** display, utilize **8** brandish, exercise, flourish **10** manipulate

wife **3** rib **4** mate **5** bride, squaw, woman **6** missus, spouse **7** consort, old lady **8** helpmate, helpmeet **9** companion
French: **5** femme
German: **4** frau

Wife of Bath
character in: **18** The Canterbury Tales
author: **7** Chaucer

Wifey
author: **9** Judy Blume

wig **3** rug **4** fall **6** carpet, peruke, switch, topper, toupee, wiglet **7** periwig **9** hairpiece

Wiggin, Kate Douglas
author of: **23** Rebecca of Sunnybrook Farm

wiggle **3** wag **4** jerk **5** shake, twist **6** quiver, squirm, twitch, writhe **7** flutter **8** writhing **9** squirming

wigwam, Wigwam **3** hut **4** tent, tipi **5** hogan, lodge, tepee **6** teepee **7** weekwam, wickiup **11** Tammany Hall

Wilcox family
characters in: **10** Howard's End
members: **4** Paul, Ruth **5** Henry **7** Charles
author: **7** Forster

wild, wilds, the wild **3** mad **4** bush, rash **5** bleak, feral, giddy, madly, nutty, rabid, rough, waste **6** choppy, crazed, fierce, insane, madcap, raging, raving, rugged, savage, unruly, wooded **7** berserk, bizarre, flighty, frantic, furious, howling, lawless, natural, untamed, violent **8** barbaric, blustery, demented, desolate, fanciful, forested, frenzied, insanely, maniacal, reckless, unbroken, unhinged **9** abandoned, fanatical, fantastic, ferocious, furiously, illogical, lawlessly, naturally, overgrown, primitive, rampantly, screwball, turbulent, violently, wasteland **10** disorderly, maniacally, uninformed **11** harebrained, impractical, tempestuous, uncivilized, uninhabited **12** uncultivated, ungovernable, unrestrained **13** rattlebrained, undisciplined **14** undomesticated

wild animal **5** beast, brute

Wild Ass's Skin
author: **14** Honore de Balzac

Wild Bunch, The
director: **12** Sam Peckinpah
cast: **10** Ben Johnson, Robert Ryan **11** Warren Oates **12** Edmond O'Brien **13** William Holden **14** Ernest Borgnine

wildcat **3** cat **4** lynx **6** ocelot

Wild Duck, The
author: **11** Henrik Ibsen
character: **5** Werle **8** Old Ekdal **9** Gina Ekdal **12** Gregers Werle, Hjalmar Ekdal **13** Hedvig Relling

Wilde, Cornel
real name: **19** Cornelius Louis Wilde
born: **9** New York NY
wife: **11** Jean Wallace
roles: **9** Maracaibo **11** Omar Khayyam **12** Forever Amber, The Naked Prey **15** A Song to Remember **21** A Thousand and One Nights **22** The Greatest Show on Earth

Wilde, Oscar
author of: **6** Salome **17** The Critic as Artist **18** Lady Windermere's Fan **22** The Ballad of Reading Gaol, The Picture of Dorian Gray **27** The Importance of Being Earnest

Wilder, Billy
director of: **11** One Two Three **12** The Apartment (Oscar) **13** Some Like It Hot **14** The Lost Weekend (Oscar) **15** Double Indemnity, Stalag Seventeen, Sunset Boulevard **16** The Seven Year Itch **18** Love in the Afternoon **24** Witness for the Prosecution

Wilder, Gene
real name: **14** Jerry Silberman
born: **11** Milwaukee WI
roles: **12** Silver Streak, The Producers **14** Blazing Saddles, Bonnie and Clyde **17** Young Frankenstein **22** The World's Greatest Lover **27** Start the Revolution Without Me **43** The Adventures of Sherlock Holmes' Smarter Brother

Wilder, Laura Ingalls
author of: **26** The Little House on the Prairie

Wilder, Thornton
author of: **7** Our Town **9** The Cabala **13** The Matchmaker **14** The Ides of March **16** The Woman of Andros **17** The Skin of Our Teeth **20** Heaven's My Destination **21** The Bridge of San Luis Rey

wilderness **4** bush **5** waste **6** barren, desert, forest, plains, tundra **7** barrens **8** badlands, wasteland **9** mountains

Wildeve, Damon
character in: **17** Return of the Native
author: **5** Hardy

Wild Is the River
author: **14** Louis Bromfield

Wild Kingdom
host/narrator: **9** Jim Fowler, Stan Brock **13** Marlin Perkins

Wild One, The
director: **12** Laslo Benedek
cast: **9** Lee Marvin **10** Mary Murphy **12** Marlon Brando

Wild Strawberries
director: **13** Ingmar Bergman
cast: **12** Ingrid Thulin **13** Bibi Andersson **14** Victor Sjostrom **17** Gunnar Bjornstrand

Wild Wild West
character: **10** James T West **13** Artemus Gordon
cast: **10** Ross Martin **12** Robert Conrad
traveled by: **5** train

wile, wiles **4** coax, lure, ploy, ruse, trap **5** charm, guile **6** cajole, entice, gambit, seduce **7** cunning **8** artifice, maneuver, persuade, subtlety, trickery **9** chicanery, expedient, stratagem **10** artfulness, craftiness, subterfuge **11** contrivance, machination

Wilfer, Bella
character in: **15** Our Mutual Friend
author: **7** Dickens

Wilhelm, Kate
author of: **10** City of Cain, Fault Lines **11** The Planners **14** The Infinity Box **16** The Clewiston Test **19** More Bitter than Death **26** Where Late the Sweet Birds Sang

Wilhelm Meister
author: **6** Goethe

Wilhelm Tell
also: **11** William Tell
author: **17** Johann von Schiller

wiliness **5** guile **7** cunning, slyness **8** artifice, foxiness, scheming, trickery **10** artfulness, craftiness **11** machination

Wilkes family
characters in: 15 Gone With the Wind
members: 4 John **5** Honey, India **6** Ashley **15** Melanie Hamilton
author: 8 Mitchell

will 4 want, wish **5** endow **6** bestow, confer, desire **7** craving, feeling, longing, resolve, wish for **8** attitude, bequeath, pleasure, yearning **9** hankering, testament **10** conviction, preference, resolution **11** disposition, inclination **12** resoluteness **13** determination

Willard, Frank
creator/artist of: 11 Moon Mullins

Willet, John
character in: 12 Barnaby Rudge
author: 7 Dickens

willful 6 mulish, unruly **7** planned, studied **8** designed, intended, obdurate, perverse, stubborn **9** obstinate, pigheaded **10** bullheaded, deliberate, determined, headstrong, inflexible, persistent, purposeful, unyielding **11** intentional, intractable **12** contemplated, premeditated, ungovernable **13** undisciplined **14** uncompromising

Williams, Esther
nickname: 13 Mermaid Tycoon **14** Queen of the Surf **17** Hollywood's Mermaid
born: 12 Los Angeles CA
husband: 13 Fernando Lamas
roles: 13 Bathing Beauty **15** Jupiter's Darling, Ziegfeld Follies **16** Dangerous When Wet, Neptune's Daughter **20** Million Dollar Mermaid

Williams, Janey
character in: 3 USA
author: 9 Dos Passos

Williams, Myrna
real name of: 8 Myrna Loy

Williams, Robin
born: 9 Chicago IL
roles: 6 Popeye **12** Mork and Mindy **18** Good Morning Vietnam **23** The World According to Garp

Williams, Ted
nickname: 6 the Kid **16** Splendid Splinter
sport: 8 baseball
position: 8 outfield
team: 12 Boston Red Sox

Williams, Tennessee
author of: 10 Camino Real **13** The Rose Tattoo **14** Summer and Smoke **16** Cat on a Hot Tin Roof, Night of the Iguana, Sweet Bird of Youth **17** Orpheus Descending, The Glass Menagerie **18** Small Craft Warnings, Suddenly Last Summer **21** A Streetcar Named Desire **24** The Roman Spring of Mrs Stone

Williams, William Carlos
author of: 7 Tempers **8** Paterson **9** White Mule **11** Al Que Quiere **20** Pictures from Brueghel

William Tell
also: 13 Guillaume Tell
opera by: 7 Rossini
character: 6 Arnold **7** Gessler

William the Conqueror
also: 17 William of Normandy **21** William I King of England
fought against: 8 Harold II
battle: 8 Hastings
succeeded by: 6 Henry I **9** William II

Willie and Joe
creator: 11 Bill Mauldin

willing 4 game **5** ready **7** content **8** amenable **9** agreeable, compliant, not averse **10** responsive

willingly 4 gain, lief, soon **6** freely, gladly, liefly **7** eagerly, happily, readily **8** by choice **10** cheerfully, graciously **11** voluntarily **12** with pleasure

willingness 4 zeal **8** alacrity **9** eagerness, readiness **10** enthusiasm **11** inclination

Willoughby, John
character in: 19 Sense and Sensibility
author: 6 Austen

willow 5 Salix
varieties: 3 bay, red **4** bush, goat, gray, seep **5** black, crack, false, Niobe, Pekin, pussy, silky, water, white **6** Arctic, arroyo, basket, desert, golden, laurel, puzzle, woolly, yellow **7** brittle, prairie, sandbar, scouler, shining, weeping **8** creeping, florist's, polished, Virginia **9** bay-leaved, bearberry, flowering, sprouting **10** cricket-bat, dragon-claw, large pussy, small pussy **11** green-scaled, heart-leaved, peach-leaved, Port Jackson **13** halberd-leaved **16** Wisconsin weeping

willowy 5 lithe **6** limber, pliant, supple, svelte **7** lissome **8** flexible **9** sylphlike

Wills, Chill
born: 12 Seagoville TX
group: 26 Chill Wills and the Avalon Boys
voice of: 21 Francis the Talking Mule
roles: 5 Giant **8** The Alamo **10** Way Out West **11** The Yearling **15** Meet Me in St Louis

Wills, Garry
author of: 14 Nixon Agonistes, Reagan's America **16** Inventing America

Will Scarlet
character in: 9 Robin Hood

willy-nilly 8 perforce **10** helplessly, inevitably **11** inescapably, unavoidably **12** compulsively, irresistibly **14** uncontrollably
Latin: 12 nolens volens

Wilmer
character in: 16 The Maltese Falcon
author: 7 Hammett

Wilson, Edmund
author of: 11 Axel's Castle **19** To the Finland Station

Wilson, Myrtle
character in: 14 The Great Gatsby
author: 10 Fitzgerald

Wilson, Sloan
author of: 26 The Man in the Gray Flannel Suit

Wilson, Woodrow ***see box***

wilt 3 die, ebb, sag **4** fade, flag, sink, wane **5** droop **6** recede, weaken, wither **7** decline, dwindle, shrivel, subside **8** decrease, diminish, languish **10** degenerate **11** deteriorate

Wilt the Stilt
nickname of: 15 Wilt Chamberlain

wily 3 sly **4** foxy **5** alert, sharp **6** artful, crafty, shifty, shrewd, tricky **7** crooked, cunning, devious **8** guileful, scheming **9** deceitful, deceptive, designing, underhand **10** intriguing **11** calculating, treacherous

win 3 bag, get, net **4** earn, gain, sway **6** attain, induce, master, obtain, pick up, secure **7** achieve, acquire, collect, conquer, convert, prevail, procure, realize, receive, success, triumph, victory **8** conquest, convince, overcome, persuade, vanquish **9** influence **10** accomplish

win acceptance 9 establish **10** ingratiate

Wilson, Woodrow
name at birth: 19 Thomas Woodrow Wilson
nickname: 5 Tommy
presidential rank: 12 twenty-eighth
party: 10 Democratic
state represented: 2 NJ
defeated: 4 (Eugene Victor) Debs, (William Howard) Taft **5** (James Franklin) Hanly **6** (Allen Louis) Benson, (Arthur Edward) Reimer, (Charles Evans) Hughes, (Eugene Wilder) Chafin **9** (Theodore) Roosevelt
vice president: 8 (Thomas Riley) Marshall
cabinet:
***state:* 5** (Bainbridge) Colby, (William Jennings) Bryan **7** (Robert) Lansing
***treasury:* 5** (Carter) Glass **6** (William Gibbs) McAdoo **7** (David Franklin) Houston
***war:* 5** (Newton Diehl) Baker **8** (Lindley Miller) Garrison
***attorney general:* 6** (Alexander Mitchell) Palmer **7** (Thomas Watt) Gregory **10** (James Clark) McReynolds
***navy:* 7** (Josephus) Daniels
***postmaster general:* 8** (Albert Sidney) Burleson
***interior:* 4** (Franklin Knight) Lane **5** (John Barton) Payne
***agriculture:* 7** (David Franklin) Houston **8** (Edwin Thomas) Meredith
***commerce:* 8** (William Cox) Redfield **9** (Joshua Willis) Alexander
***labor:* 6** (William Bauchop) Wilson
born: 2 VA **8** Staunton
died/buried: 2 DC **10** Washington
education:
***college:* 8** Davidson **18** College of New Jersey (later known as Princeton U)
***law School:* 20** University of Virginia
***university:* 12** Johns Hopkins
religion: 12 Presbyterian
author: 8 The State **16** George Washington **18** Division and Reunion **27** A History of the American People **28** More Literature and Other Essays **34** An Old Master and Other Political Essays **41** President Wilson's Case for the League of Nations **47** Congressional Government: A Study in American Politics
political career:
***governor of:* 9** New Jersey
civilian career: 6 lawyer
***professor of history:* 15** Bryn Mawr College **18** Wesleyan University
***professor of jurisprudence:* 9** Princeton
***president of:* 9** Princeton
notable events of lifetime/term: 14 Fourteen Points **15** League of Nations
***Act:* 7** Adamson **8** Sedition **9** Espionage **10** Child Labor **11** Liberty Loan, Panama Canal **14** Federal Reserve **15** Federal Farm Loan **16** Clayton Antitrust, Selective Service **22** Federal Trade Commission
***conference:* 3** ABC **10** Paris Peace
***18th Amendment:* 11** Prohibition
***program:* 10** New Freedom
***sinking of:* 9** Lusitania
***Treaty:* 10** Versailles
***won:* 15** Nobel Peace Prize
quote: 34 The world must be made safe for democracy
father: 13 Joseph Ruggles
mother: 5 Janet (Woodrow)
siblings: 13 Joseph Ruggles **14** Annie Josephson **16** Marion Williamson
wife: 5 Edith (Bolling Galt), Ellen (Louise Axson)
children: 13 Jessie Woodrow **15** Eleanor Randolph, Margaret Woodrow

wince 5 cower, quail **6** cringe, flinch, recoil, shrink **7** grimace, shudder **8** cowering, cringing, draw back, quailing **9** shrinking

wind 3 air, lap **4** bend, blow, clue, coil, curl, fold, gale, gust, hint, loop, news, puff, roll **5** blast, bluff, curve, draft, scent, smell, snake, twine, twirl, twist, whiff **6** breath, breeze, hot air, ramble, report, wander, zephyr, zigzag **7** bluster, bombast, cyclone, entwine, inkling, meander, sinuate, tempest, tidings, tornado, twaddle, twister, typhoon, whisper **8** boasting, idle talk **9** aerophone, hurricane, knowledge, whirlwind **10** intimation, suggestion **11** braggadocio, fanfaronade, information **12** intelligence
god of: 5 Eurus, Niord, Njord, Notus **6** Aquilo, Auster, Boreas **8** Favonius, Zephyrus
father: 8 Astraeus
mother: 3 Eos

windfall 7 bonanza

Windhoek
capital of: 7 Namibia

Wind in the Willows, The
author: 14 Kenneth Grahame
character: 4 Mole, Toad **6** Badger **8** Water Rat

windless **4** calm **5** still **8** stifling

window **3** bay **5** oriel **6** dormer **7** opening, orifice, transom **8** aperture, casement, porthole, skylight

Winds of War, The
author: **10** Herman Wouk

windstorm **4** gale **6** squall **7** cyclone, tempest, tornado, twister, typhoon **9** hurricane, whirlwind

windswept **4** bare **5** bleak **6** barren **8** desolate **13** weatherbeaten

windup **3** end **5** close **6** ending, finish **10** completion, conclusion, expiration **11** termination

wind up **3** end **4** halt, stop **5** cease, close **6** finish, settle **8** complete, conclude **9** terminate

windy **5** blowy, empty, gabby, gusty, wordy **6** breezy **7** verbose **8** blustery, rambling **9** bombastic, garrulous, talkative **10** loquacious, meandering, rhetorical **13** grandiloquent

wine
French: **3** vin
Italian: **4** vino
god of: **7** Bacchus
goddess of: **6** Libera

wine-colored **6** claret **8** burgundy, cardinal

winemaking
god of: **9** Aristaeus

Winesburg, Ohio
author: **16** Sherwood Anderson

wing **3** ala, fly, set **4** band, clip, flap, knot, nick, soar, zoom **5** annex, graze, group **6** circle, clique, pennon, pinion **7** adjunct, aileron, coterie, faction, section, segment **8** addition, coulisse **9** appendage, extension **10** fraternity

Winged Horse
constellation of: **7** Pegasus

Winger, Debra
husband: **13** Timothy Hutton
roles: **10** Black Widow, Cannery Row **11** Urban Cowboy **17** Terms of Endearment **22** An Officer and a Gentleman

Wingert, Dick
creator/artist of: **6** Hubert

Wingfield family
characters in: **17** The Glass Menagerie
member: **3** Tom **5** Laura **6** Amanda
author: **8** Williams

Wings
director: **15** William A Wellman
cast: **8** Clara Bow **10** Gary Cooper **12** Richard Arlen **18** Charles Buddy Rogers
Oscar for: **7** picture

Wings of the Dove, The
author: **10** Henry James
character: **8** Kate Croy, Lord Mark **9** Mrs Lowder **11** Milly Theale **12** Mrs Stringham **13** Merton Densher, Sir Luke Strett

wink at **6** ignore **7** condone, let pass **8** overlook **9** disregard

Winkle
character in: **14** Pickwick Papers
author: **7** Dickens

winner **5** champ **6** master, victor **8** champion **9** conqueror **10** vanquisher

Winnie-the-Pooh
author: **7** A A Milne
character: **3** Owl **5** Kanga **6** Eeyore, Piglet, Rabbit, Tigger **7** Baby Roo **16** Christopher Robin

winning **7** amiable **8** charming, engaging, pleasing **9** appealing, beguiling, disarming **10** attractive, bewitching, entrancing **11** captivating **12** ingratiating, irresistible

Winnipeg
hockey team: **3** Jets

win over **4** beat, best **5** charm **6** defeat, seduce **7** convert **8** overcome, vanquish **9** captivate, overpower

winsome **5** sweet **6** comely **7** amiable, likable, lovable **8** charming, cheerful, engaging, pleasing **9** agreeable, appealing, endearing **10** attractive, bewitching, delightful

Winter, Lady de
character in: **18** The Three Musketeers
author: **5** Dumas (pere)

Winter, Maxim de
character in: **7** Rebecca
author: **9** Du Maurier

Winterbourne
character in: **11** Daisy Miller
author: **5** James

Winter of Our Discontent, The
author: **13** John Steinbeck

Winters, Shelley
real name: **14** Shirley Schrift
born: **9** St Louis IL
husband: **13** Tony Franciosa **15** Vittorio Gassman
roles: **11** A Double Life **12** A Patch of Blue **14** A Place in the Sun **16** A House Is Not a Home **19** The Diary of Anne Frank **20** The Poseidon Adventure

Winterset
author: **15** Maxwell Anderson

winter sports
god of: **4** Ullr **5** Uller

Winter's Tale, The
author: **18** William Shakespeare
character: **7** Camillo, Leontes, Paulina, Perdita **8** Florizel, Hermione **9** Autolycus, Polixenes

Winter Wonderland
nickname of: **8** Michigan

wintry **3** icy, raw **4** cold **5** bleak, chilly, harsh, polar, snowy, stark **6** arctic, chilly, dreary, frigid, frosty, frozen, gloomy, stormy **7** glacial **8** Siberian **9** cheerless

wipe **3** dry, mop, rub **4** swab **5** apply, brush, clean, erase, rub on, scour, scrub, swipe, towel **6** banish, remove, rub off, sponge, stroke

wiped out **5** broke **6** failed, ruined **8** bankrupt, indigent, strapped **9** destitute, insolvent, penniless **12** impoverished

wipe out **4** ruin **5** erase **7** abolish, destroy, eclipse **8** bankrupt **9** devastate, eliminate, eradicate, extirpate, liquidate **10** annihilate, obliterate **11** exterminate

wiping out **7** erasing **9** eclipsing, expunging **10** abolishing, destroying **11** eliminating, eradicating **12** annihilating, obliterating

wire **5** cable **8** filament, telegram **9** cablegram, telegraph

wiry **4** lean **5** agile, kinky, lanky, spare, stiff **6** limber, pliant, sinewy **7** brittle

Wisconsin ***see box***

wisdom **6** brains **8** sagacity **9** teachings **10** philosophy, principles, profundity **11** discernment, penetration **12** apperception, intelligence **13** comprehension, judiciousness, understanding
god of: **2** Ea **4** Enki, Odin **5** Othin, Thoth
goddess of: **6** Athena, Athene, Brigit, Pallas, Saitis

Wisconsin
abbreviation: **2** WI **3** Wis
nickname: **6** Badger
capital: **7** Madison
largest city: **9** Milwaukee
others: **5** Ripon **6** Antigo, Beloit, Cudahy, Neenag, Racine, Wausau **7** Ashland, Baraboo, Bloomer, Kenosha, Menasha, Oshkosh, Portage, Shawano **8** Appleton, Boscobel, Green Bay, Lacrosse, Superior, Waukesha **9** Eau Claire, Fond du Lac, Sheboygan, Shorewood, Wauwatosa, West Allis **10** Brookfield, Janesville **12** Steven's Point
college: **5** Ripon **6** Beloit **7** Alverno, Carroll, Viterbo **8** Carthage, Lawrence **9** Marquette, Northland
feature:
fort: **6** Howard **8** Crawford **9** Winnebago
national lakeshore: **14** Apostle Islands
tribe: **3** Fox, Sac **4** Sauk **5** Huron **6** Oneida, Ottawa **8** Chippewa, Kickapoo **9** Winnebago **10** Potawatomi
people: **11** Orson Welles **12** Fredric March, Harry Houdini, Spencer Tracy **13** Hamlin Garland **14** Joseph McCarthy, Georgia O'Keeffe, Thornton Wilder **16** Frank Lloyd Wright **17** Robert M LaFollette
explorer: **6** Joliet **7** Allouez, Nicolet **8** Radisson **9** Marquette **12** Groseilliers
island: **8** Madeline
lake: **6** Geneva, Poygan **7** Kenosha, Mendota, Wissota **8** Michigan, Superior **9** Winnebago
land rank: **11** twenty-sixth
mountain: **7** Baraboo **9** Sugarbush **10** Blue Mounds
highest point: **9** Timm's Hill
physical feature:
glacial hills: **13** Kettle Moraine
rock formations: **8** The Dells
river: **3** Fox **4** Wolf **7** St Croix **8** Chippewa **9** Black Rock, Wisconsin **11** Mississippi
state admission: **9** thirtieth
state bird: **5** robin
state fish: **11** muskellunge
state flower: **5** pansy **6** violet **10** wood violet
state motto: **7** Forward
state song: **11** On Wisconsin
state tree: **10** sugar maple

7 Minerva **11** Tritogeneia **12** Pallas Athena **18** Alalcomenean Athena

wise **3** way **4** sage **6** manner **7** knowing, respect, sapient **8** profound **9** judicious, sagacious **10** discerning, perceptive **11** intelligent **13** knowledgeable, perspicacious, understanding

Wise, Robert
director of: **11** I Want to Live **13** West Side Story (with Jerome Robbins, Oscar) **15** The Sound of Music (Oscar)

wiseacre **4** fool, sage **5** idiot **7** tomfool **9** know-it-all, simpleton **10** smart aleck

Wise Blood
author: **15** Flannery O'Connor

wisecrack **4** jest, joke, quip **5** flash, sally **8** cut jokes **9** witticism **11** smart saying

Wise men *see* **4** Magi

wise up **5** edify **6** advise, inform **7** apprise **9** enlighten, make aware

wish **3** yen **4** hope, long, love, pine, want, whim, will **5** crave, yearn **6** aspire, desire, hunger, thirst **7** command, craving, leaning, longing, request **8** ambition, appetite, fondness, penchant, yearning **10** aspiration, partiality **11** inclination **12** predilection

wishes **11** compliments **13** felicitations **15** congratulations

wish for **4** want **5** covet, crave **6** desire

Wishfort, Lady
character in: **16** The Way of the World
author: **8** Congreve

wishful **4** avid **5** eager **6** keen on, pining **7** anxious, craving, hopeful, longing, wanting, wistful **8** aspiring, bent upon, desirous, fanciful, yearning **9** ambitious, expectant

wish well **10** felicitate **12** congratulate

wishy-washy **4** dull, weak **5** inane, vapid, wimpy **6** jejune **7** insipid **8** wavering **10** indecisive, irresolute **11** ineffective, ineffectual, vacillating **12** equivocating, noncommittal **14** tergiversating **15** shilly-shallying

wisp **4** lock, tuft **5** bunch, shred, torch, twist **6** bundle, rumple **8** fragment **10** whisk broom **11** ignis fatuus **13** friar's lantern

wispy **4** thin **5** frail **6** slight **8** fleeting, nebulous

wistaria, wisteria
varieties: **4** pink, wild **5** silky, water **7** Chinese **8** Japanese **9** Rhodesian

Wister, Owen
author of: **12** The Virginian

wistful **3** sad **6** musing, pining **7** craving, doleful, forlorn, longing, pensive **8** desirous, mournful, yearning **9** hankering, sorrowful, woebegone **10** meditative, melancholy, reflective **12** disconsolate **13** contemplative, introspective

wit **3** wag **4** gags **5** comic, humor, joker, jokes, quips, sense **6** acumen, banter, brains, jester, joking, levity, wisdom **7** cunning, funster, gagster, insight, punster, sparkle, waggery **8** comedian, drollery, humorist, jokester, judgment, raillery, sagacity, satirist, vivacity **9** funniness, intellect **10** astuteness, brightness, cleverness, jocularity, perception, shrewdness, witticisms **11** discernment, penetration, wisecracker **12** intelligence, perspicacity **13** comprehension, epigrammatist, sagaciousness, understanding
French: **8** badinage **9** bel-esprit **10** persiflage

witch **3** hag **4** fury **5** crone, scold, shrew, vixen **6** ogress, virago **7** seeress **8** battle-ax, harridan **9** sorceress, temptress, termagant **10** prophetess **11** enchantress
French: **6** beldam

witchcraft **6** hoodoo, voodoo **7** sorcery **8** black art, witchery, wizardry **9** diabolism, fetishism, voodooism **10** black magic, divination, necromancy **11** conjuration, enchantment

with
French: 4 avec, chez

with a grain of salt
Latin: 13 cum grano salis

with a lawsuit pending
Latin: 12 pendente lite

with authority
Latin: 10 ex cathedra

withdraw 2 go **5** leave, split **6** depart, go away, recall, recant, remove, retire **7** extract, rescind, retract, retreat, take off, vamoose **9** disappear, unsheathe

withdrawal 4 exit **6** egress **7** leaving, retreat **9** departure **10** retirement, retraction **14** discontinuance

withdrawn 3 shy **5** quiet **8** reserved, retiring, unsocial **9** reclusive **10** unfriendly **11** introverted **15** uncommunicative

wither 4 fade, wilt **5** abash, blast, droop, dry up, shame **7** cut down, mortify, shrivel **9** dehydrate, desiccate, humiliate

withered 3 dry **4** arid, sere **5** dried, faded **6** shrunk, wilted **7** decayed, dried up, drooped, stunned, wizened **9** petrified, shriveled **10** languished

withering 6 biting **7** caustic **8** scathing **9** shrinkage, shrinking, wrinkling **10** shriveling **11** contracting, contraction, devastating

with few words
Latin: 12 paucis verbis

with force and with arms
Latin: 9 vi et armis

with great praise
Latin: 13 magna cum laude

withheld 4 kept **7** checked, forbore, refused, starved **8** kept back **9** boycotted, refrained

with highest praise
Latin: 13 summa cum laude

withhold 4 hide, keep **6** hush up, retain **7** conceal, cover up **8** suppress

withhold from 4 deny **6** refuse

within 2 on **4** into **5** inner **6** during, inside **7** indoors **8** inwardly
combining form: 3 eso **4** endo
prefix: 5 intra

within an inch of 4 near **6** all but, almost, nearly

with-it 7 current **8** up-to-date
French: 9 au courant

with one's own two hands 7 oneself, unaided **10** unassisted

without 4 save **5** minus **6** beyond, except, unless **7** lacking, nowhere, outside, wanting **8** exterior, external, free from, outdoors **9** excepting **10** externally
appointment: 7 sine die
care: 8 sine cure
charge: 4 free **6** gratis **8** sine cure
combining form: 4 ecto
doubt: 9 sine dubio
feet: 4 apod **6** apodal
French: 4 sans
horns: 7 acerous
Latin: 4 sine
law: 8 anarchic
light: 7 aphotic
life: 5 amort **9** inanimate
luster: 3 mat **5** matte
offspring: 9 sine prole
prefix: 2 in
roads: 7 invious
saddles: 8 asellate, bareback
subcalyx leaves: 9 bractless
teeth: 5 morne **8** edentate
this: 7 sine hoc
tongue, teeth, or claws: 5 morne
which not: 10 sine qua non
wings: 7 apteral **8** apterous

without a doubt 6 surely **8** of course **9** certainly **10** absolutely, positively **11** indubitably **12** indisputably **14** unquestionably

without basis 7 unsound **9** unfounded **10** groundless, ungrounded **11** unjustified, unsupported **15** unsubstantiated

without care
French: 9 sans souci

without charge 4 free **10** gratuitous, on the house **13** complimentary
Latin: 6 gratis

without doubt
French: 9 sans doute

without end 7 endless, eternal, forever **8** immortal, infinite, timeless, unending **9** ceaseless, continual, endlessly, eternally, perpetual **10** immortally, infinitely, timelessly, unendingly **11** ceaselessly, continually, everlasting, never-ending **13** everlastingly **14** lasting forever

without equal
French: 10 sans pareil

without error 4 true **5** exact, right **7** correct, perfect, precise, sinless **8** accurate, truthful, unerring **9** faultless **10** infallible

without exception 5 never **6** always, wholly **8** entirely **10** absolutely, completely, invariably, positively

without fear and without reproach
French: 22 sans peur et sans reproche

Without Feathers
author: 10 Woody Allen

without funds 5 broke **6** ruined **8** bankrupt, indigent, strapped, wiped out **9** destitute, flat broke, insolvent, penniless **10** stone broke **12** impoverished

without light 3 dim **4** dark **5** black, dusky, murky, shady **6** opaque **7** obscure, shadowy, stygian, sunless

without limit
Latin: 11 ad infinitum

without limitation 6 wholly **7** totally, utterly **8** entirely **9** endlessly **10** absolutely, completely, definitely, positively, thoroughly **11** boundlessly **13** unequivocally **15** unconditionally
French: 12 carte blanche

without notice 5 ad-lib **9** impromptu **10** improvised **11** extemporary **14** extemporaneous
Latin: 9 extempore

without offspring, without progeny
Latin: 9 sine prole

without the day
Latin: 7 sine die

without which not
Latin: 10 sine qua non

with praise
Latin: 8 cum laude

withstand 4 bear, defy **5** brave **6** endure, resist, suffer **7** weather **8** confront, cope with, tolerate

witless 3 mad **5** crazy **6** insane, stupid **7** fatuous, foolish, unaware **9** slaphappy

witness 3 see **4** mark, note, sign, view **5** proof **6** attend, behold, look on, notice, verify **7** bear out, certify, confirm, endorse, initial, observe **8** attester, attest to, beholder, deponent, document, evidence, looker-on, observer, onlooker, perceive, validate, vouch for **9** establish, spectator, testifier, testimony **10** validation

11 corroborate, countersign **12** authenticate, confirmation, substantiate, verification **13** corroboration, documentation **14** authentication, substantiation

Witness for the Prosecution
director: **11** Billy Wilder
based on play by: **14** Agatha Christie
cast: **11** Tyrone Power **14** Elsa Lanchester **15** Charles Laughton, Marlene Dietrich

wits **4** mind **6** sanity **9** composure **14** coolheadedness

witticism **4** jest, joke, quip **5** sally **7** epigram
French: **6** bon mot **10** jeu d'esprit

witty **5** comic, droll, funny **6** bright, clever, jocose **7** amusing, jocular, waggish **8** humorous, mirthful **9** brilliant, sparkling, whimsical **11** quick-witted **13** scintillating

witty saying **4** jest, quip **6** bon mot **7** epigram **9** witticism **13** clever comment

Witwoud, Sir Wilfull
character in: **16** The Way of the World
author: **8** Congreve

wizard **4** sage, seer, whiz **5** adept, shark **6** expert, genius, oracle **7** diviner, prodigy, wise man **8** conjurer, magician, sorcerer, virtuoso **9** enchanter **10** soothsayer **11** clairvoyant, necromancer

Wizard of Id, The
creator: **10** Johnny Hart **11** Brant Parker
character: **4** King **5** Spook **6** jester, Rodney, Tyrant

Wizard of Oz, The
director: **13** Victor Fleming
author: **10** L Frank Baum
cast: **4** Toto **8** Bert Lahr (Cowardly Lion) **9** Jack Haley (Tin Woodsman), Ray Bolger (Scarecrow) **11** Billie Burke (Good Witch of the North), Frank Morgan (wizard), Judy Garland (Dorothy) **13** Clara Blandick **15** Charley Grapewin **16** Margaret Hamilton (Wicked Witch of the West), The Singer Midgets (Munchkins)
score: **9** E Y Harburg **11** Harold Arlen
remade as: **6** The Wiz
place: **6** Kansas **8** Land of Oz **11** Emerald City
Dorothy wore: **8** red shoes

wizened **3** dry **5** dried **7** dried up **8** shrunken, withered, wrinkled **9** shriveled

WKRP in Cincinnati
character: **10** Andy Travis, Herb Tarlek, Les Nessman **12** Venus Flytrap **13** Arthur Carlson, Dr Johnny Fever **14** Bailey Quarters **15** Jennifer Marlowe
cast: **7** Tim Reid **9** Gary Sandy **10** Gordon Jump **11** Frank Bonner, Jan Smithers **12** Loni Anderson **14** Howard Hesseman, Richard Sanders

wobble **4** reel, sway **5** quake, shake, waver **6** shimmy, teeter, totter **7** quaking, shaking, stagger, swaying **8** wavering **9** shimmying, teetering, tottering **12** unsteadiness

wobbly, Wobbly **5** loose, shaky **7** doubtful **8** hesitant, insecure, unstable, unsteady, wavering **9** quavering, trembling **11** vacillating
union: **17** Industrial Workers

Wodehouse, P G (Pelham Grenville)
author of: **8** Full Moon **14** Thank You Jeeves **15** The Mating Season
character: **6** Jeeves **13** Bertie Wooster

Woden
origin: **10** Anglo-Saxon
chief of: **4** gods

woe **5** agony, gloom, grief, trial, worry **6** misery, sorrow **7** anguish, anxiety, despair, torment, torture, trouble **8** calamity, distress **9** adversity, dejection, heartache, suffering **10** affliction, depression, melancholy, misfortune **11** tribulation **12** wretchedness

woebegone **3** sad **4** glum **6** gloomy **7** doleful, forlorn **8** dejected, funereal, mournful, tortured, troubled, wretched **9** agonizing, anguished, miserable, sorrowful, suffering **10** distressed

woeful **3** bad, sad **5** awful, cruel **6** tragic **7** doleful, painful, unhappy **8** crushing, dreadful, grievous, hopeless, horrible, terrible, unlikely, wretched **9** agonizing, appalling, miserable, sorrowful **10** calamitous, deplorable, depressing, disastrous, lamentable **11** distressing, unpromising **12** catastrophic, heartrending **13** disheartening, heartbreaking

woe to the vanquished
Latin: **9** vae victis

Wofford, Chloe Anthony
real name of: **12** Toni Morrison

Wojtyla, Karol
real name of: **14** Pope John Paul II **18** Archbishop of Krakow

wolf **4** bolt, gulp **5** scarf **6** devour, gobble **7** consume
constellation of: **5** Lupus
group of: **4** pack

Wolf, The
author: **11** Frank Norris

Wolfe, Thomas
author of: **14** The Hills Beyond **16** The Web and the Rock **17** Look Homeward Angel, Of Time and the River **18** You Can't Go Home Again
character: **10** Eugene Gant **12** George Webber

Wolfe, Tom
author of: **11** Radical Chic **13** The Right Stuff **14** The Painted Word **16** The Pump House Gang **21** From Bauhaus to Our House **23** The Bonfire of the Vanities **24** Mau-mauing the Flak Catchers **26** The Electric Kool-Aid Acid Test **43** The Kandy Kolored Tangerine Flake Streamline Baby

Wollstonecraft, Mary
husband: **13** William Godwin
daughter: **25** Mary Wollstonecraft Shelley
author of: **30** A Vindication of the Rights of Women

Wolverine State
nickname of: **8** Michigan

woman **4** girl, lady, maid, wife **5** flame, lover **6** damsel, maiden, matron **7** beloved, darling, dowager, females, fiancee, sweetie **8** ladylove, mistress **9** charwoman, concubine **10** girlfriend, handmaiden, sweetheart, sweetie pie **11** chambermaid, housekeeper, maidservant
French: **5** femme **8** paramour
Latin: **9** inamorata

Woman, first
Scandinavian: **5** Embla

Woman in White, A
author: **13** Wilkie Collins

womanish **7** unmanly **8** feminine, ladylike **9** sissified **10** effeminate

womanlike **8** feminine **10** effeminate

womanly **8** feminine, matronly

Woman of Substance, A
author: **21** Barbara Taylor Bradford

Woman of the Year
director: **13** George Stevens
cast: **10** Fay Bainter **12** Reginald Owen, Spencer Tracy **16** Katharine Hepburn

Woman's Life, A
author: **15** Guy de Maupassant

Women, The
director: **11** George Cukor
based on play by: **15** Clare Boothe Luce
cast: **11** Hedda Hopper **12** Joan Crawford, Joan Fontaine, Marjorie Main, Norma Shearer **15** Paulette Goddard, Rosalind Russell
remade as: **14** The Opposite Sex

Women at Point Sur, The
author: **15** Robinson Jeffers

Women in Love
director: **10** Ken Russell
based on novel by: **10** DH Lawrence
character: **11** Gerald Crich **12** Rupert Birkin **14** Gudrun Brangwen, Ursula Brangwen
cast: **9** Alan Bates **10** Oliver Reed **11** Eleanor Bron **12** Jennie Linden **13** Glenda Jackson
Oscar for: **7** actress (Jackson)

wonder **3** awe **4** gape **5** sight, stare **6** marvel, ponder, rarity **7** miracle **8** cogitate, meditate, question **9** amazement, spectacle, speculate **10** conjecture, phenomenon **11** fascination **12** astonishment, stupefaction

wonder child
German: **10** wunderkind

wonderful **4** fine, good **5** great, super **6** divine, superb, tiptop, unique **7** amazing, capital **8** fabulous, singular, smashing, striking, terrific **9** admirable, excellent, fantastic, marvelous **10** astounding, incredible, miraculous, phenomenal, staggering, surprising **11** astonishing, crackerjack, fascinating, magnificent, sensational, spectacular **13** extraordinary

Wonderland State
nickname of: **5** Maine

wonderstruck **4** agog **6** amazed **8** thrilled **9** astounded, stupefied **10** astonished, enthralled, spellbound **11** dumbfounded **13** flabbergasted

Wonder Woman
character: **9** (Corp) Etta Candy **11** Diana Prince, Joe Atkinson, (Maj) Steve Trevor **13** Gen Blankenship
cast: **11** Lynda Carter **12** Lyle Waggoner **13** Beatrice Colen, Normann Burton **14** Richard Eastham

wont **3** apt, use **4** used, vain **5** habit, haunt, usage **6** custom, desire **8** accustom, inclined, practice **10** accustomed

wonted **3** apt **5** prone **6** likely **7** given to **10** accustomed, habituated

woo **3** sue **5** chase, court **6** cajole, pursue **7** address, entreat, solicit **8** petition **9** importune

wood **3** log **4** bush **5** brake, brush, copse, grove **6** boards, forest, lumber, planks, siding, timber **7** thicket **8** firewood, kindling **9** clapboard, wallboard **10** timberland

Wood, Grant
born: **9** Anamosa IA
artwork: **12** Spring in Town **13** Stone City Iowa **14** American Gothic **15** Woman with Plants **16** Parson Weems' Fable **18** Dinner for Threshers, John B Turner Pioneer **21** Daughters of Revolution

Wood, John, Sr
architect of: **6** Circus (Bath)

Wood, Natalie
real name: **13** Natasha Gurdin
born: **14** San Francisco CA
husband: **12** Robert Wagner
roles: **5** Gypsy **10** Brainstorm **12** The Great Race, The Searchers **13** West Side Story **17** Inside Daisy Clover **18** Rebel Without a Cause, Splendor in the Grass **19** Sex and the Single Girl **23** This Property Is Condemned **25** Love with the Proper Stranger **27** Miracle on Thirty-fourth Street

wooded **5** treed **8** forested

wooden **4** dull **5** frame, rigid, stiff **6** clumsy, vacant **7** awkward, deadpan **8** lifeless, ungainly **9** impassive, unbending **10** inflexible, ungraceful **11** unemotional **14** expressionless

Woodhouse, Emma
character in: **4** Emma
author: **6** Austen

woodland **5** copse, grove, treed **6** forest **7** coppice, thicket **8** forested

wood of life
Latin: **11** lignum vitae

woods
god of: **8** Silvanus, Sylvanus

Woods, Sara
real name: **13** Sara Bowen-Judd
author of: **11** Done to Death **12** My Life Is Done **13** Yet She Must Die **15** A Show of Violence, Knives Have Edges **16** And Shame the Devil **17** The Third Encounter, Trusted Like the Fox **18** Bloody Instructions
character: **15** Anthony Maitland

Woodstock
also called: **11** The Cavalier
author: **14** Sir Walter Scott

Woodstock
director: **15** Michael Wadleigh
cast: **6** The Who **7** Santana **8** Joan Baez **9** Joe Cocker **12** Richie Havens **13** John Sebastian, Ten Years After **17** Jefferson Airplane **19** Crosby Stills and Nash **20** Country Joe and the Fish, Sly and the Family Stone
Oscar for: **11** documentary

Woodward, Bob
author of: **4** Veil **19** All the President's Men (with Carl Bernstein)

Woodward, Joanne
born: **13** Thomasville GA
husband: **10** Paul Newman
roles: **12** A Fine Madness, Rachel Rachel **15** Three Faces of Eve (Oscar) **16** The Long Hot Summer **43** The Effect of Gamma Rays on Man-in-the-Moon Marigolds

woodwind instrument **4** oboe **5** flute **7** bassoon, piccolo **8** clarinet **9** bass flute **10** cor anglais **12** bass clarinet **13** double bassoon

wooer **4** beau, love **5** flame, lover, swain **6** adorer, suitor **7** admirer, courter **8** paramour **10** sweetheart

wool
fabric: **4** felt **5** crepe, llama, serge, tweed, twill **6** alpaca, angora, boucle, covert, faille, melton, vicuna, woolen **7** challis, doeskin, Donegal, worsted **8** cashmere, homespun, shetland **9** Astrakhan, camelhair, gabardine, sharkskin **10** hopsacking **11** Harris tweed, herringbone

Woolf, Virginia
author of: **7** Orlando **8** The Waves, The Years **10** Jacob's Room **11** Mrs Dalloway

14 A Room of One's Own **15** To the Lighthouse
member of: 15 Bloomsbury Group

wool-gather 8 daydream, muse idly

woolly, wooly 5 downy, furry, fuzzy, hairy, sheep, vague **6** fleecy, lanate, lanose **7** blurred, muddled, unclear **8** confused, floccose, peronate **10** flocculent, indistinct **12** disorganized

woozy 4 hazy **5** dizzy, faint, foggy, fuzzy, giddy, shaky **6** punchy **7** muddled **9** befuddled **11** light-headed

word, words 3 vow **4** chat, dirt, news, poop, term **5** edict, order, rumor, set-to, voice **6** advice, avowal, decree, gossip, letter, notice, phrase, pledge, remark, report, ruling, signal **7** command, comment, dictate, dispute, explain, express, hearsay, lowdown, mandate, message, promise, quarrel, summons, tidings **8** argument, audience, bulletin, chitchat, colloquy, decision, describe, dialogue, dispatch, locution, telegram **9** assertion, assurance, bickering, direction, discourse, interview, sobriquet, ultimatum, utterance, wrangling **10** articulate, communique, conference, contention, discussion, expression **11** altercation, appellation, declaration, designation, information, scuttlebutt **12** consultation, intelligence, tittle-tattle **13** communication, pronouncement
French: 9 tete-a-tete

word for word and letter for letter
Latin: 19 verbatim et literatim

wordiness 9 diffusion, prolixity, verbosity **11** diffuseness, profuseness

wording 8 language, phrasing **11** phraseology

wordless 4 dumb, mute **5** tacit **6** silent **8** implicit, taciturn **10** speechless **11** unexpressed

word of honor 3 vow **4** oath **6** pledge **9** assurance

word play 6 banter **7** jesting, kidding
French: 8 badinage, repartee

Words, The
author: 14 Jean-Paul Sartre

Wordsworth, William
author of: 7 Michael **9** Ode to Duty **10** The Prelude **12** Tintern Abbey **14** Lyrical Ballads (with Coleridge) **16** The Ruined Cottage **24** Intimations of Immortality **25** Resolution and Independence
home: 11 Dove Cottage

wordy 5 windy **6** prolix, turgid **7** fustian, gushing, verbose **8** effusive, mumbling **9** bombastic, garrulous, redundant, talkative **10** discursive, loquacious, rhetorical, roundabout **12** tautological **13** grandiloquent

work, works 2 do, go **3** act, job, run, win **4** book, deed, duty, feat, form, gain, line, make, mill, mold, move, shop, song, task, toil, yard **5** beget, cause, chore, craft, enact, labor, opera, piece, plant, shape, slave, solve, sweat, trade **6** drudge, effect, effort, office, output **7** achieve, calling, drawing, execute, exploit, factory, fashion, foundry, innards, insides, operate, perform, produce, product, pursuit, succeed, trouble **8** building, business, concerto, contents, creation, drudgery, endeavor, engender, exertion, function, industry, maneuver, painting, progress, symphony, transmit, vocation **9** originate, sculpture, structure **10** assignment, employment, enterprise, manipulate, occupation, production, profession **11** achievement, composition, performance, transaction
Latin: 4 opus
French: 6 metier

work, artistic or literary
French: 6 oeuvre

workaday 5 plain **6** common **7** humdrum, prosaic, routine **8** ordinary **10** unexciting **11** commonplace

work at 3 try **5** essay **6** tackle **7** attempt **8** endeavor

workbench 5 board, table **7** counter

work conquers all
Latin: 16 labor omnia vincit
motto of: 8 Oklahoma

worker 4 doer, hand **5** grind **6** drudge, toiler **7** artisan, hustler, laborer, plodder **8** achiever, employee, producer **9** craftsman, performer **11** breadwinner, eager beaver, proletarian

work for 6 assist **7** support **8** champion

working 3 job **4** duty, toil **5** labor, tasks **6** action, chores, fluent, usable, useful **8** business, drudgery, employed, exertion, industry, laboring **9** effective, operation, operative, practical **10** employment, occupation, profession **11** assignments, functioning, performance

Working
author: 11 Studs Terkel

working-class 5 labor **8** plebeian **10** blue-collar **11** proletarian

working class 9 commoners, common man **11** blue collars, proletariat
Greek: 9 hoi polloi

workmanlike 5 adept **8** skillful **9** efficient **10** productive

workmanship 5 skill **9** handcraft, handiwork, technique **10** handicraft **11** manufacture **12** construction

work out 5 solve, train **6** figure, reckon **7** compute, resolve **8** exercise, practice **9** ascertain, calculate, determine

Works and Days
author: 6 Hesiod

work saver 9 appliance **11** convenience

work-saving 4 easy **6** simple **9** efficient

worktable 4 desk **5** bench, board, table **7** counter

work together 5 unite **7** pitch in, share in **8** take part **9** cooperate **11** collaborate, participate

work toward 3 try **4** seek **6** aim for **7** attempt **8** aspire to, endeavor, reach for

work up 4 goad, urge **5** upset **6** excite **7** agitate, ferment, provoke

work with 5 coach, drill, teach, train **6** assist **8** exercise, instruct **9** cooperate **11** collaborate

world 3 age, era, orb **4** gobs, lots, star **5** class, Earth, epoch, globe, group, heaps, realm, times **6** domain, nature, oodles, people, period, planet, sphere, system **7** mankind, society **8** creation, division, du-

ration, everyone, humanity, industry, universe **9** everybody, humankind, macrocosm **10** profession
Latin: **6** cosmos
Russian: **3** mir

World According to Garp, The
author: **10** John Irving
director: **13** George Roy Hill
cast: **10** Glenn Close, Hume Cronyn **11** John Lithgow **12** Jessica Tandy, Mary Beth Hurt **13** Robin Williams

World Enough and Time
author: **16** Robert Penn Warren

worldly **5** blase **6** astute, shrewd, urbane **7** callous, earthly, fleshly, knowing, mundane, profane, secular **8** material, physical, temporal **9** corporeal, mercenary **11** experienced, terrestrial **12** cosmopolitan **13** sophisticated

world pain
German: **11** Weltschmerz

world view
German: **11** Weltansicht

world-weary **5** blase, bored, jaded **9** unexcited

worldwide **4** rife **6** global **8** catholic, ecumenic, globular, planetal, sweeping **9** universal

worm **4** edge, inch **5** crawl, creep, steal **6** writhe **7** wriggle **9** penetrate **10** infiltrate
kinds: **4** inch, tape **5** angle, earth

worn **4** weak **5** dingy, drawn, faded, seedy, spent, tired, weary **6** frayed, shabby, wasted **7** abraded, haggard, pinched, rickety, wearied **8** battered, decrepit, dog-tired, drooping, fatigued **9** enfeebled, exhausted **10** threadbare, tumbledown **11** debilitated, dilapidated

worn-out **4** dead, shot **5** spent, tired **6** beat-up, effete, shabby, used-up **7** run-down **9** exhausted **10** threadbare **11** dilapidated **12** deteriorated

worn thin **9** motheaten **10** threadbare **11** dilapidated

worried **6** afraid, scared **7** anxious, fearful **9** concerned **10** distressed **12** apprehensive

worrisome **5** fussy, pesty **6** trying, uneasy, vexing **7** anxious, fretful, irksome **8** annoying **10** bothersome, despairing, disturbing, irritating, tormenting **11** aggravating, troublesome **12** apprehensive

worry **3** vex, woe **4** care, fret, stew **5** agony, beset, dread, grief, harry, upset **6** badger, bother, dismay, harass, hector, misery, pester, plague **7** agitate, agonize, anguish, anxiety, bugaboo, concern, despair, disturb, perturb, problem, torment, trouble **8** distress, vexation **9** misgiving, persecute **10** difficulty, uneasiness **12** apprehension **13** consternation

worsen **4** fail, slip **5** erode, lapse, slide **7** decline **10** degenerate, retrogress **11** deteriorate **12** disintegrate

worsening **7** setback **9** inflaming **10** increasing, regressing, regression **11** aggravating, heightening **12** exacerbating, intensifying **13** retrogressing, retrogression

worship **5** adore, exalt, extol **6** admire, esteem, praise, pray to, revere **7** adulate, glorify, idolize, lionize **8** dote upon, venerate **9** adoration, reverence **10** exaltation, veneration **11** devotionals

worshipful **5** pious **6** devout **8** reverent

worshiping **7** adoring **8** exalting **9** adoration, adulation, adulating, idolizing, reverence **10** exaltation, glorifying, magnifying, venerating, veneration **11** idolization **13** glorification, magnification

worst **3** bad **4** beat, best, rout **5** floor, outdo **6** defeat, lowest, outwit **7** conquer, poorest, triumph **8** inferior, overcome, vanquish **9** discomfit **10** overmaster, unpleasant

worth **3** use **4** cost, good **5** merit, price, value **6** assets, estate, wealth **7** benefit, effects, utility **8** holdings **9** appraisal, resources, valuation **10** importance, usefulness **11** consequence, possessions

worth having **8** valuable **9** desirable

Worthing, Jack
character in: **27** The Importance of Being Earnest
author: **5** Wilde

worthless **6** futile, paltry **7** trivial, useless **8** bootless, piddling, unusable **9** fruitless, meritless, pointless **10** unavailing **11** ineffectual, undeserving, unimportant **12** meretricious, unproductive **13** insignificant **14** good-for-nothing

worthless objects **4** junk **5** trash **7** garbage, rubbish **8** discards **11** odds and ends

worthwhile **4** good **6** usable, useful **8** valuable **9** rewarding **10** beneficial, profitable

worthy **3** fit, VIP **4** good, name **5** moral, noble **6** bigwig, decent, honest, leader, proper **7** big shot, ethical, fitting, notable, upright **8** big wheel, great man, immortal, laudable, luminary, official, reliable, suitable, virtuous **9** admirable, befitting, deserving, dignitary, estimable, excellent, honorable, personage, reputable **10** creditable **11** appropriate, commendable, meritorious, respectable

worthy of imitation **5** model **9** emulative, exemplary

Wotan
origin: **8** Germanic
chief of: **4** gods
corresponds to: **4** Odin **5** Othin

Wouk, Herman
author of: **13** The Winds of War **14** The Caine Mutiny **17** War and Remembrance **19** Marjorie Morningstar
character: **12** Captain Queeg

wound **3** cut **4** gash, harm, hurt, pain, slit, tear **5** slash, sting **6** bruise, damage, grieve, injure, injury, lesion, offend, pierce, trauma **7** anguish, mortify, torment **8** distress, lacerate, vexation **9** contusion **10** affliction, irritation, laceration **11** provocation

wounded **3** cut **4** hurt **6** mauled **7** damaged, injured, pierced, stabbed **8** impaired, ruptured, stricken **11** traumatized

wrack **4** kelp, ruin **5** ruins, trash **6** clouds, refuse **7** destroy, seaweed, torment **8** downfall, eelgrass, wreckage **9** cloud rack **11** destruction, storm clouds

wraith **5** ghost, shade, spook **6** spirit **7** phantom, specter **8** phantasm **10** apparition **15** materialization
Irish: **7** banshee
German: **12** doppelganger
French: **8** revenant

wrangle **4** tiff **5** argue, brawl **6** bicker **7** dispute, quarrel **8** squabble

wrangling **6** strife **7** arguing, discord **8** clashing, friction **9** bickering **10** contention **11** quarrelling

wrap **4** bind, cape, coat, fold, gird, hide, mask, veil, wind

5 cloak, cover, scarf, shawl, stole **6** bundle, clothe, encase, enfold, girdle, jacket, mantle, shroud, swathe **7** conceal, enclose, envelop, sweater **8** surround

wrapper, wrapping paper **4** case **6** casing, jacket, sheath **8** covering, envelope, slipcase **9** container

wrapping **6** caping, hiding **7** veiling **8** cerement, bundling, swathing **9** embracing, packaging, shrouding **10** engrossing, enswathing, enveloping **11** enshrouding, surrounding

wrap up **3** end **4** pack **6** finish, wind up **7** engross, envelop, involve, package **8** bundle up, complete, conclude **9** polish off **11** dress warmly

wrath **3** ire **4** bile, fury, gall, rage **5** anger **6** animus, choler, rancor, spleen **8** vexation **9** animosity, hostility **10** irritation, resentment **11** displeasure, indignation **13** irritableness

wrathful **3** mad **5** angry, irate **6** bitter, raging **7** furious **8** incensed, virulent

wreak **4** vent, work **5** visit **7** execute, indulge, inflict, unleash

wreak vengeance **6** avenge **7** get even, revenge **9** retaliate

wreath **5** crown **6** diadem, laurel **7** chaplet, coronet, festoon, garland
Hawaiian: **3** lei

wreathe **4** bend, coil, wind **5** curve, twist **7** entwine, envelop **8** encircle **10** intertwine, interweave

wreck **3** end **4** mess, raze, ruin **5** break, crash, death, level, ruins, smash, total, upset **6** finish, ravage, wretch **7** breakup, crack-up, destroy, shatter, undoing **8** demolish, derelict **9** devastate, overthrow **10** disruption **11** destruction, devastation, dissolution **12** annihilation

wreckage **4** ruin **5** ruins **6** jetsam **7** flotsam, remains **8** shambles **11** destruction

Wren, P C
author of: **9** Beau Geste

wrench **3** rip **4** jerk, pull, tear, warp **5** force, twist, wrest, wring **6** sprain, strain **7** distort, pervert **12** misrepresent
type: **6** monkey, socket **7** spanner

wrest **3** get, rip **4** earn, gain, grab, jerk, make, pull, take, tear **5** force, glean, twist, wring **6** attain, obtain, secure, wrench **7** achieve, extract, squeeze

wrestle **4** toil **5** labor **6** battle, strive, tussle **7** contend, grapple, scuffle **8** struggle **10** struggling

wrestling
athlete: **8** Dan Gable

wretch **3** cur, pig, rat **4** hobo, waif, worm **5** knave, louse, rogue, swine, tramp **6** misfit, rascal, rotter, varlet **7** castoff, outcast, stinker, villain **8** derelict, scalawag, sufferer, vagabond **9** scoundrel **10** blackguard **11** unfortunate

wretched **3** low **4** base, mean, vile **5** awful, lousy, sorry **6** abject, gloomy, rotten, shabby, sleazy **7** crushed, doleful, forlorn, hapless, pitiful, scruffy, unhappy, worried **8** dejected, downcast, dreadful, hopeless, inferior, pathetic, pitiable, terrible **9** cheerless, depressed, miserable, niggardly, sorrowful, woebegone, worthless **10** abominable, despairing, despicable, despondent, melancholy **11** crestfallen, unfortunate **12** contemptible, disconsolate, disheartened, inconsolable **13** brokenhearted

wretchedness **4** pain **6** misery, sorrow **7** despair, torment, trouble **8** distress, hardship **9** adversity **10** affliction, melancholy, misfortune **11** unhappiness **12** hopelessness

wriggle **5** twist **6** squirm, wangle, writhe **7** meander

Wright, Archibald Lee
real name of: **11** Archie Moore

Wright, Frank Lloyd
architect of: **8** Taliesin (Spring Green WI) **10** Robie House (Chicago) **11** Martin House (Buffalo NY), Unity Church (Oak Park IL) **12** Fallingwater (Kaufmann House Bear Run PA), Taliesin West (near Phoenix AZ) **13** Imperial Hotel (Tokyo) **16** Guggenheim Museum (NYC) **22** Marin County Civic Center (CA) **35** Larkin Company Administration Building (Buffalo NY) **45** S C Johnson and Son Wax Company Administration Center (Racine WI)
style: **6** Modern **7** Organic, Prairie

Wright, Orville and Wilbur
invented: **8** airplane
first plane: **6** Flyer I **9** Kitty Hawk

Wright, Richard
author of: **8** Black Boy **9** Native Son **17** Uncle Tom's Children

wring **4** hurt, pain, rend, stab **5** choke, force, press, twist, wrest **6** coerce, grieve, pierce, sadden, wrench **7** agonize, extract, squeeze, torture **8** compress, distress

wrinkle **4** fold, idea **5** crimp, fancy, pleat, slant, trick **6** crease, device, furrow, gather, notion, pucker, rimple, rumple **7** crumple, gimmick **9** crow's-feet, viewpoint **11** corrugation

wrinkled **3** old **4** aged **5** lined **6** folded, ridged, rucked, rugate, rugose, rugous, seamed **7** creased, crimped, rimpled, rippled, ruckled, rumpled **8** crimpled, furrowed, puckered **9** shriveled

writ **10** court order **11** sealed order **14** mandatory order

write **3** pen **4** copy, show **5** draft **6** author, draw up, record, scrawl **7** compose, dash off, jot down, make out, produce, set down, turn out **8** inscribe, scribble **10** transcribe

write down **3** jot **4** note, post **5** enter **6** record

write in full **5** add to **6** expand, extend, pad out **7** amplify, augment, stretch **9** expatiate

write out **6** expand, extend **7** amplify, enlarge, stretch **8** lengthen

writer **4** hack, poet **6** author, critic, penman, scribe **7** copyist **8** essayist, novelist, reporter, reviewer, scrawler **9** columnist, dramatist, scribbler **10** journalist, librettist, playwright, songwriter **11** penny-a-liner **12** calligrapher, newspaperman **13** correspondent **14** newspaperwoman
French: **11** litterateur

write to **7** address **8** send word **9** drop a line, send a card, send a note **10** correspond **11** send a letter

write-up **4** item **5** piece, story **7** article

write up **5** cover **6** report

writhe **4** jerk **5** flail **6** squirm, thrash, thresh, wiggle **7** contort, wriggle

writing **4** book, play, poem,

tome, work **5** diary, essay, novel, print, story **6** column, letter, report, script, volume **7** article, copying, journal, penning **8** critique, document, drafting, libretto, longhand **9** authoring, composing, editorial, recording **10** inscribing, manuscript, penmanship **11** calligraphy, composition, publication **12** transcribing
Latin: **4** opus

writings
Hebrew: **7** Ketubim

written agreement **6** treaty **7** compact **8** contract

written law
Latin: **10** lex scripta

written-out form **9** extension **12** augmentation **13** amplification

wrong **3** bad, sin **4** awry, bilk, evil, harm, hurt, ruin, vice **5** abuse, amiss, cheat, crime, false, inapt, kaput, unfit **6** faulty, fleece, injure, injury, ruined, sinful, unfair, unjust, untrue, wicked **7** crooked, defraud, illegal, illicit, immoral, inexact, inverse, misdeed, offense, reverse, swindle, unhappy, unsound **8** criminal, dishonor, evil deed, ill-treat, immodest, improper, iniquity, maltreat, mistaken, mistreat, opposite, trespass, unlawful, unseemly, villain **9** dishonest, erroneous, felonious, illogical, incorrect, injustice, unethical, unfitting **10** dishonesty, fallacious, illegality, immorality, inaccurate, indecorous, indelicate, iniquitous, malapropos, mistakenly, sinfulness, unbecoming, unfairness, unsuitable, wickedness, wrongdoing **11** blameworthy, erroneously, incongruous, incorrectly, inexcusable, unbefitting, undesirable, unwarranted **12** dishonorable, inaccurately, infelicitous, unlawfulness **13** inappropriate, reprehensible, transgression, unjustifiable **15** unrighteousness

wrongdoer **5** crook, felon, knave, rogue **6** rascal, sinner **7** culprit, misdoer, villain **8** evildoer, offender **9** miscreant, scoundrel **10** blackguard, delinquent, lawbreaker, malefactor, trespasser **11** perpetrator **12** transgressor

wrongdoing **3** sin **4** evil, vice **5** crime **8** misdeeds **10** misconduct **11** delinquency, malfeasance, misbehavior

wrongful **3** bad **6** unfair, unjust **7** illegal **8** criminal, unlawful **10** iniquitous, inequitable **12** illegitimate
act: **4** tort
dispossession: **6** ouster

wrongheaded **3** wry **8** perverse, stubborn **9** misguided

wrong side out **9** backwards **10** topsy-turvy

wrought **4** made **6** beaten, formed, worked **7** crafted **8** hammered **9** fashioned **11** constructed, handcrafted

wrought-up **7** excited **8** agitated **9** emotional **10** hysterical

wry **3** dry **5** askew, droll **6** bitter, ironic, warped **7** amusing, caustic, crooked, cynical, satiric, twisted **8** perverse, sardonic **9** contorted, distorted, sarcastic

Wunderkind **11** wonder child **12** child prodigy

Wurster, William
architect of: **13** Cowell College (UC Berkeley) **17** Ghirardelli Square (San Francisco CA)

Wuthering Heights
character: **9** Ellen Dean **10** Heathcliff, Mr Lockwood **11** Edgar Linton **14** Isabella Linton **15** Catherine Linton, Frances Earnshaw, Hareton Earnshaw, Hindley Earnshaw **16** Linton Heathcliff **17** Catherine Earnshaw
director: **12** William Wyler
author: **11** Emily Bronte
cast: **10** David Niven **11** Donald Crisp, Flora Robson, Leo G Carroll, Merle Oberon (Cathy) **15** Laurence Olivier (Heathcliff) **19** Geraldine Fitzgerald

Wyatt, James
architect of: **8** Pantheon

Wyoming
abbreviation: **2** WY **3** Wyo
nickname: **8** Equality
capital: **8** Cheyenne
largest city: **6** Casper
others: **4** Cody, Lusk **7** Bighorn, Buffalo, Laramie, Rawlins, Worland **8** Gillette, Greybull, Kemmerer, Riverton, Sheridan, Sundance **11** Rock Springs
feature:
center: **11** Buffalo Bill
dam: **8** Shoshone
fort: **7** Laramie
historical preserve: **11** Fort Bridger
national grassland: **11** Tunder Basin
national monument: **11** Devil's Tower, Fossil Butte
national park: **10** Grand Teton **11** Yellowstone
reservoir: **12** Flaming Gorge
tribe: **4** Crow **5** Kiowa, Sioux **7** Arapaho, Bannock **8** Cheyenne
people: **11** Buffalo Bill **14** Jackson Pollock **16** Nellie Tayloe Ross **18** Francis Emroy Warren
explorer: **6** Colter, Stuart **7** Bridger **10** Bonneville
lake: **7** Jackson **11** Yellowstone
land rank: **5** ninth
mountain: **3** Elk **5** Cloud, Moran **6** Absaro, Hoback, Tetons **7** Bighorn, Fremont, Laramie, Rockies **8** Atlantic, Sheridan **9** Wind River **10** Black Hills **11** Rattlesnake
highest point: **11** Gannett Peak
physical feature: **11** Jackson Hole
basin: **7** Wyoming
cave: **8** Shoshone
hot springs: **11** Thermopolis
plains: **5** Great
river: **4** Bear, Wind **5** Green, Snake **6** Platte, Powder, Tongue **7** Bighorn **8** Cheyenne, Shoshone **10** Sweetwater **11** Yellowstone **12** Belle Fourche
state admission: **11** forty-fourth
state bird: **17** western meadowlark
state flower: **10** painted cup **16** Indian paintbrush
state motto: **11** Equal Rights
state song: **7** Wyoming
state tree: **10** cottonwood

(London) **9** Lee Priory (Kent) **10** Stoke Poges (Buckinghamshire) **13** Fonthill Abbey (Wiltshire) **14** Dodington House (Gloucestershire) **15** Heveningham Hall (Suffolk) **16** Sandleford Priory (Berkshire)
style: 13 Gothic Revival

Wyatt, Jane
born: 9 Campgaw NJ
roles: 9 Boomerang **11** Lost Horizon **15** Father Knows Best **17** Great Expectations **19** Gentleman's Agreement **21** None But the Lonely Heart

Wyatt Earp, The Life and Legend of
character: 10 Morgan Earp, Virgil Earp **11** Ben Thompson, Doc Holliday **12** Bat Masterson, Bill Thompson **13** Old Man Clanton
cast: 9 Hal Baylor **10** Denver Pyle, Dirk London, Hugh O'Brien **12** John Anderson **13** Douglas Fowley **14** Trevor Bardette **20** Mason Alan Dinehart III
setting: 8 OK Corral **9** Dodge City, Ellsworth, Tombstone
Wyatt's pistols: 15 Buntline Special

Wyeth, Andrew Newell
born: 2 PA **10** Chadds Ford
father: 7 N C Wyeth
artwork: 9 Grape Wine, River Cove **12** Nick and Jamie **14** Christina Olson, Distant Thunder **15** Christina's World **22** Winter Nineteen Forty-six

Wyler, William
director of: 6 Ben Hur (Oscar) **7** Jezebel **9** Dodsworth, Funny Girl, The Letter **10** Mrs Miniver (Oscar), The Heiress, These Three **12** Roman Holiday **14** The Little Foxes **15** Counsellor-at-Law **16** Wuthering Heights **18** Friendly Persuasion **22** The Best Years of Our Lives (Oscar)

Wylie, Philip
author of: 13 Opus Twenty-one **19** A Generation of Vipers

Wyman, Jane
real name: 14 Sarah Jane Fulks
born: 10 St Joseph MO
husband: 12 Ronald Reagan
daughter: 13 Maureen Reagan
son: 13 Michael Reagan
roles: 5 So Big **9** Pollyanna **11** Falcon Crest, The Blue Veil, The Yearling **13** Johnny Belinda (Oscar) **14** Angela Channing, The Lost Weekend **17** The Glass Menagerie **20** Magnificent Obsession

Wyndham, John
real name: 16 John Beynon Harris
author of: 14 The Kraken Wakes **15** Consider Her Ways **17** The Midwich Cuckoos, Trouble with Lichen **19** The Day of the Triffids

Wyoming ***see box***

Wyss, Johann Rudolf
author of: 22 The Swiss Family Robinson
adaptation of: **14** Robinson Crusoe

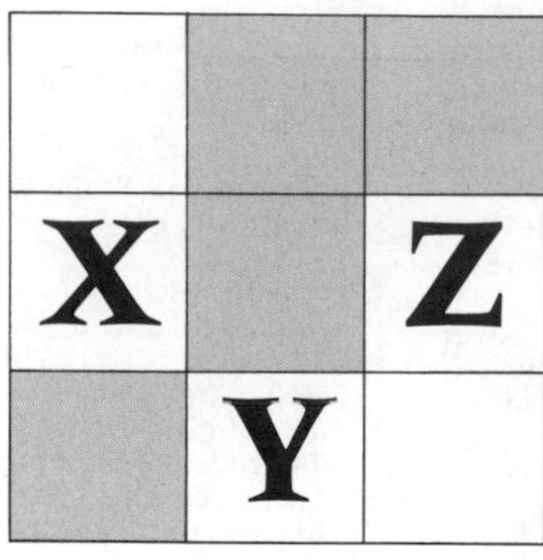

Xanthippe, Xantippe 3 hag **4** fury **5** scold, shrew, vixen **6** dragon, virago **7** scolder **8** spitfire **9** termagant
husband: 8 Socrates

Xanthus and Balius
horses of: 8 Achilles
trait: 8 immortal

Xenia
epithet of: 6 Athena
means: 10 hospitable

Xenoclea
form: 9 priestess

xenon
chemical symbol: 2 Xe

xenophobia
fear of: 9 strangers

Xerxes *see* **9** Ahasuerus

x-ray 9 radiogram **10** radiograph **13** roentgenogram **14** roentgenograph

X-ray tube
invented by: 8 Coolidge

Xuthus
father: 6 Hellen
mother: 6 Orscis
wife: 6 Creusa
son: 3 Ion **7** Achaeus

yacht 4 boat, race, sail, ship, yawl **5** ketch, sloop **6** cruise, cutter **7** catboat **8** schooner
race: 11 America's Cup

yachting
athlete: 9 Ted Turner **11** Lowell North

yahoo 4 lout **5** brute, yokel **7** lowbrow **9** barbarian, ignoramus, vulgarian

Yahoos
fictional people in: 16 Gulliver's Travels
author: 5 Swift

Yahweh 3 God **4** Lord **5** Jahve, Jahwe, Yahve **6** Author, I am I am, Jahveh **7** Creator, Eternal, Jehovah **8** Absolute, Almighty, Infinite
component: 2 he **3** yod, vav
pronunciation: 6 Adonai, Elohim **9** forbidden
transliteration: 4 YHVH

Yale, Linus, Jr
invented: 12 cylinder lock **27** dial-operated combination lock

yam 9 Dioscorea **14** Ipomoea batatas
varieties: 4 wild **5** Negro, water, white **6** Attoto, potato, yellow **7** Chinese **11** sweet potato

Yamasaki, Minoru
architect of: 14 St Louis Airport (MO) **16** World Trade Center (NYC) **21** Woodrow Wilson Building (Princeton NJ)

yammer 3 cry **4** carp, harp, howl, wail, yell **5** whine **7** grumble, whimper **8** complain

yank 3 tug **4** jerk, pull **5** pluck, wrest **6** snatch, wrench **7** draw out, extract, pull out

Yankee, Yank 2 GI **5** teddy **6** gringo **8** American, doughboy **10** Northerner
Spanish: 6 yanqui

Yankee Doodle Dandy
director: 13 Michael Curtiz
cast: 10 Joan Leslie **11** James Cagney (George M Cohan) **12** Irene Manning, Walter Huston
Oscar for: 5 actor (Cagney)

yanqui 6 Yankee **9** US citizen

Yaounde
capital of: 8 Cameroon

yap 3 yip **4** blab, gush, rave, talk, yawp, yelp **5** scold **6** babble, gabble, gossip, jabber, rave on, tattle **7** blather, chatter, lecture, palaver, prattle **8** complain, converse

Yaqui
language family: 6 Cahita
location: 6 Mexico, Sonora **7** Arizona

yard 4 lawn **5** close, court **6** garden **7** confine, grounds, pasture **8** compound **9** enclosure, three feet
abbreviation: 2 yd

yardbird 3 con **5** felon **7** convict **8** prisoner

yard goods 5 cloth **6** fabric **8** material, textiles

Yard of Sun
author: 14 Christopher Fry

yardstick 4 rule **7** measure **8** standard **9** criterion

Yaren District
capital of: 5 Nauru

yarn 4 tale **5** story **7** account **8** anecdote **9** adventure, narrative **10** experience

Yastrzemski, Carl
nickname: 3 Yaz
sport: 8 baseball
team: 12 Boston Red Sox

Yates, Peter
director of: 7 Bullitt **12** Breaking Away

yawn 3 gap **4** bore, gape **5** chasm **8** open wide, oscitate

yawp 4 roar, yelp **5** noise **6** clamor, squawk, yammer

Yaz
nickname of: 15 Carl Yastrzemski

Yazoo
author: 12 Willie Morris

year, years **3** age, era **4** time **5** cycle, epoch **6** period
abbreviation: **2** yr

Yearling, The
director: **13** Clarence Brown
author: **22** Marjorie Kinnan Rawlings
cast: **9** Jane Wyman **10** Chill Wills **11** Gregory Peck **14** Claude Jarman Jr
character: **9** Ora Baxter **10** Jody Baxter **11** Oliver Hutto, Penny Baxter **12** Grandma Hutto **14** Twink Weatherby **19** Fodder-Wing Forrester

Year of Living Dangerously, The
director: **9** Peter Weir
cast: **9** Linda Hunt (Billy Kwan), Mel Gibson **15** Sigourney Weaver
setting: **7** Jakarta
Oscar for: **17** supporting actress (Hunt)

year of wonders
Latin: **14** annus mirabilis

yearn **4** ache, long, pine, sigh, want, wish **5** crave **6** hanker, hunger, thirst **8** languish

yearning **3** yen **4** ache, want, wish **5** fancy **6** desire, hunger, thirst **7** craving, longing, passion **9** hankering **10** aspiration **11** inclination

Yeats, William Butler
author of: **7** A Vision **8** The Tower **9** Last Poems **14** Leda and the Swan **15** The Winding Stair **18** Sailing to Byzantium **19** Among School Children, The Wild Swans at Coole **21** Easter Nineteen Sixteen **22** The Lake Isle of Innisfree **29** An Irish Airman Foresees His Death

yegg **6** bomber **9** cracksman **11** safecracker

yell **3** boo, cry **4** bawl, hoot, howl, roar, yowl **5** cheer, hollo, shout, whoop **6** bellow, clamor, cry out, holler, hurrah, huzzah, outcry, scream, shriek, squall, squeal **7** screech

yellow **4** gold **5** blond, lemon, ocher **6** afraid, canary, craven, flaxen **7** chicken, fearful, saffron **8** cowardly, timorous **10** frightened **12** apprehensive, fainthearted **13** pusillanimous **14** chickenhearted

yellow-belly **6** coward **7** caitiff, chicken, dastard **8** poltroon

Yellowhammer State
nickname of: **7** Alabama

yellowish **4** buff **5** blond, cream **6** blonde, creamy, flaxen

Yemen, North
other name: **4** Sana
capital/largest city: **4** Sana **5** Sanaa
others: **4** Moka, Taiz **5** Dahhi, Damar, Jibla, Mocha, Mukha, Taizz, Umram **7** Hodeida, Hudayda
monetary unit: **4** fils, rial **5** riyal
island: **5** Zugar **6** Hanish
highest point: **6** Shuayb
river: **5** Abrad, Zabid **6** al-Jawf, Surdud
sea: **3** Red
physical feature:
desert: **10** Rub al Khali
gulf: **4** Aden
lowlands: **6** Tihama
peninsula: **7** Arabian
strait: **11** Bab el Mandeb
people: **4** Arab **5** Zaidi **6** Shafai, Yemeni **8** Yemenite
leader: **16** Ali Abdallah Saleh **19** Abd al-Aziz Abd al-Ghani
language: **6** Arabic
religion: **5** Islam
place:
ruins: **5** Marib
feature:
dagger: **7** jambiya
king: **4** imam
kingdom: **4** Saba **5** Sheba **11** Arabia Felix
tree: **3** fig **5** carob, mango, myrrh
food:
coffee: **5** mocha

Yellow Kid, The
creator: **10** R F Outcault
trademark: **10** nightshirt
place: **5** slums **11** Hogan's Alley
coined term: **16** yellow journalism
first: **10** comic strip

yelp **3** yap, yip **4** bark, howl **5** shout **6** clamor, holler, scream, shriek, squeal **7** screech

Yemen, North *see box*

Yemen, South *see box*

yen **4** ache, long, pine, sigh, want, wish **5** crave, fancy, yearn **6** aching, desire, hanker, hunger, relish, thirst **7** craving, longing, passion **8** appetite, languish, yearning **9** hankering **10** aspiration **11** inclination

Yemen, South
capital: **4** Aden **14** Madinat al-Shaab
largest city: **4** Aden
others: **5** Ahwar, Shihr, Tarim **6** Balhaf, Damqut, Seiyun, Shabwa, Shibam, Zamakh **7** Mukalla
monetary unit: **4** fils **5** dinar
island: **5** Perim **7** Kamaran, Socotra
mountain: **7** Djehaff
highest point: **6** Thamir
river: **4** Bana **6** Tibban **7** Masilah **9** Hadramaut
sea: **6** Indian **7** Arabian
physical feature:
desert: **10** Rub al Khali **12** Empty Quarter
gulf: **4** Aden
peninsula: **7** Arabian
valley: **9** Hadramawt
people: **4** Arab
language: **6** Arabic
religion: **5** Islam
feature:
animal: **4** ibex, oryx
clothing: **4** futa

yenta **3** hen **6** gossip **8** busybody **12** blabbermouth

Yentl
director: **15** Barbra Streisand
based on story by: **19** Isaac Bashevis Singer
cast: **13** Mandy Patinkin **15** Barbra Streisand

Yeobright, Thomasin and Clym
characters in: **17** Return of the Native
author: **5** Hardy

yeoman **4** chap, exon **5** churl, clerk, swain **6** farmer, fellow **7** granger, plowman, servant **8** graycoat, retainer **9** beefeater **10** freeholder **12** petty officer

Yerby, Frank
author of: **8** Fair Oaks **10** Health Card **11** Griffin's Way **12** Pride's Castle **16** The Foxes of Harrow **21** Hail the Conquering Hero

yes **3** aye, yea **4** amen, okay, true **5** truly **6** assent, indeed, it is so, just so, really, so be it, surely, verily **7** consent, exactly, granted, no doubt **8** approval, of course, to be sure **9** agreement, assuredly, certainly, doubtless, precisely **10** acceptance, positively **11** af-

firmation, undoubtedly **12** acquiescence, emphatically **13** affirmatively, authorization
French: 3 oui
German: 2 ja
Spanish: 2 si

yesterday 7 the past **10** bygone days, days of yore, olden times, time gone by **11** former times **13** the recent past **14** the good old days **17** the day before today **22** on the day preceding today

yet 3 but **4** also, even, then, up to **5** again, still, while, until **6** no less, though **7** besides, earlier, even now, further, however, thus far **8** although, hitherto, moreover **9** presently **10** eventually, ultimately **12** nevertheless **15** notwithstanding

yew 5 Taxus
varieties: 4 plum **5** Irish **6** golden **7** Chinese, English, Florida, Western **8** American, Japanese, Southern **11** Chinese plum, Plum-fruited **12** Japanese plum, Prince Albert **14** Harrington plum

Yggdrasil
also: 9 Iggdrasil
origin: 12 Scandinavian
kind of tree: 12 evergreen ash
roots: 5 three
binds: 6 Asgard **7** Midgard **8** Niflheim **10** Mithgarthr

yield 3 pay, sag **4** bear, crop, earn, gain, give **5** beget, break, burst, defer, droop, forgo, grant, spawn, split, waive **6** accede, cave in, give in, give up, kowtow, render, return, submit, supply **7** bow down, concede, forbear, furnish, give way, harvest, payment, premium, produce, product, provide, revenue, succumb, truckle **8** collapse, cry uncle, earnings, generate, interest, proceeds, renounce **9** acquiesce, gleanings, procreate, surrender **10** capitulate, relinquish

yielding 3 lax **4** soft **6** ceding, spongy **7** sagging **8** flexible, obedient **9** compliant **11** complaisant **13** accommodating

Yigdal 22 Jewish liturgical prayer
literally: 12 becomes great

Yizkor 33 Jewish service to commemorate the dead
literally: 9 be mindful

Ymir
origin: 12 Scandinavian
progenitor of: 6 giants
earth made from: 5 flesh
water made from: 5 blood
heavens made from: 5 skull

yogi 5 Hindu **6** mystic **7** ascetic

Yogi Bear
creator: 12 Hanna-Barbera
character: 6 BooBoo
setting: 14 Jellystone Park

yoke 3 tax **4** bond, join, link, load, pair, span, team **5** brace, clasp, hitch, trial, unite **6** attach, burden, collar, couple, fasten, strain, weight **7** bondage, coupler, harness, serfdom, slavery **8** distress, pressure, troubles **9** servitude, thralldom, vassalage **10** oppression **11** enslavement, tribulation

yokel 4 clod, hick, rube **7** bumpkin, hayseed, peasant, plowboy **10** clodhopper, provincial

yolk 6 yellow

yonder 3 yon **5** there **6** far-off **7** faraway, farther, thither

Yorick
skull in: 6 Hamlet
author: 11 Shakespeare

Yorick, Mr
character in: 14 Tristram Shandy
author: 6 Sterne

York, Michael
born: 6 Fulmer **7** England
roles: 6 Tybalt **7** Cabaret **11** Lost Horizon **14** Four Musketeers, Romeo and Juliet, The Forsyte Saga **15** Three Musketeers **19** The Island of Dr Moreau **24** The Last Remake of Beau Geste

York, Susannah
real name: 23 Susannah Yolande Fletcher
born: 6 London **7** England
roles: 5 Freud **6** Images **8** Jane Eyre, Tom Jones **12** The Awakening
author of: 18 In Search of Unicorns

Yossarian
character in: 14 Catch-Twenty-two
author: 6 Heller

You Asked for It
host: 8 Art Baker **9** Jack Smith

You Bet Your Life
host: 11 Groucho Marx
announcer: 14 George Fenneman

You Can't Go Home Again
author: 11 Thomas Wolfe
character: 10 Esther Jack **11** Lloyd McHarg **12** George Webber **13** Else von Kohler **14** Foxhall Edwards

You Can't Take It With You
author: 8 Moss Hart **14** George S Kaufman
director: 10 Frank Capra
cast: 10 Jean Arthur, Mischa Auer **12** Edward Arnold, James Stewart **15** Lionel Barrymore
Oscar for: 7 picture **8** director

young 3 cub, pup **4** baby, kids **5** child, issue, minor, whelp **6** boyish, callow, junior, kitten, youths **7** budding, girlish, growing, progeny, puerile, teenage **8** childish, children, immature, juvenile, underage, youthful **9** beardless, infantile, juveniles, offspring, teenagers **10** adolescent, descendant, sophomoric, youngsters **11** adolescents, undeveloped **13** inexperienced
god of: 7 Angus Og
goddess of: 4 Hebe

Young, Chic
creator/artist of: 7 Blondie

Young, Denton True
nickname: 2 Cy **7** Cyclone
sport: 8 baseball
position: 7 pitcher
team: 12 Boston Braves, Boston Red Sox **16** Cleveland Indians, St Louis Cardinals

Young, Loretta
real name: 13 Gretchen Young
husband: 12 Grant Withers
roles: 13 Cause for Alarm **14** The Bishop's Wife **15** Come to the Stable **18** The Farmer's Daughter (Oscar) **20** Rachel and the Stranger

Young, Robert
born: 9 Chicago IL
roles: 10 Relentless **11** H M Pulham Esq **13** Marcus Welby M D **15** Father Knows Best **16** Strange Interlude

Young Adventure
author: 19 Stephen Vincent Benet

Young Frankenstein
director: 9 Mel Brooks
cast: 8 Teri Garr **10** Gene Wilder, Peter Boyle **11** Gene Hackman **12** Madeline Kahn, Marty Feldman **14** Cloris Leachman
score: 10 John Morris

young girl
French: 10 jeune fille

young lady
German: 8 fraulein

Young Lonigan
author: 13 James T Farrell

Young Manhood of Studs Lonigan
author: **13** James T Farrell

youngster **3** boy, kid, tot **4** baby, girl **5** child, minor, youth **7** progeny **8** juvenile, teenager **9** fledgling, offspring **10** adolescent

young Turks **6** rebels **8** radicals, upstarts **9** activists **10** insurgents **15** revolutionaries

young woman
French: **10** demoiselle

you're welcome
German: **5** bitte

Your Show of Shows
regular: **9** Bill Hayes, Jerry Ross, Sid Caesar **10** Carl Reiner **11** Imogene Coca **12** Howard Morris, Nellie Fisher **13** James Starbuck, Robert Merrill **16** Marguerite Piazza

youth **3** boy, kid, lad **4** kids **5** bloom, child, minor, prime, teens **6** heyday **7** boyhood **8** children, girlhood, juvenile, minority, teenager **9** child-

Yugoslavia
other name: **8** Dalmatia **34** Kingdom of the Serbs Croats and Slovenes
capital/largest city: **7** Beograd **8** Belgrade
others: **3** Nis **4** Pola, Pula, Savo, Zara **5** Agram, Bosna, Budva, Fiume, Kotor, Pirot, Rieka, Rtanj, Senta, Split, Uskub, Zadar **6** Bitola, Bitolj, Ca Haro, Maglaj, Morava, Mostar, Osijek, Prilep, Ragusa, Rijeka, Skopje, Trogir, Tuzlar, Vardar, Varsac, Vixoco, Zagreb **7** Cetinje, Laibach, Maribor, Novisad, Skoplje, Spalato **8** Monastir, Pristina, Sarajevo, Subotica, Titograd **9** Banja Luka, Dubrovnik, Ljubljana, Podgorica, Smederevo **10** Mostarnish
division: **6** Bosnia, Serbia **7** Croatia **8** Crna Goro, Slovenia **9** Macedonia, Vojvodina, Voyvodina **10** Montenegro **11** Hercegovina, Herzegovina **14** Kosovo-Metohija
measure: **3** oka, rif **4** akov, ralo **5** donum, khvat, lanaz, plaze, stopa **6** motyka, ralico **9** danoranja
monetary unit: **4** para **5** dinar
weight: **3** oka **5** dramm, tovar, wagon **7** satlijk
island: **3** Rab **4** Arbe, Brac, Cres, Hvar, Pago **5** Mljet, Solta, Susac, Susak **7** Korcula
lake: **4** Bled **5** Ohrid **6** Prespa **7** Ochrida, Scutari
mountain: **5** Karst **6** Balkan **7** Rhodope **8** Crna Gora, Durmitor **9** Sar-Pindus **10** Karawanken
Alps: **6** Carnic, Julian **7** Dinaric **9** Slovenian **16** Northern Albanian
highest point: **7** Triglav
river: **3** Una **4** Drim, Drin, Ibar, Krka, Kupa, Sava, Tisa **5** Anube, Bosna, Cazma, Drava, Drina, Raska, Tamis, Timok, Tisza, Vrbas **6** Danube, Morava, Vardar, Velika **7** Neretva **9** Vojvodina
sea: **8** Adriatic
physical feature:
bay: **5** Kotor
cave: **8** Postojna
channel: **7** Narento
gulf: **5** Kotor **7** Kvarner, Trieste
hot springs: **16** Krapinske Toplice
peninsula: **6** Balkan **7** Istrian
people: **4** Serb, Slav **5** Croat **7** Slovene **8** Albanian **10** Macedonian **11** Montenegrin
author: **6** Andric, Djilas, Krleza **7** Dedijer
leader: **4** Tito **5** Dusan, Pasic **6** Djilas **7** Nemanja **9** Obrenovic **13** Mikhailovitch
ruler: **5** Peter **9** Hapsburgs **12** Ottoman Turks
sculptor: **9** Mestrovic
language: **7** Bosnian, Slovene **8** Albanian, Croatian **9** Hungarian, Slovenian **10** Macedonian **11** Montenegrin **13** Herzegovinian, Serbo-Croatian
alphabet: **5** Latin **8** Cyrillic
religion: **5** Islam **13** Roman Catholic **15** Eastern Orthodox, Serbian Orthodox
place:
amphitheater: **4** Pula
bridge: **9** Stari Most
fortress: **10** Kalemedgan
monastery: **8** Sopocani
mosque: **6** Begova **15** Bajrakli Dzamija
ruins: **14** Hadrian's Palace
square: **8** Republic
feature:
coffee house: **7** kafanas
fields: **5** polje
military governor: **7** vojvodi
musical instrument: **5** gusla
poems: **5** pesme
slippers: **6** op anki
food:
dessert: **4** pita
drink: **5** rakia **6** rakija **7** maraska **9** slivovitz **10** sljivovice **13** Turkish coffee
meat: **7** shaslik **8** cevapici **10** culbastija
soup: **6** corbas

hood, fledgling, juveniles, schoolboy, stripling, teenagers, youngster **10** adolescent, pubescence, youngsters **11** adolescence, adolescents

youthful **5** fresh, young **6** boyish, callow **7** girlish, puerile, teenage **8** childish, immature, juvenile **10** adolescent, sophomoric **12** enthusiastic, lighthearted **13** inexperienced

yowl **3** bay, cry **4** bawl, roar, wail, yelp **5** shout, whine **6** bellow, holler, scream, shriek, squeal **7** screech **9** caterwaul

yucca
varieties: **4** blue **6** banana

9 San Angelo, spineless **11** twisted-leaf

Yugoslavia ***see box, p. 1089***

Yuit *see* **6** Eskimo

Yukon Territory
border: **6** Alaska **15** British Columbia, Selwyn Mountains **18** Mackenzie Mountains
capital: **10** Whitehorse
country: **6** Canada
event: **8** gold rush (1897)
Indian: **4** Dene **6** Eskimo **7** Kutchin **8** Loucheux **9** Athabasca
lake: **6** Kluane **9** Great Bear
mineral: **4** gold **6** silver
mountain: **3** Joy **5** Logan **6** Harper **7** Kennedy **8** Campbell
region: **8** Klondike
river: **5** Pelly **9** Porcupine
sea: **8** Beaufort
town: **4** Elsa, Faro, Mayo, Snag **5** Rocky **6** Dawson **8** Franklin, Wernecke **9** Mackenzie

yule **4** Noel **9** Christmas

Yule, Joe, Jr
real name of: **12** Mickey Rooney

Yuman
tribe: **6** Mohave, Mojave **8** Hualapai

Zachariah
father: **4** Babi, Elam **9** Barachias
wife: **9** Elizabeth
son: **3** Abi **14** John the Baptist
succeeded: **8** Jeroboam
visitor: **7** Gabriel

zaddik **14** virtuous person **15** righteous person

Zadkine, Ossip
born: **6** Russia **8** Smolensk
artwork: **4** Stag **6** Christ **7** Orpheus **9** Musicians **10** The Prophet **13** Woman with a Fan **14** Mother and Child **16** The Destroyed City

Zadok
father: **5** Baana, Immer **6** Ahitub
son: **7** Shallum
daughter: **7** Jerusha
served: **5** David

zaftig **5** buxom, plump **6** bosomy

Zagreus
form: **5** child, deity
father: **4** Zeus
mother: **6** Semele **10** Persephone

Zaire ***see box***

Zambia ***see box***

zany **3** nut **4** wild **5** balmy, batty, booby, buffo, clown, comic, crazy, cutup, daffy, dizzy, goofy, inane, nutty, silly, wacky **6** jester, nitwit, screwy, weirdo **7** buffoon, half-wit, lunatic **8** bonehead, clownish, imbecile, lunkhead, numskull **9** blockhead, eccentric, harlequin, ludicrous, pantaloon, simpleton, slapstick **10** nincompoop, noodlehead, outlandish **11** nonsensical person
French: **7** farceur

Zapotec
language family: **5** Otomi **6** mixtec
location: **6** Mexico, Oaxaca

zapped **5** drunk **6** killed, soused, wasted, zonked **7** smashed **9** destroyed, plastered **10** inebriated

Zaire
other name: **5** Congo **12** Belgian Congo **13** Congo-Kinshasa **17** Congo-Leopoldville
capital/largest city: **8** Kinshasa
others: **4** Baya, Boma, Lebo **5** Aketi, Ilebo **6** Banana, Kamina, Kasaji, Kikwit, Matadi, Sandoa **7** Butembo, Kananga, Kolwezi **8** Bakwanga, Yangambi **9** Kisangani **10** Lubumbashi, Luluabourg, Mutshatsha **12** Port-Francqui, Stanleyville **14** Elisabethville
school: **5** Zaire **8** Lovanium
division: **4** Kivu **5** Kasai, Shaba **7** Equator, Katanga **8** Oriental
monetary unit: **5** zaire **6** makuta
lake: **4** Kivu **5** Mweru, Tumba **6** Albert, Edward, Upemba **9** Mai-Ndombe **10** Tanganyika
mountain: **7** Crystal, Mitumba, Virunga **9** Ruwenzori **10** Nyaragongo **18** Mountains of the Moon
highest point: **10** Margherita
river: **4** Ruki, Uele **5** Congo, Dengu, Ibina, Kasai, Lindi, Zaire **6** Likati, Lomami, Lukuga, Ubangi **7** Aruwimi, Lualaba, Lulonga
sea: **8** Atlantic
physical feature:
falls: **4** Kivu **6** Tshopo **7** Stanley
forest: **5** Ituri
valley: **9** Great Rift
people: **4** Kuba, Luba, Yaka **5** Bantu, Bashi, Bemba, Kongo, Lulue, Lunda, Mongo, Pygmy **6** Azande, Baluba, Watusi **7** Bakongo, Nilotes, Tshokwe **8** European, Mangbetu, Sudanese
explorer: **3** Cao **7** Stanley
leader: **6** Mobutu (Sese Seko) **7** Lumumba, Tshombe **8** Kasavubu
ruler: **7** Belgium, Leopold
language: **5** Bantu **6** French **7** Chiluba, Kikongo, Lingala, Swahili **8** Sudanese, Tshiluba
religion: **5** Islam **7** animism, Kimbang **10** Protestant **13** Roman Catholic
place:
dam: **4** Inga **9** Le Marinee **10** Del Commune
national park: **6** Albert, Upemba **7** Garamba
feature:
animal: **5** hyena, okapi **7** giraffe, gorilla **10** rhinoceros
fish: **11** electric eel

Zambia
other name: **16** Northern Rhodesia
capital/largest city: **6** Lusaka
others: **4** Kafu **5** Choma, Isoka, Kabwe, Kitwe, Mansa, Mbala, Mongu, Mpika, Mumba, Ndola **6** Mwenda **7** Chipata, Luapula, Mankoya **8** Balovale, Chingola, Luanshya, Mazabuka, Mufulira, Mulobezi **11** Livingstone
division: **7** Puapula **10** Copperbelt **11** Barotseland
monetary unit: **5** ngwee **6** kwacha
lake: **5** Mweru **6** Kariba **9** Bangweulu **10** Tanganyika
mountain: **8** Muchinga
highest point: **12** Mafinga Hills
river: **5** Congo, Kafue **7** Luangwa, Luapula, Zambezi **8** Chambezi **9** Chambeshi
physical feature:
cave: **5** Nsalu **14** Chifabwa Stream
falls: **7** Kalambo **8** Victoria
gorge: **6** Kariba
plateau: **7** Zambian
swamp: **7** Lukanga **9** Bangweulu **12** Mweru Wantipa
valley: **8** Chambezi **9** Great Rift
people: **4** Lozi **5** Bantu, Bemba, Ngoni, Tonga
developer: **6** Rhodes
explorer: **11** Livingstone
hero: **11** Chitimukulu
leader: **6** Kaunda
language: **4** Lozi **5** Bemba, Lunda, Tonga **6** Luvale, Nyanja **7** English **9** Afrikaans
religion: **5** Hindu, Islam **7** animism **10** Protestant **13** Roman Catholic
place:
botanical garden: **10** Munda Wanga
dam: **5** Kafue **6** Kariba
game reserve: **6** Valley
library: **20** Hammerskjold Memorial
museum: **11** Livingstone
national park: **5** Kafue, Sumbu **12** South Luangwa
feature:
canoe: **10** nalikwanda
king: **7** litunga
king's aide: **5** sungu, twite **8** inabanza
taxi: **6** zamcab

11 annihilated, intoxicated

zeal **4** fire, zest **5** ardor, gusto, verve, vigor **6** fervor, relish **7** passion **8** devotion, industry **9** animation, eagerness, intensity, vehemence **10** enthusiasm, fanaticism, fierceness, intentness **11** earnestness

zealot **3** fan, nut **4** buff **5** bigot, crank **6** pusher **7** devotee, fanatic, hustler **8** believer, champion, crackpot, go-getter, live wire, partisan **9** extremist **10** enthusiast

zealous **5** eager, rabid **6** ardent, fervid, fierce, gung ho, raging, raving **7** devoted, earnest, fanatic, fervent, intense **8** animated, vehement, vigorous **10** passionate **11** impassioned, industrious **12** enthusiastic

Zebedee
wife: **6** Salome
son: **4** John **5** James

Zeboim
destroyed with: **5** Admah, Sodom **8** Gomorrah

Zebulun
father: **5** Jacob
mother: **4** Leah
brother: **3** Dan, Gad **4** Levi **5** Asher, Judah **6** Joseph, Reuben, Simeon **8** Benjamin, Issachar, Naphtali
sister: **5** Dinah
descendant of: **10** Zebulunite

Zechariah
father: **5** Bebai, Hosah **6** Jehiel, Pashur **7** Isshiah **8** Jehoiada, Jonathan **9** Berechiah **11** Jeberechiah, Meshelemiah
grandfather: **4** Iddo
mother: **6** Merari
son: **8** Jahaziel
daughter: **6** Abijah

Zeffirelli, Franco
director of: **14** Romeo and Juliet **19** The Taming of the Shrew **20** Brother Sun Sister Moon

Zeitgeist **18** the spirit of the time

Zelos
origin: **5** Greek
personifies: **4** zeal **9** emulation
father: **11** Titan Palles
mother: **4** Styx
brother: **3** Bia **6** Cratus
sister: **4** Nike

Zemeckis, Robert
director of: **15** Back to the Future **17** Romancing the Stone

zenith **4** acme, apex, best, peak **6** apogee, climax, summit, vertex **7** maximum **8** pinnacle **11** culmination

Zenobia (Zeena)
character in: **10** Ethan Frome
author: **7** Wharton

Zephaniah
father: **8** Masseiah
son: **3** Hen **6** Josiah
succeeded: **8** Jehoiada
deathplace: **6** Riblah

zephyr **8** west wind **9** puff of air **10** gentle wind **11** breath of air, light breeze

Zephyrus
personifies: **8** west wind
father: **8** Astraeus
mother: **3** Eos
loved: **10** Hyacinthus
son: **6** Balius **7** Xanthus

Zeppelin, Ferdinand Graf von
nationality: **6** German
invented: **9** dirigible **21** rigid dirigible airship
famous ship: **10** Hindenberg

Zernbbabel
father: **7** Pedaiah **9** Shealtiel

zero **2** no **3** nil, zip **5** aught, nadir, zilch **6** cipher, naught **7** nothing **8** goose egg **11** nonexistent, nothingness

zero hour **5** onset, start **7** liftoff **9** beginning **12** commencement

zest **3** joy, zip **4** salt, tang, zeal, zing **5** gusto, savor, spice, taste, verve **6** flavor, relish, thrill **7** delight, passion **8** appetite, piquancy, pleasure **9** eagerness, flavoring, seasoning **10** enthusiasm, excitement **12** exhilaration, satisfaction

zestful **6** active, lively **7** dynamic, vibrant **8** animated, spirited, vigorous **9** vivacious **12** invigorating

zesty **5** spicy, tangy **7** piquant **9** flavorful

Zetes
origin: **5** Greek
member of: **9** Argonauts
father: **6** Boreas
mother: **8** Orithyia
twin brother: **6** Calais

Zethus
father: **4** Zeus
mother: **7** Antiope
wife: **5** Thebe
twin brother: **7** Amphion

Zeus ***see box***

zigzag **4** awry, tack **6** angles, forked, jagged **7** chevron, crankle, crooked, notched, sinuous, stagger **8** crotched, serrated, sideling, traverse **9** bifurcate **10** circuitous, deflection

Zillah
husband: **6** Lamech
son: **9** Jubal-cain, Tubul-cain

Zilpah
slave of: **4** Leah
concubine of: **5** Jacob
son: **3** Gad **5** Asher

Zimbabwe ***see box***

Zimbalist, Efrem, Jr
born: **9** New York NY
father: **14** Efrem Zimbalist
mother: **9** Alma Gluck
daughter: **18** Stephanie Zimbalist
roles: **3** FBI **13** Wait Until Dark **15** By Love Possessed **16** The Chapman Report **62** Seventy-seven Sunset Strip

Zimmerman, Ethel Agnes
real name of: **11** Ethel Merman

zinc
chemical symbol: **2** Zn

zing **3** pep, vim, zap, zip **4** dash, snap, tang, whiz, zest **5** gusto, speed, vigor, whine **6** energy, spirit **7** liven up **8** satirize, vitality **9** animation, criticize **10** enthusiasm, liveliness

zingara, zingaro **5** gypsy

Zinnemann, Fred
director of: **5** Julia **8** High Noon, Oklahoma **9** The Search **12** The Nun's Story **13** The Sundowners **17** A Man for All Seasons (Oscar) **18** From Here to Eternity (Oscar)

Zion **6** utopia **9** city of God **11** City of David **13** ancient Israel
hill in: **9** Jerusalem
built on the hill: **6** Temple

Zeus
also: **7** Cenaean **9** Atabyriam, Ithomatas **10** Anchesmius **11** Panomphaeus **12** Cithaeronian
birthplace: **5** Crete
brother: **5** Hades **8** Poseidon
corresponds to: **4** Amen, Amon, Jove **5** Ammon **6** Amen Ra, Amon Ra **7** Jupiter
daughter: **4** Hebe **6** Athene **10** Eileithyia, Persephone
epithet: **5** Areus, Arius, Sotor **6** Aqueus, Nemean, Philus **7** Alastor, Apemius, Ctesius, Lycaeus, Polieus, Stenius **8** Agoraeus, Aphesius, Apomyius, Catharius, Chthonius, Coccygius, Hecaleius, Lecheates, Mechaneus **10** Catae-bates, Coryphaeus, Homagyrius, Laphystius, Meilichius **11** Eleutherius **12** Panhellenius
father: **6** Cronus
form: **5** deity
god of: **7** heavens
lover: **4** Leto **7** Demeter
mother: **4** Rhea
position: **7** supreme
sister: **4** Hera **6** Hestia **7** Demeter
son: **4** Ares **6** Apollo, Hermes
wife: **4** Hera **5** Metis

Zimbabwe
other name: **8** Rhodesia **16** Southern Rhodesia
capital/largest city: **6** Harare **9** Salisbury
others: **5** Gwelo, Gweru **6** Kariba, KweKwe, Mutare, QueQue, Umtali **7** Gatooma, Rusambo, Selukwe, Shabani **8** Bulawayo, Zimbabwe **10** Beitbridge
monetary unit: **4** cent **6** dollar
lake: **4** Kyle **6** Kariba
mountain: **5** Vumba **6** Manica **7** Inyanga **11** Chimanimani, Matopo Hills
highest point: **9** Inyangani
river: **4** Sabi, Save **5** Lundi **6** Shashi **7** Limpopo, Umniati, Zambezi
physical feature:
falls: **8** Victoria
grassland: **4** veld
plateau: **8** Highveld **11** Mashonaland
people: **3** Ila **4** Sena **5** Asian, Bantu, Bemba, Sotho, Tongo, White **6** Indian **7** Barotse, Chinese, English, Mashoma, Mashona, Ndebele **8** Coloured, Japanese, Matabele **9** Afrikaner **10** Balokwakwa
developer: **6** Rhodes
explorer: **11** Livingstone
king: **9** Lobengula, Mzilikaze
leader: **5** Nkomo **6** Mugabe **7** Sithole **8** Muzorewa **9** Ian D Smith
language: **3** Ila **5** Bantu, Shona **7** English, Ndebele
religion: **7** animism **8** Anglican **12** Christianity, Presbyterian **13** Dutch Reformed, Roman Catholic
place:
dam: **6** Kariba
national park: **6** Hwange, Wankie **7** Matopos **9** Inyangani **13** Victoria Falls
ruins: **5** Khami **6** Temple **8** Zimbabwe **9** Acropolis **13** Valley of Ruins
feature:
cattle pen: **5** kraal
game: **5** tsoro **7** mandani
hut: **4** kaia
kingdom: **5** Rozwi **10** Monomotapa
tree: **4** teak **6** baobab, mopani

zip 3 fly, nil, pep, run, vim **4** buzz, dart, dash, hiss, life, nada, rush, zero, zest **5** aught, close, drive, force, gusto, hurry, power, punch, speed, verve, vigor, whine, zilch **6** cipher, energy, impact, naught, spirit, streak **7** nothing, whistle **8** goose egg, strength, vitality, vivacity **9** animation, intensity **10** enthusiasm, exuberance, liveliness **13** effervescence

zipper
invented by: 6 Judson

Zipporah
father: 5 Reuel **6** Jethro
husband: 5 Moses
son: 7 Eliezer, Gershom

zircon
source: 5 Burma **6** Ceylon **8** Cambodia, Sri Lanka **9** Kampuchea

zirconium
chemical symbol: 2 Zr

zodiac 4 belt, zone **5** stars **7** circuit
fire sign: 3 Leo **5** Aries **11** Sagittarius
earth sign: 5 Virgo **6** Taurus **9** Capricorn
air sign: 5 Libra **6** Gemini **8** Aquarius
water: 6 Cancer, Pisces **7** Scorpio
division: 4 sign **5** decan **6** trigon
number of houses: 6 twelve
falling between two signs: 4 cusp

Zoimo, Vincent Edward
real name of: 12 Vince Edwards

Zola, Emile
author of: 4 Nana **7** The Soil **8** Germinal **10** L'Assommoir **11** The Downfall, The Dram Shop **13** Therese Raquin **14** The Human Animal **20** The Experimental Novel

zone 4 area, belt, ward **5** tract **6** region, sector **7** quarter, section, terrain **8** district, locality, location, precinct **9** territory

zonked 5 drunk **6** soused, wasted, zapped **7** smashed **9** plastered **10** inebriated **11** intoxicated

zoo 8 vivarium **9** menagerie

zoom 3 fly, zip **4** buzz, race, rise, soar **5** climb, flash, shoot, speed **6** ascend, rocket, streak **7** advance, take off **9** skyrocket

zoophobia
fear of: 7 animals

Zophar
friend: 3 Job **5** Elihu **6** Bildad **7** Eliphaz

Zorba the Greek
director: 17 Michael Cacoyannis
based on the story by: 11 Kazantzakis
cast: 9 Alan Bates **11** Irene Pappas, Lila Kedrova **12** Anthony Quinn
score: 16 Mikis Theodorakis
Oscar for: 17 supporting actress (Kedrova)

Zosteria
epithet of: 6 Athena
means: 20 one who girds with armor

zucchini 5 gourd **6** squash **12** summer squash

Zuck, Alexandra
real name of: 9 Sandra Dee

Zuckerman Unbound
author: 10 Philip Roth

Zurich
festival: 12 Sechselanten
landmark: 8 Rietberg **9** Kunsthaus **15** CG Jung Institute **17** Centre Le Corbusier, Fraumunster Kirche **21** Grossmunster Cathedral
religious figure: 7 Zwingli **9** Bullinger
river: 6 Limmat
Roman name: 7 Turicum

Zweig, Arnold
author of: 7 Claudia **24** The Case of Sergeant Grischa